lonely p

D0194003

Australia

NO LONGER PROPERTY OF
Anythink Libraries
Rangeview Library District

Darwin &
the Northern
Territory
p797

Queensland
p272

Perth &
Western Australia
p881

Adelaide &
South Australia
p713

Sydney &
New South Wales
p68

Canberra &
the ACT
p252

Melbourne &
Victoria
p462

Tasmania
p628

Andrew Bain, Samantha Forge, Anthony Ham, Trent Holden, Hugh McNaughtan,
Charles Rawlings-Way, Andy Symington, Brett Atkinson, Fleur Bainger,
Cristian Bonetto, Paul Harding, Rachael Hocking, Anita Isalska, Anna Kaminski,
Tatyana Leonov, Sofia Levin, Virginia Maxwell, Kate Morgan, Tasmin Waby, Steve Waters

Contents

PLAN YOUR TRIP

Welcome to Australia. 6
Australia Map 8
Australia's Top 25. 10
Need to Know 22
What's New 24
If You Like 26
Month by Month 29
Itineraries 33
Family Travel 37
Your Reef Trip 40
Your Outback Trip. 47
Australia Outdoors. 54
Wildlife Watching 59
Regions at a Glance. . . . 62

ABORIGINAL CULTURE
P1036

DINGO, FRASER ISLAND
P352

GRANT FAINT/GETTY IMAGES ©

MATT MUNRO/LONELY PLANET ©

ON THE ROAD

SYDNEY &
NEW SOUTH
WALES 68
Sydney 69
Royal National Park 136
Blue Mountains 138
The Central Coast 146
Hunter Valley. 147
Newcastle 153
Mid-North Coast. 158
Port Stephens. 159
Myall Lakes
National Park 161
Port Macquarie. 162
South West Rocks 167
Bellingen 168
Coffs Harbour. 170
Byron Bay &
the Far North Coast . . . 174
Yamba & Angourie 174
Ballina 176
Byron Bay 178
Brunswick Heads. 187
North Coast
Hinterland 188
Bangalow. 188
Lismore 189
Nimbin 190
New England 193
Tamworth. 193
Armidale 194
Tenterfield 196
Northern NSW. 197
Moree 198
Lightning Ridge 199
Central NSW 200
Bathurst. 200
Orange 201
Cowra. 203
Dubbo. 205
Mudgee 206
Outback NSW 208
Bourke 209
Broken Hill. 210

Mungo National Park. . . . 214
South Coast NSW. 217
Wollongong 217
Berry. 221
Kangaroo Valley 222
Nowra. 224
Jervis Bay 225
Ulladulla & Mollymook . . .227
Batemans Bay 229
Narooma 231
Tilba Tilba &
Central Tilba 233
Sapphire Coast. 234
Southern Highlands. . . 239
Mittagong & Bowral. 239
Snowy Mountains. 241
Cooma 241
Kosciuszko
National Park 243
Riverina 246
Gundagai 246
Albury. 246
Wagga Wagga 247
Griffith 249

CANBERRA &
THE ACT. 252
Canberra 254
Around Canberra 271

QUEENSLAND. 272
Brisbane. 273
North Stradbroke
Island 305
Moreton Island 307
Toowoomba. 308
Granite Belt. 310
Gold Coast. 312
Surfers Paradise. 314
Main Beach
& The Spit 316
Broadbeach
& Mermaid Beach 318
Burleigh Heads. 319

Contents

Gold Coast Hinterland 322

Noosa & The Sunshine Coast... 324

Noosa 326

Bribie Island 331

Caloundra 332

Mooloolaba & Maroochydore.......... 334

Coolum & Peregian Beach....... 337

Cooloola Coast 338

Fraser Coast 341

Hervey Bay 342

Rainbow Beach......... 347

Gympie................ 349

Childers 349

Bundaberg............. 350

Fraser Island 352

Capricorn Coast & the Southern Reef Islands.......... 358

Agnes Water & Town of 1770 358

Southern Reef Islands 362

Rockhampton.......... 363

Yeppoon............... 366

Great Keppel Island..... 367

Whitsunday Coast 369

Mackay................ 369

Airlie Beach........... 373

The Whitsundays 377

Eungella National Park 382

Townsville to Cairns... 383

Townsville 383

Magnetic Island 389

Ingham & Around...... 391

Tully 393

Mission Beach 394

Innisfail 398

Cairns............... 399

Atherton Tablelands... 421

Kuranda 422

Atherton............... 424

Malanda & Around...... 425

Yungaburra 426

Crater Lakes National Park 426

Port Douglas to Cooktown 427

Port Douglas........... 427

Mossman.............. 432

The Daintree & Cape Tribulation........ 432

Cooktown.............. 437

Cape York Peninsula............ 439

Thursday Island & Horn Island 445

Gulf Savannah........ 446

Undara Volcanic National Park 447

Croydon 447

Normanton 448

Karumba & Karumba Point 448

Outback Queensland .. 451

Cloncurry.............. 452

Mt Isa 452

Mt Isa to Charleville..... 455

Barcaldine 458

Charleville 459

Channel Country 460

MELBOURNE & VICTORIA......... 462

Melbourne 463

The Dandenongs 516

Yarra Valley 518

Marysville & Lake Mountain 522

Daylesford & Hepburn Springs 524

Mornington Peninsula.............. 527

Phillip Island 532

Great Ocean Road 536

Geelong 536

Bellarine Peninsula 543

Torquay 546

Anglesea 548

Aireys Inlet & Around 549

Lorne 551

Apollo Bay............. 554

Cape Otway............ 556

Port Campbell.......... 557

Port Campbell National Park 559

Warrnambool 561

Port Fairy............. 564

Portland............... 567

Goldfields & Grampians 570

Ballarat................ 571

Bendigo 575

Kyneton 580

Castlemaine 581

The Grampians......... 583

Mt Arapiles State Park 588

Gippsland & Wilsons Promontory.......... 588

Wilsons Promontory National Park 589

Lakes District 592

East Gippsland & the Wilderness Coast ...596

Victorian High Country......... 601

Mansfield.............. 604

Mt Buller 605

Beechworth............ 606

Rutherglen............. 610

Bright 613

Mt Beauty & the Kiewa Valley 615

Falls Creek............. 616

Mt Hotham & Dinner Plain............ 617

The Murray 619

Mildura 619

Echuca 624

ON THE ROAD

TASMANIA........**628**
Hobart..............**634**
Richmond & Around 649
Mt Field National Park
& Around.............650
The Southeast.......**652**
Bruny Island..........652
Cygnet................655
Geeveston & Around....656
Dover.................657
**Tasman Peninsula
& Port Arthur**........**658**
Dunalley..............659
Port Arthur & Tasman
National Park..........661
The Midlands.........**663**
Ross..................664
The East Coast.......**665**
Maria Island
National Park..........665
Swansea...............668
Coles Bay & Freycinet
National Park..........669
Bicheno...............671
Binalong Bay
& the Bay of Fires......673
Derby & Around........674
Flinders Island.........676
Launceston..........**677**
Tamar Valley..........684
Longford & Around.....688
Evandale..............689
Ben Lomond
National Park..........689
**Devonport
& the Northwest**......**690**
Devonport.............690
Mole Creek............695
Penguin...............697
Burnie................698
Stanley...............700
King Island............701
The Tarkine
Wilderness............702
Corinna &
the Pieman River.......703

FREMANTLE MARKETS
P889

**Cradle Country
& The West**..........**703**
Cradle Mountain-
Lake St Clair
National Park..........704
Queenstown...........707
Strahan...............708
The Southwest.......**710**
Lake Pedder
& Strathgordon........711
Maydena..............712

**ADELAIDE &
SOUTH
AUSTRALIA**........**713**
Adelaide.............**716**
Hahndorf.............736
Stirling Area..........738
Gumeracha, Birdwood
& Lobethal............739
Fleurieu Peninsula....**739**
McLaren Vale..........740
Willunga..............742
Gulf St Vincent
Beaches..............743
Victor Harbor..........745
Port Elliot.............746
Goolwa...............747
Kangaroo Island......**748**
Barossa Valley........**757**
Clare Valley..........**762**

Murray River.........**765**
Renmark & Paringa.....769
Limestone Coast......**771**
Robe..................771
Meningie & Coorong
National Park..........773
Mount Gambier........774
Penola & the
Coonawarra
Wine Region...........776
Yorke Peninsula......**777**
Eyre Peninsula.......**780**
Port Augusta...........781
Port Lincoln...........782
Coffin Bay.............784
Streaky Bay & Around...785
Ceduna...............786
Flinders Ranges......**787**
Outback SA..........**792**
Woomera & Around.....793
Coober Pedy...........794

**DARWIN &
THE NORTHERN
TERRITORY**.......**797**
Darwin..............**800**
Batchelor.............820
Litchfield
National Park..........821
Pine Creek............823

Contents

Kakadu
National Park 824
Arnhem Land......... 834
Katherine............ 837
Nitmiluk
(Katherine Gorge)
National Park 840
Mataranka 844
Barkly Tableland
& Gulf Country 845
Carpentaria &
Tablelands Highways....846
Borroloola 847
Central NT 848
Tennant Creek......... 848
Devil's Marbles
& Around 850
Tanami Road 851
Alice Springs 852
MacDonnell Ranges ... 862
NT's Far South 867
Old South Road 867
Lasseter Highway....... 870
Kings Canyon
& Watarrka
National Park 870
Uluru-Kata Tjuta
National Park 872

PERTH &
WESTERN
AUSTRALIA 881
Perth................. 884
Rottnest Island......... 913
Swan Valley 920
Rockingham 922
Dwellingup............. 923
Mandurah 924
Perth Hills 926
Avon Valley 927
New Norcia 929
Turquoise Coast 930
Margaret
River Region 933
Bunbury............... 933

Dunsborough 937
Yallingup 940
Margaret River 942
Caves Road 945
Southern Forests 948
Manjimup............. 948
Pemberton............ 949
Southern WA......... 951
Walpole & Nornalup..... 951
Denmark 953
Albany 956
Porongurup
National Park 960
Stirling Range
National Park 961
Esperance 962
Batavia Coast 965
Geraldton.............. 965
Kalbarri 969
Shark Bay 972
Denham 972
Monkey Mia........... 974
Gascoyne Coast 976
Ningaloo Coast
& the Pilbara......... 978
Coral Bay 978
Exmouth.............. 982
Ningaloo Marine Park ... 986
Karratha.............. 989
Port Hedland.......... 991
Karijini National Park ... 993
Broome &
The Kimberley....... 995
Broome 995
Dampier Peninsula.....1004
Derby 1006
Gibb River Road 1008
Great Northern Hwy ... 1012
Kununurra 1014
Purnululu National
Park & Bungle Bungle
Range 1016
Outback WA......... 1017
Kalgoorlie-Boulder..... 1017

UNDERSTAND

History 1022
Aboriginal
Culture 1036
Environment 1041
Food & Drink 1049
Sport............... 1054

SURVIVAL GUIDE

Deadly &
Dangerous 1058
Directory A–Z 1060
Transport........... 1071

Aboriginal and Torres Strait Islander people should be aware that this book may contain images of or references to deceased people.

SPECIAL FEATURES

Family Travel.......... 37
Your Reef Trip 40
Your Outback Trip...... 47
Sydney's Beaches 93
Where to Stay
in Sydney............ 104
Great Ocean Road 538

Welcome to Australia

Australia is the unexpected: a place where the world's oldest cultures share vast ochre plains, stylish laneways and unimaginably blue waters with successive waves of new arrivals from across the globe.

An Ancient Land

Australia is a country, but also a land that encompasses many countries. To understand the latter is to walk in the footsteps of its first peoples. Whether you're tracing outlines of rock art more than 20 thousand years old in Kakadu National Park, floating in the azure waters of Rottnest Island or admiring the iconic sites of Sydney Harbour where the Eora Nation traded for centuries, you are on Indigenous land.

Urban Wonder

Nowhere builds cities quite like Australia: each is a homage to magnificent waterways or beachfronts, while offering different experiences across different geographies. Grab a bicycle from one of Melbourne's bike-share racks and tour the city's fashion districts and cafe-lined laneways. Only a city like Darwin can fuse southern-Asian influence with contemporary Aboriginal culture (and leave you with an impressive sunburn to boot). Want a bit of everything? Sydney will take your breath away with its natural beauty and bustling neighbourhoods, while Hobart strikes a chord with its Gothic history and contemporary art.

Adventurous Spirit

You only have to travel a stone's throw from any of Australia's capital cities before you've landed somewhere truly out of this world. Not scared of the deep blue? Dive into famous reefs from the Ningaloo to the Great Barrier Reef, or witness majestic southern right whales along the Great Australian Bight. And nothing will steady your sea legs more than getting on a 4WD tour and hitting one of the many dirt roads leading to rocky outcrops, from Uluru to the Kimberley.

A Foodie's Dream

Decades of migration combined with the re-emergence of native ingredients has brought Australian cuisine on to the radar of the world's best chefs. You can buy a mouth-watering kangaroo steak complemented by indigenous greens at high-end restaurants, or take a bush tucker tour outside Alice Springs and learn which local plants to taste. No trip to Tasmania would be complete without planning exactly where you'll slurp freshly shucked oysters, and don't leave South Australia without a Barossa Valley taste tour. And a word for the brave: Darwinians love their spice!

Why I Love My Country

By Rachael Hocking, Journalist

When I walk across this magnificent land, I speak to my forebears: great Warlpiri warriors, and the ancestors of each tribe that call this country home. I sing to the spirits who inhabit speckled night skies above the Tanami Desert: they look down from the stars and see circles, lines, dots; the veins of our Mother. I've shared turtle eggs with Meriam on Erub Island at the edges of the beautiful Torres Strait, and I've sighted rare rock-wallaby in the heart of the Pilbara alongside Martu Aboriginal rangers. I do not own this land, but it is a part of me.

For more about our writers, see p1104

Above: Stunning cliff scenery, Broome (p995), Western Australia

Australia

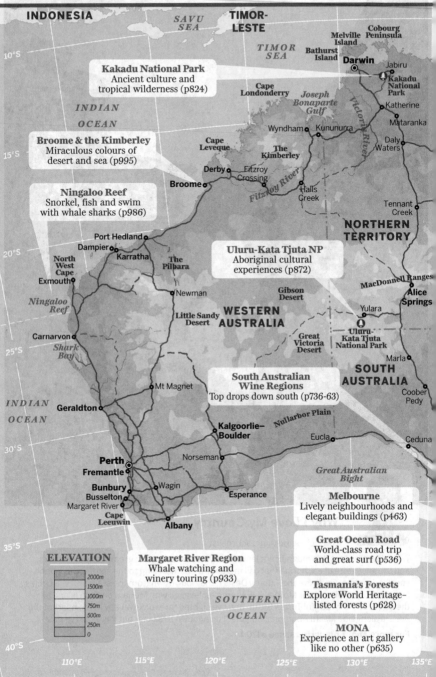

INDONESIA

SAVU SEA

TIMOR-LESTE

TIMOR SEA

Melville Island
Bathurst Island
Cobourg Peninsula

Darwin

Jabiru

Kakadu National Park
Ancient culture and
tropical wilderness (p824)

Kakadu National Park

Cape Londonderry

Joseph Bonaparte Gulf

Katherine

Mataranka

INDIAN OCEAN

Cape Leveque

The Kimberley

Wyndham

Kununurra

Victoria River

Daly Waters

Broome & the Kimberley
Miraculous colours of
desert and sea (p995)

Derby

Fitzroy Crossing

Fitzroy River

Halls Creek

Broome

Ningaloo Reef
Snorkel, fish and swim
with whale sharks (p986)

Tennant Creek

NORTHERN TERRITORY

Port Hedland

Dampier

Karratha

The Pilbara

Uluru-Kata Tjuta NP
Aboriginal cultural
experiences (p872)

North West Cape
Exmouth

Newman

Gibson Desert

MacDonnell Ranges

Alice Springs

Ningaloo Reef

Little Sandy Desert

WESTERN AUSTRALIA

Yulara

Uluru-Kata Tjuta National Park

Carnarvon

Shark Bay

Great Victoria Desert

SOUTH AUSTRALIA

Marla

INDIAN OCEAN

Mt Magnet

South Australian Wine Regions
Top drops down south (p736-63)

Coober Pedy

Geraldton

Kalgoorlie–Boulder

Nullarbor Plain

Ceduna

Norseman

Eucla

Great Australian Bight

Perth
Fremantle

Bunbury
Busselton
Margaret River
Cape Leeuwin

Wagin

Esperance

Melbourne
Lively neighbourhoods and
elegant buildings (p463)

Albany

Great Ocean Road
World-class road trip
and great surf (p536)

ELEVATION

2000m
1500m
1000m
750m
500m
250m
0

Margaret River Region
Whale watching and
winery touring (p933)

Tasmania's Forests
Explore World Heritage-
listed forests (p628)

SOUTHERN

OCEAN

MONA
Experience an art gallery
like no other (p635)

10°S   15°S   20°S   25°S   30°S   35°S   40°S

110°E   115°E   120°E   125°E   130°E   135°E

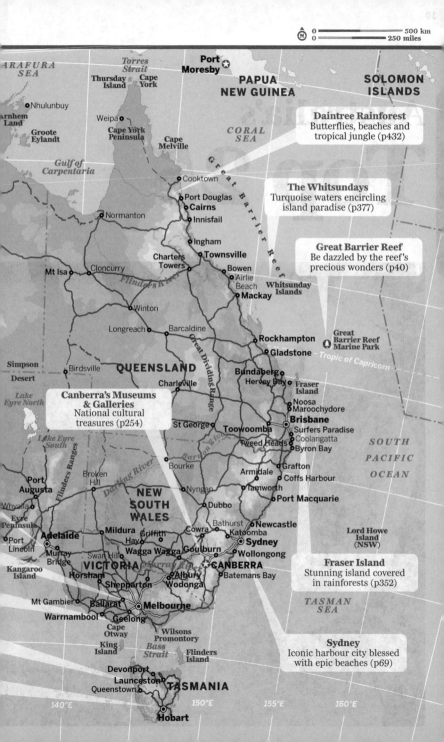

0 —— 500 km
0 —— 250 miles

ARAFURA SEA

Torres Strait

Thursday Island

Cape York

Port Moresby ★

PAPUA NEW GUINEA

SOLOMON ISLANDS

Nhulunbuy

Arnhem Land

Weipa

Cape York Peninsula

Cape Melville

CORAL SEA

Daintree Rainforest
Butterflies, beaches and tropical jungle (p432)

Groote Eylandt

Gulf of Carpentaria

Cooktown

Port Douglas

Cairns

Innisfail

Normanton

Ingham

The Whitsundays
Turquoise waters encircling island paradise (p377)

Mt Isa

Cloncurry

Charters Towers

Townsville

Bowen

Great Barrier Reef
Be dazzled by the reef's precious wonders (p40)

Flinders River

Airlie Beach

Whitsunday Islands

Mackay

Winton

Longreach

Barcaldine

Rockhampton

Gladstone

Great Barrier Reef Marine Park

Simpson Desert

Birdsville

QUEENSLAND

Charleville

Tropic of Capricorn

Lake Eyre North

Bundaberg

Hervey Bay

Fraser Island

Canberra's Museums & Galleries
National cultural treasures (p254)

St George

Toowoomba

Noosa

Maroochydore

Brisbane

Surfers Paradise

Lake Eyre South

Bourke

Coolangatta

Tweed Heads

Byron Bay

SOUTH PACIFIC OCEAN

Flinders Ranges

Broken Hill

Darling River

Nyngan

Armidale

Grafton

Coffs Harbour

Port Augusta

NEW SOUTH WALES

Dubbo

Tamworth

Port Macquarie

Whyalla

Eyre Peninsula

Bathurst

Newcastle

Lord Howe Island (NSW)

Port Lincoln

Adelaide

Mildura

Griffith

Hay

Cowra

Katoomba

Sydney

Kangaroo Island

Murray Bridge

Swan Hill

Wagga Wagga

Goulburn

Wollongong

Fraser Island
Stunning island covered in rainforests (p352)

VICTORIA

Murray River

Albury

CANBERRA

Horsham

Shepparton

Wodonga

Batemans Bay

Mt Gambier

Ballarat

Warrnambool

Melbourne

Geelong

TASMAN SEA

Cape Otway

Wilsons Promontory

King Island

Bass Strait

Flinders Island

Sydney
Iconic harbour city blessed with epic beaches (p69)

Devonport

Launceston

Queenstown

TASMANIA

Hobart

140°E 150°E 155°E 160°E

Australia's
Top 25

Aboriginal Culture

1 Australia's Aboriginal people, from over 500 different first nations, are the inheritors of the longest continuous culture on earth. Your first engagement with Aboriginal culture may be on a walking tour, via a bush-tucker experience, or while enjoying artistic expressions of art, film, music, story and dance. You don't need to visit the outback to learn about Aboriginal Australia. Whatever your introduction is, expect to have your worldview completely turned around. Post-colonial Australia is only starting to appreciate Aboriginal custodianship of the land and the humble intelligence required to thrive here for millennia.

Below left: Bush foods (p1051), central Australia

Wildlife

2 Native wildlife (p59) brings Australia's wild regions to life. You'll never forget seeing your first kangaroo bounding across a field, or encountering your first wombat in a campground. From the crocodiles of Kakadu to whale watching off the coast in winter, and adorable quokkas on Rottnest Island in Western Australia to a rainbow of birds in its cities, Australia is rich with wildlife-spotting opportunities. It's almost impossible to miss them. Did we mention koalas, dingoes, rock wallabies, platypuses, goannas and more? Don't forget to pack your binoculars.

Below right: Tasmanian echidna

HOHENHAUS/GETTY IMAGES ©

TAYLOR WILSON SMITH/SHUTTERSTOCK ©

Uluru-Kata Tjuta National Park

3 Australia's most recognised natural wonder, Uluru (p872) draws pilgrims from around the world like moths to a big red flame. No matter how many postcard images you have seen, nothing prepares you for the Rock's immense presence, character-pitted surface and spiritual gravitas. Not far away is an equally beguiling clutch of stone siblings known as Kata Tjuta. Deeply cleaved with narrow gorges sheltering tufts of vegetation, these 36 pink-red domes blush intensely at sunset.

Great Barrier Reef

4 The Great Barrier Reef (p401) is as fragile as it is beautiful. Stretching more than 2000km along the Queensland coastline, it's a complex ecosystem populated with dazzling coral, languid sea turtles, gliding rays, timid reef sharks and tropical fish of every colour and size. Whether you dive on it, snorkel over it or explore it via a scenic flight or a glass-bottomed boat, this vivid undersea kingdom and its coral-fringed islands are so unforgettable people are signing up to become a Citizen of the Great Barrier Reef to help save it.

Sydney

5 Sydney (p68) is immediately recognisable, with its iconic Opera House, the Harbour Bridge lights glistening in the night and sun worshippers lying on its famous beaches. Beyond postcard Sydney, this eclectic city has layers of history and culture to excavate as you explore neighbourhoods. Flamboyant citizens, living Aboriginal stories, Asian influences, colonial streets, old-school pubs, dramatic architecture and always the water: Sydney is defined by its relationship with the briny sea air. It's possible to witness all of this in a single Sydney moment.

The Whitsundays

6 You can hop around a whole stack of tropical islands in this seafaring life and never find anywhere with the sheer beauty of the Whitsundays (p378). Travellers of all monetary persuasions launch yachts from Airlie Beach and drift between these lush green isles in a slow search for paradise (you'll probably find it in more than one place). Don't miss Whitehaven Beach – one of Australia's (and the world's) best. Wish you were here?

Daintree Rainforest

7 Lush green fan palms, ferns and twisted mangroves tumble down towards a brilliant white-sand coastline in the ancient, World Heritage–listed Daintree (p432) rainforest. Upon entering the forest, you'll be enveloped in a cacophony of birdsong, frog croaking and the buzz of insects. Continue exploring the area on wildlife-spotting night tours, mountain treks, interpretive boardwalks, canopy walks, self-guided walking trails, 4WD trips, horse riding, kayaking, crocodile-spotting cruises, tropical-fruit orchard tours and tastings...You might even spot a prehistoric cassowary.

Melbourne

8 Why the queue? Oh, that's just the line to get into the latest 'no bookings' restaurant in Melbourne (p463). The next best restaurant, chef, cafe, barista, hidden bar may be the talk of the town, but there are things locals would never change: the leafy parks and gardens in the inner city; the crowded trams that whisk creative 'northerners' to sea-breezy southern St Kilda; and the allegiances that living in such a sports-mad city brings. The city's world-renowned street-art scene expresses Melbourne's fears, frustrations and joys. Bottom: Hosier Lane street art (p463)

CHAMELEONSEYE/SHUTTERSTOCK ©

ANDREY BAYDA/SHUTTERSTOCK ©

Margaret River & Cape Naturaliste

9 The decadent joy of drifting from winery to farm gate along eucalypt-shaded country roads is just one of the delights of Western Australia's southwest (p933). There are underground caves to explore, historic towns to visit and wildflowers to ogle. Surfers bob around in the world-class breaks near the Margaret River mouth, but it's not unusual to find yourself on a white-sand beach along the cape where the only footprints are your own. In winter and early spring, whales migrate along the 'Humpback Highway'. Above left: Margaret River wine region

MONA

10 Occupying an improbable riverside location a ferry ride from Hobart's harbourfront, the Museum of Old & New Art (p635) is an innovative, world-class institution. Described by its owner, Hobart philanthropist David Walsh, as a 'subversive adult Disneyland', three levels of astounding underground galleries – in a building (pictured) by architect Nonda Katsalidis – showcase more than 400 challenging and controversial artworks from his collections. You might not like everything you see, but a visit here is a sure-fire conversation starter and one of Australia's favourite arts experiences.

Byron Bay

11 Up there with kangaroos and Akubra hats, big-hearted Byron Bay (p178; just Byron to its mates) is one of the enduring icons of Australian culture. Families on school holidays, surfers and sun-seekers from across the globe gather by the foreshore at sunset, drawn to this spot on the world map by fabulous restaurants, a chilled pace of life and an astonishing range of activities on offer. But mostly they're here because this is one of the most beautiful stretches of coast in the country.

South Australian Wine Regions

12 Adelaide is drunk on the success of its three world-famous wine regions, all within two hours' drive: the Barossa Valley (p757) to the north, with its gutsy reds, old vines and German know-how; McLaren Vale to the south, a Mediterranean palette of sea, vines and shiraz and stunning d'Arenburg winery; and the Clare Valley, known for riesling and cycling (in that order). Better-kept secrets are the cool-climate stunners from the Adelaide Hills and the country cabernet sauvignon from the Coonawarra.

Ningaloo Reef

13 Swim beside 'gentle giant' whale sharks, snorkel among pristine coral, surf off seldom-visited reefs and dive at one of the world's premier locations at this World Heritage–listed marine park (p986), which sits off the North West Cape on the Coral Coast in Western Australia. Rivalling the Great Barrier Reef for beauty, Ningaloo has more accessible wonders: shallow, turquoise lagoons are entered straight from the beach for excellent snorkelling. Development is very low-key, so be prepared to camp, or take day trips from the access towns of Exmouth and Coral Bay. Below right: Whale shark

MILTON WORDLEY/GETTY IMAGES ©

Kakadu National Park

14 Kakadu (p824), the traditional land of the Bininj/Mungguy, is a portal into a natural and cultural landscape like no other. Weathered by relentless wet and dry seasons, the sandstone ramparts of Kakadu and neighbouring Arnhem Land have sheltered humans for millennia, and an extraordinary environmental legacy remains. Rock-art galleries depict the Dreaming, hunting stories, zoological diagrams and 'contact art' (records of visitors from Indonesia and European colonists). The Ubirr and Nourlangie galleries are World Heritage listed and are accessible to all.

Top: Gunlom waterhole (p833)

Cradle Mountain

15 A precipitous comb of rock carved out by millennia of ice and wind, crescent-shaped Cradle Mountain (p704) is Tasmania's most recognisable – and spectacular – mountain peak. It's an all-day walk (and boulder scramble) to the summit and back for unbelievable panoramas over Tasmania's alpine heart. Or you can stand in awe below and fill your camera with the perfect views across Dove Lake to the mountain. If the peak has disappeared in clouds or snow, warm yourself by the fire in one of the nearby lodges...and come back tomorrow.

Broome & the Kimberley

16 Australia's north-western frontier is one of its most beautiful corners. Broome (p995), where so many journeys out here begin, is where every evening a searing crimson sun slips into the turquoise Indian Ocean as seen from beaches that never seem to end. The far-flung Dampier Peninsula is all about extraordinary cliffs, Indigenous cultural experiences, outdoor adventures and luxury camping. And then there's the Kimberley, a world of blood-red rock formations, remote trails and unrelenting beauty, not to mention that mysterious call of the outback. Top left: Cable Beach (p998)

Great Ocean Road

17 The Twelve Apostles – craggy rock formations jutting out of wild waters – are one of Victoria's most vivid sights, but it's the 'getting there' road trip that doubles their impact. Drive slowly along roads that curl beside spectacular Bass Strait beaches, then whip inland through temperate rainforest studded with small towns and big trees. The secrets of the Great Ocean Road (p536) don't stop there; further along is maritime treasure Port Fairy and hidden Cape Bridgewater. For the ultimate in slow travel, walk the Great Ocean Walk from Apollo Bay to the Apostles. Top right: Cape Otway Lightstation (p556)

Canberra's Museums

18 Though Canberra (p254) is only a century old, Australia's purpose-built capital loves history. So it's not surprising that the major drawcard here is a portfolio of lavishly endowed museums and galleries focused on interpreting the national narrative. Institutions such as the National Gallery of Australia, National Museum of Australia, National Portrait Gallery and Australian War Memorial offer visitors a fascinating insight into the country's history and culture and do so with style and substance. Bottom right: National Museum of Australia, by architects Ashton Raggatt McDougall and Robert Peck von Hartel Trethowan (p256)

Fraser Island

19 The world's largest sand island, Fraser Island (p352) is home to dingoes, shipwrecks and all manner of birdlife. Four-wheel drive vehicles – regular cars cannot drive on sand – fan out around epic camp spots and long white beaches. The wild coastline curbs any thoughts of doing much more than wandering between pristine creeks and freshwater lakes. Beach camping under the stars will bring you back to nature. A short ferry trip away is Hervey Bay, where humpback whales shoot along the coast in winter and spring.

The Outback & Broken Hill

20 Whether you're belting along South Australia's Oodnadatta Track in a 4WD or depreciating your van on the southern section of the Birdsville Track, you'll know you're not just visiting the outback – you've become part of it. Out here, the sky is bluer and the dust redder than anywhere else. Days are measured in kilometres, spinifex mounds and tyre blowouts. Nights are spent in the five-zillion-star hotel, waiting for one to fall... If time isn't on your side, a road trip to the mining town of Broken Hill (p210) may be as far from the coast as you get.

Arnhem Land

21 The honour of visiting Arnhem Land (p834) in Australia's Top End is so more than just an opportunity to get off the beaten track. The beaches are truly pristine, and very often deserted, and the wildlife, both on land and in the sea, is abundant because of the Aboriginal approach to Country. Cobourg Peninsula has an earth's-first-morning quality. And put Injalak Arts & Crafts Centre at Gunbalanya on your itinerary – it's an important cultural hub for the remote communities living out here beyond the paved road.

Top: Palm fibre mats

Nitmiluk (Katherine Gorge)

22 While paddling a canoe upstream through one gorge and then another and leaving the crowds behind, you will be drawn into the silence of these towering cliffs, which squeeze the waters of the Katherine River (p840). Take a break on a sandy river beach, walk up to a viewpoint or take a helicopter flight for an eagle-eye view. The surrounding Nitmiluk National Park has even more to offer such as the Jatbula Trail, a five-day walk from the Gorge to the wonderful Leliyn (Edith Falls).

Wilsons Promontory

23 Victoria's southernmost point and finest coastal national park, Wilsons Promontory (p589) (or just the Prom) is heaven for bushwalkers, wildlife watchers and surfers. The bushland and coastal scenery here is out of this world; even short walks from the main base at Tidal River will take you to beautiful beaches and bays. But with more than 80km of walking trails through forests, marshes and valleys of tree ferns, over low granite mountains and along beaches backed by sand dunes, the best of the Prom requires some serious footwork.

The Ghan

24 The legendary Ghan (p1078) – named after central Australia's pioneering Afghan cameleers – is one of the world's great railway journeys. Begun in 1877, the old line from Marree to Alice Springs suffered from washouts and shoddy construction before a shiny new line replaced it in 1980. The Alice-to-Darwin section followed in 2004: now there's 2979km and 42 hours of track between Adelaide and Darwin. The Ghan isn't cheap or fast, but the journey through the vast, flat expanse of central Australia's deserts is unforgettable.

Pinnacles Desert

25 It could be mistaken for the surface of Mars, but scattered among the dunes of Nambung National Park (p931), thousands of ghostly limestone pillars rise from the surrounding plain like a vast, petrified alien army. One of the west's most bizarre landscapes, the Pinnacles Desert attracts thousands of visitors each year. Although it's easily enjoyed as a day trip from Perth, staying overnight in nearby Cervantes allows for multiple visits to experience the full spectrum of colour changes at dawn, sunset and the full moon, when most tourists are back in their hotels.

Need to Know

For more information, see Survival Guide (p1057)

Currency
Australian dollar ($)

Language
English, plus Djambarrpuyngu, Pitjantjatjara, Warlpiri, Tiwi, Murrinh-Patha, Kunwinjku among 120 Indigenous languages

Visas
All visitors to Australia need a visa, except New Zealanders. There are several different visas available from short-stay visitor visas to working-holiday visas.

Money
The Australian dollar is the only currency accepted. You won't have much trouble finding an ATM (cashpoint).

Mobile Phones
Either set up global roaming, or pick up a local SIM card with a prepaid rechargeable account on arrival.

Time
Australia has three main time zones: Australian Eastern, Central and Western Standard Time. Sydney is on AEST, which is GMT/UTC plus 10 hours.

When to Go

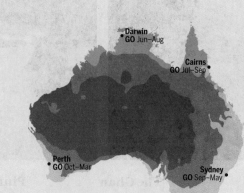

Darwin
GO Jun–Aug

Cairns
GO Jul–Sep

Perth
GO Oct–Mar

Sydney
GO Sep–May

Hobart
GO Dec–Apr

■ Desert, dry climate
■ Dry climate
■ Tropical climate, wet/dry seasons
■ Warm to hot summers, mild winters

High Season
(Dec–Feb)

➡ Summertime: wet season up north, bush fires in the south.

➡ Accommodation price rises, busy beaches.

➡ Festivals season: arts, food, film, music.

Shoulder
(Mar–May & Sep–Nov)

➡ Warm sun, clear skies, cool nights.

➡ Coastal areas busy at Easter with families.

➡ Autumn colours are atmospheric in Victoria, Tasmania and South Australia.

Low Season
(Jun–Aug)

➡ Cool wintery days down south; mild with sunny skies up north.

➡ Lower tourist numbers; some attractions keep slightly shorter hours.

➡ Head for the desert, the tropical north, or whale-watching spots.

Useful Websites

Lonely Planet (www.lonely planet.com/australia) Destination information, hotel bookings, traveller forum and more.

Tourism Australia (www.australia.com) Main government tourism site with loads of visitor info.

Bureau of Meteorology (www.bom.gov.au) Nationwide weather forecasts and weather warnings.

Parks Australia (www.environment.gov.au/topics/national-parks) Get excited about Australia's cornucopia of national parks and reserves.

Go Camping Australia (www.gocampingaustralia.com) Beginners' guide to camping in Australia; includes detailed campsite reviews.

Important Numbers

Australian landline phone numbers have a two-digit state-by-state area code, followed by an eight-digit number.

Emergency (ambulance, fire, police)	☏000
Directory assistance	☏1223

Exchange Rates

Canada	C$1	$1.06
China	Y1	$0.27
Euro-zone	€1	$1.58
Japan	¥100	$1.25
New Zealand	NZ$1	$0.97
South Korea	W1000	$1.25
UK	UK£1	$1.82
USA	US$1	$1.39

For current exchange rates, see www.xe.com

Daily Costs

Budget: Less than $200

➡ Hostel dorm bed: $40

➡ Double room in a basic motel: $100–150

➡ Simple main meal: $15–20

➡ Short bus or tram ride: $5

Midrange: $200–350

➡ Double room in a B&B or hotel: $150–250

➡ Brunch in a good cafe: $25–40

➡ Small gig or show: $30

➡ Short taxi ride: $25

Top End: More than $350

➡ Double room in a top-end hotel: from $250

➡ Three-course restaurant meal: $125 per person

➡ Theatre or festival tickets: from $100 per person

➡ City-to-city domestic flight: from $100

Opening Hours

Most attractions close Christmas Day; many also close on New Year's Day and Good Friday.

Banks & post offices 9.30am–4pm Monday to Thursday; until 5pm Friday

Cafes 7am–5pm; some close later

Petrol stations & roadhouses 8am–8pm; some open 24 hours in cities

Restaurants Lunch noon–2.30pm and dinner from 6pm; service ends early in country towns or on quiet nights

Shops 9am to 5pm Monday to Saturday; sometimes on Sunday; in larger cities, doors close at 9pm on Friday

Supermarkets 7am–9pm; some open 24 hours

Arriving in Australia

Sydney Airport AirportLink trains run to the city centre every 10 minutes from around 5am to 1am (15 minutes, $16–19). Prebooked shuttle buses service city hotels. A taxi into the city costs approximately $55 (15–40 minutes).

Melbourne Airport SkyBus services run to the city (30–45 minutes, $19.75), leaving every 6–10 minutes from 6am to midnight and at every 30 minutes through the night. A taxi into the city costs around $55 (30–40 minutes).

Brisbane Airport Airtrain trains run to the city centre (20 minutes, $19) every 15 to 30 minutes from 5am (6am weekends) to 10pm. A taxi to the city costs $35 to $45 (40 minutes).

Getting Around

Australia is the sixth-largest country in the world: how you get from A to B requires some thought. If you're short on time, consider internal flights – they're affordable (compared with petrol and car-hire costs), can usually be carbon offset, and will save you some long travel days.

Van or car Travel at your own pace, explore remote areas and visit regions with no public transport.

Plane Fast track your holiday with affordable, frequent, fast flights between major centres.

Bus Reliable, frequent long-haul services around the country. Not always cheaper than flying but you'll get a better sense of scale.

Train Slow and not inexpensive, but the scenery is great! Australia has some bucket-list rail journeys so plan ahead.

For much more on **getting around**, see p1071

What's New

Here's the low-down on what's new and interesting around Australia. From boutique big-city hotels to little bars in little towns, and from vegan eats to high-end camping retreats, there's plenty of new stuff going on here to impress first-time and repeat visitors alike.

Best in Travel

Australia's Red Centre was awarded fourth place in Lonely Planet's list of top 10 regions internationally in 2019, and Margaret River & Southern WA was awarded the number one spot in Asia Pacific.

The spiritual heart of the Red Centre is Australia's most recognised natural wonder, Uluru. In 2019, Uluru, a sacred site to local Aboriginal people, was finally closed to climbers, almost 150 years after explorers decided to 'conquer the rock'. Learn about the unique world view of the traditional custodians of this special place, and see the stars and the desert with new eyes.

Looking west, Margaret River and Southern WA has captivating coastlines, award-winning wineries, coveted food festivals, and DIY coastal hikes. And with a new 17-hour direct flight from London to Perth, Europe suddenly doesn't seem so far away.

Aboriginal Cultural Tourism

Travellers to Australia have always been thirsty for experiences with its Indigenous cultures, but now more Australians are finding out more about agriculture, astronomy and their country's ancestry through new books, apps and Aboriginal tours.

Small Towns, Small Bars

Small-bar culture has hit Australia's country towns. From Bunbury and Jurien Bay in Western Australia to Ballarat in Victoria, you'll find shopfront bars with low lighting, cosy furnishing, killer cocktail menus or extensive wine and whisky lists.

World-class Tourism Management

While the world is wringing its hands about 'overtourism', Australia gets on with building the best infrastructure to

---

LOCAL KNOWLEDGE

WHAT'S HAPPENING IN AUSTRALIA

Charles Rawlings-Way, Lonely Planet writer

To say that Australia is now familiar with political flux is an understatement. After electing just four prime ministers between 1975 and 2007, the Australian public has endured a grimy series of internal backstabbing events, delivering the nation six prime ministers in the 12 years between 2007 and 2019.

Fuelling this tumult are issues that much of the world can relate to at the moment: immigration and climate change are dividing Australian society like never before, with politicians quick to align their policies with the latest opinion polls. Fortunately, far-right and far-left politics have yet to strangle Australian societal views: despite a rather far-flung location, this has always been a relatively outward-looking, welcoming country. Whether or not new arrivals can afford to buy a house (or a coffee) is another matter...

manage its popularity. Best examples include sunrise at Uluru (p873) and the platform over The Gap near Albany.

Luxury Lodges

Australia's wilderness is astonishingly beautiful, and now travellers with coin – or anyone willing to splash out for a treat – can enjoy remote locations with oodles of 'barefoot luxury' all over the country. See Australia Tourism's website (www.luxurylodgesofaustralia.com.au) for this suite of options.

Vegan Eats

Plant-powered menus and restaurants have taken Australia's foodie scene by storm. Put Yellow (p117) in Sydney, Smith & Daughters (p492) in Melbourne or Raw Kitchen (p904) in Fremantle on your hit list.

Glamping Retreats

Australians have always loved camping, but glamping retreats – replete with wi-fi, swimming pools, yoga and wellness vibes – have taken the experience to a new level. Check out the new Discovery Rottnest Island (p917) in WA for starters.

Camping on Private Land

A host of new apps makes it easier than ever to book a space to set up camp on your Australia road trip away from the crowds; see Go Camping (www.gocamping inaustralia.com) and YouCamp (www.youcamp.com).

Sydney's West Gets Hip

Plans to turn Parramatta into a second centre for the metropolis have come to fruition. The eclectic neighbourhood also hosts Australia's premier short-film festival, Tropfest.

Winery Tourism

Australia has a number of world-class winery regions, all with tasting rooms and some with fine dining attached. A growing number offer more relaxed experiences with an environmental focus: biodynamic and organic vineyards, and pizza ovens over linen tablecloths. Take a tour through WA's Margaret River, SA's McLaren Vale

and Victoria's Mornington Peninsula wine regions and see what the buzz is about.

Hotels You Won't Want To Leave

Hotels have responded to the sharing economy by upping their game. Packed with personality and offering excellent hospitality, restaurants and bars in great locations include Alex Hotel (p896) or Como The Treasury (p895) in Perth, Old Clare Hotel (p109) and Establishment Hotel (p103) in Sydney, plus chains like QT (p483) and Ovolo (p483) in Melbourne.

LISTEN, WATCH & FOLLOW

For inspiration and up-to-date news, visit www.lonelyplanet.com/australia/travel-tips-and-articles and www.lonelyplanet.com/news/australia.

twitter.com/Australia Official Tourism Australia Twitter account (@Australia).

Q&A (www.abc.net.au/qanda/podcast) Podcast of the always-provocative ABC TV show *Q&A*, dissecting the issues (and politicians) in the firing line.

Insta @placesweswim In-the-water Australian culture; see www.placesweswim.com for info on the book.

The Real Thing (www.abc.net.au/radio national/programs/realthing) Podcast zooming in on quirky Aussie characters and stories.

FAST FACTS

Food trend Plant-based eateries

Number of languages spoken in Australian homes 300

Number of venomous snake species 100

Pop 24.4 million

population per sq km

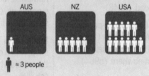

AUS NZ USA

≈ 3 people

If You Like...

Beaches

Whitehaven Beach The jewel of the Whitsundays in Queensland, with powdery white sand and crystal-clear waters. (p378)

Bondi Beach An essential Sydney experience: carve up the surf or just laze around and people-watch. (p85)

Wineglass Bay It's worth the scramble up and over the saddle to visit this gorgeous goblet of Tasmanian sand. (p669)

Bells Beach Australia's best-known surf beach is near Torquay on Victoria's Great Ocean Road. (p548)

Hellfire Bay Talcum-powder sand in WA's Cape Le Grand National Park; precisely in the middle of nowhere. (p964)

Avalon The most photogenic of Sydney's gorgeous northern beaches. (p89)

Cape Tribulation The Queensland rainforest sweeps down to kiss the long stretches of sandy beach. (p435)

Cable Beach The famous camel-strewn beach in Australia's north. (p998)

Aboriginal Culture

Kuku-Yalanji Dreamtime Walks Guided walks through Mossman Gorge in Queensland with Indigenous guides. (p433)

Uluru-Kata Tjuta Cultural Centre Understand local Aboriginal law, custom and religion on Uluru's doorstep. Book an Indigenous guide for the Rock. (p873)

Dampier Peninsula Interact with remote WA communities and learn how to spear fish and catch mudcrabs. (p1004)

Kakadu Animal Tracks Tours through Kakadu's famous Aboriginal rock-art galleries and wetlands, departing Darwin or Jabiru. (p826)

Barunga Festival Aboriginal cultural and sports festival near Katherine. Music, dance, arts, storytelling, crafts, football and spear throwing. (p844)

Injalak Arts Terrific gallery and shop, with a chance to sit with the artists while they paint. (p835)

Lurujarri Dreaming Trail Nine-day walking tours following an ancient Kimberley songline. (p999)

Koorie Heritage Trust In Melbourne: a great place to discover southeastern Aboriginal culture, with tours, and contemporary and traditional art. (p467)

Islands

Kangaroo Island A great spot in South Australia for wildlife watching and super-fresh seafood. (p748)

Bruny Island A windswept, sparsely populated retreat south of Hobart, with magical coastal scenery. (p652)

Fraser Island The world's largest sand island has giant dunes, freshwater lakes and abundant wildlife. (p352)

The Whitsundays Go sailing around this pristine Queensland archipelago. (p378)

North Stradbroke Island Brisbane's holiday playground, with surf beaches and passing whales. (p305)

Rottnest Island A ferry ride from Fremantle in WA is this atoll with adorable quokkas but a chequered history. (p913)

Lizard Island A real get-away-from-it-all isle in Far North Queensland: splash out on a resort or rough it with some camping. (p438)

Wildlife

Whale watching You can spy whales offshore in WA and Queensland. (p342)

Wombats Wilson's Prom or Cradle Mountain are two great spots to see these marsupials. (p589)

Little penguins Phillip Island hosts the world's largest little penguin colony; catch them at sunset marching up from the sea. (p532)

Top: d'Arenberg winery (p741), McLaren Vale

Bottom: Saltwater crocodile, Kakadu National Park (p822)

Quokkas Rottnest Island just off Fremantle in WA has been made famous by these adorable little creatures. (p917)

Birdlife The rich wetlands of Kakadu National Park are great for birdwatching in beautiful landscapes. (p824)

Crocodiles Cahill's Crossing, where Kakadu meets Arnhem Land, is one of many crocodile-watching spots. (p827)

Dingoes The wild dingoes on Fraser Island are the purest breed in Australia. (p356)

Dolphins At Bunbury in WA visitors can see these incredible mammals when they come into the shallows (p934)

Winery Touring

Margaret River Over 150 cellar doors, many with exquisite restaurants, close to surf beaches and towering forests. (p15)

Barossa Valley Home to Australia's greatest reds, with 80-plus cellar doors around historic German-settled villages in SA. (p757)

McLaren Vale An hour south of Adelaide, this is Mediterranean-feeling shiraz heaven with prominent architecture. (p740)

Tamar Valley Tasmania's boutique cool-climate wine area (pinot noir a favourite), a short hop from Launceston. (p684)

Clare Valley SA's Clare Valley makes riesling that rocks in a semi-arid truly Australian landscape. (p762)

Yarra Valley Just outside Melbourne, the Yarra Valley is the place for complex cabernets and farm gates interspersed with cellar doors. (p518)

Hunter Valley Dating back to the 1820s, the Hunter Valley is Australia's oldest wine region – super semillon. (p147)

Granite Belt Queensland's high-altitude wine region produces some surprisingly good wines. (p310)

Hiking

Overland Track Classic, multi-day traverse through Tasmania's heart. (p705)

Uluru Base Walk Take your time on this lap of Uluru: for such a monstrous monolith the atmosphere is surprisingly intimate. (p875)

Great Ocean Walk Walk the length of Victoria's Great Ocean Road with superb views all the way. (p556)

Cape to Cape Track Enjoy Indian Ocean views on this 135km trail from Cape Naturaliste to Cape Leeuwin in WA. (p940)

Six Foot Track The pick of many wilderness walks in the Blue Mountains of NSW. (p145)

Larapinta Trail Majestic 233.5km track along the NT's West MacDonnell Ranges. (p865)

Three Capes Walk Stunning multiday hike with high-spec huts on the Tasman Peninsula. (p662)

Jatbula Trail An intense, five-day jaunt through 66km of Nitmiluk National Park in the NT. (p841)

Bibbulmun Track This track stretches nearly 1000km from the edge of Perth through the southern forests to Albany in WA. (p958)

Solitude

Blue Mountains National Park The closest true wilderness to Sydney: spectacular canyons, cliffs and dense eucalypt forests. (p138)

Ikara-Flinders Ranges National Park Treading a line between desolation and beauty, the ancient outcrops of SA's Ikara (Wilpena Pound) are mesmerising. (p791)

Cobourg Peninsula Watch for sea turtles and whales (and crocodiles!) at this isolated stretch of paradise. (p836)

Nitmiluk National Park Tackle the epic five-day Jatbula Trail in this rugged NT wilderness, with plenty of cooling swim spots on the way. (p840)

Cradle Mountain-Lake St Clair National Park Immerse yourself in Tasmania's sometimes forbidding, ever-photogenic landscape. (p704)

The Kimberley In northern WA you'll find pounding waterfalls, spectacular gorges, barren peaks and an empty coastline. (p995)

Daintree Rainforest Explore Far North Queensland's ancient forest with abundant activities and few tourists. (p432)

Art Galleries

National Gallery of Australia This superb Canberra museum houses 7500-plus works by Aboriginal and Torres Strait Islander artists. (p254)

MONA Australia's most thematically challenging art museum is the talk of Hobart town. (p635)

National Gallery of Victoria International Home to travelling exhibitions par excellence (Monet, Dali, Caravaggio): queue up with the rest of Melbourne to get in. (p467)

Art Gallery of NSW This old-stager keeps things hip with ever-changing exhibitions, including the always-controversial Archibald Prize for portraiture. (p79)

Art Gallery of South Australia On Adelaide's North Terrace, this art gallery does things with progressive style. (p717)

Museum & Art Gallery of the Northern Territory Darwin's classy art gallery is packed full of superb Indigenous Australian art. (p801)

Art Gallery of Western Australia A treasure trove of Indigenous Australian art. (p887)

Otherworldly Landscapes

The Red Centre Expect to be moved by the spiritual significance imbued in these beautiful rock formations at Uluru and Kata Tjuta in the NT. (p872)

Karijini National Park Scramble, abseil, slide and dive through gorges on an adventure in this remote WA park. (p993)

Oodnadatta Track This historic former rail route in SA passes Kati Thanda (Lake Eyre), remote pubs and desert landscapes. (p793)

Nullarbor Plain The ultimate outback road trip: 2700km from Adelaide to Perth across the long, wide, arid Nullarbor Plain. (p786)

4WD to Cape York One of Australia's great wilderness adventures, this is an off-road journey to Queensland's most northern tip: best done on a tour unless you have all the gear. (p442)

Arnhem Land Prepare well in advance, seeking permission and guidance to take a tour of remote Arnhem Land in the NT. (p834)

Purnululu National Park It's worth the journey to wander through these ancient eroded beehive domes in WA. (p1016)

Month by Month

TOP EVENTS
....

Australian Open,
January

Adelaide Fringe,
February

WOMADelaide, March

Vivid Sydney,
May–June

Gourmet Escape,
November

January

January yawns into action as Australia recovers from its collective New Year hangover. Festival season kicks off with outdoor music festivals; Melbourne hosts the Australian Open. It's wet season up north.

⭐ Sydney Festival

The festival promo material says it all: it's big! Held over three summery weeks, this is an affiliation of music, dance, talks, theatre and visual arts in glittering Sydney. Much of it free and family-focused. (p101)

⭐ MONA FOMA

In Launceston in northern Tasmania, MONA FOMA is an annual festival bringing together international artists in the Australian answer to the Venice Biennale – but with more rock music. Edgy, progressive and unexpected performances complement the weird and wonderful museum down in Hobart. (p679)

⭐ Australia Day

The date when the First Fleet landed in 1788, 26 January, is for some Australia's 'birthday', celebrated with BBQs and fireworks. Aboriginal Australians refer to it as Invasion Day or Survival Day and a growing chorus is calling for Australia to 'change the date'.

⭐ Australian Open

Held in Melbourne, the Australian Open draws tennis fanatics from around the planet. The city centre buzzes with international visitors there to take in the courtside action. (p482)

February

February is usually Australia's hottest month: humid and sticky up north as the wet season continues, and often baking hot in South Australia and Victoria. Locals return to school and work while the sun shines on.

⭐ Adelaide Fringe

All the acts that don't (or don't want to) make the cut for the more highbrow Adelaide Festival end up in the month-long Fringe, second only to Edinburgh's version. Hyperactive comedy, music and circus acts spill from the Garden of Unearthly Delights in the parklands. (p723)

⭐ Tropfest

The world's largest short-film festival happens in Parramatta west of Sydney in February, with satellite links to locations in Melbourne, Canberra and Surfers Paradise. A compulsory prop must appear in each entry: a kiss, sneeze, balloon...

⭐ Sydney's Gay & Lesbian Mardi Gras

Mardi Gras is a decades-old festival that culminates (on the first Saturday in March) in a flamboyant parade that runs along Sydney's Oxford St and attracts 300,000 spectators. Gyms empty out and waxing emporiums tally their profits. After-party tickets are gold. (p101)

March

March is harvest time in Australia's vineyards; and in recent years it has been hot, despite its autumnal status.

✿ Adelaide Festival

Culture vultures absorb international and Australian dance, drama, opera and theatre performances at this ultra-classy annual event, Australia's biggest multi-arts festival. (p724)

☆ WOMADelaide

This annual festival of world music, arts, food and dance is held over four days in Adelaide's luscious Botanic Park, attracting crowds from around Australia, with plenty for children to enjoy too. (p724)

☆ Port Fairy Folk Festival

Past the gorgeous Great Ocean Road, southwest of Melbourne (far enough to make it a long weekender), this folksy fest spreads itself through photogenic little Port Fairy. Look for accommodation early. (p565)

☆ Australian F1 Grand Prix

Melbourne's normally tranquil Albert Park explodes with four days of Formula One action in late March. The 5.3km circuit around the lake is known for its smooth, fast surface. The city and colourful sunsets are a bonus. (p482)

April

Melbourne and the Adelaide Hills are atmospheric as European trees turn golden then maroon. Up north the rain is abating and the desert temperatures are becoming manageable. Easter means pricey accommodation everywhere.

☆ Byron Bay Bluesfest

Music erupts over the Easter weekend when 20,000 festival-goers swamp Byron Bay to hear blues and roots bands from all over the world. Held on Tyagarah Tea Tree Farm, 11km north of Byron. Some folks camp. (p183)

🍷 Barossa Vintage Festival

Biennial festival held in odd-numbered years around Easter has processions, maypole dancing, traditional dinners and much Barossa Valley wine (shoot for a sip of Penfolds' famous Grange). (p757)

✿ Tjungu Festival

The otherwise in-between month of April in the Red Centre sees the dynamic Tjungu Festival take over Yulara, with a focus on local Aboriginal culture. (p877)

May

The dry season begins in the NT, northern WA and Far North Queensland: relief from humidity. A great time of the year to visit Uluru-Kata Tjuta National Park.

🏃 Whale Watching

Between May and October along the southeastern Australian coast, migrating southern right and humpback whales come close to shore to feed, breed and calf. See them at Hervey Bay (NSW), Warrnambool (Victoria), Victor Harbor (SA), Albany (WA) and North Stradbroke Island (Queensland). (p1047)

✖ Noosa Food & Wine

One of Australia's best regional culinary fests, with cooking demonstrations, wine tastings, cheese exhibits, feasting on gourmet fare and live concerts at night. Over three days in mid-May. (p327)

☆ Uluru Camel Cup

Camel races within sight of the Rock are a fabulous if rather ungainly sight at this festival that never takes itself too seriously. It all culminates in the Frock Up & Rock Up Gala Ball. (p877)

✿ Vivid Sydney

Kicking off at the end of May, this festival of light, music and ideas brings the crowds to Sydney in winter. (p102)

June

Winter begins: snow falls across the southern Alps ski resorts and football season fills grandstands across the country. Peak season in the tropical north: waterfalls and outback tracks are accessible (accommodation prices less so).

🏃 Ski Season

When winter blows in (June to August), snow bunnies and powder hounds dust off their skis and snowboards and make for the mountains in Victoria and NSW. (p56)

✿ Laura Aboriginal Dance Festival

Sleepy Laura, 330km north of Cairns on the Cape York Peninsula in Far North

Queensland, hosts the largest traditional Indigenous gathering in Australia. Communities from the region come together for dance, song and ceremony. The Laura Races and Rodeo happen the following weekend. (p444)

Derby Boab Festival

Derby strings out its party season from late June to mid-July with concerts, mud footy, horse and mud-crab races, film festivals, poetry readings, art exhibitions, street parades and a dinner out on the mudflats. (p1006)

July

Pubs with open fires, cosy coffee shops and empty beaches down south; packed markets, tours and accommodation up north. Bring warm clothes for anywhere south of Alice Springs.

Beer Can Regatta

The NT festival calendar is studded with quirky gems like this one at Darwin's Mindil Beach, where hundreds of 'boats' constructed from empty beer cans race across the shallows. Much drinking and laughter: staying afloat is a secondary concern. (p806)

Fremantle Festival

Ten days of parades, performances, music, dance, comedy, visual arts, street theatre and workshops. Founded in 1905, it's Australia's longest-running festival. (p894)

Noosa Alive

Noosa – that affluent little beach enclave on Queensland's Sunshine Coast – stops gazing at its own gorgeous reflection in July when this 10-day festival brings in the food, music, dance, readings and workshops. (p326)

Melbourne International Film Festival

Right up there with Toronto and Cannes, MIFF has been running since 1952 and has grown into a wildly popular event; tickets sell like piping-hot chestnuts in the inner city. Myriad short films, feature-length spectaculars and documentaries flicker across city screens from late July into early August. (p507)

August

August is when southerners, sick of winter's grey-sky drear, head to Queensland for some sun. It's almost the last chance to head to the tropical Top End and outback before things get too hot and wet.

Cairns Festival

Running for three weeks from late August to early September, this massive art-and-culture fest brings a stellar program of music, theatre, dance, comedy, film, Indigenous art and public exhibitions. Outdoor events held in public plazas, parks and gardens make good use of Cairns' tropical setting. (p413)

Garma Festival

Out in remote East Arnhem Land, Yirrkala launches the Garma Festival, one of the largest and most vibrant celebrations of Indigenous culture in the Top End. (p836)

Henley-on-Todd Regatta

Alice Springs' iconic 'boat' races on the (usually) bone-dry Todd River take place on the third Saturday in August. Watch from the riverbanks or build your own boat and join in. (p858)

September

Spring heralds a rampant bloom of wildflowers across outback WA and SA, with flower festivals happening in places such as Canberra and Toowoomba. Football finishes and the Spring Racing Carnival begins.

Brisbane Festival

One of Australia's biggest arts festivals runs for 22 days in September and features an impressive line-up of concerts, plays, dance performances and fringe events around the city. It finishes off with Riverfire, an elaborate fireworks show over the river. (p281)

AFL Grand Final

The pinnacle of the Australian Football League – AFL – season is this high-flying spectacle in Melbourne, watched (on TV) by millions of impassioned Aussies. Tickets to the game are scarce, but at half-time everyone's neighbourhood BBQ moves into the local park for a little amateur kick-to-kick. (p482)

Floriade

Floriade is a florid display of spring flowers in

Canberra running from mid-September until mid-October. Locals shake off the winter chills with a look at some blooms. (p259)

☆☆ Perth Wildflower Festival

In September and early October, Kings Park and the Botanic Garden are filled with colourful wildflower displays in the annual Kings Park Festival, which celebrates WA's unique and spectacular flora. Events include guided walks, talks and live music every Sunday. (p894)

October

The weather avoids extremes everywhere: it's a good time to go camping or to hang out at some vineyards (it's a dirty job, but someone's gotta do it...). The build-up to the rains begins in the Top End – *very* humid.

☆☆ Melbourne Festival

This annual arts festival offers some of the best of opera, theatre, dance and visual arts from around Australia and the world. It starts in early October and runs through to early November.

☆ Riverland Wine & Food Festival

Sample Riverland food and drink in Berri, on the banks of the mighty, meandering Murray River (Australia's Mississippi). (p769)

☆☆ Sculpture by the Sea

From late October to early November, the cliff-top trail from Bondi Beach to Tamarama in Sydney transforms into an exquisite sculpture garden. Serious prize money is on offer for the most creative, curious or quizzical offerings from international and local sculptors. (p102)

November

Northern beaches may close due to 'stingers' – jellyfish in the shallow waters off north Queensland, the NT and WA. Outdoor events ramp up; the surf life-saving season flexes its muscles on beaches everywhere.

☆ Melbourne Cup

On the first Tuesday in November, Australia's premier horse race chews up the turf in Melbourne during the Spring Racing Carnival. The whole city takes the day off and many host picnics and put a bet on the horses. A national gambling event! (p482)

☆ Gourmet Escape

The culinary world's heavy hitters descend on regions from Margaret River to Swan Valley for four days of culinary inspiration; celebrity chefs like Nigella Lawson and Rick Stein are often on the program, as well as more accessible, family-friendly events. (p933)

☆ Wangaratta Jazz & Blues

Rural Wangaratta – population roughly 20,000, in rural northeast Victoria – fills with groovy, finger-snappin' beboppers for this esteemed annual jazz and blues fest.

December

Ring the bell, school's out! Holidays usually begin a week or two before Christmas. Cities are packed with shoppers and the weather is desirably hot. Up north, monsoon season is under way: afternoon thunderstorms bring pelting rain.

☆ Woodford Folk Festival

On the Sunshine Coast, the Woodford Folk Festival stages a diverse collection of performers playing folk sounds from across the globe. Runs from 27 December to 1 January. (p340)

☆ Sydney to Hobart Yacht Race

Pack a picnic and join the Boxing Day (26 December) crowds along Sydney's waterfront to watch the start of the Sydney to Hobart, the world's most arduous open-ocean yacht race (628 nautical miles through testing waters). (p102)

☆ Sydney Harbour Fireworks

A fantastic way to ring in the New Year: join the crowds overlooking the harbour as the Sydney Harbour Fireworks light up the night sky. There's a family display at 9pm; the main event erupts at midnight. (p102)

Itineraries

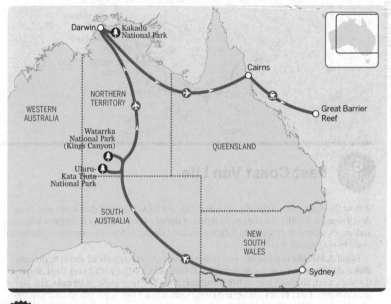

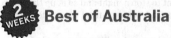

Best of Australia

Two short weeks to explore one of the largest countries on the planet will never be enough, but if you plan carefully and don't mind flying between stops, you can get a taste for Australia's greatest hits.

Fly into **Sydney** to explore one of the world's most charismatic cities. Wander the sparkling waterfront, tour the Sydney Opera House and take a ferry out to Manly, all the while enjoying outstanding museums, cocktail bars, beaches and outdoor markets. Then get out of the city to the Blue Mountains or Royal National Park. Next, fly directly to the Red Centre to spend three days exploring **Uluru-Kata Tjuta National Park** – both Uluru and Kata Tjuta deserve as much time as you can give them – with a night in **Watarrka National Park (Kings Canyon)**.

With a week left, you're heading for the Top End. Fly to **Darwin** and head straight out to **Kakadu National Park** for rock art, river cruises and fabulous wildlife. Swing over to **Cairns**, from where you can spend your last few days in Daintree rainforests at Mossman Gorge and snorkelling the **Great Barrier Reef**.

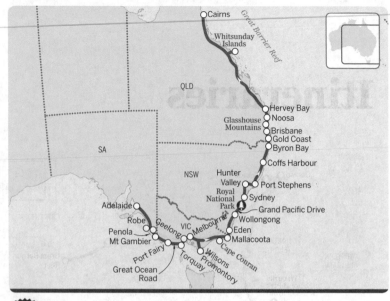

East Coast Van Life

Follow the coast from Adelaide to Cairns and you'll see every kind of Australia, from sleepy seaside hamlets to the bright lights of Sydney Harbour, plus wildlife, wilderness and waves galore. You could do it in four rushed weeks, but we recommend a minimum of six to really soak it all in.

Regal **Adelaide** is a low-key city to begin your Oz odyssey. Head south to dreamy **Robe** via the salty Coorong National Park, snapping a selfie with Larry the Lobster on the way. Next, the blue lake at **Mt Gambier**, after a winery cycle in **Penola** and you're into Victoria. **Port Fairy** is the first Great Ocean Road highlight but more await between here and **Torquay**, where you might want to stop a night and soak up the surf culture. Then it's due north to **Geelong** with its traditional seafront distractions and **Melbourne** for a city culture fix.

From Melbourne the Princess Hwy runs inland through rolling countryside, but choose a couple of spots to detour to the coast: **Wilsons Promontory**, **Cape Conran** and **Mallacoota** are all excellent. Once you enter New South Wales you're on twisting highway past ocean hamlets from **Eden** north to **Wollongong** and **Royal National Park**. Make sure you do the elevated Grand Pacific Drive during daylight hours.

A few days in **Sydney** will recharge your batteries after all that driving as you're not even halfway yet. Next, meander north along the Pacific Hwy through central and northern NSW. Quaff wines in the **Hunter Valley** and stop to splash in the sea at family-friendly **Port Stephens** and **Coffs Harbour,** home of the iconic, kitsch Big Banana. Skip up to **Byron Bay** for wellness awakenings and superb beaches, then head over the Queensland border to the surf- and sun-addled **Gold Coast**. Pause in **Brisbane** for another big-city hit, then amble up through the **Glass House Mountains** and on to the unsung gem, **Noosa** on the Sunshine Coast.

The Bruce Hwy traces the stunning coast into Far North Queensland. Spot some passing whales off the coast of **Hervey Bay** and track further north to the blissful **Whitsundays** archipelago, the coral charms of the **Great Barrier Reef** and the scuba-diving nexus of **Cairns**.

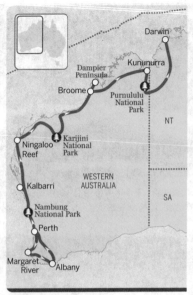

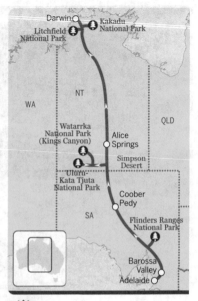

4 WEEKS West Coast Adventure

Feeling adventurous? Fly into Perth, take a quick detour south to Margaret River, then drive north up the coast until you hit Darwin!

Enjoy the laid-back charms of **Perth** and Fremantle, then head southwest for wine, surfing, forests and foodie delights from **Margaret River** to **Albany**. Hammer back past Perth and north to the otherworldly **Nambung National Park**, followed by **Kalbarri** with its soaring sea cliffs and incredible gorges. Then hug the coast for superb whale watching or snorkelling at **Ningaloo Reef**.

Inland are the ironstone hues of the Pilbara. Cool off in the gorges at **Karijini National Park**. Then follow a coastline known as the Big Empty all the way northeast to **Broome**: watch the camels on Cable Beach at sunset. Nearby **Dampier Peninsula** beckons with off-grid camping with Aboriginal communities.

Take the Great Northern Hwy to the sandstone domes of **Purnululu National Park**. Restock at **Kununurra**, then cross the border to the NT. The last leg of your road trip adventure to **Darwin** via Katherine is not too far away.

2 WEEKS Central Australia

This classic 3000km dash up the Stuart Hwy takes you into Australia's desert heart.

From the eat streets and old stone pubs of **Adelaide**, head north to the **Barossa Valley** for world-beating red wines. Next stop is the Clare Valley followed by rust-coloured **Ikara-Flinders Ranges National Park**: Ikara (Wilpena Pound) jags up from the semidesert.

Just off the Stuart Hwy are the opal-tinted dugouts of unique **Coober Pedy**. Continuing north into the desert, the Lasseter Hwy delivers you to iconic **Uluru-Kata Tjuta National Park**. The gaping chasm of **Watarrka National Park (Kings Canyon)** is 300km further north.

Overnight in the desert oasis of **Alice Springs**, then continue north (consider flying) to the wetlands and rock-scapes of World Heritage–listed **Kakadu National Park** and the waterfalls and swimming holes of **Litchfield National Park**.

Darwin is a remote but multicultural city with sunset hawker markets and the excellent Museum & Art Gallery of the Northern Territory.

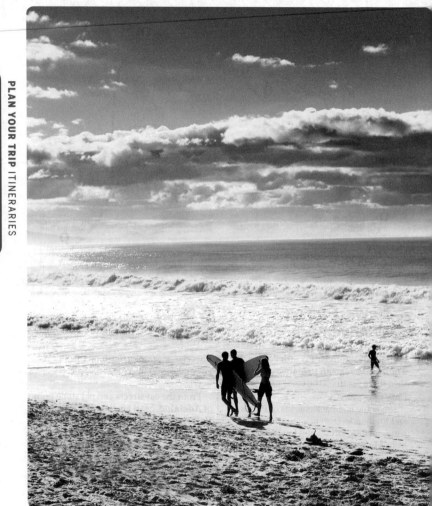

JOHN CRUX PHOTOGRAPHY/GETTY IMAGES ©

Top: Surfers at Noosa (p326), Queensland

Bottom: Pinnacles Desert (p931) stargazing, Western Australia

Plan Your Trip
Family Travel

As any Australian parent will tell you, the toughest part of any family holiday here is getting from A to B. But if you can survive the distances, travelling around Australia with the kids is terrific fun. Beaches, wildlife, museums... There's oodles of interesting stuff to see and do here, inside and out.

Children Will Love...

Beaches & Swimming

Wineglass Bay (p669; Freycinet National Park) Hike with the kids up to the lookout over the much-photographed beach, then careen down the other side for a chilly swim.

Horseshoe Bay (p746; Port Elliot) A divine golden arc on SA's Fleurieu Peninsula, with safe swimming and fab fish and chips.

South Bank Parklands (p276; Brisbane) Get splashy on a safe, sandy beach right in the centre of Brisbane – perfect for little kids.

Scarborough Ocean Pool (p888; Perth) When the Fremantle Doctor sea breeze blows in, beat a retreat to this excellent seaside pool.

Watching Wildlife

Penguin Parade (p532; Phillip Island) Watch this impossibly cute parade of little penguins returning home at dusk.

Ningaloo Marine Park (p986; Ningaloo Coast) Slow-cruising whale sharks are just one of the astonishing number of species at this spectacularly diverse WA park.

Alice Springs Desert Park (p852; Alice Springs) All the critters of central Australia in one place, including many that are extremely difficult to spy out on the trail.

Sea Life Sunshine Coast (p334; Mooloolaba) The southern hemisphere's largest oceanarium is the place to see sharks, jellyfish, stingrays, seals and dazzling fish.

Keeping Costs Down

Accommodation

Often beach-side, Australia's caravan parks are great with kids: sleep in a cute cabin (or tent!), then hit the surf/swimming pool/games room/giant trampoline/mini-golf... A family-sized cabin costs a lot less than a family-sized hotel room.

Transport

Kids receive discounts on public transport in Australian cities, or sometimes travel free. Family day-passes are also available. If you're hiring a car, BYO car seat rather than hiring one: the major domestic airlines let you carry these for free (and prams too).

Eating

In pub dining rooms, dedicated kids' menus are the norm (even if selections are unimaginative: ham-and-pineapple pizza, fish fingers, chicken nuggets...). Australia also has a proliferation of free electric BBQs in parks, or there's always fish and chips by the beach.

Activities

There's no shortage of active, interesting and amusing things for kids to experience in Australia. Museums, zoos, aquariums and science centres have interactive exhibits to get kids thinking. And of course, outdoor destinations are always a winner: hiking, swimming, surfing...

Science & Technology

Questacon (p256; Canberra) On the shores of Lake Burley Griffin, the National Science & Technology Centre delivers myriad high-tech diversions.

Sciencentre (p276; Brisbane) Visited by every Queenslander in their childhood, Brisbane's Sciencentre is popular and entertaining.

Scitech (p887; Perth) On a rainy day in Perth (it does happen, occasionally), Scitech fills with school kids riding the learning curve.

Fun Parks

Luna Park (p478; Melbourne) St Kilda's old-style amusement park, built in 1912, is a cultural icon. Creepy Mr Moon's gaping mouth swallows you up as you enter.

Luna Park (p87; Sydney) Right on Sydney Harbour, this is a magical place – as much for the spectacular ferry ride to get here as the rides.

Adventure World (p890; Perth) With plenty of preposterously fast roller coasters and splashy water-park fun, this is an exhausting day out.

Gold Coast Theme Parks (p317; Gold Coast) The gravity-defying roller coasters and water slides at these parks offer some seriously dizzying action.

Fast Food

Beerenberg Farm (p736; Hahndorf) Pick your own strawberries at this famous family-run patch in the Adelaide Hills.

Harvest (p683; Launceston) Get set for an awesome picnic with a hamper full of good stuff form this Saturday-morning market.

Central Market (p716; Adelaide) Taste-test your way through the buzzy aisles of this undercover market. Chinatown is right next door: dumplings?

Region by Region

Sydney & New South Wales

Beaches, surf lessons, salt-water pools, the Art Gallery of NSW kids' program, ferry rides... Sydney (p69) is an obvious family choice. The Blue Mountains and the NSW North and South Coasts are even better: beaches, bushwalks, wildlife parks...

Canberra & the ACT

Canberra (p257) has some of Australia's best museums, including the National Gallery of Australia and Questacon. Kangaroo-filled Namadgi National Park is nearby.

Queensland

Famous Australia Zoo and the Gold Coast theme parks are kid-pleasers – but Queensland's real kiddie-boon is the coast, especially the Gold and Sunshine Coast beaches. The Great Barrier Reef offers superb snorkelling. In Brisbane (p277) South Bank delivers super museums and safe swimming.

Melbourne & Victoria

Wilsons Promontory is a family fave, with bushwalks, swimming, surfing and wildlife. Phillip Island's Penguin Parade is another essential. Great Ocean Road offers lighthouses, beaches, kooky rock formations, koalas... In Melbourne (p463), ride the trams, go to the football or soak up some history at the Melbourne Museum.

Tasmania

Tasmania is excellent with kids: infamous Port Arthur is super-educational (ghost tours!). In Hobart (p639), don't miss a drive up kunanyi/Mt Wellington, the Salamanca Market buskers and the Tasmanian tiger exhibit at the Tasmanian Museum & Art Gallery.

Adelaide & South Australia

Adelaide (p717) has the Adelaide Zoo, artefact-rich South Australian Museum, cricket and football at the Adelaide Oval, and the Central Market for a quick-fire lunch. There are beaches and caves on the Limestone Coast, wildlife and walks in the Flinders Ranges and houseboats on the Murray River.

Darwin & the Northern Territory

Spot captive wildlife in the Territory Wildlife Park or Alice Springs Desert Park, or Kakadu National Park's wild critters. Darwin (p800) gets hot and sticky, but the Mindil Beach Market is cool-evening fun. Uluru-Kata Tjuta National Park is must.

Perth & Western Australia

Swimming with whale sharks at Ningaloo, learning about dolphins in Bunbury, spotting humpacks at Albany: uncrowded WA is perfect with kids. Perth (p897) offers free water parks and plenty of beach action.

Good to Know

Look out for the 👪 icon for family-friendly suggestions throughout this guide.

Accommodation Many hotels can supply cots and (sometimes) baby baths – larger hotels may also have child-minding services. B&Bs are often kid-free.

Breastfeeding Most Australians have a relaxed attitude about breastfeeding in public.

Change rooms All cities and most major towns have centrally located public rooms – in parks, libraries or departments stores – where parents can go to nurse their baby or change a nappy (diaper). Check with local tourist offices.

Child care Australia's numerous licensed child-care agencies offer babysitting services. Check with local tourist offices.

Child safety seats Major car-hire companies can supply child safety seats for a fee; install them yourself. Call taxi companies in advance to organise child safety seats. The rules for travelling in taxis with kids vary from state to state: in most places safety seats aren't legally required, but must be used if available.

Eating out Many cafes, pubs and restaurants offer kids' meals; many also supply high chairs.

Playgrounds Plentiful throughout Australia; see www.playgroundfinder.com.

Prams There's good pram access in most cities. Search for 'pram hire' on www.gumtree.com.au.

Useful Resources

Lonely Planet Kids (www.lonelyplanetkids.com) Loads of activities and great family travel blog content.

My Family Travel Map Australia (shop.lonely planet.com) Introduce kids to Australia and help them plan the trip with this giant fold-out continental map.

LetsGoKids (wwwletsgokids.com.au) Touring advice and highlights across Tasmania, NSW, Victoria, WA and the NT.

Kids Holidays Online (www.kidsholidaysonline.com.au/australia.htm) Bookings for kid-friendly accommodation.

Kids' Corner

Say What?

arvo	afternoon
bickie	biscuit
brekkie	breakfast
dunny	toilet
prezzie	present
servo	petrol station
undies	underpants

Did You Know? ⓘ

- Unlike ostriches, emus can't walk backwards!
- Australia has 10,685 beaches.

Have You Tried?

MPIX/SHUTTERSTOCK ©

Vegemite
Salty black sandwich spread

Plan Your Trip

Your Reef Trip

The World Heritage–listed Great Barrier Reef, stretching over 2000km from just south of the Tropic of Capricorn (near Gladstone in Queensland) to just south of Papua New Guinea, is the most extensive reef system in the world, and made entirely by living organisms.

Best Reef Experiences

Watching Wildlife

Watching sea turtles hatching on Lady Elliot or Heron Island; spying reef sharks, turtles and rays on a kayaking trip off Green Island; spotting koalas on Magnetic Island and dingoes on Fraser Island.

Snorkelling

Pack your mask, your fins and your snorkel and head to Knuckle, Hardy and Fitzroy Reefs, Magnetic Island or the Whitsunday Islands.

View from Above

Take a scenic chopper or plane ride from Cairns, Hamilton or the Whitsunday Islands. Skydiving over Airlie Beach is fun too.

Sailing Experience

Sail from Airlie Beach through the Whitsunday Islands, or explore Agincourt Reef from Port Douglas.

When to Go

High season on the Reef is from June to December. For the best underwater visibility, visit between August and January.

➡ From December to March northern Queensland (north of Townsville) is working its way through the wet season, bringing oppressive heat and monsoonal rainfall. From July to September things are much drier and cooler.

➡ Anytime is a good time to visit the Whitsundays. Winter (June to August) can be pleasantly warm, but you'll occasionally need a jumper. As per the rest of Queensland, summers here (December to March) are hot and humid.

➡ Southern and central Queensland experience mild winters (June to August) – cool enough for diving or snorkelling in a wetsuit.

Picking Your Spot

The GBR is enormous! It follows that there are myriad popular spots from which to access it, but bear in mind that the qualities of individual areas do change over time depending on the weather and recent damage.

Islands

Rising above the waterline throughout the Reef are hundreds of islands and cays, offering instant access to the undersea marvels. Here is a list of some of our favourite islands, travelling from south to north.

Lady Elliot Island A coral cay that's popular with birdwatchers: there are around 57 bird species living here. Sea turtles also nest here and it's possibly the best location on the Reef to see manta rays. There's a resort, or you can visit Lady Elliot on a day trip from Bundaberg.

Heron Island A tiny coral cay sitting in the middle of a huge spread of reef. It's a diving mecca, but the snorkelling is also good and it's possible to do a reef walk from here. Heron is a nesting ground for green and loggerhead turtles and home to some 30 species of birds.

Hamilton Island The big daddy of the Whitsunday resort islands, Hamilton is a sprawling family-friendly development laden with infrastructure. The atmosphere isn't exactly intimate, but there's a wealth of tours heading from here to outer-reef spots that can't be explored from the mainland.

Hook Island An outer Whitsunday isle fringed with reefs. There's excellent swimming and snorkelling here, and the island offers good bushwalking. There's affordable accommodation on Hook and it's easily accessed from Airlie Beach – a top choice if you're working with modest funds.

Orpheus Island A national park and one of the Reef's most exclusive and romantic hideaways. This island is great for snorkelling – you can step right off the beach and be surrounded by the Reef's colourful marine life. Clusters of fringing reefs also provide plenty of diving opportunities.

Green Island Another of the Reef's true coral cays. The fringing reefs here are considered to be among the most beautiful surrounding any island, and the diving and snorkelling are first rate. Cloaked in dense rainforest, the entire island is a national park. Bird life abounds.

Lizard Island Remote, rugged and the perfect place to beat a retreat from civilisation. Expect talcum-white beaches, remarkably blue water and very few visitors. The Reef's best-known dive site is at Cod Hole, where you can paddle up next to docile potato cod that weigh as much as 60kg each.

Mainland Gateways

The major mainland Reef access points all offer slightly different experiences or activities. Here's a brief overview, ordered from south to north.

Agnes Water & Town of 1770 Small towns and good choices if you want to beat the crowds. Tours head to Fitzroy Reef Lagoon, one of the most pristine sections of the Reef, where visitor numbers are still limited. The still-water lagoon is excellent for snorkelling and almost as impressive when viewed from a boat.

Gladstone A slightly bigger town but still a relatively small gateway. It's an exceptional choice for divers and snorkellers, being the closest access point to the Southern Reef Islands and innumerable cays, including Lady Elliot Island.

Airlie Beach A small town with a big party scene and a flotilla of sailing outfits. The major lure here is spending a few days aboard a boat and seeing some of the Whitsunday Islands' fringing coral reefs. Whether you're travelling five-star or no-star, there'll be a tour to match your budget.

Townsville A top gateway for divers. A four- or five-night live-aboard tour around numerous islands and pockets of the Reef is a great choice. In particular, Kelso Reef and the wreck of the SS *Yongala* are teeming with marine life. There are also a couple of day-trip options on glass-bottomed boats. Reef HQ Aquarium, which is basically a version of the Reef in an aquarium, is also here.

Mission Beach Closer to the Reef than any other gateway destination. It's a small, quiet town with a few boat and diving tours to sections of the outer reef. The choice isn't huge, but neither are the crowds.

Cairns The main launching pad for Reef tours with a bewildering number of operators offering inexpensive day trips on large boats to intimate five-day luxury charters. Trips cover a wide section of the Reef, with some operators travelling as far north as Lizard Island. Inexpensive tours are likely to travel to inner, less pristine reefs. Scenic flights are also an option.

Port Douglas A swanky resort town and a gateway to the Low Isles and Agincourt Reef, an outer ribbon reef featuring crystal-clear water and hyper-coloured corals. Diving, snorkelling and

---

RESOURCES

Dive Queensland (www.dive-queensland.com.au) Queensland's dive tourism association, with info on dive locations, dive operators, live-aboards and diving schools.

Great Barrier Reef Marine Park Authority (www.gbrmpa.gov.au) Reef-related info on climate change, conservation, tourism and fisheries.

Queensland Department of National Parks (https://parks.des.qld.gov.au) Info, including permits, for all national parks including marine parks.

N 0 ——— 200 km
0 ——— 100 miles

CORAL SEA

Lizard Island

○ Cooktown

○ **PORT DOUGLAS**

Green Island
○ Fitzroy Island
CAIRNS

○ Innisfail

Tully ○ **MISSION BEACH**
Dunk Island

Hinchinbrook Island

Ingham ○

Magnetic Island

TOWNSVILLE ○

○ Charters Towers

Bowen ○

Airlie ○ Beach

Hamilton Islnd
Lindeman Island

○ Mackay

GREAT BARRIER REEF

Whitsunday Islands

Tropic of Capricorn

Emerald ○

Rockhampton ○

Great Keppel Island

○ Gladstone

○ **TOWN OF 1770**

Bundaberg ○

Hervey Bay ○

Maryborough ○

Fraser Island

○ Miles

○ Noosa

PORT DOUGLAS

Book yourself onto an upmarket catamaran day trip out to Agincourt Reef. (p427)

CAIRNS

Hop over from Cairns for a luxurious sojourn on Green Island, with its rainforest and fringing coral. On a budget? Take a daytrip to Fitzroy and/or Green Island. (p399)

MISSION BEACH

Unwind on Mission Beach with rainforest walks, and overnight on nearby Dunk Island, which has good swimming, kayaking and hiking. (p394)

TOWNSVILLE

In Townsville, visit the excellent Reef HQ Aquarium for a dry-land reef encounter. If you're an experienced diver, book a trip on a live-aboard boat to dive the SS *Yongala* wreck. And don't miss the koalas on Magnetic Island. (p383)

THE WHITSUNDAYS

From backpacker-friendly Airlie Beach, explore white-sand Whitsundays beaches and encircling coral reefs via a tour or sailing cruise. (p377)

TOWN OF 1770

Head to the Town of 1770 and day trip out to Lady Musgrave Island for semisubmersible coral viewing, plus snorkelling or diving in the definitive blue lagoon. (p358)

cruising trips tend to be classier, pricier and less crowded than in Cairns. You can also take a scenic flight from here.

Camping

Pitching a tent on a tropical island is a unique and affordable way to experience the Great Barrier Reef. Campers can enjoy idyllic tropical settings at a fraction of the cost of the five-star resorts that may be just down the track. Facilities range from virtually nothing (a sandy patch in the shade) to well-established campgrounds with showers, flushing toilets, interpretive signs and picnic tables.

Most island campgrounds are remote, so ensure you're adequately prepared for medical and general emergencies. Wherever you stay, you'll need to bring your own food and drinking water (5L per day per person is recommended). Inclement weather can often prevent planned pick-ups, so bring enough supplies to last an extra three or four days in case you get stranded. Camp only in designated areas, keep to marked trails and take out everything that you bring in with you. Fires are banned – you'll need a gas stove or similar.

National park camping permits need to be booked in advance, either online or by phone through the **Queensland Department of National Parks** (https://parks.des.qld.gov.au).

Here are a few of our fave camping spots to start you dreaming:

Whitsunday Islands Nearly a dozen beautifully sited camping areas, scattered across the islands of Hook, Whitsunday and Henning.

Capricornia Cays Camping available on Masthead Island, North West Island and Lady Musgrave Island – a fantastic, uninhabited isle with boat-access camping, limited to a maximum of 40 people. Off Town of 1770.

Dunk Island Equal parts resort and national park with good swimming, kayaking and hiking. Off Mission Beach.

Fitzroy Island Resort and national park with short bushwalking trails and coral just off the sand. Off Cairns.

Frankland Islands Coral-fringed island with white-sand beaches. Off Cairns.

Lizard Island Amazing beaches, magnificent coral and abundant wildlife. Visitors mostly arrive by plane from Cairns.

Orpheus Island Secluded island (accessible by air from Townsville or Cairns) with lush tropical forest and superb fringing reef.

MAKING A POSITIVE CONTRIBUTION

The Great Barrier Reef is incredibly fragile: it's worth taking some time to educate yourself on responsible practices to minimise the impact of your visit.

➡ It is an offence to damage or remove coral in the marine park.

➡ If you touch or walk on coral, you'll damage it (and probably get some nasty cuts).

➡ Don't touch or harass marine animals, and don't enter the water near a dugong.

➡ If you have a boat, be aware of the rules in relation to anchoring around the reef, including 'no anchoring areas' to avoid coral damage.

➡ If you're diving, check that you are weighted correctly before entering the water and keep your buoyancy control well away from the reef. Ensure that equipment such as secondary regulators and gauges aren't dragging over the reef.

➡ If you're snorkelling (especially if you're a beginner), practise your technique away from coral until you've mastered control in the water.

➡ Hire a wetsuit or a 'rashie' rather than slathering on sunscreen, which can damage the reef.

➡ Watch where your fins are – try not to stir up sediment or disturb coral.

➡ Note that there are limits on the amount and types of shells that you can collect.

➡ Take all litter away with you – even biodegradable materials like apple cores – and dispose of it back on the mainland.

Diving & Snorkelling the Reef

Much of the diving and snorkelling on the Reef is boat-based, although on some islands you can walk straight off the beach and dip into the coral kingdom just offshore. Free use of snorkelling gear is usually part of any cruise to the Reef; cruises generally involve around three hours of underwater wandering. Overnight or 'liveaboard' trips provide a more in-depth experience and greater coverage of the reefs.

If you're keen to experience scuba diving but don't have a diving certificate, many operators provide introductory dives – a guided dive where an experienced diver conducts an underwater tour. A lesson in safety and procedure is given beforehand and you don't require a five-day Professional Association of Diving Instructors (PADI) course or a 'buddy'.

Boat Excursions

Unless you're staying on a coral atoll in the middle of the Great Barrier Reef, you'll need to join a boat excursion to experience the Reef's real beauty. Day trips set sail from many places along the coast, as well as from island resorts. Trips typically include the use of snorkelling gear, snacks and a buffet lunch, with scuba diving an optional extra. On some boats a naturalist or marine biologist presents a talk on Reef ecology.

Boat trips vary dramatically in passenger numbers, type of vessel and quality – which is reflected in the price – so it's worth getting all the details before committing. When selecting a tour, consider the vessel (motorised catamaran or sailing ship), the number of passengers (anywhere from six to 400), and what kind of extras are offered (food, talks, hotel transfers etc). The destination is also key: outer reefs are usually more pristine; inner reefs often show signs of damage from humans, coral bleaching and the coral-eating crown of thorns starfish. Some operators offer the option of a trip in a glass-bottomed boat or semi-submersible.

Live-Aboards

If you're keen to do as much diving as possible, a live-aboard Reef experience is an excellent option. Trips generally involve three dives per day, plus some night dives,

all in more remote parts of the Great Barrier Reef. Trip lengths generally range from one to six nights. Three-day/three-night voyages, which allow up to 11 dives (nine day and two night dives), are the most common.

It's worth checking out the various options as some boats offer specialist itineraries following marine life and events such as whale migrations or coral spawning, or offer trips to more remote spots like the far northern reefs, Pompey Complex, Coral Sea Reefs or Swain Reefs.

It's recommended to go with operators who are Dive Queensland members: see www.dive-queensland.com.au for a full list. Membership ensures that operators follow a minimum set of guidelines. Ideally, they are also accredited by Ecotourism Australia (www.ecotourism.org.au).

Popular departure points for live-aboard dive vessels, along with the locales they visit, include the following:

Bundaberg Access to the Bunker Island group, including Lady Musgrave and Lady Elliot Islands. Some trips visit the Fitzroy, Llewellyn and rarely visited Boult Reefs, or Hoskyn and Fairfax Islands.

Town of 1770 Bunker Island group.

Gladstone Swains and Bunker Island group.

Mackay Lihou Reef and the Coral Sea.

Airlie Beach The Whitsundays, Knuckle Reef and Hardy Reef.

Townsville SS *Yongala* wreck, plus canyons of Wheeler and Keeper Reefs.

Cairns Cod Hole, Ribbon Reefs, the Coral Sea and the far northern reefs.

Port Douglas Osprey Reef, Cod Hole, Ribbon Reefs, Coral Sea and the far northern reefs.

Dive Courses

In Queensland there are numerous places where you can learn to dive, take a refresher course or improve your submarine skills. Dive courses here are generally of a high standard, and all schools teach either PADI or Scuba Schools International (SSI) qualifications. Which certification you choose isn't as important as choosing a good instructor, so be sure to seek local recommendations and meet with the instructor before committing to a program.

A popular place to learn is Cairns, where you can choose between courses for the budget-minded (four-day courses from around $900) that combine pool training and reef dives; and longer, more intensive courses that include reef diving on a live-aboard boat (five-day courses including three-day/two-night live-aboard from $1500).

Other places where you can learn to dive and then head out on the Reef include Airlie Beach, Bundaberg, Hamilton Island, Magnetic Island, Mission Beach, Port Douglas and Townsville.

Diving for Nondivers

Several operators from Cairns use systems that allow nondivers to 'dive' using surface-supplied air systems. With helmet diving, hoses provide fresh surface air to divers via astronaut-like helmets so you can breathe normally and your face and hair stay dry (you can even wear glasses). There's also no need to know how to swim as you'll be walking on a submerged platform, 4m to 5m below the surface. Walks typically last 15 to 20 minutes, and are conducted under the guidance of a qualified dive instructor. Prices start at around $200. Anyone older than 12 years and over 140cm tall can participate, although as with scuba diving, certain medical conditions will prohibit participation (asthma, heart disease, pregnancy, epilepsy).

Safety Guidelines for Diving

Before embarking on a scuba-diving, skin-diving or snorkelling trip, carefully consider the following points to ensure a safe and enjoyable experience:

➡ If scuba diving, make sure you have a current diving certification card from a recognised scuba-diving instructional agency.

➡ Ensure you're healthy and feel comfortable diving.

➡ Obtain reliable information from a reputable local dive operation about the physical and environmental conditions at the dive site, such as water temperature, visibility and tidal movements, and find out how local divers deal with these considerations.

➡ Be aware that underwater conditions vary significantly from one region (or even site) to another. Seasonal changes can significantly alter any site and dive conditions. These differences influence the way divers dress for a dive and what diving techniques they use.

TOP SNORKELLING SITES

Some non-divers may wonder if it's really worth going to the Great Barrier Reef 'just to snorkel'. The answer is a resounding 'Yes!'. Much of the rich, colourful coral lies just underneath the surface (as coral needs bright sunlight to flourish) and is easily accessible. Here's a round-up of what we think are the top snorkelling sites, grouped by key access points:

Town of 1770 Fitzroy Reef Lagoon

Capricorn Coast Heron Island, Great Keppel Island, Lady Elliot Island, Lady Musgrave Island

Whitsundays Hook Island, Hayman Island, Border Island, Hardy Reef, Knuckle Reef

Cairns Lizard Island, Michaelmas Reef, Hastings Reef, Norman Reef, Saxon Reef, Green Island

Port Douglas Opal Reef, Agincourt Reef, Mackay Reef

➡ Be aware of local laws, regulations and etiquette with regard to marine life and the environment.

➡ Dive only at sites within your realm of experience. If available, engage the services of a competent, professionally trained dive instructor or divemaster.

➡ To minimise the risk of residual nitrogen in the blood that can cause decompression injury, your last dive should be completed at least 24 hours before flying anywhere – even in a balloon or for a parachute jump. It's fine to dive soon after arriving by air.

Top Reef Dive Spots

The Great Barrier Reef is home to some of the planet's best reef-diving sites. Here are a few top spots to get you started:

SS Yongala A sunken shipwreck that has been home to a vivid marine community for more than 90 years.

Cod Hole Go nose to nose with a potato cod.

Heron Island Join a crowd of colourful fish, straight off the beach.

Lady Elliot Island Has 19 highly regarded sites.

Pixie Bommie Delve into the Reef's after-five world on a night dive.

TANYA PUNTTI/SHUTTERSTOCK ©

Top: Dive instructor, Airlie Beach (p373)

Bottom: Beaked coral fish

Plan Your Trip

Your Outback Trip

Exactly where Australia's outback starts and ends is hard to pin down on a map. But you'll know you're there when the sky yawns enormously wide, the horizon is unnervingly empty, and the sparse inhabitants you encounter are incomparably resilient and distinctively Australian. Out here, enduring Indigenous culture, unique wildlife and intriguing landscapes await the modern-day adventurer.

When to Go

Best Times

Winter June through August is when the outback comes into its own. Clear skies, moderate daytime temperatures, cold nights and good driving conditions are the norm. Winter is also the best time to visit the tropical Top End, with low humidity, dry days and mild temperatures.

Spring September and October is springtime – and prime time to head into the outback, especially if you're into wildflowers. The MacDonnell Ranges near Alice Springs and the Flinders Ranges in northern South Australia erupt with colourful blooms.

Avoid

Summer Central Australia heats up over summer (December through February) – temperatures approaching 50°C aren't uncommon. With the heat comes dusty roads, overheating cars, driver fatigue, irritating flies and the need to carry extra water. In the Top End the build-up to the wet season is uncomfortably humid, with the eventual rains often flooding highways and making dirt roads impassable.

Best...

For Indigenous Culture

Kakadu National Park in the tropical Top End offers ancient rock art and cultural tours led by traditional owners.

Outback National Park

Iconic Uluru in Uluru-Kata Tjuta National Park is unmissable; nearby Kata Tjuta is just as impressive.

Outback Track

Oodnadatta Track: 620km of dust, emus, lizards, salt lakes and railroad remnants.

Outback Road Trip

The Stuart Hwy from Darwin to Port Augusta is an epic journey through the central deserts.

Season to Visit

June to October: mild temperatures, dry weather and spring wildflowers.

Things to Pack

Sunscreen, sunglasses, a hat, insect repellent, water and road-trip tunes.

Planes, Trains or Automobiles

Air The major airlines fly into Alice Springs and Yulara (for the central deserts) and Darwin (for the tropical Top End), departing from Perth, Adelaide and the major east-coast cities. From Darwin or Alice you can join a guided tour or hire a 4WD.

Car You can drive through the Red Centre from Darwin to Adelaide with detours to Uluru and Kakadu and more without ever leaving sealed roads. However, if you really want to see outback Australia, there are plenty of side routes for 4WDs that define 'off the beaten track' adventure.

Train Travelling on the *Indian Pacific* between Perth and Sydney or the legendary *Ghan* between Adelaide and Darwin is slow and expensive, but takes you through parts of the country you wouldn't see otherwise (and is a good way to beat the heat if you're travelling in summer).

Essential Outback

The Red Centre: Alice Springs, Uluru & Kings Canyon

Alice is big enough to have some great places to eat and stay. Nearby, the East and West MacDonnell Ranges offer red rocks, dramatic canyons and plenty of wildlife. Palm Valley in Finke National Park is one of the outback's least-known gems. People from all over the globe swarm to Uluru; the local Anangu people request that you didn't climb it. Watarrka (Kings Canyon), about 300km north of Uluru, is a spectacular chasm carved into the rugged landscape.

The Stuart Highway: Port Augusta to Darwin

The paved Stuart Hwy between Port Augusta and Darwin is one of Australia's greatest road trips: 2724km of red sand, scrub and galloping emus. Heading north, stop at pock-marked Coober Pedy – the opal-mining capital of the world – and detour to Uluru. The amazing gorges of Nitmiluk (Katherine Gorge) National Park are also en route. Kakadu National Park is too, with its World Heritage-listed tropical wetlands. Liquid refreshments await on Darwin's Mitchell St.

The Tropics: Darwin, Kakadu & Katherine

In the tropical Top End the wet and dry seasons determine how easy it is to get from A to B. In the Wet, roads become impassable and crocodiles move freely through the wetlands...but Kakadu resorts approach half-price! Darwin isn't technically in the outback, but it still feels like a frontier town. Big-country-town Katherine, three hours to the south, is the jumping-off point for the astonishing Nitmiluk (Katherine Gorge) National Park.

The Victoria Highway: Katherine to the Kimberley

The Victoria Hwy is a significant section of the epic Savannah Way from Cairns to Broome, the classic 'across-the-top'

ROAD TRAINS

On many outback highways you'll see thundering road trains: huge trucks with two or even three trailers, some more than 50m long. These things don't move over for anyone: it's like a scene from *Mad Max* having one bear down on you at 120km/h.

A few tips: when you see a road train approaching on a narrow bitumen road, slow down and pull over – if the truck has to put its wheels off the road to pass you, the resulting barrage of stones will almost certainly smash your windscreen. When trying to overtake one, allow plenty of room (about a kilometre) to complete the manoeuvre. Road trains throw up a lot of dust on dirt roads, so if you see one coming it's best to just pull over and stop until it's gone past.

And while you're on outback roads, don't forget to give the standard bush greeting to oncoming drivers – it's simply a matter of lifting the index finger off the steering wheel to acknowledge your fellow explorer.

route. Leaving Katherine it winds through cattle country, passing lovely river-and-escarpment country around Victoria River Crossing. Look forward to 4WD and hiking opportunities, outback camping, rock art, national parks, gorges, crocodiles and barramundi fishing. The immense Gregory National Park, Keep River National Park and legendary Gibb River Road require a 4WD.

Facilities

Outback roadhouses emerge from the heat haze with some regularity: even on the remote Oodnadatta Track or Tanami Road you'll find petrol and cold beer every few hundred kilometres. Most roadhouses sell 24-hour fuel; some have fry-up restaurants and accommodation out the back, including camp sites, air-conditioned motel-style rooms and/or basic cabins.

Organised Tours

If you don't feel like doing all the planning and driving, a guided tour is a great way to experience the Aussie outback. These range from beery backpacker jaunts between outback pubs, to Indigenous cultural tours and multiday bushwalking treks into remote wilderness.

Outback Tracks

An interesting/challenging way get from A to B in the outback is by detouring along historic cattle and rail routes. Some of these tracks are passable in a regulation 2WD, but a 4WD will make for a much more comfortable drive. Be prepared for isolation and minimal facilities, and don't attempt tougher routes during summer or if there has been recent flooding.

Unpaved Tracks
Mereenie Loop Road

Starting in Alice Springs, this well-used track is an alternative route to the big attractions of the Red Centre. The route initially follows the sealed Larapinta and

PLAN YOUR TRIP YOUR OUTBACK TRIP

> **PERMITS FOR ABORIGINAL LANDS**
> ●●●●●●●●●●●●●●●●●●●●●●●●●●●●●●
> ➡ In the outback, if you plan on driving through pastoral stations and Aboriginal communities you may need to get permission first. This is for your safety; many travellers have tackled this rugged landscape on their own and required complicated rescues after getting lost or breaking down.
>
> ➡ Permits are issued by various Aboriginal land-management authorities. Processing applications can take anywhere from a few minutes to a few days.

Namatjira Drives skirting the magnificent MacDonnell Ranges to Glen Helen Gorge. Beyond Glen Helen the route meets the Mereenie Loop Rd, which requires a permit ($5) and is usually heavily corrugated (4WD terrain) en route to Watarrka (Kings Canyon) National Park. From Watarrka the sealed Luritja Rd connects to the Lasseter Hwy and Uluru-Kata Tjuta National Park.

Oodnadatta Track

Mostly running parallel to the old *Ghan* railway line through outback SA, this iconic track is fully bypassed by the sealed Stuart Hwy to the west. Using this track, it's 429km from Marree in the northern Flinders Ranges, to Oodnadatta, then another 216km to the Stuart Hwy at Marla. If it's been dry, most well-prepared conventional vehicles should be able to manage this fascinating route, but a 4WD will do it in style.

Birdsville Track

Spanning 517km from Marree in SA to Birdsville just across the border of Queensland, this old droving trail is one of Australia's best-known outback routes – although it's not known for spectacular and varying scenery. It's often feasible to travel it in a well-prepared, conventional vehicle but not recommended.

Strzelecki Track

This track covers much of the same territory through SA as the Birdsville Track. Starting south of Marree at Lyndhurst, it

OUTBACK DRIVING & SAFETY CHECKLIST

••

Due to the lack of water, long distances between fuel stops and isolation, you need to be particularly organised and vigilant when travelling in the outback, especially on remote sandy tracks.

Communication

➡ Report your route and schedule to the police, a friend or relative.

➡ Mobile phones are useless if you venture off the highway. Consider hiring a satellite phone, high-frequency (HF) radio transceiver equipped to pick up the Royal Flying Doctor Service bases, or emergency position-indicating radio beacon (EPIRB).

➡ In an emergency, stay with your vehicle; it's easier to spot than you are, and you won't be able to carry enough drinking water very far.

➡ If you do become stranded, consider setting fire to a spare tyre (let the air out first): the smoke will be visible for kilometres.

Your Vehicle

➡ Have your vehicle serviced and checked before you leave.

➡ Load your vehicle evenly, with heavy items inside and light items on the roof rack.

➡ Carry essentials: spare fuel, spare tyre (two is preferable), fan belt, radiator hose, tyre-pressure gauge and air pump, shovel, off-road jack and a snatch strap or tow rope for extraction when you're stuck.

Supplies & Equipment

➡ Carry plenty of water: in warm weather allow 5L per person per day and an extra amount for the radiator.

➡ Bring plenty of food in case of a breakdown.

➡ Carry a first-aid kit, a good set of maps, a torch with spare batteries, a compass and a GPS.

Weather & Road Conditions

➡ Check road conditions before travelling: travelling: roads that are passable in the Dry (March to October) can disappear beneath water during the Wet.

➡ For South Australia conditions, call ☎1300 361 033 or check www.dpti.sa.gov.au/OutbackRoads.

➡ For Northern Territory, call ☎1800 246 199 or check www.roadreport.nt.gov.au.

Dirt-Road Driving

➡ Inflate your tyres to the recommended levels for the terrain you're travelling on; on desert sand, deflate your tyres to 20–25psi to avoid getting bogged.

➡ Reduce speed on unsealed roads, as traction is decreased and braking distances increase.

➡ Dirt roads are often corrugated: keeping an even speed is the best approach.

➡ Dust on outback roads can obscure your vision, so always stop and wait for it to settle.

Road Hazards

➡ Rest every few hours: driver fatigue is an all-too-common problem.

➡ Wandering cattle, sheep, emus, kangaroos, camels etc make driving fast a dangerous prospect. Take care and avoid nocturnal driving, as this is often when native animals come out. Many car-hire companies prohibit night-time driving.

➡ Road trains are ever-present: give them a wide berth.

reaches Innamincka 460km northeast and close to the Queensland border. It was close to Innamincka that the hapless explorers Burke and Wills died. A 4WD is a safe bet.

Nathan River Road

This road is a scenic section of the Savannah Way, a cobbled-together route which winds all the way from Cairns to Broome. This particular section traverses some remote country along the western edge of the Gulf of Carpentaria between Roper Bar and Borroloola, much of it protected within Limmen National Park. A high-clearance 4WD is a must; two spare tyres are recommended. There's excellent camping along the way.

Tanami Track

Turning off the Stuart Hwy just north of Alice Springs, this 1055km route runs northwest across the Tanami Desert to Halls Creek in Western Australia. The road has received extensive work so conventional vehicles are often OK, although there are sandy stretches on the WA side and it can be very corrugated. Seek advice on road conditions in Alice Springs.

Plenty & Sandover Highways

These remote routes run east from the Stuart Hwy, north of Alice Springs, to Boulia or Mt Isa in Queensland. The Plenty Hwy skirts the northern fringe of the Simpson Desert and offers the chance of gem fossicking in the Harts Range. The Sandover Hwy offers a memorable (if monotonous) experience in remote touring. Both roads are not to be taken lightly; they are often very rough going with little water and very few facilities.

Finke & Old Andado Tracks

The Finke Track follows the route of the old *Ghan* railway (long since dismantled) between Alice Springs and the Aboriginal settlement of Finke (Aputula). Chambers Pillar Historical Reserve is en route, with its colourful sandstone tower. From Finke the road heads east along the Goyder Creek, before turning north towards Andado Station and, 18km further, the homestead. At Old Andado the track swings north for the 321km trip to Alice. The Old Andado Track winds its way through the Simpson Desert to link the Homestead with Alice Springs. A high-clearance 4WD

PLAN YOUR TRIP YOUR OUTBACK TRIP

OUTBACK CYCLING

Pedalling your way through the outback is certainly not something to tackle lightly, and certainly not something you'd even consider in summer. But you do see the odd wiry, suntanned soul pushing their panniers along the Stuart Hwy between Adelaide and Darwin. Availability of drinking water is the main concern: isolated water sources (bores, tanks, creeks etc) shown on maps may be dry or undrinkable. Make sure you've got the necessary spare parts and bike-repair knowledge, and tell someone where you're headed. This is intrepid travel defined!

is essential, as are a high-frequency (HF) radio or emergency position-indicating radio beacon (EPIRB).

Simpson Desert

The route crossing the Simpson Desert from Mt Dare, near Finke, to Birdsville is a real test of both driver and vehicle. A 4WD is definitely required on the unmaintained tracks and you should be in a party of at least three vehicles equipped with sat phones, HF radio and/or EPIRB.

Paved Roads

Stuart Highway

The Stuart Hwy is one of the world's truly epic road trips, covering 2724km from Darwin in the north to Port Augusta. It's paved all the way, offering gateways to the outback's major attractions, and punctuated by roadhouses at regular intervals like outback opals on a chain.

Lasseter Highway

From Alice Springs it's a six-hour drive to Uluru-Kata Tjuta National Park along the paved Stuart and then Lasseter Hwys. The road is also paved from Lasseter Hwy up to Kings Canyon along the Luritja Rd.

Victoria Highway

The Victoria Hwy runs from Katherine to Kununurra (515km). It's the only paved road connecting the NT with WA and passes through Victoria River and Timber Creek en route.

Outback Tracks: Off the Beaten Path

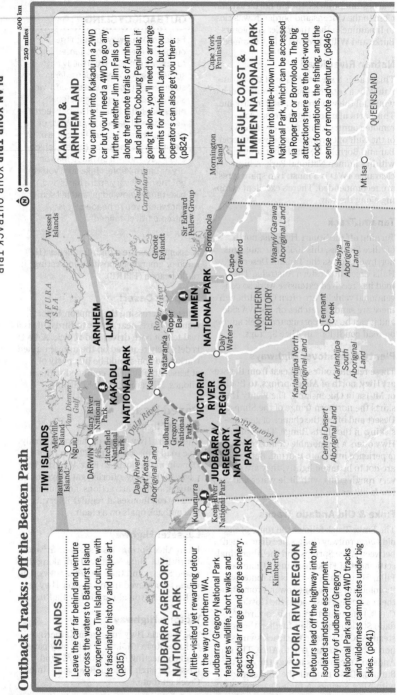

TIWI ISLANDS

Leave the car far behind and venture across the waters to Bathurst Island to experience Tiwi Island culture, with its fascinating history and unique art. (p815)

JUDBARRA/GREGORY NATIONAL PARK

A little-visited yet rewarding detour on the way to northern WA. Judbarra/Gregory National Park features wildlife, short walks and spectacular range and gorge scenery. (p842)

VICTORIA RIVER REGION

Detours lead off the highway into the isolated sandstone escarpment country of Judbarra/Gregory National Park and onto 4WD tracks and wilderness camp sites under big skies. (p841)

KAKADU & ARNHEM LAND

You can drive into Kakadu in a 2WD car but you'll need a 4WD to go any further, whether Jim Jim Falls or along the remote trails of Arnhem Land and the Cobourg Peninsula; if going it alone, you'll need to arrange permits for Arnhem Land, but tour operators can also get you there. (p824)

THE GULF COAST & LIMMEN NATIONAL PARK

Venture into little-known Limmen National Park, which can be accessed via Roper Bar or Borroloola. The big attractions here are the lost-world rock formations, the fishing, and the sense of remote adventure. (p846)

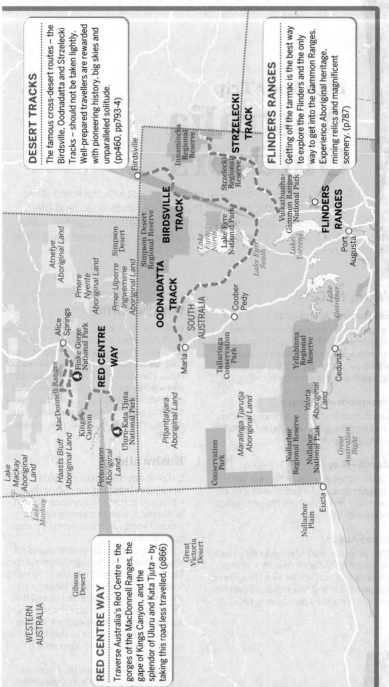

DESERT TRACKS

The famous cross-desert routes – the Birdsville, Oodnadatta and Strzelecki Tracks – should not be taken lightly. Well-prepared travellers are rewarded with pioneering history, big skies and unparalleled solitude. (pp460, pp793-4)

FLINDERS RANGES

Getting off the tarmac is the best way to explore the Flinders and the only way to get into the Gammon Ranges. Experience Aboriginal heritage, mining relics and magnificent scenery. (p787)

RED CENTRE WAY

Traverse Australia's Red Centre – the gorges of the MacDonnell Ranges, the gape of Kings Canyon, and the splendor of Uluru and Kata Tjuta – by taking this road less travelled. (p866)

Plan Your Trip
Australia Outdoors

Australia serves up plenty of excuses to just kick back and stare at incredible landscapes, but these same landscapes lend themselves to boundless outdoor pursuits – whether it's getting active on the trails and mountains on dry land, or on the swells and reefs offshore.

When to Go

September & October

Spring brings the climax of the football season, which means a lot of yelling from the grandstands. The more actively inclined rejoice in sunnier weather and warmer days, perfect for bushwalking, wildlife watching and rock climbing.

December–February

Australians hit the beach in summer: prime time for surfing, sailing, swimming, fishing, snorkelling, skydiving, paragliding...

March–May

Autumn is a nostalgic time in Australia, with cool nights and wood smoke: perfect weather for a bushwalk or perhaps a cycling trip – not too hot, not too cold.

June–August

When winter hits, make a beeline for the outback, the tropical Top End or the snow. Pack up your campervan and head into the desert for a hike or a scenic flight, or grab your snowboard and head into the mountains for some powdery fun.

On the Land

Bushwalking (hiking) is a popular pastime in all Australian states and territories. Cycling is a great way to get around, especially on off-road routes along disused rail trails. There's also skiing in the mountains and wildlife watching (p59) pretty much everywhere, especially in Australia's many national parks: wombats, wallabies, kangaroos, echidnas, emus, parrots, snakes, lizards...

Bushwalking

Bushwalking (also known as hiking, trekking or tramping, depending on where you're from) is supremely popular in Australia, with vast swathes of untouched scrub and forest providing ample opportunity.

Hikes vary from 20-minute jaunts off the roadside to week-long wilderness epics. The best time to head into the bush varies from state to state, but the further north you go the more tropical and humid the climate gets over summer (November to March), whereas in the outback and the south conditions can be baking hot, which means carrying a lot of water on your walk.

Notable walks include the Overland Track (p705) and the Three Capes Track

RESPONSIBLE CAMPING & BUSHWALKING

To help preserve the ecology and beauty of Australia that has been carefully managed for millennia by the traditional custodians, please follow this advice:

➡ Carry out all your rubbish, including sanitary products. Never bury your rubbish: digging disturbs soil and ground cover and encourages erosion. Buried rubbish will likely be dug up by animals, who may be injured or poisoned by it.

➡ Where there is a toilet, use it. Where there is none, bury your waste. Dig a small hole 15cm (6in) deep and at least 100m (320ft) from any watercourse. Cover the waste with soil and a rock. In snow, dig right down to the soil.

➡ Don't use detergents or toothpaste in or near watercourses. Spit toothpaste 50m away from a river.

➡ For personal washing, use biodegradable soap and a water container away from the watercourse. Disperse the waste water widely to allow the soil to naturally filter it.

➡ Wash cooking utensils 50m from watercourses using a scourer, sand or snow instead of detergent.

➡ Don't depend on open fires for cooking. Cook on a lightweight portable stove.

➡ In alpine areas, ensure that everyone is outfitted with enough clothing so that fires are not a necessity for warmth.

➡ If you light a fire, use an existing fireplace. Use only dead, fallen wood. Leave enough wood for the next person. Don't surround fires with rocks.

➡ Do not feed wildlife as this can lead to unbalanced populations, animals becoming dependent on humans, or the spread of diseases.

➡ Know the local laws, regulations and etiquette for the environment.

➡ Pay track fees and obtain permits, especially as these are often on an honesty system, to help maintain essential services and maintenance works.

➡ Stick to existing tracks and avoid short cuts. Walking around a muddy bog only makes it bigger – plough straight through.

(p662) in Tasmania, and the Great Ocean Walk (p556) and Great South West Walk (p568) in Victoria, as well as multiple walks at Wilsons Prom (p594). The Bibbulmun Track (p958) in Western Australia is epic, as is the Thorsborne Trail (p393) across Hinchinbrook Island and the Gold Coast Hinterland Great Walk (p324) in Queensland.

In New South Wales you can trek between Sydney and Newcastle (p153) on the Great North Walk via Lane Cove National Park (p91), tackle the Coast Track in Royal National Park (p136), the Six Foot Track (p145) in the Blue Mountains, or scale Mt Kosciuszko (p243), Australia's highest peak.

In South Australia you can bite off a chunk of the 1200km Heysen Trail (p743), while in the Northern Territory there's the majestic Larapinta Trail (p865) and remote tracks in Kakadu National Park (p824) and Nitmiluk (Katherine Gorge) National Park (p840).

Safety Guidelines for Bushwalking

Before you lace up your boots, make sure you're walking in a region – and on tracks – within your realm of experience and preparation. Check with local authorities for weather and track updates: be aware that terrain can vary significantly, weather can alter dramatically, and seasonal changes can considerably change any track. Always tell someone where you are going and when you will be back.

Cycling

Cyclists in Australia have access to plenty of cycling routes and can tour the country for days, weekends or even weeks at a time. Or just rent a bike for a few hours and cycle around a city.

Standout longer routes include the Murray to the Mountains Rail Trail (p614) and the East Gippsland Rail Trail (p599) in Victoria. In WA the Munda Biddi Trail

Hiking Tasmania's Cradle Mountain-Lake St Clair National Park (p704)

(p926) offers 900km of mountain biking, or you can rampage along the same distance on the Mawson Trail (p743) in SA. The 480km Tasmanian Trail (p695) is a north–south mountain-bike route across the length of the island state. Alice Springs (p856) in Central Australia has a prospering mountain-biking scene.

Rental rates charged by most outfits for road or mountain bikes start at around $25/50 per hour/day. Deposits range from $50 to $250, depending on the rental period. Most states have bicycle organisations that can provide maps and advice.

Buying a Bike

If you want to buy a reliable, new road or mountain bike, your bottom-level starting price will be around $600. Throw in all the requisite on-the-road equipment (panniers, helmet etc) and your starting point becomes around $1750. Secondhand bikes are worth checking out, as are the post-Christmas sales and midyear stocktakes, when last season's cycles can be heavily discounted.

To sell your bike (or buy a secondhand one), try hostel noticeboards or online at Ebay (www.ebay.com.au) or Gumtree (www.gumtree.com.au).

Resources

The following websites offers information, news and links. Each Australian state also has its own cycling information networks.

Bicycles Network Australia (www.bicycles.net.au)

Bicycle Network (www.bicyclenetwork.com.au)

Cycling & Walking Australia & NZ (www.cwanz.com.au)

MTBA (www.mtba.asn.au)

Skiing & Snowboarding

Australia has a small but enthusiastic skiing industry, with snowfields straddling the NSW–Victoria border. The season is relatively short, however, running from about mid-July to early September, and snowfalls can be unpredictable. The rest of the year these are hiking and mountain cycling hubs.

Thredbo, NSW (p244)

Perisher Valley, NSW (p244)

Snowboarder, Thredbo (p244)

Mt Buller, Victoria (p605)

Falls Creek, Victoria (p616)

Mt Hotham, Victoria (p617)

On the Water

As Australia's national anthem informs you, this land is 'girt by sea'. Surfing, fishing, sailing, diving and snorkelling are what people do here – national pastimes one and all. Inland there are vast lakes and meandering rivers, offering rafting, canoeing, kayaking and (yet more) fishing opportunities. And of course, Australia's underwater wildlife is everywhere: whales, dolphins, dugongs, turtles and myriad tropical fish. Dolphin- and whale-watching boat trips are hugely popular, although make sure you keep a respectful distance: humanity owes them a little peace and quiet!

Diving & Snorkelling

The Great Barrier Reef (p405) has more dazzling diving and snorkelling sites than you can poke a fin at. In WA, Ningaloo Reef (p986) is every bit as interesting as the east-coast reefs, but without the visitor numbers. There are spectacular artificial reefs in WA too, created by sunken ships at Albany and Dunsborough.

The Rapid Bay jetty off the Gulf St Vincent coast (p743) in SA is renowned for its abundant marine life, and in Tasmania the Bay of Fires (p673) and Eaglehawk Neck (p660) are popular spots. In NSW head for Jervis Bay (p225) and Fish Rock Cave off South West Rocks (p167).

Fishing

Barramundi fishing is hugely popular across the Top End. In the NT, these are the best fishing spots:

Cobourg Peninsula (p836)

Eastern Arnhem Land (p836)

Mary River National Park (p819)

Borroloola (p847)

Elsey National Park (p844)

Over on the Queensland coast of the Gulf of Carpentaria try Karumba (p449), and Lake Tinaroo (p427) on the Atherton Tableland in Far North Queensland.

Ocean fishing is possible right around the country, from pier or beach, or you can organise a deep-sea charter. There are magnificent glacial lakes and clear highland streams for trout fishing in Tasmania.

Before casting a line, be warned that strict limits to catches and sizes apply in Australia, and many species are threatened and therefore protected. Check local guidelines via fishing equipment stores or through the relevant state-government fishing bodies for information.

Surfing

Bells Beach, Cactus, Margaret River, the Superbank...mention any of them in the right company and stories of surfing legend will undoubtedly emerge. The Superbank and Bells Beach are mainstays on the Association of Surfing Professionals (ASP) World Tour calendar each year, with Bells the longest-serving host of an ASP event. Cactus dangles the lure of remote mystique, while Margaret River is a haunt for surfers chasing bigger waves.

While the aforementioned might be jewels, they're dot points in the sea of stars that Australia has to offer. It's little

PLAN YOUR TRIP AUSTRALIA OUTDOORS

RESOURCES

....

Bicycles Network Australia (www. bicycles.net.au) Information, news and links.

Bushwalking Australia (www.bush walkingaustralia.org) Website for the national body, with links to state and territory bushwalking clubs and federations.

Coastalwatch (www.coastalwatch. com) Surf-cams, reports and weather charts for all the best breaks.

Dive-Oz (www.diveoz.com.au) Online scuba-diving resource.

Fishing Australia (www.fishing australia.com.au) Comprehensive fishing coverage.

Ski Online (www.ski.com.au) Commercial site with holiday offers plus snow-cams, forecasts and reports.

wonder – the coastline is vast, touching the Indian, Southern and South Pacific Oceans. With that much potential swell, an intricate coastal architecture and the right conditions, you'll find anything from innocent breaks to gnarly reefs not far from all six Australian state capitals.

New South Wales

➡ Manly through to Avalon, otherwise known as Sydney's northern beaches.

➡ Byron Bay, Lennox Head and Angourie Point on the far North Coast.

➡ Nambucca Heads and Crescent Head on the mid-North Coast.

➡ The areas around Jervis Bay and Ulladulla on the South Coast.

Queensland

➡ The Superbank (a 2km-long sandbar stretching from Snapper Rocks to Kirra Point).

➡ Burleigh Heads through to Surfers Paradise on the Gold Coast.

➡ North Stradbroke Island in Moreton Bay.

➡ Caloundra, Alexandra Heads, near Maroochydore, and Noosa on the Sunshine Coast.

South Australia

➡ Cactus Beach, west of Ceduna on remote Point Sinclair – internationally recognised for quality and consistency.

➡ Greenly Beach on the western side of the Eyre Peninsula.

➡ Pennington Bay – the most consistent surf on Kangaroo Island.

➡ Pondalowie Bay and Stenhouse Bay on the Yorke Peninsula, part of Innes National Park.

➡ Victor Harbor, Port Elliot and Middleton Beach south of Adelaide.

Tasmania

➡ Marrawah on the exposed northwest coast, which can offer huge waves.

➡ St Helens and Bicheno on the east coast.

➡ Eaglehawk Neck on the Tasman Peninsula; legendary Shipstern Bluff isn't far from here – Australia's heaviest wave.

➡ Closer to Hobart, Cremorne Point and Clifton Beach.

Victoria

➡ Bells Beach, the spiritual home of Australian surfing (when the wave is on, few would argue, but the break is notoriously inconsistent).

➡ Others on the southwest coast: Barwon Heads, Point Lonsdale, Torquay and numerous spots along the Great Ocean Road.

➡ On Phillip Island, Smiths Beach for a relaxed vibe and Woolamai for bigger waves, though watch for its strong rips and currents.

➡ Point Leo, Flinders, and the back-beaches at Rye and Portsea on the Mornington Peninsula.

Western Australia

➡ Margaret River, Gracetown and Yallingup in the southwest.

➡ Trigg Point and Scarborough Beach, just north of Perth.

➡ Further north at Geraldton and Kalbarri.

➡ Down south at Denmark on the Southern Ocean.

Plan Your Trip
Wildlife Watching

Local wildlife is one of Australia's top selling points, and justifiably so. Tracking down the country's numerous iconic species can be a bit of a treasure hunt, but you just have to know where to look. National parks are great places to start, although many species are nocturnal (try camping...and BYO torch).

In the Rainforest

For those intrigued by the diversity of tropical rainforests, Queensland's World Heritage Sites are well worth visiting. Birds of paradise, cassowaries and a variety of other birds can be seen by day, while at night you can search for tree-kangaroos (yes, some kinds of kangaroo do live in the treetops). In your nocturnal wanderings you are highly likely to see curious possums, some of which look like skunks, and other marsupials that are restricted to a small area of northeast Queensland.

In the Desert

Australia's deserts are a real hit-and-miss affair as far as wildlife is concerned. If you're visiting in a drought year, all you might see are dusty plains, the odd mob of kangaroos and emus, and a few struggling trees. Return after big rains, however, and you'll encounter something close to a Garden of Eden. Fields of white and gold daisies stretch endlessly into the distance. The salt lakes fill with fresh water, and millions of water birds – pelicans, stilts, shags and gulls – can be seen feeding on the super-abundant fish and insect life of the waters. It all seems like a mirage, and like a mirage it will vanish as the land

Easy-to-get-to Zoos

Sometimes you need a quick-fire urban animal encounter.

New South Wales
Taronga Zoo Sydney (p86); Wild Life Sydney Zoo (p83)

The ACT
Tidbinbilla Nature Reserve (p271)

Queensland
Australia Zoo (p334); Wildlife Habitat Port Douglas (p429); Currumbin Wildlife Sanctuary (p321)

Victoria
Melbourne Zoo (p475); Healesville Sanctuary (p520)

Tasmania
Bonorong Wildlife Sanctuary (p649); Platypus House (p685)

South Australia
Adelaide Zoo (p720); Monarto Zoo (p765)

The Northern Territory
Crocosaurus Cove (p800); Alice Springs Desert Park (p852); Territory Wildlife Park (p820)

Western Australia
Perth Zoo (p885); Caversham Wildlife Park (p920)

dries out, only to spring to life again in a few years or a decade.

For a more reliable birdwatching spectacular, Kakadu is worth a look, especially towards the end of the dry season around November.

In the Ocean

Southern right and humpback **whales** pass close to Australia's southern coast on their migratory route between the Antarctic and warmer waters. The best spots for whale-watching are Hervey Bay in Queensland, Eden in southern NSW, the mid-north coast of NSW, Warrnambool in Victoria, Ceduna and Victor Harbor in SA, Cobourg Peninsula in the Northern Territory and Albany, Cape Naturaliste, Exmouth and the Dampier Peninsula in WA. Whale-watching season is roughly May to October. For **whale sharks** and **manta rays** try WA's Ningaloo Marine Park.

You can see **dolphins** year-round along the east coast at Jervis Bay, Port Stephens and Byron Bay in NSW; off the coast of WA at Bunbury and Rockingham; off North Stradbroke Island in Queensland; and Sorrento in Victoria. In WA, **fur seals** and **sea lions** can be seen at Rottnest Island, Esperance, Rockingham and Green Head, and all manner of beautiful sea creatures inhabit Monkey Mia (including **dugongs**). Sea lions also visit the aptly named (though not technically correct) Seal Bay on SA's Kangaroo Island.

The fragile diversity of Queensland's Great Barrier Reef is legendary, and a boat trip out to the reef from Cairns or Port Douglas is unforgettable.

Great Australian Bight

During springtime southern right whales crowd into the head of the Great Australian Bight, which is home to more kinds of marine creatures than anywhere else on earth. You can readily observe them near the remote Aboriginal community of Yalata as they mate, frolic and suckle their young. Kangaroo Island, south of Adelaide, is a fantastic place to see seals and sea lions. There are well-developed visitor centres to facilitate the viewing of wildlife, and nightly penguin parades occur at some places where the adult blue penguins make their nest burrows. Kangaroo Island's beaches are magical places, where you're able to stroll among fabulous shells, whale bones and even jewel-like leafy sea dragons amid the sea wrack.

Where to See...

For more on the best places to see Australia's mammals, get a hold of the excellent *The Complete Guide to Finding the Mammals of Australia* (2015) by David Andrew. It has a state-by-state rundown of the best locations to see various species, as well as a species-by-species overview.

Dingoes

➡ Fraser Island (Queensland)
➡ Kakadu National Park (NT)

TASMANIA

Some regions of Australia offer unique opportunities to see wildlife, and one of the most fruitful is Tasmania. The island is jam-packed with wallabies, wombats and possums, principally because foxes, which have decimated marsupial populations on the mainland, were slow to reach the island state – the first fox was found in Tasmania only as recently as 2001!

The island is also home to its eponymous Tasmanian devil. They're common on the island, and in some national parks you can watch them tear apart road-killed wombats. Their squabbling is fearsome, their shrieks ear-splitting – it's the nearest thing Australia can offer to experiencing a lion kill on the Masai Mara. Unfortunately, Tassie devil populations are being decimated by devil facial tumour disease (DFTD). Conservation projects, including establishing a disease-free population on Tasmania's Maria Island, and scientific projects aimed at building a vaccine, have offered hope that the devil may be saved, but the species remains classified as endangered.

A friendly local kangaroo, Western Australia

➡ Uluru-Kata Tjuta National Park (NT)
➡ The Kimberley Region (WA)
➡ Pungalina – Seven Emu Wildlife Sanctuary (NT)

Kangaroos

➡ Anglesea Golf Club (Victoria)
➡ Grampians (Victoria)
➡ Hattah-Kulkyne National Park (Victoria)
➡ Uluru-Kata Tjuta National Park (NT)
➡ West MacDonnell Ranges (NT)
➡ Weston Park (ACT)
➡ Namadgi National Park (ACT)

Koalas

➡ Great Ocean Road & Cape Otway (Victoria)
➡ Phillip Island (Victoria)
➡ French Island (Victoria)
➡ Gunnedah (NSW)
➡ Port Macquarie (NSW)
➡ Lismore (Queensland)
➡ Noosa National Park (Queensland)
➡ Greater Brisbane (Queensland)

Penguins

➡ Phillip Island (Victoria)
➡ Penguin (Tasmania)
➡ Kangaroo Island (SA)
➡ Victor Harbor (SA)

Platypuses

➡ Bombala River (Southeastern NSW)
➡ New England National Park (NSW)
➡ Kangaroo Island (SA)
➡ Eungella National Park (Queensland)
➡ Latrobe (Tasmania)

Saltwater Crocodiles

➡ Kakadu National Park (NT)
➡ Mary River National Park (NT)
➡ Daintree River (Queensland)

Wombats

➡ Cradle Mountain (Tasmania)
➡ Wilsons Promontory National Park (Victoria)
➡ Kangaroo Valley (NSW)
➡ Kosciuszko National Park (NSW)

Regions at a Glance

Australia's Eastern States

Queensland, New South Wales, the Australian Capital Territory and Victoria are road-tripping nirvana, with picture-perfect beaches, rainforests, hip cities and the Great Barrier Reef.

Into the Wild

Strung out for more than 18,000km, Australia's east coast is a rippling ribbon of beaches and rampant wildlife. Offshore, the astonishing Great Barrier Reef is a 2000km-long hyper-coloured haven for tropical marine life. Inland are bewitching national parks, lush rainforests, jagged peaks and native critters aplenty.

City Scenes

Home to Aboriginal peoples for millennia, Sydney was also Australia's first European settlement. Sassy and ambitious yet unpretentious, the city is a honey-pot lure for anyone looking for a good time. Melbourne is Australia's arts and coffee capital; boom-town Brisbane is a glam patchwork of inner-city neighbourhoods. And don't forget Australia's capital, Canberra – so much more than a political filing cabinet!

Action Stations

Exploring Australia's eastern states is an exercise in, well...exercise! The sun is shining and fit-looking locals are outdoors – jogging, swimming, bushwalking, surfing, cycling, kayaking, snorkelling... Why not join in? Or just head for the beach, where the locals let it all hang out.

Eat, Drink & Celebrate

Australia's big east-coast cities lift the lid on a rich culinary experience, with fantastic cafes, sprawling food markets and world-class restaurants. After dark, moody wine bars, student-filled speakeasies and boisterous Aussie pubs provide plenty of excuses to bend an elbow, chew the fat and maybe watch a bit of football.

Sydney & New South Wales

Surf Beaches
Food
Wilderness

Bondi & Beyond

Sydney's surf beaches can't be beaten. Bondi is the name on everyone's lips, but the waves here get crowded. Head south to Maroubra or Cronulla, or north to Manly, for more elbow room on the sand and the waves.

Culinary Sydney

Modern Australian dining (aka Mod Oz) is the name of the culinary game here – a pan-Pacific fusion of styles and ingredients with plenty of Sydney seafood. Serve it with a harbour view and you've got a winning combo.

National Parks

NSW has some of the best national parks in Australia. Around Sydney there's the Royal National Park, with spectacular walks and beaches; waterways and wildlife in Ku-ring-gai Chase National Park; and vast tracts of native forest in Blue Mountains National Park.

p68

Canberra &
the ACT

History & Culture
Wineries
Politics

National Treasures

Canberra offers the National Gallery of Australia, with its magnificent collections of Australian, Asian and Aboriginal and Torres Strait Islander art; the National Museum of Australia, whose imaginative exhibits provide insights into the Australian heart and soul; the moving and fascinating Australian War Memorial; and the entirely impressive National Portrait Gallery.

Capital Wines

Canberra's wine industry is relatively new, but it is winning admirers with a consistent crop of fine cool-climate wines. The Canberra vineyards are an easy and picturesque drive from downtown.

The National Debate

Politics is what really makes Canberra tick: find out for yourself at a rigorous session of Question Time at Parliament House, or visit Old Parliament House and check out the Museum of Australian Democracy.

p252

Queensland

Diving & Snorkelling
Beaches & Islands
Urban Culture

Great Barrier Reef

Blessed with the unrivalled Great Barrier Reef, Queensland is the place for world-class diving and snorkelling. The fragility of this wonder is the talk of the globe, so expect to learn more about what you can do to help it.

Lazy Day Whitsundays

There's great surf along Queensland's south coast, and reefs and rainforest-cloaked islands further north, but for picture-perfect white-sand beaches and turquoise seas, the Whitsundays are unmissable: hire a yacht and enjoy.

Brisbane Rising

Watch out Sydney and Melbourne, Brisbane is on the rise! Hip bars, a vibrant art scene and cafes to rival the best anywhere: Australia's 'new world city' is an ambitious, edgy and progressive place to be.

p272

Melbourne &
Victoria

History
City Life
Surf Beaches

Golden Days

Walk the boom-town streets of 1850s gold-rush towns. With their handsome, lace-fringed buildings, Melbourne, Bendigo and Ballarat are rich reminders of how good Victoria had it in those days.

Marvellous Melbourne

Melbourne is the spiritual home of Australian rules football: grab some friends and boot a ball around a wintry city park. Summer means cricket: locals are either watching it on TV, talking about it or out in the streets playing it.

The Surf Coast

With relentless Southern Ocean swells surging in, there's plenty of quality (if chilly) surf along Victoria's Great Ocean Road. Bells Beach is Australia's most famous break, and home to the Rip Curl Pro surfing competition every Easter.

p462

Tasmania

Food
Wildlife
History

Culinary Excellence

Tasmania produces larders full of fine food and drink. Chefs from all over Australia are increasingly besotted with Tasmania's excellent produce, including briny fresh salmon and oysters, cool-climate wines, hoppy craft beers and plump fruit and vegetables.

Native Critters

You might not spy a Tassie tiger, but you'll see wombats, wallabies, possums, pademelons and possibly a snake or two. There's also whale-, seal- and penguin-spotting along the Tasmanian coast.

Colonial Stories

Tasmania's bleak colonial history is on display in Port Arthur and along the Heritage Hwy, made all the more potent by dramatic landscapes seemingly out of proportion with the state's compact footprint.

p628

Australia's Centre & West

Australia's epic centre, South Australia and the Northern Territory is wild and beautiful country and the nation's Indigenous heartland. Further west is (surprise, surprise) Western Australia, a vast state framed by 12,500km of spectacular coastline.

The Desert & the Tropics

Call that Australia? *This* is Australia. Ever since *Crocodile Dundee* brought Kakadu to the world's attention, the outback and Top End have been on the radar for their impressive portfolio of quintessentially Aussie land forms. From Uluru and Kata Tjuta rising improbably from the desert to the pristine coastline of Arnhem Land, it's hard to escape the feeling that in this land lies eternity...

Aboriginal Connections

In the Northern Territory it's relatively easy to cross the cultural frontier and meet Indigenous Australians on their terms: on an intimate exploration of country led by an Indigenous guide, in quiet conversation with artists at work, or in the timeless rituals of a festival.

South Australia Awaits

South Australia is home to Australia's premier wine regions: the Barossa Valley, McLaren Vale, Clare Valley, Adelaide Hills and the Coonawarra. Also here is wonderful Kangaroo Island and underrated Adelaide, a hip city with amazing festivals, a simmering arts scene and great pubs, bars and foodie culture.

The Wild West

If the huge expanse of Western Australia was a separate nation, it would be the world's 10th-largest country. Most West Australians live on the coast – Perth and neighbouring Fremantle are cosmopolitan cities – yet you can wander along a WA beach without seeing another footprint, engage with abundant wildlife, or camp alone and stargaze in a national park.

Adelaide & South Australia

Wine
Festivals
National Parks

Australia's Best Wines

We challenge you to visit South Australia without inadvertently driving through a wine region. You may have heard of the Barossa Valley, Clare Valley and McLaren Vale, but what about the lesser-known Langhorne Creek, Mt Benson, Currency Creek or the Adelaide Hills regions? All produce top drops worth pulling over for.

Mad March

At the end of every summer Adelaide erupts with festivals: visual arts, world music, theatre, busking and the growl of V8 engines. The only question is, why do it all at the same time?

Ancient Landscapes

The dunes and lagoons of Coorong National Park are unique, but for sheer geologic majesty visit Ikara (Wilpena Pound), part of the craggy, russet-red Ikara-Flinders Ranges National Park in central SA.

p713

Darwin & the Northern Territory

Landscapes
Wildlife
Indigenous Culture

Iconic National Parks

The Northern Territory is blessed with some astonishing national parks, protecting the likes of Kakadu's waterways and age-old Indigenous rock-art sites, the gorgeous gorges of Nitmiluk, and must-see Uluru and Kata Tjuta.

Mammals, Birds & Crocs

The NT outback is brilliant for wildlife, from dingoes to kangaroos and wallabies to emus, while up north Kakadu also has crocodiles and even better birding.

Indigenous Meeting Places

Australia's Aboriginal communities continue to protect and celebrate their unique cultural heritage here. From wonderful community art centres to festivals and Aboriginal tours, you will learn a little about the spiritual experience of Country.

p797

Perth & Western Australia

Coastal Scenery
Adventure
Wildlife

Beaches & Reefs

There are boundless beaches along Western Australia's spectacular 12,500km-long coastline. But for sheer sandy delight, visit the isolated beaches leading down to the shallow lagoons and reefs of the World Heritage–listed Ningaloo Marine Park.

Explore the Wild

Bring it on: take the ride of your life along the bone-shaking Gibb River Road to the exceptional Mitchell Falls and remote Kalumburu. Jump on a speedboat and head full throttle for the Horizontal Waterfalls, then grab a canoe and paddle down the mighty Ord River.

Wondrous Wildlife

You can spy sharks, rays, turtles and migrating whales along WA's central west coast. Inland, birds flock to the oasis pools of Millstream-Chichester National Park, and pythons and rock wallabies hide in the shadows of Karijini National Park.

p881

YMGERMAN/GETTY IMAGES ©

Top: Blue Mountains (p138), New South Wales

Bottom: Brisbane's skyline from South Bank (p276)

On the Road

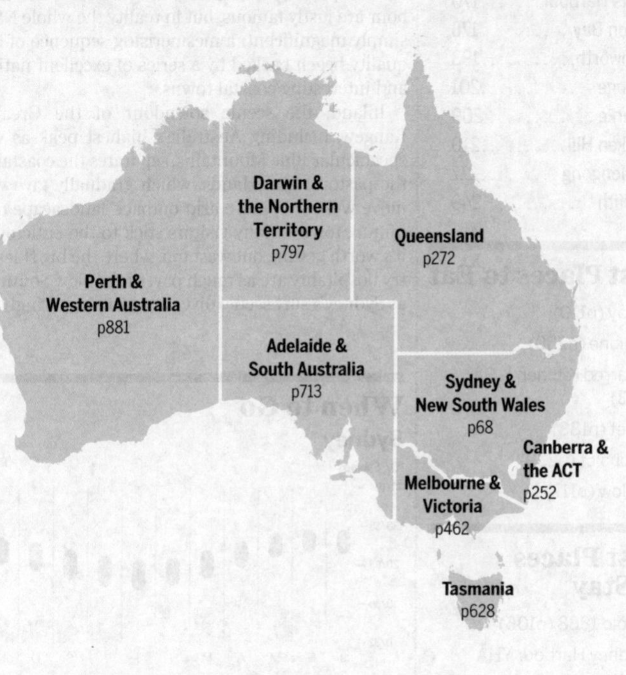

Darwin &
the Northern
Territory
p797

Queensland
p272

Perth &
Western Australia
p881

Adelaide &
South Australia
p713

Sydney &
New South Wales
p68

Canberra &
the ACT
p252

Melbourne &
Victoria
p462

Tasmania
p628

Sydney & New South Wales

🔊 02 / POP 8.1 MILLION

Includes ➜

Sydney 69
Newcastle 153
Coffs Harbour 170
Byron Bay 178
Tamworth 193
Orange 201
Bourke 209
Broken Hill 210
Wollongong 217
Griffith 249

Best Places to Eat

➜ Quay (p110)

➜ Limone (p250)

➜ Charred Kitchen & Bar (p203)

➜ Fleet (p188)

➜ Eschalot (p239)

➜ Yellow (p117)

Best Places to Stay

➜ Ovolo 1888 (p106)

➜ Sydney Harbour YHA (p102)

➜ Paperbark Camp (p227)

➜ ADGE Boutique Apartment Hotel (p106)

➜ Bannisters Pavilion (p229)

➜ 28° Byron Bay (p184)

Why Go?

Australia's most populous state is home to its largest city: glitzy, vibrant, intoxicating Sydney, an unforgettable metropolis in a privileged natural setting. Bondi Beach and the harbour are justly famous, but in reality the whole NSW coast is simply magnificent: a mesmerising sequence of beach after quality beach backed by a series of excellent national parks and interesting coastal towns.

Inland, the scenic splendour of the Great Dividing Rangew, including Australia's highest peak as well as the spectacular Blue Mountains, separates the coastal strip from the pastoral hinterlands, which gradually give way, as you move west, to a more arid outback landscape dotted with mining towns. Many visitors stick to the enticing coast, but it's worth getting out west too, where the big skies and country hospitality are as much part of the New South Wales soul as Sydney's surf scene, diversity and staggeringly good food.

When to Go
Sydney

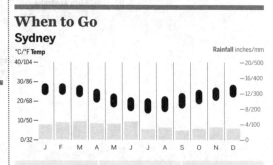

Feb Great weather but less crowded beaches, plus Mardi Gras gearing up in Sydney.

Jun Bearable temperatures out west; cosy snuggling in ski lodges and Blue Mountains guesthouses.

Oct A great month for whale-watching up and down the east coast.

ℹ️ Transport

Sydney has Australia's busiest airport, and domestic flights, many operated by **Regional Express** (REX; 📞13 17 13; www.rex.com.au), radiate out to numerous NSW airports.

NSW TrainLink (p1078) connects Sydney with northern and country NSW, Melbourne, Brisbane and Canberra.

Bus services may not be frequent, but they are reliable and cover most of the places that you can't reach by train.

SYDNEY

POP 5.2 MILLION

More laid-back than any major metropolis should rightly be, Australia's largest settlement is one of the great international cities. Blessed with outstanding natural scenery across its magnificent harbour, stunning beaches and glorious national parks, Sydney is home to three of the country's major icons – the Harbour Bridge, the Opera House and Bondi Beach. But the attractions definitely don't stop there. This is the country's oldest and most diverse city, a sun-kissed settlement that is characterised by a wonderful food culture, hedonistic attitudes, intriguing history and the brash charm of its residents.

History

What is now Greater Sydney is the ancestral home of at least three distinct Aboriginal peoples, each with their own language. Ku-ring-gai was generally spoken on the northern shore, Dharawal along the coast south of Botany Bay, and Dharug from the harbour to the Blue Mountains. The coastal area around Sydney is the ancestral home of the Eora people (which literally means 'from this place'), who were divided into clans such as the Gadigal (Cadigal) and the Wangal.

In 1770 Lieutenant (later Captain) James Cook dropped anchor at Botany Bay. The ship's arrival alarmed the local people, and Cook noted in his journal: 'All they seem'd to want was for us to be gone.'

In 1788 the British came back, this time for good. Under the command of naval captain Arthur Phillip, the 'First Fleet' included a motley crew of convicts, marines and livestock. Upon arriving at Botany Bay, Phillip was disappointed by what he saw – particularly the lack of a freshwater source – and ordered the ships to sail north, where he found 'the finest harbour in the world'. The date of the landing at Sydney Cove was 26 January, an occasion that is commemorated

each year with the Australia Day public holiday (known to many as 'Invasion Day' and focus of an increasing campaign to find a less divisive occasion to celebrate).

Armed resistance to the British was led by Aboriginal warriors including Pemulwuy (c 1750–1802), a member of the Dharug-speaking Bidjigal clan from around Botany Bay, and Musquito (c 1780–1825), an Eora man from the north shore of Port Jackson. The Aboriginal fighters were eventually crushed and the British colony wrested control. The fleet brought with them European diseases such as smallpox, which devastated the Eora people (only three of the Gadigal clan are said to have survived).

The early days of settlement were difficult, with famine a constant threat, but gradually a bustling port was established with stone houses, warehouses and streets. The surrounding bushland was gradually converted into farms, vegetable gardens and orchards.

In 1793 Phillip returned to London and self-serving military officers took control of Government House. Soon the vigorous new society that the first governor had worked so hard to establish began to unravel. Eventually London took action, dispatching a new governor, Lachlan Macquarie, to restore the rule of law. Under his rule many grand buildings were constructed (most of which still stand today), setting out a vision for Sydney that would move it from its prison-camp origins to a worthy outpost of the British Empire.

In 1813 the Blue Mountains were penetratped by explorers Blaxland, Lawson and Wentworth, opening the way for the colony to expand onto the vast fertile slopes and plains of the west. By the 1830s the Lachlan, Macquarie, Murrumbidgee and Darling river systems had been explored and the NSW colony started to thrive.

The 20th century saw an influx of new migrants from Europe (especially after WWII), Asia and the Middle East, changing the dynamics of the city as it spread westwards and became the multicultural metropolis that it is today.

◉ Sights

◉ Circular Quay & the Rocks

⭐ **Royal Botanic Garden**   GARDENS
(📞02-9231 8111; www.rbgsyd.nsw.gov.au; Mrs Macquarie's Rd; ⊙7am-dusk; 🚊Circular Quay) 🆓 Southeast of the Opera House, this garden was established in 1816 and features

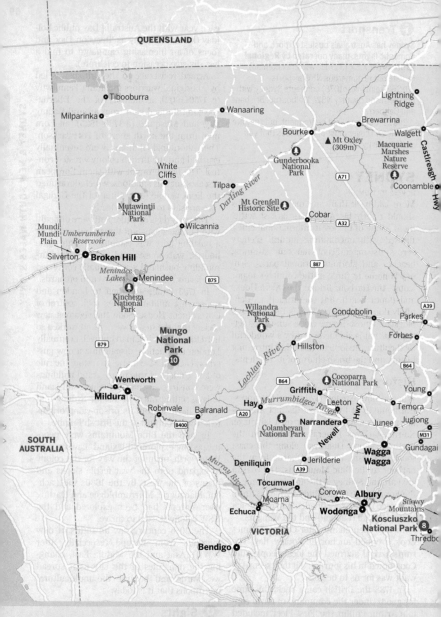

New South Wales Highlights

1 **Sydney** (p69) Living it up beachside and harbourside in this captivating, diverse city.

2 **Blue Mountains** (p138) Gazing out over sandstone cliffs to the blue-tinged eucalypt forests below.

3 **Hunter Valley** (p147) Sipping the semillon and enjoying the finer things in life in these boutique vineyards.

4 **Lord Howe Island** (p216) Climbing Mt Gower for an

unforgettable view over this island way out in the Pacific.

5 **Waterfall Way** (p168) Driving this route through some of the North Coast's most enchanting landscapes.

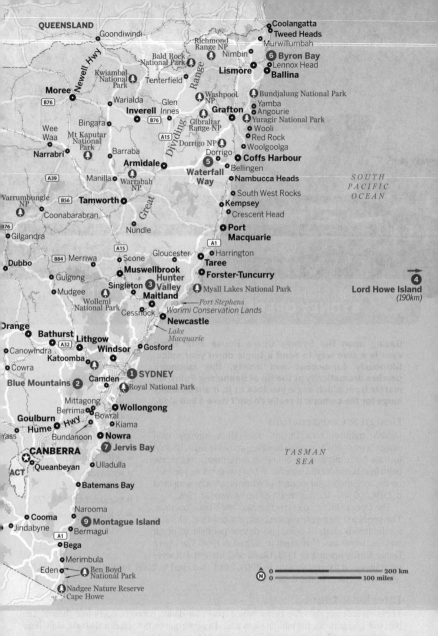

QUEENSLAND
Goondiwindi

Coolangatta
Tweed Heads
Murwillumbah

Richmond
Range NP
Nimbin
Bald Rock
National Park
Tenterfield
Kwiambal
National
Park

6 Byron Bay
Lennox Head
Ballina

Lismore

Newell Hwy

Moree

B76

Warialda

Inverell
B76

Glen
Innes

Washpool
NP
Grafton

Bundjalung National Park

Yamba
Angourie

Wee
Waa

Bingara

Mt Kaputar
National
Park

A15

Gibraltar
Range NP

Yuragir National Park
Wooli
Red Rock
Woolgoolga

Narrabri

Barraba

Dorrigo NP
Dorrigo

A39

Armidale

Coffs Harbour
Bellingen

Manilla

Waterfall
Way
5

Nambucca Heads

Warrabah
NP

Tamworth

South West Rocks

B56

Coonabarabran

Kempsey
Crescent Head

Varrumbungle
NP

Nundle

Great

Port
Macquarie

A1

376

Gilgandra

A15

Gloucester

Harrington

B84

Merriwa

Scone

Taree

Dubbo

Gulgong

Muswellbrook
Hunter
Valley

Forster-Tuncurry

Mudgee

Singleton
Maitland

3

Myall Lakes National Park

Orange

Wollemi
National Park

Cessnock

Port Stephens
Worimi Conservation Lands

Bathurst

Lithgow

A32

Windsor

Newcastle

Lake
Macquarie

Canowindra

Katoomba

Gosford

Cowra

Blue Mountains

Camden

1 SYDNEY

2

Royal National Park

Mittagong
Berrima

Wollongong

Goulburn

Bowral

Hume Hwy

Kiama

Yass

Bundanoon

Nowra

CANBERRA

7 Jervis Bay

ACT
Queanbeyan

Ulladulla

TASMAN
SEA

Dividing   Range

Great   Dividing   Range

Lord Howe Island
(190km)
4

SOUTH
PACIFIC
OCEAN

Batemans Bay

Narooma

Cooma

9 Montague Island

Jindabyne

Bermagui

A1

Bega

Merimbula

Eden

Ben Boyd
National Park

Nadgee Nature Reserve
Cape Howe

0   200 km
0   100 miles

6 **Byron Bay** (p178)
Unwinding into the unique vibe
of this iconic coastal town.

7 **Jervis Bay** (p225)
Marvelling at the white white
sands and sparkling waters of
this large, idyllic bay.

8 **Kosciuszko National Park**
(p243) Walking the trails in this
highland park so beautiful it
makes the heart sing.

9 **Montague Island** (p231)
Watching seals, penguins,

dolphins and whales at this
marvellous wildlife spot.

10 **Mungo National Park**
(p214) Appreciating the
Indigenous history and stirring
scenery of an accessible slice
of the outback.

TOOYKRUB/SHUTTERSTOCK ©

TOP SIGHT
SYDNEY OPERA HOUSE

Gazing upon the Sydney Opera House with virgin eyes is a sure way to send a tingle down your spine. Gloriously curvaceous and pointy, this landmark perches dramatically at the tip of Bennelong Point. No matter from which angle you look at it, it shamelessly mugs for the camera; it really doesn't have a bad side.

Design & Construction

Danish architect Jørn Utzon's competition-winning 1956 design is probably Australia's most recognisable sight. It's said to have been inspired by billowing sails, orange segments, palm fronds and Mayan temples. When you get close you realise the seemingly solid expanse of white is actually composed of 1,056,000 self-cleaning cream-coloured Swedish tiles.

The Opera House's construction was itself truly operatic. The predicted four-year construction started in 1959. After a tumultuous clash of egos, plus delays, politicking, death and cost blow-outs, Utzon quit in disgust in 1966. The Opera House finally opened in 1973. Utzon and his son Jan were commissioned for renovations in 2004, but Utzon died in 2008, having never seen his finished masterpiece in the flesh.

Interior & Tours

The complex comprises five performance spaces for dance, concerts, opera and theatre. The best way to experience the building is to attend a performance, but you can also take a one-hour guided tour (available in several languages), with optional food. Ongoing renovation work, scheduled to be completed in 2022, may disrupt visits.

There's also a two-hour 'access all areas' backstage tour ($175), which departs at 7am and includes breakfast in the Green Room. Other ways to experience the Opera House include a seven-minute narration of Aboriginal stories, Badu Gili, that is spectacularly projected onto the sails nightly at sunset and at 9pm; or a sunrise yoga class on the steps ($25).

DON'T MISS

➡ Catching a show
➡ Going on a guided tour
➡ Heading outside during the interval to admire the harbour

PRACTICALITIES

➡ ☑ 02-9250 7111
➡ www.sydneyopera house.com
➡ tours adult/child $40/22
➡ ⊙ tours 9am-5pm
➡ 🚇 Circular Quay

BENNY MARTY/SHUTTERSTOCKS ©

SYDNEY HARBOUR BRIDGE

Whether they're driving over it, climbing up it, jogging across it, shooting fireworks off it or sailing under it, Sydneysiders adore their bridge and swarm around it like ants on ice cream. Dubbed the 'coathanger', the harbour bridge is a spookily big object – moving around town, you'll catch sight of it out of the corner of your eye when you least expect it.

Structure

At 134m high, 1149m long, 49m wide and weighing 52,800 tonnes, Sydney Harbour Bridge is the largest and heaviest (but not the longest) steel arch in the world. It links the Rocks with North Sydney, crossing the harbour at one of its narrowest points.

The two halves of chief engineer JJC Bradfield's mighty arch were built outwards from each shore. In 1930, after seven years of merciless toil by 1400 workers, the two arches were only centimetres apart when 100km/h winds set them swaying. The coathanger hung tough, though, the arch was bolted together and the bridge finally opened to the public two years later.

Exploring the Bridge

The best way to experience this majestic structure is on foot. Don't expect much of a view crossing by train or car (driving south there's a toll). Stairs and lifts climb up the bridge from both shores, leading to a footpath on the eastern side (the western side is a bike path). The northern end of the bridge walk is very close to Milsons Point train station. Walking north to south (i.e. from Milsons Point to the city) offers the best views. You can also climb the southeastern pylon to the **Pylon Lookout** (Map p80; ☎02-9240 1100; www.pylonlookout.com.au; adult/child $15/10) or ascend the arc on the popular but expensive **BridgeClimb** (Map p80; ☎02-8274 7777; www.bridgeclimb.com; adult $263-388, child $183-278). Expect some different possibilities for interacting with the bridge over the next years as a new company has taken over the licence.

DON'T MISS

→ Sunset from the top of the bridge

→ The views from the Pylon Lookout

→ Walking across the bridge from north to south

PRACTICALITIES

→ Map p80

→ 🚆 Circular Quay, Milsons Point

Sydney Harbour

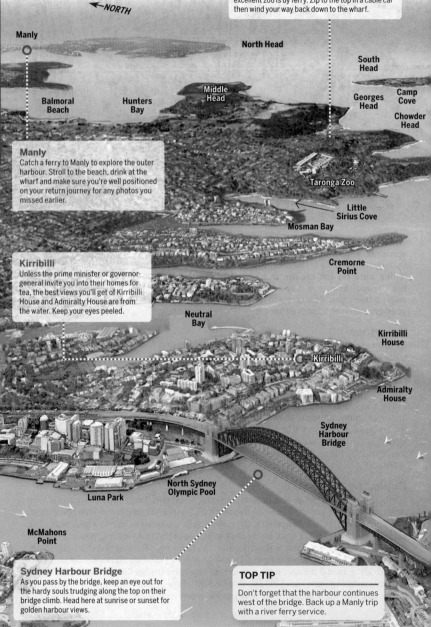

← *NORTH*

Manly

North Head

South Head

Balmoral Beach

Hunters Bay

Middle Head

Georges Head

Camp Cove

Chowder Head

Taronga Zoo
Even if you've hired a car, the best way to reach this excellent zoo is by ferry. Zip to the top in a cable car then wind your way back down to the wharf.

Taronga Zoo

Little Sirius Cove

Mosman Bay

Manly
Catch a ferry to Manly to explore the outer harbour. Stroll to the beach, drink at the wharf and make sure you're well positioned on your return journey for any photos you missed earlier.

Cremorne Point

Kirribilli
Unless the prime minister or governor-general invite you into their homes for tea, the best views you'll get of Kirribilli House and Admiralty House are from the water. Keep your eyes peeled.

Neutral Bay

Kirribilli House

Kirribilli

Admiralty House

Sydney Harbour Bridge

North Sydney Olympic Pool

Luna Park

McMahons Point

Sydney Harbour Bridge
As you pass by the bridge, keep an eye out for the hardy souls trudging along the top on their bridge climb. Head here at sunrise or sunset for golden harbour views.

TOP TIP

Don't forget that the harbour continues west of the bridge. Back up a Manly trip with a river ferry service.

Watsons Bay
Imagine Watsons Bay as the isolated fishing village it once was as you pull into its sheltered wharf. Stroll around South Head for views up the harbour and over ocean-battered cliffs.

Fort Denison
Known as Pinchgut, this fortified speck was once a place of fearsome punishment. The bodies of executed convicts were left to hang here as a grisly warning to all; the local Aboriginal people were horrified.

DINOZZAVER/SHUTTERSTOCK ©

FERRIES
Circular Quay is the hub for state-run Sydney Ferries; nine separate routes leave from here, journeying to 38 different wharves.

Watsons Bay

Macquarie Lighthouse

Vaucluse Bay

Shark Bay

Bradleys Head

Shark Island

Rose Bay

Point Piper

Double Bay

Darling Point

Clark Island

Elizabeth Bay

Garden Island

Naval Base

Fort Denison

Mrs Macquaries Point

Potts Point

Woolloomooloo Wharf

Sydney Opera House

Government House

Farm Cove

Royal Botanic Garden

Circular Quay

The Rocks

Sydney Opera House
You can clamber all over it and walk around it, but nothing beats the perspective you get as your ferry glides past the Opera House's dazzling sails. Have your camera at the ready.

Circular Quay
Circular Quay has been at the centre of Sydney life since the First Fleet dropped anchor here in 1788. Book your ferry ticket, check the indicator boards for the correct pier and get on board.

Sydney

SYDNEY & NEW SOUTH WALES SYDNEY

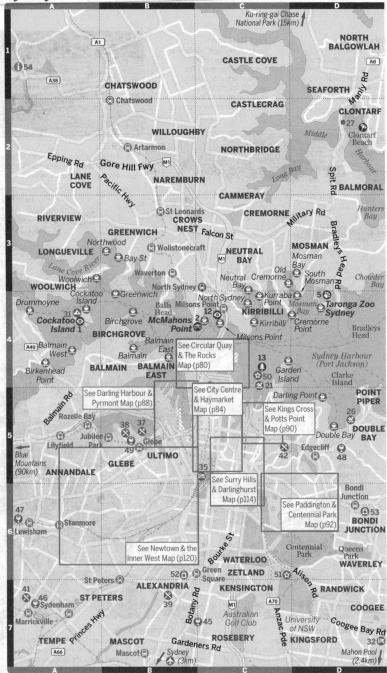

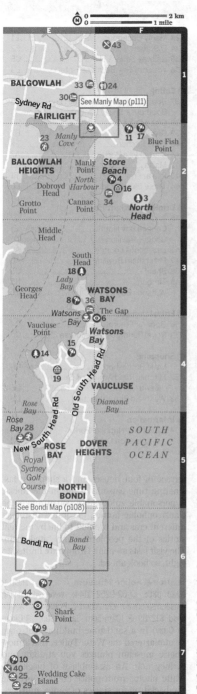

plant life from around the world. Within the gardens are hothouses with palms and ferns, as well as the **Calyx** (⊙10am-4pm; 🚇Martin Place) 🏃, a striking exhibition space featuring a curving glasshouse gallery with a wall of greenery and temporary plant-themed exhibitions. Grab a park map at any main entrance.

The gardens include the site of the colony's first paltry vegetable patch, but their history goes back much further than that; long before the convicts arrived, this was an initiation ground for the Gadigal people. Free 1½-hour guided walks depart from the visitor centre (open 10am to 3pm) at 10.30am daily, plus 1pm on March to November weekdays. Book ahead for an **Aboriginal Heritage Tour** (adult $41; ⊙10am Wed, Fri & Sat) with an Indigenous guide.

A hop-on, hop-off **tourist train** (www.choochoo.com.au; adult/child $10/5; ⊙11am-4pm May-Sep, 10am-4.30pm Oct-Apr) runs a route around the main points of interest in the garden.

★**Rocks Discovery Museum** MUSEUM
(Map p80; ☑02-9240 8680; www.therocks.com; Kendall Lane; ⊙10am-5pm; 🚇; 🚇Circular Quay) **FREE** Divided into four displays – Warrane (pre-1788), Colony (1788–1820), Port (1820–1900) and Transformations (1900 to the present) – this small, excellent museum, tucked away down a Rocks laneway, digs deep into the area's history on an artefact-rich tour. Sensitive attention is given to the Rocks' original inhabitants, the Gadigal people, and there are interesting tales of early colonial characters.

★**Sydney Observatory** OBSERVATORY
(Map p80; ☑02-9217 0111; www.maas.museum/sydney-observatory; 1003 Upper Fort St; ⊙10am-5pm; 🚇Circular Quay) **FREE** Built in the 1850s, Sydney's copper-domed, Italianate sandstone observatory squats atop Observatory Hill, overlooking the harbour. Inside is a collection of vintage apparatus, including Australia's oldest working telescope (1874), as well as background on Australian astronomy and transits of Venus. Also on offer (weekends and school holidays) are child-focused tours (adult/child $10/8), including a solar telescope viewing and planetarium show. Bookings are essential for night-time stargazing sessions, which come in family-oriented (adult/child $22/17) and adult (adult/child $27/20) versions.

Sydney

◎ **Top Sights**
1 Cockatoo Island A4
2 McMahons Point C4
3 North Head F2
4 Store Beach F2
5 Taronga Zoo Sydney D4
6 Watsons Bay F4

◎ **Sights**
7 Bronte Beach E6
8 Camp Cove E3
9 Clovelly Beach E7
10 Coogee Beach E7
11 Fairy Bower Beach F2
12 Luna Park C4
13 Mrs Macquaries Point C4
14 Nielsen Park E4
15 Parsley Bay E4
16 Q Station F2
17 Shelly Beach F2
18 South Head E3
19 Vaucluse House E4
20 Waverley Cemetery E7

🏄 **Activities, Courses & Tours**
21 Andrew (Boy) Charlton Pool C4
22 Gordons Bay Underwater Nature
   Trail E7
23 Manly Scenic Walkway E2
24 Manly Surf School F1
25 McIver's Ladies Baths E7
26 Murray Rose Pool D5
27 Sydney Harbour Kayaks D2
28 Sydney Seaplanes E5
29 Wylie's Baths E7

🛏 **Sleeping**
30 Cecil Street B&B E1
31 Cockatoo Island A4
32 Dive Hotel D7

33 Manly Bunkhouse E1
34 Q Station F2
35 Railway Square YHA C5
36 Watsons Bay Boutique Hotel E3

🍴 **Eating**
37 Boathouse on Blackwattle Bay B5
   Boathouse Shelly Beach .... (see 17)
38 Glebe Point Diner B5
39 Grounds of Alexandria B7
40 Little Kitchen E7
41 Marrickville Pork Roll A7
42 Marta C5
43 Pilu at Freshwater F1
44 Three Blue Ducks E6

🍸 **Drinking & Nightlife**
45 Archie Rose Distilling Co. C7
   Coogee Bay Hotel .... (see 32)
   Coogee Pavilion .... (see 10)
46 Lazybones Lounge A7
47 Petersham Bowling Club A6
48 Sheaf D5
49 Timbah B5
   Watsons Bay Beach Club .... (see 36)

🎭 **Entertainment**
50 OpenAir Cinema C4
51 Royal Randwick Racecourse C6

🛍 **Shopping**
   Little Bottleshop .... (see 49)
52 Mitchell Road Antique & Design
   Centre B6
53 Westfield Bondi Junction D6

ℹ **Information**
54 Lane Cove National Park
   Information Centre A1

Walsh Bay   WATERFRONT
(Map p80; www.walshbaysydney.com.au; Hickson
Rd; 🚌324, 325, 🚆Wynyard) This section of
Dawes Point waterfront was Sydney's busiest before the advent of container shipping
and the construction of port facilities at
Botany Bay. This century has seen the Federation-era wharves gentrified beyond belief,
morphing into luxury hotels, apartments,
theatre spaces, power-boat marinas and
restaurants. It's a picturesque place to stroll,
combining the wharves and harbour views
with Barangaroo Park.

Susannah Place Museum   MUSEUM
(Map p80; 🖉 bookings 02-9251 5988; www.sydney
livingmuseums.com.au; 58-64 Gloucester St; adult/
child $12/8; ⊙tours 2pm, 3pm & 4pm; 🚆 Circu-
lar Quay) Dating from 1844, this diminutive

terrace of four houses and a shop is a fascinating time capsule of life in the Rocks.
A personable guide takes you through the
claustrophobic homes, decorated to reflect
different eras and brought to life by the real
stories of the people that inhabited them.
The visit lasts an hour. Groups are limited to
eight, so book ahead.

Justice & Police Museum   MUSEUM
(Map p80; 🖉02-9252 1144; www.sydneyliving
museums.com.au; cnr Albert & Phillip Sts; adult/
child $12/8; ⊙10am-5pm Sat & Sun; 🚆Circu-
lar Quay) In a sandstone building that once
headquartered the Water Police, this atmospheric museum plunges you straight into
Sydney noir. An assemblage of black-and-
white photos from police archives provide
the backdrop for stories of gangs, murders,

bushranging and underworld figures, as well as being a fascinating window into social history. The highlight is the magnificently laconic commentary on the audiovisual features.

Museum of Contemporary Art
GALLERY

(MCA; ☏02-9245 2400; www.mca.com.au; 140 George St; ⊙10am-5pm Thu-Tue, to 9pm Wed; ⊠Circular Quay) **FREE** The MCA is a showcase for Australian and international contemporary art, with a rotating permanent collection and temporary exhibitions. Aboriginal art features prominently. The art-deco building has had a modern space grafted on to it, the highlight of which is the rooftop cafe with stunning views. There are free guided tours daily, with several languages available.

Barangaroo Reserve
PARK

(Map p80; www.barangaroo.com; Hickson Rd; ⊠324, 325, ⊠Circular Quay) Part of Barangaroo, the major redevelopment project of what was a commercial port, this park sits on a headland with wonderful harbour perspectives. The tiered space combines quarried sandstone blocks and native trees and plants to good effect. A lift connecting the park's three levels is good for weary legs. There's a car park under it, and an exhibition space.

Mrs Macquaries Point
PARK

(Map p76; Mrs Macquarie's Rd; ⊠Circular Quay) This peninsula was named in 1810 after Elizabeth, Governor Macquarie's wife, who ordered a seat to be chiselled into the rock from which she could view the harbour. **Mrs Macquaries Chair**, as it's known, is still there today. It's in the Domain but is effectively an extension of the Botanic Gardens.

Pylon Lookout
VIEWPOINT, MUSEUM

See p73.

☉ City Centre & Haymarket

★ Art Gallery of NSW
GALLERY

(Map p90; ☏1800 679 278; www.artgallery.nsw. gov.au; Art Gallery Rd; ⊙10am-5pm Thu-Tue, to 10pm Wed; ⓘ; ⊠441, ⊠St James) **FREE** With its neoclassical Greek frontage and modern rear, this much-loved institution plays a prominent and gregarious role in Sydney society. Blockbuster international touring exhibitions arrive regularly and there's an outstanding permanent collection of Australian artwa, including a substantial Indigenous section. The gallery also plays host to lectures, concerts, screenings, celebrity talks and children's activities. A range of free guided tours is offered on different themes and in various languages; enquire at the desk or check the website.

While the permanent collection has a strong collection of 19th-century European and Australian art, the highlights are the contemporary Indigenous gallery in the basement and the collection of 20th-century Australian art, with some standout canvases by the big names of the local painting scene. Look out for Albert Tucker's scary *Apocalyptic Horse,* Russell Drysdale's brilliant gold-town street *Sofala* and half a room full of Sidney Nolans, usually including one or more of his extraordinary Ned Kelly paintings. There's a good representation of female artists too, including Grace Cossington Smith's distinctively colourful scenes and several Margaret Olleys on rotation. Arthur Boyd works include one of his moving 'Bride' series and his terracotta sculpture of *Judas Kissing Christ,* while Brett Whiteley is represented by the intoxicatingly blue harbour of *The Balcony 2.*

The unfailingly controversial Archibald Prize for Australian portraiture exhibits here annually, as do the Wynne Prize (landscape or figure sculpture), the Sulman Prize (subject or mural painting) and the Artexpress exhibition of the year's best school-student art.

The cafe and **restaurant** (Map p90; ☏02-9225 1819; www.chiswickatthegallery.com.au; Art Gallery Rd; small plates $19-28, mains $30-42; ⊙noon-3pm Thu-Tue, to 9.30pm Wed; ⓘ) are fine places to hang out, with outdoor seating and views over Woolloomooloo Bay. Wednesday nights are fun too, with talks, live music and other events.

Construction of a second building is due to be completed in 2021. Occupying space to the north of the existing building, it's a major project, to be known as **Sydney Modern,** that will be centred on a new Indigenous gallery and a dedicated space for major touring exhibitions. The construction work shouldn't affect gallery visits.

★ Chinatown
AREA

(Map p84; www.sydney-chinatown.info; ⊠Paddy's Markets, ⊠Town Hall) Dixon St is the heart of Chinatown: a narrow, shady pedestrian mall with a string of restaurants and insistent spruikers. The ornate dragon gates (*paifang*) at either end have fake bamboo tiles, golden Chinese calligraphy and ornamental

Circular Quay & The Rocks

SYDNEY & NEW SOUTH WALES SYDNEY

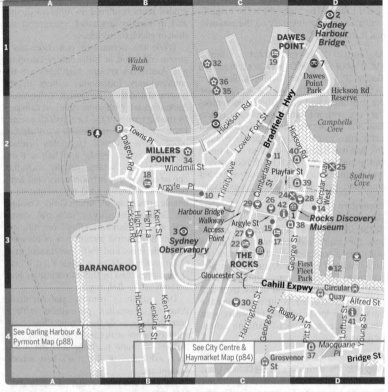

lions to keep evil spirits at bay. Chinatown in general (though not necessarily between the dragon gates) is a fabulous eating district, which effectively extends for several blocks north and south of here, and segues into Koreatown and Thaitown to the east.

Sydney Tower Eye TOWER

(Map p84; www.sydneytowereye.com.au; Level 5, Westfield Sydney, 188 Pitt St; adult/child $29/20; ⊙9am-9pm, last entry 8pm; ℝSt James) The 309m-tall Sydney Tower (still known as Centrepoint by many Sydneysiders) offers unbeatable 360-degree views from the observation level 250m up. The visit starts with the 4D Experience, a short film giving you a bird's-eye view of city, surf, harbour and what lies beneath the water, accompanied by mist sprays and bubbles. Then it's up the lift to the viewing area. The Skywalk, where you can step onto glass-floored viewing platforms outside, was suspended at time of research.

State Library of NSW LIBRARY

(Map p84; ☑02-9273 1414; www.sl.nsw.gov.au; Macquarie St; ⊙9am-8pm Mon-Thu, to 5pm Fri, 10am-5pm Sat & Sun, exhibition rooms close 5pm Mon-Wed; ℝMartin Place) **FREE** Among the State Library's over five million tomes are James Cook's and Joseph Banks' journals and William Bligh's log from the mutinous *Bounty*. It's worth dropping in to peruse the elaborately sculpted bronze doors and grand atrium of the neoclassical Mitchell Wing (1910); note the beautiful map of Tasman's journeys in the mosaic floor. The main reading room is an elegant temple of knowledge clad in milky marble. Excellent exhibition galleries highlight the collection.

Hyde Park Barracks Museum MUSEUM

(Map p84; ☑02-8239 2311; www.sydneyliving museums.com.au; Queens Sq, Macquarie St; adult/child $24/16; ⊙10am-5pm; ℝSt James) Convict architect Francis Greenway designed this squarish, decorously Georgian structure

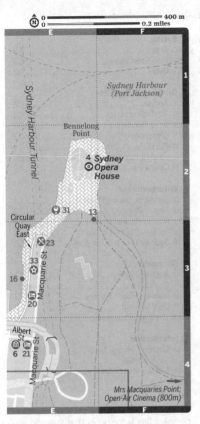

Map legend area:
- 0 — 400 m / 0.2 miles
- Sydney Harbour (Port Jackson)
- Sydney Harbour Tunnel
- Bennelong Point
- 4 Sydney Opera House
- Circular Quay East
- 31, 13, 23, 33, 16, 20
- Macquarie St
- Albert St
- 6, 21
- Mrs Macquaries Point; Open-Air Cinema (800m)

architecture are brought to life, while there's a good section on the First Fleet itself, with scale models.

Hyde Park
PARK
(Map p84; Elizabeth St; ☒St James, Museum) Formal but much-loved Hyde Park has manicured gardens and a tree-formed tunnel running down its spine, which looks particularly pretty at night, illuminated by fairy lights. The park's northern end is crowned by the richly symbolic art-deco Archibald Memorial Fountain, while at the other end is the Anzac Memorial.

Martin Place
STREET
(Map p84; ☒Wynyard, ☒Martin Place) Studded with imposing edifices, long lean Martin Place was closed to traffic in 1971, forming a terraced pedestrian mall complete with fountains and areas for public gatherings. It's the closest thing to a main civic square that Sydney has.

St Mary's Cathedral
CHURCH
(Map p84; ☎02-9220 0400; www.stmaryscathedral.org.au; St Marys Rd; crypt $5; ☺6.30am-6.30pm Mon-Fri, 8.30am-7pm Sat, 6.30am-7pm Sun; ☒St James) Sydney has traditionally been quite a Catholic city, and this is the hub of the faith. Built to last, this 106m-long sandstone Gothic Revival–style cathedral was begun in 1868, consecrated in 1905 and substantially finished in 1928, though the massive, 75m-high spires weren't added until 2000. The crypt (open 10am to 4pm weekdays) has bishops' tombs and an impressive mosaic floor depicting the Creation, inspired by the Celtic-style illuminations of the *Book of Kells*.

Anzac Memorial
MEMORIAL
(Map p84; ☎02-8262 2900; www.anzacmemorial.nsw.gov.au; Hyde Park; ☺9am-5pm; ☒Museum) **FREE** Fronted by the Pool of Reflection, this dignified art-deco memorial (1934) commemorates the soldiers of the Australia and New Zealand Army Corps (Anzacs) who served in WWI. The interior dome is studded with 120,000 stars: one for each New South Welsh soldier who served. These twinkle above Rayner Hoff's poignant sculpture *Sacrifice*. The new downstairs Hall of Service features names and soil samples of all the NSW places of origin of WWI soldiers. There's a daily 11am remembrance service here.

St James' Church
CHURCH
(Map p84; ☎02-8227 1300; www.sjks.org.au; 173 King St; ☺10am-4pm Mon-Fri, to 1pm Sat, 7.30am-2pm Sun; ☒St James) Built from

(1819) as convict quarters. Fifty thousand men and boys sentenced to transportation passed through here in 30 years. It later became an immigration depot, a women's asylum and a law court. These days it's a fascinating museum, focusing on the barracks' history and the archaeological efforts that helped reveal it. At the time of research the barracks was closed until late 2019 as the exhibition was rejigged.

Museum of Sydney
MUSEUM
(MoS; Map p84; ☎02-9251 5988; www.sydneylivingmuseums.com.au; cnr Phillip & Bridge Sts; adult/child $12/8; ☺10am-5pm; ☒Circular Quay) Built on the site of Sydney's first Government House, the MoS is a fragmented, storytelling museum, which uses installations to explore the city's history. The area's long Indigenous past is highlighted throughout, plus there's interesting coverage of the early days of contact between the Gadigal people and the colonists. Key figures in Sydney's planning and

Circular Quay & The Rocks

◎ Top Sights
1 Rocks Discovery Museum D3
2 Sydney Harbour Bridge D1
3 Sydney Observatory B3
4 Sydney Opera House E2

◎ Sights
5 Barangaroo Reserve A2
6 Justice & Police Museum E4
7 Pylon Lookout D1
8 Susannah Place Museum C3
9 Walsh Bay C2

◎ Activities, Courses & Tours
10 Bike Buffs C3
    Bonza Bike Tours .... (see 15)
11 BridgeClimb C2
12 Captain Cook Cruises D3
13 Choochoo Express E2
14 Dreamtime Southern X D3
    The Rocks Ghost Tours .... (see 15)
15 The Rocks Walking Tours C3
16 Tribal Warrior E3

◎ Sleeping
17 Harbour Rocks Hotel C3
18 Lord Nelson Brewery Hotel B2
19 Pier One C1
20 Pullman Quay Grand Sydney
    Harbour E3
21 Sir Stamford E4
22 Sydney Harbour YHA C3

◎ Eating
23 Aria E3
24 Fine Food Store D3
25 Quay D2

◎ Drinking & Nightlife
26 Argyle C3
27 Australian Hotel C3
28 Doss House D3
29 Glenmore Hotel C3
30 Harts Pub C4
    Lord Nelson Brewery Hotel .... (see 18)
31 Opera Bar E2

◎ Entertainment
32 Bangarra Dance Theatre C1
33 Dendy Opera Quays E3
34 Roslyn Packer Theatre B2
35 Sydney Dance Company C1
36 Sydney Theatre Company C1

◎ Shopping
37 Australian Wine Centre D4
    Craft NSW .... (see 18)
38 Gannon House Gallery D3
39 Opal Minded D2
40 The Rocks Markets D2

◎ Information
41 Customs House Tourist
    Information D4
42 Sydney Visitor Centre C3

convict-made bricks, Sydney's oldest church (1819) is widely considered to be architect Francis Greenway's masterpiece. It was originally designed as a courthouse, but the brief changed and the cells became the crypt. Check out the dark-wood choir loft, the sparkling copper dome, the crypt and the 1950s stained-glass 'Creation Window'. It's worth reading the marble plaques along the walls for some insights into early colonial life and exploration. A more recent plaque commemorates former prime minister Gough Whitlam and his partner Margaret.

Music is a very strong point here and classical concerts happen at 1.15pm on Wednesdays between March and December ($5 donation). See the website for details on other concerts and daily services.

◎ Darling Harbour & Pyrmont

★ Sydney Sea Life Aquarium AQUARIUM
(Map p88; ☑ 1800 614 069; www.sydneyaquar ium.com.au; Aquarium Pier, Central Sydney; adult/child $46/33; ⊙ 10am-6pm; ⓡ Town Hall) ⌀

As well as regular tanks, this impressive complex has large pools that you can walk through – safely enclosed in Perspex tunnels – as an intimidating array of sharks and rays pass overhead. Other highlights include a two-minute boat ride through a king and gentoo penguin enclosure, a dugong, disco-lit jellyfish, evolutionary throwbacks and the brilliant finale: the enormous Great Barrier Reef tank, which cycles you through different times of day in the life of coral, turtles, rare sharks and numerous fish.

★ Australian National
Maritime Museum MUSEUM
(MU-SEA-UM; Map p88; ☑ 02-9298 3777; www.sea. museum; 2 Murray St, Pyrmont; permanent collection free, temporary exhibitions adult/child $20/12; ⊙ 9.30am-5pm, to 6pm Jan; ⓟ; ☑ 389, ⓟ Pyrmont Bay) ⓕⓡⓔⓔ Beneath a soaring roof, the Maritime Museum sails through Australia's inextricable relationship with the sea. Exhibitions range from Indigenous canoes to surf culture, and from immigration to the navy. The worthwhile 'big ticket' (adult/child

$32/20) includes entry to some of the vessels moored outside, including the atmospheric submarine HMAS *Onslow* and the destroyer HMAS *Vampire*. The high-production-value short film *Action Stations* sets the mood with a re-creation of a mission event from each vessel. Excellent free guided tours explain each vessel's features.

★ **Sydney Fish Market** MARKET
(Map p88; ☑02-9004 1108; www.sydneyfish market.com.au; Bank St, Pyrmont; ⊙7am-4pm Mon-Thu, to 5pm Fri-Sun; 🚢 Fish Market) This piscatorial precinct on Blackwattle Bay shifts around 15 million kilograms of seafood annually, and has retail outlets, restaurants, sushi and oyster bars, delis and a highly regarded cooking school (Map p88; ☑02-9004 1111; www.sydneyfishmarket.com.au/seafood-school; 2/4hr courses $90/165; 🚢 Fish Market). Chefs, locals and overfed seagulls haggle over mud crabs, Balmain bugs, lobsters and salmon at the daily fish auction, which kicks off at 5.30am weekdays. Check it out on a behind-the-scenes tour (adult/child $45/20). A flash new market is being built a little further west, due to open in 2023.

★ **Chinese Garden of Friendship** GARDENS
(Map p88; ☑02-9240 8888; www.chinesegarden. com.au; Harbour St, Central Sydney; adult/child $6/3; ⊙9.30am-5pm Apr-Sep, to 5.30pm Oct-Mar; 🚉Town Hall) Built according to Taoist principles, the Chinese Garden of Friendship is usually an oasis of tranquillity – although one increasingly dwarfed by assertive modern buildings. Designed by architects from Guangzhou (Sydney's sister city) for Australia's bicentenary in 1988, the garden interweaves pavilions, waterfalls, lakes, paths and lush plant life. There's also a tea house.

Wild Life Sydney Zoo ZOO
(Map p88; ☑1800 614 069; www.wildlifesydney. com.au; Aquarium Pier, Central Sydney; adult/child $44/31; ⊙10am-5pm; 🚉Town Hall) Complementing its sister and neighbour, Sea Life, this surprisingly capacious complex houses an impressive collection of Australian native reptiles, butterflies, spiders, snakes and mammals (including koalas and a walk-through kangaroo area). The nocturnal section is particularly good, bringing out the extrovert in the quolls, potoroos, echidnas and possums. The up-close look at a sizeable saltwater croc is also memorable, while upstairs visitors queue up for cute koala selfies (from $25). Talks through the day fill you in on key species.

Surry Hills & Darlinghurst

★ **Australian Museum** MUSEUM
(Map p84; ☑02-9320 6000; www.australian museum.net.au; 6 College St, Darlinghurst; adult/child $15/free; ⊙9.30am-5pm; 🚉Museum) Under ongoing modernisation, this museum, established just 40 years after the First Fleet dropped anchor, is brilliant. A standout is the section covering Aboriginal history and spirituality, from Dreaming stories to videos of the Freedom Rides of the 1960s. The elegant Long Gallery focuses on 100 objects (from a platypus-skin rug and an Egyptian death-boat to the 'Bone Ranger') and 100 key Australians. The excellent dinosaur gallery features enormous *Jobaria* as well as local bruisers like *Muttaburrasaurus*.

★ **Sydney Jewish Museum** MUSEUM
(Map p114; ☑02-9360 7999; www.sydneyjewish museum.com.au; 148 Darlinghurst Rd, Darlinghurst; adult/teen/child $15/9/free; ⊙10am-4.30pm Mon-Thu, to 3pm Fri, to 4pm Sun; 🚉Kings Cross) One of Sydney's best museums revolves around a detailed and expertly curated exhibition on the Holocaust, with sobering personal testimonies and moving objects as well as a memorial section for the 1.5 million child victims. Other sections cover the history and practice of Judaism itself and Australian Jewish history, culture and tradition. A section on the top floor examines contemporary human rights challenges, while temporary exhibitions are always excellent. There's also a kosher cafe.

★ **Brett Whiteley Studio** GALLERY
(Map p114; ☑02-9225 1881; www.artgallery.nsw. gov.au/brett-whiteley-studio; 2 Raper St, Surry Hills; ⊙10am-4pm Fri-Sun; 🚢Surry Hills, 🚉Central) **FREE** Acclaimed local artist Brett Whiteley (1939–1992) lived fast and without restraint. His studio has been preserved as a gallery for some of his best work. Pride of place goes to his astonishing *Alchemy*, a giant multi-panel extravaganza that could absorb you for hours with its broad themes, intricate details and humorous asides. The studio room upstairs also gives great insight into the character of this masterful draughtsman and off-the-wall genius.

Kings Cross & Potts Point

★ **Elizabeth Bay House** HISTORIC BUILDING
(Map p90; ☑02-9356 3022; www.sydneyliving museums.com.au; 7 Onslow Ave, Elizabeth Bay; adult/child $12/8; ⊙11am-4pm Fri-Sun; 🚌311,

City Centre & Haymarket

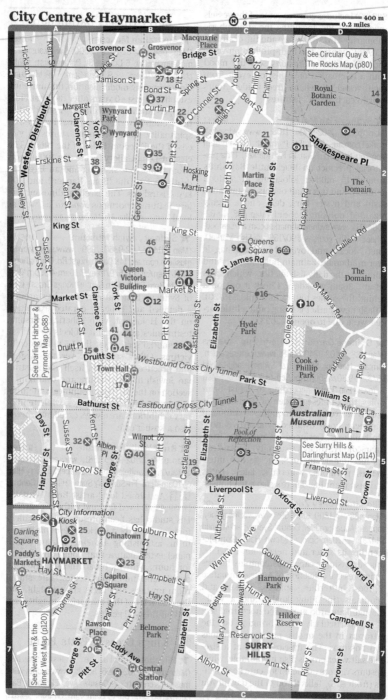

See Circular Quay &
The Rocks Map (p80)

See Darling Harbour &
Pyrmont Map (p88)

See Surry Hills &
Darlinghurst Map (p114)

See Newtown & the
Inner West Map (p120)

SYDNEY & NEW SOUTH WALES SYDNEY

City Centre & Haymarket

◎ **Top Sights**
1 Australian Museum...............................D4
2 Chinatown...A6

◎ **Sights**
3 Anzac Memorial....................................C5
4 Calyx...D2
5 Hyde Park...C4
6 Hyde Park Barracks Museum...............C3
7 Martin Place..B2
8 Museum of Sydney...............................C1
9 St James' Church..................................C3
10 St Mary's Cathedral..............................D3
11 State Library of NSW.............................D2
12 State Theatre...B3
13 Sydney Tower Eye B3

⊕ **Activities, Courses & Tours**
14 Aboriginal Heritage Tour......................D1
15 BlueBananas...A4
16 Free Tours Sydney.................................C3
17 I'm Free Walking Tours..........................B4

🛏 **Sleeping**
18 Establishment Hotel..............................B1
19 Hyde Park Inn..B5
   QT Sydney.......................................(see 12)
20 Sydney Central YHA..............................A7

✕ **Eating**
21 Azuma..C2
22 Bentley Restaurant & Bar.....................B1

23 Chat Thai..B6
24 Cross Eatery...A2
25 Golden Century......................................A6
26 Gumshara...A6
27 Mr Wong...B1
28 Pablo & Rusty's......................................B4
29 Restaurant Hubert..................................C1
30 Rockpool Bar & Grill..............................C2
31 Sydney Madang.....................................B5
32 Tetsuya's...A5

🍷 **Drinking & Nightlife**
33 Baxter Inn...A3
34 Frankie's Pizza.......................................C2
35 Ivy...B2
36 Love, Tilly Devine...................................D5
37 O Bar...B1
38 Uncle Ming's...A2

✪ **Entertainment**
39 City Recital Hall......................................B2
40 Metro Theatre..B5
   State Theatre................................(see 12)

🛍 **Shopping**
41 Abbey's...B4
42 David Jones...C3
43 Paddy's Markets.....................................A6
44 Queen Victoria Building.........................B4
45 Red Eye Records....................................B4
46 Strand Arcade..B3
47 Westfield Sydney...................................B3

🚇 Kings Cross) Now dwarfed by 20th-century apartments, Colonial Secretary Alexander Macleay's elegant Greek Revival mansion was one of the finest houses in the colony when it was completed in 1839. The architectural highlight is an exquisite oval saloon with a curved and cantilevered staircase. There are lovely views over the harbour from the upstairs rooms. Drop down to the twin cellars for an introductory audiovisual with a weird beginning.

◎ Paddington & Centennial Park

★**Centennial Park**   PARK
(Map p92; 🗷02-9339 6699; www.centennialpark lands.com.au; Oxford St; ⊗gates sunrise-sunset; 🚇Moore Park, 🚇Bondi Junction) Scratched out of the sand in 1888 in grand Victorian style, Sydney's biggest park is a rambling 189-hectare expanse full of horse riders, joggers, cyclists and in-line skaters. Grab a park map at any of the entrances or the information centre in the middle. During summer the Moonlight Cinema (p130) attracts crowds.

◎ Bondi, Coogee & the Eastern Beaches

★**Bondi Beach**   BEACH
(Map p108; Campbell Pde; 🚌333) Definitively Sydney, Bondi is one of the world's great beaches. It's the closest ocean beach to the city centre (8km away), has consistently good (though crowded) waves, and is great for a rough-and-tumble swim (the average water temperature is a considerate 21°C). If the sea's angry, try the child-friendly saltwater sea baths at either end of the beach.

Bronte Beach   BEACH
(Map p76; Bronte Rd; 🚻; 🚌379) A winning family-oriented beach hemmed in by sandstone cliffs and a grassy park, Bronte lays claims to having the oldest surf lifesaving club in the world (1903). Contrary to popular belief, the beach is named after Lord Nelson, who doubled as the Duke of Bronte (a place in Sicily), and not the famous literary sisters. There's a kiosk and a changing room attached to the surf club, and covered picnic tables near the public barbecues.

Coogee Beach BEACH
(Map p76; Arden St; ☐ 313, 314, 353, 370, 372, 373, 374, X73) Bondi without the glitz and the poseurs, Coogee (locals pronounce the 'oo' as in the word 'took') has a deep sweep of sand, historic ocean baths and plenty of green space for barbecues and Frisbee hurling. There are lockers and showers here. Between the world wars, Coogee had an English-style pier, with a 1400-seat theatre and a 600-seat ballroom...until the surf took it.

Waverley Cemetery CEMETERY
(Map p76; ☎ 02-9083 8899; www.waverleycem etery.com; St Thomas St, Bronte; ☺ 7am-5pm May-Sep, to 7pm Oct-Apr; ☐ 360, 379) Many Sydneysiders would die for these views...and that's the only way they'll get them. Blanketing the clifftops between Bronte and Clovelly beaches, the white marble gravestones here are dazzling in the sunlight. Eighty thousand people have been interred here since 1877, including writers Henry Lawson and Dorothea Mackellar, and cricketer Victor Trumper. It's an engrossing (and surprisingly uncreepy) place to explore, and maybe to spot a whale offshore during winter. The Bondi to Coogee coastal walk (p97) heads past it.

⊙ Sydney Harbourside

★ Watsons Bay AREA
(Map p76; ☐ 324, 325, 380, ⛴ Watsons Bay) Lovely Watsons Bay, east of the city centre and north of Bondi, was once a small fishing village, as evidenced by the heritage cottages that pepper the suburb's narrow streets (and now cost a fortune). It's a lovely day trip by ferry for an exploration of South Head and a leisurely lunch. While you're here, tradition demands that you sit in the pub's beer garden at sunset and watch the sun dissolve behind the Harbour Bridge, jutting above Bradley's Head.

★ Cockatoo Island ISLAND
(Map p76; ☎ 02-8969 2100; www.cockatoo island.gov.au; ⛴ Cockatoo Island) Studded with photogenic industrial relics, convict architecture and art installations, fascinating Cockatoo Island (Wareamah) opened to the public in 2007 and now has regular ferry services, a campground (p108), rental accommodation, a cafe and a bar. Information boards and audio guides ($5) explain the island's time as a prison, a shipyard and a naval base.

★ Taronga Zoo Sydney ZOO
(Map p76; ☎ 02-9969 2777; www.taronga.org.au; Bradleys Head Rd, Mosman; adult/child $47/27; ☺ 9.30am-5pm Sep-Apr, to 4.30pm May-Aug; 👶; ☐ M30, ⛴ Taronga Zoo) 🌿 A 12-minute ferry ride from Circular Quay, this bushy harbour hillside is full of kangaroos, koalas and similarly hirsute Australians, plus numerous imported guests. The zoo's critters have million-dollar harbour views, but seem blissfully unaware of the privilege. Encouragingly, Taronga sets benchmarks in animal care and welfare. Highlights include the nocturnal platypus habitat, the Great Southern Oceans section and the Asian elephant display. Feedings and encounters happen throughout the day, while in summer, twilight concerts jazz things up (see www. twilightattaronga.org.au).

★ McMahons Point VIEWPOINT
(Map p76; Henry Lawson Ave; ⛴ McMahons Point) Is there a better view of the bridge and the Opera House than from the wharf at this point, a short hop by ferry northwest of the centre? It's all unfolded before you and is a stunning spot to be when the sun is setting.

Parsley Bay BEACH
(Map p76; Vaucluse; ☐ 325) A hidden gem, this little bay has a calm swimming beach, a lawn dotted with sandstone sculptures for picnics and play, a little cafe and a cute suspension bridge. Keep an eye out for water dragons (native reptiles) as you walk down through the bush.

Vaucluse House HISTORIC BUILDING
(Map p76; ☎ 02-9388 7922; www.sydneyliving museums.com.au; Wentworth Rd, Vaucluse; adult/child $12/8; ☺ 10am-4pm Wed-Sun; ☐ 325) Construction of this imposing, turreted specimen of Gothic Australiana, set amid 10 hectares of lush gardens, commenced in 1805, but the house was tinkered with into the 1860s. Atmospheric, and decorated with beautiful European period pieces, the house offers visitors a rare glimpse into early Sydney colonial life, as lived by the well-to-do. The history of the Wentworths, who occupied it, is fascinating, and helpful guides give great background on them. In the grounds is a popular tearoom.

South Head NATIONAL PARK
(Map p76; www.nationalparks.nsw.gov.au; Cliff St, Watsons Bay; ☺ 5am-10pm; ☐ 324, 325, 380, ⛴ Watsons Bay) At the northern end of Camp Cove, the **South Head Heritage Trail**

SYDNEY IN...

Two Days

Start your first day by getting a train to Milsons Point and walking back to the **Rocks** (p77) across the **Harbour Bridge** (p73). Then explore the Rocks area, delving into all the narrow lanes. Next, follow the harbour past the **Opera House** (p72) to the **Royal Botanic Garden** (p69) and on to the **Art Gallery of NSW** (p79). That night, enjoy a performance at the Opera House or check out the action in Chinatown or Darlinghurst. Next day, spend some time soaking up the sun and scene at **Bondi** (p85) – be sure to take the cliff top walk to Coogee and then make your way back to Bondi for a sunset dinner at **Icebergs Dining Room** (p118).

Four Days

On day three, board a ferry and sail through the harbour to Manly, where you can swim at the beach or follow the **Manly Scenic Walkway** (p98). That night, head to Surry Hills for drinks and dinner. On day four, learn about Sydney's convict heritage at the **Hyde Park Barracks Museum** (p80) then spend the afternoon shopping in Paddington or Newtown.

---

kicks off, leading into a section of Sydney Harbour National Park distinguished by harbour views and crashing surf. It passes old fortifications and a path heading down to Lady Bay, before continuing on to the candy-striped Hornby Lighthouse and the sandstone Lightkeepers' Cottages (1858). Between April and November, look out to sea to where the whale-watching boats have congregated and you'll often see cetaceans.

Luna Park   AMUSEMENT PARK
(Map p76; ☑02-9922 6644; www.lunaparksyd ney.com; 1 Olympic Dr, Milsons Point; ☺11am-4pm Mon-Thu, to 10pm Fri & Sat, 10am-6pm Sun; ☷Milsons Point, ☷Milsons Point) **FREE** A sinister chip-toothed clown face (50 times life-sized) forms the entrance to this old-fashioned amusement park overlooking Sydney Harbour. It's one of several 1930s features, including the Coney Island funhouse, a pretty carousel and the nausea-inducing Rotor. You can purchase a two-ride pass ($22), or buy a height-based unlimited-ride pass (adults $55, kids $25 to $45; cheaper if purchased online). Hours are complex, and extended during school and public holidays. It also functions as a concert venue.

◉ Newtown & the Inner West

★White Rabbit   GALLERY
(Map p120; ☑02-8399 2867; www.whiterabbit collection.org; 30 Balfour St, Chippendale; ☺10am-5pm Wed-Sun, often closed Feb & Aug; ☷Central) **FREE** In many ways Sydney's best contemporary art gallery, White Rabbit is tucked away behind the Central Park development in Chippendale. There are so many works in this private collection of cutting-edge, contemporary Chinese art that only a fraction can be displayed at one time. Who knew that the People's Republic was turning out work that was so edgy, funny, sexy and idiosyncratic? An on-site cafe does speciality teas and dumplings.

University of Sydney   UNIVERSITY
(Map p120; ☑02-9351 2222; www.sydney.edu.au; Parramatta Rd, University of Sydney; ☷412, 413, 436, 438, 439, 440, 461, 480, 483, M10) Australia's oldest tertiary institution (1850) has around 50,000 students and boasts its own postcode. You don't need a PhD to grab a free campus map and wander around. Flanked by two grand halls that wouldn't be out of place in Harry Potter's Hogwarts, the sandstone Quadrangle has a Gothic Revival design that tips its mortarboard towards the stately colleges of Oxford. The excellent Nicholson Museum (Map p120; ☑02-9351 2812; www.sydney.edu.au/museums; ☺10am-4.30pm Mon-Fri, noon-4pm 1st Sat of month) **FREE** will merge with other university collections in the new Chau Chak Wing Museum in 2020.

◉ Manly

★North Head   NATIONAL PARK
(Map p76; ☑1300 072 757; www.nationalparks. nsw.gov.au; North Head Scenic Dr, Manly; ☺sunrise-sunset; ☷135) **FREE** About 3km south of central Manly, spectacular North Head offers dramatic cliffs, lookouts, secluded beaches, pretty paths through the native scrub, and sweeping views of the ocean, the harbour and the city. It's great to explore

Darling Harbour & Pyrmont

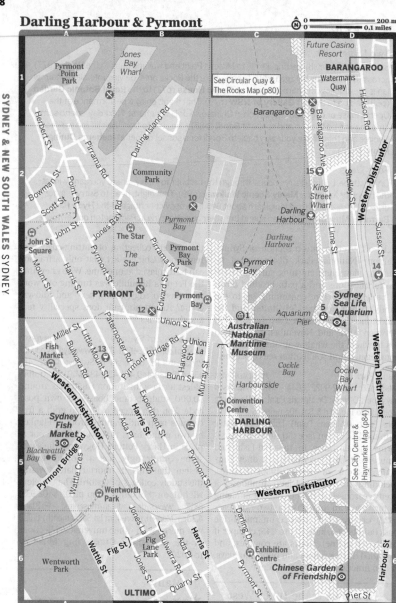

by bike or on foot, along the Manly Scenic Walkway (p98). Grab a map and plot your own path through the headland, which takes in former military barracks, WWII gun emplacements, a quarantine cemetery and a memorial walk commemorating Australia's military. At the tip, **Fairfax Lookouts** offer dramatic clifftop perspectives.

★**Manly Beach**　　　　　BEACH
(Map p111; 🚢Manly) Sydney's second most famous beach is a magnificent strand that stretches for nearly two golden kilometres,

Darling Harbour & Pyrmont

◎ **Top Sights**
1 Australian National Maritime
   Museum..C3
2 Chinese Garden of Friendship...............D6
3 Sydney Fish Market................................A5
4 Sydney Sea Life Aquarium D4

◎ **Sights**
5 Wild Life Sydney Zoo.............................D3

⊙ **Activities, Courses & Tours**
6 Sydney Seafood School.........................A5

🛌 **Sleeping**
7 Ovolo 1888 Darling Harbour B5

⊗ **Eating**
8 Cafe Morso A1
9 Cirrus...D1
10 LuMi B2
11 Momofuku Seiōbo B3
12 Sokyo...B3

⊙ **Drinking & Nightlife**
13 Edition Book Bar.....................................A4
14 Slip Inn & Chinese Laundry D3
15 Smoke D2

lined by Norfolk Island pines and midrise apartment blocks. The southern end of the beach, nearest the Corso, is known as South Steyne, with North Steyne in the centre and Queenscliff at the northern end; each has its own surf lifesaving club.

★**Store Beach**   BEACH
(Map p76; ⊙dawn-dusk; 🚢Manly) A hidden jewel on North Head, magical Store Beach can only be reached by kayak – you can hire them from Manly Kayak Centre (p92) – or boat. It's a breeding ground for **fairy penguins**, so access is prohibited from dusk, when the birds waddle in to settle down for the night.

Shelly Beach   BEACH
(Map p76; Bower St, Manly; 🚢Manly) This pretty, sheltered, north-facing ocean cove is an appealing 1km walk from the busy Manly beach strip. The tranquil waters are a protected haven for marine life, so it offers wonderful snorkelling. It's a popular place for picnickers.

Q Station   HISTORIC BUILDING
(Quarantine Station; Map p76; 🕿02-9466 1551; www.qstation.com.au; 1 North Head Scenic Dr, Manly; ⊙visitor centre 10am-4pm Sun-Thu, 10am-8pm Fri & Sat; 🚍135) FREE From 1837 to 1984 this sprawling historic complex in beautiful North Head bushland was used to isolate new arrivals suspected of carrying disease. These days it has been reborn as a tourist destination, offering appealing accommodation (p109) and tours. Shuttle buses whisk you from reception down to the wharf, where there's a lovely beach, a museum in the old luggage shop telling the site's story, an information desk and a cafe. Nearby is a bar and restaurant.

⊙ Northern Beaches

★**Palm Beach**   BEACH
(Ocean Rd, Palm Beach; 🚍199, L90) Long, lovely Palm Beach is a crescent of bliss that's famous as the setting for cheesy TV soap *Home and Away*. The 1881 Barrenjoey Lighthouse punctuates the northern tip of the headland in an annexe of Ku-ring-gai Chase National Park (p91). The suburb of Palm Beach has two sides, the magnificent ocean beach and a pleasant strip on Pittwater, where the calmer strands are good for young kids. From here you can get **ferries** (🕿02-9974 2411; www.fantasea.com.au/palmbeachferries; Barrenjoey Rd, Palm Beach; each way adult/child Pittwater ferries $8.20/4.10, Broken Bay ferries $11.80/5.90; ⊙office 9am-5pm Mon-Fri, from 10am Sat & Sun; 🚍199, L90) to other picturesque Pittwater destinations, including other park sections.

Avalon   BEACH
(Barrenjoey Rd, Avalon; 🚍188, 199, L90) Caught in a sandy '70s time warp, Avalon is the mythical Australian beach you always dreamed of but could never find. Challenging surf and sloping, tangerine-gold sand have a boutique headland for a backdrop. There's a sea pool at the southern end. Good, cheap eating options abound in the streets behind.

Barrenjoey Lighthouse   LIGHTHOUSE
(🕿02-9451 3479; www.nationalparks.nsw.gov.au; Palm Beach; 🚍199, L90) FREE This historic sandstone lighthouse (1881) sits at the northern tip of the Northern Beaches in an annexe of Ku-ring-gai Chase National Park (p91). You've got two route options – shorter stairs or a winding, convict-built track – for the steep hike to the top, but majestic views

Kings Cross & Potts Point

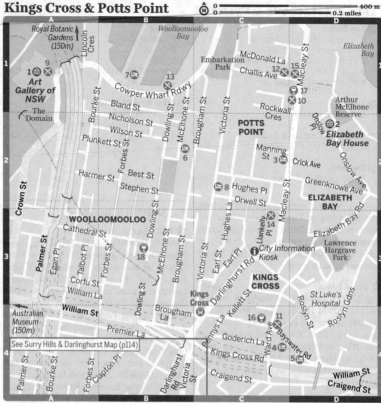

Kings Cross & Potts Point

◎ Top Sights
1 Art Gallery of NSW A1
2 Elizabeth Bay House D2

◎ Sleeping
3 Blue Parrot Backpackers C2
4 Hotel 59 ....C4
5 Kings Cross Backpackers D4
6 Mariners Court B2
7 Ovolo Hotel Woolloomooloo B1
8 Spicers C2

◎ Eating
9 Chiswick at the Gallery A1
10 Cho Cho San D1

11 Farmhouse C4
12 Fratelli Paradiso C1
13 Harry's Cafe de Wheels B1
14 Room 10 ....C3
15 Yellow D1

◎ Drinking & Nightlife
16 Crane Bar C4
17 Monopole D1
18 Old Fitzroy Hotel B3

◎ Entertainment
Old Fitz Theatre ....(see 18)

across Pittwater and down the peninsula are worth the effort. On Sundays short tours (adult/child $5/2) run half-hourly from 11am to 3pm; no need to book. The top is also good for whale watching.

◎ Parramatta

Experiment Farm Cottage   HISTORIC BUILDING
(☎02-9635 5655; www.nationaltrust.org.au; 9 Ruse St, Harris Park; adult/child $9/4; ☺guided

tours 10.30am-3.30pm Wed-Sun; ⓡHarris Park) This colonial bungalow stands on the site of Australia's first official land grant. In 1789 Governor Phillip allocated 12 hectares to emancipated convict James Ruse as an experiment to see how long it would take Ruse to wean himself off government supplies. The experiment was a success, and Ruse became Australia's first private farmer. He sold the land to surgeon John Harris, who built this house around 1835. It's decked out in period style with lovely early colonial furniture.

Entrance is by very informative guided tour; the last one begins at 3pm.

Elizabeth Farm　　　　　HISTORIC BUILDING
(✑02-9635 9488; www.sydneylivingmuseums. com.au; 70 Alice St, Rosehill; adult/child $12/8; ☺10am-4pm Wed-Sun; ⓡ909 from Parramatta station, ⓡHarris Park) Elizabeth Farm contains part of Australia's oldest surviving colonial building (1793), built by renegade pastoralist and rum trader John Macarthur. Heralded as the founder of Australia's wool industry, Macarthur was a ruthless capitalist whose politicking made him immensely wealthy and a thorn in the side of successive governors. The pretty homestead is now a hands-on museum where you can recline on the reproduction furniture and thumb voyeuristically through Elizabeth Macarthur's letters.

Old Government House　　HISTORIC BUILDING
(✑02-9635 8149; www.nationaltrust.org.au; Parramatta Park, Parramatta; adult/child $13/5; ☺10am-4pm Tue-Sun; ⓡParramatta) The country residence of the early governors, this elegant Georgian Palladian building in **Parramatta Park** (www.parrapark.com.au; cnr Pitt & Macquarie Sts; ☺6am-6pm Apr-Sep, to 8pm Oct-Mar) is now a preciously maintained museum furnished with original colonial furniture. It dates from 1799, making it the oldest remaining public building in Australia. Temporary exhibitions add to the building's interest and there's a vine-draped courtyard restaurant.

◉ Outer Sydney

★**Ku-ring-gai Chase
National Park**　　　　　NATIONAL PARK
(✑02-9472 8949; www.nationalparks.nsw.gov. au; per car per day $12, landing fee by boat adult/ child $3/2; ☺sunrise-sunset) This spectacular 14,928-hectare park, 20 to 30km from the city centre, forms Sydney's northern boundary. It's a classic mix of sandstone, bushland and water vistas, taking in over 100km of coastline along the southern edge of Broken Bay, where it heads into the Hawkesbury River. There are two unconnected principal sections, **Bobbin Head** (Bobbin Head Rd, North Turramurra; per car $12; ⓡ577 from Turramurra station, ⓡMt Colah) and the **West Head** (West Head Rd, Terrey Hills; per car $12) area. The Barrenjoey (p89) headland at Palm Beach is also part of the park. Park tours (p101) are available.

Lane Cove National Park　　NATIONAL PARK
(✑weekdays 02-8448 0400, weekends 02-9472 8949; www.nationalparks.nsw.gov.au; Lady Game Dr, Chatswood West; per car $8; ☺9am-6pm Apr-Sep, to 7pm Oct-Mar; ⓡ545, 550, ⓡNorth Ryde) This lovely park, surrounded by North Shore suburbia, flanks the Lane Cove River, which spills into the harbour. It's a great place to stretch out on some middle-sized bushwalks and is on the **Great North Walk** (www. greatnorthwalk.com) from Sydney to Newcastle. It's home to dozens of critters, including some endangered owls and toads. If you visit in spring, the water dragons will be getting frisky and the native orchids and lilies will be flowering. The **information office** (Map p76; ☺9am-4pm Mon-Fri) near the main entrance has a cafe.

🏃 Activities

Cycling
Manly Bike Tours　　　　　CYCLING
(Map p111; ✑02-8005 7368; www.manlybike tours.com.au; Belgrave St, Manly; hire per hour/day from $16/33; ☺9am-6pm Oct-Mar, to 5pm Apr-Sep; ⛴Manly) Hires out bikes and provides maps and suggested routes for self-guided tours. There's a big variety of bikes available and it's right across from the ferry wharf. Key lockers are available for you to store gear while you ride.

Diving
Dive Centre Bondi　　　　　DIVING
(Map p108; ✑02-9369 3855; www.divebondi.com. au; 198 Bondi Rd, Bondi; 2 guided dives incl equipment from shore/boat $155/195, PADI Open Water courses $495; ☺9am-6pm Mon-Fri, from 8am Sat & Sun; ⓡ333) Friendly and professional, this centre offers guided dives from shore or boat as well as equipment hire. It runs PADI Open Water courses as well as other certifications.

Paddington & Centennial Park

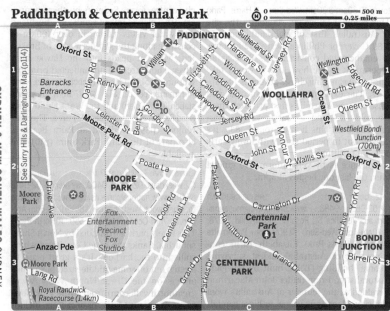

Paddington & Centennial Park

◎ **Top Sights**
1 Centennial Park....................................C3

🛏 **Sleeping**
2 Mrs Banks...B1

🍴 **Eating**
3 Chiswick..D1
4 Paddington Alimentari.........................B1
5 Saint Peter..B1

🍷 **Drinking & Nightlife**
6 10 William Street.................................B1

🎭 **Entertainment**
7 Moonlight Cinema................................D2
8 Sydney Cricket Ground........................A2

🛍 **Shopping**
9 Dinosaur Designs.................................B1
10 Paddington Markets...........................B1

Kayaking & Stand-up Paddleboarding

The harbour offers some great kayaking, with coves, islands and tributaries to explore. It's also a very busy waterway, so stick close to shore when you can. Check out Paddle Safety on Sydney Harbour on the RMS website (www.rms.nsw.gov.au). Stand-up paddleboarding (SUP) is very popular on both the harbour and ocean, with operators at several spots including Manly, Rose Bay, Coogee and Avalon hiring out boards.

Manly Kayak Centre   KAYAKING
(Map p111; ☎02-9976 5057; www.manlykayak centre.com.au; Manly Wharf, Manly; hire per 1/2/4/8hr from $25/45/55/75; ☺9am-5pm; 🚢Manly) Hire a kayak or paddleboard from

this set-up near Manly Wharf Hotel or its **street office** (Map p111; ☎02-9976 5057; 1/40 East Esplanade ☺9am-5pm). You'll be provided with a life jacket, paddling instruction and tips on secluded beaches to visit. There are large paddleboards suitable for the whole family. Four-hour kayak tours at weekends cost $109. It's best to book hires ahead.

Sydney Harbour Kayaks   KAYAKING
(Map p76; ☎02-9960 4389; www.sydneyharbour kayaks.com.au; Smiths Boat Shed, 81 Parriwi Rd, Mosman; kayak/SUP per hour from $20/25, eco-tours $125; ☺9am-5pm Mon-Fri, from 7.30am Sat & Sun, closed Mon & Tue Jun-Sep; 🚌; 🚌E66, E68, E71, E75, 76, 77) Rents out kayaks and SUPs, and leads excellent four-hour ecotours from near the Spit Bridge.

AL YOSHI/GETTY IMAGES ©

Sydney's Beaches

Whether you join the procession of the bronzed and the beautiful at Bondi, or surreptitiously slink into a deserted nook hidden within Sydney Harbour National Park, the beach is an essential part of the Sydney experience. Even in winter, watching the rollers break while you're strolling along the sand is exhilarating. Sydney's beaches broadly divide into the eastern beaches, south of the harbour, running from Bondi southwards, and the northern beaches, north of the harbour, starting at Manly.

Contents
➡ Beach Culture
➡ Need to Know
➡ Beaches by Neighbourhood
➡ Lonely Planet's Top Choices

Above Bridge to Bare Island (p96), La Perouse

Beach Culture

In the mid-1990s an enthusiastic businesswoman obtained a concession to rent loungers on Tamarama Beach and offer waiter service. Needless to say, it didn't last long. Even at what was considered at the time to be Sydney's most glamorous beach, nobody was interested in that kind of malarkey.

For Australians, going to the beach is all about rolling out a towel on the sand with a minimum of fuss. And they're certainly not prepared to pay for the privilege. Sandy-toed ice-cream vendors are acceptable; martini luggers are not. In summer one of the more unusual sights is the little coffee and ice-cream boat pulling up to Lady Bay (and other harbour beaches) and a polite queue of nude gentlemen forming to purchase their icy poles.

Surf lifesavers have a hallowed place in the culture and you'd do well to heed their instructions, not least of all because they're likely to be in your best interests. They're an Australian institution.

Ocean Pools

If you have children, or shark paranoia, or surf just isn't your thing, you'll be pleased to hear that Sydney's blessed with a string of 40 artificial ocean pools up and down the coast, most of them free. Some, like **Mahon Pool** (www.randwick.nsw.gov.au; Marine Pde, Maroubra; 📰353, 376-77) **FREE**, are what are known as bogey holes – natural-looking rock pools where you can safely splash about and snorkel, even while the surf surges in. Others are more like swimming pools; Bondi's Icebergs (p97) is a good example of this kind. They normally close one day a week so they can clean the seaweed out.

1. Bondi Icebergs Pool (p97) **2.** Surfer, Tamarama Beach **3.** A surf lifesaver on duty at Bondi

Need to Know

If you're not used to swimming at surf beaches, you may be unprepared for the dangers.

➜ Always swim between the red-and-yellow flags on lifesaver-patrolled beaches. Not only are these areas patrolled, but they're also positioned away from dangerous rips and underwater holes. Plus you're much less likely to get clobbered by a surfboard.

➜ If you get into trouble, hold up your hand to signal the lifesavers.

➜ Never swim under the influence of alcohol or other drugs.

➜ Due to pollution from stormwater drains, avoid swimming in the ocean for a day and in the harbour for three days after heavy rains. And on a related topic, don't drop rubbish – including cigarette butts – on the streets unless you don't mind swimming with it come the next rainfall.

Beaches by Region

Sydney Harbour Lots of hidden coves and secret sandy spots; the best are out near the heads and around Mosman.

Eastern Beaches High cliffs frame a string of surf beaches, with coffee and cold beer just a short stumble away.

Northern Beaches A steady succession of magical surf beaches stretching 30km north from Manly to Palm Beach.

Best for Snorkelling

Gordons Bay (Map p76; www.gordonsbay scubadivingclub.com; ☐338, 339) Probably Sydney's best spot for shore snorkelling, with an underwater nature trail.

North Bondi (p85) Plenty to see at the rocks here, but watch for surfboards.

Bronte Beach ocean pool (p85)

Camp Cove (Map p76; 🚌324, 325, 380, 🚢Watsons Bay) Interesting spot near the mouth of the harbour.

Shelly Beach (p89) One of the most sheltered of the oceanside beaches; a huge variety of fish.

Clovelly Beach (Map p76; 🚌338, 339) Clearer, calmer water than other beaches; Gordons Bay is just around the corner.

Bare Island (📞1300 072 757; www.nationalparks.nsw.gov.au; tours adult/child $15/10; ⏰tours 1.30, 2.30 & 3.30pm Sun; 🚌L94, 391, 393, 394) Pretty sponges and reefs at this Botany Bay island.

Lonely Planet's Top Choices

Bondi Beach (p85) Australia's most iconic ocean beach.

Nielsen Park (Map p76; ⏰5am-10pm; 🚌325) The pick of the harbour beaches, surrounded by beautiful national park.

Whale Beach (🚌199, L90) Peachy-coloured sand and crashing waves; you've really left the city behind at this stunning Northern Beaches haven.

Bronte Beach (p85) Family-friendly and backed by park, this is an eastern beaches gem.

Murray Rose Pool (p97) The closest beach to the city is also one of Sydney's finest.

Harbour Beaches & Pools

The pick of Sydney's harbour beaches includes Camp Cove and Lady Bay near South Head (the latter is mainly a gay nude beach), Shark Beach at Nielsen Park in Vaucluse, and Balmoral Beach on the North Shore. Also popular are the netted swimming enclosures at Cremorne Point on the North Shore and Murray Rose Pool near Double Bay. There are plenty of little sandy gems scattered about that even Sydneysiders would be hard pressed to find, including Parsley Bay and Milk Beach right in the heart of residential Vaucluse.

Surfing

Most beaches have surfboard hire available and several have companies offering surfing lessons. The southern end of Manly Beach (p88) and the northern end of Bondi (p85) are popular spots for beginners; **Freshwater** is another friendly break.

★ **Let's Go Surfing**   SURFING
(Map p108; ☑ 02-9365 1800; www.letsgosurfing. com.au; 128 Ramsgate Ave, North Bondi; board & wetsuit hire 1hr/2hr/day/week $25/30/50/200; ☑ 9am-5pm; ☑ 333) North Bondi is a great place to learn to surf, and this well-established surf school offers lessons catering to practically everyone. There are classes for 'grommets' (young surfers) aged seven to 16 (1½ hours, $49) and adults (two hours, $110; women-only classes available), or you can book a private tutor (1½ hours, $205/300 for one/two people). Prices drop outside summer.

Manly Surf School   SURFING
(Map p76; ☑ 02-9932 7000; www.manlysurf school.com; North Steyne Surf Club, Manly; surf lessons adult/child $70/60, surf safari $120; ☑ 136, 139, ☑ Manly) Reliable and well established, this outfit offers two-hour surf lessons year-round, as well as private tuition. It's a fair bit cheaper if you book a multi-class package. You can also book classes at other beaches. They run good-value surf safaris up to the Northern Beaches, including two lessons, lunch, gear and city pick-ups; a fun day out.

Swimming

Fancy a dip? Sydney has sheltered harbour coves, saltwater rock pools, more than 100 public pools and brilliant ocean beaches. Always swim between the flags on lifesaver-patrolled beaches, and avoid swimming in the ocean for a day and in the harbour for three days after heavy rains. Many outdoor pools close at the end of April for the cooler months and reopen in early October.

Bondi Icebergs Pool   SWIMMING
(Map p108; ☑ 02-9130 4804; www.icebergs.com. au; 1 Notts Ave, Bondi Beach; adult/child $8/5.50; ☑ 6am-6.30pm Mon-Wed & Fri, from 6.30am Sat & Sun; ☑ 333) Sydney's most famous pool commands the best view in Bondi and has a cute little **cafe** (Map p108; ☑ 0450 272 223; www.facebook.com/thecrabbehole; breakfasts $8-17; ☑ 7am-3pm Mon-Fri, to 5pm Sat & Sun). It's a saltwater pool that's regularly doused by the bigger breakers. There's a more sheltered pool for kids. It closes on Thursdays so they can clean the seaweed out, though it sometimes opens once the job's done.

Andrew (Boy) Charlton Pool   SWIMMING
(Map p76; ☑ 02-9358 6686; www.abcpool.org; 1c Mrs Macquaries Rd; adult/child $6.60/5; ☑ 6am-7pm Sep & Apr, to 8pm Oct-Mar; ☑; ☑ 441) One of Sydney's best saltwater pools – smack-bang next to the harbour – is a magnet for serious lap swimmers, who rule the roost (so maintain your lane). There's a cafe here looking across at the Garden Island base, great for some naval gazing. Wheelchair-accessible. **Yoga classes** (www.sydneyyogacollective.com; per class $12) are also available here, as well as other activities.

Murray Rose Pool   SWIMMING
(Redleaf Pool; Map p76; 536 New South Head Rd, Double Bay; ☑ 323-326, ☑ Double Bay) **FREE** Not a pool as such, family-friendly Murray Rose (named after a champion Olympic swimmer) is a large, shark-netted enclosure that is one of the harbour's best swimming spots. As one of the closest harbour beaches to the city, it attracts an urbane cross-section of inner-eastern locals. A boardwalk runs around it, and there's a sought-after floating pontoon.

Wylie's Baths   SWIMMING
(Map p76; ☑ 02-9665 2838; www.wylies.com.au; 4b Neptune St, Coogee; adult/child $5.50/2.60; ☑ 7am-7pm Oct-Mar, to 5pm Apr-Sep; ☑ 353, 376, 337) On the rocky coast south of Coogee Beach, this superb sea-water pool (dating from 1907) is targeted at swimmers more than splashabouts. After your swim, take a yoga class, enjoy a massage, or have a coffee at the kiosk, which has magnificent ocean views.

McIver's Ladies Baths   SWIMMING
(Map p76; www.randwick.nsw.gov.au; Beach St, Coogee; $2; ☑ sunrise-sunset; ☑ 352, 372-7) Perched against the cliffs south of Coogee Beach and well screened from passers-by, this sea pool has been popular for women's bathing since before 1876. Its strict women-only policy has made it a relaxed space popular with nuns, Muslim women and lesbians. Small children of any gender are permitted.

Walking

★ **Bondi to Coogee Clifftop Walk**   WALKING
(Map p108) The simply sensational 6km Bondi to Coogee walk leads south from Bondi Beach along the cliff tops via Tamarama, Bronte and Clovelly, interweaving

panoramic views, patrolled beaches, sea baths, waterside parks and plaques recounting local Aboriginal stories. The trail begins at the end of Notts Ave and spits you out at the north end of Coogee Beach.

★ **Manly Scenic Walkway**   WALKING
(Map p76; www.manly.nsw.gov.au; 🚇 Manly) This marvellous coastal walk has two major components: the 10km western stretch between Manly and Spit Bridge, and the 9.5km eastern loop around North Head (p87). Either download a map or pick one up from the information centre near the wharf.

The western section traces the complex harbour coastline through upmarket suburbs and then a spectacular section of unspoiled **Sydney Harbour National Park** (www.nationalparks.nsw.gov.au). It emerges in Clontarf and winds its way to the **Spit Bridge**. After crossing the bridge you can take a bus either back to Manly (buses 143 or 144) or into the city (169, 170, 178, 180 and others).

The eastern loop is known as the **North Head Circuit Track** and takes 2½ to 3½ hours. From the wharf, follow Eastern Esplanade and Stuart St to Collins Beach, head into the North Head section of Sydney Harbour National Park, and make your way through the bush to the spectacular **Fairfax Lookout** on North Head (approximately 45 minutes in total). From the lookout, walk the **Fairfax Loop** (1km, 30 minutes) and then head back via Australia's Memorial Walk and WWII gun emplacements to the **Bluefish Track**, which descends spectacularly to Shelly Beach (p89), from where you return to Manly Beach (p88) via picturesque **Fairy Bower Beach** (Map p76; Bower Lane, Manly; 🚇 Manly).

☞ Tours

Boat Tours

★ **Whale Watching Sydney**   WILDLIFE
(WWS; ☎ 02-95831199; www.whalewatchingsydney.com.au; adult/child $79/49; ☺ mid-May–early Dec) Humpback and southern right whales habitually shunt up and down the Sydney coastline, sometimes venturing into the harbour. Between mid-May and December, WWS runs three-hour tours beyond the heads. For a faster ride that also offers a more intimate whale experience, there are two-hour jet-boat expeditions ($65/49). Sunset cruises are also available.

🏃 City Walk
A Rock-Quay Road

START CADMAN'S COTTAGE
END ROYAL BOTANIC GARDEN
LENGTH 3.5KM; TWO HOURS

Start outside ❶ **Cadman's Cottage** (p100), inner-city Sydney's oldest house. It was built on a now-buried beach for John Cadman (a government boat superintendent and former convict) in 1816. Sydney Water Police also detained criminals here in the 1840s. It now sits slightly forlornly among the bustle of the surrounding area.

Head north along Circular Quay West past the ❷ **Overseas Passenger Terminal**, where multi-storey luxury cruise ships regularly dock. For a killer harbour view, if there's no ship to block it, head up to the level-four observation deck in the turret on the northern end.

Further along the quay are ❸ **Campbell's Storehouses**, which date from 1839 (construction finished in 1861, and a brick storey was added in 1890) and were built by Scottish merchant Robert Campbell, a key early trader into the colony. Such buildings were common around Circular Quay into the early 20th century, but most have been demolished since. These survivors now sustain a string of touristy restaurants in a recently refurbished precinct.

Play spot-the-bridal-party as you loop past the ❹ **Park Hyatt** (☎ 02-9256 1234; www.hyatt.com; r $1200-1800) and into the small park at the end of Dawes Point. Couples jet in from far away to have their photos taken here in front of the perfect Opera House background.

As you pass under the ❺ **Harbour Bridge** (p73), keep an eye out for Luna Park on the opposite shore. Stroll around **Walsh Bay's** (p78) gentrified ❻ **Edwardian wharves** and then cross the road and cut up the stairs (marked 'Public stairs to Windmill St') just before the Roslyn Packer Theatre. Continue up the hill on teensy Ferry Lane. Near the top you'll find the foundations of ❼ **Arthur Payne's House**; he was the first victim of the 1900 bubonic plague outbreak.

At the corner of Windmill St is the ❽ **Hero of Waterloo** (p123), a contender for the title of Sydney's oldest pub. Turn right on Lower Fort St and head to

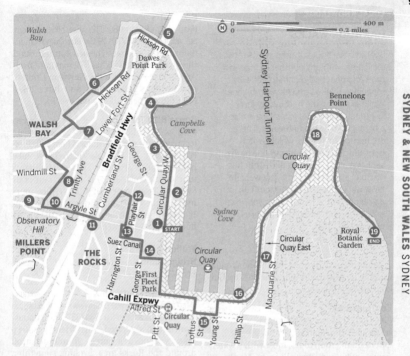

SYDNEY & NEW SOUTH WALES SYDNEY

Argyle Place, a quiet, English-style village green lined with terraced houses.

Across the road is the handsome **Garrison Church** (📞 02-9247 1071; www.churchhill anglican.com; ⏰ 9am-5pm) **FREE**, the colony's first military place of worship. Hook left into Argyle St and stroll down through the **Argyle Cut**. Convict labourers excavated this canyon-like section of road clear through the sandstone ridge that gave the Rocks its name. It was a major engineering feat of its day that connected the eastern and western sides of the Rocks, bypassing the ridge (and, these days, the freeway approaching the Harbour Bridge).

In the Cut, take the stairs up to the left and head along Gloucester Walk to **Foundation Park**, which evokes the area's cramped past. Descend through the park, duck around the building at the bottom and exit onto Playfair St where there's a row of historic terraced houses.

Cross Argyle St into Harrington St then jag left into **Suez Canal**. The narrowest of these typical Rocks lanes (hence the name, also a pun on the word 'sewers'), it is fairly salubrious these days, but was once a rat- and effluent-ridden haunt of thieves and topers, most notably street gang the Rocks Push.

Turn right into George St and cut through the **Museum of Contemporary Art** (p79), Sydney's major showcase for big-name, cutting-edge exhibitions. Exit onto Circular Quay and follow the waterline past the ferry wharves.

Walk underneath the train station to the fabulously renovated **Customs House** (📞 02-9242 8551; www.sydneycustomshouse. com.au; ⏰ 8am-midnight Mon-Fri, from 10am Sat, 11am-5pm Sun) **FREE**. Stroll back to the water to check out the buskers and the metal plaques of the **Sydney Writers Walk**. Serious and comic observations by an eclectic assemblage of authors, including Mark Twain, Germaine Greer and Clive James, cover a wide spectrum of topics, ranging from impressions of the harbour by Joseph Conrad to hopes for racial harmony in Australia by Oodgeroo Noonuccal.

Continue past the **Opera Quays** apartment and entertainment complex on Circular Quay East, which is disparagingly referred to by Sydneysiders as 'The Toaster'.

The heaven-sent sails of the **Sydney Opera House** (p72) are directly in front of you, adjacent to an unmissable perspective of the Sydney Harbour Bridge off to the left. Circumnavigate Bennelong Point, then follow the water's edge through the gates of the **Royal Botanic Garden** (p69).

LOCAL KNOWLEDGE

HARBOUR WALKS

Sydney's harbour suburbs are its most intriguing, with any number of hidden bays and beaches, quiet streets with magnificent views and local ambience. While exploring the harbour by ferry is a must, walking its foreshore is also a highlight of a visit to the city. There are numerous routes, which switch between dedicated harbourside paths, sections along beaches and stretches on quiet suburban roads. The website www.walkingcoastalsydney.com.au is a great resource for planning your own excursion, with downloadable brochures and maps.

Boats depart from Jetty 6 in Circular Quay, from Aquarium Wharf in Darling Harbour, or from Manly.

EcoTreasures
DIVING, KAYAKING

(☑0415 121 648; www.ecotreasures.com.au; snorkelling adult/child from $69/45, kayaking $89) ⬤ Offers small group tours, most with a watery focus, including snorkelling in Manly (90 minutes), kayaking in Pittwater, and other excursions to the Northern Beaches and Ku-ring-gai Chase National Park.

Captain Cook Cruises
CRUISE

(Map p80; ☑02-9206 1111; www.captaincook. com.au; Wharf 6, Circular Quay; from $35; ☒Circular Quay) As well as sightseeing ($35 to $55), lunch and dinner cruises, and whale watching, this crew offers an aquatic version of a hop-on, hop-off bus tour, with two main routes that include Watsons Bay, Taronga Zoo, Fort Denison, Shark Island and Manly. It costs $49/27 per adult/child for two days and includes some commentary. Departures from Circular Quay, Darling Harbour and Barangaroo.

Cycling Tours

BlueBananas
CYCLING

(Map p84; ☑0422 213 574; www.bluebananas. com.au; 281 Clarence St; tours from $59; ☒Town Hall) Take some of the puff out of a guided cycling tour on an electric bike. Options include the 1½-hour 'Bike the Bridge' tour ($59) and the 2½-hour Sydney City Tour ($99). The office is in a little arcade of shops.

Bike Buffs
CYCLING

(Map p80; ☑0414 960 332; www.bikebuffs.com. au; adult/child $95/70; ☒Circular Quay) Offers daily four-hour, two-wheeled tours around the harbourside sights, departing from Argyle Place opposite the Garrison Church. It also offers other tours and hires bikes ($35/60/295 per half-day/day/week).

Bonza Bike Tours
CYCLING

(Map p80; ☑02-9247 8800; www.bonzabike tours.com; 30 Harrington St; tours from $99; ⊙office 9am-5pm; ⚑; ☒Circular Quay) These bike boffins run a 2½-hour Sydney Highlights tour (adult/child $99/79) and a four-hour Sydney Classic tour ($129/99). Other tours include the Harbour Bridge and Manly. It also hires out bikes ($15/30/40/130 per hour/half-day/day/week).

Walking Tours

BridgeClimb
WALKING

See p73.

Dreamtime Southern X
WALKING

(Map p80; ☑0428 661 019; www.dreamtimesouth ernx.com.au; adult/child $44/33) Indigenous-owned and operated, this friendly set-up takes you on a leisurely 90-minute stroll around the Rocks area, evoking something of what it used to be before the First Fleet arrived, and giving insights into traditional and contemporary Aboriginal culture. Meet at **Cadman's Cottage** (☑02-9337 5511; www. nationalparks.nsw.gov.au; 110 George St; ☒Circular Quay) FREE; must be prebooked.

Sydney Architecture Walks
WALKING

(☑0403 888 390; www.sydneyarchitecture.org; adult walks $49-59, cycle not incl bike $90) These bright young archi-buffs run two 3½-hour cycling tours and six themed two-to-three hour walking tours. There's an excellent focus on explaining modern architectural principles and urban design. It's cheaper if you book in advance.

Free Tours Sydney
TOURS

(Map p84; ☑0425 291 425; www.freetourssydney. com.au; walking tour by donation, bus tour $18) Meeting at 10.30am daily at the Archibald Fountain in Hyde Park (p81), these 2½-hour tours cover historic Sydney buildings and the Rocks area; there's no set fee – you decide what to give the guide. In addition, a bus tour with a guide leaves at the same time from the same departure point for Kings Cross, Watsons Bay and Bondi Beach. It's pretty good value.

I'm Free Walking Tours
WALKING

(Map p84; ☑ 0405 515 654; www.imfree.com. au; 483 George St; walking tour by donation; ☺ 10.30am & 2.30pm; ☒ Town Hall) Departing twice daily from the square off George St, between the Town Hall and St Andrew's Cathedral (no bookings taken – just show up), these three-hour tours are nominally free but are run by enthusiastic young guides for tips. The route takes in the Rocks, Circular Quay, Martin Place, Pitt St and Hyde Park. Group sizes can be quite large. They also have a 90-minute Rocks tour, departing at 6pm outside Cadman's Cottage (p100).

The Rocks Ghost Tours
WALKING

(Map p80; ☑ 02-9241 1283; www.ghosttours. au; 28 Harrington St; adult/teen $45/35; ☺ 6.45pm Apr-Sep, 7.45pm Oct-Mar; ☒ Circular Quay) If you like your spine chilled and your pulse slightly quickened (they're more creepy than properly scary), join one of these two-hour tours, departing nightly from outside Cadman's Cottage and visiting some Rocks locations with a dark past. Tours run rain or shine (ponchos provided); bookings essential.

The Rocks Walking Tours
WALKING

(Map p80; ☑ 02-9247 6678; www.rockswalking tours.com.au; Shop 4a, cnr Argyle & Harrington Sts; adult/child/family $32/15/79; ☺ 10.30am & 1.30pm; ☒ Circular Quay) Two daily 90-minute tours through the historic Rocks, with plenty of tales and interesting minutiae. The office is in a shopping arcade; you can book online too.

Other Tours

Sydney Seaplanes
SCENIC FLIGHTS

(Map p76; ☑ 1300 732 752; www.seaplanes.com. au; Seaplane Base, Lyne Park, Rose Bay; 15/30min flights per person $200/285; ☒ Rose Bay) Based very near Rose Bay ferry wharf, this company offers scenic flights around Sydney Harbour and beaches. Aerial excitement meets epicurean delight when you take a seaplane flight to a secluded seafood restaurant such as the Berowra Waters Inn. Rose Bay has a long seaplane tradition; in fact it was Australia's first international airport.

Tribal Warrior
CULTURAL

(Map p80; ☑ 02-9699 3491; www.tribalwarrior. org; adult/child $60/40; ☒ Circular Quay) 🍃 Learn about and experience Aboriginal culture and history on this two-hour cruise, stopping at Clark Island for a cultural performance and a guided walk. You'll also be contributing to a worthwhile community self-sufficiency project. Bookings essential. Departs from the Eastern Pontoon at Circular Quay East.

Sydney OutBack
TOURS

(☑ 02-9099 4249; www.sydneyoutback.com. au; adult/child $219/159) Lovely Ku-ring-gai Chase National Park (p91) can be difficult to explore without your own transport, so Sydney OutBack's excursion is a great way to do it. Incorporating a spectacular boat tour as well as a driving visit of the park, this full-day experience has a notable focus on Aboriginal culture and engaging guides. Price includes pick-up and drop-off from city hotels.

✪ Festivals & Events

Big Bash
SPORTS

(www.bigbash.com.au; ☺ Dec-Jan) This hugely popular T20 cricket competition runs through the school holiday period and is designed to be family-friendly, with reasonable ticket prices, lots of action, fun and noise. The women's league starts a little earlier in December.

★ Sydney Festival
CULTURAL

(www.sydneyfestival.org.au; ☺ Jan) Sydney's premier arts and culture festival showcases three weeks of music, theatre and visual art.

Chinese New Year
CULTURAL

(www.sydneychinesenewyear.com) Based in Chinatown, but with elements and events right across Sydney, this 17-day celebration features food, fireworks, dragon dancers and dragon-boat races to see in the lunar new year. Actual dates vary slightly; the new year day can be from late January to mid-February.

★ Sydney Gay & Lesbian Mardi Gras
LGBT

(www.mardigras.org.au; ☺ Feb-Mar) A two-week cultural and entertainment festival celebrating all things queer and culminating in the world-famous massive parade and party on the first Saturday in March. Lots of international visitors means the city is buzzing.

Sydney Royal Easter Show
FAIR

(www.eastershow.com.au; Sydney Olympic Park) Ostensibly an agricultural show, but with a substantial commercial element, this two-week fiesta is great for families, featuring carnival rides, showbags (bags filled with promotional goodies) and sugary horrors. Crowds are massive and it can be a very pricey day out, but it's always nice to see the animals.

★ **Sydney Writers' Festival** LITERATURE
(www.swf.org.au; ☺ May) The country's pre-eminent literary shindig is held over a week in May, in various prime locations around the central city. It pulls some big names and the program is always an extremely interesting one.

★ **Vivid Sydney** LIGHT SHOW
(www.vividsydney.com; ☺ late May-mid Jun) This increasingly impressive and popular festival features spectacular immersive light installations and projections at locations right across the city. There are also performances and public talks, and debates with leading global creative thinkers. It's held over three weeks from late May.

Sydney Film Festival FILM
(www.sff.org.au; ☺ Jun) Held (mostly) at the magnificent **State Theatre** (Map p84; ☑ box office 13 61 00; www.statetheatre.com.au; 49 Market St; ☒ Town Hall), this excellent, highly regarded film festival screens art-house gems from Australia and around the world.

Sculpture by the Sea ART
(www.sculpturebythesea.com) For 17 days from late October, the clifftop trail from Bondi Beach to Tamarama transforms into a sculpture garden. Serious prize money is on offer for the most creative, curious or quizzical offerings from international and local sculptors. Try to visit midweek as it is rammed at weekends.

Sydney to Hobart Yacht Race SPORTS
(www.rolexsydneyhobart.com; ☺ 26 Dec) On 26 December Sydney Harbour is a sight to behold as hundreds of boats crowd its waters to farewell the yachts competing in this gruelling race.

★ **New Year's Eve** FIREWORKS
(www.sydneynewyearseve.com; ☺ 31 Dec) The biggest party of the year, with flamboyant firework displays on the harbour. There's a family-friendly display at 9pm then the main event at midnight. There are also any number of other events on and around the harbour. There's a variety of regulated zones to watch the fireworks from – some ticketed, some alcohol-free.

🛏 Sleeping

Sydney offers a vast quantity and variety of accommodation, especially concentrated in the city-centre, Rocks and Darling Harbour areas. Even so, the supply shrivels up under the summer sun, particularly around weekends and big events, so be sure to book ahead. Prices, even in the budget class, are high; city-centre hotels charge stratospheric rates.

🛏 Circular Quay & the Rocks

★ **Sydney Harbour YHA** HOSTEL $
(Map p80; ☑ 02-8272 0900; www.yha.com.au; 110 Cumberland St; dm $56-65, d $180-250; ❄ @ 🛜; ☒ Wynyard) 🌱 Any qualms about the unhostel-like prices will be shelved the moment you head up to the ample rooftop space of this sprawling, modern hostel and see the superb views of Circular Quay. Very well run, the hostel has spacious en-suite four- and six-berth dorms and a selection of decent-value-for-Sydney private rooms. There are also numerous sustainability initiatives in place.

★ **Harbour Rocks Hotel** BOUTIQUE HOTEL $$
(Map p80; ☑ 02-8220 9999; www.harbourrocks.com.au; 34 Harrington St; r $280-550; ❄ @ 🛜; ☒ Circular Quay) This deluxe boutique hotel on the site of Sydney's first hospital has undergone a chic and sympathetic transformation from colonial warehouse and workers' cottages to a series of New York loft–style rooms, with high ceilings, distressed brick and elegant furnishings. It maintains a historic feel and has a great little garden balcony terrace.

Pier One HOTEL $$
(Map p80; ☑ 02-8298 9999; www.pieronesydneyharbour.com.au; 11 Hickson Rd; r $280-410; P ❄ 🛜 🏊; ☒ 324, 325, ☒ Circular Quay) Offering a stunning location that's harbourside but away from the Circular Quay crowds, this ocupies one of the Walsh Bay piers with the Harbour Bridge looming very close. Decor has a light maritime theme and joists and gantries from the building's structure add character. Higher rooms have floor-to-ceiling windows that make the most of the view.

Lord Nelson Brewery Hotel PUB $$
(Map p80; ☑ 02-9251 4044; www.lordnelsonbrewery.com; 19 Kent St; r incl breakfast $210-250; ❄ 🛜; ☒ Circular Quay) Built in 1836, this atmospheric sandstone pub has a tidy set of seven upstairs rooms, with exposed

stone walls and dormer windows with harbour glimpses. They are all en suite; one is smaller and cheaper than the others. The downstairs microbrewery is a welcoming place for a pint and a meal. Rates include a continental breakfast.

Sir Stamford
HOTEL $$$

(Map p80; ☑ 02-9252 4600; www.stamford.com.au; 93 Macquarie St; r $290-450; P❄@🛜🏊; 🚇Circular Quay) With an old-fashioned ambience a world away from the city-slicker styling of most Sydney hotels, Sir Stamford leaves a grand first impression with its waistcoated staff, glittering chandeliers and gilt-framed portraits. The huge rooms – plush carpeting, sofas, marble bathrooms and pictures of English country life – are lovely, service is a strong point and there's a sundeck with a tiny pool.

Pullman Quay Grand Sydney Harbour
APARTMENT $$$

(Map p80; ☑ 02-9256 4000; www.pullmanquaygrandsydneyharbour.com; 61 Macquarie St; apt $550-800; P❄@🛜🏊; 🚇Circular Quay) With the Opera House as its neighbour, the building complex known locally as 'The Toaster' has a scorching-hot location. These large, well-equipped and well-designed contemporary apartments set you in Sydney's glitzy heart, encircled by top restaurants, cocktail bars and that attention-seeking harbour. The small number of rooms and blend of residents and visitors gives it a quiet ambience.

🛏 City Centre & Haymarket

★ Railway Square YHA
HOSTEL $

(Map p76; ☑ 02-9281 9666; www.yha.com.au; 8-10 Lee St; dm $38-44, d $113-144; ❄@🛜🏊; 🚇Central) A lovely piece of industrial renovation has converted Central station's former parcel shed into a really appealing hostel, in a great location but away from the bustle. Dorms with corrugated roofs and under-floor-heated bathrooms are spotless; some are actually in converted train carriages. There's a cafe and laundry facilities.

The future of this hostel was in some doubt at time of research as a redevelopment of Central station was potentially going to swallow it up.

Sydney Central YHA
HOSTEL $

(Map p84; ☑ 02-9218 9000; www.yha.com.au; 11 Rawson Pl; dm $37-54, d $127-160; P❄@🛜🏊; 🚇Central) 🌿 Near Central station, this

---

SYDNEY & NEW SOUTH WALES SYDNEY

ⓘ THE HOSTEL SCENE

Sydney's hostels range from the sublime to the sublimely grotty. A clump of flash-packer-style blocks encircling Central station have raised the bar, offering en-suite bathrooms, air-conditioning, rooftop decks and, in one case, a pool. Private rooms in such places are often on par with midrange hotels – and in many cases the prices aren't all that different either. You'll find smaller, cheaper hostels in Kings Cross, Glebe and at the beaches.

1913 heritage-listed monolith is the mother of all Sydney YHA properties. The hostel includes everything from a travel agency to an in-house cinema. The rooms are brightly painted and the kitchens are great, but the highlight is sweating it out in the sauna, then cooling off in the rooftop pool.

Hyde Park Inn
HOTEL $$

(Map p84; ☑ 02-9264 6001; www.hydeparkinn.com.au; 271 Elizabeth St; apt $220-360; P❄🛜; 🚇Museum) Opposite the park, this relaxed place offers brightly decorated studio rooms with kitchenettes, deluxe rooms with balconies and full kitchens, and some two-bedroom apartments. All have flat-screen TVs with cable access and some have microwaves and kitchenettes. Breakfast and parking is included in the rate, making it great value for central Sydney.

★ QT Sydney
BOUTIQUE HOTEL $$$

(Map p84; ☑ 02-8262 0000; www.qthotelsandresorts.com/sydney-cbd; 49 Market St; r $360-540; P❄@🛜; 🚇Queen Victoria Building, 🚇Town Hall) Fun, sexy and relaxed, this ultra-theatrical, effortlessly cool hotel is located in the State Theatre complex. Art-deco eccentricity is complemented by quirky extras in the rooms, which are distinct and decorated with real style and flair – there's a definite wow factor. Service is personable and upbeat; there's also a luxurious spa plus a fashionable bar and restaurant.

Establishment Hotel
BOUTIQUE HOTEL $$$

(Map p84; ☑ 02-9240 3100; www.merivale.com.au; 5 Bridge Lane; r $380-600; ❄@🛜; 🚇Wynyard) In a discreet laneway, this designer boutique hotel in a refurbished 19th-century warehouse evokes Asia with its incense aromas and dark-wood fittings. There are two principal room styles: 'light' (all white-and-tan contemporary colouring)

Where to Stay in Sydney

0 — 2 km
0 — 1 mile

Circular Quay & the Rocks
Big-ticket sights, vibrant nightlife, top hotels and restaurants but full of tourists and expensive.

Best For Honeymoons, convenience

Transport Short walk to city centre

Price Mostly top end

Sydney Harbour Bridge

Circular Quay & The Rocks

City Centre & Haymarket

Parramatta
Intriguing multicultural hub on the rise with historic sights, but far from Sydney's central areas.

Best For Budget travellers

Transport Two trains to city centre

Price Budget

Parramatta
(13km)

Darling Harbour & Pyrmont
Plenty to see and do; lively nightlife but can be a little soulless.

Best For Waterfront strollers

Transport Light rail or a short walk to the centre

Price Midrange to top end

Darling Harbour & Pyrmont

Surry Hills & Darlinghurst

Newtown & the Inner West
Bohemian zone with great cafes, cheap restaurants and interesting shops. Priced for locals.

Best For Vintage shopping, cutting-edge culture

Transport Train to city centre

Price Midrange

Newtown & the Inner West

Surry Hills & Darlinghurst
Sydney's hippest eating and drinking precinct; heart of the LGBT+ scene.

Best For LGBT+ travellers, foodies

Transport Short walk or bus to city centre

Price Midrange

Northern Beaches

A string of marvellous beaches with a buzzy summer scene, but it's a long way from the city.

Best For Camping

Transport One bus to the city

Price Budget and midrange

(5km) **Northern Beaches**

Manly

Manly

Beautiful beaches and a community feel, with both harbour and ocean on hand.

Best For Families, surfers, backpackers

Transport Ferry to the centre

Price Budget and midrange

City Centre & Haymarket

Good transport links, lots of sights, numerous bars and fantastic Asian restaurants. Can be noisy.

Best For Business travellers, shoppers

Transport Great connections to the rest of Sydney

Price Midrange to top end, some budget

Sydney Harbourside

Sydney Harbourside

Waterfront choices in a range of picturesque suburbs around the harbour.

Best For Romantic weekends

Transport Ferries to centre

Price Mostly top end

Kings Cross & Potts Point

Interesting and idiosyncratic; numerous hostels, bars and clubs; good transport links. Still some sleaze.

Best For Backpackers

Transport Short train ride to centre

Price Budget

Kings Cross & Potts Point

Bondi, Coogee & the Eastern Beaches

Sand, surf and good times at this string of brilliant beaches.

Best For Surfers, people-watchers, families

Transport Slow bus to city centre

Price Budget to top end

Paddington & Centennial Park

Paddington & Centennial Park

Leafy and genteel with boutique shopping and gourmet food. Not many accommodation options.

Best For Glitz and glamour

Transport Bus to city centre

Price Midrange

Bondi, Coogee & the Eastern Beaches

and sexier 'dark' (with wooden floorboards and a nocturnal feel). Decadent nights out are assured with the hotel's owners' numerous acclaimed bars and restaurants right around you.

Darling Harbour & Pyrmont

★ Ovolo 1888

Darling Harbour BOUTIQUE HOTEL $$

(Map p88; ☑ 02-8586 1888; www.ovolohotels.com.au; 139 Murray St, Pyrmont; r $239-539; ✳@🖙; 🖾 Convention) In a heritage-listed wool store, this stylish gem combines industrial minimalism with the warmth of ironbark-wood beams, luxury appointments and engaged staff. Rooms range from the aptly named Shoebox to airy lofts and attic suites with harbour views. The minibar is complimentary, and there's a jazzy wine bar, **Mister Percy**, downstairs with a free happy hour if you book direct.

Surry Hills & Darlinghurst

Big Hostel HOSTEL $

(Map p114; ☑ 02-9281 6030; www.bighostel.com; 212 Elizabeth St, Surry Hills; dm $35-40, s $109, d $120-130; ✳@🖙; 🖾 Central) A bright and breezy, no-frills hostel with a rooftop terrace and a crowded but decent communal area and 24-hour kitchen. Dorms do the job, with lockers, high ceilings and enough space. The four-bed ones cost a little more but have a bathroom and small TV. The price is good for central Sydney; continental breakfast is included. Free wi-fi downstairs only.

★ Little Albion BOUTIQUE HOTEL $$

(Map p114; ☑ 02-8029 7900; www.littlealbion.com.au; 21 Little Albion St, Surry Hills; r incl breakfast $260-390; ✳🖙; 🖾 Central) This boutique hotel combines an attractive heritage building with a more modern development to great design success. Rooms range from compact 'crash pads' to commodious master rooms and suites; characterful art in the public spaces leans more towards Albion Street's gangster and brothel heritage than this former convent's history. A great honesty bar area encourages socialising and service is excellent.

★ Paramount

House Hotel BOUTIQUE HOTEL $$

(Map p114; ☑ 02-9211 1222; www.paramounthousehotel.com; 80 Commonwealth St, Surry Hills; r $280-560; ✳🖙; 🖾 Museum) When reception has a rack of shirts for sale and a beer tap it's not a standard hotel. Rooms are striking, with distressed walls, quirky features and numerous designer objects; they go from cosy 'nooks' to spacious lofts and suites. You are right in the thick of it here with a great cafe and cinema in the very same building.

★ ADGE Boutique

Apartment Hotel APARTMENT $$$

(Map p114; ☑ 02-8093 9888; www.adgehotel.com.au; 222 Riley St, Surry Hills; apt $400-650; 🅿✳🖙; 🖾 301, 302, 352) Modern, catchy and bold, ADGE puts a clever, upbeat twist on the ubiquitous serviced apartment experience. The idiosyncratic but extremely comfortable two-bedroom apartments have gloriously striped liquorice-allsorts carpets, floor-to-ceiling windows, quality kitchens with Smeg fridges and appealing balconies. Little extras, including a welcome drink and turn-down service, add points. It's an ideal urban experience and great value for two couples.

Kings Cross & Potts Point

★ Blue Parrot Backpackers HOSTEL $

(Map p90; ☑ 02-9356 4888; www.blueparrot.com.au; 87 Macleay St, Potts Point; dm $35-45; @🖙; 🖾 Kings Cross) If Polly wanted a cracker of a hostel she'd head to this brilliant, colourful spot run with real enthusiasm by a pair of sisters. It's a personal experience that feels more like a share-house (but much cleaner!). There's a great back courtyard and high-ceilinged dorms with good bunks and mattresses. Netflix, Playstation, free SIM cards and a BBQ add points.

Kings Cross Backpackers HOSTEL $

(Map p90; ☑ 02-9331 0520; www.kingscrossbackpackers.com.au; 79 Bayswater Rd, Kings Cross; dm $36-48; ✳@🖙; 🖾 Kings Cross) Nicely set in a quieter part of the Cross, this is a well-run, fun-oriented place with renovated, air-conditioned dorms that sleep four to 12 and come with lockers and under-bed storage. The kitchen-lounge and sweet roof terrace are the places to hang out. Security is good and the price fair. Breakfast is included, but it's a couple of blocks away.

Hotel 59 B&B $

(Map p90; ☑ 02-9360 5900; www.hotel59.com.au; 59 Bayswater Rd, Kings Cross; s $110, d $140-150; ✳🖙; 🖾 Kings Cross) With just nine simple, spotless, comfortable rooms, family-run Hotel 59 offers great bang for your buck on the quiet but still very convenient part of Bayswater Rd. The owners are genuinely helpful and attentive and the cafe downstairs does whopping cooked breakfasts (included in the price) for those barbarous Kings Cross hangovers.

Mariners Court HOTEL $
(Map p90; ☑02-9320 3888; www.marinerscourt. com.au; 44-50 McElhone St, Woolloomooloo; r $140-170; P🅿❄@🛜; 🚪311, 🚌Kings Cross) Once a naval retirement home, this is now an under-the-radar hotel on a quiet street. It hasn't been modified much, so is solid rather than flash, but offers excellent value for this location and simple, comfortable rooms with kettle, fridge and either balcony or courtyard. Other pluses are the complimentary hot-breakfast buffet, pool table and sun deck. Good wheelchair access.

★Spicers BOUTIQUE HOTEL $$$
(Map p90; ☑02-9357 3200; www.spicerspotts point.com; 122 Victoria St, Kings Cross; r $320-760; P🅿❄🛜; 🚌Kings Cross) This expert conversion of three Victorian-era terraces adds a touch of class to leafy Victoria Street. The charming front rooms have original features and, in some cases, a balcony; the more modern back rooms are brighter and have lift access. Rates include an excellent breakfast, evening cocktail and in-room snacks. Service is faultless and personal.

★Ovolo Hotel Woolloomooloo HOTEL $$$
(Map p90; ☑02-9331 9000; www.ovolohotels. com.au; 6 Cowper Wharf Rdwy, Woolloomooloo; r $400-700; P🅿❄@🛜🏊; 🚪311, 🚌Kings Cross) Superbly set, this excellent smart-casual hotel has extremely friendly young staff and very likeable features. 'Superoo' rooms are mostly either road-facing or skylit, so for water views upgrade to a 'deluxe' (facing east) or 'city' (facing west) room. It's ultra characterful with long corridors, industrial machinery and unusually shaped, artfully designed rooms, some split-level. A Sydney standout.

🛏 Paddington & Centennial Park

Mrs Banks BOUTIQUE HOTEL $$
(Map p92; ☑02-9331 8111; www.mrsbankshotel. com.au; 259 Oxford St, Paddington; standard r incl breakfast $300-400; P🅿❄🛜; 🚪333, 352, 440, M40) A very cute conversion of a centenarian former Commonwealth Bank branch, this boutique hotel has 30 rooms that look very

sleek in shades of grey and black. The standard ones are compact but very comfortable and stylish; the more spacious studio suite doesn't usually cost a lot more. Rooms are set back from the street so noise isn't a problem.

🛏 Bondi, Coogee & the Eastern Beaches

Bondi Backpackers HOSTEL $
(Map p108; ☑02-9130 4660; www.bondiback packers.com.au; 110 Campbell Pde, Bondi Beach; dm $41-48, d without bathroom $104-119; @🛜; 🚪333) Wake up to a view of Australia's most famous beach, grab your free surfboard, cross the road and jump into the waves... you're in backpacker dreamland, right? With simple, clean, comfortable dorms and private rooms, free activities and a huge roof terrace with super vistas, this makes an excellent base. Ongoing renovations were sprucing it up when we last visited.

Bondi Beachouse YHA HOSTEL $
(Map p108; ☑02-9365 2088; www.yha.com.au; 63 Fletcher St, Tamarama; dm $30-36, tw & d without bathroom $90, d/f $110/180; 🛜; 🚪381) Perched on a hillside between Bondi and Tamarama Beaches, this 95-bed art-deco hostel has fan-cooled dorms that sleep four to eight and come with bright colours, wooden floors and spacious lockers; some of the private rooms have ocean views – all are clean and well maintained. Facilities include surfboard hire, cinema room, courtyard barbecue and a rooftop deck with top views.

Dive Hotel BOUTIQUE HOTEL $$
(Map p76; ☑02-9665 5538; www.divehotel.com.au; 234 Arden St, Coogee; standard r $240-260, oceanview r $340-400; P🅿❄@🛜🏊; 🚪313, 314, 353, 372, 373) In a cracking location right across the road from the beach, this relaxed, family-run affair is, thankfully, very inaccurately named. Simple, likeable contemporary rooms come with fridges, microwaves and small stylish bathrooms fitted with mosaic tiles and stainless steel sinks. A sociable continental buffet breakfast (included) in an appealing indoor-outdoor area is a highlight, as are the personable owners and their friendly dogs.

★QT Bondi APARTMENT $$$
(Map p108; ☑02-8362 3900; www.qtbondi. com.au; 6 Beach Rd, Bondi Beach; apt $399-720; P🅿❄🛜🏊; 🚪333) Colourful, chic and appropriately beachy, this apartment hotel is steps from the sand and offers a very appealing

Bondi

SYDNEY & NEW SOUTH WALES SYDNEY

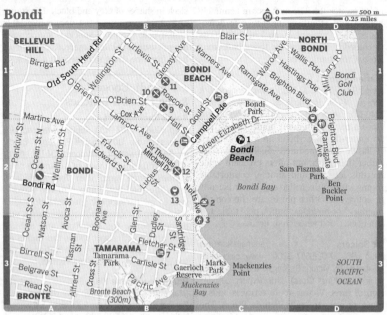

Bondi

◎ Top Sights	
1 Bondi Beach	C2

⊕ Activities, Courses & Tours	
2 Bondi Icebergs Pool	C2
3 Bondi to Coogee Clifftop Walk	C3
4 Dive Centre Bondi	A2
5 Let's Go Surfing	D2

⌂ Sleeping	
6 Bondi Backpackers	B2
7 Bondi Beachouse YHA	B3
8 QT Bondi	C1

✕ Eating	
9 Blanca	B1
Crabbe Hole	(see 2)
10 Funky Pies	B1
Icebergs Dining Room	(see 2)
11 Lox Stock & Barrel	B1
12 Trio	B2

⊙ Drinking & Nightlife	
13 Anchor	B2
14 North Bondi RSL	D1

combination of facilities, location and attitude. All the rooms and suites are exceedingly spacious, with light-coloured furniture and an airy feel. King Deluxe rooms and above have balconies, but there are no ocean views. All rooms have kitchenette, bathtub and laundry facilities.

🛏 Sydney Harbourside

★ Cockatoo Island   CAMPGROUND $
(Map p76; ☎ 02-8969 2111; www.cockatooisland. gov.au; campsites $45-50, simple tents $89-99, 2-bed tents $130-175, apt from $265, houses from $625; ☎; ⛴ Cockatoo Island) Waking up on an island in the middle of the harbour is

an extraordinary Sydney experience. Bring a tent (or just sleeping bags) or 'glamp' in a two-person tent (with double bed) on the water's edge. Non-campers will enjoy the elegant houses and apartments. For self-caters, there's a well-equipped camp kitchen; for everyone else, there are two cafes and bars.

Note that you can't take alcohol onto the island unless you are staying in one of the houses.

★ Watsons Bay
Boutique Hotel   BOUTIQUE HOTEL $$
(Map p76; ☎ 02-9337 5444; www.watsonsbay hotel.com.au; 10 Marine Pde, Watsons Bay; r $259-599; ☎✳☎; ☐ 324, 325, 380, ⛴ Watsons Bay)

The ferry pulls up right by this chic hotel in a charming beachside hamlet. Rooms are light and super-spacious with a lounge area and slick glassed-in en suites; many have balconies. Harbour-facing rooms have brilliant views, but expect some noise from the buzzing on-site Beach Club (p128); split-level duplexes are great for families. Rates include breakfast, and bikes and beach towels are provided.

Newtown & the Inner West

★ Mandelbaum House   GUESTHOUSE $

(Map p120; ✆02-9692 5200; www.mandelbaum. usyd.edu.au; 385 Abercrombie St, Darlington; s without bathroom $75, d/apt $135/170; ☺Dec-mid-Feb; ☙❋@❡; ☒Redfern) ✒ One of the University of Sydney's residential colleges, this sweet spot makes a great place to stay in summer. It's a small, genuinely friendly place with a personal welcome, a not-for-profit ethos and a range of comfortable rooms, some of which share excellent bathrooms. The location is great for exploring the cafe and bar scene of Redfern and Newtown. It's terrific value.

Mad Monkey Backpackers   HOSTEL $

(Map p120; ✆02-8705 3762; www.madmonkey broadway.com.au; 20 City Rd, Chippendale; dm $36-48; ❋❡; ☒412, 413, 422, 423, ☒Central) There's a lot to like about this friendly, well-equipped hostel in a top location. Dorms are tight but have very decent mattresses, while bathrooms are above average with hairdryers and straighteners. There's a guaranteed social life with party buses and free entry to major Saturday nightclubs, plus free comfort food to aid recovery the next day. Breakfast and Netflix included.

Urban Hotel   BOUTIQUE HOTEL $$

(Map p120; ✆02-8960 7800; www.theurban newtown.com.au; 52-60 Enmore Rd, Newtown; r $230-330; ❋@❡; ☒Newtown) ✒ A couple of minutes' walk from Newtown station and surrounded by great bars and eats, this casual hotel in a former RSL Club offers edgy industrial-styled studio accommodation. The Urban stands out from the crowd with a sustainable ethos and a slew of extras such as kitchenette with coffee-pod machine, free minibar stocked with local craft beers and relaxed check-in and -out options.

Old Clare Hotel   BOUTIQUE HOTEL $$$

(Map p120; ✆02-8277 8277; www.theoldclare hotel.com.au; 1 Kensington St, Chippendale;

r $300-600; ❋❋❡❆; ☒Central) A sensitive brewery-office conversion is now a 62-room hotel in a primo Chippendale location. Rooms are well back from noisy Broadway, high-ceilinged and easy on the eye, with artful bespoke details such as the lamps made of salvaged toolshed paraphernalia. Superior categories are appreciably larger, but the cheapest rooms still have king beds and a good sense of space.

Manly

Manly Bunkhouse   HOSTEL $

(Map p76; ✆02-9976 0472; www.bunkhouse.com. au; 35 Pine St, Manly; dm/d $45/118; ❋@❡; ☒151, 158, 159, ☒Manly) An easy walk from the beach, this laid-back hostel has a distinct surf vibe. High-ceilinged en-suite dorms have modern furnishings, plenty of room to move and lots of storage space, making them popular with long-termers. Private rooms (also en suite) are a great deal. There's a surfboard rack and bodyboards and snorkels are available, and there's a top backyard with a BBQ.

101 Addison Road   B&B $

(Map p111; ✆02-9977 6216; www.bb-manly.com; 101 Addison Rd, Manly; r $185-200; ❋❡; ☒135, ☒Manly) This sumptuously decorated 1880s cottage is perched on a quiet street close to the beach and ferry wharf. The delightful host Jill only takes bookings for one or two people at a time – meaning you'll have free rein of the antique-strewn accommodation, including many original features and a lovely guest lounge with a grand piano. Cash only.

Cecil Street B&B   B&B $

(Map p76; ✆02-9977 8036; www.cecilstreetbb. com.au; 18 Cecil St, Fairlight; s $120-160, d $140-200; ❋❡; ☒142, ☒Manly) This handsome Federation-style brick home has a quiet hillside location. Two simple but tastefully decorated rooms make the most of high ceilings, leadlight windows and polished timber floors. They share a bathroom and sitting room (with microwave and fridge), but only one booking is taken at a time. The only downside is the steep hike back from the beach.

Q Station   LODGE $$

(Map p76; ✆02-9466 1500; www.qstation.com.au; 1 North Head Scenic Dr, Manly; r $259-500; ❋❋❡; ☒135, ☒Manly) Hidden away in shrubland rolling down to a beautiful harbour beach, the former quarantine station (p89) offers a wide variety of accommodation. Minibuses shuttle you around this sizeable complex of historic buildings; rooms have their own balconies and many have harbour views. Kayaks, bikes and snorkels are available, and there's an on-site cafe and restaurant. It's an out-of-the-way, utterly relaxing spot.

✗ Eating

Sydney's cuisine is exceptional and rivals that of any great world city. The city truly celebrates Australia's place on the Pacific Rim, marrying the freshest local ingredients – excellent seafood is a particular highlight – with the flavours of Asia, the Mediterranean, the Americas and, of course, its colonial past. Sydneysiders are real foodies, always seeking out the latest hot restaurant.

Sydney's top restaurants are properly pricey, but eating out needn't be expensive. There are plenty of budget world cuisine places where you can grab a cheap, zingy pizza or a bowl of noodles. Cafes are a good bet for a solid, often adventurous and usually reasonably priced meal. Pubs either do reliable standard fare, often with excellent prices, or casual but high-quality Modern Australian dining. The numerous BYO (bring your own wine) restaurants offer a substantially cheaper eating experience; the Inner West is brimful of them.

✗ Circular Quay & The Rocks

★ Fine Food Store   CAFE $

(Map p80; ☑ 02-9252 1196; www.finefoodstore. com; cnr Mill & Kendall Lanes; light meals $9-16; ⊙ 7am-4pm Mon-Sat, from 7.30am Sun; 🗟 🖉; 🖫 Circular Quay) The Rocks sometimes seems all pubs, so it's a delight to find this contemporary cafe that works for a sightseeing stopover or a better, cheaper breakfast than your hotel. Staff are genuinely welcoming, make very respectable coffee and offer delicious panini, sandwiches and other breakfast and lunch fare. The outside tables on this narrow lane are the spot to be.

★ Quay   MODERN AUSTRALIAN $$$

(Map p80; ☑ 02-9251 5600; www.quay.com.au; Level 3, Overseas Passenger Terminal, Circular Quay West; 6/10 course degustation $210/275; ⊙ 6-9.30pm Mon-Thu, noon-1.30pm & 6-9.30pm Fri-Sun; 🖫 Circular Quay) What many consider to be Sydney's best restaurant matches a peerless bridge view with brilliant food. Chef Peter Gilmore never rests on his laurels, consistently delivering exquisitely

crafted, adventurous cuisine. A shake-up of decor and menu in 2018 has left it better than ever. Book online well in advance.

★ Aria   MODERN AUSTRALIAN $$$

(Map p80; ☑ 02-9240 2255; www.ariasydney. com.au; 1 Macquarie St; 2-/3-/4-course dinner $115/145/170, degustation $205; ⊙ noon-2.15pm & 5.30-10.30pm Mon-Fri, noon-1.30pm & 5-11pm Sat, noon-1.45pm & 5.30-10pm Sun; 🖫 Circular Quay) Aria is a star in Sydney's fine-dining firmament, an award-winning combination of chef Joel Bickford's stellar dishes, floor-to-ceiling windows staring straight at the Opera House, a stylishly renovated interior and faultless service. A good-value pre- and post-theatre menu is perfect for a special meal before or after a night at the Opera House (two/three courses $90/120).

✗ City Centre & Haymarket

Without harbour views, Sydney's central-city restaurants tend to be discreet upmarket spots – perfect for secret handshakes over million-dollar deals. Chinatown is your best bet for a cheap, satisfying meal – especially late at night. Chinese food dominates, but you'll also find superb Vietnamese, Malaysian, Japanese, Korean and Thai. There's also a Koreatown along Pitt St near Liverpool St, and Thaitown on Campbell St.

★ Gumshara   RAMEN $

(Map p84; ☑ 0410 253 180; Shop 211, 25-29 Dixon St; ramen $12-19; ⊙ 11.30am-9pm Tue-Sat, to 8.30pm Sun & Mon; 🖫 Paddy's Markets, 🖫 Central) Prepare to queue for some of Sydney's best broth at this cordial ramen house in a popular but unglamorous Chinatown budget-price food court. They boil down over 100kg of pork bones for a week to make the gloriously thick and sticky liquid. There are lots of options, including some that pack quite a punch. Ask for extra back fat for real indulgence.

Cross Eatery   CAFE $

(Map p84; ☑ 02-9279 4280; www.facebook.com/crosseatery; 155 Clarence St; light meals $10-19; ⊙ 7am-4pm Mon-Fri; 🗟 🖉; 🖫 Wynyard) There are so many tiny, jam-packed cafes around that it's very pleasant to cruise in here and enjoy a bit of elbow room. Set in the lobby of an office building, there's space to spare and a bright, luminous ambience. It does tasty coffee and good-value breakfast choices, as well as salads, deli lunches and daily sandwich specials.

Manly

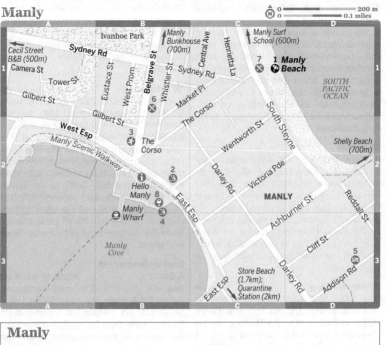

Manly

◉ Top Sights
1 Manly Beach C1

✈ Activities, Courses & Tours
2 Discover Manly.......................................B2
3 Manly Bike Tours....................................B2
4 Manly Kayak Centre...............................B2

🛏 Sleeping
5 101 Addison Road D3

🍴 Eating
6 Belgrave Cartel B1
7 The Pantry C1

🍷 Drinking & Nightlife
8 Manly Wharf Hotel..................................B2

★ **Restaurant Hubert**　　　　FRENCH **$$**
(Map p84; ☎02-9232 0881; www.restaurant
hubert.com; 15 Bligh St; mains $20-50; ☉4pm-1am
Mon-Sat, plus noon-3pm Thu & Fri; 🚇Martin Place)
The memorable descent into the sexy old-
time ambience plunges you straight into
suity Sydney into a 1930s movie. Delicious
French fare comes in old-fashioned por-
tions – think terrine, black pudding or duck,
plus a few more avant-garde creations. Can-
dlelit tables and a long whisky-backed coun-
ter provide seating. No bookings for small
groups, so wait it out in the bar area.

This is one of the few top-quality venues
in Sydney to serve food this late (kitchen
closes at midnight). The bar in itself makes a
great destination for a few cocktails – check
out the vast collection of miniature bottles
on your way down.

★ **Mr Wong**　　　　CHINESE **$$**
(Map p84; ☎02-9114 7317; www.merivale.com.au/
mrwong; 3 Bridge Lane; mains $24-44; ☉lunch
noon-3pm Mon-Fri, 10.30am-3pm Sat & Sun, dinner
5.30-11pm Mon-Wed, to midnight Thu-Sat, to 10pm
Sun; 🖥🍴; 🚇Wynyard) Classy but comfortable in an attractive, low-lit space on a CBD
laneway, this has exposed-brick colonial
warehouse chic and a huge team of staff and
hanging ducks in the open kitchen. Lunchtime dim sum offerings bristle with flavour
and the salad offerings are mouth-freshen-
ing sensations. Mains such as crispy pork
hock are sinfully sticky, while Peking duck
rolls are legendary.

Pablo & Rusty's　　　　CAFE **$$**
(Map p84; ☎02-9283 9543; www.pabloand
rustys.com.au; 161 Castlereagh St; light meals
$9-25; ☉6.30am-5pm Mon-Wed, to 7pm Thu & Fri,

8am-3pm Sat; 🛜🖊; 🚇Town Hall) Mega-busy and loud, with close-packed tables, this excellent cafe is high energy. The inviting wood-and-brick decor and seriously good coffee (several single-origins available daily) are complemented by a range of appealing breakfast and lunch specials ranging from large sourdough sandwiches to wholesome Mediterranean- and Asian-influenced combos such as tuna poke with brown rice. Try to visit off-peak.

Chat Thai
THAI $$

(Map p84; 🖊02-9211 1808; www.chatthai.com.au; 20 Campbell St; mains $13-32; ⊗10am-2am; 🖊; 🚇Capitol Square, 🚇Central) Cooler than your average Thai joint, this Thaitown linchpin is so popular that a list is posted outside for you to affix your name to should you want a table. Expat Thais flock here for the dishes that don't make it on to your average suburban Thai restaurant menu – particularly the more unusual sweets.

Sydney Madang
KOREAN $$

(Map p84; 🖊02-9264 7010; www.facebook.com/madang2006; 371a Pitt St; mains $16-28; ⊗11.30am-2am; 🚇Museum) Down a teensy Koreatown lane is this backdoor gem – an authentic BBQ joint that's low on interior charisma but high on quality and quantity. Noisy, cramped and chaotic, yes, but the chilli seafood soup will have you coming back. Try the delicious cold noodles too. Prepare to queue at weekends.

★Azuma
JAPANESE $$$

(Map p84; 🖊02-9222 9960; www.azuma.com.au; Level 1, Chifley Plaza, Hunter St; mains $29-58, tasting menus $95-130; ⊗noon-2.30pm & 6-10pm Mon-Fri, 6-10pm Sat; 🚇Martin Place) Tucked away upstairs in Chifley Plaza, this is one of Sydney's finest Japanese restaurants. Sushi and sashimi are of stellar quality and too pretty to eat – almost. Other options include sukiyaki and hot-pot DIY dishes and excellent tasting menus. It's a great place to get acquainted with high-class modern Japanese fare. It also has some moreish sake by the carafe.

★Rockpool Bar & Grill
STEAK $$$

(Map p84; 🖊02-8099 7077; www.rockpool barandgrill.com.au; 66 Hunter St; mains $37-68, bar mains $22-35; ⊗noon-3pm & 6-11pm Mon-Fri, 5.30-11pm Sat, 5.30-10pm Sun; 🚇Martin Place) You'll feel like a 1930s Manhattan stockbroker when you dine at this sleek operation in the fabulous art-deco City Mutual Building.

The bar is famous for its dry-aged, full-blood Wagyu burger (make sure you order a side of the hand-cut fat chips), but carnivores will be equally enamoured with the succulent steaks, stews and fish dishes served from the grill.

★Tetsuya's
FRENCH, JAPANESE $$$

(Map p84; 🖊02-9267 2900; www.tetsuyas.com; 529 Kent St; degustation menu $240, matching wines from $125; ⊗5.30-10pm Tue-Fri, noon-3pm & 6.30-10pm Sat; 🚇Town Hall) Concealed in a villa behind a historic cottage amid the highrises, this extraordinary restaurant is for those seeking a culinary journey rather than a simple stuffed belly. Settle in for 10-plus courses of French- and Japanese-inflected food from the genius of legendary Sydney chef Tetsuya Wakuda. It's all great, but the seafood is sublime. Excellent wine list. Book well ahead.

Bentley Restaurant & Bar
MODERN AUSTRALIAN $$$

(Map p84; 🖊02-8214 0505; www.thebentley.com.au; cnr Pitt & Hunter Sts; mains $46-70, tasting menus $140-165; ⊗noon-3pm & 6pm-midnight Mon-Fri, 6pm-midnight Sat; 🛜🖊; 🚇Wynyard) Its chic corporate veneer blending plush with industrial, Bentley has been turning heads in Sydney for the sheer quality of its imaginative dishes. Many of these have a distinctly Australian taste, with native fruits and seeds lending their unusual flavours. The bar is also a good spot to hang out, with pricey but delicious share plates of similar fare.

Golden Century
CANTONESE $$$

(Map p84; 🖊02-9212 3901; www.goldencentury.com.au; 393-399 Sussex St; mains $30-60; ⊗noon-4am; 🖊; 🚇Town Hall) The fish tank at this frenetic Cantonese place, a Chinatown classic, forms a window-wall to the street, filled with fish, crabs, lobsters and abalone cooked to order. Splash out (you can rack up huge seafood bills here) on the whole lobster cooked in ginger and shallots or try the delicious sucking pig or beef brisket with turnips. Service is brusque but attentive.

🍴 Darling Harbour & Pyrmont

Rows of restaurants line Darling Harbour, many of them pairing their sea views with seafood. Most are pricey, tourist-driven affairs that are OK but not outstanding, but Barangaroo South has upped the ante, serving quality meals to local businessfolk. Over in Pyrmont, the Star has sought to assert itself as a fine-dining destination, luring many a gifted restaurateur. There are some truly excellent restaurants here, but the shopping-mall atmosphere won't be for everyone.

Cafe Morso — CAFE $$
(Map p88; ☑02-9692 0111; www.cafemorso.com. au; Jones Bay Wharf, Pyrmont; breakfast $13-20, lunch mains $18-30; ☺7am-3.30pm Mon-Fri, 9am-2.30pm Sat, 8am-3.30pm Sun; ☏☑; ☒The Star) On pretty Jones Bay Wharf, this makes a fine venue for breakfast or lunch (though it gets busy, so you may want to book). There's a mixture of Channel 7 workers and yacht skippers. Sassy breakfasts – try the bacon gnocchi – morph into proper cooked lunches, or you can just grab a sandwich.

★LuMi — ITALIAN $$$
(Map p88; ☑02-9571 1999; www.lumidining.com; 56 Pirrama Rd, Pyrmont; tasting menus $125-185; ☺6.30-10.30pm Wed & Thu, noon-2.30pm & 6-10.30pm Fri-Sun; ☏; ☒Pyrmont Bay, ☒The Star) This wharf spot sits alongside bobbing boats, though views aren't quite knock-me-down. Hidden just steps from the Star Casino, it offers strikingly innovative Italian-Japanese cuisine in an atmosphere of casual competence. Degustations are a tour de force; memorable creations include extraordinary pasta dishes. The open kitchen is always entertaining, service is smart, and both wine and sake lists are great.

★Sokyo — JAPANESE $$$
(Map p88; ☑02-9657 9161; www.star.com.au/ sokyo; The Star, 80 Pyrmont St, Pyrmont; breakfast $38, mains $32-65; ☺7-10.30am & 5.30-10pm Mon-Thu, 7-10.30am, noon-2pm & 5.30-10.30pm Fri & Sat, 7-11.30am & 5.30-10pm Sun; ☏☑; ☒The Star) Bringing an injection of Toyko glam to the edge of the casino complex, Sokyo serves well-crafted sushi and sashimi, delicate tempura, tasty robata grills and sophisticated mains. It also dishes up Sydney's best Japanese-style breakfast options. Solo travellers should grab a counter seat by the sushi kitchen to watch all the action unfurl.

Momofuku Seiōbo — MODERN AUSTRALIAN $$$
(Map p88; ☑02-9657 9169; www.seiobo. momofuku.com; The Star, 80 Pyrmont Street, Pyrmont; degustation menu $185, pre-theatre $115; ☺6-10pm Mon-Sat; ☒The Star) The first restaurant outside the USA opened by New York's gastronomic darling David Chang, this is a key foodie favourite. Bringing together the techniques, concepts and ideas of Japanese

SYDNEY & NEW SOUTH WALES SYDNEY

LOCAL KNOWLEDGE

BREKKIE & BRUNCH IN SYDNEY

It might be something to do with long nights of partying, but breakfast and brunch is something Sydney cafes do particularly well. Many locals prefer to conduct business over a morning latte instead of a power lunch or an upmarket dinner, and friends often launch the day with scrambled eggs, smashed avocado, carrot juice and a few laughs. The prime breakfasting 'hoods are Darlinghurst, Surry Hills and the beaches, but it'd be weird not to find a decent brekky cafe in any inner-city 'burb. Yum cha in Chinatown is also a hugely popular weekend brunch option (expect to queue).

Sydney baristas have pushed the caffeine envelope in numerous directions and you'll find the inner city packed with cafes offering their own micro-roasted beans of carefully sourced single-origin coffee.

kaiseki (multi-course eating) and classical Western degustation, it's not one for the short of time, or funds. A few first-come-first-served stools allow you to order off a more casual bar menu.

Cirrus — SEAFOOD $$$
(Map p88; ☑02-9220 0111; www.cirrusdining.com. au; 10/23 Barangaroo Ave, Central Sydney; mains $38-56; ☺noon-3pm & 6-10.30pm; ☒Barangaroo, ☒Wynyard) The curved glass windows of this excellent Barangaroo seafood restaurant offer a water view more ambient than spectacular, but the tinny (simple fishing boat) suspended from the ceiling hints at another focus. Sustainably sourced fish and extremely tasty molluscs and crustaceans form the backbone of the menu, which features dishes with exquisite flavour pairings and presentation, designed to share.

✗ Surry Hills & Darlinghurst

★Le Monde — CAFE $
(Map p114; ☑02-9211 3568; www.lemondecafe. com.au; 83 Foveaux St, Surry Hills; dishes $10-18; ☺6.30am-4pm Mon-Fri, 7.30am-2pm Sat; ☏☑; ☒Central) Some of Sydney's best breakfasts are served between the demure dark wooden walls of this small street-side cafe. Top-notch coffee and a terrific selection of tea will gear you up to face the world,

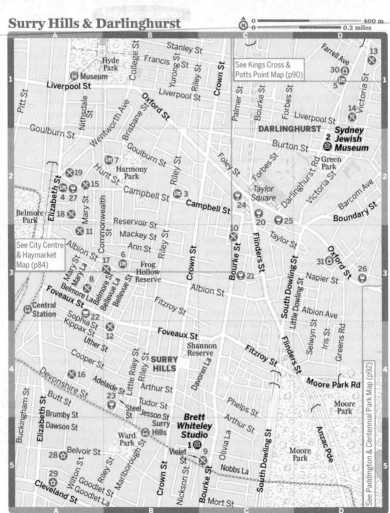

while dishes such as matcha hotcakes, truffled poached eggs, brilliant sandwiches or morning muffin specials make it worth walking up the hill for.

★ **Bourke Street Bakery** BAKERY **$**
(Map p114; ☎ 02-9699 1011; www.bourkestreet bakery.com.au; 633 Bourke St, Surry Hills; items $5-14; ⊗ 7am-6pm Mon-Fri, to 5pm Sat & Sun; ⟋; ⬛ 301, ⬛ Surry Hills, ⬛ Central) Queuing outside this teensy bakery is an essential Surry Hills experience. It sells a tempting selection of pastries, cakes, bread and sandwiches, along with near-legendary sausage rolls. There are a couple of spots to sit inside, but on a fine

day you're better off on the street. Offshoots around town offer a bit more space.

Reuben Hills CAFE **$**
(Map p114; ☎ 02-9211 5556; www.reubenhills.com. au; 61 Albion St, Surry Hills; mains $9-22; ⊗ 7am-4pm Mon-Fri, from 7.30am Sat & Sun; ⟋⟋; ⬛ Central) An industrial design and creative Latin American menu await at Reuben Hills, set in a terraced house and its former garage. There's fantastic single-origin coffee, roasted on the premises, refreshing homemade *horchata* (tiger nut milk) and stellar fried chicken, but the eggs, tacos and *baleadas* (Honduran tortillas) are no slouches either.

Surry Hills & Darlinghurst

◎ **Top Sights**
 1 Brett Whiteley Studio B5
 2 Sydney Jewish Museum........................D2

🛏 **Sleeping**
 3 ADGE Boutique Apartment Hotel.........B2
 4 Big Hostel...A2
 5 Kirketon Hotel..D1
 6 Little Albion...B3
 7 Paramount House Hotel..........................B2

✖ **Eating**
 Baccomatto Osteria ....(see 3)
 8 Bodega...A3
 9 Bourke Street Bakery.............................C5
 10 Dead Ringer C3
 11 Firedoor...A3
 12 Le Monde...B4
 13 Malabar..D1
 14 Messina D1
 15 Nomad..A2
 16 Porteño...A4
 17 Reuben Hills..B3

 18 Single O..A2
 19 Spice I Am..A2

🍷 **Drinking & Nightlife**
 20 Arq...C2
 21 Beresford Hotel.......................................C3
 Eau-de-Vie...(see 5)
 22 Reformatory Caffeine Lab......................A3
 23 Shakespeare Hotel..................................B4
 24 Stonewall Hotel.......................................C2
 25 This Must Be The Place C2
 26 Unicorn..D3
 27 Wild Rover...A2
 Wyno...(see 16)

🎭 **Entertainment**
 28 Belvoir St Theatre...................................A5
 Golden Age Cinema & Bar..............(see 7)
 29 Venue 505...A5

🛍 **Shopping**
 30 Artery D1
 31 Berkelouw Books.....................................D3

Messina ICE CREAM $

(Map p114; ☑ 02-9331 1588; www.gelatomessina. com; 241 Victoria St, Darlinghurst; 1/2/3 scoops $5/7/9; ☺ noon-11pm Sun-Thu, to 11.30pm Fri & Sat; ☑; ☒ Kings Cross) Join the queues of people who look like they never eat ice cream at the counter of the original store of Sydney's most popular gelato shop – clearly even they can't resist quirky flavours such as pear and rhubarb, or panna cotta with fig jam and amaretti biscuit. It's all delicious, and there are several dairy-free options.

Single O CAFE $

(Single Origin Roasters; Map p114; ☑ 02-9211 0665; www.singleo.com.au; 60-64 Reservoir St, Surry Hills; mains $14-25; ☺ 6.30am-4pm Mon-Fri, 7.30am-3pm Sat, 8am-3pm Sun; ☺☑; ☒ Central) 🍃 Unshaven graphic designers roll cigarettes at little outdoor tables in the bricky hollows of Surry Hills, while inside impassioned, bouncing-off-the-walls caffeine fiends prepare their beloved brews, along with a tasty selection of cafe food. A real trendsetter a few years back, this place still does coffee as good as anywhere in Sydney. The hole-in-the-wall alongside does takeaways.

★**Dead Ringer** MODERN AUSTRALIAN $$

(Map p114; ☑ 02-9331 3560; www.deadringer.wtf; 413 Bourke St, Surry Hills; share plates $17-34; ☺ 5-11pm Mon & Tue, from 4pm Wed, 4pm-midnight Thu & Fri, 10am-midnight Sat, 11am-11pm

Sun; ☺☑; ☒ 333, 440) This charcoal-fronted terrace is a laid-back haven of quality eating and drinking. Barstool it or grab an outdoor table and graze on the short, brilliant menu that changes slightly daily and runs from bar snacks through tapas to mains. Though well presented, the food's all about flavour combinations rather than airy artistry. There's always something interesting to accompany by the glass.

★**Porteño** ARGENTINE $$

(Map p114; ☑ 02-8399 1440; www.porteno.com. au; 50 Holt St, Surry Hills; sharing plates $20-50; ☺ 6pm-midnight Tue-Sat, plus noon-3pm Fri; ☒ Central) This upbeat and deservedly acclaimed Argentine restaurant is a great place to eat. The 'animal of the day' is slow-roasted for eight hours before the doors even open and is always delicious. Other highlights include homemade chorizo and morcilla, but lighter touches are also in evidence, so it's not just a meat feast. There's a decent Argentine wine list too.

Baccomatto Osteria ITALIAN $$

(Map p114; ☑ 02-9215 5140; www.baccomatto osteria.com.au; 212 Riley St, Surry Hills; mains $29-36; ☺ 6-10pm Mon-Thu, noon-3pm & 6-10pm Fri-Sun; ☺; ☒ 301, 302, 352) Sleek and modern, this smart Italian restaurant nevertheless conserves the warm and genuine welcome of your favourite trattoria. There's a real verve to the updated but faithful Italian cooking and some extraordinary flavours. The $25 meal-and-wine dinner deals from Sundays to Wednesdays are top value.

Malabar
SOUTH INDIAN $$
(Map p114; ☑02-9332 1755; www.malabar cuisine.com.au; 274 Victoria St, Darlinghurst; mains $16-29; ☺5.30-10.30pm Mon & Tue, noon-2.30pm & 5.30-10.30pm Wed-Sun, to 11.30pm Fri & Sat; ☑; ☑Kings Cross) Delicious dosas, piquant Goan curries and the soft seductive tastes of India's south make this sizeable, well-established Darlinghurst restaurant a standout. The open kitchen and decor, with large black-and-white photos adorning the walls, add atmosphere. Owner and staff are very genial and will guide you through the substantial menu. You can BYO wine. It's wise to book ahead.

Nomad
MEDITERRANEAN $$
(Map p114; ☑02-9280 3395; www.nomadwine. com.au; 16 Foster St, Surry Hills; share plates $22-48; ☺noon-2.30pm & 6-10pm Mon-Sat; ☑Central) Though this large open space has a modern industrial look, with exposed surfaces and visible ducting, the cuisine takes its inspiration from more traditional vectors. Excellent share options apply old-school techniques like pickling and marinating to a range of ingredients, creating Mediterranean masterpieces with soul. Kick things off with house charcuterie; ask for some fresh-baked focaccia bread to accompany it.

Bodega
TAPAS $$
(Map p114; ☑02-9212 7766; www.bodegatapas. com; 216 Commonwealth St, Surry Hills; share plates $16-36; ☺noon-2pm Fri, 6-10pm Tue-Sat; ☑; ☑Central) A significant scene-setter for Sydney's tapas love affair, Bodega has a casual vibe, laid-back staff and a can-do approach. Dishes vary widely in size and price and are very loosely rooted in Central American and Spanish cuisine. Wash 'em down with excellent Spanish and South American wine and finish off with a Pedro Ximénez...pure liquid indulgence for the sweet-toothed.

Spice I Am
THAI $$
(Map p114; ☑02-9280 0928; www.spiceiam. com; 90 Wentworth Ave, Surry Hills; mains $16-30; ☺11.30am-3.30pm & 5-10pm Tue-Sun; ☑; ☑Central) Once the preserve of expat Thais, this little red-hot chilli pepper now has queues out the door. It's no wonder, as everything we've tried from the 70-plus dishes on the menu is super-fragrant and super-spicy. The sign is very unobtrusive so it's easy to walk past: don't. BYO alcohol.

Firedoor
GRILL $$$
(Map p114; ☑02-8204 0800; www.firedoor.com.au; 33 Mary St, Surry Hills; share plates $24-54, degustation $90; ☺5.30-11pm Tue, Wed & Sat, noon-3pm & 5.30-11pm Thu & Fri; ☑Central) All the dishes in this moodily attractive sunken space are produced over a blazing fire, with chef Lennox Hastie matching different woods to the flavours of meat, seafood and vegetables to create extraordinary dishes with huge depth of flavour. The intriguing menu changes on a daily basis. Look out for the fleshy pipis (saltwater clams) with a garlicky sauce that's perfect for mopping.

☒ Kings Cross & Potts Point

Room 10
CAFE $
(Map p90; ☑0432 445 342; www.facebook.com/ room10espresso; 10 Llankelly Pl, Kings Cross; mains $8-15; ☺7am-4pm Mon-Fri, from 8am Sat & Sun; ☑; ☑Kings Cross) With a real neighbourhood feel, this tiny cafe is the sort of place where staff know all the locals by name. The coffee is delicious and the menu limited to sandwiches, salads and such – tasty and uncomplicated. Watch them make it in front of you as you sit at impossibly tiny tables or do some people-watching on this lovable laneway.

Harry's Cafe de Wheels
FAST FOOD $
(Map p90; ☑02-9357 3074; www.harryscafe dewheels.com.au; Cowper Wharf Roadway, Woolloomooloo; pies $5-8; ☺8.30am-1am Mon & Tue, to 2am Wed & Thu, to 3am Fri, 9am-4am Sat, 9am-1am Sun; ☑311, ☑Kings Cross) Open since 1938 (except for a few years when founder Harry 'Tiger' Edwards was on active service), Harry's has been serving meat pies to everyone from Pamela Anderson to Frank Sinatra and Colonel Sanders. You can't leave without trying a 'Tiger': a hot meat pie with sloppy peas, mashed potato, gravy and tomato sauce.

★Cho Cho San
JAPANESE $$
(Map p90; ☑02-9331 6601; www.chochosan. com.au; 73 Macleay St, Potts Point; dishes $12-33; ☺5.30-11pm Mon-Thu, from noon Fri-Sun; ☑311, ☑Kings Cross) Glide through the shiny brass sliding door and take a seat at the communal table that runs the length of this stylish Japanese restaurant, all polished concrete and blonde wood. The food is just as artful as the surrounds, with tasty izakaya-style bites emanating from both the raw bar and the hibachi grill. There's a good sake selection too.

Farmhouse

MODERN AUSTRALIAN **$$**

(Map p90; ☑0448 413 791; www.farmhousekings
cross.com.au; 4/40 Bayswater Rd, Kings Cross; set
menu $60; ☺sittings 6.30pm & 8.30pm Wed-Sat,
2pm & 6.30pm Sun; ⊠Kings Cross) Occupying
a space between restaurant and supper
club, this narrow sliver of a place has a tiny
kitchen and charming hospitality. Diners sit
at one long table and eat a set menu that fea-
tures uncomplicated, delicious dishes from
high-quality produce. There are good wines
and a buzzy, fun atmosphere. Prebooking is
essential.

Fratelli Paradiso

ITALIAN **$$**

(Map p90; ☑02-9357 1744; www.fratelliparadiso.
com; 12-16 Challis Ave, Potts Point; breakfast $12-17,
mains $25-39; ☺7am-11pm Mon-Sat, to 10pm Sun;
☐311, ⊠Kings Cross) This underlit trattoria
has them queuing at the door (especially on
weekends). The intimate room showcases
seasonal Italian dishes cooked with Mediterranean zing. Lots of busy black-clad waiters, lots of Italian chatter, lots of oversized
sunglasses. The street-side tables are the
place to be, whether for morning espresso
or night-time feasting. No bookings.

★Yellow

VEGETARIAN **$$$**

(Map p90; ☑02-9332 2344; www.yellowsydney.
com.au; 57 Macleay St, Potts Point; 5-/7-course
degustation menu $80/100; ☺5-11pm Mon-Fri,
11am-2.30pm & 5-11pm Sat & Sun; ☑; ☐311,
⊠Kings Cross) This sunflower-yellow former
artists' residence is now a top-notch con-
temporary vegetarian restaurant. Dishes are
prepared with real panache, and excellent
flavour combinations are present through-
out. The tasting menus, which can be vegan,
take the Sydney meat-free scene to new lev-
els and the service is happily not too formal.
Weekend brunch is also a highlight, as is the
wine list.

✗ Paddington & Centennial Park

Paddington Alimentari

DELI **$**

(Map p92; ☑02-9358 2142; www.facebook.com/
paddington.alimentari; 2 Hopetoun St, Paddington;
light meals $5-15; ☺7am-5pm Mon-Fri, 7.30am-4pm
Sat; ☐333, 352, 440, M40) Tucked away at the
bottom of the William St boutiques, this is
almost the soul of Paddington distilled into
one friendly cafe-deli. Super coffee, tempt-
ing Italian products and a communal feel as
well-heeled locals rub shoulders in friendly
hedonism; quite a place.

★Saint Peter

SEAFOOD **$$**

(Map p92; ☑02-8937 2530; www.saintpeter.com.
au; 362 Oxford St, Paddington; mains $28-46;
☺5.30-10pm Tue-Thu, noon-2pm & 5.30-10pm
Fri, 11am-3pm & 5.30-10pm Sat & Sun; ☐333,
352, 440, M40) Fish has sometimes been left
behind in the race for nose-to-tailery, pulled
meat and burgerisation of any land-based
beast. It reclaims its deserved pre-eminence
here, with an inspiring, innovative changing
menu. Aged cuts of fish, impeccably sourced
sustainable stock and avant-garde creations
makes this Sydney's finny tribe trailblazer.
Check out their fish butchery a few doors
up too.

★Marta

ITALIAN **$$**

(Map p76; ☑02-9361 6641; www.marta.com.
au; 30 McLachlan Ave, Darlinghurst; mains $22-
38; ☺5.30-10pm Tue-Thu, to 10.30pm Fri & Sat,
9am-9pm Sun; ⊠Kings Cross) Set back from
a showroom on its own sunny square – or
should that be piazza? – this seductive spot
focuses on traditional recipes from Rome
and its region. Fairly priced and richly fla-
voured plates blend vernacular tradition
with modern techniques to good effect.
Daily specials are hearty favourites; prepare
your palate with a drink of something sharp
at the gleaming bar.

Chiswick

MODERN AUSTRALIAN **$$**

(Map p92; ☑02-8388 8688; www.chiswickwooll
ahra.com.au; 65 Ocean St, Woollahra; mains $32-
42; ☺noon-2.30pm & 6-10pm Mon-Thu, noon-
3pm & 5.30-10pm Fri & Sat, noon-9pm Sun; ☎☑;
☐389) ✿ Though owned by celebrity chef
Matt Moran, the real star of this show here
is the kitchen garden that dictates what's on
the menu. Meat from the Moran family farm
and local seafood feature prominently too.
The setting, an airy, light pavilion in a small
park, is an especially lovely one and service
strikes an agreeably casual note.

✗ Bondi, Coogee & the Eastern Beaches

Funky Pies

VEGAN, BAKERY **$**

(Map p108; ☑0451 944 404; www.funkypies.
com.au; 144 Glenayr Ave, Bondi Beach; pies $6.50-
7.50; ☺8.30am-8.30pm Mon-Fri, from 10am Sat &
Sun; ☑; ☐379) Taking the meat out of a pie
would be considered un-Australian in some
quarters, but this tiny place does a great job
of it. Really tasty vegan combinations can be
accompanied by huge smoothies; grab one
of the two outdoor tables or take away to the

beach. The place has a social conscience too, supporting several charities.

★ Blanca
FUSION $$

(Map p108; ☑02-9365 2998; www.blanca.com.au; 75 Hall St, Bondi Beach; sharing plates $23-32; ☻5.30-11.45pm Tue-Thu, from noon Fri & Sat, noon-10pm Sun; ☑; ☑379) The crisp white minimalism of the decor here belies the food, where there's plenty going on. Marrying Japanese and European ideas along with quality Australian produce, there are some truly delicious morsels created – think seafood, slow-cooked meat, pickles, unusual mayonnaises – and lots of flavour. There are several tasting menus, including vegetarian (can be vegan) ones.

The izakaya next door does a bar menu.

★ Lox Stock & Barrel
CAFE $$

(Map p108; ☑02-9300 0368; www.loxstockandbarrel.com.au; 140 Glenayr Ave, Bondi Beach; breakfast & lunch dishes $15-22, dinner mains $30-34; ☻7am-3.30pm daily plus 6-10pm Wed & Thu, 6-11pm Fri & Sat; ☎☑♿; ☑379) Stare down the barrel of a smoking hot bagel and ask yourself one question: Wagyu corned-beef Reuben, or chicken liver with extra pickle? In the evening the menu sets its sights on the likes of steak, lamb and slow-roasted eggplant dishes. It's always busy, even on a wet Monday.

Little Kitchen
CAFE $$

(Map p76; ☑02-8021 3424; www.facebook.com/thelittlekitchencoogee; 275 Arden St, Coogee; lunch mains $19-28; ☻7am-4pm; ☑353, 376, 377) Confident modern Australian fare, strong on presentation, vibrant flavours and quality ingredients, is on offer in this tiny spot. A cheerful, family-run business with an open kitchen and some outdoor seating, it fits well with Coogee's casual beach vibe. Pre-beach breakfasts are a great option here, while brunches and a short changing lunch menu are perfect for lazy coastal days.

Trio
CAFE $$

(Map p108; ☑02-9365 6044; www.triocafe.com.au; 56 Campbell Pde, Bondi Beach; breakfast and lunch dishes $18-28; ☻7am-3pm Mon-Fri, 7.30am-3.30pm Sat & Sun; ☎☑; ☑333) Brunch in Bondi has become de rigueur in Sydney in recent years, and this friendly, unpretentious cafe is one of the top spots to do it. The menu covers several global influences, from Mexican *chilaquiles* to Middle Eastern *shakshouka* via Italian bruschetta. It's a great way to start a day by the sea.

Three Blue Ducks
CAFE $$

(Map p76; ☑02-9389 0010; www.threeblueducks.com; 141-143 Macpherson St, Bronte; breakfasts $14-24, lunches $20-33, dinners $25-43; ☻7am-2.30pm Mon & Tue, to 9pm Wed & Sat, to 3pm Sun; ☎☑; ☑379) ⌀ These ducks are a fair waddle from the water at Bronte Beach, but that doesn't stop queues forming outside the graffiti-covered walls for weekend breakfasts across two seating areas. The adventurous chefs have a strong commitment to using local, organic and fair-trade food whenever possible. It's part of a nice little eating strip.

★ Icebergs Dining Room
ITALIAN $$$

(Map p108; ☑02-9365 9000; www.idrb.com; 1 Notts Ave, Bondi Beach; mains $48-56; ☻noon-3pm & 6.30-11pm, from 10am Sun; ☑333) Poised above the famous swimming pool, Icebergs' views sweep across the Bondi Beach arc to the sea. Inside, bow-tied waiters deliver fresh, sustainably sourced seafood and steaks cooked with elan. There's also an elegant cocktail bar. In the same building, the Icebergs club has a bistro and bar with simpler, cheaper fare.

✗ Newtown & the Inner West

★ Cow & the Moon
ICE CREAM $

(Map p120; ☑02-9557 4255; www.cowandthemoon.com.au; 181 Enmore Rd, Enmore; small gelati $6.50; ☻8.30am-10.30pm Sun-Thu, to 11.30pm Fri & Sat; ☎☑♿; ☑Newtown) Forget the diet and slink into this cool corner cafe, where an array of sinful truffles and tasty tarts beckons seductively. Ignore them and head straight for the world's best gelato – the title this humble little place won in 2014 at the Gelato World Tour title in Rimini, Italy. There's decent coffee too – expect to queue.

Marrickville Pork Roll
VIETNAMESE $

(Map p76; ☑0411 167 169; 236a Illawarra Rd, Marrickville; rolls $5-6; ☻7am-5.30pm; ☑Marrickville) Some of Sydney's best *bánh mì* are served out of this little hole in the wall, where the crisp bread rolls are baked on-site. The pork rolls are delicious, bursting with flavour. There's a slightly larger outlet on the other side of Marrickville station.

Black Star Pastry
BAKERY $

(Map p120; ☑02-9557 8656; www.blackstarpastry.com.au; 277 Australia St, Newtown; snacks $4-10; ☻7am-5pm Sun-Wed, to 5.30pm Thu-Sat; ☑; ☑Newtown) Wise folks follow the black star to pay homage to excellent coffee, totally brilliant cakes and a few very good savoury things (gourmet pies and the like). There are only a couple of tables; it's more a snack-and-run or picnic-in-the-park kind of place. Prepare to queue. Other outposts have cropped up around town.

Lentil as Anything
VEGAN $

(Map p120; ☑02-8283 5580; www.lentilas anything.com; 391 King St, Newtown; meals by donation; ☺noon-3pm & 6-9pm Mon-Fri, from 10am Sat & Sun; ☑; ☑Newtown) ✔ With tasty vegan fare (the menu changes daily but often features south Asian-influenced stews and curries) on a voluntary contribution basis, this heartening project brings people together at communal tables. It's deservedly popular with everyone, from latte-sipping laptoppers to backpackers, students and some people who really need the feed.

Spice Alley
ASIAN $

(Map p120; ☑02-9281 0822; www.spicealley.com. au; Kensington St, Chippendale; dishes $8-18; ☺11am-9.30pm Sun-Wed, to 10pm Thu-Sat; ☑; ☑Central) This little laneway off Kensington St by Central Park is a picturesque outdoor eating hub serving street-foody dishes from various Asian cuisines. Grab your noodles, dumplings or pork belly and fight for a stool. Quality is reasonable rather than spectacular, but prices are low and it's fun. It's cashless: pay by card or load up a prepay card from the drinks booth.

Mary's
BURGERS $

(Map p120; www.6marystreet.com; 6 Mary St, Newtown; mains $13-18; ☺4pm-midnight Mon-Thu, from noon Fri & Sat, noon-10pm Sun; ☎☑; ☑Newtown) Not put off by the grungy aesthetics, the ear-splitting heavy metal or the fact that the graffiti-daubed building was previously a sexual health clinic and a Masonic Temple? Then head up to the mezzanine of this dimly lit hipster bar for some of the best burgers and fried chicken in town.

★ Grounds of Alexandria
CAFE $$

(Map p76; ☑02-9699 2225; www.thegrounds.com. au; 2 Huntley St, Alexandria; lunch dishes $19-25; ☺7am-4pm Mon-Fri, from 7.30am Sat & Sun; ☎⏺; ☑348, ☑Green Square) ✔ A quite extraordinary Alexandria spot, the Grounds goes well beyond converted industrial chic. This former pie factory sports futuristic coffee technology, tip-top baking and delicious food, but it's the enormous garden setting that has the biggest impact: chickens, a waste-chewing pig and greenery all around. It's

a real sight to behold. You won't behold it alone though…prepare to queue.

Bloodwood
MODERN AUSTRALIAN $$

(Map p120; ☑02-9557 7699; www.bloodwood newtown.com; 416 King St, Newtown; share plates $20-33; ☺5-11pm Mon-Fri, noon-midnight Sat, noon-10pm Sun; ☑; ☑Newtown) Relax over a few drinks and a progression of small plates (we love those polenta chips!) in the front bar, or make your way to the rear to enjoy soundly conceived and expertly cooked dishes from across the globe. The decor is industrial-chic and the vibe is alternative – very Newtown.

Koi Dessert Bar
DESSERTS $$

(Map p120; ☑02-9212 1230; www.koidessertbar. com.au; 46 Kensington St, Chippendale; dessert degustation $65; ☺10am-10pm Tue-Sun; ☑Central) Having made the nation salivate on *Master Chef Australia*, Reynold Poernomo now produces his fabulous desserts for public consumption at this two-level spot by Central Park. Downstairs is a cafe with scrumptious sweet fare on offer. Pre-book and head upstairs (6pm to 9.30pm) for the ultimate luxury: a four-course dessert degustation. It also does a savoury menu.

Maggie's
THAI $$

(Map p120; ☑02-9516 5270; www.maggiesthai. com.au; 75 Erskineville Rd, Erskineville; mains $20-30; ☺11am-2.30pm & 5-9pm Thu & Fri, 5-9pm Sat-Wed; ☑; ☑Erskineville) Worth the short stroll downhill from the Newtown strip, or as the focus of a night in pleasant Erskineville itself, this small neighbourhood Thai restaurant is a real gem. A short menu and blackboard specials offer intense, flavour-packed dishes from the open kitchen with great presentation and some unusual flavours. Intelligent service adds to the experience, as does outdoor seating.

3 Olives
GREEK $$

(Map p120; ☑02-9557 7754; 365 King St, Newtown; mains $24-29, meze dishes $13-17; ☺5.30-11pm Wed-Sun; ☑Newtown) There's something very life-affirming about a good Greek restaurant, and this family-run taverna ticks all the boxes. The decor is restrained, with olive-coloured walls, but there's nothing restrained about the portions or aromas: mounds of perfectly textured BBQ octopus, big chunks of melt-in-the-mouth lamb *kleftiko*, warm flatbread, hearty meatballs and moreish olives. It's an excellent celebration of traditional eating.

Newtown & the Inner West

Gigi Pizzeria

VEGAN $$

(Map p120; ☑02-9557 2224; www.gigipizzeria.
com.au; 379 King St, Newtown; pizzas $22-26;
⏱6-10.30pm; ✈; ☒Newtown) This block is
Sydney meat-free central and this cool cor-
ner spot turns out authentic Neapolitan
pizzas with all-vegan toppings. They are
delicious, and there are some pretty mouth-
watering non-dairy desserts on offer too.

Continental

DELI $$

(Map p120; ☑02-8624 3131; www.continental
delicatessen.com.au; 210 Australia St, Newtown;
charcuterie $10-20; ⏱noon-11pm Mon-Thu, to
midnight Fri & Sat, to 10pm Sun; ☒Newtown) It's

a pleasure to sit at the counter at this artfully designed deli and snack on charcuterie and fish preserves while quaffing a glass
of vermouth or a deeply flavoured amaro.
Staff look after you exceptionally well here.
The bistro upstairs opens for dinner and
weekend lunches and features inventive,
well-presented dishes of decent proportions,
partly based on the deli offerings.

Stinking Bishops

CHEESE $$

(Map p120; ☑02-9007 7754; www.thestinking
bishops.com; 63 Enmore Rd, Newtown; 2-/
3-/4-cheese boards $22/30/38; ⏱5-10pm Tue-
Thu, from noon Fri & Sat; ✈; ☒Newtown) A

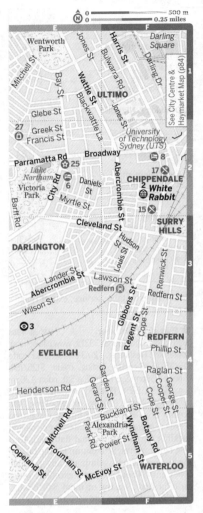

being overly gimmicky; hip, but never try-hard. The menu specialises in well-sourced Australian fish, molluscs and crustaceans prepared with a variety of global influences at play, but don't miss the blood-sausage sandwich either, or the excellent vegetarian creations. Desserts are well worth leaving room for too.

★ Boathouse on Blackwattle Bay
SEAFOOD $$$

(Map p76; ☑ 02-9518 9011; www.boathouse.net.au; 123 Ferry Rd, Glebe; mains $40-48; ⊙ 6-10pm Tue-Thu, noon-2.45pm & 6-11pm Fri-Sun; 🚢 Glebe) The best restaurant in Glebe, and one of the best seafood restaurants in Sydney. Offerings range from a selection of oysters so fresh you'd think you shucked them yourself, to a snapper pie that'll go straight to the top of your favourite-dish list. The views over the bay and Anzac Bridge are stunning. Arrive by water taxi for maximum effect.

Glebe Point Diner
MODERN AUSTRALIAN $$$

(Map p76; ☑ 02-9660 2646; www.glebepoint diner.com.au; 407 Glebe Point Rd, Glebe; mains $32-38; ⊙ noon-3pm Wed-Sun, plus 6-10pm Mon-Thu, 5.30-11pm Fri & Sat; 🚌 431, 🚢 Jubilee Park) A sensational neighbourhood bistro, where only the best local produce is used and where everything – from the home-baked bread and hand-churned butter to the nougat finale – is made from scratch. The food is creative and comforting at the same time: a rare combination. The menu changes regularly and is backed up by blackboard specials. The $45 lunch deal is top value.

✗ Manly

The Pantry
MODERN AUSTRALIAN $$

(Map p111; ☑ 02-9977 0566; www.thepantry manly.com; Ocean Promenade, North Steyne, Manly; mains $28-39; ⊙ 7.30am-10pm; 🛈; 🚢 Manly) Right on the beach, this Manly favourite is perfect for watching the goings-on in the water and on the sand while kicking back with anything from a hearty breakfast to a cocktail or something off the appealing lunch and dinner menu. The food revolves around quality Australian meats and plenty of seafood, served up with style. Some nice wines too.

Boathouse Shelly Beach
CAFE $$

(Map p76; ☑ 02-9974 5440; www.theboat housesb.com.au; 1 Marine Pde, Manly; kiosk mains $12-19, bar mains $18-29; ⊙ 7am-4pm; 🛈🚲) This sweet little spot on picturesque Shelly Beach

pungent array of artisanal cheeses is the raison d'être of this popular shop and place to eat. Choose the varieties you want, pick a wine or craft beer to accompany, and off you go. There are also very tasty charcuterie boards. All its wares are sourced from small producers and available to take home too.

★ Ester
MODERN AUSTRALIAN $$$

(Map p120; ☑ 02-8068 8279; www.ester-restaurant. com.au; 46/52 Meagher St, Chippendale; share plates $18-50; ⊙ 6-11pm Mon-Fri, from noon Sat, noon-4.30pm Sun; 🛈; 🚊 Central) Ester exemplifies Sydney's contemporary dining scene: informal but not sloppy; innovative without

Newtown & the Inner West

◎ **Top Sights**
1 Nicholson Museum D2
2 White Rabbit F2

◎ **Sights**
3 Carriageworks E4
4 Chau Chak Wing Museum D2
5 University of Sydney D2

🛏 **Sleeping**
6 Mad Monkey Backpackers E2
7 Mandelbaum House D3
8 Old Clare Hotel F2
9 Urban Hotel B5

🍴 **Eating**
10 3 Olives C5
11 Black Star Pastry C4
12 Bloodwood C5
13 Continental C4
14 Cow & the Moon B5
15 Ester F2
16 Gigi Pizzeria C5

17 Koi Dessert Bar F2
   Lentil as Anything .... (see 16)
18 Maggie's D5
19 Mary's C4
   Spice Alley .... (see 8)
20 Stinking Bishops B4

🍷 **Drinking & Nightlife**
   Courthouse Hotel .... (see 13)
21 Earl's Juke Joint C5
22 Sly Fox B5
23 Young Henry's B4

🎭 **Entertainment**
24 Enmore Theatre B5
25 Lansdowne Hotel E2

🛍 **Shopping**
   Carriageworks Farmers
   Market .... (see 3)
26 Glebe Markets D2
27 Gleebooks E2

makes a top venue for breakfast juices, brunches, fish 'n' chips, oysters, tasty flatbreads and daily fish specials, served either in the bar section or from the kiosk. There's pleasantly shady outdoor seating. No bookings. Order at the counter; last orders are strictly 3pm.

Belgrave Cartel   CAFE $$
(Map p111; ☑02-9976 6548; www.belgravecartel.com.au; 6 Belgrave St, Manly; small plates $6-18, mains $16-26; ☺6am-2pm Mon & Tue, to midnight Wed-Fri, 7am-midnight Sat, 7am-11pm Sun; 🕿; 🚢Manly) This well-established cafe serves perhaps Manly's best espresso in a soothing vintage atmosphere with a couple of laneway-style outdoor tables. Breakfasts and Sunday brunches are guaranteed to please, as is the selection of Italian share plates. By night, there's an appealing small-bar scene with cocktails and wine.

🍴 Northern Beaches

Boathouse Palm Beach   SEAFOOD $$
(☑02-9974 5440; www.theboathousepb.com.au; Governor Phillip Park, Palm Beach; lunch mains $19-28; ☺7am-4pm; 🕿🅿; 🚌199, L90) Sit on the large timber deck right by the sand at Pittwater or grab a garden table – either option is alluring at this casual seafood cafe. The food (try the legendary fish and chips or the vibrant salads) is nearly as impressive as the views – and that's really saying something.

No bookings or table service; expect queues to order.

⭐**Pilu at Freshwater**   SARDINIAN $$$
(Map p76; ☑02-9938 3331; www.pilu.com.au; Moore Rd, Freshwater; 2-/3-course à la carte $75/95, 5-/8-course tasting menu $125/154; ☺noon-2.30pm & 6-10pm Tue-Sat, noon-2.30pm Sun; 🚌139, E65) Housed within a heritage-listed beach house overlooking the ocean, this brilliant Sardinian restaurant serves specialities such as oven-roasted suckling pig and traditional flatbread. Your best bet, however, is to plump for the tasting menu and thereby eliminate any possible order envy. There are some excellent wines on offer here – many of them Sardinian – beautifully decanted and served.

⭐**Jonah's**   MODERN AUSTRALIAN $$$
(☑02-9974 5599; www.jonahs.com.au; 69 Bynya Rd, Whale Beach; 2/3 courses $89/110; ☺7.30-9am, noon-2.30pm & 6.30-11pm; 🕿; 🚌199, L90) Perched above Whale Beach, luxurious Jonah's has fabulous perspectives over the ocean. The food is easy on the eye too, with immaculate presentation and excellent fish dishes. For the ultimate Sydney indulgence, take a seaplane from Rose Bay, order the seafood platter for two and stay overnight in one of the ocean-view rooms (dinner, bed and breakfast $522 per person). There's also a bar area and terrace, which offers the same views along with cocktails and a more casual menu.

🍷 Drinking & Nightlife

In a city where rum was once the main currency, it's little wonder that drinking plays a big part in the Sydney social scene – whether it's knocking back some tinnies at the beach, schmoozing after work or warming up for a night on the town. Sydney offers plenty of choice in drinking establishments, from the flashy to the trashy.

🍷 Circular Quay & The Rocks

★ Opera Bar   BAR

(Map p80; ✆02-8587 5900; www.operabar. com.au; lower concourse, Sydney Opera House; ⊘10.30am-midnight Mon-Thu, to 1am Fri, 9am-1am Sat, to midnight Sun; 🛜; 🚉Circular Quay) Right on the harbour with the Opera House on one side and the bridge on the other, this perfectly positioned terrace manages a very Sydney marriage of the laid-back and the sophisticated. It's an iconic spot for visitors and locals alike. There's live music or DJs most nights and really excellent food, running from oysters to fabulous steaks and fish. It's a very slick operation – staff even geolocate you to know where to bring the food.

★ Hero of Waterloo   PUB

(✆02-9252 4553; www.heroofwaterloo.com.au; 81 Lower Fort St; ⊘10am-11.30pm Mon-Wed, to midnight Thu-Sat, to 10pm Sun; 🚌311, 🚉Circular Quay) Enter this rough-hewn 1843 sandstone pub to meet some locals, chat to the Irish bar staff and grab an earful of the swing, folk and Celtic bands (Friday to Sunday). Downstairs is a dungeon where, in days gone by, drinkers would sleep off a heavy night before being shanghaied to the high seas via a tunnel leading to the harbour.

★ Glenmore Hotel   PUB

(Map p80; ✆02-9247 4794; www.theglenmore. com.au; 96 Cumberland St; ⊘11am-midnight Sun-Thu, to 1am Fri & Sat; 🛜; 🚉Circular Quay) Downstairs it's a predictably nice old Rocks pub with great outdoor seating, but head to the rooftop and the views are beyond fabulous: Opera House (after the cruise ship leaves), harbour and city skyline all present and accounted for. It gets rammed up here on the weekends, with DJs and plenty of wine by the glass. The food's decent too.

★ Harts Pub   PUB

(Map p80; ✆02-9251 6030; www.hartspub.com; cnr Essex & Gloucester Sts; ⊘noon-11pm Mon-Wed, 11.30am-midnight Thu, to 1am Fri & Sat, noon-10pm

OFF THE BEATEN TRACK

MARRICKVILLE

Once the slightly frumpy western neighbour of Newtown and Enmore, the suburb of Marrickville has gradually attracted bohemians, artists, students and kooks forced out of Newtown by rising rents. Alongside a great set of pubs and bars (some of which host live music), cafes are Marrickville's new claim to fame. We suggest you explore the neighbourhood under your own steam. Jump off the train at Marrickville station, turn right and head up Illawarra Rd.

Sun; 🛜; 🚉Circular Quay) Pouring an excellent range of Sydney craft beers in a quiet corner near the beginning of the Rocks, this historical building has real character. The dishes are quality pub food, with generous salads, fish and steaks. At weekends, this is enjoyably quieter than other Rocks boozers. There are a few pleasant outdoor tables with the Shangri-La hotel looming above.

Doss House   BAR

(Map p80; ✆0457 880 180; www.thedosshouse. com.au; 77 George St; ⊘3pm-1am Tue & Wed, to 2am Thu, noon-2am Fri & Sat, 3pm-midnight Sun; 🚉Circular Quay) With a curious origin story involving two Irish pals, a lottery win and a hostel in Peru, this hidden-away jewel is an atmospheric Rocks basement space. Historic sandstone melds seamlessly with a romantic, cosy interior studded with venerable furniture and lined with whisky bottles. There's a serious malt menu as well as delicious cocktails and attractively tiled seating in the narrow courtyard.

Lord Nelson Brewery Hotel   BREWERY

(Map p80; ✆02-9251 4044; www.lordnelson brewery.com; 19 Kent St; ⊘11am-11pm Mon-Sat, noon-10pm Sun; 🛜; 🚌311, 🚉Circular Quay) This atmospheric boozer is one of three claiming to be Sydney's oldest (all using slightly different criteria). The on-site brewery cooks up its own natural ales; a pint of dark, stouty Nelson's Blood is a fine way to partake. Pub food downstairs is tasty and solid; the upstairs brasserie is an attractive space doing fancier food, including good seafood choices.

Argyle   BAR

(Map p80; ✆02-9247 5500; www.theargyle rocks.com; 18 Argyle St; ⊘11am-1am Sun-Wed, to 3am Thu-Sat; 🛜; 🚉Circular Quay) This stylish

SYDNEY & NEW SOUTH WALES SYDNEY

LOCAL KNOWLEDGE

NIGHTLIFE KNOW-HOW

Sydney's bouncers are often strict, arbitrary and immune to logic. They are usually contracted by outside security firms so have no problem in turning away business. Being questioned and searched every time you want a drink after 8pm on a weekend can definitely take the edge off a Sydney night out.

It is against the law to serve people who are intoxicated and you won't be admitted to a venue if you appear drunk. Expect to be questioned about how much you've had to drink that night: it's more to see if you're slurring your words than actual interest in the answer.

If security staff suspect that you're under the legal drinking age (18 years), you'll be asked to present photo ID with proof of your age. Some bars scan ID for everyone entering.

Plenty of places won't admit you if you are wearing tank tops, thongs (flip-flops) or sandals.

Some pubs have smoking areas, but you aren't allowed to take food into that area – even if you're happy to do so.

and wildly popular conglomeration of bars is spread through the historic Argyle Stores buildings, including a cobblestone courtyard and atmospheric wooden-floored downstairs bar. The decor ranges from rococo couches to white extruded plastic tables, all offset with kooky chandeliers and moody lighting. During the day the courtyard is a pleasant place for a drink or spot of lunch.

Australian Hotel   PUB

(Map p80; ☑02-9247 2229; www.australian heritagehotel.com; 100 Cumberland St; ☺11am-midnight; ☎; ☒Circular Quay) With its wide awning shading lots of outdoor seating, this handsome early 20th-century pub is a favoured pit stop for a cooling ale; it was doing micro-brewed beer long before it became trendy and has a great selection. The kitchen also does a nice line in gourmet pizzas ($17 to $28), including ever-popular toppings of kangaroo, emu and crocodile.

🍷 City Centre & Haymarket

The city centre has long been known for upmarket, after-work booze rooms, none of which you would describe as cosy locals.

Much more interesting is the wide network of 'small bars', which are speakeasy-style places lurking in the most unlikely back alleys and basements.

The entire city centre is subject to 1.30am lockouts and a complete ban on alcohol sales after 3am. These are extended by 30 minutes for certain places.

★Uncle Ming's   COCKTAIL BAR

(Map p84; www.unclemings.com.au; 55 York St; ☺noon-midnight Mon-Thu, to 1am Fri, from 4pm Sat; ☒Wynyard) We love the dark romantic opium-den atmosphere of this small bar secreted away in a basement by a shirt shop. It's an atmospheric spot for anything from a quick beer before jumping on a train to a leisurely exploration of the cocktail menu. It also does an excellent line in dumplings and, usually, has very welcoming bar staff.

★Frankie's Pizza   BAR

(Map p84; www.frankiespizzabytheslice.com; 50 Hunter St; ☺4pm-3am Sat-Thu, from noon Fri; ☎; ☒Martin Place) Descend the stairs and you'll think you're in a 1970s pizzeria, complete with plastic grapevines, snapshots covering the walls and tasty pizza slices ($6). But open the nondescript door in the corner and an indie wonderland reveals itself. Bands play here at least four nights a week (join them on Tuesdays for live karaoke) and there's another bar hidden below.

Baxter Inn   BAR

(Map p84; www.thebaxterinn.com; 152-156 Clarence St; ☺4pm-1am Mon-Sat; ☒Town Hall) Yes, it really is down that dark lane and through that unmarked door (there are two easily spotted bars on this courtyard, but this is through a door to your right). Whisky's the main poison and the friendly bar staff really know their stuff. There's an elegant speakeasy atmosphere and a mighty impressive choir of bottles behind the bar.

Ivy   CLUB

(Map p84; ☑02-9240 3000; www.merivale.com/ ivy; Level 1, 330 George St; ☺noon-midnight Mon-Fri, to 3.30am Sat, plus pool party 1pm-midnight Sun Oct-Mar; ☎; ☒Wynyard) Hidden down a lane off George St, Ivy is the HQ of the all-pervading Merivale Group. It's a fashionable complex of bars, restaurants – and even a swimming pool. It's also Sydney's most hyped venue; expect lengthy queues of suburban kids teetering on unfeasibly high heels on a Saturday for Sydney's hottest club night, run by Ministry of Sound.

Slip Inn & Chinese Laundry   CLUB

(Map p88; ☑02-9114 7327; www.merivale.com.
au/chineselaundry; 111 Sussex St; club $28-43;
⊙11am-1am Mon-Thu, to 3am Fri, 2pm-3am Sat,
Chinese Laundry 9pm-3.30am Fri & Sat; ☎; ⓡWy-
nyard) Slip in to this cheerfully colourful
atmospheric warren on the edge of Darling
Harbour and bump hips with the kids. There
are bars, pool tables, a pleasantly packed
beer garden and Mexican food, courtesy of
El Loco. On Friday and Saturday nights the
bass cranks up at the long-running attached
Chinese Laundry nightclub, accessed via
Slip St below.

Bassic on Friday nights spins dubstep
and bass music, while Lndry on Saturdays is
usually more house-y. Buy advance purchase
discounted tickets via the website.

O Bar   COCKTAIL BAR

(Map p84; ☑02-9247 9777; www.obardining.
com.au; Level 47, Australia Square, 264 George St;
⊙5pm-midnight Sat-Thu, noon-midnight Fri; ☎;
ⓡWynyard) The cocktails at this 47th-floor
revolving bar aren't cheap, but they're still
substantially cheaper than admission to
Sydney Tower (p80) – and it's considerably
more glamorous. The views are truly wonderful; get up there shortly after opening
time, and kick back to enjoy the sunset and
transition into night.

🍷 Darling Harbour & Pyrmont

Edition Book Bar   BAR

(Map p88; ☑02-7900 3831; http://editionbook
bar.com; 181 Harris St, Pyrmont; ⊙10am-10pm
Tue-Thu, to midnight Fri & Sat; ⓠ389, ⓡPyrmont
Bay) Roomy industrial decor, book-lined
walls, killer cocktails and great deals at
happy hour (4pm to 7pm Tuesday to Friday)
make Edition a relaxed spot to kick off your
night. Owned by New Holland, the publisher
of Taschen art books, there's also a regular
program of author talks, book launches and
other literary events.

Smoke   COCKTAIL BAR

(Map p88; ☑02-8587 5400; www.barangaroo
house.com.au; 35 Barangaroo Ave, Central Sydney;
⊙3pm-midnight Mon-Wed, from noon Thu-Sun; ☎;
🚢Barangaroo, ⓡWynyard) On the top floor of
the Barangaroo House building, Smoke has
a most pleasant outlook over the busy com-
ings and goings at the ferry wharf below. It
takes cocktails seriously – the seasonal G&T
is a standout dose of refreshment. Get here
early to bag one of the outdoor tables before
the 5pm office crowd invades.

🍸 Surry Hills & Darlinghurst

★ Love, Tilly Devine   WINE BAR

(Map p84; ☑02-9326 9297; www.lovetillydevine.
com; 91 Crown Lane, Darlinghurst; ⊙5pm-midnight
Mon-Sat, to 10pm Sun; ⓡMuseum) This dark
and good-looking split-level laneway bar is
pretty compact, but the wine list certainly
isn't. It's an extraordinary document, with
some exceptionally well-chosen wines and a
mission to get people away from their tried-
and-tested favourites and explore. Take a
friend and crack open a leisurely bottle
of something. Italian deli bites and fuller
plates are on hand too.

★ Wild Rover   BAR

(Map p114; ☑02-9280 2235; www.thewildrover.
com.au; 75 Campbell St, Surry Hills; ⊙4pm-mid-
night Mon-Sat; ⓡCentral) Look for the unsigned
wide door and enter this supremely cool
brick-lined speakeasy, where a big range of
craft beer is served in chrome steins and
jungle animals peer benevolently from the
green walls. The upstairs bar opens for trivia
and live bands. Irish folk music at weekends
gets the place pumping.

★ Shakespeare Hotel   PUB

(Map p114; ☑02-9319 6883; www.shakespeare
hotel.com.au; 200 Devonshire St, Surry Hills;
⊙10am-midnight Mon-Sat, to 10pm Sun; ⓡSurry
Hills, ⓡCentral) This is a classic Sydney pub
(1879) with art-nouveau tiled walls, scuzzy
carpet, the horses on the TV and cheap bar
meals. There are plenty of cosy hidey holes
upstairs and a cast of local characters. It's a
proper convivial all-welcome place that's the
antithesis of the more gentrified Surry Hills
drinking establishments.

Wyno   WINE BAR

(Map p114; ☑02-8399 1440; www.porteno.com.
au; 4/50 Holt St, Surry Hills; ⊙noon-11pm Tue-
Fri, 5pm-midnight Sat; ☎; ⓡCentral) Run by
Porteño (p115) next door, this wine bar has
its own character. Seat yourself at the long
communal bar and ask the welcoming
waitstaff to suggest delicious drops from
their wine selection (ask the price to avoid
a shock) and tasty snacks and larger plates
to suit your inclinations. Juicy empanadas,
cold cuts, crisp calamari or zingy salads regularly feature.

Eau-de-Vie   COCKTAIL BAR

(Map p114; ☑02-8646 4930; www.eaudevie.com.
au; 229 Darlinghurst Rd, Darlinghurst; ⊙6pm-1am
Mon-Sat, to midnight Sun; ☎; ⓡKings Cross) Take

the door marked 'restrooms' at the back of the main bar at the **Kirketon Hotel** (Map p114; ☑ 02-9332 2011; www.kirketon.com.au; 229 Darlinghurst Rd, Darlinghurst; r $149-389; ❊ ☎; ℞ Kings Cross) and enter this sophisticated, black-walled speakeasy, where a team of dedicated shirt-and-tie-wearing mixologists concoct the sort of beverages that win best-cocktail gongs.

Beresford Hotel
PUB

(Map p114; ☑ 02-9114 7328; www.merivale. au/theberesfordhotel; 354 Bourke St, Surry Hills; ⏲ noon-midnight Mon & Tue, to 1am Wed-Sun; ☎; ℞ 374, 397, 399) The well-polished tiles of the facade and interior are a real feature at this elegantly refurbished historic pub. It's a popular pre-club venue for an upmarket mixed crowd at weekends, but midweek makes for a quieter retreat. The front bar is as handsome as they come; out the back is one of the area's best beer gardens.

This Must Be The Place
COCKTAIL BAR

(Map p114; ☑ 02-9331 8063; www.tmbtp.com. au; 239 Oxford St, Darlinghurst; ⏲ 3pm-midnight; ℞ 333, 352) All Sydney's small bars seem to be dark, candlelit speakeasies with a dash of gangster chic, so it's refreshing to find this light, bright cocktail spot half a block from the Oxford Street strip. It specialises in something equally refreshing in spritzes: citric, perky blends of summery flavours. Tinned seafood conserves provide an offbeat accompaniment.

You may come across a pop-up theme. On our last visit it was all about bunker bartending: 'trying to maintain cocktail excellence in a post-apocalypse scenario'.

Reformatory Caffeine Lab
COFFEE

(Map p114; ☑ 0422 011 565; www.thereformatory lab.coffee; 51 Foveaux St, Surry Hills; ⏲ 6.30am-4pm Mon-Fri, 8am-2pm Sat; ℞ Central) Coffee is a serious business in Sydney, and this corridor's dark industrial decor and cell-block lighting cage combines with cartoon-noir wall illustrations to create a brooding atmosphere. The coffee is delicious, and though there's no seating, it's worth drinking inside for the exquisite presentation on wooden boards. The cold drip comes in chilled test tubes.

Stonewall Hotel
GAY

(Map p114; ☑ 02-9360 1963; www.stonewallhotel. com; 175 Oxford St, Darlinghurst; ⏲ noon-4am; ℞ 333) A stalwart of the Oxford Street LGBT strip, Stonewall, in a good-looking building,

has three levels of bars and dance floors. Cabaret, karaoke and quiz nights spice things up; there's something on every night of the week. Wednesday's Malebox is an inventive way to bag yourself a boy.

Arq
GAY

(Map p114; ☑ 02-9380 8700; www.arqsydney.com. au; 16 Flinders St, Darlinghurst; ⏲ 9pm-late Thu-Sun; ℞ 333) If Noah had to fill his Arq with groovy gay clubbers, he'd head here with a big net and some tranquillisers. This flash megaclub has a cocktail bar, a recovery room and two dance floors with high-energy house, drag shows and a hyperactive smoke machine.

🍷 Kings Cross & Potts Point

★ Old Fitzroy Hotel
PUB

(Map p90; ☑ 02-9356 3848; www.oldfitzroy.com. au; 129 Dowling St, Woolloomooloo; ⏲ 11am-midnight Mon-Fri, noon-11pm Sat, 3-10pm Sun; ☎; ℞ Kings Cross) A gem hidden in the backstreets of Woolloomooloo, this totally unpretentious **theatre pub** (Map p90; ☑ 0416 044 413; www.redlineproductions.com.au; 129 Dowling St, Woolloomooloo; tickets $25-48; ℞ Kings Cross) is also a decent old-fashioned boozer in its own right, with a great variety of beers on tap and a convivial welcome. Prop up the bar, grab a seat at a street-side table or head upstairs to the bistro, pool table and couches.

Monopole
WINE BAR

(Map p90; ☑ 02-9360 4410; www.monopole sydney.com.au; 71a Macleay St, Potts Point; ⏲ 5pm-midnight Mon-Fri, from noon Sat, noon-10pm Sun; ☎; ℞ 311, ℞ Kings Cross) Dark and sexy, Monopole seduces with its stylish interior, complete with hanging strips of black sound-absorption material and discreet front screen. A fabulous wine list of small Australian and international producers offers over 20 vintages by the glass or carafe, so an impromptu tasting session is easy. The food is great too, with house-cured charcuterie and intriguing cheeses a highlight.

Crane Bar
BAR

(Map p90; ☑ 02-9357 3414; www.cranebar.com. au; 32 Bayswater Rd, Kings Cross; ⏲ noon-2am Wed-Sun; ℞ Kings Cross) With origami in mind rather than the construction that is so rapidly gentrifying the Cross, Crane is a likeably different creature. The visual highlight is the extravagantly furnished conservatory lounge awash with colour and antique sofas.

There's a tasty range of casual Japanese-inspired finger food on offer, as well as decent cocktails and plenty of character.

Paddington & Centennial Park

10 William Street   WINE BAR
(Map p92; ☑02-9360 3310; www.10williamst.com.au; 10 William St; ☺5pm-midnight Mon-Thu, from noon Fri & Sat; ☑333, 352, 440, M40) Paddington loves its quality Italian food and eagerly indulges in this *minuscolo* slice of la dolce vita on the fashion strip. There are excellent imported wines, many of them by the glass, and equally impressive food. No bookings, but the very welcoming staff will do their utmost to squeeze you in.

Unicorn   PUB
(Map p114; www.theunicornhotel.com.au; 106 Oxford St, Paddington; ☺4pm-midnight Mon, to 1am Tue, to 3am Wed, 11am-3am Thu-Sat, 11am-midnight Sun; ☎; ☑333, 352, 440, M40) This spacious art-deco pub is casual and unpretentious, and a fine place to sink a few craft beers, sip some Australian wines or try out the pool table atop a Persian-style rug. Burgers are the highlight of the OK eating offerings. There's a cosy downstairs bistro and small beer garden off it. More than the sum of its parts.

Bondi, Coogee & the Eastern Beaches

★Coogee Pavilion   BAR
(Map p76; ☑02-9114 7321; www.merivale.com.au/coogeepavilion; 169 Dolphin St, Coogee; ☺7.30am-midnight Sun-Thu, to 3am Fri & Sat; ☎♿; ☑313, 314, 353, 370-4) With numerous indoor and outdoor bars, a kids' play area and a glorious adults-only rooftop, this vast complex has brought a touch of inner-city glam to Coogee. Built in 1887, the building originally housed an aquarium and swimming pools. Now, space, light and white wood give a breezy feel. It gets totally packed at weekends.

Great eating options run from Mediterranean-inspired bar food to fish 'n' chips and sashimi.

Anchor   BAR
(Map p108; ☑02-8084 3145; www.anchorbarbondi.com; 8 Campbell Pde, Bondi Beach; ☺5pm-1am Tue-Fri, from 1pm Sat & Sun; ☎; ☑333) Surfers, backpackers and the local

SYDNEY & NEW SOUTH WALES SYDNEY

LOCKOUT LAWS

In an effort to cut down on alcohol-fuelled violence, tough licensing laws have been introduced to a large area of the central city bounded by the Rocks, Circular Quay, Woolloomooloo, Kings Cross, Darlinghurst, Haymarket and the eastern shores of Darling Harbour.

Within this zone, licensed venues are not permitted to admit people after 1.30am. However, if you arrive before then, the venue is permitted to continue serving you alcohol until 3am, or 3.30am in the case of certain venues that you can enter until 2am. This latter amendment was announced after widespread protest from the public and industry over the severity of the laws. The change was too little, too late for many venues, which had already closed down. At time of research, the government was considering further amendments.

Lockout laws have seen to a shift in late-night drinking to places outside the zone, with southern Surry Hills, Chippendale, Newtown and Marrickville popular targets.

cool kids slurp down icy margaritas at this bustling bar at the south end of the Bondi strip. It sports a dark-wood nautical-piratey feel; the chunky street-side seating is tops. The two-hour happy hour from 5pm weekdays is a good way to start the post-surf debrief.

North Bondi RSL   BAR
(Map p108; ☑02-9130 3152; www.northbondirsl.com.au; 120 Ramsgate Ave, North Bondi; ☺noon-10pm Mon-Thu, to 11pm Fri, 10am-11pm Sat, 10am-10pm Sun; ♿; ☑333) This Returned and Services League bar ain't fancy, but with views no one can afford and drinks that everyone can, who cares? The kitchen serves decent nosh, including a dedicated kids' menu. Bring ID, as nonmembers theoretically need to prove that they live at least 5km away. Grab a balcony seat for the perfect beach vistas.

Coogee Bay Hotel   PUB
(Map p76; ☑02-9665 0000; www.coogeebayhotel.com.au; 253 Coogee Bay Rd, Coogee; ☺bar 9.30am-4am Mon-Thu, to 6am Fri, 9am-6am Sat, 9am-10pm Sun; ☎; ☑313, 314, 353, 372, 373, 374)

LGBTIQ+ SYDNEY

LGBTIQ+ folk have migrated to Oz's Emerald City from all over Australia, New Zealand and the world, adding to a community that is visible, vibrant and an integral part of the city's social fabric. Partly because gay and straight communities are so well integrated in central Sydney, and partly because of smartphone apps facilitating contact, the gay-specific nightlife scene has died off substantially. But the action's still going on and Sydney is indisputably one of the world's great queer cities.

The famous Sydney Gay & Lesbian Mardi Gras (p101) is now the biggest annual tourist-attracting date on the Australian calendar. While the straights focus on the parade, the gay and lesbian community throws itself wholeheartedly into the entire festival, including the blitzkrieg of partying that surrounds it. There's no better time for the gay traveller to visit Sydney than the two-week lead-up to the parade and party, held on the first Saturday in March.

Darlinghurst, Kings Cross and Newtown have traditionally been the gayest neighbourhoods, although all of the inner suburbs have a higher than average proportion of LGBT residents. Most of the gay venues are on the Darlinghurst section of Oxford St, with classic spots like Stonewall (p126) and Arq (p126). However, some of the best events are held at mixed pubs, such as the **Sly Fox** (Map p120; ☑ 02-9557 2917; www.slyfox.sydney; 199 Enmore Rd, Enmore; ☺ 6pm-3am Wed & Thu, to 6am Fri & Sat; ⬚ 423, 426, 428, M30) and the legendary Sunday afternoon session at the Beresford (p126).

Beach scenes include the north end of Bondi (p85); Lady Bay, a pretty nudist beach tucked under South Head; Obelisk, a secluded nude beach with a bush hinterland; and Murray Rose Pool (p97), another harbour beach. Women-only McIver's Baths (p97) is extremely popular with the Sapphic set.

This enormous, rambling, rowdy complex packs in the backpackers for live music, open-mic nights, comedy and big-screen sports in the beaut beer garden, sports bar and Selina's nightclub. Sit on a stool at the window overlooking the beach and sip on a cold one.

🍺 Sydney Harbourside

⭐ **Watsons Bay Beach Club** PUB
(Map p76; ☑ 02-9337 5444; www.watsonsbay hotel.com.au; 1 Military Rd, Watsons Bay; ☺ 10am-10pm Sun-Thu, to 11.30pm Fri & Sat; ⬚ 324, 325, 380, 🛥 Watsons Bay) One of the great pleasures in life is languoring in the pumping beer garden of the Watsons Bay Hotel, mere metres from the ferry wharf, after a day at the beach. It goes off here at weekends, with a rowdy good time had by all. Stay to watch the sun go down over the city. Food is pricey if OK.

⭐ **Sheaf** PUB
(Golden Sheaf Hotel; Map p76; ☑ 02-9327 5877; www.thesheaf.com.au; 429 New South Head Rd, Double Bay; ☺ 10am-1am Mon-Wed, to 2am Thu-Sat, to midnight Sun; 🛜; ⬚ 323-327, 🛥 Double Bay, 🚆 Edgecliff) A cracking pub, especially at weekends when it thrums with life all day, this is a real Eastern Suburbs favourite. The beer garden is among Sydney's best: large, with good wines by the glass, heaters, evening entertainment and brilliant pub food (all-day service Friday to Sunday). Lots of other spaces mean there's something for all.

🍺 Newtown & the Inner West

⭐ **Archie Rose Distilling Co.** BAR
(Map p76; ☑ 02-8458 2300; www.archierose.com. au; 85 Dunning Ave, Rosebery; ☺ noon-10pm Sun & Mon, to midnight Tue-Sat; 🛜; ⬚ 343, 🚆 Green Square) This distillery has made quite an impact with its excellent gins – where better to try them than the place itself? The bar is appropriately industrial chic; the mezzanine is a great spot to sit and observe the action. Try different gins in a flight, or pick your perfect G&T combination or cocktail. It also has some decent wine and beer.

⭐ **Lazybones Lounge** BAR
(Map p76; ☑ 0450 008 563; www.lazybones lounge.com.au; 294 Marrickville Rd, Marrickville; ☺ 7pm-midnight Mon-Wed, 5pm-3am Thu-Sat, 5-10pm Sun; 🛜; 🚆 Marrickville) Roomy and extravagantly decorated, Lazybones is an excellent bar-lounge with live music nightly and a decent line in cocktails and food. At weekends it gets likeably louche, with a happy crowd dancing until late. Even the

bouncers are friendly. There's a cover charge for the bands ($10 to $20); it's free later on. Enter from Illawarra Rd.

★**Timbah** WINE BAR
(Map p76; ☑02-9571 7005; www.facebook.com/TimbahWineBar; 375 Glebe Point Rd, entrance on Forsyth St, Glebe; ◷4-10pm Tue-Thu, to 10.30pm Fri, 3.30-10.30pm Sat; ▣431, ▣Glebe) ⚑ Quite a way down Glebe Point Rd is an excellent independent bottle shop; turn right to find the convivial wine bar it runs downstairs. It's a lovely space decked out in wood; there's always something interesting available by the glass, and staff are open to cracking something on demand. Tapas-style food is tasty, with Australian native flavours and home-grown herbs.

★**Earl's Juke Joint** BAR
(Map p120; www.facebook.com/earlsjukejoint; 407 King St, Newtown; ◷4pm-midnight Mon-Sat, to 10pm Sun; ▣Newtown) Swinging Earl's serves craft beers and killer cocktails to the Newtown hip-erati. It's hidden behind the down-at-heel facade of the butcher's shop it used to be, but once in, you're in downtown New Orleans, with a bar as long as the Mississippi.

Young Henry's BREWERY
(Map p120; ☑02-9519 0048; www.younghenrys.com; 76 Wilford St, Newtown; ◷noon-7pm; ▣Newtown) Conviviality is assured in this brewery bar, where the beer is as fresh as you'll get. Basically, they've filled a bit of warehouse with high tables, a loud stereo system and a counter to serve their delicious beer, then opened the roller door and filled it with happy locals. It doesn't do eats, but there's a different food truck outside each weekend.

Courthouse Hotel PUB
(Map p120; ☑02-9519 8273; www.solotel.com.au; 202 Australia St, Newtown; ◷10am-midnight Mon-Sat, to 10pm Sun; ▣Newtown) A block back from the King St fray, the 150-year-old Courthouse is one of Newtown's best pubs, the kind of place where everyone from goth lesbians to magistrates can have a beer and feel at home. It packs out for Sydney Swans games. The beer garden is one of Sydney's best: spacious, sheltered and cheerful, with decent pub food available.

Petersham Bowling Club BEER GARDEN
(Map p76; ☑02-9569 4639; www.thepbc.org.au; 77 Brighton St, Petersham; ◷5-10pm Tue-Thu, 4-11pm Fri, noon-varies Sat, noon-10pm Sun; ▣Petersham) Fancy a place where you can sip on a craft beer while your kids play safely and make lots of local friends? This is it. A former bowling club (though you can still play) is now a community-focused spot doing good beer and simple food. Parents rock up in droves at the weekends and the children romp on the grass.

🍺 Manly

★**Manly Wharf Hotel** PUB
(Map p111; ☑02-9977 1266; www.manlywharfhotel.com.au; East Esplanade, Manly; ◷11.30am-midnight Mon-Fri, 11am-1am Sat, 11am-midnight Sun; ⚹▥; ▣Manly) Just along the wharf from the ferry, this remodelled pub is all glass and water vistas, with loads of seating so you've a good chance of grabbing a share of the view. It's a perfect spot for sunny afternoon beers. There's good pub food too (mains $22 to $30), with pizzas, fried fish and succulent rotisserie chicken all worthwhile.

🌊 Northern Beaches

★**Newport** PUB
(Newport Arms Hotel; ☑02-9114 7337; www.merivale.com.au/thenewport; cnr Beaconsfield & Kalinya Sts, Newport; ◷9.30am-midnight Mon-Fri, from 9am Sat, 9am-11pm Sun; ⚹▥; ▣188, 199, L90) This legendary Northern Beaches pub actually overlooks not the ocean but the Pittwater side, with bobbing boats and quiet strands the outlook. It's an absolutely enormous complex, with acres of appealing outdoor seating, several bars, good food from various kitchens, table tennis and all sorts of stuff going on. It's a great, family-friendly place to while away a sunny afternoon.

☆ Entertainment

Cinema

★**Golden Age Cinema & Bar** CINEMA
(Map p114; ☑02-9211 1556; www.ourgoldenage.com.au; 80 Commonwealth St, Surry Hills; adult/concession tickets $22/17; ◷4pm-midnight Tue-Fri, from 2.30pm Sat, 2.30-11pm Sun; ▣Museum) In what was once the Sydney HQ of Paramount Pictures, a heart-warming small cinema occupies the former screening room downstairs. It shows old favourites, arthouse classics and a few recherché gems. There's a great small bar here too, with free gigs on Thursdays and Saturdays. All up, it's a fabulous place for a night out.

ℹ WHAT'S ON LISTINGS

Sydney Morning Herald (www.smh. com.au) Online and in Friday's 'Shortlist' section.

What's On Sydney (www.whatson sydney.com)

What's On City of Sydney (http:// whatson.cityofsydney.nsw.gov.au)

Time Out Sydney (www.timeout.com/ sydney)

Eventbrite (www.eventbrite.com.au)

The Music (www.themusic.com.au) Online and printed guide to the live music scene.

Moonlight Cinema   CINEMA
(Map p92; www.moonlight.com.au; Belvedere Amphitheatre, cnr Loch & Broome Aves, Centennial Park; adult/child $20/15; ⊗ sunset Dec-Mar; 🚍333, 352, 440, M40, 🚊 Bondi Junction) Take a picnic and join the bats under the stars in magnificent Centennial Park; enter via the Woollahra Gate on Oxford St. A mix of new-release blockbuster, art-house and classic films is screened.

OpenAir Cinema   CINEMA
(Map p76; ☑ 1300 366 649; www.stgeorge openair.com.au; Mrs Macquaries Rd; tickets $40; ⊗ early Jan–mid-Feb; 🚊 Circular Quay) Right on the harbour, the outdoor three-storey screen here comes with surround-sound, sunsets, skyline views and swanky food and wine. Most tickets are purchased in advance – look out for the dates in early December as they go fast – but a limited number go on sale at the door each night at 6.30pm; check the website for details.

Classical Music

★ **Sydney Opera House**   PERFORMING ARTS
(Map p80; ☑ 02-9250 7777; www.sydneyopera house.com; Bennelong Point; 🚊 Circular Quay) The glamorous jewel of Australian performance, Sydney's famous Opera House has five main stages. Opera may have star billing, but it's also an important venue for theatre, dance and classical concerts, while big-name bands sometimes rock the forecourt. Ongoing renovation works through to 2022 will close the concert hall for a period, but in other theatres the show goes on.

★ **City Recital Hall**   CLASSICAL MUSIC
(Map p84; ☑ 02-8256 2222; www.cityrecitalhall. com; 2 Angel Pl; ⊗ box office 9am-5pm Mon-Fri; 🚊 Wynyard) Based on the classic configuration of the 19th-century European concert hall, this custom-built 1200-seat venue boasts near-perfect acoustics. Catch top-flight companies such as **Musica Viva** (☑ 1800 688 482; www.musicaviva.com.au), the **Australian Brandenburg Orchestra** (ABO; ☑ 02-9328 7581; www.brandenburg.com.au; tickets $70-170) and the **Australian Chamber Orchestra** (ACO; ☑ 02-8274 3888; www.aco. com.au) here.

Dance

Sydney Dance Company   DANCE
(SDC; Map p80; ☑ 02-9221 4811; www.sydney dancecompany.com; Pier 4, 15 Hickson Rd; 🚍324, 325, 🚊 Circular Quay) Australia's number-one contemporary-dance company has been staging wildly modern, sexy and sometimes shocking works since 1979. Performances are usually held at the **Roslyn Packer Theatre** (Map p80; ☑ 02-9250 1999; www. roslynpackertheatre.com.au; 22 Hickson Rd) or **Carriageworks** (Map p120; ☑ 02-8571 9099; www.carriageworks.com.au; 245 Wilson St, Eveleigh; ⊗ 10am-6pm; 🚊 Redfern).

Bangarra Dance Theatre   DANCE
(Map p80; ☑ 02-9251 5333; www.bangarra.com. au; Pier 4, 15 Hickson Rd; 🚍324, 325, 🚊 Circular Quay) Bangarra is hailed as Australia's finest Aboriginal performance company. Artistic director Stephen Page conjures a fusion of contemporary themes, Indigenous traditions and Western technique. When not touring internationally, the company performs at the Opera House or at Walsh Bay.

Live Music

★ **Metro Theatre**   LIVE MUSIC
(Map p84; ☑ 02-9550 3666; www.metrotheatre. com.au; 624 George St; 🚊 Town Hall) The Metro is easily Sydney's best mid-sized venue for catching alternative local and international acts in intimate, well-ventilated, easy-seeing comfort. Other offerings include comedy, cabaret and dance parties.

Venue 505   LIVE MUSIC
(Map p114; ☑ SMS only 0419 294 755; www. venue505.com; 280 Cleveland St, Surry Hills; ⊗ 6pm-midnight Mon-Sat; 🚍372, 🚊 Central) Focusing on jazz, roots, reggae, funk, gypsy and Latin music, this small, relaxed venue is run by artists and thoughtfully programmed.

The space features comfortable couches and murals by a local painter. It does pasta, pizza and share plates so you can munch along to the music.

Enmore Theatre
LIVE MUSIC

(Map p120; ☑ 02-9550 3666; www.enmore theatre.com.au; 130 Enmore Rd, Newtown; ⊙ box office 9am-6pm Mon-Fri, 10am-4pm Sat; ☐ 423, 426, 428, ☐ Newtown) Originally a vaudeville playhouse, the bohemian art-deco Enmore now hosts medium-sized touring bands, plus theatre, ballet and comedy.

Lansdowne Hotel
LIVE MUSIC

(Map p120; ☑ 02-8218 2333; www.thelansdowne pub.com.au; 2 City Rd, Chippendale; ⊙ noon-3am Mon-Sat, to midnight Sun; ☐ 412, 413, 422, 423, ☐ Central) This famous Sydney venue is back in action after a period of closure. It's a like-ably no-frills rock pub downstairs, with graf-fiti on the walls and food served until 2am. Upstairs there are gigs most nights; prepare for around $20 cover charge at weekends, depending on the band(s).

Spectator Sport

★ Sydney Cricket Ground
SPECTATOR SPORT

(SCG; Map p92; ☑ 02-9360 6601; www.scgt.nsw. gov.au; Driver Ave, Moore Park; ☐ 373-377, ☐ Moore Park) During the cricket season (October to March), the stately SCG is the venue for interstate cricket matches (featuring the NSW Blues), family-friendly Big Bash (p101) extravaganzas and sell-out international five-day Test, one-day and T20 limited-over cricket matches. As the cricket season ends, the Australian rules football (AFL) season starts, and the stadium becomes a blur of red-and-white-clad Sydney Swans (www. sydneyswans.com.au) fans.

★ Royal Randwick Racecourse
HORSE RACING

(Map p76; ☑ 02-9663 8400; www.australian turfclub.com.au; Alison Rd, Randwick; ☐ 338, 339, ☐ Alison Rd) The action at Sydney's most famous racecourse peaks in April with sev-eral high-profile races, including the Queen Elizabeth Stakes; check the online calendar

SPORTS-CRAZY SYDNEY

Sydneysiders are sports crazy. Getting to a match is a great way to absorb some local culture and atmosphere.

Rugby league Sydney's all-consuming passion is rugby league, a superfast, supermacho game with a frenzied atmosphere for spectators. The National Rugby League (NRL; www. nrl.com) comp runs from March to October, climaxing in the sell-out Grand Final. You can catch games every weekend during the season, played at the home grounds of Sydney's various tribes. Tickets start around $25 via www.tickets.nrl.com.

Rugby union Despite its punishing physical component, rugby union (www.rugby.com. au) has a more upper-class rep than rugby league and a less fanatical following in Sydney. The annual southern hemisphere Rugby Championship provokes plenty of passion – par-ticularly the matches against New Zealand, which determine the holders of the ultimate symbol of Trans-Tasman rivalry, the Bledisloe Cup (the Aussies haven't won it since 2002). In the Super Rugby competition, the NSW Waratahs bang heads with other teams from Australia, New Zealand, Argentina, Japan and South Africa.

Australian Football League (AFL) See the Sydney Swans in their red and white splen-dour from March to September at the Sydney Cricket Ground. Sydney's other team, the Greater Western Sydney Giants, play most home games at a stadium in the Olympic Park complex. Tickets start at around $25, available via www.afl.com.au.

Soccer The A-League bucks convention, playing games from October to May rather than through the depths of winter. Sydney FC (www.sydneyfc.com) won the championship in 2006, 2010 and 2017. The newer Western Sydney Wanderers haven't won a grand final yet but landed an even bigger prize in 2014, the Asian Champions League. The W-League is the parallel women's equivalent, and is garnering rapidly increasing support. The same two Sydney clubs participate.

Cricket Major international Test, one-day and T20 matches take place at the Sydney Crick-et Ground in summer. NSW plays sparsely supported four-day Sheffield Shield matches here and at other Sydney grounds, while the all-action Big Bash draws huge crowds.

for race days, which are normally every second Saturday. The spring races are also a major event. It's always a fun day out, with Sydney fashion on show. Race-day shuttle buses run from Eddy Ave by Central station.

Theatre

⭐ **Belvoir St Theatre**   THEATRE
(Map p114; ☑02-9699 3444; www.belvoir.com.au; 25 Belvoir St, Surry Hills; 🚌372, 🚊Surry Hills, 🚊Central) In a quiet corner of Surry Hills, this intimate venue, with two small stages, is the home of an often-experimental and consistently excellent theatre company that specialises in quality Australian drama. It often commissions new works and is a vital cog in the Sydney theatre scene.

Sydney Theatre Company   THEATRE
(STC; Map p80; ☑02-9250 1777; www.sydneytheatre.com.au; Pier 4, 15 Hickson Rd; ⊘box office 9am-7.30pm Mon, to 8.30pm Tue-Fri, 11am-8.30pm Sat, 2hr before show Sun; 🚌324, 325, 🚊Circular Quay) Established in 1978, the STC is Sydney theatre's top dog and has played an important part in the careers of many famous Australian actors (especially Cate Blanchett, co-artistic director from 2008 to 2013). Performances are also staged at the Opera House. Redevelopment of the Walsh Bay precinct means they will be in the nearby Roslyn Packer Theatre (p130) until 2020.

🛍 Shopping

Sydney's city centre is brimming over with department, chain and international fashion stores and arcades – shopping here is about as fast and furious as Australia gets. Paddington is the place for art and fashion, while new and secondhand boutiques around Newtown and Surry Hills cater to a hipper, more alternative crowd. Double Bay, Mosman and Balmain are a bit more 'mother of the bride', and if you're chasing bargains, head to Chinatown or the Alexandria factory outlets.

Newtown and Glebe have the lion's share of book and record shops, though the city centre has good options too. For surf gear, head to Bondi or Manly. Woollahra, Newtown (around St Peters station) and Surry Hills are good for antiques. For souvenirs – from exquisite opals to tacky T-shirts – try the Rocks, Circular Quay and Darling Harbour.

🏛 Circular Quay & The Rocks

⭐ **Gannon House Gallery**   ART
(Map p80; ☑02-9251 4474; www.gannonhousegallery.com; 45 Argyle St; ⊘10am-6pm; 🚊Circular Quay) Specialising in contemporary Australian and Aboriginal art, Gannon House purchases works directly from artists and Aboriginal communities. You'll find the work of prominent artists such as Gloria Petyarre here, alongside lesser-known names. There are always some striking and wonderful pieces.

⭐ **Australian Wine Centre**   WINE
(Map p80; ☑02-9247 2755; www.australianwinecentre.com; 42 Pitt St; ⊘9.30am-8pm Mon-Thu & Sat, to 9pm Fri, 10am-7pm Sun; 🚊Circular Quay) This shop, with multilingual staff, is packed with quality Australian wine, beer and spirits. Smaller producers are well represented, along with a staggering range of prestigious Penfolds Grange wines and other bottle-aged gems. Service is excellent and international shipping can be arranged.

Craft NSW   ARTS & CRAFTS
(Map p80; ☑02-9241 5825; www.artsandcraftsnsw.com.au; 12 Argyle Pl; ⊘10am-5pm) This craft association gallery at the quiet end of the Rocks is full of beautiful and original creations. It's the perfect spot to pick up a unique gift for someone special.

Opal Minded   JEWELLERY
(Map p80; ☑02-9247 9885; www.opalminded.com; 55 George St; ⊘9am-6.30pm; 🚊Circular Quay) This shop in the Rocks is one of several spots around here where you can stock up on opal, that quintessential piece of Aussie bling. The quality and service are both excellent.

The Rocks Markets   MARKET
(Map p80; www.therocks.com/markets; George St; ⊘9am-3pm Fri, 10am-5pm Sat & Sun; 🚊Circular Quay) Under a long white canopy, the stalls at this market are a focus for tourists, but some excellent handicrafts outweigh the amount of koala tat. Pick up tasty treats at the 'Foodies Market' on Fridays or gifts at the weekends.

🏛 City Centre & Haymarket

⭐ **Strand Arcade**   SHOPPING CENTRE
(Map p84; ☑02-9265 6800; www.strandarcade.com.au; 412 George St; ⊘9am-5.30pm Mon-Wed & Fri, to 9pm Thu, to 4pm Sat, 11am-4pm Sun;

(⌂ Town Hall) Constructed in 1891, the beautiful Strand rivals the QVB in the ornateness stakes. The three floors of designer fashions, Australiana and old-world coffee shops will make your shortcut through here considerably longer. Some of the top Australian designers and other iconic brands have shops here – chocolatiers included! Aesop, Haighs, Leona Edmiston, Dinosaur Designs and more are all present.

★**Queen Victoria Building** SHOPPING CENTRE

(QVB; Map p84; ✆02-9265 6800; www.qvb.com. au; 455 George St; ⊙9am-6pm Mon-Wed, Fri & Sat, to 9pm Thu, 11am-5pm Sun; ⊛; ⌂ Town Hall) The magnificent QVB takes up a whole block and boasts nearly 200 shops on five levels. It's a High Victorian neo-Gothic masterpiece – without doubt Sydney's most beautiful shopping centre.

★**Abbey's** BOOKS

(Map p84; ✆02-9264 3111; www.abbeys.com. au; 131 York St; ⊙8.30am-6pm Mon-Wed & Fri, to 8pm Thu, 9am-5pm Sat, 10am-5pm Sun; ⌂ Town Hall) Easily central Sydney's best bookshop, Abbey's has many strengths. It's good on social sciences and has excellent resources for language learning, including a great selection of foreign films on DVD. There's also a big sci-fi and fantasy section. Staff are great and generally very experienced.

Westfield Sydney MALL

(Map p84; ✆02-8236 9200; www.westfield.com. au/sydney; 188 Pitt St Mall; ⊙9.30am-7pm Mon-Wed, Fri & Sat, to 9pm Thu, from 10am Sun; ⊛; ⌂ St James) The centre's behemoth shopping centre is a bafflingly large complex gobbling up Sydney Tower and a fair chunk of Pitt St Mall. The 5th-floor food court is close to Sydney's best. Shops include Calibre, Carla Zampatti, Jurlique, Oroton, RM Williams, Sass & Bide and Zimmermann.

Red Eye Records MUSIC

(Map p84; ✆02-9267 7440; www.redeye.com. au; 143 York St; ⊙9am-6pm Mon-Wed, Fri & Sat, to 9pm Thu, 10am-5pm Sun; ⌂ Town Hall) Partners of music freaks beware: don't let them descend the stairs into this shop unless you are prepared for a lengthy delay. The shelves are stocked with an irresistible collection of new, classic, rare and collectable LPs, CDs, crass rock T-shirts, books, posters and music DVDs.

David Jones DEPARTMENT STORE

(Map p84; ✆02-9266 5544; www.davidjones.com. au; 86-108 Castlereagh St; ⊙9.30am-7pm Sun-Wed, to 9pm Thu & Fri, from 9am Sat; ⌂ St James) DJs is Sydney's premier department store, with high-quality clothing and a highbrow food court. A revamp has added a flashy new designer shoe floor on level 7, while a new kids' area and rooftop Champagne bar were also in the works at the time of research. David Jones also takes up a sizeable chunk of **Westfield Bondi Junction** (Map p76; ✆02-9947 8000; www.westfield.com. au; 500 Oxford St, Bondi Junction; ⊙9.30am-6pm Mon-Wed & Sat, to 9pm Thu, to 7pm Fri, from 10am Sun; ⊛; ⌂ Bondi Junction).

Paddy's Markets MARKET

(Map p84; www.paddysmarkets.com.au; 9-13 Hay St; ⊙10am-6pm Wed-Sun; ⌂ Paddy's Markets, ⌂ Central) Cavernous Paddy's is a covered market of mostly mass-produced tat, including stall after stall flogging cheap souvenirs – great if you've got an extensive list of friends wanting clinging koalas or novelty T-shirts. There's also a mediocre fruit and vegetable section and a selection of outlet shops in the upstairs shopping centre, Market City.

Surry Hills & Darlinghurst

★**Artery** ART

(Map p114; ✆02-9380 8234; www.artery.com.au; 221 Darlinghurst Rd, Darlinghurst; ⊙10am-5pm; ⌂ Kings Cross) Step into a world of mesmerising dots and swirls at this small gallery devoted to Aboriginal art. Artery's motto is 'ethical, contemporary, affordable', and while large canvases by more established artists cost in the thousands, small, unstretched canvases start at around $35. There's also a good range of giftware as well as an offbeat sideline in preserved insects.

Paddington & Centennial Park

★**Dinosaur Designs** JEWELLERY, HOMEWARES

(Map p92; ✆02-9361 3776; www.dinosaurdes igns.com.au; 339 Oxford St, Paddington; ⊙9.30am-5.30pm Mon-Sat, 11am-4pm Sun; ⌂ 333, 352, 440, M40) This tiny shop is a visual treat. Richly coloured, translucent resin bangles and baubles sit among technicoloured vases and bowls, and chunky sterling-silver rings and necklaces. It's all beautiful and handmade in Sydney, and makes for a great present.

Paddington Markets
MARKET

(Map p92; ☑02-9331 2923; www.paddington markets.com.au; 395 Oxford St, Paddington; ◉10am-4pm Sat; 🚍333, 352, 440, M40) Originating in the 1970s, when they were drenched in the scent of patchouli oil, these markets are considerably more mainstream these days. They're still worth exploring for their new and vintage clothing, crafts and jewellery. Expect a crush.

Berkelouw Books
BOOKS

(Map p114; ☑02-9360 3200; www.berkelouw. com.au; 19 Oxford St, Paddington; ◉9.30am-9pm Sun-Thu, to 10pm Fri & Sat; 🚍333, 352, 440, M40) Expecting the dank aroma of second-hand books? Forget it! Follow your nose up to the cafe, then browse through three floors of pre-loved tomes, new releases, antique maps and Australia's largest collection of rare books. The Berkelouws have specialised in second-hand books and printed rarities over six generations since setting up shop in Holland in 1812.

🏠 Newtown & the Inner West

★ Mitchell Road Antique & Design Centre
ANTIQUES, VINTAGE

(Map p76; ☑02-9698 0907; www.mitchellroad. wordpress.com; 17 Bourke Rd, Alexandria; ◉10am-6pm; 🚉Green Square) This extraordinary vintage and antique market is a warehouse full of retro chic, whether you are after original 1970s Lego, pre-loved rocking horses, a Georgian coronation tea set or Bakelite telephones. For some it will be a dive into a past known only from movies, for others a trip down memory lane.

★ Carriageworks Farmers Market
MARKET

(Map p120; www.carriageworks.com.au; Carriageworks, 245 Wilson St, Eveleigh; ◉8am-1pm Sat; 🚉Redfern) 🌿 Over 70 regular stallholders sell their goodies at Sydney's best farmers market, held in a heritage-listed railway workshop (p130). Food and coffee stands do a brisk business and vegetables, fruit, meat and seafood from all over the state are sold in a convivial atmosphere.

Little Bottleshop
WINE

(Glebe Liquor; Map p76; ☑02-9660 1984; 375 Glebe Point Rd, Glebe; ◉11am-8pm Mon-Thu, 10am-9pm Fri & Sat, 10am-7pm Sun; 🚍431, 🚉Glebe) One of Sydney's best bottle shops for those interested in Australian wine, this unassuming place features an excellent curated selection of small-vineyard wines from quality regions. Look out for their own 2037 (Glebe's postcode) bottlings. It runs a wine bar (p129) downstairs.

Gleebooks
BOOKS

(Map p120; ☑02-9660 2333; www.gleebooks.com. au; 49 Glebe Point Rd, Glebe; ◉9am-7pm Mon-Sat, 10am-6pm Sun; 🚍431, 433, 🚉Glebe) One of Sydney's best bookshops, Gleebooks' aisles are full of politics, arts and general fiction, and staff really know their stuff. Check its calendar for author talks and book launches.

Glebe Markets
MARKET

(Map p120; www.glebemarkets.com.au; Glebe Public School, cnr Glebe Point Rd & Derby Pl; ◉10am-4pm Sat; 🚍431, 433, 🚉Glebe) The best of the west: Sydney's bohemian inner-city contingent beats a course to this crowded retro-chic market. There are some great handicrafts and designer pieces on sale, as well as an inclusive, community atmosphere.

ℹ Information

DANGERS & ANNOYANCES

➡ Sydney's wonderful beaches must be treated with healthy respect. People drown every year from rips and currents. Swim between the flags (p95).

➡ Police in Sydney have little tolerance for minor transgressions or drug use. Random searches are common in clubs and random drug testing is now conducted on drivers.

➡ Sydney's sun is fierce in summer – do as the locals do, applying a hat and plenty of sunscreen.

TOURIST INFORMATION

Sydney Visitor Centre – The Rocks (Map p80; ☑02-8273 0000; www.sydney.com; cnr Argyle & Playfair Sts; ◉9am-5.30pm; 🚉Circular Quay) Sydney's principal tourist office is in the heart of the historic Rocks district

City of Sydney Information The council operates a good tourist information desk in the Customs House (p1069) as well as kiosks in Martin Place, **Chinatown** (Map p84; www. cityofsydney.nsw.gov.au; Dixon St, Haymarket; ◉11am-7pm; 🚉Town Hall) and **Kings Cross** (Map p90; ☑0477 344 125; www.cityofsydney. nsw.gov.au; cnr Darlinghurst Rd & Springfield Ave, Kings Cross; ◉9am-5pm; 🚉Kings Cross).

Hello Manly (Map p111; ☑02-9976 1430; www.hellomanly.com.au; East Esplanade, Manly; ◉9am-5pm Mon-Fri, 10am-4pm Sat & Sun; 🚤Manly) This helpful visitor centre, just outside the ferry wharf and alongside the bus interchange, has free pamphlets covering the

ℹ OPAL CARDS

Sydney's public transport network runs on a smartcard system called Opal (www.opal. com.au). The card can be obtained (for free) and loaded with credit (minimum $10) at numerous newsagencies and convenience stores across Sydney. When commencing a journey you'll need to touch the card to an electronic reader, which are located at the train station gates, near the doors of buses and light-rail carriages, and at the ferry wharves. You then need to touch a reader when you complete your journey so that the system can deduct the correct fare. You get a discount when transferring between services, and after a certain number of journeys in the week, and daily charges are capped at $15.80 ($2.70 on Sundays). Weekly charges are capped at $63.20. You can use the Opal card at the airport train stations, but none of the aforementioned bonuses apply.

You can still buy single tickets (Opal single trip tickets) from machines at train stations, ferry wharves and light-rail stops. These are more expensive than the same fare using the Opal card, so there's not much point unless you don't think you'll use $10 worth of transport during your Sydney stay.

You can purchase a child/youth Opal card for those aged four to 15 years; they travel for half price. For student and pensioner discount Opal cards, you have to apply online.

You can also use contactless credit/debit cards on train, light rail and ferry services, but you won't get discounts for off-peak travel or transfers.

Manly Scenic Walkway (p98) and other Manly attractions, plus loads of local bus information.

Parramatta Heritage & Visitor Information Centre (☑02-8839 3311; www. discoverparramatta.com; 346a Church St, Parramatta; ☉9am-5pm; ⛴Parramatta) Knowledgeable staff will point you in the right direction with loads of brochures and leaflets, info on access for visitors with impaired mobility, and details on local Aboriginal cultural sites.

ℹ Getting There & Away

The vast majority of visitors to Sydney arrive at Sydney Airport (www.sydneyairport.com.au), 10km south of the city centre. Numerous airlines fly here from destinations throughout Australia, Asia, Oceania, Europe (with a stopover), North America and elsewhere. A second Sydney airport is due to open in the west of the city in 2026.

Trains chug into Sydney's Central station from as far north as Brisbane (13½ hours), as far south as Melbourne (11½ hours) and as far west as Perth (three days; only a luxury service now); see **NSW TrainLink** (☑13 22 32; www.nswtrainlink.info) and the **Indian Pacific** (☑1800 703 357; www.greatsouthernrail.com. au) for details.

Long-distance buses pull up to the Sydney Coach Terminal at Central station. Direct buses head here from as far afield as Adelaide and Cairns, although you can connect via Greyhound to services reaching all major cities. Operators include the following:

Australia Wide Coaches (☑02-9516 1300; www.austwidecoaches.com.au)

Firefly (☑1300 730 740; www.fireflyexpress. com.au)

Greyhound (☑1300 473 946; www.greyhound. com.au)

Murrays (☑13 22 51; www.murrays.com.au)

Port Stephens Coaches (☑02-4982 2940; www.pscoaches.com.au)

Premier Motor Service (p1072).

Flights, cars and tours can be booked online at lonelyplanet.com/bookings.

ℹ Getting Around

Transport NSW (☑13 15 00; www.transport nsw.info) coordinates all of the state-run bus, ferry, train and light-rail services. You'll find a useful journey planner on its website. The system-wide Opal transport card is used for travel, though you can also use contactless credit cards for trains, light rail and ferries. The TripView app is very useful for real-time public transport info and journey planning.

Train The linchpin of the network, with lines radiating out from Central station.

Buses Particularly useful for getting to the beaches and parts of the Inner West.

Ferries Head all around the harbour and up the river to Parramatta.

Light rail (tram) Useful for Pyrmont and Glebe; and from 2020, city-hopping, Surry Hills, Moore Park and Randwick.

Metro Under construction. The first line opened in May 2019, linking northwestern Sydney with Chatswood; the second phase will extend it through the centre of the city and out to the southwest by 2024.

AROUND SYDNEY

Royal National Park

This prime stretch of wilderness is at the city's doorstep, and encompasses secluded beaches, vertiginous cliffs, scrub, heath, rainforest, swamp wallabies, lyrebirds and raucous flocks of yellow-tailed black cockatoos.

This wonderful coastal park, protecting 15,091 hectares and stretching inland from 32km of beautiful coast, is the world's third-oldest national park (1879).

◉ Sights

Figure Eight Pools NATURAL POOL
(www.nationalparks.nsw.gov.au/figure8pools) This eight-shaped pool on a rock shelf near Burning Palms Beach is an Instagram favourite. However, park authorities recommend not visiting for safety reasons and it is imperative to pay attention to conditions: tides and weather mean that the shelf is frequently far too dangerous to visit, if not wholly submerged. Read the website forecast in detail before planning a trip here. If you aren't on the coastal walk, it's a tough 6km return walk from Garrawarra Farm car park, off Garie Road. Allow two hours each way and take plenty of water. A safe way to visit the pools is with a **Barefoot Downunder** (☑ 0476 951 741; www.barefootdownunder.com.au; half/full day $118/138; ☻ 8am-7pm) tour.

Wattamolla Beach BEACH
(www.nationalparks.nsw.gov.au; Wattamolla Rd) About halfway along the coast, Wattamolla Beach is one of the park's favourite picnic spots and gets pretty busy in summer. It has the great advantage of having both a surf beach and a lagoon, allowing for safe swimming. There's also a waterfall; jumping is strictly prohibited as shifting water levels make it deadly dangerous. The beach is 3.3km from the main road, accessed from very near the Bundeena turn-off.

Garie Beach BEACH
(Garie Beach Rd) Three kilometres down a turn-off from the main road, this excellent surf beach is a picturesque spot. Like all of the Royal National Park surf beaches, swimming can be treacherous. There's a toilet block but no other facilities despite the large building complex, though the beach is patrolled on summer weekends and daily from late December to late January. At these times, there's a food kiosk open.

Bundeena TOWN
(Bundeena Dr) The town of Bundeena, on the southern shore of Port Hacking opposite Sydney's southern suburb of Cronulla, is surrounded by the Royal National Park and has a lovely curving beach. From here you can walk 30 minutes towards the ocean to **Jibbon Head**, which has another good beach and interesting Aboriginal rock art. Bundeena is the starting point of the coastal walk.

♣ Activities

Coast Track HIKING
(www.nationalparks.nsw.gov.au) This spectacular walk traces the coastline of the Royal National Park between Bundeena and Otford, both of which are accessible by public transport. It is a tough 26km and usually tackled in two days with an overnight at North Era campground (prebook via the website). Doing it north to south offers the best perspectives and keeps the sun at your back.

In winter you may well spot whales from the spectacular clifftop lookout points, while summer hikers can reward themselves with a dip at one of the numerous beaches.

Water availability on the walk is very limited, so carry plenty and pack some purification tablets. There's a tap at Garie Beach but no water at the campground.

Audley Boat Shed KAYAKING
(☑ 02-9545 4967; www.audleyboatshed.com; 150 Audley Rd, Audley; boats per hour/day $25/50, aqua bikes per half-hour $20, mountain bikes per hour/day $16/34; ☻ 9am-5pm) At this historic boat shed near the visitor centre you can hire rowboats, canoes and kayaks for a paddle up Kangaroo Creek or the Hacking River. It also rents out aqua bikes and mountain bikes.

⌷ Sleeping

Bonnie Vale Campground CAMPGROUND **$**
(☑ 1300 072 757; www.nationalparks.nsw.gov.au; Sea Breeze Lane, Bundeena; 2-person site $34; ℗) This campground 1.5km west of central Bundeena is the largest of the national park sites and has pleasant, flat, grassy pitches. It's right by the water, with both sheltered bay beach and river estuary for swimming. It is well equipped, with flush toilets, hot showers, drinking water, electric barbecues and picnic tables.

At time of research it was closed for an environmental clean-up; check the park website for up-to-date info.

Around Sydney

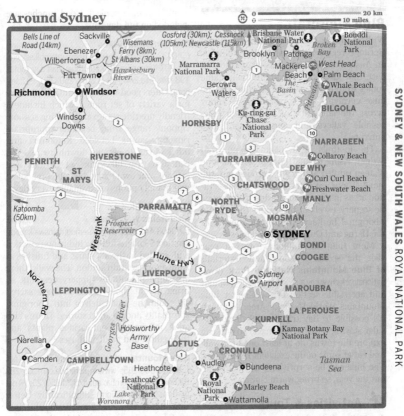

⭐ **Beachhaven**   B&B $$$
(☎ 02-9544 1333; www.beachhavenbnb.com.au;
13 Bundeena Dr, Bundeena; r $300-325; P ❄ 🛜)
Right on gorgeous Hordens Beach, this
classy B&B is run by a welcoming couple
who offer two fabulous rooms. Both have
kitchenettes, king beds with plush fabrics,
and some fine antique furnishings, as well
as a generously stocked fridge and lovely
patio area. Beach House is right by the sand,
while Tudor Suite is tucked away in a little
subtropical garden.

Other highlights include a romantic out-
door spa bath overlooking the beach, with
kayak and stand-up paddleboard on hand.
Prices drop markedly for multi-night stays.

Weemalah Cottage   COTTAGE $$$
(☎ 1300 072 757; www.nationalparks.nsw.gov.
au; Warumbul Rd, Warumbul; cottage $350-600;
P) One of three cottages rented out by the
National Parks office is this beautiful timber
place by the river at Warumbul. Once kept
for visiting dignitaries, this fully self-contained house has wide verandahs and sleeps
six. It's 4km off the main road, the last
bit along a rutted fire trail. Weekdays are
cheapest.

ℹ Information

The **visitor centre** (☎ 02-9542 6000; www.
nationalparks.nsw.gov.au; 2 Lady Carrington
Dr, Audley; ⊘ 8.30am-4.30pm) is at Audley,
2km inside the northeastern entrance, off the
Princes Hwy.

ℹ Getting There & Away

Cronulla Ferries (☎ 02-9523 2990;
www.cronullaferries.com.au; adult/child
$6.60/3.30) travels to **Bundeena** from Cro-
nulla, which is accessible by train from Sydney.

You can also get a train to Waterfall or Otford
and hike into the park from there.

Blue Mountains

With stunning natural beauty, the World Heritage region of the Blue Mountains is an Australian highlight. The slate-coloured haze that gives the mountains their name comes from a fine mist of oil exuded by the huge eucalypts that form a dense canopy across the landscape of deep, often inaccessible valleys and chiselled sandstone outcrops.

The foothills begin 65km inland from Sydney, rising to an 1100m-high sandstone plateau riddled with valleys eroded into the stone. There are eight connected conservation areas in the region offering truly fantastic scenery, excellent bushwalks (hikes) and Aboriginal heritage: this is the country of the Darug and Gundungurra peoples.

More than six million visitors a year visit the scenic lookouts and waterfalls of **Blue Mountains National Park** (www.nationalparks.nsw.gov.au), the most popular and accessible section of the Greater Blue Mountains World Heritage Area. Although it's possible to day trip from Sydney, consider staying a night (or longer) so you can explore the towns, do at least one bushwalk and eat at some of the excellent restaurants. The hills can be surprisingly cool throughout the year, so bring warm clothes.

🏃 Activities & Tours

Australian School of Mountaineering   ADVENTURE
(☑02-4782 2014; www.climbingadventures.com.au; 166 Katoomba St, Katoomba) Professional and reliable, this company, based in an equipment shop, offers guided excursions as well as training courses. It tackles rock climbing, abseiling and canyoning as well as bushcraft, mountaineering and cross-country skiing. Their one-day GPS course and two-day Wilderness Navigation course are excellent prep if you want to do some serious hiking.

Blue Mountains Adventure Company   ADVENTURE
(☑02-4782 1271; www.bmac.com.au; 84a Bathurst Rd, Katoomba; abseiling from $185, canyoning $275; ⊗8am-6pm Oct-Mar, 9am-5pm Apr-Sep) Located opposite Katoomba station, this competent and very welcoming set-up offers year-round abseiling, canyoning, bushwalking and rock climbing. They'll leave any day with two

or more people booked. Good lunches are included on full-day trips.

Blue Mountain Bikes   MOUNTAIN BIKING
(☑0432 699 212; www.bluemountainbikes.com.au; 207 Katoomba St, Katoomba; half-day routes $98, bike hire 2/4/7 days $165/250/350; ⊗8am-8pm) Offers good-quality mountain-bike hire for a variety of set routes, which include a friendly pre-ride set-up and briefing session. Options range from beginner-appropriate ridgetop jaunts between Katoomba and other towns, to serious downhill runs. You can also take bikes for set periods and explore your own paths. Must be prebooked and not all options are available every day.

Aboriginal Blue Mountains Walkabout   CULTURAL
(☑0408 443 822; www.bluemountainswalkabout.com; tour $95) This full-day Indigenous-owned and -guided bushwalk starts and finishes at Faulconbridge train station. The walk (there are some potentially slippery descents, so bring decent shoes) takes in some sacred sites and the guide delves into Aboriginal spirituality and creation stories. There's also good information on various plants and their edible and medicinal uses.

Blue Mountains Explorer Bus   BUS
(☑1300 300 915; www.explorerbus.com.au; 283 Bathurst Rd, Katoomba; adult/child $50/25; ⊗departures 9.15am-4.15pm) Significantly better than its average city equivalents, this is a useful way to get around the most popular Blue Mountains attractions. It offers a hop-on, hop-off service on a Katoomba–Leura loop. Buses leave from Katoomba station every 30 minutes and feature entertaining live commentary. Various packages include admission to attractions.

You can buy tickets online, on board, from the office at Katoomba station or from a variety of participating shops.

High 'n' Wild Australian Adventures   ADVENTURE
(☑02-4782 6224; www.highandwild.com.au; 207 Katoomba St, Katoomba; abseiling $150-260, canyoning $250-290, rock climbing $190-250) 🚣 Based at the Blue Mountains YHA (p143), this outfit runs daily tours, offering abseiling, rock climbing, canyoning and various bushwalking and survival courses.

Blue Mountains 4WD   DRIVING
(☑0414 405 974; www.bluemountains4wd.com.au; tours from $320) An experienced guide

will show you lots of Blue Mountains beauty spots on a fully customisable driving tour. You can start in Katoomba, or be picked up from Sydney.

✨ Festivals & Events

Yulefest CHRISTMAS
(☺ Jun-Aug) These Christmas-style celebrations between June and August are held in hotels and restaurants across the region. While you can't expect snow and reindeer, it's as wintry as things get in this part of Australia.

🛏 Sleeping

There's a good range of accommodation, but book ahead during winter and for Friday and Saturday nights. Leafy Leura is your best bet for romance, while Blackheath is a good base for hikers; larger Katoomba has excellent hostels and some good B&Bs. Two-night minimum stays are standard at weekends, when prices are higher.

There are bush campgrounds in the parks, some free. Tourist offices have a comprehensive list.

ⓘ Information

For more information on the national parks (including walking and camping), contact the NPWS Visitors Centre at **Blackheath** (☑ 02-4787 8877; www.nationalparks.nsw.gov.au; Govetts Leap Rd; ☺ 9am-4.30pm; ☎), about 2.5km off the Great Western Hwy and 10km north of Katoomba.

There are information centres on the Great Western Hwy at **Glenbrook** (☑ 1300 653 408; www.bluemountainscitytourism.com.au; Great Western Hwy; ☺ 8.30am-4pm Mon-Sat, to 3pm Sun; ☎), opposite the station in **Katoomba** (www.visitbluemountains.com.au; 76 Bathurst Rd; ☺ 8.45am-2pm) and at Echo Point (p142) (also in Katoomba). All can provide plenty of information on the region.

ⓘ Getting There & Away

Trains (☑ 13 15 00; www.transportnsw.info) run hourly from Sydney's Central Station to Katoomba and beyond via a string of Blue Mountains towns. The journey takes two hours to Katoomba and costs $8.69 on an Opal card.

To reach the Blue Mountains by road, leave Sydney via Parramatta Rd. At Strathfield detour onto the toll-free M4, which becomes the Great Western Hwy west of Penrith and takes you to all of the Blue Mountains towns. It takes approximately 1½ hours to drive from central Sydney to Katoomba. A scenic alternative is the Bells Line of Road (p142).

ⓘ Getting Around

There are limited local bus services run by **Blue Mountains Transit** (☑ 02-4751 1077; www.cdcbus.com.au), but it's often easiest to take the train between towns. In Katoomba and Leura, the hop-on, hop-off bus service is a good way to get around the main sights with little fuss, but walking between most of them isn't too burdensome either.

Wentworth Falls

POP 6100 / ELEV 867M
As you head into the town of Wentworth Falls, you'll get your first real taste of Blue Mountains scenery: views to the south open out across the majestic Jamison Valley. The village itself is pleasant for a short potter along the main street.

Wentworth Falls is a stop on the Blue Mountains train line. The Great Western Hwy passes through town.

Wentworth Falls Reserve NATURE RESERVE
(Falls Rd; ☒ Wentworth Falls) The falls that lend the town its name launch a plume of spray over a 300m drop. This is the starting point of several walking tracks that delve into the sublime Valley of the Waters, with waterfalls, gorges, woodlands and rainforests. Be sure to stretch your legs along the 1km return to **Princes Rock**, which offers excellent views of Wentworth Falls and the Jamison Valley. The reserve is 2.5km from Wentworth Falls station on the other side of the highway.

Fed CAFE $$
(☑ 02-4757 1429; 6 Station St; light meals $12-20; ☺ 7.30am-2pm Mon, to 4pm Tue-Fri, to 3pm Sat & Sun; ☎✍) A top spot for a pre-walk breakfast or post-falls lunch, this handsome place strikes you on entry with its display cabinets bulging with good-looking food. Homemade pies, delicious daily salads, good-value sandwiches, salmon cakes, vegan rice balls, plus hot meals and decent coffee mean there's something for everyone. Sit in the cosy ferny interior or out on the street.

Leura

POP 4600 / ELEV 985M
Leura is the Blue Mountains' prettiest town, fashioned around undulating streets, well-tended gardens and sweeping Victorian verandahs. Leura Mall, the tree-lined main street, offers rows of country craft shops

Blue Mountains

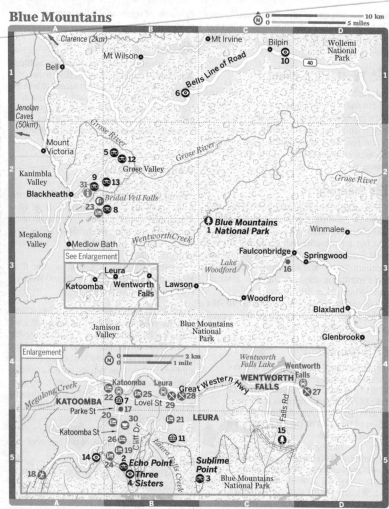

and cafes for the daily tourist influx. Leura adjoins Katoomba, which is slightly higher into the range.

⊙ Sights

★ Sublime Point   VIEWPOINT
(Sublime Point Rd) Southeast of Leura, this sharp, triangular outcrop narrows to a dramatic lookout with sheer cliffs on each side. It's much, much quieter than Katoomba's more famous Echo Point, and on sunny days cloud shadows dance across the vast blue valley below. You can spot the backside of the Three Sisters (p142) from here too.

Leuralla NSW Toy
& Railway Museum   MUSEUM
(☑ 02-4784 1169; www.toyandrailwaymuseum.com. au; 36 Olympian Pde; adult/child $15/5, gardens only $10/5; ⊙ 10am-5pm) The striking art-deco mansion that was once home to HV 'Doc' Evatt, the third president of the UN General Assembly, is jam-packed with an incredible array of collectables – from grumpy Edwardian baby dolls and *Dr Who* figurines to a rare set of Nazi propaganda toys. Model trains are a highlight and railway memorabilia is scattered throughout the handsome gardens.

Blue Mountains

◎ Top Sights
1 Blue Mountains National Park..............C3
2 Echo Point...B5
3 Sublime Point...C5
4 Three Sisters..B5

◎ Sights
5 Anvil Rock..B2
6 Blue Mountains Botanic Garden
  Mount Tomah...B1
7 Blue Mountains Cultural Centre...........B4
8 Evans Lookout...B2
9 Govetts Leap Lookout.............................A2
10 Hillbilly Cider Shed..................................C1
11 Leuralla NSW Toy & Railway
  Museum...B5
12 Perrys Lookdown......................................B2
13 Pulpit Rock...B2
14 Scenic World..A5
15 Wentworth Falls Reserve......................C5

◎ Activities, Courses & Tours
16 Aboriginal Blue Mountains
  Walkabout...C3
17 Australian School of
  Mountaineering.......................................B4
  Blue Mountain Bikes.....................(see 17)
  Blue Mountains Adventure
  Company..(see 7)
  Blue Mountains Explorer Bus.........(see 7)
18 Golden Stairs Walk..................................A5
  Grand Canyon Walk.......................(see 8)

High 'n' Wild Australian
  Adventures ....(see 17)

◎ Sleeping
19 3 Explorers Motel.....................................B5
20 Blue Mountains YHA................................B5
21 Broomelea...B5
22 Flying Fox..B4
  Greens of Leura ....(see 28)
23 Jemby-Rinjah Eco Lodge....................... A2
24 Lilianfels...B5
25 No 14..B4
26 Shelton-Lea..B5

◎ Eating
27 Fed..D4
  Hominy Bakery .... (see 17)
28 Leura Garage..B4
29 Leura Gourmet Cafe & Deli B4
  Palette Dining..................................(see 7)
  Silk's Brasserie...............................(see 28)
  Station Bar & Woodfired Pizza......(see 7)

◎ Drinking & Nightlife
30 Cassiopeia B5

◎ Information
31 Blue Mountains Heritage Centre.......... A2
  Blue Mountains Visitor
  Information Katoomba ....(see 7)
  Echo Point Visitors Centre.............(see 4)

🛏 Sleeping & Eating

★ Greens of Leura
B&B $$

(☑ 02-4784 3241; www.thegreensleura.com.au; 24-26 Grose St; r $180-230; P 🅿 🅢) On a quiet street parallel to the Mall, this pretty centenarian house set in a lovely garden offers genuine hospitality and five rooms named after British literary figures. All are individually decorated; some have four-poster beds and spas. There's a great lounge with attached courtyard. Rates include breakfast as well as afternoon tea with sparkling wine and other goodies.

★ Broomelea
B&B $$

(☑ 02-4784 2940; www.broomelea.com.au; 273 Leura Mall; r $170-240; P @ 🅢) A consummately romantic Blue Mountains B&B, this fine Edwardian house offers a cheery welcome, four-poster beds, lovely gardens, a great verandah, in-room fireplaces and a snug lounge with port, sherry and snacks on offer. Two of the four rooms have spa baths. There's also a self-contained cottage for families and plenty of other comforts. Two-night minimum stay at weekends.

Leura Gourmet Cafe & Deli
DELI $

(☑ 02-4784 1438; 159 Leura Mall; mains breakfast $12-18, lunch $14-27; ⊙ 8am-5pm; 🅢 🅿) Perfect picnic prep, with gourmet salads, pies and quiches to take away. Foodies will want to stock up on local jams, olive oils and vinegars. The great gelato selection is brilliant for bribing kids on a bushwalk and the attached cafe has impressive views.

Leura Garage
MEDITERRANEAN $$

(☑ 02-4784 3391; www.leuragarage.com.au; 84 Railway Pde; lunches $18-24, mains $22-38; ⊙ noon-9pm or later; 🅢 🅿) In case you were in any doubt that this hip cafe-bar was once a garage, the suspended mufflers, stacks of old tyres and staff in overalls press the point. The menu shifts gears from burgers to rustic shared plates served on wooden slabs, deli-treat-laden pizzas and substantial mains.

Silk's Brasserie
MODERN AUSTRALIAN $$$

(☑ 02-4784 2534; www.silksleura.com; 128 Leura Mall; lunch mains $26-41, 2-course dinner $59-75; ⊙ noon-3pm & 6-10pm) A warm welcome awaits at Leura's long-standing fine diner.

BELLS LINE OF ROAD

The stretch of road between North Richmond and Lithgow is the most scenic route across the Blue Mountains and is highly recommended if you have your own transport. It's far quieter than the highway and offers bountiful views.

Bilpin, at the base of the mountains, is known for its apple orchards; check out the **Hillbilly Cider Shed** (☑ 02-4567 2662; www.hillbillycider.com.au; 2270 Bells Line of Road, Bilpin; ☺ noon-5pm Fri, from 11am Sat & Sun; ⊞) FREE and try their brews. The Bilpin Markets are held at the district hall every Saturday from 10am to noon.

Midway between Bilpin and Bell, the **Blue Mountains Botanic Garden Mount Tomah** (☑ 02-4567 3000; www.bluemountainsbotanicgarden.com.au; Bells Line of Road, Mount Tomah; ☺ 9am-5.30pm Mon-Fri, from 9.30am Sat & Sun) ✐ FREE is a cool-climate annexe of Sydney's Royal Botanic Garden where native plants cuddle up to exotic species, including some magnificent rhododendrons.

To access Bells Line from central Sydney, head over the Harbour Bridge and take the M2 and then the M7 (both have tolls). Exit at Richmond Rd, which becomes Blacktown Rd, then Lennox Rd, then (after a short dog-leg) Kurrajong Rd and finally Bells Line of Road.

Despite its contemporary approach, it's a brasserie at heart, so the food is generous and flavoursome. It's a comfortable space, its chessboard tiles and parchment-coloured walls creating an inviting semiformal atmosphere. Make sure you save room for the decadent desserts.

ⓘ Getting There & Away

Leura is on the Sydney–Blue Mountains train line, just a three-minute ride short of Katoomba.

Katoomba

POP 8000 / ELEV 1017M

Swirling, otherworldly mists, steep streets lined with art-deco buildings, astonishing valley views, and a quirky miscellany of restaurants, buskers, artists, bawdy pubs and classy hotels – Katoomba, the biggest town in the mountains, manages to be bohemian and bourgeois all at once. It's got a great selection of accommodation and is a logical base, particularly if you're on a budget or travelling by public transport.

◉ Sights & Activities

★ **Echo Point** VIEWPOINT
(Echo Point Rd) Echo Point's clifftop viewing platform offers a magical prospect of the area's most essential sight, a rocky trio called the Three Sisters. Warning: the point draws vast, serenity-spoiling tourist gaggles, their idling buses farting fumes into the mountain air – arrive early or late to avoid them. The surrounding parking is charged and congested, so it's not a bad idea to park a few streets back and walk.

There's a **tourist office** (☑ 1300 653 408; www.bluemountainscitytourism.com.au; Echo Point Road; ☺ 9am-5pm) here.

★ **Three Sisters** LANDMARK
(Echo Point Rd) The Blue Mountains' essential sight is a rocky trio called the Three Sisters. The story goes that the sisters were turned to stone by a sorcerer to protect them from the unwanted advances of three young men, but the sorcerer died before he could turn them back into humans. A 500m trail from the main Echo Point lookout platform leads to more lookouts and a bridge across to the first Sister.

Blue Mountains Cultural Centre GALLERY
(☑ 02-4780 5410; www.bluemountainscultural centre.com.au; 30 Parke St; adult/child $5/free; ☺ 10am-5pm Mon-Fri, to 4pm Sat & Sun) It's a captivating experience to walk through the main display here, with a satellite image of the Blue Mountains beneath your feet, mountain scenery projected on the walls and ceiling, and bush sounds surrounding you. The neighbouring gallery hosts interesting exhibitions and there's a great viewing platform. There's also a decent cafe and gift shop.

Scenic World CABLE CAR
(☑ 02-4780 0200; www.scenicworld.com.au; Violet St; adult/child $43/23; ☺ 9am-5pm) This longtime favourite, the Blue Mountains' most touristy attraction, offers spectacular views. Ride the glass-floored **Skyway** gondola across the gorge and then take the vertiginously steep **Scenic Railway**, billed as the steepest railway in the world, down the

52-degree incline to the Jamison Valley floor. From here you can wander a 2.5km forest boardwalk (or hike the 12km, six-hour-return track to the **Ruined Castle** rock formation) before catching a cable car back up the slope.

The 686 bus stops at Echo Point and here, and this is on the hop-on, hop-off bus route, but it's only a 2.5km walk from Echo Point, and quite a pleasant one too.

★ **Golden Stairs Walk**   HIKING

(Glenraphael Dr) If you have your own transport, you can tackle the Golden Stairs Walk, a less congested route down to the Ruined Castle (a famous rock formation) than the track leading from Scenic World. It's a steep, exhilarating trail leading down into the valley (about 7km, five hours return). Take plenty of water.

🛌 Sleeping

★ **Blue Mountains YHA**   HOSTEL $

(📞 02-4782 1416; www.yha.com.au; 207 Katoomba St; dm $22-30, d without bathroom $118; 🅿️ @ 🛜) Behind the art-deco brick exterior of this popular 200-bed hostel are dorms and family rooms that are comfortable, light filled and spotlessly clean. Facilities include a lounge (with an open fire), a pool table, an excellent communal kitchen and an outdoor space with barbecue. Staff can book activities and tours for you and there's an on-site canyoning and abseiling operator.

Flying Fox   HOSTEL $

(📞 02-4782 4226; www.theflyingfox.com.au; 190 Bathurst Rd; campsites per person $20, dm $30-35, r $82-84; 🅿️ 🛜) 🧭 The owners are travellers at heart and bend over backwards to give this hostel an endearing home-away-from-home feel. There's free breakfast, regular free dinners and a technology-free period to encourage chat in the lounge. Dorms are high-ceilinged and spacious; private rooms are pleasant and a decent deal. The garden has spaces to pitch tents and a nice outlook.

No 14   HOSTEL $

(📞 02-4782 7104; www.14lovelst.com; 14 Lovel St; dm $31, r with/without bathroom $105/79; @ 🛜) In a rather lovely centenarian house, this cosy hostel has a friendly vibe, colourful interiors, polished floorboards and helpful managers. There's a no-music policy and no TV, so guests tend to talk to actually each other. A basic breakfast is included. The verandah deck is a top spot to chill out.

Shelton-Lea   B&B $$

(📞 02-4782 9883; www.sheltonlea.com; 159 Lurline St; r $170-240; 🅿️ 🛜) 🧭 This sweet bungalow has four spacious suites, each with its own entrance and sitting area, some with spa bathtub and three with kitchenette. There's a hint of art deco in the decor and lots of plush furnishings. There's a two-night minimum stay at weekends, when you get a cooked breakfast (midweek it's continental).

3 Explorers Motel   MOTEL $$

(📞 02-4782 1733; www.3explorers.com.au; 197 Lurline St; r $140-200; 🅿️ ❄️ 🛜) Close to Echo Point, this well-run motel has comfortable rooms with a light Japanese touch to the decor. Some of them come with a spa bath and there are good family options.

Lilianfels   HOTEL $$$

(📞 02-4780 1200; www.lilianfels.com; 5-19 Lilianfels Ave; r $420-620; 🅿️ ❄️ @ 🛜 🐕 🏊) Very close to Echo Point and enjoying spectacular views, this luxury resort set in a lush garden sports an array of facilities including a spa, heated indoor and outdoor pools, a tennis court, a billiards/games room, a library and a gym. Rooms come in a variety of categories; some have excellent vistas. Decor is classical with floral fabrics and tasteful wallpaper.

🍴 Eating & Drinking

Hominy Bakery   BAKERY $

(📞 02-4782 9816; 185 Katoomba St; loaves $7-8; ⏰ 6.30am-5pm; 🍴) Brilliant pies, delicious wholemeal sourdough loaves and tempting sweet treats make this organic bakery an excellent stop.

Station Bar & Woodfired Pizza   PIZZA $$

(📞 02-4782 4782; www.stationbar.com.au; 287 Bathurst Rd; pizzas $18-26; ⏰ noon-midnight; 🛜) Bringing visitors and locals together, this is an upbeat spot that combines three happy things – craft beer, pizza and live music – in a very likeable space next to the train station. It only does pizzas (plus a couple of salads), but they're delicious, with unusual gourmet toppings. The compact trackside courtyard is great for a summer pint in good company.

Palette Dining   MODERN AUSTRALIAN $$$

(📞 02-4782 9530; www.palettedining.com; 92 Bathurst Rd; diner mains $17-22, restaurant 2/3 courses $55/70; ⏰ bar-diner noon-3pm & 5.30-9pm Wed-Sun, restaurant dinner only; 🍴) This historic building has two distinct spaces.

Comfortably eclectic decor in the upstairs bar-diner inspires lounging around enjoying the cocktails and burgers on offer. Downstairs, a short, quality seasonal menu makes for pleasurable dinners among rotating art exhibitions. Personable service, good vegetarian/vegan choices and a big effort to source both food and drinks locally add appeal.

Cassiopeia CAFE
(☐ 02-4782 9299; www.cassiopeia.com.au; 79 Lurline St; ⊙ 7am-3pm Mon-Fri, to 2pm Sat, 8am-2pm Sun; ☎) Katoomba's most serious coffee experience, Cassiopeia roasts their own delicious single-origin beans, served in an attractive floorboarded space appealingly removed from the main drag.

ⓘ Information

Echo Point Visitors Centre (p142) A sizeable centre with can-do staff and a gift shop.

Blue Mountains Visitor Information Katoomba (p139) Friendly office handily located right opposite the station.

ⓘ Getting There & Around

Trains run from Sydney Central to Katoomba every hour ($8.69, two hours). By car, it's about 100km from central Sydney via the M4 and the Great Western Hwy. Local buses run around Katoomba itself, including the 686 that connects central Katoomba, Echo Point and Scenic World ($2.70), while a hop-on, hop-off service (p138) shuttles around the area's major tourist attractions.

Blackheath

POP 4400 / ELEV 1065M

The crowds and commercial frenzy fizzle considerably 11km north of Katoomba in neat, petite Blackheath. The town measures up in the scenery stakes, and it's an excellent base for visiting the Grose and Megalong Valleys. There are several memorable lookouts around town, and trailheads for some top hikes.

◉ Sights & Activities

The clifftop lookouts around Blackheath are among the finest in the Blue Mountains. Govetts Leap and Evans Lookout are the classic ones, while remoter Perrys Lookdown, Pulpit Rock and Anvil Rock are all accessed via Hat Hill Road and offer equally stunning perspectives over cliffs and valleys. Several of these are hiking trailheads too.

Evans Lookout VIEWPOINT
(Evans Lookout Rd) Signposted 4km from the highway in Blackheath, this lookout presents a magnificent perspective of sandstone cliffs dropping to the valley and canyon below. It's one of the most scenic of the Blue Mountains lookouts, and is also a trailhead for the majestic Grand Canyon bushwalk, perhaps the area's best half-day excursion.

★ Grand Canyon Walk HIKING
This spectacular 5km circuit plunges you from Evans Lookout into the valley for a memorable walk along the 'Grand Canyon' before looping back up to the road about 1.5km short of the lookout (where there's a car park). Though strenuous on the descent and ascent, it's one of the area's shadier walks and takes most people around three hours.

🛏 Sleeping & Eating

Glenella Guesthouse GUESTHOUSE $$
(☐ 02-4787 8352; www.glenella.com.au; 56 Govetts Leap Rd; r $120-195; ❋ ☎) Gorgeous Glenella has been a guesthouse since 1912 and is most welcoming. There are several attractive lounge spaces and a stunning dining room where optional breakfast is served. Marvellous period features include ceiling mouldings and lead lighting. Rooms range from en-suite heritage rooms (the ones with verandah access are best) to more modern, basic ones with shared bathroom downstairs.

Jemby-Rinjah Eco Lodge CABIN $$
(☐ 02-4787 7622; www.jemby.com.au; 336 Evans Lookout Rd; cabins $225-265; P ☎) ✦ Near Evans Lookout, these attractive, rustic eco-cabins are lodged so deeply in the gums and bottlebrush that it feels as though you're in very remote bushland, with just the rustle of leaves and the chirp of birds for company. All the one- and two-bedroom weatherboard cabins are equipped with kitchenettes and crockery; the deluxe model has a Japanese hot tub.

Anonymous CAFE $$
(www.anonymouscafeblackheath.com.au; 237 Great Western Hwy; meals $15-20; ⊙ 7am-3pm Mon, Wed & Thu, to 4pm Fri & Sat, from 7.30am Sun; ☎) It's hard to stay anonymous when you do the best coffee in town, so you might only just squeeze into this bijou two-roomed cafe. There's an appetising array of breakfast fare on offer, along with a few lunch mains (go for the daily specials). Upbeat service keeps things buzzy.

LOCAL KNOWLEDGE

WALKING IN THE BLUE MOUNTAINS

For tips on walks to suit your level of experience and fitness, call the National Parks' Blue Mountains Heritage Centre (p139) in Blackheath, or the information centres in Glenbrook (p139) or Katoomba (p142). All three sell a variety of walk pamphlets, maps and books.

Note that the bush here is dense and that it can be easy to become lost – there have been deaths. Always leave your name and walk plan with your accommodation, the Katoomba police or at the national parks centre. You can do this online via the National Parks website (www.nationalparks.gov.au). The police and the national parks and information centres all lend personal locator beacons and it's strongly suggested you take one with you, especially for longer hikes. Take plenty of food and, whatever you do, take lots of water; it can get powerfully hot in summer, and the steep gradients can dehydrate you fast at any time of year.

The two most popular bushwalking areas are the Jamison Valley, south of Katoomba, and the Grose Valley, northeast of Katoomba and east of Blackheath. Some top choices include the Golden Stairs Walk (p143) and the Grand Canyon Walk (p144).

One of the most rewarding long-distance walks is the 46km, three-day **Six Foot Track** from Katoomba along the Megalong Valley to Cox's River and on to the Jenolan Caves. It has campgrounds along the way.

Fumo   MODERN AUSTRALIAN **$$$**
(☑ 02-4787 6899; www.fumorestaurant.com.au; 33 Govetts Leap Rd; mains $35-38; ⊙ noon-3pm & 5.30-10.30pm Fri-Sun) The Fumo site has seen a few restaurants in recent years, but this has ingredients for longevity, with a convivial, high-volume interior and a short, punchy menu of generously proportioned dishes that marry Australian meats with Japanese-influenced marinades to good effect. Some interesting small-producer wines and understated but pleasing decor add appeal.

ℹ Information

Blue Mountains Heritage Centre (p139) The helpful, official NPWS visitor centre has information about local walks and national parks.

ℹ Getting There & Away

Blackheath is 11km further into the mountains from Katoomba. It's a stop on the Blue Mountains railway line.

Beyond Blackheath

Mt Victoria   VILLAGE
With its isolated, unadulterated village vibe, National Trust-classified Mt Victoria was once more influential than Katoomba. At 1044m, it's the highest town in the mountains. Crisp air, solitude, towering foliage and historic buildings are what bring you here, but there's also a **museum** (☑ 0407 248 620; Station St; adult/child $5/1; ⊙ noon-3pm Sat & Sun, daily in school holidays) and an

appealing vintage **cinema** (☑ 02-4787 1577; www.mountvicflicks.com.au; Harley Ave; adult/senior/child $12/11/10).

★ Jenolan Caves   CAVE
(☑ 02-6359 3911; www.jenolancaves.org.au; Jenolan Caves Rd, Jenolan; adult/child from $42/28; ⊙ tours 9am-5pm) Far from other Blue Mountains attractions, the limestone Jenolan Caves is one of the most extensive, accessible and complex systems in the world – a vast network that's still being explored. The numerous caverns are a spectacular sight with vast subterranean spaces, otherworldly limestone formations and an underground river. Cave visits run throughout the day but book up fast, so it's worth reserving in advance online. If you don't, you may face a substantial wait at busy periods, especially if you are a group.

Named Binoomea (Dark Places) by the Gundungurra tribe, the caves took shape 400 million years ago. White explorers first passed through in 1813 and the caves were a major attraction by the 1860s.

Cave tours cycle between different spaces. There are three standard tours: **Chifley Cave**, suitable for everyone, with spectacular formations and lots of crystal; **Imperial Cave**, the easiest on the legs; and **Lucas Cave**, which has more steps but lots of visual highlights. All three are suitable for children. Guides are informative and humorous, pointing out the inevitable nicknames of unusual formations.

WORTH A TRIP

HAWKESBURY RIVER

Less than an hour from Sydney, the tranquil Hawkesbury River flows past honeycomb-coloured cliffs, historic townships and riverside hamlets into bays and inlets and between a series of national parks, including Ku-ring-gai Chase (p91) and Brisbane Water .

Accessible by train, the riverside township of **Brooklyn** is a good place to hire a houseboat and explore the river. Further upstream, a narrow forested waterway diverts from the Hawkesbury and peters down to the chilled-out river town of **Berowra Waters**, where a handful of businesses, boat sheds and residences cluster around the free, 24-hour ferry across Berowra Creek.

Less frequent tours head to Orient Cave, Temple of Baal and Diamond Cave, while small group visits head to the River Cave, Ribbon Cave and the Off the Track Tour. Beyond this, there are numerous packages and other special visits available.

The caves are about an hour's drive from Katoomba and the road is not suitable for caravans. On arrival, you pass through the Grand Arch, a spectacular rock tunnel from which the principal caves are accessed. Most car parking is a long walk from the caves, so you might want to let off some passengers just beyond the tunnel by the main Caves House complex, which includes a hotel, cafe and the ticket office. The return road through the tunnel is closed from 11.45am to 1.15pm, but you can make your way back by continuing past the caves towards Oberon. The closest fuel to the caves is in Oberon or Mount Victoria.

Various accommodation options, including dormitories, are on offer at the dated but characterful Caves House – check the website for details – but there are good choices not far away that offer more peace and quiet, such as **Jenolan Cabins** (📲 02-6335 6239; www.jenolancabins.com.au; 42 Edith Rd, Jenolan Caves; d/q $165/195).

There is no public transport to the caves, but several tour companies offer trips. Otherwise you could walk here from Katoomba via the Megalong Valley along the 46km Six Foot Track, normally undertaken as a three-day hike.

The Central Coast

The Central Coast runs between Sydney and Newcastle and includes some gorgeous beaches, swaths of national park and a series of inlets and saltwater lagoons that makes the geography hereabouts a fascinating one. There's demographic diversity too, with working-class coastal communities combined with weekending Sydney socialites and a solid corpus of lifestyle retirees and property-price refugee commuters.

The area's largest town is the transport and services hub of **Gosford**, but visitors tend to head to the iconic nearby beaches of **Avoca** or **Terrigal**. Further south towards the mouth of the Hawkesbury are national park enclaves such as **Killcare** or Pearl Beach.

Further north, a series of salt 'lakes' spreads up the coast; good stopping points include the pelican-infested town of The Entrance and deep, placid **Lake Macquarie**.

The southernmost points of the Central Coast can be accessed by ferry from Sydney's Palm Beach.

⊙ Sights & Activities

Pearl Beach　　　　　　　　　　BEACH
This secluded beach is perhaps the Central Coast's most beautiful; a seductive curve of sand lapped by gentle waves with a lovely outlook across the bay. The village here is deep in vegetation and very laid-back, with holiday lets popular with summering families. The likeably few facilities include a shop/cafe and upmarket **restaurant** (📲 02-4342 4400; www.pearlsonthebeach.com.au; 1 Tourmaline Ave, Pearl Beach; small plates $23-25, large plates $43-45; ⊙ noon-2.30pm & 6-10pm Thu-Sun). A 4.2km bush track heads through national park from here to Patonga, accessible by ferry from Palm Beach.

Bouddi National Park　　　NATIONAL PARK
(📲 02-4320 4200; www.nationalparks.nsw.gov.au; vehicle access $8) At this spectacular park, short walking trails lead to isolated beaches and dramatic lookouts from where you can experience the annual whale migration between June and November. There are campgrounds ($25 to $34 for two people) at Little Beach, Putty Beach and Tallow Beach; book ahead. Only the Putty Beach site has drinkable water. From Putty Beach, the **Bouddi Coastal Walk** runs eight easy and picturesque kilometres to Macmasters

Beach. There are also good mountain-biking options in the park.

The Entrance
AREA

The Entrance has sprawled beyond its origins at the mouth of Tuggerah lake to become one of the Central Coast's main centres. With excellent beaches, including landside family-friendly paddling, it's a popular destination. The daily pelican feeding in the town centre draws crowds at 3.30pm.

Australian Reptile Park
ZOO

(☑ 02-4340 1022; www.reptilepark.com.au; Pacific Hwy, Somersby; adult/child $39/21; ☺ 9am-5pm) Get up close to koalas and pythons, gaze in awe at big crocs and watch funnel-web spiders being milked (for the production of antivenom) and a Galapagos tortoise being fed. There are wonderful tours for kids. It's signposted off the M1 Pacific Motorway, or you could get a cab from Gosford station.

Brisbane Water
National Park
NATIONAL PARK

(☑ 02-4320 4200; www.nationalparks.nsw.gov.au; Woy Woy Rd, Kariong; vehicle access at Girrakool & Somersby Falls picnic areas $8) Bordering the Hawkesbury River, 9km southwest of Gosford, this park, despite its name, is mostly sandstone outcrops and forest, with only a short Brisbane Water frontage. It's famed for its explosions of spring wildflowers and Guringai stone engravings, the most impressive gallery of which is the **Bulgandry Aboriginal Engraving Site**, 3km south of the Pacific Hwy on Woy Woy Rd. Pearl Beach is on the southeastern edge of the park and is a favourite retreat for Sydneysiders.

Central Coast
Mountain Bike Tours
MOUNTAIN BIKING

(☑ 0410 523 612; www.ccmtbtours.com.au; 2hr/half day ride $99/149) There's some great mountain biking to be done in the Central Coast's national parks and state forests, and these guys will take you out there. From two-hour leisure rides to more challenging halfdays, there are options for all abilities. They also do other rentals and pick-ups.

🛏 Sleeping & Eating

There are numerous holiday lets right up and down the coast, as well as a wide selection of hotel and motel accommodation. National parks offer rustic camping, while better-equipped sites are dotted around the population centres.

Kims Beachside Retreat
BUNGALOW $$$

(☑ 02-4332 1566; www.kims.com.au; Charlton St, Toowoon Bay; bungalow incl breakfast and dinner from $650; ⓟ❀ⓡⓧ) Boardwalks through a beachside forest of bamboo, palms and pines connect luxurious wooden bungalows at Kims, in business for over 130 years. The beach here, a short drive south of The Entrance, is beautiful, and the accommodation, which includes buffet dinner and breakfast, is ultra-relaxing. The most upmarket villas have their own pool and spa.

Boathouse Hotel Patonga
SEAFOOD $$

(☑ 02-9974 5440; www.theboathousehotelpatonga. com.au; 6 Patonga Dr, Patonga; mains $23-31; ☺ 7am-3pm Mon & Tue, to 9pm Wed-Sun; ☎) In a privileged position by the water at peaceful Patonga, looking across to West Head, this sprawling indoor-outdoor order-at-thecounter restaurant is all white maritime minimalism as far as the decor goes, but the colour comes out in the delicious seafood platters, flatbreads, fish 'n' chips and cocktails. It's a good-time place that packs out at weekends. No bookings taken.

ℹ Information

The Entrance Visitor Centre (☑ 02-4334 4213; www.visitcentralcoast.com.au; 46 Marine Pde, The Entrance; ☺ 9am-5pm) The Central Coast's tourist office is by the water in The Entrance. Around the region some hotels and other tourist sites have maps and brochures.

Hunter Valley

A filigree of picturesque roads criss-crosses this verdant valley, but a pleasant country drive isn't the main motivator for visitors – sheer decadence is. The Hunter is one big gorge fest: fine wine, gourmet restaurants, boutique beer, chocolate, cheese, olives, you name it. Bacchus would surely approve.

The Hunter wineries – over 150 at last count – are refreshingly attitude free and welcoming to novices. They nearly all have a cellar door with cheap or free tastings.

While some deride the Disneyland aspect of the Hunter Valley, the region also offers everything from hot-air balloons and horse riding to open-air concerts. Accordingly, it is a hugely popular weekender for Sydney couples, wedding parties and groups of friends wanting to drink hard while someone else drives. Every Friday they descend and prices leap accordingly.

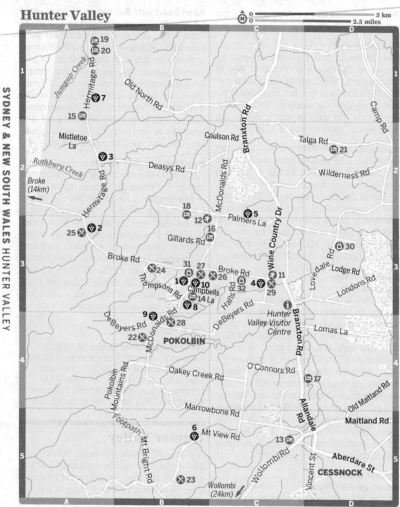

The Hunter Valley gets exceedingly hot during summer, so – like its shiraz – it's best enjoyed in the cooler months.

◉ Sights

Tulloch Wines
WINERY

(☑ 02-4998 7580; www.tullochwines.com; cnr De Beyers & McDonalds Rds, Pokolbin; ⊙ 10am-5pm) The flexibility offered is a particularly appealing aspect of the tastings at this upmarket winery. Pick from around 30 bottles on the free tasting of six wines, or kick back with charcuterie or chocolate matches. Better still is the option to pay ($8 for one or $24 for four) for fabulous cellar-aged 'museum' drops – it's great to contrast these awesome wines with their younger siblings.

Petersons
WINERY

(☑ 02-4990 1704; www.petersonswines.com.au; 552 Mt View Rd, Mount View; ⊙ 9am-5pm Mon-Sat, from 10am Sun) Though this winery has a cellar door on the main road in Pokolbin, it's worth heading up to this location, where the ultra-friendly staff have more time for a chat and to guide you through the tasty, classically styled wines. It's a very welcoming experience. The Back Block shiraz is particularly delicious.

Hunter Valley

◎ **Sights**
1 Brokenwood.................................B3
2 Glandore Estate............................A3
3 Keith Tulloch Winery.....................A2
4 Lake's Folly.................................C3
5 Moorebank Vineyard.....................C2
6 Petersons..................................B5
7 Piggs Peake................................A1
8 Tamburlaine...............................B3
9 Tulloch Wines.............................B4
10 Wine House...............................B3

◎ **Activities, Courses & Tours**
11 Balloon Aloft.............................C3
12 Grapemobile..............................B3
   Two Fat Blokes....................(see 7)

◎ **Sleeping**
13 Australia Hotel...........................C5
14 Cam Way Estate..........................B3
15 Grange on Hermitage....................A1
16 Hermitage Lodge.........................C3
17 Hunter Valley YHA.......................D4

18 Longhouse...............................B2
19 Spicers Vineyards Estate...............A1
20 Thistle Hill...............................A1
21 Tonic.....................................D2

◎ **Eating**
22 Baumé.....................................B4
23 Bistro Molines............................B5
24 Enzo......................................B3
25 EXP.......................................A3
26 Fawk Foods...............................C3
27 Hunter Valley Smelly Cheese
   Shop.....................................B3
28 Hunters Quarter..........................B4
   Muse Kitchen.......................(see 3)
29 Muse Restaurant.........................C3
   Restaurant Botanica................(see 19)

◎ **Shopping**
30 Binnorie Dairy............................D3
31 Hunter Valley Cheese Company........B3
32 Hunter Valley Chocolate Company....C3

Lake's Folly WINERY
(☏02-4998 7507; www.lakesfolly.wine; 2416 Broke Rd, Pokolbin; redeemable tasting fee $5; ☺10am-4pm) Try the highly acclaimed cabernet blend and chardonnay, which are both grown, vintaged and bottled on the estate, one of the Hunter's finest wineries. These small-production wines tend to sell out, so the cellar door is closed for four to six months of the year, normally from mid-December. Call ahead.

Keith Tulloch Winery WINERY
(☏02-4998 7500; www.keithtullochwine.com.au; cnr Hermitage & Deasys Rds, Pokolbin; redeemable tasting fee $5; ☺10am-5pm) Keith Tulloch is a fourth-generation winemaker who creates small-batch premium drops. His estate has one of the most inviting tasting settings in the region: upstairs overlooking the vineyard. They invite you to take your time over the nine or so wines in the basic tasting and to linger to enjoy the atmosphere. You can taste premium wines for $25. There's also a chocolate shop and the excellent Muse Kitchen (p152) restaurant here.

Moorebank Vineyard WINERY
(☏02-4998 7610; www.moorebankvineyard.com; 150 Palmers Lane, Pokolbin; redeemable tasting fee $5; ☺10am-5pm) 🍃 This off-the-beaten-track family-run winery makes a great visit; it's a picturesque spot and the owners are warmly welcoming. As well as the tasty wine, there's a great range of homemade condiments including spicy grape sauce, perfect for a bit of pre-barbecue glazing.

Brokenwood WINERY
(☏02-4998 7559; www.brokenwood.com.au; 401-427 McDonalds Rd, Pokolbin; tasting $10-25; ☺9.30am-5pm Mon-Sat, from 10am Sun) Known for semillon and shiraz, plus the popular 'Cricket Pitch' range, this acclaimed winery has a slick new visitor centre appropriately decked out in wood. Gather round a sociable circular tasting pod and try the range. It's well worth investing in the $25 tasting, which covers lots of high-quality single-vineyard wines. There's also a viewpoint over the barrel room, a cafe – **Cru** – doing deli plates, and a restaurant, **The Wood**. The latter underwhelmed when we visited but was newly opened.

Wine House WINERY
(☏02-4998 7668; www.winehouse.com.au; 426 McDonalds Rd, Pokolbin; redeemable tasting fee $10; ☺10am-5pm Sun-Thu, to 7pm Fri & Sat) With a sweet location by a little dam, this has a good attitude and showcases numerous varieties of wine from five great little estates, some of which don't have cellar doors. The upbeat tasting sessions include up to eight wines. There's also a casual eatery here.

Glandore Estate WINERY
(☏02-4998 7140; www.glandorewines.com; 1595 Broke Rd, Pokolbin; redeemable tasting fee $5;

10am-5pm) This sweet spot has a smartly kitted-out tasting area and some under-the-radar but rather tasty whites and reds, including a couple with the unusual white grape savagnin. Staff members are knowledgeable and make it fun. Try to book one of the wine and chocolate matchings in the afternoon.

Tamburlaine WINERY
(02-4998 4200; www.tamburlaine.com.au; 358 McDonalds Rd, Pokolbin; free tasting; 9am-5pm)
Australia's largest producer of certified organic wines, Tamburlaine has a busy, attractively rustic cellar door. It does a full range of white varietals, some tasty cabernet and shiraz, and a couple of dessert wines. Vegan options are available, and the winery also produces preservative-free drops (not usually available for tasting).

Piggs Peake WINERY
(02-6574 7000; www.piggspeake.com; 697 Hermitage Rd, Pokolbin; 10am-5pm) Priding itself on nontraditional winemaking practices, this winery is one to watch, producing limited-edition, unwooded wines that are fresh, upfront, juicy and enjoyable. The names of the wines come straight from the pig-pun: try the prosecco-style Prosciutto or, for those on a tight budget, the $10-a-bottle Swill.

Activities & Tours

Balloon Aloft BALLOONING
(02-4990 9242; www.balloonaloft.com; adult/child $339/235) Take to the skies for a sunrise hot-air-balloon ride over the vineyards. The jaunt lasts for about an hour and is followed up with bubbles and breakfast at Peterson House Winery.

★ Two Fat Blokes FOOD & DRINK
(deli 02-4998 6699; tours 0414 316 859; www.twofatblokes.com.au; 691 Hermitage Rd, Pokolbin; half-day $69-85, full day $169-259) These stand-out immersive gourmet experiences are a great way to discover the region. Upbeat guided tours take you to some excellent vineyards, but there's plenty more besides the wine, with cheese, beer, delicious lunches and plenty of entertaining background. Even if you're not doing a tour, their deli and cafe is well worth a breakfast or lunch stop.

Kangarrific Tours WINE
(0431 894 471; www.kangarrifictours.com; full day $155) This small-group tour departs from Sydney and promises the Hunter's most diverse itinerary. Taste everything from

wine to gelato and have morning tea with the eponymous roos.

Hunter Valley Boutique Wine Tours WINE
(0419 419 931; www.huntervalleytours.com.au; per person from $80) Reliable and knowledgeable small-group tours from $80 for a half-day (three cellars) and from $125 for a full day including lunch.

Festivals & Events

Big international names (think Springsteen, the Stones) drop by for weekend concerts at the larger vineyards. If there's something special on, accommodation books up well in advance. Check for info at www.winecountry.com.au.

Sleeping

Numerous wineries offer accommodation, and there are lots of boutique self-catering places. There are literally hundreds of places to stay. Prices shoot up savagely on Friday and Saturday nights, when two-night minimum stays are common and weddings also put a strain on available accommodation. Many places don't accept children.

★ Hunter Valley YHA HOSTEL $
(02-4991 3278; www.yha.com.au; 100 Wine Country Dr, Nulkaba; dm $34-40, r with/without bathroom $115/96; P 🚗 ⊛) After a long day's wine tasting or grape picking, there's plenty of bonhomie around the barbecue and pool at this attractive hostel at the northern outskirts of Cessnock. It's set in a characterful wooden building on spacious grounds; dorms are four-berth and spotless, and there's a sweet verandah, as well as hire bikes and a nearby brewery pub. Rooms can get hot.

Australia Hotel PUB $
(02-4990 1256; www.australiahotel.com.au; 136 Wollombi Rd, Cessnock; s/tw with shared bathroom midweek $45/60, r weekends $95; P 🛜) The warren of rooms above this local watering hole look a bit weary but are perfectly adequate for resting your woozy wine head. The more modern bathrooms will make you feel much better in the morning.

★ Tonic BOUTIQUE HOTEL $$$
(02-4930 9999; www.tonichotel.com.au; 251 Talga Rd, Lovedale; d incl breakfast $270-380, apt $500-700; P 🚗 🛜 ⊛ 🐾) The polished concrete floors and urban minimalist style of this handsome complex work a treat in the vivid Hunter light. There's a lovely outlook

over a dam into the sunset from the impressive rooms and two-bedroom apartment. Bathrooms and beds are great, breakfast supplies are placed in your room, and an excellent common area and genial host make for an exceptional experience.

Grange on Hermitage
B&B $$$

(☑02-4998 7388; www.thegrangeonhermitage.com.au; 820 Hermitage Rd, Pokolbin; r $215-270, cottages $430-470; P ☀ �) Spacious grounds, eucalypts and vines make this a most appealing place to relax. Rooms are enormous, with modern amenities, kitchenette and spa bath, and there are lots of lovely touches by the friendly owners, like fresh flowers and just-baked muffins delivered to your door as part of breakfast. There are also two cottages sleeping four to six.

Spicers Vineyards Estate
RESORT $$$

(☑02-6574 7229; www.spicersretreats.com; 555 Hermitage Rd, Pokolbin; ste $599-699; P ☀ � ☷) ✿ Surrounded by bushland, these 12 modern high-end spa suites have king-size beds and cosy lounge areas with open fireplace: perfect for sipping shiraz in winter. The luxury suites are worth the extra $100 a night, with balconies or private courtyards, and particularly stunning bathrooms. Unwind at the day spa or in the pool before a meal at the top-notch **Restaurant Botanica** (2/3 courses $69/79, degustation $110; ⊙6-8.30pm Wed-Fri, noon-2.30pm & 6-8.30pm Sat & Sun, plus 8-10am daily).

Service is cheerful and excellent and there are nice touches in the rooms and a pleasant guest lounge with honesty bar. No children.

Thistle Hill
B&B $$$

(☑02-6574 7217; www.thill.com.au; 591 Hermitage Rd, Pokolbin; r $295; P ☀ � ☷) This idyllic 8-hectare property features rose gardens, a lime orchard, a vineyard, a self-contained cottage sleeping five and a luxurious guesthouse with six double rooms. Rooms and common areas have an elegant French provincial sensibility and are strikingly attractive. There's a great lounge and deck by the pool. Breakfast is included: continental midweek, cooked at weekends.

Longhouse
APARTMENT $$$

(☑0402 101 551; www.thelonghouse.com.au; 385 Palmers Lane, Pokolbin; apt $500-800; P ☀ �) ✿ More than 50 architecture students designed this chic avant-garde pad, based on a traditional Australian wool shed. Made from concrete, corrugated iron and reclaimed timber, it is divided into three enormous, stylishly furnished two-bed apartments with an incredible 48m deck.

Cam Way Estate
CABIN $$$

(☑02-4998 7655; www.camwayestate.com.au; Campbells Lane, Pokolbin; r $225-295; P ☀ �) Though very central and within walking distance of several wineries, this is a peaceful spot, with well-spaced cabins surrounding a typically Australian rural scene with grazing kangaroos and laughing kookaburras. Studios and apartments are spacious and comfortable; there are flexible interlinking options, making it good for any size of family. There's a swimming pool and tennis court. Wi-fi doesn't reach most rooms.

Hermitage Lodge
CABIN $$$

(☑02-4998 7639; www.hermitagelodge.com.au; 609 McDonalds Rd, Pokolbin; r $225-475; P ☀ � ☷) Ideally located within walking distance of a variety of cellar doors, this well-run spot has rooms ranging from fairly basic motel-style doubles to bright, modern, spacious studios and suites, with sunny decks overlooking a shiraz vineyard; two have a secluded upstairs deck with spa bath. There's a good northern Italian restaurant on-site, as well as a guest laundry.

✕ Eating

Hunter Valley Smelly Cheese Shop
DELI $

(☑02-4998 6713; www.smellycheese.net.au; Roche Estate, 2144 Broke Rd, Pokolbin; light meals $10-16; ⊙10am-5pm Mon-Thu, to 5.30pm Fri, 9am-5.30pm Sat, 9am-5pm Sun, kitchen 10am-3pm) Along with the great range of stinky desirables filling the cheese counter and gloriously whiffy fromagerie fridge, there are deli platters, pizzas, burgers and baguettes to take away or eat on the deck, as well as superb gelato. Good daily specials and a cheery attitude prevail despite the besieging hordes. There's another branch in Pokolbin Village.

Fawk Foods
CAFE $$

(☑02-4998 6585; www.fawkfoods.com; 2188 Broke Rd, Pokolbin; breakfasts $18-24; ⊙7am-3pm; � ☑) Pokolbin needed an open-daily breakfast option and this stellar bakery and cafe lays down perfect foundations for a day of tasting. Dishes like beetroot hummus or smoked ocean trout are absolutely beautifully presented, and sandwiches (also takeaway) are delicious in their home-baked breads. This is the best bacon-and-egg-roll in a substantial radius. Outdoor deck seating is a pleasure too.

Enzo
CAFE $$

(☑02-4998 7233; www.enzohuntervalley.com.au; cnr Broke & Ekerts Rds, Pokolbin; breakfast mains $16-28, lunch $23-38; ☺8am-4pm Sun-Thu, to 5pm Fri & Sat; 🐾🅿) Claim a table by the fireside in winter or in the garden in summer to enjoy the rustic dishes served at this deservedly popular Italian-inflected cafe in a picturebook setting. The food is reliably excellent (succulent lamb, splendid salads), service is casually friendly and a David Hook cellar door is here, so you can add a tasting to your visit.

Baumé
MEDITERRANEAN $$

(☑02-4993 3705; www.baumeatbenean.com; Ben Ean Winery, 119 McDonalds Rd, Pokolbin; starters $20, pizzas $30, mains to share $40; ☺11am-4pm, plus 6-11pm Thu-Mon; 🅿🧒) If you need a solid feed to prep for an afternoon's wine tasting, this casual winery spot fits the bill. Food is designed for sharing, which is just as well, as anything larger than an starter will defeat one person. Upfront Mediterranean flavours dominate – cheeses, garlic, marinates – in a menu that covers wood-fired pizzas, enormous salads and whole-fish or roast-joint mains.

Service is fast and the place caters well for families.

★ Bistro Molines
FRENCH $$$

(☑02-4990 9553; www.bistromolines.com.au; Tallavera Grove, 749 Mt View Rd, Mount View; mains $42-46; ☺noon-3pm Thu-Mon, plus 7-9pm Fri & Sat) Set in Carillion's Tallavera Grove winery, this French restaurant run by the Hunter Valley's most storied chef has a carefully crafted, seasonally driven menu that is nearly as impressive as the vineyard views. It's a wonderfully romantic location with lovely seating in the paved courtyard. Daily specials supplement the menu.

Robert and Sally Molines have been doing their thing in the Hunter since the 1970s when the only foodie scene hereabouts was what came out of their kitchen.

★ EXP.
MODERN AUSTRALIAN $$$

(☑02-4998 7264; www.exprestaurant.com.au; 1596 Broke Rd, Pokolbin; 2/3 courses $63/80; ☺noon-2.30pm & 6-8.30pm Wed-Sat, noon-2.30pm Sun; 🅿) Local lad Frank Fawkner's compact space tucked into a corner of Oakvale winery makes you feel you are all – chefs, waiters, diners – on a convivial shared mission. There are some impressive bravura touches (homemade gummy bears!) but the

entrees and mains are all about deep flavours and texture contrasts; go for the more unusual offerings like quail or take on the degustation ($110).

★ Muse Restaurant
MODERN AUSTRALIAN $$$

(☑02-4998 6777; www.musedining.com.au; 1 Broke Rd, Pokolbin; 2-course lunch $75, 4-course dinner $110; ☺noon-3pm Sat & Sun, 6-9pm Wed-Sat; 🅿) Inside the Hungerford Hill winery complex is the area's highest-rated restaurant, offering assured contemporary fare and stellar service in an attractive glass-walled, high-ceilinged space. Presentation is exquisite; this is reliably impressive fine dining without pushing boundaries. Their trademark coconut dessert is sensational. Vegetarians get their own menu (same prices) and children are also decently catered for. Book well ahead at weekends.

Muse Kitchen
EUROPEAN $$$

(☑02-4998 7899; www.musedining.com.au; Keith Tulloch Winery, cnr Hermitage & Deasys Rds, Pokolbin; 2/3 courses $65/80; ☺noon-3pm Wed-Sun, plus 6-9pm Fri & Sat; 🐾🅿) For a fabulous lunch, head to this relaxed younger-sibling incarnation of the Hunter's top restaurant, Muse. Dine outside on a seasonal menu of European bistro food inspired by the vegetables, fruit and herbs grown up the road. Save room for the exquisite dessert selection as well as wine tasting at the adjacent Keith Tulloch (p149) cellar door.

Hunters Quarter
MODERN AUSTRALIAN $$$

(☑02-4998 7776; www.huntersquarter.com; Cockfighter's Ghost, 576 De Beyers Rd, Pokolbin; mains $36-44; ☺6-10pm Mon, noon-3.30pm & 6-10pm Thu-Sat, noon-3.30pm Sun; 🐾) With a lovely outlook over the vines from the array of floor-to-ceiling windows, this place is bustling but intimate. Flavoursome dishes are produced from high-quality ingredients; a good range of wines by the glass lets you taste your way around this and nearby vineyards. Monday is 'locals' night', when two/three courses are $65/80.

Margan
MODERN AUSTRALIAN $$$

(☑02-6579 1317; www.margan.com.au; Margan Wines, 1238 Milbrodale Rd, Broke; 2/3/5 courses $65/85/110; ☺6-9.30pm Thu, noon-3pm & 6-9.30pm Fri & Sat, noon-3pm Sun) 🍃 There's a tempting array of dishes at this Broke restaurant, where much of the produce is sourced from the kitchen garden and farm; the rest comes from local providores whenever possible. The luscious food is beautifully accompanied by the excellent estate-made wines. Views stretch across the vines to the Brokenback Range.

🛍 Shopping

Binnorie Dairy   CHEESE
(☎ 02-4998 6660; www.binnorie.com.au; 25 Lodge Rd, Lovedale; ⊗10am-5pm) Offers an exceptional range of handcrafted creamy soft cheeses from a little factory where you can peer in and watch the process. The goat's-cheese log, labne and marinated feta are particularly moreish. There's also a cafe here doing soups, quiches, ploughmans' lunches and the like (light meals $14 to $22).

Hunter Valley Cheese Company   CHEESE
(☎ 02-4998 7744; www.huntervalleycheese.com. au; McGuigans Winery, 447 McDonalds Rd, Pokolbin; ⊗9am-5.30pm) Staff will chat about cheesy comestibles all day long, especially during the daily 11am and 3pm cheese talks. There's a variety of styles available for purchase and you can sit down and enjoy a tasting ($8 to $15) or a more substantial cheeseboard. By the time you read this, it may have moved 500m further north up McDonalds Rd, past the roundabout.

Hunter Valley Chocolate Company   CHOCOLATE
(☎ 02-4998 6999; www.hvchocolate.com.au; 2320 Broke Rd, Pokolbin; ⊗9am-5pm) This warehouse stocks the numerous chocolatey and fudgey goodies of this company, as well as preserves and the like from other providers. There's a cafe here with pleasant verandah seating.

ℹ Information

Hunter Valley Visitor Centre (☎ 02-4993 6700; www.huntervalleyvisitorcentre.com.au; 455 Wine Country Dr, Pokolbin; ⊗9am-5pm Mon-Sat, to 4pm Sun; 🎧) Has a huge stock of leaflets and info on valley accommodation, attractions and dining.

ℹ Getting There & Away

From Sydney, you can head straight up the M1 motorway, then head to the valley via the exit near Gosford (which allows you to take the scenic route up through Wollombi), the Cessnock turn-off, or the Hunter Expressway (which begins near Newcastle).

Rover Coaches (☎ 02-4990 1699; www. rovercoaches.com.au) Has four buses heading between Newcastle and Cessnock (1¼ hours) on weekdays and two on Saturday; no Sunday service. Other buses head to Cessnock from the train stations at Morisset (one hour, two daily) and Maitland (50 minutes, hourly or better Monday to Saturday, six Sunday).

Sydney Trains (☎13 15 00; www.transport. nsw.gov.au) has a line heading through the Hunter Valley from Newcastle ($5.05, 50 minutes). Branxton is the closest station to the vineyards, although only Maitland has bus services to Cessnock.

ℹ Getting Around

There are several options for exploring without a car. The YHA hostel (p150) hires our bikes, as does **Hunter Valley Cycling** (☎ 0418 281 480; www.huntervalleycycling.com.au; per 1/2 days $35/50). **Grapemobile** (☎ 02-4998 7660; www.grapemobile.com.au; 307 Palmers Lane, Pokolbin; day route $45; ⊗10am-6pm) rents out bikes for a set circuit around several wineries. **Sutton Estate** (☎ 0448 600 288; www.suttonstateelectricbikehire.com; 381 Deasys Rd, Pokolbin; half/full day $50/65) rents out electric bikes. The other choices are to take a tour or a **taxi** (☎ 02-6572 1133; www.taxico. com.au).

iHop Hunter Valley (☎ 0455 535 035; www. ihophuntervalley.com.au; half/full day $39/59; ⊗Thu-Mon) This friendly hop-on hop-off service has 16 stops around the Hunter Valley, allowing you to plan your own flexible winery exploration. A second loop around Lovedale operates only on Saturdays.

Vineyard Shuttle (☎ 02-4991 3655; www. vineyardshuttle.com.au; ⊗6pm-midnight Tue-Sat) Offers a door-to-door service between Pokolbin accommodation and restaurants.

NEWCASTLE

POP 322,300

The port city of Newcastle may be a fraction of the size of Sydney, but Australia's second-oldest city punches well above its weight. Superb surf beaches, historical architecture and a sun-drenched climate are only part of its charm. Fine dining, hip bars, quirky boutiques, a diverse arts scene and a laid-back attitude combine to make 'Newy' well worth a couple of days of your time.

Newcastle, located on traditional Awabakal and Worimi lands, had a rough trot at the end of the 20th century, with a major earthquake and the closure of its steel and shipbuilding industries. Its other important industry, shipping coal, has a decidedly sketchy future too, but Novocastrians always seem to get by with creative entrepreneurship and a positive attitude.

Newcastle

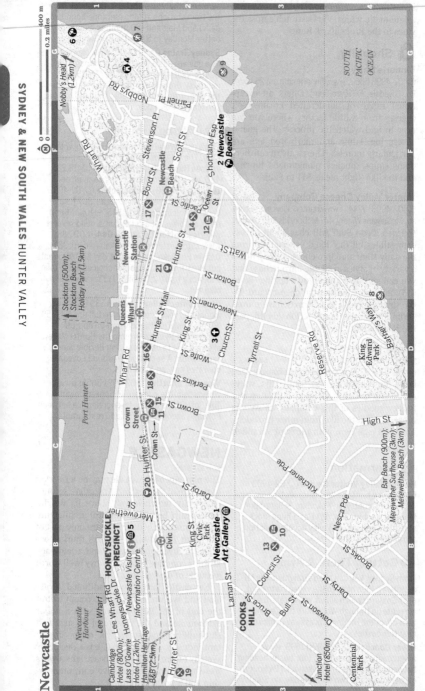

Newcastle Harbour

Port Hunter

SOUTH PACIFIC OCEAN

Stockton (500m);
Stockton Beach
Holiday Park (1.5km)

Nobby's Head
(1.2km)

Cambridge
Hotel (800m);
Lass O'Gowrie
Hotel (1.2km);
Hamilton Heritage
B&B (2.5km)

Bar Beach (900m);
Merewether Surfhouse (3km);
Merewether Beach (3km)

Junction
Hotel (850m)

HONEYSUCKLE PRECINCT

COOKS HILL

Lee Wharf

Lee Wharf Rd

Honeysuckle Dr

Newcastle Visitor
Information Centre

Wharf Rd

Crown Street

Hunter St

Merewether St

Hunter St Mall

Queens Wharf

Former
Newcastle
Station

Wharf Rd

Nobbys Rd

Parnell Pl

Stevenson Pl

Bond St

Newcastle
Beach

Pacific St

Ocean St

Scott St

Shortland Esp

Watt St

Hunter St

King St

Newcomen St

Church St

Bolton St

Wolfe St

Perkins St

Brown St

Darby St

King St
Civic Park

Laman St

Council St

Bruce St

Bull St

Dawson St

Darby St

Brooks St

Nesca Pde

Kitchener Pde

Tyrrell St

Reserve Rd

Bathers Way

King Edward Park

High St

Centennial Park

Newcastle 1
Art Gallery

Civic

Newcastle 2
Beach

Newcastle Station

400 m
0.2 miles

Newcastle

◉ Top Sights
| 1 Newcastle Art Gallery | B2 |
| 2 Newcastle Beach | F2 |

◉ Sights
3 Christ Church Cathedral	D2
4 Fort Scratchley	G1
5 Newcastle Museum	B1
6 Nobby's Beach	G1

➕ Activities, Courses & Tours
7 Bathers Way	G1
8 Bogey Hole	E4
9 Newcastle Ocean Baths	G2

🛏 Sleeping
10 Crown on Darby	B3
11 Lucky Hotel	C2
12 Newcastle Beach YHA	E2

❎ Eating
13 Coal River & Co	B3
14 Mason	E2
15 Momo	C2
16 One Penny Black	D2
17 Paymasters	E2
18 Sprout	D2
19 Subo	A2

❷ Drinking & Nightlife
20 Coal & Cedar	C2
21 Reserve Wine Bar	E2
The Koutetsu	(see 19)

SYDNEY & NEW SOUTH WALES HUNTER VALLEY

◉ Sights & Activities

★ Newcastle Art Gallery   GALLERY
(☑ 02-4974 5100; www.nag.org.au; 1 Laman St; ⊙ 10am-5pm Tue-Sun, plus Mon school holidays) FREE Ignore the brutalist exterior, as inside this remarkable regional gallery are some wonderful works. There's no permanent exhibition; displays rotate the gallery's excellent collection, whose highlights include art by Newcastle-born William Dobell and John Olsen as well as Brett Whiteley and modernist Grace Cossington Smith.

Olsen's works, in particular, bring an explosive vibrancy to the gallery, with his generative organic swirls flamboyantly representing water-based Australian landscapes. Look out for his ceiling painting by the central stairwell and his brilliant *King Sun and the Hunter*, a tribute to the essence of his native city, painted at age 88 in 2016.

Newcastle Museum   MUSEUM
(☑ 02-4974 1400; www.newcastlemuseum.com.au; 6 Workshop Way; ⊙ 10am-5pm Tue-Sun, plus Mon school holidays; 🖈) FREE This attractive museum in the restored Honeysuckle rail workshops tells a tale of the city from its Indigenous Awabakal origins to its rough-and-tumble social history, shaped by a cast of convicts, coal miners and steelworkers. Exhibitions are interactive and engaging, ranging from geology to local icons like Silverchair and the Newcastle Knights rugby league club. If you're travelling with kids, check out hands-on science centre Supernova and the hourly sound-and-light show on the steelmaking process. There's also a cafe.

Merewether Aquarium   PUBLIC ART
(Henderson Pde, Merewether) Not an aquarium in the traditional sense, this pedestrian underpass has been charmingly transformed into a pop-art underwater world by local artist Trevor Dickinson. There are numerous quirky details, including the artist himself as a diver. Find it at the southern end of Merewether Beach, opposite the Surfhouse top entrance.

Christ Church Cathedral   CATHEDRAL
(☑ 02-4929 2052; www.newcastlecathedral.org.au; 52 Church St; ⊙ 7am-6pm, tower 10.15am-3.15pm Mon-Sat, 11.15am-4.15pm Sun) FREE Dominating the city skyline, Newcastle's Anglican cathedral is filled with treasures like a gold chalice and a remembrance book made from jewellery donated by locals who lost loved ones in WWI. The self-guided tour offers an insight into special features such as the fine pre-Raphaelite stained-glass window by Edward Burne-Jones and William Morris. Climb the claustrophobic spiral stairs to the tower ($10 donation) for splendid views across the mouth of the Hunter and the long dunes beyond.

Nobby's Head   VIEWPOINT
Originally an island, this headland at the entrance to Newcastle's harbour was joined to the mainland by a stone breakwater built by convicts between 1818 and 1846; many of those poor souls were lost to the wild seas during construction. The walk along the spit towards the lighthouse and meteorological station (open on Sundays) and beyond along

DON'T MISS

NEWCASTLE'S BEACHES

At the eastern end of town, easily reached on the light rail, surfers and swimmers adore **Newcastle Beach**; the **ocean baths** (www.newcastle.nsw. gov.au; Shortland Esplanade) FREE are a mellow alternative, encased in wonderful multicoloured art-deco architecture. There's a shallow pool for toddlers and a backdrop of heaving ocean and chugging cargo ships. Surfers should goofyfoot it to **Nobby's Beach**, just north of the baths – the fast left-hander known as the Wedge is at its northern end.

South of Newcastle Beach, below King Edward Park, is Australia's oldest ocean bath, the convict-carved **Bogey Hole**. It's an atmospheric place to splash about in when the surf's crashing over its edge. The most popular surfing breaks are at **Bar Beach** and **Merewether Beach**, two ends of the same beach a bit further south. Merewether has huge **ocean baths** (www.newcastle.nsw.gov.au; Frederick St, Merewether) of its own.

The city's famous surfing festival, **Surfest** (www.surfest.com; Merewether Beach; ☉ Feb), takes place in February each year.

the long breakwater is exhilarating, but don't do it in high seas.

Fort Scratchley FORT
(☑ 02-4974 1422; www.newcastle.nsw.gov.au/ Fort-Scratchley; Nobbys Rd; tunnel tour adult/ child $12.50/6.50, full tour $16/8; ☉ 10am-4pm Wed-Mon, last tour 2.30pm) FREE Perched above Newcastle Harbour, this intriguing military site was constructed during the Crimean War to protect the city against a feared Russian invasion. During WWII the fort returned fire on a Japanese submarine, making it the only Australian fort to have engaged in a maritime attack. It's free to enter, but the guided tours are worth taking, as you venture into the fort's labyrinth of underground tunnels. Head to the shop for tickets or for a self-guided-tour brochure.

★ Bathers Way WALKING
(www.visitnewcastle.com.au) This scenic coastal path from Nobby's Beach to Glenrock Reserve winds past swaths of beach and

fascinating historical sites including Fort Scratchley and the Convict Lumber Yard. Interpretative signs describing Indigenous, convict and natural history dot the 5km trail. North of Bar Beach, it connects with the spectacular **Memorial Walk**, which offers magical sea views.

🛏 Sleeping

Newcastle Beach YHA HOSTEL $
(☑ 02-4925 3544; www.yha.com.au; 30 Pacific St; dm $30-39, s/d $70/93; @ ☎) It may have the look of a grand English mansion, but this sprawling, brick, heritage-listed YHA has the ambience of a laid-back beach bungalow, with great common spaces and airy, comfortable dorms in varying sizes. Just a minute away from the surf, it offers complimentary bodyboards, surfboards, barbecue nights and weekly pub meals.

Stockton Beach Holiday Park CAMPGROUND $
(☑ 1800 778 562; www.nrmaparksandresorts.com. au; 3 Pitt St, Stockton; unpowered/powered sites Feb-Dec $39/48, Jan $53/67, cabins $190-340; P ✿ @ ☎ ☎) ⬦ The beach is at your doorstep (or should that be tent flap?) at this tourist park behind the dunes in Stockton, a short ferry ride from Newcastle (or 20km by road). With large, grassy campsites, en suites for vans and smart, modern villas, it's a flash place to park yourself. There's a public pool next door.

★ Junction Hotel BOUTIQUE HOTEL $$
(☑ 02-4962 8888; www.junctionhotel.com.au; 204 Corlette St, The Junction; r $149-169; ✿ ☎) The upstairs of this stylishly modernised pub has been transformed with nine flamboyantly appointed rooms featuring moody lighting, lush fabrics and offbeat colours. All have generous-sized beds, coffee machines and flashy bathrooms with disco lights and (in some) little privacy. Well located among the Junction's boutiques and cafes, it's just a 10-minute walk to the beach.

★ Lucky Hotel BOUTIQUE HOTEL $$
(☑ 02-4925 8888; www.theluckyhotel.com.au; 237 Hunter St; r $145-190; ✿ ☎) A slick but sympathetic revamp of this grand old 1880s dame means it's an upbeat, modern place to stay above a great pub. The 28 light-filled rooms are smallish but tastefully decorated, with pleasing touches like luxe bedding and toiletries, not to mention a hand-painted quote about luck in case you need the inspiration.

Corridors showcase black-and-white photos of old Newcastle.

Crown on Darby
APARTMENT $$

(☑02-4941 6777; www.crownondarby.com.au; 101 Darby St; apt midweek $176-286; ▣✳🛜) Close to cafes and restaurants, this excellent modern complex of 38 apartments is right on Newcastle's coolest street. Studios are reasonably sized and have kitchenettes. One-bedroom apartments are a worthwhile upgrade, with interconnecting options, full kitchens and huge living rooms; some have spa baths. Both open and closed balconies are available, so request your preference.

Hamilton Heritage B&B
B&B $$

(☑02-49611242; www.accommodationinnewcastle. com.au; 178 Denison St, Hamilton; r $140-175; ▣✳🛜🐾) Offering genuine courtesy and a cosy atmosphere, this Federation-era home near the Beaumont St cafe strip makes for a characterful stay. The house some beautiful original features, and the three old-style rooms (including a family suite sleeping six) have en suites, fridges and tea- and coffee-making facilities. Guests can use the kitchen and back deck overlooking a lovely subtropical garden.

Lots of buses from the centre, including 13, 21, 23, 26 and 28, can drop you close by.

🍴 Eating

Newcastle has a thriving eating scene. Darby St is a local icon for cafes, Thai and Vietnamese restaurants and pizza, while the harbourfront has lots of options, particularly in the Honeysuckle Precinct near the tourist office and at Queens Wharf near the Stockton ferry. In Hamilton, places to eat cluster along Beaumont St, while the Junction is well stocked and the beaches have plenty of nearby options too.

One Penny Black
CAFE $

(☑02-4929 3169; 196 Hunter St; mains $14-20; ◔7am-4.30pm; 🛜🐾) It's perpetually popular for a reason – here you'll probably have to queue for an excellent espresso or filter coffee, served by staff who know their stuff. Devotees also rave about the toasties and fabulous breakfast platters.

Coal River & Co
ITALIAN $$

(☑02-4929 4265; www.coalriverandco.com.au; 120 Darby St; pasta $24-29; ◔6-9pm Tue-Thu, noon-2.30pm & 6-9pm Fri-Sun; 🐾) The focus here is on delicious homemade pasta dishes, which are the only main courses available,

though there are some good starters and salads designed to share. The pasta is super-fresh and tasty, and there are some interesting wines available to accompany it.

Sprout
MODERN AUSTRALIAN $$

(☑02-49271138; www.thecrownandanchor.com.au; 189 Hunter St; mains $28, pastas $20; ◔6-8.30pm Tue-Thu, noon-2.30pm & 6-10pm Fri & Sat) What at first glance appears to be a generic Aussie sports pub has a gourmet secret going. Upstairs in the Crown and Anchor Hotel an airy space with an open kitchen turns out a short, quality menu of delicious creations, including standout homemade gnocchi and other vaguely Italian-influenced dishes.

Momo
CAFE, VEGAN $$

(☑02-4926 3310; www.facebook.com/momo newcastle; 227 Hunter St; dishes $12-22; ◔7.30am-3pm; 🛜🐾) In a striking, high-ceilinged former bank building that at first seems too big for it, this friendly cafe specialises in wholefoods, offering mostly vegetarian and vegan choices. Textures, colours and flavours make the dishes very appealing, and influences range from Himalayan to local.

★Subo
MODERN AUSTRALIAN, VEGAN $$$

(☑02-4023 4048; www.subo.com.au; 551d Hunter St; 5 courses $95; ◔6-10pm Wed-Sat; 🐾) Book in advance for a table at tiny Subo, an innovative, highly lauded restaurant serving light, exquisite food with a flair for presentation but no frippery. The restaurant exclusively serves a five-course menu that changes seasonally. Vegetarian and vegan options are available.

Mason
MODERN AUSTRALIAN $$$

(☑02-4926 1014; www.restaurantmason.com; 3/35 Hunter St; 2-/3-/5-/7-course meals $75/ 92/105/130; ◔6-9pm Wed-Sat, plus noon-2.30pm Fri; 🐾) This elegant dining room near the beach opens pleasantly to the street, where extra tables sit under the plane trees. The cuisine is refined and stylishly presented, focusing on subtle flavour and texture combinations with a Japanese inflection to several of the dishes. Service is notably pleasant and helpful and there are separate tasting menus for vegetarians.

Paymasters
FUSION $$$

(☑02-4925 2600; www.paymasters.com.au; 18 Bond St; breakfast dishes $20-26, lunch & dinner mains $34-43; ◔noon-2pm & 6-10pm Wed-Fri, from 9.30am Sat, 9.30am-2pm Sun; 🐾) In a heritage weatherboard cottage overlooking a park and the river, this is a charming spot indeed. It packs out for weekend breakfasts and offers classy, creative à la carte dishes with a sizeable Asian influence at other meals. It feels a mite overpriced, but the setting is divine. There are good vegan choices.

Drinking & Nightlife

★ Coal & Cedar
COCKTAIL BAR

(☑0499 345 663; www.coalandcedar.com; 380-382 Hunter St; ⊙4pm-midnight Mon-Sat) Pull up a stool at the long wooden bar in this Prohibition-style speakeasy where you'll find Newcastle's finest drinking Old Fashioneds to the blues. Cocktails are great; let the expert bartenders guide you. Normal procedure is to text them to open up: instructions are at the entrance.

Reserve Wine Bar
WINE BAR

(☑02-4929 3393; www.reservenewcastle.com.au; 102 Hunter St; ⊙5-11pm Tue-Fri, from 4pm Sat & Sun; ☜) Run with great enthusiasm for wine but zero pretension, this bar, in a former bank, has numerous wines available from all over the world, and of course many from Newcastle's Hunter Valley backyard. As well as weekly by-the-glass selections, you can try premium drops preserved with Coravin technology. Enjoy your tipple with a bite from the interesting grazing menu.

The Koutetsu
COCKTAIL BAR

(☑0431 760 025; www.facebook.com/thekoutetsu; 555 Hunter St; ⊙4pm-midnight Wed-Sat) Wire mesh and upside-down lampshades give an offbeat industrial vibe to this dark and atmospheric speakeasy-style West End bar. A sizeable choir of carefully selected spirits, including some fine Japanese whiskies, backs the helpful bartenders, who shake some brilliant house cocktails off the CD-box menu. Atmospheric and likeable.

☆ Entertainment

Newcastle Knights
SPECTATOR SPORT

(☑02-4028 9100; www.newcastleknights.com.au; McDonald Jones Stadium, New Lambton) The pride of Newcastle, the Knights are the local rugby league side. They've had a rough trot of late, but there's plenty of passion around them here, and going to a game is a great experience. In summer, the stadium is used by the Newcastle Jets A-League soccer team.

Cambridge Hotel
LIVE MUSIC

(☑02-4962 2459; www.thecambridgehotel.com.au; 789 Hunter St) A backpacker favourite that launched Silverchair, Newcastle's most famous cultural export, this West End pub continues to showcase touring bands and local acts. Check the website for upcoming gigs.

ℹ Information

Visitor Information Centre (☑02-4974 2109; www.visitnewcastle.com.au; 6 Workshop Way; ⊙9am-5pm; ☜) Set in the shop of the Newcastle Museum at time of research, but possibly moving to a nearby location in 2020.

ℹ Getting There & Away

Newcastle's **airport** (NTL; ☑02-4928 9800; www.newcastleairport.com.au; 1 Williamtown Dr, Williamtown) is serviced from several eastern Australian cities.

Sydney Trains (p153) runs regular services to Newcastle Interchange, 2km west of the centre and easily accessed on the light rail, from Gosford ($8.69, 1½ hours) and Sydney ($8.69, 3 hours). A line also heads to the Hunter Valley; Branxton ($6.76, 50 minutes) is the closest stop to wine country.

Several bus companies run services up the coast as far as Brisbane. Sydney services are significantly pricier than the train.

ℹ Getting Around

The new light rail service runs from the **Newcastle Interchange** (Stewart Ave, Wickham) through the centre of town and on to the beach. Tickets cost $2.20 with an Opal card, or just 20¢ if you're transferring from the train or ferry.

Newcastle has an extensive network of **local buses** (☑13 15 00; www.newcastletransport.info). There's a fare-free bus zone in the inner city between 7.30am and 6pm. Otherwise you need to tap on and off with an Opal card. The main hub is next to the former Newcastle train station in the east of the city.

MID-NORTH COAST

Between Nelson Bay and Woolgoolga, the coast is riddled with lakes and shot through with swaths of coastal eucalypt and rainforest, much of it protected in national parks. The joy here is forsaking the Pacific Hwy for leafy roads that cut across to the coast, taking detours and switching back. What you'll find at the end of the road are wonderfully unpretentious beach towns, basic campgrounds beside dunes and rivers, and miles and miles of lush nothing. The big towns here are Port Macquarie and Coffs Harbour, which can appear busy and built-up but nevertheless manage to maintain a languid holiday pace.

The Worimi people are the traditional custodians of much of the land in this region and a visit to the Worimi Conservation Lands at Stockton Bight is a beautiful spot to learn about their cultural heritage.

Port Stephens

POP 69,556

An hour's drive north of Newcastle, the sheltered harbour of Port Stephens is blessed with near-deserted beaches, extraordinary national parks and a unique sand-dune system. The main centre, Nelson Bay, is home to both a fishing fleet and an armada of tourist vessels, the latter trading on the town's status as the 'dolphin capital of Australia'.

Just east of Nelson Bay is slightly smaller Shoal Bay, which has a long swimming beach; a short drive south is Fingal Bay, with another lovely beach on the fringes of Tomaree National Park. The park stretches west around the clothing-optional Samurai Beach, a popular surfing spot, and One Mile Beach, a gorgeous semicircle of the softest sand and bluest water.

The park ends at somnolent surfside village Anna Bay, which is also the gateway into the incredible Worimi Conservation Lands.

◉ Sights

★Worimi
Conservation Lands   NATURE RESERVE
(www.worimiconservationlands.com; 3-day driving permit $33) Located at Stockton Bight, these are the longest moving sand dunes in the southern hemisphere, stretching more than 35km. Thanks to the generosity of the Worimi people, the traditional owners who now manage the area, you're able to roam around and drive along the beach (4WD only, and always check conditions). You can get permits from a number of places including the Port Stephens visitor centre (p161), the NPWS office in Nelson Bay and the Anna Bay BP petrol station.

It's possible to become so surrounded by shimmering sand that you'll lose sight of the ocean or any sign of life. As spectacular as this might be, it's the rich cultural heritage of the Worimi that makes this a truly special place to visit. The area includes numerous

shell middens, some dating back tens of thousands of years. At the far western end of the beach, the wreck of the *Sygna* founders in the water. Plenty of tour operators offer experiences such as camel rides (☑0429 664 172; www.oakfieldranch.com.au; Birubi Point Car Park, James Patterson St, Anna Bay; adult/child $30/25, sunset rides $80; ◷10am-4pm) and sandboarding.

Tomaree National Park   NATIONAL PARK
(www.nationalparks.nsw.gov.au/tomaree-national-park) This wonderfully wild expanse offers beautiful hiking in an area that can feel far more remote than it actually is. The park harbours angophora forests and several threatened species, including the spotted-tailed quoll and powerful owl, and you can spot outcrops of the rare volcanic rock rhyodacite. In spring, the Morna Point trail (5.5km return, 2½ hours) is strewn with wildflowers.

🏃 Activities & Tours

There are dozens of operators offering various action-packed ways to spend your day in the area, from whale-watching (p162) to camel rides. The visitor information centre in Nelson Bay can help with bookings.

Port Stephens Surf School   SURFING
(☑0411 419 576; www.portstephenssurfschool.com.au; 1½hr group surf lessons $60) Offers both group and private surf lessons at One Mile and Fingal Bay Beaches, and stand-up paddleboarding lessons by appointment ($45 per person, minimum four people). Board hire is also available (one/two hours $20/30).

Port Stephens 4WD Tours   TOURS
(☑02-4984 4760; www.portstephens4wd.com.au; James Patterson St, Anna Bay) Offers a 1½-hour Beach & Dune tour (adult/child $52/31) and a sandboarding experience ($28/20) out on the magnificent dunes of the Worimi Conservation Lands. You can stay as long as you like if sandboarding; just jump on the shuttle when you want to go home.

Port Stephens Paddlesports   KAYAKING
(☑0405 033 518; www.paddleportstephens.com.au; 35 Shoal Bay Rd, Shoal Bay; kayak/paddleboard hire per hour $30; ◷Sep-May) Offers a range of kayak and stand-up-paddleboard hire as well as excursions, including 1½-hour sunset tours (adult/child $50/40) and 2½-hour discovery tours ($60/50).

CONNECTING WITH THE ABORIGINAL SPIRIT OF THE LAND

The area from the Tomaree Peninsula to Forster and as far west as Gloucester is the land of the Worimi people. Very little of the land is now in their possession, but in 2001 the sand dunes of the Stockton Bight were returned to them, creating the Worimi Conservation Lands (p159). Dark Point Aboriginal Place (p161) in Myall Lakes National Park has been significant to the Worimi for around 4000 years.

Heading north from Worimi land, you enter **Birpai** country, which includes Taree and Port Macquarie. The Sea Acres Rainforest Centre (p163) has a section devoted to the local people called the 'Spirit of the Land'.

After travelling through the lands of the **Dainggatti** people (roughly equivalent to Kempsey Shire) you then enter **Gumbaynggirr** country, which stretches up to the Clarence River. Places such as Nambucca Heads retain a sizeable Aboriginal community. Nearby, the village of Red Rock is the site of another 19th-century massacre. Learn more about the local Gumbaynggirr people, taste some bush tucker and see some Aboriginal artwork at the **Yarrawarra Aboriginal Cultural Centre** (☑02-6640 7104; www.yarrawarra.org; 170 Red Rock Rd, Corindi Beach; ◷10am-4pm Tue-Fri, to 1pm Sat & Sun, cafe closes at 2pm Tue-Fri) at Corindi Beach outside Yuraygir National Park. Another great insight into Gumbaynggirr culture and history is available on one of the excellent stand-up paddleboard tours operated by Wajaana Yaam Adventure Tours (p172) from Coffs Harbour.

The northern part of the NSW coast and much of the Gold Coast is the domain of the **Bundjalung** nation, including their sacred mountain Wollumbin/Mt Warning (p192). Tours run by Aboriginal Cultural Concepts (p176) offer an introduction to Bundjalung life. The **Minjungbal Aboriginal Cultural Centre** (☑07-5524 2275; www.facebook.com/ MinjungbalMuseum; Kirkwood Rd, South Tweed Heads; adult/child $15/7.50; ◷9am-3pm Mon-Fri) at Tweed Heads is also worth visiting.

🛏 Sleeping

Melaleuca Surfside Backpackers   HOSTEL $
(☑02-4981 9422; www.melaleucabackpackers. com.au; 2 Koala Pl, One Mile Beach; sites $20, dm $32-36, d tent/cabin $70/120; @🛜) Architect-designed cabins are set amid peaceful scrub inhabited by koalas, kookaburras and sugar gliders at this friendly, well-run place. You can also pitch your own tent among bushland (the whole site is blissfully car-free) or book one of the bed-equipped tents. There's a welcoming lounge area and a kitchen, along with surfboard hire, sandboarding and other excursions.

The Oasis   BUNGALOW $$
(☑02-4982 2801; www.theoasisonemile.com.au; 5 Koala Pl, One Mile Beach; bungalows $190-310; 🛠🛜🏊) Nine two-bedroom, self-contained loft bungalows (two with hot tubs and some designed for families; all wheelchair-accessible) nestle around a billabong in 2 hectares of landscaped garden. Guests also have use of garden BBQs, fire pits and outdoor dining tables. Various wellness treatments are available at the **on-site wellness centre** (www.wellnesscentreportstephens.com.au; 75min yoga class $20, massages from $80; ◷8am-6pm), which also has an infrared sauna.

★**Anchorage**   RESORT $$$
(☑02-4984 2555; www.anchorageportstephens. com.au; Corlette Point Rd, Corlette; d $299-499; 🅿🛠🛜🏊) Facing an expansive sweep of bay, this marina-fronted resort is Port Stephens' most stylish place to stay. Rooms have a crisp, coastal charm, with super-comfortable, relaxed interiors, and all have either a balcony or a terrace. There are larger suites and apartments for those after the added luxury of space or for families.

Bannisters   BOUTIQUE HOTEL $$$
(☑02-4919 3800; www.bannisters.com.au/port-stephens; 147 Soldiers Point Rd, Soldiers Point; d $275-450, ocean deck $330-454; 🅿🛠🛜🏊) After the success of its Mollymook location, Bannisters has expanded with this move north to give a old 78-room motel a bit of polish, and it's come up trumps. The design takes advantage of its waterfront location, the infinity pool is a knockout, and the rooms are light and airy, though somewhat lacking the level of luxury expected at this price.

Guests can dine on fresh seafood courtesy of the on-site **Rick Stein restaurant**, or spend the evening with a few drinks in the **Tavern** beer garden or at the poolside **Terrace Bar**.

✕ Eating

Red Ned's Gourmet Pie Bar　　PIES $
(☑02-4984 1355; www.redneds.com.au; Shop 3, 17-19 Stockton St, Nelson Bay; pies from $6; ⊙6.30am-5pm, to 4pm Sun; ♫) More than 50 varieties of pies ranging from flavours such as macadamia-nut Thai satay chicken to the classic savoury mince or old-school lamb's fry and bacon. Occasionally crocodile in mushroom-and-white-wine sauce features on the menu, and there's a good range of vegetarian options too. The beef is sourced from the Hunter Valley and the chickens are free-range.

★ Little Beach Boathouse　　SEAFOOD $$
(☑02-4984 9420; www.littlebeachboathouse.com.au; Little Beach Marina, 4 Victoria Pde, Nelson Bay; mains $29-38; ⊙noon-2pm & 5-9pm Tue-Sat, 11.30am-2.30pm Sun) In an airy but intimate dining room, right on the water, you can order fabulous seafood dishes such as Hervey Bay scallops, Port Stephens oysters and lightly battered squid, all with a side of truffle and parmesan fries. If you're not a seafood lover, go for the crispy pork belly or ravioli of the day. Service is fantastic. Book ahead for dinner.

★ Wild Herring　　SEAFOOD, AUSTRALIAN $$$
(☑02-4984 2555; www.anchorageportstephens.com.au; Corlette Point Rd, Corlette Point; mains $40-46; ⊙6-9pm) The Anchorage resort's Galley Kitchen morphs into a resolutely fine-dining restaurant in the evening, but the simple waterfront space still vibes holiday calm. Dishes range from starters of poached lobster bisque and blue swimmer crab to second courses of king prawns in a miso emulsion and snapper fillet with creamy almond sauce. Staff, attentive but chilled, can advise on the excellent wine list.

ℹ Information

National Parks & Wildlife Service Office
(NPWS; ☑02-4984 8200; www.nationalparks.nsw.gov.au; 12b Teramby Rd, Nelson Bay; ⊙8.30am-4.30pm Mon-Fri)

Visitor Information Centre (☑1800 808 900; www.portstephens.org.au; 60 Victoria Pde, Nelson Bay; ⊙9am-5pm) Has interesting displays about the marine park and can help book tours and excursions.

ℹ Getting There & Away

Port Stephens Coaches (☑02-4982 2940; www.pscoaches.com.au) Zips around Port Stephens' townships heading to Newcastle and Newcastle Airport ($4.70, one hour). A daily service runs to/from Sydney (one way/return $39/61, four hours) stopping at Nelson Bay and Shoal Bay, and on weekdays at Anna Bay.

Port Stephens Ferry Service (☑0412 682 117; www.portstephensferryservice.com.au; return adult/child $26/13) Runs two services a day on a historic timber ferry between Nelson Bay and Tea Gardens (stopping at Hawks Nest en route), with more services running from November to January and over Easter. The journey takes one hour and there's a good chance of seeing dolphins. Bookings are necessary.

Myall Lakes National Park

On an extravagantly pretty section of the coast that feels deliciously remote, this large national park incorporates a patchwork of lakes, islands, dense littoral rainforest and beaches. **Seal Rocks**, a bush-clad hamlet hugging Sugarloaf Bay, is one of Australia's most epic surf destinations. Further south, the lakes support an incredible quantity and variety of bird life, including bowerbirds, white-bellied sea eagles and tawny frogmouths. The coastal rainforest is cut through with fire trails and beach tracks that lead to the beach dunes at **Mungo Brush**, perfect territory for spotting wildflowers and surprising dingoes.

⊙ Sights

Seal Rocks　　BEACH
(www.nationalparks.nsw.gov.au/myall-lakes-national-park) This remarkably undeveloped town and its collection of beaches has long held mythic status among the global surfing community. There's plenty to enjoy even if you're not here for the idyllic, secluded breaks. **Number One Beach** has beautiful rock pools, usually mellow waves and beautiful sand. Or take the 660m walk to the **Sugarloaf Point Lighthouse** for epic ocean views, with a detour to lonely **Lighthouse Beach**, a popular surfing spot.

Near the lighthouse is a lookout over the actual Seal Rocks – islets where Australian fur seals can sometimes be spotted. Humpback whales swim past during their annual migration.

Dark Point Aboriginal Place　　DUNES
(Mungo Brush Rd) On a rocky headland in the southern part of Myall Lakes National Park near Hawks Nest, Dark Point was an important gathering place for the Worimi people

to feast on the abundant food sources in the area, and has been a culturally significant site for at least 4000 years. Local lore has it that in the late 19th century it was the site of one of many massacres at the hands of white settlers, when a community was herded onto the rocks and pushed off.

From the car park you can walk onto the surreal landscape of the blinding sand dunes, which contain Aboriginal artefacts and shell midden (there is a protected fenced-off area). The point has stunning scenic views out to Broughton Island.

Broughton Island
BIRD SANCTUARY

(www.nationalparks.nsw.gov.au/myall-lakes-national-park) This island is uninhabited except for muttonbirds and little penguins, and its surrounding waters are home to an enormous diversity of fish. The diving is excellent, and the beaches are secluded. **Moonshadow** (☑02-4984 9388; https://moonshadow-tqc.com.au; 35 Stockton St, Nelson Bay) 🛥 runs full-day trips to the island from Nelson Bay on Sundays and some Wednesdays between late September and Easter, which include snorkelling and boom-net rides (adult/child $95/55).

🛏 Sleeping

Reflections Holiday Park Seal Rocks
CAMPGROUND $

(☑02-4997 6164; www.reflectionsholidayparks.com.au; Kinka Rd, Seal Rocks; sites/cabins from $55/122; 🛜) This well-maintained holiday park is a treat and offers grassed camping and caravan sites, glamping beach tents with bathroom, and a range of cabins from budget to architecturally designed villas (complete with ocean views, contemporary decor, rainfall shower, coffee pod machine and BBQs on the decks). Facilities include a camp kitchen and a breezy common lounge with Foxtel.

NPWS Campgrounds
CAMPGROUND $

(☑1300 072 757; www.nationalparks.nsw.gov.au/myall-lakes-national-park; sites per 2 people $25-35) There are 19 basic campgrounds dotted around the park; only some have drinking water and flush toilets. All locations can be booked via the website. Mungo Brush is a popular large campground right by the lake, while Johnsons Beach is favoured for its boat-based camping and remote tranquil setting (it's very basic so you'll need to come fully prepared).

★ Bombah Point Eco Cottages
COTTAGE $$$

(☑02-4997 4401; www.bombah.com.au; 969 Bombah Point Rd, Bombah Point; cottages $300-325; ❄) 🛥 In the heart of the national park, these architect-designed glass-fronted cottages sleep up to six guests. The 'eco' in the name is well deserved: sewage is treated on-site using a bio-reactor system; electricity comes courtesy of solar panels; and filtered rainwater tanks provide water. Cottages are quietly luxurious with huge rainwater spa baths and stylish cast-iron fireplaces.

Sugarloaf Point Lighthouse
COTTAGE $$$

(☑02-4997 6590; www.nationalparks.nsw.gov.au/camping-and-accommodation; Kinka Rd, Seal Rocks; cottages from $360; 🐾) Watch the crashing waves and wandering wildlife from one of three fully renovated 19th-century lighthouse-keeper's cottages. Each is self-contained and has two or three bedrooms and a barbecue. Ceilings are high and the heritage-style interiors are mercifully unfussy. The location, as you might imagine, is extraordinary. There's a two-night minimum stay.

❶ Getting There & Away

From Hawks Nest the scenic Mungo Brush Rd heads through the park to Bombah Broadwater, where the **Bombah Point ferry** makes the five-minute crossing every half-hour from 8am to 6pm ($6.50 per car). Continuing north, a 10km section of Bombah Point Rd heading to the Pacific Hwy at Bulahdelah is unsealed.

Busways (☑02-4983 1560; www.busways.com.au) route 150 from Newcastle to Taree stops at Bluey's Beach and is the closest public transport option.

Port Macquarie

POP 44,814

Making the most of its position at the entrance to the subtropical coast, Port, as it's commonly known, might be a mini-metropolis but it remains overwhelmingly holiday focused. A string of beautiful beaches fans out either side of town, all a short driving distance from the centre. Most are great for swimming and surfing, and they seldom get crowded. There are enough interesting museums and attractions, plus a decent culinary scene, to warrant a stay of at least a couple of nights.

The local Birpai people are the traditional custodians of this land.

⊙ Sights

★ Tacking Point Lighthouse   VIEWPOINT

(Lighthouse Rd) This little lighthouse (1879) commands a headland offering immense views along the coast. It's a great spot from which to watch the waves roll in to long, beautiful Lighthouse Beach; it's particularly lovely at sunset. The viewpoint looks out to the **Three Brothers Mountains**, a place of spiritual importance to the local Birpai Aboriginal people.

Koala Hospital   WILDLIFE RESERVE

(www.koalahospital.org.au; Lord St; by donation; ⊙8am-4.30pm) Chlamydia, traffic accidents and dog attacks are the biggest causes of illness and injury for koalas living near urban areas; about 250 end up in this shelter each year. You can walk around the open-air enclosures any time of the day, but you'll learn more on a free 40-minute tour and have the chance to see them being fed (3pm).

Dooragan National Park   NATIONAL PARK

(www.nationalparks.nsw.gov.au/dooragan-national-park) FREE This little park immediately north of Crowdy Bay National Park and on the shores of Watson Taylor Lake is dominated by North Brother Mountain. A sealed road leads to the lookout at the top, which offers incredible views of the coast. Or you can try the challenging 3km **Laurieton Track** walk (one way) through blackbutt and eucalyptus forest to the summit.

Crowdy Bay National Park   NATIONAL PARK

(www.nationalparks.nsw.gov.au/crowdy-bay-national-park; vehicles $8) Known for its rock formations and rugged cliffs, this park backs onto a long and beautiful beach. A 4.8km (two-hour) loop track heads over the Diamond headland. The roads running through the park are unsealed and full of potholes, but the dappled light through the gum trees makes it a lovely drive. There is camping available at a few spots including the popular **Diamond Head** (☑02-6552 4097; www.nationalparks.nsw.gov.au/camping-and-accommodation; adult/child $12/6), Kylie's Hut (p164) and **Crowdy Gap** (adult/child $12/6).

Sea Acres Rainforest Centre   NATIONAL PARK

(☑02-6582 3355; www.nationalparks.nsw.gov.au/sea-acres-national-park; 159 Pacific Dr; boardwalk adult/child $9/5; ⊙9am-4.30pm) The 72-hectare pocket of Sea Acres National Park protects the state's largest and most diverse stand of coastal rainforest. At the Rainforest Centre you can take a self-guided tour on the wheelchair-accessible 1.3km-long elevated boardwalk through the forest, keeping an eye out for water dragons, brush turkeys, diamond pythons and birdlife, or join a fascinating free one-hour guided tour run by knowledgeable volunteers. The centre also has audiovisual displays about the local Birpai people ($2 entry), and a great cafe (p165).

Port Macquarie Historical Museum   MUSEUM

(☑02-6583 1108; https://portmuseum.org.au; 22 Clarence St; adult/child $7/3; ⊙9.30am-4.30pm Mon-Sat) An 1830s house has been transformed into this surprisingly interesting and detailed museum. Aboriginal and convict history are given due regard before moving on to everything from archaeological artefacts to a 'street of shops' and a display of beautiful old clothes in the costume gallery.

🏃 Activities

Surfing is particularly good at **Town**, **Flynn's** and **Lighthouse** beaches – all patrolled in summer. The rainforest runs to the sand at **Shelly** and **Miners** beaches, the latter of which is an unofficial nudist beach.

Whale season is from approximately May to November; there are numerous vantage points around town, or you can get a closer look on a **whale-watching cruise** (☑02-6583 8811; www.portjet.com.au; 1 Short St).

★ Port Macquarie Coastal Walk   WALKING

This wonderful coastal walk begins at Westport Park near the Town Green foreshore and winds for about 9km along the coast to Tracking Point Lighthouse in Sea Acres National Park. There are plenty of opportunities for swimming (it takes in eight beaches) and between May and November you can often view the whale migration. The walk can be divided into shorter 2km to 3km sections.

Soul Surfing   SURFING

(☑02-6582 0114; www.soulsurfing.com.au; 2hr class $50, 1-day workshop $245) A family-run school that is particularly good for nervous beginners. Also runs school-holiday intensives, as well as day-long women's workshops that include yoga, relaxation and food along with the surf lessons.

Port Macquarie Surf School   SURFING

(☑02-6584 7733; www.portmacquariesurfschool.com.au; 46 Pacific Dr; 2hr lessons $45) Offers a wide range of lessons for all ability levels and has a super-flexible daily class.

Port Macquarie

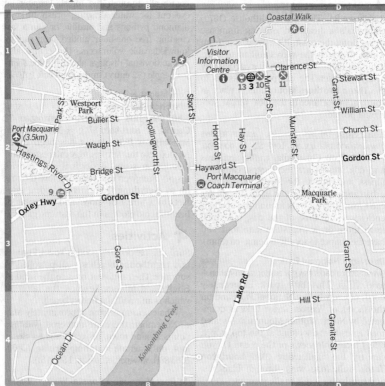

Port Macquarie

⊚ Top Sights
1 Flynn's Beach............................F4

◎ Sights
2 Koala Hospital............................E4
3 Port Macquarie Historical Museum......C1
4 Town Beach............................E1

✈ Activities, Courses & Tours
5 Port Cruise Adventures...................B1
6 Port Macquarie Coastal Walk..............D1
7 Port Macquarie Surf School.................F4

🛏 Sleeping
8 Flynns on Surf..........................F4
9 Port Macquarie Backpackers...............A2

✖ Eating
10 Bill's Fishhouse...........................C1
11 Burger Rebellion...........................C1
12 Stunned Mullet............................E2

🍷 Drinking & Nightlife
13 Botanic Wine Garden.........................C1

🛏 Sleeping

★**Kylie's Hut Campground**   CAMPGROUND $
(www.nationalparks.nsw.gov.au/camping-and-acc
ommodation; Crowdy Bay National Park; adult/child
$12/6) There are no marked sites or running
water at this walk-in campground, but it's a
delightful (and shady) place to spend a few
days under canvas. At its centre is a timber

slab hut built for Australian author Kylie
Tennant as a writers' retreat during WWII.
You're welcome to use the hut for writing
too, although it's not for overnighting.

Port Macquarie Backpackers   HOSTEL $
(☑ 02-6583 1791; www.portmacquariebackpackers.
com.au; 2 Hastings River Dr; dm/s/d from $36/
72/82; @ 🖸 ⊠) This heritage-listed house has

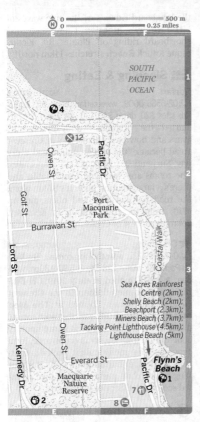

SOUTH
PACIFIC
OCEAN

Owen St

Pacific Dr

Golf St

Port
Macquarie
Park

Burrawan St

Lord St

Coastal Walk

Sea Acres Rainforest
Centre (2km);
Shelly Beach (2km);
Beachport (2.3km);
Miners Beach (3.7km);
Tacking Point Lighthouse (4.5km);
Lighthouse Beach (5km)

Owen St

Kennedy Dr

Everard St

Flynn's
Beach

Macquarie
Nature
Reserve

Pacific Dr

pressed-tin walls and a leafy backyard with a small pool. Traffic can be noisy, but the freebies (including bikes and bodyboards) and a relaxed attitude more than compensate.

Flynns on Surf
VILLA **$$**
(☑ 02-6584 2244; www.flynns.com.au; 25 Surf St; 1-/2-/3-bedroom villas $180/240/280; P✳︎⊛◱) These smart one-, two- and three-bedroom villas are set on their own private estate. Each has a gorgeous bush outlook and is fully self-contained, with extra comforts such as Nespresso machines and iPod docks.

Beachport
B&B **$$**
(☑ 0423 072 669; www.beachportbnb.com.au; 155 Pacific Dr; d $80-200; ✳︎⊛) At this excellent B&B the two downstairs rooms open onto private terraces, while the upstairs unit is more spacious. A basic do-it-yourself breakfast is provided, and Rainforest Cafe is across the road. Prices include afternoon tea on arrival, when booked directly with the B&B.

✖️ Eating

Burger Rebellion
BURGERS **$**
(☑ 02-6584 1403; www.theburgerrebellion.com.au; 14/6 Clarence St; burgers $12-16; ⊙ 11.30am-3pm & 5-9pm) A smart space with wooden communal counters, booths and street-side tables, it delivers tasty gourmet burgers, craft beer and friendly service. Vegetarians are not overlooked here – any burger can be substituted by a mushroom, a veggie pattie or halloumi – and you can ditch the bun and replace it with a burger bowl. Gluten-free options too.

Rainforest Cafe
CAFE **$$**
(☑ 02-6582 4444; www.rainforestcafe.com.au; Sea Acres Rainforest Centre, 159 Pacific Dr; mains $16-28; ⊙ 9am-4pm) You're surrounded by lush foliage at this delightful spot, whether you choose a terrace seat or inside the atrium-style cafe. The menu doesn't offer many surprises, mainly just classics done well, such as French toast, fish and chips, Caesar salad and healthy sandwiches. The homemade cakes and desserts are a highlight.

★ Stunned Mullet
INTERNATIONAL **$$$**
(☑ 02-6584 7757; www.thestunnedmullet.com.au; 24 William St; mains $35-49; ⊙ noon-2.30pm & 6-10pm) This fresh, seaside spot is one serious dining destination. The inspired contemporary menu features dishes like award-winning Tajima Wagyu beef, alongside exotic listings such as Patagonian toothfish. Note, all fish is wild caught. The extensive international wine list befits Port's best restaurant and there's a small but super-impressive wine-by-the-glass and half-bottle selection.

★ Bill's Fishhouse
AUSTRALIAN **$$$**
(☑ 02-6584 7228; www.billsfishhouse.com.au; 2/18-20 Clarence St; mains $34-36; ⊙ 5.30pm-late, closed Sun) A super-light and pretty space to escape the heat and eat the freshest of seafood. The menu changes regularly and might include local snapper fillet in a shiitake broth or blue swimmer crab risotto. It's augmented daily with the chef's pick from the fish market. The wine list is similarly tight. Bookings are advised for dinner.

🍷 Drinking & Nightlife

★ Botanic Wine Garden
WINE BAR
(☑ 02-6584 3685; www.botanicwinegarden.com. au; Shop 3, 26 Clarence St; ⊙ 4-10pm Tue-Thu & Sun, to 11pm Fri & Sat) Sit under the fairy lights debating whether the food or the wine is better here at Botanic. Short answer: too close to call. The al fresco setting invites

relaxed balmy evenings pairing cheese and cured meat platters, or mains of 16-hour pork belly and fish of the day, with a bottle of wine from the impressive list highlighting Australian small producers.

❶ Information

Visitor Information Centre (☏02-6581 8000; www.portmacquarieinfo.com.au; Glasshouse, cnr Hay & Clarence Sts; ☉9am-5.30pm Mon-Fri, to 4pm Sat & Sun) Helpful staff with plenty of brochures; inside the Glasshouse building.

❶ Getting There & Away

AIR

Port Macquarie Airport (☏02-6581 8111; www.portmacquarieairport.com.au; Oliver Dr) is 5km west from the town centre; it's served by regular local buses and a taxi will cost around $25. Regular flights run to/from Sydney with **QantasLink** (☏13 13 13; www.qantas.com. au), and Sydney and Brisbane with **Virgin** (☏13 67 89; www.virginaustralia.com).

BUS

Regional buses depart from **Port Macquarie Coach Terminal** (Gordon St).

Busways (☏02-6583 2499; www.busways. com.au) Runs local bus services from outside the Glasshouse to Port Macquarie Airport ($3.50, 30 minutes) and Kempsey ($9.80, one hour).

Greyhound (☏1300 473 946; www.greyhound. com.au) Buses head to/from Sydney (from $58, six hours, twice daily), Newcastle (from $61, 3¾ hours, twice daily), Coffs Harbour (from $40, 2½ hours, three daily), Byron Bay (from $84, 6½ hours, three daily), Surfers Paradise (from $116, 8½ hours, three daily) and Brisbane (from $128, 9½ hours, three daily).

Premier (☏13 34 10; www.premierms.com.au) Daily coaches to/from Sydney ($62, 6½ hours), Newcastle ($48, 3¾ hours), Coffs Harbour ($48, 2¼ hours), Byron Bay ($68, 7½ hours), Surfers Paradise ($69, 8½ hours) and Brisbane ($69, 11 hours).

TRAIN

The closest train station is at Wauchope, 18km west of Port Macquarie. Buses connect with arriving trains.

Crescent Head

POP 917

This beachside palm-tree-filled hideaway has a quiet relaxed coastal village feel and one of the best right-hand surf breaks in the country. Many come simply to watch the longboard riders surf the epic waves of **Little Nobby's Junction**. There's also good shortboard riding off Plomer Rd. Picturesque **Killick Beach** stretches 14km north.

🛏 Sleeping & Eating

Surfari HOSTEL, MOTEL $
(☏02-6566 0009; www.surfaris.com; 353 Loftus Rd; sites $20, dm/d $40/130; @🛜🏊) Surfari started the original Sydney–Byron surf tours and now base themselves in Crescent Head because 'the surf is guaranteed every day'. Surf-and-stay packages are a speciality. The rooms are clean and comfortable, and there's a large inviting pool. It's 3.5km along the road to Gladstone and offers pick-up ($10) from the train station in Kempsey, 25km northwest of Crescent Head.

★CH Dining AUSTRALIAN $$$
(☏0437 959 227; www.chdining.com.au; The Med, 35 Pacific St; mains $28-34; ☉5.30-9.30pm Wed-Sun; P🍽🛜) Opened in early 2019, CH Dining is a welcome addition to the Crescent Head dining scene. Located at **The Med motel** (☏0409 968 076; www.themedch.com.au; d from $195; 🏊), the space is contemporary cool and the philosophy is on organic, local produce. The menu might include char-grilled saltwater barramundi, Coffs Harbour king prawn chilli pasta or free-range grain-fed scotch fillet. Service is first-rate.

❶ Getting There & Away

Busways (☏02-6562 4724; www.busways. com.au) runs between Crescent Head and Kempsey ($5, 30 minutes), with three services per day on weekdays, one on Saturdays and no services on Sundays.

Hat Head National Park

Covering almost the entire coast from Crescent Head to South West Rocks, this 74-sq-km national park (vehicle entry $8) protects scrubland, swamps and some amazing beaches, backed by one of the largest dune systems in NSW.

The isolated beachside village of **Hat Head** (population 326) sits at its centre. At the far end of town, behind the holiday park, a picturesque wooden footbridge crosses the Korogoro Creek estuary. The water is so clear you can see fish darting around.

The best views can be had from **Smoky Cape Lighthouse** (www.nationalparks.nsw. gov.au/things-to-do/historic-buildings-places/

smoky-cape-lighthouse; Lighthouse Rd), at the northern end of the park. During the annual whale migration (May to September) it's a prime place from which to spot them.

🛏 Sleeping

NPWS campgrounds CAMPGROUND $
(www.nationalparks.nsw.gov.au/hat-head-national-park; sites per adult/child $6/3.50) Hungry Gate, 5km south of Hat Head, offers a beautifully back-to-basics holiday among native figs and paperbarks. The campground operates on a first-in basis; a ranger will come around and collect fees. There are non-flush toilets, but bring your own drinking water and gas cooker/BBQ. Kangaroos provide entertainment, but be sure to keep your food secure from them. The beach is a 20-minute walk.

★ Smoky Cape Lighthouse B&B B&B, COTTAGE $$$
(☑ 02-6566 6301; www.smokycapelighthouse.com; Lighthouse Rd; s/d from $170/220, 3-bedroom cottages per 2 nights $520-620; P) Romantic evenings can be spent gazing out to sea while the wind whips around the historic lighthouse-keeper's residence and kangaroos come out to graze high up on the headland. Views are ridiculously beautiful; rooms are traditional. Rates jump on weekends.

❶ Getting There & Away

There is no public transport to Hat Head, but you can arrange transfers from Port Macquarie or Kempsey with **Busy Bus Tours** (☑ 02-6559 9864; www.busybustours.com.au).

South West Rocks
POP 5009

One of many pretty seaside towns on this stretch of coast, South West Rocks has great beaches and enough interesting diversions for at least a night.

The lovely curve of **Trial Bay**, stretching east from the township, takes its name from the *Trial*, a boat that sank here during a storm in 1816 after being stolen by convicts fleeing Sydney. The eastern half of the bay is now protected by **Arakoon National Park**, centred on a headland that's popular with kangaroos, kookaburras and campers. On its eastern flank, **Little Bay Beach** is a small grin of sand sheltered from the surf by a rocky barricade. It's both a great place for a swim and also the starting point for some lovely walks.

◎ Sights

Trial Bay Gaol MUSEUM
(☑ 02-6566 6168; www.nationalparks.nsw.gov.au/things-to-do; Cardwell St; adult/child $11/8; ⊙ 9am-4.30pm) Occupying Trial Bay's eastern headland, this sandstone prison was built between 1877 and 1886 to house convicts brought in to build a breakwater. When nature intervened and the breakwater washed away, the imposing structure fell into disuse, aside from a brief, rather tragic, interlude in WWI when men of German and Austrian heritage were interned. Today it contains a museum devoted to its unusual history; even if you don't visit within, it's worth a detour for the views and the resident roos.

It's a pleasant 4km dawdle along the beach from South West Rocks.

🛏 Sleeping & Eating

Trial Bay Gaol Campground CAMPGROUND $
(☑ 02-6566 6168; www.nationalparks.nsw.gov.au/arakoon-national-park; Cardwell St, Arakon National Park; sites per 2 people $31-61.50) Behind the Trial Bay Gaol, this stunning NPWS campground affords generous beach views from most campsites and hosts ever-present kangaroos. Amenities include drinking water, a coin-operated laundry, flush toilets, hot showers, a camp kitchen and gas BBQs. There's a **cafe** (☑ 02-6566 7100; www.trialbaykiosk.com.au; Cardwell St, Arakon National Park; mains breakfast $10-22, lunch $20-35, dinner $26-35; ⊙ 8am-2pm Tue-Sun & 5.30-8.30pm Fri & Sat) nearby too.

Heritage Guesthouse B&B $$
(☑ 02-6566 6625; www.heritageguesthouse.com.au; 21-23 Livingstone St; d $125-175; ❈ 🛜) This renovated 1880s house has lovely, old-fashioned rooms, some with spa baths. Choose from the simpler downstairs rooms or the more lavish upstairs versions, with ocean views and air-conditioning. Rates include continental breakfast.

★ Malt & Honey CAFE $
(☑ 02-6566 5200; 5-7 Livingstone St; mains $10-22; ⊙ 7.30am-4pm Wed-Sun) An urban sensibility combines with beach-town charm at this busy cafe. Pick up an early-morning latte or grab a seat for crumpets with macadamia crumble, house-made muesli or French toast with maple-glazed bacon and banana. Big salads and other healthy but satisfying options appear on the lunch menu. The cakes are the bomb: moist and moreish.

ℹ️ Information

Visitor Information Centre (www.macleay valleycoast.com.au; 1 Ocean Ave; ⊙9am-4pm)

ℹ️ Getting There & Away

Busways (☑02-6562 4724; www.busways. com.au) Runs to/from Kempsey ($7.40, 50 minutes). Three services daily Monday to Friday, two services Saturdays and no services on Sundays.

Bellingen

POP 3074

Buried in deep foliage on a hillside above the Bellinger River, this gorgeous town dances to the beat of its own bongo drum. 'Bello' is flush with organic produce, and the creative community has an urban sensibility. Located inland between the spectacular rainforest of **Dorrigo National Park** and a spoiled-for-choice selection of beaches, it is easily accessible from Coffs Harbour and a definite jewel on the East Coast route. Bellingen is also a natural starting point for a number of scenic drives, including the spectacular Waterfall Way.

⊙ Sights

Bellingen Island   WILDLIFE RESERVE
(www.bellingen.com/flyingfoxes) This little semi-attached island on the Bellinger River (it's only completely cut off when the river is in flood) is home to a huge colony of grey-headed flying foxes. For a closer look, take the ramp down from the Old Caravan Park on Dowle St at the northern end. The best months to visit are October to January, when the babies are being born and nursed. Wear long trousers and use insect repellent to ward off stinging nettles, leeches, ticks and mosquitoes.

At dusk the flying foxes fly out in their thousands to feed, though this impressive sight is best viewed from the bridge in the centre of town.

✨ Festivals & Events

Bellingen Readers & Writers Festival   LITERATURE
(www.bellingenwritersfestival.com.au; ⊙Jun) Established and emerging writers appear at talks, panels, readings, poetry slams and workshops over the Queen's Birthday long weekend.

Bello Winter Music   MUSIC
(www.bellowintermusic.com; ⊙mid-Jul) A nicely chilled music festival with local and international folk, roots, blues, world, hip-hop and pop acts, along with great food.

🛏️ Sleeping

Much of the region's accommodation is in small B&Bs and cottages scattered across the hillsides, and riverside cabins and cottages

---

WORTH A TRIP

WATERFALL WAY

Considered NSW's most scenic drive, the 200km Waterfall Way links a number of beautiful national parks between Bellingen and Armidale, taking you through pristine subtropical rainforest, Edenic valleys and, naturally, spectacular waterfalls. As you emerge into the tablelands, there is green countryside and wide plains.

➡ **Guy Fawkes River National Park** (www.nationalparks.nsw.gov.au/guy-fawkes-river-national-park) is a rugged wilderness popular with experienced bushwalkers and campers. The dramatic **Ebor Falls** and the large climbable rock called **Lucifer's Thumb** are particular highlights. From Bellingen to Dorrigo it's a 30-minute drive, then another 40 minutes from Dorrigo to access Ebor Falls, which lies at the southern end of the park. To access Lucifer's Thumb further north, allow around 2½ hours from Bellingen.

➡ Make your way into the **Cathedral Rock National Park** (www.nationalparks.nsw.gov.au/cathedral-rock-national-park) or take a detour down Point Lookout Rd to **New England National Park** (www.nationalparks.nsw.gov.au/new-england-national-park), a section of the Gondwana Rainforests World Heritage Area.

➡ Further west **Oxley Wild Rivers National Park** (www.nationalparks.nsw.gov.au/oxley-wild-rivers-national-park) is home to the towering plunge waterfall beauty of Wollomombi Falls. These are about 1½ hours west of Bellingen.

just outside of Bellingen. In town, there is a choice of the YHA, pub accommodation and a couple of guesthouses.

Bellingen YHA
HOSTEL **$**

(Belfry Guesthouse; ☑02-6655 1116; www.yha. com.au; 2 Short St; dm $35, r with/without bathroom from $150/90; @ 🛜) A tranquil, homey atmosphere pervades this lovely renovated weatherboard house, with impressive hinterland views from the swinging hammocks hanging on the broad verandah. Pick-ups from the bus stop and train station in Urunga are sometimes possible if you call ahead ($20).

Bellingen Riverside Cottages
CABIN **$$**

(☑0413 317 635; www.bellingenriversidecottages. com.au; 224 North Bank Rd; cottages from $160; P ✳ 🛜 📶) These four polished cabins have cosy interiors with country furnishings and big windows. Timber balconies overlook the river, which you can tackle on a complimentary kayak. Friendly hosts, Margaret and John, go out of their way to make your stay comfortable and your first night includes a sizeable DIY breakfast hamper.

★Promised Land Retreat
CABIN **$$$**

(☑02-6655 9578; www.promisedlandretreat.com. au; 934 Promised Land Rd, Gleniffer; cabins $300-350; P ✳ 🛜) A 10-minute drive from town over the evocatively named Never Never River, these three stylish and private cottages feature spa baths and open-plan living areas attached to decks with dramatic views to the Dorrigo escarpment. Two of the chalets are suitable for families. Facilities include a tennis court, a games room and complimentary use of mountain bikes.

✕ Eating & Drinking

Eating in Bellingen is a pleasure: it has a large and ever-growing number of cafes and casual restaurants, most of which make use of local and organic produce.

★Hearthfire Bakery
BAKERY **$**

(☑02-6655 0767; www.hearthfire.com.au; 73 Hyde St; mains from $10; ⊘7am-5pm Mon-Fri, to 2pm Sat & Sun) Follow the smell of hot-from-the-woodfire organic sourdough and you'll find this outstanding country bakery and cafe. Try the famous macadamia fruit loaf or settle in with a coffee and a beautiful savoury pie. There is a full breakfast menu daily, and lunch dishes – including meze plates, soups and salads – are served during the week.

Bellingen Gelato Bar
ICE CREAM **$**

(www.bellingengelato.com.au; 101 Hyde St; scoop from $5; ⊘10am-6pm daily Oct-Apr, closed Mon & Tue May-Sep) Robert Sebes, the former owner of a legendary inner-Sydney cafe, has been scooping out stellar gelato in Bellingen since 2006. It's all made from scratch, with minimal added sugar. Expect traditional Italian flavours, such as zabaglione and pistachio, along with Sebes' own inventive creations – perhaps Persian date or burnt orange marmalade.

★Qudo Cafe & Sake
JAPANESE **$$**

(☑02-6655 9757; 121 Hyde St; mains $19-30; ⊘11.30am-2.30pm & 6-8.30pm Wed-Sat) Japanese chefs work their magic in this imposing and beautifully rustic two-storey former Freemason building. It's run by the same owners as Federal's Doma Cafe (p189), and the menu offers delicious delights such as sushi and sashimi, miso-glazed lamb cooked on a grill over bincho charcoal, tempura halloumi and kingfish carpaccio with wasabi oil.

★Popla
AUSTRALIAN **$$$**

(☑02-6655 9000; www.poplabellingen.com; 2 Oak St; dishes $18-35; ⊘6pm-late Wed-Sat, noon-3pm Sun) 🍴 Settle in on the candlelit verandah or cosy into a table inside the smart contemporary fit-out of this humble weatherboard house, where sophisticated open-hearted cooking is the name of the game. The menu focuses on seasonal local produce, designed as share-style plates, complemented by an all-Australian wine list, cocktails and mocktails, like the refreshing nogin and tonic. Book ahead.

★Bellingen Brewery & Co
MICROBREWERY

(☑02-6655 2210; www.bellingenbrewery.com.au; 3/5 Church St; ⊘5-11pm Wed-Fri, from noon Sat & Sun) Tucked away in a car park with a plant-strewn facade, the Bellingen Brewery packs punters in for its range of brews – from English-style bitters to a popular summer ale – along with organic wine, excellent wood-fired pizzas ($18) and a soundtrack of live music.

🔒 Shopping

While no one in these parts thinks of themselves as consumerist in the slightest, Bellingen has some decent shopping opportunities, with an emphasis on artisanal products and secondhand and boho boutiques. Markets here are also great: the **community market** (www.bellingenmarkets.com.au; Bellingen

Park, Church St; ⊙ 8am-2pm 3rd Sat of month) has more than 260 stalls and there's also a **growers' market** (www.bellingengrowersmarket.com; Bellingen Showgrounds, cnr Hammond & Black Sts; ⊙ 8am-1pm 2nd & 4th Sat of month).

ℹ Information

Waterfall Way Information Centre
(☎ 02-6655 1522; www.visitnsw.com/visitor-information-centres/waterfall-way-visitor-centre-bellingen; 29-31 Hyde St; ⊙ 9am-4.30pm Mon-Sat, 9.30am- 2.30pm Sun) Stocks brochures on scenic drives, walks and an arts trail.

ℹ Getting There & Away

Bellingen is a short drive inland from the coast. Local buses service the town from Coffs Harbour, via Sawtell.

Busways (☎ 02-6655 7410; www.busways. com.au) Bus 361 runs to/from Coffs Harbour on weekdays ($7.40, 1¼ hours).

New England Coaches (☎ 02-6732 1051; www. newenglandcoaches.com.au) Three coaches per week to Urunga ($40) and Coffs Harbour ($35).

Coffs Harbour

POP 72,944

Despite its inland city centre, Coffs has a string of fabulous beaches. Equally popular with families and backpackers, the town offers plenty of water-based activities, action sports and wildlife encounters, not to mention the kitsch yellow beacon that is the Big Banana. It also makes an easy base for exploring the quaint towns and beautiful drives of the hinterland. Coffs is located on Gumbaynggirr country and there are a few important sites where you can learn about the cultures and traditions of the Gumbaynggirr people.

◎ Sights

Park Beach is a long, lovely stretch of sand backed by dense shrubbery and sand dunes, which conceal the buildings beyond. **Jetty Beach** is somewhat more sheltered and protected by a breakwater, creating calm swimming conditions. **Diggers Beach**, reached by turning off the highway near the Big Banana, is popular with surfers, with swells averaging 1m to 1.5m. Naturists let it all hang out at **Little Diggers Beach**, just inside the northern headland.

★ **Muttonbird Island**   ISLAND
(☎ 1300 072 757; www.nationalparks.nsw.gov. au/muttonbird-island-nature-reserve; tour adult/child/family $20/10/50) The Gumbaynggirr people knew this island as Giidany Miirlarl (Place of the Moon). It was joined to Coffs Harbour by the northern breakwater in 1935. The walk to the top (steep at the end) provides sweeping vistas. From late August to early April it's occupied by thousands of wedge-tailed shearwaters (muttonbirds). Muttonbirds by Moonlight tours – led by respected Gumbaynggirr Elder Uncle Mark Flanders – are a great way to see them and to learn about the Aboriginal significance of the island.

The island is also a great spot to see the humpback whale migration between May and November.

Solitary Islands Aquarium   AQUARIUM
(www.solitaryislandsaquarium.com; Bay Dr, Charlesworth Bay; adult/child $12/8; ⊙ 10am-4pm Sat & Sun, daily in school holidays) On weekends this small aquarium belonging to Southern Cross University's Marine Science Centre is open to the public. Touch tanks and enthusiastic, well-qualified guides provide close encounters with an octopus and the fish and coral that inhabit the waters of the Solitary Islands Marine Park.

Big Banana   AMUSEMENT PARK
(☎ 02-6652 4355; www.bigbanana.com; 351 Pacific Hwy; ⊙ 9am-5pm) FREE Built in 1964, the Big Banana started the craze for 'Big Things' in Australia. Admission is free, with charges for associated attractions, such as ice skating, toboggan rides, mini-golf, the waterpark, plantation tours and the irresistibly named 'World of Bananas Experience'. Beyond the kitsch appeal there's really little to see, but kids might get a kick out of it.

🏃 Activities & Tours

Coffs offers an abundance of action-packed adventure, both in and out of the water. The nearby Solitary Islands Marine Park provides an excellent environment for diving (p172), and a number of surf schools offer lessons for all levels.

East Coast Surf School   SURFING
(☎ 0429 444 028; www.eastcoastsurfschool. com.au; Diggers Beach; 2hr lessons from $55) A particularly female-friendly outfit run by former pro surfer Helene Enevoldson.

Coffs Harbour

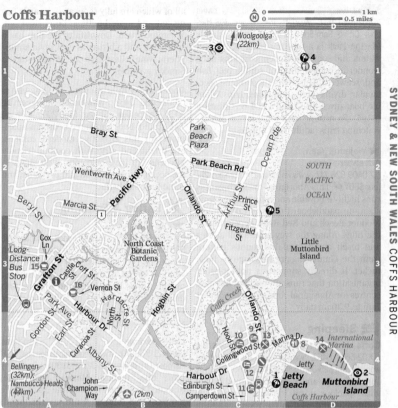

N 0 ——————————— 1 km
0 ——————————— 0.5 miles

Coffs Harbour

◎ Top Sights
1 Jetty Beach C4
2 Muttonbird Island D4

◎ Sights
3 Big Banana C1
4 Diggers Beach D1
5 Park Beach C2

✈ Activities, Courses & Tours
6 East Coast Surf School D1
7 Jetty Dive C4
8 Lee Winkler's Surf School D4

⌂ Sleeping
9 Coffs Harbour YHA C4
10 Coffs Jetty BnB C4
11 Observatory Apartments C4
12 Pier Hotel C4

✖ Eating
13 Fiasco C4
14 Latitude 30 .... D4
Lime Mexican .... (see 12)
Old John's .... (see 12)

◗ Drinking & Nightlife
15 Dark Arts Brew & Bar A3
16 Palate & Ply A3

Lee Winkler's Surf School SURFING
(☎0438 535 560; http://surfschoolcoffsharbour.
com.au; Coffs Harbour Yacht Club, 30 Marina Dr;
2hr lessons from $50) One of the oldest surf
schools in Coffs. Group and private lessons
available.

Valery Trails HORSE RIDING
(☎02-6653 4301; www.valerytrails.com.au; 758
Valery Rd, Valery; 2hr rides adult/child $80/70)
A stable of horses and plenty of acreage to
explore; it's 15km northeast of town. Rides
daily at 10am and 2pm.

Jetty Dive
DIVING

(☑02-6651 1611; www.jettydive.com.au; 398 Harbour Dr; ⊘8am-5pm) The Solitary Islands Marine Park is a meeting place of tropical waters and southern currents, making for a wonderful combination of corals, reef fish and seaweed. This dive shop offers spectacular diving and snorkelling trips (double boat dives $195) and PADI certification ($495). From June to October it runs whale-watching trips (adult/child $65/55).

★Wajaana Yaam Adventure Tours
WATER SPORTS

(☑0409 926 747; www.wajaanayaam.com.au; 2hr tour $80) ✐ This Aboriginal-owned business runs highly enjoyable and informative scenic stand-up paddleboard tours of Coffs Creek, Moonee Beach and Red Rock, depending on the tides. Along the way guides tell stories and teach about local Indigenous culture from the Gumbaynggirr language to bush tucker. It directly supports a not-for-profit organisation that runs after-school learning centres for Aboriginal children. Tours depart 7am to 9.30am daily.

🛏 Sleeping

Coffs Harbour YHA
HOSTEL $

(☑02-6652 6462; www.yha.com.au; 51 Collingwood St; dm $25-35, d $80-90, f $85-160; @ ⚛) A super-friendly and nicely positioned hostel with spacious dorms. Private rooms have bathrooms and wi-fi in the rooms, and the TV lounge (with Netflix) and kitchen are clean and colourful. You can use the free surfboards and hire bikes ($10 per day). A favourite with both families and young travellers on the fruit-picking circuit.

★Coffs Jetty BnB
B&B $$

(☑02-6651 4587; www.coffsjetty.com.au; 41a Collingwood St; d $135-170; ⚛🕸) A cut above your average B&B, this homey town house has private, tastefully decorated, spacious rooms with walk-in wardrobes and terrific bathrooms. Enjoy your continental breakfast, with fresh fruits, on the balcony, then make the easy stroll to the beach and jetty restaurants. One of the suites has a kitchenette, while all have microwaves and fridges.

Pier Hotel
PUB $$

(☑02-6652 2110; www.pierhotelcoffs.com.au; 356 Harbour Dr; s without bathroom from $89, d from $149, d without bathroom from $109; 🅿🕸) A mix of rooms with shared and private bathroom occupies the lovely, airy 1st floor of this pub, all of which are fully renovated, smartly furnished and more boutique hotel than pub accommodation. Downstairs the pub has a sports bar and a bistro, as well as an atmospheric wine cellar that's open Wednesday to Sunday evenings.

Observatory Apartments
APARTMENT $$

(☑02-6650 0462; www.theobservatory.com.au; 30-36 Camperdown St; apt $160-200; ⚛🕸⚛) The studio, two- and three-bedroom apartments in this attractive modern complex are bright and airy, with cook-up-friendly kitchens. All have balconies, with views to the ocean across the road and parkland, and some have spa baths.

🍴 Eating & Drinking

★Old John's
CAFE $

(☑02-6699 2909; www.facebook.com/oldjohns; 360 Harbour Dr; mains $10-17.50; ⊘7am-3.30pm) Join Coffs' cool kids propped up at the open window or on a street-side table sipping on the town's best coffee and digging into delights from a menu of chia 'pud', eggy breakfasts, and superfood bowls or lunch salads and toasted sandwiches.

Lime Mexican
MEXICAN $$

(☑0421 573 570; www.limemexican.com.au; 366 Harbour Dr; dishes $13-32; ⊘11.30am-9pm; 🕸) Lime does modern Mexican tapas-style, designed to share. The taco line-up includes tempura fish, braised lamb and halloumi, and there are share plates of pork belly on spicy rice, cheese-stuffed jalapeño peppers and smoky paprika corn. Choose between the dark, moody interior or grab a street-side table. Daily happy hour is 5pm to 6pm for $10 cocktails and $5 beers.

★Fiasco
ITALIAN $$$

(☑02-6651 2006; www.fiascorestaurant.com.au; 22 Orlando St; pizzas $21-28, mains $29-45; ⊘5-9pm Tue-Sat) Upmarket Italian fare is prepared in an open kitchen using produce from the best local suppliers and herbs from the restaurant's own garden. Expect authentic delights such as wood-grilled octopus, homemade gnocchi with beef and pork ragu, and well-done pizzas.

Latitude 30
SEAFOOD $$$

(☑02-6651 6888; www.latitude30.com.au; 1 Marina Dr; mains $27-42; ⊘11am-9pm) Views take in the charming working harbour to the jetty and Muttonbird Island, or across to the Pacific Ocean at this popular seafood spot. Gorge on seafood platters – available for one ($130) or two people ($240) – or tuck into mains such as seafood chowder, paella or beer-battered sustainable fish and chips. There are steaks and pasta dishes for non-seafood eaters too.

Palate & Ply COFFEE
(www.palateandply.com.au; 37 Vernon St; coffee from $3.30; ⊙6.30am-4pm Mon-Fri, to 2pm Sat) The aroma of coffee hits you as you enter this vast cafe with high ceilings and hessian sacks of coffee beans lying around. The barista on hand will deliver your brew however you take it, from V60 and Aeropress to siphon, espresso or nitro on tap, using beans roasted locally by Artisti. Also does great cafe fare.

Dark Arts Brew & Bar COFFEE, BAR
(www.facebook.com/darkartsbrewandbar; Cox Lane; ⊙6am-3pm Mon-Thu & Sun, to 9.30pm Fri & Sat) Inspired by Melbourne's laneway bars, Dark Arts is set in a nondescript CBD lane with a moody Goth interior and splashes of '80s-style graffiti on the walls. It operates as a cafe doing well-made coffee by day then transitions into an intimate cocktail bar come the weekend, with, of course, espresso martinis on the menu.

ⓘ Information

Visitor Information Centre (www.coffscoast. com.au; Coffs Central, 35-61 Harbour Dr; ⊙9am-5pm) There is no proper dedicated visitor information in Coffs Harbour anymore, but this hub in the Coffs Central shopping mall has some brochures.

ⓘ Getting There & Away

AIR

QantasLink (☑13 13 13; www.qantas.com.au), **Virgin** (☑13 67 89; www.virginaustralia.com) and **Tigerair** (☑1300 174 266; www.tigerair. com.au) all fly to **Coffs Harbour Airport** (☑02-6648 4767; www.coffsharbourairport. com.au; Airport Dr), 4km southwest of town. Qantas, Virgin and Tigerair fly to/from Sydney; Tigerair also flies to/from Melbourne. There are **Fly Corporate** (☑1300 851 269; https:// flycorporate.com.au) services to Brisbane.

BUS

Long-distance and regional buses operated by Greyhound, Premier and New England Coaches leave from the **bus stop** on the corner of McLean St and the Pacific Hwy.

Premier (☑13 34 10; www.premierms.com.au) Daily coaches to Sydney ($68, nine hours), Port Macquarie ($48, 2¼ hours), Nambucca Heads ($35, 40 minutes), Byron Bay ($52, five hours),

NORTH OF COFFS HARBOUR

Around 25km north of Coffs, Woolgoolga (locally known as Woopi) is famous for its surf-and-Sikh community. If you're driving by on the highway, you're sure to notice the impressive Guru Nanak Temple, a Sikh *gurdwara* (place of worship), and it's worth stopping by. In addition to a superb beach, Woopi has a twice-monthly Saturday **Bollywood Beach Bazaar** (☑02-6654 7673; www.facebook.com/bollywoodmarket; Woolgoolga Beach Reserve; ⊙8am-2pm, 1st & 4th Sat of month), and in September the town goes all out with the annual **Curryfest** (www.curryfest.com.au; ⊙Sep) celebration. About 10km south of town is surfing hotspot Emerald Beach, with a winning southern left-hand reef break, and the appropriately named Look at Me Now headland.

Yuraygir National Park (www.nationalparks.nsw.gov.au/yuraygir-national-park; vehicle entry $8) is fronted by a 65km stretch of varied coastline that's backed with littoral rainforest, eucalypts, pandanus and wetlands. It is an important habitat for many native species, including the endangered coastal emu. The **Yuraygir Coastal Walk**, a four-day 65km waymarked trail from Angourie to Red Rock, follows a series of tracks, trails, beaches and rock platforms, and passes through Brooms Head, Minnie Water and Wooli. It's best walked north to south with the sun at your back. Download maps of the park and the walk from www.nationalparks.nsw.gov.au/yuraygir-national-park.

At Corindi Beach, the Yarrawarra Aboriginal Cultural Centre (p160) is well worth a detour to learn about the local Gumbaynggirr people.

Wooli (population 414) occupies an isthmus within the park's southern half; a river estuary to one side and the ocean the other only adds to its isolated charm. In early October it hosts the **Australian National Goanna Pulling Championships** (www. goannapulling.com.au; Wooli; ⊙Oct), where (human) participants squat on all fours, attach leather harnesses to their heads and engage in a cranial tug of war.

Surfers Paradise ($61, six hours) and Brisbane ($61, seven hours).

Greyhound (📞1300 473 946; www.greyhound.com.au) Coaches to/from Sydney (from $87, nine hours, three daily), Port Macquarie (from $40, three hours, two daily), Nambucca Heads ($16, 1½ hours, one daily), Byron Bay (from $52, four hours, three daily), Surfers Paradise (from $83, 5½ hours, three daily) and Brisbane (from $78, seven hours, three daily).

New England Coaches (📞02-6732 1051; www.newenglandcoaches.com.au) This Tamworth service has two coaches per week to/from Dorrigo ($45, 1½ hours) and Bellingen ($35, 50 minutes).

TRAIN

NSW TrainLink (📞13 22 32; www.nswtrainlink.info) Trains head to/from Sydney ($95, nine hours), Kempsey ($18, 1¾ hours), Nambucca Heads ($7, 40 minutes) and Grafton ($16, 1¼ hours) daily, and one continues to Brisbane ($84, 5½ hours).

Sawtell

POP 3682

The mellow beach community of Sawtell is spiritually closer to glamorous Noosa further north than to its neighbour, Coffs Harbour, just 15 minutes' drive away, and it also makes a good quiet base to explore the inland towns of Dorrigo and Bellingen. Heritage-listed fig trees shade the main street, which is crammed with upmarket cafes, bars and restaurants, as well as a lovely local cinema. The town is also the home of the hugely popular Sawtell Chilli Festival.

🎊 Festivals & Events

Sawtell Chilli Festival FOOD & DRINK
(☉early Jul) The hottest food festival on the Coffs Coast draws thousands of visitors for spicy food, cooking demonstrations, street entertainment and dancing off the (mild) winter chill.

🛏 Sleeping & Eating

Sawtell Motor Inn MOTEL $$
(📞02-6658 9872; www.sawtellmotorinn.com.au; 57 Boronia St; d $160-200; 🅿❄🛜☎) Just off the main street and a five-minute walk to the beach, this quiet and clean motel has bright, spacious rooms decked out in cane furniture. Some rooms have balconies, kitchenettes and spa baths, plus there's a free guest laundry. Overall, it has a homier feel than most motels.

★**Hilltop Store** CAFE $$
(📞02-6658 5615; www.thehilltopstore.com.au; 114 First Ave; dishes $14-28; ☉6am-3pm Tue-Fri, from 7am Sat & Sun; 🛜) As the name suggests, this cute cafe is perched on a hill in a lovely old weatherboard building that was the general store back in the day. Prop yourself on a stool at an open window to sip on excellent coffee while you peruse the seasonal menu that goes above and beyond the usual cafe fare, and there's plenty you can take away too.

★**Treeo** CAFE $$
(📞0417 933 107; www.treeo.com.au; 18 First Ave; mains breakfast & lunch $15-22, dinner $29-34; ☉6.30am-4.30pm Mon, to late Tue-Sun; 🛜) Beneath one of First Ave's giant fig trees, this popular cafe turns out great coffee, delicious homemade cakes (raw and gluten-free options too) and excellent cafe fare. Corn fritters are a winner in the morning, while dining on slow-roasted lamb shoulder with a glass of wine is the perfect bookend to the day.

ℹ Getting There & Away

Sawtell is a 15-minute drive south of Coffs Harbour. **Forest Coach Lines** (📞02-9450 2277; https://forestcoachlines.com.au) runs between Coffs Harbour and Sawtell ($6.90).

BYRON BAY & THE FAR NORTH COAST

Where back-to-nature and surf-or-die lifestyles meet, this stretch of coast offers family-friendly destinations and some of the world's most stunning beaches. Towns such as Brunswick Heads and Yamba are being touted as the new Byron; though both can only be pretenders to the crown, they do have enormous appeal all of their own – some of that appeal is actually owing to the fact that they are not Byron but a more relaxed, traffic-free version.

Much of this coastline is situated on Bundjalung country, which stretches inland from Grafton to Tweed Heads and over the border into Queensland.

Yamba & Angourie

At the mouth of the Clarence River, the fishing town of Yamba is rapidly growing in popularity thanks to its gently bohemian lifestyle, splendid beaches, and excellent cafes and restaurants. Oft-heard descriptions such as 'Byron Bay 20 years ago' are not unfounded. Neighbour Angourie, 5km to the south, is a tiny, chilled-out place that has long been a draw for experienced surfers and was proudly one of Australia's first surf reserves.

◉ Sights & Activities

Angourie Blue Pools   SPRING
(The Crescent) These springwater-fed waterholes south of Spooky Beach are the remains of the quarry used for the breakwater. Daring folk climb the cliff faces and plunge to the depths. The saner can slip silently into the water, surrounded by bush, only metres from the surf.

Bundjalung National Park   NATIONAL PARK
(www.nationalparks.nsw.gov.au/visit-a-park/parks/bundjalung-national-park; vehicle entry $8) Stretching for 25km along the coast north of the Clarence River to South Evans Head, this national park is largely untouched. Most of it is best explored with a 4WD. However, the southern reaches can be easily reached from Yamba via the passenger-only **Clarence River Ferries** (☑ 0408 664 556; www.clarenceriverferries.com.au; return adult/child $8.30/4.20; ⊙11am-3pm) to Iluka (at least four daily). This section of the park includes **Iluka Nature Reserve**, a stand of rainforest facing Iluka Beach, part of the Gondwana Rainforests World Heritage Area.

On the other side of Iluka Bluff the literally named **Ten Mile Beach** unfurls.

Angourie Point   SURFING
Highly experienced surfers can tackle the world-famous right-hand break at Angourie Point.

Yamba Kayak   KAYAKING
(☑ 02-6646 0065; www.yambakayak.com; 2hr tour adult/child from $60/40) Explore the Clarence River on one of these highly recommended kayaking tours. The popular three-hour River Islands tour includes a morning tea stop (adult/child $75/50), or head out on the two-hour sunset oyster tour to the nearby oyster farm (adult/child $75/40). Kayak hire is also available.

Bike Shop Yamba   CYCLING
(☑ 02-6645 8879; www.facebook.com/YambaBikeHire; 34 Coldstream St, Yamba; bike hire per half-/full day $20/25; ⊙9.30am-4.30pm

Mon-Fri, to 12.30pm Sat) Great family-run shop that offers bike hire for adults and kids.

🛏 Sleeping

Pacific Hotel   PUB $
(www.pacifichotelyamba.com.au/accommodation; 18 Pilot St, Yamba; dm $30-40, d $130, without bathroom $80; ℗ 🛜) 'Motel-style' rooms in this lovely old pub have lots of charm. If you don't mind sharing a bathroom and you snare a corner cheapie, you've hit the view jackpot of a lighthouse out one window and the sea out the other. Rooms with bathroom have balconies as well as a fridge and a TV, and there's backpacker bunk rooms for the budget conscious.

Yamba YHA   HOSTEL $
(☑ 02-6646 3997; www.yha.com.au; 26 Coldstream St, Yamba; dm $32-36, d $95; @🛜) This sociable, family-run hostel has light-filled dorms, a popular bar and restaurant downstairs, and a barbecue area on the roof that doubles as a workout/yoga spot. Owner Shane runs three-hour guided tours of Yamba ($20), and there's surfboard hire, surf lessons, Friday night BBQs and poker nights.

Seascape Ocean Front Apartments   APARTMENT $$
(☑ 0429 664 311; www.seascapeunits.com.au; 4 Ocean St, Yamba; apt $175-200; ℗ 🛜) Four ocean-view apartments and a riverside cottage are all furnished in bright, contemporary nautical style. Apartment views are spectacular and each space has retained its '50s Australian coastal bones. Prices are cheaper for multiple-night stays.

🍴 Eating & Drinking

★**Beachwood Cafe**   TURKISH $$
(☑ 02-6646 9781; www.beachwoodcafe.com.au; 22 High St, Yamba; mains $12-26; ⊙7am-2pm closed Mon) Cookbook author Sevtap Yüce steps out of the pages to deliver her bold *Turkish Flavours* to the plate at this wonderful little cafe. Most of the tables are outside, where the grass verge has been commandeered for a kitchen garden. The seasonal menu might include treats such as organic mandarin juice and passion fruit polenta cake to braised octopus for lunch.

Sandbar   SEAFOOD $$
(☑ 02-6646 1425; www.sandbaryamba.com.au; 30 Clarence St, Yamba; dishes $20-35; ⊙7am-11.30am & 6-10pm Mon-Fri, 7am-1.30pm & 6-10pm Sat, 7am-11.30am Sun) Downstairs from the

Yamba Beach Motel (☑ 02-6646 9411; www.yambabeachmotel.com.au; 30 Clarence St, Yamba; r $149-199; P ✲ ☎ ☀ ✉), this casual eatery serves as a cafe in the morning and morphs into a popular seafood restaurant in the evening. Tapas-style plates are designed for sharing and feature the freshest of local seafood – yes, those famous sweet Yamba prawns are on the menu. Try for an early booking as some of the dishes sell out.

French Pan Tree   FRENCH $$$
(☑ 02-6646 2335; www.thefrenchpantree.com.au; 15 Clarence St, Yamba; 2-/3-course menu $40/50; ☺ 6-10pm, closed Tue) ✍ Dusky pink walls and candlelight set the scene at this atmospheric restaurant on the hill. Traditional French cuisine is tweaked with a modern approach by the Parisian chef, using the best of the Clarence Valley's local produce, including seafood straight from the trawlers. The short and regularly changing menu features beautifully presented dishes. Book ahead.

ℹ Information

There is no visitor centre (as yet), but Yamba YHA (p175) has the low-down on everything.

ℹ Getting There & Away

Yamba is 15km east of the Pacific Hwy; turn off at the Yamba Rd intersection just south of the Clarence River.

Busways (☑ 02-6645 8941; www.busways.com.au) There are four to eight buses from Yamba to Angourie ($3.50, 15 minutes), Maclean ($5, 25 minutes) and Grafton ($9.80, 1¼ hours) daily.

Greyhound (☑ 1300 473 946; www.greyhound.com.au) Has a daily coach to/from Sydney ($149, 11 hours), Coffs Harbour ($30, two hours), Byron Bay ($20, 2¼ hours), Surfers Paradise ($48, four hours) and Brisbane ($55, five hours).

NSW TrainLink (☑ 13 22 32; www.nswtrainlink.info) Has a daily coach to Maclean ($7, 25 minutes), Grafton ($12, one hour), Lennox Head ($17, 2½ hours), Ballina ($15, 2¼ hours) and Byron Bay ($17, 2¾ hours).

Ballina

POP 16,506

At the mouth of the Richmond River, Ballina is spoilt for white sandy beaches and crystal-clear waters, though overall it tends to lack a proper coastal charm, perhaps owing to its commercial centre. There are a few good eating options, a small but excellent regional art gallery, and a scattering of gracious historic buildings can still be found on its backstreets thanks to its late-19th-century history as a rich lumber town. Today Ballina is popular with family holidaymakers and retirees, and home to the region's airport.

◎ Sights & Tours

**Northern Rivers
Community Gallery**   GALLERY
(NRCG; ☑ 02-6681 6167; www.nrcgballina.com; 44 Cherry St; ☺ 10am-4pm Wed-Fri, 9.30am-2.30pm Sat & Sun) FREE An excellent regional gallery representing the strong creative community that is an essential part of this region. Housed in the historic former Ballina Municipal Council Chambers, built in 1927, it hosts a rota of shows that showcase local artists and craftspeople, and also includes edgy, contemporary works and interesting events. There's a lovely cafe (☑ 02-6681 3888; www.ballinagallerycafe.com.au; 46 Cherry St; mains breakfast $11-20, lunch $19-30; ☺ 7.30am-3pm Wed-Sun) too.

Big Prawn   LANDMARK
(Ballina Bunnings, 507 River St) Ballina's big prawn was nearly thrown on the BBQ in 2009, but no one had the stomach to dispatch it. After a 5000-signature pro-prawn petition and a $400,000 restoration in 2013, the 9m, 35-tonne, 30-year-old crustacean is looking as fetching as ever.

Aboriginal Cultural Concepts   CULTURAL
(☑ 0405 654 280; www.aboriginalculturalconcepts.com; half-/full-day tours per person $95/190; ☺ Wed-Sat) Gain an Indigenous Australian perspective on the local area with heritage tours exploring mythological sites and sampling bush tucker along the Bundjalung coast. You can also do a self-drive tour meeting up with your guide at middens, former campgrounds, contact sites, fertility sites, fish traps and hunting areas along the way.

🛏 Sleeping

Ballina Travellers Lodge   MOTEL $
(☑ 02-6686 6737; www.ballinatravellerslodge.com.au; 36-38 Tamar St; d $119-129, without bathroom $79; ✲ ☎ ✉) The motel rooms here are surprisingly plush, with feature walls, pretty bedside lamps and nice linen. Budget rooms (that is, the ones that share a bathroom) are a rung down in the decor stakes but represent good value. There's also a guest laundry and a very handy kitchen with cooking facilities.

Ballina Palms Boutique Motel
MOTEL $$

(☑02-6686 4477; www.ballinapalms.info; cnr Bentinck & Owen Sts; d from $135, 2-bed studio from $275; P✳🖤🛏️) With its lush garden setting and considered decor, this little place is a great-value motel. The rooms aren't overly large, but they all have kitchenettes, floorboards, marble tops in the super-fresh bathrooms and high comfort levels. Traffic noise can be an issue in rooms towards the front of the property, though.

Ballina Manor
HOTEL $$$

(☑02-6681 5888; www.ballinamanor.com.au; 25 Norton St; d $195-290; ✳🛜) This former boarding school has been converted into a guesthouse filled with restored 1920s furnishings. Heritage rooms are super-plumped: the most grand has a four-poster bed and a spa bath, while attic rooms are light and airy with a small balcony. Even if you're not staying, you can stop by from 10am to 5pm for a free guided tour.

🍴 Eating & Drinking

⭐ Belle General
CAFE $

(☑0411 361 453; www.bellegeneral.com; 12 Shelly Beach Rd; dishes $12-19; ⊙8am-3pm) The perfect beachside cafe and local favourite for good reason, Belle specialises in gluten-free dishes – everything from eggs on kale and blueberry hotcakes to lamb burgers, paleo veggie lasagne and fish tacos. You can even sub in some quinoa loaf instead of sourdough toast. There are plenty of dairy-free alternatives for your smoothie or latte, and everything is available for takeaway.

Lighthouse Beach Cafe
CAFE $$

(☑02-6686 4380; www.lighthousebeachcafe.com.au; 65 Lighthouse Pde; mains $12-25; ⊙7.30am-3pm, to 10pm Fri & Sat during summer; 👶) With terrific views of East Ballina's Lighthouse Beach, this family-friendly cafe at the surf club turns out hearty breakfasts and some good comfort food for lunch, including beer battered fish and chips, and a range of burgers. It's open for dinner on Friday and Saturday nights during summer with tapas dishes or pub-style mains.

⭐ Che Bon
FRENCH $$$

(☑02-6687 8221; www.chebonrestaurant.com; 37-41 Cherry St; 3-course set menu $51; ⊙5.30-10.30pm Tue-Sat) Relocating from the country to the centre of Ballina, Che Bon, headed up by chef Rodolphe who hails from Burgundy, has quickly become a firm favourite for its well-executed French cuisine – to the extent that it's consistently booked out, so plan ahead.

⭐ Seven Mile Brewing
BREWERY

(☑0421 841 373; www.sevenmilebrewing.com.au; 188-202 Southern Cross Dr; ⊙noon-6pm Wed-Sun) Flight delayed? Lucky you. Located next to Ballina airport, Seven Mile Brewing may be new on the scene but this family-run business is already receiving well-deserved praise. The warehouse brewery usually has eight beers on tap, four of which are core, including the popular West Coast IPA made with four different hops. Tasting flights get you four beers for $14.

Food trucks keep the hunger at bay.

ℹ️ Information

Ballina Airport Services Desk (www.discoverballina.com.au; Ballina Byron Gateway Airport) A small outpost of the main information centre in town; opening hours are synced with flights.

Ballina Visitor Information Centre (☑1800 777 666; www.discoverballina.com.au; 6 River St; ⊙9am-5pm Mon-Sat, 10am-2pm Sun)

ℹ️ Getting There & Away

AIR

Ballina Byron Gateway Airport (☑02-6681 1858; www.ballinabyronairport.com.au; Southern Cross Dr) is 5km north of the town centre. **Jetstar** (☑13 15 38; www.jetstar.com.au), **Virgin** (☑13 67 89; www.virginaustralia.com) and **Regional Express** (Rex; ☑13 17 13; www.regionalexpress.com.au) run services to/from Sydney; Jetstar also has services to Melbourne. **Fly Pelican** (☑02-4965 0111; https://flypelican.com.au) runs services to/from Newcastle. A taxi to central Ballina should cost roughly $15. There are regular buses and shuttle services and rental-car options for Ballina and beyond.

BUS

A number of bus lines service local towns and beyond, linking to Sydney and Brisbane, including NSW TrainLink buses that link to rail services in Casino, 33km west from Lismore.

Blanch's (☑02-6686 2144; www.blanchs.com.au) Local buses, including services to Lennox Head ($5, 25 minutes), Bangalow ($7.40, 35 minutes), Byron Bay ($7.40, 55 minutes) and Mullumbimby ($9.80, 1½ hours).

Greyhound (☑1300 473 946; www.greyhound.com.au) Has coaches to/from Sydney ($162, 12½ hours, twice daily), Coffs Harbour ($43, three hours, twice daily), Byron Bay ($7, 45 minutes, three daily), Surfers Paradise ($36, two to three hours, three daily) and Brisbane ($44, four hours, three daily).

NSW TrainLink (☑ 13 22 32; https://transportnsw.info/regional) Coaches to Byron Bay ($7, 40 minutes).

Premier (☑ 13 34 10; www.premierms.com.au) Daily coaches to/from Sydney ($95, 13¼ hours), Port Macquarie ($68, seven hours), Coffs Harbour ($48, 4½ hours), Surfers Paradise ($40, three hours) and Brisbane ($40, 4½ hours).

Northern Rivers Buslines (☑ 02-6626 1499; www.nrbuslines.com.au) Buses to Lismore ($7, 1¼ hours).

Lennox Head

POP 6407

A protected National Surfing Reserve, Lennox Head's picturesque coastline has some of the best surf on the coast, with a world-class point break. Its sleepy village atmosphere and laid-back locals make it a mellow alternative to its boisterous and well-touristed neighbour, Byron, 17km north, and you can also get well-made coffee and a rather good feed.

⊙ Sights

Seven Mile Beach BEACH
Long and lovely Seven Mile Beach starts at the township and stretches north. It's accessible to 4WDs, but you will need a permit from the automated kiosk on Camp Drewe Rd (one day $14). The best place for a dip is near the surf club at the northern end of town.

🛏 Sleeping & Eating

Reflections Holiday Park Lennox Head CAMPGROUND $
(☑ 02-6687 7249; www.reflectionsholidayparks.com.au; Pacific Pde; sites/cabins from $42/116; ☎) By the lake and near the beach, this family-friendly holiday park has a wide range of units, from rustic cabins without bathrooms to a deluxe villa sleeping six. There are fresh amenities and a kitchen for campers.

Lennox Holiday Apartments APARTMENT $$$
(☑ 02-6687 5900; www.lennoxholidayapartments.com; 20-21 Pacific Pde; apt $195-250; ✳☎✳) Gaze at the surf from your airy apartment in this stylish complex, then take a splash with a borrowed board from reception. The one-bedroom apartments are the same size as the two-bedrooms, so they feel more

spacious. Take your pick of apartments with big balconies or enclosed patios.

Penny Lane CAFE $
(☑ 02-6687 6458; 90-92 Ballina St; dishes $9.50-19; ⊙ 6.30am-4pm; ☎) Down the back of an arcade you'll find this hip, popular cafe turning out well-prepared food from a seasonal menu. Turn breakfast into dessert with French toast featuring smashed raspberries and vanilla bean mascarpone or keep it simple with eggs on sourdough ($9.50). The slow roasted lamb is a lunch favourite.

★**Shelter** AUSTRALIAN $$
(☑ 02-6687 7757; www.shelterlennox.com.au; 41 Pacific Pde; mains $21-42; ⊙ 6.30am-3pm Mon-Wed & Sun, 6.30am-3pm & 5-9pm Thu-Sat) 🍃 With its Seven Mile Beach views and luxury beach-house atmosphere, Shelter is the perfect spot to drop by for a good feed paired with an excellent single-origin coffee, a craft beer or cocktails. Eggs get a creative twist at breakfast served with tangy fish cakes, while lunch and dinner might include Spencer Gulf mussels or a 600g T-bone steak.

❶ Getting There & Away

Ballina airport is around 14km away and is serviced by local bus company **Blanch's** (☑ 02-6686 2144; www.blanchs.com.au), with coaches to Byron Bay ($5, 25 minutes), Ballina ($5, 25 minutes) and Mullumbimby ($7.40, 40 minutes), as well as local taxis.

Byron Bay

POP 5521

When it comes to Byron these days, cries of 'Paradise lost' echo in the surrounding hills, while nearby unassuming beach towns puff out their chests in pride of being dubbed 'the new Byron'. Sure, this is a place suffering under the weight of its intense popularity – traffic-choked streets, no car spaces and lengthy cafe queues – but while it might not be what it used to be, it's still pretty special.

The local Arakwal people know it as Cavanbah, which translates to 'meeting place', a fitting name when you consider its wonderful mishmash of young international backpackers, holidaying families, ageing hippies, boho-clad seachangers, property developers, models and musicians. Come here to surf epic breaks at dawn and sigh at the enchanting sunsets, refine your yoga moves and hang with beach buskers, idle at

BYRON BEACHES

One of the toughest choices you'll need to make in Byron is deciding which beach it is for the day. Northwest of the town centre, wild **Belongil Beach** with its high dunes avoids the worst of the crowds and is clothing-optional in parts. At its eastern end lies the **Wreck**, a powerful right-hand surf break.

Immediately in front of town, lifesaver-patrolled **Main Beach** is busy from sunrise to sunset with yoga classes, buskers and, occasionally, fire dancers. As it stretches east it merges into **Clarkes Beach**. The most popular surf break is at the **Pass** near the eastern headland.

Around the rocks is gorgeous **Watego's Beach**, a wide crescent of white sand surrounded by rainforest that fringes Byron's most affluent enclave. A further 400m walk brings you to secluded **Little Watego's** (inaccessible by car; accessible by steps leading down from the lighthouse), another lovely patch of sand directly under rocky Cape Byron. Head here at sunset for an impressive moonrise. Tucked under the south side of the Cape (entry via Tallow Beach Rd) is **Cosy Corner**, which offers a decent-sized wave and a sheltered beach when the northerlies are blowing elsewhere.

Tallow Beach is an incredible, deserted sandy stretch that extends for 7km south from Cape Byron. This is the place to flee the crowds. Much of the beach is backed by **Arakwal National Park**, but the suburb of **Suffolk Park** sprawls along the sand near its southern end. **Kings Beach** is a popular gay-friendly beach, just off Seven Mile Beach Rd past the Broken Head Holiday Park.

cafes, gorge on good food, then kick on at the pub. Wake up, hit repeat.

⊙ Sights

★ The Farm
FARM

(www.thefarmbyronbay.com.au; 11 Ewingsdale Rd, Ewingsdale; tours adult/child $20/15; ⊘ 7am-4pm) **FREE** A community of growers and producers shares this photogenic, 32-hectare green oasis just outside Byron, along with the Three Blue Ducks restaurant (p185), a produce store, a bakery, an ice-creamery and a florist. The passionate dedication to traditional and sustainable practices here is both a working ethos and an educational mission. Pick up a self-guided-tour map and roam the veggie plots and cattle-and-pig-dotted fields. One-hour guided tours run at 9am Friday to Sunday during summer, and horseback tours happen at 7am Saturdays ($65).

Cape Byron State Conservation Park
STATE PARK

(www.nationalparks.nsw.gov.au/cape-byron-state-conservation-area; ⊘ 8.30am-sunset) The Cape Byron State Conservation Park is home to the Cape Byron lighthouse, plenty of stunning lookouts (including from the most eastern point of the Australia mainland) and the excellent Cape Byron Walking Track (p180). There is parking available at the lighthouse ($8).

Cape Byron Distillery
DISTILLERY

(☑ 02-6684 7961; www.capebyrondistillery.com; 80 St Helena Rd, McLeods Shoot; 1½hr tour $35; ⊘ Fri-Sun) Set on the Brook family's scenic farm in Byron's hinterland is the Cape Byron Distillery, home to a much-lauded Brookie's dry gin. It's created with 26 Australian native botanicals (aniseed myrtle, macadamia, finger lime), 18 of which are sourced locally and many from the rainforest surrounding the distillery. Book a tour that will take you through the distilling process and the rainforest to learn about the botanicals and, of course, taste the end result. Price includes a G&T on arrival.

Cape Byron Lighthouse
LIGHTHOUSE

(www.nationalparks.nsw.gov.au; Lighthouse Rd; ⊘ museum 10am-4pm) **FREE** This 1901 lighthouse is Australia's most easterly and also its most powerful shipping beacon. Inside there are maritime and nature displays. If you want to venture to the top, you'll need to take one of the volunteer-run tours, which operate from 8.45am to 3.30pm weekdays ($10). There's also a cafe here and self-contained accommodation in the lighthouse-keeper's cottages. Parking $8; gate opens at 8am.

Captain Cook Lookout
VIEWPOINT

(Lighthouse Rd) Start your 3.7km walking track around Cape Byron from the Captain

Byron Bay

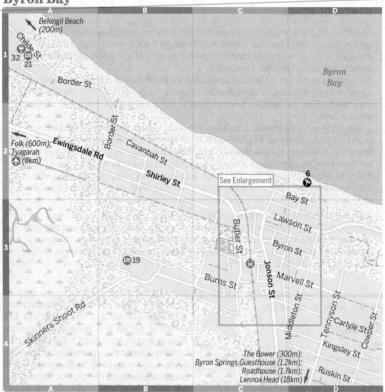

Belongil Beach (200m)

Childe St

32 21

Border St

Border St

Folk (600m); Tyagarah (8km)

Ewingsdale Rd

Cavanbah St

Shirley St

See Enlargement

Byron Bay

Bay St

Lawson St

Byron St

Butler St

Jonson St

Marvell St

19

Burns St

Skinners Shoot Rd

Middleton St

Tennyson St

Carlyle St

Cowper St

Kingsley St

The Bower (300m); Byron Springs Guesthouse (1.2km); Roadhouse (1.7km); Lennox Head (18km)

Ruskin St

6

Cook Lookout. The rainforest stretch near the lookout has the best wildlife-spotting chances.

🏃 Activities

Adventure sports abound in Byron Bay, from hang gliding and mountain biking to hot-air ballooning and kayaking, though surfing and diving are the biggest draws. Most operators offer a free pick-up service from local accommodation.

★ Gaia Retreat & Spa   SPA

(☎ 02-6687 1670; www.gaiaretreat.com.au; 933 Fernleigh Rd, Brooklet; massage & treatments $140-520) 🌿 Sure, Byron is packed with places for pampering, but none is quite like Gaia – famously co-owned by Olivia Newton John. This luxurious retreat – consistently topping world's bests lists – is tucked away in the verdant hinterland in Bundjalung country. If you don't have the cash to overnight here, a visit to the day spa is the next best thing.

★ Cape Byron Walking Track   WALKING

(www.nationalparks.nsw.gov.au/things-to-do/walk ing-tracks/cape-byron-walking-track) Spectacular views reward those who climb up from the Captain Cook Lookout (p179) on the Cape Byron Walking Track. Ribboning around the headland and through rainforest, the track dips and (mostly) soars its way to the lighthouse. Look out for dolphins (year-round) and whales (June to November). Allow about two hours for the entire 3.7km loop.

Byron Yoga Centre   YOGA

(☎ 02-6685 8327; www.byronyoga.com; 6 Byron St; class $18) One of the longest-running yoga schools in Australia, the Byron Yoga Centre offers daily classes in the Purna style – integrating physical postures with breath control and meditation. Monday to Saturday there are 4pm classes for $5, taught by teachers in training, where the money goes towards different charities. It also runs a variety of yoga retreats.

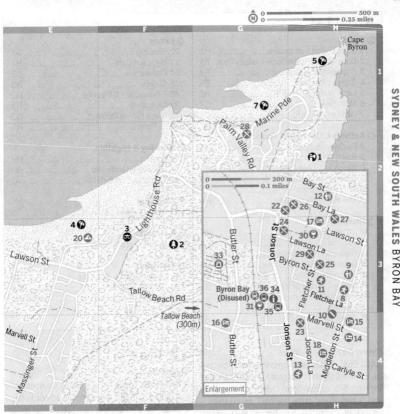

Soul Surf School
SURFING

(📞1800 089 699; www.soulsurfschool.com.au; 14 Bay St; 4hr group lesson $69) Half-day to five-day courses for beginners with small groups of up to six people, or opt for a private lesson ($160 for 2½ hours). It also offers Surf and Stay packages at the **Byron Bay Beach Hostel** (📞02-6685 8750; www.byronbaybeachhostel. com; 23 Lawson St; dm from $30, d $130-220; P🛜).

Comma
SPA

(📞02 6685 8878; www.commabyron.com; 7a, 11 Banksia Dr; treatments $120-180; ⏰10am-6pm Mon-Fri, 8am-5pm Sat, 10am-4pm Sun) Head to this day spa for treatments with a refreshing tinge of humour – there's a 'last resort' massage for aching backs, while aromatherapy oils are categorised as 'uppers' and 'downers'. The modern decor is also on point, with polished concrete and an earthy palette, while the soundtrack forgoes the usual panpipes for atmospheric beats.

Be Salon & Spa
SPA

(📞0413 432 584; www.besalonspa.com.au; 14 Middleton St; 30min/1hr massages $60/110) Manicures, pedicures, facials and waxing are offered alongside 'metaphysical' healing, massage, rebalancing and naturopathy. Highly recommended.

Go Sea Kayaks
KAYAKING

(📞0416 222 344; www.goseakayakbyronbay.com. au; adult/child $75/50) 🌿 Reputable 2½-hour sea kayak tours in Cape Byron Marine Park led by a team of local surf lifesavers daily at 9.30am and 2pm. Whale, dolphin or turtle sightings are guaranteed; otherwise you can book again for free.

Byron Bay Ballooning
BALLOONING

(📞1300 889 660; www.byronbayballooning.com. au; Tyagarah Airfield; adult/child $350/175) One-hour sunrise flights including Champagne breakfast; Byron's a wonderful place to balloon over.

Byron Bay

⊙ Sights
1 Cape Byron Lighthouse	H2
2 Cape Byron State Conservation Park	F3
3 Captain Cook Lookout	F3
4 Clarkes Beach	E3
5 Little Watego's Beach	H1
6 Main Beach	D2
7 Watego's Beach	G1

⊛ Activities, Courses & Tours
8 Be Salon & Spa	H3
9 Black Dog Surfing	H3
10 Byron Bay Dive Centre	H4
11 Byron Yoga Centre	H3
12 Soul Surf School	H2
13 The Haven Byron Bay	H4

🛏 Sleeping
14 28° Byron Bay	H4
15 Atlantic	H4
16 Barbara's Guesthouse	G4
17 Byron Bay Beach Hostel	H3
18 Byron Bay YHA	H4
19 Nomads Arts Factory Lodge	B3
20 Reflections Holiday Park Clarkes Beach	E3
21 Wake Up! Byron Bay	A1

⊗ Eating
22 Balcony Bar	G2
23 Bay Leaf Café	H4
24 Chihuahua	G3
25 Combi	H3
26 Il Buco Cafe & Pizzeria	H2
27 No Bones	H3
28 Rae's Dining Room	G2
29 St Elmo	H3

⊙ Drinking & Nightlife
30 Locura	H3
31 Railway Friendly Bar	G3
32 Treehouse on Belongil	A1

⊜ Shopping
33 Byron Farmers Market	G3

⊙ Information
34 Byron Visitor Centre	G3

⊙ Transport
35 Long Distance Bus Stop	G3
36 NSW TrainLink	G3
Skybus	(see 35)

Byron Bay Dive Centre DIVING

(☐02-6685 8333; www.byronbaydivecentre.com.au; 9 Marvell St; dives incl gear from $100, snorkelling tours $75; ☉9am-5pm) Offers guided dives and snorkelling trips as well as courses – introductory ($195), freediving ($550), open water ($595) and Professional Association of Diving Instructors (PADI; from $1595) courses.

The Haven Byron Bay MASSAGE

(☐02-6685 8304; https://thehavenbyronbay.com; 107 Jonson St; ☉10am-6.30pm Mon-Sat, 11am-4pm Sun) True to its name, the Haven offers brilliant massages by skilled therapists (one hour, $90), magnesium flotation tanks (one hour, $80) and facials (one hour, $110), as well as acupuncture, and a detoxifying infrared sauna (one hour, $50).

Black Dog Surfing SURFING

(☐02-6680 9828; www.blackdogsurfing.com; 11 Byron St; 3½hr group lesson $65, 3hr private lesson $140) One of four Byron Bay–based surf schools that can hold lessons at a Byron Bay beach, rather than further afield. Intimate (seven people max) group lessons, including women's and kids' courses. Highly rated.

👉 Tours

Byron Bay Adventure Tours HIKING, MOUNTAIN BIKING

(☐1300 120 028; www.byronbayadventuretours.com.au; half-/full-day tours from $89/149) Guided walking tours around Byron, in the hinterland and overnight camping tours to Wollumbin/Mt Warning for a sunrise summit. It also offers half-day easy mountain-bike tours in Nightcap National Park including a BBQ lunch ($169).

Aboriginal Cultural Concepts CULTURAL

(☐0405 654 280; www.aboriginalculturalconcepts.com; half-/full-day tours $95/190; ☉tours run Wed-Sat) Heritage tours led by Lois Cook – a traditional custodian of Nyangbul country in the region – explore cultural and mythological sights, and sample bush tucker along the Bundjalung coast.

Vision Walks WILDLIFE

(☐0405 275 743; www.visionwalks.com; full-day tours adult/child $145/110) See all manner of creatures in their natural habitat, including nocturnal animals (on the Night Vision Walk) and hippies (on the Hippy Hinterland Trail that takes you to Nimbin).

✴ Festivals & Events

Byron Bay Bluesfest   MUSIC
(www.bluesfest.com.au; Tyagarah Tea Tree Farm; ⊗Apr) Held over the Easter long weekend at the Tyagarah Tea Tree Farm in between Byron Bay and Brunswick Heads, this popular festival attracts high-calibre international performers (Iggy Pop, Brian Wilson and Patti Smith in recent years) and local heavyweights.

Splendour in the Grass   MUSIC
(www.splendourinthegrass.com; North Byron Parklands, 126 Tweed Valley Way, Yelgun; ⊗late Jul) Huge three-day festival featuring big-name artists. Recent past acts include Lorde, The Cure, Chvrches and LCD Soundsystem.

Byron Bay Writers' Festival   LITERATURE
(https://byronwritersfestival.com; ⊗early Aug) Gathers together big-name writers and literary followers from across Australia.

Falls Festival   MUSIC
(https://fallsfestival.com; North Byron Parklands, 126 Tweed Valley Way, Yelgun; ⊗Dec-Jan) Three-day indie music festival that runs over NYE and attracts international and Australian artists. Past acts include Interpol, King Gizzard & the Lizard Wizard, and Liam Gallagher.

🛏 Sleeping

By any standards, Byron accommodation is expensive. If you're in the market for 'barefoot luxury' – relaxed but stylish – you're in luck. Backpackers are also catered for well, but it's the middle bracket that can be hard to find, though there are some decent motels that can offer good value. Book well in advance for January, during festival times, school holidays and mid-to-late November for Schoolies Week (p316).

★ Nomads Arts Factory Lodge   HOSTEL $
(☎02-6685 7709; www.nomadsworld.com/artsfactory; Skinners Shoot Rd; sites $17-20, dm $25-32, d $70-90; @🖥🔊) 🏊 For an archetypal Byron experience, try this rambling mini-village next to a picturesque swamp set on 2 hectares, 15 minutes' walk from town. Choose from colourful four- to 10-bed dorms, campsites, a female-only lakeside cottage or a shared tepee. Couples can opt for aptly titled 'cube' rooms, island-retreat glamping-style canvas huts or the pricier 'love shack' with private bathroom.

Byron Bay YHA   HOSTEL $
(☎02-6685 8853; www.yha.com.au; 7 Carlyle St; dm $25-50, d $75-180; 🔊🖥) Having undergone a multi-million-dollar revamp in early 2018, this YHA is now more flashpacker resort than backpacker hostel. There's a heated pool with a backdrop of murals by Sydney street artist Mulga, beanbags for lounging on the deck, and a mix of bright dorms and private rooms spread out between three buildings linked by open-air walkways.

Wake Up! Byron Bay   HOSTEL $
(☎02-6685 7868; www.wakeup.com.au; 25 Childe St; dm $36-56, d $89-170; P🖥🔊) This fabulous, well-managed hostel-resort opposite Belongil Beach is a terrific and affordable alternative to staying in central Byron. Attractive dorms and private rooms are scattered through the hammock-filled gardens. There's daily yoga, free bikes and the fun Treehouse (p186) pub next door. It's a 15-minute walk (or a free shuttle ride) down Belongil Beach into town.

Reflections Holiday Park Clarkes Beach   CAMPGROUND $
(☎02-6685 6496; www.reflectionsholidayparks.com.au; 1 Lighthouse Rd; sites/cabins from $61/202; 🖥🔊) The cabins might be tightly packed but they, along with shady tent sites, sit within attractive bush in what must be one of the town's most spectacular settings, high up above the beach and overlooked by the Cape Byron lighthouse. New architecturally designed premium villas and superior cabins are a real treat with a 'boutique hotel' feel.

★ Barbara's Guesthouse   GUESTHOUSE $$
(☎0401 580 899; www.byronbayvacancy.com; 5 Burns St; d $170-330; P🖥🔊) This pretty 1920s weatherboard house, in a quiet residential street a short walk from town, has four elegant guest rooms with private bathroom and TV. The owner is an interior decorator and it shows in the smart beachy style and attention to detail. There's a communal kitchen with breakfast supplies and a coffee machine, and a lovely back deck for relaxing.

Byron Springs Guesthouse   GUESTHOUSE $$
(☎0457 808 101; www.byronsprings.com.au; 2 Oodgeroo Garden; r $150-350; P🔊) Polished floorboards, big verandahs and a leafy setting a couple of kilometres south of town make this a lovely choice if you like to be removed from the throng. There are just six rooms plus a self-contained studio; includes

a continental breakfast and there are complimentary bikes for guest use.

★ 28° Byron Bay
GUESTHOUSE $$$

(☑02-6665 7775; www.28byronbay.com.au; 12 Marvell St; d from $550; [P][※][🛜][⊛]) A perfect combination of absolute luxury and personal warmth make this gorgeous guesthouse a rare find. The three private rooms, either with a deep bath or a plunge pool, lend a bolthole appeal, while the four rooms in the main house share a relaxing common area, a lap pool and a kitchen.

Elements
RESORT $$$

(☑02-6639 1500; www.elementsofbyron.com.au; 144 Bayshore Dr; 1-bedroom villa from $380; [P][※][🛜][⊛]) 🏊 Behind 2km of Belongil dunes, this is Byron's most luxurious resort. Over 200 private villas nestle in coastal bushland and, while there are no ocean views, the sound of the surf, and cicadas, is ever-present. Split-level villas are spacious, tasteful and soothing. The main pavilion, pool and restaurant have a relaxed, almost ironic Australian glamour, plus there's a hip caravan-on-the-sand beach bar.

Byron Beach Abodes
VILLA $$$

(☑0419 490 010; www.byronbeachabodes.com.au; cottages & apt $295-1095) A handpicked collection of Byron's best design-driven properties, Byron Beach Abodes attracts overseas guests, honeymooners and Sydney's fashion set. Each has its own unique style and is nestled in the town's most upmarket enclave. You're close to the beach, lighthouse walks and the coffee hub of Top Shop.

Atlantic
BOUTIQUE HOTEL $$$

(☑02-6685 5118; www.atlanticbyronbay.com.au; 13 Marvell St; r from $240; [※][🛜]) This stylish enclave set among tropical gardens is home to four smartly decorated beach houses offering different sizing, from small beach-shack spaces to larger rooms with private verandah and outdoor shower. Or you can do some Californian dreaming in the Airstream (max two nights). Guests can hang out by the communal fire pit or throw together dinner in the shared open-air kitchens.

The Bower
BOUTIQUE HOTEL $$$

(☑02-6680 9577; www.thebowerbyronbay.com.au; 28 Bangalow Rd; ste/barn from $240/450; [P][※][🛜][⊛]) The Bower – inspired by a trip to NYC – is a former motel that's undergone a luxury makeover straight from the pages of an interior design magazine. Choose from 14 guest suites or the Bower House, the Cottage (in the original 100-year-old building) or the Barn for families and groups, all decked out with luxury linen, smart TVs and one-off artworks.

✖ Eating

Byron is a dream destination for food-focused travellers. This could well be the clean-eating capital of the country: golden lattes are ubiquitous and açaí bowls are more common than bacon and eggs. Plenty of upmarket restaurants serve Modern Australian dishes, and more casual eateries travel the globe with tacos, meze, tapas and sushi. Ingredients are usually local and sourced from small, organic producers.

★ Chihuahua
MEXICAN $

(☑02-6685 6777; Feros Arcade, 25 Jonson St; tacos $7.50-8.50; ⊙11am-8.30pm) Follow the holy Virgin to this arcade hole-in-the-wall taqueria that serves Byron's most authentic and good-value Mexican food. It's ripe for takeaway (and also delivers within central Byron), but you can eat in if there's a spare fold-out chair and table available. Don't miss the slow-roasted brisket and battered halloumi tacos.

100 Mile Table
CAFE $

(☑02-6680 9814; www.100miletable.com; Unit 4, Banksia Dr; mains $10-15; ⊙7am-3pm Mon-Fri) One of Byron Bay's most feted cafes, in the Arts & Industry Estate (www.byronartstrail.com), 100 Mile Table's locavore ethos, produce-led menu and relaxed industrial styling are a hit with both locals and out-of-towners. Settle in to a communal table with a bowl of chicken and ginger congee or soba noodle salad – flavour-packed meals reflecting the owner's 14-year tenure with renowned chef Neil Perry.

Combi
CAFE $

(www.wearecombi.com.au; 21-25 Fletcher St; mains $12-19; ⊙7am-4pm) Melbourne clean-eating icon Combi has brought its signature raw, organic and highly Instagrammable drinks, cakes and breakfast and lunch bowls to this pale-bubble-gum-coloured cafe in Byron. House-made mylk (coconut or almond milk) can be had in coffee, or made into fruit, matcha or turmeric lattes, and in matcha or raw cacao mylkshakes or superfood smoothies.

★ il Buco Café & Pizzeria   PIZZA $$

(☑02-6680 9186; www.ilbucobyronbay.com; 4/4 Bay Lane; pizza $15-28; ⊘5.30pm-late) The best pizza in town is thanks to a group of friends from Tuscany who've set up shop in Byron. Authentic thin-crust wood-fired pizzas are sparingly topped with outstanding flavours using as much local produce as possible. The delicious prosciutto funghi features Bangalow sweet pork ham, while the simple margherita is made with a deliciously slurpable homemade passata and *fior di latte* mozzarella. BYO (no corkage!). Also does takeaway.

★ Three Blue Ducks at the Farm   CAFE, AUSTRALIAN $$

(☑02-6684 7888; www.thefarmbyronbay.com. au; 11 Ewingsdale Rd, Ewingsdale; breakfast $18-25, lunch & dinner $27-36; ⊘7am-3pm Mon-Thu, to 10pm Fri-Sun) The legendary Sydney team behind Three Blue Ducks moved up north to showcase its paddock-to-plate food philosophy. Their rustic barn cafe and restaurant forms the beating heart of The Farm (p179). Breakfast features typical Byron healthy options, as well as a streaky bacon and egg roll, and slow-roasted brisket, while the lunch and dinner menus step it up to bring a gentle sophistication to the menu.

Daytime crowds can be overwhelming on weekends; steel yourself, or come during the week, super-early or for dinner.

★ Balcony Bar   INTERNATIONAL $$

(☑02-6680 9666; www.balcony.com.au; cnr Lawson & Jonson Sts; mains $22-32; ⊘noon-11pm Mon-Thu, to late Fri, 9am-late Sat & Sun; ☏) The eponymous architectural feature here wraps around the building and gives you tremendous views of the passing Byron parade (and the ever-busy traffic circle). Decor is an appealing postcolonial pastiche, while the food is a great mix of tasty tapas-style dishes, Med-inflected warm-weather-appropriate salads and sophisticated main meals from chilli crab linguine to a dry-aged beef burger on brioche.

★ Bay Leaf Café   CAFE $$

(www.facebook.com/bayleafcoffee; 2 Marvell St; mains $17-24; ⊘7am-2pm) There's a raft of Byron clichés on offer at this hip, busy cafe (golden lattes, kombucha, a '70s psych rock soundtrack), but everything is made with remarkable attention to detail and a passion for produce. Breakfasts are fantastic from the granola or Bircher muesli to the poached eggs with house-made dukkah or young Australia's national dish: avocado on sourdough.

No Bones   VEGAN $$

(☑02-6680 7418; www.lovenobones.com; 11 Fletcher St; mains $22-27; ⊘5-9pm Mon-Fri, to 10pm Sat & Sun; ☏) No bones, no problem at this plant-based restaurant that doesn't compromise on flavour. It's not your typical Buddha bowls and tofu here – dine al fresco under fairy lights on share dishes of comfort food from mac 'n' cheese and seitan Peking duck pancakes to tasty 'calamari' strips made from konjac, and homemade gnocchi. Excellent cocktails to boot.

★ St Elmo   SPANISH $$$

(☑02-6680 7426; www.stelmodining.com; cnr Fletcher St & Lawson Lane; dishes $16-29; ⊘5-11pm Mon-Sat, to 10pm Sun) Perch on a stool at this moody modern tapas restaurant, where bar staff can whip up inventive cocktails or pour you a glass of wine from the largely Australian and Spanish list (including natural and minimal intervention drops). The solidly Iberian menu is bold and broad, with traditional favourites mixing it up with contemporary flourishes.

Rae's Dining Room   SEAFOOD $$$

(☑02-6685 5366; www.raesonwategos.com; 8 Marine Pde, Watego's Beach; mains $36-44; ⊘noon-3pm & 6-11pm) The sound of the surf perfectly sets off the excellent Mediterranean-influenced dishes at this exclusive little retreat overlooking Watego's Beach. Headed up by chef Jason Barratt, formerly at Melbourne's acclaimed Attica restaurant, seafood features heavily on the menu with a strong focus on sourcing local produce from the Northern Rivers region.

🍷 Drinking & Nightlife

Byron is becoming more and more known for its after-dark scene, whether it's sundowner beers overlooking the beach and natural wines served by serious (and seriously good-looking) waitstaff, to big indie names at a sweaty pub gig or backpacker-filled bars. But at some point, *everyone* ends up at the Rails (p186).

★ Locura   BAR, CLUB

(☑02-6675 9140; www.locura.com.au; 6 Lawson St; ⊘5pm-late) No strangers to Byron's hospitality scene, the guys from Three Blue Ducks are weaving their magic on the town's bar scene with the opening of Locura, a sleek and sophisticated bar. The decor leans towards minimalist/industrial, while the menu is Latin-American inspired, with plenty of tequila and mezcal paired with shredded pork tacos, oysters with hot sauce, and ceviche.

★ Treehouse on Belongil   PUB
(☑02-6680 9452; www.treehouseonbelongil. com; 25 Childe St; ⊗7.30am-11pm) A home-spun beach bar where wooden decks spill out among the trees, afternoons are for drinking, and live, original music is played Thursday to Sunday. Soak up the beer with a menu of well-made pizzas, burgers, steaks and seafood.

Railway Friendly Bar   PUB
(The Rails; ☑02-6685 7662; www.therailsbyronbay. com; 86 Jonson St; ⊗11am-midnight, from noon Sun) The Rails' indoor-outdoor mayhem draws everyone from lobster-red British tourists to high-on-life earth mothers and babyboomer tourists. The front beer garden – conducive to long, beery afternoons – has free live music, while the kitchen pumps out excellent burgers, with variants including roo, grilled fish and pork belly with slaw.

Stone & Wood   BREWERY
(☑02-6685 5173; www.stoneandwood.com.au; 100 Centennial Circuit; ⊗tasting room 10am-5pm Mon-Fri, noon-6pm Sat & Sun) This independent and proudly local brewery, with a core family of ales, experimental pilot batches and seasonal beers, upgraded to a huge new space in late 2018. You can still drop by for a paddle and to pick up a few beers or a carton; or book online for a 1½-hour in-depth tour (three daily, except Tuesdays; $25 per person).

🛍 Shopping

★ Byron Farmers Market   MARKET
(www.byronfarmersmarket.com.au; Butler Street Reserve; ⊗8-11am Thu) Both a market and a symbol of the strength of the local community, this weekly market has a wide variety of mainly organic stalls, with both fresh produce and all manner of local products. Come early and hang with the locals for great coffee and breakfast, then linger for live music.

ⓘ Information

Byron Visitor Centre (☑02-6680 8558; www.visitbyronbay.com; Old Stationmaster's Cottage, 80 Jonson St; ⊗9am-5pm Mon-Sat, 10am-4pm Sun; 🔊) is the place for accurate tourist information, and last-minute accommodation and bus bookings.

The website www.byron-bay.com is a helpful resource.

ⓘ Getting There & Away

AIR

The closest airport is in Ballina (p177). Jetstar, Virgin and Rex run services to/from Sydney, and Jetstar also has services to Melbourne. Easy shuttle services and rental cars are at the airport for Byron travellers. **Byron Easy Bus** (☑02-6685 7447; www.byronbayshuttle.com. au; adult/child $20/12), **Steve's Airport Transfers** (☑0414 660 031; https://stevestransport. com.au; one way/return $20/35) and **Xcede** (https://byronbay.xcede.com.au; one way $20) all serve Ballina airport (20 minutes).

Gold Coast Airport (p1071) at Coolangatta has a greater range of services. **Skybus** (www. skybus.com.au/byron-bay-express; one way adult/child $28/14) runs daily services between Byron Bay and Gold Coast Airport ($28, 55 minutes), as does Byron Easy Bus ($32) and Xcede ($40).

Brisbane Airport (p1071) is served by all domestic airlines and most international carriers. The **Brisbane 2 Byron Express bus** (☑1800 626 222; www.brisbane2byron.com) ($56) and Byron Easy Bus ($60) both travel from Brisbane Airport to Byron in around three hours.

BUS

Coaches stop on **Jonson St** near the Byron Visitor Centre. Operators include **Premier** (☑13 34 10; www.premierms.com.au), **Greyhound** (☑1300 473 946; www.greyhound.com.au) and **NSW TrainLink** (☑13 22 32; www.nswtrainlink. info).

Blanch's (☑02-6686 2144; www.blanchs. com.au) Regular buses to/from Ballina Byron Gateway Airport ($7.40, one hour), Ballina ($9.60, 55 minutes), Lennox Head ($5, 25 minutes), Bangalow ($5, 25 minutes) and Mullumbimby ($5, 25 minutes).

Brisbane 2 Byron Express Bus has three daily buses to/from Brisbane (adult/child $40/36, two hours).

Byron Bay Express (www.byronbayexpress. com.au; one way/return $30/55) Four buses daily to/from Gold Coast Airport (45 minutes) and Surfers Paradise (1½ hours) for $30/55 one way/return.

Byron Easy Bus has a minibus service to Brisbane ($44, three hours).

Northern Rivers Buslines (☑02-6626 1499; www.nrbuslines.com.au) Buses to/from Lismore ($12, 1½ hours), Bangalow (30 minutes) and Mullumbimby (20 minutes), both $9.70.

TRAIN

People still mourn the loss of the popular CountryLink train service that ran from Sydney. NSW Trainlink (p186) now has buses connecting to trains at the Casino train station (70 minutes), which is 33km west of Lismore.

ℹ Getting Around

Making use of all that Byron sunshine, a restored vintage 'red rattler' is billed as the world's first **solar train** (☑ 02-8123 2130; www.byronbay train.com.au; North Beach Station, 54 Bayshore Dr, Byron Beach Station, 1b Butler St; adult/child $4/$2, 0-5yr free) and operates a 3km service between north Byron and central Byron, running hourly from 10am to 5pm daily.

Brunswick Heads

POP 1737

Long thought of as Byron's quiet little sibling, Brunswick Heads (or 'Bruns') has come into its own. The town's neat grid of streets has an almost unfairly fine selection of cafes, restaurants and shops. It's increasingly and obviously affluent too, though its hippy heart remains, with clinics offering reiki and other healing modalities, and bulk crystals for sale at the markets.

A beautiful, long surf beach and a tiny sheltered river cove are separated from the town by the wide and clear Brunswick River, crossed via a sturdy, weathered footbridge. It's a place where you still get the best of both worlds: a relaxed, archetypal Australian beach holiday of sunburn and seafood, but one that also has you eating and drinking at least as well as you would in a big city.

🛏 Sleeping

Reflections Holiday Parks Terrace Reserve   CARAVAN PARK $

(☑ 02-6685 1233; https://reflectionsholidayparks. com.au/park/terrace-reserve; Fingal St; sites/ cabins from $49/177; 🐾) Lined up along the high river bank, the cabins here have a lot of charm and are strolling distance from both the beach and the shops. Some tent sites are also riverside and all are set beneath established trees.

★Sails Motel   MOTEL $$

(☑ 02-6685 1353; www.thesailsmotel.com.au; 26-28 Tweed St; d from $125-155, 2-bed apt

LOCAL KNOWLEDGE

NORTH COAST MARKETS

Local life in the region revolves around a seemingly endless rota of markets, which bring together farmers, foragers, foodies, makers, musicians and just about anyone else you can imagine. Expect to find plenty of seasonal organic produce along with farmhouse cheeses, honey and baked goods, and arts, crafts and vintage goods. There's usually live music, especially at the weekend meets. Visit NSW (www. visitnsw.com/events-markets) has a list of market dates.

Top picks:

Byron Farmers Market (p186)

Brunswick Heads Riverside Market (Memorial Park, Fawcett St; ⊙ 7.30am-2pm 1st Sat of month)

Bellingen Community Market (p169)

Mullumbimby Farmers Market (www.mullumfarmersmarket.org.au; Mullumbimby Showground, 51 Main Arm Rd; ⊙ 7-11am Fri)

$195-225; P❋🛜🏊) This 1960s navy-and-white motel has been transformed: its 22 rooms are light and simple with the occasional design piece, great eco toiletries, comfortable beds and microwaves. The recently renovated pool, with poolside bar, is hard to resist, and the owners Amanda and Simon know everyone in town and can help you decide where to eat or swim or hike.

Brunswick Heads Motel   MOTEL $$

(☑ 02-6685 1860; www.brunswickheadsmotel. com.au; 2-6 Old Pacific Hwy; d from $125; P❋🛜🏊) A black-and-white boutique beauty, the Brunswick Heads Motel has whitewashed rooms with pops of colour in the palm-tree-print cushions, comfy beds, craft-beer-stocked minibars and an inviting pool. Explore town on a complimentary bike, or hit the water with a free paddleboard.

🍴 Eating & Drinking

One of the fastest growing food scenes in Australia has transformed happily sleepy Bruns into a food and coffee lover's dream destination.

★ **Yami** MIDDLE EASTERN **$**
(☏ 02-6685 0186; www.yami.com.au; 2/1 Park St; dishes $10.50-20; ⏱ 7am-3pm Mon & Tue, to 8pm Wed-Sat, to 4pm Sun; ☑) Yami, appropriately pronounced 'yummy', dishes up some of the crispiest felafel and most flavoursome Middle Eastern vegetarian food you'd never expect to find in a quiet seaside town. Everything is made on-site, including the creamy hummus you'll go dollop-crazy with, and felafel share platters are heaving with fresh salads, dips, pickles, the works. Enjoy it on the raised street-side deck.

★ **Fleet** GASTRONOMY **$$$**
(☏ 02-6685 1363; www.fleet-restaurant.com.au; Shop 2/16 The Terrace; dishes $16-24, degustation $85; ⏱ 3-11pm Thu-Sun) Fleet, one of Australia's most cultish dining destinations, seats just 14 guests for communal dining in its effortlessly stylish space – its genuine hospitality ensures diners feel they're among friends. The menu sometimes includes foraged ingredients, and the series of small dishes that appear from the open kitchen are punchy in flavour and beautifully presented. Book at least one month in advance online.

★ **Hotel Brunswick** PUB
(☏ 02-6685 1236; www.hotelbrunswick.com.au; 4 Mullumbimbi St; ⏱ 9am-late) The 1940s Hotel Brunswick is a destination unto itself, with a magnificent beer garden fanning out from its heritage facade beneath flourishing poincianas. There's live music at weekends, and pub grub that includes burgers and pizza. Sunday sessions attract locals from miles around. There is simple, sweetly old-fashioned upstairs accommodation too (rooms without bathroom $60 to $90).

❶ Information

Brunswick Heads Visitor Information Centre
(☏ 02-6685 1002; www.brunswickheads.org. au; 7 Park St; ⏱ 9.30am-4.30pm Mon-Fri, 10am-2pm Sat & Sun)

❶ Getting There & Away

Brunswick Heads is around 35 minutes north or south of Ballina and Gold Coast airports respectively. Byron Easy Bus (p186) operates a shuttle from Gold Coast airport ($40).

Blanch's (p186) bus lines operates a service (some are connecting services) to and from Byron Bay three times daily Monday to Friday. Buses depart from in front of the visitor information centre on Park St.

NORTH COAST HINTERLAND

Away from the coast, the lush scenery and a large population that embraces alternative lifestyles make this an exceptionally alluring region – for locals and visitors alike (real-estate prices are now as common an overhear as chakra cleansing once was). Stay up here for deep relaxation, good food and lively markets. Or day-trip from the coast, visiting beautiful towns such as Bangalow or hitting the hiking trails and swimming holes of one of the region's extraordinary national parks.

The Bundjalung people are the traditional custodians of much of this hinterland region, while the Widjabul people are the traditional owners of the Nightcap National Park land.

Bangalow

POP 2021

Surrounded by subtropical forest and rolling green farmland 14km from Byron, Bangalow (Bangers to friends) is home to a flourishing creative community, a dynamic, sustainable food scene and a range of urbane boutiques. A small arts precinct, which houses community arts organisations plus a number of cute shops and a lovely cafe, is but a stroll up the hill on Station St. The little town heaves during the monthly **Bangalow Market** (www.bangalowmarket.com.au; Bangalow Showgrounds, Market St; ⏱ 9am-3pm 4th Sun of month), but it's well worth making a trip at any time for a dose of its languid sophistication. The nearby tiny country towns of Federal and Newrybar are worth stopping by for some surprising, excellent restaurants.

✦ Festivals & Events

Sample Food Festival FOOD & DRINK
(https://samplefoodevents.com; Bangalow Showgrounds, Market St; ⏱ Sep; ♿) Brings together local growers, chefs, restaurateurs and food lovers to celebrate the amazing produce of northern NSW. There are cooking demonstrations, workshops by celebrated chefs, and food – plenty of food.

🛏 Sleeping & Eating

★ **Bangalow Guesthouse** B&B **$$$**
(☏ 02-6687 1317; www.bangalowguesthouse.com. au; 99 Byron St; r $195-285; 🅿) This stately old wooden villa sits on the river's edge, so

guests can spot platypuses and oversized lizards as they enjoy breakfast. It's the stuff of B&B dreams, with spacious private rooms and elegant, soulful decor that works well with the original architecture.

Doma Cafe JAPANESE $$

(✆02-6688 4711; 3-6 Albert St, Federal; mains $16-28; ◷7.30am-2.30pm Mon-Fri, to 3pm Sat & Sun) ✐ In a wooden building in the tiny town of Federal is not where you'd expect to find some of the region's best Japanese cuisine being served, yet here it is. There's a full breakfast menu with Japanese twists, *temaki*-style sushi (cone-shaped) made with organic brown rice, and lunch mains like the chicken *katsu* burger, all to be enjoyed at the garden tables.

★Harvest CAFE $$$

(✆02-6687 2644; https://harvestnewrybar.com. au; 18-22 Old Pacific Hwy, Newrybar; breakfast $14-23, lunch $28-42, dinner $19-44; ◷noon-11pm Mon-Fri, from 8am Sat & Sun) ✐ Responsible for putting the hinterland town of Newrybar on the map, Harvest is one part restaurant and one part deli-bakery housed in a rustic Queenslander and serving a showcase of local produce, much of which comes from its own garden. Sourdough is cranked out from the 100-year-old wood-fired oven, while foraged native ingredients are a feature in the lunch and dinner offerings.

★Town Restaurant & Cafe AUSTRALIAN $$$

(✆02-6687 2555; www.facebook.com/town bangalow; 33 Byron St; cafe mains $16-24, restaurant degustation $95; ◷cafe 7.30am-3pm Mon-Sat, from 9am Sun, restaurant 7-9.30pm Thu-Sat) Upstairs (Uptown, if you will) is one of northern NSW's perennially excellent restaurants, serving a seven-course degustation menu carefully and imaginatively constructed from seasonal local produce. There's a vegetarian option too, and both menus can be had with matched wines (add $65). Head Downtown for simple but beautifully done cafe breakfasts, light lunches and a counter that's heavy with sweet baked things.

ⓘ Getting There & Away

Blanch's (✆02-6686 2144; www.blanchs.com. au) Weekday buses to/from Ballina ($7.40, 35 minutes) and Byron Bay ($5, 25 minutes).

Northern Rivers Buslines (✆02-6626 1499; www.nrbuslines.com.au; 🕾) Weekday buses to/from Lismore ($7, 1¼ hours).

NSW TrainLink (✆13 22 32; www.nswtrainlink. info) Daily coaches to/from Byron Bay ($7, 15 minutes), Murwillumbah ($14, 1¼ hours), Tweed Heads ($16, 2¼ hours), Burleigh Heads ($20, 1½ hours) and Surfers Paradise ($22, two hours).

Lismore

POP 27,569

Lismore is the unassuming commercial centre of the Northern Rivers region, full of heritage buildings and possessing a country-town saunter. A vibrant community of creatives, the Southern Cross University student population and a larger than average gay and lesbian presence provide the town with an unexpected eclecticism. It can be an interesting place to visit, though most travellers prefer to stay on the coast or venture deeper into the hinterland.

The Bundjalung people are the traditional custodians of this land.

⊙ Sights

Lismore Regional Gallery GALLERY

(✆02-6627 4600; www.lismoregallery.org; 11 Rural St; ◷10am-4pm Tue-Sun, to 6pm Thu) FREE Having relocated to a new space in 2017, Lismore's gallery has long been a cultural force in the town and a real centre of creative life in the region. It holds excellent regularly changing exhibitions, there are free 30-minute guided tours at 10am Wednesdays and 1pm Sundays, and an on-site cafe.

✸ Festivals & Events

Tropical Fruits LGBT

(www.tropicalfruits.org.au; ◷31 Dec) This legendary New Year's bash is country NSW's biggest gay and lesbian event. There are also parties at Easter and on the Queen's Birthday holiday in June.

Lismore Lantern Parade PARADE

(www.lanternparade.com; ◷Jun) Thousands of people line the streets to watch giant illuminated creatures glide past on the Saturday closest to the winter solstice.

⌂ Sleeping & Eating

★Melville House B&B $$

(✆02-6621 5778; www.melvillehouselismore.com; 267 Ballina St; s $40-140, d $50-165; ✳☀🕾) This grand country home was built in 1942 by the owner's grandfather and features the area's largest private swimming pool. The

DON'T MISS

KOALA-SPOTTING IN LISMORE

Lismore has a high concentration of koalas living in and around the city, so it's a great place to see these adorable creatures in the wild. First stop on your koala-spotting excursion should be a tour of the **Koala Care Centre** (☑ 02-6621 4664; www.friendsofthekoala.org; 23 Rifle Range Rd; adult/family $5/10; ☺ tours 10am & 2pm Mon-Fri, 10am Sat), where donations help support the volunteer service that looks after sick and injured koalas. Just nearby is **Robinson's Lookout** (Robinson Ave, Girard's Hill), a picnic area where koalas are often spotted. Other places to scope out are the **Lismore Workers Golf Club** and **Tucki Tucki Nature Reserve**, 15km outside the city.

six rooms offer superb value and are decorated with local art, cut glass and antiques. Some have external bathrooms, but even the small 'struggling writer's room' has its own. Breakfast is included for the larger rooms; otherwise it's $10 extra.

Elindale House   B&B $$
(☑ 02-6622 2533; www.elindale.com.au; 34 Second Ave; d $160; P ❋ ☎) Any apparent chintziness is tempered by good-quality furnishings at this excellent B&B set in a characterful weatherboard house. The four rooms each have their own bathroom and pretty four-poster bed. A fantastic breakfast is included featuring blueberry pancakes and organic eggs.

Goanna Bakery & Cafe   BAKERY, CAFE $
(www.facebook.com/GoannaBakeryandCafe; 171 Keen St; dishes $7-14; ☺ 7.30am-5.30pm Mon-Fri; ☑) As well as baking organic sourdough bread and a delectable array of sweet things (gluten-free options too), this cavernous bakery-cafe serves a great selection of vegetarian and vegan meals.

★**Loft**   AUSTRALIAN $$$
(☑ 02-6622 0252; 6 Nesbitt Lane; mains $34-38; ☺ 5pm-late Wed-Sat) Slink into this split-level, dark, moody and intimate laneway spot to dine on fine Modern Australian dishes to a backdrop of street-art mural feature walls. Start with some Sydney rock oysters before moving onto a main of goat-cheese-stuffed zucchini flowers and house-made gnocchi or

the firm favourite: slow roasted lamb shoulder. The bar crowd often spills out into the laneway.

🛍 Shopping

Lismore has more markets than anywhere else in the region, with a weekly **organic market** (Lismore Showground; ☺ 7.30-11am Tue), a **produce market** (Magellan St; ☺ 2.30-6.30pm Thu), a **farmers market** (Lismore Showground; ☺ 8-11.30am Sat) and a **car-boot market** (Lismore Shopping Sq, Uralba St; ☺ 7.30am-2pm 1st Sun of month).

ℹ Information

Lismore Visitor Information Centre (☑ 1300 369 795, 02-6626 0100; www.visitlismore.com.au; 207 Molesworth St; ☺ 9.30am-4pm) Helpful and knowledgeable staff, a walk-through rainforest display, and a small exhibition on the local Bundjalung Aboriginal people and culture.

ℹ Getting There & Away

Regional Express (Rex; ☑ 13 17 13; www.regionalexpress.com.au) flies to/from Sydney. Buses stop at the **Lismore City Transit Centre** (cnr Molesworth & Magellan Sts).

Northern Rivers Buslines (☑ 02-6622 1499; www.nrbuslines.com.au) Local buses plus services to/from Grafton (three hours), Ballina (1¼ hours), Lennox Head (one hour), Bangalow (1¼ hours) and Byron Bay (1½ hours); all fares are $7.

NSW TrainLink (☑ 13 22 32; www.nswtrainlink.info) Coaches to/from Byron Bay ($9, one hour), Mullumbimby ($18, 1½ hours), Brunswick Heads ($14, 1½ hours) and Brisbane ($40, three hours).

Waller's (☑ 02-6622 6266; www.wallersbus.com) Three buses weekdays to/from Nimbin ($9.50, 30 minutes).

Nimbin
POP 1477

Welcome to Australia's alternative-lifestyle capital, a little town famous for its marijuana culture that almost drowns under the weight of its own clichés. Set in an impossibly pretty valley, Nimbin was once an unremarkable dairy village, but was changed forever in May 1973. Thousands of counter-culture kids and back-to-earth-movement types descended on the town for the Aquarius Festival. Many stayed on and created new communities in the beautiful countryside, hoping to continue the ideals expressed during the 10-day celebration.

Genuine remnants of the peace-and-love generation remain – psychedelic murals of the rainbow-serpent Dreaming still line the main street – though the town has become somewhat shadier since its heyday and can feel threatening in areas. But dig a little deeper and you'll find a strong community spirit and a focus on sustainability. A targeted police crackdown of late means Nimbin may just be losing its hold as the weed capital of Australia.

◉ Sights

Hemp Embassy   CULTURAL CENTRE
(☎02-6689 1842; www.hempembassy.net; 51 Cullen St; ⊙10am-5pm) Part shop, part stronghold for minor political group the Hemp Party, this colourful place raises consciousness about impending marijuana legalisation, and sells all the paraphernalia you'll need to attract police attention. The embassy organises the **MardiGrass festival** (www.nimbinmardigrass.com) in May and there's an attached cafe-bar selling teas, smoothies and snacks.

Djanbung Gardens   GARDENS
(☎02-6689 1755; www.permaculture.com.au; 74 Cecil St; ⊙10.30am-4pm Wed-Sun) FREE Nimbin has been at the forefront of the organic gardening movement and this world-renowned permaculture education centre, created out of a degraded cow pasture, is home to food forests, vegetable gardens, a droughtproof system of dams, ponds and furry farm animals. Pick up a map for a self-guided wander. There's a range of short courses available too.

🛏 Sleeping & Eating

★Nimbin Rox YHA   HOSTEL $
(☎02-6689 0022; www.nimbinrox.com.au; 74 Thorburn St; dm/d/bell tents from $26/65/98; @🛜🛖) Escape the coastal crowds at this hostel perched on a lush hill at the edge of town offering dorms, private rooms and lovely bell tents. There's plenty of spots to unwind, with hammocks strung among the trees, an inviting heated pool and a nearby swimming creek. Friendly managers go out of their way to please and there's a regular shuttle into town.

Grey Gum Lodge   GUESTHOUSE $
(☎02-6689 1713; www.greygumlodge.com; 2 High St; d $89-135; @🛜) The valley views from the front verandah of this palm-draped wooden Queenslander-style house is gorgeous. Each

of the six rooms are comfortable, tastefully furnished and have its own bathroom.

Bush Theatre Cafe   CAFE $$
(https://nimbinbushtheatre.com; Nimbin Bush Theatre, 2 Blue Knob Rd; mains $10-22; ⊙9am-4pm, later on theatre event days; 🖉) At this relaxed cafe with seating under the trees amid the bush-food gardens, you can drop by to breakfast on granola and free-range eggs on toast, or come for the creative burgers at lunch, including a hempseed felafel burger or the Barramundi burger with pepperberry and finger lime aioli.

🛍 Shopping

Nimbin Organic
Food Co-op   FOOD & DRINKS
(☎02-6689 1445; https://nimbinfoodcoop.org; 50 Cullen St; ⊙9am-5.30pm Mon-Fri, 9.30am-2pm Sat, 1-5pm Sun) This volunteer-run, not-for-profit co-op stocks a range of ethically farmed organic produce from fresh fruit and veg to local honey, vegan ice cream and loaves of sourdough.

Nimbin Candle Factory   ARTS & CRAFTS
(☎02-6689 1010; www.nimbincandles.com.au; Unit 5, Old Butter Factory, 2 Blue Knob Rd; ⊙9am-5pm Mon-Fri, 11am-4pm Sat & Sun) Around for almost 30 years, this working candle factory sells hand-dipped paraffin candles shaped like marijuana leaves, rainbow pyramids, wizards and unicorns in the Old Butter Factory by the bridge. It has supplied candles for some big-name movie sets, such as *Pirates of the Caribbean* and *The Great Gatsby*.

❶ Information

Nimbin Visitor Information Centre (☎02-6689 1388; www.visitnimbin.com.au; 46 Cullen St; ⊙10am-4pm) in the heart of town has accommodation options, bus tickets and a wealth of knowledge.

The community website (www.nimbinweb.com.au) is useful.

❶ Getting There & Away

Various operators offer day tours or shuttles to Nimbin from Byron Bay, sometimes with stops at surrounding sights.

Gosel's (☎02-6677 9394) Two buses on weekdays from Murwillumbah ($9.60, 1½ hours) via Uki.

Grasshoppers (☎0438 269 076; www.grasshoppers.com.au) Tours to Nimbin ($65, including BBQ lunch).

SYDNEY & NEW SOUTH WALES NIMBIN

HINTERLAND NATIONAL PARKS

Nightcap National Park (www.nationalparks.nsw.gov.au/nightcap-national-park; vehicles $8) The spectacular waterfalls, the sheer cliff of solidified lava and the dense rainforest of 80-sq-km Nightcap National Park, the traditional land of the Widjabul people, are perhaps to be expected in an area with the highest annual rainfall in NSW. It's part of the Gondwana Rainforests World Heritage Area and home to many native birds and protected creatures.

The **Historic Nightcap Track** (18km, 1½ days), which was stomped out by postal workers in the late 19th century, runs from Mt Nardi to Rummery Park, a picnic spot and campground. The **Minyon Loop** (7.5km, 4½ hours) is a terrific half-day hike around the spectacular Minyon Falls, which are good for an icy splash. There's a lookout over the top of the falls, a 50m walk from the car park. A largely unsealed but very scenic road leads from the Channon to the Terania Creek Picnic Area, where an easy track (1.4km return, 1½ hours) heads to the base of **Protestor Falls**; swimming not permitted.

The park is around 30km west of Mullumbimby and 25km north of Lismore. From Nimbin, it's a 12km drive via Tuntable Falls Rd, from where Newton Dr leads to the edge of the park and then on to Mt Nardi (800m).

Border Ranges National Park (www.nationalparks.nsw.gov.au/visit-a-park/parks/border-ranges-national-park; vehicles $8) The vast Border Ranges National Park covers 317 sq km on the NSW side of the McPherson Range, which runs along the NSW–Queensland border. It's part of the Gondwana Rainforests World Heritage Area and it's estimated that representatives of a quarter of all bird species in Australia can be found here.

The eastern section of the park can be explored on the 64km **Tweed Range Scenic Drive** (gravel, and usable in dry weather), which loops through the park from Lillian Rock (midway between Uki and Kyogle) to Wiangaree (north of Kyogle on Summerland Way). The signposting on access roads isn't good (when in doubt take roads signposted to the national park), but it's well worth the effort.

The road runs through mountain rainforest, with steep hills and lookouts over the Tweed Valley to Wollumbin/Mt Warning and the coast. The 10-minute walk out to the **Pinnacle Lookout** is a highlight and one of the best places to see the silhouette of Wollumbin against a rising sun. At **Antarctic Beech** picnic area there is a forest of 2000-year-old beech trees. From here, a walking track (about 5km) leads down to lush rainforest, swimming holes and a picnic area at **Brindle Creek**. If you do take a dip, be sure you're not wearing sunscreen or insect repellant as the chemicals are dangerous for the local frog population.

To access the Tweed Range Scenic Drive from Murwillumbah, follow the Kyogle Rd west to Lillian Rock then turn right at Williams Rd and follow the signs. It takes around two hours. If travelling from Lismore, the drive takes around 1¼ hours.

Wollumbin National Park (www.nationalparks.nsw.gov.au/wollumbin-national-park) Northwest of Uki, 41-sq-km Wollumbin National Park surrounds Wollumbin/Mt Warning (1156m), the most dramatic feature of the hinterland, towering over the valley. Its Aboriginal name, Wollumbin, means 'cloud catcher', 'fighting chief of the mountain' or 'weather maker'. Its English name was given to it by James Cook in 1770 to warn seafarers of offshore reefs.

The summit is the first part of mainland Australia to see sunlight each day, a drawcard that encourages many to make the trek to the top. You should be aware that, under the law of the local Bundjalung people, only certain people are allowed to climb the sacred mountain; they ask you not to climb it, out of respect for this law. Instead, you can get an artist's impression of the view from the 360-degree mural at the Murwillumbah Visitor Information Centre (☎02-6672 1340; https://visitthetweed.com.au; 218 Tweed Valley Way; ⏰9am-4.30pm Mon-Sat, 9.30am-4pm Sun).

Wollumbin is part of the Gondwana Rainforests World Heritage Area. Keep an eye out for the elusive Albert's lyrebird on the Lyrebird Track (300m return through palm forest).

Happy Coach (☑ 02-6685 3996; www. happycoachbyron.com; tours $55) Runs tours to Nimbin ($55); lunch is included in the price.

Waller's (☑ 02-6622 6266; www.wallersbus. com) At least three buses on weekdays to/from Lismore ($9.50, 30 minutes).

NEW ENGLAND

Despite its unfamiliarity, and the fact the Gamilaroi people had owned this land for untold millennia, the verdant scenery of this region prompted its first British occupiers to name it 'New England'. While visitors may squint hard to see the likeness, the forested uplands of the Northern Tablelands reminded the homesick early settlers of the Scotland and Wales, and the landscape bears 'Celtic' names and the label of 'Celtic country' to this day. It's a stretch, but there's no denying its rustic beauty when mist settles in the cool-climate hilltops and fertile valleys, little churches are glimpsed in oak-studded paddocks and little-used roads wind through landscapes greener than most in Australia. Tempering this fragile idyll, regional centres such as Tamworth and Armidale are robust and dynamic towns with plenty to offer those seeking culture, food and comfort.

Tamworth

POP 33,885

Australia's country-music capital has a good deal more to it than the annual festival and a reverence for Slim Dusty. The centre of a bounteous farming district traditionally owned by the Gamilaroi people, its broad streets range back from the Peel River, laid out in a grid studded with museums, art-deco hotels, cafes and restaurants. South of town is the much-photographed Golden Guitar, a landmark proclaiming Tamworth's infatuation with the song of the cowboy, while to the northeast sit modest uplands offering comprehensive views of rich farmland spreading out in all directions.

◉ Sights & Activities

★ **Powerstation Museum**　　　MUSEUM
(☑ 02-6766 8324; www.tamworthpowerstation museum.com.au; 216 Peel St; adult/child $9/5; ⊙ 9am-1pm Wed-Sat) FREE This wonderful little volunteer-run museum commemorates Tamworth's status as 'City of Light' – the first town in Australia to get electric light.

Housed in a 1907 power station packed to the rafters with electrotherapy machines, early communications devices and other fascinating artefacts, its pride and joy are two working steam dynamos, one identical to that used to first deliver power to the town in 1888.

★ **Tamworth Marsupial Park**　　　PARK
(Endeavour Dr; ⊙ 8am-5pm; ⚡) FREE Take Brisbane St 2km east to this little haven of native fauna above Tamworth, where you can get close to wallabies, echidnas, kangaroos and other native mammals in a natural bush setting. There's also an aviary where you can walk among the carolling and squawking of king parrots, scarlet rosellas and other resplendent species, a picnic area with barbecues and an adventure playground. A walking track connects to the nearby **Botanic Gardens**.

Country Music Hall of Fame　　　MUSEUM
(☑ 02-6766 9696; www.countrymusichalloffame. com.au; 561 Peel St; adult/child $7/free; ⊙ 10am-4pm; 🅿 ⚡) Recognised as a collection of 'national and international significance', this trove of artefacts and dioramas explores Australasian country music's rich story. There are two principal exhibitions – the memorabilia-filled Walk a Country Mile, and the Country Music Hall of Fame – housed inside the giant guitar-shaped building.

Oxley Scenic Lookout　　　VIEWPOINT
(Scenic Rd; ⊙ 7am-10pm) FREE Follow Tamworth's jacaranda-lined White St to the very top, where you'll reach this viewpoint. It's the best seat in the house as the sun goes down.

**Leconfield Jackaroo
& Jillaroo School**　　　HORSE RIDING
(☑ 02-6769 4328; www.leconfield.com; 'Bimboola', Kootingal; 5-day courses $695) Keen on riding, mustering, 'natural horsemanship' and general rural skills? This fair-dinkum course, held on a ranch about 43km east of Tamworth, will teach you many of the tricks you'll need to get farm work (and can also help with job placement). Students can be collected from Tamworth YHA.

✯ Festivals & Events

★ **Tamworth
Country Music Festival**　　　MUSIC
(www.tcmf.com.au; ⊙ mid-Jan) Held over 10 rollicking days from mid-January, the TCMF is the undisputed king of Australian country

music events. Typically the festival features more than 700 performers across 120 venues, with around 2800 single events entertaining some tens of thousands of visitors. That's an awful lot of boot-scooting...

🛏 Sleeping

Rex Tamworth HOSTEL $
(☑ 02-6766 1030; www.rextamworth.com; 32 White St; d from $60; P ❄ ⓦ) Tamworth's friendliest hostel, with a hotch-potch of colourful, quirky rooms that have eclectic cheapo and vintage furnishings, sits on a quiet, leafy street away from the main drag. The open fire is a nice touch in New England winters, when the more basic outdoor rooms can get chilly.

★ CH Boutique Hotel BOUTIQUE HOTEL $$
(☑ 02-6766 7260; www.chboutiquehotel.com.au; cnr Peel & Brisbane Sts; d from $169; P @ ⓦ) With 33 rooms housed in a slate-grey modern cube built in 2018 as an annex to the handsome, art-deco Central Hotel, CH is Tamworth's swankiest hotel. Rooms, including 29 in the original building, are decorated in sleek monochrome, and feature sparkling bathrooms and quality beds with downy pillow-top mattresses and good linen. Parking is $10 per night.

Retreat at Frog-Moore Park B&B $$
(☑ 02-6766 3353; www.froogmoorepark.com.au; 78 Bligh St; d from $179; P ⓦ) Perhaps best described as 'futuristic bordello chic', the extravagant decor that greets you as you step inside the Retreat continues into five individually-styled suites, fully justifying names such as 'Moroccan Fantasy' and 'The Dungeon'. Food at this unique 'hotel' is a highlight: breakfasts ($25 per head) feature homemade-preserves and sourdough, while elaborate dinners ($60 per head) explore the globe. The Retreat isn't set up for children under 16.

🍴 Eating

★ Glasshouse at Goonoo Goonoo AUSTRALIAN $$
(☑ 0429 384 297; www.goonoogoonoostation. com; 13304 New England Hwy, Timbumburi; mains $34-35; ⊘ 8-11am Sat & Sun, noon-3.30pm Fri-Sun, 5.30-11.30pm Wed-Sat; P) The Glasshouse is just that: a stunningly designed glass-walled dining room set on the historic sheep station of Goonoo Goonoo (pronounced 'gun-oo gun-oo'). It's also head-and-shoulders above

any restaurant in the Tamworth area, with an expertly staffed open kitchen turning out delights such as tea-smoked chicken with truffled chat potatoes, or a rib-cracking Florentine steak for two, served with chimichurri.

★ Ruby's Cafe & Gift Store CAFE $$
(☑ 02-6766 9833; 494 Peel St; mains $19-21; ⊘ 8am-3pm Tue-Thu, to 4pm Fri, 9am-3pm Sat, 8am-noon Sun; ❄ ⓦ) Ruby's is a gem: a charismatic, eclectically-decorated cafe with stripped-brick walls, deft baristas and garden tables that suggest lazy brunches. The food's good too: perhaps smashed avocado and poached egg on pane di casa or savoury mince with balsamic glaze (again with a poached googy on pane di casa).

ℹ Information

Tamworth Visitor Information Centre (☑ 02-6767 5300; www.destinationtamworth.com. au; cnr New England Hwy & The Ringers Rd; ⊘ 9am-5pm; ⓦ) Look for the Big Golden Guitar (☑ 02-6765 2688; www.biggoldenguitar.com. au; New England Hwy; ⊘ 9am-5pm; P ♿) to locate this helpful local tourist office.

ℹ Getting There & Away

Tamworth is 115km southwest of Armidale on the New England Hwy.

Qantas (QF; ☑ 13 13 13; www.qantas.com.au) affiliates have at least two flights a day between Tamworth and Sydney.

Fly Corporate (https://flycorporate.com.au) runs up to four flights per day between Tamworth and Brisbane.

New England Coaches (☑ 02-6732 1051; www. newenglandcoaches.com.au) runs some useful services: Tamworth to Coffs Harbour ($90) and Tamworth to Brisbane ($115). Both run three times a week.

NSW TrainLink (☑ 13 15 00; www.nswtrainlink. info) runs a daily service between Sydney and Tamworth (from $42, six hours) that continues on to Armidale.

Armidale

POP 20,386

Sitting high on NSW's Northern Tablelands, surrounded by prime grazing country traditionally owned by the Anaiwan people, Armidale – with its broad streets, lattice-wrapped pubs and distinctive bluebrick buildings – is the de facto capital of this region. Established in the rush for

THE FOSSICKERS WAY

The Fossickers Way (www.fossickersway.com) is a scenic driving route that begins about 60km southeast of Tamworth at Nundle, continues through Tamworth, then 191km north to Warialda, and on 124km east through Inverell to Glen Innes, 100km north of Armidale. Public transport along the Fossickers Way is scarce – renting a car or driving your own will give you the freedom to explore properly.

One of Australia's original touring routes through an area rich in minerals and semi-precious stones, it passes through old country towns that saw their heyday post-1851 when gold was discovered outside Tamworth.

Abutting the Gwydir River, **Bingara** is prime horse-riding country and one of the nicest towns along the Fossickers Way. Its main street has been lovingly preserved over the years and there's a self-evident sense of community in the town. Nothing showcases this better than the **Roxy Theatre Greek Museum** (☑ 02-6724 0066; www.roxybingara. com.au; 74 Maitland Street; museum $5, theatre & museum $10; ◷ 9am-12.30pm & 1.30-4.30pm Mon-Fri, to 1pm Sat & Sun) FREE, a lovingly-restored art-deco theatre, cafe and museum that also houses the town's **tourist office** (☑ 02-6724 0066; www.bingara.com.au; 74 Maitland St; ◷ 9am-4.30pm Mon-Fri, to noon Sat & Sun; 🐦). There's plenty to do here, from swimming in the outdoor pool to trail rides with **Wade Horses** (☑ 02-6724 1562; 17 Keera St; 2hr trail ride $60, 5-day course $600). Outside of town, the **Myall Creek Memorial** (cnr Delungra & Whitlow Rds) FREE, commemorating the massacre of at least 28 Gamilaroi people in 1838, is a sobering sight.

grazing land that followed from European colonists finally finding a way through the Blue Mountains to the Australian interior, its physical charms are augmented by four distinct seasons and the proximity of ravishingly beautiful forests and highlands. Summers are mild and clear in this this dignified regional centre, autumnal foliage is spectacular, crisp winters often see light snowfalls, and manicured gardens burst to life in an explosion of bright spring colours.

◉ Sights & Activities

See p168 for sights along the Waterfall Way east of Armidale.

Saumarez Homestead   HISTORIC BUILDING
(☑ 02-6772 3616; www.nationaltrust.org.au/ places/saumarez-homestead; 230 Saumarez Rd; adult/child grounds only $8/6, tours $15/10; ◷ 10am-5pm, tours 10.30am, 2pm, 3.30pm on weekends and public holidays, not available June 15 to September 1; P) This handsome mansion was built between 1888 and 1906 on one of the first sheep stations in the Armidale area, founded by gentleman grazier Henry Dumaresq in the 1830s. Guided tours are the only way to see inside the house, and you shouldn't miss the wonderfully preserved early-20th-century farm buildings a little way downhill.

**New England
Regional Art Museum**   MUSEUM
(NERAM; ☑ 02-6772 5255; www.neram.com.au; 106-114 Kentucky St; ◷ 10am-4pm Tue-Sun; P 🐦) FREE At the southern edge of Armidale, NERAM is the home of the Howard Hinton Collection, a veritable thesaurus of Australian art from the 1880s to the 1940s including works by Arthur Streeton, Margaret Preston, Norman Lindsay, Nora Heysen and other luminaries. Tours of the collection are offered at 2pm on Friday and Sunday, and the nearby Museum of Printing opens from 1pm to 4pm on Sunday.

Gorges by Chopper   SCENIC FLIGHTS
(☑ 02-6772 2348; www.fleethelicopters.com.au; Armidale Airport, 10541 New England Hwy; 30min flight per person from $275) This experienced helicopter-charter company offers half-hour aerial tours of New England's ravishing gorge country, leaving from Armidale airport. For more adventure, book the 60-minute Ten Gorges flight, or the three-hour Wilderness Picnic Adventure.

🛏 Sleeping & Eating

★ **Lindsay House**   B&B $$
(☑ 02-6771 4554; www.lindsayhouse.com.au; 128 Faulkner St; r from $130; P 🐦) Built for a doctor in the closing years of WWI, this dignified old Armidale blue-brick house is surrounded

by shady gardens and offers some of the town's most restful and tasteful accommodation. The five en-suite rooms, decked out in Victorian and Edwardian antiques, sacrifice nothing in modern comfort.

Petersons Guesthouse GUESTHOUSE $$$
(☑02-6772 0422; www.petersonsguesthouse.com.au; Dangarsleigh Rd; r from $200; P🅿❄🛜) Built in 1911 as the summer home of local nabobs the Dangars, Petersons remains one of the finest houses in the district. Set amid rolling lawns and spreading plane trees, it contains seven guest rooms with underfloor-heated en suites, a handsome lobby where fireside glasses of port are served in winter, and a dining room open seven nights a week.

★**Goldfish Bowl** CAFE $$
(☑02-6771 5533; 3/160 Rusden St; lunch $18-20; ☺7.30am-3pm Mon-Fri, to 1pm Sat; ❄) Hands-down the best lunch-stop in Armidale, the Goldfish Bowl serves top-notch coffee alongside artisanal breads and pastries, and toothsome lunches such as Keralan mackerel curry and succulent fried chicken burger with blue-cheese dressing and jalapeños. Every Friday from noon to 2.30pm and 5.30 to 8.30pm the wood oven cranks out pizzas with next-level toppings such as 'nduja salumi with olives, anchovies and fior di latte.

Bistro on Cinders FUSION $$
(☑02-6772 2828; 14 Cinders Lane; mains $24-26; ☺7.30am-2pm Tue-Sat & 6-9pm Fri & Sat; P🅿❄) Behind Armidale's post office is this cool, contemporary, family-run bistro à la mode focused around a small courtyard. The ever-changing menu fuses a variety of Asian and Western styles to create inventive dishes like cauliflower and thyme butter soup, Moroccan spiced lamb pies and Thai calamari salad.

🍷 **Drinking & Nightlife**

Eastview Estate WINERY
(☑02-6778 7473; www.eastviewestate.com; 298 Kentucky Rd, Kentucky; ☺10.30am-3.30pm) The sleepy hamlet of Kentucky, 40km southwest of Armidale, is home to this quirky winery, distillery and restaurant. The gins are particularly well regarded, and go down well with a dollop of jazz and blues in the steampunk-themed 'speakeasy'. Lunches – perhaps blackened salmon salad or a ploughman's platter groaning with house-made

charcuterie and preserves (mains $27 to $30) – are available on weekends.

The Welder's Dog CRAFT BEER
(☑0477 545 035; 120 Marsh St; ☺2pm-midnight Tue-Sat, 2-10pm Sun, 4pm-midnight Mon) Craft beer has a home in Armidale now, with this buzzy little streetcorner bar offering its own classic brews, quality drops from around Australia, and unusual tipples such as Cherry Brut Sour Ale and Pea Blossom Lemonade. Ballast for convivial evenings comes from a deli cabinet full of local cheese and charcuterie.

ℹ️ **Information**

Armidale Visitor Information Centre (☑02-6770 3888; www.armidaletourism.com.au; 82 Marsh St; ☺9am-5pm; 🛜) Runs tours and is the fount of knowledge for all things Armidale.

ℹ️ **Getting There & Away**

Armidale is approximately 485km north of Sydney via the Pacific Motorway and New England Hwy. A good option is to take the Pacific Hwy to Coffs Harbour, then scoot inland for 190km along the wonderfully scenic Waterfall Way.

Qantas (p194) and **Rex** (☑13 17 13; www.rex.com.au) both fly the Sydney–Armidale route at least once per day.

New England Coaches (☑02-6732 1051; www.newenglandcoaches.com.au) runs services to Coffs Harbour ($70, 3¼ hours) and to Brisbane ($105, 6½ hours). Both services run three times a week.

NSW TrainLink (p194) operates daily direct rail services between Armidale and Sydney (from $47, eight hours).

Tenterfield

POP 2914

Boasting a pedigree that outstrips its undemonstrative present, the quiet highland town of Tenterfield is loosely regarded as the birthplace of the Australian nation. It was at the Tenterfield School of Arts in 1889 that Sir Henry Parkes delivered the speech that gave the most impetus to the Federation of all Australian states in 1901. Its other claim to fame is that entertainer Peter Allen (the 'Boy from Oz'), was born here: some may remember his famous song 'Tenterfield Saddler', and all can still visit the workshop that inspired the tune. Boasting a clutch of charming heritage buildings, today's Tenterfield serves as the regional hub for a smattering of villages surrounded by picturesque national parks. High altitude means cooler climes in summer, and occasional ground-snow accumulations in winter. The Bundalung are the traditional owners of this land.

⊙ Sights

Bald Rock National Park
NATIONAL PARK

(☑ 02-6736 4298; www.nationalparks.nsw.gov. au; Mount Lindesay Rd; per car per day $8; P🚻) This gorgeous eucalyptus, wattle and blackbutt forest straddles the NSW–Queensland border about 35km northeast of Tenterfield. Its eponymous feature is Australia's largest granite monolith, a 200m x 750m x 500m behemoth that looks like a stripy little Uluru. There are lovely walks in the area (including two routes up the rock for great views), plus picnic sites and a camping area (adult/child $12/6) near the base. Native mammals (quolls, swamp wallabies and grey kangaroos) and birdsong are highlights.

Sir Henry Parkes
Memorial School of Arts
HISTORIC BUILDING

(☑ 02-6736 3592; www.schoolofartstenterfield. com/museum; 201-205 Rouse St; adult/child $7/3.50; ⊙10am-4pm) This beautifully restored hall, built for the Tenterfield School of Arts in 1876, now houses an interesting museum to Sir Henry Parkes, Australia's 'Father of Federation'. Decked out with colonial-era flags and gleaming wood, it's notable as the place where Parkes delivered the 1889 Tenterfield Oration, proposing the federation of the six separate British colonies in Australia. Aside from 50-odd artefacts relating to Parkes, there's a library, cinema and courtyard cafe (mains $15).

🛏 Sleeping

Tenterfield Lodge
& Caravan Park
CARAVAN PARK $

(☑ 02-6736 1477; www.tenterfieldlodgecaravanpark. com.au; 2 Manners St; unpowered/powered sites from $29, dm/cabins from $31/70; P🐾📶🐕) This friendly (and pet-friendly) place has a range of accommodation from campsites and on-site vans to small cabins. There's a camp kitchen, laundry, book exchange, picnic area and a neat little playground for kids.

★ Commercial
Boutique Hotel
BOUTIQUE HOTEL $$

(☑ 02-6736 4870; www.thecommercialboutique hotel.com; 288 Rouse St; r from $190; P❄📶)

This handsome art-deco pub has been reinvented as a glamorous boutique hotel, with eight en-suite rooms in stylish '40s monochrome. The equally stylish downstairs bar and restaurant serves excellent gastropub fare for lunch and dinner, seven days a week. Expect dishes such as lemon-myrtle crusted salmon and risotto of local speck with asparagus, confit garlic and parmesan (mains $29 to $35).

🍷 Drinking & Nightlife

Our Place
WINE BAR

(☑ 0488 014 152; www.ourplacewinebar.com; 204 Rouse St; ⊙8.30am-8.30pm) A cosy, couchequipped cafe that morphs into a wine bar with excellent food at night, Our Place is great for a drop-in most hours of the day. An interesting list of local wines is available (mostly by the bottle) with by-the-glass choices from around Australia. Food includes sharing platters of local cheese and charcuterie alongside interesting mains ($19 to $27).

ℹ Information

Tenterfield Visitor Information Centre (☑ 02-6736 1082; www.tenterfieldtourism.com.au; 157 Rouse St; ⊙9am-4.30pm Mon-Fri, to 4pm Sat, 10am-2pm Sun; 📶)

ℹ Getting There & Away

NSW TrainLink (p194) operates a daily bus to/from Armidale (from $18, 2½ hours) that connects to the daily train between Armidale and Sydney (from $47, eight hours).

New England Coaches (☑ 02-6732 1051; www.newenglandcoaches.com.au) operates a service three times a week to Armidale ($60, 2½ hours) and Brisbane ($80, 5½ hours).

Northern Rivers Buslines (☑ 02-6626 1499; www.nrbuslines.com.au) has two buses to/from Lismore every Monday, Wednesday and Friday ($7.40, 2¼ hours), with connections to Byron Bay.

NORTHERN NSW

People tend to race through the northwest part of central NSW and its flat archetypal Australian landscape, possibly with Queensland beaches on their minds, and certainly to the detriment of the wildlife whose corpses litter many roads (be warned: driving after dark can be dangerous). If Queensland isn't on the itinerary, the chances are Lightning

Ridge is. Like other outback mining communities, the town throws up as many characters as it does gems. This land traditionally belongs to the Gamilaroi people.

Coonabarabran

POP 2537

Coonabarabran ('Coona' to locals) is widely recognised as an ideal place for stargazing thanks to its pristine air, high altitude (505m) and low humidity. Several observatories have been established in the area. Sitting on land owned traditionally by the Gamilaroi people, it's an old-fashioned, welcoming sort of a country town, where the locals are likely to strike up a conversation with travellers over icy beer in one of its main-street pubs.

Perhaps the best reason to visit is for the town's proximity to the extraordinary Warrumbungle National Park, which in 2016 was declared Australia's first Dark Sky Park.

⊙ Sights

Coonabarabran has a few private observatories offering affordable, family-friendly night-sky shows (note that you'll need to phone first, as weather conditions need to be agreeable, and start times vary according to sunset).

★ Warrumbungle
National Park   NATIONAL PARK
(☑ 02-6825 4364; www.nationalparks.nsw.gov.au; John Renshaw Pkwy; per car per day $8; ⊙24hr; ℙ) This National Heritage–listed park is the area's great attraction. Cut by the dramatic, volcanic Warrumbungles (the name means 'Crooked Mountains' in the local Gamilaroi language), it's divided into an arid, western section and the wetter, forested east, providing a great variety of terrain for fauna such as red-necked wallabies and emus. Its most spectacular feature is the 100m-high volcanic dyke known as The Breadknife, accessible on the peerless 14.5km **Breadknife and Grand High Tops Walk**, leaving from Pincham car park.

Park fees are payable at the **Warrumbungle National Park NWPS Visitor Centre** (☑ 02-6825 4364; www.nationalparks.nsw.gov.au/things-to-do/Visitor-centres/Warrumbungle-Visitor-Centre/visitor-info; off John Renshaw Parkway, Warrumbungle National Park; ⊙9am-4pm; ☎), where you can also learn the Warrumbungle creation story, and about the park's

ecology and history. There are excellent campsites nearby at Camp Blackman (adult/child $6/3.50 per night), and at Camp Wambelong.

❶ Information

Coonabarabran Visitors Centre (☑1800 242 881; www.warrumbungleregion.com.au; Newell Hwy; ⊙9am-5pm; ☎) As well as providing maps and information on the Warrumbungle National Park and surrounds, this visitor centre houses a small, free dinosaur museum (check out the skull of the Diprotodon, a rhinoceros-sized marsupial found in the area until 46,000 years ago) and an Aboriginal keeping place showcasing art, tools and artefacts of the local Gamilaroi people.

❶ Getting There & Away

Coonabarabran is on the Newell Highway. The closest cities are Tamworth, 190km east, and Dubbo, 146km to the south.

NSW TrainLink (p194) operates a daily coach service to Lithgow (from $33, 5 hours) connecting to the Western XPT service (from $15, 2½ hours) to Sydney. The coach departs from the stop next to the Coonabarabran Visitor Information Centre.

Moree

POP 7383

Straddling the Mehi River on rich black-soil lands traditionally owned by the Gamilaroi, Moree is the largest town for some distance. It's also a focus of local Aboriginal community and culture, with a significant Indigenous population and a gallery showcasing local artists. In fact it has two very good galleries, plus broad riverside parks and a wonderful aquatic centre fed with geothermally heated water from the Great Artesian Basin.

⊙ Sights & Activities

★ Yaama Ganu Centre   GALLERY
(☑ 02-6794 3280; www.yaamaganu.com.au; 211 Balo St; ⊙8am-3pm Mon-Fri, to 1pm Sat; ℙ) **FREE** Exhibiting and selling pieces from local Aboriginal artists, plus select others from around the country, Yaama Ganu ('welcome all' in Gamilaroi) provides a window on current Indigenous artistic practice. Out the front is the **Gali Cafe**, which does breezy breakfasts such as smashed avocado on toast with feta ($12) and interesting lunches such as grilled turmeric chicken ($16).

Bank Art Museum Moree
GALLERY

(☑02-6757 3320; www.bamm.org.au; 25 Frome St; ⊙10am-5pm Mon-Fri, to 1pm Sat) FREE Occupying an elaborately facaded 1911 bank, this excellent local gallery holds one of regional NSW's most important collections of Aboriginal art. You'll see some of this exhibited over the gallery's two floors, alongside diverse examples of contemporary and local work. From 2019, the BAMM Art Fair, featuring various exhibitions, markets and 'micro-galleries', will be held here over June and July.

Moree Artesian Aquatic Centre
SWIMMING

(☑02-6752 2272; www.maacltd.com; 20 Anne St; adult/child $9/6.80; ⊙6am-8pm Mon-Fri, 7am-7pm Sat & Sun; ☻) These thermally heated baths – accidentally discovered in 1895 when a bore was sunk in the search for irrigation water – are a Moree highlight and local recreational favourite. With 41°C waters constantly seeping up from the Great Artesian Basin, the baths now boast a day spa and a modern aquatic and fitness complex.

✖ Eating

Thub Thim Thai
THAI $$

(☑02-6751 1220; cnr Adelaide & Frome Sts; mains $18-21; ⊙5-9pm) This Thai restaurant is the kind of hidden gem that you hope to stumble across in a rural town, off the tourist trail. Gracious service and indubitable authenticity in the kitchen make for a fantastic dining experience – grilled coconut chicken, yum talay seafood salad, noodles, curries: it's all fantastic.

ⓘ Information

Moree Visitor Information Centre (☑02-6757 3350; www.moreetourism.com.au; 67 Alice St; ⊙9am-5pm Mon-Fri, to 1pm Sat & Sun; ☎)

ⓘ Getting There & Away

Moree is situated at the intersection of the Gwydir and Newell Hwys.

NSW TrainLink (p194) operates a daily XPT rail service between Sydney and Moree (from $51, 8½ hours), the end of the line.

Lightning Ridge
POP 1437

This quirky outback mining town (one of the world's few sources of valuable black opals) has real frontier spirit, and is home to eccentric artisans, true-blue bushies and a generally unconventional collective. Unique and beautiful (in a sparse, dusty kind of way), 'The Ridge' is a worthwhile destination for those seeking the offbeat, if you're prepared to make the long and monotonous drive.

⊙ Sights & Activities

★ Chambers of the Black Hand
GALLERY

(☑02-6829 0221; www.chambersoftheblackhand.com.au; 3 Mile Rd, Yellow Car Door 5; adult/child $40/10; ⊙rolling tours from 9.30am-noon & 1-3pm Apr-Oct, 10am-noon Nov-Mar; P ☻) This place is remarkable, and symbolises the crazy and creative sides of the Ridge. Artist and miner Ron Canlin has turned a 40ft-deep mining claim into a cavernous gallery of over 800 sculptures of superheroes, celebrities, pharaohs, Buddhas, dinosaurs and other diverse subjects. Call to confirm tour times; courtesy-bus pick-up from your accommodation is offered.

Opal Mine Adventure
MINE

(☑02-6829 0473; www.opalmineadventure.com.au; 132 Wooloroo Rd, Blue Car Door 4; adult/child $20/8; ⊙9am-5pm; P ☻) The most easily accessible mine in Lightning Ridge, hand-dug in the 1960s, lets visitors get a feel for the type of cramped environment encountered by the average opal miner. Tours are self-guided, including a film on the process and culture of opal mining, and there's a gem showroom and unwashed fossicking heaps to search for rough opals.

★ Lightning Ridge Bore Baths
SWIMMING

(☑02-6829 1670; Pandora St; ⊙closed 10am-noon Mon-Fri) FREE The hot (41.5°C), mineral-rich water in these scenic, open-air baths is drawn from the Great Artesian Basin, 1200m below ground. Sunrise or sunset here can be magnificent, and chatting with the locals is a treat. Note: it's usually closed for cleaning from 10am to noon on weekdays, and the water's high temperatures aren't suitable for small children.

🛏 Sleeping

★ Opal Caravan Park
CARAVAN PARK $$

(☑02-6829 4884; www.opalcaravanpark.com.au; 142 Pandora St; campsites from $28, cabins from $120; P ❄ ☎ ☲) This smartly planned and run bushland caravan park near the

Lightning Ridge Bore Baths offers excellent modern facilities: self-contained cabins, a swimming pool, wi-fi, powered and unpowered sites with en suite, a camp kitchen with pizza oven and a courtesy bus to whisk you into town. There's even a small area for fossicking.

ℹ Information

Lightning Ridge Visitor Information Centre
(📞 02-6829 1670; www.lightningridgeinfo.com. au; Lions Park, Morilla St; ⊙9am-5pm Apr-Oct, 9am-1pm Sat & Sun Nov-Mar; 🛜) Informed and friendly, this tourist office closes during the week over summer.

ℹ Getting There & Away

Located 728km northwest of Sydney, Lightning Ridge is only accessible by road. The only public transport is a NSW Trainlink bus service from Dubbo.

Exercise caution if you're arriving or departing in the early morning or latter half of the day: it's easy to get sleepy or distracted on the 80km straight stretch of the Castlereagh Hwy between Walgett and the Ridge. At dawn and dusk, abundant (and we really mean abundant, here) wildlife – kangaroos, emus, birds – may dart onto the road at any time. The bodies of the many that didn't make it line the roads.

CENTRAL NSW

The relative proximity of Central New South Wales to Sydney, plus its bucolic landscapes, sees the region's agricultural communities gain popularity among weekenders, grey nomads on tour and city slickers seeking a tree-change. Getting here by road or rail, traversing the iconic Blue Mountains across the Great Dividing Range, is half the fun. Stately buildings, wide streets and well-tended parks and gardens align Central NSW's larger centres with a colonial history built on gold mining and bushranger folklore.

Both Orange and Mudgee are must-dos for foodies and winos alike, while travelling families love Dubbo, Parkes and Bathurst for their selection of kid-friendly museums and attractions. Further afield, pretty Cowra – with its Japanese gardens, peace monuments and war cemeteries – offers a glimpse into this quiet little town's unexpected and tragic role in Australia's wartime past.

Keep heading west and, soon enough, things start drying up and the rich, red outback soil takes over.

Bathurst

POP 43,428

Located on the 'other' side of the Great Dividing Range on Wiradjuri land, Bathurst is Australia's oldest inland colonial settlement, boasting a cool climate and a manicured central square where formidable Victorian buildings transport you to the past.

Bathurst's global claim to fame is its status as the home of Australian motor sport: since 1963, the 'Great Race' – the Bathurst 1000 – continues to draw massive crowds to its picturesque, twisty, turny circuit.

⊙ Sights

★**Australian Fossil and Mineral Museum** MUSEUM
(📞 02-6331 5511; www.somervillecollection.com. au; 224 Howick St; adult/child $14/7; ⊙10am-4pm Mon-Sat, to 2pm Sun; 🛗) Don't let the dry name fool you – this place is a treasure chest full of wonder. It's home to the internationally renowned Somerville Collection: rare fossils, plus gemstones and minerals in every colour of the rainbow (amethysts, diamonds, rubies, ancient insects frozen in amber) from around the world. The museum also houses Australia's only complete *Tyrannosaurus rex* skeleton cast.

National Motor Racing Museum MUSEUM
(📞 02-6332 1872; www.nmrm.com.au; 400 Panorama Ave; adult/child $15/7; ⊙9am-4.30pm; 🅿🛗) With a focus on the history of Mt Panorama and the Bathurst 1000, this museum at the base of Mt Panorama celebrates the achievements of Australian motor racing. There are plenty of touring cars, racing cars and motor bikes on display, as well as information placards about motor-racing heroes.

★**Mt Panorama** LANDMARK
(www.mount-panorama.com.au; Mountain Straight, Mt Panorama; 🅿) **FREE** Rev-heads will enjoy the 6.2km **Mt Panorama Motor Racing Circuit**, venue for the epic Bathurst 1000 Supercar race each October. It's a public road, so you can drive around the circuit – but only up to an unthrilling 60km/h. There's a lookout out over the Bathurst plains and a racing-themed children's playground at the top.

Abercrombie House HISTORIC BUILDING
(📞 02-6331 4929; www.abercrombiehouse.com. au; 311 Ophir Rd; adult/child $15/10; ⊙10.30am-3pm Wed-Fri, until 4pm Sat & Sun Dec-Feb; 🅿🛗)

This astonishing Tudor Gothic confection and 52-room mansion lies 7km northwest of Bathurst town centre. Admission to the heritage-listed historic house is by self-guided tour, with earlier closing times as the weather gets colder (closes half an hour earlier from March to May and September to November and one hour earlier June to August). The house and gardens frequently host special events, such as high tea parties, jazz music events and ghost tours.

🎆 Festivals & Events

★ Bathurst 1000   SPORTS
(www.supercars.com/bathurst1000; Mt Panorama; ⊘ early Oct) Over four days in October, petrolheads throng to Bathurst for this 1000km touring-car race, considered the pinnacle of Australian motor sport.

🛏 Sleeping & Eating

Governor Macquarie Motor Inn   MOTEL $
(☑ 02-6331 2211; www.governormacquarie.com. au; 19 Charlotte St; r from $90; P ❄ 🗢 ⊠) This smart motel boasts one of central Bathurst's quieter locations, set back from the busy main drag. King executive suites, a free guest laundry and saltwater pool add value.

Rydges Mount Panorama   HOTEL $$
(☑ 02-6338 1888; www.rydges.com/bathurst; 1 Conrod Straight; r from $159; P ❄ 🗢 ⊠) Boasting a trackside location at Mt Panorama, Rydges' 129 stylish studios and apartments sell out months in advance when the vroom-vrooms are in town: every room has a view over the racetrack. For the rest of the year, the location is blissfully quiet.

Annie's Old Fashioned
Ice-Cream Parlour   ICE CREAM $
(☑ 02-6331 8088; https://anniesicecream.word press.com; 82/86 George St; cones $4.80-9.30; ⊘ 8.30am-5.30pm Mon-Wed, to 9pm Thu & Fri, 10am-9pm Sat, 11am-5.30pm Sun; 🖐) Step back in time for sweet treats in a gorgeous 1950s colourful and kitsch milkbar-style shop. All the ice cream is made on-site daily, with the locally named Sofala Gold a crowd favourite.

Hub   CAFE $$
(☑ 02-6332 1565; www.thehubcafe.com.au; 52 Keppel St; mains $13-30; ⊘ 7am-3.30pm; 🖐) On a Bathurst strip with a few cool cafe options, the courtyard canopy of red umbrellas and green leaves makes this popular spot the perfect place for an al fresco meal ranging from tasty pastas to juicy burgers and decadent, freshly baked sweet treats. Early risers have a decent breakfast menu to peruse and locally roasted coffee.

9inety 2wo   MODERN AUSTRALIAN $$$
(☑ 02-6332 1757; www.9inety2wo.com; 92 Bentinck St; entrees/mains/desserts $16.50/45/16; ⊘ 6-9pm Tue-Sat) The former Temperance Hall of Bathurst (1877) sets the stage for this smart dinner-only restaurant serving Modern Australian dishes influenced by global cuisine. On warm nights, the courtyard is a lovely place to dine.

ℹ Information

Bathurst Visitor Information Centre (☑ 02-6332 1444; www.visitbathurst.com.au; 1 Kendall Ave; ⊘ 9am-5pm)

ℹ Getting There & Away

Bathurst is just over 200km west of Sydney via the Great Western Hwy. The route crosses the picturesque Blue Mountains.

Rex (p196) operates daily flights to/from Sydney.

Australia Wide Coaches (☑ 02-6362 7963; ⊘ phone reservations 6am-7pm) runs a daily express service between Sydney and Orange that stops in Bathurst ($43, 3½ hours). Coaches pick up and drop off at the Bathurst Bus Interchange at the corner of William and Howick Sts.

NSW TrainLink (p194) operates a daily XPT rail service between Sydney and Bathurst (from $40, 3½ hours) and at least four daily coach services to and from Lithgow ($8.80, one hour) to Bathurst Station.

Orange
POP 39,755

Situated on Wiradjuri land in the central west of NSW, Orange might just be the prettiest regional centre around. It has fine heritage architecture, a mild, high-elevation (863m) climate and just enough going on to make it a great place to visit, or live. Orange has become a convivial, fast-growing regional centre with a booming food-and-wine scene.

⊙ Sights

★ Heifer Station   WINERY
(www.heiferstation.com; 1034 The Escort Way; ⊘ 11am-5pm; P 🖐) Come for the chardonnay, pinot noir, pinot gris, merlot and

shiraz – best enjoyed al fresco on a warm day or inside by the fire when it's chilly. In a former life, Heifer Station was one of the biggest cattle stations in the state; today there's a small petting farm with alpacas, goats, cows, chickens and sheep, for small and big kids alike.

★ **Mt Canobolas** NATURE RESERVE
(P🚻) FREE Southwest of Orange, this conservation area encompasses waterfalls, views, walking trails and bike paths. Swimmer-friendly **Lake Canobolas** is a great place to start with plenty of picnic areas and a lakeside children's playground – the turnoff to the lake is on the extension of Coronation Rd, 8km west of town.

Ross Hill Wines WINERY
(☑02-6365 3223; www.rosshillwines.com.au; 134 Wallace Lane; ⊗10.30am-5pm; P) Sample carbon neutral wine in a stunning, new-in-2018 courtyard and cellar door space, join a 10am wine tour, indulge in a regional tasting plate ($40 for two people), then stumble home... to wherever that might be for the night.

Orange Regional Museum MUSEUM
(☑02-6393 8444; www.orangemuseum.com.au; 151 Byng St; ⊗9am-4pm; 🚻) FREE This fabulous free museum – in an architecturally designed building with a sloping grass roof – is the city's cultural pride and joy, with permanent exhibits on local history, as well as visiting exhibitions.

Stockman's Ridge WINERY
(☑02-6366 8422; www.stockmansridge.com.au; 21 Boree Lane; ⊗10am-4pm Sat & Sun; P) This beautiful vineyard is a well-respected wedding venue and offers boutique accommodation in the self-contained Swagman's Homestead (from $150 per couple). Its popular cellar door features more than 10 varieties of premium cool-climate wines.

👉 Tours

James' Vineyard Tours WINE
(☑0437 151 500; www.vineyardtours.com.au; tours from $85) Small group numbers (a maximum of 12 people) and attentive service make for a wonderful day out savouring local wine and food (lunch is not included in the price).

Orange Wine Tours WINE
(☑0458 800 174; www.orangewinetours.com.au; Summer St; tours from $90) This popular local operator knows Orange's myriad cellar doors and farm gates better than anyone.

If you can't be fussed with all the driving and navigating, why not leave it to the professionals?

✨ Festivals & Events

★ **Orange Wine Festival** WINE
(www.orangewinefestival.com.au; ⊗Oct) This popular boozy festival celebrating the region's excellent vineyards is held each October.

FOOD Week FOOD
(Food of Orange District; www.orangefoodweek.com.au; ⊗late Mar–mid-Apr) This is one of Orange's biggest weeks, with foodies coming from near and far for the festivities. Book your accommodation in advance if you plan to visit for this culinary spectacular highlighting local produce.

🛏 Sleeping

★ **de Russie**
Boutique Hotel BOUTIQUE HOTEL $$
(☑02-6360 0973; www.derussiehotels.com.au; 72 Hill St; d from $140; P❄🐾🤖) As good as anything in Sydney, this little slice of hotel heaven in Orange has boutique written all over it. It has luxe mod cons, including kitchenettes in every studio (a hamper of breakfast supplies is included).

Duntryleague GUESTHOUSE $$
(☑02-6362 3466; www.duntryleague.com.au; Woodward St; d from $130; P🤖) Orange's most stunning heritage building (built in 1876), is home to a 14-room guesthouse, function centre and golf course. Rooms have been modernised but retain their period charm, with continual upgrades taking place. It's worth popping by just to see this beautiful building.

Black Sheep Inn BOUTIQUE HOTEL $$$
(☑0404 887 849; www.blacksheepinn.com.au; 91 Heifer Station Lane, Borenore; d from $220; P❄) Black Sheep Inn is one of Orange's best transformations, a century-old shearing shed has been converted into modern accommodation. The main house has five suites and the restored shearers' quarters are a two-bedroom cottage.

🍴 Eating

Factory Espresso CAFE $
(☑02-6360 2858; www.facebook.com/factory135; 135 Kite St; meals $7-21; ⊗6am-4pm Mon-Fri, 7.30am-2pm Sat & Sun; 🖉🚻) Egg dishes with

a twist; inventive toast toppers; delicious, local-made cakes; and coffee that is worth coming back for – this industrial-style cafe hits all the high notes. There's a dedicated menu for the little ones too... babychinos are definitely a thing.

Greenhouse of Orange
PUB FOOD **$$**

(📞02-6311 1899; www.thegreenhouseoforange. com.au; 231-243 Anson St; mains $15-38; ⊙9am-10pm Thu, to 11pm Fri & Sat, to 8pm Sun; 🛜🚲👶) When this huge new venue – located on the former bowling green at the Orange Ex-Services' Club – opened in 2017 it was immediately booked out. It still brings the crowds, with à la carte dining, a wine bar with a charcuterie and pizza menu, street food, and the best kids' space in a pub in the region – really.

Agrestic Grocer
CAFE **$$**

(📞02-6360 4604; www.theagresticgrocer.com. au; 426 Mitchell Hwy/Molong Rd; lunch $18-30; ⊙8.30am-5.30pm Mon-Fri, to 4pm Sat & Sun; 🛜🚲) This rustic cafe-grocer, a few kilometres north of town on the Mitchell Hwy (also known as Molong Rd), celebrates local produce. Breakfast on house-cultured buttermilk pancakes; lunch on a beef cheek sandwich or house-made gnocchi. It's all delicious. While waiting for your food, peruse the on-site grocery store for local jams, pickles, chutneys and relishes.

★ Charred Kitchen & Bar
AUSTRALIAN **$$$**

(📞02-6363 1580; www.charred.com.au; 1-5 New St; 2/3 courses $70/85; ⊙11am-11pm Tue-Sat; 🛜👶) Beautifully executed meals starring regional produce, over 600 wines on offer (it's won many accolades for its extensive wine selection), and impeccable service position this as one of the top restaurants in the region. Save your pennies and go all out – it's worth it.

★ Lolli Redini
MODERN AUSTRALIAN **$$$**

(📞02-6361 7748; www.lolliredini.com.au; 48 Sale St; mains $40, 5-courses $115; ⊙6-9pm Tue-Sat & noon-2pm Sat; ❄🛜🚲) See Orange's finest produce wrapped in all its glory at this much-lauded restaurant (bookings essential). The matching of food with wines is well thought out, the setting and service are exemplary, and the kitchen creations (including many options for vegetarians and those needing GF) sing with flavour.

🍷 Drinking & Nightlife

★ Ferment
WINE BAR

(📞02-6360 4833; www.orangewinecentre.com. au; 87 Hill St; ⊙11am-7pm Tue-Sat) Inside a gorgeous and well-preserved heritage building, Ferment shines a spotlight on local wines (it's the cellar door for a handful of small producers around Orange). You can talk wine, graze on platters or just admire the stylish fit-out.

ℹ️ Information

In its shiny new home shared with the Orange Regional Museum, the **Orange Visitor Information Centre** (📞02-6393 8226; www. visitorange.com.au; 151 Byng St; ⊙9am-5pm; 🛜👶) is an essential first stop when you get to town.

ℹ️ Getting There & Away

Located on the Mitchell Highway, 54km west of Bathurst and 257km west of Sydney, Orange is well connected by road, rail and air.

Qantas (p194) and Rex (p196) operate daily flights to/from Sydney.

NSW TrainLink (p194) has one direct daily rail service between Sydney and Orange Station (from $26, 4¾ hours), as well as at least four coach services per day to/from Lithgow (from $13, 1¾ hours).

Australia Wide Coaches (📞02-6362 7963; www.austwidecoaches.com.au; 229 McLachlan St; ⊙9am-4pm) has one bus a day to/from Sydney ($43, four hours), via Bathurst from/to Orange Station.

Orange Buslines (📞02-6362 3197; www. buslinesgroup.com.au/orange; 120 Canobolas Rd) operates local transport services between Bathurst and Orange via Millthorpe.

Cowra

POP 10,063

Lovely little Cowra is synonymous with being the site of the only land battle fought on Australian soil during WWII, when, in August 1944, more than 1000 Japanese prisoners attempted to break out of a prisoner-of-war camp here. During the surprise attack, 231 Japanese people were killed or committed ritual suicide; four Australians were also killed.

Cowra has since aligned itself with Japan and the causes of reconciliation and world peace, and there are some poignant and worthwhile sites here to explore. An overnight visit is recommended.

DON'T MISS

MILLTHORPE

Only 20 minutes from Orange, the pioneering village of Millthorpe, with its heritage architecture, is a little slice of the mid-1800s. Its cuteness is such that the National Trust has classified the whole place. It's a quieter alternative to staying in Orange, although the town comes alive with weekenders and Sunday drivers thanks to the shopping and dining scene – and those picturesque cobbled bluestone streets.

Golden Memories Millthorpe is a wonderful volunteer-run **museum** (☑ 02-6366 3980; www.millthorpemuseum. com; 37 Park St; $8; ☉ 10am-4pm Sat & Sun, plus school & public holidays; ⊞) that has eight buildings housing a diverse collection of artefacts on a range of themes from local and Aboriginal history, farming and Australian inventions.

For a memorable meal, classy **Tonic** (☑ 02-6366 3811; www.tonicmillthorpe. com.au; cnr Pym & Victoria Sts; 2/3 courses $70/80; ☉ 6.30-10pm Thu-Sat, noon-3pm Sat & Sun; ☑) is highly lauded for its sophisticated contemporary food that celebrates the region.

Orange Buslines operates regular scheduled services between Orange and Millthorpe ($6, 30 minutes).

◉ Sights

★**Cowra Japanese Garden**
& Cultural Centre Australia GARDENS
(☑ 02-6341 2233; www.cowragarden.com.au; Ken Nakajima Pl; adult/child $15/8; ☉ 8.30am-5pm; ℗ ⊞) Built as a token of Cowra's connection with Japanese POWs (but with no overt mention of the war or the breakout), this tranquil 5-hectare garden and cultural centre is superbly presented and well worth visiting (albeit with a steep entry fee). Audio guides ($2) explain the plants, history and design of the garden. You can buy food for the koi (carp), or feed yourself at the on-site cafe (☑ 02-6342 5222; www.cowragarden.com.au; Ken Nakajima Pl; $10-27; ☉ 9am-5pm; ☜ ☑ ⊞), which serves mostly Australian fare, with a small nod to Japanese cuisine.

Cowra & Japanese
War Cemeteries CEMETERY
(Doncaster Rd; ℗) FREE These moving, well-maintained Japanese and Australian war cemeteries are signposted off the road to Canowindra, around 5km north of Cowra. The Japanese War Cemetery is the only one of its kind left in Australia.

POW Campsite
& Guard Tower MEMORIAL
(Evans St; ℗) FREE From the war cemeteries, on Doncaster Road north of Cowra, signs lead to the site of the Japanese breakout. A voice-over from the watchtower recounts the story. You can still see the camp foundations, and info panels explain the military and migrant camps of wartime Cowra.

⚘ Festivals & Events

Sakura Matsuri CULTURAL
(Cherry Blossom Festival; ☑ 02-6341 2233; www. cowragarden.com.au/events; adult/child $20/12; ☉ Sep; ⊞) Cowra's pretty and hugely popular *sakura matsuri* (cherry-blossom festival) is held over a week in late September in the beautiful grounds of the Cowra Japanese Garden, with Japanese food, culture and thousands of delicate pink cherry blossoms on show.

🛏 Sleeping & Eating

Cowra Services Club Motel MOTEL $$
(☑ 02-6341 1999; www.cowraservicesclubmotel. com.au; 105-111 Brisbane St; r from $135; ℗ ✳ ☜) Located a block from the main street, Cowra's fanciest digs are light-filled, airy and adjacent to 'the Club'. Suitable for the more discerning road-tripper, perky rooms are tastefully furnished in neutral tones with bright accents and shiny, large, flat-screen TVs.

Quarry Restaurant
& Cellar Door MODERN AUSTRALIAN $$
(☑ 02-6342 3650; www.thequarryrestaurant. com.au; 7191 Lachlan Valley Way; lunch $22-33, dinner $34; ☉ noon-2.30pm Thu-Sun, 6.30-10pm Fri & Sat) Four kilometres out of Cowra, the Quarry Restaurant is handsomely set amid the vines, and the kitchen output wins regular praise (especially the puddings!). There's a sizeable wine list too – the Quarry is the cellar door for a number of local vineyards.

ℹ Information

Start your explorations at the **Cowra Visitor Information Centre** (☑ 02-6342 4333; www. cowratourism.com.au; cnr Mid Western Hwy & Lachlan Valley Way; ☉ 9am-5pm; ⊞), which shows an excellent nine-minute holographic film about the breakout scene (it has been praised by Bill Bryson, no less). It has a small wartime museum and friendly, knowledgeable staff.

ℹ️ Getting There & Away

Cowra is 108km southwest of Bathurst along the Mid Western Hwy.

NSW TrainLink (p194) operates daily bus services between Cowra and Orange (from $12, 1½ hours). There is a direct daily rail service between Orange and Sydney (from $26, 4¾ hours).

Buses depart from and arrive at the **Cowra Coach Stop** on Macquarie St.

Dubbo

POP 38,943

Dubbo is an important rural centre on the north–south Newell Highway, on Wiradjuri land. Its name comes from the Wiradjuri word for 'red ochre'. The city has a variety of interesting, kid-friendly, educational and cultural attractions.

◉ Sights

★ Taronga Western Plains Zoo   ZOO
(☑02-6881 1400; www.taronga.org.au/dubbo-zoo; Obley Rd; 2-day pass adult/child $47/26; ⊙8.30am-4pm; P⛽) This is Dubbo's star attraction, not to mention one of the best zoos in regional Australia. You can walk the 6km circuit, ride a hire bike ($17 to $24 for full-day hire), explore in a cart ($70 for three hours) or drive your car, getting out at enclosures along the way. Free keeper talks are scheduled throughout the day and guided walks (adult/child $15/7.50) start at 6.45am on weekends, with additional walks during school holidays.

Book ahead for special animal encounters or the glorious accommodation packages – spend a night at a bush camp, in family-sized cabins, or in safari-style lodges overlooking savannah; see the website for details. There are also free barbecues and picnic grounds at the zoo, as well as cafes and kiosks.

Dubbo Observatory   OBSERVATORY
(☑0488 425 940; www.dubboobservatory.com; 17L Camp Rd; adult/child $26/12; ⊙9pm Dec-Feb, 8.30pm Mar & Nov, 7pm Apr-Sep, 8pm Oct; P⛽) Advance bookings and clear weather are essential for this fascinating chance to stargaze, which features a 90-minute presentation by local astronomer Peter Starr. You'll have access to up to six telescopes through which to explore the night sky; point out the stars, planets and constellations with a laser

pointer; and take photos of the spectacular nebula – a keepsake of your time in Dubbo.

Dubbo Regional Botanic Garden   GARDENS
(☑02-6801 4000; www.drbg.com.au; Coronation Dr, East Dubbo; ⊙9am-4pm Mon-Fri, 9.30am-4.30pm Sat & Sun; P⛽) FREE This beautiful and educational botanical garden is divided into four parts: the stunning Shoyoen Japanese Garden, the Sensory Gardens, Biodiversity Garden and the Oasis Valley, offering a real glimpse of botanical diversity thriving on the fringe of the Australian outback. Best of all, admission is free!

🛏️ Sleeping

★ Best Western Bluegum Motel   MOTEL $$
(☑02-6882 0900; www.bluegummotorinn.com; 109 Cobra St; r from $189; P❄🛜🏊) Boasting a central location, set back from the Mitchell Hwy and across from a park, this excellent motel hasn't cut corners. Choose from seven room types ranging from standard to executive and family rooms: all feature smart TVs with Foxtel, pillow-top mattresses, whisper-quiet air-conditioners, quality linen and excellent high-speed wi-fi.

Outback Cellar Dubbo   APARTMENT $$
(☑0438 872 759; www.outbackcellardubbo.com; 21 Warrie Rd; r $190; P🛜🏊) Three elegantly furnished apartments (one in a converted wine cellar) make up Outback Cellar Dubbo, 15km from the centre of town. The apartments are located on 25 acres of farming land and although city buzz is nearby, it feels a world away. Rural life at its best.

Westbury Boutique
Bed & Breakfast   GUESTHOUSE $$
(☑02-6881 6105; www.westburydubbo.com.au; cnr Brisbane & Wingewarra Sts; s/d from $150/175, incl breakfast $170/210; P❄) This lovely old heritage home (1915) has six spacious, en-suite rooms furnished in period style with modcons like flat-screen TV, bar fridge, DVD player and reverse-cycle air-conditioning. Breakfast is served in the attached restaurant, which serves spicy, aromatic Thai cuisine by night.

🍴 Eating & Drinking

Alchemy Art & Food Hub   CAFE $
(☑0491 253 663; www.facebook.com/alchemyartandfood; 200 Fitzroy St; dishes $7-19; ⊙8.30am-3pm; 🛜⛽) It's a predominantly vegetarian menu at this popular cafe, with plenty of al fresco seating in the leafy garden and

a small gallery to peruse pre- or post-meal. A second Alchemy cafe is located on 54 Victoria St.

Press Dubbo
CAFE $$

(☑02-6882 3720; www.pressdubbo.com.au; 33 Bultje St; $10-24; ☺7.30am-4pm Mon-Fri, 8am-4pm Sat, 8am-2pm Sun; ☑🖶) This buzzy cafe located in a beautiful heritage building is usually swarming with people enjoying their meals (made mostly from local produce) and the cafe's own roasted coffee – which could well be the best coffee in town.

Old Bank
BAR

(☑02-6884 7728; www.oldbankdubbo.com; 232 Macquarie St; ☺noon-midnight Mon-Sat) Occupying the former Bank of NSW building (1876), this bar-restaurant is ineffably stylish and a cut above the rest of Dubbo's offerings, with plenty of nooks and crannies in which to wine and/or dine.

ℹ Information

Dubbo Visitor Information Centre (☑02-6801 4450; www.dubbo.com.au; cnr Macquarie St & Newell Hwy; ☺9am-5pm; 🛜)

ℹ Getting There & Away

There are here are daily direct flights between Sydney and Dubbo – landing at **Dubbo City Regional Airport** (☑02-6801 4560; www.dubboairport.com; Cooreena Rd) – with Qantas (p194) and Rex (p196).

NSW TrainLink (p194) operates one daily XPT train service between Dubbo and Sydney (from $50, 6½ hours).

By road, the city is a regional hub for transport, with these major highways meeting here:

➡ A32 Mitchell Hwy between Sydney and Adelaide

➡ A39 Newell Hwy between Melbourne and Brisbane

➡ B84 Golden Hwy from Newcastle

Mudgee

POP 10,923

Situated in the fertile Cudgegong Valley, Mudgee is a handsome town with wide streets, fine old homes and historic buildings, surrounded by vineyards and rolling hills. Located on Wiradjuri land, it takes its name from the Wiradjuri word 'moothi', meaning 'nest in the hills'.

The wineries come hand-in-hand with excellent food and plenty of decent accommodation, making Mudgee a stellar weekend getaway. Beyond food and wine, the surrounding great outdoors provide a range of nature experiences for bird lovers, photographers and adventurers alike.

◉ Sights

Mudgee's more than 35 family-owned cellar doors are primarily clustered northeast of town. Some vineyards have outstanding restaurants, some have accommodation and some are open weekends only. All of Mudgee's winemakers are passionate about good wine (and usually good food too) and take great care in teaching visitors about the diversity of climate and soil and winemaking techniques.

Contact the Mudgee Visitor Information Centre (p209) for up-to-date listings, or to take a tour.

Lowe Vineyard
WINERY

(☑02-6372 0800; www.lowewine.com.au; 327 Tinja Lane; ☺10am-5pm; 🅿) 🌿 You can follow a walking and cycling trail through the orchards and vines of this idyllic biodynamic farm, past donkeys and chickens to picnic grounds. The cellar door has tastings, with preservative-free wines and vegan wines both worth trying, along with the two superb grazing platters ($35) featuring local flavours. The renowned restaurant Zin House (p208) is on the grounds. Check the website for events too.

Logan Wines
WINERY

(☑02-6373 1333; www.loganwines.com.au; 1320 Castlereagh Hwy; ☺10am-5pm; 🅿) Started in 1997 as a father-and-son outfit, and now a husband-and-wife team, Logan's is an impressive, modern, cellar-door experience 15km southeast of Mudgee, noteworthy for its fizzy (sparkling) and sticky (dessert) wines, award-winning tasting room and wonderful views.

Mudgee Observatory
OBSERVATORY

(☑02-6373 3431; www.mudgeeobservatory.com.au; 961 Old Grattai Rd; adult/child $15/10; ☺hours vary; 🅿🖶) Astronomy enthusiast John Vetter built the observatories and buildings on his own land and runs these nightly tours because he loves chatting about stars and planets. The experience is both personalised and fascinating. Call ahead for tour times as they vary with the seasons and night sky.

Robert Stein Winery & Vineyard
WINERY

(☑02-6373 3991; www.robertstein.com.au; Pipeclay Lane; ☺10am-4.30pm; 🅿) The small, rustic cellar door of this established vineyard has an eclectic and interesting range of wines to sample, including a popular riesling (a nod to Robert Stein's German heritage) and shiraz. There's also a quaint vintage motorcycle museum (free) and excellent paddock-to-plate restaurant Pipeclay Pumphouse.

Burnbrae Winery   WINERY

(☑02-6373 3504; www.burnbraewines.com.au; 548 Hill End Rd; ⊗10am-4pm; P) Established in 1968, this multi-award-winning winery has a historic winemaker's cottage where you can spend an evening (from $200 per night); but you'll likely be here to try its wide variety of cuvées from the cellar door. It also prepares fabulous antipasto boards which can be sampled under the winery's wise old peppercorn tree.

⌒ Tours

Mudgee Wine & Country Tours   TOURS

(☑02-6372 2367; www.mudgeewinetours.com. au; half-/full-day wine tours $60/95; ⊕) This local operator has been running cellar-door and sightseeing tours in the area for over 15 years – for singles, couples, families and everything in between. Better-known wineries like **di Lusso Estate** (☑02-6373 3125; www.dilusso.com.au; 162 Eurunderee Lane; ⊗cellar door 10am-5pm Mon-Sat, to 4pm Sun; trattoria noon-3pm; P) and **Pieter van Gent** (☑02-6373 3030; www.pvgwinery.com.au; 141 Black Springs Rd; ⊗9am-5pm Mon-Sat, 10.30am-4pm Sun; P) as well as lesser-known vineyards are frequently visited. Custom tours are also available.

Mudgee Tourist Bus   TOURS

(☑0428 669 945; www.mudgeetouristbus.com. au; half-/full-day wine tours $60/100) Popular vineyards like Lowe and Burnbrae, among others, are covered in these half- and full-day cellar door tours out of Mudgee. The bus picks up and returns travellers to their town accomodation.

🎉 Festivals & Events

Mudgee Food + Wine Festival   FOOD & DRINK

(☑02-6372 1020; www.mudgeewine.com.au; ⊗Sep) This popular festival celebrating the region's 35-plus wineries, local farms and paddock-to-plate restaurants runs through the month of September and features live music, cellar-door events, tastings and special lunches and dinners. Check the website for full details and book accommodation well in advance.

WORTH A TRIP

PARKES

The sleepy inland town of Parkes – on Wiradjuri land – has two wildly different claims to fame.

The **CSIRO Parkes Observatory** (☑02-6861 1777; www.csiro.au/parkes; 585 Telescope Rd; ⊗visitor centre 8.30am-4.15pm; P ⊞) FREE is a massive radio telescope about 20km north of town. The complex includes a visitor centre with space info, a 3D theatre (adult/child $7.50/6) and oodles of information on radio astronomy.

In the second week of January, Parkes' population doubles as visitors flock to celebrate Elvis' birthday in the **Parkes Elvis Festival** (www.parkeselvisfestival.com.au; ⊗Jan; 🎉). Spend five days whooping it up with impersonators, concerts, busking competitions, a zany street parade, karaoke and outdoor cinema.

There are daily flights from Sydney to Parkes. Between Orange and Parkes there's a bus service (from $10, from 1½ hours to 2½ hours depending on route). There's also a weekly direct Xplorer train service on Mondays from Sydney to Parkes and on Tuesdays from Parkes to Sydney (from $38, 6½ hours).

🛏 Sleeping

★**Perry Street Hotel**   BOUTIQUE HOTEL $$

(☑02-6372 7650; www.perrystreethotel.com.au; cnr Perry & Gladstone Sts; ste from $185; P ❄ 🛜) Stunning apartment suites make a sophisticated choice in town. The attention to detail is outstanding, right down to the kimono bathrobes, Nespresso machine and complimentary gourmet snacks.

Wildwood Guesthouse   GUESTHOUSE $$

(☑02-6373 3701; www.wildwoodmudgee.com. au; Henry Lawson Dr; r from $200; P ❄ 🛜 🎉) This rustic homestead has four comfortable bedrooms, individually styled with big downy beds, fine linens and an eclectic mix of antiques. Each opens out onto the wraparound verandah overlooking the tranquil countryside. Breakfast included.

★**Sierra Escape**   GLAMPING $$$

(☑0438 945 197; www.sierraescape.com.au; 1345 Lower Piambong Rd, Piambong; from $320; P) 🌿 Three Australian-made luxury tents sit atop 280 acres of rolling hills and valleys. The canvas walls may be thin, but the only sounds you'll hear are birds, kangaroos and the occasional sheep bleating its heart out. Mudgee's first and only glamping experience will change your thoughts on camping forever.

Mudgee Homestead
Guesthouse
GUESTHOUSE $$$

(☑02-6373 3786; www.mudgeehomestead.com. au; 3 Coorumbene Ct; s/d from $210/240, cottages from $340; P❄☎) Set amid 40 acres replete with resident kangaroos, just five minutes from town, this classic country homestead boasts sweeping rural views from its big, country-style rooms that don't skimp on comforts, with luxurious bedding, attractive antiques and fabulous bathrooms. There's a two-night minimum stay on weekends, but packages include cooked breakfasts and fine dinners.

✖ Eating & Drinking

Mudgee is known for its wineries and at many there are beautiful grazing platters available as well as main meals, usually made from local produce. In town there's also plenty of choice, with cosy cafes, country pubs, fine-dining eateries and buzzing wine bars.

Alby & Esthers
CAFE $

(☑02-6372 1555; www.albyandesthers.com.au; 61 Market St; mains $10-18; ☺8am-5pm Mon-Thu, to late Fri & Sat; ☑) Down an alleyway is this supremely pretty courtyard cafe, serving up fine local produce and good coffee. The service is exemplary and it morphs into a wine bar on Friday and Saturday nights.

Eltons Eating
+ Drinking
MODERN AUSTRALIAN $

(☑02-6372 1079; www.eltons.com.au; 81 Market St; dishes $6-20; ☺5-11pm Wed-Thu, noon-11pm Fri & Sat, 9am-3pm Sun; ☑) Share plates, tacos and decadent desserts are some of the culinary finds on the versatile food menu. A carefully curated drinks menu – predominantly regional wine and often-changing craft beer – is designed to be enjoyed alongside the food. The restaurant-bar is in a well-maintained heritage building that dates back to 1896.

★Pipeclay
Pumphouse
MODERN AUSTRALIAN $$$

(☑02-6373 3998; www.pipeclaypumphouse.com. au; 1 Pipeclay Lane; lunch $20-28, 5/8/10 courses $55/80/105; ☺noon-3pm & 6-9pm Thu & Fri,

8.30am-3pm & 6-9pm Sat & Sun; ☑) ☞ On the grounds of the Robert Stein Winery (p207), this paddock-to-plate stunner is the talk of Mudgee, serving to-die-for weekend breakfasts, à la carte and degustation lunches and degustation dinners. Book ahead... and wear stretchy pants if opting for the degustation: five courses is the minimum.

★Zin House
MODERN AUSTRALIAN $$$

(☑02-6372 1660; www.zinhouse.com.au; 329 Tinja Lane; 5-course set menu from $95; ☺noon-3pm Fri-Mon, 5-10pm Fri & Sat; ☑) ☞ The glorious Lowe Vineyard (p207) is home to this weekend highlight: long, leisurely six-course lunches of simply prepared local produce (either home-grown, or impeccably sourced from nearby). Diners share farmhouse tables in a beautifully designed home. Gather your friends; book ahead.

★Roth's
WINE BAR

(☑02-6372 1222; www.rothswinebar.com.au; 30 Market St; ☺3pm-midnight Wed-Sat) The oldest wine bar in NSW (built in 1923) sits behind a small heritage facade, and serves up great local wines (by the glass from $6), fine bar food and excellent live music. Bliss.

ⓘ Information

Mudgee Visitor Information Centre (☑02-6372 1020; www.visitmudgeeregion.com.au; 84 Market St; ☺9am-5pm; ☎)

ⓘ Getting There & Away

Mudgee is 128km north of Lithgow along the Castlereagh Hwy. From Sydney, it's a pretty 3½-hour drive through the Blue Mountains and over the Great Dividing Range.

NSW TrainLink (p194) operates one morning and one evening bus service to/from the former Mudgee train station to Lithgow train station ($26.50, 2¼ hours), where you can connect to regular scheduled trains to Sydney.

OUTBACK NSW

New South Wales is rarely credited for its far-west outback corner, but it should be. Out here, grey saltbush and red sand make it easy to imagine yourself superimposed onto the world's biggest Aboriginal dot painting, a canvas reaching as far as the eye can see. Towns with fuel and food supplies are relatively widespread and isolated, so plan accordingly, and always take the opportunity to keep your vehicle full of petrol or diesel.

● Getting Around

Outback NSW is a vast area that is geographically hard to define. While all the main highways ('A' designated roads) are sealed, local roads between isolated communities are not recommended for anything less than a 4WD. You could end up in financial hot water if you take a rental car on any road that's unsealed and it gets damaged.

Bourke

POP 2634

Sprawled along the Darling River on the edge of the outback, Bourke is miles from anywhere: this remote town is immortalised by the popular Australian expression 'back of Bourke', translating to 'in the middle of nowhere'. Further reinforcing the town's quintessential Australian credentials, the bush poet Henry Lawson once said, 'If you know Bourke, you know Australia.'

● Sights

★ Back O' Bourke Exhibition Centre   MUSEUM

(☑ 02-6872 1321; www.visitbourke.com.au; Kidman Way; adult/child $23/11; ⊙ 9am-5pm Apr-Oct, to 4pm Mon-Fri Nov-Mar; ℗) This superb exhibition space follows the legends of the back country (both Indigenous and settler) through interactive displays. The centre also houses the **Bourke Visitor Information Centre** (☑ 02-6872 1321; www.visitbourke. com.au; Kidman Way; ⊙ 9am-5pm; 🛜) and sells packages that include one or all of the town's major attractions – a river cruise on the **PV Jandra** (☑ 02-6872 1321; departs Kidman's Camp; adult/child $16/10; ⊙ 2pm Mon-Sat; 🖶), an entertaining outback show (staged at 11am) and a bus tour of the town and surrounds. Tickets can be used across two days. Note the cruise and show operate April to October only.

🛏 Sleeping & Eating

★ Kidman's Camp   CAMPGROUND, CABINS $$

(☑ 02-6872 1612; www.kidmanscamp.com.au/ bourke; Cunnamulla Rd, North Bourke; campsites/ cabins from $32/109; ℗🛜⊠) An excellent place to base yourself, on river frontage about 8km out of Bourke. The PV Jandra cruise departs from here, and Poetry on a Plate (p210) is staged in the grounds. Plus there are lush gardens, swimming pools and cabins – family-sized with shared

bathrooms, or comfy log cabins with bathroom, kitchenette and verandah.

Bourke Riverside Motel   MOTEL $$

(☑ 02-6872 2539; www.bourkeriversidemotel. com.au; 3-13 Mitchell St; r/ste from $129/169; ℗❄🛜⊠) This rambling motel has riverside gardens and a range of well-appointed rooms and suites: some have heritage overtones and antique furniture, some have kitchen, and some are family-sized. A fine choice and a short walk to good eating and drinking.

★ Poetry on a Plate   AUSTRALIAN $$

(☑ 0427 919 964; www.poetryonaplate.com. au; Kidman's Camp; adult/child $25/12; ⊙ from 6.30pm Tue, Thu & Sun Apr-Oct) A heart-warmingly unique offering here in Bourke: a well-priced night of bush ballads and storytelling around a campfire under the stars, with a simple, slow-cooked meal and dessert to boot. Dress warmly and bring your own drinks. Camp chairs and cutlery are provided. Cash only.

LOCAL KNOWLEDGE

INDIGENOUS BOURKE

This region is the traditional land of the Ngemba and Barkindji peoples. In the 1940s the arrival of displaced Aboriginal peoples from other parts of the outback – including the Wangkumara from Tibooburra – significantly increased Bourke's Indigenous population.

In recent decades the Bourke region had one of Australia's highest Indigenous incarceration rates, but since 2015 a groundbreaking Aboriginal community-led justice program called Maranguka has led to greater empowerment of the local Indigenous population. The success of Maranguka is now being seen as a model for other Indigenous communities throughout Australia.

Run by two local brothers, Jason and Joseph Dixon, **Bourke Aboriginal Cultural Tours** (☑ 0436 368 185; www. bourkeaboriginalculturaltours.com; Back O' Bourke Exhibition Centre; adult/child $30/15; ⊙ 9.30am & 11.30am Mon-Fri) are easy-going 90-minute walks along the banks of the Darling River, taking in Bourke Wharf and also an art gallery at 2CUZFM, Bourke's Indigenous radio station.

ℹ Information

The **Bourke NPWS Office** (✆ 02-6872 2744; www.nationalparks.nsw.gov.au; 51 Oxley St; ⏱ 8.30am-4.30pm Mon-Fri) can advise on visiting Aboriginal art sites at **Gundabooka National Park**, around 90 minutes southwest. Camp at Dry Tank (adult/child $6/3.50) or try the shearer's quarters (doubles $60). 2WD access is fine when the roads are dry.

For information and bookings at local accommodation and on the PV Jandra (p209), contact the Bourke Visitor Information Centre (p209).

ℹ Getting There & Away

Bourke is rather isolated: it's 760km northwest of Sydney, on the Mitchell Hwy, with not much within cooee of the town.

NSW TrainLink (p194) operates a daily Xplorer train from Sydney to Dubbo, which connects with a coach to Bourke ($75, 11½ hours).

Broken Hill

✆ 08 / POP 17,814

The massive mullock heap (of mine residue) that forms a backdrop for Broken Hill's town centre accentuates the unique character of this desert frontier town. For all its remoteness, the fine facilities and high-quality attractions can make it feel like an oasis somewhere close to the end of the earth. Some of the state's most impressive national parks are nearby, as is an intriguing near-ghost town, and everywhere there is an impressive spirit of community and creativity.

The area around Broken Hill and nearby Silverton is the traditional homeland of the Wilyakali people.

⊙ Sights

Many of Broken Hill's sights are closed sporadically over summer due to the heat and low visitor numbers; many operators close their doors at 3pm.

★ Royal Flying Doctor Service Museum   MUSEUM

(✆ 08-8080 3714; www.flyingdoctor.org.au; Airport Rd; adult/child $10/5; ⏱ 9am-5pm Mon-Fri, 10am-3pm Sat & Sun; P) This iconic Australian institution has a visitor centre at the airport. There are stirring displays and stories of health innovation and derring-do in the service of those who live and work in remote places (note: this base serves a staggeringly vast area of 640,000 sq km). It's a real eye-opener, and the video is guaranteed to stir emotions. Excellent guided tours run on the hour, providing an interesting behind-the-scenes look at the Flying Doctors' work around the outback.

★ Broken Hill Regional Art Gallery   GALLERY

(✆ 08-8080 3444; www.bhartgallery.com.au; 404-408 Argent St; gold coin donation; ⏱ 10am-4pm Tue-Sun) This impressive gallery is housed in the beautifully restored Sully's Emporium from 1885. It's the oldest regional gallery in NSW and holds 1800 works in its permanent collection. Artists featured include Australian masters such as John Olsen, Sidney Nolan and Arthur Streeton, plus there is strong representation from Aboriginal artists.

Living Desert State Park   NATURE RESERVE

(www.brokenhill.nsw.gov.au; adult/child $6/3; ⏱ 9am-sunset Mar-Nov, from 6am Dec-Feb; P 🚻) One of the most memorable experiences of Broken Hill is viewing the sunset from the **Living Desert Sculpture Symposium** (Nine Mile Rd), on the highest hilltop 12km from town. The sculptures are the work of 12 international artists who carved the huge sandstone blocks on-site. The 24-sq-km park is also home to a flora and fauna sanctuary featuring a 2.2km **Cultural Walk Trail** and a 1km **Flora Trail**.

Day Dream Mine   MINE

(✆ 0427 885 682; www.daydreammine.com.au; Silverton; underground & surface tours adult/child $32/12; ⏱ 10am & 11.30am; 🚻) The first mines were walk-in, pick-and-shovel horrors. For an eye-opening experience, tour this historic mine (dating from the 1880s) where you squeeze down the steps with your helmet-light quivering on your head. Sturdy footwear is essential. It's a scenic 13km dirt drive off the Silverton road – a total of 33km from Broken Hill. Check road conditions at the Visitor Information Centre (p213). There are additional tours during school holidays, and claustrophobes can tour the surface area only for $10. Cash only.

Pro Hart Gallery   GALLERY

(✆ 08-8087 2441; www.prohart.com.au; 108 Wyman St; adult/child $5/3; ⏱ 10am-5pm Mar-Nov, to 4pm Dec-Feb) Kevin 'Pro' Hart (1928-2006) was a former miner and is widely considered one of outback Australia's premier painters. His iconic work is spread over three storeys, his studio has been re-created, and there's a fascinating video presentation

Broken Hill

Broken Hill

◎ Top Sights
1 Broken Hill Regional Art Gallery D2

⊕ Activities, Courses & Tours
2 Tri State Safaris D2

🛏 Sleeping
3 Palace Hotel C3
4 Red Earth Motel D2

✕ Eating
5 Alfresco's D2
6 Astra D3
7 Silly Goat D2

🍸 Drinking & Nightlife
Palace Hotel .... (see 3)

---

about his life and work. You can also admire his Rolls Royce collection.

Mutawintji National Park NATIONAL PARK
(☑08-8080 3200; www.nationalparks.nsw.gov.au; Mutawintji Access Rd, Mutawintji; ℗) **FREE** This exceptional 690-sq-km park, 163km from Broken Hill, lies in the Byngnano Range – the eroded and sculptured remains of a 400-million-year-old seabed. Its stunning gorges and rock pools teem with wildlife, and the mulga plains stretch to the horizon.

The Malyangapa and Bandjigali peoples have lived in the area for thousands of years, and there are important rock engravings, stencils, paintings and scattered remains of their day-to-day life. Visit the protected Mutawintji Historic Site with a guide from Mutawintji Heritage Tours (p212).

The **Broken Hill NWPS Office** (☑08-8080 3200; 183 Argent St; ⊙8.30am-4.30pm Mon-Fri) can connect you with a guide and has park brochures that include a simple map and eight walks or drives through the park. You can camp at Homestead Creek (adult/child $6/3.50); bring all supplies. In dry weather it's generally accessible to 2WD vehicles, but always come prepared and tell someone where you're travelling. Check road-closure info on 08-8082 6660 or 08-8091 5155.

🏃 Activities & Tours

★ Outback Astronomy ASTRONOMY
(🗐 0427 055 225; www.outbackastronomy.com.au; 18817 Barrier Hwy; adult/child $45/35; 🚗) Broken Hill is surrounded by desert, making it a great place to experience inky black skies and celestial splendour. This fabulous operator runs one-hour night-sky-viewing shows from its desert base. The presenter points out constellations and various features visible to the naked eye, and through powerful binoculars (provided).

Mutawintji Heritage Tours CULTURAL
(🗐 0497 002 773; www.mutawintjiheritage.word press.com/tours; Mutawintji National Park Visitors Centre; adult/child/family $50/30/100; ⊙ 10am EST (9.30am CST)) Conducted by the traditional Indigenous owners of the Mutawintji National Park, these excellent half-day tours focus on the landscape, scenery, and flora and fauna of the Mutawintji Historic Site. Centuries-old ochre stencils and rock art are visited, and the informative tours include how the area's traditional owners harnessed native flora for traditional medicine. Booking ahead is essential, and if travelling from Broken Hill, note that Mutawintji is in a different time zone.

Tri State Safaris DRIVING
(🗐 08-8088 2389; www.tristate.com.au; 422 Argent St; day tours from $230) Well-regarded Broken Hill operator offering one- to 15-day tours to remote outback places like Mutawintji, Kinchega or Mungo National Parks, Corner Country, Birdsville and the Simpson Desert. The most popular is the one-day tour of Broken Hill and Silverton. You can also tag along with some tours in your own 4WD at reduced rates.

🛏 Sleeping

Palace Hotel HISTORIC HOTEL $
(🗐 08-8088 1699; www.thepalacehotelbrokenhill. com.au; 227 Argent St; dm/s/d with shared bathroom from $35/60/70, d from $120; 🌣) Star of the hit Australian movie *The Adventures*

of Priscilla, Queen of the Desert, this huge and ageing icon won't be to everyone's taste, but a stay here is one of the outback's most idiosyncratic sleeping experiences. Newer rooms have balcony access and en suites, but most are proudly retro. For the full experience, try the Priscilla Suite (from $225).

★ Emaroo Cottages COTTAGE $$
(🗐 08-8595 7217; www.brokenhillcottages.com. au; cottages from $190; 🅿🌣🛜) Staying in one of these four fabulous, fully self-contained, renovated two-bedroom miners cottages is a great way to experience the Hill. Each cottage is located in a different part of town, and has excellent security, undercover parking, air-conditioning, wi-fi, a full kitchen, a bathroom and a laundry, and the price can't be beat. Go for Emaroo Oxide, if you can.

★ Outback Church Stay APARTMENT $$
(🗐 0423 765 290; www.brokenhilloutbackchurch stay.com; 125 Patton St; apt from $165; 🅿🌣🛜) Broken Hill's most distinctive and luxurious lodgings can be found in this fascinating, fully self-contained church and presbytery. Its only downside is the South Broken Hill location, away from the cafes and restaurants of central BH. There's also a very comfortable self-contained cottage. Rates are cheapest from Monday to Thursday.

Red Earth Motel MOTEL $$
(🗐 08-8088 5694; www.redearthmotel.com.au; 469 Argent St; studio apt from $160, 2-/3-bedroom apt from $220/260; 🅿🌣🛜🏊) One of rural NSW's better motels, this outstanding family-run place in Broken Hill has large, stylish rooms – each with a separate lounge and kitchen facilities, making them ideal for longer stays. There's a guest laundry, plus pool and barbecue area. Three sparkling new rooms were added in September 2018, and it's a short walk to the best cafe in town.

🍴 Eating

★ Silly Goat CAFE $
(🗐 08-8088 4774; www.facebook.com/thesilly goatfamily; 425 Argent St; dishes $11-19; ⊙ 7am-4pm Mon-Fri, to 3pm Sat & Sun; 🌣🚗) What's this? Pour-overs and single-origin coffee in the outback? Nice work, Silly Goat. The menu would be at home in any big-city cafe, the array of cakes is tempting, the coffee is great, and the vibe is busy and cheerful. Cold pressed juices and a more spacious new

WORTH A TRIP

SILVERTON

Quirkiness overflows at Silverton, a former silver-mining town and now ghost town–cum–living museum. It's 25km west of Broken Hill along a sealed road. Silverton's fortunes peaked in 1885, when it had a population of 3000, but in 1889 the mines closed and the people (and some houses) moved to Broken Hill. Visiting is like walking into a Russell Drysdale painting. The town's unique appearance lends itself well to the silver screen – astute viewers will recognise locations used in films such as *Mad Max II* and *A Town Like Alice.*

When you're here, it's impossible to get lost. History buffs should beeline to the fascinating **Silverton Gaol and Historical Museum** (☑08-8088 5317; cnr Burke & Layard Sts; adult/child $4/2; ⊙9.30am-4pm), followed by the **Silverton School Museum** (☑08-8088 7481; Layard St; adult/child $2.50/1; ⊙9.30am-3.30pm Mon, Wed & Fri-Sun): both are crammed with artefacts from another age. Considerably more offbeat is the **Mad Max 2 Museum** (☑08-8088 6128; www.facebook.com/MadMaxMuseum; Stirling St; adult/child $10/5; ⊙10am-4pm), the culmination of Englishman Adrian Bennett's lifetime obsession with the theme. It's then worth driving another 5km to **Mundi Mundi Lookout** (Wilangee Rd), from where the horizon is so vast you can see the curvature of the Earth. For art lovers, there's a scattering of quirky workshops and galleries, and outdoor installations crafted from old cars and the detritus of civilisation.

After all that, you'll need to stop for a beer and a pub meal at the fabulous **Silverton Hotel** (☑08-8088 5313; www.silvertonhotel.com.au; Layard St; d $120, extra person $25; ❄ ⓢ). If you enjoy the beer garden so much that you can't drive back to the Hill, you can always spend the night in comfy, refurbished motel rooms.

Housed in the 39 Dips art gallery and shop, **Silverton Visitor Information Centre** (☑08-8088 7566; Loftus St, Silverton; ⊙9am-4pm Mon-Fri) can answer all your questions about this dusty, endearing little town.

---

location add two further ticks to easily the best cafe in town.

Astra　　　　　　　MODERN AUSTRALIAN $$
(☑08-8087 5428; www.facebook.com/theastrabrokenhill; 393 Argent St; mains $28-38; ❄ ⓘ) Multiple and consistent recommendations from locals means you won't go wrong at the Astra. Look forward to a classy menu of upmarket pub fare from juicy steaks and seafood dishes including oysters, to generous burgers and nightly chef's specials. The attached **Red Lush** cocktail bar is a busy locale for beers, pizza, bar snacks and cocktails, especially on a Friday night.

Alfresco's　　　　　MODERN AUSTRALIAN $$
(☑08-8087 5599; www.alfrescoscafe.com.au; 397 Argent St; dinner mains $15-33; ⊙7am-late; ❄ ⓘ ⓗ) This friendly place pulls an unfussy local crowd pining for its bumper portions of meat dishes (classics like steak and chicken parma) and crowd-pleasing pizza and pasta. The service is the best in town and the varied menu has something for everyone. Keep an eye on the daily specials board for surprises like Moroccan-spiced calamari.

🍷 Drinking & Nightlife

★ **Palace Hotel**　　　　　　　　PUB
(☑08-8088 1699; www.thepalacehotelbrokenhill.com.au; 227 Argent St; ⊙from 3pm Mon-Wed, from noon Thu-Sat) Built in 1889, Broken Hill's most famous pub, of *Priscilla, Queen of the Desert* fame, has an elaborate cast-iron verandah, plus wonderfully kitsch landscape murals covering almost every inch of the public areas. There's excellent pub-grub in the **Sidebar restaurant** (mains $22 to $24), but at the very least, a drink in the front bar or on the upstairs balcony is essential.

🔒 Shopping

Amanya Mitha　　　　　　　ARTS & CRAFTS
(www.facebook.com/amanyamithaindigenousarts; cnr Gypsum & Willis Sts; ⊙9.30am-4pm Mon & Tue, to 5pm Wed-Fri, 10am-1pm Sat) Home base for local Indigenous artist Clinton Kemp, a member of the Dieri mob of South Australia, this excellent gallery and shop showcases work including paintings, wood carving, handmade jewellery and wooden bowls. Miners' safety helmets and emu eggs adorned with Indigenous motifs are both

ℹ DOING IT DIFFERENTLY

When the NSW government refused to give Broken Hill the services it needed, saying the town was just a pinprick on the map, the council replied that Sydney was also a pinprick from where it was, and Broken Hill would henceforth be part of South Australia (SA). Since the town was responsible for much of NSW's wealth, Broken Hill was told it was to remain part of NSW. In protest, the town adopted SA time, phone area code, and football, playing Australian Rules from then on.

Tourists beware: time in Broken Hill is Central Standard Time (CST), 30 minutes later than the surrounding area on Eastern Standard Time (EST); you're in the 08 phone-code region; and don't talk about rugby league in the pub.

beautiful and interesting. Many of the items are compact and well priced, making good souvenirs and gifts.

ℹ Information

Broken Hill Visitor Information Centre
(☑ 08-8088 3560; www.travelin.com.au/go/broken-hill; cnr Blende & Bromide Sts; ⊗ 8.30am-5pm Mar-Nov, to 3pm Dec-Feb; 🛜) Broken Hill has much to do and a lot of it is on dusty, dangerous roads, so talk to the genuinely friendly staff and help yourself to brochures and maps to get your head around the city's outlying attractions.

ℹ Getting There & Away

Broken Hill is a long way away – wherever you are. By road, it's 1144km east to Sydney, and 512km southwest to Adelaide in South Australia.

Rex (p196) offers the quickest way to get to Broken Hill from Sydney and Adelaide, but flights are expensive. Expect to pay a minimum of around $200 one way.

NSW TrainLink (p194) runs a daily Xplorer train service from Sydney to Broken Hill (from $69, 13½ hours). Broken Hill is a stop on the iconic **Indian Pacific** (☑ 1800 703 357; www.greatsouthernrail.com.au) train between Sydney and Perth.

Buses R Us (☑ 08-8285 6900; www.busesrus.com.au) operates two to three buses per week to Adelaide ($140, seven hours) from the Broken Hill Visitor Information Centre.

Mungo National Park

This remote, beautiful and important **park** (☑ 03-5021 8900; www.visitmungo.com.au; Arumpo Rd, southwest NSW, 110km northeast of Mildura; per vehicle per day $8) covers 278.5 sq km of the Willandra Lakes Region World Heritage Area. A site of global archaeological and anthropological significance, it is one of Australia's most accessible slices of the outback.

Within the park, Lake Mungo is a dry lake and the site of the oldest archaeological finds in Australia. It also has the longest continual record of human culture: the world's oldest-recorded cremation site – thought to be over 40,000 years old – has been found here.

The area is the traditional homeland of the Barkindji, Ngyiampaa and Mutthi Mutthi peoples, and in late 2018 the remains of 105 tribal ancestors – including those of 40,000 year-old 'Mungo Man' – were returned to the park to be reinterred according to the wishes of the three local tribes.

⊙ Sights & Activities

★ **Walls of China**   ARCHAEOLOGICAL SITE
(☑ 03-5021 8900; Mungo National Park; ⊗ 24hr) A 33km semicircle ('lunette') of sand dunes, the fabulous Walls of China has been created by the unceasing westerly wind. From the visitor centre a road leads across the dry lakebed to a car park, then it's a short walk to the viewing platform. Getting up close to the formations is the preserve of guided tours only.

Lake Mungo   LAKE
(Mungo National Park) One of 17 lakes in the Willandra Lakes Region World Heritage Area, the dry lake bed of Lake Mungo, within the Mungo National Park, is home to many significant archaeological finds, including the discovery of the oldest human remains in Australia (named 'Mungo Man') and the site of the oldest ritual cremation in the world ('Mungo Lady').

Mungo Track   SCENIC DRIVE
The Mungo Track is a 70km signposted loop road around the heart of Mungo, linking the park's main attractions – you'll pass diverse landscapes, lookouts, short walks and plenty of emus and kangaroos.

Although it's unsealed, the road is generally fine for 2WD cars in dry weather; in good weather (ie not too hot), mountain-bikers may be tempted.

🏃 Tours

Day tours to the Mungo National Park are offered from the main gateway towns of Mildura, Wentworth and Balranald, plus Broken Hill. These all include food, and a walk to the Walls of China (off limits without a guide).

Companies based in Wentworth will often pick up in Mildura, and vice versa. If you prefer, operators will usually allow you to meet them in Mungo to join their tour.

Aboriginal Discovery Tours   CULTURAL
(📞03-5021 8900; www.visitmungo.com.au/discovery-tours; adult/child $50/35) For those who visit the park independently, the NPWS conducts tours from the visitor centre (p216) led by Indigenous rangers, with the most popular option being the walk to the Walls of China. Check online for schedules: tours generally run daily in school holidays, and weekends the rest of the year. Departure times depend on weather forecast, sunset time etc.

Discover Mildura   TOURS
(📞03-5024 7448; www.discovermildura.com; 14 Stockmans Dr, Mildura; tours per person $150) An excellent way to explore Mungo National Park from Mildura (Victoria; p619): day trips include pick-up from and drop-off at your Mildura accommodation, morning tea, lunch, all transport, entry fees, experienced guides and an escorted walk to the Walls of China.

🛏️ Sleeping

Fees for the park's two campgrounds must be paid at the Mungo National Park Visitor Centre.

Mungo Shearers' Quarters   HOSTEL $
(📞1300 072 757; www.nationalparks.nsw.gov.au/camping-and-accommodation/accommodation/Mungo-Shearers-Quarters; Mungo National Park; adult/child $30/10; ❄) The former shearers' quarters comprises five neat, good-value rooms (each sleeping up to six in various configurations; BYO bedding). Rooms share a communal kitchen and bathroom, and a barbecue area. Bookings can be made online.

Mungo Lodge   LODGE $$$
(📞1300 663 748; www.mungolodge.com.au; 10142 Arumpo Rd, Arumpo; dm $45, cabins

$199-295; ❄🖥️📶) 🏊 This privately managed eco-resort on the outskirts of Mungo National Park offers a range of accommodation types from campsites ($20) and dorm beds to budget and deluxe self-contained cabins: the latter are the plushest lodgings within cooee of the park. The lodge houses an inviting bar, lounge and restaurant area open for breakfast, lunch and dinner (mains $22 to $35).

ℹ️ Information

Mungo National Park Visitor Centre (📞03-5021 8900; www.visitmungo.com.au; Mailbox Rd, Mungo National Park; ⏰8.30am-4.30pm Mon-Fri) Has displays on the park's cultural and natural history, and it's here that you can pick up maps, pay park and camping fees, and enquire about tours.

ℹ️ Getting There & Away

Mungo National Park is 110km from Mildura and 150km from Balranald on good, unsealed roads that become instantly impassable after rain – a sturdy 2WD vehicle is generally fine in dry weather, but most rental-car companies prohibit taking their vehicles on unsealed roads. Be sure to check before setting out.

The closest places selling fuel are Balranald, Mildura (Victoria), Wentworth, Pooncarie and Menindee.

Contact the tourist offices in the gateway towns to see if the roads into Mungo are open and accessible.

There is no public transport in the area, and by far the safest, easiest and most rewarding way to explore the park is by guided tour, with the added benefit of knowledgeable guides.

Tibooburra & Corner Country

Out here, it's a different world: both harsh and peaceful, stretching forever to the endless sky. This far-western corner of NSW is a semidesert of red plains, heat, dust and flies – somewhere to fall off the map.

Tiny Tibooburra, the hottest town in the state, is a quintessential outback frontier town, with two pubs and a landscape of large red rock formations known as 'gibbers'.

North and northwest of Tibooburra, vast **Sturt National Park** (📞08-8091 3308; www.nationalparks.nsw.gov.au/visit-a-park/parks/Sturt-National-Park; Tibooburra; per vehicle per day $8; 🅿) encompasses over 3400 sq km of classic outback terrain. There are campgrounds

WORTH A TRIP

LORD HOWE ISLAND

Rising from the Pacific a remote 600km from the NSW mainland, little Lord Howe's tropical, World Heritage–listed beauty is surprisingly under the radar given the jaw-dropping spectacle of this former volcano. It looks like a Bond villain's lair, with two lofty mountains overlooking an idyllic lagoon, perfect crescents of beach and a verdant interior criss-crossed with walking trails.

Lord Howe's isolation and comparatively recent appearance – it was formed by hot-spot volcanic activity around seven million years ago – lends it a unique ecology, with many plant and insect species found only here. Birds rule the roost, with nesting terns noisily present and the eerie cries of muttonbirds in their burrows punctuating the night. Ongoing ecological projects are seeking to remove introduced species.

The island's restricted accommodation and flight capacity mean that a visit here doesn't come cheap, but relaxation is guaranteed: there's limited internet and no mobile-phone signal.

Activities

There's great scope for outdoors fun on Lord Howe Island. On land, walking is the main attraction, with the guided hike up **Mt Gower** the highlight. A network of well-marked trails covers the rest of the island, offering super viewpoints and secluded beaches. On the water, you can grab a kayak or paddleboard to explore the lagoon, go snorkelling or surfing, or take a turtle-spotting boat trip. Other boat excursions include fishing trips, circumnavigations of the island or journeys to magnificent **Ball's Pyramid**. Diving is also good here, with a couple of operators offering a variety of trips.

Sleeping & Eating

Book accommodation before finalising your flight, as the island fills fast. There's no budget accommodation and no campground – nor is wild camping allowed. The island website www.lordhoweisland.info lists all the accommodation choices, from lodges to holiday lets. Low-season prices are significantly cheaper, but even then rooms start at around $160. In summer the lowest prices are around double that.

Pinetrees Lodge (⏺ Lord Howe Island 02-6563 2177, reservations 02-9262 6585; www.pinetrees.com.au; Lagoon Rd; tw per person all-inclusive 5 nights from $2150; ☺ Sep-May; ℗) is a Lord Howe institution, while **Leanda Lei Apartments** (⏺ 02-6563 2195; www.leandalei.com.au; Middle Beach Rd; high/shoulder season d from $375/310; ℗ ☎) ✈ and **Beachcomber Lodge** (⏺ 02-6563 2032; www.beachcomberlhi.com.au; Anderson Rd; tw May-Sep $275, Oct-Apr $425; ☎) are other reliable choices. **Anchorage Restaurant** (⏺ 02-6563 2029; https://earlsanchorage.com; Ned's Beach Rd; dinner mains $34-45; ☺ 8am-8pm; ☎) is the island's best place to eat.

Information

There's a tourist desk in the Lord Howe Island Museum. The website www.lordhoweisland.info is very useful.

Getting There & Away

Qantaslink (www.qantas.com) flies direct to Lord Howe from Sydney and Brisbane. Flights are expensive for the distance, typically costing well over $1000 return, and a little less in low season.

and picnic areas in four locations; note that only untreated water is available in the park, so come prepared with fuel, food and water to ensure you travel safely in this hot, remote country. Definitely visit the **visitor centre** (⏺ 08-8091 3308; www.nationalparks. nsw.gov.au; 52 Briscoe St; ☺ 8.30am-4.30pm Mon-Fri; ☎) before setting out.

This region is the homeland of the Wangkumara people, but much of the community moved to around Bourke in the 1940s.

SOUTH COAST NSW

The South Coast is paradise without pretension, a place to wriggle your toes into brilliant white sand while guzzling down a meat pie. The stretch unfurls south from Sydney to Eden along coves, saw-toothed sea cliffs and bays where emerald waves lavish foam onto soft, squeaky sand. It's not as popular as NSW's North Coast and, frankly, locals couldn't be happier about that.

The Indigenous Yuin and Dharawal peoples have long enjoyed the region's bounty, for millennia gathering oysters that now grace restaurant tables up and down the coast. The land has deep significance for Aboriginal communities: Montague Island (Barranguba), with its multitude of seals and bird life; pert Pigeon House Mountain (Didthul); and ancient sites across Murramarang and Booderee National Parks.

Mass tourism has unquestionably altered destinations like Jervis Bay. But thrilling isolation isn't hard to find, especially amid the Sapphire Coast's untamed national parks and whale-rich shores.

ℹ Getting There & Away

Trains from Sydney (☑ 02-4907 7501, 13 15 00; www.sydneytrains.info) get as far as Nowra (Bomaderry) via Wollongong, Kiama and Berry, but beyond here it's buses. **Premier** (☑ 02-4423 5233, 13 34 10; www.premierms.com.au) is the major operator, linking Eden with Sydney via all coastal towns twice daily. **Murrays** (☑ 13 22 51; www.murrays.com.au) links South Coast towns with Canberra (the closest railway station to many of them), while **V/Line** (☑ 1800 800 007; www.vline.com.au) offers a bus and train connection to Melbourne.

Wollongong

POP 285,678

A seaside town with slow-burning charm, the 'Gong' lies 80km (and dozens of beauteous beaches) south of Sydney. Committed surfers and cheerful retirees are united in their love of Wollongong's beaches, while the bar and restaurant scenes effervesce with the enthusiasm of a town twice its size.

◉ Sights

★ **Wollongong Botanic Garden**   GARDENS
(☑ 02-4227 7667; www.wollongong.nsw.gov.au/botanicgarden; 61 Northfields Ave, Keiraville; ☺ 7am-5pm Apr-Sep, to 6pm Mon-Fri, to 6.45pm Sat & Sun Oct-Mar; 🅿; 🚌 55A/55C) FREE In

a region already awash in scenic spots, Wollongong's botanic gardens still delight visitors with their attractive lily ponds, manicured lawns and contrastingly gnarled gum trees, all against the rugged green backdrop of the Illawarra Escarpment. Don't miss the rose garden with its dedication to the Stolen Generations, Aboriginal Australians who, as children, were forcibly institutionalised away from their families.

North Beach   BEACH
(🅿) Stretching north from the harbour, North Beach is an excellent all-rounder: shallows for kids to splash in, breaks suitable for various levels, and conveniently close to the city centre. North Beach has lifesavers all year round at its southern end.

Wollongong City Beach   BEACH
The southern of Wollongong's two city beaches is a popular stretch of golden sand with good swimming (especially at the northern end) and, depending on the wind, surfing.

Illawarra Escarpment State Conservation Area   PARK
(www.nationalparks.nsw.gov.au) FREE Spectacular rainforest hugs the edge of the ever-eroding sandstone cliffs of the Illawarra Escarpment, a 30-million-year-old feature that rises to 534m at Mt Kembla's pointed summit. A winding, 15-minute drive from Wollongong, through knotted tunnels of trees, leads to the dramatic **Mt Keira Lookout** (464m) across Wollongong and the coast.

Signs point to the 5.5km **Mt Keira Ring Track**; it's steep with many stairs, so allow up to 4½ hours for the full loop.

🏃 Activities

HangglideOz   ADVENTURE SPORTS
(☑ 0417 939 200; www.hangglideoz.com.au; tandem flights midweek/weekend $245/295) A reliable hang-gliding operator, established in 1987 by one of the first daredevils to glide from Stanwell Park, HangglideOz offers tandem flights and courses from Bald Hill, which overlooks dazzling beaches. Pre-booking essential.

Sydney Hang Gliding Centre   ADVENTURE SPORTS
(☑ 0400 258 258; www.hanggliding.com.au; tandem flights $260-285) Decades of experience make this long-running hang-gliding operator a reliable bet for a tandem flight from

Wollongong

Wollongong

Sights
1 North Beach...C1
2 Wollongong City Beach...........................C4

Activities, Courses & Tours
3 Pines Surfing Academy............................C1

Sleeping
4 Keiraleagh...B3
5 SAGE Hotel Wollongong..........................C4

Eating
6 Babyface...B3
7 Balinese Spice Magic A3
8 Caveau...B3
9 His Boy Elroy..A3

Drinking & Nightlife
10 Humber..A3
11 Moominn...C4

breathtaking Bald Hill at Stanwell Park. Reserve ahead.

Pines Surfing Academy   SURFING
(☑ 0410 645 981; www.pinessurfingacademy. com.au; 1a Cliff Rd, North Wollongong; 2hr group lesson $50, 1hr private lesson $60, 6hr set $130) Surf lessons at either North Beach or the Farm Beach by a seasoned operator (established 1989). There are lessons year-round,

but book at least 48 hours ahead. Wetsuits included.

🛏 Sleeping & Eating

Keiraleagh   HOSTEL $
(☑ 02-4228 6765; www.backpack.net.au; 60 Kembla St; 6/4-bed dm from $25/30, s/d with shared bathroom from $65/75, d/f from $110/140; @ 🛜)
🍽 They don't make 'em like this any more. Family owned for 30 years, Keiraleagh has

a huge garden with Balinese-style benches and a barbecue area. Beyond the basic dorm rooms are spacious private doubles with quartz-effect bathrooms. There's a real community feel, with friendly dogs, a tent for overflow guests, and the owner managing security personally. Cash only.

SAGE Hotel Wollongong HOTEL $
(📞02-4201 2111; www.nexthotels.com/sage/wollongong; 60-62 Harbour St; d/ste from $149/349; P❄🐾🛜🏊) Neat and contemporary rooms at SAGE come with quality beds, fridges and coffee machines, and they feel airy and bright (with splashes of the hotel chain's signature mauve). Pleasing amenities include a small heated outdoor pool, a trim gym and a good on-site restaurant (evenings only).

His Boy Elroy BURGERS $
(📞02-4244 8221; www.hisboyelroy.com.au; 176 Keira St; burgers $13-17, mains & snacks $6-20; ⏰11am-9pm Sun-Wed, to midnight Thu-Sat) With a menu equally balanced between burgers and booze, His Boy Elroy is one of Wollongong's trendier picks for a bite. Burgers range from Wagyu beef heavy with toppings (like the bacon, egg and barbecue-sauce 'Duke') to smoky pulled pork, veggie burgers and fish patties.

The cocktail list makes use of interesting spirits (how about chia vodka or hibiscus gin), though the burgers taste best with an IPA.

★Babyface JAPANESE, AUSTRALIAN $$
(📞02-4295 0903; www.babyfacekitchen.com.au; 179 Keira St; mains $24-49, tasting menus $75-90; ⏰noon-3pm & 6-10pm or 11pm Thu-Sat, 6-10pm or 11pm Tue, Wed & Sun) The menu at this flash fusion place combines expertly prepared sashimi with quintessentially Aussie ingredients (macadamia nuts, desert quandong and local cheese). Tasting menus allow diners to sample a smorgasbord: king prawns, wattle-seed tarts, wasabi-spiked salmon and other morsels. There are some interesting wines by the glass and upbeat, friendly staff.

Balinese Spice Magic INDONESIAN, VEGAN $$
(📞02-4227 1033; http://balinesespicemagic.com.au; 130 Keira St; lunch mains $10-18, dinner mains $18-26; ⏰5.30-9.30pm Tue & Wed, 11am-2.30pm & 5.30-9.30pm Thu, 11am-2.30pm & 5.30-11pm Fri & Sat; 🌱🍴) The warmth of the welcome is only outshone by the tenderly prepared Balinese food at Spice Magic. This standout restaurant serves authentically spiced candlenut curry, chicken satay on sugar cane and a superb vegan menu of stir-fries, battered tempeh and more. Desserts like pandan roll and black sticky rice are filling but worth stretching for.

★Caveau AUSTRALIAN $$$
(📞02-4226 4855; www.caveau.com.au; 122-124 Keira St; 7-course degustation menu $110, with wine from $165; ⏰6-11pm Tue-Sat; 🍴) Heavily influenced by seasonal produce and bush tucker, this lauded restaurant serves gourmet fare such as barramundi, duck with Illawarra plums, and occasional eyebrow-raisers (crocodile ham, anyone?). There's a separate degustation for vegetarians and vegans, which is easily as inventive as the meat-eater menu.

🍷 Drinking & Nightlife

★Humber BAR
(📞02-4263 0355; www.humber.bar; 226 Crown St; ⏰4-11pm Tue & Wed, 4pm-midnight Thu & Fri, 8am-midnight Sat, 8am-10pm Sat; 🛜) Stacked into the former Humber car dealership, this multistorey bar culminates in an attractive roof terrace with retro parasols, overseen by some very competent mixologists ('Clover's Sky Club' will send you to heaven). The ground level does coffee and food before morphing into a stylish cocktail bar in the evening, and there's an art-deco-inspired bar on the 1st floor.

Moominn BAR
(📞0412 871 884; https://moominn.com.au; 68 Crown St; ⏰5-10pm Tue & Wed, 5pm-midnight Thu & Sat, 4pm-midnight Fri) With tulips, checked tablecloths and greenery dangling from the ceiling, there's no more darling setting than Moominn. Along with a bluesy soundtrack, the wide-ranging wines and cocktails can be accompanied by globe-spanning tapas like fried Czech cheese, vegan pancakes or halloumi spring rolls. Classy, a touch sentimental, and one of the Gong's best spots for a date.

ℹ Information

iHub Visitor Centre (📞02-4267 5910; www.visitwollongong.com.au; 93 Crown St; ⏰9am-5pm Mon-Fri, 10am-3pm Sat & Sun; 🛜) Local information and bookings.

Southern Gateway Centre (📞02-4267 5910; www.visitwollongong.com.au; Princes Motorway, Bulli Tops; ⏰9am-5pm; 🛜) On the clifftops north of Wollongong, this helpful centre is a worthwhile information stop if you're approaching the city by car from Sydney (and the viewing platform outside is glorious).

❶ Getting There & Away

Trains (p217) on the **South Coast Line** (Station St) undertake the scenic journey to/from Sydney's Central Station ($6.10, 90 minutes), and continue south as far as Nowra (Bomaderry; $6.10 to $8.70, 1¼ hours), via Kiama ($4.70, 45 minutes) and Berry ($4.70, 1¼ hours).

All long-distance buses leave from the eastern side of the railway station. Premier (p217) has two daily buses to Sydney ($18, two hours) and Eden ($69, 8½ hours). Murrays (p217) has buses to Canberra ($48.40, 3¼ hours).

❶ Getting Around

The free Gong Shuttle (buses 55A and 55C) runs every 10 to 20 minutes from 7am to 10pm (8am to 6pm at weekends) on a loop from the station to the university, and North Wollongong – useful for reaching North Beach, the botanic garden and Science Space.

Kiama & Around

POP 13,453

Ancient volcanic vents have given touristy Kiama a distinctively ragged coastline. Most famous for its blowhole, which launches sea spray high into the air, Kiama is also close to coastal and forest walking trails, many of them easy and family-friendly. It's a likeable place: even travellers who raise an eyebrow at the abundance of souvenir and swimwear shops are likely to be won over, especially in summer when the scent of lemon myrtle floats on the sea breeze and an easy-going ambience infuses the town.

◉ Sights

Minnamurra
Rainforest Centre   NATURE RESERVE
(☑02-4236 0469; www.nationalparks.nsw.gov.au; Minnamurra Falls Rd; car $12; ☺9am-5pm, last entry 4pm; ⊕) At the eastern edge of **Budderoo National Park**, 15km inland from Kiama via Jamberoo, this is a surprisingly lush subtropical rainforest. A 1.6km loop walk weaves through the rainforest following a cascading stream (an early section is wheelchair accessible). Look out for water dragons and lyrebirds scurrying among more than a dozen types of fern. A secondary 2.6km walk on a steepish track leads to the **Minnamurra Falls**; allow two hours to combine the walks.

The helpful visitor centre has park and ecosystem information, and an interesting display of early tools, on loan from members of local Aboriginal communities.

There's also a worthwhile cafe here, open 10am to 4pm at busy times, and 11.30am to 2.30pm on quieter days.

A weekday bus from Kiama Station gets up here, but there's six hours between arrivals.

Kiama Blowhole   NATURAL FEATURE
A tourist draw for well over a century, Kiama's blowhole sits on the point by the centre of town. It's fairly underwhelming except when the surf's up and a southeaster's blowing: then, water explodes high up out of the fissure. Girded by basalt columns and wave-thrashed rocks, the blowhole has a setting that's arguably more impressive than its occasional spurt of seawater. It's floodlit at night.

The **Little Blowhole** (Marsden Head) along the coast to the south is less impressive but much more regular.

🛏 Sleeping & Eating

Bellevue Accommodation   APARTMENT $$
(☑02-4232 4000; https://bellevueaccommodation.com.au; 21 Minnamurra St; apt from $220; 🅿❄🛜) Well-renovated modern apartments fill this 1890s manor, one of the oldest buildings in Kiama. Bay windows and palm-shaded decks with wicker chairs lend plantation-style elegance, while glossy kitchens, coral-tiled bathrooms and amenities such as washer-dryers bring apartments into the 21st century.

Kiama Harbour Cabins   CABIN $$$
(☑02-4232 2707; www.kiamacoast.com.au; Blowhole Point; cottages $300-400; 🅿❄🛜) Overlooking the beach and the nearby ocean pool, these one- to three-bedroom cabins are decorated in pleasing earth tones, with airy lounge rooms and barbecues on front verandahs.

Hungry Monkey   CAFE $
(☑0403 397 353; http://thehungrymonkeyyy.com; 5/32 Collins St; breakfasts $11-18, burgers from $12; ☺6.30am-4pm Mon & Tue, 6.30am-9pm Wed-Sat, 7.30am-4pm Sun; 🛜🍴) The most popular (read: Instagram-worthy) of Kiama's growing seam of cafes, Hungry Monkey distinguishes itself by superb coffee, gourmet burgers and a gorilla mural. Nestled among craft and souvenir shops, the cafe serves

food with plenty of zing: orange-blossom hotcakes, smoky pulled-pork burgers, and Italian-inflected dinners. You'll probably need to wait for a table for dinner or weekend brunch.

ⓘ Information

Visitor Centre (☑ 02-4232 3322; www.kiama. com.au; Blowhole Point Rd; ⊙ 9am-5pm) Helpful with finding accommodation.

ⓘ Getting There & Away

Kiama is most easily reached by train, with frequent **Sydney Trains** (☑ 13 15 00; www. sydneytrains.info; Railway Pde) departures to Wollongong ($6.80, 40 minutes), Sydney ($8.70, 2¼ hours) and Bomaderry (for Nowra; $5, 30 minutes).

Premier (p217) buses run twice daily to Eden ($69, 6¼ hours) and Sydney ($25, 2½ hours). **Kiama Coaches** (☑ 02-4232 3466; www. kiamacoaches.com.au) runs to Gerroa, Gerringong and Seven Mile Beach on weekdays ($5, twice in the morning and twice in the afternoon).

Berry

POP 2065

Idling among heritage buildings and sampling local produce are the main attractions in cute-as-a-button Berry. Most visitors pass through for immersion in the old-timey ambience, complete with wholesome B&Bs and design shops. Eight kilometres inland of stunning Seven Mile Beach, it's a pleasant way station between Kiama and Nowra on Rte 1.

◉ Sights

The town's short main street features National Trust–classified buildings and there are good-quality vineyards in the rolling countryside around Berry.

★**Silos Estate** WINERY
(☑ 02-4448 6082; www.silosestate.com; B640/ Princes Hwy, Jaspers Brush; ⊙ tastings 11am-5pm; ℗) ⎯ Beautifully set on a verdant former dairy farm between Berry and Nowra, this crowd-pleasing winery makes a range of tasty drops. Swirl a glass of bright sauvignon blanc or robust shiraz in the tasting room or linger over a meal in the excellent restaurant (p222).

The estate is carbon neutral and features lots of forward-thinking environmental initiatives (including water recycling and a charging station for electric cars).

If you can't tear yourself away, there are four utterly relaxing, and ecofriendly, boutique rooms ($205 to $275).

★**Seven Mile Beach** BEACH
(www.nationalparks.nsw.gov.au; ☝) This superlative crescent of sand, stretching south from Gerroa to Shoalhaven Heads, is one of the South Coast's most memorable beaches thanks to its pale-golden sand and sheer size. Gazetted as a national park, Seven Mile Beach has picnic areas, shaded walking tracks and kilometres of bright foam lashing the shore, making it almost impossible not to kick off your shoes and jump in.

🛏 Sleeping

Conjuring up images of cosy wood fires, Berry is a popular weekender in winter as well as summer. Upmarket B&Bs with verdant gardens and heritage features meet demand for genteel getaways, though midrange places and some unvarnished pub rooms cater to smaller budgets.

★**Berry B&B** B&B $$
(☑ 0414 433 046; http://berrybandb.com.au; 146 Kangaroo Valley Rd; r incl breakfast & with shared bathroom $200-235; ℗ ⎙) Fringed by flower gardens, this three-room charmer is tucked away in a former dairy. Genial hosts usher guests into a big, elegantly furnished lounge. The fan-cooled rooms vary in size, but all have artful features, like book-shaped nightstands and the occasional ukulele, and there's a pool in the lush back garden.

Berry Village Boutique Motel MOTEL $$
(☑ 02-4464 3570; www.berrymotel.com.au; 72 Queen St; r $160-280; ℗ ❄ ⎙ ⎙) On the main road, this exceedingly well-run motel offers 25 rooms with rococo headboards and vintage style, almost all of them with balconies. The breakfast area is equally cosy, with bold primary colours and a fireplace lit in winter. Higher-grade rooms have spa baths and towelling robes. There's a small swimming pool with a cascading water feature.

Bellawongarah at Berry B&B $$
(☑ 02-4464 1999; www.accommodation-berry. com.au; 869 Kangaroo Valley Rd, Bellawongarah; r $250-270; ℗ ❄ ⎙) Rainforest surrounds this wonderful place, 8km from Berry on the mountain road to Kangaroo Valley. There

are two rooms. One is a sumptuous loft space in the main house, which features a large spa bath overlooking the greenery, and a cosy lounge and sleeping area under the eaves. The other is a cute 1868 church with an airy, French-provincial feel.

✕ Eating

Famous Berry Donut Van
CAFE $

(📞02-4464 2753; 73 Queen St; 1/12 doughnuts $2.20/18; ⊗8am-6pm; 🖐) Parents driving the family down the South Coast for the holidays have long bribed the kids by promising a stop at this food truck if they were good along the way. The doughnuts are made fresh and rolled in cinnamon sugar. Up the ante with the 'donut & cream': split in half with a blob of vanilla ice cream ($7).

Milkwood Bakery
CAFE, BAKERY $

(📞02-4464 3033; https://berrysourdoughcafe.com.au; 109 Queen St; pies $6; ⊗6am-5.30pm Mon-Fri, 7am-5pm Sat & Sun; 🖐) Milkwood showcases baked goods from the owners' **sourdough bakery** (📞02-4464 1617; cnr Prince Alfred & Princess Sts; breakfasts from $5.50, lunch mains $16-26; ⊗8am-3pm Wed-Sun), which basks in a glowing local reputation. Every imaginable loaf and confection is here, with fig-and-walnut bread and ciabatta urging disloyalty to the flagship sourdough. Amplifying the dilemma are excellent pies and moreish friands and chocolate-almond-pear tarts.

The outdoor seating under the verandah is a very Berry place to be.

★ Silos Restaurant
AUSTRALIAN $$

(📞02-4448 6082; www.silos.com.au; B640 Princes Hwy, Jaspers Brush; 2/3-course tasting menu $60/75; ⊗noon-2pm & 6-10pm Thu-Sat, noon-2pm Sun, daily Jan; 🅿) The former grain silos that give the winery its name overlook this loveable restaurant, which has an inviting verandah space and dining room with dreamy views over the vineyard's grassy slopes. Confident and innovative flavour combinations like duck, macadamia and beetroot, and zucchini flowers with truffle honey, make this a standout.

Hungry Duck
ASIAN $$

(📞02-4464 2323; http://hungryduck.com.au; 85 Queen St; mains $16-35, 5/9-course banquet $55/85; ⊗6-9.30pm Wed-Mon) 🌿 Hungry Duck's contemporary Asian fusion menu, uniting Chinese-style duck spring rolls with kingfish sashimi and Wagyu red curry, is served tapas style, although larger mains are also available. There's a rear courtyard and kitchen garden where herbs are plucked for the plate. The menu rotates according to what's in season, and fresh fish, meat and eggs are all sourced locally.

🔒 Shopping

Treat Factory
FOOD

(📞02-4464 1112; www.treatfactory.com.au; 6 Old Creamery Lane; ⊗9.30am-4.30pm Mon-Fri, 10am-4.30pm Sat & Sun; 🖐) As much a feast for the eyes as for sweet-inclined appetites, this old-fashioned factory shop is chock-full of marshmallows, salted caramel, chocolate-covered macadamias and freckles (chocolate discs dotted with sugar sprinkles) bigger than your head.

ℹ️ Getting There & Away

Trains run every hour or two to Nowra (Bomaderry; $3.10, 10 minutes) and to Kiama ($3.50, 30 minutes), where you can change to trains heading north to Wollongong ($4.70, 1¼ hours) and Sydney ($6.10, 2¾ hours).

Premier (p217) has buses to Sydney ($25, three hours, twice daily) via Kiama, and south to Eden via all coastal towns.

Local buses run two to three times Monday to Saturday to Nowra, Gerringong and Gerroa.

Kangaroo Valley

POP 328

Cradled by mountains, the township of Kangaroo Valley has a verdant beauty that is altogether uncommon in Australia. True to its name, this is a great area to spot kangaroos and wombats (head to the Bendeela Recreation Area towards dusk) as well as hike or kayak in nearby national parks. Much as the farms, vineyards and salt-of-the-earth residents pluck at the heartstrings of visitors, this rural idyll arguably evokes more of an Australian ideal than an authentic glimpse of the past; it's lovely just the same.

◎ Sights & Activities

★ Pioneer Village Museum
MUSEUM

(📞02-4465 1306; www.kangaroovalleymuseum.com; 2029 Moss Vale Rd; adult/child $10/5; ⊗10am-4pm Fri-Mon & Wed, daily Jan & other school holidays; 🅿🖐) This open-air museum, with meticulously recreated 19th-century cottages set in seven hectares of bushland, thoroughly immerses visitors in the sounds and sights of Kangaroo Valley in the early days of European settlement. Recordings of the settlers' descendants give voice to those who gambled on starting their lives anew in Australia, and the well-preserved collection includes treasured bibles and a mouse-proof church organ.

Cambewarra Lookout
VIEWPOINT

(⊙7.30am-9pm) Signposted off the Cambewarra Lookout Rd between Kangaroo Valley and Nowra, this vantage point (678m) offers a stupendous perspective over the winding Shoalhaven River and the alluvial agricultural lands far below, and right along the coast.

Fitzroy Falls
WATERFALL

(www.nationalparks.nsw.gov.au; Morton National Park; per vehicle $4) Tumbling 81m from near-vertical sandstone cliffs, Fitzroy Falls can be a dramatic torrent or, in the heat of summer, a mere trickle. Regardless, you can rely on mesmerising views across the Yarrunga Valley (640m) from various lookouts along the easy trails in **Morton National Park** (www.nationalparks.nsw.gov.au; per vehicle at Bundanoon/Fitzroy Falls $8/4; 🖫).

The falls are about 17km northwest of the bridge in Kangaroo Valley, up a steep mountain road.

The **visitor centre** (🖉02-4887 7270; www.nationalparks.nsw.gov.au; 1301 Nowra Rd, Fitzroy Falls; per vehicle $4; ⊙9am-5pm) at the trailhead is the best resource for wildlife and walking information in the area and has a cafe.

Kangaroo Valley Canoes
KAYAKING, CANOEING

(Kangaroo Valley Safaris; 🖉02-4465 1502; www.kangaroovalleycanoes.com.au; 2031 Moss Vale Rd; canoe & kayak hire from $45; 🖫) ⫽ North of Hampden Bridge, this well-established operator offers a range of guided or self-guided canoeing and kayaking trips into Shoalhaven Gorge and the national parks, including multiday options (from $140 per person). It also does canoe, kayak and bike hire, with vessels to hold groups of three or four.

Kangaroo Valley Adventure Co
ADVENTURE SPORTS

(🖉02-4465 1372; www.kvac.com.au; Glenmack Park Campground, 215 Moss Vale Rd) Friendly Kangaroo Valley Adventure Co offers short and overnight canoeing and kayaking trips, including half-day kayaking excursions (from $40) and full-day outings biking, hiking and kayaking (from $100).

🛌 Sleeping & Eating

Glenmack Park
CAMPGROUND $

(🖉02-4465 1372; www.glenmack.com.au; 215 Moss Vale Rd; campsites adult/child $18/14, powered sites $48, cabins $75-155, cottages $185-225; 🄿 🖫 🎇 🐾) Genially run Glenmark Park has well-spaced campsites amid tall gum trees, close to Kangaroo Valley's small town centre. There's plenty of shade and a range of inviting cabins, from budget choices without bathroom to en-suite cabins with air-con (from $120) and fully equipped cottages. A pool, mini-golf, water sports and flocks of galahs make this is an appealing family option too.

★ Laurels B&B
B&B $$

(🖉02-4465 1693; www.thelaurelsbnb.com.au; 2501 Moss Vale Rd; d incl breakfast $285; 🄿 🎇 🖫) Delightfully personable hosts oversee the sumptuous Laurels, 4km north of Hampden Bridge. Walls are lined with bookshelves, and late-afternoon wine and cheese urge relaxation in the lounge. Four individually decorated rooms are similarly refined, with antiques and king-size beds. Breakfasts are cooked to order, served on fine china in a dining room that overflows with richly carved furniture. An elegant retreat.

Bistro One46
BISTRO $$

(🖉02-4465 2820; www.bistro146.com.au; 146 Moss Vale Rd; lunch mains from $15, dinner mains $25-33; ⊙11.30am-2.30pm & 5.30-8pm Mon & Tue, 5.30-8.30pm Fri, noon-3pm & 5.30-8.30pm Sat & Sun; 🖫 🖫) Personalised service makes the elegant dishes at Bistro One46 taste all the better. In the centre of the village, this vine-swathed beauty offers loosely Italian-inspired dishes and homemade specialities like pork-and-pistachio terrine and kangaroo carpaccio. Desserts encompass passion-fruit crème brûlée and intensely rich chocolate marquise. The town's top address.

Children's meal deals ($14) suit both fussy eaters (fish and chips) and refined young tastes (arancini).

❶ Getting There & Away

Nowra-based **Kennedy's** (🖉02-4421 7596; www.kennedystours.com.au) runs a few buses a week from Kangaroo Valley to central Nowra via Bomaderry train station, which has regular links to Berry and Sydney (via Kiama).

Nowra

POP 30,853

Nondescript Nowra, around 17km from the coast, acts as a service centre for the Shoalhaven area. A few urban attractions, like street art, heritage buildings and river cruises, can pleasantly while away a day. Many road trippers will simply cruise through to refuel, stock up in a winery and push on to the beaches. It's friendly and relaxed, so it makes a decent base for the surrounding attractions of Berry, Kangaroo Valley and Jervis Bay. Nowra's twin, Bomaderry, is the southern terminus of the South Coast rail line.

Yuin and Dharawal people are the traditional owners of the land. A former children's-home building on Beinda St in Bomaderry is ground zero for NSW's Stolen Generations, when Aboriginal children were torn from their families and institutionalised away from their native cultures and languages.

◉ Sights

Meroogal MUSEUM
(☑02-4421 8150; www.sydneylivingmuseums.com.au; cnr West & Worrigee Sts; adult/child $12/8; ⊙10am-4pm Sat, plus Thu & Fri Jan & other school holidays) Guided tours reveal the history behind this attractive mint-green mansion that's pretty as a picture with its gabled roof and lace-like balconies. Built in the 1880s, the house contains the artefacts accumulated by four generations of women, from diaries to photographs, painting an intimate picture of their lives. Tours leave on the hour (from 11am to 3pm).

★ Coolangatta Estate WINERY
(☑02-4448 7131; www.coolangattaestate.com.au; 1335 Bolong Rd, Shoalhaven Heads; ⊙winery 10am-5pm) FREE Founded on a 19th-century wine-growing estate, Coolangatta has been bottling its signature creamy semillons and stone-fruit scented savagnins since 1990. The wine's fantastic, and the cellar-door experience is informal and friendly. It's on the north side of the estuary, 13km east of Bomaderry and just before Shoalhaven Heads.

Stick around for a lunch plate, with nibbles of cheese, oysters and ceviche, each matched to Coolangatta wine. The estate also offers excellent accommodation in convict-built buildings.

At weekends, this is the departure point for **4WD tours** (☑0428 244 229; www.bishopsadventures.com.au; Coolangatta Estate, Shoalhaven Heads; adult/child $25/15; ⊙11.30am Sat, Sun & school holidays; ◧) up to Mt Coolangatta.

🛌 Sleeping & Eating

Nowra has sufficient motel and apartment accommodation (mostly geared towards business travellers). More cheerful options lie in the surrounding area.

There are lots of holiday lets in appealing coastal towns nearby, such as Callala Bay, Greenwell Point and Culburra Beach.

Coolangatta Estate B&B $
(☑02-4448 7131; www.coolangattaestate.com.au; 1335 Bolong Rd, Shoalhaven Heads; d $140-220; 🅿✳🛜🌊) Staying on this venerable wine-producing estate is a real treat. Rooms, spread across different buildings, vary widely, from a cute convict-built timber cottage with a high bed and a historic feel to cosy rooms in the servants' quarters or a separate lodge building.

Quest Nowra APARTMENT $$
(☑02-4421 9300; www.questnowra.com.au; 130 Kinghorne St; studios $201, 1/2-bed apt $220/334; 🅿✳🛜) Crisp, well-equipped modern apartments occupy Nowra's branch of the business Quest accommodation chain. Service is upbeat and each studio apartment is furnished with a big bed, a hotplate, a fridge and a microwave. Apartments include a full kitchen and laundry (but there are also coin-operated washing machines on the ground floor).

★ Wharf Rd AUSTRALIAN $$
(☑02-4422 6651; http://wharfrd.com.au; 10 Wharf Rd; small plates $18-21, mains $30-34; ⊙noon-3pm & 6-10pm Wed-Sat, noon-3pm Sun, 6-10pm Tue, extended hours Dec & Jan; 🅿) Big views of the river are amplified by beautifully presented seafood at understated, elegant Wharf Rd. Rich but creamy rock oysters and sashimi, brightened by yuzu granita, are highlights. Pub classics are deftly reinvented (like pork chop with pomegranate, and beer-battered fish with all the trimmings).

ℹ Information

Nowra Visitor Centre (☑02-4421 0778; www.shoalhaven.nsw.gov.au; 42 Bridge Rd; ⊙9am-5pm Mon-Sat, 10am-2pm Sun) Friendly, in-depth advice just west of the Princes Hwy in a theatre and cafe complex.

ⓘ Getting There & Away

Premier (p217) has buses to Sydney ($25, 3¼ hours, two daily), Eden ($57, five to six hours) and Ulladulla ($18, one hour, two or three daily) via other coastal towns.

Sydney Trains (p217) from Sydney to Nowra (Bomaderry) require a change in Kiama ($6 to $8.70, 2¾ hours). There's a train every hour or two. Direct trains to Berry ($3.10 to $4.40, 10 minutes) run hourly.

Local buses connect Bomaderry Station with the centre of town, and **Nowra Coaches** (☑02-4423 5244; www.nowracoaches.com.au) runs to Jervis Bay, Berry and surrounding towns. Kennedy's (p224) runs a few weekly buses between Kangaroo Valley and central Nowra via Bomaderry.

Jervis Bay

Pearl-white sand and crystalline waters have made this large, sheltered bay the darling of the South Coast. Leaping dolphins and migrating whales (May to November) add to Jervis Bay's appeal, and there's a sizeable quotient of diving, snorkelling and kayaking operators. Most development is around Huskisson and Vincentia. Beecroft Peninsula forms the northeastern side of Jervis Bay, ending in the sheer cliffs of Point Perpendicular. Most of the peninsula is navy land but is usually open to the public and harbours some beautiful, secluded beaches.

Jervis Bay's snow-white sands attract deserved hype, and summer crowds often dispel any illusion of earthly paradise. But you can skip headline-grabbing beaches for a choice of sweeping bays and, just to the south, cove-dotted Booderee National Park. In 1995 the Wreck Bay area was returned to local Aboriginal Australians, who now jointly administer it. Interestingly enough, Australian Capital Territory laws apply, a historical quirk originally devised to allow the ACT access to the sea.

⊙ Sights

★ **Booderee National Park**   NATIONAL PARK
(☑02-4443 0977; www.booderee.gov.au; 2-day car or motorcycle entry $13) Occupying Jervis Bay's southeastern spit, this sublime national park, jointly managed by the government and the local Indigenous community, offers good swimming, surfing and diving on

LOCAL KNOWLEDGE

JERVIS BAY BEACHES

South of Huskisson, the sand of sublime **Hyams Beach** is often billed as the world's whitest. This Elysian reputation brings crowds, particularly in December and January, and in recent years the traffic and overflowing car parks – unmanageable in such a small community – have forced legions of drivers to turn back. The local council is scrambling to offset the environmental impact of overtourism, which includes tourists camping illegally and leaving rubbish behind.

With more than a dozen powdery sand beaches in the bay, there's no need to follow the Hyams hype. Yes, it's a gorgeous arc of soft white sand, but it's made of much the same stuff as snowy-white **Chinamans Beach** and **Greenfield Beach** to its north and **Iluka Beach** to its south. The latter's in Booderee National Park, which has an embarrassment of postcard-perfect beaches.

both bay and ocean beaches. Much of it is heathland, with some forest, including small pockets of rainforest. Walking-trail maps and camping information are available at the **visitor centre** (☑02-4443 0977; www. booderee.gov.au; Jervis Bay Rd; ⊙9.30am-3pm Sun-Thu, 9am-4pm Fri & Sat Feb-Dec, 9am-4pm daily Jan).

Booderee Botanic Gardens (www. booderee.gov.au; ⊙8am-4pm May-Sep, longer hours Oct-Apr) FREE, managed by the Wreck Bay Aboriginal community, is within the park.

Surfing is good at **Cave Beach** and **Bherwherre Beach**, though beware the nasty rips. There's back-to-nature camping at Green Patch (p227), **Bristol Point** (☑02-4443 0977; www.booderee.gov.au; campsites $25, plus per adult/child $13/6; ℗), and secluded, tents-only **Cave Beach** (☑02-4443 0977; www.booderee.gov.au; campsites $14, plus per adult/child $13/6; ℗). Book online through the visitor centre, a month in advance if you're coming at the height of summer.

Jervis Bay Maritime Museum   MUSEUM
(☑02-4441 5675; www.jervisbaymaritimemuseum. asn.au; 11 Dent St, Huskisson; adult/child $10/free; ⊙10am-4pm; 🚻) This engaging museum tells

of Jervis Bay's ship-building past and Aboriginal history. Interesting displays explain the Wreck Bay Aboriginal community's struggle for land rights. Back rooms are filled with imagination-firing maritime miscellany like brine-splashed wooden chests and ship figureheads. The gardens, laid out like an old ship-building yard, are fun to ramble.

Clambering aboard the heritage-listed 1912 *Lady Denman* ferry is a highlight; explain to kids that they'd be in the engine room, while grown-up passengers would occupy the much-nicer saloons.

Jervis Bay National Park
NATIONAL PARK

(www.nationalparks.nsw.gov.au; ▤) **FREE** North of Huskisson, Jervis Bay National Park spreads outwards from the graceful arc of Callala Bay. More than 4850 hectares of low scrub and woodland clasp the bay, itself a marine park. There are also pockets of protected land further south, around Huskisson and white-sand Hyams Beach, which are replete with easy walking paths and family-friendly beaches. There are picnic areas (and toilets) at Red Point, Hammerhead Point and Greenfield Beach, which also has barbecue facilities and drinking water.

🏃 Activities & Tours

Huskisson is the centre for most activities on the water in Jervis Bay, including whale and dolphin watching, kayaking and kitesurfing.

Jervis Bay Kayaks & Paddlesports
KAYAKING

(☑02-4441 7157; www.jervisbaykayaks.com.au; 13 Hawke St, Huskisson; kayak hire 2hr/day from $39/69, bike hire 2hr/day $29/50, snorkel hire from $20, 2hr tours $59-79; ⊙9.30am-4.30pm Mon & Wed-Fri, to 3pm Sat & Sun Dec-Feb, hours vary Mar-Nov; ▤) This friendly, family-owned place offers rentals of simple sit-on-top kayaks, stand-up paddleboards and single and double sea kayaks on St Georges Basin or Jervis Bay (with experience). Oar-enthusiast staff can also organise various guided trips, including two-hour, kid-friendly paddles, or arrange self-guided camping and kayaking expeditions. Also hires out bikes.

Dive Jervis Bay
DIVING, SNORKELLING

(☑02-4441 5255; www.divejervisbay.com; 64 Owen St, Huskisson; 2 dives from $175, snorkelling trip $135; ⊙office 10am-3pm Mon-Wed, 10am-5pm Thu & Fri, 8am-5pm Sat, 8am-5pm Sun) The marine park's clear water offers good visibility, and this operator can arrange dives at dozens of soft-coral and cave sites visited by turtles, Port Jackson sharks and other marine life. The outfit offers PADI courses and guided dives, as well as equipment rental and bike hire.

Dolphin Watch Cruises
WILDLIFE, BOATING

(☑02-4441 6311; www.dolphinwatch.com.au; 50 Owen St, Huskisson; ⊙dolphin-/whale-watching tour $35/65; ▤) 🐾 This well-established set-up on the main street in Huskisson offers cruises in a small, fast jet-boat and a larger, more sedate double-decker. Sightings depend on the luck of the day, but it's common to see pods of dolphins frolicking around Callala Bay, and whale watching is great in season (September to November). Kids' tickets are a little over half-price.

Jervis Bay Wild
WILDLIFE, BOATING

(☑02-4441 7002; www.jervisbaywild.com.au; 58 Owen St, Huskisson; dolphin-/whale-spotting cruise $35/65, sunset river cruise $30) This operator offers 90-minute dolphin-watching cruises and two-hour trips that offer whale watching (daily from mid-May to mid-November) and a circuit of the bay's beautiful beaches, sea cliffs and lagoons. Bring your own wine and cheese for the sunset river trip, which is occasionally used as a booze cruise by locals.

🛏 Sleeping

There are options in various settlements around the bay, but Huskisson is the principal accommodation hub, offering a full spread from glamping to pub rooms. Booderee National Park offers campsites, as does the Beecroft Peninsula. Prices increase considerably at weekends and massively in January.

Green Patch
CAMPGROUND $

(☑02-4443 0977; www.booderee.gov.au; campsites $25, plus per adult/child $13/6; 🅿) The largest of the Booderee campsites and the only one to allow campervans, Green Patch is divided into two sections on either side of a lagoon. The surrounding trees are thronged with rosellas, kookaburras and other birds, and it's a short walk to the beach on Jervis Bay. There's no power, but there's water, toilets, hot-water showers and barbecue facilities.

Book at least a month ahead: it's deservedly popular.

Huskisson B&B
B&B $$

(☑02-4441 7551; www.huskissonbnb.com.au; 12 Tomerong St, Huskisson; d incl breakfast $195-275;

(P ❄ 🛜 🌐) A beachy theme and kindly service make this boutique operation one of Huskisson's most characterful places to stay. There's luxury in all the right places, like excellent mattresses, claw-foot tubs and big bath towels, while antique-effect tiles and vintage glass add charisma. The continental breakfast, complete with homemade produce, great cappuccino and lime marmalade, sweetens the package.

★ **Paperbark Camp**   LODGE $$$
(📞 02-4441 6066; www.paperbarkcamp.com.au; 571 Woollamia Rd, Woollamia; d $525-750; P 🛜) 🌿 Camp in ecofriendly style in these 12 super-luxurious safari tents with en suites, wrap-around decks and billowing mosquito nets that almost look chic. It's set in dense bush 4km from Huskisson, with only the chorus of cicadas to distract you from back-to-nature bliss. Borrow kayaks to paddle up the creek to the bay, or grab a bike to ride into town.

Sustainability underpins Paperbark's ethos, with timed lights in public areas and biodegradable cleaning products used throughout. Accordingly, there's no power in the tents except for solar lighting, but the breeze from the river is usually enough to keep things cool and there are charging points and a guest fridge in the reception complex.

There's an excellent restaurant here exclusively for guests, and an impressive breakfast is included in rates.

✗ Eating & Drinking

5 Little Pigs   CAFE $
(📞 02-4441 7056; http://5littlepigs.com.au; 64 Owen St, Huskisson; mains $11-25; ⊗ 7am-4pm; 🛜 📶) Easy-going, unvarnished and serving brunch classics and off-the-wall fusion dishes, 5 Little Pigs is a neat choice for lunch on Huskisson's main drag. Everything hits the spot, from eggy breakfast baguettes to spicy fried chicken; even the slightly incongruous combinations of halloumi, trout and zucchini fritters turn out to be delicious.

Wild Ginger   ASIAN $$
(📞 02-4441 5577; www.wild-ginger.com.au; 42 Owen St, Huskisson; mains $33; ⊗ 3-11pm Tue-Sun; 🛜 📶) Huskisson's most sophisticated restaurant, Wild Ginger is a showcase of flavours complemented by trendy decor and outdoor seating. Aroma-packed dishes dabble in recipes from Thailand, across Southeast Asia and Japan, like chilli-jam prawns, basil-tinged chicken green curry and barramundi in ginger and onion. Service isn't always slick, but a suave cocktail menu and local-leaning wine list complete an appealing package.

★ **Huskisson Hotel**   PUB
(Husky Pub; 📞 02-4441 5001; www.thehuskisson. com.au; 73 Owen St, Huskisson; ⊗ 11am-midnight Mon-Sat, to 10pm Sun; 🛜 📶) The social centre of Huskisson and indeed the whole Jervis Bay area is this light and airy pub that offers fabulous bay views from its deck, which packs out in summer. There's live music most weekends, tending towards rock, country and local DJs.

ℹ Information

Jervis Bay Visitor Information Centre (📞 02-4441 5999; www.jervisbaytourism.com.au; 11 Dent St, Huskisson; ⊗ 10am-4pm) Helpful tourist information within the Jervis Bay Maritime Museum building.

ℹ Getting There & Away

Nowra Coaches (p225) runs buses around the Jervis Bay area, with connections to Nowra and the train station at Bomaderry (1½ hours, four daily, fewer at weekends).

Ulladulla & Mollymook

POP 14,137

It's a wonder, but Ulladulla and Mollymook have kept their lack of pretension while also hosting five-star resorts, acclaimed fine dining and chic bars where glasses of chardonnay are clinked above platters of oysters. Fishing village Ulladulla has most services, while neighbour to the north Mollymook is arrayed alongside a beautiful beach.

Beyond sand and surf, Aboriginal-led guided tours, a cultural trail and a small gallery create numerous possibilities for exploring the area's Yuin heritage.

◉ Sights & Activities

Milton   VILLAGE
The town of Milton, 6km northwest of Ulladulla on the Princes Hwy, is a cheerful caricature of its 19th-century history. European settlers flocked to the area in the 1820s, lured by logging, and a township was founded some 40 years later. A courthouse, a theatre and dozens of other heritage buildings preserve Milton's lost-in-time feel. Nowadays craft shops and hipster

cafes have earned the town a spot on tourist itineraries.

Murramarang National Park NATIONAL PARK
(www.nationalparks.nsw.gov.au; per car per day $8)
Stretching along a secluded section of coast, this scenic park offers excellent beaches, opportunities to learn about Indigenous culture, and plentiful animal and bird life. Surfing is good at several beaches, and marked walking trails access views of rainforest and shore; a standout is the tough **Mt Durras** walk (up to five hours).

The enduring link between the area and Aboriginal Australians is evident at various historic sites where tools were manufactured, feasts of shellfish shared, and edible plants gathered.

★**Pigeon House Mountain (Didthul)** HIKING
(Morton National Park) One of the best South Coast walks is to the top of this iconic mountain. The steep hike involves two climbs through bush, separated by a flat phase through heathland, then an ascent up ladders to a summit with magnificent views. It's just over 5km return from the car park; allow three to four hours and look out for lyrebirds and kangaroos.

☞ Tours

★**Nura Gunyu** CULTURAL
(☑ 0405 646 911; http://nuragunyu.com.au; ⚑) ✎ Stories of Aboriginal life, present and past, roll off the tongue of Noel Butler, a Budawang Elder of the Yuin nation. His guided tours illuminate already jaw-dropping stretches of the South Coast – in particular Bawley Point, Nuggan Point and inland forest (including ancient trees in some secret locations). Bush tucker is a focus.

Ulladulla Local Aboriginal Land Council CULTURAL
(☑ 02-4455 5883; www.facebook.com/ulladullaulalc; 60 Deering St, Ulladulla; guided tours per hour adult/child $15/10; ⚑) Walks around Ulladulla's history-rich coastline are greatly enhanced by the expertise of an Aboriginal tour guide, who can point out edible plants and teach you a couple of words of the Dhurga language along the way. Book a guide through the Ulladulla Local Aboriginal Land Council. A minimum of four people is needed for a tour to go ahead; enquire in advance.

The council also hosts **Giriwa Garuwanga Aboriginal Art Gallery** (☑ 02-4455 5883; 66 Deering St, Ulladulla; ☺ 9am-3pm) FREE. Indigenous art by local creators is on display, and visitors are welcome to come in and chat to the artists, who are often found inside at work on intricate paintings.

☐ Sleeping

Mollymook Shores HOTEL $
(☑ 02-4455 5888; www.mollymookshores.com.au; 11 Golf Ave, Mollymook; d/ste from $170/180; P❄🛜🏊) Uplifted by friendly service and its location opposite a dreamy sand beach, Mollymook Shores has brightly decorated rooms arranged around a small pool. There are several room types, from commodious doubles with dining tables and balconies right up to spa suites with large living areas. Prices rise at weekends.

★**Ulladulla Guest House** B&B $$
(☑ 02-4455 1796; www.guesthouse.com.au; cnr Burrill & South Sts, Ulladulla; d incl breakfast $248-298; P❄🛜🏊) ✎ A boutique resort with all the charms of a cosy B&B, Ulladulla Guest House brims with luxuries: ample rooms in a classic style, walls laden with local art, and an exceptional wine bar. Homegrown bananas, papayas and herbs find their way to the breakfast table, and there's a barrel-shaped solar-heated sauna.

★**Bannisters Pavilion** HOTEL $$$
(☑ 02-4455 3044; www.bannisters.com.au; 87 Tallwood Ave, Mollymook; r $275-445; P❄🛜🏊) Set back from Mollymook beach, this visually striking hotel operates with breezy style. There's space to spare, with wide hallways, plush, light rooms with pleasant woody outlooks and private patio or balcony space. The two penthouses are worthy of a design magazine.

Whether or not you're staying, be sure to visit the top deck: there's a poolside bar and **restaurant** serving top-notch oysters, marvellous burgers and ribs, and desserts such as salted-caramel tart.

Bannisters by the Sea HOTEL $$$
(☑ 02-4455 3044; www.bannisters.com.au; 191 Mitchell Pde, Mollymook; r from $389, ste $410-620; P❄🛜🏊) Luxury is always most delicious when it looks effortless, and these light-flooded rooms with tastefully beachy decor perfect the art. Balconies with lovely coastal views and the sound of rolling surf are highlights, as are the can-do staff and

quality restaurant. Furled umbrellas outside every door are a nice touch: this is the South Coast, after all.

Eating

Hayden's Pies
BAKERY $

(02-4455 7798; http://haydenspies.com.au; 166 Princes Hwy, Ulladulla; pies from $5.90, sausage rolls $4.10; ⊙6am-5pm Mon-Sat, 7am-5pm Sun; ▪) With traditional pies – the likes of Sunday roast or chicken and bacon – and a range of gourmet fillings (such as goat curry), this excellent bakery is awash with crusty goodness and delicious aromas. There's a daily pie special, gluten-free options and other home-baked treats like brownies and orange-almond slices.

Tallwood
AUSTRALIAN, CAFE $$

(02-4455 5192; www.tallwoodeat.com.au; 85 Tallwood Ave, Mollymook; breakfast $12-22, dinner mains $24-52; ⊙6.30am-noon & 5.30-9.30pm, coffee served all day; ▪) ✱ Tallwood kicks off the day with excellent coffee and out-of-the-ordinary breakfasts, such as Sri Lankan hopper and asparagus on quinoa tabbouleh. For dinner, highlights to be enjoyed in the colourful and modern surroundings include roast duck made zesty with orange and sorrel, and blue cheese and beetroot tart. Desserts have unexpected flavour pairings (like thyme meringue and peach sorbet).

Cupitt's Estate
AUSTRALIAN $$$

(02-4455 7888; https://cupitt.com.au; 58 Washburton Rd, Ulladulla; 2-/3-course menu $65/80; ⊙restaurant noon-2.30pm daily, plus 6-8.30pm Fri & Sat, bar food 10am-3pm, winery 10am-5pm; P🅿) ✱ All gourmet tastes are satisfied at this restored 1851 creamery, 3km west of town. The cellar door showcases exceptional wine, accompanied by cheeseboards and bar snacks like arancini. The French-inspired fromagerie churns out blue goat, smooth brie and mature cheddar cheeses; buy at the shop. Finally, the exceptional restaurant – book ahead – serves choice cuts of Wagyu and locally sourced seafood.

Rick Stein at Bannisters
SEAFOOD $$$

(02-4455 3044; www.bannisters.com.au/rickstein; 191 Mitchell Pde, Mollymook; mains $36-48; ⊙12.30-2pm Fri-Sun, 6-10pm Tue-Sun; P🅿) Served in an elegant setting on Bannister's Point, celebrity chef Rick Stein's excellently selected and presented seafood matches the fine views. The menu is informed by local produce but has touches of French and Asian

influences; options usually include oysters, local snapper and a superb parmesan-crusted seafood pie. Book for weekends.

ℹ Information

Shoalhaven Visitor Centre (02-4444 8819; www.shoalhaven.com; Princes Hwy, Ulladulla; ⊙9am-5pm Mon-Fri, to 2pm Sat & Sun) Bookings and information in the civic centre and library, just off the highway.

ℹ Getting There & Away

Premier (p217) runs twice daily between Sydney ($35, five hours) and Eden ($50, 3½ to 4½ hours), via Batemans Bay ($14, 45 minutes) and Nowra ($18, one hour).

Batemans Bay
POP 11,294

A sparkling estuary, restaurant-lined seafront promenade and beaches within easy reach: Batemans Bay has all the ingredients for a summer holiday. As a busy service centre, replete with car dealerships and fast-food joints, it isn't as charming as other coastal towns. But make no mistake, BB is water-sports heaven. Sandy, wave-kissed beaches extending south provide countless options for surfers, while the nearby Tomaga River estuary draws SUPs and kayaks to its calm waters.

⊙ Sights & Activities

The closest beach, 3km south of town, is **Corrigans Beach**. North of the bridge, beaches lead into Murramarang National Park. Surfers flock to **Pink Rocks**, gentle, regular **Surf Beach**, **Malua Bay**, **McKenzies Beach** and long **Bengello Beach**. **Broulee** has a wide crescent of sand and no rocky surprises, but there's a strong rip at the northern end.

Batemans Bay and the coast just south have numerous operators offering lessons, hire and guided excursions with kayaks, surfboards, snorkels and stand-up paddleboards (SUPs). **Mossy Point** is ideal for kayakers, while Broulee has regular waves to suit surfers; both are 20km south of town.

Region X
KAYAKING

(1300 001 060; http://regionx.com.au; kayak rental 1hr $30, kayak tours $65-155; ▪) Rent a kayak to explore nearby waterways or take one of several paddling tours around Batemans Bay and the coast to the south. This friendly, well-organised operator is the only one offering trips in glass-bottomed kayaks, for mesmerising views of stingrays and other water life; many tours suit kids. The hire station is at Mossy Point.

It also offers cycle hire ($25 per half-day) and leads guided hikes, including day-long excursions ($135) to the top of Pigeon House Mountain (p228).

Surf the Bay Surf School
SURFING

(☑ 0432 144 220; http://surfthebay.com.au; group/private lesson $50/100) This surfing and paddle-boarding school has personable instructors and operates at Batemans Bay, Broulee and Narooma. It also has equipment for hire (from $30 for a surfboard or $40 for an SUP) and runs special courses for kids during school holidays.

Total Eco Adventures
WATER SPORTS

(☑ 02-4471 6969; www.totalecoadventures.com.au; 77 Coronation Dr, Broulee) This set-up offers various excursions on the river, including snorkelling safaris, kayaking, SUP lessons and water-sports-gear hire (from $35). Enquire ahead; departures are from Tomakin boat ramp.

🛏 Sleeping & Eating

Bay Breeze
MOTEL $$

(☑ 02-4472 7222; www.baybreezemotel.com.au; 21 Beach Rd; d $175-350; 🅿 ❄ 🛜) Balinese-style headboards and other stylish flourishes give rooms at the Bay Breeze a distinctive, luxurious air. Facilities at this boutique motel are pleasingly broad, from in-room standards like fridges and coffee-making to table tennis, laundry and massage on demand. It's discreetly shaded from the main promenade by a hedge, but the bay views from waterfront rooms (from $195) are excellent.

Zorba Waterfront Motel
MOTEL $$

(☑ 02-4472 4804; www.zorbamotel.com.au; Orient St; r $130-300; 🅿 ❄ 🛜) With blue-dappled fittings to match the bay setting, Zorba's has 17 attractive, contemporary-style motel rooms with walk-in showers. Handily located right by the string of bayside eateries, this is an accommodating, family-run place that's been a reliable option for years.

Mossy Cafe
CAFE $

(☑ 02-4471 8599; www.themossy.com.au; 31 Pacific St, Mossy Point; breakfasts from $11, lunch mains $14-21; ⏱ 7.30am-3pm; 🍴 ♿) Post-surf recovery is made much easier at this charming cafe in a converted 1930s general store. Brunch classics like smashed avo, poached eggs on sourdough and chia bowls are joined on the menu by pulled-pork tacos and Korean-spiced veg bowls, plus enticing cakes and great coffee. It's a short walk from Mossy Point's boat ramp, 1.5km north of Broulee's surf beach.

Innes' Boatshed
FISH & CHIPS $

(☑ 02-4472 4052; 1 Clyde St; fish from $10, 6 oysters $10, prawns $7; ⏱ 9am-8pm Sun-Thu, to 8.30pm Fri & Sat; ♿) Since the 1950s this has been one of the South Coast's best-loved fish-and-chip and oyster joints. Order a fish supper (in nicely crisp, light batter) or a tray of tear-'em-apart prawns and head out to the spacious deck, which hangs pleasantly over the water. Mind the pelicans. Cash only.

★ Kohli's Waterfront
INDIAN $$

(☑ 02-4472 2002; https://kohlis.com.au; 3 Orient St; mains $18-24; ⏱ 5-10pm Tue & Wed, noon-2.30pm & 5-10pm Thu-Sun; 🍴) Warm service and bay views promise a memorable meal, and the flavourful food delivers. Dishes at Kohli's positively sizzle with fresh herbs and piquant sauces. The homemade paneer cheese is a standout, but there's stiff competition from smoky tandoori prawns, butter chicken and creamy *dal* (simmered spiced lentils).

ℹ Information

Batemans Bay Visitor Centre
(☑ 02-4472 6900; www.eurobodalla.com.au; cnr Princes Hwy & Beach Rd; ⏱ 9am-5pm Oct-Apr, to 4pm May-Sep) Above-and-beyond advice and assistance for travellers in town and the wider Eurobodalla area.

ℹ Getting There & Away

Just north of Batemans Bay, the scenic Kings Hwy climbs the escarpment and heads to Canberra.

Premier (p217) runs buses to Sydney ($45, six hours) and Eden ($46, three to 3½ hours) via Ulladulla ($14, 45 minutes) and Moruya ($11, 30 minutes).

Murrays (p217) runs buses to Canberra ($37.60, 2½ hours), Moruya ($13.60, 40 minutes) and Narooma ($20.90, 1¾ hours).

V/Line (p217) runs a bus-train combination to Melbourne ($67.20, 11¾ hours), via Bairnsdale, Victoria, on Tuesday, Friday and Sunday.

Priors (☑ 02-4472 4040; www.priorsbus.com.au) runs regional services, including a bus to Broulee and Moruya via various surf beaches (bus 760; $7.40, nine times daily, less frequently at weekends).

Moruya

POP 2525

When you gaze on Sydney Habour Bridge, spare a thought for little Moruya, almost 300km south: the town's quarries supplied the granite for this Australian icon.

Other than this claim to fame, Moruya ('black swan') has Victorian buildings gathered around a broad river. There's a popular Saturday market and a couple of great places for a bed and a meal.

⊨ Sleeping & Eating

★**Post & Telegraph B&B**   B&B $
(☑ 02-4474 5745; pandtbb@hotmail.com; cnr Page & Campbell Sts; s/d incl breakfast $130/160; P ❄ 🛜) This 19th-century post and telegraph office is now an enchanting four-room B&B with great historical character. High ceilings, marble fireplaces and the occasional clawfoot tub combine with friendly, genuine hospitality and numerous thoughtful details. There's a shared verandah, decanters of port and an attractive common lounge. You couldn't ask for a lovelier spot.

The River   AUSTRALIAN $$
(☑ 02-4474 5505; www.therivermoruya.com.au; 16 Church St; mains $26-37, 5-course degustation $100, with matching wines $130; ⊙ noon-2pm & 6-8pm Wed-Sat, noon-2pm Sun) Perched right over the river and attired in nautical blue and white, this understated restaurant offers flavourful presentations of seafood. Salmon on truffled mash, saffron gnocchi and swordfish with zucchini flower impress as much as the hilly views across the water, though service can feel scattered. It's just west of the bridge.

⊕ Getting There & Away

Moruya Airport (MYA; ☑ 0409 037 520; www.esc.nsw.gov.au; George Bass Dr) is 7km east of town, near North Head. Rex (www.rex.com.au) flies to/from Merimbula and Sydney daily.

Murrays (p217) buses head to Canberra ($40.80, 3½ hours), Batemans Bay ($13.60, 40 minutes) and Narooma ($14.80, one hour), stopping in Mogo by request.

Premier (p217) runs buses to Sydney ($49, six to seven hours) via Batemans Bay ($11, 30 minutes) and in the other direction to Eden ($46, 2½ to three hours) via all coastal towns.

V/Line (p217) runs a bus-train combination to Melbourne ($60.60, 11½ hours), via Bairnsdale, Victoria, on Tuesday, Friday and Sunday.

Narooma

POP 3342

Blissfully laid-back Narooma dozes at the mouth of a tree-lined estuary, flanked by surf beaches. Much more exciting than the town itself is the marine paradise that Narooma accesses, with migrating whales and fur seals that dart daringly close to swimmers and snorkellers.

Narooma is also the jumping-off point for Montague Island (Barranguba), an offshore excursion as rich in wildlife-spotting opportunities as in history of the Yuin people, the land's traditional owners.

⊙ Sights

★**Montague Island
(Barranguba)**   NATURE RESERVE
(www.montagueisland.com.au) Wildlife thrives on this small, pest-free island, 9km offshore from Narooma, where fur seals frolic and 90 bird species wheel overhead. Little penguins nest here from September to February, while, offshore, whales are most numerous from September to November.

Book ahead for tours (p232) by park rangers. Boat operators can combine the island visit with snorkelling and whale watching. Snorkelling and diving are made even more exciting by the presence of fur seals, whose underwater acrobatics are enchanting to watch.

Be warned: seals delight in speeding towards unsuspecting snorkellers before veering off course at the last moment (boats, meanwhile, keep a respectful distance from the animals).

All tours are number and weather dependent, and independent visits to the island aren't permitted. Once ashore, the island's whale, shark and turtle rocks, named by the Aboriginal community, are off limits to most visitors.

Aboriginal Australians rowed here for millennia to conduct ceremonies initiating boys into manhood. Today the most striking landmark is the lighthouse (1881); 1m rocks were shipped from England for its construction (nowadays it's solar powered).

You can stay at the island's tastefully renovated lighthouse keepers' cottages (☑ 02-9585 683; www.nationalparks.nsw.gov.au; 3-/5-bedroom cottages $1200/1800) 🐾, but you'll need to book well ahead (at the very least seven days, to allow boat transfers to be arranged).

Underwater Safaris
DIVING

(📱 0415 805 479; www.underwatersafaris.com.au; 1/2 dives $80/120) 🕑 Unlike catch-all operators, this outfit focuses on underwater experiences amid Montague Island's marvellous wildlife. There are PADI courses, guided dives and snorkelling;the chances are good that you'll spot grey nurse sharks and bull rays gliding in the big blue. From September to November there are whale-watching excursions ($60).

Narooma Marina
BOATING

(📱 02-4476 2126; www.naroomamarina.com.au; 30 Riverside Dr; boat per 1/3hr $60/155, surfboard half-/full day $20/40, kayak 1st/subsequent hour $25/20; ▣) This chipper set-up on the river hires out canoes, kayaks, pedalos, fishing boats (with sunshades), surfboards and stand-up paddleboards. It's a one-stop shop for getting you out on the water.

Note that you aren't allowed to land at Montague Island except on an approved tour.

🧭 Tours

Montague Island Nature Reserve Tours
WALKING, CULTURAL

(📱 02-4476 2881; www.montagueisland.com.au; per person $90-125) A number of operators run boat trips to Montague Island, where you link up with a national park guide to lead you around. You'll dodge shearwater burrows on a walk across the pristine island, learn about its Aboriginal history and climb inside the lighthouse. Evening tours from September to November let you watch little penguins march ashore.

Lighthouse Charters
BOATING

(📱 0412 312 478; www.montagueislandtours.com.au; Bluewater Dr; snorkelling from $79, 4hr mixed-activity tour from $100) This friendly operator is one of several offering trips to Montague Island, whale watching and penguin-spotting (both September to November), snorkelling in the company of seals, and combinations of these.

🎉 Festivals & Events

Oyster Festival
FOOD & DRINK

(www.naroomaoysterfestival.com; adult/child $20/free; ⏱ May) A shucking good time can be had at Narooma's major festival. Oyster masterclasses, cooking demonstrations and shucking competitions fill a program of mollusc-focused hi-jinks, backed by live performances as diverse as jazz, rock and Aboriginal music. Check online for the full roll-call of events, and book accommodation well in advance.

🛏 Sleeping & Eating

⭐ Whale Motor Inn
MOTEL $

(📱 02-4476 2411; www.whalemotorinn.com; 102 Wagonga St; d from $135, ste $170-215; 🅿❄🛜🖥🐾) 🕑 From the balcony views to the comfy beds and tasteful splashes of colour, the Whale is a standout among Narooma's many motels. 'Premier' rooms are a real bargain, capacious and modern, while suites add lounges and kitchenettes. Zany decorative details increase the fun, as do the lounge bar and small pool.

Anchors Aweigh
B&B $

(📱 02-4476 4000; www.anchorsaweigh.com.au; 5 Tilba St; s/d incl breakfast from $115/165; 🅿❄🛜) 🕑 Rooms at this family-run B&B are furnished like a well-off aunt's bedroom, with heavy wooden dressers and floral decor; a couple of rooms (from $193) have spa baths. Authentic Aboriginal artwork hangs in common areas, competing for attention with garlands of teddy bears and old-fashioned toys. Breakfasts are cooked fresh from local and organic produce. No kids or pets.

Narooma Motel
MOTEL $

(📱 02-4476 3287; www.naroomamotel.com.au; 243 Princes Hwy; d/f from $100/160; 🅿🛜) Rooms are ordinary at the Narooma Motel, but the tree-shaded setting and warm welcome are anything but. Compact, budget motel-style rooms adjoin a sizeable common kitchen, but the real selling point is the back garden, complete with shaded deck, wicker chairs, barbecues and a dinky pond.

⭐ Quarterdeck Marina
CAFE, SEAFOOD $$

(📱 02-4476 2723; www.quarterdecknarooma.com.au; 13 Riverside Dr; mains $24-35; ⏱ 10am-4pm Thu, 10am-8pm Fri, 10am-3pm & 6-8pm Sat, 8am-3pm Sun; 🛜) The service is effusive, the seafood's superb, and you couldn't dream up a prettier view: pelicans playing in the crystalline waters of Forsters Bay. Whether or not you're enjoying oysters, lime-buttered scallops or Cajun-spiced catch of the day, Quarterdeck's tiki-bar theme and program of live music make it an essential stop.

Whale Restaurant
AUSTRALIAN $$

(📱 02-4476 2411; www.whalemotorinn.com; 102 Wagonga St; mains $31-39; ⏱ 6-9pm Tue-Sat;

🍽️) ⏰ The dining at this motel restaurant is as good as the dreamy coastal views. A philosophy of using quality local ingredients, some from its own vegetable garden, inspires a menu that showcases the area's magnificent oysters, homemade pasta, foraged herbs, Tilba cheeses, sustainable fish and aged beef.

ℹ️ Information

Narooma Visitor Centre and Gallery (📞 02-4476 2881; www.narooma.org.au; Princes Hwy; ⏰ 9.30am-4.30pm Mon-Fri, to 1.30pm Sat & Sun) This friendly, volunteer-run visitor centre is great for local information and also includes a gallery stocked by the local arts-and-crafts society and a free historical museum.

NPWS Office (📞 02-4476 0800; www. nationalparks.nsw.gov.au; cnr Graham & Burrawang Sts; ⏰ 10am-2pm Mon-Fri) Information on local national parks, including Montague Island.

ℹ️ Getting There & Away

Premier (p217) runs two daily buses to Eden ($41, 2½ hours) and Sydney ($58, 6½ to eight hours) via Wollongong ($56, 4½ to six hours).

V/Line (p217) runs a daily bus-train combination from Narooma to Melbourne ($67.20, 11 hours) via Bairnsdale, Victoria.

Murrays (p217) has daily buses to Moruya ($14.80, one hour), Batemans Bay ($20.90, two hours) and Canberra ($48.40, 4½ hours).

Tilba Tilba & Central Tilba

POP 383

The pocket-sized heritage town of Central Tilba is tucked away off the Princes Hwy, a charming day out from Narooma or a rest stop en route to Bega. Even tinier is Tilba Tilba, 2km down the road.

The traditional owners of the land are the Yuin people, but Central Tilba is steeped in nostalgia for its 19th-century gold-mining boom days. The heritage buildings and cafes lining its main street delight many visitors. Others may find it twee, and raise an eyebrow at the blurry line between historic buildings and antique-style homeware and souvenir shops. Either way, it's worth getting a sense of the locally made wine, cheese and art. The walk up to the water tower reveals magnificent views of Mt Gulaga (also referred to as Mt Dromedary).

OFF THE BEATEN TRACK

MYSTERY BAY

South of Narooma, just before the turn-off to the Tilbas, take the road to gorgeously undeveloped Mystery Bay and the southernmost pocket of Eurobodalla National Park. At the southern end of the main surf beach, a rock formation has created an idyllic natural swimming pool. Just by the beach, **Mystery Bay Campground** (📞 0428 622 357; www.mysterybaycampground.com.au; Mystery Bay Rd, Mystery Bay; adult/child $17/5) has pit toilets, cold showers and running water. It's first come, first served, so arrive early if you want to pitch a tent next to those emerald waves.

Foxglove Gardens GARDENS
(📞 02-4473 7375; www.thefoxglovegardens.com; 282 Corkhill Dr, Tilba Tilba; adult/child $9/2; ⏰ 9am-5pm Oct-Mar, shorter hours Apr-Sep) Attractively landscaped with tree-shaded alcoves and neoclassical statues, this 1.4-hectare English-style private garden is an enchanting place to explore. It's worth sparing an hour to amble through the rose garden and duck beneath tunnels draped in greenery. It's at the southern end of Tilba Tilba.

⭐ **Bryn at Tilba** B&B $$
(📞 02-4473 7385; www.thebrynattilba.com.au; 91 Punkalla-Tilba Rd, Central Tilba; r $260-305; P 📶) Follow Central Tilba's main street 1km out of town to this fabulous building that sits on a green-lawned hillside. It's a lovely, peaceful spot with expansive views from the rooms and wide verandah. Three rooms with hardwood floors, a light, airy feel and characterful bathrooms share sumptuous common spaces; there's also a separate self-contained cottage.

⭐ **Apma Creations** ARTS & CRAFTS
(📞 0437 617 390; 17 Corkhill Dr, Central Tilba; ⏰ 10am-4pm) ⏰ Riotously colourful and thoughtfully run, Apma Creations displays and sells eye-catching art, handicrafts and accessories by Aboriginal makers. Magical desert paintings by owner Merryn Apma take centre stage, but there's work by Indigenous Australian artists from across the country. A large canvas may tip you over your luggage limit, but there's also jewellery, decorations and toiletries scented with traditional plants.

ℹ Information

Bates Emporium (☑ 02-4473 7290; www.visittilba.com.au; 2 Bate St, Central Tilba; ⊙ 8am-5pm Mon-Fri, 8.30am-4.30pm Sat, 9am-4.30pm Sun; 🛜) There's information, fuel, groceries and postal services at Bates Emporium, at the start of the main street of Central Tilba.

ℹ Getting There & Away

Premier (p217) runs a daily bus to Sydney ($59, eight hours) via Narooma ($8, 25 minutes), and to Eden ($36, two hours). Daily services also reach Bermagui ($7, 20 minutes) and Merimbula ($28, 1½ hours).

Sapphire Coast

Unblemished beaches are dappled along the thrillingly rugged Sapphire Coast. More than six hours' drive from either Sydney or Melbourne, the coast between Bermagui and Ben Boyd National Park doesn't receive the same influx of weekenders as other parts of Australia's east coast. Thus it's all the better for seeking out empty beaches between the saw-edged sea cliffs, dense forests and lonely lighthouses. Whale watching from September to November is some of the country's best and many gastronomes visit purely for the local oysters.

Bermagui

POP 1481

The laid-back fishing port of Bermagui ('Bermie') has lagoons and shores steeped in Aboriginal history. Tucked away off the highway, it doesn't attract the same volume of road-trip tourists as other beach towns on NSW's south coast, though its reputation for breezy conditions pulls a consistent crowd of surfers.

🛏 Sleeping & Eating

Harbourview Motel MOTEL $
(☑ 02-6493 5213; www.harbourviewmotel.com.au; 56-58 Lamont St; s $160-185, d $180-205; ℗ ❋ 🛜) A standout among Bermagui's motels for its spacious, high-standard rooms, the Harbourview is run in very shipshape fashion by the helpful owner, who is a top source of local information. Each room has a full kitchenette and its own gas barbecue, and there's boat parking to boot. It's well located for the beach or Fishermen's Wharf.

Bermagui Motor Inn MOTEL $
(☑ 02-6493 4311; www.bermaguimotorinn.com.au; 38 Lamont St; s/d/f from $120/130/165; ℗ ❋ 🛜) With an excellent location right at Bermagui's principal intersection, this motel is run by a friendly couple and has spacious rooms with comfortable beds and decent facilities, including a laundry. Rooms in the budget category have just a double bed, while queen rooms offer more space and amenities.

★ **Il Passaggio** ITALIAN $$
(☑ 02-6493 5753; www.ilpassaggio.com.au; Fishermen's Wharf, 73 Lamont St; pizzas $14-23, mains $28-35; ⊙ 6-9pm Wed & Thu, noon-2pm & 6-11pm Fri-Sun) Cheerfully located on the top deck of the wharf, Il Passaggio whips up authentic pizzas and a few out-of-the-ordinary Italian dishes, like saltimbocca with silverbeet and spaghetti with purple broccolini. Well-chosen antipasti platters pair nicely with wines by the glass.

ℹ Information

Bermagui Visitor Centre (☑ 02-6493 3054; www.visitbermagui.com.au; Bunga St; ⊙ 10am-4.30pm Mon-Sat, to 2pm Sun) Near the main junction; great gift shop.

ℹ Getting There & Away

Premier (p217) buses run daily between Sydney ($60, 8½ hours) and Eden ($31, 1¾ hours).

V/Line (p217) runs four coaches a week to Bairnsdale, Victoria, connecting with a train to Melbourne (total $67.20, 10½ hours).

Merimbula & Pambula

POP 9102

Don't be fooled by the popularity of surfing, fishing and other water-bound pursuits: Merimbula is a somnolent sort of place and that's the essence of its appeal. Arrayed along a long, golden beach and a pleasant inlet, Merimbula hosts both retirees and holidaymakers – in summer, to bursting point. A few kilometres south, smaller Pambula has wetlands to cycle and a scattering of good places to eat and drink.

⊙ Sights

Panboola NATURE RESERVE
(☑ 0414 864 873; www.panboola.com; Bullara St, Pambula) 🌿 An admirable community project has protected 77 hectares of wetlands for native bird species. The well-managed realm

of mangroves and salt marshes is threaded by walking and cycling trails, including an easy 3.4km loop trail along which you can spot black swans, royal spoonbills and other bird life.

Potoroo Palace   ZOO
(☑ 02-6494 9225; www.potoroopalace.com; 2372 Princes Hwy, Yellow Pinch; adult/child $22/13; ☺ 10am-4pm; ⊕) Warmly run Potoroo Palace, a not-for-profit animal sanctuary, has a menagerie including echidnas, dingoes, koalas and native birds. Keepers have an affectionate relationship with the animals, which include free-roaming (and surprisingly shy) emus and much bolder kangaroos. It's 9km northwest of Merimbula on the road to Bega.

🏃 Activities & Tours

Surfing and kayaking are popular hereabouts, with a handful of outfits renting out gear. Several operators offer fishing charters and some run whale- and dolphin-watching tours.

Cycle 'n' Surf   CYCLING, SURFING
(☑ 02-6495 2171; www.cyclensurf.com.au; 1b Marine Pde, Merimbula; bicycle hire per hour/half-day/full day $12/25/35, surfboard hire per half-/full day $40/60; ⊕) Reliable and friendly operator near the beach. Specialises in bikes but also hires out bodyboards and surfboards.

Helmets are included with bike hire and you can add baby seats ($45 per day).

Coastlife Adventures   SURFING, KAYAKING
(☑ 02-6494 1122; www.coastlife.com.au; group/private surfing lessons $70/160, kayaking tours from $70, kayak & stand-up paddleboard rental per hour $25) Offers surfing and stand-up paddleboarding lessons and hire, plus sea-kayaking tours and kayak hire, not only in Merimbula but also at Pambula Beach and Tathra.

Merimbula Marina   WILDLIFE WATCHING
(☑ 02-6495 1686; http://merimbulamarina.com; Merimbula jetty, Market St, Merimbula; ⊕) This operator runs popular whale-watching tours (adult/child $69/50) from mid-August to late November, as well as two-hour dolphin-watching cruises (adult/child $50/30) and fishing trips ($100 for four hours, December to May).

Merimbula Divers Lodge   DIVING
(☑ 02-6495 3611; www.merimbuladiverslodge.com.au; 15 Park St, Merimbula; 1/2 boat dives $69/120, equipment for 1/2 dives $55/99) Offers basic

instruction, PADI courses and snorkelling trips – good for beginners. It runs guided dives to nearby wrecks, which include the *Empire Gladstone*, a now-collapsed 135m vessel that sank in 1950. Guided snorkelling including gear costs from $33.

★ Captain Sponge's
Magical Oyster Tours   BOATING
(☑ 0429 453 545; www.magicaloystertours.com.au; Pambula; 2hr tour adult/child $60/30; ⊕) 🐚 An experienced oyster farmer and master shucker, the charismatic Captain Sponge zips his boat around Pambula Lake, explaining mollusc mysteries along the way. The best part is the generous tasting of fresh oysters, which taste all the better on the water. Tours leave at 9am on Monday, Wednesday and Friday whenever there's demand; enquire ahead.

🛏 Sleeping

There are dozens of places to stay, catering to slim and ample budgets. Motor inns are dotted along main artery Merimbula Dr, and there are many guesthouses and holiday apartments in the streets south of the bridge, near Main Beach.

Prices often double in the January high season and drop off sharply either side of it.

Wandarrah Lodge   HOSTEL $
(☑ 02-6495 3503; www.wandarrahlodge.com.au; 8 Marine Pde, Merimbula; 6-/4-person dm $34/36, s/d/f with shared bathroom from $59/69/137; ⓟ ⓦ) All the basics are done well at Wandarrah Lodge: clean, if institutional dorm and private rooms, a lounge and TV room, and backpacker must-haves like laundry and lockers. It's a place for a peaceful night rather than a party, though the barbecue area and dining room are pleasant places to mingle ('Wandarrah' is an Aboriginal word meaning 'meeting place').

Sapphire Waters Motor Inn   MOTEL $
(☑ 02-6495 1999; www.merimbulamotel.com.au; 32-24 Merimbula Dr, Merimbula; d from $145; ⓟ ✳ ⓦ ⓢ) Resembling a row of terraced houses in England more than a motel, Sapphire Waters has ample rooms (more like suites, with separate living areas) featuring fresh decor, balconies and good shower pressure.

Coast Resort   APARTMENT $$$
(☑ 02-6495 4930; www.coastresort.com.au; 1 Elizabeth St, Merimbula; 1-/2-bedroom apt from $395/425; ⓟ ✳ ⓦ ⓢ) Ninety-eight

self-contained one- and two-bedroom apartments are stacked around this smart holiday complex, all in fetching monochrome with capacious living rooms (some with pool or town views; others facing the lake). The long list of amenities is very appealing: two pools, tennis court, covered parking and good proximity to the beach.

✕ Eating

Aboriginal middens testify to the Yuin people's use of local oysters as a food source for tens of thousands of years. Today the area remains deservedly famous for its wonderful oysters – sample them in both towns and enter into the lively debate about whether Merimbula or Pambula oysters taste better...

Dulcie's Cottage   BURGERS $

(www.dulcies.com.au; 60 Main St, Merimbula; burgers $14-17; ⊙4-11pm Mon-Wed, 4pm-midnight Thu, noon-midnight Fri & Sat, noon-10pm Sun; 🐾) Inner-city Sydney hipsterdom has arrived on the Sapphire Coast in the form of this bar and burger joint. Burgers – nothing fancy, just very good beef, chicken, mushroom or fish – on fresh milk buns are whipped up in a food truck out the front.

★ Wheelers   SEAFOOD $$

(✔02-6495 6330; www.wheelersoysters.com. au; 162 Arthur Kaine Dr, Pambula; 12 oysters from shop $15-18, restaurant mains $26-42; ⊙shop 10am-5pm Sun-Thu, 10am-6pm Fri & Sat, restaurant noon-2.30pm daily, 6pm-late Mon-Sat; 🅿🐾) At this oyster emporium and fine-dining restaurant between Merimbula and Pambula the cherished molluscs can be slurped casually from the takeaway or enjoyed with inventive garnishes (prosecco foam, wasabi aioli) in the restaurant. Beyond house-smoked fish and seafood chowder, non-pescatarians can feast on tremendous steaks and rich risottos. Tours of the oyster farm depart 11am Tuesday to Saturday ($22, 45 minutes).

Merimbula Wharf   AUSTRALIAN, SEAFOOD $$

(✔02-6495 4446; www.merimbulawharf.com.au; Lake St, Merimbula; mains $22-42; ⊙10am-5pm year-round, plus 6-9pm Wed-Sun Dec-Apr; 🐾) The views over bay and beach are just stunning from the windows of this friendly restaurant at the wharf southeast of central Merimbula. Dishes are uncomplicated and tasty but presented with flair. Seafood platters, scallops and other fish dishes dominate the menu,

but the steaks are very good too, and desserts look as good as they taste.

There's an **aquarium** (✔02-6495 4446; www.merimbulawharf.com.au; Lake St, Merimbula; adult/child $22/15; ⊙10am-5pm daily Oct-May, closed Tue Jun-Sep; 🦽) underneath the restaurant.

Ring for summer dinner opening hours, as they're a little variable.

ℹ Information

Merimbula Visitor Information Centre (✔02-6495 1129; www.sapphirecoast.com. au; 4 Beach St; ⊙9am-5pm Mon-Fri, 9am-4pm Sat, 10am-4pm Sun) In the centre of town by the lake.

NPWS Office (✔02-6495 5000; www. environment.nsw.gov.au; cnr Merimbula & Sapphire Coast Drs; ⊙10am-3pm Mon-Fri) Has information on regional national parks, walking trails and campgrounds.

ℹ Getting There & Away

Merimbula Airport (MIM; ✔02-6495 4211; www.merimbulaairport.com.au; Arthur Kaine Dr) is 1.5km south of town on the road to Pambula. Rex (www.rex.com.au) flies daily to Melbourne, Sydney, Cooma and Moruya.

Premier (p217) has two daily buses to Sydney ($69, 8½ hours) and Eden ($11, 30 minutes).

NSW TrainLink (✔13 15 00; www.nswtrainlink. info) runs a daily bus to Canberra (from $24, 4½ hours). V/Line (p217) runs buses to Bairnsdale in Victoria (five hours), from where you can connect to Melbourne (four hours) by train; full-fare tickets are around $61.

Local **buses** (Market St) run Monday to Friday to Eden, Bega and Tathra at schoolkid-friendly hours.

Eden

POP 3041

For thousands of years, whales have breached the waters of Eden's Twofold Bay. An extraordinary relationship evolved between the Yuin Thaua people and their cetacean neighbours: dolphins and killer whales helped the locals to corral their catch and bring it ashore, in return for a share of the spoils. Aboriginal Australians shared these skills with European settlers, who began whaling here in 1791.

The town of Eden is still famous for whales. Cries of 'Rusho!' – the whalers' call to action after a sighting – have fortunately fallen silent and now the annual Whale Festival welcomes the return of whales during their southern migration from Antarctic waters during September, October and November. Scenic cruises offer a closer look at whales in season, as well as dolphins and seals, while the harbour bustle and fresh-from-the-net restaurant produce add to Eden's appeal.

Sights & Tours

Killer Whale Museum MUSEUM

(☎02-6496 2094; www.killerwhalemuseum.com.au; 184 Imlay St; adult/child $10/2.50; ⏰9.15am-3.45pm Mon-Sat, 11.15am-3.45pm Sun) This long-running museum satisfies appetites for tales of seabound adventures, local Aboriginal history and blubber-based medical cures. As its centrepiece, it displays the monster skeleton of Old Tom, a killer whale and local legend.

A theatrette screens a cetacean documentary, while other exhibits trace Aboriginal whaling traditions back for thousands of years.

Old Tom, meanwhile, was a cetacean Judas who used to round up humpbacks for the local whaling fleet; his death effectively ended the industry.

Kiah Wilderness Tours KAYAKING

(☎0429 961 047; www.kiahwildernesstours.com.au; 1167 Princes Hwy, Kiah; 👪) On the Towamba River 12km south of Eden, these guided kayaking tours explore the coastal estuary, with plenty of breaks to check out seabirds, take a dip and snack on complimentary refreshments. For wildlife and tranquil waters, the pick is the leisurely morning tour ($99).

Cat Balou Cruises WILDLIFE

(☎0427 962 027; www.catbalou.com.au; Main Wharf, 253 Imlay St; adult/child $95/75; 👪) This crew operates scenic and wildlife-spotting cruises aboard a 16m catamaran. Most popular are the 3½-hour whale-spotting voyages (late September to late November); there are also shorter trips aimed at families (adult/child $79/55). At other times of the year, dolphins and seals can usually be seen during the whistle-stop bay cruise (adult/child $45/25).

Festivals & Events

Whale Festival STREET CARNIVAL

(http://edenwhalefestival.com.au; ⏰late Oct or early Nov) During the old whaling days, hunters would herald the seasonal return of their prey towards the end of the year. Fortunately these days it's all about the excitement of the start of whale-*watching* season, marked by a carnival, a street parade and stalls, plus guided whale watching and documentary screenings.

Sleeping

★Snug Cove B&B $

(☎02-6496 3123; http://snugcove.com.au; 25 Victoria Tce; incl breakfast s $120-160, d $150-220; P 📶) Is it baroque, Balinese or pirate themed? It might be all three. Snug Cove's eclectic decor succeeds in its mission to make guests smile. Between the mirrored tiles, shipwreck chic and ornamental birdcages are comfortable, individually styled rooms sharing a deck.

Cocora Cottage B&B $

(☎02-6496 1241; www.cocoracottage.com; 2 Cocora St; s/d incl breakfast $130/180; P 📶) At this heritage-listed B&B adjoining the courthouse, original features amplify the sense of intrigue, like exposed, convict-picked rock by the kitchen and the lounge's old fireplace. Two rooms are available: an attractive, antique-style room at the front, and contemporary lodgings at the back with bay windows overlooking the back garden.

Great Southern Inn PUB $

(☎02-6496 1515; www.greatsoutherninn.com.au; 121 Imlay St; r $40-100; 📶) The pub in the heart of town offers good value for its basic en-suite rooms. The cheapest just has a bunk bed and a fan, but the price is appealingly low if you're undeterred by the noise of the pub below.

Twofold Bay Motor Inn MOTEL $$

(☎02-6496 3111; www.twofoldbaymotorinn.com.au; 164-166 Imlay St; r $170-240; P ❄ 📶 🏊) Splashes of turquoise and chirpy management each do their part to enliven the ambience at Twofold Bay. The 24 rooms vary in size and bed configuration, but all are tidy and modern and have a kitchenette.

The best rooms have views of the sea. There's also a small heated indoor pool.

Seahorse Inn BOUTIQUE HOTEL $$$

(☎02-6496 1361; www.seahorseinnhotel.com.au; Boydtown Park Rd, Boydtown; r incl breakfast $240-465; P ❄ 📶) At Boydtown, 8km south of Eden, the Seahorse Inn has a majestic waterside position with lawns running to the beach on Twofold Bay. Rooms are neat in a classical style, all with king-size beds; more costly rooms have posh armoires and marble-topped desks. All top-floor rooms have balconies looking onto the beach.

✕ Eating

Sprout　　　　　　　　CAFE, VEGAN **$**
(☑02-6496 1511; www.sprouteden.com.au; 134
Imlay St; mains $11-22; ⊙7.30am-4pm Mon-Fri,
8am-2pm Sat & Sun; 🛜☑) ⌀ Among NSW's
many street cafes preparing locally sourced,
produce-heavy nosh, Sprout is a classic of
the genre. 'Nourish bowls' brim with hummus and veg, while pancakes arrive syrupy
or with berry sauce. Service can be perfunc-
tory, but the food (and, more importantly,
the coffee) is very good.

★ Drift　　　　　SEAFOOD, AUSTRALIAN **$$**
(☑02-6496 3392; www.drifteden.com.au; Main
Wharf, 253 Imlay St; snacks & share plates $9-36,
mains $18-30; ⊙5-11pm Mon-Thu, 4pm-midnight
Sat & Sun; 🛜) Eden mussels, Tilba cheeses
and Gippsland wines find their perfect
setting in this upper-floor restaurant over-
looking the wharf. The funky soundtrack
and mood lighting feel a little too trendy
for Eden (and it's pricey by local stand-
ards), but it serves up refreshing gin-
and-tonic oysters, thoughtfully garnished
mains and a charcuterie board assembled
from the best of the **smokehouse** (☑02-
6496 2331; www.edensmokehouse.com.au; 18-20
Weecoon St; ⊙7.30am-4pm Mon, Tue, Thu & Fri)
across the road.

ℹ Information

Eden Visitor Centre (☑02-6496 1953; www.
visiteden.com.au; cnr Mitchell St & Princes
Hwy; ⊙9am-5pm) Bookings and information
by the main-road roundabout in the centre.

ℹ Getting There & Away

Premier (p217) runs north to Sydney ($71,
nine to 10 hours) twice daily via all major
coastal towns. NSW TrainLink (p237) runs a
daily bus service to Canberra (from $25, 4½
hours). For Melbourne ($57, 8½ hours), V/Line
(p217) runs a bus and train combination via
Bairnsdale.

Local buses have limited services to Merim-
bula and Bega on weekdays; contact **Sapphire
Coast Buslines** (☑02-6495 6452; https://
scbuslines.com.au).

Ben Boyd National Park

With two sections either side of Eden cover-
ing almost 105 sq km, **Ben Boyd National
Park** (www.nationalparks.nsw.gov.au;
southern/northern section $8/free) has colour-
ful views, distinctive histories and one of

NSW's most photogenic multi-day hikes, the
Light to Light Walk (p239).

Ironstone cliffs give sections of Ben
Boyd's shoreline a deep orange hue. The
colour scheme is especially vivid at the **Pin-
nacles** in the northern section of the park,
where reddish clay contrasts against white
sand. Nearby, the **Pambula River Walk** fol-
lows the footsteps of the land's traditional
owners, the Yuin people, passing significant
Aboriginal sites, such as a 3000-year-old
midden.

The southern section is just as inter-
esting, with heritage buildings stand-
ing monument to 19th-century Scottish
wheeler-dealer Ben Boyd and offering a
glimpse of the area's bygone whaling indus-
try. Walking trails here are very rewarding,
running between eucalypt forests and spar-
kling blue coves.

◉ Sights & Activities

Green Cape Lightstation　　　LIGHTHOUSE
(☑02-6495 5000; www.nationalparks.nsw.gov.
au; Green Cape Rd; tours adult/child/family
$12/6/30) At the southern tip of Ben Boyd's
southern section, elegant 1883 Green Cape
Lightstation offers awesome views. There
are tours (by appointment only) and three
elegantly restored keepers' cottages. This is
a great spot to see whales in season (May
to August) and multitudes of muttonbirds
during their migration (October).

Boyd's Tower　　　　　HISTORIC BUILDING
FREE At the end of Edrom Rd is the turn-
off for Boyd's Tower, built in the late 1840s
from Sydney sandstone. It was intended
to be a lighthouse, but the government
wouldn't give Boyd permission to operate
it. Instead it served as a whaling lookout
and still stands, an enigmatic structure
surrounded by eucalypts. Step inside (it's
empty) before taking in the views of **Red
Point**'s claret-coloured shoreline.

★ Light to Light Walk　　　　HIKING
(www.nationalparks.nsw.gov.au) This 30km
coastal walk links Boyd's wannabe light-
house to the real one at Green Cape, along
russet-coloured　　shores,　　forest-backed
beaches and in view of somersaulting seals.
There are campgrounds along the route at
Saltwater Creek (12km from Boyd's Tower)
and Bittangabee Bay (22km); allow two to
three days to complete it one way.

🛏 Sleeping

Two bare-bones but beautifully located campgrounds are on the Light to Light Walk; both are accessible by road (if you can manage some unsealed sections). You can also stay at the keepers' cottages at Green Cape.

Otherwise, Eden is the logical base for exploration of the park.

ℹ Getting There & Away

There's no public transport to the park. By car, access Ben Boyd via the Princes Hwy. Take Pambula Beach Rd or Haycock Rd (between Merimbula and Eden) for the northern sections of the park or Edrom Rd (15km south of Eden) for the southern section.

SOUTHERN HIGHLANDS

With a lush, cool climate (even in summer), a wealth of historical attractions, some seriously posh nosh and luxe lodgings, the compact area known as the Southern Highlands makes for a wonderful day trip or weekend break from Sydney – especially if you've got someone special with you and you want to impress. For the low-down, see www.southern-highlands.com.au.

This region is the traditional homeland of the Gundangara people.

Mittagong & Bowral

POP 8999 (MITTAGONG), 12,949 (BOWRAL)

While the twinned towns of Mittagong and Bowral are separate entities (as locals would be keen to declare), they're so inextricably intertwined that it makes sense to look at them as a pair. Together they form the heart of the delightful Southern Highlands.

Mittagong is the smaller of the two, 5km to the north, and has a more down-to-earth vibe. Big brother Bowral has a loftier, classier feel, with some top-notch restaurants, stately heritage homes and luxury accommodation.

⊙ Sights

★ International Cricket Hall of Fame
MUSEUM

(☑02-4862 1247; www.internationalcrickethall. com; St Jude St, Bowral; adult/child $20/11; ⊙10am-5pm; ℙ) Bowral is where the late, great cricketer Sir Donald Bradman, Australia's most legendary sporting hero, spent his boyhood. Incorporating the **Bradman Museum of Cricket** (www.bradman.com. au), which has an engrossing collection of Ashes and Don-centric memorabilia, the complex has a pretty cricket oval and boasts an ever-expanding collection showcasing the international game.

Mt Gibraltar Reserve
PARK

(☑02-4871 2888; 250 Oxley Dr, Mittagong; ℙ) A drive up to this fabulous reserve (at 863m)

SYDNEY & NEW SOUTH WALES MITTAGONG & BOWRAL

WORTH A TRIP

BERRIMA

Just over 7km west of Bowral is heritage-classified Berrima, founded in 1829. Today it's like a living museum, featuring galleries, antique shops, and good food and wine. It's extremely popular with Sydney day-trippers at weekends and during public holidays.

Around 3km north of Berrima, **Berkelouw's Book Barn & Café** (☑02-4877 1370; www.berkelouw.com.au; Old Hume Hwy, Bendooley; ⊙9am-5pm) stocks more than 200,000 secondhand tomes, and also has an excellent selection of new Australia-themed books. The attached **Bendooley Bar & Grill** (☑02-4877 2235; www.bendooleyestate. com.au; 3020 Old Hume Hwy, Berrima; pizza $25, mains $26-45; ⊙10am-3pm; ℙ❄☑🍴) showcases local produce. Try the linguine and blue swimmer crab with Bendooley Estate's own sauvignon blanc or with a local Southern Highlands craft beer. There's also stylish vineyard cottage **accommodation** (☑0427 318 007; www.bendooleyestate. com.au; 3020 Old Hume Hwy; d from $295; ℙ❄🛜) here.

If you have some cash to splash and fancy yourself a foodie, a degustation at **Eschalot** (☑02-4877 1977; www.eschalot.com.au; 24 Old Hume Hwy, Berrima; mains $30-37, 5-/8-course degustation $75/110; ⊙noon-2.30pm Thu-Sun, plus 6-8.30pm Thu-Sat; ℙ❄) would round out a perfect day.

WORTH A TRIP

YASS

Laced with heritage buildings and sleepy corner pubs, and with its lazy, eponymous river meandering through parkland, Yass is quaint and unhurried. There's excellent bed and breakfast accommodation at the **Globe Inn** (☑02-6226 3680; www.theglobeinn.com.au; 70 Rossi St; d incl breakfast from $175; P ❋ 🛜) – say hi to its welcoming co-host, rescue dog Miss Patti – and top places to eat and drink include good coffee and cafe fare at **Trader & Co** (www.facebook.com/traderandco; 92 Meehan St; mains $10-19; ⊗8.30am-4pm Tue-Fri, to 2pm Sat & Sun; 🖉🖟) 🍃, innovative fine dining at **Clementine** (☑02-6226 3456; www.clementinerestaurant.com.au; 104 Meehan St; lunch 2/3 courses $42/52, dinner mains $31-33; ⊗11.30am-2pm Fri-Sun, 5.45-9pm Thu-Sat; ❋🖉) 🍃, and local wine, craft beer and Saturday night live music at **Yazzbar** (☑02-6226 3138; www.yazzbar.com.au; 81 Comur St; ⊗4pm-midnight Thu-Sat).

Visit Yass at the weekend for the best opportunity to enjoy local restaurants, bars and cafes, and also for wine tasting at the nearby vineyards of the Yass Valley.

with picnic areas and no fewer than three lookouts, offering stunning views of the valley below, is a must.

Morton National Park NATIONAL PARK
(☑02-4887 7270; www.nationalparks.nsw.gov.au; per vehicle per day $8; P) Morton National Park, one of NSW's largest, features the deep gorges and high sandstone plateaus of the Budawang Range. It's easily accessible from Bundanoon at its northern gateway. Follow the well-marked bushwalking trails, admiring waterfalls that plunge into valleys below.

🎊 Festivals & Events

Bowral Tulip Time Festival CULTURAL
(www.tuliptime.net.au; ⊗Sep) Bowral explodes with colour during the beautiful spring flower festival.

🛏 Sleeping & Eating

This area has a great foodie scene, especially around the leafy streets of Bowral and in nearby Berrima. Along Bowral's main street you'll also find a range of ethnic cuisine options including Thai, Italian and Indian. The Coles supermarket in Bowral is open to 11pm daily.

Imperial Hotel & Motel MOTEL $$
(☑02-4861 1779; www.theimperial.com.au; 228-234 Bong Bong St, Bowral; r from $125; P ❋ 🛜) This fabulous motel, set back from the eponymous and popular hotel, has stylish, modern, oversized rooms offering excellent value in pricey Bowral. Rates are cheapest on weekdays.

Links House Hotel BOUTIQUE HOTEL $$$
(☑02-4861 1977; www.linkshouse.com.au; 17 Links Rd, Bowral; r from $200; P ❋ 🛜) This boutique guesthouse has a drawing room and garden courtyard straight out of *Remains of the Day*. Prices are highest on Friday and Saturday, the same days *Vida*, the in-house restaurant, is open (two/three courses $55/70).

⭐**Press Shop** CAFE $$
(☑02-4879 9244; www.thepressshop.com.au; 391-397 Bong Bong St, Bowral; mains $13-25; ⊗7am-4pm Mon-Sat, from 8am Sun; 🖉🖟) 🍃 Harnessing produce from Southern Highlands farmers and growers, the Press Shop is the best of Bowral's excellent cafe scene. Try the super-healthy quinoa salad with a quail egg, feta, herbs and sumac, or the free-range pork Cuban sandwich with pickled cucumbers. Many other vegetarian options also feature. Don't miss checking out the workroom of the Bespoke Letterpress out the back.

Biota Dining MODERN AUSTRALIAN $$$
(☑02-4862 2005; www.biotadining.com; 18 Kangaloon Rd, Bowral; shared plates $20-35, 5-/7-course degustation $100/155; ⊗noon-11pm Thu-Mon; P ❋ 🖉) 🍃 The innovative fine-dining menus focus on produce sourced from Biota's close relationships with local farmers and growers. Menus are continually refined based on the ingredients available. Options include shared plates at Biota's bar and five- or seven-course degustation menus. See www.barnbybiota.com for details of special dining events ($195) held at a different, more rural location (twice monthly on a Friday night).

ℹ Information

Southern Highlands Visitors Centre (☑02-4871 2888; www.southern-highlands.com.au; 62-70 Main St, Mittagong; ⊗9am-5pm Mon-Fri, to 4pm Sat & Sun; 🛜) Comprehensive information on the area.

ℹ️ Getting There & Away

Mittagong is 110km from Sydney, just off the Hume Motorway. Bowral is 5km further south.

Sydney Trains (📞13 15 00; www.sydneytrains. info) operates regular services from both towns to Sydney ($8.70, 1¾ hours).

SNOWY MOUNTAINS

The 'Snowies' offer a landscape entirely different from anywhere else in Australia. This is the country's only true alpine area, where snowfall brings skiers from early June to late August (sometimes later). Though winter's peak season, the region is equally pretty under a blazing blue sky, when there are ample opportunities for hiking, cycling, kayaking and horse riding. The Australian mainland's highest peak, Mt Kosciuszko (2228m), is a memorable ascent, accessing expansive views of boulder-strewn plateaux and hills where gum trees cling on for dear life.

The Snowies form part of the Great Dividing Range where it straddles the New South Wales–Victoria border. Ski tourism began in gold-rush town Kiandra in the 1860s, hastening the growth of resorts like Thredbo and gateway town Jindabyne. For thousands of years before settlers came, the Snowies were home to Aboriginal Australians, largely the Ngarigo, most of them displaced when Europeans arrived.

ℹ️ Getting There & Away

AIR

Regional Express (www.rex.com.au) flies six times per week between Sydney and **Snowy Mountains Airport** (📞02-6452 5999; www. snowymountainsairport.com.au; 1611 Kosciuszko Rd), which is 17km southwest of Cooma on the road to Jindabyne.

BUS

NSW TrainLink (📞13 22 32; www.nswtrainlink. info) Operates coaches on the Canberra–Cooma–Merimbula–Eden (daily) and Canberra–Cooma–Jindabyne (three per week) routes; from Canberra you can connect by train to Sydney.

V/Line (p217) Coaches from Canberra stop in Cooma before continuing to Lakes Entrance and Bairnsdale (both in Victoria), where you can connect by train to Melbourne.

Greyhound (📞1300 473 946; www.greyhound. com.au) During the ski season, Greyhound operates a direct daily coach service between Sydney and Thredbo, stopping in Canberra, Cooma and Jindabyne and at the Perisher Skitube train ($90 to $99 one way from Sydney or $60 from Canberra).

Murrays (p217) Operates a seasonal Snow Express coach (July and August) between Canberra and Thredbo, stopping in Cooma and Jindabyne.

Snoexpress (📞1300 697 669; www. snoexpress.com.au; ⊙mid-Jun–mid-Sep) Has coach services from Canberra (from $99) to Thredbo and Perisher on Friday and Sunday during the ski season; services also stop in Jindabyne (from $89).

Other operators provide package trips from as far away as Sydney and Port Stephens.

ℹ️ Getting Around

Cooma Coaches (📞02-6452 4841; www. coomacoaches.com.au) and **Snowliner Coaches** (📞02-6452 1584; www.snowliner. com.au) have a twice-daily publicly accessible school run between Cooma and Jindabyne during term time (adult/child $20/12).

During the ski season various shuttle services offer private connections to the ski fields from Jindabyne. **Snowy Mountains Shuttles** (📞0497 888 444; www. snowymountainsshuttles.com.au) has a daily return service on the Cooma–Airport–Jindabyne–Skitube route.

Cooma

POP 6681

The laid-back town of Cooma acts as a gateway to the Snowy Mountains' ski resorts and hiking trails, and it's exactly the right size for a quick stopover. Motels and quality cafes abound, and there are a few historical intrigues worth investigating.

⊙ Sights

NSW Corrective
Services Museum   MUSEUM

(📞02-6452 5974; www.correctiveservices.justice. nsw.gov.au; 1 Vagg St; gold coin donation; ⊙9am–3pm Mon-Sat) At this museum devoted to Australian prison history, displays showing manacles, prison paraphernalia and an old gallows trap-door offer a bleak glimpse of the past. Guided tours led by inmates of the still-functioning prison next door add an interesting perspective, often laced with pitch-dark humour. Inmates guiding visitors are preparing for release, and their handicrafts, from denim bags to surreal artwork, are sold in the gift shop.

Snowy Hydro Discovery Centre MUSEUM

(☑1800 623 776; www.snowyhydro.com.au; Yulin Ave; ☺8am-5pm Mon-Fri, to 4pm Sat & Sun; P) **FREE** Don't write off the Snowy Hydro Discovery Centre as a niche-interest attraction. The hydroelectric power scheme explained herein is a marvel of engineering: nine power stations, 16 dams and a web of tunnels across Kosciuszko National Park – detailed in full with videos and maps at this informative and interactive museum. It's 2km north of Cooma centre.

Commenced in 1949, the scheme took 25 years and more than 100,000 people to complete. Chances are the centre's retro displays will get a makeover by the time the 'Snowy 2.0' extension, approved for construction in 2019, rolls out.

🛏 Sleeping & Eating

Ellstanmor B&B $

(☑02-6452 2402; www.ellstanmor.com.au; 32 Massie St; d incl breakfast $150-190, apt without breakfast $160-280; P🖨) Built in 1875, this charming two-storey house has four simply decorated but elegant rooms. The building's long history is revealed in features like exposed stone from the original house-front, fireplaces and French doors. Guests are encouraged to spread out in the Victorian parlour and dining room. Rates include a continental or cooked breakfast.

Cooma Snowy Mountains Tourist Park CARAVAN PARK $

(☑02-6452 1828; www.coomatouristpark.com. au; 286 Sharp St; unpowered/powered sites from $30/55, cabins from $90, without bathroom from

---

HORSING ABOUT

Perhaps due to the deep impression that Banjo Paterson's acclaimed poem 'The Man From Snowy River' (1890) has left on the Australian psyche, horse riding is a popular pursuit in these parts. You can channel your inner jackaroo on a multiday back-country trek with **Reynella Rides** (☑02-6454 2386; http://reynellarides.com.au; 699 Kingston Rd, Adaminaby; 3-/4-/5-day treks from $1550/1900/2380) or **Snowy Wilderness** (☑1800 218 171; www. snowywilderness.com.au; Barry Way, Ingebirah; 2hr ride $120, 1-/2-/3-/4-day treks $330/895/1190/1550); the latter also offers short and day-long rides.

$70; P🐕) Just off the highway, 1.5km west of town, this tree-shaded park has powered and unpowered sites, and unadorned units ranging from 'shearers' huts' (without bathroom) to en-suite cabins. Furnishings feel a little lost in the '80s, but lodgings are comfy enough and the management is kindly. Prices shoot up in winter.

Lott Foodstore CAFE $

(☑02-6452 1414; www.lott.net.au; 177 Sharp St; mains $10-18; ☺7am-3pm Mon-Fri, 8am-4pm Sat & Sun; 🍴) Enticing brunches, gourmet burgers and respectable vegetarian options make Lott Foodstore the favourite for good grub in Cooma. Recent standouts include the Wagyu burger on a charcoal bun and the falafel with beet hummus. There's good service, kid-sized portions and options to tailor some meals to become vegan or gluten-free dishes.

ℹ Information

Cooma Visitor Centre (☑1800 636 525; www. visitcooma.com.au; 119 Sharp St; ☺9am-3pm) Friendly information service offering free maps and local knowledge. Souvenirs sold too.

Jindabyne

POP 1771 / ELEV 918M

Attractive lakeside Jindabyne acts as a gateway to winter resorts Perisher and Thredbo. Ski season (June to August) brings goggle-clad boarders and skiers, who rent their gear and often base themselves in town. Activity simmers down for the rest of the year. Those who show up in summer take advantage of easy access to hiking, cycling and water sports on sapphire-blue Lake Jindabyne.

The lake was created in 1967 after the completion of a dam on the Snowy River, part of the vast Snowy Mountains Hydro-electric Scheme. The original town of Jindabyne, established in the 1840s with 250 residents at its height, lies beneath the placid waters.

🏃 Activities

Sacred Ride ADVENTURE SPORTS

(☑02-6456 1988; www.sacredride.com.au; 6 Thredbo Tce; hire per hour/day bike from $25/50, canoe or kayak $25/100; ☺9am-5pm; 🚲) For uncertain beginners and mountain-bike pros alike, the well-informed crew at Sacred Ride are the ones to see for gear rental and tips. Watery activities are catered for too, with SUPs, canoes, kayaks and fishing boats for hire. To get even wetter, you can pose on a wakeboard or waterskis while they tug you along (from $120).

Snowline Sports OUTDOORS

(☑ 02-6457 2364; www.snowlinesports.com.au; Snowline Centre, 6532 Kosciuszko Rd; skis, boots & poles per day adult/child from $45/30; ☉ 7am-7pm Jun-Sep) Good-value ski gear to buy and rent, as well as mountain-proof clothing and walking boots.

🛏 Sleeping & Eating

Jindabyne has plenty of motels, a few hotels, a couple of campgrounds and a hostel. It's cheaper than staying on the ski slopes, and catching the shuttle spares you from wrestling with chains and paying the vehicle entry charge. Winter prices increase greatly; book ahead.

Jindy Inn GUESTHOUSE $

(☑ 02-6456 1957; www.jindyinn.com.au; 18 Clyde St; d from $99; P 🛜) Though featureless from the outside, Jindy Inn has sweetly decorated rooms looked after by warm, helpful staff. Rooms are attired in tasteful charcoal grey with cushions made cute by pictures of native fauna. Organic toiletries and nice in-room teas add a dab of extra comfort, and a simple continental breakfast is included in the rate.

Snowy Mountains Backpackers HOSTEL $

(☑ 02-6456 1500; www.snowybackpackers.com.au; 2/3 Gippsland St; dm/r without bathroom from $30/75; P @ 🛜) Set above the town's best cafe, this little hostel has a central lounge, private rooms and well-spaced dorms sleeping up to eight. There's underfloor heating and fans to battle the variable mountain climate. It's sparkling clean, linen's included, and the helpful hosts can arrange after-hours check-in remotely. Rates rise during ski season (from $45/120 per bed/room).

Birchwood CAFE $

(☑ 02-6456 1880; www.birchwoodcafe.com.au; 3/3 Gippsland St; mains breakfast & lunch $11-22; ☉ 7am-3pm; 🖉 💧) As good as any of Canberra's flash brunch spots, Birchwood pours a powerful coffee, bakes its own seed-studded gluten-free bread and lovingly prepares veg bowls, tortillas and hard-to-resist apple-pie waffles. You'll feel healthier just for considering the green lentil and kale salad...though you may end up ordering the pistachio-packed Persian love cake.

Takayama JAPANESE $$

(☑ 02-6456 1133; www.takayama.com.au; level 1, Nuggets Crossing Shopping Centre, Snowy River Ave; mains $15-26; ☉ 6-9pm Tue-Sat) Takayama isn't your typical small-town Japanese restaurant; for starters, sushi isn't the focus of the menu. Beyond small plates of trout sushi and salmon sashimi, expect heartier dishes appropriate to the mountain weather: *gyoza* (dumplings), chicken *katsu* (breaded with rice and veg), beef *tataki* (seared, marinated and finely sliced), whole fish and a truly excellent ramen soup.

Café Darya PERSIAN $$

(☑ 02-6457 1867; www.cafedarya.com.au; level 1, 3 Kosciuszko Rd; mains $28-35; ☉ 6.30-9pm Tue-Sat Jan, late Jun-Sep & school holidays, hours vary rest of year) Fill up on slow-cooked beef and eggplant, chicken with nashi pear or mushroom prawns at this long-standing eatery, as beloved for its warm service as for its flavourful Persian food. BYO beer and wine. Cash only. It's best to call ahead to confirm opening hours.

❶ Information

Snowy Region Visitor Centre (☑ 02-6450 5600; www.nationalparks.nsw.gov.au; 49 Kosciuszko Rd; ☉ 8.30am-5pm) File trip-intention forms for hikes, buy national-park vehicle passes and hire a locator beacon for back-country adventures (free, but $400 if you break it). This large National Parks & Wildlife Service–run centre has displays on Kosciuszko National Park as well as a cafe and cinema.

Kosciuszko National Park

This 6940-sq-km park is a painterly landscape of subalpine meadows, twisted snow-gum trees and moraines that resemble the surface of the moon. It contains Australia's highest peak and is the source of two of the country's most legendary rivers, the Murray and the Snowy.

In winter (June to August) it's a major ski destination, while in summer travellers come to hike, drive scenic back roads, explore caves and engage in serious mountain biking. The crowning experience is climbing Mt Kosciuszko (2228m), named after a Polish national hero by explorer Paweł Strzelecki. The route's more hypnotic than high-octane, with raised walkways meandering up to a panorama of the Snowy Mountains.

Sacred to Aboriginal Australians for 20,000 years, this was the setting for inter-tribal gatherings to coincide with the edible bogong moth's annual migration. As you survey the wildflowers and glacial lakes, you'll easily see why this land has long inspired ceremony and awe.

◎ Sights & Activities

The main ski resorts are Thredbo, on the southern slopes of Kosciuszko, and Perisher, on the eastern side. The much smaller Charlotte Pass resort is approached from the Perisher side and sits higher up the slopes.

Ski season officially lasts from the Queen's Birthday weekend (early June) to Labour Day (early October). Peak season is June to August, though July and August have the best snow. Snow-making machines ensure that there's usually some cover throughout the season, though you can expect the 'white ribbon of death' – that is, a ski route fashioned from artificial snow with bare earth or muddy ground on either side – at the beginning and end of the season.

Off the slopes there's lively nightlife, good restaurants, and a plethora of facilities and activities catering to families. Both Thredbo and Perisher have a designated kids' skiing program, crèches and day care.

On the downside, resorts tend to be particularly crowded at weekends, and the limited season means that operators have to get their returns quickly, so costs are high.

Yarrangobilly Caves   CAVE

(☑02-6454 9597; www.nationalparks.nsw.gov.au; Snowy Mountains Hwy; site fee $4, self-guided visit $18, tour from $30; ☺9am-5pm) The yawning cave mouths and idyllic riverside walks of the 440-million-year-old Yarrangobilly site can consume an entire day. A highlight is the blissful 27°C mineral pool, open dawn until dusk, its green waters maintaining a constant temperature year-round (watch out for snakes nearby). The **Glory Hole Caves** are open to independently guided visits. The cave complex lies a pitted, gravelly 6km off the Snowy Mountains Hwy, which stretches northwest from Cooma to the Hume Hwy.

Thredbo Alpine Village   SNOW SPORTS

(☑1300 020 589; www.thredbo.com.au; 2-day ski-lift passes adult/child $178/97; ☺mid-Jun–Sep/Oct) On the southern flanks of Mt Kosciuszko (2228m), Thredbo is known as one of Australia's leading ski resorts,

boasting the longest runs and the highest lifted point. Around 67% of the area suits intermediate-level boarders and skiers, but there's beginner and expert-level terrain too.

Perisher   SNOW SPORTS

(☑1300 655 822; www.perisher.com.au) Four villages make up the southern hemisphere's largest ski resort. More than half the runs, attractively lined with snow gums and boulders, suit intermediate skiers and boarders, with enough for beginners and a few advanced runs too. Most of the action is in Perisher Valley. Guthega (1640m) and Mt Blue Cow (1890m) are mainly day resorts, so they're smaller and less crowded.

Thredbo Mountain
Bike Park   MOUNTAIN BIKING

(www.thredbo.com.au; Valley Terminal; day pass adult/child $77/55, mountain-bike rental $148/124; ☺mid-Nov–Apr; ⊞) Twenty-five kilometres of gravity-fuelled downhill, all-mountain and cross-country tracks start from the top of the Kosciuszko Express chairlift. There are also a couple of tracks around the village and various 2km to 3km cross-country routes, plus a skills park (and adjoining kids' area), a jump zone and a pump track. Book tickets and hire a bike in advance online for savings.

K7 Adventures   ADVENTURE SPORTS

(☑0421 862 354; www.k7adventures.com; half-day mountain biking $135, snow-climbing trip $175; ⊘) Summer and winter adventures for all levels, in the company of seasoned guides. The impressively broad offering includes rock climbing, bouldering, abseiling, cross-country and telemark skiing, snowshoeing and a guided assault on 10 peaks over four days. All activities are available to beginners. Try to book a fortnight ahead in ski season and from mid-December to January.

🛏 Sleeping & Eating

Thredbo YHA   HOSTEL $

(☑02-6457 6376; www.yha.com.au; 2 Buckwong Pl; dm summer/winter from $36/106, r from $390, without bathroom from $250; ☜) This admirable year-round hostel is run like clockwork. As in many YHA outfits, dorm rooms feel a little institutional, with metal-framed bunks. Otherwise it's friendly, homey and scrubbed clean. There are family rooms, a good-size kitchen, a barbecue area and a large, wood-beamed lounge where travellers can sink

LOCAL KNOWLEDGE

CLIMBING KOSCIUSZKO

With reasonable fitness, good weather and at least four hours to spare, Mt Kosciuszko (2228m) is relatively straightforward to climb. Reaching the top can still be strenuous, particularly in the often changeable weather.

From November until April Thredbo Alpine Village (p244) offers a range of guided walks of between four and six hours, either by day ($54), or at sunset or under the full moon ($122), head torches included. Check the website for dates and times.

Solo options include the following:

Mt Kosciuszko Track From Thredbo, take the **Kosciuszko Express Chairlift** (day pass adult/child $39/21; ⊙9am-4pm). From the top of the lift it's an uncomplicated 13km hike to the summit and back.

Summit Walk Drive to the end of the paved road above Charlotte Pass, then follow a wide gravel track. It's a 9km climb to the summit (18km return), including a steep final ascent.

Main Range Track Also beginning above Charlotte Pass, this strenuous 22km loop includes a river crossing. Check conditions before setting out, as the water level can rise quickly when it rains, and allow seven to nine hours for the circuit.

into a sofa or socialise over tales of fresh-air adventure.

Kosciuszko Tourist Park CAMPGROUND $
(☑02-6456 2224; www.kosipark.com.au; 1400 Kosciuszko Rd, Jindabyne; unpowered/powered sites from $28/39, cabins from $125, without bathroom from $85; ℗) Set amid the gums at Sawpit Creek along the road to Perisher, this campground is a good-value place to crash. Cabins (bring your own sheets) with bunk beds and kitchenettes seem to date back half a century, but there's well-disposed management and a pleasant parkland setting (often visited by kangaroos).

Snowgoose Apartments APARTMENT $$
(☑02-6457 6415; https://snowgooseapartments. com.au; 25 Diggings Tce; apt from $165; ℗ ⊛) Just above the shops but set back from the road, this luxurious set of contemporary apartments offers gas-log fireplaces, good kitchens, underfloor heating, balconies and views galore. All but the studios have a dedicated parking spot.

Sponars Chalet GUESTHOUSE $$$
(☑02-6456 1111; www.sponars.com.au; Digger's Creek; r incl half-board from $375; ℗) As worthwhile for après-ski camaraderie as for its pretty location in Kosciuszko National Park, winter-only Sponars has simple, chalet-style rooms and a merry (and good-value) bar. Established in 1909, the building has a heritage feel, though skiers will be more interested in the ski shop and the shuttle to Perisher, 8km west. There's filling half-board, efficiently served in its canteen.

Central Road 2625 CAFE $$
(☑02-6457 7271; www.facebook.com/central road2625; Village Sq; mains $14-36; ⊙8am-2pm daily Jun-Sep, Thu-Sun Oct-May; ☑) Occupying a prime spot on Village Sq, this cool corner cafe serves up an eclectic menu of sandwiches and breakfast, along with warming, Asian-inspired dishes like beef massaman, chicken with lime rice, laksa and spicy dal. The coffee is outstanding too.

Bernti's BRASSERIE $$
(☑02-6457 6332; www.berntis.com.au; 4 Mowamba Pl; mains $14-35; ⊙4pm-late Mon-Sat May-Oct, Tue-Sat Nov-Apr) Top-notch pub grub is served in the pleasant little wood-lined bar beneath this well-regarded midrange lodge. Bernti's is known for its monster steaks, but lighter fare, like ceviche, salads and soups, is also tasty and fresh. Grab a seat by the windows and take in the views. Opening days and hours can vary outside winter.

🛈 Information

NPWS Perisher Valley Information Centre
(☑02-6457 4444; www.nationalparks.nsw.gov. au; 9914 Kosciuszko Rd; ⊙8am-4pm daily Jun-Oct, Mon-Fri Nov-May) Offers information and advice on walks and other activities, including up-to-date weather forecasts. Sells vehicle passes and provides locator beacons for back-country walks (free, deposit $400). Fill out a trip-intention form here if you're planning on hiking in and around the national park.

Thredbo Information Centre (☑02-6459 4198; www.thredbo.com.au; 6 Friday Dr; ⊙9am-4.30pm) Bookings, national park passes, and weather and track information.

RIVERINA

The Riverina is NSW's most productive and agriculturally diverse region, due to its warm climate, vast plains and ample supply of water for irrigation.

Gundagai

POP 1676

Straddling the banks of the Murrumbidgee River, almost halfway between Sydney and Melbourne, little Gundagai is replete with Aussie folklore – gold rushes and bushrangers form part of its colourful history.

Immortalised in 'Along the Road to Gundagai', a folk song written by Jack O'Hagan in 1922 and made famous by country legend Slim Dusty, Gundagai today is an almost forgotten country town, but it's worth a stop here to see the Dog on the Tuckerbox and just to say that you've 'been to Gundagai'.

◎ Sights

Mt Parnassus Lookout   VIEWPOINT
(P) It's easy to see how the landscapes of the Riverina won the hearts of so many iconic Australian poets and songwriters, as you savour the sweeping 360-degree views from this lofty viewpoint.

Dog on the Tuckerbox   MONUMENT
(37 Annie Pyers Dr; P) About 7km north of town, the famous *Dog on the Tuckerbox* is a poignant sculpture of a dog from the 19th-century bush ballad.

🛏 Sleeping

Gundagai River Caravan Park   CARAVAN PARK $
(☑02-6944 1702; www.gundagairivercaravanpark.com.au; 67 Middleton Dr; unpowered/powered sites $25/35, cabins from $100; P ❄) This pleasant campground and caravan park boasts a lovely riverside location on the banks of the Murrumbidgee and has a selection of comfortable cabins, a kids' playground and good shared facilities.

★ Hillview Farmstay   COTTAGE $$
(☑02-6944 7535; www.hillviewfarmstay.com.au; 3241 Hume Hwy; 1-/2-bedroom cottages $160/200, glamping tents $260; P ❄ 🐾 ☕) Around 34km south of town and signposted off the Hume Hwy, these nicely turned out cottages are set on a 400-hectare farm and are especially good if you're fond of wildlife and birdwatching. There's a tennis court and swimming pool, and the new glamping tents added in 2018 are especially comfortable. Kids will love the menagerie.

ⓘ Information

Gundagai Visitor Information Centre (☑02-6944 0250; www.visitgundagai.com.au; 249 Sheridan St; ◎9am-12.30pm & 1-4.30pm; 🖘) Housed within the centre is **Rusconi's Marble Masterpiece** (admission $5), an intricate marble model that relentlessly plays 'Along the Road to Gundagai', so that you'll likely hum it mindlessly for days.

ⓘ Getting There & Away

Gundagai is just off the Hume Hwy midway between Sydney and Melbourne.

Firefly Express (☑1300 730 740; www.fireflyexpress.com.au) operates bus services linking Gungadai to Melbourne ($75, four hours) and Sydney ($75, 5½ hours).

Albury

POP 51,082

This major regional centre on the Murray River sits on the state border opposite its Victorian twin, Wodonga. It's a good launch pad for trips to the snowfields and High Country of both Victoria and NSW, and for exploring the upper Murray River.

The town's often overlooked by busy motorists in a hurry to get back to the big smoke, but visitors might be surprised and delighted by its pleasant layout, variety of accommodation and interesting museums and galleries.

◎ Sights & Activities

★ MAMA   GALLERY
(Murry Art Museum Albury; ☑02-6043 5800; www.alburycity.nsw.gov.au; 546 Dean St; ◎10am-5pm Mon-Fri, to 4pm Sat, noon-4pm Sun; 🐾) **FREE**
Following a $10.5 million makeover in 2015, Albury's art gallery is one of the finest NSW galleries outside of Sydney. Regular special exhibitions present an array of surprising and often challenging art, and the adjacent **Canvas Eatery** (☑02-6023 4923; www.facebook.com/canvaseatery; brunch mains $13-28, dinner mains $28-32; ◎8am-5pm Sun-Wed, 8am-late Thu-Sat; ❄ 🍴 🐾) has a very relaxed ambience. Local schools sometimes showcase art competitions at MAMA.

Albury Library Museum   MUSEUM
(☑02-6023 8333; www.alburycity.nsw.gov.au; cnr Kiewa & Swift Sts; ◎10am-7pm Mon, Wed & Thu,

to 5pm Tue & Fri, to 4pm Sat, noon-4pm Sun; ⓦ) **FREE** An excellent, state-of-the-art museum with displays on local history, including Indigenous culture and 20th-century migration into the area. Check the website for always-worthwhile special exhibitions.

Yindyamarra Sculpture Walk　　WALKING
(Kremur St; ⓦ) Meandering for 5km between the Kremur St boat ramp and the **Wonga Wetlands** (Riverina Hwy, Splitters Creek; ⊙7.30am-7.30pm; ⓦ), this riverside walking trail is enlivened with interesting sculptures telling the story Aboriginal history and the cultural significance of the Murray River to the local Wiradjuri people. Yindyamarra is a Wiradjuri word meaning 'respect, be gentle, be polite'. Keep an eye out for pelicans as you pass by Horseshoe Lagoon.

🛏 Sleeping & Eating

Hovell Tree Inn　　MOTEL **$$**
(☑02-6042 3900; www.hovelltreeinn.com.au; 614 Hovell St; d from $145; 🅿❄📶🏊) Stylishly refurbished rooms and a top location near riverside walking trails make the Hovell Tree Inn one of Albury's best motels. A spa, pool and gym provide opportunities for downtime, and the motel's own in-house grill restaurant includes tasty starters like pumpkin and parmesan arancini (Italian-style rice balls) and beetroot-cured salmon.

★**River Deck**　　CAFE **$$**
(☑02-6023 5980; www.riverdeckcafe.com.au; 48 Noreuil Pde; mains $14-34; ⊙8am-4pm daily plus 5.30-9.30pm Fri & Sat; 🅿❄🅿ⓦ) Right beside the Murray, the River Deck is a fine place for a leisurely brunch or lunch. Vegetarian options include jackfruit breakfast tacos, and Vietnamese-style salt and pepper squid is a lunch standout. Excellent shared plates and platters are the focus for evening dining on Friday and Saturday nights, and there's a convenient stand-alone booth selling ice cream and takeaway coffee

Adore on Dean　　MODERN AUSTRALIAN **$$$**
(☑02-6021 1703; www.facebook.com/adoreon dean; 492a Dean St; mains $26-33; ⊙5-10.30pm Tue-Thu, 4.30-11pm Fri & Sat; ❄🅿) European and Asian influences combine with local produce at this cosmopolitan dining room upstairs on Dean St. Try one of Albury's best pre-dinner cocktails or a tipple from its specialist gin menu, before moving on to dishes such as lamb rump with an Indonesian-style rendang sauce, roasted cashews and an

eggplant cream. The best of NSW and Asia in one dish.

ⓘ Information

Albury-Wodonga Visitor Information Centre
(☑1300 252 879; www.visitalburywodonga. com; Railway Pl; ⊙9am-5pm; 📶) Opposite the railway station. Has information about both Albury and Wodonga.

ⓘ Getting There & Away

Albury is well connected to NSW and Victoria by road, rail and air. It's 553km from Sydney and 326km from Melbourne.

Qantas (☑13 13 13; www.qantas.com.au), **Rex** (Regional Express; ☑13 17 13; www.rex.com. au) and **Virgin Australia** (☑13 67 89; www. virginaustralia.com) operate domestic flights to Sydney, Melbourne and smaller centres from **Albury Airport** (ABX; ☑02-6043 5865; www. flyalbury.com.au; 121 Airport Dr), which is 4km out of town; taxis are available (fares about $15), but there is no public transport to the airport.

Greyhound Australia (☑1300 473 946; www. greyhound.com.au) operates buses between Sydney ($91, nine hours) and Melbourne ($59, 3¾ hours) that stop in Albury.

NSW TrainLink (☑13 22 32; www.nswtrainlink. info) operates a daily and overnight XPT train service from Sydney to Albury (from $66, 7½ hours), and from Albury to Melbourne (from $44, 3¼ hours). **V/Line** (☑13 61 96; www.vline. com.au) has regular trains between Albury and Melbourne (from $39, four hours).

Wagga Wagga
POP 62,385

The Murrumbidgee River squiggles around Wagga Wagga's northern end, and riverside eucalypts complement tree-lined streets and lovely gardens. Known as 'place of many crows' to the local Wiradjuri people, 'Wagga' is NSW's largest inland city and it's a gem. Decent restaurants and cafes and an excellent art gallery all add to the appeal for visitors.

◎ Sights

Museum of the Riverina　　MUSEUM
(☑02-6926 9655; www.museumriverina.com. au; cnr Baylis & Morrow Sts; ⊙10am-4pm Tue-Sat, to 2pm Sun; 🅿ⓦ) **FREE** This interesting museum is split over two sites: this one, in the historic Council Chambers building, and the second, adjacent to the **Wagga Wagga Botanic Gardens** (Macleay

WORTH A TRIP

JUNEE

Featuring a high concentration of impressive heritage architecture, Junee makes an excellent day trip from Wagga Wagga, 43km to the south. A highlight is the **Roundhouse Railway Museum** (☑ 02-6924 2909; www. roundhousemuseum.com.au; Harold St; adult/child $6/4; ⊙10am-3pm Wed-Sun, last admission 2pm; P). Built in 1947, the Roundhouse, a giant turntable with 42 train-repair bays, is the only surviving, working one of its kind in Australia.

St; ⊙sunrise-sunset; P♿) **FREE**; the latter site focuses on Wagga's people, places and events. The Botanic Gardens site undertook a major renovation throughout 2018 and early 2019, incorporating modern exhibition spaces for many interesting items previously in storage.

🛏 Sleeping

Wagga Wagga Beach Caravan Park
CARAVAN PARK **$**

(☑ 02-6931 0603; www.wwbcp.com.au; 2 Johnston St; unpowered/powered sites $25/35, cabins from $115; P♿🖥🐾) Adjacent to the wonderful **Wagga Beach** (Tarcutta St; ♿), this van park includes its own swimming beach fashioned from the riverbank and a range of inexpensive cabins. Kids will love the playground and loads of space.

★Houston
BOUTIQUE HOTEL **$$**

(☑ 02-5908 1321; www.thehoustonwagga.com.au; 44 Kincaid St; r from $173; P♿🖥) This central, eight-room, all-suite boutique hotel is one of country NSW's best places to stay, and sumptuous original decor, luxurious linens and friendly staff all make guests feel special. Colourful design and art enlivens the decor and pricing is affordable and reasonable. Push the boat out with the bigger upstairs suite featuring a huge balcony.

Townhouse Hotel
BOUTIQUE HOTEL **$$**

(☑ 02-6921 4337; www.townhousewagga.com.au; 70 Morgan St; r $134-190; P♿🖥🐾) Fun, funky and full of flair, the Townhouse has a mish-mash of generally stylish rooms and apartments in a variety of configurations, furnished in a range of styles. The cheapest rooms lack exterior windows. If that bothers you, check with the friendly, professional staff.

🍴 Eating & Drinking

Cottontail Wines
WINERY

(☑ 02-6928 4554; www.cottontailwines.com.au; 562 Pattersons Rd, Harefield; ⊙11.30am-4pm Thu-Sun, 6pm-late Fri & Sat; P♿) Cellar-door tastings and excellent meals (mains $39 to $45) are well worth the 20-minute drive from central Wagga Wagga. Try the prosciutto-wrapped scallops or the duo of lamb from local farms. More informal menu options include wood-fired pizza ($22 to $25), and there's also a children's menu ($22).

Trail Street Coffee Shop
CAFE **$$**

(☑ 0400 753 924; www.trailstreet.com; 34 Trail St; mains $12-23; ⊙7.30am-4pm Mon-Fri, to 1pm Sat, 9am-1pm Sun; 🖥🐾) In a leafy neighbourhood on the edge of the CBD, Trail St's tattooed and Doc Marten'd crew serve up Wagga's best coffee and a concise menu of interesting variations on brunch and lunch classics. Try the sourdough-crumbed portobello mushrooms, or the Trail St eggs Benedict with sriracha hot sauce and charred corn salsa. Curbside outdoor seating seals the deal.

Oak Room Kitchen & Bar
BISTRO **$$$**

(☑ 02-6921 4337; www.townhousewagga.com/ the-oakroom; Townhouse Hotel, 70 Morgan St; bar snacks $8-24, mains $34-43; ⊙6pm-late Mon-Sat; 🖥🐾) The bustling Oak Room combines small plates, like seared Queensland scallops, with larger meals, including housemade gnocchi and roast lamb from the nearby Riverina region. The bar is open for drinks and snacks from 5pm. Booking for dinner on Friday and Saturday nights is recommended.

★Thirsty Crow Brewing Co
CRAFT BEER

(☑ 02-6921 7470; www.thirstycrow.com.au; 153 Fitzmaurice St; ⊙4pm-late Mon & Tue, noon-late Wed-Sun; 🖥) Come for the tasty beer – the hoppy Dark Alleyway IPA or the Piranha lager are both good choices – and stay for the wood-fired pizzas ($24 to $27). There's serious spicy heat in the Thai chicken pizza. Regular guest taps pour excellent beers and ciders from around Australia, and free brewery tours kick off at 2pm on Saturday and Sunday afternoons.

ℹ Information

Wagga Visitor Information Centre (☑ 1300 100 122; www.visitwagga.com; 183 Tarcutta St; ⊙9am-5pm; 🖥)

ℹ️ Getting There & Away

Wagga Wagga is midway between Young and Albury on the Olympic Hwy.

Qantas (p247) and Rex (p247) have direct flights to Sydney; Rex flights are on smaller planes and (usually) cost more.

Wagga Wagga is a stop on the twice-daily NSW TrainLink (p247) XPT service between Sydney (from $44, 6½ hours) and Melbourne (from $44, 4½ hours). The train also stops in Albury (from $13, 1¼ hours). Connecting buses to a variety of rural destinations depart from the station.

Griffith

POP 43,181

Welcome to Little Italy in the heart of NSW, where it's estimated that 60% of the town's residents have Italian ancestry. Griffith's restaurant scene makes it the food-and-wine capital of the Riverina, with two points to note: food means Italian food, and wine means cellar-door tastings – few wineries have restaurants.

The area's traditional Indigenous owners are the Wiradjuri people; 1970s tennis star Evonne Goolagong was born in Griffith and grew up in the nearby town of Barellan.

◉ Sights

Calabria Family Wines   WINERY
(☑ 02-6969 0800; www.calabriawines.com.au; 1283 Brayne Rd; ⊙ 9am-5pm Mon-Fri, 10am-4pm Sat & Sun; Ⓟ ☷) Tucked away on the edge of town, Calabria's Tuscany-style cellar door is a great place to try Italian wine varietals like Vermentino and Montepulciano. Established in 1945 and still owned by the Calabria family, the winery is regularly judged one of the Riverina's best wine-tasting experiences. Call ahead the afternoon prior to order a grazing box for lunch ($38 for two to four people).

De Bortoli   WINERY
(www.debortoli.com.au; De Bortoli Rd, Bilbul; ⊙ 9am-5pm Mon-Sat, to 4pm Sun; Ⓟ ☷) Visit the cellar door of this well-known Australian winery and be sure to try the astounding Black Noble dessert wine. Bring a picnic to enjoy the well-established gardens. There's also a good children's playground.

McWilliam's Hanwood Estate   WINERY
(☑ 02-6963 3404; www.mcwilliams.com.au; Jack McWilliam Rd, Hanwood; ⊙ tastings 10am-4pm Tue-Sat; Ⓟ) Don't miss a visit to the region's oldest (1913) and best-known winery. It's

really hard not to taste everything you possibly can.

🎊 Festivals & Events

UnWINEd   FOOD & DRINK
(www.unwined-riverina.com; ⊙ Mar-Apr) A festival of local wine and produce featuring wine tastings, lunches and live music. Check the website for specific timings of events including Rewind in the Vines (a music festival with performances from classic Aussie bands), and the Griffith Vintage Festival.

🛏️ Sleeping & Eating

★ **Ingelden Park**   FARMSTAY $$
(☑ 0457 647 964; www.ingleden.com.au; 225 Coghlan Rd; d $135-145; Ⓟ ☷) Around 18km from Griffith, Ingelden Park features two cosy cottages, both with a relaxed, rural outlook. Rose Cottage – complete with its own rose garden – is ideal for couples or smaller families, while the larger Ingelden Park Cottage sleeps up to six. There are spacious patios and barbecues for outside dining. Expect a warm welcome from the farmstay's dogs.

Griff Motel   MOTEL $$
(☑ 02-6964 0170; https://griffhotel.com.au; cnr Yambil & Kooyoo Sts; d/ste from $145/189; Ⓟ ☷ 🛜) Totally refurbished in 2018 – including spectacular wall-covering photographs of colourful vineyard scenes – the Griff Motel is the most contemporary and stylish of Griffith's central motels. With sparkling, modern kitchens ideal for self-catering, the family suites can accommodate up to four people. It's a very short stroll to great eating along Banna Ave.

Bertoldo's Bakery   BAKERY $
(☑ 02-6964 2514; www.bertoldos.com; 324 Banna Ave; desserts from $6; ⊙ 7am-5pm Mon-Fri, 7.30am-1.30pm Sat & Sun; ☷ ☷) This Italian patisserie and panetteria will have you drooling. Come for Griffith's best gelato – the pistachio flavour is especially good – and stay for the luscious cannoli (fried pastry tubes filled with ricotta cheese). Look forward to doing it all over again the following day.

★ **Zecca Handmade Italian**   ITALIAN $$
(☑ 02-6964 4050; www.zeccagriffith.com.au; 239 Banna Ave; mains $28-34; ⊙ 9.30am-4pm Tue & Wed, 9.30am-4pm & 6-11pm Thu & Fri, 11am-3pm & 6-11pm Sat; ☷ ☷) 🖊 Zecca serves up handmade pasta and Italian meals in the modern setting of a converted 1940s Rural Bank

building. The kitchen uses local ingredients where possible, working with farmers to showcase regional produce. Desserts such as coconut panna cotta are always excellent, and be sure to check out the daily blackboard specials before ordering. Local wines focus on Italian grape varieties.

★ **Limone** ITALIAN $$$

(☑02-6962 3777; www.limone.com.au; 482 Banna Ave; 2/3 courses $60/75; ☺6pm-late Tue-Sat; ❉☑) 🅿 In an elegant dining room largely constructed from recycled materials, Limone's deserved reputation as one of regional NSW's best restaurants is enhanced by two- and three-course menus showcasing intensely seasonal local produce, much of it gathered from the restaurant's own Piccolo Family Farm. The menu usually changes weekly, and is always anchored in the rustic flavours of regional Italian cuisine.

ℹ️ Information

Griffith Visitor Information Centre (☑02-6962 4145; www.visitgriffith.com.au; cnr Banna & Jondaryan Aves; ☺9am-5pm; 🛜) Excellent source of local information and includes a shop selling local artisanal produce.

Riverina NPWS Office (☑02-6966 8100; www.nationalparks.nsw.gov.au; 200 Yambil St; ☺8.30am-4.30pm Mon-Fri; 🛜) Information on nearby national parks.

ℹ️ Getting There & Away

Rex (p247) has daily flights to Sydney from Griffith Airport, 3km north of town.

Local and regional buses stop at the **Griffith Travel & Transit Centre** (☑02-6962 7199; Banna Ave) adjacent to the visitor information centre.

NSW TrainLink (p247) operates two daily bus services to Wagga Wagga ($123, three hours), where you can connect to XPT train services to Sydney ($92, 6½ hours) and Melbourne ($92, 4½ hours). Note that TrainLink buses now depart from the **Griffith Railway Station**.

Deniliquin

POP 7494

A quintessential inland Australian town, Deniliquin, also known as 'Deni', lies along a wide, lazy bend of the Edwards River. Here you'll find an attractive river beach and some appealing riverside walks amid the red gums. There's also a famed and ever-growing festival dedicated to that curious Aussie obsession, the ute.

⦿ Sights

★ **Island Sanctuary** WILDLIFE RESERVE

FREE The 16-hectare Island Sanctuary, at the junction of the Edwards River and Tarrangle Creek, has a fine walking track among the river red gums. It's home to plenty of wildlife, including eastern grey kangaroos, and almost one-fifth of all bird species recorded in Australia have been seen here. Enter via a footbridge off the southeastern end of Cressy St.

Yarkuwa Indigenous Knowledge Centre CULTURAL CENTRE

(☑03-5881 3312; www.yarkuwa.com.au; 104 End St; ☺9am-5pm Mon-Fri) Opening hours can sometimes be flexible, but it's worth dropping in to check out the museum and gallery at Yarkuwa to learn about the culture and history of the area's Wamba Wamba and Barapa Barapa Indigenous peoples.

McLean Beach BEACH

At the northern end of town, McLean Beach is one of Australia's finest river beaches, with sand, picnic facilities and a walking track. Kayak rental is available from the nearby **McLean Beach Holiday Park** (☑03-5881 2448; www.mcleanbeach.com.au; 1 Butler St; powered sites $36, cabins $135-190; 🅿🛜).

✨ Festivals & Events

★ **Deniliquin Ute Muster** MUSIC

(www.deniutemuster.com.au; adult/concession $240/125; ☺late Sep; ♿) Held on the NSW Labour Day holiday weekend in late September, the muster attracts people (and their utes) from across the country. Events include a rodeo, chainsaw sculpting, wood chopping, helicopter rides and kids' activities. The festival also draws big names in country music: US superstars Tim McGraw and Carrie Underwood have appeared in recent years.

🛏️ Sleeping & Eating

Cottages on Edward B&B $$

(☑0407 815 641; www.cottagesonedward.com.au; 304 River St; cottages incl breakfast Sun-Thu $145, Fri & Sat $175; 🅿❉) These two charming cottages, across the Edward River at the eastern end of town, are overseen by the equally charming Richard and Pat. The rooms have understated antique furnishings, spa baths and a real sense of being a home away from home.

Crossing Café
MODERN AUSTRALIAN $$

(☑03-5881 7827; www.thecrossingcafe.com.au; 295 George St; mains $18-38; ☺8am-4pm Tue-Thu, 8am-late Fri, 8.30am-late Sat, 8.30am-4pm Sun; ❋⛟) With a spacious and sunny deck, Crossing offers such dishes as Thai beef salad or salt-and-pepper calamari. Other international culinary influences showcase Italy and the Middle East, and Riverina wines and NSW craft beer complete the cafe's cosmopolitan ambience. There's a good children's menu, and kids can let steam off in an adjacent park. Also good for coffee and cake.

ℹ Information

Deniliquin Visitor Information Centre
(☑1800 650 712; www.visitdeni.com.au; George St; ☺9am-4pm; 🕾)

ℹ Getting There & Away

Deniliquin is 205km west of Albury and 74km north of Echuca/Moama, which straddles the Murray River at the Victoria–NSW border.

NSW TrainLink (p247) buses run to Albury ($20, 3½ hours), where you can connect to the XPT train to Sydney ($67, eight hours).

Hay
POP 2445

Nestled on the banks of the Murrumbidgee River, at the intersection of three major highways, little Hay is a delightful, visitor-friendly town with an interesting history and no fewer than five worthwhile museums. The traditional Indigenous owners of the area are the Nari Nari people, who, in centuries past, camped along the Murrumbidgee River where food sources like freshwater mussels and fish were plentiful.

It's a recommended overnight stop for road trips from southwestern NSW, heading further west on the Mid-Western Hwy, or south into Victoria.

★Shear Outback
MUSEUM

(Australian Shearer's Hall of Fame; ☑02-6993 4000; www.shearoutback.com.au; cnr Sturt & Cobb Hwys; adult/child $20/10; ☺9am-5pm; P⛟) Shearers, rousies, wool classers, cooks and working dogs are all under the one roof in this historic working shearing shed where you can watch a shearing demonstration and learn about the men and women who helped shape the nation. And yes, lamb burgers are available at the on-site cafe.

Dunera Museum
MUSEUM

(Hay Internment and Prisoner of War Camps Interpretive Centre; ☑02-6993 2161; Hay Railway Station; $4; ☺9am-6pm; P) Housed in two historic railway carriages of the same kind that were used to transport POWs, this sombre museum tells the story of the 'Dunera Boys' and the more than 6000 Italian, German and Japanese people who were interned in Hay prison camps during WWII.

★Saltbush Motor Inn
MOTEL $$

(☑02-6993 4555; www.saltbushmotorinn.com.au; 193 Lachlan St; r from $120; P❋🕾🌊) Right in the centre of town, this lovely, well-maintained motel has compact, simply furnished rooms and an excellent two-bedroom family suite overlooking the modern, inviting pool. Welcome to one of the best motels in regional NSW.

ℹ Information

Hay NPWS Office (☑02-6990 8200; www.nationalparks.nsw.gov.au; 339a Murray St; ☺8.30am-4.30pm Mon-Fri) Information and maps for self-guided walks and hikes through the region's Cocoparra, Mungo, Kalyarr and Colambeyan national parks.

Hay Visitor Information Centre (☑02-6993 4045; 407 Moppett St; ☺9am-5pm; 🕾) Free bike hire.

ℹ Getting There & Away

Hay is 125km north of Deniliquin at the intersection of the Sturt, Mid-Western and Cobb Hwys.

Canberra & the ACT

🗐 02 / POP 410,300

Includes →

History	254
Sights	254
Activities & Tours	258
Festivals & Events	259
Sleeping	259
Eating	263
Drinking & Nightlife	267
Entertainment	269
Shopping	269
Around Canberra	271

Best Places to Eat

→ Cupping Room (p264)

→ Lazy Su (p264)

→ Akiba (p264)

→ Pilot (p266)

→ Aubergine (p266)

→ Muse (p264)

Best Places to Stay

→ Ovolo Nishi (p263)

→ Little National Hotel (p259)

→ East Hotel (p261)

→ University House (p261)

→ Blue & White Lodge (p259)

Why Go?

With mountains, rivers, lakes and bushland all within its compact boundaries, it's easy to see how the Australian Capital Territory (ACT) came to be known as Australia's 'Bush Capital'. At the territory's heart sits the cosmopolitan city of Canberra, a well-planned, leafy city with enough cultural cachet to match Australia's larger metropolises, alongside the laid-back feel of a regional centre. Sightseeing opportunities abound within the city limits – including several world-class museums – but there's also plenty to see and do in the wider ACT as well. Whether it's bushwalking and kangaroo-spotting in the nearby wildernesses of Namadgi National Park and Tidbinbilla Nature Reserve, sipping superb shiraz at one of the many local wineries, or window-shopping in the quaint towns of Hall or Bungendore, you'll find plenty to occupy yourself among the hills and plains of this quintessential Australian region.

When to Go
Canberra

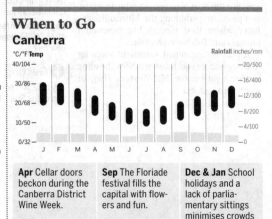

Apr Cellar doors beckon during the Canberra District Wine Week.

Sep The Floriade festival fills the capital with flowers and fun.

Dec & Jan School holidays and a lack of parliamentary sittings minimises crowds and hotel prices.

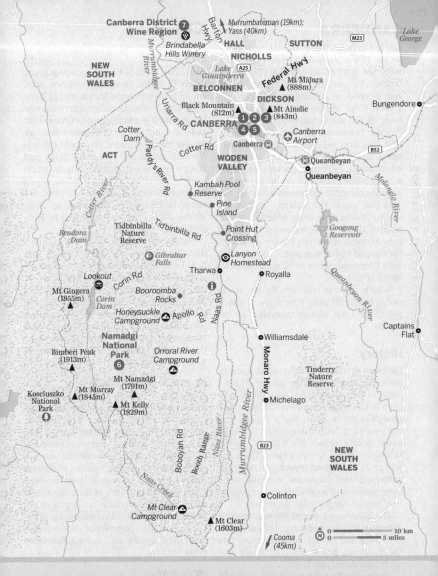

Canberra & the ACT Highlights

1 National Gallery of Australia (p254) Delving into a treasure trove of Australian and international art.

2 National Portrait Gallery (p254) Pondering the eclectic array of faces that have shaped Australian culture.

3 Australian Parliament House (p254) Witnessing democracy in action within these symbolism-laden walls.

4 Australian War Memorial (p256) Learning about how Australia's chequered military history has helped to define the national psyche.

5 Lake Burley Griffin (p257) Paddling, cycling, skating or strolling around Canberra's central water feature.

6 Namadgi National Park (p271) Spotting kangaroos and Aboriginal rock art on a walk through the wilderness.

7 Canberra District Wine Region (p268) Sampling award-winning cold-climate drops at the region's wineries.

CANBERRA

Lately Canberra has been staking a claim for the title of Australia's coolest city – and we're not just talking winter temperatures. Where else can you find superb dining and world-class cultural experiences only a short stroll from wildlife-filled bushland reserves and serene lakeshore views?

Since becoming the nation's capital in 1927, Canberra has grown into a cosmopolitan metropolis, with expansive open spaces interspersed by dense pockets of urban activity. Some of the nation's best art galleries are here, and there's plenty of history too, both past and in the making – visitors can see Australian democracy in action at Parliament House before exploring its bygone days at some of the city's many museums. Dining and nightlife opportunities abound, with Canberra's scene rivalling those of its larger neighbours.

Whether you're just here for the weekend or have a bit more time to spare, there's plenty to keep visitors occupied in the capital.

History

Canberra is built on Ngunnawal country. Rock paintings found in nearby Tharwa indicate that Indigenous Australians have lived in this region for at least 20,000 years, though evidence from nearby regions suggests an even longer duration. The Ngunnawal people called this place Kanberra, believed to mean 'Meeting Place'. The name was probably derived from huge intertribal gatherings that happened annually when large numbers of bogong moths – a popular food source – appeared in the region.

The Ngunnawal way of life was violently disrupted following the arrival of Europeans in 1820, when settlers began to move into the Canberra basin, bringing sheep and other introduced species.

During the first stage of European settlement, the Canberra area was part of the colony of New South Wales. In 1901, when Australia's separate colonies federated, the rivalry between Sydney and Melbourne meant neither could become the new nation's capital, so a location between the two cities was carved out of southern NSW as a compromise. This new city was officially named Canberra in 1913, and became the national capital in 1927.

⊙ Sights

★ National Gallery of Australia
GALLERY

(Map p260; ☑02-6240 6502; www.nga.gov.au; Parkes Pl, Parkes; temporary exhibition prices vary; ⊙10am-5pm, guided tours hourly to 2.30pm) FREE This Australian national art collection is showcased in an impressive purpose-built gallery within the parliamentary precinct. Almost every big name you could think of from Australian and international art, past and present, is represented. Famous works include one of Monet's *Waterlilies,* several of Sidney Nolan's *Ned Kelly* paintings, Salvador Dali's *Lobster Telephone,* an Andy Warhol *Elvis* print and a triptych by Francis Bacon.

Highlights include the extraordinary *Aboriginal Memorial* from Central Arnhem Land in the lobby, created for Australia's 1988 bicentenary. The work of 43 artists, this 'forest of souls' presents 200 hollow log coffins (one for every year of European settlement) and is part of an excellent collection of Aboriginal and Torres Strait Islander art. Most of the Australian art is on the 1st floor, alongside a fine collection of Asian and Pacific art.

★ National Portrait Gallery
GALLERY

(Map p260; ☑02-6102 7000; www.portrait.gov. au; King Edward Tce, Parkes; ⊙10am-5pm) FREE Occupying a flash, purpose-built building, this wonderful gallery tells the story of Australia through its faces – from wax cameos of Indigenous Australians to colonial portraits of the nation's founding families, to Howard Arkley's DayGlo portrait of musician Nick Cave. Only around 10% of the collection of more than 3500 works is on display at any one time, so there's always something different to see. New portraits of contemporary Australian figures are also commissioned every year.

★ Australian Parliament House
NOTABLE BUILDING

(Map p260; ☑02-6277 5399; www.aph.gov.au; ⊙9am-5pm) FREE Built in 1988, Australia's national parliament building is a graceful and deeply symbolic piece of architecture. Sitting atop Capital Hill, the building is crossed by two axes, north–south and east–west, representing the historical progression and legislative progression of Australian democracy. There's plenty to see inside,

Canberra

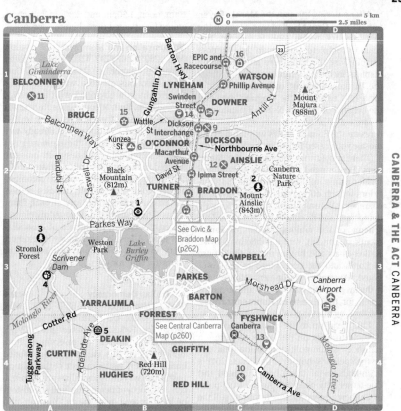

Canberra

◉ Sights
1 Australian National Botanic Gardens... B2
2 Mt Ainslie.. C2
3 National Arboretum.............................. A3
4 National Zoo & Aquarium..................... A3
5 Royal Australian Mint B4

⬤ Sleeping
6 Alvio Tourist Park B2
7 Blue & White Lodge C1
8 Vibe Canberra Airport D3

⊗ Eating
9 Asian Noodle House C2
10 Aubergine... C4

Highroad ....(see 9)
11 Malaysian Chapter A1
12 Mama Dough C2
Pilot...(see 12)

⬤ Drinking & Nightlife
13 Capital Brewing Co............................... C4
14 Old Canberra Inn................................... B1

⊛ Entertainment
15 GIO Stadium Canberra B1

⬤ Shopping
16 Capital Region Farmers Market C1

whether the politicians are haranguing each other in the chambers or not.

After passing through airport-style security, visitors are free to explore large sections of the building and watch parliamentary proceedings from the public galleries. The only time that tickets are required is for the high theatre of **Question Time** in the House of Representatives (2pm on sitting days); tickets are free but must be booked through the Serjeant-at-Arms. See the website for a calendar of sitting days.

After entering through the **Marble Foyer**, pop into the **Great Hall** to take a look at the vast tapestry, which took 14 weavers two years to complete. Upstairs in the corridors surrounding the hall, there are interesting displays including temporary exhibits from the Parliamentary art collection. Look out for a 1297 edition of the **Magna Carta** and the original of Michael Nelson Tjakamarra's *Possum & Wallaby Dreaming,* which features on the $5 note and is writ large as the mosaic you passed in Parliament's forecourt.

There are further displays in the **Members' Hall**, ringed with august portraits of former prime ministers. From the hall, corridors branch off towards the two debating chambers. Australia has a Westminster-style democracy and its chambers echo the colour scheme of the famous 'Mother of Parliaments' in London, with a subtle local twist. Rather than the bright red of the House of Lords and the deep green of the lower house, Australia's Parliament House uses a dusky pink for its **Senate** and a muted green for the **House of Representatives**, inspired by the tones of the local eucalypts.

Lifts head up to the roof. It used to be possible to walk on the lawns up here – a reminder to the politicians below that this is the 'people's house' – but since 2017 a 2.5m-high metal fence has prevented this due to security concerns. As the focal point of Canberra, however, this terrace is still the best place to get a perspective on Walter Burley Griffin's city design. Your eyes are drawn immediately along three axes, with the Australian War Memorial backed by Mt Ainslie (p258) directly ahead, the commercial centre on an angle to the left and Duntroon (representing the military) on an angle to the right. Interestingly, the church is denied a prominent place in this very 20th-century design.

Free guided tours (40 minutes) depart from the desk in the foyer at 9.30am, 11am, 1pm, 2pm and 3.30pm.

★**Questacon**   MUSEUM
(Map p260; ✆02-6270 2800; www.questacon.edu.au; King Edward Tce, Parkes; adult/child $23/17.50; ⊙9am-5pm; 🚼) A must-see for anyone travelling with kids, Canberra's science museum has stacks of fun interactive exhibits that feel nothing like what'd you learn in a classroom. From earthquake simulators to a ginormous model of the moon, there's plenty to keep even adults entertained. Time your visit to catch one of the regular science shows at the on-site theatre – usually at

11am, noon, 1.30pm and 2.30pm, but check online for updated times before your visit.

★**Australian War Memorial**   MUSEUM
(Map p260; ✆02-6243 4211; www.awm.gov.au; Treloar Cres, Campbell; ⊙10am-5pm) FREE Canberra's glorious art-deco war memorial is a highlight in a city filled with interesting architecture. Built to commemorate 'the war to end all wars', it opened its doors in 1941 when the next world war was already well under way. Attached to the memorial is a large, exceptionally well-designed museum devoted to the nation's military history.

The entrance opens onto a commemorative courtyard, which encloses a pool of remembrance where an eternal flame burns. The walls of the surrounding cloister are engraved with the names of Australia's war dead. A Last Post ceremony is held here every evening at 4.55pm, just before the doors are shut for the night.

Museum of Australian Democracy   MUSEUM
(MoAD; Map p260; ✆02-6270 8222; www.moadoph.gov.au; Old Parliament House, 18 King George Tce, Parkes; adult/child/family $2/1/5; ⊙9am-5pm) The seat of government from 1927 to 1988, this elegantly proportioned building offers visitors a taste of the political past. Displays cover Australian prime ministers, the roots of democracy and the history of local protest movements. You can also visit the old Senate and House of Representative chambers, the parliamentary library and the prime minister's office.

National Museum of Australia   MUSEUM
(Map p260; ✆02-6208 5000; www.nma.gov.au; Lawson Cres, Acton Peninsula; ⊙9am-5pm) FREE As well as telling Australia's national story, this museum hosts blockbuster touring exhibitions (admission prices vary). Highlights include the Gallery of First Australians, which explains the history and traditions of Aboriginal and Torres Strait Islander peoples, and the Garden of Australian Dreams, an interactive outdoor exhibition. The disjointed layout of the displays can sometimes be confusing; one way to get the best out of the museum is to take a one-hour guided tour (adult/child $15/10, 10am, 1pm and 3pm daily).

Australian National Botanic Gardens   GARDENS
(Map p255; ✆02-6250 9588; www.nationalbotanicgardens.gov.au; Clunies Ross St; ⊙8.30am-5pm)

CANBERRA FOR CHILDREN

Canberra is a family-friendly city, with plenty of space to roam and no huge crowds. Most of the museums and galleries have kids' programs, and many offer dedicated tours and events for little people. Kid friendly sights include the following:

➡ Questacon (p256) This excellent science museum has stacks of hands-on activities to keep little minds entertained.

➡ National Gallery of Australia (p254) The dedicated play space on the ground floor offers changing installations by Australian artists with craft activities especially designed for small hands.

➡ National Museum of Australia (p256) Download the museum Kspace app before your visit to take advantage of the Kspace Augmented Reality Trail.

➡ National Zoo & Aquarium (below) As well as spotting cheetahs, lions, tigers and rhinos, kids can let off steam at the newly opened adventure playground.

➡ National Arboretum (p258) Kids will love the tree-themed Pod Playground, with cubbies made of giant acorns, swings shaped like nests and banksia pods to climb on.

FREE On the lower slopes of Black Mountain, these sprawling gardens showcase Australian floral diversity over 35 hectares of cultivated garden and 50 hectares of remnant bushland. Various themed routes are marked out, with the best introduction being the main path (45 minutes return), which takes in the eucalypt lawn, rock garden, rainforest gully and Sydney Region garden. A 3.2km bushland nature trail leads to the garden's higher reaches.

Free hour-long guided walks (highly recommended) depart from the visitor centre at 11am and 2pm.

Aboriginal Tent Embassy   HISTORIC SITE
(Map p260; King George Tce, Parkes) First erected in 1972 as a protest against the government's approach to Indigenous land rights, this camp on the lawn in front of Old Parliament House came and went over the subsequent two decades before being re-established in 1992. It has been a constant presence since then, providing a continuing reminder of Indigenous dispossession for those visiting the symbolic heart of Australian democracy.

National Capital Exhibition   MUSEUM
(Map p260; ☎02-6272 2902; www.national capital.gov.au; Barrine Dr, Commonwealth Park; ☉9am-5pm) FREE This small but fascinating museum tells the story of how Canberra came to be Australia's capital. Displays include reproductions of the drawings entered in the international competition to design the city, including the exquisite watercolour renderings of the winning design created by Marion Mahony Griffin, the often overlooked wife and creative partner of Walter Burley Griffin.

The glass pavilion offers lovely views over the lake and Capital Hill, so you can see the real-life outcomes of the plans you're perusing.

Canberra Museum & Art Gallery   MUSEUM
(CMAG; Map p262; ☎02-6207 3968; www.cmag. com.au; cnr London Circuit & Civic Sq, Civic; ☉10am-5pm Mon-Sat) FREE This local museum is worth it for the Sidney Nolan paintings alone – 141 works, including canvases from his *Ned Kelly* series and *Burke and Wills Expedition* were gifted to the Australian government in 1974, and a rotating collection is on display here. There's also an exhibition on Canberra's own story, which is often overshadowed by 'national' stories, as well as a variety of interesting and unusual temporary exhibitions – when we last visited, there was one solely devoted to snow globes.

Lake Burley Griffin   LAKE
(Map p260) This ornamental lake was created in 1963 when the 33m-high Scrivener Dam was erected on the Molonglo River. It's lined with important institutions and monuments, including the National Carillon (Map p260; www.nca.gov.au; Aspen Island) and Captain Cook Memorial Water Jet. You can cycle the entire 28km perimeter in two hours or walk it in seven. Alternatively, you can make a smaller 'loop' by making use of the two bridges – the popular central loop is 5km and can be walked in one to 1½ hours.

National Zoo & Aquarium   ZOO
(Map p255; ☎02-6287 8400; www.nationalzoo. com.au; 999 Lady Denman Dr, Weston Creek; adult/ child $47/26; ☉9.30am-5pm) It's certainly not

CANBERRA IN TWO DAYS

Breakfast at one of the city's excellent cafes before making a beeline for the museum quarter. Check out the masterpieces at the National Gallery of Australia (p254), find familiar faces at the National Portrait Gallery (p254) or keep the kids entertained at Questacon (p256). After lunch, wander up to Parliament House (p254) for a guided tour. Grab dinner either in Kingston or on the newly developed foreshore.

On day two, breakfast in Acton then walk over to the Australian National Botanic Gardens (p256) in time for the 11am guided tour. Afterwards, head to trendy Braddon for lunch and a spot of window-shopping before spending the afternoon at the Australian War Memorial (p256). Dine at one of Civic's numerous restaurants before barhopping between some of the city's best bars.

the biggest in Australia, but Canberra's zoo is well laid out and animal friendly, with native fauna such as Tasmanian devils and dingoes to keep the kids amused. It also offers various behind-the-scenes experiences where you can help to feed the sharks, lions, tigers and bears, and interact with rhinos and cheetahs.

A new adventure playground, opened in 2019, includes life-size models of animals such as giraffes and camels and is great fun for kids.

Royal Australian Mint   MUSEUM
(Map p255; ☑02-6202 6999; www.ramint.gov. au; Denison St, Deakin; ⊙8.30am-5pm Mon-Fri, 10am-4pm Sat & Sun; P) FREE The Royal Australian Mint is Australia's biggest money-making operation. Its gallery showcases the history of Australian coinage; learn about the 1813 'holey dollar' and its enigmatic offspring, the 'dump'. There's also an observation platform where you can see coins being made (on weekdays). Engaging guided tours (30 minutes) about the history of currency in Australia run regularly throughout the day on the hour; call ahead to check times.

National Arboretum   PARK
(Map p255; ☑02-6207 8484; www.national arboretum.act.gov.au; Forest Dr, Weston Creek; ⊙6am-8.30pm Oct-Mar, 7am-5.30pm Apr-Sep, village centre 9am-4pm; P) FREE Canberra's National Arboretum is an ever-developing showcase of trees from around the world, with 94 forests of different species currently on-site. It is early days for many of the plantings, but it's still worth visiting for the spectacular visitor centre and the excellent views over the city. Regular guided tours are informative, and there is a brilliant adventure playground for kids.

National Library of Australia   LIBRARY
(Map p260; ☑02-6262 1111; www.nla.gov.au; Parkes Pl, Parkes; ⊙10am-8pm Mon-Thu, to 5pm Fri & Sat, 1.30-5pm Sun, galleries 10am-5pm daily) FREE This institution has accumulated more than 10 million items since being established in 1901 and has digitised more than nine billion files. You can pop by the **Main Reading Room** at any time to browse newspapers and magazines by the large windows. Don't miss the **Treasures Gallery**, where artefacts such as Captain Cook's *Endeavour* journal and Captain Bligh's list of mutineers are among the regularly refreshed displays; free 30-minute tours of the gallery are held at 11.30am daily.

Mt Ainslie   NATURE RESERVE
(Map p255; www.environment.act.gov.au/parks-conservation/parks-and-reserves; Ainslie Dr) Northeast of the city, 843m-high Mt Ainslie has excellent views day and night. At the top, plaques explain what the Canberra basin looked like before the city was built. You can drive to the summit, or take the walking track that starts behind the Australian War Memorial (p256; 4.5km return, 1½ hours).

🏃 Activities & Tours

Canberra's streets are perfect for cycling, and the city has an extensive network of dedicated cycle paths. The visitor centre (p270) is a good source of information, as is Pedal Power ACT (www.pedalpower.org.au).

GoBoat   BOATING
(Map p260; ☑02-6100 7776; www.goboatcan berra.com.au; Wharf 2, Trevillian Quay, Kingston Foreshore; 1/2/3hr $95/169/239; ⊙10am-8pm) Fancy pottering around Lake Burley Griffin on your own private boat? These little electric-powered dinghies can fit up to eight people and have a table in the centre just made for picnicking. You don't need a boat licence to captain your own cruise, just a sense of adventure. Bookings (via the website) are recommended.

Balloon Aloft BALLOONING

(Map p260; ☑02-6249 8660; www.balloonaloft canberra.com.au; 120 Commonwealth Ave, Yarralumla; adult/child from $330/240) Meet in the foyer of the Hyatt for an early-morning flight over Canberra – the ideal way to understand the city's unique design.

MV Southern Cross CRUISE

(Map p260; ☑02-6273 1784; www.mvsouthern cross.com.au; 1 Mariner Pl, Yarralumla; adult/child from $20/10) Offers sightseeing cruises on the lake, with three different pick-up and drop-off locations. Lunch or dinner cruises (adult/child $79/30) are also available.

Lake Burley Griffin Cruises CRUISE

(Map p260; ☑0419 418 846; www.lakecruises.com. au; adult/child $20/9; ⊙mid-Sep–May) Informative one-hour lake cruises depart from the wharf in front of the **International Flag Display** (Map p260; Queen Elizabeth Tce, Parkes).

✦ Festivals & Events

To find out what's happening during your visit, see www.events.act.gov.au.

National Multicultural Festival CULTURAL

(www.multiculturalfestival.com.au; ⊙Feb) A celebration of cultural and linguistic diversity, with three days of art, culture and food in the city centre.

Royal Canberra Show AGRICULTURAL SHOW

(www.canberrashow.org.au; Exhibition Park; ⊙late Feb) The country comes to town: pat a lamb, ride the Ferris wheel, eat some fairy floss and soak up the country-show atmosphere.

Art, Not Apart ART

(www.artnotapart.com; New Acton; ⊙Mar) This contemporary-art festival's aim is to be like no other festival you've ever seen. Held in the New Acton precinct, dance parties, art installations, live performances and 'spontaneous' acts of art are just some of what you might experience.

Enlighten CULTURAL

(www.enlightencanberra.com; ⊙Mar) For several weeks in early March, various Canberra institutions are bathed in projections and keep their doors open late, while musical performances and other outdoor events culminate in an explosive fireworks display.

Canberra Balloon Spectacular AIR SHOW

(www.enlightencanberra.com; ⊙Mar) Hot-air balloons lift off from the lawns in front of Old Parliament House every morning during this nine-day festival.

Canberra International
Music Festival MUSIC

(www.cimf.org.au; ⊙Apr or May) Eleven days of classical-music performances in significant Canberra locations and buildings.

National Folk Festival MUSIC

(www.folkfestival.org.au; Exhibition Park; ⊙Easter) One of Australia's largest folk festivals with a huge program of music, entertainment, markets and camping over five days.

★Floriade FAIR

(www.floriadeaustralia.com; Commonwealth Park) This renowned spring flower festival is one of the city's biggest events, drawing the crowds to Commonwealth Park from mid-September to mid-October to delight in elaborate floral displays.

The event includes evening events including concerts and Night Fest, promising music, comedy and more.

🛏 Sleeping

Canberra has a wide range of accommodation, though much of it is in the midrange to high-end bracket due to the constant influx of politicians and public servants. Accommodation is most expensive on parliamentary sitting days. Hotels charge peak rates midweek, but often have reduced rates at weekends. Peak rates also apply during the spring Floriade festival. Book well ahead – and usually via the hotel's website – for the best deals.

★Little National Hotel HOTEL $

(Map p260; ☑02-6188 3200; www.littlenational hotel.com.au; 21 National Circuit, Barton; r from $119; P❖@🛜) Housed within a stark black cube, this brilliant boutique hotel delivers affordable style by way of small but well-designed rooms with exceptionally comfortable beds. Compensating for the lack of cat-swinging space is an appealing 'library' and bar offering panoramic views of the city. Book early; advance bookings are a steal but prices can more than double when it's busy.

★Blue & White Lodge MOTEL $

(Map p255; ☑02-6248 0498; www.blueandwhite lodge.com.au; 524 Northbourne Ave, Downer; s/d $95/100; P❖🛜) On the main approach into Canberra from the north, this long-standing motel-style place and its indistinguishable sister, the Canberran Lodge, are reliable

Central Canberra

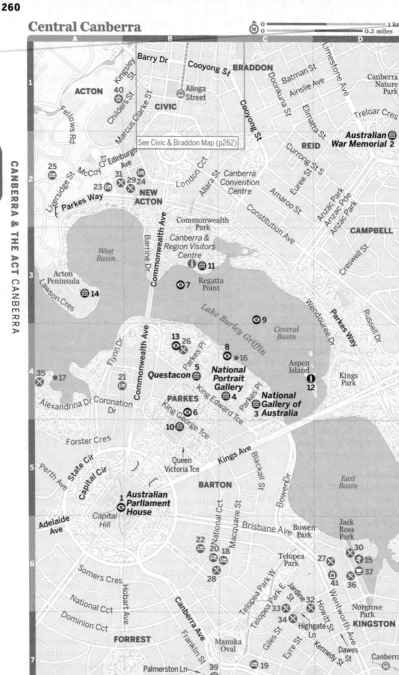

N 0 ———— 1 km
0 ———— 0.5 miles

ACTON 40

Kingsley St
Childers St
Barry Dr
Cooyong St
BRADDON
Batman St
Ainslie Ave
Limestone Ave
Canberra Nature Park

Fellows Rd
Marcus Clarke St
Alinga Street
CIVIC
Doonkuna St
Ellimatta St
Treloar Cres

Edinburgh Ave
McCoy Cct
25
23 31 29 24
NEW ACTON
London Cct
Allara St
Canberra Convention Centre
Currong St S
Euree St S
Amaroo St
REID
Australian War Memorial 2

Liversidge St
Parkes Way
Commonwealth Ave
Barrine Dr
Commonwealth Park
Constitution Ave
Anzac Park
Anzac Pde
Anzac Park
CAMPBELL

West Basin
Canberra & Region Visitors Centre
11
Creswell St

Acton Peninsula
Lawson Cres
14
7
Regatta Point
Lake Burley Griffin
9
Central Basin
Wendouree Dr
Parkes Way
Russell Dr

Flynn Dr
13 26
5
Questacon
8 16
National Portrait Gallery
Aspen Island
12
Kings Park

35
17
21
King Edward Tce
4
Parkes Pl
National Gallery of Australia 3

Alexandrina Dr
Coronation Dr
PARKES
King George Tce
6
10

Forster Cres
Queen Victoria Tce
Kings Ave
Blackall St
Bowen Dr
East Basin

Perth Ave
State Cir
Capital Cir
BARTON

Adelaide Ave
Capital Hill
Australian Parliament House 1

Somers Cres
National Cct
Hobart Ave
22
20 18
28
Macquarie St
Brisbane Ave
Bowen Park
27
41
30
15
37
36
Jack Ross Park

National Cct
Dominion Cct
FORREST
Canberra Ave
Franklin St
Telopea Park W
Telopea Park E
Telopea Park
Jardine St
Howitt St
33 32
34
Highgate Ln
Wentworth Ave
Kennedy St
Dawes St
Norgrove Park
KINGSTON

Palmerston Ln
38 39
Manuka Oval
Giles St
Eyre St
19
Canberra Ave
Bougainville St
Canberra

See Civic & Braddon Map (p262)

Central Canberra

◎ Top Sights
1 Australian Parliament House A5
2 Australian War Memorial D2
3 National Gallery of Australia................. C4
4 National Portrait Gallery C4
5 Questacon B4

◎ Sights
6 Aboriginal Tent Embassy B4
7 Captain Cook Memorial Water Jet B3
8 International Flag Display C4
9 Lake Burley Griffin C3
10 Museum of Australian Democracy B5
11 National Capital Exhibition B3
12 National Carillon C4
13 National Library of Australia B4
14 National Museum of Australia A3

⊕ Activities, Courses & Tours
Balloon Aloft .... (see 21)
15 GoBoat D6
16 Lake Burley Griffin Cruises C4
17 MV Southern Cross A4

🛏 Sleeping
18 Burbury Hotel C6
19 East Hotel C7
20 Hotel Realm B6
21 Hyatt Hotel Canberra A4
22 Little National Hotel B6
23 Ovolo Nishi A2
24 QT Canberra B2
25 University House A2

⊗ Eating
Agostini's .... (see 19)
26 Bookplate B4
27 Brodburger D6
Lilotang .... (see 18)
28 Maple & Clove B6
29 Močan & Green Grout B2
Monster Kitchen & Bar .... (see 23)
30 Morks D6
31 Morning Glory A2
Muse .... (see 19)
32 Otis C6
33 Pomegranate C6
34 Silo Bakery C7
35 Snappers A4
36 Wild Duck D6

⊕ Drinking & Nightlife
Black Market Bar .... (see 31)
Dock .... (see 37)
Joe's Bar .... (see 19)
37 Local Press D6
38 Ona B7
Parlour Wine Room .... (see 31)
39 Public Bar B7

⊕ Entertainment
Palace Electric .... (see 23)
40 Street Theatre A1

⊕ Shopping
Canberra Glassworks .... (see 27)
41 Old Bus Depot Markets D6

budget options in what can be a pricey city. It's a long walk into town, but there's a light-rail stop right out the front.

Alvio Tourist Park   CARAVAN PARK $

(Map p255; ☎02-6247 5466; www.aliviogroup. com.au; 20 Kunzea St, O'Connor; site/d/cabin from $54/125/159; P❋@🐾≋) Hidden in Canberra's bushy fringes, this well-equipped tourist park has a range of tidy cabins in various configurations and an excellent outdoor swimming pool. While it's a fair way out of town, it's on a bus route that heads straight through the heart of Civic and the parliamentary precinct.

Canberra City YHA   HOSTEL $

(Map p262; ☎02-6248 9155; www.yha.com.au; 7 Akuna St; dm $35-41, d with/without bathroom $135/115; ❋@🐾≋) You can't beat the position of this hostel, smack-bang in the city centre, although be warned: it's popular with school groups. Amenities include bike hire, a small indoor pool, a sauna, a kitchen, an outdoor terrace with a BBQ and a cafe.

★East Hotel   HOTEL $$

(Map p260; ☎02-6295 6925; www.easthotel.com. au; 69 Canberra Ave, Kingston; apt from $180; P❋@🐾) Straddling the divide between boutique and business, East offers stylish spaces and smile-inducing extras like free lollies and design magazines for loan. Even the studios have work desks, iPod docks, espresso machines and kitchenettes, and there are one- and two-bedroom suites if you need to spread out. Plus downstairs there's a dining trifecta: Joe's Bar (p267), Agostini's (p264) and Muse (p264).

★University House   HOTEL $$

(Map p260; ☎02-6125 5211; www.unihouse.anu. edu.au; 1 Balmain Cres, Acton; s/tw/d/apt from $126/162/180/200; P❋🐾) This 1950s-era building, with original custom-built furniture, resides in the tree-lined grounds of the Australian National University (ANU) and is favoured by research students, visiting academics and the occasional politician. The spacious rooms and two-bedroom apartments are unadorned but comfortable.

Civic & Braddon

Civic & Braddon

◉ **Sights**
1 Canberra Museum & Art Gallery B3

🛏 **Sleeping**
2 Avenue... B2
3 Canberra City YHA................................ B3
4 Quest... A3

🍴 **Eating**
5 Akiba... B2
6 Baby Su... A3
7 Courgette..A2
8 Cupping Room.. A3
   Doughnut Dept.............................. (see 6)
9 Greasy Monkey......................................B1
10 Lazy Su... B2
11 Les Bistronomes...................................B1
12 Mandalay..B1
   Rye.. (see 10)
13 Selli's.. B3
14 Sweet Bones... B2
15 Terra.. A3
16 Two Before Ten..................................... A3

🍷 **Drinking & Nightlife**
17 88mph A3
18 Bar Rochford.. A3
19 Barrio Collective Coffee......................B1
20 BentSpoke Brewing Co........................B1
21 Cube.. B3
22 Highball Express.................................... A3
23 Hippo Co... B3
24 Hopscotch.. B2
25 Knightsbridge Penthouse................... B2
26 Kyō Coffee Project................................B1
27 Lonsdale Street 7 Roasters B2
28 Molly A3

✪ **Entertainment**
29 Canberra Theatre Centre.................... B3
30 Dendy Canberra.................................... B2

🛍 **Shopping**
31 Bison Home..B1
32 Canberra Centre................................... B3
   Craft ACT...(see 1)

ⓘ **Transport**
33 Greyhound Australia A2
   Jolimont Centre .... (see 33)
   Murrays .... (see 33)

Vibe Canberra Airport   HOTEL **$$**
(Map p255; ☎02-6201 1500; www.vibehotels.com/hotel/canberra-airport; 1 Rogan Pl, Canberra Airport; r from $179; P❋@☎) This slick addition to the city's hotels boasts 191 rooms within walking distance of the airport. At the top end there are apartments with two bedrooms and central lounge area. Other rooms are divided into lower deck (lower levels) and upper deck, but all offer extras such as iPod docks and pod coffee machines.

Hotel Realm   HOTEL **$$**
(Map p260; ☎02-6163 1888; www.hotelrealm.com.au; 18 National Circuit, Barton; d from $160; P❋☎⊠) The luxe standard rooms here have everything you'll need for a comfy weekend break – including plush king-size beds, rainfall showers, flat-screen TVs and coffee-makers. Book in advance via the website to get the best perks, including free parking and buffet breakfast at the Buvette restaurant downstairs, which transforms into a lovely French bistro come lunchtime.

QT Canberra   BOUTIQUE HOTEL **$$**
(Map p262; ☎02-6247 6244; www.qtcanberra.com.au; 1 London Circuit, New Acton; r/ste from $184/259; ❋☎) A playful irreverence towards politics underscores the lobby, and very comfortable rooms are trimmed with cool design touches such as retro postcards

of past Aussie prime ministers. Downstairs the country's political movers and shakers do their finest *House of Cards* impressions in the Capitol Bar & Grill.

Avenue   HOTEL **$$**
(Map p262; ☎02-6246 9500; www.avenuehotel.com.au; 80 Northbourne Ave; r/apt from $144/217; P❋☎) Raw concrete offset by angled glass

provides a striking if somewhat brutal introduction to this large, contemporary hotel. Rooms are spacious and schmick; ask for one facing the central courtyard to avoid the traffic noise. Parking is free if you book directly.

Quest APARTMENT $$

(Map p262; ☑02-6243 2222; www.questapartments.com.au; 28 West Row; apt from $170; P❄✿) These tidy apartments are within easy walking distance of all the bars and restaurants of Civic, Acton and Braddon. Each comes with a comfortable lounge, big TV and modern kitchenette; some have balconies and laundry facilities.

Burbury Hotel HOTEL $$

(Map p260; ☑02-6173 2700; www.burburyhotel.com.au; 1 Burbury Cl, Barton; r/apt from $142/175; P❄✿) This business hotel offers luxe rooms, as well as one- and two-bedroom suites. The decor is neutral and relaxing, and rooms are pleasantly light-filled. Adjacent apartments are excellent for families, and the complex includes impressive Japanese and Chinese restaurants. Guests can use the spa and pool at Hotel Realm across the road.

★ Ovolo Nishi HOTEL $$$

(Map p260; ☑02-6287 6287; www.ovolohotels.com.au/ovolonishi; 25 Edinburgh Ave, New Acton; d $221-356; P❄✿) ✦ This hotel began life as an art project, and it shows, with a spectacular exterior and an equally hip interior. Rooms are quirkily decorated and have all the mod cons, from rain showers to high-tech electronics. The 'atrium' rooms can be a bit dark for some; we prefer the 'sun' side. Book direct for the best deals.

Reception is filled with nooks, crannies and minilibraries, and the Monster Kitchen & Bar (p265) is just as interesting.

★ Hyatt Hotel Canberra HOTEL $$$

(Map p260; ☑02-6270 1234; www.hyatt.com; 120 Commonwealth Ave, Yarralumla; r/ste from $295/690; P❄@✿≋) Spotting visiting heads of state is a popular activity in the foyer of Canberra's most luxurious and historic hotel. More than 200 rooms, well-used meeting spaces and a popular tea lounge mean that a constant stream of visitors passes through the building. Rooms are large and extremely well equipped, and facilities include an indoor pool, spa, sauna and gym.

✖ Eating

For such a small city, Canberra punches well above its weight on the culinary front, with a sophisticated dining scene catering to political wheelers and dealers and locals alike. Established dining hubs include Civic, Kingston and Manuka, while there are good Asian dining spots in Dickson. New Acton, the Kingston foreshore development and Lonsdale St in Braddon are the hippest new areas.

Baby Su ASIAN $

(Map p262; www.baby-su.com.au; cnr No Name Lane, West Row & Alinga St; burgers $12, other mains $15-21; ⊙noon-10pm) Neon lights and diner booths give Baby Su a more casual feel than its big sister Lazy Su (p264) in Braddon, but the same attention to detail presides. Drop in for delicious Asian-inspired burgers, fried chicken and distinctive 'waffle-cut' fries. The Lucky Pack ($20) with a burger, fries, chicken and a soft drink, is particularly good value.

Doughnut Dept BAKERY $

(Map p262; www.thedoughnutdept.com.au; No Name Lane, 2 Alinga St; doughnuts $5; ⊙7.30am-5pm Mon-Thu, to late Fri) Polished concrete and brass accents give this bright cafe a classy, industrial vibe, but we'd come here even if the floor was made of mud – the doughnuts are that good, from rhubarb and pomegranate to tiramisu and cinnamon sugar. There's also a small menu (think granola, toasties), but we all know what we're really here for.

Selli's SANDWICHES $

(Map p262; ☑02-5105 3114; www.sellicatessen.com.au; Shop 5, 88 Bunda St; mains $11-15; ⊙8am-3pm Mon-Thu, to late Sat, 10am-5pm Sun) Black-and-white tiles and neon lights give this American-style diner an air of authenticity, an impression supported by the topping-laden burgers, sandwiches, hot dogs and other mouth-watering dishes that fly out the door at lunch. At breakfast the menu switches to bagels – we like the 'Sunshine', with lemon ricotta, peach slices, blueberries and honey.

Snappers FISH & CHIPS $

(Map p260; ☑02-6273 1784; www.cscc.com.au/snapper; Mariner Pl, Yarralumla; fish & chips $14; ⊙11am-8pm Sep-May, to 3pm Mon-Fri, to 8pm Sat & Sun Jun-Aug) This tasty fish-and-chip shop on the bottom floor of a yacht club does a roaring trade on summer evenings. There is some seating available, but you may want to BYO picnic rug and find your own slice of lake view.

LOCAL KNOWLEDGE

LATE-NIGHT BITES

Canberrans know the best spot for a late-night bite is the big yellow bus of **Mandalay** (Map p262; www.facebook. com/themandalaybus; cnr Lonsdale & Girrawheen Sts, Braddon; dishes $7-10; ☺6pm-late Wed-Sat), which sits in the car park at the top of Lonsdale St. There are no white tablecloths, just superb Burmese curry and waffle fries wolfed down atop milk crates. BYO drinks.

★**Cupping Room**   CAFE **$$**
(Map p262; ☑02-6257 6412; www.thecupping room.com.au; 1 University Ave, Civic; mains $11-25; ☺7am-4pm Mon-Fri, 8am-3pm Sat & Sun; ☑) Queues often form outside this airy corner cafe, drawn by the prospect of Canberra's best coffee and an interesting menu, including great vegetarian and vegan options. The seasonal chia pudding is extraordinary, but if you prefer something a little more familiar, the burgers are equally as delicious. Choose your coffee blend from the tasting notes; we recommend the filter coffee.

★**Highroad**   CAFE **$$**
(Map p255; www.highrd.com.au; cnr Cape & Woolley Sts, Dickson; brunch $11-24, dinner $16-30; ☺7am-4pm Mon-Wed, to late Fri, 8am-late Sat, to 3pm Sun) Opened in 2017, Highroad has quickly found its groove. Locals fill the tables in the spacious corner building from lunch to dinner, supping on speciality-blend coffee in the mornings and local wines as the sun sets. The menu spans the gamut of Mod Oz cafe fare, from French toast to burgers, with a focus on local and seasonal ingredients.

Rye   CAFE **$$**
(Map p262; ☑02-6156 9694; www.ryecafe.com. au; 9 Lonsdale St, Braddon; breakfast $14-17, lunch $7-22; ☺6.30am-4pm) Charming, Scandi-inspired Rye is all blonde wood, bright lights and modish furniture, with a menu to match. Danish *smørrebrød* (open sandwiches on dark rye bread) are a popular choice at lunch, while breakfast options are variations on cafe faves like poached eggs and avocado with Danish feta and broad beans. Great coffee.

★**Lazy Su**   ASIAN **$$**
(Map p262; ☑02-5105 3812; www.lazy-su.com.au; 9 Lonsdale St, Braddon; dishes $12-29; ☺5-11pm Mon, from noon Tue-Thu & Sun, to 1am Fri & Sat)

Lazy Su's playful Asian vibe is obvious as you enter past the wall of lucky cats. You can't go far wrong with the menu, but if you can't decide between the pork-belly *bao-ger* and the yellowfin tuna tataki, opt for the seven-dish 'People's Banquet' ($49 per person).

Terra   AUSTRALIAN **$$**
(Map p262; ☑02-6230 4414; www.terracanberra. com.au; Shop G2, No Name Lane, 40 Marcus Clarke St; mains breakfast & lunch $10-16, dinner $18-30, set menu per person $58; ☺7.30am-4pm Mon-Wed, to late Thu & Fri, 10.30am-late Sat) By day this atmospheric, contemporary space churns out delectable seasonal brunch dishes and fabulous coffee. At night the rotisserie takes centre stage, with six-hour roasted meats alongside innovative sides like fried cauliflower or baked potatoes with miso. The best option, though, is the 'Feed Me' set menu (minimum two people) – trust us, you won't go home hungry.

Akiba   ASIAN **$$**
(Map p262; ☑02-6162 0602; www.akiba.com.au; 40 Bunda St; noodle & rice dishes $10-21, share plates $16-33; ☺11.30am-midnight Sun-Wed, to 2am Thu-Sat) A high-octane vibe pervades this superslick pan-Asian place, fuelled by a lively young crew that effortlessly splashes together cocktails, dispenses food recommendations and juggles orders without breaking a sweat. A raw bar serves delectable sashimi, freshly shucked oysters and zingy ceviche. Salt-and-Sichuan-pepper squid and pork-belly buns are crowd pleasers, and we love the Japanese-style eggplant.

★**Agostini's**   ITALIAN **$$**
(Map p260; ☑02-6178 0048; www.easthotel. com.au/agostinis; 69 Canberra Ave, Kingston; pizzas $21-25, mains from $25; ☺noon-3pm & 5.30pm-late) Wood-fired pizza, rosé on tap and house-made gelato are just some of the charms of this cool, millennial-pink bistro, set in the ground floor of East Hotel (p261). Holidaying families rub shoulders with Canberra's glitterati along the plush, window seating; for a real show, however, request a seat at the bar with a view of the pizza oven. Reservations recommended.

Muse   AUSTRALIAN **$$**
(Map p260; ☑02-6178 0024; www.musecanberra. com.au; 69 Canberra Ave, Kingston; mains breakfast $8-25, lunch $16-38, dinner $24-38; ☺6.30am-3pm Mon-Tue, to 10pm Wed-Fri, from 7am Sat, to noon Sun) This bibliophile restaurant-bookshop on the corner of the East Hotel

(p261) effortlessly juggles its roles. Start with a drink from the Australian-only drinks list then move on to the 'prologues', including seasonal delights such as kingfish sashimi. Larger 'chapter' dishes include a generous sharing plate of spanner crab with garlic chips. Downstairs, a well-curated bookshop makes for a charming post-meal browse.

Morks
THAI **$$**

(Map p260; ☎02-6295 0112; www.morks.com.au; 19 Eastlake Pde, Kingston; mains $18-44; ☺noon-2pm & 6-10pm Wed-Fri & Sun, 6-10pm Tue & Sat) One of our favourite restaurants on the Kingston foreshore, Morks offers a contemporary spin on Thai cuisine, with Chinese and Malay elements added to the mix. Ask for a table outside to watch the passing promenade, and tuck into multiple serves of the starters; the sweet-potato dumplings in Penang curry are staggeringly good.

Morning Glory
CAFE **$$**

(Map p260; ☎02-6257 6464; www.morning-glory. com.au; 2/15 Edinburgh Ave, New Acton; dishes $12-27; ☺6am-3pm; ⊛☎) Nestled in the heart of the New Acton complex, this sprawling cafe has a sleek, contemporary vibe and is a popular coffee stop for local office workers. The menu offers modern cafe dishes with an Asian twist, like black sesame and milk-tea pancake waffles at breakfast, or soba salad with wakame seaweed and enoki mushrooms at lunch.

Monster Kitchen & Bar
MODERN AUSTRALIAN **$$**

(Map p260; ☎02-6287 6287; www.monster kitchen.com.au; Hotel Hotel, 25 Edinburgh Ave, New Acton; breakfast $11-20, shared plates $20-34; ☺6.30am-late; Ⓟ☎) Concealed in the ubercool Nishi Building, Monster is one of Canberra's more versatile dining spots. Hotel guests, New Acton locals and politicians alike check their Instagram feeds over breakfast. Shared plates with a subtle Middle Eastern influence get everyone talking during lunch and dinner. At night it morphs into a bar (and is a good place to overhear political gossip).

Močan & Green Grout
CAFE **$$**

(Map p260; ☎02-6162 2909; www.mocanand greengrout.com; 19 Marcus Clarke St, New Acton; mains breakfast & lunch $10-18, shared plates dinner $18-30; ☺7am-6pm Mon, to 9pm Tue-Sat, 8am-4pm Sun; ☎☑) Often awash with morning sunshine, this sophisticated New Acton cafe with an open kitchen is one of Canberra's best places to start the day.

Free-range-this and local-that feature on the concise seasonal menu.

Greasy Monkey
BURGERS **$$**

(Map p262; ☎02-6174 1401; www.greasys.com.au; 19 Lonsdale St, Braddon; burgers $15-20; ☺11am-late) Don't be put off by the name – the burgers here are fresh, juicy and delicious. Vegetarians will appreciate the portobello mushroom burger, while the sides are also lots of fun, including mozzarella sticks, jalapeño poppers and loaded cheesy fries. Happy hour is from 4pm to 6pm weekdays.

Sweet Bones
VEGAN **$$**

(Map p262; ☎0413 067 890; www.sweetbones company.com; Shop 8, 18 Lonsdale St, Braddon; mains $13-20; ☺8am-4pm Mon-Sat, 8.30am-3pm Sun; ☑) ☑ Cruelty-free does not mean taste-free at this fully vegan cafe that crouches in a humble shopfront just off Lonsdale St. It does a mean all-day breakfast that could include a blueberry-pancake stack or coconut-water porridge. Its egg-free baking has scored awards for the likes of the almond and hazelnut brownie and cinnamon and sugar pretzels.

Mama Dough
PIZZA **$$**

(Map p255; ☎02-6248 0591; www.mamadough. com.au; 2 Wakefield Gardens, Ainslie; pizzas $19-25; ☺5pm-late) These folks do fabulous takeaway pizzas, but if the weather is nice an even better option is to nab a seat under the fairy lights at the handful of outdoor tables (there's no indoor seating). Options range from the 'usuals' (Margherita, hot salami) to the 'unusuals' (bolognese and ricotta or zucchini and speck). Save room for a Nutella calzone for dessert.

Asian Noodle House
ASIAN **$$**

(Map p255; ☎02-6247 6380; www.noodlehouse. net.au; 29 Woolley St, Dickson; mains $14-20; ☺11am-9pm Tue-Sun) A Canberra institution, Dickson's Noodle House is consistently chock-a-block full of converts slurping up its renowned laksa. The decor's nothing to write home about, but never mind: you're here for the food. If laksa is not your thing there are plenty of other options available, with the menu spanning Malaysian, Thai and Lao cuisine. No credit cards.

Brodburger
BURGERS **$$**

(Map p260; ☎02-6162 0793; www.brodburger. com.au; Glassworks Bldg, 11 Wentworth Ave, Kingston; burgers $14-21; ☺noon-3pm & 5.30pm-late Tue-Sat, noon-4pm Sun; ☑) Brodburger started as a lakeside caravan takeaway joint. Now it has a permanent location, but the flame-grilled burgers are as good as ever. Not only is there a good range of meat, fish and vegetarian options, but you even get to pick from four types of cheese for the cheeseburger.

Silo Bakery
BAKERY, CAFE $$

(Map p260; ☑ 02-6260 6060; www.silobakery.com. au; 36 Giles St, Kingston; mains breakfast $9-20, lunch $18-27; ⊗ 7am-4pm Tue-Sat) Top-class sourdough bread, pastries and tarts are perfect breakfast temptations, while an interesting menu of cooked dishes keeps diners happy at lunch. Good coffee and wines by the glass complete the package. Book ahead for lunch.

Bookplate
CAFE $$

(Map p260; ☑ 02-6262 1154; www.bookplate.com. au; National Library of Australia, Parkes Pl West, Parkes; dishes $16-25; ⊗ 7.30am-5pm Mon-Thu, to 4pm Fri, from 9am Sat & Sun; ⊘) In the foyer of the National Library (p258) you'll find Bookplate, an award-winning cafe with a technicolour stained-glass backdrop. It's equally good as a lunch stop – with daily specials including pulled-pork tacos or poke bowls – or just for coffee and cake after a hard day hitting the books. The wine list is also excellent.

★ Pilot
MODERN AUSTRALIAN $$$

(Map p255; ☑ 02-6257 4334; www.pilotrestaurant. com; 5/6 Wakefield Gardens, Ainslie; mains $25-45, set menu per person $90, with paired drinks non-alcoholic/alcoholic $120/150; ⊗ 6pm-late Wed-Sat, noon-3.30pm Sun) Elegant, seasonal dishes are the highlight at this classy fine-dining restaurant in suburban Ainslie. The menu changes daily but features local produce and interesting flavour combinations. À la carte options are available, but for the full experience try the 'prix fixe' tasting menu, available paired with either alcoholic or nonalcoholic beverages. There's also a Sunday 'long lunch' ($60 per person).

★ Courgette
MODERN AUSTRALIAN $$$

(Map p262; ☑ 02-6247 4042; www.courgette. com.au; 54 Marcus Clarke St; 3-course lunch $66, 4-course dinner $88; ⊗ noon-3pm & 6-11pm Mon-Sat) With its crisp white linen, impeccable service and discreet but expensive ambience, Courgette is the kind of place to bring someone you want to impress, like a date, or perhaps the Finnish ambassador. The exacting standards continue with the precisely prepared, exquisitely plated and flavour-laden food.

★ Aubergine
MODERN AUSTRALIAN $$$

(Map p255; ☑ 02-6260 8666; www.aubergine.com. au; 18 Barker St, Griffith; 4-course menu per person $98; ⊗ 6-10pm Mon-Sat) You'll need to travel to the southern suburbs to find Canberra's top-rated restaurant. While the location may be unassuming, the same can't be said for the menu, which is exciting, innovative and seasonally driven. Although only a four-course menu is offered, you can choose between a handful of options for most courses. Service and presentation are assured.

Lilotang
JAPANESE $$$

(Map p260; ☑ 02-6273 1424; www.lilotang.com.au; 1 Burbury Cl, Barton; mains $29-38; ⊗ noon-2.30pm & 6-11pm Tue-Fri, 6-11pm Sat) Artfully strung rope distracts from an industrial-looking ceiling at this upmarket Japanese restaurant in the Burbury Hotel (p263). Highlights include steamed oysters wrapped in beef tataki (seared and thinly sliced beef) and basically anything barbecued on the robata.

Otis
MODERN AUSTRALIAN $$$

(Map p260; ☑ 02-6260 6066; www.thisisotis. com.au; 29 Jardine St, Kingston; mains from $32; ⊗ noon-3pm & 5.30pm-late Tue-Sat) Sophisticated, Mod Oz cuisine is the centrepiece at Otis, with dishes like salted wallaby with vine leaves and macadamias, or roast lamb with celeriac and buckwheat. An elegant ambience, excellent local wine list and killer cocktails round out the experience. Desserts are playful takes on Australian favourites – try the signature lemon-meringue 'magnum'.

Pomegranate
MEDITERRANEAN $$$

(Map p260; ☑ 02-6295 1515; www.pomegranate kingston.com; 31 Giles St, Kingston; mains $19-36; ⊗ noon-2pm & 6pm-late Tue-Sat) Techniques from France combine with the traditions of the eastern Mediterranean, adding finesse to rustic dishes that burst with flavour. Despite the white-linen ambience, the serves are generous and the service is friendly and relaxed.

Wild Duck
SOUTHEAST ASIAN $$$

(Map p260; ☑ 02-6232 7997; www.wild-duck. com.au; 77-78/71 Giles St, Kingston; mains $27-35, banquets per person $49-99; ⊗ noon-2.30pm & 5.30pm-late Mon-Fri, 5.30pm-late Sat) Known as a favourite haunt of parliamentarians, this discreet restaurant impresses for its cuisine and its clientele. Try slow-cooked pork baked

COFFEE CAPITAL

The dense concentration of public servants, politicians, journalists, students and other caffeine hounds in Canberra means you're never very far from a really good brew.

Ona (Map p260; www.onacoffee.com.au; Shop 4, the Lawns, Manuka; ⊙7am-4pm Mon-Fri, 8am-3pm Sat & Sun) Find fabulous filter coffee at this lush cafe on a square in Manuka.

Kyō Coffee Project (Map p262; www.kyocoffeeproject.com; 5/27 Lonsdale St, Braddon; ⊙7am-4pm Tue-Sat, 7.30am-3.30pm Sun) So hip it hurts, this petite cafe in Braddon serves up perfect batch brew.

Local Press (Map p260; ☑02-6162 1422; www.local-press.com.au; 35 Eastlake Pde, Kingston; ⊙7am-3pm Mon-Fri, 8am-5pm Sat & Sun) You'll find this gem on the Kingston Foreshore.

Barrio Collective Coffee (Map p262; www.barriocollective.com; 59/30 Lonsdale St, Braddon; ⊙7am-2pm Mon-Fri, from 8am Sat & Sun, bar 5pm-late Fri) Braddonites sit at the tables here supping smooth espresso all day long.

Two Before Ten (Map p262; www.twobeforeten.com.au; 1 Hobart Pl, Acton; ⊙7am-4pm Mon-Fri, 8am-2pm Sat & Sun) Beans are roasted at their own facility in nearby Aranda.

Maple & Clove (Map p260; ☑02-6162 0777; www.mapleandclove.com.au; 7 Burbury Cl, Barton; ⊙7.30am-3pm Mon-Fri, from 8am Sat & Sun; ☑) We love this great cafe hidden in the Realm hotel precinct in Barton.

Lonsdale Street 7 Roasters (Map p262; www.facebook.com/lonsdalestroasters; 7 Lonsdale St, Braddon; ⊙6.30am-4pm Mon-Fri, from 8am Sat & Sun) An oldie but a goodie.

in lotus leaves or Massaman beef cheek – a Thai-inspired treat that ingeniously balances flavour and spice. The wine list is strong if traditional, with a Grange and Chateauneuf-Du-Pape. Vegetarian options are limited.

Les Bistronomes FRENCH $$$
(Map p262; ☑02-6248 8119; www.lesbistronomes.net; cnr Mort & Elouera Sts, Braddon; mains $31-38; ⊙noon-2pm & 6-9pm Tue-Sat) Wine bottles line the wall and the melodious French language radiates from the kitchen at this excellent little bistro. At $55, the five-course Saturday set lunch is terrific value; expect a succession of perfectly cooked, beautifully presented dishes that will leave you comfortably full without straining your belt.

🍷 Drinking & Nightlife

During the day, most of Canberra's village-like suburban centres are home to at least one excellent cafe perfect for sipping coffee and watching the world go by. In the evenings, though, nightlife tends to be concentrated in Civic and around Lonsdale and Mort Sts in Braddon. New Acton, Kingston and Mankua are also worth a look.

★**Molly** BAR
(Map p262; www.molly.bar; Odgers Lane; ⊙4pm-midnight Mon-Wed, to 2am Thu-Sat, 5pm-late Sun) The doorway to this little gem, hidden away down quiet Odgers Lane,

is illuminated only by a light bulb. It may take some courage to push through the unmarked wooden door, but have faith; inside you'll find an atmospheric 1920s-style speakeasy, with dim lighting, cosy booths and a very impressive whisky selection. Try the cocktails.

★**Bar Rochford** WINE BAR
(Map p262; ☑02-6230 6222; www.barrochford.com; 1st fl, 65 London Circuit; ⊙5pm-late Tue-Thu, 3pm-1am Fri, from 5pm Sat) Bearded barmen concentrate earnestly on their cocktail constructions and wine recommendations at this sophisticated but unstuffy bar in the Melbourne Building. Dress up and hope for a table by one of the big arched windows.

★**Joe's Bar** COCKTAIL BAR
(Map p260; ☑02-6178 0050; www.joesateast.com; 69 Canberra Ave, Kingston; ⊙4pm-late Tue-Sat) Colourful glass and draped metal beads add to the glitzy boho ambience at this attractive Italian wine bar attached to the East Hotel (p261). The extensive cocktail list includes a whole page of speciality gin and tonics, and the bar staff really know their Italian wines, too. Pace yourself with a serve of polenta chips, arancini balls or antipasti.

★**Capital Brewing Co** BREWERY
(Map p255; ☑02-5104 0915; www.capitalbrewing.co; Bldg 3, 1 Dairy Rd, Fyshwick; ⊙11.30am-late)

WORTH A TRIP

CANBERRA DISTRICT WINE REGION

Canberra's wine region produces high-country cool-climate wines, with riesling and shiraz the star performers. Most of the best wineries are actually just across the border in NSW, north of the city.

Heading north on the Barton Highway (A25), turn left near Hall onto Wallaroo Rd to get to **Brindabella Hills Winery** (☑02-6161 9154; www.brindabellahills.com.au; 156 Woodgrove Cl, Wallaroo; ⊙10am-5pm Sat & Sun). Back on the highway continue north and turn off to the right towards Springrange to visit **Wily Trout Vineyard** (☑02-6230 2487; www.wilytrout.com.au; 431 Nanima Rd, Springrange; ⊙9.50am-5pm), home to the popular smokehouse deli-restaurant **Poachers Pantry** (www.poacherspantry.com.au; mains breakfast $18-22, lunch $31-43, platters $18-36; ⊙11.30am-3pm Mon-Fri, from 9.30am Sat & Sun). Further north still there's a cluster of acclaimed wineries near Murrumbateman, including **Eden Road** (☑02-6226 8800; www.edenroadwines.com.au; 3182 Barton Hwy; ⊙11am-4.30pm Wed-Sun), **Clonakilla** (☑02-6227 5877; www.clonakilla.com.au; 3 Crisps Lane; ⊙11am-4pm Mon-Fri, 10am-5pm Sat & Sun), **Helm** (☑02-6227 5953; www.helmwines.com.au; 19 Butts Rd; ⊙10am-5pm Thu-Mon) and **Four Winds** (☑02-6227 0189; www.fourwindsvineyard.com.au; 9 Patemans Lane; ⊙10am-4pm Thu-Mon).

For further options, visit www.canberrawines.com.au.

It's worth seeking out this Fyshwick brewery offering straight-from-the-tap local craft beers in a stylishly fitted-out tap room. Get your bearings with a tasting paddle that includes the popular Coast Ale. Outside, the green is great for kids and dogs (who can sample the nonalcoholic dog brew). Hungry? The original Brodburger (p265) van serves burgers, hot dogs and snacks.

Black Market Bar   COCKTAIL BAR
(Map p260; www.blackmarket.bar; 2 Phillip Law St, New Acton; ⊙4pm-midnight Tue-Wed, to 1am Thu, to 2am Fri & Sat) Descend in the lift to the basement below **Parlour** (Map p260; ☑02-6257 7325; www.parlour.net.au; 16 Kendall Lane; ⊙noon-late) to find Black Market, a dimly lit and atmospheric basement bar with killer cocktails and a speakeasy vibe. It's the perfect spot for a late-evening digestif.

88mph   BAR
(Map p262; www.88mph.bar; 8-10 Hobart Pl, Civic; ⊙6pm-2am Tue-Wed, 4pm-4am Thu-Sat) Party like it's 1985 at 88mph (named for the speed the DeLorean had to reach to time travel in *Back to the Future*). A neon pulsing dance floor, cocktails on tap and a supremely kitsch playlist all combine to wake you up before you go-go. Wear your dancing shoes.

Hopscotch   PUB
(Map p262; ☑02-6107 3030; www.hopscotchbar.com.au; 5 Lonsdale St, Braddon; ⊙11am-late) An upmarket pub at the centre of Braddon's growing fine-dining strip. The front beer garden is the place to be on summer nights,

where regular live-music performances add to the atmosphere. A good range of beers on tap, as well as notable whisky and wine lists, complete the picture.

BentSpoke Brewing Co   MICROBREWERY
(Map p262; ☑02-6257 5220; www.bentspokebrewing.com.au; 38 Mort St, Braddon; ⊙11am-midnight) With 16 excellent beers and ciders on tap, BentSpoke is one of Australia's best craft brewers. Sit at the bike-themed bar or relax outside and kick things off with a tasting tray of four beers ($16). Our favourite is the Barley Griffin Ale, subtly tinged with a spicy Belgian yeast. Good pub food, too.

Highball Express   COCKTAIL BAR
(Map p262; www.highballexpress.com.au; Level 1, 82 Alinga St; ⊙4pm-late Tue-Sat) There's no sign, so take a punt and climb the fire escape in the lane behind Smith's Alternative to this louche tropical take on a 1920s Cuban rum bar. The highball cocktails are excellent and often come served with banana chips.

Hippo Co   BAR
(Map p262; ☑02-6247 7555; www.hippoco.com.au; Level 1, 17 Garema Pl; ⊙5pm-late Mon-Thu & Sat, from 4pm Fri) This cosy upstairs lounge-bar is popular with young whisky and cocktail slurpers who file in for Wednesday-night jazz – the turntable rules other evenings. The gin and whisky lists are more than impressive; ask the friendly bartenders for their recommendation.

Old Canberra Inn
PUB

(Map p255; ☑02-6134 6000; www.oldcanberra inn.com.au; 196 Mouat St, Lyneham; ⊙11.30am-10pm Sun-Thu, to late Fri & Sat) Coming and going a few times over the last 160 years, Canberra's oldest pub is once again thriving. Today it pours a changing roster of craft beers in sprawling beer gardens with live local music most weekends. In winter there's a crackling fire and several snug spots.

Public Bar
PUB

(Map p260; ☑02-6161 8808; 1-33 Flinders Way, Griffith; ⊙10am-late Mon-Fri, from 9am Sat & Sun) Hanging ferns and potted plants make this airy corner pub feel more oasis-like than its busy Manuka location would suggest. Street-side tables brim with locals on weekends; stop for a drink on your way to dinner, or linger longer for decent pub meals and pizzas.

Dock
PUB

(Map p260; ☑02-6239 6333; www.thedockking ston.com.au; 7/81 Giles St, Kingston; ⊙11am-late) This popular foreshore pub is packed to the brim with locals during happy hour (5pm to 6pm Monday to Thursday). There's a big screen for sports fans and live music most weekends.

Knightsbridge Penthouse
COCKTAIL BAR

(Map p262; ☑02-6262 6221; www.knightsbridge penthouse.com.au; 34 Mort St, Braddon; ⊙5pm-midnight Tue & Wed, to late Thu-Sat) Just behind the main Braddon strip, this quirky place offers good DJs, excellent cocktails and a mellow ambience. Come on Fridays before 8pm for 'Happy Friday' cheap cocktails ($10) and house wine ($5).

Cube
GAY & LESBIAN

(Map p262; ☑02-6257 1110; www.cubenightclub. com.au; 33 Petrie Plaza; ⊙10pm-late Thu-Sun) Canberra's one and only gay club has been lurking in this basement for practically forever. These days it seems to attract as many straight women as gay men. There are cheap drinks on Thirsty Thursdays; check the website for other events.

☆ Entertainment

Street Theatre
THEATRE

(Map p260; ☑02-6247 1223; www.thestreet.org. au; 15 Childers St, Civic; ⊙box office 10am-3pm Mon-Fri) Canberra's leading independent theatre stages interesting contemporary performances from new and established practitioners.

Canberra Theatre Centre
THEATRE

(Map p262; ☑02-6275 2700; www.canberratheatre centre.com.au; London Circuit, Civic Sq; ⊙box office 9am-5pm Mon-Fri, 10am-2pm Sat) Canberra's live theatre hub hosts all kinds of performances, from theatre to cabaret to comedy. Check online to see what's playing during your visit, or pop into the box office.

Palace Electric
CINEMA

(Map p260; ☑02-6222 4900; www.palacecine mas.com.au; 2 Phillip Law St, New Acton; adult/child $19/13.50; ⊙10am-10pm) A luxe cinema in the Nishi Building that screens mainly art-house and independent films.

Dendy Canberra
CINEMA

(Map p262; ☑02-6221 8900; www.dendy.com.au; 2nd fl, Canberra Centre, 148 Bunda St; adult/child $19/14) An independent and art-house cinema in the Canberra Centre (p270). Tuesday is discount day (all tickets $13).

GIO Stadium Canberra
STADIUM

(Map p255; ☑02-6256 6700; www.giostadium canberra.com.au; Battye St, Bruce) The Canberra Raiders (www.raiders.com.au) is the home-town rugby league side, and in season (from March to September) the team plays here regularly. Also laying tackles at Canberra Stadium is the ACT Brumbies (www. brumbies.com.au) rugby union team, which plays in the international Super Rugby competition (February to August).

🛍 Shopping

Craft ACT
HOMEWARES

(Map p262; ☑02-6262 9993; www.craftact.org.au; 1st fl, North Bldg, 180 London Circuit; ⊙10am-5pm Tue-Fri, noon-4pm Sat Feb-Dec) Part design shop, part museum, this beautiful space showcases art from local craftspeople and stages temporary exhibitions.

★ Bison Home
CERAMICS

(Map p262; ☑02-6128 0788; www.bisonhome. com; 14/27 Lonsdale St, Braddon; ⊙10am-5pm Mon-Fri, to 4pm Sat & Sun) A Braddon outpost of Pialligo-based ceramics label Bison, this aesthetically pleasing shop will have you rethinking every object in your kitchen, from mugs to mixing bowls. Smaller items – like tiny ceramic milk bottles in a rainbow of colours – make lovely souvenirs or gifts.

Canberra Glassworks
ARTS & CRAFTS

(Map p260; ☑02-6260 7005; www.canberra glassworks.com; 11 Wentworth Ave, Kingston; ⊙10am-4pm Wed-Sun) Call in to this converted

Edwardian power station, the young city's oldest public heritage building, to watch glass being blown in the 'hot shop' and to peruse the exquisite results in the adjacent gallery and shop.

Canberra Centre MALL

(Map p262; ☑ 02-6247 5611; www.canberracentre. com.au; Bunda St; ⊙ 9am-5.30pm Mon-Thu, to 9pm Fri, to 5pm Sat, 10am-4pm Sun) Sprawling over several city blocks, this vast shopping centre includes a multiscreen cinema, a food court and department stores, as well as design, fashion and homewares retailers.

Old Bus Depot Markets MARKET

(Map p260; ☑ 02-6295 3331; www.obdm.com.au; 21 Wentworth Ave, Kingston; ⊙ 10am-4pm Sun) A Sunday institution, this bustling market has one hall completely devoted to food and another to crafts. Self-caterers and picnickers will delight in the freshly baked goods, cheese, charcuterie and produce; come at lunch to take full advantage of the 'international' food court, with cuisine from Thailand, Ethiopia, Jordan and the USA, as well as the usual pancakes and coffee.

Capital Region Farmers Market MARKET

(Map p255; www.capitalregionfarmersmarket. com.au; Exhibition Park, off Federal Hwy, Mitchell; ⊙ 7.30am-noon Sat) Stallholders from all over the surrounding region congregate every week at this excellent farmers market, which brings the best of the countryside into the reach of suburban Canberrans. Pick up farm-fresh produce, jams, cheeses, charcuterie, baked goods and more – plan to have breakfast (or an early lunch) at one of the many excellent food and drink stalls in the market.

ℹ Information

Canberra & Region Visitor Centre (Map p260; ☑ 02-6205 0044; www.visitcanberra.com. au; Regatta Point, Barrine Dr, Commonwealth Park; ⊙ 9am-5pm Mon-Fri, to 4pm Sat & Sun) Staff at this exceptionally helpful centre can dispense masses of information and brochures, including the free quarterly *Canberra Events* brochure.

Also rents out collapsible bikes (per 2hr/day adult $20/45, child $15/30).

ℹ Getting There & Away

AIR

Canberra Airport (Map p255; ☑ 02-6275 2222; www.canberraairport.com.au; Terminal Ave, Pialligo) is located within the city itself, only 7km southeast of Civic.

Daily domestic flights service most Australian capital cities and some regional destinations. Qantas (www.qantas.com) flies to/from Adelaide, Brisbane, Melbourne, Perth and Sydney. Virgin Australia (www.virginaustralia.com.au) flies to/from Adelaide, Brisbane, Gold Coast, Melbourne and Sydney. Tigerair Australia (www. tigerair.com.au) also heads to Melbourne, while FlyPelican (www.flypelican.com.au) serves Newcastle and Dubbo.

BUS

The interstate bus terminal is in the centre of Civic at the **Jolimont Centre** (Map p262; 67 Northbourne Ave, Civic; ⊙ 5am-10.30pm), where you'll find booking desks for the major bus companies.

Greyhound Australia (Map p262; ☑ 02-6211 8545; www.greyhound.com.au; 65 Northbourne Ave) Daily coaches to Sydney (from $39, 3½ hours), Albury (from $62, 4½ hours) and Melbourne (from $69, eight hours), along with seasonal buses to the ski resorts.

Murrays (Map p262; ☑ 13 22 51; www.murrays. com.au; 65 Northbourne Ave; ⊙ 3.30am-6pm) Express services to Sydney (from $39, 3½ hours), Wollongong ($49, 3¼ hours), Batemans Bay ($38, 2½ hours), Moruya ($41, 3¼ hours) and Narooma ($49, 4½ hours), as well as the ski fields.

NSW TrainLink (☑ 13 22 32; www.nswtrainlink. info) Coaches depart Canberra Railway Station on the Canberra–Cooma–Merimbula–Eden (daily) and Canberra–Cooma–Jindabyne (three per week) routes.

CAR & MOTORCYCLE

The Hume Hwy connects Sydney and Melbourne, passing 50km north of Canberra. The Federal Hwy runs north to connect with the Hume near Goulburn, and the Barton Hwy (Rte 25) meets the Hume near Yass. To the south, the Monaro Hwy connects Canberra with Cooma.

Minimum journey times to/from Canberra include the following:

Sydney (290km, three hours)
Melbourne (670km, seven hours)
Wollongong (250km, 2½ hours)
Batemans Bay (150km, two hours)

TRAIN

NSW TrainLink (☑ 13 22 32; www.nswtrainlink. info) Services from Sydney ($28, 4¼ hours), Bowral ($17, 2½ hours), Bundanoon ($15, two hours) and Bungendore ($3.50, 40 minutes) pull into Kingston's **Canberra Railway Station** (☑ 13 22 32; Burke Cres, Kingston) three times daily.

V/Line (☑ 1800 800 007; www.vline.com.au) A daily service combines a train from Melbourne to Wodonga with a bus to Canberra (from $67, nine hours), terminating at the Jolimont Centre.

ℹ Getting Around

The bus network, operated by **Transport Canberra** (☑ 13 17 10; www.transport.act.gov.au; single adult/child $5/2.50, day pass $9.60/4.80), will get you to most places of interest in the city. A useful journey planner is available on the website.

Travellers can use the MyWay smart-card system, but if you're only here for a week or so you're better off paying the driver in cash, as a card costs a nonrefundable fee of adult/child $5/2.50. A day pass costs less than two single tickets, so purchase one on your first journey of the day.

What is referred to as the city bus interchange is actually a set of 11 bus stops scattered along Northbourne Ave, Alinga St, East Row and Mort St.

Canberra's new light-rail line from Civic to Gungahlin via Dickson is a 12km route that has 13 stops, including several along Northbourne Ave that will be of use to travellers visiting Braddon and Dickson.

AROUND CANBERRA

There are plenty of opportunities for day trips from Canberra, whether you're seeking bushwalking, cycling or relaxation. To the north of the city you'll find Canberra's wine region, while to the south hilly bushland offers excellent walking and makes a good break from the capital's museums. Just across the border in NSW, 35km east of Canberra, is **Bungendore**, an attractive village with galleries and antique shops aplenty that bustles on weekends but slumbers during the week.

⊙ Sights

⭐**Namadgi National Park** NATIONAL PARK
(☑ 02-6207 2900; www.environment.act.gov.au; Naas Rd, Tharwa; ⊙ visitor centre 9am-4pm) **FREE** Namadgi is the Ngunnawal word for the mountains southwest of Canberra, and this national park includes eight of those peaks higher than 1700m. It offers bushwalking, mountain biking, fishing and horse riding, along with the opportunity to view Aboriginal rock art. Make camping bookings online (per person $6 to $10) or at the visitor centre, 2km south of Tharwa.

Tidbinbilla Nature Reserve NATURE RESERVE
(☑ 02-6205 1233; www.tidbinbilla.act.gov.au; 141 Paddys River Rd, Paddys River; entry per car $13; ⊙ 7.30am-6pm Apr-Nov, to 8pm Oct-Mar, visitor centre 9am-5pm) Less than an hour's drive from Canberra, this nature park is a key habitat for some of Australia's best-known animals: kangaroos, koalas and emus. A predator-protected sanctuary is your best chance to spot these critters in the wild. The breeding program at the park also includes the rare brush-tailed rock wallaby and the colourful corroboree tree frog. The visitor centre offers walks and self-guided exploration.

Lanyon Homestead HISTORIC BUILDING
(☑ 02-6235 5677; www.historicplaces.com.au; Tharwa Dr, Tharwa; adult/child $7/5; ⊙ 10am-4pm Tue-Sun) In 1834, when convicts were sent in to clear this land on the edge of Murrumbidgee River for grazing, this truly was a wild frontier. Now it's a pretty slice of rural landscape, ringed by hills and with a garden that wouldn't be out of place in the Cotswolds. It's well worth the trip 25km south from Canberra to explore the gracious Victorian homestead, outbuildings and flower beds, and to ponder the improbability of it all.

✪ Festivals & Events

Canberra District Wine Week WINE
(www.canberrawines.com.au; ⊙ Apr) The 'week' stretches for 10 days during this harvest festival that features wine tastings, food and tours at wineries all around the Canberra region.

🛌 Sleeping

Old Stone House B&B **$$**
(☑ 02-6238 1888; www.theoldstonehouse.com.au; 41 Molonglo St, Bungendore; r $210-230; P ❋ 🛜) Set behind a large oak tree on Bungendore's main road, this charismatic 1867 granite-block house offers four antique-furnished rooms, all with private bathroom, although one is just across the corridor. Start your day with a three-course breakfast and a wander through the garden.

🛍 Shopping

Bungendore Wood Works Gallery ARTS & CRAFTS
(☑ 02-6238 1682; www.bungendorewoodworks.com.au; 22 Malbon St, Bungendore; ⊙ 9am-5pm) This gallery and shop showcases superb works crafted from Australian timber, as well as changing art exhibitions.

Queensland

07 / POP 5 MILLION

Includes ➡
Brisbane............273
Gold Coast.........312
Noosa.............326
Fraser Island.......352
Airlie Beach........373
The Whitsundays....377
Townsville.........383
Cairns............399
Port Douglas.......427
Cape York
Peninsula..........439
Gulf Savannah.....446
Outback
Queensland........451

Best Places to Eat

➡ Gauge (p289)

➡ Rick Shores (p320)

➡ Sum Yung Guys (p338)

➡ Spirit House (p329)

➡ My Italian Baby (p431)

➡ Ganbaranba (p414)

Best Places to Stay

➡ Ovolo Inchcolm (p284)

➡ Tryp (p285)

➡ Vacy Hall (p309)

➡ Coral Beach Lodge (p429)

➡ 1770 Getaway (p359)

Why Go?

Queensland is Australia writ large: a vast arena of natural wonders anchored by its dynamic subtropical capital, Brisbane. Many of Australia's greatest draws can be found here: the 2000km-long submarine kingdom of the Great Barrier Reef; perfect breaks spilling over boundless beaches; tropical rainforests that have thrived since the deep past; and a civilisation that has existed unbroken for over 50,000 years.

Overall, this geographic behemoth comprises 27 bioregions supporting over 1000 ecosystem-types – a natural diversity unrivalled even in Australia. It's spectacularly fecund in places, providing the exceptional produce that drives wonderful dining scenes in Brisbane, the Gold Coast, the Sunshine Coast and elsewhere. And Queensland is just as fertile culturally: from the non-stop events and world-class galleries of Brisbane to remote co-operatives showcasing contemporary Aboriginal art, there's plenty to feed the soul and spark the imagination.

When to Go
Brisbane

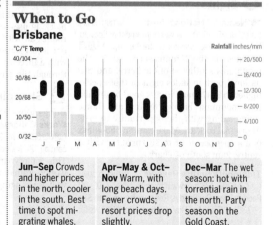

Jun–Sep Crowds and higher prices in the north, cooler in the south. Best time to spot migrating whales.

Apr–May & Oct–Nov Warm, with long beach days. Fewer crowds; resort prices drop slightly.

Dec–Mar The wet season: hot with torrential rain in the north. Party season on the Gold Coast.

BRISBANE

POP 2.5 MILLION

No longer satisfied living in the shadow of Sydney and Melbourne, Brisbane is subverting stereotypes and surprising the critics. Welcome to the new subtropical 'It kid'.

The charms of the country's third city are undeniable: the arts, the cafes, the bars, the weather, the old Queenslander houses, the go-get-'em attitude. But it's the Brisbane River that gives the city its edge. This sinuous channel carves the city into a patchwork of urban villages, each with a distinct style and topography: bohemian, low-lying West End; hip, hilltop Paddington; exclusive, peninsular New Farm; prim, pointy Kangaroo Point. Together they amount to a capital of great diversity, sophistication and charm.

⊙ Sights

Most of Brisbane's major sights lie in the city centre (CBD) and South Bank directly across the river. Behind South Bank, West End offers bohemian street life, while directly northeast of the CBD, Fortitude Valley is Brisbane's nightlife epicentre. East of it lies New Farm, home to the Brisbane Powerhouse arts centre. East of the CBD (and south of the Valley) lie the panoramic cliffs of Kangaroo Point and the antique shops and Gabba sports stadium of Woolloongabba.

⊙ Central Brisbane

★ **City Hall**   LANDMARK

(Map p282; ☑07-3339 0845; www.brisbane.qld.gov.au; King George Sq; ⊙8am-5pm, from 9am Sat & Sun, tours from 10.15am; ⓘ; ⓡCentral) FREE Fronted by a row of sequoia-sized Corinthian columns, this sandstone behemoth was built between 1920 and 1930. The Rolling Stones played their first-ever Australian gig in the building's magnificent auditorium in 1965, itself complete with a 4300-pipe organ, mahogany and blue-gum floors, and offering free concerts at noon every Tuesday from February to November. Free tours of the 85m-high clock tower run every 15 minutes; grab tickets from the excellent on-site Museum of Brisbane.

★ **Museum of Brisbane**   MUSEUM

(Map p282; ☑07-3339 0800; www.museumofbrisbane.com.au; Level 3, Brisbane City Hall, King George Sq; ⊙10am-5pm, to 7pm Fri; ⓘ; ⓡCentral) FREE On the 3rd floor of City Hall, this forward-thinking museum explores historic and modern aspects of Brisbane.

The permanent Perspectives of Brisbane exhibition includes fascinating insights into the city's ancient Indigenous culture, while temporary exhibitions have explored themes as varied as contemporary Brisbane fashion and the relationship between architecture, art, people and place. The result is a snapshot of a metropolis much more complex than you may have expected.

City Botanic Gardens   PARK

(Map p282; www.brisbane.qld.gov.au; Alice St; ⊙24hr; ⓘ; ⓢSouth Bank, ⓡCentral) FREE Originally a collection of food crops planted by convicts in 1825, this is Brisbane's favourite green space. Descending gently from the Queensland University of Technology campus to the river, its manicured lawns, tangled Moreton Bay figs, bunya pines, rainforest and mangroves are a soothing elixir for frazzled urbanites. Grab a complimentary printed guide at the rotunda, from where free one-hour guided tours leave at 11am and 1pm Monday to Saturday. On Sundays, the gardens host the popular Brisbane Riverside Markets (p302).

★ **Old Government House**   HISTORIC BUILDING

(Map p282; ☑07-3138 8005; www.ogh.qut.edu.au; 2 George St; ⊙10am-4pm Sun-Fri, tours by appt 10.30am Tue-Thu; ⓢQUT Gardens Point, ⓡCentral) FREE Queensland's most important heritage building, this 1862 showpiece was designed by estimable government architect Charles Tiffin as a residence for Sir George Bowen, Queensland's first governor. The lavish innards were restored in 2009 and the property now offers free podcast tours and one-hour guided tours; the latter must be booked in advance. The 1st floor houses the **William Robinson Gallery**, dedicated to the Australian artist and home to an impressive collection of his paintings, prints, drawings, sculpture and ceramics.

Parliament House   HISTORIC BUILDING

(Map p282; ☑07-3553 6470; www.parliament.qld.gov.au; cnr Alice & George Sts; ⊙tours non-sitting days 1pm, 2pm, 3pm & 4pm Mon-Fri; ⓢQUT Gardens Point, ⓡCentral) FREE With a roof clad in Mt Isa copper, this lovely blanched-white stone, French Renaissance–style building dates from 1868 and overlooks the City Botanic Gardens. The only way to peek inside is on one of the free 30-minute tours, which leave at the listed times (2pm only when parliament is sitting). Arrive five minutes before tours begin and don't forget to bring photo ID; no need to book.

QUEENSLAND BRISBANE

Queensland Highlights

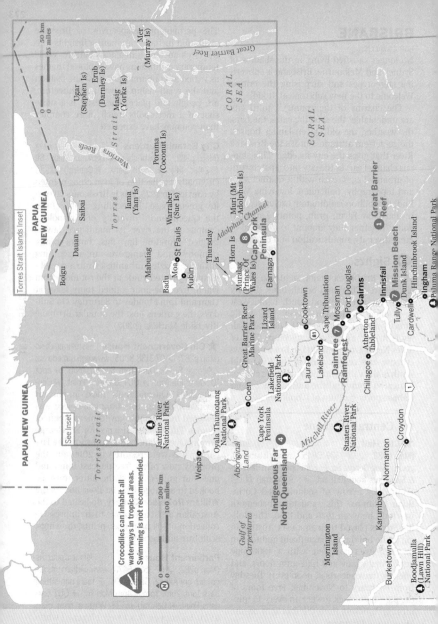

1 Great Barrier Reef
Reef (p405) Floating, rapt, through one of the planet's greatest wonders.

2 Brisbane (p273)
Getting your fill of culture, dining and nightlife in this booming subtropical metropolis.

3 Whitsunday Islands (p377)
Sailing through the warm, peaceful seas of this unrivalled yachties' paradise.

4 Indigenous Far North Queensland
(p442) Letting Australia's first peoples show you around their home of the past 60,000 years.

5 Fraser Island
(p352) Making beach tracks and snapping wild dingoes on the world's largest sand island.

Crocodiles can inhabit all waterways in tropical areas. Swimming is not recommended.

PAPUA NEW GUINEA

Torres Strait

Gulf of Carpentaria

CORAL SEA

Torres Strait Islands Inset

PAPUA NEW GUINEA

Boigu

Dauan
Saibai

Mabuiag

Badu
Moa ● St Pauls
Kubin

Ugar (Stephen Is)
Erub (Darnley Is)
Masig (Yorke Is)

Iama (Yam Is)

Poruma (Coconut Is)

Warraber (Sue Is)

Mer (Murray Is)

CORAL SEA

Warrior Reefs

Torres Strait

Muri (Mt Adolphus Is)
Thursday Is
Horn Is
Murag (Prince Of Wales Is) Cape York Peninsula
Bamaga

Great Barrier Reef

8 Cape York Peninsula
Adolphus Channel

Weipa ●

Jardine River National Park

Aboriginal Land

Ovala Thumotang National Park

Cape York Peninsula

Coen ●

Lakefield National Park

Laura ●
Lakeland ●

Cooktown ●

Great Barrier Reef Marine Park

Lizard Island

Staaten River National Park

Mitchell River

Chillagoe ●

Atherton Tableland

7 Daintree Rainforest
Cape Tribulation
Mossman
Port Douglas
Cairns ●

Innisfail ●

7 Mission Beach
Tully ● Dunk Island
Cardwell ●
Hinchinbrook Island
Ingham ●

Paluma Range National Park

Karumba ●

Croydon ●

Normanton ●

Mornington Island

Burketown ●

Boodjamulla (Lawn Hill) National Park

0   200 km
0   100 miles

0   50 km
0   25 miles

See Inset

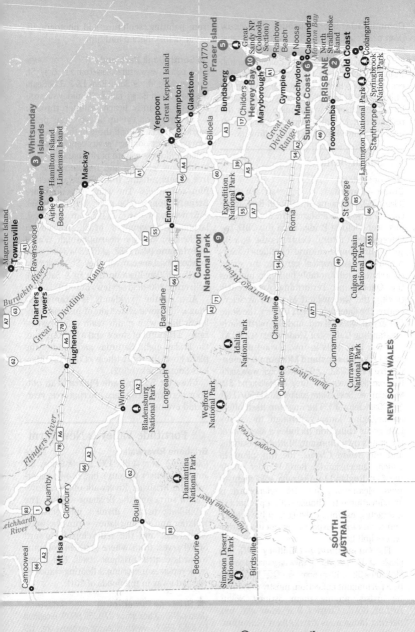

6 Sunshine Coast (p324) Surfing, sun-seeking and socialising in this playground of perpetual summer.

7 Daintree Rainforest (p432) Rambling blissfully through the verdancy of this Unesco-protected rainforest.

8 Cape York Peninsula (p439) Watching for crocs in the waterways of this northwestern wilderness.

9 Carnarvon National Park (p368) Marvelling at ancient rock art in this inland Eden.

10 Whale Watching (p342) Spotting migrating humpbacks in Hervey Bay.

Commissariat Store Museum MUSEUM
(Map p282; ☑ 07-3221 4198; www.commissariat
store.org.au; 115 William St; adult/child $7/4;
⊙ 10am-4pm Tue-Fri; ☒ North Quay, ☒ Central)
Built by convicts in 1829, this former government storehouse is the oldest occupied
building in Brisbane. Inside is an immaculate little museum whose main focus is the
region's convict and colonial history. Don't
miss the wince-inducing convict 'fingers'.

◉ South Bank

★ Queensland
Cultural Centre CULTURAL CENTRE
(Map p282; Melbourne St; ☒ South Bank Terminals 1 & 2, ☒ South Brisbane) On South Bank,
just over Victoria Bridge from the CBD, the
Queensland Cultural Centre is the epicentre of Brisbane's cultural confluence. Surrounded by subtropical gardens, the string
of architecturally notable buildings includes
the Queensland Performing Arts Centre
(p299), the Queensland Museum & Sciencentre, the Queensland Art Gallery, the State
Library of Queensland, and the particularly
outstanding Gallery of Modern Art (GOMA).

If you have kids in tow, a good place to
start is the **Queensland Museum & Sciencentre** (Map p282; ☑ 07-3840 7555; www.south
bank.qm.qld.gov.au; cnr Grey & Melbourne Sts;
Museum free, Sciencentre adult/child $14.50/11.50;
⊙ 9.30am-5pm; ☑). The museum itself offers
an engaging journey through the state's
history, its collection includes a skeleton of
the state's own dinosaur, Muttaburrasaurus,
and the *Avian Cirrus,* the tiny plane in
which Queensland's Bert Hinkler made
the first England-to-Australia solo flight in
1928. Meanwhile, the site's Sciencentre is
an educational fun house with a plethora of
interactive exhibits delving into life science
and technology. Expect long queues during
school holidays.

The **Queensland Art Gallery** (QAG; Map
p282; ☑ 07-3840 7303; www.qagoma.qld.gov.au;
Melbourne St; ⊙ 10am-5pm; ☑) FREE houses a
fine permanent collection, mostly of domestic artists, among them Sydney Nolan,
Arthur Boyd, Charles Blackman and pioneering Indigenous artist Albert Namatjira.

Occupying an award-winning contemporary building by Sydney firm Architectus,
the imposing **Gallery of Modern Art** (GOMA;
Map p282; ☑ 07-3840 7303; www.qagoma.qld.gov.
au; Stanley Pl; ⊙ 10am-5pm; ☑) FREE delivers
world-class exhibitions of both Australian
and international art in a variety of media,
from painting, sculpture and photography
to video, installation and film.

★ South Bank Parklands PARK
(Map p282; www.visitbrisbane.com.au; Grey St;
⊙ dawn-dusk; ☑; ☒ South Bank 1 & 2, 3, ☒ South
Brisbane, South Bank) FREE Should you sun-
bake on a sandy beach, saunter through
a rainforest, or eye-up a Nepalese peace
pagoda? You can do all three in this 17.5-hec-
tare park overlooking the city centre. Its can-
opied walkways lead to performance spaces,
lush lawns, eateries and bars, and regular
free events ranging from fitness classes to
film screenings. The star attractions are
Streets Beach (Map p282; ☑ 07-3156 6366;
⊙ 6am-midnight; ☑) FREE, an artificial,
lagoon-style swimming beach (packed on
weekends); and the near-60m-high **Wheel
of Brisbane** (Map p282; ☑ 07-3844 3464; www.
thewheelofbrisbane.com.au; Grey St; adult/child
$21/15; ⊙ 10am-10pm, to 11pm Fri & Sat; ☑),
delivering 360-degree views of town.

Also in the parklands is **Stanley St
Plaza**, a renovated section of historic Stanley St lined with mainstream cafes, restaurants, a handful of shops and a bustling pub.
On Friday night, Saturday and Sunday, the
plaza hosts the tourist-heavy Collective Markets South Bank (p302).

Close by, **South Bank Piazza** is an outdoor performance space offering free, year-
round events.

◉ Fortitude Valley & New Farm

Brisbane Riverwalk BRIDGE
(Map p292; ☑; ☒ 195, 196, 199, ☒ Sydney St)
Jutting out over the city's big, brown waterway, the Brisbane Riverwalk offers a novel
way of surveying the Brisbane skyline. The
870m-long path – divided into separate
walking and cycling lanes – runs between
New Farm and the redeveloped Howard
St Wharves, from where you can continue
towards central Brisbane itself. The Riverwalk replaces the original floating walkway,
washed away in the floods of 2011.

★ Brisbane Powerhouse ARTS CENTRE
(Map p278; ☑ box office 07-3358 8600, reception
07-3358 8622; www.brisbanepowerhouse.org; 119
Lamington St, New Farm; ⊙ 9am-5pm Mon, to 9pm
Tue-Sun; ☑; ☒ 196, ☒ New Farm Park) On the
eastern flank of New Farm Park stands the
Powerhouse, a once-derelict power station
superbly transformed into a contemporary
arts centre. Its innards pimped with graffiti

remnants, industrial machinery and old electrical transformers-turned-lights, the centre hosts a range of events, including art exhibitions, theatre, live music and comedy. You'll also find two buzzing riverside restaurants. Check the website to see what's on.

Chinatown
AREA
(Map p282; Duncan St, Fortitude Valley; ⓡFortitude Valley) Punctuated by a replica Tang dynasty archway at its western end, Duncan St is Brisbane's rather underwhelming Chinatown. The pedestrianised strip (and the stretch of Ann St between Duncan St and Brunswick St Mall) is home to a handful of Asian restaurants and grocery stores, none of special note. The area is at it most rambunctious during Chinese New Year (www.chinesenewyear.com.au; ⊙Jan/Feb).

⊙ Greater Brisbane

Mt Coot-tha Reserve
NATURE RESERVE
(Map p278; www.brisbane.qld.gov.au; Mt Coot-tha Rd, Mt Coot-tha; ⓐ; ⓠ471) A 15-minute drive or bus ride from the city, this huge bush reserve is topped by 287m Mt Coot-tha,

Brisbane's highest point. On the hillsides you'll find the Brisbane Botanic Gardens (Map p278; ☑07-3403 2535; www.brisbane.qld.gov.au/botanicgardens; ⊙8am-6pm, to 5pm Apr-Aug; ⓐ) FREE, the Sir Thomas Brisbane Planetarium (Map p278; ☑07-3403 2578; www.brisbane.qld.gov.au/planetarium; shows adult/child $16.10/9.80; ⊙10am-4pm Tue-Thu, to 7.30pm Fri, 10.45am-7.30pm Sat, 10.45am-4pm Sun), walking trails and the eye-popping Mt Coot-tha Lookout (Map p278; ☑07-3369 9922; www.brisbanelookout.com; 1012 Sir Samuel Griffith Dr, Mt Coot-tha; ⓐ), the latter offering a bird's-eye view of the city skyline and greater metro area. On a clear day you'll even spot the Moreton Bay islands.

🏃 Activities

CityCycle
CYCLING
(☑1300 229 253; www.citycycle.com.au; access per day/month $2/5; ⊙24hr) To use Brisbane's bike-share, purchase a 24-hour casual pass ($2 per day) on the website or at any of the 150 bike-share stations with credit-card facilities. The first 30 minutes are free, then usage fees apply. Tip: use your free time to

---

BRISBANE FOR CHILDREN

The Gold Coast may have the theme parks, but green, sun-soaked Brisbane is no slouch on the family-fun front, with plenty of diversions, many of them free.

Riverside South Bank offers abundant thrills. It's here that you'll find free, patrolled Streets Beach (p276). Australia's only artificial, inner-city beach, its combo of shallow and deeper water makes it ideal for both young ones and their adult playmates. Within walking distance is the slow-spinning, panoramic Wheel of Brisbane (p276). If it's wet (or too hot), South Bank's Queensland Museum & Sciencentre (p276) stimulates young minds with interactive exhibits, while the free Gallery of Modern Art (p276) comes with its own Children's Art Centre and (from February to November) Toddler Tuesday sessions, which use games and storytelling to explore works from the gallery's collection.

Across the river at City Hall (p273), young ones can get hands-on at the Museum of Brisbane (p273) and climb the building's soaring clock tower. For an even more spectacular view, those aged six and older can scale the city's iconic Story Bridge (Map p282; ☑07-3188 9070; https://storybridgeadventureclimb.com.au; 170 Main St, Kangaroo Point; climb from $119; ⓐ; ⓠ234, ⓢThornton St, Holman St). Flowing below the bridge, the Brisbane River offers numerous diversions, from super-affordable CityCat ferry rides (p280) to Riverlife kayak tours (Map p282; ☑07-3891 5766; www.riverlife.com.au; Naval Stores, Kangaroo Point Cliffs Dve, Kangaroo Point; bike/rollerblade hire per 4hr $39/45, kayaks per 2hr $39; ⊙9am-5pm, to 10pm Fri & Sat; ⓐ; ⓢThornton St). From the city, ferries sail downstream to the Brisbane Powerhouse (p276) arts centre, its year-round program including kids' theatre and workshops. Flanking the centre is New Farm Park (Map p278; www.newfarmpark.com.au; Brunswick St; ⊙24hr; ⓐ; ⓠ195, 196, ⓢNew Farm Park), home to a treehouse-inspired playground.

Further afield, kids can travel through the galaxy at the Sir Thomas Brisbane Planetarium (p277) and schmooze with Australia's cutest marsupial at Lone Pine Koala Sanctuary (☑07-3378 1366; www.koala.net; 708 Jesmond Rd, Fig Tree Pocket; adult/child $36/22; ⊙9am-5pm; ⓐ; ⓠ430).

Greater Brisbane

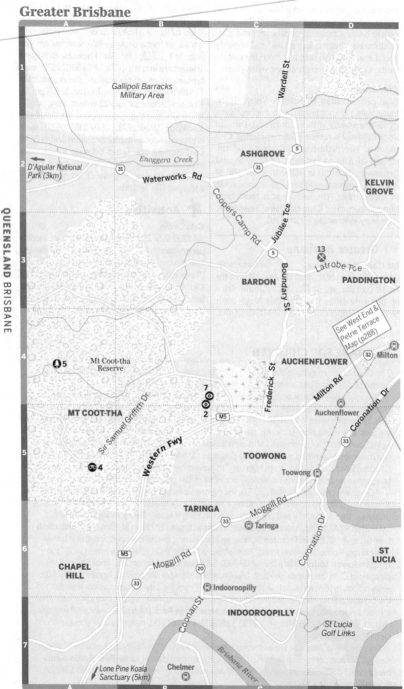

QUEENSLAND BRISBANE

Gallipoli Barracks
Military Area

Enoggera Creek

ASHGROVE

Wardell St

KELVIN
GROVE

D'Aguilar National
Park (3km)

Waterworks Rd

Coopers Camp Rd

Jubilee Tce

13

Latrobe Tce

BARDON

Boundary St

PADDINGTON

See West End &
Petrie Terrace
Map (p288)

Milton

5

AUCHENFLOWER

Frederick St

Milton Rd

Auchenflower

Coronation Dr

Mt Coot-tha
Reserve

MT COOT-THA

Sir Samuel Griffith Dr

7

2

M5

Western Fwy

TOOWONG

Toowong

4

TARINGA

Moggill Rd

33

Taringa

M5

CHAPEL
HILL

Moggill Rd

33

20

Indooroopilly

ST
LUCIA

Coronation Dr

Coonan St

INDOOROOPILLY

St Lucia
Golf Links

Lone Pine Koala
Sanctuary (5km)

Chelmer

Brisbane River

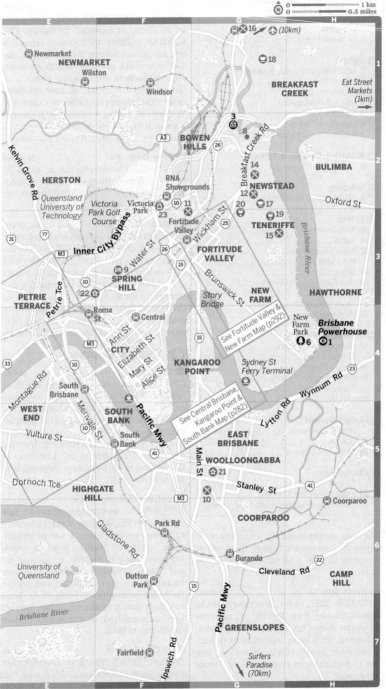

0 — 1 km
0 — 0.5 miles

Newmarket
NEWMARKET
Wilston

Windsor

BREAKFAST CREEK

Eat Street Markets (1km)

18

16 (10km)

BOWEN HILLS

A3

26

3

8

Breakfast Creek Rd

BULIMBA

HERSTON

Queensland University of Technology

Victoria Park Golf Course

Victoria Park

RNA Showgrounds

10 11

23

Fortitude Valley

14

NEWSTEAD

12

20 17

19

TENERIFFE

15

Oxford St

Brisbane River

31

77

M3

Inner City Bypass

9 Water St

SPRING HILL

26

Wickham St

25

FORTITUDE VALLEY

HAWTHORNE

Brunswick St

15

Story Bridge

NEW FARM

New Farm Park

6

Brisbane Powerhouse

1

PETRIE TERRACE

Petrie Tce

10

22

Roma St

Central

Ann St

CITY

Elizabeth St

Mary St

Alice St

33

M3

10

South Brisbane

WEST END

Montague Rd

Merivale St

SOUTH BANK

Pacific Mwy

See Fortitude Valley & New Farm Map (p292)

See Central Brisbane, Kangaroo Point & South Bank Map (p282)

KANGAROO POINT

Sydney St Ferry Terminal

Wynnum Rd

23

Lytton Rd

Vulture St

10

South Bank

41

EAST BRISBANE

Dornoch Tce

HIGHGATE HILL

WOOLLOONGABBA

21

Stanley St

41

Coorparoo

Main St

M3

10

Gladstone Rd

Park Rd

COORPAROO

University of Queensland

Buranda

Cleveland Rd

22

CAMP HILL

Dutton Park

15

Brisbane River

Fairfield

Ipswich Rd

Pacific Mwy

GREENSLOPES

Surfers Paradise (70km)

QUEENSLAND BRISBANE

Greater Brisbane

◎ **Top Sights**
1 Brisbane Powerhouse H4

◎ **Sights**
2 Brisbane Botanic Gardens Mount
     Coot-tha B4
3 Fireworks Gallery G2
4 Mt Coot-tha Lookout A5
5 Mt Coot-tha Reserve A4
6 New Farm Park H4
7 Sir Thomas Brisbane Planetarium.....B4

◎ **Activities, Courses & Tours**
8 Golden Pig G2

◎ **Sleeping**
9 Art Series – The Johnson.....................F3

◎ **Eating**
10 1889 Enoteca G5
11 Banoi F3
12 Betty's Burgers G2
     Mary Mae's....................................(see 1)
13 Naïm..D3
14 New Farm Confectionery G2
     Pearl Cafe ....(see 10)
15 Sourced Grocer G3
16 Vaquero Dining G1

◎ **Drinking & Nightlife**
17 Campos Long Island G2
     Canvas Club ....(see 10)
18 Fonzie Abbott G1
19 Green Beacon Brewing Co G3
     Range Brewing ....(see 14)
20 The Triffid G3

◎ **Entertainment**
     Brisbane Powerhouse ....(see 1)
21 Gabba G5
22 Moonlight Cinema E3

◎ **Shopping**
     Empire Revival ....(see 13)
23 Finders Keepers Markets F2
     Jan Powers Farmers Market ....(see 1)

ride from station to station, swapping bikes as you go. Inconveniently, only about half of the bikes include a helmet (compulsory to wear).

Pinnacle Sports   CLIMBING
(☑ 07-3368 3335; www.pinnaclesports.com.au; abseiling/climbing from $89/99) Climb the Kangaroo Point Cliffs or abseil down them: either way it's a lot of fun! Options include a two-hour sunset abseil, as well as full-day rock-climbing trips to the Glass House Mountains.

Q Academy   MASSAGE
(Map p292; ☑ 1300 204 080; www.qacademy.com.au; 20 Chester St, Newstead; 1hr massage $30; ☐ 393) Q Academy offers one of Brisbane's best bargains: one-hour myotherapy, relaxation or remedial massage for $30. Although the practitioners are massage students at the accredited academy, all have extensive theoretical training and enough experience to leave you feeling a lot lighter. It's a very popular spot, so book online at least a week in advance. Cards only; no cash payments.

Skydive Brisbane   SKYDIVING
(☑ 1300 815 245; www.skydive.com.au; from $279) Offers tandem skydives over Brisbane, landing on the beach in Redcliffe. Skydives are cheapest on weekdays.

Fly Me to the Moon   BALLOONING
(☑ 07-3423 0400; www.brisbanehotairballooning.com.au; adult/child from $329/250) For a bird's-eye view of the hinterland, hit the skies with early-morning hot-air balloon trip. Flights are followed by a Champagne breakfast at a vineyard in the Scenic Rim region west of the Gold Coast. Return transfers to Brisbane are available, with the whole experience from pick-up to drop-off lasting around five hours.

☞ Tours & Courses

★ CityCat   BOATING
(☑ 13 12 30; www.translink.com.au; $4.70; ⊙ 5am-midnight; ⊕) Ditch the car or bus and catch a CityCat ferry along the Brisbane River for a calmer, sometimes breathtaking perspective. Ferries run every 15 to 30 minutes between the Northshore Hamilton terminal northeast of the city to the University of Queensland in the southwest, stopping at 16 terminals en route.

BlackCard Cultural Tours   WALKING
(☑ 073899 8153; www.theblackcard.com.au; walking tours from $55; ⊕) This Aboriginal-owned and -run operator offers a trio of enlightening Indigenous walking tours in central Brisbane. Options include a 1½-hour art and culture themed tour and two three-hour walks: one also focused on art and culture, the other on traditional bush foods. Tours run daily and a minimum of two persons per tour is required; see the website for tour details and to book.

River City Cruises   CRUISE
(Map p282; ☑ 0428 278 473; www.rivercitycruises.com.au; South Bank Parklands Jetty A; adult/child $29/15; ⊕) While you can do the same route

using Brisbane's cheaper commuter ferries, these leisurely cruises include refreshments and informative commentary about Brisbane and its formidable river. Tours depart from South Bank and sail downstream to Newstead before heading back. There are two sailings daily (10.30am and 12.30pm), with the option of a cruise plus lunch at the historic Breakfast Creek Hotel ($60).

Brisbane Greeters TOURS
(Map p282; ☏07-3156 6364; www.brisbane greeters.com.au; Brisbane City Hall, King George Sq; ⊙10am; ☐Central) Free, small-group, multilingual introductory tours of Brizzy with affable volunteers. Book at least three days in advance, either online or by phone. Booking online allows you to opt for a 'Your Choice' tour (must be booked seven days in advance), based on your personal interests and schedule. While not compulsory, an online donation is appreciated.

Golden Pig COOKING
(Map p278; ☏07-3666 0884; www.goldenpig. au; 38 Ross St, Newstead; 4hr class $165; ☐300, 302, 305) In a converted motorcycle warehouse on the edge of Newstead, chefs Katrina and Mark Ryan – both of whom have worked at top Sydney restaurants – run this popular cooking-school and pan-Asian restaurant. Four-hour cooking courses span numerous themes, from sourdough baking and brunch to European, Asian and South American cuisines. See the website for class times and types, which usually run on Mondays and Sundays.

★ Festivals & Events

★**Brisbane Festival** PERFORMING ARTS
(www.brisbanefestival.com.au; ⊙Sep) One of Australia's largest and most diverse arts festivals, running for three weeks in September and featuring an impressive schedule of concerts, plays, dance and fringe events. The festival ends with the spectacular 'Riverfire', an elaborate fireworks show over the Brisbane River.

★**Bigsound Festival** MUSIC
(www.bigsound.org.au; ⊙Sep) Held over four huge nights in September, Australia's premier new-music festival draws buyers, industry experts and fans of fresh Aussie music talent. With X Cargo as its social hub, the fest features around 150 up-and-coming artists playing around 18 venues in Fortitude Valley.

Brisbane International SPORTS
(www.brisbaneinternational.com.au; Queensland Tennis Centre, Tennyson; ⊙Dec-Jan; ☐Yeerong-pilly) Featuring the world's top players, and running over eight days in late December and early January, this pro tennis tournament is a prologue to Melbourne's Grand Slam Australian Open.

Brisbane Street Art Festival ART
(www.bsafest.com.au; ⊙May) The hiss of spray cans underscores this booming two-week celebration, which sees local and international street artists transform city walls into arresting art works. Live mural art aside, the program includes exhibitions, music, theatre, workshops and street-art masterclasses.

Brisbane Comedy Festival COMEDY
(www.briscomfest.com; ⊙Feb-Mar) Feeling blue? Check yourself into this month-long laughfest, usually running from late February to March. Showcasing over 70 comedy acts from Australia and beyond, festival gigs take place at the riverside Brisbane Powerhouse (p299) arts hub as well as at Brisbane City Hall (p273) and the SunPAC performing-arts centre in suburban Sunnybank.

CMC Rocks Queensland MUSIC
(www.cmcrocks.com; ⊙Mar) The biggest country and roots festival in the southern hemisphere takes place over four days in March at Willowbank Raceway in the southwest outskirts of Brisbane. Expect a mix of prolific American acts as well as home-grown country A-listers. Note that tickets usually sell out months in advance.

'Ekka' Royal Queensland Show CULTURAL
(www.ekka.com.au; Brisbane Showgrounds, 600 Gregory Tce, Bowen Hills; ⊙Aug; ♠; ☐370, 375, ☐Exhibition) Country and city collide at this epic 10-day event in August. Head in for fireworks, showbags, theme-park rides, concerts, shearing demonstrations and prize-winning livestock by the truckload. There's also a cooking stage, with demonstrations and the odd celebrity chef.

Brisbane Pride Festival LGBT
(www.brisbanepride.org.au; ⊙Sep) Spread over four weeks in September, Australia's third-largest LGBTIQ+ festival includes the popular Pride March and Fair Day, which sees thousands march along Brunswick St from Fortitude Valley to New Farm Park in a celebration of diversity. Pride's fabulous Queen's Ball takes place in June.

QUEENSLAND BRISBANE

Central Brisbane, Kangaroo Point & South Bank

Brisbane Writers Festival   LITERATURE

(BWF; https://bwf.org.au; ⊘Sep; ⊠South Brisbane) Queensland's premier literary event has been running for over five decades. With events held at the State Library of Queensland, Queensland Art Gallery (p276) and Gallery of Modern Art (p276), the four-day program includes readings, discussions and other thought-provoking events featuring both Australian and international writers and thinkers.

Brisbane International Film Festival   FILM

(https://biff.com.au; ⊘Oct) An 11-day program of Australian and international cinema, with new-release features, documentaries, shorts and retrospectives, as well as panel discussions, conversations and more. Events take places at various venues across the city, including the Australian Cinémathèque at the Gallery of Modern Art (p276) and the Brisbane Powerhouse (p276) in New Farm.

Melt   LGBT

(www.brisbanepowerhouse.org/festivals; Brisbane Powerhouse, 119 Lamington St, New Farm; ⊘Jun/Jul; ⊠196, ⊠New Farm Park) A stimulating celebration of queer culture with 10 days of LGBTIQ+ theatre, cabaret, dance, comedy, circus acts and visual arts. The festival takes place at the Brisbane Powerhouse (p299) arts complex in inner-city New Farm.

🛏 Sleeping

In general, prices aren't seasonal in Brisbane. Rates usually reflect demand, rising midweek as well as during major events and holiday periods.

🛏 Central Brisbane

★ Next   HOTEL $

(Map p282; ☑07-3222 3222; www.snhotels.com/next/brisbane; 72 Queen St; r from $189; ❄🛜🛗; ⊠Central) Right above the Queen St Mall, Next delivers stylish, affordable accommodation. Rooms are generic though svelte and contemporary, with high-tech touchscreen technology and decent beds. The outdoor lap pool flanks a buzzing bar, itself adjacent to a handy traveller lounge (complete with massage chairs and showers) for guests who check in early or want a place to relax before a late flight.

Brisbane City YHA   HOSTEL $

(Map p282; ☑07-3236 1004; www.yha.com.au; 392 Upper Roma St; dm from $32, d with/without bathroom $97/82, f $130; ℗❄@🛜🛗; ⊠Roma St)

Central Brisbane, Kangaroo Point & South Bank

◎ Top Sights
1 City Hall C3
2 Gallery of Modern Art A2
3 Museum of Brisbane C3
4 Old Government House C5
5 Queensland Cultural Centre A3
6 South Bank Parklands A4

◎ Sights
7 Chinatown F1
8 City Botanic Gardens C5
9 Commissariat Store Museum B4
10 Parliament House C5
Queensland Art Gallery ....(see 5)
11 Queensland Museum &
Sciencentre A3
12 Stanley St Plaza A5
13 Wheel of Brisbane A4

◎ Activities, Courses & Tours
14 Brisbane Greeters C3
15 River City Cruises A4
16 Riverlife D5
17 Story Bridge Adventure Climb E4
18 Streets Beach A5

◎ Sleeping
19 Base Brisbane Uptown B2
20 Brisbane City YHA A1
21 Bunk Backpackers F1
22 Emporium Hotel A6
23 Four Points by Sheraton C4
24 Ibis Styles B3
25 Next C3
26 Ovolo Inchcolm D2
27 Westin Brisbane C4

◎ Eating
28 Donna Chang B3
29 Gauge A3
GOMA Restaurant .... (see 2)
30 Greenglass B2
31 Hello Please A3
Longtime .... (see 21)

32 Miel Container C4
33 Stokehouse Q A6
34 Strauss C3
35 Three Blue Ducks B3
36 Urbane D4

◎ Drinking & Nightlife
Birdees ....(see 21)
37 Brooklyn Standard D3
38 Café on the Goodwill Bridge B6
39 Cloakroom Bar D3
40 Coffee Anthology C4
41 Felons Brewing Co F2
42 John Mills Himself C3
43 Little Big House A6
Maker ....(see 29)
Mr Percival's ....(see 41)
44 Proud Henry F1
45 Sea Legs Brewing Co F3
46 Sportsman Hotel D1
47 The Valley Wine Bar F1

◎ Entertainment
48 American Express Openair
Cinemas A4
49 Queensland Performing Arts
Centre A4
50 Riverstage C6
51 South Bank Piazza A4

◎ Shopping
52 Apartment C3
53 Brisbane Riverside Markets C5
Collective Markets South
Bank .... (see 12)
54 Jan Powers Farmers Market B3
55 Noosa Chocolate Factory C3
56 Young Designers Market A5

◎ Information
57 Brisbane Visitor Information &
Booking Centre C3
58 South Bank Visitor Information
Centre A5

A clean, well-run hostel with good-quality facilities, including a rooftop pool. The maximum dorm size is six beds; most have bathrooms. Big on security and kitchen space (lots of fridges), the property is within walking distance of the city centre and major South Bank art galleries. Parking costs $12 per night and is best booked ahead as spots are limited.

★ **Ovolo Inchcolm** BOUTIQUE HOTEL $$
(Map p282; ☎07-3226 8888; https://ovolohotels.com.au/ovoloinchcolm; 73 Wickham Tce; d incl breakfast from $300; ❐❄🤖; ❐Central) Built in the 1920s as doctors' suites, the Inchcolm excels in contrasting heritage features with bold, modern touches, from colour-saturated wallpaper and pop-art rock-star portraits to a cabinet of curiosities in the lobby-cum-bar. Ranging from compact to spacious, rooms are plush, seductively textured and kitted out with iPad Mini, Apple TV, Alexa device, complimentary treats, Nespresso machine and super-sleek bathrooms.

Art Series – the Johnson HOTEL $$
(Map p278; ☎07-3085 7200; www.artseries hotels.com.au/johnson; 477 Boundary St, Spring Hill; r from $179; ❐❄🤖🛗; ❐321) Brisbane's first Art Series hotel is dedicated to abstract artist Michael Johnson, whose big, bold brushstrokes demand attention in the svelte

lobby. Framed works by Johnson also grace the hotel's uncluttered contemporary rooms, each with heavenly AH Beard mattresses, designer lighting and free wi-fi. There's an on-site gym as well as a sleek 50m rooftop pool designed by Olympic gold medallist Michael Klim.

Ibis Styles HOTEL **$$**

(Map p282; ☑07-3337 9000; www.ibisstyles brisbaneelizabeth.com.au; 40 Elizabeth St; d from $119; ✳@🛜; 🅡Central) Smart, contemporary digs at the world's largest Ibis hotel. Multicoloured carpets and striking geometric shapes set a playful tone in the lobby, and while the standard rooms are smallish, all are comfortable, with fantastic mattresses, smart TVs and impressive views.

Westin Brisbane LUXURY HOTEL **$$**

(Map p282; ☑07-3557 8888; www.marriott.com/ hotels/travel/bnewi-the-westin-brisbane; 111 Mary St; d from $280; P✳🛜☀; ☀Eagle St Pier, 🅡Central) The Westin has landed in Brisbane with this brand-new, 229-room property. Featuring specially commissioned photography that celebrates different aspects of the city, the luxe hotel includes Brisbane's first swim-up hotel bar, a fabulous day spa, and a high-tech gym with customised workouts. Muted hues and subtle art-deco accents underscore the rooms, which are graced with flowing white sheets, Google Chromecast TVs, Nespresso machine and intuitive climate control.

🛏 South Bank

Rydges South Bank HOTEL **$**

(Map p288; ☑07-3364 0800; www.rydges. com; 9 Glenelg St, South Brisbane; r from $169; P✳🛜☀; 🅡South Brisbane) This refurbished, 12-floor winner is within walking distance of South Bank Parklands (p276) and major galleries. In rich hues of silver, grey and purple, standard rooms are large and inviting (try to get one facing the city), with sublimely comfortable beds, smart TVs, free wi-fi, motion-sensor air-con and small but modern bathrooms.

Emporium Hotel BOUTIQUE HOTEL **$$$**

(Map p282; ☑07-3556 3333; www.emporium hotels.com.au; 267 Grey St, South Brisbane; d from $450; P✳🛜☀; 🅡South Bank) From the floor-to-ceiling glass shard panels in the lobby to the rooftop's spectacular infinity pool, South Bank's luxe new kid delivers abundant 'wow factor'. The large rooms

feature sublime beds, gilt-framed TVs, and marble bathrooms with 'magic glass' showers offering privacy at the touch of a button. Higher-priced rooms face the river, while cheaper rooms look out over leafy suburbia.

🛏 Fortitude Valley

Tryp BOUTIQUE HOTEL **$**

(Map p292; ☑07-3319 7888; www.trypbrisbane. com; 14-20 Constance St; r from $134; ✳🛜; 🅡Fortitude Valley) Fans of street art will appreciate this hip 65-room place, complete with a small gym, rooftop bar and glass-panelled lift affording views of the graffiti-strewn shaft. Each of the hotel's four floors features work by a different Brisbane street artist, and while standard rooms are small, all are comfy and feature coffee machines, interactive LSP TVs and fabulous marshmallow beds.

Bunk Backpackers HOSTEL **$**

(Map p282; ☑07-3257 3644, 1800 682 865; www. bunkbrisbane.com.au; 11-21 Gipps St; dm/tw/d/ apt from $24/85/95/190; P✳@🛜☀; 🅡Fortitude Valley) This old arts college was reborn as a backpackers over a decade ago – and the party hasn't stopped! It's a huge, five-level place with dozens of rooms (mostly eight-bed dorms), just staggering distance from the Valley nightlife. Facilities include a large communal kitchen, pool and hot tub, and in-house bar, **Birdees** (Map p282; www. katarzyna.com.au/venues/birdees; 608 Ann St; ☺3pm-late Mon-Wed, noon-late Thu-Sun), as well as a few great five-bed apartments. Not for bed-by-10pm slumberers. Parking $12.

★Calile Hotel BOUTIQUE HOTEL **$$**

(Map p292; ☑07-3607 5888; www.thecalilehotel. com; 48 James St; r from $235; 🔲470, 🅡Fortitude Valley) Worldly and sophisticated, the Calile turns many local rivals a shade of green. The statement-making, cabana-flanked pool is the stuff of fashion shoots, while its 175 uncluttered rooms come in on-trend shades of pastel blue, green and pink (the last with poolside balconies). In-room perks include gorgeous king-size beds, Nespresso machines, Bluetooth soundbars and bottled cocktails from Melbourne's cult-status bar, the Everleigh.

Ovolo the Valley BOUTIQUE HOTEL **$$**

(Map p292; ☑07-3253 6999; www.emporium hotel.com.au; 1000 Ann St; d from $280; P✳🛜☀; 🔲300, 302, 305, 306, 322, 🅡Fortitude Valley) With striking pink mesh in the lobby and inflatable flamingos in the rooftop pool,

BRISBANE'S GALLERY SCENE

While the Gallery of Modern Art (p276), aka GOMA, and the Queensland Art Gallery (p276) might steal the show, Brisbane also has a growing array of smaller, private galleries and exhibition spaces where you can mull over both the mainstream and the cutting-edge.

The Pillars Project (Map p288; www.thepillarsproject.com; Merrivale St, South Brisbane; ⊘ 24hr; ⛟; ⬚ 192, 196, 199, 202, ⬚ South Bank Terminals 1 & 2, ⬚ South Brisbane) One of Brisbane's most unexpected art spaces. A series of pillars under the South Brisbane Rail Underpass has been transformed into arresting street-art murals by numerous artists. Among these is the internationally acclaimed, Brisbane-raised Fintan Magee.

Institute of Modern Art (IMA; Map p292; ☑ 07-3252 5750; www.ima.org.au; 420 Brunswick St, Fortitude Valley; ⊘ 11am-6pm Tue-Sat; ⬚ Fortitude Valley) Located in the Judith Wright Centre of Contemporary Arts, this excellent noncommercial gallery has an industrial vibe and regular showings by both local and international names working in media as diverse as installation art, photography and painting.

TW Fine Art (Map p292; ☑ 0437 348 755; www.twfineart.com; 181 Robertson St, Fortitude Valley; ⊘ 10am-5pm Wed-Sat, to 3pm Sun; ⬚ 470, ⬚ Fortitude Valley) Easy-to-miss, this gallery eschews the 'keep it local' mantra for intellectually robust, critically acclaimed contemporary art from around the world. It also runs an innovative online gallery of limited-edition prints, which you can browse at the gallery and have couriered straight to your home.

Fireworks Gallery (Map p278; ☑ 07-3216 1250; www.fireworksgallery.com.au; 9/31 Thompson St, Bowen Hills; ⊘ 10am-6pm Tue-Fri, to 5pm Sat; ⬚ 306, 322, 393) Hidden away in an industrial corner, Fireworks is one of Brisbane's best-loved commercial galleries. With an emphasis on group exhibitions, the space showcases mainly painting and sculpture from emerging and established Australians artists, both Indigenous and non-Indigenous.

Milani (Map p288; ☑ 07-3846 6046; www.milanigallery.com.au; 270 Montague Rd, West End; ⊘ 11am-6pm Tue-Fri, to 5pm Sat; ⬚ 60, 192) **FREE** A well-regarded commercial gallery with rotating exhibitions of cutting-edge, sometimes confronting, contemporary Australian artwork. Many of the artists represented are Brisbane based, making it a good spot to savour the local scene.

Suzanne O'Connell Gallery (Map p292; ☑ 07-3358 5811; https://suzanneoconnellgallery. com; 93 James St, New Farm; ⊘ 11am-4pm Wed-Sat; ⬚ 470) **FREE** A gallery specialising in Indigenous art, with brilliant works from artists all across Australia. Check the website for regular exhibition openings.

Jan Murphy Gallery (Map p292; ☑ 07-3254 1855; www.janmurphygallery.com.au; 486 Brunswick St, New Farm; ⊘ 10am-5pm Tue-Sat; ⬚ 195, 196, 199, ⬚ Fortitude Valley) This stalwart hosts regularly changing exhibitions of contemporary Australian art from both established and emerging creatives. Expect anything from painting and sculpture to photography from names like Heidi Yardley, Fred Fowler, Adam Pyett and William Mackinnon.

it's clear that Ovolo values quirkiness. Its 103, freshly minted rooms spark wide grins with their luxe, playful takes on '70s and '80s chic, including retro bangers on the sound system. Entry-level 'Medium Rooms' are small but comfortable, while 'Valley Suites' impress with huge, hot-tub-fitted bathrooms.

✖ Eating

Brisbane's food scene is flourishing – a fact not lost on the nation's food critics and switched-on gluttons. From Mod Oz degustations to curbside food trucks, the city offers an increasingly competent, confident array of culinary highs. Particularly notable is the growing number of eateries fusing high-end culinary sophistication with an easy, casual vibe that is indelibly Brisbane. Hungry? You should be.

✖ Central Brisbane

Strauss CAFE **$**
(Map p282; ☑ 07-3236 5232; www.straussfd.com; 189 Elizabeth St; dishes $7-17; ⊘ 6.30am-3pm Mon-Fri; ⬚; ⬚ Riverside, Eagle St Pier, ⬚ Central)

Strauss shrugs off its corporate surrounds with low-key, Brooklyn-esque cool and a neighbourly vibe. Head in for pastries and banana bread, or settle in for locavore dishes that include vibrant, creative salads and toasted sandwiches (try the pastrami, sauerkraut, cheese and pickle). The place takes its coffee seriously, with espresso, filtered and bottled cold brew, mainly from local roaster Sundays.

Miel Container
BURGERS $

(Map p282; ☑07-3229 4883; cnr Mary & Albert Sts; burgers from $12.50; ⊙11am-10pm Mon-Thu & Sat, to 11pm Fri; ⬤; ᆬCentral) Miel flips delicious, rustic burgers from its red shipping-container locale. Options span the globe, with everything from tandoori-chicken and mozzarella-cheese burgers to a Korean BBQ bulgogi version that reveals the owner's own roots. If you're undecided on the sides, order wedges with confit-garlic aioli. Seating is limited, though the Botanic Gardens are two very short blocks away.

★Three Blue Ducks
AUSTRALIAN $$

(Map p282; ☑07-3556 8833; www.threeblue ducks.com/brisbane-2; Level 3, W Brisbane, 81 North Quay; breakfast $6-26, lunch & dinner mains $25-60; ⊙6.30am-10pm; 🛜🅿; ᆬNorth Quay, ᆬ) Sydney's cult-status, produce-driven eatery has checked into Brisbane's W hotel, complete with river views. Here, morning coconut chia pudding might come with honeycomb, while the in-house coal pit and wood-fired oven add complexity to dishes like fermented-chilli-glazed roast chicken with corn puree and pickled radicchio. While we love the al fresco balcony, traffic noise makes an indoor table more appealing. Book ahead.

★Greenglass
FRENCH $$

(Map p282; www.facebook.com/greenglass336; 336 George St; mains $18-35; ⊙8am-3pm Mon, to 10pm Tue-Fri; ᆬRoma St) Up a flight of stairs wedged between a discount chemist and a topless bar is this pared-back, loft-style favourite. Here, produce is king, translating into a short, chalk-scribbled menu that might offer risotto with pumpkin stock, bisque and chorizo, or a steak tartare good enough for the pickiest of French palates. The enlightened wine list champions smaller producers. Mornings are limited to coffee only.

Donna Chang
CHINESE $$

(Map p282; ☑07-3243 4888; www.donnachang. com.au; 171 George St; dishes $8-48, banquets $68-118; ⊙noon-3pm & 6-11pm; ᆬNorth Quay, ᆬCentral) Polished, contemporary Chinese in a converted 1920s bank? Count us in. Paste hued and chandelier pimped, Donna Chang peddles superbly nuanced dishes like plump prawn-and-scallop wontons with aged vinegar, coriander and chilli, and wood-fired Moreton Bay bugs with salted duck egg yolk and fermented chilli sauce. Book ahead.

★Urbane
MODERN AUSTRALIAN $$$

(Map p282; ☑07-3229 2271; www.urbanerest aurant.com; 181 Mary St; 5-/7-course menu $120/155; ⊙6-9pm Thu-Sat; 🅿; ᆬRiverside, Eagle St Pier, ᆬCentral) After working in Michelin-starred restaurants in Paris, Brisbane-born chef Andrew Gunn now steers Urbane. Widely considered Brisbane's top restaurant, its tasting menus burst with intrigue and delight, from the pairing of ingredients to the visual presentation. Choose from two tasting menus – omnivore and herbivore – offered as five- or seven-course options. Excellent wine list. Book ahead.

⅍ South Bank

★Hello Please
VIETNAMESE $

(Map p282; http://helloplease.co; 10 Fish Lane, South Brisbane; dishes $13-22; ⊙noon-3pm & 5-9.30pm Tue-Thu, to 10pm Fri & Sat, to 8.30pm Sun; ᆬSouth Brisbane) While it ticks all the It-kid prerequisites – converted shipping container, laneway address, Drapl street-art mural – shaded, outdoor Hello Please is all about punchy, knockout flavours. Vietnamese inspired and Chinese accented, options include spectacular, rice-paper spring rolls jammed with pork, crispy chicken dumplings laced with kimchi and coriander, and beautifully textured salads with combos like duck, plum, pickled vegetables and Thai basil.

Chu the Phat
ASIAN $

(Map p288; ☑07-3255 2075; https://chuthephat. com.au; 109 Melbourne St, South Brisbane; dishes $12-38; ⊙noon-late; 🚌192, 196, 199, 202, ᆬSouth Brisbane) Asian street food gets sexy at sleek, split-level Chu the Phat. Here, broth-bathed dumplings burst with smoked trout, while mung bean pancakes find their X-factor in kimchi caramel. Mains like tea-smoked duck legs with grilled pineapple, candied garlic and ginger attest to the kitchen's innovative, competent approach, while the drinks list includes an appropriate cast of Eastern-inspired cocktails.

QUEENSLAND BRISBANE

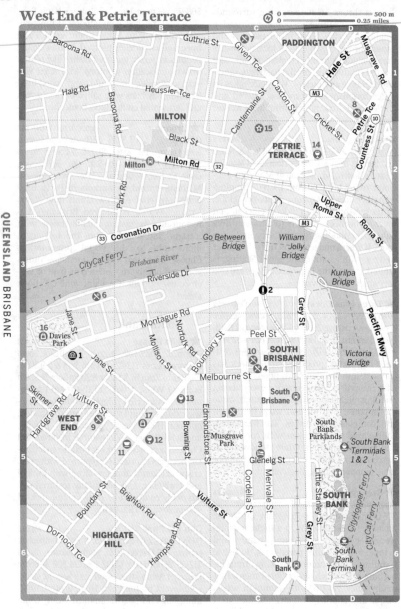

Grown VEGETARIAN $

(Map p288; ☎07-3036 7213; https://grownbne.
com; G03/21 Buchanan St, West End; dishes
$12-16; ⏱7.30am-2.30pm & 5.30-9pm Tue-Sat,
7.30am-2.30pm Sun; 🛜🍴; 🚌60, 192) 🍃 At
the western edge of West End, this luminous, relaxed cafe-restaurant champions
local produce and meat-free dining. Almost
everything is made in-house, including a
very Aussie 'Vegemite' made using black
sesame and tamari. The result is vibrant,
feel-good dishes like pearl couscous with
heirloom cherry tomatoes, refreshing watermelon and fermented pumpkin seeds.

West End & Petrie Terrace

⊚ **Sights**
1 Milani...A4
2 The Pillars Project....................................C3

⊜ **Sleeping**
3 Rydges South Bank................................C5

⊗ **Eating**
4 Chu the Phat...C4
5 Greenhouse Canteen............................C5
6 Grown...A3
7 Kettle & Tin...C1
   Messina..(see 4)
8 Scout...D1
9 Sea Fuel...A5
10 Wandering Cooks...................................C4

⊝ **Drinking & Nightlife**
11 Blackstar Coffee Roasters...................B5
12 Catchment Brewing Co........................B5
13 Cobbler..B4
   La Lune Wine Co..............................(see 4)
14 Lefty's Old Time Music Hall.................D2

⊙ **Entertainment**
15 Suncorp Stadium...................................C2

⊛ **Shopping**
16 Davies Park Market...............................A4
17 Where the Wild Things Are...................B5

Messina   GELATO $

(Map p288; ☑07-3844 0416; https://gelato
messina.com/stores/south-brisbane; 1/109 Melbourne St, South Brisbane; 1/2/3 scoops $5/7/9;
☺noon-10.30pm, to 11.30pm Fri & Sat, to 10pm
Sun; ☑⊛; ☑192, 196, 199, 202, ☒South Brisbane)
Sydney's cult-status artisanal gelateria keeps
Brisbanites cool with its rotating repertoire
of 40 freshly churned flavours. The emphasis is on fresh, natural ingredients, shining
through in options like burnt caramel and
ginger, apple pie, macadamia crunch, and
salted coconut and mango (made using
Queensland mangoes, naturally). Gluten-
free and vegan gelato available.

★ **Gauge**   AUSTRALIAN $$

(Map p282; ☑07-3638 0431; www.gaugebris
bane.com.au; 77 Grey St, South Brisbane; break-
fast & lunch dishes $7-32, dinner 2-/3-courses
$60/78; ☺5-11.45pm Wed-Sat, plus noon-3pm Fri,
8am-2.30pm Sat & Sun; ☑South Bank Terminals 1
& 2, ☒South Brisbane) In a crisp, sparse space
punctuated by black-spun aluminium lamps
and a smashing wine list, clean, contempo-
rary dishes burst with Australian confidence.
Signatures include a provocative 'blood taco'
packed with roasted bone marrow, mush-
room and native thyme, and a brilliant twist
on banana bread – black garlic bread with
burnt vanilla and brown butter.

Greenhouse Canteen   VEGAN $$

(Map p288; ☑07-3724 2761; www.greenhouse
canteen.com; 12/68 Manning St, South Brisbane;
mains $21-23; ☑; ☑192, 196, 199, ☒South Bris-
bane) It's cool to be kind at this plant-based,
gluten-free eatery, a modern, light-filled
space within walking distance of South Bank.
The menu is seasonal, comforting and split

into 'small' and 'big' eats, with bites spanning
everything from Korean rice cakes with sticky
chilli jam and cashew cheese to a gut-bust-
ing beetroot burger that even a carnivore can
appreciate. Wines are suitably organic.

Sea Fuel   FISH & CHIPS $$

(Map p288; ☑07-3844 9473; www.facebook.com/
seafuel; 57 Vulture St, West End; meals $10-26;
☺11.30am-8.30pm, from 7am Sat & Sun; ⊛; ☑199)
🖉 The only thing missing is a beach at Sea
Fuel, one of Brisbane's best fish-and-chip
pedlars. It's a polished, modern spot, with
distressed timber tabletops and blown-up
photos of coastal scenes. The fish is fresh and
sustainably caught in Australian and New
Zealand waters, and the golden chips flaw-
lessly crisp. Alternatives include fresh oysters,
Thai fish cakes and sprightly salads.

★ **Stokehouse Q**   MODERN AUSTRALIAN $$$

(Map p282; ☑07-3020 0600; https://stoke
houseq.com.au; River Quay, Sidon St; mains $37-42;
☺noon-late, from 11am Fri-Sun; ☑South Bank Terminal 3, ☒South Bank) Sophisticated bistro fare
and relaxing river views make this one of
Brisbane's destination restaurants. At crisp,
linen-clad tables, urbanites toast to locally
sourced produce, shining in polished dishes
like Fraser Isle raviolo with roasted pumpkin
or the signature soda-batter fish with triple-
cooked chips and seaweed salt.

GOMA Restaurant   AUSTRALIAN $$$

(Map p282; ☑07-3842 9916; www.qagoma.qld.
gov.au; Gallery of Modern Art, Stanley Pl; mains
$39-48, 5-course tasting menu $110; ☺noon-3pm
Wed-Sun, plus 5.30pm-late Fri & Sat; ☜; ☑South
Bank Terminals 1 & 2, ☒South Brisbane) The Gal-
lery of Modern Art's luminous, fine-dining
restaurant showcases native ingredients in

QUEENSLAND BRISBANE

a sophisticated, contemporary menu that might begin with raw Flinders Island wallaby, progress to 9Dorf Farms chicken with black rice, black vinegar and black garlic, and conclude with a combo of raw honey, white peach, honeycomb and rosemary. Wines focus on boutique Australian winemakers, including those from Queensland's Granite Belt.

✕ Fortitude Valley

★ Happy Boy — CHINESE $

(Map p292; ☑ 0413 246 890; http://happyboy.com. au; East St; dishes $6-27; ⊘ 11.30am-2pm & 5.30-8.30pm Tue-Fri, from 9am Sat & Sun; ⊘; ☒ Fortitude Valley) Fun, loud and always pumping, this places draws all types with its toothsome Chinese, good enough to make your uncle weep. Dive into smashing dishes like twice-cooked dry and sticky beef rib in sweet sauce, Chongqing chilli chicken, and smoky, burnt broccolini with black-bean butter.

★ Nodo — CAFE $

(Map p292; ☑ 07-3852 2230; www.nodo.com.au; 1 Ella St, Newstead; dishes $8-16; ⊘ 7am-3pm; 🛜⊘; ☒ 300, 302, 305, 306, 322, 470) Light-washed Nodo serves up Brisbane's poshest doughnuts, with combos like Valrhona chocolate with beetroot. They're gluten-free, baked (not fried) and sell out quickly (head in early). The rest of the cafe menu is equally good, from sourdough hotcake with cereal-milk semi-freddo, corn-milk custard and cornflake praline, to crushed avocado with pepperberry goat's cheese and freeze-dried blood orange. Great coffee too.

Banoi — VIETNAMESE $

(Map p278; ☑ 07-3607 2877; www.banoi.com.au; 20 King St, Bowen Hills; mains $14-17; ⊘ 11.30am-3pm & 5-9pm Mon-Fri, 11.30am-9pm Sat; ☒ 301, 320, ☒ Fortitude Valley) Located in the up-and-coming King St precinct, casual, contemporary Banoi stands out for its family-style Vietnamese cooking, from pillow-soft bao buns and cold noodle salads to steamed rice pancakes rolled with soy-marinated minced pork. The steamy pho (rice-noodle soup) is superb, made with perfectly chewy noodles and a complex, fragrant broth. Book ahead, especially if dining later in the week.

King Arthur Cafe — MODERN AUSTRALIAN $

(Map p292; ☑ 07-3358 1670; www.kingarthurcafe. com; 164c Arthur St; meals $12-24; ⊘ 7am-2pm, to 3pm Tue-Sat; 🛜⊘; ☒ 470, ☒ Fortitude Valley) In a barrel-vaulted former warehouse off James

St, this neighbourhood favourite serves gorgeous coffee (including batch brew), just-baked goods and creative cafe fare like chilli scramble with camel-milk cheese, fermented chilli and greens, or earthy roasted Jerusalem artichokes with mushrooms, broad beans and fennel puree. Best of all, it's all made using regional produce and ethically sourced meats.

★ Longtime — THAI $$

(Map p282; ☑ 07-3160 3123; www.longtime.com. au; 610 Ann St; mains $15-39; ⊘ 5.30-10pm Tue-Thu & Sun, to 11pm Fri & Sat; ⊘; ☒ Fortitude Valley) Blink and you'll miss the alley leading to this dim, kicking hotspot. The menu is designed for sharing, with a repertoire of Thai-inspired dishes that include a must-try soft-shell-crab bao (steamed bun) with Asian slaw and one of the best papaya salads in town. Reservations are only accepted for 5.30pm, 6pm and 6.30pm sittings, after which it's walk-ins only.

Hônto — JAPANESE $$

(Map p292; ☑ 07-3193 7392; https://honto.com.au; Alden St; larger dishes $18-65; ⊘ 5.30pm-late Mon-Sat; ☒ Fortitude Valey) An unmarked door at the end of an alley ushers you into Hônto's dramatic universe of charred-timber panels and glittering chandeliers. One of Brisbane's hottest restaurants (book ahead or go early in the week), its modern, Japanese-inspired dishes burst with creativity and flavour.

Tinderbox — ITALIAN $$

(Map p292; ☑ 07-3852 3744; www.thetinderbox. com.au; 7/31 James St; pizzas $20-24, mains $26-28; ⊘ 5pm-late Tue-Thu, from noon Fri-Sun; ⊘; ☒ 470, ☒ Fortitude Valley) Straddling a leafy laneway by the Palace Centro cinemas, this smart-casual bistro puts its wood-fired oven to good use, charring pizzas with a style somewhere between doughy Neapolitan and crispy Roman. The Italian theme extends to the starters and mains, including smoked porcini arancini and pan-seared cuttlefish with heritage tomatoes, and 'nduja, a spicy, spreadable pork salami from Calabria.

★ Little Valley — CHINESE $$$

(Map p292; ☑ 0431 619 884; https://little-valley. com.au; 6 Warner St; yum-cha $39, set dinner menus $55-75; ⊘ 5.30-10pm Wed, noon-3pm & 5.30-10pm Thu-Sun; ⊘; ☒ Fortitude Valley) The team behind celebrated Gold Coast eatery Rick Shores is the force behind this buzzing, urbane temple to regional Chinese cuisine. Order an on-point cocktail and snap your chopsticks at well-executed, modern dishes such as cured scallop with spiced pumpkin seed and chilli oil, or duck with fermented plum sauce and sheets of kohlrabi. Book ahead.

New Farm

★ Sourced Grocer
MODERN AUSTRALIAN $

(Map p278; ☑ 07-3852 6734; www.sourcedgrocer. com.au; 11 Florence St, Teneriffe; dishes $8-24; ◷ 7am-3pm, to 4pm Sat, 8am-4pm Sun; ᇦ 199, 393, 470, ᐧ Teneriffe) You can have your coconut tapioca with roasted mandarin puree, pistachio chia seeds and kaffir-lime leaf *and* buy your local Bee One Third honey at Sourced Grocer, an understatedly cool warehouse turned cafe-provedore. Decked out with a shaded front deck, its open kitchen offers seasonal dishes like standout cabbage pancake with crispy fried broccoli, soft egg and shaved goat's-milk cheese.

New Farm Confectionery
SWEETS $

(Map p278; ☑ 07-3139 0964; www.newfarmcon fectionery.com.au; 16 Waterloo St, Newstead; sweets from $3; ◷ 7am-5.30pm Tue-Fri, 8am-4pm Sat; ᇦ; ᇦ 60, ᐧ Teneriffe) For a locavore sugar rush, hit this lauded confectioner. From the macadamia brittle and chocolate-coated vanilla marshmallow to the ruby chocolate bars, all of the products are made using natural, top-tier ingredients. Nostalgic types shouldn't miss the vegan sherbet powder, made with actual freeze-dried fruit and paired with lollipops for a palate-popping dipping.

Betty's Burgers
BURGERS $

(Map p278; ☑ 07-3257 1891; www.bettysburgers. com.au; 4A/63 Skyring Tce, Newstead; burgers $10-16; ◷ 11am-9pm, to 10pm Thu-Sat; ᇦ; ᇦ 60, ᐧ Teneriffe, ᇦ Bowen Hills) Noosa's boutique burger chain is now flipping patties in hip Newstead. Sporting Betty's trademark beach-shack look, its coveted, juicy burgers include a classic cheeseburger, a southern-fried-chicken burger and a flesh-free mushroom burger. Those as body conscious as Newstead's gym boys can order their burger bun-free. That said, only a fool would skimp on Betty's famous concrete (frozen custard drink).

Dicki's
VEGAN $

(Map p292; ☑ 07-3254 2341; www.dickis.com.au; 893 Brunswick St; meals $12-24; ◷ 6am-3pm, to 5pm Sat & Sun; ᇦ ᇦ; ᇦ 195,196,199) Locals love Dicki's, a chilled, vegan cafe run by affable siblings Justine, Lexi, Choy and Diana. Buzziest at breakfast, its fresh, wholesome bites range from warm coconut rice with quinoa pudding, stewed mangoes and toasted coconut to grilled corn cakes with guacamole, pico de gallo and coriander pesto. Wash it down with decent coffee, a craft beer, vino or a classic cocktail.

★ Balfour Kitchen
MODERN AUSTRALIAN $$

(Map p292; ☑ 1300 597 540; https://spicers retreats.com/restaurants/the-balfour-kitchen; Spicers Balfour Hotel, 37 Balfour St; breakfast $12-26, lunch mains $18-26, dinner 2-/3-courses $65/75; ◷ 6.30-11am & noon-2.30pm, also 5.30-9.45pm Tue-Sat; ᇦ 195, 196, 199) Should you

QUEENSLAND BRISBANE

TRUCKS, STALLS & NIGHT MARKETS

When it comes to food trucks and street bites, Brisbane's crush has turned into a full-blown affair. Food vans roam city streets, serving up good-quality fast food, from tacos, ribs and wings to wood-fired pizza, Korean BBQ and vegan burgers. You'll find a list of offerings at www.bnefoodtrucks.com.au, a website that also includes a handy, interactive map showing the current location of food trucks across town.

South Brisbane's constantly evolving Fish Lane is home to **Wandering Cooks** (Map p288; https://wanderingcooks.com.au; cnr Fish Lane & Cordelia St, South Brisbane; lunch dishes $10-22; ◷ hours vary; ᇦ ᇦ; ᇦ 192, 196, 199, 202, ᇦ South Brisbane), an airy warehouse with a rotating roster of food stalls serving anything from authentic Egyptian *ful medames* (spiced, cooked broadbeans) to Mauritian and Indian curries, Sicilian meatballs and sustainably caught local seafood.

Further east along the Brisbane River, in suburban Hamilton, is the hugely popular **Eat Street Northshore** (☑ 1300 328 787; www.eatstreetmarkets.com; 99 MacArthur Ave; admission adult/child $3/free, meals from $10; ◷ 4-10pm Fri & Sat, noon-8pm Sun; ᐧ Bretts Wharf). Easily reached on the CityCat, it's the city's hipsterish take on the night street-food market, with a maze of upcycled shipping containers pumping out everything from freshly shucked oysters to smoky American BBQ and Turkish *gözleme* (flatbreads), all to the sound of live, rocking bands.

Fortitude Valley & New Farm

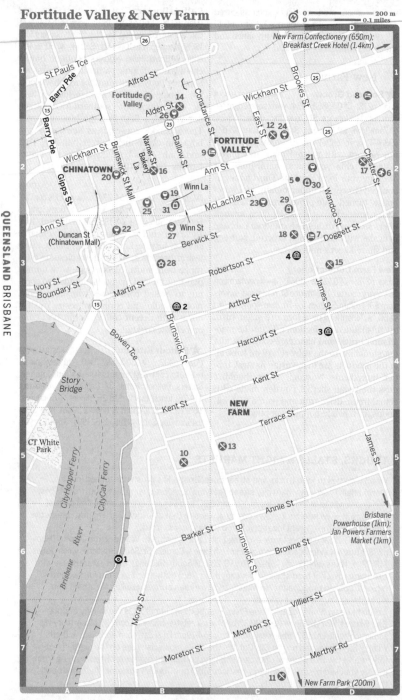

QUEENSLAND BRISBANE

New Farm Confectionery (650m);
Breakfast Creek Hotel (1.4km)

St Pauls Tce
Barry Pde
Barry Pde
Wickham St
Gipps St
CHINATOWN
Ann St
Ivory St
Boundary St

Alfred St
Fortitude Valley
Alden St
Warner St Bakery La
Brunswick St Mall
Ballow St
Constance St
Wickham St
Brookes St
East St
Ann St
Winn La
McLachlan St
Duncan St (Chinatown Mall)
Winn St
Berwick St
Robertson St
Martin St
Arthur St
Brunswick St
Bowen Tce
Harcourt St
Kent St
Story Bridge
CT White Park
CityHopper Ferry
CityCat Ferry
Brisbane River
Kent St
NEW FARM
Terrace St
Annie St
Barker St
Brunswick St
Browne St
Moray St
Moreton St
Moreton St
Villiers St
Merthyr Rd

FORTITUDE VALLEY

Wickham St
East St
Wandoo St
Chester St
Doggett St
James St
James St

Brisbane Powerhouse (1km);
Jan Powers Farmers Market (1km)

New Farm Park (200m)

Fortitude Valley & New Farm

⊙ Sights
1	Brisbane Riverwalk	B6
	Institute of Modern Art	(see 28)
2	Jan Murphy Gallery	B3
3	Suzanne O'Connell Gallery	D4
4	TW Fine Art	C3

⊙ Activities, Courses & Tours
5	James St Cooking School	C2
6	Q Academy	D2

⊜ Sleeping
7	Calile Hotel	D3
8	Ovolo the Valley	D1
9	Tryp	C2

⊗ Eating
10	Balfour Kitchen	B5
11	Dicki's	C7
12	Happy Boy	C2
13	Himalayan Cafe	C5
14	Hôntô	B1
15	King Arthur Cafe	D3
16	Little Valley	B2
17	Nodo	D2
18	Tinderbox	C3

⊙ Drinking & Nightlife
19	Beat MegaClub	B2
20	Beirne Lane	B2
21	City Winery	D2
22	Family	B3
23	Gerard's Bar	C2
24	Mr Chester	C2
25	Savile Row	B2
	Snack Man	(see 12)
26	Wickham Hotel	B1
27	X Cargo	B3

⊙ Entertainment
28	Judith Wright Centre of Contemporary Arts	B3
	Zoo	(see 19)

⊙ Shopping
29	Camilla	C2
	Jess Blak	(see 31)
	Phoebe Paradise	(see 31)
30	Standard Market Company Fruit & Deli	D2
	Tym Guitars	(see 31)
31	Winn Lane	B2

QUEENSLAND BRISBANE

nosh in the dining room, on the verandah or among the frangipani in the courtyard? This polished cafe-restaurant creates a very Queensland conundrum. From breakfast to dinner, prepare to swoon over dishes like French toast croissant with roasted stone fruit, spices and crème fraiche and ocean trout with eggplant, lotus tea, pineapple, turmeric and macadamia. Book ahead.

Himalayan Cafe NEPALI $$
(Map p292; ☑07-3358 4015; 640 Brunswick St; mains $17-29; ⊙5.30pm-late Tue-Sun; ☑; ☐195, 196,199) Awash with prayer flags, this highly atmospheric neighbourhood stalwart pulls in the punters with its authentic Tibetan and Nepalese dishes, from *phali* (oven-baked savoury pastries) to tender *fhaiya deakau* (diced lamb with vegetables, coconut milk, sour cream and spices). Some dishes impress more than others; the goat curry is a hit. Vegetarian, vegan and gluten-free options available.

Mary Mae's SOUTHERN US $$
(Map p278; ☑07-3358 5464; www.marymaes. com.au; Brisbane Powerhouse, 119 Lamington St; brunch dishes $12-17, mains $20-35; ⊙8.30am-8.30pm Mon-Thu, to 11pm Fri & Sat, to 7.30pm Sun; ☑; ☐195, 196, ☐New Farm Park) Squint and the Brisbane River becomes the Mississippi at this airy waterfront eatery. Pine

for NOLA over lighter versions of buttermilk fried chicken, poutine and oyster po' boy sliders, or start the day French-style with smoked-salmon tartine. Larger sharing plates include a seafood platter, while Saturday's four-course brunch ($45; bookings required) has the optional add-on of bottomless bubbles or Bloody Marys.

🗡 Kangaroo Point & Woolloongabba

Pearl Cafe CAFE $$
(Map p278; ☑07-3392 3300; www.facebook.com/ pearl.cafe.brisbane; 28 Logan Rd, Woolloongabba; breakfast $9-26, lunch mains $26-39; ⊙7am-3pm Tue & Sun, to 10pm Wed-Sat; ☐174,175,204) Pearl is one of Brisbane's best-loved weekend brunch spots. There are freshly baked cakes on the counter, a sophisticated selection of spirits on the shelf, and beautiful cafe fare on the menu. Snub the underwhelming avocado on corn bread for more inspiring options, which might include squid-ink risotto with pan-seared scallops. Sandwiches are chunky and generously filled.

★1889 Enoteca ITALIAN $$$
(Map p278; ☑07-3392 4315; www.1889enoteca. com.au; 10-12 Logan Rd, Woolloongabba; pasta $25-45, mains $32-55; ⊙noon-2.30pm & 6-10pm

Tue-Fri, 6-10pm Sat, noon-2.30pm Sun; 🚈174, 175, 204) Italian purists rightfully adore this moody, sophisticated bistro and wine shop, where pasta is *not* served with a spoon (unless requested) and a Roman-centric menu delivers seductive dishes such as fried zucchini flowers stuffed with mozzarella and anchovies, or pasta with *guanciale* (cured pork jowl), chilli, pecorino and a rich tomato sauce. Superlative wines include drops from lauded, smaller Italian producers.

✖ Greater Brisbane

Scout
CAFE **$**

(Map p288; 📞07-3367 2171; www.scoutcafe.com. au; 190 Petrie Tce, Petrie Terrace; meals $15-25; ⊙7am-3.30pm; 🖘🖉; 🚈379, 380, 381) This vintage neighbourhood shopfront was vacant for 17 years before Scout showed up and started selling bagels. The vibe is affable and creative, with gorgeous, all-day brunch options like cheeky French brioche toast with cinnamon baked apple and butterscotch sauce and a vegan bagel stuffed with roasted vegetables and onion jam. Great smoothies, juices and coffee too.

★ Vaquero Dining
AUSTRALIAN **$$**

(Map p278; 📞07-3862 3606; www.vaquerodining. com.au; 344 Sandgate Rd, Albion; mains $18-35; ⊙11.30am-11pm Tue-Thu, to midnight Fri & Sat; 🚈306, 322, 🚈Albion) Hidden behind its own boutique butchery, Vaquero Dining has three obsessions: local produce, pickling and charcoal cooking. Expect beautifully executed dishes like coal-fired octopus with baba ganoush, pickled garlic and smoked almonds, or Brisbane Valley quail with morcilla (blood sausage), burnt grapes and fromage blanc. A great-value lunch special ($25) – including a main and glass of wine or beer – is available Thursday to Saturday.

★ Naïm
MIDDLE EASTERN **$$**

(Map p278; 📞07-3172 1655; www.naimrestaurant. com.au; 14 Collingwood St, Paddington; dishes $18-35; ⊙8am-9pm Tue-Fri, from 7.30am Sat & Sun; 🖘🖉🖦; 🚈375) Cafe-style Naïm wins on many levels: affable staff, laid-back vibe, verdant views from the backroom and – most importantly – fresh, gorgeous dishes inspired by the Middle East. Swoon over beautiful *kusheri* (cinnamon-spiced rice with lentils, chickpeas, spiced tomato sauce, beetroot tahini and barberries) or *bastilla* (Moroccan filo-pastry pie filled with spiced roasted mushrooms, served with

caramelised almonds, pickled beetroot and dill yogurt).

Kettle & Tin
CAFE **$$**

(Map p288; 📞07-3369 3778; www.kettleandtin. com.au; 215 Given Tce, Paddington; mains $18-32; ⊙7am-3pm Mon & Tue, to 10pm Wed-Sat, to 7pm Sun; 🚈375) Behind its picket fence, homey Kettle & Tin serves up tasty cafe grub. Breakfast standards like smashed avo share the spotlight with less ubiquitous offerings, from Vietnamese-style crepes to ginger beef-cheek ramen. East also meets West on the lunch menu, which sees clean, green salads schmoozing with burgers, pastas and beef short ribs with an Asian BBQ sauce.

🍷 Drinking & Nightlife

From a booming microbrewery scene to serious new wine bars focused on artisanal winemakers and interesting varietals, Brisbane's drinking scene has grown up significantly in recent years. The city's live-music scene is also booming, with cult-status venues like Newstead's The Triffid and the Valley's new Fortitude Music Hall (opening mid-2019) serving up impressive independent talent, both homegrown and touring. Tip: always carry photo ID.

🍸 Central Brisbane

★ Felons Brewing Co
MICROBREWERY

(Map p282; 📞07-3188 9090; https://felons brewingco.com.au; Howard Smith Wharves, 5 Boundary St; ⊙11am-late; 🖘; 🚢Riverside, 🚈Central) The long timber deck at this sprawling, polished microbrewery – part of the Howard Street Wharves redevelopment – offers a knockout panorama of the river and Brisbane skyline. Drink in the view while knocking back Felons' easy-drinking pale ale, lager, IPA, or the cider made using local apples from Stanthorpe.

★ Cloakroom Bar
COCKTAIL BAR

(Map p282; 📞07-3210 1515; www.cloakroombar. co; 215 Elizabeth St; ⊙5pm-late Tue-Sat; 🚢Eagle St Pier, 🚈Central) You'll need to head down a side alley, up a fire escape and through an unmarked door to access this cocktail lounge, an intimate, grown-up affair complete with candlelit outdoor deck. There's no drinks list – just competent barkeeps who will gauge your flavour preferences and take it from there. Whatever the result, you can expect flawless, utterly drinkable revelation.

FLINDERS PEAK WINERY

This unassuming **winery** (🖉 0434 031 165; www.flinderspeakwinery.com.au; 1544-1580 Ipswich Boonah Rd, Peak Crossing; ⊙ cellar door noon-6pm Fri, to 4pm Sun) and craft distillery, around 60km southwest of Brisbane city, is home to a distinctly savoury shiraz. It's also making waves for its small-batch spirits, among them a shiraz-base gin vapour-infused with turmeric, cinnamon, clove, nutmeg, rose petals and nasturtium. Weekday distillery tours ($20; 45 minutes) should be booked a week in advance by phone or email.

The small cellar door offers wines by the glass, cocktails and generous grazing plates ($25), best enjoyed on the back patio, which comes with views of the beautiful Teviot Range.

Mr Percival's   BAR
(Map p282; www.mrpercivals.com.au; Howard Smith Wharves, 5 Boundary St; ⊙ 11am-late; 🖘; 🖻 Riverside, 🖫 Central) While the pool-boy-cute barkeeps and caviar service might scream Hamptons, the spectacular skyline view from the outdoor deck confirms otherwise. Jutting out over the Brisbane River, this breezy, pastel-hued bar is the poshest place to drink at Howard Street Wharves, pouring cocktails, spritzes, boutique wines and craft beers.

Café on the Goodwill Bridge   COFFEE
(Brendan's Café; Map p282; 🖉 0434 640 556; www.cafeonthegoodwillbridge.com.au; Goodwill Bridge; ⊙ 5am-2.30pm Mon-Sat, 5.30pm-6pm Sun; 🖫 South Bank) While the coffee at this outdoor kiosk – right on car-free Goodwill Bridge – is perfectly drinkable, it's the commanding river-and-skyline view that really makes it worth a stop. It's especially popular with early-morning cyclists and runners, here before the mid-morning heat kicks in.

Brooklyn Standard   BAR
(Map p282; 🖉 07-3221 1604; www.facebook.com/brooklynstandardbar; Eagle Lane; ⊙ 4pm-late Mon-Fri, from 6pm Sat; 🖻 Riverside, 🖫 Central) The red neon sign sets the tone: 'If the music is too loud, you are too old'. Loud, nightly live tunes is what you get at this rocking cellar bar, decked out in NYC paraphernalia, a 1940s shoe-polish dispenser and murals by local artist Dan Farmer. Slurp Brooklyn lager, Chicago root beer or a classic cocktail (either way, the pretzels are on the house).

John Mills Himself   CAFE, BAR
(Map p282; 🖉 bar 0421 959 865, cafe 0434 064 349; www.johnmillshimself.com.au; 40 Charlotte St; ⊙ cafe 6.30am-3.30pm Mon-Fri, bar 4-10pm Tue-Thu, to midnight Fri; 🖫 Central) Tiny John Mills transforms from daytime coffee shop to evening cocktail den. The latter pours outstanding

Australian artisanal spirits and local craft beers flow from six taps, while a very short wine list champions Queensland's Granite Belt. The space is accessible from both Charlotte St and an alley off Elizabeth St.

Coffee Anthology   CAFE
(Map p282; 🖉 07-3210 1881; www.facebook.com/coffeeanthology; 126 Margaret St; ⊙ 7am-3.30pm Mon-Fri, 7.30am-noon Sat; 🖘; 🖫 Central) Coffee Anthology brews a rotating selection of specialist blends from A-list Aussie roasters like Melbourne's Proud Mary and Disciple (take-home bags available). It's a contemporary, semi-al fresco space, also serving high-quality, creative breakfast and lunch dishes that range from thyme-roasted mushrooms with lentil butter and Grana Padano cheese, to noodles with peas, broad beans, chicken breast, black garlic and coffee emulsion.

🍷 South Bank

★ La Lune Wine Co   WINE BAR
(Map p288; 🖉 07-3255 0010; http://lalunewineco.com.au; 3/109 Melbourne St, entry on Fish Lane, South Brisbane; ⊙ 4pm-late Tue & Wed, from noon Thu-Sun; 🚌 192, 196, 199, 202, 🖫 South Brisbane) A favourite among local oenophiles, petite La Lune channels Europe with its intimate, moody vibe and enlightened wine list. Slip in and quaff anything from Victorian pinot noir and South Australian nebbiolo to classic Bourgogne blanc from France. Boutique charcuterie, cheeses and raw and cured bites including oysters, ceviche and crudo make for perfect grazing. Entry is from Fish Lane.

★ Maker   COCKTAIL BAR
(Map p282; 🖉 0437 338 072; 9 Fish Lane, South Brisbane; ⊙ 4pm-midnight Tue-Sun; 🖻 South Bank Terminals 1 & 2, 🖫 South Brisbane) Intimate, black-clad and spliced by a sexy brass bar, Maker crafts seasonal cocktails using house liqueurs, out-of-the-box ingredients and

a splash of whimsy. Here, classic Negronis are made with house-infused vermouth, while gin and tonics get Australian with native quandong and finger lime. Also has a selection of boutique wines by the glass and beautiful bar bites.

Little Big House   BAR
(Map p282; ✆07-3727 3999; www.littlebighouse.com.au; 271 Grey St, South Brisbane; ⊙11am-midnight, to 2am Fri & Sat; 🛜💺; 🚊South Bank) Celebrity chef Matt Moran is behind this upbeat, sprawling venue, a history-packed Queenslander with wrap-around verandah, lush foliage and festive festoon lighting. While the building may be old, the vibe is young and easy, with tropical retro cocktails, alcoholic slushies and shared punches on the drinks list. Booze-friendly bites range from chicken-parma spring rolls and jerk-spiced chicken wings to burgers (vegan burger available).

Cobbler   BAR
(Map p288; www.cobblerbar.com; 7 Browning St, West End; ⊙5pm-1am Mon, 4pm-1am Tue-Thu & Sun, 4pm-2am Fri & Sat; 🚌60, 192, 196, 198, 199, 🚊South Brisbane) Whisky fans will weep tears of joy at the sight of Cobbler's imposing bar, graced with over 400 whiskies from around the globe. Channelling a speakeasy vibe, this dimly lit West End wonder also pours a cognoscenti selection of rums, tequilas and liqueurs, not to mention a crafty selection of cocktails that add modern twists to the classics. Bottoms up!

Catchment Brewing Co   BREWERY
(Map p288; ✆07-3846 1701; www.catchment brewingco.com.au; 150 Boundary St, West End; ⊙4-10pm Mon-Thu, noon-1am Fri & Sat, noon-10pm Sun; 🚌199) A hip, two-level microbrewery with notable, seasonal nosh and live music in the courtyard. House brews include Pale Select, a nod to the signature beer of the defunct West End Brewery, with other libations including ciders and boutique wines. The best seats in the house are the two, tiny, 1st-floor balconies, serving up afternoon sun and Boundary St views.

Blackstar Coffee Roasters   CAFE
(Map p288; www.blackstarcoffee.com.au; 44 Thomas St, West End; ⊙7am-5pm; 🛜; 🚌199) One of Brisbane's top coffee roasters, laid-back Blackstar is never short of West End bookworms, hipsters and hippies. Kick back and slurp a single-origin espresso or cool down with a bottle of cold-pressed coffee.

Food options (dishes $8 to $17.50) include granola with coconut yogurt, vegan French toast, eggs and spanakopita. That said, it's the coffee that really shines here.

🍴 Fortitude Valley

★Beirne Lane   BAR
(Map p292; ✆07-3539 8820; www.beirnelane.co; T11-14/315 Brunswick St; ⊙24hr; 🛜💺; 🚊Fortitude Valey) TC Beirne would approve of this on-point yet democratic gastro-bar, housed in the Irishman's former department store. It's a great all-rounder, serving everything from excellent coffee and wine to craft and mainstream beers, and high-quality nosh. Sip $5 beers, wines and spirits from 4pm to 6pm, book to compete in Tuesday's 'Opinion Trivia' or hone your salsa moves on Wednesdays.

★Savile Row   COCKTAIL BAR
(Map p292; ✆0455 686 968; www.facebook.com/ savilerowfortitudevalley; 677 Ann St; ⊙5pm-3am; 🚊Fortitude Valley) Snug, wood-panelled Savile Row hides its secrets behind an unmarked orange door. This is one of the city's best-stocked cocktail boltholes, with around 750 spirits, including around 500 whiskies from Scotland to India and Taiwan. Cocktails are superb, inspired by a creative flavour combinations and made using cold-pressed juices.

★The Valley Wine Bar   WINE BAR
(Map p282; ✆07-3252 2224; www.thevalleywine bar.com.au; 171 Alfred St; ⊙3-9pm Mon & Tue, noon-11pm Wed-Sat; 🚊Fortitude Valley) While the tinted glass panels, moody lighting and wine-lined walls set an understatedly elegant scene, this intimate, well-versed wine bar is quintessentially Brisbane in its easy, unpretentious attitude. The focus here is on rare varietals and both low-sulphate and bio-dynamic wines from Australia and beyond. Simple, high-quality bites include marinated bush olives, toasties and a good-value cheese and charcuterie platter (from $12).

★Snack Man   BAR
(Map p292; East St, Fortitude Valley; ⊙5pm-late Wed-Sun; 🚊Fortitude Valley) Dark, moody and downright sexy, Snack Man plays little brother to Happy Boy (p290) next door. The focus is on Euro wines, sharp cocktails and beautiful, small-plate dishes that champion regional Chinese cooking. Now, should you wash down those Yunnan-style *su chai jiao* (mushroom dumplings) with a classic

LGBTIQ+ BRISBANE

While Brisbane's LGBTIQ+ scene is significantly smaller than its Sydney and Melbourne counterparts, the city has an out-and-proud queer presence. Newstead and Teneriffe have become residential epicentres for gay men, especially the upwardly mobile and buffed. Across the river, West End remains popular with artier, more alternative LGBTIQ+ folk, while other queer-friendly inner-city neighbourhoods include Fortitude Valley, Bowen Hills, New Farm and Paddington.

In Fortitude Valley, the **Wickham Hotel** (Map p292; ☑ 07-3852 1301; www.thewickham.com.au; 308 Wickham St; ☺ 6.30am-late, from 10am Sat & Sun; ⧁ Fortitude Valley) attracts a mainly mixed crowd these days, though it remains a staunchly queer-friendly pub. The Valley is also home to queer club **Beat MegaClub** (Map p292; ☑ 07-3852 2661; www.thebeatmegaclub.com.au; 677 Ann St; ☺ 8pm-late Mon-Sat, from 5pm Sun; ⧁ Fortitude Valley) and the scenier **Family** (Map p292; ☑ 07-3852 5000; www.thefamily.com.au; 8 McLachlan St; ☺ 9pm-3am Fri-Sun; ⧁ Fortitude Valley); on Sunday the latter hosts 'Fluffy'. Brisbane's biggest gay dance party. Closer to the city centre, Spring Hill's **Sportsman Hotel** (Map p282; ☑ 07-3831 2892; www.sportsmanhotel.com.au; 130 Leichhardt St; ☺ 1pm-1am, to 2.30am Fri & Sat; ⧉ 372, 373, ⧁ Central) is a blue-collar pub with pool tables, drag shows and a rather eclectic crowd.

Major events on Brisbane's queer calendar include the **Queer Film Festival** (www.brisbanepowerhouse.org/festivals/brisbane-queer-film-festival) in March, arts festival Melt (p283) in June/July and the Brisbane Pride Festival (p281) in September.

For current entertainment and events listings, interviews and articles, check out *Q News* (www.qnews.com.au). On air, tune in to *Queer Radio* (9pm to 11pm every Wednesday; www.4zzzfm.org.au), a radio show on 4ZZZ (aka FM102.1). For lesbian news and views, *Dykes on Mykes* precedes it (7pm to 9pm Wednesday).

Americano, a Puglian primitivo or a Beaujolais gamay? Decisions, decisions.

★ X Cargo
BAR

(Map p292; ☑ 07-3180 4783; http://xcargo.com.au; 37-41 McLachlan St; ☺ 7am-10pm, to late Thu-Sun; ☏; ⧁ Fortitude Valley) A virtual village of stacked shopping containers, roof decks and artificial turf, X Cargo is not your usual boozer. It feels more like a sprawling playground for grown-ups, with a trio of bars, American and Latin-inspired street food, a giant pink-flamingo mural, and moody pinks and purples that scream retro Miami. Serves everything from coffee to cocktails.

★ Mr Chester
WINE BAR

(Map p292; www.mrchesterwine.com; 2/850 Ann St, entry via Church St; ☺ 4pm-midnight; ⧁ Fortitude Valley) After years designing interiors for A-list Melbourne restaurants, Luke Reimers headed north to design his own wine bar. The result is casually elegant Mr Chester, whose passion is intriguing, experimental and lesser-known winemakers, many Australian. Let Luke guide you towards your new favourite drop, and pair it with impeccably sourced cheeses, charcuterie or pasta.

★ Gerard's Bar
WINE BAR

(Map p292; ☑ 07-3252 2606; www.gerardsbar.com.au; 13a/23 James St; ☺ 4pm-late Mon-Thu, from noon Fri & Sat; ⧉ 470, ⧁ Fortitude Valley) A stylish, grown-up bar that's one of Brisbane's best. Perch yourself at the polished concrete bar, choose from the sharply curated wine list, and couple with standout bar snacks, including prized Jamón Iberico de Belotta and beautiful cheeses. If you're craving a cocktail, try the signature 'Gerard the Drunk', a medley of vodka, passion fruit, lemon, rose and orange blossom.

City Winery
WINE BAR

(Map p292; ☑ 07-3054 7144; www.citywinery.com.au; 11 Wandoo St; ☺ 10am-late; ⧁ Fortitude Valley) City Winery is Brisbane's first urban microwinery, making vino from varietals grown in different corners of Australia. It's a sleek, industrial space, complete with cellar door and restaurant, the latter serving lunch and dinner from Wednesday to Sunday. In the kitchen is talented chef Travis Crane (formerly of the celebrated Barrelroom), cooking locally sourced produce using a 4m fire pit.

Proud Henry
BAR

(Map p282; ☑ 07-3102 1237; https://proudhenry.com.au; 153 Wickham St; ☺ 4pm-late Tue-Sat,

2-10pm Sun; 🚇 Fortitude Valley) Home to over 250 types of gin (including varieties rarely found in Australia), Proud Henry has every right to call itself a 'ginoteca'. Toast all things botanical with a classic martini or G&T, or push the boat out with a more contemporary gin-based concoction. Oenophiles won't be disappointed either, with a clued-in selection of local and international wines that preference boutique producers.

New Farm

★ The Triffid
BAR
(Map p278; ☑ 07-3171 3001; www.thetriffid.com.au; 7-9 Stratton St, Newstead; ⊘ noon-late Wed-Sun; 🚌 393) Not only does the Triffid have an awesome beer garden (complete with shipping-container bars and a cassette-themed mural honouring Brisbane bands), but it's also one of the city's top live-music venues. Acts span local, Aussie and international talent, playing in a barrel-vaulted WWII hangar with killer acoustics. It's hardly surprising given that the place is owned by former Powderfinger bassist John Collins.

★ Green Beacon Brewing Co
MICROBREWERY
(Map p278; ☑ 07-3252 8393; www.greenbeacon.com.au; 26 Helen St, Teneriffe; ⊘ noon-late; 🤟; 🚌 393, 470, 🚢 Teneriffe) In a cavernous warehouse, Green Beacon brews some of Brisbane's best beers. The liquid beauties ferment in vast stainless-steel vats behind the long bar before flowing through the taps and onto your grateful palate. Choose from five core beers or seasonal specials such as blood-orange IPA.

Campos Long Island
CAFE
(Map p278; ☑ 07-3252 3612; https://campos coffee.com; 18 Longland St, Newstead; ⊘ 6am-5pm, from 7am Sat & Sun; 🤟 🦽; 🚌 60, 393, 470, 🚢 Teneriffe) We love Campos' flagship Brisbane roastery-cafe for numerous reasons, from the spacious, tropical-chic fit out and free wi-fi to the slightly longer opening hours. Mostly, though, we love it for the coffee, sourced directly from the coffee growers and expertly brewed in numerous ways, including espresso style and cold drip.

Range Brewing
MICROBREWERY
(Map p278; ☑ 07-3310 4456; www.rangebrewing.com; 4 Byres St, Newstead; ⊘ 4-10pm Thu, noon-late Fri-Sun; 🚌 60, 🚉 Bowen Hills) High-school mates Gerard Martin and Matt McIver are behind this smart, low-key brewery. There's no core range of regular ales here. Instead,

the boys offer a changing cast of small-batch, out-of-the-box brews that might include a cherry sour ale, hazelnut milk stout, or raspberry and coconut porter. If you're peckish, sourdough pizzas are on standby.

Kangaroo Point & Woolloongabba

Sea Legs Brewing Co
MICROBREWERY
(Map p282; ☑ 0403 430 463; www.sealegs brewing.com.au; 89 Main St, Kangaroo Point; ⊘ noon-10pm, to midnight Fri & Sat; 🚌 234, 🚢 Holman St) What was an old boxing gym in the shadow of the mighty Story Bridge is now Kangaroo Point's first microbrewery. The passion project of five engineering mates, its house range includes ales, a tropical lager and milk stout. Experimental and seasonal brews, as well as guest beers from other local microbreweries, also flow from the taps. Booze-friendly bites include burgers, pizzas and charcuterie.

Canvas Club
COCKTAIL BAR
(Map p278; ☑ 07-3891 2111; www.canvasclub.com.au; 16b Logan Rd, Woolloongabba; ⊘ noon-midnight Tue-Sun; 🚌 174, 175, 204) Splashed with street-art murals by heavyweights like Fintan Magee, this vintage-inspired cocktail den mixes spirits with enviable finesse. Libations are seasonal and creative, whether it's a topical Fake News (tequila, yellow chartreuse, pernod, pineapple and lime) or an ironically Australian Bogan on Logan (rum, coconut oil, Coke reduction and Averna amaro) served in a glass bottle.

Greater Brisbane

★ Lefty's Old Time Music Hall
BAR
(Map p288; www.leftysoldtimemusichall.com; 15 Caxton St, Petrie Tce; ⊘ 5pm-late Tue-Sun; 🚌 61, 375) Paint the town and the front porch too: there's a honky-tonk bar in Brisvegas! Tarted up with chandeliers and mounted moose heads, scarlet-hued Lefty's keeps the good times rolling with close to 200 whiskies and the sweet twang of live country music. The venue includes a pop-up of top-notch Valley burger joint, Ben's Burgers, open 5pm to 10pm Wednesday to Sunday.

Fonzie Abbott
COFFEE
(Map p278; ☑ 07-3162 7552; www.fonzieabbott.com; 40 Fox St, Albion; ⊘ 6am-3pm Mon-Fri, 7am-1pm Sat & Sun; 🚌 301, 🚉 Albion) Hidden away in industrial Albion, this is one of the

D'AGUILAR NATIONAL PARK

Suburban malaise? Slake your wilderness cravings at this 36,000-hectare **national park** (www.nprsr.qld.gov.au/parks/daguilar; 60 Mount Nebo Rd, The Gap; 🚌385), just 10km northwest of central Brisbane. Pronounced 'dee-ag-lar', its mix of open eucalypt woodlands, scribbly gum forests and subtropical rainforests harbour over 800 plant species, including rare and threatened species. Maps are available at the **Walkabout Creek Discovery Centre** (🕿07-3164 3600; www.walkaboutcreek.com.au; 60 Mount Nebo Rd, The Gap; wildlife centre adult/child $8/4; ⊙9am-4.30pm) at the park's entrance. Also here is a cafe and the **South East Queensland Wildlife Centre**, where you can observe a number of local critters, including reptiles, nocturnal marsupials and a platypus.

Walking trails in the park range from a few hundred metres to a 24km-long loop. Among them is the 6km-return **Morelia Track** at the Manorina day-use area and the 4.3km **Greenes Falls Track** at Mt Glorious. Mountain biking and horse riding are also options. You can camp in the park too, in remote, walk-in bush **campsites** (🕿13 74 68; www.npsr.qld.gov.au/parks/daguilar/camping.html; per person/family $7/26). There are a couple of walks (1.5km and 5km return) kicking off from the visitor centre, but other walks are a fair distance away (so you'll need your own wheels).

To get here, catch bus 385 ($5.70, 25 minutes) from Roma St Station to The Gap Park 'n' Ride, then continue walking 650m up the road.

city's top micro-roasteries, with a trio of signature blends and a handful of single origins sourced from across the globe, including directly from family-run farms.

☆ Entertainment

Most big-ticket international bands have Brisbane on their radar, and the city regularly hosts top-tier DJ talent. World-class cultural venues offer a year-round program of theatre, dance, music and comedy.

Qtix (🕿136 246; www.qtix.com.au) is a booking agency, usually for more high-brow entertainment.

Riverstage   LIVE MUSIC
(Map p282; 🕿07-3403 7921; www.brisbane.qld. gov.au/facilities-recreation/arts-and-culture/river stage; 59 Gardens Point Rd; 🚌QUT Gardens Point, 🚉South Bank) Evocatively set in the Botanic Gardens, this outdoor arena hosts plenty of prolific national and international music acts. See the website for upcoming acts.

**Queensland Performing
Arts Centre**   PERFORMING ARTS
(QPAC; Map p282; 🕿guided tours 07-3840 7444, tickets 136 246; www.qpac.com.au; Queensland Cultural Centre, cnr Grey & Melbourne Sts; ⊙box office 9am-8.30pm Mon-Sat; 🚉South Bank Terminals 1 & 2, 🚉South Brisbane) Brisbane's main performing arts centre comprises four venues and a small exhibition space focused on aspects of the performing arts. The centre's busy calendar includes ballet, concerts, theatre and

comedy, from both Australian and international acts.

Zoo   LIVE MUSIC
(Map p292; 🕿07-3854 1381; www.thezoo.com.au; 711 Ann St; ⊙6pm-late Thu-Sat; 🚉Fortitude Valley) Going strong since 1992, the Zoo remains a grungy spot for indie rock, folk, acoustic, hip-hop, reggae and electronic acts, with no shortage of raw talent. Recent names to have hit the stage include Californian rockers Trapt and indie musician Phoebe Bridgers, alt-indie Perth band Great Gable, and Brisbane hip-hop outfit Butterfingers. Book tickets directly on the website.

**Judith Wright Centre
of Contemporary Arts**   PERFORMING ARTS
(Map p292; 🕿07-3872 9000; www.judithwright centre.com; 420 Brunswick St, Fortitude Valley; 🛜; 🚉Fortitude Valley) Home to both a medium-sized and intimate performance space, this free-thinking arts incubator hosts an eclectic array of cultural treats, including contemporary dance, circus and visual arts. It's also the hub for the hugely popular Bigsound Festival (p281), a four-night music fest held each September. Scan the website for upcoming performances and exhibitions.

Brisbane Powerhouse   PERFORMING ARTS
(Map p278; 🕿box office 07-3358 8600; www.bris banepowerhouse.org; 119 Lamington St, New Farm; 🚌196, 🚉New Farm Park) What was a 1920s power station is now a buzzing hub of nationally and internationally acclaimed

theatre, music, comedy, dance and more. Also hosts a number of special series, festivals and exhibitions through the year, some of which are free, and is a great place to kick back with a drink and bite. See the website for what's on.

Gabba   STADIUM

(Brisbane Cricket Ground; Map p278; ☑1300 843 422; www.thegabba.com.au; 411 Vulture St, Woolloongabba; ☐174, 175, 184, 185, 200, 234) You can cheer both AFL football and interstate and international cricket at the Gabba in Woolloongabba, south of Kangaroo Point. If you're new to cricket, try to get along to a Twenty20 match, which sees the game in its most explosive form. The cricket season runs from late September to March; the football from late March to September.

Suncorp Stadium   STADIUM

(Map p288; ☑07-3331 5000; www.suncorp stadium.com.au; 40 Castlemaine St, Milton; ☐61, 375, 377, 470, 475, ☒Milton) In winter, rugby league is the big spectator sport here and local team the Brisbane Broncos call this stadium home. The stadium also hosts the odd major rock concert. Guided tours (adult/child $16/10) run on Thursdays at 10.30am (public holidays excepted); book online.

🛍 Shopping

Brisbane's retail landscape is deliciously eclectic, stretching from Vogue-indexed, high-end handbags to weekend-market arts and crafts.

🏠 Central Brisbane

Apartment   FASHION & ACCESSORIES

(Map p282; ☑07-3012 9725; https://aptmnt.com; Level 1, 115 Queen St; ⊘11am-6pm, to 8pm Fri, to 5pm Sat, noon-4pm Sun; ☒Central) An easy-to-miss lift takes the cognoscenti up to Apartment, quite possibly the city's edgiest fashion boutique. Its unisex edit of youthful, street-smart clothing and accessories celebrates progressive, high-end labels such as Italy's Neul, Denmark's Norse Projects and Japan's Comme des Garçons.

Noosa Chocolate Factory   FOOD

(Map p282; ☑1300 720 668; www.noosachocolate factory.com.au; 144 Adelaide St; ⊘7am-7pm Mon-Wed, to 8pm Fri, 9am-6pm Sat, 10am-5pm Sun; ☝; ☒Central) ✏ Don't delude yourself: the small-batch, artisanal chocolates from this Sunshine Coast Willy Wonka will override any self-control. Best sellers include generous, marshmallowy Rocky Road and a very Queensland concoction of unroasted macadamias covered in Bowen mango-flavoured chocolate. Varieties rotate frequently and, best of all, none contain palm oil. A second branch at No 156 serves speciality coffee and hot chocolate.

Jan Powers Farmers Market   MARKET

(Map p282; www.janpowersfarmersmarkets.com. au; Reddacliff Pl, George St; ⊘8am-6pm Wed; ☒North Quay, ☒Central) Central Brisbane lives out its bucolic village fantasies when local growers and artisans descend on Reddacliff Pl to sell their prized goods. Fill your shopping bags with fresh fruit and vegetables, meats and seafood, fresh pasta, fragrant breads, pastries and more. Stock up for a picnic in the City Botanic Gardens, or simply grab a coffee and a ready-to-eat, multiculti bite.

🏠 South Bank

Where the Wild Things Are   BOOKS

(Map p288; ☑07-3255 3987; www.wherethewild thingsare.com.au; 191 Boundary St, West End; ⊘8.30am-6pm, to 5pm Sun; ☝; ☐199) Little sister to Avid Reader next door, Where the Wild Things Are stocks a whimsical collection of books for toddlers, older kids and teens. The bookshop also runs regular activities, from weekly story-time sessions to book launches, signings and crafty workshops covering topics such as book illustration. Scan the bookshop's website and Facebook page for upcoming events.

🏠 Fortitude Valley & New Farm

Camilla   FASHION & ACCESSORIES

(Map p292; ☑07-3852 6030; www.camilla.com/au; 1/19 James St; ⊘9.30am-5pm Mon-Sat, 10am-4pm Sun; ☐470, ☒Fortitude Valley) Fans of Camilla's statement-making silk kaftans include Beyoncé and Oprah Winfrey. And while the label may be Bondi based, its wildly patterned, resort-style creations – which also include frocks, tops, jumpsuits and swimwear – are just the ticket for languid lounging in chi-chi Brisbane restaurants and bars. Fierce and fabulous, these pieces aren't cheap – kaftans from $500, bikinis around $300.

Winn Lane   FASHION & ACCESSORIES

(Map p292; www.winnlane.com.au; Winn Lane; ☒Fortitude Valley) Duck behind Ann St (off

OUTDOOR CINEMA

One of the best ways to spend a warm summer night in Brisbane is with a picnic basket and some friends at an outdoor cinema. **Moonlight Cinema** (Map p278; www.moonlight. com.au; The Amphitheatre, Roma Street Parkland, 1 Parkland Blvd; adult/child $20/15; ⊘ Tue-Sun late Nov-Mar; �ℝ Roma Street) is held at Roma Street Parkland, on the edge of the CBD. Films, which include current mainstream releases and the odd cult classic, usually screen from Tuesday to Sunday, flickering into life around 7pm; arrive early to get a good spot. Food and drink (including alcohol) are available for purchase (card payments only).

A parallel option is **American Express Openair Cinemas** (Map p282; www.open aircinemas.com.au; Rainforest Green, South Bank Parklands; adult/reduced from $20/17; ⊘ from 5.30pm Tue-Sat, from 5pm Sun; ⛴ South Bank Terminals 1 & 2, ℝ South Brisbane), where from early October to mid-November you can watch recent-release films and retro favourites under the stars (or clouds).

Winn St) and discover this pocket-sized cul-de-sac of indie cool. A handful of offerings includes **Phoebe Paradise** (Map p292; https://phoebeparadise.com; 5d Winn Lane; ⊘ 10am-5pm Wed-Sun), stamping ground of artist-musician Phoebe Sheehy and her deliciously subversive, Queensland-inspired fashion creations. For striking handmade jewellery, check out Jess Blak's eponymous **studio** (Map p292; ☑ 0401 235 272; https://jessblak.com; 5g Winn Lane; ⊘ 10am-5pm Wed-Sat, to 4pm Sun), while just off Winn Lane, hit **Tym Guitars** (Map p292; ☑ 07-3161 5863; www.tymguitars. au; 5 Winn St; ⊘ Mon-Thu & Sat 10am-5pm, to 7pm Fri, 11am-4pm Sun) for handmade guitar pedals, vintage guitars and a punk-heavy vinyl collection.

Standard Market Company Fruit & Deli   FOOD

(Map p292; www.jamesst.com.au/james-st-market; 22 James St; ⊘ 8.30am-7pm, to 6pm Sat & Sun; ☐ 470, ℝ Fortitude Valley) Part of the James St Market precinct, this upscale provedore draws locals with its sophisticated fridge and pantry fare. While the fresh produce is exorbitantly priced, it's a great spot to pick up local and interstate artisanal fare, from organic cheeses and wild olives to ravioli filled with combinations such as duck, star anise, cinnamon and Sichuan pepper.

The space includes a bakery and florist, with the **James St Cooking School** (Map p292; ☑ 07-3252 8850; www.jamesstcookingschool. com.au; 3hr class $145-195) upstairs.

Jan Powers Farmers Market   MARKET

(Map p278; www.janpowersfarmersmarkets. com.au; Brisbane Powerhouse, 119 Lamington St; ⊘ 6am-noon Sat; ☐ 195, 196, ⛴ New Farm Park) Hankering for some purple heirloom carrots or blue bananas? The chances are you'll find

them at this abundant, appetite-piquing farmers market. Grab a coffee and pastry and soak up the spectacle of beautiful fruit and vegetables, cheeses, fish, silky olives, coffee and colourful flowers. Best of all, the CityCat will take you straight there.

Greater Brisbane

Empire Revival   ANTIQUES

(Map p278; ☑ 07-3369 8088; www.empirerevival. com.au; 167 Latrobe Tce, Paddington; ⊘ 10am-5pm, to 4pm Sun; ☐ 375) Built in 1929, this former art-deco theatre is now a sprawling antiques emporium. Over 50 dealers sell all manner of treasures and trash under a peeling, midnight-blue ceiling, from flouncy English crockery to retro fashion, lamps, toys, film posters, even the odd 17th-century Chinese vase. Take your time and pay attention – you never know what you might find.

Davies Park Market   MARKET

(Map p288; www.daviesparkmarket.com.au; Davies Park, West End; ⊘ 6am-2pm Sat; ☐ 60, 192) Shaded by huge Moreton Bay fig trees, this popular, laid-back market heaves with fresh produce, not to mention a gut-rumbling booty of multicultural food stalls. Grab an organic coffee from **Gyspy Vardo**, sip it on a milk crate, then scour the place for organic fruit and veg, herbs, flowers, handmade jewellery and even the odd bonsai.

ℹ Information

INTERNET ACCESS

Brisbane Square Library (☑ 07-3403 4166; www.brisbane.qld.gov.au; 266 George St; ⊘ 9am-6pm, to 7pm Fri, to 4pm Sat, 10am-3pm Sun; ☏; ⛴ North Quay, ℝ Central) Contemporary public library with free wi-fi access.

TO MARKET, TO MARKET

Beyond the weekly farmers markets that feed the masses in central Brisbane (p300), New Farm (p301) and West End (p301) is a string of other fantastic local markets, peddling anything from handmade local fashion and bling to art, skincare and out-of-the-box giftware. Hit the stalls at the following options.

Young Designers Market (Map p282; ☑ 07-3844 2440; www.youngdesignersmarket.com. au; Little Stanley St; ⏰ 10am-4pm, 1st Sun of the month; 🚌 South Bank Terminal 3, 🚉 South Bank) Explore the work of up to 80 of the city's best emerging designers and artists, selling mostly women's fashion, accessories and jewellery, as well as art, homewares and the occasional furniture piece. Held beside South Bank Parklands, the market generally runs on the first Sunday of the month.

Finders Keepers Markets (Map p278; www.thefinderskeepers.com/brisbane-markets; Brisbane Showgrounds, 600 Gregory Tce, Bowen Hills; adult/child $5/free; ⏰ Jun & Nov; 🚌 370, 375, 🚉 Fortitude Valley) A cool, biannual market with live music, street food and over 200 stalls showcasing the wares of independent Australian designers, artists and craftspeople. It's a great spot to score high-quality, one-off fashion pieces, jewellery, bags and more from local and interstate creatives. The three-day event usually takes place at the Brisbane Showgrounds in Bowen Hills.

Collective Markets South Bank (Map p282; www.collectivemarkets.com.au; Stanley St Plaza; ⏰ 5-9pm Fri, 10am-9pm Sat, 9am-4pm Sun; 🚌 South Bank Terminal 3, 🚉 South Bank) South Bank's Collective Markets may draw the tourist hordes, but its modest sweep of stalls do sell some great items, most notably breezy summer frocks. Other offerings include contemporary handmade jewellery, candles, skincare and (somewhat kitschy) art and prints.

Brisbane Riverside Markets (Map p282; ☑ 07-3870 2807; www.theriversidemarkets.com. au; City Botanic Gardens, Alice St; ⏰ 8am-3pm Sun; 🚌 QUT Gardens Point, 🚉 Central) Come Sunday, chilled-out peeps gather at the northern end of the City Botanic Gardens to browse this weekly food and craft market. While it's not somewhere you'd go out of your way for, it's worth a browse if you're in the area; the selection of handmade and independent womenswear, accessories and jewellery is a particular strength.

MEDICAL SERVICES

CBD Medical Centre (☑ 07-3211 3611; www. cbdmedical.com.au; Level 1, 245 Albert St; ⏰ 7am-7pm Mon-Fri, 9am-5pm Sat & Sun; 🚉 Central) General medical services and vaccinations.

Royal Brisbane & Women's Hospital (☑ 07-3646 8111; https://metronorth.health.qld.gov. au/rbwh; cnr Butterfield St & Bowen Bridge Rd, Herston; 🚌 66, 310, 330, 340, 370) 3km north of the city centre. Has a 24-hour casualty ward. In case of emergency, call 000 for an ambulance.

MONEY

Travelex (☑ 07-3174 1018; www.travelex.com. au; 300 Queen St; ⏰ 9.30am-4pm Mon-Thu, to 5pm Fri; 🚌 Riverside, Eagle St Pier, 🚉 Central) Money exchange. Currency can be ordered online, commission free, and picked up at the branch.

POST

Main Post Office (GPO; Map p282; ☑ 13 76 78; www.auspost.com.au; 261 Queen St; ⏰ 7am-6pm Mon-Fri, 9am-12.30pm Sat; 🚌 Riverside, Eagle St Pier, 🚉 Central) Brisbane's main post office offers foreign-currency exchange.

TOURIST INFORMATION

Brisbane Visitor Information & Booking Centre (Map p282; ☑ 07-3006 6290; www. visitbrisbane.com.au; The Regent, 167 Queen St; ⏰ 9am-5.30pm, to 7pm Fri, to 5pm Sat, 10am-5pm Sun; 🚉 Central) Terrific one-stop info counter for all things Brisbane, with brochures, maps and information on city attractions and events. Staff can also book a range of tours.

South Bank Visitor Information Centre (Map p282; ☑ 07-3156 6366; www.visitbrisbane.com. au; Stanley St Plaza; ⏰ 9am-5pm; 🚌 South Bank Terminal 3, 🚉 South Bank) One of Brisbane's official tourist information hubs, with brochures, maps and festival guides, plus tour and accommodation bookings, and tickets to entertainment events. Free wi-fi is available, though you'll get a more reliable signal at the State Library of Queensland, further north on South Bank.

ⓘ Getting There & Away

AIR

Sixteen kilometres northeast of the city centre, Brisbane Airport (p1071) is the third-busiest airport in Australia and the main international airport serving southeastern Queensland.

It has separate international and domestic terminals about 2km apart, linked by the Airtrain, which runs every 15 to 30 minutes from 5am (6am on weekends) to 10pm (between terminals $5/free per adult/child).

It's a busy hub, with frequent domestic connections to other Australian capital cities and regional towns, as well as nonstop international flights to New Zealand, the Pacific islands, North America and Asia (with onward connections to Europe and Africa).

BUS

Brisbane's main bus terminus and booking office for long-distance buses is the **Brisbane Transit Centre** (Roma St Station; www. brisbanetransitcentre.com.au; Roma St; ⊙information desk 8am-4pm, to 2pm Sat, to 9.30am Sun; 🛜), about 500m northwest of the city centre. It also incorporates Roma St train station, which services both long-distance and suburban trains.

Booking desks for Greyhound (☑1300 473 946; www.greyhound.com.au), **Murrays** (☑132 251; www.murrays.com.au) and **Premier Motor Service** (☑13 34 10; www.premierms.com. au) are here. Long-haul routes include Cairns, Darwin and Sydney, though it's usually just as affordable to fly, not to mention a lot quicker.

CAR & MOTORCYCLE

Brisbane has an extensive network of motorways, tunnels and bridges (some of them tolled) run by **Transurban** (☑13 33 31; www. govianetwork.com.au). The Gateway Motorway (M1) runs through Brisbane's eastern suburbs, shooting north towards the Sunshine Coast and northern Queensland and south towards the Gold Coast and Sydney. See the Transurban website for toll details and fees.

Major car-rental companies have offices at Brisbane Airport and in the city. Smaller rental companies with branches near the airport (and shuttles to get you to/from there) include **Ace Rental Cars** (☑1800 620 408; www. acerentalcars.com.au; 330 Nudgee Rd, Hendra; ⊙8am-5pm), **Apex Car Rentals** (☑1800 2739 2277; www.apexrentacar.com.au; 400 Nudgee Rd, Hendra; ⊙7am-6pm) and **East Coast Car Rentals** (☑1800 327 826; www. eastcoastcarrentals.com.au; 504 Nudgee Rd, Hendra; ⊙7am-10pm).

TRAIN

Brisbane's main station for long-distance trains is Roma St Station (essentially the same complex as the Brisbane Transit Centre). For reservations and information contact **Queensland Rail** (☑13 16 17; www.queenslandrail.com. au). For services between Brisbane and Sydney see https://transportnsw.info/regional.

Spirit of Queensland Brisbane to Cairns

Spirit of the Outback Brisbane to Longreach via Bundaberg, Gladstone and Rockhampton

Tilt Train Brisbane to Rockhampton via Bundaberg and Gladstone

Westlander Brisbane to Charleville

ⓘ Getting Around

Brisbane's excellent public transport network – bus, train and ferry – is run by TransLink, which runs a Transit Information Centre at Roma St Station (Brisbane Transit Centre). The tourist offices in the city centre and South Bank can also help with public transport information. Complementing the network is a nifty network of bike paths.

TO/FROM THE AIRPORT

Airtrain (☑1800 119 091; www.airtrain.com. au; adult one way/return $18.50/35) services run every 15 to 30 minutes from 5am (6am on weekends) to 10pm, connecting Brisbane airport's two terminals to central Brisbane. Handy stops include Bowen Hills, Fortitude Valley, Central Station, Roma St Station (Brisbane Transit Centre), South Brisbane and South Bank (one way/return $18.50/35). Translink Go Cards can be used on Airtrain services.

Con-X-ion (☑1300 631 064, 07-5556 9888; www.con-x-ion.com) runs regular shuttle buses between the airport and hotels in the Brisbane city centre (one way/return $20/38). It also connects Brisbane Airport to Gold Coast hotels and private residences (one way/return $49/92), as well as to Sunshine Coast hotels and private residences (one way/return around $54/99). Book tickets online.

A taxi to central Brisbane costs $50 to $60.

CAR & MOTORCYCLE

Brisbane's comprehensive public transport system will make driving altogether unnecessary for most visitors. If you do decide to get behind the wheel, however, consider investing in a GPS; the city's convoluted and one-way streets can quickly cause frustration.

➡ Ticketed two-hour parking is available on many streets in the CBD and the inner suburbs. Heed the signs: Brisbane's parking inspectors can be ruthless.

➡ During the day, parking is cheaper around South Bank and the West End than in the city centre, but it's free in the CBD in the evening from 6pm weekdays (from noon on Saturday).

➡ For more detailed information on parking, see www.visitbrisbane.com.au/parking.

BICYCLE

Brisbane has an extensive network of bike-ways and shared pathways across the city and suburbs.

Brisbane's bike-share program is called CityCycle (p277). To use it, purchase a 24-hour casual pass ($2 per day) on the website or at any of the 150 bike-share stations with credit-card facilities. It's pricey to hire for more than an hour, so make use of the free first 30 minutes per bike and ride from station to station, swapping bikes as you go. Inconveniently, only about half of the bikes include a helmet (compulsory to wear). For real-time information on bike availability at each station, download the official CityCycle app 'AllBikesNow'.

PUBLIC TRANSPORT

Buses, trains and ferries operate on an eight-zone system: all of the inner-city suburbs are in Zone 1, which translates into a single fare per adult/child of $4.70/2.40. If travelling into Zone 2, tickets are $5.70/2.90.

If you plan to use public transport for more than a few trips, you'll save money by purchasing a **Go Card** (www.translink.com.au/tickets-and-fares/go-card; starting balance adult/child $10/5). Purchase the card, add credit and then use it on city buses, trains and ferries, and you'll save more than 30% off individual fares. Go Cards are sold (and can be recharged) at transit stations, 7-Eleven convenience stores, newsagents, by phone or online. You can also top-up on CityCat ferry services (cash only). Go Cards can also be used on local transport on the Gold Coast and Sunshine Coast.

Boat

CityCat (p280) catamarans service 18 ferry terminals between the University of Queensland in St Lucia and Northshore Hamilton. Handy stops include South Bank (Terminal 1 & 2), the three CBD terminals, New Farm Park (for Brisbane Powerhouse), Teneriffe (for Teneriffe and Newstead microbreweries and eateries) and Bretts Wharf (for Eat Street Markets). Services run every 15 to 30 minutes from around 5am to around midnight. Tickets can be bought on board or, if you have one, use your electronic Go Card.

CityHopper Ferries are free but slower, zigzagging back and forth across the water between North Quay, South Bank (Terminal 3), Maritime Museum, the CBD, Kangaroo Point and New Farm. These additional services run roughly every 40 minutes from about 6am to around midnight.

Cross River Ferries connect Kangaroo Point (Thornton St and Holman St) with the CBD, and Kangaroo Point (Norman Park) with New Farm (Sydney St). These ferries run from around 6am to around 11pm, roughly every 12 to 35 minutes to/from the CBD and every 20 minutes to/from New Farm. Further downstream, a third service connects Teneriffe with Bulimba. This service runs every 15 minutes from about 6am to around 10pm. Standard TransLink fares/zones apply as per all other Brisbane transport.

For more information, including timetables, see www.brisbaneferries.com.au.

Bus

Brisbane's bus network is extensive and especially handy for reaching West End, Paddington, Kangaroo Point, Woolloongabba, Fortitude Valley and Newstead.

In the city centre, the main stops for local buses are the underground **Queen Street Bus Station** (Map p282) and **King George Square Bus Station** (Map p282). You can also pick up many buses from the stops along Adelaide St, between George and Edward Sts.

➡ Buses generally run every 10 to 30 minutes, from around 5am (around 6am or later Saturday and Sunday) till about 11pm. Special NightLink buses run all night on some routes on Friday and Saturday.

➡ CityGlider and BUZ services are high-frequency services along busy routes. Tickets cannot be purchased on board CityGlider and BUZ services; use a Go Card. CityGlider services run all night on Friday and Saturday.

➡ Free, hop-on, hop-off City Loop and Spring Hill Loop bus services circle the CBD and Spring Hill, stopping at key spots like QUT, Queen St Mall, City Botanic Gardens, Central Station and Roma Street Parkland. Buses run every 10 to 20 minutes on weekdays between 7am and 6pm (to 7pm on the Spring Hill Loop).

Train

TransLink's (☑13 12 30; www.translink.com.au) Citytrain network has six main, colour-coded lines, which run as far north as Gympie on the Sunshine Coast and as far south as Varsity Lakes on the Gold Coast. All trains go through Roma St Station, Central Station and Fortitude Valley Station; three of the lines (Ferny Grove and Beenleigh, Shorncliffe and Cleveland, Airport and Gold Coast) also run through South Brisbane and South Bank Station.

The Airtrain (p303) service integrates with the Citytrain network in the city centre and along the Gold Coast line.

Trains run from around 4am, with the last train on each line leaving Central Station between 11pm and midnight (later on Friday and Saturday). On Sunday, the last train can depart as early as 9.30pm or 10.30pm on some lines.

Single train tickets can be bought at train stations, or use your Go Card (p304).

For timetables and a network map, see www.translink.com.au.

TAXI

There are numerous taxi ranks in the city centre, including at Roma St Station, Treasury (corner of George and Queen Sts), Albert St (corner of Elizabeth St) and Edward St (near Elizabeth St). You might have a tough time hailing one late at night in Fortitude Valley: there's a rank near the corner of Brunswick St and Ann St, but expect long queues. The main taxi companies are **Black & White** (☑ 13 32 22; www.blackandwhitecabs.com.au) and **Yellow Cab Co** (☑ 13 19 24; www.yellowcab.com.au).

NightLink flat-fare taxis run on Friday and Saturday nights and can be hailed from three dedicated ranks: Eagle St in the CBD (at the Eagle St secure rank) and, in Fortitude Valley, Ann St (outside X&Y nightclub) and Warner St (approaching Wickham St). Pay your fare at the beginning of the journey (cash only).

AROUND BRISBANE

North Stradbroke Island

POP 2100

An easy 30-minute ferry chug from the Brisbane suburb of Cleveland, unpretentious North Stradbroke Island (Minjerribah) is like Noosa and Byron Bay rolled into one. There's a string of glorious powdery white beaches, great surf and some quality places to stay. It's also a hotspot for spying dolphins, turtles, manta rays and, between June and November, humpback whales. 'Straddie' also offers freshwater lakes and 4WD tracks.

There are only a few small settlements on the island, with a handful of accommodation and eating options – mostly near **Point Lookout** in the northeast. On the west coast, **Dunwich** is where the ferries dock. **Amity** is a small village on the northwestern corner. Much of the island's southern section is closed to visitors due to sand mining.

Interestingly, North and South Stradbroke Islands used to be one single island, but a savage storm blew through the sand spit between the two in 1896.

⊙ Sights & Activities

★ Cylinder Beach   BEACH

(🐾) Bordered by Cylinder and Home Beach Headlands, this broad, beautiful beach is patrolled by lifesavers, offers easy access from the car park, and generally has smaller waves than neighbouring beaches like the ominously named Deadman's Beach. As you'd expect, it's popular with families. Remember to swim between the flags.

Naree Budjong Djara
National Park   NATIONAL PARK

(www.nprsr.qld.gov.au/parks/naree-budjong-djara; Alfred Martin Way) Naree Budjong Djara National Park is Straddie's heartland, home to the glittering **Blue Lake (Kaboora)**. To access the park and the lake, head 6.5km east of Dunwich on Alfred Martin Way. From the roadside national park car park, follow the marked walking track, a 5.2km return trip. Keep an eye out for forest birds, skittish lizards and swamp wallabies along the way. There's a wooden viewing platform at the lake, which is encircled by a forest of paperbarks, eucalypts and banksias.

North Gorge Walk   NATURE RESERVE

(Moloomba Rd, Point Lookout; 🐾) At Point Lookout, this breathtaking 1.2km walk is a must. It's an easy 20-minute loop around the headland along boardwalks, with the thrum of cicadas as your soundtrack. Keep an eye out for turtles, dolphins and manta rays offshore. From June to November, this is also the best vantage point on the island to view humpback whales on their migration route. Topping it off is an epic view of Main Beach and its roaring surf.

★ Straddie Adventures   KAYAKING

(☑ 0433 171 477; www.straddieadventures.com.au; adult/child sea-kayaking trips from $75/40, sandboarding $35/30; 🐾) Operated by the area's traditional Aboriginal owners, this outfit runs highly recommended sea-kayaking trips with an Indigenous cultural bent, meaning fascinating insight into the island's ancient cultural history and its rich wildlife. Sandboarding sessions are also run, as well as combo trips (adult/child from $100/65) that include both activities.

Manta Lodge & Scuba Centre   DIVING

(☑ 07-3409 8888; www.mantalodge.com.au; 132 Dickson Way, Point Lookout; wetsuit/surfboard/bike hire per day $15/50/33, scuba diving course from $299) Based at the YHA, Manta Scuba Centre offers a broad range of options. You can hire wetsuits, snorkelling gear, surfboards and bikes, or take the plunge with a diving course. To explore Moreton Bay Marine Park's rich marine life, sign up for one of the popular snorkelling or scuba-diving trips ($99 and $140 respectively).

North Stradbroke Island
Surf School   SURFING

(☑ 0400 443 591, 0407 642 616; www.northstradbrokeislandsurfschool.com.au; Cylinder Beach

Brisbane & Around

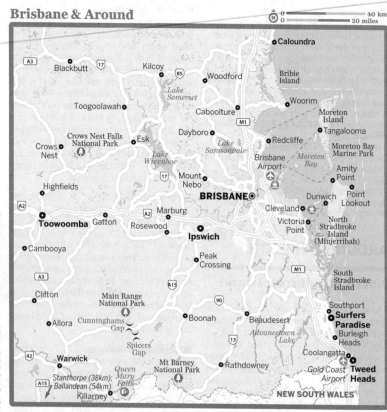

Car Park, Mooloomba Rd, Point Lookout; group/private lesson $50/100) Small-group, 1½-hour surf lessons for rookies, intermediate and advanced wave riders. One-hour solo lessons are also available if you're feeling bashful.

🛏 Sleeping & Eating

Cylinder Beach
Campground
CAMPGROUND $

(www.minjerribahcamping.com.au; powered/unpowered sites from $53/37; 🛜) Located in in Point Lookout and just steps away from beautiful Cylinder Beach, this is one of the island's top camp grounds. Facilities include power and running water, showers and toilets, as well as communal kitchen, BBQ and laundry facilities. Book well in advance, especially in summer and during school holidays.

⭐ Sea Shanties
CABIN $$

(☎07-3409 7161; www.seashanties.com.au; 9a Cook St, Amity Point; cabins $155-200; 🛜🐾)

Dotted with upcycled sculptures and tropical plants, this waterfront oasis offers seven gorgeous, self-contained cabins. Lime-washed timbers floors and stylish furnishings deliver a chic, nautical look, and each comes with fridge, hotplates, microwave and coffee machine (BYO grinds). Facilities include a well-equipped outdoor kitchen and BBQ area, lounge, private jetty (complimentary snorkelling gear available) and laundry.

⭐ Allure
APARTMENT $$$

(☎07-3415 0000, 1800 555 200; www.allurestradbroke.com.au; 43-57 East Coast Rd, Point Lookout; bungalows/villas from $245/290; 🅿🌸🛜🏊) Set in a leafy compound with a pool, gym and kitchen garden for guests, Allure offers large, clean, contemporary bungalows and villas. Bungalows are studio-style affairs with kitchenettes and mezzanine bedrooms, while villas offer full kitchens and separate bedrooms. All have private laundry facilities and outdoor deck with BBQs. While there isn't much space between the shacks, they're cleverly designed with privacy in mind.

Rufus King Seafoods
SEAFOOD $

(07-3409 7224; https://rufuskingseafoods.com.au; 44 Sovereign Rd, Amity Point; prawns per kg $25, oysters per dozen $18; 9am-5pm) For reasonably priced local fish and seafood, stop by this family-run fishmonger. You'll find everything from fresh fish fillets and Moreton Bay bugs to shucked oysters and juicy prawns. The prawns are especially good: buy a bag and devour them on the beach (cold beers optional). As to be expected, the early birds get the biggest choice and freshest produce. Also sells bait.

Blue Room Cafe
CAFE $

(0438 281 666; 27 Mooloomba Rd, Point Lookout; dishes $10-18; 7.30am-3pm;) This youthful, beach-shack-chic cafe has a small al fresco terrace, good coffee and dishes such as organic paleo granola with stewed fruit compote and natural yogurt, and a swordfish burger with house-made tartare, slaw, beetroot and pickled cucumber. Small bites include cookies and yummy vegan snacks. The adjoining provedore is aptly named the Green Room.

❶ Getting There & Away

The hub for ferries to North Stradbroke Island is the Brisbane bayside suburb of Cleveland.

Stradbroke Ferries (07-3488 5300; www.stradbrokeferries.com.au; Toondah Harbour, 12 Emmett Dve, Cleveland; one way per vehicle incl passengers from $58, walk-on adult/child $7/4) runs passenger/vehicle services between Cleveland and Dunwich on North Stradbroke Island (45 to 50 minutes, 12 to 15 times daily). If travelling with a vehicle, always book online to secure a place; there is no need to print tickets.

Stradbroke Flyer Gold Cats (07-3286 1964; www.flyer.com.au; Middle St, Cleveland; return adult/child $20/10) operates passenger-only trips between Cleveland and Dunwich (30 minutes, 14 to 15 times daily). A free Stradbroke Flyer courtesy bus picks up water-taxi passengers from the Cleveland train station 10 minutes prior to most water taxi departures (see the website for exclusions).

Citytrain (p304) services run regularly from Brisbane's Central and Roma St Stations (as well as the inner-city stations of South Bank, South Brisbane and Fortitude Valley) to Cleveland station ($8.90, one hour). Buses to the ferry terminal meet the trains at Cleveland station (seven minutes).

❶ Getting Around

Bicycle Hire out mountain bikes in Dunwich at **Straddie Super Sports** (07-3409 9252; www.facebook.com/StraddieSuperSports; 18 Bingle Rd; equipment hire per hour/day $10/50; 8am-4.30pm, to 3pm Sat, 9am-2pm Sun).

Bus Services by **Stradbroke Island Buses** (07-3415 2417; www.stradbrokeislandbuses.com.au; one way/return $4.80/9.60) meet the ferries at Dunwich and run to Amity Point and Point Lookout. They run roughly every hour and the last bus to Dunwich leaves Point Lookout at 6.20pm. Cash only.

Car Straddie is big: it's best to have your own wheels to explore it properly. If you plan to go off-road, you can get information and buy a 4WD permit ($46.80) from **Minjerribah Camping** (07-3409 9668; www.minjerribahcamping.com.au; 1 Junner St, Dunwich; 8am-4pm Mon-Fri, to 1pm Sat).

Scooter Rent out 50cc scooters from **Scooters on Straddie** (0497 777 933; https://scootersonstraddie.com.au; 9 Sturt St, Dunwich; scooter hire per day $75; 8.30am-5pm). Drop-off and pick-up in Amity Point and Point Lookout is available for an extra $10 (return).

Taxi The **Stradbroke Cab Service** (0408 193 685) charges around $60 from Dunwich to Point Lookout.

Moreton Island
POP 245

If you're not going further north in Queensland than Brisbane but fancy an island getaway, sail over to Moreton Island (Moorgumpin). The third-largest sand island in the world, its unspoilt beaches, dunes, bushland and lagoons are protected, with 95% of the isle comprising the **Moreton Island National Park & Recreation Area** (www.nprsr.qld.gov.au/parks/moreton-island). Off the west coast are the rusty, hulking Tangalooma Wrecks, which provide excellent snorkelling and diving.

Moreton Island has a rich history. Shell middens and bone scatters speak of the island's original inhabitants, the Ngugi people, a clan belonging to the Quandamooka group. The island is also the site of Queensland's first and only whaling station at Tangalooma, which operated between 1952 and 1962.

There are four small settlements, all on the west coast: **Tangalooma** (home to the island's only resort), **Bulwer** near the northwestern tip, **Cowan Cowan** between Bulwer and Tangalooma, and **Kooringal** near the southern tip.

◉ Sights & Activities

Island bushwalks include a desert trail (two hours) leaving from Tangalooma Island Resort, as well as the strenuous trek up **Mt Tempest**, 3km inland from Eagers Creek – worthwhile, but you'll need transport to reach the start.

Cape Moreton Lighthouse offers great views, particularly when the whales are passing by.

Guests staying at the Tangalooma Island Resort can pick up a map of island walking trails at the Tangalooma Eco Centre.

Just north of the resort, off the coast, are the famous **Tangalooma Wrecks** – 15 sunken ships forming a sheltered boat mooring and a brilliant snorkelling and kayaking spot. **Australian Sunset Safaris** (☑ 07-3287 1644, 1300 553 606; www.sunsetsafaris.com.au; tours from Brisbane from adult/child $199/164; ⛴) runs kayaking trips around the Tangalooma Wrecks, as well as other water activities.

Tangalooma Eco Centre   WILDLIFE RESERVE
(☑ 1300 652 250; www.tangalooma.com; Tangalooma Island Resort; ⊙ 10am-noon & 1-4pm; ⛴) Aside from providing Moreton Island walking-trail maps and displays on the island's diverse marine and bird life, this centre is a launching pad for numerous eco-tours and experiences, including a marine discovery cruise, sand-tobogganing trips and seasonal whale-watching tours (generally June to October). Currently open only to guests of the **Tangalooma Island Resort** (d/apt from $209/399; ❄ @ 🛜 🏊).

🛏 Sleeping & Eating

Tangalooma hosts the island's sole resort. There are also five national park camping areas on Moreton Island: North Point, Blue Lagoon, Ben-Ewa, the Wrecks and Comboyuro Point. All have toilets, cold showers and running water (treat before using). Book before you get to the island.

There's a small convenience store plus cafes, restaurants and bars for guests staying at the island's resort, as well as (expensive) shops at Kooringal and Bulwer. Otherwise, bring food and drink supplies with you from the mainland.

❶ Getting There & Away

Several ferries operate from the mainland. To explore once you get to the island, bring a 4WD or take a tour. Most tours are ex-Brisbane, and include ferry transfers. Timetables are available on each ferry's website.

Amity Trader (☑ 07-3820 6557; www.amitytrader.com; Victoria Point Jetty, Masters Ave, Victoria Point; 4WD/walk-on passengers return $280/40) Runs vehicle barges for 4WD vehicles and walk-on passengers from the Brisbane suburb of Victoria Point to Kooringal on Moreton Island several times monthly. Sailing time is roughly two hours one way.

Micat (☑ 07-3909 3333; www.moretonisland adventures.com.au; 14 Howard Smith Dr, Port of Brisbane; one way 4WD from $128, adult/child $28/18) Vehicle ferry service from the Port of Brisbane to Tangalooma. Bookings are essential and service frequency is based on demand, with one to two sailings daily in quiet periods and between one and five sailings daily in busy periods, such as local school holidays. Journey time is around 1½ hours one way; see the website for current sailing times.

Tangalooma Flyer (☑ 07-3637 2000; www.tangalooma.com; Holt Street Wharf, Pinkenba; return adult/child $80/45) Fast passenger catamaran operated by Tangalooma Island Resort. It makes the 1¼-hour trip to the resort three to four times daily from Holt St Wharf in the Brisbane suburb of Pinkenba.

Toowoomba

POP 100,030

Not only is the 'Garden City' Queensland's largest and oldest inland city, but it is also the birthplace of two national icons: the archetypal Aussie cake, the lamington, and Oscar-winner Geoffrey Rush. Squatting on the edge of the Great Dividing Range, 700m above sea level, Toowoomba is a sprawling country hub with wide tree-lined streets, stately homes and brisk winters made for red wine and crackling fires.

While it isn't a see-it-before-you-die kind of place, it does have a few surprises up its sleeve for those who stay a day or two. Among these is one of Australia's largest traditional Japanese gardens, a nationally renowned collection of horse-drawn vehicles, and a small regional gallery with a jewel-box library. Perhaps the biggest surprise, however, is Toowoomba's burgeoning cool factor, reflected in its growing number of hip cafes and bars, not to mention a slew of street art by nationally and globally recognised talent.

◉ Sights

Cobb & Co Museum   MUSEUM
(☑ 07-4659 4900; www.cobbandco.qm.qld.gov.au; 27 Lindsay St; adult/child $12.50/6.50; ⊙ 9.30am-4pm; ⛴) This engaging museum houses Australia's finest collection of horse-drawn

vehicles, including beautiful 19th-century Cobb & Co Royal Mail coaches and an omnibus used in Brisbane until 1924. Hands-on displays depict town life and outback travel during the horse-powered days, and the museum also houses a blacksmith forge and an interesting Indigenous section, with shields, axe heads and boomerangs, plus animated films relating Dreaming stories. Look for the spinning windmills out the front.

Ju Raku En Japanese Garden GARDENS
(www.toowoombarc.qld.gov.au; West St; ☉6am-dusk; ⊕) FREE One of Australia's largest and most traditional Japanese gardens, Ju Raku En is around 4km south of the centre at the University of Southern Queensland. The 5-hectare oasis was designed by a Japanese professor in Kyoto and contains all the expected elements, from rippling lake and carefully aligned boulders to conifers, cherry blossom trees and photogenic bridges.

Toowoomba Regional Art Gallery GALLERY
(☏07-4688 6652; www.tr.qld.gov.au/facilities-recreation/theatres-galleries/galleries; 531 Ruthven St; ☉10am-4pm Tue-Sat, 1-4pm Sun) FREE Toowoomba's modestly sized art gallery houses an interesting collection of paintings, ceramics and drawings. Its permanent collection includes works by Australian greats such as Tom Roberts, Arthur Streeton and Rupert Bunny, as well as European decorative arts from the 17th to 19th centuries. Call ahead to view the gallery's notable library (11am to 3pm Tuesday to Thursday and 1pm to 4pm Sunday), a treat of rare books, maps and travel journals, including letters written by early European explorers to Australia.

🛏 Sleeping & Eating

★Ecoridge Hideaway CHALET $$
(☏07-4630 9636; www.ecoridgehideaway.com.au; 712 Rockmount Rd, Preston; r from $145; ⓟ🛜) Ecoridge is an excellent alternative to the often unremarkable accommodation in Toowoomba. Around 15km from the city on a back road to Gatton, its three self-contained cabins are simple yet smart, with heavenly mattresses, wood heater, full kitchen, BBQ, and breathtaking sunrise views across the Great Dividing Range. Rates are cheaper for stays of three nights or more and wi-fi is available at reception only.

★Vacy Hall GUESTHOUSE $$
(☏0439 004 000; www.vacyhall.com.au; 135 Russell St; d from $133; ⓟ🛜) Uphill from the town

WORTH A TRIP

WOOLSHED AT JONDARYAN

About 45km west of Toowoomba, the **Woolshed at Jondaryan** (☏07-4692 2229; www.jondaryanwoolshed.com.au; 264 Jondaryan-Evanslea Rd; adult/child $10/5; ☉8.30am-4.30pm; ⊕) is the oldest and largest operating woolshed of its kind in the world. The place offers an interesting glimpse into rural Australian life, with a collection of antique tractors and obscure farm machinery, as well as an animal nursery and regular blacksmithing and shearing demonstrations – call ahead or ask at reception. There's rustic accommodation here too.

centre, this magnificent, heritage-listed 1899 mansion with wrap-around verandah offers 12 period-style rooms with no shortage of authentic charm, whether it be a chesterfield lounge, four-poster bed or clawfoot bathtub. All rooms have en suites or private bathrooms across the hall, and most have working fireplaces. Super-high ceilings make some rooms taller than they are wide.

★The Bakers Duck BAKERY $
(https://thebakersduck.com.au; 124 Campbell St; pastries from $4.50, lunch items $8-10; ☉7am-1pm Wed-Sun; ⊕) A hip, pared-down, urbane cafe-bakery, the Bakers Duck is a local legend, famed for its artisanal sourdough bread and pastries. These include gorgeous almond croissants and a cult-status strawberry cheesecake pastry. The generous, flaky pies, sausage rolls and quiches make for a cheap, good-quality lunch, while the coffee is some of the best you'll slurp in the state.

★Zev's Bistro MODERN AUSTRALIAN $$$
(☏07-4564 8636; www.zevsbistro.com; 517 Ruthven St; dishes $12-65, 4-/6-course tasting menu $59/89; ☉5pm-late Tue-Sat) Chef Kyle Zevenbergen has catapulted Toowoomba's dining scene to a whole new level with this lauded bistro, a burnt-orange-and-charcoal space pimped with contemporary artworks. Dishes range from very good to excellent, packed with global accents and texture. The wine list is interesting and reasonably priced.

ℹ Information

Toowoomba Visitor Information Centre
(☏1800 331 155, 07-4639 3797; www.southernqueenslandcountry.com.au; 86 James St; ☉9am-5pm; 🛜) Toowoomba's friendly,

well-stocked tourist office is southeast of the centre, at the junction with Kitchener St. Peel yourself off a vast bed-sheet-sized map of town and pick up some themed walking-tour brochures. The centre also stocks a self-guided tourist-drive map.

❶ Getting There & Away

Toowoomba lies 126km west of Brisbane on the Warrego Hwy. Toowoomba's **main bus station** (cnr Neil St & Bell St Mall) serves both city and long-distance routes. Translink Go Cards are valid on Toowoomba city buses.

Greyhound (☑ 07-4690 9868; www. greyhound.com.au; Heritage Plaza Arcade, 28 Bell St; ⊙ 5am-6pm, from 5.15am Sat & Sun) services run eight times daily between central Brisbane and Toowoomba (from $26, 1¾ hours). Six direct daily services also run from Brisbane Airport (from $30, 2½ hours).

Murrays (p303) runs five daily services between Brisbane Airport, central Brisbane and Toowoomba (central Brisbane from $26, Brisbane Airport from $30).

Airport Flyer (☑ 1300 304 350, 07-4630 1444; www.theairportflyer.com.au; one way/return $75/140) runs six daily door-to-door services each way between Brisbane Airport and Toowoomba. The cost is cheaper for more than one passenger.

Granite Belt

Dappling the western flanks of the Great Dividing Range about 210km southwest of Brisbane, the Granite Belt subverts the southeast Queensland clichés of sun and surf. Here, rolling hillsides are lined with vineyards, olive groves and orchards growing apples, pears, plums and peaches. This is Queensland's only real wine region – the only place in the state where it's cool enough to grow commercial quantities of grapes. It's also one of Australia's most exciting and underrated wine regions, known for its intimate, small-scale cellar doors and alternative grape varieties. Bracing winters lure coastal Queenslanders thrilled by the novelty of rugging up and sipping local nebbiolo by a crackling fire. Further south, on the NSW border, balancing boulders and spring wildflowers draw bushwalkers to photogenic Girraween National Park.

Stanthorpe & Ballandean

Queensland's coolest town (literally), Stanthorpe is one of the state's lesser-known drawcards. To the locals, the chilly winter months are known as 'Brass Monkey Season', with events including Christmas in July and no shortage of Queenslanders snuggling up with a vino rosso from one of the numerous local wineries.

In 1860 an Italian priest planted the first grapevines here, but it wasn't until the influx of Italian immigrants in the 1940s that the wine industry really took off. Today functional Stanthorpe and the tiny village of Ballandean, about 20km to the south, claim a flourishing wine industry, with cellar-door sales, on-site dining and boutique accommodation. The region also claims numerous food artisans, selling everything from olive oils and chutneys to cheeses and cider.

But it's not all wine and song: the Granite Belt's changing seasons also make it a prime fruit-growing area, with plenty of fruit picking available for backpackers.

Most of the Granite Belt wineries are south of Stanthorpe around Ballandean. Pick up a map and brochure from the **Stanthorpe Visitor Information Centre** (☑ 1800 762 665, 07-4681 2057; www.granitebeltwinecountry. com.au; 28 Leslie Pde; ⊙ 9am-4pm; ☎).

Aside from wineries, you can find craft ales at the **Granite Belt Brewery** (☑ 07-4681 1370; www.granitebeltbrewery.com.au; 146 Glenlyon Dr; ⊙ 10am-8pm, to 5pm Tue, Thu & Sun), spend a pleasant hour at the **Stanthorpe Regional Art Gallery** (☑ 07-4681 1874; www.srag.org.au; cnr Lock & Marsh Sts; ⊙ 10am-4pm Tue-Fri, to 1pm Sat & Sun) or take in the local wineries with **Stanthorpe Tours** (☑ 0437 707 765; www. stanthorpetours.com.au; tours from $90).

🛏 Sleeping & Eating

★ **Diamondvale B&B Cottages**　COTTAGE $$
(☑ 07-4681 3367; www.diamondvalecottages.com. au; 26 Diamondvale Rd, Stanthorpe; 1-/2-/4-bed cottage from $150/265/440; ☎) In atmospheric bushland outside of Stanthorpe, Diamondvale offers four refreshed, self-contained cottages and a four-bedroom lodge. One-bedroom cottages have kitchenettes, two-bedroom cottages offer full kitchen with oven, and all come with smart TV. You'll find a four-poster bed in the romantic 'Forget Me Not' cottage, plus a fabulous, communal BBQ hut with fireplace by the creek. No wi-fi in the lodge.

★ **Ridgemill Estate**　CABIN $$$
(☑ 07-4683 5211; https://ridgemillestate.com/stay; 218 Donges Rd, Severnlea; cabins $180-285, house $395; ❄☎) Slumber among the vines at one of Ridgemill Estate's eight contemporary

DON'T MISS

TOP VINEYARDS OF THE GRANITE BELT

You could easily spend a week wading through the wines of the region, with scores of well-known and more obscure wineries offering tastings. Or you could simply spend a day or two visiting a select few. It's usually worth an advance phone call to the smaller cellar doors to make sure they're open.

Ballandean Estate (☑07-4684 1226; www.ballandeanestate.com; 354 Sundown Rd, Ballandean; ☺9am-5pm) This is Queensland's oldest family-run winery, with 50-year-old shiraz vines and award-winning vintages. Rated four stars by prolific Australian wine critic James Halliday, the winery includes a provedore selling artisanal local foods and celebrated gourmet restaurant Barrelroom & Larder (p312). Winery tours ($5) run at 11am.

Bent Road Wine (☑0418 190 101; https://bentroadwine.com.au; 535 Bents Rd, Ballandean; ☺by appt) Principal winemaker Glen Robert thrives on pushing boundaries, and his winery ferments some of its wines in traditional terracotta amphorae imported from the Caucasus. There's no official cellar door, so email or call ahead to arrange a visit and tasting, which might see you swilling a viognier, marsanne and roussanne blend with Glen himself.

Boireann Wines (☑07-4683 2194; www.boireannwinery.com.au; 26 Donnellys Castle Rd, The Summit; ☺10am-4pm Fri-Mon; ℗) Peter Stark is one of the Granite Belt's top winemakers and his handmade premium reds – which include shiraz and viognier, grenache and mourvèdre, and tannat – rank among the finest in the region. Not surprisingly, the winery gets a five-star tick of approval from Halliday.

Golden Grove Estate (☑07-4684 1291; www.goldengroveestate.com.au; 337 Sundown Rd, Ballandean; ☺9am-4pm, to 5pm Sat) A third-generation, family-run estate established in 1946, Golden Grove grows numerous alternative varieties, including barbera, durif, malbec, mourvèdre and vermentino. It's especially known for its vermentino, though its tempranillo is also worth seeking out. Another Halliday five-star winery, it's right opposite Ballandean Estate.

Heritage Estate (☑07-4685 2197; www.heritagewines.com.au; 747 Granite Belt Dr, Cottonvale; ☺10am-4pm Wed-Fri, from 9am Sat & Sun) Also claiming five coveted stars, Heritage operates two cellar doors just north of Stanthorpe; the one at Cottonvale – set in a converted cold stores with log fire – is the more atmospheric. Notable drops include shiraz, a shiraz, mourvèdre and grenache blend, and pinot gris. Our favourite, however, is the bootleggers tawny port, aged in French oak for a decade.

Ridgemill Estate (☑07-4683 5211; https://ridgemillestate.com; 218 Donges Rd, Severnlea; ☺10am-5pm, to 3pm Sun) Ridgemill has some notable industry credentials: co-owner Martin Cooper project-managed construction of Stanthorpe's Queensland College of Wine Tourism, while winemaker Peter McGlashan co-established the region's Strange Birds Wine Trail. Ridgemill itself is the Granite Belt's only riesling producer, and both its saperavi and chardonnay have swagged awards. The winery also offers standout cabin accommodation (p310).

Symphony Wines (☑07-4684 1388; https://symphonyhill.com.au; 2017 Eukey Rd, Ballandean; ☺10am-4pm) A five-star, family-owned estate with Australia's highest-elevation pinot vines, Symphony has won numerous awards for its 2017 gewürztraminer, including Best Alternative White Wine at the National Wine Show of Australia. Both its 2016 reserve cabernet sauvignon and nero d'avola are considered quaffable enough for the business-class wine list on Qantas.

cabins offering unobstructed vineyard and mountain views and compact timber decks to soak up the vista. Interiors are stylish in hues of silvery-grey and tan, and each comes equipped with sublime king-size bed, contemporary artwork, cushy sofa, log fire, small kitchenette (with coffee-pod machine) and spacious shower.

★ **Brinx Deli & Cafe**   CAFE $
(☑07-4681 3321; www.facebook.com/brinx deli; 18 Maryland St, Stanthorpe; dishes $7.50-22; ☺8am-3pm Tue-Fri, to noon Sat & Sun; ☷) Cheery, new-school Brinx 'gets it'. The coffee is excellent and the cafe grub fresh, honest and made using products from the in-house gourmet deli. Offerings range from

rich brownies and tangy lemon tarts to açai bowls, brioche French toast, gourmet frittatas, burgers and grazing boards. The deli itself is worth a browse, especially for its French cheeses and local provisions.

★ **Jamworks of Glen Aplin**   FOOD $$
(☑ 07-4683 4171; www.jamworks.com.au; 7 Townsend Rd, Glen Aplin; mains $17-21; ☺ 9.30am-4.30pm Fri-Tue; 🛜🅿️) A modern, warehouse-style space, Jamworks serves up quality, produce-driven cafe grub, from poached eggs with chilli cornbread, baby spinach, sautéed mushrooms and cherry tomatoes, to apple pie and platters ($21), the latter laden with award-winning cheeses, locally smoked meats and marinated vegetables. Once fed, shop for Jamworks' prized relishes, chutneys, marmalades and jams, plus products from other artisanal Queensland producers.

★ **Barrelroom & Larder**   MODERN AUSTRALIAN $$$
(☑ 07-4684 1326; www.barrelroom.com.au; Ballandean Estate, 354 Sundown Rd, Ballandean; mains $34-38, 7-course tasting menu $100; ☺ noon-2.30pm & 6-8.30pm Thu-Mon) Massive 150-year-old wine barrels (filled with port and muscat) flank the dining room at the Granite Belt's top dining destination. Located at Ballandean Estate winery, the kitchen makes regional produce sing in sophisticated, soulful dishes like organic bullock pastrami with crumbed hen egg, and wild Ballandean venison leg with venison pithivier, cauliflower and fig. Book ahead, especially on weekends.

ℹ️ Getting There & Away

Stanthorpe is easily reached from Brisbane by bus, with **Crisps Coaches** (☑ 07-4661 8333; www.crisps.com.au) running one to two services daily. The afternoon service continues to Ballandean, a pleasant 20km drive southwest of Stanthorpe on the New England Hwy. A bus service between Toowoomba and Stanthorpe runs once daily on weekdays only.

GOLD COAST

Built for pleasure and remaining a place dedicated to sun, surf and the body beautiful, this strip of coast is possibly Australia's most iconic holiday destination. Its shimmering high-rises can, when glimpsed from afar, resemble a make-believe city, and its reputation for tackiness is occasionally deserved. But this is far outstripped by the area's youthful spirit and startling physical beauty: some

52km of pristine sand with countless epic surf breaks, stunning sunsets, blissful water temperatures and 300 sunny days a year.

While Surfers Paradise's malls and mega-clubs entertain the party-hard kids, the other neighbourhoods have distinct charms of their own, from booming culinary scenes and coastal chic to retro beach holiday nostalgia and laid-back local flavour. Not to be overlooked is the lush, misty subtropical rainforest of the hinterland – a good place to get in touch with the spirit of the traditional owners of this land, the Yugambeh people.

ℹ️ Getting There & Away

AIR

Gold Coast Airport (p1071) is in Coolangatta, 25km south of Surfers Paradise. All the main Australian domestic airlines fly here. **Scoot** (www.flyscoot.com), **Air Asia** (www.airasia.com) and **Air New Zealand** (www.airnewzealand.com.au) fly in from overseas.

Brisbane Airport (p1071) is 85km northwest of Surfers Paradise and accessible by train. It is a useful arrival point for the Gold Coast, especially for international visitors.

BUS

Greyhound (☑ 1300 473 946; www.greyhound.com.au) Has frequent services to/from Brisbane ($15, 1¼ hours), Byron Bay ($25, three hours) and beyond.

Premier Motor Service (☑ 13 34 10; www.premierms.com.au) A couple of daily services head to Brisbane ($20, 1½ hours) and Byron Bay ($29, 4½ hours) from Surfers Paradise, with connections up to Cairns and down to Melbourne.

TRAIN

TransLink (☑ 13 12 30; http://translink.com.au) Citytrain services connect Brisbane with Nerang, Robina and Varsity Lakes stations on the Gold Coast (75 minutes) roughly every half-hour. The same line extends north of Brisbane to Brisbane Airport. Note if you're heading to Brisbane that trains can get very crowded in peak hour.

ℹ️ Getting Around

TO/FROM THE AIRPORT

Skybus (☑ 1300 759 287; www.skybus.com.au) Meets all major flights into Gold Coast Airport and transfers to most Gold Coast accommodation (adult/child $38/22).

Con-X-ion Airport Transfers (☑ 1300 953 168; www.con-x-ion.com) Door-to-door transfers to/from Gold Coast Airport and your hotel (adult/child $22/13), as well as from Brisbane Airport (adult/child $54/17). Private pick-ups also available.

Gold Coast & Hinterland

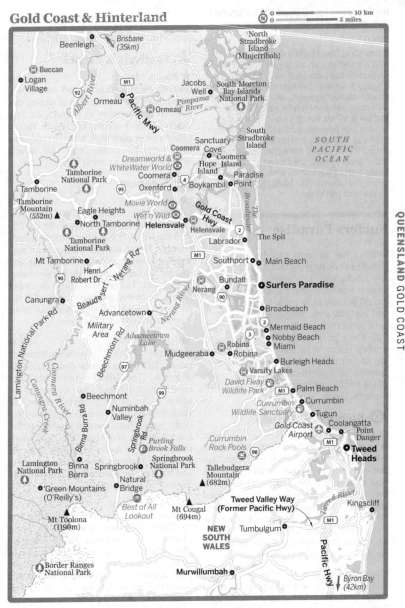

Xcede (byronbay.xcede.com.au) Shuttle between Gold Coast Airport and Byron Bay ($40).

Surfside Buslines (☑13 12 30; www.surfside. com.au) From the Gold Coast Airport, route 777 is a limited-stop service running every 15 minutes from 5.15am to 11.36pm. It takes you to Broadbeach South tram station (30 minutes), where you can transfer to the G:link tram for Surfers Paradise, Southport or other bus routes.

BUS

Surfside Buslines, a subsidiary of Brisbane's main TransLink operation, runs regular buses up and down the Gold Coast, plus shuttles from the Gold Coast train stations into Surfers Paradise and beyond (including the theme parks).

TRAM

G:link (Gold Coast Light Rail; ☑13 12 30; http://translink.com.au; tickets from $4.80, Go Explore day pass adult/child $10/5) is a handy if rather pricey light rail and tram service connecting Helensvale and Broadbeach with stops along the way including Southport and Surfers Paradise. It's worth buying a 'go explore' day pass (adult/child $10/5; available online, at tram stops and from some 7-Eleven shops) if you're doing more than one very short trip. It gives you unlimited travel on TransLink buses and the tram. Otherwise, you can buy single-trip tickets (from $4.80) from a machine on the tram platform.

Surfers Paradise

POP 23,689

While it has its seedy and downright ugly side, there's no denying that Surfers' frenetic few blocks and its glorious strip of sand attracts a phenomenal number of visitors – 20,000 per day at its peak. Party-hard teens and early-20-somethings come here for a heady dose of clubs, bars and malls, perhaps fitting in a bit of beach time as a hangover remedy before it all starts again. Families are attracted by the ready availability of spacious and affordable apartments, loads of kid-friendly eating options and, yes, that beautiful beach.

◉ Sights & Activities

SkyPoint Observation Deck   VIEWPOINT
(www.skypoint.com.au; Level 77, Q1 Bldg, Hamilton Ave; adult/child/family $25/15/65; ☉ 7.30am-10pm Sun-Thu, to 11pm Fri & Sat) Surfers Paradise's best sight is best observed from your beach towel, but for an eagle-eye view of the coast and hinterland, zip up to this 230m-high observation deck near the top of Q1, one of the world's notably tall buildings. You can also tackle the **SkyPoint Climb** (from $75) up the spire to a height of 270m.

Cheyne Horan School of Surf   SURFING
(☑1800 227 873; www.cheynehoran.com.au; 3 Trickett St; 2hr lesson $49; ☉lessons 10am & 2pm) Learn to carve up the waves at this school, run by former pro surfer Cheyne Horan. Multi-lesson packages reduce the cost per class.

Go Vertical Stand Up Paddle   WATER SPORTS
(☑0423 716 625; www.govertical.com.au; Shop 4, 19 River Dr, Budds Beach; 2hr SUP tour adult/child $65/60) The friendly instructor, Linda,

runs two-hour stand-up paddleboard tours of Surfers Paradise and Main Beach at 9am daily, with the chance to spot dolphins.

✦ Festivals & Events

★ **Bleach Festival**   CULTURAL
(www.bleachfestival.com.au; ☉ Apr) Art shows, contemporary dance, music of all genres, theatre and performances all feature, held in a variety of indoor and outdoor spaces. There's a late-summer party vibe, with the occasional superstar performer heading the bill, as well as some edgy and provocative work.

⌨ Sleeping

★ **Bunk**   HOSTEL $
(☑07-5676 6418, freecall 1800 692 865; www. bunksurfersparadise.com.au; 6 Beach Rd; dm $25-40, d $99-175; ❉@☎☱) Retro motel turned boutique hostel, Bunk features private pod-style bunks equipped with reading light and charger, and all dorms come with en suite, in-room safe, balcony and, a rarity in a lot of hostels, much-needed air-con. Cool off in the pool, soak it up in the spa or hang out in the downstairs **Dukes Parlour** bar.

★ **Island**   HOTEL $$
(☑07-5538 8000; www.theislandgoldcoast. com.au; 3128 Surfers Paradise Blvd; d $150-200; 🅿❉☎☱) The Islander Hotel has been reborn as the Island and it's indeed an island of contemporary style – more LA/ Palm Springs vibe than Gold Coast. Spacious rooms have natural timber, matte-black tapware and king-sized beds, while there's plenty of spaces to be seen, from the street-side **Goldie's** restaurant to the red-and-white-striped umbrella-lined pool and the rooftop bar (p316).

Surfers Beachside Holiday Apartments   APARTMENT $$
(☑07-5570 3000; www.surfersbeachside.com.au; 10 Vista St; 1-/2-bedroom apt $150/185; 🅿☎☱) The delightful management is a huge plus at this unpretentious, family-friendly spot. Each apartment is individually owned and decorated, but all interiors are clean, comfortable and unfussy. Minimum three-night stay in high season, but that's sometimes open to negotiation.

★ **QT**   HOTEL $$$
(☑07-5584 1200; www.qtgoldcoast.com.au; 7 Staghorn Ave; d $199-369; ❉☎☱) Acapulco chairs, retro bikes and preppy-styled staff are a deliberate take on the mid-century-design

Surfers Paradise

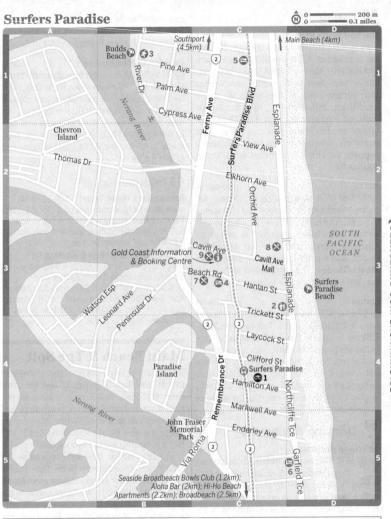

Surfers Paradise

◉ Sights
1 SkyPoint Observation Deck...................C4

✈ Activities, Courses & Tours
2 Cheyne Horan School of Surf...............C3
3 Go Vertical Stand Up Paddle................B1

🛏 Sleeping
4 Bunk..C3
  Island..(see 4)
5 QT...C1

6 Surfers Beachside Holiday
  Apartments D5

✕ Eating
7 4217 ....C3
8 Elston..C3
9 The Sandwich Bros................................C3

🍸 Drinking & Nightlife
  Island Rooftop................................(see 4)
  Paradox Coffee Roasters...............(see 7)

glory days of Surfers. The clever transformation of what was yet another bland '80s tower really does work, with an airy lobby you'll be happy to hang about in. Room interiors are less nostalgic, but have plenty of colour pops.

✗ Eating

The Sandwich Bros SANDWICHES $
(www.facebook.com/thesandwichbrosgc; 38 Cavill
Ave; sandwiches & burgers $10-12; ⊙6.30am-
5pm Mon-Fri, 7.30am-2pm Sat & Sun) Wrap your
lips around these tasty toasted sandwiches
and burgers with fillings such as garlic
mushroom grilled cheese, BBQ brisket or
southern fried chicken with slaw. The house
sauces are tasty and you can order your
sandwich or burger with a side of jalapeño
poppers, fat chips or eggplant fries. Vegan
options too.

4217 FOOD HALL $$
(☑07-5561 0555; www.the4217.com; 10 Beach Rd;
⊙7am-10pm) A lovely concept that still seems
to be finding its feet, the 4217 is home to a
serious coffee haunt, Paradox, as well as an
American burger and beer bar, **Brooklyn
Depot**, and a good Italian provedore, **Salts
Meats Cheese**. The latter also does Neapol-
itan-style puffy pizzas to take away.

Elston AUSTRALIAN $$
(☑07-5631 5935; www.elstonbar.com.au; Peppers
Soul, 8 Esplanade; mains $18-40; ⊙6.30am-
9.30pm) Its name harking back to Surfers
Paradise's pre-1933 identity, this atmospheric
spot mixes beach views with a cool industrial feel. Come for big breakfasts; juicy
burgers, steaks, seafood and salads at lunch;
or pop by in the early evening for a jug of
Pimm's and tapas plates.

🍷 Drinking & Nightlife

★**Island Rooftop** BAR
(☑07-5538 8000; www.theislandgoldcoast.com.au;
3128 Surfers Paradise Blvd; ⊙3pm-late Thu-Sun)
It may be surrounded by Surfers' high-rises
rather than perched atop one (on level 1 of
the Island hotel), but this plant-filled open-
air rooftop bar swaps sweeping views for
sophistication, attracting the Gold Coast's
cool crowd to mingle under the fairy lights.
There's gin cocktails and live jazz Thursday
nights, and DJ sets Fridays and Saturdays.

Paradox Coffee Roasters COFFEE
(☑07-5538 3235; http://paradoxroasters.com;
10 Beach Rd; ⊙7am-3pm Mon-Fri, to 2pm Sat &
Sun) Sustainably sourced beans are roasted
on-site in a Brambati Italian roaster to produce some seriously good brews at this cafe
in the 4217 food hall. It also does a fine food
menu of all-day breakfasts, and burgers and
salads for lunch.

ℹ️ Information

Backpackers World Travel (☑07-5538 7417;
www.backpackerworldtravel.com; 3063 Surfers
Paradise Blvd; ⊙10am-6pm Mon-Fri, to 5pm
Sat; 🛜) Accommodation, tour and transport
bookings and internet access.

**Gold Coast Information & Booking Cen-
tre** (☑07-5570 3259, 1300 309 440; www.
destinationgoldcoast.com; 2 Cavill Ave;
⊙8.30am-5pm Mon-Fri, 9am-6pm Sat, 9am-
4pm Sun) The main Gold Coast tourist information booth; also sells theme-park tickets and
has public transport info.

Main Beach & The Spit

North of Surfers Paradise, the apartment
towers are slightly less lofty and the pace
eases up. Main Beach makes for a serene
base if you're here for views, beach time and
generally taking it easy. Tedder Ave may no
longer possess place-to-be cache, but it still
has a pleasantly village-like atmosphere.

Further north, the Spit separates the
Southport Broadwater from the Pacific
Ocean, stretching 5km to almost meet South
Stradbroke Island. Its southern end is home
to Marina Mirage, an upmarket shopping
centre with a few waterfront dining options,
along with Mariner's Cove, a base for aquatic
activities.

The beach up here, backed as it is with
dunes and native parkland, has a startling
sublimity. It also has some very uncrowded
surf breaks that deliver when nothing else
does.

◎ Sights & Activities

Main Beach Pavilion ARCHITECTURE
(Macarthur Pde) FREE The lovely Spanish Mis-
sion-style Main Beach Pavilion (1934) is a
remnant from pre-boom days. It houses a
cafe and inside are some fabulous old photos of the Gold Coast before the skyscrapers.

ℹ️ SCHOOLIES ON THE LOOSE

Every year in November, thousands of
teenagers flock to Surfers Paradise to
celebrate the end of their high-school
education in a three-week party known
as Schoolies Week. Although local
authorities have stepped in to regulate
excesses, boozed-up and drug-addled
teens are still the norm. It's not pretty.
For more info, see www.schoolies.com.

GOLD COAST THEME PARKS

The gravity-defying roller coasters and water slides at the Gold Coast's American-style parks offer some seriously dizzying action and, although recently beset with a number of accidents, including a tragic fatal one at Dreamworld in 2016, they still attract huge crowds. Discounted tickets are sold in most of the tourist offices on the Gold Coast or can be bought online. The Mega Pass ($179 per person for 14-day entry) grants unlimited entry to Sea World, Warner Bros Movie World, Wet'n'Wild and the little-kid-friendly farm-park **Paradise Country** (http://paradisecountry.com.au), all owned by **Village Roadshow** (☑13 33 86; www.themeparks.com.au).

A couple of tips: the parks can get insanely crowded, so arrive early or face a long walk from the far side of the car park. Also note that the parks don't let you bring your own food or drinks.

Dreamworld (☑1800 073 300, 07-5588 1111; www.dreamworld.com.au; Dreamworld Pkwy, Coomera; adult/child $95/85; ⊙10am-5pm) Touts itself as the Gold Coast's biggest theme park. There are the 'Big 9 Thrill Rides', plus Wiggles World and the DreamWorks experience, both for younger kids. Other attractions include Tiger Island and a range of interactive animal encounters. A one-day pass gives you entry to both Dreamworld and neighbouring WhiteWater World.

Warner Bros Movie World (☑07-5573 3999, 13 33 86; www.movieworld.com.au; Pacific Hwy, Oxenford; adult/child $95/89; ⊙9.30am-5pm) Offers movie-themed shows, rides and attractions, including the DC Rivals Hypercoaster, Batwing Spaceshot, Justice League 3D Ride and Scooby-Doo Spooky Coaster. Actors dressed as Batman, Austin Powers, Porky Pig et al roam through the crowds.

Wet'n'Wild (☑13 33 86, 07-5556 1660; www.wetnwild.com.au; Pacific Hwy, Oxenford; adult/child $79/74; ⊙10am-5pm) The ultimate water slide here is the Kamikaze, where you plunge down an 11m drop in a two-person tube at 50km/h. This vast water park also has pitch-black slides, white-water rapids and wave pools.

WhiteWater World (☑07-5588 1111, 1800 073 300; www.dreamworld.com.au/whitewaterworld; Dreamworld Pkwy, Coomera; adult/child $95/85; ⊙11am-4pm Mon-Fri, 10am-5pm Sat & Sun) This water park, next door to Dreamworld, features the Cave of Waves, Pipeline Plunge and more than 140 water activities and slides. All passes include Dreamworld too.

Sea World continues to attract controversy for its marine shows, where dolphins and sea lions perform tricks for the crowd. While Sea World claims the animals lead a good life, welfare groups argue that keeping such sensitive sea mammals in captivity is harmful, and is exacerbated when mixed with human interaction. The park also displays penguins and polar bears, and has water slides and roller coasters.

Skybus (p312) runs to/from Gold Coast theme parks from nine pick-up points in Surfers Paradise and Broadbeach (adult/child from $11/9). Con-X-ion Airport Transfers (p312) and Surfside Buslines (p313) also serve the theme parks.

★**Federation Walk**　　　　WALKING
(www.federationwalk.org) This pretty 3.7km trail takes you through patches of fragrant littoral rainforest, flush with beautiful bird life, and runs parallel to one of the world's most beautiful strips of surf beach. Along the way, it connects to the Gold Coast Oceanway, which heads 36km to Coolangatta.

Australian Kayaking Adventures　　KAYAKING
(☑0412 940 135; www.australiankayakingadventures.com.au; Labrador; half-day tours adult/child $85/75, sunset tours $55/45) Paddle out to underrated South Stradbroke Island on a morning tour, or take a dusk paddle around Chevron Island in the calm canals behind Surfers.

🛏 Sleeping & Eating

Surfers Paradise

YHA at Main Beach　　　　HOSTEL $
(☑07-5571 1776; www.yha.com.au; 70 Sea World Dr, Main Beach; dm $25-30, d & tw $75; @ 🕏) Despite being called Surfers Paradise YHA, this is actually a great 1st-floor spot overlooking the Main Beach marina, with sky-blue dorms kitted out with basic metal bunks. There's a

QUEENSLAND MAIN BEACH & THE SPIT

free shuttle bus, pub crawl Saturday nights, and the hostel is within wobbling distance of the Fisherman's Wharf Tavern (☑07-5571 0566; http://fishermanswharftavern.com.au; Mariner's Cove, 60-70 Sea World Dr, Main Beach; ☺10am-midnight). They can also arrange tours and activities.

Pacific Views APARTMENT $$
(☑07-5527 0300; www.pacificviews.com.au; cnr Main Beach Pde & Woodroffe Ave, Main Beach; 1-bedroom apt $190-250, 2-bed apt $235-300; P✳️🛜❄️) If you can cope with decor surprises, these individually owned and furnished apartments have amazing floor-to-ceiling views, spacious balconies and helpful staff. They're just one block back from the beach, and there's a cafe downstairs that will make you coffee from 5am if you're up for an early beach wander.

★**Sheraton Grand Mirage Resort** RESORT $$$
(☑07-5577 0000; www.sheratongrandmirage goldcoast.com; 71 Sea World Dr, Main Beach; d $280-400; P✳️🛜❄️) This 295-room absolute-beachfront hotel has a relaxed glamour, and rooms are nicely low-slung and set among 6 hectares of tropical gardens. The large oasis pool has a swim-up bar, and a delicious strip of Spit beach is accessible down a little path. Discounted rates can often be found online.

Peter's Fish Market SEAFOOD $
(☑07-5591 7747; www.petersfish.com.au; 120 Sea World Dr, Main Beach; meals $9-16; ☺shop 9am-7.30pm, kitchen noon-7.30pm Mon-Sat, 11am-7.30pm Sun) A no-nonsense fish market–cum–fish and chip shop selling fresh and cooked seafood, which can be eaten on a few tables out the front by the river. Some of the seafood comes fresh from the trawlers.

Kokum FUSION $$$
(☑07-5646 7314; www.kokum.com.au; 94 Sea World Dr, Palazzo Versace, Main Beach; mains $24-55; ☺11.30am-9.30pm; 🍽️) This collaboration between Michelin-starred chef Mural and Sridhar Penumechu of the Saffron restaurant brings an exciting Indian-Asian fusion to Palazzo Versace's waterfront dining scene. The space is stylish and upmarket without being stuffy, and the menu delivers familiar dishes, including curries and biryani, alongside experimental offerings incorporating Australian native spices such as lemon myrtle and Kakadu plum.

Broadbeach & Mermaid Beach

Directly south of Surfers Paradise, Mermaid Beach and Broadbeach may be all about apartment towers and pedestrian malls, but the area is decidedly more upmarket than its northern neighbour, with carefully landscaped streets and smart places to eat, drink and shop. To the south, the low-rise blocks and rambling beach shacks look rather like the Gold Coast of old, but nestled in these suburban streets and strip malls you'll find some of the region's most innovative eating and drinking options. Of course, the gorgeous stretch of golden shore is beguiling too.

Miami Marketta (www.miamimarketta.com; 23 Hillcrest Pde, Miami; ☺5-10pm Wed, 5-11pm Fri, 4-11pm Sat), a hawker-style street market in a previously abandoned warehouse in Miami, just south of Mermaid, is a lively space offering food, fashion, art and live music. Work your way through stalls hawking Japanese tempura, tacos, homemade pasta and home-baked cakes.

🛏️ Sleeping & Eating

Hi-Ho Beach Apartments APARTMENT $$
(☑07-5538 2777; www.hihobeach.com.au; 2 Queensland Ave, Broadbeach; 1-/2-bedroom apt $140/190; P✳️🛜❄️) A top choice for location, close to the beach and cafes. You're not paying for glitzy lobbies here, but the recently refurbished rooms are comfortable with bright artworks by the owner and splashes of colour in the decor, plus it's well managed, clean and quiet. And, hey, the Vegas-esque sign!

Peppers Broadbeach APARTMENT $$$
(☑07-5635 1000; www.peppers.com.au/broad beach; 21 Elizabeth Ave, Broadbeach; 1-/2-/3-bedroom apt from $250/330/680; ✳️🛜❄️) When you want flawless, if unexciting, comfort, this Peppers apartment hotel is for you. Think marble dining tables, European kitchen appliances, wrap-around balconies and high-thread-count linen. The three-bedroom 'sky homes' really take the luxury to town. There are indoor and outdoor pools, and an Endota day spa for all your pampering needs.

★**Bam Bam Bakehouse** CAFE, BAKERY $$
(☑07-5526 5218; www.bambambakehouse.com; 2519 Gold Coast Hwy, Mermaid Beach; mains $14-21; ☺7am-3pm) Watch artisanal bakers at work through the windows at Bam

Bam – part bakehouse, part cafe, all amazing. Sitting on the edge of a park, the breezy, buzzing cafe is filled with plants and in-the-know locals. Get here early to snap up sweet treats and pastries – including Nutella 'cruffins' and flaky croissants that take three days to perfect – before they sell out.

⭐ **Etsu Izakaya**   JAPANESE **$$$**
(🕿 07-5526 0944; www.etsu.com.au; 2440 Gold Coast Hwy, Mermaid Beach; dishes $12-30; ⊘ 5pm-late) Transport yourself to Tokyo at this mysterious and moody yet fun and vibrant space reminiscent of a Japanese izakaya. Prop up the bar or nab a seat under the curved feature wall to sample share dishes from fresh sashimi and Wagyu steak to delicious *kushiyaki* skewers charred on the Robata grill. Look for the red lantern.

⭐ **Social Eating House & Bar** AUSTRALIAN **$$$**
(🕿 07-5504 5210; www.socialeatinghouse.com.au; 3 Oracle Blvd, Broadbeach; dishes $23-40; ⊘ noon-4pm & 6-11pm Mon-Thu, noon-5pm & 6-11pm Fri-Sun) These simple, elegant dishes show you what Modern Australian cooking is all about. The menu ranges from soft-shell crab with green mango, peanuts and chilli caramel to a shareable 1kg boned lamb shoulder, slow-roasted in sheep's-milk yogurt. The mid-century-meets-industrial space is a favourite with the business crowd, but there's a casualness too, with footpath tables and young, friendly staff.

🍸 Drinking & Nightlife

Aloha Bar   COCKTAIL BAR
(🕿 07-5592 5000; www.alohabaranddining.com.au; 18 Main Pl, Broadbeach; ⊘ 5pm-1am) A gritty laneway opens into this pumping tiki bar, decked out with a palm-tree ceiling and pineapple wallpaper, where hip young things knock back rum-based cocktails while DJs do their thing. Hawaiian-shirted waitstaff will deliver drinks to your table, along with poke bowls, Cuban sandwiches and Kalua pork wontons.

Seaside Broadbeach Bowls Club   CLUB
(🕿 07-5531 5913; www.broadbeachbowlsclub.com; 169 Surf Pde, Broadbeach; ⊘ 11.30am-8pm) Home to the best bowling greens in Australia – some say, the world. Far from a tired old space, this traditional club has had a modern makeover with bright, breezy and beachy bars and restaurants. Come for a sunset beer on the huge terrace, and barefoot bowls.

Burleigh Heads

The super-chilled surfie enclave of Burleigh (drop the 'Heads' if you don't want to out yourself as a tourist) has long been a family favourite, but is definitely enjoying its moment in the sun on a broader scale. The town's gently retro vibe and palpable youthful energy epitomise both the Gold Coast's timeless appeal and its new, increasingly interesting spirit. You'll find some of the region's best cafes and restaurants dotted around its little grid and, yes, that famous right-hand point break still pumps, while the beautiful pine-backed beach continues to charm everyone who lays eyes on it.

◎ Sights & Activities

Burleigh Head National Park   PARK
(www.npsr.qld.gov.au/parks/burleigh-head; Goodwin Tce; ⊘ 24hr) **FREE** Walk the headland through this 27-hectare rainforest reserve with plenty of bird life, including sea eagles, and the chance to spot whales from May to November. There are a couple of walking trails to Tallebudgera creek or the headland itself. Great views of the Burleigh surf.

⭐ **Village Markets**   MARKET
(🕿 0487 711 850; www.thevillagemarkets.co; Burleigh Heads State School, 1750 Gold Coast Hwy; ⊘ 8.30am-1pm 1st & 3rd Sun of month) A long-running market that highlights local designers, makers and collectors, with fashion and lifestyle stalls, lots of live music and a strong local following.

David Fleay Wildlife Park   WILDLIFE RESERVE
(🕿 07-5576 2411; www.npsr.qld.gov.au/parks/david-fleay; cnr Loman Lane & West Burleigh Rd, West Burleigh; adult/child/family $23/10.50/58.75; ⊘ 9am-5pm) Opened by the doctor who first succeeded in breeding platypuses, this wildlife park has 4km of walking tracks through mangroves and rainforest to use in search of animals, including cassowaries, emus, crocs, kangaroos and the platypus. There are plenty of informative native wildlife shows throughout the day.

During school holidays, on certain dates you can book the Twilight Experience ($25, 6pm to 8.45pm), for which the park collaborates with the **Jellurgal Cultural Centre** (🕿 07-5525 5955; www.jellurgal.com.au; 1711 Gold Coast Hwy; tours adult/child from $30/15; ⊘ 8am-3.30pm Mon-Fri) 🚶 **FREE**, offering an evening of Aboriginal storytelling, song and dance, and the chance to see wildlife at night.

GOLD COAST'S BEST SURF BREAKS

The Gold Coast possesses some of the longest, hollowest and best waves in the world, and is lauded for its epic consistency. The creation of the Superbank – a sand bar that's formed as part of anti-erosion efforts, stretching 2km from the Queensland–NSW border up to Kirra – has made for even better waves, even more often.

Gentle waves for a body bash or some white wash for learning the ropes are easy to find, but here is a list legendary surf breaks.

It's worth noting you won't be alone out the back. Local surfers have a reputation for being territorial and once you've seen the cut-ins, you'll understand why. Be respectful.

Snapper Rocks A highly advanced point break at Coolangatta's far south; home to the Quiksilver & Roxy Pro World Surfing League; and home break to Australian pro surfers Stephanie Gilmore and Joel Parkinson. It's so good it gets ridiculously overcrowded.

Duranbah Universally known as D-bah (and, officially, *just* over the Queensland–NSW border from Point Danger), this point and peaky beach break is good for those who like their waves technical and punchy.

Greenmount Classic beach break that benefits from a southerly swell – sightings of pro surfers Mick Fanning and Joel Parkinson are not uncommon.

Kirra Beautiful beach break that doesn't work that often, but, oh, when it does... Expect long barrels that are some of the world's best.

Burleigh Heads Strong currents and boulders to watch out for, but a perfect break that's on more often than not.

The Spit One of north Goldie's stalwarts, this peaky beach break can work even when the surf is small. From here, locals often make the precarious paddle (boats! marine life!) over to TOS ('the other side') – South Stradbroke Island – where the barrels are better than big.

Greenhouse the Bathhouse BATHHOUSE
(☑ 0435 137 364; www.greenhousethebathhouse. com; 7/37 Tallebudgera Creek Rd; 90min session from $40; ☉ noon-5.30pm by appointment only Wed-Sun) The owners of vegan restaurant **Greenhouse Canteen** (☑ 07-5601 0178; www. greenhousecanteen.com; 1/140 Griffith St; dishes $9-23; ☉ 5-10pm Tue-Sun; ☑) ✆ continue to look after the well-being of Gold Coastians by providing this relaxed haven. Beautifully designed, it offers hydrotherapy spas, eucalyptus steam room, sauna and plunge pool. If you book a massage or treatment, it includes a 90-minute session using the bathhouse's facilities.

🛏 Sleeping & Eating

Burleigh Beach Tourist Park CARAVAN PARK $
(☑ 07-5667 2750; www.goldcoasttouristparks.com. au; 36 Goodwin Tce; powered sites/cabins from $48/148; ❄ @ 🛜 ⛱) This park is snug, but it's well run and in a good spot near the beach. Aim for one of the blue cabins at the front of the park. There's a minimum two-night stay for cabins.

Burleigh Break MOTEL $$
(☑ 0418 113 411; www.burleighbreak.com.au; 1935 Gold Coast Hwy; d $130-180; P 🛜) A progressive renovation has seen one of the Gold Coast's beloved mid-century motels transformed into a friendly and great-value place to stay. Classic motel design means highway views, but you're still just a minute's amble from the beach. Rooms have retained vintage features where possible, but otherwise are fresh and simple.

★ Rick Shores FUSION $$
(☑ 07-5630 6611; www.rickshores.com.au; 43 Goodwin Tce; mains $29-55; ☉ noon-midnight Tue-Sun) Feet-in-the-sand dining often plays it safe, but while this Modern Asian spot sends out absolute crowd-pleasing dishes, it's also pleasingly inventive. The space is all about the view, the sound of the nearby waves, the salty breeze and relaxed feel. Serves are huge and designed for sharing, but be sure to start with the sensational fried Moreton Bay bug roll all to yourself.

★ Justin Lane PIZZA $$
(☑ 07-5576 8517; www.justinlane.com.au; 1708-1710 Gold Coast Hwy; mains $20-27; ☉ 5pm-late Mon-Wed, from noon Thu-Sun) One of the seminal players in Burleigh's food and drinking scene, Justin Lane has colonised most of an old shopping arcade with a downstairs

pizzeria and upstairs rooftop bar offering lovely foreshore views. Great pizzas, simple but flavour-packed pasta dishes and a fantastic wine list make it a must, even if you're not here for the party vibe.

Jimmy Wah's VIETNAMESE $$
(☑07-5659 1180; www.jimmywahs.com.au; 1724 Gold Coast Hwy; dishes $12-38; ⊘noon-late) Modern Vietnamese is dished up in a relaxed yet stylish setting, featuring a wall mural of the man himself (Jimmy Wah is a character in the film *Good Morning Vietnam*). Tuck into soft-shell crab bánh mì, snapper and crab dumplings, and sticky confit pork belly, paired with fresh, vibrant cocktails.

★Harry's Steak Bistro & Bar STEAK $$$
(☑07-5535 2699; www.harryssteakbistro.com.au; 1744 Gold Coast Hwy; mains $20-56; ⊘5pm-late Mon-Thu, from noon Fri-Sun) Don't misread the menu – a mix-and-match steak-and-sauce affair – as belonging to a chain restaurant. Harry's, a stylish paean to 'beef, booze and banter', is super-serious about its steaks, with each accredited with the name of its farm and region. Sweet staff will go out of their way to make sure you get a cut you'll enjoy.

🍷 Drinking & Nightlife

Lockwood BAR
(☑0488 111 030; www.lockwoodbar.com; 7b Justin Lane; ⊘5pm-late) Find your way to the rear laneway, look for the red door, text the number to get in – yes, a speakeasy bar has landed in Burleigh. Once you get inside, you'll find an intimate room with exposed brick, mood lighting and a great choice of fine classic cocktails.

Black Hops Brewing BREWERY
(☑0423 585 032; www.blackhops.com.au; 15 Gardenia Grove; ⊘noon-7pm Wed-Fri, to 6pm Sat & Sun) The Black Hops boys run a friendly and fun tap room, where you can enjoy a tasting paddle or sample whatever craft delight they've currently got on their 14 taps. You can also pick up bottles of beer to take home, plus there's a short menu of dishes to soak up the booze.

Currumbin & Palm Beach

Around the point from Burleigh, Palm Beach has a particularly lovely stretch of sand, backed with a few old-style beach shacks. Its numbered streets are also home to some great coffee stops and dining ops.

Further south again, Currumbin is a sleepy family-focused town, with a beautiful surf beach, safe swimming in Currumbin Creek and some evocative mid-century architecture worth seeking out. It's also home to the iconic eponymous wildlife sanctuary.

👁 Sights & Activities

Kids will enjoy a swim at **Currumbin Rock Pools** (Currumbin Creek Rd, Currumbin Valley).

The **Currumbin Wildlife Sanctuary** (☑1300 886 511; www.cws.org.au; 28 Tomewin St; adult/child/family $50/40/150) includes Australia's biggest rainforest aviary, where you can hand-feed a technicolour blur of rainbow lorikeets. There's also kangaroo and crocodile feeding, photo ops with koalas, reptile shows, a treetop ropes course and Aboriginal dance displays (some activities have fees). There's often an adults-at-kids-prices special during school holidays.

🍴 Eating & Drinking

Salt Mill CAFE $
(☑07-5525 7198; www.thesaltmillcurrumbin.cafe leader.com; 784 Pacific Pde, Currumbin; dishes $7-13; ⊘5.30am-3pm Mon-Fri, 6.30am-4pm Sat & Sun) Tiny hole-in-the-wall Salt Mill, across the road from the beach, keeps surfers and sunbathers refreshed with well-made coffee, delicious smoothies and healthy juices, along with a menu of toasted sandwiches, bagels and aai bowls.

Collective INTERNATIONAL $$
(☑07-5618 8229; www.thecollectivepalmbeach. com.au; 1128 Gold Coast Hwy, Palm Beach; mains $17-24; ⊘noon-late) Five kitchens here serve one rambling indoor-outdoor communal dining space, strung with fairy lights, flush with pot plants and packed with happy eaters. There are two bars, one of them a balmy rooftop affair. Choose from burgers, pizza, Asian fusion, Mexican and Mod Oz share plates; there are also gluten-free and vegan options. Book a table online.

★Balter BREWERY
(☑07-5525 6916; www.balter.com.au; 14 Traders Way, Currumbin; ⊘3-9pm Wed-Fri, noon-8pm Sat & Sun) Surf star Mick Fanning (the guy who punched a shark, right?) and his fellow circuit legends Joel Parkinson, Bede Durbidge and Josh Kerr are all partners in this wonderful brewery, hidden away at the back of a Currumbin industrial estate. Come and sample the already sought-after Balter XPA or a seasonal special (tasting paddles go for $15).

Coolangatta

POP 5948

A down-to-earth beach town on Queensland's far southern border, 'Coolie' has quality surf beaches, including the legendary Superbank, and a tight-knit, very real community that makes it feel less touristy. The legendary **Coolangatta Gold** (www.sls.com.au/coolangattagold) surf lifesaving comp takes place here each October, while the **Quiksilver & Roxy Pro** (www.aspworldtour.com; Point Danger) kicks off surfing's most prestigious world tour at Snapper Rocks each March. Follow the boardwalk north around Kirra Point for another beautiful long stretch of beach, sometimes challenging surf, and locally loved indie-atmosphere cafes and bars.

Point Danger Light, the lighthouse sitting between Coolangatta and Tweed Heads, marks the border between Queensland and NSW, with amazing views in both directions.

For local surfing lessons, try **Gold Coast Surfing Centre** (07 0417 191 629; www.goldcoastsurfingcentre.com; group lessons $45) or **Walkin' on Water** (07 0418 780 311, 07-5534 1886; www.walkinonwater.com; Greenmount Beach; 2hr surfing lessons $50).

🛏 Sleeping & Eating

Coolangatta Sands Backpackers   HOSTEL $
(07 07-5536 7472; http://coolangattasandshotel.com.au; cnr Griffith & McLean Sts; dm/s/d from $29/70/76; ❄ @ 🛜) Above the boozy Coolangatta Sands Hotel, this hostel is a warren of rooms and corridors with basic dorms and pub rooms, but there's a fab wrap-around balcony above the street. No alcohol allowed, unfortunately – go downstairs to the pub.

★**La Costa Motel**   MOTEL $$
(07 07-5599 2149; www.lacostamotel.com.au; 127 Golden Four Dr, Bilinga; d $130-185; ❄ 🛜) One of the few motels of 1950s 'highway heritage', this mint-green weatherboard just off the Gold Coast Hwy has stayed true to its roots on the outside, while the interiors are neat, comfortable and include kitchenettes. A lovely apartment with a private deck suits longer stays. Prices are significantly lower outside high season.

★**The Pink Hotel**   BOUTIQUE HOTEL $$$
(07 0499 746 545; http://thepinkhotelcoolangatta.com; 171 Griffith St; r from $295) Above Eddie's Grub House bar, this candy-pink mid-century motel has been transformed into a good-time boutique hotel with coastal Californian vibes and a bit of rock 'n' roll. Rooms and suites are pimped up with murals designed by a local tattoo artist, neon signs, record players, and Smeg bar fridges.

Gelato Messina   ICE CREAM $
(07 07-5536 5488; http://gelatomessina.com; 33/72-80 Marine Pde; ⊗11am-9pm Sun-Thu, to 9.30pm Fri & Sat) Get lickin' on gelato and sorbet flavours such as salted coconut and mango salsa; dulce de leche; pistachio made with Sicilian pistachios; and classics like chocolate chip.

★**Tasca**   ITALIAN $$
(07 0457 230 921; www.tascacoolangatta.com; 114 Griffith St; mains $23-29; ⊗3pm-late, closed Mon in winter) Tasca, Italian for pocket, sums up this tiny, intimate and sophisticated wine bar that not only pours from an impressive wine list but also does fantastic modern Italian dishes to match. Start off with an antipasto plate before some flash-fried squid and pappardelle with beef-cheek ragu. Excellent cocktails too.

🍷 Drinking & Nightlife

★**Eddie's Grub House**   BAR
(07 07-5599 2177; www.eddiesgrubhouse.com; 171 Griffith St; ⊗noon-10.30pm Tue-Thu & Sun, to midnight Fri & Sat) The walls are covered in photos of rock legends, from Bowie to Motörhead, at this totally old-school rock bar, summed up by one sign on display: 'The only punk in the village'. Yes, there's grub to be had, and Eddie's 'dive bar comfort food' is exactly that, but this is predominantly a place for drinking, dancing and catching local bands.

★**Black Sheep Espresso Baa**   CAFE
(07 07-5536 9947; 72-80 Marine Pde; ⊗5am-2pm) A passionate crew of coffee obsessives runs this cute little cafe right in the heart of the Marine Pde shopping strip. Perfect espresso, filter coffee and that Gold Coast necessity, iced latte, are joined by a small but creative breakfast and lunch menu.

Gold Coast Hinterland

Inland from the surf, sand and half-nakedness of the Gold Coast, the densely forested mountains of the McPherson Range feel a million miles away and are a good spot to connect with the spirit of the local Yugambeh people. There are some brilliant national parks here, with subtropical jungle,

SOUTH STRADBROKE ISLAND
·····················

A narrow, 21km-long sand island, 'Straddie' is largely undeveloped and car-free – the perfect antidote to the Gold Coast's busyness. At its northern end, the narrow channel separating it from North Stradbroke Island is a top fishing spot; at its southern end, where the Spit is only 200m away, you'll find breaks so good they have Gold Coast surfers braving the swim over.

South Stradbroke was once attached to North Stradbroke, until a huge storm in 1896 blasted through the isthmus that joined them. The ensuing isolation has been a boon for South Stradbroke's natural habitat, with wallabies aplenty and pristine bush, sand and sea to explore.

There are a few rustic campgrounds and the family-friendly **Couran Cove Island Resort** (☑ 07-5597 9999; www.courancove.com.au; studios $179-230, eco-cabins $249; ❋ ☒), but if you wish to just visit for the day, you can take the Couran Cove **ferry** (☑ 07-5597 9999; www.courancove.com.au; Hope Harbour Marina, 60 Sickle Ave, Hope Island; return adult/child $38/18) to the resort, or charter a boat to Couran Cove or **Tipplers Campground** (☑ 07-5577 2849; www.goldcoasttouristparks.com.au/straddie-park-home; sites/huts from $26/70) with **Cove Water Taxi** (☑ 0419 724 630; www.covewatertaxi.com.au).

waterfalls, lookouts and rampant wildlife. Springbrook National Park is arguably the wettest place in southeast Queensland, with cool air and a dense sea of forest. Lamington National Park attracts birdwatchers and hikers, while the kitschy Tamborine Mountain area lures craftwork hunters and cottage weekenders.

Tamborine Mountain

The mountaintop rainforest community of Tamborine Mountain – comprising Eagle Heights, North Tamborine and Mt Tamborine – is 45km inland from the Gold Coast beaches. It has cornered the arts-and-craft, Germanic-kitsch, package-tour, chocolate-fudge-liqueur market in a big way – if this is your bag, **Gallery Walk** (☑ 07-5545 2006; 197 Long Rd; ⊙ most shops 10am-4pm) in Eagle Heights is the place to stock up.

Tamborine National Park (www.nprsr. qld.gov.au/parks/tamborine) park comprises 13 sections stretching across the 8km plateau, offering waterfalls and super views of the Gold Coast. Accessed via easy-to-moderate walking trails are Witches Falls, Curtis Falls, Cedar Creek Falls and Cameron Falls. Pick up a map at the visitor centre in North Tamborine.

With **Skywalk** (☑ 07-5545 2222; www. rainforestskywalk.com.au; 333 Geissman Dr, North Tamborine; adult/child/family $19.50/9.50/49; ⊙ 9.30am-4pm) you can take a 1.5km walk along forest floor trails to pretty Cedar Creek, with spectacular elevated steel viewpoints and bridges cutting through the upper

canopy along the way. Look out for rare Richmond birdwing butterflies en route.

Lamington National Park

Australia's largest remnant of subtropical rainforest cloaks the deep valleys and steep cliffs of the McPherson Range, reaching elevations of 1100m on the Lamington Plateau. Here, the 200-sq-km **Lamington National Park** (www.nprsr.qld.gov.au/parks/lamington) is a Unesco World Heritage Site with more than 160km of walking trails. The park is known as Woonoongoora to the local Yugambeh people, meaning 'quiet and timeless', and you can spend days exploring this stunning part of the hinterland, but it also offers plenty of short walks, waterfalls, birdwatching and picnic areas for day trippers too. The two most accessible sections of the park are **Binna Burra** on the eastern side and **Green Mountains (O'Reilly's)** on the western side.

Green Mountains Campground (☑ 13 74 68; www.nprsr.qld.gov.au/parks/lamington; Green Mountains (O'Reilly's); sites per person/family $6.55/26.20), at the end of Lamington National Park Rd, is adjacent to the day-use visitor car park. There are plenty of spots for tents (and a toilet-and-shower block) but book in advance.

Binna Burra Mountain Lodge (☑ 07-5533 3622; www.binnaburralodge.com.au; 1069 Binna Burra Rd, Beechmont; powered/unpowered sites $35/30, apt from $314, cabin d with/without bathroom $160/140; P ⊖) is the nearest thing to a ski lodge in the bush and offers absolute offline peace. You can stay in rustic log cabins, well-appointed apartments (known as 'sky lodges') with spectacular Scenic Rim views, or in a tent surrounded by forest.

The famous **O'Reilly's Rainforest Retreat** (☎1800 688 722; www.oreillys.com.au; Lamington National Park Rd, Green Mountains; d $160-270, 1-bedroom villas from $350; @☎≋) has lost much of its original grandeur but retains a rustic charm – and sensational views. Rooms are super-comfortable and light-filled, while the luxury villas are slick with stunning views; two-night minimum stay applies. There are plenty of organised wildlife activities and guided walks, plus a day spa, a cafe, a bar and a restaurant (mains $26 to $40).

Springbrook National Park

A wonderland for hikers, **Springbrook National Park** (☎13 74 68; www.nprsr.qld.gov.au/parks/springbrook) has excellent trails through cool-temperate, subtropical and eucalypt forests offering a mosaic of gorges, cliffs and waterfalls. The park is a steep remnant of the huge Tweed Shield volcano that centred on nearby Wollumbin/Mt Warning in NSW more than 20 million years ago. It's

The park is divided into four sections. The 900m-high **Springbrook Plateau** is home to the township of Springbrook, which fans out along Springbrook Rd. Laced with waterfalls, trails and eye-catching lookouts, this section receives the most visitors. **Mt Cougal**, accessed via Currumbin Creek Rd, has several waterfalls and swimming holes (watch for submerged logs and slippery rocks). **Natural Bridge** section has a walking circuit leading to a scenic waterfall-cave formation, while **Numinbah Valley** to the north is the most heavily forested section of the park.

Excellent viewpoints in the park include the appropriately named **Best of All Lookout** (Repeater Station Rd), **Canyon Lookout** (Canyon Pde), which is also the start of a 4km circuit walk to Twin Falls, and the superb lookout beside the 60m **Goomoolahra Falls** (Springbrook Rd).

There are 11 grassy sites at the pretty **Settlement Campground** (☎13 74 68; www.nprsr.qld.gov.au/parks/springbrook; 52 Carricks Rd, Springbrook; sites per person/family $6.55/26.20) which has toilets and gas BBQs, but no showers. Book ahead.

The **Gold Coast Hinterland Great Walk** (www.parks.des.qld.gov.au/parks/great-walks-gold-coast-hinterland) runs through here. This epic three-day 54km trip takes walkers though Antarctic beech forests and past waterfalls from the Green Mountains aka O'Reilly's section of Lamington National Park to the Springbrook Plateau.

NOOSA & THE SUNSHINE COAST

A place of flawless beaches, coveted surf and laid-back, sun-kissed locals, the Sunshine Coast spreads a golden 100km from the tip of Bribie Island to the Cooloola Coast. Resort towns dot the coast, each with its own appeal and vibe, from chic, cosmopolitan Noosa to easy, hip Caloundra. For tens of thousands of years, these coastal plains have belonged to the Kabi Kabi (Gubbi Gubbi) people, known as the *mwoirnewar* (the saltwater people) to the Jinibara people of the neighbouring hinterland.

Lush and cool, the Sunshine Coast hinterland is where you'll find the ethereal Glass House Mountains, dramatic volcanic plugs shrouded in ancient mythology. The spirit of modern Australian icon Steve Irwin lives on at nearby Australia Zoo, while further north, the Blackall Range serves up thick forests, lush pastures and quaint villages alive with artisanal food shops and crafty boutiques.

ℹ Getting There & Around

AIR

Sunshine Coast Airport (☎07-5453 1500; www.sunshinecoastairport.com; Friendship Ave) is at Marcoola, 10km north of Maroochydore and 26km south of Noosa. Jetstar (www.jetstar.com) and Virgin Australia (www.virginaustralia.com) have daily direct flights from Sydney and Melbourne; Jetstar also runs direct flights from Adelaide three times weekly. Qantas (www.qantas.com.au) flies direct from Sydney.

Sunshine Coast Airport also hosts seasonal direct flights to Auckland, New Zealand. Once current expansion works are completed in late 2020, the airport is expected to introduce new international routes to Asia, the West Pacific and possibly Hawaii.

BUS

Greyhound Australia (p1072) has several direct daily connections between Brisbane and Mooloolaba/Maroochydore (from $21/22, 1¼ to 2¾ hours) and Noosa (from $22, 2¼ to 3 hours). It runs a daily morning service from Brisbane to Caloundra ($21, 2¼ hours), though passengers must transfer at Australia Zoo. It runs a direct morning service from Caloundra to Brisbane (from $20, 80 minutes).

Sunshine Coast

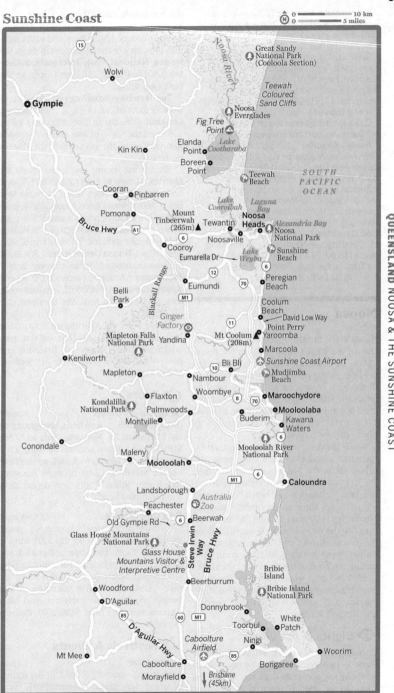

Premier Motor Service (p303) runs one daily service each way between Brisbane and Noosa ($24, 2½ hours) via Mooloolaba and Maroochydore ($24, 1½ hours).

Several companies offer transfers from Sunshine Coast Airport and Brisbane to points along the coast. Fares from Brisbane cost from around $60 to $65 and from Sunshine Coast Airport from around $18 to $35. (Fares are roughly half-price for children.)

Con-X-ion (p303) does airport transfers from the Sunshine Coast and Brisbane Airports.

Henry's Airporter (☑ 07-5474 0199, 1300 954 199; www.henrys.com.au) runs a door-to-door service from Sunshine Coast Airport to points north as far as Noosa Heads and Tewantin.

Sunbus (www.sunbus.com.au) Local routes include Caloundra to Maroochydore ($5.80, 55 minutes) and Maroochydore to Noosa ($8.90, 1¼ hours). Services also run between Nambour train station and Maroochydore ($4.80, 35 minutes) and between Nambour train station and Noosa ($8.90, 1¼ hour). The last of these travels via Yandina, Eumundi, Cooroy and Tewantin. Translink Go Cards are accepted.

Noosa

POP 52,125

Noosa is the Sunshine Coast's golden child. One of Australia's most fashionable resort towns, it's lush, low-rise centre backs onto pristine subtropical rainforest and relatively calm, crystalline waters. The result is intimate, relaxed and exclusive. The town itself is within the Noosa Biosphere Reserve, a Unesco-recognised area famous for its highly diverse ecosystem.

While the designer boutiques, destination restaurants and canal-side villas draw the urban elites, the beach and bush are free, leading to a healthy intermingling of urbanites, laid-back surfers and beach bods. Noosa encompasses three main zones: upmarket Noosa Heads (around Laguna Bay and Hastings St), the more relaxed Noosaville (along the Noosa River) and the administrative hub of Noosa Junction. All three occupy the traditional land of the Kabi Kabi (or Gubbi Gubbi) people, whose territory stretches from Fraser Island south to the Pumicestone Passage and west towards the Conondale and Blackall Ranges.

◉ Sights & Activities

Covering the headland, **Noosa National Park** (www.noosanationalpark.com; Noosa Heads; ♿) is one of Noosa's top sights; the most scenic way to reach it is to follow the boardwalk along the coast from town. The park's walking tracks lead to stunning coastal scenery, idyllic bays and great surfing. Pick up a walking-track map from the **Noosa National Park Information Centre** (☑ 07-5447 3522; ⊙ 9.15am-4.45pm) at the park's entrance.

Tea Tree Bay (Noosa National Park) is one of Noosa's most idyllic beaches, while **Laguna Lookout** (Viewland Dr, Noosa Junction) offers a panoramic view of the densely wooded national park, the ocean and the distant hinterland.

For surfing lessons and water sports try **Merrick's Learn to Surf** (☑ 0418 787 577; www.learntosurf.com.au; Beach Access 14, Noosa Main Beach, Noosa Heads; group lesson $65; ⊙ group lessons 9am & 1.30pm, private lessons 11.15am; ♿), **Foam and Resin** (☑ 0424 985 687; 53 Hastings St, Noosa Heads; surfboard/SUP rental from $25/30; ⊙ 9am-5pm), **Noosa Ocean Rider** (☑ 0438 386 255; www.facebook.com/NoosaOceanrider; Jetty 17, 248 Gympie Tce, Noosaville; per person $70; ♿) and **Kayak Noosa** (☑ 07-5455 5651; www.kayaknoosa.com; 194 Gympie Tce, Noosaville; tours adult/child $60/45; ♿).

Noosa Ferry (p330) runs an informative hop-on, hop-off Classic Tour (all-day pass adult/child $25/7) between Tewantin and the Sofitel Noosa Pacific Resort jetty in Noosa Heads.

⊙ Tours

★ **Discovery Group**   DRIVING
(☑ 07-5449 0393; www.thediscoverygroup.com.au; 186 Gympie Tce, Noosaville; tours adult/child $185/130; ♿) Runs a great one-day, 4WD tour of Fraser Island, with pick-up available on the Sunshine Coast between Sunshine Beach and Noosa. Tours also depart daily from Rainbow Beach.

Bike On Australia   MOUNTAIN BIKING
(☑ 07-5474 3322; www.bikeon.com.au; guided tours from $65, bike hire per day $30) Runs a variety of tours, including self-guided and adventurous eco-jaunts. The fun, half-day Off the Top Tour – downhill on a mountain bike – costs $79, with a minimum of four people required. Also rents out road bikes (three/seven days from $120/250). Delivery available.

✦ Festivals & Events

Noosa Alive   CULTURAL
(www.noosaalive.com.au; ⊙ Jul) A 10-day festival of world-class music, dance, theatre, visual

Noosa Heads

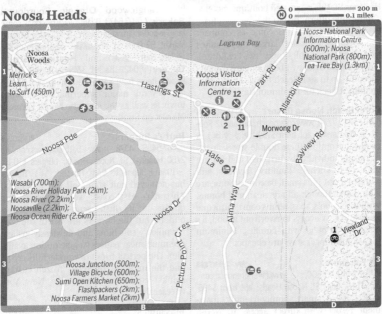

Noosa Heads

◎ Sights
1 Laguna Lookout...............................D3

✪ Activities, Courses & Tours
2 Foam and Resin...............................C1
3 Noosa Ferry.....................................A1

🛏 Sleeping
4 10 Hastings.....................................A1
5 Accom Noosa...................................B1
  Fairshore.....................................(see 5)

6 Peppers Noosa Resort & Villas............C3
7 YHA Halse Lodge................................C2

🍽 Eating
8 Betty's Burgers................................C1
  El Capitano..................................(see 8)
9 Hastings Street Bakery.....................B1
10 Kaali...A1
11 Locale...C2
12 Massimo's.......................................C1
13 Noosa Beach House...........................B1

arts, literature and more. The program includes both local and world premieres, as well as prolific festival guests.

Noosa Food & Wine FOOD & DRINK
(www.noosafoodandwine.com.au; ⊙May) A five-day tribute to all manner of gastronomic delights, featuring prolific chefs, masterclasses, special lunches and dinners, as well as themed food and wine tours.

🛏 Sleeping

For an extensive list of short-term holiday rentals, try Noosa Visitor Information Centre (p330) and the privately run **Accom Noosa** (☑1800 072 078, 07-5447 5374; www.accomnoosa.com.au; Shop 5/41 Hastings St, Noosa Heads).

★ YHA Halse Lodge HOSTEL **$**
(☑07-5447 3377; https://halselodge.com.au; 2 Halse Lane, Noosa Heads; dm/r from $32/88; **P @ ⍟**) This splendid, colonial-era Queenslander is a legendary backpacker stopover and well worth the clamber up its steep drive. There are four-, six- and 16-bed dorms, twins, doubles and a lovely wide verandah. Popular with locals, the bar is a mix-and-meet bonanza, offering great meals (mains $17 to $27) and (extra) cheap happy-hour drinks from 5pm to 6.30pm. Close to the Main Beach action.

★ 10 Hastings MOTEL **$$**
(☑07-5455 3340; www.10hastingsstreet.com.au; 10 Hastings St, Noosa Heads; studio/apt from $170/350; **❋ ⍟**) A rarity along Noosa's central

Hastings St, this renovated boutique motel is a refreshing alternative to the resorts. Clean, fresh, beach-chic rooms come as compact two-person studios and larger studio suites (sleeping two adults and two children). Larger still are the two-bedroom apartments (sleeping up to six). Beach towels are complimentary. Check for minimum stays.

Coral Beach Noosa Resort APARTMENT $$
(☑ 07-5449 7777; www.coralbeach.com.au; 12 Robert St, Noosaville; apt from $199; P ✳ 🗢 🖭) A good-value option, these double-storey apartments are individually furnished and feature their own kitchen, laundry facilities and patch of grass, plus small balconies. Some are a bit dated, though all are clean and homey. With three pools, spas, tennis court, barbeque areas and easy access to riverfront action, it's especially popular with families. Minimum two nights; longer stays are cheaper.

★ Fairshore APARTMENT $$$
(☑ 07-5449 4500; www.fairshorenoosa.com. au; 41 Hastings St, Noosa Heads; apt from $495; P ✳ 🗢 🖭) A smart, family-friendly apartment resort with direct access to Noosa Main Beach and buzzing Hastings St, Fairshore comes with a magazine-worthy, palm-fringed pool area. Two-bedroom apartments offer one or two bathrooms; though each apartment varies in style, all have laundry facilities and most are airy and contemporary. There's also a small gym. Parking is free (vehicle height restriction 1.85m).

Peppers Noosa Resort & Villas RESORT $$$
(☑ 1300 737 444; www.peppers.com.au/noosa; 33a Viewland Dr, Noosa Heads; studio/apt/villa from $185/219/600; ✳ 🗢 🖭) Backing onto Noosa National Park, this discreet resort offers three pools, an award-winning day spa, well-equipped gym and choice of studio rooms, apartments and villas. One-bedroom apartments (request a refurbished one) have kitchenettes, while both two-bedroom apartments and the three-bedroom penthouse offer fully equipped kitchen and spa bath. The airy, luxurious three- and four-bedroom villas offer the most seclusion.

✕ Eating

Noosa is a culinary hub, with no shortage of renowned and on-point restaurants. That said, dining in Noosa is rarely cheap, with mains commonly north of $30. If you're watching your budget, lunch at casual cafes and burger joints, or grab a bite at bakeries

like **Tanglewood Organic Sourdough Bakery** (☑ 07-5473 0215; www.facebook.com/tanglewoodorganicsourdough; Belmondos Organic Market, 59 Rene St, Noosaville; pastries from $5; ⊘ 7am-2pm; 🗢 🖭) and **Hastings Street Bakery** (☑ 0429 183 391; 3/49 Hastings St, Noosa Heads; items from $4; ⊘ 6am-4pm; 🖭). There are several major supermarkets around town, as well as the fantastic Noosa Farmers Market on Sundays.

Betty's Burgers BURGERS $
(☑ 07-5455 4378; www.bettysburgers.com.au; 2/50 Hastings St, Noosa Heads; burgers $10-16; ⊘ 10am-8.30pm, to 9pm Thu-Sat; 🖭) Betty's has achieved cult status all the way down Australia's east coast, which explains the queues at its lush, semi-al-fresco Noosa outlet – but the burgers are worth the wait for pillowy soft buns and flawlessly grilled, premium-meat patties (veggie option available). The perfect fries are wonderfully crispy and the moreish concretes (frozen custard drinks) come in flavours like New York cheesecake.

Massimo's GELATO $
(☑ 07-5474 8033; 75 Hastings St, Noosa Heads; gelato from $5.50; ⊘ 9.30am-9.30pm, to 10pm Fri & Sat; 🖭) While the 'no tastings' policy seems a little mean-spirited, rest assured that Massimo's icy treats are creamy and natural in flavour. You'll find both milk-based and sorbet options, from cinnamon and macadamia to climate-appropriate options like mango and passion fruit.

★ Sumi Open Kitchen JAPANESE $$
(☑ 07-5447 3270; www.sumiopenkitchen.com. au; 4/19-21 Sunshine Beach Rd, Noosa Junction; 4-/6-course menu $55/75; ⊘ 5.30-10pm, last orders around 8pm) Intimate, gracious Sumi offers a set-course menu from chef Giles Hohnen, who owns the place with partner Tomoko. From delicate dashi soup with prawn dumpling to grilled salmon served with tofu skin, pea sprouts and sun-dried daikon, flavours are clean, nuanced and a testament to high-quality produce. Libations include minimum-intervention wines and organic sake from family-owned breweries. Book ahead.

El Capitano PIZZA $$
(☑ 07-5474 9990; www.elcapitano.com.au; 52 Hastings St, Noosa Heads; pizzas $22-25; ⊘ 5-10pm, to 11pm Fri & Sat) Down an easy-to-miss path and up a set of stairs is one of Noosa's best pizzerias, a hip spot with bar seating, louvred

SUNSHINE COAST ON A PLATE

When packing for the Sunshine Coast, remember three essentials: swimsuit, sunscreen and ravenous appetite. The third is no surprise to local gourmets, well aware of the area's quiet evolution into a culinary hotspot.

The 2019 launch of region-wide food festival **The Curated Plate** (www.thecurated plate.com.au/sunshine-coast; ☉ Aug) is just one of numerous buzz-inducing additions to the area's booming food scene. Another is casual, southeast-Asian-inspired eatery Sum Yung Guys (p338), stamping ground of *Masterchef Australia* runner-up Matt Sinclair. Just up the road in Noosa, fellow high-profile chef Peter Kuravita fuses impeccable produce and his Sri Lankan heritage at fine-dining Noosa Beach House. While Noosa's most famous restaurant remains high-end Wasabi, it's worth reserving a table at newer, lesser-known Sumi Open Kitchen, an intimate Japanese restaurant whose owner-chef once worked at renowned restaurant Longrain. If you're in Noosa on a Sunday morning, hit **Noosa Farmers Market** (☑ 0418 769 374; www.noosafarmersmarket.com.au; Noosa Australian Football Club Grounds, 155 Weyba Rd, Noosaville; ☉ 6am-noon Sun) for local artisanal produce, among its cult-status buffalo mozzarella from Cedar Street Cheeserie.

Further south, the Maroochydore suburb of Kuluin harbours Lola's Pantry (p335), a hole-in-the-wall, outdoor cafe pumping out simple, exceptional vegan nosh by Alejando Cancino, former executive chef at Brisbane's celebrated Urbane. Further south still, Mooloolaba has lifted its own culinary game with numerous on-point debuts, among them contemporary Australian restaurant-bar Pier 33 (p336). The river views are free.

Inland, Yandina claims long-standing Thai powerhouse **Spirit House** (☑ 07-5446 8994; www.spirithouse.com.au; 20 Nindery Rd; mains $37-48, banquet per person $80-115; ☉ noon-3pm, plus 6-9pm Wed-Sat; ☑), one of Queensland's destination restaurants, while further uphill, cafe **Maleny Food Co** (☑ 07-5494 2860; www.malenyfoodco.com; 37 Maple St; meals $14-24, boards $26-35; ☉ 8am-4pm; ☑) seduces cheese lovers with its in-store fromagerie, a good place to pick up some black-ash brie from the hinterland's own **Kenilworth Dairies** (☑ 07-5446 0144; www.kenilworthdairies.com.au; 45 Charles St, Kenilworth; ☉ 9am-3pm; ☑).

windows and marine-themed street art. The light, fluffy pizzas are gorgeous, made with sourdough bases, topped with artisanal ingredients, and divided into *pizza rossa* (with tomato-sauce base) and *pizza bianca* (without). Book ahead.

Kaali
INDIAN $$
(☑ 07-5474 8989; www.kaaligourmetindian.com; 2/2 Hastings St, Noosa Heads; mains $19-33; ☉ 4.30-9.30pm Mon, 12.30-2.30pm & 4.30-9.30pm Tue-Sun; ☑) After all the Mod Oz cuisine on offer in Noosa Heads, this touch of India offers some spicy relief. At the western end of Hastings St, it's a casual spot, cooking up excellent curries, great tandoori breads and must-have decadent Camembert wedges in a tempura-style batter of crispy fennel, ginger and coriander.

★ Noosa Beach House
MODERN AUSTRALIAN $$$
(☑ 07-5449 4754; www.noosabeachhousepk.com. au; 16 Hastings St, Noosa Heads; dinner mains $38-48, 3-/6-course menu $80/115; ☉ 6.30-10.30am & 5.30-9.30pm, plus noon-2.30pm Sat & Sun; ☑) White walls, glass and timber set an uncluttered scene at this effortlessly chic restaurant, the stamping ground of celebrity chef Peter Kuravita. Seasonal ingredients and fresh local seafood underscore a contemporary menu whose deeply seductive Sri Lankan snapper curry with tamarind and *aloo chop* (potato croquette) nods to Kuravita's heritage. Herbivorous foodies can opt for a seven-course degustation ($100).

★ Little Humid
MODERN AUSTRALIAN $$$
(☑ 07-5449 9755; www.humid.com.au; 2/235 Gympie Tce, Noosaville; dinner mains $33-44; ☉ noon-2pm & 6pm-midnight Wed-Sun; ☑) This deservedly popular place serves up beautiful bistro fare with subtle twists: think flash-fried cuttlefish with green papaya, avocado salsa, palm sugar and chilli; orange-glaze confit duck with caramelised pumpkin, plum, walnuts and goat's curd; and roasted mushroom vol-au-vent with a white-wine and cavolo nero cream sauce. Book for dinner (up to a week ahead during peak periods).

★ Wasabi
JAPANESE $$$
(☑ 07-5449 2443; www.wasabisb.com; 2 Quamby Pl, Noosa Heads; 4 courses from $90, 7-/9-course

omakase menu $145/165; ⊙5-9.30pm Wed, Thu & Sat, noon-9.30pm Fri & Sun) An award-winning, waterside destination restaurant, Wasabi is well known to visiting gourmets. Premium produce from the region and Wasabi's own farm sings in delicate, technically brilliant dishes like handmade bunya- and soba-flour noodles with local sand crab, egg yolk, smoked sand-crab dashi and duck fat, or chocolate sorbet with black kinako milk gelée, sake poached cherry and barrel-aged rice wine. Book ahead.

Locale ITALIAN $$$
(☑07-5447 5111; www.localenoosa.com.au; 62 Hastings St, Noosa Heads; pizzas $24-27, mains $39-46; ⊙noon-late; 🖥) Dark, glossy and buzzing, upmarket Locale takes Manhattan glamour and gives it a lush tropical twist. In our opinion, the best seat is at the bar, where polished barkeeps mix flawless cocktails. The smart Italian menu – showcasing produce from Locale's own farm – includes less ubiquitous pasta options. The pizzas, however, are less impressive.

Drinking & Nightlife

★**Land & Sea Brewery** MICROBREWERY
(☑07-5455 6128; www.landandseabrewery.com; 19 Venture Dr, Noosaville; ⊙7am-10pm, to 11pm Fri-Sun; 🖥) British ex-pat Tim Crabtree is the charmer behind Noosa's first microbrewery, an impressive warehouse space off the tourist track. The town's easy living inspires head brewer Shane Fairweather, whose creations are balanced, easy-drinking and mostly vegan. There are eight to 10 beers on rotation, with regularly rotating IPAs, occasional collaborations and more unusual creations (think Japanese rice lager).

★**Clandestino Roasters** COFFEE
(☑1300 656 022; www.clandestino.com.au; Belmondos Organic Market, 59 Rene St, Noosaville; ⊙7am-4pm Mon-Fri, to 3pm Sat; 🖥) It might be off the tourist radar, but this lush warehouse microroastery packs in hipsters, surfers and suits, all here for Noosa's top coffee. Choose from three blends and six single origins served a number of ways, including espresso-style, cold-drip, pour-over and batch brew. The place also serves nitro cold brew and health-promoting elixirs created by an on-site naturopath.

★**Village Bicycle** BAR
(☑07-5474 5343; https://villagebicyclenoosa.com; 16 Sunshine Beach Rd, Noosa Junction;

⊙4pm-midnight, from 3pm Fri-Sun) Village Bicycle is run by young mates Luke and Trevor. Splashed with street art, it's a convivial, indie-spirited space, packed nightly with loyal regulars here to knock back beers (mainstream as well as local craft brews), cocktails and vino, and tuck into quality tacos, burgers and hot dogs. Best of all, the kitchen is open until 11pm.

❶ Information

Noosa Visitor Information Centre (☑07-5430 5000; www.visitnoosa.com.au; 61 Hastings St, Noosa Heads; ⊙9am-5pm; 🖥) Helpful tourist office covering Noosa and surrounds.

❶ Getting There & Away

Long-distance bus services stop at the **Noosa Junction Bus Station** on Sunshine Beach Rd. Greyhound Australia (p1072) has several daily bus connections from Brisbane to Noosa (from $22, 2¼ to 3 hours), while Premier Motor Service (p303) has one ($24, 2½ hours).

Most hostels have courtesy pick-ups.

Sunbus (www.sunbus.com.au) operates frequent services from Noosa to Maroochydore ($8.90, 1¼ hours) and Nambour train station ($8.90, 1¼ hours). Journeys to Nambour may require a transfer in Maroochydore. Translink Go Cards are valid on these services.

❶ Getting Around

BICYCLE

Bike On Australia (p326) rents out bicycles from several locations in Noosa, including the **Noosa River Holiday Park** (☑07-5449 7050; www.noosaholidayparks.com.au; 4 Russell St; powered sites $48; 🖥) in Noosaville and **Flashpackers** (☑07-5455 4088; www.flashpackersnoosa.com; 102 Pacific Ave; dm from $38, d with/without bathroom from $100/125; 🖥🖥🖥) in Sunshine Beach. Alternatively, bikes can be delivered to and from your door for $35 (or free if the booking is over $100).

BOAT

Noosa Ferry (☑07-5449 8442; www.noosaferry.com; cruise adult/child from $25/10;) operates ferries between Noosa Heads and Tewantin several times a day (all-day pass adult/child $25/7). **Noosa Water Taxi** (☑0411 136 810; www.noosawatertaxi.com; one way per person $10; ⊙9am to late) operates a water-taxi service around Noosa Sound from 9am to late; call or text to book. The service is also available for private charters.

BUS

Sunbus (www.sunbus.com.au) has local services that link Noosa Heads, Noosaville, Noosa

Junction and Tewantin. Translink Go Cards can be used on these services.

CAR & MOTORCYCLE

Most of the major car-rental brands can be found in Noosa; rentals start at around $70 per day.

Noosa Car Rentals (☑ 0429 053 728; www.noosacarrentals.com.au) A good local option; delivers to your accommodation. Both delivery and pick-up are free if staying in Noosa Heads, Noosaville, Noosa Junction, Noosa Springs, Tewantin, Sunshine Beach, Sunrise Beach, Marcus Beach, Peregian Beach or Peregian Springs. Three-day minimum hire period on most cars.

Scooter Hire Noosa (☑ 0404 086 462; www.scooterhirenoosa.com; 4/24hr from $35/65) Rents out 50cc and 150cc scooters. Scooters can be booked online and (in most cases) delivered directly to your accommodation, or rented from Scooter Mania's numerous agencies in Noosa. Riders require a full Australian or international driving licence.

Bribie Island

POP 18,190

Known as Yarun ('hunting ground') to the island's original inhabitants, the Joondoobarrie people, Bribie Island lies at the northern end of Moreton Bay. For thousands of years the Joondoobarrie lived sustainably on the island, having even trained dolphins to herd fish towards them. The first documented encounter between the Joondoobarrie and Europeans was in 1799, when British navigator Matthew Flinders landed briefly on the island. In 1823 castaways Thomas Pamphlett, John Finnegan and Richard Parsons spent seven months living on Yarun with the Joondoobarrie before being discovered by British surveyor John Oxley.

The only island in the bay linked to the mainland by bridge, Bribie today is a sedate place, popular with young families, retirees and those with a cool million (or three) to spend on a waterfront property. While it's far more developed than Stradbroke and Moreton Islands, the island does harbour some beautiful, sweeping sandy beaches.

The **Abbey Museum** (☑ 07-5495 1652; www.abbeymuseum.com; 63 The Abbey Pl, off Old Toorbul Point Rd, Caboolture; adult/child $12/7; ☉ 10am-4pm Mon-Sat) houses an extraordinary collection of art and archaeology, once the collection of Englishman 'Reverend' John Ward. The **Abbey Medieval Festival** (☑ 07-5495 1652; www.abbeymedievalfestival.com; Abbey Museum, 63 The Abbey Pl, Caboolture; ☉ Jul; 🏛) is held here in June or July.

The nearby **Caboolture Warplane Museum** (☑ 07-5499 1144; www.cabooolturewarplanemuseum.com; Hangar 104, Caboolture Airfield, McNaught Rd, Caboolture; adult/child $10/5; ☉ 9am-3pm) houses a booty of restored WWII planes, including a P51D Mustang, CAC Wirraway and Cessna Bird Dog.

Pick up maps and information at **Bribie Island Visitor Information Centre** (☑ 07-3408 9026; http://visitbribieisland.com.au; Benabrow Ave, Bellara; ☉ 9am-4pm).

🛏 Sleeping & Eating

Bribie Island

National Park Camping CAMPGROUND $
(☑ 13 74 68; www.npsr.qld.gov.au/parks/bribie-island; campsites per person $6.55) On the island's west coast, **Poverty Creek** is a large, grassy campground; facilities include toilets, a waste disposal facility and cold showers. Just south, **Ocean Beach** offers similar facilities. On the east coast, the **Gallagher Point** camping area has a few bush campsites, with no toilets or other facilities. All three sites are accessible by 4WD.

Sandstone Point Hotel PUB FOOD $$
(☑ 07-3475 3001; https://sandstonepointhotel.com.au; 1800 Bribie Island Rd, Sandstone Point; mains $18-38; ☉ 8am-9pm, to 9.30pm Sat; 🛜🏛) The best place to eat round here is on the mainland side of the bridge. This sprawling, modern waterfront pub is divided into numerous bars and dining areas, including a spacious outdoor deck. Good-quality, globally inspired bites range from breakfast egg-based classics to graze-friendly oysters, charcuterie boards and pizzas, and more substantial grilled steaks and seasonal Australian seafood dishes.

❶ Getting There & Away

There is no 4WD hire on Bribie, and you'll need a vehicle access permit ($49.50 per week) for the island's more off-track spots. Pick up one at **Gateway Bait & Tackle** (☑ 07-5497 5253; www.gatewaybaitandtackle.com.au; 1383 Bribie Island Rd, Ningi; ☉ 5.30am-5pm, to 2pm Wed, 4.30am-5pm Sat, 4.30am-3pm Sun) or online (https://parks.des.qld.gov.au).

Frequent Citytrain services run from Brisbane to Caboolture, from where **Bribie Island Coaches** (☑ 07-3408 2562; www.bribiecoaches.com.au) route 640 runs to Bribie Island via Ningi and Sandstone Point. Buses run roughly every hour, stopping in Bongaree and continuing through to Woorim. Regular Brisbane Translink fares apply (one way from central Brisbane $11.80).

GLASS HOUSE MOUNTAINS

The Glass House Mountains rise abruptly from the plains 20km northwest of Caboolture. Australia's finest example of an eroded central volcano complex, they are listed on the National Heritage Register.

The traditional owners, the Jinibara people and Kabi Kabi (Gubbi Gubbi) people, have inhabited the area for millennia. According to Dreaming legend, these looming volcanic plugs – formed some 24–27 million years ago – are a family of mountain spirits. To British explorer James Cook, their shapes recalled the conical glass-making furnaces of his native Yorkshire. Not surprisingly, they have inspired countless artists and writers.

The national park is broken into several sections (all within cooee of Beerwah), with picnic grounds and lookouts but no campgrounds. The peaks themselves are reached by a series of roads, some unsealed, that head inland from Steve Irwin Way, itself home to Australia Zoo, founded by the world-famous Crocodile Hunter himself.

The small township of Glass House Mountains is home to the **Glass House Mountains Visitor & Interpretive Centre** (☑07-5458 8848; www.visitsunshinecoast.com.au; cnr Bruce Pde & Reed St; ⊙9am-4pm; 🗢), while the mountains themselves lie a short drive to the southwest.

The easiest and most stunning panoramic viewing point is the **Glass House Mountains Lookout** (Glasshouse-Woodford Rd; 🛋) on Glasshouse-Woodford Rd, 9km from the visitor information centre. The lookout includes BBQ facilities and toilets. On clear days, you can even (just) see the Brisbane skyline.

Accommodation in the immediate area is relatively limited, with worthy options including luxe **Glass on Glasshouse** (☑0431 101 208, 07-5496 9608; www.glassonglasshouse.com.au; 182 Glasshouse-Woodford Rd; cottages incl breakfast $325-425; ❊🗢) and quirky **Glass House Mountains Ecolodge** (☑07-5493 0008; www.glasshouseecolodge.com; 198 Barrs Rd; r from $128; ❊🗢) 🏊. Campers can pitch their tent (or park their caravan) at the basic **Coochin Creek camping area** in nearby Beerwah State Forest; book ahead at https://qpws.usedirect.com/qpws. The Glass House Mountains are an easy day trip from Brisbane and the Sunshine Coast, where you'll find a plethora of accommodation options.

Caloundra

POP 51,095

Straddling a headland at the southern end of the Sunshine Coast, Caloundra has reinvented itself as an unexpected centre of cool. Beyond its golden beaches, water sports and beautiful Coastal Pathway walking track is a low-key creative scene, spanning everything from top-notch coffee shops and bars to impressive street art and a microbrewery, not to mention the coast's most sharply curated regional art galleries. The cherry on top of the proverbial cake is the **Caloundra Music Festival** (www.caloundramusicfestival.com; ⊙Sep-Oct), one of Queensland's biggest, best-loved annual music events. The town's name derives from the Aboriginal word *Kal'owen-dha* (or *cullawanda*), meaning place of beech trees. The native specimen was prolific in the area before timber-hungry lumberjacks saw their numbers decline.

👁 Sights & Activities

On Sunday mornings, crowds flock to Bulcock St to browse the market stalls at **Caloundra Street Fair** (www.caloundrastreetfair.com.au; ⊙8am-1pm Sun).

Caloundra Regional Gallery   GALLERY
(☑07-5420 8299; http://gallery.sunshinecoast.qld.gov.au; 22 Omrah Ave; ⊙10am-4pm Tue-Fri, to 2pm Sat & Sun) **FREE** When you're done with catching rays and waves, sidestep to this small, sophisticated gallery. Rotating exhibitions showcase quality local and national artists, with a number of notable Art Prize shows each year. The gallery stays up late for **Friday³Live** on the third Friday of the month, with music, talks, performances, drinks and bites.

Queensland Air Museum   MUSEUM
(☑07-5492 5930; www.qam.com.au; 7 Pathfinder Dr; adult/child $20/10; ⊙10am-4pm) Occupying two hangars beside Caloundra airport, the volunteer-run QAM houses about 80

civilian and military aircraft, including a mid-century Douglas DC-3 (the world's first mass-produced all-metal airliner) and a supersonic F-111 fighter jet belonging to the Royal Australian Air Force. Displays shed light on various aspects of Australian and international aviation history, including wartime battles and women in aviation, and there's a small collection of fabulously retro brochures, cabin bags and in-flight crockery from Australian airlines past and present.

Silky Surf
SURFING

(☑ 0402 375 681; http://silkysurf.com; 1½-hr lessons from $70) Former Aussie champion surfer Ben Silky offers private lessons for both intermediate and hardcore wave riders.

Caloundra Jet Ski
OUTDOORS

(☑ 0434 330 660; www.caloundrajetski.com.au; cnr Esplanade & Otranto Ave; rides $150-290) Affable, joke-cracking local Ken Jeffrey owns and operates these thrilling jet-ski tours of the Pumicestone Passage, the narrow waterway separating Caloundra and the northern tip of Bribie Island. Tours offer interesting insight into the area's ecosystem and are suitable for both novice and experienced jet-skiers (even the most nervous newbies will end up zipping across the blue like pros).

Sunshine Coast Skydivers
SKYDIVING

(☑ 1300 759 348, 07-3067 0715; www.sunshine coastskydivers.com.au; Caloundra Aerodrome, 1 Pathfinder Dr; tandem jumps from $239) Send your adrenaline into overdrive as you scan Caloundra and the Pacific Ocean from a brain-squeezing 4570m. If that puts a lump in your throat, consider one of the lower jumps.

🛏 Sleeping & Eating

City Centre Motel
MOTEL $

(☑ 07-5491 3301; www.caloundracitycentremotel. com.au; 20 Orsova Tce; s/d from $90/125; 🅿️ ❄️ 🛜) Spick and span, this modest, friendly motel (the closest to the city centre) offers simple, beige-hued rooms with comfortable beds, in-room microwaves and spotless bathrooms.

Monaco
APARTMENT $$$

(☑ 07-5490 5490; www.monacocaloundra.com.au; 12 Otranto Ave; apt from $180; 🅿️ ❄️ 🛜 🏊) Modern, good-sized apartments one block from Bulcock Beach. They're individually owned, so styles vary; the more expensive apartments offer full water vistas. Wi-fi is free but capped, and apartments are serviced every eight days. Property perks include a stylish,

heated lap pool, separate kids' pool, spa, sauna, gym and games rooms. Minimum two-night stay, with cheaper rates for longer stays.

Beau's
CAFE $

(☑ 07-5438 0048; www.beauskb.com.au; 32 Esplanade Headland; dishes $10-21; ❄️ 6.30am-3pm; 🚻) White and aqua tiles keep things fresh at Beau's, one of the best cafes on the Sunny Coast. Almost everything here is made from scratch, with a short, high-quality menu that might see you tossing up between maple-roasted almond granola with coconut and black sesame panna cotta, and slow-braised BBQ beef brisket with wood-smoked bacon and house-made pickle relish.

Green House Cafe
VEGETARIAN $$

(☑ 07-5438 1647; www.greenhousecafe.com.au; 5/8 Orumuz Ave; mains $15-19; ❄️ 8am-3pm, to 2pm Sat & Sun; 🚲🚻) A showcase for local ingredients, this chilled laneway spot serves up fresh, organic and filling vegetarian grub such as avocado on toast with cashew cheese, and crunchy waffles with seasonal fresh fruit and coconut nutmeg ice cream. Lighter bites and baked treats are also available, alongside virtuous smoothies, cold-pressed juices, kombucha and Hinterland-roasted organic coffee.

Tides
MODERN AUSTRALIAN $$$

(☑ 07-5438 2304; www.tideswaterfront.com.au; 26 Esplanade, Bulcock Beach; 2-/3-course lunch $39/50, dinner mains $35-55; ❄️ noon-2.30pm & 5.30-8.30pm; 🛜) Polished yet relaxed, Tides showcases local seafood and regional produce. Set lunches offer a pared-back version of the dinner menu, which might include local scallop ceviche with tomato, puffed wild rice and basil. The notable wine list includes top-tier Australian drops. Book a week ahead for a table on the sea-fronting balcony, the prime dining spot.

🍸 Drinking & Nightlife

Lamkin Lane Espresso Bar
CAFE

(www.facebook.com/lamkinlane; 31 Lamkin Lane; ❄️ 6am-4pm, 7am-noon Sat & Sun) The hearts of coffee snobs sing at minimalist Lamkin Lane, where affable baristas like nothing more than chatting about their two speciality blends and rotating trio of single origins (try their beautifully nuanced cold brew). The team here have a strong relationship with their coffee farmers, which means your brew is as ethical as it is smooth and aromatic.

DON'T MISS

AUSTRALIA ZOO

Roughly 30km inland from Caloundra is one of Queensland's most famous tourist attractions. **Australia Zoo** (☑07-5436 2000; www.australiazoo.com.au; 1638 Steve Irwin Way, Beerwah; adult/child $59/35; ⊙9am-5pm; ⊕) is a fitting homage to its founder, wildlife enthusiast Steve Irwin. The park has an amazing menagerie, with a Cambodian-style Tiger Temple, the famous Crocoseum and a dizzying array of critters, including native dingoes, Tasmanian devils and hairy-nosed wombats.

Various companies offer tours from Brisbane and the Sunshine Coast. The zoo operates a free bus to/from the nearby Beerwah train station.

Plan to spend a full day here.

Moffat Beach
Brewing Company   MICROBREWERY

(☑07-5491 4023; www.moffatbeachbrewingco.beer; 12 Seaview Tce, Moffat Beach; ⊙6.30am-5pm, to 9pm Wed-Sun) This award-winning microbrewery offers a rotating cast of house brews on tap, from a cult-status double IPA Iggy Hop to a chilli-and-chocolate Dragon's Breath stout. There's a four-brew paddle ($20) for the curious, as well as low-alcohol and gluten-free bottled beers. Live tunes add atmosphere on Fridays from 5pm, Saturdays from 4pm and Sundays from 3pm.

❶ Information

The **Caloundra Road Visitor Information Centre** (☑07-5458 8846; www.visitsunshinecoast.com; 7 Caloundra Rd; ⊙9am-4pm, to 3pm Sat & Sun; ☎) is on the roundabout at the town's entrance; there's also a central kiosk on **Bulcock St** (☑07-5458 8847; ⊙9am-3pm; ☎).

❶ Getting There & Away

The **Caloundra Transit Centre** (23 Cooma Tce) is the main bus station for both long-distance and local buses, a short walk south of Bulcock St.

Greyhound Australia (p1072) runs a daily morning service from Brisbane to Caloundra ($21, 2¼ hours); passengers must transfer at Australia Zoo. It also operates a direct morning service from Caloundra to Brisbane (from $20, 80 minutes).

Sunbus (www.sunbus.com.au) has frequent services between Caloundra and Maroochydore ($5.80, one hour). Transfer in Maroochydore for buses to Noosa. Translink Go Cards can be used on Sunbus services.

Mooloolaba & Maroochydore

Mooloolaba has seduced many with its sublime climate, family-friendly beaches and laid-back lifestyle. Once a humble fishing village, it's now one of the Sunshine Coast's main holiday hubs, its lively esplanade and riverfront lined with cafes, bars, boutiques and a recently improved dining scene. The town is also a launching pad for numerous day activities and tours, including diving and snorkelling trips.

Further north, booming Maroochydore takes care of the business end, with a brand-new city centre, a sprawling shopping centre, and its own stretch of buzzing eateries and bars. And while the vibe here may be more workaday, it too claims a stretch of sandy beachfront.

◎ Sights & Activities

Mooloolaba's north-facing main beach is one of the region's safest, most sheltered beaches. There are good surf breaks along the strip – one of Queensland's best for longboarders is the **Bluff**, the prominent point at Alexandra Headland. **Pincushion** near the Maroochy River mouth can provide an excellent break in the winter offshore winds. **Robbie Sherwell's XL Surfing Academy** (☑0423 039 505; www.xlsurfingacademy.com; 1hr private/group lessons $105/53) runs group and private surf lessons for both rookie and experienced surfers.

Sea Life Sunshine Coast   AQUARIUM

(www.underwaterworld.com.au; Wharf Marina, Parkyn Pde, Mooloolaba; adult/child $40/28; ⊙9am-3pm; ⊕) Kids will love this tropical oceanarium, complete with an 80m-long transparent underwater tunnel for close-up views of rays, reef fish and several species of shark. There's interactive exhibits, live shows, presentations and – during school holidays – the option of sleeping at the aquarium overnight ($99 per person). Check the website for discounted admission offers.

While visitors can also swim with seals, it's worth considering that animal-welfare groups believe captivity is debilitating and stressful for marine animals and exacerbated by human interaction.

Wildlife HQ   ZOO

(☑0428 660 671; www.whqzoo.com; 76 Nambour Connection Rd, Woombye; adult/child $29/15; ⊙9am-4pm; ⊕) Located at the **Big**

Pineapple ([☑]1800 132 289; www.bigpineapple.
com.au) [FREE], this 8-hectare zoo houses
native Australian, African, South American
and rare Asian critters, among them bin-
turongs, red pandas and tahrs (Himalayan
mountain goats).

Sunreef   DIVING
([☑]07-5444 5656; www.sunreef.com.au; Shop 11-12,
The Wharf, Parkyn Pde, Mooloolaba; dives from $99;
[☺]8am-5pm, to 4pm Sun) Offers numerous dives
at the wreck of sunken warship HMAS *Brisbane,* including daytime double dives (from
$165) and single night dives (from $99). It
also runs a snorkelling day trip to Flinders
Reef (from $159), which claims the highest
number of coral species of any subtropical
reef system along Australia's east coast. The
trip includes equipment and lunch.

Sunreef Hire   WATER SPORTS
([☑]07-5444 5656; www.hirehut.com.au; Shop
11-12, The Wharf, Parkyn Pde, Mooloolaba; kayak/
jet ski hire from $35/180) Hires out kayaks (two
hours $35), stand-up paddleboards (two
hours $35), jet skis (one hour $180) and
boats (first hour/additional hours $50/20).
Also hires out numerous types of bicycles
(one hour/day $10/50), including mountain
bikes, hybrids and kids' bikes.

[☞] Tours

Coastal Cruises Mooloolaba   CRUISE
([☑]0419 704 797; www.cruisemooloolaba.com.au;
Wharf Marina, 123 Parkyn Pde, Mooloolaba; cruises
from $35) Two-hour sunset and 1½-hour sea-
food lunch cruises through Mooloolaba Harbour, the river and canals.

Whale One   WILDLIFE
([☑]1300 942 531; www.whaleone.com.au; Shop
11-12, The Wharf, Parkyn Pde, Mooloolaba; whale-
watching tours adult/child $69/49; [♣]) Between
June and early November, Whale One runs
cruises that get you close to the spectacular acrobatic displays of humpback whales,
which migrate north from Antarctica to
mate and give birth. From late December
to March, sunset river cruises (adult/child
from $25/20) are also offered, with pre-
ordered food options and a licensed bar
onboard.

[✦✦] Festivals & Events

Big Pineapple Music Festival   MUSIC
(www.bigpineapplemusicfestival.com;   [☺]May)
The one-day 'Piney Festival' is one of the
region's top music events, with four stages

showcasing titans of the current Aussie
music scene. Campsites and pre-pitched
tents are available and sell out quickly.

[🛏] Sleeping

Cotton Tree Holiday Park   CAMPGROUND $
([☑]07-5459 9070; www.sunshinecoastholidayparks.
com.au; Cotton Tree Pde, Cotton Tree, Maroochydore; campsites/villas from $43/163; [🛜]) In
this popular area of Maroochydore, Cotton
Tree Holiday Park enjoys direct access to
the beach and Maroochy River. Facilities
include BBQs and laundry. Both the one-
and two-bedroom villas are air-conditioned;
each has private kitchen, bathroom and
linen supplied. Weekly rates are cheaper; see
the website for details.

[★] Oceans   RESORT $$$
([☑]07-5444 5777; www.oceansmooloolaba.com.
au; 101-105 Mooloolaba Esplanade, Mooloolaba;
2-/3-bedroom apt from $625/925; [P][❄][🛜][≋])
Cascading water greets guests at this superlative apartment resort, directly across
from the beach and in the heart of Mooloolaba. Ocean views are de rigueur in the
apartments, which are sleek, sparklingly
clean and contemporary, with Nespresso
machines, spas and quality appliances.
Apartments are serviced daily, with property
perks including adults' and children's pools
and a gym. Free parking and wi-fi.

Dockside Apartments   APARTMENT $$$
([☑]07-5478 2044; www.docksidemooloolaba.com.
au; 50 Burnett St, Mooloolaba; 2-/3-bedroom apt
from $210/260; [P][❄][🛜][≋]) The fully equipped
apartments here are all privately owned,
meaning that decor and appeal can vary
significantly. That said, you can expect neat,
clean, comfortable digs and friendly management. It sits in a quiet spot away from the
hubbub, but is an easy walk from Mooloolaba's main strip, surf club, beach and wharf
precinct. Minimum two- to three-night stay.

[✕] Eating

Lola's Pantry   VEGAN $
(4 Melaleuca St, Kuluin; meals $12-22; [☺]9am-
4pm Wed-Fri, 8am-3pm Sat & Sun; [♣]) Prioritis-
ing personal values over fame, Alejandro
Cancino resigned as executive chef at Brisbane's lauded Urbane to open this simple,
outdoor vegan cafe. While the setting is
underwhelming, the mostly organic food is
not, with a knockout meat-free burger even
omnivores will drool over. Indeed, Alejandro's succulent, lust-inducing patties are

making serious waves, with clients as far flung as China.

Riceboi
ASIAN $

(☑ 07-5444 1297; The Wharf, 123 Parkyn Pde, Mooloolaba; dishes $8-22; ☺11.30am-9pm) Neon signs, red lanterns and aerosol art collide to hip effect at loud, buzzing, riverside Riceboi. The izakaya-inspired menu peddles mouth-watering pan-Asian bites, such as juicy dumplings jammed with master-stock braised pork belly, pickled cucumber and hoisin sauce. Larger dishes include a justifiably popular 10-hour coconut braised beef. Great cocktails too.

★Velo Project
CAFE $$

(☑ 07-5444 8693; www.thevelorproject.com.au; 19 Careela St, Mooloolaba; dishes $10-23; ☺7am-3pm; 🛜🚼) A mishmash of recycled furniture and vintage ephemera, side-street Velo is an easy, breezy affair. Here, locals play board games while munching on the likes of date-and-macadamia compote with fresh banana, salted butterscotch and ice cream, or toasted ciabatta topped with Fraser Isle spanner crab, tomato salsa, asparagus, avocado and wasabi-and-turmeric mayo. Great, locally roasted coffee too.

★Pier 33
AUSTRALIAN $$$

(www.pier33.com.au; 33-45 Parkyn Pde, Mooloolaba; small dishes $10-18, sharing plates $43-62; ☺11.30am-9.30pm Tue-Sun; 🅿🚼) Crisp, luminous and casually sophisticated, waterfront Pier 33 serves up beautifully textured, produce-focused dishes, both large and small. Indeed, the place is as fabulous for bar bites as it is for a feast, its repertoire including standout spanner-crab roll and a sultry, 12-hour lamb shoulder. The cracking wine list includes natural and less-ubiquitous drops.

🍸 Drinking & Nightlife

Frank & Lotti
WINE BAR

(☑ 07-5477 7343; www.frankandlotti.com.au; 13 Mooloolaba Esplanade, Mooloolaba; ☺3pm-late Wed-Sun) This easy-to-miss wine bar and merchant, adorned with mismatched vintage chandeliers, has a sharp, Italian-focused wine list that revels in fresh, unexpected varietals, including fiano and garganega. Most offerings by the glass lie just north of $10 – excellent value given the quality. Tasty comestibles include smoked-duck prosciutto, kangaroo salami, pecorino cheese, and zucchini flowers stuffed with spinach and ricotta.

Kiki Bar & Eatery
BAR

(☑ 07-5451 0698; www.kikibar.com.au; 51 Duporth Ave, Maroochydore; ☺4pm-midnight Wed-Sun) Palm-print wallpaper and herringbone carpet set a striking scene at Kiki. Casual yet sophisticated, its wines include less obvious offerings, whether it be an Aussie montepulciano or an amber blend from Riverland. There are also Australia craft gins, while the five taps flow with local craft beers. Peckish? Try the seriously addictive honey truffle prawns.

Wax Buildup
COFFEE

(☑ 07-5326 2413; www.wax-buildup.com; 99-101 Aerodrome Rd, Maroochydore; ☺8am-4pm Tue-Sat, 10am-2pm Sun) Musician Mark Grounds and award-winning barista Cara Madden combine their passions at this neighbourly record store-meets-coffee shop. Slurp a brew and flip through an eclectic selection of (mostly pre-loved) vinyl spanning anything from rare and limited-edition treasures to rock, retro pop, jazz and local Queensland artists. Stock is graded according to quality, so you know exactly what you're getting.

ℹ Information

The **Mooloolaba Visitor Information Centre** (☑ 07-5458 8844; www.visitsunshinecoast.com.au; cnr Brisbane Rd & First Ave; ☺9am-3pm; 🛜) is a block away from the Esplanade in the heart of town. The **Maroochydore Visitor Information Centre** (☑ 07-5458 8842; www.visitsunshinecoast.com.au; cnr Sixth Ave & Melrose St; ☺9am-4pm, to 3pm Sat & Sun; 🛜) also lies one block from the beach.

Further north in Marcoola, Sunshine Coast Airport (p324) also houses a **tourist information centre** (☑ 07-5448 9088; www.visitsunshinecoast.com.au; Friendship Dr, Marcoola; ☺9am-3pm; 🛜).

ℹ Getting There & Away

AIR

Sunshine Coast Airport (p324) Gateway airport for the Sunshine Coast, with direct daily flights to Sydney and Melbourne and thrice-weekly non-stop flights to Adelaide. Also hosts seasonal direct flights to Auckland, New Zealand. Once current expansion works are completed in late 2020, the airport is expected to introduce new international routes to Asia, the West Pacific and possibly Hawaii.

BUS

In Mooloolaba, the **bus stop** for long-distance buses is in front of the Mooloolaba Bowls Club on Brisbane Rd. In Maroochydore, the **bus stop** is in front of the Sunshine Coast Visitor Information Centre. Maroochydore is also the main interchange hub for local buses heading either north or south along the Sunshine Coast or further inland. The **interchange station** (Horton Pde, Maroochydore) is outside Sunshine Plaza shopping centre.

Greyhound Australia (p1072) buses run several times daily to Brisbane (departing Mooloolaba/Maroochydore from $21/22, 1¼ to 2¾ hours).

Premier Motor Services runs daily to and from Brisbane (one way $24, 1½ hours).

Sunbus (www.sunbus.com.au) has frequent services between Mooloolaba and Maroochydore ($4.80, 20 minutes) and on to Noosa ($8.90, 55 to 80 minutes). Translink Go Cards are valid on these services.

Coolum & Peregian Beach

POP 8500 (COOLUM), 3530 (PEREGIAN)

Rocky headlands create a number of secluded coves before spilling into the fabulously long stretch of golden sand and rolling surf of Coolum Beach. Like much of the coast along here, the backdrop is spreading suburbia, but thanks to a reasonable cafe scene and easy access to the coast's hotspots, it's a useful escape from the more popular and overcrowded holiday scenes at Noosa, Mooloolaba and Maroochydore. Looming 4km south of Coolum Beach is **Mt Coolum** (https://parks.des.qld.gov.au/parks/mount-coolum; Tanah St West, Mount Coolum), an ancient volcanic dome whose peak offers spectacular views of the Sunshine Coast and its hinterland.

The low-rise, low-key beach suburbs of Peregian Beach and Sunshine Beach punctuate a 15km stretch of uncrowded, unobstructed beach that shoots north from Coolum to the rocky northeast headland of Noosa National Park. At the southern end, Peregian Beach is all about long, solitary beach walks, excellent surf breaks and the not-so-uncommon spotting of whales breaking offshore. It's also popular with 'yummy mummies' catching up at breezy local cafes with strollers and yoga mats in tow. Further north, the laid-back-latte ethos of Sunshine Beach attracts Noosa locals and surfies escaping the summer hordes.

🏃 Activities

Skydive Ramblers   SKYDIVING
(📞1300 663 634; www.skydiveforfun.com; Sunshine Coast Airport, 4 Kittyhawk Cl, Marcoola; jump from $239) Reputable operator Skydive Ramblers offers jumps above the Sunshine Coast. Soak up the sweeping coastal view before a spectacular beach landing. Free return transfers from Noosa available.

Coolum Surf School   SURFING
(📞0438 731 503; www.coolumsurfschool.com.au; Tickle Park, David Low Way, Coolum Beach; 2hr lesson $60) Coolum Surf School will have you riding the waves in no time. Instructors are friendly, enthusiastic and patient, so even the most awkward of rookies won't feel embarrassed. The outfit also hires out surfboards/bodyboards ($50/25 for 24 hours).

🛏 Sleeping & Eating

Coolum Beach
Holiday Park   CARAVAN PARK $
(📞07-5446 1474; www.sunshinecoastholidayparks.com.au; 1827 David Low Way, Coolum Beach; powered sites $48, cabins from $163; 🛜) Location, location, location: this dog-friendly park not only has absolute frontage to a patrolled beach, but is also just across the road from Coolum's main restaurant and cafe strip. Communal facilities include showers with good water pressure, a camp kitchen with TV, fridge, hotplates and BBQs, as well as laundries. On the downside, staff receive mixed reviews from guests.

Coolum Seaside   RESORT $$$
(📞07-5455 7200; www.coolumseaside.com; 6-8 Perry St, Coolum Beach; studio/apt from $230/250; 🅿❄@🛜🏊) Two blocks from the surf, this immaculately maintained, spacious resort has three pools, a tennis court, BBQs and a small gym. Both the studios and two-bedroom apartments are wonderfully clean, the latter coming with fully equipped kitchen and laundry facilities. The huge, impressive five-bedroom penthouse (from $900; minimum four-night stay) sleeps 10.

Raw Energy   CAFE $
(📞07-5471 6197; www.rawenergy.com.au; Shop 16, 1776 David Low Way, Coolum Beach; dishes $10-20; ⏱6am-4pm; 🛜🚭♿) 🅿 Tuck into brekkie or lunch at this bright, easy chain. The focus is on healthy, nutritious grub, from a 'super muesli' bowl laden with seeds, goji berries, fresh fruit, yogurt and honey, to quinoa fritters, burgers, sandwiches and wraps with combos like lentil and macadamia. It's also handy if you're craving a freshly squeezed juice or smoothie.

Hand of Fatima
CAFE **$$**

(✒ 0434 364 328; www.facebook.com/handof fatimacafe; 2/4 Kingfisher Dr, Peregian Beach; mains $18.50; ⊙ 5am-2pm) A friendly, lo-fi cafe where barefoot beach-goers banter with the staff while waiting for their impeccable macchiatos. In one corner is the tiny open kitchen, pumping out a short menu of Middle Eastern–inspired dishes like breakfast *sujuk* (a dry, spicy sausage) with tomatoes, peppers, poached eggs and tahini yogurt, or lunchtime smoked-chicken salad with avocado, pumpkin and roasted macadamia.

★ Sum Yung Guys
ASIAN **$$$**

(✒ 07-5324 1391; www.sumyungguys.com.au; 8/46 Duke St, Sunshine Beach; dishes $24-36; ⊙ noon-2.30pm & 5-8.30pm) Flavours explode and thrill at this fun and popular place, co-owned by 2016 *Masterchef Australia* runner-up Matt Sinclair. He's usually in the kitchen, whipping up knockout dishes inspired by the tang, heat and intrigue of Southeast Asia. The result: anything from hiramasa kingfish with green scud, laksa oil and coconut, to Malay-style BBQ chicken with green mango, chilli and mint.

Embassy XO
CHINESE **$$$**

(✒ 07-5455 4460; www.embassyxo.com.au; 56 Duke St, Sunshine Beach; mains $36-40; ⊙ 3-9.30pm Wed & Thu, from noon Fri-Sun) Embassy XO is not your average suburban Chinese joint, with a smashing wine list and quality produce driving dishes like pan-seared scallops with taro gnocchi and chargrilled octopus with *lop chong* (Chinese sausage), red kimchi, quinoa, nashi pear and a Thai-style coconut dressing. Other options include gorgeous banquets (vegetarian/omnivore $70/80), yum cha banquet lunch ($38) Friday to Sunday and moreish bar snacks from 3pm.

ⓘ Information

Coolum Visitor Information Centre (✒ 07-5458 8841; www.visitsunshinecoast.com.au; Tickle Park, David Low Way, Coolum Beach; ⊙ 9am-3pm; ⊛) Coolum's tourist information kiosk is in beachside Tickle Park, right beside the Coolum Surf Club. Free wi-fi available.

ⓘ Getting There & Away

Sunbus (www.sunbus.com.au) bus route 620 runs every 30 to 60 minutes from Coolum south to Maroochydore ($5.80, 30 minutes). It also runs north to Noosa ($5.80, 25 minutes). Route 622 runs hourly between Maroochydore and Noosa, stopping in Coolum en route.

Cooloola Coast

Stretching for 50km between Noosa and Rainbow Beach, the Cooloola Coast is a remote strip of long sandy beach backed by the Cooloola Section of the **Great Sandy National Park**. Although it's undeveloped, the 4WD and tin-boat set flock here in droves, so it's not always as peaceful as you might imagine. If you head off on foot or by canoe along one of the many inlets or waterways, however, you'll soon escape the crowds. The coast is famous for the **Teewah coloured sand cliffs**, estimated to be about 40,000 years old.

Great Sandy National Park: Cooloola Section

North of Noosa, the **Cooloola Section of Great Sandy National Park** (www.australiasnaturecoast.com) is not short of natural aces. Here ancient coastal cliffs bleed rich earthy hues, ocean waters teem with marine life and silent waterways stream through pristine forests. The possibilities are dizzying, from drives along wild ocean beaches to soaking in crystal-clear lagoons, canoeing down silent river tributaries or trekking through deep subtropical bushland. Stay a while or simply dabble on an easy day trip from Noosa.

Extending from Lake Cootharaba north to Rainbow Beach, the national park offers wide ocean beaches, soaring cliffs of richly coloured sands, pristine bushland, heathland, mangroves and rainforest, all of which are rich in bird life, including rarities such as the red goshawk and the grass owl. One of the most extraordinary experiences here is driving along the beach from Noosa North Shore to **Double Island Point**, around 50km to the north.

Great Beach Drive 4WD Tours (✒ 07-5486 3131; www.greatbeachdrive4wdtours.com; tours adult/child $195/120; ⊛) runs intimate, eco-centric 4WD tours of the spectacular Great Beach Drive from Noosa to Rainbow Beach. **Epic Ocean Adventure** (✒ 0408 738 192; www.epicoceanadventures.com.au; 1/6 Rainbow Beach Rd, Rainbow Beach; 3hr surfing/kayaking trip $65/79; ⊙ 8am-6pm) runs adventure tours departing both Rainbow Beach and Noosa, and including dolphin- and turtle-spotting kayaking trips.

Rainbow Beach Horse Rides (✒ 0412 174 337; www.rainbowbeachhorserides.com.au; Clarkson

Dr, Rainbow Beach; rides from $150) offers a number of horse rides on the beach, including an evocative, two-hour Full Moon Ride ($250) and, for experienced riders, a 1½-hour bareback ride in the ocean itself ($300).

The most popular (and best-equipped) **campgrounds** (☑ 13 74 68; https://parks.des. qld.gov.au/parks/cooloola/camping.html; sites per person $6.55) are Fig Tree Point, Harry's and Freshwater. If you're driving up to Rainbow Beach, you can camp on Teewah Beach in a 15km zone between the Sunshine Coast Regional Council boundary and Little Freshwater Creek. Apart from Harry's, Freshwater and Teewah Beach, all sites are accessible by hiking or river only.

Rainbow Beach Ultimate Camping (☑ 0419 464 254; www.rainbow-beach-hire-a-camp.com.au; per night from $313) takes all the hard work out of camping by providing most of the equipment and setting it up for you, from the tent, mattresses, stretchers and crockery to the dining table, BBQ, private toilet and shower.

The **QPWS Great Sandy Information Centre** (☑ 07-5449 7792; 240 Moorindil St, Tewantin; ☉ 7.30am-3.30pm) provides information on park access, tide times and fire bans within the park. The centre also issues car and camping permits for both Fraser Island and the Great Sandy National Park, but these are best booked online via https://parks.des.qld.gov.au.

Lake Cooroibah

A couple of kilometres north of Tewantin, the Noosa River widens into Lake Cooroibah. Surrounded by lush bushland, the glassy, relatively shallow lake is an idyllic spot to push out a canoe or kayak and relish the silence. The lake was once a favourite fishing location for the indigenous Kabi Kabi (Gubbi Gubbi) people and its waters continue to ripple with sand crabs and numerous types of fish.

A resort and a scattering of holidays houses are among the limited accommodation options in the area. If you take the Noosa North Shore Ferry, you can drive up to the lake in a conventional vehicle and camp along sections of the beach. That said, you'll find a much greater choice of accommodation to the south in Noosa.

The **Noosa North Shore Retreat** (☑ 07-5447 1225; www.noosanorthshoreretreat.com.au; Beach Rd; camp sites from $32, r/cottage from $140/170; ✳ @ ⊠) is home to a bar

and restaurant, though opening times are limited outside peak holiday periods. For more choice head south to Noosaville or Noosa Heads. Self-caterers will find a major supermarket in Tewantin, and quality local produce at the weekly Noosa Farmers Market (p329), held on Sunday mornings in Noosaville.

From the end of Moorindil St in Tewantin, cash-only **Noosa North Shore Ferries** (☑ 07-5447 1321; www.noosanorthshoreferries.com.au; one way per pedestrian/car $1/7; ☉ 5.30am-10.20pm, to 12.20am Fri & Sat) shuttle across the river to Noosa North Shore, from where the eastern shore of the lake is accessible. To reach the lake's western shore from Noosa, follow the signs to Tewantin and head west out of town on McKinnon Dr. Turn right into Lake Cooroibah Rd, which winds its way north towards the lake.

Lake Cootharaba & Boreen Point

Relatively shallow and warm, Cootharaba is the largest lake in the Cooloola Section of Great Sandy National Park, measuring about 5km in width and 10km in length. The area's traditional owners and custodians are the Kabi Kabi (Gubbi Gubbi) people, for whom the lake – graced with stingrays, sand crabs and fish – was traditionally an important source of sustenance. Perched on its western shore is the sleepy hamlet of Boreen Point, itself home to one of Queensland's oldest and most atmospheric pubs, the Apollonian Hotel. Lake Cootharaba is also the gateway to the glassy, ethereal **Noosa Everglades** (www.australiasnaturecoast.com). One of only two everglades systems in the world, these pristine wetlands make for an exceptional escape, with canoeing, bushwalking and tranquil bush camping all possibilities.

Discovery Group (☑ 07-5449 0393; www.thediscoverygroup.com.au; cruise adult/child $120/85, canoe tour $135/95; ⛵) and **Kanu Kapers** (☑ 07-5485 3328; www.kanukapersaustralia.com; 11 Toolara St, Boreen Point; guided tours from adult/child $155/95) are two outfits running fantastic tours of the Everglades.

Boreen Point has very limited accommodation options, among them a lakeside campground and small motel. Campsites, dorm tents and luxe glamping tents are offered at lakeside **Habitat Noosa** (☑ 07-5485 3165; www.habitatnoosa.com.au; Lake Flat Rd, Elanda Point; camp sites from $33, dm/tent per person $33/65, glamping tents $250), a further

4km north of town. Those after more luxurious digs will find a much greater choice in Noosa, around 23km further south.

Boreen Point is home to the historic **Apollonian Hotel** (☑ 07-5485 3100; www. apollonianhotel.com.au; 19 Laguna St; mains $20-29; ⊙ 10am-9pm, to 10pm Fri, to 9.30pm Sat, to 6pm Sun; ⊛), which offers standard pub grub and a popular Sunday spit roast. Around 4km further north lies polished bistro-microbrewery **Cootharabar** (☑ 07-5447 1333; www.habitatnoosa.com.au/bistro-bar; Lake Flat Rd, Elanda Point; mains $25-40; ⊙ bar from 11am daily, kitchen noon-2pm Mon-Wed, noon-2pm & 6pm-8pm Thu-Sun; ⊛).

Boreen Point lies around 23km north of Noosaville (and 26km north of Noosa Heads). From Noosaville, drive west along Gibson Rd and Hilton Tce to Tewantin. From here, McKinnon Dr heads north towards Boreen Heads.

Sunshine Coast Hinterland

Inland from Nambour, the **Blackall Range** forms a stunning backdrop to the Sunshine Coast's beaches a short 50km away. A relaxed half- or full-day circuit drive from the coast follows a winding road along the razorback line of the escarpment, passing through quaint mountain villages and offering spectacular views of the coastal lowlands.

Home to the Gubbi Gubbi people for thousands of years, the Blackall Range is of significant importance to Aboriginal people, being one of only two ranges in which the native Queensland *bonyi* (bunya pine) originally grew. The trees' nuts were considered a delicacy, and their harvest celebrated with great feasts that would draw Aboriginal groups from as far north as Townsville and as far south as Lismore in NSW.

Connecting Landsborough to Nambour, the 55km Blackall Range Tourist Drive (also known as Tourist Drive 23) winds its way along the escarpment, peering out at lush rolling hills, distant ocean blue and the striking, surreal peaks of the Glass House Mountains. It's an easy, rewarding route, passing through a string of snug, quaint townships. Among these is arty, alternative **Maleny**, home to the acclaimed **Brouhaha Brewery** (☑ 07-5435 2018; www.brouhahabrewery.com.au; 6/39 Coral St; ⊙ 11am-10pm Wed, Thu & Sun, to midnight Fri & Sat; ☎) and, just outside town, the unmissable **Mary Cairncross Scenic**

Reserve (☑ 07-5429 6122; www.mary-cairncross. com.au; 148 Mountain View Rd; by donation; ⊙ rainforest walking tracks 7am-6pm daily, Discovery Centre 9am-4.30pm; ⊛), an ancient rainforest inhabited by pademelons.

The route continues north to **Montville**, a throughly pleasant, if slightly chintzy, mountain town of fudge emporiums, Devonshire tearooms and cottage crafts. To work off that excess fudge, take a rainforest hike in **Kondalilla National Park** (https://parks.des.qld. gov.au/parks/kondalila; Kondalilla Falls Rd, Flaxton), less than 3km northwest of town. Home to soaring Kondalilla Falls, its rock pools are a popular swimming spot. (After a refreshing dip, check for leeches!)

From Montville, the Blackall Range Tourist Drive continues north to the tiny village of **Mapleton** before heading downhill to Nambour. If you're a cheese lover, however, take a detour left onto Obi Obi Rd. After 18km, you'll reach **Kenilworth**, a small country town in the pretty Mary River Valley. It's here that you'll find Kenilworth Dairies (p329), a boutique cheese factory with creamy yogurt and wickedly good cheese. If you plan to camp in the Kenilworth State Forest or Conondale National Park you'll need a permit (https://parks.des.qld.gov.au). The **Kenilworth Showgrounds** (☑ 0438 849 947; www.kenilworthshowgrounds.org.au; Elizabeth St; unpowered/powered sites from $15/20) has both unpowered and powered campsites.

Otherwise, continue northeast on the Eumundi–Kenilworth Rd for a scenic drive through rolling pastureland dotted with traditional old farmhouses and floods of jacaranda trees. After 30km you'll reach the Bruce Hwy near Eumundi, from where the Sunshine Coast is easily reached.

If you're within shouting distance of the Sunshine Coast just after Christmas, do yourself a favour and unplug at the **Woodford Folk Festival** (www.woodfordfolkfestival. com; ⊙ Dec-Jan; ⊛), a six-day cavalcade of soulful vibes, world-class musical performances, crafty workshops and thought-provoking talks. It even has its own dedicated children's festival. It takes place just southwest of Maleny.

Montville offers two very pleasant places to stay: **Altitude on Montville** (☑ 07-5478 5889; http://altitudeonmontville.com.au; 94-96 Main St; studio/2-/3-bedroom apt from $195/265/380; ᴾ❄☎) and **Secrets on the Lake** (☑ 07-5478 5888; www.secretsonthelake. com.au; 207 Narrows Rd; treehouse cabins from $425; ᴾ❄).

EUMUNDI

While the weatherboard pubs, broad verandahs and tin-roof cottages evoke classic rural Queensland, historic Eumundi is a sensitive soul. Here, utes, weathered faces and XXXX beer live side by side with chai lattes, free-spirited artists and one of the region's best bookshops. The hilly hamlet is most famous for its Eumundi Markets, a twice-weekly, hippy-hearted sprawl of crafts, clothing, produce and artisanal bites, shaded under heritage-listed fig trees. The town's name is believed to derive from 'Ngumundi' or 'Huomundy', the name of a local Aboriginal elder said to have adopted escaped convict David Bracewell as his son in 1831.

Eumundi's one main attraction is the outstanding **Eumundi Markets** (☏ 07-5442 7106; www.eumundimarkets.com.au; 80 Memorial Dr; ◷ 8am-1.30pm Wed, 7am-2pm Sat; ⛒), which run on Wednesdays and Saturdays fronting the town's main strip. The quainter supporting act is its small **local history museum** (admission free) at the nearby **Discover Eumundi Heritage & Visitor Centre** (☏ 07-5442 8762; www.discovereumundi. com; 73 Memorial Dr; ◷ 10am-3pm Mon-Fri, to 2pm Sat).

About 10km northwest of Eumundi, the little village of **Pomona** sits in the shadow of looming Mt Cooroora (440m) and is home to the wonderful **Majestic Theatre** (☏ 07-5485 2330; www.themajestictheatre.com.au; 5 Factory St; tickets adult/child $15/10; ◷ screenings noon 2nd & 4th Sat of month; ⛒), billed as the country's longest-running commercial theatre.

The modest scattering of B&Bs and guesthouses in town and the surrounding area includes **Eumundi Dairy** (https://eumundidairy.com.au; 33 Grasstree Rd; homestead/dairy per night $200/300; ⛒⛒) and **Harmony Hill** (☏ 07-5442 8685, 0418 750 643; www.airbnb. com.au/rooms/9636472; 81 Seib Rd; tent/carriage/homestead $105/110/300; ⛒⛒).

Pubs, cafes and a microbrewery flank Memorial Dr, Eumundi's main street. The Eumundi Markets offer a plethora of international street food and organic pastries from standout local bakery **Ten Acres** (www.tenacres.com.au; pastries from $4).

Eleven kilometres south of Eumundi, **Yandina** is home to Spirit House (p329), a high-end restaurant with an evocative, jungle-like setting and a contemporary, Thai-inspired menu widely considered one of Queensland's culinary highlights.

Sunbus (www.sunbus.com.au) route 630 runs from Eumundi to Noosa Junction four times daily Monday to Friday and eight times daily on Saturday ($5.80, 45 minutes). Services from Noosa Junction to Eumundi depart one to four times daily on weekdays and eight times on Saturday.

A number of tour operators in the area offer visits to the Eumundi Markets as well.

Villages such as Maleny and Montville offer a healthy number of cafes and restaurants; Maleny is especially known for its love all things organic and ethical. The hinterland also harbours a number of well-known, high-quality food and drink producers, including **Maleny Dairies** (☏ 07-5494 2392; www.malenydairies.com; 70 McCarthy Rd; tours $11; ◷ 8.30am-4.30pm Mon-Sat, tours 10am, 11.30am, 1pm & 2.30pm; ⛒) and Brouhaha Brewery.

Although buses do run through the hinterland, the most convenient and reliable way to explore the Sunshine Coast hinterland is by car. From Landsborough, Landsborough Maleny Rd shoots west to Maleny. Just to the east of Maleny, Maleny-Montville Rd breaks off Landsborough-Maleny Rd and heads north to the hinterland towns of Montville and Mapleton.

Bus 890 runs from Nambour train station (Sunshine Coast line) to Maleny ($4.70, 55 minutes) via Mapleton ($3.20, 24 minutes), Flaxton Barn ($3.70, 30 minutes) and Montville ($4.20, 34 minutes) four times daily each way from Monday to Friday. Buy tickets on board.

FRASER COAST

While Fraser Island rightfully commands the majority of traveller interest in this region, there's plenty to entice visitors to linger on the mainland. The Fraser Coast is worth lingering over for its coastal beauty, beachfront national parks, tiny seaside villages and sugar-cane fields surrounding old-fashioned country towns. This land is traditionally owned by the Butchulla, Kabi Kabi (Gubbi Gubbi) and Gureng Gureng people.

Hervey Bay

POP 52,073

One of the Fraser Coast's most alluring honeypots, Hervey Bay unfurls itself lazily along a seemingly endless bayside shorefront, packing plenty of apartments, restaurants, pubs and tour operators into the streets behind. Young travellers with an eye on Fraser Island rub shoulders with grey nomads passing languidly through campgrounds and serious fisherfolk recharging in pursuit of the one that got away. Throw in the chance to see majestic humpback whales frolicking here from July to October, and the town's convenient access to the Unesco–listed Fraser Island, and it's easy to understand how Hervey Bay has become an unflashy, yet undeniably appealing, tourist hotspot.

Fraser Island shelters Hervey Bay from the ocean surf and the sea here is shallow and completely flat – perfect for kiddies and summer holiday snapshots. The Butchulla are the traditional owners here.

◎ Sights

**Fraser Coast
Cultural Centre** MUSEUM, GALLERY
(☑07-4197 4206; www.ourfrasercoast.com.au; 166 Old Maryborough Rd; ⊙10am-4pm; ℗♿) FREE
Home to both the **Fraser Coast Discovery Sphere** and **Hervey Bay Regional Gallery**, this boldly designed cultural centre is landmarked by 'Nala', the 20-tonne humpback-whale sculpture that 'breaches' 12m into the air from its forecourt. Especially enjoyable for kids, the Discovery Sphere educates visitors about the Unesco-listed Great Sandy Biosphere through captivating and interactive exhibits, while the Gallery gives space to local artists.

Wetside Water Park AMUSEMENT PARK
(☑1300 79 49 29; www.frasercoast.qld.gov.au/ Wetside; cnr Main St & the Esplanade, Pialba; ⊙10am-5pm Wed-Sun, daily during school holidays) FREE On hot days, this watery playground on the foreshore can't be beaten. There's plenty of shade, gorgeous old trees, a cafe, fountains, tipping buckets and a boardwalk with water infotainment. Paid attractions include a waterslide ($5 for 10 slides) and a wave pool ($6 per person). Opening hours vary so check the website for updates.

Reefworld AQUARIUM
(☑07-4128 9828; www.reefworldherveybay.com; Dayman Park, cnr Kent & Pulgul Sts, Urangan; adult/ child $20/10, shark dives from $50; ⊙9.30am-4pm; ℗♿) In operation since 1979, this small family-run aquarium is popular for its interactive fish-feeding sessions at 11am and 2.30pm. You can also take a 30-minute dip with their catsharks, whalers, cod, turtles and other species – come in the morning for best visibility.

🏃 Activities & Tours

Whale-Watching

Whale-watching tours operate out of Hervey Bay every day (weather permitting) during the annual migrations between late July and early November. While you can never predict the behaviour of wild animals, around 7000 humpbacks pass through here each year, allowing operators to 'guarantee' sightings from August to the end of October (a subsequent trip is free if the whales don't show). Outside of the peak season, many boats offer dolphin-spotting tours. Boats cruise from **Sandy Straits Marina** (☑07-4125 3822; http://greatsandystraitsmarina.com. au; Buccaneer Dr, Urangan) out to Platypus Bay in the lee of Fraser Island, then zip around from pod to pod to find the most active whales. Most vessels offer half-day tours, and most include lunch and/or morning or afternoon tea. Tour bookings can often be made through your accommodation, or through the information centres.

Whale-watching operators include the following:

Blue Dolphin Marine Tours (☑07-4124 9600; www.bluedolphintours.com.au; berth B47, Great Sandy Straits Marina, Urangan; adult/child $160/130; ♿) 🐋

Freedom Whale Watch (☑1300 879 960; www.freedomwhalewatch.com.au; Great Sandy Straits Marina, Urangan; adult/child $140/100; ♿)

Spirit of Hervey Bay (☑1800 642 544; www.spiritofherveybay.com; Great Sandy Straits Marina, Buccaneer Dr, Urangan; adult/child from $90/60; ⊙8.30am & 1.30pm)

Tasman Venture (☑1800 620 322; www. tasmanventure.com.au; Great Sandy Straits Marina, Buccaneer Dr, Urangan; whale-watching adult/child $115/60; ⊙8.30am & 1.30pm Jul-early Nov; ♿)

Other Activities

Air Fraser Island SCENIC FLIGHTS
(☑1300 172 706; www.airfraserisland.com.au; scenic flights, 30/60min $135/220) Air Fraser offers scenic flights over Fraser Island and chances to land and explore. Leaving from either

Hervey Bay or Sunshine Coast Airport, they sell packages including accommodation and 4WD (from $575 per person for two nights).

Aquavue WATER SPORTS
(☑ 07-4125 5528; www.aquavue.com.au; 415a Charlton Esplanade, Torquay; ▣) Operating from a prime spot on the Torquay foreshore, Aquavue hires out paddleboards and kayaks ($20 per hour) and jet skis ($50 per 15 minutes). A more involved option is a jet-ski tour across the Great Sandy Strait to explore Fraser Island's less-visited west cost, with lunch served at Aquavue Cafe on return ($450, 3½ hours).

Skydive Hervey Bay SKYDIVING
(☑ 0458 064 703; www.skydiveherveybay.com.au) Skydives from $280 at 4270m (the highest legal altitude in Australia) with up to 60 mouth-flapping seconds of free fall. Immortalise your terror on Go-Pro for an extra $100.

Hervey Bay Ecomarine Tours CRUISE
(☑ 07-4125 6888; www.herveybayecomarinetours.com.au; Great Sandy Straits Marina, Urangan; 4hr tours adult/child from $85/45) Cruise on the 12m, glass-bottomed boat *Milbi* ('sea turtle' in the local Butchulla language) for snorkelling and coral viewing in the clear waters of the Great Sandy Strait, followed by an island barbecue. Milbi also takes whale-watching cruises in season, and transfers to nearby Weenandin ('Round Island'). Tours are designed for minimal ecological impact, and some involve education from Butchulla guides.

MV Princess II FISHING
(☑ 07-4124 0400; Berth B3, Great Sandy Straits Marina, Buccaneer Drive, Urangan; adult/child $170/110) The *Princess II*, a 45-foot vessel built specifically for fishing, is run by a crew with decades of experience and local knowledge.

Fraser Explorer Tours TOURS
(☑ 07-4194 9222; www.fraserexplorertours.com.au; 1-/2-day tours $210/385; ▣) Very experienced drivers take daily trips to Fraser Island leaving from Hervey Bay or Rainbow Beach. Premium tours include lunch at Euorng Resort and sunset drinks, while two-day tourists overnight at Eurong Resort.

✲ Festivals & Events

Hervey Bay Ocean Festival CULTURAL
(www.herveybayoceanfestival.com.au; ☉ Aug) Held to coincide with a pit stop taken every year in Hervey Bay by humpback whales migrating north, this festival offers music, talks, food, parties and the chance to get out on the water to commune with the giant mammals. Conservation and education are key foci.

🛏 Sleeping

Hervey Bay has an abundance of good hostels, motels and apartments, plus three excellent **caravan parks** (www.beachfronttouristparks.com.au; unpowered/powered sites from $34/42) strung out along Charlton Esplanade as it runs through the suburbs of Pialba, Scarness and Torquay.

Hervey Bay YHA HOSTEL $
(☑ 07-4125 1844; www.yha.com.au; 820 Boat Harbour Dr, Urangan; dm/d/cabins from $23/48/149; ❋@🛜☒) This excellent YHA is set on 8 hectares of tranquil bushland close to the Great Sandy Straits Marina and the beach. It's a lovely spot, thick with ambience, possums and parrots. Facilities include a pool, tennis and basketball courts, and a sociable bar-restaurant. All dorm rooms come with their own dining tables and desks, and stand-alone single beds.

Mango Tourist Hostel HOSTEL $
(☑ 07-4124 2832; www.mangohostel.com; 110 Torquay Rd, Scarness; dm/d $26/56; ▣❋🛜) ✐ A small and discerning hostel run by knowledgeable local Phil, who can arrange tailored Hervey Bay and Fraser Island itineraries, and put guests in contact with yachts seeking crew. Intimate and loaded with character (and geckos), the old Queenslander, set on a quiet street away from the beach, sleeps guests in a four-bed dorm room and two very homey doubles.

★ Colonial Lodge APARTMENT $$
(☑ 07-4125 1073; www.herveybaycoloniallodge.com.au; 94 Cypress St, Torquay; 1-/2-bedroom apt $120/160; ❋🛜☒) With just self-contained apartments at this hacienda-style lodge across from the water, guests sometimes get to know each other hanging out by the pool or communal BBQ area. Staff are friendly and the apartments are bigger than average, with a lovely place to sit out the front.

Emeraldene Inn & Eco-Lodge INN $$
(☑ 07-4124 5500; www.emeraldene.com.au; 166 Urraween Rd, Urraween; d from $120; ▣❋🛜☒) ✐ This family-run inn with 14 rooms is impeccably presented, sitting in a huge garden with a pool, BBQ area and plenty of visiting wildlife.

Hervey Bay

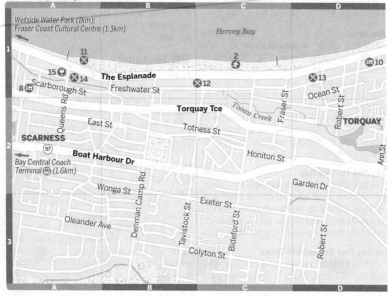

Wetside Water Park (1km);
Fraser Coast Cultural Centre (1.3km)

Hervey Bay

The Esplanade

Freshwater St

Scarborough St

Queens Rd

East St

Torquay Tce

Tooan Creek

Fraser St

Ocean St

Robert St

TORQUAY

Totness St

SCARNESS

Boat Harbour Dr

Honiton St

Ann St

Bay Central Coach
Terminal (1.6km)

Wonga St

Denman Camp Rd

Garden Dr

Oleander Ave

Tavistock St

Exeter St

Bideford St

Robert St

Colyton St

QUEENSLAND HERVEY BAY

Pier One
RESORT $$

(☑1300 213 792; 558-559 Charlton Esplanade, Urangan; 1-/2-bedroom apt $189/259; P❋🛜🏊) Pier One sits suits short-term travellers looking for a view of the sea in the background and the pool in the foreground. The apartments are bigger than most and come with two bathrooms, shiny surfaces, modern furniture and a very reasonable price tag.

Best Western Plus
Quarterdecks Retreat
APARTMENT $$

(☑07-4197 0888; www.quarterdecksretreat.com. au; 80 Moolyyir St, Urangan; 1-/2-/3-bedroom villas $149/209/249; P❋🛜🏊) These excellent villas are stylishly furnished and have a private courtyard, all the mod cons and little luxuries such as fluffy bathrobes, spa and sauna. Backing onto a nature reserve, it's quiet apart from the wonderful bird life, and is only a cooee from the beach. The accommodation-and-tour packages are great value.

Shelly Bay Resort
APARTMENT $$

(☑1800 240 797, 07-4125 4533; www.shellybay resort.com.au; 466 Charlton Esplanade, Torquay; 1-/2-bedroom units $147/180; ❋🛜🏊) The bright, breezy beach-facing apartments at Shelly Bay Resort are some of the best value in town, especially the two-bedroom ones, which have prime corner locations

overlooking the lagoon-style pool. There's a half-sized tennis court and BBQ area, and customer service is first class.

🍴 Eating & Drinking

Urangan Fisheries
FOOD

(☑07-4125 2621; http://uranganfisheries.com.au; 860 Boat Harbour Dr, Urangan; ⊙8.30am-5.30pm Mon-Sat, 9am-3pm Sun) Ideal for self-catering pescatarians, the retail outlet of this wholesale fishery is the place to go for locally caught barramundi, black-tip shark, whiting, scallops and other spanking-fresh seafood. Supplementing the catch from their own trawlers, they buy from other boats that dock in Urangan Harbour to unload the fruits of the Coral Sea.

Maddigan's Seafood
FISH & CHIPS $

(☑07-4128 4202; 1/401 Charlton Esplanade, Torquay; fish & chips $11-14; ⊙11am-8pm Thu-Tue, from 9am Wed) Deservedly popular with the locals, Maddigan's is an old-school Australian seaside fish and chippery that fries fresh. Grab flake and chips, or perhaps a burstingly full family pack ($36) and eat your spoils across the road on Torquay Beach. The catch is displayed on ice at the front of the shop if you'd prefer to cook it yourself.

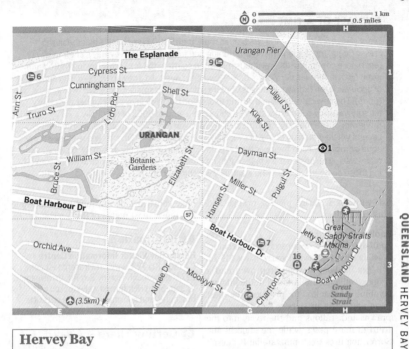

Hervey Bay

Sights
1 Reefworld H2

Activities, Courses & Tours
2 Aquavue C1
Blue Dolphin Marine Tours .... (see 4)
Freedom Whale Watch .... (see 4)
3 Hervey Bay Ecomarine Tours H3
4 MV Princess II H2
Spirit of Hervey Bay .... (see 4)
Tasman Venture .... (see 4)

Sleeping
5 Best Western Plus Quarterdecks Retreat G3
6 Colonial Lodge E1
7 Hervey Bay YHA G3
8 Mango Tourist Hostel A1
9 Pier One G1
10 Shelly Bay Resort D1

Eating
Coast .... (see 10)
11 Enzo's on the Beach A1
12 Maddigan's Seafood C1
13 Paolo's Pizza Bar D1
14 Tanto A1

Drinking & Nightlife
15 Beach House Hotel A1

Shopping
16 Urangan Fisheries G3

★Tanto
JAPANESE $$

(348 Charlton Esplanade; mains $15-22; ⏲11.30am-2pm & 5.30-8pm Tue, Wed & Fri-Sun) Great ingredients and expert charcoal-grilling are the winning formula employed by this simple shopfront restaurant on the Esplanade in Scarness. Three different proteins are offered – perhaps sweet, soy-glazed chicken, Kingaroy pork belly in honey and salt, or marinated Hervey Bay cuttlefish with nori paste – then each is cooked to order and served with rice and pickles.

★Coast
AUSTRALIAN $$

(☎07-4125 5454; https://coastherveybay.com.au; 469 Charlton Esplanade, Torquay; mains $23-32; ⏲5.30pm-late Tue-Sun & 11.30am- 2.30pm Thu-Sun) The finest restaurant in Hervey Bay, Coast brings a contemporary big-city sensibility to its food, which is designed to share and straddles cultural divides in an effort to turn great produce into great dishes. Smaller plates such as Hervey Bay scallops with lemon, caper and parsley butter are followed by larger ones such as hay-smoked

A WHALE OF A TIME

Every year, from July to early November, more than 7000 humpback whales visit the Fraser Coast, most spending time fattening and frolicking in Hervey Bay's sheltered waters before continuing their arduous migration south to the Antarctic. Having mated and given birth in the warmer waters off northeastern Australia, they arrive here in groups of about a dozen (known as pulses), before splitting into smaller groups of two or three (pods). The new calves utilise the time to develop the thick layers of blubber necessary for survival in icy southern waters by consuming around 600L of milk daily.

Viewing these majestic creatures, many of which are now accustomed to the presence of whale-watching boats, is simply awe-inspiring. You'll most likely see these showy aqua-acrobats waving their pectoral fins, tail slapping, breaching or simply 'blowing', and many will roll up beside the whale-watching boats with one eye clear of the water...making those on board wonder who's actually watching whom.

fish with black garlic, pickles, orange and pork scratchings.

Paolo's Pizza Bar
ITALIAN $$

(☑07-4125 3100; www.paolospizzabar.com.au; 2/446 Charlton Esplanade, Torquay; mains $19-23; ⊘5-9pm Thu-Mon) A wood-fired oven and a proper feeling for Italian food in the kitchen combine at Paolo's to produce the best pizza and pasta in Hervey Bay. Fresh local prawns and scallops find their way into the frutti di mare pizza, while the gnocchi alla Sorrentina uses fresh mozzarella. It doesn't take bookings and is deservedly popular, so arrive early.

Enzo's on the Beach
CAFE $$

(☑07-4124 6375; www.enzosonthebeach.com.au; 351a Charlton Esplanade, Scarness; mains around $20; ⊘6.30am-5pm Mon-Wed, to 7pm Thu & Sun, to late Fri & Sat) Opening onto the beach, this sleek and inviting cafe-restaurant offers different pleasures throughout the day: breakfast might be smashed avocado on rye with smoked salmon, feta and capers; lunch might be crispy 'southern-fried' barramundi with pickles, rocket and slaw. Dinner dishes such as Thai fish-fritter salad are offered Thursday to Sunday. Also lovely for coffee or wine.

Beach House Hotel
PUB

(☑07-4196 9366; www.beachhousehotel.com.au; 344 Charlton Esplanade, Scarness; ⊘10am-10pm Mon-Wed, 10am-11pm Thu, 10-2am Fri, 9-2am Sat, 9am-10pm Sun; 🛜🅿) The Beach House is perhaps Hervey's most popular pub, thanks to an expensive fit-out, a prime viewpoint on Scarness Beach and a willingness to give the people what they want: bristling beer taps, gambling, big-screen sport, picture windows that open to let in the offshore breeze, a

huge courtyard, decent food and accessible live music most nights of the week.

ℹ Information

Hervey Bay Visitor Information Centre

(☑1800 811 728; www.visitfrasercoast.com; 227 Maryborough-Hervey Bay Rd, Urraween; ⊘9am-5pm) Helpful and well-stocked with brochures and information. On the outskirts of town.

ℹ Getting There & Away

AIR

Hervey Bay airport is on Don Adams Dr, just off Booral Rd. **Qantas** (☑13 13 13; www. qantas.com.au) and **Virgin** (☑13 67 89; www. virginaustralia.com) have regular flights to/from Sydney and Brisbane.

BOAT

Ferries to Fraser Island leave from River Heads, about 10km south of town, and various whale-watching and tour boats leave from Great Sandy Straits Marina (p342).

BUS

Buses depart **Hervey Bay Coach Terminal** (6 Central Ave, Stockland Shopping Centre, Pialba). **Greyhound** (☑1300 473 946; www.greyhound. com.au) and **Premier Motor Service** (☑13 34 10; www.premierms.com.au) have several services daily to/from Brisbane ($41 to $65, 5¼ to 7½ hours), Maroochydore ($27 to $90, five to six hours), Bundaberg ($18 to $27, 1¾ to 2½ hours) and Rockhampton ($53 to $97, 5¼ to 7¼ hours). **Tory's Tours** (☑07-4128 6611; www. torystours.com.au) has twice daily services to Brisbane airport (adult/child $80/68). **Wide Bay Transit** (☑07-4121 3719; www. widebaytransit.com.au) runs buses from the Stockland Shopping Centre (6 Central Avenue, Pialba) to meet the Rockhampton and Bundaberg Tilt Trains in Maryborough ($8, one hour).

ⓘ Getting Around

Hervey Bay is the best place to hire a 4WD for Fraser Island.

Aussie Trax (☑ 07-4124 4433; www.fraserisland4wd.com.au; 56 Boat Harbour Dr, Pialba)

Fraser Magic 4WD Hire (☑ 07-4125 6612; www.fraser4wdhire.com.au; 5 Kruger Ct, Urangan; ⊙ 6.30am-6.15pm)

Hervey Bay Rent A Car (☑ 0417 340 574, 07-4194 6626; www.herveybayrentacar.com.au; 6 Pier St, Urangan; ⊙ 8am-4.30pm Mon-Sat)

Safari 4WD Hire (☑ 07-4124 4244; www.safari4wdhire.com.au; 28 Southern Cross Circuit, Urangan; ⊙ 7am-5.30pm Mon-Fri, 8am-4pm Sat & Sun)

Rainbow Beach

POP 1214

Named for cliffs of colourful, mineral-rich sand, Rainbow Beach is an idyllic Australian beach town on Butchulla land at the base of the Inskip Peninsula. Beloved of European backpackers and the chief contender to Hervey Bay as a base for excursions to Fraser Island, it's a generally low-key place that nonetheless offers a few hostels hot-housing all the frenetic action a young, fun-seeking clientele could want. Ideally reached via the Cooloola Section of the Great Sandy National Park (p338), a dramatic approach possible only for 4WDs, it's more easily and conventionally accessed by excellent roads from Gympie, 73km southwest. It's a great place to try your hand at different outdoor activities, tap into the backpacker party scene, or just chill out with family and friends.

◉ Sights & Activities

★ **Carlo Sandblow**   NATURAL FEATURE
(🏛) This great bowl of wind-blown sand above Rainbow Beach is arrestingly beautiful. Named for a crew-member on Cook's first voyage to these parts, it's reached by a short climb through subtropical forest, after which the foliage parts to reveal a vast scoop of golden sand, with views to Fraser Island and Inskip Point to the north, and Rainbow Beach and Double Island Point to the south. Sliding down the flanks of the environmentally fragile Sand Blow just damages them.

Take Cooloola Drive to its highest point to reach the car park and short walking track, and try to time your visit for sunrise or sunset: either will take your breath away.

Wolf Rock Dive Centre   DIVING
(☑ 07-5486 8004, 0498 743 795; www.wolfrockdive.com.au; 2 Goondi St; double-dive charters $255) Wolf Rock, a quartet of volcanic pinnacles off Double Island Point, is regarded as one of Queensland's best scuba-diving sites. This shop takes divers here to swim with the endangered grey-nurse shark year-round, and you may also see turtles, rays, giant gropers and even whales.

Rainbow Paragliding   PARAGLIDING
(☑ 0418 754 157; www.paraglidingrainbow.com; glides $200) Rainbow Beach is recognised as one of the best coastal places in the world for paragliding, with its safe launch and landing, smooth air flows and spectacular sights. Experienced operator Jean Luc has been taking tandem flights with exhilarated customers here since 1995.

Epic Ocean Adventures   SURFING
(☑ 0408 738 192; www.epicoceanadventures.com.au; 1/6 Rainbow Beach Rd; 3hr surf lessons $65, 3½hr kayak tours $79; ⊙ 8am-6pm) With a shopfront on the main drag in Rainbow Beach, this surf school has experienced instructors to guide beginners through nearby Double Island Point's sometimes-challenging breaks. Their fantastic dolphin-spotting sea-kayak tours also leave from this gorgeous, 4WD-accessible beach.

Fraser's on Rainbow   ADVENTURE SPORTS
(☑ 02 6685 2620, 07-5486 8885; www.fraserson rainbow.com; 18 Spectrum St; 3-day tours $514) A number of Rainbow Beach operators organise 'tag-along' tours to Fraser Island, where participants drive 4WDs in convoy. Fraser's tours take in principal sights and activities such as Lakes McKenzie and Wabby, the *Maheno* shipwreck and Indian Point, and are seriously fun. Meals, camping, permits and barge fees are all included.

Skydive Ramblers   SKYDIVING
(☑ 1300 663 634; www.skydiveforfun.com.au; 3048/4267m dives $239/299) Get great view of Fraser Island and the coast, jumping in tandem with experienced instructors. The 4267m dive involves a heart-bursting 65-second free-fall.

🛏 Sleeping

Rainbow Beach Hire-a-Camp   CAMPGROUND $
(☑ 0419 464 254; https://ultimatecamp.com.au; all-inclusive camping 2 people $313) 🏕 Rainbow Beach Hire-a-Camp is a great option for those who'd like to camp on the beach

and leave no trace, but aren't travelling with the necessary gear. They'll set up your camp on one of several blissful beachside sites around Inskip Peninsula, provide everything you could possibly need (including food, toilets and showers) then pack everything away once you're done.Two-night minimum.

Dingo's Backpacker's Resort HOSTEL $
(☑08-8131 5750, 1800 111 126; www.dingosresort. com; 20 Spectrum St; dm from $30; ⚑❄🛜🏊) This party hostel with a busy public bar is not for those in need of a good rest. It has loud music (live or otherwise) and events such as karaoke, trivia and bingo most nights, a chill-out gazebo for a temporary escape, free pancake breakfasts and $7 dinners. Dorms are clean and adequate, and Fraser Island tours can be arranged.

Pippies Beach House HOSTEL $
(☑07-5486 8503; www.pippiesbeachhouse.com. au; 22 Spectrum St; dm/d from $25/75; 🅿❄🛜🏊) This hostel is not as raucous as some in Rainbow Beach, but still caters mainly to young backpackers from Europe and North America. It offers decent kitchen and laundry facilities, free toast-and-jam breakfasts, a pool and organised group activities including Fraser Island tours. Extra touches such as thumb drives loaded with current films, loaned to guests on check-in, demonstrate an above-and-beyond attitude.

Fraser's on Rainbow HOSTEL $
(☑02-6685 2620, 1800 100 170; www.fraserson rainbow.com; 18 Spectrum St; dm/d/q from $32/99/120; 🅿❄🛜🏊) A classically gregarious and youthful hostel, Fraser's accommodation is basic but acceptable, with twins, doubles and four-bed 'family' rooms augmenting dorms. There's a pool, bar, laundry, BBQs, pool- and table-tennis tables, and a front desk organising tours to Fraser Island. Nightly entertainments include music, games and karaoke.

★ Debbie's Place B&B $$
(☑07-5486 3506, 0423 815 980; www.rainbow beachaccommodation.com.au; 30 Kurana St; d/ ste from $150/180, 3-bedroom apt from $340; 🅿❄🛜🏊) Debbie's meticulously kept Queenslander is the standard bearer for Rainbow Beach holiday accommodation. The motel- and apartment-style rooms are fully self-contained, with private entrances and verandahs, the effervescent Debbie is a mine of information, and the gardens are verdant with hanging baskets and tropical

blooms. There's one wheelchair-friendly room, and several with excellent outdoor cooking facilities.

🍴 Eating

Rainbow Fruit CAFE $
(☑07-5486 3126; 13B/1 Rainbow Beach Rd; wraps from $8; ⏰7.30am-5pm Mon-Fri, to 4pm Sat, to 3pm Sun; 🥗) Rainbow-fresh fruit and vegetables are sliced, diced and pureed for a range of juices, wraps and salads at this humble cafe and greengrocer just off the main strip. Breakfasts and Thai curries ($10) are well worth a try too.

The Deck at Sea Salt BISTRO $$
(☑0499 008 624; 2 Rainbow Beach Rd; mains $17; ⏰8am-6pm Sun & Mon, to 7pm Tue, to 9pm Wed & Thu, to 11pm Fri & Sat) The prime corner location – a deck open to the ocean breeze in the heart of town – is the obvious draw here, but the food's not bad either. If you don't fancy a full meal such as sticky ribs or a halloumi burger, there are always drinks, and tapas options like spicy Spanish potatoes and grilled paprika octopus to share.

Arcobaleno on the Beach ITALIAN $$
(☑07-5486 8000; 1/19 Rainbow Beach Rd; mains & pizzas $23-29; ⏰8am-10pm) Not actually on the beach (although not far from it) this welcoming, open-fronted Italian restaurant is set back from Rainbow Beach's main drag, behind the swish apartments of the Plantation Resort. Breakfasts such as savoury mince ragu with poached eggs ring in the day, while wood-fired pizzas and housemade pastas are great evening options. BYO wine.

ℹ Information

Rainbow Beach Visitor Centre (☑07-5486
3227; www.rainbowbeachinfo.com.au; 3/6 Rainbow Beach Rd; ⏰7am-5pm) This privately operated tourist desk is in a beachwear and souvenir shop.

ℹ Getting There & Away

Greyhound (☑1300 473 946; www.greyhound. com.au) and **Premier Motor Service** (☑13 34 10; www.premierms.com.au) are the two principal bus companies offering daily services to/ from Brisbane ($31 to $54, five to 5½ hours), Noosa ($20 to $37, 2½ to 2¾ hours) and Hervey Bay ($16 to $29, two hours); all stop on Spectrum St near the Rainbow Beach Community Centre. **Active Tours and Transfers** (☑07 5313 6631; www.activetransfers.com.au) runs a shuttle bus to Rainbow Beach from Brisbane

Airport ($135, three hours) and Sunshine Coast Airport ($95, two hours).

Most 4WD-hire companies will also arrange permits and barge costs to Fraser Island ($120 per vehicle return), and hire out camping gear. Try **All Trax** (🗾 07-5486 8300; www. fraserisland4x4.com.au; 66 Rainbow Beach Rd; 1 day $300; ⊙ 8.30am-4.30pm) or **Rainbow Beach Adventure Centre** (🗾 0419 663 271, 07-5486 3288; www.adventurecentre.com.au; 13 Spectrum St; per day $270; ⊙ 7am-5pm).

Maryborough

POP 22,206

Founded in 1847 to take advantage of the broad Mary River, on land belonging to the Butchulla people, Maryborough is one of Queensland's oldest towns. As a major 19th-century river port, it welcomed thousands of 19th-century free settlers looking for a better life in the young colony. This substantial heritage is self-evident in the many fine Heritage-listed buildings, Victorian parks and handsome Queenslanders that line Maryborough's broad streets, and is explicitly celebrated in a clutch of intriguing local museums and historic sites around Wharf St, including the **Military & Colonial Museum** (🗾 07-4123 5900; www.maryboroughmuseum. org; 106 Wharf St; adult/couple/family $10/18/24; ⊙ 9am-3.30pm Mon-Fri, to 12.30 Sat & Sun; 🖰) and the **Bond Store Museum** (🗾 07-4190 5722; www.ourfrasercoast.com.au/Portside; Wharf St; Portside pass $15). Just outside the centre is the excellent **Brennan & Geraghty's Store** (🗾 07-4121 2250; www.nationaltrust.org. au; 64 Lennox St; adult/family $5.50/13.50; ⊙ 10am-3pm; 🖰), a National Trust–classified former general store with exhibits stretching back to the 1870s.

Adding to this historical heft, Maryborough is the birthplace of Pamela Lyndon (PL) Travers, creator of the umbrella-wielding Mary Poppins. You can take part in Poppins-themed **walks** (🗾 07-4190 5722; $20; ⊙ 9.30am Thu & Fri), there's a life-sized **statue** of the world's most famous nanny on the corner of Richmond and Wharf Sts, and the **Mary Poppins Festival** (🗾 07-4196 9630; www.mary poppinsfestival.com.au; 🖰) enlivens the town in late June and early July.

Advice and guided tours of the town's handsome architecture can be found at the **Visitor Information Centre** (🗾 1800 214 789; www.visitfrasercoast.com; 388 Kent St, City Hall; ⊙ 9am-5pm Mon-Fri, to 1pm Sat & Sun), while pleasant B&B accommodation is offered at two adjacent Queenslanders: **Le Piaf** (🗾 0438 195 443; www.piaftreasure.com. au; 13 Treasure St; d incl breakfast $130; 🗟) and **Eco Queenslander** (🗾 0438 195 443; www. ecoqueenslander.com; 15 Treasure St; per couple from $140; 🗟) 🖗.

Gympie

POP 18,267

Founded on land traditionally owned by the Kabi Kbai (Gubbi Gubbi) people, Gympie is a pleasant former gold-rush town with some fine heritage architecture, lush parkland, a friendly main street and some interesting relics of the days when gold and timber fuelled a more fevered pitch of life. Come in August for the **Gympie Music Muster** (www. muster.com.au), one of the best country music festivals in Australia.

The **Gympie Gold Mining & Historical Museum** (🗾 07-5482 3995; www.gympiegold museum.com.au; 215 Brisbane Rd; adult/child/family $10/5/25; ⊙ 9am-4pm; P 🖰) holds a diverse collection of mining equipment and steam engines, while the **Woodworks Museum** (🗾 07-5483 7691; www.woodworksmuseum.com. au; 8 Fraser Rd, cnr Bruce Hwy; $5; ⊙ 10am-4pm Mon-Sat; P) displays memorabilia and equipment from the region's old logging days. Steam-train enthusiasts will love the 1920s **Mary Valley Rattler** (🗾 07-5482 2750; www.maryvalleyrattler.com.au; Historic Gympie Station, Tozer St; adult/child $55/30; ⊙ trains 9.30am & 2pm, Wed, Sat & Sun), and you can't beat the multiple pools and water-play areas of the shiny **Gympie Aquatic Centre** (🗾 07-5482 5594; https://gympiearc.com.au; Tozer Park Rd; swim, adult/child $5.20/3.60; ⊙ 5.30am-8pm Mon-Thu, 5.30am-7pm Fri, 6am-5pm Sat, 8am-5pm Sun; 🖰) for cooling off.

All the information you could need on the area is available at the friendly **Visitor Information Centre** (🗾 1800 444 222, 07-5481 5181; www.visitgympieregion.com.au; 24 Geordie Rd; ⊙ 9am-4pm Mon-Sat), while the **Gympie Muster Inn** (🗾 07-5482 8666; 21 Wickham St; d from $140; P 🕸 🗟) is a decent choice for over-nighters.

Childers

POP 1310

Surrounded by lush green fields and the rich red soil of an area traditionally owned by the Dunaburra of the Kabi Kabi (Gubbi Gubbi) people, Childers is a charming little town. Easily imagined in its formative Victorian years, its main street is lined with tall, shady trees and lattice-trimmed historical buildings. Most notable are the early-20th-century Federal Hotel, and the rebuilt Palace Hotel, burnt down by an arsonist in 2000 and now home to a memorial to the 15 backpackers that perished in the blaze. Backpackers still flock to Childers for fruit-picking and farm work.

The **Childers Palace Memorial & Art Gallery** (⏺07-4130 4876; www.bundabergregional galleries.com.au; 72 Churchill St; ⏲9am-4pm Mon-Fri, to 3pm Sat & Sun) FREE provides moving tribute to those who died in the fire, while the **Old Pharmacy Museum** (⏺0400 376 359; 90 Churchill St; adult/child $5/3; ⏲9am-3pm Mon-Fri, to 1pm Sat) exhibits potions, snake oils and medical equipment dating back to the 19th century. Each July over 50,000 people come for the music and stalls of the **Childers Festival** (www.childersfestival. com.au), about which the **Visitor Information Centre** (⏺1300 722 099, 07-4126 3886; 72 Churchill St; ⏲9am-4pm Mon-Fri, to 1pm Sat & Sun) can supply further details. **Mango Hill B&B** (⏺0408 875 305, 1800 816 020; www. mangohillcottages.com; 8 Mango Hill Dr; d incl breakfast from $150; ❄), attached to the Hill of Promise winery, is comfortably the nicest place to stay in town.

Childers is 50km south of Bundaberg. **Greyhound Australia** (⏺1300 473 946; www. greyhound.com.au) and **Premier Motor Service** (⏺13 34 10; www.premierms.com.au) both stop on Crescent St, behind the Post Office, and have at least one daily service to/from Brisbane ($47 to $95, 5½ to 8½ hours), Hervey Bay ($11 to $19, one to 1¾ hours) and Bundaberg ($11 to $28, 50 minutes to 1½ hours).

Bundaberg

POP 50,148

Its name an amalgam of Aboriginal and Saxon nomenclature (the Bunda were a kinship group of the traditional owners of this land, the Taribelang; while 'berg' means 'town') Bundaberg is the largest centre on the Fraser Coast. It's known throughout Australia for its sugar-cane fields, eponymous dark rum, tongue-tingling ginger beer and fruit-farming backpackers. The town proper is an agricultural centre with some friendly pubs, good dining and a decent regional art gallery. However, in many people's eyes, the beach hamlets around 'Bundy' are more attractive than the town itself. Some 25km to the north are the wide, flat beaches of **Moore Park**; to the east, families, retirees and nesting loggerhead turtles make themselves at home in the sands of **Bargara** and **Mon Repos**; while to the south the very popular **Elliott Heads** has a nice beach, rocky foreshore and good fishing.

⏺ Sights & Activities

⭐ Bundaberg Rum Distillery   DISTILLERY

(⏺07-4131 2999; www.bundabergrum.com.au; Hills St; adult/child self-guided tours $19/9.50, guided tours $29/14; ⏲10am-5pm Mon-Fri, to 4pm Sat & Sun) Bundaberg's biggest claim to fame is the iconic Bundaberg Rum: you'll see the brand's unmistakable polar bear on billboards and bumper stickers all over town. Choose from either a self-guided tour through the museum or a guided tour of the distillery, which commenced production in 1889. Tours depart on the hour, and both include a tasting for the over-18-year-olds. Wear closed shoes.

Bundaberg Barrel   BREWERY

(⏺07-4154 5480; www.bundaberg.com; 147 Bargara Rd; adult/child $12/free; ⏲9am-4.30pm Mon-Sat, 10am-3pm Sun) Bundaberg's nonalcoholic ginger beer and other soft drinks aren't as famous as Bundy Rum, but they run a deserved close second. Visit the Barrel to take an audio tour of the small museum, learn the history and processes involved, taste 14 flavours and take a six-pack home with you.

Bundaberg Regional Arts Gallery   GALLERY

(⏺07-4130 4750; www.bundabergregionalgalleries. com.au; 1 Barolin St; ⏲10am-5pm Mon-Fri, 11am-3pm Sat & Sun) FREE Known by the acronym BRAG, this small (and vividly purple) gallery has surprisingly good exhibitions, representing the local area and various 20th-century Australian schools. There's a sister gallery 50km south in Childers, the Childers Arts Space.

Anzac Park Pool   SWIMMING

(⏺07-4151 5640; 19 Quay St; adult/child $4/3; ⏲5.30am-6pm Mon-Fri, 6am-6pm Sat, 9am-5pm Sun Sep-Apr; ⏺) This boisterous public swimming pool is a Bundaberg institution on a hot summer's day. The gloriously old-fashioned Olympic-sized pool is surrounded by lawns and shady palms.

Bundaberg Aqua Scuba DIVING
(📞07-4153 5761; www.aquascuba.com.au; 239 Bourbong St; diving courses from $349; ⏱shop 9am-5pm Mon-Sat) This experienced operator leads dives to nearby sites around Coral Cove, plus longer cruises to Lady Musgrave Island (one/two dives $296/346) and interesting wrecks in the area. Also offers basic accommodation for $20/115 per night/week.

★**Lady Elliot Day Trip** TOURS
(📞1800 072 200, 07-5536 3644; www.ladyelliot. com.au; adult/child $445/299; 🚹) Fly to Lady Elliot Island, spend five hours on the Great Barrier Reef, use the resort's facilities, take free guided reef walks and snorkel in the lagoon. Lunch and a glass-bottom boat tour are also included. Flights leave Bundaberg at 8.40am and return at 4.30pm; flight time is 30 minutes.

🛏 Sleeping

Hideaway Haven B&B $$
(📞07-4155 0448, 0403 873 129; www.hideaway haven.com.au; 72 Tysons Rd; r incl breakfast $145-195; 🅿) This welcoming B&B offers four rooms in a charming bric-a-brac-filled house secreted away on a peaceful 4.8-hectare bush block 16km southwest of Bundaberg. Continental and cooked breakfasts are available, there's a BBQ for guest use, and the property is often visited by local wildlife.

Bundaberg Spanish Motor Inn MOTEL $$
(📞07-41525444; www.bundabergspanishmotorinn. com; 134 Woongarra St; r from $115; 🅿❄🛜🏊) A Spanish hacienda-style motel does not feel out of place in the hot Bundaberg climate, and this old-fashioned motor inn in a quiet side street off the main drag is *muy bueno.* Spotless units are self-contained and all overlook the central pool, and there's a BBQ for guest use.

Burnett Riverside Motel MOTEL $$
(📞07-4155 8777; www.burnettmotel.com.au; 7 Quay St; d from $150; 🅿❄🛜🏊) Popular with travelling business folk, this garish green-and-yellow motel on the banks of the Burnett has surprisingly good rooms, an above-average restaurant (mains $32 to $36) plus a pool, laundry and gym. Riverview rooms cost more, naturally.

🍴 Eating

★**Alowishus Delicious** CAFE $
(📞07-4154 2233; www.alowishus.com.au; 4/176 Bourbong St; Earl's Court; mains $13-16;

Q

TURTLE TOTS

Each summer, the largest population of marine turtles on Australia's east coast arrives on the beach at Mon Repos, 15km northeast of Bundaberg. The pregnant loggerheads drag themselves ashore to lay between November and January, and the hatchlings struggle out of the sand and towards the sea eight weeks later. The beach is off limits to humans from 6pm to 6am in this period, but you can see the tiny testudines do their thing from 7pm in guided Turtle Encounters (bookings essential). The **Mon Repos Turtle Centre** (📞07-4159 1652, 1300 722 099; https://parks. des.qld.gov.au/parks/mon-repos/turtle-centre.html; 141 Mon Repos Rd; adult/child $13/6.65; ⏱8am-5pm daily Nov-Mar & 8am-3.30pm Mon-Fri Apr-Oct; 🚹), open daily during turtle season, houses illuminating displays on the turtles and their environment.

⏱7am-6pm Mon-Wed, 7am-9pm Thu, 7am-11pm Fri, 8am-11pm Sat, 8am-5pm Sun) This slick, upbeat cafe down an arcade off Bourbong St is the place to go for well-made coffee in Bundaberg. The food's great too: breakfasts such as corn-and-zucchini fritters with poached egg, guacamole and salsa and lunches such as a crispy sweet-chilli chicken burger always hit the mark. Alowishus also does homemade ice cream (two scoops $5).

★**Oodies Cafe** CAFE $$
(📞07-4153 5340; www.oodies.com.au; 103 Gavin St; mains $14-16; ⏱6.30am-3pm Mon-Fri, to 2am Sat & Sun; 🛜) A double garage on the edge of Bundaberg's city centre is the unlikely venue for Bundaberg's most cosmopolitan cafe. Lounge on leather armchairs under art-spangled walls, surveying the bric-a-brac as you sip an expertly made coffee and wait for your super salad or breakfast bruschetta. The stream of takeaway custom is constant, as is the relaxed buzz inside.

★**Spicy Tonight** THAI $$
(📞07-4154 3320; www.spicytonight.com.au; 1 Targo St; dishes $20-22; ⏱11am-2.30pm Mon-Sat, 5-9pm daily; 🍴) Step behind the grand, columned facade of this former bank to discover a delightful family-run restaurant serving both Indian and Thai food. While the Indian offerings are fine, you should

QUEENSLAND BUNDABERG

stick to the superb Thai dishes, which betray the origins of the chef. Tom yum soup with great fat prawns, or pad cha (spicy seafood stir-fry) will delight pescatarians.

Ensoku
JAPANESE $$

(☑ 0402 291 965; 91 Bourbong St; mains $19-29; ◷ 9am-2pm & 5-9pm; ✈) Treading a line somewhere between Japanese, Korean and Western, this glass-sided corner restaurant serves some of Bundaberg's most interesting food. Never tried 'Korean Carbonara Chicken' (a Korean-style crumbed fillet topped with creamy bacon sauce)? This is your chance. Gyoza, donburi rice bowls and other more recognisable fare completes the menu.

Meekak
KOREAN $$

(☑ 07-4335 4428; 222 Bourbong St; mains $19-29; ◷ 11am-2.30pm & 5-8.30pm) This big, bustling Korean restaurant gives you the choice of barbecuing your own Wagyu, tongue, chicken and other meats at your table, ordering à la carte, dipping into a buffet of traditional dishes, or trying a medley of the three.

🍷 Drinking & Nightlife

Bargara Brewing Company
MICROBREWERY

(☑ 07-4152 1675; www.bargarabrewingco.com.au; 10 Tantitha St; ◷ 11am-9pm Wed & Thu, to 10pm Sat, to 5pm Sun) This buzzing craft brewery and taproom serves pizzas, sliders, jerky and other thoughtfully chosen drinking food ($14 to $17) to accompany pints of Drunk Fish, Thirsty Turtle and Hip Hop. Occasionally has live music too.

Spotted Dog Tavern
PUB

(☑ 07-4198 1044; www.spotteddogtavern.com.au; 217 Bourbong St; ◷ 8am-midnight) Bundaberg's most popular hotel-restaurant is busy all day. The pub food (mains $25 to $32) is serviceable, but it's really the bar, beer garden and live music that the locals come for.

ⓘ Information

Bundaberg Information Centre
(☑ 07-4153 8888, 1300 722 099; www.bundabergregion. org; 36 Avenue St; ◷ 9am-5pm) This reliable information centre has helpful staff and reams of brochures.

ⓘ Getting There & Away

AIR

Daily **Virgin** (☑ 13 67 89; https://virginaustralia. com) and **Qantas** (☑ 13 13 13; www.qantas.com. au) flight connect Bundaberg to Brisbane.

BUS

The **coach terminal** (☑ 07-4153 2646) is on Targo St. Both **Greyhound** (☑ 1300 473 946; www. greyhound.com.au) and **Premier Motor Service** (☑ 13 34 10; www.premierms.com.au) have daily services connecting Bundaberg with Brisbane ($53 to $94, eight to nine hours), Hervey Bay ($18 to $29, two to 2½ hours) and Rockhampton ($41 to $54, 3½ to five hours).

Duffy's City Buses (☑ 1300 383 397; www. duffysbuses.com.au) has nine services every weekday (and four on Saturday) to Bargara ($4, 20 minutes), leaving from behind Target on Woongarra St.

TRAIN

The **Queensland Rail** (☑ 1300 131 722; www. queenslandrailtravel.com.au) Tilt Train stops at Bundaberg en route to Brisbane (from $53, 4½ hours). The *Spirit of Queensland* (from $81, 5½ hours, five weekly) also stops here between Brisbane and Cairns.

Fraser Island

The local Butchulla people call it K'gari – 'paradise' – and for good reason. Sculpted by wind, sand and surf, the striking blue freshwater lakes, crystalline creeks, giant dunes and lush rainforests of this gigantic sandbar form an enigmatic island paradise unlike any other. Fraser Island is the largest sand island in the world (measuring 120km by 15km) and the only known place where rainforest grows on sand.

Inland, the vegetation varies from dense tropical rainforest and wild heath to wetlands and wallum scrub, with sandblows, mineral streams and 'perched' freshwater lakes opening onto long sandy beaches. The island, most of which is protected as part of the Great Sandy National Park, is home to a profusion of bird life and wildlife, including the famous dingo, while offshore waters teem with dugong, dolphins, manta rays, sharks and migrating humpback whales.

◉ Sights & Activities

Starting at Fraser''s southern tip, where the ferry leaves on Inskip Point on the mainland, a high-tide access track cuts inland, avoiding sometimes-dangerous Hook Point, and leads to the eastern beach, which serves as the main thoroughfare for an island with no paved roads. Heading north, the first settlement is Dilli Village (p357), a former sand-mining centre now home to

SAND SAFARIS

The only way to explore Fraser Island (besides walking) is with a 4WD. For most travellers, there are three realistic options: tours (tag-along or fully guided); hiring a 4WD; or skipping to a resort on Fraser and taking a day tour from there. Bear in mind this sandy miracle is fragile – the greater the number of vehicles driving on the island, the greater the environmental damage. With an average of more than 1000 people visiting the island each day over the course of the year, Fraser can sometimes feel like a giant sandpit with its own peak hour and congested beach highway.

Tag-Along Tours

Popular with backpackers, tag-along tours see groups of travellers pile into a 4WD convoy and follow a lead vehicle with an experienced guide and driver. Travellers take turns driving the other vehicles, which can be great fun, but has also led to accidents. Rates hover around $400 to $450; be sure to check if your tour includes food, fuel, alcohol, etc. Accommodation is often in tents.

Advantages: you can make new friends fast; driving the beaches is exhilarating. Disadvantages: if food isn't included, you'll have to cook; groups can be even bigger than on bus tours.

Fraser's on Rainbow (p347) Departs from Rainbow Beach.

Dropbear Adventures (☏1800 061 156; www.dropbearadventures.com.au) Lots of departures from Rainbow Beach and Noosa; easy to get a spot.

Nomads (☏07-5447 3355; www.nomadsfraserisland.com) Departs from Noosa.

Pippies Beach House (☏07-5486 8503; www.pippiesbeachhouse.com.au) Departs Rainbow Beach; well organised and has small convoys with high safety standards.

Organised Tours

Most organised tours cover Fraser's hot spots: rainforests, Eli Creek, Lakes McKenzie and Wabby, the coloured Pinnacles and the *Maheno* shipwreck.

Advantages: expert commentary; decent food and comfortable accommodation; often the most economical choice. Disadvantages: day-tour buses often arrive en masse at the same place at the same time; less social.

Fraser Explorer Tours (p343) Very experienced drivers; lots of departures.

Cool Dingo Tours (☏07-4120 3333; www.cooldingotour.com; 2-/3-day tours from $385/510) Overnight at lodges with the option to stay extra nights on the island. The party option, Cool Dingo leaves from Hervey Bay or Rainbow Beach.

Fraser Experience (☏07-4124 4244; https://fraserexperiencetours.com.au; 28 Southern Cross Circuit, Urangan; adult/child from $205/145; ⊗7am-5pm) Small group tours offer greater freedom with the itinerary; departing from Hervey Bay.

Remote Fraser (☏1800 620 322; www.tasmanventure.com.au; tours adult/child $175/100) Day tours from Hervey Bay to the less-visited west coast.

4WD Hire

You can hire a 4WD from Hervey Bay, Rainbow Beach or on Fraser Island itself. All companies require a hefty bond, usually in the form of a credit-card imprint, which you will lose if you drive in salt water – don't even think about running the waves!

When planning your trip, reckon on covering 20km an hour on the inland tracks and 40km an hour on the eastern beach. Most companies will help arrange ferries, permits and camping gear. Rates range from $270 to $300 for one day, falling for multiday hires.

Advantages: complete freedom to roam the island and escape the crowds. Disadvantages: you may encounter beach and track conditions that even experienced drivers find challenging; expensive.

There are rental companies in Hervey Bay (p347) and Rainbow Beach (p348). On the island, **Aussie Trax** (☏07-4124 4433; www.fraserisland4wd.com.au; full-day hire from $310) hires out 4WDs from Kingfisher Bay Resort on the west coast; the cheaper vehicles start at $310 per person per day, with lower daily rates for longer hires.

Fraser Island

CORAL
SEA

Sandy Cape

Sandy Cape
Lighthouse

Lake Marong

Manann
Beach

Rooney
Point

Lake Wanhar

Marloo
Bay

Hervey Bay
Marine
Park

Lake Carree

Lake Minker

Hervey
Bay

Orchid
Beach 14

Platypus
Bay

19 Waddy Point
Ranger Station 3

Middle
Rocks
8
Indian
Head

Triangle
Cliff

Yathon
Cliffs

Arch
Cliff

Lake
Gnarann

Corroboree
Beach

Bimjella Hill
(174m)

Lake
Bowarrady

Coongul
Point

Bowarrady
(244m)

13

Dundubara
Ranger
Station

K'gari (Fraser Island)
Great Sandy
National Park

10
Cathedral Beach

Point
Vernon

See Hervey Bay
Map (p344)

2 6

Hervey Bay
Visitor
Information
Centre 15

20

Hervey
Bay 9

Blackfellow
Point

Big Woody
Island

5

4

Eli Creek

Lake
Garawongera

Kingfisher
Bay

Valley of
the Giants

Happy Valley
7

River
Heads

21

Leading Hill
(184m)

Rainbow Gorge

Poyungan Valley

16 Lake
McKenzie

Poyungan Rocks

Wanggoolba Creek

22

Lake Wabby

Central Station 11

Lake Jennings

Eurong Ranger Centre

18

Boomanjin Hill
(211m)

Eurong

Maryborough

1

Poona National
Park

17

Lake Birrabeen

Lake Benaroon

Lake Boomanjin

SOUTH
PACIFIC
OCEAN

12
Dilli Village

Maaroom

Figtree Lake
(Lake Goo Mboor)

Tuan

Great Sandy Strait

Tuan State
Forest

The Bluff
(64m)

Hook Point

Inskip Point

Rainbow Beach (3km)

Fraser Island

◎ **Top Sights**
1 Brennan & Geraghty's Store A6

◎ **Sights**
2 Fraser Coast Cultural Centre A4
3 Indian Head D3
4 Maheno Wreck C4
  Mary Poppins Statue .... (see 1)
  Maryborough Military &
    Colonial Museum .... (see 1)
5 Pinnacles D4
  Portside Heritage Precinct .... (see 1)
6 Wetside Water Park A4
7 Yidney Rocks C5

◎ **Activities, Courses & Tours**
8 Champagne Pools D2
9 Fraser Experience B4

◎ **Sleeping**
10 Cathedrals on Fraser C4
11 Central Station Camp Site C5
12 Dilli Village C6
13 Dundubara Camping Ground D3
  Eco Queenslander .... (see 1)
14 Eliza Fraser Lodge D2
15 Emeraldene Inn & Eco-Lodge A4
16 Kingfisher Bay Resort B5
17 Lake Boomanjin Camping Area C6
  Le Piaf on Treasure .... (see 1)
18 Ungowa Camping Ground B6
  Waddy Point Camping
    Ground .... (see 14)
19 Wathumba Spit Camping
    Ground C2

◎ **Information**
  Maryborough Fraser Island
    Visitor Information Centre .... (see 1)

◎ **Transport**
20 Bay Central Coach Terminal A4
21 Kingfisher Bay Ferry Terminal B5
22 River Heads B5

a campground and research centre, while **Eurong**, with shops, fuel, an inexpensive resort (p357) and places to eat, is another 9km north. From here, an inland track crosses to **Wanggoolba Creek** (for the ferry to River Heads).

Right in the middle of the island is the ranger centre and forest campground at **Central Station** (☑13 74 68; http://parks. des.qld.gov.au; per person/family $6.55/26), the starting point for numerous walking trails. From here you can drive (or walk, if you have abundant time) to the beautiful **McKenzie, Jennings, Birrabeen** and **Boomanjin Lakes**. Lake McKenzie is spectacularly clear and ringed by white-sand beaches, making it a great place to swim. Lake Birrabeen sees fewer tour and backpacker groups, but is no less inviting.

About 4km along the beach north of Eurong, a signposted walking trail leads across sandblows to the beautiful **Lake Wabby**, the most accessible of Fraser's lakes. An easier route is from the Lake Wabby Lookout, off Cornwell's Break Rd from the inland side. Lake Wabby is surrounded on three sides by eucalyptus forest, while the fourth side is a massive sandblow that encroaches on the lake at a rate of about 3m a year. Wabby is deceptively shallow, so be warned that diving is very dangerous.

As you drive further north along the eastern beach, consider times of high tide as you approach **Poyungan** and **Yidney Rocks**, which may require a deviation inland. North of here is **Happy Valley**, with places to stay, a shop and a bistro; about 10km further north again is **Eli Creek**, a fast-moving, crystal-clear waterway that also requires care due to the many streams that bisect Fraser's eastern shore. About 2km after Eli Creek is the salt-rotted hulk of the **Maheno**, a condemned passenger liner blown ashore by a cyclone in 1935; its oxidised ribs now provide Fraser's classic photo opportunity.

Roughly 5km north of the *Maheno* you'll find the **Pinnacles**, an eroded section of coloured sand cliffs, and about 10km beyond those, **Dundubara** (☑13 74 68; http:// parks.des.qld.gov.au; per person/family $6.55/26), with a ranger station and an excellent campground. There is then a 20km stretch of beach before you come to the rocky prominence of **Indian Head**, named by Captain Cook for the 'Indians' who gathered here to watch him sail past in 1770. Sharks, manta rays, dolphins and (during the migration season) whales can often be seen from the top of this headland.

Between Indian Head and Waddy Point, the trail branches inland, passing **Champagne Pools**, a natural swimming site that offers the only wholly safe saltwater dip on the island. There's good beach camping at **Waddy Point** (☑13 74 68; http://parks.des.qld. gov.au; per person/family $6.55/26) near Orchid Beach, the island's most northerly settlement. Many tracks north of here are closed for environmental protection, and to 4WDs hired from companies that don't want to see their vehicles stranded in impossible terrain.

QUEENSLAND FRASER ISLAND

Meandering 90km through the island's interior from Dilli Village to Happy Valley, the **Fraser Island Great Walk** is a stunning way to experience this unique environment. Broken up into seven sections of around 6km to 16km each, plus some side trails, the walk follows the pathways of Fraser Island's original inhabitants, the Butchulla people. En route it passes underneath rainforest canopies, circles around some of the island's vibrantly blue 'perched' lakes, and courses through shifting dunes.

It's imperative that you visit the **Queensland Parks** (⌨ 13 74 68; http://parks.des.qld.gov. au) website for maps, dingo safety advice, updates on the track (which can close when conditions are bad) and camping permits.

🛏 Sleeping

Camping permits are required to camp at the 45 Queensland Parks campgrounds across Fraser. The most developed sites, with coin-operated hot showers, toilets and BBQs, are at Waddy Point, Dundubara and Central Station. Campers with vehicles can also use the smaller campgrounds with fewer facilities at **Lake Boomanjin** (⌨ 13 74 68; http://parks.des.qld.gov.au; per person/family $6.55/26), and at **Ungowa** and **Wathumba** on the west coast. Walkers' camps are set away from the main campgrounds, along the **Fraser Island Great Walk** trail. The trail map, available from Queensland Parks, lists the campsites and their facilities. Camping is permitted on designated stretches of the eastern beach, but there are no facilities. Fires are prohibited except in communal fire rings at Waddy Point and Dundubara – bring your own firewood in the form of untreated, milled timber, and ensure no fire ban is in place.

Supplies on the island are limited and costly. Stock up well before arriving, and be prepared for mosquitoes and March flies.

Dilli Village CAMPGROUND $
(⌨ 07-4127 9130; www.usc.edu.au; sites per person $10, dm/cabins $50/120) Managed by the University of the Sunshine Coast, which uses this precinct as a base for environmental education and research purposes, Dilli Village offers good sites on a softly sloping, dingo-fenced campground. The self-contained cabins, which can sleep five, are particularly good value.

Cathedrals on Fraser CARAVAN PARK $$
(⌨ 07-4127 9177; www.cathedralsonfraser.com. au; Cathedral Beach; powered/unpowered sites for two $39/29, 2-bed cabins with/without bathroom $200/180; @) This spacious dingo-fenced park offers abundant, flat, grassy sites and a range of cabins. There's a shop selling fuel, alcohol, food and groceries on-site, two camp kitchens, a laundry, communal fire pits and plenty of picnic areas.

Eurong Beach Resort RESORT $$
(⌨ 07-4120 1600, 1800 678 623; www.eurong. com.au; Eurong; r from $179, 2-bedroom apt $269; ✳ @ 🛱 🌊) While Eurong is starting to show

---

DEALING WITH DINGOES

Despite its many natural attractions and opportunities for adventure, there's nothing on Fraser Island that gives a thrill comparable to your first glimpse of a dingo. Believed to be among the most genetically pure in the world, the dingoes of Fraser are sleek, spry and utterly beautiful. They're also wild beasts that can become aggressive at the drop of a hat (or a strong-smelling food sack). While attacks are rare, there are precautions that must be taken by every visitor to the island.

➡ However skinny they appear, or whatever woebegone look they give you, never feed dingoes. Dingoes that are human-fed quickly lose their shyness and can become combative and competitive. Feeding dingoes is illegal and carries heavy fines.

➡ Don't leave any food scraps lying around, and don't take food to the lakes: eating on the shore puts your food at 'dingo level', an easy target for scrounging scavengers.

➡ Stay in groups, and keep any children within arm's reach at all times.

➡ Teasing dingoes is not only cruel, but dangerous. Leave them alone, and they'll do the same.

➡ Dingoes are best observed at a distance. Pack a zoom lens and practise some silence, and you'll come away with some brilliant photographs...and all your limbs intact.

signs of deterioration, it allows you to stay close to conveniences, and with an abundance of stunning landscape within a dingo's bark. Accommodation is either simple motel rooms or comfortable, self-contained apartments, and facilities include a shop, two pools, tennis courts, a petrol station and restaurant-bar **McKenzie's**, offering a buffet or menu for every meal.

★**Eliza Fraser Lodge**   LODGE $$$
(☑ 0418 981 610; www.elizafraserlodge.com.au; 8 Eliza Av, Orchid Beach; per person $410) Occupying a stunning purpose-built house, Eliza Fraser is the island's finest lodging. Serviced directly by Air Fraser Island and Brisbane Helicopters, the two-level house is perfect for families or small groups. The hosts are expert guides and will organise fishing trips, nature hikes and 4WD adventures, or just let you enjoy the house and its spectacular surrounds.

★**Kingfisher Bay Resort**   RESORT $$$
(☑ 1800 072 555, 07-4194 9300; www.king fisherbay.com; Kingfisher Bay; d from $199, 2-bedroom villas $405; ✳@⊛) ✎ Set in delightful native gardens, this elegant eco-resort has hotel rooms with private balconies, and sophisticated two- and three-bedroom timber villas designed to minimise environmental impact (three-night minimum stay in high season). The **Seabelle Restaurant** is terrific (mains $35 to $39), while the three bars are great fun in summer at sunset, especially the backpacker-friendly **Dingo**.

ℹ Information

Ranger stations at **Eurong** (☑ 07-4127 9128), **Dundubara** (☑ 07-4127 9138) and **Waddy Point** (☑ 07-4127 9190) are not public-facing offices, open in scheduled hours – they're often unattended, as the rangers are out on patrol.

ℹ Getting There & Away

AIR

Air Fraser Island (☑ 1300 172 706; www.air fraserisland.com.au) charges from $150 for a one-way flight to the island's eastern beach, departing Hervey Bay airport.

BOAT

Vehicle ferries connect Fraser Island with **River Heads**, about 10km south of Hervey Bay, or further south at **Inskip Point**, near Rainbow Beach.

Fraser Venture Barge (☑ 07-4194 9300, 1800 227 437; www.fraserislandferry.com.au) Makes

ℹ FRASER ISLAND PERMITS

You must purchase permits from Queensland Parks & Wildlife Service (www. parks.des.qld.gov.au) for vehicles (up to one month $51) and to camp in QPWS campgrounds (adult/family per night $6.55/26) before you arrive. Permits aren't required for private campgrounds or resorts. Buy permits online or check with visitor centres for up-to-date lists of where to buy them.

the 30-minute crossing from River Heads to Wanggoolba Creek on the west coast of Fraser Island (return fares: pedestrian adult/child $60/30, vehicle and four passengers $215). It departs daily from River Heads at 8.30am, 10.15am and 4pm, and returns from the island at 9am, 3pm and 5pm.

Kingfisher Bay Ferry (☑ 07-4194 9300, 1800 227 437; www.fraserislandferry.com) Operates a daily 50-minute vehicle and passenger service (pedestrian adult/child return $60/30; vehicle and four passengers return $215) from River Heads to **Kingfisher Bay**, departing at 6.45am, 9am, 12.30pm, 3.30pm and 6.45pm (plus 9.30pm in peak periods) and returning 7.50am, 10.30am, 2pm, 5pm and 8.30pm (plus 11pm in peak periods).

Manta Ray (☑ 0418 872 599, 07-5486 3935; www.mantarayfraserislandbarge.com.au) Leaving from Inskip Point near Rainbow Beach, Manta Ray has two ferries continuously running the 15-minute crossing to a beach just west of Hook Point on Fraser Island, from about 6am to 5.15pm daily (vehicle return $120).

ℹ Getting Around

A 4WD is necessary if you're driving on Fraser Island and you must have a vehicle permit from Queensland Parks (p356), which costs $51 for up to one month. Expensive fuel is available from shops at Cathedral Beach, Eurong, Kingfisher Bay, Happy Valley and Orchid Beach. If your vehicle breaks down, call the tow-truck service in Eurong, **Fraser Island Towing** (0428 353 164, 07-4127 9449).

The 4WD **Fraser Island Taxi Service** (☑ 0429 379 188, 07-4127 9188; www.fraserservice.com. au) operates all over the island. Bookings are essential, as there's only one cab for the whole island.

If you want to hire a 4WD while on Fraser, Aussie Trax (p353) has a medium-sized fleet, from Suzuki Jimnys to Toyota Land Cruisers, available at the Kingfisher Bay Resort.

CAPRICORN COAST & THE SOUTHERN REEF ISLANDS

This less-heralded stretch of Queensland's coast straddles the Tropic of Capricorn, and comprises the southernmost islands of the Great Barrier Reef. Here, local families seek escape from the inland heat of centres such as beef capital Rockhampton among dreamy beaches, mangroves and reef-fringed islands, while the less-accessible coast and hinterland hold some of the state's most arrestingly beautiful national parks. School holidays can be busy in the main cooling-off spots, but for most of the year you needn't travel far to find a deserted beach.

The beachy-dreamy twin towns of Agnes Water and 1770 naturally capture traveller interest, with hostels, connections to the southern reef islands, and perfect fishing, surfing and kayaking. Visitors with more time won't regret exploring less-frequented coastal attractions such as Yeppoon and the Eurimbula and Deepwater national parks, or heading inland to wander the ancient gorges of Carnarvon National Park.

Agnes Water & Town of 1770

POP 2210

Happily tucked away a decent distance from Bundaberg or Gladstone, on gorgeous coastal lands owned traditionally by the Gureng Gureng people, these two idyllic little beach towns have been tipped by property speculators as Australia's next Noosa or Gold Coast. Thankfully, and despite the love showered on them by European backpackers, such change has been slow, and they retain an unfussy charm.

Bordered by national parks, red rock coves and the rolling Pacific, Agnes Water has a surf beach, a sleepy commercial centre and some excellent hostels. Just 8km up the road is the site of Captain Cook's first landing in Queensland, in 1770. The town's short bluff walks are outstanding, and its campground one of the best in the state, a launching point for kayaking, paddleboarding and fishing excursions around the inlets of the 'Discovery Coast'.

◉ Sights & Activities

Agnes Water is Queensland's northernmost surf beach. A surf lifesaving club patrols the main beach on Sundays and public holidays from September to early May, and there are often good breaks along the coast. There's also good fishing and mud-crabbing upstream on Round Hill Creek. Charter boats are available for fishing, surfing, snorkelling and diving trips to the reef.

Agnes Water Museum MUSEUM
(☑ 07-4974 9511; www.agneswatermuseum.com. au; Springs Rd, near cnr Captain Cook Dr, Agnes Water; adult/child $3/free; ☉ 1-4pm Mon & Wed-Sat, 10am-1pm Sun) The museum displays extracts from Cook's journal, the original telescope from the first lighthouse built on the Queensland coast, Aboriginal art from Arnhem Land and a wealth of curious flotsam and jetsam.

★ Scooter Roo Tours ADVENTURE SPORTS
(☑ 07-4974 7697; www.scooterrootours.com; 2694 Round Hill Rd, Agnes Water; per person $85) You don't need to be a petrolhead to absolutely love this hilarious and informative 50km, three-hour tour of the Agnes Water area. Better yet, you only need a car licence to get low and dirty on a mini, single-gear 'chopper' bike. All routes are on-road and long pants and closed-in shoes are mandatory; they'll supply the tough-guy leather jackets.

Lazy Lizard Surf School SURFING
(☑ 0488 177 000; www.lazylizardsurfschool.com. au; 7 Agnes St, Agnes Water; 2hr lesson $35; ⬛) Offering lessons for smaller groups (six students per coach, minimum age 14) Lazy Lizard will be sure to get you up in the gentle surf in front of the clubhouse. Private lessons for groups ($150 for four) and individuals ($60 per hour) can also be arranged.

1770 Liquid Adventures KAYAKING
(☑ 0428 956 630; www.1770liquidadventures.com. au) This experienced outfit makes the most of 1770's delightful surrounds on its sunset tours (from $55). You'll be guided around the usually placid waters off Eurimbula National Park, before retiring to Bustard Bay beach for drinks and snacks in the gloaming – keep an eye out for dolphins. You can also rent kayaks for self-directed fun (single/ double kayaks per hour $20/25).

1770 Larc Tours TOURS
(☑ 07-4974 9422; www.1770larctours.com.au; 1770 Marina, 535 Captain Cook Dr, Town of 1770; day trips adult/child $160/99) ⬭ The ex-military Lighter Amphibious Resupply Cargo (LARC) vehicle makes a comfortable ride for

EURIMBULA & DEEPWATER NATIONAL PARKS

Agnes Water and 1770 are flanked by two gorgeous national parks, accessible only by 4WD.

The 78-sq-km **Eurimbula National Park** (http://parks.des.qld.gov.au/parks/eurimbula), on the northern side of Round Hill Creek, harbours an unspoilt landscape of dunes, mangroves and eucalypt forest. You'll also find delightful beaches, hikes at many levels of difficulty and splendid, and relatively accessible isolation in the Australian bush. There are basic campgrounds at **Eurimbula Creek** (limited rainwater), **Middle Creek** (no water), Bustard Head and **Rodds Peninsula** (no facilities).

To the south, equally lovely **Deepwater National Park** (http://parks.des.qld.gov.au/parks/deepwater) offers long sandy beaches, walking trails, freshwater creeks, good fishing spots and two campgrounds. It's also a major breeding ground for loggerhead turtles, which lay eggs on the beaches between November and February; hatchlings emerge at night between January and April. The northern park entrance to Deepwater is 8km south of Agnes Water and is only accessible by 4WD. From the northern entrance, it's 5km to the basic campground at Middle Rock and a further 2km to **Wreck Rock**. Wreck Rock can also be accessed from the south by 2WD vehicles via Baffle Creek.

Buy permits to camp in either park online from Queensland Parks & Wildlife (p356) beforehand (adult/family per night $6.55/26).

If you don't have your own 4WD, **Moondoggie Beach & Bush Tours** (☑0407 118 390, 07-4974 7916; http://moondoggietours.wordpress.com; day tour per person $95) can get you to either park, or both.

exploring the natural joys of Bustard Headland and Eurimbula National Park. Guides know their stuff and will entertain all ages. Aside from the signature seven-hour day trip (lunch included), they also run hourlong afternoon tours (adult/child $40/18) and the Goolimbil Walkabout ($85/45).

1770 Reef BOATING
(☑07-4972 7222; www.1770reef.com.au; 1770 Marina, 535 Captain Cook Dr, Town of 1770; day trip adult/child/family $200/99/558; 🚗) This shipshape outfit runs day trips to the 14-hectare coral cay Lady Musgrave Island in the Capricorn Bunker Group. Following the 90-minute cruise through the waters of the Great Barrier Reef, you can snorkel a coral-skirted lagoon, kick back in a glass-bottomed boat, or spot nesting bird life on guided land tours. Departs 1770 Marina at 8.30am and returns at 5pm.

🛏 Sleeping

★**Backpackers @ 1770** HOSTEL $
(☑0408 533 851; www.backpackers1770.com.au; 20-22 Grahame Colyer Dr, main entry from Captain Cook Dr, Agnes Water; dm/d $27/70; ❄🖤) Actually in Agnes Water, this gregarious, great-value hostel is a model of the genre. Family-built and -run, it offers spotless dorms, three smart doubles and a lush communal garden where meals are taken, guitars strummed and stories shared. Add

nightly events such as trivia, beer pong and movies, and this hostel becomes an east-coast must for many young travellers.

★**Cool Bananas** HOSTEL $
(☑07-4974 7660; http://coolbananasbackpackers.com; 2 Springs Rd, Agnes Water; dm $29; 🖤) The young and sociable go bananas for this funky, open-minded backpacker hangout, with a questionable colour scheme but an irresistible vibe cultivated by the friendly owners. Roomy eight-bed dorms are perfectly comfortable, and management encourages mingling during 'family time' each evening from 6pm to 8pm. Further fraternisation occurs during nightly events such as Aloha Mondays (leis and cocktails).

1770 Camping Ground CAMPGROUND $
(☑07-4974 9286; www.1770campingground.com.au; 641 Captain Cook Dr, Town of 1770; powered/unpowered sites from $41/36, beachfront sites $46; 🖤) This campground, with its absolute beach frontage and western aspect, must be a contender for best location on the east coast. The site is well shaded with palm and fig trees, and there's a laundry, cafe and camp kitchen available. Campfires are allowed on the beachfront, and sunsets can be stunning.

★**1770 Getaway** VILLA $$
(☑07-4974 9323; www.1770getaway.com.au; 303 Bicentennial Dve, Agnes Water; villas from $170;

Capricorn Coast

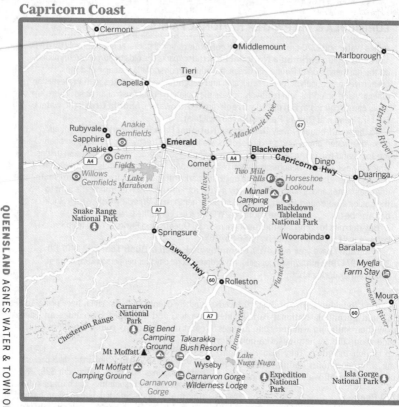

) These five delightful villas are set among 1.5 hectares of tropical gardens just out of the centre of Agnes. Decorated in soothing creams, each has an airy, open feel, well-appointed kitchens, good laundry facilities and shady private verandahs with BBQs. Breakfast by the pond at the lovely **Getaway Garden Cafe** can be included ($40 for two).

Agnes Water Beach Club　　　APARTMENT **$$**
(☑ 07-4974 7355; www.agneswaterbeachclub.com. au; 3 Agnes St, Agnes Water; 1-/2-bedroom apt from $200/250; ❄❂☎) This modern, three-storey block of holiday apartments is midway between the shops and the patrolled beach in Agnes. The one- and two-bedroom apartments themselves are bright and comfortable, facing onto a good-sized pool and spa area that buzzes with a good-humoured family atmosphere. A two-night minimum applies in school holidays, and specials are advertised on the website.

Lagoons 1770 Resort　　　RESORT **$$$**
(☑ 07-4902 1600; www.lagoons1770.com.au; 2 Beaches Village Circuit, Agnes Water; apt from $212; ℙ❄❂☎) With sleek contemporary apartments set among tropical gardens, an on-site restaurant, **Plantations**, and the relaxing **Anjea** day spa (massages from $110), this cruisy resort on the edge of Agnes Water is an all-in-one escape. If you do need to break bounds, the beach is just a few minutes' walk away.

✗ Eating

Agnes Water Bakery　　　BAKERY **$**
(☑ 07-4974 9500; Round Hill Rd, Agnes Water; pies $5.50; ◷ 6am-3.30pm Mon-Sat, to 2pm Sun) This popular bakery is known for its killer pies – expect gourmet fillings such as lamb shank or chilli, plus a couple of vegetarian selections. On the sweet side, the chocolate éclairs, jam scrolls and apple turnovers are usually gone by noon. Oh, and there is bread too.

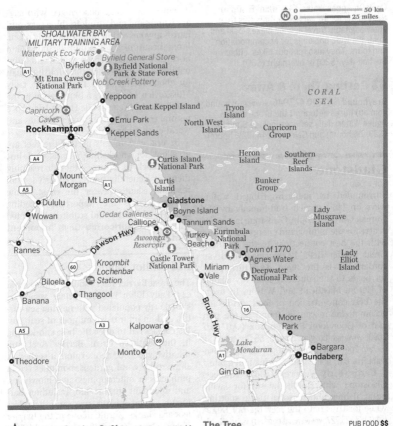

★ **Getaway Garden Café** CAFE $$
(☑ 07-4974 9323; www.1770getaway.com.au;
303 Bicentennial Dr, Agnes Water; breakfast
& lunch mains $18-20, dinner per person $28;
☺ 8am-2.30pm Sun-Fri, with booking 5.30-7.30pm
Wed & Sun; ☎) This open-sided, teak-doored
pavilion, set in restful tropical gardens
popular with local wildlife, is the venue for
some of the best food in Agnes. Dealing pri-
marily in breakfast and lunch (eggs Bene-
dict with brisket on brioche will set you up;
a vibrant salad with grilled halloumi will
keep you going), it also does a mean coffee
and cake.

Off the Hook FISH & CHIPS $$
(☑ 07-4974 7050; Shop 1, Endeavour Plaza, cnr
Captain Cook Dr & Springs Rd, Agnes Water; meals
$16-18; ☺ 11am-7.30pm Mon-Sat, to 4pm Sun) A
classic Australian seaside chippy, Off the
Hook has all the burgers, prawns, scallops,
fish fillets and other battered delights you'll
need for an al fresco dinner on the sand.

The Tree PUB FOOD $$
(☑ 07-4974 7446; www.1770beachhotel.com.au;
1770 Beach Hotel, 576 Captain Cook Dr, Town of 1770;
mains $24-26; ☺ 10.30am-10pm) Facing west
towards the sea through a curtain of green,
this indoor-outdoor pub-bistro has the best
outlook for a sundowner in 1770. Part of the
salty, laid-back 1770 Beach Hotel – the town's
main meeting place – the Tree offers pub
food appropriate to the subtropical latitude,
including pan-fried barramundi and squid
salad with crispy noodles.

ⓘ Information

Agnes Water Visitor Information Centre
(☑ 07-4902 1533; www.visitagnes1770.com.au;
71 Springs Rd, Agnes Water; ☺ 8.30am-4.30pm
Mon-Fri, 9am-4pm Sat, to 1pm Sun) Staffed by
above-and-beyond volunteers who even leave
out information and brochures when it's closed,
just in case a lost soul blows into town.

Discover 1770 (☑ 07-4974 7557; www.discover
1770.com.au; cnr Round Hill Rd & Captain

Cook Dr, Agnes Water; ⊙8.30am-5.30pm) Next to the Caltex service station, this friendly, knowledgeable travel agency makes local and Australia-wide bookings for accommodation and tours. They also rent out bikes, either by the half-day ($20) or overnight ($30).

ⓘ Getting There & Away

Greyhound (☑1300 473 946; www.greyhound. com.au) buses detour off the Bruce Hwy to Agnes Water; daily services include Bundaberg ($29, 1½ hours) and Cairns ($244, 22½ hours).

Gladstone

POP 33,418

Surrounded by mangrove-fringed waterways on land owned traditionally by the Gureng Gureng people, Gladstone is a major centre for the mining and energy industries, with the best connections to the southern Great Barrier Reef. Its marina (on Bryan Jordan Dr) is the main departure point for boats to the southern coral cay islands of Heron, Masthead and Wilson. In town, the best concentration of food, drink and accommodation can be found at the port end of Goondoon St. **Lightbox** (☑07-4972 2698; www.lightboxgladstone.co; 56 Goondoon St; ⊙7am-2pm Mon & Sun, to 10pm Tue-Thu, to midnight Fri & Sat) is ideal for a drink and a bite.

Curtis Ferry Services (p363) connects Gladstone with **Curtis Island** for swimming, fishing and seasonal turtle spotting, while for trips onto the reef, the **MV Mikat** (☑0427 125 727; www.mikat.com.au) is available for charter. Inland, artificial **Lake Awoonga** offers **boat hire** (☑0457 929 889; www.lake awoongaboatingandleisurehire.com; tinnies halfday $80, kayaks 1hr $25) and a **caravan park** (☑07-4975 0155; www.lakeawoongacaravanpark. com; 865 Awoonga Dam Rd, Benaraby; 2-person unpowered/powered site $25/34, cabins from $85), while the **Calliope River Historical Village** (☑07-4975 6764; www.callioperiverhistoricalvillage. com; Dawson Hwy, Calliope; adult/child $5/free; ⊙10am-4pm) hosts a popular market five or six times a year. More information can be had from the **Visitor Information Centre** (☑07-4972 9000; www.gladstoneregion.info; 72 Bryan Jordan Dr; ⊙8.30am-4.30pm Mon-Fri, 9am-4pm Sat, 9.30am-2pm Sun) at the marina.

Southern Reef Islands

While much hype surrounds the Great Barrier Reef's northern splendour, the Southern Reef Islands are the place of 'castaway' dreams: tiny coral atolls fringed with sugary white sand and turquoise-blue seas, and hardly anyone within flipper-flapping reach. From beautiful Lady Elliot Island, 85km northeast of Bundaberg, secluded and uninhabited coral reefs and atolls dot the ocean for about 140km up to Tryon Island. Lady Musgrave is essentially a blue lagoon in the middle of the ocean, while Heron Island is a natural escape for adventurous families and world-class scuba diving.

Several cays in this part of the reef are excellent for snorkelling, diving and just getting back to nature – though reaching them is generally more expensive than reaching islands nearer the coast. Some of the islands are important breeding grounds for turtles and seabirds, protected within the **Capricornia Cays Important Bird Area**.

Lady Elliot Island

The Great Barrier Reef's southernmost coral cay, Lady Elliot is a 45-hectare vegetated shingle cay populated with nesting sea turtles and an impressive number of seabirds. It's considered to offer the best snorkelling in the southern Great Barrier Reef and the diving is good too: explore a seabed of shipwrecks, coral gardens, bommies (coral pinnacles or outcroppings) and blowholes, and abundant marine life, including barracuda, giant manta rays and harmless leopard sharks. Sitting in one of the Barrier Reef's 'Green Zones', it enjoys the highest level of environmental protection – which is also enjoyed by the humpback whales that migrate through these waters between June and October.

Lady Elliot Island is not a national park, and camping is not allowed; your only option is the low-key **Eco Resort** (☑1800 072 200; www.ladyelliot.com.au; r with half board & activities $185-450, child $130). Accommodation here is in tent cabins, simple motelstyle units or more expensive two-bedroom, self-contained suites. Rates include breakfast and dinner, snorkelling gear and some tours.

The only way to reach the island is by light aircraft. Guests of the Lady Elliot Island Eco Resort are flown in from Bundaberg and Hervey Bay (adult/child $349/220) or the Gold Coast and Brisbane (adult/child $730/430). The resort also offers fantastic, great-value day trips from the same mainland centres, starting at

$445/299 for adults/children and including a scenic flight, a snorkelling tour and lunch – see their website for more info.

Heron & Wilson Islands

Part of the Capricornia Cays, Heron Island is ranked among the world's finest scuba-diving regions, with a majority of the Reef's fish and coral species found here. Visitors generally come to dive and snorkel the wonderful, 34-sq-km Heron Reef, but the island's rugged beauty is reason enough to stay above the surface. A true coral cay, with excellent beaches, superb snorkelling and turtle-watching in season, it's densely vegetated with pisonia and casuarina trees. There's a resort and research station on the northeastern third of the island; the remainder is national park. Note that 200,000 birds call the island home at different stages of the year, so there can be a lot of guano at times.

Tiny, private Wilson Island is a miniature version of Heron, an idyllic coral blob accessible on day trips from Heron, 15km away. It's off limits from 29 January to 1 March for turtle nesting.

Heron Island Resort (☑1800 875 343; www.heronisland.com; d/ste from $347/589; ❄) is your only accommodation choice.

The **Heron Islander** (☑1800 875 343; www.heronisland.com; one way adult/child $64/32) ferry departs Gladstone at 10am every day except Tuesday and Thursday. The trip takes two hours.

For a more glamorous approach, take a **seaplane** (☑1800 875 343; www.heronisland.com; one way $349) from Gladstone. Departures are daily subject to demand, and times can vary.

Lady Musgrave Island

Part of the Capricornia Cays National Park, this tiny cay – no more than 14 hectares of coral, sand, shingle and pisonia, 100km northeast of Bundaberg – sits on the western rim of a stunning, turquoise-blue reef lagoon renowned for its safe swimming, snorkelling and diving. A squeaky, white-sand beach fringes a dense canopy of pisonia forest brimming with roosting bird life, including terns, shearwaters and white-capped noddies. Birds nest from October to April, while green turtles nest from November to February. But with nearly 2000 hectares of reef surrounding this tiny green

dot, what's below the surface will always be the main event.

There is a Queensland Parks & Wildlife (p356) campground on the island's west side. Numbers are limited to 40 at any one time, so apply online for a permit well ahead of time (adult/family per night $6.55/26).

If you don't have your own boat, day trips leave from Town of 1770; try 1770 Reef (p359). If you're leaving from Bundaberg, try a day trip with the **Lady Musgrave Experience** (☑0427 009 922; www.ladymusgraveexperience.com.au; Shop 5, 15-17 Marina Drive, Burnett Heads, Bundaberg Port Marina; adult/child/family $218/118/599; ♿), which also offers camping transfers (adult/child $440/220). **Curtis Ferry Services** (☑07-4972 6990; www.curtisferryservices.com.au; 215 Alf O'Rouke Dr, Gladstone Marina) offers ferries from Gladstone (adult return $350).

Rockhampton

POP 61,214

Welcome to Rockhampton ('Rocky' to its mates), where the hats, boots and utes are big, and the bulls are even bigger. With over 2.5 million cattle within a 250km radius, this riverside city, founded in 1858 on land owned by the Darumbal people, calls itself Australia's Beef Capital with some justification. Despite rustic touches such as cane trains running down the centre of wide streets, it's the administrative and commercial centre of Central Queensland, with fine Victorian buildings reflecting the region's 19th-century mining and beef-rearing heyday.

Straddling the tropic of Capricorn 40km inland, far from coastal breezes, Rocky can be scorching hot and unbearably humid in summer. It has a smattering of attractions, including a fine regional gallery, but appeals most to travellers as a gateway to the coastal gems of Yeppoon and Great Keppel Island, and the Byfield National Park to the north.

◎ Sights

★**Botanic Gardens**   GARDENS
(☑1300 225 577; www.rockhamptonregion.qld.gov.au; 100 Spencer St; ◷6am-sunset; ℗♿) FREE
These Heritage-listed gardens, begun in 1873, are a beautiful escape from often-sweltering Rockhampton, with tropical and subtropical rainforest, landscaped gardens and lily-covered lagoons. The formal Japanese

DON'T MISS

CAPRICORN CAVES

Riddling the Berserker Range some 24km north of Rockhampton, **Capricorn Caves** (☑07-4934 2883; www.capricorncaves.com.au; 30 Olsens Caves Rd; adult/child/family $33/16/81; ☺tours 9am-4pm; P 🚻) is one of the Capricorn Coast's foremost attractions. Though this vast cave complex is technically not subterranean (the caves were formed by water working on the limestone of an ancient reef, thrust upward by tectonic pressure) it contains cave coral, stalactites, dangling fig-tree roots and little insectivorous bats. The most popular (one-hour) tour showcases the remarkable acoustics, with a classical music recording in Cathedral Cave, and is suitable for all ages and most fitness levels.

garden is delightfully restful, there's a cafe (open 8am to 5pm), and the small, well-kept **zoo** (open 8am to 4.30pm, admission free) has koalas, lion-tailed macaques, Asian small-clawed otters, dingoes, chimpanzees, a walk-through aviary and more.

Kershaw Gardens
GARDENS
(www.rockhamptonregion.qld.gov.au; Moores Creek Rd; ☺24hr; P 🚻) **FREE** Just north of the Fitzroy River, this excellent botanical park showcases Australian native plants and is a great spot for a picnic or play with the kids. Its attractions include the 9m-high adventure playground **Wyatt's Wonder Web** (originally designed for New York's Central Park), and a 200mm-deep watercourse that mimics the flow of the Fitzroy River and comes equipped with a working barrage. There are also BBQs, a flying fox, wi-fi and even 48-hour sites for fully self-contained RVs.

Quay Street
STREET
This historic streetscape, where grand sandstone Victorian-era buildings face the broad Fitzroy River, is Rockhampton's most beautiful area. You can pick up leaflets that map out buildings of particular note from the visitor centre.

Dreamtime Cultural Centre
CULTURAL CENTRE
(☑07-4936 1655; www.dreamtimecentre.com.au; 703-751 Yaamba Rd, Parkhurst; adult/child $16/7.50; ☺9am-3pm Mon-Fri, tours 10.30am & 1pm; P 🚻) The story of the local Darumbal people is well conveyed in this easily accessible insight into Aboriginal heritage and history. You can self-guide through exhibits such as 'The Vanishing Culture of the Sandstone Belt' – 34m of recreated sandstone caves – or join an excellent, 90-minute, hands-on tour with a knowledgeable guide. The Centre is on the Bruce Hwy, 7km north of central Rockhampton, on a landscaped site significant to the Darumbal.

Rockhampton Art Gallery
GALLERY
(☑07-4936 8248; www.rockhamptonartgallery.com.au; 62 Victoria Pde; ☺9am-4pm Mon-Fri, from 10am Sat & Sun; P) **FREE** Founded in 1967, this great regional gallery owns an impressive collection of modernist Australian paintings, including works by Russell Drysdale, Arthur Boyd, John Brack and Sidney Nolan. You'll also find important pieces by Aboriginal artists, significant British and Japanese works, and thoughtfully curated temporary exhibitions.

🛌 Sleeping

Southside Holiday Village
CARAVAN PARK $
(☑07-4927 3013; http://southsidevillage.com.au; Lower Dawson Rd; powered/unpowered sites $38/30, cabins/villas $93/103; P 🅿️🌳🛜🏊🐾) This smartly run caravan park offers neat, self-contained cabins and villas, and large grassy campsites with access to a good kitchen. There's also a fish-filleting station and a gorgeous 100-year-old fig tree. Sheltered by tropical foliage, it's about 3km south of central Rockhampton on the busy Bruce Hwy. Prices are for two people.

★ Denison Boutique Hotel
HOTEL $$
(☑07-4923 7378; www.denisonhotel.com.au; 233 Denison St; d incl breakfast $200; P 🌳🛜) Occupying a handsome, wrought-iron-wrapped, two-storey Victorian, built in 1886 for the railway administration and now on the National Heritage register, the Denison is Rockhampton's best hotel. Rooms have king-size four-poster beds with pillow-top mattresses, high ceilings and small spa baths in each en suite. Discounts are sometimes available online.

Criterion
HOTEL $$
(☑07-4922 1225; www.thecriterion.com.au; 150 Quay St; pub/motel r from $70/135; ☺pub 6.30am-midnight Sun-Thu, to 3am Fri & Sat; P 🌳🛜) Dating from 1889, with one of

the finest facades on historic Quay St, the Criterion is Rockhampton's grandest old pub. Replacing an earlier pub built in 1867, it retains its elegant foyer and well-worn period rooms, while out the front is a friendly bar and a well-respected steakhouse (mains $20 to $24, steaks $32 to $34). Live music, poker tournaments and sport are frequent diversions.

✕ Eating & Drinking

Ginger Mule   STEAK $
(📞 07-4927 7255; www.gingermule.com.au; 8 William St; mains $12-14; ⊙ noon-2am Wed-Fri, from 4pm Sat) This laid-back place bills itself as a tapas bar, but there's not much Spanish about it, and in reality everyone's here for the steak (and the drinks). The steak sandwich ($12) has to be among the best bargain meals in Queensland, while the $12 sirloin flies out of the busy kitchen. It morphs into a cocktail bar late in the evening.

Boathouse   AUSTRALIAN $$
(📞 07-4927 1683; http://boathouserockhampton. co; 189 Quay St; mains $16-19; ⊙ kitchen 7am-9pm) Occupying the most scenic position on Rockie's historic riverfront Quay St, Boathouse doesn't rest on its photogenic laurels, but augments them by providing very good food and drink throughout the day. Serving breakfast (7am to 11.30am), lunch and dinner (11.30am to 9pm), it's as reliable for a morning crab omelette as it is for panko-crumbed calamari in the evening.

★ Headrick's Lane   AUSTRALIAN $$$
(📞 07-4922 1985; www.headrickslane.co; 189 East St; mains $33-35; ⊙ kitchen 7am-9pm Tue-Sat, to 2pm Mon & Sun; 🛜) This architect-repurposed, high-ceilinged bar, restaurant and microbrewery, making intelligent use of a heritage-protected merchant's store in central Rockhampton, became the most urbane place to eat in town the instant it opened. Just as a big-city equivalent might, it morphs to meet needs throughout the day, serving inventive breakfasts, calorific bar food and more refined dinners, depending on the hour.

★ Great Western Hotel   PUB
(📞 07-4922 3888; www.greatwesternhotel.com.au; 39 Stanley St; ⊙ 11am-midnight Mon-Thu, to 3am Fri & Sat) Dating from 1862, the GWH is part country pub, part concert venue, and part of Rockhampton's social fabric. Out the back

WORTH A TRIP

MYELLA FARM STAY

Take a taste of the outback life at **Myella Farm Stay** (📞 07-4998 1290; www.myella.weebly.com; Baralaba Rd; s/d with meals $120/150, unpowered campsite $40; ❄🛜🏊), a 10.6-sq-km cattle farm 125km southwest of Rockhampton, where guests are invited to get their hands dirty. Lots of different accommodation and activity packages are available, from basic camping to farm experiences where you'll help to sort and milk cows, ride horses and take 4WD tours.

is an undercover bullring – try to time your visit for a Wednesday or Friday night, when you can watch brave cattlefolk being tossed in the air by bucking bulls and broncos in events such as the 'Bad Boy Mowdown'.

❶ Information

Tropic of Capricorn Spire Visitor Centre
(📞 1800 676 701; www.advancerockhampton. com.au; 176 Gladstone Rd; ⊙ 9am-5pm Mon-Sat, to 3pm Sun) This helpful centre sits on the highway right beside the Tropic of Capricorn marker, 3km south of central Rockhampton. Brochures include guides to fishing on the Fitzroy River.

❶ Getting There & Away

AIR
Qantas (📞 13 13 13; www.qantas.com.au) and **Virgin** (📞 13 67 89; www.virginaustralia.com) connect Rockhampton with Brisbane, Mackay, Townsville and Cairns. The airport is about 4km west of the centre of town.

BUS
Greyhound (📞 1300 473 946; www.greyhound. com.au) buses run from Rockhampton to Brisbane ($179, 11 to 15 hours) and Mackay ($69, four hours), among other destinations.

Premier Motor Service (📞 13 34 10; www. premierms.com.au) also runs to Cairns ($143, 17 hours) and Brisbane ($93, 12 hours) every day. Buses stop at the **Puma** (93/101 George St) petrol station.

TRAIN
Queensland Rail (📞 1800 872 467; www. queenslandrailtravel.com.au) runs a daily service to Brisbane ($135, 7½ to 10½ hours) and Gladstone ($49, 1½ hours).

BYFIELD

Byfield itself is a blink-and-you'll-miss-it hamlet in the heart of the **Byfield National Park**, a captivating landscape of semitropical rainforest, sand dunes, waterways, wetlands and rocky uplands, traditionally owned by the Darumbal people. It's difficult to get a sense of the place from the winding main roads that cut through pine tree plantations, but a 4WD will get you to remote hiking paths and isolated beaches beautiful enough to inspire a longer stay.

Offering appealing, basic campsites and a soothing sense of disconnectedness, the park is a 40km drive north from Yeppoon.

Established in 1980, **Nob Creek Pottery** (📞 0428 192 601, 07-4935 1161; www.nobcreek pottery.com.au; 216 Arnolds Rd; ⏱ 10am-4pm Thu-Mon) **FREE** is a working pottery and gallery nestled in 10 hectares of lovely rainforest, the natural habitat of the rare Byfield Fern. Run by the same people, **Byfield Mountain Retreat** (📞 07-4935 1161, 0428 192 601; www.byfieldmountainretreat.com; 140 Flanders Rd; house per night/week $250/1300) is a blissfully-located rental house.

There's also **Waterpark Farm and Eco-Tours** (📞 0488 351 171; www.waterparkfarm. com.au; 201 Waterpark Rd; 2½hr tour $28; 👶), offering cabins and boat trips along Waterpark Creek, a few **campgrounds** (📞 13 74 68; http://parks.des.qld.gov.au; per person/family $6.55/26) in the national park, and **Byfield General Store** (📞 07-4935 1190; 2234 Byfield Rd; mains $15-16; ⏱ 8am-4pm Mon-Fri, to 5pm Sat & Sun) for fuel, groceries, information and tasty light meals.

Yeppoon

POP 16,350

The natural point of embarkation for the Keppel Bay Islands, Yeppoon has evolved from a sleepy seaside village to a built-up town with good sleeping, eating and shopping options. With a long, beautiful beach backed by apartments and restaurants, it's a holiday destination for graziers, miners and many other folk seeking to escape the inland heat of Rockhampton. Its warm, subtropical skies are also the setting for a nightly migration of black-and-red flying foxes, which pass over the main beach and beyond in a startling sunset display. If you're here on the first Sunday of the month, drop in on the **Figtree Creek Markets**, a craft-and-produce market held in the grounds outside the **Capricorn Coast Visitor Information Centre** (📞 1800 675 785; www.capricorncoast.com.au; 1 Scenic Hwy; ⏱ 9am-5pm). Nearby, a hinterland of volcanic outcrops and pineapple patches and the wonderful **Byfield National Park** complete the picture of a lively, sun-soaked and appealing destination. Its traditional owners are the Darumbal people.

🔍 Sights & Activities

Yeppoon Lagoon   LAGOON
(http://yeppooncapricorncoast.com.au; 3 Lagoon Pl; ⏱ 6am-9pm Sep-Apr, 9am-6pm May-Aug; 👶) **FREE** The focus of Yeppoon's foreshore, this 2500-sq-metre 'resort-style' swimming lagoon features an infinity edge blending into vistas of the open ocean and Keppel Bay Islands. With kids' play areas, abundant grassy banks, lifesavers on patrol, BBQs, shade and a cafe, it's an all-in-one summer destination for families.

🛏 Sleeping & Eating

⭐ **Keppel Bay Beach House**   B&B $
(📞 0407 353 748; 19 Power St; s/d incl breakfast $75/90; 🅿 ❄ 🛜 🏊) This beautifully appointed prewar Queenslander, set in calming gardens on a quiet backstreet of Yeppoon, is the setting for an outstanding B&B that offers amazing value. There are two queen bedrooms, a studio with kitchenette and a saltwater pool and BBQ for guest use. Breakfasts are indulgent, and the hospitality warm and attentive.

⭐ **Coral Inn Yeppoon**   INN $$
(📞 07-4939 2925; www.coralinn.com.au; 14 Maple St; r from $139; ❄ 🛜 🏊) Beautiful lawns and reef-bright colours in the rooms, all with bathrooms and mod-cons, make German-run Coral Inn a great find in Yeppoon's quiet backstreets. Families in particular will enjoy the quad room, communal kitchen, BBQ, pizza oven, aviary, fishtank and mini 'beach' area with hammocks and an inviting pool. Buffet breakfast is $12 extra, and there's an open bar from 5pm to 6pm.

Surfside Motel
MOTEL **$$**

(📞 07-4939 1272; www.yeppoonsurfsidemotel.com. au; 30 Anzac Pde; r from $155; ✹ 🎧 ⛱) Location and service lift the Surfside to the top of the tree in Yeppoon. Across the road from the beach and close to town, this retro strip of lime-green motel units, built in 1962, epitomises summer holidays at the beach. And it's terrific value – the rooms are spacious and well equipped, complete with toaster, hairdryer and free cable TV and wi-fi.

While Away B&B
B&B **$$**

(📞 07-4939 5719; www.whileawaybandb.com.au; 44 Todd Ave; s/d incl breakfast $115/140; ✹ 🎧) This perennially popular B&B has good-sized, immaculately clean rooms (one with wheelchair access) and a quiet location 100m back from the beach. The bubbly owners offer complimentary nibbles, tea, coffee, port and sherry, as well as generous breakfasts with cooked options. All four rooms on the ground floor can be group-booked for $400.

Flour
CAFE **$$**

(📞 07-4925 0725; 9 Normanby St; mains $16-19; ⊙ 7am-2.30pm Mon-Fri, to 2pm Sat) Flour does a great line in home baking, alongside set-you-up-for-the-day breakfasts such as golden smashed potatoes with bacon, poached eggs, rocket, feta and 'Persian carrot jam', and lunches such as house-made tortilla with spicy chicken, halloumi, avocado, cherry tomatoes and salsa verde. The service and coffee are terrific too.

★Megalomania
FUSION **$$$**

(📞 07-4939 2333; www.megalomaniabarandbistro. com.au; cnr James & Arthur Sts; mains $36; ⊙ 11.30am-2pm & 6-10pm Tue-Sat) The chef at Megalomania is a real globetrotter, offering Moroccan-style goat curry on the same menu as grilled barramundi with panko-coated rösti, wild mushroom and truffle risotto and palm-sugar-cured Wagyu with citrus segments and basil/mango sorbet. Such eclecticism might ring alarm bells, but the cooking's spot on, and both the indoor and outdoor dining areas are stylish and relaxing.

🍸 Drinking & Nightlife

Pie Alley Blues
BAR

(📞 0403 214 818; http://piealleyblues.com.au; 14 Normanby St; ⊙ noon-10pm Wed & Sun, to 11pm Thu, to midnight Fri & Sat) Bringing the blues to central Yeppoon, together with a dash of jazz and reggae, this friendly little alley-side bar stages frequent live music, makes good coffee, and sells craft beer and whiskey. The 'New Orleans style' menu's not bad either, offering red beans and rice, chicken and waffles, and po' boys stuffed with pulled pork, Cajun shrimp and smoked brisket (mains $17 to $18).

ℹ Getting There & Away

Yeppoon is 43km northeast of Rockhampton, and 7km north of Keppel Bay Marina at Rosslyn Bay. **Young's Bus Service** (📞 07-4922 3813; www. youngsbusservice.com.au; 171 Bolsover St) runs frequent buses throughout the week from Rockhampton to Yeppoon ($6.10, 40 minutes) and down to Keppel Bay Marina ($6.10, one hour).

If you're driving, there's a free daytime car park at Keppel Bay Marina. For longer, secure undercover parking, the **Great Keppel Island Security Car Park** (📞 07-4933 6670; 422 Scenic Hwy; per day from $15) is by the turn-off to the marina, south of Yeppoon.

Keppel Konnections (📞 0484 241 505; www. keppelkonnections.com.au; Red Pier, Keppel Bay Marina, Rosslyn Bay; adult/child return $45/30) and **Funtastic Cruises** (📞 0438 909 502; www.funtasticcruises.com; Red Pier, Keppel Bay Marina, Rosslyn Bay; day cruise adult/child $115/90; ♿) both leave from Keppel Bay Marina daily to Great Keppel Island and the Keppel Bay Islands National Park.

Great Keppel Island

Known as Wop-pa to its Woppaburra traditional owners, Great Keppel is the largest of the island group that bears its name. Once home to one of Australia's most iconic resorts, the 4-sq-km island has been associated with desert-islands dreams in the country since the 1960s. Natural bushland covers 90% of its interior, rocky headlands divide its 27km coastline into 17 bone-white beaches, and it's fringed by coral in every direction. The site of the old resort, which closed in 2012, has been acquired by a developer with plans for a new mega-resort, complete with golf course, marina, airport and environmental research centre – get here soon if you prefer to do your islands in solitude.

⊙ Sights & Activities

The beaches of Great Keppel rate among Queensland's best. There are several bush-walking tracks from **Fisherman's Beach** (the main one) – the longest and perhaps most difficult leads to the 2.5m 'lighthouse' near Bald Rock Point on the far side of the island (three hours return). A steep 45-minute walk via the track, or 25 minutes south across the rocky headland, brings you to Monkey Beach, where there's very good snorkelling. A walking trail from the southern end of the airfield takes you to **Long Beach**, perhaps the best on the island.

Keppel Watersports (☑0415 076 644; Fisherman's Beach; ☺8am-3.30 Sat, Sun & school holidays; ⊞), in a hut on the main beach, hires out snorkelling equipment, kayaks and paddleboards, and runs jet-ski tours.

🛏 Sleeping & Eating

Great Keppel Island

Holiday Village   CABIN $

(☑1800 537 735, 07-4939 8655; www.gkiholiday village.com.au; 80 the Esplanade; unpowered sites $25, s & d tents $110, cabins $160) The village offers various types of good budget accommodation (dorms, cabins, decked tents), as well as entire houses (from $205). It's a friendly, relaxed place with shared bathrooms, a decent communal kitchen, an honesty shop and a barbecue area. Snorkelling gear is rented for $15, and they run motorised canoe trips to top snorkelling spots.

★ Svendsen's Beach   CABIN $$

(☑07-4938 3717; www.svendsensbeach.com; 2 people tent/studio/house $115/150/220) 🍃 The three-night minimum stays are barely enough at this secluded boutique retreat on the 'other' side of Great Keppel. Run by knowledgeable owners, this eco-friendly retreat runs on solar and wind power, and has a bush-bucket shower. The perfect place for snorkelling, bushwalking and romantic getaways, it's BYO food (although you may be able to buy fresh fish here).

Keppel Lodge   GUESTHOUSE $$

(☑07-4939 4251; www.keppellodge.com.au; Fisherman's Beach; d per person from $60, entire lodge $750; 🛜) Run by a veteran of the island's tourism industry, Keppel Lodge is terrific value and a short, sandy walk from Fisherman's Beach. The open octagonal house has four large bedrooms (with bathrooms) branching from a large communal lounge and kitchen. It's available in its entirety – ideal for a group booking of up to eight – or as individual suites.

Tropical Vibes   CAFE $

(☑07-4939 5596; burgers & wraps $14-15; ☺8am-4pm) More general store than 'pure' cafe, Tropical Vibes sells beachwear, hats, sunglasses, sunscreen and souvenirs, alongside coffee, cold beer and excellent burgers.

❶ Getting There & Away

Regular ferries make the 30-minute trip from Keppel Bay Marina in Rosslyn Bay, 7km south of Yeppoon, to **Fisherman's Beach** on Great Keppel. Keppel Konnections (p367) has twice-daily services to the island, departing Rosslyn Bay at 9am and 3pm and returning at 10am and 4pm, with an extra service from Friday to Sunday. **Freedom Fast Cats** (☑07-4933 6888; www. freedomfastcats.com; Pier 1, John Howes Dr, Keppel Bay Marina, Rosslyn Bay) leaves Rosslyn Bay between 7.30am and 10.30am and returns between 8am and 3.45pm, depending on the day and the season (adult/child/family return $45/30/135). No flights use the island **airstrip** at present.

Capricorn Hinterland

The central highlands, west of Rockhampton and the traditional lands of the Ghungalu people, are home to two stunning national parks. Blackdown Tableland National Park is a brooding, powerful place, while visitors to Carnarvon National Park will be gobsmacked by its spectacular gorges, unique flora and Aboriginal rock art.

In the Gemfields beyond Emerald, 270km inland, try fossicking for gems in the heat and rubble – you'll be surrounded by the good people and vibe of the outback, but only if you stick to the cooler months between April and November.

Carnarvon National Park

Significant to the Bidjara, Karingbal and Kara Kara people, Carnarvon Gorge and the surrounding national park are a dramatic rendition of Australian natural beauty.

This 30km-long, 200m-high fissure was carved out over millions of years by Carnarvon Creek and its tributaries twisting through soft sedimentary rock. What was left behind is a lush, otherworldly oasis, where life flourishes, shielded from the stark terrain. You'll find giant cycads, king ferns, river oaks, flooded gums, cabbage palms, deep pools, and platypuses in the creek. Escaped convicts once took refuge here, among caves that still bear ancient rock paintings.

The area was made a national park in 1932, after defeated farmers forfeited their pastoral lease.

BLACKDOWN TABLELAND NATIONAL PARK

Blackdown Tableland, traditional home of the Ghungalu people, shimmers from the highway like a spaceship, drawing travellers to its steep sandstone precipices, ancient flora and Indigenous spiritual and artistic presence. It's a bushwalker's heaven, with a number of Central Queensland's premier trails, most within easy access of the one campground.

The 23km gravel road, which begins at the base of the tableland, isn't suitable for caravans and can be unsafe in wet weather – the first 8km stretch is steep, winding and often slippery. At the top you'll come to the breathtaking **Horseshoe Lookout**, with picnic tables, barbecues and toilets. There's a walking trail to **Two Mile Creek** (1.8km) starting here.

Munall Campground (📱13 74 68; http://parks.des.qld.gov.au; per person/family $6.55/26) is the only option for campers in the park. The turn-off to Blackdown Tableland is on the A4, 12km west of Dingo. You'll need your own car to get here.

For most people, Carnarvon Gorge *is* the Carnarvon National Park, because the other sections – including Mt Moffatt (where Indigenous groups lived some 19,000 years ago), Ka Ka Mundi and Salvator Rosa – are difficult to access.

The main walking track follows Carnarvon Creek through the gorge, with detours to various points of interest. These include the **Moss Garden** (3.6km from the picnic area), **Ward's Canyon** (4.8km), the **Art Gallery** (5.6km) and **Cathedral Cave** (9.3km). Allow at least a whole day for a visit.

Australian Nature Guides (📱07-4984 4652; www.carnarvongorge.info; tours per person $25-75) takes small groups through this singular landscape on a range of day and night tours, while **Sunrover Expeditions** (📱07-3203 4241, 1800 353 717; www.sunrover.com.au; 5-day tour per person incl all meals from $940) runs five-day camping safaris here between August and October.

Sleeping options in the national park comprise two Queensland Parks campgrounds (http://parks.des.qld.gov.au), the **Carnarvon Gorge Wilderness Lodge** (📱1800 644 150, 07-4984 4503; www.carnarvongorge.com; Wyseby Rd; cabins from $220; ☉closed Dec–mid-Feb; @🛜🏊) and the **Takarakka Bush Resort** (📱07-4984 4535; www.takarakka.com.au; O'Briens Rd; unpowered/powered sites from $30/36, cabins $165-215) 🐾. Book ahead even if camping.

Basic groceries and ice are available at Takarakka; longer-term self-caterers should stock up at Rolleston.

There are no bus services to Carnarvon – you'll need to hire a car or take an overnight tour from the coast.

WHITSUNDAY COAST

Many travellers to Australia, especially those with a sailing pedigree, head straight for the Whitsundays – a stunning, white-fringed archipelago in the Coral Sea – and struggle to leave. Opal-jade waters and pure-white beaches fringe the forested isles, while around them fish swarm through the world's largest coral garden – the Great Barrier Reef Marine Park. The gateway to the islands, Airlie Beach, is a backpacker hub with a parade of tanned faces zinging between boats, beaches and nightclubs. This is as close to the islands as some budget travellers will get.

South of Airlie, Mackay is a typical coastal Queensland town with palm-lined streets framed by a jumble of art-deco buildings. It's a handy base for trips to Eungella National Park – a lush hinterland oasis where platypuses cavort in the wild. North of Airlie Beach is cute Bowen, a low-key alternative for backpackers working through their holiday.

Mackay

POP 75,710

Sitting at the heart of vast cane plantations covering land owned traditionally by the Yuibera people, Mackay is a prosperous, confident regional hub with good connections to major Australian centres, Eungella National Park and the southern Whitsunday Islands. Those who have the time or inclination to linger will find broad streets studded with handsome art-deco facades, a healthy nightlife and the region's best dining. Nestled between protected mangroves and a smart, beachy marina, Mackay has an unmistakably tropical feel that may

Whitsunday Coast

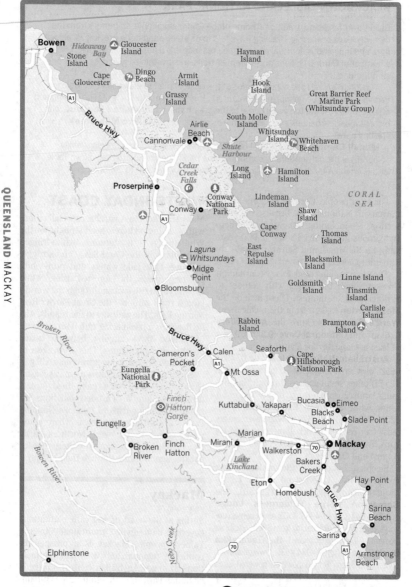

encourage you to check in at one of its many excellent-value motels. North of town, a gorgeous, winding coastline rambles up to the wilds of Cape Hillsborough. A series of headlands and bays shelter small residential communities that welcome kitesurfers and caravanners to the area's best beaches.

⊙ Sights & Activities

Mackay's impressive art-deco architecture owes much to a devastating cyclone in 1918, which flattened many of the town's buildings. Enthusiasts should pick up a copy of the pamphlet *Art Deco in Mackay* from the visitor centre.

There are good views over the harbour from **Rotary Lookout** in North Mackay and over the beach at **Lampert's Lookout**.

Mackay has plenty of beaches, although not all are ideal for swimming.

The best option near town is **Harbour Beach**, 6km north of the centre and just south of the Mackay Marina. The beach here is patrolled and there's a foreshore reserve with picnic tables and barbecues.

Even better are the beaches about 16km north of Mackay. At long, flat, residence-encroached **Blacks Beach**, the sand stretches out for 6km, while **Bucasia** is the most undeveloped and arguably the prettiest of the lot. For easy access, stay at **Blacks Beach Holiday Park** (☑ 07-4954 9334; www.mackayblacksbeachholidaypark.com.au; 16 Bourke St; powered sites from $44, villas from $160; P ❀ ❀) or **Bucasia Beachfront Caravan Resort** (☑ 07-4954 6375; www.bucasiabeach.com.au; 2 Bucasia Esplanade; powered sites $35-45; ❀ ❀).

Bluewater Lagoon   LAGOON
(Caneland Park, River St; ⊙ 9am-5.45pm Sep-Mar, to 4.45pm Apr–mid-Jul; ♠) **FREE** Backed by the Pioneer River and reassuringly stinger-free, this pleasant three-tiered artificial lagoon has kids' play areas, water slides, grassed picnic areas, free wi-fi and a cafe. A great place for families to while away a hot day, the water gets as deep as 1.8m in places.

**Mackay Regional
Botanical Gardens**   GARDENS
(☑ 07-4952 7300; www.mackayregionalbotanicgardens.com.au; 9 Lagoon St; ⊙ 5am-9pm, cafe 9am-3pm Mon-Fri, 8am-4pm Sat & Sun; P ♠) **FREE** Set on 33 hectares, 3km south of central Mackay, these gardens were first envisioned in 1878 yet didn't open until 2003. Taking their names from pioneer settlements that once stood here, and from the freshwater lagoon at their heart ('Kaliguil' to the local Yuibera people), these six themed gardens feature native plants from the Central Queensland Coast and further afield. There's a playground, walking trails, a cafe (mains $15-18) and an amphitheatre hosting regular events.

🛏 Sleeping

Coral Sands Motel   MOTEL $
(☑ 07-4951 1244; www.coralsandsmotel.com.au; 44 Macalister St; r from $99; ❀ ❀ ❀) One of Mackay's better midrange options, the Coral Sands boasts ultra-friendly management

and large rooms in a central location. Popular with the transient workforce, it's a bit tropi-kitsch, but with a saltwater pool, high-speed internet and free pay-TV, plus the river, shops, pubs and cafes on your doorstep, you won't care. Great value.

★ **Stoney Creek Farmstay**   FARMSTAY $$
(☑ 07-4954 1177; 180 Stoney Creek Rd, Eton, off Peak Downs Hwy; dm/stables/cottages $25/150/195; P) ✐ Head 32km south of McKay to stay in an endearingly ramshackle cottage, a rustic livery stable or the charismatic **Dead Horse Hostel**, and forget all about the mod-cons: this is dead-set bush livin'. Three-hour horse rides cost $115 per person, lots of other activities are available, and hostel accommodation is free if you ride for two consecutive days.

🍴 Eating & Drinking

BNW Asian Cuisine   MALAYSIAN $$
(☑ 07-4953 2804; Shop 17, Sydney Street Markets, cnr Sydney & Gordon Sts; mains $16-20; ⊙ 10am-9pm Mon-Sat, to 2.30pm Sun) This little hole-in-the-shopping-centre-wall restaurant is a dead cert for authentic Malaysian and Cantonese food. Staples such as seafood laksa and char kuay teow (rice noodles wok-charred with cockles, egg and Chinese sausage) are great value as lunch deals, or go for a chef's special such as fat king prawns with sambal and green beans.

Paddock & Brew Company   BARBECUE $$
(☑ 0487 222 880; 94 Wood St; mains $16-22; ⊙ 5pm-midnight Mon-Wed, from noon Thu & Fri, from 7am Sat & Sun) This US-style smokehouse and craft-beer bar serves up a variety of burgers – including buttermilk-marinated fried chicken and beer-battered fish – alongside pulled pork, brisket, ribs, sausage and buffalo wings. Weekend breakfasts include pancake stacks with maple syrup and a New York–style bagel bursting with bacon, hash brown, egg and house BBQ sauce.

Eimeo Pacific Hotel   PUB FOOD $$
(☑ 07-4954 6106; www.eimeohotel.com.au; 1 Mango Ave, Eimeo; mains $20-32; ⊙ 10am-8pm Sun-Thu, to 8.30pm Fri & Sat) Serving typical Australian pub fare of seafood, steak and pasta, the old Eimeo is more than the meals on its menu. The property has watched the sun set here since 1870 – the current structure has been up since 1954 – and the photos in the public bar show Mackay's past in vivid detail. Paths wind down to the beach below.

Mackay

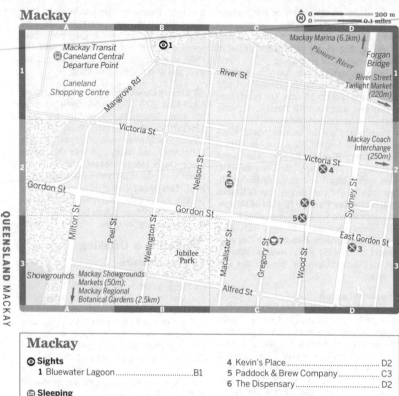

Mackay

Sights
1 Bluewater Lagoon B1

Sleeping
2 Coral Sands Motel...................................C2

Eating
3 BNW Asian Cuisine D3

4 Kevin's Place D2
5 Paddock & Brew Company C3
6 The Dispensary D2

Drinking & Nightlife
7 Woodsman's Axe Coffee C3

Kevin's Place   SINGAPOREAN $$
(07-4953 5835; http://kevinsplace.com.au; 79 Victoria St; mains $25-30; 11.30am-2pm Mon-Fri & 6-11.30pm Mon-Sat) At Kevin's, housed in a marvellous deco building on Victoria St, large groups gather at round tables and share sizzling, spicy Singaporean dishes. It's difficult to go past classics such as mee goreng (fried noodles) and Singapore chilli prawns, or lunch specials from as little as $12.

⭐ **The Dispensary**   MODERN AUSTRALIAN $$$
(07-4951 3546; http://thedispensary.nefood.com.au; 84 Wood St; mains $36-40; 6am-2.30pm Mon, to 10pm Tue-Sat) Divided into dining, cafe and bar spaces, this smart Mod Oz operation also has a divided menu: choose either individual mains (perhaps blackened salmon with ginger-passion fruit sauce or lamb rack with eggplant pickle) or share plates (pork rillettes with pickles; scallops with apple butter). Breakfasts, such as the açaí bowl with fresh fruit and toasted coconut or smoked-trout bruschetta, more than hold their own.

Woodsman's Axe Coffee   COFFEE
(0437 773 776; www.woodmansaxe.com; 47 Gordon St; 6am-3pm Mon-Fri, to 2pm Sat) The best coffee in town (from $4.30) – either espresso or filter, made from ever-changing single-origin beans – is bulked out with light eats at this self-styled 'eclectic hipster' coffee bar.

🔒 Shopping

They like their markets in Mackay, with a surprisingly varied bunch of bazaars selling everything from bric-a-brac to one-off duds and organic fruit. Try the **Mackay Showgrounds Markets** (Milton St; ⊙ 6.30am-10am Sat), the **River Street Twilight Market** (Bluewater Quay, River St; ⊙ 4-8pm 2nd Fri of the month) and the **Troppo Treasure Market** (www.troppomarket.com.au; Mt Pleasant Shopping Centre car park; ⊙ from 7.30am 2nd Sun of the month).

ℹ️ Information

Mackay Visitor Centre (📞 07-4837 1228, 1300 130 001; www.mackayregion.com; 320 Nebo Rd; ⊙ 9am-5pm Mon-Fri; 🛜) About 3km south of the centre, this visitor centre offers information, internet access and wi-fi.

The Mackay region's main visitor information centre is in **Sarina** (📞 07-4837 1228; www.mackayregion.com; Field of Dreams, Bruce Hwy; ⊙ 9am-5pm May-Oct, 9am-5pm Mon-Fri, to 3pm Sat, to 1pm Sun Nov-Apr).

ℹ️ Getting There & Away

AIR

Mackay Airport (www.mackayairport.com.au; Boundary Rd East, East Mackay) is about 3km south of the centre of Mackay.

Jetstar (📞 13 15 38; www.jetstar.com.au), **Qantas** (📞 13 13 13; www.qantas.com.au) and **Virgin** (📞 13 67 89; www.virginaustralia.com) have daily flights to/from Brisbane.

BUS

Buses stop at the **Mackay Coach Interchange** (Caltex, cnr Victoria & Tennyson Sts), where tickets can also be booked. **Greyhound** (📞 1300 473 946; www.greyhound.com.au) travels up and down the coast, connecting Mackay to Airlie Beach ($35, two hours), Townsville ($91, 6¾ hours), Cairns ($151, 12½ hours) and Brisbane ($238, 17½ hours).

Premier Motor Service (📞 13 34 10; www.premierms.com.au) runs to the same destinations for less money, but has fewer services.

TRAIN

The *Spirit of Queensland*, operated by **Queensland Rail** (📞 1300 131 722; www.queenslandrailtravel.com.au), runs from Mackay to Brisbane ($269, 13½ hours), Cairns ($215, 11½ hours) and cities between. The train station is in Paget, 5km south of the city centre.

ℹ️ Getting Around

Major car-rental firms have desks at Mackay Airport – see www.mackayairport.com.au for listings. **NQ Car & Truck Rental** (📞 1800 736 828, 07-4953 2353; www.nqcartruckrentals.com.au; 6 Malcomson St, North Mackay; ⊙ 8.30am-5pm Mon-Fri) is a reliable local operator.

Mackay Transit Coaches (📞 07-4957 3330; www.mackaytransit.com.au) has several

services around the city, many leaving from **Caneland Central shopping centre** and connecting the city with the harbour, airport and northern beaches; pick up a timetable at the visitor centre or look online.

For a taxi, call **Mackay Taxis** (📞 13 10 08; www.mackaytaxi.com.au).

Airlie Beach
POP 9334

Sitting on lovely undulating coastline traditionally owned by the Ngaro and Gia peoples, Airlie is the gateway to the unparalleled Whitsunday Islands and an essential stop on most east-coast road trips. Its multiple hostels, sprawling beer gardens and myriad tour operators are strung along Shute Harbour Rd, separated from Pioneer Bay by a lovely lawn-fringed swimming lagoon.

Between the swanky cafes and clinking masts of the Abell Point and Port of Airlie marinas, you'll find all you need in this beachside holiday hub: bars, restaurants, supermarkets, hotels and a seemingly unending string of flawlessly tanned European backpackers. Those looking to avoid the party scene – families especially – will have no trouble finding quieter lodgings close enough to the centre of town. And if that's still too hectic, the forests and walking trails of Conway National Park lie just south and east of town.

🏃 Activities

Lagoon   SWIMMING
(Shute Harbour Rd) **FREE** Take a dip year-round in the stinger-, croc-, and tropical nasties-free lagoon in the centre of town.

Airlie Beach Skydivers   SKYDIVING
(📞 1300 759 348; www.airliebeachskydivers.com.au; 2/273 Shute Harbour Rd; 3048m/4267m jump $244/295; ⊙ 8am-5.30pm) This friendly team with a shopfront on Shute Harbour Rd can take you as high as 4267m for tandem jumps landing on Airlie Beach.

Whitsunday Fishing Charters   FISHING
(📞 0457 822 553; www.whitsundayfishingcharters.com.au; half-day adult/child $145/125) Leaving every day from Abell Point Marina at 7.30am and 1pm, this outfit takes anglers out among the islands in search of cod, trevally, sweet lip, mackerel, queen fish and other species. Offering both half- and full-day trips aboard the 7.5m custom-built *Reel Deal*, they include tackle, bait and either morning or afternoon tea.

WORTH A TRIP

CONWAY NATIONAL PARK

On the Conway Peninsula you'll find the serene **Conway National Park** (http://parks.des.qld.gov.au/parks/conway), once the hunting grounds of the Giru Dala and still home to large swaths of lowland tropical rainforest, remote mangroves, rocky uplands, and pandanus and paperbark woodlands. Most easily accessed from the Conway National Park day-use area, 6.5km east of Airlie, it offers a range of easy-to-moderate walking trails (including the 5.4km **Mt Rooper Circuit**, with good views of the Whitsunday Passage and Islands), mountain biking and several Queensland Parks campsites.

Pioneer Jet Whitsundays   BOATING
(☑1800 335 975; www.pioneerjet.com.au; South Village, Abell Point Marina, Shingley Dr; adult/child $69/49) The Ultimate Bay Blast is a thunderous 30-minute spin around Pioneer Bay aboard the 6.5m jetboat *Cheeky Bee,* which can clock 38 knots even with a full load. Fun and informative guides round off the experience. Expect to get very wet.

☞ Tours

Red Cat Adventures   BOATING
(☑07-4946 4444; www.redcatadventures.com.au; tours from $179) Excellent family-owned operation with three distinct tours. Our pick is the Ride to Paradise (one/two nights $309/599), which takes in several Whitsunday highlights before overnighting in Paradise Cove, a 16.2-sq-km resort north of Airlie. Departures are from Abell Point Marina.

Air Whitsunday Seaplanes   TOURS
(☑07-4946 9111; www.airwhitsunday.com.au; Terminal 1, Whitsunday Airport; tours from $295) Air Whitsunday offers a range of tours aboard Cessna and de Havilland seaplanes, from flyovers of the Outer Reef, where you don't leave the aircraft (which nonetheless performs a 'touch-n-go' water landing en route, just for thrills) to excursions landing at Whitehaven Beach and Heart Reef, where passengers disembark to snorkel, sightsee and bliss out.

Whitsunday Crocodile Safari   SAFARI
(☑07-4948 3310; www.crocodilesafari.com.au; adult $129, child $39-69) This day-long tour heads out to the Proserpine River, Goorganga Plains wetlands and coastal mangroves in all weather, getting gawping visitors close to the 150-odd estuarine crocodiles that live here. Guides are knowledgeable, and lunch and bus transfers to Airlie are provided.

★⁂ Festivals & Events

Airlie Beach Race Week   SAILING
(www.airlieraceweek.com; ⊘Aug) Held during the mild, calm subtropical winter, this week-long regatta sees over 100 sports boats from around the world descend on Airlie to compete in paradise. On-shore diversions include live music, food and drink and a fun run. Festivities centre on the **Whitsunday Sailing Club** (☑07-4946 6138; www.whitsundaysailingclub.com.au; Airlie Point, 11 Ocean Rd; ⊘10am-10pm).

Airlie Beach Festival of Music   MUSIC
(www.airliebeachfestivalofmusic.com.au; 3-day pass $270; ⊘Nov) First held in 2012, this sunny music festival spans 18 venues and three days in November. With the principal marquee beautifully located waterside at the Whitsunday Sailing Club, its mainly Australian line-up blends new acts with established legends such as The Church.

⬒ Sleeping

★Kipara   RESORT $
(☑07-4946 6483; www.kipara.com.au; 2614 Shute Harbour Rd, Jubilee Pocket; r/cabins/villas from $85/130/150; ❄ 🞱 🏊) Tucked away in the lush, green environs of Jubilee Pocket, east of Airlie, this budget resort can be reached by Whitsunday Transit buses, so you don't need a car. Well kept and great value, it offers double rooms, spacious cabins, and even-bigger villas, equipped to accommodate families. There's also a pool, BBQ area, camp kitchens and laundry.

★Sunlit Waters   APARTMENT $
(☑07-4946 6352; www.sunlitwaters.com; 20 Airlie Cres; studios from $105, 1-bedroom apt $125; 🅿❄🞱🏊) Representing some of the best value in Airlie, these spick-and-span studios and apartments are smartly presented and have everything you need, including basic kitchenettes and stunning views from the long balconies. There's even a good swimming pool.

Airlie Beach YHA   HOSTEL $
(☑07-4946 6312; www.yha.com.au; 394 Shute Harbour Rd; dm $32, d from $90; ❄@🞱🏊) Trust YHA to provide a genuine alternative

Airlie Beach

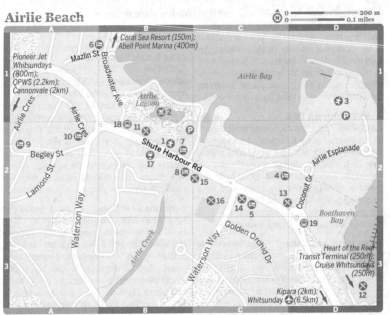

Airlie Beach

⊕ Activities, Courses & Tours
1 Airlie Beach Skydivers	B2
2 Lagoon	B1
3 Whitsunday Sailing Club	D1

🛏 Sleeping
4 Airlie Beach Hotel	C2
5 Airlie Beach YHA	C2
6 Airlie Waterfront B&B	B1
7 Heart Hotel and Gallery	B2
8 Magnums Backpackers	B2
9 Sunlit Waters	A2
10 Waterview	A2

✕ Eating
11 Airlie Beach Treehouse	B2
12 Denmans Beer Cafe	D3
13 Fish D'vine	C2
14 Sushi Hi	C2
15 Village Cafe	C2
16 Woolworths	C2

⊕ Drinking & Nightlife
17 Paddy's Shenanigans	B2

⊕ Transport
18 Whitsunday Transit Bus Stop	B2
19 Whitsunday Transit Bus Stop	D3

for young budget travellers to sordid hostels and inconvenient bush dumps. Central and reasonably quiet with a sparkling pool and great kitchen facilities, this is the best budget hostel in Airlie Beach, with six- and eight-bed en-suite dorms and plain but serviceable doubles.

Waterview   APARTMENT $$
(☑ 07-4948 1748; www.waterviewairliebeach.com. au; 42 Airlie Cres; studios from $150, 1-bedroom units from $170; P❄🛜) Waterview's small units are an excellent choice for location and comfort, with glimpses of the main street and gorgeous views of the bay. The rooms are modern, airy and spacious, and have

kitchenettes for self-caterers. Top value for a couple who can do without a pool.

Airlie Beach Hotel   HOTEL $$
(☑ 07-4964 1999; www.airliebeachhotel.com.au; cnr Airlie Esplanade & Coconut Gr; motel/hotel r from $149/229; P❄🛜♨) Given the ideal central location, the sea-facing hotel rooms here are some of the best in town at this price. With airy, smartly furnished rooms and a pool, restaurant and bottle shop on-site, you could do far worse than stay here.

Coral Sea Resort   RESORT $$$
(☑ 07-4964 1300, 1800 075 061; www.coralsea resort.com; 25 Ocean View Ave; d from $298;

P ✳ @ 🛜 🛈) Coral Sea Resort is an excellent option for families and older folk wanting quality service, spacious tiled rooms and one of the best pool settings in Queensland. An easy stroll to Abell Point Marina, it's just west of the town centre. Many rooms have stunning views, but you'll save plenty by going for a garden view and just lingering poolside.

Airlie Waterfront B&B
B&B $$$

(📋 07-4946 7631; http://airliewaterfrontbnb.com.au; cnr Broadwater Ave & Mazlin St; 1-bedroom apt from $237; P ✳ 🛜 🛈) This wonderful waterside B&B, that's more like a small resort, is for adults only. Views are superb from the position slightly above town, accessed by a five-minute stroll along the boardwalk, and the two-bedroom apartments are the best value in Airlie. Some rooms have a spa.

Heart Hotel and Gallery
BOUTIQUE HOTEL $$$

(📋 1300 847 244; www.hearthotelwhitsundays.com.au; 277 Shute Harbour Rd; d $180-270; ✳🛜) This luxury hotel in the heart of Airlie couldn't be more central. Architecturally inspired by early Queensland homes, the rooms are smallish but elegant, with top-quality bedding, up-to-date tech fittings and luxurious bathrooms. The gallery, on the top floor, shows the work of local artists.

🍴 Eating

Port of Airlie and Abell Point Marina are good hunting grounds for upmarket dining with water views, while central Airlie offers everything from cheap takeaway kebab shops to fancier restaurants. Self-caterers will find a massive **Woolworths** (cnr Shute Harbour Rd & Waterson Way; ⏰8am-9pm Mon-Fri, 8am-6pm Sat, 9am-6pm Sun) supermarket behind the main strip in the centre of town.

Bohemian Raw Cafe
HEALTH FOOD $

(📋 07-4948 0274; www.bohemianraw.com.au; Abell Point Marina, Shingley Dr; mains $12-14; ⏰7am-3pm Mon-Sat, 8am-2pm Sun; 🍴) Blessed with dazzling views across Pioneer Bay, this health-conscious marina cafe does açai bowls, superfood breakfast bowls, delicious nut-meat-stuffed wraps, salads, and an abundance of smoothies, 'naked' cakes and raw 'boho' balls in flavours such as goji bliss and cacao bliss.

Sushi Hi
SUSHI $

(📋 07-4948 0400; 390 Shute Harbour Rd; sushi $3.70-6.40, mains $10-12; ⏰11am-8pm) Super-friendly and super-fresh, this little shopfront sushi joint has a self-service train with dishes made before your eyes, but consider ordering a poke bowl, packed with rice, fresh fish and pickles.

Airlie Beach Treehouse
CAFE $$

(📋 07-4946 5550; www.facebook.com/airliebeachtreehouse; 6a/263 Shute Harbour Rd; mains $18-25; ⏰8.30am-3.30pm Wed-Sun) This laid-back restaurant by the lagoon has a reputation for uncomplicated service and quality food in a shady setting. Open for breakfast and lunch, its menu pulls surprises such as pizza with BBQ sauce, feta, onions and spicy crocodile sausage, alongside more conventional choices such as smoky American-style pork ribs with slaw.

Denmans Beer Cafe
PUB FOOD $$

(📋 07-4990 6701; www.denmans.com.au; Shop 15, 33 Port of Airlie Dr; mains $24-27; ⏰kitchen 11.30am-8.30pm Mon & Thu, 4-8.30pm Tue & Wed, 11.30am-9pm Fri-Sun) Regular live music and a convivial mood are found in this bar, which stocks more craft beers than the rest of town combined. The food – such as a shared paella ($55) or grilled local fish with sweet-potato puree ($27) – is decent, with 'tapas' including soft-shelled crab tacos and chicken-leek croquettes available as drinking food.

Fish D'vine
SEAFOOD $$

(📋 07-4948 0088; www.fishdvine.com.au; 303 Shute Harbour Rd; mains $30-33; ⏰5-11pm) The nautical staples of seafood and rum are the fortes of this bustling, upmarket, corner-side restaurant in central Airlie. Locally caught barramundi, red emperor and other fish star in the more elaborate mains, while fish and chips and seafood pasta maintain the high standards. Plus, the rum bar has an absurd 560-plus cane distillations to experience.

Village Cafe
CAFE $$$

(📋 07-4946 5745; www.villagecafe.com.au; 366 Shute Harbour Rd; mains $32-34; ⏰7.30am-9.30pm) Set back from the main drag in central Airlie, this handsomely timbered, open-sided cafe is known for its all-day breakfasts (the rösti with smoked salmon and poached eggs is top notch) and 'hot rock' cuisine, where diners cook their own meat and seafood on hot stone slabs. Beers and house wine are $5 during daily happy hour (2pm to 5pm).

🍷 Drinking & Nightlife

It's said that Airlie Beach is a drinking town with a sailing problem. The bar at **Magnums** (📋 1800 624 634; www.magnums.com.

au; 366 Shute Harbour Rd; powered/unpowered sites from $35/30, dm/d from $27/57; ✴@🛜), a huge hostel in the centre of town, is always crowded, and a popular place to kick off a raucous evening.

⭐**Northerlies Beach Bar & Grill**   BAR
(🗓1800 682 277; www.northerlies.com.au; 116 Pringle Rd, Woodwark; ⊙10am-8.30pm Sun-Thu, to 9pm Fri & Sat) Tucked away on a lovely tranquil shore-front in Woodwark, facing Airlie across Pioneer Bay, Northerlies is just the place for a sundowner. The broad, timber-floored bar and restaurant, open-sided to get the most of the views and the bay breezes, is set up to linger over crafts beers, cocktails and well-chosen wines from Australia, New Zealand and Europe.

Paddy's Shenanigans   IRISH PUB
(352 Shute Harbour Rd; ⊙7pm-3am) Airlie's inevitable Irish bar has live music every night, with occasional events, cold Guinness and plenty of backpackers enjoying a session.

ℹ Information

Whitsunday Bookings (🗓07-4948 2201; www.whitsundaybookings.com.au; 5/263 Shute Harbour Rd; ⊙8am-6pm) This office has been helping travellers book the right tour for years. Call for out-of-hours service.

AirlieBeach.com (Whitsundays Central Reservation Centre; 🗓1800 677 119; www.airliebeach.com; 259 Shute Harbour Rd; ⊙8am-7pm Mon-Fri, to 6pm Sat & Sun) This agency can help with accommodation, sailing, tours and more.

ℹ Getting There & Away

AIR

The closest major airports, **Whitsunday Coast** (Proserpine Airport; www.whitsundaycoastairport.com.au; Lascelles Ave, Gunyarra) at Proserpine and **Hamilton Island** (Great Barrier Reef Airport; 🗓07-4946 8620; www.hamiltonisland.com.au; Airport Dr) aka

Great Barrier Reef Airport, have regular connections with Sydney, Melbourne and Brisbane. Whitsunday Airport (p381), a small airfield 6km east of Airlie Beach (midway between Airlie Beach and Shute Harbour), doesn't have regular scheduled flights, but helicopter flights operate from here.

BOAT

Transfers between the **Port of Airlie** (🗓1800 676 526; www.portofairlie.com.au; 13 The Cove Rd) and Hamilton and Daydream Islands (per person $55) are provided by **Cruise Whitsundays** (🗓07-4846 7000; www.cruisewhitsundays.com; Port of Airlie, 24 The Cove Rd; half-day cruise adult/child from $115/45).

BUS

Greyhound (🗓1300 473 946; www.greyhound.com.au) buses detour off the Bruce Hwy, connecting Airlie Beach to all of the major centres along the coast, including Brisbane ($262, 19 hours), Mackay ($31, two hours), Townsville ($49, four hours) and Cairns ($99, nine hours). **Premier Motor Service** (🗓13 34 10; www.premierms.com.au) offers lower fares to the same destinations.

Long-distance buses stop at the **Heart of the Reef Transit Terminal** (Port of Airlie, Cove Rd). **Whitsunday Transit** (🗓07-4946 1800; www.whitsundaytransit.com.au) connects Proserpine (for Whitsunday Coast Airport), Cannonvale, Abell Point Marina, Airlie Beach and Shute Harbour. There are several stops in the centre along Shute Harbour Rd, at the junction with **Broadwater Ave**, and at **Port of Airlie**.

The Whitsundays

Scattered like emeralds on aquamarine velvet, the Whitsunday Islands are one of Australia's loveliest destinations, an unmatched playground for boaters, divers, campers, fishers and resort-loungers. Sheltered by the Great Barrier Reef, these warm, rarely ruffled waters are particularly perfect for sailing, as exploited by the 100-plus yachts that gather here each August for Airlie Beach Race Week (p374). Traditional home

(side tab) **QUEENSLAND THE WHITSUNDAYS**

ℹ **CYCLONE WARNING**

In Queensland's far north, between November and April each year, cyclones – known in the northern hemisphere as hurricanes – are a part of life, with an average of four or five forming each season. It's rare for these cyclones to hit the land as full-blown destructive storms, but keep a sharp ear out for predictions and alerts during the season. If a cyclone watch or warning is issued, stay tuned to local radio and monitor the Bureau of Meteorology website (www.bom.gov.au) for updates and advice. Locals tend to be complacent about cyclones, but will still buy out the bottle shop when a threat is imminent!

of the Ngaro people, these 74 islands also shelter some of the oldest archaeological sites on Australia's east coast. Five of them have resorts, but most are uninhabited, and several offer back-to-nature beach camping and bushwalking. Whitehaven Beach on Whitsunday Island is acknowledged as the finest beach in the Whitsundays (some say the world), while mainland hub Airlie Beach, the major gateway to the islands, offers a wealth of tours and activities, plenty of eating and sleeping choices, and a hard-partying backpacker scene.

◉ Sights

Whitsunday, Hook, Lindeman, Armit and Gloucester Islands all have campgrounds. Book online with Queensland Parks & Wildlife (p381), and see Scamper (p381) for transfers ($105 to $160 per person).

Whitsunday Island   ISLAND
Largest of the paradisiacal group to which it gives its name, Whitsunday Island is a forested beauty surrounded by warm, shallow, coral-rich seas. Its most photographed site is the dazzling 7km-long **Whitehaven Beach**, visited by pretty much every tour from Airlie Beach and Shute Harbour. The more intrepid will also enjoy the Hill Inlet, Solway and Chance Bay walking trails, and the island's six basic campgrounds.

Hook Island   ISLAND
The 53-sq-km Hook Island, the second-largest island in the Whitsunday group, is predominantly national park and rises to 450m at Hook Peak. There are a number of good beaches dotted around the island, and some of the region's best diving and snorkelling locations. There are Queensland Parks campgrounds at Maureen's Cove, Steen's Beach, Curlew Beach and Crayfish Beach. Although basic, they provide some wonderful back-to-nature opportunities.

Lindeman Island   ISLAND
The best known of the 13 coral-fringed specks in the **Lindeman Islands National Park**, this island is traditionally owned by the Ngaro, an Aboriginal seafaring people. The Club Med resort that opened here in 1992 closed 20 years later, and awaits redevelopment by its new owners. Now nature photographers and hikers are the main visitors, exploring a sea-claimed volcano mostly covered by national park, with splendid empty bays, reefs for snorkelling, and over 16km of walking trails.

Daydream Island   ISLAND
Just 5km from Shute Harbour, the rainforest-cloaked, reef-fringed Daydream Island is only 1km long and 200m wide, allowing it to be explored in an hour or two. For most visitors, the natural port of call is the 277-room **Daydream Island Resort & Spa** (☑07-3259 2350; www.daydreamisland.com; d from $392; ❄ ⊕ ☒). **Cruise Whitsundays** (☑07-4846 7000; www.cruisewhitsundays.com; one way per person $55) ferries stop here on their way between Shute Harbour and Hamilton Island.

South Molle Island   ISLAND
The largest of its group, South Molle is virtually joined to its reef-fringed siblings, Mid and North Molle Islands. Hit hard by Cyclone Debbie in March 2017, its resort in Bauer Bay was yet to reopen at the time of writing. Beyond this, the island is all national park and is criss-crossed by 15km of walking tracks, with some superb lookout points. The Queensland Parks campgrounds at Sandy and Paddle Bays are the only places to overnight.

Hayman Island   ISLAND
The most northerly of the Whitsunday group, little Hayman is just 4 sq km in area and rises to 250m above sea level. It has forested hills, valleys and beaches, and a luxury five-star resort – one of Australia's most celebrated, and long a stage for the lifestyles of the rich and famous.

🏃 Activities

Diving
You'll notice a lack of dedicated dive shops in Airlie Beach and the Whitsundays. While the Great Barrier Reef may beckon, most dives in this area visit the fringing reefs around the Whitsundays (especially on their northern tips) because they are much easier to reach and often hold more abundant soft corals. PADI open-water courses start at around $750, while one/two dives for those already certified cost around $80/140.

Based in Airlie, **Whitsunday Dive Adventures** (☑07-4948 1239; http://whitsundaydivecentre.com) is your best bet.

A number of **sailing cruises** include diving as an optional extra. Prices start from $95 for introductory or certified dives. Cruise Whitsundays offers dives (from $119) on day trips to its reef pontoon.

Most of the island resorts also have dive schools and free snorkelling gear.

TOP 5 WHITSUNDAY BEACHES

If the Whitsundays have some of Australia's finest beaches, and Australian beaches are some of the best in the world, then beach connoisseurs have hit the jackpot. Although there are plenty of secluded, postcard-perfect, sandy bays in this tropical paradise, the following are reasonably accessible for most tour companies:

Whitehaven Beach With azure-blue waters lapping the pure-white silica sand, Whitehaven on Whitsunday Island is absolutely stunning.

Chalkies Beach Opposite Whitehaven Beach, on Haslewood Island, this is another idyllic, white-sanded beach. It's not on the usual tourist circuit, though some operators do stop there. Otherwise, charter a boat yourself.

Langford Island At high tide, Langford is a thin strip of sand on the rim of a ludicrously picturesque, coral-filled turquoise lagoon. It's more a sandbank than a beach, but surreally beautiful nonetheless.

Butterfly Bay On the northern side of Hook Island is this protected bay, which flutters with butterfly song each winter. It's popular with discerning bareboat-charter-goers, who snorkel in the shallows and lob on the sand like happy beached whales.

Catseye Beach Hamilton Island was chosen for development for good reason. Catseye Beach is a busy-ish spot by Whitsunday standards, but its palm-shaded sand and turquoise waters are social-media ready. Plus you can rent kayaks and buy a drink!

Kayaking

Paddling with dolphins and turtles is one of the best ways to experience the Whitsundays. **Salty Dog Sea Kayaking** (☑ 07-4946 1388; www.saltydog.com.au; Shute Harbour; half/full day trips $90/145, half/full day kayak rental $60/90) offers guided tours, plus a brilliant six-day kayak and camping expedition ($1850) that's manageable even for beginners.

👉 Tours

Ocean Rafting   BOATING
(☑ 07-4946 6848; www.oceanrafting.com.au; adult/child/family from $159/102/476; 👶) Jump aboard a speedy banana-yellow semi-rigid speedboat to visit some of the less-accessed spots in the Whitsundays. After the obligatory swim at Whitehaven Beach, regain your land legs with a guided national park walk, or snorkel the reef at Mantaray Bay and Border Island. Buffet meals are an extra $16 per person.

Whitehaven Xpress   BOATING
(☑ 07-4946 1585; www.whitehavenxpress.com.au; day trips adult/child $185/120) This operator offers various boat excursions, the most popular being its daily trip to Whitehaven Beach, which includes snorkelling, a glass-bottomed boat and beach BBQ. It departs from Airlie Beach's Abell Point Marina at 8.45am, returning around 4.45pm, with courtesy bus connection to your accommodation in Airlie.

Ecojet Safari   TOURS
(☑ 0409 649 115; http://ecojetsafari.com; tours per person $195) Explore the islands, mangroves and marine life of Edgecumbe Bay in the northern Whitsundays on these three-hour, small-group jet-ski safaris (two people per jet ski).

HeliReef   SCENIC FLIGHTS
(☑ 07-4946 9102; www.helireef.com.au) Departing from **Whitsunday Airport** (☑ 07-4946 9180; www.whitsundayairport.com.au; Shute Harbour Rd, Flametree), HeliReef runs scenic helicopter flights of between 10 minutes ($135 per person) and an hour ($699 per person) over the Whitsunday Islands and Great Barrier Reef. Third-seat tickets are half the price.

🛏 Sleeping

Queensland Parks & Wildlife (☑ 13 74 68; http://parks.des.qld.gov.au) manages the **Whitsunday Islands National Park** campgrounds on several islands for both independent campers as well as groups on commercial trips, including the campgrounds on Armit, Gloucester, Hook, Lindeman, Saddleback, South Molle and Whitsunday Islands. Camping permits (per person/family $6.55/26) are available online or at Queensland Parks' **Airlie Beach office** (☑ 07-4946 1480, 13 74 68; http://parks.des.qld. gov.au; cnr Shute Harbour & Mandalay Rds; ⊙ 9am-4.30pm Mon-Fri).

You must be self-sufficient and are advised to take 5L of water per person per day, plus three days' extra supply in case you get stuck. You should also have a fuel stove, as wood fires are banned on all islands.

If Cruise Whitsundays (p378) doesn't service the island you want to access, try **Scamper** (☑ 0487 226 737, 07-4946 6285; www.whitsundaycamping.com.au). It leaves from Shute Harbour and can drop you at South Molle Island ($65 return), Whitsunday Island ($105), Whitehaven Beach ($155) and Hook Island ($160). Camping transfers include complimentary 5L water containers. You can also hire camp kits ($50 first night; $25 subsequent nights), which include a tent, gas stove, esky and more. The website is full of more details and helpful information.

SAILING THE WHITSUNDAYS

The Whitsundays are the place to skim across fantasy-blue waters on a tropical breeze. If you're flexible with dates, last-minute stand-by rates can considerably reduce the price and you'll also have a better idea of weather conditions. Many travellers hang out in Airlie Beach for a few days for this exact purpose, although you may end up spending your savings in the pub!

Most vessels offer snorkelling on the fringing reefs, where the colourful soft corals are often more abundant than on the outer reef. Equipment and meals are always included; diving and other activities nearly always cost extra.

Some of the better-known boats berthing in Airlie Beach are as follows. Once you've decided, book at one of the many booking agencies in Airlie Beach.

Atlantic Clipper (☑ 07-4946 5755; www.atlanticclipper.com.au; 2-day, 2-night trips from $489) A 53-berth party boat offering two-day cruises to Whitehaven Beach, Langford Island and other highlights.

Derwent Hunter (☑ 1800 334 773; www.tallshipadventures.com.au; day trips adult/child $195/99) A classic 90ft (27m) schooner built in Tasmania in 1946, this boat offers day cruises to Hook Island.

Prima Sailing (☑ 1800 550 751; www.primasailing.com.au; 2-day, 2-night tours from $499) This 47ft (14m) sloop, custom-built to cruise these waters, takes parties of up to 12 on two-night trips to sites only smaller boats can reach.

SV Domino (☑ 0428 631 571, 07-4948 0084; www.aussieyachting.com; day trips $195) A racing yacht crafted from New Zealand kauri, the *Domino* takes small groups on day trips to the little green island of Bali Hai.

Bareboating

Rent a boat without skipper, crew or provisions. You don't need formal qualifications, but you (or one of your party) have to prove that you can competently operate a vessel.

Expect to pay between $680 and $1000 a day in high season (roughly June to August, when the weather is mild and calm) for a yacht sleeping four to six people, plus a booking deposit and a security bond (refunded when the boat is returned undamaged). Most companies have a minimum hire period of three to five days.

There are a number of bareboat charter companies around Airlie Beach.

Charter Yachts Australia (☑ 1800 639 520; www.cya.com.au; Abell Point Marina, Shingley Dr; per night from $620)

Cumberland Charter Yachts (☑ 1800 075 101; www.ccy.com.au; Suite 18, Abell Point Marina, Shingley Dr; yachts per night from $782)

Queensland Yacht Charters (☑ 1800 075 013; www.yachtcharters.com.au; Abell Point Marina, Shingley Dr; per night from $690)

Whitsunday Escape (☑ 1800 075 145; www.whitsundayescape.com; Suite 16, Abell Point Marina, Shingley Dr; charters per night from $780)

Whitsunday Rent A Yacht (☑ 1800 075 000; www.rentayacht.com.au; 6 Bay Tce, Shute Harbour; per night from $695)

Hamilton Island

POP 1867

Welcome to a little slice of resort paradise, where the road is ruled by golf buggies, the forested interior is criss-crossed by steep, rocky walking trails, and the white beaches are buzzing with water-sports action. Though such an all-sufficing resort experience is not for everyone, it's hard not to be impressed by the selection of high-end accommodation, restaurants, bars and activities – if you've got the cash, there's something for everyone.

Day trippers can use some resort facilities – including tennis courts, a golf driving range and a minigolf course – and enjoy the island on a relatively economical budget. A few shops by the harbour also organise dives and certificate courses, and just about everyone can sign you up for a variety of cruises to other islands and the outer reef. If you only have time for one walk, clamber up scenic **Passage Peak** (239m) on the northeastern corner of the island.

🛏 Sleeping & Eating

★ Qualia   RESORT $$$

(☑ 1300 780 959; www.qualia.com.au; 20 Whitsunday Blvd; villas from $1250; ❋ @ ☎ ☲) Forced to rebuild after 2017's Cyclone Debbie, Hamilton's premier resort has come back strongly. Its 60 blissful 'pavilions' (timber-rich, luxuriously furnished villas) are better than ever, scattered among (reduced) tropical foliage on the island's secluded northern peninsular. Qualia has a private beach, two really good restaurants (mains at the **Long Pavilion** cost $42 to $46), a day spa and two swimming pools.

Reef View Hotel   HOTEL $$$

(☑ 02-9007 0009; www.hamiltonisland.com.au; 12 Resort Dr; d from $370; ❋ ☎ ☲) Aptly named, this hilltop resort has spectacular views of Hamilton's forested hills on one side, and the beach and fringing reef on the other. Central and popular with families and groups, it's a mid-priced hotel (for Hamilton) with a low-key atmosphere and all you need on-site.

Popeye's Fish n' Chips   FISH & CHIPS $

(☑ 07-4946 9999; Front St; fish & chips $12; ☻ 10am-9pm) Popeye's serves massive boxes of fish and chips that can comfortably feed two people. It also sells burgers, chicken and even frozen fishing bait.

Bommie Restaurant   AUSTRALIAN $$$

(☑ 07-4946 9999; Hamilton Island Yacht Club, Front St; 4-course/tasting menus $125/150; ☻ 6pm-late Tue-Sat) With a great peninsular location overlooking the clinking masts of Hamilton Yacht Club, the oddly named Bommie is Hamilton's swankiest restaurant. Delights stud both the four-course and tasting menus, including master-stock-braised pork cheek with barbecued eel, smoked labne (yogurt cheese), carrot and shiitake. Only the tasting menu is offered on Saturday.

❶ Getting There & Away

Hamilton Island Airport (p377), the main arrival centre for the Whitsundays, is serviced by Qantas (p373) to/from Sydney, Melbourne, Brisbane and Cairns, Virgin (p373) to/from Sydney, Melbourne and Brisbane, and Jetstar (p373) to/from Sydney.

Cruise Whitsundays (☑ 07-4846 7000; www.cruisewhitsundays.com) connects Hamilton Island Airport and the marina with the Port of Airlie in Airlie Beach (adult/child one way $62/40).

Long Island

Mostly classified as national park, thickly forested Long Island has secluded, pretty white beaches, lots of adorable wild rock wallabies and 17km of walking tracks, which connect some fine lookouts and beauty spots. Nine kilometres long, it narrows to a neck just 400m wide – hence the name.

Long Island has seen two resorts, hit by cyclones and the vagaries of tourism, close down in recent years. **Palm Bay Resort** (☑ 1300 655 126; www.palmbayresort.com.au; villas/bures/bungalows from $269/299/370; ☲) fills a void at the high end, while campers can stay at Sandy Bay's Queensland Parks **campground** (☑ 13 74 68; http://parks.des.qld.gov.au; sites per person/family $6.55/26) – not to be confused with the Sandy Bay campground at South Molle.

Two water taxis run scheduled services to Long Island's Palm Bay Resort: **Island Transfers** (☑ 0488 022 868; www.islandtransfers.com) from Proserpine, Airlie and Shute Harbour, and **Mars Charters** (☑ 1800 202 909; www.marscharters.com.au) from Hamilton Island.

Bowen

POP 8854

A small coastal town set on a hill north of Airlie Beach, Bowen is famous around Australia for its mangoes – it gets busy during fruit-picking season – and known locally for its secret bays and inlets. Its wide, quiet streets, classic stilted Queenslander houses and laid-back, friendly locals all contribute to a relaxed and dignified air. The foreshore, with its landscaped esplanade, picnic tables and BBQs, is a focal point, but there are some truly stunning – and little-visited – beaches and bays northeast of the town centre. The Ngaro and Gia peoples are the traditional owners of the land Bowen stands on.

Keep an eye out for the 'Bowenwood' sign on the town's water tower; Baz Luhrmann's epic movie *Australia* was shot here in 2007 and the locals are still a little star-struck.

🛏️ Sleeping & Eating

Rose Bay Resort RESORT **$$**
(☑ 07-4786 9000; www.rosebayresort.com.au; 2 Pandanus St; studio from $160, 1-/2-bed apt from $200/280; 🅿️ ❄️ 🛜 ♨️) Rose Bay is a seriously underrated beach, especially for snorkelling, and guests at this friendly resort have it pretty much all to themselves. Spacious studios sleep two, and comfy apartments sleep up to six guests quite comfortably. You'll need a car to reach Bowen central.

★ Bird's Fish Bar FISH & CHIPS **$**
(☑ 07-4786 1188; Henry Darwen Dr; fish & chips $10-15; ☺ 8.30am-8pm Mon-Sat, from 11am Sun) The retail shopfront and fish 'n' chip dispensary at the Bowen Fisherman's Seafood Company, this is the place to get just-landed seafood cooked to order. Ask for whatever's best that day, or just get a butcher's-paper parcel of local bug tails (the meatiest part of this toothsome Australian crustacean) with chips and lemon, and enjoy one of the best seafood meals imaginable.

Jochheims Pies BAKERY **$**
(☑ 07-4786 1227; 49 George St; pies $6.25; ☺ 5am-3.30pm Mon-Fri, to 12.30pm Sat) Jochheims has been keeping Bowen bellies full of home-made pies and other baked treats since 1963. Pies, including innovative varieties such as prawn in garlic-and-white-wine sauce (sold on Thursdays), are naturally the main stock in trade, but quiches, robust breakfasts (served until 11.30am), salads, rolls and bread are also top-notch.

Cove ASIAN **$$**
(☑ 07-4786 3842; http://thecoverestaurant.com.au; Coral Cove Apts, 2b Horseshoe Bay Rd; mains $19-24; ☺ 11am-3pm & 5-9.30pm Wed-Mon) A bustling, popular Chinese and Southeast Asian restaurant with unbroken views of the Coral Sea from its timber deck. Chef's specials, such as seafood stir-fried with chilli and basil, are the standouts.

Eungella National Park

Mystical, mountainous Eungella National Park covers nearly 500 sq km of the lofty Clarke Range, but is largely inaccessible except for the walking tracks around Broken River and Finch Hatton Gorge. The large tracts of tropical and subtropical vegetation have been isolated from other rainforest areas for thousands of years and now boast several unique species, including the orange-sided skink and the charming Eungella gastric-brooding frog, which incubates its eggs in its stomach and gives birth by spitting out the tadpoles. Home to some unique bush accommodation and atypical adventure pursuits, Finch Hatton Gorge repays the curiosity of travellers tempted off the Eungella–Mackay Road. The Birra Gubba are the traditional owners of this land.

👁️ Sights

👁️ Finch Hatton Gorge

Finch Hatton Gorge is a remarkable, prehistoric place set in a rugged subtropical rainforest. Hills of farmland disappear into a lush gorge dotted with volcanic boulders and buzzing with bird and insect life. It can feel like you've stepped through a geographical black hole into another physical dimension.

A gorgeous 1.6km walking trail leads to **Araluen Falls**, with its tumbling waterfalls and swimming holes, and a further 1km hike takes you to the **Wheel of Fire Falls**, another cascade with a deep swimming hole. Both tend to be busy with locals on weekends.

👁️ Broken River

Most days of the year, you can be pretty sure of seeing a platypus or two in Broken River at the rightfully renowned **platypus-viewing platforms** (across the street from the information office next to the bridge). It's reputedly one of the most reliable spots on earth to catch these meek monotremes at play and we can vouch for it – few people leave disappointed. The best times are the hours immediately after dawn and before dark. You must remain patient, silent and still. Platypus activity is at its peak from May to August, when the females are fattening themselves up in preparation for gestating their young. Other river life you're sure to see are large northern snapping turtles and brilliant azure kingfishers.

Don't miss the 20km of excellent **rainforest walking trails** between the Broken River picnic ground and Eungella. Maps are available from the information office by the platypus-viewing platforms in Broken River. It's sporadically staffed, but luckily there are information boards with maps at the trailheads.

🏃 Activities

Rainforest Scuba   DIVING
(📞 0434 455 040; www.rainforestscuba.com; 55 Anzac Pde, Finch Hatton; per diver certified/non-certified $115/160) Claiming to be the world's first rainforest dive operator, these guys run a tight operation. Expect to submerge in crystal-clear creeks where eels, platypus, turtles and fish share the habitat. Dives are generally held at 2pm, with no time limit, and are available as part of various packages (see the website).

Forest Flying   ADVENTURE SPORTS
(📞 07-4958 3359; www.forestflying.com; 18 Oliver's Rd, Finch Hatton; $60; ♿) Explore the rainforest at bird's-eye level, gliding through the canopy with Forest Flying. Guided tours see you harnessed to a 350m-long cable and suspended up to 25m above the ground; you control your speed via a pulley system. Bookings are essential, and you must weigh 18kg to 120kg.

🛏 Sleeping

There are a few places to stay, the best for budgeteers being the eccentric and rustic **Platypus Bushcamp** (📞 07-4958 3204; www.bushcamp.net; 672 Gorge Rd, Finch Hatton; sites/huts $10/100; P❄️🐾) 🌿 in the lush, rainforest-covered lowlands of Finch Hatton Gorge. Those with a little more cash should head straight to the friendly, comfortable **Broken River Mountain Resort** (📞 07-4958 4000; www.brokenrivermr.com.au; Eungella Dam Rd; d

$140-200; P❄️🛜🏊), right across from Broken River's platypus-viewing platform high up in the mountains.

Visit Queensland Parks (p381) online for camping information and permits.

❶ Getting There & Away

The park is 84km west of Mackay. There are no buses to Eungella or Finch Hatton, but **Reeforest Adventure Tours** (📞 07-4959 8360, 1800 500 353; www.reeforest.com; tours adult/child from $130/90) runs day trips from Mackay and will drop off and pick up those who want to linger. However, tours don't run every day so your stay may wind up being longer than intended.

Finch Hatton Gorge is reached from Mackay via the Peak Downs Rd. About 27km west of Mirani, just before the town of Finch Hatton, the turn-off. The last 2km of the 10km drive from the main road is on unsealed roads, with several creek crossings that can become impassable after heavy rain.

TOWNSVILLE TO CAIRNS

Spread between the tourist darlings of Cairns and the Whitsunday Islands, this lesser-known, rainforested stretch of quiet, palm-edged beaches is where giant endangered cassowary graze for seeds, and koalas nap in gum trees on islands encircled by turquoise seas. Oft-overlooked Townsville is the urban centre and offers pleasant, wide, modern streets, a landscaped seaside promenade, gracious 19th-century architecture, and a host of cultural venues and sporting events. It's also the jumping-off point for Magnetic Island, a great budget alternative to the Whitsundays and with far more wildlife – hand-feed wild wallabies, spot an incredible range of bird life on fantastic bushwalking trails and look for koalas.

North of Townsville beautiful Mission Beach is a laid-back village that ironically attracts thrill seekers by the busload, all eager to skydive over the reef and on to white-sand beaches, or go on an adrenaline-pumping white-water rafting trip along the Tully River.

Townsville
POP 193,601

Northern Queensland's often-overlooked major city is easy on the eye: at Townsville's heart is its handsome, endless esplanade, an ideal viewing platform to fabulous Magnetic Island, a mere ferry ride offshore. A

Townsville

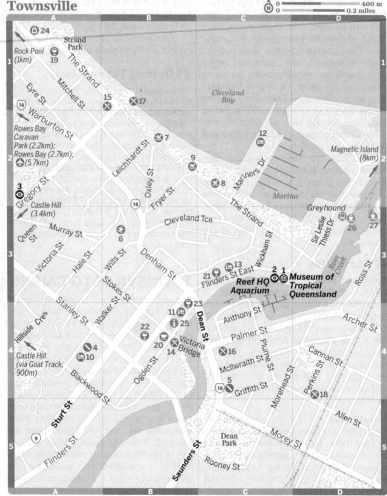

QUEENSLAND TOWNSVILLE

better museum and aquarium you'll struggle to find in Queensland, and it's a pedestrian-friendly city, its grand, refurbished 19th-century buildings offering loads of landmarks. If in doubt, join the throngs of the fit and fabulous marching up bright red Castle Hill to gaze across the city's dry environs.

Townsville has a lively, young populace, with thousands of students and armed forces members intermingling with old-school locals, fly-in, fly-out mine workers, and summer-seekers lapping up the average 320 days of sunshine per year. Needless to say, the nightlife is often full throttle.

The Wulgurukaba Indigenous people claim to be the traditional owners of the Townsville city area, but these are also the traditional lands of the Bindal, Girrugubba, Warakamai and Nawagi.

◉ Sights

★ Reef HQ Aquarium   AQUARIUM

(☎07-4750 0800; www.reefhq.com.au; Flinders St E; adult/child/family $28/14/70; ⊙9.30am-5pm) A staggering 2.5 million litres of water flow through the coral-reef tank here, home to 130 coral and 120 fish species. Kids will love seeing, feeding and touching turtles at the

Townsville

◎ **Top Sights**
1 Museum of Tropical Queensland..........C3
2 Reef HQ Aquarium.................................C3

◎ **Sights**
  Cultural Centre...............................(see 1)
3 Queens Gardens......................................A2

◐ **Activities, Courses & Tours**
4 Adrenalin Dive...A4
5 Remote Area Dive....................................C4
6 Skydive Townsville..................................B3
7 Strand...B2
8 Tobruk Memorial Baths.........................C2
9 Water Playground....................................B2

▣ **Sleeping**
10 Civic Guest House..................................A4
11 Hotel Grand Chancellor
    Townsville..B4
12 Mariners North...C2
13 Rambutan..C3

✴ **Eating**
14 A Touch of Salt.......................................B4
15 Harold's Seafood.....................................B1
16 Jam...C4

17 Longboard Bar & Grill.............................B1
18 Wayne & Adele's Garden of Eating.......D4

◓ **Drinking & Nightlife**
19 Beach Bar..A1
20 Coffee Dominion.....................................B4
21 Hooch & Fellow.......................................C3
    Rambutan......................................(see 13)
22 The Taphouse..B4
23 Townsville Brewery................................B4

⊜ **Shopping**
  Cotters Market..............................(see 20)
24 Strand Night Market...............................A1

ⓘ **Information**
  Great Barrier Reef Marine
    Park Authority...........................(see 25)
25 Visitor Information Centre....................B4

ⓘ **Transport**
26 Breakwater Ferry Terminal...................D3
27 Fantasea Car Ferry Terminal...............D3
    Magnetic Island Ferries................(see 27)
    Premier...(see 27)
    SeaLink...(see 26)

turtle hospital. Talks and tours (included with admission) throughout the day focus on different aspects of the reef and the aquarium.

★ **Museum of Tropical Queensland**   MUSEUM
(☑07-4726 0600; www.mtq.qm.qld.gov.au; 70-102 Flinders St E; adult/child/family $15/8.80/38; ◷9.30am-5pm) The award-winning Museum of Tropical Queensland provides a snapshot of this diverse region, from World Heritage–listed rainforest and reefs to the story of the shipwrecked HMS *Pandora,* the ship sent to capture the *Bounty* mutineers. The museum's family-friendly exhibitions explore life in the tropics from prehistoric times to the modern day. School holiday programs offer something for kids of all ages.

Queens Gardens   GARDENS
(cnr Gregory & Paxton Sts; ◷sunrise-sunset) FREE If you fancy a lazy picnic, head to these formal, ornamental gardens at the base of Castle Hill, 1km northwest of town.

Queens Gardens are part of Townsville's botanic gardens, which are spread across three locations: each has its own character, but all have tropical plants and are abundantly green.

Cultural Centre   CULTURAL CENTRE
(☑07-4772 7679; www.cctownsville.com.au; 2-68 Flinders St E; adult/child $5/2; ◷9.30am-4.30pm Mon-Sat) Showcases the history, traditions and customs of the local Wulgurukaba and Bindal peoples with performances and exhibitions. Call for guided-tour times.

Billabong Sanctuary   WILDLIFE RESERVE
(☑07-4778 8344; www.billabongsanctuary.com. au; Bruce Hwy; adult/child $37/24; ◷9am-5pm) 🐾 Just 17km south of Townsville, this eco-certified wildlife park offers up-close-and-personal encounters with Australian wildlife – from dingoes to cassowaries – in their natural habitat. You could easily spend all day at the 11-hectare park, with feedings, shows and talks every half-hour or so.

🏃 Activities

Strand   SWIMMING
Stretching 2.2km, Townsville's waterfront is interspersed with parks, pools, cafes and playgrounds – with hundreds of palm trees providing shade. Its golden-sand beach is patrolled and protected by two stinger enclosures.

At the northern tip is the **rock pool** (◷24hr) FREE, an enormous artificial swimming pool surrounded by lawns and sandy

RAVENSWOOD & CHARTERS TOWERS

Detour inland from the coast to taste a bit of Queensland's outback character at these two old prospecting towns.

Ravenswood is a tiny gold-mining town whose fortunes have fluctuated over the past century. Accommodation, food and of course drinks can be found in the town's two pubs, the **Imperial Hotel** (☑07-4770 2131; 23 Macrossan St; s/d $45/72; P❖❄🐾🛜) and the **Railway Hotel** (☑07-4770 2144; www.facebook.com/railwayhotelravenswood/; 66 Macrossan St; s/tw/d $45/85/98; P❖❄🛜).

The 19th-century gold-rush settlement of **Charters Towers** sits 137km southwest of Townsville. With a long main street lined with verandahs and covered walkways, it's a fine example of a rural Aussie town that owes its current form to gold (although prior to its discovery, these were the traditional lands of the Gudjal Indigenous people).

The **Stock Exchange Arcade** (☑07-3223 6666; www.nationaltrust.org.au/qld; 76 Mosman St; ◷9am-5pm) is a gorgeous little open-ended arcade (1888) that was the commercial hub of the second-largest town in Queensland in the late 19th century. Come nightfall, panoramic **Towers Hill**, the site where gold was first discovered, is the atmospheric setting for an open-air cinema showing the 20-minute film *Ghosts After Dark*.

Staying at the atmospheric and friendly **Royal Private Hotel** (☑07-4787 8688; www.royalprivate-hotel.com.au; 100 Mosman St; s/d from $75/125; ❄🛜) feels like something between time travel and visiting a museum. Those looking for a real-life cattle station experience should contact the friendly Rhonda at **Bluff Downs** (☑07-4770 4084; rhonda.bluffdowns@activ8.net.au; off Lynd Hwy; dm $20, d $90-300, campsites $20).

The excellent **Charters Towers Visitor Centre** (☑07-4761 5533; www.visitcharters towers.com.au; 74 Mosman St; ◷9.30am-5pm) books all tours in town, and has numerous brochures on attractions here and in the wider area.

beaches. Alternatively, head to the chlorinated safety of the heritage-listed, Olympic-size swimming pool, **Tobruk Memorial Baths** (☑07-4772 6550; www.townsville.qld.gov. au; adult/child $5/3; ◷5am-7pm Mon-Thu, 5am-6pm Fri, 7am-4pm Sat, 8am-5pm Sun May-Sep, open an hour earlier Sat & Sun Oct-Apr). There's also a fantastic **water playground** (◷10am-8pm Dec-Mar, to 6pm Sep-Nov, Apr & May, to 5pm Jun-Aug) FREE for the kids.

Skydive Townsville   SKYDIVING
(☑07-4721 4721; www.skydivetownsville.com.au; 182 Denham St; 3050/4270m tandem dives from $395/445) Hurl yourself from a perfectly good plane and land right on the Strand, or over on Magnetic Island.

✩ Festivals & Events

The city has a packed calendar of festivals and events, including the home games of its cherished **North Queensland Cowboys** (www.cowboys.com.au) National Rugby League team, who won the competition in 2015.

**Australian Festival
of Chamber Music**   MUSIC
(☑07-4771 4144; www.afcm.com.au; ◷Jul-Aug) Townsville gets cultural during this internationally renowned festival at various venues across the city. It's usually held in August, but can begin in late July.

🛏 Sleeping

★**Rambutan**   HOSTEL $
(☑07-4771 6915; www.rambutantownsville.com. au; 113-119 Flinders St; dm/d from $24/120) One of the coolest places to stay in Far North Queensland, central Rambutan has swish accommodation, from spick-and-span dorms to tastefully decorated rooms; groups might want to consider the villas. There's a terrific **rooftop bar** (◷noon-late) that also serves food and a street-side cafe, which may mean some struggle to find a reason to leave the premises.

★**Civic Guest House**   HOSTEL $
(☑07-4771 5381; www.civicguesthousetownsville. com.au; 262 Walker St; dm/d from $21/56; @🛜) This old-fashioned hostel respects the independent traveller's needs for cleanliness, comfort, security and easy company. The mustard-coloured, colonial-tinged Civic is a welcome change.

Hotel Grand Chancellor   HOTEL $$
(☑07-4729 2000; www.grandchancellorhotels. com/hotel-grand-chancellor-townsville; 334

Flinders St; r/apt from $110/124; ❄☎🖥) Large, spacious rooms and apartments, many with water and/or city views, in a fine central location attract numerous repeat visitors – with the perfect mix whether you're here for business or pleasure, and with eminently reasonable prices, what's not to like? The look is contemporary and there's a rooftop swimming pool.

Mariners North APARTMENT $$$

(☑07-4722 0777; www.marinersnorth.com.au; 7 Mariners Dr; 2-/3-bedroom apt from $215/375; P⊖❄☎🖥) The pick for families in Townsville is Mariners North, in the newer section of the marina, with a sandy stretch out the front and a delightful pool. The apartments are very good, particularly the ground-floor ones with direct pool and garden access; others may prefer views over Cleveland Bay.

✖ Eating

Perpendicular to the Strand, Gregory St has a clutch of cafes and takeaway joints. The Palmer St dining strip offers a diverse range of cuisines: wander along and take your pick. Many of Townsville's bars and pubs also serve food.

Harold's Seafood SEAFOOD $

(☑07-4724 1322; http://haroldseafood.com.au/; cnr the Strand & Gregory St; mains $8-15; ⊙8am-9pm Mon-Thu, to 9.30pm Fri-Sun) The big fish-and-chip joint on the corner whips up fish burgers and large serves of barramundi and salad.

★Longboard Bar & Grill AUSTRALIAN $$

(☑07-4724 1234; www.longboardbarandgrill.com; the Strand, opp Gregory St; mains $16-37; ⊙11am-3pm & 5.30pm-late Mon-Sat, 11am-3pm Sun) The coolest place in Townsville for a light meal and a light party overlooking the water is this surf-themed pub-restaurant, which does terrific nightly specials including tacos and buffalo wings. The regular steak, seafood and pasta menu is very reliable. Orders are taken at the bar, the vibe is right most nights and staff are fast and efficient.

Wayne & Adele's Garden of Eating AUSTRALIAN $$

(☑07-4772 2984; 11 Allen St; mains from $18.50; ⊙6.30-10.30pm Mon, to 11pm Thu-Sat, noon-3pm Sun) There's irreverence at every turn in this husband-and-wife-run gourmet restaurant situated in an Aussie backyard (well, courtyard at least). Those who like a side serving of quirky with their grub shouldn't

miss mains including duck ricotta gnocchi or kangaroo fillet with curried field mushrooms and bacon mash. And on no account bypass the cashew cheesecake if it's on the menu.

Jam AUSTRALIAN $$

(☑07-4721 4900; https://jamcorner.com.au/; 1 Palmer St; breakfast $10-22, mains $20-38; ⊙6.30-10am, noon-2pm & 5.30-9.30pm Tue-Fri, from 7am Sat, from 7.30am Sun; 🖋) This neat midrange restaurant, on happening Palmer St, understands its casual northern Queensland clientele. Jam serves a wide menu with celebratory breakfasts and desserts, as well as everything from lunch bento boxes to steaks and vegetarian choices.

A Touch of Salt AUSTRALIAN $$$

(☑07-4724 4441; www.atouchofsalt.com.au; 86 Ogden St; mains lunch $24-34, dinner $32-40; ⊙noon-3pm & 5.30-11pm Fri, 5.30-11pm Tue-Thu & Sat; 🖋) Although the favoured high-end dining experience for Townsville's posh set doesn't look very stylish upon entry, the bar is slick, the service is fussy and the sophisticated fusion cuisine is ambitious (though can overreach at times). Try the baked scallops with jalapeños, followed by goat's-milk cheese gnocchi or harissa-roasted lamb. Vegetarians get their own menu.

🍷 Drinking & Nightlife

★Townsville Brewery BREWERY

(☑07-4724 2999; www.townsvillebrewery.com.au; 252 Flinders St; ⊙11.30am-midnight Mon-Sat) Craft brews are made on-site at this hopping, stunningly restored 1880s former post office. Soak up a Townsville Bitter or Bandito Loco, and take a brewery tour ($48 including tasting) at noon on Wednesday or Friday.

Hooch & Fellow COCKTAIL BAR

(☑07-4721 0225; www.facebook.com/hoochandfellow; 183 Flinders St E; ⊙5pm-midnight Tue-Sat) Cocktails with Melbourne-esque cool deep in the tropics. A small drinks list, perhaps, but every cocktail is perfectly chosen and the bartenders are Townsville's best.

Beach Bar BAR

(☑07-4724 4281; www.watermarktownsville.com.au/bar; Watermark Hotel, 72-74 The Strand; ⊙11am-late) The place to be seen in Townsville. Well, if it's good enough for Missy Higgins and Silverchair, then it's good enough for the rest of us. Some serious Sunday sessions take place in the tavern bar with prime ocean views down the flash end of the Strand.

WORTH A TRIP

AUSTRALIAN INSTITUTE OF MARINE SCIENCE

Fascinating and free two-hour tours run weekly from April to November at the **Australian Institute of Marine Science** (AIMS; ☑ 07-4753 4444; www.aims.gov.au; 1526 Cape Cleveland Rd, Cape Ferguson; ⊙10am Fri Apr-Nov). This marine-research facility conducts crucial research into issues such as coral bleaching and management of the Great Barrier Reef, and how it relates to the community. Advance bookings are essential. The turn-off from the Bruce Hwy is 37km southeast of Townsville; the institute is 13km from the turn-off.

The Taphouse BAR
(☑ 07-4772 2301; www.facebook.com/thetaphousetsv; 373 Flinders St; ⊙10am-midnight) Eight craft beers on tap should be reason enough to come, but this is one place where you're allowed to pour your own. Buy your prepaid card, tap next to the beer you want and start pouring. They have cocktails too, but mixing your own is, sadly, not yet possible...

Coffee Dominion CAFE
(☑ 07-4724 0767; www.coffeedominion.com.au; cnr Stokes & Ogden Sts; ⊙6am-3pm Mon-Fri, 7am-1pm Sat & Sun) 🍃 An eco-conscious establishment roasting beans sourced from the Atherton Tablelands to Mombasa. If you don't find a blend you like, invent your own and they'll grind it fresh.

🛍 Shopping

Check out the weekly **Cotters Market** (www.facebook.com/SundayonFlinders.CottersMarket; 320 Flinders St; ⊙8.30am-1pm Sun) or monthly **Strand Night Market** (☑0477 477 040; www.townsvillerotarymarkets.com.au; The Strand; ⊙5-9pm 1st Fri of month Feb-Dec).

ℹ Information

Great Barrier Reef Marine Park Authority (☑07-4750 0700; www.gbrmpa.gov.au; 280 Flinders St) National body overseeing the Great Barrier Reef.

Visitor Information Centre (☑07-4721 3660; www.townsvilleholidays.info; 280 Flinders St; ⊙9am-5pm) Extensive visitor information on Townsville, Magnetic Island and nearby national parks. There's another branch on the Bruce Hwy 10km south of the city.

ℹ Getting There & Away

AIR

Airlines flying to/from **Townsville Airport** (☑ 07-4727 3211; www.townsvilleairport.com.au) include the following:

Airnorth (☑1800 627 474; www.airnorth.com.au) Darwin

Jetstar (☑13 15 38; www.jetstar.com.au) Melbourne, Sydney and Brisbane

Qantas (☑13 13 13; www.qantas.com.au) Melbourne, Sydney, Brisbane, Cairns, Mackay, Mt Isa and Cloncurry; dozens of connections

Virgin (☑13 67 89; www.virginaustralia.com) Sydney and Brisbane

BOAT

SeaLink (☑07-4726 0800; www.sealinkqld.com.au) runs Magnetic Island ferries almost hourly from **Breakwater** (2/14 Sir Leslie Thiess Dr; lockers per day $4-6) in Townsville (return adult/child including all-day bus pass $33/16.50, 25 minutes) between 5.30am and 11.30pm. Car parking is available in Townsville.

Magnetic Island Ferries (☑07-4796 9300; www.magneticislandferry.com.au) operates a car ferry from **Fantasea Car Ferry Terminal** (Ross St, South Townsville), crossing eight times daily (seven on weekends) from the south side of Ross Creek, taking 35 minutes. It costs $226 (return) for a car and up to three passengers, and $28/16 (adult/child return) for foot passengers only. Bookings are essential.

BUS

Greyhound (☑1300 473 946; www.greyhound.com.au; The Breakwater, Sealink Travel Centre, Sir Leslie Thiess Dr) has three daily services to Brisbane ($285, 24 hours), Rockhampton ($130, 12½ hours), Airlie Beach ($35, 4¾ hours), Mission Beach ($44, four hours) and Cairns ($55, six hours). Buses pick up and drop off at the Breakwater Ferry Terminal.

Premier (☑13 34 10; www.premierms.com.au) has one service a day to/from Brisbane ($190, 23½ hours) and Cairns ($57, 5½ hours), stopping at the Fantasea Car Ferry Terminal.

TRAIN

Townsville's **train station** (Charters Towers Rd) is 1km south of the centre.

The Brisbane–Cairns *Spirit of Queensland* travels through Townsville five times a week. Journey time between Brisbane and Townsville is 18½ hours (one way $189 to $442), while tickets to Cairns (6½ hours) cost $50 to $109. Contact **Queensland Rail** (☑1300 131 722; www.queenslandrailtravel.com.au).

ℹ Getting Around

Townsville Airport is 5km northwest of the city centre, in Garbutt. A taxi to the centre costs about $24, while **Townsville Shuttle Services** (☑0478 160 036; http://shuttletsv.com.au; Townsville Airport; per person $5-10) runs between the airport, Townsville hotels and the Magnetic Island Ferry Terminal.

Sunbus (☑07-4771 9800; www.sunbus.com.au) runs local bus services around Townsville – single/daily tickets cost $1.80/3.60. Route maps and timetables are available at the visitor information centre and online.

Magnetic Island

POP 2650

Sitting almost within swimming distance offshore from Townsville, Magnetic Island (Maggie to her friends) is a verdant island and one of Queensland's most laid-back residential addresses. The local population, who mostly commute to Townsville or cater for the tourist trade, must pinch themselves as they come home to the stunning coastal walking trails, gum trees full of dozing koalas and surrounding bright turquoise seas.

Over half of this mountainous, triangular-shaped island's 52 sq km is national park, with cycling, scenic walks and abundant wildlife, including a large (and adorable) allied rock wallaby population. Inviting beaches and waters close to shore offer water sports, or simply the chance to bask in the sunshine. The granite boulders, hoop pines and eucalyptus are a fresh change from the clichéd tropical-island paradise.

Prior to white settlement, Magnetic Island was known as Yunbenun and was home to the island's traditional owners, the Wulgarukaba people.

◉ Sights

There's one main road across the island, which goes from Picnic Bay, past Nelly and Geoffrey Bays, to Horseshoe Bay. Local buses ply the route regularly. Walking trails through the bush also link the main towns. Maps are available at the ferry terminal ticket desk.

Picnic Bay   BAY
Picnic Bay is one of the most low-key spots on the island, dominated more by a community of friendly locals than anything else. There's a stinger net during the season (November to May) and the swimming is superb. There's also a fine jetty, if you like to throw in a line or simply contemplate the sea.

Nelly Bay   BAY
Magnetic Harbour in Nelly Bay is your first taste of life on the island. There's a wide

range of busy but relaxing eating and sleeping options and a decent beach. There's also a children's playground towards the northern end of the beach, and good snorkelling on the fringing coral reef.

Arcadia   VILLAGE
Arcadia village is a conglomerate of shops, eateries and accommodation. Its main beach, **Geoffrey Bay**, has a reef at its southern end (reef walking at low tide is discouraged). By far its prettiest beach is the cove at **Alma Bay**, with huge boulders tumbling into the sea. There's plenty of shade here, along with picnic tables and a children's playground.

Horseshoe Bay   BAY
Horseshoe Bay, on the north coast, is the best of Maggie's accessible beaches and attracts its share of young, hippy-ish nature lovers and older day trippers. You'll find watersports gear for hire, a stinger net, a row of cafes and a fantastic pub. Bungalow Bay Koala Village has a **wildlife park** (☑07-4778 5577; www.bungalowbay.com.au; 40 Horseshoe Bay Rd; adult/child $29/13; ☺2hr tours 10am, noon & 2.30pm), where you can cuddle koalas. Pick up local arts and crafts at Horseshoe Bay's **market** (☑0457 023 095; Pacific Dr Foreshore; ☺9am-2pm 2nd & last Sun of month), which sets up along the beachfront.

🏃 Activities

★**Forts Walk**   WALKING
Townsville was a supply base for the Pacific during WWII, and the forts were designed to protect the town from naval attack. If you're going to do just one walk, then the **Forts Walk** (2.8km, 1½ hours return) is a must. It starts near the Radical Bay turn-off, passing lots of ex-military sites, gun emplacements and false 'rocks'.

Big Mama Sailing   BOATING
(☑0437 206 360; www.bigmamasailing.com; Pacific Dr; full-day cruises adult/child $195/110) Hit the water on an 18m ketch with passionate boaties Stu, Lisa and Fletcher, who made their name with the *Big Mama* before moving here from Mission Beach.

Tropicana Tours   DRIVING
(☑0448 58 1800; www.facebook.com/tropicana guidedadventurecompany; 10 Bayside Crt, Horseshoe Bay; full day adult/child $199/99) Ziggy and Co run magnificent tours that take in the island's best spots in their stretch 4WD. Prices include close encounters with

QUEENSLAND MAGNETIC ISLAND

DIVING THE YONGALA WRECK

Widely considered one of Australia's top wreck dives, the **SS Yongala Wreck** is left from a steamship that sank in a cyclone while passing through the Great Barrier Reef in 1911 (one year before the *Titanic* met a similar fate); 122 passengers lost their lives. Diving here involves prolific marine life, more so than almost anywhere else on the reef.

Almost guaranteed are giant gropers, giant marble rays, eagle rays, trevally, barracuda, eagle rays, turtles, sea snakes, bull sharks and more against a backdrop of a coral-crusted wreck. Yongala Dive (07-4783 1519; www.yongaladive.com.au; 56 Narrah St), in Alva Beach, organises dives out here, as do a number of Townsville-based operators, such as Adrenalin Dive (07-4724 0600; www.adrenalinedive.com.au; 252 Walker St) and Remote Area Dive (RAD; 07-4721 4425; www.remoteareadive.com.au; 16 Dean St). From Magnetic Island, try Pleasure Divers (07-4778 5788; www.pleasuredivers.com.au; 10 Marine Pde, Arcadia; open-water courses per person from $350; 8.30am-5pm) and Pro Dive Magnetic (0424 822 450; www.prodivemagnetic.com; 43 Sooning St, Nelly Bay).

wildlife, lunch at a local cafe and a sunset cocktail. Shorter tours are also available, but the eight-hour version is a hit.

Magnetic Island Sea Kayaks   KAYAKING
(07-4778 5424; www.seakayak.com.au; 93 Horseshoe Bay Rd, Horseshoe Bay; morning tours adult/child $95/75, evening $65/50; 8am & 3.45pm & 4.30pm) Magnetic Island is a perfect destination for sea kayaking, with plenty of launching points, secret beaches, marine life, and laid-back cafes to recharge in after your paddle. Join an eco-certified morning or sunset tour, or go it alone on a rented kayak.

🛏 Sleeping

★ Base Backpackers   HOSTEL $
(1800 242 273; www.stayatbase.com; 1 Nelly Bay Rd, Nelly Bay; camping per person $15, dm $31-37, d from $109; @ 🛜 ⛱) Base must be one of the best-located hostels in Australia, situated between Nelly and Picnic Bays. It's famous for wild full-moon parties, and things can get raucous at any time at the infamous on-site **Island Bar**. Sleep, food and transport package deals are available. Dorms and double rooms are serviceable and clean, but it's all about the action at Base.

Arcadia Beach Guest House   GUESTHOUSE $
(07-4778 5668; www.arcadiabeachguesthouse.com.au; 27 Marine Pde, Arcadia; dm from $35, r with private/shared bathroom from $135/75; ✳🛜⛱) Well priced and staffed by effusive professionals, Arcadia Beach Guest House does a lot right, including providing an enormous variety of sleeping quarters. Will you stay in a bright, beachy room (named after one of Magnetic Island's bays) or a

dorm? Go turtle-spotting from the balcony, rent a canoe, a Moke, a 4WD...or all of the above?

Magnetic Island B&B   B&B $$
(07-4758 1203; www.magneticislandbedandbreakfast.com; 11 Dolphin Ct, Horseshoe Bay; d $165; 🛜⛱) The double rooms here book up quickly, but the Bush Retreat ($200) sleeps four and is a great deal for some natural seclusion. Rooms are bright and breezy, and the hosts are astutely professional. There's a neat saltwater pool, and the included breakfasts are wholesome and delicious. Minimum two-night stay applies.

Shambhala Retreat   BUNGALOW $$
(0448 160 580; www.shambhala-retreat-magnetic-island.com.au; 11 Barton St, Nelly Bay; d from $115-135; ✳⛱) With some of the best-value, self-contained, tropical units on the island, Shambhala is a green-powered property with distinct Buddhist influences evident in the wall hangings and water features. Two units have outdoor courtyard showers; all have fully equipped kitchens, large bathrooms and laundry facilities. Local wildlife is often drawn to the patios. Minimum stay is two nights.

Peppers Blue on Blue Resort   RESORT $$$
(07-4758 2400; www.peppers.com.au/blue-on-blue/; 123 Sooning St, Nelly Bay; d/apt from $219/295; ✳🛜⛱) Overlooking the Nelly Bay marina, Peppers Blue on Blue is one of the island's premier addresses. Rooms are stylishly turned out, with fresh, muted colours and island photographs on the walls for when you can tear yourself away from the water views. The swimming pool seems to go on forever.

✕ Eating & Drinking

There are a few terrific pubs on the island and a definite culture of 'sundowners' (ie watching the sun cross the horizon while you nurse a drink). Head to Base Backpackers for more hedonistic parties.

★ Cafe Nourish
CAFE $

(☑07-4758 1885; www.facebook.com/cafenourishhsb; 3/6 Pacific Dr, Horsehoe Bay; mains $12-19; ⊙7.30am-2.30pm) Horseshoe Bay has become quite the hip cafe strip and this favourite cafe does the small things well: fresh healthy wraps, breakfasts, smoothies and energy balls. Try the Vietnamese chicken salad or the salmon bruschetta. Great coffee too. Service is energetic and heartfelt.

Early Bird
CAFE $$

(☑07-4758 1195; www.facebook.com/theearlyb; 2/11 Pacific Dr, Horseshoe Bay; breakfasts $10-18, mains from $16; ⊙7am-2pm Fri-Tue) With a devoted local following, the Early Bird well deserves its place along the popular Horseshoe Bay cafe strip. There is a certain echo of paradise in having breakfast under a frangipani tree while gazing out upon a turquoise tropical sea. The Hawaiian French toast is almost as intriguing as the pear and ricotta bruschetta, and the halloumi and mango salad is pretty special too.

Gilligan's Cafe
CAFE $$

(☑07-4778 5313; www.facebook.com/Gilligans CafeBar; 2/5 Bright Ave, Arcadia; burgers $11-18; ⊙8am-3pm Wed-Sun) A fun, licensed cafe in Arcadia that pumps out massive breakfasts and the finest burgers on Maggie. The owners have a *Gilligan's Island* thing going on – most people pretend to have grown out of it, but secretly love the stroll down memory lane. Get stranded while you enjoy the decent booze selection over lunch.

Picnic Bay Hotel
PUB FOOD $$

(☑07-4778 5166; www.picnicbayhotel.com.au; 1 The Esplanade, Picnic Bay; mains $12-28; ⊙9.30am-10pm) There are worse places to settle in at for a drink than the very quiet Picnic Bay, with Townsville's city lights sparkling across the bay. There's an all-day grazing menu and huge salads. Wednesday is $14 schnitzel night.

ⓘ Getting There & Away

SeaLink (www.sealinkqld.com.au) runs an excellent ferry service to Magnetic Island from Townsville (return adult/child including all-day bus pass $33/16.50, 25 minutes). There's roughly one trip per hour between 5.30am and 11.30pm. All ferries arrive and depart Magnetic Island from the terminal at Nelly Bay.

Magnetic Island Ferries (www.magneticislandferry.com.au) operates a car ferry crossing eight times daily (seven on weekends) from the south side of Townsville's Ross Creek to Magnetic Island (35 minutes). It costs $226 (return) for a car and up to three passengers, and $28/16 (adult/child return) for foot passengers only. Bookings are essential and bicycles are transported free.

ⓘ Getting Around

Sunbus (www.sunbus.com.au/magnetic-island/) ploughs between Picnic and Horseshoe Bays, meeting all ferries and stopping at major accommodation places. A day pass covering all zones is $7.20, or you can include it in your ferry ticket price. Be sure to talk to the bus drivers, who love chatting about everything to do with the island.

Moke- ('topless' car) and scooter-rental places abound. You'll need to be over 21 years old, have a current driving licence and leave a credit-card deposit. Scooter hire starts at around $40 per day and Mokes at about $75. Try **Tropical Topless Car Rentals** (☑07-4758 1111; www.tropicaltopless.com; 138 Sooning St, Nelly Bay; ⊙8am-5pm) for a classic Moke, or **Roadrunner Scooter Hire** (☑07-4778 5222; 56a Kelly St, Nelly Bay; ⊙8.30am-5pm) for scooters and trail bikes.

Ingham & Around

POP 4426

Ingham is a cane-cutting centre with a proud Italian heritage, to go with the far longer history of the Nywaigi, the traditional owners of the land around Ingham. It's also the guardian of the 120-hectare **Tyto Wetlands** (☑07-4776 4792; www.tyto.com.au; Cooper St; ⊙8.45am-5pm Mon-Fri, 9am-4pm Sat & Sun), which has 4km of walking trails and attracts around 240 species of bird, including far-flung guests from Siberia and Japan. The locals – hundreds of agile wallabies – love it too, converging at dawn and dusk. The town is the jumping-off point for the majestic **Wallaman Falls** (https://parks.des.qld.gov.au/parks/girringun-wallaman); at 305m, it's the longest single-drop waterfall in Australia.

Mungalla Station (☑0428 710 907, 07-4777 8718; www.mungallaaboriginaltours.com.au; 2hr tours adult/child $75/40) 🍃, 15km east of Ingham, runs insightful Aboriginal-led tours, including boomerang throwing and stories

ORPHEUS ISLAND

Orpheus, the traditional homeland of the Manbarra people, is a heavenly 13-sq km island 80km north of Townsville, with a national park that's part of the Great Barrier Reef Marine Park. Its dry sclerophyll forest is a geographical anomaly this far north, one where bandicoots, green tree frogs, echidnas, ospreys and pesky feral goats roam free, the latter as part of a madcap 19th-century scheme to provide food for potential shipwreck survivors. Visitors gravitate towards the eucalyptus-scented hiking trails and crystal-clear snorkelling.

Part of the Palm Islands group, Orpheus is surrounded by magnificent fringing reef that's home to a mind-blowing collection of fish (1100 species) and a mammoth variety of both hard and soft corals. While the island is great for snorkellers and divers year-round (pack a stinger suit in summer), seasonal treats such as manta-ray migration (August to November) and coral spawning (mid-November) make the trip out here even more worthwhile.

Choose between two distinct worlds: stay at one of the flashiest **resorts** (☑07-4839 7937; www.orpheus.com.au; d incl full board from $1500) in all of Queensland or go bare-bones **camping** (☑bookings 13 74 68; https://qpws.usedirect.com/qpws; adult/family $6.55/26.20) at Yank's Jetty , Pioneer Bay or South Beach. The three campgrounds can be reached only by private boat; the first two have toilets and picnic tables.

There are no scheduled ferry services to Orpheus Island, which leaves two options. The first is to ask around the town of Lucinda to arrange a boat ride or water taxi over. **Absolute North Charters** (☑0419 712 577; return transfers $90-175) is a good place to start – it has an office in Lucinda but leaves from the Cardwell jetty. You'll need to arrange a pick-up time.

Otherwise, you might be able to get a ride with **SeaLink Queensland** (☑07-4726 0800; www.sealinkqld.com.au; half-day tours per adult/child/family from $119/89/359).

from the local Nywaigi culture, plus a traditional Kupmurri lunch.

In August the **Australian Italian Festival** (☑07-4776 5288; www.australianitalianfestival. com.au) celebrates the fact that 60% of Ingham residents are of Italian descent with the motto, 'eat, drink and celebrate'.

The poem that inspired the iconic Slim Dusty hit 'Pub With No Beer' (1957) was written in the **Lees Hotel** (☑07-4776 1577; www.leeshotel.com.au; 58 Lannercost St; s/d from $95/110; ❋⊜) by Ingham cane-cutter Dan Sheahan, after American soldiers drank the place dry. The en-suite rooms here are very comfortable, while the busy bistro does fine steak and pasta dishes (mains from $15).

Alternatively, you can camp at **Wallaman Falls** (☑13 74 68; sites per person/family $6.55/26.20) or stay at award-winning **Hinchinbrook Marine Cove Resort** (☑07-4777 8395; www.hinchinbrook-marine-cove-resort. com.au; 54 Dungeness Rd, Lucinda; d $145, bungalows $175, 3-bedroom apt $350; ❋▨).

Eating options are strong too: try the fantastic **JK's Delicatessen** (☑07-4776 2828; 78 Lannercost St; mains $5-16.50; ⊗8am-5pm Mon-Fri, 8.30am-2.30pm Sat; ☑), or **Enrico's @ Tyto** (☑07-4776 1109; https://enricosrestaurant. com.au/; 73 Mcilwraith St, Tyto Precinct; mains $29-38; ⊗6-9pm Tue-Sat), the town's best Italian.

Ingham sits along the Brisbane–Cairns train line. Services with **Queensland Rail's** (☑1300 131 722; www.queenslandrailtravel.com. au) *Spirit of Queensland* include Cairns ($50 to $95, five hours) and Brisbane ($207 to $495 for a sleeper, 20½ hours).

Cardwell

POP 1309

Unusually for much of Queensland's northern coast, the Bruce Hwy runs right by the coast at Cardwell, making it both busier and more accessible than most other coastal towns in these parts. For all the passing traffic, Cardwell is an appealing place with plenty of sand, a walkable foreshore and a jetty with uninterrupted views of Hinchinbrook Island. Travellers linger here for seasonal fruit picking – if you're looking for this kind of work, there are far worse places in the world to do it (check at the backpackers for information). For everyone else, sit back and enjoy one of the town's famous crab sandwiches while gazing out at the view. The Girramay are the land's traditional owners.

Traditional woven baskets, paintings and colourful wooden sculptures are among the works for sale at **Girringun Aboriginal Art Centre** (☑07-4066 8300; www.art.girringun. com.au; 235 Victoria St; ☺8.30am-5pm Mon-Thu, 9am-2pm Fri) 🏊, a cooperative of Aboriginal artists from nine different Indigenous groups that cover 25,000 sq km.

The **Rainforest & Reef Centre** (☑07-4066 8601; www.greatgreenwaytourism.com; 142 Victoria St; ☺8.30am-5pm Mon-Fri, 9am-1pm Sat & Sun), next to Cardwell's jetty, has an interactive rainforest display and detailed info on Hinchinbrook Island and other nearby national parks, while the **Historic Cardwell Post Office & Telegraph Station** (53 Victoria St; ☺10am-1pm Mon-Fri, 9am-noon Sat) FREE has withstood cyclones and termites since 1870.

Cardwell Beachcomber Motel & Tourist Park (☑07-4066 8550; www.cardwellbeachcomber.com.au; 43a Marine Pde; powered/unpowered sites $40/32, motel d $98-135, cabins & studios from $125; ❉@🐾🛜🛊) and **Cardwell Central Backpackers** (☑07-4066 8404; www.cardwellbackpackers.com.au; 6 Brasenose St; dm $25-28; @🛜🛊) are decent sleeping options, while **Vivia Cafe** (☑07-4066 8030; 135 Victoria St; mains $12-22; ☺7.30am-3.30pm Sat-Wed, to 7pm Thu & Fri) is the town's best.

Hinchinbrook Island

Australia's largest island national park (399 sq km) is a holy grail for walkers, particularly those tackling the challenging, three-to five-day **Thorsborne Trail** (www.npsr.qld. gov.au), but getting here requires advance planning. Granite mountains rise dramatically from the sea and wildlife creeps through the foliage. The mainland side is dense with lush tropical vegetation, while long sandy beaches and tangles of mangrove curve around the eastern shore. Hinchinbrook forms part of the traditional lands of the Biyaygiri people, who called the island Pouandai.

Camping is your only option and it's not for the rank novice – you'll need to come fully equipped and be self-sufficient. There are 12 campsites on the island, each costing $6.55/26.20 per site. See https://parks.des. qld.gov.au/parks/hinchinbrook/camping. html or call 13 74 68 for more details.

Hinchinbrook Island Cruises (☑0499 335 383; www.hinchinbrookislandcruises.com.au) runs a service from Cardwell to Hinchinbrook (one way per person $99, 1½ hours). It also operates a four-hour cruise to Hinchinbrook (per adult/child $110/99, minimum four people): book through Cardwell's Rainforest & Reef Centre.

Tully

POP 2390

It may look like just another sleepy sugarcane village, but Tully is a burg with a boast, calling itself the 'wettest town in Australia'. A gigantic golden gumboot at Tully's entrance is as high as the waters rose (7.9m) in 1950: climb the spiral staircase to the viewing platform up top to get a sense of just how much that is! And while boggy Babinda challenges Tully's claim, the fact remains that all that rain ensures plenty of raftable rapids on the nearby Tully River, and shimmering fruit farms in need of travelling labour.

Indigenous **Ingan Tours** (☑07-4068 0189; www.ingan.com.au; Bruce Hwy) visits sacred story places on its full-day Spirit of the Rainforest tours (Tuesdays, Thursdays and Saturdays).

Reinsdown Horse Riding (☑0438 375 989; https://reinsdown.com.au/; 75 Aerodrome Rd; 3hr trail rides $100; ☺8.30-11.30am & 1.30-4.30pm) takes small groups on trail rides through the surrounding rainforest.

🛏 Sleeping & Eating

Mount Tyson Hotel PUB $
(☑07-4068 1088; www.mttysonhotel.com.au; 23 Butler St; s/d $60/105; ❉🛜) This pub was renovated after Cyclone Yasi hit in 2011 and is a bit bland in terms of ambience, but the motel rooms are fresh and clean and provide good value for a short stay. You're also right in the heart of town.

Ripe Harvest Cafe CAFE $
(☑07-4068 0606; www.facebook.com/ripeharvest cafetully; shop 1, 18 Butler St; mains from $7; ☺5.30am-2pm Mon-Fri, 8am-noon Sat; 🍴) Fresh tastes and friendly service go nicely with the all-day breakfasts and premade lunches. It's all about healthy eating with plenty of vegetarian and gluten-free options, and an emphasis on organic, fresh produce straight from the farmer.

❶ Information

Tully Visitor & Heritage Centre (☑07-4068 2288; Bruce Hwy; ☺9am-4.30pm Mon-Fri, 9am-1pm Sat, 10am-1pm Sun) has a brochure outlining a self-guided heritage walk around

QUEENSLAND HINCHINBROOK ISLAND

PALUMA RANGE NATIONAL PARK

It's worth making time to venture off the Bruce Hwy via the Paluma Range National Park, southern gateway to the Wet Tropics World Heritage Area. The park is divided into two parts: the Mt Spec section and the northern Jourama Falls section. Both offer a variety of waterholes, inland beaches, hiking and mountain-biking trails, and a gentle introduction to tropical north Queensland. This glorious parallel universe, running alongside the Bruce Hwy from roughly Ingham to Townsville, is also prime platypus-spotting territory. The traditional owners of the park are the Nywaigi people.

Up in the tiny village of Paluma is the cool **Rainforest Inn** (☑ 07-4770 8688; www.rainforestinnpaluma.com; 1 Mt Spec Rd; d $125; ❄), with well-designed rooms and a nearby restaurant-bar.

Mt Spec

The Mt Spec part of the park (61km north of Townsville, 40km south of Ingham) is a misty Eden of rainforest and eucalyptus trees criss-crossed by a variety of walking tracks. This range of habitats houses an incredibly diverse population of birds, from golden bowerbirds to black cockatoos.

From the northern access route of the Bruce Hwy, take the 4km-long partially sealed Spiegelhauer Rd to **Big Crystal Creek**; from there, it's an easy 100m walk from the car park to **Paradise Waterhole**, a popular spot with a sandy beach and lofty mountain views. The combination of rocks and trees make a lovely backdrop, but we couldn't take our eyes off the transparent water when the sun came out. The **Big Crystal Creek Camping Ground** (☑ 13 74 68; https://parks.des.qld.gov.au/parks; sites per person/family $6.55/26.20) has gas BBQs, toilets, cold showers and picnic tables; get here early to secure a site.

The southern access route (Mt Spec Rd) is a sealed, albeit twisty, road that writhes up the mountains to **Paluma Village**. Beware: though you may have come up here 'just for a drive', the village's cool air and warm populace may tempt you to stay longer.

En route to Paluma, be sure to stop off at **Little Crystal Creek**, a picturesque swimming hole with a cute stone bridge, picnic area and waterfalls.

Jourama Falls

Waterview Creek tumbles down these eponymous falls, past palms and umbrella trees, making this northern section of the park a fine place for a picnic and a stroll. There's bush camping with no facilities in the area.

This part of the park is reached via a 6km sealed road (though the creek at the entrance can be impassable in the Wet), 91km north of Townsville and 24km south of Ingham. Be sure to fuel up before veering off the highway.

town, with 17 interpretative panels (including one dedicated to Tully's higher-than-average tally of UFO sightings), and walking-trail maps for the nearby national parks. The centre also has free wi-fi and a book exchange.

❶ Getting There & Away

Buses stop alongside Tully's Banyan Park on the Brisbane–Cairns route.

Greyhound (☑ 1300 473 946; www.greyhound.com.au) Cairns ($28, 2½ hours) and Townsville ($43, 3½ hours)

Premier (☑ 13 34 10; www.premierms.com.au) Cairns ($27, 2½ hours) and Townsville ($31, 3¼ hours)

Mission Beach

POP 815

The rainforest meets the Coral Sea at Mission Beach, a tropical enclave of beach hamlets that has long threatened to take the Australian getaway circuit by storm, but never quite gets overrun. Somehow, this Coral Sea bolthole has maintained a beautiful balance between yoga living, backpacker bravado and eco-escape, plus it has Australia's highest density of cassowaries – this is your best chance to see this extraordinary bird. Hidden among World Heritage rainforest, a short 30km detour from the Bruce Hwy, Mission Beach is also one of the closest access points to the Great Barrier Reef, and is the gateway to Dunk Island. These are the traditional lands of the Djiru people.

While Mission's coastline seems to scream 'toe dip!', don't just fling yourself into the water any old where: stick to the swimming enclosures, lest you have a nasty encounter with a marine stinger...or a croc.

🏃 Activities

There's white-water rafting on the Tully River or, if you've your own board, Bingil Bay is one of few spots inside the reef where it's possible to surf, with small, consistent 1m swells. Stinger enclosures at Mission Beach and South Mission Beach provide safe year-round swimming.

Local walking and cycling trails abound– pick up the *Rotary Mission Beach Walk & Ride Map* from the visitor centre (p397).

★ **Charley's Chocolate Tour** TOURS
(Charley's Chocolate Factory; ☑ 07-4068 5011; www.charleys.com.au; 388 Cassowary Dr, Mt Edna; adult/child/family $34/22/98; ⊙ 10.30am Thu & Sun) Follow the trail from cocoa tree to chocolate at this terrific chocolate factory, where you'll learn the history of chocolate, learn all about how chocolate is made and get to taste the final product. An Aussie Farm Lunch is included in the tour, and there's a shop where you can buy chocolate. Advance bookings essential.

Altitude Skydivers SKYDIVING
(☑ 07-4088 6635; www.altitudeskydive.com.au; 4/46 Porter Promenade; tandem jumps $399) This small, highly experienced and fun-loving jump team has very competitive pricing.

🛌 Sleeping

★ **Jackaroo Treehouse Hostel** HOSTEL $
(☑ 07-4210 6008; www.jackarootreehouse.com; 13 Frizelle Rd; sites $12-15, dm/d incl breakfast from $25/68; 🅿 @ 🛜 ⛱) Oh to be young enough to justify whiling away the days in a timber pole-frame retreat deep in the rainforest by a huge jungle pool overlooking the Coral Sea. Bugger it: just drive inland past Clump Mountain, find a quiet double room and wander around the communal areas granting silent, wise nods to those young rascals bronzing in the tropical sun.

Dunk Island View Caravan Park CARAVAN PARK $
(☑ 07-40688248; www.dunkislandviewcaravanpark.com; 21-35 Webb Rd, Wongaling Beach; sites $35, 1-/2-bedroom units $115/145; ❄ 🛜 ⛱ ⛱) One of the best caravan parks in northern Queensland; its views of Dunk Island are stupendous and the grounds are impeccably kept. The small pool is welcome in stinger season, and there's also an on-site cafe (fish and chips $11).

Sanctuary CABIN $
(☑ 07-4088 6064, 1800 777 012; www.sanctuaryatmission.com; 72 Holt Rd; dm $40, huts with shared bathroom from $65, cabins from $135; ⊙ mid-Apr–mid-Dec; @ 🛜 ⛱) 🍃 This popular group retreat centre is reached via a steep 600m-long rainforest walking track from the car park (4WD pick-up available). At Sanctuary you can sleep surrounded only by fly screen on a platform in a simple hut, or opt for an en-suite cabin where the shower has floor-to-ceiling rainforest views. Yoga, night walks and massage are all available to guests at a cost.

★ **Licuala Lodge** B&B $$
(☑ 07-4068 8194; www.licualalodge.com.au; 11 Mission Circle; s/d/tr incl breakfast from $120/140/190; 🛜 ⛱) You'll need your own car at this peaceful B&B 1.5km from the beach and pretty much everything else.

TULLY RIVER RAFTING

The Tully River provides thrilling white water year-round thanks to Tully's trademark downpours and the river's hydroelectric floodgates. Rafting trips are timed to coincide with the daily release of the gates, resulting in Grade IV rapids foaming against a backdrop of stunning rainforest scenery.

Day trips with **Raging Thunder Adventures** (☑ 07-4030 7990; www.ragingthunder.com.au; half-/full-day rafting $129/194) or **R'n'R White Water Rafting** (☑ 07-4041 9444; www.raft.com.au; full-day rafting from $185) include a BBQ lunch and transport from Tully or nearby Mission Beach. **Wildside Adventures** (☑ 07-4088 6212; www.wildsideadventures.com.au; half-/full-day rafting from $129/189) is another option out of Mission Beach.

BANANA FARM TOURS

Bananas are a mainstay of local life in these parts and where some towns in Australia build a Big Banana and call it an attraction, these two-hour **Banana Farm Tours** (☎ 07-4065 4823; www.bananafarmtours.com.au; 132 Cowley Creek Rd, Silkwood; adult/child/family $25/10/60; ☺ 9am Tue & Wed) go to the heart of the matter. It's a fantastic behind-the-scenes look at growing, harvesting and packing, with a light lunch to finish things off.

Guests alternate between the wonderful verandah, where a terrific breakfast can be taken overlooking landscaped gardens, and the swimming pool surrounded by a rock garden. Cassowaries pop by regularly to check out the scene. Sue and Mick are welcoming hosts.

Boutique Bungalows B&B $$
(☎ 07-4068 9996; www.boutiquebungalows.com.au; 3 Spurwood Cl, Wongaling Beach; bungalows $110-130; P ☺ ❋ ☎ ⛱) This welcoming B&B has large and stylish accommodation not far from Wongaling Beach. Steve and Sharon are welcoming hosts and travellers consistently give it the thumbs-up.

Hibiscus Lodge B&B B&B $$
(☎ 07-4068 9096; www.hibiscuslodge.com.au; 5 Kurrajong Cl; r $115-155; ☎) The main homestead of this charming Mission Beach property forms the backdrop for a local fauna roll-call. Hibiscus Lodge is a discerning choice; you can taste the self-satisfaction at the breakfast table. With only three (very private) rooms, bookings are essential. Generous online discounts are available. No kids.

★ Sejala CABIN $$$
(☎ 07-4088 6699; www.sejala.com.au; 26 Pacific Pde; d from $290; ❋ ⛱) Choose from 'Waves', 'Coral' and 'Beaches': three self-contained beach 'huts' within snoring sound of the coconut palms. Each one comes with rainforest shower, deck with private BBQ and loads of character. Perfect for hiding away with a partner.

Castaways Resort & Spa RESORT $$$
(☎ 07-4068 7444; www.castaways.com.au; Pacific Pde; d $124-279, 1-/2-bedroom apt $299/329;

❋ @ ☎ ⛱) Stare longingly out to sea from your apartment in this mainstay of the Mission Beach family-holiday scene. Travellers on a budget can play it smart in a simple rainforest room (from $124) and take advantage of the two elongated pools, a luxurious spa and stunning beach views from its tropical-style bar-restaurant. Come on Tuesday for tropical high tea.

✖ Eating

Shanti Cafe CAFE $
(☎ 0467 584 017; www.facebook.com/shanticafemissionbeach/; 37 Porter Promenade; mains $6-17; ☺ 7am-2pm) Arguably Mission Beach's best coffee, matched by a better-than-average range of breakfast choices and light lunches (artful pitta wraps), make this a classy choice.

★ Tusker's Tuckerbox AUSTRALIAN $$
(☎ 0414 395 164; www.tuskers.com.au; 154 Kennedy Esplanade, South Mission Beach; mains lunch from $16, dinner $18-48; ☺ noon-9pm Fri-Sun) Something of a South Mission Beach institution as the week winds down, Tusker's does beef rump enchilada, goat casserole and a range of steaks and burgers, sometimes with everything on one epic platter. Lunch options are much lighter.

★ Bingil Bay Cafe CAFE $$
(☎ 07-4068 7146; 29 Bingil Bay Rd; mains $19-32, pizzas $25; ☺ 7am-10pm; ☎) Sunshine, rainbows, coffee and gourmet grub make up the experience at this lavender landmark with a great porch for watching the world drift by. Breakfast is a highlight, but it's open all day. The tiger prawn and Spanish mackerel linguini is excellent, and the sirloin is well priced and deservedly popular. Regular art displays and live music ensure a creative clientele.

Garage AUSTRALIAN $$
(☎ 07-4088 6280; www.facebook.com/TheGarageMissionBeach; 41 Donkin Lane; share plates $8-26, pizzas $18-25; ☺ 5-10pm Wed-Sun; ❋ ☎) A hotspot in Mission with the 20-something set, the Garage is famous for its delicious sliders (mini burgers) and free-pour cocktails ($14). The hard-working chef mixes up the menu regularly and the management ensures there's a festive vibe in the beer garden, with an eclectic playlist and tapas specials.

Chippy FISH & CHIPS $$
(☎ 07-4088 6353; shop 1, 43 Porter Promenade; mains $12-16.50; ☺ 11am-7pm Wed & Thu, to

7.30pm Fri-Sun) Mission Beach's best fish and chips? Plenty of locals think so. The barra, a seafood basket or the tropical burger (with pineapple)? Take your pick – as Gwyneth would say, it's all good.

Pippi's on the Beach   SEAFOOD $$
(📞 07-4088 6150; 42 Donkin Lane; mains $26-41; 🕐 noon-2.30pm & 5-9.30pm Fri-Tue) This beach-front venue has the best beach views in Mission Beach (get here early for a front-row table). It serves up a small range of mains from tiger prawn risotto to twice-cooked pork belly.

★**PepperVine**   AUSTRALIAN $$$
(📞 07-4088 6538; https://peppervine.com.au/; shop 2, 4 David St; tapas from $12, mains $24-44; 🕐 4.30pm-late Mon, Thu & Fri, 10am-late Sat & Sun) On the Village Green, PepperVine is an uncomplicated contemporary restaurant borrowing from Italian, Spanish and Mod Oz culinary influences, and nailing atmosphere and service. Wood-fired pizza and a glass of Australian wine is the early evening staple; the fine dining (premium steaks) announces itself after sunset as the crowd descends.

🛍 Shopping

Between them, **Mission Beach Markets** (Porter Promenade; 🕐 8am-1pm 1st & 3rd Sun of month) and **Mission Beach Rotary Monster Market** (📞 07-4068 7220; Marcs Park, Cassowary Dr, Wongaling Beach; 🕐 7.30am-12.30pm last Sun of month Easter-Nov) operate three Sundays a month.

ℹ Information

Mission Beach Visitor Centre (📞 07-4068 7099; https://missionbeachtourism.com/; 55 Porter Promenade; 🕐 9am-5pm Mon-Sat, 10am-2pm Sun) The main visitor centre in town has reams of information in multiple languages.

Wet Tropics Environment Centre (📞 07-4068 7197; www.wettropics.gov.au; Porter Promenade; 🕐 10am-5pm Mon-Sat, to 2pm Sun) Next door to the Mission Beach Visitor Centre you'll find displays and movies about the local environment, including, of course, the cassowary.

THE CASSOWARY: ENDANGERED NATIVE

Like something out of *Jurassic Park*, this flightless prehistoric bird struts through the rainforest. It's as tall as a fully grown adult, has three razor-sharp, dagger-style clawed toes, a bright-blue head, red wattles (the lobes hanging from its neck), a helmetlike horn and shaggy black feathers similar to an emu's. Meet the cassowary, an important link in the rainforest ecosystem. It's the only animal capable of dispersing the seeds of more than 70 species of trees whose fruit is too large for other rainforest animals to digest and pass (the end product also acts as fertiliser).

It is estimated that there are anywhere between 1500 and 6000 cassowaries left in the wilds of northern Queensland. An endangered species, the cassowary's biggest threat is loss of habitat, and most recently the cause has been natural. Tropical Cyclone Yasi stripped much of the rainforest around Mission Beach bare, threatening the struggling population with starvation. The cyclone also left the birds exposed to the elements, and more vulnerable to dog attacks and cars as they venture out in search of food.

The Mission Beach area has the highest density of cassowaries in Australia, and you're most likely to see cassowaries in the wild around **South Mission Beach** (watch for them around the caravan park and along South Mission Beach Rd in particular), **Etty Bay** (where you might see them on the beach) and the Cape Tribulation section of the **Daintree National Park** (p432). Cassowaries, sometimes with young, frequently wander through the garden at Licuala Lodge (p395) in Mission Beach. Cassowaries can be aggressive, particularly if they have chicks, although attacks on human beings are extremely rare. Do not approach them; if one threatens you, don't run – give the bird right-of-way and try to keep something solid between you and it, preferably a tree.

Next to the Mission Beach Visitor Centre, there are cassowary conservation displays at the Wet Tropics Environment Centre, staffed by volunteers from the Community for Coastal & Cassowary Conservation (www.cassowaryconservation.asn.au). Proceeds from gift-shop purchases go towards buying cassowary habitat. The website www.savethecassowary.org.au is also a good source of info.

WORTH A TRIP

PARONELLA PARK

Set beside a series of creeks and water-falls 50km northwest of Mission Beach (and with at least one resident croc) is **Paronella Park** (☑ 07-4065 0000; www.paronellapark.com.au; 1671 Japoonvale Rd, Mena Creek; adult/child $46/25; ☺ 9am-7.30pm). This unusual tropical park is a romantic, Dalí-esque escape from reality. Day trippers wander dreamily among its moss-covered steps, lush tropical foliage and huge palatial structures straight from some Victorian-Mayan movie set. Tours run every hour, starting at 9.30am and with the last at 4.30pm.

❶ Getting There & Away

Greyhound (☑ 1300 473 946; www.greyhound.com.au) and **Premier** (☑ 13 34 10; www.premierms.com.au) buses stop in Wongaling Beach next to the 'big cassowary'. Fares with Greyhound/Premier are $26/20 to Cairns (2¼ hours) $44/47 to Townsville (3½ to four hours).
Mission Beach Dunk Island Water Taxi (☑ 07-4068 8310; www.missionbeachwatertaxi.com; Banfield Pde, Wongaling Beach; adult/child return $40/20, 3hr tours $50/25) makes the 20-minute trip from Mission Beach's Wongaling Beach to Dunk Island at 9am, 10am and 11am. Return trips are at noon, 3.30pm or by arrangement.

Dunk Island

Dunk is known to the Djiru people, the traditional owners of this land, as Coonanglebah (the island of peace and plenty). They're not wrong: this is pretty much your ideal tropical island, with lush jungle, white-sand beaches and impossibly blue water.

Walking trails criss-cross (and almost circumnavigate) Dunk: the **circuit track** (9.2km) is the best way to explore the island's interior and encounter wildlife. There's snorkelling over bommies (coral pinnacles or outcroppings) at **Muggy Muggy** and great swimming at beautiful **Coconut Beach**. On weekends in high season there are often special events such as bongo lessons or a ukulele band – check with the Mission Beach Visitor Centre (p397).

Dunk Island was battered by Cyclone Yasi in 2011 and tourist infrastructure has yet to recover: there are no places to eat or, apart from the campground, sleep. As late as 2018 the old resort remained off limits and a real eyesore.

~~Mission Beach Charters~~ (☑ 07-4068 7009; www.missionbeachcharters.com.au; adult/child return $40/20, 3hr tours $50) runs a shuttle and a range of camping, fishing and diving trips, and you can overnight at **Dunk Island Campground** (☑ 0417 873 390; per person/family $6.35/25.40).

Innisfail

POP 7775

Innisfail is a handsome, unhurried north Queensland town known for river fishing, farming and a remarkable collection of art-deco edifices. Only 80km south of Cairns, but not a tourist in sight, here you can join the locals on the wide Johnstone River, dodge tractors along the pretty main street, or discuss the fortunes of the North Queensland Cowboys rugby league team.

Relaxing, beachside **Flying Fish Point** is 8km northeast of Innisfail's town centre, while national parks, including the fun **Mamu Tropical Skywalk** (☑ 07-4064 5294; www.mamutropicalskywalk.com.au; Palmerston Hwy; adult/child/family $25/14/72; ☺ 9.30am-5.30pm, last entry 4.30pm) (a 2.5km, wheelchair-accessible walking circuit through the canopy), are within a short drive. Turn-offs south of town lead to different beach communities including exquisite **Etty Bay**, with its wandering cassowaries, rocky headlands, rainforest, large stinger enclosure and a simple but superbly sited caravan park.

These are the traditional lands of the Ma:Mu people, who still make up nearly 20% of the population.

Snapping Tours (☑ 0448 814 655; www.snappingtours.com.au; Fitzgerald Esplanade, Innisfail Jetty; adult/child/family $40/20/110; ☺ 8.30am, 10.30am, 3.30pm & 5.30pm) runs two-hour boat trips up the Johnstone River primarily in search of saltwater crocs.

Each March the tropical-food festival **Feast of the Senses** (☑ 0447 037 476; www.feastofthesenses.com.au) provides a highlight of the northern Queensland culinary calendar.

Although there are a couple of motels catering to a more general travelling public, Innisfail's hostels primarily cater to banana pickers working the surrounding plantations (they are also the places you should enquire with if you're looking for work); weekly rates average below $200 (for a bed in a dorm). The friendly and helpful visitor information centre (📞0428 228 962; www.tropicalcoasttourism.com.au/innisfail; Anzac Park, Bruce Hwy; ⊙9am-3pm Mon-Fri, to 1pm Sat) has a full list of accommodation options that can help with finding work.

Seafood is the order of the day in Innisfail, and there's a distinctly Italian influence in the modest local dining scene. Try the huge seafood baskets and breezy seaside setting at **Flying Fish Point Cafe** (📞07-4061 2180; 9 Elizabeth St, Flying Fish Point; mains $12-27; ⊙7.30am-8pm) or the European cheeses and smallgoods at local institution **Oliveri's Continental Deli** (📞07-4061 3354; www.oliverisdeli.com.au; 41 Edith St; sandwiches $8.50-11; ⊙8.30am-5.15pm Mon-Fri, to 12.30pm Sat; 🖉).

Innisfail to Cairns

Part of the Wet Tropics World Heritage Area, steamy, dreamy **Wooroonooran National Park's** (www.parks.des.qld.gov.au/parks/wooroonooran) Palmerston (Doongan) Section is home to some of the oldest continuously surviving rainforest in Australia; visit the website for details of campgrounds and walking trails.

On the traditional tribal lands of the Yidinji people, **Babinda** is a small working-class town on the highway about 60km south of Cairns. The main attraction is the **Babinda Boulders** (🖼) FREE, 7km inland, where a photogenic creek rushes between 4m-high granite rocks. There's free camping at **Babinda Boulders Camping Area** FREE.

CAIRNS & AROUND

Far North Queensland is a remote tropical adventure where the Great Barrier Reef is tantalisingly close. It's a cliché, but the rainforest really does meet the reef up here. Steamy Cairns is the main traveller base and an obligatory stop on any east-coast itinerary. Divers and snorkellers swarm here – and to more upmarket Port Douglas – for easy access to the Great Barrier Reef. The cooler Atherton Tablelands – with volcanic craters, jungly waterfalls and gourmet food producers – is a short, scenic drive inland.

Beyond Port Douglas is the mighty Daintree River, crossed by the charming cable ferry to Cape Tribulation – one of the world's last great wilderness areas. The road beyond heads to Cooktown and Cape York, a remote land where authentic Aboriginal culture can readily be experienced.

This region is the traditional home of numerous Aboriginal groups, including the Yirrganydji, Yidinji, Djabugay, Kuku Yalanji, Guugu Yimithirr and Djirrbal.

Cairns

POP 240,190

Cairns (pronounced 'cans') has come a long way since its humble beginnings as a boggy swamp and rollicking goldfields port. As the number-one base for Far North Queensland and the Great Barrier Reef, today Cairns heaves under the weight of an ever-growing number of resorts, tour agencies, souvenir shops, backpacker bars and reef boats. This is a tourist town, and unashamedly so – luxury hotel development in 2018 and an increasingly busy cruise-ship port suggest it's only growing busier.

The city centre is more boardshorts than briefcases, and you'll find yourself throwing away all notions of speed and schedules here, thanks to heady humidity and a hearty hospitality. There's no beach in town, but spend time at the Esplanade lagoon or the Pier marina and you'll understand why many travellers fall for Cairns.

◉ Sights

Cairns has plenty of attractions that don't involve the reef or adventure, including a thriving arts and cultural scene. Check out Cairns Arts & Culture Map (www.cairnsartsandculturemap.com.au) for more information.

★Cairns Esplanade,
Boardwalk & Lagoon   WATERFRONT
(www.cairns.qld.gov.au/esplanade;   ⊙lagoon 6am-9pm Thu-Tue, noon-9pm Wed; 🖼) FREE
Sunseekers and fun-lovers flock to Cairns Esplanade's spectacular swimming lagoon on the city's reclaimed foreshore. The artificial, sandy-edged, 4800-sq-metre saltwater pool with its *Woven Fish* sculptures, is lifeguard patrolled and illuminated nightly. The adjacent 3km foreshore boardwalk has picnic areas, birdwatching vantage points, free barbecues and fitness equipment. Follow the signposts for the excellent **Muddy's** which has playgrounds and water fun for little kids, and the skate ramp, beach volleyball courts, bouldering park and Fun Ship playground.

QUEENSLAND CAIRNS

Cairns

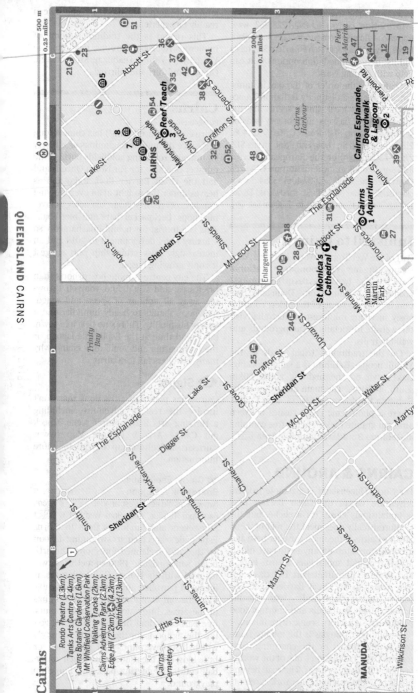

Rondo Theatre (1.3km);
Tanks Arts Centre (1.4km);
Cairns Botanic Gardens (1.6km);
Mt Whitfield Conservation Park
Walking Tracks (2km);
Cairns Adventure Park (2.1km);
Edge Hill (2.2km);
Smithfield (13km)

Cairns
Cemetery

MANUDA

Trinity
Bay

Cairns Harbour

Pier
14 Marina

Cairns Esplanade,
Boardwalk
& Lagoon

Cairns
Aquarium

St Monica's
Cathedral

Munro
Martin
Park

CAIRNS

Reef Teach

Enlargement

★**Cairns Aquarium** AQUARIUM

(☎07-4044 7300; www.cairnsaquarium.com.
au; 5 Florence St; adult/child/family $42/28/126;
⊗9am-5.30pm; ⊕) Cairns' multi-million-
dollar aquarium opened in mid-2017, with a
vast range of marine life, the Great Barrier
Reef in miniature and unique experiences
such as 'sleeping with the sharks'. Fittingly
the displays focus on the marine habitats of
Far North Queensland – not only the reef,
but also rivers, estuaries and billabongs.

Free talks and shows are held throughout
the day, covering everything from sea turtles
to reef conservation.

★**Reef Teach** CULTURAL CENTRE

(☎07-4031 7794; www.reefteach.com.au; 2nd fl,
Mainstreet Arcade, 85 Lake St; adult/child/family
$23/14/60; ⊗lectures 6.30-8.30pm Mon, Wed, Fri)
Take your knowledge to new depths at
this fun, informative centre, where marine
experts explain how to identify specific species of fish and coral, and how to approach
the reef respectfully.

★**Cairns Botanic Gardens** GARDENS

(☎07-4032 6650; www.cairns.qld.gov.au/cbg; 64
Collins Ave; ⊗grounds 7.30am-5.30pm, visitor centre 9am-4.30pm Mon-Fri, 10am-2.30pm Sat & Sun;
⊕) FREE These gorgeous gardens are an
explosion of greenery and rainforest plants.
Highlights include a section devoted to Aboriginal plant use, the **Gondwana Heritage
Garden**, the **Flecker Garden** and an excellent conservatory filled with butterflies and
exotic flowers. Visitor centre staff can advise
on free guided walks (daily from 10am).

Follow the **Rainforest Boardwalk** to Saltwater Creek and Centenary Lakes, a bird-
watcher's delight. Uphill from the gardens,
Mt Whitfield Conservation Park (www.
cairns.qld.gov.au; Edge Hill) has walking tracks
through the rainforest to city viewpoints.

★**Tjapukai Aboriginal
Cultural Park** CULTURAL CENTRE

(☎07-4042 9999; www.tjapukai.com.au; Cairns
Western Arterial Rd; adult/child/family $62/42/166;
⊗9am-4.30pm & 7-9.30pm; ⊕) Man-
aged by the area's original custodians, this
award-winning cultural extravaganza tells
the story of creation using giant holograms
and actors. There's a dance theatre, a gallery,
boomerang- and spear-throwing demonstrations and turtle-spotting canoe rides. The
Nightfire dinner-and-show package (adult/
child/family $123/75/321, from 7pm to
9.30pm) culminates in a fireside corroboree.

Cairns

◎ **Top Sights**
1 Cairns Aquarium E4
2 Cairns Esplanade, Boardwalk &
   Lagoon F4
3 Reef Teach F2
4 St Monica's Cathedral E4

◎ **Sights**
5 Cairns Art Gallery G1
6 Cairns Museum F2
7 KickArts Contemporary Arts F1
8 Samurai Gallery F1

● **Activities, Courses & Tours**
9 Cairns Dive Centre G1
10 Cairns Zoom & Wildlife Dome G5
11 Deep Sea Divers Den C5
12 Falla Reef Trips G4
13 Flyboard Cairns G5
14 GBR Helicopters G4
   Great Adventures .... (see 15)
15 Hot Air Cairns G5
16 Kuranda Scenic Railway E6
17 Mike Ball Dive Expeditions G5
18 Muddy's E3
19 NQ Watersports G4
20 Pro-Dive E6
21 Raging Thunder G1
   Reef Encounter .... (see 7)
   Reef Magic .... (see 15)
   Savannahlander .... (see 16)
22 Sunlover Reef Cruises G5
23 Tusa Dive G1

◎ **Sleeping**
24 201 Lake Street D3
25 Bay Village Tropical Retreat D3
26 Bounce F2
27 Cairns Girls Hostel E4
28 Cairns Plaza Hotel E3
29 Cairns Sharehouse D6
30 Caravella Backpackers E3
31 Doubletree by Hilton E4
32 Gilligan's Backpacker's Hotel &
   Resort F2
33 Pacific Hotel G5
34 Travellers Oasis E6

◎ **Eating**
   Bayleaf Balinese Restaurant .... (see 25)
   Bushfire Flame Grill .... (see 33)
35 Corea Corea G2
36 Fusion Art Bar & Tapas G2
37 Ganbaranba G2
38 Jafflehead G2
39 Night Markets F4
   Ochre .... (see 15)
   Perrotta's at the Gallery .... (see 5)
40 Prawn Star G4
   Roti Shack .... (see 7)
   Spicy Bite .... (see 23)
41 The Chambers G2

◎ **Drinking & Nightlife**
42 Bang & Grind G2
43 Cape York Hotel E6
44 Conservatory Bar G6
   Gilligan's .... (see 32)
45 Green Ant Cantina E6
46 Hemingway's Cairns G6
47 Salt House G4
48 The Jack F3
49 Three Wolves G1

◎ **Entertainment**
   Centre of Contemporary Arts .... (see 7)
   Reef Hotel Casino .... (see 10)

◎ **Shopping**
50 Cairns Central Shopping Centre E6
51 Doongal Aboriginal Art G1
52 Rusty's Markets F2

◎ **Transport**
53 Cairns Cooktown Express E6
54 Cairns Transit Mall F2
55 Interstate Coach Terminal G5
   John's Kuranda Bus .... (see 54)
   Trans North .... (see 53)

★ **St Monica's Cathedral** CATHEDRAL
(☑ 07-4046 5620; www.cairns.catholic.org.au; 183 Abbott St; ☺ 7am-5pm Mon-Fri, 7am-8pm Sat, 6am-6pm Sun) FREE Cairns' main Catholic church is famous for its themed stained-glass windows, the largest of their type in the world. There are 24 windows depicting the creation story from Genesis and another series known as the Peace Windows, commemorating the end of World War II.

Cairns Museum MUSEUM
(☑ 07-4051 5582; www.cairnsmuseum.org.au; cnr Lake & Shields St; adult/child $10/5; ☺ 10am-4pm Mon-Sat) The Cairns Museum reopened in 2017 after a contemporary renovation with four galleries covering the history of Cairns and Far North Queensland in pictures, exhibits and local stories. Also here is the Cairns Historical Society research centre.

Australian Armour & Artillery Museum MUSEUM
(☑ 07-4038 1665; www.ausarmour.com; 2 Skyrail Dr, Smithfield; adult/child/family $25/15/65; ☺ 9.30am-4.30pm) Military and history buffs will love the largest display of armoured vehicles and artillery in the southern

hemisphere. Go for a ride in a tank (adult/child $15/10, 11am and 2pm) or fire off bolt-action rifles in the underground bunker (from $80).

Crystal Cascades WATERFALL
(via Redlynch) FREE About 14km from Cairns, the Crystal Cascades is a series of beautiful waterfalls and idyllic, croc-free swimming holes that locals would rather keep to themselves. The area is accessed by a 1.2km (30-minute) pathway. Crystal Cascades is linked to Lake Morris (the city's reservoir) by a steep rainforest walking trail (allow three hours return); it starts near the picnic area. There is no public transport to the pools. Drive to the suburb of Redlynch, then follow the signs.

🏃 Activities

★ Cairns Zoom & Wildlife Dome ADVENTURE SPORTS, WILDLIFE
(☑07-4031 7250; www.cairnszoom.com.au; Wharf St; wildlife entry adult/child $24/12, wildlife & zoom from $45/28; ⊙9am-6pm; 🖐) Cards, croupiers and...crocodiles? Sitting on top of the Reef Hotel Casino (☑07-4030 8888; www.reefcasino.com.au; ⊙9am-5am Fri & Sat, to 3am Sun-Thu), this unusual park brings the best of Far North Queensland's outdoors inside, under a giant atrium, with a native-creatures zoo, aviary and recreated rainforest. The complex is criss-crossed with zip lines, swings, obstacle courses and more; the truly adventurous can even venture outside for a nerve-testing dome climb.

★ Skyrail Rainforest Cableway CABLE CAR
(☑07-4038 5555; www.skyrail.com.au; cnr Cook Hwy & Cairns Western Arterial Rd, Smithfield; adult/child one way from $53/26.50, return $79/39.50; ⊙9am-5.15pm; 🖐) 🖉 At 7.5km long, Skyrail is one of the world's longest gondola cableways, offering a bird's-eye view over the tropical rainforest between Cairns and Kuranda. Allow about 90 minutes for the one-way trip, including two stops en route, featuring rainforest boardwalks with interpretive panels and lookouts over the mighty Barron Falls.

★ Kuranda Scenic Railway RAIL
(☑07-4036 9333; www.ksr.com.au; adult/child one way from $50/25, return from $76/38; 🖐) Winding 34km from Cairns to Kuranda through picturesque mountains, the track used by the Kuranda Scenic Railway was completed in 1891: workers dug tunnels by hand, battling sickness, steep terrain and venomous

creatures. The two-hour pleasure trip includes seating in heritage-style carriages, audio commentary, souvenir trip guide and a stop at the Barron Falls viewing platform.

Trains depart Cairns Central train station (p417) at 8.30am and 9.30am daily, returning from the delightful, flower-strewn Kuranda station at 2pm and 3.30pm. Kuranda Scenic Railway and Skyrail offer combination tickets.

Smithfield Mountain Bike Park MOUNTAIN BIKING
(https://parks.des.qld.gov.au) Smithfield Mountain Bike Park, 20km north of Cairns, is a world-class championship course with more than 30 linked cross-country trails graded easy, intermediate, difficult and extreme. This is also home to the Cairns Mountain Bike Club.

Sugarworld WATER PARK
(☑07-4055 5477; https://sugarworldwaterpark.com.au; Hambledon Dr, Edmonton; adult/child/family $19.75/16.75/61.50; ⊙10am-4pm Sat & Sun, open daily during Qld school holidays; 🖐) Beat the heat at this locally loved weekend water park, with three big water slides and an excellent collection of pools and interactive splashy play areas for children; the littlies will also get a kick out of Sugarworld's many wandering peacocks. There's a food kiosk on-site, or make use of the barbecue facilities. It's a 15-minute drive south from Cairns.

Cairns Adventure Park ADVENTURE SPORTS
(☑07-4053 3726; www.cairnsadventurepark.com.au; Lot 82 Aeroglen Dr, Aeroglen; packages $39-146; ⊙9am-5pm) Zip-line, rock climb or abseil in rainforest surrounds with views to the sea as breathtaking as the high-energy activities themselves. For something a little more sedate, Cairns Adventure Park also offers bushwalks and birdwatching. Contact the office about pick-ups from your accommodation; it's opposite Cairns Airport (p417).

Hot Air Cairns BALLOONING
(☑07-4039 9900; www.hotair.com.au/cairns; Reef Fleet Terminal; 30min flights adult/child from $260/229) Balloons take off from Mareeba to float through dawn over the Atherton Tablelands. Prices include return transfers from Cairns. These trips are worth the 4am wake-up call.

Skydive Cairns ADVENTURE
(☑1300 821 628; www.skydive.com.au/cairns; 52-54 Fearnley St; tandem jumps $199-309) Tandem

jumps from 4500m or 2100m with serene views of the reef and rainforest. Transfers available from accommodation in Cairns or Port Douglas.

Dive Courses & Trips

Cairns, the scuba-dive capital of the Great Barrier Reef, is a popular place to attain Professional Association of Diving Instructors (PADI) open-water certification. A staggering number of courses (many multilingual) are available; check inclusions thoroughly. All operators require you to have a dive medical certificate, which they can arrange (around $60).

Keen, certified divers should look for specialised dive opportunities such as night diving, annual coral spawning, and trips to Cod Hole, near Lizard Island, one of Australia's premier diving locations. Recommended dive schools and operators include the following:

Mike Ball Dive Expeditions (☑ 07-4053 0500; www.mikeball.com; 3 Abbott St; 3-night Cod Hole $1939, 7-night liveaboard safari from $3910, PADI courses from $395)

Tusa Dive (☑ 07-4047 9100; www.tusadive. com; cnr Shields St & Esplanade; adult/child day trips from $215/140, introductory dive $285/210)

Cairns Dive Centre (CDC; ☑ 07-4051 0294; www.cairnsdive.com.au; 121 Abbott St; liveaboard 1-/2-nights from $435/555, day trips from $120, dive courses from $520)

Deep Sea Divers Den (☑ 07-4046 7333; www.diversden.com.au; 319 Draper St; day trips from $140)

Pro-Dive (☑ 07-4031 5255; www.prodive cairns.com.au; 116 Spence St; day trips from $226, PADI courses from $975)

Water Sports

From jetpack jaunts and jet-ski tours to river tubing and stand-up paddling, there are plenty of ways to get wet and wild in Cairns. Take the plunge with these recommended operators:

Aussie Drifterz (☑ 07-4031 3460; www.aussie drifterz.com.au; 19-21 Barry St; tubing adult/child $84/64)

Flyboard Cairns (☑ 0439 386 955, 0487 921 714; 30/60min session $169/299)

NQ Watersports (☑ 0411 739 069; www.nq watersports.com.au; B-Finger, Pier Marina; jet-ski croc tours solo/tandem $190/260)

What'SUP (☑ 0435-836 282; www.whatsup cairns.com.au)

Cairns Wake Park (☑ 07-4038 1304; www.cairnswakepark.com; Captain Cook Hwy, Smithfield; adult/child per hour $39/34, per day $74/69; ☺ 10am-6pm)

CORAL BLEACHING

Like coral reefs all around the world, the Great Barrier Reef is facing some big environmental challenges. Around the turn of the last century (1998 and 2002) and again in 2016, spikes in water temperature around the GBR caused the densely packed zooxanthellae to go into metabolic overdrive, producing free radicals and other chemicals that are toxic to the coral host. The corals' response was to expel their zooxanthellae, to rid themselves of the damaging toxins. Water temperatures must return to normal before the small numbers of remaining zooxanthellae start to reproduce and thus reinstate the corals' live-in food factory. But if the heat wave persists for more than a few weeks, the highly stressed corals succumb to disease and die, their skeletons soon becoming carpeted with fine, shaggy algal turfs. This is known as coral bleaching.

It takes one to two decades for a healthy coral reef to bounce back after being wiped out. So far, damaged GBR sites have shown remarkable resilience, but the future might not be so rosy, as more frequent events driven by climate change repeatedly decimate reefs before they can fully recover. In other parts of the world, some reefs have suffered the added insults of decades of pollution and overfishing. By those means, former coral areas have become persistent landscapes of rubble and seaweed.

It is an unfortunate reality that damaged reefs are easier to find now than they were 30 years ago, but the GBR is still one of the best places in the world to see coral reefs, especially if you have one of the hundreds of accredited tourism operators show you around. Like every reef around the world, the GBR is in trouble, but scientists, reef managers, coastal residents and even visitors are joining forces to help the reef through the challenges of the century ahead.

TANYA PUNTTI/SHUTTERSTOCK ©

The Great Barrier Reef

Each year, more than 1.6 million visitors experience the World Heritage–listed Great Barrier Reef – a brilliant underwater ecosystem that traces 2000km of Australia's coastline. However you experience it, expect to hear more about the challenges the reef faces and ways you can help protect this world asset for generations to come.

Contents
➡ Gateways to the Reef
➡ Top Reef Encounters
➡ Nature's Theme Park

Above A clownfish emerges from a sea anemone

MATT MUNRO/LONELY PLANET ©

1. Snorkelling off Port Douglas (p427) **2.** Townsville (p383)
3. A sunset beach stroll in Cairns (p399) **4.** Heart reef, the
Whitsundays (p377)

AUTAU/SHUTTERSTOCK ©

Gateways to the Reef

There are numerous ways to approach this massive technicolour wonder: head to a gateway town and join an organised tour; sign up for a multi-day sailing or diving trip exploring the reef's less-travelled outer reaches; or fly to a remote island, where you'll have the reef largely to yourself.

Cairns

The most popular gateway to the reef, Cairns has dozens of operators offering snorkelling day trips and multi-day reef explorations on live-aboard vessels. Ask about passenger numbers and onboard facilities before choosing a tour.

Port Douglas

An hour's drive north of Cairns, Port Douglas is an affluent beach town with great dining and accommodation options. From here, diving and snorkelling boats head to over a dozen sites, including outer reefs like Agincourt Reef.

Southern Reef Islands

For an idyllic getaway off the tourist trail, book a trip to one of the remote islands on the southern edge of the Great Barrier Reef. Look forward to fantastic snorkelling and diving right off the beach.

The Whitsundays

Fringed by turquoise waters, coral gardens and palm-backed beaches, the Whitsundays are a heaven-sent archipelago. Base yourself on an island, tour the islands on a self-skippered sailing boat, or stay at Airlie Beach on the mainland and island-hop on a day trip.

Townsville

Australia's largest tropical city is a fair hike from the outer reef (2½ hours by boat), but it has other virtues: access to Australia's best wreck dive, SS *Yongala*, an excellent aquarium and marine-themed museums, plus several live-aboard dive boats embarking on multi-day trips.

Top Reef Encounters

For an up-close look at this wet spectacle, slip on a mask and some fins and jump in. Glass-bottomed boats are fine if you want to stay dry, but to fully engage with the reef you have to get underwater. Other options include scenic flights and land-based reef walks.

Diving & Snorkelling

The classic way to see the Great Barrier Reef is to clamber aboard a catamaran and explore several coral-clad spots on a long day trip. Nothing quite compares to that first hyper-coloured underwater moment, whether diving or snorkelling.

Reef Walking

Around the southern sections of the Great Barrier Reef, many reefs are exposed at low tide. Visitors can walk across the reef tops on sandy tracks between living coral – a fabulous way to learn about reef life, especially with a naturalist guide by your side.

Sailing

Sailing off on a yacht is a great way to beat the crowds and check out some spectacular reef scenery. Experienced mariners can hire a bareboat; others can join a sailing tour – both are easily arranged from Airlie Beach or Port Douglas.

Scenic Flights

Get a bird's-eye perspective on the vast coral reef and its islands onboard a scenic flight. Sign up for a helicopter tour from Cairns, or a seaplane tour (particularly memorable over the Whitsundays).

Semi-submersibles

A growing number of reef operators (especially around Cairns) offer semi-submersible or glass-bottomed boat tours, which give cinematic views of coral, rays, fish, turtles and sharks – without you ever having to get wet.

1. A school of sweetlip emporers 2. Stony coral
3. Whitsunday Island (p378) 4. Snorkelling the reef

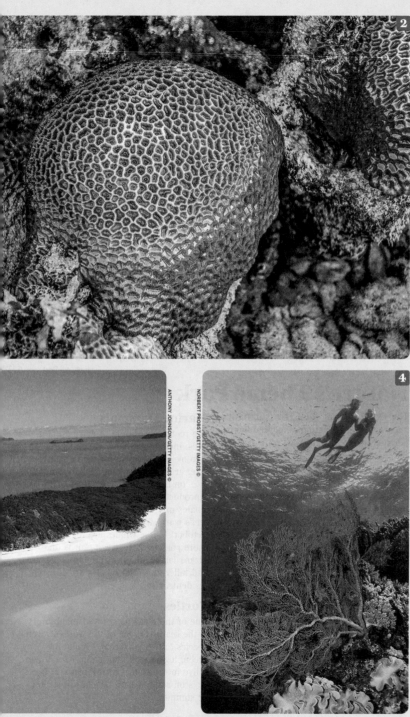

Turtle off Lady Elliot Island (p362)

Nature's Theme Park

The Great Barrier Reef is a submarine spectacular – an astoundingly biodiverse ecosystem. You'll find 30-plus species of marine mammals here, along with countless species of fish, coral, molluscs and sponges. Above the water, 200 bird species and 118 butterfly species have been recorded on reef islands and cays.

Fish

Common reef fish species include dusky butterfly fish, which are a rich navy blue with sulphur-yellow noses and back fins; large graphic turkfish, with luminescent pastel coats; teeny neon damsels, with darting flecks of electric blue; and six-banded angelfish, with blue tails, yellow bodies and tiger stripes. Rays including the spotted eagle ray are often seen gliding about.

Marine Mammals

The reef is also home to marine mammals, including whales, dolphins and dugongs. Dugongs are listed as vulnerable: around 15% of the global population lives on the Great Barrier Reef. With reproduction on their minds, humpback whales migrate from Antarctica to the reef's warm waters between May and October. Minke whales are regular offshore passers-by between Cairns and Lizard Island in June and July. Porpoises and killer and pilot whales are also reef residents.

Turtles

One of the reef's most-loved inhabitants is the sea turtle. Six of the world's seven species (all endangered) – including green, loggerhead and leatherback turtles – live in the waters of the reef and lay eggs on sandy island beaches in spring or summer.

🗘 Tours

A staggering 800-plus tours drive, chug, sail and fly out of Cairns daily, making the selection process almost overwhelming. We recommend operators with years of experience, who cover the bases of what visitors are generally looking for. Shop around for special deals. Most offer transfers to/from your accommodation.

★ **Behana Canyoning**   OUTDOORS
(☑07-4030 7940; www.behanacanyoning.com; tours $179) Give the salty stuff a break and join this fantastic freshwater expedition to beautiful Behana Gorge, a rainforest oasis of pools, waterfalls and canyons 45 minutes south of Cairns. The all-day tours include abseiling, ziplining, cliff jumping, snorkelling and swimming; you'll be shown the ropes (literally) on the day. Transfers and lunch included.

★ **Savannahlander**   RAIL
(☑07-4053 6848; www.savannahlander.com.au; tours adult/child from $380/260) All aboard for Woop Woop! This classic 1960s train chugs out of Cairns or Almadan on a variety of overnight and multiday outback tours to Chillagoe, Mt Surprise and Forsayth. Tours include the three-day Savannah Rail Runner from Cairns to Forsayth.

Billy Tea Safaris   OUTDOORS
(☑07-4032 0077; www.billytea.com.au; day trips $175-205) 🖉 This reliable bunch offers comprehensive 4WD small-group day trips to Cape Trib, the Tablelands and Chillagoe, as well as multiday safaris.

On the Wallaby   OUTDOORS
(☑07-4033 6575; www.onthewallaby.com; day tours $40-109) Excellent activity-based tours of the Tablelands' rainforests and waterfalls including swimming, cycling, hiking and canoeing. Based in Yungaburra but has daily morning pick-ups from Cairns.

Catcha Crab Tours   FISHING
(☑07-4051 7992; www.cairnscatchacrab.com.au; adult/child $95/75; 🖼) These long-running tours not only offer visitors the chance to catch tasty mud crabs, but are also a relaxing way to take in the mangroves and mudflats of Trinity Inlet. The four-hour tours, which include morning or afternoon tea plus a fresh crab lunch, depart at 8.30am and 1pm. There are free pick-ups if you're staying in the city centre.

GBR Helicopters   SCENIC FLIGHTS
(☑07-4081 8888; www.gbrhelicopters.com.au; Helipad, Pierpoint Rd; flights per person from $189) Offers a range of scenic helicopter flights, from a 10-minute soar above Cairns city to an hour-long hover over the reef and rainforest ($699).

Foaming Fury   RAFTING
(☑07-4031 3460; www.foamingfury.com.au; 19-21 Barry St; half-/full-day trips from $138/200; 🖼) Full-day trips on the Russell River, and half-day trips down the Barron. Prices include transfers and pick-up. Family rafting and multiday package options are also available.

Great Barrier Reef

Reef trips generally include transport, lunch, stinger-suits and snorkelling gear. When choosing a tour, consider the vessel type, its capacity, inclusions and destination: outer reefs are more pristine but further afield; inner reefs can be patchy and show signs of decay. Some prefer smaller, less-crowded vessels, while others go for the wide range of inclusions bigger boats promise.

Vendors with their own pontoon offer all-round value. Pontoons are a great way for families to experience the reef – those who aren't keen on getting in the water can enjoy the pontoon's facilities, or a trip in a glass-bottomed boat or semi-submersible.

Almost all boats depart from the Marlin Wharf – with check-in and booking facilities inside the **Reef Fleet Terminal** (Pierpoint Rd) – around 8am, returning around 6pm. Smaller operators may check-in boat-side at their berth on the wharf itself; check with your operator.

★ **Reef Magic**   DIVING, SNORKELLING
(☑07-4031 1588; www.reefmagiccruises.com; Reef Fleet Terminal; adult/child/family day trips from $220/110/557; 🖼) A long-time family favourite, Reef Magic's high-speed catamaran sails to its all-weather Marine World pontoon moored on the edge of the outer reef. If you're water shy, try a glass-bottomed boat ride, chat with the marine biologist or have a massage!

★ **Falla Reef Trips**   BOATING, SNORKELLING
(☑0400 195 264; www.fallareeftrips.com.au; D-Finger, Marlin Marina; adult/child/family from $145/90/420, intro dives $85) Reach the reef in inimitable style on this graceful 1950s pearl lugger. The tours, which spend time at Coral Gardens and Upolu Cay, have an exclusive

SEX ON THE REEF

If you're a keen diver or just a romantic at heart, try to time your visit with the annual coral spawning, an all-in orgy in which reef corals simultaneously release millions of eggs and sperm into the water. The ejaculatory event has been described as looking like a psychedelic snowstorm, with trails of reproductive matter streaking the sea in rainbow colours visible from miles away.

The spawning occurs sometime in November or December; the exact date depends on factors including water temperature (must be 26°C or above), the date of the full moon, the stillness of the water and the perfect balance between light and dark (who doesn't appreciate a bit of mood lighting?). Most Cairns-based diving outfits offer special spawning night dives for those looking to get in on the action. Even if you're on land, you may notice an, um, 'amorous' aroma on the night of the mass love-in.

feel. There's a maximum of 22 guests (who can help with the sailing), personalised snorkel tours and the old-school boat is the polar opposite of the sleek fibreglass vessels bobbing elsewhere on the reef.

Reef Encounter　　DIVING, SNORKELLING
(☑ 07-4037 2700; http://reefencounter. com.au; 100 Abbott St; 2-day live-aboards from $695) If one day on the reef isn't enough, try an overnight 'reef sleep' with Reef Encounter. Twenty-seven air-conditioned en-suite cabins accommodate a maximum of 42 guests; you don't even have to snorkel or dive to appreciate this floating hotel. A wide range of programs, including meals and daily departures from Cairns, make this excellent value for those wanting something a little different.

✦✦ Festivals & Events

Cairns Show　　CARNIVAL
(https://cairnsshow.com.au; Bruce Hwy, Cairns Showgrounds; ☉ Jul) Three days of carnival rides, agricultural exhibits, enthralling events (dancing diggers and wood-chopping competitions) and all the deep-fried delights and fairy floss you can stomach. The last day of the Show is a public holiday in Cairns.

Cairns Festival　　FAIR
(www.cairns.qld.gov.au/festival; ☉ end Aug-early Sep) The Cairns Festival takes over the city with a packed program of performing arts, visual arts, music and family events.

🛏 Sleeping

Families and groups should check out **Cairns Holiday Homes** (☑ 0438 134173; www. cairnsholidayhomes.com.au). If you plan to stick around for a while for work, **Cairns Sharehouse** (☑ 07-4041 1875; www.cairns-sharehouse.

com; 17 Scott St; per week $120-260; ❄ 🛜 🍴) has around 200 long-stay rooms strewn across the city.

★**Caravella Backpackers**　　HOSTEL $
(☑ 07-4051 2431; www.caravella.com.au; 149 Esplanade; dm $17-22, s/d $58/63, d with bathroom $73-83; ❄ 🛜 🍴) Caravella nicely blurs the lines between backpacker hostel and budget guesthouse – if you don't want a dorm bed there's a good range of clean, private rooms available and it's not a 20-something party joint. Add a nice pool and common area, cheerful staff and waterfront location for a winning combination.

★**Cairns Coconut Holiday Resort**　　CARAVAN PARK $
(☑ 07-4054 6644; www.coconut.com.au; cnr Bruce Hwy & Anderson Rd, Woree; powered/unpowered sites $37/35, cabins/villas/condos from $119/159/239; 🅿 ❄ 🛜 🍴) If you're travelling with kids and don't mind being a bit out of town (8km), this holiday park is a destination unto itself. It's got a massive water park, two pools with slides, playgrounds, a humungous jumping pillow, tennis courts, minigolf, spas, an outdoor cinema and much more, all spread over 11 immaculate hectares.

★**Travellers Oasis**　　HOSTEL $
(☑ 07-4052 1377; www.travellersoasis.com.au; 8 Scott St; dm/s/d from $29/60/70; 🅿 ❄ @ 🛜 🍴) Folks love this little hippy hostel, hidden away in a side street behind Cairns Central Shopping Centre. It's intimate, inviting and less party-centric than many of Cairns' other offerings. A range of room types – from three-, four- and six-bed dorms to single, twin and deluxe double rooms – are available. Air-conditioning is $1 for three hours.

★ **Tropic Days**   HOSTEL $
(☑ 07-4041 1521; www.tropicdays.com.au; 28 Bunting St, Bungalow; camping per person $15, tents $18, dm/d from $18/56; P ✴ @ ⓢ ☒) Tucked behind the showgrounds (with a courtesy bus into town), this popular hostel has a tropical garden with hammocks, pool table, bunk-free dorms, fresh linen and towels, free wi-fi and a relaxed vibe. Its Monday night croc, emu and roo barbecues are legendary. Air-conditioning is $1 for three hours. There's space for campervans.

★ **Bounce**   HOSTEL $
(☑ 07-4047 7200; 117 Grafton St; dm/apt from $21/129; P ✴ ⓢ ☒) Formerly Northern Greenhouse, refurbished Bounce is a cut above many budget guesthouses, with tidy dorms and neat studio-style apartments with kitchens and balconies, sleeping four. The central deck, pool and games room are great for socialising. Free breakfast and Sunday BBQ seal the deal.

★ **Lake Placid Tourist Park**   CARAVAN PARK $
(☑ 07-4039 2509; www.lakeplacidtouristpark. com; Lake Placid Rd; powered sites/bungalows/ en-suite cabins/cottages from $88/85/99/140; P ✴ ⓢ ☒ ☒) A 15-minute drive from the city centre, but far enough away to revel in rainforesty repose, this delightful spot overlooks the aptly named Lake Placid: it's an excellent alternative to staying centrally if you're driving. Camping and a variety of well priced, tasteful accommodation options are available. It's within striking distance of a wide range of attractions and the northern beaches.

Cairns Girls Hostel   HOSTEL $
(☑ 07-4051 2016; www.cairnsgirlshostel.com. au; 147 Lake St; dm/tw $20/50; ⓢ) Sorry lads! This white-glove-test-clean hostel is the only female-only hostel in Queensland. Rooms are plain but clean (most have no bunks) and there's a shared kitchen, lounge and patio area.

★ **Cairns Plaza Hotel**   HOTEL $$
(☑ 07-4051 4688; www.cairnsplaza.com.au; 145 Esplanade; d/studios/ste from $140/160/180; P ✴ @ ⓢ ☒) One of Cairns' original high-rise hotels, the Plaza is – thanks to a full makeover and professional staff – one of the best in its price range. Rooms have crisp, clean decor and functional kitchenettes; many enjoy stunning views over Trinity Bay. A guest laundry and friendly round-the-clock reception staff make it an excellent choice. Directly across from Muddy's (p399).

Bay Village Tropical Retreat   APARTMENT $$
(☑ 07-4051 4622; www.bayvillage.com.au; cnr Lake & Gatton Sts; d $160-175, apt $310-350; P ✴ ⓢ ☒) Sleek, shiny and ever-so-slightly removed from the Cairns hubbub, this complex offers large, cool apartments (one to three bedrooms) and spacious serviced rooms. It's a lovely place to hang your hat; it's attached to the award-winning Bayleaf Balinese Restaurant (p414).

★ **201 Lake Street**   HOTEL $$$
(☑ 07-4053 0100, 1800 628 929; www.201lake street.com.au; 201 Lake St; r from $250, apt $320-375; ✴ ⓢ ☒) Lifted from the pages of a trendy magazine, this gorgeous apartment complex has a stellar pool and a whiff of exclusivity. Grecian white predominates and guests can choose between smooth hotel rooms or contemporary apartments with an entertainment area, a large-screen TV and a balcony.

Doubletree by Hilton   HOTEL $$$
(☑ 07-4050 6070; www.doubletree3.hilton.com; 121-123 Esplanade; d $205-245; P ✴ ⓢ ☒) An enviable location on the northern end of the Esplanade, 24-hour room service and stylish, modern guest rooms with floor-to-ceiling windows define this well presented chain hotel. Balcony sea-facing rooms are at the premium.

Pacific Hotel   HOTEL $$$
(☑ 07-4051 788; www.pacifichotelcairns.com; cnr Esplanade & Spence St; d $225-265; P ✴ ⓢ ☒) In a prime location at the southern-end start of the Esplanade, this iconic hotel has been lovingly maintained and refurbished. There's a fun blend of original '70s features and woodwork, with fresh, modern amenities. All rooms have balconies. Friendly, helpful staff help to make this an excellent midrange choice. The fun **Bushfire Flame Grill** (☑ 07-4044 1879; www.bushfirecairns. com; mains $35-49, churrasco per person $55; ☺ 5.30pm-late) restaurant is attached.

🍴 **Eating**

For fresh fruit, veg and other local treats, hit Rusty's Markets (p416) on the weekend; for groceries, try **Cairns Central Shopping Centre** (☑ 07-4041 4111; www.cairnscentral.com. au; cnr McLeod & Spence Sts; ☺ 9am-5.30pm Mon-Wed, Fri & Sat, to 9pm Thu, 10.30am-4pm Sun).

Cairrns has several large supermarkets, including the central Woolworths.

★ **Ganbaranba** JAPANESE $
(☑07-4031 2522; 14 Spence St; mains $10-14; ☺11.30am-2.30pm & 5.30-8.30pm) Ganbaranba is a cult joint, and without a doubt the best place for ramen noodles and gyoza in Cairns. Slurpers can watch the chefs making noodles; if the view proves too tempting, you can ask for a refill for a mere $1.50. Absolutely worth the wait.

Jafflehead SANDWICHES $
(☑0459 622 452; 39 Lake St; jaffles $5.50-10.50; ☺7.30am-4pm Mon-Fri, 8am-3pm Sat & Sat) If you're not familiar with the term, a jaffle is a filled and sealed toasted sandwich made in a jaffle iron and that's just what Jafflehead makes. Fillings range from Aussie vegemite and cheese or egg and bacon to more unusual flavours such as Chinese braised pork or tuna and corn mornay. Good fresh juices and coffee. Cheap, simple and very Aussie.

Roti Shack CARIBBEAN $
(☑07-4253 5560; https://therotishack.com.au; shop 4/93 Lake St; roti $8.50-12; ☺11am-8pm Tue-Sun) Caribbean-Indian street-food-style roti (flatbread) curry wraps are on the menu at this cheap and tasty joint. Choose from chicken or beef curries or the vegan-friendly potato, dhal or chickpea curry wraps, spiced up with homegrown Trinidad chillies.

Corea Corea KOREAN $
(☑07-4031 6655; Orchid Plaza, 58 Lake St; mains $12-16; ☺11am-9pm) Disregard the empty-mall atmosphere at Orchid Plaza and head upstairs to dig into sizzling, spicy Korean fare at this popular takeaway.

Night Markets HAWKER $
(www.nightmarkets.com.au; Esplanade; dishes $10-18; ☺10am-11pm; 🎔) The Night Markets have a cheap, busy Asian-style food court; despite the name, the eateries here are open all day.

★ **Fusion Art Bar & Tapas** TAPAS $$
(☑07-4051 3888; www.fusionartbar.com.au; 12 Spence St; tapas $9-20, mains $19-35; ☺3-10pm Tue-Thu, 11am-11pm Fri & Sat; 🎔) Every item in this crazy cool cafe is a piece of art, and there's a real eclectic charm to everything from the furniture to the thoughtfully designed tapas menu of cured kangaroo tartare or pumpkin ravioli. Share plates feature vegan paella and pork ribs with mash and pineapple. Good wine list and coffee.

★ **Spicy Bite** INDIAN, FUSION $$
(☑07-4041 3700; 6/53 Esplanade; mains $19-30; ☺noon-3pm & 5-10.30pm; 🎔) Cairns has plenty of good Indian restaurants, but none is quite as innovative as this unassuming place, where fusion food and curries have been turned into an experience: where else could you try crocodile masala or kangaroo tikka? The classic curries are divine, and there are loads of vegetarian and vegan options.

★ **Bayleaf Balinese Restaurant** BALINESE $$
(☑07-4047 7599; www.bayvillage.com.au; cnr Lake & Gatton Sts; mains $19-34; ☺noon-2pm Mon-Fri, 6pm-late nightly) One of Cairns' best restaurants isn't along the waterfront or in the lobby of a flash hotel, but attached to a midrange apartment complex. It's unexceptional from the outside, but the Balinese food created inside by specialist chefs is wholly authentic. Order a ton of starters, go for the banquet or share mains such as gado gado or bebek kalas (duck curry with green papaya).

★ **Perrotta's at the Gallery** MEDITERRANEAN $$
(☑07-4031 5899; 38 Abbott St; mains $13-29; ☺6.30am-10pm; 🎔) This unmissable eatery, attached to the Cairns Art Gallery (p415), tempts you onto its covered deck with splendid gourmet breakfasts (6.30am to 3pm), fresh juices, barista coffees and an inventive Mediterranean-inspired lunch and dinner menu. It's a chic spot with an interesting crowd and ideal people-watching perches.

★ **Prawn Star** SEAFOOD $$$
(☑0456 421 172; www.facebook.com/prawnstarcairns; E-Finger, Berth 31, Marlin Marina; seafood $25-90; ☺10am-9pm) Trawler restaurant Prawn Star is tropical dining perfection: clamber aboard and fill yourself with prawns, mud crabs, oysters and whatever else was caught that day, while taking in equally delicious harbour views. A second boat – Prawn Star Too – was added to the eat-fleet in mid-2017, but seating is still limited and much in demand: get there early.

★ **Ochre** MODERN AUSTRALIAN $$$
(☑07-4051 0100; www.ochrerestaurant.com.au; Marlin Pde; mains $20-42; ☺11.30am-3pm & 5.30-9.30pm) The menu at this innovative waterfront restaurant utilises native Aussie fauna (such as salt and native pepper-leaf crocodile and prawns or wallaby fillet) and

flora (wattle-seed, lemon myrtle or Davidson plum glaze). Tablelands steaks are cooked to perfection. Can't decide? Order a tasting plate (six courses from $105) or a platter ($30 to $76).

The Chambers   MODERN AUSTRALIAN $$$
(☎07-4041 7302; www.the-chambers.com.au; 21 Spence St; mains $18-42; ☺cafe 7am-3pm, restaurant 5.30-10pm Tue-Sat, bar 3pm-late Tue-Sat) In an old refurbished bank building, the Chambers is three charming venues in one: a cafe, a restaurant and a bar. SoMa is the signature dinner-only fine-dining restaurant where Wagyu beef sits alongside bay bugs tagliatelle. Tattle is the casual breakfast-and-lunch cafe and Esters the sophisticated cocktail bar.

🍷 Drinking & Nightlife

★ Three Wolves   BAR
(☎07-4031 8040; www.threewolves.com.au; Red Brick Laneway, 32 Abbott St; ☺4-10pm Mon-Thu & Sun, to midnight Fri & Sat) Intimate, understated and bang on trend (think Edison bulbs, copper mugs and mixologists in old-timey barkeep aprons), this laneway bar delivers a welcome dash of Melbourne to the tropics. It's got an excellent selection of speciality spirits, cocktails and beers, plus a bar menu

including hip faves like pulled-pork tortillas, sliders and New York–style hot dogs.

★ Green Ant Cantina   MICROBREWERY
(☎07-4041 5061; www.greenantcantina.com; 183 Bunda St; ☺4pm-late Tue-Sat) Behind the train station, this grungy, rockin' Tex-Mex bar is an ace and arty alternative hang-out. Smothered in bright murals, the Green Ant brews its own beers (seven varieties, including a strong brown ale) and hosts regular music events. It also does fab food, including pulled-pork quesadillas, jambalaya and the infamous, blistering Wings of Death.

★ Salt House   BAR
(☎07-4041 7733; www.salthouse.com.au; 6/2 Pierpoint Rd; ☺6.30am-2am) On the waterfront by the yacht club, Cairns' coolest, classiest bar caters to a hip and happy crowd. With killer cocktails, tremendous views, live music and DJs, and a superb mod-Oz nibbles-and-mains menu, the Salt House is absolutely not to be missed. The pizzeria here is justifiably popular.

★ Conservatory Bar   WINE BAR
(☎0467 466 980; www.theconservatorybar.com.au; 12-14 Lake St; ☺4-10pm Wed-Sat) Tucked away in a little room in a little laneway, this is Cairns' best wine bar, and one of the city's

---

CAIRNS GALLERIES

Cairns Art Gallery (☎07-4046 4800; www.cairnsregionalgallery.com.au; cnr Abbott & Shields Sts; ☺9am-5pm Mon-Fri, 10am-5pm Sat, 10am-2pm Sun) The permanent collection of this acclaimed gallery, housed in the heritage-listed former State Government Insurance Office (1936), has an emphasis on local and Indigenous work. It also hosts prominent visiting exhibitions and workshops; attached is an excellent gift shop and Perrotta's (p414) cafe.

KickArts Contemporary Arts (☎07-4050 9496; https://kickarts.org.au; School of the Arts, 93-105 Lake St; ☺10am-5pm Mon-Fri, 10am-1pm Sat) These galleries showcase cutting-edge local and regional artworks, plus touring exhibitions. KickArts has moved to the School of the Arts while the Centre of Contemporary Arts (p416) is being refurbished.

Samurai Gallery (☎0417 642 921; http://samuraigalleryaustralia.com; 22 Shields St; adult/child $10/5; ☺11am-2pm Tue & Thu, 11am-3.30pm Wed & Fri, 10am-2pm Sat) This unusual gallery and museum displays genuine armour, swords and arts from the Japanese samurai. Owner John Grasso has been collecting swords and martial arts fittings for many years and continues to develop his unique exhibition.

Tanks Arts Centre (☎07-4032 6600; www.tanksartscentre.com; 46 Collins Ave; ☺8.30am-4.30pm Mon-Fri) Three gigantic, ex-WWII fuel-storage tanks have been transformed into art galleries; it's also an inspired performing-arts venue (p416). Check the website for upcoming events. Tanks hosts lively market days on the last Sunday of the month (April to November).

top places for a low-key tipple, whatever your flavour. It also makes fabulous cocktails and has loads of craft beers. It's relaxed, friendly and oozes a tropical sophistication all its own. The Conservatory regularly hosts exhibitions and live (mellow) music.

★**The Jack**   PUB
(☑07-4051 2490; www.thejack.com.au; cnr Spence & Sheridan Sts; ⊙10am-late) The Jack is a kick-arse pub by any standards, housed in an unmissable heritage Queenslander with an enormous shaded beer garden. There are nightly events, including live music and DJs, great pub grub, and an adjacent hostel for those who just can't tear themselves away. The live music events here are usually free entry.

Bang & Grind   COFFEE
(☑07-4051 7770; 8/14 Spence St; ⊙6am-3pm Mon-Fri, 6.30am-2.30pm Sat, 7.30am-12.30pm Sun; 🖥) Locals rate this as some of the best coffee in Cairns, so pull up a seat in the retro space for a Ransom caffeine fix. Serves breakfast and lunch.

Hemingway's Cairns   BREWERY
(⊙10am-10.30pm Sun-Thu, 10am-midnight Fri & Sat) Housed in a revamped shed on the Cairns Wharf, the ginormous Hemingway's is the second coming of the popular Port Douglas brewery, only much bigger; check out the shiny vats and brewing pipes while enjoying a tasting paddle ($15). Meals also available.

Cape York Hotel   PUB
(☑07-4031 6924; cnr Spence & Bunda Sts; ⊙10am-midnight) It may not be on the favoured backpacker circuit, but this iconic pub has retained all the knockabout charm it's been famous for since opening in 1926. Loved by larrikins and locals of all stripes, the Cape York feels a million miles away from Cairns' sleeker, tourist-oriented offerings.

Gilligan's   BAR, CLUB
(☑07-4040 2777; www.gilligans.com.au; 57-89 Grafton St; ⊙11am-late) Attached to the **hostel** (☑07-4041 6566; dm $18-39, s $137-147; ❄@🖥❄) of the same name but open to all comers, this sprawling, bawdy bar is synonymous with 'having a big one' in Cairns-speak. Throngs of party-minded backpackers and up-for-it locals pack the place out nightly for theme events and general good-timery, though annoyingly there's

often a cover charge if you're not staying here. The attached (more upmarket) Attic nightclub opens its gilded doors on Fridays and Saturdays (7pm to 3am).

☆ Entertainment

Tanks Arts Centre   LIVE PERFORMANCE
(☑07-4032 6600; www.tanksartscentre.com; 46 Collins Ave) Next to the Botanic Gardens, Tanks is one of Cairns premier live music and performance venues with a regular line-up of touring bands, theatre and comedy acts. See the website for what's on.

Rondo Theatre   THEATRE
(☑1300 855 835; www.therondo.com.au; 46 Greenslopes St) Community plays and musicals hit the stage regularly at this small theatre opposite Centenary Lakes in Edge Hill. It's 4.5km northwest of the city centre (take Sheridan St to Greenslopes St).

Starry Night Cinema   CINEMA
(☑0427 717 271; www.starrynightcinema.com.au; Collins Ave, Edge Hill, Cairns Botanic Gardens; adult/child from $13/5; ■) Enjoy classic films amid the foliage and finery of the Botanic Gardens (p401). Check the website for upcoming showings (there are usually two a month).

Centre of Contemporary Arts   GALLERY, THEATRE
(CoCA; www.centre-of-contemporary-arts-cairns.com.au; 96 Abbott St; ⊙10am-5pm Mon-Sat) CoCA was undergoing a major refurbishment in 2018, but should reopen in late 2019 – check the website for updates.

🛍 Shopping

★**Rusty's Markets**   MARKET
(☑07-4040 2705; www.rustysmarkets.com.au; 57-89 Grafton St; ⊙5am-6pm Fri & Sat, to 3pm Sun) No weekend in Cairns is complete without a visit to this busy and vibrant multicultural market. Weave (and taste) your way through piles of seasonal tropical fruits, veggies and herbs, plus farm-fresh honey, locally grown flowers, excellent coffees, curries, cold drinks, antiques and more.

Doongal Aboriginal Art   ART
(☑07-4041 4249; www.doongal.com.au; 49 Esplanade; ⊙9am-6pm) Stocks authentic artworks, boomerangs, didgeridoos and other traditional artefacts by local and Central Australian Indigenous artists. Worldwide shipping available.

ⓘ Information

The Cairns Regional Council's website (www.cairns.qld.gov.au/region/tourist-information) has tonnes of details on events, activities and transport in the region.

The government-run but volunteer-staffed visitor centre has surprisingly closed. There are many private information and booking offices around town – they all book the same trips at similar prices, but you can usually get better deals booking through your accommodation, especially at backpacker hostels.

Cairns 24 Hour Medical Centre (☑ 07-4052 1119; cnr Grafton & Florence Sts; ☺ 24hr) Centrally located medical centre; it also does dive medicals.

Post Office (☑ 13 13 18; www.auspost.com.au; 38 Sheridan St; ☺ 8.30am-5.30pm Mon-Fri, 9am-12.30pm Sat)

ⓘ Getting There & Away

AIR

Qantas (☑ 13 13 13; www.qantas.com.au), **Virgin Australia** (☑ 13 67 89; www.virginaustralia.com) and **Jetstar** (☑ 13 15 38; www.jetstar.com.au), and a handful of international carriers, arrive in and depart from **Cairns Airport** (☑ 07-4080 6703; www.cairnsairport.com; Airport Ave), with direct services to all Australian capital cities except Canberra and Hobart, and to regional centres including Townsville, Weipa and Horn Island. Direct international connections include Bali, Singapore, Manila, Tokyo and Port Moresby.

Hinterland Aviation (☑ 07-4040 1333; www.hinterlandaviation.com.au) has at least two flights daily from Cairns to Cooktown.

Skytrans (☑ 1300 759 872; www.skytrans.com.au) services Cape York communities and the Torres Strait Islands.

BOAT

Almost all reef trips from Cairns depart the Marlin Wharf (sometimes called the Marlin Jetty), with booking and check-in facilities inside the Reef Fleet Terminal (p411). A handful of smaller operators may have their check-in facilities boatside, on the wharf itself. Be sure to ask for the correct berth number.

International cruise ships and **SeaSwift** (☑ 07-4035 1234, 1800 424 422; www.seaswift.com.au; 41-45 Tingira St, Portsmith; one way/return from $670/1065) ferries to Seisia on Cape York dock at and depart from the **Cairns Seaport** (☑ 07-4052 3888; www.portsnorth.com.au/cairns; cnr Wharf & Lake Sts).

BUS

Long-distance buses arrive at and depart from the **Interstate Coach Terminal** (Reef Fleet Terminal), Cairns Central train station and the **Cairns Transit Mall** (Lake St).

CAR & MOTORCYCLE

Major car-rental companies have airport and city (usually on Sheridan St) branches. Daily rates start at around $30 for a compact auto and $80 for a 4WD. **Cruising Car Rental** (☑ 07-4041 4666; https://cruisingcarrental.com.au; 196 Sheridan St; per day from $35) and **Rent-a-Bomb** (☑ 07-4031 4477; www.rentabomb.com.au; 144 Sheridan St; per day from $33) have cheap rates on older model vehicles.

If you're looking for a cheap campervan, **Jucy** (☑ 1800 150 850; www.jucy.com.au; 55 Dutton St, Portsmith; per day $35-75), **Spaceships** (☑ 1300 132 469; www.spaceshipsrentals.com.au; 397 Sheridan St; per day from $40), **Lucky Campervan Rentals** (☑ 1800-808 881; www.lucky-rentals.com.au; 107 Bunda St; ☺ vans from $35 per day) and **Hippie Camper Hire** (☑ 1800 777 779; www.hippiecamper.com; 432 Sheridan St; per day from $20) have quality wheels at budget prices.

If you're in for the long haul, check hostels and www.gumtree.com.au for used campervans and ex-backpackers' cars.

If you prefer two wheels to four, try **Choppers Motorcycle Tours & Hire** (☑ 07-4051 6288; www.choppersmotorcycles.com.au; 150 Sheridan St; 90min ride $130; motorcycle hire per day from $150) or **Cairns Scooter & Bicycle Hire** (☑ 07-4031 3444; www.cairnsbicyclehire.com.au; 47 Shields St; scooters/bikes per day from $50/15; ☺ 8am-5pm Mon-Fri, 9am-4.30pm Sat). Note that you need a full licence for this option though.

TRAIN

The Kuranda Scenic Railway (p403) runs daily; the Savannahlander (p411) offers a miscellany of rail journeys into the outback from **Cairns Central train station** (Bunda St).

Queensland Rail (☑ 1300 131 722; www.queenslandrailtravel.com.au) operates services between Brisbane and Cairns.

ⓘ Getting Around

TO/FROM THE AIRPORT

The airport is about 6km north of central Cairns; many hotels and hostels offer courtesy pick-up. **Sun Palm** (☑ 07-4087 2900; www.sunpalmtransport.com.au; Cairns Airport) meets incoming flights until about 6.30pm and runs a shuttle (adult/child $15/7.50) directly to your accommodation; its **Airport Connect Shuttle** ($6) runs between the airport and a stop on Sheridan St just north of town. **Cairns Airport Shuttle** (☑ 0432 488 783; www.cairnsairportshuttle.com.au) is a good option for groups; the more passengers, the cheaper the fare.

Taxis to the city centre cost around $25 (plus $4 airport surcharge).

BICYCLE

Cairns is criss-crossed with cycling paths and circuits; some of the most popular routes take in the Esplanade, Botanic Gardens and Centenary Lakes. There's a detailed list of routes and maps at www.cairns.qld.gov.au/region/tourist-information/things-to-do/cycle. Some backpacker hostels rent out bikes. Otherwise try Cairns Scooter & Bicycle Hire.

BUS

Cairns has a fairy efficient and comprehensive city bus system run by **Translink** (https://translink.com.au/cairns) (formerly called Sunbus).

Islands off Cairns

Green Island

Showing some of the scars that come with fame and popularity, this pretty coral cay, 45 minutes from Cairns, nevertheless retains much of its beauty. The island has a rainforest interior with interpretive walks, a fringe of white-sand beach, and superb snorkelling just offshore; it's great for kids. You can walk around the island (which, along with its surrounding waters, is protected by national- and marine-park status) in about 30 minutes.

Before the island was named after Captain Cook's astronomer, the Gunggandji people used it as a retreat to perform initiation ceremonies for the young men of their group. In the mid-1850s, the waters around Green Island were heavily fished for bêche-de-mer (sea cucumbers); the animals were cured here for export and many of the island's trees were logged in the process. Today Green is studded with coconut palms, planted in 1889 to provide nourishment and shelter for shipwreck survivors.

While plenty of fish, turtles and beautiful artefacts are on display at family-owned **Marineland Crocodile Park** (☑ 07-4051 4032; www.greenislandcrocs.com.au; adult/child $20/9.50; ☺ 9.30am-4pm; ☺), it's Cassius, the largest croc in captivity, that's the star attraction. He's believed to be over 110 years old and is 5.5m long.

Luxurious **Green Island Resort** (☑ 07-4031 3300; www.greenislandresort.com.au; ste $745-845; ☀ @ ☎ ☎) maintains a sense of privacy and exclusivity despite having sections opened to the general public, including restaurants, bars, an ice-cream parlour and water-sports facilities.

Great Adventures (☑ 07-4044 9944; www.greatadventures.com.au; Reef Fleet Terminal; adult/child/family day trips from $236/125/597; ☺) offers resort transfers daily from Cairns' Reef Fleet Terminal (p411).

Fitzroy Island

A steep mountaintop rising from the sea, fabulous Fitzroy Island has coral beaches, giant boulders and rainforest walking tracks, one of which ends at a now-inactive lighthouse. It's a top spot for swimming and snorkelling; one of the best places to lay your towel is **Nudey Beach**, which, despite its name, is not officially clothing-optional. Unlike the rest of the island away from the resort, Nudey actually has some sand on it.

The Indigenous Gunggandji people hunted and fished from the island for centuries; in 1877, it was used to quarantine Chinese immigrants bound for the Palmer River goldfields. Today Fitzroy is a national park, with a **resort** (☑ 07-4044 6700; www.fitzroyisland.com; studios/cabins/ste/apt from $170/380/250/305; ☀ ☎ ☎) occupying but a small section on the western coast. It's popular as both a day trip from Cairns and as an overnight getaway from the mainland.

The **Cairns Turtle Rehabilitation Centre** (www.saveourseaturtles.com.au; adult/child $8.80/5.50; ☺ tours 1pm; ☺) looks after sick and injured sea turtles before releasing them back into the wild. Daily educational tours (45 minutes, maximum 15 guests) take visitors through the turtle hospital to meet recovering residents. Bookings through the Fitzroy Island Resort are essential.

Fitzroy Island Resort's tropi-cool accommodation ranges from sleek studios, suites and beachfront cabins through to luxurious apartments; the apartments and suites have kitchens. The restaurant, bar and kiosk are open to day trippers. Budgeteers can opt for the **Fitzroy Island Camping Ground** (☑ 07-4044 6700; www.fitzroyisland.com; sites $36).

The following companies offer daily transfers to Fitzroy Island from Cairns. Prices are for return tickets.

Fitzroy Island Flyer (www.fitzroyisland.com; return adult/child/family $79/39.50/209) Departs Cairns' Marlin Wharf at 8am, 11am and 1.30pm (bookings essential) and whisks you to Fitzroy Island in just 45 minutes. It returns to Cairns at 9.30am, 12.15pm and 5pm. It's run by the Fitzroy Island Resort and docks right outside the resort.

Raging Thunder (📞07-4030 7990; www.ragingthunder.com.au; 59-63 Esplanade; rafting $199) Half-day trip (adult/child/family $79/49/212) departs the Reef Fleet Terminal (p411) at 11am, and returns at 2pm; the full-day trip ($84/54/227) departs at 9am and returns at 4pm.

Sunlover Reef Cruises (📞07-4050 1333; www.sunlover.com.au; ⛵) Adult/child $80/40. Departs the Reef Fleet Terminal at 9.30am and returns at 4.20pm.

Cairns' Northern Beaches

Yorkeys Knob

POP 2760

On the traditional land of the Yirrganydji people, Yorkeys Knob is a laid-back beach community best known for its marina and **golf course** (📞07-4055 7933; www.halfmoonbaygolf.com.au; 9/18 holes $26/42, club hire $25), and the cheeky crocs that frequent it. Yorkeys has a stinger net in summer.

Blazing Saddles (📞07-4055 7400; www.blazingsaddles.com.au; 154 Yorkeys Knob Rd; horse rides from $130, quad bikes from $140; ⛵) runs three-hour horse-riding tours that meander through rainforest, mangroves and sugar-cane fields.

Half Moon Bay Resort (📞07-4055 8059; www.halfmoonbayresort.com.au; 101/103 Wattle St; apt from $130; P ❄ 🛜 🏊) is basically a collection of one-bedroom apartments directly opposite the golf course, while **Boaties Bar & Grill** (📞07-4055 7711; www.ykbc.com.au; 25-29 Buckley St; mains $16-36; ⊙noon-3pm & 6-9pm; 🌿), the restaurant at Yorkey's Knob Boating Club, is a diamond find for fresh seafood.

Trinity Beach

Trinity Beach, with its gorgeous stretch of sheltered sand, pretty esplanade and sensibly priced dining and accommodation, has managed to stave off the tourist vibe, despite being a holiday hotspot and popular dining destination for locals in the know.

One of the most handsome blocks on the beachfront, **Sea Point** (📞07-4057 9544; www.seapointontrinitybeach.com; 63 Vasey Esplanade; apt $170-400; P ❄ 🛜 🏊) has alluring indoor-outdoor balconies, tiled floors and breezy outlooks.

Blue Moon Grill (📞07-4057 8957; www.bluemoongrill.com.au; Shop 6, 22-24 Trinity Beach Rd; mains $24-36; ⊙4-10pm Mon-Thu, 7-11am

& 4-10pm Fri-Sun) is a cosy family-run bistro offering an inventive and slightly overwhelming menu of original dishes, presented with passion. And don't let the easy-breezy beach-shack vibe fool you into thinking the food at **Fratelli on Trinity** (📞07-4057 5775; www.fratelli.net.au; 47 Vasey Esplanade; mains $22-35; ⊙7am-10pm Wed-Sun, from 5.30pm Tue) is anything less than top class.

Palm Cove

POP 1215

The best known and easily most sophisticated and touristy of Cairns' northern beaches, Palm Cove has rightfully grown into a destination in its own right. More intimate than Port Douglas and more upmarket than its southern neighbours, Palm Cove is a cloistered coastal community with a beautiful promenade along the melaleuca-lined Williams Esplanade. Its gorgeous stretch of white-sand beach and its sprinkling of fancy restaurants do their best to lure young lovers from their luxury resorts.

Beach strolls, wining, dining and doing lots of sweet nothing are chief activities here, but water-sports operators offer kayaking, snorkelling, sailing and stand-up paddleboarding (SUP).

Recommended operators include **Beach Fun Co** (📞0411 848 580; www.beachfunco.com; cnr Williams Esplanade & Harpa St) for catamarans, SUPs and kayaks, **Pacific Watersports** (📞0413 721 999; www.pacificwatersports.com.au; 41 Williams Esplanade) for kiteboarding and SUPs, and **Palm Cove Watersports** (📞0402 861 011; www.palmcovewatersports.com; 149 Williams Esplanade; kayak hire per hour s/d $25/35, SUP hire $25) for kayaking, SUP and snorkelling. If that all sounds too much, drop in to a hatha yoga class with **Hartig Yoga** (📞0421 322 691; www.hartigyoga.com; per class $17; ⊙Mon-Sat).

🛏 Sleeping

⭐**Cairns Beaches Flashpackers** HOSTEL $
(📞07-4055 3797; www.cairnsbeachesflashpackers.com; 19 Veivers Rd; dm/d $39/89; P ❄ 🛜 🏊) Palm Cove's first and only hostel is a breath of budget fresh air. This splendid, spotless place 100m from the beach (opposite the tavern) is more restful retreat than party palace. The bunk-free dorms are tidy and comfortable; the private rooms have bathrooms and sliding-door access to the pool. Cook in the immaculate communal kitchen. Scooter and bike hire available.

QUEENSLAND CAIRNS' NORTHERN BEACHES

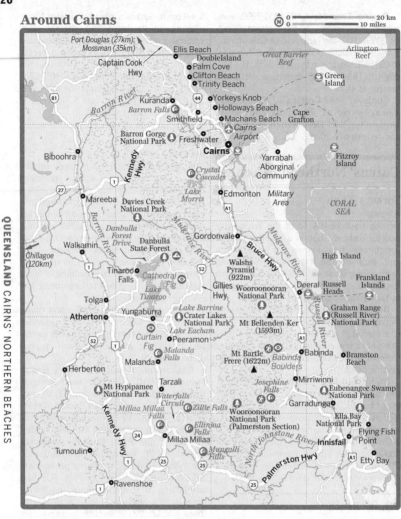

0   20 km
0   10 miles

Port Douglas (27km);
Mossman (35km)

Ellis Beach
Double Island
Captain Cook Hwy
Palm Cove
Clifton Beach
Trinity Beach
Great Barrier Reef
Arlington Reef
Green Island

Kuranda
Barron River
Barron Falls
Smithfield
Yorkeys Knob
Holloways Beach
Machans Beach
Cape Grafton

Barron Gorge National Park
Freshwater
Cairns
Cairns Airport
Yarrabah Aboriginal Community
Fitzroy Island

Biboohra
Kennedy Hwy
Crystal Cascades
Lake Morris
Edmonton
Military Area
CORAL SEA

Mareeba
Davies Creek National Park
Barron River

Danbulla Forest Drive
Danbulla State Forest
Gordonvale
Bruce Hwy
High Island

Walkamin
Tinaroo Falls
Cathedral Fig
Lake Tinaroo
Walshs Pyramid (922m)
Gillies Hwy
Wooroonooran National Park
Deeral
Russell Heads
Frankland Islands

Chillagoe (120km)
Tolga
Atherton
Yungaburra
Lake Barrine
Crater Lakes National Park
Lake Eacham
Peeramon
Mt Bellenden Ker (1593m)
Graham Range (Russell River) National Park

Curtain Fig
Malanda Falls
Malanda
Mt Bartle Frere (1622m)
Babinda Boulders
Babinda
Bramston Beach

Herberton
Mt Hypipamee National Park
Tarzali
Waterfalls Circuit
Josephine Falls
Mirriwinni
Eubenangee Swamp National Park
Garradunga

Millaa Millaa Falls
Zillie Falls
Ellinjaa Falls
Millaa Millaa
Wooroonooran National Park (Palmerston Section)
Ella Bay National Park
Flying Fish Point

Tumoulin
Mungalli Falls
Innisfail
Etty Bay

Ravenshoe
Palmerston Hwy
North Johnstone River

★ Sarayi
BOUTIQUE HOTEL $$

(☑ 07-4059 5600; www.sarayi.com.au; 95 Williams Esplanade; d $120-140, apt $190-210; P ❋ 🕏 ☒) Beachfront motel rooms in Palm Cove for under $120? White, bright and perfectly located among a grove of melaleucas across from the beach, Sarayi is a wonderful, affordable choice for couples, families and the growing number of visitors choosing to get married on its rooftop terrace.

★ Salty Souls
RENTAL HOUSE $$$

(☑ 0438 091 905; www.saltysoulspalmcove.com; 15 Lambus St; house from $350; P ❋ 🕏 ☒) If you want to linger longer in Palm Cove,

make yourself at home in this gorgeous tropical-style house. The decor and facilities are second to none, with lovely furniture, a fantastic kitchen and resort-style pool. The home sleeps eight, and children are very welcome. Everything from games and pool toys to high chairs and cots are available. Minimum five-night stay.

★ Reef House Resort & Spa
BOUTIQUE HOTEL $$$

(☑ 07-4080 2600; www.reefhouse.com.au; 99 Williams Esplanade; d $320-540; P ❋ 🕏 ☒) Once the private residence of an army brigadier, Reef House is more intimate and understated than most of Palm Cove's resorts. The white-washed walls, wicker furniture and big beds romantically draped in muslin add to the air of refinement, while the day spa adds a dose of luxury. The **Brigadier's Bar** works on an honesty system; complimentary punch is served by candlelight at twilight.

✖ Eating

★ Lucky Fish FISH & CHIPS $
(☑07-4231 9622; www.luckyfish.online; Shop 18, 111 Williams Esplanade; mains $9-15; ◷11am-8.30pm; ✹) For good old-fashioned fish and chips (barramundi, coral trout or reef fish), along with fish or prawn tacos, burgers and salads, Lucky Fish is a welcome bargain on the Palm Cove strip. Take away or eat in the casual dining space in Paradise Village shops.

★ Chill Cafe CAFE $$
(☑0439 361 122; 41 Williams Esplanade; mains $21-34; ◷6am-late) The primo position on the corner of the waterfront Esplanade, combined with friendly and attentive service, cool tunes and an airy deck, are all great reasons to try the oversized, tasty treats (think fish tacos and chunky club sandwiches) offered by this hip cafe. Opens early for breakfast, though the Bloody Marys start at 10am.

★ Vivo MODERN AUSTRALIAN $$$
(☑07-4059 0944; www.vivo.com.au; 49 Williams Esplanade; mains $33-49; ◷6.30am-9pm) The most beautiful-looking restaurant on the Esplanade is also one of the finest. Menus (breakfast, lunch and dinner) are inventive and well executed using fresh local ingredients. The speciality is seafood – even breakfast features crab omelette – while dinner might feature spaghetti marinara or coral trout. Daily set menus are excellent value.

★ Beach Almond SEAFOOD $$$
(☑07-4059 1908; www.beachalmond.com; 145 Williams Esplanade; mains $34-48; ◷5-11pm Mon-Sat, noon-3pm & 5-11pm Sun) The rustic, ramshackle, beach-house-on-sticks exterior belies the exceptional fine-dining experience that awaits within. Black-pepper mud crab, char-grilled Bali prawn and Sumatran rendang curry are among the fragrant innovations here, combining Asian flavours and spices with Modern Australian imaginings.

🍷 Drinking & Nightlife

Apres Beach Bar & Grill BAR
(☑07-4059 2000; www.apresbeachbar.com.au; 119 Williams Esplanade; ◷8am-11pm) The most

happening place in Palm Cove, with a zany interior of old motorcycles, racing cars, and a biplane hanging from the ceiling, plus regular live music. Big on steaks of all sorts too.

Surf Club Palm Cove BAR
(☑07-4059 1244; www.surfclubpalmcove.com.au; 135 Williams Esplanade; ◷11am-10pm Mon & Tue, to midnight Wed-Sat, 8am-midnight Sun; ✹) This local hang-out is great for a drink in the sunny garden bar, bargain-priced seafood and decent kids' meals.

Ellis Beach

Little Ellis Beach is the last of Cairns' northern beaches and the closest to the highway, which runs right past it. The long sheltered bay is a stunner, with a palm-fringed, patrolled swimming beach, and a stinger net in summer. Cairns' only (unofficial) clothing-optional beach, **Buchans Point**, is at the southern end of Ellis; there's no stinger net here, so consider your valuable assets before diving in in your birthday suit.

North of Ellis Beach, towards Port Douglas, **Hartley's Crocodile Adventures** (☑07-4055 3576; www.crocodileadventures.com; Captain Cook Hwy, Wangetti Beach; adult/child/family $39/19.50/97.50; ◷8.30am-5pm; ✹) 🖉 is the best place in North Queensland to see big crocs.

Ellis Beach Oceanfront Bungalows (☑07-4055 3538, 1800 637 036; www.ellisbeach.com; Captain Cook Hwy; powered/unpowered sites from $43/36, cabins with shared bathroom from $115, bungalow d $170-210; ✱🖥✱) is a low-key, palm-shaded beachfront slice of paradise with camping, cabins and contemporary bungalows.

Just try to drive past the rightfully popular **Ellis Beach Bar 'n' Grill** (☑07-4055 3534; www.ellisbeachbarandgrill.com.au; Captain Cook Hwy; mains $15-19; ◷8am-8pm) and not stop for a beer and a burger.

ATHERTON TABLELANDS

Climbing back from the coast between Innisfail and Cairns is the fertile food bowl of the far north, the Atherton Tablelands. Quaint country towns, eco-wilderness lodges and luxurious B&Bs dot greener-than-green hills between patchwork fields, pockets of rainforest, spectacular lakes, waterfalls and Queensland's highest mountains, Bartle Frere (1622m) and Bellenden Ker (1593m).

This region makes for a great getaway from the swelter of the coast: it's almost always a few degrees cooler than Cairns, and on winter nights things get downright chilly.

The Tablelands is the traditional home of the Djirrbal and Ngadjonji tribes of the Djirrbalngan language group, while the area around Kuranda and Yungaburra is the land of the Djabugay (Tjapukai) and Yidinji peoples.

❶ Getting There & Away

Four main roads lead in from the coast: the Palmerston Hwy from Innisfail, Gillies Hwy (turn-off just before Gordonvale), Kennedy Hwy (known locally as the Kuranda Range) from Smithfield, and Rex Range Rd between Mossman and Port Douglas. Though there are frequent buses from Cairns to the main towns on the Tablelands, it's worth hiring your own wheels to fully explore the area.

Trans North (☑ 07-4095 8644; www.trans northbus.com; Cairns Central train station) has regular bus services connecting Cairns with various towns on the Tablelands, including Kuranda ($6.70, 30 minutes), Mareeba ($19.60, one hour), Atherton ($25.30, 1¾ hours) and Herberton/Ravenshoe ($32/37.40, two/2½ hours, Monday, Wednesday, Friday).

John's Kuranda Bus (☑ 0418 772 953) runs a service between Cairns and Kuranda two to five times daily ($5, 30 minutes). Departs Lake Street Transit Centre.

Kuranda

POP 3008

Tucked away in thick rainforest, arty, alternative Kuranda is one of Cairns' most popular day trips, and for good reason. During the day, this hippy haven swarms with tourists soaking up the vibe, visiting animal sanctuaries and poking around its famous markets and souvenir shops; after the markets close at 3pm, you can almost hear the village sigh as the streets and pubs are reclaimed by mellow locals (and the occasional street-hopping wallaby).

Kuranda and the Barron Gorge region are the traditional home of the Djabugay (Tjapukai) people, many of whom are involved in the local arts and cultural scene. In 2004 the Djabugay successfully gained native title over the Barron Gorge National Park.

Just getting here is an experience: choose between driving a winding forest road, chugging up on a train or soaring over the treetops on Skyrail – Australia's longest gondola cableway (p403).

◉ Sights & Activities

The **Kuranda Wildlife Experience Pass** (adult/child $49.50/24.75) offers discounted entry to **Birdworld** (☑ 07-4093 9188; www. birdworldkuranda.com; Heritage Markets, Rob Veivers Dr; adult/child $18/9; ☺ 9am-4pm; ◉), the **Australian Butterfly Sanctuary** (☑ 07-4093 7575; www.australianbutterflies.com; Heritage Markets, Rob Veivers Dr; adult/child/family $20/10/50; ☺ 9.45am-4pm; ◉) and **Kuranda Koala Gardens** (☑ 07-4093 9953; www.koalagardens. com; Heritage Markets, Rob Veivers Dr; adult/child $19/9.50; ☺ 9am-4pm; ◉). Enquire at any of these attractions or at the **Kuranda Visitor Information Centre** (☑ 07-4093 9311; www. kuranda.org; Centenary Park; ☺ 10am-4pm).

During the wet season, the mighty, must-see **Barron Falls** are in full thunder; they're a 3km walk or drive down Barron Falls Rd.

★ **Kuranda Original**
Rainforest Markets MARKET
(☑ 07-4093 9440; www.kurandaoriginalrainforest market.com.au; 7-11 Therwine St; ☺ 9.30am-3pm) Follow the clouds of incense down to these atmospheric village markets. Operating since 1978, they're still the best place to see artists at work and hippies at play. Pick up everything from avocado ice cream to organic lingerie and sample local produce such as honey and fruit wines.

Rainforestation PARK
(☑ 07-4085 5008; www.rainforest.com.au; Kennedy Hwy; adult/child/family $50/25/125; ☺ 9am-4pm; ◉) You'll need a full day to properly explore this enormous complex, divided into three sections: a **koala and wildlife park**, the interactive **Pamagirri Aboriginal Experience**, and a **river and rainforest tour** aboard the amphibious Army Duck boat-truck.

The park is 3km east of Kuranda. Shuttles (one way/return adult $7.50/12.50, child $3.50/6) run every half-hour between the park and Kuranda village.

Rainforestation is included in the Capta 4 Park Pass (www.capta.com.au), which offers discounted entry to four Far North Queensland attractions.

BatReach ANIMAL SANCTUARY
(☑ 07-4093 8858; www.batreach.com; 13 Barang St; by donation; ☺ 10.30am-2.30pm Tue-Thu &

Sun; 🐾) Visitors are welcome at this rescue and rehabilitation centre for injured and orphaned bats, possums and gliders. Passionate volunteers are more than happy to show folks around and explain the work they do. It's possible to volunteer at BatReach provided you have been vaccinated for the Australian bat lyssavirus. BatReach is down the hill next to the fire station.

Doongal Ark Gallery — GALLERY
(☑ 07-4093 9999; https://doongal.com.au; 22 Coondoo St; ⊙ 9am-4pm) FREE This unmissable boat-shaped building houses a gorgeous and authentic collection of Indigenous artworks and artefacts by local artists under the Doongal association; many are available for purchase.

Kuranda Riverboat — CRUISE
(☑ 07-4093 0082; www.kurandariverboat.com.au; adult/child/family $20/10/50; ⊙ hourly 10.45am-2.30pm; 🐾) Hop aboard for a 45-minute calm-water cruise along the Barron River in search of freshwater crocodiles, or opt for an hour-long interpretive rainforest walk in a secluded spot accessible only by boat.

You'll find Kuranda Riverboat on the jetty behind the train station; buy tickets for the cruise on board, or book online for the walk.

🛏 Sleeping

Kuranda Rainforest Park — CARAVAN PARK $
(☑ 07-4093 7316; www.kurandarainforestpark.com.au; 88 Kuranda Heights Rd; powered/unpowered sites $35/30, s/d without bathroom $35/70, cabins $90-110; 🅿❄🛜🏊) This well-tended park lives up to its name, with grassy campsites enveloped in rainforest. The basic but cosy 'backpacker rooms' open onto a tin-roofed timber deck, cabins come with poolside or garden views, and there's an excellent restaurant (mains $15-27; ⊙ 5.30-8.30pm Wed-Sun; 🍴🐾) serving local produce on-site. It's a 10-minute walk from town via a forest trail.

Fairyland House — B&B $
(☑ 07-4093 9194; www.fairylandhouse.com.au; 13 Fairyland Rd; dm $55, r per person $75-80; 🅿) With a vegan raw-food restaurant, tarot readings, yoga classes, abundant fruit garden and wellness workshops, this bush retreat is about as 'Kuranda' as they come. All rooms are airy and open onto the garden. It's a 4km walk to the village; no cooked or animal food products, cigarettes, alcohol, pets or drugs allowed.

★ Cedar Park Rainforest Resort — RESORT $$
(☑ 07-4093 7892; www.cedarparkresort.com.au; 250 Cedar Park Rd, Koah; r $210-330; 🅿❄🛜) 🌱 Set deep in the bush (a 20-minute drive from Kuranda towards Mareeba), this unusual property is part Euro-castle, part Aussie-bush-retreat. In lieu of TV, guests look out for wallabies, peacocks and dozens of native birds. Breakfast is included, plus there are hammocks aplenty, creek access, a fireplace, and a gourmet restaurant with well-priced meals and free port.

🍴 Eating

Honey House — FOOD
(☑ 07-4093 7261; www.honeyhousekuranda.com; 7 Therwine St; ⊙ 9am-3pm; 🐾) A Kuranda institution since 1959, this heavenly honey shop is worth a look, whether or not you have a sweet tooth. Kids will marvel at the glass-enclosed hives, there's a beekeeper on hand to answer any questions and visitors are welcome to have a no-pressure taste of the dozens of high-quality raw local honeys on offer.

German Tucker — GERMAN $
(www.germantucker.com; Therwine St; sausages $6.50-11; ⊙ 10am-3pm) Fill up on classic würste or try the tasty emu and crocodile sausages at this amusing eatery, where they blast oompah music and splash out steins of top-notch German beer.

Warung Bamboo Indonesia — INDONESIAN $
(Shop 7, 7-11 Therwine St; mains $13-15; ⊙ 10.30am-3pm Mon-Sat; 🍴) Make a quick trip to Java or Bali at this authentic little Indonesian eatery serving up inexpensive satay skewers, bakso (meatballs), mie goreng (friend noodles) and soto ayam (chicken soup). It's in the original markets.

★ Kuranda Hotel — PUB FOOD $$
(☑ 07-4093 7206; https://kurandahotel.com; 16 Arara St; mains $16-26; ⊙ 10.30am-3.30pm; 🅿❄🛜) Locally known as the 'bottom pub', the Kuranda Hotel has been remodelled into a gastropub with a focus on generous, good-value pub meals. The broad deck overlooking the train station is usually busy at lunchtime, when hungry tourists tuck into local barramundi, kangaroo hotpots, enormous burgers and chicken parmas.

❶ Getting There & Away

Kuranda is as much about the journey (from Cairns) as the destination: choose between the Skyrail Rainforest Cableway (p403) and the

DON'T MISS

TABLELANDS MARKETS

As is seemingly obligatory for any quaint country region, the tiny towns of the Tablelands host a miscellany of monthly markets. Kuranda's blockbuster bazaars are legendary, but for something a bit more down-home, check out the following:

Atherton Undercover Markets (Merriland Hall, Robert St; ⊘7am-noon 2nd Sun of month)

Malanda Markets (www.facebook.com/malandamarkets; Malanda Showgrounds; ⊘7am-noon 3rd Sat of month)

Tumoulin Country Markets (Tumoulin Rd; ⊘8am-noon 4th Sun of month)

Yungaburra Markets (www.yungaburramarkets.com; Gillies Hwy; ⊘7.30am-12.30pm 4th Sat of month)

Kuranda Scenic Railway (p403), or do both with a combination return ticket.

Fares to Kuranda from Cairns are $6.70 with Trans North (p422), $16 on the **Cairns Cooktown Express** (☑07-4059 1423; www.cairnsbuscharters.com/services/cairns-cooktown-express) and $5 with John's Kuranda Bus (p422).

Kuranda is a 25km drive up the Kuranda Range from Cairns.

Mareeba

POP 11,079

Well known in these parts for being home to one of Australia's biggest **rodeos** (www.mareebarodeo.com.au; tickets $20-50; ⊘Jul), Mareeba has lately turned into the coffee capital of Far North Queensland, with several plantations and an impressive coffee museum – 70% of Australia's coffee crop is reportedly grown here.

This region was once the heart of the country's main tobacco-growing region, but these days Mareeba has turned its soil to more wholesome produce, with fruit orchards and distilleries in addition to the coffee farms. Mareeba's landscape differs dramatically from the higher-altitude central Tablelands and this is the last major town before making the long trips north to Cape York or west to Chillagoe.

Mareeba ('Meeting of the Waters') is the traditional home of the Muluridji people, whose territory stretched north towards Mt Molloy and Mt Carbine. Other tribes in this area included the Bar-Barrum and Walkamin peoples living to the west and Kuku Yalanji to the north.

If you love your coffee, it's well worth the trip to **Jacques Coffee Plantation** (☑07-4093 3284; www.jaquescoffee.com.au; 137 Leotta Rd; tours adult/child from $15/8; ⊘10am-4pm), a third-generation plantation with a cafe, restaurant and tours. There's also comprehensive displays on the area's history at **Mareeba Heritage Museum & Visitor Information Centre** (☑07-4092 5674; www.mareebaheritagecentre.com.au; Centenary Park, 345 Byrnes St; ⊘9am-5pm; ⊕) FREE.

For a piece of real country nostalgia, head to the **Mareeba Drive-In** (☑0429 056 615; www.mareebadrivein.com; 5303 Kennedy Hwy; adult/child $14/8; ⊘7.30pm Fri & Sat; ⊕), the only old-school drive-in cinema left in Far North Queensland.

The privately owned **Granite Gorge Nature Park** (☑07-4093 2259; www.granitegorge.com.au; 332 Paglietta Rd, Chewko; adult/child $13/6; ⊘9am-6pm; ⊕) ⚑, 12km from Mareeba, occupies an alien landscape of humungous granite boulders, caves and turtle-inhabited swimming holes. Stay at the on-site **Granite Gorge Caravan Park** (☑07-4093 2259; www.granitegorge.com.au; 332 Paglietta Rd, Chewko; powered/unpowered sites $18/16 per adult, cabin/safari tent from $95/65), if you're looking for family-friendly accommodation.

Atherton

POP 7331

The largest settlement and unofficial capital of the namesake Tablelands, Atherton is a spirited country town that makes a decent base for exploring the region's highlights and is the best place to shop for supplies. It's also a big draw for mountain-bikers.

Many backpackers head up to the Tablelands for year-round fruit-picking work; the **Atherton Visitor Information Centre** (☑07-4091 4222; cnr Main & Silo Sts; ⊘9am-5pm) can help with up-to-date work info.

This region is the traditional home of the Djirrbal and Ngadjonji tribes of the Djirrbalngan language group.

Tolga Bat Hospital (☑07-4091 2683; https://tolgabathospital.org; 134 Carrington Rd; adult/child $20/10; ⊘guided tour 3-6pm; ⊕) ⚑, a bat rehabilitation centre south of

Atherton, runs excellent guided tours every afternoon.

Thousands of Chinese migrants came to the region in search of gold in the late 1800s. All that's left of Atherton's Chinatown now is the fascinating 1903 timber and corrugated-iron **Hou Wang Miau Temple** (📞07-4091 6945; www.houwang.org.au; 86 Herberton Rd; adult/child/family $10/5/20; ⊙9am-4pm Wed-Fri, 9am-1pm Sat), now a museum run by the National Trust.

Also worth a visit is **Crystal Caves** (📞07-4091 2365; www.crystalcaves.com.au; 69 Main St; adult/child/family $25/12.50/65; ⊙9am-5pm Mon-Fri, to 4pm Sat & Sun; ⓘ), a gaudy mineralogical museum that houses more than 600 other crystals and glittering rocks.

Atherton Forest Mountain Bike Park (https://parks.des.qld.gov.au/parks/herberton-range/mountain-bike.html) FREE, an excellent network of some 55km of trails in the Herberton Range State Forest, is easily accessed from the trailhead in Atherton town centre (Vernon St) via a link track or from Rifle Range Rd. Rent a ride from **Atherton Bike Hire** (📞0408 911 854; www.bikehireatherton.com.au; 5 Robert St; half/full day from $45/55; ⊙8.30am-5pm Mon-Fri, 8.30am-1pm Sat, 9am-1pm Sun).

If you're staying, **Atherton Woodlands** (📞07-4091 1407; www.woodlandscp.com.au; 141 Herberton Rd; powered/unpowered sites from $42/30, villas & cottages $135-175; 🅿📶�ⓘ) is a beautifully maintained caravan park in gorgeous surrounds with facilities galore. Definitely have breakfast or lunch at fun cafe-gallery **Petals & Pinecones** (P&P; 📞0436 412 559; www.petalsandpineconesatherton.wordpress.com; 6-8 Herberton Rd; coffee/shakes $4.50/9; ⊙9am-4.30pm Mon-Fri, to 4pm Sat & Sun; ⓘ).

Millaa Millaa

Evocatively nicknamed the 'Village in the Mist', charming Millaa Millaa is a small and gloriously green dairy community famous for its wonderful waterfalls. Surrounded by rolling farmland dotted with black-and-white cows, it's a picturesque spot to stop for lunch or to spend a few quaint and quiet nights.

You'll find information on the town and surrounds online at www.millaamillaa.com or by dropping into the **Malanda Falls Visitor Centre** (📞07-4096 6957; www.malandafalls.com; 132 Malanda-Atherton Rd; ⊙9am-4.30pm).

This region was the traditional land of the Ngadjonji and Mamu peoples.

There's accommodation at the **Millaa Millaa Hotel** (📞07-4097 2212; 15 Main St; s/d $85/95; 🅿🛎📶) and **Millaa Millaa Tourist Park** (📞07-4097 2290; www.millaacaravanpark.com.au; cnr Malanda Rd & Lodge Ave; powered/unpowered sites $30/25, cabins $65-90; 🅿🛎📶🛁), while the **Mungalli Creek Dairy** (📞07-4097 2232; www.mungallicreekdairy.com.au; 254 Brooks Rd; meals $13-20; ⊙10am-4pm), a biodynamic dairy with attached farmhouse cafe 6km southeast of town, is ideal for a ploughman's lunch, cheese platter, smoked fish pie or slice of legendary cheesecake.

Malanda & Around

Malanda has been a byword for 'milk' in north Queensland ever since 560 cattle made the 16-month overland journey from NSW in 1908. There's still a working dairy here, and the **Malanda Dairy Centre** (📞07-4095 1234; www.malandadairycentrecafe.com; 8 James St; ⊙8am-3pm Wed-Sun; ⓘ) FREE, which has a kid-friendly museum highlighting the region's bovine history.

Rainforest-shrouded Malanda and its surrounds – including the other-worldly **Mt Hypipamee** (Crater Rd) FREE crater – are also home to shy, rare Lumholtz's tree-kangaroos; bring a low-wattage torch for an evening of spotlighting.

This region was the traditional land of the Ngadjonji people.

Guided **Rainforest Dreaming** (www.malandafalls.com/walks; adult/child/family $20/10/50; ⊙9.30am & 11am Fri, Sat & Sun) walks, led by members of the Ngadjonji community, can be booked ahead through the Malanda Falls Visitor Centre. You'll also have a great chance of spotting a wild platypus at **Australian Platypus Park & Tarzali Lakes** (📞07-4097 2713; www.australianplatypuspark.com; 912 Millaa Millaa-Malanda Rd, Tarzali; guided tour adult/child $8.50/6; ⊙9am-4pm, tours every half-hour; ⓘ). Spread your towel at the shady, croc-free **Malanda Falls** (Malanda-Atherton Rd; ⓘ) FREE, which have been tamed into a kind of public swimming pool.

If you're staying, boutique eco-accommodation doesn't get much better than **Canopy Treehouses & Wildlife Sanctuary** (📞07-4096 5364; www.canopytreehouses.com.au; Hogan Rd, Tarzali; tree house $269-479; 🅿📶) ⓘ.

Yungaburra

Yungaburra is the chocolate-box-cute country town of the Tablelands; within one lap of its tree-lined streets, you'll find 19 heritage-listed sites, a welcoming 1910 corner pub, boho-boutiques and cafes, and a dedicated platypus-watching platform. Its proximity to Lake Tinaroo and some of the region's top natural attractions makes Yungaburra a contender for best base on the Tablelands.

The town's lyrical name is thought to mean 'place of questioning' in the local Yidinyji language.

The sacred, 500-year-old **Curtain Fig** (Fig Tree Rd, East Barron) `FREE` tree (signposted 3km out of town) is a must-see for its gigantic, otherworldly aerial roots that hang down to create an enormous 'curtain'. If you're very quiet, you might catch a glimpse of a timid monotreme at the platypus-viewing **platform** (Gillies Hwy; [🚗]) `FREE` on Peterson Creek.

Explore the wild wonders of Yungaburra and around on an excellent expedition with **Alan** (☑07-4095 3784; www.alanswildlife tours.com.au; day tours \$110-550), a local naturalist of whopping passion and experience, and stay for the **Tablelands Folk Festival** (www.tablelandsfolkfestival.org.au), if here in October.

🛏 Sleeping & Eating

★ **On the Wallaby** HOSTEL **\$**
(☑07-4095 2031; www.onthewallaby.com; 34 Eacham Rd; van sites per person \$15, dm/d with shared bathroom \$28/65; [🛜]) 🍃 This cosy ecofriendly hostel features handmade timber furniture, lots of green energy touches (solar, rainwater tanks), spotless rooms and no TV. Nature-based tours (\$40) include night canoeing and mountain-biking; tour packages and transfers are available from Cairns. Cook for yourself in the communal kitchen, or join the nightly barbecue.

★ **Yungaburra Hotel** PUB FOOD **\$\$**
(Lake Eacham Hotel; ☑07-4095 3515; www.yunga burrahotel.com.au; 6-8 Kehoe Pl; mains \$15-32; ⊙restaurant noon-2pm & 6-8.30pm) This wonderful, welcoming, original-timber country pub is one of the most evocative in the state, let alone on the Tablelands. It often hosts live jams and bands, or just order a schooner, meet the locals and soak up the old-school atmosphere. The restaurant does huge, wholesome meals, including a Saturday night buffet.

❶ Information

Yungaburra Information Centre (☑07-4095 2416; www.yungaburra.com; Maud Kehoe Park; ⊙9am-5pm Mon-Sat, 10am-4pm Sun) The delightful volunteers at this immaculate centre can help recommend accommodation, provide info on walks and tours and generally yarn about all things Yungaburra.

Lake Tinaroo

Lake Tinaroo, also known as Tinaroo Dam, was allegedly named when a prospector stumbled across a deposit of alluvial tin and, in a fit of excitement, shouted 'Tin! Hurroo!'. These days locals flee the swelter of the coast for boating, waterskiing and shoreline lolling. **Barramundi fishing** (☑0438 012 775; www.tinaroobarra.com; half-/full-day fishing \$350/600) is permitted year-round, though if you're not joining a charter, you'll need to pick up a permit from local businesses.

The 28km **Danbulla Forest Drive** winds its way through rainforest and softwood plantations along the north side of the lake. The unsealed but well-maintained road passes the pretty **Lake Euramoo** and the boardwalk-encircled **Cathedral Fig**, a gigantic 500-year-old strangler fig similar to the Curtain Fig in nearby Yungaburra; it's also accessible via a signposted road off the Gillies Hwy.

This region is the traditional land of the Ngadjonji people.

There are five **Queensland Parks** (☑13 74 68; https://parks.des.qld.gov.au; camping permits per person/family \$6.55/26.20) campgrounds in the Danbulla State Forest. All have water, barbecues and toilets; advance bookings are essential. An alternative is the modern, well-equipped and shady **Lake Tinaroo Holiday Park** (☑07-4095 8232; www. laketinarooholidaypark.com.au; 3 Tinaroo Falls Dam Rd, Tinaroo Falls; powered/unpowered sites \$39/29, cabins \$135-150; [P][❄][🛜][🏊]).

Crater Lakes National Park

Part of the Wet Tropics World Heritage Area, the two mirrorlike, rainforest-fringed crater lakes of Lake Eacham and Lake Barrine are believed to have formed more than 12,000 years ago following a volcanic eruption. Both have an average depth of 65m. **Lake Barrine** is the larger of the two, and is cloaked in old-growth rainforest; a 5km walking track around its edge takes about 1½ hours. Look for the enormous 1000-year-old kauri pines.

On a hot day, folks from the coast swarm up to **Lake Eacham** for a dip – and some turtle-spotting – in its cool, clear waters. There are sheltered picnic areas, a pontoon and a boat ramp. The 3km lake-circuit track is an easy one-hour walk.

You won't have to worry about saltwater crocs, though a freshie occasionally cruises around Eacham.

To the local Ngadjonji and Yidinji people the lakes were known as Barany (Barrine) and Yidyam (Eacham)

Spot water dragons and tortoises or simply relax and soak up the views on a 45-minute **cruise** (www.lakebarrine.com.au/cruises; adult/child/family $18/8/40; ⊙ 9.30am, 11.30am & 1.30pm; 🖫) around the lake; book and board at the **Lake Barrine Teahouse** (☑ 07-4095 3847; www.lakebarrine.com.au; Gillies Hwy; Devonshire teas from $11; ⊙ 9am-4pm).

A favourite with nature lovers of all stripes, **Chambers Wildlife Rainforest Lodges** (☑ 07-4095 3754; www.chamberslodges.com.au; Eacham Close; lodge $140-210; 🅿🛜🏊) offers 10 self-contained lodges hidden among thick rainforest.

Pop into the **Rainforest Display Centre** (McLeish Rd, Lake Eacham; ⊙ 9am-1pm Mon, Wed & Fri) 🌿 for information on the area, the history of the timber industry and the ongoing rejuvenation of the rainforest.

PORT DOUGLAS TO COOKTOWN

Port Douglas

POP 3500

Welcome to your holiday. Port Douglas (Port or PD) is equal parts flash and fun, from the million-dollar marina to the dreamy Four Mile Beach and the five-star resorts big enough to warrant their own postcode.

The peninsula was the traditional home of the Yirrganydji people until European settlement turned it into a remote port and fishing village. Port Douglas really developed in the 1980s, thanks largely to the late entrepeneur Christopher Skase, becoming a sophisticated and upmarket resort town that's quite a contrast to Cairns' tourist scene. PD is well connected: the outer Great Barrier Reef is less than an hour offshore, the Dickson Inlet and estuary is packed with fish and crocs, and sunset sailing from the marina is too good to pass up.

A growing number of flashpackers, cashed-up couples and fiscally flush families choose Port Douglas over Cairns as their Far North base, and for good reason.

⊙ Sights

★**Wildlife Habitat Port Douglas**   ZOO
(☑ 07-4099 3235; www.wildlifehabitat.com.au; Port Douglas Rd; adult/child/family $36/18/90; ⊙ 8am-5pm; 🖫) 🌿 This sanctuary endeavours to keep and showcase native animals in enclosures that mimic their natural environment, while allowing you to get up close to koalas, kangaroos, crocs, cassowaries and more. Tickets are valid for three days. For an extra special experience book for **Breakfast with the Birds** ($56 incl admission; ⊙ 9-10.30am; 🖫) or **Lunch with the Lorikeets** ($58 incl admission; ⊙ noon-2pm; 🖫). The latest addition is the Predator Plank – a walkway across the saltwater croc enclosure. It's 5km from town ($5 by shuttle bus).

★**Trinity Bay Lookout**   VIEWPOINT
(Island Point Rd) FREE Head up to Flagstaff Hill for sensational views over **Four Mile Beach** (🖫) and the Coral Sea. Drive or walk up via Wharf St, or there's a walking path leading up from the north end of Four Mile Beach.

Court House Museum   MUSEUM
(☑ 07-4098 1284; www.douglashistory.org.au; Wharf St; adult/child $2/free; ⊙ 10am-1pm Tue, Thu, Sat & Sun) The 1879 Court House contains historical exhibits, including the story of Ellen Thompson, who was tried for murdering her husband in 1887 and the only woman ever hanged in Queensland.

🏃 Activities

Port Douglas has crafted an industry with a smorgasbord of activities and tours, both on water and land. For golfers the **Mirage Country Club** (☑ 07-4099 5537; www.miragecountryclub.com.au; 9/18 holes with cart $75/95, driving range from $11) and **Palmer Sea Reef** (☑ 07-4087 2222; www.palmergolf.com.au; 9/18 holes with cart $95/135) are two of north Queensland's top resort courses.

Port Douglas

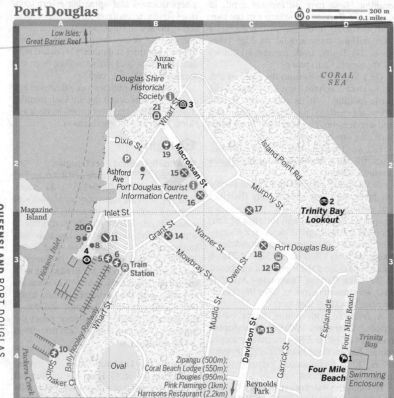

QUEENSLAND PORT DOUGLAS

Port Douglas

◎ Top Sights
1 Four Mile Beach	D4
2 Trinity Bay Lookout	D2

◎ Sights
3 Court House Museum	B1
4 Crystalbrook Superyacht Marina	A3

✦ Activities, Courses & Tours
5 Aquarius Sunset Sailing	A3
6 Bally Hooley Steam Railway	B3
7 Bike N Hike	B2
8 Blue Dive	A3
9 Lady Douglas	A3
10 Port Douglas Yacht Club	A4
Quicksilver	(see 5)
11 Tech Dive Academy	A3

🛏 Sleeping
12 Mantra Aqueous on Port	C3
13 Peppers Beach Club	C4

✖ Eating
14 Chilly's Pizza & Trattoria	B3
15 Coles Supermarket	B2
16 Grant Street Kitchen	B2
17 Little Larder	C2
18 My Italian Baby	C3
Seabean	(see 7)
Shakes Gelati Bar	(see 18)
Yachty	(see 10)

🍸 Drinking & Nightlife
19 Hemingway's	A3
20 Iron Bar	B2

🛍 Shopping
21 Crystalbrook Marina Market	A3
22 Port Douglas Markets	B1

Several companies offer PADI open-water certification as well as advanced dive certificates, including **Blue Dive** (☑ 0427 983 907; www.bluedive.com.au; 3-day dive courses $855). For one-on-one instruction, learn with **Tech Dive Academy** (☑ 07-4015 2915; www.tech-dive-academy.com; Crystalbrook Marina; 2-/4-day open-water courses from $1250/1950) ✎. The hub for cruises and other water-based activities is the impressive **Crystalbrook Superyacht Marina** (☑ 07-4099 5775; https://crystalbrookmarina.com; 44 Wharf St) [FREE].

★ **Wind Swell** WATER SPORTS
(☑ 0427 498 042; www.windswell.com.au; Barrier St; lessons from $50) Kitesurfing and stand-up paddleboarding for everyone from beginners to high-flyers. Kitesurfing lessons and paddleboarding tours from the beach start at $50, but there are also plenty of advanced options. Find them in action at the southern end of Four Mile Beach (p427).

Port Douglas Yacht Club BOATING
(☑ 07-4099 4386; www.portdouglasyachtclub.com.au; 1 Spinnaker Close; ⊙ from 4pm Wed) Free sailing with club members every Wednesday afternoon: sign on from 4pm. Those chosen to go sailing are expected to stay for dinner and drinks in the club afterwards.

Aquarius Sunset Sailing CRUISE
(☑ 07-4099 6999; www.tropicaljourneys.com; adult/child $60/50; ⊙ cruises depart 4.45pm) Twilight sailing is practically de rigueur in Port Douglas. This 1½-hour catamaran cruise includes canapés, and BYO alcohol is encouraged.

Bally Hooley Steam Railway RAIL
(☑ 0403 068 505; www.ballyhooleyrail.com.au; 46 Wharf St; adult/child return $20/10; ⊙ 9.30am-3.30pm Sun & Wed; ⊕) Kids will get a kick out of this cute miniature steam train. Every Sunday (and some public holidays), it runs from the little station at Crystalbrook Marina to St Crispins Station at 11am, 12.30pm and 2pm. A return trip takes about one hour; one way is half price. On Wednesday a diesel engine does the same trip.

☞ **Tours**

The outer reef is closer to Port Douglas than it is to Cairns, and the unrelenting surge of visitors has inevitably had a detrimental impact on its condition here in places. You will still see colourful corals and marine life, but it is patchy in parts.

Most day tours depart from Crystalbrook Marina. Tour prices usually include reef tax, snorkelling, transfers from your accommodation, lunch and refreshments.

★ **Quicksilver** CRUISE
(☑ 07-4087 2100; www.quicksilver-cruises.com; Crystalbrook Marina; adult/child/family $257/132/625) Major operator with fast cruises to its private pontoon on Agincourt Reef. Additional activities include an 'ocean walk' helmet dive ($170) on a submerged platform, introductory diving ($172), certified dive ($124) or snorkelling with a marine biologist (from $64). Also offers 10-minute scenic helicopter flights ($189, minimum two passengers).

Lady Douglas BOATING
(☑ 0408 986 127; www.ladydouglas.com.au; Crystalbrook Marina, Wharf St; 1½hr cruises adult/child/family $35/20/100; ⊙ cruises 10.30am, 12.30pm, 2.30pm & 4.30pm; ⊕) A lovely paddle steamer running four daily croc-spotting river tours (plus an evening cruise on Fridays) along the Dickson Inlet.

★ **Tony's Tropical Tours** TOURS
(☑ 07-4099 3230; www.tropicaltours.com.au; day tours adult/child from $198/178) ✎ This luxury, small-group (eight to 10 passengers) eco-tour operator specialises in day trips to out-of-the-way sections of the Mossman Gorge and Daintree Rainforest (adult/child $185/160), and Bloomfield Falls and Cape Trib (adults only $235 – good mobility required). A third tour heads south to the Tablelands. Highly recommended.

Bike N Hike CYCLING
(☑ 0477 774 443; www.bikenhiketours.com.au; 3 Warner St; tours $120-128; ⊙ 9am-5pm) Mountain-bike down the aptly named Bump Track on a cross-country bike tour, or take on an action-packed berserk night tour. Also does half-day cycling and hiking trips.

✦★ **Festivals & Events**

Port Douglas Carnivale CARNIVAL
(www.carnivale.com.au; ⊙ May) Port is packed for this 10-day festival, which includes a colourful street parade featuring live music, and lashings of good food and wine.

🛏 **Sleeping**

★ **Coral Beach Lodge** HOSTEL **$**
(☑ 07-4099 5422; http://coralbeachlodge.com; 1 Craven Close; dm $25-39, d $115; ❈ @ 🛜 ☒)

A cut above most backpacker places, this chilled-out hostel has well-equipped en-suite dorms (with four or five beds) and double or triple rooms that put some motels in the shade – flat-screen TVs, modern bathrooms and comfy beds. Each room has an outdoor area with hammocks, and there's a lovely pool, a games room, a kitchen and helpful owners.

Dougies
HOSTEL **$**

(📞 07-4099 6200, 1800 996 200; www.dougies.com.au; 111 Davidson St; tent/bungalow per person $28/30, dm/d $30/75; ✳ @ 🎝 ☲) It's easy to hang about Dougies' sprawling grounds in a hammock or pool by day and move to the bar at night. If you can summon the energy, bikes and fishing gear are available for rent and the beach is a 300m walk east. Free pick-up from Cairns on Monday, Wednesday and Saturday.

Pink Flamingo
BOUTIQUE HOTEL **$$**

(📞 07-4099 6622; www.pinkflamingo.com.au; 115 Davidson St; d studio/villa $150/210; ✳ @ 🎝 ☲) Flamboyantly painted rooms, private walled courtyards and a groovy al fresco pool-bar make the Pink Flamingo Port Douglas' hippest gay-friendly digs. With just two studios and 10 villas, it's an intimate stay in a sea of mega-resorts. Heated pool, a gym and bike rental are also on offer.

★ Peppers Beach Club
RESORT **$$$**

(📞 1300 737 444; www.peppers.com.au/beachclub; 20-22 Davidson St; spa ste from $315, 1-/2-bedoom ste from $450/515; ✳ 🎝 ☲) A killer location and an exceptional, enormous, sandy lagoon pool, combined with luxurious, airy apartments with high-end furnishings and amenities, put Peppers right up there with Port Douglas' best in its price range. Some rooms have balcony spas, others swim-up decks or full kitchens. Family friendly, but recommended for young romantics.

Mantra Aqueous on Port
APARTMENT **$$$**

(📞 07-4099 0000; www.mantraaqueousonport.com.au; 3-5 Davidson St; d from $240, 1-/2-bed apt from $235/399; ✳ 🎝 ☲) You can't beat the central town location of this resort with rooms and apartments arranged around four individual pools. The pricier ground-floor rooms have swim-up balconies, and all rooms have outdoor spa tubs. Studio and one- and two-bedroom apartments are available. Longer stays attract cheaper rates.

Turtle Cove Beach Resort
RESORT **$$$**

(📞 07-4059 1800; www.turtlecove.com; Captain Cook Hwy; d $225-360; 🅿 ✳ 🎝 ☲) Midway between Palm Cove and Port Douglas, Turtle Cove is one of the few LGBTIQ+ resorts in Far North Queensland. Refurbished rooms all have sea views, but the best are the beachfront suites and apartments. There's a beautiful pool shaded by gum trees, lazy hammocks and a relaxed, welcoming vibe. Clothing is optional.

Oaks Resort
RESORT **$$$**

(📞 07-4099 8900; www.oakshotels.com; 87-109 Port Douglas Rd; d $212-230; ✳ @ 🎝 ☲) Formerly QT, Oaks has had a makeover but is still fun and aimed at a trendy, 20- to 30-something crowd, though families will find a lot to like. There's a lagoon pool and swim-up bar, a gym, a spa and tidy minimalist rooms. The breakfast buffet is highly rated.

Thala Beach Nature Reserve
RESORT **$$$**

(📞 07-4098 5700; www.thalabeach.com.au; Captain Cook Hwy; d $400-800; ✳ 🎝 ☲) On a private coastal headland 15km south of Port Douglas, Thala Beach is a sublime upmarket eco-retreat so relaxing that even locals come here to splash out and chill for the weekend. Luxurious tree-house-style bungalows are scattered throughout the jungle with easy access to a private stretch of beach, two pools, walking trails and the treetop **Osprey's** restaurant.

🍴 Eating

Port Douglas' compact centre is awash with sophisticated cafes and restaurants, many with a tropical al fresco setting. All of the resorts have restaurants.

Self-caterers can stock up on supplies at the large **Coles Supermarket** (11 Macrossan St; ⊙ 7am-6pm) in the Port Village shopping centre.

Shakes Gelati Bar
ICE CREAM **$**

(📞 07-4099 4010; Shop 9 53 Macrossan St; 1/2 scoops $5/7; ⊙ 11am-9.30pm; 🚼) Cool off with Port Douglas' best ice cream and gelati with all the classics represented and some tropical twists: sea-salted caramel, coconut and lime sorbet, macadamia and banoffee.

Zipangu
JAPANESE **$**

(📞 07-4099 6718; 6/79 Davidson St; sushi $13-15, mains $18-25; ⊙ 11.30am-2pm & 5.30-8pm Tue-Sat) There's often a queue for takeaway at this simple little Japanese sushi and teriyaki joint. Rolled sushi comes in serves of eight pieces, sashimi plates are fresh and bowls of udon noodle soup are filling.

Grant Street Kitchen BAKERY **$**

(📷 0478-769 987; shop 4/5 Grant St; mains $7-12; ⊙ 6am-3pm; 🐾) Delicious egg-and-bacon rolls, ham-and-cheese croissants or fruit salads are breakfast treats at this awesome little artisanal bakery. For lunch try the homemade pies or loaded sandwiches.

★ **Yachty** MODERN AUSTRALIAN **$$**

(📷 07-4099 4386; www.portdouglasyachtclub. com.au; 1 Spinnaker Close; mains $20-32; ⊙ noon-2.30pm & 5.30-8pm) One of the best-value nights out is the local yacht club, where well-crafted meals, from seafood pie to Thai green curry, are served nightly with sunset views over Dickson Inlet. The lunch menu is similar but cheaper.

★ **My Italian Baby** ITALIAN **$$**

(📷 07-4099 5433; http://italianbaby.cc; 17 Macrossan St; mains $18-35; ⊙ 7.30am-10pm) Port's newest Italian restaurant, My Italian Baby is a sophisticated but down-to-earth main street eatery that gets rave reviews from locals and visitors alike. The day starts early with breakfast, while lunch and dinner features classic pasta dishes and novel, locally themed pizzas. Look out for specials nights (like two-for-one Monday).

★ **Seabean** SPANISH **$$**

(📷 07-4099 5558; www.seabean.com.au; 3/28 Wharf St; tapas $9-19, paella from $37; ⊙ 3-9pm Mon-Thu, noon-9pm Fri-Sun) This cool little tapas bar with bright red stools and attentive staff brings quality Spanish plates and paella to PD. Authentic share plates include grilled octopus and sherry-infused chorizo.

Little Larder CAFE **$$**

(📷 07-4099 6450; Shop 2, 40 Macrossan St; mains $13-22; ⊙ 7.30am-3pm; 🖥🐾) Breakfast on açai coconut bowls or Persian waffles until 11.30am, then it's gourmet sandwiches and killer cocktails from noon. Good coffee, or try freshly brewed and super-healthy kombucha tea. Little Larder is effortless cool and mostly healthy.

Chilly's Pizza & Trattoria ITALIAN **$$**

(📷 07-4099 4444; www.chillyspizza.com; 2 Mowbray St; mains $17-30; ⊙ 5-10pm) This sociable garden restaurant and bar specialises in wood-fired pizza – the seafood pizza is something to behold – and classic pasta dishes. Toppings are generous and service is efficient.

★ **Flames of the Forest** MODERN AUSTRALIAN **$$$**

(📷 07-4099 3144; www.flamesoftheforest. au; dinner with show, drinks & transfers per person $192-220; ⊙ Tue, Thu & Sat) This unique experience goes way beyond the traditional concept of 'dinner and a show', with diners escorted deep into the rainforest for a truly immersive night of theatre, culture and gourmet cuisine. Transport provided from Port Douglas or Cairns (no self-drive). Bookings essential.

★ **Harrisons Restaurant** MODERN AUSTRALIAN **$$$**

(📷 0455 594 011; www.harrisonsrestaurant.com. au; Sheraton Grand Mirage, Port Douglas Rd; mains $38-54; ⊙ 4pm-midnight) Marco Pierre White–trained chef-owner Spencer Patrick whips up culinary gems that stand toe to toe with Australia's best. Fresh, locally sourced produce is turned into dishes such as smoked duck breast and tamarind beef cheeks. Originally on Wharf St, Harrisons is now ensconced in the flash Sheraton Grand Mirage.

🍷 Drinking & Nightlife

★ **Hemingway's** MICROBREWERY

(📷 07-4099 6663; www.hemingwaysbrewery.com; Crystalbrook Marina, 44 Wharf St) Hemingway's makes the most of a fabulous location at the marina with a broad deck, a long bar and Dickson Inlet views. There are usually six brews on tap, including Hard Yards dark lager and Pitchfork Betty's pale ale. Naturally, food is available, but this is one for the beer connoisseurs. A tasting paddle is $15.

Iron Bar PUB

(📷 07-4099 4776; www.ironbarportdouglas.com. au; 5 Macrossan St; ⊙ 11am-3am) Wacky outback meets Wild West decor of corrugated iron and old timber, setting the scene for a wild night out. Don't miss the nightly 8pm cane-toad races ($5) for a bit of comic relief.

🔒 Shopping

Macrossan St is crammed with boutiques and souvenir shops, and there are local markets on **Wednesday** (Crystalbrook Marina, Wharf St; ⊙ 11am-5pm Wed) and **Sunday** (Anzac Park, Macrossan St; ⊙ 8am-2pm Sun).

ℹ️ Information

The *Port Douglas & Mossman Gazette* comes out every Thursday, and has heaps of local info, gig guides and more.

There's no official government-accredited visitor information centre in Port Douglas, but private bookings agents abound, such as **Port Douglas Tourist Information Centre** (☑ 07-4099 5599; www.infoportdouglas.com.au; 23 Macrossan St; ⊙ 8am-6.30pm).

Douglas Shire Historical Society (☑ 07-4098 1284; www.douglashistory.org.au; Wharf St; ⊙ 10am-1pm Tue, Thu, Sat & Sun) Download DIY historical walks through Port Douglas, Mossman and Daintree, or chat with a local at the on-site Court House Museum (p427).

ℹ️ Getting There & Away

Port Douglas Bus (☑ 07-4099 5665; www.portdouglasbus.com.au; 53-61 Macrossan St) and Sun Palm (p416) operate daily between Port Douglas, Cairns and Cairns Airport (p417).

Trans North (☑ 07-4095 8644; www.transnorthbus.com.au) picks up in Port Douglas on the coastal drive between Cairns and Cooktown.

ℹ️ Getting Around

Hire bikes at **Bike Shop & Hire** (☑ 07-4099 5799; www.portdouglasbikehire.com.au; 3 Warner St; half/full day from $16/20; ⊙ 9am-5pm); backpackers hostels also have bikes for hire.

Minibuses, such as those run by **Coral Reef Coaches** (☑ 07-4098 2800; www.coralreefcoaches.com.au) and **SR Coaches** (☑ 0469 723 071; https://srcoaches.com.au/local_shuttle; shuttle between town and the highway for around $5.

Major car-rental chains have branches here, or try **Comet Car Hire** (☑ 07-4099 6407; www.cometcarhire.com.au; 3/11 Warner St) and keep it local.

Port Douglas Taxi (☑ 13 10 08) offers 24-hour service.

Mossman

POP 1733

Surrounded by sugar-cane fields, the workaday town of Mossman, 20km north of Port Douglas, is best known for beautiful Mossman Gorge, part of the Daintree National Park. The town itself is worth a stop to get a feel for a Far North Queensland working community and to stock up if you're heading further north.

This is Kuku Yalanji Aboriginal country and three of Far North Queensland's best Indigenous tours are based here and at nearby Cooya Beach. In town is an excellent Indigenous art gallery.

◉ Sights & Activities

★ Mossman Gorge   GORGE
(www.mossmangorge.com.au; ⊙ 8am-6pm; 🚻)

FREE In the southeast corner of Daintree National Park, 5km west of Mossman town, Mossman Gorge forms part of the traditional lands of the Kuku Yalanji people. The gorge is a boulder-strewn valley where sparkling water washes over ancient rocks. It's 3km by road from the **visitor centre** (☑ 07-4099 7000; www.mossmangorge.com.au; ⊙ 8am-6pm) to a viewpoint and refreshing swimming hole – take care as the currents can be swift. You can walk the 4km, but visitors are encouraged to take the shuttle (adult/child/family return $9.80/4.85/24.20, every 15 minutes).

★ Kuku-Yalanji
Dreamtime Walks   OUTDOORS
(adult/child $75/37; ⊙ 10am, 11am, noon, 1pm & 3pm) 🚶 These unforgettable 1½-hour Indigenous-guided walks of Mossman Gorge include a smoking ceremony, bush tea and damper. Book through the Mossman Gorge Centre.

🛏️ Sleeping & Eating

★ Silky Oaks Lodge   RESORT $$$
(☑ 07-4098 1666; www.silkyoakslodge.com.au; Finlayvale Rd; tree houses $620-800, ste $1000-1250; ❄️ 🛜 🏊) This international eco-resort on the Mossman River woos honeymooners and stressed-out execs with amazing architecturally designed tree houses, riverside lodge suites, luxury hammocks, rejuvenation treatments, polished-timber interiors and private spa baths. Activities include tennis, gym, yoga classes and canoeing. Its stunning **Treehouse Restaurant & Bar** (mains $32-45; ⊙ 7-10am, noon-2.30pm & 6-8.30pm) is open to interlopers with advance reservation.

The Daintree & Cape Tribulation

The Daintree represents many things: Unesco World Heritage–listed **rainforest** (www.daintreerainforest.com), a river, a reef, laid-back villages and the home of its traditional custodians, the Kuku Yalanji people. It encompasses the coastal lowland area between the Daintree and Bloomfield Rivers, where the rainforest tumbles right down to the coast. It's a fragile, ancient ecosystem, once threatened by logging but now protected as a national park.

Part of the Wet Tropics World Heritage Area, the spectacular region from the Daintree River north to Cape Tribulation features ancient rainforest, sandy beaches and rugged mountains. North of the Daintree River, electricity is supplied by generators or, increasingly, solar power. Shops and services are limited, and mobile-phone reception is patchy at best. The **Daintree River Ferry** (www.douglas.qld.gov.au/community/daintree-ferry; car one way/return $16/28, motorcycle $6/11, pedestrian & bicycle $1/2; ☺6am-midnight), one of the few cable ferries of its kind in Australia, carries wanderers and their wheels across the river every 15 minutes or so.

Cow Bay & Around

Tiny Cow Bay is the first community you reach after the Daintree ferry crossing. On the steep, winding road between Cape Kimberley and Cow Bay, the **Walu Wugirriga Lookout** (Alexandra Range Lookout) offers sweeping views beyond the Daintree River inlet; it's especially breathtaking at sunset.

The white-sand and mostly deserted **Cow Bay Beach**, 5km east of the main road at the end of Buchanan Creek Rd, rivals any coastal paradise.

The award-winning **Daintree Discovery Centre** (☏07-4098 9171; www.discoverthedaintree.com; Tulip Oak Rd; adult/child/family $35/16/85; ☺8.30am-5pm; ⚑) ⚐ has an aerial walkway which includes a 23m tower used to study carbon levels, taking you high into the forest canopy. A theatre screens films on cassowaries, crocodiles, conservation and climate change.

Get closer to nature on a boat trip with **Cape Tribulation Wilderness Cruises** (☏0457 731 000; www.capetribcruises.com; Cape Tribulation Rd; adult/child from $34/24) or a walking tour with **Cooper Creek Wilderness** (☏07-4098 9126; www.coopercreek.com.au; 2333 Cape Tribulation Rd; guided walks $70-185).

🛏 Sleeping & Eating

★ Epiphyte B&B   B&B $

(☏07-4098 9039; www.rainforestbb.com; 22 Silkwood Rd; s/d/cabins from $80/130/170) This lovingly built, laid-back place is set on a lush 3.5-hectare property. Individually styled rooms are of varying sizes, but all have their own verandah. A spacious, private cabin features a patio, kitchenette and sunken bathroom. Minimum two-night stay.

★ Heritage
Lodge & Spa   LODGE $$$

(☏07-4098 9321; www.heritagelodge.net.au; Lot 236/R96 Turpentine Rd, Diwan; cabins $330; ❉ 🛜 ⛱) The friendly, accommodating owners of this wonderful retreat will do their best to make sure you feel at home. Their cute but comfortable renovated cabins are well spaced and ensconced in rainforest. A highlight is swimming in the crystal-clear waters of their gorgeous croc-free Cooper Creek swimming hole. The on-site **dining** (mains $26-38; ☺12-2pm & 5.30-9pm) and day spa are superb.

★ Daintree Ice
Cream Company   ICE CREAM $

(☏07-4098 9114; www.daintreeicecream.com.au; Lot 100, Cape Tribulation Rd; ice-cream tasting cup $7.50; ☺11am-5pm) We dare you to drive past this all-natural ice-cream producer with a range of flavours that changes daily. The tasting cup includes four flavours – you might get macadamia, black sapote, wattleseed or soursop, but they're all delicious.

Cape Tribulation

POP 330

Cape Trib is at the end of the winding sealed road from the Daintree River and, with its two magnificent beaches, laid-back vibe and rainforest walks, it's a little slice of tropical paradise. The traditional custodians of the Cape Trib area are the Kuku Yalanji people.

Despite the backpacker bars and tour operators, Cape Trib retains a frontier quality, with road signs alerting drivers to cassowary crossings, and croc warnings making evening beach strolls a little less relaxing. That there's no reliable mobile-phone reception or network internet adds to the remoteness – although there's now (since 2018) pricey roaming internet in the village.

The rainforest skirts beautiful **Myall** and **Cape Tribulation** beaches, which are separated by a knobby cape. The village here marks the end of the sealed road: beyond, the strictly 4WD-only Bloomfield Track continues north to Wujal Wujal.

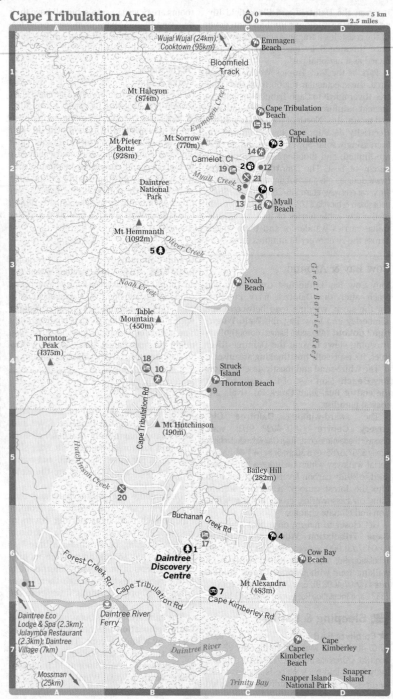

Cape Tribulation Area

Cape Tribulation Area

◎ Top Sights
1 Daintree Discovery Centre B6

◎ Sights
2 Bat House.. C2
3 Cape Tribulation Beach...................... C2
4 Cow Bay Beach..................................... C6
5 Daintree Rainforest............................. B3
6 Myall Beach.. C2
7 Walu Wugirriga Lookout..................... C6

✪ Activities, Courses & Tours
8 Cape Trib Horse Rides........................ C2
9 Cape Tribulation Wilderness
   Cruises.. C4
10 Cooper Creek Wilderness B4
11 Daintree River Cruise Centre............. A6
   Fruit Tasting Tours .... (see 2)
12 Jungle Surfing Canopy Tours C2
13 Masons Tours C2
14 Mt Sorrow Ridge Walk C2
   Ocean Safari .... (see 2)

🛏 Sleeping
15 Cape Trib Beach House........................ C2
16 Cape Tribulation Camping C2
17 Epiphyte B&B C6
18 Heritage Lodge & Spa.......................... B4
19 Rainforest Hideaway C2

✕ Eating
20 Daintree Ice Cream Company B5
   Mason's Store & Cafe................. (see 13)
   On the Turps .... (see 18)
   Sand Bar...................................... (see 16)
   Tides Bar & Restaurant .... (see 15)
21 Whet.. C2

ⓘ Information
   Mason's Store............................. (see 13)

◎ Sights & Activities

Bat House WILDLIFE RESERVE
(☑07-4098 0063; www.austrop.org.au; Cape Tribulation Rd; $5; ⊗10.30am-3.30pm Tue-Sun) This
nursery and research station for injured or
orphaned fruit bats (flying foxes), run by
conservation organisation Austrop, welcomes visitors.

Mt Sorrow Ridge Walk WALKING
Mt Sorrow is a demanding day hike for fit
walkers. The ridge-walk trail starts about
150m north of the Kulki picnic area car
park, just off the Bloomfield Rd. The strenuous walk (7km, five to six hours return, start
no later than 10am), offers spectacular views
over the rainforest and reef.

☞ Tours

★Ocean Safari SNORKELLING
(☑07-4098 0006; www.oceansafari.com.au; Cape
Tribulation Rd; adult/child/family $149/97/447;
⊗8am & noon) Ocean Safari leads small
groups (25 people maximum) on morning
and afternoon snorkelling cruises to the
Great Barrier Reef, just half an hour offshore
by fast inflatable. Swimming with sea turtles
is a highlight. Wetsuit hire ($8) available.

Fruit Tasting Tours FOOD & DRINK
(Cape Trib Farm; adult/child/family $30/20/90;
⊗2pm, closed Tue & Thu Oct-May) The orchard
at Cape Trib Farm hosts 1½-hour exotic
fruit-tasting tours with tropical delights
from breadfruit to sapote.

Masons Tours WALKING, DRIVING
(☑07-4098 0070; www.masonstours.com.au;
Mason's Store, Cape Tribulation Rd; walks up to 4
people half/full day $300/500) Long-time local
Lawrence Mason conducts enlightening
rainforest walks, including a night walk;
4WD tours up the Bloomfield Track to Cooktown are also available (groups up to five
people half/full day $800/1250). Find out
more at the popular Mason's Cafe (p436).

Jungle Surfing Canopy Tours OUTDOORS
(☑07-4098 0043; www.junglesurfing.com.au;
Cape Tribulation Rd; zip lines $105, night walks $45;
⊗8am-5.30pm, night walks 7.30pm) Get right
up into the rainforest on an exhilarating
two-hour flying-fox (zip line) surf through
the canopy. Guided night walks follow biol-
ogist-guides who shed light on the rainforest after dark. Rates include pick-up from
Cape Trib accommodation (self-drive not
permitted).

Cape Trib Horse Rides HORSE RIDING
(☑07-4098 0043; www.capetribhorserides.com.
au; rides adult/child from $110/70; ⊗8am &
2.30pm) Leisurely morning and afternoon
rides along the beach and into the forest.

🛏 Sleeping & Eating

Restaurants at Cape Trib's resorts are all
open to nonguests. There's a supermarket
stocking very basic supplies for self-caterers
– fussy shoppers should stock up in Cairns
or Port Douglas.

★Cape Trib Beach House HOSTEL, RESORT $
(☑07-4098 0030; www.capetribbeach.com.
au; 152 Rykers Rd; dm $31-41, cabins $160-275;
❅@≋) The Beach House is everything

DAINTREE VILLAGE

For wildlife lovers and birdwatchers, it's well worth taking the 20km each-way detour from the Mossman-Daintree Rd to tiny Daintree Village, set on a plateau of farmland on the Upper Daintree River on the traditional lands of the Kuku Yalanji people. Croc-spotting cruises are the main event: try long-running **Crocodile Express** (☑07-4098 6120; www.crocodileexpress.com; 1hr cruises adult/child/family $28/14/65; ⊙cruises 8.30am; 🔾), **Daintree River Wild Watch** (☑0447 734 933; www.daintreeriverwildwatch.com.au; 2hr cruises adult/child $60/35; 🔾) or **Daintree River Cruise Centre** (☑07-4098 6115; www.daintreerivercruisecentre.com.au; 2914 Mossman-Daintree Rd; adult/child $30/15/80; ⊙9.30am-4pm; 🔾).

The sublime boutique 'banyans' (pole cabins) at **Daintree Eco Lodge & Spa** (☑07-4777 7377; www.daintree-ecolodge.com.au; 3189 Mossman-Daintree Rd; tree houses $380-480; ✳@🔾🏊) 🌿 sit in seclusion high in the rainforest canopy a few kilometres south of Daintree Village. Nonguests are welcome at its superb **Julaymba Restaurant** (☑07-4098 6100; mains $30-39; ⊙dinner from 4.30pm), which uses local produce, including indigenous berries, nuts, leaves and flowers.

In the village, **Big Barramundi Garden** (☑07-4098 6186; www.bigbarra.daintree.info; 12 Stewart St; mains $18-25, burgers $8-10; ⊙10am-4pm) serves exotic burgers (barra, crocodile and kangaroo), pies and smoothies or fruit juices (black sapote, paw paw) as well as Devonshire teas.

that's great about Cape Trib – a secluded patch of rainforest facing a pristine beach and a friendly vibe that welcomes backpackers, couples and families. Clean dorms and rustic almost-beachfront cabins make the most of the location. The open-deck licensed **restaurant** (mains $15-26; ⊙7-9.30am, noon-2.30pm & 6-8pm; 🔾) and bar is well regarded enough that locals often eat and drink here.

Cape Tribulation Camping CAMPGROUND $
(☑07-4098 0077; www.capetribcamping.com.au; Lot 11, Cape Tribulation Rd; powered/unpowered sites per person $22/17) Myall Beach is just steps away from this lovely laid-back campground. Grassy sites are fairly well spaced, facilities are good (unless you want a pool) and the **Sand Bar** (☑07-4098 0077; Lot 11, Cape Tribulation Rd; pizzas $15-20; ⊙5-8pm Mon-Sat Apr-Nov) is a sociable verandah restaurant serving Cape Trib's best wood-fired pizzas.

Rainforest Hideaway B&B $$
(☑07-4098 0108; www.rainforesthideaway.com; 19 Camelot Close; d $150) 🌿 This colourful B&B, consisting of one room in the main house and a separate cabin, was single-handedly built by its owner, artist and sculptor 'Dutch Rob' – even the furniture and beds are handmade. A sculpture trail winds through the property and traditional Thai massage is available (one hour $75). Minimum two nights.

⭐ **Whet** AUSTRALIAN $$
(☑07-4098 0007; www.whet.net.au; 1 Cape Tribulation Rd; lunch $16-20, dinner $20-35; ⊙11am-3pm & 6-8pm) 🌿 Whet is regarded as Cape Trib's most sophisticated place to eat, with a loungey cocktail-bar feel and romantic, candlelit, al fresco dining. Tempura wild barramundi and house chicken curry grace the menu; all lunch dishes are under $20. You'll often find locals at the bar and the owners pride themselves on fresh produce and eco-friendly processes.

⭐ **Mason's Store & Cafe** CAFE $
(☑07-4098 0016; 3781 Cape Tribulation Rd; mains $9-18, tasting plates from $29; ⊙10am-4pm) Everyone calls into Mason's for **tourist info** (☑07-4098 0070; ⊙8am-5pm), for the liquor store (open until 5.30pm), or to dine out on exotic meats. Pride of place on the menu at this laid-back al fresco cafe goes to the croc burger, but you can also try camel, emu and kangaroo in burgers or tasting plates. A short walk away is a crystal-clear, croc-free swimming hole ($1).

North to Cooktown

The historic Cooktown region is the southernmost base for Cape York Peninsula, a wild and remote part of the north Queensland coast with a significant past of Indigenous territory and European impact – the latter starting with Cook himself. There are two routes to Cooktown from the south: the coastal route from Cape Tribulation via the 4WD-only Bloomfield Track, and the inland route, sealed all the way via the Mulligan Hwy.

The Cooktown region, including northwest to Hopevale and Rinyirru (Lakefield) National Park, is the traditional home of the Guugu Yimithirr people. South of Cooktown, to Wujal Wujal and the Daintree, is home to the rainforest Kuku Yalanji people. In both areas there are excellent opportunities to tour the land with Indigenous guides.

Bloomfield Track

No so long ago the legendary Bloomfield Track was a full-day 4WD adventure connecting Cape Tribulation to the Mulligan Hwy just short of Cooktown. Since 2014 the road has been sealed all the way from the north to the Aboriginal community at Wujal Wujal on the Bloomfield River and the river itself now has an all-season bridge.

This means you can explore from Cooktown down to Bloomfield Falls with a conventional vehicle – a trip into previously remote Kuku Yulanji country that's well worth pencilling in.

You still need a 4WD to travel from Cape Tribulation to the Bloomfield River on roughly 32km of unsealed and diabolically steep terrain traversing a couple of creek crossings – it can be impassable for weeks on end during the Wet, so check conditions at Mason's Store (p436). Although some try it, this section of road is not recommended for trailers.

Starting at Cape Trib, it's 8km to the first water crossing at **Emmagen Creek**. From here the road climbs and dips steeply, and turns sharp corners, then follows the broad Bloomfield River before reaching it 24km further in at the Indigenous community of Wujal Wujal. Here you'll find the wonderful **Bana Yirriji Art Centre** (☑07-4060 8333; www.wujalwujalartcentre.com.au; Bloomfield Rd; ☺9am-4pm Mon-Thu, to 2pm Friday; P) ☞ FREE.

Continue along the river for 1km to the impressive **Bloomfield Falls**. The half-hour **Walker Family Walking Tours** (☑07-4040 7500; adult/child $25/12.50; ☺by reservation) ☞ of the falls and surrounding forest are highly recommended.

About 7km north of Wujal Wujal is the small community of **Ayton**, with a shop,

cafes, beach access and some great places to stay, including **Bloomfield Beach Camp** (☑07-4060 8207; www.bloomfieldbeach.com.au; 20 Bloomfield Rd; powered/unpowered sites $38/32, cabin d & safari tents $95, cottage $165) and **Bloomfield Escape** (☑07-4060 8346; www.bloomfieldescape.com.au; 9 Weary Bay Rd; cabins from $125; ✳ ☎).

The sealed road continues for another 25km north to Rossville, where a rough 3km driveway leads to **Home Rule Rainforest Lodge** (☑07-4060 3925; https://homerule.com.au; unpowered sites per adult/child $10/5, s/d $20/35), ground zero for the **Wallaby Creek Festival** (www.wallabycreekfestival.org.au; ☺end Sep; ☝), a three-day, multicultural, family-ly-friendly event featuring roots, blues and Indigenous music.

It's another 9km to the iconic **Lion's Den Hotel** (☑07-4060 3911; 398 Shiptons Flat Rd, Helenvale; camping per person $12, powered sites $30, s/d dongas $60/80, pole tents $110; ✳ ☒), a legendary oasis with a tangible history dating back to 1875. Don't miss a swim in the croc-free creek.

Nearby, explore the surrounding rainforest and waterfall of **Mungumby Lodge** (☑07-4060 3158; www.mungumby.com; s/d/f $260/279/339; ☎ ☒) rates include breakfast and nature tours are available. About 4km further north, the road meets the sealed Mulligan Hwy, from where it's 28km to Cooktown.

Cooktown

POP 2630

Coastal, remote Cooktown is a small place with a big history: for thousands of years, Waymbuurr was the place the local Guugu Yimithirr and Kuku Yalanji people used as a meeting ground, and it was here that on 17 June 1770, Lieutenant (later Captain) Cook beached the *Endeavour,* which had earlier struck a reef offshore from Cape Tribulation.

Cook's crew spent 48 days here repairing the damage, making Cooktown Australia's first (albeit transient) non-Indigenous settlement.

Today Cooktown makes the most of its colonial and Indigenous history – and its pristine natural environment. It's also an easy-going place to recharge with good accommodation, dining, beaches and gardens. This is a starting base for trips to the Cape and serious fishing expeditions.

LIZARD ISLAND

The five islands of the Lizard Island Group lie 33km off the coast about 100km north of Cooktown. Lizard, the main island, has rocky, mountainous terrain, glistening white beaches and spectacular fringing reefs for snorkelling and diving. Most of the island is national park and teeming with wildlife, but most people visit for the sumptuous accommodation and dining epitomised by the five-star luxury at the ultra-exclusive **Lizard Island Resort** (☑1300 863 248; www.lizardisland.com.au; Anchor Bay; d $1970-3700; 🌢@🛜🛗). The resort was devastated by Cyclone Ita in April 2014, then again by Cyclone Nathan in 2015, but was painstakingly rebuilt and refurbished by end of 2015.

Lizard Island has historically been a sacred place used by the Dingaal (Walmbaria) people for initiation ceremonies and for hunting turtles and dugong.

The only alternative to the resort is basic **camping** (☑13 74 68; https://parks.des.qld. gov.au/parks/lizard-island/camping.html; Watsons Bay; per adult/family $6.55/26.20) 🏕 at Watson's Bay.

👁 Sights & Activities

⭐ James Cook Museum
MUSEUM

(☑07-4069 6004; www.nationaltrust.org.au/places/james-cook-museum; 50 Helen St; adult/child/family $15/5/35; ⊙9am-4pm May-Sep, 10am-1pm Tue-Sat Oct-Apr) Cooktown's finest building (an 1899 convent), this National Trust museum houses well-preserved relics including journal entries, the cannon and anchor from the *Endeavour,* and excellent displays on local Indigenous culture.

Cooktown Botanic Gardens
GARDENS

(off Walker St; ⊙24hr; P🚻) 🏕FREE The 62-hectare botanical gardens contain a large number of plant species, including the Cooktown orchid. Marked walking trails lead to the beaches at Finch Bay and Cherry Tree Bay. Download the free smartphone app 'Cook 1770', which provides a self-guided audio tour or pick up a map at the visitor centre at **Nature's Powerhouse** (☑07-4069 5763; www.cooktownandcapeyork.com; 1 Walker St; ⊙9.30am-4pm).

Grassy Hill Lookout
VIEWPOINT

(P) FREE Captain Cook climbed this 162m-high hill looking for a passage through the reefs. The 360-degree views of the town, river and ocean are wonderful, especially at sunset. Easy vehicle access is up a steep sealed road (Hope St) from town. Walkers can ascend via a bush trail from Cherry Tree Bay.

Keatings Lagoon Conservation Park
BIRD SANCTUARY

🏕FREE About 5km south of Cooktown, this 47-hectare wetland is a favourite among birdwatchers and walkers. The waterlily-filled lagoon is home to thousands of waterbirds, especially in the dry season (May to October). There are walking trails and a bird hide.

Kuku Bulkaway Gallery
GALLERY

(☑07-4069 6957; 142 Charlotte St) FREE Cooktown and the surrounding area has a strong tradition of Indigenous art. This main street gallery represents the Yuku Baja Muliku people, with all works produced by local Indigenous artists.

⭐ Cooktown Cultural Aboriginal Tours
CULTURAL

(☑07-4069 6967; 113 Charlotte St; tours $120-160, self-drive $100-140; ⊙Mon-Fri) 🏕 Nugal-warra family Elder Willie Gordon runs two humbling tours using the physical landscape to describe the spiritual one, providing a powerful insight into Aboriginal culture and lore. The four-hour Rainbow Serpent tour departs Monday, Wednesday and Friday morning and the three-hour Great Emu Rock Art tour departs in the morning and afternoon on Tuesday and Thursday.

🛏 Sleeping & Eating

⭐ Cooktown Motel
MOTEL $

(Pam's Place; ☑07-4069 5166; www.cooktown motel.com; cnr Charlotte & Boundary Sts; tw & d without bathroom $60, motel d $95, unit $110; 🌢@🛜🛗) Also known as Pam's Place, Cooktown Motel is no longer YHA affiliated but is still one of the best budget places in town, with a big communal kitchen, free lockers and relaxing tropical garden. The motel side is clean and comfortable and there are self-contained units with full kitchen.

★ **Milkwood Lodge**   COTTAGE $$
(☏07-4069 5007; www.milkwoodlodge.com; Annan Rd; d $150; P❋☲) The six split-level pole cabins here have a wonderfully secluded rainforest feel. Beautifully designed with large balconies and modern amenities, they make the ultimate romantic getaway, 2.5km south of Cooktown.

Sovereign Resort Hotel   HOTEL $$$
(☏07-4043 0500; www.sovereignresort.com.au; 128 Charlotte St; d $249-269, 2-bedroom apt $349; P❋@☏☲) Cooktown's most stylish accommodation features breezy tropical-style rooms and spacious two-bedroom apartments, gorgeous gardens enveloping the biggest pool on the Cape, and quality on-site wining and dining.

★ **Driftwood Cafe**   CAFE $
(☏07-4069 5737; 160 Charlotte St; meals $7-19; ☺6am-4pm Tue-Sun; ☏) Cooktown's coolest cafe looks out over Bicentennial Park and the harbour. It serves fine coffee and smoothies, and excels in all-day breakfast and light lunches. Eat inside or on the small street-front deck.

Cook's Landing Kiosk   DINER $
(☏07-4069 5101; Fisherman's Wharf, Webber Esplanade; mains $6.50-20; ☺6.30am-3pm & 5.30-9pm Thu-Sun; ▦) This simple over-water cafe is great for fresh seafood off the boat, as well as sandwiches and rolls – combine the two with a prawn and avocado roll or fish burger. From Thursday to Sunday you can usually see the giant grouper being hand-fed around 5.30pm.

★ **Balcony Restaurant**   MODERN AUSTRALIAN $$$
(☏07-4069 5400; 128 Charlotte St; mains $28-45; ☺7-10am & 5.30-10pm; ❋☏) Sovereign Resort's formal Balcony Restaurant serves Mod Oz cuisine such as Atherton eye fillet and crispy skinned coral trout, as well as share plates such as seafood and bush-tucker platters. The less formal street-level Cafe Bar (10am to 10pm) has reasonably priced fish and chips, steak and burgers, as well as pool tables and a full bar.

ⓘ **Information**

The website www.tourismcapeyork.com has information on the town and surrounding areas. The Cooktown Visitor Centre is at Nature's Powerhouse in the Botanic Gardens (p438).

ⓘ **Getting There & Away**

Cooktown's airfield is 7.5km west of town along McIvor Rd. **Hinterland Aviation** (☏1300 359 428; www.hinterlandaviation.com.au) has up to three flights daily (Monday to Saturday) to Cairns (one way from $137, 45 minutes).

The daily **Cairns Cooktown Express** (☏07-4059 1423; www.cairnsbuscharters.com/services/cairns-cooktown-express) travels along the inland route to Cairns (adult/child $80/40, five hours). Trans North (p432) travels to Cooktown on both the inland route ($84, 5¼ hours) and the more interesting coastal route ($85, 5½ hours).

CAPE YORK PENINSULA

Rugged, remote Cape York Peninsula has one of the wildest tropical environments on the planet. The Great Dividing Range forms the spine of the Cape: tropical rainforests and palm-fringed beaches flank its eastern side, and sweeping savannah woodlands, eucalyptus forests and coastal mangroves its west. This untamed landscape undergoes a spectacular transformation each year when the torrential rains of the monsoonal wet season set in: rough, dry earth turns to rich, red mud and trickling creek-beds swell to raging rivers.

Generally only possible in the Dry, the overland pilgrimage to the Tip is an exhilarating 4WD trek into one of Australia's last great frontiers, but if sticking to the main track, anyone with a 4WD and a sense of adventure can travel to the Tip.

Large areas of Cape York are Aboriginal land, almost half under Native Title, with more than 40 traditional tribal groups represented across some dozen communities.

☞ **Tours**

If you're travelling solo, nervous about hiring a 4WD and going it alone, or just short on time, a tour is probably your best (but not cheapest) option for exploring the Cape.

Tour operators run Cape expeditions from Cairns and Cooktown; most run between April and October and range from seven to 14 days with no more than 20 passengers. An early or late wet season may affect dates. Places typically visited include Laura, Rinyirru (Lakefield) National Park, Coen, Weipa, the Eliot River system (including Twin Falls), Bamaga, Somerset and Cape York. Thursday and Horn Islands are usually optional extras. Transport can be by land, air

Cape York Peninsula

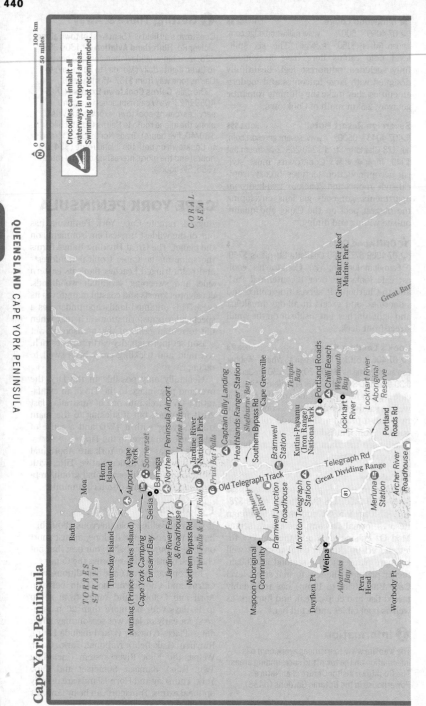

100 km
50 miles

Crocodiles can inhabit all waterways in tropical areas. Swimming is not recommended.

TORRES STRAIT

Badu

Moa

Thursday Island

Muralag (Prince of Wales Island)

Horn Island

Airport

Cape York

Sorceret

Seisia

Bamaga

Cape York Camping Punsand Bay

Northern Peninsula Airport

Jardine River

Jardine River Ferry & Roadhouse

Jardine River National Park

Fruit Bat Falls

Northern Bypass Rd

Twin Falls & Eliot Falls

Captain Billy Landing

Heathlands Ranger Station

Shelburne Bay

Southern Bypass Rd

Cape Grenville

Bramwell Station

Old Telegraph Track

Temple Bay

Portland Roads

Chilli Beach

Weymouth Bay

Kutini-Payamu (Iron Range) National Park

Lockhart River

Lockhart River Aboriginal Reserve

Portland Roads Rd

Mapoon Aboriginal Community

Ducie River

Bramwell Junction Roadhouse

Moreton Telegraph Station

Telegraph Rd

Great Dividing Range

Merluna Station

Archer River Roadhouse

Weipa

Duyfken Pt

Albatross Bay

Pera Head

Worbody Pt

81

CORAL SEA

Great Barrier Reef Marine Park

Great Barr

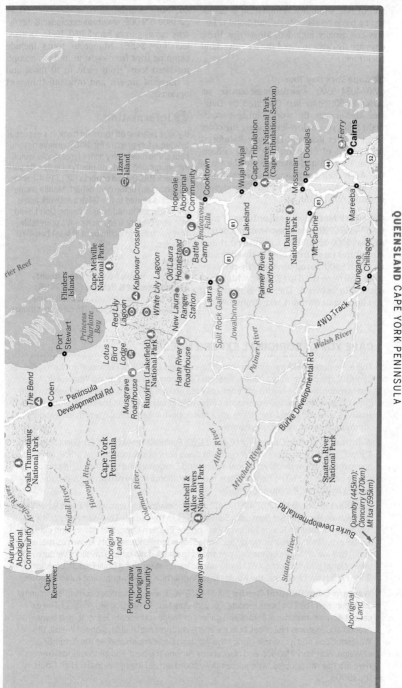

and/or sea, while accommodation is camping or basic motels. Meals and hotel transfers are usually included. Most trips these days are fly-drive to avoid the long overland backtrack.

★ **Cape York Day Tour** TOURS

(☎ 07-4034 9300; www.daintreeair.com.au; per person $1590; ◷ Apr-Jan) Operated by Daintree Air Services, the world's longest scenic flight takes you, at low-level, along the outer Great Barrier Reef and Daintree Rainforest up to parts of Cape York. A 4WD collects you in Bamaga and takes you to the tip of the Australian continent before returning to Cairns. Meals are included. Operates on demand, outside the Wet.

Cape York Motorcycle Adventures TOURS

(☎ 07-4059 0220; www.capeyorkmotorcycles.com. au; tours $500-5550) Fully supported dirt-bike adventures range from one- or two-day safaris (from $500) to the seven-day fly-ride trips from Cairns to the Tip ($5050), with lots of options in between. The trip is cheaper if you bring your own dirt bike (from $3950).

Oz Tours Safaris TOURS

(☎ 1800 079 006; www.oztours.com.au; 8-day fly-drive camping tours from $3150, 16-day overland tours from $4195) Numerous tours include camping trips from eight to 16 days, accommodated tours from eight to 10 days, and a range of air, sea and overland transport options.

ℹ️ Information

If you're heading off the main track, it's essential to adequately prepare for 4WD journeys beyond Laura. You must carry spare tyres, tools, winching equipment, food and plenty of water. Be sure to check **RACQ road reports** (☎ 13 19 40; www. racq.com.au) before you depart. Mobile phone service is limited to the Telstra network and is only available in and around towns. Don't head into very remote areas alone – it's preferable that you travel in a convoy of at least two 4WD vehicles.

PERMITS

Permits, available from the **Department of Environment & Science** (☎ 13 74 68; https://parks.des.qld.gov.au; adult/family $6.55/26.20), are required to camp in national

---

CAPE YORK ABORIGINAL EXPERIENCES

There are dozens of Aboriginal communities around Cape York Peninsula, including the Central Cape community in Coen, Western Cape communities around Weipa, Aurukun and Mapoon, and the Northern Peninsula Area groups around Bamaga and Seisia. While most organised tours and experiences into Aboriginal land are in the south of the Cape, around Laura and Cooktown, there are a few opportunities to engage with Indigenous communities in more remote regions.

Wunthulpu Visitor Centre (☎ 07-4060 1282; Peninsula Development Rd, Coen; ◷ 8.30am-4.30pm) **FREE** This small cultural centre in Coen acts as the local tourist office, but also has some excellent displays of local mining and Indigenous history, including photos dating back to 1933. The Central Cape is the traditional home of numerous groups, including Ayapathu, Kaanju and Umpila.

Lockhart River Arts (☎ 07-4060 7341; http://lockhartriverart.com.au; 1 Piiramo Rd; ◷ 9am-5pm Mon-Fri, 9am-1pm Sat, 9am-noon Sun) 🅿 **FREE** In the remote Lockhart River community south of the Iron Range National Park on the Eastern Cape, this gallery and cultural centre exhibits and sells works by acclaimed local Indigenous artists known as the 'art gang'. Browse artworks online, but call ahead to check if it's open. Travellers venture into the national park for some 4WD thrills and to camp at far-flung Chilli Beach. Lockhart River First Nations include the Kuuku Ya'u, Wuthathi, Kanthanumpu and Kaanju peoples.

Western Cape Cultural Centre (☎ 07-4069 9821; www.westerncape.com.au/community/ achimbun; Kerr Point Dr, Evans Landing; ◷ 10am-2pm Mon-Fri Apr-Oct; 🅿) 🅿 **FREE** The excellent Achimbun cultural centre and gallery in Weipa represents 11 traditional owner groups and features historical, cultural and environmental displays about Weipa, the Western Cape and its people. Today the Western Cape encompasses the communities of Weipa, Aurukun, Mapoon and Napranum. Among the best-known traditional owners here are the Wik peoples, who successfully took Native Title rights to the High Court in the 1990s.

parks or on Aboriginal land, which includes most land north of the Dulhunty River. The Injinoo Aboriginal Community, which runs the ferry across the Jardine River, includes a camping permit in the ferry fee.

Travelling across Aboriginal land elsewhere on the Cape may require an additional permit, which you can obtain by contacting the relevant community council. See the Cape York Sustainable Futures website (www.cysf.com.au) for details. Permits can take up to six weeks to be issued.

ALCOHOL RESTRICTIONS

On the way up to the Cape you'll see signs warning of alcohol restrictions, which apply to all visitors. In some communities alcohol is banned completely and cannot be carried in. In the Northern Peninsula Area (north of the Jardine River) you can carry a maximum of 11.25L of beer (or 9L of premixed spirits) and 2L of wine per vehicle (not per person). Fines for breaking the restrictions are huge – up to $49,000 for a first offence. In practice it's unlikely your vehicle will be searched, but the restrictions and fines are in place to prevent people smuggling in large quantities of grog and are taken very seriously. For up-to-date information see https://www.datsip.qld.gov.au/programs-initiatives/community-alcohol-limits.

ⓘ Getting There & Away

AIR

QantasLink (☑ 13 13 13; www.qantas.com.au) Daily flights from Cairns to Weipa and Horn Island.

Rex (☑ 13 17 13; www.rex.com.au) Regional Express flies the Cairns–Bamaga route five days a week.

Skytrans (☑ 1300 759 872; www.skytrans.com.au) Links Cairns with communities in Cape York, including Coen, Weipa and Bamaga, as well as servicing the Torres Strait Islands.

BOAT

SeaSwift (p417) is a weekly passenger and cargo ferry running between Cairns and Thursday Island (and Seisia).

CAR & MOTORCYCLE

Several rental companies in Cairns hire out 4WDs for the trip to the Tip, but you're generally restricted to the main track – none will permit you to go on the Old Telegraph Track.

A good option is to hire a vehicle fitted out as a bush camper.

Bear Rentals (☑ 1300 462 327; https://bearrentals.com.au; 71 Mulgrave Rd, Parramatta Park, Cairns; rentals per day $205-295)

Cairns 4WD Hire (☑ 07-5527 6191, 1300 360 339; www.cairns4wdhire.net.au; 57 Morehead St)

Captain Billy's Bushranger (☑ 07-4041 2191; www.captainbilly4wdhire.com.au; 80 Scott St)

WORTH A TRIP

RINYIRRU (LAKEFIELD) NATIONAL PARK

Queensland's second-largest national park is renowned for its 537,000 hectares of vast river systems, spectacular wetlands and prolific bird life. This extensive river system drains into Princess Charlotte Bay on the park's northern perimeter. The best camping (with toilets and showers) is at **Kalpowar Crossing**. The picturesque **Red Lily Lagoon**, with its red lotus lilies (best appreciated in the morning), and **White Lily Lagoon** attract masses of bird life.

The only accommodation other than bush camping is **Lotus Bird Lodge** (☑ 07-4060 3400; www.lotusbird.com.au; Marina Plains Rd; s/d incl meals $500/660; ☺ May-Nov; 🖭), a favourite with birdwatchers.

From Cooktown to Musgrave Roadhouse via the national park is 275km. Beyond Endeavour Falls and the Hopevale Aboriginal Community, it's a rugged 4WD-only road.

Laura

POP 228

Laura is considered the gateway to Cape York Peninsula and has been easily accessible since the road from Lakeland was sealed in 2013. The tiny town is worth a visit in its own right thanks to the nearby Quinkan Country rock art sites – listed by Unesco in the world's top 10 rock-art sites – and the biennial three-day **Laura Aboriginal Dance Festival** (☑ 07-4019 6212; ☺ Jun, odd years), Australia's largest celebration of Indigenous dance and culture.

The **Quinkan & Regional Cultural Centre** (☑ 07-4060 3457; www.quinkancc.com.au; Lot 2, Peninsula Developmental Rd; exhibition adult/child $6/3; ☺ 8.30am-3pm; 🅿) 🖉 covers the history of the region. Insightful tours of Quinkan Country rock-art sites with an Indigenous guide (price on application) can be booked here.

The Laura region is the traditional home of the Ang Gnarra people, who are the custodians of the Quinkan sites. European miners set up a staging post here after gold was discovered at Palmer River in 1872.

About 12km south of Laura look out for the badly signposted turn-off to the **Split Rock Gallery** (Peninsula Developmental Rd; by donation; P) ✍, the only rock-art site open to the public without a guide. The sandstone escarpments here are covered with paintings thought to date back 14,000 years.

With a **pub** (☑07-4060 3393; https://thepeninsulahotel.com.au; Deighton Rd; camping per person $10, power $4, s/d $79/99; ☺10am-midnight; P❄), **motel** (☑07-4060 3238; Terminus St; s/d $95/130; P❄) and **roadhouse** (☑07-4060 2211; Peninsula Developmental Rd; meals from $10; ☺6am-8pm) camping, Laura is a reasonable overnighter before hitting the dirt.

Laura to Weipa

The Peninsula Developmental Rd (PDR) from Laura to Weipa is the easiest Cape road to drive, with long stretches of sealed sections, thanks in part to the Rio Tinto mine in Weipa. Eventually this road will be sealed all the way, making it accessible to all vehicles in the Dry. For now, there are enough rough corrugated sections, bull-dust-filled potholes and (mostly dry) creek crossings to require a high-clearance, preferably 4WD vehicle. The landscape here is largely flat and featureless, broken only by sweeping grasslands, giant termite mounds, bone-white eucalypts and wandering cattle.

There are evenly spaced roadhouses along the route so you're never too far from fuel, food, accommodation and emergency supplies. They include **Hann River Roadhouse**, 76km north of Laura, **Musgrave Roadhouse**, a further 80km on, and **Archer River Roadhouse**, 66km north of Coen.

As the only town along this entire 500km stretch, **Coen** (pop 364) is an obligatory stop with a **pub** (☑07-4060 1133; www.coencapeyork.com.au; Regent St; ☺10am-11pm), cultural centre (p442), general store, camping areas and a small **museum** (Regent St; by donation; ☺10am-5pm) (gold was first discovered here in 1876).

Another excellent stop on the long drive between Coen and Weipa is **Merluna Station** (☑07-4060 3209; www.merlunastation.com.au; camping adult/child $13/5, s/d from $90/110,

units from $130; ❄), a working cattle station and farmstay with camping and accommodation in converted workers' quarters.

Weipa (pop 3900), the largest town on the Cape, is essentially a mining town – the site of the world's largest bauxite mine (the ore from which aluminium is processed). Don't let that put you off though: many Cape travellers venture out this way for a taste of the Gulf waters, for the legendary barramundi fishing and to explore camping opportunities north to Mapoon. Weipa is a full-service town with a large supermarket, golf course, bowls club, cafes and motels. **Weipa Caravan Park & Camping Ground** (☑07-4069 7871; www.campweipa.com.au; Lot 172, Kerr Point Dr; powered/unpowered sites $44/35, cabins $70-180, lodge r $180; ❄❄) is an excellent waterfront spot; book here for the fascinating **Town & Mine Tours** (adult/child $40/15; ☺8.30am & 2.30pm) visiting the massive mine site. For a sunset drink or meal, head to the **Albatross Bay Resort** (☑1800 240 663; www.albatrossbayresort.com.au; 10 Duyfken Cres; d $165-235; P❄📶❄). The region south and north of Weipa, from Aurukun to Mapoon, is home to a number of Aboriginal communities (p442).

Telegraph Rd: PDR to Seisia

The Telegraph Rd north to the Tip turns off the PDR about 50km north of Archer River Roadhouse and continues its rugged journey of around 330km via the main track. Across the Wenlock River (which often floods in the Wet), is the historic **Moreton Telegraph Station** (☑07-4060 3360; www.moretonstation.com.au; camping adult/child $10/5, d safari tent $140; ☺8am-6pm), with photographic displays, camping and meals. About 40km further north is **Bramwell Station** (☑07-4060 3300; www.bramwellstationcapeyork.com.au; camping per person $10), Australia's northernmost cattle station and a popular stop for camping and evening bush entertainment.

From the station turn-off it's only 5km north on the Telegraph Rd to the **Bramwell Junction Roadhouse**, which marks the intersection of the Southern Bypass Rd and the rugged 4WD-only Old Telegraph Track – only well-equipped 4WD convoys should attempt the latter. The roadhouse has the last fuel and supplies before the Jardine River Ferry.

The Southern and Northern Bypass roads (bypassing the Old Telegraph Track) are wide and regularly graded but still rough and corrugated in places. The highlight along here is stunning **Fruit Bat Falls** (🅭) **FREE**, a must-see and must-swim on the way up to the Tip. Bring a picnic and your bathers for a dip in the croc-free swimming hole. Nearby, the awesome national park **Eliot Falls Campground** (📞13 74 68; https://parks.des.qld.gov.au; per person/family $6.55/26.20) accesses beautiful Eliot and Twin Falls.

From here it's about 50km north to the **Jardine River Ferry** (📞07-4069 1369; return with/without trailer $130/100, motorbike $40; ⏰8am-5pm) (the only way to cross the croc-infested Jardine), then another easy 50km to the coast at **Seisia** (pop 260), where you can stay at **Seisia Holiday Park** (📞07-4203 0992; www.seisiaholidaypark.com; Koraba Rd; powered/unpowered site $20/12, s/d lodge from $90/125; ▦) or **Loyalty Beach Campground & Fishing Lodge** (📞07-4069 3372; 1 Loyalty Beach Rd; camp sites adult/child $12/6, powered sites per vehicle extra $5, lodge s/d $145/165). This is also the departure point for the **Peddells ferry** (📞07-4069 1551; www.peddellsferry.com.au; adult/child return $120/60; ⏰8am & 4pm Mon-Sat Jun-Sep, Mon, Wed & Fri Oct-May) to Thursday Island.

North of the Jardine River are the Aboriginal communities of Injinoo, Umagico and New Mapoon, traditional lands of numerous groups including the Anggamuthi, Atambaya, Wuthathi, Yadaigana and Gudang peoples. Bamaga and Seisia are largely settled by Saibai Islanders from Torres Strait.

To the Tip

The final part of the epic journey to the Tip of Cape York Peninsula is only about 40km from Seisia or 34km from Bamaga. En route pull into the **Croc Tent** (📞07-4069 3210; www.croctent.com.au; cnr Punsand Bay & Pajinka Rds; ⏰8am-6pm) to browse the Aussie souvenirs and pick up a free map of the area. Turning left here, it's 11km on a rough road to the idyllic oasis of **Cape York Camping** (📞07-4069 1722; www.capeyorkcamping.com.au; Punsand Bay Rd; powered/unpowered sites per person $38/18, safari tents $115-160; ▦☒) on beautiful Punsand Bay.

Staying on the main (single-lane) track it's about a 40 minute drive from the Croc Tent to the car park, from where a short trail leads over rocks to the northernmost

OFF THE BEATEN TRACK

KUTINI-PAYAMU (IRON RANGE) NATIONAL PARK

Roughly 36km north of the Archer River Roadhouse, a turn-off leads 135km through the Kutini-Payamu (Iron Range) National Park – comprising Australia's largest area of lowland rainforest, with animals found no further south in Australia – to the tiny coastal settlement of Portland Roads. Camp just south of here at **Chilli Beach**.

About 40km south of Portland Roads is the **Lockhart River Aboriginal Community**, where you can get fuel and groceries (no alcohol) or visit the gallery at Lockhart River Art (p442).

There are four official camping areas in the national park. Only Chilli Beach and Cooks Hut have toilet facilities. All sites must be booked in advance.

It's about 100km on a mostly unsealed 4WD road from the Peninsula Developmental Rd turn-off to the Lockhart River junction, then a further 20km to Portland Roads or Chilli Beach.

point of mainland Australia, marked by a signpost, a cairn, crashing waves and views of endless blue ocean. The rocky outcrop directly across from the Tip is York Island.

Thursday Island & Horn Island

POP THURSDAY ISLAND 2938, HORN ISLAND 531

Thursday and Horn Islands are the most visited of the remote Torres Strait Islands, Australia's most northerly frontier. The archipelago consists of more than 100 islands stretching like stepping stones for 150km from the tip of Cape York Peninsula to Papua New Guinea.

The islands have a fascinating history of Indigenous seafaring inhabitants distinct from mainland Aboriginal people, pearling and WWII defence, and a relaxed island culture. Horn Island (Ngurupai) is the air hub for the islands and the Cape, connected by regular ferries to nearby Thursday Island (TI; Waibene), the tiny administrative capital and main population hub. Prince of Wales Island (Muralag) is the largest of the group, but is inhabited by only around 20 souls. Friday Island and tiny Roko Island can be visited for their pearl farms.

These 'inner islands' are the traditional home of the Kaurareg people, one of four island groups in the Torres Strait.

⊙ Sights & Activities

★ Gab Titui Cultural Centre GALLERY
(�.07-4069 0888; www.gabtitui.com.au; cnr Victoria Pde & Blackall St, Thursday Island; ⊙9am-4.30pm Mon-Fri, 10am-3pm Sat) ⊘ FREE The superb Gab Titui Cultural Centre, near the ferry dock on Thursday Island, houses a contemporary gallery displaying the cultural history of the Torres Strait, and hosts cultural events and changing exhibitions by local artists.

★ Torres Strait
Heritage Museum MUSEUM
(⊘07-4090 3333; www.torresstraitheritage.com; 24 Outie St, Horn Island; museum adult/child $7/3.50, tours from $48/24; ⊙9am-5pm) Fascinating educational tours revealing the island's significant and all-but-forgotten military history, including fixed gun sites and aircraft wrecks, are run by the friendly folk at this wonderful local history museum on Horn Island. Book ahead from June to September.

Green Hill Fort FORT
(Moa Lane, Thursday Island; ⊙24hr) The highest point on Thursday Island, Green Hill is home to the well-preserved remains of a 19th-century fort, built in 1891 in preparation for a possible Russian invasion. You can still see gun emplacements and underground bunkers, and there's a small museum. This is also the place for a sunset picnic with views over surrounding islands. Follow Moa Lane up to the car park.

LAX Tours CULTURAL
(⊘0427 856 287; Thursday Island; tours per person from $60) Friendly Thursday Island local Dirk will show you around his island, including Green Hill Fort and the Japanese Pearl Divers Memorial, on personalised one-hour tours. Charter fishing trips are also available. Pick-up from accommodation.

🛏 Sleeping & Eating

Grand Hotel HOTEL $$
(⊘07-4069 1557; www.grandhotelti.com.au; 6 Victoria Pde, Thursday Island; s $150-230, d $190-300; ❄ @) On the small hill directly opposite the wharf, the Grand is TI's best all-round accommodation choice. Rooms range from

the 'budget' ones buried at the back, which are still clean with en suite, TV and air-con, to larger front rooms with ocean and mountain views. Rates include a very generous buffet breakfast. The restaurant (mains $15-25; ⊙noon-2pm & 6-8pm) consistently serves some of TI's best meals and the terrace is a popular sunset gathering spot.

Gateway Torres Strait Resort RESORT $$$
(⊘07-4069 2222; www.torresstrait.com.au; 24 Outie St, Horn Island; r from $200; ❄ @ ≋) This friendly resort has 22 self-contained retro units, a saltwater pool and a licensed restaurant. Breakfast is included. It's a five-minute walk from the Horn Island wharf.

❶ Getting There & Away

QantasLink (p443) flies twice daily from Cairns to Horn Island, while Skytrans (⊘1300 759 872; www.skytrans.com.au) flies there from Cairns most weekdays.

Peddells Ferry Service (⊘07-4069 1551; www.peddellsferry.com.au; Engineers Jetty, Thursday Island; adult/child one way $60/30) runs regular ferries from Seisia jetty to Thursday Island, and McDonald Charter Boats (⊘1300 664 875; www.tiferry.com.au; adult/child return $18/9; ⊙office 9am-4pm Mon-Fri) and Rebel Tours (⊘07-4069 1586; www.rebeltours.com.au; Douglas St, Rebel Wharf, Thursday Island; ferry only adult/child each way $10/5, with bus $40/20; ⊙6am-6pm) operate ferries between the islands.

GULF SAVANNAH

The epic Savannah Way runs all the way from Cairns to Broome, skirting the top of the country. The Queensland section, linking the east coast with the Gulf of Carpentaria, from Cairns to Burketown, is one of the state's great road trips.

The world has a different tint out here: the east coast's green, cloud-tipped mountains and sugar-cane fields give way to a flat, red dust–coated landscape of sweeping grass plains, termite mounds, scrubby forest and mangroves engraved by an intricate network of seasonal rivers and croc-filled tidal creeks that drain into the Gulf of Carpentaria. The fishing here is legendary, particularly for barramundi ('barra' season is February to September).

With detours to Karumba, Boodjamulla (Lawn Hill) National Park and Burke & Wills' northernmost campsite, this is a real outback adventure, and you don't even need a 4WD to explore most of this route in the Dry.

🛈 Getting There & Away

Rex (Regional Express; ☑13 17 13; www.rex.com.au) flies on weekdays between Cairns and Normanton and twice weekly from Cairns to Burketown.

Trans North (☑07-4096 8644; www.transnorthbus.com) runs a bus three times a week between Cairns and Karumba ($156, 11 hours), stopping at all towns, including the Undara turn-off ($68, 4½ hours) and Normanton ($150, 10 hours). It departs at 6.30am from Cairns Monday, Wednesday and Friday, and Karumba Tuesday, Thursday and Saturday. No public buses link Normanton with Mt Isa or Burketown.

Undara Volcanic National Park

Welcome to one of inland Queensland's most dramatic natural features. About 190,000 years ago, the Undara shield volcano erupted, sending molten lava coursing through the surrounding landscape. While the surface of the lava cooled and hardened, hot lava continued to race through the centre of the flows, eventually leaving the world's longest continuous (though fragmented) lava tubes from a single vent. Seen from above it's a series of perfectly formed volcanic craters rising above the forest. Down at ground level, it's an intricate, fascinating world ripe for exploration.

Opera in the Outback (www.undara.com.au/events/opera-in-the-outback; day tickets from $55; ☉Sep/Oct) and **Outback Rock & Blues** (www.undara.com.au/events/rock-and-blues; weekend passes $165; ☉Apr) are two annual very different music events staged at **Undara Experience Resort** (☑1800 990 992; www.undara.com.au; Undara Rd; powered/unpowered sites per adult $19/16, swag tent d $78, railway carriage d $180; ☉mid-Mar–mid-Nov; ☀☒); the former's future was in doubt at the time of writing.

The Undara lava tubes can only be visited by guided tour with **Undara Experience** (tours adult/child/family from $58/29/174), and there are three main daily tours leaving from the resort. A worthwhile detour if you're in the area is the signposted drive west to **Kalkani Crater**. There is a number of lava tubes in the area, most dating back close to 190,000 years.

Undara lies on the traditional lands of the Ewamian Indigenous people, and is 15km south of the Savannah Way on a sealed road.

Undara to Croydon

About 32km west of the gem and fossicking base of Mt Surprise, the partly sealed **Explorers' Loop** (check road conditions) takes you on a 150km circuit through old gold-mining towns. At **Einasleigh** have a drink at the local pub and admire amazing miniature doll's house collection before strolling to the Copperfield Gorge. For **sayth**, the terminus of the *Savannahlander* train, also has a pub and a colourful history filled with gold-mining boom-bust tales and picaresque characters.

But the real highlight out here is around 40km from Forsayth via a dirt road. On a private cattle station, the startling private spring-fed oasis of **Cobbold Gorge** is one of those unexpectedly beautiful outback finds. **Cobbold Gorge Village** (powered/unpowered sites $41/30, with en suite $57, cabins $129-185; ☉Apr-Oct; ☀☒) runs three-hour bushwalking **tours** (☑1800 669 922, 07-4062 5470; www.cobboldgorge.com.au; Cobbold Gorge; adult/child/family $92/46/232; ☉10am Apr-Oct, plus 1.30pm Jun-Aug) that culminate in a boat cruise through the stunning narrow gorge.

Back on the Savannah Way, **Georgetown** is the endpoint of the loop, with a handful of attractions, including a dazzling minerals exhibition.

Croydon

POP 258

Incredibly, little Croydon was once the biggest town in the Gulf thanks to a short but lucrative gold rush. Gold was discovered in Croydon in 1885, but by the end of WWI it had run out and the place became little more than a ghost town. Even so, this short-lived period of settlement was sufficient to drive the Bugulmara and Tagalaka peoples from their lands.

Today there's a small but well-preserved historic precinct; Croydon's **visitor information centre** (☑07-4748 7152; www.croydon.qld.gov.au/visitors; 51-59 Samwell St; ☉9am-4.30pm daily Apr-Sep, Mon-Fri Oct-Mar) has a

HISTORIC GULF TRAINS

The historic Gulflander departs Normanton at 8.30am Wednesday, arriving in Croydon at 1.30pm. It returns from Croydon at 8.30am on Thursday.

Take the **Savannahlander** (⟟ 07-4053 6848, 1800 793 848; www.savannahlander.com.au; one-way/return adult $268/457, child $134/229) on a four-day train tour departing Cairns every Wednesday at 6.30am, travelling to Forsayth (one way/return $268/457) and returning on Saturday at 6.40pm. Packages, including accommodation and add-on tours, are available. If there are spare seats you can book a short stage, such as Mt Surprise to Forsayth.

map of the main sights, a small museum and a movie about the town. **Lake Belmore** (Lake Belmore Rd), 4km north of the centre, is stocked with barramundi if you feel like fishing – or swimming.

Croydon's **historic precinct** (Samwell St; ⊙ 9am-4.30pm daily Apr-Sep, Mon-Fri Oct-Mar) **FREE** runs along the north side of Samwell St, between Sircom and Alldridge Sts, in a series of timber buildings that date from gold-rush days. Join Patrick Wheeler from the local Tagalaka people on a 90-minute **walk** (⟟ 0472 618 055; www.croydonwalkingtours.com.au; adult/child $25/free; ⊙ Mon-Sat) around Croydon, taking in plenty of history from gold rush days and from the far longer Indigenous history in these parts.

The 1887 **Club Hotel** (⟟ 07-4745 6184; www.croydonclubhotel.com.au; cnr Brown & Sircom Sts; r with shared/private bathroom $80/115; ✳ ☲) is the only pub left from Croydon's mining heyday, and has the best range of accommodation in town, including self-contained units and simple poolside rooms with shared facilities. The pub's **restaurant** (mains lunch $14-22, dinner $16-30, pizza $18-20; ⊙ noon-2pm & 6-8.30pm) serves up good counter food including pizzas, steaks and stir-fries.

Normanton

POP 1257

Once the port for Croydon's gold rush, Normanton boasts a broad and rather long main street lined with some colourful old buildings. These days it's a handy junction for Karumba- and Burketown-bound

travellers, and is the terminus for the *Gulflander* train. The Norman River produces whopping barramundi, with competitions and barra-focused events in April and May.

The traditional owners of the Normanton area are the Kukatj, Gkuthaarn and Kurtijar peoples, and they still make up nearly 60% of the population.

Everyone stops to take a photo of **Krys the Crocodile** on Landsborough St. It's a supposedly life-size statue of an 8.64m saltie shot by croc hunter Krystina Pawloski on the Norman River in 1958 – the largest recorded croc in the world.

The **Normanton train station** (⟟ 07-4745 1391; Matilda St) **FREE** has a small museum and is home to the **Gulflander** (⟟ 1800 577 245, Normanton 07-4745 1391; www.gulflander.com.au; one way/return adult $69/115, child $34.50/57.50; ⊙ mid-Feb–mid-Dec) when it's not journeying out to Croydon.

A map on the wall outside the visitor information centre details a *Town Walk*, with 29 attractions scattered around the town centre. Definitely one for early morning or late afternoon.

In the historic Burns Philp building, Normanton's excellent **Visitor information & Heritage Centre** (⟟ 07-4745 8444; www.carpentaria.qld.gov.au; cnr Caroline & Landsborough Sts; ⊙ 9am-4.30pm Mon-Fri, 10am-3pm Sat & Sun Apr-Sep, 9am-1pm Mon-Fri Oct-Mar) has a library, historical displays and lots of regional information.

For a cold drink, it's hard to miss the **Purple Pub** (⟟ 07-4745 1324; 92 Landsborough St; mains $16-29; ⊙ noon-2.30pm & 6-8.30pm), but there are two other watering holes in town in case the lurid colour threatens to do your head in after you've had a few

Karumba & Karumba Point

POP 531

A fishing mecca and winter base of many a southern retiree, Karumba is on the traditional lands of the Kareldi. It's a little piece of outback paradise where you can watch the sun sink into the Gulf of Carpentaria in a fiery ball of burnt orange. Even if you don't like fishing, Karumba is the only town accessible by sealed road on the entire gulf coast, and it's a great place to kick back for a few days.

The actual town is on the Norman River, while Karumba Point – the better place to stay – is about 6km away by road and right on the beach. Karumba's small **visitor information centre** (②07-4747 7522; www.carpentaria.qld.gov.au; 149 Yappar St, Karumba Town; ⊙9am-4.30pm Mon-Fri, 10am-3pm Sat & Sun Apr-Sep, 9am-1pm Mon-Fri Oct-Mar; 🐾) moved to the Barramundi Discovery Centre in late 2018, but no-one could confirm that this is where it would stay. It has details of fishing charters and cruises.

◉ Sights & Activities

★ Les Wilson Barramundi

Discovery Centre HATCHERY
(②07-4745 9359; www.carpentaria.qld.gov.au/barramundi-discovery-centre; 149 Yappar St, Karumba Town; adult/child $20/10; ⊙9am-1pm Mon-Fri) Big things are happening here. A shiny new centre was due to open in April 2019, and it promises to be one of the gulf region's major attractions. Everything you ever wanted to know about barramundi can be learned on the fascinating guided tours (10.30am Monday to Friday April to October, by appointment November to March) at this hatchery and breeding centre for the Southern Gulf barramundi subspecies. You can also hand-feed 'barra'. Expect a vastly improved exhibition space, longer opening hours and higher entry fees.

The gift shop stocks locally made bags and wallets fashioned from barramundi, crocodile and cane-toad leather.

Croc & Crab Tours TOURS
(②0417 011 411; www.crocandcrab.com.au; 40 Col Kitching Dr, Karumba Point; half-day tours adult/child $120/60, cruises adult/child $80/40) These excellent half-day tours include crab-catching and croc-spotting on the Norman River, and a lunch of mud crabs and local prawns. Also offers sunset cruises to Sand Island. The business was up for sale at the time of writing, so the set-up could change by the time you read this.

Ferryman CRUISE
(②07-4745 9155; www.ferryman.net.au; Gilbert St, Karumba Town; sunset cruises adult/child $60/30, wildlife cruises $80/40) A sunset cruise on the Norman River and gulf is just about de rigueur in Karumba. During the Dry, Ferryman operates regular sunset cruises that include cold drinks and prawn, fruit and cheese platters; their birdwatching guides are among the best in town. Boats depart from Gilbert St pontoon in Karumba Town.

🛏 Sleeping & Eating

Savannah Shores GUESTHOUSE $
(②07-4745 9126; www.savannahshores.com.au; 6-8 Esplanade, Karumba Point; r from $70; ❄🐾⚟) The simple cabins and units here are nicely looked after, but the location is the real winner – just walk out the front door for some of the best sunsets anywhere in the gulf region. Rates are very reasonable.

End of the Road Motel MOTEL $$
(②07-4745 9599; www.endoftheroadmotel.com.au; 26 Palmer St, Karumba Point; d $165-200, 2-bedroom apt $210; ❄🐾⚟) Karumba's best all-round motel has a range of rooms from large studios to self-contained one- and two-bedroom apartments, and sunset views from the garden. The best rooms have gulf views, of course.

Ash's Holiday Units MOTEL $$
(②07-4745 9132; www.ashsholidayunits.com.au; 21 Palmer St, Karumba Point; s/d/tr $112/122/130, cottage d/tr $160/195; ❄@🐾⚟) Six self-contained motel-style cabins surround a small pool and sleep up to six people each. There's also a great-value two-bedroom cottage and an attached cafe. It's a two-minute walk to a fine sunset point.

Karumba Point

Seafood Market SEAFOOD $
(Boat Shed; ②07-4745 9501; www.facebook.com/karumbapointseafoodmarket; 14-16 Col Kitching Dr, Karumba Point; dishes $7-17; ⊙8am-7pm) You know the fish is fresh here as the owners catch it themselves. Buy local seafood to take away, or dine in on some of the best fish and chips around.

★ Sunset Tavern PUB FOOD $$
(②07-4745 9183; www.sunsettavern.com.au; Esplanade, Karumba Point; mains $15-35, pizza $20-30; ⊙noon-2pm & 5.30-8.30pm) This big open-sided place is the hub of Karumba Point at sunset; watch the sun sink into the gulf over a glass of wine and a seafood platter. The food is reasonably good, especially the locally caught barra (best grilled), but the view from the garden tables is better – arrive early to snag a seat at an outdoor table.

Northwest Corner

Queensland's remote Northwest Corner is real frontier territory, with a number of reasons to visit, among them Boodjamulla, one of Queensland's most beautiful national

MORNING GLORY

Roughly between August and November, when 'morning glory' clouds frequently (but unpredictably) roll in, Burketown becomes the home of intrepid cloud-spotters. A rare meteorological phenomenon, these tubular clouds come in wavelike sets of up to eight. Each can be up to 1000km long and 2km high. They travel at speeds of up to 60km per hour. As the sun rises, gliders head up in the hope of catching one; ask around and the chances are someone will take you along for the ride. For a close-up look at the clouds aboard a light plane, contact Gulf-wide charter company **Savannah Aviation** (☑07-4745 5177; www.savannah-aviation. com; Burketown; 20min from $250).

parks, and **Burke & Wills Camp 119**. Burketown, too, has a real end-of-the-road feel to it. If you're out this way, there's a fair chance you're travelling along the Cairns-to-Broome Savannah Way, which in these parts is a 4WD-only adventure route where small outposts can feel like oases. If you're coming from the south, one of these is likely to be the **Burke & Wills Roadhouse** (☑07-4742 5909; Normanton-Cloncurry Rd; sites per person $12, s/d with shared bathroom $70/80, r with private bathroom $110; ⊙6am-10pm; ❋), ideal for a cold drink or to refuel.

If you, like Burke and Wills, dream of seeing the waters of the Gulf of Carpentaria, you'll need to head for Karumba Point, 74km northwest of Karumba.

If you're travelling from outback Queensland to the Northern Territory (NT), there are two main routes. The easy way is the sealed Barkly Hwy from Mt Isa to Three Ways (640km), from where you can head south to Alice Springs or north to Darwin on the sealed Stuart Hwy.

The more adventurous route is the continuation of the Savannah Way west of Burketown. It's almost 500km of partly sealed but more often unsealed (and sometimes rough, 4WD-only) territory from Burketown to Borroloola (NT) and beyond. This road is usually impassable in the Wet. Along the way you'll pass the **Doomadgee Aboriginal Community** (☑07-4745 8351), where you're welcome to buy fuel and supplies; village access is subject to council permission, and alcohol is restricted. It's another mostly sealed 80km of melaleuca scrub to well-run **Hell's Gate Roadhouse** (☑07-4745 8258; www.hellsgateroadhouse.com. au; unpowered site per person $10, powered sites $45, cabins $70-145; ❋), 50km from the NT border. The roadhouse has fuel, camping, cabins and meals.

Burketown

POP 238

Burketown can feel like the end of the earth – it's a long drive from anywhere, a quiet old place where the horizon starts at the end of each street, and when the sun or rain beats down with the full force of the north, you won't find a soul on the streets. And therein lies its charm. It's isolated but accessible – the road in from Gregory is sealed and the road from Normanton is in good condition in the Dry.

There are two more reasons to come. The barra fishing, either on the Albert River or 30km north at the Gulf, is legendary (the season runs from mid-January to the end of September). And along with Karumba, this is the best place in the world to witness the extraordinary 'morning glory' cloud phenomenon.

These are the traditional lands of the Gangalidda and Garawa peoples.

Yagurli Tours (☑07-4745 5111; www.burke town.com.au/tours; per person $65-180) lets you pre-arrange fishing, stargazing and other tours with members of the Gangalidda and Garawa traditional owners of this land: contact the **Burketown Visitor Centre** (☑07-4745 5111; www.burketown.com.au; cnr Musgrave & Burke Sts; ⊙11am-4pm Mon-Fri). There's also a pleasant **caravan park** (☑07-4745 5118; www.burketowncaravanpark.net.au; 23 Sloman St; powered sites s/d $30/36, r with shared bathroom $80, cabins d $98-135; ❋) and the excellent **Burketown Pub** (☑07-4745 5104; www. burketownpub.com; cnr Beames & Musgrave Sts; unit s/d $135/145; ❋), with rooms and meals.

Boodjamulla National Park

Boodjamulla is one of the most beautiful, pristine places in Outback Queensland. A series of deep flame-red sandstone gorges towers above the spring-fed, luminous green Lawn Hill Creek. Lush vegetation, including cabbage-leaf palms, pandanus and turkey bush, line the gorge, providing a haven for wildlife in this outback oasis. The Waanyi people, for whom Lawn Hill Gorge is sacred, have inhabited the area for 30,000 years, leaving traces of rock art. The park's name comes from the local Waanyi word for Rainbow Serpent.

In the southern part of the park is the World Heritage–listed **Riversleigh fossil field** (https://parks.des.qld.gov.au; Booddjamulla National Park), with a small **campground** (☑13 74 68; https://parks.des.qld.gov.au; Riversleigh Rd; sites per person/family $6.55/26.20; ☉Mar-Oct), 4km south of the Riversleigh D site (the only part of the fossil field open to the public). This is one of the richest fossil mammal sites in Australia, with everything from carnivorous kangaroos to pocket-size koalas. Campers must book ahead and be entirely self-sufficient.

🛏 Sleeping & Eating

Adel's Grove (☑07-4748 5502; www.adelsgrove.com.au; camping d/f $40/55, s/d safari tents with half-board from $175/270, s/d with private bathroom $245/340) is an excellent mini-resort 10km east of the park entrance. There's an on-site bar and **restaurant** (mains $10-18, 2-course dinners $35; ☉7-8am, noon-2pm & 4-10pm) with a big open-air deck.

OUTBACK QUEENSLAND

Beyond the Great Dividing Range the sky opens up over tough country that's both relentless and beautiful. Travellers come for the exotic and intimate Australian experience, their restlessness tamed by the sheer size of the place, its luminous colours and its silence. It's a place that echoes with Indigenous stories down through the ages, and tales from Burke and Wills to Waltzing Matilda. Towns like Winton, Longreach and Birdsville in particular capture the essence of this vast place.

In the dry season, endless blue skies hover over stony deserts, matched only by the brilliant velvety clarity of the Milky Way at night. It's a long way between drinks out here, but it's well worth the drive.

❶ Getting There & Away

The main driving routes include Townsville to Mt Isa on the Overlanders Way and Brisbane to Mt Isa on the Matilda Hwy.

Bus Queensland (☑1300 287 537; http://busqld.com.au) and **Greyhound** (☑1300 473 946; www.greyhound.com.au) cover the major routes from Brisbane and Townsville.

QUEENSLAND OUTBACK QUEENSLAND

NATIONAL PARKS OF OUTBACK QUEENSLAND

This vast region has numerous national parks that are worth exploring for those with plenty of time to diverge from the well-travelled routes *and* a high-clearance 4WD. In addition to the more popular parks listed here, consider also **Idalia National Park** (www.npsr.qld.gov.au/parks/idalia/) and **Mariala National Park** (www.npsr.qld.gov.au/parks/mariala/), both of which are northwest of Charleville. Self-sufficient camping is possible in each of the following parks.

Bladensburg National Park (www.npsr.qld.gov.au/parks/bladensburg/) South of Winton, this park has a beguiling mix of plains, watercourses and rocky outcrops, with wildlife a highlight too.

Diamantina National Park (www.npsr.qld.gov.au/parks/diamantina/) A remote, beautiful park with stirring scenery including sand dunes, escarpments, river courses and plains. It's southeast of Boulia and southwest of Winton.

Hell Hole Gorge National Park (www.npsr.qld.gov.au/parks/hell-hole-gorge/) A deep gorge with vertical cliffs north of Quilpie.

Lochern National Park (www.npsr.qld.gov.au/parks/lochern/) Has vast grassy or rocky plains, snaking watercourses lined with classic outback vegetation, and good wildlife. Accessible from Windorah and Longreach, it lies along the Quilpie–Jundah road, south of Longreach.

Munga-Thirri National Park (www.npsr.qld.gov.au/parks/munga-thirri/) Experience deep-desert immersion in the beautiful, difficult sand dune country of the Simpson Desert, west of Birdsville.

Welford National Park (www.npsr.qld.gov.au/parks/welford/) Offers red-sand dunes, red-rock escarpments and good wildlife along three main driving tracks.

Queensland Rail (☑13 16 17, 1800 872 467; www.queenslandrailtravel.com.au) operates three major rail routes from the coast into the outback. *Spirit of the Outback* runs from Brisbane to Longreach, the *Westlander* from Brisbane to Charleville, and the *Inlander* from Townsville to Mt Isa.

Charters Towers to Cloncurry

The Flinders Hwy runs a gruelling but sealed and straight 775km from Charters Towers west to little Cloncurry. The highway was originally a Cobb & Co coach run, and along its length are small towns established as coach stopovers. The main towns are Prairie, Hughenden, Richmond and Julia Creek.

The first stop on the dinosaur trail when heading west from the coast, **Hughenden** is well worth a look for its **Flinders Discovery Centre** (☑07-4741 2970; www.visithughenden.com.au; 37 Gray St; adult/child $5/2; ⊙9am-5pm daily Apr-Oct, 9am-5pm Mon-Fri & to 2pm Sat & Sun Nov-Mar), which houses a replica skeleton of the Muttaburrasaurus, a dinosaur found south of here in the 1960s. The town itself is a fairly standard provincial place with everything you'd need and little to detain you – when temperatures here get close to 40°C, it can feel like the earth's anvil.

The relatively lush **Porcupine Gorge National Park** (☑07-4741 1113; www.parks.des.qld.gov.au/parks/porcupine-gorge) is an oasis in the dry country 70km north of Hughenden. Camp by a (usually) running creek at Pyramid Lookout, and hike into the gorge.

The Yirandali people are the land's traditional owners.

Tiny **Richmond**, on the traditional lands of the Wanamara people, is the heartland of outback Queensland's dinosaur country, and is best known for **Kronosaurus Korner** (☑07-4741 3429; www.kronosauruskorner.com.au; 91-93 Goldring St; adult/child/family $25/15/60; ⊙8.30am-5pm Apr-Oct, to 4pm Mon-Fri, to 3pm Sat & Sun Nov-Mar) and a couple of easily accessible fossil sites. It's otherwise a blip on the Flinders Hwy, with a single main street and a couple of pubs.

Cloncurry

POP 2719

The 'Curry' is renowned as the birthplace of the Royal Flying Doctor Service, and **John Flynn Place** (☑07-4742 2778; www.john flynnplace.com.au; cnr Daintree & King Sts; adult/child/family $11.50/7.50/30; ⊙9am-4pm Mon-Fri year-round, to 3pm Sat & Sun May-Sep) is a must-see museum celebrating Dr Flynn's work in setting up this invaluable outback service. It's the only town of any real size between Charters Towers and Mt Isa. Built upon the traditional lands of the Mayi-Thanurti and Kalkadoon peoples, Cloncurry became, in the 19th century, the largest producer of copper in the British Empire. Today it's a busy pastoral centre with a reinvigorated mining industry.

On 16 January 1889 a temperature of 53.1°C (127.6°F) was recorded at Cloncurry. It remains unofficially the hottest temperature recorded in Australia, but no longer forms a part of the official record – apparently, the actual temperature was a few degrees lower than this because the thermometer was located inside a beer crate (!) at the time the temperature was recorded. The official hottest temperature comes from South Australia: 50.7°C (123.3°F) at Oodnadatta on 2 January 1960. But Cloncurry locals won't have a bar of it and, if you come here in summer, you might be inclined to agree with them. Either way, it's pretty damned hot out here.

There's information and historical displays at **Cloncurry Unearthed** (☑07-4742 1361; www.cloncurry.qld.gov.au; Flinders Hwy; museum admission by donation; ⊙8.30am-4.30pm Mon-Fri year-round, 9am-4.30pm Sat & Sun May-Oct, 9am-2pm Sat & Sun Nov & Feb-Apr, 9am-noon Dec & Jan; ☎) in the Mary Kathleen Memorial Park.

Cloncurry has ample accommodation those who don't fancy larger Mt Isa just up the road. As well as van parks and motels, there are budget rooms in the local pubs. Constructed of rammed red earth, the **Gidgee Inn** (☑07-4742 1599; www.gidgeeinn.com.au; cnr McIlwraith & Railway Sts; d $150-185; ❋☎✉) is Cloncurry's most upmarket accommodation, with reasonably plush and comfortable rooms for these parts, a pool and a good restaurant and bar.

Mt Isa

POP 32,588

You can't miss the smelter stacks from the zinc mine as you drive into Mt Isa, one of Queensland's longest-running mining towns and a real provincial hub for outback Queensland. Whether you've come to work, play or just pass through, a night spent in

Mt Isa

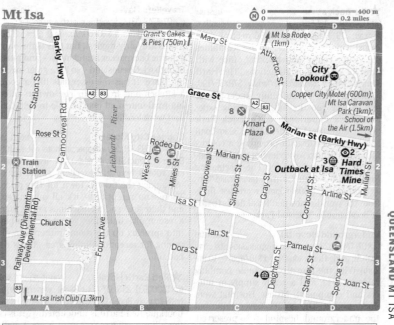

Mt Isa

◎ Top Sights
1 City Lookout................................D1
2 Hard Times Mine..........................D2
3 Outback at Isa.............................D2

◎ Sights
Isa Experience & Outback
    Park..................................(see 3)
Riversleigh Fossil Centre................(see 3)
4 Underground Hospital.....................C3

🛏 Sleeping
5 Isa Hotel.................................B2
6 Red Earth Hotel..........................B2
7 Travellers Haven.........................D3

✖ Eating
8 Frog & Toad Bistro.......................C1
Outback at Isa Cafe......................(see 2)
Red Earth Thai
    Restaurant............................(see 6)

🍷 Drinking & Nightlife
Buffs Club...............................(see 8)

ℹ Information
Mt Isa Visitor Information
    Centre................................(see 2)

ℹ Transport
Bus Queensland...........................(see 2)
Greyhound................................(see 2)

one of Isa's clubs will help you understand the town's appeal.

At night the surrounding cliffs glow and zing with industry; the view of the twinkling mine lights and silhouetted smokestacks from City Lookout is strangely pretty. The surrounding country has a stark red beauty too.

Proud locals embrace life in the dusty heat and the geographical isolation – often over multiple beers – and the sense of community is palpable. There's a similarly proud (not to mention far longer and unbroken) Indigenous history here; these are the traditional lands of the Kalkadoon, and Aboriginal people comprise nearly a quarter of the town's population.

◎ Sights & Activities

★ City Lookout   VIEWPOINT
(Lookout Rd; ⊙24hr) FREE Everyone should make the short trip up to the City Lookout for excellent 360-degree views of Mt Isa. The best time is sunset, when the smelter stacks are silhouetted and the mine lights begin to twinkle.

★**Outback at Isa**   MUSEUM

(☏07-4749 1555; www.experiencemountisa.com.au; 19 Marian St; ⊙8.30am-5pm) The award-winning Outback at Isa combines the visitor centre and booking office with three of Isa's major attractions. The **Hard Times Mine** (adult/child/family $79/35/199; ⊙tours daily) is an authentic underground trip to give you the full Isa mining experience. **Isa Experience & Outback Park** (adult/child/family $20/10/50; ⊙8.30am-5pm) is a hands-on museum providing a colourful and articulate overview of mining, pioneering and local history. The fascinating **Riversleigh Fossil Centre** (adult/child/family $15/6/33; ⊙8.30am-5pm) recreates finds from the world-renowned fossil fields (p451) at Boodjamulla National Park.

Underground Hospital   MUSEUM

(☏07-4749 0281; www.undergroundhospital.com; Joan St; guided tours adult/child $16/free; ⊙10am-2pm) With the threat of Japanese bombing raids in 1942, and a ready supply of miners and equipment, Mt Isa Hospital went underground. The bombs never came but the underground hospital was preserved. You can also see an example of a tent house, once common in Mt Isa, here.

School of the Air   TOURS

(☏07-4744 8333; www.mtisasde.eq.edu.au; 137-143 Abel Smith Pde; tours per person $2; ⊙tours 10am Mon-Fri school days) These one-hour tours during school term demonstrate the outback's isolation and innovation in catering to the educational needs of students in remote communities, from kindergarten to Year 10.

⭐ **Festivals & Events**

Mt Isa Rodeo   RODEO

(☏07-4743 2706; www.isarodeo.com.au; ⊙2nd weekend in Aug) Mt Isa is the rodeo capital of Australia and this is the biggest event of the year. Don't miss it if you're in town, and book ahead for accommodation.

🛏️ **Sleeping**

Mt Isa Caravan Park   CARAVAN PARK $

(☏07-4743 3252; www.mtisacaravanpark.com.au; 112 Marian St; powered/unpowered sites $35/28, cabins $80-140; P ⊛) The closest caravan park to the town centre is an impressive tourist village with a swag of sleeping options, including self-contained units. There's also a small pool, shady grassed areas and friendly management.

Travellers Haven   HOSTEL $

(☏07-4743 0313; www.travellershaven.com.au; 75 Spence St; dm/s/d $30/60/75; ⊛@🛜⊛) The rooms are fairly modest, but this is the only genuine backpacker hostel in Isa – and most of outback Queensland – so it's a great meeting place. It has the essentials like a pool, a kitchen and free wi-fi. The owners offer informal tours and may be able to help you find work locally.

Copper City Motel   MOTEL $$

(☏0459 593 371; www.coppercitymotel.net.au; 105 Butler St; r from $159; P ⊛ 🛜) The stylish modern rooms here are excellent value, ranking among the best in town for this price. There's no reception – it's all automated, and there are vending machines rather than a restaurant – but if they've put their money into sprucing up the rooms rather than on paying for reception/dining areas, that's no bad thing.

⭐ **Red Earth Hotel**   BOUTIQUE HOTEL $$$

(☏1800 931 235, 07-4749 8888; www.redearth-hotel.com.au; Rodeo Dr; r $166-249; ⊛@🛜) The boutique Red Earth is undoubtedly Mt Isa's top address (unless you want a pool), with period-style furniture, claw-foot baths and uniformed staff. It's worth paying a little extra for a private balcony, spa and huge TV. There's a cocktail bar, and an excellent restaurant in the lobby. Online discounts available.

The **Isa Hotel** (☏07-4749 8888, 1800 931 235; www.isahotel.com.au; 11 Miles St; s/d $129/139; ⊛🛜) is part of the same hotel complex, with cheaper rooms. The 40 rooms of Isa Hotel are nevertheless well-furnished with modern stylings in a good central location.

🍴 **Eating & Drinking**

Grant's Cakes & Pies   PIES $

(☏07-4743 9050; shop 6, 179 Camooweal St; pies from $6; ⊙6am-5pm Mon-Fri, 8am-2pm Sat) All manner of pastries and pies in the finest Aussie tradition, as well as yummy cakes, make this a fine place to pull over. The curry pie with peas and mash is something of a local favourite, but the steak and cracked pepper pie is good too.

Red Earth Thai Restaurant   THAI $

(☏07-4749 8888; http://redearthhotel.com.au/thai-restaurant/; 20 West St; mains $18; ⊙6-9pm Tue-Sat) Most things they do at this boutique hotel they do well, and this is no exception – well-regarded Thai cooking (stir-fries, curry, laksa and the like) at very reasonable prices, whether you eat in the restaurant or get takeaway.

Outback at Isa Cafe
CAFE $

(☑ 07-4743 2225; www.facebook.com/Outback atIsa; 19 Marian St; mains $13-18; ⊙ 8.30am-5pm) Light meals, decent breakfasts, snacks such as quiche and sandwiches and even a seafood basket – this cafe is a welcome break from the attractions on the premises.

Mt Isa Irish Club
BAR

(☑ 07-4743 2577, courtesy bus 0411 427 256; www. theirishclub.com.au; 1 19th Ave; ⊙ 10am-2am, to 3am Fri & Sat) A couple of kilometres south of town, the Irish Club feels a bit more sophisticated than Isa's other clubs and is a truly multipurpose venue. There's a gaming room, a piano bar, the cavernous **Blarney Bar**, coffee, the slightly tacky but heaving **Rish** nightclub, a decent restaurant and even a gym. There's also a courtesy bus to make sure you get home safely.

Buffs Club
BAR

(☑ 07-4743 2365; www.buffs.com.au; 35 Simpson St; ⊙ 8am-3am Mon-Fri, 7.30am-3am Sat & Sun, bars open 10am) The most central and enduringly popular of Isa's clubs, Buffs has the **Blue Tongue** sports bar, **Boomerang** coffee shop, a cocktail bar, a sun deck and live entertainment on weekends. You can eat well at the **Frog & Toad Bistro** (mains $15-39; ⊙ 11.30am-2pm & 6-9pm Mon-Fri, 7.30am-2pm & 6-9pm Sat & Sun; ⊕).

ℹ️ Information

The helpful visitor and booking centre is inside Outback at Isa (p454).

ℹ️ Getting There & Away

AIR

Rex (☑ 13 17 13; www.rex.com.au) flies direct from Mt Isa to Townsville daily and services many outback destinations, including Birdsville and Burketown. **Qantas** (☑ 13 13 13; www. qantas.com.au) has flights to Brisbane and Townsville, while **Virgin Australia** (☑ 13 67 89) has a daily flight to Brisbane.

The **airport** (☑ 07-4409 3000; www. mountisaairport.com.au; Barkly Hwy) is 8km north of the town centre.

BUS

Bus Queensland (p451) has a daily service from Mt Isa to Brisbane ($175, 22 hours) via Charleville and Longreach, and travels three times a week to Townsville ($99, 12 hours) via Charters Towers.

Greyhound (p451) offers twice-weekly services to Townsville ($99, 11½ hours).

Both companies have depots at Outback at Isa (p454).

TRAIN

Queensland Rail runs the **Inlander** (☑ 1800 872 467; www.queenslandrailtravel.com.au) train between Mt Isa and Townsville ($108, 21 hours) twice a week.

Mt Isa to Charleville

The Barkly and Landsborough Hwys cut through central Queensland, which encompasses a large area of largely flat cattle farming country. For travellers it's by turns dinosaur country, Waltzing Matilda country, Qantas country and even Crocodile Dundee country.

The first place to stop after the Cloncurry turn-off is tiny **McKinlay**. It's over 30 years since *Crocodile Dundee* hit the screens, but the McKinlay pub, aka **Walkabout Creek Hotel** (☑ 07-4746 8424; www.facebook.com/walkaboutcreekhotel; Landsborough Hwy; ⊙ 10am-midnight), is still trading off its success. There's a campground out the back.

Further along, **Kynuna** is also worth a stop for the atmospheric **Blue Heeler Hotel** (☑ 07-4746 8683; Landsborough Hwy; ⊙ 10am-9pm). Banjo Paterson is said to have performed *Waltzing Matilda* here after visiting nearby Combo Waterhole, possibly the inspiration for the song's billabong.

Winton

POP 875

Winton is a satisfying and friendly country town in the heart of cattle, sheep and dinosaur country – this is the best base from which to explore central Queensland's remarkable prehistoric fossil finds. The town, on the traditional lands of the Koa people, also does its best to make the most of its Waltzing Matilda connections, most notably a new **Waltzing Matilda Centre** (☑ 1300 665 115, 07-4657 1466; www.matildacentre.com. au; 50 Elderslie St; adult/child/family $30/15/65; ⊙ 9am-5pm Apr-Sep, 9am-5pm Mon-Fri & to 3pm Sat & Sun Oct-Mar), opened in 2018. Banjo Paterson reputedly wrote the Aussie anthem after a visit to a nearby **billabong** (www. parks.des.qld.gov.au/parks/combo-waterhole; off Landsborough Hwy), and it was first performed at the North Gregory Hotel (p457).

THE DINOSAUR TRAIL

Fossil fiends, amateur palaeontologists and those who are simply fans of *Jurassic Park* will love outback Queensland's triangular Dinosaur Trail. The northern points are Richmond (p452), home of Australia's richest collection of marine dinosaur fossils, and Hughenden (p452), home of the Muttaburrasaurus. In July 2018 an excavation during the annual Big Dig organised by Kronosaurus Korner (p452) unearthed a 100-million-year-old Ichthyosaur, a car-size, dolphin-esque dinosaur. At the southern tip of the triangle, the Winton region offers two premier prehistoric attractions of its own.

About 95 million years ago – give or take a few million – a herd of small dinosaurs got spooked by a predator and scattered. The resulting stampede left thousands of footprints in the stream bed, which nature remarkably conspired to fossilise and preserve. The **Dinosaur Stampede National Monument** (07-4657 0078; www. dinosaurtrackways.com.au; Winton–Jundah Rd; guided tours adult/child $25/12.50; 8.30am-5pm daily Apr-Oct, closed Sun Nov-Mar), at Lark Quarry 110km southwest of Winton, is outback Queensland's mini Jurassic Park, where you can see the remnants of the prehistoric event. Protected by a sheltered walkway, the site can only be visited by guided tour (9.30am, 11am, noon, 1pm, 2pm and 3pm), where guides will explain what scientists have deduced happened that day. There are no places to stay or eat, but it's a well-signposted drive on the partly unsealed Winton–Jundah road, suitable for 2WD vehicles in the Dry (allow 1½ hours from Winton).

The **Australian Age of Dinosaurs Museum** (07-4657 0712; www.australianageofdinosaurs.com; Lot 1, Dinosaur Dr; adult/child/family $55/30/115; 8.30am-5pm daily Apr-Oct, closed Sun Nov-Mar), 15km east of Winton on the Landsborough Hwy, is a fascinating interactive dinosaur research museum housed on a local cattle station atop a rugged plateau known as the 'Jump Up'. There are two sides to the museum – the laboratory and the collection, the latter comprising original dinosaur fossils found in the region that make up the incomplete skeletons of 'Matilda' and 'Banjo'. The latest discovery, announced in 2016, is a new species and genus of titanosaur named *Savannasaurus elliottorum*. Each side is visited on a 30-minute tour (9am, 10am, 11am, noon, 1pm and 2pm) with a half-hour break in between. Fossil enthusiasts can book in advance for two days of working with technicians cleaning dinosaur bones (from $189), or book well in advance for one of the annual three-week digs ($3500 per week).

Matilda Country Tours (07-4657 1607; www.matildacountrytouristpark.com; 43 Chirnside St; tours $45-85; 8am) offers daily bus transport to both the monument and museum.

Ask at visitor centres in the region about the **Australian Dinosaur Trail Pass** (www. australiasdinosaurtrail.com), which covers entry to the Australian Age of Dinosaurs Museum and Dinosaur Stampede National Monument, as well as Kronosaurus Korner (p452) in Richmond, and the Flinders Discovery Centre (p452) in Hughenden for a reduced rate of $95/50/215 per adult/child/family.

Elderslie St is a colourful streetscape of old timber pubs, historic buildings and opal shops, so there's plenty of photogenic period charm here.

Sights

Royal Theatre THEATRE
(73 Elderslie St; Opal Walk $5, screenings $7; 9am-5pm) There's an old-movie-world charm in the canvas-slung chairs, corrugated tin walls and star-studded ceiling at this classic semioutdoor theatre (1918), complete with the world's biggest deckchair. Enter via the Opal Walk gallery or come for the nostalgic film on Wednesday night (8pm April to September).

Arno's Wall SCULPTURE
(Vindex St) FREE Arno's Wall is one of Winton's quirky outback attractions – a 70m-long work-in-progress by artist Arno Grotjahn, featuring a huge range of industrial and household items, from TVs to motorcycles, ensnared in mortar.

Diamantina Heritage Truck & Machinery Museum MUSEUM
(0429 806 140; www.wintontruckmuseum.com. au; Kennedy Developmental Rd; $5; 8am-5pm)

Fans of trucks and old vehicles will love the collection of old Macks, Chevys and Model T Fords in this big shed. A special exhibit is the MAN truck belonging to legendary Cape York female trucker 'Toots' Holzheimer.

🛏 Sleeping & Eating

⭐ **Cottage on Cork**   COTTAGE $$
(📞0409 916 634; www.cottageoncork.com.au; 92-94 Cork St; cottages $140-185; 🅿❄🛜) One of the best places to stay anywhere out west in Queensland, Cottages on Cork has four cottages, ranging from one to three bedrooms, with plans for more. The decor is cool and stylish (vibrant artworks, wood floors and classy furnishings). Two of the cottages are at the main address, and two are down the same street not far away.

⭐ **North Gregory Hotel**   HOTEL $$
(📞07-4657 0647; www.northgregoryhotel.com; 67 Elderslie St; r $120-150; ❄🛜) This historic art-deco beauty has plenty of stories and is the pick of the town's pubs for accommodation in pub-style or en-suite rooms. The lobby is like a glamorous film-noir set and the rooms are styled somewhere between the pub's heyday and 20th-century Brisbane. Waltzing Matilda was allegedly first performed by Banjo Paterson in the hotel on 6 April 1895.

⭐ **Tuckerbox Cafe**   CAFE $$
(📞07-4657 1466; 50 Elderslie St, Waltzing Matilda Centre; mains $15-22; ⏱8am-5pm) This lovely cafe attached to the Waltzing Matilda Centre (p455) opened in 2018, and serves up the usual cafe light meals as well as garlic prawns and the enticing ploughman's platter (cold meats, cheese and a roast pumpkin salad).

ℹ Information

Winton Visitor Centre (📞1300 665 115, 07-4657 1466; www.experiencewinton.com. au; 50 Elderslie St, Waltzing Matilda Centre; ⏱9am-5pm) shares premises with the Waltzing Matilda Centre (p455).

ℹ Getting There & Away

Rex (📞13 17 13; www.rex.com.au) flies between Longreach and Townsville via Winton twice weekly. The airstrip is about 8km northeast of town.

Bus Queensland (📞1300 287 537; http:// busqld.com.au) stops at Winton on the daily run between Brisbane ($185, 22 hours) and Mt Isa (from $113, six hours).

Longreach
POP 2970

Longreach is an iconic, pioneering outback town, at once a long way from anywhere and filled with quintessentially outback attractions. The traditional lands of the Malintji, Iningai and Kunngkari peoples, Longreach was the home of Qantas early last century, but these days it's equally famous for the Australian Stockman's Hall of Fame & Outback Heritage Centre, one of Queensland's best museums, and Cobb & Co stagecoach tours. The tropic of Capricorn passes through here – look for the marker near the **visitor centre** (📞07-4658 4150; www.longreachtourism.com.au; 99 Eagle St; ⏱9am-4.45pm Mon-Fri, to noon Sat & Sun), which points to the torrid (north) and temperate (south) zones.

⊙ Sights & Activities

⭐ **Australian Stockman's Hall of Fame & Outback Heritage Centre**   MUSEUM
(📞07-4658 2166; www.outbackheritage.com.au; Landsborough Hwy; adult/child/family $32/15/80; ⏱9am-5pm) In a beautifully conceived building with an impressive multiarched design, this is a fine museum, and also a tribute to outback pioneers, early explorers, stockmen and Indigenous Australians. Five themed galleries, some featuring interactive touch-screen displays, cover Aboriginal culture; European exploration (there's a nifty map showing the trails of Burke and Wills, Ludwig Leichhardt, Ernest Giles and co); pioneers and pastoralists; 'Life in the Outback'; and the stockman's gallery.

⭐ **Qantas Founders Outback Museum**   MUSEUM
(📞07-4658 3737; www.qfom.com.au; Landsborough Hwy; adult/child/family $28/18/80; ⏱9am-5pm Apr-Oct, to 4pm Nov-Mar) Qantas Founders Outback Museum houses a life-size replica of an Avro 504K, the first aircraft owned by the fledgling airline. Interactive multimedia and working displays tell the history of Qantas. Next door the original 1921 Qantas hangar houses a mint-condition DH-61. Towering over everything outside is a bright and shiny retired 1979 **Boeing 747-200B Jumbo** (museum & jet tours adult/child/family $63/43/190, wing walks adult/child $65/55; ⏱jet tours 9.30am, 11am, 1pm & 2.30pm, wing walks 11am, 12.30pm & 2.30pm). The tour of the Jumbo Jet and nearby Boeing 707 is

QUEENSLAND MT ISA TO CHARLEVILLE

fascinating, and you can do a wing-walk with safety harness (bookings essential).

Outback Pioneers   TOURS

(☑07-4658 1776; www.outbackpioneers.com.au; 128 Eagle St; ⊘8am-5pm Mon-Sat) The main tour operator in Longreach runs a sunset paddle-wheeler cruise, followed by dinner under the stars and campfire entertainment (adult/child/family $99/69/299). The Cobb & Co Stagecoach Experience ($99/69/269) is a highlight, combining a 45-minute horse-drawn stagecoach ride with a theatre show, lunch and a film. Book ahead.

🛏 Sleeping & Eating

Longreach Tourist Park   CARAVAN PARK $

(☑07-4658 1781; www.longreachtouristpark.com. au; 12 Thrush Rd; powered/unpowered sites $37/28, sites with bathroom $49, cabins from $115; ❄☀) This large, spacious park lacks grass but has a small grotto of spa pools, a new swimming pool and the **Woolshed** restaurant and bar.

★ Salt Bush Retreat   LODGE $$

(☑07-4658 3811; www.saltbushretreat.com.au; 63-65 Ilfracombe Rd; r $145-195, slab huts from $165; ❄☀) The comfortable self-contained lodges here are excellent value – a step up from the town's motels – and the fabulous timber slab huts and homestead stables offer a rustic pioneer outback feel, brimful of character. There's a palm-shaded pool, native gardens and a large covered communal area. It's opposite the Qantas Founders Outback Museum (p457).

★ CCD Restaurant
& Beer Garden   BISTRO $$

(☑07-4658 2798; www.facebook.com/CCDRBG; 110 Eagle St; breakfast from $10, mains $15-31; ⊘11.30am-2pm & 5.30pm-late Mon-Thu, 7.30am-2pm & 5.30pm-late Fri-Sun) The narrow, darkened dining room gives way to a shady beer garden out the back at this stylish and deservedly popular main-street bistro. Steaks, pasta dishes and calamari salad are complemented by Moroccan salads, Vietnamese-style sticky pork belly, and tapas plates such as chilli prawns and mini hot dogs. Later in the evening they serve cocktails.

Stone Grill   STEAK $$$

(The Welcome Home Cafe & Tearoom; ☑07-4658 1776; www.outbackpioneers.com.au/experience/ the-welcome-home/the-stonegrill; 128 Eagle St; adult/child $55/25; ⊘6-9pm Tue, Thu & Fri, cafe 8am-4pm Mon-Fri Apr-Oct) This classy dinner option lets you choose your meat (from steak, chicken or seafood to kangaroo or crocodile; there's even a vegetarian patty), and you cook it to your liking on a hot-stone slab. It comes with potatoes, a side and salad, and there's an all-you-can-eat dessert buffet if you make it that far.

🛍 Shopping

Kinnon & Co
Station Store   FASHION & ACCESSORIES

(☑07-4658 2006; www.outbackpioneers.com.au; 126 Eagle St; ⊘8.30am-5pm Mon-Fri, 9am-1pm Sat) The fabulous Station Store is crammed with Aussie outback fashion – boots, Akubra hats, leather bags, clothing, saddles and stockman's whips, along with unusual gifts and souvenirs. Worth a look even if you're not buying. Cafe attached.

ℹ Getting There & Away

Bus Queensland (☑1300 287 537; http:// busqld.com.au) stops daily on its run between Brisbane ($170, 18 hours) and Mt Isa ($115, seven hours).

Greyhound (☑1300 473 946; www.greyhound. com.au) has a twice-weekly bus service between Longreach and Rockhampton ($107, 9½ hours) on Tuesday and Thursday. All buses stop opposite the Commercial Hotel.

Queensland Rail operates the twice-weekly **Spirit of the Outback** (☑1800 872 467, 13 16 17; www.queenslandrailtravel.com.au) service between Longreach and Brisbane ($141, 26 hours), via Rockhampton ($87, 15 hours).

Barcaldine

POP 2865

Barcaldine (bar-*call*-din), a historic little outback town at the junction of the Landsborough and Capricorn Hwys (Rte 66), gained its place in Australian history in 1891 when it became the headquarters of a major shearers' strike. The confrontation led to the formation of the Australian Workers' Party, forerunner of the Australian Labor Party. The organisers' meeting place was the Tree of Knowledge, a ghost gum that was planted near the train station and long stood as a monument to workers and their rights. It was mysteriously poisoned in 2006, but a radical and impressive memorial now stands as a testament to those days.

The original inhabitants of Barcaldine were the Inningai, encountered by explorer Thomas Mitchell when he passed through in 1824. Coming into conflict with European settlers, they were forced off their lands by the time the Barcaldine township was established in the mid-19th century.

The **Tree of Knowledge Memorial** (Oak St), a $5 million contemporary art installation outside the train station – labelled an 'upside down milk crate' by one disgruntled local – is best seen at night when dappled light filters through the wooden wind chimes. Love it or not, it certainly makes art critics of the pubs' patrons across the road, but most locals claim it's grown on them. The tree itself is a preserved version of the original eucalyptus that striking shearers would meet under during the strike of 1891.

The excellent **Australian Workers Heritage Centre** (☑07-4651 1579; www.australianworkersheritagecentre.com.au; Ash St; adult/child/family $17/10/43; ⊙10am-4pm) is dedicated to the Australian social, political and industrial movements so intertwined with Barcaldine's past. There's a variety of permanent and changing exhibits celebrating working women, shearers, the formation of the Australian Workers Union and more.

Barcaldine's flash new **visitor centre** (☑07-4651 1724; 149 Oak St; ⊙8.15am-4.30pm Mar-Oct, 9am-2pm Sat & Sun Nov-Feb), in the refurbished former Globe Hotel, offers local information and historical exhibits.

Charleville

POP 3335

Charleville is the grand old dame of central Queensland. Part of the Bidjara traditional lands, it's the largest town in mulga country, and gateway to the outback from the south. Due largely to its prime location on the Warrego River, the town was an important centre for early explorers – Cobb & Co had its largest coach-making factory here. Despite a seemingly endless cycle of drought, the town has maintained its prosperity as a major Australian wool centre and has some fascinating attractions for travellers involving the night sky and the rare bilby.

⊙ Sights

★**Charleville**
Bilby Experience   WILDLIFE RESERVE
(☑07-4654 3681; www.savethebilbyfund.org; King St; ⊙9am-4pm) FREE This interpretive centre offers a rare opportunity to learn about the native marsupial bilby and the long-running captive breeding and conservation program here. Book ahead for one of the 3pm guided tours (adult/child $30/20) or the more intimate 9am 'Up Close and Personal Encounter' (adult/child $15/10); the bilbys tend to be more active in the morning. You can visit at other times, but you'll only be able to access the shop and information boards. Advance bookings required for the tours and encounters.

Cosmos Centre   OBSERVATORY
(☑07-4654 7771; www.cosmoscentre.com; 1 Milky Way Rd; night observatory adult/child $28/19, sun viewing $15/10; ⊙9am-5pm, observatory session 7.30pm Apr-Sep, 9am-5pm Mon-Fri, to noon Sat, observatory sessions 7.30pm Mon, Wed & Fri Oct-Mar) See the outback night sky in all its glory via a high-powered telescope and an expert guide. The 90-minute sessions start at 7.30pm, soon after sunset in summer. There's also a solar telescope here for daytime sun viewing. Both are dependent on cloudless skies, which are frequent out here. There are a range of prices and packages depending on your level of interest. Bring warm clothes if you're here for the evening session.

🛏 Sleeping & Eating

★**Evening Star**   FARMSTAY $
(Thurlby Station; ☑07-4654 2430; www.evening star.com.au; 818 Adavale Rd; powered/unpowered sites $35/25, cabins $120; ⊙Apr-Oct) This welcoming station property, one of the few station-stays left in outback Queensland, is only 8km northwest of Charleville but feels a world away. There's plenty of space for camping, a single en-suite cabin, a rustic bar and regular music around the campfire. Station **tours** (per person incl morning tea $50; ⊙9am Wed & Sat Apr-Oct) are run on Wednesday and Saturday.

★**On the Rocks Restaurant**   AUSTRALIAN $$
(☑07-4654 2888; www.rocksmotel.com.au/restaurant; 74 Wills St; mains $25-39; ⊙6-9pm Mon-Sat; ▣) Charleville's best restaurant is a cut above your average outback eatery. Dishes include lamb with native spices, pork ribs and barramundi, plus a few Indian and Lebanese influences. It's a classy place with good service and there's a kids' menu.

ℹ Information

Charleville Visitor Centre (☑07-4654 3057; www.murweh.qld.gov.au; Warrego Hwy/King St; ⊙9am-5pm Mon-Fri, 10am-2pm Sat & Sun) In the old train station and next door to Charleville Bilby Experience; can book tours in the region.

ⓘ Getting There & Away

Bus Queensland (☑ 1300 287 537; http://busqld.com.au) has a direct overnight service between Charleville and Brisbane ($122, 11½ hours); a second bus stops here on the Brisbane–Mt Isa run.

The **Westlander** (☑ 1800 872 467, 13 16 17; www.queenslandrailtravel.com.au) train links Brisbane with Charleville (from $90, 17 hours) twice a week.

Channel Country

This vast region stretches south from Mt Isa to Birdsville via Boulia and Bedourie. It's named for the channels carved out by summer rains further north – in good years, these channels extend all the way to Lake Eyre in South Australia, and they water some of Australia's most prized cattle-grazing country. At the same time, the Simpson Desert encroaches on the south, with spinifex and sand-dune country reaching deep into the Australian interior from here. Much of Channel Country falls within the administrative purview of Diamantina Shire, an area larger than Tasmania but with a population of fewer than 400 people.

Boulia

POP 301

The unofficial 'capital' of the Channel Country is a peaceful, appealing little outback outpost on the cusp of the great Simpson Desert. It occupies the land of the Pitta Pitta people, who were granted native title to 30,000 sq km in the surrounding area; a **waddi tree** (Diamantina St) on the northern edge of town was the traditional meeting place and corroboree site for the Pitta Pitta.

At the southern end of town a bridge crosses the Burke River, rich in brolgas and galahs, and so named after Burke and Wills paused here on their ill-starred journey north in 1860. Nowadays the world's longest mail run ends here, having travelled some 3000km from Port Augusta in South Australia.

The most famous residents of Boulia are the mysterious min-min lights, a supposedly natural phenomenon that occurs when the temperature plummets after dark, and erratic lights appear on the unusually flat horizon. They're out there, perhaps, or at least there's sci-fi animatronic gadgetry and eerie lighting in an hourly 'alien' show at the **Min Min Encounter** (☑ 07-4746 3386; Herbert St; adult/child/family $25/20/60; ☺ hourly 9am-4pm daily Apr-Sep, 9am-4pm Mon-Fri, to noon Sat & Sun Oct-Mar), where you'll also find the **Boulia Visitor Centre** (☺ 8.45am-5pm Apr-Sep, 8.45am-5pm Mon-Fri, 9am-1pm Sat & Sun Oct-Mar; ☎).

Boulia hosts Queensland's premier **camel races** (day/weekend passes from $10/40; ☺ 3rd weekend in Jul), while the **Stone House Museum** (cnr Pituri & Hamilton Sts; adult/child $15/5; ☺ 8.30am-5pm Mon-Fri, 10am-2pm Sat & Sun), the preserved 1888 home of the pioneering Jones family, is full of local history memorabilia and Aboriginal artefacts.

Boulia Caravan Park (☑ 07-4746 3320; www.facebook.com/bouliacaravanpark; Diamantina Developmental Rd; camp sites per person $12, powered sites $29, cabins $75-100), on the banks of the Burke River, has some shady sites, surprisingly grassy areas and just a few cabins,

---

THE BIRDSVILLE TRACK

The 517km Birdsville Track, one of outback Australia's most celebrated 4WD tracks, stretches south of Birdsville to Marree in South Australia, taking a desolate course between the Simpson Desert to the west and Sturt Stony Desert to the east. The first stretch from Birdsville has two possible routes, but only the longer, more easterly Outside Track is consistently open these days.

Taking this route in your own vehicle is a serious, potentially dangerous undertaking, and only for those with fully equipped, high-clearance 4WD vehicles. You will need to be fully self-sufficient in food and water, and you should carry a satellite phone with you at all times. Inform someone of your travel plans, especially the **Birdsville Police** (☑ 07-4656 3310, 13 14 44; MacDonald St) and/or **Marree Police** (☑ 08-8675 8346; First St, Marree, SA). If heading south, check road conditions at Birdsville's **Wirrarri Centre** (☑ 0477 680 700, 07-4564 2000; www.thediamantina.com.au; 29 Burt St; ☺ 8.30am-5pm; ☎); all three also rent out satellite phones.

while the **Desert Sands Motel** (☑07-4746 3000; www.desertsandsmotel.com.au; 50 Herbert St; s/d/tw & tr $132/140/149; Ⓟ❋☎) offers modern and spacious air-con units.

Boulia's only pub, the **Australian Hotel** (☑07-4746 3144; www.facebook.com/australianhotelboulia; 22 Herbert St; s/d $50/60, motel units $130; ❋), is a classic outback watering hole with cold beer, a decent restaurant (mains $18 to $25), basic pub rooms upstairs and comfy en-suite motel units at the back.

Bedourie

POP 122

Bedourie is the administrative centre for the huge Diamantina Shire. That may be its official title, but the reality for travellers is that it lies halfway between Birdsville and Boulia and is a tiny outback outpost where you can break up the journey. Coming from Boulia, it's 192km south on a sealed road. From here to Birdsville, it's 191km, around 70km of which is unsealed (fine in a 2WD vehicle except after heavy rain). A big attraction is the free public swimming pool and **artesian spa** (Nappa St; ⊙7am-7pm) FREE. The Karanja are the traditional owners of the land around Bedourie.

Drop in to the visitor centre for local information, including road conditions to Birdsville. Next door is the **Mud Hut**: built with compressed mud from nearby Eyre Creek in the 1880s, this is, along with the **Bedourie Royal Hotel** (☑07-4746 1201; www.bedouriehotel.com; Herbert St; r from $110; ❋), one of the oldest buildings in outback Queensland

Birdsville

POP 140

A *very* long way from anywhere, Birdsville is perhaps the ultimate outback icon, a remote, storied settlement on the fringe of the Simpson Desert, in the very inland corner of outback Queensland. Although the town itself carries a certain cachet, for many it's the journey to get here that gives Birdsville its charm. Reasons to come are many, from its iconic race meeting, to one of Australia's most famous pubs, to the experience of outback eternity that begins as soon as you leave the town limits. Birdsville occupies the country of the Wangkangurru and Yarluyandi peoples.

During the first weekend in September, the annual **Birdsville Cup** (www.birdsvilleraces.com; general entry $25-30) horse races draw up to 10,000 fans from all over the country to drink, dance and punt on the horses for three dusty days.

On the edge of the Simpson Desert, about 35km west of Birdsville, **Big Red** is a photogenic 30m-high sand dune that offers a big challenge for 4WDers.

Standing strong in sandstone since 1884 is the much-loved **Birdsville Hotel** (☑07-4656 3244; www.birdsvillehotel.com.au; Adelaide St; ⊙10am-late). There are few more famous pubs in Australia, and a beer in the Front Bar, its walls crammed with memorabilia, is a rite of outback passage. The Hotel also does rooms and meals.

Melbourne & Victoria

Includes ➡

Melbourne 463
Yarra Valley 518
Phillip Island 532
Great Ocean Road . . .536
Geelong 536
Ballarat. 571
Bendigo 575
The Grampians 583
Wilsons Promontory
National Park 589
Mildura. 619
Echuca 624

Best Places to Eat

- ➡ Brae (p553)
- ➡ Sunda (p487)
- ➡ IGNI (p541)
- ➡ Attica (p499)
- ➡ Oakridge (p520)
- ➡ Reed & Co (p614)

Best Places to Stay

- ➡ QT (p483)
- ➡ Drift House (p566)
- ➡ Jackalope (p530)
- ➡ Lake House (p525)
- ➡ Spring Spur (p615)
- ➡ Lon (p546)

Why Go?

Melbourne is food-obsessed and a showpiece for Australian culture. Beyond the city limits, Victoria offers rich history, stunning wilderness and culinary excellence. In the 19th century, gold-rich Melbourne and small towns in Victoria were stamped with architectural wonders. These days many of those grand buildings survive as luxury hotels, theatres, top-notch restaurants and bars, and state-of-the-art galleries. Spread throughout the state, many small towns' epicurean credentials go from strength to strength with local-produce-driven restaurants, craft breweries, coffee roasters and excellent wineries. Victorians are also spoiled for scenery. The Great Ocean Road snaking along one of the world's most spectacular coastlines, wildlife-rich Wilsons Promontory, the picturesque mountains of the High Country, the ethereal landscape of the Grampians and the desert-like national parks of the northwest – opportunities to explore are endless, whether on two legs or skis, two wheels or four.

When to Go
Melbourne

Dec–Jan Beaches are packed with holidaymakers; book months ahead for coastal accommodation.

Feb–Mar Quieter, more accommodation options. Late summer weather can be particularly hot.

Apr–Nov Whale watching July to September in Warrnambool; ski season is June to August.

MELBOURNE

POP 4.49 MILLION

Equal parts dynamic, cosmopolitan, sports-mad and arty, Melbourne simultaneously exudes style and keeps its best spots hidden, inviting discovery by food and culture lovers.

Melbourne is often dubbed the most 'European' of Australian cities – indeed the eastern, designer section of Collins St was crowned the 'Paris End' in the 1950s. There's also a mini New York vibe here, thanks to the city's well-ordered grid and scattering of art-deco high-rises. But Melbourne is uniquely Melbourne too. Much of that is due to the 230-plus laneways that penetrate into the heart of city blocks, which are recognised for world-class street art, restaurants and bars.

While central Melbourne has its own allure, the city's charm lies in its diverse suburbs, each of which tells a different tale. Despite the long-standing north–south divide (glitzy South Yarra versus hipster Fitzroy), there's an effortless, laid-back appeal surrounding Melbourne's bars, cafes, festivals and people that transcends borders.

⦿ Sights

◉ City Centre

★ Hosier Lane   PUBLIC ART

(Map p472; Hosier Lane, Melbourne; ⊘24h; 🚊Flinders St) FREE Melbourne's most celebrated laneway for street art, Hosier Lane's cobbled length draws camera-wielding crowds and wannabe Instagram models posing in front of edgy graffiti, stencils and art installations (watch them from the comfort of the window seats at **Bar Tini**). Subject matter runs to the mostly political and countercultural, spiced with irreverent humour. Be sure to also see **Rutledge Lane**, which horseshoes around Hosier.

★ Queen Victoria Market   MARKET

(Map p495; 🗐9320 5822; www.qvm.com.au; cnr Elizabeth & Victoria Sts, Melbourne; ⊘6am-2pm Tue & Thu, to 5pm Fri, to 3pm Sat, 9am-4pm Sun; 🅿; 🚋58, 🚊Flagstaff) With more than 600 traders, 'Vic Market' is the largest open-air market in the southern hemisphere. Visit early morning to shop for fresh produce, accepting tasters and dodging the booming cries of spruiking stall holders. The wonderful deli hall with art-deco features is lined with everything from soft cheeses and Polish sausages to Greek dips and kangaroo biltong. Check if the Wednesday **Summer**

Night Market or **Winter Night Market** are on for hawker food, bars, entertainment and shopping.

Saturday morning is particularly buzzing, with market-goers breakfasting to the sounds and shows of buskers. Clothing and knick-knack stalls dominate on Sunday; they're big on variety, but don't come looking for style (if you're in the market for sheepskin moccasins or cheap T-shirts, you'll be in luck).

The market has been here for more than 130 years; before that, from 1837 to 1854, it was the old Melbourne Cemetery. Remarkably, around 9000 bodies remain buried here from underneath Shed F to the car park leading to Franklin St. There's a small memorial on the corner of Queen and Therry Sts.

Controversial redevelopment works are planned that are likely to run for several years – if they ever commence.

Various tours are run from the market including heritage, cultural and food tours; check the website for details.

★ Federation Square   SQUARE

(Map p472; 🗐03-9655 1900; www.fedsquare. com; cnr Flinders & Swanston Sts, Melbourne; ◼; 🚊Flinders St) FREE Whether they love or hate the architecture, Melburnians embrace Federation Sq as a place to meet, celebrate, protest, watch major sporting events or simply hang out on deckchairs. Occupying a prominent city block, 'Fed Square' is far from square: its undulating and patterned forecourt is paved with 460,000 hand-laid cobblestones from the Kimberley region in WA, with sight lines to important landmarks. Its buildings are clad in a fractal-patterned reptilian skin. Check the website to see what's on.

★ Ian Potter Centre: NGV Australia   GALLERY

(Map p472; 🗐03-8620 2222; www.ngv.vic.gov.au; Federation Sq, Melbourne; ⊘10am-5pm; 🚊Flinders St) FREE The National Gallery of Victoria's impressive Fed Sq offshoot was set up to showcase its extraordinary collection of Australian works. Set over three levels, it's a mix of permanent (free) and temporary (ticketed) exhibitions, comprising paintings, decorative arts, photography, prints, sculpture and fashion. Free 50-minute tours are conducted daily at 11am, noon, 1pm and 2pm.

Indigenous art is prominently featured and there are permanent displays of colonial

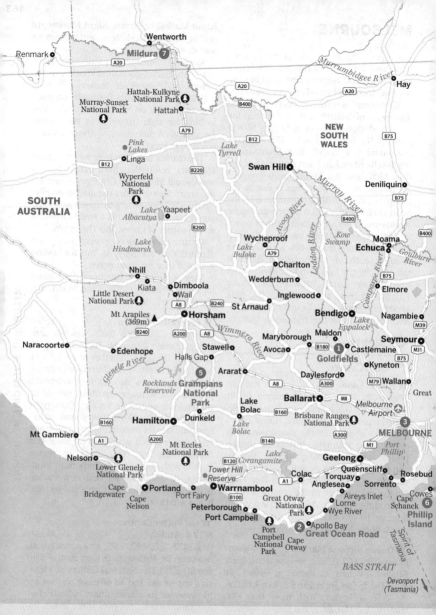

Victoria Highlights

1 **Goldfields** (p570)
Exploring the streetscapes of gold-rush towns with eateries, galleries and markets.

2 **Great Ocean Road** (p536) Taking it slow on a road that curls beside spectacular beaches then whips inland through rainforests.

3 **Melbourne** (p463) Seeking out cool cafes, hidden bars and the hottest restaurants.

4 **Wilsons Promontory** (p589) Strapping on your hiking boots to admire the sheer natural beauty.

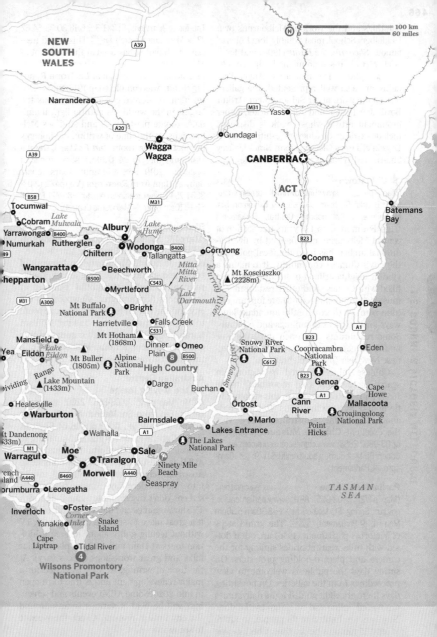

NEW SOUTH WALES

Narrandera

Yass

Gundagai

Wagga Wagga

CANBERRA

ACT

Batemans Bay

Tocumwal

Cobram

Yarrawonga

Numurkah

Rutherglen

Chiltern

Albury

Lake Mulwala

Lake Hume

Wodonga

Corryong

Cooma

Wangaratta

Beechworth

Tallangatta

Mitta Mitta River

Mt Kosciuszko (2228m)

hepparton

Myrtleford

Lake Dartmouth

Murray River

Bega

Mt Buffalo National Park

Bright

Harrietville

Falls Creek

Mt Hotham (1868m)

Dinner Plain

Omeo

Snowy River National Park

Coopracambra National Park

Eden

Mansfield

Yea

Eildon

Lake Eildon

Mt Buller (1805m)

Alpine National Park

High Country

Dargo

Buchan

Snowy River

Genoa

Cape Howe

Lake Mountain (1433m)

ividing

Range

Healesville

Warburton

Bairnsdale

Orbost

Marlo

Cann River

Mallacoota

Croajingolong National Park

t Dandenong 33m)

Walhalla

Lakes Entrance

Point Hicks

Moe

Traralgon

Sale

The Lakes National Park

Warragul

Morwell

Ninety Mile Beach

ench sland

Leongatha

Seaspray

TASMAN SEA

orumburra

Inverloch

Foster

Corner Inlet

Snake Island

Yanakie

Cape Liptrap

Tidal River

Wilsons Promontory National Park

100 km
60 miles

5 Grampians National Park (p583) Rock climbing, abseiling or bushwalking the stunning sandstone and granite outcrops.

6 Phillip Island (p532) Enjoying the nightly parade of cute little penguins.

7 Mildura (p619) Cruising on the Murray to a winery

lunch on a restored paddle steamer.

8 High Country (p601) Skiing the slopes on a high-adrenaline adventure.

paintings and the work of Melbourne's own Heidelberg School, most notably Tom Roberts' famous *Shearing the Rams* (1890) and Frederick McCubbin's monumental triptych *The Pioneer* (1904). The modernist 'Angry Penguins' are also well represented: the gallery houses the work of Sir Sidney Nolan, Arthur Boyd, Joy Hester and Albert Tucker. Other prominent artists whose work is displayed include Grace Cossington Smith, Russell Drysdale, James Gleeson, John Brack, Jeffrey Smart, Fred Williams and Brett Whiteley.

★ **Chinatown**   AREA
(Map p472; www.chinatownmelbourne.com.au; Little Bourke St, btwn Swanston & Exhibition Sts, Melbourne; 🚊 Melbourne Central, Parliament) FREE For more than 150 years this section of central Melbourne, now flanked by five traditional arches, has been the focal point for the city's Chinese community. It remains a vibrant neighbourhood of historic buildings filled with Chinese and other restaurants. A must-visit for foodies, come here for yum cha (dim sum) or to explore the attendant laneways for late-night dumplings and cocktails. Some restaurants stay open until the wee hours. Chinatown also hosts the city's Chinese New Year (p482) celebrations.

Chinese miners arrived in Victoria in search of the 'new gold mountain' in the 1850s and started to settle in this strip of Little Bourke St from the 1860s. To learn more about the Chinese-Australian story, visit the excellent **Chinese Museum** (Map p472; 🖉 03-9662 2888; www.chinesemuseum.com.au; 22 Cohen Pl, Melbourne; adult/child $11/9; ⊙ 10am-4pm; 🚊 Parliament).

Parliament House   HISTORIC BUILDING
(Map p472; 🖉 03-9651 8911; www.parliament.vic. gov.au; Spring St, Melbourne; ⊙ 8.30am-5.30pm Mon-Fri; 🚊 Parliament) FREE The grand steps of Victoria's parliament (1856) are often dotted with tulle-wearing brides smiling for the camera and placard-holding protesters. On sitting days the public is welcome to view proceedings from the galleries. On nonsitting days there are eight guided tours daily; times are posted online and on a sign by the door. Numbers are limited to 25 people, so arrive at least 15 minutes before time. Check online to book architecture or art tours in advance.

State Library of Victoria   LIBRARY
(Map p472; 🖉 03-8664 7000; www.slv.vic.gov.au; cnr Russell & La Trobe Sts, Melbourne; ⊙ 10am-9pm Mon-Thu, to 6pm Fri-Sun, galleries 10am-6pm

Thu-Tue, to 9pm Wed; 🖈; 🚊 1, 3, 5, 6, 16, 30, 35, 64, 67, 72, 🚊 Melbourne Central) FREE This grand neo-classical building has been at the forefront of Melbourne's literary scene since 1856. When its epicentre, the octagonal **La Trobe Reading Room**, was completed in 1913, the six-storey-high, reinforced-concrete dome was the largest in the world; its natural light illuminates ornate plasterwork and studious Melburnians. At the time of writing the library's original reading room, **Ian Potter Queen's Hall**, and the **Dome Galleries**, were set to open late 2019. Free 45-minute tours depart daily at 11am from **Readings** (Map p472; 🖉 03-8664 7540; www.readings.com.au; 285-321 Russell St; ⊙ 10am-6pm; 🚊 Melbourne Central).

Birrarung Marr   PARK
(Map p472; Batman Ave, Melbourne; 🚊 Flinders St) FREE Multi-terraced Birrarung Marr is a welcome addition to Melbourne's patchwork of parks and gardens, featuring grassy knolls, river promenades, thoughtful planting of Indigenous flora and great viewpoints of the city and the river. There's also a scenic route to the MCG (p470) via the 'talking' William Barak Bridge – listen out for songs, words and sounds representing Melbourne's cultural diversity as you walk.

**Australian Centre
for the Moving Image**   MUSEUM
(ACMI; Map p472; 🖉 03-8663 2200; www.acmi. net.au; Federation Sq, Melbourne; ⊙ 10am-5pm, cinemas until late; 🖈; 🚊 1, 3, 5, 6, 16, 64, 67, 70, 72, 75, City Circle, 🚊 Flinders St) FREE Managing to educate, enthral and entertain in equal parts, ACMI is a visual feast that pays homage to Australian cinema and TV, offering insight into the modern-day Aussie psyche. Its screens don't discriminate against age with TV shows, games and movies on call, making it a great place to spend a day watching TV without feeling guilty about it. Free exhibition tours at 11am and 2.30pm, plus regular talks and great workshops (prices vary). At the time of writing, ACMI was closed for a major redevelopment and is due to re-open in mid 2020. Some ACMI events and screenings will be held at various venues around the city until it reopens. Check the website to see what's on.

Flinders Street Station   HISTORIC BUILDING
(Map p472; cnr Flinders & Swanston Sts, Melbourne; 🚊 Flinders Street) Turning 100 years old in 2010, Melbourne's first railway station is also its most iconic building. You'd be hard-pressed to find a Melburnian who hasn't

uttered the phrase, 'meet me under the clocks' – the popular rendezvous spot at the front entrance. Stretching along the Yarra, the neoclassical building crowned with a striking octagonal dome contains an abandoned ballroom, closed to the public.

Old Melbourne Gaol   HISTORIC BUILDING
(Map p472; ☑ 03-9656 9889; www.oldmelbourne gaol.com.au; 337 Russell St, Melbourne; adult/child $28/15; ⊙ 9.30am-5pm; ♿; ☒ 30, 35, ☒ Melbourne Central) Dating back to 1841, this bluestone prison was in operation until 1924 and decommissioned in 1929. It's now a museum where you can tour the tiny, bleak cells. It was the scene of 133 hangings – including that of Ned Kelly, Australia's most infamous bushranger, in 1880 – and you can also attend spooky night tours (not recommended for under 16s) or take part in the Police Watch House Experience, where you get 'arrested' and thrown in the slammer (more fun than it sounds).

Old Treasury Building   MUSEUM
(Map p472; ☑ 03-9651 2233; www.oldtreasury building.org.au; 20 Spring St, Melbourne; ⊙ 10am-4pm Sun-Fri; ☒ Parliament) FREE The fine neoclassical architecture of the Old Treasury Building (1862), designed by 19-year old JJ Clarke, is a telling mix of hubris and functionality. The basement vaults were built to house the millions of pounds' worth of loot and gold bullion bars during Victoria's goldrush era, and now feature multimedia displays telling those stories. Also downstairs is the 1920s caretaker's flat and a reproduction of the 70kg 'Welcome Stranger' nugget, found in 1869.

Melbourne Town Hall   NOTABLE BUILDING
(Map p472; ☑ 03-9658 9658; www.melbourne.vic. gov.au; 90-130 Swanston St, Melbourne; ⊙ tours 11am & 1pm, Wed-Fri & Mon; ☒ Flinders St) FREE Since opening in 1870, this grand neoclassical civic building has welcomed everyone from Queen Elizabeth II, who took tea here in 1954, to the Beatles, who waved to thousands of screaming fans from the balcony in 1964. Take the free one-hour tour to see the Grand Organ (built in 1929 and the largest in the southern hemisphere) and sit in the Lord Mayor's chair. Book via phone or email and arrive 15 minutes early with photo ID.

St Paul's Cathedral   CHURCH
(Map p472; ☑ 03-9653 4333; www.cathedral. org.au; cnr Flinders & Swanston Sts, Melbourne; ⊙ 8.30am-6pm Mon-Fri, 9am-4pm Sat, 7.30am-7pm Sun; ☒ Flinders St) Once a corn market for the growing city of Melbourne, services were celebrated on this prominent site from the city's first days, but work on Melbourne's Anglican cathedral didn't commenced until 1880. Consecrated in 1891, the present Gothic Revival church is the work of distinguished ecclesiastical architect William Butterfield (a case of architecture by proxy, as he sent the drawings from England). It features ornate stained-glass windows, Victorian-era tiling and cream and grey stone.

Koorie Heritage Trust   CULTURAL CENTRE
(Map p472; ☑ 03-8662 6300; www.koorieheri tagetrust.com; Level 1 & 3, Yarra Building, Federation Sq, cnr Swanston & Flinders Sts, Melbourne; tours adult/child $30/15; ⊙ 10am-5pm; ☒ Flinders St) FREE Devoted to southeastern Aboriginal culture, this centre houses interesting artefacts and oral history. There's a shop and gallery downstairs; upstairs, carefully preserved significant objects can be viewed in display cases and drawers. It also runs hour-long tours along the Yarra (subject to weather conditions) led by Koorie guides that evoke the history and memories that lie beneath the modern city. You can book online or in person.

◉ Southbank & Docklands

What was previously a gritty industrial zone supporting a major port pre-1980s is now the glitzy tourist precinct of Southbank. This riverside promenade is peppered with big-name international restaurants, hotels and the distinct whiff of 'casino', but its Yarra River view and the presence of top arts institutions make it an essential part of any Melbourne itinerary. To the west, the once working wharves of Docklands have birthed a mini city of apartments, offices, restaurants, plazas and public art – but the somewhat soulless area remains the butt of many a Melburnian joke.

★ NGV International   GALLERY
(National Gallery of Victoria International; Map p468; ☑ 03-8620 2222; www.ngv.vic.gov.au; 180 St Kilda Rd, Southbank; ⊙ 10am-5pm; ☒ Flinders St) FREE Housed in a vast, brutally beautiful, bunker-like building, the international branch of NGV has an expansive collection, from ancient artefacts to the cutting edge. Regular blockbuster exhibitions (prices vary) draw crowds, and there are free

Melbourne

MELBOURNE & VICTORIA MELBOURNE

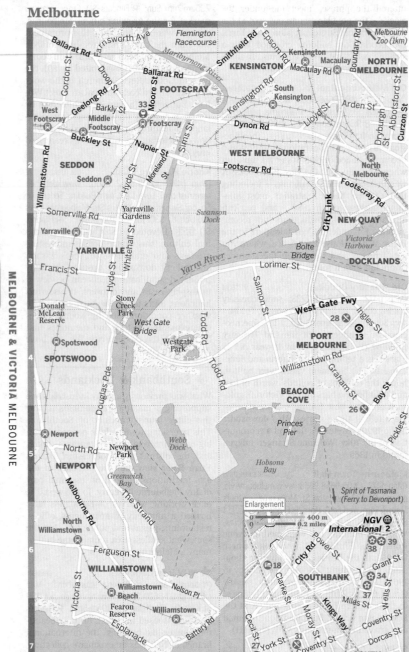

Ballarat Rd
Farnsworth Ave
Flemington Racecourse
Smithfield Rd
Epsom Rd
Melbourne Zoo (1km)
Boundary Rd
Maribyrnong River
Kensington
Macaulay
KENSINGTON
Macaulay Rd
NORTH MELBOURNE
Gordon St
Droop St
Ballarat Rd
Moore St
FOOTSCRAY
Kensington Rd
South Kensington
Arden St
Lloyd St
Dryburgh St
Abbotsford St
Curzon St
Geelong Rd
Barkly St
33
West Footscray
Middle Footscray
Footscray
Sims St
Dynon Rd
North Melbourne
Williamstown Rd
Buckley St
Napier St
Moreland St
WEST MELBOURNE
SEDDON
Hyde St
Footscray Rd
Footscray Rd
Seddon
CityLink
Somerville Rd
Yarraville Gardens
Whitehall St
Swanson Dock
NEW QUAY
Yarraville
YARRAVILLE
Hyde St
Victoria Harbour
Bolte Bridge
DOCKLANDS
Francis St
Yarra River
Lorimer St
Donald McLean Reserve
Stony Creek Park
Salmon St
West Gate Fwy
Ingles St
Spotswood
West Gate Bridge
Todd Rd
28
13
SPOTSWOOD
Westgate Park
PORT MELBOURNE
Douglas Pde
Williamstown Rd
Graham St
Bay St
Newport
BEACON COVE
26
Pickles St
North Rd
Newport Park
Princes Pier
NEWPORT
Webb Dock
Melbourne Rd
Greenwich Bay
Hobsons Bay
Spirit of Tasmania (Ferry to Devonport)
North Williamstown
The Strand
Enlargement
0   400 m
0   0.2 miles
NGV International 2
Ferguson St
City Rd
Power St
38
39
WILLIAMSTOWN
Victoria St
Williamstown Beach
18
Clarke St
SOUTHBANK
Grant St
34
Nelson Pl
Kings Way
Miles St
37
Fearon Reserve
Williamstown
Moray St
Wells St
Esplanade
Battery Rd
Cecil St
27
York St
31
Coventry St
Coventry St
Dorcas St
11
43
Dorcas St
SOUTH MELBOURNE

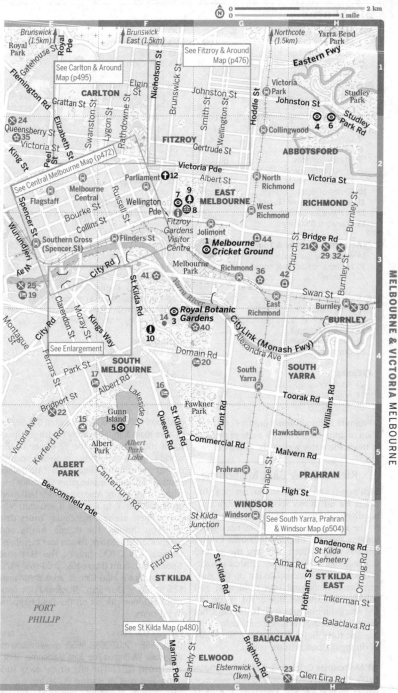

Melbourne

◎ Top Sights

1 Melbourne Cricket Ground G3
2 NGV International D6
3 Royal Botanic Gardens..........................F4

◎ Sights

4 Abbotsford Convent H2
5 Albert Park Lake....................................F5
6 Collingwood Children's Farm H2
  Collingwood Farmers Market........ (see 6)
7 Conservatory...F2
8 Cooks' Cottage......................................F2
9 Fitzroy Gardens.....................................F2
  Government House.........................(see 3)
  National Sports Museum ....(see 1)
10 Shrine of Remembrance......................F4
11 South Melbourne Market......................C7
12 St Patrick's Cathedral..........................F2
13 Starward Distillery D4

⊕ Activities, Courses & Tours

14 Aboriginal Cultural Heritage Walk F4
15 Melbourne Sports & Aquatic
   Centre...E5

⊜ Sleeping

16 Blackman F4
17 Coppersmith...E4
18 Crown Metropol.....................................C6
19 Pan Pacific Melbourne...........................E3
20 United Places..G4

⊗ Eating

21 Anchovy..H3
22 Andrew's Burgers E5

23 Attica...H7
24 Auction Rooms.....................................E2
25 Bangpop..E3
26 Ciao Cielo..D5
27 Claypots Evening Star..........................C7
28 Colonial Brewery Co.............................D4
  Convent Bakery ....(see 4)
  Farm Cafe ....(see 6)
  Lentil as Anything.........................(see 4)
  Matilda 159 ....(see 20)
29 Minamishima..H3
30 Serotonin Eatery...................................H3
  Simply Spanish.............................(see 27)
31 St Ali..C7
32 Touchwood..H3

⊜ Drinking & Nightlife

33 Pride of our Footscray B1

⊕ Entertainment

34 Chunky Move...D6
35 Comic's Lounge.....................................E2
36 Corner..G3
37 Malthouse Theatre D6
38 Melbourne Recital Centre.....................D6
39 Melbourne Theatre Company..............D6
40 Moonlight Cinema.................................G4
41 Sidney Myer Music Bowl........................F3

⊜ Shopping

42 Lily and the Weasel...............................G3
43 Nest C7
44 Pookipoiga..G3

MELBOURNE & VICTORIA MELBOURNE

50-minute highlight tours on the hour from 11am to 2pm daily. PSA: it's a rite of passage to touch the water wall at the entrance.

◎ Richmond & East Melbourne

Richmond and East Melbourne are the nexus for all things sport. The neighbourhood's southeastern skyline is dominated by the angular shapes of stadia, none more hulking than the mighty Melbourne Cricket Ground. North from here are the genteel streets of East Melbourne, centred on gorgeous Fitzroy Gardens. Taking up the eastern flank, Richmond is a residential and commercial expanse. Bridge Rd, its declining shopping hub, has seen better days, but grittier Victoria St is a destination for Vietnamese food. Beyond that there are plenty of dining diamonds in the rough.

★ **Melbourne Cricket Ground**　　STADIUM
(MCG; Map p468; ☑03-9657 8888; www.mcg.org.au; Brunton Ave, East Melbourne; tour adult/child/family $25/14/60, incl museum $35/18/76; ☉tours 10am-3pm; ☒Jolimont) With a capacity of 100,000 people, the 'G' is one of the world's great sporting venues, hosting cricket in summer and AFL (Australian Football League, Aussie rules or 'footy') in winter – for many Australians it's hallowed ground. Make it to a game if you can, otherwise there are non-match-day **tours** that take you through the stands, media and coaches' areas, change rooms and members' lounges. The MCG houses the **National Sports Museum** (Map p468; ☑03-9657 8879; www.nsm.org.au; MCG Gate 3; adult/child/family $25/14/60; ☉10am-5pm; ☒Jolimont). A two-night outdoor cinema on the field happens in February.

Fitzroy Gardens　　PARK
(Map p468; ☑03-9658 9658; www.melbourne.vic.gov.au; Wellington Pde, East Melbourne; ☒☒; ☒Jolimont) FREE The city drops away suddenly just east of Spring St, giving way to Melbourne's beautiful backyard, Fitzroy

Gardens. The park's stately avenues are lined with English elms, flowerbeds, expansive lawns, fountains and a creek. There's a playground with a dragon slide, but history buffs will love **Cooks' Cottage** (Map p468; adult/child $6.70/3.60; ☉9am-5pm), which belonged to the parents of Captain Cook. Nearby is a **visitor centre** (Map p468; ☉9am-5pm) with a cafe attached and the delightful 1930s **Conservatory** (Map p468; ✆03-8625 8888; www.serco.com; ☉9am-5pm) **FREE**.

Fitzroy, Collingwood & Abbotsford

A short tram ride from the centre delivers you to Melbourne's trendiest enclaves, where a flurry of cafes and restaurants continuously open and close; vinyl and midcentury furniture shops sit beside century-old pubs; and you can slurp ramen before heading to a divey live-music venue or gay club. Gentrification is rife in Fitzroy (Melbourne's first suburb) and Collingwood, but surrounding government housing reminds millennial renters to appreciate their cold brew coffee. Beyond Collingwood is largely industrial Abbotsford, bordered by a scenic stretch of the Yarra River with ever more cafes.

Abbotsford Convent   HISTORIC SITE
(Map p468; ✆03-9415 3600; www.abbotsford convent.com.au; 1 St Heliers St, Abbotsford; tours $15; ☉7.30am-10pm; 🚗; 🚌200, 207, 🚆Victoria Park) **FREE** This former convent, dating back to 1861, is a rambling collection of ecclesiastical architecture that's home to a thriving arts community of galleries, studios, cafes – including **Convent Bakery** (Map p468; ✆03-9419 9426; www.conventbakery. com; mains $14-19.50; ☉7am-5pm; 🚗) and vegetarian **Lentil as Anything** (Map p468; ✆03-9419 6444; www.lentilasanything.com; by donation; ☉9am-9pm; 🚗) – spread over nearly 7 hectares of riverside land. Tours of the complex run at 2pm on Sunday, or download the Abbotsford Convent app for a self-guided walking tour in which Wurundjeri elders, musicians and artists have created soundscapes that tell the story of traditional owners.

Collingwood Children's Farm   FARM
(Map p468; ✆03-9417 5806; www.farm.org.au; 18 St Heliers St, Abbotsford; adult/child/family $12/7/25; ☉9.15am-4.45pm; 🚗🚼; 🚌200, 207, 🚆Victoria Park) The inner city melts away at this rustic riverside retreat that's much beloved, and not just by children. There are frolicking farm animals that kids can help feed, as well as cow milking and guinea-pig cuddles. The fantastic, open-air cafe (p492) opens at 9am and can be visited without entering the farm itself, while the monthly **farmers market** (Map p468; www.mfm.com.au/markets/collingwood-childrens-farm; adult/child $2/free; ☉8am-1pm 2nd Sat of month; 🚗🚼) is a local highlight.

Stomping Ground Brewery & Beer Hall   BREWERY
(Map p476; ✆03-9415 1944; www.stomping ground.beer; 100 Gipps St, Collingwood; ☉11.30am-11pm Sun-Thu, to 1am Fri & Sat; 🚗; 🚆Collingwood) This inviting brewery-beer hall set in a former textile factory is a relaxed, leafy retreat with exposed-brick walls, hanging plants, a kids' play area (featuring a cubby) and a large central bar. There's a 30-tap bar with rotating guest beers and a menu of wood-fired pizzas and share dishes. Free brewery tours at noon on weekends.

Carlton & Brunswick

Home to Melbourne's Italian community and the University of Melbourne, there's as much history to absorb in Carlton as there is pasta. Until recently there was cultural cringe associated with 'tourist-trap' Lygon St, but the strip has been reinvigorated thanks to next-generation Australian-born Italians and restaurateurs opening venues inspired by the area's heritage.

Head west to multicultural-meets-hipster Brunswick to feast on affordable and filling Middle Eastern cuisine. Most establishments are clustered on or near Sydney Rd, with plenty of cafes and secondhand shopping during the day, followed by bar-hopping come nightfall.

★Royal Exhibition Building   HISTORIC BUILDING
(Map p495; ✆13 11 02; www.museumvictoria. com.au/reb; 9 Nicholson St, Carlton; tours adult/child $10/7; 🚌Tourist Shuttle, 🚋City Circle, 86, 96, 🚆Parliament) Built for the 1880 International Exhibition, this Victorian edifice in Carlton Gardens symbolises the glory days of 19th-century Melbourne's economic supremacy. It was the first Australian building to fly the country's flag, house an aquarium, hold parliament (in 1901) and receive Unesco World Heritage Status (in 2004). Tours of the building leave from Melbourne Museum (p474) at 2pm; call to confirm.

Central Melbourne

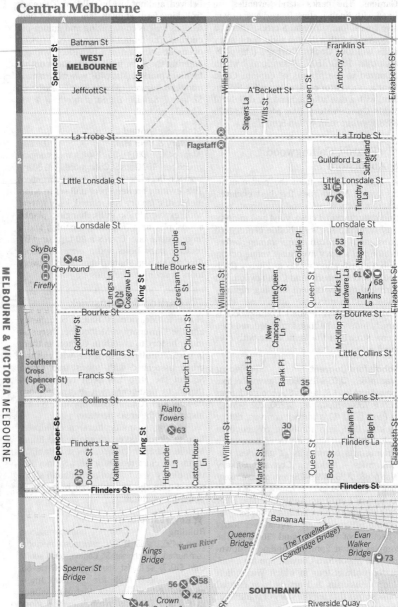

Batman St

WEST
MELBOURNE

Spencer St

King St

JeffcottSt

Franklin St

Anthony St

Elizabeth St

Queen St

A'Beckett St

Singers La

Wills St

William St

La Trobe St

La Trobe St

Flagstaff

Guildford La

Sutherland St

Little Lonsdale St

Little Lonsdale St

31
47

Lonsdale St

Gresham St

Crombie La

Little Bourke St

Lonsdale St

53

Goldie Pl

Niagara La

SkyBus

Greyhound

Firefly

48

Langs Ln

Cosgrave Ln

25

King St

William St

Little Queen St

Queen St

Kirks Ln

Hardware La

61

Rankins La

68

Bourke St

Bourke St

Godfrey St

Little Collins St

Church Ln

Church St

New Chancery Ln

Gurners La

Bank Pl

McKillop St

Little Collins St

Southern
Cross
(Spencer St)

Francis St

35

Collins St

Collins St

Spencer St

Rialto
Towers

63

30

Fulham Pl

Bligh Pl

Elizabeth St

Flinders La

Flinders La

Downie St

Katherine Pl

Highlander La

Custom House Ln

William St

Market St

Queen St

Bond St

29

Flinders St

Flinders St

Banana Al

Yarra River

Queens
Bridge

The Travellers
(Sandridge Bridge)

Evan
Walker
Bridge

73

Kings
Bridge

Spencer St
Bridge

56

58

SOUTHBANK

42

44

Crown
Casino &
Entertainment
Complex

Queensbridge St

Riverside Quay
Eureka
Tower

10

Clarendon St

Whiteman St

City Rd

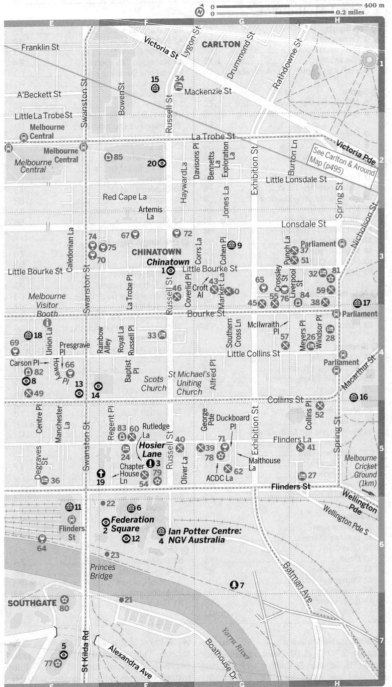

0 ———————— 400 m
0 ———————— 0.2 miles

Franklin St

CARLTON

Victoria St

Lygon St

Drummond St

Rathdowne St

15
34

A'Beckett St

BowerSt

Russell St

Mackenzie St

Little La Trobe St

La Trobe St

See Carlton & Around
Map (p495)

Victoria Pde

Melbourne
Central

Swanston St

Melbourne
Central

Melbourne
Central

85
20

Haywards La

Davisons Pl

Bennetts La

Exploration La

Exhibition St

Burton Ln

Little Lonsdale St

Spring St

Nicholson St

Red Cape La

Jones La

Artemis
La

Lonsdale St

74
67
72

Caledonian La

Swanston St

La Trobe Pl

Corrs La

Cohen Pl

9

Punch Ln

Parliament
37
51

Little Bourke St

CHINATOWN
Chinatown

75
70

Little Bourke St

1

Croft
Al

43
50

65

Crossley St

Liverpool St

32
81

59
84

Little Bourke St

46

Market La

55
76

45
38

17

Melbourne
Visitor
Booth

Bourke St

Mcllwraith
Pl

Parliament

18
69

Union La

Presgrave
Pl

33

Southern
Cross Ln

Little Collins St

Meyers Pl

57
26
28

Windsor Pl

Parliament

Carson Pl
82
66
8

Howey Pl

Rainbow
Alley

Royal La

Russell Pl

Baptist
Pl

St Michael's
Uniting
Church

Alfred Pl

Macarthur St

13
49
14

Scots
Church

Collins St

16

52

Centre Pl

Manchester
La

Swanston St

Regent Pl

83
60

Rutledge
La

George
Pde

Duckboard
Pl

Collins Pl

Collins St

Spring St

24

*Hosier
Lane*

40

71

Flinders La

41

Degraves
La

Chapter
House Ln

3
79
54

Oliver La

39
78

Malthouse
La

62

Melbourne
Cricket
Ground
(1km)

36

19

ACDC La

27

Flinders St

11

Flinders
St

64

22

6

Federation
2 Square
12

Ian Potter Centre:
4 NGV Australia

Wellington
Pde

Wellington Pde S

23

Princes
Bridge

7

Batman Ave

SOUTHGATE
80

21

5
77

St Kilda Rd

Alexandra Ave

Yarra River

Boathouse Dr

MELBOURNE & VICTORIA MELBOURNE

Central Melbourne

◎ Top Sights
1 Chinatown F3
2 Federation Square F6
3 Hosier Lane F5
4 Ian Potter Centre: NGV Australia......... F6

◎ Sights
5 Arts Centre Melbourne......................... E7
6 Australian Centre for the Moving
   Image F6
7 Birrarung Marr......................................G6
8 Block Arcade... E4
9 Chinese Museum G3
10 Eureka Skydeck....................................D7
11 Flinders Street Station E6
12 Koorie Heritage Trust F6
13 Manchester Unity Building E4
14 Melbourne Town Hall E4
15 Old Melbourne Gaol F1
16 Old Treasury Building H4
17 Parliament House H3
18 Royal Arcade... E4
19 St Paul's Cathedral F5
20 State Library of Victoria F2

⊕ Activities, Courses & Tours
21 Kayak Melbourne F7
22 Melbourne By Foot............................... F6
23 Rentabike F6

⊜ Sleeping
24 Adelphi Hotel F5
25 Alto Hotel on Bourke B3
26 City Centre Budget Hotel......................H4
27 Hotel Lindrum H5
28 Hotel Windsor.......................................H4
29 Melbourne Central YHA A5
30 Notel..C5
31 Novotel and Ibis Melbourne
   Central D2
32 Ovolo Laneways H3
33 QT Melbourne F4
34 Space Hotel...F1
35 Treasury on Collins D4
36 United Backpackers E5

⊗ Eating
37 Bar Saracen H3
38 Butcher's Diner.....................................H3
39 Chin Chin G5
40 Coda F5
41 Cumulus Inc H5
42 Dinner by Heston B7
43 Flower Drum G3
44 Gradi Crown B7
45 Grossi Florentino.................................G3
46 Hakata Gensuke....................................F3
47 Hardware Societe D2
48 Higher Ground...................................... A3
49 Hopetoun Tea Rooms E4
50 HuTong Dumpling Bar G3
51 Longrain H3
52 Mamasita H5
53 Miznon D3
54 MoVida F5
55 Pellegrini's Espresso Bar G3
56 Rockpool Bar & Grill B6
57 Soi 38 ....G4
58 Spice Temple...B6
59 Spring Street Grocer H3
   Sunda..(see 37)
60 Supernormal F5
61 Tipo 00 ....D3
62 Tonka...G5
63 Vue de Monde B5

⊖ Drinking & Nightlife
64 Arbory E6
65 Arlechin G3
66 Bar Americano.......................................E4
67 Boilermaker House.................................F3
68 Brother Baba Budan D3
69 Chuckle Park E4
70 Cookie E3
71 Garden State Hotel G5
72 Heartbreaker F3
   Longsong .... (see 51)
   Lui Bar ....(see 63)
   Melbourne Supper Club...............(see 59)
73 Ponyfish Island......................................D6
   Rooftop at QT..(see 33)
74 Rooftop Bar E3
75 Section 8..F3
   Siglo..(see 59)
76 Traveller G3

⊙ Entertainment
77 Australian Ballet...................................E7
78 Cherry..G5
79 Forum.. F5
80 Hamer Hall..E7
   Melbourne Symphony
     Orchestra..................................... (see 80)
81 Princess Theatre...................................H3

⊙ Shopping
82 Basement Discs.....................................E4
83 Craft Victoria..F5
   Hill of Content ....(see 45)
84 Melbournalia...H3
85 Readings F2

★ **Melbourne Museum**   MUSEUM
(Map p495; ☏13 11 02; www.museumvictoria.
com.au; 11 Nicholson St, Carlton; adult $15, child
& student free, exhibitions extra; ⊙10am-5pm;

⍟; ⍟Tourist Shuttle, ⍟City Circle, 86, 96, ⍟Par-
liament) This museum provides a grand
sweep of Victoria's natural and cultural
histories, incorporating dinosaur skeletons,

a 600-species-strong taxidermy hall, 3D volcano and an open-air forest atrium of Victorian flora. There's a children's gallery, and the excellent **Bunjilaka** on the ground floor presents Indigenous Australian history told through objects and Aboriginal voices with state-of-the-art technology. There's also an **IMAX cinema**.

⊙ North Melbourne, Parkville & West Melbourne

★**Melbourne Zoo**   ZOO
(🖉1300 966 784; www.zoo.org.au; Elliott Ave, Parkville; adult/child $37/19, child weekends & holidays free; ⊙9am-5pm, from 8am summer holidays; 🖮; 🚌58, 🚃Royal Park) 🖉 Established in 1862, this compact zoo is the oldest in Australia and the third oldest in the world. It remains one of the city's most popular attractions and continues to innovate, becoming the world's first carbon-neutral zoo. Set in prettily landscaped gardens, the enclosures aim to simulate the animals' natural habitats and give them the option to hide if they want to (the gorillas and tigers are particularly good at playing hard to get).

⊙ South Melbourne, Port Melbourne & Albert Park

Hugging Port Phillip Bay, this well-heeled trio of suburbs are leafy and sedate. You'll spot ladies lunching with prams, AFL stars and Porsches pulled up beside Victorian terraces and grandiose bayside condos – the area boasts beautiful heritage architecture. South Melbourne is the busiest neighbourhood, centred on its namesake market surrounded by cafes and curated design shops. Albert Park offers culture in a former gasworks and the world-renowned Grand Prix in March, while near the end of shop-studded Bay St in Port Melbourne is Station Pier, from where ferries cruise south to Tasmania.

South Melbourne Market   MARKET
(Map p468; 🖉03-9209 6295; www.southmelbournemarket.com.au; cnr Coventry & Cecil Sts, South Melbourne; ⊙8am-4pm Wed, Sat & Sun, to 5pm Fri; 🅿🖮; 🚌1, 12, 96, 109) Trading since 1867, this market is an institution, its labyrinthine guts packed with a brilliant collection of stalls selling everything from organic produce and arts and crafts to Indigenous Australian deli products. It's famed for dim sims (sold here since 1949), and there's no shortage of atmospheric restaurants. From

early January to late February, the lively **South Melbourne Night Market** runs from 5.30pm on Thursdays. It's also home to a cooking school. See the website for details.

Albert Park Lake   LAKE
(Map p468; btwn Lakeside Dr & Aughtie Dr, Albert Park; 🚌96) Elegant black swans give their inimitable bottoms-up salute as you jog, cycle or walk the 5km perimeter of this artificial lake. Lakeside Dr was used as an international motor-racing circuit in the 1950s, and since 1996 the revamped track has been the venue for the Australian F1 Grand Prix (p482) come March. Also on the periphery is the Melbourne Sports & Aquatic Centre (p479), with an Olympic-size pool and child-delighting wave machine.

Starward Distillery   DISTILLERY
(Map p468; www.starward.com.au; 50 Bertie St, Port Melbourne; tours $10; ⊙3-10pm Wed & Thu, noon-10pm Fri & Sat, to 8pm Sun; 🚌235, 🚌109) This sleek distillery-warehouse-bar is massive, with a public area up the front and copper stills at the rear. Sample the Distillery's Selection flight ($13) or cocktails over cheese and charcuterie. Tours ($10 including two 15mL pours) run on Fridays at 7pm and weekends at 2pm, 3.30pm and 5pm. Book via the website, where you can also lock in masterclasses.

⊙ South Yarra, Prahran & Windsor

★**Royal Botanic Gardens**   GARDENS
(Melbourne Gardens; Map p468; 🖉03-9252 2300; www.rbg.vic.gov.au; Birdwood Ave, South Yarra; ⊙7.30am-sunset; 🖮🚌; 🚃Tourist Shuttle, 🚌1, 3, 5, 6, 16, 64, 67, 72) FREE From the air, these stunning, 94-acre gardens evoke a giant green lung in the middle of the city. Drawing nearly two million visitors annually, they're considered one of the finest examples of Victorian-era landscaping in the world. Here you'll find global plantings and a range of Australian flora. Mini ecosystems, a herb garden and an Indigenous rainforest are set amid vast, picnic-friendly lawns and black-swan-spotted ponds. Be sure to book the Aboriginal Heritage Walk (p481).

Shrine of Remembrance   MONUMENT
(Map p468; 🖉03-9661 8100; www.shrine.org.au; Birdwood Ave, South Yarra; ⊙10am-5pm, last entry 4.30pm; 🖮; 🚃Tourist Shuttle, 🚌3, 5, 6, 16, 64, 67, 72) FREE One of Melbourne's icons, the Shrine of Remembrance is a commanding

Fitzroy & Around

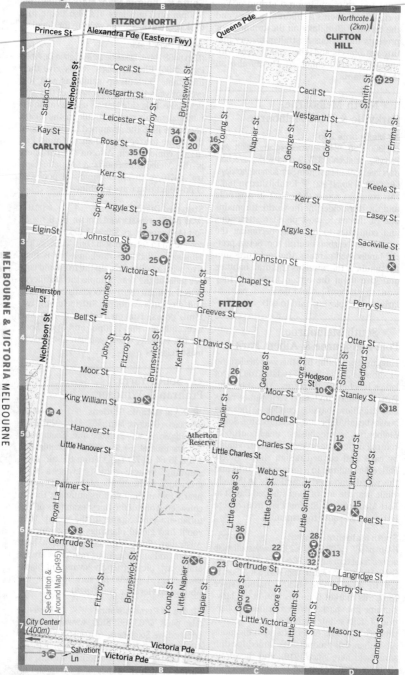

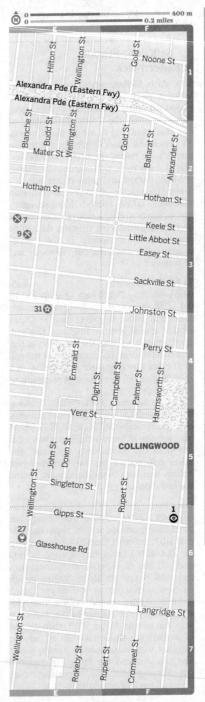

Fitzroy & Around

⊙ Sights
1 Stomping Ground Brewery &
  Beer Hall F6

🛏 Sleeping
2 Brooklyn Arts Hotel C7
3 Home @ The Mansion A7
4 Nunnery A5
5 Tyrian Serviced Apartments B3

🍽 Eating
6 Charcoal Lane B6
7 CIBI E3
8 Cutler & Co A6
9 Easey's E3
10 Gelato Messina D5
11 Horn D3
12 Hotel Jesus D5
13 IDES D6
14 Industry Beans B2
15 Lazerpig D6
16 Lune Croissanterie C2
17 Marios B3
18 Proud Mary D5
19 Smith & Daughters B5
20 Vegie Bar B2

🍸 Drinking & Nightlife
21 Black Pearl B3
22 Builders Arms Hotel C6
23 Everleigh C6
24 Grace Darling D6
25 Naked for Satan B3
26 Napier Hotel C4
27 Peel Hotel E6
28 Sircuit D6

🎭 Entertainment
29 Gasometer D1
30 Old Bar B3
31 The Tote E3
32 Yah Yah's D6

🛍 Shopping
33 Lore Perfumery B3
34 Polyester Records B2
35 Rose Street Artists' Market B2
36 Third Drawer Down C6

memorial to Victorians who have served
in war and peacekeeping, especially those
killed in WWI. Built between 1928 and
1934, much of it with Depression-relief, or
'susso' (sustenance) labour, its stoic, classical design is partly based on the Mausoleum of Halicarnassus, one of the seven
ancient wonders of the world. The shrine's
upper balcony affords epic panoramic views
of Melbourne's skyline and all the way up
tram-studded Swanston St.

MELBOURNE & VICTORIA MELBOURNE

Government House
HISTORIC BUILDING

(Map p468; ☑03-9656 9889; www.governor.vic.
gov.au; Kings Domain, South Yarra; tours adult/child
$18/10; ⊙tours subject to availability 10am Mon &
Thu; ☒Tourist Shuttle, ☒1, 3, 5, 6, 16, 58, 64, 67, 72)
On the outer edge of the Botanic Gardens,
this Italianate Government House dates
from 1872. A replica of Queen Victoria's
Osborne House on England's Isle of Wight,
it's served as the residence of all Victorian
governors, as well as being the royal pied-
à-terre. It remains the largest residential
building in Australia. The two-hour tour
only runs with 10 or more people and permission from Government House, so enquiries should be made at least two weeks ahead,
by phone or email.

Prahran Market
MARKET

(Map p504; ☑03-8290 8220; www.prahran
market.com.au; 163 Commercial Rd, South Yarra;
⊙7am-5pm Tue & Thu-Sat, 10am-3pm Sun; ☒;
☒72, 78, ☒Prahran) Prahran Market is a
Melbourne institution and foodie paradise.
The facade – designed by Charles D'Ebro
in Queen Anne–revival style – dates back
to 1891. Grab a speciality coffee from Market Lane (p505) and trawl produce stalls,
pop into culinary shop and cooking school
Essential Ingredient (Map p504; ☑03-9827
9047; www.essentialingredient.com.au; classes per
person $95-275; ⊙classes vary, shop 9am-5pm
Tue, Thu & Fri, 10am-4pm Wed & Sun, 8am-5pm Sat)
and soak up live music on Saturday. Don't
miss Maker & Monger (p497) for a 'flam-
ing reuben', $1 sushi rolls at Claringbold's
Quality Seafood or mushroom man Damian
Pike, awarded the Order of Australia for his
services.

Como House & Garden
HISTORIC BUILDING

(Map p504; ☑03-9827 2500, tour bookings
03-9656 9889; www.nationaltrust.org.au; cnr Williams Rd & Lechlade Ave, South Yarra; adult/child
$15/9; ⊙gardens & cafe 9am-5pm daily, house
tours 11am, 12.30pm & 2pm Sat & Sun; ☒☒; ☒58)
A wedding cake of Australian Regency and
Italianate architecture, this elegant colonial
residence is among Melbourne's heritage
royalty. Dating from 1847, it houses numerous belongings of the high-society Armytage
family, the last and longest owners, who
lived in the house for 95 years. House tours
run every Saturday and Sunday and tickets
can be purchased online or by phone.

The Stables of Como cafe, located in the
former stables, can pack a picnic hamper

for you to enjoy on the stately lawns; it also
hosts high tea.

⊙ St Kilda, Elwood
& Elsternwick

St Kilda is Melbourne's tattered bohemian
heart, a place where a young Nick Cave
played gloriously chaotic gigs at the George
Hotel (formerly the Crystal Ballroom) and
one that's featured in songs, plays, novels,
TV series and films. Originally a 19th-cen-
tury seaside resort, the neighbourhood has
played many roles: post-war Jewish enclave,
red-light district and punk-rocker hub. It's
a complex jumble of boom-style Victorian
mansions, raffish Spanish Moorish apartments, seedy streets, a rickety roller coaster
and nostalgia-inducing theatres, flanked by
wonderful dining options in the friendly
neighbouring suburbs of Elwood and
Elsternwick

St Kilda Foreshore
BEACH

(Map p480; Jacka Blvd, St Kilda; ☒☒; ☒3, 12, 16,
96) FREE Despite the palm-fringed promenades and golden stretch of sand, St Kilda's
seaside appeal is more Brighton, England,
than Venice, LA – with the exception of regular rollerbladers. There's a kiosk at the end
of St Kilda Pier (Map p480; Jacka Blvd; ☒; ☒3,
12, 16, 96) that offers a knockout panorama of
Melbourne's skyline.

During summer, Port Phillip EcoCentre (Map p480; ☑03-9534 0670; www.ecocentre.
com; 55a Blessington St; ☒3, 16, 67, 78, 79, 96) ⦿
runs a range of tours including urban wildlife walks and coastal discovery walks, and
offers information on the little-penguin
colony that lives in the breakwater behind
the pier's kiosk.

Luna Park
AMUSEMENT PARK

(Map p480; ☑03-9525 5033; www.lunapark.com.
au; 18 Lower Esplanade, St Kilda; single ride adult/
child $11/10, unlimited rides $50/40; ⊙hours vary;
☒; ☒3, 16, 96) Luna Park opened in 1912
and still has an old-style amusement-park
feel, with creepy Mr Moon's gaping mouth
swallowing you up as you enter. There's
a heritage-listed scenic railway (the oldest wooden roller coaster in the world – it
stayed in motion during WWI when the rest
of the park was closed); a beautiful baroque
carousel with hand-painted horses, swans
and chariots; and the full complement of
gut-churning rides, with something for all
ages and levels of adrenaline-seeker.

MELBOURNE IN...

Two Days

Grab a coffee at **Arbory** (p500) then head over to check out the **Ian Potter Centre: NGV Australia** (p463) art collection and have a look around **Federation Square** (p463) before joining a **walking tour** (p481) to see Melbourne's street art. Find a rooftop bar to test the city's cocktails and take in the views before dining at one of Melbourne's best restaurants. Start day two with a stroll along **Birrarung Marr** (p466) and into the **Royal Botanic Gardens** (p475), then discover the gastronomic delights of the **Queen Victoria Market** (p463). Catch a tram to **St Kilda** (p478) to wander along the foreshore and pier before propping up at a bar in lively Acland Street for the evening.

Four Days

On day three, spend a couple of hours at **Melbourne Museum** (p474) then head into Fitzroy to boutique-shop alongGertrude Street and Smith Streetand grab lunch and coffee at **Proud Mary** (p492) in Collingwood. Back in the city centre, wander through **Chinatown** (p466) and check out Ned Kelly's armour at the **State Library** (p466) before grabbing some dumplings for dinner. Spend day four shopping and cafe-hopping in hip Windsor and Prahran then take a tram back over the river to explore **Abbotsford Convent** (p471) and the Yarra Trail.

Jewish Museum of Australia MUSEUM
(Map p480; ☑03-9834 3600; www.jewishmuseum.com.au; 26 Alma Rd, St Kilda; adult/child $12/6; ☺10am-4pm Tue-Thu, to 3pm Fri, to 5pm Sun, closed Jewish holy days; 🚋3, 67) Interactive displays and timelines tell the history of Australia's Jewish community from the earliest days of European settlement, while permanent exhibitions celebrate Judaism's rich cycle of festivals, traditions and holy days. Past exhibits featured Amy Winehouse and a storyteller series; check the website to see what's on.

St Kilda Botanical Gardens GARDENS
(Map p480; ☑03-9209 6777; www.portphillip.vic.gov.au; cnr Blessington & Tennyson Sts, St Kilda; ☺gardens sunrise-sunset, conservatory 10.30am-3.30pm Mon-Fri, sunrise-sunset Sat & Sun; 🚋67, 96) Taking pride of place on the southern line of the Barkly St, Carlisle St and Blessington St triangle, the Botanical Gardens are an unexpected haven from St Kilda's hustle. Wide gravel paths invite a leisurely stroll, and there are plenty of shady spots for sprawling on the open lawns. Features include local indigenous plants, a subtropical-rainforest conservatory and a giant chessboard (smaller ones are built into adjoining tables).

🏃 Activities

Kite Republic KITESURFING
(Map p480; ☑03-9537 0644; www.kiterepublic.com.au; St Kilda Sea Baths, 4/10-18 Jacka Blvd,

St Kilda; 1hr lesson kite surfing/SUP $95/85; ☺10am-6pm Mon-Fri, to 5pm Sat & Sun; 🚋96) Offers kiteboarding lessons, tours and equipment; also a good source of info. Most people opt for a two-hour kite-surfing lesson for $175. In winter it can arrange snow-kiting at Mt Hotham. Also rents stand-up paddleboards (SUPs) for $25 per hour.

Stand Up Paddle HQ WATER SPORTS
(Map p480; ☑0416 184 994; www.supb.com.au; St Kilda Pier, St Kilda; hire per hour $30, 1.5hr private/group lesson $99/60; ☺8am-3.30pm Nov-Feb, weather permitting; 👶; 🚋96) Arrange a lesson or hire SUP equipment from Vincent, about 200m from St Kilda Pier towards the city. Look for the flags.

Melbourne Sports & Aquatic Centre SWIMMING
(MSAC; Map p468; ☑03-9926 1555; www.msac.com.au; 30 Aughtie Dr, Albert Park; adult/child from $8.50/5.80; ☺5.30am-10pm Mon-Fri, 7am-8pm Sat & Sun; 👶; 🚋96, 112) Flanking Albert Park Lake (p475), Melbourne's premier aquatic centre was a venue for the 2006 Commonwealth Games. Facilities include indoor and outdoor 50m pools, an indoor 25m pool, sauna and steam room, and spacious common areas. Kids will love SplashOUT, with inflatables, a wave pool, waterslide and more (adults and kids cost $10.20 and $7.10 respectively). Childcare available.

MELBOURNE & VICTORIA MELBOURNE

St Kilda & Around

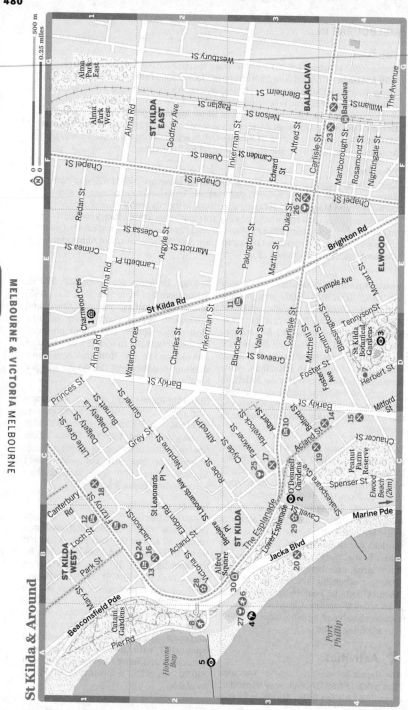

St Kilda & Around

⊙ Sights
1 Jewish Museum of Australia.................D1
2 Luna Park C3
3 St Kilda Botanical Gardens D4
4 St Kilda Foreshore A3
5 St Kilda Pier...A2

⊕ Activities, Courses & Tours
Aurora Spa Retreat.....................(see 13)
6 Kite Republic B3
7 Port Phillip EcoCentre D4
8 Stand Up Paddle HQ...............................A2

⊜ Sleeping
9 Abode St Kilda B1
10 Base Backpackers C3
11 Habitat HQ...E3
12 Hotel Tolarno B1
13 Prince Hotel..B2

⊗ Eating
14 Cicciolina C4
15 Claypots C4
16 Lau's Family Kitchen B2

17 Matcha Mylkbar C3
18 Miss Jackson C1
19 Monarch Cake Shop................................C4
20 Stokehouse B3
21 Tulum G4
22 Uncle..F3
23 Ziggy's Eatery F4

⊙ Drinking & Nightlife
24 Bar Di Stasio B2
25 Dogs Bar..C3
26 Local Taphouse...F3
Misery Guts.................................(see 18)
Pontoon.......................................(see 20)
27 Republica A3

⊙ Entertainment
28 Esplanade Hotel B2
29 Palais Theatre...B3
Prince Bandroom ....(see 13)

⊙ Shopping
Readings ....(see 14)
30 St Kilda Esplanade Market...................B3

🕝 Tours

★ Rentabike
CYCLING

(Map p472; 📞 0417 339 203, 03-9654 2762; www.
rentabike.net.au; Vault 14, Federation Wharf, Federation Sq, Melbourne; rental per hour/day $15/40,
4hr tour incl lunch adult/child $120/79; ⊙10am–
5pm; 🚶; 🚆Flinders St) 🏃 Renting out bikes
for more than 40 years, this outfit also
runs **Real Melbourne Bike Tours**, offering
a local's insight into the city with a foodie
focus. Tours max out at eight people. Electric
bikes are also available.

★ Kayak Melbourne
KAYAKING

(Map p472; 📞 0418 106 427; www.kayakmelb
ourne.com.au; Community Hub at The Dock, 912
Collins St, Docklands; tours $75–110; 🚶; 🚆11, 48)
🏃 Ninety-minute City Sights tours paddle
past Southbank to Docklands, while two-
hour River to Sky tours include entry to the
Eureka Skydeck (Map p472; 📞 03-9693 8888;
www.eurekaskydeck.com.au; 7 Riverside Quay,
Southbank; adult/child $23/19, Edge extra $12/8;
⊙10am–10pm; 🚆Flinders St). You can start
your day saluting the sun on a two-hour
Yoga Sunrise tour or end it with a 2½-hour
Moonlight tour starting from Docklands.
Other tours start at Boathouse Dr, directly
across the Yarra River from Federation Sq.

Melbourne Street Art Tours
TOURS

(📞 03-9328 5556; www.melbournestreettours.
com; tours adult/child $69/34.50; ⊙ city centre
1.30pm Tue, Thu & Sat, Fitzroy 11am Sat) Three-
hour tours exploring the street art that
makes Melbourne's laneways and buildings
famous. Tours take place either in the city
centre or Fitzroy – meet out the front of
ACMI (p466) or Easey's (p492) respectively –
and the guides are street artists themselves,
so you'll leave with a much better insight
into this art form.

Aboriginal Cultural Heritage Walk
WALKING

(Map p468; 📞 03-9252 2429; www.rbg.vic.gov.au;
Royal Botanic Gardens, Birdwood Ave, South Yarra;
adult/child $35/12; ⊙ tours from 11am Sun–Fri; 🚶;
🚆3, 5, 6, 8, 16, 64, 67, 72) 🏃 The Royal Botanic
Gardens (p475) is a significant cultural
site for the Kulin people. This the 90-min-
ute Aboriginal Heritage Walk starts with a
smoking ceremony (don't take photos without asking) and continues with a leisurely,
informative stroll led by an Aboriginal guide.
Learn about traditional uses for plants and
animals, before finishing with a lemon myrtle tea. Not suitable for wheelchairs.

Melbourne By Foot
WALKING

(Map p472; 📞 1300 311 081; www.melbourneby
foot.com; departs Federation Sq, Melbourne; tours
$50; ⊙1pm; 🚆Flinders St) Take a few hours
out and experience a mellow, informative,
three-hour walking tour that covers laneway art, politics, Melbourne's history and

diversity – highly recommended. There's even a Beer Lovers tour ($90). Book online.

⛩ Festivals & Events

Australian Open
SPORTS
(www.australianopen.com; Melbourne Park, Olympic Blvd, Melbourne; ☉ Jan; ⛹) The world's top tennis players and huge, merry-making crowds descend for Australia's grand-slam tennis championship. Check out the AO Live Stage at Birrarung Marr (p466) for international music acts, the mini theme park for kids and dining options from local restaurants that improve each year.

St Jerome's
Laneway Festival
MUSIC
(www.lanewayfestival.com; 40 Maribyrnong Blvd, Footscray; ☉ Jan or Feb) The one-day 'Laneway Fest' – which moved to Footscray Park in 2019 – keeps getting better, scheduling international and local alternative artists just as they're starting to break through.

★ Chinese New Year
CULTURAL
(www.melbournechinesenewyear.com; Little Bourke St, Melbourne; ☉ Jan/Feb; ⛹) FREE The lunar new year goes off with a bang in Chinatown, where the world's biggest processional dragon makes its way down Little Bourke St, food stalls set up, and events and celebrations continue for a few weeks.

★ Melbourne Food
& Wine Festival
FOOD & DRINK
(www.melbournefoodandwine.com.au; ☉ Mar) Food lovers travel to Melbourne especially for this festival, which celebrates the city's world-class food and wine scene with more than 200 unique events. From the sell-out Longest Lunch – served on a table that snakes through a different iconic Melbourne location each year – to international Michelin-starred chefs taking over restaurants, masterclasses and free events, there's something for every gastronome.

Australian Formula 1
Grand Prix
SPORTS
(Australian F1 Grand Prix; ☏ 03-9258 7100, 1800 100 030; www.grandprix.com.au; Albert Park Lake, Albert Park; general admission from $35; ☉ Mar) The 5.3km circuit around the normally tranquil Albert Park Lake is known for its smooth, fast surface. The buzz, both on the streets and in your ears, takes over Melbourne for four days of rev-head action. Listen out for the cars and jets.

Melbourne International
Comedy Festival
COMEDY
(www.comedyfestival.com.au; ☉ Mar-Apr) An enormous range of local and international comic talent hits town with four weeks of laughs in Melbourne venues, whether at Melbourne Town Hall (p467), a spiegeltent or a nightclub. Tickets average $30, but there is free entertainment too. Check the website for details.

AFL Grand Final
SPORTS
(www.afl.com.au; MCG, Brunton Ave, East Melbourne; ☉ Sep) It's easier to kick a goal from the boundary line than to pick up sought-after tickets to the Aussie rules Grand Final, usually held on the final Saturday in September – but it's not hard to get your share of finals fever anywhere in Melbourne (particularly at pubs).

Melbourne Cup
SPORTS
(www.springracingcarnival.com.au; Flemington Racecourse; ☉ Nov) Culminating in the prestigious Melbourne Cup, the Spring Racing Carnival is as much a social event as a sporting one. The Cup, held on the first Tuesday in November, is a public holiday here. Expect to see Melburnians frocked up in their finest during the horse races – before getting frocked up at bars around town later on.

🛏 Sleeping

As in any big city, accommodation in Melbourne can be expensive. You'll need to book ahead if your trip coincides with a major event, such as the Australian Open or Melbourne Cup. Note that prices shoot up on Friday and Saturday nights. Hostels are scattered around popular suburbs, while four- and five-star hotels are clustered in the city. Boutique hotels book up fast, as does rental and home-sharing accommodation.

🛏 City Centre

United Backpackers
HOSTEL $
(Map p472; ☏ 03-9654 2616; www.unitedbackpackers.com.au; 250 Flinders St, Melbourne; dm from $40, r with/without bathroom from $140/110; ❄🛜; ☒ Flinders St) Occupying an Edwardian building in the heart of the action opposite Flinders St station, this perpetually buzzing backpackers has been thoughtfully renovated throughout. The prices are steep for a hostel, but the location is fantastic. Wi-fi is only available in communal areas unless you

pay, but there's a bar downstairs, free pancakes and city tours every morning.

Space Hotel HOSTEL $

(Map p472; ☎03-9662 3888; www.spacehotel.com.au; 380 Russell St, Melbourne; dm from $37, r with/without bathroom from $130/105; ❄ 📶; 🚆Melbourne Central) This sleek place walks the line between hostel and budget hotel. Private rooms have iPod docks and flat-screen TVs, while dorms have touches like large lockers with sensor lights and lockable adapters. Some doubles have en suites and balconies. The rooftop hot tub and free St Kilda shuttle (summer only) are big ticks. Shame you have to pay for wi-fi.

Melbourne Central YHA HOSTEL $

(Map p472; ☎03-9621 2523; www.yha.com.au; 562 Flinders St, Melbourne; dm from $32, d with/without bathroom from $137/114; 📶; 🚆Southern Cross) 🌿 Expect a lively reception, clean rooms and kitchens, and common areas on each level. Entertainment's high on the agenda and there's a cafe-bar on the ground floor, plus a communal rooftop. There are two private en-suite rooms on the roof and guests can opt in to free Melbourne tours and weekly environmental programs run through the Port Phillip EcoCentre (p478).

Home @ The Mansion HOSTEL $

(Map p476; ☎03-9663 4212; www.homeatthemansion.com; 80 Victoria Pde, East Melbourne; dm/r from $29/85; 📶; 🚆Parliament) Located within a castle-like former Salvation Army building with grand double staircases, this hostel has genuine character. There are 92 dorm beds and four doubles. Rooms are basic but with high ceilings. There are two tiny TV areas, an unkempt courtyard out the front and a sunny kitchen.

Alto Hotel on Bourke HOTEL $

(Map p472; ☎1800 135 123, 03-8608 5500; www.altohotel.com.au; 636 Bourke St, Melbourne; r/apt from $176/206; P ❄ 📶; 🚆Southern Cross) 🌿 Environmentally minded (and awarded) Alto has water-saving showers, energy-efficient lights and double-glazed windows. Recycling is encouraged and there's free parking for electric and hybrid vehicles that fit its Tesla charger. Rooms have good light and neutral decor, and even the 'petite' rooms are reasonably sized. Studios have kitchenettes, while larger apartments have full kitchens. Prices fluctuate considerably throughout the year.

Guests have access to a nearby gym.

★Ovolo Laneways BOUTIQUE HOTEL $$

(Map p472; ☎03-8692 0777; www.ovolohotels.com.au; 19 Little Bourke St, Melbourne; r from $275; ❄ 📶; 🚆Parliament) This 42-room boutique hotel has a funky city vibe. It's friendly, fun and loaded with goodies – on the free list are self-service laundry, minibar, Nespresso machines, a candy bar in the lobby and, for direct bookings, happy-hour booze and breakfast. Suites are more impressive than studios; all have Amazon's Alexa. We love the personalised welcome messages and treats.

Novotel and Ibis Melbourne Central HOTEL $$

(Map p472; ☎03-9929 8888; www.accorhotels.com; 399 Little Lonsdale St, Melbourne; Ibis r $160-220, Novotel r $240-300; ❄ 📶; 🚌19, 57, 59, 🚆Melbourne Central) Once you get your head around this sparkling dual hotel in the city centre, you'll realise it's a fabulous option for its location, cleanliness and design. Ibis rooms are on floors 4 to 18, with the more luxurious Novotel between levels 20 to 35. From the 3rd floor down are common areas, including a bar and two fantastic restaurants.

Treasury on Collins APARTMENT $$

(Map p472; ☎03-8535 8535; www.treasuryoncollins.com.au; 394 Collins St, Melbourne; apt from $241; ❄ @ 📶; 🚌11, 12, 48, 109) This imposing neoclassical building (1876) once housed a branch of the Bank of Australia. A lofty public bar now fills downstairs, leading up to a guests-only mezzanine serving complimentary wine and nibbles between 4pm and 6pm, its high ceiling supported by gilt-edged columns. The apartments are modern, restrained and spacious. Winning extras include coffee machines, Netflix and Molton Brown toiletries.

★QT Melbourne HOTEL $$$

(Map p472; ☎03-8636 8800; www.qtmelbourne.com.au; 133 Russell St, Melbourne; r from $350; ❄ @ 📶; 🚌86, 96) Arty vibes, industrial surfaces, brass trim, lifts with tapestry light boxes that spurt random utterances in a Russian accent – this is one of Melbourne's quirkiest and best boutique hotels. The 188 rooms are beautifully kitted out – a contrast of concrete and soft, colourful fabrics – and there's a guide to the artwork in the building. Don't miss the rooftop (p500) bar.

Adelphi Hotel HOTEL $$$

(Map p472; ☎03-8080 8888; www.adelphi.com.au; 187 Flinders Lane, Melbourne; r from $350;

HEIDE MUSEUM OF MODERN ART

The former home of John and Sunday Reed, the **Heide Museum of Modern Art** (☑ 03-9850 1500; www.heide.com.au; 7 Templestowe Rd, Bulleen; adult/child $20/free; ☺ 10am-5pm Tue-Sun; ☐; ☐ 903, ☐ Heidelberg) is a prestigious not-for-profit art gallery with a stunning sculpture garden. It holds regularly changing exhibitions, many of which include works by the famous artists that called Heide home, including Sidney Nolan and Albert Tucker. The collection is spread over three buildings: a large purpose-built gallery, the Reeds' original farmhouse and the wonderful modernist house built in 1963 as 'a gallery to be lived in'.

There's also a cafe, or you can pack a picnic to eat by the Yarra. Tours are free with entry tickets and run regularly – check the website for details. Also check for the Makers' Market, a collaboration between Heide and the Rose Street Artists' Market (p510), held monthly. There are also 'detective' and 'sculpture sounds' trail maps to keep the kids busy.

Bulleen is 14km northeast of the city centre and Heide is located next to Banksia Park, which is part of the Main Yarra Trail, a flat, 33km bike trail from Westerfolds Park in Templestowe to Southbank, which passes native trees and billabongs.

❇ 🛜 ⊠; ☐ Flinders St) This discreet Flinders Lane property has a glam European feel with design touches throughout. The lobby looks good enough to eat, although it could just be the jelly beans at reception and dessert-themed **Om Nom** restaurant making us salivate. Look for the iconic glass-bottomed pool hanging nine-storeys above Flinders Lane (access available to non-guests for $35 subject to availability).

Bonus: there are free lollies and non-alcoholic beverages in the well-stocked minibars.

Notel
GLAMPING $$$

(Map p472; www.notelmelbourne.com.au; cnr Harper & Flinders Lanes (look up at Fry's Fast Car Park), Melbourne; airstreams $395-440; P ⊖ ❇ 🛜; ☐ 11, 12, 48, 58, 109) Experience one of six, funky 1970s Airstream caravans on top of a nondescript car park. Each has a deck sharing a communal area; one has a private spa overlooking Flinders Lane. There's no front desk – use your smartphone as a key – but there are pink showers, free minibars and parking, and an iPad with a virtual concierge and Netflix.

Hotel Lindrum
BOUTIQUE HOTEL $$$

(Map p472; ☑ 03-9668 1111; www.hotellindrum.com.au; 26 Flinders St, Melbourne; r $270-390; ❇ 🛜; ☐ Parliament) Formerly a billiards hall named for the legendary billiards-and-snooker-playing family that included the unbeatable Walter Lindrum, this hotel is recognisable from its stunning facade and arched windows. Inside is

minimalist with tactile fabrics, although the beige colour scheme falls flat and bathrooms can look tired. Best opt for a deluxe room with marvellous Melbourne views. **Felt Restaurant** and a bar on-site.

Hotel Windsor
HOTEL $$$

(Map p472; ☑ 03-9633 6000; www.thehotelwindsor.com.au; 111 Spring St, Melbourne; r from $200; ❇ @ 🛜; ☐ Parliament) Sparkling chandeliers and a grand piano in the lobby set the scene for this opulent, heritage-listed 1883 building that's one of Australia's most famous and self-consciously grand hotels. Adding to its English quaintness is high tea service and the historic Cricketers Bar, decked out in cricketing memorabilia.

🛏 Southbank & Docklands

Pan Pacific Melbourne
HOTEL $$

(Map p468; ☑ 1800 049 610, 03-9027 2000; www.panpacific.com; 2 Convention Centre Pl, South Wharf; r from $259; P ❇ @ 🛜; ☐ 35, 70, 75) Polished wood and natural fibres provide an earthy feel in this luxurious hotel. Suites are huge and some offer dazzling views across Melbourne. **Red Desert Dreamings Gallery**, an independent Aboriginal art gallery, is on the 4th floor, with art for sale. On the ground floor is a restaurant, a cafe and impressive artwork made from scourers depicting a coral reef.

Crown Metropol
HOTEL $$$

(Map p468; ☑ 1800 056 662, 03-9292 6211; www.crownmetropolmelbourne.com.au; 8 Whiteman St,

Southbank; r from $268; P ✳ @ 🛇 ≋; 🚍12, 96, 109) Welcome to one of the biggest hotels in the southern hemisphere, with a staggering 658 rooms over 28 floors. Guests have access to Skybar on the top floor and an extraordinary indoor infinity pool one floor down, offering views over the city to the Dandenongs. Rooms are suitably plush and there's a gym, fabulous restaurants and a luxury spa nearby.

Fitzroy, Collingwood & Abbotsford

Brooklyn Arts Hotel   B&B $
(Map p476; ☎03-9419 9328; www.brooklynarts hotel.com.au; 48-50 George St, Fitzroy; s/d from $115/155; 🛇; 🚍86) There are seven rooms in this character-filled hotel owned by filmmaker and artist Maggie Fooke. Set in a terrace house, they vary in size but are all clean, quirky and decorated with worldly treasures. Spacious upstairs rooms with high ceilings and balconies are the pick (from $200). Expect lively conversation over the included breakfast and attention from Badger the dog.

Nunnery   HOSTEL $
(Map p476; ☎1800 032 635; www.nunnery.com.au; 116 Nicholson St, Fitzroy; dm/s/d from $36/95/130; 🛇; 🚍96) Built in 1888, the Nunnery oozes atmosphere, with sweeping staircases and many original features plus religious works of art and ornate stained-glass windows. The next-door Nunnery Guesthouse has larger rooms in a private setting (from $140). It can be popular with long-term guests, so book ahead. All rates include breakfast. Free bike hire.

Ask about movie nights, pub crawls, BBQs and events.

**★Tyrian Serviced
Apartments**   APARTMENT $$
(Map p476; ☎03-9415 1900; www.tyrian.com.au; 91 Johnston St, Fitzroy; apt from $209; P ✳ 🛇; 🚍11) Big couches, flat-screen TVs, European laundries and balconies add to the appeal of these spacious, self-contained serviced apartments, while plenty of restaurants and bars are right at your door. It's rounded off with free wi-fi and parking. Rooms facing Johnston St can get noisy, but room 301 has an especially huge balcony with city views.

There's a supermarket right next door.

Carlton & Brunswick

169 Drummond   B&B $
(Map p495; ☎03-9663 3081; www.169drummond. com.au; 169 Drummond St, Carlton; d incl breakfast $135-145; P ⊖ ✳ 🛇; 🚍1, 8) This privately owned, four-room guesthouse in a renovated, 19th-century terrace is well located, just a block from vibrant Lygon St. Rooms feature fireplaces and Persian rugs, and there's a homey dining area and kitchenette for guests' use. It's gay-friendly and welcoming to all.

South Melbourne, Port Melbourne & Albert Park

★Coppersmith   BOUTIQUE HOTEL $$
(Map p468; ☎03-8696 7777; www.coppersmith hotel.com.au; 435 Clarendon St, South Melbourne; r from $235; ✳ 🛇; 🚍12) Low-key, contemporary and elegant, 15-room Coppersmith has every right to call itself a boutique property. Designer furniture, heavenly beds and fine woollen rugs set a seductive tone in muted rooms, each with a Nespresso machine, work desk, free wi-fi, recordable cable TV and minibar customisable to your dietary preferences. There's also a smart bistro-bar and rooftop deck with skyline views.

Blackman   BOUTIQUE HOTEL $$
(Map p468; ☎03-9039 1444, 1800 278 468; www. artserieshotels.com.au/blackman; 452 St Kilda Rd, Melbourne; r from $209; ✳ 🛇; 🚍3, 5, 6, 16, 64, 67, 72) While it may not have original Charles Blackman paintings (though there are loads of gallery-quality prints and room decals), it boasts a superb outlook. The bathrooms are somewhat dated, but the beds are luxurious. Aim for a corner suite for views of Albert Park Lake (p475) and the city skyline – the word 'Bay' in front of room names is a giveaway.

South Yarra, Prahran & Windsor

Hotel Claremont   GUESTHOUSE $
(Map p504; ☎03-9826 8000; www.hotelclare mont.com; 189 Toorak Rd, South Yarra; dm/d from $44/90; 🛇; 🚍58, 78, ℝSouth Yarra) In an 1886 heritage building, Claremont offers good value on an exclusive strip. Popular with travelling student groups, it's not exactly a party atmosphere, and the 75 rooms are simple and small, but clean and

comfortable, with wooden floorboards and shared bathrooms. There's a guest laundry and 24-hour reception. It's steps from Chapel St and South Yarra station. Rates include breakfast.

SoYa
BOUTIQUE HOTEL $$

(Map p504; ☑03-9820 0377; www.soyahotel.com.au; 4 Darling St, South Yarra; r from $150; ☻❋☎☜; ☒58, 78, ☒South Yarra) Short for 'South Yarra', SoYa was refurbished in 2018. Staff are friendly and the king 1960s apartments are spotless and tastefully decorated, some with entertaining wall art. Two-bedrooms suites and a designated pet-friendly room are available, while amenities include tablets, TVs with Netflix, laundry, full kitchen with coffee machine and more. Rent an electric bike for $15 per day.

Cullen
BOUTIQUE HOTEL $$

(Map p504; ☑03-9098 1555; www.artserieshotels.com.au/cullen; 164 Commercial Rd, Prahran; r from $229; ❋☎; ☒72, 78, ☒Prahran) Late grunge painter Adam Cullen's vibrant and often graphic art provides such visions as Ned Kelly shooting you from the opaque bedroom-bathroom dividers. Rooms are stylish and comfy with handy kitchenettes, but you can order room service from HuTong and Gramercy Social downstairs. Standard studios are small. Rooms facing north and west from level four up offer the best views.

United Places
BOUTIQUE HOTEL $$$

(Map p468; ☑03-9866 6467; www.unitedplaces.com.au; 157 Domain Rd, South Yarra; ste $650-1100; ❋☎; ☒248, ☒58) This exclusive spot across from the Botanic Gardens spares no detail – or expense. Quiet and with Le Labo toiletries, the price includes breakfast byMatilda 159 (p498) downstairs served in one of 12 stunning, terraced suites. The kitchen has custom ceramics, you can watch Netflix from plush velvet designer couches and sip Sullivans Cove whisky from the minibar.

🛏 St Kilda, Elwood & Elsternwick

★ Base Backpackers
HOSTEL $

(Map p480; ☑03-8598 6200; www.stayatbase.com; 17 Carlisle St, St Kilda; dm/d from $25/90; ❋☎; ☒3, 16, 96) Provides streamlined dorms with en suites and slick doubles, although cleanliness can be an issue. There's a floor complete with hair straighteners and

champagne deals set aside for female travellers, plus free continental breakfast, and a bar that hosts nightly events and live music. Ask about free walking tours and 'boozy bingo'. Buy a pint on Thursday to score a free steak.

Abode St Kilda
MOTEL $

(Map p480; ☑03-8598 0200, 1300 301 730; www.easystay.com.au; 63 Fitzroy St, St Kilda; d from $134; ☒❋☎; ☒3, 12, 16, 96) A great choice for those who've outgrown hostels but want an affordable private room in the heart of the action. Although the exterior suggests 'dodgy motel', the rooms are clean and upbeat, with images of iconic St Kilda on the walls, free wi-fi, microwaves, and bathrooms with underfloor heating. St Kilda Foreshore (p478) is 300m away.

Habitat HQ
HOSTEL $

(Map p480; ☑1800 202 500, 03-9537 3777; www.habitathq.com.au; 333 St Kilda Rd, St Kilda; dm/d from $34/129; ☒❋@☎; ☒3, 67) There's not much this clean, carbon-neutral hostel doesn't have. Check off open-plan communal spaces, a fully equipped kitchen, a bar, a beer garden, honey bees, a travel agent and a pool table, for starters. There's even a piano and a guitar available to play. Parking available on the property for $4 per day.

Hotel Tolarno
HOTEL $

(Map p480; ☑03-9537 0200; www.tolarnohotel.com.au; 42 Fitzroy St, St Kilda; s/d/ste from $115/135/220; ❋@☎; ☒3, 12, 16, 96) Previously the site of art dealer Georges Mora's namesake gallery, no two rooms here are the same, but all come eclectically furnished with good beds, bold artwork, Nespresso machines and free wi-fi. Squishy piccolo rooms are a lot smaller than standard – 9 sq metres versus 17 sq metres. Those at the front of the building can get a bit noisy.

Prince Hotel
HOTEL $$

(Map p480; ☑03-9536 1111; www.theprince.com.au; 2 Acland St, St Kilda; r from $189; ☒❋☎; ☒3, 12, 16, 96) Recent renovations have re-created this iconic space. The 39 rooms, all muted pastels and velvet green cushions, feature custom furniture, Bose SoundTouch speakers and photography (ask for a deluxe room with a bath). Mediterranean-inspired restaurant Prince Dining Room (open 7am to 11pm), celebrated Prince Bandroom (p507) (be prepared for weekend noise) and Aurora Spa Retreat (Map p480; ☑03-9536 1130; www.auroraspartreat.com; 1hr massage $175;

10am-6pm Mon, Tue, Thu & Fri, 11.30am-7.30pm Wed, 9am-5.30pm Sat, 10am-2pm Sun) are here. Stairs only.

✖ Eating

⚔ City Centre

★ Miznon
ISRAELI $

(Map p472; ✆ 03-9670 2861; www.miznonaustralia.com; 99 Hardware Lane, Melbourne; gourmet pitas $12-19, dinner share plates $6-19; ⊙ noon-10pm Mon-Sat; ✐; 🚊 86, 96) Originating in Tel Aviv, Miznon is as fun and as fresh as it gets. Book seats on iconic Hardware Lane, or sit on the 'steps' inside or up at the mezzanine level. Order pitas stuffed with everything from hot chickpeas to ocean trout belly and share roasted whole cauliflower. Help yourself to the pita, tahini and pickle bar while you wait.

★ Hakata Gensuke
RAMEN $

(Map p472; ✆ 03-9663 6342; www.gensuke.com.au; 168 Russell St, Melbourne; ramen $13.50-15; ⊙ 11.30am-10pm Mon-Thu, 11.30am-1am Fri, noon-1am Sat, to 10pm Sun; 🚊 Parliament) The original of four locations, Gensuke only does one thing and does it extraordinarily well: *tonkotsu* (pork broth) ramen. Choose from four types (signature, garlic and sesame-infused 'black' broth, spicy 'god fire' or the lighter *shio*) and then order extra toppings like marinated *cha shu* pork, egg, seaweed and black fungus. Worth queuing for.

Soi 38
THAI $

(Map p472; ✆ 0402 422 573; www.soi38.com; 38 McIlwraith Pl, inside Wilson car park, Melbourne; noodle soup from $10; ⊙ 11am-3pm Mon-Sat; 🚊 86, 96, 🚊 Parliament) This tiny shop inside a multi-level city car park is straight out of Bangkok. DIY condiments adorn blue and red fold-away tables, where customers order traditional boat noodles from tick-box menus. The city's best-kept secret (at least before this was published) is that it turns into **Nana Moojum & Thai BBQ** between 6pm and 1am from Tuesday to Sunday.

Spring Street Grocer
DELI $

(Map p472; ✆ 03-9639 0335; www.springstreetgrocer.com.au; 157 Spring St, Melbourne; sandwiches $8-11, gelato from $5; ⊙ grocer 8am-9pm Mon-Fri, from 9am Sun, gelateria 7am-11pm Mon-Thu, to midnight Fri, 9am-midnight Sat, 9am-11pm Sun; 🚊 Parliament) Join the queue at **Gelateria Primavera** for gelati scooped from traditional *pozzetti* (metal tubs fitted into the bench). Next door the **sandwich bar** serves coffee and gourmet made-to-order rolls (weekdays 11am to 3pm). Head down the winding staircase to reach the pungent **cheese cave**, an atmospheric maturation cellar in a former car park with an impressive selection.

Butcher's Diner
DINER $

(Map p472; ✆ 03-9639 7324; www.butchersdiner.com; 10 Bourke St, Melbourne; mains $10-19, daily specials $16-25; ⊙ 24hr; 🚊 Parliament) Open nonstop, offering breakfasts of steak and eggs between 6am and 11pm; and classic burgers, hand-made dim sims and offal yakitori any time. A curved glass cabinet displays cuts of meat, but if it's all too much, there's a vegan vending machine (and an ATM) out the front.

Pellegrini's Espresso Bar
ITALIAN $

(Map p472; ✆ 03-9662 1885; 66 Bourke St, Melbourne; mains $18; ⊙ 8am-11.30pm Mon-Sat, noon-8pm Sun; 🚊 Parliament) The Italian equivalent of a diner, locally famed Pellegrini's has remained unchanged since 1954. There's no menu; staff tell you what's available. Expect Italian comfort food: sloppy lasagne, spaghetti bolognese, watermelon granita and big slabs of cake. Service can be brusque, but that's all part of the experience. A photo under the neon sign outside is a rite of passage.

Pellegrini's is so important to Melbourne's cultural fabric that after the tragic death of co-owner Sisto Malaspina in 2018 during a terror attack in Bourke St, the 74 year old was given a state funeral.

★ Sunda
ASIAN $$

(Map p472; ✆ 03-9654 8190; www.sunda.com.au; 18 Punch Lane, Melbourne; set menu $85, share dishes $22-42; ⊙ 6pm-late Mon-Thu, noon-3pm & 5.30pm-late Fri, 5.30pm-late Sat; 🚊 Parliament) This contemporary Southeast Asian restaurant is in a former car park down a laneway. Slick with metal scaffolding, raw brick, a long communal table and mezzanine level, the calm kitchen plates modern Indonesian, Vietnamese and Malaysian dishes spiked with native Australian ingredients. Bar seats are best, while the off-menu roti with Vegemite curry is essential – and far better than it sounds.

★ Higher Ground
CAFE $$

(Map p472; ✆ 03-8899 6219; www.highergroundmelbourne.com.au; 650 Little Bourke St, Melbourne; mains day $16.50-28.50, night $27-45; ⊙ 7am-4pm

Mon-Wed, 8am-11pm Thu-Sat, 8am-4pm Sum; ☎; ⓡ Southern Cross) Melbourne's most impressive cafe looks more like an industrial designer hotel as it's housed in a former power station. Within 15m-high ceilings are nooks, crannies and a mezzanine level – all flooded with light from arched windows. Diners queue to order from the innovative brunch menu, but it's also open for dinner Thursday to Saturday.

★ Supernormal   ASIAN $$

(Map p472; ☑ 03-9650 8688; www.supernormal. net.au; 180 Flinders Lane, Melbourne; dishes $14-36; ⊙ 11am-11pm Sun-Thu, to midnight Fri & Sat; ⓡ Flinders St) From the man behind Cumulus Inc (p490), Andrew McConnell, comes this creative selection of pan-Asian sharing dishes, from dumplings to raw seafood to slow-cooked Sichuan lamb. The New England lobster roll is famous, but we prefer the lunchtime *tonkatsu* sandwich special. No dinner bookings after 5.30pm, so arrive early to put your name on the list. Look for the neon cherries.

★ Chin Chin   SOUTHEAST ASIAN $$

(Map p472; ☑ 03-8663 2000; www.chinchin restaurant.com.au; 125 Flinders Lane, Melbourne; mains $27.50-38.50; ⊙ 11am-late; ⓡ Flinders St) Insanely popular, bustling Chin Chin serves Southeast Asian hawker-style food with big flavours, designed to share. It's housed in a glammed-up warehouse that's all marble, white tiles and neon. Arrive on the dot at 11am or 5pm to avoid queues, otherwise fill in time at Go Go Bar downstairs until there's space. No bookings.

Longrain   THAI $$

(Map p472; ☑ 03-9653 1600; www.longrain.com; 40-44 Little Bourke St, Melbourne; mains $24-38; ⊙ 6pm-late Mon-Thu, 5.30pm-late Fri-Sun; ⓡ Parliament) Get in early or expect a long wait – upstairs, Longsong is a beautiful holding space – before sampling this delicious Thai cuisine. Communal tables don't exactly work for a romantic date, but they're great for checking out everyone else's meals. Dishes are designed to share; try the pork-and-prawn eggnet and contorted whole fried fish, sweet with tamarind.

Bar Saracen   MIDDLE EASTERN $$

(Map p472; ☑ 03-8639 0265; www.barsaracen. com.au; 22 Punch Lane, Melbourne; bar snacks $4-8, share mains $15-35; ⊙ noon-late Tue-Fri, from 5.30pm Sat, plus lunch & dinner Mon Dec; ⓡ Parliament) A more recent addition from the team behind Rumi (p496), this restaurant-wine-bar 'of Middle Eastern appearance' is the ultimate pre- and post-show spot, just minutes on foot from major theatres. With the kind of service that makes you feel special and dishes such as '*nduja* (spreadable salami) egg and cheese borek and lamb and pistachio *kofte*, it's worth dinner without the show.

Tipo 00   ITALIAN $$

(Map p472; ☑ 03-9942 3946; www.tipo00.com. au; 361 Little Bourke St, Melbourne; starters $16-21, pasta $26-38; ⊙ 11.30am-10pm Mon-Sat; ☐ 19, 57, 59) Melbourne's best pasta is served at this small Italian restaurant within a palette of muted teal and earthy shades against concrete and white-marble finishes. The wine list is a trip around Italy and Victoria – a treat with hand-made spaghettini infused with saffron and tossed with spanner crab, confit tomato and zucchini. Next door, sister restaurant Osteria Ilaria is also wonderful.

Mamasita   MEXICAN $$

(Map p472; ☑ 03-9650 3821; www.mamasita.com. au; 1st fl, 11 Collins St, Melbourne; tacos & quesadillas $14-18, shared plates $22-39; ⊙ 5pm-late Sat-Thu, noon-late Fri; ⓡ Parliament) Up a staircase above a 7-Eleven is the restaurant responsible for kicking off Melbourne's obsession with Mexican food. Mamasita remains one of the best. Chargrilled corn sprinkled with cheese and chipotle mayo is a legendary starter and there's a fantastic range of corn-tortilla tacos. Instead of a sommelier, there's a mezcalier. Now taking bookings.

Hardware Societe   CAFE $$

(Map p472; ☑ 03-9078 5992; 123 Hardware St, Melbourne; brunch $15-26; ⊙ 7.30am-3pm Mon-Fri, from 8am Sat & Sun; ⓡ Melbourne Central) If you're not prepared for a lengthy queue, go elsewhere, as this wonderful little cafe is always heaving. It's an offshoot of the original across the lane at 120 Hardware St, which in February 2019 moved to a 100-seat, more grown-up venue at 10 Katherine Pl. Both have an inventive menu of mouth-watering French-influenced cafe fare.

HuTong Dumpling Bar   CHINESE $$

(Map p472; ☑ 03-9650 8128; www.hutong.com. au; 14-16 Market Lane, Melbourne; dumplings $8-15, mains $14-39; ⊙ 11.30am-3pm & 5.30-10.30pm; ⓡ Parliament) Are these Melbourne's best *xiao long bao* (soup dumplings)? We think so, which is why getting a seat in this

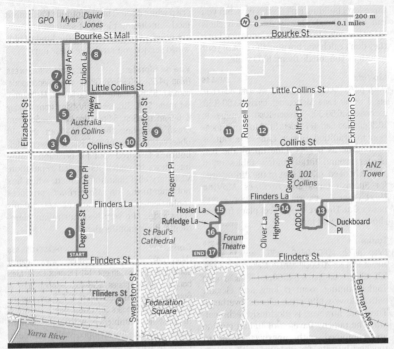

🚶 City Walk
Arcades & Laneways

START DEGRAVES ST
END RUTLEDGE LANE
LENGTH 3KM; 2½ HOURS

Central Melbourne is a warren of 19th-century arcades and gritty-turned-hip cobbled bluestone laneways featuring street art, basement restaurants, boutiques and bars.

Start on ❶ **Degraves St**, an archetypal Melbourne lane lined with interesting shops and cafes. Continue north, crossing over Flinders Lane to cafe-filled ❷ **Centre Pl**, good for spotting street art and grabbing a coffee.

Cross Collins St and enter ❸ **Block Arcade**. Built in 1892 and featuring ornate plasterwork and mosaic floors, it's based on Milan's Galleria Vittorio Emanuele II arcade. Ogle the window display at the ❹ **Hopetoun Tea Rooms** (www.hopetountearooms.com.au; ⊙8am-5pm Mon-Sat, from 9am Sun) before continuing to the basement of Block Pl to browse vinyl at ❺ **Basement Discs** (p509).

As you exit the arcade at Little Collins St you could stop for an afternoon tipple at kooky ❻ **Chuckle Park** (www.chucklepark.com.au; ⊙3pm-1am), before continuing on to the won-derfully ornate ❼ **Royal Arcade**; look out for Gog and Magog, hammering away under the dome. Wander through to Bourke St Mall, then turn right and continue until you find street-art-covered ❽ **Union Lane** on the right.

Follow Union Lane south to the end, turn left onto Little Collins St, then take a right on Swanston St. Walk past ❾ **Melbourne Town Hall** (p467), on the other side of the street, and pop into the 1932 ❿ **Manchester Unity Building** to see its impressive foyer, then cross Swanston St and head up the hill to the 'Paris End' of Collins St. Along the way you'll pass the 1873 Gothic ⓫ **Scots Church** and the 1866 ⓬ **St Michael's Uniting Church**, built in an unusual Lombardic Romanesque style.

Turn right into Exhibition St, then into Flinders Lane, and continue to ⓭ **Duckboard Pl**. Take your time soaking up the street art before horseshoeing around into AC/DC Lane. If there's no queue at ⓮ **Chin Chin** (p488), it might be worth ending the tour here, otherwise continue down Flinders Lane to see the street art of ⓯ **Hosier Lane** (p463) and ⓰ **Rutledge Lane** before finishing with tapas or a hard-earned drink at ⓱ **MoVida** (p490).

three-level building isn't always easy, but you can book ahead. Downstairs, watch chefs make the delicate dumplings, and then hope they don't catch you burning the roof of your mouth as you inhale them. BYO wine.

MoVida
TAPAS $$

(Map p472; ☑ 03-9663 3038; www.movida.com. au; 1 Hosier Lane, Melbourne; tapas $3.80-9.50, raciones $16.50-30; ⊙ noon-10pm Sun-Tue, to 10.30pm Wed-Sat; ☒ Flinders St) MoVida's location in graffitied Hosier Lane is about as Melbourne as it gets. Line up by the bar, cluster around little window tables or, if you've booked, take a seat in the dining area for Spanish tapas and *raciones*. **MoVida Next Door** – yes, right next door – and newer **Bar Tini** are the perfect place for pre-show drinks and tapas.

Tonka
INDIAN $$$

(Map p472; ☑ 03-9650 3155; www.tonkarest aurant.com.au; 20 Duckboard Pl, Melbourne; mains $25-43; ⊙ noon-3pm & 6-10.30pm; ☒ Parliament) Tonka's dining room is long and elegant with billowy white mesh 'clouds' overhead. The food, however, is gloriously technicolour. The punchy flavours of Italian cuisine are combined with unexpected Indian touches; burrata, for instance, with coriander relish and charred roti. Get the clued-up sommelier to recommend appropriate wine matches or visit for an express *thali* lunch for $23.

Cumulus Inc
MODERN AUSTRALIAN $$$

(Map p472; ☑ 03-9650 1445; www.cumulusinc. com.au; 45 Flinders Lane, Melbourne; breakfast $14-18, mains $36-44; ⊙ restaurant 7am-11pm Mon-Fri, from 8am Sat & Sun, wine bar 5pm-late Tue-Thu, from 4pm Fri & Sat; ☒ Parliament) Quintessentially Melbourne, Cumulus is famed for its generous slow-roast lamb shoulder. It's all about beautiful produce and artful cooking, served at the long marble bar and little round tables. Reservations are for groups only and **Cumulus Up** wine bar upstairs is worth a visit alone – peruse the tome of a wine list and order duck waffles.

Flower Drum
CHINESE $$$

(Map p472; ☑ 03-9662 3655; www.flowerdrum. melbourne; 1st fl, 17 Market Lane, Melbourne; mains $20-48; ⊙ noon-3pm & 6-11pm Mon-Sat, 6-10.30pm Sun; ☎; ☒ Parliament) Established in 1975, Flower Drum continues to be Melbourne's most celebrated Chinese restaurant, imparting a charmingly old-fashioned ambience through its dark wood, lacquerwork and crisp white linen. The sumptuous Cantonese food – including plenty of seafood at 'market price' – is delivered with the kind of old-world service you rarely see these days.

Vue de Monde
MODERN AUSTRALIAN $$$

(Map p472; ☑ 03-9691 3888; www.vuedemonde. com.au; 55th fl, Rialto, 525 Collins St, Melbourne; set menu $275-310; ⊙ reservations from midday & 6-9pm Thu-Sun, 6-9pm Mon-Wed; ☒ Southern Cross) Surveying the world from the old observation deck of the Rialto tower, Melbourne's favoured spot for occasion dining has views to match its storied reputation. Visionary chef Shannon Bennett, when he's not mentoring on *MasterChef*, produces sophisticated and theatrical set menus showcasing the very best Australian ingredients. Book months ahead.

Coda
SOUTHEAST ASIAN $$$

(Map p472; ☑ 03-9650 3155; www.codarest aurant.com.au; basement, 141 Flinders Lane, Melbourne; larger plates $36-45; ⊙ noon-3pm & 6pm-late Sun-Thu, noon-3pm & 5.30pm-late Fri & Sat; ☒; ☒ Flinders St) Coda has a wonderful basement ambience, with exposed light bulbs and roughly stripped walls. Its menu leans heavily towards Southeast Asian flavours, but Japanese, Korean, French and Italian influences are also there. Larger dishes are made for sharing, but single-serve bites – like crispy prawn and tapioca betel leaf – are particularly good. The $65 set lunch is great value.

✗ Southbank & Docklands

Gradi Crown
PIZZA $$

(Map p472; ☑ 03-9292 5730; www.crownmelb ourne.com.au/restaurants/casual/gradi; Ground fl, Crown Riverwalk, 8 Whiteman St, Southbank; pizza $19-35; ⊙ noon-10.30pm Mon-Fri, to 11pm Sat & Sun; ☑; ☒ 58, ☒ Flinders Street) A branch of the Brunswick East **original** (☑ 03-9380 2320; www.400gradi.com.au; 99 Lygon St, Brunswick East; pizza $14-32, mains $32-48; ⊙ noon-11pm; ☒ 1, 6), this is a solid bet for a good, reasonably priced meal in a complex that can be overpriced and underwhelming. The award-winning margherita pizza is on the menu, along with a handful of pastas, *secondi* and desserts including gelato from **Zero Gradi**. Outdoor seats are best.

Bangpop
THAI $$

(Map p468; ☑ 03-9245 9800; www.bangpop.com. au; 35s South Wharf Promenade, South Wharf;

noodles $17-19, mains $17-30; ⊗noon-late; 🖉; 🚇35, 70, 75) Bangpop breathes the colour, vibrancy and flavour of Thailand into otherwise grey surrounds with its bar made from Lego and dangling filament bulbs. Flavourful, hawker-style dishes and curries are served at communal cafe tables and accompanied by Thai-inflected cocktails. Check the website for monthly Thai cooking classes.

Spice Temple CHINESE $$$
(Map p472; 🖉03-8679 1888; www.spicetemple. com.au; Crown, Yarra Promenade, Southbank; mains $42-60, yum cha lunch banquet from $55; ⊗6-11pm Mon-Wed, noon-3pm & 6-11pm Thu-Sun; 🖉; 🚇55) When he's not at **Rockpool** (Map p472; 🖉03-8648 1900; www.rockpoolbarandgrill.com.au; Crown, Yarra Promenade, Southbank; mains $35-55, grill $55-125, bar mains $12-39; ⊗noon-3pm & 6-11pm Sun-Fri, 6-11pm Sat) or in one of his Sydney restaurants, chef Neil Perry pays homage to the spicy cuisines of China's central provinces on the waterfront (hot dishes printed in red on the menu). By day you can gaze at the river while tucking into a yum cha banquet. By night, descend to the atmospheric, darkened tabernacle beneath.

Dinner by Heston BRITISH $$$
(Map p472; 🖉03-9292 5779; www.crownmelbourne.com.au/restaurants; Level 3, 8 Whiteman St, Southbank; 3-/5-course set menu $140/170; ⊗6-10pm Mon-Thu, from 5.30pm Fri, noon-2pm & 5.30-10pm Sat & Sun; 🖉; 🚇58, 🚋Flinders St) Heston Blumenthal needs no introduction, and while he's not in the kitchen here, his head chef and team serve creative takes on historical recipes, with dates printed on the menu. Perhaps the most famous is the 'meat fruit', a flawless chicken liver disguised as a mandarin. The nitro ice-cream trolley is just as worthy. Opposite Crown Spa.

🍴 Richmond & East Melbourne

Richmond's main draw has traditionally been restaurant-packed Victoria St, with its long strip of cheap, cheerful and traditional Vietnamese restaurants. Food is decent if not a little beige on Swan St, Church St and Bridge Rd, but there are a few brilliant cafes to be found – along with what is arguably Melbourne's best (and most expensive) Japanese restaurant.

Touchwood CAFE $$
(Map p468; 🖉03-9429 9347; www.touchwood cafe.com; 480 Bridge Rd, Richmond; dishes $15-20;

⊗7am-4pm Mon-Fri, from 7.30am Sat & Sun; 🚇48, 75) There's plenty of space both indoors and in the courtyard of this light, airy cafe housed in a former recycled-furniture shop (hence the name). The coffee is single origin (unless you order a pink, golden or green latte) and breakfast ranges from kaiserfleish eggs Benedict to 'nourish bowls'.

★ Serotonin Eatery VEGAN, VEGETARIAN $$
(Map p468; 🖉03-9108 1507; www.serotonin dealer.com; 52 Madden Grove, Burnley; dishes $17-23; ⊗8am-3pm Wed-Fri, 8.30am-4pm Sat & Sun; 🖉🚻; 🚉Burnley) This plant-based cafe (eggs and feta are on the menu, but a lot is vegan) on the cusp of Richmond is centred on happiness – the joy that comes from seeing a coconut 'Magnum' in your galaxy açaí bowl, sitting on indoor swings or sunken cushioned seating sipping an iced gingerbread latte, and from how smug you feel after filling 'positive pancakes'. Kids' menu available.

Anchovy VIETNAMESE $$
(Map p468; 🖉03-9428 3526; www.anchovy.net. au; 338 Bridge Rd, Richmond; dishes from $18, degustation per person $68; ⊗5.30-9.30pm Wed, noon-2.30pm & 5.30-9.30pm Thu, to 10pm Fri & Sat; 🚇48, 75) A wonderful amalgamation of Southeast Asian and Australian cuisine, Anchovy is a gem on an underwhelming strip. The elegant space features comfortable banquette seating, stools at the bar and window, lacquered floors and a stone feature table. Dishes might include anything from whole crab with kaffir lime, tamarind and coconut to BBQ snail skewers in lemongrass *sate* butter.

★ Minamishima JAPANESE $$$
(Map p468; 🖉03-9429 5180; www.minamishima. com.au; 4 Lord St, Richmond; per person $185; ⊗6-10pm Tue-Sat; 🚇48, 75) Arguably Australia's best Japanese restaurant – if you care to empty your pockets and book two months in advance. Hidden down a side street, the best seats are at the bar, where sushi master Koichi Minamishima prepares seafood with surgical precision and serves it one piece at a time. Sake or wine pairings available for an additional $125 per head.

🍴 Fitzroy, Collingwood & Abbotsford

Skip Fitzroy and Collingwood and you'll miss a big part of what gives Melbourne its global culinary reputation. By the time this is published, Smith St's astounding food scene will have evolved again – the bar raised too high for some to handle. Brunswick St is more hit-and-miss, with a bohemian air thanks to lots of vegan-friendly options. Connecting Brunswick and Smith Sts are Gertrude St – spitting distance from the city and lined with fantastic restaurants and bars – and Johnston St, also peppered with dining and drinking gems. Take a day and explore the four streets, which make a big square.

★ **Lune Croissanterie** BAKERY $
(Map p476; ☑03-9419 2320; www.lunecroissanterie.com; 119 Rose St, Fitzroy; pastries $5.90-12.50; ⊙7.30am-3pm Mon-Fri, from 8am Sat & Sun; 🖬11) Good things come to those who queue, and here they come in the form of unrivalled pastries, from innovative cruffins to plain croissants often dubbed the world's best. In the centre of this warehouse space is a glass, climate-controlled cube where the magic happens. Book well in advance for the Lune Lab experience, an innovative three-course pastry flight ($65).

★ **Gelato Messina** GELATO $
(Map p476; www.gelatomessina.com; 237 Smith St, Fitzroy; 1 scoop $5.30; ⊙noon-11pm Sun-Thu, to 11.30pm Fri & Sat; 🖬86) Messina is hyped as Melbourne's ice cream creamery, and while purists might gawk at specials like peanut butter gelato with white chocolate covered potato chips, its popularity is evident in the queues of people, irrespective of the weather. You can watch the ice-cream makers at work through glass windows inside.

★ **Proud Mary** CAFE $
(Map p476; ☑03-9417 5930; www.proudmarycoffee.com.au; 172 Oxford St, Collingwood; dishes $15-22; ⊙7am-4pm Mon-Fri, from 8am Sat & Sun; 🖘; 🖬86) A champion of direct-trade, single-origin coffee, this quintessential industrial Collingwood red-brick space takes its caffeine seriously. It's consistently packed, not only for its excellent brews but also for top-notch food, such as breakfast dan dan noodles, and hotcakes with lemon curd, cream-cheese whip and eucalyptus.

★ **Farm Cafe** CAFE $
(Map p468; ☑03-9415 6581; www.farmcafe.com.au; Collingwood Children's Farm, 18 St Heliers St, Abbotsford; dishes $13-21; ⊙9am-3pm Mon-Fri, to 4pm Sat & Sun; 🚴🖬🖼; 🖬200, 207) Just 4km from the city's edge is this oasis of a cafe,

where you can watch children pull faces at goats at Collingwood Children's Farm (p471) and pet cute dogs while enjoying brunch *en plein air*. Farm produce is used in the dishes, from breakfast dhal and a filling super salad to the kitchen's unbeatable sausage roll.

CIBI JAPANESE $
(Map p476; ☑03-9077 3941; www.cibi.com.au; 33-39 Keele St, Collingwood; dishes $14-21.50; ⊙7.30am-5pm Mon-Fri, from 8am Sat & Sun, kitchen closes 3.30pm; 🖉; 🖬89) It's ironic that 'Cibi' translates to 'little one' in Japanese given this incredibly aesthetically pleasing and zen cafe has expanded into a massive, airy warehouse. Along with traditional Japanese breakfasts you can browse the adjoining plant nursery and shop stocking beautifully made products, from Japanese knives and sake sets to selected pantry items and vases.

Easey's BURGERS $
(Map p476; ☑03-9417 2250; www.easeys.com.au; 3/48 Easey St, Collingwood; burgers $12-17; ⊙11am-10pm Sun-Thu, to 11pm Fri & Sat; 🖘🖉; 🖬86) Biting into burgers and gulping down beers in an old graffiti-covered train carriage perched on top of a backstreet rooftop – it doesn't get much more Collingwood than this. Easey's does a handful of no-holds-barred burgers that will have your cholesterol rising faster than you can say, 'gimme a side of triple-fried dim sims'.

Lazerpig PIZZA $$
(Map p476; ☑03-9417 1177; www.lazerpig.com.au; 9-11 Peel St, Collingwood; pizza $16-27; ⊙noon-late; 🖬86) From the neon-pink pig sign out the front to the disco ball and red-gingham tablecloths, hip Lazerpig is where northsiders go to let their hair down. It's a rock 'n' roll disco meets trattoria, where people pile in to scoff excellent wood-fired pizzas and craft beer to DJs doing their thing. Come early to get a seat.

Smith & Daughters LATIN AMERICAN, VEGAN $$
(Map p476; ☑03-9939 3293; www.smithanddaughters.com; 175 Brunswick St, Fitzroy; dinner $16-26, brunch $12-22; ⊙6pm-late Mon-Fri, 10am-late Sat, to 3pm Sun; 🖉; 🖬11) This busy corner restaurant has an all-vegan menu and punk sensibility. Italian dishes like 'beef' ragu on 'cheesy' polenta will have you swearing it's meat, while rich *cacio e pepe* ('parmesan' and pepper pasta) will kick any carb cravings. Also open for weekend brunch

(try the breakfast pizza). For brilliant vegan sandwiches, takeaway from **Smith & Deli** nearby.

Industry Beans
CAFE **$$**
(Map p476; ☎ 03-9417 1034; www.industrybeans. com; 3/62 Rose St, Fitzroy; mains $18-25; ☺ 7am-4pm Mon-Fri, from 8am Sat & Sun; ☎; ☒ 96, 11) With something for both food and coffee lovers, this warehouse cafe tucked down a side street offers a coffee guide that takes you through speciality styles roasted on-site and an innovative, all-day menu. Dishes like brioche with tonka bean ice cream, maple peanuts, blackberry coulis, manuka sherbert and coffee caviar are commonplace. Try a coffee bubble cup.

Charcoal Lane
MODERN AUSTRALIAN **$$**
(Map p476; ☎ 03-9418 3400; www.charcoallane. com.au; 136 Gertrude St, Fitzroy; starters $20-30, mains $31-36; ☺ noon-3pm & 6-9pm Tue-Sat; ☒ 86) ☝ Housed in an old bluestone former bank, this training restaurant for Indigenous and disadvantaged young people is one of the best places to try native flora and fauna, and the chef's tasting plate for two ($30) is a great place to start. Weekend bookings advised, especially now that Prince Harry and Meghan Markle have dined here.

Moroccan Soup Bar
MOROCCAN **$$**
(☎ 03-9482 4240; www.moroccansoupbar.com. au; 183 St Georges Rd, North Fitzroy; banquet per person $28-33; ☺ 6-10pm Tue-Sun; ☝; ☒ 11) Prepare to queue before being seated by stalwart Hana, who goes through the vegetarian menu verbally while you sip mint tea (it's an alcohol-free zone). The banquet's great value and includes a sublime chickpea bake.

Hotel Jesus
MEXICAN **$$**
(Map p476; www.hoteljesus.com.au; 174 Smith St, Collingwood; tacos & quesadillas $11-16, mains $19-28; ☺ 5.30pm-late Tue-Fri, from 8am Sat, from 9am Sun; ☒ 86) Set in an old post-office building, this retro cantina is going for fun with gleaming tiles, red folding chairs and a picture menu. Street food is the focus, particularly tostadas – some better than others. Service can be lacking despite the tick-box paper ordering system, but street-side tables are a good place to linger with a mojito.

Horn
AFRICAN **$$**
(Map p476; ☎ 03-9417 4670; www.thehorncafe. com.au; 20 Johnston St, Collingwood; mains $16-24; ☺ 6pm-late Wed-Sat, 3-10pm Sun; ☝; ☒ 86) Straight outta Addis Ababa, the flavours and feel of this Ethiopian restaurant are as authentic as its homemade *injera* (fermented, pancake-like bread; prepared fresh daily). Use it to scoop up your food with your fingers and wash it down with Ethiopian beer. There's jazz on Thursday evening, and on Sunday the eight-piece Black Jesus Experiment plays traditional Ethiopian music with a modern take.

Call ahead if you'd like to arrange a coffee ceremony.

Vegie Bar
VEGAN, VEGETARIAN **$$**
(Map p476; ☎ 03-9417 6935; www.vegiebar.com.au; 380 Brunswick St, Fitzroy; mains $16-24; ☺ 11am-10pm Mon-Thu & Sun, to 10.30pm Fri & Sat; ☝; ☒ 11) An oldie but a goodie, this cavernous warehouse eatery has been feeding droves of Melbourne's veggie-loving residents for 30 years. Expect inventive fare and big servings from its menu of thin-crust pizzas, tasty salads, burgers and curries, as well as smoothies and fresh juices. Plenty of vegan choices with a dedicated vegan dessert place, **Girls & Boys**, next door.

Marios
CAFE **$$**
(Map p476; ☎ 03-9417 3343; www.marioscafe.com. au; 303 Brunswick St, Fitzroy; breakfast $10-19.50, mains $17.50-31.50; ☺ 7am-10pm Mon-Wed, to 10.30pm Thu-Sat, 8am-10pm Sun; ☒ 11) Mooching at Marios is part of the Melbourne 101 curriculum. Started by two Italian waiters in the '80s, breakfasts here are big and served all day, the service is swift, the dishes classically Italian and the coffee old-school strong.

★ Cutler & Co
MODERN AUSTRALIAN **$$$**
(Map p476; ☎ 03-9419 4888; www.cutlerandco. com.au; 55-57 Gertrude St, Fitzroy; mains $46-54; ☺ 6pm-late Tue-Sun, lunch from noon Sun; ☒ 86) Hyped for all the right reasons, this is Andrew McConnell's flagship Melbourne restaurant and its attentive, informed staff and joy-inducing dishes make it one of Melbourne's top places for fine dining. The menu incorporates the best seasonal produce across the à la carte offering, degustation menu (from $170), and casual Sunday lunch designed for sharing ($75).

IDES
MODERN AUSTRALIAN **$$$**
(Map p476; ☎ 03-9939 9542; www.idesmelbourne.com.au; 92 Smith St, Collingwood; degustation $180, 4-course menu $100; ☺ from 6pm Tue-Fri, from noon Sat & Sun; ☒ 86) Word spread quickly when Attica (p499) sous chef Peter Gunn started his own establishment, where he does the term 'creative' justice with a

contemporary take on fine dining, focusing on Australian ingredients. It's a multi-course, seasonal affair preceded by hot bread with dangerously good house 'peanut butter butter'. Inside it's dark but comfortable, with tactile leather-covered tables and felt-adorned walls that muffle chatter.

Carlton & Brunswick

Sydney Rd in Brunswick is Melbourne's Middle Eastern hub, with bakeries and long-standing restaurants spread out along the thoroughfare. Since the arrival of Mediterranean immigrants in the 1950s, Lygon St in Carlton has been synonymous with Italian cuisine. For a little of both, head to the trendy Brunswick East end of Lygon St, where excellent Italian and Middle Eastern restaurants sit side by side, along with some popular coffee spots and newer establishments. Middle Eastern cuisine is great for both vegetarians and carnivores.

★ King and Godfrey
DELI, ITALIAN

(Map p495; ☑03-9347 1619; www.kingandgodfree.com.au; cnr Faraday & Lygon Sts, 293-297 Lygon St, Carlton; ☺rooftop & restaurant noonlate, deli 8am-8pm, espresso bar 7am-late; ☒1, 6) It took three years to transform King and Godfrey, an Italian grocer since 1884, into this multi-venue wonder. There's **Johnny's Green Room** with 360-degree rooftop views and a glitterati cocktail vibe; a deli with cold cuts, cheese and food to take away; **Agostino** wine bar and restaurant; and the all-day espresso bar for coffee, panini, pasta or a negroni or two.

Lanzhou Beef Noodle
CHINESE $

(Map p495; ☑0404 848 468; www.beefnoodle.com.au; Shop 3, 743-751 Swanston St, Carlton; noodle dishes $12.80, dumplings $3-6; ☺10.30am-3pm & 4-10pm; ☒1, 3, 5, 6, 16, 64, 67, 72) Lanzhou has developed a cult following for its numbingly spicy, rich beef noodle soups. Pick up cold side dishes and interesting Chinese drinks from the counter, before choosing your noodle type, thickness and extras. Good for a quick, cheap slurp among uni students and foodies in the know. Also in the city centre, South Yarra and beyond. All are excellent.

Pidapipo
GELATO $

(Map p495; ☑03-9347 4596; www.pidapipo.com.au; 299 Lygon St, Carlton; 1/2/3 scoops $4.80/6.80/8.80; ☺noon-11pm; ☒Tourist Shuttle, ☒1, 6) Pidapipo is the perfect pre-cinema, pre-theatre, post-pizza treat when hanging out on Lygon St. Owner Lisa Valmorbida learned from the best at the Carpigiani Gelato University and now whips up her own flavours on-site from local and imported ingredients. Italian-accented staff rightly recommend pistachio and salted caramel. Add Nutella on tap, amarena cherries or whipped cream for $1.

East Elevation
CAFE $

(☑03-9381 5575; www.eastelevation.com.au; 351 Lygon St, Brunswick East; mains $15-23; ☺9am-4pm, kitchen closes 3pm; ☒☐☐; ☒1, 6) ☞ Part warehouse cafe and part chocolate factory, watch organic, fair-trade **Monsieur Truffe** chocolates come to life behind glass while you tuck into vibrant dishes made with produce grown in a friendly neighbour's garden– complete with quails and honey bees. If you can get past single-origin hot chocolates, coffee is great here too. Look for the red door.

Killiney Kopitam
SINGAPOREAN $

(Map p495; ☑03-9650 9880; www.killiney-kopitiam.com.au; 114 Lygon St, Carlton; meal deal $16, starters $3-10, mains $8-18; ☺11.30am-10pm Mon-Fri, from 11am Sat & Sun; ☒200, 207, ☒1, 3, 5, 6, 16, 64, 67, 72) The first of these Singaporean hawker-style shops opened in the motherland in 1919. Today there are three shops – also in the city and Abbotsford (p471) – but this one is by far the best, serving food as tasty as it is good value. There are classics like Hainanese chicken, laksa and nasi lemak, and the spicy XO clams are packed with flavour.

Heartattack and Vine
ITALIAN $

(Map p495; www.heartattackandvine.com.au; 329 Lygon St, Carlton; lunch $14-15.50, cicchetti $4.50; ☺7am-11pm Mon-Fri, from 8am Sat & Sun; ☒Tourist Shuttle, ☒1, 6) Heartattack and Vine is a relaxed space with a neighbourhood feel, all centred on a long, wooden bar. Drop in for coffee morning or night, prop up at the bar for an Aperol spritz or spend the evening nibbling cicchetti, a Venetian take on tapas, which you pay for at the bar.

Very Good Falafel
FELAFEL $

(☑03-9383 6479; www.shukiandlouisa.com; 629 Sydney Rd, Brunswick; falafel from $9; ☺11am-10pm Mon-Sat; ☒; ☒19, ☒Anstey) We're calling it: this is Melbourne's best felafel. What started as a venture selling dips at markets is now a small, clean shop that's popular with locals for a reason. On offer are Israeli-style pitas with falafel and other fillings, Middle Eastern salads and filter coffee.

MELBOURNE & VICTORIA MELBOURNE

Carlton & Around

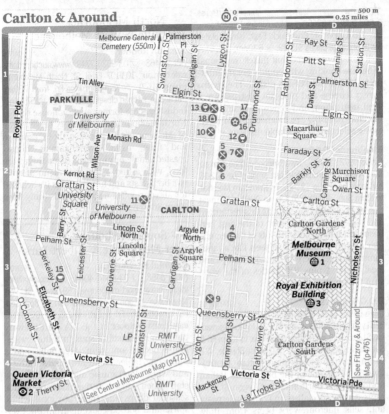

Carlton & Around

◎ Top Sights
1 Melbourne Museum	D3
2 Queen Victoria Market	A4
3 Royal Exhibition Building	D3

🛏 Sleeping
4 169 Drummond	C3

✴ Eating
5 D.O.C. Delicatessen	C2
6 D.O.C. Espresso	C2
7 D.O.C. Pizza & Mozzarella Bar	C2
8 Heartattack and Vine	C1
9 Killiney Kopitam	C3
10 King and Godfrey	C2
11 Lanzhou Beef Noodle	B2
Pidapipo	(see 10)

☕ Drinking & Nightlife
12 Carlton Wine Room	C2
13 Jimmy Watson's	C1
14 Market Lane Coffee	A4
15 Seven Seeds	A3

✴ Entertainment
16 Cinema Nova	C2
17 La Mama Courthouse	C1

🛍 Shopping
18 Readings	C1

★ **Hellenic Republic**　　　　　GREEK $$
(☏03-9381 1222; www.hellenicrepublic.com.au;
434 Lygon St, Brunswick East; starters $7-17, shared
mains $19-48; ⊙5.30-9.30pm Mon-Thu, noon-4pm
& 5.30-late Fri-Sun; 🖍; 🚋1, 6) The ironbark
charcoal grill at George Calombaris' north-
ern outpost works overtime as staff serve
and chat with ease. The slow-roasted lamb
shoulder is the signature here, but tara-
masalata and grilled saganaki with sticky
figs make an unbelievably good start. Wash
it all down with ouzo from the long list.

★ **Rumi** MIDDLE EASTERN **$$**
(☑ 03-9388 8255; www.rumirestaurant.com.
au; 116 Lygon St, Brunswick East; small plates
$9-16.50, large plates $15-29; ⏰ 6-10pm; 🚋 1, 6) A
well-considered place that mixes traditional
Lebanese cooking with contemporary inter-
pretations of old Persian dishes. The *sigara
boregi* (cheese and pine-nut pastries) are a
local institution, and generous mains from
the charcoal BBQ are balanced by an inter-
esting selection of vegetable dishes.

Bluebonnet BBQ BARBECUE **$$**
(☑ 03-9972 1815; www.bluebonnetbbq.com.au;
124-6 Lygon St, Brunswick East; small plates $12-16,
barbecue per 200g $23-25; ⏰ 11am-1am Mon-Sat,
to 11pm Sun; 📶; 🚋 1, 6) Up to 280kg of meat
can be cooked in the tank at this restaurant
and bar, which serves some of the best barbecue in Melbourne. With lots of timber, taxidermy and a pool table, it feels like a fancy
hunting lodge. There's a bar with 12 taps and
local 'tinnies', plus 100 bottles of the good
stuff for whisky lovers.

D.O.C. Espresso ITALIAN **$$**
(Map p495; ☑ 03-9347 8482; www.docgroup.net;
326 Lygon St, Carlton; pasta $19-26, focaccia & piad-
ina $12-16; ⏰ 7am-9.30pm Mon-Thu, to 10pm Fri &
Sat, 8am-9.30pm Sun; 🅿; 🚌 Tourist Shuttle, 🚋 1,
6) Run by third-generation Italian Austral-
ians, D.O.C. is one of the best casual Italian
options at the Carlton end of Lygon St. The
espresso bar specialises in homemade pasta
and sells microbrewery beers from Italy.
During *aperitivo* (4pm to 7pm), you can
enjoy a complimentary nibble board with
your negroni.

The affiliated **deli** (Map p495; 330 Lygon St;
panini $5-16; ⏰ 9am-7pm Mon-Sat, from 10am Sun)
next door offers cheese boards and panini,
while around the corner is the original **piz-
zeria** (Map p495; ☑ 03-9347 2998; 295 Drum-
mond St; pizzas $18-25; ⏰ 5pm-10.30pm Mon-Wed,
noon-10.30pm Thu & Sun, to 11pm Fri & Sat).

Bar Idda ITALIAN **$$**
(☑ 03-9380 5339; www.baridda.com.au; 132 Lygon
St, Brunswick East; mains $22-30, set menu $55-
75; ⏰ 6-10pm Mon-Sat, from 5.30pm Sun; 🚋 1, 6)
This cosy Sicilian restaurant with hanging
pot-plants inside is intimate and relaxed,
with a share-plate menu ranging from *coto-
lette* Sicilian fried pork to *gnocchetti* with
broccoli and anchovy, not to mention classic Italian desserts like *cassata*, a layered
ricotta cake and sponge cake with chocolate,
amarena cherries and marzipan.

✕ North Melbourne, Parkville & West Melbourne

Auction Rooms CAFE **$**
(Map p468; ☑ 03-9326 7749; www.auctionrooms
cafe.com.au; 103-107 Errol St, North Melbourne;
mains $11-21; ⏰ 7am-5pm Mon-Fri, from 7.30am
Sat & Sun, kitchen closes 3.30pm; 📶; 🚋 57) This
industrial-chic former auction house turned
North Melbourne success story serves some
of Melbourne's best coffee, both espresso
and filter, using ever-changing, house-
roasted, single-origin beans. Then there's the
food, with a highly seasonal menu of creative breakfasts and lunches. Plus it's licensed
for all your coffee negroni needs (only from
10am Sundays).

✕ South Melbourne, Port Melbourne & Albert Park

Colonial Brewery Co BREWERY
(Map p468; ☑ 03-8644 4044; www.colonialbrew
ingco.com.au/port-melbourne; 89 Bertie St, Port
Melbourne; ⏰ noon-6pm Thu & Sun (to 8pm Sep-
Feb), noon-11pm Fri & Sat; 🚋 235, 🚋 109) This
east-coast outpost of the WA craft brewery
pours thirst-crushing suds in a huge warehouse decked out with steel tanks and a
ping-pong table. There are pizzas, burgers
and wings, loud music and knowledgeable
staff (when you catch them). Beers include
seasonal drops and there are local wines,
spirits and bottled cocktails from the Everleigh (p502).

Andrew's Burgers BURGERS **$**
(Map p468; ☑ 03-9690 2126; www.andrewsham
burgers.com.au; 144 Bridport St, Albert Park; burgers from $10.50; ⏰ 11am-9pm Mon-Sat; 🅿; 🚋 1)
Andrew's is a family-run, wildly popular
institution that's been around since 1939. Its
walls are wood-panelled and covered with
photos of local celebs who, like many, drop
in for an old-school burger and a big bag of
chips. Veg options and kids' burger available. There's a newer, more modern location
in the city.

Ciao Cielo ITALIAN **$$**
(Map p468; ☑ 03-9646 7697; www.ciaocielo.com.
au; 115 Bay St, Port Melbourne; antipasti from $6,
mains $28-36, steak from $48; ⏰ noon-3pm &
6-9pm Sun-Wed, to 10pm Fri & Sat; 🚋 234) Set in
Melbourne's first courthouse, this roman-
tic Italian restaurant has soaring ceilings
with rustically peeling walls, powder-blue
banquettes and a regional Italian menu.

Spanner crab spaghettini, oxtail ragu with potato gnocchi and salt-baked whole fish are signatures. Don't leave without trying Nonna's tiramisu. More casual **Ciao Cucina** next door offers thin-crust pizzas and a spritz menu in a covered courtyard.

Simply Spanish
SPANISH $$

(Map p468; ☑ 03-9682 6100; www.simplyspanish.com.au; South Melbourne Market, cnr Coventry & Cecil Sts, South Melbourne; tapas $8-17, paellas $14.50-48; ☺ 8am-9pm Wed, 10am-9pm Thu, 8am-10pm Fri & Sat, 8am-4pm Sun; ☐ 12, 96) When a Melbourne restaurant repeatedly wins the title of 'Best Paella Outside of Spain' in Valencia, you know you're on to a good thing. This casual market eatery is *the* place for paella, available here in numerous combos, although tapas can be hit and miss.

St Ali
CAFE $$

(Map p468; ☑ 03-9132 8960; www.stali.com.au; 12-18 Yarra Pl, South Melbourne; mains $16-25; ☺ 7am-6pm; ☎; ☐ 12) The coffee is guaranteed to be good at this Melbourne cafe original in a hideaway warehouse conversion. If you can't decide between house blend, speciality, black or white, there's a six-coffee tasting 'adventure' ($25). The food menu covers all bases with competence and creativity, from secret-recipe corn fritters with poached eggs and halloumi to a panko-crumbed fish-finger sandwich.

Claypots Evening Star
SEAFOOD $$

(Map p468; ☑ 03-9645 5779; www.claypots eveningstar.net; cnr Cecil & York Sts, South Melbourne Market; whole fish from $15, pintxos $5-20; ☺ 11am-11pm; ☐ 236, ☐ 96, 12) This seafood spot at South Melbourne Market (p475) is bustling towards the end of the week. Diners pounce on outdoor tables and soak up live music Friday through Sunday. Order tapas-like dishes or check the blackboard for fresh seafood specials. There's also the **Seafood Peddler**, a portable stall selling fish sandwiches for $12 from Wednesday through Sunday, 11am to 3pm.

✕ South Yarra, Prahran & Windsor

★ Maker & Monger
CHEESE $

(Map p504; ☑ 0413 900 490; www.makerand monger.com.au; Prahran Market; toasted sandwiches from $12; ☺ 7am-5pm Tue & Thu-Sat, 8am-3pm Sun; ☒; ☐ 72, 78, ☐ Prahran) What was a small cart now has a shop complete with 40 seats, neon, pretty sage-colour tiling and Savignac-inspired posters. Cheap eats favourite Maker & Monger continues to sell *raclette* in winter and blow-torched reuben sandwiches oozing with cheese year-round, but now also makes cheese on-site as well as sells it. Try the luxurious *fontin bleu* for breakfast.

Darling Cafe
CAFE $

(Map p504; ☑ 03-9820 9222; www.darlingcafe.com.au; 2 Darling St, South Yarra; dishes $15-22; ☺ 7am-4pm; ☐ 58, 78, ☐ South Yarra) This busy cafe is the best this end of South Yarra. At the bottom of an office block with concrete pillars and shiny metal finishes, it remains bright with sliding glass windows that open in warmer weather. Opt for beetroot and ricotta fritters or tackle the sticky date pancakes.

Dainty Sichuan
SICHUAN $$

(Map p504; ☑ 03-9078 1686; www.daintysichuan food.com.au; 176 Toorak Rd, South Yarra; starters from $13, shared mains $21-50; ☺ 11.30am-3pm & 5-9.30pm Sun-Thu, to 10pm Fri & Sat; ☐ 58, 78, ☐ South Yarra) A favourite among spice lovers and chefs since 2009, there's nothing Dainty about the numbing chilli effects of the food here. Among more challenging dishes like offal and periwinkles (or, as it says on the menu, 'periwrinkles') are pork ribs, cumin lamb and *ma po* tofu. Start with the famed 'Ants Climbing the Trees' dish – it ain't what you think.

Grand Lafeyette
CAFE $$

(Map p504; ☑ 03-9510 0501; www.grandlafayette.com.au; 9 Clifton St, Prahran; bao $10, mains $15-27, dinner all you can eat per person $32.80; ☺ 8am-3pm Mon, 8am-3pm & 5.30-9pm Tue-Thu & Sun, to 10pm Fri & Sat; ☐ 6, 78) If you eat to Instagram, this cafe spread over two shopfronts has the brunch for you. Think Japanese 'raindrop cakes' and 'freakshii' (a creative take on sushi that will trouble traditionalists). At night there's an all-you-can eat option with dishes such as chicken karaage and miso salmon for $32.80 per person – although restrictions make sure there's no waste.

Hawker Hall
SOUTHEAST ASIAN $$

(Map p504; ☑ 03-8560 0090; www.hawkerhall.com.au; 98 Chapel St, Windsor; snacks $9.50-16.50, noodles $13.50-18.50, shared mains $28.50-38.50; ☺ 11am-late; ☐ 5, 6, 64, 78, ☐ Windsor) Brought to you by the team behind ever-popular Chin Chin (p488), this hipster take on a Southeast Asian food hall attracts shorter lines. With playful Tokyo-style signage, it serves punchy

MELBOURNE & VICTORIA MELBOURNE

share-style dishes such as economy noodles (a mix of whatever's going with sambal), pork and ginger dumplings and salt and pepper tofu fries. Reservations accepted for small groups Sunday to Thursday.

Matilda 159 AUSTRALIAN $$$
(Map p468; ☑03-9089 6668; www.matilda159. com; 159 Domain Rd, South Yarra; starters $25-34, mains $33-58; ◷noon-3pm & 6-10pm; ☐246, ☐58) Across from Botanic Gardens (p475) and beneath United Places (p486), this classy restaurant focuses on cooking over flames, whether whole tiger flathead or Wagyu beef with smoked bone marrow. Starters steal the spotlight, especially spanner crab with prawn butter served in its shell. With glass cabinets containing seasonal botanic installations, plus smooth surfaces and slick service, this is what Australian fine-dining looks like.

Woodland House MODERN AUSTRALIAN $$$
(Map p504; ☑03-9525 2178; www.woodland house.com.au; 78 Williams Rd, Prahran; 5-/8-course dinner $145/175; ◷6.30-9pm Tue, Wed & Sat, noon-3pm & 6.30-9pm Thu & Fri; ☑☑; ☐6) In a glorious Victorian villa, Woodland House is home turf for young-gun chefs Thomas Woods and Hayden McFarland, former sous chefs to lauded Melbourne restaurateur Jacques Reymond. The menu spotlights local produce, cooked confidently in dishes such as grilled scampi with pickled mushroom and saltbush. On Thursday and Friday there's a smashing-value $60 three-course lunch with a glass of wine.

St Kilda, Elwood & Elsternwick

Despite having lost its shine, Fitzroy St remains a popular eating strip. Along it's length you'll find the good, the bad and the downright ugly, so it's best not to leave it to chance. Acland St's historical cake shops now sit beside new-generation gelato shops, while over the Nepean Hwy, Carlisle St in Balaclava has some worthy restaurants and hipster cafes, catering to a mostly local crowd. Stray a little further to Ripponlea for Australia's most highly awarded restaurant (assuming you've booked months ago), nestled among Jewish grocers, butchers and deli-inspired cafes.

★Penta CAFE $
(☑03-9523 0716; www.pentaelsternwick.com. au; 28 Riddell Pde, Elsternwick; $17.50-22.50;

◷7am-4pm Mon-Fri, from 7.30am Sat, from 8am Sun; ☒☜; ☐Elsternwick) Pumping Penta might be all polished concrete and muted tones inside, but the food here is a rainbow of colours, textures and technique usually reserved for dinner. The Nutella panna cotta must be one of Melbourne's most Instagrammed brunches, planted in a flowerbed of toasted marshmallows, edible blooms and banana slices coated in nut butter.

Ziggy's Eatery BURGERS $
(Map p480; ☑1300 944 497; www.ziggyseatery. com.au; 195 Carlisle St, Balaclava; burgers from $13; ◷11.30am-9.30pm Mon-Thu, to 10pm Fri-Sun; ☐Balaclava) This chef-owned burger joint uses Aussie produce and makes its own sauces. If you visit on a Friday there are two-for-one beers and wines between 5pm and 7pm, but the burgers are good any time. The biggest challenge is finishing the Recovery Burger: two 150g patties and double cheese, bacon, tomato, pickles and lettuce.

Monarch Cake Shop DESSERTS $
(Map p480; ☑03-9534 2972; www.monarch cakes.com.au; 103 Acland St, St Kilda; slice of cake from $5; ◷8am-10pm; ☐96) Family-owned Monarch is a favourite among St Kilda's Eastern European cake shops and its *kugelhopf* (marble cake), plum cake and Polish baked cheesecake can't be beaten. In business since 1934, the shop hasn't changed much, with a soft, old-time atmosphere and wonderful, buttery aroma – not to mention framed snaps of local football players who've visited.

Tulum TURKISH $$
(Map p480; ☑03-9525 9127; www.tulumrest aurant.com.au; 217 Carlisle St, Balaclava; starters $8-19, mains $29-34; ◷5pm-late Tue-Fri, noon-3pm & 5pm-late Sat; ☑; ☐3, 16, ☐Balaclava) With Nigella Lawson singing Tulum's praise during her Melbourne travels, this contemporary Turkish restaurant uses Australian ingredients and modern cooking techniques to reinterpret cuisine from the Ottoman Empire. Depending on the season, you might start with meze like *manti* (Turkish dumplings), before sharing *kaburga*, beef short ribs served with smoked eggplant, cumin, tahini and preserved lemon and date jam.

Matcha Mylkbar CAFE, VEGAN $$
(Map p480; ☑03-9534 1111; www.matchamylkbar. com; 72a Acland St, St Kilda; dishes $17-25; ◷8am-3pm Mon-Fri, to 4pm Sat & Sun; ☜☑; ☐3, 16, 96)

If you've spied Matcha Mylkbar on Instagram, it's likely you've been green with envy. This small, contemporary cafe is known for its creative, 100% plant-based menu. Order social-media-tailored smoothies with names like 'free the nibs' in glass skull mugs, nourishing bowls and the trade-marked vegan eggs made from agar, sweet potato, coconut milk and linseed protein.

Uncle
VIETNAMESE $$

(Map p480; ☑03-9041 2668; www.unclestkilda. com.au; 188 Carlisle St, St Kilda; pho $16, share dishes $33-37; ☺5pm-late Tue-Thu, from noon Fri & Sat; ☑3, 16, 78, ⓡBalaclava) Uncle delivers stellar Vietnamese cooking in a space complete with colourful, upside-down baskets and a rooftop dining area. Pho (noodle soup) is fragrant and herbaceous, best ordered as a small portion so you have room to try rich Wagyu brisket with bone marrow, pomelo heirloom tomato salad and kampot pepper sauce. There's another venue in the city centre.

Miss Jackson
CAFE $$

(Map p480; ☑03-9534 8415; www.facebook.com/ missjacksoncafe; 2/19 Grey St, St Kilda; dishes $12-25; ☺7am-4pm Tue-Sun; ☑3, 16, 96) The casual set-up and atmosphere here makes it feel like you've been invited to a friend's house for brunch – a friend with good enough taste to serve coconut ricotta hotcakes with kaffir lime–poached mango and honeycomb butter, or eggs Benedict with potato doughnuts and smoked pork belly. Slow but friendly service – worth the wait.

Claypots
SEAFOOD $$

(Map p480; ☑03-9534 1282; www.facebook.com/ claypotsstkilda; 213 Barkly St, St Kilda; claypots $25, mains from $35; ☺noon-1am; ☑96) A local favourite, compact Claypots serves share-style plates of fresh seafood. Its namesake dish is available in a number of options, including a spiced Moroccan mussels and fish fillet cooked with couscous, tomato, eggplant, harissa, zaatar and chickpeas. Get in early to nab a seat and ensure the good stuff is still available – hot items go fast.

★ Attica
MODERN AUSTRALIAN $$$

(Map p468; ☑03-9530 0111; www.attica.com.au; 74 Glen Eira Rd, Ripponlea; tasting menu $295; ☺6pm-late Tue-Sat; ☑67, ⓡRipponlea) Attica is Australia's only restaurant on San Pellegrino's World's Top 50 Restaurants list. Here Ben Shewry creates contemporary dishes with native ingredients, like saltwater crocodile rib glazed with soured honey and peppermint gum, and dessert served in emu eggs. Even more popular since starring in Netflix's *Chef's Table;* reservations are taken on the first Wednesday of the month for the following three months.

Lau's Family Kitchen
CHINESE $$$

(Map p480; ☑03-8598 9880; www.lauskitchen. com.au; 4 Acland St, St Kilda; mains $26-49; ☺noon-3pm & 6-10pm Mon-Fri, 6-10pm Sat, 12.30-3.30pm & 6-10pm Sun; ☑16, 96) This polished spot with service to match offers beautiful, home-style Cantonese with a few Sichuan surprises. Start with delicate dumplings and spanner crab and sweet corn soup, then order one of Melbourne's best *ma po* tofu dishes with minced pork and steamed rice. Reserve ahead and check out the elegant wall panels, made from 1930s kimonos.

Stokehouse
SEAFOOD $$$

(Map p480; ☑03-9525 5555; www.stokehouse. com.au; upstairs, 30 Jacka Blvd, St Kilda; mains $39-55; ☺noon-2.30pm & 6pm-late; ☑3a, 16, 96) After a devastating fire, lauded Stokehouse rebuilt better and brighter. Striking contemporary architecture and floor-to-ceiling bay views set the tone for modern, seafood-centric dishes and a devilishly good bombe. This is one of Melbourne's most-loved occasion restaurants, so book ahead. For a cheaper view, watch the sunset from adjoining **Stokebar** with a cocktail and snacks.

Cicciolina
ITALIAN $$$

(Map p480; ☑03-9525 3333; www.cicciolina stkilda.com.au; 130 Acland St, St Kilda; mains lunch $18-30, dinner $32-49; ☺restaurant noon-late, back bar from 5pm; ☑3, 16, 96) This hideaway of dark wood, subdued lighting and pencil sketches is a St Kilda institution. The menu is Italian, with dishes that might see signature linguini twirled with salmon, braised leek, capers, baby spinach, lemon and olive oil. Bookings for lunch only; for dinner eat early or start in the moody back bar, worth a visit on its own.

🍷 Drinking & Nightlife

Melbourne's drinking scene is easily the best in Australia and a major player on the world stage. There's a huge diversity of venues, from basement dives hidden down laneways and rooftop cocktail perches to wine-bar locals and urban breweries and distilleries. Many pubs have pulled up beer-stained carpet and polished the concrete, but don't dismiss the character-filled oldies that still exist.

City Centre

★ Heartbreaker
BAR

(Map p472; ☑03-9041 0856; www.heartbreaker bar.com.au; 234a Russell St, Melbourne; ☺3pm-3am Mon-Thu, from noon Fri & Sat, noon-1am Sun; ☒Melbourne Central) Black walls, red lights, skeleton handles on the beer taps, random taxidermy, craft beer, a big selection of bourbon, a jukebox and tough-looking sweethearts behind the bar – it's always a good time at Heartbreaker. Cocktails are pre-batch only. Order **Connie's Pizza** slices from the bar and pick up behind the pool table.

★ Rooftop Bar
ROOFTOP BAR

(Map p472; ☑03-9654 5394; www.rooftopbar.co; 7th fl, Curtin House, 252 Swanston St, Melbourne; ☺noon-1am Apr-Nov, from 11am Dec-Mar; ☒Melbourne Central) This bar sits atop happening Curtin House. In summer (December to March) there are daily DJs and it transforms into an outdoor cinema with striped deckchairs and a calendar of new and classic favourite flicks. Hit up the burger shack, order a cocktail jug and make some new friends.

★ Bar Americano
COCKTAIL BAR

(Map p472; www.baramericano.com.au; 20 Presgrave Pl, Melbourne; ☺5pm-1am Mon-Sat; ☒Flinders St) A hideaway bar in a lane off Howey Pl, Bar Americano is a teensy standing-room-only affair with black-and-white chequered floors complemented by classic 'do not spit' subway-tiled walls and a subtle air of speakeasy. Once it hits its 14-person max, the grille gets pulled shut. The cocktails here don't come cheap, but they do come classic and superb.

★ Siglo
ROOFTOP BAR

(Map p472; ☑03-9654 6631; www.siglobar.com. au; 2nd fl, 161 Spring St, Melbourne; ☺5pm-3am; ☒Parliament) Siglo's sought-after terrace comes with Parisian flair, wafting cigar smoke and serious drinks. It fills with suits on Friday night, but any time is good to mull over a classic cocktail and admire the 19th-century vista over Parliament (p466) and **St Patrick's Cathedral** (Map p468; ☑03-9662 2233; www.stpatrickscathedral.org.au; 1 Cathedral Pl, East Melbourne; ☺9am-5pm Mon-Fri; ☒Parliament). With Melbourne's strict smoking laws, food is limited to snacks. Entry is via the similarly unsigned Supper Club (p501).

★ Arbory
BAR

(Map p472; ☑03-8648 7644; www.arbory.com.au; 1 Flinders Walk, Melbourne; ☺7.30am-late; ☒Flinders St) Situated as close as a venue can get to the Yarra without toppling in, Arbory occupies the decommissioned platform for the Sandridge train line at the edge of Flinders St Station. At over 100m long, it's Melbourne's longest bar. Come for the view of the Arts Centre (p508) across the water, stay for the espresso martinis. The food's not bad.

Rooftop at QT
ROOFTOP BAR

(Map p472; ☑03-8636 8800; www.qthotels andresorts.com/melbourne/eat-drink; 11th floor, 133 Russell St, Melbourne; ☺noon-midnight Mon-Fri, from 2pm Sat & Sun; ☒86, 96) Nestled among the CBD's high-rise buildings is this fantastic spot for a drink, with a retractable awning and efficient heating system. With a green-tiled bar, wooden deck with wide chairs and designer feel, it's easy to see why it's popular. Snack on fried kingfish wings or a burger (vegetarian available) and order the signature G&T made with elderflower quinine.

Arlechin
COCKTAIL BAR

(Map p472; www.arlechin.com.au; Mornane Pl, Melbourne; ☺5pm-late Tue-Sat; ☒86, 96, ☒Parliament) Look for the festoon lights illuminating the laneway to Arlechin, a bar from the **Grossi** (Map p472; ☑03-9662 1811; www. grossiflorentino.com; 1st fl, 80 Bourke St, Melbourne; 2-course lunch $65, 3-course dinner $150, degustation $180; ☺noon-3pm & 6-10pm Mon-Fri, 6pm-late Sat; ☒Parliament) family of Melbourne hospitality fame. Sit among a glass-walled cellar beneath a curved ceiling and order spot-on cocktails and brilliant bar snacks – including a sloppy joe and 'midnight spaghetti'. Great for late-night hunger pangs.

Boilermaker House
BAR

(Map p472; ☑03-8393 9367; www.boilermaker house.com.au; 209-211 Lonsdale St, Melbourne; ☺4pm-3am Mon-Wed, from 3pm Thu & Sun, from noon Fri & Sat; ☒Melbourne Central) A real surprise on busy, workaday Lonsdale St, this dimly lit haven of urbanity has a phenomenal 900 whiskies on its list, along with 12 craft beers on tap and a further 30 by the can and bottle. Snack on cheese and charcuterie as you make your way through them, or order a wallaby burger (yes, we eat them).

Cookie
BAR

(Map p472; 📞03-9663 7660; www.cookie.net.au; 1st fl, Curtin House, 252 Swanston St, Melbourne; ⏰noon-3am; 🚇Melbourne Central) Part bar, part Thai restaurant, this kooky-cool venue with grand bones is one of the more enduring rites of passage of the Melbourne night. The bar is unbelievably well stocked with fine whiskies, wines and plenty of craft beers, among them more than 200 brews on offer. The staff also know how to make a serious cocktail.

Lui Bar
COCKTAIL BAR

(Map p472; 📞03-9691 3888; www.luibar.com. au; 55th fl, Rialto, 525 Collins St, Melbourne; ⏰5.30pm-midnight Mon-Wed, 11.30am-1am Thu, 11.30am-3am Fri & Sat, 11.30am-midnight Sun; 🚇Southern Cross) Some people are happy to shell out $27 for the view from the 120m-high Melbourne Star, but we'd much rather spend $25 on a cocktail at this sophisticated bar perched 236m up the Rialto tower. Beside and owned by Vue de Monde (p490), it's Vue's view and liquid creativity without the price tag. Arrive early (and nicely dressed) for a table.

Melbourne Supper Club
BAR

(Map p472; 📞03-9654 6300; www.melbourne supperclub.com.au; 1st fl, 161 Spring St, Melbourne; ⏰5pm-4am Sun-Thu, to 6am Fri & Sat; 🚇Parliament) This sophisticated hideaway and the **Princess Theatre** (Map p472; 📞Ticketmaster 1300 111 011; www.marrinertheatres.com.au; 163 Spring St), entered via an unsigned wooden door, is a favoured after-work destination for performers and hospitality types. Cosy into a chesterfield, browse the encyclopaedic wine menu and relax; the sommeliers will cater to any liquid desire.

Garden State Hotel
BAR

(Map p472; 📞03-8396 5777; www.gardenstate hotel.com.au; 101 Flinders Lane, Melbourne; ⏰11am-late; 🚇; 🚇Flinders St) Just as in a grand English garden, there are orderly bits and wild bits in this so-hot-right-now multi-purpose venue. Shuffle past the suits into the main bar area, backed by shiny copper vats and a three-storey void filled with mature trees. The best part is the chandelier-adorned Rose Garden cocktail bar in the basement. The food is solid too.

Market Lane Coffee
CAFE

(Map p495; 📞03-9804 7434; www.marketlane. com.au; 83-85 Victoria St, Queen Victoria Market, Melbourne; ⏰7am-4pm Mon-Thu, to 5pm Fri & Sat, 8am-5pm Sun; 🚌19, 57, 58, 59) It's all about the super-strong coffee at this branch of Market Lane. It serves a few pastries too, but as it's on the corner of Queen Victoria Market (p463) there's no shortage of snacks at hand to enjoy with your takeaway cup. There's another branch in the market's deli hall.

Section 8
BAR

(Map p472; 📞0430 291 588; www.section8.com. au; 27-29 Tattersalls Lane, Melbourne; ⏰10am-11pm Mon-Wed, to 1am Thu-Sat, noon-11pm Sun; 🚇; 🚇Melbourne Central) Enclosed within a cage full of graffiti, wooden-pallet seating and a shipping-container bar, Section 8 is makeshift-cool. It's quite a scene, packing out with DJs playing nightly. During the day you can play giant chess and Jenga.

🍴 Southbank & Docklands

Ponyfish Island
BAR

(Map p472; www.ponyfish.com.au; Southbank Pedestrian Bridge, Southbank; ⏰11am-late; 🚇Flinders St) Not content with hiding bars down laneways or on rooftops, Melburnians are finding ever more creative spots to do their drinking. Where better than a little open-air nook on the pylon of a bridge arcing over the Yarra? It's a surprisingly good spot to knock back beers while snacking on beer-friendly food and cheese platters. Packs out in good weather.

🍴 Richmond & East Melbourne

Royal Saxon
BAR

(Map p504; 📞03-9429 5277; www.royalsaxon. com; 545 Church St, Richmond; ⏰noon-late; 🚇East Richmond) With a spotless heritage-listed facade and glass-filled, architecturally designed interior, there are different spots to eat and drink here. On a nice day the outdoor tables beneath the Moreton Bay fig tree are the place to eat, but come Friday and Saturday from 8pm, DJs turn upstairs into a dance-fuelled party with 'pornstar' martinis.

🍴 Fitzroy, Collingwood & Abbotsford

★Black Pearl
COCKTAIL BAR

(Map p476; 📞03-9417 0455; www.blackpearlbar. com.au; 304 Brunswick St, Fitzroy; ⏰5pm-3am, Attic Bar 7pm-1am Thu, to 3am Fri & Sat; 🚌11) After more than 15 years in the game, Black

Pearl goes from strength to strength, winning awards and receiving global accolades. Low lighting, leather banquettes and candles set the mood downstairs. Prop at the bar to study the extensive cocktail list or let the expert bartenders concoct something to your tastes. Upstairs is table-service **Attic Bar**; book ahead.

★ **Everleigh**   COCKTAIL BAR

(Map p476; ☑ 03-9416 2229; www.theeverleigh. com; Upstairs, 150-156 Gertrude St, Fitzroy; ⊙ 5pm-1am; ⓐ 86) Sophistication is off the charts at this hidden, upstairs nook. Settle into a leather booth in the intimate setting with a few friends for conversation and classic cocktails, or sidle up to the bar for a solo martini. The Bartender's Choice is encouraged: state your flavour and alcohol preferences and a tailored cocktail will appear soon after.

★ **Naked for Satan**   BAR

(Map p476; ☑ 03-9416 2238; www.nakedforsatan. com.au; 285 Brunswick St, Fitzroy; ⊙ noon-midnight Sun-Thu, to 1am Fri & Sat; ⓐ 11) Reviving an apparent Brunswick St legend (a man nicknamed Satan who would get naked because of the heat of his illegal vodka distillery), this place is packed with travellers vying for a seat on the roof terrace with wrap-around balcony, **Naked in the Sky**. Food is disappointing compared with nearby options, but the view is a standout.

Grace Darling   PUB

(Map p476; ☑ 03-9416 0055; www.thegracedarl inghotel.com.au; 114 Smith St, Collingwood; mains $19.50-34; ⊙ noon-1am Mon-Sat, to 11pm Sun; ⓐ 86) Adored by Collingwood football fans as the birthplace of the club, the Grace has been given a spit-and-polish and attracts a clientele of pretty young things. The

LGBTIQ+ MELBOURNE

While there's still a handful of specifically LGBTIQ+ venues scattered around the city, some of the best hang-outs are weekly takeovers of mainstream bars, especially Sunday afternoon at the **Railway Hotel** (Map p504; ☑ 03-9510 4050; www.therailway.com. au; 29 Chapel St, Windsor; ⊙ main bar and deck noon-late Tue-Sun; ⓐ 5, 64, 78, ⓡ Windsor) in Windsor, Sunday evening at the **Emerson** (Map p504; ☑ 03-9825 0900; www.theemer son.com.au; 141-145 Commercial Rd, South Yarra; ⊙ rooftop 5pm-late Thu, from noon Fri-Sun, nightclub 10pm-late Thu, from 9pm Fri & Sat; ⓐ 72, 78, ⓡ Prahran) in South Yarra, Thursday night at **Yah Yah's** (Map p476; www.yahyahs.com.au; 99 Smith St, Fitzroy; ⊙ 8pm-5am Thu-Sat; ⓐ 86) in Fitzroy and next door at **The 86** for Honcho Disko.

There's lots of fun to be had at Saturday-night drag at **Pride of our Footscray** (Map p468; ☑ 0417 219 899; www.prideofourfootscray.bar; 1st fl, 86-88 Hopkins St, Footscray; ⊙ 5pm-1am Tue-Thu, to 3am Fri, noon-3am Sat, noon-midnight Sun; ⓡ Footscray). The **Peel** (Map p476; ☑ 03-9419 4762; www.thepeel.com.au; 46 Peel St, cnr Wellington St, Collingwood; ⊙ 10pm-7am Fri & Sat; ⓐ 86) in Collingwood is a much-loved local institution that's also worth a look; nearby **Sircuit** (Map p476; www.sircuit.com.au; 103 Smith St, Fitzroy; ⊙ 9pm-late Wed-Sun; ⓐ 86) is popular too and has regular drag shows.

Semi-regular themed gay party nights are also popular, like Woof (www.woofclub. com), DILF (www.iwantadilf.com), Closet (www.facebook.com/closetpartyoz), Fabuland (www.facebook.com/fabulandmelb) and Swagger (www.facebook.com/swaggerparty). For lesbians, there's Fannys at Franny's (www.francescasbar.com.au) and Mother Party (www.facebook.com/motherqueergirlsparty).

The big event on the queer calendar is the annual **Midsumma Festival** (www.mid summa.org.au; ⊙ Jan-Feb). It has a diverse program of cultural, community and sporting events, including the popular Midsumma Carnival at Alexandra Gardens, St Kilda's Pride March and much more. The **Melbourne Queer Film Festival** (www.mqff.com.au; ⊙ Mar), Australia's largest, also screens more than 100 films from around the world.

For more local info, pick up a copy of free magazine *Star Observer* (www. starobserver.com.au) from gay-friendly bookshops, venues and some libraries (check online for distribution), or digitally subscribe to LOTL (formerly Lesbians on the Loose; www.lotl.com). Gay and lesbian radio station JOY 94.9FM (www.joy.org.au) is another important resource for visitors and locals.

bluestone beauty has a cosy restaurant, street-side tables and live music, mainly aimed at the young indie crowd. Check the website for weeknight deals, like $15 parma, burger and curry nights.

Builders Arms Hotel   PUB

(Map p476; ☑ 03-9417 7700; www.buildersarms hotel.com.au; 211 Gertrude St, Fitzroy; ⊗ noon-late; ☐ 86) A reimagined old boozer that's retained its charm. Come for a pot by all means, but there's also decent wine by the glass and fancy versions of pub grub at the bistro (think chicken parma and a great fish pie). Picnic-style tables on the footpath outside are perfect for taking in Gertrude St.

Napier Hotel   PUB

(Map p476; ☑ 03-9419 4240; www.thenapierhotel. com; 210 Napier St, Fitzroy; ⊗ 3-11pm Mon-Thu, noon-1am Fri, to 11pm Sat, 1-11pm Sun; ☐ 11, 86) The friendly Napier has stood on this corner for more than a century. Worm your way around the central bar to the boisterous dining room for an iconic Bogan burger. Lesser-known is that this place is the biggest seller of kangaroo in Victoria, thanks to a pepper-crusted steak. There's a fireplace for winter and beer garden for summer.

🍸 Carlton & Brunswick

Carlton Wine Room   WINE BAR, BISTRO

(Map p495; ☑ 03-9347 2626; www.thecarltonwine room.com.au; cnr Drummond & Faraday Sts, Carlton; ⊗ 4-11pm Tue & Wed, from noon Thu-Mon; ☐ 200, 207, 955, 966, ☐ 1, 6) There's no better place for a pre- or post-Nova (p507) tipple than this neighbourhood gem. It has a distinctly Melbourne-European vibe: a marble bar and raised communal table downstairs, more dining space upstairs and food ranging from small share dishes to a daily pasta. Knowledgeable staff guide you through the 100-bottle list and reserve wines. Ask for the 'staff choice'.

Wide Open Road   CAFE

(☑ 03-9010 9298; www.wideopenroad.com.au; 274 Barkly St, Brunswick; ⊗ 7am-4pm Mon-Fri, to 5pm Sat, 8am-5pm Sun (kitchen shuts 1hr prior); 🖤; ☐ 19, ☐ Jewell) Wide Open in name translates to wide open in space at this converted-warehouse cafe-roastery, just off hectic Sydney Rd. There's plenty of elbow room at the communal tables, where you can tuck into dishes like eggs Benedict with truffle hollandaise or a seared salmon 'nourish

bowl' while sipping house-blend espresso and filter coffee.

Seven Seeds   CAFE

(Map p495; ☑ 03-9347 8664; www.sevenseeds. com.au; 114 Berkeley St, Carlton; ⊗ 7am-5pm Mon-Sat, from 8am Sun; ☐ 19, 58, 59) This inconspicuous warehouse a little north of Queen Victoria Market (p463) has plenty of room to store your bike and sip a splendid coffee with something from the all-day menu. Public coffee classes are held 8.30am Wednesday for a $5 charitable donation. It also owns **Traveller** (Map p472; 2/14 Crossley St, Melbourne; bagels from $7; ⊗ 7am-5pm Mon-Fri; ☐ 86, 96) and **Brother Baba Budan** (Map p472; ☑ 03-9347 8664; 359 Little Bourke St, Melbourne; ⊗ 7am-5pm Mon-Thu, to 7pm Fri & Sat, 8am-5pm Sun; 🛜; ☐ Melbourne Central) in the CBD.

Alehouse Project   BAR

(☑ 03-9387 1218; www.thealehouseproject.com.au; 98-100 Lygon St, Brunswick East; ⊗ 3pm-late Mon-Fri, from noon Sat & Sun; 🛜🐾; ☐ 1, 6) A Brunswick venue for beer snobs to convene and compare notes, or for those who just want to rock up and taste test a great selection of 12 rotating craft beers on tap. In its first six years, the venue had tapped 2000 beers. There's also a pool table and beer garden.

Padre Coffee   CAFE

(☑ 03-9381 1881; www.padrecoffee.com.au; 438-440 Lygon St, Brunswick East; ⊗ 7am-4pm Mon-Sat, from 8am Sun; 🛜; ☐ 1, 6) A big player in Melbourne's third-wave coffee movement, this warehouse cafe is the original roaster for Padre Coffee and brews its premium single origins and blends. There are pastries and snacks to complement your coffee, and you can purchase beans and brewing equipment. Holds workshops on Mondays (check the website).

Jimmy Watson's   WINE BAR

(Map p495; ☑ 03-9347 3985; www.jimmywatsons. com.au; 333 Lygon St, Carlton; ⊗ restaurant & wine bar 11.30am-late; ☐ Tourist Shuttle, ☐ 1, 6) If this Robin Boyd–designed midcentury building had ears, there'd be a few generations of writers and academics in trouble. There's something for all ages, whether a bottle of something special in the handsome indoor space to accompany a long lunch, the sunny courtyard or **Wolf's Lair** rooftop, a great spot for cocktails.

South Yarra, Prahran & Windsor

N
0 _____ 500 m
0 _____ 0.25 miles

RICHMOND
CREMORNE
CityLink (Monash Fwy)
Yarra River
Alexandra Ave
Como Park
TOORAK
SOUTH YARRA
South Yarra
PRAHRAN
Hawksburn
WINDSOR
ST KILDA

The Tan (350m)
Albert Park Lake (2km)

Punt Rd
Alexandra Ave
Caroline St
Domain Rd
Caroline St
Avoca St
Murphy St
Darling St
Yarra St
Cubitt St
Green St
Balmain St
Church St
Chapel St
Cotter St
Brighton St
Mary St
Williams Rd North
Verdant Ave
Bruce St
Washington St
Lechlade Ave
Toorak Rd
Malcolm St
River St
Tivoli Rd
Rockley Rd
Kensington Rd
Como Ave
Williams Rd
Rockley Gardens
Toorak Rd
Claremont St
Daly St
Oxford St
Clara St
Cromwell Rd
Hawksburn Rd
Cassell St
Gordon St
Alexandra St
Lang St
Powell St
Davis St
William St
Chambers St
Arthur St
Palermo St
Fawkner St
Nicholson St
Albion St
Argo St
Tyrone St
Moore St
Hardy St
Osborne St
Portland Pl
Phoenix St
Balmoral St
Fitzgerald St
Cliff St
Grosvenor St
Chapel St
Garden St
Wilson St
Ellis St
Simmons St
Surrey St
Cromwell Rd
Motherwell St
Joy St
Howitt St
McKillop St
Luxton Rd
Williams Rd
May Rd
Barry St
Commercial Rd
Porter St
Grattan St
Izett St
Cato St
Malvern Rd
Malvern Rd
Moss St
Greville St
Perth St
Charles St
Prahran
Little Chapel St
Essex St
Princes Gardens
King St
Clifton St
Mount St
Bangs St
York St
Lewisham Rd N
Clarke St
Mackay St
Murray St
Victoria Gardens
Spring St
Wrights Tce
Pridham St
Bayview St
Aberdeen Rd
High St
High St
Andrew St
Raleigh St
Upton Rd
Green St
Artists La
Chapel St
Anchor Pl
Victoria St
Eastbourne St
Earl St
Duke St
James St
Gertrude St
The Avenue
Lewisham Rd
Newry St
Jessamine Ave
Chomley St
Union St
Henry St
Peel St Windsor
Albert St
Mcilwrick St
Hornby St
Wrexham Rd
Gooch St
Lumley Park
Dandenong Rd
Wellington St

19
1
6
8
5
7
15
3
11
14
2
16
4
25
18
23
9
13
24
20
10
17
21
22
12

South Yarra, Prahran & Windsor

◉ **Sights**
1 Como House & Garden..........................D3
2 Prahran Market B5

◎ **Activities, Courses & Tours**
3 Essential Ingredient..............................B4

◎ **Sleeping**
4 Cullen..B5
5 Hotel Claremont....................................B3
6 SoYa...A3

◎ **Eating**
7 Dainty Sichuan B3
8 Darling Cafe A3
9 Grand Lafeyette B6
10 Hawker Hall..B7
11 Maker & Monger.....................................B4
12 Woodland House.....................................D6

◎ **Drinking & Nightlife**
13 Borsch, Vodka & Tears B6
14 Emerson..A5
15 Leonard's House of Love.......................B4
16 Market Lane Coffee...............................B4
17 Railway Hotel..B7
18 Revolver Upstairs B6
19 Royal Saxon..C1
20 Yellow Bird..B6

◎ **Entertainment**
21 Astor...B7
22 Red Stitch Actors Theatre....................B7

◎ **Shopping**
23 Chapel Street Bazaar............................B6
24 Design a Space.......................................B6
25 Greville Records.....................................B5

South Yarra, Prahran & Windsor

★**Leonard's House of Love** BAR
(Map p504; ☑0428 066 778; http://leonardshouse
oflove.com.au; 3 Wilson St, South Yarra; ⊙noon-
1am Sun-Thu, to 3am Fri & Sat; ☒; ☐78) Inside
what appears to be someone's '70s love-
shack party house, you'll find this American
bar touting 'free love and cold beer'. The
menu is mostly burgers, fried chicken and
loaded fries, which can be scoffed outside
when warm or by the fire when chilly. Challenge a stranger to a game of pool and try
the house Bathtub Lager.

Market Lane Coffee CAFE
(Map p504; ☑03-9804 7434; www.marketlane.
com.au; Shop 13 Prahran Market, 163 Commercial
Rd, South Yarra; ⊙7am-4pm Mon & Wed, to 5pm
Tue & Thu-Sat, 8am-5pm Sun; ☐72, 78, ☐Prah-
ran) The first Market Lane speciality coffee shop and roastery hides at the back of
Prahran Market. The beans here are strictly
seasonal, producing cups of coffee that are
beautifully nuanced and best paired with
a scrumptious pastry. There's only whole,
organic milk or nothing here. On weekends
the cafe serves locally famous mushroom
burgers.

Yellow Bird BAR
(Map p504; ☑03-9533 8983; www.yellowbird.
com.au; 122 Chapel St, Windsor; ⊙8am-late; ☐6,
78, ☐Windsor) Somewhere between Mexican
kitsch and band-poster grunge, this little
bird keeps Windsor's cool kids happy with
all-day drinks, breakfast and diner-style
food. It's owned by the drummer from
Something for Kate, so the rock 'n' roll
ambience is legit. Mingle with a passing
cast of musos, listen to the playlist of underground bands and munch on burgers.

Borsch, Vodka & Tears BAR
(Map p504; ☑03-9530 2694; www.borschvodka
andtears.com; 173 Chapel St, Windsor; ⊙8am-late
Mon, 3pm-late Tue-Thu, 8am-3am Fri, 9am-3am
Sat, 9am-10.30pm Sun; ☐6, 78, ☐Prahran)
A Chapel St classic and nod to the area's
Eastern European influences. With up to
200 vodkas available, you can try drops like
clear, oak-matured, fruit-infused and traditional *nalewka kresowa* (made according
to old Russian and Polish recipes). Staff
are knowledgeable and the menu includes
borscht and blintzes good enough to make
your Polish grandpa weep. *Na zdrowie!*
(Cheers!)

Revolver Upstairs CLUB
(Map p504; ☑03-9521 5985; www.revolver
upstairs.com.au; 229 Chapel St, Prahran; ⊙5pm-
late Tue & Wed, 5pm-6am Thu, noon Fri-noon Sat,
5pm Sat-9am Mon; ☐6, 78, ☐Prahran) Rowdy
Revolver – or 'Revs', if you're local – can feel
like an enormous version of your lounge
room. But with nonstop music come the
weekend and the ability to party for 24
hours straight, you're probably glad it's not.
Live music, art exhibitions and interesting
local, national and international DJs and
bands keep the mixed crowd wide awake.

🍷 St Kilda, Elwood & Elsternwick

⭐ Bar Di Stasio
WINE BAR

(Map p480; ☑03-9525 3999; www.distasio.com.
au; 31 Fitzroy St, St Kilda; ⊙11.30am-midnight;
🚌3, 12. 16, 96) Within red Pompidou-style
scaffolding – the work of artist Callum Morton – lies this buzzing, sophisticated spot,
dominated by a grand marble bar and plas-
ter-chipped walls behind lit glass. Waiters
seemingly plucked from Venice's Caffè Flo-
rian mix perfect spritzes while dishing out
bites, from lightly fried local seafood to elegant pastas (available until 11pm). Book; it's
extremely popular.

⭐ Pontoon
BAR

(Map p480; ☑03-9525 5445; www.pontoonstkilda
beach.com.au; 30 Jacka Blvd, St Kilda; ⊙noon-late
Mon-Fri, from 11am Sat & Sun; 🚌3, 16, 96) Beneath
fine-diner Stokehouse (p499) is its casual,
buzzing bar-bistro, a light-soaked space with
floor-to-ceiling windows and a deck over the
beach, looking out to sunset. Shared-plates
deliver some decent bites, including pizzas,
grain salads and the namesake cheeseburger
(mains $16 to $32). Slip on the shades and
sip craft suds or a local prosecco.

Dogs Bar
BAR

(Map p480; ☑03-9593 9535; www.dogsbar.com.
au; 54 Acland St, St Kilda; ⊙3pm-1am Mon-Wed,
from noon Thu-Sun; 🕿; 🚌3, 16, 96) You're guaranteed a good time at this St Kilda veteran, a
joint that hasn't been short of berets, boozy
debates and raucous banter from locals
since it opened in 1989. Soaked in afternoon
sunshine, the outdoor tables are a prime
people-watching spot (especially at weekends), while the golden-hued interior is the
setting for live blues, rock or funk, nightly
from around 9pm.

Misery Guts
BAR

(Map p480; www.miserygutsbar.com; 19 Grey St,
St Kilda; ⊙4-11pm Tue & Wed, to midnight Thu,
3pm-1am Fri & Sat, 3pm-midnight Sun; 🚌3, 16, 96)
There's nothing cantankerous about this
unruffled local, a few steps (and a million
miles) away from Fitzroy St's backpacker
bars. Punctuated with various oddities –
including a vintage police sign – it's where
the locals lounge, gossiping over decent
beers, interesting wines by the glass and
cheese toasties. There's live music from 6pm
Sunday.

Republica
BAR

(Map p480; ☑03-8598 9055; www.republica.
net.au; St Kilda Sea Baths, 10-18 Jacka Blvd, St
Kilda; ⊙11.30am-late Mon-Fri, from 9am Sat &
Sun; 🕿; 🚌3, 16, 96) Opening right up to St
Kilda Beach with palm trees and astroturf,
Republica is about as close as you'll get to a
beach bar in Melbourne. Ditch the food and
head in later in the afternoon or evening for
sunset beers, cocktail lounging and the odd
flirtatious glance.

Local Taphouse
BAR

(Map p480; ☑03-9537 2633; www.thelocal.com.
au; 184 Carlisle St, St Kilda; ⊙noon-late, kitchen
closes 10pm; 🚌3, 16, 78, 🚃Balaclava) Reminiscent of an old-school Brooklyn bar, this
warm, wooden local has a rotating cast of
20 craft tap beers and an impressive bottle
list, with more than 400 tapped each year.
There's a beer garden upstairs and snug mix
of leather couches and open fires inside.
Weekly events include comedy on Monday
and live music on Friday and Saturday.

☆ Entertainment

Cinema

⭐ Moonlight Cinema
CINEMA

(Map p468; www.moonlight.com.au; Gate D, Royal
Botanic Gardens, Birdwood Ave, South Yarra; adult/
child $20/15; ⊙Nov-Mar; 👪👹; 🚌1, 3, 5, 6, 16, 64,
67, 72) Melbourne's original outdoor cinema
hits Royal Botanic Gardens (p475) from the
end of November through March, screening
current releases and retro classics. Bring a
picnic hamper and booze, or buy some from
cashless operators at the venue. 'Gold Grass'
tickets ($35) include waitstaff service and a
beanbag in the premium viewing area. Look
up to see bats and bring warm clothes.

It's easiest and best to pre-purchase tickets online.

Astor
CINEMA

(Map p504; ☑03-9510 1414; www.astortheatre.
net.au; cnr Chapel St & Dandenong Rd, Windsor;
tickets $14-17.50; 🚌5, 64, 78, 🚃Windsor) This
1936 art-deco darling has had more ups and
downs than a Hollywood diva. Saved from
permanent closure, it's one of Melbourne's
best-loved landmarks, with double features
most nights and a mix of recent releases, art-
house films and cult classics. Discount tickets ($14) are available Monday, Wednesday
and Thursday. Look out for movie marathon
events, some lasting 24 hours.

MELBOURNE & VICTORIA MELBOURNE

Cinema Nova CINEMA
(Map p495; 03-9347 5331; www.cinemanova.
com.au; 380 Lygon St, Carlton; adult/student/
child $21/16/13; ; Tourist Shuttle, 1, 6)
See the latest in art-house, docos and foreign films at this cinema, a locals' favourite.
Cheap Monday screenings ($7/10 before/
after 4pm).

Live Music

★**Esplanade Hotel** LIVE MUSIC
(Map p480; 03-9534 0211; www.hotelespl
anade.com.au; 11 The Esplanade, St Kilda; 11am-
late) You could spend a day going from room
to room now the beloved 'Espy' is back, following a $15 million renovation. Antiques
complement its Victorian bones and there
are three food and beverage offerings, plus
about 10 bars, including the **Ghost of Alfred
Felton**. There's also the **Espy Kitchen**, modern Cantonese restaurant **Mya Tiger**, a pod-
casting studio and band rooms.

The Tote LIVE MUSIC
(Map p476; 03-9419 5320; www.thetotehotel.
com; cnr Johnston & Wellington Sts, Collingwood; 4pm-1am Wed, to 3am Thu-Sat, to 11pm
Sun; 86) One of Melbourne's most iconic
live-music venues, this divey pub has been
hosting a roster of local and international
punk, heavy metal and hardcore bands since
the '80s. It has one of the best jukeboxes in
the universe and its temporary closure in
2010 saw people fiercely protest against the
liquor-licensing laws that were blamed for
the closure.

Corner LIVE MUSIC
(Map p468; 03-9427 7300; www.cornerhotel.
com; 57 Swan St, Richmond; 4pm-late Mon,
noon-late Tue-Thu & Sun, to 3am Fri & Sat; ;
Richmond) The band room here is one of
Melbourne's most popular midsize venues.
It's seen plenty of action over the years, from
Dinosaur Jr to the Buzzcocks. If your ears
need a break, there's a friendly front bar.
The rooftop has city views but gets packed
with a different crowd from the music fans
below. Kitchen closes between 9.30pm and
10.30pm.

Prince Bandroom LIVE MUSIC
(Map p480; 03-9536 1168; www.princeband
room.com.au; 29 Fitzroy St, St Kilda; 12, 16, 96)
The Prince is a legendary St Kilda venue,
with a solid line-up of local and international acts spanning hip-hop, dance, rock
and indie. It's been going for more than 75
years with an eclectic mix of guests, from

Lenny Kravitz and Coldplay to UK rapper
Tinie Tempah and Nordic hardcore-punk
outfit Refused.

Palais Theatre CONCERT VENUE
(Map p480; 03-8537 7677, tickets 13 61 00; www.
palaistheatre.com.au; cnr Lower Esplanade & Cavell
St, St Kilda; 3, 16, 96) Standing gracefully
next to Luna Park, the heritage-listed Palais
(c 1927) is a St Kilda icon, with the Rolling
Stones, Beach Boys, Rufus Wainwright and
others gracing its stage. At the time of writing the building was undergoing multi-million-dollar renovations, with the deco giant
already repainted in its original colours,
upgraded lighting and electronics, restora-
tion of the ceiling domes and more.

Old Bar LIVE MUSIC
(Map p476; 03-9417 4155; www.theoldbar.com.
au; 74-76 Johnston St, Fitzroy; 2pm-3am; ;
11, 96) With live bands seven days a week
and a licence 'til 3am, the Old Bar's proof
that Melbourne is the rock 'n' roll capital of
Australia. It gets great local bands and a few
internationals in its grungy band room with
a house-party vibe.

Gasometer LIVE MUSIC
(Map p476; 03-9416 3335; www.thegasometer
hotel.com.au; 484 Smith St, Collingwood;
4pm-midnight Tue & Wed, to 2am Thu, to 3am
Fri, 1pm-3am Sat, to 1am Sun; 86) This bright
red corner pub features a cosy front bar,
an excellent line-up of bands most nights –
from up-and-coming local acts to punk and
indie big names – and one of the best band
rooms in the city, holding 350 fans with a
mezzanine level and a retractable roof for
open-air gigs.

Forum CONCERT VENUE
(Map p472; 1300 111 011; www.forummelbourne.
com.au; 154 Flinders St, Melbourne; Flinders
St) One of the city's most atmospheric live-
music venues, the Forum does double duty
as a cinema during the **Melbourne International Film Festival** (MIFF; www.miff.com.
au; Aug). The striking Moorish exterior (an
over-the-top fantasia with minarets, domes
and dragons) houses an equally interesting
interior, with the southern night sky rendered on the domed ceiling.

Theatre & Arts

Red Stitch Actors Theatre THEATRE
(Map p504; 03-9533 8082, tickets 03-9533
8083; www.redstitch.net; rear 2 Chapel St, Windsor; box office 10am-5pm Mon-Fri; 5, 64, 78,

Windsor) Featuring prolific national talent, Red Stitch is one of Australia's most respected actors' ensembles, staging new international works that are often premieres in Australia. The company's intimate black-box theatre is opposite the historic Astor (p506) cinema, down the end of a driveway.

La Mama Courthouse
THEATRE
(Map p495; 03-9347 6948; www.lamama.com.au; 349 Drummond St, Carlton; tickets $10-25; box office 10.30am-5pm Mon-Fri, 2-3pm Sat & Sun; Tourist Shuttle, 1, 6) As visitors wait for La Mama Theatre (205 Faraday St) to rebuild following a fire in 2018, it's business as usual at the larger venue, La Mama Courthouse, built in 1887. The group is known for producing new Australian works and experimental theatre and has a reputation for developing emerging playwrights.

Malthouse Theatre
THEATRE
(Map p468; 03-9685 5111; www.malthousetheatre.com.au; 113 Sturt St, Southbank; box office 9.30am-5pm Mon, to late Tue-Fri, 10.30am-late Sat, 1hr before performances Sun; 1) Dedicated to promoting Australian works, this exciting company stages interesting productions in its own theatre, converted from an atmospheric old brick malthouse. Both Australian and international acts play here, with the intention of sparking conversation and debate.

Melbourne Theatre Company
THEATRE
(MTC; Map p468; 03-8688 0800; www.mtc.com.au; 140 Southbank Blvd, Southbank; box office 9am-5pm or start of evening performance Mon-Sat, 2hr prior to performance Sun; 1) Founded in 1953, MTC is the oldest professional theatre company in Australia. It stages up to a dozen productions each year, ranging from contemporary (including many new Australian works) to Shakespeare and other classics. Performances take place in its award-winning Southbank Theatre, a striking black building enclosed within angular white tubing.

Comedy

Comic's Lounge
COMEDY
(Map p468; 03-9348 9488; www.thecomicslounge.com.au; 26 Errol St, North Melbourne; doors open btwn 5.30pm & 7.30pm; 57) There's stand-up featuring Melbourne's best-known funny people most nights of the week here. If you like to live dangerously, Tuesday's when professional comedians try out new material. Admission prices vary.

Classical Music

Melbourne Symphony Orchestra
LIVE PERFORMANCE
(MSO; 03-9929 9600; www.mso.com.au; box office 10am-6pm Mon-Fri) The MSO has a broad reach: while not afraid to be populist (it's done sell-out performances with Burt Bacharach and Kiss), it usually performs classical symphonic master works. It plays regularly at its Hamer Hall (Map p472; 1300 182 183; www.artscentremelbourne.com.au; 100 St Kilda Rd, Southbank; box office 10am-5.45pm; 1, 3, 6, 16, 64, 67, 72, Flinders St) home at the Arts Centre, but also has a popular summer series of free concerts at the Sidney Myer Music Bowl (Map p468; 136 100; www.artscentremelbourne.com.au; Kings Domain, 21 Linlithgow Ave, Southbank; 3, 5, 6, 8, 16, 64, 67, 72) (BYO picnic).

Melbourne Recital Centre
CLASSICAL MUSIC
(Map p468; 03-9699 3333; www.melbournerecital.com.au; 31 Sturt St, Southbank; 9am-5pm Mon-Fri, 2hr prior events Sat & Sun; ; 1) This building may look like a framed piece of giant honeycomb, but it's actually home (or hive?) to Melbourne Chamber Orchestra (www.mco.org.au), with lots of other ensembles performing regularly. Its two halls are said to have some of the best acoustics in the southern hemisphere. Performances range from chamber music to contemporary, classical, jazz, world music and dance.

Dance

Australian Ballet
BALLET
(1300 369 741; www.australianballet.com.au; 9am-5pm Mon-Fri) More than 50 years old, Melbourne-based Australian Ballet performs traditional and new works in the Arts Centre (Map p472; 9281 8000, tickets 1300 182 183; www.artscentremelbourne.com.au; 100 St Kilda Rd, Southbank; box office Theatres Building 9am-8.30pm Mon-Sat, 10am-5pm Sun, box office Hamer Hall 10am-5.45pm; Flinders St) and around the country. Take an hour-long Primrose Potter Australian Ballet Centre tour ($39) that includes a visit to the wardrobe department and dancer studios, or a two-hour production centre tour through a treasure trove of costumes, sets and props ($160). Bookings essential.

Chunky Move
DANCE
(Map p468; 03-9645 5188; www.chunkymove.com; 111 Sturt St, Southbank; 1) This acclaimed contemporary-dance company performs mainly at the Malthouse Theatre.

It also runs a variety of public dance classes and contemporary yoga; check the website.

🛍 Shopping

Melbourne is proud of its makers. Despite empty shops on once-booming strips like Bridge Rd (Richmond) and Chapel St (South Yarra), passionate, dedicated retailers still cater to a broad range of tastes. City laneways and Gertrude St (Fitzroy) are great for small, independent clothing boutiques, but keep your eye out for finds in arcades, vintage shops and markets too.

🏠 City Centre

★Melbournalia GIFTS & SOUVENIRS
(Map p472; ☑03-9663 3751; www.melbournalia. com.au; Shop 5/50 Bourke St, Melbourne; ⊙10am-7pm Mon-Thu, to 8pm Fri, 11am-6pm Sat & Sun; ☒Parliament) This is the place to stock up on interesting souvenirs by more than 100 local designers – prints featuring city icons, tram socks, native Aussie-inspired earrings and great books on Melbourne, as well as maps and guides, gift cards, postcards and more. The friendly staff can help you send excess shopping home. Extended December hours.

★Craft Victoria ARTS & CRAFTS
(Map p472; ☑03-9650 7775; www.craft.org.au; Watson Pl, off Flinders Lane, Melbourne; ⊙11am-6pm Mon-Fri, to 5pm Sat; ☒Parliament) This retail arm of Craft Victoria showcases goods handmade exclusively by Victorian artists and artisans. Its range of jewellery, textiles, accessories, glass and ceramics bridges the art-craft divide and makes for some wonderful Melbourne mementos. There are also a few galleries with changing exhibitions; admission is free. Pop in for a guide to the **Craft Cubed Festival** in August.

Hill of Content BOOKS
(Map p472; ☑03-9662 9472; www.hillofcontent bookshop.com; 86 Bourke St, Melbourne; ⊙9am-6pm Mon-Thu, to 8pm Fri, 10am-6pm Sat, 11am-5pm Sun; 👪; ☒Parliament) Melbourne's oldest bookshop (established 1922) has a range of general titles and an extensive stock of books on art, classics and poetry.

Basement Discs MUSIC
(Map p472; ☑03-9654 1110; www.basementdiscs. com.au; 24 Block Pl, Melbourne; ⊙10am-6pm Mon-Fri, to 5pm Sat, 11am-5pm Sun; ☒Flinders St) In addition to a range of CD titles and vinyl across all genres, Basement Discs has regular in-store lunchtime performances by big-name touring and local acts. There's also vintage fashion, DVDs and music posters and books. Descend to the basement for a browse; you never know who you might find playing.

🏠 Richmond & East Melbourne

Pookipoiga GIFTS & SOUVENIRS
(Map p468; ☑03-8589 4317; www.pookipoiga.com; 64 Bridge Rd, Richmond; ⊙10.30am-5.30pm Mon-Sat, 11am-3pm Sun; ☒48, 75) 🌿 Everything is ethically produced, sustainable and animal friendly at this cute little gift shop. There's a great selection of quirky greeting cards, ceramic planters in the shape of giraffes, bamboo sunglasses, tea in test tubes and more.

Lily and the Weasel GIFTS & SOUVENIRS
(Map p468; ☑03-9421 1008; www.lilyandthe weasel.com.au; 173 Swan St, Richmond; ⊙11am-6pm Tue-Fri, 10am-5pm Sat, 11am-4pm Mon & Sun; ☒70, 78) A curated mix of beautiful, mostly hand-made things from around the globe is stocked at this interesting shop, such as earrings, bags and wallets, children's toys, scarves, toiletries, ceramics and the work of local designers.

🏠 Fitzroy, Collingwood & Abbotsford

★Third Drawer Down HOMEWARES
(Map p476; ☑03-9534 4088; www.thirddrawer down.com; 93 George St, Fitzroy; ⊙10am-5pm Mon-Thu, to 6pm Fri & Sat, 11am-5pm Sun; 👪; ☒86) This 'museum of art souvenirs' stocks both beautiful and absurdist pieces with a sense of humour, many of which are collaborations with well-known designers and artists. Watermelon stools sit next to ceramic plates, silk scarves and squeezy stress bananas. There are plans to swap the giant yellow blow-up duck out the front to an oversized David Shrigly 'Ridiculous Inflatable Swan-Thing'.

There's a dedicated kids' room in the shop.

Lore Perfumery COSMETICS
(Map p476; ☑03-9416 1221; www.loreperfumery. com.au; 313 Brunswick St, Fitzroy; ⊙10am-6.30pm Mon-Thu & Sat, to 7pm Fri, to 6pm Sun; ☒11) This shop stocks more than 500 fragrances from $25 through to $500. A lot of it is Australian – the vegan body products made with native

botanicals make a great souvenir. Look out for other goodies like nostalgic Australian soaps shaped like Bubble O'Bill ice creams and scents like 'dirt' and 'clean sheets'.

Polyester Records
MUSIC

(Map p476; ☑03-9419 5137; www.polyester records.com; 387 Brunswick St, Fitzroy; ☺11am-7pm Mon-Wed, to 10pm Thu-Sat, to 5pm Sun; ☐11) Opening in 1981, this popular record shop has been selling independent music for decades, with a great range of local stuff. The knowledgeable staff will help you find what you're looking for and can offer suggestions, while there are often free gigs (check their social media). In-house bar **Crazy Arms** is open 4pm to 10pm Thursday to Saturday.

Rose Street Artists' Market
MARKET

(Map p476; ☑03-9419 5529; www.rosestmarket. com.au; 60 Rose St, Fitzroy; ☺11am-5pm Sat & Sun; ☐11) One of Melbourne's most popular art-and-craft markets showcases the best of local designers. Here you'll find up to 120 creatives selling jewellery, clothing, ceramics and iconic Melbourne screen prints. Nearby you can find local produce from **Fitzroy Mills Market** (9am to 2pm Saturday) or head to Industry Beans (p493) around the corner for a coffee fix.

Carlton & Brunswick

★Dejour Jeans
CLOTHING

(☑03-9939 0667; 542 Sydney Rd, Brunswick; ☺9.30am-4.30pm Mon-Fri, 10am-4pm Sat; ☐19) This store-workshop custom fits denim jeans, skirts and jackets for a steal. Men's and women's jeans cost between $55 and $60. Pick your style and colour, then have a pair altered to your body, usually within 60 minutes (two hours on weekends). It's always busy, so arrive early. The ultimate souvenir, the badge on the back says 'Made in Australia'.

Mediterranean Wholesalers
FOOD & DRINKS

(☑03-9380 4777; www.mediterraneanwholesalers. com.au; 482 Sydney Rd, Brunswick; ☺9am-5.30pm Mon-Fri, 8.30am to 2pm Sat, 9am to 1pm Sun; ☐19, ☐Brunswick) This Mediterranean haven founded in 1961 is Australia's largest continental food shop. Shop for supplies with your nonna or a picnic with friends, get lost in the aisles, or have an espresso and cannoli at the bar for less than $5. Think cheese, charcuterie, olive oils, more than 250 varieties of pasta, kitchenware, Italian wines and so much more.

Readings
BOOKS

(Map p495; ☑03-9347 6633; www.readings.com. au; 309 Lygon St, Carlton; ☺9am-11pm Mon-Sat, 10am-9pm Sun; ☐; ☐Tourist Shuttle, ☐1, 6) A potter around this defiantly prosperous indie bookshop can occupy an entire afternoon, if you're so inclined. There's a dangerously loaded (and good-value) specials table and switched-on, helpful staff. Just next door is its speciality children's shop.

Also in the city centre (p466) and **St Kilda** (Map p480; ☑03-9525 3852; www.readings.com. au/st-kilda; 112 Acland St, St Kilda; ☺10am-9pm; ☐3, 16, 96).

South Melbourne, Port Melbourne & Albert Park

Nest
HOMEWARES

(Map p468; ☑03-9699 8277; www.nesthome wares.com.au; 289 Coventry St, South Melbourne; ☺9.30am-5.30pm Mon-Sat, to 5pm Sun; ☐12, 96) In a soothing, light-filled space, Nest stocks a gorgeous range of homewares and gifts, from 100% linen bedding to soy candles, Aesop skincare and a range of cotton-knit 'comfort wear' that's too nice to hide in at home. The artistic installation of tiny bells hanging from the ceiling doesn't jingle – we tried.

South Yarra, Prahran & Windsor

Design a Space
CLOTHING

(Map p504; ☑03-9510 0144; www.designaspace. com.au; 142 Chapel St, Windsor; ☺10am-6pm Tue-Sat, noon-4pm Sun, to 5pm Mon; ☐78, ☐Windsor) You know the disappointment you feel when someone tells you they bought an incredible item of clothing overseas? Your payback is now at this colourful, quirky and unique fashion shop. Around 60 up-and-coming independent Australian designers have their own section selling clothing, jewellery and accessories. There are also shops in the city and Fitzroy, supporting more than 100 designers in total.

Chapel Street Bazaar
VINTAGE

(Map p504; ☑03-9529 1727; www.facebook. com/ChapelStreetBazaar; 217 Chapel St, Prahran; ☺10am-6pm; ☐6, 78, ☐Prahran) This old arcade is a sprawling, retro-obsessive riot and the closest thing you'll find to Aladdin's 'Cave of Wonders'. There are trinkets, jewellery and treasures, but you'll also pick up everything from modernist furniture and classic Hollywood posters to Noddy eggcups, vintage clothing, cameras, vinyl and old toys. Prepare to lose track of time.

Greville Records
MUSIC
(Map p504; ☑ 03-9510 3012; www.grevillerecords.com.au; 152 Greville St, Prahran; ☺10am-6pm Mon-Thu & Sat, to 7pm Fri, 11am-5pm Sun; 🚋72, 78, 🚉Prahran) One of the last bastions of the 'old' Greville St, this banging music shop from 1979 has such a loyal following that Neil Young invited the owners on stage during a Melbourne concert. The forte here is vinyl, with no shortage of eclectic and limited-edition discs (a super-limited Bob Dylan *Live in Sydney 1966* double vinyl has been discovered here).

St Kilda, Elwood & Elsternwick

St Kilda Esplanade Market
MARKET
(Map p480; www.stkildaesplanademarket.com.au; Esplanade, St Kilda; ☺10am-4pm Sun May-Sep, to 5pm Oct-Apr; 👶; 🚋3, 12, 16, 96) Fancy a Sunday shop by the seaside? This is the place, with a kilometre of trestle tables joined end to end. Pick up everything from local ceramics, sculpture, glassware and woodwork to photographic prints, organic soaps, jewellery and tongue-in-cheek tea towels.

ℹ Information

DANGERS & ANNOYANCES
Melbourne is a safe city, but as is the case anywhere, common sense goes a long way.
➡ There are occasional reports of alcohol-fuelled violence in the city centre late at night, particularly on King St. Steer clear of the heavily intoxicated and don't linger outside clubs.
➡ Screaming matches between those struggling to kick a habit are not uncommon in Collingwood's backstreets and on Fitzroy St, St Kilda. Ignore those involved and they'll most likely ignore you too.

INTERNET ACCESS
Free wi-fi is available at central city spots such as Federation Sq, Flinders St Station, Crown Casino and the State Library. It's also the norm in most midrange accommodation, although you sometimes have to pay for access in both budget and top-end stays. Many cafes also offer free wi-fi.

If you're not travelling with your own device, there are plenty of libraries around Melbourne with computer terminals, though you'll need to bring ID to sign up and pre-booking is recommended. The **City** (☑ 03-9658 9500; www.melbourne.vic.gov.au/libraries; 253 Flinders Lane; ☺8am-8pm Mon-Thu, to 6pm Fri, 10am-5pm Sat, noon-5pm Sun; 🛜👶; 🚉Flinders St), **St Kilda** (☑ 03-9209 6655; http://library.portphillip.vic.gov.au; 150 Carlisle St; ☺10am-8pm Mon-Thu, to 6pm Fri, to 5pm Sat & Sun; 🚋3, 16, 78, 🚉Balaclava) and **Prahran** (☑ 03-8290 3344; www.stonnington.vic.gov.au/library/Visit-us/Prahran-Library; 180 Greville St; ☺10am-6pm Mon-Fri, to 1pm Sat; 🚋; 🚋78, 79, 🚉Prahran) libraries all offer access.

MEDICAL SERVICES
La Trobe St Medical (☑ 03-9650 0023; www.melbournecentralpharmacy.com.au; Melbourne Central, 211 La Trobe St, Melbourne; ☺8.30am-5pm Mon-Fri; 🚉Melbourne Central)

QV Medical Centre (☑ 03-9662 2256; www.qvmedical.com.au; L7, 1 Elizabeth St, Melbourne; ☺9am-6pm Mon, Thu, Fri & Sun, to 11pm Tue, Wed & Sat)

Travel Doctor (TVMC; ☑ 03-9935 8100; www.traveldoctor.com.au; L3, 393 Little Bourke St, Melbourne; ☺9am-5pm Mon-Wed & Fri, to 8pm Thu, by appointment Sat)

Travel Doctor (☑ 03-9690 1433; www.traveldoctor.com.au; 3 Southgate Ave, Southbank; ☺8.30am-5.30pm Mon-Fri)

Wellnation Clinic (☑1300 859 785; www.wellnationclinics.com.au; Level 3, 368 Elizabeth St, Melbourne; ☺by appointment Mon-Sat)

Royal Children's Hospital (☑ 03-9345 5522; www.rch.org.au; 50 Flemington Rd, Parkville; ☺7.30am-5.30pm Mon-Fri, 10am-2pm Sat, emergency 24hr; 🚋57)

Royal Melbourne Hospital (☑ 03-9342 7000; www.thermh.org.au; 300 Grattan St, Parkville; ☺24hr; 🚋19, 58, 59)

ℹ Getting There & Away

Most travellers arrive via Melbourne Airport, which is well connected to the city by shuttle bus and taxi, although not by public transport. There are also interstate trains and buses, a direct boat from Tasmania and two minor domestic airports nearby.

Flights, cars and tours can be booked online at lonelyplanet.com/bookings.

AIR
Melbourne Airport
Melbourne Airport (MEL; ☑ 03-9297 1600; www.melbourneairport.com.au), 22km northwest of the city centre in Tullamarine, is the city's only international and main domestic airport. It has all of the facilities you'd expect from a major airport, including **baggage storage** (☑ 03-9338 3119; www.baggagestorage.com.au; Terminal 2, International Arrivals, Melbourne Airport; large bag per 4/8/24hr $12/14/17; ☺5am-12.30am).

Dozens of airlines fly here from destinations in the South Pacific, Asia, the Middle East and the Americas. The main domestic airlines are **Qantas** (☑131 313; www.qantas.com), **Jetstar** (☑131 538; www.jetstar.com), **Virgin Australia** (☑13 67 89; www.virginaustralia.com), Tigerair (☑1300 174 266; www.tigerair.com.au) and **Regional Express** (Rex; ☑131 713; www.rex.com.au).

Avalon

Jetstar flights to and from Sydney, Adelaide and Gold Coast, as well as as AirAsia flights to and from Kuala Lumpur, use **Avalon Airport** (☑03-5227 9100; www.avalonairport.com.au; 80 Beach Rd, Lara), around 55km southwest of Melbourne's city centre.

BOAT

The **Spirit of Tasmania** b(Map p468; ☑1800 634 906, 03-6419 9320; www.spiritoftasmania.com.au; Station Pier, Port Melbourne; adult/car one way from $89/99; 🛜🅿️) ferry crosses Bass Strait from Melbourne to Devonport, Tasmania, at least nightly; there are also day sailings during peak season. The crossing takes between nine and 11 hours.

BUS

The main terminus for long-distance buses is within the northern half of Southern Cross station. Here you'll find counters for all the main bus companies, along with **luggage lockers** (☑03-9619 2588; www.southerncrossstation.net.au; Southern Cross Station, 99 Spencer St; per 3/24hr from $6/12; ⊙ during train-service hours).

Firefly (Map p472; ☑03-8318 0318, 1300 730 740; www.fireflyexpress.com.au; Southern Cross station, 99 Spencer St, Coach Terminal) Overnight coaches to and from Sydney ($70, 12 hours), Albury ($70, 3½ hours), Ballarat ($65, 1¾ hours) and Adelaide ($60, 9¾ hours).

Greyhound (Map p472; ☑1300 473 946; www.greyhound.com.au) Coaches to Albury (from $56, 3½ hours), Sydney (from $113, 12 hours) and Canberra (from $65, eight hours).

V/Line (☑1800 800 007; www.vline.com.au; Southern Cross Station, Spencer St, Docklands) Services destinations within Victoria, including Korumburra ($15.60, two hours), Mansfield ($30.40, three hours) and Echuca ($30.40, three hours).

CAR & MOTORCYCLE

The most direct (and boring) route between Melbourne and Sydney is the Hume Hwy (870km). The Princes Hwy hugs the coast and is much more scenic but also much longer (1040km) and slower. Likewise, the main route to and from Adelaide is the Western/Dukes Hwy (730km), but this bypasses the Great Ocean Road.

TRAIN

Southern Cross station (Spencer St, Docklands) is the terminus for intercity and interstate trains.

Great Southern Rail (☑1800 703 357; www.greatsouthernrail.com.au) Runs the *Overland* between Melbourne and Adelaide ($164, 10 to 11 hours, twice weekly).

NSW TrainLink (☑bookings 13 22 32; www.nswtrainlink.info) Twice-daily services to and from Sydney ($89, 11½ hours) via Benalla ($21, 2¼ hours), Wangaratta ($30, 2½ hours), Albury ($44, 3¼ hours) and Wagga Wagga ($58, 4½ hours).

V/Line Operates the Victorian train and bus networks. Trains head to and from Warrnambool ($38.60, 3¾ hours) and Albury ($40.20, four hours), among others. Fares to Geelong ($13.40, one hour), Ballarat ($22.20,1½ hours), Bendigo ($33.40, 2 hours), and Traralgon ($31.20, 2¼ hours) must be paid with a myki.

ℹ️ Getting Around

TO/FROM THE AIRPORT

Melbourne Airport The SkyBus (Map p472; ☑1300 SKYBUS, 03-9335 2811; www.skybus.com.au; Southern Cross Station, 99 Spencer St; adult/child one way $19.75/10, return $38/20; 🚆Southern Cross) departs regularly and connects the airport to Southern Cross station 24 hours a day. There are also services to other parts of Melbourne, including St Kilda.

Avalon Airport Near the neighbouring city of Geelong, but connected to Melbourne's Southern Cross station by the **SkyBus** (☑1300 SKYBUS/03-9335 2811; www.skybus.com.au; adult/child one way $19.75/10, return $38/20; 🛜) Avalon City Express service.

Southern Cross Station Long-distance trains and buses arrive at this large station on the Docklands side of the city centre. From here it's easy to connect to metropolitan trains, buses and trams.

CAR & MOTORCYCLE

Driving in Melbourne presents its own set of challenges, due to the need to share the road with trams.

➡ Where trams run along the centre of the road, drivers cannot pass them once they indicate that they're stopping, as passengers board and alight from the street.

➡ In the city centre many intersections are marked 'right turn from left only'. This is the counter-intuitive 'hook turn', devised to stop vehicles blocking trams and other cars. Right-turning drivers are required to move into the far left of the intersection (it's marked) and then turn right once the lights on that side of the intersection turn green (or in other words, just after the lights in front of you turn red). See www.vicroads.vic.gov.au for further details.

ⓘ TICKETS & PASSES

Melbourne's buses, trams and trains use **myki**, a 'touch on, touch off' travel-pass system. It's not particularly convenient for short-term visitors as it requires you to purchase a $6 plastic myki card and then add credit before you travel. For more information, see **PTV** (Public Transport Victoria; ☑ 1800 800 007; www.ptv.vic.gov.au).

Note that myki cards are not needed within the free tram zone, bordered by Flinders St, Spring St, La Trobe St and Harbour Esplanade, and extending further around the Queen Victoria Market and Docklands. See www.ptv.vic.gov.au if you're unsure, and listen out for announcements on the tram for when you're entering and exiting the free zone.

Travellers should consider buying a **myki Explorer** ($15), which includes the card, one day's travel and discounts on various sights; it's available from SkyBus terminals, PTV hubs and some hotels. Otherwise, standard myki cards can be purchased at 7-Elevens, newsagents and major train stations.

The myki can be topped up at 7-Eleven stores, machines at most train stations and at some tram stops in the city centre; online top-ups take some time to process. You can either top up with pay-as-you-go **myki Money** or purchase a seven-day unlimited **myki Pass** ($44); if you're staying more than 28 days, longer passes are available.

For travel within metropolitan Melbourne (zones 1 and 2), the pay-as-you-go fare is $4.40 for two hours, capped at $8.80 for the day ($6.40 on weekends and public holidays). There are large fines for travelling without having touched on a valid myki card; ticket inspectors are vigilant, unforgiving and sometimes undercover.

Car Hire

Most car and campervan hire places have offices at Melbourne Airport and in the city or central suburbs. There are some great comparison websites if you're looking for a bargain in advance.

Aussie Campervans (☑ 03-9317 4991; www.aussiecampervans.com; 189a South Centre Rd, Tullamarine; ☺ 8am-4pm)

Avis (☑ 03-136 333; www.avis.com.au)

Britz Australia (☑ 1300 738 087; www.britz.com.au; Central West Business Park, 2/9 Ashley St, Braybrook; ☺ 7.30am-4pm Sep-Apr, 10am-4pm Mon-Sat May-Aug)

Budget (☑ 1300 362 848; www.budget.com.au)

Europcar (☑ 1300 131 390; www.europcar.com.au)

Hertz (☑ 13 30 39; www.hertz.com.au)

Rent a Bomb (☑ 03-9428 0088; www.rentabomb.com.au; 452 Bridge Rd, Richmond; ☺ 8am-6pm Mon-Fri, 9am-3pm Sat & Sun; ☑ 48, 75)

Thrifty (☑ 1300 367 227; www.thrifty.com.au)

Travellers Autobarn (☑ 1800 674 374; www.travellers-autobarn.com.au; 55 King St, Airport West; ☺ 9am-5pm Mon-Fri, to 1pm Sat Sep-May, 10am-4pm Mon-Fri Jun-Aug) Rents out and sells vehicles.

Parking

Parking inspectors are particularly vigilant in the city centre and popular suburbs, like St Kilda, Collingwood and Fitzroy. Most street parking is metered and it's more likely than not that you'll be fined if you overstay your metered time. Many places, including the city, now have PayStay as an option, an intuitive app linked to your credit card to pay for parking.

Keep an eye out for 'clearway' zones (prohibited kerb-side parking indicated by signs), which can result in sizeable fines and vehicles being towed. There are plenty of parking garages in the city, but rates vary and can be exorbitant during the day from Monday to Friday. Motorcyclists are allowed to park on the footpath except in some parts of the city centre where there are signs.

Toll Roads

Both drivers and motorcyclists will need to purchase a Melbourne Pass ($5.50 start-up fee, plus tolls and a 55c or 30c vehicle-matching fee per trip, depending on the toll road) if planning on using one of the two toll roads: **CityLink** (☑ 13 33 31; www.citylink.com.au), from Tullamarine Airport to the city and eastern suburbs, or **EastLink** (☑ 03-9955 1400; www.eastlink.com.au), which runs from Ringwood to Frankston. Pay online or via phone – but pay within three days of using the toll road to avoid a fine.

Rental cars are sometimes set up for automatic toll payments; check when you hire.

TAXI

Melbourne's taxis are metered and require an estimated prepaid fare when hailed between 10pm and 5am (you may need to pay more or get a refund depending on the final fare). Toll charges are added to fares. Two of the largest taxi companies are **Silver Top** (☑ 131 008;

JODIE JOHNSON/SHUTTERSTOCK ©

1. Espresso city
Fuel up for the day ahead like a true Melburnian.

2. Street art
Australian folklore legend Ned Kelly depicted by artist Haha.

3. Night market, Queen Victoria Market (p463)
A wonderland of food, culture and shopping.

4. NGV International (p467)
One of the largest and most-visited art museums in the country, designed by architect Roy Grounds.

JAX10289/GETTY IMAGES ©

www.silvertop.com.au) and **13 Cabs** (🗖13 22 27; www.13cabs.com.au). **Uber** (www.uber.com) also operates in Melbourne and is often cheaper and easier if you're familiar with the service.

TRAIN

Flinders St Station is the main city hub for Melbourne's 17 train lines. Trains start around 5am weekdays, run until midnight Sunday to Thursday, and all night on Friday and Saturday nights. Trains generally run every 10 to 20 minutes during the day and every 20 to 30 minutes in the evening – although during peak hour (7am to 9am into the city and 4pm to 6pm out), trains run every three to five minutes.

Payment is via myki card; PTV (p513) has timetables, maps and a journey planner on its website.

TRAM

Trams are intertwined with the Melbourne identity and an extensive network covers the city. They run roughly every 10 minutes during the day (more frequently in peak periods), and every 20 minutes in the evening. Services run until around 12.30am Sunday to Thursday, 1am Friday and Saturday, and some major lines run all night on weekends.

The entire city centre is a free tram zone. The zone is signposted on tram stops, with announcements made when you're nearing its edge to warn you that you should either hop off or pay with a myki card. Note that there's no need to 'touch off' your myki on the trams, as all zone 1 journeys are charged at the same rate – although it won't matter if you do.

PTV (p513) has timetables, maps and a journey planner on its website. There's also a handy app called tramTRACKER that will help organise your outings.

MELBOURNE REGION

The Dandenongs

These lush and tranquil ranges (Mt Dandenong at 633m is the tallest peak) are just 35km east of Melbourne, but feel worlds away from the hustle and bustle of the city. Originally inhabited by the Wurundjeri and Boon Wurrung nations, the landscape is now a patchwork of exotic and native flora with an understorey of tree ferns. Take care driving on the winding roads – you may well see lyrebirds and other wildlife crossing.

The consumption of tea and scones is de rigueur in the area's many cafes, but decent restaurants are hard to find; the best are clustered in and around Olinda and Sassafras.

On summer weekends, the hills are alive with day trippers – visit midweek to escape the crowds and traffic jams.

🔘 Sights & Activities

Burrinja Cultural Centre   CULTURAL CENTRE
(🗖03-9754 8723; www.burrinja.org.au; 351 Glenfern Rd, Upwey; ⏰10am-4pm Tue-Sun; 🅿🚻; 🚌699 from Upwey) FREE A multi-purpose space incorporating gallery spaces where local Indigenous art is often showcased as well as artists' studios, Burrinja also has a theatre and a cafe/bar where live music is staged. Its garden features Indigenous plants and artwork reflective of Victorian Koorie culture. A planned redevelopment in 2019–20 will see many spaces temporarily closed, although the theatre will remain open.

Dandenong Ranges National Park   NATIONAL PARK
(www.parkweb.vic.gov.au/explore/parks/dandenong-ranges-national-park; ⏰24hr; 🚉Upper Ferntree Gully, Belgrave) This national park protects the largest areas of remaining forest in the Dandenongs, which are home to lush fern gullies and huge stands of mountain ash. There are a number of popular walks, including a two-hour return walk along **1000 Steps** up to **One Tree Hill Picnic Ground** (Lord Somers Rd, Tremont; ⏰7.30am-9pm). This is part of **Kokoda Memorial Track**, which commemorates Australian WWII servicemen who served in New Guinea. Other walks include the 17km **Dandenong Ranges Tourist Track** between Sassafras and Emerald.

William Ricketts Sanctuary   GARDENS
(🗖03-8427 2138; www.parkweb.vic.gov.au/explore/parks/william-ricketts-sanctuary-gardens-of-the-dandenongs; 1402 Mt Dandenong Tourist Rd, Mt Dandenong; ⏰10am-4.30pm; 🚌688 from Croydon) FREE This tranquil garden features 90+ sculptures of Indigenous Australians created by potter and sculptor William Ricketts (1898–1993). Ricketts, who lived with Indigenous communities in Central Australia for periods in the 1950s, believed that all Australians should emulate Aboriginal philosophies respecting the spirituality of mother earth and the sanctity of all things in the natural world. His garden celebrates those beliefs. Audio tours can be downloaded from the website.

Around Melbourne

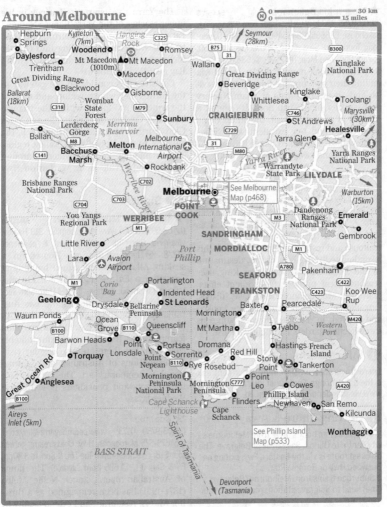

Puffing Billy

RAIL

(📞 03-9757 0700; www.puffingbilly.com.au; 1 Old Monbulk Rd, Belgrave; return adult/child/family Belgrave-Gembrooke $77.50/39/155; ⊗ schedules change daily; 👶; 🚃 Belgrave) Holding fond memories for many Melburnians, popular Puffing Billy is an iconic restored steam train that toots its way from Belgrave to Emerald Lake Park and Gembrook on a five-hour return trip. It's possible to hop on and hop off en route to enjoy a picnic or walk. A diesel locomotive replaces the steam engine on total fire ban days.

🛏 Sleeping & Eating

The Dandenongs are an easy day trip from the city, but there's plenty of accommodation – most of it chintzy B&Bs. **Valley Ranges Getaways** (📞 1300 488 448; www.vrgetaways.com.au; 361-363 Mt Dandenong Tourist Rd, Sassafras; ⊗ 9.30am-5.30pm Sat-Thu, to 8pm Fri; 👶; 🚌 688 from Croydon) can help you to find B&Bs. Camping is not permitted in the national parks.

Keep an eye on developments at Burnham Beeches, where the owners are proposing to open a luxury hotel retreat in 2020.

★**Proserpina Bakehouse** BAKERY $
(☑03-9755 3332; www.facebook.com/Proserpina-Bakehouse-683565208465496; 361 Mt Dandenong Tourist Rd, Sassafras; sandwiches $10-11.50; ⏰7am-5pm Wed-Mon; P🅿🚲; 🚌688 from Croydon) There aren't many bakeries in Victoria milling their own organic flour, but this stylish and always busy cafe at Loam Nursery on Sassafras' main strip does. It's one of a number of reasons to visit, the others being good coffee and tea, excellent sandwiches made with freshly baked house loaves, hefty pizza slices and sweet temptations galore.

★**Coonara Springs** AUSTRALIAN $$
(☑03-9751 1686; www.coonarasprings.com; 129 Olinda-Monbulk Rd, Olinda; shared plates $16-36; ⏰noon-3pm & 6-9pm Wed-Sat, to 3pm Sun; P🅿🚲; 🚌663, then 696 from Lilydale) Built as a residence in the 1890s and operating as a teahouse and restaurant since the 1930s, this is undoubtedly the best dining destination in the Dandenongs. Chef Luke King uses seasonal local produce to excellent effect, delivering well-balanced and tasty dishes. On summer weekends, pizzas are cooked and served in the restaurant's gorgeous three-hectare garden. Excellent wine list.

ℹ Information

There are no staffed visitor information centres in the Dandenongs. For tourist information go to www.visitdandenongranges.com.au.

ℹ Getting There & Away

It's just under an hour's drive from Melbourne's city centre to Olinda, Sassafras or Belgrave. The quickest route is via the Eastern Fwy, exiting on Burwood Hwy or Boronia Rd.

Suburban trains from Melbourne (Belgrave Line) head to Belgrave station; you can use your myki card.

AAT Kings (www.aatkings.com) operates day tours from Melbourne that include a ride on Puffing Billy and a Devonshire tea.

Yarra Valley

The traditional land of the Wurundjeri people, scenic Yarra Valley is now Victoria's premier wine region and weekend getaway – partly for its close proximity to Melbourne, but mainly for its wineries, superb restaurants, national parks and wildlife-viewing opportunities. This is the place to rise at dawn in a hot-air balloon and to kick back at world-class wineries in the afternoon.

The Yarra river starts its journey in the upper reaches of the Yarra Ranges National Park, passing through Warburton and close to Healesville before winding into Greater Melbourne and emptying into Port Phillip Bay near Williamstown.

Coldstream is considered the gateway to the Yarra Valley winery region, and most of the wineries are found within the triangle bound by Coldstream, Healesville and Yarra Glen. Further southeast, Warburton is the gateway to the Upper Yarra Valley region. There's another knot of wineries around Wandin and Seville along Warburton Hwy (B380).

⊙ Sights

★**TarraWarra Museum of Art** GALLERY
(☑03-5957 3100; www.twma.com.au; 313 Healesville-Yarra Glen Rd; adult/student & pensioner $12/8; ⏰11am-5pm Tue-Sun) Housed in a striking Allan Powell–designed building at **TarraWarra Estate** (☑03-5957 3510; www.tarrawarra.com.au; tastings $5; ⏰11am-5pm Tue-Sun), this excellent gallery showcases Australian art from the second half of the 20th century to the present day. Exhibitions often feature works from the museum's notable collection, but there are also regular visiting exhibitions of Australian and international contemporary art. The entrance fee for students and pensioners is waived on Wednesdays.

★**Coombe** WINERY
(☑03-9739 0173; www.coombeyarravalley.com.au; 673-675 Maroondah Hwy, Coldstream; garden tour $18; ⏰9.30am-5pm Tue-Thu & Sun, to 3.30pm Fri & Sat; P; 🚌685 from Lilydale) The home of Australian opera singer Nellie Melba (1871–1931) has been reimagined as a thriving winery, restaurant and events facility by her descendants. Book in for a tour of the seven-acre garden, designed in parts by both William Guilfoyle and Edna Walling and planted between 1909 and 1931. Afterwards, you can taste the estate's wines at the cellar door or stay for lunch in the elegant restaurant (mains $30 to $39). A small multimedia exhibition space tells Melba's story.

★**Yering Station** WINERY
(☑03-9730 0100; www.yering.com; 38 Melba Hwy, Yering; ⏰10am-5pm Mon-Fri, to 6pm Sat & Sun; P) Dating from 1838, Yering Station was home to Victoria's first vineyard. Reinvented as a wine and events estate, it has a Mod Oz restaurant in a contemporary glass pavilion

(two-/three-course set lunch $63/78) and a hybrid cellar door and gallery space set in the historic 1859 winery building (free tastings of up to five wines). The Yarra Valley Farmers Market is held here every third Sunday.

★ Domain Chandon
WINERY

(📞 03-9738 9200; www.chandon.com; 727 Maroondah Hwy, Coldstream; tastings $12; ⏱ 10.30am-4.30pm; 🅿) Chandon is an example of mass wine tourism done well. The winery – a subsidiary of Moët & Chandon – produces sparkling wines and has a restaurant, lounge bar and cellar door complex with a stunning vineyard vista; the lounge terrace is particularly alluring. Three-hour wine classes ($125 per person) are held on Sundays. The free self-guided tours of the winery are interactive and informative.

Yarra Valley Chocolaterie & Ice Creamery
FACTORY

(📞 03-9730 2777; www.yvci.com.au; 35 Old Healesville Rd, Yarra Glen; ⏱ 9am-5pm; 🅿 ♿) If you're exploring Yarra Valley with kids, this is an essential stop. Staff proffer trays piled high with free samples made with imported Belgian chocolate and you can watch the chocolatiers at work through floor-to-ceiling glass windows before enjoying an ice cream, cake or coffee in the cafe. The Bushtucker range of chocolate bars makes for great souvenirs.

Fergusson Winery
WINERY

(📞 03-5965 2237; www.fergussonwinery.com.au; 82 Wills Rd, Dixon's Creek; ⏱ 11am-4.30pm Wed-Mon May-Aug, daily Sep-Apr; 🅿) This family-run winery has been producing quality cool-climate reds and whites since 1968. It offers free wine tastings and also has a restaurant (mains $23 to $29) and rustic accommodation (double $225, suite $325 including a cooked breakfast).

👉 Tours

Yarra Valley Winery Tours
TOURS

(📞 1300 496 766; www.yarravalleywinerytours.com.au; tours from Yarra Valley/Melbourne per person $390/555) Private tours taking in four or five wineries, plus lunch. Prices cited are based on a group of two; they drop as group sizes increase.

🛏 Sleeping & Eating

Chateau Yering Hotel
BOUTIQUE HOTEL $$$

(📞 03-9237 3333; www.chateauyering.com.au; 42 Melba Hwy, Yering; r $395-845; 🅿 ❄ 🅦 ⚏)

YARRA VALLEY WINERIES

The Yarra Valley (www.wineyarravalley.com.au) has more than 300 wineries and approximately 100 cellar doors scattered around its rolling, vine-cloaked hills, and is recognised as Victoria's oldest wine region – the first vines were planted at Yering Station in 1838. The region produces cool-climate, food-friendly drops, such as chardonnay, pinot noir and pinot gris, as well as full-bodied reds.

The smaller family-run wineries are equal to the large-scale producers, offering a less pretentious experience; visit www.yarravalleysmallerwineries.com.au for a list.

Some cellars charge a fee for tasting, but this is usually redeemable upon purchase.

The epitome of a country house hotel, this slightly faded but still tempting heritage-listed hulk set in gorgeous gardens is one of the best accommodation options in the valley. Rooms are comfortable and well sized, with attractive marble bathrooms. Facilities include a tennis court, swimming pool, on-site cafe and **restaurant** (2-/3-course menus $85/98; ⏱ 6-9pm). Breakfast is eaten in the cafe.

Zonzo
ITALIAN $$

(📞 03-9730 2500; www.zonzo.com.au; 957 Healesville-Yarra Glen Rd; pizzas $24; ⏱ noon-3pm Wed-Sun & 6pm-late Fri-Sun; 🅿 ♿) Serving Italian home-style food, this eatery has superb views of the valley and a casual vibe. Order a pizza or opt for the shared menu ($50 per person) of antipasti, pizzas and a meat main. There's also a well-priced and well-pitched kids' menu. The estate's wines can be tasted in the cellar door, which was converted from old horse stables.

Yarra Valley Dairy
CHEESE, WINE $$

(📞 03-9739 0023; www.yvd.com.au; 70-80 McMeikans Rd, Yering; cheese platters from $25; ⏱ 10.30am-5pm) 🧀 This renowned cheesemaker sells creamy handmade cheeses, produce and wine from its farm gate – the ashed chevre is particularly delicious. Take part in the free cheese tasting, pick your favourites and order a platter to eat in the dairy's refurbished milking shed.

★ **Oakridge** AUSTRALIAN $$$

(☑ 03-9738 9900; www.oakridgewines.com.au; 864 Maroondah Hwy, Coldstream; 2-/3-course menus $70/85; ⊙ cellar door 10am-5pm, restaurant 11.30am-3pm Thu-Mon; P ✳ 🐾) Head here to taste Oakridge's acclaimed chardonnay in one of the most stunning cellar door set-ups in the valley (and that's really saying something). Then stay for what is probably the best food in the region. Chefs Matt Stone and Jo Barrett present assured Mod Oz menus built around local seasonal produce and the results are simply inspired. Bookings essential.

ezard at
Levantine Hill MODERN AUSTRALIAN $$$

(☑ 03-5962 1333; www.levantinehill.com.au; 882 Maroondah Hwy, Coldstream; shared plates $18-59; ⊙ 11am-5pm Wed-Fri, dinner Sat with advance reservation; P ☑) Moving outside his usual inner-Melbourne patch, multi-hatted chef Teage Ezard has collaborated with the Levantine Hill winery to open this upmarket restaurant, which has a distinctive design featuring floor-to-ceiling windows overlooking the vineyard. Opt for tasting menus in the signature restaurant (vegetarian available) or order à la carte in the more casual area, which offers both indoor and outdoor seating.

❶ Getting There & Away

The area is easily reached from Melbourne, being only an hour's drive by car along Maroondah Hwy.

Metro trains travel to Lilydale, from where McKenzies buses continue to Healesville, Coldstream, Yarra Glen and Marysville. Myki cards can be used.

A number of operators run winery tours from Melbourne.

Healesville

POP 7461

There's a lot more to Healesville than immediately meets the eye. Within its historic town centre, a swag of craft breweries and distilleries, contemporary cafes, wine bars and restaurants are waiting to be discovered. Indeed, it's not an exaggeration to say that this is one of the state's pre-eminent food and wine destinations. Other attractions include the famed Healesville Sanctuary and unsung Sandra Bardas Art Gallery, an impressive showcase of contemporary Indigenous art. Outside town, the triangular area of Lower Yarra Valley is home to gently sloped terrain where some of the region's finest wineries grow their grapes and welcome visitors to cellar doors and restaurants.

⦿ Sights

★ **Healesville Sanctuary** ZOO

(☑ 1300 966 784; www.zoo.org.au/healesville; Badger Creek Rd; adult/child 5-15 yrs/family $37/19/from $93; ⊙ 9am-5pm; P 🦽; 🚌 685 then 686 from Lilydale) One of the best places in southern Australia to see native fauna, this wildlife park is home to kangaroos, wallabies, dingoes, Tasmanian devils, echidnas, wombats and koalas. Highlights include Platypus House, where the shy underwater creatures can be observed, and the exciting Spirits of the Sky presentation, which features huge wedge-tailed eagles and colourful parrots soaring through the air (check the website for daily session times). Admission to the sanctuary for kids is free on weekends and holidays.

Sandra Bardas Art Gallery GALLERY

(☑ 03-5962 4344; www.worawa.vic.edu.au; 60-80 Barak Lane, Worawa Aboriginal College, Healesville; by donation; ⊙ by appointment; P) Located on the former site of the Corenderk Mission, a government reserve for Indigenous Victorians who had been dispossessed of their traditional lands, Worawa College is Victoria's first and only Aboriginal school. This impressive gallery on the school grounds shows and sells affordable art produced in the remote communities that many of the students come from. Also here is a Dreaming Trail of 21 white poles commemorating influential Indigenous Victorians and 38 white poles representing groups of the Kulin nation.

🛏 Sleeping

BIG4 Yarra Valley
Park Lane Holiday Park CAMPGROUND $

(☑ 03-5962 4328; www.parklaneholidayparks.com.au/yarravalley; 419 Don Rd; sites from $45, d cabins, pods & tents $195-245; P ✳ ☰) Set on a well-treed 24-hectare block that has Badger Creek running through it, this holiday park offers comfortable cabins, glamping pods and tents, en-suite caravan sites and a variety of campsites. It's a great spot for kids, with facilities including an inflatable water park in a small lake, jumping cushion and jump pad, swimming pool and tennis courts.

YARRA VALLEY CIDER & ALE TRAIL

While it's wine that brings most visitors to Yarra Valley, the **Cider & Ale Trail** (www.ciderandaletrail.com.au) will lead you on a fantastic route visiting local microbreweries and cider producers. Melbourne-based **Aussie Brewery Tours** (☑ 1300 787 039; www.aussiebrewerytours.com.au; tour incl transport, lunch & tastings $160; ☺ Wed-Mon) offers popular day trips. Breweries, brewpubs and cideries to visit include the following:

Buckley's Beer (☑ 0466 823 808; www.buckleysbeer.com.au; 30 Hunter Rd; ☺ 11am-5pm Sat & Sun; ☖ 685 from Lilydale) 🍃, Healesville

Hargreaves Hill Brewing Co (☑ 03-9730 1905; www.hargreaveshill.com.au; 25 Bell St, Yarra Glen; ☺ 11.30am-8pm Mon-Sat, to 4pm Sun; ☖ 685 from Lilydale)

Napoleone Brewery & Ciderhouse (☑ 03-9738 9100; www.napoleonecider.com.au; 12 St Huberts Rd, Coldstream; ☺ 10am-5pm)

Kellybrook Winery & Distillery (☑ 03-9722 1304; www.kellybrookwinery.com.au; Fulford Rd, Wonga Park; tastings $5; ☺ 10am-5pm Fri-Mon)

Coldstream Brewery (☑ 03-9739 1794; www.coldstreambrewery.com.au; 694 Maroondah Hwy, Coldstream; ☺ 11am-late; ♿)

Watts River Brewing (☑ 03-5962 1409; www.wattsriverbrewing.com.au; 7 Hunter Rd; ☺ 11am-5pm Thu, Sun & Mon, to 9pm Fri & Sat; ☗; ☖ 685 from Lilydale), Healesville

Yering Farm (☑ 03-9739 0461; www.yeringfarmwines.com; 19-21 St Huberts Rd, Yering; ☺ 10am-5pm) Produces apple cider and juice as well as wines.

Healesville Hotel
HOTEL **$**

(☑ 03-5962 4002; www.yarravalleyharvest.com.au; 256 Maroondah Hwy; d without bathroom $115-195; ☀☗; ☖ 685 from Lilydale) This restored 1910 hotel in Healesville's main street offers attractive rooms on the floor above the bar and restaurant; some have sinks and all share a spotless bathroom at the end of the corridor. The hotel also manages chic en-suite apartments behind the hotel in Furmston House (double from $190). No breakfast, but there are plenty of cafes nearby.

Tuck Inn
B&B **$$**

(☑ 03-5962 3600; www.tuckinn.com.au; 2 Church St; d week/weekend incl breakfast from $160/180; ℗☀☗; ☖ 685 from Lilydale) This former Masonic lodge in the centre of town has been refitted as a contemporary guesthouse with a lovely communal lounge/dining room where a generous breakfast is served. Guest rooms are light and airy, albeit frills-free; opt for the king-sized options as the queen-sized alternatives are cramped. No children under 14 years.

✖ Eating

★ Habituel
CAFE **$**

(☑ 03-5957 3230; www.habituel.com.au; 314 Maroondah Hwy; sandwiches $14-16; ☺ 7am-4pm; ☀☗♿; ☖ 685 from Lilydale) Its name is taken from the French term *L'habituel* (the things one does every day), and this excellent cafe does everyday things, such as coffee and sandwiches, extremely well. Of note are the brews made with small-batch, house-roasted beans; sandwiches made with house-baked natural levin sourdough; and quality reading matter (*New York Review of Books*, *Guardian Weekly*) provided for customers.

★ Healesville Hotel
MODERN AUSTRALIAN **$$**

(☑ 03-5962 4002; www.yarravalleyharvest.com.au; 256 Maroondah Hwy; mains $26-39; ☺ noon-9pm; ☗; ☖ 685 from Lilydale) One of the area's culinary showstoppers, historic Healesville Hotel is split into a formal dining room and a casual front bar – the same delicious Mod Oz menu featuring top-quality local and imported produce is served in both spaces. On spring and summer weekends a popular wood-fired BBQ spread is on offer in the hotel garden ($28 per person, from noon).

★ Giant Steps
MODERN AUSTRALIAN, WINE **$$**

(☑ 03-5962 6111; www.giantstepswine.com.au; 336 Maroondah Hwy; mains $16-32; ☺ 11am-6pm Mon-Wed, to 9pm Thu-Sun; ℗☀☗♿☗; ☖ 685 from Lilydale) Known for both its cellar door and buzzing restaurant, this slick operation takes the quality of its food and wine seriously and is a great choice for a casual meal. The pizza menu is authentically Italian, with *rosso* (red) and *bianco* (white) options, and the wood-grilled meats are satisfyingly succulent. Top marks go to the ultra-affordable kids' menu ($8 to $9).

🍷 Drinking & Nightlife

★ Four Pillars
DISTILLERY

(☑03-5962 2791; www.fourpillarsgin.com.au; 2a Lilydale Rd; ☺10.30am-5.30pm Sun-Thu, to 9pm Fri & Sat; 🚍685 from Lilydale) The heady aroma of spices and botanicals greets visitors to this hugely successful gin distillery. You can watch the unusual range of gins being made while enjoying a tasting ($10) or G&T paddle ($12). Enthusiastic staff members will explain the distilling process on request.

Alchemy Distillers
DISTILLERY

(☑0434 446 387; www.alchemydistillers.com; 242 Maroondah Hwy; ☺11am-6pm Thu & Sun, to 9pm Fri & Sat; 🚍685 from Lilydale) Adding to Healesville's reputation as a centre of excellence for craft beer and liquors, this boutique distillery in a laneway off the main street concocts intriguing tipples including chamomile gin, quinoa vodka and knock-your-socks-off moonshine. Head here on Saturdays in summer, when musicians play in the small courtyard and locals down the house spirits and Victorian beers and wines with alacrity.

🛍 Shopping

★ Kitchen & Butcher
FOOD

(☑03-5962 2866; www.yarravalleyharvest.com.au; 258 Maroondah Hwy; ☺9.30am-6pm Mon-Fri, from 9am Sat, 10am-5pm Sun; 🚍685 from Lilydale) Melbourne is well-endowed with gourmet delis, but it's not unheard of for its residents to make the trek to this wonderful shop when their pantry shelves need to be reprovisioned. The selection of Australian and European cheeses and cured meats is particularly noteworthy, but the jams, sauces, ready-made meals and other comestibles on offer are also highly desirable.

ⓘ Getting There & Away

Healesville is 65km north of Melbourne, an easy one-hour drive via the Eastern Fwy and Maroondah Hwy/B360.

McKenzie's Bus Lines (☑03-5962 5088; www.mckenzies.com.au) operates a daily wheelchair-accessible V/Line bus service from Melbourne's Southern Cross station to Healesville (1½ hours, $12.46) en route to Marysville and Eildon; check website for schedule. The company also runs regular Metro bus services to/from Lilydale Train Station (30 minutes, $4.30). Myki cards can be used for both trips.

Marysville & Lake Mountain
POP 394

Located in the foothills of Lake Mountain and surrounded by the towering mountain ashes, majestic waterfalls and scenic lookouts of Marysville State Forest, this little town has a proud history as a holiday retreat – Melburnians have been holidaying here since the 1860s, and by the 1920s the town was known as Melbourne's honeymoon capital. Despite losing much of its historic fabric in the 2009 Black Saturday fires, it's still a popular holiday destination due to the natural beauty of its surroundings and its proximity to the cross-country ski fields, high-adrenaline mountain-bike trails and summer wildflowers on Lake Mountain.

Part of Yarra Ranges National Park, family-friendly **Lake Mountain** (1433m) is the premier cross-country skiing resort in Australia, with 37km of trails and several toboggan runs. It's almost as popular outside the ski season, when hikers, road cyclists and mountain bike riders take to its wildflower-edged trails and roads.

◉ Sights & Activities

Phoenix Museum
MUSEUM

(Black Saturday Museum; www.blacksaturdaymuseum.com; 11 Murchison St; $5; ☺10am-4pm; Ⓟ; 🚍684 from Lilydale) Housed in the Marysville Information & Regional Artspace (p524) (MIRA), this sobering exhibition shows the devastating impact the 2009 Black Saturday bushfires had on the town. Displays include photos, video footage and salvaged artefacts.

Steavenson Falls
WATERFALL

(Falls Rd) Spectacular Steavenson Falls is one of Victoria's highest waterfalls (84m). A viewing platform beneath the falls spans Steavenson River. To get here, drive to Steavenson Falls car park 3km southeast of the town centre, or follow the **Tree Fern Gully Trail**, a scenic 3.4km one-way walk from the heart of town to the base of the falls.

Keppel Lookout Trail
WALKING

The 15km Keppel Lookout Trail is a well-signed but challenging walk that climbs up through a mountain ash and stringybark forest, passing lookouts across Marysville, Cathedral Range State Park and Steavenson Falls. Most people start the walk from Marysville Information & Regional Artspace (p524), where it is possible to park cars.

🛏 Sleeping

Marysville Garden Cottages COTTAGE $

(☑03-5774 7664; www.marysvillegardencottages. com.au; 2 Barton Ave; d $150-260; 🚍684 from Lilydale) These eight garden cottages have an old-fashioned ambience; features in each can include claw-foot baths, window seats, timber floors, stained-glass windows and gas log fires. All have kitchenettes and lounge areas. No children, no breakfast and no reception.

Black Spur Inn INN $

(☑03-5963 7121; www.blackspurinn.com.au; 436 Maroondah Hwy, Narbethong; d cabins $110-125, d rooms $165-210; ⊘restaurant noon-3pm & 5.30-7.30pm Mon-Fri, to 8.30pm Sat & Sun; P❄�🈂) Just the kind of place every weary traveller hopes to stumble upon, this 1863 inn is set in forest 14km from Marysville. The main building has comfortable but bland rooms and there are basic cabins out the back. The atmospheric bar and restaurant (mains $25 to $38) has a roaring fireplace that's perfect for winter meals.

🍴 Eating & Drinking

Elevation 423 INTERNATIONAL $$

(☑03-5963 3312, 0422 620 871; www.elevation 423marysville.com.au; 41 Murchison St; mains $18-33; ⊘noon-9pm; 🚍684 from Lilydale) Named for Marysville's elevation above sea level in metres, this family-run cafe, bar and restaurant rates higher than most of its town competitors when it comes to friendliness and menu diversity. There are plenty of Indian-style dishes, including a rich goat curry, as well as pizzas, Singapore-style noodles and Middle Eastern dips. Vegan, vegetarian, MSG-free and halal options available.

Fraga's Café Restaurant CAFE $$

(☑03-5963 3216; www.facebook.com/FragasCafe; 19 Murchison St; mains $10-29; ⊘9am-4pm

BLACK SATURDAY

Victoria is no stranger to bushfires. In 1939, 71 people died in Black Friday fires; in 1983 Ash Wednesday claimed 75 lives in Victoria and South Australia. But no one was prepared for the utter devastation of the 2009 bushfires that became known as Black Saturday.

On 7 February, 2009, Victoria recorded some of its hottest temperatures on record, with Melbourne exceeding 46°C and some parts of the state topping 48°C. Strong winds and tinder-dry undergrowth from years of drought, combined with the record-high temperatures, created conditions in which the risk of bushfires was extreme. The first recorded fires began near Kilmore and strong winds from a southerly change fanned the flames towards the Yarra Ranges. Within a few devastating hours a ferocious firestorm engulfed the tiny bush towns of Marysville, Kinglake, Strathewen, Flowerdale and Narbethong, while separate fires started at Horsham, Bendigo and an area southeast of Beechworth. The fires virtually razed the towns of Marysville and Kinglake, and moved so quickly that many residents had no chance to escape. Many victims of the fires died in their homes or were trapped in their cars, some blocked by trees that had fallen across the road.

Fires raged across the state for more than a month, with high temperatures, winds and practically no rainfall making it impossible for fire crews to contain the worst blazes. New fires began at Wilsons Promontory National Park (burning more than 50% of the park area), Dandenong Ranges and in the Daylesford area.

The statistics tell a tragic tale: 173 people died, more than 2000 homes were destroyed, an estimated 7500 people were left homeless and more than 4500 sq km were burned. What followed from the shell-shocked state and nation was a huge outpouring of grief, humanitarian aid and charity. Strangers donated tonnes of clothing, toys, food, caravans and even houses to bushfire survivors, while an appeal set up by the Australian Red Cross raised more than $300 million.

Today the blackened forests around Kinglake and Marysville have regenerated, and the communities are still rebuilding. Tourism remains a big part of the economy, and visiting the shops, cafes and hotels in the area continues to boost their recovery.

Mon-Fri, to 4.30pm Sat & Sun; 🚌684 from Lilydale) Generally acknowledged as the home of Marysville's best coffee (beans from Great Divide Roastery), this bustling cafe on the main strip has a large outdoor area where regulars enjoy hearty breakfasts of free-range eggs and Thornton smoked bacon, and lunches featuring local specialities such as smoked Buxton trout.

The Duck Inn
PUB

(📞03-5963 3437; www.facebook.com/theduck innmarysvillepub; 6 Murchison St; ⊙11am-11pm; 🚻; 🚌684 from Lilydale) Rebuilt after being destroyed during Black Saturday, the town's much-loved pub has a bar with local beers on tap, a pool table and a bistro serving a menu of pub classics with a few gluten-free and vegetarian wildcards thrown into the mix (mains $17 to $35). It's very family friendly.

❶ Information

Marysville Information & Regional Artspace
(MIRA; 📞03-5963 4567; www.marysvilletourism.com; 11 Murchison St; ⊙10am-4pm; 🛜; 🚌684 from Lilydale) This modern complex houses an information centre staffed by enthusiastic and knowlegeable volunteers, an art gallery, an events space and the Phoenix Museum (p522). It provides information, maps and brochures; free wi-fi; and clean toilets.

Lake Mountain Alpine Resort
(📞03-5957 7201, snow sports 03-5957 7256; www.lakemountainresort.com.au; 1071 Lake Mountain Rd; car entry in ski season $56; ⊙8am-4.30pm early Jun–mid-Sep, to 4pm Mon-Fri mid-Sep–early Jun) Offers general info and daily hire of ski equipment ($35.50), snowshoes (adult/child $25/30) and toboggans (adult/child $45/50). A one-hour ski lesson costs adult/child $70/65 including all-day equipment hire. Mountain bikes can be hired in the green season from Lake Mountain Café (📞03-5957 7201; www.lakemountainresort.com.au; Lake Mountain Alpine Resort; mains $12; ⊙9.30am-4.30pm Fri-Sun Oct–Dec & Feb–mid-Jun, 10am-5pm daily mid-Jun–Oct & Jan) (half/full day $25/50 including helmet); bike trails are closed during ski season.

❶ Getting There & Away

Marysville is 100km from Melbourne, a 1½-hour drive via Maroondah Hwy. It's a 40-minute drive from Healesville via a beautiful drive over Black Spur; look out for lyrebirds on the way.

McKenzie's Bus Line (p522) runs a daily service to/from Melbourne ($12.46, 2¼ hours) via Marysville and Healesville.

Daylesford & Hepburn Springs
POP DAYLESFORD 2548, HEPBURN SPRINGS 329

Marketed as the 'spa centre of Victoria', this couplet of conjoined towns is a hugely popular weekend getaway for Melburnians. Set among the scenic hills, lakes and forests of Central Highlands, it's a fabulous year-round destination where you can soak away your troubles in warm, mineral-rich waters and dine in some of regional Victoria's best eateries. The local population is an interesting blend of New Agers, urbanites and down-to-earth farmers. There's also a thriving gay and lesbian scene here.

The health-giving properties of the area's mineral springs were first claimed in the 1870s, attracting droves of fashionable Melburnians. The well-preserved and restored buildings show the prosperity of these towns, as well as the lasting influence of the many Swiss-Italian miners who came to work the tunnel mines in the surrounding hills.

◎ Sights & Activities

Hepburn Mineral Springs Reserve
NATURE RESERVE

(Mineral Springs Reserve Rd; ⊙24hr) **FREE** Located in Hepburn Springs, this 30-hectare nature reserve is known for its historic bathhouse (📞03-5321 6000; www.hepburnbathhouse.com; Mineral Springs Reserve Rd, Hepburn Springs; 2hr bathhouse entry Tue-Thu/Fri-Mon adult $42/52, child $24/27; ⊙9am-6.30pm Mon-Thu, to 9pm Fri, from 8am Sat, to 6.30pm Sun), which allows you to gaze out on the bush setting while soaking in the public pool and has a spa offering various treatments or a soak in a private mineral-springs pool. The Reserve is also home to the Soda, Sulphur, Locano, Wyuna and Argyle mineral springs; pumps at each let you fill your water bottles. There are also picnic spots, BBQ areas, children's playgrounds and walking trails.

Convent Gallery
GALLERY

(📞03-5348 3211; www.conventgallery.com.au; 7 Daly St, Daylesford; $5; ⊙10am-4pm) Surrounded by pretty, flower-filled gardens, the 19th-century Holy Cross Convent on Wombat Hill now functions as an art gallery. Its **Bad Habits Café** (www.theconvent.com.au; high tea adult/child $49/39 weekdays, $65/55 weekends; ⊙10am-3.30pm; 🖊🚻) and a huge gift shop take up much of the ground floor,

MELBOURNE & VICTORIA DAYLESFORD & HEPBURN SPRINGS

and accommodation is offered in a spacious penthouse apartment (d including breakfast $350). Head up the garden path behind the convent for sweeping views over the town. On winter weekends, ghost tours are occasionally held.

Wombat
Discovery Tours WILDLIFE WATCHING
(☑ 0484 792 212; www.wombatdiscoverytours.com.au; tours adult/child from $35/20; ☺ Saturday evening) These night tours in Wombat State Forest are a wonderful opportunity to spot Australian wildlife in its natural habitat (as opposed to enclosures). You're likely to see wombats, kangaroos and wallabies, along with the occasional koala, echidna and glider. Group tours are held on Saturday nights; private tours ($350) can be arranged at other times. Rates include pick-up from Daylesford.

🛏 Sleeping

Mt Franklin Campground CAMPGROUND
(www.parkweb.vic.gov.au) `FREE` An excellent option for budget travellers and campers is this free short-term camping on top of Mt Franklin's volcanic crater, 10km north of Hepburn Springs. There are toilets, fireplaces for cooking and water for washing, but you'll need to bring drinking water and everything else. No reservations, so it's first come, first served. It gets busy during holidays.

2 Dukes GUESTHOUSE $
(☑ 03-5348 4848; www.2dukesdaylesford.com; 2 Duke St, Daylesford; r with shared bathroom from $99; P ✳ 🛜) Flying the flag for affordable accommodation in Daylesford is this clean and comfortable former doctor's surgery turned guesthouse, which is kitted out with vintage finds and original bright artworks. The five rooms each have their own personalities and share bathrooms. A communal lounge and kitchen are available. Breakfast is not provided and children are not welcome.

★**Lake House** BOUTIQUE HOTEL $$$
(☑ 03-5348 3329; www.lakehouse.com.au; King St, Daylesford; d incl half board from $670, ste from $930; ✳ 🛜) Regularly nominated as Victoria's best regional hotel, this boutique choice overlooking Lake Daylesford is set in rambling gardens featuring bridges and waterfalls. Accommodation is offered in studios, suites and a villa, some of which have lake views. Rates include breakfast and a three-course dinner at the Lake House (p526) restaurant; facilities include a tennis court, library, bar, and spa with sauna.

★**Holyrood House** B&B $$$
(☑ 03-5348 1063; www.holyrooddaylesford.com.au; 51 Stanbridge St, Daylesford; r $325-495; P 🛜) A boutique B&B in a pretty timber house in the centre of town, Holyrood gets rave reviews for its many added extras, which include Floris toiletries, a lavish à la carte breakfast, elegant afternoon teas and pre-dinner drinks with cheese. The six rooms feature top-quality alpaca blankets, open fires and antique furniture. It's deservedly popular, so book well in advance.

★**Clifftop at Hepburn** VILLA $$$
(☑ 1300 112 114; www.clifftopathepburn.com.au; 209-219 Main Rd, Hepburn; d $395-483, extra person $126; P 🛜) Three villas with kitchens, laundries and fireplaces have been joined by four chalets converted from shipping containers, with kitchenettes and fireplaces. The villas sleep up to four (children welcome), while the shipping containers sleep two (no children permitted). There are also en-suite glamping tents available. Basic breakfast supplies are included; there's a two-night minimum stay on weekends.

Shizuka Ryokan GUESTHOUSE $$$
(☑ 03-5348 2030; www.shizuka.com.au; 7 Lakeside Dr, Hepburn Springs; d $265-389; 🛜) Inspired by traditional places of renewal and rejuvenation in Japan, this spa getaway has six rooms surrounding a serene Zen garden. Each room has tatami matting and futon bedding. Host and Japanophile Catherine offers a traditional Japanese or continental breakfast (included) as well as multi-course dinners three nights per week ($90 per person). Children are not welcome.

🍴 Eating

★**Pancho** CAFE $
(www.panchocafe.com.au; 117 Vincent St, Daylesford; mains $12-18; ☺ 7.30am-3.30pm Mon & Wed-Fri, 8am-4pm Sat & Sun; 🛜 🍴 🐾) Daylesford's best coffee, made using Wide Open Road beans and Inglenook Dairy milk, is served here. It's the perfect accompaniment to the all-day breakfast dishes on offer, but there are also salads, soups and filled rolls at lunch – all made with local produce. Grab a table upstairs, downstairs or in the dog-friendly courtyard.

★ Blue Bean Cafe
CAFE $$

(☎03-5348 2297; www.facebook.com/bluebean hepburn; 115 Main Rd, Hepburn Springs; mains $16-24; ⊙8am-3pm Mon-Thu, to 9pm Fri-Sun; 🛜🍴🦽) The Bluebeanies take their coffee seriously, offering a weekly rotating single-origin coffee alongside a crowd-pleasing menu of breakfast dishes, light lunch dishes and ever-popular Devonshire teas ($12). Burgers, steaks and vegan options are offered for dinner Friday to Sunday, when live music is staged (6pm to 8pm) and plenty of local craft beer and cider is poured. Kids love the toy corner.

Surly Goat
BISTRO $$

(☑03-5348 4628; www.thesurlygoat.com.au; 3 Tenth St, Hepburn Springs; shared plates $12-32; ⊙from 6pm Wed & Thu, noon-3.30pm & from 6pm Fri & Sat, noon-3.30pm Sun; 🦽) Just off the main road in the heart of Hepburn Springs, this contemporary bistro has a deceiving name, as no one seems at all cranky. At lunch, $40 gets you a two-course meal and glass of wine. At night, the à la carte menu offers a tantalising array of globally diverse dishes – from pigs-ear croquettes to mussels marinière and baba ganoush.

Wombat Hill House
CAFE $$

(☑03-4373 0099; www.wombathillhouse.com.au; Wombat Hill Botanic Gardens, off Central Springs Rd, Daylesford; mains $15-23; ⊙9am-4pm Thu-Mon; 🅿🍴🦽) Associated with Lake House, this cute cafe in Wombat Hill Botanic Gardens is popular for breakfast and lunch. Sit near the fireplace in winter or in the kitchen garden in summer. There's high tea from 2pm ($40 per person) and picnic lunch hampers are available ($59 to $95 for two). Advance booking is required for the high tea and hampers.

Farmers Arms
PUB FOOD $$

(☑03-5348 2091; www.thefarmersarms.com.au; 1 East St, Daylesford; mains $22-46; ⊙noon-10pm) Modern and rustic surroundings and food meld tastefully in this classic corner pub. There's a welcoming front bar with a beer garden for summer days. The attractive rear dining room serves a menu of Aussie pub classics with a few global wildcard dishes thrown in to spice up the culinary action. There's a good list of wines by the glass.

★ Lake House
MODERN AUSTRALIAN $$$

(☑03-5348 3329; www.lakehouse.com.au; 4 King St, Daylesford; 3-/4-course à la carte menus $130/155; ⊙noon-2.30pm & 6-9pm; 🅿❄🛜🍴) You can't talk about Daylesford without waxing lyrical about Alla Wolf Tasker's Lake House restaurant, long regarded as the region's top dining experience. It features picture windows showing off Lake Daylesford, a superb seasonal menu, an award-winning wine list and impressive service. Book well ahead for weekends.

🍺 Drinking & Nightlife

★ Old Hepburn Hotel
PUB

(☑03-5348 2207; www.oldhepburnhotel.com.au; 236 Main Rd, Hepburn Springs; ⊙5pm-11pm Mon, Thu & Fri, noon-late Sat & Sun; 🛜) A country pub with both character and taste, Old Hepburn makes for a great night out with live music on weekends (usually free). The pub food hits the spot, and it has a ripper beer garden. Monday night is parma night; on Thursday night burgers take centre stage.

It's a bit out of town, but there's a courtesy bus from Daylesford and Hepburn Springs if you book for dinner.

Daylesford Cider
CIDER HOUSE

(☑03-5348 2275; www.daylesfordcider.com.au; 155 Dairy Flat Rd, Musk; ⊙11am-4pm Wed-Fri, 10am-5pm Sat & Sun; 🦽🐾) A 10-minute drive east of Daylesford, this sweet-smelling cider house produces English-style ciders from the 17 heritage-listed varieties of apples grown on its organic orchard. Opt for a tasting paddle ($15) to sample the seven varieties produced here or order a glass ($7 to $10) and enjoy it in the outdoor courtyard or inside by the fire.

Palais-Hepburn
CABARET

(☑02-5348 1000; www.palais-hepburn.com; 111 Main Rd, Hepburn Springs; ⊙hours vary) Dating from 1926, this iconic venue has recently been restored. It re-opened in 2018 in time to host performances during the **World Circus & Cabaret Festival** (www.worldcircuscabaretfestival.com; ⊙mid-Nov) and its stated aim is to become one of regional Victoria's major live-music venues. The lounge bar is a lovely spot for a drink before or after performances.

🔒 Shopping

Daylesford is jam-packed with shops selling antiques as well as vintage and new-age paraphernalia. The long-standing **Daylesford Sunday Market** (www.facebook.com/daylesfordmarket; 18 Raglan St; ⊙8am-1.30pm Sun; 🦽🐾) FREE at the old train station is one of the state's most popular street markets.

WORTH A TRIP

HANGING ROCK

An ancient and evocative feature in the landscape, the extinct volcano formation known as **Hanging Rock** (☑03-5421 1468, 1800 244 711; www.mrsc.vic.gov.au/See-Do/Our-Region/Natural-Attractions/Hanging-Rock; South Rock Rd; per vehicle/pedestrian or cyclist $10/4; ⊙9am-5pm, later hours apply in high summer; P⊞🛝) is a sacred site for its traditional owners, the Wurundjeri people, but everyone is welcome to take the strenuous 50-minute climb up and down the path to the 1800m summit. Many myths and legends surround the rock – the most enduring being its association with the Joan Lindsay novel *Picnic at Hanging Rock* – and many feel an eerie energy when they visit here.

Joan Lindsay's novel was written in 1967 and was subsequently made into a hugely successful film by Australian director Peter Weir in 1975. It chronicles the lead-up and fallout from the disappearance of a group of schoolgirls at the rock on Valentine's Day in 1900. Though entirely fictional, the story has become folkloric since its publication and many visitors to the rock feel as if they are following in the actual footsteps of Miranda and the other girls.

The walk-through **Hanging Rock Discovery Centre** explains the rock's history and geology. Although there is a cafe on-site, most visitors choose to emulate the schoolgirls and bring a picnic; there are plenty of picnic tables and a number of gas barbecues that are free to use.

The rock is a 10-minute drive from the lovely town of Woodend or a 15-minute drive from Kyneton (p580). There's no public transport; a taxi from the railway station in Woodend will cost around $40 one way, or about $50 from the station in Kyneton.

ℹ Information

Daylesford Visitor Centre (☑03-5321 6123, 1800 454 891; www.visitdaylesford.com; 98 Vincent St; ⊙9am-5pm) Located within an old fire station, this excellent tourist centre has good information on the area and mineral springs. It also has a self-guided walking-tour map for Daylesford. There's a history **museum** (☑03-5348 1453; www.daylesfordhistory.com.au; 100 Vincent St; adult/child $4/1; ⊙1.30-4.30pm Sat & Sun) next door too.

ℹ Getting There & Away

Daylesford is 115km from Melbourne, a 1½-hour drive via the National Hwy (M8) and Ballan-Daylesford Rd.

Daily **V/Line** (☑1800 800 007; www.vline.com.au) train and coach services connect Melbourne by train to Woodend, from where there's a coach to Daylesford ($5.20, 45 minutes, two daily). The buses run from Bridport St opposite the fire station.

Local buses operate the 3km journey between Daylesford (from Bridport St) and Hepburn Springs ($2.40); it's a 10- to 15-minute journey.

Mornington Peninsula

A string of communities curling around the southeastern flank of Port Phillip Bay to Western Port Bay, the Mornington Peninsula (traditionally Boon Wurrung country)

is a favourite summer holiday patch for beach-loving Melburnians. Truth be told, the road along the rocky stretch of Port Phillip Bay foreshore that stretches south from Mornington to Rye doesn't highlight the Peninsula's many beauty spots. Along Point Nepean Rd, suburban shopping strips house a battalion of takeaway food shops that service the thousands of daytripping families who head to the bay's beaches in summer – fortunately the beaches themselves are attractive, clean and safe.

At the tip of the peninsula, a world of rugged ocean surf beaches, sublime links golf courses and coastal bushwalks opens up. Away from the coast, the peninsula's interior is a wine- and food-lover's paradise, with an ever-growing number of cellar doors and some of Victoria's finest restaurants. Away to the east, it's a short ferry ride to wild and isolated French Island and then on to Phillip Island, one of Victoria's premier tourist attractions.

◉ Sights & Activities

★**Point Nepean National Park** NATIONAL PARK
(www.parkweb.vic.gov.au/explore/parks/point-nepean-national-park; Point Nepean Rd; ⊙8am-5pm, to 6pm late Dec-Mar; P; 🚌788 from Frankston) Commanding expansive ocean

DON'T MISS

PENINSULA HOT SPRINGS

There are lots of spas and massage centres popping up along the peninsula, but none is better than the **Peninsula Hot Springs** (☑03-5950 8777; www.peninsulahotsprings.com; Springs Lane, Fingal; bathhouse adult/child Mon-Fri $45/25, Sat & Sun $55/35; ☺bathhouse 7am-10pm). This large and luxurious complex utilises hot, mineral-rich waters pumped from deep underground. There's a huge menu of spa, private bathing and massage treatments and packages available, or you can just relax in the bathhouse. Bookings essential.

views, this windswept national park on the peninsula's western tip was a seasonal base of its traditional owners, the Boon Wurrung people. After colonisation, a Quarantine Station was established here in 1852. **Fort Nepean** (☺8am-5pm, to 6pm late Dec-Mar), which played an important role in defending Australia from military threat, was built in stages from the late 1870s. Original gun emplacements remain there, as do the 50-odd heritage buildings that made up the Quarantine Station.

Arthurs Seat Eagle CABLE CAR
(☑03-5987 0600; www.aseagle.com.au; 795 Arthurs Seat Rd, Arthurs Seat; adult/child one way $17.50/11, return $24/15; ☺10am-4pm, extended hours late spring, summer & autumn) Climb aboard one of the modern Swiss-built gondolas on this iconic chairlift to enjoy an all-encompassing view stretching as far as Melbourne's city skyline and even to Mt Macedon. While most opt for return tickets, the trek back down (45 minutes) is along a steep but scenic route through state forest.

The base station is at 1085 Arthurs Seat Rd in Dromana; you can start your journey there or from the summit.

★**Mornington Peninsula National Park** NATIONAL PARK
(www.parkweb.vic.gov.au/explore/parks/mornington-peninsula-national-park) Stretching from Portsea along a long sliver of coastline to Cape Schanck and then inland to the Greens Bush area, this national park showcases the peninsula's most beautiful and rugged coastline, including spectacular surf beaches. The traditional land of the Boon

Wurrung, who gathered shellfish and other foods along this coastline for thousands of years, the park has colonial additions including the picturesque **Cape Schanck Lighthouse** (☑0407 348 478; www.facebook.com/lighthousecapeschanck; 420 Cape Schanck Lighthouse Rd; tours incl museum & lighthouse adult/child/family $13/7/38; ☺select weekends; ♿), built in 1859.

Bass & Flinders DISTILLERY
(☑03-5989 3154; www.bassandflindersdistillery.com; 40 Collins Rd, Dromana; ☺11am-5pm Fri-Sun; ℗) Drop by this boutique distillery to taste its range of unique gins, which includes everything from the likeable Smooth & Soft to Angry Ant – distilled using botanicals sourced from outback WA and infused with bull-ant pheromone! Tasting flights cost from $15. The distillery also offers gin master classes ($160 per person) where you can make up your own batch from a choice of botanicals.

☆ Entertainment

Dromana Drive-In CINEMA
(☑03-5987 2492, office 03-5931 0022; www.dromanadrivein.com.au; 133 Nepean Hwy, Dromana; adult/child $17/11; ☺7.30pm & 10pm Thu-Sun) A relic of the 1960s, when there were more than 330 drive-in cinemas across Australia, this National Trust-listed drive-in cinema is one of just a handful that remains open. It's greatly loved by local residents who came here as children in the family sedan to watch films in their pyjamas on sultry summer evenings. There's also deckchair seating.

ⓘ Information

Peninsula Visitor Information Centre
(☑03-5950 1579, 1800 804 009; www.visitmorningtonpeninsula.org; 359b Nepean Hwy, Dromana; ☺9am-5pm; ☎) The visitor information centre along the peninsula can book accommodation and tours, and stocks an abundance of brochures.

Point Nepean Visitor Information Centre
(☑03-8427 2099; www.parkweb.vic.gov.au/explore/parks/point-nepean-national-park; Quarantine Station; ☺10am-1pm & 1.30-4pm) This information point in the Quarantine Station at Point Nepean National Park supplies advice and walking maps, and also rents out bikes.

Love the Pen (www.lovethepen.com.au) Has a website offering food reviews, along with local tips and experiences.

ℹ Getting There & Away

The fastest way to Mornington Peninsula is via the tollway Eastlink (M3) and exiting at the Mornington Peninsula Fwy (M11) via Peninsula Link. Point Nepean Rd (B110) also feeds into the Mornington Peninsula Fwy (M11), the main peninsula access. Alternatively, exit Moorooduc Hwy to Mornington and take the coast road around Port Phillip Bay.

Frequent Metro trains run from Melbourne to Frankston, Hastings and Stony Point.

BOAT

Westernport Ferries (☑ 03-5257 4565; www. westernportferries.com.au; adult/child/bicycle return $26/12/8) Runs between Stony Point and Cowes via French Island.

Queenscliff–Sorrento Ferry (☑ 03-5257 4500; www.searoad.com.au; foot or car passenger 1-way adult/child $13/9, driver & car 1-way/return $67/124; ⊙ hourly 7am-6pm, to 7pm Jan & long weekends) Sails between Sorrento and Queenscliff, enabling you to cross Port Phillip Bay by car or bicycle.

BUS

Ventura Bus Lines (☑ 03-9771 4300; www. venturabus.com.au) Offers public transport across the peninsula.

788 From Frankston to Portsea via Mornington, Dromana and Sorrento.

786 From Rye to St Andrews Beach.

787 From Dromana to Sorrento.

782 From Frankston train station to Flinders via Hastings and Balnarring.

Sorrento

POP 1592

As charming as its namesake on the Italian Riviera, Sorrento wears its history with pride, carefully maintaining its historic limestone buildings and reminding visitors that this was the first place in Victoria settled by Europeans (in 1803). It's also a place of great natural beauty, with ocean and bay beaches, stands of Norfolk pines and a pretty-as-a-picture jetty. Heaving with visitors in summer, it remains relatively busy year-round and is an excellent base if you're exploring the Peninsula.

🛏 Sleeping

Sorrento Foreshore Camping Ground　　　CAMPGROUND $
(☑ 03-5950 1011; www.mornpen.vic.gov.au/ activities/camping; Nepean Hwy; unpowered sites $26-50, powered sites $40-56; ⊙ late Oct-Apr; P; ☑ 788 from Frankston) Hilly, bush-clad sites

between the bay beach and the main road into Sorrento.

Hotel Sorrento　　　HERITAGE HOTEL $$
(☑ 03-5984 8000; www.hotelsorrento.com.au; 5-15 Hotham Rd, Sorrento; d weekdays/weekends from $150/195, apt weekdays/weekends from $250/295; P✳🛜; ☑ 788 from Frankston) Dating from 1871, the legendary Hotel Sorrento has well-equipped rooms in the main building and 'On the Hill' double and family apartments in an adjoining modern block. The latter have airy living spaces, spacious bathrooms and private balconies with water views. The pub also has great views and is a good spot for a drink. Breakfast costs $25.

🍴 Eating & Drinking

Hotel Sorrento is the only one of the town's historic pubs currently operating, although the Continental on Ocean Beach Rd is undergoing a major renovation and is due to reopen in 2020. **Sorrento Brewhouse** (☑ 03-5972 2483; www.sorrentobrewhouse.com. au; 154-164 Ocean Beach Rd; burger with chips $20; ⊙ noon-3pm & 5.30-9.30pm) has stepped into the breach, and is a popular drinking spot.

★**Bistro Elba**　　　AUSTRALIAN $$
(☑ 03-5984 4995; www.bistroelba.com.au; 100-102 Ocean Beach Rd; mains $30-38; ⊙ noon-9.30pm; 🛜; ☑ 788 from Frankston) Its name references the sun-kissed Tuscan island, and Bistro Elba's menu reflects this Mediterranean inspiration. Stylishly casual, it's undoubtedly Sorrento's best eatery and is sure to offer something to suit most palates. There's a fixed-price lunch of a main with glass of wine ($29.50) and a popular happy hour when freshly shucked oysters are half price. Excellent wine list.

Itali.co　　　ITALIAN $$
(☑ 03-5984 4004; www.italicosorrento.com; 1 Esplanade; mains $9.50-27; ⊙ 8am-3pm & 5pm-late Mon-Fri, 8am-late Sat & Sun; ✳🖐; ☑ 788 from Frankston) Located within a heritage 1878 building on Sorrento's Esplanade, this noisy, family-friendly pizzeria offers filled *piadine* (Italian flatbread) and panini during the day. It's best loved for the Neapolitan-style pizzas and assorted pastas and risottos that fly out of the open kitchen at night and are perfect washed down with a Peroni or two.

Red Hill & Around

POP 924

The undulating hills around Red Hill and Main Ridge are a real highlight of Mornington Peninsula. The centre of the region's viticulture and wine-making industries, this area is also home to farm gates, boutique cheese factories and tempting cafes. You can spend a sublime afternoon visiting cellar doors, restaurants and local producers before bunking down in a luxurious boutique hotel for the night. Life doesn't get much better.

🛏 Sleeping

Point Leo Foreshore Reserve   CAMPGROUND $
(☑03-5989 8333; www.pointleo.com; 1 Point Leo Ring Rd, Point Leo; unpowered sites $30-40, powered sites $35-50; P) This sprawling campground on the foreshore of Point Leo has a mix of seasonal and year-round sites right next to the beach; in winter only the powered sites are offered. It's a great spot for surfers and those wanting to learn. There are free barbecues, clean amenities blocks with hot water, a camp kitchen and a laundry. Online bookings only.

★ Jackalope   BOUTIQUE HOTEL $$$
(☑03-5931 2500; www.jackalopehotels.com; 166 Balnarring Rd, Merricks North; r incl breakfast $675-1500; P✷🛜🏊) This hotel for the Instagram generation offers a heavily curated and visually arresting accommodation experience. Rooms are as luxe as their hefty price tags indicate, and facilities include an infinity pool overlooking the Willow Creek vineyard, a cocktail bar and the **Doot Doot Doot** (5-course tasting menu $110; ⏱6.30-9pm Sun-Thu, 12.30-2pm & 6-10pm Fri & Sat; P✷🛜) fine-dining restaurant. A two-night minimum stay applies on some weekends. Rates include breakfast.

🍴 Eating & Drinking

Green Olive at Red Hill   MODERN AUSTRALIAN $
(☑03-5989 2992; www.greenolive.com.au; 1180 Mornington-Flinders Rd, Main Ridge; tapas $13.50; ⏱9am-4pm; P🛜🐾🏊) Set on a 27-acre farm, this always-bustling family-run enterprise revolves around its modern, light-drenched restaurant, which has outdoor tables overlooking the pastoral surroundings. Food is from the farm or locally sourced, with a tapas-style menu of olives, dips, cheese and frittatas. The farm produces five types of

olive oil, which can be purchased to take home.

★ Merricks General Wine Store   CAFE $$
(☑03-5989 8088; www.mgwinestore.com.au; 3460 Frankston-Flinders Rd, Merricks; mains $28-38; ⏱8.30am-5pm) Dating back to the 1920s, this place is the heart of the district, frequented by locals and visitors alike. Its La Marzocco espresso machine is used to make excellent coffee (Little Rebel beans) and food options range from baked goods to hearty mains. Local produce is sold, and wines from the Elgee Park and Baillieu Vineyard wineries can be tasted.

Rare Hare   AUSTRALIAN $$
(☑03-5931 2500; www.rarehare.com.au; 166 Balnarring Rd, Merricks Nth; mains $16-38; ⏱11am-5pm Sun-Thu, to 9pm Fri & Sat) So on-trend that it's almost a parody, the casual eatery in the Jackalope winery features communal tables overlooking the Willow Creek vineyard. The space adjoins a dramatic glass-walled barrel hall where free wine tastings are offered. The menu of artfully plated shared dishes relies on produce from the on-site kitchen garden, and there are plenty of vegetarian options on offer.

Montalto   MODERN AUSTRALIAN $$
(☑03-5989 8412; www.montalto.com.au; 33 Shoreham Rd, Red Hill South; mains $17-48; ⏱cafe 11am-5pm, restaurant noon-2.30pm Fri-Tue, 6.30-10pm Fri & Sat, extended hours summer; P🐾) Wander alongside the vines to view the 31 permanent works in Montaldo's sculpture garden and then relax over a meal in the well-regarded Mod Oz restaurant or in the al fresco cafe, which specialises in pizzas. Both venues source their veggies from the on-site kitchen garden. Bookings are accepted for the restaurant, but it's first come, first served in the cafe.

★ Port Phillip Estate   MODERN AUSTRALIAN $$$
(☑03-5989 4444; www.portphillipestate.com.au; 263 Red Hill Rd, Red Hill South; 2-/3-course meal $68/85; ⏱noon-3pm Wed-Sun & 6.30-8.30pm Fri & Sat; P✷) Home of the acclaimed Kooyong Estate pinot noir and chardonnay, this stunning Wood Marsh–designed winery resembles the lair of a Bond villain. Its restaurant is one of the peninsula's best, offering Mod Oz dishes and stunning views of the vineyards. Those who choose not to eat can enjoy a wine tasting ($5, redeemable with purchase) at the sleek cellar bar.

MORNINGTON PENINSULA WINERIES

Most of the peninsula's wineries are located in the hills between Red Hill and Merricks, and most have excellent cafes or restaurants attached. The cool climate means that pinot noir and chardonnay are the predominant varietals. Several companies offer winery tours – ask at the visitor centre (p528). For an overview, check out **Mornington Peninsula Wineries & Region** (www.mpva.com.au). Wineries with cellar doors worth a visit include the following:

Red Hill Estate (☑03-5989 2838; www.redhillestate.com.au; 53 Shoreham Rd, Red Hill South; ⊙cellar door 11am-5pm; P) One of the Peninsula's most picturesque wineries, Red Hill Estate boasts spectacular views of Western Port Bay, and has a highly regarded restaurant.

Pt. Leo Estate (☑03-5989 9011; www.ptleoestate.com.au; 3649 Frankston-Flinders Rd, Merricks; tastings $6, sculpture park adult/concession/family $10/5/25; ⊙11am-5pm; P🚻) Among the largest vineyards on the peninsula, this state-of-the-art estate has two highly regarded restaurants and a huge sculpture garden.

Lindenderry at Red Hill (☑03-5989 2933; www.lancemore.com.au/lindenderry; 142 Arthurs Seat Rd, Red Hill; mains $22-24; ⊙11.30am-3.30pm Sat & Sun) Gorgeous gardens, a fine-dining restaurant, a pizzeria and a luxurious hotel.

Main Ridge Estate (☑03-5989 2686; www.mre.com.au; 80 William Rd, Red Hill; ⊙cellar door noon-5pm Fri-Mon, restaurant to 3pm Fri-Sun; P) One of the Peninsula's oldest wineries, offering casual meals on weekends.

Montalto (p530) One of the Peninsula's best winery restaurants. There's also the piazza and garden cafe for casual dining, as well as a sculpture garden.

Port Phillip Estate (p530) Inside an architecturally resplendent winery building is a restaurant, bistro, magnificent cellar door and boutique accommodation.

Ten Minutes By Tractor (☑03-5989 6080; www.tenminutesbytractor.com.au; 1333 Mornington-Flinders Rd, Main Ridge) The unusual name comes from the three vineyards, which are each 10 minutes apart by tractor.

T'Gallant (☑03-5931 1300; www.tgallant.com.au; 1385 Mornington-Flinders Rd, Main Ridge; mains $17-33; ⊙11.30am-4pm; P🚻) A rustic trattoria with delicious antipasti, pastas and wood-fired pizzas. Its cellar door offers generous free tastings of its pinot grigio and pinot gris.

Petit Tracteur Bistro   FRENCH $$$
(☑03-5989 2510; www.petittracteur.com.au; 1208 Mornington Flinders Rd, Main Ridge; mains $30-39; ⊙noon-2.30pm Wed-Fri, 6-8pm Thu & Fri, 9-10.45am, noon-2.30pm & 6-8.30pm Sat & Sun; P🚻) Uncompromisingly French, the Little Tractor is associated with nearby Ten Minutes by Tractor. You'll dine on Gallic delights such as steak tartare, escargot, duck à l'orange and fish meunière – vegans should steer clear as there's almost nothing suitable on the menu. The bar menu offers small plates ($9 to $15) and cheese and charcuterie plates ($29 to $35). *Très délicieux.*

Red Hill Cheese   CHEESE $
(☑0418 138 123; www.redhillcheese.com.au; 81 William Rd, Red Hill; tasting plates $10-20; ⊙11am-5pm Fri-Sun; P) Specialising in artisanal cheeses made from sheep, goat and buffalo milk, this farm has a picturesque cellar door surrounded by bush. Stop in for a tasting or to purchase picnic provisions.

Red Hill Brewery   BREWERY
(☑03-5989 2959; www.redhillbrewery.com.au; 88 Shoreham Rd, Red Hill South; ⊙11am-6pm Thu-Sun, extended hours summer; P) Established in 2005, this popular microbrewery produces small batch craft beers (golden ale, pilsner, wheat beer, scotch ale and more) that can be sampled by the tasting paddle ($12 for four beers). In summer you can nosh on Texan-style wood-smoked BBQ (from $12) while you tipple.

🧭 Tours

Salty Surf School   SURFING
(☑0475 910 032; www.saltysurfschool.com; 10 Marine Pde, Shoreham; public/private surf lesson

per 2hr from $65/100; 🚍782 from Frankston) Homegrown company offering lessons for all levels at Point Leo and Shoreham beaches. Also offers surfboard and wetsuit hire (half/full day $50/70).

Phillip Island

POP 10,387

Synonymous with penguins and petrolheads, Phillip Island attracts a curious mix of holidaymakers and tourists. At its heart, the island is still a farming community, but nature has conspired to turn it into one of Victoria's most popular tourist destinations. Apart from the major draws of the Penguin Parade and the annual Motorcycle Grand Prix, there's rich Indigenous history here (the Boon Wurrung people are the traditional custodians), as well as abundant bird life and fauna. And there are also wonderful beaches, which are a major attraction in summer.

⊙ Sights

★ Penguin Parade   WILDLIFE RESERVE

(☑03-5951 2800; www.penguins.org.au; 1019 Ventnor Rd, Summerland Beach; general viewing adult/child/family $26.20/13/65.40; ⊘parade times vary, access doors open 1hr before; ℗⏣) One of Victoria's major tourist draws, this parade of little penguins (*Eudyptula minor*) showcases the world's smallest, and probably cutest, penguins. The main complex, which was under renovation when we visited, includes amphitheatres that hold up to 3800 spectators who come to see the little fellas just after sunset as they waddle from the sea to their land-based nests. An underground viewing section, premium seats and VIP platforms are available for those wanting prime views; book well in advance.

Penguin numbers swell after breeding in summer, with as many as 32,000 arriving on a given night, but they're in residence year-round. After the parade, hang around the boardwalks for a closer view as the stragglers search for their burrows and mates. Bring warm clothing, and take note there's strictly no photography or videoing. Be sure to arrive an hour beforehand – check the website for their ETA.

There are a variety of specialised tours where you can be accompanied by rangers to explain the behaviour of penguins; check the website for details. If you plan to see other attractions on the island, consider purchasing a Parks Pass.

At the time of research, the popular tours led by Indigenous rangers had been postponed; staff were hopeful that these would resume in 2019.

★ Antarctic Journey   OBSERVATORY, THEATRE

(☑03-5951 2800; www.penguins.org.au/attractions/recreational-areas/the-nobbies; 1320 Ventnor Rd, Nobbies Centre, Summerlands; adult/child/family $18/9/45; ⊘10am-2hrs before sunset) Developed with the World Wide Fund for Nature (WWF), this cutting-edge multimedia exhibition at Nobbies Centre spotlights the shared waters between this coast and Antarctica. Its interactive displays are highly informative, with clever augmented reality features. There are 20-minute guided tours (included in ticket price) at 11am, 1pm and 3pm daily. Nobbies Centre is only a five-minute drive from the Penguin Parade, so aim to visit in mid-afternoon if you're seeing the penguins.

Churchill Island   FARM

(☑03-5951 2800; www.penguins.org.au; Phillip Island Rd, Newhaven; adult/child/family $13/6.50/32.50; ⊘10am-4.30pm Mon-Fri, from 9am Sat & Sun; ℗⏣) Regarded as a sacred site by its traditional owners, this island is connected to Phillip Island by a bridge near Newhaven. Excavated middens suggest that it was a place where the Boon Wurrung people came in summer to feast on shellfish and short-tailed shearwaters. European settlers subsequently planted Victoria's first non-Indigenous crops here in 1860. These days the historic homestead and farm is a popular tourist attraction where activities including sheep shearing and cow milking are demonstrated.

Nobbies Centre & Boardwalk   VIEWPOINT

(☑03-5951 2800; Summerlands; ⊘10am-1hr before sunset) FREE The cafe and souvenir shop known as **Nobbies Centre** on the island's southwestern tip is home to the multimedia Antarctic Journey. In front of the centre, a **boardwalk** winds down to vantage points to view the Nobbies offshore rock formations and the offshore Seal Rocks, which are inhabited by one of Australia's largest colonies of fur seals; the boardwalk's one in 14 gradient makes it reasonably disability friendly. Coin-operated binoculars ($2) allow you to view the seals.

On the drive here you'll pass by memorable landscapes of windswept grassy plateaus and rugged coastal scenery. The area

Phillip Island

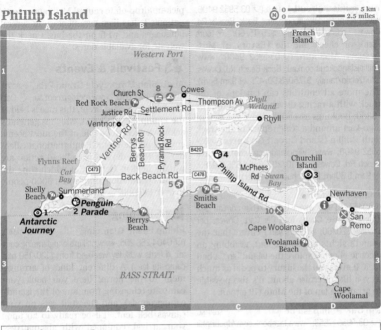

MELBOURNE & VICTORIA PHILLIP ISLAND

Phillip Island

◎ **Top Sights**
1 Antarctic Journey......................................A2
2 Penguin Parade..A2

◎ **Sights**
3 Churchill Island.......................................D2
  History of Motorsport
  Museum...(see 5)
4 Koala Conservation Centre....................C2
  Nobbies Centre & Boardwalk.........(see 1)

◎ **Activities, Courses & Tours**
  Grand Prix Guided Circuit
  Tours...(see 5)

5 Phillip Island Circuit..............................B2
  Phillip Island Circuit Go Karts.......(see 5)

🛏 **Sleeping**
6 Clifftop..C2
7 Cowes Foreshore Tourist Park..............B1
8 Glen Isla House B1

🍴 **Eating**
9 BEANd...D3
10 Cape Kitchen..C2

is a protected wildlife reserve, where penguins come to nest nightly (look for their purpose-built burrows); however, everyone is required to leave the site one hour before sunset. There's an abundance of wildlife on the roads, particularly Cape Barren geese, so take care driving – usually they won't budge.

Koala Conservation Centre   ZOO
(☎03-5951 2800; www.penguins.org.au; 1810 Phillip Island Rd, Cowes; adult/child/family $13/6.50/32.50; ⊙10am-5pm, extended hours in summer; 🅿) There are only 20 to 30 of these furry marsupials left in the wild on the island, but if you take to the treetop

boardwalks or the easily accessible trails on the ground at this conservation centre you're guaranteed to see some. Wallabies, echidnas and colourful native birds can also be spotted.

🏃 Activities

Phillip Island Circuit   ADVENTURE SPORTS
(☎03-5952 9400; www.phillipislandcircuit.com. au; Back Beach Rd, Cowes) Petrolheads love the Island's motor racing circuit, home to the annual Australian Motor Grand Prix and a host of other motor racing events, on two wheels and four. The visitor centre

runs **guided circuit tours** (☑03-5952 9400; www.phillipislandcircuit.com.au; Back Beach Rd, Cowes; adult/child/family $25/15/60; ⊙tours 2pm), or check out the **History of Motorsport Museum** (☑03-5952 9400; www.phillipislandcircuit.com.au; Back Beach Rd, Cowes; adult/child/family $17.50/8.50/42; ⊙9am-5pm). The more adventurous can cut laps of the track with a racing driver in hotted-up V8s ($360; bookings essential). Drive yourself in a go-kart around a scale replica of the track with **Phillip Island Circuit Go Karts** (☑03-5952 9400; www.phillipislandcircuit.com.au; Back Beach Rd, Cowes; per 10/20/30min $35/60/80; ⊙9am-5.30pm, longer hours summer).

Island E Bike Hire CYCLING
(☑0457 281 965; www.islandebikehire.com.au; 142 Thompson Ave, Cowes Total Car Care, Cowes; per 1hr/day $20/60; ⊙hours vary) Given that the island's sights are spread out, grabbing an electric bike to explore the island isn't a bad idea. It gives you the luxury to pedal as much as you like or cruise about; it's also possible to arrange a lap of the Moto GP circuit.

Rip Curl Phillip Island SURFING
(☑03-5956 7553; www.facebook.com/ripcurlphilipisland/; 10-12 Phillip Island Tourist Rd, Newhaven; ⊙9am-5pm) As well as selling surf apparel and running a surf **museum** (☑03-5956 7553; www.theislantissurfexperience.com.au; 10-12 Phillip Island Rd, Big Wave Complex, Newhaven; adult/child/family $4.50/2.50/12; ⊙9am-5pm), Rip Curl also rents out boards ($12.50/40 per hour/day) and wetsuits.

☞ Tours

Wild Ocean Eco Boat WILDLIFE WATCHING
(☑03-5952 3501, 1300 763 739; www.wildlifecoastcruises.com.au/cruises/express-eco-boat-tour; 11-13 Jetty Triangle, Cowes; adult/child/family $85/65/235; ⊙office 8.30am-4.30pm Jun-Aug, 9am-5pm Sep-May) 🐾 Operated by **Wildlife Coast Cruises** (☑03-5952 3501, 1300 763 739; www.wildlifecoastcruises.com.au; 11-13 Jetty Triangle, Cowes; ⊙office 8.30am-4.30pm Jun-Aug, 9am-5pm Sep-May) 🐾, these high-speed boat tours visit the Australian fur seal colony at Seal Rocks and pass by the blowhole and 'pirate's cave' at Nobbies. Check the website for the daily schedule.

Go West TOURS
(☑03-9485 5290; www.gowest.com.au; adult/child $135/115) This one-day tour from Melbourne includes entry to the Penguin Parade (p532), lunch, wildlife encounters, wine-tasting and pick-up/drop-off to central Melbourne destinations. It has iPod commentary in several languages and wi-fi on the bus. Check the website for available dates.

★☆ Festivals & Events

Australian Motorcycle Grand Prix SPORTS
(☑1800 100 030; www.motogp.com.au; ⊙Oct) The island's biggest event, this race is held at the Phillip Island Circuit, which is generally acknowledged to be one of the most scenic circuits on the MotoGP international calendar. Its three days of petrolhead action are usually held in October, at which time the island's population jumps from 8000 people to over 150,000.

🛏 Sleeping

Phillip Island Glamping TENTED CAMP $
(☑0404 258 205; www.phillipislandglamping.com.au; d tents weekday/weekend from $120/150 plus campsite fees) A different kind of arrangement to the norm: here you book your campsite (choosing from any of the island's campgrounds), and the staff sets up your canvas bell tent. It'll be ready to go upon your arrival, equipped with air mattress, bedding, towels, heater, outdoor table and chairs, esky and cooking utensils. You'll use communal bathroom facilities.

Cowes Foreshore Tourist Park CAMPGROUND $
(☑03-5952 2211; www.cowesforeshoretouristpark.com.au; 164 Church St, Cowes; sites/cabins from $40/95; [P][🚿][🛜][🐾]) Located right next to the beach, this park offers a range of powered and unpowered campsites as well as en-suite cabins sleeping up to six guests – the better ones have air-con and water views. Facilities include a children's playground and a camp kitchen. It's an easy walk into the centre of Cowes.

Island Accommodation HOSTEL $
(☑03-5956 6123; www.theislandaccommodation.com.au; 10-12 Phillip Island Rd, Newhaven; dm/d from $29/99; [P][🚿][@][🛜]) 🐾 This YHA-affiliated backpackers has two living areas complete with air-con in summer and fireplaces for winter. There are also two communal kitchens and a rooftop deck with terrific views. The cheapest dorms sleep 12 and doubles are motel-standard; sadly, beds are uncomfortable. The location isn't the best – you'll need your own transport to do any exploring. In summer, book ahead.

★ **Clifftop** BOUTIQUE HOTEL $$
(☑03-5952 1033; www.clifftop.com.au; 1 Marlin St, Smiths Beach; d $235-290; P ❋ 🛜) It's hard to imagine a better location for your island escape than this classy place perched above Smiths Beach. Of the eight luxurious suites, the top four have ocean views and private balconies, while the downstairs rooms open onto gardens – all have comfortable beds and an attractive 'boho-luxe' decor. The communal lounge has a wood fire and pool table.

Glen Isla House BOUTIQUE HOTEL $$
(☑03-5952 1882; www.glenisla.com; 230 Church St, Cowes; d/ste/q cottages from $250/360/550; P ❋ 🛜) Set in the well-tended gardens of an 1870 homestead, this place offers rooms in modern timber outbuildings as well as a self-catering cottage and one heritage suite in the original homestead. The decor and feel are tasteful but old-fashioned; rooms are well set up and there's a communal lounge, but breakfast is only available occasionally. No children under 12.

✖ Eating

Nordic Kantine CAFE $
(☑0403 651 257; www.nordic-kantine.com.au; 113b Thompson Ave, Cowes; mains $15-18; ⊙8.30am-3pm Thu-Mon; ❋ 🅿 🚲) 🥐 Moving from the Baltic Sea island of Bornholm to this island on the other side of the globe was a major step for the family who runs this friendly cafe, but Bornholm's loss was undoubtedly Phillip Island's gain. Come here to enjoy hearty breakfasts, decadent waffles or Danish open-sandwiches – produce is often foraged and organic. Kids love the Lego table.

The cafe was likely to move premises some time in 2019; check the website for updates.

Youki's JAPANESE $
(☑03-5952 6444; www.youkis.com.au; Shop 1, 68-80 Thompson Ave, Cowes; mains $6-15; ⊙10am-3.30pm Mon-Fri, to 4.30pm Sat, to 2.30pm Sun) Forget the greasy fish and chip shops that are found everywhere in Cowes – the best fast food in town is served at this spick and span Japanese joint. Grab a table to enjoy udon, ramen, don bowls, okonomiyaki, sushi and sashimi, or order a bento box or sushi pack to go.

BEANd CAFE $
(☑0407 717 588; www.beand.com.au; 157 Marine Pde, Shop 4, San Remo; breakfast $8-18; ⊙7.30am-3pm Thu-Tue) On the mainland side of the bridge heading into Phillip Island is this vibrant and friendly little cafe serving topnotch pour-over, espresso and cold brew coffees using single-origin beans roasted in Wonthaggi. Its all-day breakfasts are popular, as are the burgers and toasted sangas on offer at lunch.

★ **Bani's Kitchen** MEDITERRANEAN $$
(☑03-5932 0710; www.baniskitchen.com.au; 69b Chapel St, Cowes; mains $12-32; ⊙noon-3pm & 5-9pm Wed-Fri, 10am-9pm Sat & Sun; ❋ 🛜) Chef Manpreet Singh Tung seems an unlikely candidate to be operating this eatery as his cooking pedigree includes stints with acclaimed chefs Guy Grossi and Pam Talimanidis. But here on Phillip Island he is, and tiny Bani's is a delight. Meat eaters should opt for the slow-cooked lamb or a souvlaki; vegetarians for the herb-laden vegan bowl. BYO (corkage $5).

Cape Kitchen MODERN AUSTRALIAN $$$
(☑03-5956 7200; www.thecapekitchen.com.au; 1215 Phillip Island Rd, Newhaven; mains $19-44; ⊙8.30am-4.30pm Fri-Mon; P 🛜 🚲) Book a window table so that you can admire the ocean vistas while enjoying the contemporary bistro food served at the island's most fashionable dining option. Service is far better than most places in town, as is the wine list. It's a great breakfast choice.

🍷 Drinking & Nightlife

Ocean Reach Brewing BREWERY
(☑03-5952 5274; www.oceanreach.beer; 47 Thompson Ave, Cowes; ⊙4-9pm Wed & Thu, noon-10pm Fri & Sat, to 7pm Sun) Close to the main beach in Cowes, this popular family-owned taphouse serves regular and seasonal beers brewed in-house – try the fruity and hoppy Island Pale Ale, or hedge your bets and opt for a tasting paddle ($20). The on-site food truck serves American-style burgers ($15 to $20), tacos ($7) and buffalo wings ($14). In summer, opening hours are noon to 10pm daily.

ℹ Information

Phillip Island Visitor Information Centre
(☑1300 366 422; www.visitbasscoast.com.au; 895 Phillip Island Tourist Rd, Newhaven; ⊙9am-5pm, to 6pm summer school holidays; 🛜) The main visitor centre on the island has a wall of brochures and maps. It sells tickets to the Penguin Parade, as well as discounted sights packages. It also offers a helpful accommodation booking service.

Cowes Visitor Information Centre (🖋1300 366 422; www.visitphillipisland.com; cnr Thompson Ave & Church St, Cowes; ⊙9am-5pm) An alternative to the info centre in Newhaven in the Bass Coast Shire Council complex.

❶ Getting There & Away

Located about 140km from Melbourne by car, Phillip Island can only be accessed by crossing the bridge between San Remo and Newhaven. From Melbourne take Monash Fwy (M1) and exit at Pakenham, joining South Gippsland Hwy at Koo Wee Rup.

If you're on foot or bicycle, you can get here by ferry from Stony Point to Cowes.

Once on the island it's easy and quick to get around by car or bike – it's just a 15-minute drive from Cowes to the Penguin Parade or Grand Prix circuit.

GREAT OCEAN ROAD

The Great Ocean Road (B100) is one of Australia's most famous touring routes. It takes travellers past world-class surfing breaks, through pockets of rainforest and calm seaside towns, and under koala-filled tree canopies. It shows off sheer limestone cliffs, dairy farms and heathland, and gets you up close and personal with the crashing waves of the Southern Ocean.

Hunt out the isolated beaches and lighthouses in between the towns and the thick eucalyptus forest of the Otway hinterlands to really escape the crowds. Rather than heading straight to the Great Ocean Road, a fork in the road at Geelong can take you the long, leisurely way there, through the Bellarine Peninsula, with visits to charming Queenscliff and wineries en route.

Day-tripping tourists from Melbourne rush in and out of the area in less than 12 hours, but in a perfect world you'd spend at least a week here.

Geelong

POP 157,104

As Victoria's second-largest city, Geelong is a proud town with an interesting history and pockets of charm. While Melburnians love to deride their little cousin as a boring backwater, in reality few of the knockers have veered off its main thoroughfare enough to know what makes the town tick. Geelong's new bypass means travellers can skip the city and head straight to the Great Ocean Road; however, there are lots of reasons to stop here.

Great Ocean Road & Southwest Coast

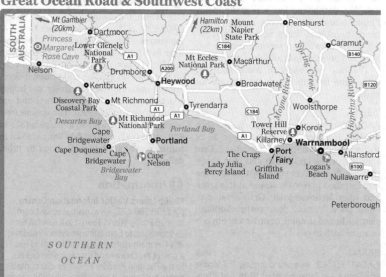

With the recent closure of major industry, Geelong is in the process of reinventing itself as a tourist town. It's centred on the sparkling Corio Bay waterfront and the city centre, where heritage buildings from the boom days of the gold rush-era and the thriving wool industry have been converted into swanky restaurants and bars. It's also a footy-mad town, passionate about its AFL team, the Cats.

The Wathaurung people are Geelong's original inhabitants and traditional custodians.

☉ Sights

Geelong Waterfront   WATERFRONT
(Beach Rd) Geelong's sparkling revamped waterfront precinct is a great place to stroll, with plenty of restaurants set on scenic piers, plus historical landmarks, a 19th-century **carousel** (☑03-5224 1547; www.geelong australia.com.au/carousel; $5; ☉11am-4.30pm Mon-Fri, 10.30am-5pm Sat & Sun, longer hours summer), sculptures, grand homes, swimming areas, playgrounds and grassy sections ideal for picnics. In summer you can cool off at popular **Eastern Beach**, with an art-deco bathing pavilion complete with diving boards, sunbathing area and toddler pool. Jan Mitchell's 100-plus painted **Baywalk**

Bollards are scattered the length of the waterfront.

Botanic Gardens   GARDENS
(☑03-5272 4379; www.geelongaustralia.com.au/gbg; cnr Podbury & Eastern Park Drs; ☉gardens 8am-5pm, longer hours summer, cafe 10am-3pm Mon-Fri, to 5pm Sat & Sun) **FREE** Geelong's botanic gardens (established in 1851) are the fourth oldest in Australia and make for a peaceful stroll or picnic. Aim to get here for a volunteer-run tour (weather permitting), held Wednesday at 11am or Sunday at 2pm. At other times pick up a self-guided map from the cafe, which does Devonshire tea ($9), as well as sandwiches and the like.

Geelong Art Gallery   GALLERY
(☑03-5229 3645; www.geelonggallery.org.au; 55 Little Malop St; ☉10am-5pm) **FREE** With over 6000 works in its collection, this excellent gallery has celebrated Australian paintings such as Eugene von Guérard's *View of Geelong* and Frederick McCubbin's *A Bush Burial*. It also exhibits contemporary works and has free tours on Sunday at 2pm.

National Wool Museum   MUSEUM
(☑03-5272 4701; www.geelongaustralia.com.au/nwm; 26 Moorabool St; adult/child/family $10/6/30; ☉9.30am-5pm Mon-Fri, 10am-5pm Sat

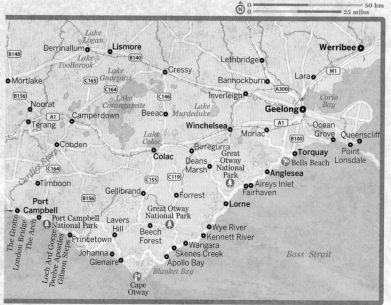

MELBOURNE & VICTORIA GEELONG

The Great Ocean Road

The Great Ocean Road begins in Australia's surf capital Torquay, swings past Bells Beach, then winds its way along the coast to the wild and windswept koala heaven of Cape Otway. The Twelve Apostles and Loch Ard Gorge are obligatory stops before the road sweeps on towards Warrnambool with its whales, and Port Fairy with its fine buildings and folk festival, and the natural drama peaks again close to the South Australian border.

Road trippin' (p536)
ectacular scenery on Victoria's most iconic road

Otway Fly Treetop Adventures (p554)
perience the Otway rainforest on a walk through
e treetops

Port Fairy (p564)
e perfect seaside village sits at the western end of the
eat Ocean Road

Koala spotting (p557)
ep an eye out for one of the country's best-loved
tive creatures

Geelong

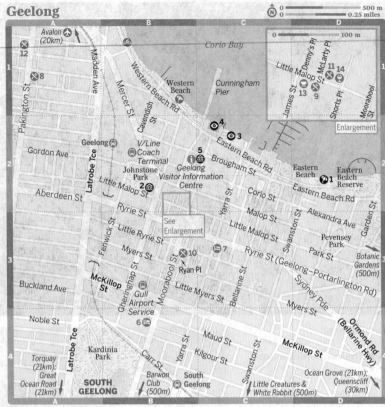

MELBOURNE & VICTORIA GEELONG

Geelong

⊚ Sights
1 Eastern Beach	D2
2 Geelong Art Gallery	B2
3 Geelong Waterfront	C2
4 Geelong Waterfront Carousel	C2
5 National Wool Museum	C2

⊟ Sleeping
6 Devlin Apartments	B4
7 Gatehouse on Ryrie	C3

⊗ Eating
8 Box Office	A1
9 Hot Chicken Project	D1
10 IGNI	B3
11 Pistol Pete's Food n Blues	D1
12 Tulip	A1

⊙ Drinking & Nightlife
13 Cartel Coffee Roaster	D1
14 Geelong Cellar Door	D1

& Sun) More interesting than it may sound, this museum showcases the importance of the wool industry in shaping Geelong economically, socially and architecturally – many of the grand buildings in the area are former wool-store buildings, including the museum's 1872 bluestone edifice. There's a sock-making machine and a massive 1910 Axminster carpet loom that gets chugging at regular intervals throughout the day.

**Narana Aboriginal
Cultural Centre** CULTURAL CENTRE
(☏ 03-5241 5700; www.narana.com.au; 410 Torquay Rd, Grovedale; ⊙ 9am-5pm Mon-Fri, to 4pm Sat, cafe 9am-4pm Mon-Fri, to 3pm Sat) FREE The Wathaurung people – the original inhabitants and traditional custodians of Geelong – called the area Jillong, and this precinct on its outskirts offers a fascinating insight into their culture. There's a range of things going on: a **gallery** featuring Victoria's largest

collection of Aboriginal art; a fusion cafe that offers contemporary dishes using indigenous ingredients; didgeridoo performances (or play it yourself); a boomerang-throwing gallery; and a native garden (admission by donation) that features emus and wallabies. Call ahead for daily tours.

🛏 Sleeping

As the city has become a destination in its own right over the past few years, a number of modern hotels and apartments have opened up. There are a few historical guesthouses but no real budget options – for a room under $50, try Airbnb. There are plenty of motels too, but it's best to avoid the outer suburbs.

Gatehouse on Ryrie   GUESTHOUSE $
(📞0417 545 196; www.gatehouseonryrie.com.au; 83 Yarra St; d incl breakfast $120-155; P@🛜) In a prime location in the centre of town, this guesthouse is one of Geelong's best midrange choices. Built in 1897, it features gorgeous timber floorboards throughout, spacious rooms (most with shared facilities), and a communal kitchen and lounge area. Breakfast is in the glorious front room.

Devlin Apartments   APARTMENT $$
(📞03-5222 1560; www.devlinapartments.com.au; 312 Moorabool St; r $170-500; ❄🛜) Geelong's most stylish offerings are these boutique apartments, housed in a 1926 heritage-listed building (the former Gordon Tech school). Many of the apartments feature themed design, including 'New Yorker' loft-style apartments with arched windows; 'Modernist', furnished with Danish designer chairs; and 'Industrial', featuring wrought iron, rustic wood and tiled brick bathrooms. There are motel-style rooms too.

🍴 Eating & Drinking

Box Office   CAFE $
(📞0417 603 323; www.boxofficecafe.com.au; 77 Preston St, Geelong West; dishes $12-24; ⏱6.30am-4pm Mon-Fri, from 7.30am Sat & Sun; 🛜) Tucked just off Pakington St, Box Office is a standout along a celebrated cafe strip. Amid industrial decor featuring handmade furniture, it serves a contemporary menu with a distinct indigenous twist. Avo smash is infused with desert lime and chilli, the bacon cheeseburger has pepperberry relish, and smoothie bowls feature anything from wattle seed and lemon myrtle to Kakadu plum.

Hot Chicken Project   AMERICAN $
(📞03-5221 8977; www.thehotchickenproject.com.au; 84a Little Malop St; mains from $18; ⏱noon-10pm) A fixture along Little Malop is this welcoming diner specialising in authentic Nashville chicken. Choose from a menu of wings, tenders or dark meats – or hot fish or tofu – in a spectrum of heat levels peaking at 'Evil Chicken', served with a side of slaw or turnip greens.

Pistol Pete's Food n Blues   AMERICAN $
(📞03-5221 0287; www.pistolpetesfoodnblues.com.au; 93a Little Malop St; mains $12-24; ⏱noon-9.30pm Tue & Wed, to 11pm Thu, to midnight Fri & Sat, to 9pm Sun) Divey hang-out Pistol Pete's serves up Cajun-style burgers, shrimp po'boys, Southern fried chicken, gumbo, swamp fries and baloney sandwiches. Live music is also a feature, with regular bluesy, Americana twang bands to enjoy with a US craft beer or a bourbon.

Tulip   AUSTRALIAN $$
(📞03-5229 6953; www.tuliprestaurant.com.au; 9/111 Pakington St, Geelong West; smaller/larger dishes from $15/35; ⏱5.30pm-late Tue, noon-2.30pm & 5.30pm-late Wed-Sat) One of only two Geelong restaurants to earn a prestigious *Good Food Guide* chef's hat, unassuming Tulip delivers a gastronomic experience with its mix of inventive small and large plates designed to share. Dishes may include cured Spanish leg ham, whole lamb shoulder, poached ocean trout with grilled peas and mussels or native items such as kangaroo tartare with pepperberry oil.

⭐IGNI   AUSTRALIAN $$$
(📞03-5222 2266; www.restarantigni.com; Ryan Pl; 8 courses $150, with wine pairing $245; ⏱6-10pm Thu, noon-2.30pm & 6-10pm Fri & Sat) Creating a buzz among food lovers across Melbourne is this latest venture by lauded chef (and local boy) Aaron Turner. The set tasting menus change on a whim, incorporating a mix of indigenous and European flavours from saltbush to oyster leaf, or marron to squab, using a wood-fired grill fuelled by ironbark and red gum.

🍷 Drinking & Nightlife

⭐Cartel Coffee Roaster   COFFEE
(📞03-5221 4757; www.coffeecartel.com.au; 1-80 Little Malop St; coffee from $4.50; ⏱7am-5pm Mon-Fri, 8am-4pm Sat, 9am-2.30pm Sun) A big player in Australia's third-wave coffee

movement is this single-origin roaster run by a passionate owner who forges relationships with farmers across Africa, Asia and Latin America. The result is well-sourced beans, expertly roasted and prepared in its smart space on happening Little Malop. Its impressive high-tech BKON filter machine puts it at the forefront of Australian coffee-making innovation.

★ Little Creatures & White Rabbit
BREWERY

(☑ Little Creatures 03-5202 4009, White Rabbit 03-5202 4050; www.littlecreatures.com.au; cnr Fyans & Swanston Sts; mains from $18; ☺ 11am-5pm Mon & Tue, to 9pm Wed-Fri, 8am-9pm Sat, to 5pm Sun; ☏) Sharing space within the historic red-brick woollen-mill complex are these two separate, well-respected breweries that have come together to create a giant playground for beer-lovers. Little Creatures is the bigger operation, a vast, vibrant indoor-outdoor space, while White Rabbit, relocated from Healesville in 2015, is the more boutique offering, with a chic set-up among its brewing equipment.

Geelong Cellar Door
WINE BAR

(☑ 03-5229 9568; www.geelongcellardoor.com. au; 97-99 Little Malop St; ☺ noon-11pm Tue-Sun) A wonderful spot to sample local wines is this tasteful wine bar on fashionable Little Malop. Of its wines, 99% come from Geelong, the Bellarine, Moorabool and the Great Ocean Road. Come winter it's a cosy spot for a drink indoors by the fire; at other times head to its brick courtyard, a space shared with neighbouring restaurants, which you're welcome to order from.

Barwon Club
LIVE MUSIC

(☑ 03-5221 4584; www.barwonclub.com.au; 509 Moorabool St; ☺ 11am-late) The BC has long been Geelong's premier live-music venue, and has spawned the likes of Magic Dirt, Bored! and Warped, seminal bands in the 'Geetroit' rock scene. As well as a place to catch local and international bands, it's great for a beer.

❶ Information

Geelong Visitor Information Centre

(☑ 03-5283 1735, 1800 755 611; www. visitgreatoceanroad.org.au; 26 Moorabool St; ☺ 9am-5pm; ☏) is the city's main tourist office, with brochures on Geelong, the Bellarine Peninsula and the Otways, as well as free wi-fi.

❶ Getting There & Away

Geelong is 75km south of Melbourne along the Geelong Rd (Princes Fwy; M1). The 25km Geelong Ring Rd runs from Corio to Waurn Ponds, bypassing Geelong entirely. To get to Geelong city, be careful not to miss the Princes Hwy exit from the left lanes.

AIR

Avalon Airport (p512) is around a 20-minute drive from Geelong. Jetstar (p512) has services from Avalon to Adelaide, Sydney, the Gold Coast and Brisbane. AirAsia (☑ 02-8188 2133; www.airasia.com) has also introduced direct international flights to Kuala Lumpur (Malaysia) and Osaka (Japan).

Skybus (☑ 1300 759 287; www.skybus.com. au) meets most flights at Avalon and goes to Geelong ($18, 35 minutes).

BUS

Gull Airport Service (☑ 03-5222 4966; www. gull.com.au; 45 McKillop St; ☺ office 9am-5pm Mon-Fri, 10am-noon Sat) Has regular services between Geelong and Melbourne Airport (adult/child $34/22, 1¼ hours), departing from the city centre and Geelong Station.

McHarry's Buslines (☑ 03-5223 2111; www. mcharrys.com.au) Runs frequent buses from Geelong Station to Torquay ($3.40, 40 minutes) and the Bellarine Peninsula.

V/Line (☑ 1800 800 007; www.vline.com. au; Geelong Station, Gordon Ave) Buses run from Geelong Station to Apollo Bay ($20.40, 2½ hours, four daily) via Torquay ($3.40, 25 minutes), Anglesea ($6.80, 45 minutes), Lorne ($12.40, 1½ hours) and Wye River ($15.60, two hours). On Monday, Wednesday and Friday a bus continues to Port Campbell ($35.60, 5¼ hours) and Warrnambool ($40.20, 6½ hours); both services involve a transfer at Apollo Bay. The train is a much quicker and cheaper option for those heading direct to Warrnambool, though you'll miss out on the Great Ocean Road experience. Heading inland, there's a bus to Ballarat ($11, 1½ hours).

TRAIN

V/Line trains run frequently from Geelong Station (☑ 1800 800 007; www.vline.com.au; Gordon Ave) to Melbourne's Southern Cross Station ($9.40 to $13.40, one hour). Trains also head from Geelong to Warrnambool ($27.60, 2½ hours, three daily).

FERRY

There were plans to trial a new ferry (☑ 03-9514 8959; www.portphillipferries.com.au) in late 2019 that would link Geelong with Melbourne's Docklands – this would certainly be a more scenic way of getting between the two cities. Check the website for updates.

Bellarine Peninsula

Melburnians have been making the drive down the Princes Hwy (Geelong Rd) to the seaside villages along the Bellarine Peninsula for more than a century. It's known for family-friendly and surf beaches, historic towns, and wonderful cool-climate wineries.

As well as linking up with the Great Ocean Road, it's just a short ferry trip from here over to the Mornington Peninsula.

The Wathaurong people, who resided here and along the coast to Lorne for over 25,000 years, are the traditional custodians of the Bellarine Peninsula.

❶ Information

Bellarine Visitor Information Centre
(☑ 1800 755 611, 03-5250 6861; www.visitgeelongbellarine.com.au; 1251 Bellarine Hwy, Wallington; ◷ 9am-5pm) Located within the premises of Flying Brick Cider Co. (p544), this visitor centre has a heap of brochures and ideas on what to do in the area.

❶ Getting There & Away

BUS

McHarry's Buslines (p542) Connects Geelong with Barwon Heads (30 minutes), Ocean Grove (45 minutes), Portarlington (45 minutes), Point Lonsdale (55 minutes) and Queenscliff (one hour). A two-hour/day ticket costs $3.40/6.80; myki card required.

CAR

From Melbourne the Bellarine Peninsula is easily accessible via the Princes Fwy (M1) to Geelong. Be sure not to take the Geelong bypass; instead, take the Geelong exit and follow the signs to the Bellarine Hwy (B110).

FERRY

Port Phillip Ferries (☑ 03-9514 8959; www.portphillipferries.com.au; Portarlington Pier, Portarlington; one way adult/child $16/8) A serious boon for the region is the introduction of a ferry service linking Portarlington with Melbourne (one way adult/child $16/8, 1½ hours). There are two departures per day from Portarlington to Melbourne's Docklands.

Queenscliff–Sorrento Ferry (☑ 03-5257 4500; www.searoad.com.au; 1 Wharf St East, Queenscliff; one way foot passenger adult/child $13/9, car incl driver $67, bicycle free; ◷ hourly 6am-6pm) Runs between Queenscliff and Sorrento (40 minutes); till 7pm at peak times.

BICYCLE

Bring along your bike from Melbourne on the train and get off at South Geelong Station to pedal the **Bellarine Rail Trail** (www.railtrails.org.au) for 35km to Queenscliff. The path follows the historical train line, away from the road.

Queenscliff

POP 1315

Historic Queenscliff is a charming seaside town that mixes a salty maritime character with one of Victoria's most picturesque streetscapes. Many of its heritage-listed 19th-century buildings have been converted into hotels, restaurants and art galleries. It's a great base from which to explore the nearby wineries and beaches, along with the various historical sites and museums in town. The views across the Port Phillip Heads and Bass Strait are glorious.

◉ Sights

Queenscliff Maritime Museum   MUSEUM
(☑ 03-5258 3440; www.maritimequeenscliffe.org.au; 2 Wharf St; adult/child $8/5; ◷ 11am-4pm) Home to the last lifeboat to serve the Rip, this recommended museum has displays on the intriguing current-day pilot-boat process, shipwrecks, lighthouses and steamships. Head out the back to see the historic 1895 boat shed, with paintings that served as a record of passing ships in the bay.

Fort Queenscliff   HISTORIC SITE
(☑ 03-5258 1488; www.fortqueenscliff.com.au; cnr Gellibrand & King Sts; 90min tours adult/child/family $15/7/35; ◷ 11am, 1.45pm & 3pm daily school holidays, 11am Mon-Fri, 11am & 1.45pm Sat & Sun rest of year) Queencliff's fort was first used as a coastal defence in 1882 to protect Melbourne from a feared Russian invasion. It remained a base until 1946, and was then used as the Army Staff College until late 2012; today it functions as the defence department's archive. Tours take in the military museum (not always accessible), the magazine, cells and the twin lighthouses (including the iconic black lighthouse). It's a defence area, so bring ID for entry and arrive 10 minutes early.

Queenscliff Gallery   GALLERY
(☑ 03-4202 0942; www.qgw.com.au; 81 Hesse St; ◷ 10am-5pm Wed-Mon, daily summer) **FREE** A lovely space inside a historic stone church (c 1868), this worthwhile gallery exhibits works by contemporary Australian artists

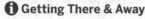

MELBOURNE & VICTORIA BELLARINE PENINSULA

BELLARINE WINERIES

Well known for its cool-climate pinot noir, chardonnay and shiraz, the Bellarine/Geelong region has more than 50 wineries. If you don't have your own transport, consider a winery tour with **For the Love of Grape** (📞0408 388 332; www.fortheloveofgrape.com. au; half-/full-day tours from Geelong $85/149, from Melbourne $95/159), or visit during the **Toast to the Coast** (www.toasttothecoast.com.au; tickets per day $40; ☉early Nov) festival in November.

Most wineries listed here are open weekends only (daily during summer); at other times call ahead. For a full list of the region's wineries, check out www.winegeelong.com. au.

The area is also famous for its produce, from goat's-milk cheese and olives to mussels and blueberries. Combine a winery hop with the **Bellarine Taste Trail** (www. thebellarinetastetrail.com.au) and you've got yourself a fantastic day out.

Scotchmans Hill (📞03-5251 3176; www.scotchmans.com.au; 190 Scotchmans Rd, Drysdale; mains $18-26; ☉10.30am-4.30pm) One of the Bellarine's first wineries remains one of its very best, with a new winery-restaurant that is another reason to visit.

Jack Rabbit (📞03-5251 2223; www.jackrabbitvineyard.com.au; 85 McAdams Lane, Bellarine; restaurant mains from $20; ☉noon-3pm Sun-Thu, noon-3pm & 6-11pm Fri & Sat) Come to this boutique winery to take in stunning bay views from its deck while enjoying a glass of pinot and a bowl of mussels.

Basils Farm (📞03-5258 4280; www.basilsfarm.com.au; 43-53 Nye Rd, Swan Bay; ☉10am-4pm Wed-Sun, daily Jan) Enjoy a bottle of prosecco, a produce platter and fabulous views of Swan Bay at this boutique winery.

Banks Road (📞0431 896 331; www.banksroad.com.au; 600 Banks Rd, Marcus Hill; ☉cellar door 11am-5pm Thu-Sun, or by appointment) Come for a glass of pinot gris while looking out to open-air sculptures in a pastoral setting shared with a quality restaurant.

Oakdene (📞03-5256 3886; www.oakdene.com.au; 255 Grubb Rd, Wallington; ☉cellar door 10am-4pm, cafe noon-3.30pm & 5-7.30pm Mon-Fri, 8.30am-7.30pm Sat & Sun, restaurant 6.30pm-late Wed-Fri, from noon Sat & Sun) Set in a quirky upside-down barn and surrounded by arty objects, this is a vineyard with a difference. It's also popular for its fine and casual dining.

Flying Brick Cider Co. (📞03-5250 6577; www.flyingbrickciderco.com.au; 1251-1269 Bellarine Hwy, Wallington; tasting paddles $14; ☉bar 10am-5pm Sun-Thu, to late Fri & Sat, restaurant 11.30am-3pm Mon-Thu, 11.30am-3pm & 6-9pm Fri & Sat, noon-4pm Sun) Not a winery, but worth a stop, this popular cider house produces a range of quality alcoholic apple and pear ciders, to be enjoyed in its grassy outdoor area.

Terindah Estate (📞03-5251 5536; www.terindahestate.com; 90 McAdams Lane, Bellarine; breakfast $11-15, mains $27-39; ☉tastings 10am-4pm daily, Shed noon-4pm Thu, Fri & Mon, 8-10am, noon-4pm & 6-10pm Sat, 8-10am & noon-4pm Sun) This winery has incredible views, quality pinots and fine dining in its glasshouse shed.

McGlashan's Wallington Estate (📞03-5250 5760; www.mcglashans.com.au; 225 Swan Bay Rd, Wallington; platters for 2-4 people $19-48; ☉11am-5pm Thu-Sun, daily Jan) This unpretentious winery offers tastings of its quality shiraz (and its ales) in a barn decorated with motor memorabilia.

who work on paper. Lithography is the main focus, and all works are available for purchase.

🏃 Activities

Scubabo Dive Victoria　　　　DIVING
(Queenscliff Dive Centre; 📞0499 588 846, 0431 336 866, 03-5258 4188; www.dive.scubabo.com/ melbourne; Queenscliff Harbour; per dive with/without gear $135/65) Scubabo offers SSI diving courses and trips for all levels, from intro to technical. There are some 200 sites in the area, taking in rich marine life and shipwrecks from the past three centuries, including ex-HMAS *Canberra*, scuttled in 2009, and WWI submarines. Snorkel

trips are also possible. Visit the website for upcoming trips and training courses.

Sea-All Dolphin Swims
WILDLIFE

(☎03-5258 3889; www.dolphinswims.com.au; Queenscliff Harbour; adult/child sightseeing tours $89/69, 3½hr snorkel $149/129; ⊘9am & 1.30pm 9 Oct-9 May) Offers sightseeing tours and swims with seals and dolphins in Port Phillip Heads Marine National Park. Seal sightings are guaranteed; dolphins aren't always, but there's a good chance. Snorkelling trips take in Pope's Eye (an unfinished military fort), which is home to abundant fish and an Australasian gannet breeding colony, before visiting a permanent Australian fur seal colony at Chinaman's Hat. Note that some animal welfare organisations counsel against swimming with wild marine animals.

★✦ Festivals & Events

Queenscliff Music Festival
MUSIC

(☎03-5258 4816; www.qmf.net.au; ⊘last weekend Nov) One of the coast's best festivals features big-name Australian and international musos with a folksy, bluesy bent. It's held at numerous stages and venues around town.

🛏 Sleeping

Twomey's Cottage
B&B $

(☎0400 265 877; www.classiccottages.com.au; 13 St Andrews St; d weekday/weekend from $130/140) Just the place to soak up Queenscliff's historical atmosphere, this heritage fisher's cottage is fantastic value. Its claim to fame is as the residence of artist Fred Williams when he painted his Queenscliff series. Renowned recitalist Keith Humble also composed music here, so creative vibes abound.

Sister property nearby **Albion Cottage** (☎0400 265 877; www.classiccottages.com.au; 43 Stevens St; d midweek/weekend from $140/185) is a similarly charming option.

Cobb & Co Lodge
HOSTEL $

(☎03-5258 4188; 37 Learmonth St; dm/d with shared bathroom $55/140; 🛜🏊) While this hostel-style accommodation is primarily for divers, if there are rooms available it's a good option for budget travellers too. The modern shared kitchen and lounge facilities are bright and airy, while the simple rooms are out the back. It was built in 1864, when it was used as Cobb & Co stable.

★ Vue Grand
HOTEL $$

(☎03-5258 1544; www.vuegrand.com.au; 46-48 Hesse St; r incl breakfast $198-495; ❄🛜) One

of Queenscliff's most elegant historic buildings, the Vue has everything from standard pub rooms to a modern turret suite (boasting 360-degree views) and bay-view rooms (with freestanding baths in their lounges).

Athelstane House
BOUTIQUE HOTEL $$

(☎03-5258 1024; www.athelstane.com.au; 4 Hobson St; r incl breakfast $160-310; ❄🛜) Dating back to 1860, beautifully kept, double-storey Athelstane House is notable as Queenscliff's oldest guesthouse. Its rooms are spotless, mixing period touches with modern comforts such as corner spa baths, iPod docks, DVD players and fast wi-fi. Its front lounge is a good place to hang out, with a vintage record player and a stack of vinyl.

🍴 Eating & Drinking

Charlie Noble
CAFE $

(☎03-5258 5161; www.charlienoble.com.au; Shop 5, 4 Wharf St; mains breakfast $10-22, lunch $12-23; ⊘9am-3.30pm Mon-Fri, 8am-3.30 Sat & Sun) With a prime location on the sparkling marina overlooking luxury yachts, this good all-rounder does tasty, hearty breakfasts, pizzas, burgers and seafood spaghetti.

Athelstane House
AUSTRALIAN $$

(☎03-5258 1024; www.athelstane.com.au; 4 Hobson St; breakfast $10-22, mains $32-40; ⊘8-11.30am & 6-8.30pm; 🛜) Come for breakfast or dinner inside this lovely heritage home, or outside on the pretty garden deck. For dinner choose from a daily seasonal menu that may include chargrilled eye fillet or tempura-battered fish. In the morning there's homemade oven-baked muesli as well as hot breakfasts.

Circa 1902
INTERNATIONAL $$

(☎0499 771 674; www.circa1902.com.au; 59 Hesse St; mains $18-20, tapas $7-13.50; ⊘noon-2.30pm & 6-8.30pm Mon-Fri, 11.30am-3pm & 5.30-9pm Sat & Sun; 🛜) On the main street, this historic hotel (c 1902) is a popular place to soak up Queenscliff's heritage atmosphere. It does multinational cuisine ranging from Goan chicken curry to seafood pies, but it's best known for its tapas. It's a good spot to sample regional wines and beers too.

Queenscliff Brewhouse
PUB

(☎03-5258 1717; www.queenscliffbrewhouse.com.au; 2 Gellibrand St; ⊘11am-late) Branching out from its Otways base (p555), Prickly Moses has set up a second brewhouse here in Queenscliff. The full range is showcased on tap, plus there are a few of its own local

LON RETREAT

In the same family for seven generations since the 19th century, this farm underwent a dramatic redevelopment in 2018 to become the upmarket **Lon Retreat** (☑ 03-5258 2990; www.lonretreat.com.au; 25 Gill Rd, Point Lonsdale; r $395-850; treatments from $165; ❋). It's still run by the family, with hosts Claire and Rob offering a tasteful brand of informal luxury. Villas feature stylish, understated design, with handmade furniture and works by local artists. Minimum two-night stay.

beers, as well as a selection of guest brewers, best enjoyed in the beer garden. It's also started distilling gin, and there's an upstairs whisky bar.

☆ Entertainment

Blues Train LIVE MUSIC
(☑ 1300 885 993; www.thebluestrain.com.au; Queenscliff Station; tickets incl dinner from $118; ⊙ departures 6.30pm Fri & Sat Sep-May) Get your foot tapping with train trips that feature not one but four quality blues and roots bands on different carriages, along with dinner. The historic train leaves Queenscliff Station most weeks; it's popular, so book well ahead. Check the website for performers.

ⓘ Information

Queenscliff Visitor Centre (☑ 03-5258 4843; www.queenscliff.com.au; 55 Hesse St; ⊙ 9am-5pm; ☎) Has plenty of brochures on the area and sells the self-guided walking-tour map *Queenscliff – A Living Heritage*. Wi-fi and internet access next door at the library.

Torquay

POP 13,258

In the 1960s and '70s Torquay was just another sleepy seaside town. Back then, surfing in Australia was a decidedly countercultural pursuit, its devotees crusty hippy dropouts living in clapped-out Kombis, smoking pot and making off with your daughters. These days it's become unabashedly mainstream, and the town's proximity to world-famous Bells Beach and its status as the home of two iconic surf brands – Rip Curl and Quiksilver, both initially wetsuit makers – ensure Torquay's place as the undisputed capital of the country's surf industry. It's one of Australia's fastest-growing towns, experiencing a population increase of 67% between 2001 and 2013 that these days makes it feel almost like an outer suburb of Geelong.

It has some lovely beaches, plus a growing number of hip cafes and restaurants, and one of Victoria's more innovative breweries.

◉ Sights & Activities

★ **Australian National Surfing Museum** MUSEUM
(☑ 03-5261 4606; www.australiannationalsurfing museum.com; Surf City Plaza, 77 Beach Rd; adult/child/family $12/8/25; ⊙ 9am-5pm) The perfect starting point for those embarking on a surfing safari, this superbly curated museum pays homage to Australian surfing. Here you'll see Simon Anderson's ground-breaking 1981 thruster, Mark Richard's awesome airbrushed board-art collection and, most notably, Australia's Surfing Hall of Fame. It's full of great memorabilia (including Duke Kahanamoku's wooden longboard), videos and displays on surf culture from the 1960s to the '80s. Its themed shows throughout the year are always quality too.

Torquay Surf Academy SURFING
(☑ 03-5261 2022; www.torquaysurf.com.au; 34a Bell St; 2hr group/private lesson $60/180) Offers one-on-one and group surfing lessons. Also hires surfboards (from $25), stand-up paddleboards (from $35) and bodyboards ($20); it's $5 extra for a wetsuit. It also rents out bikes (half-/full day $25/30) and kayaks ($40/50).

⌂ Sleeping

Bells Beach Backpackers HOSTEL $
(☑ 03-5261 4029; www.bellsbeachbackpackers. com.au; 51-53 Surfcoast Hwy; van sites per double $24-30, dm $28-36, d with shared bathroom $80-100; @☎) On the main highway in Torquay (not Bells Beach), this friendly backpackers does a great job of fitting into the fabric of this surf town. It has a casual, relaxed atmosphere, with basic rooms that are clean and in good nick, and a large kitchen that 'van packers' can also use.

**Beachside
Accommodation** APARTMENT $

(☑ 03-5261 5258, 0419 587 445; www.beachside accommodationtorquay.com.au; 24 Felix Cres; d $110-160; ❋ 🕲) Only a five-minute stroll to the beach, this relaxed residential-style accommodation is owned by a German-English couple. You'll get a private patio with a barbecue and an Aussie-backyard atmosphere.

**Torquay Foreshore
Caravan Park** CAMPGROUND $

(☑ 03-5261 2496, 1300 736 533; www.torquaycaravanpark.com.au; 35 Bell St; powered sites $55-100, cabins $95-400; 🕲) Just behind the Back Beach is the largest campground on the Surf Coast. It has good facilities and premium-priced cabins with sea views. Wi-fi is limited.

✖ Eating & Drinking

Cafe Moby CAFE $

(☑ 03-5261 2339; www.cafemoby.com.au; 41 The Esplanade; dishes $8-25; ☺ 6.30am-4pm; 🕲🍴) This old weatherboard house on The Esplanade harks back to a time when Torquay was simple – which isn't to say its meals aren't modern. Fill up on smoked-bacon breakfast burgers, spiced-duck tacos or slow-cooked lamb souvlaki. There's a whopping great playground for kids, and a little bar out the front doing local beers.

Quiksilver Bar 61 CAFE $

(☑ 03-5261 7592; www.facebook.com/board ridersbar61; Surf City Plaza, 61 Surf Coast Hwy; mains $10-22; ☺ 7am-4pm Sun-Thu, to 10.30pm Fri & Sat; 🕲) Part of the home-grown Quiksilver brand, this flagship surf shop has a cool rooftop cafe-bar that screens surf vids while you feast on flathead-tail tacos and sip cold local brews. There's also a barber, free yoga at 6.45am on Thursday, and live music at weekends.

Fisho's SEAFOOD $$

(☑ 0474 342 124; www.facebook.com/fishos torquay; 36 The Esplanade; mains from $21; ☺ noon-3pm & 5-8pm) Not your average fish-and-chip shop, this oceanfront joint does original takes on the classics, such as gummy-shark tacos, sticky-fried-snapper wings and sweet-potato cakes. It's set up in an atmospheric weatherboard house with AstroTurf front seating, and local beer and cider on tap.

★**Blackman's Brewery** MICROBREWERY

(☑ 03-5261 5310; www.blackmansbrewery.com.au; 26 Bell St; ☺ noon-10pm Wed-Sun, daily summer) One of Victoria's best microbreweries is this brewpub, where you can taste all eight Blackman's beers, which are produced on-site. Go the tasting paddle ($16) to sample the range of IPAs, unfiltered lager, pale ale and inventive seasonals – enjoy by a roaring fire or in the AstroTurf beer garden. A gun chef does a menu of modern European shared plates.

★**Bomboras** BAR

(www.bomboras.com.au; 48 The Esplanade, Fisherman's Beach; ☺ noon-9.30pm 1 Oct–Easter) The place to be in summer, this pop-up rooftop beach bar has prime ocean views. Enjoy local brews on tap, cocktails, pizza, and live music or DJs.

It also has a **pizzeria** (☑ 03-5264 7881; 37 The Esplanade; pizzas $12-21; ☺ 6am-late) up the road.

Ocean Grind COFFEE

(☑ 0448 884 099; www.oceangrind.com.au; 10b Sawmills Way; ☺ 7am-2pm Mon-Sat) ✎ Torquay's best coffee is in its outskirts, where this third-wave micro-roaster in an industrial space serves up single-origin batch brews and espresso coffees. There are pastries, plus a food truck Wednesday and Thursday.

🛍 Shopping

**Rip Curl Surf
Factory Outlet** FASHION & ACCESSORIES

(Baines Surf Seconds; 16 Baines Cres; ☺ 9am-5.30pm) Rip Curl's shiny main outlet is in Surf City Plaza, but head round the back to the industrial estate for the factory outlet, where you'll get 30% off the price of last season's clothing and wetsuits. A big-name global brand these days, Rip Curl was founded in Torquay in 1969.

ℹ Information

Torquay Visitor Information Centre (www.torquaylife.com.au; Surf City Plaza, Beach Rd; ☺ 9am-5pm) The well-resourced tourist office next to the Australian National Surfing Museum (p546) makes a good starting point along the Great Ocean Road to fine-tune your itinerary. There's free wi-fi and internet access at the library next door.

ℹ Getting There & Away

Torquay is 15 minutes' drive south of Geelong on the B100.

McHarry's Buslines (p542) Bus 51 runs hourly from 9am to 8pm (around 5pm weekends) between Geelong and Torquay ($3.40, 40 minutes).

V/Line (p542) Buses run four times daily from Geelong to Torquay ($3.40, 25 minutes).

Bells Beach & Point Addis

The Great Ocean Road officially begins on the stretch between Torquay and Anglesea. A slight detour takes you to famous **Bells Beach**, the powerful point break that's part of international surfing folklore; it has hosted Australia's premier surfing event, the Bells Classic, since 1973. (It was here too, in name only, that Keanu Reeves and Patrick Swayze had their ultimate showdown in the film *Point Break*.)

Around 3km away, on the outskirts of Torquay, is the surf town of **Jan Juc**, a local hang-out for surfers, with a mellow, sleepy vibe. Nine kilometres southwest of Torquay is the turn-off to spectacular **Point Addis**, a vast sweep of pristine, clothing-optional beach that attracts surfers, nudists, hang-gliders and swimmers.

The Wathaurong people are the traditional custodians of this stretch of coast, and you can learn about their culture on the recommended Koorie Cultural Walk.

Activities

★Koorie Cultural Walk WALKING

A highly recommended detour signposted off the Great Ocean Road is the fantastic Koorie Cultural Walk, a 2km trail (one hour return) that details how the Indigenous Wathaurung people lived here for millennia. It's a lovely bushwalk through Great Otway National Park, with echidnas and wallabies, and spectacular coastal outlooks of dramatic cliffs and pristine beaches, including **Addiscott Beach**.

In 1836 a community of some 700 Wathaurung people resided in the immediate area; tragically, by 1853 this number had been reduced to a mere 35 as a direct result of European settlement. In the car park at the top of the hill there's a plaque about William Buckley (p550), an escaped convict who spent 32 years living with the Wathaurung from 1803.

★Surf Coast Walk WALKING

(www.surfcoastwalk.com.au) This epic walks follows the scenic coastline for 44km from Torquay to Fairhaven, just outside Aireys Inlet. The route is divided into 12 distinct walks (see the website for the breakdown), which cover an impressive diversity of landscapes along ocean clifftops, past empty beaches and through the bushland of Great Otway National Park.

Getting There & Away

Catch bus 51 from Geelong Station to Jan Juc ($3.40, 50 minutes, hourly till around 8pm) via Torquay.

For Bells Beach you'll need a car. The beach is about 4km east of the Great Ocean Road; follow the signs after the roundabout in Bellbrae.

Anglesea

POP 2538

Mix sheer orange cliffs falling into the ocean with hilly, tree-filled 'burbs and a population that booms in summer and you've got Anglesea, where sharing fish and chips with seagulls by the Anglesea River is a decades-long family tradition for many.

Activities

Anglesea Golf Club Kangaroo Tours WILDLIFE WATCHING

(☎03-5263 1582; www.angleseagolfclub.com.au; Anglesea Golf Club, Golf Links Rd; 20min kangaroo tours adult/child/family $12.50/5/30, 9/18 holes from $30/50, club hire 9/18 holes $25/35; ⏲10am-4pm) Get up close to eastern grey kangaroos on a tour of Anglesea's golf course, famous for its mob of resident roos that have lived here for many a year. Tours are informative and offer good photo ops.

Go Ride a Wave SURFING

(☎03-5263 2111, 1300 132 441; www.gorideawave.com.au; 143b Great Ocean Rd; 2hr lesson adult/child from $72/62, 2hr board hire from $25; ⏲9am-5pm) Long-established surf school that runs lessons and hires out boards, stand-up paddleboards and kayaks. Operates at different locations down the Bellarine Peninsula and along the Great Ocean Road.

Sleeping

Anglesea Backpackers HOSTEL $

(☎03-5263 2664; www.angleseabackpackers.com; 40 Noble St; dm $32-35, d/tr $95/150; @ 📶) While most hostels like to cram 'em in, this simple, homey backpackers has just two dorm rooms and one double/triple, and is clean, bright and welcoming. In winter the fire glows warmly in the cosy living room. There are free bikes for guests and the owner can pick you up from town or as far away as Torquay.

Anglesea Rivergums B&B $
(✓0414 855 014, 03-5263 3066; www.angleseariver gums.com.au; 10 Bingley Pde; d $140-150; ✱) Tucked by the river with tranquil views, these two spacious, tastefully furnished rooms (a self-contained bungalow and a room attached to the house) are excellent value and a good option for self-caterers. Two-night minimum.

Great Ocean Properties ACCOMMODATION SERVICES $$
(✓03-5263 1100; www.greatoceanproperties.com. au; 101 Great Ocean Rd) Has a range of beach-house rentals; two-night minimum.

✖ Eating

Hot Chicken Project CHICKEN $
(✓03-5263 1365; www.thehotchickenproject. com; 143a Great Ocean Rd; mains $18; ⊙noon-9pm) Anglesea's dining scene just got a little hotter with the arrival of this spicy-chicken joint from Geelong (p541).

Four Kings CAFE $
(www.facebook.com/4kingscoffee; 143a Great Ocean Rd; breakfast from $10; ⊙6am-3pm) Set up by a youthful local team, this quality cafe has excellent coffee from Padre in Melbourne, good-value all-day brekkies, and gourmet toasties and lunch options. Daily specials are also worth checking out. It has plenty of plants, artwork and reclaimed-wood finishes, including menus made from the decking of Anglesea beach houses.

★ **Captain Moonlite** AUSTRALIAN $$
(✓03-5263 2454; www.captainmoonlite.com.au; 100 Great Ocean Rd; breakfast $8-16, lunch & dinner from $26; ⊙8am-10pm Fri-Sun, to 3pm Mon, 5.30-10pm Thu) Sharing space with the life-saving club – and with unbeatable beach views – Moonlite is Anglesea's first restaurant to earn a *Good Food Guide* chef's hat. It mixes an unpretentious atmosphere with a quality menu it describes as 'coastal European'. Expect tasty breakfasts such as ocean trout on rye with a soft-boiled egg, meze-style plates, and mains such as slow-roasted lamb and fresh seafood.

❶ Information

Anglesea Visitor Information Centre (www. visitgreatoceanroad.org.au; Great Ocean Rd;

⊙9am-5pm; ☎) Located at the lake, this tiny volunteer-run information centre has a heap of brochures on the area, including walks in the surrounding Great Otway National Park.

❶ Getting There & Away

The Geelong bypass has reduced the time it takes to drive from Melbourne to Anglesea to around 1½ hours.

There are four to six daily V/Line buses between Geelong and Anglesea ($6.80, 45 mins).

Aireys Inlet & Around

POP 1116

Midway between Anglesea and Lorne, Aireys Inlet is an attractive coastal hamlet that makes for an essential stop along the Great Ocean Road. It's home to a historic lighthouse that forms the backdrop to glorious stretches of beach, including **Fairhaven** and **Moggs Creek**. Its microbrewery, gin distillery and acclaimed restaurant are other reasons to stop.

◎ Sights & Activities

★ **Split Point Lighthouse** LIGHTHOUSE
(✓03-5263 1133, 1800 174 045; www.splitpoint lighthouse.com.au; Federal St; 40min tours adult/child/family $14/8/40; ⊙tours hourly 11am-2pm, 10am-4pm summer) Scale the 136 steps to the top of the beautiful 'White Queen' lighthouse for sensational 360-degree views. Built in 1891, the 34m-high lighthouse is still operational, though it's now fully automated. A guide will accompany you to the top, recounting the area's history and local stories. The lighthouse was used as a setting for the popular TV show *Round the Twist*.

Great Ocean Road Gin DISTILLERY
(✓03-5210 5705; www.greatoceanroadgin.com. au; 32 Great Ocean Rd; tastings/cocktails $15/18; ⊙12.30-8pm Wed-Sun) Gin distilleries are popping up everywhere, but Aireys is the first Great Ocean Road town to get one. Though it distills off-site, you can stop by its bar to sample the gins (a navy strength and a citrus-driven classic dry), both featuring indigenous botanicals, including coastal succulents, kelp and surf-coast honey. There are G&Ts and cocktails to go with bar snacks. Call ahead to confirm it's open.

Blazing Saddles HORSE RIDING
(✓03-5289 7322, 0418 508 647; www.blazingsaddles trailrides.com; Lot 1, Bimbadeen Dr; 1½hr bush rides from $60, 2½hr beach & bush rides $130) People

THE WATHAURUNG & WILLIAM BUCKLEY

As you tour this stretch of coast from the Bellarine Peninsula to the Great Ocean Road, consider the Wathaurung people who inhabited the area from Geelong to Aireys Inlet.

A unique insight into their lives emerges through the remarkable story of William Buckley, an escaped convict who lived with the Wathaurung for 32 years (1803 to 1835). They accepted this 'wild white man' as one of their own, and he lived, hunted and camped with them through Point Lonsdale, Torquay, Point Addis, Anglesea and Aireys Inlet. The period is detailed in his autobiography, *The Life and Adventures of William Buckley*.

His story is believed by many to lend its name to the colloquialism 'you've got Buckley's chance' – meaning you've got little to no chance – entrenched in the Australian vernacular as a tribute to Buckley's survival against the odds.

In the Geelong or Bellarine visitor centres, pick up the *William Buckley Discovery Trail* map to visit 19 sites that he passed through, each with interpretative plaques.

come from around the world to hop on a Blazing Saddles horse and head along stunning Fairhaven Beach or into the bush.

🛏 Sleeping

Hammond Road Campground　CAMPGROUND
(☑ 13 19 63; www.parkweb.vic.gov.au; Hammond Rd, Wensleydale) FREE You'll need your own wheels to reach it, but this free bush campground is an excellent option for travellers who are here with a van or tent. Located 13km inland northwest of Aireys on the road to Bambra, its 20 sites are offered on a first-come, first-served basis. It has non-flushing toilets, and fireplaces (use prohibited in summer).

Aireys Inlet Holiday Park　CABIN $
(☑ 03-5289 6230; www.aicp.com.au; 19-25 Great Ocean Rd; unpowered sites $34-68, powered sites $39-80, cabins $105-285; @ 🕸 🏊) The only budget option in Aireys itself is this well-maintained caravan park that's more cabin town than tent city. Facilities are all spick and span, and it's conveniently located for the pub, top shops and beach.

Aireys Inlet Getaway　VILLA $$
(☑ 03-5289 7021; www.aireysinletgetaway.com.au; 2-4 Barton Ct; d low/high season from $140/250; 🕸 🕸) These self-contained villas, great for families or couples, are well placed a short walk from the beach, pub and shops. Rooms range from studios to two-bedroom lofts, all set in a complex featuring pool, tennis court and heated spa. It's often booked out during busy times, but it's excellent value if you're visiting midweek.

Pole House　RENTAL HOUSE $$$
(☑ 03-5220 0200; www.greatoceanroadholidays.com.au; 60 Banool Rd, Fairhaven; per night from $540) One of the most iconic houses along the Great Ocean Road, the Pole House is a unique architectural creation that, as the name suggests, sits atop a pole, with extraordinary ocean views. Access to the house is via an external pedestrian bridge. It's not suitable for children.

🍴 Eating & Drinking

Willows Tea House　CAFE $
(☑ 03-5289 6830; 7 Federal St; scones $4, breakfast & lunch $8-16; ⏱ 9am-4pm; 🕸) Soak up Aireys' seafaring atmosphere at this teahouse set up within a historic weatherboard cottage a few steps from the lighthouse. Stop by for morning or afternoon tea to indulge in homemade scones with jam and cream, enjoyed in the cosy interior or at outdoor tables. Its bacon-and-egg muffins are a good way to start the day.

★ **a la grecque**　GREEK $$
(☑ 03-5289 6922; www.alagrecque.com.au; 60 Great Ocean Rd; mains $28-40; ⏱ noon-2.30pm & 6-9.30pm Wed-Sun, closed winter) Be whisked away to the Mediterranean at this outstanding modern Greek taverna. Mezze such as seared scallops or chargrilled octopus with apple, celery and a lime dressing and mains such as grilled rack of lamb with *melitzanosalata* (eggplant dip) are sensational. So is the wine list.

★ **Aireys Pub**　PUB, BREWERY
(☑ 03-5289 6804; www.aireyspub.com.au; 45 Great Ocean Rd; ⏱ 11.30am-late; 🕸) 🍺 Established in 1904, this pub is a survivor, twice burning down before closing in 2011, only to be revived by locals chipping in to save it. Now it's better than ever, with an on-site brewery, **Salt Brewing Co** (www.saltbrewing.co). The food's fantastic (mains $17 to $42), and there's a meat smoker, a roaring fire, live music and a sprawling beer garden.

❶ Getting There & Away

From Melbourne, count on a 1¾-hour drive for the 123km trip to Aireys Inlet, or a bit longer if you're heading via Torquay (27km, 25 minutes).

Departing from Geelong Station, V/Line has four to six daily buses to Aireys Inlet ($9.40, one hour), which continue to nearby stops at Fairhaven, Moggs Creek and Eastern View for the same fare.

Lorne

POP 1026

One of the Great Ocean Road's original resort towns, Lorne may be a tad overdeveloped these days, but it retains all the charms that have lured visitors here since the 19th century. Beyond its main strip it has an incredible natural beauty: tall old gum trees line its hilly streets, and Loutit Bay gleams irresistibly. It backs onto the lovely eucalyptus forest, fern gullies and waterfalls that inspired Rudyard Kipling to pen his poem 'Flowers' in 1891.

It gets busy; in summer you'll be competing with day trippers for restaurant seats and lattes, but, thronged by tourists or not, it's a lovely place to hang out.

◎ Sights

★ Qdos Art Gallery   GALLERY
(📋 03-5289 1989; www.qdosarts.com; 35 Allenvale Rd; ⊙9am-5pm Thu-Mon, daily Jan, Fri-Mon winter) FREE Set amid the lush forest behind Lorne, Qdos always has something interesting showing at its contemporary gallery, to go with its open-air sculpture garden. There's also a lovely little cafe doing wood-fired pizzas and *ryokan*-style accommodation (p552).

Great Ocean Road Story   MUSEUM
(15 Mountjoy Pde; ⊙9am-5pm) FREE Inside Lorne Visitor Centre (p553), this permanent exhibition of displays, videos and books offers informative background to the Great Ocean Road's construction. There are multimedia displays, and the opportunity to get yourself superimposed into a picture of an old automobile chugging along the magnificent road.

Erskine Falls   WATERFALL
(Erskine Falls Access Rd) Head out of town to see this lovely 30m waterfall. It's an easy walk from the Erskine Falls car park to the viewing platform (15 minutes return) or 300, often slippery, steps down to its base (30 minutes return), from where you can explore further or head back up.

🏃 Activities

Live Wire Park   CLIMBING
(📋1300 548 394; www.livewirepark.com.au; 180 Erskine Falls Rd; adult/child $12/8, zip coaster $36/32, rope circuit from $52/45; ⊙9am-5pm, to 6pm summer) This park with a state-of-the-art zip line and high-ropes tree courses is in the rainforest 900m from town. Its most thrilling feature is the Shockwave Zip Coaster, a zip line that flies through a twisting eucalyptus-canopy circuit, covering 525m in 1½ minutes. The two rope circuits (lasting from one to two hours) encompass swings, zip lines, tree climbs, obstacles and suspension bridges.

Sharkys   SURFING
(📋03-5289 2421; www.sharkys.com.au; Shop 12, 150 Mountjoy Pde; 2hr surfboard rental incl wetsuit $25; ⊙9am-5pm) Long-established local surf shop that rents out boards and wetsuits.

🎆 Festivals & Events

Falls Festival   MUSIC
(www.fallsfestival.com; 2-/3-/4-day tickets $259/340/349; ⊙28 Dec-1 Jan) A four-day knees-up over New Year's on a farm just out of town, this stellar music festival attracts a top line-up of international rock and indie groups. Past headliners include Iggy Pop, the Kings of Leon and the Black Keys. Sells out fast (usually within an hour); camping ($139) and parking ($40) is additional.

🛏 Sleeping

Allenvale Mill
Site Campground   CAMPGROUND
(📋13 19 63; www.parkweb.vic.gov.au) FREE At the back of Lorne, off Allenvale Rd, this free bush campground has picnic tables and non-flushing toilets but no fires; bring along a gas stove if you plan to cook. It has 16 sites, but it's not possible to book; if it's full, try Big Hill Track (📋13 19 63; www.parkweb.vic.gov. au; 1265 Deans Marsh-Lorne Rd, Benwerrin) FREE.

Great Ocean Road Cottages   HOSTEL $
(📋03-5289 1070; www.greatoceanroadcottages. com; 10 Erskine Ave; dm $35-50, d $100-180; ❄🛜) On a lovely garden property replete with trees and bird life, this friendly backpackers has dorm and private double options, both with cooking facilities. It's a five-minute

walk from town, up a steep road running past the IGA supermarket.

Cash bookings bring discounted rates.

Lorne Foreshore
Caravan Park
CAMPGROUND $

(☑1300 364 797, 03-5289 1382; www.lornecaravan park.com.au; 2 Great Ocean Rd; unpowered sites $40-80, powered sites $45-95, cabins $135-195; ❄️☎️) Book at the Foreshore for all of Lorne's five caravan parks. Of these, **Erskine River Caravan Park** is the prettiest, though note that there's no swimming in the river. It's on the left-hand side as you enter Lorne, just before the bridge. Book well ahead for peak-season stays. Wi-fi is limited.

Grand Pacific Hotel
HISTORIC HOTEL $$

(☑03-5289 1609; www.grandpacific.com.au; 268 Mountjoy Pde; d $130-250; ❄️☎️) A Lorne landmark harking back to 1875, the Grand Pacific has been restored and now boasts sleek modern decor that retains some classic period features. The best rooms have balconies and stunning sea views out to the pier. Plainer rooms are boxy but still top value, and there are self-contained apartments too.

★ Qdos
RYOKAN $$$

(☑03-5289 1989; www.qdosarts.com; 35 Allenvale Rd; r incl breakfast $325-495; ☎️) The perfect choice for those seeking a romantic getaway or forest retreat, Qdos' luxury Zen tree houses are fitted with tatami mats, rice-paper screens and no TV. Two-night minimum at weekends; no kids.

✖️ Eating & Drinking

HAH
CAFE $

(Health & Hire Lorne Beach; ☑0406 453 131, 0437 759 469; www.hahlornebeach.com.au; 81 Mountjoy Pde; mains from $10; ⊘8am-5.30pm, longer hours summer; ☎️) This health-conscious cafe has a prime location on the foreshore and a menu loaded with superfoods, protein balls, salads, vegan and paleo dishes, and leafy smoothies. There are also gourmet toasties and home-baked banana bread drizzled with Lorne honey.

Swing Bridge Cafe & Boathouse
CAFE $

(☑0423 814 770; 30 Great Ocean Rd; dishes $10-22; ⊘8am-2.30pm, 7am-10pm summer) This tiny cafe at the historic swing bridge (c 1934) has an appealing retro vibe. It's the place for single-origin coffee to go with a brioche filled with anything from pulled pork to beef brisket to jerk tofu with salsa verde. On summer evenings it does Argentine-style charcoal

barbecues or paella on the lawn, paired beautifully with a carafe of wine ($28).

Pizza Pizza
PIZZA $

(☑03-5289 1007; www.pizzapizzalorne.com; 2 Mountjoy Pde; pizzas $16-21; ⊘3-8.30pm) Set up in a weatherboard cottage, this is easily Lorne's best spot for authentic thin-crust pizza.

★ Ipsos
GREEK $$

(☑03-5289 1883; www.ipsosrestaurant.com.au; 48 Mountjoy Pde; sharing plates $5-26, larger plates $28-66; ⊘noon-3pm & 6-10pm Thu-Mon, longer hours summer) From the same family that ran Kosta – a Lorne institution that's relocated to Aireys Inlet as a la grecque (p550) – comes this smart, casual taverna that occupies the same location where it all started in 1974. The menu comprises mainly Greek-influenced sharing plates, or go for the signature slow-roasted lamb shoulder ($66 for two people).

It earned a *Good Food Guide* hat in 2018.

★ Lorne Beach Pavilion
AUSTRALIAN $$

(☑03-5289 2882; www.lornebeachpavilion.com. au; 81 Mountjoy Pde; breakfast $8-24, mains $18-45; ⊘9am-5pm Mon-Thu, to 9pm Fri, 8am-9pm Sat & Sun) With its unbeatable foreshore location, life here is a beach, especially with a cold drink in hand. Cafe-style breakfasts and lunches hit the spot, while a more upmarket modern Australian menu of seafood and rib-eye steaks is on for dinner. Come at happy hour (3pm to 6pm) for $7 pints, or swing by at sunset for a bottle of prosecco.

★ Movida Lorne
SPANISH $$$

(☑03-5289 1042; www.movida.com.au; 176 Mountjoy Pde; tapas $4-8.50, raciones $15-70; ⊘noon-3pm & 5.30-10pm) One of Melbourne's hottest restaurants has gone for a sea change: setting up on the ground floor of the **Lorne Hotel** (☑03-5289 1409; www.lornehotel.com.au; 176 Mountjoy Pde; r $160-300; ❄️☎️), Movida has brought its authentic Spanish cuisine to the Great Ocean Road. The menu features a mix of classic dishes made with flair using regional produce.

❶ Information

Lorne Visitor Centre (☑1300 891 152, 03-5289 1152; www.lovelorne.com.au; 15 Mountjoy Pde; ⊘9am-5pm; ☎️) Stacks of information (including heaps of ideas for walks in the area), helpful staff, fishing licences, bus tickets and accommodation referrals. Also has a gift shop,

BRAE IN BIRREGURRA

Regarded as one of Australia's best restaurants, Brae (☑03-5236 2226; www.brae restaurant.com; 4285 Cape Otway Rd; 8-course tasting plates per person $275, matched wines additional $175; ⊙from 6pm Thu, noon-3pm & from 6pm Fri & Sat, noon-3pm Sun & Mon) was established by acclaimed chef Dan Hunter – who made his name at Dunkeld's Royal Mail Hotel – in 2012. The restaurant mostly uses whatever's growing in its 12 hectares of organic gardens to create delightful gastronomic concoctions, all masterfully presented and with plenty of surprises.

Set within an attractive farmhouse cottage, Brae serves an eight-course tasting menu that changes daily, with flavours reflecting what traditionally grows in the area, including many indigenous ingredients, which are arguably the highlight. Food is matched with regional wines, as well as offerings from local breweries and distilleries. For good reason the restaurant is a regular on the list of the World's Best 100 Restaurants; it reached number 44 in 2017. Reservations are essential, and need to be made well in advance.

internet access, free wi-fi and a charger out the front for electric cars.

❶ Getting There & Away

If you're driving from Melbourne allow just under two hours for the 143km journey. Birregurra and Forrest, inland, are both around a 45-minute drive away.

V/Line buses pass through daily from Geelong ($12.40, 1½ hours) en route to Apollo Bay ($5.40, from one hour and five minutes).

Wye River

POP 63

The Great Ocean Road snakes spectacularly around the cliff from Cumberland River before reaching the tiny township of Wye River. Nestled discreetly in the pretty (steep) hillsides, just across from the ocean, it's a ripper of a community, and despite its small size it boasts one of the best pubs and one of the best cafes on the entire coast.

On Christmas Day 2015 major bushfires destroyed 116 homes in the area, and the entire town was evacuated; fortunately, no deaths were recorded.

🛏 Sleeping

Scully Mill Studios   GUESTHOUSE $
(☑0409 813 255, 03-5289 0462; www.scullymill. com.au; 27 Stanway Dr, Separation Creek; r from $130) A smidge outside Wye River is this tranquil beach-and-bush retreat run by husband-and-wife owners Peter and Bronwen Jacobs, both established artists. Choose between a contemporary loft suite with handmade furniture and a wood heater, and well-priced, cosy units, all with cooking facilities. It's an 800m walk to Wye River and only 200m from the beach. There's a two-night minimum stay.

Big4 Wye River Holiday Park   CAMPGROUND $
(☑1800 890 241, 03-5289 0241; www.big4wyeriver. com.au; 25 Great Ocean Rd; unpowered sites $30-98, powered sites $48-105, cabins $135-185, houses $310-395; ❋⚡) Just back from the beach, this popular caravan park sprawls over 10 hectares. Featuring an Otways forest backdrop, its grassy sites are great for camping, and there's a range of comfortable units for couples and groups.

✕ Eating & Drinking

★**Wye General**   CAFE $$
(☑03-5289 0247; www.thewyegeneral.com; 35 Great Ocean Rd; mains $15-26; ⊙8am-5pm Mon-Sat, to 4pm Sun) This well-loved general store has provisions and groceries, but it's most noteworthy for its smart indoor-outdoor cafe-bar. With polished-concrete floors, timber accents and a sophisticated retro ambience, it does old-fashioned cocktails, beers on tap and a menu of breakfasts, burgers and sourdough toasties made in-house. It stays open later in summer for dinner.

★**Wye Beach Hotel**   PUB
(☑03-5289 0240; www.wyebeachhotel.com.au; 19 Great Ocean Rd; ⊙11.30am-11pm; 🛜) This is undoubtedly one of the finest coastal pubs in Victoria, if not Australia – the ocean views just don't get much better. It has an unpretentious, local vibe and an all-regional craft-beer selection on tap, with brews from Forrest, Torquay and Aireys Inlet as well as one of its own. There's pub food too, though it's a bit pricey (mains from $27).

❶ Getting There & Away

Wye River is 159km from Melbourne, around a 2½-hour drive. It's positioned approximately halfway between Lorne and Apollo Bay on the Great Ocean Road.

There are several buses a day from Geelong ($15.60, two hours).

Apollo Bay

POP 1366

One of the larger towns along the Great Ocean Road, Apollo Bay has a tight-knit community of fisherfolk, artists, musicians and sea changers. Rolling hills provide a postcard backdrop to the town, while broad, white-sand beaches dominate the foreground. It's an ideal base for exploring magical Cape Otway and the adjoining national park. There are some decent restaurants and several lively pubs, and it's one of the best towns on the Great Ocean Road for budget travellers, with numerous hostels and ready transport access. It's also a popular stop for package bus tourists.

The Gadubanud people are the traditional custodians of Apollo Bay and the Otways region.

◉ Sights & Activities

Marriners Lookout VIEWPOINT

(155 Marriners Lookout Rd) Located 1.5km from town back towards Cape Patton, this scenic walk offers wonderful panoramic views over town and the ocean. If you have a car it's a steep five-minute walk from the lookout car park; otherwise, it's around a 45-minute walk (one way) from the centre of town.

Surf'n'Fish DIVING

(📞 03-5237 6426; www.surf-n-fish.com.au; 157 Great Ocean Rd) This authorised PADI dive centre can hire out equipment to certified divers. It can also recommend a number of offshore dives to nearby reefs and wrecks, including the SS *Casino*, which sank in 1932. It rents out snorkelling equipment for the nearby **Marengo Reef Marine Sanctuary**; get the low-down on the best tides before setting out.

It also rents out surfboards ($35/60 per half/full day), stand-up paddleboards ($40/75) and fishing tackle (from $15 per day), plus metal detectors ($40) too!

Otway Fly ADVENTURE SPORTS

(📞 03-5235 9200; www.otwayfly.com; 360 Phillips Track; adult/child treetop walks $25/15, zip-line tours $120/85; ⊘ 9.30am-4pm Mon-Fri, last entry 2.45pm, 9am-5pm Sat & Sun, last entry 4pm) The popular Otway Fly is an elevated steel walkway suspended among the forest canopy, and includes a swaying lookout tower 50m above the forest floor. Kids will enjoy the 'prehistoric path' loaded with dinosaurs, and everyone can test their bravery on the guided 2½-hour zip-line tour – including a 120m run. It's cheaper to buy tickets online.

☞ Tours

★ Mark's Walking Tours WALKING

(📞 0417 983 985; tours $20) Take a walk around the area with local Mark Brack, son of the Cape Otway lighthouse keeper. He knows this stretch of coast, its history and its ghosts better than anyone around. Daily options include shipwreck tours, historical tours, glow-worm tours and Great Ocean Walk (p556) treks. Minimum two people – prices drop the more people join the tour.

★ Apollo Bay Surf & Kayak ADVENTURE

(📞 0405 495 909, 03-5237 1189; www.apollobay surfkayak.com.au; 157-159 Great Ocean Rd; 2hr kayak tours $75, 1½hr SUP/surfing lesson $70/75) For a cool wildlife encounter, grab a paddle and head out by kayak to visit an Australian fur-seal colony on these well-run tours. They depart from Marengo Beach (south of the town centre); children need to be over 12 years old. Also offers surfing and stand-up paddleboard lessons, plus board and mountain-bike hire ($35 per half-day).

⌇ Sleeping

YHA Eco Beach HOSTEL $

(📞 03-5237 7899; www.yha.com.au/hostels/vic/great-ocean-road/apollo-bay; 5 Pascoe St; dm $30-45, d $85-120, f $120-180; @☎) 🍃 This architect-designed hostel is an outstanding place to stay, with eco credentials, great lounge areas, kitchens, a boules pit and rooftop terraces. Rooms are generic but spotless. It's a block behind the beach.

Surfside Backpacker HOSTEL $

(📞 0419 322 595, 03-5237 7263; www.surfsideback packer.com; cnr Great Ocean Rd & Gambier St; dm from $30, d with shared/private bathroom $85/95; ☎) Right across from the sand, this fantastic, sprawling 1940s beach house will appeal to those looking for budget accommodation with true Apollo Bay character. Run by delightful owner Robyn, it has a homey lounge with couches, board games and huge windows looking out onto the ocean.

FORREST

Tucked away in the hinterland of the Otways, a 30-minute drive from Apollo Bay, the former logging town of Forrest has emerged as a tourist hotspot.

Since the closure of the logging industry the town has reinvented itself as one of the best **mountain-biking** destinations in the state. Parks Victoria and the state's environment department have opened 16 cross-country trails (adding up to more than 50km) ranging from beginner to highly advanced; download a trail map at www.rideforrest.com.au/trails. In addition to renting out mountain bikes, **Forrest Hire Bikes** (☑ 0448 843 236; www.forresthirebikes.com.au; 33 Grant St; bike hire half/full day $50/80; ⊘ 8am-5pm Sat & Sun or by appointment) has a wealth of info, arranges tours, and stocks accessories, maps and repair kits. The town hosts the **Otway Odyssey Mountain Bike Marathon** (www.rapidascent.com.au/otwayodyssey) in late February.

The town is also known for its food and drink spots, including the **Forrest Brewing Company** (☑ 03-5236 6170; www.forrestbrewing.com.au; 26 Grant St; 7-beer tasting paddles $14, pots/pints from $5.50/10; ⊘ 9am-5pm Sun-Wed, to 11pm Thu-Sat, daily Dec & Jan; 🗢), the **Forrest General Store** (☑ 03-5236 6496; 33 Grant St; dishes $7-10; ⊘ 8am-5pm) and **Platypi Chocolate** (☑ 0433 362 639; www.platypichocolate.com.au; 73 Grant St; dishes $6.50-17; ⊘ 10am-5pm).

There are plenty of B&Bs in town, and the **Wonky Stables Holiday Park** (☑ 03-5236 6275; www.wonkystables.com.au; 1 Station St; unpowered sites $25-48, powered sites $30-54, cabins with shared/private bathroom from $69/105; ❄) or a free campground at **Stevensons Falls** (www.delwp.vic.gov.au) FREE, about 12km southwest of town.

Koalas are often spotted in the trees. It's a 15-minute walk from the bus stop.

Pisces Big4 Apollo Bay CAMPGROUND $
(☑ 03-5237 6749; www.piscespark.com.au; 311 Great Ocean Rd; unpowered sites $39-75, powered sites $48-115, cabins $107-389; 🗢🏊) It's the unbeatable views from the oceanfront villas (from $180) that set this family-oriented park apart from the others. It's a sprawling site, with a suburbia-like layout, complete with street signs.

★**Beacon Point Ocean View Villas** VILLA $$
(☑ 03-5237 6218; www.beaconpoint.com.au; 270 Skenes Creek Rd, Skenes Creek; r incl breakfast $170-370; ❄🗢) With a commanding hill location among the trees, this wonderful collection of comfortable one- and two-bedroom villas is a luxurious yet affordable bush retreat. Most villas have sensational coast views, balcony and wood-fired heater. There's also a popular restaurant. It's in Skenes Creek, 6km east of Apollo Bay.

🍴 Eating & Drinking

Apollo Bay Fishermen's Co-op SEAFOOD $
(☑ 03-5237 1067; www.facebook.com/apollobay fishcoop; Breakwater Rd; flake $7; ⊘ 11am-8pm) The best fish and chips in town is at the local fisherman's co-op, directly on the wharf.

Most of its fish and crayfish is caught locally; check the Facebook page for the latest catch.

Bay Leaf Cafe CAFE $$
(☑ 03-5237 6470; www.facebook.com/bayleafcafe apollobay; 131 Great Ocean Rd; meals $10-26; ⊘ 7.30am-2pm; 🗢) A local favourite for its innovative menu, good coffee, breakfast bagels, lobster rolls (in summer), Wagyu-beef burgers and chargrilled squid. Add a boutique-beer selection and a friendly atmosphere, and you have a winner.

★**Chris's Beacon Point Restaurant** GREEK $$$
(☑ 03-5237 6411; www.chriss.com.au; 280 Skenes Creek Rd; breakfast $13-21, mains from $42-55; ⊘ 8.30-10.40am & 6pm-late daily, plus noon-2pm Sat & Sun; 🗢) Feast on memorable ocean views, deliciously fresh seafood and Greek-influenced dishes at Chris's hilltop fine-dining sanctuary among the treetops. Reservations recommended. You can also stay in its wonderful stilted villas.

★**Great Ocean Road Brewhouse** PUB
(☑ 03-5237 6240; www.greatoceanroadbrewhouse. com.au; 29 Great Ocean Rd; beer from $5; ⊘ pub 11am-11pm Mon-Thu, to 1am Fri & Sat, Tastes of the Region noon-7pm Mon-Fri, from 11am Sat & Sun) Set up by renowned Otways brewery Prickly Moses, this taphouse pours an impressive range of its own and guest ales. The front

DON'T MISS

GREAT OCEAN WALK

The superb multiday Great Ocean Walk (www.greatoceanwalk.com.au) starts at Apollo Bay and runs all the way to the Twelve Apostles (p559). It takes you through ever-changing landscapes – along spectacular clifftops, past deserted beaches and into the dense eucalypt forests of Great Otway National Park.

It's possible to start at one point and arrange a pick-up at another (public-transport options are few and far between). You can do shorter walks or the whole 104km trek over eight days. Designated campgrounds are spread along the walk, catering for registered walkers only; bring cooking equipment and tents (no fires are allowed). Otherwise, there are plenty of comfortable accommodation options, from luxury lodges to caravan parks. Check out the helpful FAQ page on the website for all the info.

Walk 91 (☑03-5237 1189; www.walk91.com.au; 157-159 Great Ocean Rd; 3-day & 4-night guided walks from $659) and Hike2Camp (☑0497 132 047; www.hike2camp.com.au; per person 2-/4-/6-day walks from $240/630/840) can arrange your itinerary, and transport and equipment hire, and can shuttle your backpack to your destination.

---

bar is a classic pub and bistro, but through the back is the 'Taste of the Region' room, with 14 of its own beers on tap to enjoy with local-produce tasting platters.

ℹ Information

Great Ocean Road Visitor Centre (☑1300 689 297; www.visitapollobay.com; 100 Great Ocean Rd; ☺9am-5pm) Modern and professional tourist office with a heap of info on the area. Has free wi-fi and can book bus tickets too.

ℹ Getting There & Away

From Melbourne the fastest route is inland via the Geelong bypass that leads to Birregurra and Forrest, a 200km drive. If you're taking the scenic route along the Great Ocean Road (highly recommended), count on a 4½-hour trip.

Apollo Bay is easily reached by public transport from Melbourne ($30.40, 3¾ hours) via train to Geelong and then transfer to a connecting bus. There are three daily buses to/from Apollo Bay; stops include Torquay ($17, two hours and 10 minutes), Anglesea ($12.40, 1¾ hours) and Lorne ($5.40, 65 minutes). Heading west, there are buses to Port Campbell ($12.40, two hours and 10 minutes) and Warrnambool ($23.40, 3½ hours), both departing on Monday, Wednesday and Friday.

Cape Otway

If you thought the Great Ocean Road was one long coastal drive, then this leg through the Otways may surprise you. Here the road heads inland, through shady rainforest with towering trees and fern gullies; it's home to a plethora of wildlife, most notably koalas.

Cape Otway is the second-most-southerly point in mainland Australia (after Wilsons Promontory), and features a lighthouse that overlooks a beautiful, rugged coastline that's notoriously treacherous for shipping.

After Cape Otway the road enters the fertile Horden Vale flats, returning briefly to the coast at tiny Glenaire. Six kilometres north of Glenaire, a 5km detour goes to Johanna Beach, known for its massive surf; swimming here is not advised. From here the road heads inland again and north to the historic logging township of Lavers Hill.

The Otway region is home to the Gadubanud people; you can learn about their culture at the Cape Otway Lightstation.

◉ Sights

★ **Cape Otway Lightstation**   LIGHTHOUSE (☑03-5237 9240; www.lightstation.com; Lighthouse Rd; adult/child/family $19.50/7.50/49.50; ☺9am-5pm) The oldest surviving lighthouse in mainland Australia, Cape Otway Lightstation was built in 1848 without mortar by more than 40 stonemasons. There are sublime coastal views from its observation deck, while the Telegraph Station has fascinating displays on the 250km undersea telegraph-cable link with Tasmania, laid in 1859. It's a sprawling complex with plenty to see, from Aboriginal cultural sites to a WWII radar bunker built to detect potential Japanese threats.

⌂ Sleeping

★ **Bimbi Park**   CARAVAN PARK $ (☑03-5237 9246; www.bimbipark.com.au; 90 Manna Gum Dr; unpowered sites $25-40, powered sites $30-45, cabins $45-215; ☎) ✎ Down a dirt road 3km from the lighthouse is this character-filled caravan park with bush sites, cabins, bunkhouses, pods and old-school caravans. It's fantastic for families, and also for hikers on the Great Ocean Walk. There's plenty of wildlife about, including koalas, plus horse rides (adult/child $65/55 per hour) and a rock-climbing wall ($15). Good use of water-saving initiatives too.

For the cheaper rooms you'll need to bring your own linen, or you can rent it here.

Cape Otway Lightstation   B&B $$$
(☑03-5237 9240; www.lightstation.com; Lighthouse Rd; r incl breakfast & entry to lighthouse $295-395) There's a range of options at this romantic, windswept lighthouse (p556). You can book out the whole Head Lightkeeper's House (sleeps 16) or the smaller Lighthouse Lodge (sleeps two), as well as other two-bedroom options for larger groups.

Great Ocean Ecolodge   LODGE $$$
(☑03-5237 9297; www.greatoceanecolodge.com; 635 Lighthouse Rd; r incl activities from $395; ⊜) ✎ Reminiscent of a luxury African safari lodge, this mud-brick homestead stands in pastoral surrounds with plenty of wildlife. It's all solar powered and rates go towards the on-site **Centre for Conservation Ecology** (www.conservationecologycentre.org). Prices include a dusk wildlife walk with an ecologist, where you'll visit a tiger-quoll and potoroo enclosure. Bookings are only available for weekdays.

❶ Getting There & Away

V/Line runs a coach service from Apollo Bay to Lavers Hill ($5.40, 40 minutes) on Monday, Wednesday and Friday, en route to Princetown and Warrnambool. However, unless you're traversing this stretch on foot via the Great Ocean Walk you'll need a car to get around: there's no public transport to Cape Otway, and all the main sights and accommodation are found off the Great Ocean Road.

Port Campbell

POP 267

This small, laid-back coastal town was named after Scottish captain Alexander Campbell, a whaler who took refuge here on trading voyages between Tasmania and Port Fairy. It's a friendly town with some nice little eateries and drinking spots, which make ideal places to debrief after visiting the

KOALA SPOTTING

The forested road leading to Cape Otway is a terrific spot for koala sightings. Where are they? Look for the cars parked on the side of the road and people looking up into the trees.

Unfortunately, in recent years koala numbers have declined dramatically. This is due to both starvation and relocation, as an overpopulation of the marsupials led to the death of many of the park's manna gums – the koalas' sole food source. Despite this sad turn of events, you still have a very good chance of spotting koalas out this way.

Twelve Apostles. Its pretty bay has a lovely sandy beach, and is one of the few safe places for swimming along this tempestuous stretch of coast.

◉ Sights & Activities

The 4.4km **Discovery Walk** follows a clifftop trail through heathland, giving an introduction to the area's natural and historical features. It's accessed via the stairs on the far-right (western) side of the bay; in high tide it can be reached via another trailhead signed off the main highway above town.

★**Port Campbell**
Visitor Centre   VISITOR CENTRE
(☑1300 137 255; www.visit12apostles.com.au; 26 Morris St; ⊙9am-5pm) As well as invaluable tourist info and a fascinating display of items salvaged from historic shipwrecks (including the *Loch Ard* and the *Fiji*), this visitor centre offers a heap of activities. There's free hire of binoculars (for those visiting the penguins at the Twelve Apostles or doing some whale watching), a massive Newtonian reflector telescope for stargazing, as well as cameras, GPS gadgets and even an anemometer to measure wind speeds.

Port Campbell Boat Charters   FISHING
(☑0428 986 366; www.portcampbellboatcharters. com.au; scenic tours/diving/fishing per person from $60/100/100) Get up close and personal with the Twelve Apostles (p559) on a boat tour, or join a group dive or fishing charter. Trips go year-round but are weather dependent. There's a minimum of five people for trips to run, but they'll add you to another group if you don't have the numbers.

🛏 Sleeping

★ Port Campbell Hostel
HOSTEL **$**

(☑03-5598 6305; www.portcampbellhostel.com.au; 18 Tregea St; dm/d/tr/q from $36/170/190/200; @ 🛜) This impressive, modern, double-storey backpackers has a range of clean mixed dorms and private rooms, along with a huge shared kitchen and an even bigger lounge area. It's a short stroll to the beach, and there's a bar with Sow & Piglets (p559) ales on tap (open 4pm to 10pm) and pizzas in the evenings ($10). Wi-fi in the lobby only.

Port Campbell
Guesthouse Flashpackers
GUESTHOUSE **$**

(☑0407 696 559; www.portcampbellguesthouse andflashpackers.com.au; 54 Lord St; r from $110, s/d without bathroom from $70/100; 🅿 🛜) A place for independent-minded budget travellers who aren't into the hostel scene, this guesthouse feels more like going around to a mate's place. Set up within a historic cottage are four cosy rooms, a comfy lounge and a country kitchen with filter coffee. Its ultrarelaxed owner, Mark, is knowledgeable about the area.

Port Campbell
Recreation Reserve
CAMPGROUND **$**

(☑0407 666 610, 0431 128 790; www.facebook.com/PortCampbellRecReserve; 90 Hennessy St; per person $10; 🛜) For those with tents or campervans, this is the cheapest option in town. Head up just past the footy oval, where you'll find the tin-shed reception to check in; if no one's around there's an honour system. There are no powered sites, but there's a kitchen, laundry facilities, a toilet and shower block, and wi-fi.

Sea Foam Villas
APARTMENT **$$**

(☑03-5598 6413; www.seafoamvillas.com.au; 14 Lord St; r $185-570) Located directly across from the water, Sea Foam undoubtedly has the best views in town. It's only really worth it, however, if you can snag one of the bayview apartments, which are large, comfortable and luxurious.

🍴 Eating & Drinking

★ Forage on the Foreshore
CAFE **$$**

(☑03-5598 6202; www.forageontheforeshore.com.au; 32 Cairns St; dishes $12-32; ⊙9am-4pm; 🛜) In the old post office is this seafront cottage cafe with wooden floorboards, art on the walls, an open fireplace and a vintage record player spinning vinyl. There's an all-day breakfast menu, gourmet sandwiches, burgers, duck-fat-fried chips, and items featuring fresh abalone and regional produce.

12 Rocks Cafe Bar
CAFE **$$**

(☑03-5598 6123; www.12rocksbeachbar.com.au; 19 Lord St; mains $12-35; ⊙9.30am-11pm) Your classic coastal beachside bistro, 12 Rocks is just about perfect for those who want a feed and a drink with waterfront views. Try an Otways beer with modern Australian pub fare such as beer-battered fish and chips, paprika-spiced calamari or a pulled-pork

---

THE SHIPWRECK COAST

In the era of sailing ships, Victoria's beautiful and rugged southwestern coastline was one of the most treacherous on earth, due to hidden reefs and frequent heavy fog. Between the 1830s and the 1930s, more than 200 ships were torn asunder along the so-called Shipwreck Coast between Cape Otway and Port Fairy. From the early 1850s to the late 1880s, Victoria's gold rush and the subsequent economic boom brought countless shiploads of prospectors and hopefuls from Europe, North America and China. After spending months at sea, many vessels (and lives) were lost on the 'home straight'.

The **lighthouses** at Aireys Inlet, Cape Otway, Port Fairy and Warrnambool are still operating, and you'll find shipwreck museums, memorial plaques and anchors that tell the story of wrecks along this coast. The most famous is that of the iron-hulled clipper **Loch Ard**, which foundered off Mutton Bird Island (near Port Campbell) at 4am on the final night of its long voyage from England in 1878. Of the 37 crew and 19 passengers on board, only two survived. Eva Carmichael, who couldn't swim, clung to wreckage and was washed into a gorge – since renamed Loch Ard Gorge (p560) – where apprentice officer Tom Pearce rescued her. Tom heroically climbed the sheer cliff and raised the alarm, but no other survivors were found. Eva and Tom were both 19 years old, leading to speculation in the press about a romance, but nothing actually happened – they never saw each other again and Eva soon returned to Ireland (this time, perhaps not surprisingly, via steamship).

HOW MANY APOSTLES?

The Twelve Apostles are not 12 in number and, from all records, never have been. From the viewing platform you can clearly count seven, but maybe some obscure others. We consulted widely with Parks Victoria officers, tourist-office staff and even the cleaner at the lookout, but it's still not clear. Locals tend to say, 'It depends where you look from', which really is true.

The apostles are known as 'stacks' in geological parlance, and they were originally called the 'Sow and Piglets'. In the 1960s someone (nobody can recall who) thought they might attract some tourists with a more venerable name, so the formations were renamed 'the Apostles'. Since apostles come in a dozen, the number 12 was added sometime later. The two stacks on the eastern (Otway) side of the viewing platform are not technically among the apostles – they're Gog and Magog.

The soft limestone cliffs are dynamic and changeable, with constant erosion from the unceasing waves – one 70m-high stack collapsed into the sea in July 2005 and the Island Archway lost its archway in June 2009.

burger, or enjoy the hearty breakfasts and decent coffee. It also serves ice cream from nearby Timboon.

Sow & Piglets MICROBREWERY
(☑ 03-5598 6305; 18 Tregea St; ☺ 4-10pm) The taproom for Sow & Piglets is inside the Port Campbell Hostel (p558). Overseen by a German brewer, it serves four beers on tap, all unfiltered and unpasteurised, including a Kölsch, an IPA and a few seasonals made using local ingredients. It also cooks up frozen pizzas for $10.

❶ Getting There & Away

V/Line buses leave Geelong on Monday, Wednesday and Friday and travel through to Port Campbell ($35.60, 5¼ hours), but you'll need to transfer to a different bus in Apollo Bay (two hours and 15 minutes), which generally leaves 30 minutes later. There's also a bus from Port Campbell to Warrnambool ($8.40, 1¼ hours) that leaves on the same days.

Port Campbell National Park

East of the Otways, the Great Ocean Road levels out and enters narrow, flat, scrubby escarpment lands that fall away to sheer, 70m-high cliffs along the coast between Princetown and Peterborough – a distinct change of scene. This is Port Campbell National Park, home to the Twelve Apostles, the most famous and most photographed stretch of the Great Ocean Road.

However, don't for a moment think that the Twelve Apostles constitute the road's end point. There's a string of iconic rock

stacks west of Port Campbell, some arguably more scenic than the apostles themselves, among them the Bay of Islands and London Bridge.

Other than the bay at Port Campbell, none of the beaches along this stretch is suitable for swimming because of strong currents and undertows.

The Kirrae Whurrong are the traditional custodians of this coastline.

◉ Sights

★ **Twelve Apostles** LANDMARK
(Great Ocean Rd) The most iconic sight and enduring image for most visitors to the Great Ocean Road, the Twelve Apostles provide a fitting climax to the journey. Jutting out from the ocean in spectacular fashion, these rocky stacks stand as if they've been abandoned to the waves by the retreating headland. Today only seven apostles can be seen from a network of viewing platforms connected by timber boardwalks around the clifftops.

There's pedestrian access to the viewing platforms from the car park at the Twelve Apostles Visitor Centre – more a kiosk and toilets than an info centre – via a tunnel beneath the Great Ocean Road.

The best time to visit is sunset, not only for optimum photographic opportunities and to beat the tour buses but also to see little penguins returning ashore. Sightings vary, but generally the penguins arrive 20 to 40 minutes after sunset. You'll spot them from about 60m away, so you'll need binoculars, which can be borrowed from the **Port Campbell Visitor Centre** (☑ 1300 137 255; www.visit12apostles.com.au; 26 Morris St; ☺ 9am-5pm).

TWELVE APOSTLES GOURMET TRAIL

Head through the Corangamite hinterland on the 12 Apostles Gourmet Trail (www.12 apostlesfoodartisans.com) to taste cheeses, chocolate, wine, ice cream and single-malt whiskies, among other fine regional produce.

Start at **Timboon**, a former logging town 15km from Point Campbell, home to **Timboon Railway Shed Distillery** (☑03-5598 3555; www.timboondistillery.com.au; 1 Bailey St; share plates from $19; ☉10am-4.30pm), a historic railway shed converted into a whisky distillery and vibrant cafe. Inspired by Timboon's illegal 19th-century whisky trade, it produces single malts and vodkas. Watch the distillery process, sample a few whiskies and infused vodkas, and nab some keepsakes. The restaurant's big on local produce and does shared plates to enjoy on its terrace. Across from here is **Timboon Fine Ice Cream** (☑03-5501 9736; www.timboonfineicecream.com.au; 1a Barrett St; ice cream from $4; ☉11am-5pm), offering classic and seasonal flavours made using local dairy produce. Keep an eye out for its 'Sundae School', where you can make up your own ice cream.

Up the road you can pick your own strawberries and blackberries at **Berry World** (☑03-5598 3240; www.facebook.com/berryworldtimboon; 26 Egan St; scones $4.50; ☉10am-4.30pm Tue-Sun Nov-Apr), or just stop by for a cup of strawberries and cream, a spot of high tea or scones with cream and homemade jam.

Further along is **Timboon Cheesery** (☑03-5598 3322; www.timbooncheesery.com.au; 23 Ford & Fells Rd; ☉11am-4pm) 🌿, a lovely garden cafe owned by Schulz Organic Dairy, a third-generation German cheesemaker, offering free tastings of its organic cheeses, as well as platters, wine, and scones with cream. **Apostle Whey Cheese** (☑0437 894 337; www.apostlewheycheese.com.au; 9 Gallum Rd, Cooriemungle; toasties $3.50; ☉8am-5pm Mon-Fri, from 10am Sat & Sun) also has tastings of delectable award-winning blue cheeses, bries and gumtree-smoked cheddar on its dairy farm. Midweek you can watch cheese-making in action.

En route schedule a beer stop at the **Sow & Piglets** (☑0490 665 810; www.sowand piglets.com; 1170 Cooriemungle Rd, Cooriemungle; ☉11am-4pm), where a German brewer crafts a range of European ales. Grab a pint or a tasting paddle ($10), and if the weather's nice enjoy it on the terrace with a bratwurst barbecue ($18 for four people).

The day wouldn't be complete without chocolate. With plenty of goodies and samples, **GORGE** (☑0488 557 252; www.gorgechocolates.com.au; 1432 Princetown Rd, Cooriemungle; ☉10am-5pm) is an essential stop for its handmade Belgian chocolates. **Dairylicious Fudge Farm** (☑03-5594 6370; www.farmfudge.com.au; 1281 Timboon-Colac Rd, Jancourt East; ☉11am-5pm), a 15-minute drive north, offers a delicious array of fudges you can sample – all made on-site using local ingredients.

After all this you may feel a little bloated, but luckily the **Camperdown–Timboon Rail Trail** offers a 34km track for cyclists and walkers, following the historical railway line. You can hire mountain bikes from **Ride with Us** (☑0428 407 777; www.ridewithus. com.au; Bailey St; bike hire per hour/half-/full day $15/20/30).

If you don't have your own wheels you can take a tour of the area with **Timboon Taxi Service** (☑0438 407 777; www.ridewithus.com.au/taxis.html).

Loch Ard Gorge
BEACH

Close to the Twelve Apostles (p559), Loch Ard Gorge is where the Shipwreck Coast's most famous and haunting tale (p558) unfolded when two young survivors of the wrecked iron clipper *Loch Ard* made it to shore. There are several walks in the area, the most popular being the path down to the picturesque beach and cave where the pair took shelter. Further trails from here lead to scenic viewpoints, a cemetery, a blowhole and a rugged beach.

London Bridge
LANDMARK

Just outside Port Campbell, en route to Peterborough, London Bridge has indeed fallen down. It was once a double-arched rock platform linked to the mainland, but in January 1990 the bridge collapsed, leaving two terrified tourists marooned on the world's newest island – they were eventually rescued by helicopter. It remains a spectacular sight nevertheless. At dusk keep an eye out for penguins, which are often spotted on the beach, generally about 40m away.

Gibson Steps
BEACH

Follow 86 steps, hacked by hand into the cliffs by 19th-century landowner Hugh Gibson (and more recently replaced by concrete ones), down to wild Gibson Beach. You can walk along the beach, but be careful not to get stranded by high tides. It's a 50m walk from the car park, or a 2.2km return walk along a trail that sets out from the Twelve Apostles Visitor Centre.

Bay of Islands Coastal Park
VIEWPOINT

Past Peterborough (12km west of Port Campbell), the lesser-visited **Bay of Martyrs** and **Bay of Islands** have spectacular lookout points from which to see rock stacks and sweeping views. Both bays have fantastic coastal walks, and there's a great beach at **Crofts Bay**.

The Arch
LANDMARK

Offshore from Point Hesse, and well worth stopping for, the Arch is an intact bridge-like rock formation. It's believed that it will, one day – imminently – break into two separate rock stacks. There are some good photo ops from the various viewing points looking down on it.

The Grotto
VIEWPOINT

A scenic stopover heading west from Port Campbell is the Grotto, where steep stairs lead down to a hollowed-out cavelike formation where waves crash. It's approximately halfway between Port Campbell and Peterborough, a short drive from London Bridge.

Tours

Port Campbell Boat Charters (p557) allows you to see the Apostles from out on the water. You can also arrange a **helicopter flight** (☑03-5598 8283; www.12apostleshelicopters.com.au; per person 15min flights $145) to take you over this dramatic stretch of coast.

Go West Tours (☑03-9485 5290; www.gowest.com.au; $135) and **Ride Tours** (☑0427 180 357; www.ridetours.com.au; tours $225) make the trip here from Melbourne.

Information

Twelve Apostles Visitor Centre Kiosk

(☺10am-5pm Sun-Fri, to 5.30pm Sat) Across the road from the Twelve Apostles, this tourist office has toilets, a kiosk and interpretative panels. Park here, then access the Apostles via a tunnel that passes under the road. In late 2018 the federal government announced $154 million in funding to revamp the site's entire viewing area, allowing for all-weather views.

Getting There & Away

V/Line runs a coach service from Apollo Bay to Princetown ($11, 70 minutes) on Monday, Wednesday and Friday, en route to Warrnambool. However, having your own car is pretty much the only way to go in terms of exploring this area, unless you're going with one of the tours above. The Apostles are 15km east of Port Campbell, with Loch Ard Gorge a little closer to town (around 12km). Other rock formations stretch 18km west of Port Campbell.

Warrnambool
POP 30,709

Once a whaling and sealing station, Warrnambool is booming these days as a regional commercial and whale-watching centre. It's an attractive city, with heritage buildings, beaches, gardens and tree-lined streets, but the major housing and commercial development at the city fringes has rendered these areas much like city suburbs anywhere in Australia.

It's the whales that Warrnambool is most famous for, but it also has some great art galleries and historical sights. The sizeable population of uni students gives the town some spark, and you'll find some cool bars and cafes about.

The Gunditjmara people are the traditional owners of the land.

Sights & Activities

★ **Warrnambool Art Gallery**
GALLERY

(WAG; ☑03-5559 4949; www.thewag.com.au; 165 Timor St; ☺10am-5pm Mon-Fri, to 3pm Sat & Sun) **FREE** One of Australia's oldest art galleries (established 1886), Warrnambool has a collection of works by prominent Australian painters. Its most famous piece is Eugene von Guérard's landscape *Tower Hill*, which is so detailed that it was used by botanists as a historical record when regenerating the Tower Hill area. There are contemporary pieces too, and several exhibitions run concurrently.

★ **Flagstaff Hill Maritime Village**
HISTORIC SITE

(☑03-5559 4600; www.flagstaffhill.com; 89 Merri St; adult/child/family $18/8.50/43.20; ☺9am-5pm, last entry 4pm) The world-class Flagstaff Hill precinct is of equal interest for its shipwreck museum, heritage-listed lighthouses and garrison as for its reproduction of an 1870s port town. It also has the nightly **Tales of the Shipwreck Coast** (adult/

WHALES AT WARRNAMBOOL

In the 19th century Warrnambool's whale industry involved hunting with harpoons, but these days the cetaceans are a major tourist attraction, with crowds gathering to see them frolic offshore on their migration between May and September. Southern right whales (named thus due to being the 'right' whales to hunt) are the most common visitors, heading from Antarctica to these more temperate waters.

Although whales can be seen between Portland and Anglesea, undoubtedly the best place to see them is at Warrnambool's **Logan's Beach whale-watching platform** (Warrnambool Foreshore Promenade) – they use the waters here as a nursery. Sightings aren't guaranteed, but you've got a very good chance of spotting them breaching and slapping their tails as they nurse their calves in the waters. Call the visitor centre (p564) ahead of your visit to see whether the whales are about, or consult www.visitwarrnambool.com.au or the Great Ocean Road Whales Facebook page for info on the latest sightings.

child/family $30/12/69.30), an engaging 70-minute sound-and-light show telling the story of the *Loch Ard*'s plunge (p558). The village has ye olde shoppes such as blacksmiths, candle makers and shipbuilders. If you're lucky the Maremma dogs (p563) will be around for you to meet.

★ **F Project Gallery**   GALLERY
(www.thefproject.org.au; 224 Timor St; ⊙10am-4pm Wed-Sun) Set up in a former funeral home by local art collective the F Project, this contemporary gallery always has something interesting showing at its monthly exhibitions. Pop round the back to say g'day to the artists in residence. Its shop is another reason to visit, with some wonderful jewellery, accessories, artworks, books and music, all produced by Warrnambool locals. There's inexpensive **accommodation** (☑0419 395 875; www.thefproject.org.au; 224 Timor St; r with shared bathroom $90; ☎) too, and some cool street-art murals outside.

Rundell's Mahogany Trail Rides   HORSE RIDING
(☑0408 589 546; www.rundellshorseriding.com.au; Millers Lane; 1½hr beach rides $70) Get to know some of Warrnambool's quiet beach spots on horseback. Riders need to be over seven years of age for the beach ride, but younger is OK for the shorter rides. Check the website for the schedule.

🛏 Sleeping

Cally Hotel   PUB $
(☑03-5561 3932; www.callyhotel.com.au; 112-114 Fairy St; dm from $35, d with shared bathroom $50-90; ☎) The Cally (c 1892) has undergone a modern refit to reopen as one of the city's best pubs, with upstairs rooms that are

excellent value. Don't expect anything too flash, though: these are simply a much nicer version of your usual pub rooms.

Downstairs has live music, a selection of craft beers and good food, with discounts for those staying here.

Warrnambool Beach Backpackers   HOSTEL $
(☑03-5562 4874; www.beachbackpackers.com.au; 17 Stanley St; camping per person $15, dm $28-36, d from $90; @☎) A short stroll from the beach, this hostel meets all backpackers' needs, with a huge living area, a kitschy Aussie-themed bar, free wi-fi, a kitchen and free pick-up from the train station. Rooms are basic but clean. 'Vanpackers' can stay here for $15 per person. There's bike, surfboard, stand-up paddleboard, wetsuit, kayak and fishing-equipment hire, and free use of boogie boards.

It's a 25-minute walk into the city, or there's a bus from here. It can also assist foreign backpackers looking for work in the area.

✖ Eating

Graze   CAFE $
(☑1300 105 590; www.graze.net.au; 52a Kepler St; mains $11-22; ⊙7am-4pm Mon-Fri, to 2.30pm Sat; ☎) A hipster-centric deli doing the likes of smoked bacon and poached eggs with sriracha mayo for brekkie, and slow-cooked lamb-shoulder tacos or gourmet steak sandwiches for lunch. There's also single-origin coffees and a good selection of wines from the Bellarine Peninsula.

Kermond's Hamburgers   BURGERS $
(☑03-5562 4854; www.facebook.com/kermonds hamburgers; 151 Lava St; burgers $6.50-12.50;

⊙9am-9.30pm) Likely not much has changed at this burger joint since it opened in 1949, with Laminex tables, wood-panelled walls and classic milkshakes served in stainless-steel tumblers. Its burgers are an institution.

Simon's Waterfront CAFE $$
(☑03-5562 1234; www.simonswaterfront.com.au; Level 1, 80 Pertobe Rd; ⊙8.30am-3pm Sun-Tue, to 10pm Wed-Sat; ☎) Feeling more Bondi than Warrnambool, this uber-trendy cafe has killer seafront views. It does a breakfast pizza among the usual cooked-egg options, while for lunch there's a pleasing choice of *moules frites*, seafood chowder and burgers. It's also a great place for a beer or coffee from Melbourne roaster Seven Seeds.

Standard Dave PIZZA $$
(☑03-5562 8659; www.standarddavepizza.com; 218 Timor St; pizza $16-24; ⊙5-10pm Tue-Fri, 2-10pm Sat, 4-10pm Sun) Standard Dave attracts a young indie crowd, here for awesome pizzas, a drink and decent music. Its thin-crust pizzas use quality ingredients made from scratch or sourced locally. Be sure to head next door to bar Dart & Marlin.

🍷 Drinking & Nightlife

Rough Diamond CAFE
(☑03-5560 5707; www.roughdiamondcoffee.com.au; 203 Koroit St; coffee from $4.20; ⊙7am-2pm Mon-Fri, 8am-2pm Sat) So cool that it rocks an ugly brick 1970s motel-style facade – done out with AstroTurf and hipster signage – Rough Diamond does awesome single-origin coffee. Choose between African and Latin American beans for pourover coffees, and order from a menu featuring brioche buns, banana on sourdough, and Turkish rolls stuffed with peppery pulled pork.

Dart & Marlin BAR
(216-218 Timor St; ⊙5-10pm Tue-Fri, 2-10pm Sat, 4-10pm Sun) The city's coolest drinking den, this old-fashioned-style bar has plenty of character – from church-pew booth seating, art-deco features and distressed walls to a battered piano that beckons to be played. Pull up a stool at the wooden bar to order from the quality selection.

Hotel Warrnambool PUB
(www.hotelwarrnambool.com.au; cnr Koroit & Kepler Sts; ⊙noon-late; ☎) One of Victoria's best coastal boozers, the Hotel Warrnambool mixes pub charm with bohemian character and serves a range of beers and wines, along with wood-fired pizzas and other gastropub fare (mains $12 to $34). Also a decent place to sleep, with rooms (incl breakfast d $140, without bathroom $110) upgraded to the more boutique end of the scale while keeping a classic pub-accommodation feel.

Loft LIVE MUSIC
(☑0417 169 073; www.theloftbar.com.au; 58 Liebig St; ⊙8pm-late Tue-Sun) Warrnambool's premier live-music venue, Loft hosts Aussie

---

MAREMMAS, FOXES & LITTLE PENGUINS

One of the more interesting conservation efforts taking place in Australia, the Maremma Project has worked wonders in restoring Warrnambool's once-fledgling penguin colony. Maremmas (pure bred white sheepdogs from Italy) were introduced to Middle Island in 2006 to protect little penguins from predators – namely foxes, which had decimated the penguin population. In 1999 some 600 penguins lived on Middle Island, but there were as few as 10 by 2005, as foxes had found a way to reach the island at low tide.

Remarkably, after the project was launched not a single fox was sighted on Middle Island, and the penguin population grew to just under 200. Unfortunately, in August 2017 a major setback occurred when the Maremmas were unable to get to the island due to high tides and poor weather: some 140 penguins were killed by foxes. Since then, however, penguin numbers have slowly recovered to around 100 birds.

The Maremmas recently found fame as the subject of the popular 2015 film *Oddball*, a quirky Aussie film based on the true story of the dogs and their owner, Swampy, a local chicken farmer.

On **Meet the Maremma Tours** (☑1800 637 725; www.warrnamboolpenguins.com.au; adult/child/family $18/5/38) you can interact with the canines and learn about their role, from December to April on a trip to Middle Island – 150m from Warrnambool's foreshore – or at other times at Flagstaff Hill Maritime Village (p561); visit the tour website for the schedule.

indie bands like You Am I as well as DJs and local acts.

🔒 Shopping

Fletcher Jones Market VINTAGE
(✍03-5562 9936; www.facebook.com/fjmarket; 61-77 Flaxman St; ⊙10am-5pm) The iconic Fletcher Jones clothing factory – recognisable by its 40m-high orb-topped water tower – now houses a sprawling, eclectic mix of collectables and vintage clothing, with 30 stalls set up over two levels. Take a stroll in its heritage-listed 1940s garden.

ℹ Information

Warrnambool Visitor Centre (✍1800 555 111, 1800 637 725; www.visitwarrnambool.com. au; 89 Merri St; ⊙9am-5pm) For the latest on whale sightings, local tour and accommodation bookings, and walking-trail maps.

ℹ Getting There & Away

Warrnambool is an hour's drive west of Port Campbell on the Great Ocean Road, and about three hours' drive from Melbourne on the Princes Hwy (A1).

V/Line (✍03-5562 9432, 1800 800 007; www. vline.com.au; Merri St) trains run to Melbourne ($37.60, 3¼ hours, three or four daily) via Geelong ($27, 2½ hours).

There are two V/Line buses a week along the Great Ocean Road to Apollo Bay ($22.80, two hours), as well as four daily **buses** (✍03-5562 1866; www.transitsw.com.au) to both Port Fairy ($5, 35 minutes) and Portland ($13.40, 1½ hours). There's also a bus to Halls Gap ($29.60, three hours) three days a week, via Dunkeld ($19.80, two hours), en route to Ararat ($34.80, three hours and 40 minutes). A coach to Ballarat ($19.80, two hours and 50 minutes) departs Warrnambool at 6.40am Monday to Friday. Buses are run by **Christian's Bus Co** (✍1800 800 007; www.christiansbus.com.au).

ℹ Getting Around

Cycling is a good way of getting to Port Fairy or Tower Hill (via Koroit) on the **rail trail**.

Otherwise there's a local **taxi** (✍13 10 08) to get around.

Tower Hill Reserve

Tower Hill, 15km west of Warrnambool, is a vast caldera born in a volcanic eruption 35,000 years ago. Aboriginal artefacts unearthed in the ash show that Indigenous people lived in the area at the time, and today the Worn Gundidj Aboriginal

Cooperative runs the **Tower Hill Natural History Centre** (✍03-5565 9202, 0448 509 522; www.towerhill.org.au; 1½hr walks adult/child $25.50/11.50; ⊙10am-4pm, guided walks 11am & 1pm).

The centre – housed within a UFO-like 1962 building designed by renowned Australian architect Robin Boyd – runs daily bushwalks led by Indigenous guides that include boomerang throwing and bushtucker demonstrations. With 24 hours' notice, spotlighting (wildlife watching by torchlight; adult/child/family $28.95/14/65) is available too. It also sells Aboriginal handicrafts, artwork and accessories.

After a century of deforestation and environmental degradation, a detailed 1855 painting of Tower Hill by Eugene von Guérard (now exhibited in the Warrnambool Art Gallery; p561) was used to identify species for a replanting program; over 300,000 trees have been replanted since 1961.

Parks Victoria manages the park and it's one of the few places where you'll spot wild emus, kangaroos and koalas hanging out together. It's also home to over 200 avian species, with its wetland habitat attracting both resident and migratory birds.

ℹ Getting There & Away

Four or five daily buses ($3.40, 15 minutes) pass Tower Hill en route to Port Fairy, Koroit and Warrnambool, but it's much more feasible to visit with your own vehicle. Cycling here along the rail trail is also an option.

Port Fairy

POP 3029

Established as a whaling and sealing station in 1833, Port Fairy has retained its historic 19th-century maritime charm. Here it's all about heritage bluestone and sandstone buildings, whitewashed cottages, colourful fishing boats and wide, tree-lined streets.

There are also several nice beaches, surfing, fishing and plenty of wildlife to see. And then there are the festivals, a packed schedule of events throughout the year, most notably the Port Fairy Folk Festival in March.

In 2012 the town was voted the world's most liveable small community, and it's not hard to see why.

The Gunditjmara are the traditional custodians of this southwestern Victorian region.

◎ Sights & Activities

Wharf
PORT

Back in the 1850s the town's port was one of the busiest in Australia, serving as the main departure point for ships heading to England laden with wool, gold and wheat. Today there's still plenty going on at this charming marina, from luxury yachts to the weather-worn fishing boats moored here.

Griffiths Island
ISLAND

Where the Moyne River meets the ocean, Griffiths Island is home to a protected short-tailed shearwater (mutton-bird) colony; they descend on the town each October and stay until April (dusk is the best time to visit) before commencing their 15,000km northern migration to near Alaska. The 3km circuit makes for a lovely one-hour walk, passing the lighthouse (c 1859) and some swimming spots along the way.

Battery Hill
HISTORIC SITE

Located across the bridge from Port Fairy's picturesque harbour, Battery Hill is worthy of exploration, with cannons and fortifications positioned here in 1887 to protect the town from the then perceived threat of Russian warships. You'll also encounter resident black wallabies. It was originally used as a flagstaff, so the commanding views don't disappoint.

East Beach
BEACH

Safe for swimming, East Beach has a surf life-saving club and small waves to suit beginners.

Basalt Wines
WINERY

(☑ 0429 682 251; www.basaltwines.com; 1131 Princes Hwy, Killarney; dishes $9-24; ☺ 10am-4pm, longer hours summer) Just outside Port Fairy is this family-run biodynamic winery that does free tastings in its tin shed, with a glass atrium so you can enjoy the views. There are tasty tapas dishes too, such as locally smoked eel or gin-cured ocean trout, as well as regional cheeses, charcuterie and locally distilled gins, single malts and vermouths. Grab a Cuban cigar to round things out.

Eco Tuk Port Fairy
TOURS

(☑ 0456 269 536; www.ecotukportfairy.com; 30min tour per person adult/child/family $17/12/55) Get zipped around in the back of an electric tuk tuk for a unique tour of Port Fairy. Tours take in the town's rich maritime history, architecture and natural sights, with plenty of interesting stories along the way. Even in the depths of winter, tours go ahead – heating is provided.

Southern Coast Charters
WILDLIFE WATCHING

(☑ 0429 983 112; www.southerncoastcharters.com.au; seal trips adult/child $100/80) As well as offering a range of fishing trips, Southern Coast Charters can take you to visit a nearby seal colony on Lady Julia Percy Island, an underwater (dormant) volcano. Trips last around four hours.

Mulloka Cruises Boat
CRUISE

(☑ 0408 514 382; cruises adult/child $15/5) Runs half-hour cruises of the port, the bay and Griffiths Island.

✦ Festivals & Events

★ Port Fairy Folk Festival
MUSIC

(www.portfairyfolkfestival.com; tickets $290-310, free events in town; ☺ Mar) Australia's premier folk-music festival is held on the Labour Day long weekend in March. It includes an excellent mix of international and national acts, and the streets are abuzz with buskers. Accommodation can book out a year in advance.

🛏 Sleeping

Port Fairy YHA
HOSTEL $

(☑ 03-5568 2468; www.portfairyhostel.com.au; 8 Cox St; dm/s/d/f from $27/47/79/125; @ 🛜) Easily the best budget option in town, in the rambling 1844 home of merchant William Rutledge, this friendly, well-run hostel has a large kitchen, a pool table, free cable TV and peaceful gardens. The owners have excellent local info.

Seacombe House
GUESTHOUSE $

(☑ 03-5568 1082; www.seacombehouse.com.au; 22 Sackville St; r from $120, without bathroom from $90, cottages $200; ❄ 🛜) Built in 1847, historic Seacombe House has cosy (OK, tiny) rooms, but it offers all the atmosphere and romance you'd hope for from this seafaring town. Modern motel rooms are available in its rear wing. It's above the acclaimed Gladioli restaurant (p566).

Pelican Waters
CABIN $

(☑ 0438 827 607, 03-5568 1002; www.pelicanwatersportfairy.com.au; 34 Regent St; cabins from $110; ❄ 🛜) One of Port Fairy's more interesting places to stay is this rustic farm with old windmills, roaming chickens and resident alpacas and llamas. There's a range of choices, but it's most known for its rooms within converted old-school Melbourne suburban train carriages (weekday/weekend $120/140 per double), fitted with all mod cons (DVD players, air-con, kitchens).

Merrijig Inn   HOTEL $
(☑ 03-5568 2324; www.merrijiginn.com; 1 Campbell St; d from $130; ⊚) At the heritage-listed Merrijig, one of Victoria's oldest inns, you can choose between the quaint doll's-house 'attic' rooms upstairs and roomier, more comfortable rooms downstairs. There's a wonderful back lawn with veggie garden and silkie bantam chickens, plus comfy lounges with fireplaces throughout. Its restaurant is another reason to stay; add $30 for a delicious breakfast.

★**Drift House**   BOUTIQUE HOTEL $$$
(☑ 03-5568 3309, 0417 782 495; www.drifthouse. com.au; 98 Gipps St; d from $395; ⊛⊚) An intriguing mix of 19th-century grandeur and 21st-century design, Drift House is a must for architecture-lovers. Its grand frontage is that of the original 1860 double Victorian terrace, yet rooms feature ultra-slick open-plan designs and are decked out with boutique fittings. It's won a bunch of awards and is undoubtedly *the* spot to treat yourself in town.

🍴 Eating & Drinking

★**Coffin Sally**   PIZZA $
(☑ 03-5568 2618; www.coffinsally.com.au; 33 Sackville St; pizzas $13-20; ⊘ 4.30-11pm) This historic building, once used by a coffin maker, is now well regarded for traditional thin-crust pizzas, cooked in an open kitchen and wolfed down on street-side stools or in dimly lit dining nooks out the back next to an open fire. Its bar is one of Port Fairy's best spots for those into craft beers and cocktails.

Farmer's Wife   CAFE $
(☑ 03-5568 2843; www.facebook.com/farmerswife portfairy; 47a Sackville St; mains $10-20; ⊘ 8am-2pm) Hidden down a walkway in a modern lot, Farmer's Wife doesn't need a heritage building to impress, and instead lets its food do the talking. Overseen by the chef previously at acclaimed Stag, the seasonal brunch menu features tempting items such as porkbelly Benedict brioche, chilli fried eggs with pork quesadilla and salsa, and sourdough fruit toast.

Port of Mexico   MEXICAN $
(☑ 03-5568 1285; www.portofmexico.com. au; 3/32 Bank St; tacos from $7; ⊘ 5.30-10pm Wed-Sun) Bringing some much-needed colour and flair to Port Fairy's austere bluestone buildings is this modern taqueria decked out with vibrant mosaics and Frida Kahlo murals. It does soft corn tacos filled with anything from slow-cooked pork shoulder to Tijuana-style fish, along with burrito bowls and a good choice of Mexican beers and cocktails.

★**Gladioli**   AUSTRALIAN $$$
(☑ 03-5539 7523; www.gladiolirestaurant.com.au; 22 Sackville St; 2/3/5/8 courses $70/90/110/130; ⊘ 12.30-3pm Fri & Sat, 6-10pm Wed-Sat; ⊛⊚) Moving into historic Seacombe House – an esteemed address home to Port Fairy's premier fine dining over the years – in late 2018 is this acclaimed restaurant famed for its original Inverleigh location. Its regularly changing, European-influenced menu is driven primarily by locally sourced ingredients, ordered as two-course à la carte or a range of tasting menus paired with local wines.

It also has **Conlan's Wine Store** (☑ 03-5568 2582; www.conlanswinestore.com.au; 34 Bank St; small/large dishes from $14/28; ⊘ 5-10pm Mon & Tue, noon-10pm Wed-Sun) around the corner.

Merrijig Kitchen   AUSTRALIAN $$$
(☑ 03-5568 2324; www.merrijiginn.com; 1 Campbell St; mains from $36; ⊘ 6-9pm Thu-Mon; ⊚🍽) Here at Port Fairy's most atmospheric restaurant you can warm yourself by the open fire and enjoy superb dining with a menu that owner-chef Tanya Connellan changes daily according to what's seasonal. It has a kitchen garden, house-cured meats and home-smoked fish, and features an award-winning wine list. Delectable food with great service.

Stump   PUB
(Caledonian Inn; ☑ 03-5568 1044; 41 Bank St; ⊘ 11am-late) Victoria's oldest continuously licensed pub (1844), the Stump, aka Caledonian Inn, is very much a local institution. It's a no-frills drinking den but has an open fireplace, and a beer garden when the sun's shining. It does pub grub (mains $15 to $35) and has motel rooms ($120) too.

❶ Information

Port Fairy Visitor Centre (☑ 1300 656 564; www.portfairyaustralia.com.au; Railway Pl, Bank St; ⊘ 9am-5pm; ⊚) Provides spot-on tourist information, walking-tour brochures (20 to 50 cents), free wi-fi, V/Line tickets, tourism brochures and publications. There's

CAPE NELSON & CAPE BRIDGEWATER

Only a 10-minute drive from Portland is the historic 1884 Cape Nelson Lighthouse (☑ 0438 012 352; www.capenelsonlighthouse.com.au; adult/child/family $15/10/40; ⊘ tours 11.30am & 2pm). It's still operational, but twice-daily tours allow you climb to its top and be shown around the premises while hearing tales of shipwrecks.

While you're here pop in for a bite or a drink at Margaret & Agnes @ Isabella's (☑ 03-5523 5119; Cape Nelson Lighthouse; mains $12-20; ⊘ 10am-4pm), at the lighthouse's blustery base, which offers excellent deli-style food within its thick bluestone walls. Those who want to stay can book into the self-contained lighthouse keepers' cottage (☑ 0428 131 253; www.capenelsonlighthouse.com.au; Cape Nelson Lighthouse; 1/2-bedroom cottages incl breakfast from $220/270; ☒ ☎). The cottages have all mod cons while retaining their historic charm.

Home to one of Australia's finest stretches of white-sand surf beach, Cape Bridgewater makes for an essential 21km detour off the Portland–Nelson Rd. Its powdery white sands and turquoise waters resemble Queensland's shores more than a remote Victorian beach. Though the beach is the main drawcard, there are also a number of walks featuring dramatic scenery and an opportunity to swim with Australian fur seals, which makes this destination one of the coast's best-kept secrets.

also bike hire (half/full day $20/30), as well as free beach wheelchairs for travellers with disabilities.

❶ Getting There & Away

Port Fairy is 20 minutes' drive west of Warrnambool on the A1 and just under an hour's drive to Portland in the other direction. If you're coming from Melbourne it's a 288km journey, with the most direct route along the B140 highway from Geelong.

From Melbourne you can catch a train to Warrnambool, from where V/Line (☑ 1800 800 007; www.vline.com.au; ⊘ ticket office 9.15am-3.15pm & 4.45-5pm Mon-Fri) runs four to five connecting buses a day ($5, 35 minutes). The bus also heads to Tower Hill ($4.20) and Koroit ($4.20). There's also a bus from Port Fairy to Portland ($9.20, 55 minutes).

❶ Getting Around

Port Fairy is small enough to get about on foot, but hiring a bike is also a good way to go – they're available from the tourist office. There's also a local taxi (☑ 0419 764 983) and an electric tuk tuk (p565) if you get stuck.

Portland

POP 10,061

Portland's claim to fame is as Victoria's first European settlement, founded as a whaling and sealing base in the early 1800s. Despite its colonial history, appealing architecture and beaches, blue-collared Portland feels much more like a regional hub than a tourist town.

Though with that said, there's a lot on offer. The Great South West Walk (p568) is a big attraction, as are seafood and fishing, whale watching in winter, plus other excellent wildlife encounters, and some good surf breaks outside town. It's also a good base for visiting the surrounding region.

The Gunditjmara people are the traditional custodians of this land. A visit to nearby Tyrendarra (p569) is a must to learn about their culture.

◉ Sights

Historic Waterfront WATERFRONT
(Cliff St) The grassy precinct overlooking the harbour has several heritage bluestone buildings. The Customs House (1850) is still a working office, but on weekdays you can ask to see its fascinating display of confiscated booty in the cellar, including a stuffed black bear. Also here is the 1845 courthouse and the 1886 Rocket Shed, with a display of ship rescue equipment.

Up the hill is the 1889 battery with its cannons, built as a defence against feared Russian invasion.

Portland Maritime
Discovery Centre MUSEUM
(☑ 1800 035 567; Lee Breakwater Rd; adult/child under 15yr $7.50/free; ⊘ 9am-5pm) Visit for excellent displays on shipwrecks and Portland's whaling history. Other highlights

include a sperm-whale skeleton that washed ashore, a giant squid caught in 1997 and the original 1858 wooden lifeboat used to save 19 passengers after the disastrous wreck of the SS *Admella*. The **cafe** (📞03-5521 7341; www.facebook.com/thecaptainsgalleyportland; mains $18-22; ⊙9.30am-3.30pm) has one of the best views in town.

Portland Cable Tram   LANDMARK
(📞03-5523 2831; www.portlandcabletrams.com. au; 2a Bentinck St; adult/child/family $18/7/45; ⊙departures 10am, 11.15am, 12.30pm, 1.45pm & 3pm, museum 9am-4pm) This restored 1886 cable tram (now diesel powered) does four to five trips a day, plying a circular 7.4km route on a track laid in 2002 that links the **vintage-car museum** (📞03-5523 5795; cnr Glenelg & Percy Sts; adult/child/family $8/1/16; ⊙10am-4pm), **botanical gardens** (⊙sunrise-sunset), Maritime Discovery Centre and **WWII memorial water tower** (1/2 Wade St; adult/child $4/3; ⊙10am-4pm). Hop on and off as you please. Also here are a tram museum, historical photographs, a rock exhibit and a toy-train exhibit.

🛏 Sleeping

Sawpit Campground   CAMPGROUND
(Mount Clay State Forest) **FREE** Located 3.5km from Narrawong, around 20km east of Portland, this free campground occupies the site of a disused sawmill, surrounded by forest and wildlife. There are six sites, as well as fireplaces, barbecues and drop toilets; you'll need to bring your own drinking water.

GREAT SOUTH WEST WALK

The 250km signposted loop that is the **Great South West Walk** begins and ends at Portland's visitor centre. It takes in some of the southwest's most stunning natural scenery: from the remote, blustery coast, through the river system of Lower Glenelg National Park, and back through the hinterland to Portland. The whole loop takes at least 10 days, but it can be tackled in sections, and parts can be done as day walks or even a two-hour loop. Maps are available from visitor centres in Portland and Nelson (p566).

Visit www.greatsouthwestwalk.com for information and registration details.

The area's popular with bushwalkers and mountain-bikers.

★**Clifftop**
Accommodation   GUESTHOUSE $
(📞03-5523 1126; www.portlandaccommodation. com.au; 13 Clifton Ct; d from $150; ❊🐾) The panoramic ocean views from the balconies here are incredible. The three self-contained rooms are huge, with big brass beds, telescopes and a modern maritime feel.

Hotel Bentinck   HISTORIC HOTEL $
(📞03-5523 2188; cnr Bentinck & Gawler Sts; motel s/d from $80/95, hotel r from $170; ❊🐾) A rather grand historic pub (c 1856) on the main street, the Bentinck offers local character, comfort and overall good value. Room 27 is the pick, with water views, a spa bath and chesterfield couches. There are also motel rooms around the back; they're generic but get the job done.

🍴 Eating & Drinking

Deegan Seafoods   FISH & CHIPS $
(📞03-5523 4749; 106 Percy St; fish from $6; ⊙9am-6pm Mon-Fri) This fish-and-chip shop famously serves the freshest fish in Victoria, caught daily off its boat. Whether you go the flake or the calamari rings, you're in for a treat. It sells fresh fish at weekends, but only cooks it up weekdays.

Mac's Hotel   PUB FOOD $
(Bentinck Hotel; 41 Bentinck St; lunch $10; ⊙11am-1am) Portland's best pub for a cold beer and a feed is this historic hotel that's most popular for its $10 counter lunches. There's also its more upmarket Admella's dining room, with historic charm and an impressive variety of schnitzels.

Bahloo Portland   CAFE $$
(📞03-5548 4749; www.facebook.com/bahloo portland; 85 Cliff St; mains $14-39; ⊙7.30am-4.30pm Mon-Fri, from 8am Sat & Sun; 🐾) Housed in the original bluestone watchkeeper's house, across from the harbour, is one of Portland's best spots for hearty cooked breakfasts, loaded salad bowls, steak sandwiches and the like. Its terrace is perfect for a coffee or glass of wine.

ℹ Information

Portland Visitor Centre (📞1800 035 567; www.iamportland.com.au; Lee Breakwater Rd; ⊙9am-5pm) In a modern building on the waterfront, this excellent information centre has a stack of suggestions for things to do and see.

BUDJ BIM CULTURAL LANDSCAPE

The traditional homeland of the Gunditjmara people, the Budj Bim region offers a fascinating insight into the ancient settlements of the Aboriginal people who've resided here for tens of thousands of years.

Part of an ancient volcanic region – the Kanawinka Geotrail, which stretches across southwestern Victoria and southeastern South Australia – Budj Bim's landscape is characterised by lava flows from the now dormant Mt Eccles, which erupted an estimated 30,000 years ago.

Of most interest to visitors is the Tyrendarra Indigenous Protected Area, the site of some of the oldest constructed aquaculture systems in the world, built by the Gunditjmara some 6600 years ago. A nature trail loops around the lava flow and wetlands, where you'll see a system of eel and fish traps and channels, as well as reproductions of the traditional round stone-and-thatch dwellings found in the region. In July 2019 the area became a Unesco World Heritage Site.

The best way to visit is through Budj Bim Tours (☑ 0458 999 315, 03-5527 0000, 03-5527 1427; www.budjbimtours.net; 12 Lindsay St, Heywood; tours from $40), an organisation run by the Gunditjmara that will guide you through the area, explaining the culture, traditions and land. However, the outfit is often difficult to get hold of, so book well ahead. Otherwise, it's possible to visit independently, with useful information boards along the way offering details of the trail. The access point is prone to flooding, so be prepared to take off your shoes and get your feet wet! It's on Taylors Rd, off Tyrendarra–Ettrick Rd, 2.5km north of the Princes Hwy (A1) and 32km northeast of Portland.

Also in the area is Budj Bim National Park (formerly known as Mt Eccles National Park), 45km northeast of Tyrendarra. The park is co-managed by the Gunditjmara and Parks Victoria, and its main feature is the dormant Mt Eccles, covered in manna-gum forest and offering a number of walks. The best is the 2.6km crater-rim walk, with koalas, bird life and lovely views, as well as a tunnel cave formed by the lava flow. At the park's entrance is a visitor centre with good info on the area, as well as a campground with toilets, hot showers, fireplaces and gas barbecues.

There's free camping at the recreation reserve in Macarthur, a small town 11km east of the national park. Here you'll find a general store and a historic pub. Also of interest is Suffoir Winery & Brewery (☑ 0430 382 432; www.suffoirwines.com.au; 144 Mount Eccles Rd, Macarthur; ⊙ 11am-6pm Fri, 10am-6pm Sat, 2-6pm Sun, daily school holidays), a rustic cellar door in a tin shed where you can sample pinot noir, craft beers and ciders. It's on the road between the national park and Macarthur.

ⓘ Getting There & Away

Portland is an hour's drive west of Port Fairy on the Princes Hwy (A1).

V/Line buses connect Portland with Port Fairy (from $9.20, 55 minutes) and Warrnambool (from $13.40, one hour and 25 minutes) four times daily on weekdays and twice a day at weekends. Buses depart from Henty St.

Nelson

☑ 08 / POP 190

Tiny Nelson is the last outpost before the South Australian border – just a general store, a pub and a handful of accommodation places. It's a popular holiday and fishing spot at the mouth of the Glenelg River, which flows through Lower Glenelg National Park. It's pretty much the halfway mark between

Melbourne and Adelaide, and likes to think of itself as the beginning of the Great Ocean Road. Note that Nelson uses South Australia's 08 telephone area code.

⊙ Sights & Activities

★ Princess Margaret Rose Cave   CAVE
(☑ 08-8738 4171; www.princessmargaretrosecave. com; Princess Margaret Rose Caves Rd, Mumbannar, Lower Glenelg National Park; adult/child/family $22/15/48; ⊙ tours depart 10am, 11am, noon, 1.30pm, 2.30pm, 3.30pm & 4.30pm, reduced hours winter) Opened to the public in 1940, this limestone cave with surreal, gleaming calcite formations remains one of Australia's finest show caves. It can only be visited as part of a guided tour, which takes 45 minutes and is totally illuminated, with clear

walkways. The interpretative centre has good info on the cave's history. It's within Lower Glenelg National Park, 17km north of Nelson, and crosses the border before looping back over; it's best to get here via **Nelson River Cruises** ([📞]08-8738 4191, 0448 887 1225; www.glenelgrivercruises.com.au; cruises adult/child/family $32.50/10/75; ⏷Sep-Jun).

There's a campground here too, along with numerous walking trails.

Lower Glenelg National Park NATIONAL PARK
Hidden away in Victoria's far southwestern corner is one of the state's most scenic national parks, of which the Glenelg River is the most prominent feature. It's a popular spot to hit the water, whether by houseboat, kayak or tinnie, and makes for a relaxing destination for fishing and swimming. There are plenty of bushwalking trails and campsites, and it's home to the stunning Princess Margaret Rose Cave (p569). If you're lucky you'll spot the rare southeastern red-tailed black cockatoo.

★**Nelson Canoe Hire** CANOEING
([📞]0409 104 798; hire per half-/full day canoe $40/65, kayak $45/60) Exploring the 65km stretch of scenic river along Lower Glenelg National Park on a multiday canoe trip is one of Victoria's best secret adventures. This outfit can kit you out for leisurely paddles or serious river-camping expeditions (three days including waterproof barrels). There's no office, but it'll deliver all the gear; BYO tent and supplies.

★**Nelson Boat Hire** BOATING
([📞]08-8738 4048; www.nelsonboathire.com.au; dinghy per 1/4hr $55/130, motorboat per hour $65, houseboat per 2 nights $450-490; ⏷Sep-Jul) Whether you head out for a few hours' fishing or hire a self-contained houseboat, cruising along the scenic waters of Lower Glenelg National Park will likely be the most relaxing part of your trip. The best bit is you don't need a boat licence. Houseboats sleep six and have bathroom, fridge and kitchen; there's a two-night minimum hire period.

🛏 **Sleeping & Eating**

River Vu CAMPGROUND $
([📞]08-8738 4123; www.rivervupark.com.au; 31 Kellett St; unpowered/powered/en-suite sites $21/28/29) Overlooking the Glenelg River, this campground is conveniently close to the water, the pub and the kiosk next door.

Kywong Caravan Park CAMPGROUND $
([📞]08-8738 4174; www.kywongcaravanpark.com.au; 92 North Nelson Rd; unpowered sites $23-28, powered sites $28-35, cabins $95-105; ❇🐾) Set 1km north of town, this 10-hectare park is next to the national park and the Glenelg River, with plenty of wildlife (including bandicoots) and great birdwatching.

★**Nelson Hotel** PUB
([📞]08-8738 4011; Kellett St; ⏷11am-late; 🐾) As real as outback pubs come, the Nelson Hotel (established 1855) is an essential stop for a beer and a friendly yarn with locals. It's got a character-filled front bar, featuring a dusty stuffed pelican, and a bistro serving hearty meals (mains from $15).

There are basic room too, which, while in need of a refurb, are perfectly fine for the night (singles/doubles with shared bathroom $45/75).

ℹ Information

Nelson Visitor Centre ([📞]08-8738 4051; www.nelsonvictoria.com.au; ⏷10am-12.30pm & 1.30-5pm; 🐾) Good info on both sides of the border; particularly helpful for the parks and the Great South West Walk (p568). Also has wi-fi. During summer it has longer opening hours; otherwise, it leaves tourist packages for visitors after hours.

ℹ Getting There & Away

Nelson is 65km from Portland, and 4km from the South Australian border.

There's no public transport, so you'll need your own wheels. You could also walk here on the Great South West Walk (p568).

GOLDFIELDS & GRAMPIANS

History, nature and culture combine spectacularly in Victoria's regional heart. In the mid-19th century more than a third of the world's gold came out of Victoria and today the spoils of that brief boom time can be seen in the grand regional cities of Bendigo and Ballarat and the charming towns of Castlemaine, Kyneton and Maldon. Fantastic for touring, the area has landscapes ranging from pretty countryside and green forests to red earth and granite country to farmland, orchards and wineries. The region's also rich in the arts, home to some of the state's finest galleries.

Further west, there's a different type of history to experience at Grampians National Park, one of Victoria's great natural wonders. Some 80% of Victoria's Aboriginal rock-art sites are found here, and the majestic ranges are an adventurer's paradise, lording it over the idyllic Wartook Valley and the towns of Halls Gap and Dunkeld.

Ballarat

POP 93,759

Ballarat is one of the greatest gold-mining towns on earth, and the mineral continues to provide most of the town's major attractions, even long after the end of the gold rush. It's easy to see the proceeds of that boom time in the monumental Victorian-era buildings around the city centre.

The single biggest attraction here is the fabulous re-created gold-mining village at Sovereign Hill, but there's plenty more in this busy provincial city to keep you occupied, including art galleries and microbreweries. Rug up if you visit in winter – Ballarat's renowned for being chilly.

The Wathaurung people are the traditional custodians of this land.

◉ Sights

★ Sovereign Hill   HISTORIC SITE
(☑03-5337 1199; www.sovereignhill.com.au; Bradshaw St; adult/child/family $57/25.60/144; ⊙10am-5pm, to 5.30pm during daylight saving) You'll need to set aside at least half a day to visit this fascinating re-creation of Ballarat's 1860s gold-mining township. The site was mined in the gold-rush era and much of the equipment is original, as is the mine shaft. Kids love panning for gold in the stream, watching the hourly gold pour and browsing ye olde lolly shop. While it's especially popular with children and families, it'll be enjoyed by all.

★ Art Gallery of Ballarat   GALLERY
(☑03-5320 5858; www.artgalleryofballarat.com.au; 40 Lydiard St N; ⊙10am-5pm, tour 2pm) FREE Established in 1884 and moved to its current location in 1890, the Art Gallery of Ballarat is the oldest provincial gallery in Australia. The architectural gem houses a wonderful collection of early colonial paintings and modern art, with works by noted Australian artists (including Tom Roberts, Sidney Nolan, Russell Drysdale, Albert Tucker, Fred Williams and Howard Arkley). It also hosts contemporary, ticketed shows by national and international artists.

Eureka Centre   MUSEUM
(102 Stawell St; adult/child/family $6/4/18; ⊙10am-5pm) Standing on the commemorative site of the Eureka Rebellion, this modern museum focuses on the momentous 1854 Battle of the Eureka Stockade. Multimedia displays re-create the events of this famous uprising, where gold prospectors clashed with colonial troopers over reforms to miners' rights, resulting in 27 deaths. Pride of place goes to the preserved remnants of the original Eureka flag, which remains an enduring symbol of democracy in Australia.

Lost Ones Gallery   GALLERY
(☑03-4343 1754; www.thelostones.com.au; 14 Camp St) FREE Putting Ballarat's ornate architecture to good use, this contemporary gallery is set up inside an 1870s Masonic temple with a colonnaded facade. It's a lovely space with a diverse program showing cutting-edge works by local and international artists. There's an atmospheric basement bar (⊙4pm-late Wed-Fri, from 7pm Sat & Sun).

Botanic Gardens   GARDENS
(Wendouree Pde; ⊙sunrise-sunset) FREE On the western side of the lake, Ballarat's beautiful and serene gardens were first planted in 1858. The 40 hectares include immaculately maintained rose gardens, wide lawns and a colourful conservatory. Visit the cottage of poet Adam Lindsay Gordon or walk along the Prime Ministers' Ave, a collection of bronze busts of all of Australia's prime ministers up until Tony Abbott.

★ Red Duck Brewery
& Kilderkin Distillery   BREWERY, DISTILLERY
(☑03-5332 0723, 0407 526 540, 0424 791 790; www.redduckbeer.com.au; 11a Michaels Dr, Alfredton; ⊙10am-4pm Mon-Fri, noon-5pm Sat & Sun) These guys have been brewing craft beer since 2005 – way before it was cool – and continue today with ever-changing, inventive seasonal brews to complement their core range. They were likewise ahead of the game with their gins, distilled using indigenous botanicals that you can sample at the no-frills cellar door in an industrial estate on the town outskirts.

☂ Activities

Mining Exchange Gold Shop   OUTDOORS
(☑03-5333 4242; www.thegoldshop.com.au; 8a Lydiard St N; ⊙10.30am-5pm Mon & Wed-Fri, to

Ballarat

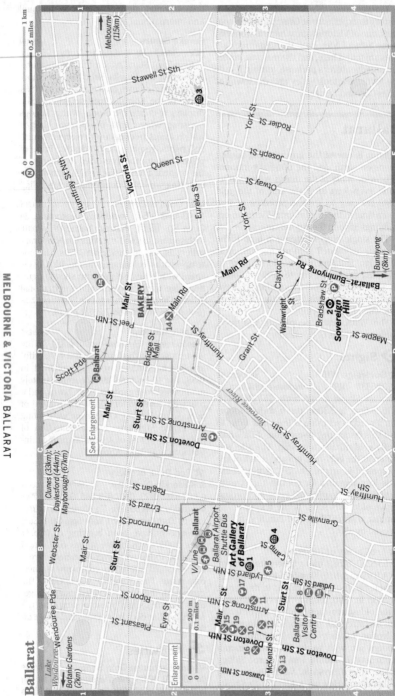

1 km
0.5 miles

Melbourne (115km)

Stawell St Sth

3

York St

Rodier St

Joseph St

Queen St

Otway St

Humffray St Nth

Victoria St

Eureka St

York St

Mair St

Peel St Nth

BAKERY HILL

Main Rd

Clayton St

Main Rd

9

14 Main Rd

Humffray St

Wainwright St

Ballarat–Buninyong Rd

Buninyong (8km)

Bradshaw St

Sovereign Hill

2

Magpie St

Grant St

Scott Pde

Ballarat

Bridge St Mall

Sturt St

Mair St

Armstrong St Sth

Doveton St Sth

18

Yarrowee River

Humffray St Sth

See Enlargement

Clunes (33km);
Daylesford (44km);
Maryborough (67km)

Webster St

Mair St

Sturt St

Ripon St

Eyre St

Pleasant St

Raglan St

Errard St

Drummond St

Lake Wendouree Wendouree Pde

Botanic Gardens (2km)

Enlargement

200 m
0.1 miles

Ballarat

V/Line
6

Ballarat Airport
Shuttle Bus

Lydiard St Nth

Art Gallery
of Ballarat
1

Camp St

4

5

Greenville St

17

Mair St

Armstrong St Nth

11

Sturt St

Lydiard St Sth

8

7

Ballarat
Visitor
Centre

15

19

Doveton St Nth

10

16

McKenzie St

12

Dawson St Nth

13

Humffray St Sth

3.30pm Sat) Hopeful prospectors can pick up miners' rights and rent metal detectors at the Gold Shop in the historic Mining Exchange. It also has gold nuggets and jewellery for sale, and owner Cornell is a wealth of knowledge on everything to do with gold in the region.

⚑ Festivals & Events

★ White Night Ballarat CULTURAL
(www.whitenightballarat.com.au; ⊘7pm-7am Oct) FREE Ballarat is the latest city in the world to be blessed by this wonderful all-night arts festival. It features a packed program of performances, exhibitions and patterned projections over the city's historical streetscape.

Winter Wonderlights CHRISTMAS
(www.winterwonderlights.com.au; Bradshaw St, Sovereign Hill; adult/child/family $62/27.80/157; ⊘Jul) Debuting in 2016, this wildly successful family festival held at Sovereign Hill (p571) celebrates Christmas in July. Expect carols, snowfalls and colourful light projections on the old buildings.

🛏 Sleeping

Ansonia on Lydiard B&B $
(☑03-5332 4678; www.theansoniaonlydiard.com.au; 32 Lydiard St S; r $120-220; ❄ 🔊) In a heritage building that was originally a bank, the Ansonia exudes calm with its minimalist design, polished floors, dark-wood furnishings and light-filled atrium. The stylish rooms have large-screen TVs and range from studio apartments to family suites. No parking.

Eastern Hotel PUB $
(☑0427 440 661; www.easternhotelaccommodation.com.au; 81 Humffray St N; s/d with shared bathroom from $50/75; 🔊) Sharing space with a lovely corner pub that's good for live music, this former backpackers hostel remains one of Ballarat's few budget options. These days it offers tasteful pub-style accommodation, with nicely furnished doubles and a kitchen for self-catering. Rooms 6, 7 and 8 are best for light sleepers. The phone is rarely attended, so online bookings are best.

Craig's Royal Hotel HOTEL $$
(☑03-5331 1377; www.craigsroyal.com; 10 Lydiard St S; s/d incl breakfast from $200/260; ❄ 🔊) The best of Ballarat's Victorian-era pubs was so named after it hosted the Prince of Wales and the Duke of Edinburgh, as well as literary royalty: Mark Twain. It's full of

---

Ballarat

◉ Top Sights
1	Art Gallery of Ballarat	B3
2	Sovereign Hill	D4

◉ Sights
3	Eureka Centre	G2
4	Lost Ones Gallery	B3

◉ Activities, Courses & Tours
5	Mining Exchange Gold Shop	B3
6	Welcome Nugget	B2

◉ Sleeping
7	Ansonia on Lydiard	B4
8	Craig's Royal Hotel	B3
9	Eastern Hotel	E1

◉ Eating
	Craig's Royal Hotel	(see 8)
10	Fika Coffee Brewers	A3
11	Forge Pizzeria	A3
12	Hydrant Food Hall	A3
13	L'Espresso	A3
14	Mr Jones	D2
15	Pub with Two Names	A3
16	Underbar	A3

◉ Drinking & Nightlife
17	Hop Temple	B3
	Lost Ones Basement Bar	(see 4)
	Main Bar	(see 14)
18	Mallow Hotel	C2
19	Mitchell Harris	A3

old-fashioned opulence – including a grand staircase and an elegant 1930s lift – and the rooms have been beautifully refurbished with heritage furnishings and marble bathrooms.

🍽 Eating

Fika Coffee Brewers CAFE $
(☑0427 527 447; www.fikacoffeebrewers.com.au; 36a Doveton St N; dishes $10-24; ⊘6.30am-3pm Mon-Fri, 7.30am-3pm Sat) One of Ballarat's best cafes, this smart, urban-chic space has dangling light bulbs and wood-panelled walls. Here you can expect an inventive brunch menu offering the likes of pulled-pork bagels, waffles with espresso-maple-drizzled bacon, or steak sandwiches with onion-and-whiskey relish on sourdough. There's fantastic coffee, made using St Ali beans from Melbourne.

Mr Jones ASIAN $$
(☑03-5331 5248; www.mrjonesdining.com.au; 42-44 Main Rd; small dishes $7-21, larger plates

THE EUREKA STOCKADE

On 29 November 1854, about 800 miners tossed their licences into a bonfire during a meeting, then, led by Irishman Peter Lalor, they built a stockade at Eureka, where they prepared to fight for their rights. A veteran of Italy's independence struggle named Raffaello Carboni called on the crowd, 'irrespective of nationality, religion and colour', to salute the Southern Cross as the 'refuge of all the oppressed from all the countries on Earth'.

On 3 December the government ordered troopers (the mounted colonial police) to attack the stockade. There were only 150 miners within the makeshift barricades and the fight lasted a short but devastating 20 minutes, leaving 25 miners and four troopers dead.

Though the rebellion was short-lived, the miners won the sympathy and support of many Victorians. The government deemed it wise to acquit the leaders of the charge of high treason. It's interesting to note that only four of the miners were Australian born; the others hailed from Ireland, Britain, Italy, Corsica, Greece, Germany, Russia, Holland, France, Switzerland, Spain, Portugal, Sweden, the USA, Canada and the Caribbean.

The licence fee was abolished and replaced by a Miners' Right, which cost one pound a year. This gave miners the right to search for gold; to fence in, cultivate and build a dwelling on a piece of land; and to vote for members of the Legislative Assembly. The rebel miner Peter Lalor became a member of parliament some years later. Eureka remains a powerful symbol in Australian culture, standing as it does for the treasured notions of workers' rights, democracy and 'a fair go for all'.

Goldfield brotherhood in 1854, sadly, had its limits. The 40,000 miners who arrived from southern China to try their luck on the 'new gold mountain' were often a target of individual violence and systemic prejudice. Still, the Chinese community persevered, and it has to this day been a strong and enduring presence in the city of Melbourne and throughout regional Victoria.

$24-45; ⊘ 6-9.30pm Wed-Sat, plus noon-2pm Fri) Ballarat's most respected restaurant, Catfish, reincarnated as Mr Jones in late 2018. Looking for a new challenge, the proprietors turned their hand to casual fine-dining with creative dishes shaped by what's local and seasonal. Offerings on the changing menu range from house-made chorizo and smoked duck breast to caramelised pork belly and wood-grilled spiced vegetables.

Craig's Royal Hotel
AUSTRALIAN $$

(☑ 03-5331 1377; www.craigsroyal.com.au; 10 Lydiard St S; mains $24-42; ⊘ 7am-10pm; 🕾) Even if you're not staying here, you can experience some royal treatment by dining in the sumptuous, light-filled Gallery Bistro, which serves European-inspired cuisine. Otherwise, come for a cocktail in the historic, wood-panelled Craig's Bar, or a coffee in the cafe. The hotel also hosts high tea ($65; 3pm Sunday) in its elegant Victorian banquet room; reservations essential.

L'Espresso
ITALIAN $$

(☑ 03-5333 1789; www.facebook.com/lespresso ballarat; 417 Sturt St; mains $13.50-25; ⊘ 7am-5pm Sat-Thu, to late Fri) A mainstay on Ballarat's cafe scene for over 30 years, this old-school European-style cafe doubles as a cool record shop – choose from the impeccable selection of indie, jazz, blues and world vinyl while you wait for your espresso or Tuscan bean soup. Also has fabulous risotto and house-made pastas.

Pub with Two Names
GASTROPUB $$

(☑ 03-4373 2432; www.thepwtn.com.au; 331 Mair St; mains $23-46; ⊘ 11.30am-9pm, to 10pm Fri & Sat) The latest chapter in the history of this long-standing pub (established 1842) sees contemporary Australian artist David Bromley take over the reins, revamping it as an art-filled gastropub. Here it's all about the *parrilla* (grill), with succulent rib-eye steak, Peruvian chicken and charred seafood. Alternatively, keep it simple and grab a burger with a pot of local beer.

Hydrant Food Hall
CAFE $$

(☑ 0478 638 202; www.thehydrant.com.au; 3 McKenzie St; dishes $16-26; ⊘ 7am-4pm Mon-Fri, from 8am Sat & Sun) Sneakily hidden down a city laneway is this industrial-chic cafe in a converted heritage warehouse, full of in-the-know patrons sipping Seven Seeds–roasted coffees. The menu offers contemporary cafe fare: bagels with grilled sardines and ricotta; leafy salad and quinoa bowls; and mushroom ragu baguettes.

Forge Pizzeria
ITALIAN $$

(☑ 03-5337 6635; www.theforgepizzeria.com.au; 14 Armstrong St N; pizzas $19-24; ☺ noon-10pm) Ballarat's go-to place for both authentic and inventive wood-fired pizza is this smart-casual brick-walled restaurant. It's also great for wine and fine charcuterie boards of Italian cured meats, along with homemade gelato.

★ Underbar
GASTRONOMY $$$

(www.underbar.com.au; 3 Doveton St N; 5-course set dinner $150; ☺ 7-11pm Fri & Sat) The current darling of the Goldfields food scene, this intimate, minimalist 12 seater only opens for a handful of seatings – and it's booked out for months. Chef Derek Boath (formerly of New York's Michelin-starred Per Se) takes you through his degustation works of art, comprising cutting-edge fare that's all locally sourced or foraged.

🍷 Drinking & Nightlife

★ Hop Temple
BEER HALL

(☑ 03-5317 7158; www.hoptemple.com.au; rear, 24-28 Armstrong St N; ☺ 4-11pm Wed-Fri, noon-11pm Sat, noon-9pm Sun) Symbolic of Ballarat's meteoric rise from unglamorous country town to happening city is this converted red-brick warehouse tucked down a lane. There are 19 craft beers on tap (plus 200 kinds in the fridge) and artisanal cocktails to go with a menu of buttermilk-fried-chicken drumsticks, smoked barbecue meats and panko-fried mac-and-cheese-patty burgers.

★ Mitchell Harris
WINE BAR

(☑ 03-5331 8931; www.mitchellharris.com.au; 38 Doveton St N; ☺ 11am-9pm Sun-Wed, to 11pm Thu-Sat) This stylish red-brick space without a hint of pretension is set up by local winemakers Mitchell Harris. It showcases their own range as well as wines from across the Victorian Pyrenees region. Tastings ($10 for four wines) and wines by the glass complement the local-produce-driven menu, also a big draw.

★ Mallow Hotel
PUB

(☑ 03-5331 1073; www.themallow.com.au; 20 Skipton St; ☺ 4pm-late Wed & Thu, noon-late Fri-Sun) One of the first pubs in town to start serving decent beer, the Mallow remains a cherished, divey local. It has a dozen local beers and ciders on tap, and the food's good too: craft-beer-battered fish-and-chips, Southern-fried cauliflower and the signature Mallow burger (mains from $18).

Main Bar
BAR

(☑ 0439 311 668; 28 Main Rd, Bakery Hill; ☺ 5.30-10pm Wed-Sat) A refined, old-fashioned boozer, the revamped Main Bar adds another layer of charm to a villagey strip in Bakery Hill. Its intimate wood-panelled decor suits Ballarat to a tee, and it's a perfect spot to soak up the town's history while getting stuck into quality regional wines and a menu of wood-fired sourdough pizza ($12 to $16.50).

ℹ Information

Ballarat Visitor Centre (☑ 03-5337 4337, 1800 446 633; www.visitballarat.com.au; Town Hall, 225 Sturt St; ☺ 9am-5pm; 🛜) This modern and well-equipped info centre sells the Ballarat Pass, stocks free self-guided walking-tour maps and offers complimentary internet access.

ℹ Getting There & Away

Ballarat is 116km (1½ hours) west of Melbourne via the Western Hwy.

Ballarat Airport Shuttle Bus (☑ 03-5333 4181; www.airportshuttlebus.com.au; Ballarat Railway Station; ☺ office 8.30am-5.30pm Mon-Fri, 9am-1pm Sat) Goes direct from Melbourne Airport to Ballarat train station (adult/child $37/18, 1½ hours, 12 daily weekdays, seven on weekends). Can book online.

Firefly (☑ 1300 730 740; www.fireflyexpress.com.au) Buses to Adelaide ($65, eight hours).

V/Line (☑ 1800 800 007; www.vline.com.au) Has frequent direct trains between Melbourne (Southern Cross Station) and Ballarat (from $15.54, 1½ hours) and at least three services from Geelong ($15.54, 1½ hours).

ℹ Getting Around

Ballarat has a number of handy bus lines starting from the main train station; for routes and timetables visit www.cdcvictoria.com.au.

Next to the train station, **Welcome Nugget** (☑ 0468 339 116, 0423 268 618; www.ballarat.com/ballaratonabike.html; 128 Lydiard St N; bike hire 3hr/day/24hr from $15/20/26; ☺ 10am-5pm) hires out bicycles, but you'll need to provide 24 hours' notice.

Otherwise there are Uber and taxis to get about town.

Bendigo

POP 92,379

One of regional Victoria's largest cities, and an 1850s boom town, Bendigo is firmly on the map as a must-see Goldfields destination. It's doing great things: dynamic dining

Bendigo

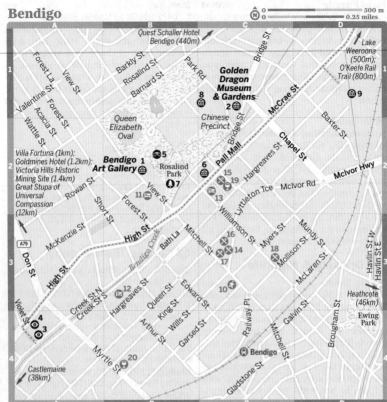

Bendigo

◎ Top Sights
1 Bendigo Art Gallery B2
2 Golden Dragon Museum & Gardens C1

◎ Sights
3 Bendigo Talking Tram A4
4 Central Deborah Gold Mine A4
5 Poppet Head Lookout B2
6 Post Office Gallery C2
7 Rosalind Park B2
8 Sandhurst Gaol C1
9 Tramways Depot D1

◎ Activities, Courses & Tours
10 Moronis Bike Shop C3

◎ Sleeping
11 Allawah Bendigo B2
12 Bendigo Backpackers B3
13 Shamrock Hotel C2

◎ Eating
14 Bendigo Wholefoods C3
15 El Gordo.. C2
16 Mason's of Bendigo C3
17 Toi Shan C3
   Wine Bank on View .... (see 11)
18 Woodhouse... C3

◎ Drinking & Nightlife
19 Dispensary Bar & Diner......................... C2
   Get Naked Espresso....................... (see 17)
20 Golden Vine Hotel.................................. B4
   Handle Bar .... (see 17)

◎ Entertainment
   Ulumbarra Theatre........................... (see 8)

◎ Information
   Bendigo Visitor Centre.................... (see 6)

and arts scenes, cool bars and a stunning reimagining of historic spaces have joined an already formidable array of attractions.

The city's stately gold-rush-era architecture is reminiscent of a pocket-size London, and the world-class art gallery, fascinating Chinese history and Tibetan Buddhist temples come alive during multicultural festivals. It's a good spot for the outdoors too, whether you're exploring the city surrounds by bike, indulging in a spot of gold prospecting or hitting the nearby vineyards.

The Dja Dja Wurrung and the Taungurung peoples of the Kulin Nation are the traditional custodians of the Greater Bendigo region.

⊙ Sights & Activities

★ Bendigo Art Gallery   GALLERY
(✓ 03-5434 6088; www.bendigoartgallery.com.au; 42 View St; ⊙ 10am-5pm, tour 2pm) FREE One of Victoria's finest regional galleries (founded in 1887), Bendigo Art Gallery has a permanent collection that includes outstanding colonial and contemporary Australian art. It showcases works by the likes of Russell Drysdale, Arthur Boyd, Brett Whiteley and Fred Williams. Aim to visit at 2pm for a free tour. The equally impressive temporary exhibitions (both ticketed and free) are cutting edge and have been an important part of Bendigo's revival, bringing big numbers through the doors.

★ Golden Dragon
Museum & Gardens   MUSEUM
(✓ 03-5441 5044; www.goldendragonmuseum.org; 1-11 Bridge St; adult/child/family $12/7/30; ⊙ 9.30am-5pm Tue-Sun, daily school holidays) Bendigo's Chinese heritage sets it apart from other goldfields towns, and this fantastic museum is the place to experience it. Walk through a huge wooden door into an awesome chamber filled with dragons and amazing Chinese cultural items and costumes. The highlight for many are the imperial dragons, including Old Loong (the oldest in the world) and the recently retired Sun Loong (100m long); its replacement, Dai Gum Loong (the longest in the world at 120m), was unveiled in 2019.

Bendigo Talking Tram   LANDMARK
(✓ 03-5443 8117; www.bendigotramways.com; adult/child/family $18/11/53; ⊙ 10am-3.30pm, to 4pm school holidays) For an interesting city tour, hop aboard a restored 'talking' tram. The hop-on, hop-off trip runs from the Central Deborah Gold Mine (p578) to the **Tramways Depot** (✓ 03-5442 2821; www.bendigotramways.com; 1 Tramways Rd; ⊙ 10am-4pm) FREE every half-hour, making several stops, including at the Golden Dragon Museum and **Lake Weeroona** (cnr Nolan & Napier Sts). Tickets are valid all day (a $2 upgrade secures two days), so aim for the 10am themed trams – including the **Dja Dja Wurrung tram** (Monday, Wednesday, Friday, Sunday) and the **Anzac Centenary Tram** (Tuesday, Thursday, Saturday), covering Aboriginal and WWI history, respectively.

Bendigo Pottery   ARTS CENTRE
(✓ 03-5448 4404; www.bendigopottery.com.au; 146 Midland Hwy; ⊙ 9am-5pm) FREE Australia's oldest pottery works, Bendigo Pottery was founded in 1857 and is classified by the National Trust. The historic kilns are still used; watch potters at work, admire the gorgeous ceramic pieces (all for sale) or throw a pot yourself ($20 for 30 minutes; it's an extra $10 to glaze the item and have it posted home – bookings essential). The **museum** (adult/child $8/4) tells the story of pottery through the ages. It's just over 4km north of the town centre.

Villa Fortuna   HISTORIC BUILDING
(✓ 1800 813 153; www.fortuna-villa.com; 22 Chum St; tour per person incl high tea $90; ⊙ 10am & 2pm afternoon Sat) Of all Bendigo's beautiful heritage buildings, none is more extravagant than Villa Fortuna. Set on a 7.5-hectare property, this opulent Victorian-era mansion is the former residence of Bendigo mining entrepreneur George Lansell (1823–1906), who was then one of the world's wealthiest men. The building opened to the public in 2015, and tours take in the lavishly furnished interior and stately curated gardens, along with its lake, elaborate Pompeii Fountain and Roman bath. High tea's taken in the dining room.

Sandhurst Gaol   HISTORIC BUILDING
(Ulumbarra Theatre; ✓ 1800 813 153; www.bendigotourism.com/tours/bendigo/sandhurst-gaol-tour; 10 Gaol Rd; adult/child $15/10; ⊙ tours 11am Tue & 2pm Sun) Opened in 1863, this Pentonville-designed prison (decommissioned in 2005) has been converted into the slick **Ulumbarra Theatre** (✓ 03-5434 6100; www.ulumbarratheatre.com.au; 10 Gaol Rd). You'll need to sign up for a tour to see its intact

cells and learn about its notorious inmates and the executions that took place here; book online or through the visitor centre (p576). Otherwise, if there's an evening show you can have a poke around then.

Great Stupa of Universal Compassion
BUDDHIST SITE

(☑ 03-5446 7568; www.stupa.org.au; 25 Sandhurst Town Rd, Myers Flat; by donation; ⊙ 9am-5pm Mon-Fri, from 10.30am Sat & Sun) In Myers Flat, just beyond Bendigo's city limits, this Buddhist stupa was blessed by the Dalai Lama in 2007 and promises to be the largest stupa in the Western world: it's 50m high with a 50m base. Inside sits a 2.5m jade Buddha statue, the world's largest that's carved out of the precious stone, weighing a hefty 4 tonnes. Grab a self-guided-tour handout and stroll the gardens, with Bodhi tree, Buddhist sculptures and Tibetan prayer wheels lining the stupa.

There's a cafe serving vegetarian and vegan dishes from $6.50.

Central Deborah Gold Mine
HISTORIC SITE

(☑ 03-5443 8255, 03-5443 8322; www.central-deborah.com; 76 Violet St; adult/child/family mine experience from $32/17/88; ⊙ 9.30am-5pm) Don your hard hat and get ready to descend with a geologist into this 412m-deep mine. Operating in 1939–54, the mine has been worked on 17 levels and has yielded 925kg of gold. The 'Mine Experience' tours (75 minutes) that descend 61m are the most popular option; others include the 2½-hour 85m underground adventure (adult/child/family $85/52.50/245) and 'nine levels of darkness' ($200 per person), which heads 228m underground, where you can enjoy lunch and work the drill.

Rosalind Park
PARK

In the city centre, this lovely green space is reminiscent of a London park, with lawns, grand old trees, a fernery, 19th-century statues and the fabulous **Cascades Fountain**, excavated after having been buried for 120 years. Climb to the top of the poppet-head **lookout tower** (Rosalind Park) at the back of Bendigo Art Gallery for sensational 360-degree views or wander through the 19th-century **Conservatory Gardens Building**. You can download a walking-tour map from Bendigo Tourism's website (www.bendigotourism.com).

🏃 Activities

O'Keefe Rail Trail
CYCLING

(www.railtrails.org.au) Completed in 2015, this bike path follows a disused railway line for 49km from Lake Weeroona to Heathcote. There's a heap of wineries and eateries along the way; the Bendigo tourism website (www.bendigotourism.com) has a useful map. Bikes and tours can be arranged through **Moronis Bike Shop** (☑ 03-5443 9644; www.moronisbikes.com; 104-106 Mitchell St; bike hire per day $40; ⊙ 9am-5.30pm Mon-Thu, to 6pm Fri, to 4pm Sat, 10.30am-4pm Sun).

🛏 Sleeping

Bendigo Backpackers
HOSTEL $

(☑ 0429 078 955, 03-5443 7680; www.bendigobackpackers.com.au; 33 Creek St S; dm/d/f with shared bathroom from $29/45/70; ❊ 🛜) This small and friendly hostel is in a cosy weatherboard cottage with a handy central location. It has bright, cheery rooms with all the usual amenities plus a few extras, and a lovely courtyard.

★ Quest Schaller Hotel Bendigo
BOUTIQUE HOTEL $

(☑ 03-4433 6100; www.questschallerhotelbendigo.com.au; cnr Bayne & Lucan Sts; d from $125; 🅿 ❊ 🛜) At the forefront of Bendigo's style makeover, the Schaller art hotel takes its inspiration from Australian artist Mark Schaller, and his signed works feature in all their colourful glory. Public areas are edgy and cool, while most of the rooms have a playful energy. The foyer doubles as a vibrant cafe-bar, and there's a tiny gym too.

Shamrock Hotel
HOTEL $

(☑ 03-5443 0333; www.hotelshamrock.com.au; cnr Pall Mall & Williamson St; d incl breakfast $150-205, ste $255-285; ❊ 🛜) One of Bendigo's historic icons, the Shamrock is a stunning Victorian building with stained glass, original paintings, fancy columns and a *Gone with the Wind*–style staircase. The refurbished upstairs rooms range from small standards to spacious deluxe and spa suites.

★ Allawah Bendigo
APARTMENT $$

(☑ 03-5441 7003; www.allawahbendigo.com; 45 View St; r $125-260; ❊ 🛜) Allawah offers two lovely options in the heart of Bendigo's historic centre, both in heritage former bank buildings. The maisonette rooms at the rear of the stunning **Wine Bank** (☑ 03-5444 4655; www.winebankonview.com; breakfast $9-25, mains $20-42; ⊙ 10am-11pm Mon-Fri, from 8.30am Sat,

8.30am-4pm Sun) are the more affordable choice, while the more boutique **Fountain Suites** are across the road in a splendid 19th-century building. For both, check-in is at the Wine Bank.

Eating

El Gordo
SPANISH **$**

(☑ 0466 432 156, 0401 412 894; www.elgordo bendigo.com; 14 Chancery Lane; dishes $11-20; ⊘ 8am-4pm Tue-Sat, 6-10pm Fri & Sat) Hidden down a city lane is this Spanish cafe doing authentic tapas such as *patatas bravas* as well as *bocadillos* (baguettes) and a good menu of *raciones* and Western brunch items. It also has Spanish beers, sangria and Industry Beans (p493) coffee from Melbourne.

Toi Shan
CHINESE **$**

(☑ 03-5443 5811; www.toishan.com.au; 65 Mitchell St; mains $8-23; ⊘ 11.30am-9.30pm Sun-Fri, from 4.30pm Sat) Opening its doors in 1892, cheap and cheerful Toi Shan has been around since the gold rush – it's reportedly Australia's oldest Chinese restaurant. Fill up on an excellent-value lunchtime smorgasbord ($13 on weekdays). BYO wine.

★ Goldmines Hotel
GASTROPUB **$$**

(☑ 03-5443 3004; www.goldmineshotel.com; 49-57 Marong Rd; smaller dishes $16-27, mains $22-60; ⊘ 5-10pm Wed, noon-10pm Thu-Sat, noon-8pm Sun) A remnant of the lucrative **Victoria Hills** (24-32 Happy Valley Rd) **FREE** goldfields, this grand heritage hotel (1857) just west of central Bendigo has been taken over by the folk from Source Dining (p580). There's a similar focus on local-produce-driven fine dining, but here it sits alongside well-prepared takes on pub classics. Enjoy your meal in the tastefully decorated indoor space or the famous, leafy beer garden.

★ Mason's of Bendigo
AUSTRALIAN **$$**

(☑ 03-5443 3877; www.masonsofbendigo.com. au; 25 Queen St; small plates $15.50-18.50, large plates $33-65; ⊘ noon-2.30pm & 6-8.30pm Tue-Sat) Casual yet sophisticated, the acclaimed Mason's has an agreeable mix of inventive, beautifully plated fine food and great atmosphere. Order several tasting dishes to go with larger shared plates such as the signature roast lamb loin with crispy belly and rolled shoulder.

Bendigo Wholefoods
CAFE **$$**

(☑ 03-5443 9492; www.bendigowholefoods. com.au; 314 Lyttleton Tce; mains $12-25; ⊘ cafe 7am-4pm Mon-Fri, to 3pm Sat, store 8.30am-6pm Mon-Fri, to 3pm Sat) 🍴 Come by this wholefoods centre's cafe to pick up a vegan milkshake, a superfood açai bowl, a cleansing, detoxifying green blend or perhaps a paleo brekky. There are also cafe mainstays, along with global dishes such as West African chicken stew or Israeli slow-cooked lamb salad.

★ Woodhouse
STEAK **$$$**

(☑ 03-5443 8671; www.thewoodhouse.com.au; 101 Williamson St; pizza $20-25, mains $38-65; ⊘ noon-2.30pm & 5.30pm-late Tue-Fri, noon-late Sat) In a warehouse-style space clad in warm brick tones, Woodhouse has some of the finest steaks you'll find in regional Victoria – all cooked on a red-gum wood-fired grill. The Wagyu tasting plate ($68) is pricey but close to heaven for dedicated (and hungry) carnivores. The smoky Wagyu burger also comes off the grill, while the thin-crust pizzas are seriously gourmet.

Drinking & Nightlife

★ Dispensary Bar & Diner
BAR

(☑ 03-5444 5885; www.dispensarybendigo.com; 9 Chancery Lane; ⊘ 4pm-late Mon, noon-late Tue-Sat, noon-4pm Sun) With its sneaky lane location and intimate den-like space, the Dispensary is equal to any of Melbourne's hip city bars. It has a selection of 100-plus craft beers, 40 gins and 60 whiskies, along with quality cocktails. The food's equally appealing, with plates of confit-duck steamed buns, blue-swimmer-crab spaghetti and Black Angus eye fillet.

Golden Vine Hotel
PUB

(☑ 03-5443 6063; www.facebook.com/golden vinebendigo; 135 King St; mains $10-29; ⊘ 11am-11pm Tue-Thu, to 1am Fri-Sun) This divey inner-suburban pub is one of Bendigo's best, with rock 'n' roll, $10 counter meals, quality beers on tap and a cool beer garden. Opening its doors in 1877, it has some serious history too.

Get Naked Espresso
CAFE

(☑ 0411 950 044; www.getnakedespressobar.com; 73 Mitchell St; ⊘ 6.30am-2pm; 🛜) A cool little city spot, Get Naked Espresso is a great place to hang out and taste quality Mt Beauty–roasted coffee. There's a second location across from Bendigo Art Gallery (p577).

For booze, head out the back to its **Handle Bar** (☑ 0417 477 825; www.handlebarbendigo. com; 73 Mitchell St; ⊘ 2-11pm Thu-Sun; 🛜).

ⓘ Information

Bendigo Visitor Centre (📞 03-5434 6060, 1800 813 153; www.bendigotourism.com; 51-67 Pall Mall; ⏰ 9am-5pm; 🛜) In the historic former post office, this helpful centre can book tickets for sights and tours, provides accommodation referrals and has a bazillion brochures. Also here is the **Post Office Gallery** (📞 03-5434 6179; www.bendigoartgallery.com.au; 51-67 Pall Mall; gold coin donation; ⏰ 9am-5pm).

ⓘ Getting There & Away

Bendigo is a 1¾-hour drive (150km) northwest of Melbourne along the Calder Fwy (M79).

Bendigo Airport (📞 0417 448 328; www.bendigo.vic.gov.au/services/bendigo-airport) In March 2019 Qantas Link announced that it would commence six flights a week between Sydney and Bendigo airport.

Bendigo Airport Service (📞 03-5444 3939; www.bendigoairportservice.com.au; Platform 2, Bendigo Railway Station; adult/child $47/23; ⏰ office 9am-5pm Mon-Fri) Runs direct between Melbourne's Tullamarine Airport and Bendigo train station. Bookings essential.

V/Line (📞 1800 800 007; www.vline.com.au) Has frequent trains between Melbourne (Southern Cross Station) and Bendigo (from $23.38, two hours, around 20 daily) via Castlemaine ($4.70, 20 minutes) and Kyneton ($8.40, 40 minutes).

Kyneton

POP 4866

Kyneton, established in 1850, a year before gold was discovered in the region, was the main coach stop between Melbourne and Bendigo and the centre for the farmers who supplied the diggings with fresh produce. Today its historic Piper St is a destination in itself, as Melbourne foodies flock here at weekends to sample its golden quarter-mile of restaurants, bars, cafes and gin distillery in a precinct lined with heritage buildings. The rest of Kyneton remains steadfastly blue collar, with a built-up shopping area around Mollison and High Sts.

The Taungurung, Dja Dja Wurrung and Wurundjeri people are the traditional custodians of this region.

🛏 Sleeping

⭐ **Flop House**   ACCOMMODATION SERVICES **$$**
(📞 0438 160 671; www.flophouse.com.au; 1/58-60 Piper St; d $185-750; ❄🛜) A boutique accommodation-booking service, Flop House has nine wonderful options around

town that are decked out with style and charm. Choose between renovated weatherboard cottages, riverside farmhouses and an open-plan Scandinavian-style studio. The hosts go to great lengths in offering tips for around town, and there's free bike rental and hampers of local, seasonal goods. Two-night minimum stay.

🍴 Eating & Drinking

Dhaba at the Mill   INDIAN **$**
(📞 03-5422 6225; www.dhaba.com.au; 18 Piper St; mains $14-20; ⏰ 5-9pm Thu-Sat, noon-2.30pm & 5-9pm Sun; 🅿) Behind the heavy wooden doors at the old bluestone steam mill, you can tuck into authentic, affordable curries – classics such as butter chicken, coconut blue grenadier curry and smoky lamb yoghurt curries. It's an appealing space decked out in retro Bollywood film posters and jars of spices.

⭐ **Source Dining**   AUSTRALIAN **$$$**
(📞 03-5422 2039; www.sourcedining.com.au; 72 Piper St; mains $38-45; ⏰ noon-2.30pm & 6-9pm Thu-Sat, noon-2.30pm Sun) One of central Victoria's best restaurants, this fine place has a menu that changes with the seasons and dish descriptions that read like a culinary short story about regional produce and carefully conceived taste combinations.

Major Tom's   BAR
(📞 03-5422 6395; www.majortoms.com.au; 57 Piper St; ⏰ 5-10pm Tue-Fri, noon-late Sat & Sun) Bringing a bit of Castlemaine hipster cool to Piper St is this rock 'n' roll diner with beers, burgers and live bands.

Animus Distillery   DISTILLERY
(📞 03-5403 2431; www.animusdistillery.com; 1/89a Piper St; gin tasting $15; ⏰ noon-8pm Sun & Mon, 4-9pm Wed & Thu, noon-11pm Fri & Sat) We're living in a golden age for booze-lovers when small country towns are getting their own gin distilleries. Slotting in effortlessly along Piper St is Kyneton's new gin bar, where all three of Animus' varietals are produced on-site using botanicals such as bush tomato, strawberry gum and lemon myrtle.

Do a tasting, or grab a G&T to enjoy on the street terrace.

ⓘ Information

Kyneton Visitor Centre (📞 1800 244 711, 03-5422 6110; www.visitmacedonranges.com; 127 High St; ⏰ 9am-5pm) On the southeastern entry to town, with a large selection of brochures, including self-guided town and nature walks, and scenic driving routes.

ℹ️ Getting There & Away

Kyneton is just off the Calder Hwy about 90km northwest of Melbourne.

Regular V/Line trains on the Bendigo line run here from Melbourne (from $12.46, 1¼ hours) and on to Castlemaine ($3.64, 20 minutes) and Bendigo ($8.40, 50 minutes). The train station is 1km south of the town centre.

Castlemaine

POP 9932

At the heart of the central Victorian goldfields, picturesque Castlemaine is home to stirring examples of late-19th-century architecture and gardens. While its goldfields backdrop has always been a lure for tourists (along with antique shopping and Castlemaine Rock lollies), these days visitors are drawn here more for its vibrant arts and food scene. It has two wonderful galleries, a lovely historical theatre and a heap of talented chefs and artisans.

As well as being a proud working-class town with a tight-knit rural community, Castlemaine's known for attracting a left-leaning bohemian crowd. The last 10 years especially have seen an influx of Melburnian tree-changers, bringing with them inner-city style, cafe culture, bars and live-music venues. It's an intriguing dynamic: folks in Hard Yakka workwear getting stuck into a pie alongside a set of fedora-wearing musos, artists and freelancers.

The Dja Dja Wurrung people are the traditional custodians of this region.

⊙ Sights & Activities

★ Castlemaine Art Museum GALLERY
(☑03-5472 2292; www.castlemainegallery.com; 14 Lyttleton St; ☉noon-5pm Thu-Sun) FREE
Housed in a superb art deco building, this gallery (established in 1913) features colonial and contemporary Australian art, including works by such well-known artists as Frederick McCubbin, Arthur Streeton, Russell Drysdale, Fred Williams and Sidney Nolan. There are guided tours on Saturday. A basement museum provides insights into Aboriginal and colonial history, with period costumes, porcelain, silverware and gold-mining relics. The gallery was set to close in 2017, but an anonymous donor chipped in $250,000 to save the day.

★ Old Castlemaine Gaol GALLERY
(36-48 Bowden St) Looming from its commanding hilltop location, the Old Castlemaine Gaol is the town's most notable historical landmark; dating from 1861, it closed its doors in 1990. Today the cells that once held some of the state's most feared criminals are home to the whimsical works and sculptures of esteemed Australian artist David Bromley. He bought the site in 2018 with the aim of beautifying the once-fearsome Pentonville-style prison into his latest canvas.

Mill HISTORIC BUILDING
(www.millcastlemaine.com.au; 1/9 Walker St) Originally the Castlemaine Woollen Mills (1875), this red-brick industrial complex has been developed into one of the town's coolest precincts. It's worth dropping in for a look around; a number of local businesses have set up here, including a brewery (p583), **vintage shops** (☑03-5470 6555; www.castlemainebazaar.com.au; ☉10am-5pm), **designer wares** (☑0409 520 840; www.platformno5.com; ☉10am-5pm), an artisanal meat smoker, a **winery** (☑0417 237 155, 0432 382 454; www.boomtownwine.com.au; ☉by appointment Mon-Thu, 5-11pm Fri, noon-5pm Sat & Sun) and an Austrian-inspired coffee house.

Castlemaine to Maldon Rail Trail CYCLING
(www.railtrails.org.au) Running parallel to the historic **Goldfields Railway** (☑03-5470 6658; www.vgr.com.au; adult/child return $50/20, 1st class $70/65), this well-maintained bike track heads 18km from Castlemaine to Maldon through farming and bushland scenery. It passes Muckleford Railway Station at the halfway mark. Count on around two hours one way.

🛏️ Sleeping

Rembrandts Retreat B&B $
(☑0418 534 490, 03-5470 6724; www.rembrandtsretreat.wordpress.com; 40-42 Campbell St; r $75) At the back of a historic convent (c 1860), this self-contained bungalow surrounded by garden is a great choice for artists, writers and art-lovers. The main building is the family residence and studio of painter Brian Nunan; for more on his work, see www.nunangallery.com.

Castlemaine Colonial Motel MOTEL $
(☑03-5472 4000; www.castlemainemotel.com.au; 252 Barker St; r $100-195; ❄️🐾) Conveniently central and the best of Castlemaine's motels,

MALDON

Like a pop-up folk museum, the whole of tiny Maldon is a well-preserved relic of the gold-rush era, with many fine buildings constructed from local stone. The population is significantly lower than the 20,000 who used to work the goldfields, but this is still a living, working town – packed with tourists at weekends but reverting to its sleepy self during the week.

Evidence of those heady mining days can be seen around town – you can't miss the 24m-high **Beehive Chimney**, just east of Main St. A short trip south along High St reveals the remains of the **North British Mine**, where interpretative boards tell the story of what was once one of the world's richest mines. Here also is the **Parkins Reef Circuit**, a 2.3km loop that takes you through the alluvial gold diggings.

Maldon is 19km northwest of Castlemaine along the Bridgewater–Maldon Rd (C282). From Castlemaine you can ride to Maldon along the 18km rail trail (p581) or take a train on the Victorian Goldfields Railway (p581).

Castlemaine Bus Lines (📞 03-5472 1455; www.castlemainebuslines.com.au) runs three to four buses a day between Maldon and Castlemaine ($3.70, 20 minutes); the last bus back to Castlemaine leaves around 3.20pm on weekdays and 5.15pm at weekends.

the Colonial has a choice of high-ceilinged apartments in a beautifully converted school building (c 1852) or more retro but comfortable motel rooms, some with spa.

★ **Newnorthern** BOUTIQUE HOTEL $$
(📞 03-5472 3787; www.newnorthern.com.au; 359 Barker St; incl breakfast r from $209, without en suite $179; ❄🔊) The old Northern Hotel (c 1870) has been beautifully restored and decorated by renowned furniture maker and artist Nicholas Dattner. The spacious, comfortable rooms feature artwork, antiques and designer furniture. Though not all rooms are en suite, each room is allocated its own private bathroom. There's a lovely lounge and bar downstairs, where breakfast is served, along with complimentary port.

✕ Eating

★ **Johnny Baker** BAKERY $
(📞 03-5470 5695; www.johnnybaker.com.au; 359 Barker St; pies & pastries from $5; ⊙6.30am-4pm) Not your usual country bakery, here it's all about hand-rolled croissants baked with Belgian butter, among other mind-blowing sugary pastries. Its pies are equally popular, with favourites including the vegan lentil-and-eggplant shepherd's pie, or Wagyu sherry, and a heap of baguettes that you can wolf down on the milk-crate seating out the front. Coffee is locally roasted too.

Icecream Social ICE CREAM $
(📞 0468 729 743; www.icecreamsocial.com.au; 12 Hargraves St; ice creams $3-8; ⊙noon-6pm Thu-Sun, daily summer) Moving into a new shop

along the main drag in late 2018, this artisanal ice creamery offers seasonal 'one-off' flavours, including gin garden, lemon, lime and bitters or olive oil and thyme. Other reasons to visit include the cherry pie and the damn fine coffee, along with burgers and Suntory beer on tap.

In summer it also operates out of its original hole-in-the-wall site down at the old Mill (p581).

★ **Bistro Lola** ITALIAN $$
(📞 03-5472 1196; www.bistrolola.com.au; Theatre Royal, 30 Hargraves St; mains $16-30; ⊙5.30-10.30pm Tue-Fri, noon-10.30pm Sat, noon-3pm Sun) A contributing factor to the buzz about the reopened Theatre Royal, Bistro Lola features a menu of classy Italian mains rarely seen in this neck of the woods. Expect the likes of anchovy-and-herb slow-roasted lamb or leek-and-pumpkin tortellini with brown butter, sage and hazelnuts. Chef Carly Lauder has spent time at Trentham's well-respected du Fermier.

If you'd rather keep things casual, downstairs does authentic pizzas, charcuterie and Italian-style bar food you can enjoy on the street-side seating, as well as a good selection of *aperitivos*, wine and beer.

Red Hill Hotel GASTROPUB $$
(📞 03-5416 1133; www.redhillhotel.com.au; 163 Main Rd, Chewton; mains $18-35; ⊙5-11pm Thu, from 3pm Fri, from noon Sat, noon-9pm Sun) In Chewton, 5km east of Castlemaine, this beautiful 19th-century pub has a new Scottish owner who's given it polish while

retaining its classic country-pub character. The menu has nods to the UK in its cheesy curry 'pub chips' and Chewton charcuterie plate featuring blood sausage and pork pies, plus there are such pub staples as schnitzels and roasts.

🍷 Drinking & Nightlife

Taproom
BREWERY

(Shedshaker; 📞0425 323 005, 0438 042 901; www.shedshakerbrewing.com; The Mill, 9 Walker St; ⏰2-8pm Tue & Wed, to 10pm Thu, to 11pm Fri, noon-11pm Sat, noon-9pm Sun) It's been a long time between drinks, but finally Castlemaine has a brewery again. One good one too, set up within the Mill (p581) complex, with 10 of its beers on tap and a bar looking onto the vats. There are pizzas and platters to go with its IPAs and pale, red and golden ales, plus a heap of interesting seasonals.

☆ Entertainment

★ Theatre Royal
THEATRE

(📞03-5472 1196; www.theatreroyalcastlemaine.com.au; 30 Hargreaves St) In operation since the 1850s, the Theatre Royal is a Castlemaine landmark that hosts a fantastic range of cinema as well as touring live bands. Recent headliners include Cat Power, J Mascis, the Cosmic Psychos and local lad DD Dumbo. Consult the website for the program. Be sure to check out the quality Bistro Lola too.

Bridge Hotel
LIVE MUSIC

(📞03-4406 6730; www.thebridgehotelcastlemaine.com; 21-23 Walker St; ⏰3-10pm Mon-Wed, to 11pm Thu, to 1am Fri, noon-1am Sat, noon-9pm Sun) The new owners of this much-loved grungy band room have made food (mains mains $23-29) a big feature, but thankfully they're still booking quality Aussie indie bands: there are two to three gigs a week. The Bridge remains one of regional Victoria's best live-music venues, and it has a killer beer garden for a brew any other time.

ℹ Information

Castlemaine Visitor Centre (📞03-5471 1795, 1800 171 888; www.maldoncastlemaine.com; 44 Mostyn St; ⏰9am-5pm; 📶) In the magnificent **Old Castlemaine Market** (44 Mostyn St), this handy tourist office has brochures, downloadable walking tours, books, and bikes for rent (from $20/30 per half-/full day). It also offers an online accommodation-booking service.

ℹ Getting There & Away

V/Line trains run hourly between Castlemaine and Melbourne (from $17, 1½ hours), passing through Kyneton ($3.65, 20 minutes) and continuing to Bendigo ($4.75, 30 minutes).

Bendigo Airport Service (📞03-5444 3939; www.bendigoairportservice.com.au; adult/child $55/28) Runs direct between Melbourne's Tullamarine Airport and Castlemaine train station. Bookings essential.

The Grampians

Rising up from the western Victorian plains, and acting as a haven for bushwalkers, rock climbers and nature-lovers, the Grampians are one of the state's most significant natural and cultural features. The rich diversity of wildlife and flora, the unique rock formations, the Aboriginal rock art, the spectacular viewpoints and an extensive network of trails and bush campsites offer something for everyone. The local Indigenous Jardwadjali people called the mountains Gariwerd – in the local language 'gari' means 'pointed mountain' and 'werd' means

---

THE GRAMPIANS PEAKS TRAIL

The **Grampians Peaks Trail** (www.grampianspeakstrail.com.au) looms as a flagship trek: an epic 13-day, 12-night expedition that will span the entire length of the park when it's complete in 2020.

At the time of research, only stage 1 had been launched: a 36km, three-day, two-night loop through the Wonderland Ranges. First you'll need to book your campsites – the first night is spent at **Bugiga Hiker Camp** (📞03-5361 4000, 13 19 63; www.parkweb.vic.gov.au; Silverband Rd; sites $32.80) and the second at **Borough Huts Campground** (📞13 19 63, 03-5361 4000; www.parkweb.vic.gov.au; Grampians Rd; sites $26.80) – and then you'll need to register your hike; both can be done online at www.parkweb.vic.gov.au or in person at the **Parks Victoria office** (📞13 19 63, 03-5361 4000; www.parkweb.vic.gov.au; Brambuk Cultural Centre, 277 Grampians Tourist Rd, Halls Gap), 2.5km from Halls Gap Visitor Centre.

The Grampians (Gariwerd)

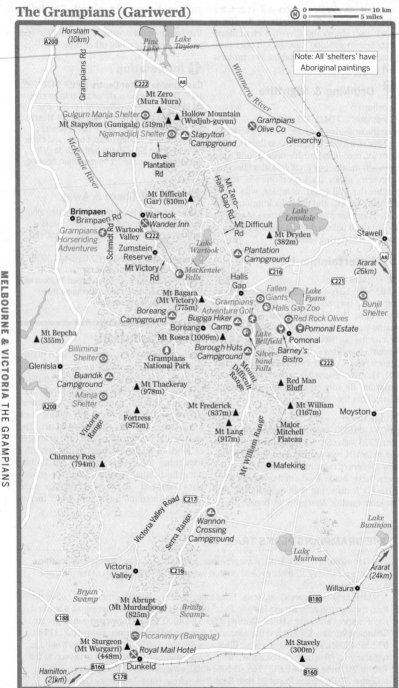

N 0 |——————————| 10 km
0 |——————————| 5 miles

Note: All 'shelters' have
Aboriginal paintings

Horsham
(10km)
A200

Grampians Rd

Pine
Lake

Lake
Taylors

Wimmera River

C222

Mt Zero
(Mura Mura)

A8

Gulgurn Manja Shelter
Mt Stapylton (Gunigalg) (519m)
Ngamadjidj Shelter

Hollow Mountain
(Wudjub-guyun)

Grampians
Olive Co

Glenorchy

Stapylton
Campground

Laharum

Olive
Plantation
Rd

McKenzie River

Mt Zero–
Halls Gap Rd

Mt Difficult
(Gar) (810m)

Brimpaen
Brimpaen Rd

Wartook
Wander Inn

Mt Difficult
Rd

Lake
Lonsdale

Mt Dryden
(382m)

Stawell

Grampians
Horseriding
Adventures

Schmidt Rd

Wartook
Valley
C222

Zumstein
Reserve

Lake
Wartook

Plantation
Campground

Ararat
(26km)
A8

Mt Victory
Rd

MacKenzie
Falls

Halls
Gap

C216

Mt Bagara
(Mt Victory)
(775m)

Fallen
Giants

Lake
Fyans

C221

Boreang
Campground

Grampians
Adventure Golf

Halls Gap Zoo

Bunjil
Shelter

Mt Bepcha
(355m)

Bugiga Hiker
Camp

Boreang

Red Rock Olives

Billimina
Shelter

Mt Rosea (1009m)

Lake
Bellfield

Pomonal Estate

Pomonal

Glenisla

Borough Huts
Campground

Silver-
band
Falls

Barney's
Bistro

C222

Buandik
Campground

Grampians
National Park

Mount
Difficult
Range

Red Man
Bluff

Manja
Shelter
A200

Mt Thackeray
(978m)

Mt William
(1167m)

Moyston

Victoria Range

Fortress
(875m)

Mt Frederick
(837m)

Major
Mitchell
Plateau

Mt Lang
(917m)

Mt William Range

Chimney Pots
(794m)

Mafeking

Victoria Valley Road
C217

Serra Range

Wannon
Crossing
Campground

Lake
Buninjon

Lake
Muirhead

Victoria
Valley
C216

Ararat
(24km)

Willaura
B180

Bryan
Swamp

Mt Abrupt
(Mt Murdadjoog)
(825m)

Brady
Swamp

C188

Mt Sturgeon
(Mt Wurgarri)
(448m)

Piccaninny (Bainggug)

Royal Mail Hotel

Mt Stavely
(300m)

Hamilton
(21km)
B160

Dunkeld
C178

B160

'shoulder'. Explorer Thomas Mitchell named the ranges the Grampians after the mountains in Scotland.

The Jardwadjali and Djab Wurrung people are the traditional custodians of this country.

❶ Getting There & Away

The Grampians are around 260km from Melbourne, with Halls Gap the main access point. If you're coming from the Great Ocean Road you'll pass through Dunkeld into the southern region of the Grampians. From the Goldfields it's a 1½- to two-hour drive, depending on where you're coming from. From the west, count on a five-hour drive from Adelaide.

You can reach Halls Gap by train-bus combo from Melbourne, Ballarat, Warrnambool and Adelaide.

Halls Gap

POP 316

Nudging up against the craggy Wonderland Range, Halls Gap is a pretty little town – you might even say sleepy if you visit midweek in winter, but boy does it get busy during holidays. This is the main accommodation base and easiest access for the best of the Grampians. The single street through town has a neat little knot of shops, a supermarket, adventure-activity offices, restaurants and cafes.

There are plenty of kangaroos in its grassy surrounds – the football oval is a favourite hang-out. Emus are also often spotted.

◉ Sights & Activities

As well as walks (p586) into the Grampians, there's also a designated **cycling path** through town that leads to Lake Bellfield. For climbing, abseiling, mountain biking or guided overnight treks, get in touch with **Absolute Outdoors** (☏1300 526 258; www.absoluteoutdoors.com.au; 105 Grampians Rd).

★ Brambuk
Cultural Centre   CULTURAL CENTRE

(☏03-8427 2058, 03-8427 2311; www.brambuk.com.au; 277 Grampians Rd; gold-coin donation; ⊗9am-5pm) 🎗 FREE Don't leave Halls Gap without visiting the superb cultural centre at Brambuk, 2.5km south of town. Run by five Koorie communities (including the Jardwadjali and Djab Wurrung people, the traditional custodians of the region) in conjunction with Parks Victoria, the centre offers insights into local culture and history through traditional stories, art, music, dance, weapons, tools and photographs.

🛏 Sleeping

★ Tim's Place   HOSTEL $

(☏03-5356 4288; www.timsplace.com.au; 44 Grampians Rd; dm/s/d/tr from $30/60/75/100, apt from $120; @ 🛜) This spotless eco backpackers has a friendly, cosy feel. Owner Tim has run the place for 25 years and is a fantastic source of local info. There are free mountain bikes, ping pong, pétanque and a community food garden that you're welcome to, as long as you do a spot of weeding. There's a great deck for a sunset drink too.

Grampians YHA Eco-Hostel   HOSTEL $

(☏03-5356 4544; www.yha.com.au; cnr Grampians & Buckler Rds; dm/d/f from $33/90/118; @ 🛜) 🎗 This architecturally designed and ecofriendly hostel utilises solar power and rainwater tanks and makes the most of light and space. It's beautifully equipped, with a spacious lounge, a top-notch kitchen and spotless rooms.

Plantation Campground   CAMPGROUND

(☏13 19 63; www.parkweb.vic.gov.au; Mt Zero Rd) FREE Only 9.5km north of Halls Gap, accessed via an unsealed road, this free campground is on an old pine plantation at the edge of the Mt Difficult Range. The 30 campsites operate on a first-come, first served basis – ie there are no pre-bookings, so you'll have to chance your luck. It has non-flushing toilets, bush showers and fire pits.

★ D'Altons Resort   COTTAGE $

(☏03-5356 4666; www.daltonsresort.com.au; 8 Glen St; studio/deluxe/family cottages from $125/130/170; ❄🛜🏊) These delightful timber cottages, with cosy lounge chairs, cute verandahs and log fires, spread up the hill from the main road amid gum trees and kangaroos. The cottages are immaculately kept and have cooking facilities for self-caterers, and the friendly owners are a mine of local information. There's even a tennis court and a saltwater pool.

🍴 Eating & Drinking

Harvest   CAFE $

(☏03-5356 4782; www.harvesthg.com.au; 2 Heath St; day menu $10.50-22; ⊗8am-4pm) Utilising the region's rich bounty of produce, the menu here focuses on locally grown food and wine. There are all-day gourmet breakfasts, and bites like sourdough steak sandwiches for lunch. The on-site provedore stocks a range of items such as local olives, wines and fruit preserves.

Brambuk Bushfood Cafe
AUSTRALIAN $

(☑03-5361 4000; www.brambuk.com.au; Brambruk Cultural Centre, 277 Grampians Rd; mains $9-25; ☺9.30am-3.30pm) Within the Brambuk Cultural Centre (p585), this cafe is a must for those who have yet to sample native Australian flavours such as wattle seed, lemon myrtle and bush tomato. Expect items such as saltbush lasagne, kangaroo pies, grilled emu and wattle-seed damper. The bush-food platter ($25) is a good choice if you'd like to sample a bit of everything.

Spirit of Punjab
INDIAN $$

(☑03-5356 4234; www.spiritofpunjabrestaurant. com; 161-163 Grampians Rd; mains $14.50-26; ☺5-9pm Mon-Thu, noon-2.30pm & 5-9pm Fri-Sun; ⓟ) For a taste of the subcontinent in an Aussie bush setting, head to this excellent Punjabi restaurant with an array of authentically flavoured dishes, including a good tandoori selection. There are cheap bottles of wine, Kingfisher and local beers on tap, and a deck overlooking a natural clearing frequented by roos. There's some fairly bizarre folk sculpture out the front.

★ Pomonal Estate
WINERY, BREWERY

(☑0448 983 248, 0408 564 501; www.pomonal estate.com.au; 2079 Pomonal Rd, Pomonal; ☺10am-5pm Wed, Thu, Sat & Sun, to 7pm Fri) Whatever your tipple, this popular winery, microbrewery and cider producer has you covered. It boasts a fantastic location within an architecturally designed space looking out to pastoral surrounds and a Grampians backdrop. It's still developing its vineyards, but all its wines are created using locally sourced grapes, and it does excellent craft beers and ciders. The food's good too, including tasty local-lamb burgers.

Paper Scissors Rock Brew Co.
MICROBREWERY

(www.paperscissorsrock.beer; 119 Grampians Rd; ☺noon-late) Halls Gap's first microbrewery was about to open its doors at the time of research. Expect the usual crafty selections, including some interesting seasonals such as beers made using locally grown hops. As well as beer tasting, drop in for a menu of brewpub comfort food (pizzas, wings).

ⓘ Information

Halls Gap Visitor Centre (☑1800 065 599; www.visitgrampians.com.au; 117-119 Grampians Rd; ☺9am-5pm; ☎) Staff members here can book tours, accommodation and activities. However, if you want more detailed info on walks you'll have to buy a map ($3.50).

ⓘ Getting There & Away

Halls Gap is 254km (three hours) from Melbourne along the Western Hwy; you'll pass through Ballarat (142km) around the halfway mark. If you're coming from the Great Ocean Road, Halls Gap is 156km north of Port Fairy.

The town is well served by public transport. V/Line connects it with Melbourne ($35.60 to $40.20, 3½ to four hours) via Ballarat ($18.40 to $27.60, around two hours); connecting buses await at Ararat or Stawell stations. There's also a bus from Warrnambool ($30.40, three hours) on Tuesday, Friday and Sunday.

Dunkeld & Around

The southern point of access for the Grampians, Dunkeld (population 508) is a sleepy little town with a very big-name restaurant. The setting is superb, with Mt Abrupt and Mt Sturgeon rising up to the north, while the

---

WALKS FROM HALLS GAP

If you're based in Halls Gap and have time for only one walk, the **Wonderland Loop** is what you're after. The most popular hike in the park, the loop takes you through the evocative landscapes of the Wonderland Ranges, with spectacular canyons, rock pools, shelters and the stunning endpoint at **Pinnacle Lookout**, with its timeless vistas over the park. The walk starts from town (9.6km return) or from the Wonderland car park (5.5km return).

A 15-minute drive further west brings you to the **Balconies Lookout**, one of the Grampians' most iconic spots; it's a 2km return walk from the Reed Lookout car park.

Otherwise, several other walks, lasting anywhere from 30 minutes to a full day, leave from Halls Gap. They will lead you to surrounding waterfalls and peaks – including to the top of **Mt Rosea** (8.6km return) for some of the best views in the park. For longer walks, let someone – preferably Parks Victoria rangers – know where you're going.

ROCK ART

Traditional Aboriginal owners – namely the Jardwadjali and Djab Wurrung – have been occupying Gariwerd for more than 20,000 years and this is the most accessible place in Victoria to see Indigenous rock art. These paintings, in rock overhangs (protected by cage fences), mostly consist of handprints, animal tracks and stick figures. They indicate the esteem in which these mountains are held by local Aboriginal communities and should be treated with respect. The paintings are spread across the Gariwerd region, and you'll need a car to access them; better yet, join a guided tour with the Brambuk Cultural Centre (p585).

Sites include **Bunjil Shelter**, one of southeastern Australia's most sacred Aboriginal sites. It's the only known rock art to depict Bunjil – the Kulin people's spiritual creator and protector of the natural world – and is painted here in clay ochre accompanied by two dingoes. It's 33km east of Halls Gap in the Black Range Scenic Reserve, 10km south of Stawell.

In the west of the park is the **Manja Shelter** ('manja' means 'hands of young people'), with wonderful hand stencils, a 2.6km return walk from the Harrop Track car park. The **Billimina Shelter**, a 1.1km walk from Buandik Campground, is where the Jardwadjali resided and features human figures and patterned swirls. In the far north of the Grampians is the **Ngamadjidj Shelter**, a short walk from Stapylton Campground; 'ngamadjidj' translates to 'white people', and the art here depicts what are assumed to be Europeans who came into contact with the Jardwadjali in the 1830s. A further 7km north is the **Gulgurn Manja Shelter**, with more children's handprints and emu tracks.

Grampians Tourist Rd to Halls Gap gives you a glorious passage into the park, with cliffs and sky opening up as you pass between the Serra and Mt William Ranges. Fit hikers can walk to the summit of Mt Abrupt and Mt Sturgeon for panoramic views of the ranges. Both walks leave from signposted car parks off the Grampians Tourist Rd.

The Djab Wurrung and Gunditjmara are the traditional custodians of this region, and it was a meeting point for these two warring clans.

🛏 Sleeping & Eating

Wannon Crossing Campground　　　　　CAMPGROUND
(www.parkweb.vic.gov.au; Mafeking) FREE An option for budget travellers, this free campground in the southern part of the Grampians is located 30km north of Dunkeld, off Grampians Rd. It's a scenic site running next to the Wannon River, but it can be noisy with passing traffic. There are fireplaces and non-flushing toilets; BYO firewood and drinking water.

★**Bunyip Hotel**　　　　　GASTROPUB $$
(☑03-5574 2205; www.bunyiphotelcavendish.com; 17-25 Scott St, Cavendish; shared plates $7.50-16.50, mains $27.50-33.50; ⊘restaurant 5.30-10pm Wed & Thu, noon-2pm & 5.30-10pm Fri & Sat, noon-2pm Sun, pub noon-late Wed-Sat, to 6pm Sun) After a

successful stint as head chef at the lauded Movida Sydney, local-boy-made-good James Campbell has returned to his home town of Cavendish to open his own place. Setting up inside the old Bunyip pub (c 1842), with its appealing art-deco facade, he pays tribute to home-style Aussie cooking with tasty versions of egg and chips, saltbush lamb shoulder and golden-syrup dumplings.

★**Royal Mail Hotel**　　　　　GASTRONOMY $$$
(☑03-5577 2241; www.royalmail.com.au; 98 Parker St, Dunkeld; bistro mains $24-40, restaurant 5/8 courses $170/195; ⊘bar & bistro noon-3pm & 6-9pm, restaurant 6-10pm Wed-Fri, noon-2.30pm & 6-10pm Sat) Dunkeld's main attraction is the **Wickens at the Royal Mail**, awarded two coveted *Good Food Guide* chef's hats and long regarded as one of Victoria's finest restaurants. The kitchen is overseen by Robin Wickens, who's behind its daily-changing menu of local, seasonal produce. Also here is the **Parker St Project bistro**, a more affordable option that doesn't skimp on quality.

ℹ Information

Dunkeld Visitor Centre (☑03-5577 2558, 1800 807 056; www.visitgreaterhamilton. com.au; 55 Parker St, Dunkeld; 9am-5pm) Has useful information about this small town south of the Grampians.

❶ Getting There & Away

Dunkeld is 64km south of Halls Gap, so if you're coming specifically to eat at the Royal Mail (p587) you can theoretically make it as a day trip. The town is 269km (three hours) from Melbourne. If you're coming from the Great Ocean Road you can head through Warrnambool, from where it's 100km to Dunkeld.

There are three weekly buses to Dunkeld from Warrnambool ($20.40, two hours), departing Tuesday, Friday and Sunday; these continue to Halls Gap.

NORTHWEST OF THE GRAMPIANS

Mt Arapiles State Park

Mt Arapiles is Australia's premier rock-climbing destination. Topping out at 369m, it's not an especially big mountain, but with more than 2000 routes to scale, it attracts climbers from around the world. Popular climbs include the Bard Buttress, Tiger Wall and the Pharos. In the tiny nearby farming town of Natimuk, a community of avid climbers has set up to equip visitors, and the town has also developed into something of a centre for artists.

🏃 Activities

Natimuk Climbing Company CLIMBING
(☑ 03-5387 1329, 0400 871 328; www.climbco. com.au; 6 Jory St, Natimuk) For over 30 years this outfit has run climbing, bouldering and abseiling instruction.

🛏 Sleeping & Eating

National Hotel HOTEL $
(☑ 03-5387 1300; www.natimukhotel.com.au; 65 Main St, Natimuk; 2/3-person units $85/100, s/d/tr with shared bathroom $35/55/70; ⊙ 11am-late Tue-Sat, 3pm-late Sun & Mon; ❈ 🛜) Nati's pub has tidy motel-style self-contained units with air-con or classic pub rooms upstairs with shared bathrooms – but minus air-con, so it gets hot in summer. Discounts are available for stays over a week. It's a good spot for a counter meal and a beer too (meals from $14).

Centenary Park Campground CAMPGROUND $
(☑ 13 19 63; www.parkweb.vic.gov.au; Centenary Park Rd, Mt Arapiles; sites per person $5.30) Most climbers head for this popular campground

at the base of the mountain, with three separate sites – the Lower Gums, Pines and Upper Gums areas. There are toilets, communal fireplaces and picnic tables, but you'll need to bring your own drinking water and firewood.

Natimuk Cafe CAFE $
(☑ 03-5387 1316; 2 Jory St, Natimuk; dishes $10-17; ⊙ 8.30am-10pm Fri, to 4.30pm Sat, to 1pm Mon) This lovely, rustic little cafe has a menu of locally sourced, homemade goods, including big breakfasts, Turkish pizzas and daily specials. Great coffee too. It's a top hangout for climbers, with lots of rock-climbing magazines and books. It also has a modern self-contained apartment ($110 per night).

It often closes over January; check the Facebook page for updates.

❶ Getting There & Away

Mt Arapiles is 37km west of Horsham and 12km west of Natimuk.

Wimmera Roadways (☑ coach pick-up 0428 861 160, office 03-5381 1548; www.wimmeraroadways.com.au) runs a bus service from Horsham to Mt Arapiles ($7, 30 minutes) from Monday to Friday, passing through Natimuk ($5.20). It leaves Natimuk at 9.30am and Horsham at 2.20pm.

GIPPSLAND & WILSONS PROMONTORY

The Great Ocean Road may get the crowds, but Gippsland hides all the secrets. Gippsland is one region where it pays to avoid the cities – the towns along the Princes Hwy are barely worth a traveller's glance. But beyond the highway are some of the state's most absorbing, unspoiled and beautiful wilderness areas and beaches.

Along the coast there's Wilsons Promontory National Park, a fabulous destination for hikers and sightseers alike. This is only the start when it comes to stirring beaches. Epic Ninety Mile Beach yields to Cape Conran Coastal Park and Croajingolong National Park. Put them together and it's one of the wildest, most beautiful coastlines on Earth.

Inland, the Buchan Caves are a mustsee attraction, while the national parks at Snowy River and Errinundra are as deeply forested, remote and pristine as any in the country.

SILO ART TRAIL

The 200km **Silo Art Trail** (www.siloarttrail.com) runs through the remote Wimmera–Mallee region, leading to a series of giant murals on disused grain silos that depict local identities. There are six silos in total, scattered among the tiny farming towns of **Rupanyup**, **Sheep Hills**, **Brim**, **Rosebery**, **Lascelles** and **Patchewollock**. Despite its out-of-the-way location, the trail is fast gaining recognition as one of the region's most popular road trips, all while breathing life into isolated towns that previously received few visitors.

With an early start, it's feasible to cover the entire route in a day from Halls Gap. Otherwise, Grampians Wine Tours (☑ 0487 401 699; www.grampianswinetours.com.au; per person from $79) offers trips or you can visit by helicopter (☑ 0438 981 438; www.grampianshelicopters.com.au; Stawell Airport, Aerodrome Rd, Stawell; flights from $60).

Fish Creek

POP 199

Travellers in the know have been stopping for a bite to eat at Fish Creek on their way to the coast or Wilsons Promontory for years. These days it has developed into a little bohemian community, with craft shops, galleries, studios, bookshops and some great cafes. The Great Southern Rail Trail passes through too.

⊙ Sights

★ **Gurneys Cider**   CIDER HOUSE
(☑ 0423 039 863; www.gurneyscider.com.au; 343 Fish Creek-Foster Rd; tastings $10-14; ⊙ 11am-5pm Wed-Sun, daily summer, Fri-Sun winter) Run by a family of expat Brits, Gurneys is an impressive, hands-on team of cider-makers who are passionate about producing real dry English ciders. Everything is made on-site using 30 types of apples that grow in its orchards. Tasting paddles are available, or you can buy cider by the bottle to enjoy the pastoral views with a produce platter.

Celia Rosser Gallery   GALLERY
(☑ 0455 777 334; www.celiarossergallery.com.au; Promontory Rd; ⊙ 10am-4pm Fri-Sun) FREE A bright art space, this gallery features the works of renowned botanical artist Celia Rosser, who's most famous for her banksia watercolours. The *Banksia rosserae* was named after her; Queen Victoria is the only other woman to have a banksia named in her honour.

🛏 Sleeping & Eating

Fish Creek Hotel   PUB $
(☑ 03-5683 2404; www.fishcreekhotel.com.au; 1 Old Waratah Rd; d with shared bathroom $85-95, with private bathroom $110-130; ⊙ noon-2pm & 6-9pm) The striking art deco Fish Creek Hotel, universally known as the Fishy Pub, is an essential stop for a beer or **bistro meal** (mains $23-34; ⊙ kitchen 11.45am-2.30pm & 5.30-8.30pm) and serves as a handy base for trips into Wilsons Prom. There's a choice of comfortable pub rooms (upstairs; no TV or kettle) with shared bathrooms, and self-contained motel accommodation at the back.

🛈 Getting There & Away

Follow the signs off the South Gippsland Hwy at Foster (13km away) or Meeniyan (28km). Fish Creek is 24km (20 minutes) from the Wilsons Prom entrance gate.

There are three direct daily buses from Melbourne's Southern Cross Station ($21.80, 2¾ hours), and a few services with a transfer at Dandenong (3½ hours). Fish Creek is also along the Korumburra–Foster bus line, with at least three departures daily.

Wilsons Promontory National Park

If you like wilderness bushwalking, stunning coastal scenery and secluded white-sand beaches, you'll absolutely love the Prom – one of the most popular national parks in Australia. That's hardly surprising, given its accessibility from Melbourne, its network of more than 80km of walking tracks, its swimming and surf beaches, and its abundant wildlife. The southernmost part of mainland Australia, the Prom once formed part of a land bridge that allowed people to walk to Tasmania.

Tidal River, 30km from the park entrance, is the hub, home to the Parks Victoria office, a general store, a cafe and accommodation,

Gippsland

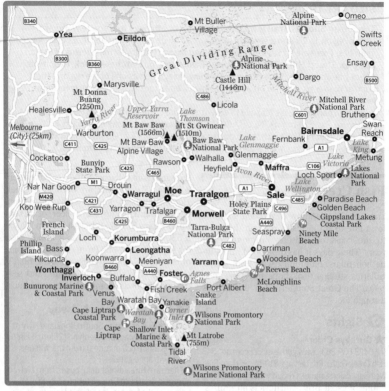

but there's no fuel here. The wildlife around Tidal River is incredibly tame, but to prevent disease, don't feed the animals or birds.

The Brataualung clan from the Gunai and Kurnai nation are the traditional custodians of this land.

⊙ Sights

Norman Beach
BEACH

(Tidal River) The Prom's most popular beach is this beautiful stretch of golden sand, conveniently located at Tidal River campground. It's patrolled by surf life savers in January; at other times, don't swim beyond waist depth as there are rips.

Wilsons Promontory Lighthouse
LIGHTHOUSE

Close to being on the southernmost tip of mainland Australia, this 19m granite lighthouse dates back to 1859. It's only accessible on foot, via a 19.2km (one-way) walk from Telegraph Saddle car park, so most visitors

stay overnight at the lighthouse keepers' cottages (p592), or **Roaring Meg campground**, 5.2km away. Tours are available daily; contact the park office to make arrangements.

⌖ Tours

Wildlife Coast Cruises
CRUISE

(☏1300 763 739; www.wildlifecoastcruises.com.au; adult/child Prom $250/195, whale watching $168/120; ☺cruises Prom 9.30am Nov-Apr, whale watching 10am Tue, Thu, Sat & Sun Sep-Nov) For a different perspective on the Prom, get out on the water for a cruise to the lighthouse and Skull Island, with a stopover at lovely Refuge Cove for a swim. Visits also take in seal colonies, and there's a good chance you'll spot dolphins. Cruises depart from Welshpool.

First Track Adventures
ADVENTURE

(☏0427 342 761; www.firsttrack.com.au; ☺closed winter) This Yarragon-based company organises customised bushwalking, canoeing, abseiling, stand-up paddleboard and surf

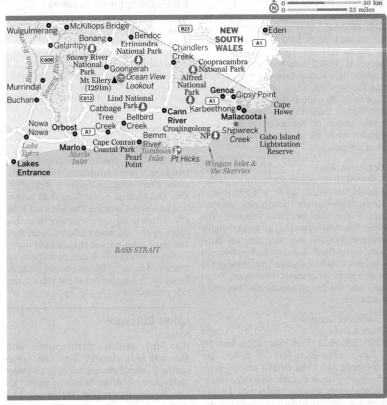

trips to the Prom for individuals and groups. Prices vary according to group size and activity.

🛌 Sleeping & Eating

The main accommodation base is Tidal River, comprising campsites and cabins. There are bush sites in the southern and northern sections of the park. Book online or through the visitor centre (p588) at Tidal River.

Surrounding towns have B&Bs and motels that you can use as a base for visiting the park on a day trip.

Park Campsites – Tidal River
CAMPGROUND **$**

(📞 13 19 63, 03-8427 2122; www.parkweb.vic.gov.au; Tidal River; unpowered/powered sites from $59/66) Campsites are sprawled across the Tidal River precinct and along the foreshore close to the beach. A maximum of eight campers are allowed at each site. There's access to hot showers, flush toilets, a dish-washing area, rubbish-disposal points and gas barbecues. No campfires permitted.

Park Huts – Tidal River
HUT **$**

(📞 03-8427 2122, 13 19 63; www.parkstay.vic.gov.au; Tidal River; 4-/6-bed huts from $106/161) If you're travelling tent free, these cosy wooden huts are a decent option, with bunks, mini-bar, kitchenette and cooking utensils. Bathrooms are shared. Bring your own linen, pillows and towels.

Top of the Prom at Promview Farm
COTTAGE **$**

(📞 0407 804 055, 03-5687 1232; 4295 Meeniyan-Promontory Rd, Yanakie; d $140-165, extra person $20; 🕐) Only 200m from the park entrance, this two-bedroom dairy cottage is the closest private accommodation to the Prom. It has a kitchen, wi-fi, a DVD player and views over the paddocks; BYO linen and towels.

★ **Wilsons Promontory Lightstation** COTTAGE $$$

(📞 03-5680 9555, 13 19 63; www.parkweb.vic.gov.au; double cottages $370-411, 12-bed cottages per person $134-148) These isolated, heritage-listed 1850s cottages, attached to a working light station on a small dot of land that juts into the ocean, are a real getaway. Kick back after the 19km hike (around six hours) from Tidal River and watch ships or whales passing by. Banks Cottage is ideal for couples, while the other cottage has bunks ideal for groups.

★ **Limosa Rise** COTTAGE $$$

(📞 03-5687 1135; www.limosarise.com.au; 40 Dalgleish Rd, Yanakie; s $335-470; ✳️ 🛜) The views are stupendous from these luxury self-contained digs near the Prom entrance. The three tastefully appointed cottages (studio, one bedroom and two bedroom) are fitted with wood-fired heaters, and full-length windows to take complete advantage of the sweeping views across Corner Inlet, farmland and the Prom's mountains. Two-night minimum.

Tidal River General Store & Cafe CAFE $

(📞 03-5680 8520; Tidal River; dishes from $6; ⊗ 9am-5pm Mon-Fri, to 6pm Sat, to 4pm Sun, longer hours Jan) Tidal River's general store has grocery items and ice, and some camping equipment and gas bottles, but if you're hiking or staying a while it's cheaper to stock up in Foster. The cafe serves takeaway food such as pies, burgers, fish and chips and sandwiches, as well as all-day breakfasts, and meats and bread for a barbecue. No alcohol sold here.

ℹ Information

Prom Country Visitor Information Centre (📞 03-5682 2469; www.visitpromcountry.com.au; cnr McDonald & Main St, Foster; ⊗ 9am-5pm) Helpful info for those heading into the Prom, as well as ideas for the surrounding region.

Tidal River Visitors Centre (📞 13 19 63, 03-8427 2122, 03-5680 9555; www.parkweb.vic.gov.au; ⊗ 8.30am-4.30pm, to 4pm winter) Handles all park accommodation (including permits for camping away from Tidal River) and offers info on the area's hiking options. It also has lockers for campers to charge devices, and a range of equipment, including all-terrain and beach wheelchairs, for travellers with limited mobility.

Park Entrance Booth (⊗ 9am-sunset)

ℹ Getting There & Away

Tidal River is approximately 224km southeast of Melbourne. There's no fuel here; the closest petrol station is at Yanakie.

There's no direct public transport between Melbourne and the Prom. The closest towns accessible by direct V/Line bus are Fish Creek ($21.80, 2¾ hours) and Foster ($24.60, two hours and 50 minutes, three daily). From there you'll need to find a lift by other means.

Lakes District

The Gippsland Lakes form the largest inland waterway system in Australia, with the three main interconnecting lakes – Wellington, King and Victoria – stretching from Sale to beyond Lakes Entrance. The lakes are actually saltwater lagoons, separated from the ocean by the Gippsland Lakes Coastal Park and the narrow coastal strip of sand dunes known as Ninety Mile Beach. Apart from the beach and taking to the water, the highlights here involve hanging out at the relaxed seaside communities.

Lakes Entrance

POP 6071

With the shallow Cunninghame Arm waterway separating the town from ocean beaches, Lakes Entrance basks in an undeniably pretty location. In holiday season it's a packed-out tourist town with a graceless strip of motels, caravan parks, mini-golf courses and souvenir shops lining the Esplanade. Still, the bobbing fishing boats, fresh seafood, endless beaches, and cruises out to Metung and Wyanga Park Winery should win you over.

The Tatungalung and Krauatungalung clans from the Gunai and Kurnai nation are the traditional custodians of this land. The Aboriginal community that lives both here and at nearby Lake Tyers is the second largest in the state behind that of Shepparton.

◉ Sights & Activities

Wyanga Park Winery WINERY

(📞 03-5155 1508; 248 Baades Rd; ⊗ 9am-5pm) Pop by for a tasting at this quirky, art-filled, family-owned winery, the oldest in Gippsland. It's most known for its chardonnay, but it's all good and available for free sampling. There's a restaurant (meals $12 to $34) with a cosy fireplace in winter, and a deck for enjoying a platter when the sun's shining.

Wilsons Promontory National Park

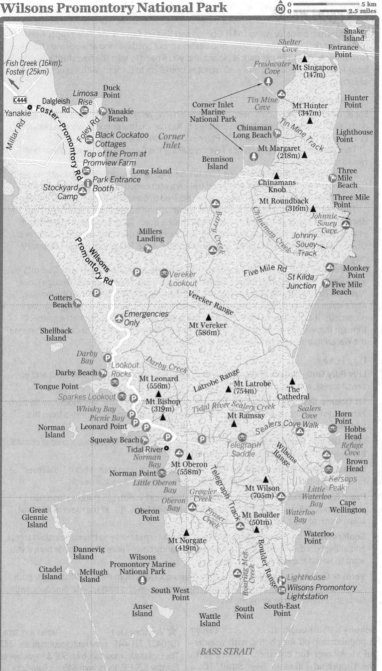

TOP PROM WALKS

The departure point for walks to Mt Oberon and Sealers Cove is the **Telegraph Saddle car park.** During the summer and Easter school holidays, and at weekends from November to April, the car park is closed and you'll need to take the free shuttle bus from Tidal River, departing every 30 minutes from 9am to 5.45pm, with a break for lunch at 1pm.

Overnight Walks

For all overnight walks you'll need to arrange a hiking permit ($13 per person per night) and pay for camp bookings before setting off. You can do this online at www.parks.vic. gov.au/stay or in person at the Tidal River information centre.

The most popular long-distance hikes are along the **Southern Circuit**; these last two to seven days.

Overnight walks in the **Northern Circuit** are through remote wilderness with no set trails. They're suitable only for seasoned trekkers with honed navigational skills. Before setting off on the Northern Circuit you'll be required to complete a hiker self-assessment.

The best overnight hike, the **Southern Prom Hike (Southern Circuit)** is a two-day walk that starts at Telegraph Saddle and heads down Telegraph Track to overnight at beautiful **Little Waterloo Bay** (12km, 4½ hours). The next day, walk on to **Sealers Cove** via the lovely beach at **Refuge Cove** and return to Telegraph Saddle (20km, 7½ hours).

The most popular long-distance hike, the **Lighthouse Walk (Southern Circuit)** is a moderate 51km circuit across to Sealers Cove from Tidal River, down to Refuge Cove, Waterloo Bay and the lighthouse (p590), and then back to Tidal River via Oberon Bay. Allow three days and coordinate your walk with tide times, as creek crossings can be hazardous. It's possible to visit or stay at the lighthouse (p592) by prior arrangement through the website or the park office. If you want do a longer hike, you can head here via the Waterloo trek, which makes a five-day hike in total.

Day Hikes

Lilly Pilly Gully Nature Walk An easy 5km (two-hour) walk through heathland and eucalypt forest, with lots of wildlife.

Mt Oberon Summit Starting from the Telegraph Saddle car park, this moderate-to-hard 7km-return walk is an ideal introduction to the Prom, with panoramic views from the summit.

Little Oberon Bay A moderate 19km (six-hour) walk over sand dunes covered in coastal tea trees, with beautiful views over Little Oberon Bay.

Squeaky Beach Nature Walk An easy 5km return stroll (two hours) from Tidal River through coastal tea trees and banksias to a sensational white-sand beach.

Prom Wildlife Walk In the north of the park, this short 2.3km (45-minute) loop trail yields good potential kangaroo, wallaby and emu sightings. It's off the main road about 14km south of the park entrance.

Sealers Cove This popular 19km hike (six hours return) takes you through pristine forest and along boardwalks that lead to a gorgeous sandy cove. There's a campsite here if you want to spend the night.

Vereker Outlook In the north of the park, this walk leads from the Five Mile Rd car park (6km return, 2½ hours) through varied bush landscapes and past granite boulders, with fantastic coastal views along the way.

Jemmy's Point Lookout   VIEWPOINT

A popular stop-off for photos, with wonderful views over the entrance – which links the Gippsland Lakes to Bass Strait. It's a 20-minute walk up here from town.

⭐ **Venture Out**   ADVENTURE SPORTS

(☑ 0427 731 441; www.ventureout.com.au; 347b The Esplanade; mountain-bike, SUP & kayak hire per 2hr/day $29/59, tours from $49; ☺ 9am-5pm Tue-Sat Feb-Apr & Sep-Nov, daily Dec & Jan, 10am-4pm

Tue-Sat May-Aug) This is a definitive stop for anyone looking to get active in Lakes Entrance. Owner Sarah offers excellent mountain-bike tours and sunset SUP and kayak trips, including one that paddles to a local winery ($69 including lunch). Mountain bikes and e-bikes are available for rent, perfect for tackling the Gippsland Lakes Discovery Trail (www.railtrails.org.au).

Peels Lake Cruises CRUISE
(☑0409 946 292, 03-5155 1246; www.peelscruises.com.au; Post Office Jetty; 4hr Metung lunch cruises adult/child $59/16, 1¼hr cruises adult/child $33/16.50) This long-running operator has been going since the 1920s, across four generations. It offers daily lunch cruises aboard the *Stormbird* to Metung and 1¼-hour cruises on the *Thunderbird* through the entrance and to Metung, often passing dolphins.

🛏 Sleeping

Kalimna Woods COTTAGE $
(☑03-5155 1957; www.kalimnawoods.com.au; Kalimna Jetty Rd; d $144-169; ❄🐾) Retreat 2km from town to Kalimna Woods, set on a large bush-garden property complete with friendly resident sugar gliders and parrots. The self-contained country-style cottages (some with spas) are spacious, private and cosy, and come with barbecues and wood-burning fireplaces.

**Eastern Beach
Tourist Park** CARAVAN PARK $
(☑03-5155 1581, 1800 761 762; www.easternbeach.com.au; 42 Eastern Beach Rd; unpowered sites $28-52, powered sites $32-73, cabins $122-318; @🐾🏊🐕) Most caravan parks in Lakes pack 'em in, but this one has space, grassy sites and a great location away from the hubbub in a bush setting close to the beach. A walking track takes you into town (30 minutes). New facilities are excellent, including a camp kitchen, barbecues and a playground. It sells beer at reception too.

Bellevue on the Lakes HOTEL $$
(☑03-5155 3055; www.bellevuelakes.com; 201 The Esplanade; d from $179, 2-bedroom apt from $249; ❄🐾🏊) Right in the heart of the Esplanade, Bellevue is Lakes Entrance's plushest option, with neatly furnished earth-toned rooms, most with water views. For extra luxury, go for the spacious spa suites or two-bedroom self-contained apartments. The foyer **bar** (☑03-5155 1209; www.facebook.com/albertand

cocatering; dishes $12-34; ⊙7am-3pm & 6pm-late) is another reason to stay here.

🍴 Eating & Drinking

Miriam's Restaurant STEAK, SEAFOOD $$
(☑03-5155 3999; www.miriamsrestaurant.com.au; cnr The Esplanade & Bulmer St; small plates $8.50-17.50, large plates $20-38; ⊙noon-late) The upstairs dining room at Miriam's overlooks the waterfront, and the Gippsland steaks, local-seafood dishes and casual cocktail-bar atmosphere are excellent. Try the epic 'Greek fisherman's plate': 1kg of local seafood for $75. There's a good choice of local wines and craft beers too. Happy-hour oysters ($2 each) are available from 4pm to 5pm.

Ferryman's Seafood Cafe SEAFOOD $$
(☑03-5155 3000; www.ferrymans.com.au; Middle Harbour, The Esplanade; mains $20-33; ⊙noon-3pm & 6pm-late Thu-Mon) It's hard to beat the ambience of dining on the deck of this floating cafe-restaurant (an old Paynesville–Raymond Island passenger ferry), which will fill you to the gills with fish and seafood dishes. The seafood pie, fish and chips, and seafood platter ($77) are popular orders.

★Waterwheel Beach Tavern PUB
(☑03-5156 5855; www.thewaterwheel.com.au; 577 Lake Tyers Beach Rd, Lake Tyers Beach; ⊙10am-late; 🐾) Head to the adjoining township of Lake Tyers, 9km east of Lakes Entrance, for this wonderfully relaxed coastal pub looking out to Ninety Mile Beach. There are Lakes Entrance craft beers on tap and local fish and chips to wolf down on its waterfront terrace. Call ahead for the courtesy bus from Lakes.

ℹ Information

Lakes Entrance Visitor Centre (☑03-5155 1966, 1800 637 060; www.discovereast gippsland.com.au; cnr Princes Hwy & Marine Pde; ⊙9am-5pm, 10am-4pm winter; 🐾) Free accommodation- and tour-booking services. Also check out www.lakesentrance.com.

ℹ Getting There & Away

Lakes Entrance is 314km from Melbourne along the Princes Hwy.

V/Line (☑1800 800 007; www.vline.com.au) runs a train-bus service from Melbourne to Lakes Entrance ($42.60, from 4½ hours, three to four daily) via Bairnsdale.

BATALUK CULTURAL TRAIL

The Gunai and Kurnai people have lived in the East Gippsland region for 30,000 years; Borun the pelican and Tuk the musk duck are their Dreaming ancestor creators. The **Bataluk Cultural Trail** (www.batalukculturaltrail.com.au) follows the traditional routes taken by the Gunai and Kurnai, who consist of five clans: the Brataualung, Brayakaulung, Brabralung, Tatungalung and Krauatun-galung. The trail takes in sacred natural landmarks, 10,000-year-old shell middens and scarred trees whose bark was used to make dugout canoes. Evocative stories detail the sites' significance and history.

East Gippsland & the Wilderness Coast

Beyond Lakes Entrance stretches a wilderness area of spectacular coastal national parks and old-growth forest. Much of this region has never been cleared for agriculture, and it contains some of the most remote and pristine national parks in the state, making logging in these ancient forests a contentious issue.

Buchan

POP 236

The sleepy town of Buchan, in the foothills of the Snowy Mountains, is famous for the spectacular and intricate limestone cave system at the Buchan Caves Reserve, open to visitors for almost a century. Underground rivers cutting through ancient limestone rock formed the caves and caverns, and they provided shelter for Aboriginal people as far back as 18,000 years ago.

The Krauatungalung clan from the Gunai and Kurnai nation are the traditional owners of this land; the Buchan Caves are featured on the Bataluk Cultural Trail.

◎ Sights

★ **Buchan Caves**   CAVE
(☑13 19 63; www.parks.vic.gov.au; Caves Rd; tours adult/child/family $22.80/13/63.10, 2 caves $34.20/19.80/94.20; ☉tours 10am, 11.15am, 1pm, 2.15pm & 3.30pm, hours vary seasonally) Since they were unveiled to Melburnians as a blockbuster sight in the early 1900s the Buchan Caves have been dazzling visitors with their fantasy world of glistening calcite formations. Parks Victoria runs guided cave tours daily, alternating between **Royal** and **Fairy Caves**. They're both super-impressive: Royal has more colour, a higher chamber and dripping candle-like formations; Fairy has more delicate decorations and potential fairy sightings.

🛏 Sleeping & Eating

Buchan Lodge   HOSTEL $
(Buchan Backpackers; ☑03-5155 9421; www.buchanlodge.com.au; 9 Saleyard Rd; dm $25; ☎) While the backpacker tour buses don't come through town any more, this old-school hostel remains as an excellent budget option, with dorms and a massive open-plan kitchen and lounge space. It's been run by the same owner, Dick, for over 25 years, so he's a great source of local info.

Buchan Caves Motel   LODGE $
(☑03-5155 9419; www.buchanmotel.com.au; 67 Main Rd; d/tr/q $140/160/180; ❄☎) Enjoy views of the bucolic countryside from your balcony at this comfortable hilltop lodge. Its modern rooms feature boutique touches.

Buchan Caves Hotel   PUB
(☑03-5155 9203; www.facebook.com/buchancaveshotel; 49 Main Rd; ☉11am-late) Risen from the ashes, the 125-year-old Buchan pub reopened in December 2016 after burning to the ground in 2014. Its rebirth came about via the world's first crowd-funding campaign to build a pub, with contributions from around the globe. Celebrate its return by stopping in for a chicken parma and a cold frothy (mains $22 to $26).

❶ Getting There & Away

Buchan is an easy 56km drive north of Lakes Entrance. **Dyson's** (☑03-5152 1711) runs a bus service from Bairnsdale to Buchan on Wednesday and Friday at 2.50pm ($3.40, two hours). The bus meets the train at Bairnsdale. At other times you'll need your own transport.

Snowy River National Park

Northeast of Buchan, this is one of Victoria's most isolated and spectacular national parks, dominated by deep gorges carved through limestone and sandstone by the Snowy River on its route from the Snowy Mountains in New South Wales to its mouth

MELBOURNE & VICTORIA EAST GIPPSLAND & THE WILDERNESS COAST

NINETY MILE BEACH

To paraphrase the immortal words of Crocodile Dundee...that's not a beach, *this* is a beach. Isolated Ninety Mile Beach is a narrow strip of dune-backed sand punctuated by lagoons and stretching unbroken for more or less 90 miles (150km) from near McLoughlins Beach to the channel at Lakes Entrance. The area is great for surf fishing, camping and *long* beach walks, though the crashing surf can be dangerous for swimming, except where patrolled at Seaspray, Woodside Beach and Lakes Entrance.

The main access road to Ninety Mile Beach is the South Gippsland Hwy from Sale or Foster, turning off to Seaspray, Golden Beach and Loch Sport. Other than to Lakes Entrance, there's no public transport out this way.

at Marlo. The park is a smorgasbord of unspoilt, superb bush and mountain scenery. It covers more than 950 sq km and includes a huge diversity of vegetation, ranging from alpine woodland to eucalypt forest to rainforest.

The Gunai and Kurnai people are the traditional custodians of this land, and as of 2018 co-manage the national park in conjunction with Parks Victoria (www.parkweb.vic.gov.au). The Bidawal and Nindi-Ngudjam Ngarigu Monero people are also from the area.

🛏 Sleeping

McKillops Bridge   CAMPGROUND
(📞13 19 63, 02-8427 2024; www.parkweb.vic.gov.au; sites free) **FREE** The most popular of the park's free campgrounds, this beautiful spot lies along the Snowy River. Sites have fireplaces and non-flushing toilets. It's a popular launching place for canoeists, and a range of hikes start here.

Karoonda Park   FARMSTAY $
(📞03-5155 0220; www.karoondapark.com; 3558 Gelantipy Rd; dm/r $40/135; ❄@🛜🏊) Just south of Gelantipy, 40km north of Buchan on the road to Snowy River National Park, is this 1800-acre cattle-and-sheep property with comfortable backpacker and cabin digs. Meals are available with notice, and there's a kitchen for self-caterers. There's also an indoor climbing wall, a swimming pool and a heap of wildlife.

ℹ Getting There & Away

The two main access roads to the park are the Buchan–Jindabyne Rd from Buchan, and Bonang Rd north from Orbost. These roads are joined by McKillops Rd (also known as Deddick Valley Rd), which runs across the northern border of the park. Various minor access roads and scenic routes run into and alongside the park

from these three main roads. The 43km Deddick Trail, which runs through the middle of the park, is only suitable for 4WDs.

Dyson's (📞03-5152 1711) operates a bus service from Bairnsdale to Gelantipy (via Buchan) on Wednesday and Friday (2.50pm, $3.40, 2¾ hours), which can drop you at Karoonda Park.

Errinundra National Park

Errinundra National Park contains Victoria's largest cool-temperate rainforest and is one of East Gippsland's most outstanding natural areas. The forests surrounding the park are a constant battleground for loggers and environmentalists. The park was gazetted in the 1980s largely due to the efforts of environmental campaigners.

Covering 256 sq km, the park has three granite outcrops that extend into the cloud, resulting in high rainfall, deep, fertile soils, and a network of creeks and rivers that flow north, south and east. Errinundra has several climatic zones – some areas are quite dry, while the peaks regularly receive snow. This is a rich habitat for native birds and animals, which include many rare and endangered species such as the potoroo. Lyrebirds are common too.

The traditional custodians of the region are the Bidawal, Krauatungalung and Nindi-Ngudjam Ngarigu Monero people.

🛏 Sleeping

Goongerah Camp Site   CAMPGROUND
(sites free) **FREE** The most accessible of the park's free campgrounds is in Goongerah, an hour's drive north of Orbost. It's within a state forest at the edge of the park, set along the Brodribb River, from which you're able to drink. There are drop toilets but no other facilities.

WORTH A TRIP

RAYMOND ISLAND

Home to a colony of around 250 koalas, Raymond Island offers pretty much guaranteed sightings of the cute, cuddly marsupials in the wild. Directly across from Paynesville, the island (population 548) is easily accessed by a five-minute ferry ride, from where there's a signed 1.2km **Koala Trail** (20 minutes) leading you through the residential streets and a tract of forest; look up in the trees to spot koalas snoozing or munching eucalyptus leaves. Echidnas are also regularly seen.

There's also a waterfront boardwalk that's wonderful for a scenic stroll.

Most of the koalas were relocated here from Phillip Island in the 1950s. Sadly, in recent years the koalas have faced starvation due to dry conditions, clearing of forest for bushfire protection and an increase in the human population.

The flat-bottom car-and-passenger ferry operates every 20 minutes from 6.40am to midnight. It's free for pedestrians and cyclists; cars cost $13 and motorcycles $6.

★ Tin Chalet
COTTAGE $

(☑03-5154 0145; Goongerah; house $110) 🍽 A genuine off-the-grid getaway, this solar-powered double-storey cottage is constructed from corrugated iron. Its charming interior features a wood-fired stove, reclaimed timber and plenty of quirky, old-fashioned character. By the river and surrounded by forest, it occupies an organic farm and orchard run by Jill Redwood, the inspiring environmentalist who set up **Environment East Gippsland**. There's a two-night minimum stay.

ℹ Information

Environment East Gippsland (☑03-5154 0145; www.eastgippsland.net.au) 🍽 Local community group lobbying extensively on forest issues. There's detailed information about park drives and walks on its website.

Goongerah Environment Centre (GECO; ☑03-5154 0174, 0414 199 645; www.geco.org. au; 7203 Bonang Rd) Visit the website of this grassroots environmental group to download a self-drive guided tour of the park.

ℹ Getting There & Away

Errinundra National Park lies approximately 490km east of Melbourne. The main access roads are Bonang Rd from Orbost and Errinundra Rd from Club Terrace. Bonang Rd passes along the western side of the park, while Errinundra Rd passes through its centre. Roads within the park are all unsealed but 2WD accessible. Road conditions are variable. Expect seasonal closures between June and November, though roads can deteriorate quickly at any time of year after rain and are often closed or impassable after floods (check with Parks Victoria in Orbost or Bendoc). Watch out for logging trucks and sambar deer when driving here.

Cape Conran Coastal Park

This blissfully undeveloped part of the coast is one of Gippsland's most beautiful corners, with long stretches of remote white-sand beach. The 19km coastal route from Marlo to Cape Conran is particularly pretty, bordered by banksia trees, grass plains, sand dunes and the ocean.

The region offers fantastic fishing, good surf and some lovely walks – it's one for those seeking long, lazy days spent between the campsite and the beach. There's no internet or mobile coverage out this way, so bring a good book!

The Aboriginal Gunai and Kurnai people are the traditional custodians of Cape Conran. The Krauatungalung clan lived here for tens of thousands of years, as evidenced by midden sites you can visit.

🛏 Sleeping

Cape Conran
Coastal Park Cabins
CABIN $

(☑03-5154 8438; www.parkweb.vic.gov.au; cabins $180.40-189.30) These self-contained cabins, which can sleep up to eight, are surrounded by bush and just 200m from the beach. Built from local timbers, the cabins are like oversize cubby houses, with cooking facilities and lofty mezzanines for sleeping. There's a minimum stay of two nights (seven in peak season).

Banksia Bluff
Camping Area
CAMPGROUND $

(☑03-5154 8438; www.parkweb.vic.gov.au; Marlo-Conran Rd; unpowered sites $37.80-41.30) Run by Parks Victoria, this excellent campground is right by the foreshore. Its generous sites are surrounded by banksia woodlands offering shade and privacy. It has flush toilets, cold showers and a few fireplaces, but you'll need to bring drinking water. A ballot is held to allocate sites over the Christmas period.

ℹ️ Getting There & Away

Cape Conran Coastal Park lies south of the Princes Hwy, 405km from Melbourne. The well-signposted turn-off from the highway lies just east of the small settlement of Cabbage Tree. The park is around 15km south of the turn-off along Cabbage Tree–Conran Rd. There's no public transport, so you'll need a car to get here.

Mallacoota

POP 1005

One of Gippsland's, and indeed Victoria's, little gems, Mallacoota is the state's most easterly town, snuggled on the vast Mallacoota Inlet and surrounded by the tumbling hills and beachside dunes of beautiful Croajingolong National Park. Those prepared to come this far are treated to long, empty ocean-surf beaches, tidal estuaries, and swimming, fishing and boating on the inlet.

It's a good place for wildlife too, with plentiful kangaroos, as well as koalas and echidnas.

⊙ Sights & Activities

★ **Gabo Island**   ISLAND

On Gabo Island, 14km offshore from Mallacoota, the windswept 154-hectare **Gabo Island Lightstation Reserve** is home to seabirds and one of the world's largest colonies of little penguins (you'll only see them if you stay overnight). There's also a significant fur-seal colony, and whales and dolphins are regularly sighted offshore. The snorkelling here is outstanding. The island has an operating red-granite **lighthouse** (1862) that's one of the tallest in the southern hemisphere – you can stay in the old keepers' cottages (p600).

Mallacoota Bunker Museum   MUSEUM

(☑️ 0459 437 474, Tue morning 03-5158 0725; www.mallacootabunker.com.au; Airport Rd; adult/child $5/1; ⊙ 9.30-11.30am Tue & 1-3pm Sun) Concealed in the bush just outside Mallacoota, this RAAF military bunker makes for a somewhat surreal visit. A high-security communication installation during WWII, the bunker is now a museum and details its history through various displays. Even if you're not here during the limited opening hours, it's worth coming down for a look from the outside, as there are exterior information panels.

Mallacoota Hire Boats   BOATING

(☑️ 0438 447 558; www.mallacootahireboats.com; 10 Buckland Dr; motorboats per 2/8hr $90/180, kayaks 1/2 people per 2hr $30/40; ⊙ 7.30am-6pm) Hires out kayaks, motorboats, pedal boats and fishing equipment. No boat licence required; cash only. Houseboats can also be arranged. It's based at Mallacoota Foreshore Holiday Park (p600).

MV Loch-Ard   CRUISE

(☑️ 0438 580 708; www.mallacootacruises.com; Main Wharf, 1 Buckland Dr; 2hr cruise adult/child $40/10) Several inlet cruises are available on the beautiful MV *Loch-Ard*, a 1910 passenger boat built from Tasmanian Huon pine. Trips include an interesting commentary on Mallacoota's history (as well as tea and biscuits). Sightings of white-breasted sea eagles and other birdlife are likely.

EAST GIPPSLAND RAIL TRAIL

The 96km **East Gippsland Rail Trail** (www.eastgipplandrailtrail.com.au) is a walking and cycling path that runs along the former railway line between Bairnsdale and Orbost, passing through Bruthen and Nowa Nowa, and close to several other small communities. By bike the trail can comfortably be done in two days, but allow longer to explore the countryside and perhaps detour on the Gippsland Lakes Discovery Trail (p595) to Lakes Entrance.

The East Gippsland Rail Trail takes in undulating farmland, temperate rainforest, the Colquhoun Forest mountain-bike park and some impressive timber bridges. From Nowa Nowa to Orbost the path is quite stony, so a mountain bike is the way to go.

For those without their own bike, **Snowy River Cycling** (☑️ 0428 556 088; www.snowyrivercycling.com.au; 7 Forest Rd; bike hire per 2hr/day $30/45) offers self-guided tours with map and bike ($45), plus luggage transport ($16.50); return transport is $50. It also runs guided cycle adventures.

🛌 Sleeping

★ Adobe Abodes
APARTMENT $

(📞 0499 777 968; www.adobeabodes.com.au; 17-19 Karbeethong Ave; q $110-150) 🏠 These handmade mud-brick units are something special. With an emphasis on recycling and eco-friendliness, the whimsical flats (sleeping up to four) have solar hot water, and guests are encouraged to compost their kitchen scraps. The apartments are comfortable and well equipped, and come with wonderful water views and welcome baskets of wine and chocolate. BYO linen and towels.

Mallacoota Foreshore Holiday Park
CARAVAN PARK $

(📞 03-5158 0300; cnr Allan Dr & Maurice Ave; unpowered sites $18.50-50, powered sites $26-60; 🛜) Curling around the waterfront, the grassy sites here constitute one of Victoria's largest, most sociable and scenic caravan parks, with sublime views of the inlet and its population of black swans and pelicans. There are no cabins, but this is the best of Mallacoota's many parks for campers. Reception is across the road in the same building as the visitor centre.

★ Karbeethong Lodge
GUESTHOUSE $$

(📞 03-5158 0411; www.karbeethonglodge.com.au; 16 Schnapper Point Dr; r incl breakfast $120-220; 🛜) It's hard not to be overcome by serenity as you sit on the broad verandah of this early-1900s timber guesthouse and take in uninterrupted views over Mallacoota Inlet and the expansive gardens. The large guest lounge and dining room have an open fire and period furnishings, there's a mammoth kitchen, and the pastel-toned bedrooms are small but tastefully decorated.

★ Gabo Island Lighthouse
COTTAGE $$

(📞 03-5158 0255, Parks Victoria 13 19 63; www.parkweb.vic.gov.au; cottages $350-382) This remote lighthouse offers accommodation in the historic assistant keeper's residence. The three bedrooms sleep up to eight. There's a two-night minimum stay and a ballot for use during the Christmas and Easter holidays. Note that there are no refunds if you're unable to reach the island (or get stranded there) during inclement weather.

🍴 Eating & Drinking

Croajingolong Cafe
CAFE $

(📞 03-5158 0098; Shop 3, 14 Allan Dr; mains $10-19; ⊙ 8am-4pm Tue-Sun) Overlooking the inlet, this cafe has a vintage nautical theme and a terrace with views over the water; it's the place to read the newspaper over coffee, toasted sandwiches or an all-day breakfast.

★ Lucy's
ASIAN $$

(📞 03-5158 0666; 64 Maurice Ave; mains $8-28; ⊙ 8am-8pm) Lucy's is popular for delicious and great-value homemade rice noodles with chicken, prawn or abalone, as well as dumplings stuffed with ingredients from the garden. Cash only, and order at the counter; be prepared for pandemonium when things get busy.

Mallacoota Hotel
PUB

(📞 03-5158 0455; www.mallacootahotel.com.au; 51-55 Maurice Ave; ⊙ 10am-10pm; 🛜) The local pub is a popular spot for a drink, with a cosy indoor bar and a ripper outdoor beer garden full of palm trees – wonderful on a balmy evening. Its bistro serves hearty meals (mains $18 to $33) from a varied menu, with reliable favourites the chicken parma, Gippsland steak and pale-ale fish and chips. Bands play regularly in summer.

There's motel accommodation (doubles from $110) here too.

ℹ️ Information

Mallacoota Visitor Centre (📞 03-5158 0800; www.visitmallacoota.com.au; cnr Allan Dr & Maurice Ave; ⊙ 9am-5pm; 🛜) On the main strip across from the water, this extremely helpful tourist centre has a tonne of info on the area and its walking trails, and a handy updated booklet on local sights ($1). Free 24-hour wi-fi and internet access too.

Parks Victoria (📞 03-8427 2123; www.parkweb.vic.gov.au) Contact this office for information on Gabo Island, road conditions, overnight hiking, camping permits and track notes.

ℹ️ Getting There & Away

Mallacoota is 23km southeast of Genoa (on the Princes Hwy), which is 492km from Melbourne.

Taking public transport from Melbourne to Mallacoota entails a long journey ($55.40, 8½ hours): from Southern Cross Station, take the train to Bairnsdale, then the V/Line bus to Genoa (3½ hours); the Mallacoota–Genoa bus meets the V/Line bus on Monday, Thursday and Friday, plus Sunday during school holidays, and runs to Mallacoota (30 minutes).

A number of local boats head to Gabo Island, but boat access to the island is often restricted due to bad weather; **Wilderness Coast Ocean Charters** (📞 0417 398 068), **Gabo Island Escapes** (📞 03-5158 0605, 0437 221 694; per person $130) and **Mallacoota Fishing**

Charters & Tours (☑ 0419 223 101; www.mallacootafishingcharters.com) are your best bets. If you have a boat you can head out independently, but you'll need to be experienced in these waters.

Otherwise, you can take a plane there: **Merimbula Air Services** (☑ 02-6495 1074; www.mairserv.com.au) offers tours to the island (half/full day $325/375) that depart a 1½-hour drive north of Mallacoota. From Mallacoota, a four-seater charter plane costs $750 one way.

Croajingolong National Park

Croajingolong is one of Australia's finest coastal-wilderness parks, recognised by its listing as a Unesco World Biosphere Reserve (one of nine in Australia). The park covers 875 sq km, stretching for about 100km from the town of Bemm River to the NSW border. Magnificent, unspoilt beaches, inlets, estuaries and forests make it ideal for camping, walking, swimming and surfing. The five inlets, **Sydenham**, **Tamboon**, **Mueller**, **Wingan** and **Mallacoota** (the largest and most accessible), are popular canoeing and fishing spots.

Two sections have been declared wilderness areas (which means no vehicles, access for a limited number of walkers only and permits required): the **Cape Howe Wilderness Area**, between Mallacoota Inlet and the NSW border, and the **Sandpatch Wilderness Area**, between Wingan Inlet and Shipwreck Creek.

The area is the country of the Bidwell, and Gunai and Kurnai Indigenous people, along with the Monero-Ngarigo people from across the NSW border.

◉ Sights

★ **Point Hicks Lighthouse**   LIGHTHOUSE
(☑ 13 19 63; www.parkweb.vic.gov.au; Lighthouse Track, Tamboon; ☺ tours 1pm Fri-Mon) **FREE** Climb 162 stairs that spiral to the top of this remote lighthouse (1890) for dizzying coastal views and plenty of interesting stories. Tours are free for the moment, but this is under review by Parks Victoria. Note that there's no vehicle access to the lighthouse, so it's a 2.2km walk (one way) to get here from the car park. There are lots of wombats out this way (but they're only active at night), and you'll likely see wallabies.

The road from Cann River is sealed for the first 16km, but it's *very* rough going for the remaining 30km; it's possible for smaller cars, but you'll need to take it slowly, as people have flipped their cars in the past.

▒ Sleeping

Thurra River   CAMPGROUND **$**
(☑ 13 19 63; www.parkstay.vic.gov.au; unpowered sites from $27.20) This is the largest of the park's campgrounds, with 46 well-designed sites stretching along the foreshore from the river towards the lighthouse. Most of the sites are separated by bush, and there are communal fireplaces and pit toilets. From here there are several walks, including to some impressive dunes (4km return).

Point Hicks Lighthouse   COTTAGE **$$**
(☑ 13 19 63; www.parkstay.vic.gov.au/point-hicks-lighthouse; bungalows $126-146, cottages $332-388) This remote lighthouse has two comfortable, heritage-listed cottages and one double bungalow, which originally housed the assistant lighthouse keepers. The cottages sleep eight to 12, and have sensational ocean views, fireplaces and kitchens. Bring your own food, bedding and towels, or you can hire linen from $18 per person. To get here you'll need to walk 2.2km from the car park.

ℹ Information

There's no phone or internet service in the park. **Parks Victoria** (☑ 13 19 63, 03-5158 6351; www.parkweb.vic.gov.au) Information on road conditions, overnight hiking, camping permits and track notes.

ℹ Getting There & Away

Croajingolong National Park lies 492km east of Melbourne. Access roads of varying quality lead south off the Princes Hwy and into the park from various points between Cann River and the NSW border. Among these are tracks leading to campgrounds at Wingan Inlet, Mueller Inlet, Thurra River and Shipwreck Creek.

Apart from Mallacoota Rd, all of the access roads are unsealed and can be very rough (especially after heavy rains), so check road conditions with Parks Victoria in Cann River or Mallacoota before venturing on.

VICTORIAN HIGH COUNTRY

With its enticing mix of history, adventure and culinary temptations, Victoria's High Country is a wonderful place to spend some time. The Great Dividing Range – Australia's eastern mountain spine – curls around eastern Victoria from the Snowy Mountains to the Grampians, peaking in the spectacular High Country. These are Victoria's alps – a

High Country

MELBOURNE & VICTORIA VICTORIAN HIGH COUNTRY

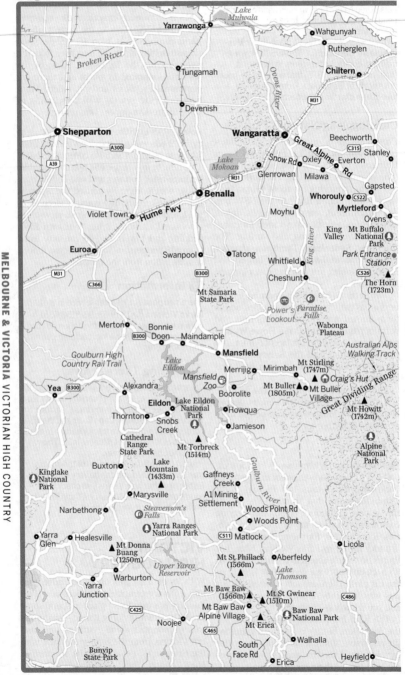

Lake Mulwala

Yarrawonga

Wahgunyah

Rutherglen

Broken River

Tungamah

Ovens River

Chiltern

M31

Devenish

Shepparton

A300

A39

Wangaratta

Great Alpine Rd

Beechworth

C315

Stanley

Snow Rd

Oxley

Everton

Lake Mokoan

Glenrowan

Milawa

Gapsted

M31

Whorouly

C522

Benalla

Moyhu

Myrtleford

Violet Town

Hume Fwy

Ovens

King Valley

Mt Buffalo National Park

Euroa

Swanpool

Tatong

Whitfield

Park Entrance Station

C526

M31

C366

Cheshunt

The Horn (1723m)

Mt Samaria State Park

B300

Power's Lookout

Paradise Falls

Wabonga Plateau

Merton

Bonnie Doon

Maindample

Australian Alps Walking Track

Goulburn High Country Rail Trail

B300

Lake Eildon

Mansfield

Mt Stirling (1747m)

Merrijig

Mirimbah

Craig's Hut

Yea

B300

Alexandra

Mansfield Zoo

Mt Buller (1805m)

Mt Buller Village

Great Dividing Range

Eildon

Boorolite

Lake Eildon National Park

Thornton

Snobs Creek

Howqua

Mt Howitt (1742m)

Cathedral Range State Park

Jamieson

Buxton

Mt Torbreck (1514m)

Alpine National Park

Kinglake National Park

Lake Mountain (1433m)

Gaffneys Creek

Goulburn River

Marysville

A1 Mining Settlement

Narbethong

Steavenson's Falls

Woods Point Rd

Yarra Ranges National Park

Woods Point

Yarra Glen

Healesville

C511

Matlock

Licola

Mt Donna Buang (1250m)

Mt St Phillack (1566m)

Aberfeldy

Upper Yarra Reservoir

Lake Thomson

Warburton

Yarra Junction

Mt Baw Baw (1566m)

Mt St Gwinear (1510m)

C486

C425

Baw Baw Alpine Village

Baw Baw National Park

Noojee

C465

Mt Erica

Bunyip State Park

South Face Rd

Walhalla

Heyfield

Erica

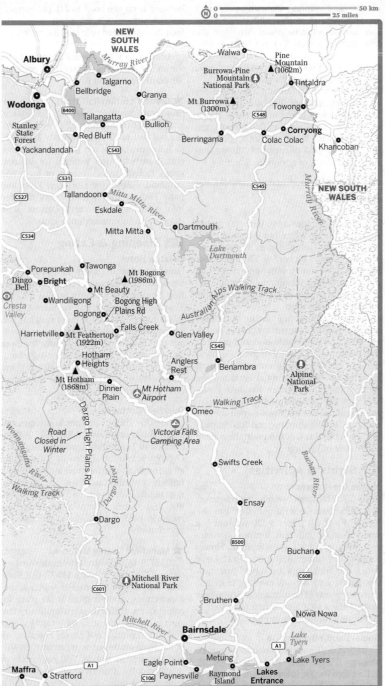

mountain playground attracting skiers and snowboarders in winter and bushwalkers and mountain bikers in summer. Here the mountain air is clear and invigorating, winter snowfalls at the resorts of Mt Buller, Mt Hotham and Falls Creek are fairly reliable, and the scenery is spectacular.

Away from the mountain tops, there are activities aplenty and Bright is one of the loveliest gateway towns in the state. Throw in historic towns such as Beechworth, the wineries of King Valley and Rutherglen, and the gourmet food offerings of Milawa and you'll find plenty of reasons to linger.

Mansfield

POP 4787

Mansfield is the gateway to Victoria's largest snowfields at Mt Buller, but is also an exciting all-seasons destination in its own right. There's plenty to do here in *The Man from Snowy River* country, with horse riding and mountain biking popular in summer, and a buzzing atmosphere in winter when the snow bunnies hit town.

Mansfield and around is the traditional homeland of the Taungurung people, and in late 2018 an agreement was signed between the Taungurung Clans Aboriginal Corporation and the Victorian government, covering areas of the Alpine National Park and the Buffalo and Lake Eildon National Parks. The agreement gives around 3000 Taungurung people access to Crown-owned land for hunting, fishing, camping and food gathering, and covers 11% of the entire land mass of the state of Victoria.

⊙ Sights & Activities

Howes Creek Farm   FARM

(☑ 03-5775 1246; www.facebook.com/howescreek farm; 1195 Howes Creek Rd; ⊙ 8.30am-4pm Thu-Sun; ℗ 🖶) 🍽 Sit under a 120-year-old oak tree and enjoy pork pies, terrines, sausages and pâté, all made on-site from Howes Creek's free-range Berkshire pigs. Local wines and craft beers are served with tasting plates, and for self-catering travellers there are plenty of farmgate products to take away. Time a visit for the free farm tour at 11am every Saturday morning.

Social Bandit Brewing Co   BREWERY

(☑ 03-5775 3281; www.facebook.com/socialbandit brewing; 223 Mt Buller Rd; pizzas from $18; ⊙ 11am-9pm Thu-Sat, to 8pm Sun) In a commercial estate on Mansfield's outskirts, this craft brewery is on the road to Mt Buller. Sample the numerous beers produced on-site, including American pale ales and refreshing sour beers, all accompanied by pizzas and pretzels. Grab a few bottles to enjoy up on the mountain. Tasting trays of four beers are served in mini mason jars.

★**Great Victorian Rail Trail**   CYCLING

(www.greatvictorianrailtrail.com.au) This 134km-long cycling trail is Australia's longest continuous rail trail, running from Mansfield to Tallarook, taking you through some less-visited parts of rural Victoria. Its different stages include varied scenery of bush and farmland, valleys, the Goulburn River and Lake Eildon. The website offers detailed info, along with itinerary planners, with stopover and accommodation ideas.

🛏 Sleeping & Eating

Delatite Hotel   PUB $

(www.thedelatitehotel.com.au; 95 High St; r $120, s/d with shared bathroom from $65/89; 🕸 🛜) Run by a friendly owner who also runs the Mansfield Regional Produce Store (p605), this country hotel on the main road has pub accommodation upstairs. Rooms are basic, but they're spacious and adequate for those on a budget. One room has an en-suite bathroom. Downstairs has an atmospheric bistro and there's often live blues and folk music on Friday nights.

Overflow Cottages   COTTAGE $$

(☑ 03-5775 2869; www.overflowcottages.com. au; 3458 Maroondah Hwy; d $140-160; ℗ 🕸 🛜) Located in Mansfield's semi-rural outskirts, Overflow's four two-bedroom cottages are all surprisingly spacious and kitted out with full kitchens and laundries. The charming host family lives on-site in a separate building, and there's usually a few easygoing sheep in nearby paddocks to enhance the agrarian vibe.

★**Mansfield Coffee Merchant**   CAFE $$

(☑ 03-5779 1703; www.mansfieldcoffeemerchant. com.au; 23 Highett St; mains $14-22; ⊙ 6.30am-3pm; 🕸 🖉 🖶) 🍽 This roaster set-up within a cavernous, modern space is *the* place for coffee lovers. It also does contemporary fare such as Bircher muesli, chilli-scrambled eggs and apple crumble and ricotta hotcakes. All of its single-origin beans are roasted on-site, and prepared as siphon, V60 pour overs or machine coffee. Otherwise pop in for a local wine or craft beer.

★**Mansfield Regional Produce Store** CAFE $$

(☑03-5779 1404; www.theproducestore.com.au; 68 High St; mains $14-32; ☺8.30am-5pm; 🖉🖮) 🖉 Wildly popular with Mansfield folk for breakfast and brunch is this rustic store-cafe with mismatched furniture and an array of local produce and wine. The ever-changing menu offers full breakfasts, locally made sourdough baguettes and coffee. The cafe also acts as Mansfield's informal cultural centre, so check the window for information on occasional music, art and cultural events held here.

ℹ️ **Information**

Mansfield & Mt Buller High Country Visitor Centre (☑1800 039 049; www.mansfield mtbuller.com.au; 173 High St; ☺9am-5pm) In a modern building next to the town's original railway station, the visitor centre books accommodation for the region and sells lift tickets.

ℹ️ **Getting There & Away**

Mansfield is 209km northeast of Melbourne, but allow at least 2½ hours if you're driving; take the Tallarook or Euroa exits from the Hume Hwy.

V/Line (☑1800 800 007; www.vline.com.au) coaches run between Melbourne's Southern Cross station and Mansfield ($29.60, three hours) at least once daily, with more frequent departures during the ski season.

There's a winter bus service to Mt Buller with **Mansfield–Mt Buller Buslines** (☑03-5775 2606; www.mmbl.com.au; 137 High St, Mansfield) (adult/child return $68/47).

Mt Buller

ELEV 1805M

Victoria's largest and busiest ski resort is also the closest major resort to Melbourne, so it buzzes all winter long. It's also developing into a popular summer destination for mountain bikers and hikers, with a range of cross-country and downhill trails. The downhill-skiing area covers 180 hectares, with a vertical drop of 400m.

🛏️ **Sleeping**

There are over 7000 beds on the mountain. Rates vary throughout the ski season, with cheaper rates midweek. A handful of places are open year-round. **Mt Buller Alpine Reservations** (☑03-5777 6633; www.mtbullerreservations.com.au) and **High Country Reservations** (☑1800 039 049; www.mansfieldmtbuller.com.au) book

accommodation; there's generally a two-night minimum stay on weekends.

ABOM Hotel & Apartments APARTMENTS $$

(☑1800 810 200; www.abom.com.au; 16 Athletes Walk; d summer/winter $154/330, q $132/368; 🅿🌀🛜) Shared four-bed rooms, doubles and family apartments are all on offer at this central option that's conveniently open all year round. There's also a good cafe and bar. Drop in for happy hour from 4pm to 6pm. Note that weekend and apartment bookings all have a two-night minimum stay.

Hotel Enzian CHALET $$$

(☑03-5777 6996; www.enzian.com.au; 69 Chamois Rd; r/apt from $180/415; 🛜) Enzian has a good range of lodge rooms and apartments (sleeping up to 10) with all the facilities, alpine charm and an in-house restaurant and bar. Breakfast is included for the rooms, but not for the apartments that have cooking facilities. Check online for midweek prices.

🍴 **Eating & Drinking**

Snowpony LATIN AMERICAN $$

(☑03-5777 6010; www.snowponybuller.com.au; 231 Summit Rd; mains $17-43, tapas $12-24; ☺9am-late Mon-Fri, from 8am Sat & Sun Jun-Sep; 🌀🖉) Hearty Latin American flavours feature at one of Mt Buller's most versatile restaurants. Kick off with the eggy delights of a breakfast burrito or *huevos rancheros*, before returning at night for tapas including tacos, ceviche and grilled prawns. An excellent wine list and cocktails (a pricey $18 to $26) all make Snowpony one of the mountain's most fun after-dark destinations.

Kooroora Hotel PUB

(☑03-5777 6050; www.facebook.com/thekoor oorahotel; Village Sq, 3-5 The Avenue; ☺10am-3am Jun-Sep) Redeveloped and modernised in time for the 2019 winter sports season, Kooroora is still the mountain's best option to rock hard and late. There's live music and pumping DJs around five nights a week, usually from Wednesday to Sunday. Serves good bistro meals. Planned for 2020 is further redevelopment including the addition of upmarket apartments.

ℹ️ **Information**

Mt Buller Resort Management Board (☑03-5777 6077; www.mtbuller.com.au; Community Centre, Summit Rd; ☺8.30am-5pm Mon-Fri, 10am-4pm Sat & Sun) Also runs an information office in the village square clock tower during winter.

❶ Getting There & Away

Mansfield–Mt Buller Buslines (p605) runs a winter bus service from Mansfield (adult/child return $68/47).

In winter there are numerous shuttles from Melbourne; visit www.mtbuller.com.au for the current operators.

V/Line operates at least one daily bus between Melbourne and Mansfield ($29.60, three hours), but has no connecting service to Mt Buller; however, there's a shuttle ($20) from the Mirimbah Park, at the foot of the mountain, daily in January and weekends from February to the end of April. See www.allterraincycles.com.au/shuttles for departure times.

❶ Getting Around

Ski-season car parking is below the village. A 4WD taxi service transports people to their village accommodation.

Day trippers park in the Horse Hill car park and take the quad chairlift into the skiing area, or there's a free day-tripper shuttle-bus service between the day car park and the village. Ski hire and lift tickets are available at the base of the chairlift.

Milawa Gourmet Region

The Milawa/Oxley gourmet region is the place to indulge your taste buds. As well as wine tasting, you can sample cheese, olives, mustards and marinades, or dine in some of the region's best restaurants. If you're self-catering, it's a great area to pick local artisanal produce for on-the-road picnics.

✗ Eating & Drinking

Milawa Cheese Company   CHEESE $
(☏ 03-5727 3589; www.milawacheese.com. au; 17 Factory Lane, Milawa; ☉ 9am-5pm, meals 11.30am-3pm) From humble origins, the Milawa Cheese Company now produces a mouth-watering array of cheeses to sample or buy. It excels at soft farmhouse brie (from goat or cow) and pungent washed-rind cheeses. There's a bakery here and an excellent restaurant doing bistro food and sourdough toasties using Milawa cheese. It's 2km north of Milawa.

Gamze Smokehouse   BARBECUE $$
(☏ 03-5722 4253; www.gamzesmokehouse.com. au; Shop 1/1594 Snow Rd, Milawa; mains $24-29, pizza $16-21; ☉ 8am-3pm Sun-Wed, to 9pm Thu-Sat; ℗) Self-catering travellers can stock up on bacon, ham and other European-style smallgoods at this country-style smokehouse, but it's also a good location for lunch daily or dinner on weekends. Pair ribs, burgers and steaks with local wine or craft beers from the nearby King Valley. Leave room for dessert of Gundowring ice cream, just maybe Victoria's best.

★ Patricia's Table   MODERN AUSTRALIAN $$$
(☏ 03-5720 5540; www.brownbrothers.com.au/ visit-us/victoria/eat; 239 Milawa-Bobinawarrah Rd, Milawa; 2-course meal & wine pairing $75; ☉ noon-3pm) Break up your travels with lunch at this fine-dining restaurant at the picturesque **Brown Brothers** (☏ 03-5720 5500; www. brownbrothers.com.au; ☉ cellar door 9am-5pm, 1hr tour 11am & 2pm daily; ♿) winery. Regarded as one of the region's very best, expect beautifully presented, contemporary dishes featuring the likes of blackened barramundi and grilled honey-glazed pork paired with earthy seasonal flavours. All the set-course combinations are accompanied with wines, which makes this hatted restaurant excellent value.

Hurdle Creek Still   DISTILLERY
(☏ 0411 156 773, 0427 331 145; www.hurdlecreekstill. com.au; 216 Whorouly-Bobinawarrah Rd, Bobinawarrah; ☉ 10am-4pm Mon, Tue & Thu, to 5pm Sat & Sun) This rural, small-scale, family-run distillery produces all its gins from a tin shed; drop by for tastings and pick up a bottle.

❶ Information

See www.milawagourmet.com.au for local information on accommodation and eating options.

❶ Getting There & Away

Milawa lies along the Snow Rd, between Wangaratta and Myrtleford. There's no public transport through the region.

Beechworth

POP 3859

Beechworth's historic honey-coloured granite buildings and wonderful gourmet offerings make it one of northeast Victoria's most enjoyable towns. It's also listed by the National Trust as one of Victoria's two 'notable' towns (the other is Maldon), and you'll soon see why. Other highlights include its position on the Murray to Mountains Rail Trail, and good local craft beer and wine.

Traditionally the Beechworth area is the ancestral homeland of the Dhudhuroa people, and ancient Indigenous cave paintings can be seen at the Yeddonba Aboriginal Cultural Site 20km north of town.

⊙ Sights & Activities

★ Ned Kelly Vault
MUSEUM

(☑03-5728 8067; www.burkemuseum.com.au; 101 Ford St; entry with Beechworth Heritage Pass; ☺11am-4pm) Within the original subtreasury building (c 1858) where gold was stored is this exhibition space dedicated to Australia's most infamous bushranger, Ned Kelly. There's detailed info on the Kelly story, as well as one of his original death masks, a Sidney Nolan painting, rare photographs and an early manuscript of Peter Carey's *True History of the Kelly Gang*. There's also an exhibit on the iconic bulletproof suits, and a mask you can wear for a photo op.

★ Burke Museum
MUSEUM

(☑03-5728 8067; www.burkemuseum.com.au; 28 Loch St; entry with Beechworth Heritage Pass; ☺10am-5pm) Dating from 1857, when it was the Beechworth Athenaeum, this is one of Australia's oldest museums. It was renamed in 1861 in tribute to the famous explorer Robert O'Hara Burke – police superintendent at Beechworth from 1854 to 1858 – following the ill-fated Burke and Wills expedition. It shows gold-rush relics and an arcade of shopfronts preserved as they were around 150 years ago. Highlights include a taxidermied thylacine (Tasmanian tiger), Charles Dickens' writing desk, Burke's pistol and 'trench art' bullets from WWI.

★ Bridge Road Brewers
BREWERY

(☑03-5728 2703; www.bridgeroadbrewers.com.au; Old Coach House Brewers Lane, 50 Ford St; pizza $16-24; ☺11am-10pm Wed-Sun, to 5pm Mon & Tue; ⓐ) Beechworth's gem of a microbrewery produces some excellent beer; our favourites are the Chevalier saison and the Bling IPA. All go beautifully with freshly baked pretzels, gourmet house-made pizzas and burgers. Free bike hire, a playground and a kids' menu seal the deal for families.There's a brewery tour every Saturday at 11am ($15) including tastings of four beers.

Yeddonba Aboriginal Cultural Site
HISTORIC SITE

(Yeddonba Rd, Chiltern-Mt Pilot National Park; ⓟ) Located within the heart of the **Chiltern-Mt Pilot National Park** (Chiltern Box-Ironbark National Park; ☑13 19 63; www.parks.vic.gov.au) – around 20km north of Beechworth – this 40-minute trail traverses a rocky and scrubby hillside and wooden boardwalks to reach a viewing platform sheltering three centuries-old Aboriginal cave paintings. The faint red ochre representations of a snake, goanna and thylacine (Tasmanian tiger) are sacred to the Dhudhuroa people, the dominant Indigenous clan of the area around Beechworth. Note the rocky track can be slippery after rain.

Old Beechworth Gaol
HISTORIC BUILDING

(www.oldbeechworthgaol.com.au; cnr Ford & Williams Sts; adult/child/family $15/10/40; ☺tours 11am Mon-Fri, 11am & 1pm Sat & Sun) In 2016 a consortium of locals banded together to buy the historic 1860 Beechworth prison in order to save it from being developed. Entry to the gaol is only possible by taking a 'Rogues, Rat Bags and Mongrel Dogs' tour, packed with fascinating tales of its most infamous inmates – namely Ned Kelly, his family and sympathisers. There's a good cafe housed in a retro Airstream caravan (open 9am to 2pm), and bikes can be hired from a kiosk just outside.

Beechworth Asylum
HISTORIC SITE

(Albert Rd) One for those into dark tourism is this creepy, old 'lunatic' asylum, decommissioned in 1995, which sits on Mayday Hill overlooking town. While a lot of the buildings have been redeveloped into hotels, residential properties, and the studios of the Mayday Hills Art Society, a lot remains abandoned and downright spooky. You can't access inside any of the buildings, unless you sign up with **Asylum Ghost Tours** (☑0473 376 848; www.asylumghosttours.com; tours adult/child $38/28; ⓐ), which operates historical tours by day and ghost tours by night.

☀ Activities & Tours

Bike Hire Company
CYCLING

(☑0400 345 648; www.thebikehirecompany.com.au; bikes/e-bikes per day $38/78; ⓐ) This Beechworth-based company offers bike hire, convenient shuttle services along the Murray to Mountains Rail Trail linking Beechworth, Bright, Millawa, Myrtleford, Wangaratta and Yackandandah, and authoritative advice on self-guided bicycle tours throughout the region. Check the website for excellent day-ride itineraries and downloadable trail maps. Also has plenty of family-friendly accessories such as kids' bike trailers and toddlers' seats.

Beechworth Honey Experience
FOOD

(☑03-5728 1433; www.beechworthhoney.com.au; 31 Ford St; ☺9am-5.30pm; ⓐ) **FREE** Beechworth Honey's owners, a fourth-generation

MELBOURNE & VICTORIA BEECHWORTH

ⓘ COMBINED TICKET

To access the best of the town's museums and also join two excellent historical walking tours, visitors must purchase a good-value **Beechworth Heritage Pass** (adult/child/family $15/15/40). The pass provides entry to the **Beechworth Courthouse** (☑ 03-5728 8067; www.burkemuseum.com.au; 94 Ford St; ⊙ 9.30am-5pm). Burke Museum (p607), Ned Kelly Vault (p607) and **Telegraph Station** (☑ 03-5728 8067; www.burkemuseum.com.au; 92 Ford St; ⊙ 10am-5pm), and can be purchased at the visitor centre (p609).

family of honey producers, showcase the world of bees with self-guided tours, a live hive, educational displays and honey tastings. Try the huge variety of honeys and pick up honey-infused treats like ginger and honey soda. Interesting for overseas visitors are honeys made from Indigenous Australian trees like ironbark and lemon myrtle.

★ **Walking Tours** TOURS
(included in Beechworth Heritage Pass; ⊙ 10.15am & 1.15pm) Daily guided walking tours leave from the visitor centre and feature lots of gossip and interesting details. The Echoes of History tour starts at 10.15am and the Ned Kelly–themed tour at 1.15pm. The good-value Beechworth Heritage Pass includes both walking tours.

🛏 Sleeping

Lake Sambell Caravan Park CARAVAN PARK $
(☑ 03-5728 1421; www.caravanparkbeechworth. com.au; 20 Peach Dr; unpowered/powered sites from $32/38, cabins & units $98-180; ❄ �) This shady park next to beautiful Lake Sambell has great facilities, including a camp kitchen, playground, mountain-bike hire (half-/full day $22/33) and canoe and kayak hire (from $45). The sunsets reflected in the lake are spectacular. The newer deluxe villas are particularly comfortable, and mini-golf and a playground are good for holidaying families.

★ **Woolshed Cabins** COTTAGE $$
(☑ 03-5728 1035; www.thewoolshedcabins.com; cnr Chiltern & McFeeters Rds; s/d from $150/170; 🅿 ❄) Shaded by bushland around 5km north of Beechworth, the four cottages at Woolshed Cabins combine rustic materials

like corrugated iron and rough-sawn timber with designer furnishings and a stylish retro vibe. Verandahs are ideal for end-of-day relaxation, and full kitchens and the ability to accommodate up to four make them a good choice for families or travelling couples.

Old Priory GUESTHOUSE $$
(☑ 03-5728 1024; www.oldpriory.com.au; 8 Priory Lane; dm/s/d incl breakfast $50/70/100, cottages s $150, d $150-170, q $200; 🐾) This historic convent dating from 1904 is a spooky but charming old place. It's often used by school groups, but it's the best budget choice in Beechworth, with lovely gardens and a range of rooms, including beautifully renovated miners' cottages. The self-contained flat is good for groups and families.

★ **Freeman on Ford** B&B $$$
(☑ 03-5728 2371; www.freemanonford.com.au; 97 Ford St; s/d incl breakfast from $285/370; 🅿 ❄ 🐾 ▦) In the 1876 Oriental Bank, this sumptuous but homey place offers five-star Victorian luxury in six beautifully renovated rooms, right in the heart of town. The owner, Heidi, will make you feel very special.

🍴 Eating & Drinking

Beechworth Bakery BAKERY $
(☑ 1300 233 784; www.beechworthbakery.com.au; 27 Camp St; pies from $5; ⊙ 6am-6.30pm; 🖉 🖽) This popular place is the original in a well-known, statewide bakery chain. It's great for pies and pastries, cakes and sandwiches. Its signature pie is the Ned Kelly, topped with an egg and bacon, but the veggie cauliflower pie is also a winner.

Press Room TAPAS $$
(☑ 03-5728 2360; www.thepressroomwinebar.com. au; 37 Camp St; tapas $5-12, shared plates $16-38; ⊙ 6-11pm Wed-Fri, 8.30am-11.30am & 6-11pm Sat & Sun; ❄) Originally the location of Beechworth's historic printing press, the Press Room is now a stylish and cosy Spanish tapas and wine bar. Seasonal menu highlights could include chargrilled lamb with hummus and pomegranate, or ricotta and spinach dumplings with a chorizo sauce. The brunch burrito with bacon and chipotle mayo is a good way to kick off Saturday or Sunday.

Blynzz Coffee Roasters CAFE $$
(☑ 0423 589 962; www.coffeeroastersbeechworth. com.au; 43 Ford St; mains $15-19; ⊙ 8.30am-2pm Thu-Sun) This inner-city-chic micro-roastery

cafe on Beechworth's main strip has polished concrete floors and designer fittings along with great breakfasts and brunches. However, it's best known for its coffee, roasting all of its single-origin beans on-site, with hessian sacks of green beans stacked at the back.

★**Provenance** MODERN AUSTRALIAN $$$
(☑03-5728 1786; www.theprovenance.com.au; 86 Ford St; 2-/3-course meals $73/95, degustation menu without/with matching wines $125/200; ⊙6.30-9pm Wed-Sun; ☑) In an 1856 bank building, Provenance has elegant but contemporary fine dining. Under the guidance of local chef Michael Ryan, the innovative menu features modern Australian fare with Japanese influences, such as smoked wallaby tartare with *umeboshi*, egg yolk and miso sauce. If you can't decide, go for the degustation menu. Bookings are essential. There's also a vegetarian degustation menu.

Accommodation-wise there are four boutique rooms ($200 to $310) here in what were once horse stables.

Empire Hotel PUB
(☑03-5728 2743; www.empirehotelbeechworth.com.au; 10 Camp St; mains $26-38; ⊙11am-late) Following a stylish makeover, one of Beechworth's most historic pubs now celebrates a distinctly modern and urban vibe. There's a diverse selection of local wines, craft beers and cocktails, and the regular curry specials ($20) are a firm menu favourite. Beechworth locals are also lured by live gigs from 4pm on Sundays, usually with a blues, folk or alt-country bent.

Cellar Door Wine Store WINE BAR
(www.cellardoorwinestore.com.au; 62 Ford St; ⊙9am-5pm Thu-Sun, to late Fri & Sat) Along Beechworth's atmospheric main street is this elegant yet casual wine bar that's perfect for a pre-dinner tipple. Wines are available by the glass, carafe or bottle, along with craft beers, to go with select French cheeses. The tables out the front are a favourite of beer-quaffing local winemakers. Planned for 2019 was a bold expansion to include an adjacent stand-alone bistro.

🛈 **Information**

Beechworth Visitor Centre (☑1300 366 321; www.explorebeechworth.com.au; 103 Ford St; ⊙9am-5pm; 🕏) Information and an accommodation and activity booking service in the town hall. Includes free wi-fi, complimentary

use of a tablet, and a handy charging station for your own electronic devices.

🛈 **Getting There & Away**

Beechworth is just off the Great Alpine Rd, 36km east of Wangaratta and 280km northeast of Melbourne.

V/Line (☑1800 800 007; www.vline.com.au) runs a train/bus service between Melbourne and Beechworth ($37.60, 3½ hours, three daily), with a change at Wangaratta. There are direct buses from Wangaratta ($5.40, 35 minutes, five daily) and Bright ($5, 50 minutes, two daily).

Yackandandah

☑02 / POP 1811
An old gold-mining town nestled in beautiful hills and valleys east of Beechworth, 'Yack', as it's universally known, is original enough to be classified by the National Trust. Essentially a one-street town – bookended by two pubs (the 'Bottom Pub' and the 'Top Pub') – its historic streetscape is one of the most charming you'll find in country Australia.

⊙ **Sights & Activities**

Yackandandah Museum MUSEUM
(☑02-6027 0627; www.yackandandahmuseum.wordpress.com; 21 High St; gold coin donation; ⊙11am-4pm Wed-Sun, daily school holidays; 🖮) In a former bank building, this interesting museum has changing historical exhibitions on Yackandandah. Out the back is an original 1850s cottage that's furnished in period style and includes a unique outdoor 'double dunny' (toilet). A few interactive and participatory exhibits make it a good kids' destination. There's also a good selection of themed walking-tour maps in its gift shop.

Karrs Reef Goldmine Tour TOURS
(☑0408 975 991; adult/child $25/20; ⊙10am, 1pm & 4pm Sat & Sun or by appointment) Don a hard hat and descend into the original tunnels of this gold mine that dates from 1857. On the 1½-hour guided tour you'll learn all about the mine's history. Bookings can be made through the visitor centre (p610).

🛏 **Sleeping & Eating**

Yackandandah Holiday Park CARAVAN PARK $
(☑02-6027 1380; www.yhp.com.au; 1 Dederang Rd; powered sites $32-35, cabins $100-130; 🅿🕏🐾) Beside pretty Yackandandah Creek, but close to town, this well-equipped park is a little oasis of greenery and autumn colours.

Gum Tree Pies BAKERY $
(☑02-6027 1233; www.gumtreepies.com.au; 11 High St; pies $6.50; ☺9am-4pm; ☑) Fuel up with just maybe our favourite pies in all of Victoria. Steak and mushroom and Thai-style pumpkin are our top flavours.

★ **Saint Monday** CAFE $$
(☑02-6027 1202; www.saintmondaycafe.com.au; 26 High St; mains $15-26; ☺7am-4pm Wed-Sun; ☑) ☞ Deconstructed sushi and vegan doughnuts are definitely items you once couldn't order in Yackandandah, but those days are gone since the arrival of this lovely little cafe with art on the walls. The kitchen uses locally sourced ingredients to create delicious vegetarian and ethical cuisine. Seasonal dishes could include treats like smoked Harrietville trout with fennel panna cotta.

Star Hotel PUB FOOD $$
(☑02-6027 1493; www.facebook.com/starhotelyack; 30 High St; mains $17-28; ☺11am-late) Known locally as the 'Top Pub', this 1863 hotel does classic counter meals, but of more interest is its American-style BBQ using a red-gum smoker. It's also the place for craft beer, being the home of Yack's very own Two Pot Brewing. On Wednesday and Thursday nights local musos crowd in for regular gigs. Check Facebook for other regular events.

🛍 Shopping

Kirby's Flat Pottery CERAMICS
(☑02-6027 1416; www.johndermer.com.au; 225 Kirby's Flat Rd; ☺10.30am-5pm Sat & Sun or by appointment) The studio-cum-gallery-cum-shop of internationally renowned potter John Dermer, Kirby's Flat Pottery is a great place to pick up affordable, original pieces, or just browse the gallery with its stunning collection of salt-glazed ceramics. It's set in a lovely garden retreat 4km south of Yackandandah.

🛈 Information

Yackandandah Visitor Centre (☑02-6027 1988; www.exploreyackandandah.com.au; 37 High St; ☺9am-5pm) Stocks a good selection of brochures and has information on walking tours and accommodation for Yack and beyond. Also sells mining licences for those who fancy prospecting for gold.

🛈 Getting There & Away

Yackandandah is 307km northeast of Melbourne – take the Hume Hwy to the Great Alpine Rd exit north of Wangaratta then follow the signs to Beechworth. From here it's a further 22km to Yackandandah.

On weekdays there are daily buses to/from Beechworth ($2.80) en route to Albury Wodonga.

Rutherglen
☑02 / POP 2109

Rutherglen combines some marvellous gold-rush-era buildings (gold was discovered here in 1860) with northern Victoria's most celebrated winemaking tradition. The town itself has all the essential ingredients that merit a stopover, among them a great pie shop, antique dealers and classic country pubs. Factor in excellent B&B accommodation and a good craft brewery, and Rutherglen is also a great base for exploring the Murray River's Victorian hinterland.

Rutherglen is the traditional homeland of the Bangerang and Wiradjuri peoples, and an excellent new Indigenous art gallery opened in late 2017 in the centre of town.

◉ Sights & Activities

An extension of the Murray to Mountains Rail Trail (p614) passes through Rutherglen and Wahgunyah and leads to a few local wineries. Hire bicycles (half-/full day $35/50) and tandem bikes ($50/85) from the Rutherglen Visitor Information Centre. Ask for the *Pedal to Produce* brochure and biking and walking maps.

★ **Aboriginal Exhibitions Gallery** GALLERY
(☑02-6032 7999; www.aboriginalexhibitions.com.au; Tuileries, 13-35 Drummond St, Rutherglen Estates; ☺10am-5.30pm; P) Opened in late 2017, this Indigenous gallery at Rutherglen Estates presents an ongoing and evolving showcase of work by some of Australia's leading Aboriginal artists. Painting, mixed media and sculpture are all featured, and exhibitions are usually refreshed around every three months. The spectacular gallery is housed amid a modern architectural reboot of Seppelts' wine warehouses that date from the late 19th century.

Rutherglen Brewery BREWERY
(☑02-6032 9765; www.rutherglenbrewery.com; 121b Main St; mains $15-25; ☺10am-3pm & 5.30pm-late Wed-Sat, 10am-3pm Sun) With an atmospheric courtyard and cosy taproom, this craft brewery offers 10 beers and ciders to team with grills, burgers and pizzas. The

RUTHERGLEN WINERIES

Rutherglen's wineries produce superb fortifieds (port, muscat and tokay) and some potent durifs and shirazes – among the biggest, baddest and strongest reds. Many wineries date back to the 1860s, and are still run by fifth- or sixth-generation winemakers.

Most of the wineries don't distribute beyond the area, so it makes visiting all the more worthwhile. Most offer free tastings. See www.winemakers.com.au for more information.

All Saints (☑02-6035 2222, 1800 021 621; www.allsaintswine.com.au; All Saints Rd, Wahgunyah; ☉10am-5pm Sun-Fri, to 5.30pm Sat; 🅿) With its aristocratic gardens and heritage-listed 19th-century castle, All Saints is a classy affair.

Buller Wines (☑02-6032 9660; www.bullerwines.com.au; 2804 Federation Way; ☉10am-5pm; 🅿) Making fine shiraz since 1921 and now including bistro dining at Ripe@Buller Wines.

Rutherglen Estates (☑02-6032 7999; www.rutherglenestates.com.au; Tuileries, 13-35 Drummond St; ☉10am-5.30pm) The closest winery to town with shiraz, grenache and table red and white wines.

Stanton & Killeen Wines (☑02-6032 9457; www.stantonandkilleenwines.com.au; 440 Jacks Rd; ☉9am-5pm Mon-Fri, from 10am Sat & Sun) This century-old winery is known for its durif-shiraz blend, rosé and vintage ports.

Warrabilla Wines (☑02-6035 7242; www.warrabillawines.com.au; 6152 Murray Valley Hwy; ☉10am-5pm) Run by a sixth-generation winemaker, this is one for those who like their reds big, brash and full of oak.

Morris (☑02-6026 7303; www.morriswines.com.au; 154 Mia Mia Rd; ☉9am-5pm Mon-Sat, from 10am Sun) Rutherglen's oldest winery with a dusty cellar door designed by esteemed architect Robin Boyd.

Pfeiffer (☑02-6033 2805; www.pfeifferwinesrutherglen.com.au; 167 Distillery Rd, Wahgunyah; ☉9am-5pm Mon-Sat, from 10am Sun) This atmospheric cellar door known for its gamay is run by a father-daughter winemaker team.

Chambers Rosewood (☑02-6032 8641; www.chambersrosewood.com.au; Barkly St; ☉9am-5pm Mon-Sat, from 10am Sun) One of Rutherglen's originals, this ramshackle tin-shed cellar door's wine tasting is all self-serve.

Cofield Wines (☑02-6033 3798; www.cofieldwines.com.au; Distillery Rd, Wahgunyah; ☉9am-5pm Mon-Sat, from 10am Sun; 🍴) Stop by to sample Champagne-style sparkling wines, produced using a traditional method.

St Leonard's Vineyard (☑02-6035 2222; www.stleonardswine.com.au; 201 St Leonards Rd, Wahgunyah; ☉10am-5pm Thu-Sun; 🍴) Head through its dark barrel room to enter a modern light-filled cellar door with grassy outdoors area and lagoon.

Campbells Winery (☑02-6033 6000; www.campbellswines.com.au; 4603 Murray Valley Hwy; ☉9am-5pm Mon-Sat, from 10am Sun; 🍴) Spanning five generations of winemakers, this well-respected family-owned winery is 3km west of Rutherglen.

Scion Vineyard (☑02-6032 8844; www.scionvineyard.com; 74 Slaughterhouse Rd; ☉10am-5pm) A more contemporary affair than Rutherglen's more traditional offerings, this boutique cellar door is close to town.

Valhalla Wines (☑02-6033 1438; www.valhallawines.com.au; 163 All Saints Rd, Wahgunyah; ☉10am-4pm Fri-Mon or by appointment) 🖉 Set up by a passionate winemaker, Valhalla adopts a modern approach using sustainable, renewable practices.

al fresco fairy-lit beer garden is the place to be on a balmy evening, especially if there's a band playing on Saturday night or Sunday afternoon. Standout brews are the Hoppy Saison and the Turon Widow IPA.

Behind the Scenes TOURS
(☑1800 622 871; www.explorerutherglen.com.au/behind-the-scenes-tours; ☉2pm Mon & Thu, 11am Sat & Sun) FREE A few local wineries offer fantastic, free 'Behind the Scenes' winery

tours that take you into the world of the winemaking process. Advance bookings are essential. Check the website to match your day with a winery and then book directly with the wineries.

🛏 Sleeping & Eating

★ Amberesque
B&B $$

(☑02-6032 7000; www.amberesque.com.au; 80 Main St; d from $185; ❄🐾) Named after host Amber, who, along with her husband, has set up this B&B in a historic bank in the heart of town. Upstairs rooms are lovely, with king-sized beds and spa baths, and a patio overlooking the garden. The highlight is the beautiful downstairs space where you can enjoy a lavish personalised breakfast, complimentary port and welcome cheese-and-wine platter.

Tuileries
BOUTIQUE HOTEL $$

(☑02-6032 9033; www.tuileriesrutherglen.com. au; 13 Drummond St; d $199, incl dinner $299; ❄🐾🏊) Looking out to the vineyards, all rooms at this luxurious place are individually decorated in bright contemporary tones. There's a guest lounge, tennis court, pool and fine-dining restaurant (lunch mains $22-25, dinner $29-43; ⊙7am--9.30am, noon-2pm & 6.30-9pm) and cafe. Located next to Rutherglen Estates (p611); rates include breakfast.

★ Parker Pies
BAKERY $

(☑02-6032 9605; www.parkerpies.com.au; 86-88 Main St; pies $5-9.50; ⊙8.30am-5pm) If you think a pie is just a pie, this award-winning local institution might change your mind. Try the gourmet pastries – emu, venison, crocodile, buffalo or the lovely Jolly Jumbuck (a lamb pastry with rosemary and mint).

Pickled Sisters Café
MODERN EUROPEAN $$

(☑02-6033 2377; www.pickledsisters.com.au; Cofield Wines, Distillery Rd, Wahgunyah; mains $16-35; ⊙10am-3pm Mon & Wed-Fri, 9am-4pm Sat & Sun) Attached to the Cofield (p611) winery, this popular little eatery does some interesting dishes such as honey-and-muscat-glazed confit duck, and twice-baked Milawa goats-milk cheese soufflé, along with various platters to go with wine. There's also the opportunity to spend the night in a luxury tent (☑02-6033 3798; www.cofieldwines.com.au/glamping.aspx; Cofield Wines, Distillery Rd, Wahgunyah; d from $260). Check the website for

monthly cooking classes where meals are teamed with Cofield wines.

★ Jones Winery Restaurant
FRENCH $$$

(☑02-6032 8496; www.joneswinery.com.au; 61 Jones Rd; menus $36-68; ⊙cellar door 10am-4pm Mon, Thu & Fri, to 5pm Sat & Sun, restaurant noon-3pm Thu-Sun; 🅿❄) This French-style cellar door specialises in shiraz, marsanne and durif wines crafted from historic well-established vines, and the relaxed bistro is also a fine place for lunch. Sit in the shade under Jones' sprawling grape arbour or in the cosy interior and enjoy French classics infused with local Australian ingredients. Menu highlights include kangaroo tartare with pepperberry or paperbark-roasted duck.

★ Terrace Restaurant
MODERN AUSTRALIAN $$$

(☑02-6035 2209; www.allsaintswine.com.au/terrace-restaurant; All Saints Estate, All Saints Rd, Wahgunyah; 2-/3-course meal $60/80; ⊙noon-3pm Wed-Fri & Sun, noon-3pm & 6-11pm Sat; 🍴) One of the region's best restaurants, this classy bistro serves inventive and modern seasonal European cuisine, overlooking the stately grounds of All Saints (p611) wine estate. Local Victorian ingredients are proudly showcased and seasonal menu highlights could include house-smoked duck croquettes. The attached Indigo cafe sells cheese, cured meat platters and gourmet produce for self-catering or al fresco picnics.

🍷 Drinking & Nightlife

★ Thousand Pound
WINE BAR

(☑02-6035 2222; www.thousandpound.com.au; 82 Main St; mains $27-35; ⊙5pm-late Fri & Sat) If ever there were a place suited to a wine bar, it's Rutherglen's picturesque main street. Grab a stool at the long tiled bar, by the window or on the communal table to select from 140 local and international family-owned wineries. Its food is also excellent, with charcoal-grilled steaks and roast barramundi among the highlights.

ℹ Information

Rutherglen Visitor Information Centre (☑1800 622 871; www.explorerutherglen.com.au; 57 Main St; ⊙9am-5pm Mon-Sat, 10am-4pm Sun; 🐾) In the same complex as the Rutherglen Wine Experience; has good info on accommodation, wineries and sights. Also rents bikes and has wi-fi access.

ⓘ Getting There & Away

Rutherglen is 295km northeast of Melbourne. To get there by car, take the Hume Hwy (M31) and turn off at Chiltern.

V/Line (☑1800 800 007; www.vline.com. au) has a train and coach service between Melbourne and Rutherglen ($37.60, 3½ hours, daily), with a change at Wangaratta. During festivals, bus transport to wineries can be organised through the visitor centre (p610).

The Murray to Mountains Rail Trail (p614) has an extension to Rutherglen, which means you can get here and around by bike.

Bright

POP 2165

Famous for its glorious autumn colours, Bright is a popular year-round destination in the foothills of the alps and a gateway to Mt Hotham and Falls Creek. Skiers make a beeline through Bright in winter, but it's a lovely base for exploring the Alpine National Park, paragliding, fishing and kayaking on the Ovens River, bushwalking and exploring the region's wineries.

It's a big cycling destination too, with the Murray to Mountains Rail Trail, as well as single-track mountain-bike and alpine road trails. Plentiful accommodation and some sophisticated restaurants and cafes complete the appealing picture.

The region around Bright is the traditional ancestral homeland of the Dhudhuroa people.

⊙ Sights & Activities

The Murray to Mountains Rail Trail (p614) starts behind the old train station. Rent bikes at **Cyclepath** (☑03-5750 1442; www. cyclepath.com.au; 74 Gavan St; per half-/full day recreational bikes from $30/40, e-bikes from $58/75, mountain/road bikes per day from $55/75; ⊙9am-5.30pm Mon-Fri, to 5pm Sat & Sun; 🖫) or **Bright Electric Bikes** (☑03-5755 1309; www.brightelectricbikes.com.au; 2 Delany Ave; per hour/half-/full day e-bike rental $39/49/69, bicycle from $20/25/35; ⊙9am-6pm daily Sep-May, Fri-Sun Jun-Aug; 🖫). The **Mystic MTB Park** (www.alpinecommunityplantation. com.au/mystic) is popular with mountainbikers. See **Bright Adventure Company** (☑03-5756 2486; www.brightadventure company.com.au; 9 Ireland St, Bright Outdoor Centre; adult/child from $110; ⊙9am-5pm Mon-Fri, to 3pm Sat & Sun; 🖫) for abseiling, kayaking and underground river caving. Bright is also

a base for fly-fishing, hiking, cycling and paragliding.

Bright Brewery BREWERY
(☑03-5755 1301; www.brightbrewery.com.au; 121 Gavan St; ⊙11am-10pm; 🖫) This brewery produces quality craft beers (sample six for $12) and beer-friendly food such as pizzas, beef burgers and meze boards. Guided tours and tastings occur at 3pm on Monday, Friday and Saturday ($18), and there's live blues on Sunday from 3pm. With 24 beer taps there's always seasonal brews and craft beers and ciders from around Victoria on offer.

🛏 Sleeping

Bright Holiday Park CARAVAN PARK $
(☑1800 706 685, 03-5755 1141; www. brightholidaypark.com.au; Cherry Lane; unpowered sites $33-50, powered sites $35-60, cabins $130-284; 🅿🟦🖫🛇) Straddling pretty Morses Creek, this lovely park is five minutes' walk to the shops. The riverside spa cabins are very nice and feature pay TV channels. It's a great spot for families with a pool, mini-golf and a playground.

★**Odd Frog** BOUTIQUE HOTEL $$
(☑0418 362 791; www.theoddfrog.com.au; 3 McFadyens Lane; d $165-214, q $275; 🟦🛇) 🌿 Designed and built by the architect–interior designer owners, these contemporary, ecofriendly studios feature light, breezy spaces and fabulous outdoor decks with a telescope for stargazing. The design features clever use of the hilly site with sculptural steel-frame foundations and flying balconies. Kangaroos often graze on a nearby hillside.

Bright Velo APARTMENT $$
(☑03-5755 1074; www.brightvelo.weebly.com; 2 Ireland St; r $100-169, apt $250; 🅿🟦) Run by Kiwi ex-professional cyclist Wayne Hildred, a veteran of the European pro-cycling tour, options at this centrally located accommodation spot include heritage rooms, motel units and a self-contained apartment sleeping up to seven.

★**Aalborg** APARTMENT $$$
(☑0401 357 329; www.aalborgbright.com.au; 6 Orchard Ct; r $220-240; 🅿🟦🛇) Clean-lined Scandinavian design with plenty of pine-and-white furnishings dominates this gorgeous place. Every fitting is perfectly chosen and abundant glass opens out onto sweeping bush views. There's a minimum two-night stay.

MURRAY TO MOUNTAINS RAIL TRAIL

The **Murray to Mountains Rail Trail** (www.murraytomountains.com.au) is Victoria's second-longest bike path and one of the High Country's best walking/cycling trails for families or casual riders. It's sealed and relatively flat much of the way, and passes through spectacular rural scenery of farms, forest and vineyards, with views of the alpine ranges.

The 94km trail runs from Wangaratta to Bright via Myrtleford and Porepunkah. A section of the trail then heads northwest from Wangaratta to Wahgunyah via Rutherglen, completing the true Murray to Mountains experience.

Aficionados say the 16km between Everton and Beechworth, which detours off the main trail, is the best part of the ride (despite a challenging uphill section), as you're cycling through bush. Bikes can be hired in Wangaratta, Beechworth and Bright, as well as towns in between.

✖ Eating

★ Dumu Balcony Cafe   CAFE $
(☑03-5755 1489; www.facebook.com/pg/dumu balconycafe; 4 Ireland St; snacks & light meals $7-14; ☺9am-3pm; 🕸🐾👶) 🍴 Set up to train Indigenous youth from the Wadeye community in Australia's Northern Territory, Dumu – translating to 'Pacific black duck' in Bright's local Dhudhuroa language – is an excellent social enterprise cafe with a strong focus on healthy, sustainable ingredients and snacks. Relax on the breezy upstairs balcony and take in the infectious laughter usually coming from the kitchen.

Ginger Baker   CAFE $
(☑03-5755 2300; www.gingerbaker.com.au; 127 Gavan St; breakfast mains $8-18, shared plates $12-20; ☺8am-3pm Sun-Thu, to 9pm Fri & Sat; 🕸🐾) 🍴 This rightfully popular cafe within a cute rustic weatherboard cottage opens up to an expansive garden with seating overlooking the river. Locally roasted coffee from Sixpence goes well with potato rösti, poached eggs and salmon for breakfast, while Bridge Road (p607) beers complement lunch and dinner shared plates such as gnocchi with gorgonzola and walnuts, goat tagliatelle or pork and fennel meatballs.

★ Reed & Co   MODERN AUSTRALIAN $$
(☑03-5750 1304; www.reedandcodistillery.com; 15 Wills St; shared plates $8-20, set menu $57; ☺3pm-late Sun, Mon & Fri, from noon Sat; 🐾) 🍴 Combining a gin distillery with delicious wood-fired food, Reed & Co is an essential Victorian High Country destination. Native Australian bush botanicals are harnessed for Reed's excellent gin, best enjoyed as a tasting flight as you take in the culinary theatre of the tiny open kitchen. The menu includes many Australian ingredients including wallaby tartare and smoked Murray river cod.

🍷 Drinking & Nightlife

★ Wandi Pub   PUB
(☑03-5750 1050; www.thewandipub.com; 580 Morses Creek Rd, Wandiligong; ☺noon-late; 👶) Voted one of Victoria's best country pubs, it's definitely worth making the 7km journey out to Wandiligong. Aussie craft beers and High Country wines feature on the drinks list, and there's live music most weekend afternoons in the leafy beer garden. Wandi's excellent pub meals (mains $24 to $29) are also a cut above. Try the brisket tacos or the chicken parmigiana.

Sixpence   COFFEE
(☑0423 262 386; www.sixpencecoffee.com.au; 15 Wills Street; ☺8am-3pm Tue-Fri, 8am-2pm Sat) A short stroll from Bright's main strip is this cool cafe that will excite coffee enthusiasts who love their Ethiopian, Colombian and Sumatran beans. It's all roasted at Sixpence's roastery on the outskirts of town, and perfectly enjoyed inside the hip interior along with panini and fresh brioches and croissants. Sourdough bread is also available some days.

ℹ Information

Alpine Visitor Information Centre (☑1800 111 885, 03-5755 0584; www.visitbright.com. au; 119 Gavan St; ☺9am-5pm) Has a busy accommodation booking service, along with useful brochures and an attached cafe. And because Bright is such a biking hub, there's even a bike pump to borrow.

ℹ Getting There & Away

Bright is 310km northeast of Melbourne, around a 3½-hour journey that's mostly via the Hume Hwy (M31).

V/Line (p609) runs train/coach services from Melbourne ($39.40, 4½ hours, two daily) with a change at Wangaratta.

Dyson Group (☑ 0477 991 377; www.dyson group.com.au/alps-link; Day Ave) has a handy year-round service three times a week that heads from Bright to Harrietville ($4.40, 15 minutes) and Mt Hotham ($5.40, one hour) en route to Omeo ($13.40, two hours).

During the ski season the **Snowball Express** (☑ 1300 656 546; www.snowballexpress.com. au) operates from Bright to Mt Hotham (adult/ child return $60/50, 1½ hours). Some departures continue to Dinner Plain ($75/57.50).

Mt Beauty & the Kiewa Valley

POP 824

Huddled at the foot of Victoria's highest mountain, Mt Bogong (1986m), on the Kiewa River, Mt Beauty and its twin villages of Tawonga and Tawonga South are the gateways to Falls Creek ski resort. It's reached by a steep and winding road from Bright, with some lovely alpine views. This region is the traditional homeland of the Dhudhuroa Indigenous people.

⊙ Sights & Activities

The 2km **Tree Fern Walk** and the longer **Peppermint Walk** both start from Mountain Creek Picnic Area, on Mountain Creek Rd, off the Kiewa Valley Hwy (C531). About 1km south of Bogong Village (towards Falls Creek), the 1.5km return **Fainter Falls Walk** takes you to a pretty cascade. For information on longer walks in the area, visit the **Mt Beauty Visitor Centre** (☑ 1800 111 885, 03-5755 0596; www.visitmountbeauty.com.au; 31 Bogong High Plains Rd; ⊙ 10am-4pm Mon-Fri, from 9am Sat & Sun).

Kiewa Valley Historical Museum   MUSEUM
(☑ 03-5755 0596; www.kiewavalleyhs.wixsite.com/kvhs-museum; 31 Bogong High Plains Rd; gold coin donation; ⊙ 9am-5pm; 🅿) Within the Mt Beauty Visitor Centre is this interesting little museum that covers the history of the Kiewa Valley and Bogong High Plains, from the area's Indigenous Dhudhuroa people through to the colonial highland cattlemen. There's a replica of an old mountain hut, historical background on skiing in the region, and info on the **Bogong Power Station** (☑ 03-5754 3318; Bogong High Plains Rd; ⊙ 10.30am-2.30pm Sun; 🅿) **FREE**.

Sweetwater Brewing Company   BREWERY
(☑ 03-5754 1881; www.sweetwaterbrewing.com. au; 211 Kiewa Valley Hwy; ⊙ 1-7pm Fri, to 6pm Sat & Sun) This highway microbrewery in Mt Beauty utilises the fresh mountain water of the Kiewa River for its range of beers brewed on-site – including pale, golden and summer ales, IPA, wheat beer and porter. To sample its range, grab a tasting paddle, served on a cool, mini ski paddle. Look forward to live music from 3pm on Sunday afternoons.

Bogong Horseback Adventures   HORSE RIDING
(☑ 03-5754 4849; www.bogonghorse.com.au; 52 Fredas Lane, off Mountain Creek Rd, Tawonga; 2/4hr ride $98/125, full day with lunch $275; 🐴) Horse riders can experience this beautiful area on short two-hour jaunts, day-long trips with a delicious lunch, or week-long pack-horse camping trips to remote alpine regions over Mt Bogong. It's 12km northwest of Tawonga, and includes the delightful Spring Spur homestay.

🛏 Sleeping & Eating

★ **Spring Spur**   HOMESTAY $
(☑ 03-5754 4849; www.springspurstay.com.au; 52 Fredas Lane, off Mountain Creek Rd, Tawonga; per person from $95; 🅿🐾) A wonderful place to soak up the High Country atmosphere is this family-run farm on a property known for its horse-riding tours. The well-designed, modern rooms (minimum two-night stay) have private verandahs looking out to Mt Feathertop and the Kiewa Valley. Meals are a highlight (three courses $50), shared with the Baird family and featuring paddock-to-plate cuisine.

Expect homemade pastas, home-baked sourdough bread and homegrown veggies, with regular faves including the duck-prosciutto wood-fired pizza and pulled-pork tacos with soft corn tortillas. Much of the spectacular artwork in the accommodation is by co-founder Steve Baird.

The Park   CARAVAN PARK $
(☑ 03-5754 4396; www.theparkmountbeauty.com. au; 222-226 Kiewa Valley Hwy; unpowered/powered sites from $32/37, cabins & yurts $90-155; 🅿🐾) This family caravan park close to Mt Beauty town centre has river frontage, kids' games and a playground, and an interesting range of cabins, including hexagonal 'yurts'.

★ **Templar Lodge**   MODERN AUSTRALIAN $$
(☑ 03-5754 4415; www.facebook.com/templar lodgebyemmahandley; 181-183 Kiewa Valley Hwy, Tawonga; mains $26-42; ⊙ 6pm-11pm Thu-Sun; 🅿) Housed in a former Masonic hall,

Templar Lodge is a showcase for well-known Victorian chef Emma Handley. Secure a table on the verandah and feast on homemade pasta, kangaroo tartare and French-style rillettes made from local High Country trout. Subtle Asian and European influences underpin a menu that's further evidence of Mt Beauty as an emerging regional Victorian dining hotspot.

Roi's Diner Restaurant ITALIAN $$$

(📞03-5754 4495; 177 Kiewa Valley Hwy; mains from $30; ⊙6.30-11pm Thu-Sun, 7-9pm Mon) It's hard to believe this unassuming timber shack on the highway 5km from Mt Beauty is an award-winning restaurant, specialising in exceptional modern northern Italian cuisine. Expect great risotto, eye fillet carpaccio, its signature roasted pork chops, homemade or imported pasta and handmade ice cream.

❶ Getting There & Away

V/Line (📞1800 800 007; www.vline.com.au) operates a train/bus service from Melbourne to Mt Beauty ($44.60, 5½ hours) on Monday, Wednesday and Friday, via Wangaratta and Bright.

In winter **Falls Creek Coach Service** (📞03-5754 4024; www.fallscreekcoachservice.com.au) operates daily direct buses from Melbourne to Mt Beauty (one way/return $95/154) and Falls Creek ($63/126) from 30 June to 17 September; prices include resort entry to Falls Creek. In early June and late September there are less frequent services.

Falls Creek

POP 293 / ELEV 1780M

Victoria's glitzy, fashion-conscious resort, Falls Creek combines a picturesque alpine setting with impressive skiing and infamous après-ski entertainment. It offers some of the best downhill skiing, snowboarding and cross-country skiing in Victoria, and plenty of snow activities for non-skiers. Summer is also a good time to visit, with scenic hiking and a fast-emerging mountain-biking scene attracting outdoor enthusiasts in droves.

🛏 Sleeping

Falls Creek Central
Reservations ACCOMMODATION SERVICES

(📞1800 033 079; www.fallscreekreservations.com.au) Accommodation bookings on the mountain.

Alpha Ski Lodge LODGE $

(📞03-5758 3488; www.alphaskilodge.com.au; 5 Parallel St; summer dm/s/d $59/84/112, winter dm $84-171, d $188-378; ❋ 🛜) A spacious, affordable lodge with a sauna, a large lounge with panoramic views and a communal kitchen. Rates per night decrease significantly with multi-night stays. Open year-round except from October to mid-November and the first three weeks of May.

QT Falls Creek RESORT $$$

(📞03-5732 8000; www.qthotelsandresorts.com/falls-creek; 17 Bogong High Plains Rd; 1-bedroom apt $235-1180; ❋ 🛜) Open year-round, QT is a large-scale resort along the main road. Its self-contained apartments are modern and stylish, with wi-fi, pay TV, a kitchen and a balcony with outdoor hot tub looking out to spectacular alpine views. Within the complex is a day spa, a pub and two restaurants. Check online for good spring and summer deals.

🍴 Eating & Drinking

★ Milch Café CAFE $$

(📞03-5758 3407; www.fvfallscreek.com.au/milch-cafe; 4 Schuss St; mains from $20; ⊙8am-late; 🛜) A vibrant, art-filled cafe run by a friendly owner, Milch does a good menu of breakfast rolls, house-baked breads and slow-cooked meats. Its bar is lined with a dangerous selection of schnapps bottles, and the coffee is specially roasted and best enjoyed on the AstroTurf terrace. It closes for a few months after winter but usually reopens in December.

★ Summit Ridge MODERN AUSTRALIAN $$$

(📞03-5758 3800; www.summitridge.com.au/resturant; 8 Schuss St; mains $35-41, degustation menu with/without wine matches $175/125; ⊙6-10pm mid-Jun–late Sep; 🖥) One of the best restaurants for fine dining on the mountain, Summit Ridge does a menu of alpine-inspired modern Australian dishes using local produce, such as wild-boar terrine, scotch fillet with truffle mash and wild mushrooms, and Milawa cheese platters. There's a very good wine list, a children's menu, and the High Country's best craft beers from Dinner Plain's Blizzard Brewing.

Man Hotel PUB

(📞03-5758 3362; www.themanfallscreek.com; 20 Slalom St; ⊙4pm-late Jun-Sep) 'The Man' has been around forever, and is the heart of Falls' nightlife. It's only open in winter, when it fires up as a club, cocktail bar and live-music venue featuring popular Aussie bands. Good pub dinners and pizzas are available.

ℹ Information

For all the latest prices, packages and online tickets, visit www.fallscreek.com.au. Ski season daily resort entry is from $49.50 per car. It's cheaper to buy tickets online in advance. From 5pm to midnight is free if you're in Falls Creek for night skiing or for dining. One-day lift tickets per adult/child cost from $126/70. Buying online in advance offers the best pricing. Group ski lessons are $77 per day.

Falls Creek Resort Management (☑ 03-5758 1202; www.fallscreek.com.au; 1 Slalom St; ⊙ 9am-5pm Mon-Fri Nov-Jun, daily Jul-Oct) Offers excellent information, as well as pamphlets on trails for skiing, hiking and mountain biking. Its website is useful too.

Activities Hotline (☑ 1800 204 424) Also handy for info on mountain activities.

ℹ Getting There & Away

Falls Creek is 375km from Melbourne, around a 4½-hour drive. The Hume Hwy (M31) to Wangaratta is the fastest route before heading through Milawa, Myrtleford, Bright and Mt Beauty. If coming from Gippsland, note that the road to Omeo is only open when there's no snow – generally November to April.

During winter the **Falls Creek Coach Service** (☑ 03-5754 4024; www.fallscreekcoachservice. com.au) operates daily between Falls Creek and Melbourne (one way/return from $63/126) and also runs services to and from Albury and Mt Beauty. There's a reduced service in early June and late September.

Falls Bus (☑ 1300 781 221; www.fallsbus.com. au; 🛜) A bus service during winter that heads from Melbourne to Falls Creek (return from $129, six hours).

If you've got camping gear you can hike here from Mt Hotham along the **Falls to Hotham Alpine Crossing** (www.parkweb.vic.gov.au; ⊙ Nov-Apr) trail.

ℹ Getting Around

No vehicles are permitted into the Falls Creek Village during winter, so you'll have to walk (or better, ski) between your lodge and the car park; however, for families an Accommodation Transfer Service – an over-snow taxi service – operates between the car parks and the lodges (adult/child return $37/23) from 7am to midnight daily (to 2am Friday, to 1am Saturday and Sunday). Car parking for day visitors is at the base of the village, next to the ski lifts.

Mt Hotham & Dinner Plain

ELEV 1868M

The conjoined-twin ski resort towns of Mt Hotham and Dinner Plain together provide the quintessential alpine experience, offering quality skiing mixed with a charming atmosphere. Serious hikers, skiers and snowboarders make tracks for Mt Hotham, which has some of the best and most challenging downhill runs in the country.

Over at Dinner Plain, 10km from Hotham village and linked by a shuttle, there are excellent cross-country trails around the village, including the Hotham–Dinner Plain Ski Trail. There's also a growing mountain-biking scene, with the **local bike club** (☑ 0409 538 935, 0439 559 010; www.dpriders. com.au; bike hire per day $25; ⊙ Nov-Jun) developing new trails in the area.

◉ Sights & Activities

**Howling Husky
Sled Dog Tours** DOG SLEDDING
(☑ 0488 040 308; www.facebook.com/pg/howling. huskys; 2 people from $300; ⊙ Apr-Sep) Offering a unique experience are these dog-sled tours where you'll glide through snow with a team of energetic Siberian huskies. Options include a short 30-minute ride through to a 75-minute family experience ($550 for two adults and two children). Weather permitting, tours are offered at both Dinner Plain (April to September) and Mt Hotham (June to September).

★ Blizzard Brewing Co BREWERY
(☑ 0447 847 029; www.blizzardbrewing.com; 5 Cattle Pen Dr, Dinner Plain; ⊙ 2-8pm Fri & Sat, to 6pm Sun Sep-May, noon-late daily Jun-Aug) An unexpected find in the outskirts of Dinner Plain alpine village is this awesome little brewery that produces all of its American-style craft beers on-site. The warehouse set-up has a taphouse pouring all of its range of core and seasonal ales, with the option of tasting paddles. There are no meals, but there is a menu of beer snacks and platters.

🛏 Sleeping & Eating

While the bulk of lodges only operate during the ski season, a few stay open year-round. For a comprehensive list, get in touch with accommodation booking services such as **Dinner Plain Accommodation** (☑ 1800 444 066, 03-5159 6696; www.accommdinnerplain.com.

au; 19 Big Muster Dr, Dinner Plain), **Dinner Plain Central Reservations** (☑1800 670 019, 03-5159 6451; www.dinnerplain.com; 6 Big Muster Dr, Dinner Plain) and **Mt Hotham Accommodation Service** (☑1800 657 547; www.mthothamaccommodation.com.au). During the ski season, accommodation places generally stipulate a minimum two-night stay.

★ **General Lodge**   LODGE $$$

(☑03-5759 3523; www.thegeneral.com.au; Great Alpine Rd, Mt Hotham; studio/1-/2-bedroom apt Oct-May from $204/220/305; ☑ 🎧) Attached to the General (meals $15-26; ⊙9.30am-late Mon-Sat, to 4pm Sun, open late Sun winter; 🎧) pub are these modern and stylish fully self-contained apartments with lounge, gas fireplaces and kitchen, and fantastic views from the balcony. Accommodation is open year-round, but prices double (and more) in winter when there's also a two-night minimum stay.

Mountain Kitchen   CAFE $

(☑03-5159 6560; www.mountainkitchen.com.au; 1 Big Muster Dr, Dinner Plain; dishes $10-19; ⊙9am-4pm Wed-Sun Oct-May, daily Jun-Sep; 🌶) A popular cafe-restaurant at the entrance to the Dinner Plain alpine village, Mountain Kitchen's menu is focused squarely on homemade items using regional produce. Excellent breakfasts, coffee, sandwiches, fresh juices and mulled wine. It also operates as a deli and provedore selling honey, chutney and mustard.

★ **Stone's Throw**   PUB FOOD $$

(☑03-5159 6324; www.hotelhighplains.com.au; Hotel High Plains, 185 Big Muster Dr, Dinner Plain; mains $19-33; ⊙5pm-late; 🌶) One of the mountain's best restaurants, Stone's Throw specialises in produce from regional Victoria. The menu is seasonal, but expect the likes of smoked trout linguine, Blizzard-beer-battered fish and chips, and excellent gourmet wood-fired pizzas. It's located within the Hotel High Plains pub, which has local beers on tap, an open fire and accommodation (rooms $150) over summer only.

ⓘ Information

The ski-season admission fee is $50 per car per day, and $15 for bus passengers (this may be included in your fare). Lift tickets (peak) per adult/student/child cost $120/100/58. Passes are cheaper in September and there are packages that include gear hire and lessons.

Dinner Plain Visitor Centre (☑03-5755 0555; www.visitdinnerplain.com; Big Muster Dr, Dinner Plain; ⊙10am-5pm Mon-Fri, 9am-5pm daily winter) In the Dinner Plain Alpine Village is this centre for chalet bookings, trail maps and general info. Its website is an excellent source of information too.

Mt Hotham Alpine Resort Management Board (☑03-5759 3550; www.mthotham.com.au; Great Alpine Rd, Mt Hotham; ⊙8am-4.30pm Mon-Fri, 7am-6pm daily winter) At the village administration centre, this visitor centre has a range of brochures with maps for short, eco, heritage and village walks. Also has an app with stop-off points for driving in the area.

Mt Hotham Central Guest Services (☑03-5759 4470) Can assist with general tourist info on the mountain, from ski lessons to bus timetables.

ⓘ Getting There & Away

Mt Hotham is 360km northeast of Melbourne. By car take the Hume Hwy to Wangaratta, then follow the Great Alpine Rd to Mt Hotham. Alternatively you can take the Princes Hwy to Omeo, before continuing on the Great Alpine Rd to Hotham via Dinner Plain.

In winter all vehicles must carry diamond-patterned snow chains, to be fitted at the designated fitting bays. During ski season all vehicles will need to purchase a resort pass ($50 per day); if you're just passing through you're only permitted to stay for 30 minutes. The winding drive down to Harrietville is on a knife's edge so take it easy if there's snow on the road.

During the ski season, both **Hotham Bus** (☑1300 781 221; www.hothambus.com.au; one way/return $109/178; ⊙late Jun-early Sep, mainly Fri-Sun; 🎧) and **Snowball Express** (☑1300 656 546; www.snowballexpress.com.au; one way/return from $110/150; ⊙daily during ski season) run buses here from Melbourne.

Dyson's Alpine Link (☑0428 591 377; www.dysongroup.com.au/alps-link) has three buses a week connecting Mt Hotham and Dinner Plain with Bright ($8.20, two hours) and Omeo ($6.80, one hour); check its website for the schedule.

For hikers, there's the Falls to Hotham Alpine Crossing (p617), a two-night, three-day 37km trek that links Hotham with Falls Creek.

There's an **airport** (MHU; www.mthotham.com.au) at Mt Hotham that's only used by private charter flights.

ⓘ Getting Around

In winter, a shuttle service operates between Dinner Plain and Mt Hotham (return ticket adult/child $15/7.50) every 30 minutes between 7am and 5.30pm; you'll need to secure a SmartCard

THE MALLEE

Occupying the vast northwestern corner of Victoria, the Mallee appears as a flat horizon and endless, undulating, twisted mallee scrub and desert. The attractions – other than the sheer solitude – are the semi-arid wilderness areas, including Wyperfeld National Park and Big Desert Wilderness Park. Collectively these parks cover more than 750,000 hectares, and are notable for their abundance of native plants, spring wildflowers and birds. Nature lovers might delight in it, but much of it is inaccessible to all but experienced 4WD enthusiasts. Visiting this, the Victorian outback, is best avoided in the hot summer months.

The main route through the Mallee is the Sunraysia Hwy (B220), via the towns of Birchip and Ouyen, but if you want to explore the region's national parks, turn off to the historic farming towns of Jeparit (birthplace of Sir Robert Menzies and the jumping-off point for Lake Hindmarsh), Rainbow, Yaapeet and Hopetoun.

---

from local businesses and add credit to the card to access this service.

In Mt Hotham itself a free shuttle runs frequently around the resort from 6.45am to 2am.

THE MURRAY

The mighty Murray River is Australia's longest and most important inland waterway, and arrayed along its banks are some of Victoria's most historic and captivating towns. The region is a stirring place of wineries and orchards, bush camping, balmy weather and river red gum forests. The Murray changes character constantly along its 2400km route. History looms large in towns such as Echuca; food and wine dominate proceedings around Mildura; and national parks enclose soulful desert expanses in the far northwest. It's a world of picturesque river beaches, of paddle steamers that were once the lifeblood of Victoria's inland settlements, and of unending horizons that serve as a precursor to the true outback not far away. It's an intriguing if relatively far-flung mix, which enables you to follow in the footsteps of some of Australia's earliest explorers who travelled along the river.

❶ Getting There & Away

Towns along the Hume Fwy are well serviced by V/Line trains (often in combination with bus travel). Having your own wheels allows you to explore country locations more easily, however.

V/Line also services the Murray Valley Hwy that runs alongside the Murray River.

Once you are in the Mallee region, you'll need your own car, especially if you plan to visit the national parks. Note: many national parks require 4WD.

Mildura

POP 53,878

On the banks of the Murray River, sunny Mildura is a leafy oasis enlivening an often very dry surrounding region. Now a cosmopolitan and bustling provincial city, Mildura also celebrates its historic roots in the grand old era of hardworking pastoralists. Other highlights for travellers include heritage art-deco buildings and some of provincial Victoria's best cafes and restaurants. Explore nearby wilderness national parks and go fishing, swimming, canoeing, waterskiing or houseboating on the Murray River. Other activities include paddle-steamer cruises or negotiating riverside golf courses. Expect warm and sunny weather, even in midwinter, and blue-sky days throughout the year. Note that in January and February, the temperature can regularly exceed 40°C.

The Mildura region is the traditional homeland of the Latje Latje and Paakantyi peoples.

◉ Sights

★ **Rio Vista & Mildura Arts Centre** HISTORIC BUILDING

(☑ 03-5018 8330; www.milduraartscentre.com.au; 199 Cureton Ave; ◉ 10am-5pm; ℙ) **FREE**
The grand homestead of William B Chaffey (a Mildura founder), historic Queen Anne-style Rio Vista has been preserved and restored. Each room has historical displays depicting colonial life in the 19th century, with period furnishings, costumes, photos and a collection of letters and memorabilia. The Mildura Arts Centre, in the same complex, combines a modern-art gallery with

Murray River

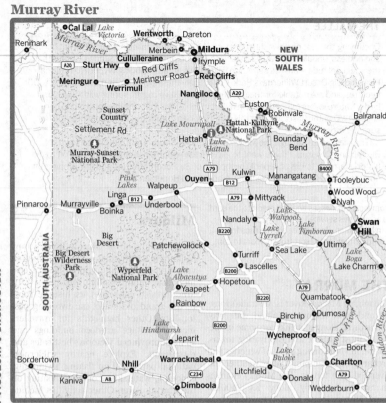

changing exhibitions and a theatre showing cutting-edge productions (thanks to its involvement on the regional performance circuit). There's a small cafe on-site.

Sunraysia Cellar Door WINERY
(☑ 03-5021 0794; www.sunraysiacellardoor.com.
au; 125 Lime Ave; ⊗ 9am-5pm Mon-Thu, 9am-9pm
Fri, 11am-5pm Sat & Sun) Sunraysia Cellar Door has free tastings and sales for around 250 local wines from 22 different wineries from the Murray–Darling region, as well as a few local craft beers and local edible products for purchase. Cheese platters are available, and on Friday nights the Cellar Door's outdoor tables become one of Mildura's best ways to end the working week.

Old Mildura Station Homestead HISTORIC SITE
(Cureton Ave; by donation; ⊗ 9am-6pm) Along the river, near the historic Rio Vista & Mildura Arts Centre, this cottage was the first home of William B Chaffey. The heritage park here contains a few other historic log buildings, and has picnic and barbecue facilities.

☞ Tours

Wild Side Outdoors ADVENTURE
(☑ 0428 242 852, 03-5024 3721; www.wildside
outdoors.com.au; canoes/kayaks/mountain bikes per hour $35/25/25) ⚓ For more than 20 years this ecofriendly outfit has offered a range of activities, including a sunset kayaking tour at Kings Billabong ($120 for two people). Handily for independent travellers, it will support three-day river trips, supplying maps, gear and transport (from $450 for two people). Will deliver and collect gear too.

Murray Offroad Adventures TOURS
(☑ Jeanie Kelly 0417 500 131, Peter Kelly 0428 224 368; www.murrayoffroadadventures.com.au;

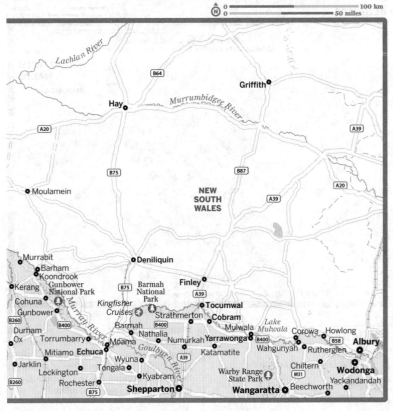

per person half-/full day $100/180) Various tours include the Hattah-Kulkyne National Park, and the history and environment of the Murray River. Guide and driver Peter Kelly has worked closely on regional environmental issues and with local Indigenous communities for 30 years, and he brings this unique and considered perspective to the tours.

Moontongue Eco-Adventures KAYAKING
(☑0427 898 317; www.moontongue.com.au; kayak tours $35-65) 🍃 A sunset kayaking trip is a great way to see the river and its wildlife. Local guide Ian will tell you about the landscape and birdlife as you work those muscles in the magnificent, peaceful surroundings of Gol Gol Creek and the Murray. Operates by appointment only.

PS Melbourne BOATING
(☑03-5023 2200; www.paddlesteamers.com. au; 2hr cruises adult/child $32/14; ⏱10.50am

& 1.50pm; ⛴) One of the original paddle steamers (built in 1925), and the only one still driven by steam power. Watch the operator stoke the original boiler with wood.

🛌 Sleeping

Apex RiverBeach Holiday Park CARAVAN PARK $
(☑03-5023 6879; www.apexriverbeach.com. au; Cureton Ave; unpowered/powered sites from $32/34, cabins from $95; ❄🛜) Thanks to a fantastic location on sandy Apex Beach, just outside town, this bush park is always popular – prices are 25% higher during school holidays. There are campfires, a bush kitchen, a barbecue area, a boat ramp, good swimming and a cafe. Kids can enjoy the huge bouncy pillow.

Seven Pines Motor Inn MOTEL $$
(☑03-5021 1931; www.sevenpines.com.au; 157 Seventh St; r from $120; 🅿❄🛜) Given a

Mildura

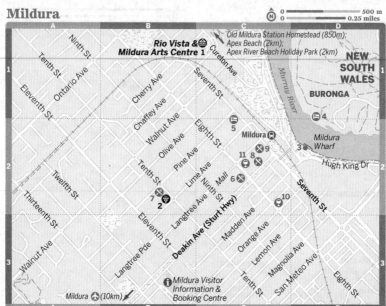

Old Mildura Station Homestead (850m);
Apex Beach (2km);
Apex River Beach Holiday Park (2km)

NEW SOUTH WALES

BURONGA

Murray River

Mildura Wharf

Hugh King Dr

Mildura Visitor Information & Booking Centre

Mildura ✈ (10km)

Mildura

◉ Top Sights
1 Rio Vista & Mildura Arts Centre C1

◎ Sights
2 Sunraysia Cellar Door B2

✪ Activities, Courses & Tours
3 PS Melbourne D2
   PV Rothbury .... (see 3)

⬤ Sleeping
4 Mildura Houseboats D1
5 Seven Pines Motor Inn C2

⊗ Eating
6 Blk.Mlk C2
7 Nash Lane B2
8 Stefano's Cafe C2
9 Stefano's Cantina C2

◉ Drinking & Nightlife
10 Fossey's Ginporium C2
11 Sip C2

MELBOURNE & VICTORIA MILDURA

modern and stylish makeover in 2018, this Mildura motel is well positioned just a short walk from riverside parks and the town's eating and drinking precinct. If you're arriving by train or bus, the railway station is right across the road.

Mildura Houseboats　　HOUSEBOAT **$$**
(☑1800 800 842, 03-5024 7770; www.mildura houseboats.com.au; 2- to 6-berth for 7 nights $1850-2000) Choose from a fleet of around 15 houseboats sleeping two to 12 people. Gourmet and golf packages also offered.

✗ Eating

Blk.Mlk　　　　CAFE **$**
(☑03-5023 1811; www.facebook.com/blk.mlk. specialty.coffee; 51 Deakin Ave; mains $10-21; ⊙7am-3pm Mon-Fri, 8am-3pm Sat, 8am-2pm Sun) The deconstructed name might be a tad pretentious (black milk, get it?) but the coffee and food are anything but. If you're like us, you'll find yourself sitting for a coffee, and an hour later you may have polished off Mildura's best breakfast granola, gourmet burgers or a pork belly salad. A great choice for gourmands and java hounds alike.

★ Nash Lane　　　　CAFE **$$**
(☑03-5051 9978; www.facebook.com/NashLane Mildura; 163-165 Tenth St; mains $14-18; ⊙7am-4pm Mon-Fri, 7.30am-3pm Sat; 🖉🌢) 🖉 Attached to a coffee roastery, Nash Lane's shared tables are popular with savvy locals enjoying brunch and lunch classics. Grab a spot under the spectacular living wall and

try the breakfast cannoli with spiced apple, or the Nash stack with hash browns and poached eggs. Hip and attentive waitstaff and tasty vegetarian dishes make Nash Lane a keeper.

Trentham Estate Winery AUSTRALIAN $$$
(☑03-5024 8888; www.trenthamestate.com.au; 6531 Sturt Hwy; ⊘platters & barbecue $16-30, mains $36-48; P🅿🐾) A versatile vineyard dining option right on the Murray, scenic Trentham Estate is often the answer when you ask locals where to dine. Most informal are shared platters or the 'Cook Your Own' barbecue option – including a salad bar – enjoyed on the terrace, but there's also a classier menu with hearty dishes including Murray River cod, pork belly and confit duck.

Stefano's Cantina ITALIAN $$$
(☑03-5023 0511; www.stefano.com.au; Quality Hotel Mildura Grand, Seventh St; 5-course dinner set menu $99; ⊘6-11pm Tue-Sat; 🐾) Stefano de Pieri was a celebrity chef before the term was invented. The Italian-Australian introduced fresh and simple farm-to-plate cuisine to households via his popular TV program and at this delightful cellar restaurant. It's an intimate, candlelit experience and very popular – book well in advance. Upstairs is a more informal bistro (mains $28 to $39), also offering special dishes for younger diners. Around the corner is a casual daytime cafe and bakery (☑03-5021 3627; www.stefano.com.au; 27 Deakin Ave; meals $14-23; ⊘7am-3pm Mon-Fri, 8am-3pm Sat, 8am-noon Sun).

🍷 Drinking & Nightlife

Fossey's Ginporium DISTILLERY
(☑03-5023 1341; www.fosseysgin.com.au; 110 Eighth St; ⊘2-8pm Thu, Fri & Sun) Gin tasting flights, cocktails, cold beers and cheese platters all combine at this quirky and welcoming spot housed in Mildura's historic Settlers Club. Interesting additions to its self-described 'gin elixirs' include kaffir lime, native Australian pepperberry and rose petals. Fossey's closes relatively early, so consider popping in for an aperitif before heading on somewhere else for dinner.

Sip WINE BAR
(☑03-5021 0680; www.sipcocktailbar.com; 138 Eighth St; ⊘3pm-midnight Wed-Sun) Scandi styling blends with retro 1970s sofas at this friendly spot proving there's more to Mildura than pubs and sports bars. Excellent cocktails and four changing taps of craft beer combine with local wines and bar snacks and platters imbued with global flavours. Cool music too, with classic Motown tunes providing the soulful soundtrack to our visit.

ℹ Information

Mildura Visitor Information & Booking Centre (☑03-5018 8380, 1800 039 043; www.visitmildura.com.au; cnr Deakin Ave & Twelfth St; ⊘9am-5.30pm Mon-Fri, to 5pm Sat & Sun; 🛜) Free service for booking accommodation, with interesting displays, local produce, a cafe, a library, and very helpful staff who book tours and activities.

ℹ Getting There & Away

Mildura is 542km northwest of Melbourne along the Calder Hwy (A79).

AIR

Victoria's busiest regional airport, **Mildura Airport** (☑03-5055 0500; www.milduraairport.com.au; Alan Mathews Dr) is about 10km west of the town centre off the Sturt Hwy. Mildura–Melbourne flights are served by **Qantas** (☑13 13 13; www.qantas.com.au) and **Virgin Australia** (☑13 67 89; www.virginaustralia.com). **Regional Express Airlines** (Rex; ☑13 17 13; www.regionalexpress.com.au) has flights to/from Melbourne, Adelaide and Broken Hill.

BUS & TRAIN

V/Line (☑1800 800 007; www.vline.com.au) Combination train-coach services operate from the train station on Seventh St. There are no direct passenger trains to/from Mildura; change from V/Line trains to coaches at Ballarat, Bendigo or Swan Hill. Services ply the Mildura–Melbourne route ($54, seven to 10 hours, three to four daily).

NSW Trainlink (☑13 22 32; www.nswtrainlink.info) A coach-train combination covers the Mildura–Sydney route, with a coach to Cootamundra then Southern Express train to Sydney ($117, 13½ hours, once daily).

ℹ Getting Around

BOAT

A paddle-steamer cruise here is a must. Mildura Paddlesteamers runs the three main vessels that paddle along: PS Melbourne (p621), **PV Rothbury** (☑03-5023 2200; www.paddlesteamers.com.au; cruises adult/child winery $75/35, dinner $75/35, lunch $37/17;

⊞) and **PV Mundoo** (the latter is for groups and weddings only). Check which services pass through the locks. You can enjoy sunset or even meal cruises.

BUS

Even without your own wheels you can see some of the Sunraysia District via a good local bus system. The visitor information centre has the latest bus timetables.

Echuca

POP 12,906

One of the loveliest towns in rural Victoria, Echuca is the state's paddle-steamer capital and a classic Murray River town, bursting with history, nostalgia and, of course, riverboats. Echuca lies within the traditional boundaries of the Bangerang people, and the Aboriginal name translates as 'meeting of the waters'. It's here that three rivers meet: the Goulburn, the Campaspe and the Murray.

In the 1800s Echuca was an important crossing point between NSW and Victoria, and the ensuing river trade and transport ensured its success.

The highlight of Echuca is unquestionably its historic port area and the rivers themselves, best enjoyed on a riverboat cruise or a sunset stroll as cockatoos and corellas screech overhead. Some good cafes, restaurants and a new craft distillery are all combining to also boost the town's foodie credentials.

◎ Sights & Activities

★ Port of Echuca
Discovery Centre   MUSEUM
(☑ 03-5481 0500; www.portofechuca.org.au; 74 Murray Esplanade; adult/child/family $14/8/45; ☉ 9am-5pm; ⊞) At the northern end of Murray Esplanade, the stunning Port of Echuca Discovery Centre is your gateway to the Echuca wharf area. It presents excellent displays (some of them interactive) on the port's history, the paddle steamers and the riverboat trade. Informative and fun free guided tours set out from the discovery centre twice daily (11.30am and 1.30pm).

★ National Holden Museum   MUSEUM
(☑ 03-5480 2033; www.holdenmuseum.com. au; 7 Warren St; adult/child/family $10/5/25; ☉ 9am-5pm) Car buffs should check out this museum dedicated to Australia's

four-wheeled icon, with more than 40 beautifully restored Holdens, from the FJ to the Monaro. There's also racing footage and memorabilia.

Great Aussie Beer Shed   MUSEUM
(☑ 03-5480 6904; www.greataussiebeershed. com.au; 377 Mary Ann Rd; adult/child/family $14/5/30; ☉ 9.30am-5pm Sat, Sun & holidays) This is a wall-to-wall shrine of more than 17,000 beer cans in a huge shed. It's the result of 30 years of collecting – one can dates back to Federation (1901). Guided tours will take you through the history of beer. Very Aussie. A recent addition is an interesting display of heritage farming machinery.

River Country Adventours   CANOEING
(☑ 0428 585 227; www.adventours.com.au; half-/full-day safaris $75/110; ⊞) For organised canoe safaris on the Goulburn River, this Kyabram-based team is the expert in this part of the world. It offers canoe and camping safaris around the Barmah and Goulburn regions, as well as on the Murray.

🛏 Sleeping

High Street Motel   MOTEL $
(☑ 03-5482 1013; www.highstreetmotelechuca. com.au; 439 High St; d $120; P ❄ 🛜) The current owners have done a good job at this motel makeover. Rooms are simple and as neat as a pin, and prices are fair for what you get. The decent mattresses will guarantee good slumber, and toasters and microwaves are handy for self-caterers. It's walking distance to Echuca's centre and good cafes. Very friendly owners.

★ Cock 'n' Bull
Boutique Hotel   BOUTIQUE HOTEL $$
(☑ 03-5480 6988; www.cocknbullechuca.com; 17-21 Warren St; s/d from $159/189; P ❄ 🛜 ❄) These luxury apartments add a touch of class to Echuca's central motel-style options. The building's older section (once a bustling pub from the 1870s) looks out over the Campaspe River, while a newer, modern section is at the rear. All apartments differ in mood and design, and all are tasteful.

★ Elinike Guest Cottages   COTTAGE $$$
(☑ 03-5480 6311; www.elinike.com.au; 209 Latham Rd; d $190-210; P ❄ ❄) These excellent self-contained cottages are set in

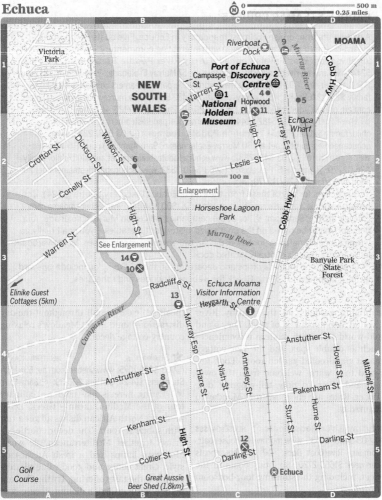

Echuca

MELBOURNE & VICTORIA ECHUCA

Echuca

◎ Top Sights
1 National Holden Museum	C1
2 Port of Echuca Discovery Centre	C1

✦ Activities, Courses & Tours
3 Echuca Paddlesteamers	D2
4 Murray River Paddle Steamers	C1
5 PS Alexander Arbuthnot	D1
PS Canberra	(see 5)
6 PS Emmylou	B2
PS Pevensey	(see 5)
PS Pride of the Murray	(see 5)

🛏 Sleeping
7 Cock 'n Bull Boutique Hotel	B2
8 High Street Motel	B4
9 Murray River Houseboats	C1

✦ Eating
10 Shebani's	B3
11 Sweet Meadow	C1
12 The Mill	C5

◑ Drinking & Nightlife
13 American Hotel	B3
14 Echuca Distillery & Cafe	B3

PADDLE-STEAMER CRUISES

A paddle-steamer cruise is almost mandatory in Echuca. Five boats – wood-fired, steam-driven (one is electric diesel) with interesting commentary – offer trips operating at various times. Privately owned **Murray River Paddle Steamers** (☑03-5482 5244; www.murrayriverpaddlesteamers.com.au; 57 Murray Esplanade; ☺9am-5pm; 🖟) runs **PS Canberra** (☑03-5482 5244; www.murrayriverpaddlesteamers.com.au; adult/child/family $26/12/68; 🖟), **PS Emmylou** (☑03-5482 5244; www.murrayriverpaddlesteamers.com.au; cruises adult/child/family 1hr $30/20/91, 2hr $40/29/125; 🖟) and **PS Pride of the Murray** (☑03-5482 5244; www.murrayriverpaddlesteamers.com.au; adult/child/family $20/10/50; 🖟); **Echuca Paddlesteamers** (☑03-5481 2832; www.echucapaddlesteamers.net.au; 30 Murray Esplanade; ☺9am-4pm; 🖟) runs **PS Alexander Arbuthnot** (☑03-5481 2832; www.echucapaddlesteamers.net.au; adult/child/family $26/12/70; 🖟) and **PS Pevensey** (☑03-5481 2832; www.echucapaddlesteamers.net.au; adult/child/family $26/112/70; 🖟).

Buy tickets for any of these from the Port of Echuca Discovery Centre (p624), **Echuca Moama visitor information centre** (☑1800 804 446; www.echucamoama.com; 2 Heygarth St; ☺9am-5pm; 🕿) or at the companies' offices on Murray Esplanade. Your decision might be based on the boat's size, history or timetables – you can't really go wrong. Check timetables for lunch, dinner, twilight and sunset cruises. Most riverboats leave from Echuca's centrally located dock.

Overnight and multi-day trips and departures on the PS *Emmylou* include vineyard visits, glamping and golfing. Check the website for prices and schedules.

rambling gardens on the Murray River around 5km northwest of town. They blend old-world style with modern conveniences such as double spas, and the lilac cottage has a glass-roofed garden room. Look forward to a warm welcome from the owners and their friendly tail-wagging dog, Dozer. Rates are cheapest from Monday to Thursday.

Murray River Houseboats HOUSEBOAT $$$
(☑03-5480 2343; www.murrayriverhouseboats.com.au; Riverboat Dock; 2-7 bed houseboats per week $1650-2720) Six houseboats in the fleet, including the stunning four-bedroom *Indulgence*.

✕ Eating

★ **Sweet Meadow** VEGAN $$
(☑03-5482 4099; www.thesweetmeadow.com; 640 High St; mains $14-22; ☺7.30am-4pm Mon, Tue, Thu & Fri, from 8am Sat & Sun; 🖉🖟) 🍃
There's absolutely no trade-off for flavour in Sweet Meadow's great vegan and plant-based menu. Overflowing with seasonal fruit, quite possibly Australia's best granola is a breakfast standout, while corn fritters with house-made baked beans and avocado are ideal for brunch. Cold-pressed juices, superfood smoothies and coffee and

(healthy!) cake are all throughout-the-day distractions amid Sweet Meadow's relaxing country-cottage decor.

★ **Shebani's** MEDITERRANEAN $$
(☑03-5480 7075; www.shebani.com.au; 535 High St; mains $14-24, platters $20-39; ☺8am-4pm; 🖉) Eating here is like taking a culinary tour of the Mediterranean – Greek, Lebanese and North African dishes all get a run with subtle flavours. The decor effortlessly brings together Mediterranean tile work, Moroccan lamps and a fresh Aussie-cafe style. Great coffee and good-value platters complete the tasty offering. Try the Shebani platter with grilled halloumi cheese and goat sausage.

Johnny & Lyle CAFE $$
(☑03-5480 3133; www.facebook.com/johnnyandlyle; 433 High St; mains $12-25; ☺6am-3pm Mon-Fri, from 7am Sat & Sun) This ticks the right boxes in terms of colour: not only the cups (an array of bright hues), but the lovely courtyard and the vibrant dishes – granola with berries and yoghurt ($15), brekky burgers ($15), and fabulous lunch dishes including a Thai beef salad ($19) and steak sandwiches ($21). Worth the short stroll a few blocks south of the centre.

The Mill
INTERNATIONAL $$$

(📞03-5480 1619; www.themillechuca.com; 2-8 Nish St; shared plates $12-28, mains $28-42; ⊘4pm-late; 🍴) A former flour mill (built in 1881) has been transformed into a gathering space for locals. Rustic style and industrial chic combine for a buzzing bar and a sun-filled lounge-restaurant. Modern Australian dishes and shared plates are substantial and varied, and craft beers from Echuca-based Bandicoot Brewing are on tap. Devour good cocktails and a fine wine list too.

🍷 Drinking & Nightlife

★ American Hotel
PUB

(📞03-5480 0969; www.americanhotelechuca. com.au; 239-249 Hare St; ⊘8am-late; 🍴) Dubbed the 'Yank' by locals, the American is a modern reinvention of the classic Aussie pub. A glass atrium shades the beer garden, while the best beer selection in town is partnered by good pizza and food tinged with the flavours of the southern USA – think tacos, ribs and burgers. Check Facebook for regular weekend gigs and DJs.

Echuca Distillery & Cafe
DISTILLERY

(📞0428 317 384; www.echucadistillery.com.au; 555 High St; ⊘11am-10pm Thu-Su) Craft spirits (including gin and vodka) and liqueurs all feature at this addition to Echuca's main street. There's also snacks and local craft beers available, all best enjoyed on the spacious upstairs deck.

ℹ️ Information

Echuca Moama Visitor Information Centre (p626) In the old pump station; has helpful staff, brochures and offers booking services for accommodation and paddle steamers. Be sure to grab *Heritage Walk Echuca* brochure, which points out historic buildings and sites.

ℹ️ Getting There & Away

Echuca lies 222km north of Melbourne. Take the Hume Fwy (M31) then the well-signposted turn-off to the B75, which passes through Heathcote and Rochester en route to Echuca.

V/Line (📞1800 800 007; www.vline.com. au) runs combined train and coach services between Melbourne and Echuca ($30, three to 3½ hours, regular departures) with a change at Bendigo, Shepparton or Murchison.

Tasmania

☎ 03 / POP 529,900

Includes ➡

Hobart	634
Bruny Island	652
Port Arthur	661
Freycinet National Park	669
Binalong Bay & the Bay of Fires	673
Flinders Island	676
Launceston	677
Devonport	690
Stanley	700
Cradle Mountain-Lake St Clair National Park	704

Best Places to Eat

➡ Templo (p644)

➡ Coal River Farm (p650)

➡ Agrarian Eatery (p651)

➡ Stillwater (p682)

➡ CharlotteJack (p691)

Best Places to Stay

➡ MACq 01 (p642)

➡ Pumphouse Point (p706)

➡ @VDL (p700)

➡ Peppers Silo (p681)

➡ Port Arthur Holiday Park (p663)

Why Go?

Some say islands are a metaphor for the heart. Isolation mightn't be too good for romance, but Tasmania has turned remoteness into an asset. From the lichen-splashed granite of the east coast to the bleak alpine plateaus of Cradle Mountain-Lake St Clair National Park, Tasmania has a unique beauty. Tragic stories of the island's Indigenous and colonial history play out through this haunting, Gothic landscape: the sublime scenery around Port Arthur only reinforces the site's grim convict history. It's just as easy to conjure up visions of the raffish past in Hobart's Battery Point and atmospheric harbourside pubs. And then there's the food, the wine and the parties: Tasmania is seemingly custom-built for a driving holiday spent shuffling between farm-gate suppliers, boozy cellar doors and hip festivals. Yes, this is still Australia, but Tasmania is bewitchingly different.

When to Go
Hobart

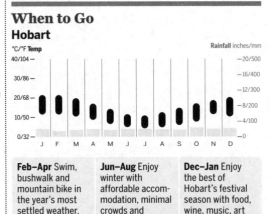

Feb–Apr Swim, bushwalk and mountain bike in the year's most settled weather.

Jun–Aug Enjoy winter with affordable accommodation, minimal crowds and brooding vibes.

Dec–Jan Enjoy the best of Hobart's festival season with food, wine, music, art and culture.

History

The first European to spy Tasmania was Dutch navigator Abel Tasman, who bumped into it in 1642. He named this new place Van Diemen's Land after the Dutch East Indies' governor. It's estimated there were between 5000 and 10,000 indigenous people in Tasmania when Europeans arrived, living in 'bands' of around 50 people, each claiming rights over a specific area of land and being part of one of nine main language groups.

European sealers began to work Bass Strait in 1798, raiding tribal communities along the coast and kidnapping Aboriginal women to act as forced labour and sex slaves. The sealers were uninterested in Aboriginal land and eventually formed commercial relationships, trading dogs and other items.

In the late 1790s Governor King of NSW decided to establish a second settlement in Australia, south of Sydney Cove. The Mornington Peninsula in Victoria was initially considered, but the proposed site was rejected due to a lack of water and, in 1803, Tasmania's Risdon Cove was chosen. One year later the settlement relocated to Sullivans Cove, the site of present-day Hobart, where the Hobart Rivulet offered a reliable water supply.

That same year 74 convicts were shipped out to Van Diemen's Land, with 71 soldiers, plus their 21 wives and 14 children, and by 1833 roughly 2000 convicts a year were sent to Tasmania as punishment for often-trivial crimes. The community quickly developed a very particular character: lawlessness and debauchery were rife.

Although it was ignored in the initial federal ministry, Tasmania officially became a state when Australia's Federation took place in 1901. For Tasmanians, as for mainlanders in the new Commonwealth of Australia, the first half of the 20th century was dominated by war.

Since the early 1970s, the key influence on Tasmanian history has been the ongoing battle between pro-logging companies and environmental groups. In 1972, concerned groups got together to form the United Tasmania Group. Ten years later, thousands of people acted to stop the damming of the Franklin River. Leaders in these movements became a force in Australian federal politics, including Greens party leader Bob Brown, who was a senator from 1996 until 2012.

Aboriginal Tasmania

The culture of the Tasmanian Aboriginal peoples diverged from the way people were living on the mainland, as they developed a sustainable, seasonal culture of hunting, fishing and gathering.

Europeans arrived in 1804 and despite initial friendly exchanges and trade, an unknown number of peaceable Aboriginal people were killed during this early period. In return Aboriginal people began to carry out their own raids. In 1816 Governor Thomas Davey produced his 'Proclamation to the Aborigines', which represented settlers and Indigenous Tasmanians living together amicably – in direct contrast to the realities of a brutal conflict.

By the 1820s these territorial disputes had developed into the so-called Black War, as Aboriginal people increasingly refused to surrender their lands without a fight. In 1828 martial law was declared by Lieutenant-Governor Arthur. Aboriginal groups were systematically murdered, arrested or forced at gunpoint from districts settled by whites – arsenic on bread and steel traps designed to catch humans were used. Many more succumbed to European diseases against which they had no immunity.

As the Black War continued, Lieutenant-Governor Arthur consented to George Augustus Robinson's plan to 'conciliate' the Aboriginal people. In effect Robinson enticed and cajoled virtually all of the Aboriginal people in mainland Tasmania to lay down their arms, leave their traditional lands and accompany him to new settlements. There is strong historical evidence that the people of Oyster Bay followed him to a succession of settlements in the Furneaux Islands based on the promise of sanctuary and land. Instead they were subjected to attempts to 'civilise' and Christianise them, and made to work for the government.

After enduring a number of moves, Tasmania's indigenous inhabitants were finally settled at Wybalenna (Black Man's Houses) on Flinders Island. The people began to die from a potent mixture of despair, homesickness, poor food and respiratory disease. In 1847 those who had managed to survive petitioned Queen Victoria, referring to the 'agreement' they thought Robinson had made with Lieutenant-Governor Arthur on their behalf. Wybalenna was eventually abandoned and the survivors transferred to mainland Tasmania. Of the 135 who had

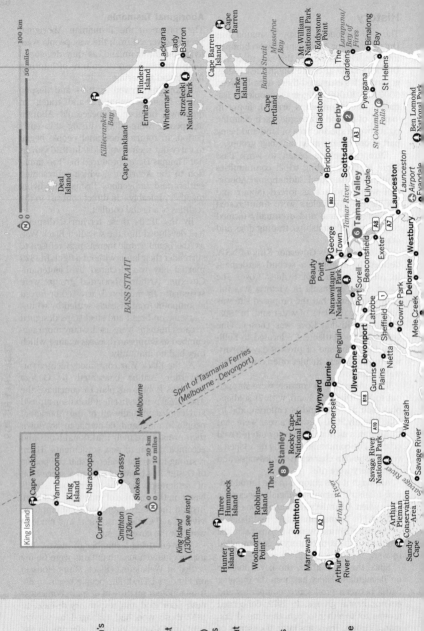

Tasmania Highlights

① MONA (p635)
Being inspired, turned on, appalled, educated and amused at Tasmania's unique art gallery.

② Derby (p674)
Getting down and Derby on the world-class mountain-bike trails in his northeast mining town.

③ Port Arthur Historic Site (p661)
Paying your respects to the past, both distant and recent, at these sombre ruins.

④ Wineglass Bay (p669) Hiking through the Hazards to this fabled bay, then cooling off in the sea.

⑤ Salamanca Market (p648)
Losing yourself in the crowds at Hobart's all-things-to-all-people market.

⑥ Tamar Valley

Wine Route (p684)

Sampling sparkling wine and pinot noir at a series of ridiculously picturesque vineyards on both sides of the Tamar River.

7 Bruny Island

(p652) Dropping in and out of mobile-phone reception for a couple of days while exploring the island's magical coastline.

8 Stanley (p700)

Summiting the Nut and watching penguins shuffle ashore in the evening.

9 Overland Track

(p705) Walking among Tasmania's most striking peaks on a week-long hike from Cradle Mountain to Lake St Clair.

10 Rafting the Franklin River (p710)

Shooting the rapids on a rafting journey down Tasmania's wildest river.

been sent to Flinders Island, only 47 lived to return. The new accommodation again proved to be substandard and within a decade, half of the 47 were dead. The 1876 death of Truganini, the last of these people, instigated the widely propagated myth that the Aboriginal peoples of Tasmania were extinct. However, there were local Aboriginal people in the Furneaux Group of islands and other descendants remained in Tasmania. In the 1970s a movement for Aboriginal land rights began to gain momentum, with community and government groups today still working to restore land rights and preserve Tasmanian Aboriginal language and heritage.

☞ Tours

Mountain Bike & Rock Climbing Tasmania
ADVENTURE

(☎ 0447 712 638; www.mountainbiketasmania. au) Rock-climbing and abseiling adventures in Launceston's Cataract Gorge, Freycinet Peninsula's cliffs and (for the more experienced) the Organ Pipes on kunanyi/Mt Wellington. Also mountain biking at Derby, Ben Lomond, Launceston and Hobart.

Under Down Under Tours
TOURS

(☎ 1800 444 442; www.underdownunder.com. au) Nature-based, backpacker-friendly trips ranging from one to nine days, heading all over the state: Bruny Island, Port Arthur, Wineglass Bay, Richmond, Cradle Mountain... The company also runs the Mt Wellington Descent (p637).

✸✸ Festivals & Events

Ten Days on the Island
CULTURAL

(www.tendays.org.au; ☺ Mar) Australia's only statewide multi-arts festival is a biennial event (odd-numbered years) celebrating Tasmanian arts, music and culture at multiple venues, from the big cities to small towns. Expect concerts, exhibitions, dance, film, theatre and workshops.

ⓘ Information

Tourism Tasmania (www.discovertasmania. com) Tasmania's official tourism promoter.

Hobart Visitor Information Centre (p648) A helpful spot for planning statewide travel, and can handle bookings of all sorts.

Parks & Wildlife Service (☎ 1300 827 727; www.parks.tas.gov.au) Manages Tasmania's parks and reserves. Contact it for park passes, and to book bushwalking permits on the Overland and Three Capes Tracks.

ⓘ Getting There & Away

There are no direct international flights to Tasmania. Visitors need to get to one of Australia's mainland cities and connect to a Tasmania-bound domestic flight to Hobart, Launceston or Devonport. Melbourne and Sydney (and, to a lesser extent, Brisbane) airports have the most frequent direct air links. Also popular is the *Spirit of Tasmania* passenger and car ferry, sailing between Melbourne and Devonport in Tasmania's north.

Flights, cars and tours can be booked online at www.lonelyplanet.com/bookings.

AIR

Jetstar (☎ 13 15 38; www.jetstar.com.au) Qantas' low-cost airline flies from Melbourne, Sydney and Brisbane to Hobart and Launceston. Also flies from Adelaide to Hobart.

Qantas (☎ 13 13 13; www.qantas.com.au) Flights from Sydney, Brisbane and Melbourne to Launceston, and from Sydney and Melbourne to Hobart. Also flies between Melbourne and Devonport.

Regional Express (Rex; ☎ 13 17 13; www. regionalexpress.com.au) Flies from Melbourne to Burnie and King Island.

Tiger Air (☎ 1300 174 266; www.tigerair. au) Flies from Melbourne and the Gold Coast direct to Hobart.

Virgin Australia (☎ 13 67 89; www.virgin australia.com) Flights from Melbourne, Sydney, Brisbane and Perth to Hobart, and from Melbourne, Brisbane and Sydney to Launceston.

BOAT

Two big, red **Spirit of Tasmania** (☎ 03-6419 9320, 1800 634 906; www.spiritoftasmania. com.au; ☜) ferries ply Bass Strait nightly in each direction between Melbourne and Devonport on Tasmania's north coast. The crossing takes around 10½ hours, departing both Melbourne and Devonport at 7.30pm and arriving at 6am. During peak periods – including Christmas, Easter, key holiday weekends and many Saturdays – the schedule is ramped up to two sailings per day, departing at 9am or 9.30am and 9pm or 9.30pm. Check the website for details.

Each ferry can accommodate 1400 passengers and around 500 vehicles and has restaurants, bars, two cinemas and games facilities. The whole experience is a bit of an adventure for Australians, who are used to flying or driving everywhere; kids especially get a kick out of it – daytime sailings even have children's entertainers on board.

The ships' public areas have been designed to cater for wheelchair access, as have a handful of cabins.

ℹ Getting Around

BICYCLE

Tasmania's compact shape makes it arguably Australia's finest state for bicycle travel – there are bikes aplenty down the east coast during summer, and a trickle of cyclists along the hillier and wetter west coast. Roads are generally in good shape, and traffic outside the cities is light. There aren't many areas that can be described as flat, and it's an island...which means island winds.

Transport It's worth bringing your own bike, especially if you're coming via ferry: bike transport on the *Spirit of Tasmania* can cost as little as $19. Another option is buying a bike in Hobart or Launceston and reselling it at the end of your trip – hit the bike shops or the noticeboards at backpacker hostels.

Rental Bike rental is available in the larger cities, and a number of operators offer multi-day cycling tours or experiences such as rolling down kunanyi/Mt Wellington in Hobart or the spectacular Jacobs Ladder on Ben Lomond.

Road rules Bicycle helmets are compulsory in Tasmania, as are white front lights and red rear lights if you're riding in the dark. See www.biketas.org.au for more information.

BUS

Redline Coaches (☑1300 360 000; www.tasredline.com.au) Daily buses between Hobart and Smithton (between Hobart and Burnie only on weekends), servicing the Midland Hwy between Hobart and Launceston, and north-coast towns between Launceston and Smithton, including Mole Creek, Devonport, Penguin, Burnie and Stanley.

Tassielink (☑1300 300 520, 03-6235 7300; www.tassielink.com.au) The main player in the bus game, with extensive statewide services, including express services from the *Spirit of Tasmania* ferry terminal in Devonport to Launceston and Hobart.

From Hobart buses run to Dover (via the Huon Valley), Port Arthur, Richmond, Launceston (via the Midlands Hwy), the east coast as far as Bicheno, and Strahan via Lake St Clair. From Launceston buses run to Cressy, Hobart (via the Midlands Hwy), and Strahan via Devonport, Cradle Mountain and Queenstown. Buses also link Burnie with Strahan via a (relatively) wild northwest route.

CAR & MOTORCYCLE

With limited bus schedules (and no passenger train services), Tasmania is best explored with your own wheels...and you can crank up the music as loud as you like! You can bring vehicles from the mainland to Tasmania on the *Spirit of Tasmania* ferries, so renting may only be cheaper

for shorter trips. Tasmania has the usual slew of international and local car-rental agencies.

Motorcycles are a great way to get around the island, but be prepared for all kinds of weather in any season.

Rental

Practicalities Before hiring a car, ask about any kilometre limitations and find out exactly what the insurance covers. Note that some companies don't cover accidents on unsealed roads, and hike up the excess in the case of any damage on the dirt – a considerable disadvantage, as many of the top Tasmanian destinations are definitely off-piste! Some companies also don't allow their vehicles to be taken across to Bruny Island.

Costs International company rates are pricey in Tasmania: expect to pay upwards of $90 per day for a week's hire of a small car in any season. Book in advance for the best prices. Small Tasmanian and Australian firms rent cars for as little as $25 a day, depending on the season and the duration of the hire. The smaller companies don't often have desks at arrival points, but can usually arrange for your car to be picked up at airports and the ferry terminal in Devonport.

Autorent-Hertz (☑1800 030 500; www.autorent.com.au) Also has campervans for hire and sale.

Avis (☑13 63 33; www.avis.com.au) Also has 4WDs.

Bargain Select (☑1800 300 102; www.selectivecarrentals.com.au) Branches in Hobart, Hobart Airport, Launceston Airport and Devonport.

Budget (☑1300 362 848; www.budget.com.au) Car rental.

Europcar (☑1300 131 390; www.europcar.com.au) Car and 4WD rental.

Lo-Cost Auto Rent (☑03-6231 0550; www.locostautorent.com) Branches in Hobart, Hobart and Launceston airports and the Devonport ferry terminal.

Rent For Less (☑1300 883 728; www.rentforless.com.au) Hobart, Hobart Airport, Launceston Airport and Devonport locations.

Thrifty (☑1300 367 227; www.thrifty.com.au) Car and 4WD rental.

Campervans

Companies offering campervan hire include the following. Rates can be found from around $60 (two berth) or $75 (four berth) per day, usually with minimum five-day hire and unlimited kilometres. For rate comparisons, see www.fetchcampervanhire.com.au.

Apollo (☑1800 777 779; www.apollocamper.com) Also has a backpacker-focused brand called Hippie Camper.

Britz (☎1300 738 087; www.britz.com.au) Also has 4WDs.

Cruisin' Tasmania (☎1300 664 485; www. cruisintasmania.com.au; 3 Runway Pl, Cambridge)

Leisure Rent (☎0429 727 277; www.leisure rent.com.au) At the airports in Hobart, Launceston and Devonport, as well as the *Spirit of Tasmania* ferry terminal in Devonport.

Maui (☎1800 827 821; www.maui.com.au)

Tasmanian Campervan Hire (☎0438 807 118; www.tascamper.com; 2/105 Mornington Rd, Mornington) Hobart-based; specialises in two-berth vans.

Tasmanian Campervan Rentals (☎03-6248 4418; www.tasmaniacampervanrentals.com.au; 12 Aqua Pl, Seven Mile Beach) Based in Hobart.

HOBART

POP 222,356

Australia's second-oldest city and southernmost capital, Hobart is a city where nature rules. It stretches along the foot of kunanyi/ Mt Wellington, angling down to the slate-grey Derwent River, which forms one edge of the city centre. The town's colonial architecture and natural charms are complemented by world-class food and drink, innovative festivals and art experiences – Australia's first-ever art exhibition was held here in 1837 and MONA, Hobart's Museum of Old and New Art, has stamped Tasmania onto the global cultural map.

It's a gorgeous place, and though there's the sobering fact that it's closer to Antarctica than Cairns, Hobart is Australia's second-driest capital city. Weather consequently stops few visitors from exploring the gorgeous surrounds – not far past the outskirts of the city are some great beaches, alpine areas and historic villages.

Hobart was the country of the South East Aboriginal nation, including the muwinina people, to whom Mt Wellington was known as kunanyi.

⊙ Sights

⊙ Central Hobart & the Waterfront

★**Tasmanian Museum & Art Gallery**   MUSEUM
(TMAG; Map p640; ☎03-6165 7000; www.tmag. tas.gov.au; Dunn Pl; ⊙10am-4pm, closed Mon Apr-Dec) **FREE** Incorporating Tasmania's oldest surviving public building, the Commissariat Store (1808), TMAG features Aboriginal and colonial relics and an excellent Antarctic and Southern Ocean display. The gallery curates a collection of Tasmanian colonial and modern art, and there are changing temporary exhibitions. Free guided tours run at 1pm and 2pm from Wednesday to Sunday, plus special themed tours at 11am; check the website to see what's on. There's a cool courtyard cafe and shop too.

Mawson's Huts Replica Museum   MUSEUM
(Map p640; ☎03-6231 1518, 1300 551 422; www. mawsons-huts-replica.org.au; cnr Morrison & Argyle Sts; adult/child/family $15/5/35; ⊙9am-6pm Oct-Apr, 10am-5pm May-Sep) This excellent waterfront installation is a model of one of the huts in which Sir Douglas Mawson's Australasian Antarctic Expedition team, which set sail from Hobart, hunkered down from 1911 to 1914. The replica is painstakingly exact (Mawson's tiny keyboard, a sledge and an ice axe are actually originals) and a knowledgeable guide is on hand to answer your Antarctic enquiries. Imagine 18 men living here, dining on penguin stew...

Waterfront   AREA
(Map p640) Hobartians flock to the city's waterfront like seagulls to chips. Centred on **Victoria Dock** (a working fishing harbour) and **Constitution Dock** (full of floating fish punts and the odd wayward seal), it's a brilliant place to explore. The obligatory Hobart experience is to sit in the sun, munch some fish and chips and watch the harbour hubbub. If you'd prefer something with a knife and fork, there are some superb restaurants here too – head for **Elizabeth Street Pier** or Mures (p644).

Hobart Convict Penitentiary   HISTORIC SITE
(Map p636; ☎03-6231 0911; www.nationaltrust. org.au/places/penitentiary; cnr Brisbane & Campbell Sts; tours adult/child/family $25/15/65; ⊙tours 10am, noon, 2pm, 5.30pm & 7pm Tue-Sun) The courtrooms, cells and gallows at 'the Tench' had a hellish reputation in the 1800s, and every convict in Tasmania passed through here. The barracks are all gone, but the red-brick chapel remains solidly intact. Visits are by tour only, and include a 40-minute film, *Pandemonium*, projected onto the walls of the chapel, where convicts sat for church – it held up to 1500 people and was built atop 36 solitary-confinement cells. Book ahead for night-time ghost tours.

☉ MONA & Northern Hobart

★MONA
MUSEUM, GALLERY

(Museum of Old & New Art; ☑03-6277 9900; www.
mona.net.au; 655 Main Rd, Berriedale; adult/child
$28/free, Tasmanian residents free; ☉10am-6pm
Jan, 10am-6pm Wed-Mon Feb-Apr & Dec, to 5pm
Wed-Mon May-Nov) Twelve kilometres north
of Hobart's city centre, MONA is burrowed
into the Triassic sandstone of a peninsula
jutting into the Derwent River. Arrayed
across three underground levels, the
$75-million museum created by local philan-
thropist-owner David Walsh mixes ancient
antiquities among contemporary artworks.
It's sexy, provocative, disturbing and deeply
engaging – don't miss it.

To get here, catch the MONA ferry (return
standard/posh $22/55) or MONA Roma
shuttle bus ($22) from Hobart's Brooke
St Pier.

★North Hobart
AREA

(Map p636) Hobart at its most bohemian,
the Elizabeth St strip in North Hobart (aka
NoHo) is lined with dozens of cafes, restaurants, bars and pubs – enough to keep you
coming back meal after drink after meal.
Also here is the excellent art-house State
Cinema (p647), and Hobart's staunchest
live-music room, the Republic Bar & Café
(p647). Must-do Hobart!

Royal Tasmanian
Botanical Gardens
GARDENS

(Map p636; ☑03-6166 0451; www.rtbg.tas.gov.au;
Lower Domain Rd, Queen's Domain; ☉8am-6.30pm
Oct-Mar, to 5.30pm Apr & Sep, to 5pm May-Aug)
FREE On the eastern side of the Queen's
Domain park, these beguiling 200-year-old
gardens feature more than 6000 exotic and
native plant species. Picnic on the lawns,
check out the Subantarctic House or grab
a bite at the restaurant or cafe. Call to ask
about guided tours. Down the hill from
the main entrance, opposite Government
House, is the site of the former Beaumaris
Zoo, where the last captive Tasmanian tiger
died in 1936; a couple of dilapidated enclosures remain.

☉ Salamanca Place
& Battery Point

★Salamanca Place
STREET

(Map p640) This picturesque row of three-
and four-storey sandstone warehouses is
a classic example of Australian colonial

architecture. Dating back to the whaling
days of the 1830s, Salamanca Pl was then
the waterfront – goods were winched from
the upper levels of the warehouses directly
onto ships. By the mid-20th century many of
the warehouses had fallen into ruin, before
restorations began in the 1970s. These days
Salamanca hosts myriad restaurants, cafes,
bars and shops, and the unmissable Saturday Salamanca Market (p648).

★Salamanca Arts Centre
ARTS CENTRE

(SAC; Map p640; ☑03-6234 8414; www.salarts.
org.au; 65-77 Salamanca Pl; ☉shops & galleries
9am-5pm) The nonprofit Salamanca Arts
Centre has been here since 1977 and occupies seven Salamanca warehouses. It's home
to dozens of arts organisations and individuals, including excellent shops, galleries,
theatres, studios, performing-arts venues,
a cheese shop, a couple of cafes and public
spaces.

★Battery Point
HISTORIC SITE

(Map p640) Tucked in behind Salamanca Pl,
the old maritime village of Battery Point is
a tight nest of lanes and 19th-century cottages. Spend an afternoon exploring: stumble up Kelly's Steps (Map p640; Kelly St, via
Salamanca Pl) from Salamanca Pl and wander through Princes Park, where the gun
battery of the suburb's name stood, protecting Hobart Town from nautical threats
both real and imagined. Spin around picturesque Arthur Circus, refuel in Hampden
Rd's cafes, then ogle St George's Anglican
Church (Map p636; ☑03-6223 2146; www.
stgeorgesbatterypoint.org; 30 Cromwell St; ☉of-
fice 9.15am-2.15pm Mon-Thu, services 8am & 10am
Sun) – the tower was designed by a convict
architect.

☉ Sandy Bay & South Hobart

★Kunanyi/Mt Wellington
MOUNTAIN

(www.wellingtonpark.org.au; Pinnacle Rd, via Fern
Tree) Ribbed with its striking Organ Pipes
cliffs, kunanyi/Mt Wellington (1271m) towers over Hobart like a benevolent overlord. The view from the top stretches over
Hobart and much of the state's south, and
the slopes are laced with walking trails.
Mountain bikers come for the North South
Track, descending from the Springs to
Glenorchy, while you can also coast down
the sealed summit road on a bike with Mt
Wellington Descent. The Hobart Shuttle Bus Company (☑0408 341 804; www.

TASMANIA HOBART

Hobart

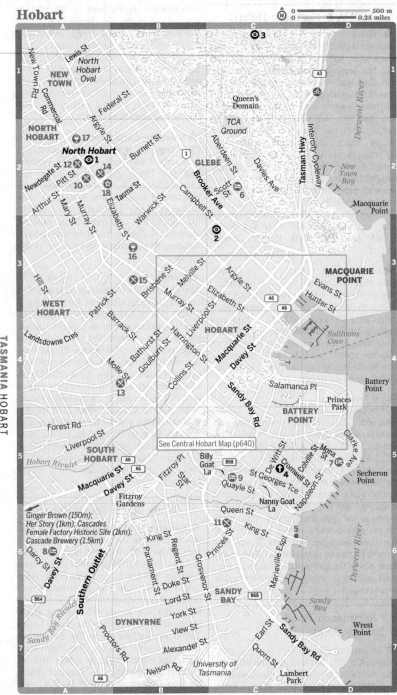

Hobart

◎ **Top Sights**
1 North Hobart A2

◎ **Sights**
2 Hobart Convict Penitentiary C3
3 Royal Tasmanian Botanical
   Gardens C1
4 St George's Anglican Church............... C5

◉ **Activities, Courses & Tours**
   Penitentiary Chapel Ghost
   Tour .... (see 2)
5 Roaring 40s Kayaking C6

◉ **Sleeping**
6 Corinda C2
7 Grande Vue Private Hotel D5
8 Islington A6
9 Quayle Terrace.................................... C5

◎ **Eating**
10 Burger Haus.. A2
11 Don Camillo.. C6
12 Pancho Villa A2
13 Pigeon Hole B4
14 Roaring Grill A2
15 Templo B3

◎ **Drinking & Nightlife**
16 Shambles Brewery B3
17 The Winston... A2
   Willing Bros .... (see 12)

◉ **Entertainment**
18 Republic Bar & Café A2
   State Cinema .... (see 17)

◎ **Shopping**
   State Bookstore .... (see 17)

hobartshuttlebus.com) also runs daily two-hour tours to the summit.

★ **Cascade Brewery** BREWERY
(☏03-6212 7801; www.cascadebrewery.com.au; 140 Cascade Rd, South Hobart; brewery tour adult/child 16-18yr $30/15, Beer School adult/child $15/10) Standing in startling, Gothic isolation next to the clean-running Hobart Rivulet, Australia's oldest brewery (1824) is still pumping out superb beers. The daily one-hour tours involve plenty of history, with tastings at the end. Note that under-16s aren't permitted on the main brewery tour (take the family-friendly Beer School tour instead), and that brewery machinery might not be running if you're here on a weekend (brewers have weekends too). To get here, take bus 446, 447 or 449.

★ **Cascades Female Factory Historic Site** HISTORIC SITE
(☏03-6233 6656, 1800 139 478; www.femalefactory.org.au; 16 Degraves St, South Hobart; adult/child/family $8/5/20, Heritage Tour $18/12/45; ◷9.30am-4pm, tours 10am, 11am, 1pm, 2pm & 3pm) This World Heritage Site was where Hobart's female convicts were incarcerated and put to work. Around 12,500 women were transported to Tasmania, and at its height the Cascades Female Factory held 1200 women – more convicts than Port Arthur ever held at a time. You can explore the hauntingly spare yards with their interpretive installations independently, or take a guided Heritage Tour or the excellent Her Story (p639) dramatisation. To get here by public transport, take bus 446, 447 or 449.

🏃 Activities

Hobart Bike Hire CYCLING
(Map p640; ☏0447 556 189; www.hobartbikehire.com.au; 1a Brooke St; bike/e-bike hire per day from $25/45; ◷9am-5pm) Just in from the Brooke Street Pier, this bike-hire shop has lots of ideas for self-guided tours around the city or along the Derwent River to MONA museum. Maps, locks and helmets are included; kids' trailers, tag-alongs, electric bikes and tandems are available, and you can keep the bike overnight (extra $10) if you're missing your dawn rides.

☞ Tours

★ **Mt Wellington Descent** CYCLING
(Map p640; ☏1800 444 442; www.underdownunder.com.au/tour/mount-wellington-descent; adult/child $85/65; ◷10am & 1pm year-round, plus 4pm Dec-Feb) Take a van ride to the summit of kunanyi/Mt Wellington, and follow with 21km of downhill cruising on a mountain bike. It's terrific fun, with minimal energy output and maximum views. If you want to up the adventure, there's an off-road option. Tours start and end on Elizabeth St, opposite the visitor centre, and last 2½ hours. No kids under eight.

★ **Pennicott Wilderness Journeys** BOATING
(Map p640; ☏03-6234 4270; www.pennicottjourneys.com.au; Dock Head Bldg, Franklin Wharf; tours adult/child from $125/100; ◷7am-6.30pm) Pennicott offers several outstanding boat trips around key southern Tasmanian sights, including trips along Bruny Island, the Tasman Peninsula and the Iron Pot

HOBART IN...

One Day

Get your head into history mode with an amble around **Battery Point** (p635), the storied precinct on the headland southeast of the city centre. Don't miss the photogenic cottages on compact Arthur Circus, the cafes on Hampden Rd and the sleek tower of St George's Anglican Church on Cromwell St. Stop for a pie or pastry at **Jackman & McRoss** (p645), a neighbourhood favourite. After lunch wander down Kelly's Steps to the historic warehouses on Salamanca Pl. If it's Saturday, the **Salamanca Market** (p648) will still be rolling on; otherwise check out the craft shops and galleries in the **Salamanca Arts Centre** (p635) and get caffeinated at **Machine Laundry Café** (p645). Delve into Hobart's Antarctic links at the **Mawson's Huts Replica Museum** (p634) on the waterfront. For dinner, feast on fish and chips at **Flippers** or **Mures** (p644) and then head to the floating Brooke Street Pier for a tipple with a view at the **Glass House** (p646).If you're feeling more earthy, duck back in behind Salamanca Pl for a beer in the garden (or bus) at **Preachers** (p647). End the night with a drink aeons in the making at the refined **Evolve** (p646) spirits bar inside the MACq 01 hotel.

Two Days

On day two stop for breakfast at **Ginger Brown** (p645) as you head up Hobart's overlord mountain, **kunanyi/Mt Wellington** (p635) – you can run a weather check on the summit from the cafe's front window. Then head up and take in the massive view over Hobart and far beyond from the tower-topped summit. Descend the mountain to the floating Brooke Street Pier and catch the ferry out to **MONA** (p635). Grab lunch here at the Source or the casual Faro Wing restaurant and then delve into the gallery's amazing subterranean spaces – a multilevel maze of surprise encounters, quiet moments, hilarious installations, a poo machine and a wall of plaster-cast vulvas. Grab a cab to North Hobart and beef things up for dinner at **Roaring Grill** or go Mex mad at **Pancho Villa** (p645). For a craft beer or three after dinner, try the bohemian **Winston** or **Shambles Brewery** (p646), then see what's screening at the art-house **State Cinema** or wander down to **Republic Bar & Café** (p647) for some live tunes.

Lighthouse south of Hobart. The 7½-hour Tasmanian Seafood Seduction trip, replete with a Neptune's bounty of abalone, lobster, oysters and salmon, is a winner for fans of all things fishy.

★ **Roaring 40s Kayaking**   KAYAKING
(Map p636; ☑0455 949 777; www.roaring 40skayaking.com.au; Marieville Esplanade, Sandy Bay; adult/child $90/60; ☺10am Oct-Apr, 10am & 4pm Nov-Mar) Hobart looks its prettiest from the water. Take a safe, steady, 2½-hour guided paddle with Roaring 40s, named after the prevailing winds at these latitudes. You'll cruise from Sandy Bay, rounding Battery Point and heading into Constitution Dock for some fish and chips while you float, before returning to Sandy Bay.

Above & Beyond   SCENIC FLIGHTS
(Map p640; ☑1300 338 303; www.aboveand beyond.flights; Kings Pier Marina, Franklin Wharf; ☺8am-6pm) This seaplane operator took flight at the end of 2018, offering two main scenic jaunts from Hobart's waterfront: a

25-minute City Scenic tour ($229), looping over the city and as far south as Bruny Island; and a 90-minute Port Arthur & Three Capes Panorama ($545), landing in Port Arthur and flying back out over Cape Pillar and Tasman Island.

Drink Tasmania   DISTILLERY
(☑0475 000 120; www.drinktasmania.com.au; whisky tour per person from $299; ☺Fri & Sun) Tasmanian whisky is riding a wave of awards and popularity, and a day tour with this passionate outfit visits three or four southern distilleries for tastings of top Tassie single malts. Minimum four people. Wine and beer tours also available.

Gourmania   FOOD & DRINK
(☑0419 180 113; www.gourmaniafoodtours.com. au; tours $129-139) Fabulous, flavour-filled walking tours run by passionate local foodies, taking in Salamanca Pl and central Hobart. Expect plenty of tasting opportunities and chats with restaurant, cafe and

shop owners. Saturday sees a two-hour Salamanca Market tour ($95).

Her Story
HISTORY

(☑03-6233 6656; www.livehistoryhobart.com.au/her-story; 16 Degraves St, South Hobart; adult/child/family $25/15/70) An engaging and interactive dramatisation that brings to life the story of a female convict – Mary James – as you roam one of the yards at the Cascades Female Factory Historic Site (p637). The two-actor performance begins at midday daily. Bookings not required.

Red Decker
BUS

(☑03-6236 9116; www.reddecker.com.au; 20-stop pass adult/child/family 24hr $35/20/90, 48hr $40/25/110) Commentated sightseeing on an old London double-decker bus. Buy a 20-stop, hop-on-hop-off pass (valid for one or two days) or do the tour as a 90-minute loop. You can also add a Cascade Brewery tour ($65, including the bus loop) or minibus trip to the summit of kunanyi/Mt Wellington (adult/child $70/45) to the deal.

Lady Nelson
BOATING

(Map p640; ☑03-6234 3348; www.ladynelson.org.au; Elizabeth St Pier; adult/child $30/15; ⊙11am & 1pm Sat & Sun) Sail around the harbour on a 1½-hour tour aboard a replica of the surprisingly compact brig *Lady Nelson,* one of the first colonial ships to sail to Tasmania. Multiday trips are occasionally on offer; check the website. There's an extra 3pm sailing on Saturday and Sunday from mid-December to April.

★ Festivals & Events

★ Dark MOFO
CULTURAL

(www.darkmofo.net.au; ⊙Jun) The sinister sister of Launceston's MONA FOMA (p679), Dark MOFO broods in the half-light of June's winter solstice. Expect live music, installations, readings, film noir, bonfires, red wine and the dark and delightful Winter Feast each night.

★ Sydney to Hobart Yacht Race
SPORTS

(www.rolexsydneyhobart.com; ⊙Dec) After leaving Sydney on Boxing Day, maxi-yachts competing in the world's most gruelling open-ocean race start arriving in Hobart around 28 December – just in time for New Year's Eve. (Yachties sure can party...) Check the yachts out in Constitution Dock.

Festival of Voices
MUSIC

(www.festivalofvoices.com; ⊙Jul) Sing to keep the winter chills at bay during Australia's largest vocal festival, featuring myriad performances, workshops, cabaret and choirs at venues around town. Things get warmest at the Big Sing Bonfire.

Taste of Tasmania
FOOD & DRINK

(www.thetasteoftasmania.com.au; Princes Wharf; ⊙Dec-Jan) On either side of New Year's Eve, this week-long harbourside event is a celebration of Tassie's gastronomic prowess. The seafood, wines and cheeses are predictably fab, or you can branch out into mushrooms, truffles, raspberries and much more. Live music, and a private New Year's Eve party.

HOBART FOR CHILDREN

Parents won't break the bank keeping the troops entertained in Hobart. The Salamanca Place area abounds in diversions, with the street performers, buskers and visual smorgasbord of Saturday's Salamanca Market (p635) captivating kids of all ages. The free Friday-night Rektango (p647) music event in the courtyard at the Salamanca Arts Centre is also a family-friendly affair. Drive the kids up the wall for a change, belaying them as they fearlessly scale the indoor walls (or crawl through the caving tunnels) at the city-centre **Rockit Climbing** (Map p640; ☑03-6234 1090; www.rockitclimbing.com.au; 54 Bathurst St; adult/child/family $17/15/50, incl gear $25/18/60; ⊙noon-9pm Mon-Fri, to 6pm Sat & Sun) gym.

There are plenty of rainy-day attractions to satisfy your child (or inner child). The Tasmanian Museum & Art Gallery (p634) give kids the chance to understand Aboriginal history, get the low-down on the Tasmanian tiger, and ogle shiny stones. Give the little blighters a concept of true hardship at the Mawson's Huts Replica Museum (p634). It's life, Antarctic-style.

Pick up the free *LetsGoKids* (www.letsgokids.com.au) magazine at the Hobart Visitor Information Centre for activity ideas.

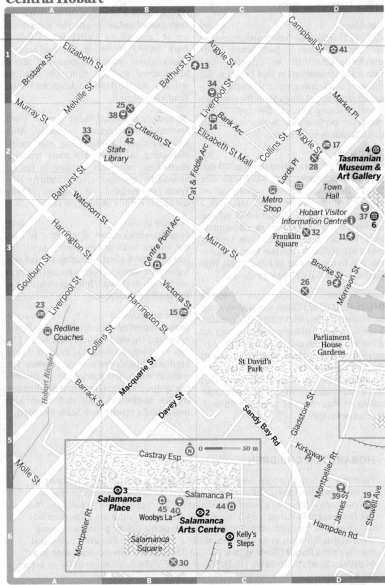

Australian Wooden Boat Festival CULTURAL
(☎03-6223 3375; www.australianwoodenboatfest
ival.com.au; ⊙Feb) A biennial event (odd-
numbered years) showcasing Tasmania's
boat-building heritage and maritime traditions. You can almost smell the Huon pine.
Coincides with the Royal Hobart Regatta.

🛏 Sleeping

BIG4 Hobart Airport
Tourist Park   CARAVAN PARK $
(☎1800 441 184; www.hobartairporttouristpark.
com.au; 2 Flight St, Cambridge; powered sites/cab-
ins from $40/145; ❄⑨) Plane-spot from your

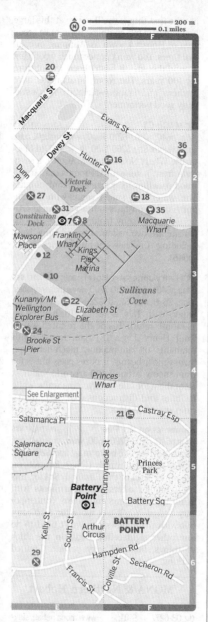

Central Hobart

◉ Top Sights
1 Battery Point	E5
2 Salamanca Arts Centre	C6
3 Salamanca Place	B6
4 Tasmanian Museum & Art Gallery	D2

◎ Sights
5 Kelly's Steps	C6
6 Mawson's Huts Replica Museum	D3
7 Waterfront	E2

⊕ Activities, Courses & Tours
8 Above & Beyond	E2
9 Hobart Bike Hire	D3
10 Lady Nelson	E3
11 Mt Wellington Descent	D3
12 Pennicott Wilderness Journeys	E3
13 Rockit Climbing	C1

⊜ Sleeping
14 Alabama Hotel	C2
15 Astor Private Hotel	B4
16 Henry Jones Art Hotel	F2
17 Hobart Central YHA	D2
18 MACq 01	F2
19 Montacute	D6
20 Old Woolstore Apartment Hotel	E1
21 Salamanca Wharf Hotel	F4
22 Somerset on the Pier	E3
23 The Nook	A4

⊗ Eating
24 Aløft	E4
25 Bury Me Standing	B2
26 Daci & Daci	D3
27 Flippers	E2
28 Franklin	D2
29 Jackman & McRoss	E6
30 Machine Laundry Café	B6
31 Mures	E2
32 Street Eats @ Franko	D3
33 Urban Greek	A2

⊜ Drinking & Nightlife
34 Brunswick Hotel	C1
35 Evolve	F2
Glass House	(see 24)
36 Hobart Brewing Company	F2
37 Lark Distillery	D3
38 New Sydney Hotel	B2
39 Preachers	D6
40 The Den	B6

⊛ Entertainment
Rektango	(see 2)
41 Theatre Royal	D1

⊜ Shopping
42 Farm Gate Market	B2
43 Fullers Bookshop	B3
44 Handmark Gallery	C6
45 Salamanca Market	B6

TASMANIA HOBART

cabin or caravan at this big, clean and grassy caravan park beside Hobart Airport. Space at each campsite is generous and there are four rows of cabins, a camp kitchen and an undercover BBQ area, with plenty of local travel info posted around. Perfectly located if you've got an early flight.

🛏 Central Hobart & the Waterfront

⭐ Alabama Hotel
HOTEL **$**

(Map p640; 📞 0499 987 698; www.alabama hobart.com.au; L1, 72 Liverpool St; d/tw $100/110; 📶) 🎵 Sweet home Alabama! This old art-deco boozer – once a grim, sticky-carpet lush magnet – has settled into a new life as a boutique budget hotel. None of the 17 rooms has a bathroom, but the shared facilities are immaculate. Decor is funky and colourful with retro-deco flourishes, and there's an all-day bar with a sunny balcony.

The Nook
HOSTEL **$**

(Map p640; 📞 03-6135 4044; www.thenookback packers.com; 251 Liverpool St; dm/d from $26/85; 📶) It's less of a nook and more of a reconfigured old pub, but the Nook is doing things right. Fourteen tidy rooms extend above a sociable, sun-lit living space, with a large BBQ deck area out the back. There are free bus tours to kunanyi/Mt Wellington and MONA twice a week, and a couple of bikes for hire (half/full day $8/14).

Hobart Central YHA
HOSTEL **$**

(Map p640; 📞 03-6231 2660; www.yha.com.au; 9 Argyle St; dm from $25, d & tw with/without bathroom from $132/104, f from $163; 📶) Adjoining a historic hotel, this simple but clean YHA offers bright, secure accommodation right in the middle of town. Spread over three maze-like levels are dorms of all sizes, including nifty en-suite rooms and family-sized rooms. No parking, but you're within walking distance of everything here.

⭐ Astor Private Hotel
HOTEL **$$**

(Map p640; 📞 03-6234 6611; www.astorprivate hotel.com.au; 157 Macquarie St; d from $150, s/d with shared bathroom from $89/110, all incl breakfast; 📶) A rambling central 1920s charmer, the Astor is probably Hobart's most characterful hotel, from the stained-glass windows (and seemingly stained-glass carpets) to the lofty ceilings (complete with ceiling roses) and the irrepressible Tildy, who runs it all like a family home. Older-style rooms have shared bathrooms, while more recently refurbished rooms have en suites.

Old Woolstore Apartment Hotel
HOTEL **$$**

(Map p640; 📞 1800 814 676, 03-6235 5355; www. oldwoolstore.com.au; 1 Macquarie St; d from $149, 1-/2-bedroom apt from $189/239; 📶) Oodles of parking and super-friendly staff

are the first things you'll notice at this large hotel-apartment complex in a once-seedy area of Hobart known as Wapping in colonial times. You won't notice much wool lying around though – it hasn't been a wool store for 100 years. The roomy apartments have kitchens and laundry facilities. A consistently good performer.

⭐ MACq 01
HOTEL **$$$**

(Map p640; 📞 03-6210 7600; www.macq01.com. au; 18 Hunter St; r $260-1400; 📶) Old Macquarie Wharf No 1 is now MACq 01, a sassy waterfront hotel with 114 rooms that are all wood panelling, concrete and jaunty angles. The waterfront suites come with private butlers, and upstairs suites get a huge artificial-grass balcony looking over the docks. On-site are two restaurants and three bars, including the new-yet-prehistoric Evolve (p646).

⭐ Henry Jones Art Hotel
BOUTIQUE HOTEL **$$$**

(Map p640; 📞 03-6210 7700; www.thehenryjones. com; 25 Hunter St; d $280-1200; 📶) Super-swish HJs is feeling fresh after an 18-month refurb. Inside the restored waterfront Henry Jones IXL jam factory, with remnants of jam-making machinery and huge timber beams, it oozes class but is far from snooty. Around 400 artworks – almost all of them for sale – enliven the walls, while facilities and distractions (bar, restaurants, cafe) are world class.

Somerset on the Pier
APARTMENT **$$$**

(Map p640; 📞 03-6220 6600; www.somerset.com; Elizabeth St Pier; 1-/2-bedroom apt from $255/340; 📶) In a definitively Hobart location, on the upper level of the Elizabeth St Pier, this cool complex offers luxe apartments with beaut harbour views and breezy, contemporary design. You'll pay more for a balcony, but with these views you won't need to do any other sightseeing. Right in the thick of things, but still very private. Limited parking.

🛏 MONA & Northern Hobart

MONA Pavilions
BOUTIQUE HOTEL **$$$**

(📞 03-6277 9911; www.mona.net.au/stay/mona-pavilions; MONA, 655 Main Rd, Berriedale; d from $750; 📶) For a slice of artistic luxury, book an uber-chic pavilion at MONA, 12km north of the city. The eight mod, self-contained chalets (one- and two-bedroom) are dressed to the nines, with private balconies, wine cellars, river views, private artworks from the MONA gallery's collection and oh-so-discreet service. The indoor swimming pool is an aid to relaxation, and MONA is in your backyard.

A tip: stay over on a Tuesday, when MONA is closed, and you can get a private, exclusive tour of the gallery.

Corinda B&B $$$
(Map p636; ☑03-6234 1590; http://corinda.com. au; 17 Glebe St, Glebe; r & cottages incl breakfast from $250; P☎) This gorgeous renovated Victorian mansion built by the owner's great-great grandfather, a former Hobart mayor, sits high on the Glebe hillside a short (steep!) walk from town. Each room is different – the loo with a view in the Verandah Room is a winner – and there are three cottages and two ultra-modern pavilions sprinkled through the meticulously maintained parterre gardens.

Salamanca Place & Battery Point

★**Montacute** HOSTEL $
(Map p640; ☑03-6212 0474; www.montacute. com.au; 1 Stowell Ave, Battery Point; dm/tw/d from $40/105/115; P☎) Many Hobart hostels are cheap remodellings of old pubs, but Montacute – a renovated house in Battery Point – sets the bar a mile higher, with immaculate rooms and shared bathrooms, appealing art, quality linen and mattresses, a lovely lounge with the feel of a salon, and bikes ($10) for guests. It's in a quiet street, but just steps away from the Salamanca action.

★**Quayle Terrace** RENTAL HOUSE $$
(Map p636; ☑0418 395 543; 51 Quayle St, Battery Point; d $190-220, extra person $20; P✱☎) With no signage, this tastefully renovated terrace house will make you feel as though you're part of the neighbourhood. On a residential street tracing the boundary between Battery Point and Sandy Bay, the two-storey, two-bedroom house is contemporarily furnished, with a cosy gas fire and stone-walled courtyard. Free street parking; minimum three-night stay.

★**Grande Vue Private Hotel** B&B $$$
(Map p636; ☑03-6223 8216; www.grandevue hotel.com.au; 8 Mona St, Battery Point; 1-bedroom unit $265-295, 2-bedroom unit $350; P☎) 'Vues' from the best rooms at this tastefully restored 1906 mansion take in a broad sweep of the Derwent River, or kunanyi/ Mt Wellington in the other direction – only room 1 lacks a full water or mountain view. Sleek bathrooms, kitchenettes and super-friendly service lift Grande Vue to the top of the Battery Point B&B pile. Continental breakfast costs $15.

Salamanca Wharf Hotel APARTMENT $$$
(Map p640; ☑03-6224 7007; www.salamanca wharfhotel.com; 17a Castray Esplanade, Battery Point; d from $265; P✱☎) Filling a gap between historic sandstone ordnance stores just east of Salamanca Pl, these 22 slick studios and one-bedroom apartments offer nifty kitchens, cool Antarctic photos and an unbeatable location (though views are mixed). Units at the front have balconies; those at the back have baths. Penthouse suites are also available (from $395) and there's a cool cafe downstairs.

Sandy Bay & South Hobart

★**Islington** BOUTIQUE HOTEL $$$
(Map p636; ☑03-6220 2123; www.islingtonhotel. com; 321 Davey St, South Hobart; d from $425; P✱☎) Classy Islington is one of Hobart's finest hotels, but it might also be the city's second-best art gallery – those are indeed works by Hockney, Matisse, Warhol and Whiteley, plus a sketch by Picasso. Service is attentive but understated, with breakfast served in an expansive conservatory overlooking the glorious garden. Exquisite private dinners are also available. No children aged under 15.

Eating

Central Hobart & the Waterfront

★**Bury Me Standing** CAFE $
(Map p640; ☑0424 365 027; www.facebook. com/burymestandinghobarttown; 83-85 Bathurst St; bagels $5-13; ☉6am-4pm Mon-Fri, 7am-2pm Sat & Sun) Stepping into this brilliant little coffee-and-bagel joint, run by a chipper Minnesotan who ended up in Hobart accidentally, is like waking into an old-time curiosity shop – skeleton wallpaper one side, bright swatches of paisley wrapping paper on the other. Seats are few and bagels are pot-boiled in the traditional method – don't go past the meat-free bagel dogs.

★**Flippers**   FISH & CHIPS **$**
(Map p640; ☑03-6234 3101; www.flippersfish
andchips.com.au; 1 Constitution Wharf; fish & chips
$12-17; ◷9am-9.30pm; 🌶) There are four
floating fish punts moored in Constitution
Dock, selling fresh-caught seafood either
uncooked or cooked. Our pick is Flippers, an
enduring favourite with a voluptuous fish-
shaped profile. Fillets of flathead and curls
of calamari come straight from the deep
blue sea and into the deep fryer. The local
seagulls will adore you.

Grab dessert from the floating ice-cream
punt next door.

Street Eats @ Franko   MARKET **$**
(Map p640; ☑03-6234 5625, 0408 543 179; www.
streeteatsfranko.com.au; Franklin Sq, 70 Macquarie
St; ◷4.30-9pm Fri Nov-Apr) This buzzy night
market showcases fabulous southern Tasmanian food, with stalls ringed around the
fountain in Franklin Sq. There's live music
and plenty to drink too. Look for **palawa
kipli**, serving up bush tucker with a twist
– think crickets (yes,crickets!) with guaca-
mole, mushrooms and saltbush.

Daci & Daci   BAKERY **$**
(Map p640; ☑03-6224 9237; www.dacianddaci
bakers.com.au; 11 Murray St; mains $10-18;
◷7am-5pm) A 2018 refurb has this stylish
bakery-cafe looking all leather and latte, and
suitably slick for the steady flow of public
servants and parliamentary folk. The seasonal soup with house bread is great value
at $12.50, and the dessert list is extensive.
Sit inside if it's wet, or on the split-level deck
jutting out into Murray St if it's not.

★**Templo**   ITALIAN **$$**
(Map p636; ☑03-6234 7659; www.templo.com.
au; 98 Patrick St; plates $14-32; ◷6pm-late Thu &
Fri, noon-2.30pm & 6pm-late Sat-Mon) Unpreten-
tious little Templo, on a nondescript reach
of Patrick St, is a Hobart dining treasure.
With only 20 seats (bookings essential),
most of them around a communal table, and
only three or four Italian-inspired mains to
choose from, it's an exercise in selectivity
and sharing (your personal space, and your
food). Survey the pricey-but-memorable
wine list at the cute bar.

Mures   SEAFOOD **$$**
(Map p640; ☑Lower Deck 03-6231 2009, Upper
Deck 03-6231 1999; www.mures.com.au; Victoria Dock; mains Lower Deck $15-29, Upper Deck
$36-42; ◷Lower Deck 7am-10pm, Upper Deck
11am-late; 🐟) The big fish in Hobart's seafood

scene, bottle-green Mures has a **Lower Deck**
with fishmonger, fish-and-chip shop and ice
cream, while the **Upper Deck** is a sassier,
bookable affair, with silvery dockside views
and à la carte seafood dishes. The seafood
comes direct from Mures' own boat.

★**Aløft**   MODERN AUSTRALIAN **$$$**
(Map p640; ☑03-6223 1619; www.aloftrestaurant.
com; Brooke St Pier; plates $14-36, banquets from
$80; ◷6pm-late Tue-Sat; 🌶) Boldly claiming
itself as Hobart's top restaurant, angular
Aløft occupies a lofty eyrie atop the floating
Brooke St Pier. Menu hits include silken tofu
with burnt onion and baby leeks, and crispy
duck leg with kimchi. If you can drag your
gaze away from the view, service and pres-
entation are both excellent, in an unpreten-
tious Hobart kinda way.

Franklin   MODERN AUSTRALIAN **$$$**
(Map p640; ☑03-6234 3375; www.franklinhobart.
com.au; 30 Argyle St; shared plates $16-40;
◷5pm-late Tue-Sat) Regularly on lists of Australia's top restaurants, Franklin fills a lofty
industrial space (the former *Hobart Mercury* newspaper printing room) and is all
concrete, steel beams, cowhide and curtains.
Everything is on show in the central kitchen,
as the likes of wood-roasted octopus and Lit-
tlewood Farm lamb slip in and out of the
10-tonne oven.

Urban Greek   GREEK **$$$**
(Map p640; ☑03-6109 4712; www.urbangreek
hobart.com; 103 Murray St; mains $30-49;
◷5-10pm Mon-Thu & Sat, noon-2.30pm & 5-10pm
Fri & Sun) Fancy Mediterranean offerings in
a former garage fitted out with bent copper
lighting conduits, a timber bar, polished con-
crete floors and an intimidating Minotaur
etched into the copper-plate wall. Expect
generous Greek classics done to perfection
(moussaka, saganaki, charcoal-grilled octo-
pus), family-style hospitality and imported
Greek beers and wines.

🍴 MONA & Northern Hobart

★**Burger Haus**   BURGERS **$**
(Map p636; ☑03-6234 9507; www.theburger
haus.com.au; 364a Elizabeth St, North Hobart;
burgers $13-16; ◷11.30am-late) Boasting big
beefy burgers, a little outdoor terrace, craft
beers and ciders, and a view that combines
a concrete car park with the moody hues
of kunanyi/Mt Wellington, this back-lane
burger bar has it all! The Haus Burger (with

bacon, onion rings, caramelised pineapple and mustard mayo) reigns supreme.

★ Pigeon Hole
CAFE $$

(Map p636; ☑ 03-6236 9306; www.pigeonhole cafe.com.au; 93 Goulburn St, West Hobart; mains $12-22; ⊙ 7.30am-4pm Mon-Fri, 8am-3.30pm Sat & Sun) This compact bakery-cafe is the kind of place every inner-city neighbourhood should have. The love child of a family farm at Hobart's edge, its menu is filled with farm produce that merges into the likes of whipped sweet corn tofu with roasted asparagus, or potato and smoked eel rösti covered in abundant greens.

Myu
ASIAN $$

(☑ 03-6228 7777; www.facebook.com/Myu.easy bites; 2/93 New Town Rd, New Town; mains $19-28; ⊙ 5.30-8.30pm Tue-Sat) Let yourself in on a little Hobart secret at this unsigned, unadulterated dining room in an unprepossessing strip of shops where the ever-changing menu rolls straight off the home printer each night. Expect a pan-Asian journey – the night's menu might include beef rendang, Hainanese chicken, bao and momos.

Pancho Villa
MEXICAN $$

(Map p636; ☑ 03-6234 4161; www.panchovilla. au; cnr Elizabeth & Pitt Sts, North Hobart; small plates $16-25, large plates $26-38; ⊙ 5.30pm-late) A red-brick bank turned super-moody tequila bar and restaurant with Day of the Dead skulls, pressed metal lanterns and stained-glass windows – it's like stepping into a Gothic novel. Choose from creative tacos, quesadillas and BBQ jerk chicken (with churros dulce de leche to sweeten the finish), with 40 tequilas to fire things up.

The Source
MODERN AUSTRALIAN $$$

(☑ 03-6277 9904; www.mona.net.au/eat-drink/ the-source-restaurant; MONA, 655 Main Rd, Berriedale; mains $22-40; ⊙ 7.30-10am & noon-2pm Wed-Mon, 6pm-late Fri & Sat) The Source is an excellent (and not overpriced) restaurant at MONA (p635), named after a painting by John Olsen hanging in the entryway. It's a stylish affair (lots of glass), especially in the evening as the shadows march across the Derwent River just below. Hope the abalone with mushrooms and chicken skin is on the menu.

Roaring Grill
STEAK $$$

(Map p636; ☑ 03-6231 1301; www.roaringgrill. com; 301 Elizabeth St, North Hobart; mains $26-60; ⊙ 5pm-late Mon & Tue, from noon Wed-Sun)

Beefing up the offerings in NoHo is this sassy steakhouse named for the Roaring Forties winds that wash and dry Tasmania. It's a stylish split-level fit-out – exposed brickwork, dark-wood tables and globular glassware – with the usual cuts (eye fillet, scotch fillet, rib eye, fillet mignon) done well rather than well done. Also serves up fish, ceviche and oysters.

🍴 Salamanca Place & Battery Point

★ Jackman & McRoss
BAKERY $

(Map p640; ☑ 03-6223 3186; 57-59 Hampden Rd, Battery Point; items $4-14, breakfast $6-15; ⊙ 7am-5pm) Make sure you stop by this enduring Hobart favourite, even if it's just to gawk at the display cabinet full of delectable pies, tarts, baguettes and pastries. Breakfasts involve scrambled egg, bacon and avocado panini or potato, asparagus and brie frittatas, or perhaps just grab a duck, cranberry and walnut sausage roll.

Machine Laundry Café
CAFE $

(Map p640; ☑ 03-6224 9922; 12 Salamanca Sq; mains $11-23; ⊙ 7.30am-5pm Mon-Sat, from 8am Sun) Washing machines and dryers; pavement chessboard; retro styling; parmesan, caramelised onion and spinach pancakes; and the 'mental lentil' panini...breakfast or lunch is never dull at this brilliant and bright cafe squished into a corner of Salamanca Sq.

🍴 Sandy Bay & South Hobart

★ Ginger Brown
CAFE $

(☑ 03-6223 3531; 464 Macquarie St, South Hobart; mains $10-20; ⊙ 7.30am-4pm Mon-Fri, from 8.30am Sat & Sun; 🚗 👶) This perennially popular and well-run cafe presents a wide-ranging menu, including a house crumpet with raspberry mascarpone and lemon curd, a black quinoa salad and a poke bowl. It's very kid- and cyclist-friendly, and the coffee is the best in South Hobart. Last orders 3pm. Grab the window bench for fine views of kunanyi/Mt Wellington.

Don Camillo
ITALIAN $$$

(Map p636; ☑ 03-6234 1006; www.doncamillo restaurant.com; 5 Magnet Ct, Sandy Bay; mains $28-42; ⊙ 11.30am-2.30pm Thu & Fri, 5.30-9.30pm Tue-Sat) Claiming to be Hobart's oldest restaurant (since 1965), venerable Don Camillo is still turning out a tight menu of classic

Italian pastas, risottos, meat dishes and Mama's cassata – no pizzas here – on red-checked tablecloths. Look for the red Vespa parked out the front.

🍷 Drinking & Nightlife

Central Hobart & the Waterfront

★ New Sydney Hotel   PUB
(Map p640; ☑ 03-6234 4516; www.newsydney hotel.com.au; 87 Bathurst St; ⊙ noon-10pm Mon, to midnight Tue-Sat, 4-9pm Sun) This low-key city pub is the best boozer in the CBD, with open fires, creative pub food (such as trout Kiev, or hazelnut and beetroot gnocchi; mains $15 to $38) and more than a dozen island craft beers and ciders on tap. No poker machines!

Glass House   COCKTAIL BAR
(Map p640; ☑ 03-6223 1032; www.theglass.house; Brooke St Pier; ⊙ noon-late) The very fancy Glass House sits in the prow of the floating Brooke St Pier, sandwiched between Aløft (p644) and Brooke St Larder, with a huge window-wall affording uninterrupted views across the Derwent River. Put on your best duds, order a martini with sheep-whey vodka and soak it all in. Fab bar food too (small plates $12 to $36).

Evolve   LOUNGE
(Map p640; ☑ 03-6210 7656; http://evolve spiritsbar.com.au; MACq 01, 18 Hunter St; ⊙ 5pm-1am) What's prehistorically old is new at this sophisticated spirits bar inside the MACq 01 hotel, where you'll drink among an array of fossils, including a mammoth tusk and a Russian cave bear. Some of the whiskies – including the 1950 Glen Grant single malt (got a spare $7000?) – are almost museum pieces themselves.

Brunswick Hotel   PUB
(Map p640; ☑ 03-6234 4981; www.brunswick hotelhobart.com.au; 67 Liverpool St; ⊙ 9am-midnight Mon-Sat) Purportedly Australia's second-oldest pub (pouring since 1827), the convict-built Brunswick has the city centre's best beer garden in the form of its Grill steakhouse in the rear courtyard. 'Parmi and pint' night segues nicely into trivia night on Wednesday.

Hobart Brewing Company   CRAFT BEER
(Map p640; ☑ 03-6231 9779; www.hobart brewingco.com.au; 16 Evans St; ⊙ 3-10pm Wed & Thu, to 11pm Fri, 2-11pm Sat, 2-5.30pm Sun) In a big red shed on Macquarie Point, fronted by the Red Square community space (fancy a haircut from a caravan hair salon?), Hobart Brewing Company is doing good things with craft beer. There are up to a dozen creative brews on tap, plus regular live music and the **Hobart Blues, Brews and Barbecues** festival around February or March.

Lark Distillery   DISTILLERY
(Map p640; ☑ 03-6231 9088; www.larkdistillery. com; 14 Davey St; ⊙ noon-8pm Sun-Thu, to 11pm Fri & Sat) The pioneer and patriarch of Tasmanian distilleries, Lark has a moody, low-slung cellar door and whisky bar at the water's edge (the actual distillery is in the Coal River Valley, 20 minutes' drive away). Work your way along the whisky wall, and if the weather's right, sit out the back in the whisky garden overlooking Constitution Dock.

🍺 MONA & Northern Hobart

★ Shambles Brewery   CRAFT BEER
(Map p636; ☑ 03-6289 5639; www.shambles brewery.com.au; 222 Elizabeth St, North Hobart; ⊙ 4pm-late Wed & Thu, from noon Fri-Sun) An excellent brewery just south of the NoHo strip, with minimalist interiors and a concrete-block bar. Head out the back to drink among the vats (and have a hit of table tennis). Tasting paddles are $14, or refill your 'growler' (1.9L bottle) to take home and savour. Terrific beery bar food too: burgers, wallaby drumsticks, fried chicken and the like.

★ The Winston   PUB
(Map p636; ☑ 03-6231 2299; www.thewinstonbar. com; 381 Elizabeth St, North Hobart; ⊙ 4pm-late) The grim old art-deco Eaglehawk pub has been transformed into the Winston, a craftbeery, US-style alehouse. Grab a pint of the house stout from one of the beardy guys behind the bar and check out the wall of US registration plates near the pool table. The food flavours – buffalo wings, grilled corn, brisket – match the setting.

Willing Bros   WINE BAR
(Map p636; ☑ 03-6234 3053; www.facebook.com/ willingbros; 390 Elizabeth St, North Hobart; ⊙ 3pm-late Tue-Sun) This classy wine bar is NoHo's most sophisticated resident. Pull up a window seat at the front of the skinny room and sip something hip from the tightly edited menu of reds, whites and bubbles. Food

drifts from goat curd ravioli to bangers and mash – perfect fodder for a post-movie debrief.

Salamanca Place & Battery Point

The Den   BAR
(Map p640; ☑0499 888 233; http://theden.com.au; 63 Salamanca Pl; ☺11am-late) Among the string of dark drinking dens along Salamanca Pl, this Den has emerged as a shaft of light. Framed around a central fireplace and ranging over two levels, it's all lodge-in-the-woods style in non-woodsy Salamanca. There's a menu of share plates ($14 to $22) and bao buns, and gin rules the roost, with more than 60 on offer.

Preachers   BAR
(Map p640; ☑03-6223 3621; www.facebook.com/preachershobart; 5 Knopwood St, Battery Point; ☺noon-11.30pm) Hipster beards are optional but preferred at this 1849 sailmaker's cottage turned bar. The ramshackle beer garden is the place to be in Hobart on a summer evening, while the retro sofa inside is a warm hibernation den in winter. Great list of craft beers and wine, while the burgers keep the inebriation in vague check.

☆ Entertainment

★ Republic Bar & Café   LIVE MUSIC
(Map p636; ☑03-6234 6954; www.republicbar.com; 299 Elizabeth St, North Hobart; ☺3pm-late Mon & Tue, from noon Wed-Sun; ☎) The Republic is a raucous art-deco pub hosting live music every night (often with free entry). It's the number-one live-music pub around town, with an always interesting line-up, including international acts. Loads of different beers and excellent food (mains $20 to $33; try the Jack Daniel's–marinated rump steak). Just the kind of place you'd love to call your local.

★ State Cinema   CINEMA
(Map p636; ☑03-6234 6318; www.statecinema.com.au; 375 Elizabeth St, North Hobart; tickets adult/child $20/16) Saved from the wrecking ball in the 1980s, the 11-screen State (built in 1913) shows independent and art-house flicks. There's a great cafe and bar on-site, plus a summertime rooftop screen (with another bar!), a browse-worthy bookshop (p648) and the foodie temptations of North Hobart's restaurants right outside. Magic.

Theatre Royal   THEATRE
(Map p640; ☑03-6233 2299, box office 03-6146 3300; www.theatreroyal.com.au; 29 Campbell St; ☺box office 10am-4pm Tue-Sun) This venerable old stager is Australia's oldest continuously operating theatre, with actors first treading the boards here back in 1837 (the foundation stone says 1834, but it took them a few years to finish it). Theatregoers can expect an eclectic range of music plus ballet, theatre, opera, comedy and university revues.

Guided **tours** are available (one-hour tour adult/child $15/10) at 11am Monday, Wednesday and Friday. At the time of writing, the theatre was closed for renovations, and set to reopen as part of the Hedberg performing arts centre in mid-2019, so call ahead to check on the status of its backstage tours.

Rektango   LIVE MUSIC
(Map p640; ☑03-6234 8414; www.salarts.org.au/rektango; Salamanca Arts Centre Courtyard, Salamanca Pl; ☺5.30-7.30pm Fri) Some of Hobart's best live tunes get an airing every Friday night in the Salamanca Arts Centre Courtyard, best reached off Woobys Lane. It's a free community event that started with the current millennium, adopting its name from a band that sometimes graces the stage. Acts vary month to month – expect anything from African beats to rockabilly, folk and gypsy-Latino.

Blundstone Arena   SPECTATOR SPORT
(Bellerive Oval; ☑tickets 13 28 49, tours 03-6282 0400; www.blundstonearena.com.au; 15 Derwent St, Bellerive; tours adult/chld $15/5; ☺tours 10am Tue & Wed, 1pm Thu) Hobart's home of cricket and football is across the Derwent River from the city in Bellerive. The AFL's North Melbourne Football Club plays four home games here a year, while international Test, one-day and T20 cricket matches also pull good crowds. Guided arena tours run if there's no game happening, also taking in the **Tasmanian Cricket Museum** (☑03-6282 0433; adult/child $2/1; ☺10am-3pm Tue-Thu).

🛍 Shopping

★ Farm Gate Market   MARKET
(Map p640; ☑03-6234 5625; www.farmgatemarket.com.au; Bathurst St, btwn Elizabeth & Murray Sts; ☺8.30am-1pm Sun) 🌿 Bathurst St turns organic at this weekly foodie favourite that brings in primary producers from across the state – expect fresh fruit and veg, raw

SALAMANCA MARKET

Every Saturday since 1972, the open-air Salamanca Market (Map p640; ☑03-6238 2843; www.salamancamarket.com.au; ⊘8am-3pm Sat) has filled the tree-lined expanses of Salamanca Pl with more than 300 stalls. Fresh organic produce, secondhand clothes and books, tacky tourist souvenirs, ceramics and woodwork, cheap sunglasses, antiques, exuberant buskers, quality food and drink... it's all here, but people-watching is the real name of the game.

A free shuttle bus runs between various stops in the city and the market every 10 minutes between 9am and 2pm (see the website for stop details). On foot, the market is around 10 minutes from the city centre. Rain or shine – don't miss it!

honey, BBQ octopus, cut flowers and organic kimchi and yoghurt. A seat in the sun on the road with a Lady Hester sourdough doughnut is the place to be on a Sunday morning.

★ **Fullers Bookshop** BOOKS
(Map p640; ☑03-6234 3800; www.fullersbookshop.com.au; 131 Collins St; ⊘8.30am-6pm Mon-Fri, 9am-5pm Sat, 10am-4pm Sun) Hobart's best bookshop has a great range of literature and travel guides, plus regular book launches, signings and readings, and the writerly Afterword Café in the corner. Fullers has been a true hub of the Hobart literary scene for almost a century.

★ **State Bookstore** BOOKS
(Map p636; ☑03-6169 0720; www.state cinemabookstore.com.au; 377 Elizabeth St, North Hobart; ⊘9.30am-7pm Sun & Mon, to 9pm Tue-Sat) Usually the movie is adapted from the book, but in this case the bookshop is adapted from the adjoining State Cinema (p647). Recently relocated into a larger space, its mainstays are art, architecture, literary fiction and high-quality cookbooks – all the good things.

★ **Handmark Gallery** ART
(Map p640; ☑03-6223 7895; www.handmark.com.au; 77 Salamanca Pl; ⊘10am-5pm Mon-Fri, to 4pm Sat & Sun) A key tenant at the Salamanca Arts Centre (p635), Handmark has been here for 30 years, displaying unique

ceramics, glass, woodwork and jewellery, plus paintings and sculpture – 100% Tasmanian, 100% exquisite.

ℹ️ Information

EMERGENCY

Hobart Police Station (☑03-6230 2111, nonemergency assistance 13 14 44; www.police.tas.gov.au; 37-43 Liverpool St; ⊘24hr) Hobart's main cop shop.

INTERNET ACCESS

State Library of Tasmania (☑03-6165 5597; http://libraries.tas.gov.au; 91 Murray St; ⊘9.30am-6pm Mon-Thu, to 7pm Fri, to 2pm Sat) Free wi-fi and pre-booked internet terminals.

MEDICAL SERVICES

My Chemist Salamanca (☑03-6224 9994; www.mychemist.com.au; 6 Montpelier Retreat, Battery Point; ⊘8.30am-6pm Mon-Fri, to 5pm Sat, 10am-4pm Sun) Handy pharmacy just off Salamanca Pl.

Royal Hobart Hospital (☑03-6166 8308; www.dhhs.tas.gov.au; 48 Liverpool St; ⊘24hr) Accident and emergency, running round the clock.

Salamanca Medical Centre (☑03-6223 8181; www.salamancamc.com.au; 5a Gladstone St, Battery Point; ⊘8am-4pm Mon-Fri, 10am-3pm Sat, 10am-1pm Sun) General medical appointments, just off Salamanca Pl.

MONEY

Major banks have branches and ATMs around Elizabeth St Mall, with more ATMs around Salamanca Pl, Salamanca Sq and along Elizabeth St in North Hobart.

POST

General Post Office (GPO; Map p640; ☑03-6236 3575; www.auspost.com.au; 9 Elizabeth St; ⊘8.30am-6pm Mon-Fri, 9am-12.30pm Sat) Forget about the bus mall and check out the heritage architecture! It was built in 1905 in lavish Edwardian baroque style.

TOURIST INFORMATION

Hobart Visitor Information Centre (Map p640; ☑03-6238 4222; www.hobarttravelcentre.com.au; 20 Davey St; ⊘8.30am-5pm Mon-Fri, from 9am Sat & Sun) Poised perfectly between the CBD and the waterfront, the visitor centre offers information, maps and statewide tour, transport and accommodation bookings.

ℹ️ Getting There & Away

AIR

Don't get excited by the signs – Hobart's 'international' airport (☑03-6216 1600; www.hobart

airport.com.au; 6 Hinkler Rd, Cambridge) has only domestic flights, with services operated by Qantas, Virgin Australia, Jetstar and Tiger Air. Direct flights arrive from Melbourne, Sydney, Brisbane and (less regularly) Adelaide, Perth and Gold Coast. The airport is in Cambridge, 19km east of the city.

BUS

In the absence of passenger trains, buses are the mainstay of public transport to/from Hobart. There are two main intrastate bus companies, **Redline Coaches** (Map p640; ☑1300 360 000; www.tasredline.com.au; 230 Liverpool St; ⊙9am-1.15pm & 2.15-6pm Mon-Fri, 9am-noon & 12.30-3.30pm Sat, 9am-noon, 1-4pm & 4.30-6pm Sun) and Tassielink (p633). Redline runs between Hobart and Burnie via Launceston and Devonport (and towns in between), while Tassielink has statewide routes. Check online for fares, routes, arrival/departure locations and timetables. Tassielink buses leave from various points around Hobart's city centre – call or check the website for updates.

ⓘ Getting Around

TO/FROM THE AIRPORT

A taxi into the city will cost around $45 and take about 20 minutes.

SkyBus (☑1300 759 287; www.skybus.com.au; adult/senior/child $19.50/16.50/10; ☎) Airport shuttle service (30 minutes) running from three destinations in the city: Brooke St Pier, Franklin Sq and the Grand Chancellor Hotel (buses from the airport don't stop at Franklin Sq). The first bus leaves the city at 4.45am, in time for 6am flights, and services continue until the day's final flight.

BUS

The local bus network is operated by **Metro Tasmania** (☑13 22 01; www.metrotas.com.au), which is reliable but infrequent outside of business hours. The **Metro Shop** (Map p640; ☑13 22 01; www.metrotas.com.au; 22 Elizabeth St; ⊙8am-5.30pm Mon-Fri) handles ticketing and enquiries: most buses depart from this section of Elizabeth St, or from nearby Franklin Sq.

Alternatively, the Hobart Shuttle Bus Company (p637) has minibus transfers and tours from Hobart to Richmond and the summit of kunanyi/Mt Wellington, while the **kunanyi/Mt Wellington Explorer Bus** (Map p640; ☑03-6236 9116; www.mtwellingtonexplorer.com.au; Brooke St Pier; one way pass adult/child $25/15, all-day pass $35/25; ⊙9am, 10am, 11am, 1pm, 2pm & 3pm Nov-Apr, 9.30am, 11.30am & 2.30pm May-Oct) can also haul you (and your bike) up the mountain.

TAXI

Hobart Maxis (☑13 32 22; www.hobartmaxitaxi.com) Taxi vans that are wheelchair accessible and suited to groups.

Yellow Cab Co (☑13 19 24; http://hobart.yellowcab.com.au) Standard cabs (not all of which are yellow).

AROUND HOBART

Richmond & Around

POP 858

Straddling the Coal River 27km northeast of Hobart, Richmond is the colonial spirit set in stone. It was once a strategic military post and convict station on the road to Port Arthur, and is clipped together by Australia's oldest road bridge. Riddled with 19th-century buildings, it's arguably Tasmania's premier historic town, but businesses here tend to err on the 'kitsch colonial' side of tourism – it's either terrific or twee, depending on your perspective.

That said, Richmond is certainly a picturesque little town and the kids will love chasing the ducks around the riverbanks. It's a good place to tumble back into at night, after a wine crawl through the Coal River Valley.

⊙ Sights

★**Sullivans Cove Distillery** DISTILLERY
(☑03-6248 5399; www.sullivanscove.com; 1/10 Lamb Pl, Cambridge; tour/tasting $30/20; ⊙10am-4pm) Remarkable things come from this unremarkable-looking tin shed. Sullivans Cove has managed to produce the world's best single-malt whisky and the best single-cask single malt, as adjudged at the 2014 and 2018 World Whiskies Awards. Tours run at 11am and 3pm daily (bookings essential) or you can just drop in for a tasting.

★**Bonorong Wildlife Sanctuary** WILDLIFE RESERVE
(☑03-6268 1184; www.bonorong.com.au; 593 Briggs Rd, Brighton; adult/child/family $30/16/85; ⊙9am-5pm) In spacious enclosures ringed around a large grassy area, Forester kangaroos lounge about like beach-goers at this impressive wildlife park – its name derives from an Aboriginal word meaning 'native compcape bruny light anion'. You'll see Tasmanian devils, wombats, echidnas, quolls and a couple of mainland imports – koalas and emus – and you can watch vets working at the hospital, treating

resident and rescued wildlife. Nocturnal tours available (adult/child from $160/85). Bonorong is 18km west of Richmond, well signed on the edge of Brighton.

Richmond Bridge BRIDGE

(Wellington St, Richmond) This stately and shapely sandstone bridge, with its four arches, is the town's proud centrepiece. The oldest road bridge in Australia, it was built by convicts in 1823 and still funnels traffic across the Coal River. It's purportedly haunted by the 'Flagellator of Richmond', George Grover, who was murdered here in 1832.

Frogmore Creek WINERY

(☑03-6274 5844; www.frogmorecreek.com.au; 699 Richmond Rd, Cambridge; ◷10am-5pm, restaurant 11.30am-3pm) Overlooking the Mt Pleasant Observatory, flashy Frogmore Creek has a smart restaurant serving lunch, along with excellent chardonnay, pinot noir and sticky botrytis riesling. Head upstairs to see *A Flawed History of Tasmanian Wine*, an in-floor jigsaw by local artist Tom Samek, and the oldest-known bottles of Tasmanian sparkling, dating from the 1840s. Restaurant bookings recommended (mains $18 to $27).

Pooseum MUSEUM

(☑0413 802 206; http://pooseum.com.au; 22 Bridge St, Richmond; adult/child $16/8; ◷10am-5pm Wed-Sun; 🐾) This new science museum takes its scat seriously, with interactive displays on animal poo, from beaches made up entirely of parrotfish poo, to the work of paleo-scatologists – more faeces facts than you can poke a toilet brush at. Kids will think the 'Pootube' videos disgustingly good.

Puddleduck Vineyard WINERY

(☑03-6260 2301; www.puddleduck.com.au; 992 Richmond Rd, Richmond; ◷10am-5pm; 🐾) There's no mistaking the theme: push past the rubber ducks, souvenir ducks, duck socks and duck greeting cards to find this small, family-run vineyard producing just 1500 cases per year, including the 'Bubbleduck' sparkling white. Its wines are sold exclusively at the cellar door – this duck doesn't wander far. Tastings start at $5.

🛏 Sleeping & Eating

Daisy Bank Cottages COTTAGE $$

(☑0417 202 963; www.daisybankcottages.com.au; 78 Middle Tea Tree Rd, Richmond; d from $175, spa cottage from $185, extra person $30; 🛜) A rural delight: two spotless, stylish, self-contained

units (one with spa) in a converted 1840s sandstone barn on a working sheep farm at Richmond's very edge. There are loft bedrooms, farmhouse-style interiors, views of the Richmond rooftops and plenty of bucolic distractions for kids. Full farm breakfast, including eggs from the property, costs $10.

Richmond Bakery BAKERY $

(☑03-6260 2628; 50 Bridge St, off Edward St, Richmond; items $4-8; ◷7am-6pm) Come for takeaway pies, pastries, sandwiches, croissants, muffins and cakes, or munch on them in the courtyard. Their version of the Tasmanian classic, curried scallop pie, is as generous on the scallops as they come.

★ Coal River Farm BISTRO $$

(☑03-6248 4960, 1300 455 196; www.coalriverfarm.com.au; 634 Richmond Rd, Cambridge; mains breakfast $14-22, lunch $18-29; ◷9am-5pm; 🐾) A snappy piece of hillside architecture, Coal River Farm is a family-friendly spot to try some artisanal cheese and chocolate or grab some breakfast or lunch in the bistro – perhaps some roasted pork belly with tomato-braised white beans. You can also pick berries in season, feed the goats and collect eggs from the chooks.

There's 'high cheese' at 2.30pm each day, and you can bundle up your lunch order into a picnic (blanket supplied) at the top of the orchard.

❶ Getting There & Away

Tassielink (p633) runs multiple services daily (Monday to Saturday) from Hobart to Richmond ($7.60, 45 minutes), departing Hobart from outside the town hall on Elizabeth St.

Richmond Tourist Bus (Hobart Shuttle Bus; ☑0408 341 804; www.hobartshuttlebus.com; adult/child return $30/20) runs a daily (except Saturday) service from Hobart, with three hours to explore Richmond (unguided) before returning. It departs from the Hobart Visitor Information Centre at noon.

Mt Field National Park & Around

Proclaimed in 1916, Mt Field is Tasmania's oldest national park (along with Freycinet) and sits little more than an hour's drive north of Hobart. There's an upstairs, downstairs structure to the park, with its rainforest-covered lower slopes leaking waterfalls, while its tips hold exposed alpine moorlands, a laid-back ski field and the wonderful Tarn

Shelf, which turns on one of Tasmania's finest autumn spectacles when the native fagus (beech) glows gold.

It's an accessible day trip from Hobart, or you can bunk down overnight. Either way, things can get mighty chilly here – bring warm clothing!

◉ Sights & Activities

Russell Falls   WATERFALL
(www.parks.tas.gov.au; off Lake Dobson Rd) The park's star water feature is the magnificently tiered, 45m-high Russell Falls, an easy 20-minute return amble from behind the Mt Field National Park visitor info centre. The sealed path, through a beautiful section of rainforest, is suitable for prams and wheelchairs.

Salmon Ponds   FARM
(☑03-6261 5663; www.salmonponds.com.au; 70 Salmon Ponds Rd, Plenty; adult/child/family $8/6/22; ☺9am-4pm Nov-Apr, 10am-3pm May-Oct; ♦) In 1864 rainbow and brown trout were bred for the first time in the southern hemisphere at this hatchery, 9km west of New Norfolk. You can feed the fish in the display ponds, which are strung through a Victorian-style English garden, visit the hatchery and check out the angling museum's rods, reels and flies. The restaurant (mains $19 to $21) specialises in sweet and savoury pancakes (try the smoked salmon and Camembert) plus Tasmanian wines, and serves decent coffee.

Agrarian Kitchen   COOKING
(☑03-6261 1099; www.theagrariankitchen.com; 650 Lachlan Rd, Lachlan; classes from $385) Located in a 19th-century schoolhouse in the Derwent Valley village of Lachlan, about a 40-minute drive from Hobart, is Tasmania's first hands-on, farm-based cookery school. The Kitchen's working farm provides organically grown vegetables, fruit, berries and herbs for the classes. Other ingredients are sourced from local farmers, fishers and artisanal producers.

Tassie Bound   KAYAKING
(☑0417 008 422; www.tassiebound.com.au; all trips adult/child $150/100) Float serenely downstream before splashing through grade II rapids on this three-hour Derwent River kayak trip, with lunch on the riverbank. The trip departs from Bushy Park. Other Tassie Bound offerings include an evening platypus-spotting paddle and a two-hour kayak trip on Lake Pedder.

🛏 Sleeping & Eating

★**Duffy's Country Accommodation**   COTTAGE $$
(☑03-6288 1373; www.duffyscountry.com; 49 Clark's Rd, Westerway; d $135-165, extra adult/child $25/20; ❋🐾) Overlooking a strawberry field at Westerway (8km east of Mt Field National Park) are these great-value, immaculate self-contained cottages: one studio-style cabin for couples, and one two-bedroom rangers' hut, relocated from Mt Field National Park, for families. There are also a couple of cute two-bed bunkhouses, and wallaby sightings are a distinct possibility.

Possum Shed   CAFE $$
(☑03-6288 1364; www.thepossumshed.com.au; 1654 Gordon River Rd, Westerway; mains $15-20; ☺10am-4pm Mon-Fri, 9am-5pm Sat & Sun; ♦) Walking into the Possum Shed is a bit like stumbling into a CWA (Country Women's Association) meeting. Knitted goodies and other crafts line the walls, and staff get about in kitchen aprons as they dish out great Devonshire teas, burgers and salads. Sit out on the rear deck and scan the Tyenna River below for a platypus.

★**Agrarian Eatery**   MODERN AUSTRALIAN $$$
(☑03-6262 0011; www.theagrariankitchen.com; 11a The Avenue, New Norfolk; small plates $18-22, large plates $36-44; ☺11am-3pm Thu-Mon) This classy love child of the Agrarian Kitchen sits inside a cavernous former ward of the Willow Court psychiatric hospital. The main wall is lined with jars of preserved fruits, and produce comes predominantly from the community garden across the road or the Agrarian Kitchen's garden. Expect the likes of wood-roasted suckling pig and rich farmers' cheese dumpling.

❶ Information

Mt Field National Park Visitor Centre (☑03-6288 1149; www.parks.tas.gov.au; 66 Lake Dobson Rd; park day pass per vehicle/person $24/12; ☺9am-4pm) This visitor centre houses the Waterfalls Cafe and the Curiosity Room with touch-and-feel exhibits on the landscape. It sells park passes, and has reams of information on walks and ranger-led summer activities. There are excellent day-use facilities around the centre, including BBQs, shelters, lawns and a children's playground.

❶ Getting There & Away

The 70km drive from Hobart to Mt Field through the Derwent Valley and Bushy Park is an absolute stunner, with river rapids, hop fields, old oast houses, rows of poplars and hawthorn hedgerows. There's no public transport to the park, but some Hobart-based tour operators offer Mt Field day trips; try Tours Tasmania (p658).

Derwent Valley Link (☎ 03-6261 4653; www.derwentvalleylink.com.au) can get you close to the park, with buses from Hobart to New Norfolk ($8.30) three to 13 times daily, and one service daily continuing to Westerway ($13.30), 8km from the park entrance.

THE SOUTHEAST

Still harbours, misty valleys, a fringe of wilderness – Tasmania's southeast has much to entice. The apple-producing heartland of the Apple Isle, this fertile area also churns out cherries, apricots, Atlantic salmon, wines, mushrooms, cheeses, vodka...and apple cider! The wide, tea-coloured Huon River remains the region's lifeblood and pretty much everything that claims 'southernmost in Australia' is here.

As you head south, the fruity hillsides of the Huon Valley give way to the sparkling inlets of the D'Entrecasteaux Channel, with Bruny Island afloat just offshore. Hartz Mountains National Park rises a short way inland, providing a grandstand view into the depths of Tasmania's southwest wilderness, and, further south, the epic South Coast Track kicks off at magnificent Recherche Bay.

The plethora of French names here reflects the fact that French explorers Bruni d'Entrecasteaux and Nicolas Baudin charted much of the region's coastline in the 1790s and early 1800s.

❶ Getting There & Away

Tassielink (p633) Runs daily buses from Hobart through Huonville ($10.40, 45 minutes), Franklin ($10.40, one hour) and Geeveston ($13.70, 1¼ hours) to Dover ($21, 1¾ hours). Also runs a service from Hobart through Huonville to Cygnet ($11, one hour).

Bruny Island

POP 620

Bruny Island is effectively two islands tied together by a string-thin, 5km-long sandy isthmus called the Neck. Renowned for its wildlife (little penguins, echidnas, muttonbirds), the island's two halves – North Bruny and South Bruny – exude very different characters: the rural north and, luring most visitors, the rugged south with its high cliffs, beaches and national park, which runs a frame around much of South Bruny's coast. Access is via a short car-ferry chug from Kettering to North Bruny.

Bruny's coastal scenery is magical, showing itself off on beautiful walking tracks around Fluted Cape, Labillardiere Peninsula, Cape Queen Elizabeth and surf-slapped Cloudy Bay. The calories are quickly replenished by the island's revered cheeses, oysters, wine and whisky. Too many visitors cram their Bruny experience into one day: if you can handle the peace and quiet, stay a few days. Bruny Island takes hold slowly, then tends not to let go.

❂ Sights

The Neck   NATURE RESERVE
(www.brunyisland.org.au/about-bruny-island/the-neck; Bruny Island Main Rd) `FREE` Park midway across the isthmus – aka the Neck – between North and South Bruny and climb to the **Truganini Memorial** for broad views of both ends of the island. Another timber walkway crosses the Neck to the beach on the ocean side, where you can watch little penguins shuffling ashore at dusk, politely sharing their burrows with clumsy muttonbirds.

South Bruny National Park   NATIONAL PARK
(☎ 03-6293 1419; www.parks.tas.gov.au; South Bruny; park day pass per vehicle/person $24/12) This national park comprises extensive coastal and wooded hinterland areas. Near Adventure Bay an easy trail leads to the old whaling station at **Grass Point** (1½ hours return), with possible sightings of Bruny's unusual white wallabies. From here, you can climb to **Fluted Cape** (2½ hours return), atop some of Australia's highest sea cliffs.

The park's southwestern portion covers the **Labillardiere Peninsula**, **Cloudy Bay** and Cape Bruny Lighthouse, with walks ranging from leisurely beach rambles to a six-hour peninsula circuit.

Cape Bruny Lighthouse   LIGHTHOUSE
(☎ 03-6293 1419; www.parks.tas.gov.au; Lighthouse Rd, South Bruny; park day pass per vehicle/person $24/12; ☺ lighthouse tours 10am-3.45pm) Designed by colonial architect John Lee Archer, the 1836, 13m-high stone lighthouse on one of Bruny's southern tips overlooks a particularly rugged section of coast. It was

The Southeast

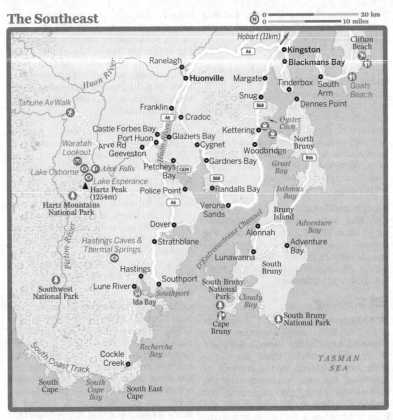

Australia's longest-serving lighthouse – 158 years when it was decommissioned in the 1990s. The lamps were originally powered by sperm-whale oil. You can check out the inside of the lighthouse with **Bruny Island Lighthouse Tours** (☎ 0437 499 795; www.bruny islandlighthousetours.com.au; adult/child $15/10; ☺ 10am-3.45pm), or just wander around the surrounding reserve. National park entry fees apply.

Bligh Museum of
Pacific Exploration MUSEUM
(☎ 03-6293 1117; www.southcom.com.au/~jontan/index.html; 876 Adventure Bay Rd, Adventure Bay; adult/senior/child $4/3/2; ☺ 10am-4pm) This curio-crammed, windowless, church-like museum details the local exploits of explorers Bligh, Cook, Furneaux, Baudin and, of course, Bruni d'Entrecasteaux. The engaging collection includes maps, charts and manuscripts – crowned by the remains of the tree to which Cook is said to have tied up his

ship, and Bligh's original diary from his stop in Adventure Bay in 1792.

🖝 Tours

★ **Bruny Island Cruises** BOATING
(Pennicott Wilderness Journeys; ☎ 03-6293 1465; www.brunycruises.com.au; 1005 Adventure Bay Rd, Adventure Bay; adult/child/family $135/85/430) This excellent three-hour tour skims along the island's awesome southeast coastline, taking in seal colonies, bays, caves and towering sea cliffs, with chances of spotting migrating whales. Trips depart Adventure Bay at 11am daily, with an extra 2pm cruise in summer.

You can also take the tour as a full-day trip from Hobart (departs Hobart 7.45am), or leave your car at Kettering and take the tour bus (departs 8.30am), which goes onto the ferry and down to Adventure Bay (additional charges apply).

The company's large Adventure Bay base features a decent seafood restaurant (mains $11 to $38, open 10am to 3pm).

Bruny Island Long Weekend
WALKING

(📞 0437 256 270; www.brunyislandlongweekend. com.au; per person $1895) Indulgent but active three-day tours around Bruny's best bits, with expert guides and staying in a private campground – tents have king-size beds and there's a decadent hot outdoor shower. Activities include wading out to an oyster farm, and walks on Cloudy Bay and Mt Mangana, Bruny's highest point. Trips depart from Hobart each Tuesday and Friday, October to April.

Bruny Island Safaris
TOURS

(📞 03-6144 3045; www.brunyislandsafaris.com. au; per person $155) Full-day tours departing Hobart, focusing on Bruny's landscapes and its culinary bounty, including oysters, salmon, cheese, wine and berries, plus a visit to Cape Bruny Lighthouse.

🛏 Sleeping

★ 43 Degrees
APARTMENT $$

(📞 03-6293 1018; www.43degrees.com.au; 1 Lumeah Rd, Adventure Bay; studio/ste $190/240) 🏖 At 43°S latitude, these five hangar-shaped apartments at the entrance to Adventure Bay were constructed by the owner-builder and have impeccable eco credentials. They are doubled-glazed and triple-insulated, with plantation or recycled timbers throughout and waste water treated and released into the thriving garden. Suites have freestanding spa baths; studios have corner spas.

★ Adventure Bay Retreat
COTTAGE $$$

(📞 0419 300 392; www.adventurebayretreat.com. au; 49 Hayes Rd, Adventure Bay; cottages from $260; 🐾) Four discreet and very individual houses are sprinkled around a rural setting at Adventure Bay's edge. The spa Cottage is all cuteness, while the flash Lair (double $600) is ultra-contemporary and filled with bespoke Tasmanian furnishings and fittings. The large Lodge is perfect for families, with its mezzanine filled with toys and games, and an outdoor playground.

🍴 Eating & Drinking

★ Bruny Island Cheese Co
CHEESE $

(📞 03-6260 6353; www.brunyislandcheese.com. au; 1807 Bruny Island Main Rd, Great Bay; tastings free, meals from $12; ⊙ 9.30am-5pm) Hankering for a quivering sliver of cheese? Head to the Bruny Island Cheese Co, where Kiwi cheesemaker Nick Haddow produces eight varieties of fromage. The in-house Bruny Island Beer Co operates under the same auspices: try the Cloudy Bay pale ale and some artisanal wood-fired sourdough bread with your cheese platter, eaten under the eucalypts and blackwoods.

★ Get Shucked Oyster Farm
SEAFOOD $$

(📞 0439 303 597; www.getshucked.com.au; 1735 Bruny Island Main Rd, Great Bay; 6 oysters unshucked/shucked from $12/15, 12 oysters from $20/23; ⊙ 9.30am-4.30pm) Get Shucked cultivates the 'fuel for love'. Visit the tasting room, or sit out on the wooden deck overlooking the leases in Great Bay, and wolf down a briny dozen with wasabi sour cream and a cold flute of Jansz bubbles. Shucking brilliant.

There's even a drive-through window if you want your bivalves in a hurry.

Hotel Bruny
PUB FOOD $$

(📞 03-6293 1148; www.hotelbruny.com; 3959 Bruny Island Main Rd, Alonnah, South Bruny; mains $22-36; ⊙ 11am-late; 🐾) If you're staying the night on Bruny, your dinner choices are singular: Hotel Bruny. The menu at this shoreline pub is tastily parochial – the oysters come seven ways, the lamb shoulder is roasted in Moo Brew pale ale and Bruny honey, the chicken parma is covered in Bruny Island cheese, and there's Bruny beer and cider on tap.

Bruny Island House of Whisky
BAR

(📞 03-6260 6344; www.tasmanianhouseofwhisky. com.au; 360 Lennon Rd, North Bruny; ⊙ 9.30am-5.30pm, reduced winter hours) Stand in awe before this lustrous, dazzling bar, full of bottles containing Tasmania's best single malt whiskies (including the house Trappers Hut whisky) and a lone, limited-release gin – Seclusion – distilled exclusively for the House of Whisky. Get a single tasting (from $12) or a flight of four (from $40). Gourmet platters are also available.

It's just 3km from the ferry terminal, so a perfect way to end a Bruny visit, but don't blame us if you miss the last ferry back...

ℹ Information

Bruny D'Entrecasteaux Visitor Centre (📞 03-6267 4494; www.brunyislandaccommodation andtours.com; Ferry Rd; ⊙ 9am-5pm) The main Bruny Island visitor centre is actually at the ferry terminal in Kettering (ie not on the island). At the rear of the **Bruny Island Gateway** cafe and provedore (cafe open 7am to 5pm), the centre is a one-stop shop for info on island accommodation and services.

ℹ Getting There & Away

Bruny Island Ferry (☑1300 127 869; www.sealinkbrunyisland.com.au; Ferry Rd, Kettering; car return $32-38, motorcycle/bike/foot passenger return $6/6/free) Vehicles are ferried from Kettering to Roberts Point on North Bruny (20 minutes) on three boats. The first ferry leaves Kettering at 6.30am (7.30am Sunday); the last one at 7pm, with departures almost every half-hour. The first ferry from Bruny sails at 7am (8am Sunday); the last one at 7.15pm. No bookings – queue up at the jetties.

Cygnet

POP 1556

Groovy Cygnet likes to wear its hair long. Originally named Port de Cygne Noir (Port of the Black Swan) by Bruni d'Entrecasteaux, after the big *noir* birds that cruise around the bay, it's been youthfully reincarnated as Cygnet (a baby swan) and is a town where free-flight living is the norm – a dreadlocked, arty enclave that also functions as a major fruit-producing centre. Weathered farmers and banjo-carrying hippies chat amiably outside vegetarian cafes in the main street and share blanket space at the annual folk festival.

◉ Sights

Pagan Cider   BREWERY
(☑0448 688 809; www.pagancider.com.au; 7891 Channel Hwy; tastings free; ☺11am-5pm) Get fruity at this cider-maker outside of Cygnet that uses eating apples and pears, as well as squeezing out Australia's first natural cherry-apple cider and seasonal ciders, such as blueberry, strawberry and quince. Mop up the tasting with a crepe or galette from the **Pandemonium** food van outside.

🛏 Sleeping & Eating

Cygnet's Secret Garden   B&B $$
(☑03-6295 0223; www.cygnets-secret-garden.com.au; 7 Mary St; r $160-210; 🛜) Dating from 1913, this lovely Federation-style weatherboard house sits at the bottom of the main street (across from the pub – handy) and has four B&B rooms with plenty of heritage charm. There are sofas aplenty on the veranda deck, and the continental breakfasts feature homemade jams and fruit from the owners' orchard.

★**Red Velvet Lounge**   VEGETARIAN $$
(☑03-6295 0730; www.redvelvetlounge.com.au; 24 Mary St; mains $13-24; ☺9am-4pm Wed, Sat & Sun, to 8pm Thu, to 9pm Fri; 🍴) 🌱 The journey hasn't been as smooth as velvet for this hippy-happy cafe – it burned down in 2014 – but its reincarnation as a vegetarian and vegan eatery is a good one. Enjoy cauliflower steak, vegan salad plates and halloumi fries. There's a curry night on Thursday, with live music and wood-fired pizzas on Friday nights.

Huon Valley

The biggest town in the southeast, agrarian Huonville flanks the Huon River 40km south of Hobart, not far from some lovely vineyards, cider-makers and small villages. Having made its name as Tasmania's apple-growing powerhouse, it remains a functional, working town – low on charm but with all the services you need. Nearby Ranelagh is an agricultural hub with a couple of stellar foodie stops.

The Huon Hwy traces the Huon River south, passing the settlements of Franklin and Port Huon. These were once important shipping ports for apples, but nowadays the old wharves and packing sheds are decaying like old fruit. Strung-out, boatie-central Franklin is the oldest town in the Huon Valley, and the wide, shallow, reedy riverscape here is one of Australia's best rowing courses.

◉ Sights & Activities

★**Willie Smith's Apple Shed**   BREWERY
(☑03-6266 4345; www.williesmiths.com.au; 2064 Huon Hwy, Grove; ☺10am-5pm Mon-Thu & Sat, to 9pm Fri, to 6pm Sun) At Grove, 5km north of Huonville, this barn-like wooden shed is home to Willie Smith's Organic Apple Cider, and functions as a cafe-cum-provedore-cum-museum. Swing by for a coffee, a cheese plate, meals ($12 to $34), or a cider-tasting paddle ($12). The museum (gold coin donation) zooms in on Huonville's appley heritage, with old cider presses and an amazing wall of different apple varieties. Peek in also at the apple brandy distillery (tours 2pm Thursday to Monday).

TASMANIA CYGNET

Wooden Boat Centre
WORKSHOP

(☑03-6266 3586; www.woodenboatcentre.com; 3333 Huon Hwy, Franklin; adult/child/family $15/5/30; ⊘9.30am-4.30pm Mon-Fri, 10.30am-4pm Sun) This engaging, sea-centric spot is a unique institution running accredited courses in traditional boat building (from one week to build a kayak, up to eight weeks for a dinghy), using Tasmanian timbers. A volunteer guide will walk you through the centre, where you can watch boats being cobbled together and catch a glorious whiff of Huon pine.

Huon Bikes
CYCLING

(☑0447 270 669; www.huonbikes.com; 105 Wilmot Rd, Huonville; per day $36; ⊘10am-4pm Tue-Thu, to 3pm Fri, to 5pm Sat) Saddle up for a day ride on a vintage, retro or mountain bike and go exploring around Huonville. Helmets and locks are provided. See the website for some ideas on local routes to follow, from 12km to 34km.

🛏 Sleeping & Eating

Huon Valley Caravan Park
CARAVAN PARK $

(☑0438 304 383; www.huonvalleycaravanpark.com.au; 177 Wilmot Rd, Huonville; unpowered/powered sites from $36/39, en-suite sites $65) At the junction of the Huon and Mountain Rivers is this lush, grassy patch on a working farm. There are no cabins, but there's a fabulous camp kitchen with a pizza oven, tidy amenities, and nifty powered sites with elevated, brightly painted en suites. You're free to pick from the strawberry patch, herb garden and orchard.

The farm is part of the Devil Recovery Program, and at 4pm each day it runs a devil feeding and farm show for guests, with working dogs, chicks for the kids to handle and so on.

Huon Bush Retreats
CABIN, CAMPGROUND $$

(☑03-6264 2233; www.huonbushretreats.com; 300 Browns Rd, Ranelagh; unpowered sites $30, tepees $145, cabins $185-420) 🦘 This private habitat reserve sits deep in the forest on the flanks of not-so-miserable Mt Misery. There are five modern, self-contained, one- and two-bedroom cabins, two tepees (with fireplace), tent and campervan sites, a fantastic BBQ camp kitchen, plus 5km of walking tracks beneath 70m-high gum trees. It's 12km from Huonville – beware of the steep unsealed road!

★ Ranelagh General Store
CAFE $

(☑03-6264 2316; www.facebook.com/ranelagh generalstore; 31 Marguerite St, Ranelagh; burgers $16-18; ⊘10am-4pm Mon, 11am-8pm Thu-Sun) The tame old Ranelagh General Store has been reborn as an inventive burger bar. Furnished like your great-grandparents' farmhouse, its burgers rely on local produce – the buns are made on-site – with a menu of all-day snacks also available. The Stanley burger (wallaby with popcorn furikake slaw, pickled ginger and wasabi) is a real winner.

★ Summer Kitchen Bakery
BAKERY $

(☑03-6264 3388; 1 Marguerite St, Ranelagh; pies $7-7.50; ⊘7.30am-4pm Mon-Fri, from 8am Sat & Sun) Head to the side courtyard of this tucked-away treasure, on a street corner in Ranelagh a few kilometres out of Huonville, for a wide-ranging selection of pies – from wallaby to mushroom and quinoa – as well as fiendishly good cakes and the best coffee in the Huon. Locals come from kilometres around just for the bread.

❶ Information

Huon Valley Visitor Centre (☑03-6264 0326; www.huonvalleyvisitorcentre.com.au; 23-25 Main Rd, Huonville; ⊘9am-5pm) Timber-clad visitor centre in the heart of Huonville. Has a great little gift shop of local woodwork, artisanal items, food and wine.

Geeveston & Around
POP 1302

A utilitarian town 31km south of Huonville, Geeveston was built by bushmen who came to extract timber from the surrounding forests – the twin tree trunks that serve as the town's gateway still declare it the 'Forest Town'. Its main attractions, the Hartz Mountains National Park and Tahune Adventures, are within easy day-trip range of Hobart or the Huon Valley, but Geeveston makes a good stop along the way – especially if you come on a Friday or Saturday, when Tasmania's best sushi is on the menu.

Founded in the mid-19th century by the Geeves family, Geeveston has more recently been the filming location for the fictional town of 'Rosehaven' for the ABC TV comedy series of the same name – a quirky and surprisingly tender insight into small-town Tasmania.

◉ Sights

★**Hartz Mountains National Park** NATIONAL PARK

(✆03-6121 7026; www.parks.tas.gov.au; park day pass per vehicle (up to 8 people) $24) A favourite southern national park for its proximity to Hobart, 80km away, and the relative ease of reaching its vast alpine views, Hartz Mountains forms one edge of the Tasmanian Wilderness World Heritage Area. Most visitors come to walk to the park's highest point, 1254m **Hartz Peak** (7.4km, four hours return), with its superb outlook onto two of Tasmania's most dramatic mountains: Federation Peak and Precipitous Bluff. Rapid weather changes bluster through – bring waterproofs and warm clothing regardless of the forecast.

⋏ Activities

Tahune Adventures OUTDOORS

(✆03-6251 3903; http://tahuneadventures.com.au; Arve Rd; adult/child/family $30/15/60; ⊙9am-5pm Oct-Mar, 10am-4pm Apr-Sep) About 29km west of Geeveston, Tahune Adventures' centrepiece is the Tahune AirWalk, a 600m-long, wheelchair-accessible steel walkway suspended 20m above the forest floor. One 24m cantilevered section, all but dangling over the Huon River, is designed to sway disconcertingly with approaching footsteps. Vertigo? Ground-level walks include a 20-minute riverside stroll through stands of young Huon pine.

Other activities at Tahune Adventures include rafting or kayaking the Huon and Picton Rivers ($125), and the **Eagle Hang Glider** (✆03-6251 3903; http://tahune adventures.com.au; Tahune Adventures, Arve Rd; adult/child/family $19/17/58; ⊙9.30am-4.30pm Oct-Mar, 10.30am-3.30pm Apr-Sep). There's also a cafe, lodge accommodation (dorms/doubles/families from $64/128/160) and a lone cabin (from $190) that gives you exclusive night-time entry to the AirWalk.

The name Tahune derives from Tahune-Linah, the Aboriginal name for the area around the Huon and Kermandie Rivers.

The AirWalk was damaged by a bushfire in January 2019.

✗ Eating

★**Masaaki's Sushi** JAPANESE $

(✆0408 712 340; 20b Church St; 6/12 sushi $9/18; ⊙11.30am-3pm Fri-Sun) What a surprise! Tasmania's best sushi – including fresh Tasmanian wasabi – is in sleepy Geeveston. Opening hours are disappointingly limited (and he usually sells out by 2pm), so book a table ahead or join the long queue for takeaway. You'll also find Masaaki (from Osaka) and his outstanding sushi at Hobart's Sunday-morning Farm Gate Market (p647).

ⓘ Information

Geeveston Visitor Information Centre (✆03-6264 0334; www.facebook.com/geeveston visitorcentre; 15 Church St; ⊙9am-5pm, reduced winter hours) In Geeveston's old redbrick town hall, this official visitor centre sells tickets to the Tahune AirWalk and Hastings Caves & Thermal Springs (p658), as well as Hartz Mountains National Park passes.

Dover

POP 854

A fishing town with a beach and a pier (but sadly no pub – it burned down in 2013), Dover is a chilled-out spot to while away a few deep-south days. The town was originally called Port Esperance after a ship in Bruni d'Entrecasteaux's fleet, but that moniker now only applies to the bay. The bay's three small islands are optimistically called Faith, Hope and Charity, and unlike its English namesake, this Dover sports no white cliffs but plenty of white sand.

In the 19th century this was timber territory. Huon pine and local hardwoods were milled and shipped from here (and from nearby Strathblane and Raminea), heading to China, India and Germany for use as railway sleepers. Today the major industries are fruit growing and aquaculture – around half of Dover's working population is employed in salmon farming.

⊨ Sleeping & Eating

★**Peninsula Experience** RENTAL HOUSE $$$

(✆03-6298 1441; www.peninsulatas.com; Blubber Head Rd; d from $525; ☏) Atop a private peninsula, beyond some steely gates and a long wiggly driveway, this stately old farmhouse now exudes 21st-century luxury. Asian-chic design infuses the three bedrooms (it sleeps six) and the elegant kitchen. At dusk pademelons, wallabies and echidnas patrol the grounds. The Boat House (from $425) is a slick little waterside cottage for two.

★**Post>Office 6985** PIZZA $$

(✆03-6298 1905; 6985 Huon Hwy; mains $16-30; ⊙4-8pm Thu-Sat) With cool decor, foodie

TASMANIA DOVER

magazines and a bewildering number of specials boards, this Post Office delivers excellent wood-fired pizzas (try the scallop, caramelised onion and pancetta version). There's a sterling beer and wine list too, and about the only chance to stay out after dark in Dover.

Southport & Around

Southport was once called Baie des Moules (Bay of Mussels), one of several names it's had over the years. Many travellers don't take the 2km detour off the main road to visit Australia's most southerly town, but it's a worthy diversion if only to stay in one of its B&Bs, which make good use of the waterside locale. The nearby Hastings Caves & Thermal Springs reserve and the frayed shores of even-more-southerly Recherche Bay are worthwhile detours. Unfortunately public transport won't get you here.

☉ Sights

Hastings Caves & Thermal Springs CAVE
(☑ 03-6298 3209; www.parks.tas.gov.au/reserves/hastings; 754 Hastings Caves Rd, Hastings; caves & pool adult/child/family $24/12/60, pool only $5/2.50/12; ☺ 9am-5pm Jan, 10am-4pm Feb-Apr & Oct-Dec, 10.30am-4pm May-Sep) A 7.5km drive inland from the Southport turn-off on the Huon Hwy are the amazing Hastings Caves and their adjunct thermal springs. Cave tours (45 minutes) take you into the impressive dolomite Newdegate Cave, with the option of a dip in the thermal pool behind the visitor centre, filled with 28°C spring water. Tour times change across the year, but there are at least four tours a day.

⊨ Sleeping

★ Jetty House B&B $$
(☑ 03-6298 3139; www.endoftheroadtasmania.com; Main Rd, Southport; d/f from $190/240, entire house from $380; ☜☺) This family-run guesthouse near the wharf is a rustic, verandah-encircled homestead, built in 1876 for the local sawmill boss. Rates include full cooked breakfast and afternoon tea. Open fires, interesting art and the total absence of doilies complete the package. Dinner by arrangement, cheaper long-stay rates offered, and kids and pets welcome. Lovely!

★ The Shackeau RENTAL HOUSE $$$
(☑ 03-6298 1441; www.shackeau.com; 223 Kingfish Beach Rd, Southport; house from $190; ❄) Any more waterfront and this lovely shack would be a houseboat. Almost the last in a long row of quirky little beach shacks, it's a cream-coloured weatherboard affair, with mod, beachy interiors, a fabulous deck and an infinity-edge spa tub, offering unbeatable views as far across the water as Cape Bruny Lighthouse. Sleeps four.

TASMAN PENINSULA & PORT ARTHUR

Just an hour from Hobart lie the staggering coastal landscapes, sandy beaches and historic sites of the Tasman Peninsula. Bushwalking, surfing, sea kayaking, diving and rock-climbing opportunities abound – all good reasons to extend your visit beyond a hurried day trip from Hobart.

Don't miss visiting the peninsula's vertiginous 300m-high sea cliffs – the tallest in the southern hemisphere – studded with natural add-ons such as the legendary Totem Pole sea stack. Most of the cliffs are protected by Tasman National Park, which is best explored on the fabulous, four-day Three Capes Track that has fast become Tasmania's go-to coastal hike.

Waiting portentously at the end of Arthur Hwy is Port Arthur, the infamous and allegedly escape-proof 19th-century penal colony. Today kids kick footballs and families cook sausages on the BBQs here, but it's impossible to totally blank out the tragedy of this place, both historically and more recently.

↺ Tours

Under Down Under Tours TOURS
(☑ 1800 444 442; www.underdownunder.com.au; $125) Guided backpacker-style day trips to Port Arthur from Hobart, including accommodation pick-up, admission fees, a guided walk and a harbour cruise. There's also a quick look at Richmond en route, as well as stops at Tasman Arch and Devils Kitchen.

Tours Tasmania TOURS
(☑ 1800 777 103; www.tourstas.com.au; $125) Good-value, small-group day tours to the Tasman Peninsula from Hobart, with a four-hour stop at Port Arthur, as well as visiting Devil's Kitchen, Tasman Arch and the Waterfall Bay bushwalk. Backpacker focused.

❶ Getting There & Away

The Tassielink (p633) Tasman Peninsula service will take you from Hobart to Dunalley ($13.70,

Tasman Peninsula

one hour), Eaglehawk Neck ($21, 1½ hours) and Port Arthur ($24.20, two hours).

Dunalley

POP 316

Strung along one edge of the 895m-long Denison Canal, a boating shortcut that effectively turns the Forestier and Tasman Peninsulas into an island, the small town of Dunalley wears a few historic stars and scars. The only place where Abel Tasman made landfall in Tasmania in 1642 was near the town, and the first contact between Europeans and Aboriginal people in Tasmania was here, while memories run strong from the 2013 bushfire that destroyed a third of Dunalley's homes. The town has well and truly bounced back, and though there's not a whole lot to do here, nor anywhere outstanding to stay, there are a couple of good foodie haunts if you're hungry. If you're here around New Year and it seems noisy, Tasmania's most rocking music festival – Falls Festival – takes place just down the road at Marion Bay.

🤏 Tours

Tasmanian E-bike Adventures CYCLING
(☎0438 072 453; http://tasmanianebikeadventures.com.au; from $550) Cycle with push-of-a-button assistance on flexible e-bike day tours on history-rich Bangor farm. Make a gentle ride out to Cape Frederick Hendrick, or extend things with a pedal (tide permitting) along the sands of Two Mile Beach to Monument Bay, where Abel Tasman made his only Tasmanian landing. Gourmet picnic lunch included and Indigenous cultural experiences available.

🎪 Festivals & Events

Falls Festival MUSIC
(http://fallsfestival.com; ⊙29-31 Dec) The Tasmanian version of the Victorian rock festival

RECHERCHE BAY & COCKLE CREEK

The gorgeous, tree-lined Recherche Bay was the spot where, in 1792, two French ships captained by Bruni d'Entrecasteaux – L'Espérance and La Recherche – dropped anchor and set about exploring. These days it's still a tranquil spot, with some sheltered beaches and campsites. From the road's end at Cockle Creek – the southernmost bit of road in Australia – there's an easy 10-minute walk to a bronze **whale sculpture**, commemorating the days when there were four whaling stations here.

The challenging six- to eight-day **South Coast Track** also starts (or ends) at Cockle Creek, tracking between here and remote Melaleuca in the Southwest National Park (p711). Combined with the **Port Davey Track** you can walk all the way to Lake Pedder, though it'd take about two weeks. Shorter walks from Cockle Creek include ambles along the shoreline to the lighthouse at **Fishers Point** (4km, two hours return; best done at low tide), and a section of the South Coast Track to **South Cape Bay** (15.4km, four to five hours return). National park entry fees apply; self-register at Cockle Creek.

is a winner. Three days and two nights of live Oz and international tunes (Fleet Foxes, Liam Gallagher, Amy Shark and Hilltop Hoods have all played) at Marion Bay, around 10km north of Dunalley.

✖ Eating

★ **Bangor Vineyard Shed** SEAFOOD $$
(☑ 03-6253 5558; www.bangorshed.com.au; 20 Blackman Bay Rd; 12 oysters from $29, mains $18-35; ⏰ 10am-5pm; 🔊) Turn left 1km beyond the Denison Canal to discover this excellent vineyard cafe, sitting atop an open rise on one of Tasmania's oldest family farms – it's been in the Dunbabin family for five generations. The cellar door doubles as a restaurant with local oysters and more substantial mains.

Eaglehawk Neck

Eaglehawk Neck is less a town than a smattering of holiday homes amid an assortment of natural coastal curiosities. It's the second isthmus crossed as you head south to Port Arthur, this one connecting the Forestier Peninsula to the Tasman Peninsula. In convict days, the 100m-wide Neck had a row of ornery dogs chained across it to prevent convicts from escaping – the infamous Dogline. Timber platforms were also built in narrow Eaglehawk Bay to the west, and stocked with more dogs to prevent convicts from wading around the Dogline, while rumours were circulated that the waters were shark infested. Remarkably, despite these measures, several convicts made successful bids for freedom.

These days it's a far more inviting place, with the coast immediately north and south

of the Neck strung with fascinating rock formations – huge stone arches, blowholes, cliffs, strange natural pavement – while the Neck itself has a superb surf beach.

⊙ Sights

Blowhole, Tasman Arch & Devil's Kitchen LANDMARK
(www.eaglehawkneck.org/attractions; off Blowhole Rd, Doo Town) FREE For a close look at the spectacular coastline just south of Eaglehawk Neck, head through quirky **Doo Town** (www.eaglehawkneck.org/attractions/doo-town) to the Blowhole (which wheezes sporadic bursts when seas are fierce), Tasman Arch (a cavern-like natural bridge) and Devil's Kitchen (a rugged 60m-deep cleft). At the Devil's Kitchen car park, a walking trail (3.4km, 1½ hours return) heads along the top of the sea cliffs to **Waterfall Bay** (☑ 03-6250 3980; www.parks.tas.gov.au; park day pass per vehicle/person $24/12), which has further photo-worthy views.

Tessellated Pavement NATURAL FEATURE
(off Pirates Bay Dr) FREE At the northern end of Pirates Bay, a 10-minute trail leads to a rocky coastal terrace that has curiously eroded into what looks like tiled paving – it's geology as geometry.

✖ Eating

★ **Doo-Lishus** FISH & CHIPS $
(☑ 0437 469 412; www.tasmanregion.com.au/doo-lishus; Blowhole Rd, Doo Town; meals $8-19; ⏰ 9am-6pm, to 7pm in summer) Sometimes rated as Tasmania's best fish and chips, this unexpected caravan at the Blowhole

car park in Doo Town serves up the usual range of battered swimming things, plus good ice cream, fresh berry smoothies and interesting pies (eg curried-scallop, venison and rabbit).

★ **Cubed** CAFE $
(☑ 0400 059 061; www.cubedespresso.com.au; Pirates Bay Lookout, Pirates Bay Dr; snacks $3.50-5; ⊙ 9am-noon Mon, to 3pm Thu-Sun) ◢ Drink in the views as well as the coffee at this restored, solar-powered 1957 caravan at the Pirates Bay Lookout that doles out fastidiously prepared coffee and snacks. There's a Persian rug, blankets and cushions spread out at the roadside, and you'll want to train the van's telescope at the famed Totem Pole and Candlestick across the bay.

Port Arthur & Tasman National Park

POP 251

History sits heavily at Port Arthur. Founded as a timber station in 1830, it quickly gained its continuing notoriety when it was chosen as the site of what would become Australia's most infamous convict settlement. It was a 'natural penitentiary' – the peninsula is connected to the mainland by Eaglehawk Neck, a strip of land less than 100m wide, where ferocious guard dogs and tales of shark-infested waters deterred escape.

Despite its redemption as a major tourist site (the structures and ruins here are undeniably amazing), Port Arthur remains a sombre place. Don't expect to remain unaffected by what you see: there's a sadness here that's palpable, compounded by the continuing memory of the day in April 1996 when a young gunman fired bullets indiscriminately around the site, murdering 35 people and injuring 37 more. After burning down a guesthouse, he was finally captured and remains imprisoned in Hobart.

Port Arthur is surrounded by some of Tasman National Park's finest features – Remarkable Cave, Fortescue Bay and Crescent Bay – and the clifftop Three Capes Track also begins here.

◉ Sights

★ **Port Arthur Historic Site** HISTORIC SITE
(☑ 03-6251 2310, 1800 659 101; www.portarthur. org.au; 6973 Arthur Hwy; adult/child/family $39/17/99; ⊙ tours & buildings 10am-5pm, grounds 9am-dusk) This amazing World Heritage–listed convict site is one of Tasmania's big-ticket attractions. The dozens of structures here are best understood via guided tour (included with admission). The feared **Separate Prison** (site admission adult/child/family $39/17/99; ⊙ 10am-5pm) was built to punish prisoners through 23-hours-a-day isolation and sensory deprivation. The 1836 **church** (site admission adult/child/family $39/17/99; ⊙ 9am-5pm) burned down in 1884, and the **penitentiary** (site admission adult/child/family $39/17/99; ⊙ 10am-5pm) was originally a granary and flour mill. The shell of the Broad Arrow Café, scene of many of the 1996 shootings, has been preserved as a **memorial garden** (site admission adult/child/family $39/17/99; ⊙ 9am-dusk).

Inside the main entrance is a daytime cafe, the 1830 (p663) restaurant and a gift shop, which stocks some interesting convict-focused publications. There's also a cafe at the Visiting Magistrates House inside the site.

A guided 40-minute walking tour of the site and a 25-minute harbour cruise are included in admission prices. Additional tours include those to the **Isle of the Dead Cemetery** (combined site entry & tour adult/child/family $59/27/144; ⊙ 11am & 1pm) and **Point Puer Boys' Prison** combined site entry

DON'T MISS

TASMANIAN DEVIL UNZOO

The prime attraction in Taranna, 9km south of Eaglehawk Neck, is the **Tasmanian Devil Unzoo** (☑ 1800 641 641; www.tasmaniandevilunzoo.com.au; 5990 Arthur Hwy; adult/child/family $36/20/89, tour incl admission $110/60/280; ⊙ 9am-6pm), an unfenced enclave of native bushland where wildlife comes and goes of its own accord. Species you might encounter include native hens, wallabies, quolls, eagles, wattlebirds, pademelons and, of course, Tasmanian devils. Relax: the devils aren't free roaming, but you can see them being fed six times a day. Devil Tracker 4WD tours have you monitoring devils to help in the fight against the insidious Devil Facial Tumour Disease (DFTD).

Pick up a bird or plant checklist before you go walking to help you identify species.

& tour adult/child/family $59/27/144; ⊙11.40am & 1.40pm Sep-Jul), and the **Escape from Port Arthur** (adult/child/family $15/5/35; ⊙11am, 12.30pm & 2.30pm), **Commandant's Carriage** (combined site entry & tour adult/child $69/47; ⊙10.30am, 12.45pm & 2.15pm) and after-dark **ghost tours** (adult/child/family $26.50/15/75; ⊙dusk).

Buggy transport around the site (10am to 3.30pm) can be arranged for people with restricted mobility; ask at the information counter. The ferry plying the harbour is also wheelchair accessible.

★**Remarkable Cave** CAVE
(www.eaglehawkneck.org/gateway-to/remarkable-cave; Safety Cove Rd) FREE About 7km south of Port Arthur is Remarkable Cave, a long tunnel eroded from the base of a collapsed gully, under a cliff and out to sea. The waves surge through the tunnel and fill the gully with sea spray (and sometimes water – watch out!). A boardwalk and 115 steps provide access to a metal viewing platform. Hardcore surfers often brave the cave, paddling out through the opening to surf the offshore reefs beyond.

From the car park, a walking track heads east to **Crescent Bay** (four hours return), a magical arc of white sand backed by some of Tasmania's most impressive dunes. Just

OFF THE BEATEN TRACK

COAL MINES HISTORIC SITE

The least known of Tasmania's World Heritage–listed convict sites, the **Coal Mines Historic Site** (☎1800 659 101, 03-6251 2310; www.coalmines.org.au; Coal Mine Rd) FREE provides a wonderfully low-key experience. The state's first operational mine, it began excavation in 1833 and was worked by convicts in abominable conditions before closing in 1848 on 'moral and financial grounds'. Walking tracks loop through the ruins of the site. The crumbled sandstone barracks, overlooking the water, are particularly evocative, and the solitary confinement cells are torturously small and dark.

At Premaydena, take the signposted turn-off (the C341) 13km northwest to Saltwater River and the historic site. There's a popular, basic and beautiful campground 4km past the Coal Mines at Lime Bay State Reserve.

before reaching the beach, a short sidetrack climbs to low **Mt Brown,** from which there are good views of Crescent Bay, Cape Pillar and Tasman Island.

🏃 Activities & Tours

★**Three Capes Track** HIKING
(☎1300 827 727; www.threecapestrack.com.au; adult/child $495/396) Now rivalling Tasmania's famous Overland Track for popularity, the 46km Three Capes Track traverses Tasman National Park's lofty clifftops, culminating high on Cape Pillar on the well-named Blade rock formation. It's a four-day, three-night hike, with a boat trip from Port Arthur Historic Site to the trailhead, excellent hut accommodation, and a bus back to Port Arthur at the end.

★**Tasman Island Cruises** BOATING
(Pennicott Wilderness Journeys; ☎03-6250 2200; www.tasmancruises.com.au; 6961 Arthur Hwy; adult/child/family $135/85/430; ⊙9.15am year-round, plus 1.15pm mid-Dec–mid-Apr) Boat trips departing the Pennicott Wilderness Journeys office near Port Arthur incorporate a three-hour adventure cruise past the Tasman Peninsula's most spectacular coastal scenery. Trips pass beneath Australia's highest sea cliffs at Cape Pillar, float among the seals of Tasman Island and peep at natural rock stars around Cape Hauy and Eaglehawk Neck.

★**Roaring 40s Kayaking** KAYAKING
(☎0455 949 777; www.roaring40skayaking.com.au; $220; ⊙8am Mon & Fri Nov-Apr) Paddle among seals and sea stacks on this epic sea-kayaking day tour, which launches at Fortescue Bay and heads to Cape Hauy and the famed Totem Pole sea stack – a legendary rock-climbing site. Prices include equipment, lunch and transfers from Hobart. Minimum age 16.

Three Capes Lodge Walk HIKING
(☎03-6392 2211; www.taswalkingco.com.au/three-capes-lodge-walk; from $2895) A four-day guided walk on the Three Capes Track, staying in plush private lodges. Spend the first night at Crescent Lodge and two nights at Cape Pillar Lodge (thus you don't have to pack up your gear one of the days), which has a solar-heated outdoor bathtub and a 'relaxation pavilion' with masseuse. Fine Tasmanian food and wine round out the days.

🛏 Sleeping & Eating

★ Port Arthur Holiday Park　CARAVAN PARK **$**
(📞1800 607 057; www.nrmaparksandresorts.com.
au/port-arthur; Garden Point Rd, Port Arthur; unpow-
ered/powered/en-suite sites from $26/30/41, cab-
ins $90-175; ❄️ 🛜) Hidden deep in the trees,
this spacious park, 2km before Port Arthur
Historic Site, is like bush camping with a
few civilised luxuries: camp kitchen, wood-
fired pizza oven, petrol pump, shop, and
even a pump track for kids with bikes and
scooters. The cabins are well designed, and
there's a walking track to Port Arthur.

Brick Point Cottage　RENTAL HOUSE **$**
(📞0438 070 498; www.brickpointcottage.com.au;
241 Safety Cove Rd; up to 4 people $99) Fronted
by a dinky little white garage, this old-school
Tassie shack has two bedrooms, a compact
kitchen, wood fire and lawn arcing down
to a sheltered reach of Carnarvon Bay. The
BBQ on the sunny rear deck completes the
Aussie seaside-holiday dream. There are few
more unpretentious and affordable places to
stay on the whole Tasman Peninsula.

Fortescue Bay Camp Site　CAMPGROUND **$**
(📞03-6250 2433; www.parks.tas.gov.au; Fortescue Bay Rd; unpowered sites per 2 people/fam-
ily $13/16, extra adult/child $5/2.50) Dream
the night away to the sound of gentle surf
within Tasman National Park. There are no
powered sites but there's a hot shower, fireplaces and gas BBQs (in the day-use area).
National-park fees apply in addition to
camping fees. Bookings essential November
to Easter. BYO supplies; there's a basic shop.

Stewarts Bay Lodge　RESORT **$$**
(📞03-6250 2888; www.stewartsbaylodge.com.
au; 6955 Arthur Hwy; d from $160, 1-/2-bedroom
spa chalet $236/329; 🛜) Arrayed around
a gorgeous hidden cove, one bay round
from Port Arthur Historic Site, Stewarts
Bay Lodge combines rustic log cabins with
newer deluxe units, some with private spa
baths and uninterrupted water views. You
can cook up in your contemporary kitchen,
but you'll probably spend more time in the
sleek **On the Bay** (📞03-6250 2771; mains lunch
$22-33, dinner $24-44; ⏱8-11am, noon-3pm &
5.30-8.30pm) restaurant.

1830　MODERN AUSTRALIAN **$$$**
(📞1800 659 101, 03-6251 2310; www.portarthur.
org.au; Port Arthur Historic Site, 6973 Arthur Hwy;
mains $28-60; ⏱5pm-late, from 6pm summer)
The food is anything but prison rations at

this swish restaurant inside the main visitor
centre at the Port Arthur Historic Site. Looking through slit windows to the penitentiary
(which is lit at night) and serving the likes
of Cape Grim beef and a lasagne of Cygnet
mushrooms, 1830 is as slick and dark as a
city wine bar.

❶ Getting There & Away

In addition to the Tassielink service, **Tassie
Tours** (📞0487 163 624; http://tassietours.
com) runs a twice-daily shuttle ($55) between
Hobart and the Port Arthur Historic Site. Buses
pick up from seven locations around Hobart,
including the Hobart visitor centre (p648),
departing the city at around 8am and noon.
The shuttle schedule allows you four hours at
Port Arthur.

THE MIDLANDS

Tracking north–south between Launceston and Hobart, the convict-built Midland
Hwy – now also nostalgically known as the
'Heritage Hwy' – has been Tasmania's main
thoroughfare since it opened to horse-and-
carriage traffic around 1821. It's a journey
through rural Tasmania, with towns that
were established as garrisons for prisoners and guards, protecting travellers from
the menace of bushrangers. These days
the towns are open-air galleries of colo-
nial-era architecture, offering plenty of
places to stop and eat, drink and absorb
the history. Before Europeans arrived, the
Midlands were predominantly inhabited
by the Midland Plain and Oyster Bay Aboriginal nations. Find out more at www.
heritagehighway.com.au.

❶ Getting There & Away

Redline Coaches (📞1300 360 000; www.
tasredline.com.au) power between Hobart
and Launceston two to four times daily, via
Kempton, Oatlands, Ross and Campbell Town.
The Tassielink service plying the same route
doesn't stop at the Midlands towns.

Oatlands & the Southern Midlands
POP 683

A small town built on a grand scale, Oatlands contains Australia's largest single
collection of Georgian architecture. On the
stately main street alone (which feels like a
film set) there are 87 historic buildings.

GOLFING WITH CONVICTS

Australia's oldest golf course, **Ratho Farm** (☑ 03-6259 5553, 0497 644 916; www.rathofarm.com; 2122 Highland Lakes Rd, Bothwell; 9/18 holes $25/40, club/trolley hire $10/5; ⊙ 8am-dusk), was rolled out of the dust in 1822 by the Scottish settlers who built Bothwell. It's an eccentric course: sheep do much of the green-keeping work and, more than bunkers, hay bales are the hazards. No bookings needed.

The rambling old homestead at Ratho Farm has also been transformed into fabulous boutique **accommodation** (☑ 0497 644 916, 03-6259 5553; www.rathofarm.com; 2122 Highland Lakes Rd; 1-/2-bedroom units from $185/235; ✳ ☎). The same family has owned this place for generations, and their convict-built outbuildings host 20 rooms, all with different configurations. The original timbers, shingles and stone have been retained wherever possible, and there's a chance of spotting platypuses in the stream.

Dinner, bed and breakfast packages are available, with meals in the main homestead.

The site for the town was chosen in 1821 as one of four military posts on the Hobart–George Town road, and in 1832 an optimistic surveyor marked out 80km of streets – on the assumption that Oatlands would become the Midlands' capital. Many folks made the town home in the 1830s, erecting solid buildings with the help of former convicts and soldiers who were skilled carpenters and stonemasons.

These days the town has a few decent places to stay and eat. Bypassed by the highway, it retains a sense of colonial calm and makes for a history-soaked stopover.

◉ Sights

Callington Mill   HISTORIC BUILDING
(☑ 03-6254 5000; www.callingtonmill.com.au; 1 Mill Lane; ⊙ grounds 9am-5pm) Spinning above the Oatlands rooftops, the Callington Mill was built in 1837 and ground flour until 1891. After decades of neglect, with the innards collecting pigeon poo and the stonework crumbling, it's been fully restored and is once again producing high-grade organic flour. It's an amazing piece of engineering – the only working Lincolnshire-style windmill in Australia. Visitors are free to wander around the grounds.

Old Kempton Distillery   DISTILLERY
(☑ 03-6259 3058; www.oldkemptondistillery.com.au; 26 Main St; tours $35, tastings $20-28; ⊙ 10am-4pm) Kempton's manorial Dysart House, an 1842 colonial classic, is a suitably noble setting for a single malt experience. Pull off the highway for a whisky tasting, a bite to eat in the cafe (mains $14 to $18), or a tour (including four tastings) of the distillery and lovely old homestead (1.30pm).

Nant Distillery   DISTILLERY
(☑ 03-6111 6110; www.nant.com.au; 254 Nant Lane; tours with/without tastings $35/15, tastings $25; ⊙ 10am-4pm, closed Tue & Wed Jun-Aug) A key component of Bothwell's Scotland-in-the-south ambience is this distillery, where superb single malt whisky is crafted in an 1820s flour mill. There are tours (11am, 1.30pm and 2.30pm) and tastings, and the Atrium restaurant serves burgers ($20), pies ($8) and platters ($25 to $30).

🛏 Sleeping & Eating

Blossoms Cottage   B&B $
(☑ 03-6254 1516; www.blossomscottageoatlands.com.au; 116-118 High St; d $110; ☎) In a self-contained garden studio, Blossoms is bright and cheerful, with a cast-iron bed, blackwood floors, lead-light windows, a small kitchen and a couple of easy chairs under a silver birch. Great value. Generous breakfast basket provided.

Feisty Hen Pantry   CAFE $
(☑ 0411 232 776; www.feistyhenpantry.com.au; 94 High St; mains $6-20; ⊙ 9am-3.30pm Wed-Sun) This likeable little hen has a very small roost out the back of Oatlands Lodge. It feels like a farmhouse kitchen and serves up all-day breakfasts, Devonshire teas, toasted sandwiches, slabs of quiche and slices of carrot cake – using all-local, all-seasonal ingredients. Good coffee too. There are a couple of sunny tables out the front if the Midlands wind isn't howling.

Ross

POP 404

Immaculate Ross was established in 1812 to protect Hobart–Launceston travellers from bushrangers. The town became an important coach staging post at the centre of Tasmania's burgeoning wool industry and, before the famous Ross Bridge was built in 1836, a fording point across the Macquarie River.

These days the town's elm-lined streets are veritably awash with colonial charm and, in autumn, golden colours. Plenty of tourist accommodation keeps Ross buzzing along.

◎ Sights

Ross Bridge   BRIDGE
(Bridge St) FREE The oft-photographed 1836 Ross Bridge is the third-oldest bridge in Australia. Designed by colonial architect John Lee Archer, it was built by two convict stonemasons, James Colbeck and Daniel Herbert, who were granted pardons for their efforts. Herbert chiselled the 184 intricate carvings decorating the arches, including Celtic symbols, animals and notable people (including Governor Arthur and Anglo-Danish convict Jorgen Jorgensen, the farcical ex-king of Iceland). At night the bridge is lit up – the carvings shimmer with spooky shadows.

🛏 Sleeping & Eating

Ross B&B   B&B $$
(☑ 0417 522 354, 03-6381 5354; www.rossaccomm odation.com.au; 12 Church St; d/retreat from $155/162; ☕) Choose from two en-suite rooms in a one-time blacksmith's home at the very heart of town, or a two-bedroom garden retreat in a separate wing. This outfit also manages four carefully restored, self-contained cottages dotted around Ross, including a former convict barracks; see the website for details.

★Ross Village Bakery   BAKERY $
(☑ 03-6381 5246; www.rossbakery.com.au; 15 Church St; pies $5-9; ⊗ 8.30am-4.30pm Wed-Mon; ☕) Overdose on pies and astonishingly tall vanilla slices. The owners get up before dawn every day to set the 1860 wood oven blazing. Wood-fired pizzas on Saturday nights in summer, and fresh-baked sour-dough loaves for that Midlands picnic.

ℹ Information

Ross Visitor Information Centre (☑ 03-6381 5466; www.visitross.com.au; 48 Church St; ⊗ 9.30am-5pm Mon-Fri, 10am-4.30pm Sat & Sun) Inside the Tasmanian Wool Centre.

THE EAST COAST

Tasmania's east coast is sea-salted and rejuvenating – a land of quiet bays and sandy shores, punctuated by granite headlands splashed with flaming orange lichen. The sand is white-blonde and the water is gin-clear. It looks as inviting as a tropical post-card, but when you strip off and plunge in, you'll probably be quickly out again – even in summer the water temperatures here can leave you breathless.

This coast sits in a rain shadow – by the time the clouds make it out here from the west, they're virtually empty! It's no surprise, then, that this is prime holiday terrain for Tasmanians, with plenty of opportunities to hike, cycle, kayak, surf, dive and fish – set up your beachside camp and get into it. At day's end, fish and chips on the beach is a sure-fire winner. And if luxury is more your thing, you'll find hip lodges and top-flight eateries aplenty.

ℹ Getting There & Away

Tassielink (p633) runs up the coast from Hobart as far as Bicheno, stopping at all the towns along the way. From Bicheno, Calow's Coaches (p671) head as far north as St Helens, and run from Bicheno to Launceston via St Marys. Calow's also operates a bus from Bicheno to Coles Bay, connecting with Tassielink buses to/from Hobart on Monday, Wednesday and Friday at the Coles Bay turn-off.

Maria Island National Park

Captivating Maria (muh-*rye*-uh) Island is a carefree, car-free haven – a top spot for walking, wildlife watching, mountain biking, camping, delving into history and reading a book on the beach.

Maria is laced with impressive scenery: curious cliffs, fern-draped forests, squeaky-sand beaches and azure seas. Forester (eastern grey) kangaroos, wombats and wallabies wander around; grey-plumed Cape Barren geese honk about on the grasslands; and an insurance population of Tasmanian devils (they're beset with disease on the mainland) has been released here and is thriving – more than 100 devils at last count. Below water there's also lots to see, with good snorkelling and diving in the clear, shallow marine reserve.

In 1972 Maria became a **national park** (☑ 03-6257 1420; www.parks.tas.gov.au; park day

East Coast

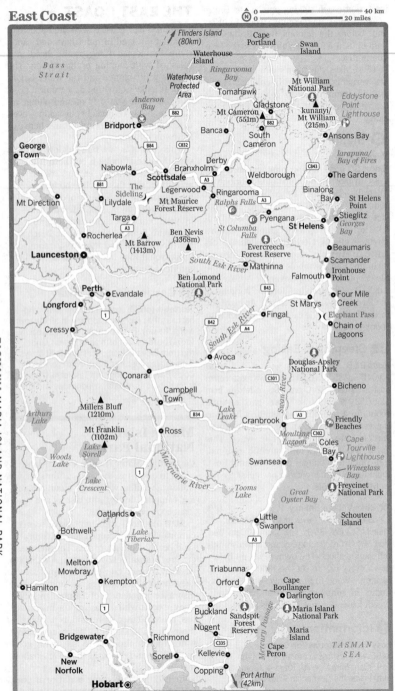

pass per person $12), as much for its history as for its natural assets, and Darlington is now also a World Heritage–listed site.

The island doesn't have any shops: BYO food and gear.

◉ Sights & Tours

Darlington HISTORIC SITE
(☑ 03-6257 1420; www.parks.tas.gov.au; park day pass per person $12) The township of Darlington (officially the World Heritage–listed Darlington Probation Station) is where you'll start your time on the island. Close to the ferry jetty are some tall **silos** and the historic **Commissariat Store**, now the national park **visitor centre** (◷ 9am-5pm). Through an avenue of gnarled macrocarpa trees lies the **penitentiary**, which once housed convicts and now offers bunkhouse-style accommodation, as well as the restored **Coffee Palace** and **mess hall**.

Maria Island Walk HIKING
(☑ 03-6234 2999; www.mariaislandwalk.com. au; $2550) Redefine your concept of bushwalking on this luxury guided four-day hike along the island's length – Haunted Bay to the Fossil Cliffs. The first two nights are spent at secluded bush camps, with the third at the historic former home of entrepreneur Diego Bernacchi in Darlington. The price includes fine Tasmanian food and wines, park fees and transport from Hobart.

East Coast Cruises CRUISE
(☑ 03-6257 1300; www.eastcoastcruises.com.au; adult/child/family $225/90/545; ◷ Oct-May, Fri-Sun only Oct & May) 🏊 Full-day boat trips from Triabunna to Maria Island, cruising past the island's Painted Cliffs and Fossil Cliffs, with a guided walk around the old convict settlement at Darlington. The boat then either heads to the Ile des Phoques seal colony or circumnavigates the island – ask which itinerary when you book.

🛏 Sleeping

Darlington Camp Site CAMPGROUND $
(☑ 03-6257 1420; www.parks.tas.gov.au; Darlington; unpowered sites s/d/f $7/13/16) Grassy unpowered sites behind the dunes of Darlington beach. The camp shelter has gas barbecues and a fireplace, and there are toilets and showers ($1). Expect more wallabies and wombats (and likely a Tasmanian devil or two) than humans as neighbours. National park fees apply. Fees are payable at the island visitor centre; no bookings.

WORTH A TRIP

THOUSAND LAKES LODGE
Truly in the wilderness, this wooden, barn-like **lodge** (☑ 03-6346 1990, 0418 342 694; www.thousandlakeslodge.com.au; 1247 Lake Auga Rd, Liawenee; d $305-385) was once a training facility for Antarctic expeditions. The nine rooms are simple, but the fire-warmed lounge is addictive, especially when wind, rain or snow is beating at the walls. There are e-bikes to hire, and you're in the midst of some of the world's finest trout-fishing lakes – guides available.

There's nothing around for miles, so you'll be glad of the fine dinners (two/three courses $55/66), the well-stocked larder and the bars of quality Tassie wines, craft beers and ciders.

Penitentiary LODGE $
(☑ 03-6256 4772; www.parks.tas.gov.au; Darlington; dm adult/child $25/15, d/f $44/50) Darlington's brick penitentiary once housed the island's convicts. These days it's simple accommodation, with mostly six-bunk rooms, shared bathrooms and coin-operated showers ($1). BYO bedding, lighting (there's no electricity), food, cooking gear and ghost stories. It's often full of school groups, so plan ahead. Book via the Triabunna Visitor Information Centre.

❶ Information
Triabunna Visitor Information Centre (☑ 03-6257 4772; http://eastcoasttasmania.com; cnr Charles St & Esplanade W; ◷ 8.30am-6pm Oct-Apr, 10am-4pm May-Sep) Cheerily delivered information on the whole east-coast region, plus Maria Island ferry tickets and accommodation bookings.

❶ Getting There & Away
Encounter Maria Island (☑ 03-6256 4772; www.encountermaria.com.au; Charles St, Triabunna; return incl national park entry adult/child $50/33, per bicycle/kayak $10/20; ◷ 9am, 10.30am, noon, 2.45pm & 4.15pm Sep-Apr, 10.30am, noon & 2.45pm Wed & Fri-Mon May-Aug) Encounter Maria Island runs three ferries in each direction between Triabunna and Darlington, extending to five sailings daily from September to April. The last ferry back from the island is 5pm (3.30pm May to August). Bike hire per day is adult/child $33/20.

Swansea

POP 866

Unhurried Swansea graces the western shore of sheltered Great Oyster Bay, with sweeping views across the water to the peaks of the Freycinet Peninsula. Founded in 1820 as 'Great Swanport', Swansea also delivers some interesting historic buildings and a museum.

The town is strung along behind Jubilee and Waterloo Beaches, and it manages to retain a laid-back holiday vibe. There are plenty of enticements for visitors in and around town, including myriad accommodation options, restaurants, cafes and some impressive wineries to the north. If you're planning to spend time along the east coast, it's a good midway base.

⊙ Sights

★ **Spiky Bridge**   BRIDGE
(Tasman Hwy) About 7km south of Swansea is the rather amazing Spiky Bridge, built by convicts in the early 1840s using thousands of local fieldstones (yes, they're spiky). The main east-coast road used to truck right across it, but these days it's set beside the highway. Nearby **Kelvedon Beach**, **Spiky Beach** and **Cressy Beach** have deep golden sand and rarely a footprint.

East Coast Heritage Museum   MUSEUM
(✐03-6256 5066; www.eastcoastheritage.org.au; 22 Franklin St; gold coin donation; ☉10am-4pm) Inside Swansea's original schoolhouse, this engaging little museum covers Aboriginal artefacts, colonial and convict history, whaling and the plight of the thylacine (including a tiger trap from the late 19th century). It's worth stopping in just to see the diorama of old Swansea, and eggs from the now-extinct Tasmanian emu.

⌊⌈ Sleeping

Swansea Backpackers   HOSTEL $
(✐03-6257 8650; www.swanseabackpackers.com.au; 98 Tasman Hwy; unpowered sites $25, dm/d/tr/q from $39/85/85/90; ☞) This hip backpackers was the first in Tasmania to introduce capsules (rather than bunk beds) to its dorm. It has smart, spacious public areas, and the clean, shipshape rooms surround a shady deck. There's camping out the back.

★ **Schouten House**   B&B $$
(✐03-6257 8564; www.schoutenhouse.com.au; 1 Waterloo Rd; d incl breakfast $160-200; ☞) This brick-and-sandstone 1844 mansion was built by convicts, and was the centre of 'Great Swanport' before the action shifted a little further north. Decorated in frill-free Georgian style, its rooms now house 19th-century half-tester beds and other antiques. The attentive owners offer a large breakfast menu that includes a vegan ratatouille, bacon butties and great pancakes.

★ **Piermont**   COTTAGE $$$
(✐03-6257 8131; www.piermont.com.au; 12990 Tasman Hwy; 1-/2-bedroom cottage from $375/495; ☞⚊) Down a hawthorn-hedged driveway, 4km south of Swansea, these 21 stylish stone cabins fan out from an old farmhouse close to the sea and beside a lagoon-like river pool. Most units have a fireplace and spa. There's also a pool, tennis court, free bikes and kayaks, and the highly regarded **Homestead Restaurant** (1/2/3 courses $45/65/80, degustation without/with wine $110/165; ☉noon-2pm mid-Dec–Easter, 6-8pm year-round).

At the time of writing, eight chic new villas were in the works.

✗ Eating

★ **Melshell Oyster Shack**   SEAFOOD $$
(✐0428 570 334, 03-6257 0269; www.melshell oysters.com.au; 9 Yellow Sandbanks Rd, Dolphin Sands; 12 oysters unshucked/shucked from $15/20; ☉10am-4pm) On the Dolphin Sands sand spit, about 16km from Swansea (and well signposted from the highway north of town), Melshell is a quirky caravan on a working oyster farm. Grab your dozen and head for the seats atop the dunes overlooking Melshell's leases in the Swan River. It has glasses if you BYO wine.

Bark Mill Tavern & Bakery   PUB FOOD, BAKERY $$
(✐03-6257 8094; www.barkmilltavern.com.au; 96 Tasman Hwy; mains bakery $6-18, tavern $20-42; ☉bakery 6am-4pm, tavern noon-2pm & 5.30-8pm) The Bark Mill has two foodie faces: a busy bakery-cafe and a pub, both doing a roaring trade. The bakery serves cooked breakfasts, filled rolls almost as large as Tasmania itself, sweet temptations, neat quiches and good coffee; the tavern does pizzas and voluminous mains (try the kangaroo-and-cheese sausages).

❶ Information

Swansea Visitor Information Centre (✐03-6256 5072; http://eastcoasttasmania.com; 22

Franklin St; ⌚9am-5pm; 📶) In the old school building on the corner of Noyes St (sharing space with the East Coast Heritage Museum).

Coles Bay & Freycinet National Park

POP 353

Touching shoulders with Freycinet National Park, Coles Bay township has been a holiday town for generations and yet it remains remarkably low key – a couple of shops, a restaurant, a caravan park, a tavern – for a town that sits on the cusp of arguably Tasmania's most famous natural feature: Wineglass Bay. This bay and the sublime **Freycinet National Park** (☎03-6256 7000; www.parks.tas.gov.au; via Coles Bay; park day pass per vehicle/person $24/12), which is a wild domain of sugar-white beaches, pinkish granite mountains and utterly transparent water, are the reasons everyone is here.

The park encompasses the whole of the peninsula south of Coles Bay, including Schouten Island to the south of Freycinet, and a stretch of coastal scrub around the Friendly Beaches further north. To see the gorgeous goblet of Wineglass Bay, take the short hike up to the saddle lookout, or continue down to the sand on the other side for a nippy dip in the sea.

Sights

★Friendly Beaches BEACH

(☎03-6256 7000; www.parks.tas.gov.au; Friendly Beaches Rd, Freycinet National Park; day pass per vehicle/person $24/12) Take a break from all those curvy little bays further down the peninsula and wander the sands of this windswept ocean beach, signposted from the main road 18km north of Coles Bay. There's a lookout point right beside the main car park, while a walk to the beaches' southern end and back could take up to five hours.

Cape Tourville NATURAL FEATURE

(☎03-6256 7000; www.parks.tas.gov.au; via Cape Tourville Rd, Freycinet National Park; day pass per vehicle/person $24/12) There's an easy 20-minute, wheelchair-accessible circuit here for beautiful panoramas of Freycinet Peninsula's eastern coastline. Along the way you can peer into the mouth of Wineglass Bay, and look out for migrating whales.

The cape is topped by **Cape Tourville Lighthouse**, built in 1971 and a magical spot to watch sunrise.

DON'T MISS

WINEGLASS BAY WALK

Curvaceous Wineglass Bay is the big-ticket walk on Tasmania's east coast. The climb to the Wineglass Bay Lookout (1½ hours return), for a super view over the bay and peninsula, is fairly gentle, but to step onto Wineglass' white sands, make the steeper descent from the lookout to the bay (30 minutes, or 2½ to three hours return from the car park).

Bring your bathers if you want to take a dip in the brine once you make it to Wineglass. Park passes can be purchased with eftpos at the Wineglass Bay walk car park.

Tours

★Freycinet Adventures KAYAKING

(☎03-6257 0500; www.freycinetadventures.com.au; 2 Freycinet Dr, Coles Bay; adult/child $105/95; 👪) Get an eyeful of the peninsula as you paddle along the foot of the Hazards and into Honeymoon Bay on these terrific three-hour paddles. Trips run morning and evening through summer, and mornings only outside the busy season; start times change with the seasons. No experience necessary. An overnight trip to Hazards Beach (adult/child $345/330) also runs weekly through summer.

Offering the quickest approach to Wineglass Bay, Freycinet Adventures also operates the Aqua Taxi, delivering you to Hazards Beach (adult/child $35/30) – from where it's a short, flat walk across the isthmus.

Freycinet Experience Walk WALKING

(☎1800 506 003, 03-6223 7565; www.freycinet.com.au; adult/child from $2550/2450; ⌚Oct-Apr) 🍃 For those who like their wilderness more mild and less wild, Freycinet Experience Walk offers a four-day, fully catered exploration of the peninsula. Walkers return each evening to the secluded, environmentally attuned Friendly Beaches Lodge for superb meals, local wine, hot showers and baths, and comfortable beds. The walk covers around 39km, from Schouten Island to the Friendly Beaches.

Wineglass Bay Cruises BOATING

(☎03-6257 0355; www.wineglassbaycruises.com; Esplanade, Coles Bay; adult/child $150/95;

EAST COAST WINERIES

Along the Tasman Hwy, around Cranbrook and Swansea, you'll encounter a string of terrific wineries where the producers are making the most of sunny east-coast days and cool nights.

Freycinet Vineyard (☑03-6257 8574; www.freycinetvineyard.com.au; 15919 Tasman Hwy, Apslawn; ☉10am-5pm) The Bull family has been growing grapes beneath the east-coast sun since 1980 – it was the first vineyard on the coast. The vibe at the cellar door is agricultural, not flashy – we like it! Super sauvignon blanc.

Devil's Corner (☑03-6257 8881; www.devilscorner.com.au; 1 Sherbourne Rd, Apslawn; ☉10am-5pm) Wine with a widescreen view at this cutting-edge cellar door (Eyesore or delight? You decide.) overlooking Moulting Lagoon and the Hazards mountains on Freycinet Peninsula, complete with jaunty lookout tower.

Gala Estate Vineyard (☑03-6257 8641; www.galaestate.com.au; 14891 Tasman Hwy, Cranbrook; ☉10am-4pm Sep-May) Enjoy a red in retroville in this funky pistachio-coloured cellar door – once a post office – right on the main road through Cranbrook.

Spring Vale Wines (☑03-6257 8208; www.springvalewines.com; 130 Spring Vale Rd, Cranbrook; ☉11am-4pm) Down a long driveway in Cranbrook this winery is on land owned by the same family since 1875. The cellar door is housed in a convict-built 1842 stable. Don't miss the pinot gris.

Milton Vineyard (☑03-6257 8298; www.miltonvineyard.com.au; 14635 Tasman Hwy; ☉10am-5pm) Worth a stop alone for the bizarre twin trees at the entrance – a eucalyptus and macrocarpa seemingly growing out of the same trunk. Tastings are in an elegant, white weatherboard pavilion presiding over the vines.

☉10am Sep-May, 10am Tue, Thu & Sat Jun & Jul, 10am Tue & Thu Aug) Sedate, four-hour cruises from Coles Bay to Wineglass Bay, including a bento-box lunch. The boat chugs around the peninsula's southern end, passing Hazards Beach and Schouten Island en route. You'll likely see dolphins, sea eagles, seals and perhaps even migrating whales. Book ahead. The kid-free Sky Lounge ($220) gives you free canapés, freshly shucked oysters, beer, wine and bubbly.

🛏 Sleeping & Eating

BIG4 Iluka on Freycinet Holiday Park CARAVAN PARK, HOSTEL $
(☑1800 786 512, 03-6257 0115; www.big4.com.au; Reserve Rd, Coles Bay; unpowered/powered sites $30/40, hostel dm/tw $30/80, cabins & units $120-215; 🛜) Iluka is a big, rambling park that's been here forever and is an unfaltering favourite with local holidaymakers – book well ahead. The backpackers section is managed by YHA; there's room for only 32 (refreshingly small) in dorms, twins and doubles, and a predictably decent kitchen. The local shop, bakery, tavern and Muirs Beach are just steps away.

Freycinet Rentals ACCOMMODATION SERVICES $$
(☑03-6257 0320; www.freycinetrentals.com; 5 East Esplanade, Coles Bay; house from $185) Your hub for renting (mostly older-style) holiday houses and beach 'shacks' in and around Coles Bay. Prices swing wildly between summer and winter, and minimum stays apply for long weekends and Christmas holidays. One option, Beaulieu is a modern apartment with floor-to-ceiling windows full of the Hazards (double from $250).

★Saffire Freycinet RESORT $$$
(☑1800 723 347, 03-6256 7888; www.saffire-freycinet.com.au; 2352 Coles Bay Rd, Coles Bay; d incl meals from $2200; ✳@🛜) Tasmanian travel glamour lives here. This architectural, gastronomic and wallet-slimming marvel has 20 luxe suites, with the curvaceous main building housing a swanky restaurant, bar, library, art gallery and spa. There's also a menu of activity options, many included in the price, and the views are the best in the land. Two-night minimum stay.

★Freycinet Marine Farm SEAFOOD $$
(☑03-6257 0140; www.freycinetmarinefarm.com; 1784 Coles Bay Rd, Coles Bay; plates $20-30, 12 oysters $22-25; ☉9am-5pm Sep-May, 10am-4pm Jun-Aug) Super-popular Freycinet Marine

Farm grows huge, succulent oysters in the waters around Coles Bay, while its farm-gate cafe also dishes up fish and chips, mussels, scallops and abalone. Sit on the deck, sip some chardonnay and dig into your seafood picnic, as fresh as the Freycinet air.

Tours (☑ 0444 519 288; www.oysterbaytours.com; Freycinet Marine Farm, 1784 Coles Bay Rd; $80; ☺ 10am & 1pm) of the oyster farm run daily.

Géographe   CAFE $$
(☑ 03-6257 0124; www.geographecolesbay.com; 6 Garnet Ave, Coles Bay; breakfast $12-19, mains $20-27; ☺ 8am-8pm) The only hazards here are the view – of the Hazards – and the possibility of lingering too long over breakfast. Mornings are eggy and evenings are pizza-focused, but in interesting ways: poached eggs with beetroot hummus and dukkah; smoked salmon, gummy shark and bocconcini. Most of the seating is on the Hazards-facing deck, but would you want to be anywhere else?

❶ Information

Freycinet National Park Visitor Information Centre (☑ 03-6256 7000; www.parks.tas.gov.au; Freycinet Dr, Freycinet National Park; ☺ 8am-5pm Oct-Apr, 9am-4pm May-Sep; ☎) At the park entrance, you can get your parks passes here (passes can also be purchased with eftpos at the Wineglass Bay walk car park). The centre has good displays on the park, its activities and natural and human histories. Ask about free ranger-led activities from Christmas through January.

❶ Getting There & Away

Coles Bay is 27km from the Tasman Hwy turn-off. Traverse this stretch slowly between dusk and dawn to avoid hitting any wildlife on the road.

Calow's Coaches (☑ 03-6376 2161, 0400 570 036; www.calowscoaches.com.au) runs buses from Bicheno to Coles Bay ($11.50, 30 to 50 minutes). These buses also pick up passengers from Tassielink (p633) east-coast buses at the Coles Bay turn-off (from Hobart $35.60, three hours).

Bicheno
POP 943

Despite boasting beaches and ocean colours worthy of framing, Bicheno (*bish*-uh-no) is very much a functioning fishing port with a holiday habit. With brilliant ocean views and lovely beaches, it's madly popular with holidaymakers, but it retains an appealing lack of polish. A busy fishing fleet still comes home to harbour in the Gulch with pots of lobsters and scaly loot. Accommodation prices here will seem realistic if you're heading north from Coles Bay.

European settlement began here when whalers and sealers came to the Gulch in 1803. The town became known as Waubs Bay Harbour, to honour an Aboriginal woman, Waubedebar, who rescued two drowning men when their boat was wrecked offshore. After her death in 1832, the settlement bore her name until the 1840s, when it was renamed after James Ebenezer Bicheno, once colonial secretary of Van Diemen's Land.

◉ Sights

★ **Blowhole**   NATURAL FEATURE
(off Esplanade) One of those rare blowholes that still plies its trade, even on fairly benign days, with geysers of white water surging up through a crack in the coastal rocks with a thunderous boom when waves roll in. Don't get too close: you can be unexpectedly drenched.

Diamond Island   ISLAND
Off the northern end of **Redbill Beach** (off Gordon St) is this photogenic granite outcrop, connected to the mainland via a short, semi-submerged, sandy isthmus – at low tide you can wade across to the island.

Bicheno Motorcycle Museum   MUSEUM
(☑ 0419 883 736, 03-6375 1485; 35 Burgess St; adult/child $9/free; ☺ 9am-5pm Mon-Fri, to 4pm Sat, to 3pm Sun) Andrew Quin got his first Honda at age four, and has been hooked on motorbikes ever since. You don't have to know your Benellis from your Bultacos to enjoy his wonderful museum out the back of his bike-repair shop. There are more than 60 immaculately restored bikes on display, including the only Noriel 4 Café Racer in the world. A few of the bikes are usually up for sale if you want to buy the dream.

Natureworld   ZOO
(☑ 03-6375 1311; www.natureworld.com.au; 18356 Tasman Hwy; adult/child/family $26.50/12/68; ☺ 9am-5pm) About 7km north of Bicheno, this wildlife park is overrun with native and non-native wildlife, including Tasmanian devils, wallabies, quolls, snakes, wombats and enormous 'roos. There are devil feedings daily at 10am, 12.30pm and 3.30pm, and you can get a glimpse of devil nightlife

on a dusk tour with Devils in the Dark. There's a cafe here too.

🏃 Activities & Tours

★ **Foreshore Footway**   WALKING
(via Gordon St) This lovely 3km seaside stroll extends from Redbill Beach (p671) to the Blowhole (p671) via **Waubedebar's Grave** (off Old Tram Rd) and the **Gulch** (off Esplanade). Return along the path up **Whalers Hill** (off Foster St) for broad views over the town and coast.

Bicheno Penguin Tours   BIRDWATCHING
(📞03-6375 1333; www.bichenopenguintours.com. au; 70 Burgess St; adult/child $40/20; ⊙booking office 9am-5pm) Spy some of Bicheno's many little penguins on these one-hour dusk tours, as the birds waddle back to their burrows. Departure times vary across the year, depending on when dusk falls. Photos aren't allowed, but the company can send you free photos after your tour. Penguin numbers peak from November to January. Bookings essential.

Devils in the Dark   WILDLIFE
(📞0401 246 777; www.devilsinthedark.com.au; $65; ⊙dusk) Get a secret look into Tasmanian devil life with a nocturnal tour to the free-range enclosure at Natureworld. From a low-angle hide, you'll watch them feeding and feuding...as you tuck into your own wine and cheese. Pick-ups offered from various locations around town (ask when you book). No kids under seven.

🛏 Sleeping & Eating

Bicheno Backpackers   HOSTEL $
(📞03-6375 1651; www.bichenobackpackers.com; 11 Morrison St; dm/tw/house from $31/75/110; 🛜) This congenial backpackers has dorms spread across two mural-painted buildings, plus a 12-berth self-contained house nearby, set up as six doubles. Room 5 gets a private deck overlooking the town centre and Diamond Island. The communal kitchen is the place to be, and there's a walking track to Lookout Rock at the top of the street.

★ **Beach Path House**   RENTAL HOUSE $$
(📞03-6375 1400; www.beachpathhouse.com.au; 2 Gordon St; house $225-420; ❄) Painted cream and navy, this mid-century beach shack has been reborn as a contemporary holiday house, with three bedrooms, an open fire and a little deck from where you can peer out over Diamond Island. A couple of old cray pots are strewn about for good nautical measure. Sleeps up to eight. Prices change dramatically with the seasons.

★ **Pasinis**   ITALIAN $$
(📞03-6375 1076; www.facebook.com/pasinis; 70 Burgess St; mains $22-32, pizza $13-33; ⊙8am-8pm) This expertly managed outfit does Italian staples much better than most – homemade pasta, wood-fired pizzas and *arancini* for example, with the occasional Nepali curry sneaking on board. The breakfasts border on artisanal, and east-coast beers, wines and oysters also make the cut. Winner! Book ahead for dinner; takeaways also available.

Lobster Shack   SEAFOOD $$
(📞03-6375 1588; www.lobstershacktasmania.com. au; 40 Esplanade; fish & chips $12-20, half-lobster from $65; ⊙10am-7pm) Sit on the outside deck of this waterside shack and you'll think you're at the railings of a ship. The lobster comes myriad ways – baked, grilled, inside rolls – and there's a host of other briny bites, including oysters and chowder. Head upstairs for a wide Gulch view and a tankful of live lobsters.

❶ Information

Bicheno Visitor Information Centre (📞03-6375 1500; www.eastcoasttasmania.com; 41b Foster St; ⊙9am-5pm Oct-Apr, 10am-4pm May-Sep) Local information and accommodation bookings. Free mobile-phone charging.

❶ Getting There & Away

Tassielink buses (p633) run from Hobart to Bicheno ($37.80, 3¼ hours) on Monday, Wednesday, Friday and Sunday. North of here, Calow's Coaches (p671) runs to St Helens ($14, 1½ hours) and to Launceston ($34, three hours), both daily except Saturday. Calow's also does the trip into Coles Bay from Bicheno ($11.50, 30 to 50 minutes).

St Helens

POP 2070

On the broad, protected sweep of Georges Bay, St Helens began life as a whaling and sealing settlement in the 1830s. Soon the 'swanners' came to plunder, harvesting the bay's black swans for their downy underfeathers. By the 1850s the town was a permanent farming settlement, which swelled in 1874 when tin was discovered nearby.

Today the town, suitably named after a ship, harbours the state's largest fishing fleet. This equates to plenty for anglers to get excited about – charter boats will take you out to where the big game fish play – while St Helens will likely also figure soon on the mountain-bike map, with plans for a 66km extension of Derby's trail network to be added here.

◉ Sights & Activities

St Helens History Room   MUSEUM
(☑ 03-6376 1479; www.sthelenshistoryroom.com; 61 Cecilia St; adult/child/family $3/free/5; ☺ 9am-5pm) Out the back of the town visitor centre is this unexpected little museum, with more than 1000 items cataloguing the town's social and natural history. Farming, exploring, schooling, whaling, fishing, mining, religion and east-coast wildlife all get the once-over, accompanied by the tick-tick-tick of an antique clock. Don't miss the amazing old funeral buggy, and the cheesy but interesting film introducing the Trail of the Tin Dragon tourist route, which focuses on Chinese tin mining in Tasmania's northeast.

Gone Fishing Charters   FISHING
(☑ 03-6376 1553; www.breamfishing.com.au; per person for 1/2/3/4 people $200/125/100/85) Hook a bream or two on a close-to-shore fishing trip with an expert local guide. No fish, no pay (you have to admire the confidence).

🛏 Sleeping & Eating

★ BIG4 St Helens Holiday Park   CARAVAN PARK $
(☑ 1300 559 745; www.big4sthelens.com.au; 2 Penelope St; unpowered/powered sites from $25/37, cabin & villa $115-225; 🅿🛜) Rolled across a green hillside 1.5km south of town, this park has plenty of family-centric amenities (games room with cinema, jumping pillow, playground) and a smart row of blue-and-cream villas racked up the hill. Decent camp kitchen, with grassy tent sites up top.

The park's new mountain-biker Bunkhouse (single/double $45/90) is like a little self-contained village inside the park. Rooms are in black shipping containers ringed around a fire pit, sun loungers and open-air kitchen with pizza oven. It has a bike wash-down bay, maintenance area, bike storage and shuttles to the Blue Tier trail (p675) above Derby. A winning addition.

The French House   B&B $$
(☑ 0414 264 258, 03-6376 2602; www.thefrenchhousesthelens.com.au; 197 Ansons Bay Rd; d $150-180; 🅿🛜) About 4km from St Helens, this B&B, built in the 1980s by a Frenchman homesick for his country home, exudes Gallic charm. Upstairs are four compact en-suite rooms with TV and fridge; downstairs is a country kitchen and fire-warmed guest lounge. Not frilly or kitsch, just simple and stylish. Breakfasts are generous cooked affairs. *Oui, oui!*

Nina Restaurant & Bar   MODERN AUSTRALIAN $$$
(☑ 03-6441 5007; www.ninarestaurantandbar.com; 55 Cecilia St; breakfast & lunch mains $25-36, dinner $28-43; ☺ 9am-late Tue-Sat) Oh look, a slick urban nook! With a sunny front terrace, sleek inner-city styling and sexy soundtrack, Nina is a global food journey in little old St Helens – from fish and chips with green pea mash to steamed bao with pork belly. Good for an evening drink too.

ⓘ Information

St Helens Visitor Information Centre (☑ 03-6376 1479; 61 Cecilia St; ☺ 9am-5pm) Just off the main street behind the library. Sells national parks passes.

ⓘ Getting There & Away

Calow's Coaches (p671) run between Launceston and St Helens ($32.50, 2½ hours), with connections at Epping Forest to Redline's Hobart service.

Binalong Bay & the Bay of Fires

POP 290

Larapuna/Bay of Fires could easily have taken its name from the fiery orange lichen that lights up almost every granite headland along this 29km-long sweep of powder-white sand and crystal-clear seas (though it was named for the fires of Aboriginal people sighted by Tobias Furneaux in 1773).

There's no road that runs the length of the bay, which is actually a string of superb beaches: the C850 heads out of St Helens to the gorgeous beachside holiday settlement of Binalong Bay, which marks the southern end of the bay, with the C848 continuing 11km further north to the smattering of houses at the Gardens. At the bay's northern end are Ansons Bay, a quiet holiday hamlet, and the southern sections of Mt William

National Park, including Eddystone Point, which marks the larapuna/Bay of Fires' northern extremity. The granite Eddystone Point Lighthouse stands here as a symbolic exclamation mark.

Sights & Activities

Mt William National Park NATIONAL PARK
(☎03-6387 5510; www.parks.tas.gov.au; day pass per vehicle/person $24/12, camping from $13) Little-known, isolated Mt William National Park features long sandy beaches, prolific wildlife and the eponymous wukalina/Mt William, reached on a one-hour return walk. Standing 216m above sea level, it's more a glorified hill, but still affords view over the stunning coastline and the southern Furneaux Group islands. The area was declared a national park in 1973, primarily to protect Tasmania's remaining Forester (eastern grey) kangaroos, which faced extinction in the 1950s and '60s (they've been breeding themselves silly ever since).

Bay of Fires Lodge Walk WALKING
(☎03-6392 2211; www.taswalkingco.com.au/bay-of-fires-lodge-walk; from $2395; ⊙Oct-May) A four-day, three-night guided adventure along this glorious coastline. A maximum of 10 guests wander south from Mt William National Park, led by knowledgeable guides, with a day of kayaking on Ansons River. The first night is spent at a secluded beach camp, with the next two at the sublime Bay of Fires Lodge. Fine food and wine included. Magic!

Bay of Fires Eco Tours BOATING
(☎0499 209 756; www.bayoffiresecotours.com.au; Titley's Shack, Main Rd; ⊙Gardens Explorer tour 9.30am Tue, Thu, Fri & Sun; 👪) A coast this vibrant deserves to be seen from the water. Based in a little wooden shack beside the Binalong Bay boat ramp, this outfit runs a series of tours to see dunes, dolphins, Aboriginal sites and the lichen-covered coast between Binalong Bay and Eddystone Point. The two-hour Gardens Explorer (adult/child $105/65) is the most popular trip.

wukalina walk WALKING
(☎0447 244 727; www.wukalinawalk.com.au; from $2495; ⊙Oct-Apr) Hike the coastline from wukalina/Mt William to Eddystone Point on this four-day, three-night guided hike run by the *palawa* (Tasmanian Aboriginal) community. It explores bush tucker, middens, *palawa* culture and history and the striking beauty of the coastline. Two nights are spent at an award-winning standing camp behind the beaches, and one night in the Eddystone Point lighthouse keeper cottages.

Sleeping & Eating

Kingfisher Cottage RENTAL HOUSE $$
(☎0467 808 738; www.kingfishercottage.com.au; 74 Main Rd; house from $195; 📶) Not gregarious, not making a statement, not flashy or pretentious – just the perfect little beach house in a primo location, right in the sandy heart of Binalong Bay, next to Lichen and a pebble's toss from the perfect beach. Sleeps up to six in two bedrooms.

Bay of Fires Bush Retreat TENTED CAMP $$
(☎0439 343 066; www.bayoffiresbushretreat.com.au; 795 Reids Rd; d from $165, safari tent d & tw $185; ⊙mid-Sep–mid-Jul; 📶) On the outskirts of town, near the turn-off to the Gardens, this rustic, hippy-goes-boutique bush-camping retreat involves interesting 'bell tents' with shared bathrooms and cooking facilities. Cooked breakfasts ($24) and two-course chef's-choice dinners ($42) are available, with an honesty bar of Tassie tipples. The vibe is chilled-out and wholesome. Book well ahead.

★Lichen Restaurant & Cafe MODERN AUSTRALIAN $$
(☎03-6376 8086; www.lichenrestaurant.com; 66 Main Rd; mains $22-42; ⊙9am-3pm & 6pm-late Tue-Sat, 9am-3pm Sun) We're likin' what they're doing here – good coffee, casual days that slide into fine-dining evenings, leisurely weekend breakfasts and locally caught fish, even in the tempura Tokyo tacos. Perhaps best of all is the view from the elevated wooden deck peering along the length of the bay.

Getting There & Away

At the southern end of larapuna/Bay of Fires is Binalong Bay, an easy 15-minute drive from St Helens. The northern end of the bay is flagged by Ansons Bay and Eddystone Point Lighthouse, both accessed via Ansons Bay Rd tracking north from St Helens. In between, other than the road from Binalong Bay to the Gardens holiday settlement, there's no road access, and certainly no public transport.

Derby & Around

POP 173

Derby once shone as a tough tin-mining centre, but today it's the town that mountain biking rebuilt. In the decades after the tin mines closed in the 1940s, Derby all but slipped from the map, but with the opening of the Blue Derby mountain-bike trail network in 2015, the air was pumped back into Derby's tyres. The town quickly became one of the world's most revered mountain-bike destinations – in 2017 and 2019, it hosted a round of the Enduro World Series. Trails radiate in all directions from the centre of town, and the main street often holds more bikes than cars, even though the Tasman Hwy trucks straight through the middle of it all.

Accommodation fills up quickly when the mountain-bike urge hits. About 8km west of Derby is **Branxholm** (population 267) with further sleeping and eating options.

⊙ Sights & Activities

Bridestowe Lavender Estate   FARM
(📞 03-6352 8182; www.bridestowelavender.com. au; 296 Gillespies Rd, Nabowla; $10 Dec & Jan, free Feb-Nov; ⊗ 9am-5pm Sep-Apr, 10am-4pm May-Aug) Near Nabowla, 22km west of Scottsdale, is the southern hemisphere's largest lavender farm. In the flowering season (mid-December to late January), the farm's slopes become rolling waves of purple. There's also a cafe and gift shop that sells all things lavender: soap, eye pillows, teas (lavender and mint, anyone?) and 'Bobbie Bears' – lavender-stuffed teddy bears that sell by the thousands.

In December and January, the entry fee includes a guided tour of the blooms.

★ **Blue Derby**
Mountain Bike Trails   MOUNTAIN BIKING
(www.ridebluederby.com.au) **FREE** Derby has become synonymous with mountain biking through its ever-growing Blue Derby trail network. Trails range from easy to extremely difficult, and from 1km tootles to 40km all-day epics. Standout trails include Blue Tier, Atlas and Return to Sender. The signboard at the main trailhead, at the bottom of Christopher St, below the post office, has maps and ride suggestions.

Vertigo MTB   MOUNTAIN BIKING
(📞 0488 463 333; www.vertigomtb.com.au; 66 Main St; bike hire per day incl equipment $59-125; ⊗ 8am-5pm, closed Aug) A one-stop shop for all your MTB needs in Derby: bike hire, trail info, repairs and maintenance and shuttles to trailheads. There are several shuttle options, including the Blue Tier and Atlas Day (shuttle to the top of the Blue Tier track, a lunch stop at the Weldborough Hotel, then transported to the start of Atlas) for $75.

Blue Derby Pods Ride   MOUNTAIN BIKING
(📞 0407 090 904; http://bluederbypodsride.com. au; $2150) A three-day guided mountain-biking trip around the Blue Derby trails, staying in wooden sleeping pods ingeniously hidden within the trail network, with any muscle soreness soothed by fine Tassie food and wine.

🛏 Sleeping & Eating

Almost every home in Derby seems to have become a rental house aimed at mountain bikers. The option of choice for many

---

THE MOUNTAIN BIKING REVOLUTION

It began with a forgotten and forlorn tin-mining town. When Derby, in Tasmania's northeast, was fitted with a scribble of mountain bike tracks in 2015, the town and Tasmania suddenly found themselves at the centre of the mountain-biking world. Two rounds of the Enduro World Series have now been held along the Blue Derby trail network, and there are many who rate tracks such as Blue Tier as among the finest on the planet.

Blue Derby has well and truly set the mountain bike rolling for Tasmania. In January 2018, the Maydena Bike Park (p712) opened in the state's southwest, with more than 50 trails plummeting 800m down the area's rainforest-covered slopes. Despite its reputation for steep and challenging runs, Maydena launched the world's biggest beginner descent – the Regnans Ride – at the end of 2018.

At around the same time, the **Wild Mersey** (http://ridewildmersey.com.au) mountain bike trail network opened in the state's northwest. Centred on Latrobe and the Badgers Range, its plans include more than 100km of trails – stage one features 15km of predominantly green (easy) and blue (intermediate) trails in Latrobe's Warrawee Reserve.

Nor is Derby itself finished with its development, with stage two of its development to see a 66km extension of the trail network created near St Helens.

though is the free short-term camping in Derby Park by the Ringarooma River, with unpowered sites, a toilet block, a BBQ hut and the option of a dunk in the river. There are coin-operated showers ($3) at the Blue Derby network trailhead at the bottom of Christopher St.

Tin Dragon Trail Cottages
COTTAGE $$

(✆0407 501 137; www.tindragontrailcottages.com. au; 3 Cox's Lane, Branxholm; cottage from $170) ♪ These five neat, sustainably built cottages sit near the Ringarooma River on a property that has an interesting story to tell from the Chinese mining past. The cottages are fully self-sufficient in power, running on a micro-hydro station, solar and Tesla batteries. Three cottages have outdoor spas.

Weldborough Hotel
PUB $

(✆03-6354 2223; www.weldborough.com.au; 12 Main Rd; unpowered sites per person $10, d/f without bathroom from $100/150; ☉pub 11.30am-late) This remote and characterful 1876 pub – it basically *is* the township of Weldborough – has basic rooms, but its true treats are the park-like camping area (with hot showers) and the exhaustive selection of Tasmanian craft beers and ciders. The kitchen does decent pub grub (mains $22 to $34).

The Hub
PIZZA $$

(✆0434 445 809; www.thehubderby.com.au; 72 Main St; pizza $12-22; ☉noon-9pm Wed-Sun; 🛜) Mountain biking, pizza and beer are a perfect marriage, and Derby's finest eatery, reopened under new owners in late 2018, brings it all together. Wrapped around a central fireplace (grab the chesterfield sofa!), the friendly place serves up mighty fine wood-fired pizzas and Tassie craft beers.

❶ Getting There & Away

Sainty's North East Bus Service (Map p680; ✆0400 791 076, 0437 469 186; www. saintysnortheastbusservice.com.au) Twice-daily (weekdays) buses between Launceston and Lilydale, Scottsdale, Derby and Bridport in the northeast. Departs the Cornwall Square Transit Centre.

Flinders Island

POP 906

Distil Tasmania into an even smaller parcel and you have Flinders Island, the largest of the 52 Furneaux Group islands that sprinkle the eastern edge of Bass Strait. The island is the remains of the land bridge that connected Tasmania with mainland Australia 10,000 years ago, with coastlines resembling the Bay of Fires and granite mountains that could have been borrowed from the Freycinet Peninsula.

Sparsely populated and naturally gorgeous, Flinders is a rural community that lives mostly from fishing and agriculture. For visitors there's great bushwalking, copious wildlife, fishing, mountain biking, kayaking, snorkelling, diving and safe swimming in its curvaceous bays. Or you can spend a few leisurely hours combing the beaches for elusive Killiecrankie diamonds (topaz, technically) and nautilus shells.

◉ Sights & Activities

Even by Tasmanian standards, Flinders Island punches above its weight as a bushwalking destination, with three of the state's 60 Great Short Walks on the island: a 1½-hour (1.9km) circuit around the bewilderingly named and bewitchingly beautiful **Trousers Point**; a 1½-hour (6.6km) beach hop to the hulking **Castle Rock**; and the 5.6km, four- to five-hour (return) climb to the island's highest point, the 756m **Strzelecki Peaks**.

Wybalenna Historic Site
HISTORIC SITE

(Port Davies Rd, Emita; ☉dawn-dusk) FREE A chapel and cemetery are about all that remain of this misguided settlement, built to 'care for' relocated mainland Tasmanian Aboriginal people. Between 1834 and 1847, more than 150 people died here from poor food, disease and despair. Among them was Manalargena, chief of the Trawlwoolway tribe, whose headstone can be seen. The site is on Aboriginal land: be respectful.

Furneaux Museum
MUSEUM

(✆03-6359 8434; www.furneauxmuseum.org.au; 8 Fowlers Rd, Emita; adult/child $5/free; ☉1-5pm Christmas-Easter, 1-4pm Sat & Sun Easter-Christmas) The grounds around the volunteer-run Furneaux Museum are strewn with whalebones, blubber pots and rusty ship propellers. Inside are Aboriginal artefacts (including beautiful shell necklaces), plus sealing, sailing and muttonbird industry relics, occupying buildings that include century-old prison cells. Cash only.

🛏 Sleeping & Eating

West End Beach House
RENTAL HOUSE $$$

(✆0488 089 955; www.westendbeachhouse.com. au; 801 West End Rd, Leeka; house for up to 4 people

$205-395) ✐ Architect-designed to have a minimal environmental footprint, this fabulous, roll-roofed holiday house en route to Mt Tanner has a very Australian vibe: corrugated iron, lots of fold-back glass, sunny decks and an outdoor post-beach shower, all a short stroll from the sand. And the sunken bath is something to cherish! Four-night minimum stay in peak summer. Sleeps up to seven.

Flinders Wharf　　MODERN AUSTRALIAN $$
(☑0474 889 236; http://theflinderswharf.com.au; 16 Esplanade, Whitemark; mains breakfast & lunch $10-30, dinner $18-38; ☺7am-8pm Mon-Fri, 8am-8pm Sat & Sun Oct-Apr, shorter hours winter) Flinders Island's finest restaurant opened in March 2019 beside Whitemark's wharf. To the menu of local produce, including a drinks list featuring the likes of Kunzea cordial, add Bass Strait views, a live crayfish tank, a working beehive (bring a jar and you can leave with honey) and, from the middle of 2019, a whisky distillery.

Furneaux Tavern　　PUB FOOD $$
(☑03-6359 3521; www.furneauxtavern.com.au; 11 Franklin Pde, Lady Barron; mains $23-40; ☺noon-1.30pm & 6-7.30pm) Excellent pub bistro food, striving for minimal intervention between paddock and plate. The menu features the likes of wallaby pies, plus an unsurprising and entirely pleasing seafood bent. Island wines too. Short kitchen hours, so don't be late.

The tavern also offers an array of nicely updated motel-style cabins (double/family $150/165), set amid native gardens and with wrap-around decks looking out over Franklin Sound. The restaurant is a major bonus given the lack of other eating options at this end of the island.

ⓘ Information

Flinders Island Visitor Information Centre
(☑03-6359 5001; www.visitflindersisland.com.au; 4 Davies St, Whitemark; ☺9am-5pm Mon-Fri) The main hub for island advice.

ⓘ Getting There & Around

Sharp Airlines (☑1300 556 694; www.sharpairlines.com; Flinders Island Airport, Palana Rd, Whitemark) Flies between Melbourne (Essendon Airport) and Flinders Island Airport at Whitemark (one way $255), and between Launceston and Flinders Island ($188). Packages with car hire and accommodation start at $484 per person.

Flinders Island Car Rentals (☑0415 505 655, 03-6359 2168; www.ficr.com.au; Flinders Island Airport, Palana Rd, Whitemark) Flinders Island Car Rentals has vehicles from $80 per day, and operates an electric-powered shuttle between the airport and your accommodation ($15 per person to Whitemark). It can also arrange national park passes and hiking guidebooks to the island.

LAUNCESTON

POP 84,153

Tasmania's second city (pronounced 'lonsess-ton') has forever been locked in rivalry with big-smoke Hobart to the south. Launcestonians argue that their architecture is more elegant, their parks more beautiful, their surrounding hills more verdant and their food scene zestier. It is indeed a city where art and design are highly valued, the locals embrace the outdoors, and food and coffee culture thrives. A striking new hotel inside the city's tallest building – repurposing grain silos, of all things – has opened, while Cataract Gorge remains the sort of natural adornment you rarely find inside cities, and it's an easy and endearing base for those exploring the Tamar Valley or other parts of the north. There's a lot to like about 'Lonnie'.

Launceston was once part of the country belonging to the Midland Plain Aboriginal people.

◉ Sights

★**Cataract Gorge**　　PARK
(Map p678; www.launcestoncataractgorge.com.au; ☺24hr) At magnificent Cataract Gorge, right at the city centre's edge, the bushland, cliffs and ice-cold South Esk River feel a million miles from town. At First Basin there's a free (chilly) outdoor **swimming pool** (November to March), the world's longest single-span **chairlift** (adult/child one way $13/8; 9am to 5.30pm, to 4.30pm in winter) and Victorian-era gardens where peacocks strut. Elsewhere there are walking tracks and various lookouts. Eating options include a cafe and the Gorge Restaurant (p682).

Two walking tracks straddle the gorgeous gorge (**Cataract Walk** is level; the **Zig Zag Track** is steep), leading from Kings Bridge up to First Basin. You can also drive to the First Basin car park – follow the signs from York St to Hillside Cres, Brougham St and Basin Rd.

Just upstream from First Basin is the **Alexandra Suspension Bridge**, from where

Launceston

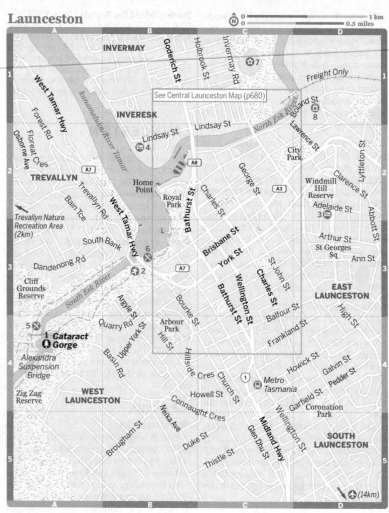

See Central Launceston Map (p680)

Launceston

◎ Top Sights
1 Cataract Gorge A4

✦ Activities, Courses & Tours
2 Penny Royal Adventures B3

⬛ Sleeping
3 Kurrajong House D2
4 Peppers Silo B2

✕ Eating
5 Gorge Restaurant A4
6 Stillwater B3

★ Entertainment
7 York Park C1

⬛ Shopping
8 Autobarn D1

another walking track (45 minutes one way) heads further up the gorge to **Duck Reach**, the earliest municipal hydroelectric power station in Australia (1895).

You can also explore the gorge on a **guided walk** (☏ 0434 359 818; www.walkcata ractgorge.com.au) or a boat trip with Tamar River Cruises.

★**Queen Victoria Museum**   MUSEUM
(QVMAG; Map p680; ☑ 03-6323 3777; www.qvmag.
tas.gov.au; 2 Invermay Rd, Inveresk; ⊙10am-4pm,
planetarium shows 1pm & 3pm Tue-Fri, 2pm & 3pm
Sat; 🚻) FREE Inside the restored and reinvented Inveresk railway yards, QVMAG has
the usual assembly of dinosaurs and stuffed
animals, but they sit alongside historic
treasures such as bushranger Martin Cash's
revolver, the tortoise-shell workbasket of
Lady Jane Franklin, and a section devoted to
the Tasmanian tiger. Kids will love the interactive gadgetry of the Phenomena Factory,
and the **planetarium** (adult/child/family
$7/5/18) is perennially popular. There's also
a cafe and museum shop. Get here on the
free Tiger Bus (p683).

Free museum tours on Sundays at 1pm.

★**Queen Victoria Art Gallery**   GALLERY
(QVMAG; Map p680; ☑ 03-6323 3777; www.qvmag.
tas.gov.au; 2 Wellington St; ⊙10am-4pm Feb-Dec,
to 5pm Jan) FREE Colonial paintings, including works by John Glover, are the pride of
the collection at this art gallery in a meticulously restored 19th-century building on the
edge of Royal Park. Be sure to check out the
ground-level First Tasmanians Gallery, featuring stone tools, Indigenous history, a basket weaved by the famous Truganini and a
map of Tasmania's Aboriginal nations to get
your ancient bearings on the island. There's
also a cafe and a gallery shop.

Boag's Brewery   BREWERY
(Map p680; ☑ 03-6332 6300; www.jamesboag.
com.au; 39 William St; adult/child $33/15; ⊙tours
11am, 1pm & 3pm) James Boag's beer has
been brewed on William St since 1881. See
the amber alchemy in action on 90-min-
ute guided tours, which include a beer and
cheese tasting. Alternatively, order a beer
paddle ($12) and take your drink upstairs
to the free on-site museum, which is a toast
to brewing history, from the Boag family
story to the brewery's Helmut Newton ad
campaigns.

🏃 **Activities & Tours**

Penny Royal Adventures   ADVENTURE SPORTS
(Map p678; ☑ 03-6332 1000; www.pennyroyal
launceston.com.au; 1 Bridge Rd; adult/child $59/39;
⊙10am-4pm Mon-Fri, 9.30am-5pm Sat & Sun;
🚻) Kids driving you up the wall? Let them
climb up a cliff wall at the mouth of Cataract
Gorge instead, or walk across it (and over a
waterfall) on rope bridges, or leap from it on
a 20m controlled-descent jump.

Tamar River Cruises   BOATING
(Map p680; ☑ 03-6334 9900; www.tamar
rivercruises.com.au; Home Point Pde) Runs up to
12 boat trips a day, ranging from 50-minute
squeezes into Cataract Gorge aboard the
electric-driven, 1890s-style *Lady Launceston* (adult/child/family $33/15/80), to four-
hour lunch trips on kanamaluka/Tamar
River to Batman Bridge ($135/70/325). The
2½-hour *Tamar Odyssey* ($89/40/195) trips
head as far downstream as Rosevears.

⭐ **Festivals & Events**

★**MONA FOMA**   PERFORMING ARTS
(Museum of Old & New Art Festival of Music & Art;
www.mofo.net.au; ⊙Jan) MONA FOMA, run
by Hobart's fabulous MONA (p635), upped
stumps in 2019, shifting from Hobart to
Launceston and bringing its wonderfully
eclectic collection of performances to the
north. The festival is under the stewardship
of Brian Ritchie, the bass-man from the Violent Femmes.

Junction Arts Festival   PERFORMING ARTS
(www.junctionartsfestival.com.au; ⊙Sep) Five
excellent days of offbeat and interesting arts
performances, installations and gigs in or
around Princes Sq.

Festivale   FOOD & DRINK, ART
(www.festivale.com.au; daily entry adult $15-25,
child $7.50, family $40-60; ⊙Feb) Launceston's
foodie-cultural highlight is three festive days
in City Park, with eating, drinking, arts and
live music. Tasmanian food and wine get an
appropriate airing, including through masterclasses in the likes of pinot noir appreciation and beer-and-cheese pairing.

🛏 **Sleeping**

Launceston Backpackers   HOSTEL $
(Map p680; ☑ 03-6334 2327; www.launceston
backpackers.com.au; 103 Canning St; dm $27-28, s/
tw/tr $65/69/90, d with/without bathroom $75/65;
P🖥🛜) 🍃 Overlooking Brickfields Reserve,
this cavernous Federation-era house is the
pick of Launceston's scant budget offerings. Dorms have a mix of bunks and single
beds; en-suite doubles have comfy beds. The
public areas have copious space, including
an industrial-size kitchen. Management is
eco-attuned, proudly backing local environmental activities, and it's a no-party
hostel – you'll be asked to do your drinking
elsewhere.

Central Launceston

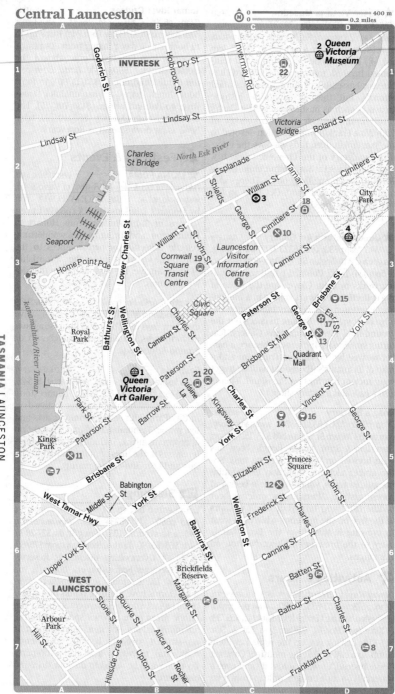

0 — 400 m
0 — 0.2 miles

INVERESK

Goderich St
Holbrook St
Dry St
Invermay Rd

Queen Victoria Museum
2

22

Lindsay St
Lindsay St

Victoria Bridge
Boland St

Charles St Bridge
North Esk River
Esplanade
Cimitiere St

Lindsay St

Shields St
William St
3

Tamar St
Cimitiere St

City Park

Seaport

Home Point Pde

William St
St John St
George St
18

Launceston Visitor Information Centre
4

Lower Charles St

Cornwall Square Transit Centre
19

10

Cameron St

Civic Square

Paterson St

Brisbane St
15

Bathurst St
Wellington St

Charles St
Cameron St

George St
Earl St
17
13

York St

Paterson St

Brisbane St Mall

Quadrant Mall

Queen Victoria Art Gallery
1

21 20
Cuisine La

Charles St

Barrow St

Kingsway

York St

Vincent St
14   16

Park St
Paterson St

Brisbane St

Kings Park
11

Elizabeth St

Princes Square

St John St

George St

7

Babington St

Middle St
York St

West Tamar Hwy

12

Frederick St

Charles St

Bathurst St

Wellington St

Upper York St

Canning St

WEST LAUNCESTON

Stone St
Bourke St

Brickfields Reserve
Margaret St

Batten St
9

6

Balfour St

Charles St

Arbour Park

Hill St

Hillside Cres
Upton St
Alice Pl
Rocher St

Frankland St
8

Central Launceston

◎ **Top Sights**
1 Queen Victoria Art Gallery B4
2 Queen Victoria Museum D1

◎ **Sights**
3 Boag's Brewery C2
4 Design Tasmania D3

◉ **Activities, Courses & Tours**
5 Tamar River Cruises A3

◉ **Sleeping**
6 Launceston Backpackers C7
7 Leisure Inn Penny Royal A5
8 Mantra Charles Hotel D7
9 Two Four Two D6

◉ **Eating**
10 Bread & Butter C3
11 Cataract on Paterson A5
12 Geronimo C5
13 Sweetbrew D4

◎ **Drinking & Nightlife**
14 Bakers Lane C5
15 Bar Two D3
16 Saint John D5

◎ **Entertainment**
17 Princess Theatre D4

◎ **Shopping**
Design Tasmania Shop .... (see 4)
18 Harvest D2

❶ **Transport**
Calow's Coaches .... (see 19)
19 Cornwall Square Transit Centre B3
20 Lee's Coaches C4
21 Manions' Coaches B4
Redline Coaches .... (see 19)
Sainty's North East Bus
Service .... (see 19)
22 Tiger Bus C1

★ **Peppers Silo**   HOTEL $$
(Map p678; ☑ 1300 987 600, 03-6700 0600; www.
peppers.com.au/silo; 89-91 Lindsay St; d $240-
305, ste $540-600; ❉ 🛜) Peppers is one of
Launceston's newest and most ambitious
hotels. Filling the city's former silos (together
forming Launceston's highest building), it's
now stuffed with character instead of grain.
Room walls curve with the silos' shape, and
you're free to take the hotel dog – Archie the
black Labrador – for a walk. Silo-side rooms
have views to Seaport and Cataract Gorge.

★ **Two Four Two**   APARTMENT $$
(Map p680; ☑ 03-6331 9242; www.twofourtwo.
com.au; 242 Charles St; studio/apt from $230/270;
P ❉ 🛜) Launceston's best self-catering
accommodation, super-stylish Two Four
Two is wrapped around one of the cafes
on the hip Charles St strip. Two double
studios and an apartment sleeping up to
four feature fully equipped kitchens with
coffee machines, spacious bathrooms (with
bathrobes) and comfortable beds sheathed
in quality linen. All have books, DVDs, Tasmanian wines and art...and there are free
bicycles!

Mantra Charles Hotel   HOTEL $$
(Map p680; ☑ 03-6337 4100, 1300 987 604; www.
hotelcharles.com.au; 287 Charles St; d/apt from
$169/249; P ❉ @ 🛜) Grab a curative sleep at
this former hospital, which has been given a
funky facelift and now rightfully claims the
title of Launceston's savviest business hotel.

Room types include king rooms, one-bed-
room spa apartments and studios with
kitchenette. All are spacious, stylish and
utterly comfortable, with bright splashes of
colour.

Leisure Inn Penny Royal   HOTEL $$
(Map p680; ☑ 03-6335 6600; www.leisureinn
pennyroyal.com.au; 147 Paterson St; d/apt
from $130/150) You might wish you'd
packed your jousting sticks in these faux-
medieval rooms, but you can't stay any
closer to Cataract Gorge. Apartments (which
are more colonial than Dark Age) back right
up against the cliffs at the gorge's mouth,
while hotel rooms are just down the road
inside an 1825 water-mill complex. Good
value, great location.

Kurrajong House   B&B $$
(Map p678; ☑ 03-6331 6655; www.kurrajong
house.com.au; cnr High & Adelaide Sts; d $159-214;
P 🛜) This fastidiously run B&B in a hand-
some 1879 house offers five rooms in the
main house and a self-contained cottage in
the former stables. The Adelaide room is
huge, while the Emily room sports a glass
chandelier. The pitch is squarely towards
'mature' guests (no kids...and no under-21s),
and a cooked breakfast is served.

✗ Eating

★ **Bread & Butter**   CAFE $
(Map p680; ☑ 03-6124 2299; http://breadand
buttertasmania.com.au; 89 Cimitiere St; items

$5-11.50; ⊙7am-3pm Mon-Sat, from 8am Sun) Go to the source (or the butter, in this case) in this cavernous new cafe inside a former motorcycle warehouse turned butter factory. With its black walls, funky art and toasters on the tables, it's all inner-city hipster styling with good coffee and wonderful fresh-baked sweet treats.

★Sweetbrew   CAFE $$
(Map p680; ☑03-6333 0443; www.facebook.com/sweetbrewespresso; 93a George St; breakfast $14-19; ⊙7am-3pm Mon-Fri, 8am-3pm Sat, 8am-2pm Sun; 🛜🅿) Sweet indeed is this cafe – the best in the city centre – cooking up an interesting breakfast and brunch menu, including miso wild mushrooms, turmeric pancakes, and lentil and mushroom burgers. We love the sneaky booth rooms out the back and the warming throws on the footpath tables.

Cataract on Paterson   STEAK $$
(Map p680; ☑03-6331 4446; www.cataractonpaterson.com.au; 135 Paterson St; mains $26-45; ⊙5pm-late Mon & Tue, noon-2pm & 5pm-late Wed-Sun) Beef is big in Launceston (as you'd expect with Cape Grim so close). A mod-industrial space near Cataract Gorge, C on P specialises in steaks cooked on 400°C stones at the tables. Not now for cow? Chicken, pork, lamb and seafood also pass muster, plus a couple of vegetarian dishes if you feel like bucking the trend. Can get noisy.

Gorge Restaurant   MODERN AUSTRALIAN $$
(Map p678; ☑03-6331 3330; www.launcestoncataractgorge.com.au; Cataract Gorge; lunch mains $22-46, dinner $38-46; ⊙noon-2.30pm & 6.30-9pm Tue-Sat, noon-2.30pm Sun) It's worth eating here for the photogenic setting alone, especially when sitting outside in summer watching the peacocks strut their stuff. Walk off your deep-fried brie and your twice-cooked duck on the stroll back to town through Cataract Gorge. Super-romantic at night.

★Geronimo   MODERN AUSTRALIAN $$$
(Map p680; ☑03-6331 3652; www.geronimorestaurant.com.au; 186 Charles St; shared plates $17-42, pizzas $22-26; ⊙5pm-late Mon-Thu, from 3pm Fri-Sun; 🅿) Arrive early and begin with an *aperitivo* at the bar of Launceston's most savvy restaurant. There's an up-to-the-moment menu of shared plates, wood-fired pizzas, a formidable wine list and bright interiors. The food is great – think pan-fried gnocchi with leeks, blue cheese and

walnuts – and there's a snack menu ($9 to $17) to go with the *aperitivi*.

★Stillwater   MODERN AUSTRALIAN $$$
(Map p678; ☑03-6331 4153; www.stillwater.net.au; 2 Bridge Rd; breakfast $9-26, mains $37-60; ⊙8.30am-3pm Mon & Sun, to late Tue-Sat; 🅿) The much-awarded Stillwater, inside a historic flour mill on the Tamar (parts of which date back to 1832), has long been at the top of Launceston's dining tree. It serves laid-back breakfasts and lunches...then puts on the Ritz for dinner. The menu changes with the seasons and, like the thoughtful wine list, zeros in on local produce.

🍷 Drinking & Nightlife

★Saint John   BAR
(Map p680; ☑03-6333 0340; www.saintjohncraftbeer.com.au; 133 St John St; ⊙noon-late Mon-Sat, from 2pm Sun) The 10 taps get busy at this dark and delightful bar, pouring a vast range of craft beers for regulars of every age and social category. Food – fried chicken and burgers – comes from a caravan hidden out the back (from 5pm). Settle into one of the chesterfield lounges if you're here for a session.

Bakers Lane   BAR
(Map p680; ☑03-6334 2414; www.bakerslanebar.com; 81 York St; ⊙11.30am-late Wed-Sat, 3-8.30pm Sun) Launceston's coolest bar delivers bar food (fried chicken, pork ribs, burgers), cocktails and craft beer beneath a faux hanging garden. Thursday is vegan curry night. It also stays open later than most venues in town.

Bar Two   WINE BAR
(Map p680; ☑0405 323 125; www.facebook.com/bartwolaunceston; 47a Brisbane St; ⊙4pm-late Mon-Thu, noon-midnight Fri & Sat) This new little wine bar, tucked into a city alcove, is as cosy as they come. Wines and spirits are exclusively Tasmanian and exhaustive – there's more than 50 pinot noirs alone – and the soundtrack is as smooth as a good shiraz. The design is simple; it's all about the wine. Cheese boards ($19) and small plates ($6 to $12) are available.

☆ Entertainment

York Park   SPECTATOR SPORT
(University of Tasmania Stadium; Map p678; www.launceston.tas.gov.au/University-of-Tasmania-Stadium; Invermay Rd, Invermay) If you're in town during the Australian Football League

(AFL) season (April to August), come here to see the big men fly. Melbourne-based AFL team Hawthorn (www.hawthornfc.com.au) plays four home games here each season. The AFL Women's North Melbourne team also play one game a season here.

Princess Theatre THEATRE
(Map p680; ☑ 03-6323 3666; www.theatrenorth. com.au/princess-theatre; 57 Brisbane St; ☺ box office 9am-5pm Mon-Fri, 10am-1pm Sat) Built in 1911 and incorporating the smaller Earl Arts Centre, the old Princess stages an eclectic schedule of drama, dance and comedy.

🛍 Shopping

⭐**Design Tasmania Shop** ARTS & CRAFTS
(Map p680; ☑ 03-6331 5506; www.designtas mania.com.au/shop; cnr Brisbane & Tamar Sts; ☺ 9.30am-5.30pm Mon-Fri, 10am-4pm Sat & Sun Oct-Apr, shorter hours rest of year) The beautiful shop at **Design Tasmania** stocks a huge array of artisan-made objects, with a particular emphasis on furniture and homewares made from local wood – a veritable hymn to Huon pine. With jewellery, ceramics and clothing, you'll find no finer souvenirs in Tasmania.

⭐**Harvest** MARKET
(Map p680; ☑ 0417 352 780; www.harvestmarket. org.au; 71 Cimitiere St; ☺ 8.30am-12.30pm Sat) An excellent weekly gathering of organic producers and sustainable suppliers from around Tasmania. Craft beer and cider, artisanal baked goods, cheese, olives, truffles, salmon from 41° Degrees South, honey and veggies are all on offer, plus food trucks and stalls selling treats including *bolani* (filled Afghan flatbread).

ℹ Information

Launceston General Hospital (☑ 03-6777 6777; www.dhhs.tas.gov.au; 274-280 Charles St; ☺ 24hr) Accident and emergency.

Launceston Visitor Information Centre (Map p680; ☑ 1800 651 827; www.destination launceston.com.au; 68-72 Cameron St; ☺ 9am-5pm Mon-Fri, to 1pm Sat & Sun) Helpful tourist office that can book accommodation and tours, supply a city map and offer information about the city and region. Ask for the map of self-guided historic walks around the city.

ℹ Getting There & Away

AIR

Launceston Airport (☑ 03-6391 6222; www. launcestonairport.com.au; 201 Evandale Rd,

Western Junction) is on the road to Evandale, 15km south of the city. Qantas, Virgin Australia and Jetstar fly direct from Melbourne, Sydney and Brisbane.

BUS

Tassielink (p633) is the prime bus service, with coaches running to Hobart ($35, 2½ hours) via the Midlands Hwy, and Devonport ($24.50, 1½ hours).

Calow's Coaches (Map p680; ☑ 03-6376 2161, 0400 570 036; www.calowscoaches.com.au) Services the east coast (St Marys, St Helens, Bicheno) from Launceston. Also runs into Coles Bay and Freycinet National Park, connecting with Tassielink buses to/from Hobart on Monday, Wednesday and Friday at the Coles Bay turn-off.

Redline Coaches (Map p680; ☑ 1300 360 000; www.tasredline.com.au) From Launceston west to Westbury, Deloraine, Mole Creek, Devonport, Ulverstone, Penguin, Burnie, Wynyard, Stanley and Smithton. Also runs south to Hobart via Campbell Town, Ross, Oatlands and Kempton. Departs the Cornwall Square Transit Centre.

ℹ Getting Around

TO/FROM THE AIRPORT

The **airport shuttle** (☑ 0488 200 700; adult/child $15/10, from Airbnb properties $20) runs door-to-door services (book at least four hours before pick-up for departures). A taxi into the city costs about $35.

BUS

Tiger Bus (Map p680; ☑ 03-6323 3000; www. metrotas.com.au) Free bus service running in a loop from the Inveresk Queen Victoria Museum on two routes every 30 minutes. The **City Explorer** goes to Princes Sq, Launceston General Hospital, Windmill Hill Reserve and City Park between 10am and 3pm weekdays. The **River Explorer** goes to Princes Sq, Paterson St near the Queen Victoria Art Gallery, and Home Point (for Tamar River Cruises) between 10.30am and 3.30pm.

Metro Tasmania (Map p678; ☑ 13 22 01; www.metrotas.com.au; 168 Wellington St; ☺ 8.30am-5pm Mon-Fri) Runs Launceston's suburban bus network. One-way fares vary with distances ('zones') travelled (from $3.40 to $4.70). Buses depart from the two blocks of St John St between Paterson and York Sts. Some routes don't operate in the evenings or on Sundays. Route maps and timetables can be found on the Metro website.

TAXI

Taxi Combined (☑ 13 10 08; www.taxi combined.com.au)

AROUND LAUNCESTON

Tamar Valley

A terrain of undulating emerald hills covered with vineyards, orchards and stands of native forest, this valley is intersected by the wide kanamaluka/Tamar River, a tidal waterway running 64km north from Launceston towards Bass Strait. The valley forms Tasmania's prime wine region, with more than 30 vineyards connected by the Tamar Valley Wine Route (www.tamarvalleywineroute.com.au). kanamaluka/Tamar's western bank is the prettier of the two, but the eastern bank holds some of the bigger-name vineyards. The Batman Bridge (named for John Batman, who sailed out from kanamaluka/Tamar to found Melbourne, rather than the superhero) unites the two shores near Deviot.

☞ Tours

Tamar Valley Wine Tours WINE
(☑ 0447 472 177; www.tamarvalleywinetours.com.au; tours per person $125; ⊙ 11am Mon-Sat, noon Sun) Highly regarded small-group tours that pick up and drop off in Launceston and visit four cellar doors on a half-day tour. Includes lunch.

❶ Information

Tamar Visitor Information Centre (☑ 03-6394 4454, 1800 637 989; www.wtc.tas.gov.au/tourism/tamar-visitor-centre; 81 Main Rd, Exeter; ⊙ 9am-4pm Apr-Sep, 8.30am-5pm Mon-Fri & 9am-5pm Sat & Sun Oct-Mar; 🛜) This extremely helpful information centre sells national parks passes and the Tamar Triple Pass (adult/family $49/135), which gives entry to Seahorse World (p686), Platypus House (p685) and the Beaconsfield Mine (☑ 03-6383 1473; www.beaconsfieldheritage.com.au; West St, Beaconsfield; adult/child/family $15/5/38; ⊙ 9.30am-4.30pm). Also stocks a huge array of brochures and offering free wi-fi.

❶ Getting There & Away

Lee's Coaches (Map p680; ☑ 0400 937 440; www.leescoaches.com) Services the East Tamar region between Launceston and George Town (adult/child $13.80/1.70). Buses depart from 152 Brisbane St.

Manions' Coaches (Map p680; ☑ 03-6383 1221; www.manionscoaches.com.au) Services the West Tamar region (Exeter, Beaconsfield, Beauty Point etc) from Launceston. Buses

stop at 168 Brisbane St, opposite Village Cinemas.

Legana & Rosevears

It's often deceptive to refer to vineyards as 'Tamar Valley' since many sit so far from the river, but this is not the case in Rosevears, where the vines almost tumble into the water. Rosevears and Legana offer the first pit stops, and the first vines, heading north out of Launceston along the West Tamar Hwy (A7) – they're almost suburbs of Launceston, they're so darn proximal. Legana is right on the highway, while Rosevears adheres to narrow Rosevears Dr, where the road runs closer to the river than almost anywhere else in the region.

◉ Sights

Tamar Ridge WINERY
(☑ 03-6330 0300; www.tamarridge.com.au; 1a Waldhorn Dr, Rosevears; ⊙ 10am-5pm; 🚗) Tamar Ridge is best known for its quaffable Pirie sparkling wine (named after the brothers who pioneered the Tamar wine industry). Begin with a free tasting, choose a bottle to buy then hit the scenic terrace, which overlooks kanamaluka/Tamar River, to enjoy a cheese, salmon and charcuterie platter from the on-site Hubert & Dan. The kids can spin hula hoops on the lawn, or scrawl on the blackboard wall.

🛏 Sleeping & Eating

Rosevears Hotel HOTEL $$
(☑ 03-6394 4074; www.rosevearshotel.com.au; 215 Rosevears Dr, Rosevears; d without/with spa $195/255, ste $245; ❋🛜) 🖉 This progressive pub has stylish units crouched on the slope above the hotel. All have king beds and river-facing balconies (rooms 27 and 28 get the best of the view); spa rooms have an outdoor spa. Tesla batteries feed back into the grid, there's an attached art gallery and meals (☑ 03-6394 4074; www.rosevearshotel.com.au; 215 Rosevears Dr, Rosevears; mains $27-33; ⊙ 11.30am-3pm & 5.30pm-late) are available at the hotel.

Timbre Kitchen MODERN AUSTRALIAN $$
(☑ 03-6330 3677; www.timbrekitchen.com; Vélo Wines, 755 West Tamar Hwy, Legana; small plates $10-20, large plates $32, banquets per person $40-65; ⊙ 11am-4pm Wed, Thu & Sun, to late Fri & Sat; 🅿) Timbre's kitchen is the ultimate in seasonal menu design – the menu changes at least weekly, and is dependent on what

Around Launceston

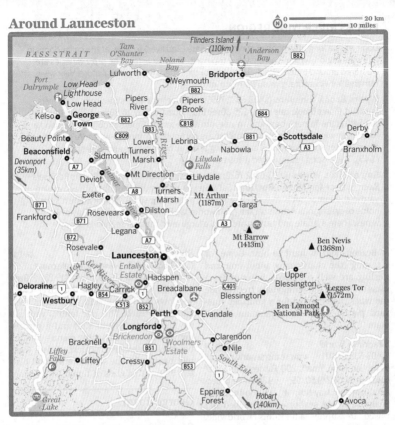

produce local growers have delivered in a swap for wine from the attached vineyard. Vegan and gluten-free options are available. Decor is Scandinavian-chic, there's a large wine list and you can sit inside or on the large deck overlooking the vines.

Book ahead for the set-menu dinner ($44) on the weekend, as it's always popular.

Beauty Point & Around

POP 1222

While the surrounding hillsides and riverscapes are certainly beautiful, the name of this town actually derives from winsomeness of the bovine variety: a now-immortalised bullock called Beauty. These days, visitors come here to visit other animals: Platypus House and Seahorse World, filling a pair of large sheds on Inspection Head Wharf. It's also a good base for exploring the Tamar Valley Wine Route.

◉ Sights

★ **Platypus House**   ZOO
(☏ 03-6383 4884; www.platypushouse.com.au; Inspection Head Wharf, 200 Flinders St; adult/child/family $25/11/60; ☺ 9.30am-4.30pm Nov-Apr, 10am-3.30pm May-Oct) Cute Platypus House puts the world's only two monotremes – the platypus and the echidna – on display for your viewing pleasure. Platypuses (including Jupiter, the largest platypus in captivity) swim about in glass-sided tanks, while in the 'echidna garden', the spiky critters wander around your feet as guides dish out scientific facts and feed. Guided tours depart on the hour.

Goaty Hill Wines   VINEYARD
(☏ 1300 819 997; www.goatyhill.com; 530 Auburn Rd, Kayena; tastings per person $3; ☺ 11am-5pm) The view from the corrugated-iron cellar door at this scenic vineyard, 7km east

PIPERS RIVER WINE REGION

Don't miss a long afternoon putting your palate (and liver) to work at the cellar doors in this wine region, which is an easy day trip north of Launceston. The prize wineries are clustered around Pipers Brook, 11km east of the Pipers River general store. Visit www.tamarvalleywineroute.com.au for more info.

Pipers Brook Vineyard (☎ 03-6382 7555; www.kreglingerwineestates.com; 1216 Pipers Brook Rd, Pipers Brook; cafe mains $25-30; ⊘ 10am-5pm Oct-May, 10.30am-4.30pm Thu-Mon Jun-Sep) is the Tamar's best-known vineyard and home to Pipers Brook, Ninth Island and Kreglinger wines (the Kreglinger sparkling is particularly impressive). There's a tasting room ($5 for six wines) and a cafe serving arancini balls, pizzas and cheese boards ($45). The tasting fee is waived if you buy a bottle.

Bay of Fires Wines (☎ 03-6382 7622; www.bayoffireswines.com.au; 40 Baxters Rd, Pipers River; ⊘ 11am-4pm Mon-Fri, from 10am Sat & Sun; 🖢) is perhaps the most attractive vineyard in the Tamar, set between tall deciduous trees and a slope of thick bush. It's the home of prestigious Arras sparkling and workaday Eddystone Point and Bay of Fires wines. There's a cafe and tasting area and a large lawn that will keep kids happy.

of Beaconsfield, is hard to beat. Come for a tasting (the chardonnay, pinot noir and riesling are well regarded), but stay for a glass under the tall stringybark trees beside the vines. Book ahead for a gourmet vineyard platter ($60) or Tasmanian cheese plate ($25).

Seahorse World AQUARIUM
(☎ 03-6383 4111; www.seahorseworld.com.au; Inspection Head Wharf, 200 Flinders St; adult/child/family $22/9.50/55; ⊘ 9.30am-4pm Dec-Apr, 10am-3pm May-Nov; 🖢) At coo-inducing Seahorse World, seahorses are hatched and raised to supply aquariums worldwide. Compulsory 45-minute guided tours run on the hour and take you through the farm, where up to 90,000 seahorses drift about. Among other bizarre sea creatures here are the critically endangered spotted handfish (found only in Hobart's Derwent estuary) and a Tasmanian giant crab, the world's second-largest crab species.

🛌 Sleeping & Eating

★ **Jensens Bed & Breakfast** B&B $$
(☎ 0410 615 678; www.jensensbedandbreakfast.com.au; 77 Flinders St; r $180-210; 🅿 🖢) Occupying a handsome Federation-style house surrounded by apple and pear trees and a manicured garden, Jensens has a communal lounge with an open fire, two stylish en-suite rooms – the Blue Room has the river views and the Rose Room has the claw-foot bath – and a large verandah with a distinctive rotunda and river views. Helpful host Carol cooks guests a full breakfast.

River Cafe CAFE $$
(☎ 03-6383 4099; www.therivercafe.com.au; 225 Flinders St; pizzas $10-19, mains $19-22; ⊘ 9am-4pm; 🖢) On sunny days, the River Cafe's windows fold back and the water feels almost in reach. The cafe tempts with all-day breakfasts ($10 to $22) and a surprisingly varied and interesting menu – Buddha bowls, dukkah-crusted chicken salad, gourmet panini. Try the signature seafood platter ($39) with a glass of Tamar Valley wine.

George Town
POP 4347
George Town stands sentinel on kanamaluka/Tamar River's eastern shore, close to where it empties into Bass Strait. Originally the territory of the Leterremairrener people, it was occupied by Europeans in 1804 as part of the British attempt to stave off settlement by the French, who had been reconnoitring the area. It was the third British town established in the new colony after Sydney and Hobart. A number of buildings in the town centre date from the 1830s and 1840s, when George Town prospered as the port linking Tasmania with Victoria. With its economic links to the smelters at nearby Bell Bay, George Town's fortunes fluctuate, but it's a good place to bunker down among history and explore Low Head and the lower reaches of the Tamar Valley.

◉ Sights

★ **Bass & Flinders Centre** MUSEUM
(☎ 03-6382 3792; www.bassandflinders.org.au; 8 Elizabeth St; adult/child/family $10/4/24;

⊙10am-4pm, closed Sat & Sun Jun-Oct) Undoubtedly the highlight of a visit to George Town, this small museum in a former cinema houses a red-sailed, full-size replica of the *Norfolk,* the sloop in which Bass and Flinders circumnavigated Tasmania in 1798. You can climb aboard the replica (and go below deck), which re-created the famous circumnavigation in 1998. There are other boats here too, including a replica of Bass and Flinders' wooden dinghy, *Tom Thumb* – it's altogether a rather fabulous collection. There's also a cafe.

🛏 Sleeping & Eating

⭐**York Cove**   HOTEL **$$**
(☑03-6382 9900; http://yorkcove.com.au; 2 Ferry Blvd; r $119-179, apt from $209; 🛜🏊) An unexpected bit of marina life in George Town, this waterfront resort has three downstairs suites and two upstairs apartments with views. The rooms are huge; the apartments even bigger. There's an outdoor swimming pool and hot tub, plus a gym and **restaurant** (mains $18-33; ⊙7-10am, noon-3pm & 5-8pm Mon-Sat, 7-10am & noon-3pm Sun; 🛜) looking over the marina to the town centre.

Gunn Deck Cafe   CAFE **$**
(☑03-6382 3792; www.facebook.com/gunndeck; 8 Elizabeth St; mains $7-15; ⊙10am-4pm Mon-Fri) Hidden in an upstairs mezzanine in the nautical Bass & Flinders Centre, overlooking the *Norfolk* sloop replica, this cafe is a pleasant surprise. Delicious cakes, a soup of the day, sandwiches, comfort food such as ploughman's platters and Devonshire teas, and wine (to give you that rolling feeling of the sea...) make it George Town's best lunch choice.

ℹ Information

George Town Visitor Information Centre
(☑03-6382 1700; www.georgetown.tas.gov. au/visitor-information; 92-96 Main Rd; ⊙9am-4pm) This volunteer-staffed centre is on the main road as you enter from the south. It supplies brochures and maps, makes accommodation bookings and hires bikes (half/full day $15/20) – the 6km Kanamaluka bike path runs from George Town to Low Head.

Low Head

POP 572

Strung along the northernmost banks of kanamaluka/Tamar River, Low Head sits shoulder-to-shoulder with George Town

– you'll barely have time to take a breath as you leave one before you hit the other. The historic town is in a spectacular setting, looking out over the swirling – and treacherous – waters of kanamaluka/Tamar as it empties into the sea. Lighthouses dominate the scene, with a couple of navigational lead lights standing tall before it all comes to an end – the town and Tasmania – at the Low Head Lighthouse. There's good surf at East Beach on Bass Strait, and safe swimming at the well-named Lagoon Beach on kanamaluka/Tamar.

⊙ Sights & Tours

Low Head
Maritime Museum   MUSEUM
(☑03-6382 1143; 399 Low Head Rd; adult/child/family $5/3/15; ⊙10am-4pm) In the Low Head historic pilot station precinct, this museum occupies the cottages that once housed Low Head's pilot. A series of rooms contains a weird and wonderful array of exhibits about the maritime history of this part of Tasmania – displays include a deep-sea diving suit, salvaged items from shipwrecks and an old homemade surfboard.

Coxswain's Cottage Café (p688) is next door, and Low Head Pilot Station Accommodation (p687) occupies a number of cottages in the precinct.

Low Head Penguin Tours   BIRDWATCHING
(☑0418 361 860; www.penguintourstasmania. com.au; 485 Low Head Rd; adult/child $22/10; ⊙sunset) Check out the little penguins that come ashore around the Low Head Lighthouse. Wheelchair-friendly guided tours leave nightly at sunset from a signposted spot between the Low Head historic pilot station precinct and the lighthouse. Bookings advised.

🛏 Sleeping & Eating

⭐**Low Head Pilot**
Station Accommodation   COTTAGE **$$**
(☑03-6382 2826; 399 Low Head Rd; cottage from $195) Low Head's historic pilot station precinct and lighthouse offer nine smartly refurbished, self-contained cottages sleeping between two and nine. The Lighthouse Cottage and Queenslander, by the lighthouse, have the best views, looking over Bass Strait and the river mouth. The cottages are great for families, with plenty of grass where kids can play. Wi-fi is available in the nearby cafe (and the reception).

WORTH A TRIP

HOLLYBANK WILDERNESS ADVENTURES

Swing through the trees with the greatest of ease on the rope and zip-line course at this **outdoor adventure centre** (☑03-6395 1390; www.holly bankadventures.com.au; 66 Hollybank Rd, Underwood; ☺9am-5pm; ⚑), 21km northeast of Launceston. Scramble along ropes and nets through pine trees on the supervised two-hour ropes course (seven levels of difficulty, adult/child $48/38), or take to the air on a guided 2½-hour zip-line tour (adult/child $125/90) through the forest.

You can also take a 1½-hour guided exploration of the forest reserve on a Segway ($100), and the centre has three mountain-bike trails, ranging in levels of difficulty – the easy No Sweat trail (5km) is ideal for families. Mountain bikes are available for hire, starting at $30 for two hours.

Coxswain's Cottage Café   CAFE $
(☑03-6382 2826; 399 Low Head Rd; sandwiches $6.50, mains $13-20, pizzas $18.50; ☺10am-4pm mid-Dec–Mar, to 3pm Mar–mid-Dec; ☜) The only place to eat in Low Head, this simple cafe in an 1847 cottage at the Low Head historic pilot station precinct serves hot and cold drinks, homemade pies, soup, toasted sandwiches, fish and chips and stone-baked pizzas. You can also order food to take away.

Longford & Around

POP 3863

Longford was founded in 1807 when free landholding farmers were moved to Van Diemen's Land from Norfolk Island. It's one of the few Tasmanian towns not established by convicts. Two farms on the far edge of town, Woolmers Estate and Brickendon, should be on your must-see list when visiting this area. Longford is also the birthplace of Man Booker Prize–winning Tasmanian author Richard Flanagan, who picked up the award in 2014 for his novel *The Narrow Road to the Deep North*. The town's other claim to fame is its role as host to the Australian Grand Prix from 1953 to 1968.

☉ Sights

★ **Woolmers Estate**   HISTORIC SITE
(☑03-6391 2230; www.woolmers.com.au; 658 Woolmers Lane; adult/child/family $16/5/35, with homestead tour $22/7/50; ☺9.30am-4pm, tours 10am, 11.15am, 12.30pm, 2pm & 3.30pm) Part of the Unesco World Heritage Australian Convict Sites listing, this pastoral estate on the Macquarie River was built by Thomas Archer in 1817 and remained in the ownership of the Archer family until 1994. You can freely wander the grounds, which include a striking **rose garden** and the oldest shearing shed in use in Australia, or take a guided 45-minute tour through the homestead, still furnished with the family's possessions.

It's possible to overnight in self-contained **cottages** (cottage from $150) on the site, and you can stroll like the gentry to neighbouring Brickendon estate on the 2.8km **Convict Trail Walk**. The visitor centre contains a decent cafe (mains $10 to $17).

Brickendon   HISTORIC SITE
(☑03-6391 1383; www.brickendon.com.au; 236 Wellington St; adult/child/family $12.50/5/38; ☺9.30am-5pm Tue-Sun Oct-May, to 4pm Jun-Sep) Wander through the convict-built farm village and gorgeous heritage gardens at Brickendon, a property that has been in the Archer family since 1824 and is also a Unesco World Heritage Australian Convict Site. There's animal feeding for the kids at 10.15am, the 2.8km Convict Trail Walk to adjoining Woolmers Estate, and on-site **accommodation** (cottage $190-225; ☜⚒).

🛌 Sleeping

★ **Quamby Estate**   BOUTIQUE HOTEL $$$
(☑03-6392 2135; www.quambyestate.com.au; 1145 Westwood Rd, Hagley; d $140-349, breakfast $25; ⚒☜) Few hotels can match the setting of this classy country-house hotel, which offers 10 stylish rooms (opt for a downstairs deluxe suite) in a pastoral 1828 homestead. Dinners (two/three courses $60/75) are in a formal ballroom setting with an informal atmosphere, and you can play golf, grab one of the free bikes, or just pretend you're 'to the manor born'.

★ **Red Feather Inn**   BOUTIQUE HOTEL $$$
(☑03-6393 6506; www.redfeatherinn.com. au; 42 Main St, Hadspen; d/q incl breakfast from $250/450; ⚒☜) Hadspen's unreservedly gorgeous 1844 Red Feather Inn offers French Provincial–style boutique

accommodation, with rooms ranging from attic doubles to a cottage sleeping eight. The Library and Garden Suites are particularly attractive. Full-day, well-regarded cooking classes (from $195) are held through winter in the country kitchen, which also services the in-house restaurant (three courses $85; open by appointment).

No kids under 16, except in the three cottages.

Evandale

POP 1124

Walking down the main street of Evandale is like stepping into a period film set, which is precisely why the entire town is National Trust classified. There are antiques, homewares and artworks aplenty behind the historic facades of Russell St, while the heritage atmosphere wheels to life each February, when Evandale hosts the **National Penny Farthing Championships** – the large penny farthing statue on Russell St plays proxy for the rest of the year. If you visit on a Sunday, the Evandale Market offers light commercial entertainment.

◉ Sights

★ Clarendon   HISTORIC BUILDING
(☑ 03-6398 6220; www.nationaltrust.org.au/places/clarendon; 234 Clarendon Station Rd, Nile; adult/child $20/free; ◷ 10am-4pm Thu-Sun Sep-Mar, Thu, Sat & Sun Apr-Jun) This 1838 mansion on the banks of the South Esk River, built for wealthy wool grower and merchant James Cox, is a Georgian gem that looks like it's stepped straight out of *Gone with the Wind*. Long the grandest house in the colony, it's open for self-guided visits, though National Trust volunteers are also usually on hand to steer you through the antique-furnished home.

⊨ Sleeping & Eating

Old Wesleyan Chapel   COTTAGE $
(☑ 0427 548 726; 28 Russell St; cottage $95) Built in 1835, this tiny brick chapel has been used variously as a Druids hall, RSL hall and scout hall. Now it's self-contained accommodation. There's a washing machine and fully equipped kitchen with homemade breakfast provisions, and a pull-out sofa bed for the kids. A recent refurbishment has given the interior a surprisingly contemporary look. Fantastic value.

Ingleside Bakery Cafe   CAFE $
(☑ 03-6391 8682; www.facebook.com/ingleside bakery; 4 Russell St; mains $8-23; ◷ 8.30am-5pm Mon-Fri, to 4pm Sat & Sun; 🖈) Sit out under the roses in the Tuscan-styled courtyard, or under the high ceiling inside this former council chambers building (1867). Expect delicious pies and pasties, a hefty ploughman's lunch and all manner of sweet treats, including superb strudels and Devonshire teas. The shelves are packed with Tasmanian products and, sealing the deal, it's licensed.

ℹ Information

Evandale Visitor Information Centre (☑ 03-6391 8128; www.evandaletasmania.com; 18 High St; ◷ 10am-4pm) Offers local info and accommodation bookings and stocks the *Evandale Heritage Walk* pamphlet ($3), detailing the town's historic riches. The history room has a display on Victoria Cross–winning WWI soldier Harry Murray and artist John Glover, who lived 20km from town. Both are commemorated with statues near the town centre.

Ben Lomond National Park

Home to Tassie's best-equipped ski field, this 181-sq-km **park** (☑ 03-6777 2179; www.parks.tas.gov.au; Ben Lomond Rd; pass vehicle/person per day $24/12) takes in the whole of the Ben Lomond massif: a craggy alpine plateau whose loftiest point, Legges Tor (1572m), is the second-highest spot on the island (the highest is the 1617m Mt Ossa). Bushwalkers make the short stroll to Legges Tor, which is really just a bump in the plateau, when the snow melts, wandering through alpine wildflowers, or marvelling at the views from the precipitous escarpments elsewhere along the plateau's edge. The drive to the plateau alone, through the tortuous Jacobs Ladder, is likely to provide the most dramatic few minutes you'll experience in a vehicle in Tasmania.

⊨ Sleeping

There's a small Parks & Wildlife Service–maintained camping area at the base of Jacobs Ladder, near the park entrance: six unpowered sites with flushing toilets, drinking water, a shelter and super views. National park entry fees apply (no camping fees or bookings).

TASMANIA EVANDALE

SKIING AT BEN LOMOND

Ben Lomond is considered Tasmania's Aspen – well, not quite, but it is the most reliable of the state's ski options. Snow coverage can be patchy, but the ski season generally runs from early July to late September. Three 'snow guns' top up the natural snow. Full-day ski-lift passes cost $70/50/30 per adult/teenager/child, while half-day passes cost $45/35/20. Under-sevens ride free. There are three T-bars and four Poma lifts. For snow reports and cams, see www.benlomond.org.au.

Ben Lomond Snow Sports runs a kiosk selling takeaway food and a shop doing ski, snowboard and toboggan rental, and associated gear. Skis, boots, poles and a lesson cost $90/70 per adult/child; just skis, boots and poles cost $65/45. Toboggan hire costs $15.

National park entry fees apply; buy your pass at self-registration booths at the park (cash only) or online.

❶ Getting There & Away

There's no public transport to the mountain, so driving is your only option.

Note that the road up to the plateau is unsealed and includes Jacobs Ladder, a sensationally steep climb with six white-knuckle hairpin bends. During the snow season, chains are standard issue – hire them from **Autobarn** (Map p678; ☑ 03-6334 5601; www.autobarn. com.au/stores/launceston; 6 Innes St; ⊙ 8am-5.30pm Mon-Fri, 9am-5pm Sat, 9am-4pm Sun) in Launceston ($40 per day, plus $60 deposit). Don't forget antifreeze.

During the ski season, **Ben Lomond Snow Sports** (☑ 03-6390 6185, out of season 0427 318 984; www.skibenlomond.com.au; Ben Lomond Rd, Ben Lomond National Park; ⊙ 9am-4.30pm in ski season) runs a shuttle bus ($15/50 per person/family return) from the bottom car park at the Parks & Wildlife Service registration booth, 7km from the ski field. If you're catching the shuttle, you don't need to hire chains for your car. Call for pick-ups.

DEVONPORT & THE NORTHWEST

Washed pure by the cleanest air on earth, and with soils so fertile they almost look edible themselves, Tasmania's northwest is rich in wilderness and poor in tourists – out here you'll have many sites, landscapes and beaches to yourself. The northwest is home to two national parks – Rocky Cape and Savage River – and is smothered in one of the largest temperate rainforests on the planet: the great, green Tarkine wilderness, known as takayna to the Tarkininer Aboriginal people, who were part of the North and Northwest groups that lived across this region prior to European settlement. Out here are also some of the best places in Australia to see platypuses and penguins, and to enjoy rustic meals featuring world-class local produce. Burnie and Devonport meanwhile maintain a gritty presence that feels as genuine and natural as the landscape that cradles them.

Devonport

POP 29,381

Tasmania's third-largest city is the port for the red-and-white *Spirit of Tasmania* ferries that connect the island state with the mainland. It's an evocative sight when, after three deep blasts of the horn, these huge ships cruise past the end of the main street to begin their voyage north. Most passengers arriving on the ferry typically scatter immediately to other destinations on the island, but there's a watch-this-space feeling about Devonport, with the city undergoing an ambitious redevelopment. It's embodied for now by Providore Place, which is planned to become the heart of the local food scene, and the Paranaple Arts Centre, with a waterfront hotel to come.

◉ Sights & Tours

★ **Bass Strait Maritime Centre** MUSEUM
(☑ 03-6424 7100; www.bassstraitmaritimecentre. com.au; 6 Gloucester Ave; adult/child/family $10/5/25; ⊙ 10am-5pm) Housed in the former harbour master's residence (c 1920), this small but impressive museum is home to displays about the maritime history of Bass Strait and Devonport. Its large collection of ship and ferry models is impressive, but the knockout exhibit is the interactive simulator ($2) that allows museum-goers to steer (or crash) a steamer into the Mersey River docks.

Mersey Bluff LANDMARK
(Bluff Rd; ⊙ access road 7.30am-9.30pm) Light-house-topped Mersey Bluff is Devonport's most striking natural feature. The Tiagarra Centre (Australia's second-oldest Aboriginal keeping place) atop the bluff opens infrequent hours, but the **Tiagarra Walking Track** (10 minutes), which begins from the shingled hut behind the centre, passes several petroglyphs of unknown origin as it loops around the bluff to the red-and-white-striped lighthouse. There are views over Bass Strait from beside the lighthouse, which was built in 1889 to aid navigation into the port.

★ **Julie Burgess** CRUISE
(☑ 03-6424 7100; www.bassstraitmaritimecentre. com.au/julie-burgess; 2hr cruise $50; ⊙ Sun) Purpose-built in 1936 to work the rich crayfish fields of Bass Strait and Tasmania, this meticulously restored fishing ketch offers a two-hour journey into Bass Strait towards Don Heads, as well as infrequent overnight trips. Book in advance through the Bass Strait Maritime Centre, as tours only operate with minimum numbers and in favourable weather conditions.

The cruises depart from Reg Hope Park next to the Mersey Yacht Club in East Devonport.

🛏 **Sleeping**

Mersey Bluff
Caravan Park CARAVAN PARK $
(☑ 03-6424 8655; www.merseybluffcaravanpark. com.au; 41 Bluff Rd; unpowered/powered sites from $25/35, cabins $150-180; 🐾) Nestled behind a stand of Norfolk Pines on Mersey Bluff, this basic, pleasantly green park is just steps from Bluff Beach and is immaculately presented. There's a campers' kitchen, laundry and excellent ablutions blocks. A couple of new cabins were installed at the end of 2018 and there's a wonderful children's playground nearby. Classic seaside camping.

★ **The Grand on Macfie** B&B $$$
(☑ 03-6424 2000; www.thegrandonmacfie.com.au; 44a Macfie St; r incl breakfast $225-300; 🛜) Built in 1899, the highly regarded Grand is just that – a well-located, large and extremely handsome mansion, offering five elegant antique-filled rooms, a guest lounge, a balcony with views over the city centre, and a dining room where a full cooked breakfast is served. On weekend afternoons, high tea

($39.50, or $49.50 with sparkling wine) is offered.

🍴 **Eating & Drinking**

Laneway CAFE $$
(☑ 03-6424 4333; www.lane-way.com.au; 2/38 Steele St; mains $12-25; ⊙ 7am-5pm Mon-Fri, to 4pm Sat & Sun; 🛜♿) Occupying a former bakery, this retro cafe accessed from Rooke St is as hip as Devonport gets. Large all-day breakfast plates (eggs, beans, waffles, coconut chia pudding) are the order of choice for a loyal local clientele, accompanied by well-made coffee or T2 tea. Check the website for occasional evening events with special dinner menus.

★ **CharlotteJack** MODERN AUSTRALIAN $$$
(www.charlottejack.com.au; Providore Place, 13-17 Oldaker St; plates $14-38; ⊙ 5pm-late) The flagship of the Providore Place complex is this glass-walled restaurant from (and named after the children of) TV celebrity chef Ben Milbourne. Select from around a dozen shared plates focused on local produce, and if you nab a bar stool you're pretty much sitting in the kitchen with the chefs. No bookings; just walk in.

Milbourne's TV studio is immediately next door; take a peek through the glass to watch the filming.

★ **Mrs Jones** MODERN AUSTRALIAN $$$
(☑ 03-6423 3881; www.mrsjonesrbl.com.au; 1st fl, 35-39 Bluff Rd; lunch mains $23-34, dinner $36-48; ⊙ noon-late Wed-Sun; 🛜♿♿) Head upstairs at the surf lifesaving club at Bluff Beach for fine food with an equally fine beach view. The ambitious menu cherry-picks highlights from global cuisines, but is particularly strong on Asian dishes – think red duck curry, Japanese-style pork dumplings and Vietnamese spanner-crab salad. Decor is casual chic, service is polished and the excellent wine list is predominantly Tasmanian.

Dedicated vegan, dairy-free, gluten-free and children's menus available.

Empress Craft Beer CRAFT BEER
(☑ 03-6423 3648; www.empresscraftbeer.com.au; 48-54 Oldaker St; ⊙ 11am-late Mon & Wed-Sat, from 2pm Sun) Devonport's most interesting bar is as dark as stout inside, but has craft beer and cider pouring from 11 taps, as well as a strong spirits collection. It sits unusually inside a grocer's complex, which perhaps explains the enlightened idea of shelves of

TASMANIA DEVONPORT

The Northwest

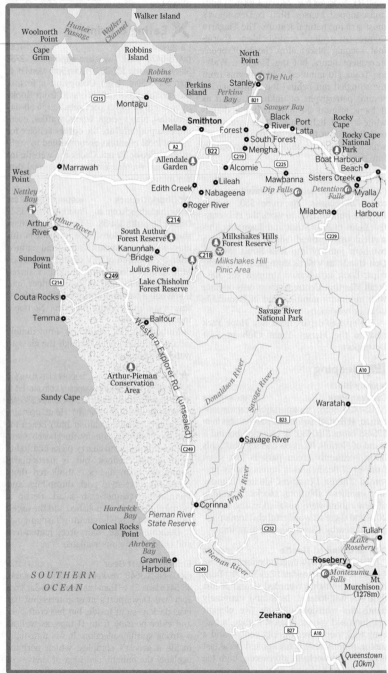

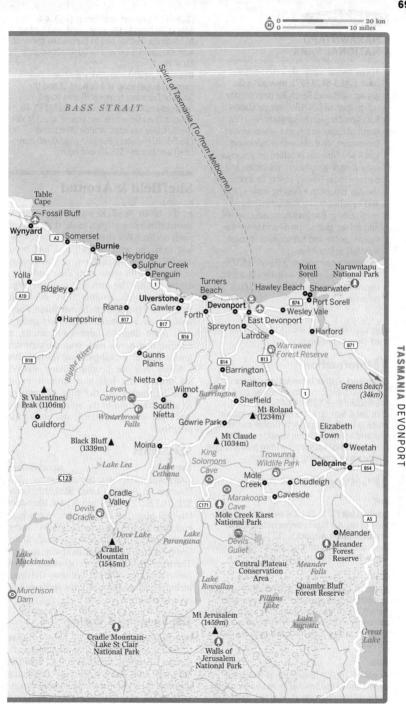

WORTH A TRIP

NARAWNTAPU NATIONAL PARK

There's wildlife aplenty in this coastal park (☏03-6428 6277; www.parks.tas. gov.au; via Bakers Beach Rd; pass per day vehicle/person $24/12; ☉ranger station 9am-4pm Dec-Apr, to 3pm May-Nov) 95km north of Launceston and 40km east of Devonport. Visit at dawn or dusk and you'll see Forester (eastern grey)kangaroos, foraging wombats, wallabies and pademelons. There's plenty to do during the day too, from following walking trails and beachcombing to swimming and horse riding. Rangers run guided walks and activities in summer and there's a visitor centre and full picnic and toilet facilities at Springlawn.

There's **camping** (☏03-6428 6277; www.parks.tas.gov.au; via Bakers Beach Rd; unpowered/powered sites from $13/16) here too.

cheeses, olives and meats so you can make your own in-bar platter.

ℹ Information

Devonport Visitor Information Centre (☏03-6420 2900; http://visitcradlecoast.com.au; 145 Rooke St; ☉7.30am-4.45pm Mon-Fri, to 2pm Sat & Sun; 🖥) This helpful information office in the Paranaple Arts Centre can make tour and accommodation bookings, sell national park passes, supply a town map and give advice about travelling in the region.

ℹ Getting There & Away

AIR

QantasLink (☏13 13 13; www.qantas.com. au) has regular flights between Melbourne and **Devonport Airport** (☏13 13 13; www. devonportairport.com.au; Airport Rd), which is about 9km east of the town centre.

BOAT

Spirit of Tasmania (☏1800 634 906; www. spiritoftasmania.com.au; ☉customer info 8am-8.30pm Mon-Sat, 9am-8pm Sun) Ferries sail between Station Pier in Melbourne and the ferry terminal on the Esplanade in East Devonport.

BUS

Tassielink (p633) Buses stop at the visitor centre and at the *Spirit of Tasmania* terminal. Services from Devonport head to Launceston

($24.50, 1½ hours) and Hobart ($59, 4¼ hours). To head to the west coast, you'll need to catch the Redline bus to Burnie and connect with Tassielink's service to Queenstown and Strahan.

Redline (☏1300 360 000; www.tasredline. com.au) Buses stop at 9 Edward St and the *Spirit of Tasmania* terminal. Buses travel between Launceston and Devonport ($25.40, 1½ hours) via Deloraine and (sometimes) Mole Creek. Other services include Ulverstone ($6.50, 30 minutes), Penguin ($8.50, 40 minutes) and Burnie ($11.20, one hour).

Sheffield & Around

POP 1552

In the 1980s Sheffield was a typical small Tasmanian country town in the doldrums of rural decline. But then some astute townsfolk came up with an idea that had been applied to the small town of Chemainus in Canada, with some surprising and wonderful results. The plan was to paint large murals on walls around town, depicting scenes from the district's pioneer days. Sheffield is now a veritable outdoor art gallery, with more than 80 large-scale murals, a number that grows each year through the town's annual mural-painting festival. It's a handy base for people walking around Mt Roland and splashing around in/on Lake Barrington. At the time of writing, an app with a tour of the murals was being developed – check at the visitor centre for progress.

◉ Sights

Tasmazia   AMUSEMENT PARK
(☏03-6491 1934; www.tasmazia.com.au; 500 Staverton Rd, Promised Land; adult/child/family $27.50/13.75/77; ☉9am-5pm Oct-Apr, 10am-4pm May-Sep) Sugar up on pancakes in the cafe and then let the kids run themselves dizzy in this wacky complex's eight mazes (four hedge mazes and four footpath mazes). There's also a whimsical model village called Lower Crackpot, and the Embassy Gardens, including 60 model buildings representing over 40 countries.

🛏 Sleeping & Eating

Acacia B&B   B&B $$
(☏0437 911 502, 0413 149 691; www.acacia-bandb. com.au; 113 High St; tw $120-125, d & f $140-170; 🖥) Ann and Nigel Beeke are justifiably proud of their quiet and meticulously maintained B&B, with four rooms on offer. Three

have en-suite bathrooms, while the twin has a private but separate bathroom; the king room with its four-poster bed is the best. A generous continental breakfast, including eggs from the owners' chickens, is served.

The owners live off-site but nearby, and are happy to supply information about touring the region. They can also store bikes in a garage – Sheffield is on the **Tasmanian Trail** (www.tasmaniantrail.com.au).

★**T's Chinese Restaurant**   CHINESE $$
(☑️03-6491 2244; 83 Main St; mains $25-34; ☺noon-2pm Tue-Sat, 5.30-9pm) Country Chinese restaurants never used to be as good as this unassuming treasure. T's delivers a full paddock-to-plate experience, with the free-range lamb and pork coming direct from the Zhao family's farm. Divine dumplings too. Anthony Liu, chef at Melbourne's celebrated Flower Drum restaurant, once rated T's among his favourite Chinese eateries... enough said? Bookings essential.

ℹ️ Information

Kentish Visitor Information Centre (☑️03-6491 1179; www.sheffieldcradleinfo.com.au; 5 Pioneer Cres; ☺9am-5pm Mon-Fri, 10am-4pm Sat & Sun Nov-Apr, 9am-5pm Mon-Fri, 11am-3pm Sat & Sun May-Oct; 📶) Sheffield's helpful visitor centre supplies information on Sheffield and the greater Kentish region. It also provides maps, can make accommodation and tour bookings, and sells national park passes and fishing licences.

ℹ️ Getting There & Away

Tassielink's bus service through Sheffield was cut in March 2019; the only way here now is with your own wheels.

Deloraine

POP 2432

At the base of the Great Western Tiers, Deloraine commands wonderful views at almost every turn. Blessed with the photo gene, the town is bisected by the winding Meander River, with Georgian and Victorian buildings scattered around the main street, Emu Bay Rd. It's a crafty town – in the artistic sense – at the doorstep to one of Tasmania's most beautiful waterfalls.

⦿ Sights

41° South Tasmania   FARM
(☑️03-6362 4130; www.41southtasmania.com; 323 Montana Rd; self-guided tour adult/child/family $10/5/25; ☺9am-5pm Nov-Mar, to 4pm Apr-Oct) ⚑**FREE** Salmon are reared in raised tanks and a wetland is used as a natural bio-filter at 41° South Tasmania – a no-waste, no-chemical method of fish farming. Take a self-guided walk, feeding the fish and heading through the wetlands to the low Montana Falls Cascades, before enjoying a free tasting of superb hot-smoked salmon or lunch in the terrace cafe (mains $10 to $20). The farm is 8km out of town towards Mole Creek (signposted down Montana Rd).

🍴 Eating

Cycles @ The Empire   AUSTRALIAN $$
(☑️03-6362 1029; www.theempiredeloraine.com. au; 19 Emu Bay Rd; mains $19-33; ☺10am-10pm Tue-Sat, to 9pm Sun, kitchen noon-3pm Tue-Sun, 6-8.30pm Sun-Thu & 6-9pm Fri & Sat; 📶) Housed in a former bicycle factory attached to the heritage-listed Empire Hotel, Cycles presents a cafe-style vibe within a pub. There are treats such as New Orleans gumbo and cauliflower fritters among the usual parmas, shanks and salt-and-pepper squid.

ℹ️ Information

Great Western Tiers Visitor Information Centre (☑️03-6362 5280; www.greatwesterntiers. net.au; 98-100 Emu Bay Rd; ☺9am-5pm) Behind the statue of 1884 Melbourne Cup winner Malua, sharing premises with the Deloraine Museum. Helpful staff can supply plenty of information about activities in the region and book accommodation.

ℹ️ Getting There & Away

Redline (☑️1300 360 000; www.tasredline. com.au) Redline buses run to Launceston ($14.30, 45 minutes, three daily), Devonport ($8.50, 40 minutes, two daily) and Mole Creek ($6.50, 30 minutes, one daily). Buses depart from the visitor centre on Emu Bay Rd, but only stop if booked.

Mole Creek

POP 514

If the name 'Mole' has you thinking of underground things, you're not far wrong about this diminutive rural town. Mole Creek sits at the edge of a karst landscape riddled with caves, and makes a fine base for forays into nearby national parks such as Cradle Mountain-Lake St Clair and Walls of Jerusalem. There's a good chance of seeing platypuses (rather than moles) in the town's waterways – keep an eye out just after sunrise and just

LIFFEY FALLS

Pouring through Liffey Falls State Reserve, part of the Tasmanian Wilderness World Heritage Area, is one of Tasmania's most classically beautiful **waterfalls** (www.parks.tas.gov.au; C513). A gentle 45-minute return walk descends through temperate rainforest and past a series of cascades on the Liffey River to reach the base of the waterfall. The start of the track is 29km south of Deloraine, reached along Highland Lakes Rd (A5).

before sunset – and the town pub has a bit of a thing about Tassie tigers.

◉ Sights & Tours

★ Marakoopa Cave   CAVE
(☑ 03-6363 5182; www.parks.tas.gov.au; 330 Mayberry Rd, Mayberry; adult/child/family $19/9.50/47.50; ⊙ tours hourly 10am-3pm, plus 4pm Oct-May) The name Marakoopa derives from an Aboriginal word meaning 'handsome' and this cave well and truly lives up to its moniker, featuring a subterranean world of straws, stalactites, glowworms and sparkling crystals. Two tours are available: the easy Underground Rivers & Glowworms Tour (10am, noon and 2pm, plus 4pm October to May) visits the lower chamber with its crystals and glowworms, while the Great Cathedral & Glowworms Tour (11am, 1pm and 3pm) includes a climb to the vast Great Cathedral cavern.

King Solomons Cave   CAVE
(☑ 03-6363 5182; www.parks.tas.gov.au; Liena Rd, Liena; adult/child/family $19/9.50/47.50; ⊙ tours 11.30am, 12.30pm, 2.30pm & 3.30pm, plus 10.30am & 4.30pm Dec-Apr) Guided 45-minute tours of this compact cave, approximately 17km west of Mole Creek, reveal its lavish colours and formations. To get here, take Liena Rd (B12). Tickets can be purchased at the Mole Creek Caves office at Marakoopa Cave, 11km away, or at King Solomons Cave itself (no cash sales).

Trowunna Wildlife Park   WILDLIFE RESERVE
(☑ 03-6363 6162; www.trowunna.com.au; 1892 Mole Creek Rd; adult/child/family $26/16/75; ⊙ 9am-5pm, guided tours 11am, 1pm & 3pm) This privately owned wildlife park with a focus on conservation and education has Tasmanian devils, wombats, quolls and a raptor

rehabilitation centre, and you can wander among the kangaroos. The informative, no-nonsense tour (40 minutes) will get you up close to a devil and a wombat, and you will see devils being fed. To find Trowunna, look for the big Tasmanian devil by the side of the road to Deloraine.

Wild Cave Tours   ADVENTURE
(☑ 03-6367 8142; www.wildcavetours.com; half-/full-day tours $150/300) Operated by enthusiastic and knowledgeable environmental scientist Deb, this company offers caving tours beyond Mole Creek's two show caves. Guides can take you into Cyclops, Baldocks and other wild caves in the area – no paths, steps or ladders. Prices include lunch but you'll need to purchase a national parks pass separately. Children must be aged 4 or over.

🛏 Sleeping & Eating

Mole Creek Hotel   PUB FOOD $$
(☑ 03-6363 1102; www.molecreekhotel.com; 90 Pioneer Dr; mains $21-38; ⊙ 11am-late, kitchen noon-2pm & 6-8pm; 🛜) Old-fashioned pub food – the sort that still believes in coleslaw and a slice of beetroot – isn't extinct in this hotel's Tassie Tiger Bar, where dishes include schnitzels, reef and beef, and seafood baskets. The menu is big on fish but light on veggie options. Try the Tassie Tiger pies or burgers if you've bought into the bar's theme.

There are 10 basic, yesteryear-furnished rooms (single $50, double $85 to $105) upstairs, all but one with a shared bathroom.

ℹ Information

Mole Creek Caves Office (☑ 03-6363 5182; www.parks.tas.gov.au; 330 Mayberry Rd, Mayberry; ⊙ 9am-4.30pm) Tour tickets for Marakoopa Cave and King Solomons Cave are available at this helpful office with a small gift shop, close to the Marakoopa Cave entrance.

Mole Creek Community & Information Centre (☑ 03-6363 2030; www.molecreek.info; 48 Pioneer Dr; ⊙ 10am-4pm; 🛜) This small community and information centre inside the brightly signed Cafe Bozzey offers wi-fi ($2 for 500MB) and internet access on fixed computers. Staff can help with information about the area, and it stocks a small range of tourist brochures and maps.

ℹ Getting There & Away

Redline (☑ 1300 360 000; www.tasredline.com.au) One daily Redline bus service travels between Mole Creek and Deloraine ($6.50, 30 minutes), Westbury ($8.50, 45 minutes) and Launceston ($22.30, 1½ hours).

Walls of Jerusalem National Park

The mountains of the Walls of Jerusalem National Park (☑03-6701 2104; www.parks.tas. gov.au; via Mersey Forest Rd to Lake Rowallan; day pass per vehicle/person $24/12) are so spectacular it took biblical names to describe them: Solomons Throne, King Davids Peak, Mt Jerusalem, the Temple. It's a glacier-scoured landscape of spectacularly craggy dolerite peaks, alpine tarns and forests of ancient pines. The park adjoins the lake-spangled wilderness of the Central Plateau and is part of the Tasmanian Wilderness World Heritage Area. The only way in is on foot, with walking tracks approaching the Walls from several directions.

🏃 Activities & Tours

The main trailhead for walks into the park is on Mersey Forest Rd, near Lake Rowallan, where a steep walking track leads from the car park to Trappers Hut (two hours). From Trappers Hut it's two hours to the Wild Dog Creek camping area and nearby Herods Gate, the entrance to the surround of mountains that form the 'walls' of Jerusalem. From Wild Dog Creek it's three hours return to Solomons Throne or 3½ hours return to the old Dixons Kingdom hut and camping area, which is surrounded by hauntingly beautiful pencil-pine forests. From Dixons Kingdom the walk to the top of Mt Jerusalem takes 2½ hours return. You can walk into the Walls in a day, but to allow exploration (especially if you plan to walk to Dixons Kingdom or Mt Jerusalem) it's better to camp overnight.

Be prepared for harsh weather conditions: it snows a substantial amount here, and not only in winter. Walks across the park are described in *Cradle Mountain Lake St Clair & Walls of Jerusalem National Parks*, by John Chapman, Monica Chapman and John Siseman.

Tasmanian Expeditions　　　WALKING
(☑1300 666 856; www.tasmanianexpeditions.com. au) Tasmanian Expeditions leads a four-day Walls of Jerusalem Experience (from $1495), taking in the park's highlights from a base camp. It also offers a truncated three-day self-guided version (from $1095), a six-day circuit (from $1895) and a four-day winter hike (from $1495).

❶ Getting There & Away

Cradle Mountain Coaches (☑0448 800 599, 03-6427 7626; www.cradlemountaincoaches. com.au) This bushwalker shuttle service, operated by Devonport-based Merseylink, runs to either the Lake Rowallan or Higgs Track trailheads from Launceston ($320, or $80 per person for four or more passengers) or Devonport ($260/65). The shuttles collect passengers from Launceston or Devonport airport, the *Spirit of Tasmania* terminal or accommodation.

Penguin
POP 3849

There's an old joke on Tasmania's north coast that you can find penguins anywhere along the coast, except in Penguin. That hasn't stopped this pretty town working its name – there's a 3m-high Big Penguin between the main beach and shopping strip, as well as penguin bollards, statues and rubbish bins dotted around town. Little penguins do actually shuffle ashore within easy reach of Penguin, but if you look beyond the birds, you'll discover a seaside town with a vibrant cafe culture, fronted by a beautiful caramel-coloured beach and backed by the Dial Range, which has several fine walks.

🛏 Sleeping & Eating

⭐**The Madsen**　　　BOUTIQUE HOTEL $$
(☑03-6437 2588; www.themadsen.com; 64 Main Rd; d $129-199, penthouse d $270, extra adult/child $40/20; ☎) Housed in a grand former bank building on the beachfront, this friendly and well-managed boutique hotel offers six well-sized rooms with comfortable beds. All are decorated tastefully, but the luxurious penthouse and beachfront spa suites are the most impressive. The honesty bar has Tasmanian wines and Hellyers Road whisky – the port and sherry are free.

⭐**Jo & Co Cafe**　　　CAFE $$
(☑0447 617 215; www.facebook.com/joandcocafe; 74 Main Rd; mains $14-18; ☺8.30am-3pm Tue-Fri, 8am-3.30pm Sat & Sun; ☎🍴) On fine days, the windows at this retro-laminex cafe pull back and you can eyeball the Big Penguin across the road. Its quirky vibe and the tasty menu, catering to vegetarians and vegans, are a winning combination. Breakfast involves everything from smashed avocado to the full

cooked production, while lunch focuses on burgers and salad.

ℹ Information

Penguin Visitor Information Centre (☎ 03-6437 1421; www.coasttocanyon.com.au; 78 Main Rd; ⊙ 9am-4pm Oct-May, 9.30am-3.30pm Jun-Sep) Staffed by volunteers, the friendly Penguin visitor centre can supply brochures and advice about visiting nearby attractions. Pick up a copy of the *Discover Penguin on Foot* brochure for a self-guided walking tour past more than 30 historic buildings.

ℹ Getting There & Away

Redline (☎ 1300 360 000; www.tasredline.com.au) Redline buses go to Burnie ($6.50, 20 minutes) and Devonport ($8.50, 45 minutes) twice daily. Buses stop at Johnsons Beach, opposite the Penguin Caravan Park, and in Crescent St in the town centre.

Burnie

POP 19,385

Burnie is like Tasmania's naughty child, the one that used to smoke, belch and foul the waters. All grown up now, it's trying hard to reinvent itself as a 'City of Makers', referring both to its heavy manufacturing past and its present creative flair. The things being made here these days include paper, cheese and whisky – an unusual but interesting

---

WHERE TO SEE PENGUINS

True to its name, Penguin can make a good base for viewing the little (or fairy) penguins that come ashore nightly along Tasmania's north coast from about October to March. There are two good places to see them. **Lillico Beach**, 25km east of Penguin, is home to Tasmania's second-largest little penguin breeding colony, with the birds arriving ashore around sunset. There's a viewing platform and, on most nights in season, there are volunteer guides in residence to answer any questions. Contact Penguin's visitor information centre (above) for more details. A smaller colony comes ashore around the Little Penguin Observation Centre (next page) in the centre of Burnie, behind the Makers' Workshop (19km west of Penguin).

---

mix. Its penguin centre, Makers' Workshop and distillery are well worth a visit, and if you pause to look around, the coast is undeniably beautiful and the beach is pretty good.

⊙ Sights & Activities

★ **Burnie Regional Museum**   MUSEUM
(☎ 03-6430 5746; www.burnieregionalmuseum.net; Little Alexander St; adult/child $8.50/free; ⊙ 10am-4.30pm Mon-Fri, 1.30-4pm Sat & Sun) The centrepiece of this absorbing museum is the lovingly crafted Federation St, a re-creation of a 1900 Burnie streetscape, including blacksmith's forge and farrier's shop, wash house, general store, post and telegraph office, stagecoach depot, inn, dentist's surgery, newspaper office and boot maker. Each is based on an actual business that existed in Burnie, incorporates multimedia elements and features excellent interpretative panels. Interesting temporary exhibitions feature in an adjoining room.

Hellyers Road Distillery   DISTILLERY
(☎ 03-6433 0439; www.hellyersroaddistillery.com.au; 153 Old Surrey Rd; tours $19.50; ⊙ 10am-4.30pm) Take a stroll through the angel's share at Australia's largest distillery; the tour is also the only way to get a tasting of Hellyers' cask-strength whisky. Tours depart at 10.30am, 11.30am, 2pm and 3pm daily. There's a cafe and you can work through a flight of three nips of the good stuff ($17 to $37).

Makers' Workshop   MUSEUM
(☎ 03-6430 5831; www.facebook.com/makersworkshopburnie; 2-4 Bass Hwy; ⊙ 9am-5pm) **FREE** Part museum and part arts centre, this dramatic structure dominating the western end of Burnie's main beach is a good place to get acquainted with the city's creative heart. The life-size **paper people** in odd corners of the workshop's cavernous interior are the work of **Creative Paper** (www.creativepapertas.com.au; tours adult/child/family $15/8/40; ⊙ tours 10am-3.45pm), Burnie's hand-made-paper producers. Its tours take you through the production process of making paper from such unusual raw materials as kangaroo poo, apple fibres and forest-floor leaves.

There are also **makers' studios** stationed throughout the centre, where you can watch local producers at work on handicrafts from jewellery to violins, ceramics to glass, and felt to papier-mâché. You can buy some of the products produced in the shop, and enjoy a coffee in the on-site cafe.

★ **Little Penguin Observation Centre**   BIRDWATCHING

(☑0437 436 803; www.facebook.com/Burnie PenguinObservationCentre; Parsonage Point; ☉dusk Oct-Mar) **FREE** Who knew penguins would come ashore this close to a city centre? From October to March, you can take a free Penguin Interpretation Tour about one hour after dusk, when the penguins emerge from the sea and waddle back to their burrows. Volunteer wildlife guides are present to talk about the birds and their habits. Wear dark clothing.

🛏 Sleeping & Eating

Duck House   COTTAGE **$$**

(☑03-6431 1712; www.duckhousecottage.com. au; 26 Queen St; s/d $140/180, extra adult/child $40/20, all incl breakfast; ☎🖳) Though it's named after Salvation Army stalwarts Bill and Winifred Duck, who lived here for 30 years, this charming self-contained two-bedroom cottage works the ducky decor, from duck slippers to 'duck-ted' heating. It sleeps up to five, and is a five-minute walk from the city centre and the Makers' Workshop arts centre.

A three-bedroom property next door, **Mrs Philpott's** (s/d $140/180, extra adult/child $40/20, all incl breakfast; ☎🖳), sleeps up to seven and a third house, **Amelia's** (s/d $140/180, extra adult/child $40/20, all incl breakfast; ☎🖳), sleeps up to six and is located immediately around the corner. All three share an abundant vegetable garden from which you have freedom to pick.

★ **Ikon Hotel**   BOUTIQUE HOTEL **$$$**

(☑03-6432 4566; www.ikonhotel.com.au; 22 Mount St; d incl breakfast $230-260; ☀☎) Boutique hotel chic comes to Burnie at this centrally located property. Situated on the 1st floor of a city-centre heritage hotel, it subscribes to the everything-is-big-in-Burnie ethos: large TVs and bathrooms, huge rooms, enormous mirrors, and massive prints on the hallway walls. Only the breakfast provisions are modest.

★ **The Chapel**   CAFE **$$**

(☑03-6432 3460; www.chapelcafe.com.au; 50 Cattley St; mains $12-22; ☉7.30am-3pm Mon-Thu, 7.30am-3pm & 7-10pm Fri, 8am-3pm Sat) This hipsterish cafe is housed in a handsome decommissioned chapel and the quality of

DON'T MISS

TABLE CAPE TULIP FARM

The volcanic, chocolate-red soils of Table Cape are extraordinarily fertile, so it's a perfect spot to grow tulips. In October, when the bulbs flower at **Table Cape Tulip Farm** (☑03-6442 2012; www.tablecapetulipfarm.com.au; 363 Table Cape Rd; adult/child $12/free; ☉9am-4.30pm late-Sep–Oct), there's a mesmerising array of colours to marvel at and a canteen serving Devonshire teas. Blooming dates are never certain, but the best time is likely during the second week in October. At other times of the year it's possible to buy bulbs in the farm's shop – call ahead.

the food certainly matches the surrounds. The best cafe in Burnie (and probably the best on the north coast), it serves excellent house-roasted coffee, house-made chai and brilliant breakfasts. There are good pastries, muffins and cakes too.

Fish Frenzy   SEAFOOD **$$**

(☑03-6432 1111; http://fishfrenzyburnie.com.au; 2 North Tce; mains $10-27; ☉8-late; ♿) This modern, bustling fish and chippery crumbs its super-fresh fish or douses it in a beer or tempura batter before frying, ensuring that its creations are a cut above the competition. It also serves oysters and lavish seafood platters ($75 for two). Any closer to the sea and you could pluck the fish out of the water yourself.

ℹ Information

Visitor Information Centre (☑03-6430 5831; www.discoverburnie.net; Makers' Workshop, 2 Bass Hwy; ☉9am-5pm) A desk in the foyer of the Makers' Workshop, this volunteer-staffed information centre can provide advice, brochures and a city map.

ℹ Getting There & Away

AIR

Burnie Airport (☑03-6442 1133; www.burnieairport.com.au; 3 Airport St, Wynyard) is 19km northwest of Burnie. Regular flights travel to/from Melbourne (75 minutes) with **Regional Express** (Rex; ☑13 17 13; www.regionalexpress.com.au), and to/from King Island (40 minutes) and Launceston (30 minutes) with **Sharp Airlines** (☑1300 556 694; www.sharpairlines.com).

DON'T MISS

BOAT HARBOUR BEACH

This may well be paradise. Picture-perfect Boat Harbour Beach has the kind of pristine white sand and sapphire-blue waters that make you feel like you've taken a wrong turn off the Bass Hwy and ended up somewhere in the Caribbean. The usually calm seas are patrolled in summer and perfect for kids, and one of the north coast's best casual eateries is located in the surf lifesaving club. The beach is 3km north of the Bass Hwy, across the edge of Table Cape.

BUS

Metro ([phone] 13 22 01; www.metrotas.com.au) Regular local buses run to Penguin ($6.50, 35 minutes), Devonport ($11, 70 minutes) and Wynyard ($6.50, 40 minutes), departing from the bus interchange on Cattley St, between Mount and Wilson Sts.

Redline ([phone] 1300 360 000; www.tasredline. com.au) Redline buses stop on Wilmot St, opposite the Metro Cinemas. Useful destinations include Devonport ($11.20, one hour), Launceston ($39.30, 2½ hours) and Smithton ($24, 1½ hours).

Stanley

POP 553

At a glance, Stanley could easily just be a line of buildings huddled along the base of the ancient volcano, the Nut, but the town has an undeniable magnetism. Fishing boats piled high with cray pots bob in the harbour, penguins amble ashore and the blast of the Roaring Forties ensures that the air is exhilaratingly clear. With a couple of top-drawer tourist attractions (Highfield homestead and the Nut), an array of excellent accommodation options and a few good eateries, it's an understandably popular place to while away a day or two. In 2018 a penguin-viewing platform and boardwalk were installed at the town end of Godfreys Beach; come at dusk and you can watch little penguins wandering ashore directly beneath you.

◎ Sights & Tours

★**Highfield Historic Site**   HISTORIC BUILDING
([phone] 03-6458 1100; www.parks.tas.gov.au/highfield; 143 Green Hills Rd; adult/child/family $12/6/30; ⊙9.30am-4.30pm) Built in 1835 for the chief agent of the Van Diemen's Land Company, this homestead, poised 2km north of town, is an exceptional example of domestic architecture of the Regency period in Tasmania. Managed by the Tasmanian Parks & Wildlife Service, it can be visited on a self-guided tour that covers the house, pretty garden and outbuildings, including stables, grain stores, workers' cottages and the chapel.

The Nut   MOUNTAIN
(off Browns Rd) FREE Known to the area's Indigenous people as Moo-Nut-Re-Ker and labelled 'Circular Head' by explorer Matthew Flinders, this striking 143m-high, 12-million-year-old core of an extinct volcano can be seen for many kilometres around Stanley. To get to the summit it's a steep 20-minute climb or a ride on the **chairlift** ([phone] 03-6458 1482; www.thenutchairlift.com.au; Browns Rd; adult one way/return $11/17, child $6/12, family $32/48; ⊙from 9.30am Sep-May, last chairlift 4.30-5.30pm). The best **lookout** is a short walk to the south of the chairlift. At the top is a 2km circuit walk (about one hour) around the summit plateau.

Stanley Seal Cruises   WILDLIFE
([phone] 0419 550 134, 03-6458 1294; www.stanley sealcruises.com.au; Fisherman's Dock, Wharf Rd; adult/child/family $55/18/150; ⊙10am & 3pm Sep-Apr, 1pm May–mid-Jul) These excellent 75-minute cruises on the MC *Sylvia C* take passengers to see hundreds of Australian fur seals sunning themselves on Bull Rock, just off the coast north of Stanley. Departures are dependent on sea conditions – book ahead to make sure they're running.

🛏 Sleeping & Eating

**Stanley Cabin
& Tourist Park**   CARAVAN PARK $
([phone] 03-6458 1266, 1800 444 818; www.stanley cabinpark.com.au; 23a Wharf Rd; unpowered/powered sites per 2 people $28/35, cabins d $85-180; 🛜) If location is everything, this spacious park is pretty complete, with the Nut rising from one edge and gorgeous Sawyer Bay along another. It offers waterfront campsites, a large camp kitchen and laundry, a games room with ping-pong and foosball, and neat but basic self-contained cabins, including waterfront cabins with spa.

★**@VDL**   BOUTIQUE HOTEL $$
([phone] 03-6458 2032; www.atvdlstanley.com.au; 16 Wharf Rd; ste $160-220, loft apt from $285; 🛜) What's been done within the bluestone

walls of this 1840s warehouse near the port is quite incredible. The ultra-hip boutique offering has two suites and a self-contained loft apartment. The decor and amenities are top class, featuring designer furniture, contemporary art, sleek bathrooms and bikes for guest use.

★ Cable Station Accommodation
B&B $$

(☑ 03-6458 1312; www.cablestationstanley.com.au; 435 Green Hills Rd; d/tr $165/195; ☎ ☀) Keep cute company at this property built to carry Tasmania's first telephone link to the mainland. Little penguins come ashore within walking distance and the two beautifully furnished guest units (sleeping two or three) have some fabulous touches: claw-foot tubs with bath salts and robes; and homemade bread and jams at breakfast.

Hursey Seafoods
FISH & CHIPS $

(☑ 03-6458 1103; www.hurseyseafoods.com.au; 2 Alexander Tce; takeaway fish & chips $12-21; ☺ restaurant noon-2.45pm & 5.45-7.45pm, takeaways 11.30am-7.30pm) Stanley is a fishing town, so it'd be a crime not to eat seafood here. Hursey's fleet of nine fishing boats supplies fish, crayfish and scallops to the clinical-looking restaurant upstairs – locals recommend ordering takeaway from the ground-floor shop instead.

❶ Information

Stanley Visitor Information Centre (☑ 1300 138 229, 03-6458 1330; www.stanley.com.au; 45 Main Rd; ☺ noon-5pm; ☎) A mine of information on Stanley and the surrounding areas. Offers bicycle hire (adult half/full day $22/34, child $15/22) and free wi-fi.

❶ Getting There & Away

Redline (☑ 1300 360 000; www.tasredline.com.au) Redline buses stop at the visitor centre on Main Rd en route between Burnie ($21.10, 80 minutes) and Smithton ($6.10, 25 minutes) on weekdays.

Marrawah & Around

POP 131

Untamed and unspoilt, Marrawah is both wild and pure at once, with vast ocean beaches, abundant signs of Aboriginal Tasmania (especially in the fascinating Preminghana Indigenous Protected Area just north of town), mind-blowing sunsets and green, rural hills. A nearby scientific station has decreed that the world's cleanest air blows through here on the relentless Roaring Forties. Beloved by surfers for its challenging breaks, Marrawah is home to the West Coast Classic surfing event each March.

❂ Sights

Gardiner Point
VIEWPOINT

(Edge of the World; off Airey St) Gardiner Point is Tasmania's official 'edge of the world': the sea here stretches uninterrupted all the way to Argentina, 15,000km away over the wild seas. There's a plaque at the point and the stunningly jagged coastline is smothered in logs washed in by the Southern Ocean. It's a great place to take those leaning-into-the-wind, world's-end photos.

It's signposted off the main road on the southern side of Arthur River.

🛏 Sleeping

Marrawah Beach House
RENTAL HOUSE $$

(☑ 03-6457 1285, 0428 571 285; 19 Beach Rd; d from $180, extra person $28) If being too far from the world is not far enough, these two well-maintained, self-contained houses are perfection. Perched on a working farm overlooking Green Point Beach to Woolnorth's wind turbines, one house sleeps four in two bedrooms, while the second is a studio sleeping two. Surfboard hire and summer surf lessons can be arranged. No wi-fi or TV reception.

King Island

POP 1585

King Island (or 'KI', as the locals call it) is 64km long and 26km wide – a fabulously laid-back place where everyone knows everyone and wallabies outnumber the human population by about 300 to one. The island's windswept green pastures famously produce a rich bounty of beef and dairy (you'll be testing how much cheese it's actually possible to ingest over the space of a few days) and its seas supply fabulously fresh seafood. Surfers are drawn here by one of the world's best breaks, and golfers by the pair of links golf courses rated among the top five public courses in Australia. The island's main town is **Currie** (population 770) on the west coast, and there are tiny east-coast settlements at **Grassy** (population 140) and **Naracoopa** (population 60).

ROCKY CAPE NATIONAL PARK

Tasmania's smallest national park, pinmatik/Rocky Cape (☑03-6458 1480; www.parks.tas.gov.au; day pass per vehicle/person $24/12), stretches 12km along Bass Strait's shoreline. It has great significance to the local Indigenous people, who made their homes in the sea caves here 8000 years before European occupation. You can drive out to a squat lighthouse on the cape's tip and enjoy fine Bass Strait views, while a 20-minute return walk from here leads down towards North Cave. Parks passes are available at the Sisters Beach General Store.

◉ Sights

King Island Dairy   DAIRY
(☑03-6462 0947; www.kingislanddairy.com.au; 869 North Rd, Loorana; ⊙10am-5pm) FREE Low-key but top quality, King Island Dairy's *fromagerie* is 8km north of Currie (just beyond the airport). Visit its attached shop to taste award-winning bries, cheddars and feisty blues, learn about the cheesemaking process and grab a cheese platter (with matching beer or wine) to fuel your King Island exploring.

🛏 Sleeping & Eating

Island Breeze Motel   MOTEL $$
(☑0475 351 807, 03-6462 1260; www.island breezemotel.com.au; 95 Main St, Currie; d $180, 2- & 3-bedroom units $210; 🖻) Popular with those playing King Island's trio of highly rated golf courses, this motel offers attractive, well-heated rooms with comfortable beds and views of the coast and Currie Lighthouse. It also has self-catering units and cabins sleeping up to six. The friendly and efficient manager can supply plenty of advice about touring the island. Continental breakfast included in the price.

King Island Accommodation Cottages   COTTAGE $$
(☑0427 002 397, 03-6461 1326; www.kingisland accommodationcottages.com.au; 149 Esplanade, Naracoopa; 1-/2-bedroom cottages from $130/140, extra adult/child $25/15; 🖻) Right on the coast and beautifully maintained, these quiet self-catering cottages are an excellent choice. If they were on the mainland, they'd

cost double this price. Wi-fi in public areas only.

Wild Harvest   MODERN AUSTRALIAN $$$
(☑0408 546 469, 03-6461 1176; www.wildharvest kingisland.com.au; 4 Bluegum Dr, Grassy; mains $32-55; ⊙6pm-late Fri-Sun) King Island on a plate – most of the produce used by the chefs at this eatery overlooking Grassy Harbour is local, seasonal and fresh. The result is a menu of dishes such as seafood chowder with crayfish, and muttonbird and wallaby. Winter meals are enjoyed in front of a roaring log fire; in summer, guests can dine outside.

ℹ Information

King Island Tourism (☑1800 645 014, 03-6462 1355; www.kingisland.org.au; 5 George St, Currie; ⊙10.30am-5pm Mon-Fri, 10am-noon Sat) Supplies brochures and information at both the airport and its office in Currie. The website is an excellent planning resource, with suggested itineraries and loads of information about accommodation, activities and tours – accommodation can be booked direct through the website.

ℹ Getting There & Away

Three airlines fly into King Island's small airport, 8km northeast of Currie. **King Island Airlines** (☑03-6462 1000; www.kingislandair.com.au) flies to/from Melbourne's Moorabbin airport (one way/return $210/376, one hour) once or twice daily; **Regional Express** (Rex; ☑13 17 13; www.regionalexpress.com.au) flies daily to/from Melbourne's Tullamarine airport (one way from $133, 55 minutes); and **Sharp Airlines** (☑1300 556 694; www.sharpairlines.com) flies daily to/from Melbourne's Essendon airport (one way from $150, 45 minutes), Burnie (one way from $219, 40 minutes) and Launceston (one way from $286, 1½ hours).

ℹ Getting Around

There's no public transport on the island. **King Island Car Rental** (☑03-6462 1282; King Island Airport, 102 Morrison Ave; ⊙office 8am-5pm Mon-Fri, to noon Sat) and **P&A Car Rental** (☑03-6462 1603; King Island Airport, 102 Morrison Ave; ⊙office 8am-5pm Mon-Fri, to noon Sat) offer car hire.

The Tarkine Wilderness

Known as takayna in local Aboriginal dialect, the Tarkine is a 4470-sq-km stretch of temperate rainforest between the Arthur River in the north, the Pieman River in the south, the Murchison Hwy to the east and the Southern Ocean to the west. It's a globally significant ecosystem, sometimes claimed as the world's second-largest expanse of temperate rainforest, that encompasses vast forests of myrtle, leatherwood and pine trees, endless horizons of buttongrass plains, savage ocean beaches, sand dunes and extensive coastal heathland. Because of its remoteness, ferocious weather and isolation, the takayna/Tarkine survived almost untouched by modernity well into the 20th century, and the region still offers a frontier-style experience for those keen to explore it.

The easiest look at takayna/Tarkine comes on the 213km sealed Tarkine Drive, a tourist route that cuts through the forest's north, beginning in Arthur River. Pick up a Tarkine Drive brochure at the Stanley Visitor Information Centre (p701).

🏃 Activities & Tours

★ Tarkine Forest Adventures
ADVENTURE SPORTS

(☑ 03-6456 7138; www.dismalswamptasmania. com.au; 26,059 Bass Hwy, Togari; adult/child 8-12yr/child under 7yr $20/10/free, plus per slide $2; ⊙10am-4pm; 🖑) Framed around the Dismal Swamp sinkhole (the largest sinkhole in the southern hemisphere), this adventure centre 32km southwest of Smithton is home to a 110m-long 'serpent slide', which provides a thrilling descent through the dense old-growth canopy to more than 1km of boardwalks on the forest floor. Sliders must be over eight years of age and at least 90cm tall.

★ Tarkine Trails
WALKING

(☑ 0405 255 537; www.tarkinetrails.com.au; per person $1849) Tarkine Trails takes bushwalkers on a four-day Tarkine Rainforest Walk, including all meals and accommodation in fab rainforest safari tents. Hikers venture out on day walks from the exclusive and deliciously remote Tiger Ridge base camp, where you can ogle the surrounding giant tree ferns from the lodge's cantilevered verandah.

Corinna & the Pieman River

Corinna is the green and gold of Australia made literal – a former gold-mining town inside the deep rainforest of takayna/Tarkine. As a humming mining settlement in the late 1800s, it had two hotels, a post office, shops, a slaughter yard and a population of 2500. These days, it's a tranquil place with only one business – Corinna Wilderness Experience – providing accommodation in campsites and cabins, a restaurant, cruises down the Pieman River to one of the wildest beaches in Australia, kayak hire and a number of good walks. There are no TVs, no phone signal and no wi-fi; there's just living.

☞ Tours

Pieman River Cruises
BOATING

(☑ 03-6446 1170; www.corinna.com.au/river-cruises; adult/child $95/55; ⊙10am Dec-Apr, 10am Mon, Wed & Sat May-Nov) Cruise the dark, mirror-flat Pieman River on the only Huon-pine-built river cruiser still operating in the world. The 4½-hour trip sails downstream to the river mouth at the wild and windblown Pieman Heads. Packed lunch is included. Also on offer is a 3pm, one-hour Sweetwater Cruise (adult/child $35/20) to fern-packed Lovers' Falls and the SS *Croydon* shipwreck. Book well ahead.

🛏 Sleeping & Eating

Corinna Wilderness Experience
COTTAGE $$

(☑ 03-6446 1170; www.corinna.com.au; Corinna Rd; unpowered sites $40, cottage d/f $230/290) Corinna's tranquil wilderness village offers accommodation in one- and two-bedroom timber cottages scattered through the attractive rainforest above the riverside lodge. They sleep either two or four and are solar powered; all have a kitchen or kitchenette, a wood stove or fire, and a deck. The campsites, arrayed along the riverbank, get the best views.

The lodge's Tannin Restaurant (mains lunch $14-19, dinner $28-35; ⊙noon-2pm & 6-8pm mid-Sep–mid-May) offers hearty meals, and there are kayaks for hire (half-day $35).

CRADLE COUNTRY & THE WEST

Welcome to the island's wild west, a land of endless ocean beaches, ancient mossy rainforests, tannin-tinted rivers, glacier-sculpted mountains and wildflower-strewn high plains – a place where you'll often feel like you're the only soul on earth. This is Tasmania's vast outdoor playground, replete with national parks, conservation reserves

TASMANIA CORINNA & THE PIEMAN RIVER

and World Heritage–protected wilderness, where your options for adventure are varied and plentiful.

Come here for the toughest multiday hikes (or gentle rainforest wanders); come to shoot rapids on untamed rivers (or cruise mirror-calm waters); and come to kayak into some of the last untouched temperate wilderness on earth (or fly over it all in a light plane). You can visit independently or with a guided group – however you choose to arrive, one thing is sure: you won't want to leave.

Cradle Mountain and the western areas of the state were home to the Big River, Northwest and Southwest Aboriginal nations.

Cradle Mountain-Lake St Clair National Park

Part of the World Heritage–listed Tasmanian Wilderness, this 1262-sq-km **national park** (☑03-6492 1110; www.parks.tas.gov.au; vehicle/person per day $24/12) incorporates glacier-sculpted mountains, river gorges, lakes, tarns and wild alpine moorland. Though it extends from the Great Western Tiers in the north to Derwent Bridge in the south, its most beloved landscapes and walks – including the start of the world-renowned 65km Overland Track – are around Cradle Mountain. The park encompasses seven of Tasmania's 10 highest mountains, including the tallest, Mt Ossa (1617m), as well as Lake St Clair, the deepest (200m) lake in Australia. Wildlife is also plentiful, including wombats, Bennett's wallabies, pademelons and platypuses. The main tourist hubs are Cradle Valley, a tourist settlement scattered along Cradle Mountain Rd, and smaller Derwent Bridge, near the southern end of Lake St Clair.

Before European settlement, the traditional owners of the Cradle Mountain area were the Big River Aboriginal people, who lived across much of the Central Highlands.

◉ Sights

Devils@Cradle   WILDLIFE RESERVE
(☑03-6492 1491; www.devilsatcradle.com; 3950 Cradle Mountain Rd; adult/child $20/12, family from $60, night feeding tours adult/child $30/15, family from $80; ☺10am-4pm Apr-Sep, to 5pm Oct-Mar) A refuge for around 55 Tasmanian devils, this excellent wildlife sanctuary also

plays host to eastern and spotted-tail quolls. Although it's open all day for self-guided visits, try to sign up for a night tour, when the mainly nocturnal animals are best observed. Day tours (45 minutes) run at 10.30am, 1pm and 3pm, with night tours (1¼ hours) at 5.30pm year-round and 8.30pm October to April. Extra information about the animals is given in an interesting Attenborough DVD presentation.

As well as the standard tours, the sanctuary offers a 'Dine with the Devil' experience ($99) between 7pm and 8pm daily from November to April. This includes drinks and snacks and gives participants an opportunity to interact with the animals.

✇ Activities

Cradle Mountain Walks
The Cradle Mountain area has some of the most accessible trailheads in the park. The following is by no means an exhaustive list.

Knyvet Falls (45 minutes return) Begins opposite Cradle Mountain Lodge and follows Pencil Pine Creek to a lookout over the falls.

Marions Lookout (three hours return) Climb past Lilla Lake and Wombat Pool to an eyeball-to-eyeball view of Cradle Mountain's summit.

Cradle Valley Boardwalk (1½ hours one way) An easy 5km walk from the interpretation centre to Ronny Creek at the start of the Overland Track.

Dove Lake Circuit (6km, two hours) Lap the lake, setting out from Dove Lake car park, with near-and-far Cradle Mountain views.

Cradle Mountain Summit (13km, six to eight hours return) A tough but spectacular climb with incredible views in fine weather. Some scrambling acrobatics are required as you near the summit. It's not recommended in poor visibility or when it's snowy and icy in winter. Begin at either Dove Lake car park or Ronny Creek.

Lake St Clair Walks
If you're at the southern, Lake St Clair end of the national park, these are our top picks of the day hikes on offer. Always check weather and other conditions with the Lake St Clair Visitor Information Centre (p707) at Cynthia Bay before setting out.

Larmairremener tabelti & Platypus Bay (4.5km, 1½ hours return) Aborig-

THE OVERLAND TRACK

Tasmania's alpine Overland Track, arguably the most famous multiday walk in Australia, is a 65km, five- to seven-day odyssey (with backpack) through incredible World Heritage–listed mountainscapes, from Ronny Creek near Cradle Mountain to the shores of Lake St Clair. If you have experience with multiday hikes, solid fitness and are well prepared for Tasmania's erratic weather, it's a very achievable independent adventure, with the track threading between mountains rather than grinding over them. Inexperienced walkers should consider signing up with a guided walking group.

Most hikers walk the Overland Track during summer, when alpine plants are fragrantly in flower, daylight hours are long and you can work up enough heat to swim in one of the frigid alpine tarns. The track is very busy at this time and is subject to a crowd-limiting permit system between October and May. During the permit season, you can only walk the track in one direction – north to south. Outside of the booking season (ie through winter) a growing number of hardy folk walk the track, savouring the solitude and the icy beauty – it can be hiked in either direction during this time.

The trail is well marked for its entire length. Side trips lead to features such as Mt Ossa (Tasmania's loftiest peak at 1617m) and some fantastic waterfalls, so it's worth budgeting time for some of these. You can expect to meet many walkers each day except in the dead of winter. The walk itself is extremely varied, negotiating high alpine moors, rocky scree, gorges and tall rainforest. Guided walks are operated by the following:

Cradle Mountain Huts Walk (☑03-6392 2211; www.taswalkingco.com.au/overland-track; Overland Track from $3695; ⊙Oct-May) This well-regarded company runs six-day guided walks along the length of the Overland Track, staying in private huts equipped with hot showers, private bedrooms and drying rooms. Perhaps even better, the days are fuelled with fine food and Tasmanian wine, and you need only carry about 8kg on your back.

Tasmanian Expeditions (☑1300 666 856; www.tasmanianexpeditions.com.au; 6-day hike from $2195) This long-operating company offers a six-day, camping-based Overland Track guided walk, as well as winter crossings (from $2495) and a self-guided option (from $1390) that includes your food, equipment and transport to and from the track.

inal cultural-interpretative walk that winds through the traditional lands of the Larmairremener, the region's Indigenous people who know Lake St Clair as Leeawuleena (Sleeping Water). The walk starts at the visitor information centre and loops through the lakeside forest before returning along the shore.

Shadow Lake Circuit (11.5km, four to five hours return) Mixture of bush tracks and boardwalks through rainforest, stringy-bark trees and subalpine forests. A good extension continues on to the summit of Little Hugel, overlooking the lake.

Mt Rufus Circuit (18km, seven to eight hours return) Climbs Mt Rufus through alpine meadows and past lakes and sandstone outcrops with fine views over Lake St Clair.

Lake St Clair Lakeside Walk Catch the ferry from Cynthia Bay to Echo Point (11km, three to four hours' walk back) or Narcissus Hut (16.5km, five to seven hours back) and walk back along the lakeshore.

⛰ Tours

★**Cradle Mountain Canyons** ADVENTURE (☑1300 032 384; www.cradlemountaincanyons.com.au; 3845 Cradle Mountain Rd, Cradle Valley; adult $125-245, child $100; ⊙departures 8.30am & 9.30am Nov-Apr) Squeeze into a wetsuit and swim, wade, jump, walk, float and abseil your way past six waterfalls inside Dove Canyon – the Laundry Chute rock slide is incredible! There's also the Lost World Canyon for beginners and kids, and an on-demand trip through Machinery Creek, with higher abseils but fewer leaps.

Lake St Clair Scenic Cruise CRUISE (☑03-6289 1137; www.lakestclairlodge.com.au; adult/child $70/35; ⊙9am, 12.30pm & 3pm Oct-Apr, on demand May-Sep) Hop aboard the *Ida Clair* for a 1½-hour ferry trip from Cynthia Bay to Echo Point and Narcissus Bay and back, admiring pristine Lake St Clair and peaks such as Mt Olympus and sharp-tipped Mt Ida along the way. Advance bookings are advised since the boat doubles as the pick-up service for Overland Track bushwalkers.

🛏 Sleeping & Eating

🛏 Cradle Mountain

Discovery Holiday Parks
Cradle Mountain CAMPGROUND $
(☑ 03-6492 1395; www.discoveryholidayparks.com.au; 3832 Cradle Mountain Rd; unpowered/powered sites for 2 $47/58, dm $39, cabin d $150-$290; ☎) Bush camping at its best, with options aplenty. Campsites are well spaced; single-sex dorms sleep four; basic cabins include kitchens and small bathrooms; and larger versions have gas fires and TVs with DVD player. Communal facilities include a laundry, squeaky-clean ablutions blocks and camp kitchens with stoves, BBQs and pizza ovens. Reception doubles as the valley's best-equipped store.

Cradle Mountain Highlanders CABIN $$
(☑ 03-6492 1116; www.cradlehighlander.com.au; 3876 Cradle Mountain Rd; d $155-290, extra adult/child $35/25; ☎) Everything is rustic-alpine in these 16 immaculately kept timber cottages sleeping between two and seven people. All have wood or gas fires, electric blankets, TV and DVD and equipped kitchens. Four cabins include a spa, and the two premium cabins have a view of Cradle Mountain. There's a communal BBQ area and laundry. On-site wi-fi is intermittent.

The surrounding bush is peaceful and filled with wildlife that will most likely pay you a visit. Breakfast provisions must be ordered in advance ($12 to $15 per person).

★ Cradle Mountain Wilderness Village CABIN $$$
(☑ 03-6492 1500; www.cradlevillage.com.au; 3816 Cradle Mountain Rd; d cabins $240-390; ☎) Cleverly camouflaged in the bush, the 45 cabins here are clean, comfortable and well equipped. All have TV with DVD player and the top-of-the-line cabins are wrapped around a central spa with views out of a picture window – particularly beautiful when the waratahs are flowering in summer. Wi-fi is available in the main building only. Hellyers Restaurant serves the area's best food.

Hellyers Restaurant MODERN AUSTRALIAN $$$
(☑ 03-6492 1500; www.cradlevillage.com.au; Cradle Mountain Wilderness Village, 3816 Cradle Mountain Rd; plates $19-29; ☉dinner 6-10pm Tue-Sat, lounge bar 2-10pm) Small plates come with a big view over Cradle Valley and the treetops at this fine restaurant in the Cradle Mountain Wilderness Village. Try the Tasmanian carpaccio with smoked salmon and wasabi pea puree, and some Spring Bay mussels and beer-battered fries. Bookings not needed.

🛏 Lake St Clair

Derwent Bridge Chalets & Studios COTTAGE $$
(☑ 03-6289 1000; www.derwent-bridge.com; 15,478 Lyell Hwy, Derwent Bridge; studio d $185, chalet d $230-255; ☎) There's a range of tightly clustered studios and small chalets on offer here – think caravan-park cabins with a bit of panache. Five have wood fires, two have spas and one is set up for guests with disabilities. Some have a kitchenette, others have a full kitchen; chalets have a laundry. Expect wallabies and wombats on the lawns in the evening.

★ Pumphouse Point BOUTIQUE HOTEL $$$
(☑ 0428 090 436; www.pumphousepoint.com.au; 1 Lake St Clair Rd; shorehouse r $295-495, pumphouse r $495-610, retreat $1440; P☺) Unique and impressive, Pumphouse Point occupies a three-tier hydroelectric pump house built in 1940 atop Lake St Clair, accessed via a narrow pier, as well as a smaller art-deco substation and a hidden retreat on the shoreline. Pumphouse rooms are best, though you'll gravitate to its sun-drenched lounges even if you're staying in the Shorehouse. Everything about the place is world-class.

Derwent Bridge Wilderness Hotel PUB FOOD $$
(☑ 03-6289 1144; www.derwentbridgewilderness hotel.com.au; Lyell Hwy, Derwent Bridge; lunch mains $11-20, dinner mains $27-42) This large, barn-shaped hotel offers the best eating and the warmest welcome (thanks to possibly the largest fireplace in Tasmania) around Lake St Clair. There are pub staples such as parmigiana and roast, plus curries from the Sri Lankan chef and, if you've really hiked up an appetite, the 350g King Billy steak with prawns and scallops ($67).

ℹ Information

Cradle Mountain Visitor Information Centre
(☑ 03-6492 1110; www.parks.tas.gov.au; 4057 Cradle Mountain Rd; ☉8.30am-4.30pm; ☎) Located just outside the park boundary, this visitor information centre sells park passes and some bushwalking clothing and equipment, offers free wi-fi, and supplies detailed

bushwalking information and maps. The helpful staff can also provide weather condition updates and advice on bush safety and etiquette. There's an on-site cafe (✆03-6492 1110; www.parks.tas.gov.au; Cradle Mountain Visitor Information Centre, 4057 Cradle Mountain Rd; mains $9-20; ☺8.30am-5pm) and petrol station.

Lake St Clair Visitor Information Centre
(✆03-6289 1172; www.parks.tas.gov.au; Cynthia Bay; ☺9am-4pm summer, hours vary rest of year) Located at Cynthia Bay, on the park's southern boundary. Helpful rangers provide park and walking information and a small shop sells a limited range of souvenirs and bushwalking equipment and clothing. There are also displays on the area's geology, fauna, Aboriginal heritage and historic huts. An attached privately operated cafe offers coffee and meals of average quality.

❶ Getting There & Away

Cradle Mountain Coaches (✆0448 800 599, 03-6427 7626; www.cradlemountaincoaches.com.au) Operated by Devonport-based Merseylink, these bushwalker shuttle services run between Launceston and Cradle Mountain ($320, or $80 per person for four or more passengers), Devonport and Cradle Mountain ($260/65) and Lake St Clair (Cynthia Bay) and Cradle Mountain ($400/100).

The company also runs shuttles between Lake St Clair and Hobart, Launceston or Devonport (each $360/90). The shuttles collect passengers from Launceston, Hobart and Devonport airports, the *Spirit of Tasmania* ferry terminal or accommodation.

Queenstown

POP 1790

Queenstown was once a place totally devoid of trees, with a moonscape of bare, dusty hills and eroded gullies where rainforest had proliferated. Copper was discovered here in the 1890s, with mining quickly poisoning the land. Today the trees are finally returning, but the landscape remains a patchwork of mineral colours – red, orange, yellow, purple – riven by the pumpkin-orange flow of the Queen River. The town has always had a hard edge – its heritage-listed football ground famously has a gravel surface, with every player guaranteed to bleed – but it's a likeable grittiness. Though clearly still suffering the economic aftershocks of the mine closure in 2014, it's trying hard to reinvent itself as a tourism destination.

◉ Sights & Activities

Iron Blow Lookout VIEWPOINT
(off Lyell Hwy) On top of Gormanston Hill on the Lyell Hwy, just before the final descent along hairpin bends west into Queenstown, is a sealed side road leading 900m to an utterly spectacular lookout over the geological wound of Iron Blow. This awesomely deep decommissioned open-cut mine, where Queenstown's illustrious mining career began, is now filled with emerald water. You can get an eagle's-eye view from the 'springboard' walkway projecting out into thin air above the mine pit.

★ **West Coast Wilderness Railway** RAIL
(✆03-6471 0100; www.wcwr.com.au; Queenstown Station, 1 Driffield St; standard carriage adult/child/family $110/55/245, wilderness carriage adult/child $179/100; ☺ticket office 8am-4.30pm) Hop on board this historic railway line and take an unforgettable journey through the thick rainforest that stretches between Strahan and Queenstown. The half-day Rack & Gorge trip departs from Queenstown, climbing over Rinadeena Saddle to Dubbil Barril station, skirting the King River Gorge, and then returning to Queenstown.

King River Rafting RAFTING
(✆0409 664 268; www.kingriverrafting.com.au) Splash through the wild King River Gorge, with its grade III rapids, before floating serenely downriver for a few hours (adult/child $250/190), or go from wild to mild by rafting the gorge and then riding the West Coast Wilderness Railway back to Queenstown (adult/child $300/200). Trips depart from the Queenstown railway station.

RoamWild HISTORY
(✆0407 049 612; www.roamwild.com.au; Paragon Theatre, 11 McNamara St; tours adult $85-115, child $55-80; ☺tours 9am & 1.30pm) Operated by the knowledgeable Anthony Coulson, this company runs a range of history-focused tours. Visit blockade sites from the Franklin Dam protests, or an early 20th-century hydro-electricity plant on Lake Margaret, or go underground at old copper and gold mines and visit a commercial sawmill and stand of Huon-pine rainforest.

🛏 Sleeping & Eating

★ **Penghana** GUESTHOUSE $$
(✆03-6471 2560; www.penghana.com.au; 32 Esplanade; d $180-225, 2-bedroom apt from $185; 🛜) Built in 1898 for the general manager

of the Mt Lyell Mining & Railway Co, this National Trust–owned mansion commands the loftiest position in town. All rooms are en suite, and guests get the run of the place with its two sitting rooms and ballroom with championship-size snooker table. The Owen room gets the grandstand view over Queenstown.

Mt Lyell Anchorage
B&B $$

(☑0428 429 962; www.mtlyellanchorage.com; 17 Cutten St; r $170-180; 🛜) Though you wouldn't guess it from outside, this 1890s weatherboard home has been transformed into a welcoming guesthouse with comfortable rooms featuring excellent beds. Three of the rooms have stylish bathrooms (a fourth has private facilities across the hall) and there's a shared fully equipped kitchen next to a comfortable communal lounge. Owner Joy is a mine of local information.

Empire Hotel
PUB FOOD $$

(☑03-6471 1699; www.empirehotel.net.au; 2 Orr St; mains $18-30; ⊙meals noon-2pm & 5.30-8pm) The 'grand old lady of the west coast' delivers hearty pub standards, including parmas, pastas and steaks, with a hefty side serve of atmosphere. The dining room feels like a true relic of Queenstown's mining heyday, as does the signature lamb's fry and bacon. The bar is the town's major meeting place.

ⓘ Information

Visitor Information Counter (☑03-6471 1483; Galley Museum, 1-7 Driffield St; ⊙9am-5pm Oct-Apr, 10am-4pm May-Sep) Unofficial, volunteer-run information counter inside the Galley Museum, with plenty of good advice on local accommodation, walks and tours.

ⓘ Getting There & Away

Tassielink (p633) buses run between Queenstown and Burnie ($36.60, three hours) and Strahan ($10.60, 50 minutes).

Strahan

POP 708

The tyranny of distance has been kind to Strahan. More than four hours' drive from Hobart and 3½ hours from Launceston, it retains the sense of purity that led a US newspaper to dub it 'the best little town in the world'. Nestled between Macquarie Harbour (a body of water six times the size of Sydney Harbour) and the rainforest, it combines top-drawer tourist attractions – Gordon River cruises and the West Coast Wilderness Railway (p707) – with beach life and the lingering feel of a time-forgotten fishing town.

⊙ Sights & Tours

Morrison's Huon Pine Sawmill FACTORY

(☑03-6471 7235; www.facebook.com/morrisons huonpinesawmill; Esplanade; ⊙10am-4pm) **FREE** You hear a lot about Huon pine in Strahan... now see it, smell it and touch it at this working waterfront sawmill. Milling demonstrations take place daily at 3pm (coinciding with the return of the Gordon River boats), and there's a small gift shop selling Huon-pine chopping boards, jewellery, wood shavings and offcuts.

If you want a heftier Huon-pine souvenir, **Wilderness Woodworks** (☑03-6471 7244; www.wildernesswoodworks.com.au; 12 Esplanade; ⊙9am-5pm Mon-Fri, 10am-4.30pm Sat & Sun) is directly in front of the sawmill.

Ocean Beach BEACH

(via Ocean Beach Rd) Head 6km west of Strahan's town centre to find Ocean Beach, Tasmania's longest beach (40km), which is fiercely pounded by surf. It runs uninterrupted from Trial Harbour in the north to Macquarie Heads in the south and is an evocative place to watch the sun dip into the sea. The water is treacherous: don't swim here. Around 14km north of Strahan are the spectacular **Henty Dunes**, a series of 30m-high sugar-fine sand dunes backing Ocean Beach. From the picnic area, you can wander around the tops of the dunes, or take the 1½-hour return walk through them and out to Ocean Beach; remember to carry drinking water.

★Gordon River Cruises CRUISE

(☑03-6471 4300; www.gordonrivercruises.com.au; 24 Esplanade; cruise incl buffet lunch adult $135-265, child $65-265, family from $310) The sleek hybrid (diesel and electric) *Spirit of the Wild* catamaran heads to Hells Gates (the entrance to Macquarie Harbour) and is the first of the boats into the Gordon River, giving you the best chance of catching the river's reflections. On return, it stops at Sarah Island. There are standard packages, window seating or the lavishly catered 'premier upper deck' experience.

World Heritage Cruises CRUISE

(☑03-6471 7174; www.worldheritagecruises.com. au; 18 Esplanade; adult $125-175, child $60-95, family $300-380; ⊙9am mid-Aug–mid-Jul) The Grining family have been taking visitors to the Gordon River since 1896 and they are true river experts. Join them aboard their low-wash, environmentally sensitive catamaran, the *Harbour Master,* for a six-hour cruise through Macquarie Harbour, out through Hells Gates, to Sarah Island and up the Gordon River. All prices include a buffet meal.

West Coast Yacht Charters BOATING
(☑03-6471 7422; www.westcoastyachtcharters. com.au; 59 Esplanade; cruise adult/child $380/190; ⊙Oct-Apr) If you'd like your Gordon River experience with a little adventure (and fewer people), sailing on the *Stormbreaker* may be the way to go. This 20m ketch departs Strahan at 1pm, spending the night on the Gordon before returning at noon the next day (minimum four people, meals and accommodation on board included). It includes a visit to Sarah Island.

🛏 Sleeping & Eating

Strahan Holiday Retreat CARAVAN PARK $
(☑03-6471 7442; www.strahanretreat.com.au; 8-10 Innes St; unpowered/powered sites from $24/38, cabins & cottages from $120; ☎) Close to Strahan's West Beach, this sprawling village within a village – caravan park, cafe, bottle shop, tour desk and ATM – offers tent and caravan sites, self-contained cabins and multi-room cottages. There's not much grass and accommodation is cheek-by-jowl, but there's a stream with platypuses, a games room, camp kitchen, laundries and kayak/bicycle/toboggan/golf club hire ($45/35/10/10 per day).

Strahan Bungalows APARTMENT $$
(☑03-6471 7268, 0412 870 684; www.strahan bungalows.com.au; cnr Andrew & Harvey Sts; d $160-240; ☎) Decorated with a nautical theme, these curvaceous two-bedroom bungalows are clean, well maintained and fully equipped for a self-contained stay. They sleep up to five people, though that would be a squeeze. There's also a hidden granny-flat-like suite out the back that feels more suburban but fills with birdsong. It's near the beach, about a 15-minute walk from the town centre.

★Wheelhouse Apartments RENTAL HOUSE $$$
(☑0429 356 117; www.wheelhouseapartments. com.au; 4 Frazer St; d $295-350; ❄) Talk about

a room with a view! Perched above the town centre, this pair of swish town houses has wrap-around walls of glass framing a jaw-dropping view over Macquarie Harbour. Each features a fully equipped kitchen with espresso machine, lounge with TV (though the view is better than any TV programming) and a spiral staircase leading to a bedroom with spa.

The Coffee Shack CAFE $
(☑03-6471 7095; www.facebook.com/thecoffee shackstrahan; 19 Esplanade; items from $5; ⊙6am-3pm) If you want a feed or some caffeine before getting on that Gordon River boat, this little tin shed is perfectly positioned across the road from the docks. The menu is as simple as the shack itself – toasties, muffins (vegan-virtuous strawberry and coconut, perhaps?) and the coffee is life-sustaining. A fine start to any Strahan day.

★Bushman's MODERN AUSTRALIAN $$$
(☑03-6471 7612; www.bushmanscafe.com.au; 1 Harold St; mains $17-39; ⊙11am-late Mon-Fri, from 5.30pm Sat; ☑) A focus on local produce, including Petuna salmon, Spring Bay scallops and Sassafras steak, is the defining feature of the menu at Strahan's best restaurant. Lunch is a laid-back affair featuring salads, pasta dishes and burgers. Dinner is a wider-ranging proposition, with dishes such as rib eye, braised duck leg and a variety of vegetarian options. Book ahead for dinner.

☆ Entertainment

★The Ship That Never Was THEATRE
(☑03-6471 7700; www.roundearth.com.au; West Coast Visitor Information Centre, Esplanade; adult/child/concession $25/2.50/12.50; ⊙performance 5.30pm Sep-May, movie 5.30pm Jun-Aug) Billed as Australia's longest-running play (it celebrated its 25th anniversary in Strahan in January 2019), this 1¼-hour, two-actor performance tells the picaresque tale of a group of convicts who escaped from Sarah Island in 1834 by hijacking a ship they were building. It's hugely entertaining, suitable for all age groups and involves audience participation.

ℹ Information

West Coast Visitor Information Centre
(☑1800 352 200; www.westernwilderness. com.au; Esplanade; ⊙10am-5.30pm; ☎) This extremely friendly and helpful visitor centre

supplies information about Strahan and other destinations on the west coast. Staff can also make tour and accommodation bookings.

❶ Getting There & Away

Tassielink (p633) buses run to/from Strahan and Queenstown ($10.60, 50 minutes) and Burnie ($47.20, 3¾ hours).

Franklin-Gordon Wild Rivers National Park

Named after the wild rivers that twist and cascade their way through its infinitely rugged landscapes, this magnificent national park (www.parks.tas.gov.au; vehicle/person per day $24/12) is part of the Tasmanian Wilderness World Heritage Area and encompasses the catchments of the Franklin, Olga and Gordon Rivers. Proclaimed a national park in 1981, it's a place as wild as the name suggests. Bushwalkers head to the imposing white-quartzite tip of Frenchmans Cap (1443m), while rafters bump down the emblematic Franklin River on one of the world's great rafting trips.

🕈 Activities

Rafting the Franklin River is about as wild and thrilling a journey as it's possible to make in Tasmania. This is really extreme adventure and a world-class rafting experience. Experienced rafters can tackle it independently if they're fully equipped and prepared, but for anyone who's less than completely river savvy (and that's about 99% of all Franklin rafters), there are tour companies offering complete rafting packages.

If you go with an independent group, you should read the Franklin rafting notes on the Parks & Wildlife Service website, and all expeditions should register at the booth located where the Lyell Hwy crosses the Collingwood River, 49km west of Derwent Bridge.

Guided trips down the Franklin, starting at Collingwood River and ending at Sir John Falls on the Gordon River, typically take between seven and 10 days. From the exit point at Sir John Falls, groups are normally picked up by the West Coast Yacht Charters (p709) yacht, *Stormbreaker*, for the trip back to civilisation at Strahan.

The upper Franklin, from Collingwood River to the Fincham Track, passes through the bewitchingly beautiful Irenabyss Gorge and you can scale Frenchmans Cap as a side trip. The lower Franklin, from the Fincham Track to Sir John Falls, passes through the wild Great Ravine, which requires several portages.

Tasmanian Expeditions RAFTING, HIKING
(☑ 1300 666 856; www.tasmanianexpeditions.com.au; ☺ Frenchmans Cap trek from $1795, 9-/11-day rafting trips from $2895/2995) Tasmanian Expeditions offers bushwalks to Frenchmans Cap and rafting trips on the Franklin River. The Franklin trips are guided and fully catered, with the final leg to Strahan on the *Stormbreaker*. The longer option includes a Frenchmans Cap climb. On the five-day, 46km guided Frenchmans Cap walk, you camp at Lakes Vera and Tahune before climbing the 1446m mountain.

Franklin River Rafting RAFTING
(☑ 0422 642 190; www.franklinriverrafting.com; 8-/10-day trip $2970/3300; ☺ Nov-Apr) Excellent eight- and 10-day guided and fully catered trips from Collingwood Bridge, with the final leg also on the *Stormbreaker*. .

THE SOUTHWEST

Tasmania's wild southwest corner is an edge-of-the-world domain made up of primordial forests, rugged mountains and endless heathland, all fringed by untamed, often unvisited beaches and turbulent seas. It's among the last great wilderness areas on earth: an isolated, magisterial place that's ripe for adventure.

Once inhabited by the Southwest Aboriginal people, Southwest National Park is the largest national park in Tasmania and the biggest slice of the Unesco-listed Tasmanian Wilderness World Heritage Area. Just one road cuts through the 6183-sq-km park, and this only goes as far as the hydroelectric station on the Gordon Dam. Otherwise all access is by light plane to the gravel airstrip at Melaleuca, by sailing boat around the tempestuous coastline, or on foot.

🕝 Tours

Wild Pedder HIKING, KAYAKING
(☑ 0456 869 092; www.wildpedder.com.au; from $2490) Lake Pedder has immense stories as well as volume, and this four-day trip led by two passionate young guides reveals many

of them – including Pedder's long-lost pink beach, and the Florentine Valley site of the last captured Tasmanian tiger – over three days of hiking and one day of kayaking on the lake.

ℹ Information

To pick up national park passes and information about the southwest, stop at the Mt Field National Park Visitor Centre (p651) or, if entering at Cockle Creek, at the **Parks & Wildlife Service** (☑ 03-6121 7026; www.parks.tas.gov.au; 22 Main St, Huonville; ☺ 10am-4pm Mon-Fri) office in Huonville.

ℹ Getting There & Away

The two major access points for Southwest National Park are the small town of Southport (Australia's most southerly town), 97km south of Hobart on the A6; and the tiny settlement of Strathgordon on Lake Pedder, accessed via the B61. Strathgordon is a 2½-hour, 155km drive west of Hobart; there's no fuel available past Maydena on this drive, and even there you may not have any luck – it's best to fill the tank at Westerway or New Norfolk. Neither Strathgordon nor Southport are serviced by public transport.

Par Avion (p712) flies bushwalkers into remote Melaleuca from Hobart.

Lake Pedder & Strathgordon

This vast flooded valley system covers the area that once cradled the original Lake Pedder, a spectacularly beautiful natural lake that was the region's ecological jewel. Its shallow, whisky-coloured waters covered 10 sq km, with one end fringed by a spectacular pink-tinged beach on which light aircraft could famously land. The lake was the first part of the southwest to be protected within its own national park, a status that failed to preserve it when Lake Pedder (and the pink beach) disappeared beneath hydroelectric dam waters in 1972. The protests surrounding the damming are often claimed as giving birth to the world's first green political party.

These days the artificial replacement is 242 sq km and, while its history has created a love-hate relationship for many people, it remains unquestionably spectacular. At its northern tip is the tiny settlement of Strathgordon.

🏃 Activities

Aardvark Adventures ADVENTURE SPORTS (☑ 03-6273 7722; www.aardvarkadventures.com.au; $210) Abseil over the edge of the Gordon Dam wall on what's billed as the world's highest commercial abseil – 140m from top to very distant bottom. Suitable for beginners; minimum two people.

🛏 Sleeping

There are two campgrounds near the lake's southern shore, the exposed **Edgar Camping Ground** (☑ 03-6288 1149; www.parks.tas.gov.au; off Scotts Peak Rd) and the more protected **Huon Campground** (☑ 03-6288 1149; www.parks.tas.gov.au; off Scotts Peak Rd), as well as **Ted's Beach Campground** (☑ 03-6288 1149; www.parks.tas.gov.au; Gordon River Rd) near Strathgordon. All three are free; no advance bookings can be made.

Pedder Wilderness Lodge LODGE $$ (☑ 03-6280 1166; www.pedderwildernesslodge.com.au; Gordon River Rd; d/tr from $149/179, units $239-269, ste $389; ☎ ☒) There's a wide range of comfortable accommodation at this former hydro-workers' lodge, from budget rooms to spa suites. If you've come this far from civilisation, it's worth plumping for at least a lake-view room (even if the walls are a bit thin). Otherwise, the **Twelvetrees Restaurant** (mains $25 to $36) has a bar, open fire and the same view.

Southwest National Park

The state's largest **national park** (☑ 03-6121 7026, 03-6288 1283; www.parks.tas.gov.au; vehicle/person per day $24/12) is made up of remote, wild country: forests, mountains, grassy plains and seascapes. Home to both the Huon pine, which lives for 3000 years, and the swamp gum, the world's tallest flowering plant, it also hosts about 300 species of lichen, moss and fern – some very rare. These festoon the rainforests, while the alpine meadows are replete with wildflowers and flowering shrubs. Through it all run wild rivers, their rapids tearing through deep gorges. Combining these sights with majestic Mt Anne, the jagged crest of the Western Arthur Range and the fang-like appearance of Australia's most dramatic mountain, Federation Peak, the park is irresistible to photographers, bushwalkers and nature enthusiasts.

☆ Activities & Tours

The best-known walk in the southwest is the 85km **South Coast Track**, running along the wild southern edge of Tasmania between Melaleuca and Cockle Creek, near Southport close to the park's southeastern edge; it takes six to eight days. Joining it at Melaleuca, but stretching north to Scotts Peak Dam on Lake Pedder, is the **Port Davey Track**, a 70km walk (five to six days) originally cut as an escape route for shipwrecked sailors.

Of the more difficult walks that require a high degree of bushwalking skill, the shortest is the three-day circuit of the **Mt Anne Range**, a challenging walk with some difficult scrambling. The walk to scarily exposed **Federation Peak** (four to five days) has earned a reputation as the most difficult bushwalking ascent in Australia, while the spectacular **Western Arthur Range** is an extremely complex and difficult traverse, for which seven to 11 days are recommended.

Roaring 40s Kayaking   KAYAKING
(☑0455 949 777; www.roaring40skayaking.com. au; 3-/7-day trip from $2350/3295) The most intimate way to experience the southwestern wilderness is by kayak. From November to April, Hobart-based Roaring 40s Kayaking offers camp-based kayaking trips exploring Port Davey and Bathurst Harbour, with access by light plane to/from Hobart.

Par Avion   SCENIC FLIGHTS
(☑03-6248 5390; www.paravion.com.au; 115 Kennedy Dr, Cambridge; adult/child $599/549) You can swoop over the southwest on a scenic small-plane day trip with this operator based in Cambridge, near Hobart Airport. On a clear, day you can see the whole of this corner of Tasmania as you buzz over wild beaches and jagged peaks before landing at Melaleuca, where you head out to explore remote Bathurst Harbour on a boat.

Maydena

POP 222

The once-maligned forestry town of Maydena went from zero to hero in 2018, when the Maydena Bike Park opened, giving southern Tasmania a counterbalance to the runaway success of the Blue Derby mountain-bike trails (p675) in the northeast. Though Maydena is in easy day-trip reach of Hobart, about 1½ hours' drive away, accommodation options have started to sprout like mushrooms. It's also the final vestige of civilisation before the road disappears into the World Heritage wilderness of the Southwest National Park and Lake Pedder.

☆ Activities

Maydena Bike Park   MOUNTAIN BIKING
(☑1300 399 664; www.maydenabikepark.com; 34 Kallista Rd; shuttle-bus day pass adult/child $80/75, dual-suspension bike hire per day $125; ⊙shuttles 9.30am-4pm) Opened in January 2018, this mountain-bike park's typical run is steep and challenging (and muddy in winter), plunging 800m from summit to the park hub inside Maydena's old school. Trails are accessed by shuttle buses, with a climbing trail for those who prefer some hurt in their legs.

There's a cafe and bar at the park hub serving burgers, pizzas ($18 to $23) and power bowls, and a bar-restaurant at the summit.

🛏 Sleeping

Trails End   RENTAL HOUSE $$
(☑0413 544 449; www.trailsendmaydena.com; 1 West St; house $165) Created for mountain bikers, this large house, 300m from Maydena Bike Park, sleeps up to eight (10 at a pinch) and has a lock-up bike shed with bike stand and tools, as well as a bike-washing area. It's perfectly designed for post-ride sprawling.

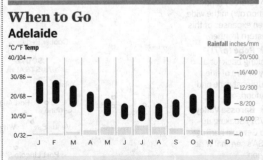

Adelaide & South Australia

♪ 08 / POP 1.72 MILLION

Includes ➡

Adelaide 716
Fleurieu Peninsula 739
Kangaroo Island 748
Barossa Valley 757
Clare Valley 762
Murray River 765
Limestone Coast 771
Yorke Peninsula 777
Eyre Peninsula 780
Flinders Ranges 787
Outback South
Australia 792

Best Places to Eat

➡ Peel Street (p726)

➡ Star of Greece (p745)

➡ d'Arenberg Cube (p742)

➡ Dudley Wines Cellar Door (p752)

➡ Fino Seppeltsfield (p760)

Best Places to Stay

➡ Port Elliot Beach House YHA (p747)

➡ Tanonga (p784)

➡ Mayfair Hotel (p725)

➡ Prairie Hotel (p792)

➡ Lush Pastures (p744)

Why Go?

Escape the frenzy of Australia's east coast with a few days in gracious, relaxed South Australia (SA). The driest state in the planet's driest inhabited continent, SA beats the heat by celebrating life's finer things: fine landscapes, fine festivals, fine food, and (...OK, forget the other three) fine wine.

It's true – almost everywhere you go in SA you'll find cellar doors vying for your attention. Succumb to temptation in SA's famous wine regions: the Barossa Valley, Clare Valley, Coonawarra, McLaren Vale and the Adelaide Hills. But don't miss Kangaroo Island's wildlife and seafood; big-sky, wild-west landscapes on the Yorke and Eyre peninsulas; the photogenic Flinders Ranges; the fertile terrain around the snaking Murray River; and the craggy shores and caves in the beach-strewn Limestone Coast. At the heart of it all, Adelaide delivers as many high-brow festivals as it does dive bars.

When to Go
Adelaide

| **Feb–Mar** SA's festival season hits its straps: the Adelaide Fringe and WOMADelaide are highlights. | **Mar–May** Beat the summer city heat in shoulder season (also September to November). | **Sep** Football finals time: yell yourself silly in the stands, beer and pie in hand(s). |

South Australia Highlights

1 **Adelaide**
(p716) Settling in for a cricket match or some Australian rules football at the magnificent Adelaide Oval, then catching some live tunes in this Unesco 'City of Music'.

2 **McLaren Vale Wine Region** (p741) Swirling and quaffing your way through SA's most popular wine region.

3 **Adelaide Hills**
(p734) Day-tripping through Adelaide's backyard, with cellar doors, markets and historic towns.

4 **Kangaroo Island**
(p748) Listening to snorting seals and sampling super seafood on 'KI'.

5 **Flinders Ranges**
(p787) Watching sunset colours shift across the rocky walls of 80-sq-km natural basin Ikara (Wilpena Pound).

6 **Eyre Peninsula**
(p780) Losing sight of yesterday (and tomorrow) in the wide open expanses of this western frontier.

7 **Robe** (p771)
Kicking back for a day or two of fine southeast wine and seafood.

8 **Barossa Valley**
(p757) Soaking up the German heritage in SA's seminal wine region.

9 **Yorke Peninsula**
(p777) Exploring low-key beach towns, surf breaks and waterside pubs not far from Adelaide.

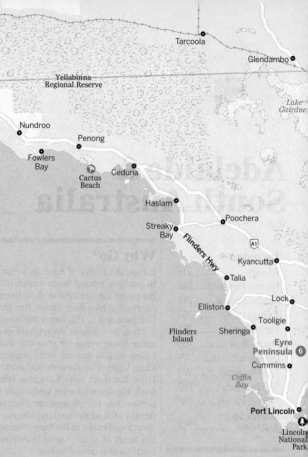

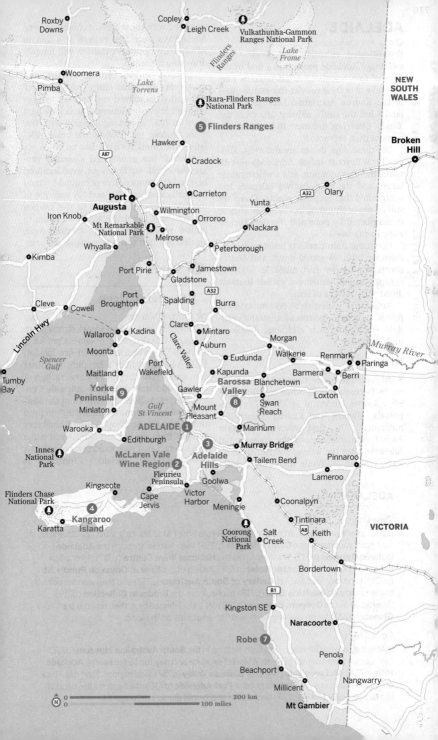

ADELAIDE

📞 08 / POP 1.34 MILLION

Sophisticated, cultured, neat-casual – the self-image Adelaide projects is a nod to the days of free colonisation. Adelaidians may remind you of their convict-free status – and of the Kaurna Aboriginal heritage of this land – but the stuffy, affluent origins of the 'City of Churches' did more to inhibit development than promote it.

But these days things are different. Multicultural flavours infuse Adelaide's restaurants; there's a pumping arts and live-music scene; and the city's festival calendar has vanquished dull Saturday nights. There are still plenty of church spires here, but they're outnumbered by pubs and hip bars tucked away in city lanes.

Down the tram tracks is beachy Glenelg: Adelaide with its guard down and boardshorts up. Nearby Port Adelaide is slowly gentrifying but remains a raffish harbour 'hood with buckets of soul.

Note that Adelaide's accommodation prices lag behind the rest of Australia's capitals – a high season midrange double is under $200.

History

South Australia was declared a province on 28 December 1836, when the first British colonists landed at Holdfast Bay (current-day Glenelg, and Kaurna country for millennia). The first governor, Captain John Hindmarsh, named the state capital Adelaide, after the wife of the British monarch, William IV. While the eastern states struggled with the stigma of convict society, Adelaidians were free citizens – a fact to which many South Australians will happily draw your attention.

Adelaide, unlike Sydney, Hobart and many other Australian cities, was a 'planned' city – sited, conceived and laid out by government Surveyor-General Colonel William Light in 1837. A rectangular grid with five main squares, encircled by the broad Adelaide Park Lands, it's a city like no other.

Adelaide has maintained a socially progressive creed: trade unions were legalised here in 1876; women were permitted to stand for parliament in 1894; and SA was one of the first places in the world to give women the vote, and the first state in Australia to outlaw racial and gender discrimination, legalise abortion and decriminalise gay sex.

👁 Sights

👁 Central Adelaide

⭐ **Central Market**　　　　　　　MARKET
(📞08-8203 7494; www.adelaidecentralmarket.com.au; 44-60 Gouger St; ⏰7am-5.30pm Tue & Thu, 9am-5.30pm Wed, 7am-9pm Fri, 7am-3pm Sat) **FREE** A tourist sight or a shopping op? Either way, satisfy your deepest culinary cravings at the 250-odd stalls in superb Adelaide Central Market. A sliver of salami from the Mettwurst Shop, a crumb of English Stilton from the Smelly Cheese Shop, a tub of blueberry yoghurt from the Yoghurt Shop – you name it, it's here. Good luck making it out without eating anything. Adelaide's Chinatown is

---

ADELAIDE IN...

Two Days

If you're here at Festival, WOMADelaide or Fringe time ('Mad March'), lap it up. Otherwise, kick-start your day at the **Central Market** (p716) then wander through the **Adelaide Botanic Gardens** (p717), finishing up at the **National Wine Centre** (p717). After a few bohemian beers at the **Exeter Hotel** (p728), have a ritzy dinner at **Orana on Rundle St** (p727). Next day, visit the **Art Gallery of South Australia** (p717) and then wander down to the revamped **Adelaide Oval** (p718) to check out the **Bradman Collection** (p719). Grab a cab out to **Coopers Brewery** (p720) for a beer-tinged tour, then ride the tram to **Glenelg** (p720) for an evening swim and fish and chips on the sand.

Four Days

Follow the two-day itinerary – perhaps slotting in the **South Australian Museum** (p717) – then pack a picnic basket of Central Market produce and day-trip to the nearby **Adelaide Hills** (p734), **McLaren Vale** (p740) or **Barossa Valley** (p757) wine regions. Next day, truck out to the museums and historic pubs of **Port Adelaide** (p730), then catch a live band at the **Grace Emily Hotel** (p728) back in the city, before dinner on Gouger St.

ADELAIDE FOR CHILDREN

There are few kids who won't love the tram ride from the city down to Glenelg (p720); kids under five ride free. You may have trouble getting them off the tram – the lure of a splash in the shallows at Glenelg Beach then some fish and chips on the lawn should do the trick.

During school holidays, the South Australian Museum (p717), State Library of South Australia (p732), Art Gallery of South Australia (p717), Adelaide Zoo (p720) and Adelaide Botanic Gardens (p717) run inspired kid- and family-oriented programs with accessible and interactive general displays. The Art Gallery also runs a START at the Gallery kids' program (tours, music, activities) from 11am to 3pm on the first Sunday of the month.

Down on the River Torrens there are Popeye (p722) river cruises and Paddle Boats (p722), which make a satisfying splash.

The free street press *Kiddo* (www.kiddomag.com.au) and *Child* (www.childmags.com. au), available at cafes and libraries, are largely advertorial but do contain event and activity listings. For babysitters, try **Hessel Group** (08-8462 0222; www.hesselgroup.com.au; 4/224 Glen Osmond Rd, Fullarton).

right next door. Adelaide's Top Food & Wine Tours (p723) offers guided tours.

Eateries of note within the market complex include the long-running **Lucia's Pizza & Spaghetti Bar** (08-8231 2303; www. lucias.com.au; Central Market, 44-60 Gouger St; mains $8-15; 7am-3pm Mon-Thu & Sat, to 9pm Fri) and **Asian Gourmet** (08-8203 7494; www.adelaidecentralmarket.com.au/traders/asian-gourmet; Central Market, 44-60 Gouger St, Adelaide; mains $10-15; 9am-5.30pm Mon, Wed & Thu, 7am-5.30pm Tue, 7am-9pm Fri, 7am-3pm Sat), serving the best laksa in town.

★ **South Australian Museum**   MUSEUM
(08-8207 7500; www.samuseum.sa.gov.au; North Tce; 10am-5pm) FREE Dig into Australia's natural history with the museum's special exhibits on whales and Antarctic explorer Sir Douglas Mawson. Over two levels, the amazing Australian Aboriginal Cultures gallery is one of the largest collections of Aboriginal artefacts in the world. Elsewhere, the giant squid and the lion with the twitchy tail are definite highlights. Free one-hour tours depart at 11am. The cafe here is a handy spot for lunch/recaffeination.

★ **Art Gallery of South Australia**   GALLERY
(08-8207 7000; www.artgallery.sa.gov.au; North Tce; 10am-5pm) FREE Spend a few hushed hours in the vaulted, parquetry-floored gallery that represents the big names in Australian art. Permanent exhibitions include Australian, Aboriginal and Torres Strait Islander, Asian, European and North American art (20 bronze Rodins!). Progressive visiting exhibitions occupy the basement. There are free guided tours (11am and 2pm daily) and lunchtime talks (12.30pm every day except Tuesday). There's a lovely cafe out the back too.

Adelaide Botanic Gardens   GARDENS
(08-8222 9311; www.botanicgardens.sa.gov.au; cnr North Tce & East Tce; 7.15am-sunset Mon-Fri, from 9am Sat & Sun) FREE Meander, jog or chew through your trashy airport novel in these lush city-fringe gardens. Highlights include a restored 1877 palm house, the water-lily pavilion (housing the gigantic *Victoria amazonica*), the First Creek wetlands, the engrossing **Museum of Economic Botany** and the fabulous steel-and-glass arc of the **Bicentennial Conservatory** (10am to 4pm), which re-creates a tropical rainforest. Free 1½-hour guided walks depart the Schomburgk Pavilion at 10.30am daily. The classy **Botanic Gardens Restaurant** (08-8223 3526; www.botanicgardensrestaurant.com.au; off Plane Tree Dr; 3-/4-courses $70/90; noon-2.30pm Tue-Sun, 6.30-9pm Fri & Sat) is here too.

National Wine Centre of Australia   WINERY
(08-8313 3355; www.wineaustralia.com.au; cnr Botanic & Hackney Rds; 9am-6pm) FREE Check out the free self-guided, interactive Wine Discovery Journey exhibition at this very sexy wine centre (doubling as a research facility for the University of Adelaide, as well as a visitor centre). It's a great way to understand the issues winemakers contend with, and you can even have your own virtual vintage rated. Explore the Cellar Door (the largest in Australia!) and get stuck into some cleverly automated tastings (from $2.50). Free guided tours run at 11.30am daily.

Adelaide

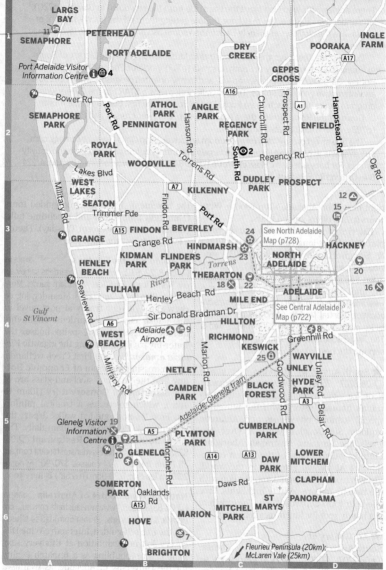

Port Adelaide Visitor Information Centre

North Adelaide

★ **Adelaide Oval**   SPECTATOR SPORT
(☎08-8205 4700; www.adelaideoval.com.au; King William Rd, North Adelaide; tours adult/child $25/15; ☉tours 10am, 11am & 2pm daily, plus 1pm Sat &

Sun) Hailed as the world's prettiest cricket ground, the Adelaide Oval hosts interstate and international cricket matches in summer, plus national AFL and state football matches in winter. A wholesale redevelopment has boosted seating capacity to 53,000 – when they're all yelling, it's a serious home-town

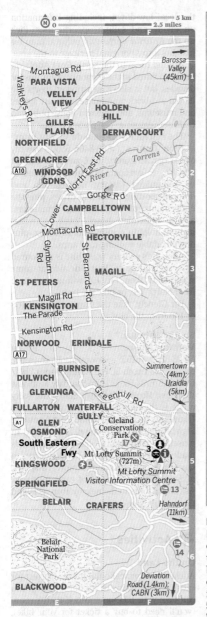

Adelaide

⊙ Sights
1 Cleland Conservation Park F5
2 Coopers Brewery C2
3 Mt Lofty Summit F5
4 South Australian Maritime
   Museum..B1

⊕ Activities, Courses & Tours
5 Eagle Mountain Bike Park E5
6 Glenelg Bicycle Hire B5
7 SA Aquatic & Leisure Centre.............B6
8 Tree Climb Adelaide D4

⊜ Sleeping
9 Atura Adelaide Airport.......................B4
10 Glenelg Beach Hostel B5
11 Largs Pier Hotel..................................A1
12 Levi Park Caravan Park D3
13 Mt Lofty House F5
14 Stirling Hotel......................................F6
15 Watson..D3

⊗ Eating
16 Argo on the Parade D4
17 Cleland Café.......................................F5
   Low & Slow American BBQ..........(see 4)
   Mt Lofty Summit
   Restaurant.................................(see 3)
18 Parwana Afghan Kitchen....................C4
19 Zucca..B5

⊙ Drinking & Nightlife
20 Little Bang Brewing Company............D3
21 Moseley B5
   Port Admiral Hotel ....(see 4)
22 Wheatsheaf..C3

⊗ Entertainment
23 Adelaide Entertainment Centre C3
24 Governor Hindmarsh Hotel................C3

⊟ Shopping
25 Adelaide Farmers Market C4
   Stirling Markets ....(see 14)

North Adelaide; ⊙ 9am-4pm non-playing days) FREE, where devotees of Don Bradman, cricket's greatest batsman, can pore over the minutiae of his legend. Check out the bronze statue of 'the Don' cracking a cover drive out the front of the stadium. Also here is **Roofclimb Adelaide Oval** (☑ 08-8331 5222; www.roofclimb.com.au; Adelaide Oval, King William Rd, North Adelaide; adult day/twilight/night $104/114/119, child day/twilight $70/80), where you scale the giant roof scallops above the hallowed turf (amazing views!). A proposed hotel wrapping around the stadium's eastern flank was causing mass controversy at the time of writing. Watch this space...

advantage! Guided 90-minute tours run on non-game days, departing from the Riverbank Stand (south entrance), off War Memorial Dr; call for bookings or book online.

Also here is the **Bradman Collection** (☑ 08-8211 1100; www.adelaideoval.com.au/bradman-collection; Adelaide Oval, War Memorial Dr,

Adelaide Zoo
ZOO

(☑08-8267 3255; www.zoossa.com.au/adelaide-zoo; Frome Rd, Adelaide; adult/child/family $36/20/91.50; ☺9.30am-5pm) Around 1800 exotic and native mammals, birds and reptiles roar, growl and screech at Adelaide's wonderful zoo, dating from 1883. There are free walking tours half-hourly (plus a slew of longer and overnight tours), feeding sessions and a children's zoo. Wang Wang and Fu Ni are Australia's only giant pandas and always draw a crowd (pandamonium!). Other highlights include the nocturnal and reptile houses. You can take a river cruise to the zoo on Popeye (p722).

⊙ Inner Suburbs

Adelaide Gaol
HISTORIC BUILDING

(☑08-8231 4062; www.adelaidegaol.sa.gov.au; 18 Gaol Rd, Thebarton; self-guided tours adult/child/family $14.50/9/35.50; ☺10am-4pm) Decommissioned in 1988 after housing 300,000 inmates since 1841, this old Victorian lock-up has a grim vibe, but its displays of homemade bongs, weapons and escape devices are amazing. It's allegedly the most haunted historic site in SA – 45 prisoners were executed here, and are buried in the grounds. Ask about scheduled guided and ghost tours if you're feeling brave (www.adelaidegaol.org.au).

Coopers Brewery
BREWERY

(☑08-8440 1800; www.coopers.com.au; 461 South Rd, Regency Park; 1hr tour per person $27.50; ☺tours 1pm Tue-Fri) You can't possibly come to Adelaide without entertaining thoughts of touring Coopers Brewery. Tours take you through the brewhouse, bottling hall and history museum, where you can get stuck into samples of stouts, ales and lagers. Bookings required; minimum age 18. The brewery is in the northern suburbs; grab a cab or walk 1km from Islington train station.

⊙ Glenelg to Port Adelaide

Glenelg, or 'the Bay' – the site of SA's colonial landing – is Adelaide at its most LA. Glenelg's sandy beach faces towards the west, and as the sun sinks into the sea, the pubs and bars burgeon with surfies, backpackers and sun-damaged sexagenarians. The tram rumbles in from the city, past the Jetty Rd shopping strip to the alfresco cafes around Moseley Sq.

The Glenelg Visitor Information Centre (☑08-8294 5833; www.glenelgsa.com.au; Glenelg Town Hall, Moseley Sq, Glenelg; ☺10am-4pm) has the local low-down, including information on diving and sailing opportunities. Pick up the *Kaurna yarta-ana* cultural map for insights into Aboriginal heritage in the area.

Around 16km to the north, Port Adelaide has been mired in the economic doldrums for decades, but is slowly gentrifying, morphing its old red-brick warehouses into art spaces and museums, and its brawl-house pubs into craft-beer emporia. The place has soul!

The helpful Port Adelaide Visitor Information Centre (☑08-8405 6560; www.cityofpae.sa.gov.au/tourism; 66 Commercial Rd, Port Adelaide; ☺9am-5pm; ☎) stocks brochures on self-guided history, heritage-pub and dolphin-spotting walks and drives, plus the enticements of neighbouring Semaphore, a very bohemian beach 'burb. Activities include dolphin cruises and kayaking, plus downloadable walking-tour apps.

Adelaide's solitary tram line is rumoured to be extending to Port Adelaide at some stage. Until then, bus 150 will get you here from North Tce, or take the train.

For Glenelg, take the tram or bus 167, 168 or 190 from the city.

South Australian Maritime Museum
MUSEUM

(☑08-8207 6255; www.samaritimemuseum.com.au; 126 Lipson St, Port Adelaide; adult/child/family $15/6/34.50; ☺10am-5pm daily, lighthouse 10am-2pm Mon-Fri, 11am-4pm Sun) This salty cache is the oldest of its kind in Australia. Highlights include the iconic Port Adelaide Lighthouse ($1 on its own, or included in museum admission), busty figureheads made everywhere from Londonderry to Quebec, shipwreck and explorer displays, and a computer register of early migrants. Ask about tours to the nearby Torrens Island Quarantine Station.

🏃 Activities

On the Land

Adelaide is a pancake-flat town – perfect for cycling and walking (if it's not too hot!). You can take your bike on trains if there's room (you'll need to buy a ticket for your bike), but not on buses or trams.

Trails SA (www.southaustraliantrails.com) and Walking SA (www.walkingsa.org.au) offer loads of cycling- and hiking-trail info: pick up the *40 Great South Australian Short Walks* brochure, or download it from the Walking SA website.

ABORIGINAL SOUTH AUSTRALIA

SA offers up some great opportunities to learn about Aboriginal cultures and beliefs. Some of the best include the Aboriginal-run Bookabee Tours (p723) of Adelaide and the Flinders Ranges, Yorke Peninsula cultural tours run by Adjahdura Land (p777), and Adelaide's **Tandanya National Aboriginal Cultural Institute** (☑08-8224 3200; www. tandanya.com.au; 253 Grenfell St; ☺10am-5pm Mon-Sat) **FREE**. Also in Adelaide is the Australian Aboriginal Cultures Gallery in the South Australian Museum (p717), the largest collection of Australian Aboriginal artefacts on the planet.

SA's best-known Aboriginal language is Pitjantjatjara (also known as Pitjantjara), which is spoken throughout the Anangu-Pitjantjarjara Aboriginal Lands of northern SA, down almost to the Great Australian Bight. The traditional language of the Adelaide area is Kaurna. Many Kaurna-derived place names have survived around the city: Aldinga comes from *Ngultingga,* Onkaparinga from *Ngangkiparringga* and Noarlunga from *Nurlungga.* The Adelaide Hills region is Peramangk country.

The Coorong, in Ngarrindjeri country, is a complex series of dunes and salt pans separated from the sea by the long, thin Younghusband Peninsula. It takes its name from the Ngarrindjeri word *kurangh,* meaning 'long neck'. According to the Ngarrindjeri, their Dreaming ancestor, Ngurundjeri, created the Coorong and the Murray River.

The iconic Ikara (Wilpena Pound), a natural basin in Flinders Ranges National Park, is sacred to the Adnyamathanha people, who have lived in the area for more than 15,000 years. Dreaming stories tell of two *akurra* (giant snakes) who coiled around Ikara during an initiation ceremony, creating a whirlwind and devouring the participants. The snakes were so full after their feast they couldn't move, and willed themselves to die, thus creating the landmark.

In 1966, SA became the first state to grant Aboriginal people title to their lands. In the early 1980s most of the land west of the Stuart Hwy and north of the railway to Perth was transferred to Aboriginal ownership. Cultural clashes still sometimes occur, however, exemplified by the politically and culturally divisive Hindmarsh Bridge controversy in the 1990s, which pitted Aboriginal beliefs against development. In 2017 a monument installed at Elliston on the Eyre Peninsula caused community ructions and made international news. A massacre occurred here in 1849, when local Wirangu people were pushed to their deaths from the clifftops. Racial tensions simmered over the monument and a petition circulated in town to ask the word 'massacre' to be removed from the plaque, but the petition had only 80 signatories and the word stayed.

There are free guided walks in the Adelaide Botanic Gardens (p717). The riverside **Linear Park Trail** is a 40km walking/cycling path running from Glenelg to the foot of the Adelaide Hills, mainly along the (at times underwhelming) River Torrens: pick up the two brochures covering the route from city to the hills, and the city to the beach, or download maps from www.southaustraliantrails.com. Another popular hiking trail is the steep **Waterfall Gully Track** (three hours return) up to or down from Mt Lofty Summit.

To pick up an **Adelaide Free Bike** to explore for a day, contact Bicycle SA (p734).

★**Tree Climb Adelaide** CLIMBING
(☑0411 268 486; www.treeclimb.com.au; cnr Greenhill & Unley Rds, Adelaide; adult/child $35/29; ☺9am-4pm; ⓐ) Making brilliant use of the Adelaide Park Lands (surely Adelaide's town planner Colonel William Light didn't intend intend them only to be passively observed!), this human ropes-and-platforms spiderweb includes 70 obstacles over seven courses, strung between the boughs of some mighty huge gum trees. There's a dedicated kids' course too. Great fun!

Adelaide Kaurna Walking Tour WALKING
(☑08-8203 7203; www.cityofadelaide.com. au; Adelaide Festival Centre, King William Rd; ☺daylight hours) **FREE** Adelaide is Kaurna country: for an understanding of this ancient culture and some significant sites around the city and River Torrens, follow this 17-stop self-guided walking trail, developed by the city council. Pick up a map at the Adelaide Visitor Information Centre (p733), or download one from www.city ofadelaide.com.au. Stop 1 is at the Adelaide Festival Centre.

Central Adelaide

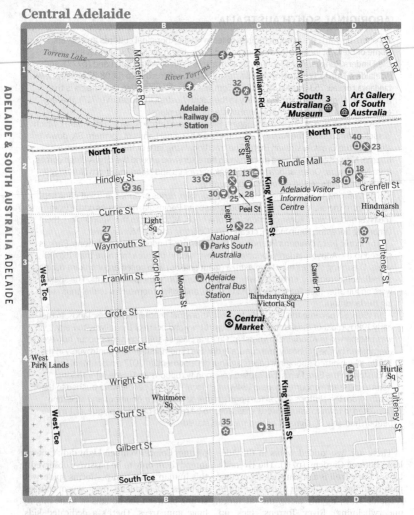

On & in the Water

Adelaide gets *reeeally* hot in summer. Hit the beach at Glenelg, or the pools at the **Adelaide Aquatic Centre** (08-8203 7665; www.adelaideaquaticcentre.com.au; Jeffcott Rd, North Adelaide; adult/child/family $8.40/6.70/23.50; 6am-9pm Mon-Fri, 7am-7pm Sat & Sun) or **SA Aquatic & Leisure Centre** (08-8198 0198; www.saaquatic.ymca.org.au; 443 Morphett Rd, Oaklands Park; adult/child/family $8.50/7/24; 5am-10pm Mon-Fri, to 8pm Sat, 7am-8pm Sun). Away from the beach, check out **Popeye** (08-8232 7994; www.thepopeye.com.au; Elder Park; return adult/child $15/8, one way $10/5; 10am-4pm, reduced

hours winter) cruises on the River Torrens and the little **Paddle Boats** (08-8232 7994; www.facebook.com/popeyeadelaide; Elder Park, Adelaide; hire per 30min 2-4 people $20; 10am-4pm, reduced hours winter) nearby, run by the same folks.

Adventure Kayaking SA   KAYAKING
(08-8295 8812; www.adventurekayak.com.au; tours adult/child from $50/25, kayak hire per 3hr 1-/2-/3-seater $40/60/80) Family-friendly guided kayak tours around the Port River estuary (dolphins, mangroves, shipwrecks). Also offers kayak and stand-up paddleboard hire, plus self-guided tours.

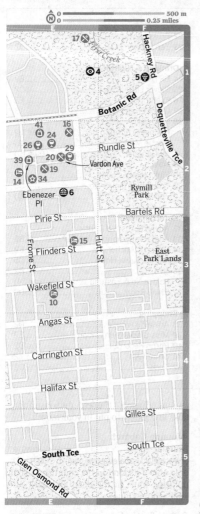

River Torrens to Henley Beach then heading along the foreshore to Glenelg, before hopping on the tram back into town ($119 including bike, helmet, morning tea and tram ticket). Waterfall walks at Morialta Conservation Park and Waterfall Gully also available.

Adelaide's Top Food & Wine Tours FOOD & DRINK
(☑ 08-8386 0888; www.topfoodandwinetours. com.au) Get out of bed early and uncover Adeaide's gastronomic soul with a dawn ($75 including breakfast) or morning ($55) tour of the buzzing Central Market (p716), where stallholders introduce their produce. Adelaide Hills, McLaren Vale, Barossa and Clare Valley wine tours are also available.

Adelaide Sightseeing TOURS
(☑ 1300 769 762; www.adelaidesightseeing.com. au) Runs a half-day city highlights tour ($58) including North Tce, Glenelg, Haigh's Chocolates and the Adelaide Oval (among other sights). Full-day city and Adelaide Hills tours also available ($112), plus jaunts to the Barossa Valley, McLaren Vale and Kangaroo Island.

Bookabee Tours CULTURAL
(☑ 08-8235 9954; www.bookabee.com.au) 🌿 Indigenous-run half-/full-day city tours (from $180/260; price on application) focusing on Tandanya National Aboriginal Cultural Institute, the South Australian Museum and bush foods in the Adelaide Botanic Gardens. A great insight into Kaurna culture.

🎊 Festivals & Events

★ Tour Down Under SPORTS
(www.tourdownunder.com.au; ⊙ Jan) The world's best cyclists sweating in their lycra: six races through SA towns, with the grand finale in central Adelaide.

★ Adelaide Fringe PERFORMING ARTS
(www.adelaidefringe.com.au; ⊙ Feb/Mar) This off-kilter and unfailingly entertaining annual independent arts festival in February and March is second only to the Edinburgh Fringe. Funky, unpredictable and downright hilarious, with hundreds of events over a very entertaining month – it's a world-class festival. There's a handy ticket booth in Rundle Mall.

🕝 Tours

★ Adelaide City Explorer WALKING
(www.adelaidecityexplorer.com.au) **FREE** Excellent downloadable walking tours around the city, cosponsored by the Adelaide City Council and the National Trust (there's a definite architectural bias here, which we like!). There are 27 themed trails in all – art deco, pubs, North Tce, outdoor art, trees etc – get 'em on your phone and get walking.

Pure SA CYCLING
(☑ 08-7226 9011; www.puresa.com.au) A guided bike ride from the city to the sea, tracing the

Central Adelaide

◉ Top Sights
1 Art Gallery of South Australia............... D1
2 Central Market.. C4
3 South Australian Museum D1

◎ Sights
4 Adelaide Botanic Gardens E1
5 National Wine Centre of Australia F1
6 Tandanya National Aboriginal
    Cultural Institute E2

◎ Activities, Courses & Tours
7 Adelaide Kaurna Walking Tour C1
8 Paddle Boats B1
9 Popeye C1

◎ Sleeping
10 Adabco Boutique Hotel E3
11 Adelaide Central YHA B3
12 Hostel 109 .... D4
13 Mayfair Hotel C2
14 Roof Garden Hotel E2
15 Soho Hotel E3

◎ Eating
16 Africola E2
    Asian Gourmet .... (see 2)
17 Botanic Gardens Restaurant E1
18 Jasmin Indian Restaurant D2
19 Kutchi Deli Parwana E2
    Lucia's Pizza & Spaghetti Bar .... (see 2)
20 Orana E2
21 Peel Street C2

22 Press C3
23 Zen Kitchen D2

◎ Drinking & Nightlife
24 BRYKLN E2
25 Clever Little Taylor C2
26 Exeter Hotel E2
27 Grace Emily Hotel A3
28 Hains & Co C2
    Hennessy Rooftop Bar .... (see 13)
    Maybe Mae .... (see 21)
    Mr Goodbar .... (see 19)
29 Nola E2
30 Pink Moon Saloon C2
31 Prohibition Liquor Co C5
    Zhivago .... (see 30)

◎ Entertainment
32 Adelaide Festival Centre C1
33 Adelaide Symphony Orchestra B2
34 Crown & Anchor E2
35 Gilbert Street Hotel C5
36 Jive B2
    Palace Nova Eastend .... (see 24)
37 Rhino Room D3

◎ Shopping
38 Adelaide Arcade D2
39 Miss Gladys Sym Choon E2
40 Rerun Records D2
41 Streetlight E2
42 Tarts D2

★ **Adelaide Festival** PERFORMING ARTS
(www.adelaidefestival.com.au; ◷ Mar) Top-flight
international and Australian dance, drama,
opera, literature and theatre performances
in March. Arguably Australia's best performing arts festival. Don't miss the Northern Lights along North Tce – old sandstone
buildings ablaze with lights – and the
hedonistic late-night club.

★ **WOMADelaide** MUSIC
(www.womadelaide.com.au; ◷ Mar) One of Australia's best live-music events, with more
than 300 musicians and performers from
around the globe, doing their thing over a
warm autumn weekend. Food, wine and
wholesome fun. Perfect for families and
those with a new-age bent. Attracts almost
100,000 folks over the weekend – fantastic!

★ **Tasting Australia** FOOD & DRINK
(www.tastingaustralia.com.au; ◷ Apr) This major
SA festival has really come of age in recent
years, with fabulous foodie experiences
around the city and its encircling wine

regions. Expect classes, demonstrations,
talks and plenty to put in your mouth.

**Adelaide Cabaret
Festival** PERFORMING ARTS
(www.adelaidecabaretfestival.com; ◷ Jun) The
only one of its kind in the country. A bright,
uplifting tonic in the deep and dark Adelaide winter (June).

OzAsia Festival CULTURAL
(www.ozasiafestival.com.au; ◷ Sep/Oct) Adelaide
celebrates Australia's relationship with Asia
– look forward to performing arts, film, conversation, music, the foodie Lucky Dumpling Market and mesmerising Moon Lantern
Festival. Two weeks in September/October.

Adelaide Film Festival FILM
(ADL Film Fest; www.adelaidefilmfestival.org;
◷ Oct) Adelaide is a city so flush with festivals that some real gems held in uneventful
months (eg October) often escape the lime-
light. The 11-day film festival is one such
fiesta – one of the top 50 film festivals in the
world, screening innovative flicks.

Feast Festival LGBT

(www.feast.org.au; ☉Nov) Adelaide's big-ticket gay-and-lesbian festival happens over two weeks in November, with a carnival, theatre, dialogue and dance.

🛏 Sleeping

🛏 Central Adelaide

Adelaide Central YHA HOSTEL $

(☎08-8414 3010; www.yha.com.au; 135 Waymouth St; dm from $25, d without/with bathroom $80/112, f from $124; P❋@⊚) The YHA isn't known for its gregariousness – you'll get plenty of sleep in the spacious and comfortable rooms here. This is a seriously schmick hostel with great security, a roomy kitchen and lounge area, and immaculate bathrooms. A real step up from the average backpacker places around town. Parking is around $12 per day, but the pancake breakfasts are free.

Hostel 109 HOSTEL $

(☎08-8223 1771; www.hostel109.com; 109 Carrington St; dm/s/d/f from $32/59/88/133; ❋@⊚) A small, well-managed hostel in a quiet corner of town, with a couple of little balconies over the street and a cosy kitchen/communal area. It's clean and super-friendly, with lockers, good security and gas cooking. The only negative: rooms open onto light wells rather than the outside world. Free on-street parking after 5pm.

★Soho Hotel HOTEL $$

(☎08-8412 5600; www.thesohohotel.com.au; 264 Flinders St; d from $159; P❋⊚☲) Attempting to conjure up the vibe of London's Soho district, these plush suites in Adelaide's East End (some with spas, most with balconies) are complemented by sumptuous linen, 24-hour room service, Italian-marble bathrooms, a rooftop jet pool and a fab restaurant. Rates take a tumble midweek. Parking from $20. Look out for 'Raid the Minibar' rates with online bookings.

Adabco Boutique Hotel BOUTIQUE HOTEL $$

(☎08-8100 7500; www.adabcohotel.com.au; 223 Wakefield St; d $160-250, f from $200; ❋⊚) This excellent, stone-clad boutique hotel – built in 1894 in high Venetian Gothic style – has at various times been an Aboriginal education facility, a rollerskating rink and an abseiling venue! These days you can expect three levels of lovely rooms with interesting art and quality linen, plus complimentary breakfast, free wi-fi and smiling staff.

Roof Garden Hotel HOTEL $$

(☎08-8100 4400; www.majestichotels.com.au; 55 Frome St; d from $185; P❋⊚) Everything looks new in this central, Japanese-toned place. Book a room facing Frome St for a balcony and the best views (Rundle St is metres away), or take a bottle of wine up to the namesake rooftop garden to watch the sunset. Good walk-in and last-minute rates. Parking from $20 per day.

★Mayfair Hotel HOTEL $$$

(☎08-8210 8888; www.mayfairhotel.com.au; 45 King William St; d $220-400; P❋⊚) The gargoyles on Adelaide's 1934 Colonial Mutual Life insurance building guarded a whole lot of empty rooms for decades (has the money gone out of insurance?), but the old dame has been reborn as the very luxe Mayfair Hotel. It's a fabulous fit-out, with the excellent **Hennessey Rooftop Bar** (www.mayfairhotel.com.au/hennessy; ☉5-11pm Mon-Thu, 3pm-2am Fri & Sat, 3-10pm Sun), eateries and smiling, friendly staff all over the place. Enjoy! Parking $20.

🛏 North Adelaide

★Minima Hotel HOTEL $

(☎08-8334 7766; www.majestichotels.com.au; 146 Melbourne St, North Adelaide; d from $105; P❋⊚) The mural-clad Minima offers compact but stylish rooms, each decorated by a different SA artist, in a prize-winning Melbourne St location (wake up and smell the coffee). Limited parking from $10.50 per night. Terrific value so close to the city, and far nicer than any of Adelaide's motels.

Greenways Apartments APARTMENT $$

(☎08-8267 5903; www.greenwaysapartments.com.au; 41-45 King William Rd, North Adelaide; 1-/2-/3-bedroom apt $138/180/250; P❋⊚) These 1938 apartments ain't flash, but if you have a pathological hatred of slick, 21st-century open-plan 'lifestyles', then Greenways is for you! And where else can you stay in apartments so close to town at these rates? A must for cricket fans, with the Adelaide Oval just a lofted hook shot away – book early for Test matches. New bathrooms.

🛏 Inner Suburbs

Levi Park Caravan Park CARAVAN PARK $

(☎08-8344 2209; www.levipark.com.au; 1a Harris Rd, Vale Park; unpowered/powered sites from $42/44, cabin/apt from $118/159; P❋⊚) This leafy, grassy Torrens-side park is about 4km northeast of town and loaded with facilities, including tennis courts and a palm-fringed cricket oval. Apartments are in the restored Vale House, purportedly Adelaide's oldest residence (mid-1850s). If you don't have wheels, Adelaide Metro bus W90 runs into the city from Harris St. The closest unpowered sites to the city.

Atura Adelaide Airport HOTEL **$$**
(☑ 08-7099 3300; www.aturahotels.com/adelaide-airport; 1 Atura Circuit, Adelaide Airport; d/tr/q from $185/245/305; P❖❄@⊛) Got an early flight? Atura is a sleek, seven-level airport hotel – a bit 'Eastern Bloc' externally, but a designer's delight on the inside. Splashed with playful pastels, retro aviation prints, exposed air-con ducts and industrial lighting, the vibe is downright playful. The best rooms have runway views, but the oversized pool table in the bar is where you want to be.

Watson BOUTIQUE HOTEL **$$**
(☑ 1800 278 468, 08-7087 9666; www.artserieshotels.com.au/watson; 33 Warwick St, Walkerville; d from $200, 1-/2-bedroom ste from $230/260; P❄⊛⊠) The Watson (named after indigenous artist Tommy Watson, whose works dazzle here) is a sassy, multilevel 115-unit complex 4km north of the CBD in Walkerville (an easy commute). Once upon a time these rooms were government Department of Infrastructure offices. Today's infrastructure includes a gym, a lap pool, 24-hour concierge, free bikes, free parking and car hire... Nice one!

🛏 Glenelg to Port Adelaide

Glenelg Beach Hostel HOSTEL **$**
(☑ 08-8376 0007; www.glenelgbeachhostel.com.au; 1-7 Moseley St, Glenelg; dm/s/d/f from $28/60/70/110; ☎) A couple of streets back from the beach, this beaut old terrace (1878) is Adelaide's budget golden child. Fan-cooled rooms maintain period details and are mostly bunk-free. There's cold Coopers in the basement bar (live music/DJs on weekends), open fireplaces, lofty ceilings, female-only dorms, free on-street parking and a courtyard beer garden. Book *waaay* in advance in summer.

★ Largs Pier Hotel HOTEL **$$**
(☑ 08-8449 5666; www.largspierhotel.com.au; 198 Esplanade, Largs Bay; d/f/apt from $164/220/240; P❄☎) Surprise! In the snoozy beach 'burb of Largs Bay, 5km north of Port Adelaide, is this gorgeous, 130-year-old, three-storey wedding-cake hotel with sky-high ceilings, big beds, taupe-and-chocolate colours and beach views. There's a low-slung wing of motel rooms off to one side; apartments are across the street. Pub trivia: AC/DC and Cold Chisel often played here in the bad old days.

🍴 Eating

Central Adelaide

★ Zen Kitchen VIETNAMESE **$**
(☑ 08-8232 3542; www.facebook.com/zenkitchenadelaide; Renaissance Arcade, 23 Austin St; mains $7-15; ⊙ 10.30am-4.30pm Mon-Fri; ☑) Superb, freshly constructed rice paper rolls, *pho* and super-crunchy barbecue-pork *bánh mì*, eat-in or take away. Wash it all down with a cold coconut milk or a teeth-grindingly strong Vietnamese coffee with sugary condensed milk. Authentic, affordable and absolutely delicious.

★ Africola AFRICAN **$$**
(☑ 08-8223 3885; www.africola.com.au; 4 East Tce; mains $19-38; ⊙ 6pm-late Tue-Sat) Adelaide's most hyped restaurant deserves the limelight: its fun, generous, irreverent attitude has challenged haughty fine-dining norms across the city. Inside a lovely old bluestone building, expect plenty of colour and noise, and the likes of charred pork neck with anchovy sauce and massive grilled peppers. Book way in advance; sit at the bar to watch the kitchen do its thing.

★ Peel Street MODERN AUSTRALIAN, ASIAN **$$**
(☑ 08-8231 8887; www.peelst.com.au; 9 Peel St; mains $20-35; ⊙ 7.30am-10.30pm Mon & Wed-Fri, 7.30am-4.30pm Tues, 6-10.30pm Sat) Peel St itself – a long-neglected service lane in Adelaide's West End – is now Adelaide's after-dark epicentre, lined with hip bars and eateries, the best of which is this one. It's a super-cool cafe/bistro/wine bar that just keeps packing 'em in: glam urbanites sit at window seats nibbling parmesan-crumbed parsnips and turkey meatballs with preserved lemon. Killer wine list.

★ Jasmin Indian Restaurant NORTH INDIAN **$$**
(☑ 08-8223 7837; www.jasmin.com.au; Basement level, 31 Hindmarsh Sq; mains $18-31; ⊙ noon-2.30pm Thu & Fri, 5.30-9pm Tue-Sat; ☑) Enter this basement wonderland for magical north Indian curries and consummately professional staff (they might remember your name from when you ate here in 2011).

There's nothing too surprising about the menu, but it's done to absolute perfection and (in a world changing too fast) is utterly consistent. Bookings essential.

★**Orana**　MODERN AUSTRALIAN $$$

(☑08-8232 3444; www.restaurantorana.com; Level 1, 285 Rundle St; tasting menus lunch/dinner $120/240, with wine $210/410; ☻noon-2pm Fri, 6-9pm Tue-Sat) Racking up recent 'Australia's Best Restaurant' awards, Orana is a secretive beast, with minimal signage and access via a black staircase at the back of Bistro Blackwood restaurant on Rundle St. Upstairs rockstar chef Jock Zonfrillo's tasting menu awaits: at least seven courses for lunch, and 18 for dinner (18!). Add wine to the experience to fully immerse yourself in SA's top offerings.

★**Press**　BISTRO $$$

(☑08-8211 8048; www.pressfoodandwine.com.au; 40 Waymouth St; mains $18-48; ☻noon-late Mon-Sat) The pick of the restaurants on office-heavy Waymouth St. Press is super stylish (brick, glass, lemon-coloured chairs) and not afraid of offal (pan-fried lamb's brains, sweetbreads) or things raw (beef carpaccio, gravlax salmon). Tasting menu $75 per person. Book a table upstairs, or they'll fit you in downstairs near the bar, alongside journos from the *Advertiser* across the street.

✕ North Adelaide

Bakery on O'Connell　BAKERY $

(☑08-8361 7377; www.bakeryonoconnell.com.au; 128-130 O'Connell St, North Adelaide; items $4-8; ☻24hr) Hunger pangs at 3am? Roll on into the Bakery on O'Connell for pizza slices, cakes, buns, pies, pasties and doughnuts as big as your face. Or perhaps a classic SA 'pie floater' is more to your taste (a meat pie adrift in a bowl of warm pea soup, smothered in tomato sauce – awesome!).

★**Gin Long Canteen**　ASIAN $$

(☑08-7120 2897; www.ginlongcanteen.com.au; 42 O'Connell St, North Adelaide; small plates $8-16, mains $18-45; ☻noon-2.30pm Tue-Fri, 5.30pm-late Tue-Sat) This energetic food room is a winner. Chipper staff allocate you a space at the communal tables (bookings only for six or more) and take your order pronto. The food arrives just as fast: fab curries, slow-braised Thai beef and pork, netted spring rolls, Malay curry puffs... It's a pan-Asian vibe, bolstered by jumbo bottles of Vietnamese beer and smiles all round.

Lucky Lupitas　MEXICAN $$

(☑08-8267 3082; www.luckylupitas.com; Shop 1, 163 O'Connell St, North Adelaide; tacos $8-10, mains $16-25; ☻noon-2pm Thu, Fri & Sun, 5.30-9pm Sun-Thu, 5.30-10pm Fri & Sat) Nifty plywood panelling, stacks of hot-sauce boxes by the door and unbelievably good spicy King George whiting tacos, beef brisket nachos and braised lamb enchiladas – any meal at Lucky Lupitas is a lucky one indeed. Cold *cerveza* by the gallon. When can we come here again?

✕ Inner Suburbs

★**Argo on the Parade**　CAFE $

(☑08-8431 1387; www.argo.love; 212 The Parade, Norwood; mains $10-24; ☻6am-5pm Mon-Fri, 6.30am-5pm Sat, 7am-5pm Sun) The best cafe in affluent, eastern-suburbs Norwood is arguably the best cafe in Adelaide too. It *is* in Norwood, so by default it's a bit thin on soul. But the food, coffee, service and quirky design all take the cake. As does the breakfast burrito. And the marinated tuna bowl. And the coffee. And the sweet potato fries...

Parwana Afghan Kitchen　AFGHANI $$

(☑08-8443 9001; www.parwana.com.au; 124b Henley Beach Rd, Torrensville; mains $14-25; ☻6-10pm Tue-Thu & Sun, to 10.30pm Fri & Sat) Nutty, spicy, slippery and a little bit funky: Afghan food is unique, and this authentic restaurant, west of the CBD across the parklands, is a great place to try it. The signature *banjaan borani* eggplant dish is a knockout. There's also a lunchtime branch just off Rundle St in the city called **Kutchi Deli Parwana** (☑08-7225 8586; www.kutchi.com.au; 7 Ebenezer Pl, Adelaide; mains $14-25; ☻11.30am-3pm Mon-Sat). BYO; cash only.

✕ Glenelg to Port Adelaide

Low & Slow American BBQ　AMERICAN $$

(☑0402 589 722; www.lowandslowamericanbbq.com; 17 Commercial Rd, Port Adelaide; mains $10-29; ☻noon-2pm Fri & Sun, 6-8.30pm Wed-Sun) Give your arteries something to do: this woody food room plates up succulent US-style BBQ meats, with a slew of slaws, beans, greens and grits on the side. Wash it all down with a Brooklyn Lager and a couple of Wild Turkey shots. Hip!

Zucca　GREEK $$

(☑08-8376 8222; www.zucca.com.au; Shop 5, Marina Pier, Holdfast Shores, Glenelg; mains $13-36; ☻noon-3pm daily, 6pm-late Mon-Sat)

North Adelaide

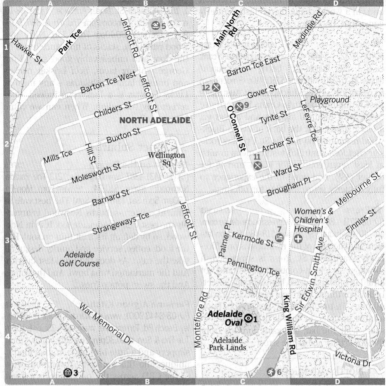

Multicoloured tables, marina views, super service and a contemporary menu of meze plates – you'd struggle to find anything this appealing on Santorini. The grilled Hindmarsh Valley halloumi with spiced raisins and the seared scallops with feta and pistachio are sublime.

🍷 Drinking & Nightlife

🍷 Central Adelaide

⭐ **Exeter Hotel**   PUB

(📞 08-8223 2623; www.theexeter.com.au; 246 Rundle St; ⏱ 11am-late) Adelaide's best pub, this legendary boozer attracts an eclectic brew of postwork, punk and uni drinkers, shaking the day off their backs. Pull up a bar stool or nab a table in the grungy beer garden and settle in for the evening. Original music nightly (indie, electronica, acoustic); no pokies. Book for curry nights in the upstairs restaurant (Wednesdays).

⭐ **Maybe Mae**   BAR

(📞 0421 405 039; www.maybemae.com; 15 Peel St; ⏱ 5pm-late Mon-Sat, 6pm-late Sun) Down some stairs down an alleyway off a laneway, Maybe Mae doesn't proclaim its virtues loudly to the world. In fact, if you can't find the door, you won't be the first thirsty punter to wander back upstairs looking confused. But once you're inside, let the good times roll: classic rock, cool staff, booth seats and brilliant beers. Love it!

⭐ **Grace Emily Hotel**   PUB

(📞 08-8231 5500; www.graceemilyhotel.com.au; 232 Waymouth St; ⏱ 4pm-late) A true contender for the title of 'Adelaide's Best Pub', the Grace has live music most nights (alt-rock, country, acoustic, open-mic nights), kooky '50s-meets-voodoo decor, open fires and great beers. Regular cult cinema; no pokies. Are the Bastard Sons of Ruination playing tonight?

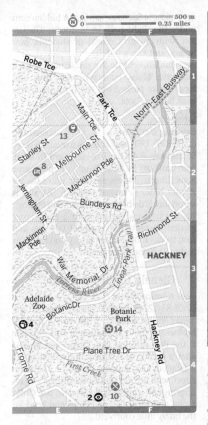

North Adelaide

◎ Top Sights
1 Adelaide Oval	C4

◎ Sights
2 Adelaide Botanic Gardens	F4
3 Adelaide Gaol	A4
4 Adelaide Zoo	E4
Bradman Collection	(see 1)

✪ Activities, Courses & Tours
5 Adelaide Aquatic Centre	B1
6 Popeye	C4
RoofClimb Adelaide Oval	(see 1)

⊨ Sleeping
7 Greenways Apartments	C3
8 Minima Hotel	E2

⊗ Eating
9 Bakery on O'Connell	C2
10 Botanic Gardens Restaurant	F4
11 Gin Long Canteen	C2
12 Lucky Lupitas	C1

◎ Drinking & Nightlife
13 Kentish Hotel	E2

⊕ Entertainment
14 Moonlight Cinema	F4

★ Nola
BAR

(www.nolaadelaide.com; 28 Vardon Ave; ⊘4pm-midnight Tue-Thu, noon-2am Fri & Sat, noon-midnight Sun) This hidden back-lane space was once the stables for the adjacent Stag Hotel. Out with the horse poo, in with 16 craft beers on tap, American and Australian whiskies (no Scotch!), Cajun cooking (gumbo, oysters, jambalaya) and regular live jazz. A saucy bit of Deep South in the East End.

★ Mr Goodbar
BAR

(☑08-8223 7574; www.mrgoodbar.com.au; 12 Union St; ⊘5pm-late Wed-Sun) If you're looking for Mr Goodbar, you'll find him at this excellent red-brick cocktail bar just off Rundle St in Adelaide's East End. Super-attentive staff really know their product, and can navigate you towards a gin to suit your mood, a high-end Japanese single malt, or perhaps a dark ale to fend off the weather. Soul, funk and '90s hip-hop.

Pink Moon Saloon
BAR

(www.pinkmoonsaloon.com.au; 21 Leigh St; ⊘4pm-late) Now this place is ace! Wedged into an impossibly tight alleyway space off Leigh St (only a couple of metres wide), Pink Moon Saloon has a bar in its front room, a little courtyard behind it, then a neat BBQ shack out the back. Cocktails and craft beer are why you're here. The same folks run **Clever Little Taylor** (☑0407 111 857; www.cleverlittletailor.com. au; 19 Peel St, Adelaide; ⊘4pm-late Mon-Sat).

Prohibition Liquor Co
DISTILLERY

(☑08-8155 6007; www.prohibitionliquor.co; 22 Gilbert St; ⊘11.30am-10pm Thu-Sat, 11.30am-7pm Sun) Forget the pious 'City of Churches' moniker: Adelaide has always been a hard-drinking town. 'Gin City' might be a better tag these days, with 21 brands of mother's ruin now made in SA. Prohibition Liquor Co is at the forefront of the boom: a sassy central distiller operating out of an industrial space on increasingly interesting Gilbert St.

Hains & Co
BAR

(☑08-8410 7088; www.hainsco.com.au; 23 Gilbert Pl; ⊘4pm-late) The nautical vibe might seem incongruous on a hot Adelaide night this far from the ocean (diving helmets, barometers,

ⓘ PINT OF COOPERS PLEASE!

Things can get confusing at the bar in Adelaide. Aside from the 200ml (7oz) 'butchers' – the choice of old men in dim, sticky-carpet pubs – there are three main beer sizes: 285ml (10oz) 'schooners' (pots or middies elsewhere in Australia), 425ml (15oz) 'pints' (schooners elsewhere) and 568ml (20oz) 'imperial pints' (traditional English pints). Now go forth and order with confidence!

anchors etc) – but somehow it works. A really clever fit-out of a tight laneway space, with the focus on all things gin and rum. Get a few under your belt and belt out a sea shanty.

Zhivago   CLUB
(☏08-8212 0569; www.zhivago.com.au; 54 Currie St; ⊙10pm-late Sat & Sun) The pick of the West End clubs, Zhivago is all muscles and manscaping vs high heels and short skirts, with DJs pumping out everything from reggae and dub to quality house.

BRYKLN   BAR
(www.brklyn-adl.com; 260a Rundle St; ⊙4pm-late Tue-Fri, 6pm-late Sat) Adelaide is a long way from NYC, but above the Rundle St fray, BRYKLN does (if you squint a little bit) conjure up a vague vibe of the Big Apple. There's a barber trimming heads in one corner, a DJ spinning soul in another, and artfully tattooed staff maintaining a passing interest in serving customers. Super-cool interior design; fab pastrami-on-rye.

☕ North Adelaide

Kentish Hotel   PUB
(☏08-8267 1173; www.thekentish.com.au; 23 Stanley St, North Adelaide; ⊙11.30am-11pm Mon-Thu, to midnight Fri & Sat, to 10pm Sun) They don't make 'em like they used to. Actually, these days, when it comes to handsome two-storey sandstone pubs, they don't make 'em at all. This backstreet beauty is great for a cold one on a hot afternoon, or gastronomic delights including a funky fish stew and a 'Memphis Burger' with fried chicken and smoked bourbon barbecue sauce.

☕ Inner Suburbs

★ Wheatsheaf   PUB
(☏08-8443 4546; www.wheatsheafhotel.com.au; 39 George St, Thebarton; ⊙1pm-midnight Mon-Fri,

noon-midnight Sat, noon-9pm Sun) A hidden gem under the flight path in industrial Thebarton, with an arty crowd of students, jazz musos and the gainfully unemployed. Tidy beer garden, eclectic live music out the back (acoustic, blues, country), open fires and food trucks parked out the front. Kick-arse craft beers to boot.

Little Bang
Brewing Company   MICROBREWERY
(☏08-8362 7761; www.littlebang.com.au; 25 Henry St, Stepney; ⊙4-10pm Thu, noon-10pm Fri & Sat, noon-6pm Sun) Is 'little bang' a euphemism? Something to discuss as you sip into a Geezer Pleaser bitter or Naked Objector IPA at this surprising little brewery in suburban Stepney. It's a warehouse set-up, with a sunny beer garden, 21 taps (!), occasional DJs sets and food trucks rolling up on Friday and Saturday nights. Deliciously subversive.

☕ Glenelg to Port Adelaide

Port Admiral Hotel   PUB
(☏08-8341 2249; www.portadmiral.com.au; 55 Commercial Rd, Port Adelaide; ⊙11am-late) A flagship business in the rejuvenation of Port Adelaide is the Port Admiral Hotel, reopened in 2017 after a decade of boarded-up dereliction. It's a fabulous old building (1849) on the main street, with bearded craft-beer drinkers swanning around a curvaceous art-deco bar. Order a pint and some fish and chips and head for the buzzy little courtyard.

Moseley   PUB
(☏08-8295 3966; www.themoseley.com.au; Moseley Sq, Glenelg; ⊙11am-late Mon-Fri, 8am-late Sat & Sun) This old boozer was an Irish pub for years, but a fancy refit has purged all the dark wood and replaced it with wicker. The upstairs balcony is where you want to be, sipping a G&T as the tram rumbles into Moseley Sq from the city. Classy pub mains $24 to $42. Also runs a beach bar down on the Glenelg sand in summer.

☆ Entertainment

Arty Adelaide has a rich cultural life that stacks up favourably against much larger cities. For listings and reviews, see *Adelaide Now* (www.adelaidenow.com.au) and *Adelaide Review* (www.adelaidereview.com.au). Agencies for big-ticket event bookings include **BASS** (☏13 12 46; www.bass.net.au) and **Moshtix** (☏1300 438 849; www.moshtix.com.au).

Live Music

Adelaide knows how to kick out the jams! Top pub venues around town include the **Crown & Anchor** (⌨08-8223 3212; www. facebook.com/thecrankerhotel; 196 Grenfell St; ⊙noon-late Mon-Sat, 2pm-midnight Sun), Wheatsheaf (p730), Grace Emily Hotel (p728) and Exeter Hotel (p728).

For gig listings check out the following:

➡ *Adelaide Review* (www.adelaidereview. com.au/guides)

➡ *Music SA* (www.musicsa.com.au)

➡ *Jazz Adelaide* (www.jazz.adelaide.onau. net)

➡ *Scenestr* (www.scenestr.com.au/gig-guides/adelaide-gig-guide)

⭐ **Governor Hindmarsh Hotel**   LIVE MUSIC
(⌨08-8340 0744; www.thegov.com.au; 59 Port Rd, Hindmarsh; ⊙11am-late) Ground zero for live music in Adelaide, 'The Gov' hosts some legendary local and international acts. The odd Irish band fiddles around in the bar, while the main venue features rock, folk, jazz, blues, salsa, reggae and dance. A huge place with an inexplicably personal vibe, it's far enough from the city to sidestep any noise complaints from the neighbours. Good food too.

Gilbert Street Hotel   JAZZ
(⌨08-8231 9909; www.gilbertsthotel.com.au; 88 Gilbert St; ⊙11am-late) The best place in Adelaide to catch some live jazz (on Tuesday nights, at any rate) the Gilbert is a renovated old pub but continues to ooze soul. Order a *vin rouge* at the bar and dig the scene with the goateed regulars. Soul and acoustic acts Thursday and Sunday.

Jive   LIVE MUSIC
(⌨08-8211 6683; www.jivevenue.com; 181 Hindley St) In a converted theatre spangled with a brilliant mural, Jive caters to an off-beat crowd of student types who like their tunes funky, left-field and removed from the mainstream. Top marks for endurance in a fast-changing world. See if you can get a seat on the balcony for the best views in the house.

Adelaide Entertainment Centre   CONCERT VENUE
(⌨08-8208 2222; www.theaec.net; 98 Port Rd, Hindmarsh; ⊙box office 9am-5pm Mon-Fri) Around 12,000 indoor bums on seats for everyone from the Wiggles to Keith Urban to Stevie Wonder.

Adelaide Symphony Orchestra   CLASSICAL MUSIC
(ASO; ⌨08-8233 6233; www.aso.com.au; 91 Hindley St; ⊙box office 9am-4.30pm Mon-Fri) The estimable ASO has gigs at various venues including the Grainger Studio on Hindley St, the Festival Theatre and Adelaide Town Hall. Check the website for performance info.

Film

Moonlight Cinema   CINEMA
(⌨1300 551 908; www.moonlight.com.au/adelaide; Botanic Park, Hackney Rd; adult/child $17/12.50; ⊙7pm daily Dec-Feb) In summer pack a picnic and mosquito repellent, and sprawl out on the lawn to watch old and new classics under the stars. 'Gold Grass' tickets, which cost a little more, secure you a prime-viewing beanbag.

Palace Nova Eastend   CINEMA
(⌨08-8125 9312; www.palacenova.com.au; 3 Cinema Pl; adult/child $20/16; ⊙10am-late) Just off Rundle St, handily poised down the alley next to the Exeter Hotel, this plush city complex screens new-release art-house, foreign-language and independent films, as well as some mainstream flicks. Fully licensed.

Theatre & Comedy

See *Adelaide Theatre Guide* (www.theatre guide.com.au) for booking details, venues and reviews for comedy, drama and musicals. Larger performances happen at the **Adelaide Festival Centre** (⌨08-8216 8600; www.adelaidefestivalcentre.com.au; King William Rd; ⊙box office 9am-6pm Mon-Fri), the city's iconic cultural hub.

Adelaide's long-running comedy club is the **Rhino Room** (⌨08-8227 1611; www.rhino room.com.au; 1/131 Pirie St, Adelaide; ⊙7.30-11pm Mon, 7.30pm-3am Fri, 9pm-3am Sat) on Pirie St.

Sport

As most Australian cities do, Adelaide hangs its hat on the successes of its sporting teams. In the **Australian Football League** (www. afl.com.au), the Adelaide Crows and Port Adelaide Power have sporadic success and play at the Adelaide Oval between March and September. The **AFL Women's** league (www. afl.com.au/womens) runs through the summer months. Suburban Adelaide men's teams compete in the confusingly named **South Australian National Football League** (www. sanfl.com.au), also over winter.

In the summertime **National Basketball League** (www.nbl.com.au), the Adelaide 36ers have been a force for decades (lately, not so much). In netball, the Adelaide Thunderbirds play in the **Super Netball** comp (www.super netball.com.au) with regular success. In soccer, Adelaide United ('the Reds') kick the round ball around in the men's **A-League** (www. a-league.com.au) and women's **W-League** (www.w-league.com.au) comps over summer.

Also in summer, under the auspices of **Cricket SA** (www.cricketsa.com.au), the Redbacks play one-day and multiday state matches at the Adelaide Oval. The Redbacks rebrand as the Adelaide Strikers in the national **T20 Big Bash** (www.bigbash.com. au) competition. There's also a women's Strikers team who play in the **Women's Big Bash League** (WBBL; www.bigbash.com.au/wbbl). International cricket also happens at the Adelaide Oval (www.cricketaustralia.com.au).

🔒 Shopping

Shops and department stores line Rundle Mall (www.rundlemall.com). The beautiful old arcades running between the mall and Grenfell St, most notably **Adelaide Arcade**, (☑08-8223 5522; www.adelaidearcade.com.au; 112-118 Grenfell St; ⊙9am-7pm Mon-Thu, to 9pm Fri, 9am-5pm Sat, 11am-5pm Sun) retain their original splendour and house eclectic little shops. Rundle St and the adjunct **Ebenezer Pl** (www.ebenezerplace.com.au) are home to boutique and retro clothing shops.

★**Streetlight** BOOKS, MUSIC
(☑08-8227 0667; www.facebook.com/streetlight adelaide; 2/15 Vaughan Pl; ⊙10am-6pm Mon-Thu & Sat, to 9pm Fri, noon-5pm Sun) Lefty, arty and subversive in the best possible way, Streetlight is the place to find that elusive Miles Davis disc, Del Amitri rock biography or Charles Bukowski poetry compilation.

Rerun Records MUSIC
(☑08-8223 6299; www.rerun.com.au; Renaissance Arc, 32 & 35, 128 Rundle Mall; ⊙10am-5pm Sat-Thu, to 9pm Fri) Packed full of racks of records and dressed to the nines with rock posters, old copies of *Rolling Stone*, picture discs, vintage Elvis record sleeves and a distressingly big photo of Gene Simmons and his tongue, Rerun is a vinyl-lover's paradise. Don't expect anything post-2000.

Adelaide Farmers Market MARKET
(☑08-8231 8155; www.adelaidefarmersmarket. com; Adelaide Showground, Leader St, Wayville; ⊙8am-1pm Sun) 🍴 Don't mind dragging yourself out of bed too early on a Sunday and paying $6 for an organic parsnip? Then the

Adelaide Farmers Market is for you! Actually, ignore our cynicism – the food offerings here are fabulous: fresh, organic, local and sustainable, to take home or cooked into delicious things you can eat on the spot. Good coffee too.

Miss Gladys Sym Choon FASHION & ACCESSORIES
(☑08-8223 1500; www.missgladyssymchoon.com. au; 235a Rundle St; ⊙9.30am-6pm Mon-Thu, to 9pm Fri, 10am-5.30pm Sat, 11am-5pm Sun) Named after a famed Rundle St trader from the 1920s (the first woman in SA to incorporate a business) this hip shop is the place for fab frocks, rockin' boots, street-beating sneakers, jewellery, watches and hats. Guys and gals.

Tarts ARTS & CRAFTS
(☑08-8232 0265; www.tartscollective.com.au; 10g Gays Arcade, Adelaide Arcade, Rundle Mall; ⊙10am-5pm Mon-Sat) 🍴 Textiles, jewellery, bags, cards and canvases from a 35-member local arts co-op: prime gifts-for-the-folks-back-home terrain. Meet the artists in-store.

ℹ️ Information

EMERGENCY & IMPORTANT NUMBERS

Ambulance, Fire, Police	☑000
RAA Emergency Roadside Assistance	☑13 11 11

INTERNET ACCESS

Adelaide cafes and pubs have been slow to adopt free wi-fi for customers, though you can find it (you might have to ask). Most Adelaide accommodation has free wi-fi these days. You can also hook up to the Adelaide City Council's free wi-fi in the CBD and North Adelaide: see www.adelaidefree wifi.com.au for details. Beyond the city centre, if you're travelling here from overseas, you'll probably be better off buying a local SIM card with a data allowance you can top up, rather than relying on free access. At a pinch, try the free terminals at the **State Library of South Australia** (☑08-8207 7250; www.slsa.sa.gov.au; cnr North Tce & Kintore Ave; ⊙10am-8pm Mon-Wed, to 6pm Thu & Fri, to 5pm Sat & Sun; 🛜).

MEDICAL SERVICES

SA Dental Service (☑1300 008 222; www. sadental.sa.gov.au) Sore tooth?

Midnight Pharmacy (☑08-8232 4445; www. healthdirect.gov.au; 192-198 Wakefield St; ⊙9am-midnight) Late-night presciptions.

Royal Adelaide Hospital (☑08-7074 0000; www.rah.sa.gov.au; Port Rd; ⊙24hr) Emergency department (not for blisters!) and STD clinic in this impressive hospital, opened in 2018 – the most expensive public building in Australian history!

Women's & Children's Hospital (☏08-8161 7000; www.wch.sa.gov.au; 72 King William Rd, North Adelaide; ⊙24hr) Emergency and sexual-assault services.

MONEY

There are ATMs and banks all over the Adelaide CBD and suburbs. Visit **Travelex** (☏08-8231 6977; www.travelex.com.au; Shop 4, Beehive Corner, Rundle Mall; ⊙8.30am-7pm Mon-Thu, to 9pm Fri, 9am-5pm Sat, 11am-5pm Sun) for foreign currency exchange.

TOURIST INFORMATION

Adelaide Visitor Information Centre (☏1300 588 140; www.adelaidecitycouncil.com; 9 James Pl, off Rundle Mall; ⊙9am-5pm Mon-Fri, 10am-4pm Sat & Sun) Adelaide-specific information, plus abundant info on SA, including fab regional booklets.

National Parks South Australia (☏08-8204 1910; www.parks.sa.gov.au; Ground Fl, 81-95 Waymouth St; ⊙9am-4.30pm Mon-Fri) National parks information and bookings.

There are also helpful visitor centres in Glenelg (p720) and Port Adelaide (p720).

ⓘ Getting There & Away

AIR

International, interstate and regional flights via a number of airlines service Adelaide Airport (p1071), 7km west of the city centre. Domestic services include:

Jetstar (www.jetstar.com.au) Direct flights between Adelaide and Perth, Darwin, Cairns, Brisbane, Gold Coast, Sunshine Coast, Sydney, Melbourne and Hobart.

Qantas (www.qantas.com.au) Direct flights between Adelaide and Perth, Alice Springs, Darwin, Cairns, Gold Coast, Brisbane, Sydney, Canberra and Melbourne.

Regional Express (Rex; www.regionalexpress.com.au) Flies from Adelaide to regional centres around SA – Kingscote, Coober Pedy, Ceduna, Mount Gambier, Port Lincoln and Whyalla – plus Broken Hill in NSW and Mildura in Victoria.

Tigerair Australia (www.tigerair.com.au) Direct flights between Adelaide and Melbourne, Sydney and Brisbane.

Virgin Australia (www.virginaustralia.com) Direct flights between Adelaide and Perth, Alice Springs, Brisbane, Gold Coast, Sydney, Canberra and Melbourne.

BUS

Adelaide Central Bus Station (☏08-8203 7532; www.cityofadelaide.com.au; 85 Franklin St; ⊙6am-9.30pm) is the hub for all major interstate and statewide bus services. Note: there is no Adelaide–Perth bus service.

Firefly Express (☏1300 730 740; www.fireflyexpress.com.au) Runs between Sydney and Adelaide via Melbourne.

Greyhound Australia (☏1300 473 946; www.greyhound.com.au) Australia's main long-distance player, with services from Adelaide to Melbourne and Alice Springs, with onward connections.

Premier Stateliner (☏1300 851 345; www.premierstateliner.com.au) Statewide bus services, connecting the major dots (as far west as Ceduna).

V/Line (☏1800 800 007; www.vline.com.au) Bus and bus/train services between Adelaide and Melbourne.

CAR & MOTORCYCLE

The major international car-rental companies have offices at Adelaide Airport and in the city. There's also a crew of local operators. Note that some companies don't allow vehicles to be taken to Kangaroo Island.

Access Rent-a-Car (☏08-8340 0400; www.accessrentacar.com; 464 Port Rd, West Hindmarsh; ⊙8am-5pm Mon-Fri, to noon Sat & Sun) Kangaroo Island travel permitted; 4WDs available.

Cut Price Car & Truck Rentals (☏08-8443 7788; www.cutprice.com.au; cnr Sir Donald Bradman Dr & South Rd, Mile End; ⊙7.30am-5pm Mon-Fri, to 3pm Sat & Sun)

Royal Automobile Association of South Australia (RAA; ☏08-8202 4600; www.raa.com.au; 41 Hindmarsh Sq; ⊙8.30am-5pm Mon-Fri, 9am-4pm Sat) Provides auto advice (including road conditions in outback areas) and plenty of maps.

TRAIN

Interstate trains run by **Great Southern Rail** (☏08-8213 4401; www.greatsouthernrail.com.au) grind into the **Adelaide Parklands Terminal** (☏13 21 47; www.greatsouthernrail.com.au; Railway Tce, Keswick; ⊙6am-3pm Mon & Tue, 9am-3pm Wed, 9am-9.30pm Thu, 6am-3pm Fri, noon-12.30pm Sat, 8.30am-12.30pm Sun), 1km southwest of the city centre. The following trains depart Adelaide regularly; fares include all meals, booze and off-train excursions en route:
→ *The Ghan* to Alice Springs (from $1059, 26 hours)
→ *The Ghan* to Darwin (from $1959, 54 hours)
→ *The Indian Pacific* to Perth (from $1599, 42 hours)
→ *The Indian Pacific* to Sydney (from $779, 25 hours)
→ *The Great Southern* to Brisbane (from $1649, 55 hours)

ℹ Getting Around

TO/FROM THE AIRPORT & TRAIN STATION

Prebooked private **Adelaide Airport Flyer** (☑ 08-8385 9967; www.adelaideairportflyer. com) minibuses run door-to-door between the airport and anywhere around Adelaide; get a quote and book online (into the city from the airport for one to three people costs $45). Public Adelaide Metro **JetExpress and JetBus** (☑ 1300 311 108; www.adelaidemetro.com.au/time tables/special-services; $3.60-5.50; ⊙ 4.30am-11.30pm) bus services – routes J1, J1X, J3, J7 and J8 – connect the airport with Glenelg and the CBD; standard Metro fares apply.

Taxis charge around $30 into the city from the airport (15 minutes); or about $15 from Adelaide Parklands Terminal (10 minutes). Many hostels will pick you up and drop you off if you're staying with them. **Adelaide Transport** (☑ 08-8212 1861; www.adelaidetransport.com.au) also offers shuttle transfers. **Uber** also operates at Adelaide Airport; see www.uber.com/en-au/airports/adl.

BICYCLE

Adelaide is pizza-flat: great for cycling! With a valid passport or driving licence you can borrow an **Adelaide Free Bike** from **Bicycle SA** (☑ 08-8168 9999; www.bikesa.asn.au; 53 Carrington St, Adelaide; ⊙ 9am-4.30pm); helmet and lock provided. There are a couple of dozen locations around town: you can collect a bike at any of them, provided you return it to the same place. Multiday hires also available.

Down at the beach, hire a bike from **Glenelg Bicycle Hire** (☑ 08-8376 1934; www.glenelg bicyclehire.com.au; Norfolk Motel, 71 Broadway, Glenelg South; bikes per half-/full-day $15/25; ⊙ 8.30am-7pm).

PUBLIC TRANSPORT

Adelaide Metro (☑ 1300 311 108; www.adelaide metro.com.au; cnr King William & Currie Sts; ⊙ 9am-5pm Mon-Fri, 9am-4pm Sat) runs Adelaide's decent and integrated bus, train and tram network.

Tickets can be purchased on board, at staffed train stations and in delis and newsagents across the city. Ticket types include day-trip ($10.40), two-hour peak ($5.50) and two-hour off-peak ($3.60) tickets. Peak travel time is before 9am and after 3pm. Kids under five ride free! There's also a three-day, unlimited-travel visitor pass ($25). If you're here for longer, save at least $1 per trip with a rechargable multi-trip Metrocard.

Bus

Adelaide's buses are clean, air-conditioned and reliable (if a little infrequent). Most services start around 6am and run until midnight.

Every 30 minutes daily, Adelaide Metro's free **City Connector** (☑ 1300 311 108; www.adelaide metro.com.au/timetables/special-services; ⊙ 9am-7.15pm Sat-Thu, to 9.15pm Fri) buses – routes 98A and 98C – run clockwise and anti-clockwise around the CBD fringe, passing North Tce, Victoria Sq, Hutt St and Central Market and winding through North Adelaide en route. The 99A and 99C buses ply the same route (minus North Adelaide) Monday to Friday – the net effect is a free bus every 15 minutes Monday to Friday.

Train

Adelaide's hokey old diesel trains are slowly being electrified. Trains depart from **Adelaide Station** (www.railmaps.com.au/adelaide.htm; North Tce), plying five suburban routes (Belair, Gawler, Grange, Seaford and Outer Harbour). Trains generally run between 6am and midnight (some services start at 4.30am).

Tram

Adelaide's state-of-the-art trams rumble to/ from Moseley Sq in Glenelg, through Victoria Sq in the city and along North Tce to the Adelaide Entertainment Centre. A 2018 line extension runs east along North Tce to the Adelaide Botanic Gardens. Trams run approximately every 10 minutes on weekdays (every 15 minutes on weekends) from 6am to midnight daily. Standard Metro ticket prices apply, but the sections between South Tce and the Adelaide Entertainment Centre, and along Glenelg's Jetty Rd, are free.

TAXI

Adelaide Independent Taxis (☑ 13 22 11; www.aitaxis.com.au) Regular and wheelchair-access cabs.

Adelaide Transport has minibus taxis for four or more people, plus airport-to-city transfers.

Suburban Taxis (☑ 13 10 08; www.suburban taxis.com.au) Taxis, all suburbs.

Yellow Cabs (☑ 13 22 27; www.yellowcabgroup. com.au) Regular cabs (most of which are white).

ADELAIDE HILLS

When the Adelaide plains are desert-hot in the summer months, the Adelaide Hills (technically the Mt Lofty Ranges – the traditional lands of the Peramangk people) are always a few degrees cooler, with crisp air, woodland shade and labyrinthine valleys. Early colonists built stately summer houses around Stirling and Aldgate, and German settlers escaping religious persecution also arrived, infusing towns like Hahndorf and Lobethal with European values and architecture.

Adelaide Hills

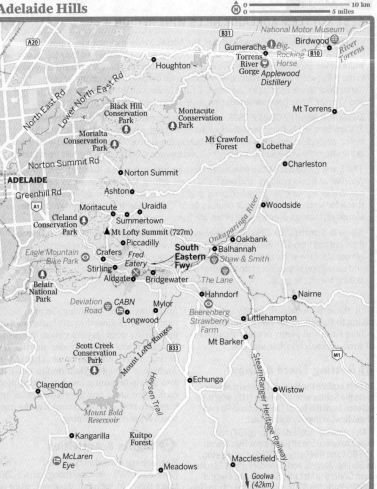

The Hills make a brilliant day trip from Adelaide: hop from town to town (all with at least one pub), passing carts of fresh produce for sale, stone cottages, olive groves and cool-climate wineries along the way.

🏃 Activities & Tours

Eagle Mountain Bike Park   MOUNTAIN BIKING

(☑ 08-8226 5833; www.ors.sa.gov.au/our_venues/ eagle_mountain_bike_park; Mt Barker Rd, Leawood Gardens; ⊙ daylight hours) **FREE** Mountain bikers should wheel themselves to the Eagle Mountain Bike Park in the Adelaide Hills, pronto; it has 21km of gnarly trails plus a

jumps park and trials area. Check the website for directions.

Trailhopper   WINE

(☑ 08-8271 4485; www.trailhopper.com.au; per person $45) A hop-on/hop-off winery tour bus, looping around to nine different Hills wineries – including The Lane, Shaw & Smith and Nepenthe – on a fixed schedule? What a great idea! Pick-up and drop-off in Hahndorf.

Ambler Touring   TOURS

(☑ 0414 447 134; www.ambler.net.au; half-/full day per person from $99/155) See the Hills in style

DON'T MISS

BEST BOTTLES: ADELAIDE HILLS WINE REGION

With night mists and reasonable rainfall, the Adelaide Hills' mid-altitude slopes sustain one of SA's cooler climates – perfect for producing some complex and truly top-notch white wines, especially chardonnays and sauvignon blancs. There are dozens of wineries in the Hills (see www.adelaidehillswine.com.au for details, or pick up the *Adelaide Hills Cellar Door Guide* brochure); January's **Crush** (www.crushfestival.com.au; ⊙ Jan) festival and **Winter Reds** (www.winterreds.com.au; ⊙ Jul) in July celebrate this rich bounty.

Deviation Road (☑ 08-8339 2633; www.deviationroad.com; 207 Scott Creek Rd, Longwood; ⊙ 10am-5pm; 🖪) Nothing deviant about the wines here: sublime pinot noir, substantial shiraz, zingy pinot gris and a very decent bubbly too. Grab a cheese platter and wind down in the afternoon in the sun. Unpretentious and lovely, a short hop over the hills from Stirling.

The Lane (☑ 08-8388 1250; www.thelane.com.au; 5 Ravenswood La, Hahndorf; ⊙ 10am-4pm) Wow! What a cool building, and what a fabulous setting. Camera-conducive views and contemporary varietals (viognier, pinot grigio, pinot gris), plus an outstanding restaurant (book for lunch: two/three/four courses $65/75/85, serving noon to 3pm Wednesday to Monday). Tastings of entry-level wines are free.

Shaw & Smith (☑ 08-8398 0500; www.shawandsmith.com; 136 Jones Rd, Balhannah; wine-flight tastings from $20; ⊙ 11am-5pm) Picture-perfect Mt Lofty Ranges and lake views almost steal the show at this mod winery, run by two cousins. Outstanding chardonnays and sauvignon blancs hold hands with grand shiraz. If you buy a bottle they'll knock the tasting fee off the price.

with these personalised, locally run tours taking in Hahndorf, Mt Lofty Summit, Beerenberg Farm and plenty of other sights. Lots of wine, cheese, chocolate and arts.

ⓘ Getting There & Away

To best explore the Hills, BYO wheels: access is via the Southeastern Freeway (M1), which extends from the top of Glen Osmond Rd (aka Motel Row) in the city's southeast.

Alternatively, Adelaide Metro (p734) runs buses between the city and most Hills towns. The 864 and 864F city–Mt Barker buses stop at Stirling, Aldgate and Hahndorf; the 823 runs from Crafers to Mt Lofty Summit and Cleland Wildlife Park; the 830F runs from the city to Oakbank, Woodside and Lobethal. Buses 835 and 835A connect Lobethal with Mt Barker. Standard Metro fares apply (one-way from $3.70).

Hahndorf

☑ 08 / POP 2670

Like the Rocks in Sydney, and Richmond near Hobart, Hahndorf is a 'ye olde worlde' colonial enclave that trades ruthlessly on its history: it's something of a kitsch parody of itself.

That said, Hahndorf is undeniably pretty, with Teutonic sandstone architecture, European trees, and flowers overflowing from half wine barrels. And it *is* interesting:

Australia's oldest surviving German settlement (1839), founded by 50 Lutheran families fleeing religious persecution in Prussia. Hahndorf was placed under martial law during WWI, and its name changed to 'Ambleside' (renamed Hahndorf in 1935). It's also slowly becoming less kitsch and more cool: there are a few interesting cafes and bars here now, and on a sunny day the main street is positively pumping.

◉ Sights & Activities

Beerenberg Strawberry Farm FARM
(☑ 08-8388 7272; www.beerenberg.com.au; 2106 Mount Barker Rd, Hahndorf; strawberry picking per adult/child $4/free, strawberries per kg $11; ⊙ 9am-5pm) 🖉 Pick your own strawberries between November and April from this famous, family-run farm, also noted for its myriad jams, chutneys and sauces. Last entry for picking 4.15pm. Strawberry ice cream to take away.

Hahndorf Walking Tours WALKING
(☑ 0477 288 011; www.facebook.com/hahndorf walkingtours; adult/child $35/15; ⊙ tours 2pm daily) Short on distance but big on insight, these history-soaked, 90-minute walks are a great way to get a feel for the old town. Bookings essential; tours depart Hahndorf Academy. Spooky night-time tours run at 8pm April to September and 9pm October to March, departing the Manna.

🛌 Sleeping

★ Hahndorf Resort
CARAVAN PARK **$**

(☑1300 763 836, 08-8388 7921; www.hahndorf resort.com.au; 145a Mount Barker Rd, Hahndorf; powered sites from $40, cabins & villas from $140; ⓟ❄📶⅏) It may feel a bit odd camping this close to Adelaide – not really in it, not really out of it – but if the sun is setting and you want to park your van, there are super-tidy grassy terraced sites here. Wander into Hahndorf for a meal, or hit the impressive camp kitchen. Lots of cabin/villa configurations too, all totally immaculate.

Manna
MOTEL, APARTMENTS **$$**

(☑08-8388 1000; www.themanna.com.au; 25 & 35a Main St, Hahndorf; d/ste from $149/199; ⓟ❄📶⅏) The Manna is a stylish, contemporary maze of rather corporate-feeling motel suites on the main street, spread over several buildings. There are also older units nearby at the affiliated, refurbished Hahndorf Motor Lodge, an exposed-brick complex set back from the street (cheaper rates...and where the pool is). The house restaurant – predicatably called the **Haus** (☑08-8388 7555; www.haushahndorf.com.au; 38 Main St, Hahndorf; breakfast $7-23, lunch & dinner mains $20-42; ⊙7.30am-11pm) – is across the street.

The Manna also runs the self-contained **Haus Studio Apartments** (☑08-8388 1000; www.hausstudioapartments.com.au; 34 Main St, Hahndorf; 1-/2-bedroom apt from $170/330; ⓟ❄📶), nearby.

🍴 Eating & Drinking

Seasonal Garden Cafe
CAFE **$$**

(☑08-8388 7714; www.facebook.com/theseasonal gardencafe; 100 Main St, Hahndorf; mains $8-20; ⊙7am-5pm; 🚗) 🌿 Swimming against Hahndorf's mainstream currents, this zero-waste cafe is adorned with strings of dried chillies and rustic old-wood tables. Menu-wise it's good coffee, grass-green smoothies and lots of local, seasonal and organic ingredients (try the potted baked eggs with house-made beans, goat curd and dukkah). Sunny lawn and deck out the back.

Ambleside Distillers
DISTILLERY

(☑0408 834 010; www.amblesidedistillers.com; cnr Ambleside & Mt Barker Rds, Hahndorf; ⊙noon-6pm Thu & Fri, 11am-6pm Sat & Sun) Taking its name from Hahndorf's pseudonym during WWI ('Hahndorf' was deemed to be unpatriotic), Ambleside occupies a stylish,

purpose-built shed on the outskirts of town, overlooking a creek and a cow-filled paddock – ideal environs to sit and sip a few G&Ts and chew into a share plate of local edibles ($18 to $28). The 'No.8 Botanical' is a citrus-soaked winner.

★ Prancing Pony
CRAFT BEER

(☑08-8398 3881; www.prancingponybrewery.com. au; 42 Mt Barker Rd, Totness; ⊙10am-6pm Mon, 4-10pm Wed & Thu, 10.30am-10pm Fri-Sun) Trophy-winning craft beers, burgers, platters, bar snacks and live troubadours all make an appearance at this funky beer shed, on the road out of Mt Barker heading for Hahndorf. Kick back with an Indie Kid Pilsener or three and revel in the fact that you're not in a winery or a pub.

ℹ Information

Adelaide Hills Visitor Information Centre

(☑08-8393 7600; www.adelaidehills.org.au; 68 Main St, Hahndorf; ⊙9am-5pm Mon-Fri, 10am-5pm Sat & Sun) The usual barrage of brochures, plus accommodation bookings and lots of Hills winery info on the main street in Hahndorf. The interesting Hahndorf Academy (☑08-8388 7250; www.hahndorfacademy. org.au; 68 Main St, Hahndorf; ⊙10am-5pm) is here too.

OFF THE BEATEN TRACK

URAIDLA

Just a few short years ago, the little Hills town of Uraidla was neglected, overlooked, bypassed and forgotten (we could think of plenty more grim adjectives, but you get the picture). Then, the old **Uraidla Hotel** (☑08-8390 0500; www.uraidlahotel.com.au; 1198 Greenhill Rd, Uraidla; ⊙11am-late) was tarted-up and started brewing craft beer out the back of the cafe next door, and pizza joint called **Lost in a Forest** (☑08-8390 3444; www.lostinaforest.com.au; 1203 Greenhill Rd, Uraidla; mains $15-28; ⊙5pm-late Thu, noon-late Fri & Sat, noon-9pm Sun) found itself in the old church across the road. BOOM! Now there are few more pleasant places in the Hills to while away an afternoon, an evening, or both.

Greenhill Rd is a main line to the Adelaide Hills from the city – it's 13km to Uraidla. Alternatively, take Adelaide Metro (p734) buses 821 or 822 (one way from $3.70).

Stirling Area

The photogenic little villages of old-school Stirling (population 2970) and one-horse Aldgate (population 3350) are famed for their dazzling autumn colours, thanks to the deciduous trees the early residents saw fit to plant. Oddly, Aldgate has also been home to both Bon Scott and Mel Gibson over the years. On a less rock 'n' roll tack, the 6km Aldgate Valley Nature Walk runs from Aldgate to nearby Mylor; follow the bandicoot signs from the little park across the road from the Aldgate shops (map from www.ahc.sa.gov.au).

Towards the city from Stirling, Crafers (population 1940) has a drive-through vibe but a seriously good pub...and access to lofty Mt Lofty Summit.

◉ Sights

Cleland Wildlife Park   WILDLIFE RESERVE
(☑ 08-8339 2444; www.clelandwildlifepark.sa.gov.au; 365 Mt Lofty Summit Rd, Crafers; adult/child/family $25.50/12/61; ⊙ 9.30am-5pm, last entry 4.30pm) Within the steep Cleland Conservation Park (www.parks.sa.gov.au; ⊙ 24hr) FREE, this place lets you interact with all kinds of Australian beasts. There are keeper talks and feeding sessions throughout the day, plus occasional Night Walks (adult/child $51/40.50) and you can have your mugshot taken with a koala ($30.50; 2pm to 3pm daily, plus 11am to noon Sundays). There's a cafe (www.environment. sa.gov.au/clelandwildlife; mains $5-15; ⊙ 9.30am-5pm) here too. From the city, take bus 864 or 864F from Grenfell St to Crafers for connecting bus 823 to the park.

Mt Lofty Summit   VIEWPOINT
From Cleland Wildlife Park you can bushwalk (2km) or drive up to Mt Lofty Summit (727m), which has show-stopping views across the Adelaide plains to the shimmering Gulf St Vincent. Mt Lofty Summit Visitor Information Centre (☑ 08-8370 1054; www.parks.sa.gov.au; Mt Lofty Summit Rd, Crafers; ⊙ 9am-5pm) has info on local attractions and walking tracks, including the steep Waterfall Gully Track (8km return, 2½ hours) and Mt Lofty Botanic Gardens Loop Trail (7km loop, two hours). There's a decent cafe (☑ 08-8839 2600; www.mountloftysummit.com; mains $9-25; ⊙ 9am-5pm Mon-Fri, 8.30am-5pm Sat & Sun) here too. Parking is an irritating $2.

Mt Lofty Botanic Garden   GARDENS
(☑ 08-8222 9311; www.botanicgardens.sa.gov. au; gates on Mawson Dr & Lampert Rd, Crafers; ⊙ 8.30am-4pm Mon-Fri, 10am-5pm Sat & Sun) FREE From Mt Lofty, truck south 1.5km to the cool-climate slopes of this botanic garden. Nature trails wind past a lovely looking lake, exotic temperate plants, native stringybark forest and eye-popping ranks of rhododendron blooms. Free guided walks depart the lower Lampert Rd car park at 10.30am every Thursday.

🛏 Sleeping & Eating

★ CABN   CABIN $$
(☑ 0409 572 367; www.cabn.life/adelaide-hills; off Longwood Rd, Longwood; d $190-395, extra adult/ child $45/free; 🅿 🐾) 🔌 This snappy-looking bush eco-cabin is in an undisclosed locale behind Stirling (you'll find out the exact address when you book). But until then, we can tell you that it's sustainable (off-grid, composting toilet, no air-con), architecturally handsome, sleeps two (four at a pinch) and comes with a sense of humour ('ironing is forbidden'). Disconnect from the city; reconnect with nature.

★ Mt Lofty House   HISTORIC HOTEL $$$
(☑ 08-8339 6777; www.mtloftyhouse.com.au; 74 Mt Lofty Summit Rd, Crafers; d/ste/cottage from $299/399/499; 🅿 ❄ 🐾 🏊) Proprietorially poised above Mt Lofty Botanic Garden (awesome views), this 1852 stone baronial mansion has lavish heritage rooms and garden suites, plus the upmarket Hardy's restaurant (also with killer views; two/three courses $79/95) and moody Arthur Waterhouse lounge bar. There's been an absolute mint spent on this place recently, and it's looking superb. The perfect honeymooner/naughty weekender.

★ Stirling Hotel   BOUTIQUE HOTEL $$$
(☑ 08-8339 2345; www.stirlinghotel.com.au; 52 Mt Barker Rd, Stirling; d from $230; 🅿 ❄ 🐾) The owners spent so much money tarting up this gorgeous old dame, it's a wonder they can pay the staff. Upstairs are five guest suites: plush, contemporary and stylish. Downstairs is a free-flowing, all-day bistro (classy pub grub and pizzas) and a romantic restaurant (upmarket regional cuisine). The whole shebang is a runaway success story.

★ Fred Eatery   CAFE $$
(☑ 08-8339 1899; www.fredeatery.com.au; 220 Mt Barker Rd, Aldgate; mains $12-26; ⊙ 7.30am-4pm Tue-Fri, 7.30am-3.15pm Sat & Sun, plus 6-9pm Fri; 🍴) Build it, and they will come... For decades Aldgate eked out a cafe lifestyle with no quality cafe offerings. Then along came

Fred, a rather urbane fellow, decked out in green, black and white, with a savvy cityside menu, killer coffee and great staff. The house bircher muesli makes a solid start to the day, while the bodacious Reuben sandwich is calorific heaven.

🔒 Shopping

Stirling Markets MARKET

(☑0488 770 166; www.stirlingmarket.com.au; Druid Ave, Stirling; ⊙10am-4pm 4th Sun of the month, 3rd Sun in Dec) 'Bustling' is such a corny, overused adjective...but in this case it applies! Market stalls fill oak-lined Druid Ave: much plant life, busking, pies, cakes, affluent locals with dogs and Hills knick-knackery.

Gumeracha, Birdwood & Lobethal

A scenic drive from Adelaide to Birdwood leads through the **Torrens River Gorge** to Gumeracha (gum-er-ack-a; population 1020), a hardy hillside town with a pub at the bottom (making it hard to roll home). Nearby Birdwood (population 1300) marks the finishing line for September's **Bay to Birdwood** (www.baytobirdwood.com.au; ⊙Sep) classic-car rally. The rest of the year it makes a perfectly soporific Hills detour, with an excellent automotive musuem.

Back towards Woodside, Lobethal (population 2530), was established by Lutheran Pastor Fritzsche and his followers in 1842. Like Hahndorf, Lobethal was renamed during WWI – 'Tweedale' was the unfortunate choice. It's still a pious sort of town: church life plays a leading role in many locals' day-to-day lives, though the local craft-beer brewery and some excellent wineries in the surrounding hills demand reverence of a different kind.

National Motor Museum MUSEUM

(☑08-8568 4000; www.nationalmotormuseum.com.au; Shannon St, Birdwood; adult/child/family $15.50/6.50/35; ⊙10am-5pm) Behind an impressive 1852 stone flour mill in Birdwood, the National Motor Museum has a collection of 300-plus immaculate vintage, modern and classic cars (check out the DeLorean!) and motorcycles.

Big Rocking Horse MONUMENT

(☑08-8389 1085; www.thetoyfactory.com.au; 452 Torrens Rd, Gumeracha; $2; ⊙9am-5pm)

Gumeracha's main attraction is climbing the 18.3m-high Big Rocking Horse, which doesn't actually rock, but is unusually tasteful as far as Australia's 'big' tourist attractions go. You can also buy nifty wooden kids' toys at the shop below, and take the kids into the fenced compound next door ($1) to see tame kangaroos, geese, ducks, sheep, llamas and the odd emu.

★Applewood Distillery DISTILLERY

(☑08-8389 1250; www.applewooddistillery.com.au; 24 Victoria St, Gumeracha; ⊙11am-4pm) A leading light in the burgeoning South Australian distilling scene, Applewood has turned a chilly old 1920s cold store on the outskirts of Gumeracha into a warm-your-heart gin palace with a gritty industrial aesthetic. Run by a couple of former wine-makers, the emphasis is on terroir and the spirit of the land. Tasting flights start at $15; cheese platters available.

FLEURIEU PENINSULA

Patterned with vineyards, olive groves and almond plantations running down to the sea, the Fleurieu (*floo*-ree-oh) is Adelaide's weekend playground. The McLaren Vale wine region is booming, producing gutsy reds (salubrious shiraz) to rival those from the Barossa Valley (actually, we think McLaren Vale wins hands down). Like the Adelaide area, this land is Kaurna country. Further east, the Fleurieu's Encounter Coast is Ngarrindjeri country, with an engaging mix of surf beaches, historic towns and whales cavorting offshore. Forget the weekend playground – there's enough here to keep you entertained for months.

ℹ Getting There & Away

Your own vehicle is the best way to explore the Fleurieu, but several bus companies service the towns here.

➡ Adelaide Metro (p734) Suburban trains run between Adelaide and Seaford (one hour). From here, bus 751 runs to McLaren Vale and Willunga (45 minutes). Regular Adelaide Metro ticket prices apply (from $3.60).

➡ LinkSA (☑08-8555 2500; www.linksa.com.au) Runs daily buses from Adelaide to Victor Harbor ($27.20, one hour), continuing on to Port Elliot and Goolwa for the same fare.

➡ SeaLink (p751) On the Gulf St Vincent coast, the Kangaroo Island ferry company runs daily buses between Adelaide and Cape Jervis on the Fleurieu, from where the ferry departs. The bus

Fleurieu Peninsula

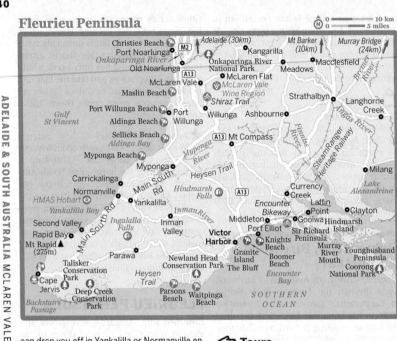

can drop you off in Yankalilla or Normanville en route ($21.50, 1¼ hours).

McLaren Vale

📞 08 / POP 3840

Flanked by the wheat-coloured Willunga Scarp and striated with vines, McLaren Vale is just 40 minutes south of Adelaide. Servicing the famed **McLaren Vale Wine Region**, it's a businesslike, utilitarian town strung along an endless main street – but it has some terrific cafes and eateries, both centrally and in the back blocks, and a few handy places to stay. But more critically, the town offers easy access to some truly excellent winery cellar doors.

◉ Sights & Activities

Shiraz Trail　　　　　　　　　CYCLING
(www.walkingsa.org.au; ⏲24hr) **FREE** Get the McLaren Vale vibe on this 8km walking/cycling track, along an old railway line between McLaren Vale and Willunga. If you're up for it, the trail continues another 30km to Marino Rocks along the **Coast to Vines Rail Trail**. Hire a bike from Oxygen Cycles (p742) or McLaren Vintage Bike Hire (p742); ask the visitor centre for a map or download one from the website.

☞ Tours

Trailhopper　　　　　　　　　　WINE
(📞08-8271 4485; www.trailhopper.com.au; per person $50) Remove the hassle of driving between cellar doors from your McLaren Vale equation with these hop-on/hop-off tour services, departing Adelaide then the McLaren Vale & Fleurieu Visitor Information Centre before wheeling past 15 McLaren Vale wineries on a scheduled loop. Five departures per day; spend as long as you like anywhere along the route. What a good idea!

Adelaide's Top Food & Wine Tours　　FOOD & DRINK
(📞08-8386 0888; www.topfoodandwinetours.com.au) Either a full-day winery tour ex-Adelaide ($165 per person) or a more detailed cheese-and-wine trail through the Vale ($320).

Chook's Little Winery Tours　　　WINE
(📞0414 922 200; www.chookslittlewinerytours.com.au; per person incl lunch $120-160) Small-group, full-day tours visiting some of the lesser-known boutique McLaren Vale wineries, ex-Adelaide (or McLaren Vale pick-up), run by the irrepressible Chook McCoy.

BEST BOTTLES: MCLAREN VALE WINE REGION

If the Barossa Valley is SA wine's old school, then McLaren Vale is the upstart teenager smoking cigarettes behind the shed and stealing nips from mum's sherry bottle. The luscious vineyards around here have a Tuscan haze in summer, rippling down to a calm coastline that's positively Ligurian. This is shiraz country, producing wines that are solid, punchy and seriously good. Some tastings are free, some are pricey, but often redeemable if you buy a bottle.

Alpha Box & Dice (☑08-8323 7750; www.alphaboxdice.com; 8 Olivers Rd, McLaren Vale; ☺11am-5pm Mon-Fri, 10am-6pm Sat & Sun) One out of the box, this refreshing little gambler wins top billing for interesting blends, funky furnishings, quirky labels and laid-back staff. On a warm afternoon, a bottle of AB&D prosecco goes unnaturally well with a cheese platter.

Coriole (☑08-8323 8305; www.coriole.com; Chaffeys Rd, McLaren Vale; ☺10am-5pm Mon-Fri, 11am-5pm Sat & Sun) Duck into the Farm Shop at this beautiful stone-cottage cellar door (1860) and assemble a regional tasting platter to share on the lawns, made lovelier by multiple swills of Redstone shiraz or the flagship chenin blanc. Gather at Coriole is the excellent slate-floored restaurant here (mains $30 to $40), taking a hunter-gatherer approach to lunch. Definitively McLaren Vale; book ahead.

d'Arenberg (☑08-8329 4888; www.darenberg.com.au; 58 Osborn Rd, McLaren Vale; ☺10am-5pm) 'd'Arry's' relaxes atop a hillside with mighty fine views. The wine labels are part of the character of this place: the Dead Arm shiraz and the Broken Fishplate sauvignon blanc are our faves. Book for lunch at the excellent d'Arry's Verandah restaurant (mains $36 to $38), or the sensational d'Arenberg Cube (p742), winemaker Chester Osborne's architectural oddity.

🎇 Festivals & Events

Sea & Vines Festival FOOD & DRINK
(www.seaandvines.com.au; ☺Jun) It seems like most of Adelaide gets tizzed-up and buses down to the annual Sea & Vines Festival over the June long weekend. Local wineries cook up seafood, splash wine around and host live bands. Can get messy later in the evening.

🛏 Sleeping

McLaren Vale Backpackers HOSTEL $
(☑08-8323 0916; www.mclarenvalebackpackers.com.au; 106 Main Rd, McLaren Vale; dm $27-30, s & d from $80; 🅿❄@🛜) McLaren Vale's boisterous backpackers fills out an old health club at the top end of the main street, with winery workers' beds in the old squash courts and regular dorms and private rooms out the front. Health-club remnants include a sauna, spa and plunge pool. Good weekly rates.

Red Poles B&B $$
(☑08-8323 8994; www.redpoles.com.au; 190 McMurtrie Rd, McLaren Vale; d with/without bathroom $125/115, extra adult/child $25/15; 🅿❄) Bushy, eccentric Red Poles is a great place to stay (and eat!). Aim for the rustic en-suite room (bigger than its two counterparts). Order some gnocchi with pesto and truffle salsa or other dishes (weekend breakfast mains $10 to $20, Wednesday to Sunday lunch $28 to $38), and check out some local artwork while you wait.

McLaren Eye RENTAL HOUSE $$$
(☑08-8383 7122; www.mclareneye.com.au; 36a Peters Creek Rd, Kangarilla; 1-/2-bedroom $520/900; 🅿❄🛜) Super-luxe hillside architectural splendour with an outlook from here to eternity, McLaren Eye has everything you need for a decadent stay – and every room has a view, even the bathroom (slip into the fancy two-person bath). In Kangarilla, 13km from McLaren Vale township. Two-night minimum.

🍴 Eating & Drinking

⭐ **Pizzateca** PIZZA $$
(☑0431 700 183; www.pizza-teca.com; 319 Chalk Hill Rd, McLaren Vale; pizzas $20-28, set menu $38-55; ☺noon-4pm Mon, noon-9pm Fri & Sat, noon-5pm Sun; 🖐) Crazy-busy-popular Pizzateca occupies a little back-blocks cottage, with a broad deck beneath a couple of huge old redgum trees. Generously sized pizzas wheel out from the wood-fired oven, as kids careen across the lawns – it's an effervescent scene. Try the devilishly hot 'Diablo' (sugo, dried chilli, *fontina* cheese, salami and housemade chilli honey). More prosecco, anyone?

★ **d'Arenberg Cube**   FUSION $$$

(🖉 08-8329 4888; www.darenberg.com.au/daren berg-cube-restaurant; d'Arenberg, 58 Osborn Rd, McLaren Vale; degustation menu from $190, wine pairings from $95, museum $10; ☺ noon-3pm Thu-Sun, museum 10am-5pm) The product of d'Arenberg winemaker Chester Osborne's vision, the d'Arenberg Cube is an eccentric, surprising place – a towering, multi-tiered, black-and-white Rubik's Cube, educating with a museum ($10), stimulating with wine tastings, and satisfying with a fabulous regional degustation restaurant. There are lounge areas, viewing platforms, artful installations and McLaren Vale's only lift! Failing to enjoy yourself here just isn't an option.

★ **Salopian Inn**   BISTRO $$$

(🖉 08-8323 8769; www.salopian.com.au; cnr Main & McMurtrie Rds, McLaren Vale; mains $28-67; ☺ noon-3.30pm daily, 6pm-late Thu-Sat) This old vine-covered inn has been here since 1851. Its latest incarnation features super Mod Oz offerings with an Asian twist: launch into the Berkshire pork buns or blue swimmer crab and prawn dumplings, with a bottle of something local that you can hand-select from the cellar. And there are 170 gins with which to construct your G&T! Outstanding.

Goodieson Brewery   BREWERY

(🖉 0409 676 542; www.goodiesonbrewery.com.au; 194 Sand Rd, McLaren Vale; tastings $6; ☺ 11am-5.30pm) Anyone for a beer? This family-run outfit brews pale ale, pilsner, wheat beer and brown ale, plus brilliant seasonal beers. Sip a few on the sunny terrace.

ⓘ Information

McLaren Vale & Fleurieu Visitor Information Centre (🖉 08-8323 9944; www.mclarenvale. info; 796 Main Rd, McLaren Vale; ☺ 9am-5pm Mon-Fri, 10am-4pm Sat & Sun) At the northern end of McLaren Vale's main strip. Winery info, plus accommodation assistance and Sealink bus/ferry bookings for Kangaroo Island. Pick up the *McLaren Vale Heritage Trail* brochure for an historic walk around the main street (or download it from www.walkingsa.org.au/walk/find-a-place-to-walk/mclaren-vale-heritage-trail). Bike hire also available (half-/full day $22/33).

ⓘ Getting Around

Once you're in McLaren Vale, take a tour to see the wineries, or tackle them with your own transport.

For bike hire, see **Oxygen Cycles** (🖉 08-8323 7345; www.oxygencycles.com; 143 Main Rd,

McLaren Vale; bike hire per 3hr single/tandem $20/40; ☺ 10am-6pm Tue-Fri, 9am-5pm Sat) or **McLaren Vintage Bike Hire** (🖉 0410 067 199; www.mclarenvintagebikehire.com; 189 Main Rd, McLaren Vale; per day $45; ☺ 9am-5pm). Helmet, lock and basket (for bottles!) included.

Willunga

🖉 08 / POP 2310

A one-horse town with *three* pubs (a winning combo!), arty Willunga took off in 1840 when high-quality slate was discovered nearby and exported across Australia (used for everything from flagstones to billiard tables). Today, the town's early buildings along sloping High St are occupied by some excellent eateries, B&B accommodation and galleries. The Kidman Trail (p743) kicks off here, winding north to beyond the Barossa Valley. There's also a terrific farmers market here, plus a couple of craft-beer breweries doing good things.

⊙ Sights

Willunga Slate Museum   MUSEUM

(🖉 08-8556 2195; www.nationaltrust.org.au/sa/willunga-slate-museum; 61 High St; adult/child $5/1; ☺ 1-4pm Sun & 1st Tue of the month) At the top end of Willunga's ascending high street is this cluster of old stone buildings, which at various times have housed a police station, a courthouse, a prison and a boys' school. These days the emphasis is on Willunga's slate-mining history and the Cornish miners who did all the dirty work. Pick up the *Willunga Slate Trail & Museum* brochure and tour the town's top slate spots.

★ **Willunga Farmers Market**   MARKET

(🖉 08-8556 4297; www.willungafarmersmarket. com; Willunga Town Sq; ☺ 8am-12.30pm Sat) Heavy on the organic, the bespoke and the locally sourced, Willunga Farmers Market happens every Saturday morning on the corner of High St and Main Rd. Buskers, coffee, breakfast and hamper-filling goodies. Brilliant.

🛏 Sleeping & Eating

Farm   B&B $$$

(🖉 0434 125 172; www.thefarmwillunga.com.au; 11 Martin Rd; d from $320; 🅿 ❋ 🛜) High on the hill behind Willunga (great views!), Farm is a cafe-providore and working organic farm, with two ritzy accommodation suites out the back, one atop the other. You'll pay a bit more to be upstairs, but really, both suites are stylish, contemporary and utterly comfortable.

DIY breakfast from the fridge, or have it cooked in the cafe. Helipad available(!).

Russell's Pizza   PIZZA $$
(☑ 08-8556 2571; www.russellspizza.com; 13 High St; pizzas from $26, 2/3 courses $39/44; ⊙ 6-11pm Thu-Sat) It may look like a rustic, ramshackle chicken coop, but Russell's is the place to be on weekends for sensational wood-fired pizza. No one minds the wait for a meal (which could be an hour) – it's all about the atmosphere. It's perennially popular, so book way ahead.

Shifty Lizard   CRAFT BEER
(☑ 08-7079 2471; www.shiftylizard.com; 33 High St; ⊙ 2-8pm Thu, 11am-10pm Fri & Sat, 11am-7pm Sun) Polished concrete, white subway tiles, '90s rock, tricky lighting, pizzas and a couple of bearded local lads – put it all together inside a former butcher's shop on Willunga's main street, add some pints of 'Bruce Lee-zard IPA' and 'Stouty McStout Face' and you've got yourself an evening out.

Gulf St Vincent Beaches

There are some ace swimming beaches (but no surf) along the Gulf St Vincent coastline, starting with suburban **Christies Beach** and **Port Noarlunga**, where there's a fabulous snorkelling reef (☑ 08-8384 0666; www.southaustraliantrails.com/trails/port-noarlunga-reef; via Port Noarlunga Jetty, Esplanade; ⊙ daylight hours) FREE and access to the walking trails and wetlands of **Onkaparinga River National Park** (☑ 08-8550 3400; www.parks.sa.gov.au; via Piggott Range Rd, Old Noarlunga; ⊙ 24hr) FREE. A few kilometres up the river from Port Noarlunga, **Old Noarlunga** (via Patapinda Rd; ⊙ 24hr) FREE is a surprising diversion: a well-preserved historic village dating back to 1840, studded with heritage stone cottages revolving around a village green (with a playground and BBQs) and overseen by an austere church on the hillside.

Maslin Beach is further south again, the southern end of which is a nudist and gay hang-out. Maslin is 45 minutes from Adelaide by car – just far enough to escape the sprawling shopping centres and new housing developments trickling south from the city.

Port Willunga is the closest sand to McLaren Vale and is the best swimming spot along this stretch of coast. There's a superb cafe on the clifftops here, with the remnant piers of what once was a 145m-long jetty down below.

TAKE THE LONG WAY HOME

South Australia has three epic long-distance trails for hiking and cycling, all running through or past Adelaide.

Heysen Trail (www.heysentrail.asn.au) Australia's longest walking trail: 1200km between Cape Jervis on the Fleurieu Peninsula and Parachilna Gorge in the Flinders Ranges. Access points along the way make it ideal for half- and full-day walks. Note that due to fire restrictions, some sections of the trail are closed between December and April.

Kidman Trail (www.southaustralian trails.com/trails/kidman-trail) A 10-section cycling, horse-riding and walking trail between Willunga on the Fleurieu Peninsula and Kapunda, north of the Barossa Valley.

Mawson Trail (www.southaustralian trails.com/trails/mawson-trail) A 900km bike trail between Adelaide and Blinman in the Flinders Ranges, via the Adelaide Hills and Clare Valley.

Keep trucking south to cute little **Myponga** (population 540), where the craft beer at **Smiling Samoyed Brewery** (☑ 08-8558 6166; www.smilingsamoyed.com.au; 46 Main South Rd, via Hansen St, Myponga; ⊙ noon-4pm Mon-Thu, 11am-9pm Fri, 11am-6pm Sat & Sun) will have you smiling like a hound. There are four main brews to try – a kolsch, an APA, an IPA and a dark ale – plus seasonal efforts. In 1971 Myponga hosted the one-off Myponga Pop Festival, featuring Black Sabbath and legendary Australian bands Daddy Cool, Spectrum and Billy Thorpe and the Aztecs (Cat Stevens was booked to play too, but he cancelled). **Myponga Beach** (www.southaustralia.com; via Myponga Beach Rd, Myponga; ⊙ 24hr; ⊛) FREE is nearby – a quaint, almost Grecian spot.

Further south is soporific **Yankalilla** (population 5160), which has the regional **Yankalilla Bay Visitor Information Centre** (☑ 08-8558 0240; www.yankalilla.sa.gov.au; 163 Main South Rd, Yankalilla; ⊙ 9am-5pm Mon-Fri, 10am-4pm Sat & Sun; ☎). There's a small local history **museum** (☑ 1300 965 842; www.yankalilla.sa.gov.au; Yankalilla Bay Visitor Information Centre, 169 Main South Rd, Yankalilla; adult/child/family $7/2/15; ⊙ 9am-5pm Mon-Fri, 10am-4pm Sat & Sun) out the back; look for the radar antenna from the scuttled HMAS *Hobart* (www.south

RAPID BAY

Take the turn-off about 19km south of Normanville and follow the signs to Rapid Bay. This was the site of Adelaide founder Colonel William Light's first landing in SA in 1836, in his ship the *Rapid*. There's a stone down by the shore with 'WL 1836' carved into it. Then, in the 1950s, Rapid Bay became a boom town, the local limestone quarry shipping 60,000 tonnes of lime per month from the enormous jetty. Production ceased in 1981; since then Rapid Bay has assumed a gothic, ghost-town atmosphere. Empty '50s villas and workers' quarters line the streets, and the local shop (closed) has signs advertising soft drinks they don't make anymore. The jetty (recently rebuilt; www.rapidbayjetty.org) has become a popular fishing and diving site. **Adventure Kayaking SA** (☑08-8295 8812; www.adventurekayak.com.au; tours from $200) 🏄 runs kayak trips around the coast here, checking out sea caves, beaches and wildlife.

australiantrails.com/trails/ex-hmas-hobart), now a dive site not far offshore.

About 60km south of Adelaide is **Carrickalinga** (population 370), which has a gorgeous arc of white sandy beach: it's a very chilled spot with no shops. For supplies and accommodation, head to neighbouring **Normanville** (population 1630). Here you'll find a rambling pub, a supermarket and a couple of caravan parks. About 10km out of Normanville along Hay Flat Rd are the picturesque little **Ingalalla Falls** (follow the signs from the Yankalilla side of town). Along similar lines, the **Hindmarsh Falls** are off Hindmarsh Tiers Rd, inland from Myponga.

About 14km south of Normanville is little **Second Valley** (population 160). The beach here is good for a sheltered swim. Another 5km south is the turn-off to **Rapid Bay**, an eerie semi-ghost town with a *looong* fishing jetty.

There's not much at **Cape Jervis**, 107km from Adelaide, other than the Kangaroo Island ferry terminal, and the start point for the Heysen Trail (p743). Nearby, **Deep Creek Conservation Park** (☑08-8598 0263; www.parks.sa.gov.au; via Main South Rd, Deep Creek; per car $10; ⊕24hr) has sweeping coastal views, a wicked waterfall, human-size yakkas (*Xanthorrhoea semiplana tateana*), sandy beaches, kangaroos, kookaburras and popular bush-camping areas ($9 to $27 per vehicle).

🛏 Sleeping

Coast Motel & Apartments   MOTEL $$
(☑08-8386 3311; www.coastmotelandapartments.com.au; 153 Esplanade, Port Noarlunga South; d/2-bedroom apt from $149/199; P❋🛜) This two-storey motel on the clifftops above the Onkaparinga River mouth wins points for

enthusiasm: the new owners are doing a great job of reviving what was a weary old motel, renovating rooms with beachy colours and adding new blinds, carpets and beds. The upstairs rooms have fab sunset views; downstairs are larger apartments. Bike hire per day $15.

Jetty Carvan Park   CARAVAN PARK $
(☑08-8558 2038; www.jettycaravanparknormanville.com.au; 34 Jetty Rd, Normanville; unpowered/powered sites $38/48, cabins with/without bathroom from $128/85, extra person $10; P❋🛜) The pick of the two caravan parks in 'Normy', split into two sections either side of the Bungala River, Jetty CP has grassy sites, towering Norfolk Island pines and trim cabins. The beachfront kiosk across the car park does a mean fish and chips.

★**Lush Pastures**   B&B $$$
(☑0411 286 377; www.lushpastures.com.au; 29 Coomooloo Rd, Bald Hills; d incl breakfast $320; P❋🛜) Esteemed South Australian architect Max Pritchard has done it again! This time he's concocted a neat sequence of three private, contemporary villas on a hillside 11km inland from Yankalilla, with aeronautical V-shaped roofs and show-stopping sunset views across fields to the sea (the business is owned by Mr and Mrs Lush, if you were thinking the name is a bit naff).

🍴 Eating & Drinking

Victory Hotel   PUB FOOD $$
(☑08-8556 3083; www.victoryhotel.com.au; Main South Rd, Sellicks Beach; mains $19-34; ⊕noon-2.30pm & 6-8.30pm) On the highway above Sellicks Beach, the Victory is an excellent pub, parts of which hark back to 1858. There are awesome views of the silvery Gulf St Vincent, a cheery, laid-back vibe and a beaut

beer garden. Factor in inspired meals, an impressive cellar and wines by the glass and you'll be feeling victorious. Book ahead.

Three hillside cabins available too (doubles $150, or $165 including breakfast).

★ Star of Greece   BISTRO $$$

(☑ 08-8557 7420; www.starofgreece.com.au; 1 The Esplanade, Port Willunga; mains $29-38; ⊘noon-3pm Wed-Sun, 6pm-late Fri & Sat, daily Jan) Port Willunga hosts the justifiably busy, clifftop seafood shack the Star of Greece. Named after a shipwreck, it has funky decor, great staff and a sunny patio. We asked the waiter where the whiting was caught: he gazed across the bay and said, 'See that boat out there?' There's also a takeaway kiosk (snacks $7 to $15, open weekends and school holidays).

Victor's Place   CRAFT BEER

(☑ 0467 466 212; www.victorsplace.com.au; 62 Victor Harbor Rd, Old Noarlunga; ⊘11am-9pm Thu-Mon) Inside a renovated 1870s stone shearing shed (check out the bottomless well!), Victor's is a stylish brew-house run by an ex–McLaren Vale winemaker. There's pale ale, IPA, stout and special bitter: grab a pint or a tasting paddle ($14) and head for the sunny terrace. Small-plate edibles ($10 to $22) run the gamut from lamb-fat hashbrowns to kangaroo loin. Takeaway cans.

ⓘ Getting There & Away

This strip of coastline deserves your time and attention: explore with your own vehicle to make the most of it. At a pinch, Adelaide Metro (p734) trains and buses can get you as far as Port Noarlunga; while the Kangaroo Island ferry company SeaLink (p751) runs daily buses between Adelaide and Cape Jervis (from where the ferry departs), and can drop you off in Yankalilla or Normanville en route ($21.50, 1¼ hours).

Victor Harbor

☑ 08 / POP 14,670

The biggest town on the Encounter Coast is Victor Harbor (yes, that's the correct spelling: blame one of SA's poorly schooled early Surveyor Generals). It's a raggedy, brawling holiday destination with three huge pubs and migrating whales offshore. It's a handy spot to stay if you're exploring the Encounter Coast, but comes up a little short on urban virtues. Still, the locals seem to love it: 'Another day in paradise', says a pony-tailed pensioner to no one in particular, as he shuffles along Ocean St in the sun.

◉ Sights & Activities

Granite Island   ISLAND

(☑ 08-8552 0300; www.parks.sa.gov.au; via Causeway; ⊘24hr) **FREE** Take a wander (or ride the famed horse-drawn tram) over Victor Harbor's historic waterfront causeway to Granite Island. This compact craggy outcrop has resident penguins and a great 1.5km walking trail looping around the cliffs and shoreline (a 40-minute circuit).

South Australian Whale Centre   MUSEUM

(☑ 08-8551 0750; www.sawhalecentre.com; 2 Railway Tce; adult/child/family $9/4.50/24; ⊘10.30am-5pm) Victor Harbor is on the migratory path of southern right whales (May to October). The multilevel South Australian Whale Centre has impressive whale displays (including a big stinky skull) and can give you the low-down on where to see them. Not whale season? Check out the big mammals in the 3D-cinema, and the exhibit on Aboriginal whale stories. For whale sightings info, call the Whale Information Hotline (☑ 1900 942 537).

★ Encounter Bikeway   CYCLING

(☑ 08-8551 0777; www.victor.sa.gov.au/web data/resources/files/bikeway.pdf) The much-wheeled Encounter Bikeway extends 30km from Victor Harbor to Laffin Point beyond Goolwa, past beaches, lookouts and the odd visiting whale. The visitor centre stocks maps (or download one); pick up the trail nearby. Perplexingly, there's nowhere to hire a bike in Victor Harbor, or Goolwa: the nearest option is Surf & Sun (p747) in Middleton.

Horse-Drawn Tram   OUTDOORS

(☑ 08-8551 0720; www.horsedrawntram.com.au; Esplanade; return adult/child/family $10/7/25, one way $7/5/19; ⊘hourly 10am-4pm) Just offshore is the boulder-strewn Granite Island, connected to the mainland by a 632m causeway built in 1875. You can walk to the island, but it's much more fun to take the 1894 double-decker tram pulled by a big Clydesdale. It's the definitive Victor Harbor experience. Tickets are available from the driver or visitor information centre.

ⓒ Tours

Oceanic Victor   WILDLIFE

(☑ 08-8552 7137; www.oceanicvictor.com. au; via Granite Island; tours adult/child/family $120/95/400; ⊘9am-5pm Mon-Fri, 10am-5pm Sat & Sun) Two-hour boat tours head to a floating marine aquarium not far offshore, full of swift-moving Southern Bluefin tuna (the 'Ferraris of the sea'). You can either jump in and swim with the fish, or stay dry and feed them from a platform. Guided two-hour penguin-spotting tours on Granite Island also available (adult/child/family $25/20/75).

Big Duck　　　　　　　　　　　BOATING

(☎ 08-8555 2203; www.thebigduck.com.au; Esplanade; 45min tour adult/child/family $40/25/115, 90min $65/50/200) Do a lap of Granite Island and cruise along the coast to check out seals, dolphins and whales (in season) on the rigid inflatable Big Duck boat. Call or go online for times and bookings. Strict guidelines about proximity to whales are adhered to, although research suggests that human interaction with sea mammals potentially alters their behavioural and breeding patterns.

🛏 Sleeping & Eating

Anchorage Hotel　　　　　GUESTHOUSE $

(☎ 08-8552 5970; www.anchoragehotel.com; 21 Flinders Pde; s/d/apt from $85/100/265; P ❋ 🤝) This grand old guesthouse exudes seaside charm. Immaculately maintained, great-value rooms open off long corridors. Most rooms face the beach, and some have a balcony (you'd pay through the nose for this in Sydney!). There are myriad room configurations; the cheapest ones are view-free and share bathrooms. The cafe-bar (mains breakfast $10-19, lunch & dinner $24-35; ⊗ 8am-late) downstairs is a winner.

⭐ **Kings Beach Retreats**　RENTAL HOUSE $$$

(☎ 0407 183 905; www.kingsbeachretreats.com.au; 60 Dump Rd, Waitpinga; d/house up to 10 people from $290/1000, extra person $35/50; P ❋ 🤝) On a spectacular rocky promontory 10km south of Victor Harbor, these three cottages – from one to five bedrooms – are sublimely positioned. A sense of isolation is what you're paying for here: the ocean collides with the rocky shoreline, whales cruise by and petrels circle overhead. The architecture combines rammed earth, huge recycled jetty timbers and broad view-capturing windows. Marvellous!

⭐ **Nino's**　　　　　　　　　　ITALIAN $$

(☎ 08-8552 3501; www.ninoscafe.com.au; 17 Albert Pl; mains $16-39; ⊗ 8.30am-9pm; 🚸) Nino's cafe has been here since 1974 (the building longer), but it manages to put a contemporary sheen on central VH. Hip young staff and a mod interior set the scene for gourmet

pizzas, burgers, pasta, salads, risottos and meaty Italian mains. Excellent coffee, cakes and takeaways. Good kids' stuff too, plus dinner-and-a-movie deals with Victa Cinema.

❶ Information

Victor Harbor Visitor Information Centre

(☎ 08-8551 0777; www.tourismvictorharbor. com.au; Esplanade; ⊗ 9am-5pm) Handles tour and accommodation bookings. If you're feeling fit, nostalgic or both, pick up the *Walks In & Around Victor Harbor* and *Town Centre Heritage Trail Victor Harbor* brochures and pound the pavement.

❶ Getting There & Away

On the first and third Sundays from June to November inclusive, **SteamRanger Heritage Railway** (☎ 1300 655 991, 08-8263 5621; www. steamranger.org.au) operates the *Southern Encounter* (adult/child return $73/38) tourist train from Mt Barker in the Adelaide Hills to Victor Harbor via Strathalbyn, Goolwa and Port Elliot. The **Cockle Train** (adult/child return $30/16) runs along the Encounter Coast between Victor Harbor and Goolwa via Port Elliot every Sunday and Wednesday, and daily during school holidays. Several other trains ply shorter, less prominent routes: see the website for details.

Port Elliot

⌖ 08 / POP 2100

About 8km east of Victor Harbor, historic (and today, rather affluent) Port Elliot is set back from **Horseshoe Bay**, a gorgeous orange-sand arc with gentle surf and good swimming. Norfolk Island pines reach for the sky, holidaying city-siders shuffle between cafes, and there are whale-spotting updates posted on the pub wall. If there are whales around, wander out to **Freemans Knob** lookout at the end of the Strand and peer through the free telescope.

🏃 Activities

Commodore Point, at the eastern end of Horseshoe Bay, and nearby **Boomer Beach** and **Knights Beach**, have reliable waves for experienced surfers, with swells often holding around 2m. The beach at otherwise-missable **Middleton**, the next town towards Goolwa, also has solid breaks. Further afield, try wild **Waitpinga Beach** and **Parsons Beach**, 12km southwest of Victor Harbor (not for beginners).

The best surfing season is March to June, when the northerlies doth blow. See www.

southaustralia.com for info, and www.surf southoz.com for surf reports. There are a couple of good surfing schools in Middleton.

Surf & Sun SURFING
(☎1800 786 386; www.surfandsun.com.au; 44 Goolwa Rd, Middleton; ☜) Offers board/wetsuit hire ($30/15 per half-day) and surfing lessons ($55 for a two-hour lesson, including gear). Very kid friendly (two-hour family lessons $240). Is also the only place along the Encounter Bikeway (p745) between Victor Harbor and Middleton to offer **bike hire** ($30/45 per half-/full day). Book online or call.

🛏 Sleeping & Eating

★**Port Elliot Beach House YHA** HOSTEL $
(☎08-8554 1885; www.yha.com.au; 13 The Strand; dm/tw/d/f from $30/35/90/130; P❈@✿) Built in 1910 (the old Arcadia Hotel), this sandstone beauty has sweeping views across the Port Elliot coastline. Drag your eyes away from the scenery and you'll find polished floorboards, en-suite rooms, nice linen and contemporary colour schemes: a million-dollar fit-out (maybe more). Surf lessons are almost mandatory.

BIG4 Port Elliot Holiday Park CARAVAN PARK $
(☎08-8554 2134; www.portelliotholidaypark.com. au; off Port Elliot Rd; unpowered/powered sites from $33/36, cabins/units/cottages from $90/115/145; P❈✿) In an unbeatable position behind the Horseshoe Bay dunes (it can be a touch windy), this grassy, 5-hectare park has all the requisite facilities, including a shiny camp kitchen and all-weather barbecue area. Lush grass and healthy-looking trees. Prices plummet in winter.

Port Elliot Bakery BAKERY $
(☎08-8554 2475; www.portelliotbakery.com; 31 North Tce; items $5-10; ☺7am-5.30pm) It's standing room only at Port Elliot's little bakery, with queues out the door on sunny afternoons. Wraps, pies, donuts, pasties, pizza slices, big quiches and killer custard tarts – it's all here. Scoff a chicken-and-camembert pie at the shady terrace tables.

★**Flying Fish Cafe** MODERN AUSTRALIAN $$
(☎08-8554 3504; www.flyingfishcafe.com.au; 1 The Foreshore; mains cafe $12-16, restaurant $26-32; ☺cafe 9am-4pm daily, restaurant noon-3pm daily & 6-8pm Fri & Sat; ☜) Sit down for a cafe breakfast and you'll be here all day – the views of Horseshoe Bay are sublime. Otherwise grab some takeaway Coopers-battered flathead and chips and head for the sand. At night things get classy, with à la carte mains focusing on independent SA producers. One of SA's must-visit foodie haunts.

Goolwa
☎08 / POP 2350
Much more low-key and elegant than kissing-cousin Victor Harbor, Goolwa is an unassuming historic river port where the Murray River spills into the sea. Beyond the dunes is a broad surf beach with ranks of breakers rolling in from the ocean.

☞ Tours

Canoe the Coorong CANOEING
(☎0424 826 008; www.canoethecoorong. com; adult/child $135/85) ☞ Full-day paddles around the Coorong and Murray River mouth, departing Goolwa. Includes lunch and a bush-tucker walk through the dunes. Three-hour sunset tours (adult/child $90/65) and overnight expeditions also available ($390 per person). Kayak hire (all sorts) starts at $50 per day.

Cruise the Coorong CRUISE
(☎08-8555 1984; www.cruisethecoorong.com.au; Goolwa Wharf; adult/child $140/110) Small-boat, six-hour 'Coorong Ultimate' cruises with walks, bush tucker, seal spotting and digging for *pipis* (shellfish) on the beach. Lunch, snacks, beer and wine included. A great way to see Coorong National Park.

Spirit of the Coorong CRUISE
(☎08-8555 2203; www.coorongcruises.com.au; Goolwa Wharf) ☞ Excellent eco-cruises on the Murray River and into the Coorong National Park, including lunch and guided walks. The 3.5-hour Coorong Discovery Cruise (adult/ child $95/69) runs on Thursdays all year, plus Mondays and Saturdays from October to May. The six-hour Coorong Adventure Cruise ($115/80) runs on Sundays all year, plus Wednesdays from October to May. Lunch included; bookings essential.

✵ Festivals & Events

South Australian Wooden Boat Festival SPORTS
(www.woodenboatfestival.com.au; ☺Apr) Wooden boats of all sizes, configurations and degrees of quaintness make a splash in the Murray River. Held in April in odd-numbered years.

🛏 Sleeping & Eating

Captains Quarters   RENTAL HOUSE $$
(☎0402 254 742; www.facebook.com/captains
quartersgoolwa; 15 Wildman St; d from $200, extra
person $20; ⓟ✱) It looks like an oldie, but
it's actually a newie. Built in 2010, Cap-
tains Quarters is a super-cute cottage in the
Goolwa backstreets, just a short walk from
the shops and cafes. Sleeps six in three bed-
rooms – a very clever use of space on a tight
block of land.

★Australasian   BOUTIQUE HOTEL $$$
(☎08-8555 1088; www.australasian1858.com; 1
Porter St; d incl breakfast from $395; ⓟ✱🛜)
This gorgeous 1858 stone hotel at the head
of Goolwa's main street has been reborn as
a sassy B&B, with a sequence of Japanese-
inspired decks and glazed extensions, and
an upmarket dining room (open to non-
guests Saturday nights; $89 per person).
The five plush suites all have views, and the
breakfast will make you want to wake up
here again. Two-night minimum.

★Motherduck   CAFE $$
(☎08-8555 1462; www.motherduckcafe.com.au;
1/13 Cadell St; mains $12-20; ⊗8am-4pm Tue-Sun;
🖍) A buzzy highlight of the Goolwa shop-
ping strip is this crafty little cafe, which
always seems busier than anywhere else in
Goolwa. Exposed stone walls, bravely strong
coffee, pulled-pork eggs Benedict, Lang-
horne Creek wines, curries, pancakes, happy
staff and Jack Johnson on the stereo – the
perfect small-town cafe?

ℹ Information

Goolwa Visitor Information Centre (☎1300
466 592; www.visitalexandrina.com; 4 Goolwa
Tce, Goolwa; ⊗9am-5pm Mon-Fri, 10am-4pm
Sat & Sun) Inside an 1857 post office, with
detailed local info (including accommodation).

KANGAROO ISLAND

From Cape Jervis, car ferries chug across the
swells of the Backstairs Passage to Kangaroo
Island (KI). Uninhabited when Brit explorer
Matthew Flinders named the island in 1802
and long devoid of tourist trappings, KI is
today a booming destination for wilderness
and wildlife fans. It's a veritable zoo of seals,
birds, dolphins, echidnas and (of course)
kangaroos. Still, the island remains rurally
paced and underdeveloped – the kind of
place where kids ride bikes to school and
farmers advertise for wives on noticeboards.
Island wine and produce is a highlight.

History

Many KI place names are French, attrib-
utable to Gallic explorer Nicholas Baudin
who surveyed the coast in 1802 and 1803.
Baudin's English rival, Matthew Flinders,
named the island in 1802 after his crew
feasted on kangaroo meat here. By this stage
the island was uninhabited, but archaeol-
ogists think Indigenous Australians lived
here as recently as 2000 years ago. Why
they deserted KI is a matter of conjecture,
though the answer is hinted at in the Indige-
nous name for KI: Karta (Land of the Dead).
In the early 1800s an Indigenous presence
(albeit a tragically displaced one) was re-
established on KI when whalers and sealers
abducted Aboriginal women from Tasmania
and brought them here.

🏃 Activities

There's plenty to see under your own steam
on KI, including bushwalking trails ranging
from 1km to the epic 61km, five-day Kanga-
roo Island Wilderness Trail (p756). Check
out www.tourkangarooisland.com.au/walks-
and-hikes for more trail info.

The safest swimming is along the north
coast, where the water is warmer and there
are fewer rips than down south. Try Emu
Bay, Stokes Bay, Snelling Beach or Western
River Cove.

For surfing, hit the uncrowded swells
along the south coast. Pennington Bay has
strong, reliable breaks; Vivonne Bay and
Hanson Bay in the southwest also serve up
some tasty waves. Pick up the *Kangaroo
Island Surfing Guide* brochure from island
visitor info centres.

Cycling is a great way to see KI, although
road distances can be surprisingly, well...
distant. Bring your bike on the ferry (return
$22) then pick up the handy *Kangaroo
Island Cycling* brochures form the Gateway
Visitor Information Centre (p752).

�) Tours

Hot tip: say at least one night on the island
if you can (one-day tours from Adelaide are
hectic).

Kangaroo Island Trails   FOOD & DRINK
(☎0458 471 419; www.kangarooislandtrails.com.
au) Foodie-focused half-day tours, sipping
and chewing into the best of KI (adult/

Kangaroo Island

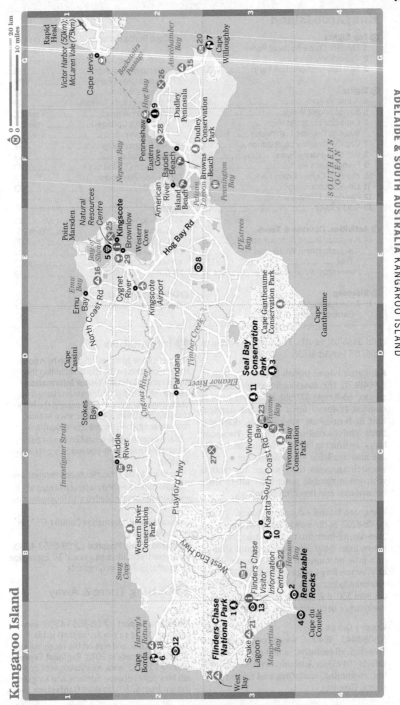

Kangaroo Island

⊙ Top Sights
1 Flinders Chase National Park A3
2 Remarkable Rocks B3
3 Seal Bay Conservation Park D3

⊙ Sights
4 Admirals Arch A4
5 Bay of Shoals Wines E1
6 Cape Borda Lightstation A2
   Cape du Couedic Lighthouse .... (see 4)
7 Cape Willoughby Lightstation G3
8 Clifford's Honey Farm E2
9 Frenchman's Rock F2
10 Kelly Hill Conservation Park B3
11 Little Sahara D3
12 Ravine des Casoars A2
13 Rocky River A3

⊙ Activities, Courses & Tours
14 Kangaroo Island Outdoor Action C3
   Kangaroo Island Wilderness
      Trail ....(see 13)
   Penneshaw Penguin Centre .... (see 9)

⊙ Sleeping
15 Antechamber Bay South
   Campground G2

Cape Borda Cottages .... (see 6)
Cape du Couedic Lodges .... (see 4)
16 Discovery Lagoon Caravan &
   Camping Grounds E1
17 Flinders Chase Farm B3
18 Harvey's Return A2
19 Lifetime Private Rentals C2
   May's Homestead .... (see 13)
   Postman's Cottage .... (see 13)
   Rocky River .... (see 13)
20 Sea Dragon Lodge G2
21 Snake Lagoon A3
22 Southern Ocean Lodge B3
23 Vivonne Bay Lodge C3
24 West Bay A3

⊗ Eating
25 Amadio Wines E1
   Cactus ....(see 25)
   Chase Cafe .... (see 13)
26 Dudley Wines Cellar Door G2
27 Marron Café C3
28 Sunset Food & Wine F2

⊙ Drinking & Nightlife
29 Kangaroo Island Brewery E2

child $165/55; ex-KI). The full-day option is $296/178 (ex-Adelaide).

Kangaroo Island Ocean Safari WILDLIFE
(☑ 0419 772 175; www.kangarooislandoceansafari.com.au; adult/child $77/55) Hop aboard this buoyant 12-seater for a 75-minute nautical tour ex-Penneshaw, spying seals, dolphins, birds and (sometimes) whales. Two-hour tours swimming with dolphins and seals are also available – it's worth noting that research suggests that human interaction with sea mammals potentially alters their behavioural and breeding patterns.

Kangaroo Island Adventure Tours TOURS
(☑ 08-8202 8678; www.kiadventuretours.com.au) Two-day, all-inclusive tours ex-Adelaide, with prices from $459 for dorm accommodation, or a little bit more for private rooms – both at Vivonne Bay Lodge (☑ 08-8559 4232; www.vivonnebaylodge.com.au; 66 Knofel Dr, Vivonne Bay; dm from $30, d & tw from $120; P�). Has a backpacker bent and plenty of activities.

Groovy Grape TOURS
(☑ 08-8440 1640; www.groovygrape.com.au) Two-day, all-inclusive, small-group wildlife safaris ($445) ex-Adelaide, with sandboarding, swimming, campfires and all the main sights. Groovy.

ⓘ Information

There are a few agencies which can help book accommodation on the island, including the island's main **Gateway Visitor Information Centre** (☑ 1800 811 080; www.tourkangarooisland.com.au/accommodation) and the ferry company **SeaLink** (☑ 13 13 01; www.sealink.com.au/kangaroo-island-accommodation).

Island mobile phone reception can be patchy outside the main towns (reception is best with Telstra).

There are ATMs in Kingscote and Penneshaw.

Online, there's a handy interactive map at www.kimap.com.au, loaded with foodie-touring info.

Gateway Visitor Information Centre (p752) In Penneshaw.

Kangaroo Island Hospital (☑ 08-8553 4200; www.countryhealthsa.sa.gov.au; 3-7 Esplanade, Kingscote; ◔ 24hr) In Kingscote.

ⓘ Getting There & Away

AIR

Kingscote Airport (☑ 08-8553 4500; www.kangarooisland.sa.gov.au/airport) is 14km from Kingscote, and was on the receiving end of a major upgrade in 2018. **Regional Express** (Rex; ☑ 13 17 13; www.regionalexpress.com.au) flies daily between Adelaide and Kingscote (return from $280), as does **QantasLink** (www.

qantas.com; return from $295), the Qantas regional brand.

Car-hire companies and some accommodation providers will meet you when you land. **Kangaroo Island Transfers** (☑ 0427 887 575; www.kitransfers.com.au) connects the airport with Kingscote (from $25 per person), American River (from $70 for one or two people) and Penneshaw (from $90 for one or two people). Bookings essential. Sealink also offers transfers; call for details.

FERRY

SeaLink (☑ 13 13 01; www.sealink.com.au) operates the car ferry between **Cape Jervis** (Main South Rd, Cape Jervis) and **Penneshaw** (Bay Tce, Penneshaw) on KI, with multiple ferries each way daily (return adult/child from $98/50, motorcycles/cars/campervans $66/196/196, 45 minutes one way).

There's also a passenger-only ferry run by **Kangaroo Island Connect** (KIC; ☑ 0419 100 100; www.kic.com.au), running from Cape Jervis to Penneshaw (return adult/child $55/40, 30 minutes). There are five sailings per day to and from Penneshaw; the first and last services daily run from/to American River via Penneshaw ($77/55, 45 minutes).

BUS

SeaLink runs daily buses (return adult/child $56/30, 2¼ hours one way) between Adelaide and Cape Jervis on the Fleurieu Peninsula, where the ferry departs.

Kangaroo Island Connect also runs buses from Adelaide to Cape Jervis (return adult/child $64/30).

❶ Getting Around

Forget public transport: you're gonna need some wheels. The island's main roads are sealed, but the rest are gravel, including those to Cape Willoughby, Cape Borda and the North Coast Rd (take it slowly, especially at night). There's petrol at Kingscote, Penneshaw, Parndana and Vivonne Bay.

BUS

Once they roll off the ferry, SeaLink coaches run from Penneshaw to Kingscote (one way adult/child $20/10). Call for times and bookings.

Rockhopper (☑ 13 13 01; www.kangarooisland.sa.gov.au/rockhopper) is a community bus service traversing eastern and western routes from Kingscote. The eastern service runs three times each way on Wednesdays, stopping at American River and Penneshaw; the western service runs twice daily on Tuesdays and Fridays, visiting Cygnet River, Parndana and Vivonne Bay. Flat-rate fares are one-way adult/child $10/5. Call for bookings.

---

❶ KI TOUR PASS

If you plan on seeing most of the main sights, save some cash with a **Kangaroo Island Tour Pass** (☑ 08-8553 4444; www.parks.sa.gov.au/book-and-pay/parks-passes/kangaroo-island-tour-pass; adult/child/family $74.50/43.50/197), which covers all KI park and conservation area entry fees, plus ranger-guided tours at Seal Bay, Kelly Hill Caves, Cape Borda and Cape Willoughby. Available online, at visitor centres or at most sights.

For minibus hire, A-to-B transfers or customised touring, check out **KI 24/7 Bus Charters** (☑ 0473 672 139; www.ki247buscharters.com.au).

Penneshaw & Dudley Peninsula

Looking across Backstairs Passage to the Fleurieu Peninsula, Penneshaw (population 300), on the north shore of the Dudley Peninsula, is the ferry arrival point and KI's second-biggest town. The passing tourist trade, including thousands of wandering cruise-ship passengers in summer, lends a certain transience to the businesses here, but the pub and the backpacker joint remain authentically grounded.

◉ Sights & Activities

Frenchman's Rock   MONUMENT
(Frenchman's Tce; ☺ 24hr) **FREE** When intrepid French explorer Nicholas Baudin surveyed the KI coast in 1803, he came ashore at what's now Penneshaw for a look around. He left his mark: under a white concrete dome on the shoreline is a replica of KI's first graffiti – a rock engraved with *'Expedition De Decouverte par le Commendant Baudin sur Le Geographe 1803'* ('Expedition of discovery by Commander Baudin on *Le Geographe* 1803'). The original rock can be seen safely preserved at the Gateway Visitor Information Centre (p752) nearby.

Kangaroo Island Farmers Market   MARKET
(☑ 08-8553 1237; www.facebook.com/pg/kangaroo islandfarmersmarket; Lloyd Collins Reserve, 99 Middle Tce; ☺ 9am-1pm 1st Sun of the month) Has baked goods, chutneys, seafood, olive oil, honey, eggs, cheese, yoghurt and of course wine and dodgy buskers (including, once,

a certain Lonely Planet writer who shall remain unnamed). SeaLink (p751) offers dedicated passenger-only return tickets (adult/child $42/32) from the mainland if you'd like to visit the market for the day. Additional market days happen when cruise-ship passengers are in town.

Cape Willoughby Lightstation LIGHTHOUSE
(☑ 08-8553 4410, 08-8553 4466; www.parks. sa.gov.au; Cape Willoughby Rd, Cape Willoughby; tours adult/child/family $16/10/42, self-guided tour not incl lighthouse $5; ⊙ guided tours 11am, 12.30pm & 2pm Thu-Mon, daily during school holidays) About 28km southeast of Penneshaw (via an unsealed road) on a treeless headland, this tidy white turret started shining out in 1852 (SA's first lighthouse) and is now used as a weather station. Inside is lots of shipwreck info, with basic cottage accommodation adjacent (doubles $225, extra adult/ child $30/15). Extra tours at 3pm and 4pm during school holidays. Interesting stuff.

**Penneshaw Penguin
Centre** WILDLIFE WATCHING
(☑ 08-8553 7407; www.penneshawpenguincentre. com; Foreshore, via Middle Tce; tours adult/child/ family $13/10/35; ⊙ dusk Wed-Sun) Seemingly unfazed by the massive vehicle ferries chugging into the jetty just metres away, Penneshaw's little colony of Little Penguins (about 15 breeding pairs) is a sweet sight to behold. They come waddling into shore every evening around dusk: these small-group, unintrusive guided tours are the only way to see them. Hours vary year-round – call ahead.

🛏 Sleeping & Eating

★ **Antechamber Bay
South Campground** CAMPGROUND $
(☑ 08-8204 1910; www.parks.sa.gov.au; off Creek Bay Rd, Antechamber Bay; unpowered sites per person/car $9/15) Within Lashmar Conservation Park where the Chapman River runs into Antechamber Bay, these dozen marvellously low-key campsites are right on the riverbank, with fire pits, a BBQ hut and silvery bream on the end of your fishing line. There are more sites on the north bank of the river.

Kangaroo Island Backpackers HOSTEL $
(☑ 0439 750 727; www.kangarooislandbackpackers. com; 43 North Tce; dm/s/tw $28/38/58, f $120-180; ℙ✳) A tidy, affable independent hostel a short wander from both the pub and the ferry dock – proximity is the main asset here. It's a simple, compact set-up, but hey, you're

on holiday on an island – who needs interior design? Dangle a line off the jetty instead.

Sea Dragon Lodge LODGE $$$
(☑ 0401 727 234; www.seadragonlodge.com.au; 2575 Willoughby Rd, Willoughby; d incl breakfast $780-1260, extra person $70; ℙ✳🛜) This beautiful three-bedroom timber lodge near Cape Willoughby is a high-end paradise, with polished timber floors, lofty ceilings, a mod kitchen and a broad BBQ deck with glorious coastal views. Airport and ferry transfers, 4WD tours and fishing trips also on offer. Breakfast hampers included; two-night minimum stay. Plush one-bedroom villas also available (doubles $535 to $859; single-night stays OK).

★ **Dudley Wines Cellar Door** CAFE $$
(☑ 08-8553 1333; www.dudleywines.com.au; 1153 Cape Willoughby Rd, Cuttlefish Bay; mains $15-44; ⊙ noon-3pm, bar 10am-5pm) About 12km east of Penneshaw, KI's pioneering winery has a winning cellar door – a fancy corrugated-iron shed, with astonishing views over a deep ravine and back to the mainland. On the menu are superb pizzas (big enough for two: try the King George whiting version), dips and KI produce platters – perfect with a bottle of chardonnay on the deck. Unbeatable.

Sunset Food & Wine BISTRO $$$
(☑ 08-8553 1378; www.sunsetfoodandwine.com; 4564 Hog Bay Rd; mains $31-37; ⊙ noon-3pm Tue & Wed, noon-2.30pm & 6-8.30pm Thu-Sat) Awesome view! If you can't make it up the steep driveway, there's another access around the back. Either way, expect brilliant modern bistro fare. Expect the likes of KI squid with pickled carrot, chorizo, cucumber and fennel salad. Saturday night is a six-course degustation menu ($89, plus $59 for wines).

ℹ Information

Gateway Visitor Information Centre (☑ 08-8553 1185; www.tourkangarooisland.com.au; 3 Howard Dr, Penneshaw; ⊙ 9am-5pm Mon-Fri, 10am-4pm Sat & Sun; 🛜) Just outside Penneshaw on the road to Kingscote, this centre is brimming with brochures and maps. Also books accommodation, and sells park entry tickets and the Kangaroo Island Tour Pass (p751).

Kingscote
☑ 08 / POP 1830
Once slated as the future capital city of the South Australian colony, snoozy seaside Kingscote (kings-coat) is the main settlement on KI, and the hub of island life. It's

ALL CREATURES GREAT & SMALL

You bump into a lot of wildlife on KI (sometimes literally). Kangaroos, wallabies, bandicoots and possums come out at night, especially in wilderness areas such as Flinders Chase National Park. Koalas and platypuses were introduced to Flinders Chase in the 1920s when it was feared they would become extinct on the mainland. Echidnas mooch around in the undergrowth, while goannas and tiger snakes keep KI suitably scaly.

Of the island's 267 bird species, several are rare or endangered. One notable species – the dwarf emu – has gone the way of the dodo. Glossy black cockatoos may soon follow it out the door due to habitat depletion.

Offshore, dolphins and southern right whales are often seen cavorting, and there are colonies of little penguins, New Zealand fur seals and Australian sea lions here too.

a photogenic town with swaying Norfolk Island pines, a couple of pubs and some decent eateries – but even in peak summer season it can be deathly (or pleasantly) quiet.

◉ Sights

Bay of Shoals Wines
WINERY

(☏08-8553 0289; www.bayofshoalswines.com. au; 49 Cordes Rd; ⊙11am-5pm) 🥢 Out past Kingscote's cemetery, overlooking the shallow Bay of Shoals itself (yes, plenty of shoals), this established winery instills confidence with its rows of mature vines and arrays of solar panels. Sip some pinot gris and munch into a tasting platter ($8 to $20).

Island Beehive
FARM

(☏08-8553 0080; www.island-beehive.com.au; 59 Playford Hwy; tours adult/child/family $6/5/18; ⊙9am-5pm, tours every 30min 10.30am-3.30pm) Runs 20-minute factory tours where you can study up on passive, hard-working Ligurian bees and bee-keeping, then stock up on by-products (bee-products?) including delicious organic honey and honeycomb ice cream. Tour-bus crowds aplenty.

🛏 Sleeping

KI Dragonfly Guesthouse
GUESTHOUSE $

(☏0400 197 231; www.kidragonfly.com; 19 Murray St; tw/d/f/cabin from $99/99/109/119; 🅿❄🛜) Just a couple of blocks from Kingscote's main strip, this small, bright-yellow guesthouse is clean and affordable, and has a cosy lounge, lush lawns, and a beaut en-suite double cabin out the back. It feels like staying at someone's house – good or bad, depending on how sociable you're feeling. Shared bathrooms; two-night minimum stay.

Ozone Hotel
HOTEL $$

(☏08-8553 2011; www.ozonehotelki.com.au; 67 Chapman Tce; d $195-245, 1-/2-/3-bedroom apt

from $275/445/515; 🅿❄🛜🌊) Opposite the foreshore with killer views, the 100-year-old Ozone has quality pub rooms upstairs, motel rooms, and stylish deluxe apartments in a new wing across the street. The eternally busy bistro (mains $19 to $36) serves meaty grills (KI lamb) and seafood (KI whiting), and you can pickle yourself on KI wines at the bar.

🍴 Eating & Drinking

★Amadio Wines
ITALIAN $$

(☏08-8553 3235; www.amadiowines.com/ki-cellar door; 1 Commercial St; pizzas $14-25; ⊙4pm-late) In a handsome corner shopfront with a lace-trimmed balcony, Amadio blasts reggae and retro Brit-pop into Kingscote's sleepy streets. It's a mainland-SA winery that also grows grapes on KI (try the sauvignon blanc and shiraz). Authentic Italian pizzas are baked in an imported Italian wood oven by an imported Italian chef. Share plates also available; head for the outdoor tables.

Cactus
CAFE $$

(☏0419 400 107; www.facebook.com/cactus.ki.59; 59 Dauncey St; mains $10-20; ⊙7.30am-2.30pm) Occupying a former Mexican restaurant (glad they kept the 'Day of the Dead' mural!), Cactus is a progressive Kingscote cafe run by a couple of ex-Southern Ocean Lodge employees. KI wines and beer complement interesting cafe fare – the likes of homemade Portuguese custard tarts and a prosciutto-and-pear open sandwich with salsa verde, goats' curd and rocket. Buzzy street-side terrace.

Kangaroo Island Brewery
BREWERY

(☏0409 264 817; www.kangarooislandbrewery. com.au; 61 North Coast Rd; ⊙11am-7pm Fri-Sun) Here a brewery, there a brewery... Seems you can't go anywhere in Australia these days without being tempted by craft beer, and KI is no exception. This neat, black roadside shack pours some tasty drops, including a ginger wheat bear and Sheoak Stout. Retro/rustic interiors set the scene.

North Coast Road

Exquisite beaches (calmer than the south coast), bushland and undulating pastures dapple the North Coast Rd, running from Kingscote along the coast to the Playford Hwy 85km west. There's not a whole lot to do here other than swan around on the beach – sounds good!

⊙ Sights

About 18km from Kingscote, Emu Bay is a holiday hamlet with a sensational, 5km-long, white-sand beach flanked by dunes – one of KI's best swimming spots (a fact surely not overlooked by the developers of a sprawling new subdivision not far from the sand). Around 36km further west, Stokes Bay has a penguin rookery and broad rock pool, accessible by scrambling through a 20m tunnel in the cliffs at the bay's eastern end (mind your head!). Beware the rip outside the pool.

Further west along North Coast Rd, the view as you look back over Snelling Beach from atop Constitution Hill is awesome. Continue 7km west and you'll hit the turn-off to Western River Cove, where a small beach is crowded in by sombre basalt cliffs. The ridgetop road in is utterly scenic (and steep).

🛏 Sleeping & Eating

Discovery Lagoon Caravan & Camping Grounds   CARAVAN PARK $
(☑0412 422 618; www.discoverycamping.com.au; 948 North Coast Rd, Emu Bay; unpowered sites $23-28, cabins incl linen $65; ℗) Not far along the road into Emu Bay after you turn off the North Coast Rd (all up, about 12km from Kingscote), this simple lakeside campground has lots of grass and shade, a neat camp kitchen and toilets, and the lake itself (or rather, lagoon – mostly dry when we visited) to look at, with ghostly white trunks standing resolute. Check in at 948 North Coast Rd.

Lifetime Private Rentals   RENTAL HOUSE $$$
(☑08-8559 2248; www.life-time.com.au; Snelling Beach, North Coast Rd, Middle River; d from $430, extra person $30; ℗❋⊛) Pricey but worth every penny, these four gorgeous self-contained stone-and-timber houses dot the hillsides above beautiful Snelling Beach (actually, they're not that pricey if

there's a few of you: from $600 for six people in three bedrooms). Expect decks, big windows, quirky artworks and knock-out views. Food-and-accommodation packages also available, including dining under the ancient Enchanted Fig Tree.

Rockpool Café   CAFE $$
(☑08-8559 2277; www.facebook.com/therockpool cafe; off North Coast Rd, Stokes Bay; mains $15-28; ◷11am-5pm Tue-Sun mid-Sep–mid-May) Don't worry about sandy feet at this casual, al fresco joint by the beach in Stokes Bay. 'What's the house special?', we asked. 'Whatever I feel like doin'!', said the chef (usually seafood, washed down with local wines and decent espresso). Occasionally open Friday nights.

Cygnet River & South Coast Road

Tracking from Kingscote through Cygnet River (population 80) to Flinders Chase National Park, the South Coast Rd doesn't often come close to the coast (at the Cygnet River end, at any rate). But if it did, you'd see that the wave-swept shores here are much less sheltered than those on the northern side of KI. This is wild country, and a great place to meet some island wildlife. And don't miss Vivonne Bay, one of SA's most beautiful beaches.

⊙ Sights & Activities

★ **Seal Bay Conservation Park**   NATURE RESERVE
(☑08-8553 4463; www.sealbay.sa.gov.au; Seal Bay Rd, Seal Bay; guided tours adult/child/family $35/20/86.50; ◷9am-5pm, to 6pm mid-Dec–Jan) ⊘ 'Observation, not interaction' is the mentality here. Guided tours stroll along the beach (or boardwalk on self-guided tours; adult/child/family $16/13/42.50) to a colony of (mostly sleeping) Australian sea lions, endemic to SA and WA (there are only about 14,700 of them left in the wild). Book tours in advance; lots of extra tour times during school holidays. Last entry 45 minutes before closing time.

Kangaroo Island Spirits   DISTILLERY
(KIS; ☑08-8553 9211; www.kispirits.com.au; 856 Playford Hwy, Cygnet River; bottles from $47; ◷11am-5.30pm Wed-Mon, daily during school holidays) One of SA's original gin distillers (there are now more than 20!), this fiesty little moonshiner makes small-batch gin with KI native juniper

berries, plus vodka, brandy and liqueurs (pray the organic honey-and-walnut version hasn't sold out).

Clifford's Honey Farm   FARM

(📞 08-8553 8295; www.cliffordshoney.com.au; 1157 Elsegood Rd, Haines; ⏰ 9am-5pm) **FREE** It's worth swimming the Backstairs Passage for the honey ice cream (sourced from rare Ligurian bees) at this charming, uncommercial farm, which is a bit off the tourist radar. Honey-infused drinks, biscuits, mead, cosmetics and candles are also available. Look for the queen bee in the glass-fronted beehive. There's often a food truck on-site (burgers, fries, arancini balls; items $14 to $16); and **Drunken Drone Brewery** (www.facebook.com/drunkendrone brewery) is here too, bottling up yeasty Honey Wheat Ale.

Kelly Hill Conservation Park   NATURE RESERVE

(📞 08-8553 4464; www.parks.sa.gov.au; South Coast Rd, Hanson Bay; tours adult/child/family $20/11/52, adventure caving adult/child $76.50/45.50; ⏰ visitor centre 10.15am-4.30pm) This series of dry limestone caves was 'discovered' in the 1880s by a horse named Kelly, who fell into them through a hole. Take the standard show cave tour (10.30am, then hourly 11am to 4pm); or add on an adventure caving tour (2.15pm; bookings essential). The **Hanson Bay Walk** (9km one way) runs from the caves past freshwater wetlands. There are extra show cave tours during school holidays.

Kangaroo Island Outdoor Action   KAYAKING

(📞 08-8559 4296; www.kioutdooraction.com.au; 188 Jetty Rd, Vivonne Bay; ⏰ 9am-5pm Oct-Apr, 10am-4pm May-Sep) Rents out single/double kayaks ($47/77 for four hours). Two-hour kayak tours also available ($97 per person). Also has an outlet at **Little Sahara** (off South Coast Rd, Vivonne Bay; ⏰ 24hr) **FREE** near Seal Bay on the South Coast Rd, from which it proffers sandboards and toboggans ($47 per day) to skid down the amazing dunes.

🛏 Sleeping & Eating

Flinders Chase Farm   LODGE $

(📞 0447 021 494; www.flinderschasefarm.com.au; 1561 West End Hwy, Karatta; dm/cabin/d/f from $30/82/112/214; 🅿) A working farm with charm, a short drive from Flinders Chase National Park. Accommodation includes tidy dorms, a couple of cosy cabins and en-suite rooms in a lodge. There's also a terrific camp kitchen, fire pits and 'tropical' outdoor showers.

ℹ NATIONAL PARKS PASS

Around 22% of SA's land area is under some form of official conservation management, including national parks, recreation parks, conservation parks and wildlife reserves. National Parks South Australia (www.parks.sa.gov.au) manages the state's conservation areas and sells park passes and camping permits. A handy two-month multiple-entry vehicle pass ($40) covers entry to 11 of SA's key national and conservation parks, excluding the desert parks and Flinders Chase on Kangaroo Island. Purchase online or at park offices.

★ Southern Ocean Lodge   LUXURY HOTEL $$$

(📞 08-8559 7347; www.southernoceanlodge.com.au; Hanson Bay Rd, Hanson Bay; d from $1450; 🅿✳@🛜🏊) Looking for a place to woo your sweetheart? The shining star in the SA tourism galaxy is Southern Ocean Lodge, a sexy, low-profile snake tracing the Hanson Bay cliff-top – a really lovely piece of architecture, and an utterly lovely place to stay. Two-night minimum; prices include airport transfers, all meals and drinks, and guided tours of KI. World-class luxury.

Sunken lounges, opulent king-sized beds, glass-walled bathrooms, complimentary mini-bar, twice-daily housekeeping, day spa... The facilities list here is as lengthy as the view. The vibe is exclusive and super-private but still down-to-earth, attracting everyone from 50th-wedding-anniversary couples to Hollywood celebs.

★ SupaShak   RENTAL HOUSE $$$

(📞 08-8410 4557; www.sealink.com.au/kangaroo-island-accommodation/470-supashak; Flinders St, Vivonne Bay; d from $360, extra person $30; 🅿) Oh look, a lunar landing pod has touched down in the Vivonne Bay dunes... This angular architectural spacecraft is future-fantastic, responding to the bushfire-prone locale with steel and fibre-cement construction and lots of water storage. Geared towards longer stays (minimum three nights), with room for six bods. The wood fire cranks in winter; ceiling fans spin in summer.

Marron Café   MODERN AUSTRALIAN $$

(📞 08-8559 4114; www.andermel.com/cafe; 804 Harriet Rd, Central Kangaroo Island; mains $18-46; ⏰ 11am-4.30pm Oct-Apr, noon-3.30pm May-Sep) Around 15km north of Vivonne Bay, you can check out marron (naive freshwater cray-fish) in breeding tanks, then eat some! It's a subtle taste, not always enhanced by the heavy sauces issued by the kitchen. There are salads, steak and chicken dishes too, for the crustacean-shy. Last orders 30 minutes before closing. Two Wheeler Creek winery cellar door is here too.

Flinders Chase National Park

Occupying the western end of the island, Flinders Chase National Park is one of SA's top national parks. Much of the park is mallee scrub, and there are also some beautiful, tall sugar-gum forests, particularly around Rocky River and the Ravine des Casoars, 5km south of Cape Borda. Sadly, around 100,000 acres of bush were burned out by bushfires in 2007, but the park is making a steady recovery. Kooky rock formations and brilliant bushwalks are the highlights. Pay your park entry fees online or at the Flinders Chase Visitor Information Centre.

◉ Sights & Activities

Once a farm, Rocky River (☑ 08-8553 4470; www.parks.sa.gov.au; South Coast Rd, Flinders Chase National Park; park entry 1/2 days $22/32; ⊙ daylight hours), the area around the visitor centre, is now a rampant hotbed of wildlife, with kangaroos, wallabies and Cape Barren geese competing for your affections. A slew of good walks launch from behind the visitor centre, including the Rocky River Hike (9km loop, three hours), on which you might spy a platypus. There's also camping and accommodation here.

From Rocky River, a road runs south to a remote 1906 lighthouse (☑ 08-8553 4470; www.parks.sa.gov.au; via Cape du Couedic Rd, Flinders Chase National Park; park entry 1/2 days $22/32; ⊙ daylight hours) atop wild Cape du Couedic (de *coo*-dik). You can't access the lighthouse, but it's nice to look at. There's cottage accommodation here too. Not far away, a boardwalk weaves down to Admirals Arch, a huge archway ground out by heavy seas, and passes a colony of New Zealand fur seals (sweet smelling they ain't...).

At Kirkpatrick Point, a few kilometres east of Cape du Couedic, the much-photographed, rather Dalí-esque Remarkable Rocks are a cluster of hefty, weather-gouged granite boulders atop a rocky dome that arcs 75m down to the sea.

On the northwestern corner of the island, the square 1858 Cape Borda Lightstation (☑ 08-8553 4465; Playford Hwy; tours adult/child/family $16/10/42, self-guided tour $5; ⊙ 9am-5pm Fri-Tue, daily during school holidays, tours 11am, 12.30pm & 2pm) stands tall above the rippling iron surface of the Southern Ocean. There are walks here from 1.5km to 9km, and extra tours at 3.15pm and 4pm during summer holidays. The cannon is fired at 12.30pm! There's accommodation here too.

At nearby Harvey's Return, a cemetery speaks poignant volumes about the reality of isolation in the early days. From here you can drive to Ravine des Casoars (via Ravine Rd), literally 'Ravine of the Cassowaries', referring to the now-extinct dwarf emus seen here by Baudin's expedition. The challenging Ravine des Casoars Hike (8km return, four hours) tracks through the ravine to the coast.

★ Kangaroo Island
Wilderness Trail   HIKING
(☑ 08-8553 4410; www.kangarooislandwilderness trail.sa.gov.au; Flinders Chase Visitor Information Centre, South Coast Rd, Flinders Chase; adult/child $164.50/98) The big-ticket bushwalk in Flinders Chase NP is this five-day, four-night wilderness trail – an excellent 61km adventure through the park wilds, with dedicated campsites or beds off-trail if you're in need of some comfort. The trail starts at the park visitor centre and ends at Kelly Hill Conservation Park on the south coast. Maximum numbers apply; book online.

⨳ Sleeping & Eating

There are campgrounds at Rocky River (via Cape de Couedic Rd, Flinders Chase National Park; per vehicle $30.50), Snake Lagoon (Snake Lagoon Rd, Flinders Chase National Park; per vehicle $15), West Bay (West Bay Rd, Flinders Chase National Park; per vehicle $15) and Harvey's Return (Ravine Rd, Flinders Chase National Park; per vehicle $15). You'll need a 4WD for Harvey's Return and West Bay.

There's also refurbished cottage accommodation at Rocky River – budget Postman's Cottage (South Coast Rd,; d $76.50, extra person $26) and family-friendly May's Homestead (South Coast Rd; d $179.50, extra adult/child $30/15) – and lightkeepers' cottages at Cape du Couedic (via Cape du Couedic Rd; d $225, extra adult/child $30/15) and Cape Borda (Playford Hwy; d $50-225, extra adult/child $30/15).

Book park accommodation at www.parks. sa.gov.au/booking, through the Flinders Chase Visitor Information Centre, or at the

Natural Resources Centre (☑ 08-8553 4444; www.naturalresources.sa.gov.au/kangarooisland; 37 Dauncey St; ⊙ 9am-5pm Mon-Fri) in Kingscote.

Chase Cafe
CAFE $$

(☑ 08-8559 7339; www.thechasecafe.net; 442 Cape du Couedic Rd, Flinders Chase National Park; snacks from $6, mains $12-30; ⊙ 9am-5pm) On the food front, if you're not self-catering the only option within Flinders Chase National Park is the buzzy, daytime Chase Cafe at the visitor centre, serving burgers, wraps, soup, pizzas, big salads, Kangaroo Island whiting, coffee and KI wines by the glass.

❶ Information

Flinders Chase Visitor Information Centre (☑ 08-8553 4470, accommodation 08-8553 4410, camping 08-8553 4471; www.parks. sa.gov.au; 442 Cape du Couedic Rd, Flinders Chase; park entry 1/2 days $22/32; ⊙ 9am-5pm) Info, park passes, maps and camping/ accommodation bookings, plus the Chase Cafe and displays on island ecology.

BAROSSA VALLEY

With hot, dry summers and cool, moderate winters, the Barossa is one of the world's great wine regions and an absolute must for wine fans. It's a compact valley – just 25km long – but the Barossa produces 21% of Australia's wine, and it makes a no-fuss day trip from Adelaide, 65km away.

Dating back to 1842, Barossa towns have a distinctly German feel. Fleeing religious persecution in Prussia and Silesia, settlers (bringing their vine cuttings with them) created a Lutheran heartland where German traditions endure today. Cultural legacies of the early days include a dubious passion for oompah bands, and an appetite for wurst, sauerkraut and pretzels.

And of course, before the shiraz, this was – and is – Peramangk country, bordering on Ngadjuri lands further north. There's little to see regarding the traditional owners today, other than Peramangk Rd in Nuriootpa and an underwhelming display at Tanunda's Barossa Museum.

☞ Tours

Barossa Valley Ambler
TOURS

(☑ 0414 447 134; www.ambler.net.au; full day from $129) Door-to-door small group Barossa explorations ex-Adelaide, Hahndorf or Glenelg, stopping at wineries big and small, Mengler's Hill Lookout, the Whispering Wall and Maggie Beer's Farm Shop for lunch (not included). Visits Rockford Winery (our fave).

Barossa Taste Sensations
FOOD & DRINK

(☑ 0457 101 487; www.barossatours.com.au; half-/ full day from $160/250) Flavour-packed small-group tours in a comfy VW, focusing on food as much as wine. The half-day 'fast-track' tour (ex-Barossa only) is a zippy oversight of the whole valley.

Bums on Seats Tours
TOURS

(☑ 0438 808 253; www.bumsonseatstours.com.au; adult/child from $99/45) Plant your buttocks on a seat on these good-fun minibus tours, visiting Lyndoch, Tanunda, Nuriootpa and Angaston, and all the good bits in between. Ex-Adelaide.

✵ Festivals & Events

Barossa Gourmet Weekend
FOOD & DRINK

(www.barossagourmet.com; ⊙ Sep) Fab food matched with winning wines at select wineries; usually happens in September. The number-one event in the valley (book your beds *waaay* in advance).

Barossa Vintage Festival
FOOD & DRINK

(www.barossavintagefestival.com.au; ⊙ Apr) A weeklong festival with music, maypole dancing, tug-of-war contests etc; around Easter (harvest time – very atmospheric) in odd-numbered years.

❶ Getting There & Away

The Barossa Valley makes an easy day-trip from Adelaide, just 65km southwest of the region. If you're driving, consider the slightly longer route through the Adelaide Hills (via Woodside, Birdwood, Mt Pleasant and Springton), which is super-scenic and infinitely more appealing than the traffic snarl of Main North Rd (A20).

Adelaide Metro (www.adelaidemetro.com.au) runs regular daily trains from Adelaide to Gawler ($5.50, one hour), from where LinkSA (www. linksa.com.au) buses run to Lyndoch ($5.90, 30 minutes), Tanunda ($10.70, 45 minutes), Nuriootpa ($13.50, one hour) and Angaston ($16.40, 1¼ hours).

No public transport runs to Greenock – DIY.

❶ Getting Around

BICYCLE

The 27km **Jack Bobridge Track** runs from Gawler to Tanunda, with a 14km **rail trail** continuing through Nuriootpa to Angaston, passing plenty of wineries. It's part of the longer (40km)

Barossa Valley

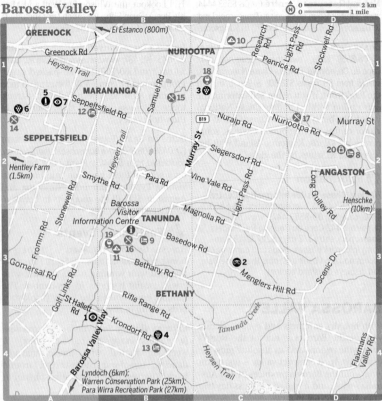

El Estanco (800m)

Barossa Valley

⊙ Sights
1 Keg Factory A4
2 Mengler's Hill Lookout C3
3 Penfolds C1
4 Rockford Wines B4
5 Seppelt Family Mausoleum A1
6 Seppeltsfield A1
7 Seppeltsfield Road A1

🛏 Sleeping
8 Angaston Masonic Lodge D2
9 Barossa Backpackers B3
10 BIG4 Barossa Tourist Park C1
11 Discover Holiday Parks Barossa
    Valley B3
12 Louise A1
13 The Kirche @ Charles Melton B4

⊗ Eating
14 Fino Seppeltsfield A2
15 Maggie Beer's Farm Shop &
    Eatery B1
16 Red Door Espresso B3
17 Vintners Bar & Grill D2

⊖ Drinking & Nightlife
18 Barossa Distilling Company C1
19 Barossa Valley Brewing B3
    Stein's Taphouse .... (see 18)

🛍 Shopping
    Barossa Farmers Market .... (see 17)
20 Barossa Valley Cheese Company D2

north–south **Barossa Trail**. Pick up the *Barossa by Bike* brochure at the Barossa Visitor Information Centre (p760) in Tanunda, or download one from its website.

Based in Nuriootpa, **Barossa Bike Hire** (☎0400 537 770; www.barossabikehire.com; 5 South Tce, Nuriootpa; ⊗9am-5pm) rents out quality cycles/tandems from $40/80 per day (pick-up price: bikes can be delivered for $10/20

ADELAIDE & SOUTH AUSTRALIA BAROSSA VALLEY

DON'T MISS

BEST BOTTLES: BAROSSA VALLEY WINE REGION

The Barossa is best known for shiraz, with riesling the dominant white. There are 80-plus vineyards here and around 60 cellar doors, ranging from boutique wine rooms to monstrous complexes. The long-established 'Barossa Barons' hold sway – big, ballsy and brassy – while spritely young boutique wineries are harder to sniff out.

Penfolds (☎08-8568 8408; www.penfolds.com; 30 Tanunda Rd, Nuriootpa; ⏲9am-5pm) You know the name: Penfolds is a Barossa legend. Book ahead for the Make Your Own Blend tour ($65), or the Taste of Grange tour ($150), which allows you to slide some luscious Grange Hermitage across your lips (if you want to buy a bottle, prices kick off at around $900).

Rockford Wines (☎08-8563 2720; www.rockfordwines.com.au; 131 Krondorf Rd, Tanunda; ⏲11am-5pm) One of our favourite boutique Barossa wineries (OK, so it is our favourite), this 1850s cellar door sells traditionally made, small-range wines, including sparkling reds. The Black Shiraz is a sparkling, spicy killer.

Seppeltsfield (☎08-8568 6200; www.seppeltsfield.com.au; 730 Seppeltsfield Rd, Maranaga; ⏲10.30am-5pm) The atmospheric, bluestone Seppletsfield estate started life in 1851 when Joe Seppelt stuck some vines in the dirt and came up trumps. Now it's one of Australia's most esteemed wine brands, most famous for its 100-year-old Para Tawny. Not into port? Everything else here is similarly rich and luscious, including the food at Fino (p760), one of Australia's top restaurants.

extra). Electric bikes, foodie hampers and guided half-day bike tours are also available. In Tanunda, run by the visitor centre, the **Barossa Cycle Hub** (☎1300 852 982; www.barossa.com/visit/see-do/cycling/barossa-cycle-hub; 70 Murray St, Tanunda; ⏲9am-5pm Mon-Fri, 9am-4pm Sat, 10am-4pm Sun) has bikes per half-/full day for $30/45. **Angaston Hardware** (☎08-8564 2055; www.angastonhardware.com.au; 5 Sturt St, Angaston; ⏲8.30am-5.30pm Mon-Fri, 9am-4pm Sat, 10am-4pm Sun) also rents out bikes for $25/35 per half-/full day.

TAXI

Barossa Taxis (☎0411 150 850; www.barossataxis.com.au; ⏲24hr) Taxis for up to nine people.

Tanunda

☎08 / POP 4560

At the centre of the valley both geographically and socially, Tanunda is the Barossa's main tourist town. Tanunda manages to morph the practicality of Nuriootpa with the charm of Angaston without a sniff of self-importance. There are some great eateries around town, but the wineries are what you're here for – sip, sip, sip!

Sights

Mengler's Hill Lookout VIEWPOINT
(Menglers Hill Rd; ⏲24hr) FREE From Tanunda, take the scenic route to Angaston via Bethany for hazy valley views (just ignore the naff sculptures in the foreground). The road tracks through beautiful rural country, studded with huge eucalyptus trees.

Keg Factory FACTORY
(☎08-8563 3012; www.thekegfactory.com.au; 25 St Hallett Rd; ⏲8am-4pm Mon-Fri, 11am-4pm Sat) FREE Watch honest-to-goodness coopers make and repair wine barrels, 4km south of town. Amazing! If you want to roll one home, kegs start at $325.

Sleeping

Discover Holiday Parks Barossa Valley CARAVAN PARK $
(☎08-8563 2784; www.discoveryholidayparks.com.au; Barossa Valley Way; unpowered/powered sites from $38/47, cabins with/without bathroom from $162/119, safari tents $180, villas from $266; ❄📶🏊) This spacious park just south of town is dotted with mature trees offering a little shade to ease your hangover. Facilities include a playground, BBQs, a laundry and bike hire for guests ($35 per day). The flashy two- and three-bedroom villas sleep up to six. Our pick are the new, and rather glamorous, en-suite safari tents with trim little decks.

Barossa Backpackers HOSTEL $
(☎08-8563 0198; www.barossabackpackers.com.au; 9 Basedow Rd; dm/s/d from $28/80/80;

P @ 🛜) Occupying a converted, U-shaped winery office building 500m from Tanunda's main street, Barossa Backpackers is a clean, secure and shipshape affair (if a little soulless), with good weekly rates. Management can help you find local picking/pruning work.

★ **The Kirche @ Charles Melton** B&B $$$
(🛜08-8563 3606; www.charlesmeltonwines.com.au/the-kirche; 192 Krondorf Rd; d $515, extra adult/child $75/40; P ✳ 🛜) Knocked together in 1964, this old stone Lutheran church – the Zum Kripplein Christi church, in fact – is now a fabulous boutique B&B. It's a few minutes' drive south of central Tanunda, on the same road as a string of good wineries. Inside you'll find black leather couches, a marble-tiled bathroom, two bedrooms and a cranking winter wood-heater. Two-night minimum.

✖ Eating & Drinking

★ **Red Door Espresso** CAFE $$
(🛜08-8563 1181; www.reddoorespresso.com; 79 Murray St; mains $8-29; ⏱7.30am-5pm Wed-Sat, 9.30am-4pm Sun; 🛜🐾) A decent cafe shouldn't be hard to create, but it's rare in the Barossa for good food, coffee, staff, music and atmosphere to come together this well. The avocado and basil-infused eggs Benedict is a winner, best consumed with an eye-opening coffee in the pot-planted courtyard. Live music over weekend brunch; wine, cheese and antipasto in the afternoons.

★ **Fino Seppeltsfield** MODERN AUSTRALIAN $$$
(🛜08-8562 8528; www.fino.net.au; 730 Seppeltsfield Rd, Seppeltsfield; 3/4/5 plates $48/65/75, incl wine $83/115/135; ⏱noon-3pm daily, 6-8.30pm Fri & Sat) From humble beginnings in a little stone cottage on the Fleurieu Peninsula, Fino has evolved into one of Australia's best restaurants, now ensconced in the gorgeous 1851 Seppeltsfield estate west of Tanunda. Food from the understated, deceptively simple menu highlights local ingredients, and is designed to be shared. Try the dry-aged sirloin with anchovies, chard and butter.

Hentley Farm MODERN AUSTRALIAN $$$
(🛜08-8562 8427; www.hentleyfarm.com.au; cnr Gerald Roberts & Jenke Rds, Seppeltsfield; 4-/7-course menu $115/190, incl wine $160/265; ⏱noon-2.30pm Thu-Sun, 6.30-8.30pm Fri & Sat) What? Yet another of SA's best restaurants here in the Barossa? Correct. Hentley Farm is a top-quality outfit, occupying an 1880s

stables building on Hentley Farm itself, now more given over to grapevines than anything requiring a stable. Chef Lachlan Colwill's menu is regional all the way, paired with superb wines from the adjacent cellar door. Just wonderful.

Barossa Valley Brewing CRAFT BEER
(🛜08-8563 0696; www.bvbeer.com.au; 2a Murray St, Tanunda; ⏱noon-4pm Mon-Wed, noon-9pm Thu-Sunstretc) Beer! Real beer, here among all the wine! On Tanunda's southern fringe, BVB has a paved terrace beneath some astoundingly big eucalypts, just made for an afternoon with a few easy-drinking IPAs. You can also peer at the stout steel tanks in the brewery, or grab a pizza, burger or some ribs from the brasserie (mains $17 to $33).

ℹ Information

Barossa Visitor Information Centre (🛜1300 852 982, 08-8563 0600; www.barossa.com; 66-68 Murray St, Tanunda; ⏱9am-5pm Mon-Fri, 9am-4pm Sat, 10am-4pm Sun; 🛜) The low-down on the whole valley, plus bike hire and accommodation and tour bookings. Stocks the *A Town Walk of Tanunda* brochure.

Nuriootpa

🛜08 / POP 6320
Along an endless main street at the northern end of the valley, Nuriootpa is the Barossa's commercial centre. It's not as endearing as Tanunda or Angaston, but it has a certain agrarian simplicity. There's a big new supermarket complex here too, and unlike many South Australian towns, the population in 'Nuri' is actually growing. Perhaps it has something to do with Lutheran spirit: a sign says, 'God has invested in you – are you showing any interest?'

◎ Sights & Activities

Seppeltsfield Road STREET
(🛜1300 852 982; www.seppeltsfieldroad.com; Seppeltsfield Rd, Marananga; ⏱24hr) FREE Don't miss a drive along Seppeltsfield Road, an incongruous avenue of huge palm trees meandering through the vineyards behind Nuri. Beyond Marananga, the palm rows veer off the roadside and track up a hill to the **Seppelt Family Mausoleum** (🛜08-8568 6217; Lot 2 Seppeltsfield Rd) – a 1927 Grecian tomb fronted by chunky Doric columns. Great views! Quite a few ex-Seppelts are interred here – be respectful.

🛏 Sleeping

BIG4 Barossa Tourist Park CARAVAN PARK $
(☑ 08-8562 1404; www.barossatouristpark.com.
au; Penrice Rd; unpowered/powered sites from
$35/50, cabins from $100; P ✳ 🛜 ☒) There are
at least six different kinds of cabin at this
shady park lined with pine trees, next to the
Nuriootpa football oval (go Tigers!). All cabins have TVs, fridges and cooking facilities
(not all come with linen). Check out the 1930
Dodge 'House on Wheels' out the front – the
seminal caravan?

Louise BOUTIQUE HOTEL $$$
(☑ 08-8562 2722; www.thelouise.com.au; 375 Sep-
peltsfield Rd, Marananga; d from $625; P ✳ @ 🛜 ☒)
Top of the accommodation tree in the BV, the
Louise does everything with consummate
style, from the architecture and the linen to
the in-house restaurant Appellation and the
smile at the front desk. Louise might stretch
your wallet, but is worth every stretch mark.
Marananga (less a town, more an area) is
equidistant from Nuriootpa and Tanunda.

🍴 Eating & Drinking

Maggie Beer's Farm Shop & Eatery DELI $
(☑ eatery 08-8562 1902, shop 08-8562 4477; www.
maggiebeer.com.au; 50 Pheasant Farm Rd, Nuri-
ootpa; items $5-20, hampers from $25, mains $34-
38; ☺ shop 10.30am-5pm, eatery noon-3pm Mon-Fri,
11am-3pm Sat & Sun) Celebrity SA gourmet
Maggie Beer has been hugely successful with
her quality condiments, preserves and pâtés
(and TV appearances!). The vibe here isn't as
relaxed as it used to be, but stop by for some
gourmet tastings, an ice cream, a picnic ham-
per or a cooking demo (2pm daily). There's a
high-end restaurant here now too – the Farm
Eatery (www.thefarmeatery.com).

★ El Estanco SOUTH AMERICAN $$
(☑ 0438 006 552; www.elestanco.com.au; 23 Murray
St, Greenock; mains $17-26; ☺ 8am-4pm Wed-Mon,
6-10pm Fri) 🍷 Run by a charismatic couple – a
Columbian and a Brit – El Estanco is one of
the best things to happen to the Barossa in
recent times. Earthy, authentic, wholesome,
value-for-money and ethically attuned, it's a
casual eatery in a 70-year-old cottage, serving
a mash-up of Latin-influenced fare (sublime
pulled-pork tacos) and English edibles (giant
slabs of cake). Local wines galore.

★ Stein's Taphouse CRAFT BEER
(☑ 08-8562 2899; www.steinstaphouse.com.au;
18-28 Barossa Valley Way; ☺ noon-late) Inside the
old Penfolds complex is this excellent craft
beer bar (sacrilege?), also serving artisanal
spirits, small-production SA wines and food
that pairs up nicely with all three (burgers,
pork ribs, chilli con carne). There are a dozen
beer taps: study the blackboard behind the
bar and pick something local (oh look –
Greenock Brewers!). Regular live country
and blues.

Barossa Distilling Company DISTILLERY
(☑ 0498 999 934; www.barossadistilling.com; 18-28
Barossa Valley Way; ☺ 11am-5pm Mon, Wed, Thu &
Sun, 11am-10pm Fri, 11am-6pm Sat) Inside Penfolds' old decommissioned brandy distillery,
which is nothing short of *amazing* – an
Orwellian mesh of pipes, huge vats and elaborate spiral stairs, built in 1929 – Barossa Distilling Company does good things with gin,
either citrus-, fruity- or maple syrup-infused.
Sit on the sunny terrace and slurp a few G&Ts,
a welcome relief after all that shiraz.

Angaston
☑ 08 / POP 2100
Photo-worthy Angaston – the best-looking
town in the Barossa – was named after
George Fife Angas, a pioneering Barossa
pastoralist. An agricultural vibe persists, as
there are relatively few wineries on Angaston's doorstep: cows graze in paddocks at
end of the town's streets, and there's a vague
whiff of fertiliser in the air. Along the pretty
main drag are two pubs and some terrific
cafes and eateries.

🛏 Sleeping & Eating

Angaston Masonic Lodge B&B $$$
(☑ 0419 323 532; www.angastonmasoniclodge.com;
56 Murray St, Angaston; d incl breakfast from $250,
extra person $50; P ✳ 🛜) Wow, what a beauty!
Right in the middle of town, Angaston's 1910
temple of secret handshakes and clandestine
male behaviour is now a stylish two-bedroom
B&B, sleeping four in contemporary comfort.
Bonuses include lofty ceilings (hey, it's a hall),
kitchenette, pool table and free scooters to
zoom around on.

★ Vintners Bar & Grill MODERN AUSTRALIAN $$$
(☑ 08-8564 2488; www.vintners.com.au; cnr Stock-
well & Nuriootpa Rds, Angaston; mains $36-42;
☺ noon-2.30pm daily, 6.30-9pm Mon-Sat) One of
the Barossa's landmark restaurants, Vintners
emphasises simple elegance in both food and
atmosphere. The dining room has an open
fire, vineyard views and bolts of crisp white
linen; menus concentrate on local produce

(the Moroccan-spiced kangaroo with chick-peas and beets is a flavour sensation). A super-classy stayer.

🛍 Shopping

Barossa Valley Cheese Company CHEESE
(☎08-8564 3636; www.barossacheese.com.au; 67b Murray St, Angaston; ⊙10am-5pm Mon-Fri, to 4pm Sat, 11am-3pm Sun) The Barossa Valley Cheese Company is a fabulously stinky room, selling handmade cheeses from the milk of local cows and goats. Tastings are free, but it's unlikely you'll leave without buying a wedge of Washington Washed Rind. Sit outside with a wine-and-cheese flight or a camembert vs brie taste-off plate (both $20 per person). Tourist brochures and maps available.

Barossa Farmers Market MARKET
(☎0402 026 882; www.barossafarmersmarket.com; cnr Stockwell & Nuriootpa Rds, Angaston; ⊙7.30-11.30am Sat) Happens every Saturday in the big farm shed behind Vintners Bar & Grill, a few kilometres west of central Angaston. Expect hearty Germanic offerings, coffee, flowers, lots of local produce and questionable buskers.

CLARE VALLEY

At the centre of the fertile Mid North agricultural district, two hours north of Adelaide, the wine bottle–slender Clare Valley produces world-class, sweet-scented rieslings and mineral-rich reds. This is gorgeous countryside – Ngadjuri Indigenous homelands – with open skies, rounded hills, stands of large gums and wind rippling over wheat fields. Towns here date from the 1840s; many were built to service the Burra copper mines.

You can tackle the Clare Valley as a day trip from Adelaide, but when the wine and food are this good, why rush? Spend a few days exploring old-fangled towns, cycling between cellar doors, eating and revelling in the general pleasures of life.

☞ Tours

A Wine Wagon WINE
(☎0488 065 347; www.awinewagon.com.au; per person incl lunch $140) Great-value, full-day tours with an operator who's genuinely interested in wine, seeking out some of the valley's more unusual drops. Ex-Clare Valley or Barossa Valley. Maximum 10 bums on seats.

★ Festivals & Events

Clare Valley Gourmet Weekend FOOD & DRINK
(www.clarevalley.com.au; ⊙May) A fab frenzy of Clare Valley wine, food and music in May. LinkSA (www.linksa.com.au) buses get involved, with shuttles to/from Adelaide ($75). Book your B&B beds miles in advance.

ℹ Getting There & Around

Your own set of wheels is the easiest way to access the Clare Valley, affording ultimate flexibility. Note that the main Clare Valley through-route is called either the Horrocks Hwy or Main North Rd, depending on who you talk to. On a good day, it's a 117km, 90-minute drive north from Adelaide to Auburn at the valley's southern end.

If you're relying on public transport, **Yorke Peninsula Coaches** (☎08-8821 2755; www.ypcoaches.com.au) runs from Adelaide to Auburn ($38, 2¼ hours) and Clare ($46, 2¾ hours) on Monday, Wednesday, Friday and Sunday (also running in the opposite direction on these days). Services extend to Burra ($46, 3¼ hours) on Wednesday only.

THE RIESLING TRAIL

Following the course of a disused railway line between Auburn and Barinia, north of Clare, the fabulous Riesling Trail (www.rieslingtrail.com.au) is 33km of wines, wheels and wonderment. It's primarily a cycling trail, but the gentle gradient means you can walk or push a pram along it just as easily. It's a two-hour dash end to end on a bike, but why hurry? There are three loop track detours and extensions to explore, and dozens of cellar doors to tempt you along the way. The **Rattler Trail** (www.riverton.sa.com/discover/rattler-trail) continues for another 19km south of Auburn to Riverton.

For bike hire, check out **Clare Valley Cycle Hire** (☎0418 802 077; www.clarevalleycyclehire.com.au; 32 Victoria Rd, Clare; bike hire per half-/full day $20/30; ⊙9am-5pm) or **Riesling Trail Bike Hire** (☎0418 777 318; www.rieslingtrailbikehire.com.au; 10 Warenda Rd, Clare; bike hire per half-/full day $25/40, tandems $40/60, kids' bikes $15/25; ⊙8.30am-6.30pm Wed-Mon, Tue by appointment) in Clare, or **Cogwebs Hub Cafe** (☎0400 290 687; www.cogwebs.com.au; 30 Horrocks Hwy, Auburn; bike hire per half-/full day $25/40, tandems $35/60; ⊙9am-4pm) in Auburn.

DON'T MISS

BEST BOTTLES: CLARE VALLEY WINE REGION

The Clare Valley's microclimate, with cool air circulating around rivers, creeks and gullies, noticeably affects the local wines, enabling whites to be laid down for long periods and still be brilliant. The valley produces some of the world's best riesling, plus grand semillon and some challengingly flinty shiraz.

Jeanneret Wines (☑08-8843 4308; www.jeanneretwines.com; 22 Jeanneret Rd, Sevenhill; ⊗10am-5pm Mon-Sat, noon-5pm Sun) For some of the loveliest rosé you're ever likely to taste, squirrel out Jeanneret Wines, way up a bush-crowded dirt road beyond the much-better-known Skillogalee. Sip a few at the bar, select your bottle of choice, then repair to the deck with your BYO picnic. Clare Valley Brewing Co (CVBC; ☑08-8843 4308; www.cvbc.beer; 22 Jeanneret Rd, Sevenhill; ⊗10am-5pm Mon-Sat, noon-5pm Sun) is here too.

Sevenhill Cellars (☑08-8843 4222; www.sevenhill.com.au; 111c College Rd, Sevenhill; ⊗10am-5pm) Like a little religion, guilt or forgiveness with your drink? This place was established by Jesuits in 1851, making it the oldest winery in the Clare Valley (check out the incredible 1866 St Aloysius Church near the cellar door). Oh, and the wine is mighty fine too!

Skillogalee (☑08-8843 4311; www.skillogalee.com.au; 23 Trevarrick Rd, Sevenhill; ⊗7.30am-5pm) Skillogalee is a small family outfit known for its spicy shiraz, fabulous food and top-notch riesling. Kick back with a long, lazy meal on the verandah (breakfast mains $17 to $22, lunch $24 to $49; book ahead). This place just might be heaven.

In Auburn and Clare, you can hire a bike to pelt around the wineries. Rates are around $25/40 per half-/full day.

Clare Valley Taxis (☑08-8842 1400) will drop off/pick up anywhere along the Riesling Trail.

Auburn

☑08 / POP 660

Sleepy Auburn (founded 1849) – the Clare Valley's southernmost village – is a leave-the-back-door-open-and-the-keys-in-the-ignition kinda town, with a time-warp vibe that makes you feel like you're in an old black-and-white photograph. The streets are defined by beautifully preserved, hand-built stone buildings; cottage gardens overflow with untidy blooms. Pick up a copy of the *Walk with History at Auburn* brochure from the Clare Valley Wine, Food & Tourism Centre (p765).

Now on the main route to the valley's wineries, Auburn initially serviced bullock drivers and South American muleteers whose wagons – up to 100 a day – trundled between Burra's copper mines and Port Wakefield.

🛏 Sleeping & Eating

Bed in a Shed APARTMENT $$$
(☑0418 346 836; www.vineartstudio.com; cnr Leasingham Rd & Blocks Rd, Leasingham; d from $245; P☀🌐) Around 7km north of Auburn in little Leasingham, Bed in a Shed puts a different spin on the Clare Valley B&B: a rustic (but very well insulated) corrugated-iron farm shed decked out with cool art, woody built-in shelves, recycled timbers, quirky furnishings and a fridge full of breakfast stuff. Not a floral bedspread or lace curtain in sight!

Loft at Cobbler's Rest APARTMENT $$$
(☑0424 784 572; www.theloftclarevalley.com.au; 24 Main North Rd; d/q from $210/320; P☀) Upstairs in a beautiful stone building in the heart of Auburn, the Loft is a compact apartment comprising two double bedrooms, kitchen/dining and a big bathroom. There's just enough of a 'cottage' vibe for the whole set-up to feel authentic, without overdoing it. Sleeps four; providore provisions included.

★Terroir AUSTRALIAN $$$
(☑08-8849 2509; www.terroirauburn.com.au; 21 Main North Rd; mains restaurant $30-35, cafe $10-25; ⊗restaurant 6-8.30pm Wed-Sat, cafe 9am-3pm Wed-Sun; 🍴) 🖋 'Terroir' – a word often associated with the wine trade – defines the nature of a place: its altitude, its soil, its climate. At this excellent restaurant it applies to ingredients, sourced seasonally from within 100 miles, and cooked with contemporary savvy. The menu changes weekly. Terroir has also expanded into the cafe next door: more affordable, more relaxed, just as delicious.

BURRA

Bursting at the seams with historic sites, Burra (population 910), 40km northeast of Clare, was a copper-mining boom town between 1847 and 1877 with a burgeoning Cornish community. Towns like Mintaro and Auburn serviced miners travelling between Burra and Port Wakefield, from where the copper was shipped. The miners had it tough here, excavating earth dugouts for themselves and their families to live in.

Burra Visitor Information Centre (☑08-8892 2154; www.visitburra.com; 2 Market Sq; ⊙9am-5pm Mon-Fri, 10am-4pm Sat & Sun) sells the self-guided **Burra Heritage Passport** (adult/child $30/free) providing access to nine historic sights and two museums, along an 11km driving route. Many of the old mining sites are in a state of thorough dereliction, but this only adds to the sense of historic intrigue. The museums are in slightly better nick, but still atmospheric and appropriately musty. For commentary along the way, go to www.daytrippa.com.au/burra.

While you're here, check out the **Midnight Oil House** (☑08-8892 2154; www.visit burra.com/see-do/arts-cultural-hub/midnight-oil-house; cnr Barrier Hwy & West Tce; ⊙daylight hours) FREE 3km north of town. Legendary Australian rock band Midnight Oil sold millions of albums in the late 1980s, including *Diesel and Dust* (1987), which featured a photo of this derelict stone farmhouse on the front sleeve.

Not a business too easily defined, Terroir also offers three lovely suites out the back (doubles from $190).

Mintaro

☑08 / POP 190

Heritage-listed Mintaro (min-*tair*-oh; founded 1849) is a lovely stone village that could have been lifted out of the Cotswolds and plonked into the Australian bush. There are very few architectural intrusions from the 1900s – the whole place seems to have been largely left to its own devices. A fact for your next trivia night: Mintaro slate is used internationally in the manufacture of billiard tables.

Pick up the *Historic Mintaro* pamphlet around the valley.

⊙ Sights

★ **Martindale Hall** HISTORIC BUILDING
(☑08- 8843 9088; www.martindalehall-mintaro. com.au; 1 Manoora Rd; adult/child $15/8; ⊙11am-4pm Mon-Sat, daily during school holidays) Martindale Hall is an astonishing 1880 manor 3km south of Mintaro. Built for young pastoralist Edmund Bowman Jnr, who subsequently partied away the family fortune (OK, so drought and plummeting wool prices played a part), the manor features original furnishings, a magnificent blackwood staircase, Mintaro-slate billiard table and an opulent, museum-like smoking room. The hall starred as Appleyard College in the 1975 film *Picnic at Hanging Rock,* directed by Peter Weir. *Mirandaaa...*

If you also go to the **Mintaro Maze** (☑08-8843 9012; www.mintaromaze.com.au; cnr Jacka Rd & Wakefield St, Mintaro; adult/child $15/8; ⊙10am-4pm Sat & Sun, daily school holidays; ⊕), you'll get $1 off your entry here.

🛏 Sleeping & Eating

Irongate Studio B&B B&B $$$
(☑0498 998 778; www.irongatestudio.com.au; 60 Torr St; d/tr/q from $295/370/445; ℗❀📶) There's plenty of rusty old iron around this stylish B&B (it used to be a metalworker's art gallery), but inside it's all slick and contemporary. Two en-suite bedrooms extend off a generous shared living space and kitchen (good for two couples), with slate floors, tasteful ceramics and prints, and a heightened sense of the good life.

Reilly's MODERN AUSTRALIAN $$
(☑08-8843 9013; www.reillyswines.com.au; cnr Hill St & Leasingham Rd; mains $22-31; ⊙10am-4pm) Reilly's started life as a cobbler's shop in 1856. These days it's a cellar door for Reilly's Wines and a lovey restaurant, which is decorated with local art and serves creative, seasonal Mod Oz food (antipasto, rabbit terrine, platters) and the (excellent) house wines. The owners also rent out four gorgeous old stone cottages on Hill St (doubles from $175, including cook-your-own breakfast).

Clare

📵 08 / POP 3160

Named after County Clare in Ireland, this town was founded in 1842 and is the biggest in the valley. Strung out along the Horrocks Hwy, it's more practical than charming. All the requisite services are here (post office, supermarket, fuel, pubs), but you'll have a more interesting Clare Valley experience sleeping out of town. That said, the cafes and restaurants are worth the trip.

🛏 Sleeping & Eating

⭐ Mill Apartments
APARTMENT $$$

(📵 08-8842 1111; www.themill.apartments; 310 Horrocks Hwy; 1-/2-bedroom apt $290/390; 🅿 ✳ 🛜) At the northern end of Clare's long main street, the Mill Apartments are six high-end hideaways, elevated on stilts (park your car underneath) and interlinked, but with private decks and leafy outlooks backing onto the slender Hutt River. Like a motel, but so much nicer!

⭐ Umbria
ITALIAN $$

(📵 08-8812 1718; www.facebook.com/umbria restaurant; 308c Main North Rd; mains $19-29; ⊙ noon-2pm & 6-10pm Tue-Sat) Umbria looks like a high-end Melbourne Italian restaurant, lifted from Lygon St and dropped onto Main North Rd. But the exposed stonework and moody lighting is a ruse – eating here won't break the bank. Expect rustic homemade pastas made with free-range Clare Valley eggs, and a few meaty mains – perhaps a fish, beef and lamb dish, depending on the season.

ℹ Information

Clare Valley Wine, Food & Tourism Centre
(📵 08-8842 2131; www.clarevalley.com.au; cnr Horrocks Hwy & Spring Gully Rd, Clare; ⊙ 9am-5pm Sat-Thu, to 7pm Fri; 🛜) Local info, valley-wide accommodation bookings and the *Clare Historic Walk* brochure. Local produce for sale too. A Clare Valley winemaker is featured every Friday evening – drinks from $5; get social!

MURRAY RIVER

On the lowest gradient of any Australian river, the slow-flowing Murray hooks through 650 South Australian kilometres. Tamed by weirs and locks, it irrigates the fruit trees and vines of the sandy Riverland district to the north, and winds through the dairy country of the Murraylands district to the south.

Raucous flocks of white corellas and pink galahs launch from cliffs and river red gums, darting across lush vineyards and orchards.

Prior to European colonisation, the Murray was home to Meru communities, with Ngarrindjeri lands around Murray Bridge and closer to the sea. Then came shallow-draught paddle steamers, carrying wool, wheat and supplies from Murray Bridge as far as central Queensland along the Darling River. With the advent of railways, river transport declined. These days, waterskiers, jet skis and houseboats crowd the river, especially during summer. If your concept of serenity doesn't include the roar of V8 inboards, sidestep the major towns during holidays and weekends.

ℹ Getting There & Away

As with most places in regional SA, having your own vehicle will give you the most flexibility when exploring the Murray River towns. But if you are bussing it, there are a couple of options.

LinkSA (📵 08-8532 2633; www.linksa.com.au) runs several daily bus services between Adelaide and Murray Bridge ($23.50, 1¾ hours), usually via a bus change at Mt Barker in the Adelaide Hills; plus Murray Bridge to Mannum ($8, 45 minutes) from Monday to Friday. Premier Stateliner (p733) runs daily Riverland buses from Adelaide, stopping in Waikerie ($47.50, 2½ hours), Barmera ($59, 3¼ hours), Berri ($59, 3½ hours) and Renmark ($59, four hours). Change at Kingston-on-Murray for buses to Loxton ($59, 3¾ hours).

Murray Bridge

📵 08 / POP 14,560

SA's largest river town and a rambling regional hub (the fifth-biggest town in SA, if you don't count Gawler, which is more of an outer suburb of Adelaide), Murray Bridge has lots of old pubs, an under-utilised riverfront, a huge prison and charms more subtle than obvious.

◉ Sights

Monarto Zoo
ZOO

(📵 08-8534 4100; www.monartozoo.com.au; 3401 Old Princes Hwy, Monarto South; adult/child/family $36/20/91.50; ⊙ 9.30am-5pm, last entry 3pm) About 14km west of Murray Bridge, this excellent open-range zoo is home to Australian and African beasts including cheetahs, meerkats, rhino, zebras and giraffe (and the photogenic offspring thereof). A hop-on/hop-off bus tour is included in the price;

HOUSEBOATING ON THE MURRAY

Houseboating is big business on the Murray. Meandering along the river is great fun – you just need to be over 18 with a current driving licence. Boats depart most riverside towns; book ahead, especially between October and April.

The Houseboat Hirers Association (☑ 08-8346 6655; www.house boatbookings.com) is a reputable booking service, with boats available in most Murray River towns. For a three-night weekend, expect to pay anywhere from $750 for two people to $2700 for a luxury 10-bed boat. Most boats sleep at least two couples and there's generally a bond involved (starting at $200). Many provide linen – just bring food and fine wine. See also SA Tourism's *Houseboat Holidays* and The HHA's *Houseboat Holidays South Australia* booklets for detailed houseboat listings, as well as www. murrayriver.com.au/houseboats.

keeper talks happen throughout the day. There's a cafe here too, if you forget your sandwiches/thermos.

Murray Bridge Regional Gallery   GALLERY
(☑ 08-8539 1420; www.murraybridgegallery.com. au; 27 Sixth St; ⊙10am-4pm Tue-Sat, 11-4pm Sun) **FREE** This is the town's cultural epicentre, a great little space housing touring and local exhibitions: paintings, ceramics, gorgeous glassware, jewellery and prints. A terrific diversion on a rainy river afternoon.

🛏 Sleeping

Cube Murray River   HOUSEBOAT **$$$**
(☑ 0478 772 311; www.the-cube-murraybridge.com. au; Riverglen Marina, Riverglen Dr, White Sands; d from $270; ℗ ❄) Putting a rootsy, arty, off-beat spin on the mainstream houseboat theme, the Cube is a two-person timber cabin afloat on the river, moored in a quiet spot not far downstream from Murray Bridge. There's a bedroom, a kitchen and lounge area, but out on the deck is where you want to be. Sit, sip and change down to river time.

❶ Information

Murray Bridge Visitor Information Centre
(☑ 08-8339 1142; www.murraybridge.sa.gov. au; 3 South Tce, Murray Bridge; ⊙9am-5pm Mon-Fri, 10am-4pm Sat & Sun) Stocks the Murray Bridge *Accommodation Guide* and *Dining Guide* brochures, and history walk and drive pamphlets. Also has information on river cruise operators.

Mannum
☑ 08 / POP 2640

About 30km upstream from Murray Bridge, clinging to a narrow strip of riverbank, improbably cute Mannum is the unofficial houseboat capital of the world! The *Mary Ann,* Australia's first riverboat, was knocked together here in 1853 and made the first paddle-steamer trip up the Murray. Today, Mannum is unpretentious and just far enough from Adelaide to feel like holiday terrain.

◉ Sights & Activities

Mannum itself, adhering itself to the crumbling riverbanks, is quite a sight. The Mannum Visitor Information Centre incorporates the **Mannum Dock Museum of River History** (☑ 08-8569 1303; www.psmarion. com; Mannum Visitor Information Centre, 6 Randell St, Mannum; adult/child/family $7.50/4/20; ⊙9am-5pm Mon-Fri, 10am-4pm Sat & Sun), featuring info on local Ngarrindjeri Aboriginal communities, an 1876 dry dock and the restored 1897 paddle steamer *PS Marion,* on which you can occasionally chug around the river.

About 9km out of Mannum on the way to Murray Bridge, **Mannum Waterfalls** (www. adelaideexplorer.com/mannum-falls; off Cascade Rd; ⊙24hr) **FREE** surge impressively over granite boulders after it's been raining (not much action in February). Head to the top car park for the best access.

From Mannum heading north to Swan Reach, the eastern riverside road often tracks a fair way east of the river, but various lookouts en route help you scan the scene. Around 9km south of Swan Reach, the Murray takes a tight meander called **Big Bend**, a sweeping river curve with pock-marked, ochre-coloured cliffs.

Sedentary old **Swan Reach** (population 280), about 80km north of Mannum, is a bit of a misnomer: there's an old pub, a museum and plenty of pelicans here, but not many swans.

Breeze Holiday Hire   CANOEING
(☑ 0438 802 668; www.murrayriver.com.au/ breeze-holiday-hire-1052) Hires out canoes and kayaks ($75 per day), dinghies with

outboards ($95) and fishing gear ($15), and can get you waterskiing too. Based in Mannum.

PW Mayflower
BOATING

(✆08-8569 1303; www.mannum.org.au/ps-mayflower.html; Mannum Dock Museum of River History, 6 Randell St; adult/child $25/10) Take a 90-minute punt up and down the mighty Murray onboard the oldest paddle-wheeler in South Australia (1884). Seemingly as tall as she is long, the *PW Mayflower* is a delightful river conveyance, and still in tip-top working order, despite a broken crank-shaft in 1888.

🛏 Sleeping & Eating

River Shack Rentals
ACCOMMODATION SERVICES

(✆0447 263 549; www.rivershackrentals.com.au) Offers a raft of riverside properties (doubles from $120) to rent from Murray Bridge, Mannum and further upstream, sleeping two to 20 bods. Most of them are right on the water: 36 River Lane is a solid Mannum-centric option, right on the river with room for 10 (from $450). B&Bs also available.

Pretoria Hotel
PUB FOOD $$

(✆08-8569 1109; www.pretoriahotel.com.au; 50 Randell St; mains $17-36; ⊗11.30am-2.30pm & 5.30-8.30pm Mon-Sat, 11.30am-8.30pm Sun) The stone-built family-friendly Pretoria (1900) has a vast bistro and deck fronting the river, and plates up big steaks and salads, king prawn linguine and impressive parmas (amongst other delectable things). When the 1956 flood swamped the town, it kept pouring beer from the 1st-floor balcony. That's the spirit!

ℹ Information

Mannum Visitor Information Centre (✆1300 626 686, 08-8569 1303; www.psmarion.com/visitor-centre; 6 Randell St; ⊗9am-5pm Mon-Fri, 10am-4pm Sat & Sun) This is the place for cruise and houseboat bookings, the *Mannum Historic Walks* brochure and the Mannum Dock Museum of River History (p766). Bike hire also available ($25/40 per half-/full day).

Waikerie

✆08 / POP 2690

A citrus-growing centre oddly covered with TV antennas, Waikerie takes its name from the Meru Aboriginal phrase for 'anything that flies'. Indeed, there's plenty of bird life

ℹ **DON'T PAY THE FERRYMAN**

As the Murray curls abstractly across eastern SA, roads (on far more linear trajectories) invariably bump into it. Dating back to the late 19th century, a culture of free, 24-hour, winch-driven ferries has evolved to shunt vehicles across the water. Your car is guided onto the punts by burly, bearded, fluoro-clad ferry workers, who lock safety gates into position then shunt you across to the other side. There are 11 ferries in operation, the most useful of which are those at Mannum, Swan Reach and Waikerie. Turn off your headlights if you're waiting for the ferry at night so you don't dazzle the approaching skipper.

around here, plus houseboats gliding past on the river. The Waikerie vibe is utilitarian and workaday – tourism runs a distant second to fruit.

◎ Sights & Activities

★ Banrock Station
WINERY

(✆08-8583 0299; www.banrockstation.com.au; Holmes Rd, Kingston OM; ⊗9am-4pm Mon-Fri, to 5pm Sat & Sun) 🎫FREE Overlooking regenerated wetlands off the Sturt Hwy at Kingston OM (Ngawitjerook tribal country), carbon-neutral Banrock Station Wine & Wetland Centre is a stylish, rammed-earth wine-tasting centre (love the tempranillo). The jazzy restaurant (mains breakfast $10 to $20, lunch $28 to $33 – try the slow-cooked pork belly with Riverland fennel) uses ingredients sourced locally. There's a lovely 8km, three-hour wetland loop walk here too.

Nippy's Factory
FACTORY

(✆08-8541 0600; www.nippys.com.au; 2 Ian Oliver Dr; ⊗8am-4pm Mon-Fri) A long-running local fruit-juice company (since 1933) with factory-front sales. Its lip-nipping lemon juice is ace on a hot river afternoon.

Rivergum Cruises
CRUISE

(✆0477 333 896; www.rivergumcruises.com.au; Leonard Norman Dr; 2hr/3hr cruise per person from $60/90) Head out onto the river from the Waikerie waterfront in a powerboat to see some mighty Murray cliffs, during the day or at sunset with drinks. Longer cruises to visit Banrock Station, Caudo Vineyards or the Overland Corner also available.

🛌 Sleeping & Eating

Waikerie Holiday Park CARAVAN PARK $
(☑ 08-8541 2651; www.waikerieholidaypark.com.
au; 44 Peake Tce; powered sites $34, cabins $100-
170, extra person $15; ᴾ 🅿️ 🐾 📶 ☯) After a whole-
sale makeover, Waikerie's riverside caravan
park is open. It's a slick operation, with lots
of grass, sparking new amenities blocks and
camp kitchen, riverside BBQ pavilions and
loads of kids' enticements (playground, pool,
bouncy pillow, games room, resident emu).

⭐ **Wigley Retreat** B&B $$
(☑ 0417 186 364; www.wigleyretreat.com.au; Wig-
ley Flat Rd, Wigley Flat; d from $195; ᴾ 🅿️) Some
27km east of Waikerie and a couple of kilo-
metres off the Sturt Hwy, Wigley Retreat is a
simple but stylish stone cottage right on the
riverbank. It's a one-bedroom arrangement,
with a well-stocked fridge and a table for
two by the water. Super-private, super-sce-
nic. The perfect spot to de-stress for a couple
of days. No room for kids.

⭐ **Waikerie Hotel Motel** HOTEL, MOTEL $$
(☑ 08-8541 2999; www.waikeriehotel.com; 2
McCoy St; d from $120; ᴾ 🅿️ 📶) Much of this
huge pub burnt down in 2012, two days shy
of its 100th birthday. The 19 rebuilt en suite
pub rooms upstairs are awesome: fancy
linen, glowing bar fridges and big TVs, with
leather and granite everywhere. The bistro
does pub-grub classics (mains $17 to $28).
Slightly cheaper are the updated motel
rooms out the back. Bike hire available
(half-/full day $25/40).

Waikerie Bakery BAKERY $
(☑ 08-8541 2142; www.facebook.com/waikerie
bakery; 3 Peake Tce; items $4-8; ⏰ 8.30am-5.30pm
Mon-Fri, to 1pm Sat) Hey, that rhymes! This
simple little bakehouse on the lower side of
town does fabulous pumpkin-and-feta past-
ies, apricot chicken pies, jam tarts, pecan
pies and bags of biscuits. Consume them on
the sunny deck off to one side, or head for
the riverbank.

ℹ️ Information

Waikerie Visitor Information Centre (☑ 08-
8541 0708; www.waikerie.com/waikerie-
visitor-information-centre; Strangman Rd,
Waikerie; ⏰ 9am-5pm Mon-Fri, 9am-4pm Sat,
10am-4pm Sun; 📶) The modest little Waikerie
Visitor Information Centre is on the big roundabout on the way into town. Old-building fans
should look for the *Walk Waikerie History* map.

Loxton

☑ 08 / POP 4570

Sitting above a broad loop of the slow-
roaming Murray, Loxton proclaims itself the
'Garden City of the Riverland'. The vibe here
is low-key, agricultural and untouristy, with
more tyre distributors, hardware shops and
irrigation supply outlets than anything else.
It's perhaps telling that the two most interesting things in town are ancient trees.

⊙ Sights

Tree of Knowledge LANDMARK
(☑ 08-8584 8071; www.visitloxton.com.au; Grant
Schubert Dr; ⏰ 24hr) FREE Down by the river
near the caravan park, the Tree of Knowledge
is marked with flood levels from years past
when the river opted for a little inundation.
The bumper flows of 1931, '73, '74, '75, and
2011 were totally outclassed by the flood-to-
end-all-floods of 1956, marked about 4m up
the trunk.

Loxton Pepper Tree LANDMARK
(☑ 08-8202 9200; www.trusttrees.org.au; Allen
Hosking Dr; ⏰ 24hr) FREE This gnarled, weath-
er-split, termite-ravaged old pepper tree dates
back to 1878, allegedly planted by boundary
rider William Charles Loxton, after whom the
town was named. He lived near here in a little
pine hut from 1878 to 1881.

🛌 Sleeping & Eating

Loxton Hotel HOTEL, MOTEL $
(☑ 08-8584 7266; www.loxtonhotel.com.au; 45
East Tce; d hotel/motel from $110/145; ᴾ 🅿️ 📶 ☯)
With all profits put back into the Loxton
community, this large complex offers immaculate rooms with tasty weekend packages.
The original pub dates from 1908, and it has
been relentlessly extended. Bistro meals are
available for breakfast, lunch and dinner
(mains $15 to $35).

⭐ **Here's Your Beer** BAR
(☑ 0472 688 012; www.facebook.com/heresyour
beer; 2 Mill Rd; ⏰ 5-10pm Wed & Thu, 11.30am-mid-
night Fri, 5.30pm-midnight Sat, 11.30am-8pm Sun)
In a big tin shed in Loxton's back blocks, this
hipster haven pours craft beers and plates up
beaut burgers to anyone who doesn't want
to go to the local pub. The vibe is 'urbanish',
says the owner (more 'retro' by our measure:
old tables, candles, '70s rock and share-house
couches). Casual street-side terrace; occasional live tunes.

ⓘ Information

Loxton Visitor Information Centre (☑08-8584 8071; www.visitloxton.com.au; Bookpurnong Tce; ☺9am-5pm Mon-Fri, 10am-2pm Sat & Sun) A friendly place for accommodation, transport and national-park info, plus there's a bit of an art gallery off to one side. Pick up the *Discover Loxton* drive and walk brochure.

Berri

☑08 / POP 4090

The name Berri derives from the Meru Aboriginal term *berri berri,* meaning 'big bend in the river', and it was once a busy refuelling stop for wood-burning paddle steamers. These days Berri is an affluent regional hub for both state government and agricultural casual-labour agencies; it's one of the best places to chase down casual harvest jobs. The abandoned 'Big Orange' – one of Australia's iconic 'big' roadside tourist lures – awaits re-juicing on the edge of town.

⚐ Activities

Canoe Adventures   CANOEING
(☑0421 167 645; www.canoeadventure.com.au; canoe hire per day single/double $45/60, tours per adult/child half-day $125/80, full day $190/125) Canoe hire, guided half- and full-day canoe trips and camping expeditions ahoy! This outfit conducts all of the above from its Berri base, and can also deliver to most Riverland towns. A brilliant way to see the river.

✸ Festivals & Events

Riverland Wine & Food Festival   FOOD & DRINK
(RWFF; www.riverlandwineandfood.com; ☺Oct) Get festive on the banks of the Murray at the annual Riverland Wine & Food Festival, highlighting local produce and booze. It's a reasonably classy event – buy tickets in advance and dress up.

⨭ Sleeping & Eating

Berri Backpackers   HOSTEL $
(☑08-8582 3144; www.berribackpackers.com.au; 1081 Old Sturt Hwy; dm per night/week $35/160; ⓟ✳ⓢ⨊) This eclectic hostel is destination numero uno for work-seeking travellers, who chill out in quirky new-age surrounds after a hard day's manual toil. Rooms range from messy dorms to doubles, share houses, a tepee and a yurt – all for the same price. The managers can hook you up with harvest work (call in advance).

Dot's House   RENTAL HOUSE $$
(☑0427 393 789; www.dotshouse.net; 13 Verran Tce; d from $150, extra person $20; ⓟ✳ⓢ) Dot used to live in this 100-year-old stone house on the hill above the town – it's one of the oldest houses in Berri. There are two bedrooms, a full kitchen and laundry, a yard studded with citrus trees (pick your own mandarins), a chook shed (fresh eggs) and an amiable cockatoo wandering around. Sleeps four; two-night minimum.

Sprouts Café   CAFE $
(☑08-8582 1228; www.sproutscafe.com.au; 28 Wilson St; mains $6-14; ☺8.30am-4pm Mon-Fri, 9.30am-noon Sat) A cheery cafe on the hill a few blocks back from the river, with a natty lime-green colour scheme. Serves soups, quiches, burgers, pasta, curries, wraps, killer bacon-and-egg rolls with chilli chutney, and mighty fine coffee. Homemade cakes, scones and 'ultimate' chocolate pecan pudding too. The best cafe in Berri by a hefty margin.

⌂ Shopping

Riverland Farmers Market   MARKET
(☑0417 824 648; www.riverlandfarmersmarket. org.au; Senior Citizens Hall, Crawford Tce; ☺7.30-11.30am Sat) All the good stuff that grows around here in one place. A bacon-and-egg roll and some freshly squeezed orange juice will right your rudder.

ⓘ Information

Berri Visitor Information Centre (☑08-8582 5511; www.berribarmera.sa.gov.au; Riverview Dr; ☺9am-5pm Mon-Fri, 9am-2pm Sat, 10am-2pm Sun) Right by the river, with brochures, maps, waterproof canoeing guides ($10) and clued-up staff. There's a cafe next door, good for a quick caffeine fix.

Renmark & Paringa

☑08 / POP 5570

Renmark (population 4630) is the first major river town across from the Victorian border; about 254km from Adelaide. It's not a pumping tourist destination by any means, but has a relaxed vibe and a grassy waterfront, where you can pick up a houseboat. This is also the hub of the Riverland wine region: lurid signs on the roads into town scream 'Buy 6 Get 1 Free!' and 'Bulk port $6/litre!'. Local fruit also gets a roadside airing ('Mandarins $2 a Bag!').

On the other side of the river, 4km upstream, is Renmark's low-key satellite town, Paringa (population 940).

⊙ Sights & Activities

★ Twenty Third Street Distillery

DISTILLERY

(☑ 08-8586 8500; www.23rdstreetdistillery. au; cnr 23rd St & Renmark Ave, Renmark; tours & tastings from $15; ⊗ 10am-4pm) Sip your way into some heady Riverland spirits at this fabulously renovated, art-deco factory on the road into Renmark. The old distillery here closed in 2002, buckling under market pressures, but it's made one helluva comeback. Gin, whisky and brandy are the headliners: do a tasting, take a tour of the century-old copper stills, or both. It also has a bar in Adelaide (see www.23rdon melbourne.com.au).

★ Murray River Walk

HIKING

(☑ 0418 808 475; www.murrayriverwalk.com.au; per person from $2500) ⌀ Step out into the Murray River wilderness on this four-day, three-night guided hike, traversing private land through red gum forests and flood plain wetlands. Prices include all meals and houseboat accommodation, and a full day of river cruising on the final day. An intimate, low-impact and highly informative river experience. Ex-Renmark; runs May to September.

Canoe the Riverland

CANOEING

(☑ 0475 754 222; www.canoetheriverland.com; 835 Murtho Rd, Murtho, via Paringa; tours adult/child from $65/40) ⌀ Slow-paced guided sunset, moonlight and wetland canoe tours on the Murray, departing 8km north of Paringa, across the river from Renmark. Canoe/kayak hire (single/double from $35/55 per day) and on-site camping (adult/child $15/5 per night) also available.

🛏 Sleeping

Paringa Resort

HOSTEL $

(☑ 0400 659 659; www.paringaresort.com.au; 11 Hughes Ave, Paringa; dm per night/week $35/130, d per week $300; [P][❄][☎][⛱]) Not a rancid laundry, dank bathroom or crummy kitchen in sight, Paringa's sparkling highway-side 'resort' is actually a snazzy backpackers, with tidy ranks of bright en-suite dorms (eight- or 10-bed maximum), palm trees, a gym, pool, games room, BBQ terrace... What's the catch? An almost complete absence of soul.

BIG4 Renmark Riverfront Holiday Park

CARAVAN PARK $

(☑ 08-8586 8111; cnr Sturt Hwy & Patey Dr, Renmark; unpowered/powered sites from $44/47, 1-/2-/3-bedroom cabins & villas from $126/153/215; [P][❄][☎][⛱]) Highlights of this spiffy riverfront park, 1km east of town, include a camp kitchen, canoe and paddleboat hire, splashy water park for kids and absolute waterfront cabins and powered sites. The newish corrugated-iron cabins are top notch, and look a little 'Riviera' surrounded by scraggy palms. The waterskiing fraternity swarms here during holidays. Fab splash park for the kids.

Renmark Hotel

HOTEL, MOTEL $

(☑ 1800 736 627, 08-8586 6755; www.renmarkhotel. com.au; cnr Para St & Murray Ave, Renmark; d $115-140; [P][❄][☎][⛱]) The sexy art-deco curves of Renmark's humongous pub are looking good. Choose from older-style hotel rooms and upmarket motel rooms. On a sultry evening it's hard to beat a cold beer and a big steak or some Murray cod on the balcony at **Nanya Bistro** (mains $15 to $38, serving lunch and dinner daily plus weekend breakfast).

Frames

BOUTIQUE HOTEL $$$

(☑ 0418 862 260; www.theframes.com.au; 7 Panorama Ct, Paringa; d from $1150; [P][❄][☎][⛱]) If your ship has just come in, these three luxury clifftop villas are seriously stylish – architectural pods congregating on the precipice, with brilliant views, outdoor waterfall showers, private courtyards, original artworks and lavish internal appointments. Absolute luxury.

🍴 Eating & Drinking

Renmark Club

PUB FOOD $$

(☑ 08-8586 6611; www.renmarkclub.com.au; 160 Murray Ave, Renmark; mains $20-38; ⊗ noon-2.30pm & 6-9pm; ✦) Right on the river, this 110-year-old pub/club has been reborn as a shiny mod bistro, serving upmarket pub food (rustic shank pie, seared Lyrup kangaroo with bush spices and quandong jus) with unbeatable water views. Non-members (that's you) sign themselves in at the door.

★ Woolshed Brewery

BREWERY

(☑ 08-8595 8188; www.wilkadene.com.au; Wilkinson Rd, Murtho, via Paringa; ⊗ 11am-5pm) Amid the grapevines and orchards, 15km north of Renmark on a Murray River kink, the Woolshed is doing marvellous things. Part of the historic Wilkadene Homestead, the 100-year-old shed is now a craft-beer brewery, its broad riverside deck built from floorboards from Adelaide's demolished Centennial Hall (The Beatles stood here!). Dive into a tasting paddle and enjoy. Live weekend music.

ℹ Information

Renmark Paringa Visitor Information Centre
(✆ 08-8586 6704; www.renmarkparinga.sa.gov.au; 84 Murray Ave, Renmark; ⊘ 9am-5pm Mon-Fri, 10am-2pm Sat & Sun) Has the usual local info, brochures and contacts for backpacker accommodation around town, plus an interpretive centre and bike hire ($30/40 per half-/full day). The adjacent recommissioned 1911 paddle steamer PS *Industry* goes for a 90-minute chug on the first Sunday of the month (adult/child $20/10) and is open for inspection at the wharf occasionally ($2/free).

LIMESTONE COAST

The Limestone Coast – strung out along southeastern SA between the flat, olive span of the lower Murray River and the Victorian border – is a curiously engaging place. On the highways you can blow across these flatlands in under a day, no sweat – but around here the delight is in the detail. Detour off-road to check out the area's lagoons, surf beaches and sequestered bays. Also on offer are wine regions, photogenic fishing ports and snoozy agricultural towns. And what's *below* the road is even more amazing: a bizarre subterranean landscape of limestone caves, sinkholes and crater lakes – a broad, formerly volcanic area that's known as the Kanawinka Geopark.

Heading southeast, trace the Limestone Coast through the sea-salty Coorong (Ngarrindjeri country), past beachy holiday towns to Mount Gambier, SA's second city (Buandig tribal lands). And if you haven't already overdosed on wine in SA, the Coonawarra wine region is here too.

ℹ Getting There & Away

The Dukes Hwy (A8) is the most direct route between Adelaide and Melbourne (729km), but the coastal Princes Hwy (B1; about 900km), adjacent to the Coorong National Park, is infinitely more scenic.

AIR

Regional Express (p750) flies daily between Adelaide and Mount Gambier (one way from $129, 1¼ hours).

BUS

Premier Stateliner (p733) runs two bus routes – coastal and inland – from Adelaide to Mount Gambier ($85, six hours). From Adelaide along the coast (Monday, Thursday and Friday) via the Coorong, you can stop at Meningie ($42, two hours), Robe ($75, 4½ hours) and Beachport ($79, five hours). The inland bus runs Tuesday to Sunday via Naracoorte ($72, five hours) and Penola ($81, 5¾ hours). In the other direction (Limestone Coast to Adelaide), the coast bus runs on Wednesday, Friday and Sunday; and the inland bus runs Thursday to Tuesday.

TRAIN

V/Line (p733) runs a service between Mount Gambier and Melbourne ($50, 5½ hours) – you take the bus from Mount Gambier to Ballarat or Warrnambool, where you hop on a train for Melbourne.

Robe

✆ 08 / POP 1090

Robe is a cherubic little fishing port that's become a holiday hotspot for Adelaidians and Melburnians alike. The sign saying 'Drain L Outlet' as you roll into town doesn't promise much, but along the main street you'll find quality eateries and boundless accommodation, and there are some magic beaches and lakes around town. Over Christmas and Easter, Robe is packed to the heavens – book eons in advance.

◉ Sights & Activities

Obelisk   LANDMARK
(off Obelisk Rd, Robe; ⊘24hr) FREE After there were 30 shipwrecks in Guichen Bay in 1835 alone, this iconic red-and-white turret was erected atop the cliffs on Cape Dombey. From here, rockets were launched out to stricken ships, carrying lifelines back to the shore. The cliffs are steadily eroding beneath the Obelisk, and the local council has deemed it too pricey to either reinforce the cliffs, or relocate the Obelisk (it's built from many small mortared-together stones). How long the Obelisk will stand is anyone's guess.

Robe Town Brewery   BREWERY
(✆ 0415 993 693; www.robetownbrewery.com; 97 Millicent Rd; ⊘10am-5pm Mon-Fri, noon-5pm Sat) Riding the crest of Australia's craft beer wave, Robe Town uses old-fangled methods to produce its hearty Shipwreck Stout and an excellent amber ale (among other creative brews). The brewery occupies a low-key shed in the eastern outskirts of town. Heavily involved in the annual Robe Beer Fest in October. Open daily during school holidays.

Steve's Place
SURFING

(☑08-8768 2094; www.facebook.com/steves.
place.66; 26 Victoria St; ⊗9.30am-5pm Mon-Fri, to
1pm Sat, 10am-1pm Sun) Steve's Place has been
here for more than 50 years and rents out
boards ($40 per day), bodyboards ($20),
paddleboards ($50) and wetsuits ($20). It's
also the place for info on surfing lessons and
the annual Robe Easter Classic in April,
SA's longest-running surf comp (since 1968).

✰✦ Festivals & Events

Robe Beer Fest
BEER

(www.robebeerfest.com.au; Foreshore; ⊗Oct)
Local home-brewers and more established
craft beer operators such as Robe Town
Brewery strut their beery stuff over a weekend in October on the foreshore. A local
restaurant hosts the impressive 'Beer Feast'.
Much food, live music and happiness.

🛏 Sleeping & Eating

Local rental agents with properties from
as low as $100 per night in the off season
include the following:

➔ Happyshack (☑08-8768 2341; www.
happyshack.com.au)

➔ SAL Coastal Holidays (☑08-8768 2737;
www.bookrobeaccommodation.com.au; 25
Victoria St; ⊗9am-5pm Mon-Fri)

➔ Ottson Holidays (☑08-8768 2600; www.
robeholidayrentals.com.au)

➔ Robe Lifestyle (☑1300 760 629; www.
robelifestyle.com.au)

LONG WALK TO BALLARAT

Robe set up shop as a fishing port in
1846 – one of SA's earliest settlements.
During the 1850s gold rush in Victoria,
Robe came into its own when the Victorian government whacked a $10-per-
head tax on Chinese gold miners arriving to work the goldfields. Thousands of
Chinese miners dodged the tax by landing at Robe in SA, then walking the 400-
odd kilometres to Bendigo and Ballarat
in Victoria; 16,500 arrived between 1856
and 1858, with 10,000 in 1857 alone! But
the flood stalled as quickly as it started
when the SA government instituted its
own tax on the Chinese. The 'China-
men's wells' along their route (including
one in the Coorong) can still be seen
today, as can a memorial to the Chinese
arrivals on the Robe foreshore.

Lakeside Tourist Park
CARAVAN PARK $

(☑08-8768 2193; www.lakesiderobe.com.au; 24
Main Rd; unpowered/powered sites from $36/38,
cabins/villas from $85/150; P✳🛜) Right on
Lake Fellmongery (a 'fellmonger' is a wool
washer, don't you know), this abstractly
laid-out, rather boutique park has heritage-
listed pine trees and reception building
(132-year-old former stables), plenty of
grass, basic cabins and flashy villas.

★ Caledonian Inn
HOTEL $$

(☑08-8768 2029; www.caledonianinnrobe.com.
au; 1 Victoria St; r without bathroom $70-130, cot-
tages $200-250; P✳🛜) This historic inn
(1859) has a half-dozen bright and cosy
upstairs pub rooms: shared bathrooms and
no air-con, but they are great value. Out the
back are a row of lovely two-tier cottages
and a three-bedroom rental house called
Splash. The pub grub is classy too (mains
$22 to $36, serving noon to 2pm and 6pm
to 8pm). Air-con in the cottages and rental
house only.

Grey Masts
B&B $$$

(☑0411 627 146; www.greymasts.com.au; 36-38
Smillie St; d from $250, extra person $50; P✳)
This lovely, low-ceilinged 1840s stone building at the foot of the main street is one of
Robe's oldest buildings. It's divided into a
cottage (sleeps four) and a house (sleeps six),
each with kitchens, welcoming lounge areas
and flower-filled gardens. The Savage family
(Mr and Mrs Savage and their 12 sons!) once
lived here. Minimum stays apply.

★ Union Cafe
CAFE $

(☑08-8768 2627; www.facebook.com/unioncafe.
sa; 4/17-19 Victoria St; mains $9-22; ⊗8am-
2.30pm; 🛜🖶) Perennially busy, this curiously angled corner cafe with polished-glass
fragments in the floor has expanded into the
next-door shopfront. Unionise your hangover with a big cooked breakfast, lashed with
locally made hot sauce. Good coffee, pancakes, curries, salads and wraps. Billy Joel
soundtrack + plenty of outdoor seating =
hard to beat!

★ Vic St Pizza Project
PIZZA $$

(☑08-8768 2081; www.facebook.com/pizza
projectrobesa; 6 Victoria St; mains $20-30;
⊗11.30am-2pm & 5-8pm; 🖉🖶) Go for some-
thing trad (Hawaiian, margherita, pep-
peroni) or something more daring (lamb
souvlaki, squid and chorizo) – either way,
the pizzas at this bright, family-run good-
timer are definite crowd pleasers. Pastas,

OFF THE BEATEN TRACK

STILL WATERS RUN DEEP

Everyone has heard of Mount Gambier's famous Blue Lake, which glows an iridescent blue in summer. But the little version? Actually the Little Blue Lake (☑08-8724 9750; www.mountgambierpoint.com.au/attractions/lakes/little-blue-lake; Mount Salt Rd, Mount Schank; ⊙daylight hours) FREE is more greenish, but is much more accessible than Big Blue – there's a stepped walkway down the escarpment to the water. Cool off with a swim, but beware: the water is always cold and it's an estimated 45m to the bottom. It's 17km north of Port MacDonnell en route to Mount Gambier, not far off the Riddoch Hwy.

Closer to the Victorian border, the Piccaninnie Ponds (☑08-8735 1177; www.parks. sa.gov.au; Piccaninnie Ponds Rd, Wye; ⊙daylight hours) FREE are part of an amazing flooded limestone cave system, famous for its gin-clear water bubbling up from a spring far, far below. Cave diving is the sport of choice here, descending to see features such as the Cathedral and the Chasm; or, if you retain some skerrick of sanity, just take a swim across the surface. For tours and gear hire, contact Reef 2 Ridge (☑0411 519 825, 08-8707 9203; www.reef2ridge.com; 11 Caldwell St, Mount Gambier; ⊙10am-5pm Tue-Fri, 9am-5pm Sat, 9am-2pm Sun) in Mount Gambier.

risottos and salads too. Open early for dinner when you've got hungry familials in tow. Love the chunky pink-salt grinders.

❶ Information

Robe Visitor Information Centre (☑08-8768 2465; www.robe.com.au; Public Library, cnr Mundy Tce & Smillie St; ⊙9am-5pm Mon-Fri, 10am-1pm Sat & Sun) History displays, brochures and free internet. Look for the *Scenic Drive, Heritage Drive* and *A Walk Through History* pamphlets.

Meningie & Coorong National Park

In Ngarrindjeri country, the amazing Coorong National Park (☑08-8575 1200; www.parks.sa.gov.au; via Princes Hwy; ⊙24hr) FREE is a fecund lagoon landscape curving along the coast for 145km from Lake Alexandrina towards Kingston SE. A complex series of soaks and salt pans, it's separated from the sea by the chunky dunes of the Younghusband Peninsula. More than 200 waterbird species live here. *Storm Boy*, an endearing 1976 film about a young boy's friendship with a pelican (based on the 1964 novel by Colin Thiele), was filmed here, and remade for a 2019 release.

Bordering the Coorong on Lake Albert (a large arm of Lake Alexandrina), little Meningie (population 1120) was established as a minor port in 1866. The environmental health of Lake Albert – one of the 'lower lakes' – has been perilous of late, with reduced Murray River flows.

◉ Sights & Activities

The Princes Hwy scuttles through the Coorong, but you can't see much from the road. Instead, take the 13km, unsealed Coorong Scenic Drive. Signed as Seven Mile Rd, it starts 10km southwest of Meningie off the Narrung Rd, and takes you right into the landscape, with its stinky lagoons, sea mists, fishing shanties, formation-flying pelicans, black swans and wild emus. The road rejoins the Princes Hwy 10km south of Meningie.

With a 4WD you can access Ninety Mile Beach, a well-known surf-fishing spot. The easiest ocean access point is 3km off the Princes Hwy at 42 Mile Crossing, 19km south of Salt Creek – a worthy dirt-road detour.

On the southern fringe of the Coorong is Kingston SE (population 1430; www. kingstonse.com.au). The town is a hotbed of crayfishing: there's a summertime seafood festival, plus one of Australia's 'big' tourist attractions, the anatomically correct Larry the Lobster, a famed roadside resident.

For a watery perspective, try Spirit of the Coorong or Cruise the Coorong cruises, or Canoe the Coorong, all based in Goolwa (p747) on the Fleurieu Peninsula.

🛏 Sleeping

Coorong National Park Camp Sites CAMPGROUND $
(☑08-8575 1200; www.parks.sa.gov.au; Coorong National Park; per vehicle $15; ℗) There are 18 bush/beach campsites in Coorong National Park, some of them brilliantly isolated;

you'll need a permit from Parks SA, available online.

★ **Dalton on the Lake**   B&B **$$**
(☑0428 737 161; www.facebook.com/daltonon thelake; 30 Narrung Rd, Meningie; d from $200, extra person $15; P❋) Generous in spirit and unfailingly clean, this two-bedroom lakeside B&B (parts of which date back to the 1890s) goes to great lengths to ensure your stay is comfortable. There'll be fresh bread baking when you arrive, jars of homemade biscuits, and bountiful bacon and eggs for breakfast. Also a BBQ, and mulberry and pear trees out the back; *Storm Boy* DVD ready to go.

★ **Coorong Cabins**   RENTAL HOUSE **$$$**
(☑0488 724 155; www.coorongcabins.com.au; 436 Seven Mile Rd, Meningie; d/q from $200/250; P❋) Two mod, self-contained rental houses – Pelican and Wren, sleeping four and two respectively – are about 14km south of town, but right on the waterfront within the national park. Decor is beachy-chic-chi, and there are bikes and kayaks available so you can explore the Coorong beyond where the road may take you. Check in at the house out the front.

ℹ Information

Meningie Visitor Information Centre (Coorong Cottage Industries; ☑08-8575 1770; www.meningie.com.au; 14 Princes Hwy, Meningie; ⊙10am-4.30pm) The spot for local info, doubling as a craft shop.

Mount Gambier

☑08 / POP 28,670
Strung out along the flatlands below an extinct volcano, Mount Gambier is the Limestone Coast's major town and service hub. Despite some lovely historic buildings (pick up the *City Heritage Walk* brochure from the visitor centre), 'The Mount' can sometimes seem a little short on urban virtues (though you can get a good coffee here these days). But it's not what's above the streets that makes Mount Gambier special – it's the deep Blue Lake and the caves that worm their way though the limestone beneath the town. Amazing!

⊙ Sights

★ **Blue Lake**   LAKE
(☑1800 087 187; www.mountgambierpoint.com. au/attractions/blue-lake; John Watson Dr; ⊙24hr) **FREE** Mount Gambier's big-ticket item is the luminous, 75m-deep lake, which turns an insane hue of blue during summer. Perplexed scientists think it has to do with calcite crystals suspended in the water, which form at a faster rate during the warmer months. Consequently, if you visit between April and November, the lake will look much like any other – a steely grey. But in January, wow! The surface of the water is 20m below central Mt Gambier's street level.

Aquifer Tours (☑08-8723 1199; www.aquifer tours.com; cnr Bay Rd & John Watson Dr; adult/child/family $11/5/31; ⊙tours hourly 9am-5pm Nov-Jan, to 2pm Feb-May & Sep-Oct, to noon Jun-Aug) runs hourly tours, taking you down near the lake shore in a glass-panelled lift, via an 80m tunnel. Or you can just wander around the rim of the lake along a 3.6km trail.

Riddoch Art Gallery   GALLERY
(☑08-8721 2563; www.facebook.com/theriddoch; Main Corner, 1 Bay Rd; ⊙10am-5pm Mon-Fri, 10am-3pm Sat & Sun) **FREE** If Mount Gambier's famed Blue Lake isn't blue, don't feel blue – cheer yourself up at one of Australia's best regional galleries. Passionately curated, there are three main spaces here housing touring and permanent exhibitions, contemporary installations and community displays. There are over 2000 artworks in the permanent collection, dating back to the 1870s and valued at $3.5 million – be impressed!

Cave Gardens   CAVE
(☑1800 087 187; www.mountgambierpoint.com. au/attractions/cave-gardens; cnr Bay Rd & Watson Tce; ⊙24hr) **FREE** This is a 50m-deep sinkhole right in the middle of town, with the odd suicidal shopping trolley at the bottom. You can walk down into it, and watch the nightly **Sound & Light Show** (from 8.30pm) telling local Buandig Aboriginal Dreaming stories. The multicultural **Mount Gambier Farmers Market** (☑0466 155 848; www.mgfm. org.au; Cave Gardens, cnr Bay Rd & Watson Tce; ⊙9am-noon Sat) happens here on Saturday mornings.

🛏 Sleeping

Old Mount Gambier Gaol   HOTEL **$**
(☑08-8723 0032; www.theoldmountgambier-gaol.com.au; 25 Margaret St; dm $30, d with/without bathroom $100/90, f from $195; P🐾) If you can forget that this place was a prison until 1995 (either that or embrace the fact), these refurbished old buildings make for an atmospheric and comfortable stay. There are backpacker dorms available in old admin

> **WORTH A TRIP**
>
> ### NARACOORTE CAVES NATIONAL PARK
>
> About 10km southeast of Naracoorte is World Heritage–listed **Naracoorte Caves National Park** (☑ 08-8762 1210; www.naracoortecaves.sa.gov.au; 89 Wonambi Rd, Naracoorte; self-guided tours adult/child/family from $10/6/27.50, guided tours from $22/13/61, Wonambi Fossil Centre $14/8.50/38.50; ⊙ 9am-5pm). The discovery of an ancient fossilised marsupial in these limestone caves raised palaeontological eyebrows around the world, and featured in David Attenborough's 1979 BBC series *Life on Earth*. The 28 limestone caves here, including **Alexandra Cave**, curiously named **Stick-Tomato Cave** and **Victoria Fossil Cave**, have bizarre stalactite and stalagmite formations.
>
> Prospective Bruce Waynes should check out the **Bat Observation Centre** (adult/child/family $26/15.50/72) near Blanche Cave, from which thousands of endangered southern bentwing bats exit en masse at dusk during summer. You can see the Stick-Tomato Cave by self-guided tour, but the others require ranger-guided tours, with options including single-cave tours and adventure caving. The behind-the-scenes **World Heritage Tour** ($300 per two people) gives you a scientific slant on the action.
>
> The park visitor centre doubles as the impressive **Wonambi Fossil Centre** – a re-creation of the rainforest that covered this area 200,000 years ago.

buildings, or you can up the spooky stakes and sleep in a former cell. There's a bar too, in which to plot your next criminal exploit.

BIG4 Blue Lake Holiday Park CARAVAN PARK $
(☑ 08-8725 9856; www.bluelakeholidaypark.com.au; 100 Bay Rd; unpowered/powered sites $35/39, cabins/units/villas from $105/135/210; P❋ ☎ ☜) Adjacent to the Blue Lake, a golf course and walking and cycling tracks (but too far to walk into town), this amiable park has some natty grey-and-white cabins and well-weeded lawns. The spiffy contemporary, self-contained villas sleep four.

★**Colhurst House** B&B $$
(☑ 08-8723 1309; www.facebook.com/colhursthousebnb; 3 Colhurst Pl; d/ste from $170/250; P❋ ☎) Most locals don't know about Colhurst – it's up a laneway off a side street (Wyatt St), and you can't really see it from central Mount G. It's an 1878 mansion built by Welsh migrants, and manages to be old-fashioned without being overly twee. There's a gorgeous wrap-around balcony upstairs with great views over the rooftops. Cooked breakfast. Nice.

✗ Eating

★**Metro Bakery & Cafe** CAFE $$
(☑ 08-8723 3179; www.metrobakeryandcafe.com.au; 13 Commercial St E.; mains breakfast $6-20, lunch & dinner $10-22; ⊙ 8.30am-5pm Mon-Wed, to late Thu-Sat, 9am-3pm Sun) Ask a local where they go for coffee: chances are they'll say, 'the Metro, you fool!' In the thick of things on the main drag, it's an energetic cafe with black-and-white decor and serves omelettes, salads, sandwiches, pastries and meatier mains (try the chilli squid with charred lemon). There's a wine bar here too, brimming with Coonawarra cabernets. Book for dinner.

Wild Ginger THAI $$
(☑ 08-8723 6264; www.wildginger.com.au; 17 Commercial St W; mains $14-29; ⊙ 11.30am-2pm Thu & Fri, 5.30-8.30pm Tue-Sun) Locals recommend this authentic, gilt-fringed Thai nook on the main street, plating up the likes of citrus-rich larp chicken salad and menacing red beef curry. It's a classy operation, with a lot of attention to detail (food presentation, interiors, staff attire etc). Good stuff.

Mayura Station MODERN AUSTRALIAN $$$
(☑ 08-8733 4333; www.mayurastation.com/dining; Canunda Frontage Rd, off Lossie Rd, Millicent; 3/4 courses $110/130; ⊙ from 7pm Thu-Sat) Mayura Station – a cattle property in Millicent, midway between Mount Gambier and Beachport – has a serious rep for its fine Japanese full-blooded Wagyu beef. Book a table in advance at the classy/farmy dining room to try some of the best cuts, via a three- or four-course set menu, paired with seasonal vegetables.

☆ Entertainment

Morrison's Jazz Club JAZZ
(☑ 08-8723 0925; www.morrisonsjazzclub.com; 2/16 Commercial St W; admission varies; ⊙ 7.30pm-late Thu, 8pm-late Fri & Sat) Beyond a nondescript black doorway on the main street is Mt G's very own jazz club, named after legendary Australian jazz trumpeter

and all-round good guy James Morrison. Expect local and touring trios, big bands and soul singers, playing into the wee smalls.

ⓘ Information

Mount Gambier Visitor Information Centre (☑08-8724 9750, 1800 087 187; www.mount gambiertourism.com.au; 35 Jubilee Hwy E; ☺9am-5pm Mon-Fri, 10am-4pm Sat & Sun) Has details on local sights, activities, transport and accommodation, plus the *City Heritage Walk* pamphlet and a town history movie. The Lady Nelson Discovery Centre (☑1800 087 187; www.mountgambier.sa.gov.au; Mount Gambier Visitor Information Centre, 35 Jubilee Hwy E; ☺9am-5pm Mon-Fri, 10am-4pm Sat & Sun) is here too. Bike hire (☑1800 087 187; www.mountgambier.sa.gov.au; Mount Gambier Visitor Information Centre, 35 Jubilee Hwy E; ☺9am-5pm Mon-Fri, 10am-4pm Sat & Sun) available.

Penola & the Coonawarra Wine Region

A rural town on the way up (what a rarity!), Penola (population 1600) is the kind of place where you walk down the main street and three people say 'Hello!' to you before you reach the pub. The town is famous for two things: for its association with the Sisters of St Joseph of the Sacred Heart, cofounded in 1867 by Australia's first saint, Mary MacKillop; and for being smack-bang in the middle of the Coonawarra Wine Region (killer cabernets).

◉ Sights & Activities

Mary MacKillop Interpretive Centre　　　MUSEUM
(☑08-8737 2092; www.mackilloppenola.org.au; cnr Portland St & Petticoat Lane, Penola; adult/child $5/free; ☺10am-4pm) The centre occupies a jaunty building with a gregarious entrance pergola (perhaps not as modest as St Mary might have liked). There's oodles of info on Australia's first saint here, plus the Woods MacKillop Schoolhouse, the first school in Australia for children from lower socioeconomic backgrounds.

Coonawarra Experiences　　　WINE
(☑0404 092 611; www.coonawarraexperiences. com.au; half-day tour incl lunch per person $120) Small-group winery tours where you select the cellar doors you'd like to visit. Pick-up/drop-off at your accommodation; ploughman's lunch included.

🛌 Sleeping & Eating

★**Cameron's Cottage**　　　COTTAGE $$
(☑0419 373 450; www.coonawarradiscovery.com. au/camerons-cottage; 1 Davis Cres, Penola; d/f $185/265; P❄🖤) Surrounded by rampant blooms, this original whitewashed timber settler's cottage (1863) has seen some history. Inside it's cottagey without being twee, with cast-iron beds, a full kitchen, exposed historical timbers and a cranking wood heater for chilly nights. Set at a jaunty angle to the street, a short walk from town. Sleeps four.

Alexander Cameron Suites　　　MOTEL $$
(☑08-8737 2200; www.alexandercameron suites.com.au; 23 Church St, Penola; s/d/tw/f from $145/155/170/230; P❄🖤) Looking much less bleak now that some trees have matured around it, this newish motel on the Mount Gambier side of town offers stylish rooms, well-tended gardens and rural Australian architectural stylings. It's named after Penola's founder, a wiry Scottish pastoralist: check out his statue next to the pub. Three-bedroom house also available (one bedroom $180, extra bedroom $30).

★**Pipers of Penola**　　　FUSION $$$
(☑08-8737 3999; www.pipersofpenola.com.au; 58 Riddoch St, Penola; mains $38-42; ☺6-9pm Tue-Sat) A classy, intimate dining room inside a 1908 Methodist church, with friendly staff and seasonal fare. The menu fizzes with high-end culinary lingo: *tobiko* (Japanese flying fish roe), lardons (bacon cubes), *sabayon* (Italian custard sauce) – serious gourmet indicators! Prices are lofty, but so is quality. Superb wine list with lots of locals (the beer list could be craftier). One of SA's top restaurants.

ⓘ Information

Penola Visitor Information Centre (☑08-8737 2855; www.wattlerange.sa.gov.au/tourism; 27 Arthur St, Penola; ☺9am-5pm Mon-Fri, 10am-4pm Sat & Sun) Services the Coonawarra region, with info about local cycling routes and winery tours. The John Riddoch Centre (☑08-8737 2855; www.wattlerange.sa.gov.au/tourism; Penola Visitor Information Centre, 27 Arthur St, Penola; ☺9am-5pm Mon-Fri, 10am-4pm Sat & Sun) is also here. Pick up a wineries map and/or the *Coonawarra Wineries Walking Trail* brochure detailing an easy 5km walk past five wineries (www.coonawarrawalkingtrail.com.au). The *Walk With History* brochure is also here, or download it from www.wattlerange.sa.gov.au (search for 'Penola Walk with History').

DON'T MISS

BEST BOTTLES: COONAWARRA WINE REGION

When it comes to spicy cabernet sauvignon, it's just plain foolish to dispute the virtues of the Coonawarra Wine Region (www.coonawarra.org). The *terra rossa* (red earth) soils here also produce irresistible shiraz and chardonnay. Most of the wineries are just off the main highway north of Penola.

Bellwether Wines (📞0417 080 945; www.bellwetherwines.com.au; 14183 Riddoch Hwy, Coonawarra; ⏰11am-5pm Fri-Mon) Sue Bell runs Bellwether (ha-ha), an irreverent, arty cellar door in a stone 1868 shearing shed – pretty much the first Coonawarra winery you come to rolling in from the north. Camping here ranges from unpowered/powered sites ($30/45) to six rather lovely 'glamping' bell tents (single/double $100/200, including a bottle of wine) in the lush, tree-studded paddock out the back, with shared facilities. FYI, a 'bellwether' is the leading sheep in a flock, with a bell around its neck.

Majella Wines (📞08-8736 3055; www.majellawines.com.au; Lynn Rd, Coonawarra; ⏰10am-4.30pm) The family that runs Majella are fourth-generation Coonawarrans, so they know a thing or two about gutsy reds (love 'The Musician' shiraz-cabernet).

Rymill Coonawarra (📞08-8736 5001; www.rymill.com.au; 110 Clayfield Rd, Glenroy; ⏰11am-5pm) Rymill rocks the local boat by turning out some of the best sauvignon blanc you'll ever taste. The cellar door is fronted by a statue of two duelling steeds – appropriately rebellious.

YORKE PENINSULA

Narungga country since time immemorial, the boot-shaped Yorke Peninsula has since become a firm favourite with holidaying Adelaideans – it's just under two hours northwest of the city.

For history buffs, the northwestern end of 'Yorkes' has a trio of towns called the Copper Triangle: Moonta (the mine), Wallaroo (the smelter) and Kadina (the service town). Settled by Cornish miners, this area drove the regional economy following a copper boom in the early 1860s, and this is still the peninsula's commercial heartland.

In the big-sky peninsula country to the east and south, things are much more agricultural and laid-back, with sleepy holiday towns, isolated Innes National Park, remote surf breaks, ospreys, kangaroos and an empty coastline.

🏃 Tours & Activities

Walk The Yorke   WALKING
(📞1800 654 991; www.yorkepeninsula.com. au/walk-the-yorke) 🚶 Walk the Yorke is an interconnected, 500km network of coastal walking and cycling trails around the Yorke Peninsula, running between Port Wakefield and Moonta Bay. See the website for detailled planning notes, or pick up trail note brochures from the visitor centre in Kadina ($10 each, or $90 for the set of 10).

**Aboriginal Cultural
Tours South Australia**   CULTURAL
(📞0429 367 121; www.aboriginalsa.com.au; half-/1-/2-/3-day tours $100/230/420/550) 🚶 Highly regarded Indigenous cultural tours of the peninsula, exploring the incredibly long Narungga Aboriginal association with this country. Lots of culture, wilderness and camping. Tours ex-Adelaide or Yorke Peninsula; half-day tours ex-Port Victoria.

🛏 Sleeping

For holiday house rentals from as little as $100 per night, try Accommodation on Yorkes (📞08-8852 2000; www.accommodation onyorkes.com.au) or Country Getaways (📞08-8832 2623; www.countrygetaways.info).

There are 19 council-run bush campgrounds (📞08-8832 0000; www.yorke.sa.gov. au; per night/week $10/50) dotted around the coastline the peninsula, mostly in the south and west, and mostly sans toilets and water (but with loads of bushy/beachy charm). See the website for details.

ⓘ Information

There are three main visitor information centres on the peninsula. In decreasing order of size and usefulness, they are:

Copper Coast Visitor Information Centre
(📞08-8821 2333, 1800 654 991; www.yorke peninsula.com.au; 50 Mines Rd, Kadina; ⏰9am-5pm Mon-Fri, 10am-4pm Sat & Sun)
Southern Yorke Peninsula Visitor Information Centre (p780)

Yorke Peninsula Visitor Information Centre
(☑1800 202 445, 08-8853 2600; www.visit
yorkepeninsula.com.au; 29 Main St, Minlaton;
⊙10am-4pm Mon-Fri, 10am-2pm Sat & Sun)

ℹ Getting There & Away

Yorke Peninsula Coaches (☑08-8821 2755;
www.ypcoaches.com.au) Daily buses from Adelaide to Kadina ($42, 2¼ hours), Wallaroo ($42,
2½ hours) and Moonta ($42, three hours), with
another route running down the peninsula's
east coast daily except Tuesday and Thursday,
stopping at Port Vincent ($54, 3¼ hours),
Stansbury ($54, 3½ hours) and Edithburgh
($56, four hours).

West Coast

Fronting Spencer Gulf, the Yorke Peninsula's
west coast has a string of shallow swimming beaches, plus the 'Copper Triangle'
historic mining towns of Kadina, Wallaroo
and Moonta, all a short drive from each
other. **Kernewek Lowender** (www.kernewek.
org; ⊙May), aka the Copper Coast Cornish
Festival, happens around here in May of
odd-numbered years. Further south, Point
Turton and Corny Point are magical little
spots with caravan parks and taverns.

Wallaroo

☑08 / POP 4010

Still a major grain port and fishing town,
Wallaroo is on the way up: there's a huge
new subdivision north of town, a new shopping complex inserted in the middle of the
old town, and the shiny Copper Cove Marina
is full of expensive boats. There are plenty of
pubs here, and the pubs are full of drinkers.

That said, the old town area retains a
romantically weathered 'seen-better-days'
vibe: wander around the compact little
streets and old cottages in the shadows of
the huge grain silos and soak up the atmosphere (is this the place to pen your next
novel?).

Wallaroo Heritage
& Nautical Museum   MUSEUM
(☑08-8823 3015; www.nationaltrust.org.au; cnr
Jetty Rd & Emu St; adult/child $6/3; ⊙10am-4pm)
Down by the water, the stoic 1865 post office
now houses the Wallaroo Heritage & Nauti-
cal Museum. There are several of these little
National Trust museums around Yorkes – in
Port Victoria, in Ardrossan, in Milaton, in
Edithburgh – but this is the best of them,
with tales of square-rigged English ships,

the Tipara Reef Lighthouse and George the
pickled giant squid.

🛏 Sleeping & Eating

Wallaroo Marina
Apartments   APARTMENTS $$
(☑08-8823 4068; www.wallarooapartments.com.
au; 11 Heritage Dr; d/apt from $155/195; 🅿❋🛜)
Motels are horizontal, apartments are ver-
tical. Adhering to this architectural adage,
the six-storey Wallaroo Marina Apartments
at the marina on the northern edge of town
has spiffy suites, kayak hire and the pump-
ing Coopers Alehouse downstairs. The
swishest place to stay in Wallaroo by far.

Smelter   CAFE $
(☑08-8823 2329; www.facebook.com/thesmelter
cafe; 15b Owen Tce; mains $7-19; ⊙7am-3pm Tue-
Thu & Sun, 7am-late Fri & Sat) Until this mean
little bean brewer took control in Wallaroo,
the cafe scene here was mired somewhere
around 1990. But Smelter smells entirely of
the new century, with big breakfasts, won-
derful salads, steak sandwiches and proper
coffee. Hard blues on the stereo; rusty indus-
trial signage. Open early if you have to hit
highway.

Moonta

☑08 / POP 2670

In the late 19th century, the Moonta copper
mine was the richest in Australia. These
days the town, which calls itself 'Australia's
Little Cornwall', maintains a faded glory and
has a couple of decent pubs and places to
bite into a Cornish pasty. The old mine ruins
– the Moonta Heritage Site – on the edge of
town are interesting, archaeologically and
architecturally more than anything else.
Head to Moonta Bay for safe swimming and
jetty fishing.

⊙ Sights

Moonta Mines Museum   MUSEUM
(☑08-8825 1891; www.moontatourism.org.au; Ver-
ran Tce; adult/child $8/4; ⊙1-4pm, from 11am dur-
ing school holidays) This impressive 1878 stone
edifice was once the Moonta Mines Model
School and had 1100 students. These days
it's the centrepiece of the sprawling **Moonta
Heritage Site**, and captures mining life – at
work and at home – in intimately preserved
detail. A little tourist train chugs out of the
museum car park at 2pm on Wednesday,
and 1pm, 2pm and 3pm on weekends (adult/
child $12/5; daily during school holidays).

🛌 Sleeping & Eating

Serendipity Cottage
COTTAGE $$

(📞 0438 324 457; www.stayz.com.au; 155 Coast Rd; d from $155, extra person $55; ❄️ 🛜) This woody little family beach cabin occupies the back garden of the owners' house, but it has its own entrance via a rear laneway and is very private. Gardens feature vegetable beds, a brazier for marshmallow toasting and even a Coke machine! Sleeps up to six bods spread over two bedrooms and a fold-out couch. Unpretentious, beachy and quite lovely.

Taste the Yorke
CAFE $

(📞 08-8825 3121; www.facebook.com/tastethe yorke; 52b George St; mains $8-23; ⏱️ 8am-5pm) Making a splash in Moonta, this corner cafe occupies a heritage shopfront in the old town, with couches under the low eaves outside and retro timber tables within. Daily specials are written on brown paper bags and taped to the wall, or there's a regular menu of big eggy breakfasts, soups, salads, muffins, waffles, old-school milkshakes and supreme carrot cake.

Cornish Kitchen
BAKERY $

(📞 08-8825 3030; 10-12 Ellen St; items $4-12; ⏱️ 9am-3pm Mon-Fri, to 2pm Sat) After a dirty day digging down the mine, swing your pick into the Cornish Kitchen for the ultimate pasty. (The chunky steak and onion pies are pretty great too). The place is festooned with vintage Cornish tea towels.

ℹ️ Information

Moonta Visitor Information Centre (📞 08-8825 1891; www.moontatourism.org.au; Old Railway Station, Blanche Tce, Moonta; ⏱️ 9am-5pm) Stocks a smattering of history pamphlets including the *Moonta Walking Trail* map, and has details on the Moonta Heritage Site 1.5km east of town.

East Coast

About 24km south of Ardrossan is magical little Black Point, a holiday hotspot with a long row of shacks built right on the dunes above a protected, north-facing beach (perfect if you've got kids).

Further south, unpretentious Port Vincent (population 480) has lots of accommodation, a waterfront pub and a busy marina, from where yachts dart across to Adelaide. Continuing south, Stansbury is the happening-est town on the east coast, with a caravan park, visitor info centre, a great little restaurant and a beaut waterside pub.

Further south again is endearing little Edithburgh, which has a free tidal swimming pool in a small cove. From the clifftops here, views extend offshore to sandy **Troubridge Island Conservation Park** (📞 08-8854 3200; www.parks.sa.gov.au), home to much bird life including penguins, cormorants and terns. You can stay the night here at the old **lighthouse** (📞 08-8852 6290; www.environment.sa.gov.au/parks; Troubridge Island Conservation Park; per adult/child incl transfers from $120/60, min charge $360). The island is steadily eroding – what the sea wants, the sea will have...

Stansbury

📞 08 / POP 550

Little Stansbury has everything one might conceivably require on a beach holiday: a beach, a jetty, a caravan park, a pub, a takeaway shop and a progressive little bistro with a bit of an idea about what people eat and drink in the city. What more could you want? Oh yes, a neat little historical museum.

Stansbury Museum
MUSEUM

(📞 0408 142 875; www.stansburymuseum.com; North Tce, Stansbury; adult/child/family $3/1/7; ⏱️ 2-4pm daily Jan, 2-4pm Wed & Sun Feb-Dec) Lording it over the local school yard (this used to be the headmaster's house), Stansbury's museum digs into the town's post-colonial history with a proudly curated collection of rusty farm stuff, seagoing memorabilia, old clothes, bottles, photos and domestic remnants (don't get your fingers caught in the mangle).

Stansbury Caravan Park
CARAVAN PARK $

(📞 08-8852 4171; www.stansburysa.com/park; 395 Anzac Parade, Stansbury; unpowered/powered sites from $24/30, cabins $112-140; 🅿️ ❄️ 🛜) Occupying the high ground at Oyster Point on Stansbury's eastern frontier, the town caravan park is a compact, boom-gated enclave with powered sites and a small clutch of clifftop cabins. Not much shade, but if you're here for a beach holiday that might not bother you. Grassy unpowered sites are at the Oyster Point Carvan Park annex, 1km further south.

⭐ Wild Ma's Bistro
BISTRO $$

(📞 08-8852 4523; 9a St Vincent St, Stansbury; pizzas $15-26, mains $20-32; ⏱️ 11am-11pm Thu-Sun; 🍴) In a lovely old shopfront up the hill from the pub, Ma drives Stansbury wild with her superior seafood, wood-oven pizzas, craft beers, boutique wines and rebellious interior design (love the mural). Order a couple of espresso martinis and a smoked salmon and mango salad and reflect on another hard day at the beach. Check Facebook for the latest menu updates.

❶ Information

Southern Yorke Peninsula Visitor Information Centre (☑08-8852 4577; www.stansbury. com; cnr Weaver & Towler Sts, Stansbury; ◷9.30am-4pm Mon-Fri Jan-Dec, 10am-2pm Sat & Sun Sep-May) Local info, maps and accommodation advice, inside the town's old stone post office (1877).

South Coast & Innes National Park

At **Innes National Park** (☑08-8854 3200; www.environment.sa.gov.au/parks; via Stenhouse Bay Rd, Stenhouse Bay; per vehicle $10; ◷24hr) sheer cliffs plunge into indigo waters and rocky offshore islands hide small coves and sandy beaches. **Marion Bay** (www. marionbay.com.au), just outside the park, and **Stenhouse Bay** and **Pondalowie Bay**, both within the park, are the main local settlements. Pondalowie Bay has a bobbing lobster-fishing fleet and a gnarly surf beach. The rusty ribs of the 711-tonne steel barque *Ethel,* which foundered in 1904, arc forlornly from the sands just south of here.

Follow the sign past the Cape Spencer turn-off to the ghost-town ruins of **Inneston**, a gypsum-mining community abandoned in 1930.

★**Marion Bay Motel** MOTEL $$
(☑08-8854 4141; www.marionbaytavern.com. au; 5 Stenhouse Bay Rd, Marion Bay; s/d/tr $130/150/170; ❋ ❄ 🛜) A highlight of tiny Marion Bay is this wing of five spiffy motel rooms (white walls, new TVs, nice linen) – a welcome surprise if you've been camping or hanging out in sandy-floor beach shacks and are in need of a little sophistication. The Marion Bay tavern is just next door.

★**Yondah Beach House** RENTAL HOUSE $$$
(☑0417 829 010; www.yondah.com.au; off South Coast Rd, Point Yorke; 1/2/3 bedrooms from $330/380/440; ❋ ❄ 🛜 ❄) ❂ One of the stars of the SA tourism scene, Yondah is a gorgeous, architect-designed, three-bedroom beach house, way over yonder in the southern dunes east of Marion Bay. It's a wonderfully isolated spot, with lots of wildlife and luxe privacy by the bucketload. Good value for a group or a big family. And you can bring your dog!

EYRE PENINSULA

Home terrain for three Aboriginal tribal groups – the Banggarla, Nawu and Wirangu peoples – the vast, straw-coloured triangle of Eyre Peninsula is South Australia's big-sky country. It's also the promised land for seafood fans. Meals out here rarely transpire without the option of trying the local oysters, tuna or whiting. Sublime national parks punctuate the coast along with world-class surf breaks and low-key holiday towns, thinning out as you head west towards the Great Australian Bight, the Nullarbor Plain and Western Australia.

The peninsula's photogenic wild western flank is an important breeding ground for southern right whales, Australian sea lions and great white sharks (the scariest scenes in *Jaws* were shot here).

⛵ Tours

Goin' Off Safaris TOURS
(☑0428 877 488; www.goinoffsafaris.com.au; tours from $190) Check the big-ticket items off your Eyre Peninsula 'to-do' list – sharks, tuna, sea lions and seafood – with local guides. Day trips around Port Lincoln and Coffin Bay, plus overnight jaunts, seafood-focused trips and fishing expeditions.

❶ Getting There & Away

AIR

Regional Express (Rex; www.regionalexpress. com.au) operates daily flights from Adelaide to Whyalla (one way from $147), Port Lincoln (from $149) and Ceduna (from $191).

QantasLink (www.qantas.com/qantaslink) also flies from Adelaide to Port Lincoln (one way $162).

BUS

Premier Stateliner (☑1300 851 345; www. premierstateliner.com.au) has daily buses from Adelaide to Port Augusta ($63, 4¼ hours), Whyalla ($70, 5½ hours), Tumby Bay ($121, 9¼ hours), Port Lincoln ($126, 9¾ hours), Streaky Bay ($132, 10 hours) and Ceduna ($147, 11¼ hours).

FERRY

The **SeaSA** (☑08-8823 0777; www.seasa.com. au; Lucky Bay Rd, Lucky Bay; one way adult/

Eyre Peninsula & Yorke Peninsula

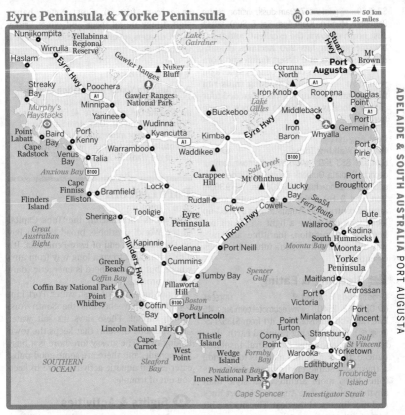

child/car from $35/10/140) car ferry running between Wallaroo on the Yorke Peninsula and Lucky Bay near Cowell on the Eyre Peninsula shaves 350km and several hours off the drive from Adelaide via Port Augusta. The voyage takes around two hours one way. Sailings have been sporadic since 2017, with terminal works at Lucky Bay disrupting services: call or check the website well in advance.

TRAIN

The famous *Ghan* train connects Adelaide with Darwin via Port Augusta; the equally celebrated *Indian Pacific* (between Perth and Sydney) crosses paths with the *Ghan* at Port Augusta. Both epic rail journeys operate as all-inclusive holiday packages these days, rather than point-to-point commuter services. See www.great southernrail.com.au for details.

Pichi Richi Railway (☑1800 777 245; www. prr.org.au; Port Augusta Train Station, Stirling Rd, Port Augusta; return adult/child/family from $53/19/127) runs historic trains from Port Augusta to Quorn in the Flinders Ranges

on most Saturdays, following the original *Ghan* train route.

Port Augusta

☑08 / POP 13,810

From utilitarian, frontier-like Port Augusta – the 'Crossroads of Australia' – highways and railways roll west across the Nullarbor into WA, north to the Flinders Ranges or Darwin, south to Adelaide or Port Lincoln, and east to Sydney. Not a bad position! The old town centre has considerable appeal, with some elegant old buildings and a revitalised waterfront: locals cast lines into the Spencer Gulf as the local kids backflip off jetties.

⊙ Sights & Activities

**Australian Arid Lands
Botanic Garden** GARDENS
(☑08-8641 9116; www.aalbg.sa.gov.au; 144 Stuart Hwy, Port Augusta West; guided tours adult/child

$8/5.50; ☺ gardens 7.30am-dusk, visitor centre 9am-5pm Mon-Fri, 10am-4pm Sat & Sun) **FREE** Just north of town, the excellent (and free!) botanic garden has 250 hectares of sandhills, clay flats and desert fauna and flora (ever seen a Sturt's desert pea?). Explore on your own – established walking trails run from 500m to 4.5km – or take a guided tour (10am Monday to Friday). There's a cafe here too.

Port Augusta
Guided Walking Tours WALKING
(☑ 0439 883 180; www.destinationtown.com.au; departs Wadlata Outback Centre, 41 Flinders Tce; adult/concession/child $25/20/free; ☺ 9.30am Mon, Wed & Fri) Take a 90-minute amble around central Port Augusta with a clued-up local, who can shine a light on Aboriginal heritage, colonisation, maritime and railway history, and the town's future. Bookings essential.

🛏 Sleeping & Eating

Crossroads Ecomotel MOTEL $$
(☑ 08-8642 2540; www.ecomotel.com.au; 45 Eyre Hwy, Port Augusta West; d/f from $135/145; P ❋ 🛜) 🅿 Built using rammed earth, double glazing and 'sips' (structural insulated panels), the aim at this motel is to provide a thermally stable environment for guests (plus 100% more architectural style than anything else in Port Augusta). Desert hues and nice linen seal the deal. The site is a bit barren but a pool is on the cards.

Oasis Apartments APARTMENT $$
(☑ 08-8648 9000; www.majestichotels.com. au; Marryatt St; d from $168, 1-/2-bedroom apt from $179/240; P ❋ 🛜 🐕) Catering largely to conventioneers, this group of 75 luxury units (from studios to two-bedroom) with jaunty designs is right by the water. All rooms have washing machines, dryers, TVs, fridges, microwaves and flashy interior design. Fortress-like security might make you feel like you're in some sort of elitist compound...which you possibly are.

★ Archers' Table CAFE $
(☑ 08-7231 5657; www.archerstable.com.au; 11b Loudon Rd, Port Augusta West; mains $12-21; ☺ 7am-4pm Mon-Thu, to 10pm Fri, to 2pm Sat, to noon Sun) Beneath an attractive vine-hung awning across the gulf from central PA, Archers is an urbane cafe with small-town prices, serving interesting cafe fare (pumpkin and black bean burritos, zucchini and

sweet corn fritters). Great coffee, happy staff, funky mural, beer and wine, Friday night dinners, open seven days...we have a winner!

ℹ Information

Port Augusta Visitor Information Centre
(☑ 08-8641 9193; www.portaugusta.sa.gov. au; Wadlata Outback Centre, 41 Flinders Tce; ☺ 9am-5pm Mon-Fri, 10am-4pm Sat & Sun) This is the major information outlet for the Eyre Peninsula, Flinders Ranges and outback. It's part of the Wadlata Outback Centre.

Port Lincoln
☑ 08 / POP 16,150
Prosperous Port Lincoln, the 'Tuna Capital of the World', overlooks broad Boston Bay on the southern end of Eyre Peninsula. It's a raffish fishing town a long way from anywhere, but the vibe here is energetic (dare we say progressive!).

If not for a lack of fresh water, Port Lincoln might have become the South Australian capital. These days it's salt water (and the tuna therein) that keeps the town ticking over. The grassy foreshore is a busy promenade, and there are some good pubs, eateries and aquatic activities here to keep you out of trouble.

◉ Sights & Activities

Lincoln National Park NATIONAL PARK
(☑ 08-8688 3111; www.parks.sa.gov.au; via Proper Bay Rd; per vehicle $11; ☺ 24hr) Sea-salty Lincoln National Park is 13km south of Port Lincoln. You'll find roaming emus, roos and brush-tailed bettongs, safe swimming coves, vast dunes and pounding surf beaches. Pay entry fees online or at the Port Lincoln Visitor Information Centre (p784), who can advise on **cottage accommodation** (☑ 0419 302 300; www. visitportlincolnaccommodation.net.au/donington-cottage; Donnington Rd; per night $104) and bush camping ($12 per vehicle) within the park, including campgrounds at Fisherman's Point, Memory Cove, September Beach and Surfleet Cove.

Axel Stenross
Maritime Museum MUSEUM
(☑ 08-86823624; www.axelstenross.com.au; 97 Lincoln Hwy, Port Lincoln; adult/child/family $8/12/16; ☺ 9.30am-4.30pm Tue, Thu & Sun, 1-4.30pm

Sat) Chart Port Lincoln's history of boat-building, sailing and whaling in this tin-shed museum on the shores of Boston Bay, just north of town (look for the marooned 1946 tug *Nabilla* by the highway). It's named after a super-capable Finnish sea-man who lived here from 1927 to 1980.

Whalers Way
SCENIC DRIVE

(🌐1300 788 378; www.visitportlincoln.net; Whalers Way Rd; 24hr pass per car incl 1 night camping $30, key deposit $10; ⊙24hr) A scenic 14km coastal drive featuring blowholes, cliffs and crevasses on a remote spit of private land, starting 32km southwest of Port Lincoln. Ever seen a 2642-million-year-old rock? Contact the Port Lincoln visitor information centre (p784) for permits.

👉 Tours

Tasting Eyre
TOURS

(🌐08-8687 0455; www.tastingeyre.com.au; adult/child $129/99) Scenery, wildlife and fishing are the names of the games on this well-planned day tour around Port Lincoln, including a walk in Lincoln National Park, a visit to Whalers Way and seafood tasting at the Fresh Fish Place. Coffin Bay day tours and multi-day Eyre Peninsula epics also available.

Adventure Bay Charters
WILDLIFE

(🌐08-8682 2979; www.adventurebaycharters.com.au; 2 South Quay Blvd) Carbon-neutral Adventure Bay Charters takes you swimming with sea lions (adult/child $205/145) and cage diving with great white sharks (observer $395/295 – add $125 if you want to actually get in the water, or view through a submerged 'aqua sub'). Multiday ocean safaris also available. Note that research suggests that human interaction with sea mammals potentially alters their behavioural and breeding patterns.

Adventure Bay Charters also runs **Fred's Marina Cruises** (🌐1300 788 378; www.adventurebaycharters.com.au/marine-adventure-tours/freds-marina-cruises; Marina Hotel Pontoon, 13 Jubilee Dr; adult/child $50/30; ⊙2pm daily) – a leisurely punt around Port Lincoln's tuna-fleet marina.

Calypso Star Charters
WILDLIFE

(🌐08-8682 3939; www.sharkcagediving.com.au; 3/10 South Quay Blvd, Port Lincoln) Runs submerged cage dives to see great white sharks around the Neptune Islands. Book

in advance (adult/child $495/395; $100 cheaper if you're just watching nervously from the boat). Also runs four-hour swimming with sea lions trips (adult/child/family $195/135/560). But it's still worth noting that research suggests that interaction with sea mammals isn't recommended.

🎉 Festivals & Events

Salt Festival
ART

(www.saltfestival.com.au; ⊙Apr) An innovative, collaborative arts and ideas festival, focused on Port Lincoln but with happenings and venues right across the southern Eyre Peninsula. Expect installations, exhibitions, performances, talks and workshops. Port Lincoln's **Nautilus Arts Centre** (🌐08-8621 2351; www.nautilusartcentre.com.au; 66 Tasman Tce, Port Lincoln; ⊙box office & shop 10am-3pm Mon-Fri, 10am-1pm Sat, performance times vary) features prominently.

Tunarama Festival
CULTURAL

(www.tunarama.net; ⊙Jan) The annual Tunarama Festival on the Australia Day weekend in January celebrates every finny facet of the tuna-fishing industry (including the ethically questionable 'tuna toss').

🛏️ Sleeping

⭐Port Lincoln YHA
HOSTEL $

(🌐08-8682 3605; www.yha.com.au; 26 London St, Port Lincoln; dm $27-35, tw/d/q/f from $75/85/130/185; 🅿❄@🛜) 🧖 Run by a high-energy couple who have spent a fortune renovating the place, this impressive 84-bed hostel occupies a former squash court complex. Thoughtful bonuses include chunky sprung mattresses, reading lights, a cafe/bar and power outlets in lockers. Outrageously clean, and with 300 movies for a rainy day (including *Jaws*). Staff can help with activities bookings too.

Port Lincoln Hotel
HOTEL $$

(🌐08-8621 2000; www.portlincolnhotel.com.au; 1 Lincoln Hwy; d/f/ste from $155/165/220; 🅿❄🛜♨) Bankrolled by a couple of ex-Adelaide Crows AFL footballers, this ritzy seven-storey hotel lifts Port Lincoln above the fray. It's a classy, contemporary affair with switched-on staff. Good on-site bars and eateries too, and it's open all day – play 'Spot Mark Ricciuto' from behind your menu (mains $16 to $34; try the local fish tacos). Bike hire is $15/20 per half-/full day.

★ **Tanonga** B&B $$$

(☑ 0427 277 417; www.tanonga.com.au; Pope Dr, Charlton Gully; d incl breakfast from $325; P ❋) ⚑ Two plush, solar-powered, architect-designed ecolodges stand in stark-white modernist isolation in the hills behind Port Lincoln. They're both super-private and surrounded by native bush, bird life and walking trails. Roll into town for dinner, or order a DIY pack of local produce. Unique and absolutely glorious. 'No frills' rates (sans breakfast) also available.

✖ Eating

★ **Fresh Fish Place** SEAFOOD $$

(☑ 08-8682 2166; www.portlincolnseafood.com.au; 20 Proper Bay Rd; mains $17-29; ⊙ 8.30am-6pm Mon-Fri, to 2pm Sat) Check the 'fish of the day' on the blackboard out the front of this fabulous seafood shack. Inside you can buy fresh local seafood straight off the boats (King George whiting, tuna, kingfish, flathead, squid etc), plus Coffin Bay oysters for $17 a dozen and superb fish and chips. Not to be missed! Seafood tasting tours and cooking classes also available.

Del Giorno's ITALIAN $$

(☑ 08-8683 0577; www.delgiornos.com.au; 80 Tasman Tce; mains breakfast $7-18, lunch & dinner $13-38; ⊙ 7.30am-9pm Mon-Sat, 8am-9pm Sun) The busiest eatery in town, and with good reason: there's decent coffee, big breakfasts and excellent local produce at prices lower than at the pubs. Expect top-notch pizzas, pastas and mains from the land or sea (go for the pot of Kinkawooka mussels with citrus, cream and white wine). Nice one.

🍷 Drinking & Nightlife

★ **Beer Garden Brewing** BREWERY

(☑ 08-8683 5303; www.beergardenbrewing. com; 28 London St; ⊙ noon-6pm Wed, noon-8pm Thu & Sun, noon-10pm Fri & Sat) ⚑ Right next door to Port Lincoln's backpacker hostel (savvy positioning), Beer Garden Brewing brings the craft-beer revolution to the Eyre Peninsula. Sustainability is the focus: it's a family-run business, utilising local wheat, barley, rainwater and hops. The venue is a big, beery barn strewn with retro furniture. The namesake garden is out the front, backed by a long, shady verandah on which you can sit and sip. Try the 6% Cage Diver IPA – hoppy heaven! Pizzas, cheese boards and live music too.

And The Rebel COCKTAIL BAR

(☑ 0413 239 960; www.andtherebel.com; Level 1, 64 Tasman Tce; ⊙ 5-10pm Thu, 5pm-midnight Fri & Sat) Inside the art-deco Nautilus Arts Centre (1923 – formerly the Soldiers' Memorial Hall), follow the curvy handrails upstairs to this sassy, blacked-out cocktail bar. Rebel is the sister operation to **Rogue & Rascal** (☑ 0467 611 086; www.facebook.com/ rogueandrascal; 62 Tasman Tce; mains $12-17; ⊙ 7am-5pm Mon-Thu, to 4pm Fri, to 3pm Sat, to 1pm Sun; ☑) cafe downstairs, and is by far the classiest place for a drink in Port Lincoln. Order a whisky sour and head for the balcony. Occasional live tunes too.

❶ Information

Port Lincoln Visitor Information Centre (☑ 1300 788 378, 08-8683 3544; www.visit portlincoln.net; 3 Adelaide Pl; ⊙ 9am-5pm Mon-Fri, 10am-4pm Sat & Sun) This mega-helpful place books accommodation, has national parks information and passes, and stocks the *Parnkalla Walking Trail* map, tracing a scenic 35km course around the Port Lincoln coastline (you don't have to walk it all at once).

Coffin Bay

☑ 08 / POP 650

Oyster lovers rejoice! Deathly sounding Coffin Bay (named in 1802 by English explorer Matthew Flinders after his buddy Sir Isaac Coffin) is a snoozy fishing village basking languidly in the warm sun...until a 4000-strong holiday horde arrives every January. Slippery, salty oysters from the nearby beds are exported worldwide – superb!

◉ Sights & Activities

Coffin Bay National Park NATIONAL PARK

(☑ 08-8688 3111; www.parks.sa.gov.au; via Coffin Bay Rd; per vehicle $10; ⊙ 24hr) Along the ocean side of Coffin Bay is wild, coastal Coffin Bay National Park, overrun with roos, emus and fat goannas. Access for conventional vehicles is limited: you can get to picturesque Point Avoid (with coastal lookouts, rocky cliffs, good surf and whales passing between May and October) and Yangie Bay (arid-looking rocky landscapes and walking trails), but otherwise you'll need a 4WD. There are some isolated campsites within the park ($12 per vehicle), generally with dirt-road access.

Pure Coffin Bay Oysters FOOD & DRINK

(☑0428 261 805; www.coffinbayoysters.com.
au; 9 Martindale St; ☺9am-5pm Mon-Fri,
9.30am-12.30pm Sat & Sun) Take a tour of a
working Coffin Bay oyster farm – either out
on the water where they're cultivated ($65,
90 minutes) or the shed in which they're
shucked ($25, one hour) – or just visit the
cute little backstreet 'Shellar Door' (ha-ha)
for takeaway bivalves shucked to order.

🛏 Sleeping & Eating

Coffin Bay

Caravan Park CARAVAN PARK $

(☑08-8685 4170; www.coffinbaycaravanpark.
com.au; 91 Esplanade; unpowered/powered sites
from $24/33, cabins without/with bathroom from
$115/80, villas from $135; Ⓟ❄🛜) Resident
cockatoos, galahs and parrots squawk
around the she-oak shaded, gently sloping
sites here, and the cabins offer reasonable bang for your buck (BYO linen). Lovely
two-bedroom family villas too. On the downside, it's all a bit exposed, public and visible
from the main street, but if you're into caravan parks, that's probably not an issue.

1802 Oyster Bar BISTRO $$

(☑08-8685 4626; www.1802oysterbar.com.au;
61 Esplanade; mains $24-42; ☺noon-late Wed-Fri,
11am-late Sat & Sun) This snappy-looking place
on the way into town, with its broad deck
and rammed-earth walls, looks out across
the boat-filled harbour. Order a Spencer
Gulf prawn and mango curry, a vegetarian
risotto or some beer-battered flathead to
accompany your crafty Long Beach Lager
(on tap). Oysters (of course) come in 12 different incarnations, chilled or grilled.

Streaky Bay & Around

☑08 / POP 1480

This endearing little seasider (actually
on Blanche Port) takes its name from the
streaks of seaweed Matt Flinders spied in
the bay as he sailed by in 1802. Visible at low
tide, the seagrass attracts ocean critters and
the bigger critters that eat them – meaning
first-class fishing.

The town itself has a terrific pub, plenty
of accommodation and a couple of good eateries, and is a lovely spot to dream away a
day or three.

◉ Sights & Activities

Murphy's Haystacks LANDMARK

(www.nullarbornet.com.au/themes/murphyshay
stacks.html; off Flinders Hwy, Point Labbatt; per
person/family $2/5; ☺daylight hours) A few kilo-
metres down the Point Labatt road are the
globular Murphy's Haystacks, an improbable congregation of 'inselbergs' – colourful,
weather-sculpted granite outcrops that are
an estimated 1500 million years old.

Cape Bauer Loop

Scenic Drive SCENIC DRIVE

(☑08-8626 1108; www.streakybay.com.au/
explore/scenic-drives-trails; Cape Bauer Rd, Streaky
Bay; ☺24hr) FREE Drive north beyond
Streaky Bay's wheat fields to the rugged
dune country around Cape Bauer – a 38km
dirt-road loop that makes a super-scenic
detour. Islands, beaches, reefs, blowholes,
crumbling limestone cliffs and the endless
ocean grinding into shore – this is isolated,
end-of-the-world terrain, and a chance
to redress your urban overload. Look for
ospreys, kangaroos and circling sea eagles
en route.

🛏 Sleeping & Eating

Streaky Bay

Motel & Villas MOTEL $$

(Streaky Bay; ☑08-8626 1126; www.streakybay
motelandvillas.com.au; 11-13 Alfred Tce; motel s/d/f
from $115/135/170, villas $180-290; Ⓟ❄🛜🏊)
A tidy row of bricky, older-style motel units
(with a Hollywood-worthy facelift), plus an
ever-expanding complex of family-size villas
that are much more 'now' (spiky pot plants,
mushroom-hued render, lime-coloured outdoor furniture). There's a not-unstylish BBQ
area and an indoor pool too, if you don't
fancy the shark-proof swimming enclosure
down at the jetty. Good off-season rates.

★Bay Funktion CAFE $$

(☑0428 861 242; www.bayfunktion.com.au; cnr
Wells St & Bay Rd, Streaky Bay; mains $14-27;
☺8am-5pm Mon-Fri, to 2pm Sat; 🛜) In a lovely
old brick-and-stone shopfront on the main
street, funky Bay Funktion is part cafe, part
florist and part wedding planner (hence the
slightly odd name). But as a cafe, it's great!
Croissants, pizzas, breakfast tacos, slabs of
cake, juices, sunny staff and killer coffee.
Head for the plant-filled courtyard out the
back if all the tables are full (likely).

ℹ️ Information

Streaky Bay Visitor Information Centre

(📞 08-8626 7033; www.streakybay.com.au; 21 Bay Rd, Streaky Bay; ⏰ 9am-12.30pm & 1.30-5pm Mon-Fri) For the local low-down, swing by the visitor info centre.

Ceduna

📞 08 / POP 1850

Despite the locals' best intentions, Ceduna remains a raggedy fishing town that just can't shake its tag as a sand-blown, edgy pit stop en route to WA (there are *five* caravan parks here). But the local oysters love it! And if you're heading west in whale season (May to October), Ceduna is the place for updates on sightings at Head of Bight. Also of interest is Maralinga, the British 1950s nuclear test site 400km north of Ceduna, which you can now visit on tours.

◉ Sights

Maralinga Atomic Bomb Test Site   HISTORIC SITE

(www.maralingatours.com.au; tour per person incl 2 nights camping/hut $230/355; ⏰ Mar-Oct) If you've got a 4WD, make your way to Maralinga, 400km northwest of Ceduna – a 9½-hour approach. It was here at Ground Zero that the British detonated seven nuclear bombs between 1956 and 1963, doing a notoriously bad job of protecting the local Maralinga Tjarutja people from fallout and cleaning up afterwards. Tour the site and hear the stories.

Thevenard   AREA

(Thevenard Rd, Ceduna; 24hr) FREE For a dose of hard-luck, weather-beaten atmosphere, take a drive out to Thevenard, Ceduna's photogenic port suburb on the peninsula south of town. Boarded-up shops, a pub with barred windows, dusty old iron-clad shacks...all loomed over by the massive silos next to the pier. If you're a painter or writer, this is fertile fuel for the imagination!

✳️ Festivals & Events

Oysterfest   FOOD

(www.facebook.com/cedunaoysterfest; ⏰ Sep/Oct) If you're passing through Ceduna in late September/early October, check out Oysterfest, the undisputed king of Australian oyster parties. Art exhibitions, cooking demonstrations, a street parade, live music and boundless bivalves.

🛏️ Sleeping & Eating

Ceduna Foreshore Hotel/Motel   MOTEL $$

(📞 08-8625 2008; www.cedunahotel.com.au; 32 O'Loughlin Tce; d $150-195; 🅿️✳️🛜) Clad in aquamarine tiles, the 54-room Foreshore is the most luxurious option in town, with water views and a bistro focused on west-coast seafood (mains $19 to $40, serving 6.30am to 9am, noon to 2pm and 6pm to 8.30pm). The view from the outdoor terrace extends through Norfolk Island pines and out across the bay.

⭐ Ceduna Oyster Barn   SEAFOOD $$

(📞 0497 085 549; www.facebook.com/ceduna oyster; Eyre Hwy,; 6 oysters from $14, mains $12-30; ⏰ 10am-6.30pm) Pick up a box of freshly shucked molluscs and head for the foreshore, or sit up on the rooftop here under an umbrella and watch the road trains rumble in from WA. Fresh as can be. Fish and chips too, plush fish burgers and sushi (probably an unnecessary menu addition).

ℹ️ Information

Ceduna Visitor Information Centre (📞 08-8625 3343; www.cedunatourism.com.au; 58 Poynton St; ⏰ 9am-5.30pm Mon-Fri, to 4.30pm Sat & Sun) The Ceduna Visitor Information Centre can help with local info, maps and current whale-sighting stats.

Ceduna to the Western Australia Border

It's 480km from Ceduna to the WA border. Along this stretch you can get a bed and a beer at **Penong** (72km from Ceduna), **Fowlers Bay** (141km), **Nundroo** (151km), the **Nullarbor Roadhouse** (295km) near Head of Bight, and at **Border Village** on the border itself.

Wheat and sheep paddocks line the road to Nundroo, after which you're in mallee scrub for another 100km. Around 20km later, the trees thin to low bluebush as you enter the true Nullarbor (Latin for 'no trees'). Road trains, caravans and cyclists of questionable sanity are your only companions as you put your foot down and career towards the setting sun.

◉ Sights & Activities

Head of Bight   LANDMARK

(📞 08-8625 6201; www.headofbight.com.au; off Eyre Hwy, Nullarbor; adult/child/family Jun-Oct

$15/6/35, Nov-May $7/5/14; ⊗8am-5pm Jun-Oct, 8.30am-4pm Nov-May) The viewing platforms and boardwalks at Head of Bight overlook a major southern right whale breeding ground. Whales migrate here from Antarctica, and you can see them cavorting from May to October. The breeding area is protected by the 45,822-sq-km **Great Australian Bight Commonwealth Marine Reserve** (☑1800 069 352; www.parksaustralia. gov.au/marine/parks/south-west/great-australian-bight; ⊗24hr), the world's second-largest marine park after the Great Barrier Reef. The info centre here has snacks.

Cactus Beach   SURFING
(☑08-8625 1036; www.nullarbornet.com.au/towns/cactusBeach.html; off Point Sinclair Rd, via Penong) Turn off the highway at Penong (population 200), and follow the 21km dirt road to Point Sinclair and Cactus Beach, which has three of Australia's most famous surf breaks. Caves is a wicked right-hand break for experienced surfers (locals don't take too kindly to tourists dropping in). There's basic bush camping on private property close to the breaks ($10 per person per night); BYO drinking water.

FLINDERS RANGES

Known simply as 'the Flinders', this ancient mountain range is an iconic South Australian environment. Jagged peaks and escarpments rise up north of Port Augusta and track 400km north to Mt Hopeless. The colours here are remarkable: as the day stretches out, the mountains shift from mauve mornings to midday chocolates and ochre-red sunsets. Emus wander across roads; yellow-footed rock wallabies bound from boulder to boulder.

Before Europeans arrived, the northern Flinders Ranges were prized by the Adnyamathanha peoples for their red ochre deposits, used in medicines and rituals. Sacred caves, rock paintings and carvings abound throughout the region. In the wake of white exploration came villages, farms, country pubs, wheat farms and cattle stations, many of which failed under the unrelenting sun.

The Southern Ranges were home to different tribal groups: the Nukuna around Port Pirie extending up to Quorn, and the Ngadjuri around Peterborough and Ororoo.

☞ Tours

Arkaba Walk   WALKING
(☑1300 790 561; www.arkabawalk.com; per person ex-Arkaba/Adelaide $2400/2900; ⊗mid-Mar–mid-Oct) Hike for four days through the Flinders in fine (guided) style. Prices include park entry fees, chef-cooked meals, luggage portage, deluxe camping and a night at the superplush Arkaba Station (p790). A once-in-a-lifetime treat! Save a few hundred by making your own way to the station.

SA Eco Tours   ECOTOUR
(☑0417 830 533; www.saecotours.com.au; tours 3 day $695-1995, 5 day $1495-2495) Three- and five-day tours into the Flinders from Adelaide, with prices sliding up the scale depending on what kind of accommodation you opt for, from camping in pre-erected tents to motels and eco-villas. The five-day tour extends to Arkaroola. Big on environmental and Indigenous information and respect.

❶ Getting There & Away

Exploring the Flinders on a tour or under your own steam is a great way to go (public transport is very limited). Or take a guided tour.

Port Pirie is an easy 226km highway drive from Adelaide. From here it's minor-road driving inland towards Laura, Melrose and Peterborough.

Premier Stateliner (p733) runs daily buses from Adelaide to Port Pirie ($50, 3½ hours). From here, **Port Pirie Bus Service** (☑08-8632 5200; www.facebook.com/pg/piriebus) buses run to Peterborough ($7, two hours) every Monday and Thursday, via Melrose ($7, 1¼ hours) on Thursday.

Genesis Transport (☑08-8552 4000; www. genesistransport.com.au) runs an Adelaide–Copley bus on Monday and Thursday, via Laura, Melrose, Quorn, Hawker, Parachilna and Leigh Creek, returning on Tuesday and Friday in the other direction. Extensions to Wilpena and Blinman on demand. See the website for times and fares.

Pichi Richi Railway (☑1800 777 245; www. prr.org.au; Flinders Ranges Visitor Information Centre, Railway Tce, Quorn; one way adult/child/family $71/24/178) runs historic trains from Port Augusta to Quorn in the Flinders Ranges on most Saturdays March to November, following the old Ghan train route.

Southern Ranges

Port Pirie is the big-smoke around these parts, but you don't enter the Southern Ranges proper until **Laura** (population

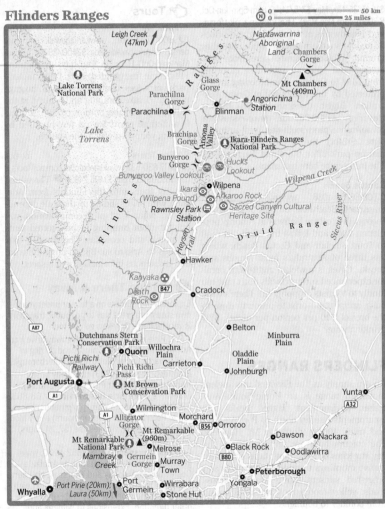

660), which emerges from the wheat fields like Superman's Smallville (all civic pride and 1950s prosperity). The long, geranium-adorned main street has a supermarket, chemist, bakery, bank, post office and even a shoe shop! Tiny **Stone Hut** is 10km north of Laura.

The Flinders' oldest (and most appealing) town is little **Melrose**, under the considerable shadow of Mt Remarkable. **Peterborough** (population 1420), 87km inland from Melrose, is a characterful place: a former service town for SA Railways trains, with a time-tunnel main street lined with old shopfronts, rickety verandahs and huge stone pubs. There were 100 steam trains a day running through Peterborough in 1923 – enough steam to change the local climate, making it hotter and more humid than surrounding towns.

Steamtown Heritage
Rail Centre   MUSEUM
(📞08-8651 3355; www.steamtown.com.au; 1 Telford Ave, Peterborough; adult/child/family $17.50/8/35, sound-and-light show per person $25; ⏰9am-5pm) nside Peterborough's original rail depot, this excellent museum takes you back to the days of steam power, when 100

trains a day were shunting through this little town. Guided tours (90 minutes) run all day, with the last one at 3.30pm. There's also a sound-and-light show at 8.30pm (7.30pm in winter). The town's visitor information centre is here too (www.visitpeterboroughsa. com.au).

ℹ Information

The visitor info centres in **Port Pirie** (📞 08-8633 8700; www.pirie.sa.gov.au; 3 Mary Elie St, Port Pirie; ⊙ 9am-5pm Mon-Fri, to 4pm Sat, 10am-4pm Sun) and Port Augusta (p782) are veritable fonts of Southern Ranges info.

Peterborough Visitor Information Centre (📞 08-8651 3355; www.visitpeterboroughsa. com.au; Steamtown Heritage Rail Centre, 1 Telford Ave, Peterborough; ⊙ 9am-5pm) Inside the Steamtown Heritage Rail Centre.

Melrose

📞 08 / POP 350

The oldest town in the Flinders is photogenic Melrose (founded 1853), snug in the elbow of the 960m Mt Remarkable (which comprises most of Mt Remarkable National Park). Melrose has the perfect mix of well-preserved architecture, a cracking good pub, quality accommodation and parks with *actual* grass (you won't see much of this further north). There are some great mountain-biking trails around here too. Pick up the *Melrose Historical Walk* brochure for a history tour. Online, check out www. melrose-mtremarkable.org.au.

⊙ Sights

Mt Remarkable
National Park   NATIONAL PARK
(📞 08-8841 3400; www.parks.sa.gov.au; National Hwy 1, via Mambray Creek; per vehicle $10; ⊙ 24hr) Bush boffins rave about the steep, jagged Mt Remarkable National Park, which straddles the Southern Flinders and rises above little Melrose like a protective overlord. Wildlife and bushwalking are the main lures, with various tracks (including part of the Heysen Trail) meandering through isolated gorges. Remarkable! The main access point is at Mambray Creek, 50km north of Port Pirie, or you can walk into the park from Alligator Gorge or Melrose.

Over The Edge   MOUNTAIN BIKING
(📞 08-8666 2222; www.otesports.com.au; 4 Stuart St, Melrose; ⊙ 9am-5pm Wed-Mon) Mountain biking is a big deal in little Melrose. Over

The Edge has spares, repairs, quality bike rental ($45 to $100 per day) and a little cafe (snacks $4 to $10).

🛏 Sleeping & Eating

Under The Mount   RENTAL HOUSE $
(📞 0409 093 649; www.underthemount.com. au; 9-11 Jacka St, Melrose; d/6-bed dm $110/180; 🅿 ❄) Run by some mountain-biking doyens, casual, rambling Under The Mount features six en-suite doubles, two six-bed dorms and a communal kitchen inside, and BBQs, fire areas, a bike workshop and hose-down areas outside. It's part share-house, part hostel, with a common love of mountain-biking good times uniting guests.

★**North Star Hotel**   PUB $$
(📞 08-8666 2110; www.northstarhotel.com.au; 43 Nott St, Melrose; d/trucks from $110/160; 🅿 ❄ 🛜) As welcome as summer rain: the North Star is a noble 1854 pub renovated in city-meets-woolshed style. Sit under spinning ceiling fans at the bistro (mains $18 to $32) for lunch, dinner or just a cold beer. Accommodation comprises plush suites upstairs, Bundaleer Cottage next door (sleeps 16) and quirky cabins lodged atop two old trucks out the back. Excellent.

Quorn

📞 08 / POP 1230

Is Quorn a film set after the crew has gone home? With more jeering crows than people, it's a cinematographic little outback town with a pub-lined main street. Wheat farming took off here in 1875, and the town prospered with the arrival of the Great Northern Railway from Port Augusta. Quorn (pronounced 'corn') remained an important railroad junction until trains into the Flinders were cut in 1970.

Death Rock   RELIGIOUS SITE
(off Quorn–Hawker Rd, via Kanyaka; ⊙ daylight hours) **FREE** From the ruins (41km north of Quorn on the Quorn–Hawker Rd), it's a 20-minute walk to a waterhole loomed over by the massive Death Rock. The story goes that local Aboriginal people once placed their dying kinfolk here to see out their last hours. Be respectful.

★**Quorn Caravan Park**   CARAVAN PARK $
(📞 08-8648 6206; www.quorncaravanpark.com.au; 8 Silo Rd, Quorn; unpowered/powered sites $28/35, dm $40, van s/d $65/75, cabins $100-140, extra

ADNYAMATHANHA DREAMING

Land and nature are integral to the culture of the traditional owners of the Flinders Ranges. The people collectively called Adnyamathanha (Hill People) are actually a collection of the Wailpi, Kuyani, Jadliaura, Piladappa and Pangkala tribes, who exchanged and elaborated on stories to explain their spectacular local geography.

The walls of Ikara (Wilpena Pound), for example, are the bodies of two *akurra* (giant snakes), who coiled around Ikara during an initiation ceremony, eating most of the participants. The snakes were so full after their feast they couldn't move and willed themselves to die, creating the landmark.

adult/child $20/15; P ❄) ✐ Fully keyed-in to climate change, this passionately run park on Pinkerton Creek is hell-bent on reducing emissions and restoring native habitat. Features include spotless cabins, a backpacker cabin (sleeps six), a camp kitchen made from recycled timbers, shady sites, rainwater tanks everywhere and a few lazy roos lounging about under the red gums. Discounts for walkers and cyclists.

★ **Great Northern Lodge** LODGE $$
(☑08-8648 6940; www.greatnorthernlodge. com.au; 45 First St, Quorn; d/apt from $110/200; P ❄ 🛜) This impressive operation comprises six buildings, with all kinds of accommodation configurations: private motel-style doubles, double bedrooms off a communal kitchen, single-level suites and two-storey apartments. All are classy, with leather couches, mod bathrooms, kitchens, nice linen and tastefully muted colour schemes. Raid the shared veggie garden for cabbages, spinach and parsley. Check in at Emily's Bistro (☑08-8648 6940; www. facebook.com/emilysbistro; 45 First St, Quorn; bakery items from $4, mains $22-28; ⊘8am-9m Tue-Sat, to 5pm Mon & Sun).

❶ Information

Flinders Ranges Visitor Information Centre
(☑08-8620 0510; www.flindersranges.com; Quorn Railway Station, Railway Tce, Quorn; ⊘9am-5pm Mon-Fri, 9am-4pm Sat & Sun) Maps, brochures and advice – the main info hub for the Flinders Ranges. Check out the little history room out the back.

Hawker

☑08 / POP 240

Hawker is the last outpost of civilisation before Ikara (Wilpena Pound), 59km to the north. Much like Quorn, Hawker has seen better days, most of which were when the old *Ghan* train stopped here. These days Hawker is a pancake-flat, pit-stop town with an ATM, a general store, a pub and the world's most helpful petrol station.

Arkaroo Rock RELIGIOUS SITE
(www.walkingsa.org.au/walk/find-a-place-to-walk/ arkaroo-rock-hike; Arkaroo Rock Rd, via Hawker; ⊘daylight hours) FREE Around 40km north of Hawker towards Wilpena, Arkaroo Rock is a sacred Aboriginal site (we don't need to lecture you about being respectful). The rock art here features reptile and human figures in charcoal, bird-lime, and yellow and red ochre. It's a short(ish) return walk from the car park (2km, one hour).

Flinders Bush Retreats FARMSTAY $$
(☑08-8648 4441; www.flindersbushretreats.com. au; Willow Waters Rd; unpowered sites per vehicle $10, eco-tent d $165, houses 1-4 people from $275; P ❄) Working hard to crack into the booming Flinders station-stay market, Flinders Bush Retreats offers private bush camping, a restored early-1900s stone homestead (three bedrooms), a fancy four-bedroom guesthouse and an excellent breezy eco-tent for two (glamp it up!). Lots of fire-pit, BBQ and stargazing action to be had. Minimum two-night stay; 21km east of Hawker.

Arkaba Station BOUTIQUE HOTEL $$$
(☑02-9571 6399, 1300 790 561; www.arkaba station.com; Wilpena Rd, via Hawker; adult/child from $1070/963; P ❄ 🛜 ≋) Flashy outback station accommodation in an 1850s homestead, between Hawker and Wilpena: it's an exercise in contemporary bush luxury. Rates include chef-cooked meals and daily guided wilderness safaris tailored to your interests (walking, driving, cultural, airborne). Transfers also available (though at these prices, you might want to save a few dollars and drive yourself). Two-night minimum stay.

Flinders Food Co CAFE $
(☑08-8648 4380; www.facebook.com/flinders foodco; 66 Elder Tce; mains $12-19; ⊘7.30am-4.30pm Tue-Sat, 7.30am-3pm Sun) At last, a decent cafe in Hawker! Taking over from an old country tearoom that was well past its use-by date, Flinders Food Co sasses things

up with kangaroo burgers, grilled saltbush lamb backstraps, smoked-salmon bagels and wattle-seed hotcakes. Good coffee, smoothies and milkshakes too. Eyeball the turtles in the tanks on your way out.

ℹ️ Information

Hawker Motors (📞 08-8648 4014; www.hawkermotors.com.au; cnr Wilpena & Cradock Rds, Hawker; ⏱️ 7.30am-6pm) The town's petrol station (fill up if you're heading north) doubles as the most helpful visitor information centre you may ever encounter.

Ikara-Flinders Ranges National Park

One of SA's most treasured parks, **Ikara-Flinders Ranges National Park** (📞 08-8648 0048; www.parks.sa.gov.au; via Wilpena Rd, Wilpena; per vehicle $10; ⏱️ 24hr) is laced with craggy gorges, saw-toothed ranges, abandoned homesteads, Aboriginal sites, native wildlife and, after it rains, carpets of wild flowers. The park's big-ticket item is the 80-sq-km natural basin Ikara (Wilpena Pound) – a sunken elliptical valley ringed by gnarled ridges (don't let anyone tell you it's a meteorite crater!).

🔆 Sights

The only vehicular access to see **Ikara** is via the Wilpena Pound Resort's **shuttle bus** (📞 08-8648 0004; www.wilpenapound.com.au; Wilpena Pound Resort, Wilpena Rd, Wilpena; return adult/child/family $5/3/12), which drops you about 1km from the old **Hills Homestead**, from where you can walk to **Wangarra Lookout** (another steep 500m). The shuttle runs at 9am, 11am, 1pm and 3pm. Otherwise, it's a three-hour, 8km return walk between the resort and lookout (guided walking tours available from the resort for $45 per person).

The 20km **Brachina Gorge Geological Trail** features an amazing layering of exposed sedimentary rock, covering 120 million years of the earth's history. Grab a brochure from the visitor centre.

The **Bunyeroo–Brachina–Aroona Scenic Drive** is a 110km round trip, passing by Bunyeroo Valley, Brachina Gorge, Aroona Valley and Stokes Hill Lookout. The drive starts north of Wilpena off the road to Blinman.

Wilpena Pound Resort (p792) itself, inside the national park, is owned and managed by a local Adnyamathanha business group.

🏃 Activities

Bushwalking in the Flinders is unforgettable. Before you make tracks, ensure you've got enough water, sunscreen and a massive hat, and tell someone where you're going. Pick up the *Bushwalking in Flinders Ranges National Park* brochure from the visitor information centre. Many walks kick off at Wilpena Pound Resort (p792).

For a really good look at Ikara, the walk up to **Tanderra Saddle** (return 15km, six hours) on the ridge of **St Mary Peak** is brilliant, though it's a thigh-pounding scramble at times. The Adnyamathanha people request that you restrict your climbing to the ridge and don't climb St Mary Peak itself, due to its traditional significance to them.

The quick, tough track up to **Mt Ohlssen Bagge** (return 6.5km, four hours) rewards the sweaty hiker with a stunning panorama. Good short walks include the stroll to **Hills Homestead** (return 6.5km, two hours) and the dash up to the **Wilpena Solar Power Station** (return 500m, 30 minutes).

Just beyond the park's southeast corner, a one-hour, 1km return walk leads to the **Sacred Canyon Cultural Heritage Site**, with Aboriginal rock-art galleries featuring animal tracks and designs.

🕝 Tours

There are **4WD tours** run by both Wilpena Pound Resort (p792; half-/full day from $189/295) and Rawnsley Park Station (half-/full day from $180/280). Some tour companies also operate from Hawker.

Both operations also offer **scenic flights** of various durations (from $169). Wilpena Pound Resort also runs **Aboriginal cultural tours** – 2km walks focusing on land, culture and heritage ($45/35 per adult/child). And there's also a traditional Welcome to Country ceremony here every night near reception, free to all-comers.

🛏️ Sleeping

⭐ Rawnsley Park Station   RESORT, CARAVAN PARK $$

(📞 08-8648 0700; www.rawnsleypark.com.au; Wilpena Rd, via Hawker; unpowered/powered sites $27/38, hostel per adult/child $40/30, cabins/units/villas/houses from $108/175/430/570; 🅿️❄️🛜🏊) This rangy homestead 35km from Hawker on the southern fringes of Ikara-Flinders Ranges

National Park offers everything from tent sites to luxe eco-villas, a 1950s self-contained house and a caravan park with cabins and dorms. Activities include mountain-bike hire (half-/full day $30/60), bushwalks, 4WD tours and scenic flights. The excellent **Woolshed Restaurant** (mains $34-42; ☺ noon-2pm Wed-Sun Mar-Nov, 6-8.30pm daily year-round) is also on-site. Great stuff.

Wilpena Pound Resort
RESORT $$

(☏08-8648 0004; www.wilpenapound.com.au; Wilpena Rd, Wilpena; unpowered/powered sites from $14/35, permanent/safari tents $90/320, motel d/f $193/223; P ❀ ☎ ☲) Owned and managed by a local Adnyamathanha business group, this far-flung resort has lost considerable sheen of late (maintenance standards have slipped, and restaurant offerings are now more pub-like – mains $26 to $38), but it remains an interesting place to stay, with motel-style rooms and a campground with plush safari tents (book in advance). Take a dip in the pool and have a drink at the bar.

Bike hire, scenic flights, guided walks and Aboriginal cultural experiences also available.

ⓘ Information

Wilpena Pound Visitor Information Centre

(☏08-8648 0048; www.wilpenapound.com.au/do/visitors-centre; Wilpena Pound Resort, Wilpena; ☺8am-6pm) At the resort's info centre you'll find a shop, petrol, park and bushwalking info and bike hire ($35/65 per half-/full day). It also handles bookings for scenic flights and 4WD tours. Pay your park entry fees here too, or online before you arrive.

Blinman & Parachilna

About an hour north of Wilpena on a sealed road, ubercute Blinman (population 30) owes its existence to the copper ore discovered here in 1859 and the smelter built in 1903. But the boom went bust and 1500 folks left town. Today Blinman's main claim to fame is as SA's highest town (610m above sea level). There are interesting tours of the old mines.

On the Hawker–Leigh Creek road, middle-of-nowhere Parachilna (population somewhere between four and seven) is an essential Flinders Ranges destination. The draw here is the legendary Prairie Hotel – a world-class stay.

Heritage Blinman Mine
HISTORIC SITE

(☏08-8648 4782; www.heritageblinmanmine.com.au; Mine Rd, Blinman; tours adult/child/family $28/11/65; ☺9am-4.30pm, reduced hours Nov-Mar) Much of Blinman's 150-year-old copper mine has been redeveloped, with lookouts, audiovisual interpretation and information boards. Excellent one-hour tours run on the hour between 10am and 3pm. If you've got a few minutes to wait, ask for the key to the amazing old 1870 haberdashery shop across the road, which is trying hard to stay vertical.

★ Prairie Hotel
HOTEL $$

(☏08-8648 4844; www.prairiehotel.com.au; cnr High St & West Tce, Parachilna; unpowered/powered sites $21/35, budget cabins d/tw/f $115/115/160, hotel s/d/tr from $125/180/350; P ❀ ☎) The Prairie Hotel (1905) has slick suites out the back, plus camping and basic cabins across the street. Don't miss a pub meal (mains breakfast $8 to $28, lunch and dinner $24 to $42): try the feral mixed grill (camel sausage, kangaroo fillet and emu). 'Too early for a beer?! Whose rules are those?' said the barman at 10.42am.

OUTBACK SOUTH AUSTRALIA

The area north of the Eyre Peninsula and the Flinders Ranges stretches into the vast, empty spaces of the South Australian outback – about 70% of the state, covering the traditional lands of dozens of Indigenous nations. If you're prepared, travelling through this sparsely populated and harsh country is utterly rewarding.

Heading into the red heart of Australia, Woomera is the first pit stop, with its dark legacy of nuclear tests and shiny collection of left-over rockets. Further north on the Stuart Hwy and along the legendary Oodnadatta and Strzelecki Tracks, eccentric outback towns such as William Creek, Innamincka and Coober Pedy emerge from the heat haze. This is no country for the faint-hearted: it's waterless, fly-blown and dizzyingly hot. No wonder the opal miners in Coober Pedy live underground.

ⓒ Tours

Sacred Earth Safaris
ADVENTURE

(☏08-8536 2234; www.sacredearthsafaris.com.au; adult/child $5575/5375) Epic 10-day outback 4WD tours trundling along the big

OODNADATTA TRACK

The legendary, lonesome Oodnadatta Track – passing mostly through Arabana country – is an unsealed, 615km road between Marla on the Stuart Hwy and Marree in the northern Flinders Ranges. The track traces the route of the old Overland Telegraph Line and the defunct Great Northern Railway, along which the famous *Ghan* train once travelled. Along the way are remote settlements, quirky desert sights and the enormous Kati Thanda-Lake Eyre (usually dry). Bring a 4WD – the track is often passable in a regular car, but it gets bumpy, muddy, dusty and potholed and is much more viable with four-wheel power. Plenty of guided 4WD tours also run along the track.

Fuel, accommodation (at least a campsite) and meals are available at Marla, Oodnadatta, William Creek and Marree. For track info, pick up the *Oodnadatta Track – String of Springs* brochure, or download it from www.roxbydowns.sa.gov.au/webdata/resources/files/string-of-springs.pdf. Also see the sketchy-but-useful 'mud maps' on the Pink Roadhouse website (www.pinkroadhouse.com.au).

Before you head off, check track conditions (and for closure after rains) with the Coober Pedy Visitor Information Centre (p796), the Royal Automobile Association (p733) in Adelaide, online at www.dpti.sa.gov.au/OutbackRoads, or call the Outback Road Report on 📞 1300 361 033.

three desert tracks – Oodnadatta, Strzelecki and Birdsville – plus Coober Pedy and the Flinders Ranges.

Arabunna Tours CULTURAL
(📞 08-8675 8351; www.arabunnatours.com.au; multiday tours ex-Adelaide from $2000) Aboriginal-owned company running cultural tours from Adelaide to the Flinders Ranges, Marree, Oodnadatta Track and Lake Eyre.

❶ Getting There & Away

AIR
Regional Express (p750) flies most days between Adelaide and Coober Pedy (from $250, two hours).

BUS
Greyhound Australia (p733) runs a daily (overnight) bus from Adelaide to Pimba ($100, 6¾ hours) and Glendambo ($115, 8¼ hours), Coober Pedy ($178, 11¼ hours) and Marla ($243, 14¼ hours), continuing to Alice Springs.

CAR
The Stuart Hwy tracks from Port Augusta to Darwin. In SA, fuel and accommodation are available at Pimba (176km from Port Augusta), Glendambo (288km), Coober Pedy (542km), Cadney Homestead (693km) and Marla (775km). Pimba, Coober Pedy and Marla have 24-hour fuel sales.

TRAIN
Operated by Great Southern Rail (p733), all-inclusive journeys on the *Ghan* train run through outback SA between Adelaide and Alice Springs, continuing to Darwin, with a stop at Coober Pedy (or rather, a rail siding near Coober Pedy, from

where tour buses ferry you into town); see the website for details.

Woomera & Around

A 6km detour off the Stuart Hwy from little truckstop **Pimba** (population 50; 481km north of Adelaide), Woomera (population 150) emerged as a settlement in 1947 as HQ for experimental British rocket and nuclear tests at notorious sites like Maralinga. The local Maralinga Tjarutja people suffered greatly from the resulting nuclear fallout. You can visit the Maralinga test site with Maralinga Atomic Bomb Test Site Tours (p786) via Ceduna on the Eyre Peninsula. Woomera itself is Kokatha tribal country.

These days Woomera remains an eerie artificial town that's still an active Department of Defence test site. Beyond Woomera, drive-through **Glendambo** and quirky **Roxby Downs** offer different takes on the outback-town experience.

🛏 Sleeping & Eating

Glendambo Hotel-Motel & Caravan Park MOTEL $
(📞 08-8672 1030; Stuart Hwy, Glendambo; unpowered/powered sites $25/30, s/d/f from $95/110/140; 🅿❄🏊) If your eyelids are drooping out on the highway, bunk down at the oasis-like Glendambo Hotel-Motel, which has bars, a restaurant, a pool (!) and a bunch of OK motel units. Outside are dusty campsites; inside are meaty mains at the

ADELAIDE & SOUTH AUSTRALIA COOBER PEDY

BIRDSVILLE & STRZELECKI TRACKS

Crossed by indigenous Australians for millennia, these two iconic, historic outback stock routes tell stories of exploration and the opening up of the Australian continent. Completing either of these tracks is a real badge of honour – journeys into Australia's red heart that you won't hurriedly forget.

The **Birdsville Track** is an old droving trail running 517km from Marree in SA to Birdsville, just across the border in Queensland. It was made famous by stockmen in the late 1800s, who drove cattle from Queensland's Channel Country to the railway at Marree. More recently, legendary outback mailman Tom Kruse (no, not that Tom Cruise) belted his mail truck along the track from 1936 until 1963.

Meandering through the sand hills of the **Strzelecki Regional Reserve**, the **Strzelecki Track** spans 460km from Lyndhurst, 80km south of Marree, to the tiny desert outpost of Innamincka. The newer Moomba–Strzelecki Track is better kept, but longer and less interesting than the old track, which follows Strzelecki Creek.

Both tracks are graded regularly, but unless you've been out in the sun too long, there's no way you'd tackle them in anything other than a rugged 4WD. Check road conditions with the Royal Automobile Association (p733) in Adelaide, online at www.dpti.sa.gov.au/Out backRoads, or call the Outback Road Report on 1300 361 033.

For a detailed guide, pick up the interesting *Birdsville Strzelecki: Legendary Tracks of the Marree-Innamincka District* brochure from regional visitor centres.

bistro ($20 to $35, serving noon to 2pm and 6pm to 8pm).

Eldo Hotel MOTEL **$$**
(☑08-8673 7867; www.facebook.com/eldo-hotel; Kotara Pl, Woomera; s/d from $90/110; [P][※]) Built to house rocket scientists, the Eldo Hotel has comfortable budget and motel-style rooms, and serves à la carte meals in the surprisingly urbane bistro (mains $20 to $35, serving 7am to 9am, noon to 2pm and 6pm to 8.30pm). Try the meaty game plate (oh, and curry nights!).

ℹ Information

Woomera Heritage & Visitor Information Centre (☑08-8673 7042; Dewrang Ave, Woomera; museum adult/child $6/3; ⊙9am-5pm Mar-Nov, 10am-2pm Dec-Feb) Rocket into the info centre, with its displays on Woomera's past and present (plus a bowling alley!). Just across the car park is the **Lions Club Aircraft & Missile Park**, studded with jets and rocket remnants.

Coober Pedy

☑08 / POP 1770
Coming into cosmopolitan Coober Pedy (yes, cosmopolitan – there are 44 nationalities represented in this little town, including the local Kokatha and Arabana peoples), the dry, barren desert suddenly becomes riddled with holes and adjunct piles of dirt

– reputedly more than a million around the township. The reason for all this rabid digging is opals. Discovered here 103 years ago, these gemstones have made this small town a mining mecca. This isn't to say it's also a tourist mecca – with swarms of flies, no trees, 50°C summer days, cave-dwelling locals and rusty car wrecks, you might think you've arrived in a postapocalyptic wasteland – but it sure is interesting! The name derives from local Aboriginal words *kupa* (white man) and *piti* (hole).

The surrounding desert is jaw-droppingly desolate, a fact not overlooked by international film-makers who've come here to shoot end-of-the-world epics like *Mad Max Beyond Thunderdome*, *Red Planet*, *Ground Zero*, *Pitch Black* and the slightly more believable *Priscilla, Queen of the Desert*.

◉ Sights & Activities

★**Old Timers Mine** MUSEUM
(☑08-8672 5555; www.cooberpedy.com/old-timers-mine; 1 Crowders Gully Rd; self-guided tours adult/child/family $15/5/40; ⊙9am-5.30pm) This interesting warren of tunnels was mined in 1916, and then hidden by the miners. The mine was rediscovered in 1968 when excavations for a dugout home punched through into the labyrinth of tunnels. As well as the great self-guided tunnel tours, there's a museum, a re-created 1920s

Coober Pedy

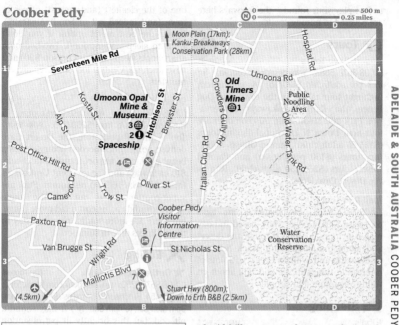

Coober Pedy

◎ Top Sights
1 Old Timers Mine	C1
2 Spaceship	B2
3 Umoona Opal Mine & Museum	B2

🛏 Sleeping
4 Desert Cave Hotel	B2
5 Mud Hut Motel	B3

🍴 Eating
6 John's Pizza Bar & Restaurant	B2
7 Outback Bar & Grill	B3
Umberto's	(see 4)

underground home, and free mining-equipment demos daily (9.30am, 1.30pm and 3.30pm).

★ **Spaceship** SCULPTURE
(Hutchinson St, Coober Pedy; ⊘ 24hr) **FREE**
Check out this amazing leftover prop from the film *Pitch Black,* which has crash-landed on Hutchinson St (a minor *Millennium Falcon*?). Intricate, creative, unexpected and somehow disquieting – words can't quite do it justice.

Kanku-Breakaways
Conservation Park NATURE RESERVE
(www.parks.sa.gov.au; off Stuart Hwy) The Breakaways Reserve is a stark but colourful area

of arid hills, mesas and scarps 32km north from Coober Pedy along a rough road – turn off the highway 22km west of town. Entry permits ($10 per vehicle per 24 hours) are available at the Coober Pedy Visitor Information Centre; note that Indigenous land owners may change this process at some stage in the future. Get some solid directions from the visitor centre too.

Umoona Opal Mine & Museum MUSEUM
(☏ 08-8672 5288; www.umoonaopalmine.com.au; 14 Hutchison St; museum free, tours adult/child $12/6; ⊘ 8am-6pm) For a terrific introduction to Coober Pedy – including history, fossils, desert habitats, Aboriginal culture, ecology and mining – take a wander through this free maze-like underground museum, run by the Umoona shop. Book yourself on a guided tour (10am, 2pm and 4pm) if you want a deeper insight.

Opal Fields Golf Club GOLF
(☏ 08 8672 5690; www.cooberpedygolfclub.com.au; Rowe Dr; 18 holes incl club hire $20; ⊘ from 12.45pm Sun, other times by arrangement) There's not much grass on Coober Pedy's golf course. Actually, there isn't any grass. But that's the appeal – and a fact that persuaded the famous St Andrews' course in Scotland to offer reciprocal playing rights to Coober Pedy members! Look for the glimmer of opal

as you play your round – the fairways here are covered in mining spoils.

👉 Tours

Desert Cave Tours   TOURS
(📞08-8672 5688; www.desertcave.com.au; 4hr tour per adult/child $120/65) A convenient highlight tour taking in the town, the Dog Fence, the Kanku-Breakaways Conservation Park and Moon Plain. Also on offer are four-hour Down 'N' Dirty opal-digging tours ($125/65 adult/child), Sunset Ghosts & History tours ($160 per person) and Painted Desert tours ($260/130 adult/child). Run by the Desert Cave Hotel.

Mail Run Tour   DRIVING
(📞08-8672 5226; www.mailruntour.com; tours per person $295) Coober Pedy–based full-day mail-run tours, looping through the desert and along the Oodnadatta Track between Oodnadatta and William Creek, with lots of interesting things to see and talk about en route. Maximum four people.

🛏 Sleeping

Riba's   CAMPGROUND $
(📞08-8672 5614; www.camp-underground.com. au; 1811 William Creek Rd; underground sites $32, above-ground unpowered/powered sites $24/30, s & d from $66; 🅿🛜) Around 5km east of town, Riba's offers a unique opportunity– underground camping! Extras include an underground TV lounge, cell-like underground budget rooms and a nightly opal-mine tour (adult/child $25/15; free for underground and unpowered-site campers; discounted for other guests). Interesting!

⭐ Down to Erth B&B   B&B $$
(📞08-8672 5762; www.downtoerth.com.au; 1795 Wedgetail Cres; d incl breakfast from $165, extra child $35; 🅿🛜🌊) A real dugout gem about 3km from town: your own subterranean two-bedroom bunker (sleeps two adults and three kids – perfect for wandering families) with a kitchen/lounge area, a shady plunge pool for cooling off after a day exploring the earth, wood-fuelled BBQ and complimentary chocolates.

⭐ Mud Hut Motel   MOTEL $$
(📞08-8672 3003; www.mudhutmotel.com.au; cnr Hutchison & St Nicholas Sts; s/d/f/2-bedroom apt $130/150/180/220; 🅿❄🛜) The rustic-looking walls here are made from rammed earth, and despite the grubby name this is one of the cleanest (and newest) places in town (and indeed, all of South Australia). By far the best motel option if you don't want to sleep underground. Two-bedroom apartments sleep six (extra person $20) and have kitchens. Central location; free airport transfers.

Desert Cave Hotel   HOTEL $$$
(📞08-8672 5688; www.desertcave.com.au; 1 Hutchison St; s/d from $200/270; 🅿❄🛜🌊) Top of the CP price tree, the Desert Cave delivers some much-needed luxury – plus a beaut pool, cafe, airport transfers (a cheeky $10 each way) and the excellent Umberto's (mains $28-43; ⏱6-9pm) restaurant. Staff are super-courteous and can organise tours. Above-ground rooms cost a tad more (huge, but there are more soulful places to stay in town). Prices dive in summer.

🍴 Eating

⭐ Outback Bar & Grill   FAST FOOD $$
(📞08-8672 3250; www.facebook.com/shellcoober pedy; 454 Hutchison St; mains $7-35; ⏱7am-9pm Mon-Sat, to 8pm Sun; 🛜) It may sound a bit odd, but this brightly lit petrol-station diner is one of the best places to eat in Coober Pedy! Roasts, pastas, burgers, lasagne, schnitzels and an awesome Greek-style lamb salad that's a bold departure from trucker norms. You can get a beer here too, if you're dry from the highway. Decent cabins out the back (single/double $99/119).

⭐ John's Pizza Bar
& Restaurant   ITALIAN $$
(📞08-8672 5561; www.jpbr.com.au; Shop 24, 1 Hutchison St; mains $9-32; ⏱10am-10pm) Hey, a fancy new sign and logo! You didn't need to go to such lengths, John – you still run the best place to eat in town. Expect table-sized pizzas, hearty pastas and heat-beating gelato, plus salads, burgers, gyros, and fish and chips. Sit inside, order some takeaways, or pull up a seat with the bedraggled pot plants by the street.

ℹ Information

Coober Pedy Visitor Information Centre
(📞08-8672 4600; www.cooberpedy.com; Council Offices, 773 Hutchison St; ⏱9am-5pm Mon-Fri, 9am-noon Sat & Sun) Free 30-minute internet access (prebooked), history displays and comprehensive tour and accommodation info.

Darwin &
the Northern Territory

08 / POP 228,833

Includes →

Darwin 800

Kakadu National
Park 824

Arnhem Land 834

Katherine 837

Nitmiluk
(Katherine Gorge) . . .840

Alice Springs 852

MacDonnell
Ranges 862

Uluru-Kata Tjuta
National Park 872

Best Places to Eat

→ Marksie's Camp Tucker (p840)

→ Sounds of Silence (p876)

→ Under the Desert Moon (p872)

→ Anbinik Restaurant (p829)

→ Black Russian Caravan Bar (p839)

Best Places to Stay

→ Cicada Lodge (p842)

→ Wildman Wilderness Lodge (p819)

→ Djakanimba Pavilions (p845)

→ Anbinik Kakadu Resort (p829)

Why Go?

The Top End is frontier country. It feels wild out here; time spent exploring the region's outer reaches will feel like exploring the Australia of childhood imaginings. This is the nation's most rewarding Indigenous homeland, a land of art centres, isolated communities and ancient rock art. It is also a world of iconic Aussie wildlife, from the jumping crocs of Mary River to the flood plains and wetlands of Kakadu. Darwin is an intriguing place with a steamy, end-of-Australia feel, excellent markets, restaurants and galleries of Indigenous art.

The remote and largely untamed chunk of the Northern Territory (NT) from Katherine to Uluru is where dreams end and adventure begins. If you enjoy off-road driving and meeting real characters of the Australian outback, then you've come to the right place. And delighting travellers with its eccentric offerings, pioneering spirit and weathered mountain setting, Alice Springs is the city at the centre of a continent.

When to Go
Darwin

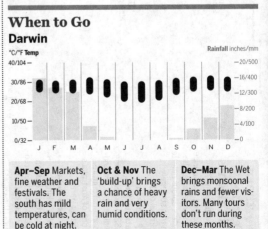

Apr–Sep Markets, fine weather and festivals. The south has mild temperatures, can be cold at night.

Oct & Nov The 'build-up' brings a chance of heavy rain and very humid conditions.

Dec–Mar The Wet brings monsoonal rains and fewer visitors. Many tours don't run during these months.

Northern Territory Highlights

1 Uluru (p873) Watching the sunrise and sunset after the earth's colour palette on this strangely spiritual rock.

2 Kakadu National Park (p824) Experiencing wildlife, rock art and Aboriginal culture in one of Australia's premier parks.

3 Kata Tjuta (p874) Hiking through the hidden valleys and deep-red monoliths of Kata Tjuta (the Olgas).

4 Litchfield National Park (p821) Plunging into a cascading, crystal-clear rock pool in this oasislike national park.

5 Arnhem Land (p834) Touring this remote and hypnotically beautiful

Crocodiles can inhabit all waterways in tropical areas. Swimming is not recommended.

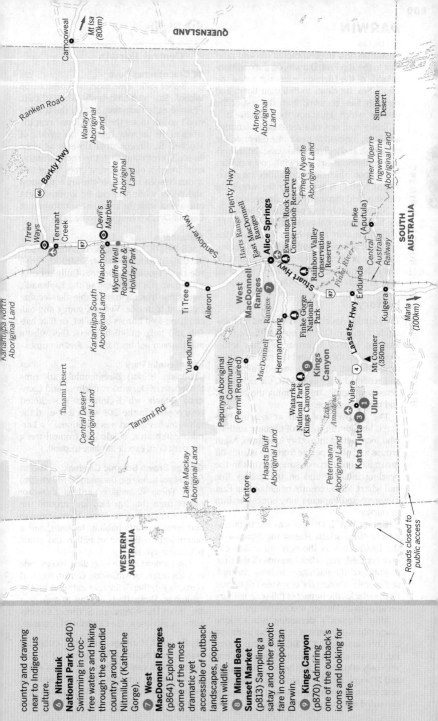

QUEENSLAND

Mt Isa
(80km)

Carnooweal

Ranken Road

Wakaya
Aboriginal
Land

Barkly Hwy

66

Three
Ways

Tennant
Creek

87

Devil's
Marbles

Wauchope

Wycliffe Well
Roadhouse &
Holiday Park

Anurrete
Aboriginal
Land

Sandover Hwy

Harts Range   Plenty Hwy

East MacDonnell
Ranges

Atnetye
Aboriginal
Land

Alice Springs

Ewaninga Rock Carvings
Conservation Reserve

Pmere Nyente
Aboriginal Land

Pmer Ulperre
Ingwemirne
Aboriginal Land

Simpson
Desert

West
MacDonnell
Ranges

Ti Tree

Aileron

Ranges: 7

Rainbow Valley
Conservation
Reserve

Finke
(Aputula)

Finke River

Central
Australia
Railway

SOUTH
AUSTRALIA

Stuart Hwy

Karlantipa North
Aboriginal Land

Karlantipa South
Aboriginal Land

Tanami Desert

Central Desert
Aboriginal Land

Yuendumu

MacDonnell

Hermannsburg

Finke Gorge
National Park

Erldunda

87

Marla
(100km)

Tanami Rd

Papunya Aboriginal
Community
(Permit Required)

Watarrka
National Park
(Kings Canyon)

Kings
Canyon 9

4

Lasseter Hwy

Mt Conner (350m)

Kulgera

Lake Mackay

Haasts Bluff
Aboriginal Land

Lake
Amadeus

Yulara

Kata Tjuta 3 1

Uluru

4

WESTERN
AUSTRALIA

Kintore

Petermann
Aboriginal Land

Roads closed
to public access

country and drawing
near to Indigenous
culture.

6 Nitmiluk
National Park (p840)
Swimming in croc-
free waters and hiking
through the splendid
country around
Nitmiluk (Katherine
Gorge).

7 West
MacDonnell Ranges
(p864) Exploring
some of the most
dramatic yet
accessible of outback
landscapes, popular
with wildlife.

8 Mindil Beach
Sunset Market
(p813) Sampling a
satay and other exotic
fare in cosmopolitan
Darwin.

9 Kings Canyon
(p870) Admiring
one of the outback's
icons and looking for
wildlife.

DARWIN

POP 136,828

Australia's only tropical capital city and gateway to the Top End, Darwin, on the traditional lands of the Larrakia, gazes out across the Timor Sea. It's closer to Bali than Bondi and certainly feels removed from the rest of the country, which is just how the locals like it.

Tables spill out of street-side restaurants and bars, innovative museums celebrate the city's past, and galleries showcase the region's rich Indigenous art. Darwin's cosmopolitan mix – more than 50 nationalities are represented here – is typified by the wonderful markets held throughout the dry season.

Nature is truly part of Darwin's backyard: the famous national parks of Kakadu and Litchfield are only a few hours' drive, and the unique Tiwi Islands are a boat ride away. For locals the perfect weekend is going fishing for barra (barramundi) in a tinny (small boat) with an esky (cooler) full of beer.

History

The Larrakia Aboriginal people lived for thousands of years in Darwin, hunting, fishing and foraging. In 1869 a permanent white settlement was established and the grid for a new town laid out. Originally called Palmerston and renamed Darwin in 1911, the new town developed rapidly, transforming the physical and social landscape.

The discovery of gold at nearby Pine Creek brought an influx of Chinese settlers, who soon settled into other industries. Asian groups and other people from the islands off Australia's north coast came to work in the pearling industry and on the railway line and wharf. More recently, neighbouring East Timorese and Papuans have sought asylum in Darwin.

During WWII, Darwin was the front line for the Allied action against the Japanese in the Pacific. It was the only Australian city ever bombed, and official reports of the time downplayed the damage – to buoy Australians' morale. Though the city wasn't destroyed by the attacks, the impact of full-scale military occupation on Darwin was enormous.

More physically damaging was Cyclone Tracy, which hit Darwin at around midnight on Christmas Eve 1974. By Christmas morning, Darwin effectively ceased to exist as a city, with only 400 of its 11,200 homes left standing and 71 people killed. The town was rebuilt to a new, stringent building code and has steadily expanded outwards and upwards.

◉ Sights

◉ Central Darwin

★ **Crocosaurus Cove**   ZOO
(🕿 08-8981 7522; www.crocosauruscove.com; 58 Mitchell St; adult/child/family $35/23/110.20; ⊙ 9am-6pm, last admission 5pm) If the tourists won't go out to see the crocs, then bring the crocs to the tourists. Right in the middle of Mitchell St, Crocosaurus Cove is as close as you'll ever want to get to these amazing creatures. Six of the largest crocs in captivity can be seen in state-of-the-art aquariums and pools, while you can be lowered right into a pool with the crocs in the transparent Cage of Death (one/two people $170/260).

Aquascene   AQUARIUM
(🕿 08-8981 7837; www.aquascene.com.au; 28 Doctors Gully Rd; adult/child/family $15/10/43; ⊙ high tide, check website) At Doctors Gully, an easy walk from the north end of the Esplanade, Aquascene runs a remarkable fish-feeding frenzy at high tide. Visitors, young and old, can hand-feed hordes of mullet, catfish, batfish and huge milkfish. Check the website and tourism publications for feeding times.

Bicentennial Park   PARK
(Esplanade; ⊙ 24hr) Bicentennial Park runs the length of Darwin's waterfront and **Lameroo Beach**, which inhabits a sheltered cove popular in the '20s when it housed the saltwater baths, and was traditionally a Larrakia camp area. Shaded by tropical trees, the park is an excellent place to stroll.

George Brown Botanic Gardens   GARDENS
(www.nt.gov.au/leisure; Geranium St; ⊙ 7am-7pm) FREE These 42-hectare gardens showcase plants from the Top End and around the world – monsoon vine forest, the mangroves and coastal plants habitat, baobabs, and a magnificent collection of native and exotic palms and cycads.

The gardens are an easy 2km bicycle ride or walk from Darwin, along Gilruth Ave and Gardens Rd; there's another entrance off Geranium St. Alternatively, city bus 10 stops near the Stuart Hwy/Geranium St corner and city bus 4 stops close to the Gardens Rd entrance.

Myilly Point Heritage Precinct   HISTORIC SITE
(www.nationaltrust.org.au/nt; Burnett Pl) At the far northern end of Smith St is this small but important precinct of four houses built between 1930 and 1939 (which means they survived both the WWII bombings and

IS IT SAFE TO SWIM?

Darwin has some fabulous beaches, but choosing whether or not to swim is not as easy as you'd think. Darwin's swimming beaches tend to be far enough away from mangrove creeks to make the threat of meeting a crocodile remote (although not so long ago the NT News, on one of its notorious front pages, showed a saltwater croc surfing the waves at Vesteys Beach...). A bigger problem is the deadly box jellyfish, which makes swimming decidedly unhealthy between October and March (and often before October and until May). Unlike in tropical Queensland, there are no stinger nets here to allow safe swimming, due to both the expense of maintaining the fence and Darwin's strong tides.

If you do decide to swim, the most popular beaches are Mindil (p806) and Vesteys (p812) on Fannie Bay. Further north, a stretch of the 7km **Casuarina Beach** is an official nude beach.

You can swim year-round without fear in the western part of **Lake Alexander**, an easy cycle from the centre at East Point Reserve (p812), and at the very popular Wave & Recreation Lagoons (p806), the centrepiece of the Darwin Waterfront Precinct. At the recreation lagoon, filtered seawater and nets provide a natural seawater swim.

Cyclone Tracy!). They're now managed by the National Trust. One of them, **Burnett House** (☑08-8981 0165; www.nationaltrust.org. au/nt; Burnett Pl; $2; ⊙10am-1pm Mon-Sat, 3-5pm Sun), operates as a museum.

◉ Darwin Waterfront Precinct

The bold redevelopment of the old Darwin Waterfront Precinct (www.waterfront.nt.gov. au) has transformed the city. The multi-million-dollar redevelopment features a cruise-ship terminal, luxury hotels, boutique restaurants and shopping, the Sky Bridge, an elevated walkway and lift at the south end of Smith St, and a Wave Lagoon (p806).

★ **Royal Flying Doctor Service** MUSEUM
(☑08-8983 5700; http://rfdsdarwin.com.au/; Stokes Hill Wharf; adult/child/family $28/16/70; ⊙9.30am-6pm, last entry 5pm Jun-Sep, 9.30am-5pm, last entry 4pm Oct-May) This outstanding museum on Stokes Hill Wharf is the way all museums should be. There's a 55-seat hologram cinema, virtual-reality glasses that enable you to relive in vivid detail the 1942 Japanese bombing raid on Darwin Harbour, a decommissioned Pilatus PC-12 aircraft from the Royal Flying Doctor Service (RFDS), a live map showing the current location of RFDS planes, and a series of touch screens that take you through the story of the RFDS and Darwin during WWII.

WWII Oil-Storage Tunnels TUNNEL
(☑08-8985 6322; www.ww2tunnelsdarwin.com. au; Kitchener Dr; self-guided tours adult/child $8/5; ⊙9am-4pm May-Oct, to 1pm Nov-Apr) You can escape from the heat of the day and relive your Hitchcockian fantasies by walking through the WWII oil-storage tunnels. They were built in 1942 to store the navy's oil supplies (but never used); now they exhibit wartime photos.

Indo-Pacific Marine Exhibition AQUARIUM
(☑08-8981 1294; www.indopacificmarine.com.au; 29 Stokes Hill Rd; adult/child/family $27/12/66; ⊙10am-2pm Apr-Oct, call for hours Nov-Mar) This excellent marine aquarium at the Waterfront Precinct gives you a close encounter with the denizens of Darwin Harbour. Each small tank is a complete ecosystem, with only the occasional extra fish introduced as food for some of the predators, such as stonefish or the bizarre anglerfish.

Also recommended here is the **Coral Reef by Night** (☑08-8981 1294; www.indopacific marine.com.au; 29 Stokes Hill Rd; adult/child $120/60; ⊙6.30pm Wed, Fri & Sun), which consists of a tour of the aquarium, a seafood dinner and an impressive show of fluorescing animals.

◉ Fannie Bay & Parap

★ **Museum & Art Gallery of the Northern Territory** MUSEUM
(MAGNT; ☑08-8999 8264; www.magnt.net.au; 19 Conacher St, Fannie Bay; ⊙10am-5pm) **FREE**
This superb museum and art gallery boasts beautifully presented galleries of Top End–centric exhibits. The **Aboriginal art collection** is a highlight, with carvings from the Tiwi Islands, bark paintings from Arnhem Land and dot paintings from the desert. An entire room is devoted to **Cyclone Tracy**, in a display that graphically illustrates life before and after the disaster. You can listen to

Greater Darwin

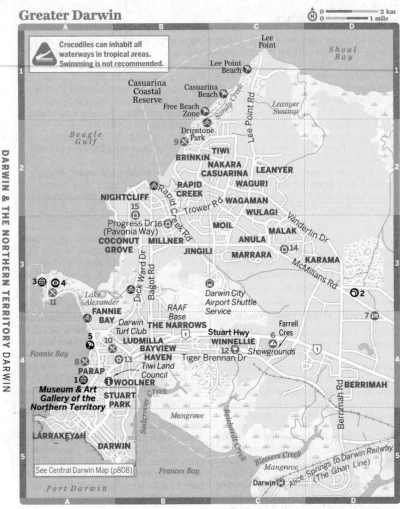

Crocodiles can inhabit all waterways in tropical areas. Swimming is not recommended.

DARWIN & THE NORTHERN TERRITORY DARWIN

the whirring sound of Tracy at full throttle – a sound you won't forget in a hurry.

Darwin Military Museum   MUSEUM
(Defence of Darwin Experience; ☑08-8981 9702; www.darwinmilitarymuseum.com.au; 5434 Alec Fong Lim Dr, East Point; adult/child/family $18/8/40; ⊙9.30am-5pm May-Oct, 10am-3.30pm Nov-Apr) At this innovative museum and multimedia experience, you can hear personal accounts of those affected by, and those who actively participated in, Australia's defence during WWII. Darwin and the Top End is the focus – the area was bombed 64 times, with 188 aircraft attacking the city

on 19 February 1942. A small theatre runs a 20-minute show bringing it all to life.

⊙ Outer East

Crocodylus Park   ZOO
(☑08-8922 4500; www.crocodyluspark.com.au; 815 McMillans Rd, Berrimah; adult/child $40/20; ⊙9am-5pm) Crocodylus Park showcases hundreds of crocs and a minizoo comprising lions, tigers and other big cats, spider monkeys, marmosets, cassowaries and large birds. Allow about two hours to look around the whole park, and you should time your visit with a tour (10am, noon and 2pm),

Greater Darwin

◎ **Top Sights**
1 Museum & Art Gallery of the
    Northern Territory A4

◎ **Sights**
2 Crocodylus Park D3
3 Darwin Military Museum A3
4 East Point Reserve A3
5 Vesteys Beach A4

◎ **Sleeping**
6 Discovery Holiday Park – Darwin C4
7 Grungle Downs B&B D4

◎ **Eating**
8 Darwin Ski Club A4
9 De la Plage B2
10 Laneway Specialty Coffee A4
    Parap Fine Foods .... (see 10)

11 Pee Wee's at the Point A3
    Saffrron Restaurant .... (see 10)

◎ **Drinking & Nightlife**
    Darwin Ski Club .... (see 8)
12 One Mile Brewing Company C4

◎ **Entertainment**
13 Darwin Railway Club B4

◎ **Shopping**
14 Malak Marketplace C3
15 Nightcliff Market B2
    Nomad Art Gallery .... (see 10)
    Outstation Gallery .... (see 10)
    Parap Village Market .... (see 10)
16 Rapid Creek Market B3
    Tiwi Art Network .... (see 10)

which includes a feeding demonstration. Croc meat BBQ packs for sale!

The park is about 15km from the city centre. Take bus 5 from Darwin.

🧭 Tours

★ Turtle Tracks   TOURS
(☏ 1300 065 022; www.seadarwin.com; Dock 2, Stokes Hill Wharf; adult/child/family $295/200/950; ⊙ 4pm May-Sep) This late-afternoon tour goes out beyond Darwin Harbour and Charles Point Lighthouse to beautiful Bare Sand Island, where you'll arrive around sunset. Guides show you around the island, explaining its history, then take you by torchlight to watch the wonderful sight of turtles laying their eggs; come late in the season and you may see the hatchlings emerge.

★ Ethical Adventures   TOURS
(☏ 0488 442 269; www.ethicaladventures.com) A cut above most of those offering day tours to Litchfield National Park from Darwin, Ethical Adventures runs sunrise-to-sunset tours (adult/child $225/185) that take in all of the main attractions, providing excellent food (including barbecued crocodile and buffalo) and good guides. Its focus on small groups, cultural engagement and ethical practices is a highlight. They cover Kakadu, Litchfield and attractions around Darwin.

★ Northern Territory
Indigenous Tours   CULTURAL TOUR
(☏ 1300 921 188; www.ntitours.com.au; cnr Esplanade & Knuckey St, Lyons Cottage; day tours adult/ child from $249/124) Upmarket Indigenous tours to Litchfield National Park and Kakadu.

Sea Darwin   OUTDOORS
(☏ 1300 065 022; www.seadarwin.com; Dock 2, Stokes Hill Wharf; 1hr tours adult/child/family $35/20/100) 🚢 Various eco tours around the city and Darwin Harbour, including a sunset fish and chips option, checking out mangroves, a crocodile trap, a shipwreck and (from May to September) turtle nesting sites.

Sacred Earth Safaris   ADVENTURE
(☏ 08-8536 2234; www.sacredearthsafaris.com. au; ⊙ May-Oct) Multiday, small-group 4WD camping tours around Kakadu, Katherine and the Kimberley. The three-day Kakadu tour starts at $1800, while the five-day Top End National Parks Safari is $3100.

Darwin Walking Tours   WALKING
(☏ 08-8981 0227; 50 Mitchell St; adult/child $50/ free) 🚶 Two-hour guided heritage walks around the city, enlivened by local anecdotes from good local guides.

Harbour Cruises

Between April and October there are plenty of boats based at the Cullen Bay Marina and Stokes Hill Wharf to take you on a cruise of the harbour.

Darwin Harbour Cruises   CRUISE
(☏ 08-8942 3131; www.darwinharbourcruises. com.au; Stokes Hill Rd; ⊙ 6pm mid-Feb–mid-Dec) Offers a variety of cruises from Stokes Hill Wharf, including evening cruise options aboard the *Charles Darwin,* a tri-level

JOHN HAY/GETTY IMAGES ©

DANIELA CONSTANTINESCU/SHUTTERSTOCK ©

DAVID WALL PHOTO/GETTY IMAGES ©

1. Mindil Beach Sunset Market (p813)

Join the locals and laze the evening away on the lawns at this Darwin classic.

2. Darwin Waterfront (p801)

A popular place for restaurants, shops, water sports and cruise ships.

3. Crocosaurus Cove (p800)

The chance to spot some crocs up close.

4. Sunset splendour

Darwin's sunsets are the stuff of legends.

catamaran. Possibilities include a 2½-hour sunset cruise (adult/child $58/35), or the same deal but with a buffet dinner ($102/68).

✶✦ Festivals & Events

Darwin Festival
ART

(📞08-8943 4200; www.darwinfestival.org.au; ⊙Aug) This mainly outdoor arts and culture festival celebrates music, theatre, visual art, dance and cabaret, and runs for 18 days in August. Festivities are centred on the large park next to Civic Sq, off Harry Chan Ave.

Darwin Aboriginal Art Fair
ART

(📞08-8981 0576; www.darwinaboriginalartfair.com.au; ⊙Aug) Held at the Darwin Convention Centre (📞08-8923 9000; www.darwinconvention.com.au), this three-day festival showcases Indigenous art from communities throughout the NT.

Darwin Fringe Festival
CULTURAL

(https://darwinfringe.org.au; ⊙Jul) Showcases eclectic, local performing and visual arts at venues such as Brown's Mart (📞08-8981 5522; www.brownsmart.com.au; 12 Smith St) theatre.

Beer Can Regatta
CULTURAL

(www.beercanregatta.org.au; ⊙Jul) An utterly insane and typically Territorian festival that features races for boats made out of beer cans. It takes place at Mindil Beach and is a good, fun day.

🛏 Sleeping

🏘 City Centre & Waterfront

Discovery Holiday Park – Darwin
CARAVAN PARK $

(📞1800 662 253, 08-8984 3330; www.discovery holidayparks.com.au; cnr Farrell Cres & Stuart Hwy, Winnellie; powered sites from $37, cabins $98-191; ❄🛜🏊) A well-treed caravan park with immaculate facilities, a camp kitchen, a licensed shop, a covered outdoor saltwater pool and friendly staff. Public bus 8 rolls into central Darwin from the corner of the street.

Chilli's
HOSTEL $

(📞08-8980 5800, 1800 351 313; www.chillis.com.au; 69a Mitchell St; dm $29, tw & d with shared bathroom from $60; ❄@🛜) Friendly Chilli's is a fun place with a small sun deck and spa (use the pool next door). There's also a pool table and a breezy kitchen/meals terrace overlooking Mitchell St. Rooms are compact but

clean. There are nice touches to this place, such as pots with scented herbs hanging from the roof of the balcony.

Melaleuca on Mitchell
HOSTEL $

(📞1300 723 437; www.momdarwin.com; 52 Mitchell St; dm $25-28, d with/without bathroom $65/60; ❄@🛜🏊) If you stay here take note: 24-hour check-in and it's plonked right in the action on Mitchell St. So, sleeping...maybe not. Partying? Oh yes! The highlight is the rooftop island bar and pool area – complete with waterfall spa and big-screen TV. Party heaven! This modern hostel is immaculate with great facilities and it's very secure. Third floor is female only.

★Vibe Hotel
HOTEL $$

(📞08-8982 9998; www.vibehotels.com; 7 Kitchener Dr; r $159-275; 🅿❄@🛜🏊) You're in for an upmarket stay at this professional set-up with friendly staff and a great location at the Darwin Waterfront Precinct. Room prices creep upward with more bed space and water views. The Wave Lagoon (📞08-8985 6588; www.waterfront.nt.gov.au; adult/child $7/5; ⊙10am-6pm) is right next door if the shady swimming pool is too placid for you.

C2 Esplanade
APARTMENT $$

(📞08-8941 1969; http://c2esplanade.com.au/; 102 Esplanade; 1-/2-/3-bedroom apt from $160/175/195; 🅿❄🛜🏊) Large and lovely apartments just across from the waterfront make this a brilliant choice, with much more reasonable prices than other similar places nearby. Upper-floor, sea-facing rooms have fabulous views and you're within walking distance of just about everything in the centre.

Darwin City B&B
B&B $$

(📞0441 442 373; www.darwinbnb.com.au; 4 Zealandia Cres, Larrakeyah; r $105-145, apt $179-250; ❄🏊) Some B&Bs are businesslike and others feel like you're staying with friends; this is one of the latter. There are three rooms in this pleasant Spanish Mission–style home, equipped with fridges, flat-screen TVs and private entrances. The owners also run apartments nearby that have excellent facilities and Indigenous art adorning the walls.

★Adina Apartment Hotel
APARTMENT $$$

(📞08-8982 9999; www.adinahotels.com; 7 Kitchener Dr; apt $165-475) The Adina is a stylish place with contemporary apartments sporting clean lines and modern art on the walls. Most rooms have excellent views out over the water and waterfront precinct. You're close to restaurants and bars, and also within walking distance of the city centre.

★Argus Apartments
APARTMENT $$$

(☑08-8925 5000; www.argusaccommodation. com.au; 6 Cardona Ct; 1-/2-/3-bedroom apt from $234/285/356; P☀@☎) Apartments are *very* spacious at Argus, and the whole place rings with quality. There are lovely bathrooms, generous expanses of cool floor tiles, simple balcony living/dining spaces and snazzy kitchens with all the requisite appliances. The pool is shady and welcoming on a sticky Top End afternoon. Wet-season prices drop considerably.

Oaks Elan Darwin
HOTEL, APARTMENT $$$

(☑08-8981 0888, 1300 542 502; www.minorhotels. com; 31-33 Woods St; r $180-309, apt $225-464; P☀☎☎) Views here are stunning and the facilities first-rate; you can even check in online, and unlock your room door via your mobile phone. It's also central without being within earshot of Mitchell St.

⛺ City Fringe & Suburbs

FreeSpirit Resort Darwin
CARAVAN PARK $

(☑08-8935 0888; www.darwinfreespiritresort. com.au; 901 Stuart Hwy, Berrimah; unpowered/powered sites from $40/53, cabins & units $99-260; ☀@☎☎) An impressive highway-side park about a 10-minute drive from the city, with loads of facilities (including three pools). With a jumping cushion, a kidz corner, a bar and live music in the Dry, adults and kids are easily entertained.

Darwin City Edge
MOTEL $$

(☑08-8981 1544; www.darwincityedge.com.au; 38 Gardens Rd; d/ste from $89/99; P☀@☎☎) There's a lot to like here: value-for-money rooms, friendly and efficient service, and a handy location. Contemporary motel rooms and larger studios with kitchenettes are on offer. It's right on the city fringe, convenient to the Gardens Park golf course, the Botanic Gardens (p800) and Mindil Beach.

Keep an eye on its website for discounts.

Grungle Downs B&B
B&B $$

(☑08-8947 4440; www.grungledowns.com.au; 945 McMillans Rd, Knuckey Lagoon; r incl breakfast $140-165, cottages $200-400; ☀☎☎) Set on a 2-hectare property, this beautiful rural retreat seems worlds away from the city (but it's only 13km). When it's hot outside, hang out in the guest lounge or by the pool. There

ⓘ BOOKING SERVICE

Track down the best Darwin deals through the professionally run booking service **More Than a Room** (☑0418 616 888; www.morethanaroom.com.au) – it can hook you up with apartments, hotel rooms, villas and holiday homes.

are four lodge rooms (one with en suite) and a gorgeous two-bedroom cottage.

✖ Eating

Darwin is the Territory's culinary capital. Cafes, restaurants and market stalls all offer outdoor seating, and the quality and diversity of produce is unrivalled. The city's multicultural make-up is reflected in its food; steaks and seafood are other mainstays. Vegetarian and vegan options are limited, although many restaurants will have a handful of choices. Large supermarkets are found across the city.

✖ City Centre & Waterfront

★Aboriginal Bush Traders Cafe
CAFE, AUSTRALIAN $

(☑09-8942 4023; www.aboriginalbushtraders. com; cnr Esplanade & Knuckey St; mains & light meals $9-17.50; ☺7.30am-3pm Mon-Fri) In historic **Lyons Cottage** (☑0488 329 933; cnr Esplanade & Knuckey St) FREE, this fine little cafe has some really tasty dishes inspired by Aboriginal bush tucker from the desert. In addition to more conventional dishes such as gourmet toasted rolls, try the damper with jam (Kakadu plum or wild rosella), the kutjera (wild tomato) and aniseed-myrtle feta damper, or the saltbush dukkah, avocado and feta smash.

★Frying Nemo
FISH & CHIPS $

(☑08-8981 2281; www.fryingnemo.com.au; Shop 10, 90 Frances Bay Dr, Stuart Park; mains from $12; ☺5pm-late Mon-Fri, 11.30am-9pm Sat & Sun) They've won various awards here and are consistently ranked among Australia's best fish and chips. Lightly battered, wild-caught NT fish are the mainstays, but the burgers (barra, croc, buffalo) are all worth considering too.

Speaker's Corner Cafe
CAFE $

(☑08-8946 1439; www.karensheldoncatering.com. au/speakers; Parliament House, Mitchell St; breakfast $5-20, mains $12-18; ☺7.30am-4pm Mon-Fri) In the grounds of Darwin's **Parliament House** (☑08-8946 1417; www.nt.gov.au/lant;

Central Darwin

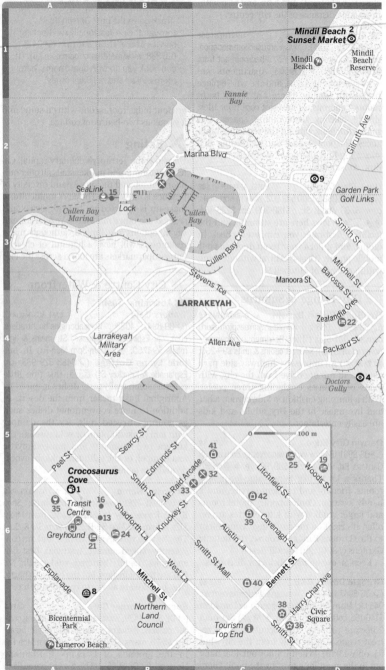

Mindil Beach Sunset Market 2

Mindil Beach

Mindil Beach Reserve

Gilruth Ave

Fannie Bay

Marina Blvd

29
27
SeaLink 15
Cullen Bay Marina
Lock
Cullen Bay

9

Garden Park Golf Links

Smith St

Cullen Bay Cres

Stevens Tce

Manoora St

Mitchell St

Barossa St

LARRAKEYAH

Zealandia Cres 22

Larrakeyah Military Area

Allen Ave

Packard St

Doctors Gully 4

0 — 100 m

Searcy St

Edmunds St

41

25
19
Woods St

Peel St

Crocosaurus Cove 1

Smith St

Air Raid Arcade

32

Litchfield St

35

Transit Centre 16

Shadforth La

33

42

13

Knuckey St

39

Cavenagh St

Greyhound 21

24

Austin La

Smith St Mall

40

Bennett St

Esplanade

8

Mitchell St

West La

Harry Chan Ave

38

Northern Land Council

Civic Square

36

Bicentennial Park

Tourism Top End

Smith St

Lameroo Beach

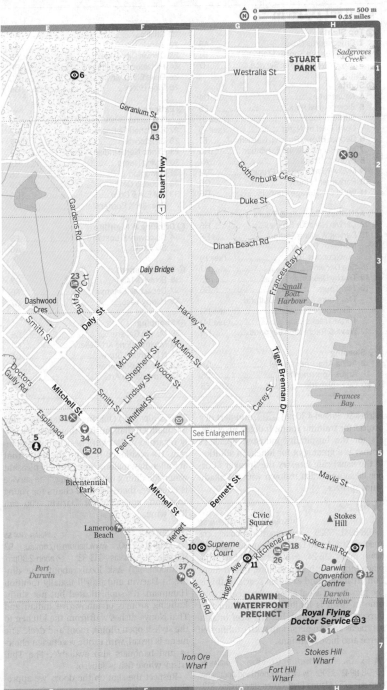

Central Darwin

⊙ Top Sights
1 Crocosaurus Cove A6
2 Mindil Beach Sunset Market............... D1
3 Royal Flying Doctor Service.................. H7

⊙ Sights
4 Aquascene D4
5 Bicentennial Park................................... E5
  Burnett House .... (see 9)
  Coral Reef by Night..........................(see 7)
6 George Brown Botanic Gardens E1
7 Indo-Pacific Marine Exhibition H6
8 Lyons Cottage A7
9 Myilly Point Heritage Precinct..............D2
10 Parliament House G6
11 WWII Oil-Storage Tunnels.....................G6

⊙ Activities, Courses & Tours
12 Darwin Harbour Cruises.......................H6
13 Darwin Walking Tours............................B6
  Northern Territory
  Indigenous Tours .... (see 8)
14 Sea Darwin H7
15 Tiwi by Design...B3
16 Tiwi Tours..B6
  Tiwi Tours Aboriginal Cultural
  Experience ....(see 15)
  Turtle Tracks....................................(see 14)
17 Wave & Recreation Lagoons H6

⊙ Sleeping
18 Adina Apartment Hotel G6
19 Argus Apartments D5
20 C2 Esplanade..E5

21 Chilli's A6
22 Darwin City B&B D4
23 Darwin City Edge E3
24 Melaleuca on Mitchell B6
25 Oaks Elan Darwin...................................D5
26 Vibe Hotel G6

⊙ Eating
  Aboriginal Bush Traders Cafe........(see 8)
27 Boatshed Coffee House......................... B2
28 Crustaceans H7
29 Exotic North Indian Cuisine.................. B2
30 Frying Nemo H2
31 Hanuman E5
32 Moorish Café C5
33 PM Eat & Drink B6
  Speaker's Corner Cafe.................(see 10)

⊙ Drinking & Nightlife
34 Discovery & Lost Arc..............................E5
35 Six Tanks... A6

⊙ Entertainment
36 Brown's Mart C7
37 Deckchair Cinema F6
38 Happy Yess..C7

⊙ Shopping
39 Mason Gallery C6
40 Mbantua Fine Art Gallery...................... C7
41 NT General Store.................................... C5
42 Paperbark Woman.................................. C6
43 Provenance Arts F2

Mitchell St; ⊙8am-4.30pm) **FREE**, and part of a project for training young Indigenous workers for the hospitality industry, Speaker's Corner is a great spot for lunch. In addition to the usual cafe fare, try the Speaker's Corner laksa and wash it down with a Kakadu plum spritzer.

★ PM Eat & Drink   AUSTRALIAN, INTERNATIONAL **$$**
(☑08-8941 3925; www.pmeatdrink.com; cnr Knuckey St & Austin Lane; lunch mains from $16, dinner mains $16-24; ⊙noon-late Tue-Sat) This place buzzes with atmosphere, not to mention great food and excellent service – this is the pick for a casual city-centre meal if your time in town is limited. The tempura fish burger is outstanding, but the beef brisket soft tacos and Angus sirloin with cauliflower puree also have their fans.

★ Exotic North Indian Cuisine   INDIAN **$$**
(☑08-8941 3396; www.exoticnorthindiancuisine. com.au; 2/52 Marina Blvd, Cullen Bay; mains $13-22; ⊙5-10pm; ⌖) Offering outstanding value for quality Indian cuisine, this place is widely regarded as Darwin's best Indian restaurant. It's positioned right on the waterfront at Cullen Bay, making for extremely pleasant waterside dining in the evening. The service is attentive, there are high chairs for young 'uns and, unusually for Darwin, you can BYO wine.

Hanuman   INDIAN, THAI **$$**
(☑08-8941 3500; www.hanuman.com.au; 93 Mitchell St; mains $13-38; ⊙noon-2.30pm, 6-10.30pm; ⌖) Ask locals about fine dining in Darwin and they'll usually mention Hanuman. It's sophisticated but not stuffy. Enticing aromas of innovative Indian and Thai Nonya dishes waft from the kitchen to the stylish open dining room and deck. The menu is broad, with exotic vegetarian choices and banquets also available. The Thai crispy whole fish is superb.

Respect the sign on the door: 'we appreciate neat attire'.

Boatshed
Coffee House
CAFE, INTERNATIONAL **$$**

(☑08-8981 0200; www.boatshedcoffeehouse.com.
au; 56 Marina Blvd; breakfast $8-23, lunch mains
$16-27; ⊘7.30am-2.30pm) If you can snaffle
one of the outdoor tables overlooking the
marina here in Cullen Bay, you'll have found
one of the best breakfast spots in Darwin.
The well-sized portions, shady setting and
gentle breeze also go well with lunch dishes
such as a bucket of prawns, a seafood platter
or simply fish and chips or a burger. Great
juices and coffee too.

★Crustaceans
SEAFOOD **$$$**

(☑08-8981 8658; www.crustaceans.net.au; Stokes
Hill Wharf; mains $19-45; ⊘5.30-11pm, last order
8.30pm; 🖫) This casual, licensed restaurant features fresh fish, Moreton Bay bugs,
lobster, oysters and even crocodile, as well
as succulent steaks. It's all about the location, perched right at the end of Stokes Hill
Wharf with sunset views over Frances Bay.
The cold beer and a first-rate wine list seal
the deal.

Moorish Café
MIDDLE EASTERN **$$$**

(☑08-8981 0010; www.moorishcafe.com.au; 37
Knuckey St; tapas & share plates $4-26, lunch mains
$17-25, dinner mains $29-45; ⊘11am-2.30pm
& 6-10pm Tue-Fri, 11am-10pm Sat) Seductive
aromas emanate from this divine terracot-
ta-tiled cafe fusing North African, Mediter-
ranean and Middle Eastern delights. The
tapas can be a bit hit-and-miss, but dishes
such as the Berber-spiced kangaroo and the
Spanish seafood hotpot are tasty and reli-
able; we loved the pistachio-crusted wild-
caught barramundi. It went up for sale in
late 2018, so hopefully little will change.

✕ City Fringe & Suburbs

De la Plage
CAFE **$**

(☑0403 623 363; www.facebook.com/delaplage
0810; Surf Lifesaving Club, Darribah Rd, Brinkin;
breakfast $5-18.50, mains $12.50-19; ⊘7am-3pm
Mon-Thu, to 8pm Fri-Sun) Boasting arguably
Darwin's best cafe views, Belgian/Austral-
ian/Turkish-run De la Plage looks out over
the Casuarina Coastal Reserve from a dis-
used surf storeroom, a 20-minute drive
north of the CBD. Outstanding breakfasts
are followed up with a fine vegan burger,
baked camembert wheel and all manner
of healthy salads and decadent crepes. If
they've the fig and dark chocolate baklava,
order it. Now.

DON'T MISS

PARAP VILLAGE

Parap Village is a foodie's heaven with
several good restaurants, bars and cafes
as well as the highly recommended deli
Parap Fine Foods (☑08-8981 8597;
www.parapfinefoods.com; 40 Parap Rd,
Parap; ⊘8am-6.30pm Mon-Fri, 8am-6pm
Sat, 9am-1pm Sun). However, it's the Sat-
urday morning **market** (☑0438 882 373;
www.parapvillage.com.au; Parap Shopping
Village, 3/3 Vickers St, Parap; ⊘8am-2pm
Sat) that attracts locals like bees to
honey. It's got a relaxed vibe as breakfast
merges into brunch and then lunch. Be-
tween visits to the takeaway food stalls
(most serving spicy Southeast Asian
snacks) shoppers stock up on tropical
fruit and vegetables – all you need to
make your own laksa or rendang. The
produce is local so you know it's fresh.

Laneway Specialty Coffee
CAFE **$**

(☑08-8941 4511; www.lanewaycoffee.com.au;
4/1 Vickers St, Parap; mains $14-22; ⊘7am-4pm
Mon-Fri, 7.30am-4pm Sat, 8am-2.30pm Sun) The
pared-back, industrial interior, corner loca-
tion and powerhouse coffee here have locals
wondering if they could be in Melbourne.
Getting rave reviews, this place is endur-
ingly popular. Its well-prepared dishes use local
and organic ingredients; the almost artistic
bacon-and-egg roll and the eggs Benedict
with pulled pork and spinach are worth the
trip here alone.

★Darwin Ski Club
AUSTRALIAN **$$**

(☑08-8981 6630; www.darwinskiclub.com.au;
Conacher St, Fannie Bay; mains $22-32; ⊘noon-
10pm) This place just keeps getting better.
Already Darwin's finest location for a sunset
beer (p812), it now does seriously good tucker too. The dishes are well prepared, and the
menu is thoughtful and enticing. The red
curry is particularly tasty. Highly recommended by locals.

★Saffrron Restaurant
INDIAN **$$**

(☑08-8981 2383; https://saffrron.com; 14/34
Parap Rd; mains lunch $20-41, dinner $17-28;
⊘5.30-9pm Tue, Wed, Sat & Sun, 11am-2pm &
5.30-9pm Thu & Fri) 🌱 At the forefront of
Parap's burgeoning culinary scene and one
of Darwin's best Indian restaurants, mul-
ti-award-winning Saffrron puts sustainabil-
ity and local ingredients front and centre.

The cooking is assured and the service attentive and knowledgeable. You could take your pick of the menu and leave happy, but the Barramundi masala and Kerala mussel curry are highly recommended.

★ **Pee Wee's at the Point** AUSTRALIAN $$$
(☑ 08-8981 6868; www.peewees.com.au; Alec Fong Lim Dr, East Point; mains $41-55; ⊙ from 6.30pm) Arguably Darwin's premier kitchen, this is indeed a place for a treat. Enjoy your double-roasted duckling or the wild-caught barramundi with macadamia, herb and lemon myrtle among tropical palms at **East Point Reserve** (⊙ mangrove boardwalk 8am-6pm), right on the waterfront.

🍸 Drinking & Nightlife

★ **Six Tanks** BAR
(☑ 08-8923 9780; www.facebook.com/sixtanks; 4/69 Mitchell St; ⊙ 10am-2am) Proof that there's some real quality along Mitchell St among the generic backpacker spots, this brewpub serves up its craft beers from 26 different taps; six are reserved for the beers brewed on-site and supplied straight from the tanks, while others are devoted to guest craft beers from elsewhere in Australia or around the world.

★ **One Mile Brewing Company** BREWERY
(☑ 0429 782 870; www.onemilebrewery.com.au; 8/111 Coonawarra Rd, Winnellie; ⊙ 5-8pm Thu & Fri, noon-7.30pm Sat) A good place to start your Darwin night out, this brewery's tasting bar showcases some of the Top End's tastiest beers. We like the 4:21, a beer cheekily named after the time Darwin's civil servants famously finish work, but the Pink Lady Cider also has its devotees. Ask about a brewery tour if you're a beer aficionado.

★ **Darwin Ski Club** PUB
(☑ 08-8981 6630; www.darwinskiclub.com.au; Conacher St, Fannie Bay; ⊙ noon-late) Leave Mitchell St behind and head for a sublime sunset at this laid-back waterski club on **Vesteys Beach**. The view through the palm trees from the beer garden is a winner, and there are often live bands. Hands down the best venue for a sunset beer in Darwin.

Discovery & Lost Arc CLUB
(☑ 08-8942 3300; www.discoverydarwin.com.au; 89 Mitchell St; ⊙ noon-late) Discovery is Darwin's biggest nightclub and dance venue, with three levels featuring hip hop, techno and house, plus bars, private booths, karaoke, an elevated dance floor and plenty of partygoers. The Lost Arc is the classy chillout bar opening on to Mitchell St, which starts to thaw after about 10pm.

☆ Entertainment

Darwin's balmy nights invite late-night exploration and while there's only a handful of nightclubs, you'll find something on every night. There's also a thriving arts and entertainment scene: theatre, films and concerts.

Off the Leash (www.offtheleash.net.au) magazine lists events happening around town. Keep an eye out for bills posted on noticeboards and electricity poles that advertise dance and full-moon parties.

★ **Deckchair Cinema** CINEMA
(☑ 08-8981 0700; www.deckchaircinema.com; Jervois Rd, Waterfront Precinct; adult/child $16/8; ⊙ box office from 6.30pm Apr-Nov) During the Dry, the Darwin Film Society runs this fabulous outdoor cinema below the southern end of the Esplanade. Watch a movie under the stars while reclining in a deckchair. There's a licensed bar serving food or you can bring a picnic (no BYO alcohol). There are usually double features on Friday and Saturday nights (adult/child $26/13).

Happy Yess LIVE MUSIC
(www.happyyess.tumblr.com; Brown's Mart, 12 Smith St; ⊙ 6pm-midnight Thu-Sat) This venue is Darwin's leading place for live music. A not-for-profit venue for musicians run by musicians, you won't hear cover bands in here. Original, sometimes weird, always fun.

Darwin Railway Club LIVE MUSIC
(☑ 08-8981 4171; www.darwinrailwayclub.org; 17 Somerville Gardens, Parap; ⊙ 4-11.30pm Mon-Fri, noon-1.30am Sat, noon-10pm Sun) Big supporters of Darwin's live music scene, this place pulls in some class acts. The nearly 20-piece band gets the place swinging on Wednesdays, with everything from up-and-coming indie acts to folk strumming possible the rest of the week.

🛍 Shopping

★ **Provenance Arts** ART
(☑ 08-6117 5515; www.provenancearts.com.au; Stuart Hwy, Stuart Park; ⊙ 10am-5pm Tue-Fri, to 3pm Sat & Sun) A fabulous initiative from Injalak Arts (p835), an outstanding Indigenous art centre in Arnhem Land, Provenance Arts is a gallery with works from over

DON'T MISS

DARWIN'S MAGICAL MARKETS

Darwin has one of the best collection of markets of any Australian city, and they're worth planning your visit around.

Mindil Beach Sunset Market (www.mindil.com.au; off Gilruth Ave; ⊙4-9pm Thu & Sun May-Oct; ☐4, 6) Food is the main attraction here. But that's only half the fun – arts and crafts stalls bulge with handmade jewellery, fabulous rainbow tie-dyed clothes, Aboriginal artefacts, and wares from Indonesia and Thailand. As the sun heads towards the horizon, half of Darwin descends on the market, with tables, chairs, rugs, grog and kids in tow. Mindil beach is about 2km from Darwin's city centre; it's an easy walk or hop on buses 4 or 6, which go past the market.

Parap Village Market (p811) This compact, crowded food-focused market is a local favourite. There's the full gamut of Southeast Asian cuisine, as well as plenty of ingredients to cook up your own tropical storm. It's open year-round.

Nightcliff Market (☑0414 368 773; 7 Pavonia Place, Nightcliff; ⊙8am-2pm Sun) A popular community market north of the city in the Nightcliff Shopping Centre. You'll find lots of secondhand goods and designer clothing.

Rapid Creek Market (☑08-8948 4866; https://rapidcreekmarkets.com.au/; 48 Trower Rd, Rapid Creek; ⊙8am-2pm Sun) Darwin's oldest market is an Asian marketplace, with a tremendous range of tropical fruit and vegetables mingled with a heady mixture of spices and swirling satay smoke.

Malak Marketplace (www.malakmarketplace.org.au; 14 Malak Cres, Malak; ⊙4-9pm Sat late Apr–late Oct) This small market (around 70 stalls) is very much food-focused with an emphasis on organic farmers' produce and healthy eating, as well as a few stalls selling arts and crafts. It's a fun place to spend a Saturday evening.

30 Aboriginal art centres from across the NT, WA and Qld, but their ambitions run further – visitors can sometimes interact with the artists themselves and there are plans for an Indigenous cultural tourism information centre.

★**Outstation Gallery** ART
(☑08-8981 4822; www.outstation.com.au; 8 Parap Pl, Parap; ⊙10am-1pm Tue, to 5pm Wed-Fri, to 2pm Sat) One of Darwin's best galleries of Indigenous art, Outstation presents the works of nine different Aboriginal art centres from across the NT, from Arnhem Land to the Western Desert.

Nomad Art Gallery ART
(☑08-8981 6382; www.nomadart.com.au; 1/3 Vickers St, Parap; ⊙10am-5pm Mon-Fri, 9am-2pm Sat) Around since 2005, this excellent high-end gallery sells contemporary Indigenous art, including limited-edition paintings, textiles, carpets, bronzes and jewellery.

Mbantua Fine Art Gallery ART
(☑08-8941 6611; www.mbantua.com.au; 2/30 Smith St Mall; ⊙9am-5pm Mon-Sat) Vivid Utopian designs painted on everything from canvases to ceramics.

Paperbark Woman TEXTILES
(☑08-8941 7142; www.paperbarkwoman.com.au; Shop 13, Arafura Plaza, 24 Cavenagh St; ⊙10am-5pm Mon-Thu, to 6pm Fri, to 2pm Sat) An extraordinary range of fabrics designed and made by Aboriginal and Torres Strait Islanders crowd this CBD shop. There's a good mix of finished articles (clothing, accessories etc) and raw materials for quilters and other creative types.

Mason Gallery ART
(☑08-8981 9622; www.masongallery.com.au; Shop 7, 21 Cavenagh St; ⊙9am-5pm Mon-Fri, 10am-3pm Sat & Sun) Features bold dot paintings from the Western and Central Desert regions, as well as works from Arnhem Land and Utopia.

NT General Store SPORTS & OUTDOORS
(☑08-8981 8242; www.thentgeneralstore.com.au; 42 Cavenagh St; ⊙8.30am-5.30pm Mon-Wed, to 6pm Thu&Fri, to 1pm Sat) This casual, corrugated-iron warehouse has shelves piled high with camping and bushwalking gear, as well as a range of maps.

Tiwi Art Network ART
(☑08-8941 3593; www.ankaaa.org.au/art-centre/tiwi-art-network-tiwi-islands; 3 Vickers St, Parap;

🕑 10am-5pm Wed-Fri, to 2pm Sat) 🎫 The office and showroom for three arts communities on the Tiwi Islands.

ℹ️ Information

DANGERS & ANNOYANCES

➻ Darwin is a generally safe city to visit, but the usual rules apply: petty crime can be a problem, particularly late at night, so avoid walking alone in unlit areas and don't leave valuables in your car.

➻ In response to several reports of drugged drinks, authorities are advising women to refuse drinks offered by strangers in bars and to drink bottled alcohol rather than from a glass.

➻ Always assume that there are crocodiles in waterholes and rivers in the Darwin area.

➻ Cyclones can happen from November to April, while heavy monsoon rains can curtail outdoor activities from December to March.

INTERNET ACCESS

Most accommodation in Darwin provides some form of internet access, and there's free wi-fi available in the Smith Street Mall, Darwin Waterfront Precinct and Mindil Beach Sunset Market (p813).

You can also get online at the **Northern Territory Library** (📞 1800 019 155; www.dtc.nt.gov. au; Parliament House, Mitchell St; 🕑 10am-5pm Tue, Thu & Fri, 10am-8pm Wed, 1-5pm Sat & Sun; 🕾).

MEDICAL SERVICES

Royal Darwin Hospital (📞 08-8920 6011; www. health.nt.gov.au; 105 Rocklands Dr, Tiwi; 🕑 24hr)

POST

General Post Office (📞 13 13 18; www.auspost.com.au; 48 Cavenagh St; 🕑 9am-5pm Mon-Fri, to 12.30pm Sat)

TOURIST INFORMATION

Ark Aid (📞 08-8932 9738; www.wildlifedarwin. org.au; 56 Georgina Cres, Yarrawonga, Palmerston; 🕑 8am-6pm Mon-Fri, 9am-1pm Sat) The people to call if you come across injured wildlife. For emergency animal rescues, call Wildcare NT on 08-8988 6121.

Northern Land Council (📞 08-8920 5100; www.nlc.org.au; 45 Mitchell St) Permits for Arnhem Land and other northern mainland areas.

Tiwi Land Council (📞 08-8981 4898; www. tiwilandcouncil.com; 162/2 Armidale St, Stuart Park) Permits for the Tiwi Islands.

Tourism Top End (📞 08-8980 6000; www. tourismtopend.com.au; cnr Smith & Bennett Sts; 8.30am-5pm Mon-Fri, 9am-3pm Sat & Sun) Helpful office with hundreds of brochures; books tours and accommodation for Darwin and beyond.

ℹ️ Getting There & Away

AIR

➻ Darwin International Airport (📞 08-8920 1811; www.darwinairport.com.au) is 12km north of the city centre, and handles both international and domestic flights.

➻ **Darwin City Airport Shuttle Service** (📞 08-8947 3979; www.darwincityairportshuttle service.com.au; per person $18) is one of a number of private airport shuttle companies who will pick up or drop off almost anywhere in the centre. When leaving Darwin book a day before departure.

➻ A taxi fare into the centre is about $40 to $45.

➻ The following airlines operate from the airport: **Airnorth** (📞 1800 627 474; www.airnorth. com.au; Darwin Airport), **Jetstar** (www.jetstar. com; Darwin Airport), **Qantas** (www.qantas. com.au; Darwin Airport) and **Virgin Australia** (www.virginaustralia.com; Darwin Airport).

BUS

Greyhound (📞 1300 473 946; www.greyhound. com.au) runs at least one service per day up and down the Stuart Hwy, the only road in and out of Darwin. Buses depart from the rear of the **Transit Centre** (www.enjoy-darwin.com; 69 Mitchell St). Stops include Pine Creek (from $67, three hours), Katherine ($77, four hours), Mataranka ($115, seven hours), Tennant Creek ($148, 14¼ hours) and Alice Springs ($209, 22 hours). For Kakadu, there's a daily return service from Darwin to Jabiru ($79, 3¾ hours).

Backpacker buses and tours can also get you to out-of-the-way places.

CAR & CAMPERVAN

For driving around Darwin, conventional vehicles are cheap enough, but most companies offer only 100km per day free, which won't get you very far out of town. Rates start at around $40 per day for a small car with 100km per day.

There are also plenty of 4WD vehicles available in Darwin, through companies like **Britz** (📞 1800 331 454; www.britz.com.au; 17 Bombing Rd, Winnellie), but you usually have to book ahead and fees/deposits are higher than for 2WD vehicles. Larger companies offer one-way rentals plus better mileage deals for more-expensive vehicles. Campervans are a great option for touring around the NT and you generally get unlimited kilometres even for short rentals. Prices start at around $60 a day for a basic camper or $100 to $120 for a three-berth high-top camper, to $250-plus for the bigger mobile homes or 4WD bushcampers. Additional insurance cover or excess reduction costs extra.

Most rental companies are open every day and have agencies in the city centre. **Avis** (📞 08-8936 0600; www.avis.com.au; 89 Smith St), **Budget** (📞 08-8981 9800; www.budget.com.au; McLachlan St), **Hertz** (📞 08-8941 0944; www.

hertz.com.au; Shop 41, Mitchell Centre, 55-59 Mitchell St; ⊙8am-5pm Mon-Fri, to noon Sat & Sun) and **Thrifty** (☑08-8924 2455; www.thrifty. com.au; 50 Mitchell St, Value Inn; ⊙8am-5pm Mon-Fri, to 1pm Sat, to noon Sun) all have offices at the airport.

Europcar (☑08-8941 0300; www.europcar. com.au; 77 Cavenagh St; ⊙8am-5pm Mon-Fri, to noon Sat & Sun)

JJ's Car Hire (☑0427 214 229; www.jjscarhire. com.au; 7-9 Goyder Rd, Parap) A good local operator.

Mighty Cars & Campervans (☑08-8981 2081; www.mightycampers.com.au; 17 Bombing Rd, Winnellie)

Travellers Autobarn (☑1800 674 374; www. travellers-autobarn.com.au; 19 Bishop St, Woolner; ⊙9am-5pm Mon-Fri, to 1pm Sat)

For assistance or information try **AANT Roadside Assistance** (☑13 11 11; www.aant.com.au).

TRAIN

The legendary **Ghan** (☑08-8213 4401; www. greatsouthernrail.com.au; Berrimah Rd, East Arm, Darwin Train Station) train, operated by Great Southern Rail, runs weekly (twice weekly May to July) between Adelaide and Darwin via Alice Springs. The Darwin terminus is on Berrimah Rd, 15km (20 minutes) from the city centre. A taxi fare into the centre is about $40, though there is a shuttle service to/from the Transit Centre.

ⓘ Getting Around

BUS

Darwinbus (☑08-8944 2444; www.nt.gov. au/driving/public-transport-cycling) runs a comprehensive bus network that departs from the **Darwin Bus Terminus** (Harry Chan Ave), opposite Brown's Mart. For timetables, check out the website at the **Department of Transport** (☑08-8924 7666; https://nt.gov.au/driving/public-transport-cycling/public-bus-timetables-maps-darwin).

A $3 adult ticket gives unlimited travel on the bus network for three hours (validate your ticket when you first get on). Daily ($7) and weekly ($20) travel cards are also available from bus interchanges, newsagents and the visitor centre.

BICYCLE

Spin Way (☑0414 296 196; www.spinwaynt. com.au; ⊙1/4/24hr $14/33/44), Darwin's public bicycle-hire system, works like similar schemes around the world – go to one of numerous stations around town, swipe your credit card, select how long you wish to rent for and then get riding. For a list of locations, pick up the Spin Way brochure *Automated Bike Hire Station* from Tourism Top End, or check online. Note that you must return the bike to the same station you took it from, and helmets and locks are included in the rental price.

AROUND DARWIN

In Darwin's hinterland you'll come across some real gems, particularly Litchfield National Park, the Mary River region and the Tiwi Islands. You're never more than a couple of hours from the capital but, with the exception of the Tiwi Islands, we recommend doing more than just a day visit from Darwin – every one of these places is worth lingering over.

Tiwi Islands

The Tiwi Islands – Bathurst Island and Melville Island – lie about 80km north of Darwin, and are home to the Tiwi Aboriginal people. A visit here is one of the cultural highlights of the Top End. The Tiwis (We People) have

DARWIN & THE NORTHERN TERRITORY TIWI ISLANDS

TIWI ISLAND CULTURE

The Tiwis' island homes kept them fairly isolated from mainland developments until the 20th century, and their culture has retained several unique features. Perhaps the best known are the *pukumani* (burial poles), carved and painted with symbolic and mythological figures, which are erected around graves. More recently the Tiwis have turned their hand to art for sale: carvings, paintings, screen-printed and batik textiles, and pottery using traditional designs and motifs. The Bima Wear textile factory (https://bimawear.com) was set up in 1969 to employ Tiwi women, and today makes many bright fabrics in distinctive designs.

Most of the 2700 Tiwi Islanders live on Bathurst Island (there are about 900 people on Melville Island). Most follow a mainly nontraditional lifestyle, but they still hunt dugong and gather turtle eggs, and hunting and gathering usually supplements the mainland diet a couple of times a week. Tiwis also go back to their traditional lands on Melville Island for a few weeks each year to teach and to learn traditional culture. Descendants of the Japanese pearl divers who regularly visited here early last century also live on Melville Island.

Around Darwin

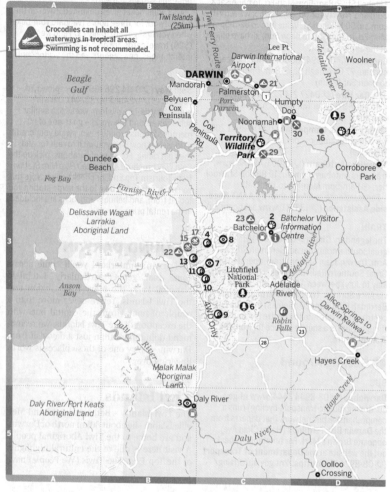

a distinct culture and today are well known for producing vibrant art and the odd champion Aussie rules football player. Tourism is restricted on the islands and for most travellers the only way to visit is on one of the daily organised tours from Darwin.

The main settlement on the islands is Wurrumiyanga in the southeast of Bathurst Island, which was founded in 1911 as a Catholic mission. On Melville Island the settlements are Pirlangimpi and Milikapiti.

☞ Tours

To get more than a passing glimpse of the islands, take a tour. SeaLink runs ferries and some excellent tours. Try also **Tiwi Tours** (☑ 08-8923 6523; Shop 6, 52 Mitchell St, Darwin).

SeaLink Tiwi Day Tour CULTURAL
(☑ 1300 130 679; www.sealinknt.com.au; adult/child $295/148; ☺ 8am-5.45pm Thu & Fri May-Oct, also Mon Jun-Aug) SeaLink offers fascinating day trips to the Tiwis, although interaction with the local community tends to be limited to your guides and the local workshops and showrooms. The day tour (adult/child $295/148) includes permit, welcome ceremony, light lunch, and visits to the early Catholic mission buildings, the Patakijiyali Museum and a *pukumani* burial site.

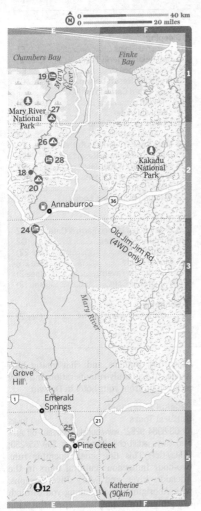

displays the Tiwis' passion for Aussie rules football. Thousands come from Darwin for the day, which coincides with the Tiwi Art Sale (www.tiwidesigns.com). Book your ferry trip well in advance, although you don't need to be on a tour or have a permit to come to this.

🛏 Sleeping & Eating

Visitors are not allowed to stay on the island without permission and there are no hotels. Visit instead on a day trip from Darwin.

Some of the tour operators provide lunch, but otherwise there are no restaurants or supermarkets so you'll need to bring your own.

❶ Getting There & Away

SeaLink (📞1300 130 679; www.sealinknt. com.au; adult/child one-way $60/30, return $120/60) ferries operate from Darwin's Cullen Bay to the Tiwi Islands daily at 8am (less often during the Wet) – check the website for timetables and departure times. The journey takes 2½ hours and departs Wurrumiyanga on Bathurst Island at 3.15pm. Unless you're on a tour, which we strongly recommend, if you want to explore beyond town you'll need a permit from the Tiwi Land Council (p814).

Arnhem Highway

The Arnhem Highway (Rte 36) connects Darwin to Kakadu National Park – it branches off towards Kakadu 34km southeast of Darwin – and while many travellers stop for little more than petrol along the way, there are a number of worthwhile sights and activities if you have the time. These include river cruises and wetland birdwatching, as well as the small agricultural hub (and gloriously named) Humpty Doo, where you can see the Big Boxing Crocodile, unmistakeable by the side of the Arnhem Hwy, close to the Humpty Doo Hotel. The highway traverses the traditional lands of numerous Aboriginal peoples and language groups.

◎ Sights

Window on the Wetlands Visitor Centre   WILDLIFE RESERVE
(📞08-8988 8188; www.nt.gov.au/leisure/parks-reserves; Arnhem Hwy; ⊙8am-5.30pm) FREE Three kilometres past the Fogg Dam (p818) turn-off, east along the Arnhem Hwy, is this dashing-looking structure full of displays explaining the wetland ecosystem, as well as

The Tiwi by Design tour (adult/child $349/295; 8am-5.45pm Thu & Fri Apr–mid-Dec, also Mon Jun-Aug) also includes permit and a welcome ceremony, as well as lunch, visits to a local museum and church, and an art workshop, where you get to create your own design for a screen print to take home.

✿ Festivals & Events

**Tiwi Grand Final
& Annual Art Sale**   SPORTS
(⊙Mar) Held at the end of March on Bathurst Island, this sporting spectacular

Around Darwin

◎ **Top Sights**
1 Territory Wildlife Park..................C2

◎ **Sights**
2 Batchelor Butterfly Farm......................C3
  Berry Springs Nature Park ....(see 1)
3 Daly River Crossing.............................B5
4 Florence Falls......................................C3
5 Fogg Dam Conservation Reserve........D2
6 Litchfield National Park.......................C4
7 Lost City...C3
8 Magnetic Termite Mounds...................C3
9 Surprise Creek Falls............................C4
10 Tjaynera Falls....................................C3
11 Tolmer Falls.......................................C3
12 Umbrawarra Gorge Nature Park..........E5
13 Wangi Falls...B3
14 Window on the Wetlands Visitor
    Centre..D2

◎ **Activities, Courses & Tours**
  Buley Rockhole................................(see 4)
15 Cascade Pools....................................B3
  NT Air..(see 13)
16 Pudakul Aboriginal Cultural Tours........D2
  Tabletop Track ....(see 4)
17 Walker Creek......................................B3
18 Wetland Cruises – Corroboree
    Billabong...E2

◎ **Sleeping**
19 Bamurru Plains E1
  Batchelor Butterfly Farm...............(see 2)
20 Couzens Lookout.................................E2
21 FreeSpirit Resort Darwin.....................C1
  Lazy Lizard Caravan Park &
    Tavern ....(see 25)
  Litchfield Motel ....(see 2)
22 Litchfield Safari Camp........................B3
23 Litchfield Tourist Park.........................C3
24 Mary River Wilderness Retreat.............E3
25 Pine Creek Railway Resort...................E5
26 Point Stuart Wilderness Lodge.............E2
  Rum Jungle Bungalows ....(see 2)
27 Shady Camp.......................................E1
28 Wildman Wilderness Lodge..................E2

◎ **Eating**
29 Crazy Acres Mango Farm & Cafe........C2
30 Humpty Doo Hotel.............................. D2
  Litchfield Cafe ....(see 22)
  Mayse's Cafe ....(see 25)
  Rum Jungle Tavern.........................(see 2)
  Wangi Falls Cafe............................(see 13)

◎ **Shopping**
  Coomalie Cultural Centre...............(see 2)

the history of the local Limilngan-Wulna Aboriginal people. There are great views over the Adelaide River flood plain from the observation deck, and binoculars for studying the waterbirds on Lake Beatrice.

Fogg Dam
Conservation Reserve　　　　NATURE RESERVE
(☑08-8988 8009; www.nt.gov.au/leisure/parks-reserves) Bring your binoculars – there are ludicrous numbers of waterbirds living at the fecund green Fogg Dam Conservation Reserve. The dam walls are closed to walkers (crocs), but there are a couple of nature walks (2.2km and 3.6km) through the forest and woodlands. Bird numbers are highest between December and July. The turn-off for the reserve is about 15km southeast along the Arnhem Hwy from Humpty Doo.

🕝 Tours

Adelaide River Tours　　　　WILDLIFE
(☑0472 786 877; www.adelaiderivertours.com.au; per person $160; ☺8am-5pm) With a focus on spotting local wildlife (rather than feeding jumping crocs), Adelaide River Tours gets our vote for the best of the tours on the Adelaide River. Yes, you'll see crocs, as well as

kangaroos, buffalos and charismatic bird species. It's a family-run operation and they pick you up from your hotel in Darwin.

Pudakul Aboriginal
Cultural Tours　　　　TOURS
(☑08-8984 9282; www.pudakul.com.au; off Arnhem Hwy; adult/child/family from $99/55/250; ☺May-Oct) This fine small operator runs two-hour Indigenous cultural tours in the Adelaide River and Mary River regions, with Aboriginal guides taking you through everything from painting, spear-throwing and didgeridoo lessons to bush-tucker and bush-medicine guided walks. They also run a seven-hour Wetland Discovery Tour or Croc and Culture Tour (either tour adult/child $165/145)

🛌 Sleeping & Eating

Humpty Doo Hotel　　　　PUB FOOD $$
(☑08-8988 1372; www.humptydoohotel.com.au; Arnhem Hwy; mains $18-33; ☺10am-9pm Sun-Wed, to 9.30am Thu-Sat; ▣) Some people stop here because, well, it's the sort of name you'd like to tell your friends about when you're back home, but there's more to this place than novelty. Darwin locals often stop by

for a trio of burgers platter (barra, buffalo and croc), or the Tuesday rump steaks and parma specials.

There are unremarkable motel rooms and cabins out the back (rooms $130 to $160).

❶ Getting There & Away

There's not much public transport along the Arnhem Hwy; most visitors either drive or visit on a tour. There's a **petrol station** (⊙6am-9pm) at Humpty Doo.

Mary River Region

Often overlooked in the rush to Kakadu, Mary River is worth dedicating some time to, with the wetlands and wildlife of the **Mary River National Park** (www.nt.gov.au/leisure/parks-reserves), north of the Arnhem Hwy, the centrepiece. This is Jawoyn country, whose traditional lands stretch south all the way to Nitmiluk (Katherine Gorge) National Park.

☞ Tours

Wetland Cruises –
Corroboree Billabong TOURS
(☑08-8985 5855; www.wetlandcruises.com.au; ⊙Mar-Oct) These excellent boat excursions show the Mary River Wetlands in all their glory. You're almost guaranteed to see salt-water crocs, as well as plenty of birdlife. There are one-hour morning cruises (adult/child $55/40) and lunch or sunset cruises, along with full-day excursions from Darwin (adult/child $140/100).

🛌 Sleeping

There are basic public campgrounds at **Couzens Lookout** (☑08-8978 8986; www.nt.gov.au/leisure/parks-reserves; Mary River National Park; adult/child/family $3.30/1.65/7.70) and **Shady Camp** (Mary River National Park; adult/child/family $3.30/1.65/7.70), where there are grassy campsites under banyan trees. Come prepared to ward off armies of mosquitoes. Elsewhere there are some lovely lodges and wilderness retreats.

⭐**Mary River**
Wilderness Retreat RESORT $$
(☑08-8978 8877; www.maryriverretreat.com.au; Mary River Crossing, Arnhem Hwy; unpowered/powered sites $30/45, dm $45, cabins & safari tents $153-240; ❋🛜🛏) Boasting 3km of Mary River frontage, this bush retreat has excellent poolside and bush cabins with decks surrounded by trees, as well as some fine safari

DARWIN & THE NORTHERN TERRITORY ARNHEM HIGHWAY

CROC-JUMPING?

One of the most popular activities in the Arnhem Hwy region involves taking travellers out on a boat and enticing otherwise wild crocodiles to leap from the water to snatch food being held above them. There are some concerns with these tours, many of which are advertised as day trips from Darwin, on animal welfare grounds. Akin to the discredited practice of leopard-baiting in Africa – food is left for leopards to come and feed on, in full view of waiting tourists – croc-feeding and croc-jumping in this way has created an unnatural dependence upon humans for food among wild crocs, thereby altering their behaviour for the sole purpose of human entertainment and profit.

tents. Pool cabins are the pick of the bunch, with high ceilings, walk-in showers and more space to knock around in; both sleep up to three people. Camping on the grassy slopes here is delightful.

Point Stuart
Wilderness Lodge CAMPGROUND $$
(☑08-8978 8914; www.pointstuart.com.au; Point Stuart Rd; camping per adult/child $17.50/6, safari tents s/d $35/50, d $130-195; ❋🛏) Accessible by 2WD and only 36km from the Arnhem Hwy, this remote lodge is part of an old cattle station and ideal for exploring the Mary River region. Accommodation ranges from campsites and simple safari tents to budget rooms and decent lodge rooms. Two-hour wetland cruises on croc-rich Rockhole Billabong cost $65/25 per adult/child, and boat hire is available.

⭐**Bamurru Plains** LODGE $$$
(☑1300 790 561; www.bamurruplains.com; Mary River Floodplains; per person from $490) This remote slice of eco-friendly luxury has canvas-topped lodgings with hardwood floors, wrap-around views and high levels of comfort. Safaris are by airboat or 4WD, there's wildlife aplenty and the sunsets here are rather extraordinary. It's almost impossible to find on your own, which is why most guests fly in from Darwin.

⭐**Wildman Wilderness Lodge** RESORT $$$
(☑08-8978 8955; www.wildmanwildernesslodge.com.au; Point Stuart Rd; safari tents/cabins half-

USEFUL NT APPS

Welcome to Country (www.welcome tocountry.mobi) Handy introduction to Indigenous cultures.

Trakka (http://trakkaapp.com.au/) Aboriginal sites and events.

Indigital Storytelling (www.indigital. net.au) Intersection between Indigenous stories and technology.

Kakadu National Park Apps (https:// parksaustralia.gov.au/kakadu/plan/ apps/) Kakadu visitor guide with park information.

Red Centre Art Trails (http://spinifex valley.com.au/red-centre-art-trails/) Art attractions and events in the Red Centre.

Field Guide to NT Fauna (www.magnt. net.au/fieldguide) Wildlife of the Northern Territory.

Uluru Birds (https://parksaustralia.gov. au/uluru/do/birdwatching/) Essential guide to birdwatching at Uluru.

board $675/795; 🐾🐾) One of the best places to stay in the Top End, Wildman Wilderness Lodge is an upmarket safari lodge with an exceptional program of optional tours and activities, not to mention some gorgeous, supremely comfortable accommodation options in a beautiful and remote setting. There are just 10 air-conditioned, stylish, architect-designed cabins and 15 fan-cooled, clean-lined luxury tents.

❶ Getting There & Away

➻ You'll need a 4WD to explore anywhere in the national park beyond the Arnhem Hwy, although a few park trails may be passable in a 2WD during the dry season.

➻ **Petrol** (⊙7am-8pm) is available along the Arnhem Hwy.

➻ Some accommodation places offer transfers from Darwin and elsewhere.

Berry Springs

The only three reasons to come to Berry Springs – and they're good ones – are to visit one of the NT's best zoos, home to a brilliant collection of Australia's native wildlife, a fine waterhole and an excellent cafe. It's an easy day trip from Darwin.

Berry Springs lies on the traditional lands of the Kungarakan, whose territory reaches from Berry Springs to Batchelor.

◉ Sights

★**Territory Wildlife Park** ZOO
(📞08-89887200; www.territorywildlifepark.com.au; 960 Cox Peninsula Rd; adult/child/family $32/ 16/54.50; ⊙9am-5pm) This excellent park showcases the best of Top End Aussie wildlife. Pride of place must go to the aquarium, where a clear walk-through tunnel puts you among giant barramundi, stingrays, sawfish and saratogas, while a separate tank holds a 3.8m saltwater crocodile.

The turn-off is 48km down the Stuart Hwy from Darwin; from here it's 12km further down Cox Peninsula Rd to the park.

Berry Springs Nature Park NATURE RESERVE
(📞08-8988 6310; www.nt.gov.au/leisure/parks-reserves; ⊙8am-6.30pm) This wonderful waterhole is the closest to Darwin and very popular with locals. It's a beautiful series of spring-fed swimming holes shaded by paperbarks and pandanus palms and serenaded by abundant birds; native flowers bloom here in March and April. Facilities include a kiosk, a picnic area with BBQs, toilets, changing sheds and showers. And there are large grassed areas to lounge around on in between swims.

Turn off the Stuart Hwy 48km south of Darwin; it's then about 10km to the park.

✕ Eating

★**Crazy Acres Mango Farm & Cafe** CAFE $
(📞0417 945 837, 08-8988 6227; www.crazyacres. com.au; Reedbeds Rd; light meals $10-17; ⊙9am-5.30pm May-Sep) Homemade ice cream, mango smoothies, local honey, Devonshire teas and a range of light meals from mango chicken (of course) to a gorgeous Farmer's Platter – what's not to like about this lovely little award-winning place, just off Cox Peninsula Rd?

❶ Getting There & Away

The turn-off to Berry Springs is 48km down the Stuart Hwy from Darwin; it's 10km from the turn-off to the nature park, and a further 2km to the wildlife park.

Batchelor

POP 507

The little town of Batchelor was once so sleepy, for a time the government gave blocks of land away to encourage settlement. That was before uranium was discovered here and the nearby Rum Jungle mine developed (it closed in 1971 after operating for almost 20 years). These days Batchelor is an important gateway and service centre for neighbouring Litchfield National Park.

This is the traditional country of the Warrai and Kungarakany Indigenous peoples.

◎ Sights

From the Visitor Information Centre, pick up a copy of the photocopied *Batchelor Heritage Walk* to guide your steps. It provides a potted history of the town and a self-guided route for a leisurely amble with a focus on local history.

🛏 Sleeping & Eating

Litchfield Tourist Park   CARAVAN PARK $
(📞08-8976 0070; www.litchfieldtouristpark.com.au; 2916 Litchfield Park Rd; sites $38, bunkhouse $79, en-suite cabins from $165; ❄@☀) Just 4km from Litchfield National Park, there's a great range of accommodation here, from shady campsites to better-than-average cabins, and it's the closest option to the park. There's also a breezy, open-sided bar-restaurant (dishes $11 to $23, open breakfast and dinner) where you can get a beer, a burger or a real coffee.

★Rum Jungle Bungalows   BUNGALOW $$
(📞08-8976 0555; www.rumjunglebungalows.com.au; 10 Meneling Rd; r $180; ❄☎☀) With more personality than most Batchelor places and rooms with warm and eclectic decor, Rum Jungle is an excellent choice. It's set in soothing and beautiful gardens and is open year-round.

Batchelor Butterfly Farm   RESORT $$
(📞08-8976 0110; www.butterflyfarm.net.au; 8 Meneling Rd; d with shared bathroom $85, d Apr-Sep $160, Oct-Mar $100; ❄@☎☀) This compact, slightly eclectic retreat divides itself between a low-key **butterfly farm** (📞08-8976 0110; www.butterflyfarm.net.au; 8 Meneling Rd; adult/child $12/6; ◷9am-4pm) and friendly tropical-style resort. They have colourful en suite cabins, a large homestay and a busy all-day cafe-restaurant (mains $18 to $32) featuring Asian-inspired dishes. It's all a bit Zen with Buddha statues, chill music and wicker chairs on the shaded deck.

Litchfield Motel   RESORT $$
(📞08-8976 0123; www.litchfieldmotel.com.au; 37-49 Rum Jungle Rd; d Apr-Oct $195-215, Nov-Mar

$150-170; ❄☎☀) On the edge of town, this sprawling orange-brick complex has decent motel rooms and energetic new managers. It's good for families, with bird feeding, two pools and two restaurants. There's also a bar and a grocery shop.

Rum Jungle Tavern   PUB FOOD $$
(📞08-8976 0811; www.rumjungletavern.com.au; 5 Nurndina St; mains $18-35; ◷noon-2.30pm & 6-8.30pm) The menu here promises the best and most varied meals in town, with burgers, wild-caught barramundi, pizzas, lamb racks and a range of schnitzels. The execution is a bit hit-and-miss, and the atmosphere falls flat many weeknights, but it gets busy on weekends.

🛍 Shopping

Coomalie Cultural Centre   ARTS & CRAFTS
(📞1800 677 095, 08-8939 7404; www.facebook.com/coomalieartcentre; cnr Awilla Rd & Nurndina St; ◷10am-5pm Tue-Sat Apr-Sep, to 4pm Tue-Fri Oct-Mar) The community-based Coomalie Cultural Centre displays and sells a range of Indigenous art and crafts from throughout the NT. It also runs an artist-in-residence program, so you may see artists at work.

ℹ Information

Batchelor Visitor Information Centre (📞08-8976 0444; Takarri Rd; ◷10am-5pm) The local tourist office is run by volunteers, so opening hours can vary, and they may not open at all some days during the Wet.

ℹ Getting There & Away

Batchelor is 98km south of Darwin and 14km west of the Stuart Hwy along a sealed road. There's a **petrol station** (◷7am-6pm Mon-Sat, 8am-5pm Sun) in the town centre, and another out at **Litchfield Motel** (Rum Jungle Rd; ◷7am-7pm).

Litchfield National Park

It may not be as well known as Kakadu, but many Territory locals rate Litchfield (📞08-8976 0282; www.nt.gov.au/leisure/parks-reserves), part of Wagait traditional Indigenous lands, even higher. Why not visit both? The rock formations and pools in the cliff shadow here are simply stunning, and Litchfield is smaller and more manageable than Kakadu. The 1500-sq-km national park encloses much of the spectacular Tabletop Range, a wide sandstone plateau mostly surrounded by cliffs. The waterfalls that pour off the edge of this plateau are a highlight of the park, feeding crystal-clear cascades and croc-free plunge pools.

The only downside is that, given its proximity to and ease of access from Darwin, it's often busy, and the only road through the park can be full of tour buses. Even so, it remains a beautiful place and certainly one of the best spots in the Top End for bushwalking, camping and especially swimming.

◎ Sights

About 17km after entering the park from Batchelor you come to what look like tombstones. But only the very tip of these magnetic termite mounds is used to bury the dead; at the bottom are the king and queen, with workers in between. They're perfectly aligned to regulate temperature, catching the morning sun, then allowing the residents to dodge the midday heat. Nearby are some giant mounds made by the aptly named cathedral termites.

Another 6km further along is the turn-off to Buley Rockhole, 2km on from the turn-off, where water cascades through a series of rock pools big enough to lodge your bod in. This turn-off also takes you to Florence Falls, 5km on, one of Litchfield's more agreeable waterholes. It's a 15-minute, 135-step descent to the deep, beautiful pool surrounded by monsoon forest. Alternatively, you can see the falls from a lookout, 120m from the car park, and if you don't fancy climbing the steep staircase back up to the car park, Shady Creek Walk (950m) begins by the waterhole and climbs gently through riverine monsoon forest then into the more open savannah woodland country. En route, watch for the shy short-eared rock wallaby. There's also a walking track (1.7km, 45 minutes) between Florence Falls and Buley Rockhole that follows Florence Creek.

If you've a 4WD, the Lost City is one of the more accessible of such rock formations in the NT. This dramatic collection of eroded rocky outcrops, some up to 500 million years old, has come to resemble a city of sandstone skyscrapers. Short walking tracks loop through the rocks. The Lost City is signposted off the main road through Litchfield, and is reached via 10km of unsealed track. It can possibly be done in a 2WD vehicle but a 4WD is recommended, especially after rain.

Back on the main road, about 18km beyond the turn-off to Florence Falls is the turn-off to the spectacular Tolmer Falls, which are for looking at only. A 1.6km loop

track (45 minutes) offers beautiful views of the valley. Tolmer Falls doesn't quite get the crowds because of the absence of swimming, and we like it all the more for that.

It's a further 7km along the main road to the turn-off for Litchfield's big-ticket attraction, Wangi Falls (pronounced wong-guy) 1.6km up a side road. The falls flow year-round, spilling either side of a huge orange-rock outcrop and filling an enormous swimming hole bordered by rainforest. Bring swimming goggles to spot local fish. It's immensely popular during the Dry (when there's a portable refreshment kiosk here, and free public wi-fi), but water levels in the Wet can make it unsafe; look for signposted warnings.

Beyond Wangi, Cascade Pools and Walker Creek are also excellent for swimming.

🏃 Activities

★ Tabletop Track   HIKING
(☉ May-Aug) The park offers plenty of bushwalking, including the Tabletop Track (39km), a moderate to challenging circuit of the park that takes three to five days to complete, depending on how many side tracks you follow. You can access (or detour from) the track at Florence Falls, Wangi Falls and Walker Creek.

You must carry a topographic map of the area, available from tourist and retail outlets in Batchelor, and you must obtain a permit prior to setting out – ring the park office (08-8976 0282) for advice on obtaining the permit. Check out also the Litchfield National Park – Tabletop Track information sheet, available online at www.nt.gov.au/leisure/recreation. The track is closed late September to April.

NT Air   SCENIC FLIGHTS
(☑ 08-8978 1423; www.ntair.com.au; 10/15/20/30min per person $110/165/220/320) Litchfield is spectacular from the ground, but even more so from the air. These helicopter flights offer fabulous views and the longer you fly, the more of the park you'll see. They're based at Wangi Falls, but you'll need to book in advance.

🛏 Sleeping & Eating

There is excellent public camping (adult/child $6.60/3.30) with toilets and fireplaces at Florence Falls; Florence Creek; Buley Rockhole; Wangi Falls, which is better for vans than tents; and Tjaynera Falls (4WD required). There are more-basic campsites at Surprise Creek Falls (4WD required) and Walker Creek.

Otherwise, most people who stay overnight do so in one of the motels or caravan parks in Batchelor or on the road into Litchfield.

Litchfield Safari Camp
CAMPGROUND $

(☑08-8978 2185; www.litchfieldsafaricamp.com.au; Litchfield Park Rd; unpowered/powered sites $28/38, dm $35, d safari tents $150; ☒) Shady grassed sites make this a good alternative to Litchfield's bush camping sites, especially if you want power and to stay inside the park. The safari tents are great value as they comfortably sleep up to four folks. There's also a ramshackle camp kitchen, a kiosk and a pint-sized pool.

Wangi Falls Cafe
CAFE $

(☑08-8978 2077; www.wangifallscentre.com.au; mains from $9.50; ☉10am-3pm May-Sep, 11am-2pm Oct-Apr; ☎) This busy cafe at Wangi Falls is one of few places in the park for a light meal. There are hot rolls, OK burgers and other bites to eat as well as a small souvenir shop. Try the smoothies made from local mangoes or the iced coffee. The kitchen closes at 2.30pm.

Litchfield Cafe
CAFE $$

(☑08-8978 2077; www.litchfieldcafe.com.au; Litchfield Park Rd; mains $14-36; ☉noon-3pm & 6-8pm Jun-Sep) Filo parcels (try the chicken, mango and macadamia) make for a super lunch at this excellent licensed cafe, or you could go for a meal of grilled local barramundi, topped off with a good coffee and some wicked mango cheesecake.

❶ Getting There & Away

The two routes to Litchfield (115km south of Darwin) from the Stuart Hwy join up and loop through the park. The southern access road via Batchelor is all sealed, while the northern access route, off the Cox Peninsula Rd, is partly unsealed, corrugated and often closed in the Wet. Many travellers visit on a day tour from Darwin.

There are numerous Litchfield tours ex-Darwin – most operate as day trips leaving soon after dawn and returning close to sunset.

Pine Creek

POP 328

A short detour off the Stuart Hwy, Pine Creek is a small settlement that was once the scene of a frantic gold rush. Before that, it stood at the meeting point of three Aboriginal peoples – the Wagiman (from the Daly River Region), the Jawoyn (around Katherine) and the Waray (north of the Kakadu Hwy). Although Pine Creek stays busy thanks to its position just off the highway, the town fell on hard times with the closure of the nearby iron-ore mine in 2015, a reminder that this has long been a boom-bust place, which somehow always seems to survive.

It's a quietly pretty little town with a nice park in the centre. Thanks to the good places to sleep and eat, and the town's proximity to the Kakadu Hwy turn-off, it's a good place to break a journey.

Umbrawarra Gorge Nature Park
NATURE RESERVE

(☑08-8976 0282; www.nt.gov.au/leisure/parks-reserves) About 3km south of Pine Creek on the Stuart Hwy is the turn-off to pretty Umbrawarra Gorge, with a safe swimming hole, a little beach and a basic campground (adult/child $3.30/1.65). It's 22km southwest on a rugged dirt road (just OK for 2WDs in the Dry; often impassable for everyone in the Wet). The walk along the water's edge is easy, but will have you clambering over boulders every now and then. Bring plenty of water and mosquito repellent.

🛏 Sleeping & Eating

Lazy Lizard Caravan Park & Tavern
CAMPGROUND $

(☑08-8976 1019; www.lazylizardpinecreek.com.au; 299 Millar Tce; unpowered/powered sites $18/30, s $60, d cabins $120; ☎☒) The small, wellgrassed camping area at the Lazy Lizard seems like an afterthought to the pulsing pub next door, but the sites are fine. The open-sided bar supported by carved ironwood pillars is a busy local watering hole, with a pool table and old saddles slung across the rafters.

★ Pine Creek Railway Resort
BOUTIQUE HOTEL $$

(☑08-8976 1001; www.pinecreekrailwayresort.com.au; s/d $90/130, cabins $150-170; ❄☎☒) This charming hotel uses raw iron, steel and wood in its modern rooms, which are easily the best for quite a distance in any direction. The dining area has been designed with romantic rail journeys of yore in mind; it's a scene-stealer with pressed-tin ceilings and elaborate chandeliers.

The menu (mains $19 to $30) is, however, modern, with steaks, pasta, ribs and risotto on offer.

Mayse's Cafe
CAFE $

(☑08-8976 1241; www.facebook.com/Maysescafe; Moule St; breakfast $5-19, mains $10-13; ☉8am-

3pm Mon-Sat, 9am-2pm Sun) Offering Pine Creek's best lunches, Mayse's does sandwiches, homemade pies, fish burgers, steak sandwiches and a mean lamb souvlaki in a cavernous dining area that feels vaguely like an American diner.

ⓘ Getting There & Away

→ The Kakadu Hwy (Rte 21) branches off the Stuart Hwy here, connecting Pine Creek to Cooinda and Jabiru. There's a **petrol station** (44 Moule St; ☉ 5.30am-8pm) in the centre of town.

→ Greyhound buses (www.greyhound.com.au) connect Pine Creek with Darwin (from $67, 2¾ to 3½ hours) and Katherine ($36, one hour) twice daily.

KAKADU NATIONAL PARK

There is more than a national park at Kakadu (www.parksaustralia.gov.au/kakadu); this place is also a vibrant, living acknowledgement of the elemental link between the Aboriginal custodians, the Bininj/Mungguy, and the country they have nurtured, endured and respected for thousands of generations. Encompassing almost 20,000 sq km (about 200km north–south and 100km east–west), it holds within its boundaries a spectacular ecosystem, periodically scorched and flooded, and mind-blowing ancient rock art.

In just a few days you can cruise on billabongs bursting with wildlife, examine 25,000-year-old rock paintings with the help of an Indigenous guide, swim in pools at the foot of tumbling waterfalls and hike through ancient sandstone escarpment country.

If Kakadu has a downside it's that it's very popular – in the Dry at least. Resorts, campgrounds and rock-art sites can be very crowded. But this is a vast park and with a little adventurous spirit you can easily leave the crowds behind.

Wildlife

Kakadu has more than 60 mammal species, more than 280 bird species, 120 recorded species of reptile, 25 species of frog, 55 freshwater fish species and at least 10,000 different kinds of insect. Most visitors see only a fraction of these creatures (except the insects), since many of them are shy, nocturnal or scarce.

Rock Art

Kakadu is one of Australia's richest, most accessible repositories of rock art. There are more than 5000 sites, which date from 20,000 years to 10 years old. The vast majority of these sites are off limits or inaccessible, but two of the finest collections are the easily visited galleries at Ubirr (p827) and Nourlangie (p829).

Rock paintings have been classified into three roughly defined periods: Pre-estuarine, which is from the earliest paintings up to around 6000 years ago; Estuarine, which covers the period from 6000 to around 2000 years ago, when rising sea levels brought the coast to its present level; and Freshwater, from 2000 years ago until the present day.

For local Aboriginal people, these rock-art sites are a major source of traditional knowledge and represent their archives. Aboriginal people rarely paint on rocks anymore, as they no longer live in rock shelters and there are fewer people with the requisite knowledge. Some older paintings are believed by many Aboriginal people to have been painted by mimi spirits, connecting people with Creation legends and the development of Aboriginal lore.

As the paintings are all rendered with natural, water-soluble ochres, they are very susceptible to water damage. Drip lines of clear silicon rubber have been laid on the rocks above the paintings to divert rain. As the most accessible sites receive up to 4000 visitors per week, boardwalks have been erected to keep the dust down and to keep people at a suitable distance from the paintings.

ⓘ KAKADU PARK ADMISSION

Admission to the park is via a seven-day Park Pass (adult/child/family April to October $40/20/100, November to March $25/12.50/65). Passes can be bought online or at various places around the park, including Bowali Visitor Information Centre (p832), where you can also pick up the excellent *Visitor Guide* booklet. Carry your pass with you at all times as rangers conduct spot checks – penalties apply for nonpayment. Other places to purchase the pass include the following:

Cooinda Lodge & Campground (p833)

Katherine Visitor Information Centre (p840)

Tourism Top End (p814)

Kakadu National Park

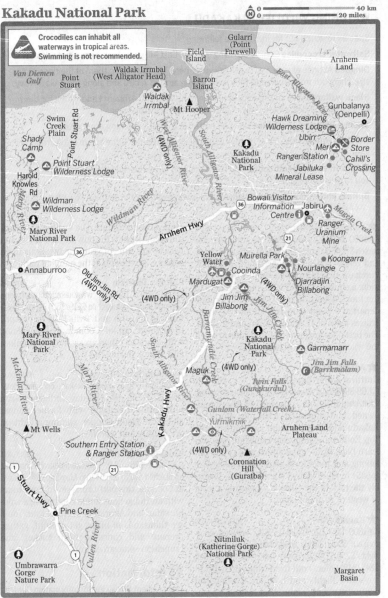

Tours

★ **Guluyambi Cultural Cruise** CULTURAL
(☎1800 525 238; www.kakaduculturaltours.com; adult/child $79/52; ◷9am, 11am, 1pm & 3pm May-Nov) Launch into an Aboriginal-led river cruise from the upstream boat ramp on the East Alligator River near Cahill's Crossing. Highly recommended by Darwin locals, it's a wonderful way to see crocodiles and a little of Arnhem Land from the riverbank, listening to Indigenous stories as you go.

WATCHING WILDLIFE IN KAKADU

Species to watch out for include the following:

Saltwater crocodiles Cahill's Crossing over the East Alligator River – you can't miss them.

Dingoes At once elusive and possible everywhere; you may seem them at the flood plains stretching out from Ubirr, and they're also seen around Jabiru and along the Kakadu Hwy.

Black wallaroo This shy species is unique to Kakadu and Arnhem Land – look for them at Nourlangie Rock, where individuals rest under rocky overhangs.

Short-eared rock wallabies Can be spotted in the early morning around Ubirr.

Northern quolls Possible at night out the back of the Border Store and in the surrounding area.

Northern brown bandicoots Find them and you've hit the jackpot; watch for them if you're driving at night.

Buffalo and wild horses Non-native species you might spot from the Yellow Water cruise.

★ **Yellow Water Cruises**　　　CRUISE
(☑1800 500 401; www.kakadutourism.com; per person $72-99) Cruise the South Alligator River and Yellow Water Billabong spotting wildlife. Purchase tickets from Gagudju Lodge, Cooinda; a shuttle bus will take you from here to the tour's departure point. Two-hour cruises depart at 6.45am, 9am and 4.30pm; 1½-hour cruises leave at 11.30am, 1.15pm and 2.45pm. The best ones are at sunrise and sunset, when the wildlife's at its most active.

★ **Arnhemlander**
Cultural & Heritage Tour　　　CULTURAL
(☑08-89792548; www.kakaduculturaltours.com.au; adult/child $273/218; ⊘May-Nov) Aboriginal-owned and -operated tour into northern Kakadu and Arnhem Land. See some of the Top End's most impressive ancient rock art, learn bush skills, enjoy lunch at a pretty billabong and meet local artists at Injalak Arts (p835) in Gunbalanya (Oenpelli). It's probably the pick of the options for getting a taste of western Arnhem Land.

★ **Kakadu Air**　　　SCENIC FLIGHTS
(☑1800 089 113, 08-8941 9611; www.kakaduair. com.au; 30min flights adult/child $150/120, 60min flights $250/200, 20/30min helicopter flights adult $245/345) Offers both fixed-wing and helicopter scenic flights and both are a wonderful way to get a sense of the sheer scale and beauty of Kakadu and Arnhem Land. Note that flights are only available over Jim Jim Falls in the wet season – traditional owners request that the 'skies are rested' in the Dry.

Kakadu Scenic Flights　　　SCENIC FLIGHTS
(☑08-8979 3432; www.scenicflight.com.au; 30/60/120min flights per person $130/240/400) A range of scenic flights. The one-hour wet season scenic flight is the only way to see Jim Jim Falls at this time of year; the two-hour flight covers a large swath of the national park.

Kakadu Tourism　　　TOURS
(☑08-8979 1500; www.kakadutourism.com; Cooinda Lodge; adult/child $219/160) Runs 4WD tours to Jim Jim and Twin Falls from April to October out of Cooinda Lodge (p833), with tours to other areas such as Gunlom and Maguk during the Wet.

Ayal Aboriginal Tours　　　CULTURAL
(☑0429 470 384; www.ayalkakadu.com.au; adult/ child $220/99) ◢ Full-day Indigenous-run tours around Kakadu with former ranger and local Victor Cooper, shining a light on art, culture and wildlife.

Kakadu Animal Tracks　　　CULTURAL
(☑0429 676 194; www.animaltracks.com.au; adult/child $220/55; ⊘1pm May-Sep) ◢ Based at Cooinda, this outfit runs seven-hour tours with an Indigenous guide combining a wildlife safari and Aboriginal cultural tour. You'll see thousands of birds, get to hunt, gather, prepare and consume bush tucker, and crunch on some green ants.

❶ Information

The excellent Bowali Visitor Information Centre (p832) has walk-through displays that sweep you across the land, explaining Kakadu's ecology from Aboriginal and non-Aboriginal perspectives. The helpful, staffed info window has 'Park Notes' flyers on all walks, with superb information about plants, animals and salient features you might encounter on each walk, plus explanations of their uses and significance. The 'What's On' flyer details where and when to catch a free and informative park ranger talk. The Marrawuddi Gallery is good for souvenirs; it stocks music, as well as high-quality paintings and craft by the countrymen and women of Kakadu and Arnhem Land. The centre is about 2.5km south of the Arnhem Hwy intersection; a 1km walking track connects it with Jabiru.

ⓘ Getting There & Around

The Arnhem Hwy and Kakadu Hwy traverse the park; both are sealed and accessible year-round. Fuel is available at Kakadu Resort, Cooinda and Jabiru.

Many people choose to access Kakadu on a tour, which shuffles them around the major sights with a minimum of hassle, but it's just as easy with your own wheels if you know what kinds of road conditions your trusty steed can handle (Jim Jim and Twin Falls, for example, are 4WD-access only).

Greyhound (p814) runs a coach service between Darwin and Jabiru ($75, 3¾ hours).

Ubirr & Around

Magnificent Ubirr is one of the jewels in Kakadu's rather well-studded crown. Even if you know what to expect, coming here feels like wandering into a lost and beautiful world that is at once playful art gallery of the ancients and soulful history book of Kakadu's extraordinary human and natural history. There are real treasures here – the NT's best sunset, a rare and accessible depiction of the Rainbow Serpent, the intriguing and improbable representation of the thylacine (Tasmanian tiger) and generally mesmerising Ubirr rock art. It's a spiritual place and very, very beautiful.

◎ Sights

★Ubirr   ROCK ART
(⊙8.30am-sunset Apr-Nov, 2pm-sunset Dec-Mar) It takes a lot more than the busloads of visitors to disturb Ubirr's inherent majesty and grace. Layers of rock-art paintings, in various styles and from various centuries, command a mesmerising stillness. Ubirr is 39km north of the Arnhem Hwy via a sealed road.

Part of the main gallery reads like a menu, with images of kangaroos, tortoises and fish painted in X-ray, which became the dominant style about 8000 years ago. Pre-dating these are the paintings of mimi spirits: cheeky, dynamic figures who, it's believed, were the first of the Creation Ancestors to paint on rock. (Given the lack of cherry-pickers in 6000 BC, you have to wonder who else but a spirit could have painted at that height and angle.) Look out for the yam-head figures, where the head is depicted as a yam on the body of a human or animal; these date back around 15,000 years.

The magnificent **Nardab Lookout** is a 250m scramble accessed from the main gallery. Surveying the exotic flood plain, watching the sun set in the west and the moon rise in the east like they're on an invisible set of scales gradually exchanging weight, is humbling to say the least.

★Cahill's Crossing   RIVER
It may be small, but there can be few more dramatic frontiers in Australia. This shallow causeway, which is impassable when the tide's in, crosses the East Alligator River from Kakadu National Park on the west bank to Arnhem Land to the east. And watching you as you cross is the river's healthy and rather prolific population of saltwater crocs. Ask at Border Store (p828) or Jabiru's Northern Land Council (p829) for tide timings.

☆ Activities

Manngarre Monsoon Forest Walk   WALKING
Mainly sticking to a boardwalk, this walk (1.5km return, 30 minutes, easy) starts by the boat ramp near the Border Store and winds through heavily shaded vegetation, palms and vines.

Bardedjilidji Sandstone Walk   WALKING
Starting from the upstream picnic-area car park, this walk (2.5km, 90 minutes, easy) takes in wetland areas of the East Alligator River and some interesting eroded sandstone outliers of the Arnhem Land escarpment. Informative track notes point out features on this walk; watch for both rock wallabies and the much-prized-among-birders chestnut-quilled rock pigeon. These are sacred rocks – no climbing.

🛏 Sleeping

Ubirr/Border Store Hostel   HOSTEL $
(☏08-8979 2474; borderstore@hotmail.com; Oenpelli Rd, Ubirr; camping per person $20, dm/f $50/240; ⊙May-Nov; P☀🐾) A most welcome addition to Kakadu's accommodation scene, this new hostel out the back of the iconic Border Store (p828) opened in May 2019, and has campsites as well as simple but good dorm rooms, a family room with a double and two single beds, and a communal kitchen and bathrooms. It's a rare backpacker outpost in this part of the world.

DARWIN & THE NORTHERN TERRITORY UBIRR & AROUND

Merl Camping Ground
CAMPGROUND $

(☑08-8938 1120; www.parksaustralia.gov.au/kakadu; adult/child/family $15/7.50/38) The turn-off to this campground is about 1km before the Border Store. It is divided into a quiet zone and a generator-use zone, each with a block of showers and toilets. It can get mighty busy at peak times and, be warned, the mosquitoes are diabolical. The site is closed in the Wet.

★ Hawk Dreaming Wilderness Lodge
LODGE $$$

(☑1800 525 238; www.kakaduculturaltours.com.au; s/d incl half-board $420/588, child $234; ⊙mid-May–mid-Oct) In a restricted area of the park (ie only guests and local Indigenous residents are allowed in), this deliciously remote lodge sits in the shadow of the stunning Hawk Dreaming sandstone escarpment and is as close to sweeping flood plains and billabongs as it is far from the clamouring crowds of Kakadu.

The safari tents are simple but nicely spread through shady grounds inhabited by wallabies, whistling kites and blue-winged kookaburras.

There's a small hot tub and rates include dinner and breakfast, transfers from the Border Store in Ubirr, sundowners and excursions to see local rock art that will be yours and yours alone to enjoy.

★ Border Store
CAFE $$

(Manbiyarra; ☑08-8979 2474; www.facebook.com/ubirrborderstore; mains $28; ⊙8.30am-8pm May-Nov) Run by Michael and Amm, charming little Border Store is full of surprises, including real coffee, sweet cakes and delicious Thai-cooked Thai food – a real treat. You can book a Guluyambi Cultural Cruise (p825) on the East Alligator River or a tour to Arnhem Land, or browse the small selection of books and artwork.

❶ Getting There & Away

Ubirr is 39km north of the Arnhem Hwy via a sealed road.

Jabiru
POP 1081

It may seem surprising to find a town of Jabiru's size and structure in the midst of a wilderness national park, but it exists solely because of the nearby Ranger uranium mine. With the closure of the mine slated for 2021, the town's future appears uncertain, dependent upon the extent to which the town can build on its other role as the national park's major service centre. In this capacity, it has just about everything you'd need, with a bank, newsagent, medical centre, supermarket, bakery and service station, as well as some good accommodation and an improving culinary scene.

⚞ Festivals & Events

Mahbilil Festival
CULTURAL

(www.mahbililfestival.com; ⊙Sep) A one-day celebration in early September (usually the first Saturday) of Indigenous culture in Jabiru. There are exhibitions showcasing local art as well as craft demonstrations, such as weaving and painting. Also on offer are competi-

---

SAVING JABIRU

Jabiru in its current manifestation was founded as a mining town back in the 1990s, and its growth in population and services has always been tied to the Ranger uranium mine just up the road. But the town is facing something of an identity crisis, with the mine due to cease operations in 2021 and close completely in 2026.

Part of the original agreement for the mine held that the mining companies – Energy Resources Australia (ERA) and its parent company Rio Tinto – had to clean up after they left. But the agreement was silent on the future of Jabiru.

In 2018 the NT government, in conjunction with the Mirarr traditional owners, finally announced a $446 million plan to build on Jabiru's role as a service centre for Kakadu National Park. Initial ideas included public art installations, turning Lake Jabiru into a croc-free tourist precinct, a new world heritage interpretive centre, a wellness centre and a five-star lodge. There was also talk of sealing roads into a number of Kakadu attractions (such as Jim Jim Falls and Gunlom) that are currently accessible only in the dry season.

Critics suggested that such a plan is years overdue. They also point out that for many of these ideas to come to fruition, as-yet-unsecured funding from the federal government and private investment will be required to supplement any funding from the NT government.

tions in spear throwing, didgeridoo blowing and magpie-goose cooking. In the evening the focus is on Indigenous music and dance.

🛌 Sleeping

★ Anbinik Kakadu Resort CABIN $$
(☑08-8979 3144; www.anbinik.com.au; 27 Lakeside Dr; en-suite powered sites $38-42, bungalows $105-140, d Apr-Nov/Dec-Mar $150/110, cabins Apr-Nov/Dec-Mar $260/210, ste Apr-Nov/Dec-Mar $250/180; ✸💻) This Aboriginal-owned park is one of Kakadu's best, with a range of tropical-design bungalows, cabins and suites in lush gardens. The doubles share a communal kitchen, bathroom and lounge and also come equipped with their own TV and fridge. The 'bush bungalows' are rustic and airy, while corrugated-iron-clad suites have a real hint of style. By far the best value in Jabiru.

Bungalows sleep up to four.

Aurora Kakadu
Lodge & Caravan Park RESORT $$
(☑08-8979 2422, 1800 811 154; www.auroraresorts.com.au; Jabiru Dr; unpowered/powered sites $30/42, r from $99, cabins $129-290; ✸🛜💻) One of the best places to camp in town with lots of grass, trees and natural barriers between camping areas, creating a sense of privacy. This sprawling, impeccable resort/caravan park also has a lagoon-style swimming pool. Self-contained cabins sleep up to five people.

Mercure Kakadu HOTEL $$$
(Crocodile Hotel; ☑08-8979 9000; www.accorhotels.com; 1 Flinders St; d from $275; ✸🛜💻) Known locally as 'the Croc', this hotel is designed in the shape of a crocodile, which, of course, is only obvious when viewed from the air. The rooms are clean and comfortable if a little pedestrian for the price. Try for one on the ground floor opening out to the central pool.

🍴 Eating

★ Anbinik Restaurant THAI $$
(☑08-8979 3144; www.anbinik.com.au; Lakeside Dr; mains $25; ☺7am-8.30pm) Easily Jabiru's best place for a meal, this outpost of Thailand in Kakadu has lovely outdoor tables (that can lack shade at lunchtime) and expertly prepared Thai soups, curries and stir-fries – both the Northern Thai–style stir-fry with basil and vegetables and the soups are particularly memorable.

Escarpment Restaurant INTERNATIONAL $$
(☑08-8979 9000; www.accorhotels.com; 1 Flinders St; mains $21-38; ☺noon-3pm & 6-9pm) This restaurant inside the Mercure Kakadu gets mixed reviews. Some love it, others hate it; the truth is somewhere in between. A good fallback, it's pretty uninspiring but you won't leave hungry. Dishes on the regularly changing menu cover the usual meat and seafood staples (steaks, burgers, barra) with the occasional nod to local bush-tucker tastes.

Brolga Bar & Bistro PUB FOOD $$
(Jabiru Sports & Social Club; ☑08-8979 2326; www.jabirusportsandsocialclub.com.au; off Lakeside Dr; mains $26-31, pizza $12; ☺noon-2pm & 6-9pm Tue-Sat) This low-slung hangar is the only place to meet locals over a beer or glass of wine, but the atmosphere is either stale or rowdy. The bistro meals, such as T-bone steak, chicken parma and fish and chips, are honest and there's an outdoor deck overlooking the lake, a kids' playground and sport on TV.

ℹ️ Information

Northern Land Council (☑1800 645 299, 08-8938 3000; www.nlc.org.au; 3 Government Bldg, Flinders St; ☺8am-4.15pm Mon-Fri) Issues permits for Arnhem Land, including Gunbalanya (Oenpelli).

ℹ️ Getting There & Away

Jabiru lies 257km from Darwin along the sealed Stuart and then Arnhem Hwys. There's no public transport out here, but nor is there any shortage of tours.

Nourlangie

The sight of this looming outlier of the Arnhem Land escarpment makes it easy to understand its ancient importance to Aboriginal people. Its long red-sandstone bulk, striped in places with orange, white and black, slopes up from surrounding woodland to fall away at one end in stepped cliffs. Below is Kakadu's best-known collection of rock art.

WHAT'S IN A NAME?

Of the 19 Aboriginal clans who are the traditional custodians of Kakadu, it is the Warramal who hold sway at Nourlangie. Traditionally, the upper area of the escarpment here was called Burrunggui, the lower reaches Anbangbang. The name Nourlangie is a corruption of *nawulandja*, an Aboriginal word that refers to an area larger than the rock itself.

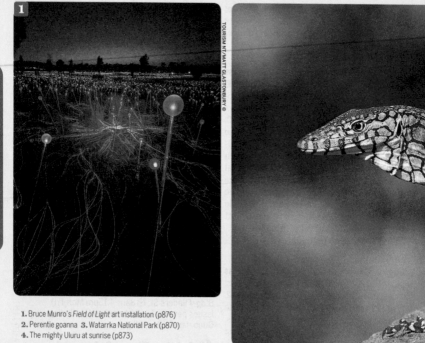

TOURISM NT/MATT GLASTONBURY ©

1. Bruce Munro's *Field of Light* art installation (p876)
2. Perentie goanna 3. Watarrka National Park (p870)
4. The mighty Uluru at sunrise (p873)

TOURISM NT/SHAANA MCNAUGHT ©

Ultimate Outback

'Outback' means different things to different people and in different parts of Australia – deserts, tropical savannah, wetlands... But what's consistent is the idea that it's far from the comforts of home. The outback is 'beyond the black stump' and holds many surprises.

Kata Tjuta

The tallest dome of Kata Tjuta is taller than Uluru (546m versus 348m), and for some people exploring these 36 mounded monoliths is a more moving experience. Trails weave in among the red rocks, leading to pockets of silent beauty where you can bear witness to its spiritual gravitas.

Kings Canyon

In Watarrka National Park, about 300km north of Uluru by road, Kings Canyon is the inverse of Uluru – as if someone had grabbed the big rock and pushed it into the desert sand. Here 100m-high sheer cliffs drop away to a palm-lined valley floor, home to 600 plant species and delighted-to-be-here native animals.

MacDonnell Ranges

The 'Macs' stretch east and west of Alice Springs. In their ancient folds are hidden worlds where rock wallabies and colourful birds can find water even on the hottest days.

Uluru

Uluru-Kata Tjuta National Park is the main draw of central Australia. And while you may have seen a hundred images of this remarkable geological feature, nothing compares to actually being in the presence of its almighty bulk. Guided walks draw out some of its spiritual significance, remarkable shapes, colours and textures. Helicopter rides, fine dining, camel treks and astronomy tours all add to the experience of visiting.

Sights & Activities

A 2km looped walking track (open 8am to sunset) takes you first to the **Anbangbang Shelter**, used for 20,000 years as a refuge and canvas. Next is the **Anbangbang Gallery**, featuring vivid Dreaming characters repainted in the 1960s. Look for the dangerous **Nabulwinjbulwinj**, a dangerous spirit who likes to eat females after banging them on the head with a yam. From here it's a short, steep walk to **Gunwarddehwarde Lookout**, with views of the Arnhem Land escarpment.

Barrk Walk
WALKING

This long day walk (12km loop, five to six hours, difficult) will take you away from the crowds on a circuit of the Nourlangie area. Barrk is a male black wallaroo and you might see this elusive marsupial if you set out early. Pick up a brochure from the **Bowali Visitor Information Centre** (08-8938 1120; www. parksaustralia.gov.au/kakadu; Kakadu Hwy, Jabiru; 8am-5pm).

Nanguluwur Gallery
WALKING

This outstanding rock-art gallery sees far fewer visitors than Nourlangie simply because it's further to walk (3.5km return, 1½ hours, easy) and has a gravel access road. Here the paintings cover most of the styles found in the park, including very early dynamic style work, X-ray work and a good example of 'contact art', a painting of a two-masted sailing ship towing a dinghy.

Sleeping

Muirella Park
CAMPGROUND $

(Djarradjin; adult/child/family $15/7.50/38) Basic campground at Djarradjin Billabong, with BBQs, excellent amenities and the 5km-return **Bubba Wetland Walk**. Look for the turn-off from the Kakadu Hwy, about 7km south from the turn-off to Nourlangie.

Getting There & Away

Nourlangie is well signposted at the end of a 12km sealed road that turns east off Kakadu Hwy.

Cooinda & Yellow Water

Cooinda is one of the main tourism hubs in Kakadu. An all-purpose resort has grown up around the wetlands, which are known as Yellow Water, or to give its rather challenging Indigenous name, Ngurrungurrundjba. The cruises, preferably taken around sunrise or sunset, are undoubted highlights of any visit to Kakadu.

Sights

Warradjan Aboriginal Cultural Centre
MUSEUM

(www.kakadutourism.com; Yellow Water Area; 9am-5pm) FREE About 1km from the Cooinda resort (an easy 15-minute walk), the Warradjan Aboriginal Cultural Centre depicts Creation stories and has an excellent permanent exhibition that includes clap sticks, sugar-bag holders and rock-art samples. You'll be introduced to the moiety system (the law of interpersonal relationships), languages and skin names, as well as the 'six seasons of Kakadu'. A mesmeric soundtrack of chants and didgeridoos plays in the background. Occasionally, Indigenous women artists weave pandanus baskets in the shade outside.

WORTH A TRIP

JIM JIM FALLS & TWIN FALLS

Remote and spectacular, these two falls epitomise the rugged Top End. **Jim Jim Falls**, a sheer 215m drop, is awesome after rain (when it can only be seen from the air), but its waters shrink to a trickle by about June. **Twin Falls** flows year-round (no swimming), but half the fun is getting here, involving a little boat trip (adult/child $15/free, 7.30am-5pm, last boat 4pm) and an over-the-water boardwalk. There's camping near Jim Jim Falls at the **Garnamarr Camping Ground** (08-8938 1120; www.parksaustralia.gov.au/kakadu; adult/child/family $15/7.50/38). You'll need to bring food supplies with you and have the necessary equipment to cook for yourself.

These two iconic waterfalls are reached via a 4WD-only track that turns south off the Kakadu Hwy between the Nourlangie and Cooinda turn-offs. Jim Jim Falls is about 56km from the turn-off (the last 1km on foot) and it's a further five corrugated kilometres to Twin Falls. The track is open in the Dry only and can still be closed into late May; it's off limits to most rental vehicles (check the fine print). A couple of tour companies make trips here in the Dry.

🛏 Sleeping

Mardugal Park Campground CAMPGROUND **$**
(www.parksaustralia.gov.au/kakadu; camping per
adult/child/family $15/7.50/38) Just south of
the Kakadu Hwy, 2km south of the Cooinda turn-off, is the National Parks Mardugal
Park campground – an excellent spot with
shower and toilets.

Cooinda Lodge & Campground RESORT **$$**
(☑1800 500 401; www.kakadutourism.com; Cooin-
da; unpowered/powered sites $38/50, budget/
lodge r from $175/200; ❄ 🛜 ⛺) This sprawling
place has a good variety of accommodation
options and is Kakadu's most popular re-
sort – even with 380 campsites, facilities can
get very stretched. The budget air-con units
share campground facilities and are com-
pact and comfy enough. The lodge rooms
are spacious and more comfortable, sleep-
ing up to four people. The swimming pool is
large and lovely.

There's a grocery shop, tour desk, fuel
pump and the excellent open-air **Barra Bar
& Bistro** (☑1800 500 401; www.kakadutour-
ism.com; Cooinda; mains $24-38; ⊙11am-3pm &
5-9pm) here too.

Ask about the 'Flash Camp @ Kakadu', a
semimobile camp of tents set up out in the
bush with all the comforts of a tented camp.

ⓘ Getting There & Away
The turn-off to the Cooinda accommodation
complex and Yellow Water wetlands is 47km
down the Kakadu Hwy from the Arnhem Hwy
intersection at Jabiru. It's then 4.5km to the
Warradjan Aboriginal Cultural Centre (p832),
a further 1km to the Yellow Water turn-off and
another 1km to Cooinda. There is no public
transport to Cooinda.

Southwestern Kakadu

Kakadu's southwestern reaches shelter two
of Kakadu's most underrated attractions –
the gorgeous waterholes at Maguk and
dramatic Gunlom. Both require a 4WD or
high-clearance 2WD and may be impassable
in the Wet – all of which is precisely why you
won't see any tour buses down here. Both
waterholes are generally considered safe for
swimming.

⊙ Sights

★**Maguk** WATERFALL
(Barramundi Gorge) Though it's unlikely you'll
have dreamy Maguk to yourself, you might

**TOP NT ABORIGINAL
CULTURAL EXPERIENCES**

➡ Ghunmarn Culture Centre (p845) &
Djakanimba Pavilions (p845), Beswick
(Wugularr)

➡ Injalak Arts (p835), Gunbalanya

➡ Dot Painting Workshop (p877),
Yulara

➡ Ancient Garlarr One Gorge Safari
(p841), Nitmiluk (Katherine Gorge)
National Park

➡ Guluyambi Cultural Cruise (p825),
Kakadu National Park

➡ Uluru Aboriginal Tours (p875), Uluru-
Kata Tjuta National Park

➡ Wira (p875), Uluru-Kata Tjuta
National Park

➡ Karrke Aboriginal Experience
(p871), Kings Canyon & Watarrka
National Park

---

time it right to have the glorious natural
pool and falls between just a few of you. The
2km-return walk in from the car park passes
through monsoon forest rich in endemic an-
binik trees and then opens out into a nicely
bouldered river section. Count on about an
hour's walking, plus swimming time. The
track in here is a rough, 10km corrugated
track lined with termite mounds.

★**Gunlom** WATERFALL
(Waterfall Creek) Gunlom is a superb escarp-
ment waterfall 40-odd kilometres south of
Maguk and 37km along an unsealed, though
well-graded, gravel road. The reward is a
gloriously large waterhole and drama-filled
scenery, and that's just 200m through the
paperbark forest from the car park. There's
also a lovely picnic area here. If you're keen
to explore more, take the steep **Lookout
Walk** (one hour, 1km), which affords incred-
ible views; when there's water, the infinity
pool at the top is Kakadu's best swim.

ⓘ Getting There & Away
Both Maguk and Gunlom are clearly signposted
off the Kakadu Hwy along unsealed tracks. The
route requires a 4WD or high-clearance 2WD and
may be impassable in the Wet. There's no public
transport to either site and few tour operators
come this way.

ARNHEM LAND

One of Australia's last wilderness areas and an Aboriginal homeland of great spiritual power – the two very often go hand in hand – Arnhem Land is a destination for dry season adventurers. This is a land of unspoilt coastlines and abundant wildlife. It's a hauntingly beautiful, even mysterious place, its red earth, azure seas and bottle-green woodlands the backdrop to a fascinating, soulful human story.

Arnhem Land's population of fewer than 20,000 people, in a land the size of Victoria, comes mostly from the Yolngu nation and traditional owners. This is their land and you're here only with their permission (permits are required). Most people live on outstations, but there are also Indigenous art centres, including some of Australia's best, and a fine festival to anchor your visit.

Travelling out here requires careful planning, but the rewards can be life-changing.

☞ Tours

★ Kakadu Cultural Tours   CULTURAL
(☑ 1800 525 238; www.kakaduculturaltours.com.au; adult/child $273/218; ☺ May-Nov) The most accessible way to explore explore Arnhem Land without launching a major expedition, this eight-hour Arnhemlander 4WD Cultural Tour is outstanding. It takes you to ancient rock-art sites, Inkiyu Billabong and Injalak Arts (p835) at Gunbalanya (Oenpelli), and includes lunch. The tour leaves from Border Store (p828) at Ubirr in Kakadu National Park.

Outback Spirit   TOURS
(☑ 1800 688 222; www.outbackspirittours.com.au) This experienced operator has an epic 13-day traverse of Arnhem Land's north, from the Cobourg Peninsula to Yirrkala. Prices start at $11,995 per person.

Venture North Australia   TOURS
(☑ 08-8927 5500; https://venturenorth.com.au; 4-/5-day tours $2990/3490; ☺ May-Oct) Four-wheel-drive tours to remote areas, featuring expert guidance on rock art. The four-day Arnhem Land and Cobourg Peninsula Tour ($2990/2590 per adult/child) is the pick of numerous Arnhem Land options. Also runs a camp with safari-style tents overlooking the water near Smith Point on the Cobourg Peninsula for the exclusive use of Venture tour guests.

Davidson's Arnhemland Safaris   CULTURAL
(☑ 08-8979 0413; www.arnhemland-safaris.com) Experienced operator taking tours to Mt Borradaile, north of Gunbalanya (Oenpelli). Meals, guided tours, fishing and safari-camp accommodation at its Safari Lodge are included in the daily price (from $800 per person); transfers from Darwin can be arranged.

🛏 Sleeping

★ Davidson's Arnhemland Safari Lodge   LODGE $$$
(www.arnhemland-safaris.com; s/d cabins all-inclusive from $1175/1600; 🅰) An oasis of good taste with high levels of comfort in western Arnhem Land, Davidson's has appealing cabins on stilts, good food and a lovely setting. It's generally worth paying a little extra for the deluxe cabins. Excursions include billabong boat trips, hikes into the nearby escarpments and birdwatching.

Barramundi Lodge   LODGE $$$
(☑ 08-8983 1544; www.barralodge.com.au; d from $600; 🅰) Out in the wilds of Arnhem Land, close to Maningrida, this lovely lodge is a haven for sport-fishers and birdwatchers from March to November. The safari-style tents are beautifully appointed in the finest African safari style, with just canvas between you and the great outdoors, but with high levels of comfort.

❶ Getting There & Away

Most visitors to Arnhem Land come as part of an organised tour.

Gunbalanya (Oenpelli)

POP 1116

Gunbalanya is a small Aboriginal community 17km into Arnhem Land across the East Alligator River from the Border Store in Kakadu. Home to one of the NT's best Indigenous art centres, Gunbalanya makes an excellent add-on to a visit to Kakadu.

The drive in itself is worth the trip, with brilliant green wetlands and spectacular escarpments lining the road. Road access is only possible between May and October; check the tides at Cahill's Crossing on the East Alligator River before setting out so you don't get stuck on the other side.

To travel to and from Injalak Arts, you'll need to obtain a permit from the Northern

ARNHEM LAND PERMITS

Visits to Arnhem Land are strictly regulated through a permit system, designed to protect the environment, rock art and ceremonial grounds, as *balanda* (white people) are unaware of the locations of burial grounds and ceremonial lands. Basically, you need a specific purpose for entering the area, usually to visit an arts centre, in order to be granted a permit. It's also worth noting that some of the permits issued are transit permits (others are called recreational permits) that allow you to travel along certain roads but not more than a few metres either side of them – check when picking up your permit. By the time you read this, hopefully the Northern Land Council will have inaugurated its online permit application system, which should make the whole process easier.

If you're travelling far enough to warrant an overnight stay, you'll need to organise accommodation (which is in short supply) in advance. It's easy to visit Gunbalanya (Oenpelli) and its arts centre on a day trip from Kakadu National Park, just over the border, either on a tour or independently. Elsewhere, it's best to travel with a tour, which will include the necessary permit(s) to enter Aboriginal lands.

If you're travelling independently, you'll need to arrange the following permits:

Place	Issued by	Cost	Duration	Processing time
Central Arnhem Hwy	Northern Land Council (p814)	free	transit	10 days to issue
East Arnhem Land	**Dhimurru Aboriginal Corporation** (☑08-8939 2700; www.dhimurru.com.au; 11 Arnhem Rd, Nhulunbuy)	$15/35	1 day/7 days	varies
Gunbalanya (Oenpelli)	Northern Land Council (p814)	$16.50	1 day	issued on the spot
West Arnhem Land (excluding Cobourg Peninsula & Garig Gunak Barlu National Park)	Northern Land Council (p814)	$88 (free with Garig Gunak Barlu NP permit)	transit	10 days to issue
Cobourg Peninsula & Garig Gunak Barlu National Park	**Parks & Wildlife** (☑08-8999 4815, 08-8999 4555; www.nt.gov.au/leisure/parks-reserves)	$232.10 per vehicle (up to 5 people)	7 days	six weeks

Land Council (p829) in Jabiru. These are the traditional lands of the Birriwinjku people.

◉ Sights & Tours

★**Injalak Arts** GALLERY
(☑08-8979 0190; www.injalak.com; ☺8am-5pm Mon-Fri, 9am-2pm Sat) FREE At this centre, artists display traditional paintings on bark and paper, plus didgeridoos, pandanus weavings and baskets, and screen-printed fabrics; the shop is excellent and half of the sale price goes directly to the artists.

Take the time to wander around and watch the artists at work (morning only): the women usually make baskets out in the shade of the trees on the centre's west side,

while the men paint on the verandah to the east. Some of the works come from remote outstations throughout Arnhem Land.

There are good views from the centre's grounds south towards the wetlands to the escarpment and Injalak Hill (Long Tom Dreaming).

Kakadu Cultural Tours and **Lord's Kakadu & Arnhemland Safaris** (☑0438 808 548; www.lords-safaris.com) both offer excellent day tours that include a visit here.

★**Rock Art Tours** TOURS
(☑08-8979 0190; www.injalak.com/rock-art-tours; adult/child $110/33; ☺9am Mon-Sat Jun-Sep) Five kilometres south of Injalak Arts, Injalak Hill (Long Tom Dreaming) is one of western

COBOURG PENINSULA

The Cobourg Peninsula is one of the Top End's hidden treasures. Accessible only by air or by 4WD, and only possible to visit with a permit, it sees very few visitors, which adds considerably to its sense of pristine beauty and isolation. If you're able to make it out here, do it.

The land's traditional owners, the Arrarrkbi, have lived here for more than 40,000 years. The waters of **Garig Gunak Barlu National Park** (www.nt.gov.au/leisure/parks-reserves; ⊙May-Oct), which covers most of the peninsula, are home to six species of marine turtle: green, loggerhead, olive ridley, hawksbill, flatback and leatherback; some of these nest on remote beaches in the later months of the year. Watch for the northern snake-necked turtle in the park's inland billabongs. Whales, dolphins, various shark species and saltwater crocodiles are all found in the waters off the coast – swimming here would be extremely dangerous.

Mammal species, though elusive, are always possible, especially around dawn, dusk and overnight. Species include dingoes, echidnas and northern brown bandicoots. The park is also home to more than 200 bird species.

The Cobourg Peninsula is well known among fishers for its fabulous barramundi fishing in March, April, October and November, while wildlife-watching is excellent during the Dry (the Peninsula is very difficult to access at other times). Fishing safaris run by Venture North Australia (p834) are outstanding.

There are two campgrounds in the park with showers, toilets, BBQs and limited bore water; generators are allowed in one area. **Wiligi Outstation** (☑08-8979 0069; www.wiligiarnhemland.com.au; camping per person $55, eco tents $275) is an excellent alternative, with lovely eco tents. **Garig Store** (☑08-8979 0455; Algarlarlgarl; ⊙4-6pm Mon-Sat) sells very basic provisions, ice and camping gas.

The track to Cobourg starts at Gunbalanya (Oenpelli) and is accessible by 4WD vehicles only from May to October. The 270km drive to Black Point from the East Alligator River takes about five hours.

Arnhem Land's best collections of rock art. To see it you'll need to join one of the three-hour tours run out of the arts centre. Expert local guides take you to rock shelters that include some stunning representations of traditional stories.

❶ Getting There & Away

There is no public transport to Gunbalanya and most travellers visit as part of an organised tour. The road here from Cahill's Crossing is only partly sealed and is impassable in the Wet (usually from October or November to March).

Eastern Arnhem Land

The wildly beautiful coast and country of eastern Arnhem Land is off the beaten track and really only for the adventurous (you'll need a 4WD to get around) and those who plan carefully (you'll need a permit to visit). About 4000 people live in the region's main settlement, Nhulunbuy, built to service the bauxite mine here. The 1963 plans to establish a manganese mine were hotly protested by the traditional owners, the Yolngu peo-

ple; though mining proceeded, the case became an important step in establishing land rights. Some of the country's most respected art comes out of this region too, including bark paintings, carved mimi figures, *yidaki* (didgeridoos), woven baskets and mats, and jewellery.

◎ Sights

★**Buku Larrnggay Mulka Art Centre & Museum**   GALLERY
(☑08-8987 1701; www.yirrkala.com; 138 Tuffin Rd, Yirrkala; by donation; ⊙8am-4.30pm Mon-Fri, 9am-noon Sat) This museum and community-run art centre, 20km southeast of Nhulunbuy in Yirrkala, is one of Arnhem Land's best; this is the heartland of some of Arnhem Land's most celebrated artists and artistic traditions, and they all come together here. No permit is required to visit from Nhulunbuy or Gove airport.

✦ Festivals & Events

★**Garma Festival**   CULTURAL
(☑08-8945 5055; www.yyf.com.au; ⊙Aug) A four-day festival in northeastern Arnhem

Land, Garma is one of the most significant regional festivals, a celebration of Yolngu culture that includes ceremonial performances, bushcraft lessons, a *yidaki* masterclass and an academic forum. Serious planning is required to attend, so start early.

🛏 Sleeping

Walkabout Lodge   MOTEL **$$**
(☑ 08-8939 2000; www.walkaboutlodge.com. au; 12 Westal St, Nhulunbuy; powered sites $40, s/d Aug & Sep $250/290, Oct-Jul $218/245) Air-conditioned, motel-style rooms in a leafy Nhulunbuy setting. They'd be overpriced elsewhere, but they're not bad value here. There are also 12 powered campsites.

BanuBanu Wilderness Retreat   LODGE **$$$**
(☑ 08-8987 8085; www.banubanu.com; Bremer Island; eco tents per person incl full board wet/dry season $450/510, beach houses $350/400, cabins $400/450) The eco tents on Bremer Island, off the Gove Peninsula, couldn't be closer to the beach – and it's the location (and the fishing) that is most memorable here. The tents themselves are fairly simple and the surrounding area a little bare and shadeless, but as you'll spend most of your day out fishing, this latter point may prove less significant.

🛍 Shopping

Nambara Arts & Crafts
Aboriginal Gallery   ART
(☑ 08-8987 2811; Melville Bay Rd, Nhulunbuy; ⊙ 10am-4pm Mon-Fri, to 2pm Sat) Sells art and crafts from northeast Arnhem Land and often has artists-in-residence.

ℹ Getting There & Away

Airnorth (☑ 1800 627 474; www.airnorth.com. au) and Qantas (p814) fly from Darwin to Gove Airport (for Nhulunbuy).

The Central Arnhem Hwy to Gove leaves the Stuart Hwy (Rte 87) 52km south of Katherine. It's a 10-hour 4WD trip and only possible in the Dry.

KATHERINE
POP 6303

Katherine is best known for the stunning Nitmiluk National Park (p840), around 30km to the east. Apart from being an obvious base for this, one of the Territory's biggest attractions, the town also has a handful of interesting outback attractions worth a day or two of your time.

Katherine has always been an important meeting place in this part of the world, standing as it does where the traditional lands of the Jawoyn, Dagoman and Wardaman Indigenous peoples come together. Roads also converge here from Darwin, WA and Alice Springs; you'll certainly feel like you've arrived somewhere if you've just made the long trip up the highway from Alice Springs (Katherine's namesake river is the first permanent running water on the road north of Alice Springs).

⊙ Sights

★**Top Didj Cultural**
Experience & Art Gallery   GALLERY
(☑ 08-8971 2751; www.topdidj.com; cnr Gorge & Jaensch Rds; cultural experiences adult/child $75/47; ⊙ 9.30am & 2.30pm May-Oct) Run by the owners of the on-site Katherine Art Gallery, Top Didj is a good place to see Aboriginal artists at work. The cultural experience is hands-on, with fire sticks, spear throwing, painting and basket weaving, and is a somewhat more dynamic take than many staged Indigenous encounters for travellers.

★**Katherine**
School of the Air   CULTURAL CENTRE
(☑ 08-8972 1833; www.ksa.nt.edu.au; Giles St; adult/child $20/free; ⊙ 9am & 1pm late Apr-late Sep) Listen into a class and learn how nearly 200 kids, from preschool to Year 9, are educated in areas where there is no physical school. The tour, run by staff members, takes you on a fascinating journey behind the scenes into the logistics of how things work in what is sometimes called the world's biggest classroom; it gives a real feel for the place. Booking ahead is recommended, especially for groups. Open during school terms two and three.

Godinymayin Yijard Rivers
Arts & Culture Centre   GALLERY
(☑ 08-8972 3751; www.gyracc.org.au; Stuart Hwy, Katherine East; ⊙ 10am-5pm Tue-Fri, to 3pm Sat) This beautiful arts and culture centre is housed in a landmark contemporary building. The centre is designed to be a meeting place for Indigenous and non-Indigenous people, and a chance to share cultures. The centre houses a gallery space hosting Territory artworks and a performing arts venue seating up to 400 people. It's 1km east of Katherine, signposted off the Stuart Hwy.

Katherine

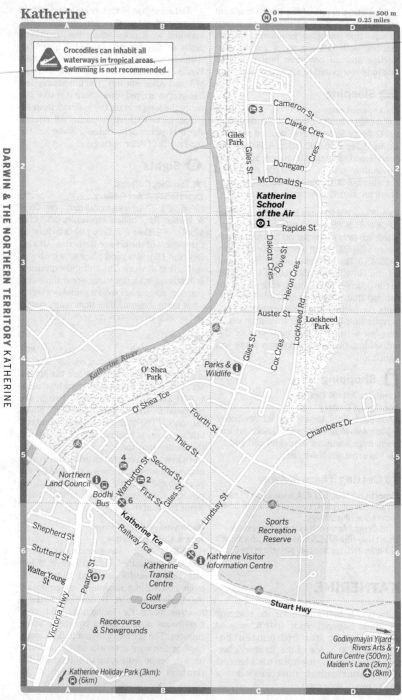

Crocodiles can inhabit all waterways in tropical areas. Swimming is not recommended.

Katherine

⊙ Top Sights
  1 Katherine School of the Air................C3

⊟ Sleeping
  2 Coco's Backpackers............................B5
  3 Knott's Crossing Resort......................C1
  4 St Andrews Apartments......................B5

⊗ Eating
  5 Black Russian Caravan Bar.................B6
  6 Coffee Club...B5
    Savannah Bar & Restaurant........(see 3)

⊙ Shopping
  7 Mimi Aboriginal Art & Craft................A6

🛏 Sleeping

Katherine Holiday Park CARAVAN PARK $
(☑08-8972 3962; www.katherineholidaypark.
com.au; 20 Shadforth Rd; unpowered/powered
sites $45/48, cabins/safari tents from $195/118;
❋🐾🏊) A well-manicured park with plenty
of shady sites, a great swimming pool adjoining a bar and an excellent bistro (mains $21
to $32) that is sheltered by a magnificent fig
tree. The amenities are first rate, making it
the pick of the town's several caravan parks.
It's about 5km along the Victoria Hwy from
town, across the Low Level bridge.

Coco's Backpackers HOSTEL $
(☑08-8971 2889; www.cocos-house.com.au; 21
First St; camping/dm per person $18/30, cabins
from $115) Travellers love this place, with In-
digenous art on the walls and didgeridoos
in the tin shed next door helping to provide
an authentic Katherine experience. Coco's is
a converted home, where the owner chats
with the guests and has great knowledge
about the town and local area. Aboriginal
artists are often here painting didgeridoos.

Knott's Crossing Resort MOTEL $$
(☑08-8972 2511; www.knottscrossing.com.au; cnr
Cameron & Giles Sts; unpowered/powered sites
$30/48, r $130-180; ❋@🏊🐾) Probably the
pick of Katherine's in-town accommodation
options, there is variety to suit most budg-
ets, a good restaurant and the whole place
is very professionally run. Everything is
packed pretty tightly into the tropical gar-
dens at Knott's, but it's easy to find your own
little nook.

St Andrews Apartments APARTMENT $$$
(☑1800 686 106, 08-8971 2288; www.standrews
apts.com.au; 27 First St; apt $240-290; ❋🏊) In
the heart of town, these serviced apartments
are great for families and those pining for a
few home comforts and a little more space.
The two-bedroom apartments sleep four (six
if you use the sofa bed) and come with fully
equipped kitchen and lounge/dining area.
Nifty little BBQ decks are attached to the
ground-floor units.

🍴 Eating

**★Black Russian
Caravan Bar** INTERNATIONAL $
(☑0409 475 115; www.facebook.com/theblack
russiancaravanbar; Stuart Hwy; mains $8-11;
⊙7am-1pm) This cutesy little caravan sits
sheltered in the western wall of the visitor centre. It serves Katherine's best coffee
and fabulous, thick-cut toasties (from tri-
ple-smoked ham to Philly cheesesteak or
Texas pork), as well as pastries and cakes.

★Maiden's Lane BURGERS, CAFE $$
(☑0429 268 018; www.facebook.com/maidens-
lane; 5/19 Crawford St; mains $17-20; ⊙6am-2pm
Mon-Fri, 7am-2pm Sat & Sun) Owned by the
people who brought you the Black Russian
Caravan Bar, this brilliant, sophisticated
cafe serves up top-notch burgers, as well as
waffles, salads, cakes, pastries and damned
good coffee. You'll need a vehicle to get here
– it's out in an industrial zone in Katherine
East – but it's well worth the detour.

Coffee Club CAFE $$
(☑08-8972 3990; www.coffeeclub.com.au; cnr
Katherine Tce & Warburton St; breakfast $5-22,
mains $12-19; ⊙6.30am-4.30pm Mon-Fri, 7am-
3pm Sat & Sun) This is the best place in town
for breakfast, as well as a good bet at lunchtime. Dining is in a light-filled contemporary space. On offer are decent coffee and
healthy all-day breakfast options including
fruit and muesli, plus burgers, sandwiches,
wraps and salads all day.

Savannah Bar & Restaurant AUSTRALIAN $$
(☑08-8972 2511; www.knottscrossing.com.au;
Knott's Crossing Resort, cnr Giles & Cameron Sts;
mains $25-42; ⊙6-9pm) Undoubtedly one of
the best dinner choices in Katherine, it's
predominantly an outdoors garden restau-
rant, with a cool breeze wafting through
the tropical vegetation. The menu includes
croc spring rolls, kangaroo loin and crispy
skinned barramundi. Service is fast and
friendly and the whole place is very well run.
From 4pm to 6.30pm on Saturdays, it's pizza
happy hour.

★ **Marksie's Camp Tucker** AUSTRALIAN $$$

(☑ 0427 112 806; www.marksiescamptucker.com.au; 363 Gorge Rd; adult/child $80/40, Stockman's Camp $50/25; ⊙ 7pm Apr-Sep) They should declare Geoff Mark (Marksie) a national treasure. Head to his re-created stockman's camp, 7km from town, for a night of fabulous food and fun storytelling. He prepares a three-course set menu that might include crocodile, wild-caught barramundi, camel, buffalo and/or kangaroo, all cooked over camp ovens and leavened with bush spices and hilarious bush yarns. Bookings essential.

Marksie, a warm and wily raconteur and one of Katherine's great characters, does a cheaper Stockman's Camp night on Tuesdays and Thursdays at 6pm. Shares an entrance with Top Didj (p837).

☆ Entertainment

Katherine Outback Experience LIVE PERFORMANCE

(☑ 0428301580; www.katherineoutbackexperience.com.au; 115 Collins Rd, Uralla; adult/student/senior $50/25/45; ⊙ 4.30pm Mon, Thu & Fri, 9.30am Tue, 2.30pm Wed, closed Nov-Mar) You get a little bit of everything for your money out here – the 90-minute show is about horse training and working station dogs, but don't be surprised if presenter Tom Curtain bursts into song at some stage during proceedings. Sometimes it falls a bit flat, but it's great when it works, which is often.

🛍 Shopping

★ **Mimi Aboriginal Art & Craft** ARTS & CRAFTS

(☑ 08-8971 0036; www.facebook.com/mimiaboriginalart; 6 Pearce St; ⊙ 8.30am-4.30pm Mon-Fri) Aboriginal owned and not-for-profit, Mimi is arguably Katherine's best Indigenous art centre. It's a small but carefully chosen collection of works from the Katherine region, the Tanami Desert and all the way up to the Kimberley.

ℹ Information

Katherine Visitor Information Centre (☑ 1800 653 142; www.visitkatherine.com.au; cnr Lindsay St & Stuart Hwy; ⊙ 8.30am-5pm daily mid-Apr–Sep, 8.30am-5pm Mon-Fri, 10am-2pm Sat & Sun Oct–mid-Apr) Modern, air-conditioned centre stocking information on all areas of the NT. Pick up the handy *Katherine Region Visitor Guide*.

Katherine Wildlife Rescue Service (☑ 0412 955 336; www.fauna.org.au/katherine-wildlife) The place to call if you come across injured wildlife.

Northern Land Council (☑ 08-8971 9899; www.nlc.org.au; 5/29 Katherine Tce; ⊙ 10am-4pm Mon-Fri) Permits for the Central Arnhem Hwy towards Gove.

Parks & Wildlife (☑ 08-8973 8888; www.nt.gov.au/leisure/parks-reserves; 32 Giles St; ⊙ 8am-4.21pm) National park information and notes.

ℹ Getting There & Away

AIR

Airnorth (☑ 1800 627 474; www.airnorth.com.au) connects Katherine with Darwin, Alice Springs and Tennant Creek a few times a week.

BUS

Greyhound (☑ 1300 473 946; www.greyhound.com.au) has regular services between Darwin and Alice Springs, Queensland or WA. Buses stop at **Katherine Transit Centre** (☑ 08-8971 9999; 6 Katherine Tce). One-way fares from Katherine include Darwin ($77, 4¼ hours), Alice Springs (from $176, 16½ hours), Tennant Creek ($151, 8½ hours) and Kununurra ($115, 4½ hours).

An alternative is the **Bodhi Bus** (☑ 08-8971 0774; www.thebodhibus.com.au; 6/27 Katherine Tce), which travels to remote communities. There's a twice-weekly service to/from Borroloola ($150, 8½ hours) via Mataranka ($50, 1½ hours), Larrimah ($60, 2¼ hours), Daly Waters ($85, 3¾ hours) and Cape Crawford ($130, 7¼ hours), and to Beswick (Wugularr; $80, two hours). Three times a week, it also plies the Katherine–Darwin route ($70, 3¾ hours) via Adelaide River ($65, 2¾ hours) and Pine Creek ($50, 1¼ hours), dropping off passengers at the Palmerston bus exchange and Darwin airport.

AROUND KATHERINE

Nitmiluk (Katherine Gorge) National Park

Spectacular **Katherine Gorge** forms the backbone of the 2920-sq-km **Nitmiluk National Park** (☑ 08-8972 1253, 08-8972 1886; www.nt.gov.au/leisure/parks-reserves), about 30km from Katherine. A series of 13 deep sandstone gorges have been carved by the Katherine River on its journey from Arnhem Land to the Timor Sea. It's a hauntingly beautiful place – although it can get crowded in peak season – and a must-do from Katherine. In the Dry the tranquil river is perfect for a paddle, but in the Wet the deep still waters and dividing rapids are engulfed by an awesome torrent that churns through the gorge.

VICTORIA RIVER CROSSING

The red sandstone cliffs surrounding the spot where the highway crosses the Victoria River (194km southwest of Katherine) create a dramatic setting. Much of this area forms the eastern section of Judbarra/Gregory National Park (p842).

Park up at the roadhouse and wander down to **Victoria River Crossing** and the old bridge for lovely river views and good birding; watch the tall grass for the prized purple-crowned fairy wren, as well as other bird species such as the star finch, chestnut-breasted mannikin and blue-winged kookaburra.

As you continue west of Victoria River in the direction of Timber Creek, you'll pass through some lovely escarpment country where the river cuts its way through. A number of signposted walks head off up into the hills around here, while the **old river crossing**, signposted off the highway, is a gorgeous spot.

There's a well-run **campground** (☑08-8975 0744; Victoria Hwy; powered/unpowered sites $28/22, r $55-160) behind the Victoria River Roadhouse with good facilities and a range of cabins, from the budget variety with shared bathrooms to more expensive options. It also has a shop and a bar and can provide meals ($12 to $38). It's on a rise on the west side of the bridge over the river.

The traditional owners are the Jawoyn Aboriginal people, who jointly manage Nitmiluk with Parks & Wildlife. The park was handed back to the Jawoyn in 1989; 'Nitmiluk' means 'Place of the Cicada Dreaming'. Nitmiluk Tours manages accommodation, cruises and activities within the park.

⊙ Sights & Activities

Leliyn
NATURE RESERVE

(Edith Falls) Reached off the Stuart Hwy 40km north of Katherine and a further 20km along a sealed road, Leliyn is an idyllic, safe haven for swimming and hiking. The moderate **Leliyn Trail** (2.6km loop, 1½ hours, medium) climbs into escarpment country through grevillea and spinifex and past scenic lookouts (Bemang is best in the afternoon) to the Upper Pool, where the moderate **Sweetwater Pool Trail** (8.6km return, three to five hours) branches off.

★ Nitmiluk Tours
TOURS

(☑08-8972 1253, 1300 146 743; www.nitmiluktours. com.au; Nitmiluk Visitor Centre) This excellent operator runs most of the park's activities, including scenic flights, a wide range of boat cruises and cultural safaris, and canoe rental. To really get a feel for the park, take the Three Gorge Cruise (from April to September, adult/child $134/67).

An Ancient Garlarr One Gorge Safari (adult/child $150/120); takes you on a more intimate journey into local rock art, crafts and the natural world.

Waleka Walk
WALKING

This challenging 14km one-way walk (two to three days) from Pat's Lookout to the eighth gorge has fabulous views of the second gorge and follows the upper contours of the escarpment.

Jatbula Trail
WALKING

This renowned walk (66km one way, five days, difficult) to Leliyn climbs the Arnhem Land escarpment, passing the swamp-fed Biddlecombe Cascades, Crystal Falls, the Amphitheatre and Sweetwater Pool. This walk can only be done one way (ie you can't walk from Leliyn to Katherine Gorge), is closed from October to April and requires a minimum of two walkers.

A ferry service takes you across the gorge to kick things off.

Baruwei Lookout & Loop
WALKING

The pick of the short walks from the visitor centre, Baruwei follows the path of a dragonlike Jawoyn Creation Ancestor. There are two options: the 1.8km (one-hour) climb to the lookout for glorious views, or the longer 4.8km (two-hour) loop. Starting with a short, steep climb, the entire loop provides good views over the Katherine River.

Butterfly Gorge
WALKING

A challenging, shady walk (12km return, 4½ hours, difficult) through a pocket of monsoon rainforest, often with butterflies, leads to midway along the second gorge and a deep-water swimming spot.

JUDBARRA/GREGORY NATIONAL PARK

The remote and rugged wilderness of the little-visited Judbarra/Gregory National Park (08-8975 0888; www.nt.gov.au/leisure/parks-reserves) will swallow you up – this is right off the beaten track and ripe for 4WD exploration. Covering 12,860 sq km, it sits at the transitional zone between the tropical and semiarid regions. The park is so large that it encompasses the traditional lands of numerous Aboriginal language groups, among them the Ngarinyman, Karrangpurru, Malngin, Wardaman, Ngaliwurru, Nungali, Bilinara, Gurindji and Jaminjung. This is croc country; swimming isn't safe.

There are numerous campgrounds, including at Big Horse Creek (adult/child $3.30/1.75), right by the Victoria River.

Parks & Wildlife (08-8975 0888; www.nt.gov.au/leisure/parks-reserves; Timber Creek; 7am-4.30pm) in Timber Creek has park and 4WD notes. It can also provide a map featuring the various walks, camping spots and tracks, as well as the historic homestead and ruggedly romantic original stockyards – a must before heading in.

Sleeping & Eating

Nitmiluk National Park

Nitmiluk National Park Campground   CAMPGROUND $
(1300 146 743, 08-8972 1253; www.nitmiluktours.com.au; unpowered/powered sites $39.50/50;) Plenty of grass and shade, hot showers, toilets, BBQs, a laundry and a kiosk by the good-lookin' swimming pool. Wallabies, goannas and night curlews are frequent visitors. Book at the Nitmiluk Visitor Centre .

Nitmiluk Chalets   CABIN $$
(08-8972 1253, 1300 146 743; www.nitmiluktours.com.au; 1-bedroom cabins $180-230, 2-bedroom chalets $225-290;) Next door to the caravan park, these cabins are a serviceable choice if you'd rather have a solid roof over your head (and a flat-screen TV). Has access to all the caravan park facilities (pool, BBQs, kiosk etc), but the wi-fi doesn't extend beyond the pool area.

★ Cicada Lodge   BOUTIQUE HOTEL $$$
(08-8974 3100, 1800 242 232; www.cicadalodge.com.au; 1 Gorge Rd, Nitmiluk National Park; r incl breakfast $519-750;) This luxury lodge has been architecturally designed to meld modern sophistication and traditional Jawoyn themes. It has 18 luxury rooms overlooking the Katherine River. Decor is tasteful and stylish and features include full-length louvred doors that open on to private balconies. Indigenous artworks decorate the walls. Breakfast is included and there's a fine-dining restaurant.

Sugarbag Café   CAFE $$
(Nitmiluk Visitor Centre; breakfast $8.50-20, mains $15.50-20; 7am-2pm) The food here at the visitor centre is excellent, with highlights including the Nitmiluk burger and the pepper berry steak sandwich. There's also pasta, kids' meals and snacks. The elevated deck looking out over the river and filled with blue-faced honeyeaters (keep an eye on your food) is a fine place to rest after a walk or cruise.

Information

The **Nitmiluk Visitor Centre** (08-8972 1253, 1300 146 743; www.nitmiluktours.com.au; 6.30am-5.30pm) has excellent displays and information on the park's geology, wildlife, the traditional owners (the Jawoyn) and European history. There's also the cafe and a desk for Parks & Wildlife, which has information sheets on a wide range of marked walking tracks that start here and traverse the picturesque country south of the gorge. Registration for overnight walks and camping permits ($3.30 per night) is from 8am to 1pm; canoeing permits are also issued.

Getting There & Away

It's 30km by sealed road from Katherine to the Nitmiluk Visitor Centre, and a few hundred metres further to the car park, where the gorge begins and the cruises start.

Katherine to Western Australia

The sealed Victoria Hwy – part of the Savannah Way (p446) – stretches 513km from Katherine to Kununurra in WA. A 4WD will get you into a few out-of-the-way national parks accessed off the Victoria Hwy, or you can meander through semiarid desert and sandstone outcrops until bloated baobab trees herald your imminent arrival in WA. They sometimes call this part of the world East Kimberley, and it is indeed a stirring precursor to the glorious red-rock landscapes of the Kimberley further west.

All fruits, vegetables, nuts and honey must be left at the quarantine inspection post on the state border.

Timber Creek

POP 249

Tiny Timber Creek is the only town between Katherine and Kununurra. It lies in the heart of spectacular country, a pre-Kimberley world of rivers and red-rock escarpments – the road here from Victoria River Crossing is especially pretty. This has long been the traditional lands of the Ngaliwurru and Nungali Aboriginal people, whose world was

turned upside down in 1855 with the arrival of a European exploration party led by AC Gregory; when repairs on their boat, *Tom Tough,* were carried out with local timber, the name took hold for the white settlement that grew up here.

Worthwhile detours just out of town include tracks to **Gregory's Tree**, where Gregory carved his name in 1855, achingly pretty **Policeman's Point**, and **Escarpment Lookout**; the latter has fine views over town and the surrounding country.

Victoria River Cruise   CRUISE
(☑ 0428 588 960; www.victoriarivercruise.com. au; sunset cruises adult/child $95/50; ⊙ 4pm daily Apr-Sep) A highlight of Timber Creek is the Victoria River Cruise, which takes you 40km downriver spotting wildlife, returning in time for a fiery sunset. There are also

DARWIN & THE NORTHERN TERRITORY KATHERINE TO WESTERN AUSTRALIA

WE OF THE NEVER NEVER

Few outback stories have captured the national imagination quite like *We of the Never Never,* Jeannie Gunn's account of life on Elsey Station at Mataranka.

Originally from Melbourne, where she ran a girls' school, Gunn arrived in the NT in 1902 with her husband, Aeneas, who had already spent some years there and was returning to take up the manager's position at Elsey Station.

At that time there were very few white women living in the NT, especially on isolated cattle stations. Station life was tough, but Jeannie adapted and interacted with the local Najig and Guyanggan Nganawirdbird Aboriginal people, a number of whom worked on the station.

Only a year after their arrival at Elsey, Aeneas contracted malarial dysentery and died. Jeannie returned to Melbourne and recorded her Top End experiences in the novel, which was published in 1908. She was a keen observer of the minutiae of station life and managed to spark the interest of people down south, who led such a different existence. These days, however, her depiction of Aboriginal people seems dated at best, and naive and patronising at worst, although she did voice the (then-unpopular) opinion that white settlers had stolen the land from Indigenous people, who deserved some kind of compensation.

Jeannie was awarded an OBE in 1939 for her contribution to Australian literature and died in Melbourne in 1961 at the age of 91. *We of the Never Never* was made into a film in 1981. Interestingly, in 2012 native title to Mataranka was granted to the Najig and Guyanggan Nganawirdbird Aboriginal groups, represented in court by Jessie Roberts, who played Nellie in the film.

A number of sites around Mataranka pay tribute to this history. Lonely **Elsey Cemetery**, around 20km south of Mataranka and signposted off the Stuart Hwy, is a poignant footnote to the story. Many of the larger-than-life characters from the book are buried here, among them Aeneas Gunn (alongside a memorial to his wife), Henry Peckham, John MacLennan and Tom Pearce. The last remains of the original Elsey Station Homestead (destroyed during roadworks in the 1940s) lie 300m to the south near the end of the gravel track. Outside the entrance to the **Mataranka Homestead Resort** (☑ 08-8975 4544; www.matarankahomestead.com.au; Homestead Rd; powered/unpowered sites $30/26, d/ cabins $89/115; ❄ ⧂ ≋) is a replica **homestead** (admission by donation; ⊙ daylight hours), constructed for the filming of *We of the Never Never,* which is screened daily at noon in the resort bar. In town, the **Never Never Museum** (120 Roper Tce; adult/child $4/2; ⊙ 9am-4pm Mon-Fri) has displays on the northern railway, WWII and local history; pay your admission fees at the post office. Life-size figures representing the story's main characters populate the the park along the Stuart Hwy in the town centre.

morning 'croc and wildlife' cruises if there are enough takers. Book your cruise through the **Croc Stock Shop** (☑08-8975 0850; Victoria Hwy; ⊗8am-6pm).

Timber Creek Hotel CARAVAN PARK $
(☑08-8975 0722; www.timbercreekhotel.com.au; Victoria Hwy; unpowered/powered sites $31/35, s/d with private bathroom from $110/120, cabins $165; ❋ ❄) The town is dominated by this roadside hotel and caravan park. Enormous trees shade parts of the camping area, which is next to a small creek. There are simple rooms, more comfortable motel rooms and cabins as well as an apartment (minimum four-nights booking). The complex includes the Timber Creek Hotel (pub) and a small supermarket.

❶ Getting There & Away

Greyhound (p840) has a daily service to/from Katherine ($83, three hours) on its way through to Kununurra ($77, four hours), but the bus usually passes through after dark.

Mataranka
POP 350

With soothing, warm thermal springs set in pockets of palms and tropical vegetation, you'd be mad not to pull into Mataranka for at least a few hours to soak off the road dust. The small settlement regularly swells with towel-toting visitors shuffling to the thermal pool. But Mataranka has more calling cards than most roadside outback towns: nearby spring-fed Elsey National Park and a history linked to one of Australia's most enjoyable outback tales, not to mention the welcoming tree-lined road through town, add considerable appeal to a stop here.

Nearly a third of the town's population is Indigenous and the town's name means 'Home of the Snake' in the local Aboriginal language.

DON'T MISS

BARUNGA FESTIVAL

For three days over a wonderful long weekend in mid-June, the **Barunga Festival** (☑08-8941 8066; www.barunga festival.com.au; ⊗Jun)80km east of Katherine, displays traditional arts and crafts, dancing, music and sporting competitions. Bring your own camping equipment; alternatively, visit for the day from Katherine.

This is the traditional lands of the Najig and Guyanggan Nganawirdbird peoples.

◉ Sights & Activities

Elsey National Park NATIONAL PARK
(☑08-8975 4560; www.nt.gov.au/leisure/parks-reserves) This national park adjoins Mataranka's thermal-pool reserve and offers peaceful camping, fishing and walking along the Waterhouse and Roper Rivers. **Bitter Springs** is a serene palm-fringed thermal pool within the national park, 3km from Mataranka along the sealed Martin Rd. The almost unnatural blue-green colour of the 34°C water is due to dissolved limestone particles.

Mataranka Thermal Pools THERMAL BATHS
Mataranka's crystal-clear thermal pool, shrouded in rainforest, is 10km from town beside the Mataranka Homestead Resort. The warm, clear water, dappled by light filtered through overhanging palms, rejuvenates a lot of bodies on any given day; it's reached via a boardwalk from the resort and can get mighty crowded.

🛏 Sleeping & Eating

Aside from one run-down cafe, you'll find a few basic takeaway joints and a supermarket along the Stuart Hwy as it makes its way through town. Otherwise, try the places to stay, most of which have restaurants.

⭐**Little Roper Stockcamp** CARAVAN PARK $
(☑0427 880 819; www.littleroperstockcamp.com. au; 547 Homestead Rd; unpowered/powered sites $20/30, s/d swags $30/45; 3-course dinners adult $50, under 5 yr free, 5-16 pay their age; 5.30pm Sat May-Sep) Des and Telka run a welcoming little caravan park here with good sites and a taste of outback station life. You can feed the cattle, but the real highlight is the Stockcamp Dinner, where you can join Des for bush yarns and food cooked over camp ovens under the stars, following a fine outback tradition. The three-course meal is ideal, but there's also camp stew and curry night (adult/child $15/10) on Tuesday and Thursday. Advance bookings essential.

**Territory Manor
Motel & Caravan Park** MOTEL $
(☑08-8975 4516; Martin Rd; unpowered/powered sites $26/30, s/d $110/120; ❋ @ ❄) Mataranka's best caravan park is well positioned and a class act – no surprise it's also popular. Smallish motel rooms are well decked out and have good-size bathrooms, and the grounds

are well shaded for camping. In the licensed bistro (mains $19 to $38) they serve barramundi, along with steaks, salad, lamb chops with a honey-mint glaze and other surprises.

Bitter Springs Cabins
CABIN $$

(☑08-8975 4838; www.bitterspringscabins.com. au; 4705 Martin Rd, Bitter Springs; unpowered/powered sites $30/35, cabins $130; ✳@🛜🐾) On the banks of the Little Roper River, only a few hundred metres from Bitter Springs thermal pool, this quiet bush setting has some amazing termite mounds adorning the front paddock. The TV-equipped, open-plan cabins have balconies with bush views. Pets welcome.

❶ Getting There & Away

Mataranka lies 108km south of Katherine and 568km north of Tennant Creek along the Stuart Hwy. Daily Greyhound buses (p840) connect Mataranka with Katherine ($38, 1¼ hours) and Tennant Creek ($136, 7¼ hours).

Beswick (Wugularr)

POP 531

If you're interested in seeing genuine Aboriginal art produced by local communities, it's worth detouring off the Stuart Hwy to the remote cultural centre and small community of Beswick (Wugularr). It's an outstanding opportunity to draw near to the great artistic traditions of Arnhem Land, without straying down detours along long and lonely dirt tracks. Staying overnight also offers a rare opportunity to experience a taste of local Indigenous life.

The settlement inhabits the traditional lands of the Jawoyn people, although members of other language groups and communities also live in the town.

◉ Sights & Festivals

★Ghunmarn Culture Centre
GALLERY

(Djilpin Arts; ☑08-8977 4250; www.djilpinarts.org. au; 2 Cameron Rd; ⊗9.30am-4pm Mon-Fri Apr-Nov) The Ghunmarn Culture Centre, opened in 2007, displays local artworks, carvings, weavings and didgeridoos from western Arnhem Land. The centre also features the Blanasi Collection, a permanent exhibition of fabulous artworks by renowned artist David Blanasi and other elders from the western Arnhem Land region; the high-tech multimedia display for some paintings is excellent. Call ahead to check that it's open.

Walking With Spirits
CULTURAL

(www.djilpinarts.org.au/walking-with-spirits-aborig inal-festival; ⊗Jul) A two-day Indigenous cultural festival at Beswick Falls, 130km from Katherine. In a magical setting, traditional dance and music are combined with theatre, films and a light show. Camping is allowed at the site (only during the festival). A 4WD is recommended for the last 20km to the falls; alternatively, a shuttle bus runs from Beswick.

🛏 Sleeping & Eating

There are no restaurants out here, so you'll need to self-cater. Beswick has a **general store** (☑08-8975 4523; Madigan Rd; ⊗8.30am-12.30pm &1.30-4pm Mon-Thu, to 1.30pm Fri & Sat) with supplies.

★Djakanimba Pavilions
GUESTHOUSE $$

(☑08-8977 4250; www.djilpinarts.org.au/accom modation-cultural-experiences; Cameron Rd,; d $140-180; ✳) These four attractive guestrooms attached to the impressive Djilpin Arts complex in Beswick are a wonderful chance to sleep overnight in a predominantly Aboriginal community. The accommodation – on stilts and with a contemporary outback aesthetic, including louvred windows to catch the prevailing breezes – is simple, stylish and smart-casual. There's a range of simple gallery pieces on display. An excellent choice.

There's also a communal kitchen, and cultural packages that revolve around the arts centre and local community are on offer. Excursions into the surrounding bush can be arranged, either with the women going in search of pandanus or the men looking for honey and didgeridoo materials (half-/full-day $165/350 per person). All profits go back into the community and the arts centre.

❶ Getting There & Away

Beswick, reached via the sealed Central Arnhem Rd, is 56km east of the Stuart Hwy on the southern fringes of Arnhem Land.

BARKLY TABLELAND & GULF COUNTRY

East of the Stuart Hwy lies some of the NT's most remote cattle country, but parts are accessible by sealed road and the rivers and inshore waters of the Gulf coast are regarded as some of the best fishing locales in the country. Other than the fishing, the reason to venture out here is to immerse yourself in the silence of this remote and empty land – travelling the entire 390km from Daly Waters to Borroloola you may pass just a couple of cars and a road train.

Roper Highway

Not far south of Mataranka on the Stuart Hwy, the mostly sealed single-lane Roper Hwy strikes 175km eastwards to **Roper Bar**, crossing the paperbark- and pandanus-lined Roper River, where freshwater meets saltwater. It's a gateway to remote and dramatic Limmen National Park. The road continues out to Numbulwar on the Gulf of Carpentaria coastline – you'll need a permit to take this road, including visiting Ngukurr, which is obtainable through the Northern Land Council (p840) in Katherine. Most of the highway is passable only in the Dry.

The Roper Hwy traverses the lands of numerous Indigenous language groups – together they go by the name Yugul Mangi.

With the closure of the Roper Bar Store, there's no organised accommodation out here. Bush camping is the only option until it reopens.

★**Limmen National Park**   NATIONAL PARK
(☑08-8975 9940; www.nt.gov.au/leisure/parks-reserves) A vast and rugged landscape, this 9608-sq-km national park is in the heart of tropical savannah country and appeals par-

> **WORTH A TRIP**
>
> ## LORELLA SPRINGS
>
> One of the best places to stay in the entire Gulf region, **Lorella Springs Wilderness Park** (☑08-8975 9917; www.lorellasprings.com.au; camping per adult/child $20/5, s $99-225, d $99-250; ☺Apr-Sep) has a marvellously isolated setting, a thermal spring and river frontage, and a restaurant and bar, as well as self-contained air-con cabins, rooms with ceiling fans and good campsites. Activities include fishing, swimming, birdwatching, bushwalking, 4WD expeditions and even helicopter scenic flights.
>
> Lorella Springs is 135km from Cape Crawford, 180km from Borroloola and 275km from Roper Bar, close to the Gulf of Carpentaria coast. You'll need a 4WD to get here, unless you have your own plane.

ticularly to fisherfolk and 4WD enthusiasts. This is home to some of the most striking sandstone-escarpment country in southern Arnhem Land and the 'lost cities' – upthrusts of rocky pinnacles that are simply spectacular and worth exploring on foot. For an aerial view, contact Heartbreak Hotel along the Carpentaria Hwy.

★**Ngukurr Arts Centre**   GALLERY
(☑08-8975 4260; www.ngukurrarts.net; ☺10am-4pm Mon-Fri) This community-owned and run Indigenous arts centre is well worth the long trip out here, showcasing as it does works by artists from local Alawa, Mara, Ngalakan, Ngandi, Nunggubuyu, Rittarrngu and Wandarang clans; 60% of the sale price goes back to the artist.

ⓘ Getting There & Away

Roper Bar is a 4WD-only access point to Borroloola, a more beautiful but more rugged alternative to the route via the sealed Stuart and Carpentaria Hwys. Not deterred? Head south along the rough-going Nathan River Rd through Limmen National Park – high-clearance, two spares and emergency fuel supplies required – and across southeastern Arnhem Land.

Bodhi Bus (p840) runs a dry-season service from Katherine to Numbulwar ($150, eight hours, twice weekly) that only goes as far as Ngukurr ($110, 5¼ hours) in the Wet.

Carpentaria & Tablelands Highways

The Carpentaria Hwy connects the deserts of the outback with the subtropical hinterland of the Gulf of Carpentaria and is one of the NT's most remote stretches of tarmac. Part of the Savannah Way (a loose network of highways from Broome to Cairns), it runs for 390km from Daly Waters, on the Stuart Hwy, to Borroloola. The only 'town' en route is Cape Crawford, which is little more than a roadhouse and petrol station.

The Tablelands Hwy is even more remote, connecting Cape Crawford to the Barkly Homestead Roadhouse, which is along the Barkly Hwy and itself in the middle of nowhere; take this route if you're heading to Tennant Creek or Mt Isa.

★**Airborne Solutions**   SCENIC FLIGHTS
(☑08-8972 2345, 1300 435 486; www.airbornesolutions.com.au/cape-crawford; Heartbreak Hotel, Cape Crawford; 15/40min flights per person from $120/290) You just don't expect to find

helicopter scenic flights out here, but you'll be glad that you did. Flights zip out over Limmen National Park and its dramatic rock formations known as 'lost cities' – you'll need to take the longer flights to get that far, while the shorter trips take in smaller versions of same.

Heartbreak Hotel   HOTEL **$**

(☑08-8975 9928; www.facebook.com/Heartbreak 695; cnr Carpentaria & Tablelands Hwys, Cape Crawford; unpowered/powered sites $22/30, s/d $80/100, deluxe cabins $175; ❄) The Heartbreak Hotel, a fairly standard outback roadhouse and expensive fuel stop, is 267km west of Daly Waters, 123km short of Borroloola and 374km from the Barkly Homestead Roadhouse...yes, you're in the middle of nowhere. Pitch the tent on the shaded grassy lawn and then nurse a cold beer on the wide verandah.

★**Barkly Homestead
Roadhouse**   CARAVAN PARK **$$**

(☑08-8964 4549; www.barklyhomestead.com.au; unpowered/powered sites $28/36, cabins & motel d $150; ❄❄) You're a *long* way from anywhere out here; to Cape Crawford it's a desolate 377km north across the Barkly Tablelands along the Tablelands Hwy (Rte 11), 210km west to Tennant Creek or 252km east to the Queensland border. And yet it's here you'll find one of the NT's best roadhouses. Meals (mostly burgers and salads) in the restaurant (6am to 8.30pm) cost $16.50 to $25

ℹ **Getting There & Away**

The only public transport along the Carpentaria Hwy (Rte 1) is the twice weekly Bodhi Bus (p840) from Katherine to Borroloola. There's no public transport along the Tablelands Hwy (Rte 11), but the single-lane road is paved.

Borroloola

POP 871

On the McArthur River, out near the Gulf of Carpentaria, Borroloola has a wonderful end-of-the-road feel to it – it's a sleepy, slightly neglected place that revels in its remoteness. There's a good Indigenous art centre, some fine wildlife and conservation reserves in neighbouring country and fabulous barramundi fishing.

The town isn't actually on the Gulf of Carpentaria – it's a further 59km to the Bing Bong port loading facility, from which you'll have obscured views of the Gulf of Carpentaria. The nearby McArthur River zinc mine is the town's lifeblood.

WORTH A TRIP

CARANBIRINI CONSERVATION RESERVE

Just off the Carpentaria Hwy, 46km south of Borroloola, the fine **Caranbirini Conservation Reserve** (☑08-8975 8792; www.nt.gov.au/leisure/parks-reserves) is good for wildlife – including euros (wallaroos), agile wallabies and water goannas – and birdwatching (prize species include the Gouldian finch, Carpentaria grasswren and sandstone rock-thrush) and plays an important role in many Aboriginal Dreaming stories. But Caranbirini is also remarkable for the drama of its sandstone spires and pinnacles – this is the most accessible of all of the 'lost-city' rock formations for which the area is renowned.

These are the traditional lands of the Yanyuwa people.

◉ Sights & Activities

★**Waralungku Arts Centre**   ARTS CENTRE

(☑08-8975 8677; www.waralungku.com; Robinson Rd, opposite McArthur River Caravan Park; ⊙8.30am-4pm Mon-Fri, 10am-1pm Sat May-Oct) This relaxed art centre on the main road through town showcases work by artists from the four different Indigenous-language groups in the area: the Yanyuwa, Garrwa, Marra and Gudanji peoples. Utterly unlike the dot-painting styles of the Western Desert or the bark paintings of Arnhem Land, the paintings here have a style all their own, with a more figurative approach.

King Ash Bay Fishing Club   FISHING

(☑08-8975 9800; www.kingashbay.com.au; 1 Batten Rd, King Ash Bay) One of the bigger operators in these parts, although still refreshingly small scale, this fishing club northeast of Borroloola has an on-site restaurant, some camping facilities and plenty of advice on where to fish for barra.

Malandarri Festival   CULTURAL

(☑08-8941 1444; https://artbacknt.com.au/what-we-do/indigenous-traditional-dance/borroloola; ⊙mid-Jun) This two-day event in June is Borroloola's biggest celebration, with traditional dance the focal point alongside artworks, markets, workshops and other activities.

🛏 Sleeping & Eating

McArthur River Caravan Park CARAVAN PARK $
(☑ 08-8975 8734; www.mcarthurcaravanpark.com.
au; Robinson Rd; unpowered/powered sites $25/30,
units s $100-140, d $110-150) This fairly simple
campground and caravan park on the main
road into town is a little dusty during the
Dry, but the owners are keen fishers and it's
a good place to stay if that's why you're here.
Ask for one of the newer cabins, which are
much better than their older counterparts.

Savannah Way Motel MOTEL $
(☑ 08-8975 8883; www.savannahwaymotel.com.
au; Robinson Rd; r & cabins $80-130; ❄ 🛜 🐾) This
motel, close to the airstrip on the main road
through town, is clean and comfortable, with
cabins and guesthouse rooms set in tropical
gardens. It's often full so book ahead.

Carpentaria Grill AUSTRALIAN $$
(☑ 08-8975 8883; Savannah Way Motel, Robinson
Rd; mains $18-30; ⏱ 11am-2pm & 6-10pm Mon-Fri,
6-10pm Sat & Sun, closed for lunch in the Wet) Easily
the best place to eat in town, the Carpentar-
ia Grill does Aussie pub staples, but the best
choice is always the barra – served grilled or
battered. There are special nights: Monday is
steak night, Wednesday schnitzel, Friday is
all about barra, while Sunday means roasts.

ℹ Getting There & Away

BUS
Bodhi Bus (☑ Katherine 08-8971 0774) has a
twice weekly bus service between Borroloola
and Katherine ($150, 8½ hours), which runs
via Mataranka, Larrimah, Daly Waters and
Cape Crawford. Borroloola's stop is outside the
Malandari General Store.

CAR & MOTORCYCLE
Under normal conditions, it's a 5½-hour drive
(390km) from Daly Waters to Borroloola, via Cape
Crawford along the Carpentaria Hwy (Route 1).
  If you're travelling to Queensland, there are two
options. It's 479km along a mostly unsealed road
to Burketown in Queensland if you travel via the
Savannah Way; parts of this route are impassable
in the Wet. Otherwise it's 950km to Mount Isa via
Cape Crawford, Barkly Homestead Roadhouse
and Camooweal, which is paved all the way.

CENTRAL NORTHERN TERRITORY

The Stuart Hwy from Katherine to Alice
Springs is still referred to as 'the Track' – as
it has been since WWII, when it was literally
a dirt track connecting the NT's two main
towns, roughly following the Overland Tel-
egraph Line. It's dead straight most of the
way and gets progressively drier and flat-
ter as you head south, but there are a few
notable diversions, notably Katherine and
the Devil's Marbles. As you head down the
Track, you'll traverse the lands of numerous
Aboriginal peoples.

Tennant Creek
POP 2991

Tennant Creek is the only town of any size
between Katherine and Alice Springs, and
is the NT's fifth-largest town (which says
more about the NT's small population than
it does about Tennant Creek). As one of few
meaningful options where you can break up
a long drive, it's more necessary than desira-

OFF THE BEATEN TRACK

PUNGALINA-SEVEN EMU WILDLIFE SANCTUARY

The **Pungalina–Seven Emu Wildlife Sanctuary** (www.australianwildlife.org) repre-
sents a groundbreaking collaboration between the Australian Wildlife Conservancy and
local traditional owners, merging wildlife conservation with a working cattle station in an
area rich in coastal rainforest, mangroves, eucalyptus woodlands, wetlands and thermal
springs.

  The sanctuary is home to a recorded 209 bird species and 48 mammals, among them
little-known species such as the Carpentarian pseudantechinus (a small carnivorous
marsupial), along with northern brown bandicoots, dingoes and a host of wallaby and
rock-wallaby species. Birds to watch out for include the Gouldian finch, red goshawk and
purple-crowned fairy wren.

  The sanctuary covers 3060 sq km and includes 55km of Gulf shoreline and 100km of
the Calvert River. Seven Emu Station (☑ 08-8975 9904, 08-8975 8307; www.sevenemustation.
com.au; camping per vehicle $50) makes a good base.

ble, though it does have at least one attraction worth an hour of your time. Tennant Creek is known as Jurnkurakurr to the local Warumungu people, and almost half of the population is of Aboriginal descent.

◉ Sights & Activities

Nyinkka Nyunyu GALLERY
(www.nyinkkanyunyu.com.au; Paterson St) Closed for extensive renovations at the time of writing, when this innovative museum and gallery reopens it will highlight the art and culture of the local Warumungu people. The displays focus on contemporary art, traditional objects (many returned from interstate museums), bush medicine and regional history. The diorama series, or bush TVs, as they became known within the community, are particularly special.

Battery Hill Mining Centre MINE
(☑08-8962 1281; www.barklytourism.com.au; Peko Rd; adult/child $30/16, combined ticket with museums $36/21; ☉9am-5pm) Experience life in Tennant Creek's 1930s gold rush at this mining centre, which doubles as the visitor information centre, 2km east of town. There are **underground mine tours** and audio tours of the 10-head **battery**. In addition there is a superb **Minerals Museum** and a **Social History Museum** as well.

Kelly's Ranch HORSE RIDING
(☑08-8962 2045; www.kellysranch.com.au; 5 Fazaldeen Rd; trail rides/lessons per person $150/50) Experience the Barkly from the back of a horse with local Warumungu man Jerry Kelly. His two-hour trail rides start with a lesson and then a ride through some superb outback scenery, with bush-tucker stops along the way. Jerry entertains with stories about Aboriginal culture and life on the cattle stations.

🛏 Sleeping & Eating

Outback Caravan Park CAMPGROUND $
(☑08-8962 2459; www.outbacktennantcreek.com.au; 71 Peko Rd; unpowered/powered sites $32/39, cabins $109-169; P❄️🛜🏊) In a town that often feels parched, it's nice to be in the shade of this grassy caravan park about 1km east of the centre. There's a well-stocked kiosk, a camp kitchen and fuel. You may even be treated to some bush poetry and tucker, courtesy of yarn spinner Jimmy Hooker, at 7.30pm ($10).

Bluestone Motor Inn MOTEL $$
(☑08-8962 2617; www.bluestonemotorinn.com.au; 1 Paterson St; r/f from $165/280; P🛜🏊)

DON'T MISS

DALY WATERS PUB

Decorated with business cards, bras, banknotes and memorabilia from passing travellers, the **Daly Waters Pub** (☑08-8975 9927; www.dalywaterspub.com; unpowered/powered sites $20/32, d $75-129, cabins $135-175; ❄️🏊) claims to be the oldest in the NT (its liquor licence has been valid since 1893). Beside the pub is a dustbowl campground with a bit of shade; book ahead or arrive early to secure a powered site.

Daly Waters is 3km off the highway; the turn-off is 160km south of Mataranka or 407km north of Tennant Creek.

At the southern end of town, this 3½-star motel has comfortable standard rooms in leafy surrounds. In addition there are spacious hexagonal deluxe rooms with queen-size beds and a sofa. There are also wheelchair-accessible units and a restaurant. It's easily the pick of the town's motels.

Tennant Creek Memorial Club AUSTRALIAN $$
(☑08-8962 2688; www.tennantcreekmemorialclub.com/dining; 48 Schmidt St; mains $16-32; ☉noon-2pm & 6-9pm) In a town where eating rarely rises above the mediocre, the Memorial Club is a reliable if generally unexciting option, and it's your best choice for lunch. It has standard rural club fare, with barramundi, burgers, steaks, pasta, chicken parma... It's also a friendly place with a courtesy bus back to your hotel.

Woks Up CHINESE $$
(☑08-8991 0183; 108 Paterson St; mains $14-26; ☉5-9pm Mon-Sat) Every town in the NT, no matter how remote, has a Chinese restaurant. After a few changes of name and management, this one's an excellent deal for dinner, with an appealing dining area that's packed with locals and tourists most nights.

ℹ Information

Central Land Council (☑08-8962 2343; www.clc.org.au; 63 Paterson St; ☉9am-4pm Mon-Fri) For Aboriginal land and transit permits.
Visitor Information Centre (☑1800 500 879; www.barklytourism.com.au; Peko Rd; ☉9am-5.30pm) At Battery Hill, 2km east of town.

❶ Getting There & Away

AIR

Airnorth (☑1800 627 474; www.airnorth.com.au) flies between Tennant Creek and Alice Springs or Darwin (via Katherine) four times a week.

BUS

All long-distance buses stop at the **Transit Centre** (☑08-8962 2727; 151 Paterson St; 9am-5pm Mon-Fri, 8.30-11.30am Sat), where you can purchase tickets. **Greyhound** (☑1300 473 946; www.greyhound.com.au) has daily buses from Tennant Creek to Alice Springs ($119, six hours), Katherine ($151, 8½ hours), Darwin (from $148, 14 hours) and Mount Isa ($169, nine hours). As few of the buses originate in Tennant Creek, departure times are sometimes 3.15am.

CAR & MOTORCYCLE

It's a long drive anywhere out here – 680km to Katherine, 511km to Alice Springs and 662km to Mt Isa. Car hire is available from **Thrifty** (☑08-8962 2207, 1800 891 125; www.thrifty.com.au; Davidson St, Safari Lodge Motel) and there's a **petrol station** (☑08-8962 2626; 218 Paterson St; ⊙6am-9pm) in the town centre.

Devil's Marbles & Around

The Stuart Hwy between Tennant Creek and Alice Springs is a long and lonely stretch of tarmac. The standout attractions are the Devil's Marbles – one of the more accessible of outback Australia's unusual rock formations. Otherwise, Stuart Hwy roadhouses, no matter how basic, can seem like oases amid the great expanses.

◉ Sights

★ **Devil's Marbles** RELIGIOUS SITE
(☑08-8962 4599; www.nt.gov.au/leisure/parks-reserves) The gigantic granite boulders piled just east of the Stuart Hwy, 105km south of Tennant Creek, are known as the Devil's Marbles (Karlu Karlu in the local Warumungu language) and they're one of the more beautiful sights out here. The Marbles are a sacred site to the traditional Aboriginal owners of the land, who believe the rocks are the eggs of the Rainbow Serpent. On 27 October 2008 ownership of the land was returned to their care.

Although the owners are the Alyawarre people, the Marbles also carry great spiritual significance for other Aboriginal groups, including the Kaytetye, Warumungu and Warlpiri people.

Such are the extremes of temperature out here that the boulders undergo a constant 24-hour cycle of expansion and contraction, hence the large cracks in many of the boulders.

There are five signposted walks around the Devil's Marbles, from the 20-minute, 400m **Karlu Karlu Walk** departing the day-use area to the 1½-hour, 4km **Nurrku Walk** that takes you away from the crowds. If you've only time for one walk, make it the 30-minute, 800m **Mayijangu Walk** from the day-use area to the campground, with a 20-minute, 350m add-on up to **Nyanjiki Lookout**. Unless specifically permitted to do so by signposts pointing you in that direction, respect local beliefs by not climbing on the rocks. A 15-minute walk loops around the main site.

Wildlife possibilities include small black-headed goannas in the rocky clefts, while birds to keep an eye out for include zebra finches, painted finches and fairy martins that build bottle-shaped mud nests on the underside of some boulders.

Complementing Aboriginal explanations for the existence of these strange formations, scientists argue that the boulders are made of granite that originated with the hardening of volcanic magma beneath the earth's surface; this could have occurred nearly two billion years ago. The granite then pushed through the surface thanks to the complex interaction beneath the granite and softer, surrounding sandstone. Once atop the earth's surface, the boulders' shapes were formed over millions and millions of years by the weathering of wind and water, as well as extremes of temperature. This process changed the outer layer, although the core of each boulder remains largely unchanged. They range in size from barely 50cm across to those with a diameter of 6m.

This geological phenomenon is particularly beautiful at sunrise and sunset, when these oddballs glow warmly. The campground has remarkably hard ground, pit toilets and fireplaces (BYO firewood).

🛏 Sleeping & Eating

**Devil's Marbles
Camping Ground** CAMPGROUND $
(☑08-8962 4599; www.nt.gov.au/leisure/parks-reserves; adult/child $3.30/1.65) The most atmospheric place to camp for a many a long outback mile, the campground at Devil's Marbles is a little exposed by day, but has toilets

STUART HWY ROADSIDE STOPS

Threeways Roadhouse (☑08-8962 2744; www.threewaysroadhouse.com.au; Stuart Hwy; unpowered/powered sites $24/32, d $120; ❉ @ ⊠) Threeways Roadhouse, 537km north of Alice Springs at the junction of the Stuart and Barkly Hwys, is a potential stopover on the Track, with a bar and restaurant. Rooms are simple but better than most roadhouse stops.

Banka Banka (☑08-8964 4511; unpowered sites per adult/child $12/6) Banka Banka is a historic cattle station 100km north of Tennant Creek, with a grassy camping area (no power), marked walking tracks (one leading to a tranquil waterhole), a mudbrick bar and a small kiosk selling basic refreshments.

Renner Springs Desert Inn (☑08-8964 4505; www.rennerspringshotel.com.au; Stuart Hwy; unpowered/powered sites $24/32, motel s/d $117/129) With the usual mix of petrol, simple motel rooms, a camping area and cold beer, Renner Springs does what it's supposed to do – serve as something of an oasis for those on long outback journeys.

and barbecues and is suitable for caravans. You'll have a front-row seat for stunning sunrise/sunset views.

Barrow Creek Hotel PUB $
(☑08-8956 9753; Stuart Hwy; powered sites $26, s/d $70/90) The Barrow Creek Hotel is one of the highway's oddball outback pubs. In the tradition of shearers who'd write their name on a banknote and pin it to the wall to ensure they could afford a drink when next they passed through, travellers have left notes, photos, bumper stickers and knick-knacks. Dinner, basic motel-style rooms and campsites are available.

Wycliffe Well
Roadhouse & Holiday Park CARAVAN PARK $
(☑1800222195, 08-89641966; unpowered/powered sites $37/40, budget s/d from $65/75, s/d cabins with bathroom $130/150; ⏲6.30am-9pm; ❉ @ ⊠) At Wycliffe Well Roadhouse & Holiday Park, 17km south of Wauchope, you can fill up with fuel and food (mains $14 to $29; open 7am to 9pm), or stay and spot the UFOs that apparently fly over with astonishing regularity. The park has a pleasant lawn campground, a kids' playground, an indoor pool, a cafe and a range of international beer.

Devils Marbles Hotel HOTEL $
(Wauchope Hotel; ☑08-8964 1963; www.devils marbleshotel.com.au; Stuart Hwy; unpowered/powered sites $10/30, s with shared bathroom $70, d/cabin with private bathroom $130/160; ❉ ⊠) At Wauchope (*war*-kup), 8km south of the Devil's Marbles, are the well-kept rooms of the Devils Marbles Hotel. The budget rooms are dongas (small, transportable buildings); the more expensive rooms are more spacious, with en suite. Meals from the restaurant are more than satisfactory.

Aileron Hotel
Roadhouse MOTEL, CAMPGROUND $$
(☑08-8956 9703; www.aileronroadhouse.com.au; Stuart Hwy; unpowered/powered sites $17/20, dm/s/d $44/125/140; ⏲5am-9pm; ❉ ⊠) Aileron Hotel Roadhouse has campsites (power available until 10pm), a 10-bed dorm and decent motel units. There's also an ATM, a bar, a shop and a licensed restaurant. The owner's collection of Namatjira watercolours (at least 10 by Albert) is displayed around the roadhouse's bar and dining area – quite the find in this otherwise standard roadside roadhouse.

Devils Marbles
Hotel Restaurant PUB FOOD $$
(☑08-8964 1963; www.wauchopehotel.com.au; Stuart Hwy; breakfast $10.50-22, mains lunch $15-27, dinner $23-43) Serves large-sized meals from an extensive menu that includes outback staples such as the barra burger, steak sandwiches and burgers. Unusually for an outback roadhouse, there's an extensive wine list too.

❶ Getting There & Away

Greyhound buses run up and down the Stuart Hwy, stopping off in the major towns along the way. The road is tarmac all the way.

Tanami Road

Welcome to one of the longest short cuts on the planet. Synonymous with isolated outback driving, the 1055km Tanami Rd connects the Stuart Hwy north of Alice Springs with Halls Creek in WA – the Red Centre with the Kimberley. The Tanami Desert and surrounding country are the homeland of the Warlpiri, Arrernte, Luritja and Pintupi peoples and much of the land has reverted to their traditional ownership. The three main attractions along the way (apart, of course, from the blissful sense of isolation) are the important Indigenous settlement of Yuendumu, the Newhaven Wildlife Sanctuary and Wolfe Creek Crater – the latter is on the WA side of the border. It's a long haul and only occasionally beautiful; watch for the termite mounds, up to 800 per hectare in places. But crossing the Tanami does have huge cachet and is a journey to remember.

The only formal accommodation is at **Tilmouth Well** (☑ 08-8956 8777; www.tilmouth well.com; powered/unpowered sites $40/30, cabins without bathroom $80; ⊘ petrol station 7am-8pm; ✽ @ ✈) or the camping at Newhaven Wildlife Sanctuary. Otherwise it's wild camping until you get to Alice Springs or Halls Creek. **Renahans Bore** (sites free) is the best site for bush camping – there's nothing more than a water tank and a picnic table here, but it's wonderfully quiet.

★**Newhaven Wildlife Sanctuary** WILDLIFE RESERVE
(☑ 08-8964 6000; www.australianwildlife.org; off Tanami Rd; ⊘ Apr-Sep) Run by the Australian Wildlife Conservancy (AWC), this ground-breaking wildlife reserve 136km south off the Tanami Track covers 2620 sq km and is on the front line of attempts to save Australia's native wildlife. By building a fence to keep out feral cats, foxes and other species that have killed countless native mammals and birds, AWC has been able to reintroduce numerous endangered native species. Camping ($10 per person, cash only) is possible, as are self-guided tours of the sanctuary.

★**Warlukurlangu Art Centre** GALLERY
(☑ 08-8956 4133; www.warlu.com; Ral Ral Ave, Yuendumu; ⊘ 9am-4pm Mon-Fri) The community arts centre Warlukurlangu is a locally owned venture representing over 150 artists working primarily in acrylics. It's one of the longest established art centres in the Territory. It's always worth ringing ahead to let them know you're coming.

ℹ️ **Getting There & Away**

In dry conditions it's possible to make it through the unsealed dust and corrugations in a well-prepared 2WD. Stay alert, as rollovers are common, and stock up with fuel, tyres, food and water.

There's a lot of mining activity in the Tanami these days, and a natural gas pipeline is under construction, so expect a lot more trucks than you'd like on this otherwise remote track. On the plus side, their constant activity and need for access ensures the track is kept well graded, especially on the NT side of the border.

The NT Government publishes a condition report for the Tanami Road, which is also available by phone; call 1800 246 199.

ALICE SPRINGS
POP 24,753

Alice Springs wouldn't win a beauty contest, but there's more going on here than first meets the eye, from the inspirational (excellent museums, a fine wildlife park and outstanding galleries of Indigenous art) to the practical (a wide range of accommodation, good dining options and travel connections).

It's the gateway to some of central Australia's most stirring landscapes: Uluru-Kata Tjuta National Park is a four-hour drive away, while closer still, the ruggedly beautiful MacDonnell Ranges stretch east and west; you don't have to venture far to find yourself among ochre-red gorges, pastel-hued hills and ghostly white gum trees.

Alice is a key touchstone for understanding Aboriginal Australia in all its complexity and its present-day challenges. The Aboriginal name for Alice Springs is Mparntwe, and the region's traditional owners are the Arrernte, although many different Aboriginal communities now call Alice Spring home.

When it's not too hot, Alice can be good for cycling.

⊙ **Sights**

★**Alice Springs Desert Park** WILDLIFE RESERVE
(☑ 08-8951 8788; www.alicespringsdesertpark.com. au; Larapinta Dr; adult/child $32/16, nocturnal tours adult/child $45.50/28.50; ⊘ 7.30am-6pm, last entry 4.30pm, nocturnal tour 7.30pm Mon-Fri) Head to Desert Park, where the creatures of central Australia are all on display in one place, including many that are extremely difficult to find out on the trail. The predominantly open-air exhibits faithfully re-create the animals' natural environments in a series of habitats: inland river, sand country and woodland. It's an easy 2.5km cycle to the park. Pick up a free audio guide (available in various languages) or join one of the free ranger-led talks throughout the day.

Araluen Arts Centre GALLERY
(☑ 08-8951 1122; www.araluenartscentre.nt.gov. au; cnr Larapinta Dr & Memorial Ave; ⊘ 10am-4pm) For a small town, Alice Springs has

a thriving arts scene and the Araluen Arts Centre is at its heart. There is a 500-seat theatre and four galleries with a focus on art from the Central Desert region. The **Albert Namatjira Gallery** features works by the artist, who began painting watercolours in the 1930s at Hermannsburg. The exhibition draws comparisons between Namatjira and his initial mentor, Rex Battarbee, and other Hermannsburg School artists.

Museum of Central Australia   MUSEUM
(✐08-8951 1121; www.magnt.net.au/museum-of-central-australia; 4 Memorial Ave; adult/child/family $8/6/20; ☺10am-4pm) The natural history collection at this compact museum is beautifully displayed, with geological exhibits such as meteorite fragments and fossils, as well as items of cultural interest and local fauna specimens. The museum houses the **Strehlow Research Centre** (http://artsandmuseums. nt.gov.au/araluen-cultural-precinct; cnr Larapinta Dr & Memorial Ave) with displays on the work of Professor TGH Strehlow, a linguist, anthropologist and avid collector of Indigenous artefacts, although most of the collection is off limits for cultural reasons. There's a new **outpost** (✐08-8951 1113; www.magnt.net.au/alcoota; Todd St; ☺10am-4pm) FREE of the museum on Todd Mall – it focuses on the region's ancient megafauna.

Olive Pink Botanic Garden   NATURE RESERVE
(✐08-8952 2154; www.opbg.com.au; Tuncks Rd; ☺8am-6pm) FREE A network of meandering trails leads through this lovely arid zone botanic garden, which was founded by the prominent anthropologist Olive Pink. The garden has more than 500 central Australian plant species and grows bush foods and medicinal plants such as native lemon grass, quandong and bush passionfruit.

Royal Flying Doctor Service Base   MUSEUM
(RFDS; ✐08-8958 8411; www.rfdsalicesprings. com.au; Stuart Tce; adult/child/family $17/10/52; ☺9am-5pm Mon-Sat, 1-5pm Sun) This excellent museum, filled with interactive information portals, is the home of the Royal Flying Doctor Service, whose dedicated health workers provide 24-hour emergency retrievals across an area of around 1.25 million sq km. State-of-the-art facilities include a hologram of John Flynn (the RFDS founder) and a look at the operational control room, as well as some ancient medical gear and a flight simulator. Guided tours leave every half hour, with the last at 4pm.

Grave of John Flynn   CEMETERY
On the western edge of Alice on the road to the West MacDonnell Ranges, the grave of John Flynn is topped by a boulder donated by the Arrernte people (the original was a since-returned Devil's Marble). Opposite the car park is the start of the sealed cycling track to Simpsons Gap, a recommended three- to four-hour return ride.

Alice Springs Reptile Centre   ZOO
(✐08-8952 8900; www.reptilecentre.com.au; 9 Stuart Tce; adult/child $18/10; ☺9.30am-5pm) It may be small, but this reptile centre packs a poisonous punch with its impressive collection of venomous snakes, thorny devils and bearded dragons. Inside the cave room are 11 species of NT geckos and outside there's Terry, a 3.3m saltwater croc, plus Bub, a magnificent perentie, Australia's largest lizard. The enthusiastic guides will happily plonk a python around your neck during the handling demonstrations (check the website for times) or let you pet a blue-tongue lizard.

Anzac Hill   LANDMARK
For a tremendous view, particularly at sunrise and sunset, take a hike (use Lions Walk from Wills Tce) or a drive up to the top of Anzac Hill, known as Untyeyetweleye in Arrernte. From the war memorial there is a 360-degree view over the town down to Heavitree Gap and the MacDonnell Ranges.

Telegraph Station   PARK
(✐08-89523993;http://alicespringstelegraphstation. com.au; adult/child $10/5; ☺reserve 8am-9pm, building 9am-5pm, guided tours 9.30am, 11.30am, 1.30pm & 3.30pm Apr-Oct) The old Telegraph Station, which used to relay messages between Darwin and Adelaide, offers a fascinating glimpse of the town's European beginnings. It's an easy 4km walk or cycle north from Todd Mall; follow the path on the riverbed's western side. Nearby is the original 'Alice' spring (Thereyurre to the Arrernte Aboriginal people), a semipermanent waterhole in the Todd River after which the town is named.

School of the Air   MUSEUM
(✐08-8951 6834; www.assoa.nt.edu.au; 80 Head St; adult/child $11/8; ☺8.30am-4.30pm Mon-Sat, 1.30-4.30pm Sun) Established in 1951, this was the first school of its type in Australia, broadcasting lessons to children over an area of 1.3 million sq km. While transmissions were originally all done over high-frequency radio, satellite broadband internet and web-cams now mean students can study in a virtual

Alice Springs

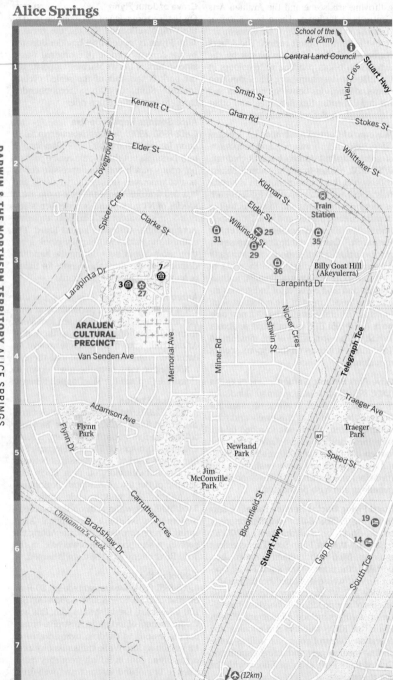

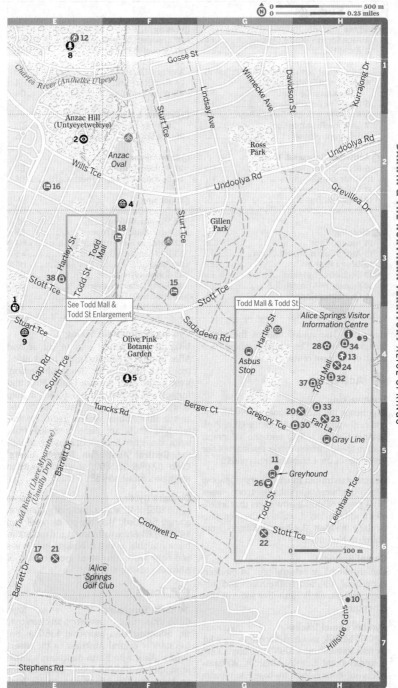

Alice Springs

◉ Sights

1	Alice Springs Reptile Centre	E4
2	Anzac Hill	E2
3	Araluen Arts Centre	B3
	Museum of Central Australia	(see 7)
4	Museum of Central Australia - Megafauna Central	F2
5	Olive Pink Botanic Garden	F4
6	Royal Flying Doctor Service Base	E4
7	Strehlow Research Centre	B3
8	Telegraph Station	E1

◉ Activities, Courses & Tours

9	Alice Springs Walking Tours	H4
10	Dreamtime Tours	H7
11	Emu Run Experience	G5
12	Larapinta Trail	E1
13	Outback Cycling	H4

◉ Sleeping

14	Alice on Todd	D6
15	Alice's Secret Traveller's Inn	F3
16	Desert Rose Inn	E2
17	Doubletree by Hilton	E6
18	Pioneer YHA Hostel	F3
19	Quest Alice Springs	D6

◉ Eating

20	Epilogue Lounge	H5
21	Hanuman Restaurant	E6
22	Montes	G6
23	Page 27 Cafe	H5
24	Red Ochre Grill	H4
25	Water Tank Cafe	C3

◉ Drinking & Nightlife

	Monte's Lounge	(see 22)
26	The Rock Bar	G5

◉ Entertainment

27	Araluen Arts Centre	B3
28	Sounds of Starlight Theatre	H4

◉ Shopping

29	Desert Dwellers	C3
30	Mbantua Gallery	H5
31	Ngurratjuta Iltja Ntjarra	C3
32	Papunya Tula Artists	H4
33	Red Kangaroo Books	H5
34	Talapi	H4
35	Tangentyere Artists	D3
36	Tjanpi Desert Weavers	C3
37	Todd Mall Market	H4
38	Yubu Napa Art Gallery	E3

classroom. The guided tour of the centre includes a video. The school is about 3km north of the town centre.

🏃 Activities

Bushwalking

Experience the bush around Alice with several easy walks radiating from the Olive Pink Botanic Garden (p853) and the Telegraph Station (p853), which marks the start of the first stage of the Larapinta Trail (p865).

Central Australian Bushwalkers WALKING
(https://centralaustralianbushwalkers.com; walks $5) A group of local bushwalkers that schedules a wide variety of walks in the area, particularly the West MacDonnell Ranges, from March to November.

Camel Riding

Camels played an integral part in pioneering central Australia before roads and railways, and travellers can relive some of that adventure.

Pyndan Camel Tracks CAMEL TOURS
(📞 0416 170 164; www.cameltracks.com; Jane Rd; 1hr rides adult/child from $79/49; ⊙ noon, 2.30pm & sunset) Local cameleer Marcus Williams offers one-hour rides at his base 17km southwest of Alice.

Cycling & Mountain Biking

Bikes are the perfect way to get around Alice Springs. There are cycle paths along the Todd River to the Telegraph Station, west to the Alice Springs Desert Park and further out to Simpsons Gap. For a map of cycling and walking paths go to the visitor information centre (p861). Mountain-bike trails are easily accessed from town or meet up for a social sunset ride with the **Central Australian Rough Riders' Club** (📞 08-8952 5800; www.centralaustralian roughriders.asn.au; rides $5).

Outback Cycling CYCLING
(📞 08-8952 1541; www.outbackcycling.com/alice-springs; 6/63 Todd Mall; hire per day/week from $40/160) Bike hire with urban and mountain bikes available, as well as baskets, kids' bikes and baby seats. Also offers cycling tours of Alice and at Uluru.

👉 Tours

★ Earth Sanctuary TOURS
(📞 08-8953 6161; www.earth-sanctuary.com. au; astronomy tours adult/child $36/25) See the stars of central Australia in the desert outside Alice with Earth Sanctuary's terrific nightly Astronomy Tours. Tours last for an hour and the informative guides have

high-powered telescopes to get you up close and personal with the stars. You'll need to ring ahead – they'll know by 4pm if clear skies are forecast.

★**Wayoutback Desert Safaris**   DRIVING

(📞1300 551 510, 08-8300 4900; www.wayoutback. com) Numerous small-group, 4WD safari tours are offered, including the chance for remote desert camping near Uluru. There are also three-day safaris that traverse 4WD tracks to Uluru and Kings Canyon and five-day safaris that top it up with the West MacDonnell Ranges.

★**RT Tours**   TOURS

(📞08-8952 0327; www.rttoursaustralia.com; tours per person from $150) Chef and Arrernte guide Bob Taylor runs a popular lunch and dinner tour at Simpsons Gap or the Telegraph Station Historical Reserve, where he whips up a bush-inspired meal. Other tours available too.

★**Trek Larapinta**   HIKING

(📞1300 133 278; www.treklarapinta.com.au; 3/6 days from $1495/2895) 🏳 Guided multiday walks along sections of the Larapinta Trail (p865). Also runs volunteer projects involving trail maintenance, and bush regeneration on Aboriginal outstations.

Rainbow Valley Cultural Tours   TOURS

(📞08-8956 0661; www.rainbowvalleyculturaltours. com; afternoon walking tours adult/child $120/60; ⏰2pm-sunset Mon, Wed & Fri) Tour beautiful Rainbow Valley with a traditional owner and visit rock art sites not open to the general public. Tours can include overnight camping and dinner for an extra $30/20 per adult/child. They also run birdwatching tours at the site upon request. You'll need your own transport to get there.

Alice Springs Walking Tours   WALKING

(📞0432 511 492; www.facebook.com/aspwalking tours; cnr Parsons St & Todd Mall; per person $28) These 90-minute walking tours around Alice are a terrific way to get to know the town. Local guide James Acklin is a mine of information. Tours leave from outside the visitor information centre.

Dreamtime Tours   CULTURAL

(📞08-8955 5095; 72 Hillside Gardens; adult/child $85/42, self-drive $66/33; ⏰8.30-11.30am) Runs the three-hour Dreamtime & Bushtucker Tour, where you meet Warlpiri Aboriginal people and learn a little about their tradi-

---

CLIMBING MT GILLEN

Climbing Mt Gillen (914m) is a popular walk for locals, but little known among visitors. That's partly because the track is unsignposted and little advertised. It's something of a local secret, but remains a favourite walk in the area. The walk begins 50m west of the grave of John Flynn (p853), around 7km west of Alice. The track passes through a gate and then climbs (a little scrambling required) the Heavitree Range, part of the West MacDonnell Ranges. Having reached the ridge line, head west for around 500m for wonderful mountain, desert and town views. You could return the way you came, but we prefer to follow the trail that continues down the southern slopes, heading southeast and then east to the Heavitree Gap, the southern gateway to town. The entire walk covers 11km and should take 3½ to four hours.

---

tions. As it caters for large bus groups it can be impersonal, but you can tag along with your own vehicle.

Emu Run Experience   TOURS

(📞1800 687 220, 08-8953 7057; www.emurun. com.au; 72 Todd St) Operates day tours to Uluru (from $219) and two-day tours to Uluru and Kings Canyon (from $490). Prices include park entry fees, meals and accommodation. There are also recommended, small-group day tours through the West MacDonnell Ranges (from $132).

🎭 Festivals & Events

★**Parrtjima**   CULTURAL

(www.parrtjimaaustralia.com.au; ⏰Apr) This Indigenous-driven festival gets better with each passing year. It showcases Arrernte culture, with art exhibitions and installations, light shows and all manner of music and dance performances. Most events take place in or around Todd Mall, or out at the Alice Springs Desert Park (p852).

★**Camel Cup**   SPORTS

(www.camelcup.com.au; ⏰mid-Jul) A carnival atmosphere prevails during the running of the Camel Cup at Blatherskite Park .

★**Henley-on-Todd Regatta**   SPORTS

(📞0417 864 085; www.henleyontodd.com.au; ⏰3rd Sat in Aug) These boat races on the dry bed of the Todd River are a typically Australian, light-hearted denial of reality. The boats are bottomless; the crews' legs stick through and they run down the course.

Alice Springs Cup Carnival   SPORTS
(www.alicespringsturfclub.org.au; ☉ Apr-May) On the first Monday in May, don a hat and gallop down to the Pioneer Park Racecourse for the main event of this carnival that runs over three weeks.

Finke Desert Race   SPORTS
(☑ 08-8952 8886; www.finkedesertrace.com.au; ☉ Jun) Motorcyclists and buggy drivers vie to take out the title of this crazy race 240km from Alice along the Old South Rd to Finke; the following day they race back again. Spectators camp along the road to cheer them on.

Alice Desert Festival   ART
(☑ 08-8952 2392; www.alicedesertfestival.com.au; ☉ late Aug–mid-Oct) A cracker of a festival, including a circus program, music, film and comedy. A colourful parade down Todd Mall marks the beginning of the festival. It's held over six weeks from late August until the middle of October.

🛏 Sleeping

Alice's Secret Traveller's Inn   HOSTEL $
(☑ 08-8952 8686; www.asecret.com.au; 6 Khalick St; dm $27-29, d from $65; ❄ @ 🖾) Get the best accommodation deals here by booking your tour to Uluru through the inn. One of the best hostels in Alice, just across the Todd River from town, this place gets a big thumbs up for cleanliness and the helpful, friendly owner. Relax around the pool, blow on a didgeridoo or lie in a hammock in the garden.

Desert Rose Inn   HOSTEL $
(☑ 08-8952 1411; www.desertroseinn.com.au; 15 Railway Tce; r $55-95; 🖾) Centrally located, the Desert Rose is a great alternative to the backpacker hostels, with its spotless budget rooms, communal kitchen and lounge. Budget rooms are two-share, with beds (no bunks) and a shower. No more walking down the corridor in your towel! There are other rooms with double beds, fridges and TVs, and motel rooms with full bathrooms.

Pioneer YHA Hostel   HOSTEL $
(☑ 08-8952 8855; www.yha.com.au; cnr Leichhardt Tce & Parsons St; dm $25-34, tw & d from $85; ❄ @ 🖾) This YHA is housed in the old Pioneer outdoor cinema and guests can still enjoy nightly screenings of movies under the stars. Location is the biggest bonus here, but it's also friendly and well run. The comfortable doubles share bathrooms. There's a good-sized kitchen and a pleasant outdoor area around a small pool. Discounted weekly rates are available.

MacDonnell Range
Holiday Park   CARAVAN PARK $
(☑ 1800 808 373, 08-8952 6111; www.macrange.com.au; Palm Pl; unpowered/powered sites $42/48, cabins d $100-250; ❄ @ 🖾) Probably Alice's biggest and best kept, this caravan park has grassy sites and spotless amenities. Accommodation ranges from simple cabins with shared bathroom to self-contained, two-bedroom villas. Kids can cavort in the adventure playground, on the BMX track and on the basketball court.

Quest Alice Springs   APARTMENT $$
(☑ 08-8959 0000; www.questapartments.com.au; 10 South Tce; d studio/1-bedroom apt from $142/210; P ❄ 🖘 🖾) These stylish modern apartments just across the road from the Todd River are an excellent choice. The Quest chain is reliably comfortable and well run, and the quality of the rooms is well above most Alice choices.

Doubletree by Hilton   HOTEL $$
(☑ 08-8950 8000, 1300 666 545; www.doubletree3.hilton.com; Barrett Dr; d from $150, ste $175-350; ❄ @ 🖘 🖾) With its spacious resort-style facilities, this is widely considered one of Alice's top hotels. Choose from the garden-view rooms or the better mountain range–view rooms – they're decked out with floor-to-ceiling windows, cane furniture and pastel colours. There's a lovely pool and spa, a well-equipped gym and sauna, tennis courts and a house peacock.

Alice on Todd   APARTMENT $$
(☑ 08-8953 8033; www.aliceontodd.com; cnr Strehlow St & South Tce; studio/1-bed apt from $120/165; ❄ @ 🖘 🖾) This place has a great set-up, with friendly and helpful staff. It's an attractive and secure apartment complex on the banks of the Todd River offering one- and two-bedroom self-contained units with kitchen and lounge. There are also studios. The balconied units sleep up to six, so they're a great option for families.

Bond Springs Outback Retreat   B&B $$
(☑ 0417 750 798; Burt Plains; cottage d $234; ❄ 🖾) Experience a taste of outback station life at this retreat, about 25km north of town.

The private self-contained cottage is a refurbished stockman's quarters. A full breakfast is included but other meals are self-catering. Have a game of tennis or mooch around the enormous property that includes the original station school, which operated through the School of the Air.

✗ Eating

★ Kungkas Cafe   CAFE $
(☑ 08-8952 3102; Shop 17, Diarama Village, Larapinta Dr; snacks & light meals from $10; ☺ 7.30am-3pm Mon-Fri) Now here's something a little different. The coffee at this Indigenous catering place is good, but we love it for its snacks that put wild-harvested bush foods (eg bush tomatoes, lemon myrtle) front and centre. Take-home treats include saltbush or wattleseed dukkah, bush tomato chutney and quandong relish.

★ Page 27 Cafe   CAFE $
(☑ 0429 003 874, 08-8952 0191; www.facebook.com/Page27Cafe; Fan Lane; mains breakfast $8-22, lunch $14-20; ☺ 7am-2.30pm Tue-Fri, 7.30am-2pm Sat & Sun; ☑) Alice's locals duck down this arcade for great coffee or fresh juice. There are wholesome homestyle breakfasts (eggs any style, pancakes), pita wraps and fancy salads such as chicken fattoush with herbed quinoa, rocket and baba ganoush. Excellent vegetarian menu.

★ Montes   AUSTRALIAN $$
(☑ 08-8952 4336; www.montes.net.au; cnr Stott Tce & Todd St; mains $13-28; ☺ 2pm-2am Wed-Sun; ☑) Travelling circus meets outback homestead. Montes is family friendly with a play area for kids, and the food ranges from gourmet burgers, pizzas and tapas to curries and seafood. Sit in the leafy beer garden (with a range of beers) or intimate booth seating. Patio heaters keep patrons warm on cool desert nights.

★ Hanuman Restaurant   THAI $$
(☑ 08-8953 7188; www.hanuman.com.au/alice-springs; Doubletree by Hilton, 82 Barrett Dr; mains $18-38; ☺ noon-2.30pm Mon-Fri, 6-10pm daily; ☑) You won't believe you're in the outback when you try the fab Thai- and Indian-influenced cuisine at this stylish restaurant. The delicate Thai starters are a real triumph, as are the seafood dishes, particularly the Hanuman prawns. Although the menu is ostensibly Thai, there are enough Indian dishes to satisfy a curry craving.

Epilogue Lounge   TAPAS $$
(☑ 08-8953 4206; www.facebook.com/epiloguelounge; 58 Todd Mall; mains $18-22; ☺ 7.30am-11.30pm Wed-Sat, 8am-3pm Sun & Mon) This urban, retro delight is definitely the coolest place to hang in town. With a decent wine list, food served all day and service with a smile, it is a real Alice Springs stand-out. Expect dishes such as halloumi burgers and steak sandwiches. They also have live music at 8pm Saturdays and open-mike comedy from 7.30pm on Thursdays.

Water Tank Cafe   CAFE $$
(☑ 0408 854 472; www.facebook.com/Watertank Cafe; 16b Wilkinson St; mains $10-21; ☺ 8am-3pm Mon-Sat, 10am-2.30pm Sun; ☎) Made from the raw materials of an outback water tank (corrugated iron, decorated with a range of recyclables), this quirky cafe serves up decent breakfasts, light meals for lunch, free wi-fi and occasional live music. Food is international, meandering through Italy and Vietnam, with a few wraps, focaccias and bowl food.

Red Ochre Grill   AUSTRALIAN $$$
(☑ 08-8952 9614; www.alicespringsaurora.com.au/red-ochre-grill; Todd Mall; mains $18-36; ☺ 6.30-10am, noon-2.30pm & 5-9pm) Offering innovative fusion dishes with a focus on outback cuisine, the menu here usually features the usual meats plus locally bred proteins, such as kangaroo and croc, sometimes matched with native herbs such as lemon myrtle, pepperberries and bush tomatoes. Keep an eye out for special deals such as tapas with a bottle of wine or discounts for an early-bird dinner.

🍺 Drinking & Nightlife

Monte's Lounge   BAR
(☑ 08-8952 4336; www.montes.net.au; 95 Todd St; ☺ 2pm-2am Wed-Sun) One of the mainstays of the Alice Springs drinking scene, Monte's is best known for its terrific beer garden and circuslike interior. Public servants share bar space with backpackers, and there are all manner of boutique beers on tap.

The Rock Bar   BAR
(☑ 08-8953 8280; 78 Todd St; ☺ noon-2am Mon-Fri, 4pm-2am Sat & Sun) There is an excellent beer selection at this Alice classic. It's blessed with a beer garden and is ideal for a cold drink by windows that open on to the street. The Rock Bar pulls in a good mix of locals and tourists, although it can get seedy in the evenings (which could be a metaphor for Alice itself).

☆ Entertainment

★ Sounds of
Starlight Theatre
LIVE MUSIC

(☑08-8953 0826; www.andrewlangford.com; 40 Todd Mall; adult/concession/family $30/25/90, dinner & show $85/75/285; ☺8pm Tue, Fri & Sat Apr-Nov) This atmospheric 1½-hour musical performance evoking the spirit of the outback with didgeridoos, drums and keyboards, plus wonderful photography and lighting, is an Alice institution. Musician Andrew Langford also runs free didgeridoo lessons (11am Monday to Friday). You can add dinner to the mix or just see the show.

🛍 Shopping

Alice is the centre for Aboriginal arts from all over central Australia. There's also a semi-regular market, an excellent bookshop and two places that sell equipment for those heading out on an outback expedition.

If you're considering purchasing an original artwork), make sure you're buying from an authentic dealer; an authentic piece will come with a certificate indicating the artist's name, language group and community, as well as the work's title, its story and when it was made.

★ Papunya Tula Artists
ART

(☑08-8952 4731; www.papunyatula.com.au; Todd Mall; ☺9am-5pm Mon-Fri, 10am-1pm Sat) This stunning gallery showcases artworks from the Western Desert communities of Papunya, Kintore and Kiwirrkurra – even if you're not buying, it's worth stopping by to see the magnificent collection.

★ Talapi
ART

(☑08-8953 6389; www.talapi.com.au; 45 Todd Mall; ☺9am-6pm Mon-Fri, 10am-5pm Sat) Talapi is a beautiful space in the heart of town, exhibiting and promoting Central Desert Indigenous art. It sources its artworks directly from Aboriginal-owned art centres and is a member of the Indigenous Art Code. Drop in to ask about upcoming exhibitions.

Yubu Napa Art Gallery
ARTS & CRAFTS

(☑0450 894 142; www.yubunapa.com; 65 Hartley St; ☺10am-6pm Mon-Fri, to 4pm Sat) One of the larger gallery shops in Alice, Yubu Napa has dot painting from the Western Desert, watercolours from the Hermannsburg School, photography, basketwork and other arts and crafts from central Australian Aboriginal communities.

Tangentyere Artists
ARTS & CRAFTS

(☑08-8951 4232; www.tangentyereartists.org.au; 16 Fogarty St; ☺10am-4pm Mon-Fri) Paintings across a range of styles, printed textiles, recycled tin jewellery – there's a real breadth of genres on offer here at this urban Indigenous art centre.

Tjanpi Desert Weavers
ART

(☑08-8958 2336; www.tjanpi.com.au; 3 Wilkinson St; ☺10am-4pm Mon-Fri, closed Jan) This small enterprise by the Ngaanyatjarra Pitjantjatjara Yankunytjatjara (NPY) Women's Council employs and supports more than 400 Central Desert female weavers from 26 remote communities. The shop is well worth a visit to see the magnificent woven baskets and quirky sculptures created from grasses collected locally – *tjanpi* means 'wild harvested grass'.

Mbantua Gallery
ART

(☑08-8952 5571; www.mbantua.com.au; 64 Todd Mall; ☺9am-6pm Mon-Fri, 9am-5pm Sat, 10am-2pm Sun) This privately owned gallery includes extensive exhibits of works from the renowned Utopia region, as well as watercolour landscapes from the Namatjira school. Collectors should ask to see their collection of bark paintings, old boomerangs and high-end works out the back.

Ngurratjuta Iltja Ntjarra
ART

(Many Hands Art Centre; ☑08-7979 3452, 08-8950 0910; www.manyhandsart.com.au; 29 Wilkinson St; ☺9am-5pm Mon-Fri) The 'many hands' art centre is a small gallery and studio for visiting artists from all over central Australia. Watercolour paintings by descendants of Albert Namatjira are the focus here. Works are reasonably priced and you buy directly from the artists. You can see artists at work from 10am to 3pm Monday to Thursday.

Red Kangaroo Books
BOOKS

(☑08-8953 2137; www.redkangaroobooks.com; 79 Todd Mall; ☺9am-5.30pm Mon-Fri, to 3pm Sat, to 1pm Sun market days) Excellent bookshop specialising in central Australian titles: history, art, travel, novels, guidebooks and more. It also has a small well-chosen wildlife section.

Desert Dwellers
SPORTS & OUTDOORS

(☑08-8953 2240; www.desertdwellers.com.au; cnr Milner Rd & Wilkinson St; ☺9am-5pm Mon-Fri, 9am-2pm Sat, 10am-2pm Sun Mar-Sep, shorter hours rest of year) For camping and hiking gear, head to this shop, which has just about everything you need to equip yourself for an outback jaunt: maps, swags, tents, portable fridges, stoves and more.

Todd Mall Market MARKET
(☑ 0458 555 506; www.toddmallmarkets.com.au; Todd Mall; ⊙ 9am-1pm) Buskers, craft stalls, sizzling woks, smoky satay stands, Aboriginal art, jewellery and knick-knacks make for a relaxed stroll at this seasonal Sunday market. The market doesn't run in January, runs once in late February, then runs two to three times monthly the rest of the year.

ℹ Information

DANGERS & ANNOYANCES
Avoid walking alone at night anywhere in town. Catch a taxi back to your accommodation if you're out late.

MEDICAL SERVICES
Alice Springs Hospital (☑ 08-8951 7777; https://nt.gov.au/wellbeing; Gap Rd)
Alice Springs Pharmacy (☑ 08-8952 1554; shop 19, Yeperenye Shopping Centre, 36 Hartley St; ⊙ 8.30am-9pm Mon-Fri, 8.30am-7pm Sat, 9am-4.30pm Sun)

POST
Main Post Office (☑ 13 13 18; www.auspost. com.au; 31-33 Hartley St; ⊙ 9am-5pm Mon-Fri, to 12.30pm Sat)

TOURIST INFORMATION
Alice Springs Visitor Information Centre (☑ 08-8952 5800, 1800 645 199; www.disc overcentralaustralia.com; cnr Todd Mall & Parsons St; ⊙ 8am-6pm Mon-Fri, 9.30am-4pm Sat & Sun; ☎) This helpful centre can load you up with stacks of brochures and the free visitors guide. Weather forecasts and road conditions are posted on the wall. National parks information is also available. Ask about the unlimited kilometre deals if you are thinking of renting a car.
Central Land Council (☑ 08-8951 6211; www. clc.org.au; PO Box 3321, 27 Stuart Hwy, Alice Springs; ⊙ 9am-5pm Mon-Fri) For Aboriginal land permits and transit permits.
Parks & Wildlife (☑ 08-8999 4555, 08-8951 8250; www.nt.gov.au/leisure/parks-reserves; Arid Zone Research Institute, off Stuart Hwy) Information on national parks and for the Larapinta Trail (p865).
Wildcare Inc Alice Springs (☑ 0419 221 128; www.wildcareasp.org.au) The people to call if you find injured wildlife.

ℹ Getting There & Away

AIR
Alice Springs is well connected, with **Qantas** (☑ 13 13 13, 08-8950 5211; www.qantas.com.au) and **Virgin Australia** (☑ 13 67 89; www.virgin australia.com) operating regular flights to/from capital cities. Airline representatives are based at **Alice Springs airport** (☑ 08-8951 1211; www. alicespringsairport.com.au; Santa Teresa Rd).

BUS
Greyhound (☑ 1300 473 946; www.greyhound. com.au; Shop 3, 113 Todd St) has regular services from Alice Springs (check the website for timetables and discounted fares). Buses arrive at, and depart from, the Greyhound office in Todd St.

Destination	One-way fare ($)	Duration (hr)
Adelaide	205	21
Coober Pedy	155	9
Darwin	209	22
Katherine	176	16½
Tennant Creek	119	6½

Emu Run (p857) runs cheap daily connections between Alice Springs and Yulara (for Uluru; one way $120). **Gray Line** (☑ 1300 858 687; www.grayline.com; Capricornia Centre 9, Gregory Tce) also runs between Alice Springs and Yulara (one way $120).

Backpacker buses roam to and from Alice providing a party atmosphere and a chance to see some of the sights along the way. **Groovy Grape Getaways Australia** (☑ 1800 661 177; www.groovygrape.com.au) plies the route from Alice to Adelaide on a six-day, backpacker camping jaunt for $945.

CAR & MOTORCYCLE
Alice Springs is a long way from everywhere. It's 1180km to Mt Isa in Queensland, 1490km to Darwin, 1531km to Adelaide and 441km (4½ hours) to Yulara (for Uluru). Although the roads to the north and south are sealed and in good condition, these are still outback roads and it's wise to have your vehicle well prepared, particularly as you'll rarely get a mobile phone signal outside Alice or Yulara. Carry plenty of drinking water and emergency food at all times.

ℹ UNLIMITED KILOMETRES

Most car-rental firms in Alice will only rent you vehicles with around 100km to 200km free per day, whereafter you'll pay around $0.20 per kilometre. But you'll usually get free unlimited kilometres if you arrange your rental through Alice's visitor information centre . Out here, the difference can be considerable.

All the major car-hire companies have offices in Alice Springs and many have counters at the airport. Prices drop by about 20% between November and April, but rentals don't come cheap, as most firms offer only 100km free per day, which won't get you far out here. Talk to the Alice Springs Visitor Information Centre (p861) about its unlimited kilometres deal before you book. A conventional (2WD) vehicle will get you to most sights in the MacDonnell Ranges and out to Uluru and Kings Canyon via sealed roads. If you want to go further afield, say to Chambers Pillar, Finke Gorge or even the Mereenie Loop Rd, a 4WD is essential.

TRAIN

➤ The train station is at the end of George Cres, off Larapinta Dr.

➤ A classic way to enter or leave the NT is by the **Ghan** (☑13 21 47; www.greatsouthernrail. com.au), which runs between Adelaide and Darwin, and can be booked through Great Southern Rail. Discounted fares are sometimes offered, especially in the low season (February to June). Bookings are essential.

❶ Getting Around

TO/FROM THE AIRPORT

Alice Springs airport is 15km south of the town; it's about $50 by taxi. A bus from **Alice Wanderer** (☑08-8952 2111, 1800 722 111; www.alice-wanderer.com.au) meets all flights and drops off passengers at city accommodation. Book a day in advance for pick-up from accommodation.

BUS

The public bus service, **AS Bus** (☑08-8944 2444), departs from outside the **Yeperenye Shopping Centre** (Hartley St). Buses run about every 1½ hours Monday to Friday and Saturday morning. There are three routes of interest to travellers: 400/401 has a detour to the cultural precinct, 100/101 passes the School of the Air, and 300/301 passes many southern hotels and caravan parks along Gap Rd and Palm Circuit. The visitor information centre (p861) has timetables.

Desert Park Transfers (☑08-8952 1731; www.tailormadetours.com.au; adult/child $40/22) offers transfers from town to the Alice Springs Desert Park (p852), five times daily during park hours. The cost includes park entry and pick-up/drop-off at your accommodation. Alice Wanderer offers a similar service.

TAXI

Taxis congregate near the visitor information centre (p861). To book one, call ☑13 10 08 or ☑08-8952 1877.

MACDONNELL RANGES

The beautiful, weather-beaten MacDonnell Ranges, within the traditional lands of the Arrernte, stretch 400km across the desert and are a hidden world of spectacular gorges, rare wildlife and poignant Aboriginal heritage – all within a day from Alice.

East MacDonnell Ranges

The East MacDonnell Ranges are extremely picturesque. Overshadowed by the more popular West Macs, the East Macs receive fewer visitors, which can make for a more enjoyable outback experience. With gorges, some stunning scenery (especially around sunset and sunrise) and the old gold-mining ruins of Arltunga, there's enough to fill a day trip from Alice.

☉ Sights

★**Arltunga Historical Reserve** HISTORIC SITE
At the eastern end of the MacDonnell Ranges, 110km east of Alice Springs, the old gold-mining ghost town of Arltunga (33km on an unsealed road from the Ross Hwy) has lonely ruins and a wonderful end-of-the-road feel. Old buildings, a couple of cemeteries and the many deserted mine sites in this parched landscape give visitors an idea of what life was like for the miners.

★**Trephina Gorge**
Nature Park NATURE RESERVE
(☑08-8956 9765; www.nt.gov.au/leisure/parks-reserves) If you only have time for a couple of stops in the East MacDonnell Ranges, make Trephina Gorge Nature Park (75km from Alice) one of them. The play between the pale sandy riverbeds, the red and purple gorge walls, the white tree trunks, the eucalyptus-green foliage and the blue sky is spectacular. Depending on the time of year, you'll also find deep swimming holes and abundant wildlife. There's a rangers station and **campground** (☑08-8956 9765; adult/child $3.30/1.65) with barbecues, water and toilets.

N'Dhala Gorge
Nature Park NATURE RESERVE
(www.nt.gov.au/leisure/parks-reserves) Just southwest of the Ross River Resort, a strictly 4WD-only track leads 11km south to N'Dhala Gorge. More than 5900 ancient Aboriginal rock carvings (some date back 10,000 years) and some rare endemic plants deco-

rate a deep, narrow gorge, although the art isn't easy to spot. There's a small, exposed **campground** (adult/child $3.30/1.65) without reliable water. From the car park, there's a 1.5km (one hour) return walk to the gorge with some signposts to rock art walls.

Ruby Gap Nature Park   NATURE RESERVE
(www.nt.gov.au/leisure/parks-reserves) This remote park rewards visitors with wild and beautiful scenery. The sandy bed of the Hale River sparkles with thousands of tiny garnets. It's an evocative place and is well worth the considerable effort required to reach it – by high-clearance 4WD. **Camping** (adult/child $3.30/1.65) is permitted anywhere along the river; make sure to BYO drinking water and a camp cooker. Allow two hours each way for the 44km trip from Arltunga.

Emily & Jessie Gaps
Nature Park   NATURE RESERVE
Both of these gaps in the rock wall of the East MacDonnells are associated with the Eastern Arrernte Caterpillar Dreaming trail. Emily Gap, 16km out of Alice, has stylised rock paintings and a fairly deep waterhole in the narrow gorge. The gap is a sacred site with some well-preserved paintings on the eastern wall, although some of the paintings have been vandalised. Jessie Gap, 8km further on, is usually much quieter. Both sites have toilets, but camping is not permitted.

Corroboree Rock
Conservation Reserve   HISTORIC SITE
(☑ 08-8956 9765; www.nt.gov.au/leisure/parks-reserves) Corroboree Rock, 51km from Alice Springs, is one of many strangely shaped dolomite outcrops scattered over the valley floor. Despite the name, it's doubtful the rock was ever used as a corroboree area, but it is associated with the Perentie Dreaming trail. The perentie lizard, Australia's largest, grows in excess of 2.5m and takes refuge within the area's rock falls. There's a short walking track (15 minutes) around the rock.

The car park is 1km along a sealed road off the Ross Hwy.

🛏 Sleeping

Most people visit on a day trip from Alice, but there are basic campgrounds at Arltunga, Trephina Gorge, John Hayes Rockhole, Ruby Gap Nature Park and N'Dhala Gorge, as well as two fine noncamping options, one at Ross River, the other along the Arltunga Tourist Dr.

CATERPILLAR DREAMING

Known to the Arrernte as Anthwerrke, Emily Gap in the East MacDonnell Ranges is one of the most important Aboriginal sites in the Alice Springs area; it was from here that the caterpillar ancestral beings of Mparntwe originated before crawling across the landscape to create the topographical features that exist today.

Arltunga Bush Hotel   CAMPGROUND $
(☑ 08-8956 9797; sites per person $7, dm $12, family cottages $55; ☺ Mar-Nov) Arltunga Bush Hotel, close to the entrance of the Arltunga Historical Reserve, has a campground with showers, toilets, barbecue pits and picnic tables. Fees are collected in the late afternoon. It's a lovely spot with plenty of shade and nicely spaced sites.

⭐**Hale River Homestead**
at Old Ambalindum   FARMSTAY $$
(☑ 08-8956 9993; www.haleriverhomestead.com.au; unpowered/powered sites from $30/35, dm $40-80, r/d cottage/homestead $190/220; ❄ ⛱) This remote spot run by NT veterans Sean and Lynne offers a great range of accommodation including a nicely renovated homestead, a cottage sleeping five people, a converted shed, simple bunkhouses and lovely campsites, all on a working cattle station. Bookings are essential and ring ahead to ask whether you need to bring your own food.

Ross River Resort   CARAVAN PARK $$
(☑ 08-8956 9711; www.rossriverresort.com.au; Ross Hwy; unpowered/powered sites $30/39, bunkhouse with/without linen $40/30, d/f cabin $155/180; ❄ 🛜 ⛱) Nine kilometres along the continuation of the Ross Hwy past the Arltunga turn-off (coming from Alice Springs) is the secluded Ross River Resort. Built around a historic stone homestead, timber cabins encircle a swimming pool.

❶ Getting There & Away

The sealed Ross Hwy runs 100km along the Ranges. Arltunga is 33km off the Ross Hwy along an unsealed road that is usually OK for 2WD vehicles; the first 13km off the Ross Hwy require careful driving as the road bucks and weaves through the hills, but the final 20km into Arltunga crosses more open floodplains.

You'll need a 4WD to access John Hayes Rockhole (in Trephina Gorge Nature Park), N'Dhala Gorge and Ruby Gap.

From Arltunga it's possible to loop back to Alice along the Arltunga Tourist Dr, which pops out at the Stuart Hwy about 50km north of town.

West MacDonnell Ranges

Looking for all the world like some gnarled desert reptile strung out across the desert, the West MacDonnell Ranges (the West Macs to their friends) are worthy desert companions to the better-known Uluru, Kata Tjuta and Kings Canyon away to the southwest. Beautiful when taken as a whole, the West Macs are nonetheless all about the detail. Below rampartlike summits, deep gashes snake into the heart of the escarpment in a series of gorges filled with water and wildlife. Part of the stirring Tjoritja/West MacDonnell Ranges National Park, a land of great beauty, filled with sacred Dreaming stories, the range can easily be visited on a day trip from Alice Springs. But you'll be rewarded a hundred times over if you stay longer.

The West MacDonnell Ranges lie within the traditional lands of the Arrernte people.

◉ Sights

★ Simpsons Gap
CANYON

One of the prettiest corners of the West MacDonnell Ranges, Simpsons Gap, 22km

---

WEST MACDONNELL WILDLIFE

The West MacDonnell Ranges offer some fine possibilities when it comes to native Australian wildlife. Species to watch out for include the following:

Black-footed rock wallaby Most easily seen at Simpsons Gap.

Common brushtail possum Any riverine woodland across the range.

Dingo Possible at Ormiston Gorge or Ellery Creek Big Hole.

Euro or common wallaroo Simpsons Gap or Ormiston Gorge.

Fat-tailed false antechinus This small, rodentlike marsupial is sometimes seen early morning around Ormiston Gorge.

Red kangaroo Around Simpsons Gap, along Larapinta Dr around sunset and Ormiston Gorge.

---

by road from Alice Springs and 8km off Larapinta Dr along a paved road, combines wonderful scenery with good wildlife-watching. Towering red-rock cliffs watch over a riverbed strewn with gums, and a few pools where the canyon narrows. The bouldered slope on the eastern side is one of the best places in the region to see black-footed rock wallabies, especially in the early morning and late afternoon.

Standley Chasm
GORGE

(Angkerle Atwatye; ☑08-8956 7440; www.standley chasm.com.au; adult/child/family $12/7/30; ☺8am-5pm, last chasm entry 4.30pm) Spectacular Standley Chasm is owned and run by the local Iwupataka community. The narrowest of the West MacDonnell defiles, it's a stunning spot with sheer rock walls rising 80m from the canyon floor. A rocky path into the gorge (20 minutes, 1.2km) follows a creek bed lined with ghost gums and cycads. There's a kiosk, camping (☑08-8956 7440; per person $18.50; ☎), picnic facilities and toilets near the car park.

The chasm is 50km west of Alice Springs and signposted off Larapinta Dr. The road is sealed all the way.

◉ Namatjira Drive

Heading west from Alice Springs, Namatjira Dr branches off Larapinta Dr then hits some of the highlights of the West Macs. Your first stop might be **Ellery Creek Big Hole**. Ninety-one kilometres from Alice Springs and with a large permanent waterhole, it's a popular place for a swim on a hot day (the water is usually freezing). It's good for wildlife and birdwatching too. About 11km further west along Namatjira Dr, a rough gravel track leads to narrow, ochre-red **Serpentine Gorge**, which has a lovely waterhole blocking the entrance and a lookout at the end of a short, steep track (30 minutes return), where you can view ancient cycads.

Ochre Pits line a dry creek bed 11km west of Serpentine and were a source of pigment for Aboriginal people. The various coloured ochres – mainly yellow, white and red-brown – are weathered limestone, with iron-oxide creating the colours.

The car park for the majestic **Ormiston Gorge** is 25km beyond the Ochre Pits. Ormiston is the most impressive chasm in the West MacDonnells. There's a waterhole shaded with ghost gums, and the gorge curls around to the enclosed Ormiston Pound. It's a haven

LARAPINTA TRAIL

The 230km **Larapinta Trail** extends along the backbone of the West MacDonnell Ranges and is one of Australia's great long-distance walks. The track is split into 12 stages of varying difficulty, stretching from the Telegraph Station in Alice Springs to the craggy 1380m summit of Mt Sonder. Trail notes and maps are available from Parks & Wildlife (p861).

Each section takes one to two days to navigate and the trail passes many of the attractions in the West MacDonnell Ranges.

Section 1 Alice Springs Telegraph Station to Simpsons Gap (23.8km)

Section 2 Simpsons Gap to Jay Creek (24.5km)

Section 3 Jay Creek to Standley Chasm (13.6km)

Section 4 Standley Chasm to Birthday Waterhole (17.7km)

Section 5 Birthday Waterhole to Hugh Gorge (16km)

Section 6 Hugh Gorge to Ellery Creek (31.2km)

Section 7 Ellery Creek to Serpentine Gorge (13.8km)

Section 8 Serpentine Gorge to Serpentine Chalet Dam (13.4km)

Section 9 Serpentine Chalet Dam to Ormiston Gorge (28.6km)

Section 10 Ormiston Gorge to Finke River (9.9km)

Section 11 Finke River to Redbank Gorge (25.2km)

Section 12 Redbank Gorge to Mt Sonder (15.8km return)

Walking groups of eight or more should contact Parks & Wildlife with a trip plan. There's no public transport out to this area, but transfers can be arranged through the Alice Wanderer (p862); see the website for the various costs. For guided walks, including transport from Alice Springs, go through Trek Larapinta (p857).

for wildlife (dingo, red kangaroo and euro are all possible, and look for the fat-tailed false antechinus near sunrise) and birds (western bowerbird, rufous-crowned emu-wren and spinifex pigeon among others). The only drawback? It's also the busiest site along Namatjira Dr. There are some excellent walking tracks – take one and you'll soon leave the crowds behind – including the **Ghost Gum Lookout** (20 minutes), which affords brilliant views down the gorge, and the excellent, circuitous **Pound Walk** (three hours, 7.5km). There's a small **visitor centre** (☑08-8956 7799; ⊙10am-4pm), a kiosk (open 10am to 4pm) and a **campground** (☑08-8954 6198; Ormiston Gorge; adult/child/family $10/5/25).

About 2km further is the turn-off to **Glen Helen Gorge**, where the Finke River cuts through the MacDonnells. Just 1km past Glen Helen is a good **lookout** over Mt Sonder; sunrise and sunset here are particularly impressive.

If you continue northwest for 25km you'll reach the turn-off (4WD only) to multi-hued, cathedral-like **Redbank Gorge**. A permanent waterhole runs for kilometres through the labyrinthine gorge and makes for an incredible swimming and scrambling adventure on a hot day. Namatjira Dr then

heads south and is sealed as far as **Tylers Pass Lookout**.

🛏 Sleeping

Most people explore the West MacDonnells on a day trip (or day trips) from Alice Springs, but there are campgrounds at **Ellery Creek Big Hole** (per adult/child/family $5/2.50/12.50), Ormiston Gorge and Redbank Gorge, as well as the Glen Helen Resort, also with camping area, at Glen Helen.

Glen Helen Resort
HOTEL $

(☑08-8956 7489, 1300 269 822; www.glenhelen lodge.com.au; Namatjira Dr; unpowered/powered sites $24/30, d without/with breakfast $195/240; ❄🛜🏊) At the western edge of the West MacDonnell Ranges National Park is the popular Glen Helen Resort, which has an idyllic back verandah slammed up against the red ochre cliffs of the spectacular gorge. There's a busy restaurant-pub serving hearty meals such as steaks and parmas (mains $25 to $35) and live music some weekend.

Wallace Rockhole
Tourist Park
CARAVAN PARK $

(☑08-8956 7993; www.wallacerockholetours.com. au; unpowered/powered sites $22/28, cabins $120;

THE RED CENTRE WAY & MEREENIE LOOP

The Red Centre Way is best known as the 'back road' from Alice Springs to Uluru, but there's more to it than that.

For some of its journey, it incorporates part of the West MacDonnell Ranges, an 'inner loop' comprising Namatjira and Larapinta Drs. The entire loop has now been paved, meaning that you take Namatjira Dr heading west, then return east along Larapinta Dr – a much-needed improvement that avoids long backtracking, as was previously the case for drivers of 2WD vehicles.

There's also the rugged Mereenie Loop Rd, the short cut to Kings Canyon. This dusty, heavily corrugated road is not to be taken lightly and hire-car companies won't permit their 2WDs to be driven on it. To travel along this route, which passes through Aboriginal land, you need a permit ($5), which is valid for one day and includes a booklet with details about the local Aboriginal culture and a route map. The pass is issued on the spot (usually only on the day of travel) at the visitor information centre in Alice Springs (p861), Glen Helen Resort (p865), Kings Canyon Resort (p872) and **Ntaria Store & Fuel** (☑ 08-8956 7480; www.ntariasupermarket.com; 59 Tjalkabota Rd; ⊙ 8.30am-5pm Mon-Fri, 9am-4pm Sat, 9am-3pm Sun) in Hermannsburg.

✳) You'll be virtually guaranteed seclusion at the Wallace Rockhole Tourist Park, situated at the end of an 18km dirt road branching off Larapinta Dr. The park has a camping area with good facilities. Tours here include a 1½-hour rock art and bush medicine tour (adult/child $12/10) with billy tea and damper (advance bookings essential).

❶ Getting There & Away

There is no public transport through the West MacDonnell Ranges, although some operators in Alice offer tours. Otherwise, you'll need your own wheels.

Hermannsburg

POP 605

The Aboriginal community of Hermannsburg (Ntaria), about 125km from Alice Springs, is famous as the one-time home of artist Albert Namatjira and as the site of the Hermannsburg Mission. It's an appealingly run-down and sleepy place, which belies its significance as one of the most important Aboriginal communities in the area. Around 90% of the population is Aboriginal, and these are the traditional lands of the Aranda, or Arrernte, people.

Hermannsburg Mission   HISTORIC SITE
(☑ 08-8956 7402; www.hermannsburg.com.au; adult/child $12/free; ⊙ 9am-5pm) The whitewashed walls of the old mission are shaded by tall river gums and date palms. This fascinating monument to the NT's early Lutheran missionaries includes a school building, a church and various outbuildings. The 'Manse'

houses an art gallery and a history of the life and times of Albert Namatjira as well as work by 39 Hermannsburg artists.

Kata-Anga Tea Rooms   CAFE $
(mains $8-15; ⊙ 9am-4pm Apr–mid-Oct) Within Hermannsburg Mission, Kata-Anga Tea Rooms, in the old missionary house, serves Devonshire teas, sandwiches and strudel, and displays historic photographs, plus a good range of paintings. There are distinctive ceramic works by the Hermannsburg potters on display and available for sale.

❶ Getting There & Away

There's no public transport to/from Hermannsburg, which is 127km southwest of Alice Springs along Larapinta Dr. Note that the road to Glen Helen Gorge and other attractions in the West MacDonnell Ranges (but not Kings Canyon) is paved.

Pick up fuel, basic groceries and permits for the road to Kings Canyon at Ntaria Store & Fuel while you're here.

Finke Gorge National Park

With its primordial landscape, the Finke Gorge National Park, south of Hermannsburg, is one of central Australia's premier wilderness reserves. It's hard going getting here and even harder getting around, but that also tends to keep the numbers of visitors down, which only adds to the park's already considerable appeal.

There's a **campground** (Finke Gorge National Park; adult/child $6.60/3.30) with basic facilities inside the national park.

★ **Palm Valley**   GORGE

Top attraction Palm Valley is famous for its red cabbage palms (up to 12,000 of them!), which exist nowhere else in the world. These relics from prehistoric times give the valley a picture-book, oasis feel. In Palm Valley, walking tracks include **Arankaia walk** (2km loop, one hour), which traverses the valley, returning via the sandstone plateau; the **Mpulungkinya track** (5km loop, two hours), heading down the gorge before joining the Arankaia walk; and the **Mpaara track** (5km loop, two hours), which takes in the Finke River, Palm Bend and a rugged natural amphitheatre (a semicircle of sandstone formations sculpted by a now-extinct meander of Palm Creek).

ℹ️ Getting There & Away

Access to the park follows the sandy bed of the Finke River and rocky tracks, so a high-clearance 4WD is essential. If you don't have one, several tour operators go to Palm Valley from Alice Springs. The turn-off to Palm Valley starts about 1km west of the Hermannsburg turn-off on Larapinta Dr.

If you are well prepared there's a challenging route through the national park along the sandy bed of the Finke River. This is a remote and scenic drive to Ernest Giles Rd, from where you can continue west to Kings Canyon (or Uluru) or east back to the Stuart Hwy, although such a trip is an expedition in itself, not a short cut. It pays to travel in a convoy (getting bogged is part of the adventure) and get a copy of the *Finke River 4WD Route* notes (www.nt.gov.au/leisure/parks-reserves).

NORTHERN TERRITORY'S FAR SOUTH

Most travellers clocking long desert kilometres along the Stuart and Lasseter Hwys do so oblivious to the fact that some fascinating and dramatic sites lie off in the hinterland. You'd need a few days to see all of them, but possibilities for those with limited time include Rainbow Valley Conservation Reserve, Henbury Meteorite Craters, the views of Mt Connor and Australia's geographical centre.

Old South Road

The Old South Road, which runs close to the old Ghan railway line, is a pretty rough 4WD track that takes you about as far off the beaten track as you can go this close to

Alice Springs. Attractions, beyond that sense of being somewhere deliciously remote, are few, but you may end up at Australia's geographical centre if you go far enough.

⊙ Sights

It's only 39km from Alice Springs to **Ewaninga**, where prehistoric Aboriginal petroglyphs are carved into sandstone. The rock carvings found here and at N'Dhala Gorge are thought to have been made by Aboriginal people who lived here before those currently in the region, between 1000 and 5000 years ago.

The eerie, sandstone **Chambers Pillar** (www.nt.gov.au/leisure/parks-reserves), southwest of Maryvale Station, towers 50m above the surrounding plain and is carved with the names and visit dates of early European explorers – and, unfortunately, some much less worthy modern-day graffiti. To the Aboriginal people of the area, Chambers Pillar is the remains of Itirkawara, a powerful gecko ancestor. Most photogenic at sunset and sunrise, it's best to stay overnight at the **campground** (adult/child $3.30/1.65). It's 160km from Alice Springs and a 4WD is required for the last 44km from the turn-off at Maryvale Station.

Back on the main track south, you eventually arrive at **Finke** (Aputula), a small Aboriginal community 230km from Alice Springs. When the old Ghan was running, Finke was a thriving town; these days it seems to have drifted into a permanent torpor, except when the Finke Desert Race (p858) is staged. Fuel and basic supplies are available here at **Aputula Store** (📞 08-8956 0968; ⊙ 9am-noon & 2-4pm Mon-Fri, 9am-noon Sat).

Just 21km west of Finke, and 12km north of the road along a signposted track, is the **Lambert Centre**. The point marks Australia's geographical centre and features a 5m-high version of the flagpole found on top of Parliament House in Canberra.

🛏️ Sleeping & Eating

The only official place to sleep along the Old South Rd is the basic campground at Chambers Pillar.

Basic supplies are available at the Aputula Store in Finke, but we strongly recommend that you carry with you everything you think you're likely to need as supplies sometimes run low and prices are high.

ℹ️ Getting There & Away

You'll need a fully equipped, high-clearance 4WD to travel this route. The road begins south of Alice

South of Alice Springs

DARWIN & THE NORTHERN TERRITORY RAINBOW VALLEY

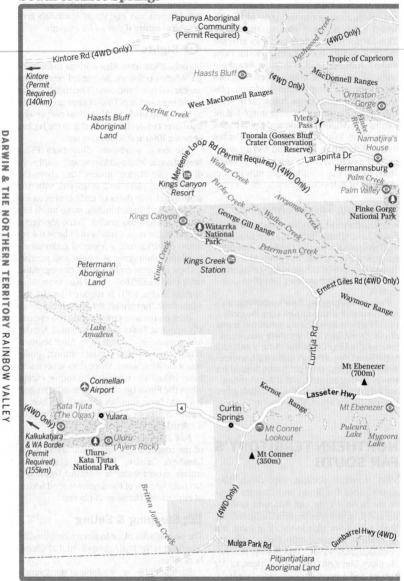

Springs, close to where the road branches to the airport and the newer Stuart Hwy. At the southern end, from Finke, you can turn west along the Goyder Stock Rte to join the Stuart Hwy at Kulgera (150km) or east to Old Andado station on the edge of the Simpson Desert (120km). (Expensive) fuel is sold at the Aputula Store (p867).

Rainbow Valley Conservation Reserve

Visit this series of free-standing sandstone bluffs and cliffs, in shades ranging from cream to red, at sunset or sunrise and you'll

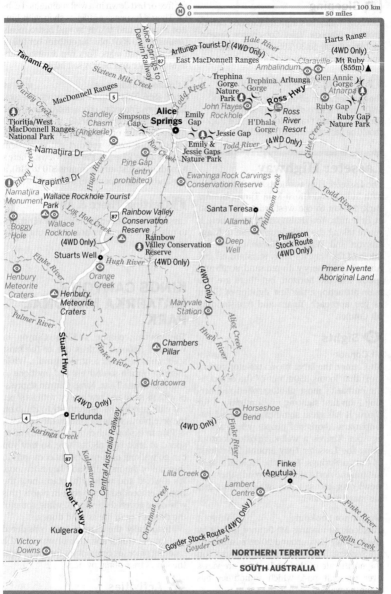

encounter one of central Australia's more underrated sights. Visit in the middle of the day and you're likely to wonder what all the fuss is about, save for one thing – deep-desert silence will overwhelm you whatever time of day you are here. A marked walking trail takes you past clay-pans and in between the multihued outcrops to the aptly named **Mushroom Rock**. The land belongs to a northern group of the Indigenous Arrernte people who call the area Wurre.

🛏 Sleeping

Rainbow Valley has a pretty exposed **campground** (Rainbow Valley Conservation Reserve; adult/child/family $3.30/1.65/7.70), but the setting is perfectly positioned for sunset viewing.

ℹ Getting There & Away

The park lies 22km off the Stuart Hwy along a 4WD track; the turn-off is 77km south of Alice Springs. If it hasn't rained for a while, the track should be passable in a 2WD vehicle.

Lasseter Highway

The Lasseter Hwy connects the Stuart Hwy with Yulara and Uluru-Kata Tjuta National Park, 244km to the west from the turn-off at Erldunda. You'll also travel along here if you're taking the sealed-road route to Kings Canyon and Watarrka National Park. For much of the way, it's fairly standard central Australian scenery with red sand, scrub and spinifex to the horizon, but there are two main attractions: the first sighting of Uluru as you approach Yulara and free-standing Mt Conner.

◉ Sights

Mt Connor   MOUNTAIN

Mt Connor, the large mesa (tabletop mountain) that looms 350m out of the desert, is the outback's most photographed red herring – on first sighting many mistake it for Uluru. It has great significance to local Pitjantjatjara Aboriginal people, who know it as Atila. There's a well-signposted lookout along the Lasseter Hwy around 20km east of Curtin Springs; from the lookout's summit (on the north side of the road), there are views over the salt pan, which sometimes has standing water.

Mt Connor Lookout   VIEWPOINT

This lookout towards Mt Connor is right by the Lasseter Hwy around 20km east of Curtin Springs; from the lookout's summit (on the north side of the road), there are views over the salt pan, which sometimes has standing water.

🛏 Sleeping

Curtin Springs Wayside Inn   MOTEL **$$**

(📞 08-8956 2906; www.curtinsprings.com; Lasseter Hwy; unpowered/powered sites free/$45, r with shared/private bathroom $105/190; ❋) They pride themselves on friendliness here. Pitch a tent for free or bed down in a well-maintained cabin. There's (expensive) fuel, a shop with limited supplies and takeaway and bistro meals (mains $18 to $35), plus an outback bar full of history and tall tales. They can arrange tours to Mt Connor and nearby salt lakes.

Erldunda Roadhouse   MOTEL **$$**

(📞 08-8956 0984; http://erldundaroadhouse.com; Stuart Hwy, Erldunda; unpowered/powered sites $11/21, motel s/d from $115/149; ❋ 🛜 🏊) Motel rooms here are of a good standard and look out on to a lovely red-dirt native garden. Rooms 23 to 27 enjoy the best views. There's a roadhouse restaurant (mains $10 to $16), a bar and (really expensive) fuel.

ℹ Getting There & Away

Lasseter Hwy is sealed all the way from Erldunda to Yulara (and beyond as far as Kata Tjuta, inside the national park).

KINGS CANYON & WATARRKA NATIONAL PARK

The yawning chasm of Kings Canyon in Watarrka National Park is one of the most spectacular sights in central Australia. While there's a certain soulfulness and mystique to Uluru and Kata Tjuta, Kings Canyon impresses with its scale and raw beauty, with its sheer red cliffs and by the opportunity to climb on the precipitous walls for fabulous aerial views.

Plan to explore the canyon on foot, and to spend at least two nights here, so that you can go walking on a number of occasions in the cool of the morning and late afternoon. It's a weird and wonderful place: note the ripples embedded in the rock in places (this was once covered in water), while some of the domes began life as sand dunes.

Historically the canyon was considered a place of refuge, a source of water and a meeting place for ceremonies for the Luritja, the land's traditional owners.

🏃 Activities

⭐ **Kings Canyon Rim Walk**   HIKING

Walkers are rewarded with awesome views on the Kings Canyon Rim Walk (6km loop, three to four hours; you must begin before 9am on days when temperatures are forecast to exceed 35°C), which many travellers rate as a highlight of their trip to the Centre.

Kings Canyon

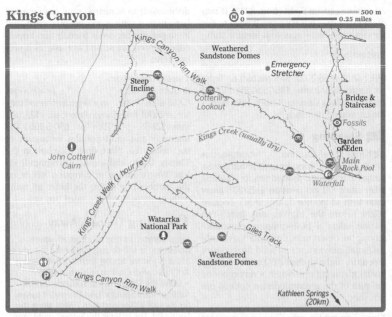

It's a challenging hike at the beginning, but is possible for anyone of reasonable fitness.

After a short but steep climb (the only 'difficult' part of the trail), the walk skirts the canyon's rim before descending wooden stairs to the Garden of Eden, a lush pocket of ferns and prehistoric cycads around a tranquil pool. The next section of the trail winds through a swarm of giant beehive domes: weathered sandstone outcrops, which to the Luritja represent the men of the Kuniya Dreaming.

There is a short version called the **Short Return Walk**, which stays open on hot days until 11am, but that's the only reason to do it – you'll miss most of the best views, but work almost as hard to get there.

Kings Creek Walk   HIKING
The Kings Creek Walk (2km return, one hour) is a short stroll along the rocky creek bed to a raised platform with views of the towering canyon rim. The platform was badly damaged in a rockfall – no one was injured – shortly before the time of research and the last 100m of the walk was closed while repairs were being made.

Giles Track   HIKING
The Giles Track (22km one way, overnight) is a marked track that meanders along

the George Gill Range between Kathleen Springs and the canyon; before setting out, fill out the logbook at Reedy Creek rangers office (signposted off Luritja Rd, south of the main Kings Canyon turn-off) so that in the event of an emergency, rangers can more easily locate you.

Kathleen Springs Walk   HIKING
About 10km east of the Kings Canyon car park, the Kathleen Springs Walk (1½ hours, 2.6km return) is a pleasant, wheelchair-accessible track leading to a waterhole at the head of a gorge.

☞ Tours

★ Karrke Aboriginal Experience   TOURS
(☑08-8956 7620; www.karrke.com.au; adult/child/family $65/45/175; ☺9am, 10.30am, 2pm & 4pm) This fine Aboriginal-run experience covers a lot of ground in an hour, from bush tucker and medicinal plants to hunting techniques and dot painting, although walking distances are small. You can book directly, or via Kings Canyon Resort (p872) or Kings Creek Station (p872).

Kings Creek Helicopters   SCENIC FLIGHTS
(☑08-8956 7474; www.kingscreekstation.com.au; flights per person $60-460) Trips from Kings Creek Station, including a breathtaking

30-minute canyon flight (from $275). It may seem expensive, but it's a small price to pay for views like this – once-in-a-lifetime stuff.

Professional Helicopter Services SCENIC FLIGHTS
(PHS; ☑08-8956 2003; www.phs.com.au; flights per person 8/15/30mins $95/150/285) Picking up from Kings Canyon Resort, PHS buzzes the canyon on demand.

🛏 Sleeping

★ **Kings Creek Station** CAMPGROUND $$
(☑08-8956 7474; www.kingscreekstation.com.au; Luritja Rd; unpowered/powered sites for 2 $40/50, safari cabins s/d incl breakfast $125/202, luxury safari tents all inclusive $1100; @🐾) Located 36km before the canyon, this family-run station offers a bush-camping experience among the desert oaks. Cosy safari-style cabins (small canvas tents on solid floors) share amenities and a kitchen-BBQ area, while the luxury glamping experience is very cool and the pick of the accommodation options out this way.

Kings Canyon Resort RESORT $$$
(☑08-8956 7442, 1800 837 168; www.kingscanyonresort.com.au; Luritja Rd; unpowered/powered sites $44/54, dm $47, d $310-500; ✳@🐾) Only 10km from the canyon, this well-designed resort boasts a wide range of accommodation, from a grassy camping area with its own pool and bar to deluxe rooms looking out on to native bushland. Eating and drinking options are as varied, with a bistro, the Thirsty Dingo bar and an outback BBQ for big steaks and live entertainment.

🍴 Eating

★ **Under the Desert Moon** AUSTRALIAN $$$
(☑08-8956 7442; www.kingscanyonresort.com.au; off Luritja Rd, Kings Canyon Resort; per person $159; ☺6pm Mon, Wed, Fri & Sat Apr-Oct) Dine out under the stars and around a campfire in great comfort and with fine food at the Kings Canyon Resort. There's a five-course set menu and the whole experience lasts from three to four hours. It's not quite as atmospheric as the Yulara versions near Uluru, but it's still a lovely night.

Carmichael's Restaurant AUSTRALIAN $$$
(☑08-8956 7442; www.kingscanyonresort.com.au; off Luritja Rd, Kings Canyon Resort; mains $28-49; ☺6-9pm) The most sophisticated dining option at Kings Canyon Resort, Carmichael's uses local ingredients where possible in

dishes such as kangaroo satay, pan-roasted barramundi with a macadamia crust and lamb pot pie. Service is friendly and knowledgeable and the setting as classy as it gets out here.

Thirsty Dingo Bar & Outback BBQ AUSTRALIAN $$$
(☑08-8956 7442; www.kingscanyonresort.com.au; Luritja Rd, Kings Canyon Resort; pizza $22, BBQ mains $28-36; ☺bar 11am-9pm, BBQ 6-9pm) The mainstay and most popular restaurant of the resort, this place does OK pizza in the Thirsty Dingo and steaks, barramundi fillets, Wagyu burger or kangaroo sirloin on the barbecue by night; the latter all come with jacket potato and a salad bar.

ℹ Getting There & Away

Kings Canyon is a long way from anywhere. Unless you're self-driving, you'll need to come on a tour. If you are driving, there are three routes to Kings Canyon, but no public transport.

➡ Leave the Stuart Hwy at Erldunda, 199km south of Alice Springs, take the sealed Lasseter Hwy for 108km and then 169km along the Luritja Rd. The latter is the longest route from Alice Springs but easily the most popular and comfortable.

➡ Drive the 4WD-only Mereenie Loop or Red Centre Way from Hermannsburg. Note that you'll need a permit for this route. They're available from Glen Helen Resort (p865), Kings Canyon Resort and Alice Springs Visitor Information Centre (p861).

➡ Along the unsealed Ernest Giles Rd, which heads west off the Stuart Hwy 140km south of Alice Springs. Note that some car-rental companies prohibit you from taking this route, even in a 4WD. If you ignore their advice, you won't be covered by the vehicle's insurance.

ULURU-KATA TJUTA NATIONAL PARK

Nothing can really prepare you for the immensity, grandeur, changing colour and stillness of 'the Rock'. It really is a sight that will sear itself on to your mind. The World Heritage–listed icon has attained the status of a pilgrimage.

Uluru, the equally impressive Kata Tjuta, formerly known as the Olgas, and the surrounding area are of deep cultural significance to the traditional owners, the Pitjantjatjara and Yankunytjatjara Aboriginal peoples (who refer to themselves as Anangu). The Anangu own **Uluru-Kata Tjuta**

Uluru

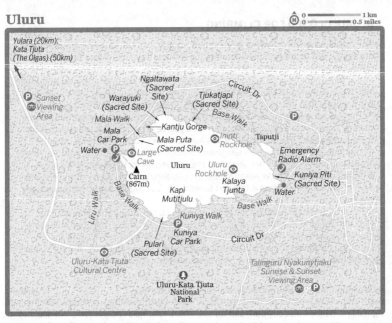

Yulara (20km);
Kata Tjuta
(The Olgas) (50km)

0 ——— 1 km
0 ——— 0.5 miles

Sunset Viewing Area

Ngaltawata (Sacred Site)

Warayuki (Sacred Site)

Tjukatjapi (Sacred Site)

Circuit Dr

Mala Walk

Base Walk

Mala Car Park

Kantju Gorge

Water

Mala Puta (Sacred Site)

Ininti Rockhole

Taputji

Large Cave

Uluru

Uluru Rockhole

Emergency Radio Alarm

Cairn (867m)

Kuniya Piti (Sacred Site)

Kalaya Tjunta

Kapi Mutitjulu

Water

Liru Walk

Base Walk

Base Walk

Kuniya Walk

Kuniya Car Park

Circuit Dr

Pulari (Sacred Site)

Uluru-Kata Tjuta Cultural Centre

Talinguru Nyakunytjaku Sunrise & Sunset Viewing Area

Uluru-Kata Tjuta National Park

National Park (https://parksaustralia.gov.au/uluru; adult/child/family 3-day passes $25/12.50/65; ☉ sunrise-sunset), which is leased to Parks Australia and jointly administered.

There's plenty to see and do. But standing and gazing in awe remains the most natural response to being here.

⊙ Sights

Uluru   LANDMARK
(Ayers Rock; https://parksaustralia.gov.au/uluru; Uluru-Kata Tjuta National Park) Uluru is a beautiful, charismatic place. Its dimensions are one thing: Uluru is 3.6km long and rises 348m from the surrounding sands (867m above sea level). If that's not sufficiently impressive, remember this: two-thirds of the rock lies beneath the sand. This is a monolith textured with layers of profound spirituality and timeless beauty, the epitome of desert stillness and, in the plays of light and shadow that dance across its surface, one of the richest shows in nature.

Sacred sites are located around the base of Uluru; entry to and knowledge of the particular significance of these areas is restricted by Anangu law. The landscape of Uluru changes dramatically with the shifting light and seasons. In the afternoon, Uluru appears as an ochre-brown colour, scored

and pitted by dark shadows. As the sun sets, it illuminates the rock in burnished orange, then a series of deeper and darker reds before it fades into charcoal. A performance in reverse, with marginally fewer spectators, is given at dawn.

★**Uluru-Kata Tjuta**
Cultural Centre   CULTURAL CENTRE
(☏ 08-8956 1128; www.parksaustralia.gov.au/uluru; ☉ 7am-6pm) Uluru-Kata Tjuta Cultural Centre, just 1km from the Rock, is a fabulous

---

SUNSET & SUNRISE VIEWING AREAS

About halfway between Yulara and Uluru, the sunset viewing area has plenty of car and coach parking for that familiar postcard view. The **Talinguru Nyakunytjaku sunrise-viewing area** is perched on a sand dune and captures both Uluru and Kata Tjuta in all their glory. It also has two great interpretive walks (1.5km) about women's and men's business. There's a shaded viewing area, toilets and a place to picnic. There is also the **sand-dune viewpoint** for a panoramic view of Kata Tjuta.

ULURU: CLOSED FOR CLIMBING

Many visitors consider climbing Uluru to be a highlight of a trip to the Centre, even a rite of passage. But for the traditional owners, the Anangu, Uluru has always been a sacred place. The path up the side is part of the route taken by the Mala ancestors on their arrival at Uluru and has great spiritual significance – and it is not to be trampled by human feet. When you arrive at Uluru you'll see a sign from the Anangu saying 'We don't climb', and a request that you don't climb either. From 26 October 2019 you won't be able to.

The Anangu are the custodians of Uluru and they take responsibility for the safety of visitors. Any injuries or deaths that occur are a source of distress and sadness to them. For similar reasons of public safety, Parks Australia has always preferred that people didn't climb, even while the walk remained open. It's a very steep ascent, not to be taken lightly, and each year there are several air rescues, mostly for people suffering heart attacks. Furthermore, Parks Australia had to constantly monitor the climb and close it on days where the temperature is forecast to reach 36°C or over, or when strong winds are expected.

For decades it was held that the climb would be closed once the number of those climbing dipped below 20% of all visitors to the park. That finally happened and a commitment was made in October 2017 to close the climb for good in 2019. Until then, it remains a personal decision and a question of respect. Before deciding, visit the cultural centre (p873) and perhaps take an Anangu guided tour (p875).

introduction to your Uluru experience. Displays and exhibits focus on tjukurpa (Aboriginal law, religion and custom), and on the natural and human history of the park. Park rangers can supply the informative *Visitor Guide,* leaflets and walking notes, as well as other park information.

Walkatjara Art Centre
GALLERY

(☑ 08-8956 2537; www.walkatjara.com; ⊙ 9am-4.30pm) A working art centre owned by the local Mutitjulu community, it has an extensive selection of paintings on display (and for sale), and most days you can watch the artists at work.

Kata Tjuta

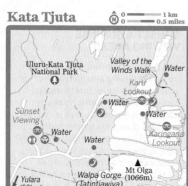

Kata Tjuta
LANDMARK

(The Olgas; www.nt.gov.au/leisure/parks-reserves; Uluru-Kata Tjuta National Park) No journey to Uluru-Kata Tjuta National Park is complete without a visit to Kata Tjuta, a striking group of domed rocks huddled together about 35km west of Uluru. There are 36 boulders shoulder to shoulder, forming deep valleys and steep-sided gorges. Many visitors find them just as captivating as their prominent neighbour.

The tallest rock, Mt Olga (546m; 1066m above sea level) is approximately 200m higher than Uluru. Kata Tjuta means 'many heads' and is of great tjukurpa significance, particularly for men, so stick to the tracks.

There's a picnic and sunset-viewing area with toilet facilities just off the access road a few kilometres west of the base of Kata Tjuta. Like Uluru, Kata Tjuta is at its glorious, blood-red best at sunset.

🏃 Activities

Cycling is a terrific way to get around Uluru. It takes around 2½ hours (around 15km, following Liru and Uluru Base walks) to circumnavigate Uluru from the Uluru-Kata Tjuta Cultural Centre.

Outback Cycling (☑ 0437 917 018, 08-8952 1541; www.outbackcycling.com; Uluru-Kata Tjuta Cultural Centre; adult/child bike for 3hrs $50/35, tag-a-longs $25, toddler seats $20; ⊙ 7am-4pm, last hire at 1pm) This cycle-hire place operates out of the Uluru-Kata Tjuta Cultural Centre.

Book in advance online or at the Tour & Information Centre (p879) in Yulara.

🖝 Tours

Desert Awakenings 4WD Tour   TOURS
(☑ 1300 134 044; www.ayersrockresort.com.au; adult/child from $179/139) Predawn tranquillity and a guided tour at the base of Uluru. Enjoy a traditional bushman's breakfast including billy tea and damper.

Wira   WALKING
(☑ 08-8956 1128; Uluru-Kata Tjuta Cultural Centre; ⊙ 4.30-6pm Mon, Wed & Fri) **FREE** This free tour is a lovely way to spend an afternoon, walking through the bush surrounding the cultural centre with a local Anangu guide who'll teach you all about bush plants. You'll never look at the desert in the same way again.

Uluru Aboriginal Tours   CULTURAL TOUR
(www.facebook.com/Uluru-Aboriginal-Tours-248457278623328/; guided tours from $99)

Owned and operated by Anangu from the Mutitjulu community, this company offers a range of trips to give you an insight into the significance of Uluru through the eyes of the traditional owners. Tours operate and depart from the cultural centre (p873) where you can make the booking, as well as from Yulara Ayers Rock Resort, through **AAT Kings** (☑ 1300 228 546, 08-8956 2171; www.aatkings.com; Tour & Information Centre, Town Sq, Yulara), and from Alice Springs.

Seit Outback Australia   BUS
(☑ 08-8956 3156; www.seitoutbackaustralia.com.au) This small-group tour operator has dozens of Uluru and Kata Tjuta tours, including sunset tours around Uluru and sunrise tours at Kata Tjuta. Food is increasingly a part of what they offer as well.

Uluru Camel Tours   OUTDOORS
(☑ 08-8956 3333; www.ulurucameltours.com.au; 90/150min camel tours $80/132, farm visits free; ⊙ farm 9am-3pm May-Oct, to 1pm Nov-Apr) View

---

HIKING ULURU & KATA-TJUTA

Uluru Walks

Uluru Base Walk This track (10.6km, three to four hours, wheelchair-accessible in dry weather) circumnavigates the rock, passing caves, paintings, sandstone folds and geological abrasions along the way. Get started early as the northern stretches in particular have little shade. Other available walks break this track into segments.

Mala Walk From the Mala car park (2km return, one hour), interpretive signs explain the tjukurpa of the Mala (hare-wallaby people), which is significant to the Anangu. There are also fine examples of rock art. A free, 1½-hour ranger-guided walk runs along this route every morning, with explanations on Indigenous rock art and other aspects of Uluru.

Liru Walk Links the cultural centre with the start of the Mala Walk and winds through strands of mulga before opening up near Uluru (4km return, 1½ hours). Watch for wildflowers after rain.

Kuniya Walk A short walk (1km return, 45 minutes) from the car park on the southern side of Uluru leads to the most permanent waterhole, Mutitjulu, home of the ancestral water snake. Great birdwatching and some excellent rock art are highlights of this walk.

Kata-Tjuta Walks

Valley of the Winds Walk The 7.4km Valley of the Winds loop (four hours, partially wheelchair-accessible) is one of the most challenging and rewarding bushwalks in the park. It winds through the gorges giving excellent views of Kata Tjuta's surreal domes and traversing varied terrain. It's not particularly arduous, but wear sturdy shoes and take plenty of water. This is a culturally sensitive area so take note of info about photos.

Starting this walk at first light often rewards you with solitude, enabling you to appreciate the sounds of the wind and bird calls carried up the valley. When the weather is forecast to reach 36°C, trail access is closed, usually by 11am.

Walpa Gorge Walk The short signposted track at Kata Tjuta, beneath towering rock walls into pretty Walpa Gorge (2.6km return, 45 minutes,) is especially beautiful in the afternoon, when sunlight floods the gorge. Watch for rock wallabies in the early morning or late afternoon.

Uluru and Kata Tjuta from a distance atop a camel (1½ hours) or take the popular Camel to Sunrise and Sunset tours (2½ hours). You can visit the farm for free.

Uluru Motorcycle Tours TOURS
(☑08-8956 2019; www.ulurucycles.com; rides $139-439) Approach Uluru on a Harley – now that's the way to arrive! Check the website for the many possible tours on offer.

Scenic Flights

Ayers Rock Helicopters SCENIC FLIGHTS
(☑08-8956 2077; www.flyuluru.com.au; 15/30/36min scenic flights per person $150/285/310) One of the most memorable ways to see Uluru; you'll need the 30-minute flight to also take in Kata Tjuta. There's also a 120-minute flight ($830 per person) that visits Uluru, Kata Tjuta and even lands on the summit of Mt Connor!

Professional Helicopter Services SCENIC FLIGHTS
(PHS; ☑08-8956 2003; www.phs.com.au; 15/30/36/120min scenic flights per person $150/245/320/950) Fabulous aerial views. The 120-minute option is part of a 4½-hour package that takes in Uluru, Kata Tjuta and Kings Canyon, including two hours' flying time.

✖ Eating

★ Sounds of Silence AUSTRALIAN $$$
(☑08-8957 7448; www.ayersrockresort.com.au/sounds-of-silence; adult/child $210/105) Waiters serve champagne and canapés on a desert dune with stunning sunset views of Uluru and Kata Tjuta. Then it's a buffet dinner (with emu, croc and roo) beneath the southern sky, which, after dinner, is dissected and explained with the help of a telescope.

Tali Wiru AUSTRALIAN $$$
(☑02-8296 8010; www.ayersrockresort.com.au/tali-wiru; per person $360; ☺Apr–mid-Oct) One way to combine sophistication with the ruggedness of the outback landscape is the Tali Wiru outdoor dining experience. Organised between April and mid-October, it involves walking to a dune-top 'restaurant' to eat a four-course meal and drink as the sun sets over timeless Uluru. An Indigenous storyteller entertains guests. Make your booking online or at the Tour & Information Centre (p879) in Yulara.

The price includes a Field of Light pass and transfer to/from your hotel.

🛍 Shopping

The cultural centre encompasses the craft outlet Maruku Arts (p877), owned by about 20 Anangu communities from across central Australia (including the local Mutitjulu community) and selling hand-crafted wooden carvings, bowls and boomerangs.

Ininti Cafe & Souvenirs (☑08-8956 2214; ☺7am-5pm) sells souvenirs such as T-shirts, ceramics, hats and CDs plus a variety of books on Uluru, Aboriginal culture, bush foods and the flora and fauna of the area. The attached cafe serves ice cream, pies and light meals.

ℹ Information

The park is open from half an hour before sunrise to sunset daily (varying slightly between months; check the website for exact times). Entry permits are valid for three days (but can be extended for an extra two days for no extra cost) and are available at the drive-through entry station on the road from Yulara or online.

ℹ Getting There & Away

➤ Yulara is the gateway to the park and has an airport with flights to/from Melbourne, Sydney and Cairns. There are also buses and tours from Alice Springs.

➤ If you're driving, the sealed route from Alice Springs (447km) is via the Stuart and then Lasseter Hwys.

Yulara

POP 1100

Yulara is the service village and necessary base for exploring Uluru-Kata Tjuta National Park, and has effectively turned one of the world's least hospitable regions into a comfortable place to stay with a full range of amenities. It lies just outside the national park, 20km from Uluru and 53km from Kata Tjuta.

◉ Sights & Activities

★ Field of Light GALLERY
(☑1300 134 044; https://northernterritory.com; Napala Rd; adult/child from $42/30) This extraordinary installation by artist Bruce Munro will be open until at least 31 December 2020. It consists of over 50,000 poppylike stems topped with lit, frosted glass, with Uluru as a backdrop. Appropriately it's known as 'Tili Wiru Tjuta Nyakutjaku' by locals, which means 'looking at lots of beautiful lights'. There are numerous ways to experience it:

at sunset or sunrise, on a camel ride or with dinner. Advance bookings essential.

Wintjiri Arts & Museum
GALLERY

(☑08-8957 7377; Yulara Dr; ☺8.30am-5pm) A fascinating overview of local natural and cultural history, with plenty of artworks, an artist-in-residence and an excellent small shop. It's up the steps, just north of reception for the Desert Gardens Hotel.

Uluru Outback Sky Journey
STARGAZING

(☑08-8956 2563; Town Sq; adult/child $50/free) Takes an informative one-hour look at the startlingly clear outback night sky with a telescope and an astronomer. Tours start at the Yulara Town Sq, 30 minutes after sunset.

🛶 Courses & Tours

★ Dot Painting Workshop
ARTS & CRAFTS

(☑0499 829 635; www.maruku.com.au; adult/child/family $72/36/198; ☺11.30am & 2pm Apr-Sep, 10.30am & 1.30pm Oct-Mar) This brilliant workshop enables you to learn from a local Anangu artist, and involves a mix of story-telling, lessons about Indigenous symbols and crafts, and the chance to create your own artwork. Although operated by **Maruku Arts** (☑08-8956 2558; www.maruku.com.au; ☺8.30am-5.30pm), it takes place at Yulara Town Sq. Make bookings at the Tour & Information Centre (p879).

Bush Food Experience
TOURS

(Wintjiri Arts & Museum; ☺1pm) **FREE** Learn about native bush foods with a cooking demonstration thrown in.

Didgeridoo Workshop
TOURS

(Town Sq; ☺11am Mon, Wed & Fri, 4pm Sat & Sun) **FREE** These half-hour workshops include a demonstration from an expert and a brief opportunity to try it for yourself.

✨ Festivals & Events

★ Tjungu Festival
CULTURAL

(www.ayersrockresort.com.au/tjungu; ☺late Apr) This festival runs over four days in late April, hosted by Ayers Rock Resort and celebrating Indigenous culture. Food, art, film and music, plus plenty to keep the kids entertained. It centres on the lawn area adjacent to the Town Sq.

Uluru Camel Cup
SPORTS

(www.ayersrockresort.com.au/events; ☺late May) Over two days in May, Yulara hosts camel racing against a desert backdrop.

🛏 Sleeping

Ayers Rock Resort Campground
CAMPGROUND $

(☑08-8957 7001; www.ayersrockresort.com.au/arrcamp; off Yulara Dr; unpowered/powered sites $43/53, cabins $184; ❋@☀) A saviour for the budget conscious, this sprawling camp ground is set among native gardens. There are good facilities including a kiosk, free BBQs, a camp kitchen and a pool. During peak season it's very busy and the inevitable predawn convoy heading for Uluru can provide an unwanted wake-up call.

Outback Pioneer Hotel & Lodge
HOSTEL $$

(☑1300 134 044; www.ayersrockresort.com.au; Yulara Dr; dm/d from $38/280; ❋@☎☀) With a lively bar, barbecue restaurant and musical entertainment, this is the budget choice for noncampers. The cheapest options are the 20-bed YHA unisex dorms and squashy four-bed budget cabins with fridge, TV and shared bathroom. There are also more spacious motel-style rooms that sleep up to four people, and for which prices drop considerably the longer you stay.

Children under 12 stay free.

★ Desert Gardens Hotel
HOTEL $$$

(☑1300 134 044; www.ayersrockresort.com.au; Yulara Dr; r from $360; ❋☎☀) One of Yulara's original hotels, four-and-a-half-star Desert Gardens has supremely comfortable rooms with a lovely Scandinavian minimalist look. Some have partial or distant Uluru views (for which you pay extra). Prices drop considerably depending on the number of nights you stay.

Lost Camel
BOUTIQUE HOTEL $$$

(☑02-8296 8010; www.ayersrockresort.com.au; off Town Sq; r $250-450; ℗❋☎☀) Billing itself as Yulara's boutique hotel option, the Lost Camel reopened in 2018 after extensive works. The contemporary rooms with steely-blue and burnt-orange decor are offset by the blinding white walls. The location is among the best in Yulara – everything's close but noise is never an issue.

Sails in the Desert
HOTEL $$$

(☑1300 134 044; www.ayersrockresort.com.au/sails; Yulara Dr; superior d from $340; ❋@☎☀) The rooms seem overpriced at the resort's flagship hotel, but they're still the most upmarket choice in Yulara. There's a lovely pool and surrounding lawn shaded by sails

Yulara (Ayers Rock Resort)

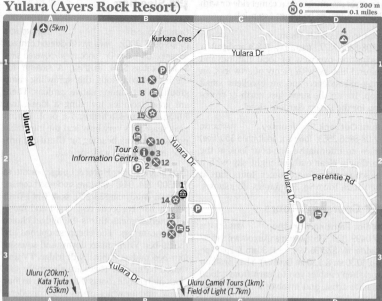

DARWIN & THE NORTHERN TERRITORY YULARA

Yulara (Ayers Rock Resort)

◎ Sights
1 Wintjiri Arts & Museum B2

✪ Activities, Courses & Tours
2 AAT Kings..B2
  Ayers Rock Helicopters.................. (see 2)
  Bush Food Experience...................... (see 1)
  Desert Awakenings 4WD Tour ...... (see 2)
3 Didgeridoo Workshop.............................B2
  Dot Painting Workshop .... (see 2)
  Professional Helicopter
    Services.. (see 2)
  Seit Outback Australia.................... (see 2)
  Uluru Motorcycle Tours .... (see 2)
  Uluru Outback Sky Journey........... (see 2)

🛏 Sleeping
4 Ayers Rock Resort Campground..........D1
5 Desert Gardens Hotel............................B3
6 Lost Camel...B2
7 Outback Pioneer Hotel & Lodge............D3
8 Sails in the Desert B1

✗ Eating
9 Arngulli Grill & Restaurant.................... B3
  Bough House..................................(see 7)
10 Geckos Cafe B2
11 Ilkari Restaurant B1
12 Kulata Academy Cafe............................B2
13 Mangata Bistro & Bar............................B3
  Outback Pioneer Barbecue...........(see 7)

🍷 Drinking & Nightlife
  Pioneer Barbecue Bar....................(see 7)

✪ Entertainment
14 Mani-Mani Indigenous Cultural
    Theatre.. B2
15 Red Desert Reptiles...............................B2

🛍 Shopping
  Mulgara Gallery...............................(see 8)
  Newsagency .... (see 12)

and trees. There are also tennis courts, several restaurants, a health spa and a piano bar. The best rooms have balcony views of Uluru – request one when you make a booking.

✗ Eating

Kulata Academy Cafe   CAFE $

(Town Sq; breakfast $4.80-8, sandwiches, pies & light meals $10.50; ☺ 7.30am-5pm) Run by trainees of Uluru's Indigenous training academy,

Kulata is a good place to pick up a coffee in the morning and a light lunch (including pies) later in the day.

Bough House
AUSTRALIAN **$$**

(Outback Pioneer Hotel & Lodge; 3-course meals $38-49; ⊘6.30-9.30pm; 🖼) This family-friendly, country-style place overlooks the pool at the Outback Pioneer (p877). Intimate candlelit dining is strangely set in a barn-like dining room. Bough House specialises in native ingredients such as lemon myrtle, Kakadu plums and bush tomatoes. The entree and dessert buffets are free with your main course, which makes it an excellent deal.

Mangata Bistro & Bar
BISTRO **$$**

(Desert Gardens Hotel; mains $23-47; ⊘noon-9pm) The lobby bar in the Desert Gardens Hotel (p877) has a cafe-bistro feel to it, with small and big plates to share, as well as burgers and barista coffee. The Mangata Charcuterie Plate is a lovely dish of cured meats, mustards and cheeses upon which to graze.

Outback Pioneer Barbecue
BARBECUE **$$**

(Outback Pioneer Hotel & Lodge; burgers/meat/salad bar $20/35/20; ⊘6-9pm) For a fun, casual night out, this lively tavern is the popular choice for everyone from backpackers to grey nomads. Choose between kangaroo skewers, prawns, veggie burgers, steaks and emu sausages, and grill them yourself at the communal BBQs. The deal includes a salad bar.

Geckos Cafe
MEDITERRANEAN **$$**

(Town Sq; mains $19-29; ⊘noon-2.30pm & 6.30-9pm) For great value, a warm atmosphere and tasty food, head to this buzzing licensed cafe. The wood-fired pizzas and kangaroo burgers go well with a carafe of sangria, and the courtyard tables are a great place to enjoy the desert night air. There are several veggie and gluten-free options, plus meals can be made to take away.

★ Arngulli Grill & Restaurant
AUSTRALIAN **$$$**

(✆08-8957 7888; Desert Gardens Hotel; mains $30-56; ⊘6-9pm) Celebrated by many as Yulara's best restaurant, Arngulli serves up fabulous, locally sourced steaks, as well as kangaroo fillet and wild mushroom risotto. It's an elegant place where you might want to dress nicely.

Ilkari Restaurant
BUFFET **$$$**

(✆02-8296 8010; Sails in the Desert; buffet $75; ⊘6-9pm; 🖼) This three-course buffet at Sails in the Desert (p877) will satisfy the hungriest of Uluru sightseers. It includes seafood, sashimi, Asian dishes, roasts and a chocolate fountain finale. Kids eat free.

🍷 Drinking & Nightlife

Pioneer Barbecue Bar
PUB

(Outback Pioneer Hotel & Lodge; ⊘10am-midnight) This rowdy bar is lined with long benches, providing plenty of opportunity to meet other travellers. It has pool tables, live music nightly (usually with a touch of twang) and a surprisingly sophisticated beer selection.

☆ Entertainment

Red Desert Reptiles
LIVE PERFORMANCE

(adult/child $25/15; ⊘10am & 2pm Mon-Sat) In the concrete amphitheatre a couple of hundred metres north of the Yulara Town Sq, Danny, the local snake catcher, runs this reptile show that introduces you to Bruce the blue-tongue lizard as well as bearded dragons and various local snakes. You can also get the obligatory photo of you with a snake draped around your neck.

Buy tickets at the gate, your hotel or the Tour & Information Centre.

Mani-Mani Indigenous Cultural Theatre
THEATRE

(Arkani Theatre; ⊘11am & 2pm Wed-Sat) **FREE** Contemporary Indigenous storytelling using sound, light and 3D visuals to tell the story of 'The Eagle, the Cockatoo & the Crow'. It's a fascinating take on Indigenous stories and well worth watching. Shows are free; book ahead through your hotel or the Tour & Information Centre at least 24 hours in advance.

🛍 Shopping

Newsagency
BOOKS

(Town Sq; ⊘8.30am-8pm) Excellent newsagents with magazines, a wide range of books with outback Australian themes and good maps.

Mulgara Gallery
ARTS & CRAFTS

(✆08-8957 7439; Sails in the Desert Hotel; ⊘8.30am-5pm) A wide range of quality, handmade Australian arts and crafts are displayed here, such as textiles, paintings and crafty Indigenous knick-knacks.

ℹ Information

The useful *Manta* flyer is available at hotel desks. Most of the village's facilities are scattered around Yulara Town Sq.

Tour & Information Centre (☎ 08-8957 7324; Resort Shopping Centre; ⊙ 8am-7pm) Most tour operators and car-hire firms have desks at this centre.

ℹ Getting There & Away

AIR

Connellan Airport (Ayers Rock Airport; ☎ 08-8956 2266; Coote Rd) About 4km north of Yulara.

Jetstar (☎ 13 15 38; www.jetstar.com) Yulara to/from Melbourne and Sydney.

Qantas (☎ 13 13 13; www.qantas.com.au) Connects Yulara with Cairns, Sydney and Melbourne.

Virgin Australia (☎ 13 67 89; www.virginaustralia.com) Flies Yulara–Sydney with onward connections.

BUS

There is no public bus transport to/from Yulara. Emu Run (p857) runs cheap daily connections between Alice Springs and Yulara (one way adult/child $135/80).

CAR & MOTORCYCLE

The main route from Alice to Yulara is sealed all the way, with regular food and petrol stops. It's 200km from Alice to Erldunda on the Stuart Hwy, where you turn west for the 245km journey along the Lasseter Hwy. The journey takes four to five hours.

There's a longer, 4WD-only route that goes via Hermannsburg and Kings Canyon. For this you'll need a permit ($5 to $5.50, depending on where you get it) from Alice Springs Visitor Information Centre (p861), Glen Helen Resort (p865) or Kings Canyon Resort (p872).

Renting a car in Alice Springs to go to Uluru and back is an excellent way to see a little of the country en route, if you have the time.

There's an expensive **Shell Petrol Station** (Yulara Drive; ⊙ 7am-9pm) along Yulara Dr, between the Campground and the Outback Pioneer Hotel & Lodge.

ℹ Getting Around

A free shuttle bus meets all flights (pick-up is 90 minutes before your flight when leaving) and drops off at all accommodation points around the resort. Another free shuttle bus loops through the resort – stopping at all accommodation points and the shopping centre – every 20 minutes from 10.30am to 6pm and from 6.30pm to 12.30am daily.

Uluru Hop-On Hop-Off (☎ 08-8956 2019; www.uluruexpress.com.au; adult 1-/2-day passes $120/160, child $40/60, Uluru return adult/child $49/15, Kata Tjuta $95/40) falls somewhere between a shuttle-bus service and an organised tour. It provides return transport from the resort to Uluru and Kata Tjuta with one- to three-day passes also available. Check the website for timetables.

Perth & Western Australia

🎵 08 / POP 2.6 MILLION

Includes ➡

Perth.............884
Rottnest Island......913
Margaret River
Region.............933
Kalbarri..........969
Exmouth..........982
Karijini
National Park.......993
Broome...........995
Kununurra........1014
Kalgoorlie-Boulder...1017

Best Places to Eat

➡ Pinchos (p901)

➡ Yarri (p939)

➡ Karijini Eco Retreat Restaurant (p995)

➡ Aarli (p1002)

➡ Loose Goose (p964)

Best Places to Stay

➡ Como The Treasury (p895)

➡ Fremantle Apartment (p897)

➡ McAlpine House (p1002)

➡ Goombaragin Eco Retreat (p1005)

➡ Beaches of Broome (p1002)

Why Go?

If the vast expanse of Western Australia (WA) was a separate nation, it would be the world's 10th-largest (bigger than Algeria, smaller than Kazakhstan). Most of WA's population clings to the coast, yet you can wander along a beach here without seeing another footprint, or be one of a few scattered campers stargazing in a national park.

There's something unfettered and alive about this place – a frontier spirit that's free from the baggage of east-coast concerns. This is also an ancient land and its Aboriginal cultures are more visibly present than in much of the rest of Australia.

The state's fertile southwest is a playground of white-sand coves, rampant wildflowers and lush forests abuzz with wildlife. Up north in the big-sky, red-dirt Pilbara and Kimberley you'll encounter gorgeous gorges and mesmerising waterfalls – and no one else for miles and miles. In between is 12,500km of truly spectacular coastline.

When to Go
Perth

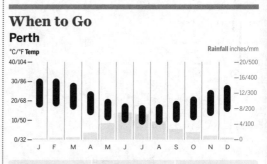

Feb–Apr Beaches empty as kids go back to school, but it's still warm. The wine harvest approaches.

Jun–Aug Peak season up north, with dry days and low humidity.

Sep–Nov WA's wildflowers bloom and humpback whales cavort offshore.

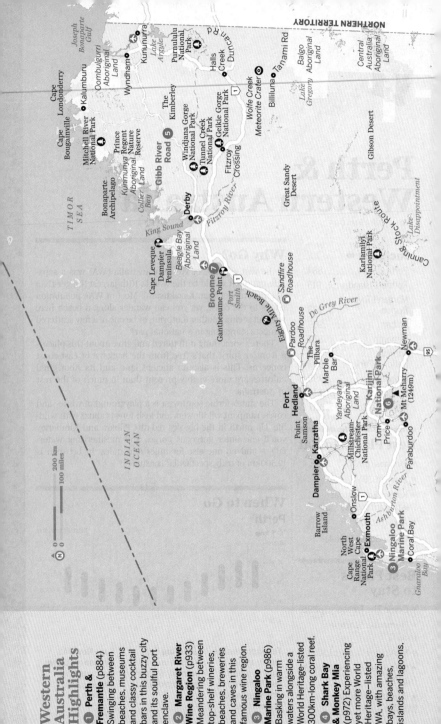

Western Australia Highlights

❶ Perth & Fremantle (p884)
Swinging between beaches, museums and classy cocktail bars in this buzzy city and its soulful port enclave.

❷ Margaret River Wine Region (p933)
Meandering between top-shelf wineries, beaches, breweries and caves in this famous wine region.

❸ Ningaloo Marine Park (p986)
Basking in warm waters alongside a World Heritage-listed 300km-long coral reef.

❹ Shark Bay & Monkey Mia (p972)
Experiencing yet more World Heritage-listed WA, with amazing bays, beaches, islands and lagoons,

---

Joseph Bonaparte Gulf

Cape Londonderry

Cape Bougainville

Kununurra

Lake Argyle

Wyndham

Oombulgurri Aboriginal Land

Kalumburu

Mitchell River National Park

Prince Regent Nature Reserve

Kununurra Aboriginal Land

Halls Creek

Purnululu National Park

Duncan Rd

Tanami Rd

Balgo Aboriginal Land

Central Australia Aboriginal Land

The Kimberley

Gibb River Road ❺

Windjana Gorge National Park

Tunnel Creek National Park

Geikie Gorge National Park

Fitzroy Crossing

Wolfe Creek Meteorite Crater

Billiluna

Lake Gregory

Bonaparte Archipelago

Collier Land

Kunmunya Aboriginal Land

Beagle Bay

King Sound

Fitzroy River

Derby

Great Sandy Desert

Gibson Desert

TIMOR SEA

Cape Leveque

Dampier Peninsula

Beagle Bay Aboriginal Land

Port Smith

Broome ❼

Gantheaume Point

Eighty Mile Beach

Sandfire Roadhouse

Karlamilyi National Park

Canning Stock Route

Lake Disappointment

INDIAN OCEAN

Pardoo Roadhouse

De Grey River

Port Hedland

Point Samson

The Pilbara

Marble Bar

Yandeyarra Aboriginal Land

Newman

95

Karratha

Dampier

Barrow Island

Onslow

Millstream-Chichester National Park

Karijini National Park

Tom Price

Paraburdoo

Mt Meharry (1249m)

❻

North West Cape

Exmouth

Cape Range National Park

Coral Bay

Ningaloo Marine Park ❸

Gnaraloo Bay

Ashburton River

N

0   200 km
0   100 miles

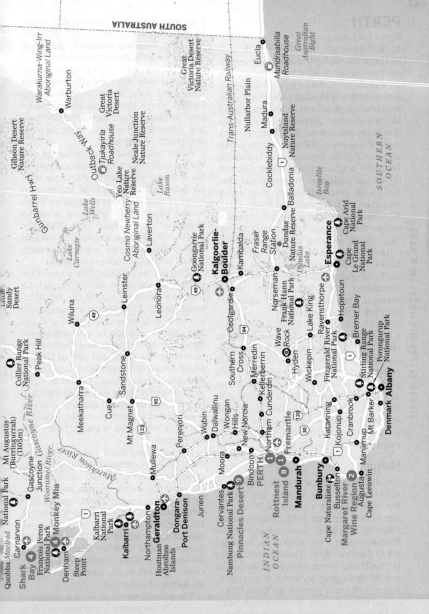

and astonishing
biodiversity.

5 Gibb River Road
(p1008) Prepping your
4WD and adventuring
down this remote
outback track through
one of Australia's
wildest regions.

**6 Karijini National
Park** (p993) Scaling
WA's highest peaks
in the Pilbara's
wildlife- and plant-rich
heartland.

7 Broome (p995)
Enjoying some luxe
downtime in WA's
premier resort town.

8 Rottnest Island
(p913) Grappling to
resolve a dark history
with contemporary
pleasures on this
fascinating island off
Perth.

9 Pinnacles Desert
(p931) Pretending
you're on a sci-fi
film set as you roam
around these bizarre
limestone formations
in the Turquoise Coast
dune country.

PERTH

📍 08 / POP 2.14 MILLION

In Wadjuk country, way out west in the Indian Ocean breeze, Perth regularly attracts that most easy-going of adjectives – 'liveable'. Under a near-permanent canopy of blue sky, life here unfolds at a pleasing pace. Throw in superb beaches, global eats and booming small-bar and street-art scenes, and Perth seems downright progressive. Free from the pressures of congestion, pollution and population afflicting Sydney, Brisbane and Melbourne, Perth and neighbouring port town Fremantle are uncomplicated, unfettered and alive. Yes, it's the most isolated city of its size on the planet, but this remoteness fosters an outward-looking world view. Instead of heading east for their holidays, locals – who suffer the ugly, geologic-sounding moniker of 'Perthites' – travel to Bali, the Maldives, Singapore, Sri Lanka... Currency-exchange reports include the Indian rupee, while the Perth-to-London 'Dreamliner' direct flight delivers Europe's virtues in a tick under 17 hours. Forget about isolation: Perth is going places.

On Perth's southern fringe, Fremantle is a boho harbour town with sea-salty soul to burn. Like Valparaiso in Chile or Littleton in New Zealand, old-town 'Freo' is a tight nest of streets with an atmospherically faded cache of Victorian and Edwardian buildings. At the same time, Fremantle thrums with live music, craft-beer bars, boutique hotels, left-field bookshops, Indian Ocean seafood shacks, buskers and beaches – it's a fabulous place to spend a few days.

History

The discovery of ancient stone implements near the Swan River suggests that Mooro, the site on which the city of Perth now stands, has been occupied for around 40,000 years. In Aboriginal Dreaming stories, the Wadjuk people, a subgroup of the Noongar, tell of the Swan River (Derbal Yaragan) and the landforms surrounding being shaped by two Wargal (giant serpent-like creatures), which lived under present-day Kings Park.

Fast-forward many thousands of years: in December 1696 three ships in the Dutch fleet commanded by Willem de Vlamingh anchored off Rottnest Island. On 5 January 1697 a well-armed party landed near present-day Cottesloe Beach. They tried to make contact with the local people to ask about survivors of the *Ridderschap van Holland*, lost in 1694, but were unsuccessful, so they sailed north.

It was de Vlamingh who bestowed the name Swan on the river.

Modern Perth was founded in 1829 when Captain James Stirling established the Swan River Colony, and (rather obsequiously) named the main settlement after the Scottish home town of the British Secretary of State for the Colonies. The original settlers paid for their own passage and that of their servants, and received 200 acres for every labourer they brought with them.

At the time, Mooro was the terrain of a Wadjuk leader called Yellagonga and his people. Relations were friendly at first, the Wadjuk believing the British to be the returned spirits of their dead, but competition for resources led to conflict. Yellagonga moved his camp first to Lake Monger, but by the time he died in 1843 his people had been dispossessed of all of their lands and were forced to camp around swamps and lakes to the north.

Midgegooroo, an Elder from south of the Swan River, along with his son Yagan, led a resistance campaign against the British invasion. In 1833 Midgegooroo was caught and executed by firing squad, while Yagan was shot a few months later by some teenage settlers whom he had befriended. Yagan's head was removed, smoked and sent to London, where it was publicly displayed as an anthropological curiosity. Yagan's head was buried in an unmarked grave in Liverpool in 1964, before being exhumed in 1993 and eventually repatriated to Australia and finally laid to rest in the Swan Valley in 2010, 177 years after his murder.

Life for the new arrivals was much harder than they had expected. The early settlement grew very slowly until 1850, when convicts alleviated the labour shortage and boosted the population. Convicts constructed the city's substantial buildings, including Government House and the Town Hall. Yet Perth's development lagged behind that of the cities in the eastern colonies until the discovery of gold inland in the 1890s. Perth's population increased by 400% within a decade and a building bonanza commenced.

The mineral wealth of WA has continued to drive Perth's growth. In the 1980s and '90s, though, the city's clean-cut, nouveau-riche image was tainted by a series of financial and political scandals.

WA's 21st-century mining boom has cooled in recent years, but there are still plenty of dollars awash in the state's economy, and Perth continues to blossom like WA's wildflowers in spring. Major civic works include a new football stadium, and visitors to Perth can witness ongoing work on two major reboots of the central city's urban landscape.

The City Link project will transform the area between Northbridge and the CBD, linking the two neighbourhoods through public spaces and new buildings. Part of this project is Yagan Sq, a new civic space that opened in 2018 – named after Yagan the Wadjuk warrior. At the opposite end of the CBD, the Elizabeth Quay development is adding parks and retail and hospitality precincts to the riverfront land between Barrack and William Sts. Having turned its back on the river for many decades, central Perth will once again link with the silvery waters of the Swan.

Too often excluded from Perth's race to riches have been the Noongar people. In 2006 the Perth Federal Court recognised native title over the city of Perth and its surrounds, but this finding was appealed by the WA and Commonwealth governments. In December 2009 an agreement was signed in WA's parliament, setting out a time frame for negotiating settlement of native-title claims across the southwest. In mid-2015, a $1.3 billion native-title deal was settled by the WA government recognising the Noongar people as the traditional owners of WA's southwest. Covering over 200,000 sq km, the settlement region stretches from Jurien Bay to Ravensthorpe, and includes the Perth metropolitan area.

⊙ Sights

⊙ Central Perth

Elizabeth Quay AREA
(Map p892; www.elizabethquay.com.au; Barrack St) A vital part of the city's urban redevelopment is Elizabeth Quay, at the bottom of Barrack St. Luxury hotels and apartments – including the Ritz – are nearing completion, joining waterfront cafes and restaurants. With a busport, train station and ferry terminal, the area is also a busy transport hub. Cross the spectacular Elizabeth Quay pedestrian bridge and splash in the water park.

Perth Zoo ZOO
(Map p886; ☑ 08-9474 0444; www.perth-zoo.wa.gov.au; 20 Labouchere Rd; adult/child $32/15.50; ⊙ 9am-5pm) Part of the fun is getting to this zoo – take a ferry across the Swan River from Elizabeth Quay Jetty (p913) to Mends St Jetty (every half-hour) and walk

up the hill. Zones include Australian Bushwalk (kangaroos, emus, koalas, dingos), Reptile Encounter (all those Aussie snakes you want to avoid), peaceful Australian Wetlands (black swans, brolgas, blue-billed ducks) and the usual international animals from giraffes and lions to elephants and orangutans. Another transport option is bus 30 or 31 from Elizabeth Quay Bus Station.

Whipper Snapper Distillery DISTILLERY
(Map p892; ☑ 08-9221 2293; www.whippersnapper distillery.com; 139 Kensington St, East Perth; tours & tastings $20-55; ⊙ 7am-5pm Mon-Fri, 8am-4pm Sat, from 11am Sun) Look for the vintage aircraft logo on the exterior wall as you visit this combination of urban whisky distillery and sunny coffee shop, in an out-of-the-way location. The whisky is crafted from 100% WA ingredients, something you'll hear a lot about on an entertaining and informative distillery tour (from $20 per person).

Bell Tower LANDMARK
(Map p892; ☑ 08-6210 0444; www.thebelltower. com.au; Barrack Sq; adult/child $18/9 incl bell-tower chiming experience; ⊙ 10am-4pm, ringing noon-1pm Mon, Thu & Sun) This pointy glass spire fronted by copper sails contains the royal bells of London's St Martin-in-the-Fields, the oldest of which dates from 1550. The 12 bells were given to WA by the British government in 1988, and are the only set known to have left England. Clamber to the top for 360-degree views of Perth by the river.

Perth Mint HISTORIC BUILDING
(Map p892; ☑ 08-9421 7222; www.perthmint.com. au; 310 Hay St; adult/child $19/8; ⊙ 9am-5pm) Dating from 1899, the compelling Mint displays a collection of coins, nuggets and gold bars. You can caress bullion worth over $700,000, mint your own coins and watch gold pours (on the half-hour, from 9.30am to 3.30pm). The Mint's Gold Exhibition features a massive, Guinness World Record–holding 1 tonne gold coin, worth a staggering $60 million.

⊙ Kings Park & Subiaco

★ Kings Park & Botanic Garden PARK
(Map p898; ☑ 08-9480 3600; www.bgpa.wa.gov. au; ⊙ free guided walks 10am, noon & 2pm) **FREE** The 400-hectare, bush-filled expanse of Kings Park, smack in the city centre and enjoying epic views, is Perth's pride and joy. The Botanic Garden contains over 3000 plant species indigenous to WA, including a giant boab tree

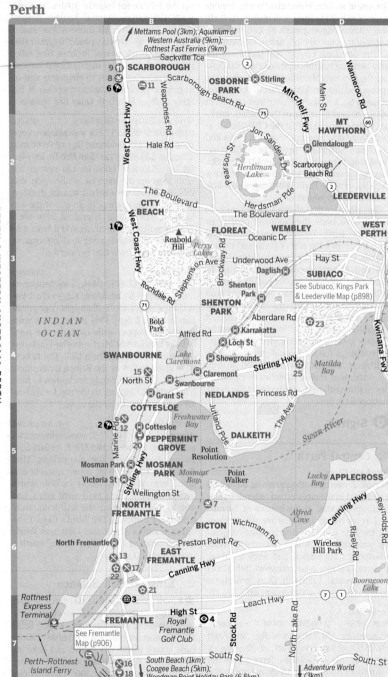

Mettams Pool (3km); Aquarium of
Western Australia (9km);
Rottnest Fast Ferries (9km)
Sackville Tce

9 ⓫ SCARBOROUGH
8 ⊗
6 ⓭

⓫ 11
Scarborough Beach Rd
Weaponess Rd

OSBORNE
PARK
⊗ Stirling

Mitchell Fwy

Main St

Wanneroo Rd

MT
HAWTHORN 60

West Coast Hwy

Hale Rd

75

Jon Sanders Dr

Pearson St

Herdsman
Lake

Glendalough

Scarborough
Beach Rd

The Boulevard

2

LEEDERVILLE

Herdsman Pde

The Boulevard

1 ⓭

West Coast Hwy

CITY
BEACH

Reabold
Hill

Perry
Lakes

FLOREAT

Herdsman Pde

WEMBLEY
Oceanic Dr

Underwood Ave
Daglish

WEST
PERTH

Hay St

SUBIACO

See Subiaco, Kings Park
& Leederville Map (p898)

Stephens on Ave

Brockway Rd

Shenton
Park

Rochdale Rd

71

SHENTON
PARK

Aberdare Rd

23

INDIAN
OCEAN

Bold
Park

Alfred Rd

Karrakatta

Loch St

Kwinana Fwy

SWANBOURNE

Lake
Claremont

Showgrounds

Stirling Hwy

Matilda
Bay

25

15 ⊗
North St

Claremont

Swanbourne

NEDLANDS

Princess Rd

The Ave

Grant St

COTTESLOE

Freshwater
Bay

Jutland Pde

DALKEITH

Swan River

2 ⓭ 12
⊗ Cottesloe

20

PEPPERMINT
GROVE

Point
Resolution

Point
Walker

Lucky
Bay

APPLECROSS

Marine Pde

Mosman Park ⊗

Victoria St ⊗

MOSMAN
PARK

Stirling Hwy

Wellington St

Mosman
Bay

Canning Hwy

Reynolds Rd

NORTH
FREMANTLE

⊗ 7

BICTON

Wichmann Rd

Alfred
Cove

Risely Rd

North Fremantle ⊗

13

EAST
FREMANTLE

Preston Point Rd

Canning Hwy

Wireless
Hill Park

Booragoon
Lake

22 ⊗ 17

21

Leach Hwy

7 1

Rottnest
Express Terminal

3

FREMANTLE

See Fremantle
Map (p906)

High St
4 ⊙
Royal
Fremantle
Golf Club

Stock Rd

North Lake Rd

Perth–Rottnest
Island Ferry

10 ⊗ 16
⊗ 18

South Beach (1km);
Coogee Beach (5km);
Woodman Point Holiday Park (6.5km)

South St

South St

Adventure World
(3km)

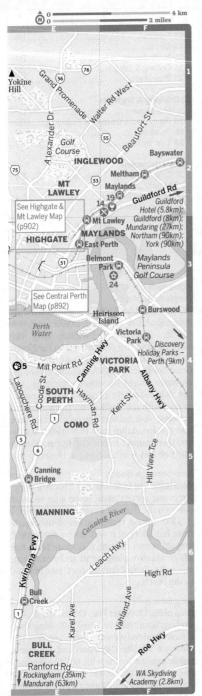

that's 750 years old. Each September there's a free festival displaying the state's famed wildflowers. A year-round highlight is the **Federation Walkway**, a 620m path leading to a 222m-long glass-and-steel sky bridge that crosses a canopy of eucalyptus trees.

Scitech MUSEUM
(Map p898; ☑ 08-9215 0700; www.scitech.org.au; City West Centre, Sutherland St; adult/child $19/12; ☺ 9am-4pm Mon-Fri, 9.30am-5pm Sat & Sun; 🖈) Scitech is an excellent rainy-day option for those travelling with children. It has over 160 hands-on, large-scale science and technology exhibits. Tickets are discounted later in the afternoon.

◎ Northbridge

★ Art Gallery of Western Australia
GALLERY
(Map p892; ☑ 08-9492 6622; www.artgallery.wa.gov. au; Perth Cultural Centre; ☺ 10am-5pm Wed-Mon) **FREE** Founded in 1895, this excellent gallery houses the state's preeminent art collection as well as regular international exhibitions that, increasingly, have a modern, approachable bent. The permanent collection is arranged into wings, from contemporary to modern, historic to local and Aboriginal. Big-name Australian artists such as Arthur Boyd, Russell Drysdale and Sidney Nolan are there, as are diverse media including canvases, bark paintings and sculpture. Check the website for info on free tours running most days at 11am and 1pm.

Nostalgia Box MUSEUM
(Map p892; ☑ 08-9227 7377; www.thenostalgia box.com.au; 16 Aberdeen St; adult/child/family $17/12/50; ☺ 11am-4pm Sun-Mon & Wed-Fri, to 5pm Sat; 🖈) Ease into poignant, low-pixel childhood memories of Atari, Nintendo and Super Mario at this surprisingly interesting collection of retro 1970s and '80s gaming consoles and arcade games. Along the way you'll learn about the history of gaming, and there are plenty of consoles to jump onto and see if the old skills are still there from a few decades back.

Perth Institute of Contemporary Arts GALLERY
(PICA; Map p892; ☑ 08-9228 6300; www.pica.org. au; Perth Cultural Centre; ☺ 10am-5pm Tue-Sun) **FREE** PICA (*pee-kah*) may look traditional – it's housed in an elegant 1896 red-brick former school – but inside it's one of Australia's principal platforms for contemporary art, including installations, performance,

Perth

Sights
1 City Beach B3
2 Cottesloe Beach B5
3 Fremantle Arts Centre B7
4 Fremantle Cemetery C7
5 Perth Zoo E4
6 Scarborough Beach B1

Activities, Courses & Tours
7 Blackwall Reach Reserve C6
Coastal Trail .... (see 8)
8 Scarborough Beach Pool B1
9 Scarborough Beach Surf School B1

Sleeping
10 Be.Fremantle A7
Cottesloe Beach Hotel .... (see 2)
11 Western Beach Lodge B1

Eating
Canvas .... (see 3)
12 Cott & Co Fish Bar B5

13 Flipside B6
14 Mrs S F2
15 North Street Store B4
16 Ootong & Lincoln B7
17 Propeller B6

Drinking & Nightlife
Mrs Browns .... (see 13)
18 Percy Flint's Boozery & Eatery B7
19 Swallow F2
20 Twenty9 .... B5

Entertainment
21 Duke of George B6
22 Mojos B6
23 Moonlight Cinema D4
24 Optus Stadium F3
25 Somerville Auditorium D4

sculpture and video. PICA actively promotes new and experimental art, and it exhibits graduate works annually. From 10am to late, Tuesday to Sunday, the **PICA Bar** is a top spot for a coffee or cocktail, and has occasional live music.

Western Australian Museum – Perth MUSEUM
(Map p892; ☑08-6552 7800; www.museum. wa.gov.au; Perth Cultural Centre; ☉9.30am-5pm) FREE The state's museum is a six-headed beast, with branches in Albany, Geraldton and Kalgoorlie as well as two in Fremantle. This main branch in Northbridge is closed for renovations and is due to reopen as the renamed New Museum for WA in 2020. See online for an outline of the project – it's going to be amazing. While the hub is closed, key exhibits are being displayed as pop-ups at other venues around town – see the website for details.

Scarborough to Cottesloe

Cottesloe Beach BEACH
(Map p886; Marine Pde; ⊞) Perth's safest swimming beach, Cottesloe has cafes, pubs, pine trees and fantastic sunsets. From Cottesloe train station (on the Fremantle line) it's 1km to the beach; there's a free shuttle that runs between the stop and the sand during the annual Sculpture by the Sea exhibition in March. Bus 102 ($4.80) from Elizabeth Quay Busport goes straight to the beach.

Aquarium of Western Australia AQUARIUM
(AQWA; ☑08-9447 7500; www.aqwa.com.au; Hillarys Boat Harbour, 91 Southside Dr; adult/child $30/18; ☉10am-5pm) Dividing WA's vast coastline into five distinct zones (Far North, Coral Coast, Shipwreck Coast, Perth and Great Southern), AQWA features a 98m underwater tunnel showcasing stingrays, turtles, fish and sharks. (The daring can snorkel or dive with the sharks with the aquarium's in-house divemaster.) By public transport, take the Joondalup train to Warwick Station and then transfer to bus 423. By car, take the Mitchell Fwy north and exit at Hepburn Ave.

Scarborough Beach BEACH
(Map p886; The Esplanade; ⊞) This is a popular young surfers' spot, so be sure to swim between the flags, as waves can be powerful. A $100 million revitalisation of the beachfront has adorned it with a new public pool, grassed sunset-viewing hill, skate park, free BBQs, massive playground and restaurants and cafes. From Perth Busport, take bus 990 to the beach.

City Beach BEACH
(Map p886; Challenger Pde) Offers swimming, surfing, lawn and amenities. Following a significant redevelopment, there are two restaurants (we like **Odyssea**) and a pizzeria, public change rooms with hot showers and free outdoor seating. On the beach's northern end, old faithful **Clancy's** pub is another

fine option with gorgeous views. Take bus 81 or 82 from Perth Busport.

☺ Fremantle

★ **Fremantle Prison** HISTORIC BUILDING
(Map p906; 📞08-9336 9200; www.fremantle prison.com.au; 1 The Terrace; day tour adult/child $22/12, combined day tour $32/22, Torchlight Tour $28/18, Tunnels Tour $65/45; ⊙9am-5pm) With its forbidding 5m-high walls, the old convict-era prison dominates Fremantle. Various daytime tours explore the jail's maximum security past, give insights into criminal minds and allow you into solitary-confinement cells. Book ahead for the Torchlight Tour through the prison, with a few scares and surprises, and the 2½-hour Tunnels Tour (minimum age 12 years), venturing into subterranean tunnels and doing an underground boat ride.

★ **WA Shipwrecks Museum** MUSEUM
(Map p906; 📞1300 134 081; www.museum.wa.gov. au; Cliff St; suggested donation $5; ⊙9.30am-5pm) Located within an 1852 commissariat store, the Shipwrecks Museum is considered the finest display of maritime archaeology in the southern hemisphere. The highlight is the **Batavia Gallery**, where a section of the hull of Dutch merchant ship *Batavia,* wrecked in 1629, is displayed. Nearby is a stone gate, intended as an entrance to Batavia Castle, which was carried by the sinking ship.

★ **Western Australian Museum – Maritime** MUSEUM
(Map p906; 📞1300 134 081; www.museum.wa.gov. au; Victoria Quay; adult/child museum $15/free, submarine $15/7.50; ⊙9.30am-5pm) Significant West Australian boats are suspended from the rafters of this sail-shaped museum building. There's the yacht that won the America's Cup race in 1983, pearl luggers and an Aboriginal bark canoe. Take an hour-long tour of the submarine HMAS *Ovens;* the vessel was part of the Australian Navy's fleet from 1969 to 1997. Tours leave every half-hour from 10am to 3.30pm. Book ahead.

Walyalup Aboriginal Cultural Centre CULTURAL CENTRE
(Map p906; 📞08-9430 7906; www.fremantle. wa.gov.au/wacc; 12 Captains Lane; ⊙10am-3pm Thu-Sat) Various classes and workshops, including language, art and crafts, are held at this interesting Aboriginal cultural centre. Booking ahead for most is encouraged, so check the program online. As it's part of the

Bathers Beach Art Precinct (Map p906; www. facebook.com/bathersbeachartsprecinct; ⊙hours vary) there are also regular Aboriginal art exhibitions, with works available for purchase and proceeds going directly to the artists.

Fremantle Markets MARKET
(Map p906; www.fremantlemarkets.com.au; cnr South Tce & Henderson St; ⊙8am-8pm Fri, to 6pm Sat & Sun) **FREE** Originally opened in 1897, these colourful markets were reopened in 1975 and today draw slow-moving crowds combing over souvenirs. A few younger designers and artists have introduced a more vibrant edge. The fresh-produce section is a good place to stock up on supplies and there's an excellent food court featuring lots of global street eats.

Bon Scott Statue STATUE
(Map p906; Carrington St & Leach Hwy, Palmyra) The most popular of Fremantle's public sculptures is Greg James's statue of Bon Scott (1946–80), strutting on a Marshall amplifier in Fishing Boat Harbour. The AC/DC singer moved to Fremantle with his family in 1956 and his ashes are interred in **Fremantle Cemetery** (Map p886; Carrington St). Enter the cemetery near the corner of High and Carrington Sts. Bon's plaque is on the left around 15m along the path.

Round House HISTORIC BUILDING
(Map p906; 📞08-9336 6897; www.fremantle roundhouse.com.au; Captains Lane; admission by donation; ⊙10.30am-3.30pm) Completed in 1831, this 12-sided stone prison is WA's oldest surviving building. It was the site of the colony's first hangings, and was later used for holding Aboriginal people before they were taken to Rottnest Island (p915). At 1pm daily, a time ball and cannon-blasting ceremony just outside reenacts a historic seamen's alert. Book ahead to fire the cannon.

Fremantle Arts Centre GALLERY
(Map p886; 📞08-9432 9555; www.fac.org.au; 1 Finnerty St; ⊙10am-5pm) **FREE** An impressive neo-Gothic building surrounded by lovely elm-shaded gardens, the Fremantle Arts Centre was constructed by convict labourers as a lunatic asylum in the 1860s. Saved from demolition in the 1960s, it houses interesting exhibitions and the excellent **Canvas** (Map p886; 📞08-9335 5685; www.fac.org.au/ about/cafe; mains $16-28; ⊙8am-3pm Mon-Fri, to 4pm Sat & Sun; 🛜⊞) cafe. During summer there are concerts (free on Sunday afternoons), courses and workshops.

⚡ Activities

⭐ Scarborough Beach Pool SWIMMING

(Map p886; ☎08-9205 7560; www.scarborough beachpool.com.au; 171 The Esplanade, Scarborough; swimming adult/child $7/4.30; ⊗5.30am-9pm Mon-Fri, 6.30am-8pm Sat, from 7.30am Sun, reduced winter hours; 🅰) This superb outdoor, ocean-side swimming pool is the place to be when the Fremantle Doctor blows in and flattens out the Scarborough surf. Bikinis, buff bods, squealing kids and general West Coast ebullience – it's quite a scene. Cafe on-site.

Blackwall Reach Reserve SWIMMING

(Map p886; ☎08-9420 7207; www.bushland perth.org.au/treasures/blackwall-reach-reserve; off Blackwall Reach Pde, Bicton; ⊗daylight hours) FREE Long a rite of passage for Perth teenagers, plunging off these craggy 8m-high limestone cliffs into the Swan River is a major thrill. The water is deep, but there's a long history of hapless cliff-jumpers expiring in the process. Watch your step, and don't underestimate your ability to not drown. Follow the pathway at the end of Blackwall Reach Pde.

Water Wanderers KAYAKING

(☎0412 101 949; www.waterwanderers.com.au) 🛶 Guided and self-guided kayak tours around the Swan River in central Perth – a watery perspective that most locals never experience. Tours run at dawn ($55, 75 minutes), in the morning ($60, 90 minutes) and at twilight ($79, two hours), departing from locations in South Perth and East Perth. Self-guided tours for experienced kayakers are $160 for two paddlers.

WA Skydiving Academy SKYDIVING

(☎1300 137 855; www.waskydiving.com.au; 2 Mustang Rd, Jandakot Airport, Jandakot) Hurl yourself out of a perfectly good aeroplane high above Perth, Mandurah or Pinjarra. Tandem jumps from 6000/8000/10,000/12,000ft start at $260/350/390/430. Flights depart from Jandakot Airport 22km south of Perth.

Beatty Park Leisure Centre SWIMMING

(Map p898; ☎08-9273 6080; www.beattypark. com.au; 220 Vincent St, North Perth; swimming adult/child $7/5; ⊗5.30am-9pm Mon-Fri, 6.30am-7pm Sat & Sun; 🅰) Built for the Commonwealth Games, hosted by Perth in 1962, this complex has indoor and outdoor pools, water slides and a huge gym. Turn left at the top of William St and continue on Vincent St to just past Charles St.

Rockface CLIMBING

(Map p892; ☎08-9328 5998; www.rockface. com.au; 63b John St; climbing with/without gear hire adult $30/20, child $27/17; ⊗10am-10pm Mon-Fri, 9am-6pm Sat & Sun; 🅰) Inside an old brick warehouse abutting the Mitchell Fwy, Rockface has an impressive array of indoor climbing walls, bouldering areas, slabs and overhangs. Don your nifty rubber shoes, clip your rope to your harness and up you go. Good fun for kids too.

Coastal Trail CYCLING

(Map p886; Scarborough Beach Foreshore, Scarborough) FREE Feel like a ride? There's a fabulous cycling/walking trail running continuously north from the Scarborough foreshore, tracing the Indian Ocean clifftops all the way to Hillarys Boat Harbour 10km to the north. The trail extends southwards too, delivering you eventually (with a few detours) to Fremantle, 20km away.

Scarborough Beach Surf School SURFING

(Map p886; ☎08-9448 9937; www.surfschool. com; Scarborough Beach, Scarborough; lessons $70; ⊗Oct-May) Longer-than-usual lessons (2½ hours) at Scarborough Beach, including boards and wetsuits; bookings essential. From June to September the operation moves to Leighton Beach just north of Fremantle.

Adventure World AMUSEMENT PARK

(☎08-9417 9666; www.adventureworld.net.au; 351 Progress Dr, Bibra Lake; adult/child/family $59.50/49.50/185; ⊗10am-7pm Sun-Fri, to 6pm Sat Dec-Jan, reduced hours mid-Sep–Nov & Feb-Apr; 🅰) Highlights of Adventure World's 28 rides are the Abyss roller coaster; the Black Widow, a G-force-defying spinning wonder; and (release) the Kraken, the world's longest and steepest funnel water slide, navigable in four-person rafts. Other water- and theme-park attractions include rapids, go-karts, Australian wildlife, a castle and the lofty Sky Lift.

👣 Tours

Oh Hey WA WALKING

(Map p892; ☎0408 995 965; www.ohheywa.com. au; 45 St Georges Tce; tours from $35) Highly rated central Perth walking tours, zeroing in on the city's booming street-art scene, hip small bars, throbbing nightlife zones and architectural heritage. Self-guided audio tours and two-hour bike tours also available.

Go Cultural Aboriginal Tours CULTURAL

(☎0459 419 778; www.gocultural.com.au) 🛶 Small-group, Aboriginal-run walking tours

PERTH IN...

Two Days

Kick off with a leisurely cafe breakfast in Mt Lawley or Central Perth, then spend your first morning exploring the Perth Cultural Centre – don't miss the superb **Art Gallery of Western Australia** (p887). Grab lunch and browse the shops in hip the Leederville 'hood before exploring verdant and view-catching **Kings Park** (p885) – a huge parkland area close to the city. The following day, discover the lustrous riches of the **Perth Mint** (p885) before catching the **Little Ferry Co** ferry (p913) from **Elizabeth Quay** (p885) to view the city from the water. A night drinking cocktails in the city's laneway bars, or craft beer in the **Northbridge** (p905) pubs awaits...

Four Days

Follow the two-day itinerary then head for the beach. Pick up provisions for a picnic at **Cottesloe** (p888) or **City Beach** (p888), or truck further north to booming **Scarborough** (p888), with its swimming pool, precipitous skate bowl and rolling surf (and surf lessons). On your final day, visit **Fremantle** (p889), Perth's raffish, soulful port town. Two of WA's best museums are here – the **Western Australian Museum – Maritime** and **WA Shipwrecks Museum** – plus the disquieting, World Heritage–listed **Fremantle Prison**. Take your pick, then conclude your Perth adventure with some chilly pints at **Little Creatures** (p908).

of Yagan Sq (one hour, $40) and Elizabeth Quay (90 minutes, $60) in central Perth. Tours peel back the layers of the city to understand the cultural and physical landscape of Aboriginal life here, now and in ancient times. Three-hour tours also available ($120).

Food Loose Tours　　FOOD & DRINK
(☑0467 542 437; www.foodloosetours.com.au; ⊙tours from $39) Entertaining, informative walking tours negotiating flavour-packed Perth routes, taking in restaurants, quick-fire cafes and hard-to-find small bars in Perth and Fremantle. Italian- and Asian-themed tours also available.

Two Feet & A Heartbeat　　WALKING
(☑1800 459 388; www.twofeet.com.au; tours from $35) Crime, culture, coffee and cocktails – these excellent guided walking tours of Perth and Fremantle cover all the bases, running both during the day and after dark. Kids will enjoy the thee-hour Scavenger Hunt ($35); three-hour nocturnal bar tours take in some lesser-known booze rooms ($55).

Perth Explorer　　BUS
(☑08-9370 1000; www.perthexplorer.com.au; 24hr ticket adult/child/family $40/12/95) Hop-on, hop-off double-decker bus tour, with a looping route taking in the central city, Kings Park and Northbridge. Buy tickets on board, or shave a few dollars off the price if you purchase online; 48-hour tickets also available. Other package options include a two-

day bus and Rottnest Island experience, and an add-on river cruise to Fremantle.

Djurandi Dreaming　　CULTURAL
(☑0458 692 455; www.djurandi.com.au; tours adult/child $45/35) ✐ Aboriginal walking tours around the booming Elizabeth Quay precinct in central Perth: 45 minutes of Nyungar cultural immersion, focusing on stories of The Dreaming, art, native flora and fauna, traditional diet, seasons and family structures.

✸ Festivals & Events

Perth Cup　　SPORTS
(www.perthracing.org.au; Ascot Racecourse; ⊙5 Jan) Perth's biggest day at the races, with the party people heading to 'Tentland' for DJs and daiquiris.

Fringe World Festival　　PERFORMING ARTS
(☑08-9227 6288; www.fringeworld.com.au; varies by performance; ⊙Jan-Feb) If you're challenged by nudity, offended by swearing and hate being drawn from the audience into a show, look away now. At Perth's cheekiest arts festival, hundreds of international and Australian artists perform in parks, pubs and playhouses for a month across January and February, delivering a party vibe with boundary-pushing comedy, circus, burlesque and theatre shows – many are free.

Australia Day Skyworks　　FIREWORKS
(www.perth.wa.gov.au; ⊙26 Jan) Around 300,000 people come to the riverside for a

Central Perth

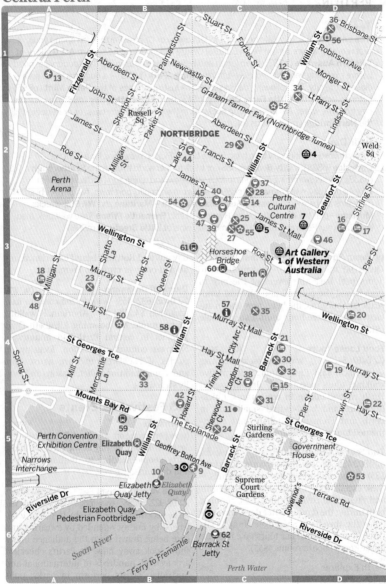

PERTH & WESTERN AUSTRALIA PERTH

whole day of largely free, family entertainment, culminating in a 30-minute firework display at 8pm. Activities spread across Langley Park and on the South Perth foreshore, while views of the fireworks are best from Kings Park.

Laneway Festival MUSIC
(http://fremantle.lanewayfestival.com; ☺ early Feb) Open-air party with the planet's up-and-coming indie acts. The ubercool festival takes place around Fremantle's West End and Esplanade Reserve.

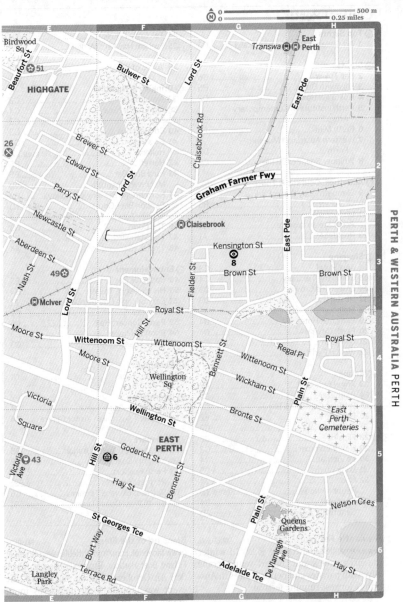

Perth Festival ART
(www.perthfestival.com.au; ⊙mid-Feb–early Mar)
Artists such as Laurie Anderson, Dead Can
Dance and Sleater-Kinney perform alongside top local talent. Held over 26 days, the
festival spans theatre, classical music, jazz,
visual arts, dance, immersive experiences
(many free), international films (held in a
beautiful outdoor cinema) and a writers'
week. Worth scheduling a trip around, especially for nocturnal types.

Central Perth

◎ **Top Sights**
1 Art Gallery of Western Australia C3

◎ **Sights**
2 Bell Tower C6
3 Elizabeth Quay.......................................B5
4 Nostalgia Box...D2
5 Perth Institute of Contemporary
   Arts...C3
6 Perth Mint F5
7 Western Australian Museum –
   Perth..D3
8 Whipper Snapper Distillery..................G3

◯ **Activities, Courses & Tours**
9 Elizabeth Quay Water Park..................B5
10 Little Ferry Co B5
11 Oh Hey WA C5
12 Perth Steam Works...............................C1
13 Rockface...A1

◉ **Sleeping**
14 Alex Hotel C3
15 Como the Treasury C4
16 Emperor's Crown D3
17 Hostel G D3
18 Melbourne Hotel....................................A3
19 Pensione Hotel D4
20 Perth City YHA.......................................D4
21 QT Perth C4
22 Westin Perth D5

✖ **Eating**
23 Angel Falls Grill A3
24 Balthazar C5
25 Bivouac Canteen & Bar C3
26 Brika..E2
27 Chicho Gelato C3
28 Flipside C2
29 Henry Summer..C2
30 Le Vietnam C4
31 Long Chim...C5
32 Nao..C4
   Petition Kitchen............................(see 31)
33 Print Hall...B4
   Santini Bar & Grill ....(see 21)

34 Tak Chee House......................................D1
35 Twilight Hawkers Market.......................C4
   Wildflower..(see 15)
36 Wines of While..D1

◯ **Drinking & Nightlife**
37 Alabama Song C2
38 Alfred's Pizzeria C4
39 Bird..C3
40 Connections C3
41 Ezra Pound C3
   Halford ....(see 15)
42 Helvetica B5
43 Hula Bula Bar..E5
   Mechanics Institute.......................(see 28)
44 Northbridge Brewing Company............B2
   Petition Beer Corner ....(see 31)
45 Sneaky Tony's C3
46 The Court..D3
47 The Standard..C3
48 Tiny's A4

✪ **Entertainment**
49 Badlands Bar...E3
50 His Majesty's Theatre B4
51 Lazy Susan's Comedy Den.....................E1
52 Moon..C2
53 Perth Concert Hall.................................D5
54 Rooftop Movies......................................B3
55 State Theatre Centre C3

◉ **Shopping**
56 William Topp..D1

ℹ **Information**
57 Perth City Visitor Kiosk.........................C4
58 Western Australian Visitor Centre B4

ℹ **Transport**
59 Elizabeth Quay Bus Station...................B5
60 Integrity Coach Lines C3
61 Perth Busport...B3
   Rottnest Express ....(see 62)
62 Rottnest Express Terminal....................C6
   South West Coach Lines...............(see 59)

Fremantle Festival
CULTURAL

(www.fremantlefestival.com.au; ⊙ Jul) In winter the city's streets and concert venues come alive with parades and performances in Australia's longest-running festival.

Kings Park Festival
CULTURAL

(www.kingsparkfestival.com.au; ⊙ Sep) Perth's largest, inner-city green space, Kings Park is planted with thousands of native wildflowers each year, which bloom each September. To coincide with the Botanic Garden displays, the festival includes live music every Sunday, nature exhibitions, guided walks and talks.

Blessing of the Fleet
RELIGIOUS

(www.facebook.com/fremantleblessingofthefleet; Fishing Boat Harbour, Esplanade Reserve; ⊙ late Oct) An October tradition since 1948, this event was brought to Fremantle by immigrants from Molfetta, Italy. It includes the procession of the Molfettese *Our Lady of Martyrs* statue (carried by men) and the Sicilian *Madonna di Capo d'Orlando* (carried by women) from St Patrick's Basilica (47 Adelaide St) to Fishing Boat Harbour, where the blessing takes place.

🛏 Sleeping

🏨 Central Perth

Pensione Hotel BOUTIQUE HOTEL $
(Map p892; ☑08-9325 2133; www.pensione.com.
au; 70 Pier St; d $105-175; P🅿❄🛜) The central-
city 98-room Pensione delivers a bit of
budget boutique sheen. The standard rooms
definitely veer towards cosy and (very) compact, but classy decor, reasonable prices and
a good location are redemptive. Spend a few
dollars more on a Premium King room for
some extra elbow room. Parking $28.

Perth City YHA HOSTEL $
(Map p892; ☑08-9287 3333; www.yha.com.au;
300 Wellington St; dm from $25, d with/without
bathroom $90/70, f with bathroom $120; ❄🛜🏊)
Occupying an impressive 1939 sandstone
art-deco building by the train tracks, Perth's
YHA corridors have a boarding-school feel,
but the rooms are clean and there's a pool,
gym and generous kitchen. The 'Fun Starts
Here' declares a sign on a faux-turf wall, but
like most YHAs the vibe is low-key after dark
(good or bad, depending on your interests).

⭐**Melbourne Hotel** BOUTIQUE HOTEL $$
(Map p892; ☑08-9320 3333; www.melbourne
hotel.com.au; 33 Milligan St; d/ste from $180/280;
P🅿❄🛜) The new section of the Melbourne
Hotel looms above the original 1897 heritage
pub like a parasitic black Darth Vader. But fear
not – it's actually an extremely stylish addition
to the old dame, itself thoroughly upgraded to
contemporary hotel specs. Room prices in ei-
ther the old or new sections are comparable:
it's just a question of taste. Parking from $18.

QT Perth DESIGN HOTEL $$
(Map p892; ☑08-9225 8000; www.qthotelsand
resorts.com/perth; 133 Murray St; d from $285;
P🅿❄🛜) With a lobby decorated with potted
cacti, polished concrete and jarrah, retro
furniture and a sparkling cafe/cocktail bar,
you'll be forgiven for feeling like you're on a
James Bond film set. Rooms dip into a similar 'industrial luxe' designer grab-bag: it's a
really funky high-end product, enhanced by
a superb rooftop bar. Valet parking $40.

⭐**Como The Treasury** BOUTIQUE HOTEL $$$
(Map p892; ☑08-6168 7888; www.comohotels.
com/thetreasury; State Bldgs, 1 Cathedral Ave; r from
$445; P🅿❄🛜🏊) A regular on lists of 'World's
Best Hotels', Como the Treasury has 48 luxury
rooms that fill the baroque splendour of the
historic State Buildings, vacant for 20 years

before the Como opened in 2016. Despite the
heritage backdrop, the property is wonder-
fully contemporary, with tasteful art, super-
courteous staff, a superb spa and indoor pool.
Valet parking from $40.

Westin Perth HOTEL $$$
(Map p892; ☑08-6559 1888; www.marriott.com;
480 Hay St; d/f/ste from $280/370/520; P🅿❄🛜)
A glam glass tower, straight outta downtown
Houston, this slick internationalist could
easily have defaulted to carbon-copy global
style. But with the breezy outdoor lounges
and cafes on adjacent Hibernian Pl, native
plantings and fabulous Aboriginal art installations (sculptures, weavings, paintings
and imprinted concrete panels), the Westin
manages to feel very 'WA'. One of Perth's top
hotels. Valet parking $55.

🏨 Highgate & Mount Lawley

Witch's Hat HOSTEL $
(Map p902; ☑08-9228 4228; www.witchs-hat.com;
148 Palmerston St, Highgate; dm $24-30, tw & d $60-
75; P🅿❄@🛜) Like something out of a fairy
tale, this 1897 building could be mistaken for
a gingerbread house, with its stained glass,
lovely old floorboards and the witch's hat
itself (a terracotta-tiled Edwardian turret)
standing proudly out the front, beckoning
the curious to step inside. Dorms are light
and uncommonly spacious, and there's a red-
brick barbecue area out the back.

Durack House B&B $$
(Map p902; ☑08-9370 4305; www.durackhouse.
com.au; 7 Almondbury Rd, Mount Lawley; r $195-
215; P🅿❄🛜) It's hard to avoid words like 'de-
lightful' when describing this white-painted
Federation house, set on a peaceful Mount
Lawley street behind a brick-paved garden
and rose-adorned picket fence. The two guest
rooms have boundless old-world charm,
paired with mod bathrooms. It's only 250m
from Mount Lawley Station. Rates include
breakfast: cooked (menu changes daily) or
continental (fruit, yoghurt, juice, cereal).

🏨 Kings Park & Subiaco

⭐**Riverview 42 Mt St Hotel** APARTMENT $
(Map p898; ☑08-9321 8963; www.riverviewperth.
com.au; 42 Mount St, West Perth; apt $110-210;
P🅿❄🛜) There's a lot of brash new money
on Mount St, but character-filled Riverview
stands out with a bit of old-school person-
ality. Its refurbished 1960s bachelor pads sit
neatly atop a buzzy cafe and foyer hung with

Persian rugs. Rooms (all with kitchenette) are sunny and simple; the ones at the front have river views, while the rear ones are quieter.

Tribe Hotel DESIGN HOTEL $$
(Map p898; ☎08-6247 3333; www.tribehotels.com.au; 4 Walker Ave, West Perth; r from $170; P ❄ 📶) Join the tribe of fans who list Tribe as their fave Perth hotel, a stylin' multistorey addition to the accommodation offerings around Kings Park, barely 100m away. Looking like the black-box flight recorder from some giant crash-landed spaceship – all black perforated-metal panels and jaunty sunshades – Tribe ticks the style boxes inside too, angling for a supermodel clintele. Hip defined.

Sage Hotel DESIGN HOTEL $$
(Map p898; ☎08-6500 9100; www.nexthotels.com/sage/west-perth; 1309 Hay St, West Perth; r from $190; P ❄ 📶) Handily placed for both the CBD and Kings Park, Sage's eccentrically patterned concrete tower offers sassy rooms with big TVs, cleverly designed bathrooms and work stations. Amenities include a gym in which to iron out your aeroplane-seat kinks, and **Julio's Italian Restaurant** in a 100-year-old heritage house out the front (mains $28 to $47). Free off-site parking.

Leederville

★Lakeside B&B B&B $
(Map p898; ☎08-9381 7257; www.lakesideperth.com.au; 130 St Leonards Ave, West Leederville; d with/without breakfast from $160/140; P ❄ 📶 ≋) Lakeside B&B is close to Lake Monger, with its ducks, jogging paths and BBQs, but once you're inside this lovely wisteria-hung Federation home you'll lose interest in lakes. The two guest rooms are tastefully styled with interesting antiques, and there's a pool and shady verandah demanding the consumption of G&Ts. The guest rooms share a bathroom, but that's the only catch.

Northbridge

★Hostel G HOSTEL $
(Map p892; ☎0402 067 099; www.hostelgperth.com; 80 Stirling St; dm/d/f from $26/96/120; ❄ 📶) Hostel G is a snappy refit of an old office block, with designer interiors by esteemed architects Woods Bagot. Beanbag-strewn communal areas revolve around a central bar/cafe (burgers, pizza, pasta), with lofty ceilings, a cinema wall, pool tables and yoga studio. The quiet en-suite rooms are graded in ascending order of niceness: good, great, glam and greatest, priced accordingly. Excellent!

Emperor's Crown HOSTEL $
(Map p892; ☎08-9227 1400; www.emperorscrown.com.au; 85 Stirling St; dm from $19, d with/without bathrooms from $75/65, tr with bathroom $99; P ❄ 📶) One of Perth's best hostels is also one of the most keenly priced, with friendly staff, high housekeeping standards and a primo position (close to the Northbridge scene without actually being in it). Over several levels and awash with orange doors, it's an entirely tidy operation. Parking $10.

★Alex Hotel BOUTIQUE HOTEL $$
(Map p892; ☎08-6430 4000; www.alexhotel.com.au; 50 James St; d from $209; ❄ 📶) A vision of robust contemporary design, the Alex is stylish evidence of Northbridge's social evolution. Classy, compact rooms are decked out in neutral colours, and stacked with fine linen and electronic gear. Relaxed shared spaces include a hip mezzanine lounge (honesty bar and muffins!) and fab city-view roof terrace. **Shadow**, Alex's street-front wine bar, channels Euro bistro vibes. Excellent stuff.

Scarborough to Cottesloe

Western Beach Lodge HOSTEL $
(Map p886; ☎08-9245 1624; www.westernbeach.com; 6 Westborough St, Scarborough; dm/d without bathroom from $28/60; P 📶) A real surfer hang-out, this sociable, rather shaggy hostel has a low-key, guitar-strumming, hammock-swinging vibe. Discounts kick in for stays of three nights or longer. Surfboards and bodyboards are ready to go ('At the beach' says the sign, if the owner's not around).

★Cottesloe Beach Hotel PUB $$
(Map p886; ☎08-9383 1000; www.cottesloebeachhotel.com.au; 104 Marine Pde, Cottesloe; d from $195; ❄ 📶) The old art-deco Cottesloe is a mighty charming pub on Cottesloe Beach, with bars and cafes downstairs (perfect Indian Ocean sunset-watching territory) and 13 lovely rooms upstairs. Far above usual pub accommodation standards, each room has a bathroom, double glazing, balcony and effortless beachy style. Angle for a sea view if you can. On-street parking only.

Fremantle

Fremantle Hostel HOSTEL $
(Map p906; ☎08-9430 6001; www.fremantlehostel.com.au; 15 Packenham St; dm $22-29;

PERTH FOR CHILDREN

With a usually clement climate and plenty of open spaces and beaches to run around on, Perth is a great place to bring the kids. Of the beaches, Cottesloe (p888) is the safest and a family favourite. Otherwise, the netted **Sorrento Beach Enclosure** (☑08-9400 4000; www.joondalup.wa.gov.au; West Coast Dr, Sorrento; ☉daylight hours; ♿) **FREE** offers waves without the risk of becoming something's lunch. With older kids, arrange two-wheeled family expeditions along Perth's riverside bike paths or Coastal Trail (p890) north or south from Scarborough. Kings Park (p885) has playgrounds and walking tracks.

The **Perth Royal Show** (www.perthroyalshow.com.au; Claremont Showground; ☉late Sep–early Oct) is an ever-popular family day out, with breakfast-reintroducing rides, kitsch show bags and proudly displayed poultry. Many of Perth's big-ticket attractions also cater well for young audiences, especially the Aquarium of Western Australia, (p888) the fabulous Perth Zoo (p885) and the Art Gallery of Western Australia (p887).

Scitech (p887) is a good rainy-day option, with more than 160 hands-on, large-scale science and technology exhibits. For artificial rain, try the squirting water jets at **Hyde Park Playground** (Map p902; ☑08-9273 6000; www.vincent.wa.gov.au/parks-and-facilities/item/hyde-park; Throssell St, Highgate; ☉daylight hours; ♿) **FREE** or the **Elizabeth Quay Water Park** (Map p892; ☑08-6557 0700; www.mra.wa.gov.au; Geoffrey Bolton Way; ☉10am-10pm daily Dec-Feb, to 6pm Wed-Mon Mar-Nov; ♿) **FREE** by the river.

Fremantle is super kid-focused, with an excellent program of events at the Fremantle Arts Centre (p889) and the awesome WA Shipwrecks Museum (p889) and Western Australian Museum – Maritime (p889). And at the end of the day, Little Creatures (p908) brewery has a big sandpit full of toy trucks.

♿@☎) A lofty warehouse encloses this bright, airy, clean hostel of dorms and shared bathrooms only. It has free bikes to borrow, a free food night, a hammock, gym, BBQ, pool table and a chilled lounge area. Street art graces the large white walls and there's an in-house cafe doing drinks and desserts. Buffet breakfast is included. Upstairs rooms have air-conditioning.

Fremantle Prison YHA Hostel   HOSTEL $
(Map p906; ☑08-9433 4305; www.yha.com.au; 6a The Terrace; dm $24-29, d & tw from $96, f/cottages from $122/250; ☉7am-11pm reception; P♿☎) Fremantle's former women's prison is a hostel with clean dorm-style accommodation, private rooms and family-friendly cottages (Map p906; ☑08-9433 4305; www.fremantlecottages.com.au; 6a The Terrace; cottages $250) (once guards' homes). Stay in one of the spartan cells and read the photo boards sharing inmate and prison stories. Well located, with excellent communal spaces and plenty of social activities such as free movies, team sports and wine nights.

★Fremantle Apartment   APARTMENT $$
(Map p906; www.thefremanteapartment.com; 7 Leake St; apt $110-160; P♿☎) Arrayed across three floors and featuring a New York–loft vibe, this spacious apartment is right in Fre-

mantle's heritage precinct. A massive leather couch and big-screen TV combine with a well-equipped kitchen, and the fridge is usually stocked with a few complimentary chocolate nibbles. Friendly owners Cam and Terri have plenty of ideas on how best to enjoy Fremantle.

★Hougoumont Hotel   BOUTIQUE HOTEL $$
(Map p906; ☑08-6160 6800; www.hougoumonthotel.com.au; 15 Bannister St; d $173-275; ♿@☎) Named after a historic convict ship, this boutique hotel's spotlessly clean rooms are cleverly constructed from sea containers. Standard 'cabins' are compact, but stylish and efficiently designed; state rooms are bigger. Top-end toiletries, a breezy ambience and complimentary late-afternoon wine and snacks reinforce the centrally located Hougoumont's refreshing approach to accommodation. Service from the multinational team is relaxed but professional.

National Hotel   BOUTIQUE HOTEL $$
(Map p906; ☑08-9335 6688; www.nationalhotelfremantle.com.au; 98 High St; d $189-376; ☺♿☎) Not only does this boutique hotel have Fremantle's best (and only) rooftop bar, but its classic, heritage-style rooms are also exceedingly comfortable. The historic hotel was burnt to the ground and restored;

Subiaco, Kings Park & Leederville

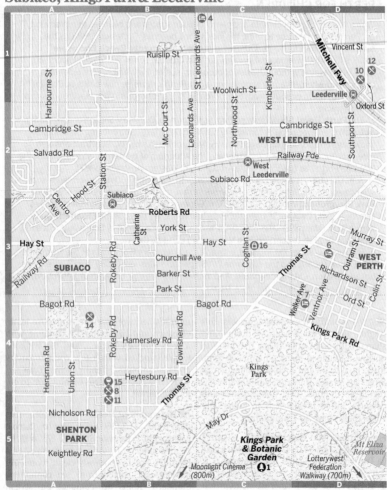

now, chic bathrooms with huge baths that face a wall TV add allure. Lower-level rooms will feel and hear the vibrations from weekend live music in the anchoring pub.

Be.Fremantle
APARTMENT **$$**

(Map p886; ☑ 08-9430 3888; www.befremantle. com.au; Challenger Harbour, 43 Mews Rd; studio/apt from $189/199; ❋ ☎) At the end of a wharf, these 4.5-star sandstone studios and one- to three-bedroom apartments have had a stylish makeover to reopen as the Be.Fremantle complex. The more expensive Marina View apartments enjoy the best ocean vistas, and bikes are available to

explore Fremantle. A further 24 new apartments opened in mid-2017, so ask about scoring one of those.

Port Mill B&B
B&B **$$**

(Map p906; ☑ 08-9433 3832; www.portmillbb. com.au; 3/17 Essex St; r $199-299; ❋ @ ☎) One of the most luxurious B&Bs in town, Port Mill is clearly the love child of Paris and Freo. Crafted from local limestone (it was built in 1862 as a mill), inside it's all modern French style, with gleaming taps, wrought-iron balconies and French doors opening out to the sun-filled decks, where the included breakfast is often served.

Subiaco, Kings Park & Leederville

◎ Top Sights
1 Kings Park & Botanic Garden C5

◎ Sights
2 Scitech E2

⊙ Activities, Courses & Tours
3 Beatty Park Leisure Centre F1

⊜ Sleeping
4 Lakeside B&B C1
5 Riverview 42 Mt St Hotel E4
6 Sage Hotel D3
7 Tribe Hotel D4

◎ Eating
8 Boucla B4
9 Duende E1
10 Kailis Bros D1
11 Meeka B5
12 Pinchos D1
13 Sayers E1
14 Subiaco Farmers Market A4

◎ Drinking & Nightlife
15 Juanita's B4

◎ Shopping
16 Mossenson Galleries –
   Indigenart C3

PERTH & WESTERN AUSTRALIA PERTH

✗ Eating

✗ Central Perth

Le Vietnam   VIETNAMESE $

(Map p892; ☑08-6114 8038; www.facebook.com/levietnamcafe; 1/80 Barrack St; snacks $7; ⊙7.30am-3pm Mon-Fri; ☑) The best bánh mì (Vietnamese baguettes) in town are served in this tiny, central spot. Classic flavour combos blend pork slivers, pâté, chilli and lemongrass, while newer spins feature pulled pork, roast pork and crackling. Interesting drinks include Vietnamese coffee and lychee lemonade, and a hearty breakfast or lunch will only cost around 10 bucks.

Nao   JAPANESE $

(Map p892; ☑08-9325 2090; www.naojapanese restaurant.com.au; Equus Arcade, shop 191/580 Hay St; mains $11-14; ⊙11.30am-6pm Mon-Thu, to 9pm Fri, noon-5pm Sat & Sun) Asian students, CBD desk jockeys and savvy foodies all gravitate to this spot serving the best Japanese-style ramen in town. At peak times you'll need to battle a small queue, but the silky combinations of broth, roast *chashu* pork and noodles are definitely worth the wait.

Twilight Hawkers Market   STREET FOOD $

(Map p892; http://twilighthawkersmarket.com; Forrest Chase; snacks & mains around $10-15; ⊙4.30-9.30pm Fri Nov-Mar) Ethnic food stalls bring the flavours and aromas of the world to central Perth on Friday nights in spring and summer. Combine your Turkish *gözleme* (savoury crepe) or Colombian empanadas (deep-fried pastries) with regular live music from local Perth bands.

Petition Kitchen   AUSTRALIAN $$

(Map p892; ☑08-6168 7771; www.petitionperth.com/kitchen; cnr St Georges Terrace & Barrack St; small plates $12-22, large plates $17-60; ⊙7am-

11pm Mon-Fri, from 8am Sat & Sun; ❀) One of Perth's most polished warehouse bistros, Petition manages to impress across all meal sittings with its inventive approach to local and seasonal ingredients, sometimes woven with indigenous produce such as finger lime or pepper berry. Breakfast is punchy, lunch wows with squid-ink linguine, pipis and Pernod, while dinner keeps the party going with charred zucchini, stracciatella and curry leaf.

Angel Falls Grill
VENEZUELAN **$$**

(Map p892; ☑08-9481 6222; www.angelfalls grill.com.au; Shop 16, Shafto Lane; mains $18-50; ⏰11am-late) The pick of Shafto Lane's ethnic restaurants, Angel Falls Grill brings a taste of South America to WA. Salads and meat dishes are served with arepas (flat breads), and starters include empanadas and savoury-topped plantains. Grilled meat dishes from the *parrillada* (barbecue) are flavour-packed, and surprising breakfast options also make Angel Falls a great place to start the day.

★ Wildflower
MODERN AUSTRALIAN **$$$**

(Map p892; ☑08-6168 7855; www.wildflowerperth. com.au; State Bldgs, 1 Cathedral Ave; mains $42-49, 5-course tasting menu without/with wine $145/240; ⏰noon-2.30pm & 6pm-late Tue-Fri, 6pm-late Sat) Filling a glass pavilion atop the restored State Buildings, Wildflower offers finedining menus inspired by the six seasons of the Indigenous Noongar people of WA. There's a passionate focus on West Australian produce: dishes often include Shark Bay scallops or kangaroo smoked over jarrah embers, as well as indigenous herbs and bush plants like lemon myrtle and wattle seed.

★ Long Chim
THAI **$$$**

(Map p892; ☑08-6168 7775; www.longchimperth. com; State Bldgs, cnr St Georges Tce & Barrack St; mains $25-45; ⏰noon-late; ☑) Australian chef David Thompson is renowned for respecting the authentic flavours of Thai street food, and with dishes like a tongue-burning chicken *laap* (warm salad with fresh herbs) and roast red-duck curry, there's definitely no dialling back the flavour for Western palates. The prawns with toasted coconut and betel leaves may well be the planet's finest appetiser.

Santini Bar & Grill
ITALIAN **$$$**

(Map p892; ☑08-9225 8000; www.santinibarand grill.com.au; QT Perth, 133 Murray St; small plates $14-24, large plates $23-58; ⏰6.30am-late; ❀) Classy, fine-dining-style Italian food is served in the undeniably cool interiors of the QT hotel (p895). The pasta is made inhouse (the duck 'Bolognese' with crackling is a thing of beauty), the fish is ocean-fresh (try the tuna crostini) and the perfectly seasoned steak sublime. The pizzas are cracking too. Have a pre or post drink across the hall.

Print Hall
MODERN AUSTRALIAN **$$$**

(Map p892; ☑08-6282 0000; www.printhall.com. au; 125 St Georges Tce; shared plates $12-20, mains $25-49; ⏰11.30am-midnight Mon-Fri, from 4pm Sat) This sprawling complex in the Brookfield Pl precinct includes the **Apple Daily**, featuring Southeast Asian–style street food, the perfect-for-leaning **Print Hall Bar** and a swish Italian restaurant called **Gazette**. Don't miss having a drink and a burger or pizza in the rooftop **Bob's Bar**, named after Australia's larrikin former prime minister Bob Hawke.

Balthazar
MODERN AUSTRALIAN **$$$**

(Map p892; ☑08-9421 1206; www.balthazar.com. au; 6 The Esplanade; small plates $21-28, large plates $36-57; ⏰noon-midnight Mon-Fri, from 6pm Sat) Low-lit, discreet and sophisticated, with a cool soundtrack and charming staff, Balthazar has an informal vibe that's matched by exquisite food and a famously excellent wine list. The menu is refreshingly original, combining European flavours with an intensely local and seasonal focus. Younger owners have reinvented Balthazar as a refined yet relaxed option with superior shared plates.

✖ Highgate & Mount Lawley

★ Sayers Sister
CAFE **$$**

(Map p902; ☑08-9227 7506; www.sayerssister. com.au; 236 Lake St, Highgate; mains $14-28; ⏰7am-4pm Mon-Fri, to 3pm Sat & Sun) Topnotch brunch options – including leek and Parmesan croquettes in dreamy leek cream with poached eggs – combine with eclectic interiors that are said to be inspired by the long-time owners' home. Plonk down in an armchair or perch on the bench table for fine quality, seasonal fare a short walk from leafy **Hyde Park** (Map p902; William St, Highgate; ☑). Breakfast cocktails add to the fun.

Mrs S
CAFE **$$**

(Map p886; ☑08-9271 6690; www.mrsscafe.com. au; 178 Whatley Cres, Maylands; mains $11-23; ⏰7am-4pm Mon-Fri, from 8am Sat & Sun) Mrs S has a quirky retro ambience, the perfect backdrop for beautifully decorated cakes, a healthy breakfast or a lazy brunch. Menus – presented in Little Golden children's books

– feature loads of innovative variations on traditional dishes. Weekends are *wildly* popular, so try to visit on a weekday. Always get the pulled-pork 'manwich'.

El Público
MEXICAN $$

(Map p902; ☑0418 187 708; www.elpublico.com. au; 511 Beaufort St, Highgate; snacks & shared plates $5-19; ⊙5pm-midnight Mon-Fri, from 4pm Sat & Sun) Interesting and authentic spins on Mexican street food, all served as small plates that are perfect for sharing. Menu standouts include duck carnitas tacos, grilled octopus, and a sweetcorn sundae with coconut and popcorn for dessert. Bring along a few friends and groove to the occasional DJs over mezcal and great cocktails.

★ Must Winebar
FRENCH $$$

(Map p902; ☑08-9328 8255; www.must.com. au; 519 Beaufort St, Highgate; bar snacks $6-23, mains $23-38; ⊙4pm-midnight Tue-Thu & Sat, from noon Fri) One of Perth's best wine bars, Must is also one of the city's slickest restaurants with a cheeky, playful vibe that particularly resonates on Fridays, when Champagne and shucked oysters flow. The menu marries smart modern-Australian numbers with excellent local produce. A French-bistro influence wafts through, particularly in the bar snacks; the house charcuterie plate is legendary.

St Michael 6003
MODERN AUSTRALIAN $$$

(Map p902; ☑08-9328 1177; www.stmichael6003. com.au; 483 Beaufort St, Highgate; entrees $18-21, mains $28-39; ⊙6-10pm Tue-Sat & noon-3pm Fri) Welcome to one of the city's classiest and most elegant restaurants. Like so many of Perth's eateries, the emphasis here is on smaller shared plates, but there's some serious culinary wizardry in the kitchen. Menu highlights could include locally sourced marron (freshwater lobster), scallops, quail and lamb. Sign up for the seven-course menu ($95 per person) for a leisurely treat.

✖ Kings Park & Subiaco

Subiaco Farmers Market
MARKET $

(Map p898; ☑0406 758 803; www.subifarmers market.com.au; Subiaco Primary School, 271 Bagot Rd; snacks & meals $7-12; ⊙8am-noon Sat; 🐾) Every Saturday morning this market fills with gourmet-food stalls, fresh fruit and veg, naturally leavened breads, fresh flowers, pretty cupcakes and live music from buskers. Bring along your dog if you want to really blend in with the locals.

Boucla
CAFE $

(Map p898; ☑08-9381 2841; www.boucla.com.au; 349 Rokeby Rd, Subiaco; mains $10-23; ⊙7am-4pm Mon-Sat, 8am-1pm Sun) A locals' secret, this Greek- and Levantine-infused haven is pleasingly isolated from the thick of the Rokeby Rd action. Baklava and cakes tempt you from the corner, and huge tarts filled with blue-vein cheese and roast vegetables spill off plates. The salads are great too.

Meeka
MIDDLE EASTERN $$$

(Map p898; ☑08-9381 1800; www.meekarestau rant.com.au; 361 Rokeby Rd, Subiaco; meze $15-18, mains $31-39; ⊙5pm-late Tue-Sat) In Subiaco's Rokeby Rd restaurant enclave, Meeka combines Modern Australian cuisine with the flavours of the Middle East and North Africa. Of the many meze dishes try the local tempura whiting (fish) with eggplant puree and pomegranate salad, while a lamb tagine will send you home full-bellied. At $60, the chef's multicourse menu is excellent value.

✖ Leederville

★ Pinchos
TAPAS $

(Map p898; ☑08-9228 3008; www.pinchos.me; 112-124 Oxford St; small plates $11-18, larger plates $25-27; ⊙8am-10pm Sun-Tue, to 10.30pm Wed-Thu, to 11pm Fri & Sat) Iberian-inspired good times constantly rock this corner location amid Leederville's many cafes, casual restaurants and bars. The must-have tapas are the pork-belly chicharrons and the Piedro Ximenez and blue-cheese mushrooms – they've never left the menu. Those and the beef cheeks are perfect drinking fodder with the attractively priced Spanish beer, wine, sherry and on-tap sangria.

Duende
TAPAS $$

(Map p898; ☑08-9228 0123; www.duende.com.au; 662 Newcastle St; tapas & mains $8-20; ⊙noon-late Mon-Fri, from 11.30am Sat & Sun) Sleek, candlelit Duende occupies a quiet corner site just off the buzzing nexus of Leederville. Stellar, modern-accented and good-value tapas offer a compelling argument to make a meal of it. Or call in for a late-night glass of dessert wine and churros. The cocktails are particularly polished here too. The six-course chef's selection menu makes so much sense ($55).

Sayers
CAFE $$

(Map p898; ☑08-9227 0429; www.sayersfood. com.au; 224 Carr Pl; mains $17-27; ⊙7am-5pm) This classy Leederville brunch cafe has a

Highgate & Mt Lawley

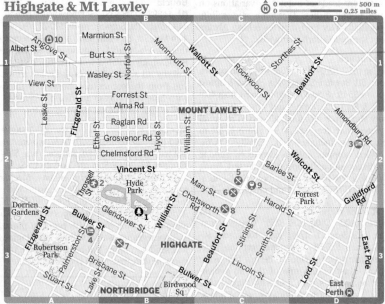

Highgate & Mt Lawley

⊙ Sights
1 Hyde Park..B3

🏃 Activities, Courses & Tours
2 Hyde Park Playground.........................A2

🛏 Sleeping
3 Durack House.......................................D2
4 Witch's Hat...A3

🍴 Eating
5 El Público..C2

6 Must Winebar.......................................C2
7 Sayers Sister..B3
8 St Michael 6003...................................C3

🍷 Drinking & Nightlife
9 Five Bar..C2
Must Winebar...............................(see 6)

🛍 Shopping
10 Future Shelter.....................................A1

counter groaning under the weight of an alluring cake selection. The excellent breakfast menu includes coffee spiced brisket with fried eggs and sesame-seed bagel, while lunch highlights include house-smoked salmon in saffron rice with poached eggs. Welcome to one of Perth's best cafes.

Kailis Bros   SEAFOOD **$$**
(Map p898; ☑08-9443 6300; www.kailisbrosleeder ville.com.au; 101 Oxford St; small plates $14-26, mains $28-60; poke bowls $16; ⊙shop 8am-6pm, cafe 7am-late, poke window 10am-2pm Mon-Sat) A big fresh-seafood supplier with attached cafe. Go in just for a stickybeak: the staff are always happy to pick up a live yabby or marron (local freshwater crayfish) to show interested

parties. The fish market also has a poke-bowl window, with sashimi-grade fish sliced from specimens brought in that morning.

🍴 Northbridge

★Wines of While   AUSTRALIAN **$**
(Map p892; ☑08-9328 3332; www.winesofwhile. com; 458 William St; mains $10-24; ⊙noon-midnight Tue-Sat, to 10pm Sun) 🌿 A 50-seater wine bar that's become known for its great value and flavoursome food. It's run by a young, qualified doctor who still works as a surgical assistant on Mondays. His true passion is natural wine, but he's a phenomenal cook. Get the ricotta-zucchini salad, the house-baked bread and zesty lemon white beans.

★**Chicho Gelato** GELATO $

(Map p892; www.chichogelato.com; 180 William St; from $5; ☺noon-10pm Sun-Wed, to 11pm Thu-Sat) Hands down Perth's best gelato. With innovative flavours like avocado with candied bacon, and everything made from real ingredients (no fake flavourings here), it's easy to see why. Expect queues in the evening – don't worry, the line moves quickly – and ask about current collaborations with local chefs. Do pay $1 extra to have melted chocolate poured into your waffle cone.

Tak Chee House MALAYSIAN $

(Map p892; ✆08-9328 9445; 1/364 William St; mains $11-18; ☺11am-9pm Tue-Sun) With Malaysian students crammed in for a taste of home, Tak Chee is one of the best Asian cheapies along William St. If you don't have a taste for satay, Hainan chicken or *char kway teo* (fried noodles), Thai, Vietnamese, Lao and Chinese flavours are all just footsteps away. Cash only; BYO wine or beer.

★**Bivouac Canteen & Bar** CAFE $$

(Map p892; ✆08-9227 0883; www.bivouac.com.au; 198 William St; small plates $9-19, large plates $28-34; ☺noon-late Tue-Sat) Flavour-jammed, Middle Eastern–influenced cuisine partners with a good wine list, craft beers and artisanal ciders. Always-busy Bivouac's white walls are adorned with a rotating roster of work from local artists. The lamb ribs in a lemon glaze are a great way to kick off the meal, followed by the Palestinian-style nine-spice chicken with toasted buckwheat and smoky yoghurt.

Henry Summer AUSTRALIAN $$

(Map p892; www.lavishhabits.com.au/venues/henry-summer; 69 Aberdeen St; ☺noon-midnight Sun-Thu, to 2am Fri & Sat; ☻; 🚍free CAT) The size of a pub with the feel of a small bar, Henry Summer woos with cascading plants and fronded canopies, open-air spaces and a welcoming vibe. The menu blends premixed cocktails with wood-fired meats and raw salads. Collect your dishes from a pink neon sign declaring 'Pick up spot' and see what – or who – else you encounter.

Brika GREEK $$

(Map p892; ✆0455 321 321; www.brika.com.au; 3/177 Stirling St; meze & mains $12-35; ☺5pm-late Mon-Thu, from noon Fri-Sun) Presenting a stylish spin on rustic Greek cuisine, off the main drag Brika is a load of fun. The whitewashed interior is enlivened by colourful traditional fabrics. Menu highlights include creamy smoked-eggplant dip, slow-cooked lamb and charred calamari. Definitely leave room for a dessert of *loukoumades* (Greek doughnuts).

🍴 **Scarborough to Cottesloe**

North Street Store BAKERY $

(Map p886; ✆08-9286 2613; www.northstreet store.com.au; 16 North St, Cottesloe; rolls $10-14; ☺8am-8pm Mon-Fri, to 3pm Sat & Sun; 🖶) If ever you have a hankering for a crispy pork roll or a cinnamon scroll, this is your happy place. Perched on a corner away from the beachfront, this place heaves from early in the morning, not least for its house-baked breads. The coffee is perhaps Cottesloe's best too.

Cott & Co Fish Bar SEAFOOD $$

(Map p886; ✆08-9383 1100; www.cottandco.com. au; 104 Marine Pde, Cottesloe; snacks & oysters $3-14, mains $26-41; ☺5pm-late Wed-Thu, from noon Fri & Sat, to 3pm Sun) This sleek seafood restaurant and wine bar is part of the renovated and historic Cottesloe Beach Hotel (p896). Order local oysters and a glass of Margaret River wine, and tumble into a relaxing reverie in front of an Indian Ocean sunset. Out the back, the pub's formerly rowdy garden bar now channels a whitewashed Cape Cod vibe as the Beach Club.

🍴 **Fremantle**

Leake St Cafe CAFE $

(Map p906; www.facebook.com/pg/leakestcafe teria; Leake St; mains $10-15; ☺7.30am-3.30pm Mon-Fri) 🌿 Access this compact courtyard space by walking through the Kakulas Sister deli (Map p906; ✆08-9430 4445; www.kakulassister. net.au; 29-31 Market St; ☺9am-5.30pm Mon-Fri, to 5pm Sat, from 11.30am Sun; 🌿), and find some of Freo's best coffee and an ever-changing menu. Healthy flavours could include a salad of roasted eggplant, chickpeas and toasted almonds, sourdough sandwiches, or good-value brown-rice bowls overflowing with Asian spiced chicken. Don't miss the savoury muffins, especially if figs are in season.

★**Manuka**
Woodfire Kitchen BARBECUE, PIZZA $$

(Map p906; ✆08-9335 3527; www.manukawood fire.com.au; 134 High St; shared plates $7-38, pizzas $19-22; ☺5-9pm Tue-Fri, noon-3pm & 5-9pm Sat & Sun) 🌿 Relying almost exclusively on a wood-fired oven, the kitchen at Manuka is tiny, but it's still big enough to turn out some of the tastiest food in town. The passionate chef has become an expert at taming the flame; his seasonal menu could include whole roasted fish, coal-grilled eggplant or peppers and basil pesto. The pizzas are also excellent.

★ **Ootong & Lincoln** CAFE $$
(Map p886; ☑ 08-9335 6109; www.facebook.com/ootongandlincoln; 258 South Tce; mains $12-23; ☺ 6am-5pm; 🚻) Catch the free CAT bus to South Fremantle for this top breakfast spot. Join the locals grabbing takeaway coffee or beavering away on their laptops, and start the day with macadamia-and-dukkah porridge, or pop in from noon for Mexican corn croquettes. Vintage 1960s furniture and loads of space make it a great place to linger.

★ **Bread in Common** BISTRO, BAKERY $$
(Map p906; ☑ 08-9336 1032; www.breadincommon.com.au; 43 Pakenham St; shared platters $15-19, mains $23-33; ☺ 11.30am-10pm Mon-Fri, 8am-late Sat & Sun; 🚻) 🍴 Be lured by the comforting aroma of the in-house bakery before staying on for cheese and charcuterie platters, or larger dishes such as lamb ribs or pork belly. The focus is on comfort food and culinary flair, while big shared tables and a chic warehouse ambience encourage conversation over WA wines and Aussie craft beers and ciders.

★ **Propeller** CAFE $$
(Map p886; ☑ 08-93359366; www.propellernorthfreo.com.au; 222 Queen Victoria St, North Fremantle; shared plates & mains $12-36; ☺ 8am-late) A blue shipping container doubles as a coffee-window and bar inside this cafe-bistro in North Fremantle, enclosed in glass from sometimes icy winds. Middle Eastern flavours inform dishes including Moorish skewers, refreshing salads, and rustic wood-fired *manoushe* (Lebanese flatbreads) spread with lamb, yoghurt and pomegranate, or mushroom and blue cheese. The chef's $49 menu is a steal.

Duck Duck Bruce CAFE $$
(Map p906; ☑ 08-6219 5216; www.duckduckbruce.com.au; 8 Collie St; $14-23; ☺ 6.30am-3pm Mon-Fri, from 7am Sat & Sun; 🚻🍴) Out of the ordinary breakfast dishes are served in this airy, homey cafe that's flanked with al fresco spaces. Think stewed strawberries and rhubarb over maple granola. Or coconut sambal with eggs and cumin raita. Then there's the vanilla pancake stack with almonds and burnt orange curd. Get there before the 11.30am breakfast cut-off. Dogs are welcome too.

Raw Kitchen VEGETARIAN $$
(Map p906; ☑ 08-9433 4647; www.therawkitchen.com.au; 181a High St; mains $17-25; ☺ 11.30am-3.30pm Mon-Thu, to 9pm Fri-Sun; 🛜🍴) 🍴 The

beautiful warehouse this vegan, organic and sustainable cafe inhabits is less hippy than you might expect. Boost your energy levels in the concrete, brick and beam surrounds with superhealthy but still tasty food. Plant-based dishes naturally feature raw ingredients – think raw pad thai or poke. Hit the boutique for zero waste and plastic-free finds, including eco cosmetics.

🍷 Drinking & Nightlife

🍺 Central Perth

★ **Petition Beer Corner** CRAFT BEER
(Map p892; ☑ 08-6168 7773; www.petitionperth.com/beer; State Bldgs, cnr St Georges Tce & Barrack St; ☺ 11.30am-late Mon-Sat, from noon Sun; 🛜) Distressed walls provide the backdrop for craft brews at this spacious bar. There's a rotating selection of 18 independent beers on tap – check out Now Tapped on Petition's website – and it's a great place to explore the more experimental side of the Australian craft-beer scene. Servings begin at just 150mL, so the curious beer fan will be in heaven.

Halford COCKTAIL BAR
(Map p892; ☑ 08-6168 7780; www.halfordbar.com.au; State Bldgs, cnr Hay St & Cathedral Ave; ☺ 4pm-2am Sat-Wed) Channelling a golden, 1950s vibe, basement bar Halford is where to come to sip Rat Pack–worthy cocktails, including expertly prepared martinis and other American bar classics. Halford's decor and furnishings combine theatre with a tinge of retro style too, with shimmering fabrics, coloured mood lighting, and vintage boxing pics lining the walls.

Tiny's BAR
(Map p892; ☑ 08-6166 9188; www.tinysbar.com.au; QV1 Plaza, cnr Hay St & Milligan St; ☺ 11.30am-late Mon-Fri, from 4pm Sat) It's hard to decide if this is a bar with excellent food, or a restaurant with a strong booze focus. Tiny's blurs the lines beautifully, starting with a punchy cocktail program, a refined wine list and a fun wine shop; and continuing with the city's best rotisserie chicken (with gravy). It has cool factor in spades and gets raucous Fridays.

Alfred's Pizzeria BAR
(Map p892; www.alfredspizzeria.com.au; 37 Barrack St; ☺ 3pm-midnight) Pizza by the slice at all hours, a dive-bar vibe (with a touch of *The*

Godfather), and craft beer and Aussie wines all combine in this improbably compact space in the CBD. Check out the cool B&W photos of heritage NYC, and don't miss the wall-covering murals featuring Axl Rose as Jesus and Madonna as the Virgin Mary.

Helvetica BAR
(Map p892; ☑08-9321 4422; www.helveticabar. com.au; rear 101 St Georges Tce; ⊙3-10pm Mon-Thu, noon-1am Fri, from 3pm Sat) Clever arty types tap their toes to delicious alternative pop in this bar named after a typeface and specialising in whisky and cocktails. The concealed entry is off Howard St; look for the chandelier in the laneway and the street-art characters by internationally renowned local artist, Stormie Mills.

Highgate & Mount Lawley

★Swallow WINE BAR
(Map p886; ☑08-9272 4428; www.swallowbar.com. au; 198 Whatley Cres, Maylands; ⊙5-10pm Wed, to 11pm Thu, 4pm-midnight Fri, noon-11pm Sat, to 9pm Sun) Channeling an art-deco ambience with funky lampshades and vintage French advertising, tiny Swallow is the kind of place you'd love as your local. Wine and cocktails are exemplary, and the drinks list includes Spanish lagers, New Zealand dark beers and WA ciders. Check the website for live music Thursday to Sunday. Excellent bar snacks ($4 to $34) are also available.

★Five Bar CRAFT BEER
(Map p902; ☑08-9227 5200; www.fivebar.com.au; 560 Beaufort St, Mount Lawley; ⊙4-10pm Mon-Thu, to midnight Fri, from noon Sat, to 10pm Sun) International and Australian craft beers – including seasonal and one-off brews from WA's best – as well as comfy lounges and funky decor make Mount Lawley's Five Bar worth seeking out, both for the discerning drinker and the social butterfly. Wine lovers are also well catered for, and the menu leans towards classy comfort food.

Must Winebar WINE BAR
(Map p902; ☑08-9328 8255; www.must.com. au; 519 Beaufort St, Highgate; ⊙noon-midnight) With cool French house music pulsing through the air and the perfect glass of wine in your hand (40 offerings by the glass, and more than 500 on the list), Must is hard to beat. It's particularly popular with mature-age bon vivants who love the bubbles and charcuterie, and upstairs is an exclusive, bookings-only Champagne bar.

THE FREMANTLE DOCTOR

Huh? Who's a doctor? And why are they the only one in Fremantle? No – this medic is actually Perth's famous summer sea breeze, which cools down the city and provides sweet relief to the gasping, sun-stroked locals. The science is simple: the air over Perth heats up in the sunshine and rises into the sky, sucking in cool air from over the Indian Ocean to fill the void – a classic sea-breeze scenario. The Doctor peaks between noon and 3pm, reaching wind speeds of up to 20 knots (about 37km/h) and blustering as far inland as York by late afternoon. Local tip: hit the beach in the morning, before the Doctor flattens out the surf and blows sand in your face.

Kings Park & Subiaco

Juanita's BAR
(Map p898; ☑08-9388 8882; www.facebook. com/juanitasbarsubiaco; 341 Rokeby Rd, Subiaco; ⊙2-10pm Tue, to 11pm Thu, from noon Fri, from 2pm Sat, 3-9pm Sun) Welcome to Perth's most neighbourly small bar. Tapas, shared platters (terrines, pâtés and fries – the co-owner chef often works the floor) and a concise selection of beer and wine partner with mismatched chairs and couches inside, and packed clusters of tables outside. It's all thoroughly local, very charming and a refreshing antidote to the flash, renovated pubs elsewhere in Subiaco.

Northbridge

★Sneaky Tony's BAR
(Map p892; www.facebook.com/sneakytonys; Nicks Lane; ⊙4pm-midnight) On Friday and Saturday you'll need the password to enter this speak-easy amid street art and Chinese restaurants – don't worry, it's revealed weekly on Sneaky Tony's Facebook page. Once inside, park yourself at the long bar and order a rum cocktail. Try the refreshing Dark & Stormy with ginger beer and lime. The hidden entrance is behind 28 Roe St.

★The Standard BAR
(Map p892; ☑08-9228 1331; www.thestandard perth.com.au; 28 Roe St; ⊙4pm-midnight Mon-Thu, from noon Fri & Sat, to 10pm Sun) Effortlessly straddling the divide between bar and restaurant, the Standard carries Northbridge's arty

Fremantle

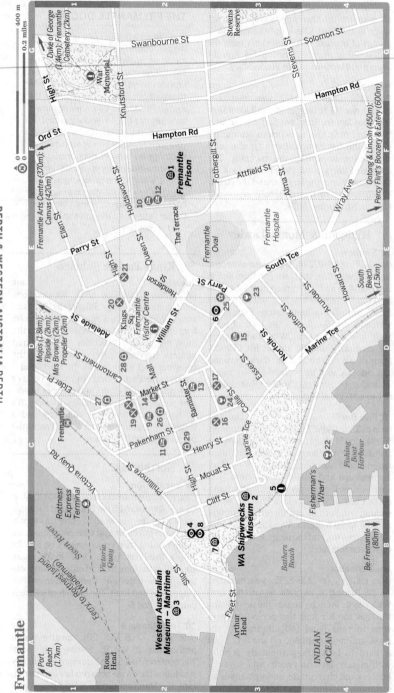

PERTH & WESTERN AUSTRALIA PERTH

400 m
0.2 miles

Swanbourne St
Stevens Reserve
Stevens St
Solomon St
Duke of George (14km); Fremantle Cemetery (2km)
High St
War Memorial
Hampton Rd
Knutsford St
Ord St
Hampton Rd
Fothergill St
Attfield St
Alma St
Wray Ave
Oatong & Lincoln (450m); Percy Flint's Boozery & Eatery (600m)
Fremantle Arts Centre (370m); Canvas (420m)
Holdsworth St
Ellen St
Fremantle Prison
Fremantle Hospital
The Terrace
Parry St
High St
Queen St
Fremantle Oval
South Tce
South Beach (1.5km)
Henderson St
Parry St
Howard St
Arundel St
Adelaide St
Fremantle Visitor Centre
Kings Sq
William St
Norfolk St
Marine Tce
Elder Pl
Cantonment St
Market St
Mall
Bannister St
Essex St
Suffolk St
Mojos (1.8km); Flipside (2km); Mrs Browns (2km); Propeller (2km)
Fremantle
Victoria Quay Rd
Pakenham St
Henry St
Cliff St
Mouat St
High St
Phillimore St
Cliff St
Marine Tce
WA Shipwrecks Museum 2
Fisherman's Wharf
Fishing Boat Harbour
Rottnest Express Terminal
Western Australian Museum – Maritime 3
Fleet St
Arthur Head
Slip St
Bathers Beach
Be.Fremantle (80m)
INDIAN OCEAN
Port Beach (1.7km)
Rous Head
Ferry to Rottnest Island (Wadjemup)
Swan River
Victoria Quay

Fremantle

⊙ **Top Sights**
1 Fremantle Prison....................................F2
2 WA Shipwrecks Museum......................B3
3 Western Australian Museum –
   Maritime...A2

⊙ **Sights**
4 Bathers Beach Art Precinct..................B2
5 Bon Scott Statue....................................C3
6 Fremantle Markets................................D3
7 Round House...B3
8 Walyalup Aboriginal Cultural
   Centre..B2

🛏 **Sleeping**
9 Fremantle Apartment............................C2
10 Fremantle Colonial Cottages................E2
11 Fremantle Hostel....................................C2
12 Fremantle Prison YHA Hostel...............E2
13 Hougoumont Hotel.................................D2
14 National Hotel...C2
15 Port Mill B&B..D3

🍴 **Eating**
16 Bread in Common...................................C3
17 Duck Duck Bruce....................................D3
18 Kakulas Sister...C2
19 Leake St Cafe..C2
20 Manuka Woodfire Kitchen....................D1
21 Raw Kitchen...E2

🍷 **Drinking & Nightlife**
22 Little Creatures......................................C4
23 Norfolk Hotel...E3
24 Strange Company...................................C3

🎭 **Entertainment**
25 Freo.Social...E3

🛍 **Shopping**
26 Common Ground Collective..................C2
27 Didgeridoo Breath..................................C1
28 Mills Records..D2
29 New Edition...C2

vibe into its colourful interior. Head through to the summery, courtyard garden and its shipping-container deck for the most raffish ambience, and partake in a Pimm's or spritz and such playful share plates as KFC cauliflower and toasted-coconut ceviche.

★ **Mechanics Institute** BAR
(Map p892; ☑08-9228 4189; www.mechanics institutebar.com.au; 222 William St; ☺noon-midnight Mon-Sat, to 10pm Sun) Negotiate the laneway entrance via the James St cul-de-sac – behind Alex Hotel (p896) – to discover one of Perth's most easy-going rooftop bars. Share one of the big, pine tables on the deck or nab a bar stool. Brilliant cocktails are readily shaken, craft beers are on tap, and you can even order in a gourmet burger from sister venue, **Flipside** (Map p892; ☑08-9228 8822; www.flipsideburgerbar.com.au; 222 William St; burgers $8-15; ☺11.30am-9.30pm Mon-Wed, to late Thu-Sat, noon-9pm Sun), downstairs.

Alabama Song BAR
(Map p892; www.facebook.com/alabamasongbar; level 1, behind 232 William St; ☺6pm-2am Wed-Sat, from 8pm Sun) Featuring over 130 rye whiskies and bourbons, Alabama Song is a fun, late-night dive bar down a back lane in Northbridge. Chicken wings and cheeseburgers are impressively good, and on Friday and Saturday nights live bands and DJs rip through rockabilly, honky tonk and country classics. Don't forget your John Deere trucker cap, worn with a side of irony.

**Northbridge
Brewing Company** MICROBREWERY
(Map p892; ☑08-6151 6481; www.northbridge brewingco.com.au; 44 Lake St; ☺11am-late Sun-Thu, to 2am Fri & Sat) The beers brewed here are decent enough, but the real attractions are the occasional on-tap guest beers from around Australia. The outdoor bar adjoining the grassy expanse of Northbridge Plaza is relaxed and easy-going, and various big screens dotted around the multilevel industrial space make this a good spot to watch live sport.

Bird BAR
(Map p892; www.williamstreetbird.com; 181 William St; ☺11.30am-midnight Mon-Sat, to 11pm Sun) A cool indie bar lined with wood and bird cages, leading to a stage regularly ruled by local bands, performers and DJs. One of Perth's few live-music venues, it has an excellent brick courtyard out the back, filled with dog-eared couches and chatterboxes.

Ezra Pound BAR
(Map p892; ☑0401 347 471; www.ezrapound. com.au; 189 William St; ☺3pm-midnight Mon-Thu, from 1pm Fri & Sat, to 10pm Sun) Down a much-graffitied laneway leading off William St, Ezra Pound is favoured by Northbridge's tattooed, arty, bohemian set. It's the kind of place where you can settle into a red-velvet chair and sip a Tom Collins out of a jam jar. Earnest conversations about Kerouac and Kafka are strictly optional.

Scarborough to Cottesloe

Twenty9   BAR

(Map p886; ☑ 08-9284 3482; 29 Napoleon St, Cottesloe; mains $20; ⊙ 7am-9pm Tue-Wed, to 10pm Thu-Sun) In the swanky retail street of Cottesloe, away from the chilled-out beach strip, Twenty9 is a casual, family-friendly joint playing Foxtel sport and serving easy-to-please dishes.

Fremantle

★ **Little Creatures**   BREWERY

(Map p906; ☑ 08-6215 1000; www.littlecreatures. com.au; Fishing Boat Harbour, 40 Mews Rd; ⊙ 10am-late Mon-Fri, from 9am Sat, to 11pm Sun; ⊕) Try everything on tap – particularly the Pale Ale and Rogers. The floor's chaotic and fun, and the wood-fired pizzas ($20 to $24) are worth the wait. Shared plates ($8 to $27) include kangaroo with tomato chutney and marinated octopus. There's a sandpit out the back for kids and free bikes for all, plus regular brewery tours ($20). No bookings.

★ **Norfolk Hotel**   PUB

(Map p906; ☑ 08-9335 5405; www.norfolkhotel. com.au; 47 South Tce; share plates $9-24, mains $19-40; ⊙ 11am-midnight Mon-Sat, to 10pm Sun) Slow down to Freo pace at this 1887 pub. Interesting guest beers wreak havoc for the indecisive drinker, and the food and pizzas are very good. The heritage limestone courtyard is a treat, especially when sunlight dapples through elms and eucalypts. Downstairs, the **Odd Fellow** channels a bohemian small-bar vibe and has live music Wednesday to Saturday from 7pm.

Strange Company   COCKTAIL BAR

(Map p906; www.strangecompany.com.au; 5 Nairn St; small plates $9-15, mains $14-23; ⊙ noon-midnight) Fabulous cocktails – try the spiced daiquiri – WA craft beers and slick, good-value food make Strange Company a sophisticated alternative to the raffish pubs along South Tce. It's still very laid-back, though – this is Freo, after all – and after-work action on the sunny terrace segues into after-dark assignations in Strange Company's cosy wooden interiors. It's worth staying for dinner.

Percy Flint's Boozery & Eatery   BAR

(Map p886; ☑ 08-9430 8976; www.facebook.com/ percyflintsouthfreo; 211 South Tce; ⊙ 4pm-midnight Tue-Thu, from noon Fri-Sun) A relaxed neighbourhood watering hole, Percy Flint is very popular with locals. The tap-beer selection is one of Freo's most interesting, with brews from around WA, and shared plates with Mediterranean or Asian flavours are best enjoyed around the big tables in the garden courtyard.

Mrs Browns   BAR

(Map p886; ☑ 08-9336 1887; www.mrsbrownbar. com.au; 241 Queen Victoria St, North Fremantle; ⊙ 4.30pm-midnight Mon-Thu, from noon Fri & Sat, to 10pm Sun) Exposed bricks and a copper bar combine with retro and antique furniture to create North Fremantle's most atmospheric drinking den. The music could include all those cult bands you thought were *your* personal secret, and an eclectic menu of beer, wine and tapas targets the more discerning, slightly older bar hound. Ordering burgers from **Flipside** (Map p886; ☑ 08-9433 2188; www.flipsideburgers.com.au; 239 Queen Victoria St; burgers $8-16; ⊙ 11.30am-9pm) next door is encouraged.

☆ Entertainment

Live Music

★ **Duke of George**   JAZZ

(Map p886; ☑ 08-9319 1618; www.dukeofgeorge. com.au; 135 George St, East Fremantle; plates $18-29; dinner show $35-65 plus gig ticket; ⊙ 5pm-midnight Thu-Fri, from noon Sat, to 10pm Sun; ⊕) Opening in early 2019 in the historic Brush Factory, this is a fun, lively, hugely approachable new jazz bar where dancing between the tables (there's no designated dance floor) is encouraged. Saturday's dinner and show is highly recommended (excellent value too), but you can keep things simple with the à la carte menu of dishes inspired by America's deep south.

Freo.Social   LIVE MUSIC

(Map p906; www.freo.social; Parry St, Fremantle; ⊙ 11am-midnight Wed-Sun; ⊕) Part live music haunt, part microbrewery, part food-truck and beer-garden hang-out, Freo.Social is difficult to pigeonhole. Opening March 2019, the evolving venue with capacity for 550 people fills a historic space in central Fremantle. It favours big-name local talent, from San Cisco to John Butler and the Waifs, but also leans towards the experimental and has DJ sets.

Badlands Bar   LIVE MUSIC

(Map p892; ☑ 0498 239 273; www.badlands.bar; 3 Aberdeen St; ⊙ 6pm-2am Fri & Sat) Located on the fringes of Northbridge, Badlands has

LGBTIQ+ PERTH

Perth is home to all of WA's gay and lesbian venues. Before you get too excited, let's clarify matters: 'all' entails a couple of bars like **The Court** (Map p892; ☑ 08-9328 5292; www.the-court.com.au; 50 Beaufort St; ⊙ noon-10pm Sun-Tue, to midnight Wed-Thu, to 2am Fri & Sat) and **Hula Bula Bar** (Map p892; ☑ 08-9225 4457; www.hulabulabar.com; 12 Victoria Ave; ⊙ 4pm-midnight Tue-Thu, to 1am Fri, from 6pm Sat, noon-midnight Sun; ☎); a club, **Connections** (Map p892; ☑ 08-9328 1870; www.connectionsnightclub.com; 81 James St; ⊙ 8pm-late Wed-Sat); and one men's **sauna** (Map p892; ☑ 08-9328 2930; www.perthsteamworks.com.au; 369 William St; $25; ⊙ noon-1am Sun-Thu, to 2am Fri & Sat). Many other bars, especially around Highgate and Mt Lawley, are somewhat gay-friendly, but it's hardly what you'd call a pumping scene.

For a head's up on what's on, pick up the free monthly newspaper *Out in Perth* (www.outinperth.com). Pride WA runs **PrideFest** (www.pridewa.com.au; ⊙ Nov), a 10-day festival from mid-November culminating in the Pride Parade.

shrugged off its previous incarnation as a retro 1950s-inspired nightclub to be reborn as an edgy rock venue. The best WA bands are regulars, and if an up-and-coming international band is touring, Badlands is the place to see them before they become really famous. Check online for listings.

Mojos LIVE MUSIC
(Map p886; ☑ 08-9430 4010; www.mojosbar.com.au; 237 Queen Victoria St, Fremantle; ⊙ 5.30pm-midnight Mon-Tue, from 5pm Wed, to 1am Thu-Sat, 4-10pm Sun) Local and national bands (mainly Aussie rock and indie) and DJs play at this small place, and there's a sociable beer garden out the back. First Friday of the month is reggae night, every Monday is open-mic night and local music stars on Tuesdays. It's slightly dingy and dog-eared in that I-want-to-settle-in-all-night kind of way. Locals love it.

Moon LIVE MUSIC
(Map p892; ☑ 08-9328 7474; www.themoon.com.au; 323 William St; ⊙ 5pm-1am Mon-Thu, noon-late Fri-Sun) A low-key, late-night cafe that's been running for more than 20 years and is regarded as a local institution, particularly by students. It has singer-songwriters on Wednesday night, jazz on Thursday and poetry slams on Saturday afternoon from 2pm.

Film

Somerville Auditorium CINEMA
(Map p886; ☑ 08-6488 2000; www.perthfestival.com.au; 35 Stirling Hwy, Crawley; ⊙ Nov-Mar) A quintessential Perth experience, the Perth Festival's international film program is held outdoors, on the University of WA's beautiful grounds, surrounded by pines and strings of lights. Picnicking before the film is a must.

Bring a cushion as the deckchair seating can be uncomfortable.

Rooftop Movies CINEMA
(Map p892; ☑ 08-9227 6288; www.rooftopmovies.com.au; 68 Roe St; online/door $16/17; ⊙ Tue-Sun late Oct-late Mar) Art-house, classic movies and new releases screen under the stars on the 6th floor of a Northbridge car park. Beanbags, wood-fired pizza and craft beer all combine for a great night out. Booking ahead online is recommended and don't be surprised if you're distracted from the on-screen action by the city views. Score $14 tickets on cheap Tuesdays.

Moonlight Cinema CINEMA
(Map p886; www.moonlight.com.au; May Dr Parklands, Kings Park; ⊙ 1 Dec-31 Mar) In summer, bring a blanket and a picnic and enjoy a romantic moonlit movie. Booking ahead online is recommended.

Theatre & Classical Music

Perth Concert Hall CONCERT VENUE
(Map p892; ☑ 08-9231 9999; www.perthconcerthall.com.au; 5 St Georges Tce) Home to the **Western Australian Symphony Orchestra** (WASO; ☑ 08-9326 0000; www.waso.com.au), this Brutalist-style building also hosts big-name international acts, musicals and comedians.

State Theatre Centre THEATRE
(Map p892; ☑ 08-6212 9292; www.ptt.wa.gov.au/venues/state-theatre-centre-of-wa; 174 William St) This stunning complex filled with gold tubes hanging from the ceiling includes the 575-seat Heath Ledger Theatre and the 234-seat Studio Underground. It hosts performances by the Black Swan State Theatre Company, Yirra Yaakin Theatre Company and the Barking Gecko young people's theatre.

Serious, challenging and deeply artistic performances are regularly held.

His Majesty's Theatre
THEATRE

(Map p892; ☑08-6212 9292; www.ptt.wa.gov.au/venues/his-majestys-theatre; 825 Hay St) The majestic home to the **West Australian Ballet** (☑08-9214 0707; www.waballet.com.au) and **West Australian Opera** (☑08-9278 8999; www.waopera.asn.au), as well as lots of theatre, comedy and cabaret.

Comedy

Lazy Susan's Comedy Den
COMEDY

(Map p892; ☑08-9328 2543; www.lazysusans.com.au; Brisbane Hotel, 292 Beaufort St, Highgate; ⊙8pm Tue, Fri & Sat) Shapiro Tuesday offers a mix of first-timers, seasoned amateurs and pros trying out new shtick (for a very reasonable $5). Friday is for more grown-up stand-ups, including some interstate visitors ($25). Saturday is the Big Hoohaa – a team-based, improv-comedy-meets-theatre laughfest ($25).

Sport

In WA, 'football' means Aussie rules. During the Australian Football League (AFL; www.afl.com.au) season (March to September), it's hard to get locals to talk about anything but the two WA teams: the West Coast Eagles (www.westcoasteagles.com.au) and the Fremantle Dockers (www.fremantlefc.com.au). West Coast have had regular success, most recently winning the competition in 2018.

In the men's National Basketball League (NBL; www.nbl.com.au), the Perth Wildcats have appeared in every finals series since 1987 and have won the league an unrivalled eight times. The West Coast Fever netball team and Perth Scorchers Big Bash League cricket team are also very successful at the national level.

Optus Stadium
STADIUM

(Perth Stadium; Map p886; www.optusstadium.com.au; Victoria Park Dr, Burswood) Perth's new 60,000-seat riverside stadium and its surrounding, family-friendly park (think playground, BBQs, sculptures) opened in January 2018. Big concerts, AFL games and international sport fixtures including cricket and rugby are held here. A new Perth Stadium train station services incoming crowds, while the Matagarup bridge links the stadium precinct with East Perth, enabling pedestrian access across the Swan River.

🛍 Shopping

Common Ground Collective
DESIGN

(Map p906; ☑0418 158 778; www.facebook.com/cmmngrnd; 82 High St, Fremantle; ⊙10am-5pm Mon-Sat, from 11am Sun) An eclectic showcase of jewellery, apparel and design, much of it limited-edition and mainly from local Fremantle artisans and designers. The coffee at the in-house cafe is pretty damn good too.

Didgeridoo Breath
ARTS & CRAFTS

(Map p906; ☑08-9430 6009; www.didgeridoobreath.com; 6 Market St, Fremantle; ⊙10.30am-5pm) The planet's biggest selection of didgeridoos, Aboriginal Australian books and CDs, and how-to-play lessons ranging from one hour to four weeks. The didgeridoos are handmade and painted.

New Edition
BOOKS

(Map p906; ☑08-9335 2383; www.newedition.com.au; cnr High & Henry Sts, Fremantle; ⊙9am-9pm) Celebrating a sunny corner location for the past 30 years, this bookworm's dream has comfy armchairs for browsing, and a superb collection of Australian fiction and nonfiction tomes for sale. Author events, poetry readings and literary launches are common.

Mills Records
MUSIC

(Map p906; ☑08-9335 1945; www.mills.com.au; 22 Adelaide St, Fremantle; ⊙9am-5.30pm Mon-Fri, to 5pm Sat, from 11am Sun) Music, including some rarities (on vinyl and CD), instruments from harmonicas to acoustic guitars, and concert tickets. Check out the 'Local's Board' for recordings by Freo and WA acts.

Mossenson Galleries – Indigenart
ART

(Map p898; ☑08-9388 2899; www.mossensongalleries.com.au; 115 Hay St, Subiaco; ⊙11am-4pm Wed-Sat) Serious Aboriginal art from around Australia but with a focus on WA artists. Works include weavings, paintings on canvas, bark and paper, and sculpture.

Future Shelter
HOMEWARES

(Map p902; ☑08-9228 4832; www.futureshelter.com; 56 Angove St, North Perth; ⊙10am-5pm Mon-Sat, noon-3pm Sun) Quirky clothing, gifts and homewares designed and manufactured locally. Surrounding Angove St is an emerging hip North Perth neighbourhood with other cafes and design shops worth browsing.

William Topp
DESIGN

(Map p892; ☑08-9228 8733; www.williamtopp.com; 452 William St; ⊙10.30am-5.30pm Mon-Fri, 10am-5pm Sat, 11am-4pm Sun) Cool designer knick-knacks, one-off finds, handmade ceramics and framed tea towels. If you need a quirky gift, this is your spot.

ℹ Information

INTERNET ACCESS

Perth City offers free wi-fi access in Murray St Mall between William St and Barrack St.

State Library of WA (☎08-9427 3111; www.slwa.wa.gov.au; Perth Cultural Centre, 25 Francis St; ⊗9am-8pm Mon-Thu, to 5.30pm Fri, from 10am Sat & Sun; 🛜) Free wi-fi and internet access.

Fremantle City Library (☎08-9432 9766; www.frelibrary.wordpress.com; Fremantle Oval, 70 Parry St; ⊗9am-6pm Mon-Thu, to 5pm Fri, to 1pm Sat, 11am-3pm Sun; 🛜)

MEDICAL SERVICES

Lifecare Dental (☎08-9221 2777; www.lifecaredental.com.au; 419 Wellington St; ⊗8am-8pm) In Forrest Chase.

Royal Perth Hospital (☎08-9224 2244; www.rph.wa.gov.au; 197 Wellington St; ⊗24hr) In central Perth.

Travel Medicine Centre (☎08-9321 7888; www.travelmed.com.au; 5 Mill St; ⊗8am-5pm Mon-Thu, to 4pm Fri, 8.30am-12.30pm Sat) Travel-specific advice and vaccinations.

Sexual Assault Resource Centre (☎08-6458 1828, free call 1800 199 888; www.kemh.health.wa.gov.au/services/sarc; ⊗24hr) Provides a 24-hour emergency service.

Chemist Discount Centre (☎08-9321 5391; www.chemistdiscountcentre.com.au; 93 William St; ⊗7am-7pm Mon-Thu, to 9pm Fri, 9am-6pm Sat, 11am-5pm Sun) Handy city pharmacy.

Fremantle Hospital (☎08-9431 3333; www.fhhs.health.wa.gov.au; Alma St; ⊗24hr) At the edge of central Fremantle.

MONEY

ATMs are plentiful, and there are currency-exchange facilities at the airport and major banks in the CBD.

TOURIST INFORMATION

Perth City Visitor Kiosk (Map p892; www.visitperth.com.au; Forrest Pl, Murray St Mall; ⊗9.30am-4.30pm Mon-Thu & Sat, to 8pm Fri, 11am-3.30pm Sun) Volunteers here answer questions and run walking tours.

WA Visitor Centre (Map p892; ☎08-9483 1111; www.wavisitorcentre.com.au; 55 William St; ⊗9am-5pm Mon-Fri, 9.30am-4pm Sat & Sun) Excellent resource for information across WA.

Fremantle Visitor Centre (Map p906; ☎08-9431 7878; www.visitfremantle.com.au; Town Hall, Kings Sq; ⊗9am-5pm Mon-Fri, to 4pm

Sat, from 10am Sun) Accommodation and tour bookings; bike rental.

ℹ Getting There & Away

AIR

Around 10km east of Perth, Perth Airport (p1071) is served by numerous airlines, including **Qantas** (QF; ☎13 13 13; www.qantas.com.au), with daily flights to and from international and Australian destinations. There are four terminals: T1 and T2 are 15 minutes' drive from T3 and T4. T1 handles most international flights, along with Virgin Australia interstate flights. T2 handles regional WA flights for Alliance Airlines, Tigerair, Virgin Australia and Regional Express. T3 handles all Jetstar flights; T4 handles all Qantas flights. A free terminal transfer bus operates round the clock.

BUS

Transwa (Map p892; ☎13 62 13; www.transwa.wa.gov.au; East Perth Station, West Pde, East Perth; ⊗office 8.30am-5pm Mon-Fri, to 4.30pm Sat, 10am-4pm Sun) operates services from the bus terminal at East Perth train station to/from many destinations around the state. These include the following.

➠ SW1 to Augusta ($55, six hours) via Mandurah, Bunbury, Busselton and Dunsborough.

➠ SW2 to Pemberton ($57, 5½ hours) via Bunbury, Balingup and Bridgetown.

➠ GS1 to Albany ($66, six hours) via Mt Barker.

➠ GE2 to Esperance ($98, 10 hours) via Mundaring, York and Hyden.

➠ N1 to Geraldton ($69, six hours) and on to Northampton and Kalbarri.

South West Coach Lines (Map p892; ☎08-9753 7700; www.southwestcoachlines.com.au) focuses on the southwestern corner of WA, running services from **Elizabeth Quay Bus Station** (Map p892; ☎13 62 13; www.transperth.wa.gov.au; Mounts Bay Rd) to most towns in the region. Destinations include Bunbury ($58, three hours), Busselton ($63, 3¾ hours), Dunsborough ($77, 4½ hours), Margaret River ($77, 4½ hours) and Manjimup ($79, five hours).

Integrity Coach Lines (Map p892; ☎08-9274 7464; www.integritycoachlines.com.au; cnr Wellington St & Horseshoe Bridge) runs northbound and southbound services linking Perth to Broome and stopping at key coastal travellers' destinations en route. It also runs inland services between Perth and Port Hedland via Mt Magnet, Cue, Meekatharra and Newman.

TRAIN

Transwa runs the following services from Perth into rural WA.

➠ *Australind* (twice daily) Perth Station to Pinjarra ($18.05, 1¼ hours) and Bunbury ($33.50, 2½ hours).

→ *MerredinLink* (daily) East Perth Station to Toodyay ($18.05, 1¼ hours), Northam ($21.15, 1½ hours) and Merredin ($48.60, 3¼ hours).

→ *Prospector* (daily) East Perth to Kalgoorlie-Boulder ($91.80, 5¾ hours).

Great Southern Rail (☑1800 703 357; www. greatsouthernrail.com.au) runs the *Indian Pacific* train between Perth and Sydney – a four-day, three-night, 4352km cross-continental epic. Fares start at $2239 one way, including all meals, drinks and off-train excursions.

ℹ Getting Around

TO/FROM THE AIRPORT

Taxi fares to the city from the airport are around $45 from all terminals.

Just Transfers (☑0400 366 893; www.just transfers.com.au) runs prebooked shuttle-buses between Perth Airport and the city/Fremantle (one way per person $25/60; cheaper for multiple travellers).

Transperth bus 40 travels regularly to T3 and T4; bus 380 runs regularly to T1 and T2, both from Elizabeth Quay Bus Station (both routes $4.80, 40 minutes).

BICYCLE

Bikes can be taken free of charge on ferries at any time and on trains outside weekday peak hours (7am to 9am and 4pm to 6.30pm) – with a bit of planning you can pedal as far as you like in one direction then return via public transport. Bikes can't be taken on buses, except some regional coaches (for a small charge). For route maps, see www.transport.wa.gov.au/cycling or call into a bike shop.

Spinway WA (☑0413 343 305; www.spin waywa.bike; per 1/4/24hr from $11/22/33) has 14 self-serve bicycle-hire kiosks in handy spots around central Perth, Kings Park, South Perth, Scarborough and Fremantle. Bikes cost $11 for one hour, $22 for four hours, or $33 for 24 hours. Swipe your credit card and follow the prompts. Helmets and locks are included, available from partner businesses (often hotel reception desks) where bikes are parked outside. Alternatively, rent a bike from **Cycle Centre** (☑08-9325 1176; www.cyclecentre.com.au; 326 Hay St; bike hire per day/week from $25/65; ☺9am-5.30pm Mon-Fri, to 4pm Sat, from 1pm Sun).

About Bike Hire (☑08-9221 2665; www. aboutbikehire.com.au; 305 Riverside Dr, East Perth; per hour/day/week from $10/24/64; ☺8am-6pm Nov-Mar, reduced hours Apr, May & Oct) Road, off-road and hybrid bikes for hire at reasonable rates. Also hires kayaks and stand-up paddleboards; see the website for details.

Free Wheeling Fremantle (☑08-9431 7878; www.fremantle.wa.gov.au/visit/getting-around/ cycling; Fremantle Visitor Centre, Kings Sq; ☺9am-5pm Wed-Sun) Bike rental.

CAR & MOTORCYCLE

Driving in the city takes a bit of practice, as some streets are one way and many aren't signposted. There are plenty of (expensive) car-parking buildings in the central city but no free places to park.

A fun way to careen about the city is on a moped. **Scootamoré** (☑08-9380 6580; www. scootamore.com.au; 356a Rokeby Rd, Subiaco; hire 1/3/7 days $60/150/300; ☺8.30am-5.30pm Mon-Fri, 9am-1pm Sat) hires out 50cc scooters with helmets (compulsory) and insurance included (for those over 21).

Car-rental companies big and small proliferate in Perth, including **Avis** (☑08-9237 0022; www. avis.com.au; 960 Hay St; ☺7.30am-6pm Mon-Fri, to 1pm Sat & Sun), **Backpacker Car Rentals** (☑08-9430 8869; www.backpackercarrentals. com.au; 284 Hampton Rd, South Fremantle), **Bayswater** (☑08-9325 1000; www.bayswater carrental.com.au; 160 Adelaide Tce; ☺7am-6pm Mon-Fri, 8am-3.30pm Sat & Sun), **Budget** (☑08-9237 0022; www.budget.com.au; 960 Hay St; ☺8am-5pm Mon-Fri, to 11am Sat, to 10am Sun), **Campabout** (☑08-9858 9126; www.campabout oz.com.au), **Hertz** (☑08-9321 7777; www.hertz. com.au; 475 Murray St; ☺7am-6pm Mon-Thu, to 6.30pm Fri, 8am-1pm Sat & Sun), **Sunset** (☑08-9245 2466; www.sunsetrentacar.com.au; 6 Scarborough Beach Rd, Scarborough; ☺8am-5pm Mon-Fri, to 1pm Sat) and **Thrifty** (☑08-9225 4466; www.thrifty.com.au; 198 Adelaide Tce; ☺8am-4.45pm Mon-Fri, to 11.45pm Sat & Sun). **Britz** (☑08-9479 5208; www.britz.com/au) hires out fully equipped 4WDs fitted out as campervans, popular on the roads of northern WA; it has offices in all the state capitals, as well as Perth and Broome, so one-way rentals are possible.

PUBLIC TRANSPORT

Transperth (☑13 62 13; www.transperth.wa.gov. au) operates Perth's excellent network of public buses, trains and ferries. There are Transperth information offices at Perth Station (Wellington St), Perth Busport (between Roe St and Wellington St), Perth Underground Station (off Murray St) and Elizabeth Quay Bus Station (Mounts Bay Rd). There's a serviceable online journey planner.

Bus

Perth's central **Free Transit Zone** (FTZ) is served by regular buses and is well covered during the day by the four free **Central Area Transit** (CAT) services. The Yellow and Red CATs operate east–west routes, with Yellow sticking mainly to Wellington St, and Red looping roughly east on Murray St and west on Hay St. The Blue CAT does a figure eight through Northbridge and the southern end of the city; this is the only one to run late – to midnight on Friday and Saturday only. The Green CAT connects Leederville Station and Elizabeth Quay Bus Station via West Perth and St Georges Tce. There are also free Red and Blue CATs in Fremantle: Red loops north of the central area, Blue to the south.

Pick up a copy of free CAT timetables (widely available on buses and elsewhere) for the exact routes and stops. Buses run roughly every five to 15 minutes, more frequently on weekdays. Digital displays at the stops advise when the next bus is due.

The broader metropolitan area is serviced by a wide network of **Transperth** (☑ 13 62 13; www. transperth.wa.gov.au) buses. Pick up timetables from any Transperth information centre or use the online journey planner. Most buses leave from the underground **Perth Busport** (Map p892; ☑ 13 62 13; www.transperth.wa.gov. au/perthbusport; via Yagan Sq; ☺ info centre 7.30am-5.30pm Mon-Fri, 8am-1pm Sat), located between the CBD and Northbridge.

Ferry

A ferry runs every 20 to 30 minutes between **Elizabeth Quay Jetty** (Map p892; ☑ 13 62 13; www.transperth.wa.gov.au; off William St, Elizabeth Quay) and Mends St Jetty in South Perth – a great way to get to Perth Zoo or for a bargain from-the-river glimpse of the Perth skyline. **Little Ferry Co** (Map p892; ☑ 0488 777 088; www.littleferryco.com.au; Elizabeth Quay; 1/2/3 stops adult $12/18/22, child $10/16/20, day pass adult/child $32/28; ☺ 10am-5.30pm) runs scheduled services linking Elizabeth Quay and Claisebrook Cove, also connecting to Perth Stadium on big-game days.

The highly professional **Rottnest Express** (Map p892; ☑ 1300 467 688; www.rottnestexpress. com.au) runs ferries to Rottnest Island from both **Elizabeth Quay** (Map p892; pier 2, Barrack St Jetty, Elizabeth Quay) and Fremantle – stops at **Victoria Quay** (Map p906; B Shed, Victoria Quay; ☺ 6.45am-5.15pm) and **Rous Head** (Map p886; 1 Emma Pl, Northport, Rous Head; ☺ 7.30am-5pm). All kinds of bike-hire, island tour and accommodation packages are available.

Train

Transperth operates five train lines from around 5.20am to midnight weekdays and to about 2am Saturday and Sunday. Your rail ticket can also be used on Transperth buses and ferries within the ticket's zone. You're free to take your bike on the train during nonpeak times. The lines and useful stops include the following:

Armadale Thornlie Line Perth, Burswood

Fremantle Line Perth, City West, West Leederville, Subiaco, Swanbourne, Cottesloe, North Fremantle, Fremantle

Joondalup Line Elizabeth Quay, Perth Underground, Leederville

Mandurah Line Perth Underground, Elizabeth Quay, Rockingham, Mandurah

Midland Line Perth, East Perth, Mt Lawley, Guildford, Midland

Perth Station (☑ 13 62 13; www.transperth. wa.gov.au; Wellington St) is the main hub with access to all lines (some via the linked Perth Underground Station).

Elizabeth Quay Station (☑ 13 62 13; www. transperth.wa.gov.au; off William St, Elizabeth Quay) is serviced by the Joondalup and Mandurah lines.

TAXI

Perth has a decent system of metered taxis, though the distances make frequent use costly and on busy nights you may have trouble flagging a taxi down in the street. The two main companies are **Swan Taxis** (☑ 13 13 30; www. swantaxis.com.au) and **Black & White Cabs** (☑ 08-9230 0440; www.blackandwhitecabs. com.au); both have wheelchair-accessible cabs. **Uber** also operates throughout Perth.

PERTH REGION

Western Australia is gargantuan, but you don't have to travel too far from Perth for a taste of the state. Just a day trip away, venturing into the lands of the Noongar nation, are the oceanic activities and breezy cafes of Mandurah, and the hyperactive winery, craft-beer and foodie scenes of the Swan Valley and Perth Hills (Wajuk tribal country). The heritage-listed towns of the underrated Avon Valley (Ballardong homelands) are also nearby. If you prefer more natural detours, head for the astonishing granite swell of Wave Rock on Nyaki-Nyaki lands; the brilliant swim spots and resident quokkas on Wadjemup/Rottnest Island; the people-free shores of the Turquoise Coast (Yuat lands); or the lonesome highways and long-lost wheat towns along Wildflower Way (also Ballardong country), which burst into a blaze of native blooms in spring.

❶ Getting There & Away

Perth is the logical gateway for exploring this area and is easily reached on flights from around Australia, New Zealand and Asia. For the independently minded (that's you, right?), hiring a car is the best way to go: local **Transwa** (☑ 1300 662 205; www.transwa.wa.gov.au) bus and train services exist, but can only get you to the main hubs and put a cap on your explorations.

Rottnest Island

☑ 08 / POP 340

'Rotto' – or Wadjemup to Noongar Aboriginal people – has long been the go-to destination for Perth families on holiday, and a coming-of-age promised land for local teens. Although it's only about 19km offshore from Fremantle, this car-free, off-the-grid slice of paradise, ringed by secluded beaches and bays, feels a million miles away

Cycling, snorkelling, fishing, surfing, diving and wildlife-spotting are excellent on the island. There's not a lot to do here that's not outdoors-oriented, so postpone your day trip if the weather isn't looking good.

History

The island was originally called Wadjemup (place across the water), but Wadjuk oral history recalls that it was joined to the mainland before being cut off by rising waters. Modern scientists date that occurrence to before 6500 years ago, making these memories some of the world's oldest. Archaeological finds suggest that the island was inhabited 30,000 years ago, but not after it was separated from the mainland.

Dutch explorer Willem de Vlamingh claimed discovery of the island in 1696 and named it Rotte-nest ('rat's nest' in Dutch) because of the king-sized 'rats' (read: quokkas) he saw there.

From 1838 the island was used as a prison for Aboriginal men and boys from all around the state. At least 3670 people were incarcerated here, in harsh conditions, with around 370 dying (at least five were hanged). Although there were no new prisoners after 1903 (by which time holidaymakers from the mainland had already discovered the island), some existing prisoners served their sentences here until 1931. Even before the prison was built, Wadjemup was considered a 'place of the spirits', and it's been rendered even more sacred to Aboriginal people because of the hundreds of their own, including prominent resistance leaders, who died here. Many avoid it to this day.

During WWI, approximately a thousand men of German and Austrian extraction were incarcerated here, their wives and children left to fend for themselves on the mainland. Ironically, most of the 'Austrians' were actually Croats who objected to Austro-Hungarian rule of their homeland. Internment resumed during WWII, although at that time it was mainly WA's Italian population that was imprisoned.

There's an ongoing push to return the island to its original name. One suggested compromise is to adopt a dual name, Wadjemup/Rottnest.

☉ Sights

Wadjemup Lighthouse   LIGHTHOUSE
(☑ 08-9372 9730; www.rottnestisland.com/see-and-do/Island-tours/wadjemup-lighthouse; Wadjemup Hill, off Digby Dr; tours adult/child $9/4; ☉ tours 10am-2.30pm) Rottnest's unmissable human-made landmark, the 20m-tall Wadjemup Lighthouse was built in 1849 and was WA's first stone lighthouse. Tours run daily every 30 minutes from 10am until 2.30pm inclusive, operated by Rottnest Voluntary Guides (p916). Take the Island Explorer (p916) bus to get here or cycle, but don't underestimate the ride: it can get windy by the salt lakes, and there are more than a few hills to conquer. There's often a coffee caravan parked here to aid recovery.

Rottnest Museum   MUSEUM
(☑ 08-9372 9703; www.rottnestisland.com/see-and-do/island-tours/museums-and-galleries; Kitson St; by donation; ☉ 10am-3.30pm) Housed in the old hay-store building built by Aboriginal prisoners in 1857, this engaging little museum tells of the island's natural and human history, not shirking from grim tales of shipwrecks and Aboriginal incarceration.

Wadjemup Aboriginal
Burial Ground   CEMETERY
(☑ 08-9372 9730; www.rottnestfoundation.org.au/aboriginal-burial-ground; off Kitson St) Adjacent to the Quod is a hushed, shady woodland area where hundreds of Aboriginal prisoners were buried in unmarked graves. Until relatively recently, this area was used as a campground, but it's now fenced off with signs asking visitors to show respect for what is regarded as a sacred site. Plans are under consideration to convert the area into a memorial, in consultation with Aboriginal Elders. Check the website for updates.

Quod   HISTORIC SITE
(☑ 08-9432 9300; www.ria.wa.gov.au/sustainability/social-sustainability/quod; Kitson St) Once an Aboriginal prison block, this hefty octagonal building with a central courtyard was built in 1864. During its time as a prison several men would share a 3m by 1.7m cell, with no sanitation (most of the 300-plus prisoner deaths here were reportedly due to disease). The site was later converted to a hostel, ignoring its deplorable past. With recognition of this, the only part of the complex that can now be visited is a small whitewashed chapel, where a weekly Sunday service is held at 9.30am.

Around Perth

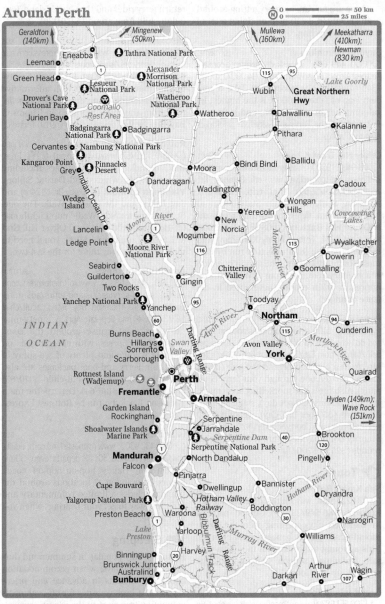

0   50 km
0   25 miles

Geraldton (140km)

Mingenew (50km)

Mullewa (160km)

Meekatharra (410km); Newman (830 km)

Eneabba

Leeman

Green Head

Tathra National Park

Alexander Morrison National Park

Wubin

Lake Goorly

Great Northern Hwy

Lesueur National Park

Drover's Cave National Park

Jurien Bay

Watheroo National Park

Coomallo Rest Area

Watheroo

Dalwallinu

Kalannie

Badgingarra National Park

Badgingarra

Pithara

Cervantes

Nambung National Park

Bindi Bindi

Ballidu

Kangaroo Point

Grey

Pinnacles Desert

Cataby

Dandaragan

Moora

Waddington

Cadoux

Wedge Island

Moore River

Yerecoin

Wongan Hills

Cowcowing Lakes

Lancelin

Ledge Point

Mogumber

New Norcia

Wyalkatchem

Seabird

Guilderton

Two Rocks

Moore River National Park

Gingin

Chittering Valley

Dowerin

Goomalling

Yanchep National Park

Yanchep

Toodyay

INDIAN OCEAN

Burns Beach

Hillarys

Sorrento

Scarborough

Swan Valley

Darling Range

Avon River

Northam

Cunderin

Rottnest Island (Wadjemup)

Perth

Fremantle

Avon Valley

York

Quairad

Garden Island

Rockingham

Armadale

Hyden (149km); Wave Rock (151km)

Shoalwater Islands Marine Park

Serpentine

Jarrahdale

Serpentine Dam

Serpentine National Park

Brookton

Mandurah

Falcon

North Dandalup

Pingelly

Cape Bouvard

Pinjarra

Dwellingup

Bannister

Hotham River

Dryandra

Yalgorup National Park

Hotham Valley Railway

Boddington

Preston Beach

Waroona

Darling Range

Narrogin

Lake Preston

Yarloop

Bibbulmun Track

Murray River

Williams

Binningup

Brunswick Junction

Australind

Harvey

Arthur River

Wagin

Bunbury

Darkan

Activities

Most visitors come for Rottnest's beaches and briny activities (there are 63 beaches here!). Protected by a ring of reefs, the Basin (off Kings Way; ⏰ 24hr; 🚻) is the most popular spot for swimming. Other good swim spots are **Longreach Bay** and **Geordie Bay**, though there are many smaller secluded beaches around the shoreline, including beautiful **Little Parakeet Bay**. There's a handy online beach guide at www.westernaustraliatravellersguide.com/rottnest-island-beaches.html.

There are no cars here, so getting around is an activity in itself: plan on doing a lot of walking and cycling.

Skydive Geronimo SKYDIVING

(2 1300 449 669; www.skydivegeronimo.com.au; Rottnest Airport, Brand Way; 10,000/14,000/15,000ft $349/449/499; ⊙by appointment) Take a tandem leap of faith (15,000ft is the highest legal jump height in Australia) and land on a Rottnest beach. Ferry-and-skydive packages also available.

Oliver Hill Train & Tour RAIL

(2 08-9432 9300; www.rottnestisland.com/see-and-do/Island-tours/oliver-hill; off Defence Rd; adult/child $29/16.50) This trip, departing from the Settlement Train Station (Brand Way) at 1.30pm, takes you by train to historic **Oliver Hill Battery** (2 08-9372 9730; tours adult/child $9/4; ⊙tours hourly 10am-2pm) and includes the Gun & Tunnels tour run by Rottnest Voluntary Guides. The gun in question is a military remnant from WWII, with an impressive 9.2in calibre (never fired in defence or anger).

Pedal & Flipper CYCLING

(2 08-9292 5105; www.rottnestisland.com/see-and-do; cnr Bedford Way & Welch Rd; bikes per half-/full day from $16/30; ⊙8am-6pm) Bikes for hire from a big shed behind the pub (if you haven't booked one through your ferry company). Also hires out snorkelling sets (mask, snorkel and fins $20 per day), stand-up paddleboards ($50 per half-day), wetsuits ($20 per half-day) and bodyboards ($20 per day). Security bond payments are required for all rentals ($25 to $200).

☞ Tours

Sea Kayak Rottnest KAYAKING

(2 08-6219 5164; www.rottnestkayak.com.au; 2hr tour adult/child $49/39; ☻) Guided paddles in sheltered bays, peering into the brine though glass panels beneath your bum (!). Kids as young as six can join in – it's a very safe, low-impact session. Call for bookings and pick-up locations.

Grand Island Tour BUS

(2 1300 551 687; www.adamspinnacletours.com.au; adult/child incl lunch $79/59; ⊙departs 10.30am or 11.30am) Run by Adams Pinnacle Tours, these 3½-hour, in-depth explorations of the island include lunch. Book online or at the visitor centre (p919) when you arrive. Buses depart from the main bus stop in Thomson Bay. The ferry companies run packages incorporating

return ferry rides and the Grand Island Tour (adult/child from around $150/130).

Discover Rottnest BUS

(2 1300 467 688; www.rottnestexpress.com.au/tours-and-services/island-tours.html; adult/child $49/25; ⊙departs 11.20am & 1.50pm) Ninety-minute tours of the island with informative and entertaining commentary. Coaches depart from the main bus stop in Thomson Bay. Run by Rottnest Express (p919) ferries.

Rottnest Voluntary Guides WALKING

(2 08-9372 9757; www.rvga.asn.au) FREE Free, themed walks daily, with topics including History, Reefs, Wrecks and Daring Sailors, **Vlamingh Lookout** (off Digby Dr; ⊙24hr) and Salt Lakes, and the Quokka Walk. The outfit also runs tours of Wadjemup Lighthouse (p914; adult/child $9/4) and Oliver Hill Gun & Tunnels (adult/child $9/4); you'll need to make your own way there for the last two.

Adventure Rottnest BOATING

(2 1300 467 688; www.rottnestexpress.com.au/tours-and-services/island-tours/adenture-boat-tour.html; Thomson Bay Jetty; adult/child $67/33.50; ⊙mid-Sep–late Apr) A ninety-minute power-boat cruise around the coast on the *Eco Express,* with an emphasis on spotting wildlife and plenty of sea-spray in your hair. Ferry-and-boat packages are also available from Perth (adult/child $170/83) and Fremantle ($136/64). Departs the main Thomson Bay jetty; run by Rottnest Express (p919) ferries.

Island Explorer BUS

(2 08-9432 9300; www.rottnestisland.com; adult/child/family $20/15/50; ⊙departs every 30min 8.30am-3pm) Handy hop-on/hop-off coach service stopping at 17 locations around the island. Includes a limited commentary and is a great way to get your bearings when you first arrive.

🛏 Sleeping

Rotto is wildly popular in summer and during school holidays, when accommodation books out months in advance and prices skyrocket. Check websites for off-peak deals combining transport to the island, especially for weekday visits. Most accommodation is in cottages, from budget to rather stylish, run by the Rottnest Island Authority: book via www.rottnestisland.com. Other privately run accommodation, including the holiday park and hotel, can also be booked via this website.

QUOKKAS

Rottnest's tame little fur-bundles have suffered a number of indignities over the years. First Willem de Vlamingh's crew mistook them for rats as big as cats. Then the British settlers misheard and mangled their name (the Noongar word was probably *quak-a* or *gwaga*). But, worst of all, a cruel trend of 'quokka soccer' by sadistic louts in the 1990s saw many kicked to death before a $10,000 fine was imposed; occasional cases are still reported. On a more positive note, the phenomenon of 'quokka selfies' has illuminated the internet since 2015, and shows no signs of abating (Margot Robbie and Roger Federer in glorious Instagram quokka-company!).

These marsupials (part of the macropod family – relatives of kangaroos and wallabies) were once found throughout WA's southwest, but are now confined to small pockets of forest between Perth and Albany on the mainland and a few offshore islands, including a population of 8000 to 10,000 on Rottnest Island. Don't be surprised if one approaches looking for a morsel. Politely decline: human food isn't good for them.

Rottnest Campground CAMPGROUND $

(⌨ 08-9432 9111; www.rottnestisland.com; off Strue Rd; unpowered sites $39) The Rottnest Island Authority runs this simple, sandy, 43-site campground close en route to the Basin (p915), with barbecue pavilions and an amenities block. Be vigilant about your belongings, especially your food – insolent quokkas have been known to help themselves.

Rottnest Hostel HOSTEL $

(⌨ 08-9432 9111; www.rottnestisland.com; Kingstown Rd; dm/f $53/117) This rather austere backpackers occupies a 1937 art-deco army barracks that still has an institutional vibe and limited good-time opportunities. The defunct clock tower is stuck in an eternal 4pm. Check in at the visitor centre (p919) before you make the 1.8km walk, bike or bus trip to Kingston. There's a simple cafe on-site.

★Discovery Rottnest Island TENTED CAMP $$

(⌨ 08-6350 6170; www.discoveryholidayparks.com.au/discovery-rottnest-island; Strue Rd; tents d/f from $150/270; ☞☒) The first accommodation option to hit Rottnest in decades, this fabulous safari-tent park is nooked into the dunes behind Pinky Beach. Accommodation takes the form of 83 en suite safari tents, with muted colour schemes, luxe beds, roll-up walls and (in the deluxe versions) sea views. There's also a brilliant swimming pool, restaurant and bar. Wonderful!

Rottnest Island Authority Cottages COTTAGE $$

(⌨ 08-9432 9111; www.rottnestisland.com; cottages $120-385; ☒) Most of the accommodation on the island is run by the Rottnest Island Authority. There are more than 250 villas and cottages for rent: some have magnificent beachfront positions and are palatial; others are more like beach shacks. Prices jump by around $60 on Fridays and Saturdays, and higher in peak season. Check online for the labyrinthine pricing schedule.

Hotel Rottnest HOTEL $$$

(⌨ 08-9292 5011; www.hotelrottnest.com.au; 1 Bedford Ave; r $249-400; ☒☞) Occupying a wing that's adjunct to the castellated former summer-holiday pad for the state's governor (built in 1864), Hotel Rottnest does things with easy seaside style. The whiter-than-white rooms are smart and modern, if a tad pricey. The Bayview rooms have beautiful bay views (unsurprisingly), but the real hit here is the excellent **pub** (mains $21-35; ☺11am-late) out the front.

🍴 Eating

Rottnest's small township has cafes, restaurants, a great pub and a bakery – daytrippers won't go hungry. Most overnight visitors to Rotto self-cater. The **general store** (⌨08-9292-5017; www.rottnestgeneralstore.com.au; Digby Dr; ☺8am-8pm) is a small supermarket (and also stocks liquor) – and there's a similar shop at **Geordie Bay** (⌨cafe 08-9292 5411, supermarket 08-9292 5068; www.rottneststore.myfoodlink.com; 1 Geordie Bay Rd; ☺8am-7pm) – but if you're staying a while, it's better to bring supplies with you.

Frankie's on Rotto PIZZA $$

(⌨0431 735 090; www.frankiesonrotto.com.au; 342 Somerville Dr; mains breakfast $6-17, lunch & dinner $16-24; ☺8am-8pm) Boasting Rotto's first home-delivery service (free from 5pm to 7pm), Frankie's does excellent sourdough

PERTH & WESTERN AUSTRALIA ROTTNEST ISLAND

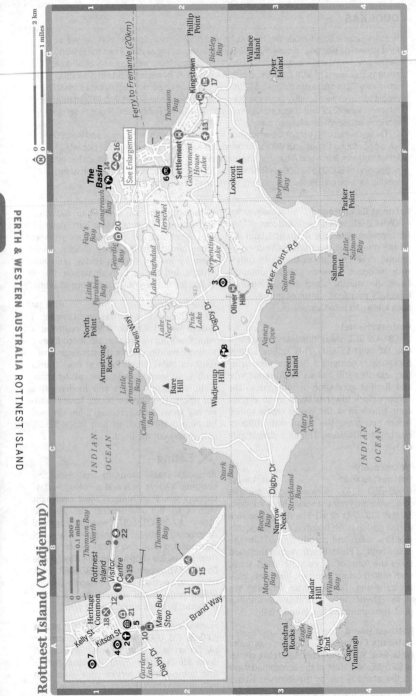

Rottnest Island (Wadjemup)

Rottnest Island (Wadjemup)

⊙ **Top Sights**
1 The Basin...................................F1

⊙ **Sights**
2 Historic Chapel............................A1
3 Oliver Hill Battery E2
4 Quod A1
5 Rottnest Museum A1
6 Vlamingh Lookout.....................F2
7 Wadjemup Aboriginal Burial
   Ground.....................................A1
8 Wadjemup Lighthouse D2

⊙ **Activities, Courses & Tours**
9 Adventure Rottnest B1
10 Discover Rottnest A2
   Grand Island Tour ....(see 10)
   Island Explorer...............(see 10)
   Oliver Hill Train & Tour ... (see 3)
11 Pedal & Flipper B2
12 Rottnest Voluntary Guides A1
13 Skydive Geronimo.....................F2

⊙ **Sleeping**
14 Discovery Rottnest Island F1
15 Hotel Rottnest..B2
16 Rottnest Campground............................F1
17 Rottnest Hostel.......................................G2

⊙ **Eating**
18 Frankie's on Rotto...................................A1
   Hotel Rottnest...............................(see 15)
19 Thomsons...B1

⊙ **Shopping**
20 Geordie Bay General Store....................E1
21 Rottnest General Store...........................A1

⊙ **Transport**
   Ferry Stop.....................................(see 22)
22 Rottnest Express B1
   Sealink...(see 22)

pizzas and a few salads and pastas, plus rejuvenating coffee and eggy breakfasts for those island mornings when memories of the pub seem far too recent. Sit on the deck under the Moreton Bay fig trees.

Thomsons SEAFOOD $$
(☑08-9292 5171; www.thomsonsrottnest.com.au; Colebatch Ave; mains $19-39; ☺11.30am-late) With mod boathouse vibes in a primo waterfront position (only compromised by netting to keep the seagulls out), Thomsons is Rotto's most upmarket option. Seafood is the name of the game: prise open some chilli mussels, dip into a chowder, or push the boat (way) out with a seafood platter for two ($160).

ℹ Information

Rottnest Island Visitor Centre (☑08-9372 9730; www.rottnestisland.com; Thomson Bay; ☺7.30am-6pm Sat-Thu, to 7pm Fri) Handles check-ins for all of the island authority's accommodation, and hands out maps, directions and general advice with good cheer. Your first point-of-call for all Rotto info.

ℹ Getting There & Away

AIR

Rottnest Air-Taxi (☑0421 389 831; www.rottnestairtaxi.com.au) Flies to Rottnest from Jandakot Airport in Perth's southern suburbs. Return prices start at around $120 per per person with a full plane (six passengers). Prices per person rise with fewer passengers.

Rotorvation Helicopters (☑08-9414 8584; www.rotorvation.com.au) Flies to Rotto from Jandakot Airport and Hillarys Boat Harbour in Perth's northern suburbs, from around $300 per person one way.

Note that the Rottnest Island Authority charges a $52.50 airport landing fee payable per landing; ask if this is included in your fare.

BOAT

Ferry services pulling into the **Thomson Bay jetty** include the following:

Rottnest Express (☑1300 467 688; www.rottnestexpress.com.au; return ex-Fremantle adult/child from $64/30, ex-Perth from $103/49) Regular ferries from Perth's Barrack Street Jetty (p913) (1¾ hours, once daily), Shed B on Victoria Quay (p913) (30 minutes, seven times daily) and Rous Head (p913) in North Fremantle (30 minutes, four times daily). A huge array of packages is on offer, including bike hire, snorkelling equipment, meals, accommodation and boat and bus tours. Services increase in summer and during school holidays.

Rottnest Fast Ferries (☑08-9246 1039; www.rottnestfastferries.com.au; adult/child return from $86.50/49) Departs from Hillarys Boat Harbour (40 minutes, four times daily), around 40 minutes' drive north of Perth. See www.hillarysboatharbour.com.au for public transport details. All kinds of gear-hire and accommodation packages also available. Reduced winter services.

Sealink (☑1300 786 552; www.sealinkrottnest.com.au; adult/child return from $64/30) A major player, with two to six daily departures from Shed B on Victoria Quay in Fremantle, year-round. Big boats, big business. Add-ons include joy flights, skydiving, electric- and regular-bike hire and lots of guided tours.

ⓘ Getting Around

BIKE

Rottnest is just big enough (and has just enough hills) to make a day's ride a good workout. The ferry companies all hire bikes and helmets (around $30/15 per adult/child per day) as part of their island packages, and have them waiting for visitors on arrival. The visitor centre (p919) hires out bikes too. Do a quick test ride before you head off to ensure your gears and brakes are working.

BUS

A free **shuttle bus** runs between Thomson Bay and the main accommodation areas (and the airport on request), departing roughly every 30 minutes from 7.30am, with the last bus at 6pm (8pm on Friday and Saturday).

The Island Explorer (p916) is a handy hop-on/hop-off coach service stopping at 19 locations around the island. Between Geordie Bay and Thomson Bay it's free.

Swan Valley

Perth locals love to swan around this semi rural vale on the city's northeastern suburban fringe. This is Wadjuk country – the inland extension of the river valley that becomes a vast estuary as it flows past Perth. Any visit to the Swan Valley inevitably revolves around wine – there are more than 40 vineyards here. Perhaps in tacit acknowledgement that its wines will never compete with the state's more prestigious regions (it doesn't really have the ideal climate), the Swan Valley compensates with plenty of galleries, breweries, providores and restaurants.

◉ Sights

Whiteman Park   PARK
(☑ 08-9209 6000; www.whitemanpark.com.au; off Lord St, West Swan; ⊙8.30am-6pm, visitor centre 10am-4pm, water park 10am-3pm; ⏩) FREE
Located in Caversham in West Swan, at 26 sq km this is Perth's heftiest park – a marvellous grassy reserve with over 30km of walkways and bike paths, a free kids' **water park**, sports ovals and dozens of picnic and barbecue spots. You'll also find the **Caversham Wildlife Park** (☑ 08-9248 1984; www.cavershamwildlife.com.au; adult/child $29/13; 9am-5.30pm, last entry 4.30pm; ⏩), **Revolutions Transport Museum** (☑ 08-9209 6040; by donation; ⊙10am-4pm; ⏩), the **Motor Museum of Western Australia** (☑ 08-9249 9457; www.motormuseumofwa.asn.au; adult/child/family $15/10/35; ⊙10am-4pm Mon-Fri, to 5pm Sat & Sun; ⏩), a **tractor museum** (☑ 08-9209 3480; www.facebook.com/tmofwa; by donation; ⊙10am-4pm Wed & Fri-Sun) and **train** (☑ 08-9534 3215; www.bbr.org.au; adult/child/family $8/4/20; ⊙11am-1pm Wed & Thu, to 4pm Sat & Sun) and **tram** (☑ 08-9443 1945; www.pets.org.au; adult/child/family return $5/2.50/13; ⊙11am-1.30pm Tue & Fri-Sun, daily in school holidays) rides for the kids. It's a massive place: pick up a map from the visitor centre.

Sandalford Wines   WINERY
(☑ 08-9374 9374; www.sandalford.com; 3210 West Swan Rd, Caversham; tours $25, mains $35-45; ⊙10am-5pm, tours noon, restaurant noon-3pm) Sandalford is one of the oldest Swan Valley wineries (1840) and hosts high-society weddings and major concerts (Sting, Tom Jones, Lionel Richie) on its expansive lawns. Sip some semillon at the cellar door, take a tour, or book a seat at the elegant restaurant for creative Mod Oz mains (the likes of barramundi with preserved lemon, pomegranate, beetroot, feta and maple dressing).

Houghton   WINERY
(☑ 08-9274 9540; www.houghton-wines.com.au; 148 Dale Rd, Middle Swan; ⊙10am-5pm) The Swan's oldest and best-known winery is surrounded by stroll-worthy grounds, including a jacaranda grove (check out the insanely purple blooms from late spring to early summer). There's a gallery in the cellar where bushranger Moondyne Joe was caught, and a small display of old winemaking equipment. Oh, and the wine's good too!

ⓒ Tours

Out & About Wine Tours   WINE
(☑ 08-9377 3376; www.outandabouttours.com.au; half-/full-day tours from $85/115) An experienced local operator running full-day, half-day and evening tours of the Swan Valley wineries, including lunch and plenty of tastings. There's a river-cruise option from Perth too ($155). Ex-Perth.

Captain Cook Cruises   CRUISE
(☑ 08-9325 3341; www.captaincookcruises.com.au/cruises/wine-cruises; full-day cruises from $169) Chug upstream from Perth along the increasingly narrow Swan River to the Swan Valley wineries, either stopping at Sandalford Wines for lunch, or jumping on a bus and exploring further.

🛌 Sleeping & Eating

Keller's B&B
B&B $$

(☑08-9274 8500; www.kellersbedandbreakfast.com.au; 104 Victoria Rd, Dayton; d $140-210; P❇🅡) Amid a remnant patch of farmland near the (it has to be said) awful Dayton suburban housing subdivision, Keller's is a charming limestone farmhouse with two en-suite guest rooms, each with a private entrance. It's a working farm with lots of cows, pigs and sheep – but it's not really set up for kids. Generous continental breakfast included.

★Rose & Crown
PUB FOOD $$

(☑08-9347 8100; www.rosecrown.com.au; 105 Swan St; mains breakfast $13-24, lunch & dinner $22-46; ⊙7am-late Mon-Fri, from 8am Sat & Sun) WA's oldest still-operating pub (1841) has a rambling beer garden and quirky heritage corners to explore inside. Have a beer in the enticingly dim cellar bar, where there's a convict-built well, and check out the sealed-off tunnel that used to connect the hotel with the river. The fat rabbit pie with a pint of Feral Brewing's 'The Local' is unbeatable.

There's also accommodation here, in the form of heritage hotel rooms in the pub and tastefully styled motel rooms out the back (with pool). Rates include breakfast and start at $170.

Lamont's
TAPAS $$

(☑08-9296 4485; www.lamonts.com.au; 85 Bisdee Rd, Millendon; tapas $9-27; ⊙10am-5pm Thu-Sun) Look forward to lazy tastings and heaving plates of tapas (shaved pastrami with black-olive salsa, coconut crumbed prawns) under the wide WA sky. The wine's top-notch too, much of it grown at Lamont's Margaret River vineyard. Little Lamont's cafe is down the road at 660 Great Northern Hwy, Herne Hill.

Cheese Barrel
CHEESE $$$

(☑08-9296 4539; www.thecheesebarrel.com.au; 920 Great Northern Hwy, Millendon; platters $35-70; ⊙10am-5pm, last orders 4.30pm) Rope together some travelling amigos for a high-end cheeseboard and wine flight from the adjacent Olive Farm Wines, then stock up on cheeses for on-the-road appetite attacks. Sign up for an enjoyable cheesemaking course (from $45) to craft Camembert or marinated feta; see www.thecheesemaker.com.au for details.

RiverBank Estate
BISTRO $$$

(☑08-9377 1805; www.riverbankestate.com.au; 126 Hamersley Rd, Caversham; mains $29-65; ⊙cellar door 10am-4pm, lunch 11.30am-2.30pm) The pick of the region's winery restaurants, rustic River Bank delivers excellent Mod Oz cuisine on its wrap-around verandah (or inside if it's hot). It's a little better dressed than the competition (hot tip: you too) and there's regular live jazz. There's also Sunday breakfast on the lawns from 7.30am to 10.30am (mains $16 to $25).

🍷 Drinking & Nightlife

★Homestead Brewery
CRAFT BEER

(☑08-6279 0500; www.mandoonestate.com.au/eat-drink/homestead-brewery; 10 Harris Rd, Caversham; ⊙10am-8.30pm Mon-Fri, 7.30am-10.30pm Sat & Sun) Located in the grounds of the award-winning Mandoon Estate winery, progressive Homestead's standout brews include Kaiser's Choice, a zingy Bavarian wheat beer, and Thunderbird, an American pale ale. Food runs all day, from baked eggs with chorizo and coriander to mussels in Homestead apple cider to chickpea and black-bean burgers with mustard mayo. Winner!

★Feral Brewing Company
CRAFT BEER

(☑08-9296 4657; www.feralbrewing.com.au; 152 Haddrill Rd, Baskerville; ⊙11am-5pm Sun-Thu, to late Fri & Sat) The regularly lauded, always-interesting craft beers at Feral include a Hop Hog pale ale and barrel-aged and sour brews that pair nicely with a robust pub-grub menu (mains $22 to $36). Try the fruity Karma Citra India black ale with some beer-fried cheese.

Mash Brewing
CRAFT BEER

(☑08-9296 5588; www.mashbrewing.com.au; 10250 West Swan Rd, Henley Brook; ⊙11am-5pm Sun-Thu, to 9pm Fri & Sat) This dude-filled Americana beer bunker at the northern end of the valley showcases craft lager, ales, wheat beer and cider. Breeze through a few Freo Doctor lagers, and contemplate the limited-edition Barley Wine – dangerously easy to drink despite clocking in at a stonking 9.5% alcohol (someone else driving?). Calorific bar food to boot (mains $22 to $38).

ℹ️ Information

Swan Valley Visitor Centre (☑08-9207 8899; www.swanvalley.com.au; Guildford Courthouse, cnr Swan & Meadow Sts, Guildford; ⊙9am-4pm) Information and maps, plus an interesting display on local history.

ℹ️ Getting There & Away

Guildford, the gateway to the Swan Valley, falls within Zone 2 of Perth's public-transport system: it costs only $4.80 to get here by bus or train on the Midland line from Perth, East Perth or Mt Lawley Station. For Whiteman Park, catch the train to Bassendean Station. Switch to the 353 or 955 bus to Ellenbrook and get off at Lord St (bus stop 15529).

If you don't want to travel under your own steam, there are myriad tour companies – ferry and minibus – that can deliver you here and show you around.

❶ Getting Around

To get around the Swan Valley your best options are to drive or take a tour.

Another option is to rent a **bike** (☑ 0401 077 405; 1235 Great Northern Hwy, Upper Swan; standard/electric bikes per day $35/45), but the area is surprisingly spread out and the roads are usually busy. Pick up the *Cycling in the Swan Valley & Guildford* brochure/map from the Swan Valley Visitor Centre (p921).

There's also the hop-on/hop-off **Swan Valley Explorer** (☑ 1300 551 687; www.adamspinnacle tours.com.au/full-day-tours/swan-valley-explorer-bus-service; adult/child/family $20/15/50) service, running two handy loops around the valley from Guildford train station, departing every 30 minutes from around 10am. Book online.

Rockingham

☑ 08 / POP 125,120

Just 46km south of Perth on Wajuk homelands, Rockingham is finding its feet as a seaside destination, and has found popularity with increasing numbers of retirees, who mooch along the waterfront. Wedged between the Shoalwater Islands Marine Park to the south, home to colonies of dolphins, sea lions and penguins, and the vast industrial estates, port works and naval facilities of Kwinana and Garden Island to the north, the town has a cheery cafe strip and a strung-out waterfront park, backing onto a lovely safe swimming beach.

Rockingham was founded in 1872 as Perth's southern port, and although you'll still see plenty of big ship silhouettes out on the bay, this function was largely taken over by Fremantle in the 1890s.

◉ Sights & Activities

Shoalwater Islands
Marine Park   NATURE RESERVE

(☑ 08-9303 7700; www.parks.dpaw.wa.gov.au/park/shoalwater-islands; off Arcadia Dr, Shoalwater; ⊙ daylight hours, closed for nesting Jun–mid-Sep) 🏃 **FREE** Just a few minutes' paddle, swim or boat ride away from the shore 5km south

of Rockingham is strictly protected **Penguin Island**, home to penguins, silver gulls, boardwalks, beaches and picnic tables. Apart from birdwatching (pied cormorants, pelicans, crested and bridled terns, oystercatchers), day visitors can also swim, paddle in the rock pools and snorkel.

It's free to wade the few hundred metres out to the island across the sandbar at low tide, but keep one eye on the sea – people have drowned here after being washed off the bar during strong winds and high tides. Otherwise, the **Penguin Island Ferry** (☑ 08-9591 1333; www.penguinisland.com.au/penguin-island-ferry; Mersey Point Jetty, 153 Arcadia Dr, Shoalwater; adult/child/family $18/14/56, with penguin feeding $27/20/85; ⊙ hourly 9am-3pm mid-Sep–May) can chug you out there and back: fares can include penguin-feeding session at the Discovery Centre on the island, run by **Rockingham Wild Encounters** (☑ 08-9591 1333; www.penguinisland.com.au; cnr Arcadia Dr & Penguin Rd, Shoalwater; ⊙ 8.30am-4.30pm mid-Sep–May). Sea-kayaking tours with **Capricorn Seakayaking** (☑ 0427 485 123; www.capricornseakayaking.com.au; adult/child $180/162; ⊙ late Sep-late Apr) explore the marine park in more depth.

🛏 Sleeping & Eating

★ Manuel Towers   B&B $$

(☑ 08-9592 2698; www.manueltowers.com.au; 32 Arcadia Dr, Shoalwater; d with/without breakfast from $205/155; 🅿 ❄ 🛜) Manuel? He's from Barcelona... *Fawlty Towers* gags aside, this five-room waterfront B&B near Penguin Island is the real deal, with rough-hewn limestone walls, terracotta tiles, chunky beams, wrought-iron balustrades, fig trees and a Spanish host (OK, he's from Morocco, but he grew up across the Med). The downstairs breakfast room is marvellously atmospheric – a little slice of Catalonia in Shoalwater.

★ Ostro Eatery   CAFE $$

(☑ 08-9592 8957; www.ostroeatery.com.au; 11a Rockingham Beach Rd; mains breakfast $13-20, lunch & dinner $16-34; ⊙ 7.30am-3pm Mon-Thu & Sun, to late Fri & Sat) This arty waterfront cafe with broad shared tables morphs into an effervescent evening option on weekends. The pulled-pork breakfast burger will kick-start your day, while nocturnal options range from house-cured salmon with apple and fennel to classy fish and chips. Cold-pressed juices, hemp-seed protein shakes and house-made sodas complement a concise beer and wine selection (Bloody Mary mix to take away).

★**Rustico** TAPAS $$

(☑08-9528 4114; www.rusticotapas.com.au; 61 Rockingham Beach Rd; tapas $12-32, 6-course degustation with/without wine from $88/59; ☺noon-10pm Tue-Thu, to midnight Fri, from 11am Sat, to 10pm Sun) This moody tapas/wine bar caps the northern end of Rockingham's beachside strip, with authentic Spanish-style food and an ocean-view corner terrace. Shared plates of *jamón*, sloe gin salmon and braised beef cheek hit the target. The six-course degustation pairs with WA wines, while cocktails, sangria and craft beer (try the Three Rivers Kolsch from Mandurah) bolster the good-time vibe.

ℹ Information

Visitor Information Centre (☑08-9592 3464; www.rockinghamvisitorcentre.com.au; 19 Kent St; ☺9am-5pm Mon-Fri, to 4pm Sat & Sun) Has accommodation listings and all the local low-down.

ℹ Getting There & Away

Rockingham is on the Mandurah line on the Transperth (p913) public transport network. Regular trains depart Perth Underground for Rockingham ($8.40, 35 minutes), continuing to Mandurah ($5.60 from Rockingham, 15 minutes).

Dwellingup

☑08 / POP 560

Dwellingup is a small, timber-shrouded township between Pinjarup and Wiilman lands 100km south of Perth, with a forest-load of character. Its rep as an activity hub has been enhanced by the hardy long-distance walkers and cyclists trucking through town on the epic Bibbulmun Track (p958) and Munda Biddi Trail (p926) respectively. There's a petrol station, a pub and a police station here too – the three pillars of society in rural WA.

◉ Sights

★**Wine Tree Cidery** WINERY

(☑08-9538 1076; www.winetreecidery.com.au; 46 Holyoake Rd; ☺1-7pm Fri, from 10am Sat & Sun) Wine, cider, apples, trees...the name almost hangs together, conceptually. Regardless, this cavernous steel space (a former apple shed) is a cheery spot for a tasting paddle of the house ciders ($16: classic, dry and fruity), a look at the vintage motorcycle collection, a cheese board ($30), or all of the above. Ben the Labrador is on duty.

Forest Discovery Centre NATURE RESERVE

(☑08-9538 1395; www.forestdiscoverycentre. com.au; 1 Acacia St; adult/child/family $5/3/13; ☺10am-3pm Mon-Fri, to 4pm Sat & Sun; 🚼) Tucked into the jarrah forest on the edge of town, this interesting rammed-earth building takes the shape of three interlinked gum leaves. Inside are displays about the forest's flora and fauna, and a shop selling beautiful pieces crafted by local and visiting woodworkers. Short trails, including an 11m-high canopy walk, meander off into the woods. There's a cafe and kids' nature-play areas here too.

🏃 Activities

Trees Adventure ADVENTURE SPORTS

(☑08-9463 4063; www.treesadventure.com.au/park/lane-poole-park; off Nanga Rd; adult/child $48/38; ☺10am-5pm Tue-Fri, from 9am Sat & Sun; 🚼) Scale the forest canopy and see what sort of condition your adrenaline gland is in at this treetop climbing course, with swings, bridges, flying-foxes and challengingly lofty obstacles aplenty. The kids will love it, even if you have very logical reservations.

Hotham Valley Railway RAIL

(☑08-6278 1111; www.hothamvalleyrailway.com. au; Dwellingup Station, off Marinup St; Forest Train adult/child $28/14, Restaurant Train $92, Steam Ranger $40/20; ☺Forest Train departs 10.30am & 2pm Sat & Sun, Restaurant Train 7.45pm Sat, Steam Ranger 10.30am & 2pm Sun May-Oct) On weekends (and Tuesday and Thursday during school holidays), the Forest Train chugs along 8km of forest track on a 90-minute return trip. Every Saturday night and some Fridays, the Restaurant Train follows the same route, serving a five-course meal in a 1919 dining car. There's also the Steam Ranger, travelling 14km via WA's steepest rail incline to Isandra Siding.

Dwellingup Adventures ADVENTURE SPORTS

(☑08-9538 1127; www.dwellingupadventures.com. au; cnr Marinup & Newton Sts; 1-person kayaks & 2-person canoes per day $50, mountain bikes $40; ☺8.30am-5pm Sat & Sun, by appointment Mon-Fri) A one-stop shop for canoe, kayak, raft, camping gear and mountain-bike hire to explore the terrain on and around the beautiful Murray River. Or sign up for a supported (but self-guided) paddling or cycling tour (from $125 per person). White-water-rafting tours are also available from June to October (from $150 per person).

Sleeping & Eating

Lewis Park Chalets
COTTAGE $$

(☑08-9538 1406; www.lewisparkchalets.com.
au; 99 Irwin Rd; d $150; P❄) These three self-
contained, iron-clad chalets with wide veran-
dahs rest inconspicuously on 16 hectares of
rolling pastureland with valley views to the
Peel Inlet and of nearby jarrah forests. Blue
wrens skitter through the foliage, horses mut-
ter in the paddocks, mobile reception drops in
and out... It's 5km west of Dwellingup.

★ Blue Wren Cafe
CAFE $$

(☑08-9538 1234; www.facebook.com/dwelling
upbluewrencafe; 53 McLarty St; mains $15-20;
⊙6am-5pm Sat-Thu, to 7.30pm Fri) Corrugated
iron, hessian hangings and rustic timber
collude to create a happy vibe at this cosy
corner cafe, offering stonking homemade
sausage rolls and regular specials (pulled-
pork pies!). The coffee is worthy of a flash
cafe in the big smoke, and there's a roaring
wood heater for chilly Dwellingup winters
(it gets down to -3°C here sometimes).

❶ Information

Dwellingup History & Visitor Information
Centre (☑08-9538 1108; www.dwellingupwa.
com.au; Marinup St; ⊙9am-3.30pm; ☎) Lots
of local info, including interesting displays
about the 1961 bushfires that wiped out the
town, destroying 75 houses but taking no lives.
The website lists accommodation options.

❶ Getting There & Away

There's no regular public transport to Dwellingup: hit the road, Jack.

Mandurah

POP 80,820

Shrugging off its fusty retirement-haven image, Mandurah – Mandjoogoordap in Pinjarup
dialect – has made a good fist of reinventing
itself as an upmarket beach enclave, taking
advantage of the easy train link to Perth. And
although the town's network of interlinked
marinas, canals and precincts is shamelessly
artificial, and despite well-documented social
problems (local rates of methamphetamine
use are some of the highest in regional Australia) most people here seem to be enjoying
themselves. Wander along the waterfront
from the Ocean Marina (boats, cafes and the
Dolphin Quay indoor market), past canals
and glitzy apartments linked by Venetian-ish
sandstone bridges and along the boardwalk

to the Cultural Precinct. Suspend cynicism
and enjoy your moment under the southern
sun – this is mainstream Australia!

Mandurah Bridge spans the Mandurah Estuary, which sits between the ocean and the
sizeable Peel Inlet. It's one of the best places
in WA for fishing, crabbing and prawning.

◉ Sights & Activities

Mandurah Museum
MUSEUM

(☑08-9550 3682; www.mandurah.wa.gov.au/
facilities/museum; 3 Pinjarra Rd; by donation;
⊙10am-4pm Tue-Fri, 11am-3pm Sat & Sun) Mandurah's community-run museum is an engaging
little repository of all things aged and olden
– it's one of WA's better regional collections.
Unless you're walking, park behind the museum in the car park off Leslie St: if you try
to drive any closer on Pinjarra Rd, there's nowhere to stop and you'll be funneled across
the Mandurah Bridge, never to return...

Town Beach
BEACH

(off Dolphin Dr; ⊙24hr) FREE Just across from
the human-made Ocean Marina, Town
Beach delivers some natural respite, with
a gentle swell surging in and out and locals
basking on the golden sand. A lovely spot.

Mandurah Cruises
CRUISE

(☑08-9581 1242; www.mandurahcruises.com.
au; 73 Mandurah Tce) Take a one-hour Dolphin & Scenic Canal Cruise (adult/child
$32/18), half-day Murray River Lunch Cruise
($89/55) or Sunset Cruise ($30/15). Fish and
chips on the canal and dolphin cruises are
$12 extra. Book online. Indo-Pacific bottle-
nose dolphins come close to the boat; note
that research suggests that human interaction with sea mammals potentially alters
their behavioural and breeding patterns.

Mandurah Boat & Bike Hire
CYCLING

(☑08-9535 5877; www.mandurahboatandbikehire.
com.au; 20a Ormsby Tce; ⊙8am-6pm) Chase the
fish in a four-seat dinghy (from $55/350 per
hour/day), or hire a bike and go exploring
(from $10/40). Kayaks and stand-up paddle-
boards also available ($25 per hour).

Mandjoogoordap Dreaming
CULTURAL

(☑0408 952 740; www.mandurahdreaming.com.
au; adult/child $35/15) ⚐ Explore Mandurah's
foreshore with local Pinjarup guide George
– a 90-minute interpretation of the land and
sea through Indigenous eyes. Book ahead;
meet at the Mandurah Performing Arts Centre (p926). Bus tours and longer explorations
around the Peel Inlet are also available.

WAVE ROCK

The multicoloured cresting swell of Wave Rock (☑ 08-9880 5182; www.waverock.com.au; Wave Rock Rd; per vehicle/adult/child $12/5/3; ☉ 24hr), 336km east of Perth, formed some 60 million years ago by weathering and water erosion. Streaked with colours created by runoff from local mineral springs, it's actually one edge of a larger granite outcrop called Hyden Rock. It's not gargantuan – just 15m high and 110m long – but it's nonetheless impressive. And when the wind is whispering in the sheoaks, it's a quietly moving place – as it has always been for the Nyaki-Nyaki people.

To get the most out of Wave Rock, pick up the *Walk Trails at Wave Rock and The Humps* brochure from the **visitor centre** (☉ 9am-5pm). A steep walk leads up around the summit of Hyden Rock, passing a dazzlingly insensitive concrete-block wall built along the crest of Wave Rock to stop stone-surfers from plunging to their deaths. There's another good trail to **Hippo's Yawn** (1km) along a shady track from the base of Wave Rock.

Parking at Wave Rock is $12 per car (pay at the parking meter); or you can save a few bucks by parking out on Wave Rock Rd or the visitor centre and walking in a few hundred metres – pay pedestrian fees at the **caravan-park** (☑ 08-9880 5022; www.waverock.com.au/business/accommodation/wave-rock-caravan-park; 1 Wave Rock Rd; unpowered/powered sites from $30/38, cabins from $130; P ❄ ☀) kiosk.

🛏 Sleeping

★ Mandurah Ocean Marina Chalets
MOTEL $$

(☑ 08-9535 8173; www.marinachalets.com.au; 6 The Lido; d/f unit from $120/140; P ❄ 🛜) Embrace Mandurah by staying right in the middle of it: pitched-roof chalets here are spotless and modern, with full-kit kitchens and little decks, all revolving around a central BBQ pavilion and crab-cooking facility. It's a tightly arranged complex, but is beautifully landscaped with eucalypts and neat hedges. There's no pool, but Mandurah's **Swimming Beach** (Keith Holmes Reserve, The Lido; ☉ daylight hours; 🚻) FREE is right across the Lido. Great value.

Seashells Resort
APARTMENT $$

(☑ 08-9550 3000; www.seashells.com.au; 16 Dolphin Dr; 1-/2-bedroom apt & villas from $225/325; P ❄ 🛜 ☀) With a rounded prow and porthole-like windows, Seashells looks like an art-deco ocean liner, but inside the apartments are cool and contemporary. Town Beach is right on the doorstep and there's a lovely infinity-lipped pool just metres away. Check into one of the luxe beachfront villas and you may not want to leave.

🍴 Eating & Drinking

★ Flic's Kitchen
BISTRO $$

(☑ 08-9535 1661; www.flicskitchen.com; 3/16 Mandurah Tce; breakfast $10-25, share plates $21-27; ☉ 8am-late; 🍷) Perfectly aligned to snare the afternoon sun, fabulous Flic's is infused with city cool, with outdoor seating and a versatile menu spanning breakfast to dinner. Consider a breakfast beer (how fabulously indecent!) to accompany your smoked pork collar with charred corn, chilli scramble and whipped feta. Vegan and paleo options too. Winner!

Peninsula
PUB FOOD $$

(☑ 08-9534 9899; www.thepenmandurah.com.au; 1 Marco Polo Dr; mains $16-36; ☉ 11am-late) There's been a pub here since 1911; the 'Pen' is the latest incarnation, a sassy 21st-century bar at the base of the **Sebel Mandurah** (☑ 08-9512 8300; www.thesebel.com/western-australia/the-sebel-mandurah; d from $210, 1-bedroom apt from $300; P ❄ 🛜 ☀), with a shady beer garden and excellent bar food. Frosty pints of Gage Roads Single Fin pale ale pair perfectly with plates of garlic and pepper soft-shell crab and house-made pork, bacon and cheese sausage rolls.

★ Three Rivers Brewing Company
CRAFT BEER

(☑ 0411 823 870; www.3riversbrewing.com.au; 2/6 Harlem Pl, Greenfields; ☉ 2-8pm Fri-Sun) 🍺 Murray, Serpentine, Harvey: Mandurah's three rivers all flow into the Peel Inlet, which in turn empties into the Indian Ocean. It's a cyclic environmental image, setting a sustainable tone at this cheery craft brewery in the industrial backblocks. There's no gimmickry here, just traditionally brewed English, European and American ales. The Tomahawk APA rules the roost. Tasting paddles $10.

☆ Entertainment

**Mandurah Performing
Arts Centre** ARTS CENTRE
(ManPAC; ☑08-9550 3900; www.manpac.com.
au; Ormsby Tce; ☺box office 9am-5pm Mon-Fri,
10am-4pm Sat, from noon Sun) The jewel of
Mandurah's Cultural Precinct, the Man-
PAC is a stylish glass-and-steel auditorium
hosting everything from twinkle-toed ballet
troupes to stand-up comics, earnest singer-
songwriters, art-house movie festivals and
touring Status Quo tribute bands.

ⓘ Information

Mandurah Visitor Centre (☑08-9550 3999;
www.visitpeel.com.au; 75 Mandurah Tce;
☺9am-4pm) On the estuary boardwalk.

ⓘ Getting There & Away

Mandurah is 72km south of central Perth; take
the Kwinana Fwy and follow the signs.

Mandurah sits within the outermost zone (7) of
the Transperth (p913) public-transport system
on the end of the Mandurah line. There are direct
trains to/from Perth Underground ($11.10, 50
minutes) and Rockingham ($5.60, 15 minutes).

Transwa (p913) SW1, SW2 and SW3 buses roll into
Mandurah most days of the week.

Perth Hills

Wait...Perth has hills? Who knew! Technically known as the Darling Range, this
forest-covered escarpment to the city's east
is Beelu country, and provides a green backdrop with some great spots for picnicking,
bushwalking, mountain biking and hanging
with the local kangaroos. Better yet, nooked
into a lush Hills' vale, the Bickley Valley plays
host to a dozen or so wineries with attendant
cellar doors, B&Bs and cafes. Perth locals are
discovering the pleasures of an indulgent
Hills weekend away.

◎ Sights

★ Core Cider WINERY
(☑08-9293 7583; www.corecider.com.au; 35 Merrivale Rd, Pickering Brook; tours adult/child tractor
$30/23, walking $25/18; ☺10am-4pm Wed-Sat,
to 5pm Sun) This hidden valley in Pickering
Brook has sustained apple orchards since
1939. Take a one-hour tour through the trees
on a tractor-pulled carriage, a 45-minute
walking tour, or book a table at the excellent bistro (mains $27 to $32) or casual cider garden (mains $12 to $25) for lunch. But

of course, the main deal here is cider: their
'Core Range' (ha-ha) includes outstanding
sparking apple and pear offings. Head to the
Harvest Room for tastings (from $10).

Perth Observatory OBSERVATORY
(☑08-9293 8255; www.perthobservatory.com.au;
337 Walnut Rd, Bickley; tours adult/child day $20/15,
night $40/30; ☺admission by tour only) Check
the website for regularly scheduled day and
night tours of the Perth Observatory, sitting
pretty atop a Perth Hills' peak near the Bickley Valley wineries. Check the website for
times and bookings. They've been stargazing
here for 120 years, over which time local as-
tronomers have discovered 29 minor plan-
ets, 30 supernovae and the rarely seen rings
around Uranus. You can also abseil down the
concrete tower (adult/child $35/25).

Brookside Vineyard WINERY
(☑08-9291 8705; www.brooksidevineyard.com.au; 5
Loaring Rd, Bickley; ☺11am-4pm Sat & Sun) Follow
the sounds of lilting jazz down a shady, poplar-
lined driveway to Brookside, a rustic farm-
shed cellar door. Enjoy a couple of glasses of
cab sav, chardonnay or sparkling white on
the terrace by the namesake babbling brook.
The **Vineyard Kitchen** (☑08-9227 7715; www.
thevineyardkitchen.net.au; Brookside Vineyard, 5
Loaring Rd, Bickley; mains $29-33; ☺noon-3pm
Thu-Sun) restaurant is here too, serving masterful Mod Oz.

Mundaring Weir DAM
(☑08-9290 6645; www.goldenpipeline.com.au;
Mundaring Weir Rd, Mundaring; ☺daylight hours)
FREE Restraining the Helena River, Mundaring Weir is a concrete dam built in 1903 to
the designs of engineer CY O'Connor as part
of a dazzlingly ambitious scheme to supply
water to the Kalgoorlie goldfields 560km to
the east (the longest freshwater pipeline in
the world...and it worked!). The reservoir is
a blissful spot, with walking trails, kangaroos and a well-positioned **pub** (☑08-9295
1106; www.mundaringweirhotel.com.au; cnr Hall &
Mundaring Wier Rds; r $125-150, extra adult/child
$40/20; [P][🐾][🛜][♨]). The best dam view is from
the lookout just off Mundaring Weir Rd near
the dam's southern end.

🏃 Activities & Tours

Munda Biddi Trail MOUNTAIN BIKING
(☑08-6336 9699; www.mundabiddi.org.au) WA's
most exciting route for mountain bikers
is the Munda Biddi Trail, meaning 'path
through the forest' in the Noongar Aborigi-

nal language. The 1000km mountain-biking equivalent of the Bibbulmun Track runs all the way from Mundaring on Perth's outskirts to Albany on the south coast. Campsites are situated a day's easy ride apart, and maps are available online and at visitor centres. Epic!

Rock 'n' Roll
Mountain Biking MOUNTAIN BIKING
(☑0410 949 182; www.facebook.com/rockandroll mtb; 361 Paulls Valley Rd, Paulls Valley; bike hire per half-/full day/weekend from $45/60/100; ⊗9am-noon Thu & Fri, 8am-2pm Sat & Sun, by appointment Mon-Wed) Right on the Bibbulmun Track, these two-wheeled rock 'n' rollers can kit you out with a top-quality mountain bike, upon which you can blaze local trails from easy to 'Black Diamond' (extremely difficult). They also run courses and have an in-house repair shop.

Up Close & Local Tours WINE
(☑0423 126 254; www.upcloseandlocaltours.com. au; half-/full-day tours $79/129) Bickley Valley specialists offering a half-day (afternoon) tour from Perth, visiting two wineries and Core Cider, with plenty of sightseeing in between. There's also a full-day option called the 'Cider, Wine & Whiskey' tour, getting a bit more of the good stuff into your glass.

🛏 Sleeping & Eating

Bickley Valley Cottage B&B $$$
(☑0437 616 869; www.bickleyvalleycottage.com; 15 Glenisla Rd, Bickley; d from $270, extra person $40; P🌐🛜) A three-bedroom heritage cottage built in 1914, this little timber B&B has valley views and buckets of charm. Breakfast comes in an overflowing DIY hamper (with a bottle of wine...not necessarily for breakfast, but why not?); while interior design is cottagey without erring on the side of chintz. There are a couple of good wineries within walking distance.

⭐ Parkerville Tavern PUB FOOD $$
(☑08-9295 4500; www.parkervilletavern.com.au; 6 Owen Rd, Parkerville; pizzas $15-20, mains $22-34; ⊗11.30am-late Mon-Sat, from 8am Sun; 🛜🍴) Built in 1896, this cheery red-brick pub 3km northwest of Mundaring is a surprising find. Pub grub is the main lure (brilliant BLTS, perfect parmas), plus there's a pool table, a blazing pizza oven in the beer garden (weekends only) and a kids' sandpit. All-day kitchen Friday to Sunday; noon to 2.30pm and 5.30pm to 8.30pm Monday to Thursday.

Kalamunda Farmers Market MARKET $
(☑0437 632 126; www.kalamundafarmersmarket. com; Central Mall, Kalamunda; ⊗8am-noon Sun) One of the Perth area's best farmers markets, with up to 70 stalls and some rather good buskers. There are lots of street eats – don't even think about breakfast beforehand. See www.kalamundanightmarket.com.au for info on its summertime Friday-night market.

ⓘ Information

The **Perth Hills Visitor Centre** (☑08-9257 9998; www.experienceperthhills.com.au; 50 Railway Rd; ⊗9am-4pm Mon-Fri, from 10am Sat & Sun) is in Kalamunda, with all the requisite maps and brochures including the handy *Kalamunda to Mundaring Self-Drive Tourist Map*, *Perth Hills Winery Guide* and *Bickley Valley Wine Trail* maps.

ⓘ Getting There & Away

The Hills are most easily accessed with your own set of wheels (great wiggly roads for motorcycle touring!) but Transwa (p913) buses and trains from Perth do link with Kalamunda and Mundaring. For Mundaring, catch a Midland Line train from Perth Station to Midland Station then bus 320 (one hour, $6.70); for Kalamunda, catch a 283, 295, 296, 298 or 299 bus from Elizabeth Quay Bus Station (50 minutes, $5.60).

Avon Valley

The meandering – and before summer takes hold, lush and green – Avon Valley is Ballardong country. European settlers moved into the area in early 1830 after food shortages forced Governor Stirling to dispatch Ensign Dale to search the Darling Range for arable land. What he found was the upper reaches of the Swan River, which he presumed was a separate waterway (which is why the river's name changes from the Swan to the Avon in Walyunga National Park). And so, just a year after Perth was founded, homesteads began to appear in the newly named Avon Valley. Many historic stone buildings still stand in the towns and countryside here: it's an atmospheric place, with Ballardong culture still esteemed and celebrated.

ⓘ Getting There & Away

Tranwa (p913) runs its GS2 buses to Northam and York from Perth, and Northam and Toodyay are both on the AvonLink, Prospector and MerredinLink train lines from Perth.

Northam

📱 08 / POP 6550

The major town in the Avon Valley and a stronghold of Ballardong culture, Northam is a busy commercial hub on the Avon River – a likeable enough place with a couple of good cafes and old pubs, but a down-on-its-luck main street and little to warrant a lengthy stay. The railway line from Perth once ended here and miners had to make the rest of the trek to the Kalgoorlie goldfields by road; the line now continues all the way to Sydney, traversed by the iconic *Indian Pacific*. The most stimulating time to be in town is during the hectic Avon Descent in early August.

◉ Sights & Activities

★ Bilya Koort Boodja   CULTURAL CENTRE
(📱 08-9622 2170; www.bilyakoortboodja.com; 2 Grey St; adult/child/family $10/5/25; ⊘ 9am-4pm) Next to the pedestrian suspension bridge over the Avon, this black-clad centre honours the history, culture and environmental know-how of local Ballardong tribes and the broader Noongar nation. A sequence of spaces includes a 'Welcome to Country' introduction, an explanation of the six Noongar seasons, artefacts, artworks and a storytelling session. It's an impressive celebration of this living culture.

Northam Silo Art   PUBLIC ART
(📱 08-9226 2799; www.publicsilotrail.com; Northam-Toodyay Rd; ⊘ 24hr) FREE Part of WA's series of seven brilliant silo-art installations, spangled across the southwest wheat-belt region, Northam's towering rank of 16 silos has a fabulously weird future-fantasy scene on one end by London artist Phlegm, and a dazzlingly colourful Aboriginal-inspired mural by Atlanta artist HENSE at the other. Head out of town on the road to Toodyay – you can't miss it.

★⋆ Festivals & Events

Avon Descent   SPORTS
(www.avondescent.com.au; ⊘ Aug) A street parade, markets and fireworks are followed by the Avon Descent, a gruelling 124km white-water event for power dinghies, kayaks and canoes down the river in all its winter-flow glory. General chaos ensues – great fun!

🛏 Sleeping & Eating

★ Dukes Inn   MOTEL $$
(📱 08-9670 3450; www.dukesinn.com.au; 197 Duke St; d with/without bathroom from $130/90, 1-/2-bedroom apt from $180/190; 🅿 ❄ 🖥)

Northam has a handful of rambling old pubs, most of which have seen better days. But the two-tier red-brick 1907 Dukes Inn in the backstreets raises the bar with a zappy renovation and superior pub grub (mains $15 to $35). Choose from upstairs rooms with shared bathrooms (and access to the balcony) or apartments in the renovated stables out the back.

Cafe Yasou   CAFE $$
(📱 08-9622 3128; www.cafeyasou.com.au; 175 Fitzgerald St; mains $14-24; ⊘ 8am-4pm Mon-Fri, to noon Sat) This sunny cafe serves excellent coffee and a Med-inspired menu, including a grilled-halloumi and peach salad, crispy fish tortillas with apple slaw and turmeric, and a stonking eggs Benedict. Sandwiches, cakes and a Greek goddess mural complete the picture. Be sure to pick up a slice of baklava to take away.

ℹ️ Information

Visitor Centre (📱 08-9622 2100; www. avonvalleywa.com.au; 2 Grey St; ⊘ 9am-4pm; 🛜) Overlooking a picturesque slice of the Avon River, with pelicans, parrots and a little island, Northam's info centre is a helpful operation.
RiversEdge Cafe (📱 08-9622 5635; www.rivers edgecafe.com.au; 2 Grey St; mains $13-25; ⊘ 7.30am-2.30pm Tue-Sun) is here too. Pick to the *Northam Walking Tracks* pamphlet detailing a few good walks around town.

York

📱 08 / POP 3610

Only 97km from Perth on Ballardong land, National Trust–listed York is the Avon Valley's most appealing town. It's the oldest inland town in WA, settled by white farmers in 1831, just two years after the Swan River Colony. The homesick settlers here drew parallels between Avon Valley and their native Yorkshire, so Governor Stirling bestowed the name York.

Convicts were brought to the town in 1851 and contributed to regional development; the local convict-hiring depot didn't close until 1872, four years after transportation of convicts to WA ceased. York boomed during the gold rush in the late 1880s and early 1890s, servicing miners who were trucking east to Southern Cross, a goldfields town 273km away. Most of the town's impressive buildings date from this time.

These days York is an affable, country town with plenty to keep you out of trouble for a day or two.

◎ Sights & Activities

Mt Brown Lookout VIEWPOINT
(off Pioneer Dr; ⊘24hr) `FREE` For a cracking view over York, the Avon River and the surrounding hills and wheatfields, find your way out past the town cemetery on the eastern side of the river, continuing to the end of Pioneer Dr and the summit of Mt Brown (342m). Pick up a map at the visitor centre.

Residency Museum MUSEUM
(✐08-9641 1751; www.york.wa.gov.au/residency museum; 4 Brook St; adult/child/family $5/3/12; ⊘1-3pm Tue, Wed & Thu, 11am-3.30pm Sat & Sun) Built in 1858, this museum houses some intriguing historical exhibits, paying respect to Ballardong culture, and has plenty of poignant old black-and-white photos of York (no, it's not inside the amazing two-storey red-brick house a bit further down Brook St!).

Skydive York SKYDIVING
(✐1300 815 241; www.skydive.com.au; 3453 Spencers Brook Rd; 14,000ft tandem jumps from $279) The Avon Valley is WA's skydiving epicentre; the drop zone is about 3km out of town. Weekdays usually offer the best rates.

✰✰ Festivals & Events

York Festival CULTURAL
(www.yorkfestival.com.au; ⊘Sep-Oct) This month-long arts and culture fest injects plenty of life (and dollars) into York every September, banishing the winter blues in favour of workshops, concerts, markets, foodie events, exhibitions and installations.

🛏 Sleeping & Eating

York Palace Hotel MOTEL $$
(✐08-9641 2454; www.theyork.com.au; 145 Avon Tce; d hotel/motel from $165/210; P ❉ ☎) Chose between lavishly restored heritage rooms upstairs at the silver-turreted York Palace (yet another of York's fine old pubs, this one built in 1909), or one of 15 very tidy, contemporary motel-style rooms in the terraces out the back. It comes down to what kind of person you are: frills, or no-frills.

Jules Cafe CAFE $
(✐08-9641 1832; 121 Avon Tce; mains $19-21; ⊘8am-4pm Mon-Fri, to 3pm Sat & Sun; ✐) 🍃 Putting a hippy spin on heritage York since 1990 (Che Guevara poster, World Wildlife Fund sticker, patchouli incense...you get the picture), Jules Cafe channels Lebanese heritage with top-notch kebabs, falafel and Middle Eastern salads, wraps and sandwiches.

Expect myriad organic, veggie and GF options, plush freshly smashed juices and summery fruit smoothies.

❶ Information

Visitor Centre (✐08-9641 1301; www.avonvalleywa.com.au; Town Hall, 81 Avon Tce; ⊘9.30am-12.30pm & 1.30-3.30pm) Closes for lunch every day (how quaint).

New Norcia
✐08 / POP 100

A bizarre architectural vision in the dry hills 132km north of Perth, the monastery settlement of New Norcia is a cluster of ornate, Spanish-style buildings cast incongruously in the Australian bush. Founded in 1847 by Spanish Benedictine monks as an Aboriginal mission, the working monastery today holds prayers and retreats, alongside a business producing boutique breads and curating a marvellous museum and art gallery. White-robed monks meet for lunch at the town's hotel, then return to their pious single-file movements from church to chambers. It's all very cinematic, and at once gloriously tranquil and deeply unnerving: looking at the faces in the old photographs on display at the museum, it's easy to believe that as many people have suffered as been saved here. Either way, it's a fascinating place.

◎ Sights

★New Norcia
Museum & Art Gallery MUSEUM
(✐08-9654 8056; www.newnorcia.wa.edu.au/museum/museum; New Norcia Rd; adult/child/family $12.50/7.50/30; ⊘9.30am-4.30pm) Over three levels, New Norcia's marvellously musty Museum & Art Gallery traces the history of the monastery and houses and has an impressive art collection. Contemporary Australian works recast traditional religious styles, alongside one of the country's largest collations of post-Renaissance religious art (including a genuine Raphael). The gift shop sells souvenirs, honeys, preserves and monk-baked breads. Town Tours (adult/child/family $13/7.50/30, with museum entry $25/15/60; ⊘11am & 1.30pm) leave from here too.

Abbey Church CHURCH
(✐08-9654 8056; www.newnorcia.wa.edu.au; Old Geraldton Rd; ⊘9.30am-4.30pm) Creak open the door of New Norcia's 1850s Georgian-meets-Latvian Abbey Church, flanked by

slender palms. Spot the kangaroos in the sgraffito murals, depicting the Stations of the Cross (look hard – there's also an astronaut). It's a sombre, hushed interior, the wind whispering in the eaves: you'll be forgiven for feeling that you're not alone in here (we made a hurried exit).

Sleeping & Eating

New Norcia Hotel   HOTEL $

(☑08-9654 8034; www.newnorcia.wa.edu.au/hotel/hotel; New Norcia Rd; s/d with shared bathroom incl breakfast from $80/100, extra person $27; ⊙meals noon-2pm & 6-8pm; P) The white colonnades of the noble New Norcia Hotel hark back to a more genteel time (1927, actually), with sweeping staircases, high ceilings, simple rooms and wide verandahs. Better-than-decent pub food (mains $20 to $28) is available at the bar or in the elegant dining room. Don't bypass the dips with New Norcia's own olive oil and wood-fired sourdough.

Monastery Guesthouse   GUESTHOUSE $

(☑08-9654 8002; www.newnorcia.wa.edu.au/accommodation/individuals-groups/guesthouse; Old Geraldton Rd; s & tw inc meals per person $80) The abbey (p929) offers lodging in the Monastery Guesthouse, within the walls of the southern cloister. Guests can join in prayers with the monks (and men can dine with them). Some rooms have bathrooms, some have shared facilities. Air-con also filters to some of the rooms. Various other cottages and colleges are also available for groups – ask when you book.

Getting There & Away

Transwa (p913) bus N2 runs in each direction between New Norcia and East Perth ($24.15, two hours) on Tuesday, Thursday, Saturday and Sunday.

Turquoise Coast

Cruising up Indian Ocean Dr from Lancelin into Cervantes and beyond, the chilled-out Turquoise Coast – traditional Yuat lands, and Amangu country further north – is studded with soporific fishing villages, sweeping stretches of beach, extraordinary geological formations, national parks and wildflower blooms. Not far offshore, marine parks and island nature reserves provide safe breeding havens for Australian sea lions, while crayfishing brings in the big bucks (there's a distinct 'have' and 'have not' social divide

here, between the crayfishers and the land-lubbers). If you've been craving some time to reconnect with the natural realm, do some beachcombing (this coastline is shipwreck central) or just chew through your airport novel, the Turquoise Coast is waiting for you.

Getting There & Away

Departing Tuesday and Thursday, Integrity Coach Lines (p911) runs along the coast between Perth and Broome, stopping at all the major towns. Also from Perth on Friday and Sunday, Transwa (p913) N5 buses stop at Cervantes, Jurien Bay, Green Head and Leeman en route to Geraldton. But really, why muck around with fares, aisle seats and timetables: having your own vehicle is the best way to go.

Lancelin

☑08 / POP 730

Afternoon offshore winds and a protective outlying reef make raffish little Lancelin a heaven-sent destination for windsurfing and kitesurfing, attracting wind-worshippers from around the planet. In January the **Lancelin Ocean Classic** (www.lancelinocean classic.com.au; ⊙Jan) windsurfing race kicks off at Ledge Point not far to the south. Back on dry land, the mountainous white dunes on the edge of town are prized sandboarding terrain.

Lancelin itself isn't much to look at – a flat, ramshackle fishing town – but there are a couple of decent places to stay, eat and drink here if you're in need of an overnighter. Online, see www.lancelin.com.au.

Activities

Have a Chat General Store   OUTDOORS

(☑08-9655 1054; 104 Gingin Rd; sandboard hire per 2hr $10; ⊙5am-5pm Mon-Fri, from 6am Sat, 7am-4pm Sun) Hires sandboards, so you can careen down the towering Lancelin dunes. Snorkelling equipment also available ($25 per half-day). Reduced winter hours.

Sleeping & Eating

★**Lancelin Lodge YHA**   HOSTEL $

(☑08-9655 2020; www.lancelinlodge.com.au; 10 Hopkins St; dm/d/f from $33/90/135; P❄🛜🏊) This laid-back, flag-adorned hostel on the edge of town is well equipped and welcoming, with deep verandahs and lots of indoor/outdoor communal spaces. Facilities include a big kitchen, BBQ, wood-fired pizza oven, enticing swimming pool, hammocks and free bikes and bodyboards. Stylistically it's big, boxy and bricky, but remains one of WA's best hostels. Self-contained suite also available (from $250).

⭐**Endeavour Tavern**   PUB FOOD **$$**
(☑08-9655 1052; www.endeavourtavern.com.au; 58 Gingin Rd; mains $19-39; ⊙10.30am-10pm Sun-Thu, to midnight Fri & Sat, meals noon-2pm & 6-8pm) The Endeavour is a classic Aussie beachfront beer bunker, with a big grassy terrace overlooking the Indian Ocean. The kitchen cooks up hefty pub-grub standards (chips with everything), including BLTs and burgers in buns from the Lancelin **bakery** (☑08-9655 1457; 8 Rock Way; items $4-8; ⊙10am-6pm Fri-Wed). As you'd expect, the seafood is magic: order the grilled sweetlip snapper (with chips). Live bands on weekends.

Lobster Trap   CAFE **$$**
(☑08-9655 1127; www.lobbstertrap.com; 91 Gingin Rd; mains $12-32; ⊙8am-3pm Thu-Mon) On Lancelin's rather aimless main street, Lobster Trap has the best coffee in town, plus wraps, salads, curries and lobster (aka crayfish) served myriad ways: lobster linguine, lobster wraps, lobster sliders... Trap yourself in the shady garden and ponder your next move. Opening hours can vary: call ahead if you're making a dedicated voyage to eat here.

Cervantes & Pinnacles Desert

☑08 / POP 530
Laid-back crayfishing town Cervantes, 198km north of Perth, makes a handy overnight stop with easy access to the Pinnacles Desert and the wildflower heaths of Lesueur National Park (p932), plus some beaut beaches. Only established in 1963, the town is scruffy, sprawling and charmless – even the Spanish street names, taking their cue from the 1844 wreck of the *Cervantes* nearby, do little to elevate the vibe. But things could be worse: the waterlogged survivors of the *Cervantes* wreck had to walk to their salvation in Fremantle, 216km away.

◎ Sights

⭐**Nambung National Park**   NATIONAL PARK
(☑08-9652 7913; www.parks.dpaw.wa.gov.au/park/nambung; Pinnacles Dr, off Indian Ocean Dr; per vehicle $13; ⊙daylight hours, visitor centre 9.30am-4.30pm) Around 14km from Cervantes, Nambung is home to the eye-popping **Pinnacles Desert**, a vast, alien-like plain studded with thousands of jaunty limestone pillars. Rising eerily from the desert floor, some of them

3.5m tall, these columns are remnants of a compacted seashell layer that once covered the plain and, over millennia, has slowly eroded. The one-way Pinnacles Desert Dr loop road runs through the formations, but it's more fun on foot, especially in the crepuscular evening light when crowds evaporate.

🧭 Tours

Many Perth-based companies offer day trips to the Pinnacles, including the following:

Explore Tours Perth (☑08-9308 2211; www.exploretoursperth.com.au; day tour adult/child $169/119)

Kandu Perth Tours (☑0419 935 677; www.kanduperthtours.com.au; day tour adult/child from $175/130)

Travel Western Australia Tours (☑08-6267 0701; www.twatours.com.au; day tour per person $165)

🛏 Sleeping & Eating

Lobster Lodge   HOSTEL **$**
(☑08-9652 7377; www.lobsterlodge.com.au; 91 Seville St; dm $35, d with/without bathroom $135/95, 3-bedroom apt $300; [P][❄][☎]) Refurbished in early 2019 and managed by the same folks who run the Lobster Shack (p932), this unhurried hostel behind the dunes near Thirsty Point has a fantastic front terrace hung with a lazy hammock or two, small and tidy dorms, a chipper communal kitchen and a snug lounge. Bright, spacious en-suite rooms, some with views, occupy the building next door.

RAC Cervantes Holiday Park   CARAVAN PARK **$**
(☑08-9652 7060; www.parksandresorts.rac.com.au/park/cervantes-holiday-park; 35 Aragon St; unpowered/powered sites $36/46, 2-/3-bedroom cabins $200/250; [P][❄][☎][≋]) In a fantastic location right behind the dunes with plenty of shady, grassy sites and an on-site **cafe** (www.parksandresorts.rac.com.au/cervantes/park-info/cafe-and-shop; mains $8-20; ⊙8am-4pm), this auto-club park is open to all-comers (RAC members receive a $5 discount). The spanking-new cabins circling around the swimming pool are a highlight. Kids scoot around pathways lined with native plants, and to the playground across the street.

Pinnacles Edge Resort   APARTMENT **$$**
(☑08-9652 7788; www.pinnaclesedgeresort.com.au; 7 Aragon St; d from $180, 1-/2-bedroom apt from $220/340; [P][❄][☎][≋]) Top of the Cervantes accommodation tree, this two-storey complex of limestone-coloured apartments revolves

around a sparkling central swimming pool, somehow reminiscent of Queensland. The best units have spa and balcony. If there's no room here, the adjoining **Cervantes Pinnacles Motel** has 40 or so cheaper, older-style doubles (also with pool). Short stroll to the pub.

★ **Lobster Shack** SEAFOOD $$
(☑ 08-9652 7010; www.lobstershack.com.au; 37 Catalonia St; mains $17-43; ⊙ shop 8am-5pm, cafe 11am-3pm, tours noon-3pm) Craving some cray? They don't come much fresher than at this lobster-factory-turned-lunch spot, where half a grilled lobster, chips and salad will set you back around $38. Fish burgers, prawn buckets, abalone, oysters, beer and wine complete the picture. Self-guided factory tours ($10) and takeaway also available; B-52s' 'Rock Lobster' sing-alongs mandatory.

Cervantes Bar & Bistro PUB FOOD $$
(☑ 08-9652 7009; www.facebook.com/cervantes barandbistro; 1 Cadiz St; mains $26-38; ⊙ 11am-midnight Mon-Sat, to 10pm Sun) Cervantes' tavern is the hub of town life, serving pub meals that are a cut above. Local seafood is the star – lobster, squid, mussels, snapper and oysters – while a decent array of tap beers pairs admirably with interesting flavours from across the Indian Ocean: chicken masala, massaman lamb, nasi goreng... Skip the macho sports bar and car-park tables.

🛈 **Information**

Visitor Information Centre (☑ 08-9652 7700; www.visitpinnaclescountry.com.au; 14-16 Cadiz St; ⊙ 9am-5pm) Grab a copy of the *Turquoise Coast Self Drive Map* from Cervantes' visitor centre, which also supplies accommodation and tour info. Doubles as the town post office, newsagent and fishing-bait shop (old newspaper wrapping supplied).

Jurien Bay
☑ 08 / POP 1760

Big enough to have an op shop, a supermarket and a tattoo parlour, rough-and-tumble Jurien Bay has been booming over the past decade, after being selected as a regional 'SuperTown' by WA's Department of Primary Industries & Regional Development in 2011 and earmarked for population growth. Home to a hefty fishing fleet and lots of garish big houses, it's already rather spread out and disjointed; however, there's a long swimming beach, a fishing jetty and some great snorkelling and diving sites.

◉ **Sights & Activities**

Lesueur National Park NATIONAL PARK
(☑ 08-9688 6000; www.parks.dpaw.wa.gov.au/park/lesueur; off Cockleshell Gully Rd, Hill River; per vehicle $13; ⊙ 24hr) This botanical nirvana, 30km northeast of Jurien Bay, protects 900 plant species, many of them rare and endemic, such as the pine banksia (*Banksia tricuspis*) and Mt Lesueur grevillea (*Grevillea batrachioides*). Late winter sees the heath erupt into a mass of colour: cruise the 18km Lesueur scenic drive and check it out, stopping at picnic areas and lookouts (maybe you'll spot an endangered Carnaby's black cockatoo). A jaunt to the flat top of **Mt Lesueur** (4km return) delivers panoramic coastal views.

Jurien Bay Adventure Tours ADVENTURE
(☑ 1300 462 383; www.jurienbayadventuretours. com.au; tours per person $29-99) Versatile one-stop shop to hire bikes ($30 per day), sandboards ($30), stand-up paddleboards ($50) and snorkelling gear ($20), plus guided tours covering everything from the Pinnacles and Mt Lesueur to WWII radar bunkers and the crayfishing industry south at Cervantes. All tours depart from the visitor centre (p933).

🛏 **Sleeping & Eating**

Jurien Bay Motel Apartments MOTEL $$
(☑ 08-9652 2062; www.jurienbayapartments.com. au; 7 Murray St; d from $140, 1-/2-bedroom apt from $180/240; 🅿 ❊ 🛜) This chunky, institutional-looking complex of motel rooms and one- and two-bedroom apartments could have used a more subtle architectural eye at the design stage, but once you're inside they're just fine, with beachy colours, plush carpets and full kitchens in the apartments (and if you're not cooking, the Murray St Grill is right across the street).

★ **Murray St Grill** BISTRO $$
(☑ 08-9652 2114; www.facebook.com/murrayst grill; 1/12 Murray St; mains $20-39; ⊙ 11am-9pm Tue-Thu, to 10pm Fri & Sat, to 8pm Sun; 🛜) This slick bistro is a breath of fresh Indian Ocean air for Jurien Bay, with savvy interior design, amiable staff, quick-fire tapas plates (cheese-stuffed jalapeños, pork-belly bites, lemon-on-pepper squid) and meatier mains (steaks, burgers, lamb cutlets, battered red-spot emperor). The double-beef burger is challengingly weighty. Full bar, all-day kitchen, good coffee and kickin' apple mojitos. Nice one!

PERTH & WESTERN AUSTRALIA TURQUOISE COAST

WILDFLOWER WAY

Extending north from the towns of Moora and Wongan Hills in WA's northern wheatfields (Ballardong lands) to meet the coast at Geraldton, WA's Wildflower Way joins the dots between a series of humble farming towns: Ballidu, Pithara, Dalwallinu, Wubin, Buntine, Latham, Perenjori and Morawa...most of which have a wheat silo, a pub and a caravan park. But you're not necessarily here to drink beer and pitch a tent: the main game here is native wildflowers, which burst into glorious bloom between August and September. Collectively, Western Australia's annual wildflower bloom is the largest such event on earth, including more than 12,000 species – more than 60% are found nowhere else. You won't see all of them along Wildflower Way – there are plenty more further north in the Pilbara and the southwest – but as the hordes of camera-wielding flower fans attest, this landscape is bloomin' marvellous.

For pre-trip inspiration, check out www.wildflowercountry.com.au.

Little C's Pizzeria PIZZA $$
(⌨ 08-9652 1229; www.sandpipertavern.com.au/menu; 12 Roberts St; pizzas $14-26; ⊗ 5-10pm Thu-Mon, to 9pm Tue & Wed) In a twin-business arrangement with the **Sandpiper Bar & Grill** (⌨ 08-9652 1229; www.sandpipertavern.com.au; 12 Roberts St; mains $23-38; ⊗ 11.30am-10pm Thu-Mon, 5-9pm Tue & Wed) next door, Little C's does takeaway small-town discs with witty, rock-and-roll names to keep you amused while you wait: Smashing Pumpkins (with pumpkin), Mushroom Records (with mushroom), Tame Impala (with impala peppercorns), Flaming Lips (spicy!)... Skip the dessert pizzas.

ⓘ Information

Turquoise Coast Visitor Centre (⌨ 08-9652 0870; www.visitturquoisecoast.com.au; 67 Bashford St; ⊗ 9am-5pm Mon-Fri, to 1pm Sat; ⓡ) Jurien Bay's excellent visitor centre can advise on activities, transport and accommodation in 'JB' and the surrounding Dandaragan Shire.

MARGARET RIVER REGION

The farmland, forests, rivers and coast of the lush, green southwestern corner of WA, traditionally the land of the Wardandi and Bibbulmun people, contrast vividly with the stark, sunburnt terrain of much of the state. On land, world-class wineries and craft breweries beckon, and tall trees provide shade for walking trails and scenic drives. Offshore, dolphins and whales frolic, and devoted surfers often find their perfect break.

Unusually for WA, distances between the many attractions are surprisingly short, making it a fantastic area to explore for a few days – you will get much more out of your stay here if you have your own wheels. Summer brings hordes of visitors, but in the wintry months from July to September the cosy pot-bellied stove rules and visitors are scarce, and while opening hours can be somewhat erratic, prices are much more reasonable.

✲ Festivals & Events

Gourmet Escape FOOD & DRINK
(www.gourmetescape.com.au; ⊗ late Nov) From Rick Stein, Nigella Lawson and Heston Blumenthal to *MasterChef Australia*'s George Calombaris and Matt Preston, the Gourmet Escape food and wine festival attracts the big names in global and Australian cuisine. Look forward to three days of food workshops, tastings, vineyard events and demonstrations.

Margaret River Pro SPORTS
(www.worldsurfleague.com; ⊗ May-Jun; ☝) FREE
Top ranked male and female surfers compete over a 12-day period, plus there's gigs, surf workshops and exhibitions.

ⓘ Getting There & Away

Transwa (⌨ 1300 662 205; www.transwa.wa.gov.au) and **South West Coach Lines** (⌨ 08-9261 7600; www.southwestcoachlines.com.au) offer comprehensive bus services to the region. Bunbury is the terminus of the Australind train line from Perth, and there is an airport at Busselton.

Bunbury

⌨ 08 / POP 81,389
Both a busy port and beachside holiday spot, Bunbury has much to recommend it. Holidaymakers mostly stop here to see the local

The Southwest

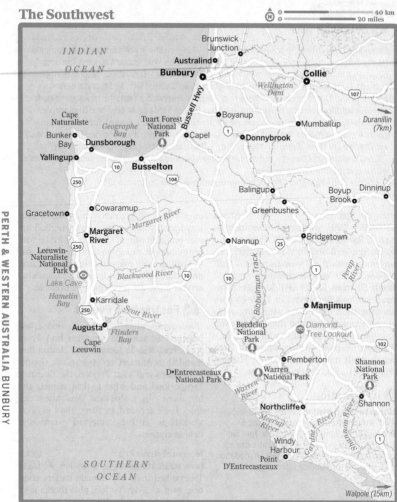

dolphins, but with an excellent local history museum, regional art gallery, street art, international cuisine and opportunities to learn about the Indigenous culture, it's definitely worth a longer visit.

Inhabited by the Wardani, before the Dutch, French and then Brits sailed in (the Brits later returning to claim ownership in 1838), the bay was named after Nicolas Baudin's ship *Le Géographe* in 1803; British Governor James Stirling renamed the township after a lieutenant in charge of the original military outpost.

👁 Sights

★ **Dolphin Discovery Centre** SCIENCE CENTRE (☎ 08-9791 3088; www.dolphindiscovery.com. au; Koombana Beach; adult/child $18/10; ☉ 9am-2pm May-Sep, 8am-4pm Oct-Apr; P 🚸) Around 60 bottlenose dolphins live in the bay year-round, their numbers increasing in summer. This community-led centre teaches visitors about the dolphins and their habitat, with lots of hands-on experiences. To meet the wild dolphins in real life, head to the beachside zone early in the day. The experience is carefully supervised by well-trained volunteers for the safety of the dolphins.

★ Bunbury Museum & Heritage Centre
MUSEUM

(www.bunburymuseum.com.au; 1 Arthur St; ⏱10am-4pm Tue-Sun; ♿) **FREE** A fabulous small museum, packed full of information on the original inhabitants here, the Wardandi people, explorers who visited and the colonisers who moved in. Relies a lot on multimedia, but there are some interesting artefacts and an old school room. Ask about the wreck buried under Bunbury somewhere.

Bunbury Regional Art Gallery
GALLERY

(☎08-9792 7323; www.brag.org.au; 64 Wittenoom St; ⏱10am-4pm; ♿) **FREE** Housed in a restored late-19th-century convent, now painted a dusty pink, this excellent gallery is arranged over two floors and exhibits new works as well as pieces from its collection.

☞ Tours

Dolphin Swim Tour & Eco Cruises
WILDLIFE WATCHING

(https://dolphindiscovery.com.au; 3hr swim tour $165, 1½hr eco tour adult/child $54/40; ⏱8am & noon; ♿) Rise early for the opportunity to swim with dolphins in what many say is a life-changing experience, although animal welfare experts are wary. Alternatively meet at midday for an informative boat cruise spotting some of Bunbury's playful dolphins in the wild.

Ngalang Wongi Aboriginal Cultural Tours
CULTURAL

(☎0457 360 517; www.ngalangwongi.com.au; Bunbury Visitor Centre; adult/child from $50/25; ♿) Don't leave Bunbury without learning its pre- and post-colonial history and sites of cultural significance. A gifted storyteller, local Noongar man Troy Bennell runs a two-hour city walking tour, plus a morning around the estuary and Collie River including wildlife and bushfoods.

🛏 Sleeping

Quality Hotel Lighthouse
BOUTIQUE HOTEL $$

(☎08-9781 2700; http://lighthousehotel.com.au; 2 Marlston Dr; r from $150; ❄🛜🏊) With a commanding location looking towards the Indian Ocean, this newish hotel is across the road from the ocean beach and a short walk to the estuary. It has excellent modern facilities, but is small enough to have a boutique vibe.

Clifton
MOTEL $$

(☎08-9721 4300; www.theclifton.com.au; 2 Molloy St; r from $135; 🛜) For heritage accommodation with a dose of luxury, go for the top-of-the-range rooms in the Clifton's historic Grittleton Lodge (1885). Good-value motel rooms are also available in a separate building.

✕ Eating & Drinking

★ Market Eating House
MODERN AUSTRALIAN $$$

(☎08-9721 6078; www.marketeatinghouse.com.au; 9 Victoria St; shared plates $12-18, mains $35-42; ⏱5.30pm-late Wed & Thu, noon-late Fri & Sat, 9am-4pm Sun) Focuses on a custom-made wood-fired grill that is used for everything from chicken and fish to pork and beef. Turkish and Middle Eastern flavours underpin many dishes, and smaller shared plates include plump ricotta dumplings and hummus topped with lamb.

★ Tokyo Jack's
JAPANESE $$$

(www.tokyo-jacks.com.au; 54 Victoria St; small share plates $5-18, large plates $29-38; ⏱11am-10pm; ❄♿) With a contemporary fit-out, polished concrete and a mural, Tokyo Jack's offers *izakaya*-style Japanese tapas. Moreish highlights include popcorn shrimp and Wagyu beef croquettes, while the broader menu includes sushi and sashimi as well as all your Japanese classics.

Lost Bills
COCKTAIL BAR

(www.lostbills.com; 41 Victoria St; ⏱4-11pm Wed-Thu, 3pm-midnight Fri & Sat, 2-8pm Sun) Lost Bills' compact brick-lined space is enlivened by quirky artwork. A good wine and cocktail list and four guest taps with beer and cider from around WA are also valid reasons to visit Bunbury's answer to the small bar in Sydney or Melbourne.

Yours or Mine
BAR

(☎08-9791 8884; www.facebook.com/yoursormine1; 26 Victoria St; ⏱noon-3pm & 5pm-midnight Mon-Thu, noon-midnight Sat & Sun) Yours or Mine continues Bunbury's small-bar scene but with tasty shared plates ($18 to $28) and chesterfield sofas. The South American–influenced menu (mains $24 to $42), including pulled-pork tacos, is worth the wait when its busy. Check the website for nightly specials and occasional live gigs.

ⓘ Information

Visitor Centre (☎08-9792 7205; www.visitbunburygeographe.com.au; Carmody Pl; ⏱9am-5pm Mon-Sat, 10am-2pm Sun) Located in the historic train station (1904). Bikes can be rented and there are free historic walking tours every Wednesday at 10am.

❶ Getting There & Away

Coaches stop at the **central bus station** (☏08-9722 7800; Carmody Pl), next to the visitor centre, or at the **train station** (Picton Rd, Woolaston).

Transwa (p933) has bus routes to most neighbouring cities and towns and down to Albany and Denmark.

South West Coach Lines (p933) runs to/from Perth's Elizabeth Quay Busport to Busselton, Dunsborough and Bridgetown.

TransBunbury runs buses (30 minutes) between the central bus station and train station ($2.90; no Sunday service). Look for bus number 827.

Bunbury is the terminus of the Transwa (p933) Australind train line, with two daily services to Perth ($31.45, 2½ hours).

Busselton

☏08 / POP 38,300

Unpretentious and uncomplicated, Busselton is what passes for the big smoke in these parts. Surrounded by calm waters and white-sand beaches, its outlandishly long jetty is its most famous attraction. The family-friendly town has plenty of diversionary activities for lively kids, including sheltered beaches, water slides and animal farms.

◎ Sights

Busselton Jetty LANDMARK
(☏08-9754 0900; www.busseltonjetty.com.au; adult/child $4/free; ⊙Oct-Apr 8.30am-6pm, May-Sep 9am-5pm; ⊕) Busselton's 1865 timber-piled jetty – the southern hemisphere's longest (1841m) – reopened in 2011 following a $27 million refurbishment. A little train (adult/child $13.50/8.50) chugs along to the Underwater Observatory (Map p938; adult/child incl train $34/20; ⊙9am-4.25pm; ⊕), where tours take place 8m below the surface; bookings essential. There's also an Interpretive Centre, an attractive building in the style of 1930s bathing sheds, about 50m along the jetty. You can also explore the underwater world around the jetty's historic piles with Dive Busselton Jetty (☏1800 994 210; www.divebusseltonjetty.com. au; underwater walks $179, snorkelling/diving from $20/99; ⊙underwater walks Dec-Apr) wearing a self-contained breathing apparatus called a SeaTREK helmet.

Tuart Forest National Park FOREST
(www.parks.dpaw.wa.gov.au; P⊕) The tuart is a type of eucalypt that only grows on coastal limestone in southwest Western Australia. This 20-sq-km strip squeezed between the Bussell Hwy and the Indian Ocean just outside Busselton is the last tuart forest left after decades of logging. There is a self-guided 1.5km walk in the forest designed for nighttime possum spotting. Bring your own torch.

Capel Vale WINERY
(☏08-9727 1986; www.capelvale.com.au; Mallokup Rd; ⊙cellar door 10am-4.30pm, restaurant 11.30am-3pm Thu-Mon) Geographe Bay wine region's best-known winery is conveniently located halfway between Bunbury and Busselton. Capel Vale offers free tastings and has a restaurant overlooking the vines. It's off the Bussell Hwy on the opposite side of the highway from Capel village.

ArtGeo Cultural Complex GALLERY
(☏08-9751 4651; www.artgeo.com.au; 6 Queen St; ⊙10am-4pm) Grouped around the old courthouse (1856), this complex includes tearooms, an artist-in-residence and the Busselton Art Society's exhibition space, selling work by local artists from ceramics to fine jewellery.

✦✦ Festivals & Events

CinéfestOZ FILM
(www.cinefestoz.com; ⊙late Aug) Busselton briefly morphs into Cannes with this oddly glamorous festival of French and Australian cinema, including lots of Australian premieres and the odd Aussie starlet.

🛏 Sleeping

Big 4 Beachlands Holiday Park CARAVAN PARK $
(Map p938; ☏08-9752 2107; www.beachlands. com.au; 10 Earnshaw Rd, West Busselton; sites per 2 people $53, chalets $145-215; ❋⑤⊛) This excellent family-friendly park offers a wide range of accommodation – grassy tent sites to deluxe villas – amid shady trees, palms and flax bushes. A playground, pool, bikes, stand-up paddleboards and pedal go-carts will keep kids happy.

Observatory Guesthouse B&B $$
(☏08-9751 3336; www.observatoryguesthouse. com; 7 Brown St; d from $150; ❋❋⑤) A five-minute walk from the jetty, this friendly B&B has four bright, cheerful rooms. They're not overly big, but you can spread out on the communal sea-facing balcony and front courtyard.

★ **Aqua** DESIGN HOTEL $$$
(Map p938; 08-9750 4200; www.theaqua
resort.com.au; 605 Bussell Hwy; apt $420-1400;
❄ 🛜 ⌨) Down a driveway framed by pep-
permint trees and with direct beach access,
the luxury beach town houses at Aqua are
a grand option for families or a pair of cou-
ples travelling together. Bedrooms and bath-
rooms are stylish and understated, but the
real wow factor comes from the stunning
lounges and living areas. Facilities include
a beachfront infinity pool and a spa and
sauna.

🍴 Eating & Drinking

Goose CAFE $$
(08-9754 7700; www.thegoose.com.au; Ge-
ographe Bay Rd; breakfast $13-22, share plates
& mains $11-35; 7am-10pm; 🛜) Next to the
jetty, stylish Goose is a cool and classy cafe,
bar and bistro. The drinks list bubbles away
with WA craft beer and wine, and a versatile
menu kicks off with eggy breakfasts, before
graduating to share plates using local ingredients including Vietnamese pulled-pork
sliders, and larger dishes such as steamed
mussels and seafood chowder.

Vasse Bar + Kitchen PUB FOOD $$
(08-9754 8560; www.vassebarkitchen.com.au;
44 Queen St; mains $17-32; 10am-late) The pub
menu mainstays include hearty pizza, pas-
ta, steaks and pale-ale-battered fish. There's
a good range of beers on tap, and the out-
door tables are perfect for people-watching.
Check out the listings for live music on the
window.

Darleen's BAR
(www.facebook.com/pg/Darleens; 43 Prince St;
noon-midnight Wed-Sat, to 8pm Sun) Taking
over from the much loved Laundry 43, Dar-
leen's brings the karaoke, vinyl and beer-yo-
ga vibes to Busselton. Exposed brick walls
form the backdrop for Margaret River beers
and wines, plus dishes.

Fire Station CRAFT BEER
(08-9752 3113; www.firestation.bar;
11.30am-9.30pm, till late Fri & Sat) Park your-
self in the cosy interior or outside under
the market umbrellas and enjoy one of the
southwest's best selections of wine and craft
beer. The tasty food menu includes classic
drinking dishes like spicy chicken wings and
cheese and chilli croquettes, and weekly spe-
cials include Thursday's Bao & Beer deal and
Asian steamed buns from 4pm.

ℹ️ Information

Visitor Centre (08-9752 5800; www.
margaretriver.com; end of Queen St, Busselton
foreshore; 9am-5pm, to 4.30pm Sat & Sun)
On the waterfront near the pier. Loans out
helmets for cycle hire.

ℹ️ Getting There & Around

South West Coach Lines and Transwa (p933)
buses link Busselton to the north and south.

Busso is fairly spread-out; if you don't have a
car, hire a **bike** (www.spinwaywa.bike; 1 hour/
day $15/33) to get around.

Dunsborough

08 / POP 5320
Dunsborough is a gentle township with a
well-heeled resident base. It's a good spot
to base yourself to explore Cape Natural-
iste's bushland and beaches, with excellent
shopping and dining options. Family hol-
iday houses line the bayside waterfront,
and its YHA has one of the best backyards
in Australia. The name Dunsborough first
appeared on maps in the 1830s, but to the
Wardandi people it was always Quedjinup,
meaning 'place of women'.

◉ Sights & Activities

Blind Corner WINERY
(Map p938; www.blindcorner.com.au/blogs/cellar-
door/cellar-door; 1105 Vasse-Yallingup Siding Rd;
10am-4pm Mon-Sat) Newcomers to the re-
gion, the winemakers at Blind Corner are
shaking things up with a super-approacha-
ble cellar door experience (no question too
embarrassing) and producing biodynamic
hand-picked wines. Plans to get a pizza oven
will see people lingering longer.

Naturaliste Charters WHALE WATCHING
(08-9750 5500; www.whales-australia.com.au;
25/27 Dunn Bay Rd; adult/child $90/50; 10am &
2pm Sep–mid-Dec) Two-hour whale-watching
cruises. From December to January, the em-
phasis switches to an Eco Wilderness Tour
showcasing beaches, limestone caves with
Aboriginal art, and wildlife, including dol-
phins and seals.

Cape Dive DIVING
(08-9756 8778; www.capedive.com; 222 Natural-
iste Tce; 9am-5pm) There is excellent diving
in Geographe Bay, especially since the de-
commissioned Navy destroyer HMAS *Swan*
was purposely scuttled in 1997 for use as a
dive wreck. Marine life has colonised the

Margaret River Wine Region

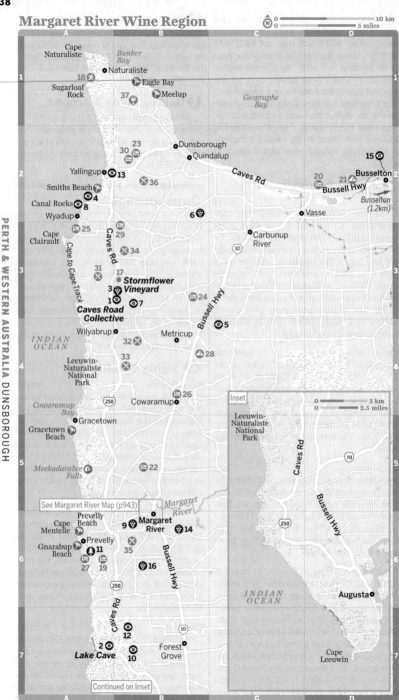

Cape
Naturaliste

*Bunker
Bay*

1

Naturaliste

18

Eagle Bay

Sugarloaf
Rock

37

Meelup

*Geographe
Bay*

23

30

Dunsborough

Quindalup

Yallingup

13

Caves Rd

Busselton

15

20

21

Busselton

36

*Busselton
(1.2km)*

Bussell Hwy

Smiths Beach

4

Canal Rocks

8

Wyadup

6

Vasse

25

Cape
Clairault

29

Carbunup
River

34

10

31

17

**Stormflower
Vineyard**

3

1

7

24

**Caves Road
Collective**

Bussell Hwy

Wilyabrup

5

*INDIAN
OCEAN*

32

Metricup

Leeuwin-
Naturaliste
National
Park

33

28

250

26

Cowaramup

*Cowaramup
Bay*

Gracetown

Gracetown
Beach

*Meekadarabee
Falls*

22

Inset

0 — 5 km
0 — 2.5 miles

Leeuwin-
Naturaliste
National
Park

Caves Rd

10

250

Bussell Hwy

See Margaret River Map (p943)

*Margaret
River*

Cape
Mentelle

Prevelly
Beach

9

**Margaret
River**

14

Prevelly

Gnarabup
Beach

11

35

27

19

16

Bussell Hwy

250

*INDIAN
OCEAN*

Augusta

Caves Rd

12

10

2

Lake Cave

10

Forest
Grove

Cape
Leeuwin

Continued on Inset

Margaret River Wine Region

◎ **Top Sights**
1 Caves Road Collective............................B3
2 Lake Cave...A7
3 Stormflower Vineyard...........................B3

◎ **Sights**
4 Aquarium..A2
5 Beer Farm..C4
6 Blind Corner...B2
7 Bootleg Brewery...................................B3
8 Canal Rocks...A2
9 Cape Mentelle......................................B6
10 Giants Cave..B7
11 Leeuwin-Naturaliste National
   Park...A6
12 Mammoth Cave.....................................B7
13 Ngilgi Cave...A2
14 Stella Bella...B6
15 Underwater Observatory.......................D2
16 Voyager Estate.....................................B6

◎ **Activities, Courses & Tours**
17 Cape Lodge...B3
18 Cape to Cape Track...............................A1
   Wildwood Valley Cooking
   School.......................................(see 29)

◎ **Sleeping**
19 Acacia Chalets......................................A6
20 Aqua...D2
21 Big 4 Beachlands Holiday Park.............D2
22 Burnside Organic Farm.........................B5
23 Empire Retreat & Spa...........................B2
24 Forest Rise...B3
25 Injidup Spa Retreat..............................A3
26 Noble Grape Guesthouse......................B4
27 Surfpoint..A6
28 Taunton Farm Holiday Park..................B4
29 Wildwood Valley Cottages....................B3
30 Yallingup Lodge & Spa..........................B2

◎ **Eating**
31 Amiria...A3
32 Rustico at Hay Shed Hill.......................B4
33 Vasse Felix...B4
34 Wills Domain..B3
35 Xanadu..B6
36 Yallingup Woodfired Bread...................B2

◎ **Drinking & Nightlife**
37 Eagle Bay Brewing Co..........................B1

◎ **Shopping**
   Margaret River Regional Wine
   Centre.......................................(see 26)

ship, which lies at a depth of 30m, 2.5km offshore. Trips include Busselton Jetty (p936) too.

🛏 Sleeping

Dunsborough Beachouse YHA
HOSTEL $

(☑08-9755 3107; www.dunsboroughbeachouse.com.au; 205 Geographe Bay Rd; dm $34-36, s/d $57/88; Ｐ🖥) This friendly, well-run hostel has lawns stretching languidly to the beach. Welcoming, though popular with longer-term stayers too, it's an easy 2km cycle from the town centre; bike hire available.

Dunsborough Central Motel
MOTEL $$

(☑08-9756 7711; www.dunsboroughmotel.com.au; 50 Dunn Bay Rd; dm $40, r $180-220; 🖥🖥) Centrally located, this motel is good value with dorm beds as well as motel rooms. A good option if you want to dine, drink or just mooch in town.

🍴 Eating & Drinking

Pourhouse Bar & Kitchen
GASTROPUB $$

(☑08-9759 1720; www.pourhouse.com.au; 26 Dunn Bay Rd; mains $19-34; ⊙11am-late) An unpretentious modern pub, with comfy couches, weekend DJs and an upstairs terrace, the **Elevator Bar**. The pizzas are varied, and

burgers come in a locally baked sourdough bun. A considered approach to beer includes rotating taps from the best of WA's craft breweries and lots of bottled surprises.

Yarri
AUSTRALIAN $$$

(https://yarri.com.au; 6/16 Cyrillean Way; mains $18-40; Ｐ) The talk of the region when we visited, this elegant restaurant serves a modern Australian menu aligned with the seasons and using indigenous ingredients. You're as likely to have dishes with emu as marron (freshwater crayfish), plus the kid-friendly yakitori. Food is paired with wines from Snake + Herring.

Blue Manna
ASIAN $$$

(☑08-9786 5051; www.bluemannabistro.com.au; 1/16 Cyrillean Way; mains $20-38; ⊙noon-late, closed public holidays; Ｐ) Pan Asian–style bistro specialising in seafood dishes with excellent staff who manage well given its buzzing popularity. Dishes range from mouth-watering salt and pepper blue manna crab to Balinese betutu duck.

Eagle Bay Brewing Co
BREWERY

(Map p938; ☑08-9755 3554; www.eaglebaybrewing.com.au; Eagle Bay Rd, Dunsborough; ⊙11am-5pm) Offers a lovely rural outlook; interesting beers and wines served in modern, spacious surroundings; and excellent food, including crisp wood-fired pizzas. Keep an eye out for Eagle Bay's single batch specials.

ℹ Information

Visitor Centre (☑08-9752 5800; www.marg aretriver.com; 1/31 Dunn Bay Rd; ☺9am-5pm, 9.30am-4.30pm Sat & Sun) Information and bookings.

ℹ Getting There & Away

Transwa and South West Coach Lines (p933) buses link Dunsborough north to Perth and further south through Margaret River to Albany and the southwest.

Cape Naturaliste

Northwest of Dunsborough, Cape Naturaliste offers the secluded white sand beaches of Meelup, Eagle Bay and Bunker Bay, a lighthouse with breathtaking views and the oft-photographed Sugarloaf Rock. There are plenty of short walks and lookouts along the cape to explore; pick up brochures from Dunsborough's visitor centre before heading out of town. Whales like to hang out on the edge of Bunker Bay, where the continental shelf drops 75m. There's also excellent snorkelling at Shelley Cove and the HMAS *Swan* wreck offshore.

◉ Sights & Activities

Ngilgi Cave   CAVE
(Map p938; ☑08-9755 2152; www.margaretriver. com; Yallingup Caves Rd; adult/child $22.50/12; ☺9am-5pm; P 🚻) This 500,000-year-old cave is associated in Wardandi spirituality with the victory of the good spirit Ngilgi over the evil spirit Wolgine. A whitefella first stumbled upon the site in 1899 while looking for his horse. Today semi-guided tours of the caves, which allow you to explore at your own pace, depart every half-hour. Last tour at 4pm.

Cape to Cape Track   WALKING
(Map p938; www.capetocapetrack.com.au) Stretching from Cape Naturaliste to Cape Leeuwin, the 135km Cape to Cape Track passes through the heath, forest and sand dunes of the Leeuwin-Naturaliste National Park (Map p938; Caves Rd), with Indian Ocean views. Most walkers take about seven days to complete the track (staying in a combination of national park campsites and commercial accommodation). You can walk it in five days, or break up the route into a series of day trips.

Southwest Eco Discoveries   ECOTOUR
(☑0477 049 722, 0477 030 322; www.southwesteco discoveries.com.au; tours $55-95) Brothers Ryan and Mick White run tours exploring Geographe Bay and Cape Naturaliste. Options include morning tours of the stunning coastline, afternoon tours with a wine and gourmet focus, and evening outings to see endangered woylies and other nocturnal marsupials. Tour pick-ups can be made from accommodation in Busselton, Dunsborough and Cowaramup, and from Margaret River by availability and arrangement.

**Geographe Alternative
Wines Trail**   WINE
(https://visitbunburygeographe.com.au/geo graphe-alternative-wine-trail) 🍷 Get off the beaten track and tour this lesser-known wine region. The visitor centre has copies of the self-drive maps, which are also available online. Meet innovative wine makers working with 12 alternative wine varieties for the region, from barbera to tempranillo.

ℹ Getting There & Away

No public transport runs to Cape Naturaliste, so visitors need their own transport, or else will need visit on a prebooked tour.

Yallingup

☑08 / POP 1029
Huddled on an ocean-facing hillside, the township of Yallingup is a quiet spot favoured by surfers and coastal walkers. It's mostly residential, with a wellness, yoga and family-holidays vibe. The dramatic surf-battered coastline is overlooked by a cascade of residential houses huddled together surrounded by trees. Yallingup means 'place of love' in the Wardandi Noongar tongue. Beautiful well-marked walking trails follow the coast over rocky outcrops and through treed hills overlooking the aquamarine ocean.

◉ Sights

Aquarium   NATURAL POOL
(Map p938; Smiths Beach Rd; ☺24hr; P) FREE
Protected from the pounding surf, this natural rock pool is a top spot for swimming and snorkelling. It's a walk along the Cape to Cape track to the rock pool – ask locally

for exact directions. Wild swimming precautions should be taken.

Canal Rocks
NATURAL FEATURE

(Map p938; https://parks.dpaw.wa.gov.au/site/canal-rocks; Canal Rocks Rd; [P]) Photo opportunities abound with the new bridge across the natural canal. The Wardani called it Winjee Sam.

Yallingup Surf School
SURFING

([J]08-9755 2755; www.yallingupsurfschool.com) Grab a 1½-hour group lesson for beginners or private coaching sessions. Also offers six-day surf and yoga safaris for women at www.escapesafaris.com.au.

🛏 Sleeping

Yallingup Beach Holiday Park
CARAVAN PARK $

([J]08-9755 2164; www.yallingupbeach.com.au; Valley Rd; sites per 2 people $32-54, cabins $90-285; [🖥]) You'll fall asleep to the sound of the surf here, with the beach just across the road. Prices vary with the seasons.

Yallingup Lodge & Spa
RETREAT $$

(Map p938; [J]08-9755 2411; https://yallinguplodge.com.au; 40 Hemsley Rd; glamping $170, r $200-550; [@🖥🌊]) On a secluded property between Dunsborough and Yallingup with the comforts of a lodge – a cosy lounge area around an open fire and a large deck overlooking trees, plus a swimming pool and day spa. Accommodation is mostly in the main residence, but the glamping option, a short walk away, includes an outdoor shower, and waking to birdsong with the sunrise.

★ Wildwood Valley Cottages
COTTAGE $$$

(Map p938; [J]08-9755 2120; www.wildwoodvalley.com.au; 1481 Wildwood Rd; cottages from $250; [🖥]) Luxury cottages trimmed by native bush are arrayed across 120 acres, and the property's main house also hosts the **Wildwood Valley Cooking School** (Map p938; classes per person $140; ⊙Dec-Mar) with Sioban and Carlo Baldini. Look out for grazing kangaroos as you meander up the unsealed road to reception.

Injidup Spa Retreat
BOUTIQUE HOTEL $$$

(Map p938; [J]08-9750 1300; www.injidupsparetreat.com.au; Cape Clairault Rd; ste from $650; [❄🌊]) ⟋ The region's most stylish and luxurious accommodation, Injidup perches atop an isolated cliff south of Yallingup. A striking carved facade fronts the car park, while inside are heated polished-concrete floors, 'eco' fires and absolute sea views. Each of the 10 suites has its own plunge pool. It's off Wyadup Rd.

RED TAILS IN THE SUNSET

Between Cape Naturaliste and Cape Leeuwin is the most southerly breeding colony of the red-tailed tropicbird (*Phaethon rubricauda*) in Australia. From September to May, look for it soaring above Sugarloaf Rock, south of Cape Naturaliste. The viewpoint can be reached by a 3.5km walk from the Cape Naturaliste lighthouse or by taking Sugarloaf Rd.

The tropicbird is distinguished by its two long, red tail streamers – almost twice its body length. Bring binoculars to watch this small colony soar, glide, dive and then swim with their disproportionately long tail feathers cocked up.

Empire Retreat & Spa
SPA HOTEL $$$

(Map p938; [J]08-9755 2065; www.empireretreat.com; Caves Rd; ste $295-575; [❄🖥]) Everything about the intimate Empire Retreat is stylish, from the cool Scandi-inspired design to the attention to detail and service. The rooms are built around a former farmhouse, and a rustic but sophisticated ambience lingers. Check online for good packages combining accommodation and spa treatments.

🍴 Eating & Drinking

Yallingup Woodfired Bread
BAKERY $

(Map p938; 189 Biddle Rd; bread from $4; ⊙7am-6pm Mon-Sat) Look out for excellent sourdough, rye bread and fruit loaves at local shops and the Margaret River Farmers Market (p944), or pick up some still-warm loaves at the bakery near Yallingup.

Wills Domain
BISTRO $$$

(Map p938; [J]08-9755 2327; www.willsdomain.com.au; cnr Brash & Abbey Farm Rds; mains $29-40, seven-course menu $110; ⊙tastings 10am-5pm, lunch noon-3pm) A restaurant and gallery with wonderful hilltop views over vines. An innovative seven-course tasting menu (with or without matching wines) is also available.

Caves House
BEER GARDEN

(Hotel Yallingup; [J]08-9750 1888; www.caveshousehotelyallingup.com.au; 18 Yallingup Beach Rd; [🖥🅿]) This restored heritage hotel is the main congregation spot for Yallingup locals. Pub food, a beer garden with plenty of shade, big screens showing Australian sport, and live music on summer afternoons draw in the families who are mostly content to let their kids run riot.

❶ Getting There & Around

Transwa (☏ 1300 662 205; www.transwa.
wa.gov.au; Proudlove Pde) buses that link Perth
and Albany stop in Yallingup, but to explore
fully you'll need your own transport.

Margaret River

☑ 08 / POP 4500

Although tourists usually outnumber locals,
Margaret River still feels like a country town.
The advantage of basing yourself here is that
after 5pm, once the wineries shut up shop,
it's one of the few places with any vital signs.
Plus, it's close to the incredible surf of Margaret River Mouth and Southside, and the swimming beaches at Prevelly and Gracetown.

Margaret River spills over with tourists
every weekend and gets very, *very* busy at
Easter and Christmas. Accommodation prices
tend to be cheaper midweek.

❍ Sights

Cape Mentelle WINERY
(Map p938; www.capementelle.com.au; 331 Walcliffe
Rd; tours from $30; ☺ 10am-5pm; ⚑) Offers a
cellar door, wine tours and tastings (with optional and food pairings), petanque, and an
outdoor cinema in summer. This Margaret
River winery is one of the originals from 1970.

**Margaret River
Distilling Company** DISTILLERY
(Map p943; ☏ 08-9757 9351; www.distillery.com.au;
Maxwell St, off Carters Rd; ☺ 10am-6pm, to 7pm Fri
& Sat; ⚑) Limeburners single malt whisky,
Tiger Snake sour mash, Great Southern gin
and White Shark vodka can all be sampled
at this edge-of-the-forest tasting room. There
are also local beers to take away with pizzas
and shared platters.

Stella Bella WINERY
(Map p938; ☏ 08-9758 5000; www.stellabella.com.
au; 205 Rosabrook Rd; ☺ 10am-5pm) Excellent
wines at a pretty cellar door (BYO picnic).
This outfit boasts the more interesting label
designs in the region.

☆ Activities

Margaret River SUP WATER SPORTS
(☏ 0419 959 053; www.margaretriversup.com.au;
adult/child $79/49) See a different side to Margs
on a two-hour stand-up paddleboarding
tour of the river in the nearby national park.
Guides teach you the skills, and provide all the
equipment required. Kids over eight welcome.

Dirt Skills MOUNTAIN BIKING
(☏ 0402 305 104; www.dirtskillsmargaretriver.
com; per person $65-70; ☺ Sat) If you're serious
about getting active amid Margaret River's
growing mountain-biking scene, consider a
training hook-up with these guys. Beginner
and intermediate riders are all welcome,
and if there's at least two of you, a special
trail-guiding session will help you find the
region's best tracks. Bikes can also be hired.

Margaret River Surf School SURFING
(☏ 0401 616 200; www.margaretriversurfschool.
com; group/individual lessons from $50/120, 3-/5-
day course from $120/185) Group and individual
lessons for both surfing and stand-up paddleboards. Three- and five-day courses are the
best option if you're serious about learning
to surf.

☞ Tours

Margaret River Brewery Tours FOOD & DRINK
(☏ 0458 450 120; www.mrbt.com.au; per person
$70-110; ☺ noon-6pm) Four craft breweries are
visited on these small-group minibus tours
helmed by the super-friendly Jules. The $70
'Mid Strength' option allows participants to
buy their own drinks as they go, while the
$110 'Full Strength' tour includes a six-brew
tasting paddle at each stop. Both options include an excellent lunch, and cider drinkers
can also be catered for.

Cape to Cape Tours WALKING
(☏ 0459 452 038; www.capetocapetours.com.au;
per couple from $1300) Negotiate the entire
route or just parts of the stunning Cape to
Cape coastal walk on self-guided and guided
itineraries. Trips include camping or lodge
accommodation and excellent meals, and
options from three to eight days are available. Various day tours exploring the Margaret
River region are also offered.

**Margaret River
Adventure Company** ADVENTURE SPORTS
(☏ 0418 808 993; www.margaretriveradventure.com.
au; half-/full day $80/160) Mountain biking, reef
snorkelling and 'coasteering' – a combination
of rock climbing, shore scrambling and leaping off cliffs into the ocean – all combine in
these fun tours with an excellent guide.

Taste the South WINE
(☏ 0438 210 373; www.tastethesouth.com.au; per
person from $95) Wine and craft-beer tours.
Up to five breweries can be visited, and
the special 'Hits with Kids' tour combines
children-friendly vineyards with activities

Margaret River

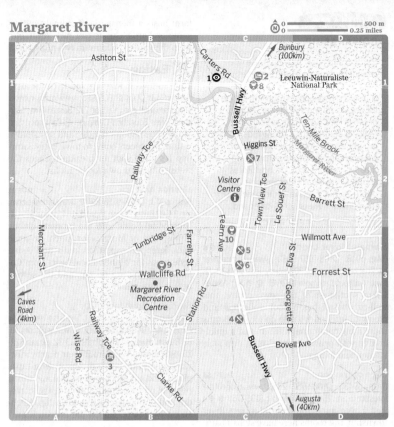

Margaret River

◉ **Sights**
1 Margaret River Distilling Company........C1

🛏 **Sleeping**
2 Edge of the Forest.................................C1
3 Margaret River Lodge...........................B4

✗ **Eating**
4 Margaret River Farmers Market..........C3
5 Miki's Open Kitchen..............................C3

6 Morries Anytime....................................C3
7 Swings & Roundabouts Taphouse.......C2

🍷 **Drinking & Nightlife**
8 Brewhouse..C1
9 The River Hotel.......................................B3
10 Yonder..C3

including lamb feeding, sheep shearing and visiting a chocolate factory.

Dirty Detours　　　　MOUNTAIN BIKING
(☑ 08-9758 8312; www.dirtydetours.com; per person $80-105) Runs guided mountain-bike rides, including through the magnificent Boranup Forest, as well as a Sip 'n' Cycle cellar-door tour. Multiday tours are also available.

🛏 Sleeping

Prevally Caravan Park　　CARAVAN PARK **$**
(☑ 08-9757 2374; http://prevellycaravanpark. com.au; sites from $30; ℗) A well-run family-friendly caravan park with shady tent sites near the beach rather than town. There's a well-stocked shop, plus the **Sea Garden** cafe on-site is a great spot for some sundowners.

WORTH A TRIP

COWARAMUP

Cowaramup (Cow Town to those who cannot pronounce it) is 10 minutes up the road from Margaret River on the Busselton Hwy and an excellent option for accommodation if Margs is full or too pricey. Cow Town is a thriving regional centre with a strong local community; check out the website (www.cowaramup.com.au) to see what we mean. Cow puns and cow sculptures abound. The area is famous for its dairy offerings, but if you're not into ice cream there's other sweets, plus cafes and local wineries to check out too.

Margaret River Lodge HOSTEL $

(Map p943; ☑08-9757 9532; www.margaretriverbackpackers.com.au; 220 Railway Tce; dm $30-32, r with/without bathroom $87/76; @🗐🎿) About 1.5km southwest of the town centre, this well-run hostel has a pool, volleyball and plenty of intel on what to do locally. Dorms share a big communal kitchen, and a quieter area with private rooms has its own little kitchen and lounge.

Edge of the Forest MOTEL $$

(Map p943; ☑08-9757 2351; www.edgeoftheforest.com.au; 25 Bussell Hwy; r $135-175; ❄🗐) Just a pleasant stroll from Margaret River township, the rooms here have stylish bathrooms and a chic Asian theme. The friendly owners have lots of local recommendations, and the leafy shared garden is perfect for an end-of-day barbecue. The spacious front unit is a good option for families. At busy times a two-night minimum stay is required.

★ Forest Rise CHALET $$$

(Map p938; www.forestrise.com.au; Yelverton Rd; cabins from $260; 🗐) 🧭 Award-winning luxury self-contained cabins are spread across a large tree-filled property. So gorgeous and relaxing you probably won't want to leave.

★ Burnside Organic Farm BUNGALOW $$$

(Map p938; ☑08-9757 2139; www.burnsideorganicfarm.com.au; 287 Burnside Rd; d from $300; ❄🗐) Welcome to the perfect private retreat after a day cruising the region's wine, beer and food highlights. Bungalows made from rammed earth and limestone have spacious decks and designer kitchens, and the surrounding farm hosts a menagerie of animals and organic orchards. Guests can pick vegetables from the garden. Minimum two-night stay.

✖️ Eating

Margaret River Farmers Market MARKET $

(Map p943; ☑0438 905 985; www.margaretriverfarmersmarket.com.au; Lot 272 Bussell Hwy, Margaret River Education Campus; ⊙8am-noon Sat; 🚗) 🧭 The region's organic and sustainable artisan producers come to town every Saturday. It's a top spot for breakfast. Check the website for your own foodie hit list.

Morries Anytime CAFE $$

(Map p943; ☑08-9758 8280; www.morries.com.au; 2/149 Bussell Hwy; tapas $11-14, mains $21-34; ⊙noon-late) Settle into the intimate clubby atmosphere of Morries for lunch, or come back later for expert cocktails and Asian style tapas for dinner. Local beers from Colonial Brewing are on tap, and the service here is impeccable.

Swings & Roundabouts Taphouse BISTRO, WINE BAR $$

(Map p943; ☑08-9758 7155; www.swings.com.au; 85 Bussell Hwy; shared plates $13-32, pizzas $22-25; ⊙3pm-late) Wine from their nearby vineyards and craft beer are served with tapas plates and gourmet pizzas, making this a popular cosmopolitan option at the northern end of Margaret River township. Kitchen closes at 9pm, but the bar is open later.

★ Miki's Open Kitchen JAPANESE $$$

(Map p943; ☑08-9758 7673; www.facebook.com/mikisopenkitchen; 131 Bussell Hwy; small plates $12-17, large plates $31-36; ⊙6pm-late Tue-Sat) Secure a spot around the open kitchen and enjoy the irresistible theatre of the Miki's team creating innovative Japanese spins on the best of Western Australia's seafood and produce. Combine a Margaret River wine with the $60 multi-course tasting menu for the most diverse experience, and settle in to watch the laid-back Zen chefs work their tempura magic. Bookings recommended.

🍺 Drinking & Nightlife

Yonder BAR

(Map p943; www.yonderbar.com; 124 Busselton Hwy; ⊙5pm-midnight Wed-Sat, to 10pm Sun) Tucked behind the shops off the Busselton Hwy, this American-style saloon bar serves up an extensive range of beers plus a classic cocktails list.

The River Hotel
PUB

(Map p943; www.theriverhotel.com.au; 40 Wallcliffe Rd; ⊙noon-late; 🛜🖶) Exposed brick walls give a warm feel inside, while tables and chairs on the grass out the front are the perfect place to catch some rays at this large country tavern that also hosts live music.

Brewhouse
MICROBREWERY

(Map p943; 🖉08-9757 2614; www.brewhouse margaretriver.com.au; 35 Bussell Hwy; ⊙11am-7pm, to 9pm Fri-Sun; 🖶) Brewhouse is nestled amid karri forest with a rustic bar and restaurant serving three guest beers and six of its own brews. Try the Inji Pale Ale with the chilli salt squid, and check out live music on Friday nights and Sunday afternoons.

🛍 Shopping

Margaret River
Regional Wine Centre
WINERY

(Map p938; 🖉08-9755 5501; www.mrwines.com; 9 Bussell Hwy, Cowaramup; ⊙10am-7pm, noon-6pm Sun) A one-stop shop for buying up a selection of 600 Margaret River wines and craft beers in nearby Cowaramup.

ℹ Information

Visitor Centre (Map p943; 🖉08-9780 5911; www.margaretriver.com; 100 Bussell Hwy; ⊙9am-5pm) Bookings and information plus displays on local wineries.

ℹ Getting There & Away

Margaret River is linked by regular buses north to Bunbury and Perth, and also further south to Pemberton, Denmark and Albany. During summer, the **Margaret River Beach Bus** (🖉08-9757 9532; www.margaretriverbackpackers.com. au) links the township with the beaches around Prevelly.

Caves Road

West of the Margaret River township, the coastline provides spectacular surfing opportunities and long coastal forest walks. Prevelly is the main settlement, with a few places to sleep and eat. Most of the sights are on Caves Rd or just off it.

◉ Sights & Activities

★ Stormflower Vineyard
WINERY

(Map p938; www.stormflower.com.au; 3503 Caves Rd, Wilyabrup; ⊙11am-5pm) Rustic and relaxed, with beautiful Australian natives in the garden, this is the antidote to some of Margaret

River's more grandiose tasting rooms and formal wine estates. The compact organic vineyard is just 9 hectares, and Stormflower's cabernet shiraz is highly regarded.

★ Lake Cave
CAVE

(Map p938; 🖉08-9757 7411; www.margaretriver. com/members/lake-cave; Conto Rd; adult/child $22.50/12; ⊙9am-5pm; 🖶) The main ticket office for Lake, **Mammoth** (Map p938; www.margaretriver.com; Caves Rd; adult/child $22.50/12; ⊙9am-5pm; 🖶) and Jewel Caves (p947) has excellent displays about caves, cave conservation and local fossil discoveries. You'll also find an authentic model cave and a 'cave crawl' experience. Behind the centre is Lake Cave, the prettiest of them all, where limestone formations are reflected in an underground stream. Tours depart hourly from 9.30am to 3.30pm

Voyager Estate
WINERY

(Map p938; 🖉08-9757 6354; www.voyagerestate. com.au; Stevens Rd; ⊙10am-5pm) The formal gardens and Cape Dutch–style buildings delight at Voyager Estate. Tours of the estate include the kitchen garden that Rick Stein also loved. Wine flight tastings start at $9 or stay for a seven-course tasting menu at the award-winning restaurant.

Giants Cave
CAVE

(Map p938; www.parks.dpaw.wa.gov.au; Caves Rd; adult/child $18/9; ⊙10am-1pm Oct-Apr, 9.30am-3.30pm school & public holidays; 🖶) This self-guided cave is managed by the Parks & Wildlife Service, which provides helmets and torches. Features steep ladders and scrambles. See it on a combined ticket with other caves on the cape.

Cape Lodge
COOKING

(Map p938; 🖉08-9755 6311; www.capelodge.com. au; 3341 Caves Rd, Wilyabrup; from $145) Cooking classes and cooking demonstrations using local produce are a hands-on foodie experience. Overnight accommodation packages at this lovely country lodge are also available.

🛏 Sleeping

Taunton Farm Holiday Park
CARAVAN PARK $

(Map p938; 🖉1800 248 777; www.tauntonfarm. com.au; Bussell Hwy, Cowaramup; sites $45, cottages $130-160; 🛜) There are plenty of farm animals for the kids to meet at one of Margaret River's best family-oriented campgrounds. For caravan and tenting buffs, the amenities blocks are spotless, and farm-style self-contained cottages are also scattered about.

CAVES ROAD CRAFT BEER

The Margaret River region's wine credentials are impeccable, but the area is also a destination for craft-beer fans. Many breweries serve bar snacks and lunch.

Caves Road Collective (Map p938; ☑ 08-9755 6500; https://cavesroadcollective.com.au; 3517 Caves Rd, Wilyabrup; tasting paddles from $20; ⊘ 11am-5pm; ℗ ⛹) A spectacular location on a private lake, Black Brewing Company, Ground to Cloud winery and Dune Distilling have joined forces at this tastings temple with an excellent restaurant, and a kids' playground to boot. Beers are approachable, try the crisp and citrusy extra pale ale (XPA). Dune boasts local botanicals, and the on-site winery produces a small but confident list.

Beer Farm (Map p938; ☑ 08-9755 7177; www.beerfarm.com.au; 8 Gale Rd, Metricup; ⊘ 11am-6pm, to 10.30pm Fri, to 7pm Sat; ⛹) Located in a former milking shed down a sleepy side road, the Beer Farm is Margaret River's most rustic brewery. Loyal locals crowd in with their children and dogs, supping on the Beer Farm's own brews – try the hoppy Rye IPA – and there's a food truck and plenty of room for the kids (and dogs) to run around.

Bootleg Brewery (Map p938; ☑ 08-9755 6300; www.bootlegbrewery.com.au; Puzey Rd, off Yelverton Rd, Wilyabrup; ⊘ 11am-5pm) More rustic than some of the area's flashier breweries, but lots of fun with a pint in the sun – especially with live bands on Saturday. Try the award-winning Raging Bull Porter – a West Australian classic – or the US West Coast–style Speakeasy IPA. The food is also very good.

Surfpoint
GUESTHOUSE $$

(Map p938; ☑ 08-9757 1777; www.surfpoint.com.au; Reidle Dr, Gnarabup; d with/without bathroom from $140/95; @🗟🛜🗲) This airy place offers the beach on a budget. The rooms are clean and well presented, and there's an enticing little pool. Private rooms with en-suite facilities are good value, and energetic new owners have done a great job with recent renovations. Shared spaces include a very comfortable lounge and a full kitchen. Stylish apartments nearby are also available.

Noble Grape Guesthouse
B&B $$

(Map p938; ☑ 08-9755 5538; www.noblegrape.com.au; 29 Bussell Hwy, Cowaramup; s $140-160, d $150-190; ❋🗟) Noble Grape is more like an upmarket motel than a traditional B&B. Rooms offer a sense of privacy and each has a verdant little garden courtyard.

★ Acacia Chalets
CHALET $$$

(Map p938; ☑ 08-9757 2718; www.acaciachalets.com.au; 113 Yates Rd; d $240-280; ❋) Private bushland – complete with marsupial locals – conceals three luxury chalets that are well located to explore the region's vineyards, caves and rugged coastline. Limestone walls and honey-coloured jarrah floors are combined in some of the area's best self-contained accommodation. Spacious decks are equipped with gas barbecues.

✖ Eating

Amiria
WINERY $$

(Map p938; ☑ 08-9755 2528; https://arimia.com.au; 242 Quininup Road; 2-course menu $55) Down an unsealed road you'll find this organic and biodynamic winery and restaurant creating excellent seasonal meals with ingredients almost entirely sourced from the property.

Rustico at Hay Shed Hill
TAPAS $$$

(Map p938; ☑ 08-9755 6455; www.rusticotapas.com.au; 511 Harmans Mill Rd, Wilyabrup; shared plates $17-28, pizzas $27-29, six-course tasting menu from $65; ⊘ 11am-5pm) Vineyard views from Rustico's deck provide the background for a Spanish-influenced menu using the best of southwest Australian produce. Albany rock oysters are paired with Margaret River riesling, pork belly comes with Pedro Ximinéz sherry, and paella is crammed with chicken from Mt Barker and local seafood. Consider a leisurely six-course tasting menu with wine matches from Hay Shed Hill vineyard.

Vasse Felix
BISTRO $$$

(Map p938; ☑ 08-9756 5050; www.vassefelix.com.au; cnr Caves Rd & Tom Cullity Dr, Cowaramup; mains $37-39; ⊘ 10am-3pm, cellar door to 5pm; ℗❋) Vasse Felix winery is considered by many to have the best fine-dining restaurant in the region, the big wooden dining room reminiscent of an extremely flash barn. The grounds are peppered with sculptures, while the gallery displaying a revolving exhibition from the Holmes à Court collection is worth a visit. Vegans catered for with 24 hours' notice.

Xanadu
BISTRO $$$

(Map p938; ☑08-9758 9531; www.xanaduwines. com; Boodjidup Rd; mains $34-38; ⊙10am-5pm, restaurant from noon) Escape into your own personal pleasure dome in the hip and chic restaurant filling Xanadu's vast space. The menu of small and larger shared plates changes seasonally – we had terrific kangaroo with black garlic, cheddar and macadamia. Definitely leave room for dessert.

❶ Getting There & Away

Buses link to Margaret River township, but to further explore the area you'll need to join a tour or have your own transport with one designated driver. As they say round here, 'Who's the Skipper?'

Augusta & Around

☑08 / POP 1392

Augusta is positioned at the mouth of the Blackwood River just north of Cape Leeuwin. The vibe is pure nostalgia as if you've stepped back in time to slowed-down beach holidays of yesteryear where kids ride bikes without supervision, families languidly fish from the pier, or puddle around on boats, and no one is trying to sell you anything but the opportunity to relax.

◉ Sights & Activities

Jewel Cave
CAVE

(☑08-9780 5911; www.margaretriver.com; Caves Rd; adult/child $22.50/12; ⊙9.30am-3.30pm) The most spectacular of the region's caves, Jewel Cave has an impressive 5.9m straw stalactite, so far the longest seen in a tourist cave. Fossil remains of a Tasmanian tiger (thylacine), believed to be 3500 years old, were discovered here. It's near the south end of Caves Rd, 8km northwest of Augusta. Access to the cave is by guided tours that run hourly.

Cape Leeuwin Lighthouse
LIGHTHOUSE

(☑08-9780 5911; www.margaretriver.com; tour adult/child $20/14; ⊙8.45am-4.30pm) Wild and windy Cape Leeuwin, where the Indian and Southern Oceans meet, is the most southwesterly point in Australia. It takes its name from a Dutch ship that passed here in 1622. The lighthouse (1896), WA's tallest, offers magnificent views of the coastline. Whale-watching opportunities abound in the migration season. There is a good cafe on-site too.

Augusta Boat Hire
WATER SPORTS

(www.margaretriver.com/members/augusta-boat-hire; Ellis St Pier; per hour $25; ☑) Next to Ellis pier you'll find this old-school outfit hiring canoes, boats and stand-up paddleboards so you can get out on the river and explore. Safety gear also provided.

Naturaliste Charters
WHALE WATCHING

(☑08-9750 5500; www.whales-australia.com.au; from $90; ⊙mid-May–Aug) 🐾 This operator runs two-hour whale-watching cruises departing Augusta from mid-May to August. During May, the emphasis switches to an Eco Wilderness Tour showcasing beaches and wildlife, including dolphins, seals and lots of seabirds.

🛏 Sleeping & Eating

Baywatch Manor
HOSTEL $

(☑08-9758 1290; www.baywatchmanor.com.au; 9 Heppingstone View; dm $38, d from $130, without bathroom $100; @🛜) Clean, modern rooms come with brick walls and antique furniture. There is a bay view from the deck and, in winter, a roaring fire in the communal lounge. Some doubles have compact balconies.

Blue Ocean Fish & Chips
FISH & CHIPS $

(73 Blackwood Ave; ⊙11.30am-2pm & 5-8pm; ☑☑) Oft-rated best fish 'n' chips ever eaten (no overstatements here obviously), this very basic blue-plastic-chairs and simple-wall-menu fast-food joint boasts excellent locally caught fish, perfectly crisp batter and optional chicken salt on your chips. At night there are not many other options in sleepy Augusta.

Colourpatch Café
CAFE $$

(☑08-9758 1295; 38 Albany Tce; snacks & mains $15-34; ⊙9am-6pm; ☑) The self-styled 'last eating house before the Antarctic' you can get breakfast, lunch or fish and chips by the Blackwood River mouth here. Note it can sometimes close earlier than the stated hours.

❶ Information

Visitor Centre (☑08-9780 5911; www.margaretriver.com; cnr Blackwood Ave & Ellis St; ⊙9am-5pm) Information and bookings. Ask about seeing local wildflowers, boat trips and local entertainment options.

❶ Getting There & Away

Augusta is on bus routes with South West Coach Lines (p933) and Transwa (p933) linking Perth with Albany.

SOUTHERN FORESTS

The tall forests of WA's southwest are simply magnificent, with towering gums (karri, jarrah, marri) sheltering cool undergrowth. Between the forests, small towns bear witness to the region's history of logging and mining. Many have redefined themselves as small-scale tourist centres where you can take walks, wine tours, canoe trips and fishing expeditions.

❶ Getting There & Away

Transwa (p933) coach routes travel between the main towns from East Perth down to Albany.

South West Coach (p933) Lines runs services between Nannup and Bunbury, plus Balingup, Bridgetown and Manjimup from Perth.

Bridgetown

📵 08 / POP 2400

Historic Bridgetown is surrounded by karri forests and farmland, and spread around the Blackwood River. Weekends are busy, and the popular Blues at Bridgetown Festival (📵08-9761 2921; www.bluesatbridgetown.com.au) occurs annually on the second weekend of November.

◉ Sights

Bridgedale House HISTORIC BUILDING
(Hampton St; by donation; ⊘10am-2pm Sat & Sun) Bridgedale House is one of Bridgetown's oldest buildings, built of mud and clay by the area's first settler in 1862, and since restored by the National Trust.

⏹ Sleeping & Eating

Bridgetown Hotel HOTEL $$
(📵08-9761 1034; www.bridgetownhotel.com.au; 157 Hampton St; r $165-250; ❈) This main-street 1920s gem features large modern bedrooms (some with balconies) with spa baths, and art-deco interior features. Also a good spot for a bite, it's open for lunch and dinner with quirky dishes like satay prawn pizzas ($24).

Bridgetown Riverside Chalets CHALET $$
(📵08-9761 1040; www.bridgetownchalets.com.au; 11347 Brockman Hwy; chalets from $150) On a rural riverside property, 5km up the road to Nannup, these four stand-alone wooden chalets (complete with stoves and washing machines) sleep up to six in two bedrooms.

Barking Cow CAFE $$
(📵08-9761 4619; www.barkingcow.com.au; 88 Hampton St; breakfast $11-18, lunch $13-21; ⊘8am-2.30pm Mon-Sat; 🖉) Colourful, cosy and serving the best coffee in town, the Barking Cow is also worth stopping at for daily vegetarian specials and world-famous-in-Bridgetown gourmet burgers.

Cidery CAFE $$
(📵08-9761 2204; www.thecidery.com.au; 43 Gifford Rd; mains $10-25; ⊘11am-4pm, to 8pm Fri) Craft beer from the Blackwood Valley Brewing Company, cider and light lunches are all enjoyed on outdoor tables. On Friday nights from 5.30pm there's live music. Our favourite brew is the easy-drinking mid-strength Summer Ale.

❶ Information

Visitor Centre (📵08-9761 1740; www.bridgetown.com.au; 154 Hampton St; ⊘9am-5pm Mon-Fri, 10am-3pm Sat, 10am-1pm Sun) Includes apple-harvesting memorabilia and a surprisingly interesting display of jigsaws from around the world in the attached heritage museum.

Manjimup

📵 08 / POP 4349

Manjimup is a regional centre for the timber and agricultural industries. It's a working town so the centre is not rich with tourist delights, but the region has much to explore. For foodies in particular it's known for something very different: truffles. During August especially, Manjimup's black Périgord truffles make their way onto top Australian menus.

◉ Sights & Activities

Truffle & Wine Co FARM
(📵08-9777 2474; www.truffleandwine.com.au; Seven Day Rd; ⊘10am-4pm) To discover how the world's most expensive produce is harvested, follow your nose to the Truffle & Wine Co. Join a 2½-hour truffle hunt with the clever truffle-hunting Labradors from Friday to Sunday (June to August only; book ahead). Throughout the year there are plenty of truffle products to sample, and the attached cafe (11am to 3pm) serves up tasting plates and truffle-laced mains ($25 to $40), including seafood ravioli and mushroom risotto.

Four Aces FOREST
(Graphite Rd) These four 300-plus-year-old karri trees sit in a straight line; stand directly

in front and they disappear into one. There's a short loop walk through the surrounding karri glade, and a 1½-hour loop bushwalking trail from the Four Aces to One Tree Bridge.

Diamond Tree Lookout   VIEWPOINT
Nine kilometres south of Manjimup along the South Western Hwy is the Diamond Tree Lookout. Metal spikes allow you to climb this 52m karri, and there's a nature trail nearby.

Great Forest Trees Drive   SCENIC DRIVE
(https://trailswa.com.au/trails/great-forest-trees-drive) A 48km one-way loop with walks that include the easy 3.5km walk to the Shannon Dam and the 8km Great Forest Trees Walk across Shannon River. On the southern section of the drive, hop out to tread boardwalks over giant karri at Snake Gully and Big Tree Grove or take the path to a lookout point over Lane Poole Falls.

🛏 Sleeping & Eating

⭐ **Fonty's Chalets & Caravan Park**   CARAVAN PARK **$**
(www.fontyspool.com.au; 699 Seven Day Rd; sites from $33; 🌊) An excellent well-run caravan park a short drive from town through busy orchards. It is blessed with a natural swimming pool for the summer months, which is also a popular day trip for locals.

Tall Timbers   BISTRO **$$**
(☑ 08-9777 2052; www.talltimbersmanjimup.com. au; 88 Giblett St; tapas $10-19, mains $19-44; ⊙ 9am-10pm, from 8am Sat & Sun) Tall Timbers' upmarket pub food stretches from gourmet burgers to confit duck, but its real point of difference is wines from all over southwest Australia. More than 40 wines are available, many from boutique vineyards that don't have cellar doors, and a special dispensing system allows visitors to purchase samples from just 25ml and pair them with tapas or cheese platters.

ℹ️ Information

Visitor Centre (☑ 08-9771 1831; www.manjim upwa.com; Giblett St; ⊙ 9am-5pm) Located in Manjim Park and offering accommodation and transport bookings.

Pemberton

☑ 08 / POP 974
Hidden deep in the karri and jarrah forests, tiny Pemberton is blessed with a multitude of activities, from canoeing and mountain-bike riding to just sipping a whisky by a wintry fire. The last whistle at the South West timber mills blew in 2016, and thankfully the national parks circling Pemberton and beyond to D'Entrecasteaux National Park remain deeply impressive. Spend a day or two driving the well-marked Karri Forest Explorer tracks, walk forest trails, and 'forest bathe' among the gigantically tall trees standing here.

Pemberton also produces excellent cooler climate wines: chardonnay and pinot noir, among other varietals. Wine tourism isn't developed here, but you can grab a free map listing cellar-door opening hours from the visitor centre (p951).

⊙ Sights

Gloucester Tree   LANDMARK
(Ⓟ) Its reputation proceeds it as an epic fire-lookout tree to admire for its height and girth, or a daring opportunity to test your vertigo and your fitness. The tree climb is closed in wet or windy conditions, but read the visitors book and you'll hear many tales of woe once climbers get to the top and realise they need to go back down the twisty ladder again, backwards.

Big Brook Arboretum   NATURE RESERVE
(⊙ 24hr) FREE A showcase of big trees from all around the world. Pick up a Karri Forest Explorer map from the Pemberton visitor centre.

🏃 Activities

Mountford Wines & Tangletoe Cidery   WINE
(☑ 08-9776 1345; www.mountfordwines.com.au; Bamess Rd; ⊙ 10am-4pm) 🍷 The wines and ciders produced here are all certified organic, plus there's a gallery on-site. It's north of Pemberton and is easily incorporated into the Karri Forest Explorer circuit.

Pemberton Pool   SWIMMING
(Swimming Pool Rd) Surrounded by karri trees, this natural pool is popular on a hot day – despite the warning sign (currents, venomous snakes). They breed them tough around here. Nearby is the trailhead for tracks making up the **Pemberton Mountain Bike Park** (www.pembertonvisitor.com.au/pages/pemberton-mountain-bike-park; 🚵).

Pemberton Tramway   RAIL
(☑ 08-9776 1322; www.pemtram.com.au; adult/child $28/14; ⊙ 10.45am & 2pm Mon-Sat; 🚂) Built between 1929 and 1933, the tram route travels through lush karri and marri forests to Warren River. A commentary is provided

and it's a fun – if noisy – 1¾-hour return trip for the whole family.

Tours

Donnelly River Cruises · CRUISE
(☑ 08-9777 1018; www.donnellyrivercruises.com.au; adult/child $75/45) 🚢 Cruises through 12km of D'Entrecasteaux National Park to the cliffs of the Southern Ocean.

Pemberton Discovery Tours · TOURS
(☑ 08-9776 0484; www.pembertondiscoverytours.com.au; 12 Brockman St; tours per person from $95) 🚢 Half-day 4WD tours to the Yeagarup sand dunes and the Warren River mouth. Other tours focus on local vineyards, breweries and cideries, and the wild coastal scenery of D'Entrecasteaux National Park. Visit its central Pemberton location for local information and mountain-bike hire, including details of nearby tracks and recommended rides.

Pemberton Hiking & Canoeing · CANOEING
(☑ 08-9776 1559; www.hikingandcanoeing.com.au; adult/child $50/25; 🧒) 🚢 Offers environmentally sound tours in Warren and D'Entrecasteaux national parks. Specialist tours (wildflowers, frogs, rare fauna) are also available, as are night canoeing trips to spot nocturnal wildlife.

Sleeping

Pemberton Backpackers YHA · HOSTEL $
(☑ 08-9776 1105; www.yha.com.au; 7 Brockman St; dm from $31.50; 🛜) Pemberton's only budget digs is sometimes busy with seasonal workers, so book ahead if you're planning to stay. There's a main building plus a cute weatherboard cottage, all of it comfortable enough for the price, and it's centrally located.

RAC Karri Valley Resort · CABIN $$
(☑ 08-9776 2020; https://parksandresorts.rac.com.au/karri-valley; Vasse Highway; cabins from $185; 🛜🏊) A recently refurbished forest resort next to a lush body of deep water where kangaroos and local fisherman also congregate. Cabins are self-contained, and not too close to each other. There's a restaurant on-site with beautiful views, especially after dark when the lakeside trees are lit up. It's a decent drive into Pemberton township for more things to see and do.

Pemberton Lodge Resort · LODGE $$
(☑ 08-9776 1113; www.forestlodgeresort.com.au; Vasse Hwy; r from $135) A well-managed lodge with accommodation in the main building, and self-contained cabins. The lounge

opens onto outdoor decks to enjoy meals or a drink overlooking the lake. Board games and DVDs available. A short walk back into town (good if you want to have a drink), but take a torch. It's dark here in the forest.

Old Picture Theatre Holiday Apartments · APARTMENT $$
(☑ 08-9776 1513; www.oldpicturetheatre.com.au; cnr Ellis & Guppy Sts; apt $170-220; ❄🛜) The town's old cinema has been revamped into well-appointed, self-contained, spacious apartments with lots of jarrah detail and black-and-white movie photos. It offers good value for money and includes an on-site spa.

Eating & Drinking

Holy Smoke · CAFE $
(https://pembertonfwg.com.au/cafe; 6 Dickinson Street; dishes $8-25; ⏰ 9.30am-3.30pm; 🧒) A gourmet cafe outpost for Holy Smoke, the food suppliers in nearby Manjimup. This small garden cafe serves the best coffee in town plus a sumptuous tasting platter of smoked salmon, chicken and trout, complemented by local goodies like strawberries, pickled walnuts, quince paste and cheeses.

Treehouse Tapas & Wine · TAPAS $$
(www.treehousewinebar.com.au; 50b Brockman St; ⏰ 4-10pm Thu-Sat, 4-9pm Sun; 🚗🧒) A relaxed owner-run tapas restaurant serving up excellent small dishes, a decent wine list and good non-alcoholic drink choices including local sparkling apple juices.Try the lightly fried cauliflower, marinated octopus, marron (a freshwater crayfish), or the local avocado options (including avocado desserts). Furnishings include formica chairs and soft armchair spaces. Board games and children's books are welcome distractions.

Jaspers · BAR
(www.jasperspemberton.com; 23 Brockman St; ⏰ 3-8pm Mon-Wed, noon-10.30pm Thu-Sat, noon-10pm Sun) The latest addition to Pemberton town centre, this stylish new whisky bar boasts an extensive list and a cosy fire for an evening in.

Jarrah Jacks · CRAFT BEER
(☑ 08-9776 1333; www.jarrahjacks.com.au; Lot 2 Kemp Rd; ⏰ 11am-5pm Thu-Sun) A popular craft brewery with vineyard views, six craft beers and tasty locally sourced food from a seasonal menu. Try the Swinging Axe Ale, a robust 6% Red Ale, or take it easy with the mid-strength 2.9% Arthur's Hop Ale. Sampling trays are also available for variety, and you can try wines from Pemberton's Woodsmoke Estate.

ℹ Information

Visitor Centre (☎08-9776 1133; www.pember tonvisitor.com.au; Brockman St; ⊙9am-4pm) Includes a pioneer museum and karri-forest discovery centre.

SOUTHERN WA

Standing above the waves and cliffs of the rugged south coast is an exhilarating experience. On calm days, the sea is aquamarine and white-sand beaches lie pristine and welcoming. Even busy summer holiday periods in the Great Southern are relaxed. Winter months bring pods of migrating whales, while the spectacular tingle trees of Walpole's Valley of the Giants are more super-sized evidence of nature's wonder.

For a change from the great outdoors, Albany – the state's earliest European settlement – has colonial and Anzac history, and Denmark has excellent wine, craft beer and good food. Inland, the peaks and plains of Stirling National Park are enlivened by wildflowers from September to November, while orca visit remote Bremer Bay from February to April.

Further west, Esperance is the gateway to some of Australia's best beaches.

ℹ Getting There & Around

Albany and Esperance can be reached by flights from Perth, and Transwa (www.transwa.wa.gov. au) offers the most comprehensive bus services to the region. This corner of Australia is an easy driving distance from Perth and distances between towns are not as extreme as elsewhere. Most visitors can easily get by with a 2WD; you only need a 4WD to explore the remote tracks and beaches of some of the coastal national park.

Walpole & Nornalup

☎08 / POP 330

On traditional Minang Noongar land, the peaceful twin inlets of Walpole and Nornalup make good bases from which to explore the heavily forested Walpole Wilderness Area – an immense wilderness incorporating a rugged coastline, several national parks, marine parks, nature reserves and forest conservation areas – covering a whopping 3630 sq km. Walpole is the bigger settlement, and it's here that the South Western Hwy (Rte 1) becomes the South Coast Hwy.

THE ROAD TO MANDALAY

About 13km west of Walpole, at Crystal Springs, is an 8km gravel road to **Mandalay Beach**, where the *Mandalay*, a Norwegian barque, was wrecked in 1911. The wreck eerily appears every 10 years or so after storms. See the photos at Walpole visitor centre (p953). The beach is glorious, often deserted, and accessed by a boardwalk across sand dunes and cliffs. It's part of D'Entrecasteaux National Park.

◉ Sights

★**Valley of the Giants**   NATURE RESERVE
(☎08-9840 8263; www.valleyofthegiants.com.au; Valley of the Giants Rd; Tree Top Walk adult/child $21/10.50; ⊙9am-5pm) In the Valley of the Giants, the spectacular Tree Top Walk consists of a 600m-long ramp rising from the valley, allowing visitors access high into the canopy of the giant tingle trees. At its highest point, the ramp is 40m above the ground. It's on a gentle incline so it's easy to walk and is accessible by assisted wheelchair. At ground level, the Ancient Empire boardwalk (admission free) meanders through veteran red tingles, up to 16m in circumference and 46m high.

Walpole-Nornalup National Park   NATIONAL PARK
(https://parks.dpaw.wa.gov.au/park/walpole-nornalup; off South Coast Hwy) Giant trees include red, yellow, and Rate's tingles (all types of eucalypt, or gum, trees). Good walking tracks include a section of the **Bibbulmun Track**, which passes through Walpole to Coalmine Beach. Scenic drives include the **Knoll Drive**, 3km east of Walpole; the Valley of the Giants Rd; and through pastoral country to Mt Frankland, 29km north of Walpole. Here you can climb to the summit for panoramic views or walk around the trail at its base.

Conspicuous Cliffs   LANDMARK
(Conspicuous Beach Rd) Midway between Nornalup and Peaceful Bay, Conspicuous Cliffs is a good spot for whale watching from July to November. It features a hilltop lookout and a steepish 800m walk to the beach.

☞ Tours

★**WOW Wilderness Ecocruises**   CRUISE
(☎08-9840 1036; www.wowwilderness.com.au; Jones Rd, Walpole, town pier; adult/child $45/15) 🌿 The dreamy landscape of Nornalup Inlet

PERTH & WESTERN AUSTRALIA WALPOLE & NORNALUP

South Coast

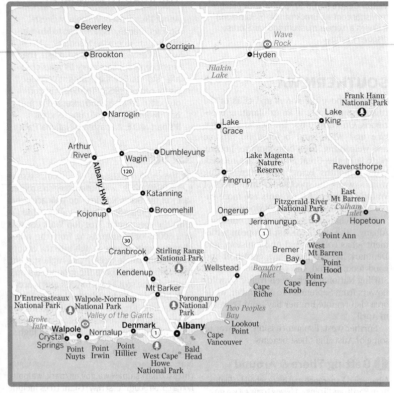

and its wildlife are brought to life through anecdotes about Aboriginal settlement, Tolstoy's Walpole connections, and shipwrecked pirates. Highlights include a stop with an optional walk to windswept Sandy Beach and the guide's mother's legendary lemon cake. The 2½-hour cruise leaves at 10am daily; book at the visitor centre (p953).

Naturally Walpole Tours ECOTOUR
(☑08-9840 1111; Walpole Visitor Centre) 🌿 Half-day tours exploring the Walpole Wilderness (adult/child $70/35) and the Tree Top Walk ($80/40).

🛏 Sleeping

★ **Tingle All Over YHA** HOSTEL $
(☑08-9840 1041; www.yha.com.au; 60 Nockolds St, Walpole; dm/s/d $30/50/70; P ❋ @ 🗢) Help yourself to lemons from the garden of this motel-style option with spotless, snug rooms, a great guest kitchen and a lounge

filled with DVDs and board games. Lots of advice on local walks is on offer and the owners are super-friendly.

Coalmine Beach CARAVAN PARK $
(☑08-9840 1026; www.coalminebeach.com.au; Coalmine Beach Rd, Walpole; camping per person $21, cabins $88-160; P ❋ @ 🗢) It's hard to imagine a more idyllic location than this, under shady trees above the sheltered waters of the inlet. A spacious recreation room and smart chalets are highlights.

Nornalup Riverside Chalets CHALET $$
(☑08-9840 1107; www.nornalupriversidechalets.com.au; Riverside Dr, Nornalup; chalets $115-190; P ❋) Stay a night in sleepy Nornalup in these comfortable, colourful self-contained chalets, just a rod's throw from the fish in the Frankland River. The chalets are well spaced out, and there are two-person canoes ($25 per hour), kayaks ($15) and stand-up paddleboards ($15) for hire.

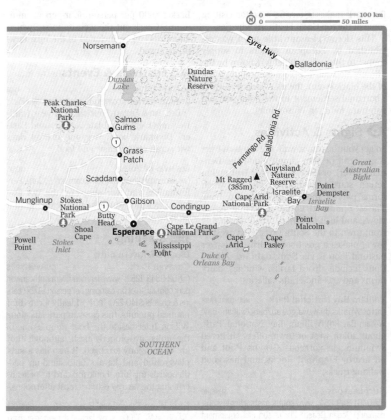

🍴 Eating

Nornabar BISTRO **$$**

(📞 08-9840 1407; http://nornabar.com; 6684 South Coast Hwy; tapas $12-16, mains $25-37; ⊘ 10am-late Wed-Sun; ❄ 🐾) This light, sunny bar and cafe soundtracked with cool jazz and enlivened by colourful local art serves playful, globally inspired dishes. There's a concise selection of local Great Southern wines available, and the menu stretches from chicken, ricotta and tarragon meatballs to spicy baby squid. A compact beer garden completes a versatile offering.

Four Sisters Cafe COFFEE

(Nockolds St, Walpole; ⊘ 7am-4pm) Come to this petrol station cafe for good coffee and muffins against a backdrop of stunning Aboriginal art.

ℹ Information

Walpole Visitor Centre (📞 08-9840 1111; www.walpole.com.au; South Coast Hwy, Wal-pole; ⊘ 9am-5pm) Plenty of info on the region. Book your WOW cruise tickets (p951) here.

ℹ Getting There & Away

Walpole and Nornalup sit on the South Coast Highway (Hwy 1).

Departing from the visitor centre, Transwa (www.transwa.wa.gov.au) bus GS3 heads daily to/from Bunbury ($49, 4½ hours), Bridgetown ($27, three hours), Pemberton ($21, 1¾ hours), Denmark ($15, one hour) and Albany ($24, 1¾ hours).

Denmark

📞 08 / POP 2557

Denmark's beaches and coastline, river and sheltered inlet, forested backdrop and hinterland have attracted a varied, arty and environmentally aware community. Farmers, fishers and families all mingle during the town's four market days each year, and

Denmark makes a terrific base for visiting some of the top Great Southern wineries.

This sleepy, pleasant little town was established by European settlers to supply timber to the early goldfields. Known by the Minang Noongar people as Koorabup (place of the black swan), there's evidence of early Aboriginal settlement in the 3000-year-old fish traps found in Wilson Inlet.

◉ Sights & Activities

To get your bearings, walk the **Mokare Heritage Trail** (a 3km circuit along the Denmark River), or the **Wilson Inlet Trail** (12km return, starting at the river mouth), which forms part of the longer **Nornalup Trail**. The **Mt Shadforth Lookout** has fine coastal views, and lush **Mt Shadforth Rd**, running from town to the South Coast Hwy west of town, makes a great scenic drive. A longer pastoral loop is via **Scotsdale Rd**. Attractions include alpaca farms, wineries, dairy farms and arts-and-crafts galleries.

William Bay National Park NATIONAL PARK
(https://parks.dpaw.wa.gov.au/park/william-bay; William Bay Rd) William Bay National Park, about 20km west of town, offers sheltered swimming in gorgeous **Greens Pool** and off nearby **Elephant Rocks**, and has good walking tracks.

Surf Lessons SURFING
(☑0401 349 854; www.southcoastsurfinglessons. com.au; Ocean Beach; 2hr lesson incl equipment from $60) Surfing lessons from recommended instructor Mike Neunuebel on Ocean Beach near Denmark. October to June is the best time to learn.

☞ Tours

Poornarti Aboriginal Tours CULTURAL
(☑0412 786 588, 0415 840 216; www.poornarti. com.au; 27 Strickland St; adult/child $150/60; ☺9.30am-5pm) Joey leads engaging day tours that focus on the Noongar cultural history of Kwoorabup (Denmark) and Stirling Range National Park, and include foraging and tasting bush tucker, as well as local art and traditional song and dance. Vibrational healing day tours are also available, incorporating ancient Noongar healing techniques.

Denmark Wine Lovers Tour WINE
(☑0427 482 400; www.denmarkwinelovers.com. au) Full-day tours taking in Denmark wineries ($88 per person, two-person minimum) or heading further afield to Porongurup/Mt Barker ($90 per person, four-person minimum). Check out the website to see which vineyards can be included in the mix. Pick-up arranged.

★彡 Festivals & Events

Market Days FAIR
(www.denmarkarts.com.au/markets; Berridge Park; ☺Dec, Jan & Easter) Four times a year (mid-December, early and late January and Easter) Denmark hosts riverside market days with craft stalls, music and food.

Festival of Voice MUSIC
(www.denmarkfestivalofvoice.com.au; ☺Jun) Performances and workshops on the WA Day long weekend, which incorporates the first Monday in June.

⊨ Sleeping

Denmark Rivermouth
Caravan Park CARAVAN PARK $
(☑08-9848 1262; www.denmarkrivermouthcaravan park.com.au; Inlet Dr; camping per person $17.50, cabins & chalets $140-220; ℗❄) Ideally located for nautical pursuits, this caravan park sits along Wilson Inlet beside the boat ramp. Some of the units are properly flash, although they are quite tightly arranged. It also has a kids' playground and kayaks and stand-up paddleboards for hire. Look forward to pelicans cruising the nearby estuary most afternoons.

Blue Wren Travellers' Rest YHA HOSTEL $
(☑08-9848 3300; www.denmarkbluewren.com.au; 17 Price St; dm/s/d/f $30/50/70/120; ❄) Great info panels cover the walls, and it's small enough (20 beds) to have a homey feel. Bikes can also be rented – $20 per day – and the owner is an affable South African who reckons Denmark is a great place to call home.

★ Denmark Waters B&B B&B $$
(☑0409 038 300; www.denmarkwaters.com. au; 9 Inlet Dr; r $180-190; ℗❄☎) Run by the delightful Maria, a treasure trove of local knowledge, this intimate, three-room B&B sits in a quiet location overlooking the sound, just south of town. Spotless rooms come with separate sleeping and living areas with complimentary decanters of port.

★ Cape Howe Cottages COTTAGE $$
(☑08-9845 1295; www.capehowe.com.au; 322 Tennessee Rd S; cottages $179-289; ℗❄☎) For a remote getaway, these five cottages in bushland southeast of Denmark really make the grade. They're all different, but all come with

DENMARK WINERIES

Denmark has the coolest climate in the Great Southern wine region, and is well known for its riesling and chardonnay, though the red cabernet blends also have an international following. There are 18 wineries in the Denmark area, some particularly renowned for their vintages, while others excel when it comes to on-site dining or cheese-making. Ones not to miss include the following:

Moombaki Wines (☑ 08-9840 8006; www.moombaki.com; 341 Parker Rd, Kentdale; ⊙ 11am-5pm) Family-run five-star winery with stellar malbec, shiraz, cabernet sauvignon and cabernet franc.

Harewood Estate (☑ 08-9840 9078; www.harewood.com.au; 1570 Scotsdale Rd; ⊙ 10am-4pm Fri-Mon) Award-winning wines that showcase the diversity of the Great Southern region.

Rising Star (☑ 08-9848 1626; www.risingstarwines.com; 46 Redman Rd; ⊙ 10.30am-5.30pm Fri-Mon; 🐾) Single-estate wines produced by friendly Texans, including sparkling chardonnay and rosé and some experimental vintages.

Rockcliffe Winery (☑ 08-9848 1951; www.rockliffe.com.au; 18 Hamilton Rd; mains from $18; ⊙ 11am-5pm) Five-star pinot noir, shiraz, cabernet sauvignon, chardonnay and rosé, plus a good restaurant.

Singlefile Wines (☑ 1 300 885 807; www.singlefilewines.com; 90 Walter Rd; ⊙ 11am-5pm) Particularly good for chardonnay, with a coffee roastery on-site and beautiful picnic grounds.

PERTH & WESTERN AUSTRALIA DENMARK

well-equipped kitchens, TVs and iPod docks. The best is only 1.5km from dolphin-favoured Lowlands Beach and is properly plush – with a BBQ on the deck.

31 on the Terrace BOUTIQUE HOTEL $$
(☑ 08-9848 1700; www.denmarkaccommodation.com.au; 31 Strickland St; r $145-165, apt $199; ❄) Travel from Windsor to Havana inside these stylish, individually decorated en-suite rooms – some with balconies – that fill this renovated corner pub in the centre of town. Compact apartments sleep up to five people.

✖ Eating & Drinking

★ Ravens Coffee CAFE $
(☑ 08-9848 1163; www.ravenscofee.com; 1/7 South Coast Hwy; mains $17-20; ⊙ 8am-6pm; ❄🐾) Denmark's best coffee, as well as the most creative breakfasts – from avo crisp to poached eggs with a spicy, Tunisian-style tomato sauce.

Pepper & Salt MODERN AUSTRALIAN, ASIAN $$
(☑ 08-9848 3053; www.pepperandsalt.com.au; 1564 South Coast Hwy, Forest Hill Vineyard; 1/2/3 courses $30/60/75; ⊙ noon-3pm Thu-Sun, from 6pm Fri; ❄) With his Fijian-Indian heritage, chef Silas Masih's knowledge of spices and herbs is wonderfully showcased in his fresh and vibrant food. Highlights may include seared scallops on pork and chive dumplings, grilled barramundi with aloo matar and tamarind tomato,

and chargrilled galangal chicken. Bookings essential.

★ Boston Brewery CRAFT BEER
(☑ 08-9848 1555; www.willoughbypark.com.au; South Coast Hwy, Willoughby Park Winery; ⊙ 11am-7pm Mon-Thu, to 10pm Fri & Sat, to 9pm Sun) The industrial chic of the brewery gives way to an absolute edge-of-vineyard location, where superb wood-fired pizzas ($21 to $26), meals (mains $21 to $39) and bar snacks go well with Boston's core portfolio of eight beers. The Willoughby Park Winery is also on-site, and there's live music from 4pm to 8pm every second Saturday. Seasonal brews usually available.

🛍 Shopping

★ Butter Factory Studios & Gallery ARTS & CRAFTS
(☑ 0410 891 136; https://butterfactorystudios.com; 10-12 Mount Shadforth Rd; ⊙ 10am-4pm Wed-Mon) Run by a local collective of women artists, this is a terrific place to pick up some fine handcrafted wooden utensils, beautiful ceramics, paintings, sculpture and other crafts. Check out the changing exhibitions.

ℹ Information

Denmark Visitor Centre (☑ 08-9848 2055; www.denmark.com.au; 73 South Coast Hwy;

⊙9am-5pm) Has information, accommodation bookings, local gourmet foodstuffs for sale and a display on the local wine scene.

🛈 Getting There & Away

Transwa (☑1300 662 205; www.transwa. wa.gov.au; Holling Rd) bus service GS3 heads daily to/from Bunbury ($54, 5¼ hours), Bridgetown ($37, four hours), Pemberton ($30, 2½ hours), Walpole ($15, one hour) and Albany ($10.20, 42 minutes).

Denmark sits on the South Coast Hwy (Hwy 1), between Walpole to the west and Albany to the east.

Albany

☑08 / POP 29,369

On the traditional lands of the Minang Noongar and Wagyl Kaip peoples, Albany is the oldest European settlement in the state; it was settled in 1826, shortly before Perth. Albany is now the bustling commercial centre of the southern region, and is a mixed bag comprising a stately and genteel decaying colonial quarter, a waterfront in the midst of sophisticated redevelopment and a hectic sprawl of malls and fast-food joints. Less ambivalent is its spectacular coastline, from Torndirrup National Park's surf-pummelled cliffs to Middleton Beach's white sands and the calm waters of King George Sound.

The town is in an area that's seen the violence of weather and whaling. Whales are still a part of the Albany experience, but these days are hunted with a camera lens.

The Bibbulmun Track (p958) ends (or starts) here, just outside the visitor centre.

History

The Minang Noongar people called this place Kinjarling (the place of rain) and believed that fighting Wargals (mystical giant serpents) created the fractured landscape.

Initial contacts with Europeans were friendly, with over 60 ships visiting between 1622 and 1826. The establishment of a British settlement was welcomed as it regulated the behaviour of sealers and whalers, who had been kidnapping, raping and murdering Minang people. Yet by the end of the 19th century, every shop in Albany refused entry to Aboriginal people, and their control over every aspect of their lives (including the right to bring up their own children) had been lost.

For the British, Albany's raison d'être was its sheltered harbour, which made it a whaling port right up to 1978. During WWI it was the mustering point for transport ships for Australian and New Zealand Army Corps (Anzac) troops heading for Egypt and the Gallipoli campaign.

In late 2014, Albany commemorated the centenary of the departure of over 40,000 Anzac soldiers to the Great War, and the opening of the National Anzac Centre has seen the city develop into an important destination for travellers interested in WWI history.

⊙ Sights

On a peninsula directly south of Albany, the **Historic Whaling Station** (☑08-9844 4021; www.discoverybay.com.au; 81 Whaling Station Rd; adult/6-15yr/family $32/12/75; ⊙9am-5pm; 🐾) and **Torndirrup National Park** (https://parks. dpaw.wa.gov.au/park/torndirrup; off Frenchman Bay Rd; per motorcycle/car $7/13) are easy and popular half-day trips from town. East of Albany, **Two Peoples Bay** (https://parks.dpaw. wa.gov.au/park/two-peoples-bay; Two Peoples Bay Rd) and **Waychinicup National Park** (https://parks.dpaw.wa.gov.au/park/waychinicup; Waychinicup South Rd; camp site adult/child $8/2.30) FREE beckon with their beaches, bushwalking and canoeing opportunities.

★**National Anzac Centre** MUSEUM
(☑08-6820 3500; www.nationalanzaccentre.com. au; 67 Forts Rd, Albany Heritage Park; adult/child $24/10; ⊙9am-5pm) Opened for Albany's Anzac centenary commemorations in late 2014, this superb museum remembers the men and women who left by convoy from Albany to fight in WWI. Excellent multimedia installations provide realism and depth to the exhibitions, and there is a profound melancholy in the museum's location overlooking the same expansive body of water the troop ships left from.

★**Museum of the Great Southern** MUSEUM
(☑08-9431 8413; www.museum.wa.gov.au; Residency Rd; by donation; ⊙10am-4pm) Encompassing the Eclipse building, the **Residency Museum** (☑08-9841 4844; www. museum.wa.gov.au; Residency Rd; by donation; ⊙10am-5pm) and **Brig Amity** (Amity Quays; adult/child $5/2; ⊙10am-4.30pm), this regional museum is a terrific introduction to Albany's history. The Eclipse building has a children's discovery section, a lighthouse exhibition and excellent visiting displays. The restored 1850s home of the resident magistrate il-

Albany

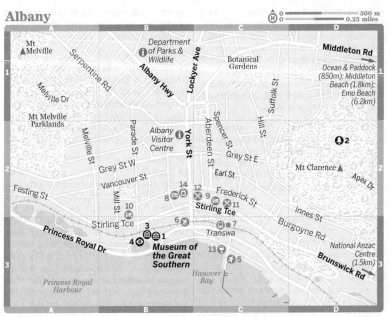

Albany

⊙ Top Sights
1 Museum of the Great Southern B3

⊙ Sights
2 Albany Heritage Park.............................D2
3 Albany Residency Museum B3
4 Brig Amity B3

⊙ Activities, Courses & Tours
5 Albany Ocean Adventures C3
  Albany Whale Tours.........................(see 5)
6 Bibbulmun Track....................................B3
7 Busy Blue Bus...C3

⊙ Sleeping
8 1849 Backpackers B2
9 Albany Foreshore Guest House............ C2
10 Albany Harbourside B2

⊗ Eating
11 Gourmandise & Co C2
12 Mean Fiddler..C2

⊙ Drinking & Nightlife
13 Due South C3
  White Star.......................................(see 11)

⊙ Shopping
14 South Coast Woodwork Gallery B2

luminates Minang Noongar history, local natural history and seafaring stories, while Amity Brig is a life-sized replica of the ship that brought the original European settlers to this region.

Albany Heritage Park   PARK
(www.nationalanzaccentre.com.au/visit/albany-heritage-park; Apex Dr) Inaugurated in 2014, the Albany Heritage Park incorporates the National Anzac Centre, Princess Royal Fortress, Padre White Lookout, Desert Mounted Corps Memorial and the Ataturk Memorial.

Great Southern Distillery   DISTILLERY
(☑ 08-9842 5363; www.distillery.com.au; 252 Frenchman Bay Rd; tours $25; ⊙ 10am-5pm, tours 11am & 2pm) Limeburners Single Malt whisky is the star at this waterfront distillery, but brandy, gin, absinthe and grappe also feature. Tours daily – check the website for timing and availability – include tastings, and there's a cafe offering tapas, local beer and snacks.

🏃 Activities & Tours

After whaling ended in 1978, whales slowly began returning to the waters of Albany. Now southern right and humpback whales gather near the bays and coves of King George Sound from July to mid-October. You can sometimes spot them from the beach. Both **Albany Ocean Adventures** (☑0428 429 876; www.whales.com.au; 5a Toll Pl; adult/child $100/60; ☺Jul-Oct) and **Albany Whale Tours** (☑08-9845 1068; www.albanywhaletours.com. au; 5d Toll Pl; adult/child $98/58; ☺Jun-Oct) run whale-watching trips in season.

SUPLime
WATER SPORTS

(☑0475 090 404; www.facebook.com/suplimewa; 6 Middleton Rd; ☺6am-7pm) Fun stand-up paddleboarding (SUP) outings, SUP lessons and SUP hire ($25 per hour). Locations vary; check their Facebook page for updates.

Bibbulmun Track
HIKING

(www.bibbulmuntrack.org.au; Princess Royal Dr) Taking around eight weeks, the 963km Bibbulmun Track runs from Albany to Kalamunda, 20km east of Perth, through mainly natural environment. Terrain includes jarrah and marri forests, wildflowers, granite outcrops, coastal heath country and spectacular coastlines. Comfortable campsites are spaced regularly along the track. The best time to do it is from August to October.

Busy Blue Bus
BUS

(☑08-9842 2133; www.busybluebus.com.au; old train station, Proudlove Pde; ☺adult/child from $109/103) Full- and half-day tours taking in Albany's Anzac history, the city's whaling heritage, or further afield to the Great Southern vineyards or Castle Rock and the Granite Skywalk in the Porongurup National Park. Pickups from the old train station.

⌕ Sleeping

★1849 Backpackers
HOSTEL $

(☑08-9842 1554; www.albanybackpackersaccom modation.com.au; 45 Peels Pl; dm/s/d $33/77/99; ✳@☜) Big flags from many nations provide a colourful international welcome at this well-run hostel. A huge, modern kitchen; info on local attractions splashed across walls; sunny rooms; and a laid-back social ambience make this one of WA's best places to stay for budget travellers. Homemade pancakes for breakfast every morning.

Albany Foreshore Guest House
B&B $

(☑08-9842 8324; http://albanyforeshoreguest house.com.au; 86 Stirling Tce; ☺s/d from $100/120; ✳☜) Housed inside a 19th-century former bank, this five-room B&B has more character than most in the region. Expect sky-high ceilings, heavy drapes, a collection of vintage

cameras and replicas of famous paintings peering out at you at every angle. Hearty breakfast included.

Albany Harbourside
APARTMENT $$

(☑08-9842 1769; www.albanyharbourside.com.au; 8 Festing St; d $169-279; P✳☜) Albany Harbourside's portfolio includes spacious and spotless apartments on Festing St, and three other self-contained options arrayed around central Albany. Decor is modern and colourful, and some apartments have ocean views.

★Beach House at Bayside
BOUTIQUE HOTEL $$$

(☑08-9844 8844; www.thebeachhouseatbayside. com.au; 33 Barry Ct, Collingwood Park; r $310-435; P✳☜) Positioned right by the beach and the golf course in a quiet cul-de-sac, midway between Middleton Beach and Emu Point, this 10-room hotel offers wonderful service. Rates include breakfast, afternoon tea, and evening port and chocolates. The friendly owners have their fingers on the pulse of Albany's dining scene, and a second property a few doors away is equally comfortable.

✗ Eating

★Gourmandise & Co
BAKERY $

(☑08-9847 4005; www.gourmandiseandco.com. au; 56 Stirling Tce; cakes from $6; ☺7.30am-3pm Mon-Sat; ✳) Squeeze inside this bright and cheerful little French bakery and help yourself to quiche, freshly baked croissants and bread, organic coffee, and all manner of sweet goodies.

★Emu Point Cafe
CAFE $

(☑08-9844 7207; http://emupointcafe.com.au; 1 Mermaid Ave; mains $8-23; ☺7.30am-4pm Mon-Fri, to 5pm Sat & Sun; ✳✍🍴) This locally legendary breakfast joint does everything right: from Albany's best cup of coffee and cold-pressed juices to imaginative morning offerings, such as poached eggs with chimichurri and garlicky yogurt, freshly baked muffins and jalapeño corn fritters. Eat inside or on the breezy seafront terrace.

Ocean & Paddock
FISH & CHIPS $

(☑08-9842 6212; www.oceanandpaddock.com.au; 116 Middleton Ave; mains $12-19; ☺3-9pm Wed & Thu, 11am-9pm Fri-Sun; ✳🍴) Winners of the 'best fish and chips in WA' award, these guys serve up perfectly cooked, lightly battered ocean goodies. Not a pescatarian? There are moreish beef brisket, pulled pork and southern chicken rolls as well. Kiddie menu too.

ALBANY WINERIES

Albany is part of the Great Southern wine-growing region, and there are four wineries dotted around the area. Don't miss the following:

Oranje Tractor (☑ 08-9842 5175; www.oranjetractor.com; 198 Link Rd, Marbelup; ☉ 11am-6pm Sun; by appointment rest of time) **FREE** Small organic winery, good riesling and sauvignon blanc and sparkling varieties, plus WOOFing opportunities.

Wignalls Wines (☑ 08-9841 2848; www.wignallswines.com.au; 448 Chester Pass Rd; ☉ 11am-4pm Thu-Mon) Family-run winery renowned for pinot noir. Also good cabernet merlot, shiraz, chardonnay and sauvignon blanc.

Montgomery's Hill (☑ 0407 424 455; www.montgomeryshill.com.au; 45821 South Coast Hwy, Kalgan; cheese platters $15; ☉ 11am-5pm) Excellent shiraz and cabernet sauvignon; cheese platters served alongside wines.

Three Anchors PUB FOOD **$$**
(☑ 08-98411 600; www.threeanchors.com.au; 2 Flinders Pde, Middleton Beach; mains $18-34; ☉ 7am-10pm; ❇) Located under towering Norfolk pines on the edge of Middleton Beach, Three Anchors is a versatile all-day eatery just metres from the sand. Enjoy a leisurely breakfast, or try such crowd-pleasers as Exmouth prawns or tandoori-spiced pork belly. Sunday sessions offer live music from 4pm to 7pm, and craft beers from Albany's Wilson Brewing Company are often on tap.

Mean Fiddler MODERN AUSTRALIAN **$$$**
(☑ 08-9841 1852; www.facebook.com/MeanFiddler Restaurant; 132 York St; mains $27-48; ☉ noon-3pm & 5.30-10pm Mon-Sat; ❇ 🍷) Making waves in Albany foodie circles, the menu at this creative new spot takes inspiration from the owner's global roamings. Expect the likes of five-spice pork belly, Vietnamese-style prawns, local oysters with a splash of strawberry vinegar and local Wilson Brewing Company craft beer.

🍷 Drinking & Nightlife

★ **Wilson Brewing Company** MICROBREWERY
(☑ 08-9842 3090; www.wilsonbrewing.com.au; 47768 South Coast Hwy; ☉ 10am-7pm) Just west of Albany, this nautically themed microbrewery is particularly popular for its Rough Seas pale ale, though the hoppy Stiff Mast and malty Dirty Oar are also well worth a try. Seasonal brews and session ales available.

★ **White Star** PUB
(☑ 08-9841 1733; www.whitestarhotel.com.au; 72 Stirling Tce; ☉ 11am-late) With the largest selection of beers on tap in town (from James Squire to the local Wilson Brewing Compa-

ny), excellent pub grub (from $20), a beer garden and lots of live music, this old pub gets a gold star. Sunday-night folk and blues gigs are a good opportunity to share a pint with Albany's laid-back locals.

Due South BAR
(☑ 08-9841 8526; www.duesouthalbany.com.au; 6 Toll Pl; ☉ 11am-late) Located inside an airy space with great sea views, Due South is the best place for a sunset drink. There are decent craft beers on tap, the wine list comprises exclusively Great Southern wines, and the pub food menu is available throughout the day – handy in a town where many places take a break between lunch and dinner.

🛍 Shopping

★ **South Coast Woodwork Gallery** ARTS & CRAFTS
(☑ 08-9845 2028; www.southcoastwoodworks.com.au; 135 York St; ☉ 10am-4pm Mon-Fri, to 1pm Sat) If you believe that everything useful should also be beautiful, you'll find plenty of fine handcrafted kitchen utensils to captivate you here. More high-end are striking vases and other wooden art, made of sustainably harvested jarrah, sheoak and other native hardwoods.

Mount Romance Sandalwood Factory PERFUME
(☑ 08-9845 6888; www.mtromance.com.au; 2 Down Rd; ☉ 9am-5pm) 🌿 Some 8km north of town, just past the airport, Australia's largest sandalwood factory welcomes you into its sweet-scented depths. Learn about its production; purchase the scents, body butters and other skincare products; and taste sandalwood nut cheesecake at the attached cafe.

ℹ Information

Albany Visitor Centre (☑ 08-6820 3700; www.amazingalbany.com; 221 York St; ⊘9am-5pm) Central; lots of helpful regional info.

Parks & Wildlife Service (☑ 08-9842 4500; https://parks.dpaw.wa.gov.au; 120 Albany Hwy; ⊘8am-4.30pm Mon-Fri) National park information.

ℹ Getting There & Away

Albany Airport (☑ 08-6820 3777; Albany Hwy) is 11km northwest of the city centre. Rex Airlines (www.rex.com.au) flies to/from Perth (70 minutes) daily.

Transwa (p942) bus services stop at the visitor centre.

Porongurup National Park

The 24-sq-km, 12km-long Porongurup National Park (https://parks.dpaw.wa.gov.au/park/porongurup; Porongurup Rd; per car/motorcycle $13/7) has 1100-million-year-old granite outcrops, panoramic views, misty scenery, large karri trees and some excellent bushwalks. Porongurup is also part of the Great Southern wine region and there are 11 wineries in the vicinity, several of them truly excellent. See www.porongurup.com.

The Wagyl Kaip people are the traditional custodians of this area.

◉ Sights

Castle Rock Estate WINERY
(☑ 08-9853 1035; www.castlerockestate.com.au; Porongurup Rd; ⊘10am-5pm) Family-owned winery producing award-winning riesling, shiraz, and chardonnay. Also great for pinot noir, as well as a sparkling della and the sweet dessert muscat. Intimate tasting sessions.

Zarephath Wines WINERY
(☑ 08-9853 1152; www.zarephathwines.com.au; 424 Moorialup Rd; mains from $20; ⊘11am-4pm Sat & Sun) A short drive east of the park, this family-run winery serves trophy-winning riesling and pinot noir, as well as excellent syrah, chardonnay and cabernet, all grown on the estate. Book ahead for tasty slow-food lunches.

Duke's Vineyard WINERY
(☑ 08-9853 1107; www.dukesvineyard.com; 1380 Porongurup Rd; ⊘10am-4.30pm) Particularly good for award-winning, single-vineyard shiraz, riesling and rosé, a fantastic reserve shiraz and sparkling riesling and shiraz. Cellar door combined with art gallery.

🏃 Activities

Trails include the following:

Granite Skywalk (4km return, two hours) Mostly gentle hike through the forest, followed by vertical climb up Castle Rock.

Wansborough Walk (4km one way) Easy walk through the forest from the Tree-in-the-Rock picnic area.

Devil's Slide Trail (5km return, two hours) Turn-off from Wansborough Walk, with great views from the rocky summit.

Hayward Peak & Nancy Peak Walk (5.5km loop, two to three hours) Moderately challenging ascents of two peaks on a loop from Tree-in-the-Rock.

Porongurup National Park

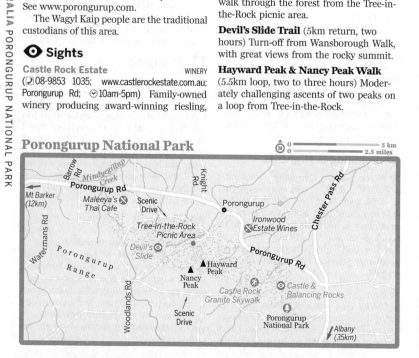

FITZGERALD RIVER NATIONAL PARK

Midway between Albany and Esperance, this gem of a **national park** (https://parks.dpaw. wa.gov.au/park/fitzgerald-river; per car/motorcycle $13/7) is the traditional home of the Wudjari people and a Unesco Biosphere Reserve. Its 3300 sq km contains half of the orchid species in WA (more than 80; 70 of which occur nowhere else), 22 mammal species, 200 species of bird and 1700 species of plant (20% of WA's described flora species).

Walkers will discover beautiful coastline, sand plains, rugged coastal hills (known as 'the Barrens') and deep, wide river valleys. In season, you'll almost certainly see whales and their calves from the shore at **Point Ann**, where there's a lookout and a heritage walk that follows a short stretch of the 1164km **No 2 rabbit-proof fence**.

Bookending the park are the sleepy coastal settlements of Bremer Bay and Hopetoun, both with white sand and shimmering waters.

You'll need your own transport to get here; a 4WD vehicle is strongly recommended.

✗ Eating

★**Maleeya's Thai Cafe** THAI $$
(☑ 08-9853 1123; www.maleeya.com.au; 1376 Porongurup Rd; mains $26-34; ⊙ 11.30am-3pm & 6-9pm Fri-Sun; ▣ ✈) ✔ Foodies venture to Porongurup for some of WA's most authentic Thai food. Curries (including the signature massaman prawn curry), soups and stir-fries all come with fresh herbs straight from Maleeya's garden. Bookings recommended.

Stirling Range National Park

Rising abruptly from surrounding flat and sandy plains, the Stirling Range's propensity to change colour through blues, reds and purples captivates photographers during the spectacular wildflower season from late August to early December. Over 1500 plant species grow in the park, including 120 species of orchids and 87 endemics. The Noongar and Wagyl Kaip peoples are the traditional custodians of Stirling Range and recognise it as a place where the spirits of the dead return.

This 1156-sq-km **national park** (https:// parks.dpaw.wa.gov.au/park/stirling-range; Chester Pass Rd; ⊙ per car/motorcycle $13/7) consists of a chain of peaks pushed up by plate tectonics to form a range 10km wide and 65km long. Running most of its length are isolated summits, some knobbly and some perfect pyramids, towering above broad valleys covered in shrubs and heath. Bluff Knoll (Bular Mai), at 1095m, is the highest point in the southwest.

Park fees are charged at the start of Bluff Knoll Rd.

🏃 Activities

The Stirlings are renowned for serious bushwalking. Trails are as follows:

Bluff Knoll (1095m; 6km return, three to four hours) The highest mountain in the park with great views.

Toolbrunup Peak (1052m; 4km return, three to four hours) Second-highest peak; some steep loose rock and scree sections near the top; 360-degree views.

Mt Hassell (848m; 3km return, three hours) Steep scramble over rock dome on approach to the summit. Great views from Toolbrunup Peak from the top.

Talyuberlup (783m; 2.6km return, three hours) Scrambles through gullies and increasingly steep climb to a rocky crag.

Mt Trio (856m; 3.5km return, two to three hours) Knee-popping steps for much of the way, then a gentle stroll; 360-degree views.

Mt Magog (856m; 7km return, three hours) Serious bushwalking through wandoo woodland and thick bush. Great summit views.

The park's most challenging trek is from Bluff Knoll to **Ellen Peak** (28.8km, three days). Alpine conditions: violent weather changes, steep ascents and descents, scrambling over rock. Two-night bivouac involved.

🛏 Sleeping & Eating

Stirling Range Retreat CARAVAN PARK $
(☑ 08-9827 9229; www.stirlingrange.com.au; 8639 Chester Pass Rd; unpowered/powered site $16/36, on-site caravan $69, cabins $95-149, units $170-195; ▣ @ ▣) ✔ On the park's northern boundary, this shaded area offers campsites, cabins and vans, and self-contained, rammed-earth

Stirling Range National Park

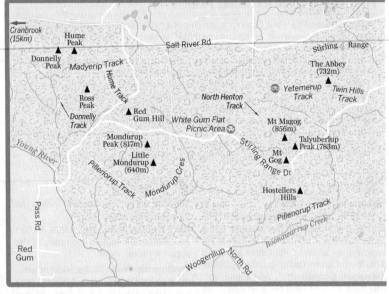

PERTH & WESTERN AUSTRALIA ESPERANCE

units. Wildflower and orchid bus tours and birdwatching walks (three hours, $49 per person) are conducted from mid-August to the end of October. The swimming pool only opens from November to April. Shuttle transport to Bluff Knoll arranged.

★ **The Lily Dutch Windmill** GUESTHOUSE $$
(☑08-9827 9205; www.thelily.com.au; Chester Pass Rd; cottages $159-189; ※) These cottages, 12km north of the park, are grouped around a working windmill. Accommodation is self-contained, and meals are available for guests at the neighbouring restaurant. Call to enquire which nights the restaurant is open to the public and to arrange mill tours ($50, minimum of four people). There's also private accommodation in a restored 1944 Dakota DC3 aircraft ($249).

Esperance

☑08 / POP 10,420

Framed by aquamarine waters and pristine white beaches, Esperance sits in solitary splendour on traditional Wudjari land on the Bay of Isles. But despite its isolation, families still travel from Perth or Kalgoorlie just to plug into the easy-going vibe and great beach life. For travellers taking the coastal route east across the continent, it's the last sizeable town before the Nullarbor.

Picture-perfect beaches dot the even more remote national parks to the town's southeast, and the pristine environment of the 105 islands of the offshore Recherche Archipelago are home to fur seals, penguins and seabirds.

◉ Sights & Activities

There are numerous stunning beaches within easy reach of Esperance, strung out along the Great Ocean Dr – all pristine white sand and crystal-clear cerulean waters. Many, including **West Beach**, **Salmon Beach**, **Fourth Beach** and **Twilight Beach**, all off Twilight Beach Rd, are great for walking and sunbathing, but swimmers must heed the rip current warnings: West Beach waters are particularly dangerous. The best beach for swimming is **Blue Haven**, but it also gets occasional strong currents.

Esperance Museum MUSEUM
(☑08-90711579; cnr James & Dempster Sts; adult/child $8.50/3.50; ⊙1.30-4.30pm)This warehouse is filled with everyday objects from yesteryear, as well as Aboriginal weaponry (spot the fishing boomerang!), a vintage locomotive and a 19th-century train carriage you can climb aboard. Other big items include

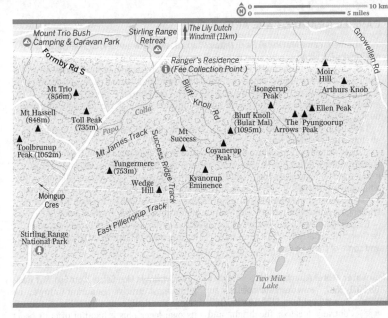

0 ——— 10 km
0 ——— 5 miles

Mount Trio Bush
Camping & Caravan Park

Stirling Range
Retreat

The Lily Dutch
Windmill (11km)

Gnowellen Rd

Formby Rd S

Ranger's Residence
(Fee Collection Point)

Mt Trio
(856m)

Mt Hassell
(848m)

Toll Peak
(735m)

Colla

Papa

Mt James Track

Success Ridge Track

Bluff Knoll Rd

Isongerup
Peak

Moir
Hill

Arthurs Knob

Ellen Peak

Bluff Knoll
(Bular Mai)
(1095m)

The
Arrows

Pyungoorup
Peak

Toolbrunup
Peak (1052m)

Mt
Success

Coyanerup
Peak

Yungermere
(753m)

Wedge
Hill

Kyanorup
Eminence

Moingup
Cres

East Pillenorup Track

Stirling Range
National Park

Two Mile
Lake

boats, a train carriage and the remains of the USA's spacecraft *Skylab,* which made its fiery re-entry at Balladonia, east of Esperance, in 1979.

★ **Great Ocean Drive**   SCENIC DRIVE
(Twilight Beach Rd) Many of Esperance's most dramatic sights can be seen on this well-signposted 40km loop. Starting from the waterfront, it heads southwest along the breathtaking stretch of coast that includes a series of popular surfing and swimming spots, including **Blue Haven Beach** (Twilight Beach Rd) and **Twilight Cove.** Stop at rugged **Observatory Point,** the lookout on **Wireless Hill** and the Lucky Bay Brewery (p964).

Great Ocean Trail   CYCLING
(Twilight Beach Rd) Stretching from Castletown Beach in Esperance proper all the way to Twilight Beach, 17km west, this is a terrific seafront trail for cycling or hiking, with wonderful sea views throughout.

Tours

Esperance Island Cruises   BOATING
(☑08-9071 5757; www.esperancecruises.com.au; 72 The Esplanade; adult/child $100/65; ☺9am-12.30pm) Scenic half-day wildlife cruises for spotting sea lions, New Zealand fur seals, dolphins, Cape Barren geese and sea eagles.

Snorkelling equipment and a light morning tea provided.

Eco-Discovery Tours   DRIVING
(☑0407 737 261; www.esperancetours.com.au) Runs 4WD tours along the sand to Cape Le Grand National Park (half-/full day $105/195, minimum two/four people) and two-hour circuits of Great Ocean Dr (adult/child $60/45).

Sleeping

Woody Island Eco-Stays   CAMPGROUND $
(☑0484 327 580; www.woodyisland.com.au; camping $42, 2-/4-person tent $100/135, safari tent $155; ☺mid-Dec–Jan, mid-Apr–early May; ✷)
🏕 Sleeping options at this appealing campground include leafy campsites (BYO camping equipment), as well as pre-prepped tents and canvas-sided two-person safari huts. Power is mostly solar, and rainwater supplies the island – both are highly valued. Allow for an $80 return ferry transfer as well.

Driftwood Apartments   APARTMENT $
(☑0428 716 677; www.driftwoodapartments.com.au; 69 The Esplanade; apt $120-260; ℗✷🛜) Each of these seven smart blue-and-yellow apartments, right across from the waterfront, has its own BBQ and outdoor table setting. The two-storey, two-bedroom units have decks and a bit more privacy.

CAPE LE GRAND & CAPE ARID

In **Cape Le Grand National Park** (https://parks.dpaw.wa.gov.au/park/cape-le-grand; off Fisheries Rd; entry per car/motorcycle $13/7, campsites adult/child $11/3) good fishing, swimming and camping can be found at **Lucky Bay** – arguably Australia's top beach, complete with beach-going kangaroos – and **Le Grand Beach**, and day-use facilities at gorgeous **Hellfire Bay**. Make the effort to climb **Frenchman Peak** (a steep 3km return, allow two hours), as the views from the top and through the rocky 'eye', especially during the late afternoon, are superb.

The beautiful 15km **Le Grand Coastal Trail** links the bay, or you can do shorter stretches between beaches.

Whales (in season), seals and Cape Barren geese are seen regularly at **Cape Arid National Park** (https://parks.dpaw.wa.gov.au/park/cape-arid; off Fisheries Rd; entry per car/ motorcycle $13/7, campsites adult/child $11/3). Much of the park is 4WD-accessible only, although the Thomas River Rd leading to the shire campground suits all vehicles and you can reach most of the beautiful, deserted beaches either via 2WD or on foot. There's a challenging walk to the top of Tower Peak on Mt Ragged (3km return, three hours).

Esperance-based Eco-Discovery Tours (p963) runs 4WD excursions exploring Cape Le Grand National Park. You'll need a 4WD to access much of Cape Arid National Park and some of Cape Le Grand.

Clearwater Motel Apartments MOTEL $
(📞08-9071 3587; www.clearwatermotel.com.au; 1a William St; s/d/f/apt from $120/140/160/160; P❄🛜) Centrally located, the bright and spacious rooms and apartments here have balconies and are fully self-contained, and there's a well-equipped shared BBQ area.

⭐ **Esperance B&B by the Sea** B&B $$
(📞08-9071 5640; www.esperancebb.com; 34 Stewart St; r $130-190, f $360; P❄🛜) This great-value beachhouse has a private guest wing and the views from the deck overlooking Blue Haven Beach are breathtaking, especially at sunset. It's just a stroll from the ocean and a five-minute drive from central Esperance.

✖ Eating & Drinking

⭐ **FishFace** SEAFOOD $
(📞08-9071 1601; www.facebook.com/FishFace Esperance; 1 James St; mains $15-20; 🕙4.30-8.30pm Thu-Tue; ❄) Seafood is the star at FishFace. One half is a busy fish-and-chip takeaway, with punters lining up for superior battered snapper, whiting and cod. The other half is a restaurant with brisk, friendly service and lively conversation around the tables fuelled by seafood risotto, with the slurping of raw oysters and the crunch of crispy batter.

⭐ **Loose Goose** MODERN AUSTRALIAN $$$
(📞08-9071 2320; www.loosegooseesperance. com.au; 9a Andrew St; 1/2/3 courses $35/60/80;

🕙4pm-midnight Mon-Sat, to 10pm Sun; ❄) Easily the most creative restaurant in town, the Goose also doubles as a lively bar that serves its own lager plus a handful of craft beers on tap. It's all minimalist black and chrome and teardrop lamps, with creative fare ranging from sashimi scallops to spicy, blackened catch of the day on fresh pasta.

⭐ **Lucky Bay Brewery** MICROBREWERY
(📞0447 631 115; www.facebook.com/luckybay brewing; Barook Rd; tastings $10-15; 🕙2-6pm) Look for Lucky Bay's beers in bars around Esperance or make the journey 12km west to this simple brewery and tasting room. Two-litre growlers are available for takeaway, and the friendly brewmasters will guide you through beers, including the refreshing Skippy Rock kölsch, award-winning Thistle Cove Scottish ale , smoky Black Jack porter or hoppy Cyclops IPA.

🔒 Shopping

⭐ **Karnpi Designs Art Gallery** ART
(📞08-9072 1688; www.facebook.com/karnpi designs; cnr Dempster & Kemp Sts, Museum Village; 🕙10am-4pm Tue-Fri, to 2pm Sat) Desert reds and ochres meet ocean blues in the stunning Aboriginal artworks displayed at this gallery by the likes of award-winning artist Sophia Ovens, as well as owner Pauline. Also for sale are silk ties and bags with Aboriginal designs, clapping sticks, maps of Aboriginal Australia and much more, with a substantial part of the sales going directly to artists.

ⓘ Information

Parks & Wildlife (☑08-9083 2100; https://parks.dpaw.wa.gov.au; 92 Dempster St; ⊙8am-4.30pm Mon-Fri) National park information.

Visitor Centre (☑08-9083 1555; www.visitesperance.com; cnr Kemp & Dempster Sts; ⊙9am-5pm Mon-Fri, to 4pm Sat, to 2pm Sun) In the museum village with handy 24-hour information on outside wall.

ⓘ Getting There & Away

Esperance Airport (www.esperance.wa.gov.au/airport; Coolgardie-Esperance Hwy) is 18km north of the town centre. Rex Airlines (www.rex.com.au) flies between Perth and Esperance daily.

Transwa (☑1300 662 205; www.transwa.wa.gov.au; cnr Kemp St & Dempster St) services stop at the visitor centre.

Destination	Cost ($)	Time (hr)	Frequency
Albany	73	6½-9½	Wed, Thu & Sat
Coolgardie	60	4¾	8am Sun
East Perth	88	10	daily except Sun
Kalgoorlie-Boulder	31	5¼	Wed, Fri & Sun
Norseman	34	2½	Wed, Fri & Sun

BATAVIA COAST

From tranquil Dongara-Port Denison to the remote, wind-scoured Zutydorp Cliffs stretches a dramatic coastline steeped in history, littered with shipwrecks and rich in marine life. While the region proved the undoing of many early European sailors, today modern fleets make the most of a lucrative crayfish industry, and travellers hunt down empty beaches.

ⓘ Getting There & Away

Regional airlines connect Perth with Geraldton, and there are frequent Transwa (www.transwa.wa.gov.au) buses between the two hubs, stopping at Dongara and offering connections to Kalbarri.

Geraldton

☑08 / POP 31,978

Capital of the midwest, sun-drenched 'Gero' is surrounded by excellent beaches offering myriad aquatic opportunities – swimming, snorkelling, surfing and, in particular, wind- and kitesurfing. The largest town between Perth and Darwin has huge wheat-handling and fishing industries that make it independent of the fickle tourist dollar, and seasonal workers flood the town during crayfish (rock lobster) season.

While many travellers pass through briefly, heading for attractions further north, Geraldton is a town with a gritty maritime history and the gateway to the stunning Abrolhos Islands, and is worth a couple of days of your time. The fantastically revamped waterfront is a masterclass in creating fun public spaces, and Gero blends big-city sophistication with small-town friendliness, offering a strong arts culture and a thriving foodie scene.

◎ Sights

★**Western Australian Museum – Geraldton** MUSEUM
(☑08-9431 8393; www.museum.wa.gov.au; 2 Museum Pl; by donation; ⊙9.30am-3pm) At one of the state's best museums, intelligent multimedia displays relate the area's natural, cultural and Aboriginal history. The Shipwreck Gallery documents the tragic story of the *Batavia*, while 3D video footage reveals the sunken wrecks of HMAS *Sydney II* and the *Kormoran*. Highlights tour daily at 11.30am.

★**HMAS Sydney II Memorial** MONUMENT
(www.hmassydneymemorial.com.au; Gummer Ave) **FREE** Commanding the hill overlooking Geraldton is this moving memorial commemorating the 1941 loss of the *Sydney* and its 645 men after a skirmish with the German raider *Kormoran*. Note the Waiting Woman, the Pool of Remembrance and the cupola over the pillared Dome of Souls – the latter comprises 645 steel gulls, representing the lives lost. Free guided tours at 10.30am daily.

Old Geraldton Gaol & Craft Centre HISTORIC BUILDING
(☑08-9921 1416; www.facebook.com/oldgeraldtongaolmuseum; 84 Chapman Rd; by donation; ⊙10am-3.30pm Mon-Fri, 9am-noon Sat) The gaol's gloomy cells held prisoners from 1856 to 1985, and framed historic documents weave a fascinating tale of daring escapes, gruesome executions, and offences punishable by forced labour in Australia (such as theft of £149 worth of cigars, cigarettes and asparagus).

Geraldton

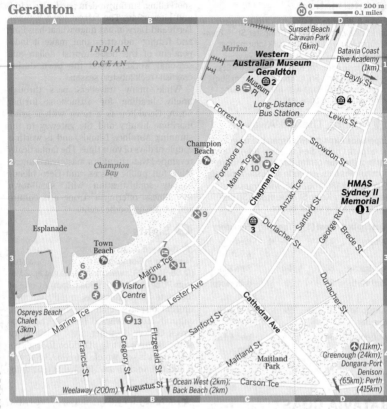

Geraldton Regional Art Gallery (GRAG)
GALLERY

(☑08-9956 6750; https://artgallery.cgg.wa.gov.au; 24 Chapman Rd; ⊙10am-4pm Mon-Sat, from 1pm holidays) FREE With an excellent permanent collection, including paintings by Norman Lindsay and Elizabeth Durack, this petite gallery also presents provocative contemporary work and regular touring exhibitions by the best local and international artists.

🏃 Activities

KiteWest
KITESURFING

(☑0449 021 784; www.kitewest.com.au; Coronation Beach; lessons per hour from $70; ⊙9am-5pm) From October to May, KiteWest offers kitesurfing courses, surfing lessons, stand-up paddleboarding tuition and yoga. You can also arrange customised water-sports and 4WD camping tours. Lessons are held on various Gero beaches, depending on the weather.

Batavia Coast Dive Academy
DIVING

(☑08-9921 4229; www.facebook.com/bataviacoast dive; 118 North West Coastal Hwy; 2-tank dive $200; ⊙8.30am-5pm Mon-Fri, 8am-2pm Sat, 10am-noon Sun) Offers PADI courses and a range of top-notch diving advice and trips, including chartered trips to the Houtman Abrolhos Islands (from $300 per person per day). Due to get a new boat in late 2019, and will be able to do day trips to the Abrolhos.

Ultimate Watersports
WATER SPORTS

(☑0427 645 362; www.ultimatewatersports.com.au; Foreshore; SUP hire per 30min/1hr $30/50; ⊙9am-4pm) Based on the Foreshore from October to April, these guys rent stand-up paddleboards and kayaks and offer flyboard X ($150), wakeboarding, kneeboarding and pretty much any kind of water sport you can think of.

Midwest Surf School
SURFING

(☑0419 988 756; www.surf2skool.com; lessons/board hire from $60/20) Year-round surfing lessons for absolute beginners and kids

Geraldton

⊚ Top Sights
1 HMAS Sydney II Memorial D3
2 Western Australian Museum –
  Geraldton C1

⊚ Sights
3 Geraldton Regional Art Gallery
  (GRAG) C3
4 Old Geraldton Gaol & Craft
  Centre D1

⊕ Activities, Courses & Tours
5 Revolutions A3
6 Ultimate Watersports A3

⊜ Sleeping
7 Geraldton Backpackers B3
8 Mantra Geraldton C1

⊗ Eating
9 Beached Barrel B3
10 Saltdish C2
   Skeetas .... (see 8)
11 The Provincial B3

⊝ Drinking & Nightlife
12 Cutler & Smith C2
13 Geraldton Hotel B4

⊜ Shopping
14 Yamaji Art B3

through to advanced surfers at Geraldton's back beaches. Stand-up paddleboarding lessons and rental also available.

Revolutions CYCLING
(☎08-9964 1399; www.revolutionsgeraldton. com.au; 268 Marine Tce; bike hire per half-/full day $25/30; ☺9am-5.30pm Mon-Fri, to 2pm Sat, 10am-2pm Sun) Bicycle rental from a handy foreshore location. A $50 deposit is required.

☞ Tours

★ Eco Abrolhos ECOTOUR
(☎08-9964 5101; www.ecoabrolhos.com.au; 5-day cruise incl meals from $2161) Offers live-aboard tours cruising the Houtman Abrolhos Islands, departing from Geraldton between March and October and including diving, fishing and shore excursions. The vessel can accommodate 38 passengers in air-con cabins with en-suite bathrooms.

Shine Aviation TOURS
(☎08-9923 3600; www.shineaviation.com.au; Geraldton Airport; 4/6hr Abrolhos tour $320/360) Offers excellent flightseeing tours, with the most popular option to land on the Abrolhos

Islands and snorkel off the beach. There's also a cheaper flyover option (90 minutes, $290), and you can combine an Abrolhos visit with flyover of Kalbarri and Hutt Lagoon (aka Pink Lake; $495). Also offers half-hour scenic flights above Geraldton and surrounds ($110).

☆ Festivals & Events

Sunshine Festival CULTURAL
(www.sunshinefestival.com.au; ☺Oct) It started in 1959 as a tomato festival, but now Geraldton's celebrations include dragon-boat races, parades, sand sculptures and parties. It's held over a week in early October. Sunshine guaranteed.

⊜ Sleeping

★ Geraldton Backpackers HOSTEL $
(☎08-9904 7342; www.geraldtonbackpackers. com.au; 172 Marine Tce; dm/s/d without bathroom $34/55/89; P❋@☎) This rambling central hostel is full of hidden nooks, sunny balconies and world-weary travellers. It's very close to beaches, bars and cafes, and is a good place to find a job, lift or travel buddy. It's well run too, with bright, fresh decor that's a cut above. Discounts for longer stays.

Weelaway B&B $
(☎08-9997 0356; www.weelaway.com.au; 104 Gregory St; r $88-125, 2-bedroom cottage $145; P❋☎) Weelaway offers four sumptuously decorated rooms (three en suite) in a heritage-listed homestead dating from 1862. There are formal lounge rooms, shady verandahs and a well-stocked library, and it's all within walking distance of the town centre and a great beach for swimming.

Ocean West APARTMENT $
(☎08-9921 1047; www.oceanwest.com.au; 1 Hadda Way; apt from $110; P❋☎❆) Don't let the 1960s brick put you off; these fully self-contained units have all been renovated in fresh monochrome, making them one of the better deals in town. Facilities are excellent and there's a wildly beautiful beach just across the road.

Mantra Geraldton APARTMENT $$
(☎08-9956 1300; www.mantra.com.au; 221 Foreshore Dr; apt from $219; P❋☎❆) This is the pick of the upmarket options, for its marina-side location and proximity to museums, the foreshore and town centre. It offers modern apartments (one- to three-bedroom, all with balcony, kitchen and laundry), polished facilities and **Skeetas** (☎08-9964 1619; www.

HOUTMAN ABROLHOS ISLANDS

Better known as 'the Abrolhos', this archipelago of 122 islands and coral reefs 60km off the coast of Geraldton is home to amazing wildlife, including sea lions, green turtles, carpet pythons, ospreys and the Tammar wallaby. Much of the flora is rare, endemic and protected, and the surrounding reefs offer great diving and snorkelling.

The name Abrolhos is thought to derive from the Portuguese expression *Abre os olhos*, meaning 'keep your eyes open'. These gnarly reefs have claimed many ships over the years, including the ill-fated Dutch East India Company's *Batavia* (1629) and *Zeewijk* (1727). Visit Geraldton's Western Australia Museum and read Peter FitzSimons' *Batavia* for the full bloody story of the Batavia shipwreck, mutiny and bloodshed.

You can visit either on a live-aboard boat as a diver or by taking a scenic flight/island landing. The Geraldton visitor centre (p969) can help with information about the islands and can book tours for you.

Good info is on the website of the WA Department of Fisheries (www.fish.wa.gov.au). Download its *Abrolhos Islands Information Guide* for information on wildlife, fishing regulations, dive trails and more.

skeetas.com.au; 3/219 Foreshore Dr; mains $24-46; ⊙7am-9.30pm; ❄) restaurant downstairs.

✖ Eating

★ Beached Barrel   AUSTRALIAN $
(www.facebook.com/BeachedBarrel; 26 Foreshore Dr; doughie $6-19; ⊙7.30am-3pm Tue-Sun) Love doughnuts? Love burgers? This beachfront shack combines the two in a genius move by using doughnuts instead of buns – from their lunchtime Angus Beef 'Cheesenut' to the Dirty Dawg, smothered in barbecue beans, sour cream and jalapeños. There are breakfast doughies as well as great coffee. Your arteries may not thank you, but your taste buds will.

★ Burnt Barrel   BARBECUE $$
(☑08-9920 5552; www.burntbarrel.com; 305 Nanson-Howatharra Rd, Nanson; mains $28-40; ⊙11am-4pm Fri-Sun, plus 6-9.30pm Sat (prior booking only); P❄) If you happen to be exploring Chapman Valley, north of Geraldton, you may be lured inside this self-proclaimed 'Outback brewBQ' by the wafting scents of pulled pork, smoked for hours on end, ribs, with the meat so tender it falls right off the bone, and the promise of ice-cold beers, brewed at the on-site microbrewery. Reservations essential.

★ Saltdish   CAFE $$
(☑08-9964 6030; www.facebook.com/saltdish cafe; 35 Marine Tce; breakfast $8-25, lunch $22-30; ⊙7am-4pm Mon-Fri, plus 6-11pm Fri & Sat; ❄🏠) The hippest cafe in town serves innovative, contemporary brekkies, light lunches and industrial-strength coffee, plus homebaked sweet treats. The menu is an ode to local produce and accomplished cooking, from Exmouth prawn and spring-pea risotto to tempura-fried Atlantic cod. Also open for dinner on Friday and Saturday nights. BYO wine or beer.

The Provincial   MODERN AUSTRALIAN $$
(☑08-9964 1887; 167 Marine Tce; pizza $15-23, mains $18-34; ⊙4.30pm-late Tue-Sat; ❄) Stencil art and a lifesize wire mesh shark adorns this cool little taste of the city, an atmospheric bar particularly renowned for its wood-fired pizzas (but also with tapas-style plates on offer). It's a loungey spot with smooth tunes, outdoor courtyard, cocktail specials, and live music most Friday and Saturday nights.

🍷 Drinking & Nightlife

Cutler & Smith   CRAFT BEER
(☑08-9921 8925; www.cutlerandsmith.com.au; 41 Chapman Rd; ⊙4pm-midnight Wed & Thu, from noon Fri & Sat, from 2pm Sun) Comfy booths, a smattering of local craft beers (including seasonal brews), a menu full of imaginative tapas (jalapeño and mozzarella arancini, pork belly with apple slaw, hot wings) and rock on the stereo make this industrial-themed joint a cool new addition to Geraldton's night scene.

Geraldton Hotel   PUB
(☑08-9921 3700; www.geraldtonhotel.com.au; 19 Gregory St; ⊙10am-10pm Sun-Thu, to midnight Fri & Sat) Winning features of this landmark old pub (dating from 1860) include a huge palm-tree-lined courtyard, $10 meal deals, and live music on weekends.

🛍 Shopping

★ Yamaji Art
ART

(☑08-9965 3440; www.yamajiart.com; 205 Marine Tce; ⊙9am-4pm Mon-Fri) This Aboriginal-owned and -operated art gallery is a terrific place to learn about Wajarri, Nyoongar, Badimaya, Wilunyu and other regional art, ranging from traditional to abstract, and to purchase paintings, painted wooden emu eggs and other crafts by the 30 or so artists who are exhibited here.

❶ Information

Visitor Centre (☑08-9956 6670; www.visit geraldton.com.au; 246 Marine Tce; ⊙9am-5pm Mon-Fri, to 1pm Sat & Sun) Helpful staff and plenty of info on the town and region. Can book Abrolhos Islands tours. Gift shop sells books on marine life and Aboriginal and military history.

❶ Getting There & Away

Geraldton is 415km north of Perth.

Virgin Australia and Qantas both fly daily between Perth and Geraldton. Geraldton Airport is 12km east of the city centre; taxis can get you into town.

The **long-distance bus station** (Chapman Rd) is at the old railway station on Chapman St; a Transwa booking office is here.

Transwa (www.transwa.wa.gov.au) runs buses between Perth and Geraldton ($68, six to 8½ hours). The most frequent service is via the Brand Hwy (Rte 1); it offers connection to Kalbarri ($30; 2½ hours) three times a week. Transwa also has a twice-weekly service from Geraldton to Meekatharra ($81, seven hours).

Integrity (www.integritycoachlines.com.au) runs three bus services per week linking Geraldton to Perth ($63, six hours), Carnarvon ($115, 6½ hours) and Exmouth ($156, 11½ hours).

Kalbarri

☑08 / POP 1351

Magnificent sandstone cliffs terminate at the Indian Ocean. The beautiful Murchison River snakes through tall, steep gorges before ending treacherously at Gantheaume Bay. Wildflowers line paths frequented by kangaroos, emus and thorny devils, while whales breach just offshore, and rare orchids struggle in the rocky ground. To the north, the towering line of the limestone Zuytdorp Cliffs remains aloof, pristine and remote.

Kalbarri is a sleepy seaside town surrounded by stunning nature, and there's great surfing, swimming, fishing, bushwalking, horse riding and canoeing both in town and in Kalbarri National Park (p971).

◉ Sights & Activities

Rainbow Jungle
BIRD SANCTUARY

(☑08-9937 1248; www.rainbowjunglekalbarri. com; Bridgeman Rd; adult/child/family $16/8/42; ⊙9am-5pm Mon-Sat, to 4pm Sun; ⊕) Bird fans and kids will enjoy this bird park south of town – it's an Australian parrot breeding centre, with other feathered creatures to admire (local lorikeets and cockatoos, and South American macaws). It has a walk-through aviary, a lookout tower, a maze (adult/child/family $15/7/40) and a small cafe. Look for outdoor movie evenings at the park's Cinema Parrotiso (adult/child $18/10), held in the school holidays.

Chinamans Beach
BEACH

(off Stiles St) Where the Murchison River meets the sea, Chinamans Beach offers calm, sheltered waters ideal for swimming. Fishing is popular from nearby Chinamans Rock, and sunset watching from the lookout here is recommended.

Pelican Feeding
WATERFRONT

(Foreshore, off Grey St; ⊙8.45-9.15am) **FREE** Kalbarri's most popular attraction takes place every morning on the waterfront. Look for the compact wooden viewing area and wait for the hungry birds to rock up.

Kalbarri Abseil
CANYONING

(☑08-9937 1618; www.kalbarriabseil.com; adult/ child $90/80) Abseil into the gorges of Kalbarri National Park, then take a dip in the river. After a morning pick-up you're driven to the Z-Bend Gorge – cliff walls range in height from 4m to 35m. A visit to Nature's Window rounds out the half-day tour. Kids need to be aged six to abseil, but all ages can join the tour (tag-alongs with no abseiling are $40).

☞ Tours

Kalbarri Scenic Flights
SCENIC FLIGHTS

(☑08-9937 1130; www.kalbarriaircharter.com. au; Kalbarri Airport, off Ajana-Kalbarri Rd; 5-hour Abrolhos Islands flight $299) Offers 20-minute scenic flights over the coastal cliffs, and a menu of longer flights over river gorges, the Zuytdorp Cliffs, Shark Bay and the Abrolhos Islands (including landing options at the latter two). The Pink Lake, River Gorges & Coastal Cliffs tour (1¾ hours, $299) is a spectacular combo.

Kalbarri

Map legend locations:
- Jetty
- Children's Playground
- Clotworthy St
- Ajana-Kalbarri Rd
- Big River Ranch (2km); Gorges (38km); Overlander Roadhouse (245km); Denham (375km)
- Auger St
- Grey St
- Mortimer St
- Smith St
- Maver St
- Hasleby St
- Coles St
- Woods St
- Patrick Cres
- Murchison River
- Gantheaume Bay
- Chinamans Rock
- Oyster Reef
- Lookout
- Swimming Beach
- Kalbarri Visitor Centre
- Transwa Bus Stop
- Smith St
- Foreshore
- Red Bluff Rd
- Grey St
- Ruston St
- Porter St
- Porter St
- Kalber St
- Hackney St
- Walker St
- Gabba Gabba Gully
- Nanda Dr
- Red Bluff Rd
- Coastal Cliffs (5km); Port Gregory (68km); Horrocks (92km)
- Nautilus Retreat Kalbarri B&B (150km)
- Magee Cres

Kalbarri

◉ Sights

1 Chinamans Beach A3
2 Pelican Feeding C2

✈ Activities, Courses & Tours

3 Reefwalker Adventure Tours C4

🛌 Sleeping

4 Gecko Lodge A4
Kalbarri Backpackers YHA ....(see 6)
5 Pelican Shore Villas B4
6 Pelican's Nest D2

🍴 Eating

7 Finlay's Fresh Fish BBQ C4
8 Grace of Kalbarri D1

Reefwalker Adventure Tours   WILDLIFE
(☎08-9937 1356; www.reefwalker.com.au; Porter St; whale-watching tour adult/child $85/55) Spot migrating humpbacks on 2½-hour whale-watching cruises (departing June to November). Reefwalker also runs ocean fishing, lobstering and sightseeing tours.

Kalbarri Adventure Tours   CANOEING
(☎08-9937 1677; www.kalbarritours.com.au; half-day canoe tour adult/child $85/60) Combine canoeing, bushwalking and swimming around the national park's Z-Bend/Loop area. Full- and half-day tours available. You can opt for more sedate half-day tours of the park highlights, and seasonal wildflower tours.

🛏 Sleeping

Pelican's Nest   MOTEL $
(☎08-9937 1598; www.pelicansnestkalbarri.com.au; 45-47 Mortimer St; r/apt from $120/140; P❋🛜🏊) In a quiet location a short walk from the beach, the Nest has a selection of neat motel-style rooms, plus apartments with kitchenette or full kitchen.

★ **Gecko Lodge** B&B $$
(📞 08-9937 1900; www.geckolodgekalbarri.com.
au; 9 Glass St; ste from $215; 🅿️ ❄️ 🛜) If you're
looking to romance your sweetie in Kalbar-
ri, there's no better place than this intimate,
luxurious B&B. The suites come with spa
baths, the penthouse has its own balcony
and kitchen, owners Paul and Lindley are
treasure troves of local knowledge, and there
are freshly baked muffins every morning.

Nautilus Retreat Kalbarri B&B B&B $$
(📞 0400 248 859; 30 Batavia Circle; r from $150;
🅿️ ❄️ 🛜 🏊) Inside this cheery, canary-yellow
house in a residential area, friendly hostess
Debbie makes guests feel exceptionally welcome. Rooms with exposed brick walls are
aligned around a greenery-shaded pool and
breakfast includes fresh fruit and fruitcake.

Pelican Shore Villas APARTMENT $$
(📞 08-9937 1708; www.pelicanshorevillas.com.au;
cnr Grey & Kaiber Sts; villas $205-295; 🅿️ ❄️ 🛜 🏊)
Eighteen modern and stylish villas are dot-
ted around a curvy pool, with the best view
in town and lovely grounds. All units have
full kitchen and laundry; choose from two-
or three-bedroom options.

Eating

★ **Grace of Kalbarri** NORTH INDIAN $$
(📞 0426 986 752; www.facebook.com/Authentic
IndianRestaurant; 4 Clotworthy St; mains $16-28;
⊘ 11am-2pm & 5-9pm Wed-Mon; ❄️ 🍽️) A first-
class Indian restaurant that would do any
large city proud, Grace serves an excellent
range of North Indian standards to please
all palates, including savoury, moreish cha-
na masala, super-fresh local fish in a punchy,
fiery vindaloo or tangy Goan fish curry, and
fragrant lamb biriyani. Portions are large,
and service is efficient and friendly.

★ **Finlay's Fresh Fish BBQ** SEAFOOD $$
(📞 0438 708 429; www.facebook.com/finlays.bbq.
palmresort; 24 Magee Cres; mains $15-45; ⊘ 5.30-
10pm Tue-Sun) Fresh local seafood (chilli
mussels, salt and pepper squid, catch of the
day) comes simply but beautifully prepared
at this super-quirky Kalbarri institution – a
junkyard strewn with farming implements,
buoys and shark sculptures. Wash it down
with Finlay's own microbrews.

❶ Information

Kalbarri Visitor Centre (📞 08-9937 1104;
www.kalbarri.org.au; Grey St; ⊘ 9am-5pm Mon-
Sat, to 1pm Sun) Plenty of info on the region.

Also sells bus tickets, fly nets and quality crafts
by Aboriginal Warlukurlangu artists.

❶ Getting There & Away

Getting to/from Perth ($85, 10 hours) and
Geraldton ($30, two hours) by bus is easiest
with **Transwa** (www.transwa.wa.gov.au; Grey
St, Kalbarri Visitor Centre), which departs from
the visitor centre on Tuesdays, Thursdays and
Saturdays.

Heading to/from points further north, the only
option is Integrity (www.integritycoachlines.
com.au), which has three departures per week
heading to Exmouth ($146, 10 hours) and on to
Broome or Port Hedland. To link with these ser-
vices, catch a shuttle ($45) linking Kalbarri with
the Ajana-Kalbarri Rd turn-off. Shuttles should
be pre-booked with Integrity or via **Kalbarri
Backpackers** (📞 08-9937 1430; www.kalbar-
ribackpackers.com; cnr Woods & Mortimer Sts;
dm/r $29/77; 🅿️ ❄️ @ 🛜 🏊).

Kalbarri National Park

With its magnificent river red gums and
Tumblagooda sandstone, rugged **Kalbarri
National Park** (www.parks.dpaw.wa.gov.au/
park/kalbarri; admission per car $13) contains al-
most 2000 sq km of wild bushland, stunning
river gorges and savagely eroded coastal
cliffs. It contains abundant wildlife, includ-
ing over 1000 species of plants, 200 species
of birds, and spectacular wildflowers in Au-
gust and September.

There are two faces to the park: coastal
cliffs line the coast south of Kalbarri, with
great lookouts and walking trails connecting
them; inland are the river gorges.

◉ Sights

A string of lookouts dots the coast south of
Kalbarri (accessed from George Grey Dr).
Most lookouts are just a short walk from
car-parking areas; Eagle Gorge, Red Bluff
and Pot Alley have trails down to beaches
below. From July to November, you may spot
migrating whales.

For an invigorating walk, take the **Big-
urda Trail** (8km one way) following the
clifftops between Natural Bridge and Eagle
Gorge; for a shorter walk, pick up the trail at
Shellhouse Grandstand.

Pot Alley, Rainbow Valley, Mushroom
Rock and Red Bluff are closer to town. **Red
Bluff** is the closest part of the park to town,
and is accessible via a walking trail from
Kalbarri (5.5km one way). From the lookout

there are wonderful views of the Zuytdorp Cliffs to the north, and sunsets here are stunning.

The river gorges are east of Kalbarri, accessed from the Ajana-Kalbarri Rd. Roads travel to car-park areas with shaded picnic facilities, basic toilets and walking paths (from 200m to 1.2km return) to dramatic lookouts.

Travel east of town for 11km to reach the first park turn-off. A sealed, 20km road grants access to the park's favourite sites.

At the T-intersection, turn left to reach **West Loop Lookout** (where a wheelchair-accessible Skywalk and cafe were due to open soon after the time of research) and the Loop Lookout. From the Loop Lookout, a 1km return path leads to the park's most iconic attraction, the photogenic **Nature's Window** (a rock formation that perfectly frames the Murchison River below).

Bring lots of water if you want to walk the unshaded **Loop Trail** (8km return, three to five hours) that continues from Nature's Window and descends into the gorge.

Turning right at the T-intersection leads to **Z-Bend** with a breathtaking viewpoint overlooking the bend in the Murchison River (1.2km return, one hour), or you can continue steeply down to the gorge bottom (2.6km return, two hours); scrambling on rocks and climbing ladders en route. The most demanding trail here is the Four Ways Trail (6km return, two to three hours), with a steep ascent up from the river.

Head back to Ajana-Kalbarri Rd and travel a further 24km east to reach the second set of sights. Turn off the road and you'll quickly reach the **Ross Graham Lookout**, with stunning gorge views and where you can access the river's edge (700m return). Nearby **Hawks Head** (200m return) has more great views – it's named after the shape of the rock structure seen from the lookout.

ⓘ Information

For information, visit the Kalbarri Visitor Centre (p971) or the Parks & Wildlife Service website (www.parks.dpaw.wa.gov.au). The Kalbarri tourist brochure (published annually) has excellent maps and details of all the walks.

Take *lots* of water if you're visiting the gorges, and note that temperatures in this part of the park can be up to ten degrees higher than on the coast; several tourists have died in recent years from heat exposure. Hiking early in the morning is best.

ⓘ Getting There & Away

There is no public transport serving the park. BYO wheels.

SHARK BAY

The World Heritage–listed area of Shark Bay, stretching from Kalbarri to Carnarvon, consists of more than 1500km of dazzling coastline: turquoise lagoons, barren finger-like peninsulas, hidden bays, white-sand beaches, towering limestone cliffs and numerous islands. It's the westernmost part of the Australian mainland, and one of WA's most biologically rich habitats, with an array of plant and animal life found nowhere else on earth. Lush beds of seagrass and sheltered bays nourish dugongs, sea turtles, humpback whales, dolphins, stingrays, sharks and more.

On land, Shark Bay's biodiversity has benefited from Project Eden, an ecosystem-regeneration program that has sought to eradicate feral animals and reintroduce endemic species. Shark Bay is also home to the amazing stromatolites of Hamelin Pool.

ⓘ Getting There & Away

Shark Bay airport is located between Denham and Monkey Mia. Rex (www.rex.com.au) flies to/from Perth a handful of times weekly.

Integrity (www.integritycoachlines.com.au) buses run along the coast between Perth and Broome a few days a week, stopping at the Overlander Roadhouse on the North West Coastal Hwy, 130km from Denham. **Shark Bay Car Hire** (☑ 0474 556 296; www.carhire.net.au; 65 Knight Tce; shuttle $72, car/4WD hire per day from $95/185) has cars and 4WDs for hire.

If you're visiting without your own wheels, **Shark Bay Coaches & Tours** (☑ 0429 110 104; www.sharkbaycoaches.com) provides useful transfers between Denham and Monkey Mia ($60), and from the Overlander Roadhouse to Denham, plus links to the airport. The Monkey Mia Dolphin Resort (p975) can also arrange airport transfers for its guests.

Denham

☑ 08 / POP 696

Beautiful, laid-back Denham, with its aquamarine sea and palm-fringed beachfront, makes a great base for trips to the surrounding Shark Bay Marine Park, nearby **François Peron** and Dirk Hartog Island national parks, and Monkey Mia, 26km away.

DIRK HARTOG ISLAND NATIONAL PARK

The slim, wind-raked island, which runs parallel to the Peron Peninsula, once attracted Dutch, British and French explorers (who left pewter plates nailed to posts as calling cards), but until recently its visitors were mostly fisherfolk. WA's largest island is now a national park, with feral goats, sheep and cats removed, native plants replanted and endemics such as the boodie, banded hare-wallaby and rufous hare-wallaby being re-introduced in a bid to restore the island to its 1616 splendour.

Only 20 high clearance 4WD vehicles are allowed on the island at any one time, so bookings are necessary. The draws are isolation, natural beauty, wildlife (from logger-head turtles to dugongs) and history – a winning combination.

The best source of information is the website www.dirkhartogisland.com. See also the Parks & Wildlife Service's site, at http://parks.dpaw.wa.gov.au/park/dirk-hartog-island.

Shark Bay 4WD (☑08-9948 1765; www.sharkbay4wd.com.au; 1 Ocean Park Rd; ⊙from $205) runs guided half- and full-day tours from Denham to Dirk Hartog Island using their own boat. Wula Gura Nyinda Eco Adventures can arrange a custom-made, multiday tours of the island.

Australia's westernmost town originated as a pearling base, and the streets were once paved with pearl shell.

◉ Sights

★**Ocean Park** AQUARIUM

(☑08-9948 1765; www.oceanpark.com.au; Shark Bay Rd; adult/child $25/18; ⊙9am-5pm; ⊕) ⌀
On a spectacular headland 8km south of Denham, this family-friendly attraction features an artificial lagoon where you can observe shark feedings, plus tanks filled with turtles, stingrays and fish (many being rehabilitated after rescue). It's all revealed on a funny and informative 60-minute guided tour.

★**Little Lagoon** LAGOON

(Little Lagoon Rd) Idyllic Little Lagoon, 4km from town, has picnic tables and barbecues along its small beach, and is good for a walk or swim.

**Shark Bay World
Heritage Discovery Centre** MUSEUM

(☑08-9948 1590; www.sharkbayvisit.com; 53 Knight Tce; ⊙9am-5pm Mon-Fri,to 1pm Sat & Sun) Shark Bay's visitor centre has a gallery (free entry) that houses stunning aerial photos of the Shark Bay area, and a superb museum (adult/child $11/6) dedicated to the Unesco World Heritage Site of Shark Bay. Informative and evocative displays showcase Shark Bay's ecosystems, marine and animal life (including rare endemics), Aboriginal culture, early explorers, settlers and shipwrecks.

⌨ Tours

★**Wula Gura Nyinda
Eco Adventures** OUTDOORS

(☑0429 708 847, 0432 029 436; www.wulagura.com.au; 2hr sunset tour adult/child $70/35) ⌀
Learn how to let the Country talk to you on these excellent tours led by local Aboriginal guide Darren 'Capes' Capewell, including the secrets of bush survival and bush tucker. The campfire-at-sunset 'Didgeridoo Dreaming' tours are magical. There are also kayaking and stand-up paddleboarding tours (adult/child $199/145), plus exciting 4WD adventures into Francois Peron National Park ($199/140). Custom tours arranged.

Shark Bay Coastal Tours OUTDOORS

(☑0407 890 409; www.sharkbaycoastaltours.com.au; Post Office, Knight Tce, Denham; half-/full day $150/195) Recommended half- and full-day tours of Francois Peron National Park, full-day ventures to Steep Point and custom tours of Shark Bay.

Shark Bay Aviation SCENIC FLIGHTS

(☑08-9948 1773; www.sharkbayaviation.com; 2 Denham Rd; flights from adult/child $120/60) Flights from Shark Bay airport range from a 20-minute Francois Peron National Park flyover to a sensational 90-minute trip over Useless Loop, Steep Point and the Zuytdorp Cliffs (adult/child $345/160). There are also tours available to Dirk Hartog Island, Coral Bay or Mt Augustus. Make bookings at the waterfront office.

🛏 Sleeping

Tradewinds APARTMENT $
(☑08-9948 1222; www.tradewindsdenham.com.
au; Knight Tce; apt from $145; P※🛜) Spa-
cious, fully self-contained, modern, one- or
two-bedroom units sit right across from the
beach. Friendly owners, plus a nice outdoor
dining area overlooking the sea.

★On The Deck @ Shark Bay B&B $$
(☑0409 481 957; www.onthedeckatsharkbay.com;
6 Oxenham Chase; r $169-186; ※🛜) Denham's
most characterful accommodation is this
luxurious B&B on the outskirts of town,
overlooking scrubland and visited daily by
local wildlife. Whether you're staying in one
of the two individually decorated, spacious
rooms upstairs, or in the garden-facing
downstairs room, you have access to the
heated spa, outdoor dining area, continental
breakfast and helpful advice from owners
Phil and Kerrie.

**Denham Seaside
Tourist Village** CARAVAN PARK $$
(☑08-9948 1242; www.sharkbayfun.com; Knight
Tce; unpowered/powered site $37/55, 1-/2-bed-
room chalet $150/159; P※🛜) This lovely,
shady park on the water's edge is the best of
the three parks in Denham, though you will
need to borrow the drill for your tent pegs.
Accommodation ranges from unpowered
campsites and to one- and two-bedroom en-
suite chalets with shady decks, sleeping up
to five/six people respectively. Handy supermarket across the road.

🍴 Eating & Drinking

★Oceans Restaurant CAFE $$
(☑08-9948 1765; www.oceanpark.com.au;
Ocean Park Rd; mains $14-34; ⊙9am-3pm)
Overlooking aquamarine waters at Ocean
Park (p973), breakfast is served here until
11am, and you can partner craft beer and
award-winning wines the the freshest sea-
food in Shark Bay (such as seared lemon
pepper calamari and crispy-skinned barra-
mundi). Romancing your other half? Look
no further than the spectacular Ocean Park
seafood platter ($60).

Old Pearler Restaurant SEAFOOD $$
(☑08-9948 1373; 71 Knight Tce; mains $26-50;
⊙from 5pm Mon-Sat; ※) Built from shell
bricks that account for the incredible acoustics, this atmospheric nautical haven serves
decent seafood. There are no outdoor tables

or view, but the hefty seafood platter ($100
for two people) features local snapper, whiting, crayfish, oysters, prawns and squid –
some grilled, some battered and fried. BYO
drinks; bookings recommended.

Shark Bay Hotel PUB
(☑08-9948 1203; www.sharkbayhotelwa.com.
au; 43 Knight Tce; ⊙10am-late; 🍴) Sunsets are
dynamite from the front beer garden of Australia's most westerly pub, lovingly called
'the Oldie' by locals. It has a decent menu of
pub classics (served noon to 2pm, and 6pm
to 9pm), plus occasional live music.

ℹ Information

For information, interactive maps and downloadable permits, check out www.sharkbay.org.au.
There's more info at www.sharkbayvisit.com.au
and www.experiencesharkbay.com.

Parks & Wildlife Service (☑08-9948 2226;
www.parks.dpaw.wa.gov.au; 61 Knight Tce;
⊙8.30am-4.30pm Mon-Fri) Park passes, drone
permits and info about Edel Land, Dirk Hartog
Island and Francois Peron National Park.

Shark Bay Visitor Centre (☑08-9948 1590;
www.sharkbayvisit.com; 53 Knight Tce; ⊙9am-
5pm Mon-Fri, to 1pm Sat & Sun) Books accommodation, tours and bush-camping permits
for South Peron. Located inside the Shark Bay
World Heritage Discovery Centre.

ℹ Getting There & Away

Tiny Shark Bay airport is located between Denham and Monkey Mia. Rex (www.rex.com.au)
flies to/from Perth six times weekly.

The closest Integrity (www.integritycoach
lines.com.au) buses get is the Overlander Roadhouse, 128km away on the North West Coastal
Hwy. **Shark Bay Coaches** (☑0429 110 104;
www.sharkbaycoaches.com.au; adult/child from
$90/40) run a connecting shuttle (book at least
24 hours ahead).

Monkey Mia

Watching the wild dolphins turning up for
a feed each morning in the shallow waters
of Monkey Mia, 26km northeast of Denham,
is a highlight of most travellers' trips to the
region.

There's not much to the place (Monkey
Mia is little more than a beach and resort),
but you don't need to rush off after the early
feeding – the beach is lovely, the area is rich
in Aboriginal history, and there are water
sports and other activities.

FRANCOIS PERON NATIONAL PARK

Covering the whole peninsula north of Denham is a spectacular area of low scrub, salt lagoons and sandy dunes, home to the rare bilby, mallee fowl and woma python. It's a breathtaking place to observe the rust-red cliffs, white-sand beaches and exquisite blue waters, but it's largely off limits unless you join a tour of have a high-clearance 4WD.

The 520-sq-km national park (http://parks.dpaw.wa.gov.au/park/francois-peron; admission per car $13) was named after the French naturalist and explorer who was the zoologist aboard Nicolas Baudin's 1801 and 1803 scientific expeditions to WA.

Two-wheel drive vehicles can travel only as far as the **Peron Heritage Precinct** (Peron Homestead Rd) FREE, which was a sheep station in the 1950s. The big attractions – **Cape Peron** with its red cliffs and dolphin population, **Skipjack Point Lookout** with rays and whales swimming below, and several gorgeous beaches, such as **Big Lagoon** and **Cattle Well** – are reachable only by high-clearance 4WD.

⊙ Sights

★ Monkey Mia
Marine Reserve
BAY

(adult/child/family $13/5/30; ⊙feeding at 7.45am; ⓘ) ∅ It's hard not to smile as Indo-Pacific bottlenose dolphins start arriving for a breakfast snack. Note that during feedings, visitors are restricted to the edge of the water, and only a lucky few people per session are selected to wade in and help feed the dolphins. The pier makes a good vantage point for it all. Rangers talk you through the history of the dolphin encounters.

★ Hamelin Pool
MARINE RESERVE

(Hamelin Pool Rd) Twenty-nine kilometres along Shark Bay Rd from the Overlander Roadhouse is the turn-off for Hamelin Pool, a marine reserve with the world's best-known colony of stromatolites. These coral-like formations consist of cyanobacteria almost identical to organisms that existed 3.5 billion years ago; through their use of photosynthesis they are considered largely responsible for creating our current atmosphere, paving the way for more complex life.

Wildsights
ADVENTURE

(✐1800 241 481; www.monkeymiawildsights.com.au; Monkey Mia; 2½hr cruise adult/child $99/50) On the small *Shotover* catamaran you're close to the action for the 2½-hour wildlife cruise (recommended). There are also 1½-hour sunset cruises (adult/child $49/25, bring your own drinks and snacks), and a full-day 4WD trip to Francois Peron National Park (adult/child $215/140); discounts are available if you do both.

🛏 Sleeping & Eating

Monkey Mia
Dolphin Resort
RESORT $

(✐1800 871 570; www.monkeymia.com.au; Monkey Mia Rd; unpowered/powered site $38/53, backpacker dm/r $34/145, r from $265; ℗⊛⊚⊠) With a stunning beachside location, the only accommodation option in Monkey Mia is a catch-all resort for campers, backpackers, package and top-end tourists. The backpacker rooms are good value (and have kitchen access), but the top-end rooms are expensive. It can also get quite crowded. The grounds are home to a restaurant, bar, two pools, shop and tour booking office.

Boughshed
MODERN AUSTRALIAN $$

(✐08-9948 1171; www.facebook.com/boughshed; Monkey Mia Resort, Monkey Mia Rd; lunch $15-24, dinner mains $26-42; ⊙7am-8pm) The views are fabulous (and the visiting birdlife is prolific – just don't feed it!). Stylish Boughshed has plenty of areas in which to nurse a coffee or drink, and menus range from buffet/à la carte breakfast to light lunches and some creative dinner options, such as Shark Bay blue swimmer crab with linguini and twice-cooked pork belly. Reservations recommended.

Monkey Bar
BAR

(Monkey Mia Resort, Monkey Mia Rd; pizzas & mains $13-20; ⊙4-10pm; ⓘ) A relaxed and informal option overlooking the sea in the backpacker section of the resort, the Monkey Bar has a pool table, happy hour from 5pm to 6pm, and a menu of pizzas and pub-style grub (fish and chips, lasagne, burgers). There are children's options too. It's open from noon during school holidays.

ℹ Information

Monkey Mia Visitor Centre (☑ 08-9948 1366; Monkey Mia Rd; ⊙7am-3.30pm) Information about the area, tour bookings, plus art for sale by local Aboriginal artist. It's close to the dolphin feeding location.

ℹ Getting There & Away

There is no public transport to Monkey Mia from Denham. Hire a car in Denham, or use the transfer service ($60 return per person) operated by Shark Bay Coaches (p974).

The resort can arrange transfers from Shark Bay airport ($15).

GASCOYNE COAST

This wild, rugged, largely unpopulated coastline stretches between two World Heritage–listed areas, Shark Bay and Ningaloo Reef, and offers excellent fishing and a killer wave that attract surfers and kitesurfers from around the world.

Subtropical Carnarvon, the region's hub, is an important fruit- and vegetable-growing district, and farms are often looking for seasonal workers. Travellers see it as a handy place to restock before heading north from Carnarvon, either towards Shark Bay or along the stunning Quobba coast.

Carnarvon

☑ 08 / POP 4429

On Yinggarda country at the mouth of the Gascoyne River, fertile Carnarvon, with its fruit and vegetable plantations and fishing industry, makes a decent stopover between Denham and Exmouth.

It's a friendly place without the tourist focus of other coastal towns, with a few quirky attractions, decent accommodation, well-stocked supermarkets and great local produce. The palm-fringed waterfront is a relaxing place to amble.

Carnarvon is also the last town of any size before you reach the turn-off for the stunning Quobba Coast.

⊙ Sights

Carnarvon Space & Technology Museum   MUSEUM
(www.carnarvonmuseum.org.au; Mahony Ave; adult/child/family $10/6/25; ⊙10am-3pm Apr-Sep, to 2pm Oct-Mar; ⓐ) Established jointly with NASA in 1966, the **OTC Satellite Earth Station** (or OTC Dish) at the edge of town tracked the Gemini and Apollo space missions, as well as Halley's Comet, before closing in 1987. The Space & Technology Museum is now here, with its fascinating, family-friendly assortment of space paraphernalia (including handprints from

OFF THE BEATEN TRACK

MT AUGUSTUS NATIONAL PARK

In Wajarri country, the huge sandstone inselberg (or 'island mountain') of **Mt Augustus**, twice as large as Uluru and a good deal more remote, rises 715m above the surrounding red sand plains.

Surrounding the monolith is **Mt Augustus National Park** (http://parks.dpaw.wa.gov.au/park/mount-augustus; $13 per vehicle). Within the park is a 49km **loop drive** around the 8km-long massif (known as Burringurrah in the local Aboriginal language) – the drive allows changing views of the rock's many faces, and is suitable for 2WD vehicles. It also gives access to walking trails and Aboriginal rock-art sites, including the superb **summit trail** (12km return, five to eight hours, requiring a high level of fitness).

Head to **Emu Lookout**, about 6km northwest of the park boundary on the Cobra-Mt Augustus Rd, for great views of the inselberg, especially at sunset.

In a 2WD it's a 465km from Carnarvon via Gascoyne Junction (the first 172km are sealed) or 340km from Meekatharra, which is the more popular route. With a 4WD there are at least three other routes, including a handy back door to Karijini National Park via Dooley Downs and Tom Price. Check on road conditions before setting out (seasonal rainfall may alter access). All of these routes see little traffic, so be prepared for the worst and carry plenty of fuel, water and supplies.

Mt Augustus Outback Tourist Park (☑08-9943 0527; www.mtaugustustouristpark.com; Dooley Downs Rd; unpowered/powered site $22/33, donga $88, units $176) sells fuel.

visitors like Buzz Aldrin and Australian astronaut Andy Thomas).

One Mile Jetty   LANDMARK

(Babbage Island Rd; adult/child $5/free) Built in 1897 and stretching 1493m, this boardwalk was built to accommodate the cattle and wool trade. Views here are terrific, especially at sunset. You used to be able to walk or take the quirky Coffee Pot Train (Babbage Island Rd, One Mile Jetty; ♿) to the end, but the jetty was closed indefinitely at the time of research due to its decrepit condition.

🛏 Sleeping & Eating

Coral Coast Tourist Park   CARAVAN PARK $

(☑08-9941 1438; www.coralcoasttouristpark.com.au; 108 Robinson St; camping per site $39, cabins $99-235; P⛅🛜🏊) This pleasant, shady park, with a pool and grassy sites, is close to the town centre. It has a variety of well-appointed cabins (the plusher ones en suite), a decent camp kitchen and excellent bathrooms, plus bicycles for hire ($25/75 per day/week).

Best Western Hospitality Inn   MOTEL $$

(☑08-9941 1600; www.hospitalityinncarnarvon.com.au; 6 West St; r $139-189; P⛅🛜🏊) This is the best of the motels in town, with spacious and spotless, carpeted rooms arranged a around a pool, plus friendly service. Wi-fi is unreliable. The on-site restaurant, Sails (mains $24-45; ⊙6-9pm; 🌿), is highly regarded.

Gascoyne Arts, Crafts
& Growers Market   MARKET $

(www.gascoynefood.com.au/growers-market; Robinson St, Civic Centre car park; ⊙8-11.30am Sat late May-early Oct) This weekly market has delicious regional produce.

Bumbak's   MARKET $

(☑0409 377 934; www.facebook.com/bumbaks; 449 North River Rd; smoothies $8; ⊙9am-4pm Mon-Fri, from 10am Sat & Sun) Bumbak's, a working banana and mango plantation about 10km north of town (signposted off the highway), sells a variety of fresh and dried fruit, preserves and delicious homemade ice cream. On the must-try list: mango smoothies, caramelised-fig ice cream and choc-coated bananas.

A Taste of Thai by Fon   THAI $$

(☑0427 722 016; www.facebook.com/ATasteOfThaiByFon; 17 Hubble St; mains $16-30; ⊙10am-9pm Mon-Fri, from 10.30am Sat, from 11am Sun; 🌿🍴) Authentic Thai flavours add spice to Carnarvon's dining scene. Ask Fon to kick the heat a notch when she makes your red, green or mussuman curry, or tuck into some local crab or noodle dishes. Vegan variations available for most dishes.

ℹ Information

Carnarvon Visitor Centre (☑08-9941 1146; www.carnarvon.org.au; Civic Centre, 21 Robinson St; ⊙9am-5pm Mon-Fri, to noon Sat) Information, internet, maps and booking service. Local chutneys and relishes for sale, plus some Aboriginal art.

ℹ Getting There & Away

Rex (www.rex.com.au) Flies a few times a week to/from Perth; some flights stop at Shark Bay en route.

Integrity (www.integritycoachlines.com.au) Runs three times a week to Exmouth ($92, 4¾ hours), Geraldton ($115, six hours) and Perth ($167, 11¾ hours). Buses arrive and depart from the visitor centre.

Bikes can be hired from Coral Coast Tourist Park.

Quobba Coast

While the North West Coastal Hwy heads inland, the coast north of Carnarvon is rugged and desolate, and a favourite haunt of surfers and fisherfolk. Those who make it this far are rewarded by huge swells, high summer temperatures, relentless winds, amazing marine life, breathtaking scenery and fire-in-the-sky sunsets. Red Bluff is the southern point of the majestic Ningaloo Reef.

The beaches, snorkelling, fishing, surfing, kiting and windsurfing possibilities are outstanding – as is the feeling that you've really stumbled across a secret, secluded destination.

◉ Sights & Activities

★ Gnaraloo Bay   BEACH

(Quobba-Gnaraloo Rd) Some 7km north of Gnaraloo Station, past the airstrip, this crescent of white sand is as gorgeous as beaches come. You can snorkel in the cerulean waters, walk around the cape at the south end of the beach if you wish to sunbathe nude, or hit the water with your kite if the wind is right.

Blowholes   LANDMARK

(Beach Rd) From the turn-off on the North West Coastal Hwy, it's 49km (on a sealed road) to this natural phenomenon. Big swells force sprays of water through sea caves and, howling, up out of narrow chimneys in the rocks.

★ **Tombstones** SURFING

Boasting one of the longest, roundest tubes in the world, Tombstones is on most surfers' must-do list. You have to be an expert, since it's a heavy, scary, left-hander reef break. Surfers come here mid-April to October; the rest of the time, conditions are best for hardcore kite- and windsurfers.

🛏 Sleeping

Quobba Station Homestead CAMPGROUND $

(☑08-9948 5098; www.quobba.com.au; off Gnaraloo Rd; unpowered/powered site per person $15/20, cottages & chalets per person $30-70) 🐾

Ten kilometres north of the blowholes is Quobba Station, a huge, ocean-front pastoral property with plenty of rustic self-catering accommodation, campsites (including some generator-powered sites), a small shop and legendary fishing. The family-sized chalets are the pick for non-campers.

Quobba Station also owns the **Red Bluff Campground** (☑08-9948 5001; www.quobba.com.au; Red Bluff Rd; unpowered site/shack per person $15/30, eco-tent per person $80) 🐾, which is some 60km north of the homestead.

★ **Gnaraloo Station** CABIN $$

(☑08-9942 5927; www.gnaraloo.com; off Quobba-Gnaraloo Rd; camping per adult/child $25/12.50, cabins $150-330; ❉🛜) 🐾 At the end of the road, around 150km from Carnarvon, Gnaraloo Station is the jewel in the crown of the Gascoyne Coast. Surfers from around the world come from April to October to ride the notorious Tombstones, while hotter months bring wind- and kitesurfers trying to catch the Carnarvon Doctor, the strong afternoon sea breeze. Camp or stay at the homestead.

❶ Getting There & Away

From the turn-off on the North West Coastal Hwy (24km north of Carnarvon), it's 49km on a sealed road to reach the blowholes. Heading north from here, an unsealed, occasionally bumpy road takes you 75km to Gnaraloo Station, passing a couple of coastal sites and campgrounds en route. You'll need to retrace your steps to join the highway again (you can't travel north of Gnaraloo to Coral Bay).

Ask locally for advice about road conditions; the unsealed road is passable by 2WD, but there are several sandy stretches, so high clearance is a boon. The website www.gnaraloo.com/getting-here has useful info.

NINGALOO COAST & THE PILBARA

Lapping languidly against Australia's second-largest reef, the shallow, turquoise waters of the Ningaloo Coast nurture a marine paradise. Lonely bays, deserted beaches and crystal-clear lagoons offer superb snorkelling and diving among myriad forms of sea life, including humpback whales, manta rays and loggerhead turtles. World Heritage–listed Ningaloo Reef is one of the very few places where you can swim with the gentle whale shark, as well as humpback whales. Development is low-key, towns few and far between, and seafood and sunsets legendary.

Inland, among the eroded ranges of the Pilbara, giant mining machinery delves into the depths of the earth, while ore trains snake down to a string of busy ports. Hidden away here are ancient Aboriginal rock art sites and two beautiful national parks, home to spectacular gorges, remote peaks, tranquil pools and abundant wildlife.

❶ Getting There & Away

Learmonth Airport (south of Exmouth) is the primary hub for Ningaloo, while there are airports enabling the ferrying of workers between Perth and the Pilbara mining towns of Port Hedland, Karratha, Paraburdoo and Newman.

Qantas (www.qantas.com.au) covers the biggest network, while Virgin Australia (www.virginaustralia.com) covers some Perth-to-Pilbara routes. Skippers Aviation (www.skippers.com.au) serves Karratha, Port Hedland and other Pilbara destinations.

Integrity (www.integritycoachlines.com.au) operates twice-weekly departures from Perth to Broome, stopping at Coral Bay, Exmouth, Karratha, Roebourne and Port Hedland. A weekly departure from Perth runs to Port Hedland via Coral Bay and Exmouth.

Coral Bay

☑08 / POP 214

Beautifully situated just north of the Tropic of Capricorn, the tiny, chilled-out seaside village of Coral Bay is one of the easiest locations from which to access the exquisite Ningaloo Marine Park (p986). Consisting of only one street and a sweeping white-sand beach, the town is small enough to enjoy on foot.

Coral reefs lie just off the town beach, making it brilliant for snorkelling and swimming. It's also a great base for outer-reef activities such as scuba diving, fishing and whale watching (June to November), and swimming with whale sharks (April to July) and manta rays.

Development is strictly limited, so expect higher prices for food and accommodation. Exmouth, 152km away, has more options. The town is particularly busy from April to October.

◉ Sights & Activities

★ Bill's Bay
BEACH

(Robinson St; 🅿) Bill's Bay is the perfectly positioned town beach at the end of Robinson St. Easy access and sheltered teal waters make this a favourite with everyone, from families to snorkellers. Keep to the southern end when snorkelling; the northern end (Skeleton Bay) is a breeding ground for reef sharks.

Purdy Point
SNORKELLING

Walk 500m south from Bill's Bay along the coast until the 8km/h marker. Snorkelling from this point allows access to some fantastic coral bommies, and you can drift with the current back to the bay. Hire snorkel gear anywhere in town.

☞ Tours

Ningaloo Marine Interactions
SNORKELLING

(☏08-9948 5190; www.mantaraycoralbay.com.au; Shopping Centre, Robinson St; whale watching $75, manta-ray interaction $170, wildlife spotting $210) ✐ Informative and sustainably run tours to the outer reef include two-hour whale watching (seasonal), half-day manta-ray interaction (year-round) and six-hour wildlife-spotting cruises with snorkelling. Child prices and family deals too.

Ningaloo Reef Dive & Snorkel
DIVING

(☏08-9942 5824; www.ningalooreefdive.com; Shopping Centre, Robinson St; diving from $300) ✐ This highly regarded PADI and eco-certified dive crew offers snorkelling with whale sharks (March to July; $390) and manta rays (all year; $155), half-day reef dives ($180) and a full range of dive courses (from $300), as well as 'humpback whale in-water interaction' tours ($355). Book scenic flights over the reef here.

Coral Bay Ecotours
SNORKELLING

(☏08-9942 5885; www.coralbayecotours.com.au; Robinson St; 1/2/3hr tours $41/57/78, full-day tour $175) ✐ Eco-certified and carbon-neutral tours include glass-bottom-boat cruises with snorkelling, and all-day wildlife-spotting trips complete with manta-ray interaction. In

ALL CREATURES GREAT & SMALL

WA's native wildlife is ever-present, and this is a place where marine wildlife and humans regularly cross paths. Each year 30,000 whales cruise the coast-hugging 'Humpback Hwy', while Bremer Bay near Albany is known for its orcas. Ningaloo Marine Park is home to the world's largest fish, the whale shark, while dolphins proliferate at Rockingham, Bunbury and Monkey Mia.

It's worth noting that some animal welfare organisations counsel against swimming with wild marine animals. With a bit of research you can make an ethical choice about how you choose to interact.

season, the company offers snorkelling with whale sharks ($395) and humpback-whale interaction ($365). The booking office is next to Fin's Cafe.

Ningaloo Kayak Adventures
WATER SPORTS

(☏08-9948 5034; www.coralbay.org/kayak.htm; off Robinson St; day package $70; ☺8am-5pm Mon-Fri, 9am-3pm Sat) From a kiosk by the main beach, you can hire a glass-bottom kayak ($30 per hour), stand-up paddleboards ($25 per hour), wetsuits and snorkelling gear ($15 per day). Kayaking tours with snorkelling are also available, plus one-hour guided snorkelling tours using underwater Sea-Doo scooters for propulsion ($70).

⌁ Sleeping

★ Bullara Station
FARMSTAY $

(☏08-9942 5938; www.bullara-station.com.au; Burkett Rd; unpowered/powered site $14/38, tw/d $110/140, cottage from $270; ☺Apr-Oct; 🅿) A great, friendly, 2WD-accessible set-up 65km north of Coral Bay, and 6km east of the Minilya-Exmouth road junction. There are several rooms in the stylishly renovated shearers' quarters (shared kitchen and bathrooms), a couple of self-contained cottages, and campsites with amenities (including laundry and open-air showers).

Ningaloo Club Backpackers
HOSTEL $

(☏08-9948 5100; www.ningalooclub.com; Robinson St; dm $29-34, r with/without bathroom $120/95; 🅿✳🛜🏊) Popular with the party crowd, this hostel is a great place to meet people, and boasts a central pool equipped for water volleyball, plus a well-equipped kitchen, an

Ningaloo Coast & the Pilbara

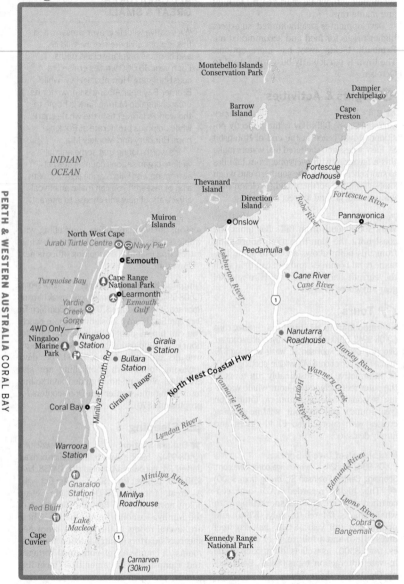

on-site bar and surprisingly swish en-suite rooms. It also sells bus tickets (Integrity coaches stop outside) and discounted tours.

Peoples Park　　　　　CARAVAN PARK $$
(☑08-9942 5933; www.peoplesparkcoralbay.com; Robinson St; sites $44-54, cabins/villas from

$232/258; P ❄) This excellent caravan park offers grassy, shaded sites and a variety of self-contained cabins and villas. Friendly staff keep the amenities and camp kitchen spotless, and it's the only place with fresh-water showers. The hilltop villas have superb views.

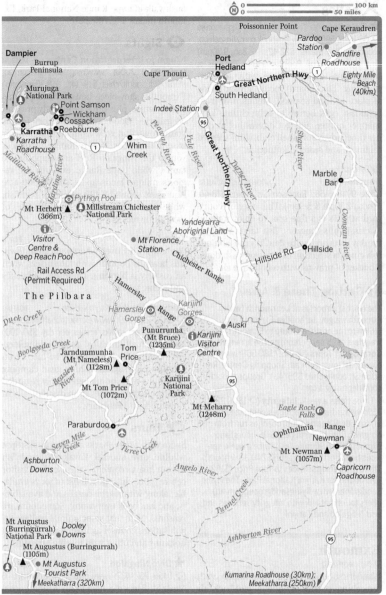

Ningaloo Reef Resort   HOTEL $$$
(☎08-9942 5934; www.ningalooreefresort.com. au; 1 Robinson St; r $280-450; P❄️📶☢️) The cream tile and blonde wood decor of this resort probably won't make your social media pics, but Coral Bay's plushest digs offer studios and various apartments (ocean views are pricier). The location is the winner: directly opposite the beach, in a slightly elevated position, making views from the outdoor areas a treat. There's a restaurant and bar here too.

✖ Eating

★ Fin's Cafe
SEAFOOD $$

(☑ 08-9942 5900; www.facebook.com/finscafecb; Robinson St; mains $22-42; ☺ 8am-9.30pm) Out the front of Peoples Park, Fin's is a super-casual outdoor place with an ever-changing blackboard menu giving pride of place to local seafood. Menus rove from breakfast eggs Benny to a lunchtime king snapper burger, and get interesting at dinner time: crispy soft-shell crab, chilli-scented calamari, and seafood fettuccine.

Bill's on the Ningaloo Reef
MODERN AUSTRALIAN $$

(☑ 08-9948 5156; Robinson St; mains $18-40; ☺ noon-2.30pm & 5-9pm) The interior courtyard at Bill's is a fine spot to enjoy a menu of classic hits (burgers, fish tacos, catch of the day) prepared with flair. Try the fabulous fish curry, a selection of tapas or wash down a bucket of prawns with a boutique ale.

❶ Getting There & Away

The closest airport is at **Learmonth** (www.exmouth.wa.gov.au; Minilya-Exmouth Rd), 116km to the north, en route to Exmouth. Airport transfers ($95 per person) can be arranged with **Coral Coast Tours** (☑ 0427 180 568; www.coralcoasttours.com.au; Shopping Centre, Robinson St; adult/child $95/48). Groups should consider hiring a car.

Three times a week, **Integrity** (☑ 1800 226 339; www.integritycoachlines.com.au; Robinson St, outside Ningaloo Club) coaches run from Ningaloo Club to Perth ($203, 16 hours) and Exmouth ($47, 90 minutes); twice a week, services head north to Broome ($240, 18½ hours). There are weekly services to Tom Price ($162, 10½ hours) for Karijini National Park. The Flying Sandgroper (www.flyingsandgroper.com.au) offers tours that link with Integrity services and visit Ningaloo and Karijini.

Exmouth

☑ 08 / POP 2207

Wandering emus, palm trees laden with screeching cockatoos, and a laid-back air give Exmouth a real Australian charm. Year-round, visitors are drawn by the nearby Ningaloo Reef, with spikes in visitor numbers during the whale shark season (from April to July) and humpback whale season (August to October).

Whether you've come to swim with the leviathans, snorkel off the Ningaloo Reef or bushwalk in Cape Range National Park, Exmouth makes a terrific base.

⊙ Sights

Ningaloo Interpretation Centre
MUSEUM

(☑ 08-9949 3000; www.ningaloocentre.com.au; Murat Rd; adult/child $19/14; ☺ 8.30am-5pm) Exmouth's showpiece houses the expanded visitor centre, plus three beautifully presented galleries. One covers the history of this young town that grew from an American air base in the 1960s. Reef to Range introduces you to the Ningaloo Reef and Cape Range fauna, while Cape Range explores the region's unique landscapes. The 55,000-litre Aquarium shows off 100 species of reef fish, while other displays regale you with tales of local shipwrecks.

Town Beach
BEACH

(Warne St) A relatively short walk from town, this beach is popular with kitesurfers when an easterly is blowing. There are barbecues and picnic tables.

Exmouth Boat & Kayak Hire
BOATING

(☑ 0438 230 269; www.exmouthboathire.com; 7 Patterson Way; kayaks/tinnies per day $50/100) Tinnies (small dinghies) or something larger (including a skipper!) can be hired; you can also hire kayaks, fishing gear, camping gear and 4WDs, or arrange highly regarded fishing charters. Prices drop dramatically in November and February.

⊙ Tours

Swim with whale sharks or humpbacks, spot wildlife, dive, snorkel, kayak, surf and fish to your heart's content – the excellent visitor centre (p985) has the full list of tours available, along with all the details and availability, and can book everything. Some tours are seasonal. Note that some animal welfare organisations counsel against swimming with dolphins and other wild marine animals.

★ Dive Ningaloo
DIVING

(☑ 0456 702 437; www.diveningaloo.com.au; 6 Nimitz St; 2-tank dive from $200) A small, local company garnering a big reputation, Dive Ningaloo offers try dives, PADI courses, snorkelling trips (including with small Sea-Doo scooters), whale-watching cruises and great dive options. It's the only diving operator licensed to dive the world-class Navy Pier (p986) site and to do four-dive overnight trips to the Muiron Islands.

Exmouth

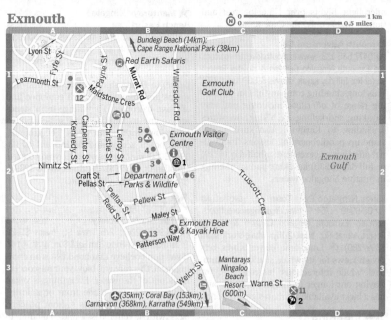

N 0 _____ 1 km
0 _____ 0.5 miles

Bundegi Beach (14km);
Cape Range National Park (38km)

Lyon St
Fyfe St
Learmonth St
Maidstone Cres
Murat Rd
Willersdorf Rd
Red Earth Safaris
Exmouth
Golf Club

Carpenter St
Kennedy St
Lefroy St
Christie St
10
5
9
4
3
Exmouth Visitor
Centre
1
6

Nimitz St
Craft St
Pellas St
Department of
Parks & Wildlife
Pellas St
Pellew St
Reid St

Exmouth
Gulf

Truscott Cres

Maley St
Exmouth Boat
& Kayak Hire

13
Patterson Way

Welch St

Mantarays
Ningaloo
Beach
Resort
(600m)
8
Warne St
11
2

(35km); Coral Bay (153km);
Carnarvon (368km), Karratha (549km);

Exmouth

⊙ Sights
1 Ningaloo Interpretation Centre.............B2
2 Town Beach...D3

⊕ Activities, Courses & Tours
3 Dive Ningaloo..B2
4 Exmouth Adventure Co.........................B2
5 Kings Ningaloo Reef Tours B2
6 Ocean Eco Adventures..........................B2
7 Three Islands Whale Shark Dive A1

⊜ Sleeping
8 Exmouth Escape C3

9 Exmouth Ningaloo Caravan &
  Holiday Resort...................................... B2
10 Ningaloo Lodge.......................................B1

⊗ Eating
  BBqFather ....(see 9)
11 Short Order Local D3
12 The Social Society A1
  Whalers Restaurant........................(see 8)

⊜ Drinking & Nightlife
  Froth Craft Brewery ....(see 7)
13 Whalebone Brewing Company B3

Ocean Eco Adventures SNORKELLING

(☑08-9949 1208; www.oceanecoadventures.com.au; Truscott Cres; whale-shark swim/observation from $379/219) ⊘ A well-set-up operator with a luxurious vessel and its own wildlife-spotting microlight. The whale-shark swim months are followed by humpback interaction and whale-watching tours.

Three Islands Whale Shark Dive SNORKELLING

(☑1800 138 501; www.whalesharkdive.com; 1 Kennedy St; whale shark swim adult/child $395/285;

⊘Mar-Oct) ⊘ This well-respected, ecologically minded outfit consistently wins awards for its whale-shark tours, which run from mid-March to July. From August to October, it also offers humpback interaction tours (adult/13-to-17-year-old $325/295); under-13s may only observe from the boat.

Birds Eye View SCENIC FLIGHTS

(☑0427 996 833; www.birdseyeview.net.au; Hangar 28, Exmouth Aerodrome, Minilya-Exmouth Rd; 30/60/90min flight $199/329/439) Don't want to get your feet wet but still after adrenaline? Get some altitude on these incredible microlight flights over Ningaloo reef and (longer flights only) the Cape Range.

Exmouth Adventure Co KAYAKING

(📞 0477 685 123; www.exmouthadventureco.com. au; Exmouth Ningaloo Caravan & Holiday Resort, Murat Rd; full-day kayak, snorkel & SUP tour $250) This long-standing company has an expanding range of offerings, including multiday kayaking, snorkelling and hiking adventures (including to Karijini). Also surfing and stand-up paddleboarding lessons. Its original offerings are excellent: a half-day ($120) or full-day ($230) kayaking and snorkelling in pristine Ningaloo waters.

Kings Ningaloo Reef Tours SNORKELLING

(📞 08-9949 1764; www.kingsningalooreeftours. com.au; Exmouth Ningaloo Caravan & Holiday Resort, Murat Rd; adult/2-16yr whale-shark swim $399/280) 🏊 Long-time player Kings gets rave reviews for its whale shark and humpback whale interactions. It's renowned for staying out longer than everyone else, and has a 'next available tour' no-sighting policy.

🛏 Sleeping

Exmouth Ningaloo
Caravan & Holiday Resort CARAVAN PARK $

(📞 08-9949 2377; www.exmouthresort.com; Murat Rd; unpowered/powered site $40/50, dm/d $40/84, chalets from $185; 🅿 ❄ 🌐 🏊 🐾) Across from the visitor centre, this friendly, spacious park has grassy sites, self-contained chalets, backpacker dorms and doubles (shared bathrooms; known as Winston's Backpackers), an on-site restaurant and even a pet section.

Exmouth Escape APARTMENT $$

(📞 08-9949 4800; www.exmouthescaperesort. com.au; 27 Murat Rd; apt from $199; 🅿 ❄ 🌐 🏊) A collection of smart, self-contained villas that range in size (up to three bedrooms). They're set around a lovely central area with pool and garden, plus the excellent Whalers restaurant. The resort also has car hire available, and package deals.

Ningaloo Lodge MOTEL $$

(📞 08-9949 4949; www.ningaloolodge.com.au; Lefroy St; r $160; 🅿 ❄ 🌐 🏊) One of the better deals in town. Motel-style rooms are compact but clean and well appointed, and the extras are great: a well-equipped communal kitchen and laundry, barbecue, shady pool and courtyard.

★ Mantarays Ningaloo
Beach Resort RESORT $$$

(📞 08-9949 0000; www.mantaraysningalooresort. com.au; Madaffari Dr; r/apt from $179/360; 🅿 ❄ @ 🌐 🏊) At the marina, this resort is at the pointy end of sophistication (and expense) in Exmouth. The tastefully designed rooms are spacious and well equipped and all have balconies. They range from standard rooms to two-bedroom self-contained bungalows with ocean views. The grounds, pool, beach access and restaurant (📞 08-9949 0000; www.mantaraysningalooresort.com.au; Madaffari Dr; lunch $17-30, dinner mains $28-43; ⏱ 6.30am-late) are all top-notch.

🍴 Eating

★ The Social Society VEGETARIAN $

(📞 08-9949 2261; 2/5 Thew St; mains $11-21; ⏱ 7am-3pm Mon-Fri, to 2pm Sat & Sun; ❄ 🌐 🍽) 🌿 If you don't believe that breakfast is an exciting meal, this cafe will blow your misconceptions out of the water. Everything is vegan or vegetarian and made from organically-sourced local ingredients – from poached eggs with green harissa and halloumi to banana pancake stacks. There's gourmet coffee and a shop stocking eco-conscious sunscreen and apparel designed by local artists.

★ Short Order Local FOOD TRUCK $

(📞 0411 149 372; www.facebook.com/theshort orderlocal; Warne St, Town Beach; snacks $5-10; ⏱ 6.30-11.30am Mon-Sat) Cute as a button, this pastel-striped food van is parked at the north end of Town Beach and rewards early risers with great coffee, toasties and fresh muffins. Tables and benches are scattered around the grassy patch next to it.

BBqFather ITALIAN $$

(Pinocchio's; 📞 08-9949 4905; www.thebbqfather. com.au; Exmouth Ningaloo Caravan & Holiday Resort, Murat Rd; mains $21-37; ⏱ 6-9pm Mon-Sat; ❄ 🍽 🍴) This popular, licensed al fresco *ristorante* serves up huge, succulent, smoky slabs of brisket and pork ribs. At the same time, the Italian owners remain true to their much-loved pizzas and homemade pastas that made them a hit originally. The servings are as legendary as ever. Locals still call it Pinocchio's. BYO wine.

★ Whalers Restaurant SEAFOOD $$$

(📞 08-9949 2416; www.whalersrestaurant.com. au; Exmouth Escape, 27 Murat Rd; mains $30-42; ⏱ 5.30pm-late; ❄ 🍽) This Exmouth institution has a pretty poolside location, smart service and a mega seafood menu (but vegetarians and vegans get some loving too). Don't miss the signature New Orleans gumbo, or spread your wings to the blackened fish tacos. Die-hard crustacean aficionados need look no further than the towering seafood medley. Whalebone craft beer graces the drinks menu. Bookings recommended.

Drinking & Nightlife

★ **Froth Craft Brewery**   MICROBREWERY
(☑08-9949 1451; www.frothcraft.com; 5 Kennedy St; ☺11am till late; ☜) Award-winning Froth wears many hats and we love them all. It's a cracking microbrewery where you can quench your post-Ningaloo-Reef thirst with a pint of pale ale, IPA, amber ale or kölsch, grab a juicy burger, rock out to live music with a beer cocktail in hand or sip an excellent coffee.

Whalebone Brewing Company   CRAFT BEER
(☑0498 554 406; www.whalebonebrewing.com.au; 27 Patterson Way; ☺4-10pm Thu-Sun; ☜) Run by two local couples who wished to share their love of good beer with the world, this friendly microbrewery entices with its nine offerings, ranging from the hoppy Big Bone IPA and German-style wheat beer to the malty amber ale and refreshing pale ale. Great pizza, plus a kids' play area.

ℹ Information

Exmouth Visitor Centre (☑08-9949 1176; www.visitningaloo.com.au; Ningaloo Centre, Murat Rd; ☺9am-5pm Apr-Oct, 9am-5pm Mon-Fri, to 1pm Sat & Sun Oct-Mar; ☜) Tour bookings, bus tickets, accommodation service and parks information. It's a great first port of call, with boards and folders outlining all the tour options in the area, and friendly, helpful staff. You can hire snorkel gear here too, and purchase local Aboriginal art and stunning photos of Ningaloo.

Parks & Wildlife Service (☑08-9947 8000; www.dpaw.wa.gov.au; 20 Nimitz St; ☺8am-5pm Mon-Fri) Supplies maps, brochures and permits for Ningaloo and Cape Range national parks and Muiron Islands, including excellent wildlife guides. Get your drone permit here. Can advise on turtle volunteering.

ℹ Getting There & Away

Learmonth Airport (p982) is 36km south of town and has regular links with Perth courtesy of Qantas.

The **airport shuttle bus** (☑08-9949 4623; adult/child $40/25) must be prebooked; it costs

adult/child $40/25 between Learmonth and Exmouth town.

On Tuesdays, Fridays and Sundays, Integrity (www.integrity.com.au) coaches run from the visitor centre to Perth ($240, 17½ hours) and Coral Bay ($47, 90 minutes); on Wednesdays and Fridays, services head north to Broome ($240, 16¾ hours). There are buses on Mondays to Tom Price ($146, eight hours) for Karijini National Park. The Flying Sandgroper (p994) offers tours that link with Integrity services and visit Ningaloo and Karijini.

Red Earth Safaris (☑1800 827 879; www.redearthsafaris.com.au; Murat Rd; $840) operates a weekly tour out of Perth, which reaches Exmouth over six days ($840, including dorm accommodation and most meals). On Sundays it departs Exmouth from the Potshot Hotel Resort at 7am, returning to Perth over two days ($200, 30 hours; price includes meals and an overnight stop).

Around Exmouth

North of Exmouth, the main road skirts the top of the **North West Cape** before turning and running south, passing glorious beaches until it reaches the entry to Cape Range National Park (p988).

Head north past Harold E Holt Naval Communication Station to an intersection before the VLF antenna array. Continue straight on for Bundegi Beach or turn left onto Yardie Creek Rd for the magnificent beaches and bays of the western cape and Ningaloo Reef.

◉ Sights

★ **Vlamingh Head Lighthouse**   LIGHTHOUSE
(Lighthouse Access Rd) It's hard to miss this hilltop lighthouse built in 1912. Spectacular views of the entire cape make it a great place for whale spotting and sunset watching.

Bundegi Beach   BEACH
(Murat Rd) In the shadow of the VLF antenna array, and within cycling range of Exmouth (13km to the south), the calm, sheltered waters of Bundegi Beach and accompanying reef provide pleasant swimming, snorkelling, diving, kayaking and fishing.

Jurabi Turtle Centre   VISITOR CENTRE
(JTC; www.ningalooturtles.org.au/jurabi.html; Yardie Creek Rd) ♿ **FREE** Visit this unstaffed interpretive centre by day to study turtle life cycles and obtain the Parks & Wildlife Service pamphlet *Marine Turtles in Ningaloo Marine Park*. Return at night to observe

nesting turtles and hatchlings (December to March), remembering to keep the correct distance and to never shine a light directly at any animal. Guided evening **turtle-viewing tours** (www.ningalooturtles.org.au/datesjurabi.html; adult/child $20/10; ☺6.30pm Mon, Wed & Fri Dec-Feb) are available.

🏃 Activities

⭐**Exmouth Navy Pier**　　　　　　DIVING
(☑0456 702 437; www.diveningaloo.com.au; Point Murat; 1-/2-tank dives $140/210) Point Murat, named after Napoleon's brother-in-law, is home to one of the world's very best shore dives, under the Navy Pier. There's a fantastic array of marine life including nudibranchs, scorpion fish, moray eels and reef sharks. As it's on Defence territory, there are strict visitation rules and you'll need to join a tour operated by Dive Ningaloo (p982).

Muiron Islands　　　　　　　SURFING
Serious surfers should grab a few mates and charter a boat to the Muiron Islands, just off Point Murat, where there are countless breaks and no one to ride them. You can camp on South Muiron with a permit from the Parks & Wildlife Service (p985). There's also excellent snorkelling and diving – this is the most northerly point of the Ningaloo World Heritage area.

Exmouth Kite Centre　　　　KITESURFING
(☑0467 906 091; www.exmouthkitecentre.com.au; Yardie Creek Rd, Ningaloo Lighthouse Caravan Park; 1/3hr kitesurf lessons $100/290) Learn to kitesurf, surf or stand-up paddleboard (SUP) with this fun, expert crew based at the Ningaloo Lighthouse Caravan Park. You can take various lessons, SUP sunset tours or just rent the gear (surfboard/SUP $40/50 per day).

Ningaloo Marine Park

You'll be hard-pressed to find words that do justice to the pristine, aquarium-like waters and pure sands of Ningaloo, Australia's largest fringing reef, which extends for over 300km of coastline. The fact that it abuts the arid, rugged Cape Range National Park for much of its length simply adds to the appeal, as do a couple of world-class beaches you'll find there.

World Heritage–listed Ningaloo Marine Park protects the full 300km length of Ningaloo Reef, from Bundegi on the eastern tip of the North West Cape to Red Bluff on

---

ℹ WHEN TO VISIT NINGALOO

Year-round marine awesomeness:

December to March Turtles – three endangered species nest and hatch in the dunes. Best seen outside Exmouth.

March and April Coral spawning – an amazing event occurring seven days after the full moon.

Mid-March to mid-August Whale sharks – the biggest fish on the planet arrive for the coral spawning. Tours out of Exmouth and Coral Bay.

May to November Manta rays – present year-round; their numbers increase dramatically over winter and spring. Snorkelling and diving tours that interact with manta rays (ie swim above them) leave from Exmouth and Coral Bay in winter, and from Coral Bay in summer.

June to November Humpback whales – breed in the warm tropics then head back south to feed in the Antarctic. Tours out of Exmouth and Coral Bay (whale watching, and also interaction tours).

September to February Reef sharks – large numbers of harmless black tip reef sharks can be found inhabiting the shallow lagoons. Skeleton Bay near Coral Bay is a well-known nursery.

Aside from marine encounters, factors to consider include: school holidays (avoid if you can, as you'll pay more and accommodation is limited) and weather. The region is dry and warm all year, but temperatures are high in summer (mid-30s to low 40s Celsius from November to March), and there is also moderate risk at this time of a tropical cyclone.

Hint: bring polarised sunglasses, which make it easier to spot marine life in the water.

North West Cape

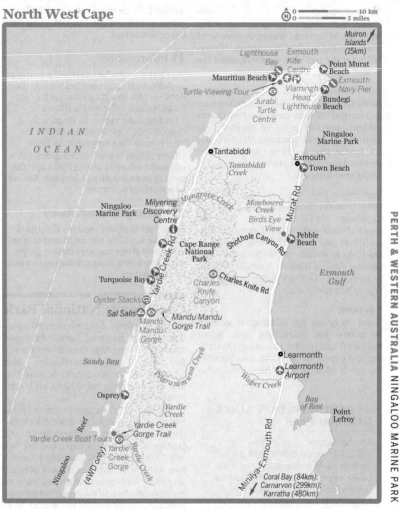

Quobba Station far to the south. It's home to a staggering array of marine life – sharks, manta rays, humpback whales, turtles, dugongs, dolphins and more than 200 coral species and 500 fish species – and it's also easily accessible; in places it's only 100m offshore.

🏃 Activities

Snorkelling & Diving

Most travellers visit Ningaloo Marine Park to snorkel. Always stop first at Milyering Discovery Centre (p989) for maps and information on the best spots and conditions.

Check the tide chart and know your limits: currents can be dangerous, the area is remote, and there's no phone coverage or lifeguards. While not common, unseasonal conditions can bring dangerous 'smacks' of irukandji jellyfish. Milyering also rents and sells snorkelling equipment (as do many other places around Exmouth and Coral Bay).

Add a new dimension to your snorkelling or diving by collecting marine data in your own time, or volunteering for reef monitoring (courses available). Visit www.reefcheckaustralia.org for more information.

★ **Turquoise Bay**   BEACH

This perfect sweep of powdery-white sand, lapped at by cerulean waters, is considered one of the top beaches in Australia. If snorkelling at the reef near the shore, mind the posted warnings about rip currents.

Oyster Stacks   SNORKELLING

(Yardie Creek Rd) These spectacular bommies (submerged offshore reefs) are just metres offshore, but they must be snorkelled at high tide to avoid damaging the reef, and reef booties are a boon since there are sharp rocks at the entry/exit point. The car park is 69km from Exmouth.

Lighthouse Bay   DIVING

(Yardie Creek Rd) There's great scuba diving at Lighthouse Bay (at the northern tip of the cape) at sites such as the Labyrinth, Blizzard Reef and Helga's Tunnels. Check out the Parks & Wildlife Service book *Dive and Snorkel Sites in Western Australia* for other ideas. Dive operators in Exmouth can set you up and take you out.

Kayaking

Kayak moorings are installed at some of Ningaloo's best snorkelling sites. Tether your craft and snorkel at Bundegi, Tantabiddi and Osprey in the north, and Maud in the south (close to Coral Bay). Kayaks can be hired off the beach in Coral Bay or in Exmouth town, or you can join a tour from either destination.

ℹ Information

The Parks & Wildlife Service (PWS) produces an invaluable visitor guide, entitled *Ningaloo Coast World Heritage Area*. It's given out at the Cape Range National Park entrance station.

The best visitor centres for Ningaloo are at Exmouth (p985) and Milyering (p989) – the latter is inside Cape Range National Park.

There's plenty of information available online, with useful websites including PWS's site http://parks.dpaw.wa.gov.au/park/ningaloo. Also see www.visitningaloo.com.au.

ℹ Getting There & Away

Get yourself to either Exmouth or Coral Bay to make your way to the reef. Both towns have an assortment of tour operators that can get you diving, snorkelling, boating, fishing and kayaking the reef's waters.

Cape Range National Park

It's the coastline of the rugged 506-sq-km **Cape Range National Park** (https://parks.dpaw.wa.gov.au/park/cape-range; admission per car $13) that gets most of the attention – after all, these are the spectacular beaches that give access to the pristine Ningaloo Marine Park (p986).

Still, the park's jagged limestone peaks and heavily incised gorges deserve acclaim – they offer relief from the otherwise flat, arid expanse of North West Cape, and are rich in wildlife, including the rare black-flanked rock wallaby, five types of bat and over 160 species of bird. Spectacular deep canyons cut dramatically into the range, before emptying out onto the wind-blown coastal dunes and turquoise waters of Ningaloo Reef.

◉ Sights & Activities

Charles Knife Canyon   GORGE

(Charles Knife Rd) On the east coast, a very scenic, partially sealed and at times dramatically narrow 11km-long road ascends a knife-edge ridge via rickety corners. A rough track (passable by 2WD) continues to **Thomas Carter lookout** (at 311m, with great views). From near the lookout, in the cooler months you can walk the 6.8km **Badjirrajirra Trail**. The signposted canyon road is 22km south of Exmouth (not suitable for caravans).

ℹ CAMPING IN CAPE RANGE NATIONAL PARK

The campgrounds (adult/child $13/2.20) are run by the Parks & Wildlife Service. All bookings must be done online, where you can also see the location and facilities of each campground: https://parkstay.dpaw.wa.gov.au.

The park's 12 campgrounds stretch from Neds Camp in the north to Yardie Creek in the south (note: there is no campground at Turquoise Bay).

Facilities and shade are minimal at the sandy grounds, though most have eco-toilets (no showers, no water) and some shelter from prevailing winds, plus possibly a picnic shelter. No campfires allowed; bring your own camp stove. There are no powered sites, though some campgrounds are for tents and camper vans only. Most campgrounds have resident caretakers during peak season.

Yardie Creek Gorge
GORGE

(Yardie Creek Rd) Two walking trails give access to excellent views above this water-filled gorge: the gentle **Nature Walk** is 1.2km return, or the longer, steeper trail is 2km return and takes you high above the creek. There's also the option of a more relaxing **boat tour** (🖉 08-9949 2920; www.yardiecreekboattours.com.au; Yardie Creek Rd; adult/child/family $40/20/90; ⊙ 11am & 12.30pm on scheduled days).

Yardie Creek is 50km from the park entry (and accessible to all vehicles).

Mandu Mandu Gorge
GORGE

(Yardie Creek Rd) There's a small car park off the main road 14km south of the Milyering Discovery Centre, and from here there's a pleasant, occasionally steep 3km return walk onto the picturesque gorge rim.

🛏 Sleeping

Sal Salis
TENTED CAMP $$$

(🖉 08-9949 1776; www.salsalis.com; off Yardie Creek Rd, South Mandu; per person per night $900-1125; ⊙ mid-Mar–Oct) 🍃 Want to watch that crimson Indian Ocean sunset from between 500-threadcount sheets? Pass the chablis! For those who want their camp without the cramp, this exclusive tented camp has a minimum two-night stay, 16 en-suite, fan-cooled tents, three gourmet meals a day, a free bar (!) and the same things to do as the folks staying nearby in the pop-up camper.

ℹ Information

Milyering Discovery Centre (🖉 08-9949 2808; Yardie Creek Rd; ⊙ 9am-3.45pm; 📶) Serving both Ningaloo Marine Park and Cape Range National Park, this visitor centre has informative natural and cultural displays, maps, tide charts, campground photos and iPads for making camping reservations. Check here for road and water conditions. It rents out snorkelling gear (day/overnight $10/15), and sells drinks, ice cream and books on wildlife and history.

ℹ Getting There & Around

The Cape Range National Park entrance station is 40km from Exmouth, and the road south is sealed as far as Yardie Creek (91km from Exmouth). Off the main road are short access roads to beaches, campgrounds and day-use sites. The park is full of wildlife – try to avoid driving between dusk and dawn.

Without your own wheels? In Exmouth there's an abundance of tour operators, although most tours focus on the waters of the adjacent reef rather than the range itself. There are also several car- and campervan rental companies in Exmouth.

Karratha
🖉 08 / POP 22,205

In the past, most travellers to Karratha ran their errands – banking, restocking, repairing stuff etc – and then got out of town before their wallet ignited. That did the town a small disservice. It's the primary base for mining and industry in the region, and it certainly has a few things worth sticking around to investigate – from excellent Aboriginal tours and ancient rock art to cafes that wouldn't look out of place in the coolest parts of Perth.

◉ Sights & Activities

Miaree Pool
LAKE

(North West Coastal Hwy) Yeah, it gets hot up here. You might have noticed. Cool off at this shady waterhole, popular with locals for picnicking and swimming. It's 30km southwest of the Karratha turn-off, on the North West Coastal Hwy (Hwy 1).

Warlu Way
SCENIC DRIVE

(www.warluway.com.au; Warlu Rd) Dotted with interpretive signage, this 2500km scenic drive follows the path of the warlu, the Dreamtime serpent who travelled through the Pilbara, creating waterways as he went along.

Follow it through Karratha, the Burrup Peninsula, Roebourne, Cossack and Point Samson before cutting across Karijini and Millstream-Chichester national parks, and on to Port Hedland, Eighty Mile Beach and Broome.

Yaburara Heritage Trail
WALKING

(off Karratha Rd) The heritage trail consists of three main trail loops (2.25km to 3.75km in length), as well as a two further trails, and can be accessed either from behind the visitor centre or a car park off Dampier Hwy. Sites include Yaburara rock art, stone quarries and shell middens, plus excellent lookout points. Bring plenty of water and start your walks early.

★ Ngurrangga Tours
CULTURAL

(🖉 08-9182 1777; www.ngurrangga.com.au; 42 Roe St, Roebourne; half-day rock art tour adult/child $160/80; ⊙ Feb-Nov) Clinton Walker, a Ngarluma man, runs cultural tours that merit rave reviews. His half-day Murujuga National Park tour explores rock-art petroglyphs on the Burrup Peninsula near Dampier, while longer day tours explore the culturally significant areas of Millstream Chichester National Park (adult/child $300/150). Three-day Millstream camping tours are also available ($1450/500).

✦ Festivals & Events

Red Earth Arts Festival CULTURAL
(www.reaf.com.au; ☺ Sep) Over 10 days in mid-September, Karratha and the surrounding coastal Pilbara towns come alive for this festival, an eclectic mix of live music (all genres), theatre, comedy, visual arts and storytelling.

🛏 Sleeping & Eating

★ Latitude20 The Dunes APARTMENT $
(☑ 1300 528 488; www.latitude20apartments.com.au; 2 Walcott Way; apt $110; P ❄ 🛜 ≋) Spacious, spotless and equipped with a full kitchen, these fantastic studio apartments are clustered around a pool with an appealing barbecue area. They're a 3km drive from central Karratha, right by the coastal mangroves.

Discovery Parks – Pilbara, Karratha CARAVAN PARK $
(☑ 08-9185 1855; www.discoveryholidayparks.com.au; 70 Rosemary Rd; camping per site $29-49, motel r/studio from $88/129; P ❄ 🛜 ≋) Neat and well run with good facilities, this park has all manner of options for all budgets, from sites with en suite to family-sized units and cabins. It's tucked away off the Dampier Hwy.

Lo's Cafe Fusion Bistro CAFE $
(☑ 0438 186 688; www.facebook.com/losbistro; 20 Sharpe Ave, The Quarter; mains $18-24; ☺ 7.30am-5pm; ❄ ☝) This bright and breezy cafe mixes local ingredients with Asian influences to create their signature sweet potato waffle with fried chicken, poached eggs with pork belly, banana pancakes and more. All-day breakfasts aside, there are also rice burgers and wraps with teriyaki fillings and great coffee.

★ Empire 6714 CAFE $$
(☑ 0427 654 045; www.empire6714.com.au; Warambie Rd; mains $13-28; ☺ 5.30am-3pm; ❄ ☝) Sure, you can get your standard bacon and eggs here, but why wouldn't you go for banana flour waffles or tuna poke? There's lots of organic, hard-to-source goodness on the menu, and we like the playful Asian touches: bibimbap and salmon katsu alongside steak sandwiches. There are also impeccable

smoothies, cold-pressed juices, coffee and kombucha (fermented tea drink).

❶ Information

Karratha Visitor Centre (☑ 08-9144 4600; www.karrathavisitorcentre.com.au; De Witt Rd; ☺ 8.30am-4.30pm Mon-Fri, 9am-2pm Sat & Sun; 🛜) Has excellent local maps and info, supplies rail access road permits (for the most direct route to Tom Price) and books tours (including to mining infrastructure). At the time of research it was in the process of either being renovated or moved to a different location.

❶ Getting There & Away

Karratha Airport (www.karrathaairport.com.au; Hood Way), halfway between Karratha and Dampier, is well connected to Perth courtesy of Virgin Australia and Qantas. Also daily flights to Port Hedland.

Integrity (www.integritycoaches.com.au) operates twice-weekly bus services from Perth to Broome, stopping at Coral Bay, Exmouth, Karratha, Roebourne and Port Hedland. Buses head north from Karratha on Wednesdays and Fridays at 10.25pm and south on Fridays and Sundays at 6.40am.

Fares from Karratha include Perth ($282, 24 hours), Exmouth ($164, 6½ hours), Port Hedland ($89, 3½ hours) and Broome ($187, 10 hours).

Dampier
☑ 08 / POP 1106

Practically a suburb of Karratha, Dampier is the region's main port. Home to heavy industry, it's spread around King Bay. Dampier's most famous resident is Red Dog (who has had books written about him, and movies made), a much-loved mutt that roved the town and surrounds in the 1970s. A statue of him is at the entry to town. North of Dampier is the Burrup Peninsula, home to a pretty beach and one of Australia's wealthiest collections of Aboriginal rock paintings.

◎ Sights

★ Murujuga National Park NATIONAL PARK
(http://parks.dpaw.wa.gov.au/park/murujuga; Burrup Peninsula Rd) FREE Murujuga is home to the world's largest concentration of rock art (dating back more than 30,000 years), stretched out along the rocky hills of the heavily industrialised Burrup Peninsula. The most accessible are at **Deep Gorge**, near Hearson's Cove. The engravings depict fish, goannas (lizards), turtles, ospreys, kangaroos and even a Tasmanian tiger.

MILLSTREAM CHICHESTER NATIONAL PARK

Among the arid, spinifex-covered plateaus and basalt ranges between Karijini and the coast, the tranquil waterholes of the Fortescue River form cool, lush oases in the 2400-sq-km **Millstream Chichester National Park** (https://parks.dpaw.wa.gov.au/park/millstream-chichester; admission per car $13), the traditional lands of the Yinjibarndi people. In the park's north are the stunning breakaways and eroded mesas of the Chichester Range. As well as a lifeline for local flora and fauna – which includes nearly 100 reptile species and around 150 bird species – the park is one of the most important Aboriginal sites in WA.

Millstream Homestead Visitor Centre (Millstream; ⊘8am-4pm) Formerly the homestead of the 19th-century sheep station established here, the unstaffed visitor centre houses historical, ecological and cultural displays. It's 22km west of the Karratha-Tom Price Rd.

Python Pool (Chichester Range) Just off the road that traverses the Chichester Range (19km east of the Karratha-Tom Price Rd), this plunge pool sits photogenically at the base of a cliff. The water is normally fine for swimming, though check for algal blooms before sliding in.

Deep Reach Pool (Nhangganggunha; Millstream) Some 4km from the visitor centre, shady picnic tables and barbecues back onto a perfect swimming hole, believed to be the resting place of the Warlu (creation serpent). The water is deep and the banks can be steep, so use the steps here. Be respectful (no shouting or splashing), as it's sacred to the Yindjibarndi people.

Mt Herbert (Chichester Range) A 10-minute climb from the car park (arrowed off the road to Roebourne) reveals a fantastic panorama of the ragged Chichester Range.

The best way to see and appreciate the importance of this art is through a half-day tour out of Karratha with Ngurrangga Tours (p989).

Dampier Archipelago NATURE RESERVE
(https://parks.dpaw.wa.gov.au/park/dampier-archipelago) Offshore from Dampier, the coral waters and pristine islands of the Dampier Archipelago support a wealth of marine life, including dugongs, plus endangered marsupials (25 of the 42 islands are nature reserves). It's a popular recreational fishing and boating destination, and plenty of boat-owning locals head here for R&R. Enquire at Karratha visitor centre (p990) about fishing charters and cruises.

❶ Getting There & Away

Dampier is 20km northwest of Karratha.

There's an twice-daily community bus between Karratha and Dampier – see www.karratha.wa.gov.au/community-bus.

Port Hedland

📱 08 / POP 13,828

Founded on traditional Kariyarra lands, Port Hedland is many things; it's mountains of gleaming white salt that turn pink during sunset, vast cargo ships and furnaces, the world's largest deep-water port, a dystopia of railway yards and iron-ore stockpiles, and the all-pervasive red dust that tints the buildings and passing road trains a uniform ochre. Under that red dust lurks a colourful 130-year history of mining booms and busts, cyclones, pearling and WWII action, juxtaposed against two galleries showcasing contemporary Aboriginal art and colourful street art. If you're heading north to Broome or south through the Outback, this is your last stop from real coffee, good food and a dip in the sea for quite some time.

◉ Sights & Activities

Collect the brochure entitled *Adventure Awaits: Your Guide to Port Hedland* from the visitor centre and take a self-guided tour around the CBD and foreshore.

Goode St, near Pretty Pool, is handy to observe Port Hedland's **Staircase to the Moon** (on full-moon nights from March to October), where water caught in sand ripples reflects the moonlight, creating the effect of a staircase to the moon.

★**Courthouse Gallery** GALLERY
(📱08-9173 1064; www.courthousegallery.com.au; 16 Edgar St; ⊘9am-4.30pm Mon-Fri, to 3pm Sat) **FREE** More than a gallery, this leafy arts HQ is the centre of all goodness in Port Hedland.

OFF THE BEATEN TRACK

MARBLE BAR

Marble Bar, a long way off everybody's beaten track, burnt itself into the Australian psyche as the country's hottest town when, back in summer of 1923–24, the mercury reached 37.8°C (100°F) for 160 consecutive days.

A service centre for nearby mines and full of quirky local characters, the town was (mistakenly) named after a bar of jasper beside a pool on the Coongan River, 5km southwest of the town centre.

Aside from poring over the minerals at the **Comet Gold Mine Museum** (☑08-9176 1015; Comet Mine Rd; $3; ◷9am-4pm), admiring the jasper at the **Marble Bar Pool** (Marble Bar Pool Rd) and checking out lofty views from the **Water Tank Lookout** (Water Tank Lookout Rd), there's not a great deal to do in town other than to prop yourself up at the bar and have a yarn with Foxy at the **Iron Clad Hotel** (☑08-9176 1066; 15 Francis St; ◷noon-close).

Marble Bar is 200km from Port Hedland via Rte 138 (a sealed road). To carry on to Newman is 300km on an unsealed road via Nullagine that sees little traffic, but is usually OK for 2WDs (check locally; carry plenty of water).

Inside are stunning, curated local contemporary and Aboriginal art exhibitions, while the shady surrounds host sporadic craft markets. Curators are happy to chat about art styles.

★**Spinifex Hill Studios** ART
(☑08-9172 1699; www.spinifexhillstudio.com.au; 18 Hedditch St, South Hedland; ◷10am-4pm Tue-Fri, to 2pm Sun) Aboriginal art from Port Hedland and a considerable range of styles from Noongar, Banjima, Innawongka, Martu, Kariyarra, Nyiyaparli and Yamatji cultural groups from across the Pilbara, plus the Torres Strait Islands, are housed inside a striking building. Saturday is the best time to visit, with artists at work and coffee offered (a kind of 'open house'). Good to call before visiting.

Harbour Tour TOURS
(☑08-9173 1315; www.phseafarers.org; cnr Wedge & Wilson Sts; adult/child $55/30; ◷9.30am Mon-Sat, 1.30pm Sun) Run by the Seafarers Centre, this hour-long tour covers the facts and figures of the port, and includes a boat tour around the harbour. Check tour times online and wear proper footwear.

🛏 Sleeping & Eating

Discovery Holiday Caravan Park CARAVAN PARK $
(☑08-9173 1271; www.discoveryholidayparks.com.au; cnr Athol & Taylor Sts; camping per site $38, backpacker r $59-89, unit r $119-169; ﾟ❄🛜🏊) At the town's eastern end, this caravan park offers lots of cabin options, backpacker rooms (with shared kitchen and bathroom)

and well-maintained amenities. There's a nice view over the mangroves.

Esplanade Hotel HISTORIC HOTEL $$
(☑08-9173 9700; www.theesplanadeporthedland.com.au; 2-4 Anderson St; tw/d incl breakfast from $199/215; ﾟ❄@🛜) One of the roughest pubs in Port Hedland in a former incarnation, the 'Nard' is now a reasonably characterful 4½-star hotel with 98 smart, well-equipped guest rooms (though they're petite and quite pricey). It's a favourite with business travellers, making the weekend rates considerably cheaper. It has good food and drink on-site.

Hedland Harbour Cafe CAFE $
(☑08-9173 2630; www.facebook.com/hedland harbourcafe; 5 Wedge St; mains $10-20; ◷4am-4pm Mon-Tue, 4.30am-8pm Wed-Sun; ❄) A favourite with early risers and dock workers, this friendly cafe serves up smashed avo with poached eggs, brekkie burritos, kebabs, grilled red emperor and chips, and other tasty fare. Good coffee and smoothies too.

★**Hai's Coffee Van** COFFEE
(www.facebook.com/haicoffeevan/; 181 Wilson St; ◷5-9am Mon-Fri, to 10.30am Sat) Hai reliably parks her van in front of the Don Rhodes Mining Museum six mornings a week to dole out tasty caffeine hits in hot and cold forms.

ℹ Information

Port Hedland Visitor Centre (☑08-9173 1711; www.visitporthedland.com; 13 Wedge St; ◷9am-5pm Mon-Fri, to 2pm Sat; 🛜) This excellent centre sells books on travel and Aboriginal culture, publishes shipping times,

Karijini National Park

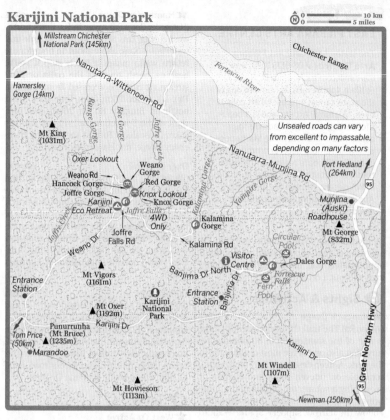

Millstream Chichester
National Park (145km)

Chichester Range

Fortescue River

Hamersley
Gorge (14km)

Nanutarra-Wittenoom Rd

Range Gorge

Bee Gorge

Mt King
(1031m)

Joffre Creek

Unsealed roads can vary
from excellent to impassable,
depending on many factors

Oxer Lookout

Weano
Gorge

Nanutarra-Munjina Rd

Port Hedland
(264km)

95

Weano Rd

Red Gorge

Hancock Gorge

Joffre Gorge

Knox Lookout

Knox Gorge

Kalamina Gorge

Yampire Gorge

Munjina
(Auski)
Roadhouse

Karijini
Eco Retreat

Joffre Falls

4WD
Only

Kalamina
Gorge

Mt George
(832m)

Joffre Creek

Joffre
Falls Rd

Kalamina Rd

Weano Dr

Visitor
Centre

Banjima Dr North

Circular
Pools

Dales Gorge

Entrance
Station

Mt Vigors
(1161m)

Karijini
National
Park

Entrance
Station

Banjima Dr

Fortescue
Falls

Fern
Pool

Mt Oxer
(1192m)

Karijini Dr

Tom Price
(50km)

Punurrunha
(Mt Bruce)
(1235m)

Marandoo

Karijini Dr

Mt Windell
(1107m)

Great Northern Hwy

95

Mt Howieson
(1113m)

Newman (150km)

arranges iron-ore plant tours, and helps with turtle monitoring (November to February). Aboriginal designs, stunning regional photos and iron ore are for sale. Salt mine tours are due to commence in late 2019.

❶ Getting There & Away

Port Hedland International Airport (www. porthedlandairport.com.au; Williamson Way) is about 12km south of town and has good connections. Virgin Australia and Qantas both fly to Perth several times daily, and Quntas also has a weekly direct flight to Brisbane. Virgin has handy weekend flights to Bali. Skippers Aviation (www.skippers.com.au) serves Karratha.

Integrity (☐1800 226 339; www.integrity coachlines.com.au; Wedge St) operates two weekly bus services from the visitor centre north to Broome ($129, 6½ hours). There are four services south to/from Perth ($274 to $293, 21½ to 28½ hours) taking various routes, coastal and inland. The quickest journey runs from Port Hedland on Thursdays via Newman and Meekatharra.

Karijini National Park

The 15 narrow, breathtaking gorges, hidden pools and spectacular waterfalls of the 6275-sq-km Karijini National Park (https:// parks.dpaw.wa.gov.au/park/karijini; admission per car $13) form one of WA's most impressive attractions. Nature lovers flock to this red slice of the Hamersley Range and its deep, dark chasms – the traditional lands of the Banyjima, Kurrama and Innawonga peoples – which is home to abundant wildlife and over 800 different plant species.

Kangaroos, snappy gums and wildflowers dot the spinifex plains, rock wallabies cling to sheer cliffs and endangered olive pythons lurk in giant figs above quiet pools. The park also contains WA's three highest peaks: Mt Meharry, Punurrunha (Mt Bruce) and Mt Frederick.

Summer temperatures reach extremes in the park (frequently over 40°C), so carry

WORTH A TRIP

EAST PILBARA ARTS CENTRE

The state-of-the-art **East Pilbara Arts Centre** (☑08-9175 1020; www.martumili.com.au; Newman Dr, Newman; ☉10am-4pm Mon-Fri) is home to one of the state's most successful art collectives, Martumili Artists, and is a beautiful setting in which to admire their acclaimed, vibrant art. The Martu people live in remote desert communities in the East Pilbara region, and are the traditional custodians of vast stretches of WA desert. For sale are authentic Aboriginal paintings, artefacts and woodcarvings.

plenty of water. Winter nights are cold. At any time of year, choose walks wisely, dress appropriately and never enter a restricted area without a certified guide.

◉ Sights & Activities

★ Hancock Gorge   GORGE
(Weano Rd) The trail through Hancock Gorge is one of the shortest (400, 80 minutes return) but also one of the most challenging in the park. A steep descent (partly on ladders), scramble on uneven rocks and fording or swimming a submerged section of the gorge brings you to the sunny **Amphitheatre**. Follow the narrow, slippery **Spider Walk** to sublime **Kermits Pool**.

★ Dales Gorge   GORGE
(Dales Rd; ⊞) From the Fortescue Falls car park, a trail descends steeply via a long staircase to stunning **Fortescue Falls** (the park's only permanent waterfall; about one hour return) and a photogenic swimming hole, behind which a leafy 300m stroll upstream reveals beautiful **Fern Pool**.

You can enjoy a 2km **gorge-rim trail** from the start of the Fortescue Falls track to Circular Pool lookout, with great views into Dales Gorge. The Circular Pool lookout is connected to Dales Campground by an easy walking trail.

★ Fern Pool   NATURAL POOL
(Jubura) Swim quietly and with respect at this lovely, shady pool – it has special significance to the local Aboriginal people. It's a 300m (roughly 10-minute) walk upstream from Fortescue Falls.

★ Hamersley Gorge   GORGE
(Hamersley Gorge Rd) Away in Karijini's northwest corner, this idyllic swimming hole and waterfall (400m; allow about an hour for the return walk) makes a lovely stop if you're heading north towards the coast or Millstream (it can't be accessed from Banjima Dr). It's about 67km from Tom Price: head north on Bingarn Rd for 26km, and turn right at the T-junction, carrying on another 41km (unsealed). Turn at the sign for Hamersley Gorge, not Hamersley Range.

Oxer Lookout   VIEWPOINT
(Weano Rd) The 13km drive (past the Karijini Eco Retreat) to the breathtaking Oxer Lookout is bumpy and unsealed, but it's worth it for the magnificent views of the junction of the Red, Weano, Joffre and Hancock gorges some 130m below. The lookout is a short walk from the car park. Nearby is the Junction Pool Lookout with views of Hancock Gorge.

Punurrunha   HIKING
(Mt Bruce; off Karijini Dr) Gorged out? Go and grab some altitude on WA's second-highest mountain (1235m), a superb ridge walk with fantastic views all the way to the summit. Start early, carry lots of water and allow six hours (9km return). The access road is off Karijini Dr, opposite Banjima Dr West.

⛯ Tours

★ West Oz Active
Adventure Tours   ADVENTURE
(☑0400 441 691; www.westozactive.com.au; Karijini Eco Retreat, Banjima Dr West; Joffre Gorge abseil $150; ☉Apr-Oct) Based at Karijini Eco Retreat, this highly regarded company offers action-packed day trips through the restricted gorges of the park and combines hiking, swimming, floating on inner tubes, climbing, sliding off waterfalls and abseiling. All equipment and lunch provided. The minimum age for tours is 14.

★ Flying Sandgroper   TOURS
(☑0438 913 713; www.flyingsandgroper.com.au; Karijini Eco Retreat, Weano Rd; 2-day Krijini package $425, 6-day Reef to Range tour $1265; ☉Apr-Oct) The Flying Sandgroper's aim is to overcome the huge distances and costs of visiting the northwest, so offers multiday tours that take in Karijini (and Ningaloo too), with the choice of bus-in bus-out and fly-in-fly-out packages, depending on your budget. It's affiliated with the excellent West Oz Active

Adventure Tours, and based at Karijini Eco Retreat.

🛏 Sleeping & Eating

Dales Gorge Campground   CAMPGROUND $
(Dales Rd; camping per adult/child $11/3) Though somewhat dusty, this large Parks & Wildlife Service campground offers shady, spacious sites with nearby toilets, gas barbecues and picnic tables. Forget tent pegs – you'll be using rocks as anchors. It's first come, first served (no bookings). The campground is 17km on sealed road from the eastern entrance station.

★ Karijini Eco Retreat   RESORT $$$
(📞 08-9425 5591; www.karijiniecoretreat.com. au; Weano Rd; camping per person $20, eco cabin $199, deluxe tent r $349; 🅿 ❄) 🍴 This 100% Aboriginal-owned retreat is a model for sustainable tourism, and the on-site **restaurant** (mains $18-39; ⊙ 7am-8pm) has fantastic food. The deluxe eco-tents have en suites; there are also cheaper tents, eco cabins with shared bathrooms, and camping spaces. Access is via the sealed Banjima Dr West, with the final 3km on Weano Rd unsealed. Campers get access to hot showers and drinking water.

❶ Information

Karijini Visitor Centre (📞 08-9189 8121; https://parks.dpaw.wa.gov.au/park/karijini; Banjima Dr North; ⊙ 9am-4pm mid-Feb–mid-Dec) Aboriginal managed with excellent interpretive displays highlighting Banyjima, Yinhawangka and Kurrama cultures, as well as displays on park wildlife, good maps and walks information, a public phone, cold drinks, books on wildlife and Aboriginal art for sale, and really great air-con. In a separate building are toilets, plus showers ($4).

It's accessed via sealed road, 10km from the eastern entrance.

❶ Getting There & Away

Bring your own vehicle or join a tour. Check out the excellent options from the Flying Sandgroper (p994) to make a visit more accessible.

The closest airports are Paraburdoo (101km) and Newman (201km).

Integrity (www.integritycoaches.com.au) operates a weekly bus service between Perth and Port Hedland along the coast, heading inland from Exmouth on Rte 136 and stopping at Paraburdoo and Tom Price, where you can pick up a tour to the park.

BROOME & THE KIMBERLEY

Australia's last frontier is a wild land of remote, spectacular scenery spread over huge distances, with a severe climate, a sparse population and minimal infrastructure. Larger than 75% of the world's countries, the Kimberley is hemmed by impenetrable coastline and unforgiving deserts. In between lie vast boab-studded spinifex plains, palm-fringed gorges, desolate mountains and magnificent waterfalls. Travelling here is an adventure and each dry season a steady flow of explorers search for the real outback along the legendary Gibb River Road.

Aboriginal culture runs deep across the region, from the Dampier Peninsula, where neat communities welcome travellers to Country, to distant Mitchell Plateau, where ancient Wandjina and Gwion Gwion stand vigil over sacred waterholes.

Swashbuckling Broome (home to iconic Cable Beach, camel-tinged sunsets and amber-hued watering holes) and practical Kununurra (with its irrigation miracle) bookend the region. Both are great places to unwind, find a job and meet other travellers.

❶ Getting There & Away

AIR

A number of airlines service Broome and the Kimberley:

Airnorth (📞 1800 627 474; www.airnorth.com. au) Broome and Kununurra to Darwin.

Qantas (📞 13 13 13; www.qantas.com.au) Broome to Perth daily and Broome to east-coast cities direct in season.

Skippers (p1003) Flies between Broome, Halls Creek and Fitzroy Crossing.

Virgin Australia (📞 13 67 89; www.virgin-australia.com) From Perth to Broome and Kununurra.

BUS

Integrity (📞 08-9274 7464; www.integritycoach lines.com.au) Perth to Broome twice a week.

Greyhound (p1003) Broome to Darwin daily (except Sunday).

Broome

📞 08 / POP 16,500

Like a paste jewel set in a tiara of natural splendour, Broome clings to a narrow strip of pindan (red-soil country) on the Kimberley's far-western edge, at the base of the

PERTH & WESTERN AUSTRALIA BROOME

The Kimberley

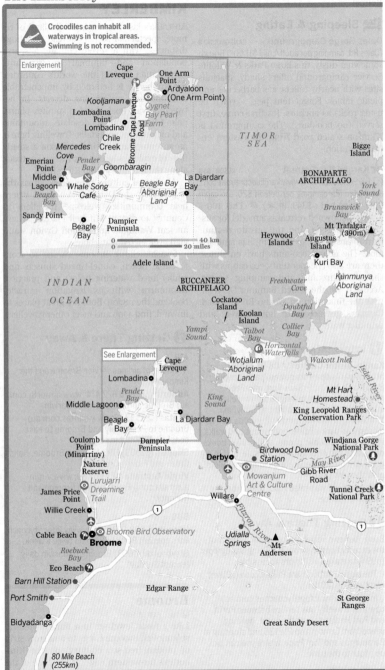

Crocodiles can inhabit all waterways in tropical areas. Swimming is not recommended.

Enlargement

Cape Leveque
One Arm Point
Ardyaloon (One Arm Point)
Kooljaman
Cygnet Bay Pearl Farm
Lombadina Point
Lombadina
Chile Creek
Mercedes Cove
Emeriau Point
Pender Bay
Goombaragin
Middle Lagoon
Whale Song Cafe
Beagle Bay Aboriginal Land
La Djadarr Bay
Sandy Point
Beagle Bay
Dampier Peninsula

0   40 km
0   20 miles

TIMOR SEA

Bigge Island

BONAPARTE ARCHIPELAGO

York Sound

Brunswick Bay

Mt Trafalgar (390m) ▲

Heywood Islands
Augustus Island

Kuri Bay

Kunmunya Aboriginal Land

Adele Island

INDIAN OCEAN

BUCCANEER ARCHIPELAGO

Freshwater Cove

Cockatoo Island
Koolan Island

Doubtful Bay

Yampi Sound

Talbot Bay

Collier Bay

Horizontal Waterfalls

Walcott Inlet

See Enlargement
Cape Leveque
Lombadina
Pender Bay
Middle Lagoon
Beagle Bay
La Djardarr Bay
Dampier Peninsula

King Sound

Wotjalum Aboriginal Land

Mt Hart Homestead

Isdell River

Coulomb Point (Minarriny)
Nature Reserve
Lurujarri Dreaming Trail
James Price Point
Willie Creek

Birdwood Downs Station

King Leopold Ranges Conservation Park

Windjana Gorge National Park

Derby
Mowanjum Art & Culture Centre
May River
Gibb River Road

Willare
Tunnel Creek National Park

Cable Beach
Broome Bird Observatory
Broome
Roebuck Bay
Eco Beach

Fitzroy River

Udialla Springs
Mt Andersen

Barn Hill Station

Port Smith

Edgar Range

St George Ranges

Bidyadanga

Great Sandy Desert

80 Mile Beach (255km)

0 ——— 100 km
0 ——— 50 miles

TIMOR SEA

Cape Londonderry

Cape Bougainville

Napier Broome Bay

Faraway Bay

King George Falls

Honeymoon Bay

Kalumburu Aboriginal Land

Cape Voltaire

Admiralty Gulf

Cape Bougainville Aboriginal Land

Berkeley River Lodge

Port Warrender

Kalumburu

Joseph Bonaparte Gulf

Walsh Point

Oombulgurri Aboriginal Land

King George River

Cambridge Gulf

Surveyor's Pool

Kimberley Coastal Camp

Mitchell Falls

Ngauwudu (Mitchell Plateau)

Munurru

Berkeley River

Mitchell River National Park

Kalumburu Road

Carson River

Drysdale River National Park

Mitchell River

Cockburn Ranges

Parry Lagoons Nature Reserve

Prince Regent Nature Reserve

King Edward River

Miner's Pool

Pentecost River

Wyndham

Ord River

King Cascades

Mirima National Park

Prince Regent River

Drysdale River

Gibb River

Home Valley Station

Ellenbrae Station

Emma Gorge

Kununurra

Argyle Homestead

Drysdale River Station

Chamberlain Gorge

Wuggubun

The Kimberley

El Questro Wilderness Park

Lake Argyle Tourist Village

Synnot Range

Mt Elizabeth Station

Zebedee Springs

Lake Argyle

Durack River

Doon Doon

Gibb River Road

Barnett River Gorge

Charnley River Station

Chamberlain River

Wilson River

Durack Range

Argyle Diamond Mine

Mt Barnett Roadhouse & Manning River Gorge

Galvans Gorge

Warmun

Bell Gorge

Adcock Gorge

Violet Hill Aboriginal Land

Hann River

Adcock River

Imintji Store

Purnululu National Park

Mt Ord (937m)

Bedford Downs

Lennard River Gorge

King Leopold Range

Mornington Wilderness Camp

Fitzroy River

Ord River

Ord River

Leopold Downs

Oscar Range

Fitzroy River

O'Donnell River

Mueller Range

Geikie Gorge National Park

Leopold River

Eitrie River

Fitzroy Crossing

Halls Creek

Margaret River

Mt Amhurst

Duncan Rd

Mimbi Caves

Yackanarra

Sawpit Gorge

Start Creek

Tanami Rd

Wangkatjungka

Yiyili

Kundat Djaru

Larrawa Station

Christmas Creek

Billiluna (40km); Canning Stock Route (40km);
Balgo (140km); Yuendumu (NT; 620km);
Alice Springs (NT; 910km)

Wolfe Creek Crater National Park

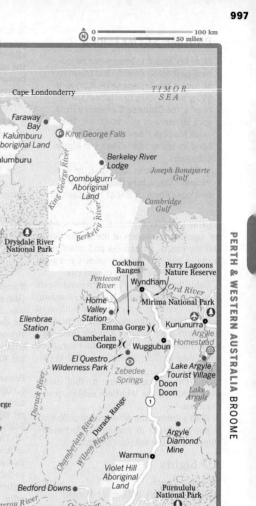

BROOME'S CEMETERIES

Mute testament to Broome's multicultural past are its cemeteries. The most striking is the **Japanese** (Port Dr) with 919 graves (mostly pearl divers) while nearby, the **Chinese Cemetery** (Frederick St) contains over 90 tombs. The small **Muslim Cemetery** (Frederick St) honours Malay pearl-divers and Afghan cameleers.

A few kilometres southeast, the small **Pioneer Cemetery** (Map p1000; P) overlooks Roebuck Bay at Town Beach.

pristine Dampier Peninsula. Surrounded by the aquamarine waters of the Indian Ocean and the creeks, mangroves and mudflats of Roebuck Bay, this Yawuru country is a good 2000km from the nearest capital city.

Cable Beach, with its luxury resorts, hauls in the tourists during high (dry) season (April to October), with romantic notions of camels, surf and sunsets. Magnificent, sure, but there's a lot more to Broome than postcards, and tourists are sometimes surprised when they scratch the surface and find pindan just below.

The Dry is a great time to find casual work, while in the Wet (low season) prices plummet.

Each evening, the whole town collectively pauses, drinks in mid-air, while the sun slinks slowly towards Madagascar.

⊙ Sights

★ Cable Beach   BEACH
(Map p1004; P🐪) WA's most famous landmark offers turquoise waters and beautiful white sand curving away to the sunset. Clothing is optional north of the rocks, while south, walking trails lead through the red dunes of **Minyirr Park**, a spiritual place for the Yawuru people. Cable Beach is synonymous with camels and an evening ride along the sand is a highlight for many visitors. Locals in their 4WDs swarm north of the rocks for sunset drinks. Stingers are common in the Wet.

Gantheaume Point
& Dinosaur Prints   VIEWPOINT
(P🐪) Beautiful at dawn or sunset when the pindan cliffs turn scarlet and the Indian Ocean brilliant turquoise, this peaceful lookout holds a 135-million-year-old secret.

Nearby lies one of the world's most varied collections of dinosaur footprints, impossible to find except at very low tides. Grab the map from the visitor centre (p1003) and beware of slippery rocks. Look out for the ospreys returning with fish to their nests on the lighthouse.

Sun Pictures   HISTORIC BUILDING
(Map p1000; ☑08-9192 1077; www.sunpictures. com.au; 27 Carnarvon St; movies adult/child $17.50/12.50, history tour $5; ⊘hours vary; 🐪) Sink back in a canvas deck chair under the stars in the world's oldest operating picture gardens, dating from 1916. The history of the Sun building is the history of Broome itself; having witnessed war, floods, low-flying aircraft (it's still on the airport flight path) and racial segregation. A short 15-minute history tour runs on request during the Dry (ring first).

Bungalow   GALLERY
(Map p1000; ☑08-9192 6118; www.shortstgallery. com; 3 Hopton St, Town Beach; ⊘10am-3pm Mon-Sat, shorter hours wet season) Short St Gallery's Hopton St stock room at Town Beach holds a stunning collection of canvases from across the Kimberley and beyond.

Broome Bird Observatory   NATURE RESERVE
(☑08-9193 5600; www.broomebirdobservatory. com; Crab Creek Rd; by donation, campsites per person $18, unit with shared bathroom s/d/f $45/60/85, chalets $140; ⊘8am-4pm; P🐪) 🕭 The RAMSAR-recognised tidal mudflats of Roebuck Bay are a vital staging post for thousands of migratory birds, coming from as far away as Siberia. In a peaceful coastal setting 25km from Broome, the 'Bird Obbie' offers quiet walking trails, secluded bush campsites and a choice of low-key rooms. There's a number of tours ($70, 2½ hours) and courses ($1400, five days) available as well as volunteering opportunities. Hardcore twitchers shouldn't miss the daily 6pm bird count.

WWII Flying Boat Wrecks   HISTORIC SITE
FREE On a very low tide (<1.3m) it's possible to walk out across the mudflats from **Town Beach** (Map p1000; P🐪) to the wrecks of Catalina and Dornier flying boats attacked by Japanese 'Zeroes' during WWII. The planes had been evacuating refugees from Java and many still had passengers aboard. Over 60 people and 15 flying boats (mostly Dutch and British) were lost. Only six wrecks are visible, with the rest in deep water.

Broome Museum
MUSEUM

(Map p1000; 08-9192 2075; www.broome museum.org.au; 67 Robinson St; adult/child $12/8; 10am-4pm Mon-Fri, to 1pm Sat & Sun dry season, to 1pm daily wet season; P) Discover Cable Beach and Chinatown's origins through exhibits devoted to the area's pearling history and WWII bombing in this quirky museum, occupying the former Customs House.

🏃 Activities

Odyssey Expeditions
DIVING

(0428 382 505; www.odysseyexpeditions.com. au; 8-day tour from $3800; Sep-Oct) Runs several eight-day, live-aboard diving tours from Broome each spring to the Rowley Shoals Marine Park. You need to be an experienced diver with your own gear (though some gear may be hired in Broome).

Turtle Monitoring
WILDLIFE

(08-9195 5500; www.roebuckbay.org.au/volun teer-activities/turtle-monitoring; Cable Beach; Nov-Feb;) Stuck in Broome over the Wet? Volunteers walk 4km along Cable Beach in the morning and record the previous night's turtle activity. Free training provided.

Fat Bike
CYCLING

(Map p1004; 0419 895 367; www.broomefat bikes.com.au; Cable Beach; 90min ride adult/child $69/55; sunset Mar-Nov) Camels passé? Ride off into the blazing Cable Beach sunset on these fat puppies from the Broome Adventure folks.

👉 Tours

Camel-riding tours along Cable Beach are a hit with the kids:

Broome Camel Safaris
(Map p1004; 0419 916 101; www.broomecamelsafaris.com.au; adult/child morning $65/45, afternoon $40/30, sunset $90/70;)

Red Sun Camels
(Map p1004; 1800 184 488; www.redsuncamels.com.au; adult/child morning $70/50, afternoon $45/30, sunset $95/70)

Sundowner Camel Tours
(Map p1004; 0477 774 297; www.sundownercameltours.com; adult/child afternoon $45/30, sunset $90/60)

⭐ Lurujarri Dreaming Trail
WALKING

(Frans 0423 817 925; www.goolarabooloo.org. au; adult/student $1600/900; hours vary May-Aug;) This incredible 82km walk follows a section of ancient songline north along

PERTH & WESTERN AUSTRALIA BROOME

DON'T MISS

STAIRCASE TO THE MOON

The reflections of a rising full moon rippling over exposed mudflats at low tide create the optical illusion of a golden stairway (www.broomemarkets.com.au/ markets; Town Beach; Apr-Oct;) leading to the moon. Between April and October Broome buzzes around the full moon, with everyone eager to see the spectacle. At Town Beach there's a lively evening market (Map p1000; www.broomemarkets. com.au/markets; full moon Apr-Oct, Thu evenings Jun-Sep;) with food stalls and people bring fold-up chairs, although the small headland at the end of Hamersley St has a better view.

While Roebuck Bay parties like nowhere else, this phenomenon happens across the Kimberley and Pilbara coasts – anywhere with some east-facing mudflats. Other good viewing spots are One Arm Point at Cape Leveque, Cooke Point in Port Hedland, Sunrise Beach at Onslow, Hearson Cove near Dampier and the lookout at Cossack. Most visitor centres publish the dates on their websites.

the coast from Gantheaume Point (Minyirr) to Coulomb Point (Minarriny). The Goolarabooloo organise several guided nine-day walking trips each dry season, staying at traditional campsites. There is a strong emphasis on sharing Aboriginal culture with activities like spear-making, bush-tucker hunting, fishing, mud-crabbing and jewellery making.

⭐ Jetty to Jetty
WALKING

(Map p1000; www.yawuru.com;) This self-guided walking tour from the local Yawuru people comes with a fantastic audio accompaniment (download the free Jetty to Jetty smartphone app), taking you past 13 points of historical and cultural significance between Chinatown's Streeter's Jetty and the Old Jetty at Town Beach. The 2.8km walk (with stops) should take around two hours.

⭐ Astro Tours
TOURS

(0417 949 958; www.astrotours.net; adult/child $95/75; Apr-Oct) Fascinating after-dark two-hour stargazing tours held by the entertaining and (incredibly!) self-taught Greg Quicke, at a 'dark site' 20 minutes from

Broome

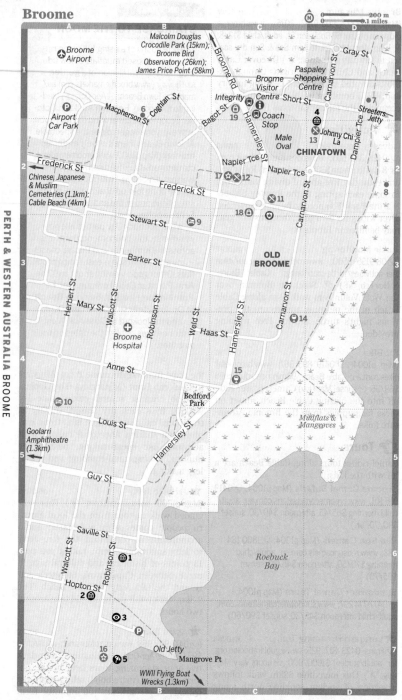

Broome Airport

Malcolm Douglas
Crocodile Park (15km);
Broome Bird
Observatory (26km);
James Price Point (58km)

Gray St

Paspaley
Shopping
Centre

Carnarvon St

Streeters
Jetty

Airport Car Park

Macpherson St

Coghlan St

Bagot St

Broome Visitor Centre

Integrity

Short St

19

Coach Stop

Hamersley St

Male Oval

Johnny Chi La

13

CHINATOWN

Dampier Tce

Frederick St

Chinese, Japanese
& Muslim
Cemeteries (1.1km);
Cable Beach (4km)

Frederick St

Napier Tce

17

12

Napier Tce

Carnarvon St

8

11

18

Stewart St

9

OLD BROOME

Barker St

Herbert St

Mary St

Walcott St

Robinson St

Weld St

Haas St

Hamersley St

Carnarvon St

14

Broome Hospital

Anne St

15

Louis St

10

Bedford Park

Mudflats &
Mangroves

Goolarri
Amphitheatre
(1.3km)

Guy St

Hamersley St

Saville St

Robinson St

1

Hopton St

2

3

Roebuck Bay

Walcott St

16

5

Old Jetty

Mangrove Pt

WWII Flying Boat
Wrecks (1.3km)

PERTH & WESTERN AUSTRALIA BROOME

Broome

⊙ Sights
1 Broome Museum B6
2 Bungalow...A6
3 Pioneer Cemetery B7
4 Sun Pictures D2
5 Town Beach B7

⊙ Activities, Courses & Tours
6 Broome Aviation......................................B1
7 Jetty to Jetty...D1
8 Narlijia Cultural Tours...........................D2

⊜ Sleeping
9 Broome Town B&B B3
10 McAlpine House A4

⊗ Eating
11 Aarli..C2
12 Good Cartel C2
13 Green Mango...D2

⊙ Drinking & Nightlife
14 Bay Club...C4
15 Matso's Broome Brewery.....................C4

⊙ Entertainment
16 Town Beach Night Markets...................A7
17 Twin Cinema...C2

⊙ Shopping
18 Courthouse Markets C2
19 Magabala Books C1

Broome. Book online early as the tours are extremely popular. Self-drive and save $20.

Narlijia Cultural Tours　　　CULTURAL
(Map p1000; ☑08-9195 0232; www.toursbroome. com.au; Chinatown; adult/child mangroves $75/35, history $55/25, Minyirr $95/65; ☺May–mid-Oct; ⊕) Yawuru local Bart Pigram runs short (two to three hour) informative cultural tours around the mangroves and historical buildings of Chinatown and Minyirr.

Broome Adventure Company　　KAYAKING
(☑0419 895 367; www.broomeadventure.com.au; 3hr trip adult/child $85/65; ☺Mar–Dec; ⊕) ⦿ Glide past turtles, hidden beaches and sea caves on these eco-certified coastal kayaking trips.

Broome Aviation　　　SCENIC FLIGHTS
(Map p1000; ☑08-91921369; www.broomeaviation. com.au; Unit 1, 2 Macpherson St; half/full-day flights from $645/1180) Half-day flights to Cape Leveque and the Horizontal Falls (p1007) from Broome. Full-day tours add-on the Devonian Reef National Parks, Bell Gorge (p1009) and Mt Hart, Mitchell Falls or even the Bungle Bungles ($1620).

Broome Historical
Walking Tours　　　WALKING
(☑0408 541 102; www.broomehistoricalwalking tours.com; adult/child $50/30; ☺twice daily Mon-Fri Apr-Nov (minimum 2 people)) This fabulous 1½-hour walking tour examines the Broome of yesteryear through site visits and photographs – from WWII back to the pearling days – with raconteur Wil telling some fabulous stories. The tour price includes admission to Broome Museum (p999). Wil also guides walks out to the flying boats on appropriate low tides (adult/child $55/45).

Hovercraft Tours　　　TOURS
(☑08-9193 5025; www.broomehovercraft.com.au; Port Drive; adult/child dinosaur $136/96, sunset $196/124, flying boats $196/124) Skim over tidal flats to visit historical sights, dinosaur footprints and, on low tides, the wrecks of flying boats (p998) sunk during WWII. The sunset tour has complimentary sparkling wine.

★★ Festivals & Events

Sea Grass Monitoring　　ENVIRONMENTAL
(☑08-9192 1922; www.environskimberley.org.au/ seagrass_project; Roebuck Bay; ☺hours vary; ⊕) ⦿ Every three months or so volunteers walk out onto the mudflats of Roebuck Bay to monitor the sea grass that marine creatures such as dugongs and turtles depend on. All are welcome and no experience is necessary. Bring a hat, water bottle and closed shoes.

Kullarri Naidoc Week　　　CULTURAL
(www.goolarri.com; ☺late Jun–mid-Jul) Celebration of Aboriginal and Torres Strait Islander culture.

A Taste of Broome　　PERFORMING ARTS
(☑08-9195 5333; www.goolarri.com; Goolarri Amphitheatre, Blackman St, Old Broome; general/VIP $35/70; ☺Jul-Sep; ⊕) Indigenous flavours, dance and music caress the senses at this ticket-only event held monthly from July to September. VIP tickets include premium seating and a tasting platter.

Shinju Matsuri

Festival of the Pearl CULTURAL
(www.shinjumatsuri.com.au; ⊙Aug/Sep;) Broome's homage to the pearl includes a week of parades, food, art, concerts, fireworks and dragon-boat races.

Mango Festival FOOD & DRINK
(www.facebook.com/broomemangofestival; ⊙last weekend Nov) Three days of mango madness in late November, including quizzes, music, alcoholic beverages and anything else vaguely fruit related.

🛏 Sleeping

⭐**Beaches of Broome** HOSTEL $
(Map p1004; ☑1300 881 031; www.beachesof broome.com.au; 4 Sanctuary Rd, Cable Beach; dm $32-45, motel d without/with bathroom $145/185; P❄@🛜🏊) More resort than hostel, its spotless, air-conditioned rooms are complemented by shady common areas, a poolside bar and a modern self-catering kitchen. Dorms come in a variety of sizes (and include female-only rooms) and the motel rooms are beautifully appointed. Both the continental breakfast and wi-fi are free. Scooter and bike hire available.

Tarangau Caravan Park CARAVAN PARK $
(☑08-9193 5084; www.tarangaucaravanpark.com; 16 Millington Rd, Cable Beach; unpowered/powered sites $40/50; ⊙office 8.30am-5pm; P🏊) A quieter alternative to the often noisy Cable Beach caravan parks, Tarangau has pleasant, grassy sites 1km from the beach.

⭐**McAlpine House** B&B $$$
(Map p1000; ☑08-9192 0588; www.mcalpine house.com.au; 55 Herbert St; d $185-485; P❄🛜🏊) Lord McAlpine made this stunning house, a former pearl master's lodge, his Broome residence during the '80s. Now renovated to its former glory, there are lovely airy rooms, open communal areas, shady tropical verandahs and a lush canopy of mango trees, tamarind and frangipanis. Escape from the heat by the pool, or travel back through time in the library.

Bali Hai Resort & Spa SPA HOTEL $$$
(Map p1004; ☑08-9191 3100, cafe 08-9191 3160; www.balihairesort.com; 6 Murray Rd, Cable Beach; r from $338; ⊙cafe 5.30pm-late Wed-Sun, breakfast 8-11am Sat & Sun; P❄🛜🏊) Lush and tranquil, this beautiful small resort has gorgeously decorated studios and villas, each with individual outside dining areas and open-roofed bathrooms. The emphasis is on

relaxation and the on-site spa offers a range of exotic therapies. There's also an Asian-themed cafe (mains $29 to $42) showcasing fresh WA produce. The off-season prices are a bargain.

Broome Town B&B B&B $$$
(Map p1000; ☑08-9192 2006; www.broome town.com.au; 15 Stewart St, Old Broome; r $285; P❄🛜🏊) This delightful, boutique-style B&B epitomises Broome-style architecture, with high-pitched roofs, wooden louvres, jarrah floors, tasteful rooms, an open communal guest lounge and lots of tropical shade.

🍴 Eating

Cable Beach General Store & Cafe CAFE $
(Map p1004; ☑08-9192 5572; www.cablebeach-store.com.au; cnr Cable Beach & Murray Rds; burgers $11-17; ⊙6am-8pm; 🛜) Cable Beach unplugged – a typical Aussie corner shop with egg breakfasts, barramundi burgers, pies, internet and no hidden charges. You can even play a round of minigolf (adult/child/family $8/6/20).

⭐**Good Cartel** CAFE $$
(Map p1000; ☑0499 335 949; 3 Weld St; breakfast $7-25, burgers $12.50-20; ⊙5am-2pm; 🅿🛜🏊) 📍 *The* hippest place in town to grab a great coffee, healthy juice and Mexican-themed brekkies. Locals queue for their fabled lunchtime burgers. Follow the line of cars behind the **Twin Cinema** (Map p1000; ☑08-9192 3199; www.broomemovies.com.au; 3 Weld St; adult/child/family $17.50/12.50/55; ⊙10am-midnight or end of last movie;) in the business park. Doggies more than welcome as the cafe is active in rehabilitating strays. Find them on Facebook (search for Good Cartel Broome).

⭐**Aarli** TAPAS $$
(Map p1000; ☑08-9192 5529; www.theaarli.com.au; 6 Hamersley St, enter via Frederick St; share plates $14-22, mains $20-38, breakfast $13-21; ⊙8am-late; 🅿) Ask any Broome local where they love eating and most will say the Aarli, with its wonderful outdoor relaxed dining and the share plates that Broome does so well. Drop in for some quick tapas (Med–Asian fusion) or a main meal, or while away the afternoon working through the excellent wine list. Also open for breakfast (8am to noon).

Green Mango CAFE $$
(Map p1000; ☑08-9192 5512; http://greenmango broome.com/; Shop 2/12 Carnarvon St, Chinatown;

breakfast $14-25, lunch $11-23; ☺kitchen 7am-2pm; 🚼♿) This great healthy brunch choice in Broome's Chinatown has a wide selection of juices, smoothies and salads, as well as more traditional breakfast fare.

Wharf Restaurant SEAFOOD $$$
(☑08-9192 5800; www.facebook.com/thewharf restaurantbroome; 401 Port Dr, Port; mains $36-120; ☺11am-late) Settle back for a long, lazy seafood lunch with waterside ambience and the chance of a whale sighting. OK, it's pricey and the service fluctuates, but the wine's cold, the sea stunning and the chilli crab and barramundi wings both sensational. Just wait until after 2pm to order oysters (when they become half-price).

🍷 Drinking & Nightlife

Bay Club BAR
(Mangrove Hotel; Map p1000; ☑08-9192 1303; www.mangrovehotel.com.au; 47 Carnarvon St; mains $17-39; ☺11am-10pm; ♿) The Mangrove Hotel's casual outdoor bar is perfect for a few early bevvies while contemplating Roebuck Bay. Sophisticated, healthy bistro meals and live music complement excellent Staircase to the Moon (p999) viewing. On Sundays, parents can drop their kids at the bouncing castle.

Matso's Broome Brewery PUB
(Map p1000; ☑08-9193 5811; www.matsos.com. au; 60 Hamersley St; share plates $8-36, mains $23-38; ☺7am-midnight; ♿) Get yourself a Chango (50/50 chilli/mango beer) and a half-kilo bucket of prawns then kick back to the lazy afternoon music on the shady verandah at Broome's finest brewery.

🛍 Shopping

Magabala Books BOOKS
(Map p1000; ☑08-9192 1991; www.magabala.com; 1 Bagot St; ☺9am-4.30pm Mon-Fri; ♿) Brilliant Indigenous publishers showcasing Kimberley storytelling with a selection of novels, social history books, biographies and children's literature.

Courthouse Markets MARKET
(Map p1000; www.broomemarkets.com.au; Hamersley St; ☺8am-1pm Sat year-round, Sun Apr-Oct; ♿) Local arts, crafts, music, hawker food and general hippy gear.

ℹ Information

Broome Visitor Centre (Map p1000; ☑08-9195 2200; www.visitbroome.com.au;

1 Hamersley St; ☺8.30am-4.30pm Mon-Sat, to 3pm Sun, shorter hours during wet season) Great for info on road conditions, Staircase to the Moon (p999) viewing, dinosaur footprints (p998), WWII wrecks (p998), tide times and souvenirs. Books accommodation and tours for businesses registered with it and is also the long-haul coach stop. It's on the roundabout entering town, opposite Male Oval.

ℹ Getting There & Away

Unless you're on a road trip, the easiest way into Broome is by air. **Broome Airport** (Map p1000; ☑08-9194 0600; www.broomeair.com.au; Macpherson St) is centrally located and serviced by **Qantas** (☑13 13 13; www.qantas.com.au), **Skippers** (☑1300 729 924; www.skippers.com. au), **Virgin** (☑13 67 89; www.virginaustralia. com) and **Airnorth** (☑08-8920 4001; www. airnorth.com.au). A **shuttle** (Airport Shuttle; ☑08-9192 5252; www.broometaxis.com; Broome/Cable Beach hotels $10/15) service meets flights and drops off passengers at most Broome hotels and Cable Beach resorts.

Long-distance **Integrity** (Map p1000; ☑08-9274 7464; www.integritycoachlines.com.au; Visitor Centre) coaches run to Perth and **Greyhound** (☑1300 473 946; www.greyhound.com. au) to Darwin, while a local bus (p1007) services Derby. All services arrive/depart from the **coach stop** (Map p1000) outside the visitor centre.

ℹ Getting Around

Most hostels will rent out bicycles and scooters.
Town Bus Service (☑08-9193 6585; www. broomebus.com.au; adult $4, 24hr pass $15; ☺7.23am-6.23pm dry season, 8.53am-5.53pm Mon-Sat, from 10.53am Sun wet season; ♿) links Town Beach, Chinatown and Cable Beach every 30 minutes during the Dry and every hour during the Wet.

Broome Broome (☑08-9192 2210; www. broomebroome.com.au; 3/15 Napier Tce; scooter/car/4WD per day from $35/75/185) is the only rental car company prepared to offer unlimited kilometres. Scooter hire is $35 per day.

Broome Cycles (☑08-9192 1871; www.broome cycles.com.au; 2 Hamersley St; day/week mountain bikes $30/100, fat bikes $60/400, deposit $150; ☺8.30am-5pm Mon-Fri, to 2pm Sat) hires mountain bikes out by the day ($30) or week ($100) from Chinatown and from a trailer at **Cable Beach** (☑0409 192 289; www. broomecycles.com.au; cnr Cable Beach & Sanctuary Rds, Cable Beach; ☺9am-noon May-Oct) in season.

For a taxi, try **Broome Taxis** (☑13 10 08), **Chinatown Taxis** (☑1800 811 772) or **Pearl Town Taxis** (☑13 13 30).

Cable Beach

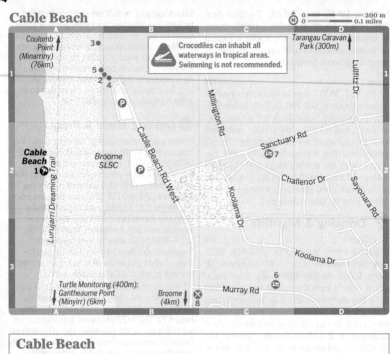

Crocodiles can inhabit all waterways in tropical areas. Swimming is not recommended.

Cable Beach

⊙ Top Sights
1 Cable Beach...A2

⊕ Activities, Courses & Tours
2 Broome Camel Safaris..........................B1
3 Fat Bike...A1
4 Red Sun Camels....................................B1
5 Sundowner Camel Tours.....................A1

⊟ Sleeping
6 Bali Hai Resort & Spa...........................C3
7 Beaches of Broome..............................C2

⊗ Eating
8 Cable Beach General Store & Cafe.....B3

Dampier Peninsula

Stretching north from Broome, the pindan (red-soil country) of the Dampier Peninsula ends abruptly above deserted beaches, secluded mangrove bays and cliffs burnished crimson by the setting sun. This remote and stunning Country is home to thriving Indigenous settlements of the Ngumbarl, Jabirr Jabirr, Nyul Nyul, Nimanburu, Bardi Jawi and Goolarabooloo peoples. Access is via the rough, 215km-long Cape Leveque Rd.

Always book ahead when visiting Aboriginal communities, ideally directly with the community hosts, though the Broome Visitor Centre (p1003) may help; check if permits and/or payments are required. Look for the informative booklet *Ardi–Dampier Peninsula Travellers Guide* ($5). You need to be self-sufficient, though limited supplies are available.

⊙ Sights

Pender Bay BAY

Exquisitely remote, this pristine bay is an important calving ground for humpback whales and many can be seen offshore from May to November. The easiest access is from either **Whale Song Cafe** (☑08-9192 4000; www.whalesongcafe.com.au; Munget, Pender Bay; light meals $13-29, campsites adult/child $20/10; ⊙8.30am-4pm Jun-Aug; ☑🖶) 🖋, if open, or via the small **Pender Bay campground** (☑0429 845 707; www.facebook.com/penderbayescape; Pender Bay; day use/campsites per person $10/15; 🖾) (between Mercedes Cove and Whale Song), where clifftop vantage points provide exceptional viewing. Simple bush campsites (and an amenity block) are available.

★ James Price Point BEACH

(Walmadan; Manari Rd; P) FREE The striking red pindan cliffs of Walmadan (named for the proud warrior who once lived here) are worth a visit even if you're not camping; they're 35km from Cape Leveque Rd. Right in the middle of the Lurujarri Songline, this important cultural site of the Goolarabooloo people has been the scene of past environmental protests. Bush campsites (three-night maximum) sit on the bluff overlooking the stunning cliffs and mesmerising Indian Ocean.

Cape Leveque (Kooljaman) BEACH

(day access per person $10; 🚻) Spectacular Cape Leveque, right on the tip of the Dampier Peninsula, has stunning red cliffs and gorgeous white beaches perfect for swimming and snorkelling. Access is via **Kooljaman** (☑ 08-9192 4970; www.kooljaman.com.au; entry per adult $10, unpowered/powered sites $50/55, dome tents $90, beach shelters $120, cabin with/without bathroom $200/170, safari tents from $310; P 🚻) resort, where there are plenty of accommodation options.

Beagle Bay Church CHURCH

(☑ 08-9192 4913; by donation; P 🚻) Around 110km from Broome, Beagle Bay is notable for the extraordinarily beautiful mother-of-pearl altar at Beagle Bay church, built by Pallottine monks in 1918. Fuel is available at the community shop (weekdays only).

Lombadina ABORIGINAL COMMUNITY

(☑ 08-9192 4936; www.lombadina.com; entry per car $10, campsites $50, s/d/cabin $100/170/220; ☺ office 8am-noon & 1-4pm Mon-Fri; P 🚻) Between Middle Lagoon and Cape Leveque, Lombadina is 200km from Broome. This beautiful tree-fringed Aboriginal community offers various tours (minimum three people), including fishing, whale watching, 4WD, mud-crabbing, kayaking and walking, which can be booked through the office. Accommodation is in backpacker-style rooms (one to five people) and self-contained cabins (maximum four people) or unpowered bush campsites. Fuel is available on weekdays and there are lovely artworks for sale at the Arts Centre (open weekdays). Don't miss the paperbark church.

☞ Tours

Cape Leveque Tour BUS

(Broome Transit; ☑ 08-9192 5252; www.broometransittours.com.au; $240) This full-day tour of Cape Leveque takes in Beagle Bay, Koolja-man, Cygnet Bay, Ardyaloon and Gumbanan. Tours pick up from Broome accommodation around 6am, returning by 7pm.

Ngarlan Yarnin' HISTORY

(☑ 0438 118 578; Beagle Bay; 2 people/family $25/40; ☺ tours 9am, 10.30am, noon, 1.50pm & 5pm Mon-Sat) Mena Lewis, a local Nyul Nyul and Bardi woman, holds fascinating one-hour storytellings on the history of the Sacred Heart Church, Beagle Bay and the community itself. Cash only.

Brian Lee Tagalong Tours TOURS

(☑ 08-9192 4970; www.brianleetagalong.com.au; Kooljaman; adult/child $98/45) Tag along (in your own 4WD) with Bardi traditional owner Brian Lee as he reveals the culture and history surrounding Hunters Creek, where you'll get a chance to fish and hunt for mud crabs.

🛏 Sleeping

Quandong Point CAMPGROUND $

(Kardilakan; Manari Rd; campsites free; 🐾 🐾) Various spread-out bush campsites on the Lurujarri Songline look down at a pristine beach. Maximum three-night stay. Located 22km from the Cape Leveque Rd junction.

Gumbanan CAMPGROUND $

(☑ 0499 330 169; www.gumbananwilderness retreat.com.au; near One Arm Point; campsites per person $15, safari tent d/f $120/140; P 🐾) On a beautifully unspoiled mangrove coast, this small outstation between Cape Leveque and **Ardyaloon** (Bardi; ☑ 08-9192 4930; per person $15, child free; ☺ office 8am-noon & 1.30-4pm Mon-Thu, 8am-noon & 1.30-3pm Fri) offers quiet, unpowered sites and simple safari tents. Immerse yourself in traditional Bardi culture with spear-making ($85), mud-crabbing ($95) or damper (camp bread) making ($40) courses.

★ Goombaragin
Eco Retreat RESORT $$

(☑ 0429 505 347; www.goombaragin.com.au; Pender Bay; campsites per person $18, tent with/without bathroom $175/80, chalets $220; ☺ Apr-Oct; P 🐾 🐾 🐾) 🍴 With a superb location overlooking the scarlet pindan cliffs and turquoise waters of Pender Bay, this eco-retreat offers several unpowered campsites, a range of safari tents and a self-contained chalet. There's a nightly communal get-together around the fire and regular pizza nights.

Mercedes Cove
CABIN $$

(☑08-9192 4687; www.mercedescove.com.au; Pender Bay; eco-tents/cabins $150/300; ⊗Apr-Sep; 🌢🛜🐾) 🏊 On a stunning, secluded cove near **Middle Lagoon** (Nature's Hideaway; ☑08-9192 4002; www.middlelagoon.com. au; campsites per person $20-22, cabins $150-300, day use $10; 🅿🛜), Mercedes offers a chilled glamping experience with beautifully appointed eco-tents and air-con cabins, all with amazing Indian Ocean views. It's the perfect spot for whale watching, beach-combing, fishing and birdwatching. A minimum stay (two/three nights) applies for weekends/long weekends.

❶ Getting There & Away

There is currently no public transport to the Dampier Peninsula, though check with Broome Visitor Centre (p1003) for the latest update. Otherwise, without your own wheels (high-clearance 4WD) you'll have to take a tour.

Derby
☑08 / POP 3600

Late at night while Derby (dur-bee) sleeps, the boabs cut loose and wander around town, the marauding mobs flailing their many limbs in battle against an army of giant, killer croc-people emerging from the encircling mudflats... If only.

There *are* crocs hiding in the mangroves, but you're more likely to see birds, over 200 varieties, while the boabs are firmly rooted along the two main parallel drags, Loch and Clarendon Sts. Derby, sitting on **King Sound**, is the West Kimberley's administrative centre and home to various Indigenous groups (eg Nykina, Dambimangari, Worrorra, Wunumbal) who comprise 50% of the population. Tours depart here for the Horizontal Waterfalls (p1007) and Buccaneer Archipelago, and it's also the western terminus of the Gibb River Road (p1008).

⊙ Sights

★ Norval Gallery
GALLERY

(☑0458 110 816; www.facebook.com/norvalgallery derby; 1 Sutherland St; ⊗hours vary) Kimberley art legends Mark and Mary Norval have set up an exciting gallery in an old tin shed on the edge of town. Featuring striking artworks, exquisite jewellery, decent coffee and 5000 vinyl records, a visit here is a delight to the senses. Note they may be moving to the other end of town in the near future.

Jetty
LANDMARK

(Jetty Rd; 🅿) Check out King Sound's colossal 11.5m tides from the circular jetty, 2km northwest of town, a popular fishing, crabbing, bird-spotting and staring-in-to-the-sunset haunt. Yep, there are crocs in the mangroves.

☞ Tours

★ Horizontal Falls
Seaplane Adventures
SCENIC FLIGHTS

(☑08-9192 1172; www.horizontalfallsadventures. com.au; 6hr tours from Derby/Broome $775/850) Flights to Horizontal Waterfalls (p1007) land on Talbot Bay before transferring to high-powered speedboats for an adrenaline-packed ride through both sets of falls. There's also an overnight-stay option (ex-Derby) from $895.

Kimberley Dreamtime
Adventure Tours
CULTURAL

(☑08-9191 7280; www.kdatjarlmadangah.word press.com; adult/child 2 days from $492/350, 3 days from $710/565; ⊗Apr-Oct) Aboriginal-owned and -operated cultural tours based in Nyikina Mangala country on Mt Anderson Station, 126km southeast of Derby. Camp under the stars, ride camels, fish, hunt, walk and learn about Aboriginal culture. Pick-ups from Broome, Willare or Derby.

Windjana Tours
CULTURAL

(☑08-9193 1502; www.windjana.com.au; adult/child $230/95; ⊗Tue, Thu & Sun Apr-Sep, also Fri Jun-Aug) Full-day cultural tours to Windjana Gorge (p1008) and Tunnel Creek (p1008) from Derby. Lunch and refreshments are included. May still run during the Wet (dependent on numbers and road conditions). Pick-up from visitor centre (p1007).

☆ Festivals & Events

★ Boab Festival
MUSIC, CULTURAL

(www.derbyboabfestival.org.au; ⊗Jul; ♿) Concerts, mud footy, horse and mud-crab races, poetry readings, art exhibitions and street parades. Try to catch the Long Table dinner out on the mudflats.

⊨ Sleeping & Eating

Kimberley Entrance
Caravan Park
CARAVAN PARK $

(☑08-9193 1055; www.kimberleyentrancecaravan park.com; 2 Rowan St; unpowered/powered sites $36/40; 🅿🛜) Not all sites are shaded, though there's always room. Amenities are

HORIZONTAL WATERFALLS

One of the most intriguing features of the Kimberley coastline is the phenomenon known as 'horizontal waterfalls'. Despite the name, the falls are simply tides gushing through narrow coastal gorges in the Buccaneer Archipelago, north of Derby. What creates such a spectacle are the huge tides, often varying up to 11m. The water flow reaches an astonishing 30 knots as it's forced through two narrow gaps 20m and 10m wide – resulting in a 'waterfall' reaching 4m in height.

Many tours leave Derby (and some Broome) each Dry, by air, sea or a combination of both. It's become de rigueur to 'ride' the tide change through the gorges on a high-powered speedboat. There is a risk element involved and accidents have occurred. Scenic flights are the quickest and cheapest option and some seaplanes will land and transfer passengers to a waiting speedboat for the adrenaline hit. If you prefer to be stirred, not shaken, then consider seeing the falls as part of a longer cruise through the archipelago. Book tours at the Derby and Broome visitor centres.

The traditional Dambimangari owners recognise that the Falls are a tourist attraction, but prefer you don't travel through them on the tide change, in respect to the Wongudd (creator snake), said to be the tide itself.

basic but clean. Expect insects this close to the mudflats.

★ Desert Rose B&B $$
(☑ 0428 332 269; twobrownies@bigpond.com; 4 Marmion St; d $225; ※ ☒) It's worth booking ahead for the best sleep in town, with spacious, individually styled rooms, a nice shady pool, lead-light windows and a sumptuous breakfast. Host Anne is a fount of local information.

Derby Lodge MOTEL $$
(☑ 08-9193 2924; www.derbylodge.com.au; 15-19 Clarendon St; r/apt $150/210; P ※ ☎) Choose between neat, clean motel rooms or self-contained apartments with cooking facilities.

The on-site Neaps Bistro (☑ 08-9191 1263; www.facebook.com/neapsbistro; mains $19-38; ☺ 7-11am & 6-9pm Mon-Sat, 7-11am Sun; ☑) does the best food in Derby.

Sampey Meats DELI $
(☑ 08-9193 2444; www.sampeymeats.com.au; 59 Rowan St; ☺ 8.30am-5pm Mon-Fri, 8am-noon Sat) Carnivores can stock up for the Gibb with homemade jerkies, biltong and succulent vacuum-sealed steaks.

Jila Gallery ITALIAN $$
(☑ 08-9193 2560; www.jilacafe.com.au; 18 Clarendon St; pizzas $20-28, mains $24-34; ☺ 6pm-late Tue-Sat; ☖) Jila's fortunes fluctuate with its chefs, who turn out wood-fired pizzas, homemade pastas and wonderful cakes, all in a shady, al fresco setting. Last orders 8.30pm.

❶ Information

Derby Visitor Centre (☑ 08-9191 1426; www.derbytourism.com.au; 30 Loch St; ☺ 8.30am-4.30pm Mon-Fri, 9am-3pm Sat & Sun dry season) Helpful centre with the low-down on road conditions, accommodation, transport and tour bookings. Buses leave from here.

❶ Getting There & Away

All buses depart from the visitor centre.

Derby Bus Service (☑ 08-9193 1550; www.derbybus.com.au; 30 Loch St; one way/return $50/80; ☺ Mon, Wed & Fri) Leaves early for Broome (2½ hours), stopping at Willare Roadhouse (and anywhere else along the way if you ask the driver), returning the same day.

Greyhound (☑ 1300 473 946; www.greyhound.com.au; 30 Loch St) Heads to Broome ($64, 2½ hours), Darwin ($289, 25 hours), Fitzroy Crossing ($72, 3 hours) and Kununurra ($144, 12 hours) daily (except Sundays).

Devonian Reef National Parks

Three national parks with three stunning gorges were once part of a western 'great barrier reef' in the Devonian era, 350 million years ago. Windjana Gorge (p1008) and Tunnel Creek (p1008) National Parks are accessed via the unsealed Fairfield-Leopold Downs Rd (linking the Great Northern Hwy with the Gibb River Road), while Geikie Gorge (p1008) National Park is 22km northeast of Fitzroy Crossing.

Sights

★ Tunnel Creek
NATIONAL PARK

(per car $13; ⊙ dry season; [P]) Sick of the sun? Then cool down underground at Tunnel Creek, which cuts through a spur of the Napier Range for almost 1km. It was famously the hideout of Jandamarra (a Bunuba man who waged an armed guerrilla war against the police and white settlers for three years before he was killed). In the Dry, the full length is walkable by wading partly through knee-deep water; watch out for bats and bring good footwear and a strong torch.

Geikie Gorge
NATIONAL PARK

(Darngku; ⊙ Apr-Dec; [P][♿]) Don't miss this magnificent limestone gorge, 20km north of Fitzroy Crossing by sealed road. The self-guided trails are sandy and hot, so take one of the informative boat cruises run by either **Parks & Wildlife staff** (☑ 08-9191 5121; https://parksandwildlife.rezdy.com/154373/geikie-gorge-boat-tour; 1hr tour adult/child $50/14; ⊙ cruises from 8am May-Oct) or local Bunuba guides.

Windjana Gorge
NATIONAL PARK

(per car $13, campsites adult/child $13/3; ⊙ dry season) The sheer walls of the Napier Range soar 100m above the Lennard River in this gorge sacred to the Bunuba people. Contracting in the Dry to a series of pools, scores of freshwater crocodiles line the riverbank, hence swimming is not recommended. Bring plenty of water for the sandy 7km return walk from the campground.

Tours

Bungoolee Tours
CULTURAL

(☑ 08-9191 5355; www.bungoolee.com.au; 2hr tour adult/child $60/30, smoking ceremony $25, full-day tour adult/child $235/150; ⊙ 2hr tour 10am & 2pm Mon, Wed & Fri, full-day tour 8am Tue, Thu & Sat dry season) Bunuba lawman Dillon Andrews runs informative two-hour Tunnel Creek tours explaining the story of Jandamarra. Also available is a traditional 'Welcome to Country' smoking ceremony ($25) and a full-day tour to both Tunnel Creek and Windjana Gorge from Fitzroy Crossing. Book through Fitzroy Crossing visitor centre (p1013).

Darngku Heritage Tours
CRUISE

(☑ 0417 907 609; www.darngku.com.au; adult/child 2hr tour $100/80, 3hr $120/90, half-day $200/165; ⊙ Apr-Dec; [♿]) Local Bunuba

guides introduce Aboriginal culture and bush tucker on these amazingly informative cruises through Geikie (Darngku) Gorge. A shorter one-hour cruise (adult/child $55/15) operates during the shoulder seasons (April and October to December).

❶ Getting There & Away

You'll need your own vehicle to visit the three parks. Geikie Gorge is easily accessed from Fitzroy Crossing, but if you only have a 2WD, check the condition of Fairfield-Leopold Downs Rd first – for Windjana Gorge and Tunnel Creek – where there's at least one permanent creek crossing. Otherwise, consider taking a day tour from Derby (p1006) or Fitzroy Crossing.

Gibb River Road

Cutting a brown swath through the scorched heart of the Kimberley, the legendary Gibb River Road ('the Gibb' or GRR) provides one of Australia's wildest outback experiences. Stretching some 660km between Derby and Kununurra, the largely unpaved road is an endless sea of red dirt, big open skies and dramatic terrain. Rough, sometimes deeply corrugated side roads lead to remote gorges, shady pools, distant waterfalls and million-acre cattle stations. Rain can close the road at any time and it's permanently closed during the Wet. This is true wilderness with minimal services, so good planning and self-sufficiency are vital.

A high-clearance 4WD is mandatory, with two spare tyres, tools, emergency water (20L minimum) and several days' food in case of breakdown. **Britz** (☑ 08-9192 2647; www.britz.com; 10 Livingston St; minimum 5-day hire van/4WD from $1000/1600) in Broome is a reputable hire outfit. Fuel is limited and expensive, mobile phone coverage is minimal and temperatures can be life-threatening.

Tours

Adventure Tours
DRIVING

(☑ 1300 654 604; www.adventuretours.com.au; from $2195) Ten-day Gibb River Road camping tours catering for a younger crowd.

Wundargoodie Aboriginal Safaris
CULTURAL

(☑ 0429 928 088; www.wundargoodie.com.au; 1707 Great Northern Hwy; tag-along per vehicle per day from $250; ⊙ Apr-Sep; [♿]) These insightful Aboriginal-run 4WD tag-along tours (ie you bring your own vehicle) showcase local

MITCHELL FALLS & DRYSDALE RIVER

In the Dry, Kalumburu Rd is normally navigable as far as Drysdale River Station (p1012), 59km from the Gibb River Road.

The **Mitchell Plateau** (Ngauwudu) turn-off is 160km from the Gibb and within 6km a deep, rocky ford crosses the **King Edward River**, which is formidable early in the season. You're now on **Wunambal Gaambera Country** and the first of two rock-art shelters is on the left, with the second just after the nearby **Munurru Campground** (campsites per adult/child $8/3; P), both to the right.

From the Kalumburu Rd it's a very rough 87km, past lookouts and forests of *Livistona* palms to the dusty campground at **Mitchell River National Park** (www.dpaw.wa.gov.au; entry per person $45, campsites adult/child $11/3; ⊙ dry season; P) 🏊. The park contains the stunning, multi-tiered **Mitchell Falls** (Punamii-unpuu), which can be seen on a lovely three-hour return walk passing inviting, shady waterholes and incredible Aboriginal rock art.

culture and rock art in the remote East Kimberley. They will also run all-inclusive women-only tours on demand, camping at special sites and sharing experiences with Aboriginal women from various communities.

Kimberley Adventure Tours DRIVING
(☑ 1800 171 616; www.kimberleyadventures.com. au; 9-day tour $2195) Small-group camping tours from Broome up the Gibb, with the nine-day tour continuing to Purnululu and Darwin. Also offers the reverse direction, starting in Darwin.

Kimberley Wild Expeditions DRIVING
(☑ 1300 738 870; www.kimberleywild.com.au; tours $245-4295) Consistent award winner. Tours from Broome range from one ($245) to 15 days ($4295) on the Gibb River Road and beyond.

ℹ Information

For tourist info head to the Derby (p1007) and Kununurra (p1015) visitor centre websites. The visitor centres also sell the *Gibb River & Kalumburu Roads* guide ($5).

An **Uunguu Visitor Pass** (UVP; www.wunambalgaambera.org.au; entry per person $45) (UVP) is required to visit Mitchell Falls and Munurru.

Mainroads Western Australia (MRWA; ☑ 13 81 38; www.mainroads.wa.gov.au) Highway and Gibb River Road conditions. Has a useful *Driving the Gibb River Road* downloadable brochure.

Parks & Wildlife Service (www.dpaw.wa.gov. au) Park permits, camping fees and information. Consider a Holiday Pass ($46) if visiting more than three parks in one month (does not cover Mitchell Falls).

Shire of Derby/West Kimberley (☑ 08-9191 0999; www.sdwk.wa.gov.au) Side-road conditions and closures for the Western and Central Gibb.

Shire of Wyndham/East Kimberley (☑ 08-9168 4100; www.swek.wa.gov.au) Kalumburu/ Mitchell Falls road conditions.

Western Gibb

Heading east from Derby, the first 100-odd kilometres of the Gibb River Road are now sealed. Don't miss **Mowanjum Art & Culture Centre** (☑ 08-9191 1008; www.mowanjumarts.com; Gibb River Rd; ⊙ 9am-5pm daily dry season, closed Sat & Sun wet season, closed Jan) FREE, only 4km along.

The Windjana Gorge turn-off at 119km is your last chance to head back to the Great Northern Hwy. Windjana is an easy 22km off the Gibb and is a popular camp site. Back on the GRR, the scenery improves after crossing the **Lennard River** into Napier Downs Station as the **King Leopold Ranges** loom ahead. Just after **Inglis Gap** is the Mount Hart Wilderness Lodge turn-off and another 7km brings the narrow **Lennard River Gorge**.

Despite its name, **March Fly Glen**, 204km from Derby, is a pleasant, shady picnic area ringed by pandanus and frequented by blue-faced honeyeaters. Don't miss stunning **Bell Gorge** (per car $13), with its waterfall and plunge pool. Refuel (diesel only), grab an ice cream and check your email at **Imintji Store** (☑ 08-9191 7227; www.imintji.com; ⊙ 8am-5pm dry season, shorter hours wet season; 📶).

You can find a bed at **Mount Hart Wilderness Lodge** (☑ 08-9191 4645; www.mounthart.com.au; campsites adult/child $18/10, r or

MUNJA TRACK

Desperately remote, the **Munja Track** (☑08-9191 4644; www.mtelizabeth stationstay.com.au; per vehicle $150, key deposit $50; ⊘dry season) – one of the most challenging 4WD tracks in the country – leads from Mt Elizabeth Station through the Kimberley's heart and soul to the Indian Ocean coastline at **Walcott Inlet**. Originally cut by the Lacy family, there's countless rocky creek crossings and 'jump ups' (steep rocky inclines), amazing rock art, sublime gorges and isolated campsites.

safari tent per person incl dinner & breakfast $295; ⊘dry season) and **Birdwood Downs Station** (☑08-9191 1275; www.birdwooddowns.com; campsites $15, huts from $110), but camping will be a lot cheaper.

Mount Hart Wilderness Lodge (p1009) and Imintji Store (p1009) both sell diesel only. If you need unleaded petrol, keep going another 78km east from Imintji to Mt Barnett Roadhouse.

Central Gibb

Heading east from Imintji, it's only 25km to the Mornington turn-off and another 5km further to the entrance of **Charnley River Station** (☑08-9191 4646; www.australianwildlife. org; campsites per person $20, entry per vehicle $25; ⊛). If heading across the wild, lonely savannah to exquisite Mornington Wilderness Camp, call first using the radio at the Gibb. Back on the GRR, most of the cattle you pass are from **Mount House Station**. Cross the **Adcock**, wave to Nev and Leonie as you pass Over the Range Repairs, then drop down to **Galvans Gorge** (Gibb River Rd) `FREE` at the 286km mark.

Fuel up at Mt Barnett Roadhouse, 300km from Derby, and get your camping permit if choosing to stay at nearby **Manning River Gorge** (7km behind Mt Barnett Roadhouse; campsites per person $22.50, gorge day access $8; ⊘dry season; ⊛), though there are better options further east. There's free camping on the **Barnett River** (29km east of Mt Barnett Roadhouse; campsites free; ⊛) at the 329km mark and if you've still got daylight, consider pushing on to historic **Mt Elizabeth Station** (☑08-9191 4644; www.mtelizabeth

stationstay.com.au; campsites per person $22, r person with/without meals $220/135, gorge pass day/overnight $20/15; ⊘dry season; ☎); turn-off at the 338km mark.

Both Mornington Wilderness Camp and Charnley River Station have lovely campsites with good amenities and attractions.

Over the Range Repairs (☑08-9191 7887; overtherangetyres@gmail.com; ⊘8am-5pm dry season), between Adcock and Galvans gorges, is your best – if not only – hope of mechanical salvation on the whole Gibb.

Mt Barnett Roadhouse (☑08-9191 7007; www.facebook.com/mtbarnettroadhouse; ⊘8am-5pm dry season, shorter hours wet season) has fuel (diesel and unleaded petrol) and groceries. If you're heading west, there's no more unleaded till Derby.

★**Mornington
Wilderness Camp**   WILDLIFE RESERVE
(☑08-9191 7406; www.australianwildlife.org/ mornington-wilderness-camp; entry per vehicle $25, campsites per adult/child $20/10, full-board safari tents s/d $335/600; ⊘May–mid-Oct; ⊛) Part of the Australian Wildlife Conservancy, the superb Mornington Wilderness Camp is as remote as it gets, lying on the Fitzroy River, an incredibly scenic 95km drive across the savannah from the Gibb's 247km mark. Nearly 400,000 hectares are devoted to conserving the Kimberley's endangered fauna and there's excellent canoeing, swimming, birdwatching and bushwalking.

Eastern Gibb

At 406km from Derby you reach the Kalumburu turn-off. Head right on the Gibb River Road and 70km later call in for scones at historic **Ellenbrae Station** (☑08-9161 4325; www.ellenbraestation.com.au; Gibb River Rd; campsites per person $17.50, cabins from $155, scones $4.50; ⊘dry season; ℗). Continue through spectacular country, crossing the mighty **Durack River** then climbing though the **Pentecost Ranges** to 579km where there are panoramic views of the Cockburn Ranges, Cambridge Gulf and Pentecost River. Shortly after is the turn-off to the lovely Home Valley Station.

Soon after Home Valley, at 589km from Derby, you'll cross the infamous **Pentecost River** – take care as water levels are unpredictable and saltwater crocs lurk nearby. El Questro Wilderness Park looms on the right. The last section of the Gibb River

KALUMBURU

Kalumburu, WA's most northerly settlement, is a picturesque mission nestled beneath giant mango trees and coconut palms on the King Edward River. There's some interesting rock art nearby and the odd WWII bomber wreck. You can stay at the **Kalumburu Mission** (☑08-9161 4333; www.kalumburumission.org.au; campsites per adult/child $20/8, donga s/d $125/175; [P][🐾][🛜]), which has a small **museum** (Fr Thomas Gill Museum; ☑08-9161 4333; www.kalumburumission.org.au; $10; ⊙11am-1pm), or camp (with a permit) at **Honeymoon Bay** (☑08-9161 4378; www.facebook.com/honeymoonbaywa; campsites per person $15; [🐾]) or **McGowan Island** (Sunset Beach; ☑08-9161 4748; www.facebook.com/mcgowanssunsetbeachcampingwa; campsites per person $20; [🐾]), 20km further out on the coast – the end of the road. Don't miss **Wongalala Falls** (www.facebook.com/kalumburu tourism; Kalumburu access permit $50; ⊙dry season) Falls, about 20km from Kalumburu and only opened to non-Indigenous tourists in 2018. These stunning hour-glass falls empty into a large, perfectly circular plunge pool.

You'll need a permit from the **Department of Aboriginal Affairs** (DAA; ☑1300 651 077; www.dplh.wa.gov.au) in Broome to visit Kalumburu and a **Kalumburu Aboriginal Community** (☑08-9161 4300, www.kalumburu.org) visitors' permit ($50 per vehicle, valid for seven days) upon entry, available from the **Community Resource Centre** (CRC, Visitor Centre; ☑08-9161 4627; www.kalumburu.org; ⊙hours vary; [🛜]).

The road to Kalumburu deteriorates quickly after the Mitchell Plateau turn-off and eventually becomes very rocky.

Fuel (☑08-9161 4333; www.kalumburumission.org.au; ⊙7-11.30am & 1.30-4pm Mon-Fri, 9-11am Sat) is available from the yard next to the mission store.

Aviair (☑08-9166 9300; www.aviair.com.au; Kununurra to Kalumburu $369) fly Mondays, Wednesdays, Fridays to/from Kunurnurra.

Road is sealed. The turn-off to beautiful **Emma Gorge** (⊙Apr-Sep; [P][🚶]) is 10km past El Questro. You'll cross **King River** 630km from Derby and, at 647km, you'll finally hit the Great Northern Hwy – turn left for Wyndham (48km) and right to Kununurra (53km).

Heading east, if you fuelled up at Mt Barnett Roadhouse, you should have enough to reach Kununurra. **Drysdale River Station** (☑08-9161 4326; www.drysdaleriver.com.au; campsites per person $12-16, d from $150; ⊙8am-5pm Apr-Sep, lunch 11am-2pm, dinner from 5pm; [P][🍴]), 59km up the Kalumburu Rd, is your only other option.

Coming from the east, 2WD vehicles should make it to El Questro; just check the water level of the permanent creek crossing between the GRR and El Questro Station Township.

Home Valley, El Questro, Drysdale River and Ellenbrae all offer tyre repairs.

El Questro Wilderness Park   PARK
(☑08-9169 1777; www.elquestro.com.au; adult permit per day/week $12/20; ⊙dry season; [🚶]) This vast 400,000-hectare former cattle station turned international resort incor-

porates scenic gorges (Amelia, **El Questro**) and **Zebedee Springs** (El Questro Wilderness Park; ⊙7am-noon; [P]). **Boat tours** (adult/child from $65/33; ⊙3pm) explore Chamberlain Gorge or you can hire your own boat ($100). There are shady campsites and air-con bungalows at **El Questro Station Township** (☑08-9169 1777; www.elquestro.com.au; campsites per person $22-30, station tent d $175, bungalow d from $339; [❄][🛜]) and also an outdoor bar and upmarket steakhouse (mains $28 to $44).

★**Home Valley Station**   FARMSTAY $
(☑08-9161 4322; www.homevalley.com.au; Gibb River Rd; campsites per person $21, eco-tent d from $165, homestead d from $295; ⊙May-Oct; [❄][@][🛜][🏊]) The privations of the Gibb are left behind after pulling into amazing Home Valley Station, a hospitality training resort for local Indigenous men and women, which has a superb range of luxurious accommodation. There are excellent grassy campsites and motel-style rooms, a fantastic open-air bistro (mains $24 to $48), tyre repairs, and activities including trail rides, bushwalks, fishing and cattle mustering.

Great Northern Hwy

One of the Kimberley's best-kept secrets is the vast subterranean labyrinth of **Mimbi Caves** (☑08-9191 5355; www.mimbicaves.com.au; Mt Pierre Station; P⛺), 90km southeast of Fitzroy Crossing, located within Mt Pierre Station on Gooniyandi land. Stay at their wonderful **Jarlarloo Riwi** (Mimbi Caves Campground; ☑08-9191 5355; www.mimbicaves.com.au; Mt Pierre Station; campsites per adult/child/family $18/15/48; P) campground at the at the base of the scenic **Emmanuel Range** or keep heading east 50km to **Larrawa Station** (Bush Camp; ☑08-9191 7025; www.larrawabushcamp.com; Great Northern Hwy; campsites per person $10; ☉Apr-Sep; @⛺), a pleasant overnight stop with hot showers, basic campsites and shearers' rooms. Another 30km towards Halls Creek is tiny Yiyili with its **Laarri Gallery** (☑08-9191 7195; www.fitzroycrossingtourism.com.au/yiyili/laarri-gallery; Yiyili; ☉9am-4pm school days Mar-Nov; P⛺).

Pushing on from Halls, the scenery becomes progressively more interesting and just after the **Ord River** bridge you'll pass the Purnululu National Park (p1016) turn-off at 108km. Warmun (162km) has a roadhouse and an amazing **gallery** (☑08-9168 7496; www.warmunart.com.au; Warmun; ☉8am-4pm Mon-Fri; P) in the nearby community. **Doon Doon Roadhouse** (☑08-9167 8004; Doon Doon; ☉6am-8pm), 91km from Warmun and 60km from the Victoria Hwy junction, is the only other blip on the landscape and your last chance to refuel before Kununurra or Wyndham. If heading to **Wuggubun** (☑08-9161 4040; campsites per vehicle $30; ☉Apr-Sep; P⛺), the signposted turn-off is 4km south of the highway junction, just before Card Creek (if heading north).

☞ Tours

Luridgii Tours　　　　　　　DRIVING
(Junama; ☑08-9168 2704; www.luridgiitours.com.au; Doon Doon; per vehicle $250) Be personally guided through the gorges, thermal pools and Dreaming stories of Miriuwung country by the traditional owners on these 4WD cultural tag-alongs (you drive your own vehicle). Tours depart from Doon Doon Roadhouse on the Great Northern Hwy and there is an overnight camping option ($50 per vehicle). BYO food.

Luridgii also offer Cultural Awareness tours ($150, 2 hrs) and a full-day fly, drive and boat tour ex Kununurra to Argyle Diamond Mine, returning by a sunset cruise across Lake Argyle ($890).

Girloorloo Tours　　　　　　CULTURAL
(☑08-9191 5355; www.mimbicaves.com.au; 2hr tour adult/child $80/40; ☉8am, 10am & 2pm Mon-Thu, 8am Fri, 8am & 10am Sat Apr-Sep; ⛺) Aboriginal-owned Girloorloo Tours runs trips to the remarkable Mimbi Caves, a vast subterranean labyrinth housing Aboriginal rock art and impressive fish fossils. The tours include an introduction to local Dreaming stories, bush tucker and traditional medicines. Book through Fitzroy Crossing or Halls Creek visitor centres.

❶ Getting There & Away

The Great Northern Hwy (GNH) is sealed and services are spaced at manageable distances. Always carry extra water, because if your vehicle breaks down, you may need to spend the night in it before help arrives.

Mainroads Western Australia (p1009) For road conditions.

Greyhound (p1003) Links the towns on the GNH with Broome and Darwin.

Skippers (☑1300 729 924; www.skippers.com.au) Flies to Broome from Fitzroy Crossing and Halls Creek.

Aviair (☑08-9166 9300; www.aviair.com.au; adult one way $325) For Kununurra from Halls Creek.

Fitzroy Crossing

☑08 / POP 1300

Gooniyandi, Bunuba, Walmajarri, Nyikina and Wangkajungka peoples populate the small settlement of Fitzroy Crossing where the Great Northern Hwy crosses the mighty Fitzroy River. There's little reason to stay other than that it's a good access point for the Devonian Reef National Parks and has some fine art and craft studios.

⊙ Sights

Mangkaja Arts　　　　　　　　GALLERY
(☑08-9191 5833; www.mangkaja.com; 8 Bell Rd; ☉11am-4pm Mon-Fri) This Fitzroy Crossing gallery is where desert and river tribes interact, producing unique acrylics, prints and baskets.

Marnin Studio　　　　　　ARTS CENTRE
(Marninwarntikura Women's Resource Centre; ☑08-9191 5284; www.mwrc.com.au; Lot 284, Balanijangarri Rd; ☉8.30am-4.30pm Mon-Fri) Marnin

is the Walmajarri word for women and this studio uses crafts such as boab-nut painting, textile printing and bush-nut jewellery-making to bind together the women of the various local language groups.

🛏 Sleeping & Eating

Fitzroy River Lodge   RESORT $$
(✆08-9191 5141; www.fitzroyriverlodge.com.au; Great Northern Hwy; campsites per person $21, tent/motel d $210/265, studios $375-530; ⊕bar noon-8.30pm, restaurant 5.30-8.30pm; 🅿❄@ 🛜🏊🐾) Across the river from town, Fitzroy River Lodge has comfortable motel rooms, safari tents, exclusive Riverview studios and grassy campsites. The friendly bar offers decent counter meals ($22 to $38) from noon to 8.30pm, while the deck of the **Riverside Restaurant** (dinner only, mains $32 to $42) is perfect for that much-needed sundowner.

⭐ Jalangurru Mayi Cafe   CAFE $$
(✆08-9191 5124; www.facebook.com/jalangurru mayi; 75 Emmanuel Way; meals $6.50-23; ⊕7am-2pm Tue-Sat; 🍴🐾) Nourishing, healthy, paleo food is the mantra behind Jalangurru Mayi ('good mood'), which eschews refined ingredients and sugars, a smart move in a town where diabetes is a growing problem. Easily the best brunch option between Broome and Kununurra, seriously good coffee complements wholesome breakfasts, lunches, salad bowls and gluten-free cakes. Offers free training to community members.

ℹ Information

Visitor Centre (✆08-9191 5355; www.fitzroy crossingtourism.com.au; ⊕8am-4pm Mon-Fri, to noon Sat) Can arrange accommodation and book tickets to Geikie Gorge (p1008) and Mimbi Caves. Greyhound (✆1300 473 946; www. greyhound.com.au) bus stop and public library.

Halls Creek
✆08 / POP 1600
On the edge of the Great Sandy Desert, Halls Creek is a small services town with communities of Kija, Jaru and Gooniyandi peoples. The excellent visitor centre (p1014) can book tours to the Bungle Bungles and tickets for Mimbi Caves. Across the highway, Yarliyil Gallery is definitely worth a look. The town regularly suffers water shortages.

👁 Sights & Activities

Sawpit Gorge   GORGE
(Duncan Rd) Great bushwalking, swimming and secluded campsites await the traveller prepared to cross the rocky Albert Edward Range to this gorge 50km from Halls Creek.

Palm Springs   OASIS
(Lugangarna; Duncan Rd) **FREE** Soak your weary, corrugations-bashed body in this beautiful, permanent pool on the Black Elvire River, 45km from Halls Creek. Free, 24-hour camping allowed.

Yarliyil Gallery   GALLERY
(✆08-9168 6723; http://yarliyil.com.au; Great Northern Hwy; ⊕9am-5pm Mon-Fri; 🅿) Halls Creek gallery showcasing talented local artists as well as some Ringer Soak mob.

Northwest Regional Airlines   SCENIC FLIGHTS
(✆08-9168 5211; www.facebook.com/northwest regional; Halls Creek Airport; flights per person 2/3/4 passengers from $580/390/295) Scenic flights from Halls Creek over Wolfe Creek Meteorite Crater and the Bungle Bungles (p1016).

🛏 Sleeping & Eating

Zebra Rock Mine   CAMPGROUND $
(Wetland Safaris; ✆0400 767 650; www.zebrarock mine.com.au; Duncan Rd, NT; unpowered sites per adult $10, safari tent $25; ⊕Apr-Sep; 🅿🏊) The only formal accommodation on Duncan Rd is 10km from the Victoria Hwy and is technically in the Northern Territory. Travellers love the rustic vibe, and the sunset bird-watching tour ($120) is not to be missed. There's also a small cafe and gift shop. It is 2WD accessible if coming from the north.

Halls Creek Motel   MOTEL $$
(✆08-9168 9600; www.hallscreekmotel.com. au; r from $200; 🅿❄🛜🏊🐾) Right on the highway, there's a variety of well-equipped rooms, from budget to deluxe with spa. **Russian Jack's** (✆08-9168 9600; www.hallscreek-motel.com.au; Halls Creek Motel; mains $25-44, kids $20; ⊕5-8.30pm; 🐾) opens for dinner.

⭐ Cafe Mungarri in the Park   CAFE $
(✆0477 552 644; 2 Hall St; toastie/curry $10/14; ⊕7.30am-3pm Mon-Sat; 🛜🐾) The nicest coffee option in Halls Creek, Mungarri serves up cheap, simple wraps, toasted sandwiches and fresh juices on a shady verandah in the same building as the visitor centre (p1014).

OFF THE BEATEN TRACK

DUNCAN ROAD

Snaking its way east from Halls Creek before eventually turning north and playing hide and seek with the Northern Territory (NT) border, Duncan Rd is a much more singular driving experience than the heavily touristed Gibb River Road. Unsealed for its entire length (445km), it receives only a trickle of travellers, but those who make the effort are rewarded with stunning scenery, beautiful gorges, tranquil billabongs and breathtakingly lonely camp sites.

There are no services on the entire Duncan, so carry fuel for at least 500km. Enquire at Halls Creek or Kununurra visitor centres about road conditions, or check online at www.hallscreek.wa.gov.au (WA) and www.ntlis.nt.gov.au/roadreport (NT).

❶ Information

Visitor Centre (☑08-9168 6262; www.hallscreektourism.com.au; 2 Hall St; ⊘8am-4pm; 🕿) This great local resource can book tours and arrange art-gallery visits, as well as tickets for the Mimbi Caves (p1012). There's free wi-fi in the council precinct outside.

Kununurra

☑08 / POP 6000

On Miriwoong country near the Northern Territory border, Kununurra is a relaxed oasis set among farmland growing superfoods, and tropical fruit and sandalwood plantations, all thanks to the Ord River irrigation scheme. With good transport and communications, excellent services and well-stocked supermarkets, it's every traveller's favourite slice of civilisation between Broome and Darwin.

Kununurra is also the departure point for most East Kimberley tours, and with all that fruit, there's plenty of seasonal work. Note that NT time is 90 minutes ahead of WA.

◉ Sights

Kelly's Knob   VIEWPOINT
(Kelly Rd) The best view in Kununurra is from this rock outcrop on the town's northern edge. Great for sunrise or sunset.

Mirima National Park   NATIONAL PARK
(per car $13) Like a mini Bungle Bungles, the eroded gorges of Hidden Valley are home to brittle red peaks, spinifex, boab trees and abundant wildlife. Several walking trails lead to lookouts; early morning or dusk are the best times for sighting fauna.

Waringarri Aboriginal Arts Centre   GALLERY
(☑08-9168 2212; www.waringarriarts.com.au; 16 Speargrass Rd; gallery tour adult/child $55/25; ⊘8.30am-4.30pm Mon-Fri year-round, 10am-2pm Sat dry season only) This excellent gallery-studio hosts local artists working with ochres in a unique abstract style. It also represents artists from Kalumburu. A 90-minute artist-led gallery tour runs Tuesday to Thursday mornings.

Lily Creek Lagoon   LAKE
Across the highway from the township, Lily Creek Lagoon is a mini-wetlands with amazing birdlife, boating and freshwater crocs.

**Kununurra Historical
Society Museum**   MUSEUM
(☑08-9169 3331; www.kununurra.org.au; Coolibah Dr; gold coin donation; ⊘noon-5.30pm Mon-Fri) Old photographs and newspaper articles document Kununurra's history, including the story of a wartime Wirraway aircraft crash and the subsequent recovery mission. The museum is opposite the country club exit. It's open whenever the gate is open.

🏃 Activities & Tours

Go Wild   ADVENTURE SPORTS
(☑1300 663 369; www.gowild.com.au; 3-day canoe trips $220) Self-guided multiday canoe trips from Lake Argyle along the Ord River, overnighting at riverside campsites. Canoes, camping equipment and transport are provided; BYO food and sleeping bag. They also run group caving, abseiling and bushwalking trips.

Yeehaa Trail Rides   HORSE RIDING
(☑0417 957 607; www.facebook.com/yeehaatrail rides; Boab Park; 1/6½hr rides $70/220) Trail rides and tuition to suit all skill levels, 8km from Kununurra. The sunset ride to Elephant Rock ($120, 2½ hours) is the perfect introduction to the Kimberley.

Waringarri Art & Culture Tours   CULTURAL
(www.waringarriarts.com.au/tours; Mirima tours adult/child $85/45, On Country adult/child half-day $255/155, full-day $375/200; ⊘10am-12.30pm Tue & Thu, 3-5.30pm Mon & Wed; ♿) The Wa-

ringarri mob run informative 2½-hour art and culture tours around Mirima National Park (including a stunning Sunset Tour) and longer 'On Country' tours at local sites with traditional custodians. All tours include a Welcome to Country, Dreaming stories and bush tucker.

Helispirit SCENIC FLIGHTS
(📞1800 180 085; www.helispirit.com.au; East Kimberley Regional Airport; 18/30/42min flights ex Bellbird $299/399/499) The Kimberley's largest chopper outfit offers scenic flights over the Bungle Bungles from Bellbird (inside the park) and Warmun ($425, 45 minutes). It also arranges flights over Mitchell Falls, Kununurra, King George Falls, Lake Argyle and anywhere else in the Kimberley.

Sunset BBQ Cruises CRUISE
(Kununurra Cruises; 📞08-9168 2882; www.kununurracruises.com.au; adult/child $95/65; ⊙May-Aug) Popular sunset BBQ dinner cruises on Lake Kununurra (Diversion Dam; 🅿) and the Ord River. Complimentary drinks and all transfers included.

✸ Festivals & Events

Ord Valley Muster CULTURAL
(📞08-9168 1177; www.ordvalleymuster.com.au; ⊙May; ♿) For 10 days each May, Kununurra hits overdrive with a collection of sporting, charity and cultural events culminating in a large outdoor concert under the full moon on the banks of the Ord River.

🛏 Sleeping

Hidden Valley Tourist Park CARAVAN PARK $
(📞08-9168 1790; www.hiddenvalleytouristpark.com; 110 Weaber Plains Rd; unpowered/powered sites $32/42, cabin d $140; @🛜🈂🍽) Under the looming crags of Mirima National Park, this relaxed campground has nice grassy sites and is popular with seasonal workers and road-trippers. The self-contained cabins are good value.

★Wunan House B&B $$
(📞08-9168 2436; www.wunanhouse.com; 167 Coolibah Dr; r from $155; 🅿🈂🛜) Aboriginal-owned and -run, this immaculate B&B offers light, airy rooms, all with en suites and TVs. There's free wi-fi, off-street parking and an ample continental breakfast.

Freshwater APARTMENT $$
(📞08-9169 2010; www.freshwaterapartments.net.au; 19 Victoria Hwy; studios $228, 1-/2-/3-bedroom

apt $272/366/433; 🅿🈂🛜🍽) Exquisite, fully self-contained units with exotic open-roofed showers surround an inviting figure-of-eight tropical pool. Once here, you won't want to leave.

Kimberley Croc Motel MOTEL $$
(📞08-9168 1411; www.kimberleycrocmotel.com.au; 2 River Fig Ave; budget/standard/deluxe d from $99/143/169; 🅿🈂🛜🍽🐾) Taken over by Gulliver's (📞08-9168 1666; www.facebook.com/gulliverstavernkununurra; 196 Cottontree Ave; burgers $12.50, mains $19-34; ⊙noon-10pm), the old Croc lodge is now a sleek motel, offering a variety of renovated budget (basically four-bed dorms), standard, deluxe (garden or balcony) and pet-friendly rooms, all with en suites and kitchenettes. Add on the central location, mandatory pool, guests' kitchen and free wi-fi and you have a winner.

✕ Eating

★Wild Mango CAFE $
(📞08-9169 2810; www.wildmangocafe.com.au; 20 Messmate Way; breakfast $7-25, lunch $15-19; ⊙7am-4pm Mon-Fri, to 1pm Sat & Sun; 🍃) 🥗 Hip and healthy offerings include breakfast burritos, succulent salads, mouth-watering pancakes, chai smoothies, real coffee and homemade gelato. The entrance is on Konkerberry Dr.

Ivanhoe Cafe CAFE $$
(📞0427 692 775; www.facebook.com/ivanhoecafe; Ivanhoe Rd; breakfast $9-23, lunch $12-24; ⊙8am-2pm Wed-Mon Apr-Sep; 🍃) Grab a table under the leafy mango trees and tuck into tasty wraps, salads, tasting plates, dips and healthy burgers, all made from fresh, local produce. Don't miss the signature mango smoothie. Vegan friendly.

★PumpHouse MODERN AUSTRALIAN $$$
(📞08-9169 3222; www.thepumphouserestaurant.com; Lot 3005, Lakeview Dr; mains lunch $21-27, dinner $29-44; ⊙4.30pm-late Tue-Fri, 8am-late Sat & Sun; 🅿🛜) Idyllically situated on Lake Kununurra, the PumpHouse creates succulent dishes featuring quality local ingredients. Watch the catfish swarm should a morsel slip off the verandah, or just have a beer and watch the sunset. There's also an excellent wine list.

ℹ Information

Visitor Centre (📞1800 586 868; www.visitkununurra.com; Coolibah Dr; ⊙8.30am-4.30pm Apr-Sep, shorter hours Oct-Mar) Can

Purnululu National Park

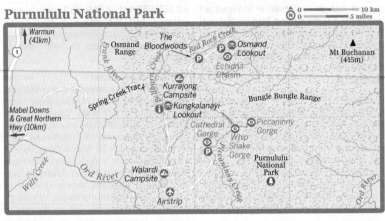

help find accommodation, tours and seasonal work.

Parks & Wildlife Service (☑08-9168 4200; www.dpaw.wa.gov.au; Lot 248, Ivanhoe Rd; ☺8.30am-4.30pm Mon-Fri) For park permits and publications.

ⓘ Getting There & Away

Airnorth (TL; ☑1800 627 474; www.airnorth. com.au; East Kimberley Regional Airport) flies to Broome and Darwin daily and to Perth on Saturdays. **Virgin Australia** (VA; ☑13 67 89; www.virginaustralia.com.au) has four flights a week to Perth.

Greyhound (☑1300 473 946; www.greyhound. com.au; 5 Messmate Way) buses depart the **BP Roadhouse** (☑08-9169 1188; 5 Messmate Way; ☺24hr) Sunday to Friday for Broome ($171, 13 hours) via Halls Creek ($108, four hours), Fitzroy Crossing ($125, 8 hours) and Derby ($146, 11 hours). The Darwin ($150, 10½ hours) via Katherine ($112, 6 hours) service runs Monday to Saturday.

ⓘ BORDER CROSSINGS

WA has strict quarantine laws and there is a permanent 24-hour checkpoint on the Victoria Hwy NT border 42km outside Kununurra where any fresh produce (including honey) will be confiscated. Most travellers coming from NT have one last big cook-up at the rest area just before the checkpoint. Check www. agric.wa.gov.au/exporting-western-australia/quarantine-information-private-travellers for further info.

Purnululu National Park & Bungle Bungle Range

The bizarre, ancient, eroded sandstone domes of the Unesco World Heritage–listed **Purnululu National Park** (per car $13; ☺Apr-Nov; ℗) will take your breath away. Known colloquially as the **Bungle Bungles**, these remote rocky ranges are recognised as the finest example of cone karst sandstone in the world.

The park is a microcosm of fauna and flora and several easy walks lead out of the baking sun into cool, shady palm-fringed gorges. Sunsets here are sublime. Facilities in the park are refreshingly minimal and visitors must be totally self-sufficient. Temperatures can be extreme. Rangers are in attendance during the high season when the small visitor centre (p1017) opens. There are two large, basic bush campgrounds at either end of the park.

Access is by a rough, unsealed, flood-prone 4WD-only track from the Great Northern Hwy north of Halls Creek, or by air on a package tour from Kununurra or Warmun.

◉ Sights & Tours

Kungkalanayi Lookout   VIEWPOINT
(℗) Sunsets and sunrises are spectacular from this hill near Three Ways. Mobile-phone reception from the top.

Piccaninny Gorge   GORGE
This 30km return trek (two to three days) from the southern car park to a remote and pristine gorge is best suited for experienced

hikers. There are plenty of opportunities for further exploration in the upper gorge. Take plenty of water and go early in the season. You must register at the visitor centre first.

Echidna Chasm
GORGE

(P) Look for tiny bats high on the walls above this palm-fringed, extremely narrow gorge in the northern park. The entrance is fringed by *Livistona* palms. Allow one hour for the 2km return walk.

Cathedral Gorge
GORGE

(P) Aptly named, this immense and inspiring circular cavern is an easy 2km (return) stroll from the southern car park.

Bungle Bungle Guided Tours
WALKING

(📱1800 899 029; www.bunglebungleguided tours.com.au; Bellburn Airstrip, Purnululu; adult/child from $299/149) Aboriginal-run half-day walking tours to Cathedral Gorge and Echidna Chasm and a full-day helicopter ride/hike ($997) to Piccaninny Gorge. Tours depart from the park airstrip at Bellburn and can be linked up with scenic flights from Kununurra, Warmun and Halls Creek.

🛏 Sleeping

Kurrajong Campsite
CAMPGROUND $

(campsites per person $13; ⊘ Apr-Nov; P) In the northern end of Purnululu National Park, there are dusty campsites with water, toilets and the odd picnic table, and thankfully no generators.

Walardi Campsite
CAMPGROUND $

(campsites per person $13; ⊘ Apr-Nov; P) Fresh water, toilets and some generator-free areas in the southern park.

ⓘ Information

Visitor Centre (📱08-9168 7300; ⊘8am-noon & 1-4pm Apr-Sep) Pay for your permit and grab a map. If closed, use the honesty envelopes.

ⓘ Getting There & Away

If you haven't got a high-clearance 4WD, consider taking a tour instead. You can fly in from Kununurra, Warmun and Halls Creek.

OUTBACK WA

The southern and western outback is an iconic Australian experience. Almost-empty roads run through a technicolour landscape of red dirt, green bush and endless

WORTH A TRIP

WALGA ROCK

Some 48km west of Cue via unsealed road, the granite monolith **Walga Rock** (Cue-Dalgaranga Rd) is Australia's second largest after Uluru (Ayers Rock). The shallow cave here is the largest gallery of Aboriginal rock paintings in WA, with 10,000-year-old images of goannas, snakes, spears, handprints and spirals. Left of the main paintings is a rigged sailing ship, etched by Sammy Hassan, a sailor from the *Xantho* pearling ship in the 1800s who came ashore and is known to have lived among the local Aboriginal people.

blue sky towards South Australia (SA) via the Nullarbor Plain, and up to the Northern Territory (NT). This was (and is) gold-rush country, with the city of Kalgoorlie-Boulder as its hub. The outback draws adventurers with its challenging 4WD routes (among the remotest on earth), eerie ghost towns, the parched scenery of this unforgiving land, rich Aboriginal culture and remote little towns populated by novel-worthy characters.

ⓘ Getting There & Away

Qantas (www.qantas.com.au) Flies Perth to Kalgoorlie.

Virgin Australia (www.virginaustralia.com) Flies Kalgoorlie to Perth and Melbourne, with connections to other cities.

Transwa (www.transwa.wa.gov.au) Operates a coach service between Kalgoorlie and Esperance three times weekly.

Transwa (www.transwa.wa.gov.au) runs the Prospector train service between East Perth and Kalgoorlie (from $92, seven hours, daily).

Kalgoorlie-Boulder

📱08 / POP 30,059

With well-preserved historic buildings, Kalgoorlie-Boulder (Karlrurla) is an outback success story and is still the centre for mining in this part of the state. Kalgoorlie-Boulder is on traditional Wongutha lands.

Historically, mine workers would come straight to town to spend up at Kalgoorlie's infamous brothels, or at pubs staffed by skimpies (scantily clad female bar staff). Today 'Kal' is definitely more family-friendly – the larger companies operating here have

OUTBACK TRACKS

Gunbarrel Highway (www.exploroz.com/treks/gunbarrel-highway) The old Gunbarrel Hwy from Wiluna to Warburton (where it joins the Outback Way) or even further – 1173km from Wiluna to Warrakurna – is one of the world's most beautiful and most remote 4WD adventures, for experienced and self-sufficient drivers only. One permit (obtained online instantly) is required from Wiluna to Warburton; an additional one is needed for the abandoned section (seven days).

Canning Stock Route (www.exploroz.com/treks/canning-stock-route) The Canning Stock Route runs 1850km northeast to Halls Creek, crossing the Great Sandy and Gibson Deserts, and is a route to be taken very seriously. If you're starting from Wiluna, pick up road and safety information from the shire office (☑ 08-9981 8000; www.wiluna.wa.gov.au; cnr Watton & Wall Sts; ⊙ 8.30am-4pm Mon-Fri). You'll need two permits to cross the Birril-burru native-title area.

Outback Way (www.outbackway.org.au) The partially sealed Outback Way links Laverton with Winton in central Queensland, via the red centre of the Northern Territory. From Laverton it's a mere 1098km to Yulara, 1541km to Alice Springs and 2720km to Winton! 'The longest shortcut' from Perth to Cairns is a tremendous road trip and by 2025, it should be completely paved. Permits required.

a policy that mine workers should reside in town rather than be transient 'fly-in-fly-out' labour.

It still feels a bit like the Wild West though, and the heritage pubs and remaining skimpies are reminders of a more turbulent past.

There are historical and modern mining sites to discover, excellent Aboriginal art galleries, a surprisingly varied dining scene and even a hip craft beer brewery. Kalgoorlie is also a good base from which to explore the ghost towns in the surrounding area.

⊙ Sights & Activities

★ **Museum of the Goldfields**   MUSEUM
(☑ 08-9021 8533; www.museum.wa.gov.au; 17 Hannan St; suggested donation $5; ⊙ 10am-3pm) The impressive Ivanhoe-mine head frame marks this excellent museum's entrance; take the lift to look over the city. An underground vault displays giant nuggets and gold bars, and there's also a fantastic exhibit on Aboriginal history and culture, as well as others on how this town grew and prospered. Look out for the Coolgardie safe – an early coolbox invention.

Super Pit Lookout   VIEWPOINT
(www.superpit.com.au/community/lookout; Outram St; ⊙ 7am-7pm) FREE The view is staggering here, with building-sized trucks zigzagging up and down the huge hole and looking like kids' toys. Gawp at the vast gold mine from above or get closer by taking a fascinating mine tour with **Kalgoorlie Tours & Charters** (☑ 1800 620 441; www.kalgoorlietours.com.au; 250 Hannan St; 2½hr tour adult/child $75/45).

Hannans North Tourist Mine   MINE
(☑ 08-9022 1664; www.hannansnorth.com.au; 130 Goldfields Hwy; adult/child/family $15/8/45; ⊙ 9am-4pm Sun-Fri; ☉) Hear Paddy Hannan's talk of how he struck gold and try your hand at panning for gold and playing two-up (a popular miners' gambling game). Check out the vast mining machinery, climb into the shovel of an immense loader, and learn all about the hardships of mining life in the 1890s. If you're not claustrophobic, visit the underground refuge chamber that can keep 12 people alive for 72 hours.

★ **Heartwalk**   WALKING
(www.heartwalkcbd.com) The largest public art project ever to take place in the Goldfields, Heartwalk is an entertaining 4km-long mural trail around central Kalgoorlie. Seek out serpents, kangaroos and other Dreaming images by local Aboriginal artists, as well as artistic endeavours by artists from all over Australia and even further afield. Download the art map from the website.

☞ Tours

★ **Bush Ghoodhu Wongutha Tours**   CULTURAL
(☑ 0474 971 548; www.bushghoodhu.com.au; day tour $250) Join Linden and his family for a

day of immersion in Wongutha culture: learn about the challenges facing Aboriginal people today, about bush tucker and how to throw a spear and boomerang, and tuck into 'roo stew warmed over a bush campfire. Overnight tours are particularly rewarding, with camping in the bush and hunting for honey ants and witchetty grubs.

Goldrush Tours CULTURAL
(☑08-9092 6000; www.goldrushtours.com.au; 19 Epis St; day tours $50-160) Heritage jaunts around Kalgoorlie-Boulder and day tours to Lake Ballard's sculptures by a local who knows the goldfields like the back of her hand. Call or check the website for upcoming tours, as they are confirmed only when there is a group booking for 10 (and more seats are then available to the general public).

⚐ Festivals & Events

Kalgoorlie-Boulder 'Race Round' SPORTS
(www.kbrc.com.au/race-round.php; 14 Meldrum Ave, Kalgoorlie-Boulder Racing Club; ☉Sep) Locals and a huge influx of visitors dress up to watch horses race over a week of festivities in September. Accommodation can be difficult to secure.

🛏 Sleeping

Palace Hotel HISTORIC HOTEL $
(☑08-9021 2788; https://palacehotelkalgoorlie.com; 137 Hannan St, Kalgoorlie; budget r $85, s/d/f/ste from $95/105/140/195; P❄) This classic 1897 hotel gets top marks for its super-central location and oodles of character: grand spiral staircase and heavy dark-wood furniture. You're also just steps away from a popular balcony bar, which is a boon or a bane, depending on your outlook. Rooms could be cleaner, though, and beds and linens could use a spruce-up.

Discovery Holiday Parks – Kalgoorlie CARAVAN PARK $
(☑08-9039 4800; www.discoveryholidayparks.com.au; 286 Burt St, Boulder; unpowered/powered site $28/37, economy s $66, cabins & chalets $140-220; P❄🌐❄) This nicely spacious park is on the edge of Boulder, 4km south of the Kal town centre. There are A-frame chalets and cabins, budget dongas, grassy tent sites, barbecue sites and an excellent camper kitchen, plus playgrounds and a pool.

Kalgoorlie Backpackers HOSTEL $
(☑08-9091 1482; www.kalgoorliebackpackers.com.au; 166 Hay St, Kalgoorlie; dm/s/d/f $33/60/85/120; P❄🌐❄) Located partially in a former brothel, this hostel is reasonably central, offers modestly sized, basic rooms and is a good place to find out about work opportunities.

Cecilia's On Hay BOUTIQUE HOTEL $$
(☑08-9021 3737; www.ceciliasonhay.com; 181 Hay St, Kalgoorlie; r $110-200; P❄🌐) Formerly a famous brothel, Cecilia's has 14 themed rooms including an Afghan boudoir or the Holden-On room that's perfect for recovering petrolheads. Some rooms come with private spa baths but share toilet facilities; others are decorated with tasteful nudes. One of the owners is also the chef who runs the popular on-site tapas and cocktail bar.

🍴 Eating & Drinking

★ Just a Little Cafe CAFE $
(☑08-9091 8585; 4 Maritana St, Kalgoorlie; mains from $12; ☉7am-3pm Mon-Fri, 8am-3pm Sat & Sun; ❄) Mismatched furniture, striking art and mining photos on the walls, and the best coffee in town all add to the appeal of Kalgoorlie's most popular cafe. Hungry? Then go for a You've Got To Be Trippin' Shroom Burger or else the Disco Pig Fries – poutine livened up with pulled pork and 'sexy sauce'.

★ Yada Thai THAI $$
(☑0403 535 201; 268 Hannan St, Kalgoorlie; mains $21-27; ☉4.30-9pm Tue-Sun; ❄) Stylishly decorated, this stellar Thai restaurant would be a credit to any world capital. The raw oysters with spicy Thai sauce are a revelation, and the basil and chilli baramundi and soft-shell crab with black pepper sauce make your taste buds sing with joy. Service can be leisurely, but after you taste their specialities, you'll be happy to linger for hours.

★ Beaten Track Brewery MICROBREWERY
(☑0429 205 516; www.beatentrackbrewery.com.au; 25a Dwyer St, South Boulder; ☉1-6pm Mon-Sat) Going strong for over a decade, this tin-shed brewery draws beer lovers with its six rotating brews on tap – from the hoppy English IPA and traditional highland ale to seasonal ales, porters and stouts. Brimming with creativity, it also hasgot small-batch session brews and excellent wood-fired pizzas.

OFF THE BEATEN TRACK

MENZIES & LAKE BALLARD

On traditional Wongutha lands, 132km north of Kalgoorlie, the tiny township of Menzies was a thriving town of 10,000 people during the gold rush and you can trace this history along the main street through interpretive panels. Today it's the gateway to the stunning Inside Australia (http://lakeballard.com; Menzies North West Rd, Lake Ballard): Antony Gormley sculptures on Lake Ballard, an eye-dazzling salt pan 52km northwest of town.

🔒 Shopping

★ **Bush Blossom Gallery**   ART
(☑ 0417 979 901; www.facebook.com/bushblossomgallery; 105 Hannan St, Kalgoorlie; ⊙ 10am-4pm Thu & Fri, to 2pm Sat) This terrific gallery of Aboriginal art stocks works by Ngaatjatjarra, Wongkathja and other regional artists, including some internationally renowned names: Dr Pantjiti Mary McLean, with her unique and instantly recognisable style, plus locally prolific Jason Dimer, Edie Ulrich and others. Styles vary from traditional to contemporary abstract art. Didgeridoos, boomerangs and clapping sticks are also for sale. Curator Monica is happy to chat.

❶ Information

Visitor Centre (☑ 08-9021 1966; www.kalgoorlietourism.com; Town Hall, 316 Hannan St; ⊙ 8.30am-5pm Mon-Fri, 9am-2pm Sat & Sun; 🛜) Plenty of info about the region and town; tour bookings; books for sale on the gold rush; also sells souvenirs, though we'd recommend buying locally-made art instead.

❶ Getting There & Away

Qantas (www.qantas.com.au) and Virgin Australia (www.virginaustralia.com) fly between Perth and Kalgoorlie-Boulder several times daily.

Transwa buses to Esperance ($62, Monday, Wednesday and Friday at 2.30pm, five hours) depart from in front of the **train station** (☑ 1300 662 205; www.transwa.wa.gov.au; Forrest St; ⊙ ticket office 6.30am-noon & 12.30-3pm Mon-Fri, 6.30-8.30am Sat, 11.30am-2.15pm Sun) that doubles as the Transwa booking office.

Transwa (www.transwa.wa.gov.au) runs the Prospector train service from East Perth to Kalgoorlie ($92, seven hours, daily).

Understand Australia

HISTORY 1022

An ancient continent, an ancient people and a few hundred years of European-style turmoil.

ABORIGINAL CULTURE 1036

Aboriginal history, arts and culture will extend your holiday by at least 50,000 years.

ENVIRONMENT 1041

Cyclones, droughts, bushfires – the resident marsupials of this wide brown land have seen it all before.

FOOD & WINE 1049

Food is an Australian religion: worship at cafes, restaurants, farmers markets and less-pious pubs and winery cellar doors.

SPORT 1054

A tapering Olympic medal count, middling soccer and deplorable cricket behaviour aside, Australia still punches above its sporting weight.

History

The story of Australia is an epic 'where the New World meets the Old' in a clash of two very different versions of history. It's only in recent years that the story of Indigenous Australians – here for more than 50,000 years before British colonisation – has come to occupy its rightful place at centre stage. It is a further sign, perhaps, that this dynamic, sometimes progressive and often laid-back country is really starting to grow up.

First Australians

Many academics believe Indigenous Australians came here from somewhere else, with scientific evidence placing them on the continent at least 40,000 to 60,000 years ago. Aboriginal people, however, believe they have always inhabited the land.

At the time of European contact the Aboriginal population was grouped into 300 or more different nations, with distinct languages and land boundaries. Most Aboriginal people did not have permanent shelters but moved within their territory and followed seasonal patterns of animal migration and plant availability. The diversity of landscapes in Australia meant that each nation varied in their lifestyles; and although they were distinct cultural groups, there were also many common elements, and each nation had several clans or family groups who were responsible for looking after specific areas. For thousands of years Aboriginal people lived within a complex kinship system that tied them to the natural environment. From the desert to the sea, Aboriginal people shaped their lives according to their environments and developed different skills and a wide body of knowledge on their territory.

Aboriginal society is a diverse group of several hundred sovereign nations. Torres Strait Islanders are a Melanesian people with a separate culture from that of Aboriginal Australians, though they have a shared history. Together these two groups form Australia's Indigenous peoples.

Strangers Arrive

Zachary Hicks was keeping sleepy watch on the British ship *Endeavour* when suddenly he was wide awake. He summoned his commander, James Cook, who climbed into the brisk morning air to a miraculous sight. Ahead of them lay an uncharted country of wooded hills and gentle valleys. It was 19 April 1770. In the coming days Cook began to draw the first European map of Australia's eastern coast (the Dutch had

TIMELINE	80 million years ago	50,000 years ago	1606
	After separating from the prehistoric Gondwana landmass about 120 million years ago, Australia breaks free from Antarctica and heads north.	The earliest record of Indigenous Australians inhabiting the land. The country is home to lush forests, teeming lakes and giant marsupials – including a wombat the size of a rhinoceros.	Dutch seaman Willem Janszoon 'discovers' Cape York on a foray from the Dutch East Indies, although he mistakes it for part of New Guinea.

arrived along the Western Australian coast more than a century before). He was also mapping the end of Aboriginal supremacy.

Two weeks later Cook led a party of men onto a narrow beach. As they waded ashore, two Aboriginal men stepped onto the sand and challenged the intruders with spears. Cook drove the men off with musket fire. For the rest of that week, the Aboriginal people and the intruders watched each other warily.

The *Endeavour* was a floating annexe of London's leading scientific organisation, the Royal Society. The ship's passengers included technical artists; scientists; a Tahitian interpreter, astronomer and navigator, Tupaia; and a wealthy botanist named Joseph Banks. As Banks and his colleagues explored the Indigenous Australians' territory, they were delighted by the mass of new plants they collected. (The showy flowers called banksia – which look like red, white or golden bottlebrushes – are named after Banks.)

The local Aboriginal people called the place Kurnell; Cook called it 'Botany Bay'. The fertile eastern coastline of Australia is now teeming with Cook's place names – including Point Hicks, Hervey Bay (after an English admiral), Endeavour River and Point Solander (after one of the scientists on the *Endeavour*).

When the *Endeavour* reached the northern tip of Cape York, blue ocean opened up to the west. Cook and his men could smell the sea-route home. And on a small, hilly island ('Possession Island'), Cook raised the Union Jack. Amid volleys of gunfire, he claimed the eastern half of the continent for King George III. Unfortunately Tupaia, who hoped to see England, died on the passage north in Batavia (modern-day Jakarta).

Cook's intention was not to steal land from the Indigenous Australians. In fact, he rather idealised them. 'They are far more happier than we Europeans', he wrote. 'They think themselves provided with all the necessaries of Life and that they have no superfluities'. At most, his patriotic ceremony was intended to contain the territorial ambitions of the French, and of the Dutch, who had visited and mapped much of the western and southern coast over the previous two centuries. Indeed, Cook knew the western half of Australia as 'New Holland'.

Convict Beginnings

In 1788, 18 years after Cook's arrival, the English were back to stay. They arrived in a fleet of 11 ships, packed with supplies including weapons, tools, building materials and livestock. The ships also contained 751 convicts – of various nationalities – and around 250 British soldiers, officials and their wives.

This motley 'First Fleet' was under the command of a humane and diligent naval captain, Arthur Phillip. As his orders dictated, Phillip

---

HISTORY CONVICT BEGINNINGS

Tasmania's Aboriginal people were separated from mainland Australia when sea levels rose after the last ice age. They subsequently developed their own entirely distinct languages and cultures.

A brilliant biography of Cook is Robert Mundle's *Captain James Cook* (2017), a cracking read that takes you right onto the decks of the *Endeavour*. Peter FitzSimon's *Batavia* (2012) relates one of the grimmest and most extraordinary tales of Dutch exploration of West Coast Australia.

1616	**1770**	**1788**	**1789**
The Dutch trading route across the Indian Ocean to Indonesia utilises winds called 'the Roaring Forties'. These winds bring Dutch Captain Dirk Hartog to the Western Australian coast.	Captain James Cook is the first European to map Australia's east coast, which he names New South Wales. He returns to England having found an ideal place for settlement at Botany Bay.	The First Fleet brings British convicts and officials to the lands of the Eora people, where Governor Arthur Phillip establishes a penal settlement that he calls Sydney.	An epidemic of smallpox devastates Indigenous peoples – who have no immunological resistance to it – around Sydney. British officers report that their bodies are rotting in every bay of the harbour.

DUTCH EXPLORERS & THE WRECK OF THE BATAVIA

Australia's history books have long focused on the arrival of Captain James Cook and the First Fleet in the 18th century. But Australia's history of white settlement could have been very different. Most authorities believe that the first European to travel any great distance to the Australian continent was a Dutchman named Willem Janszoon. In 1606 he sailed the speedy little ship *Duyfken* out of the Dutch settlement at Batavia (modern Jakarta) to scout for the Dutch East India Company, and found Cape York (the pointy bit at the top of Australia), which he thought was an extension of New Guinea.

Ten years later, another Dutch ship, the *Eendracht,* rode the mighty Atlantic trade winds, bound for the 'spice islands' of modern Indonesia. But the captain, Dirk Hartog, misjudged his position and stumbled onto the island (near Gladstone) that now bears his name. Hartog inscribed the details of his visit onto a pewter plate and nailed it to a post. In 1697 the island was visited by a second Dutch explorer, named Willem de Vlamingh, who swapped Hartog's plate for one of his own.

Other Dutch mariners were not so lucky: several ships were wrecked on the uncharted western coast of the Aboriginal continent. The most infamous of these is the *Batavia*. In 1629, after the ship struck a reef in the waters off what is today Geraldton, its commander, Francis Pelsaert, transferred the survivors to neighbouring islands in a longboat, then took several crewmembers and sailed to the Dutch East India Company's base at Batavia for help. While he was gone, some mutinous crew members massacred over 100 of the men, women and children who had been on the ship. When Pelsaert returned with a rescue vessel two months later to discover this horror, he executed the murderers, sparing only two youths, whom he marooned on the beach of the continent they knew as New Holland. (Some experts believe the legacy of these boys can be found in the sandy hair and the Dutch-sounding words of some local Aboriginal peoples.) The remains of the *Batavia* and other wrecks are now displayed at the Western Australian Museum (p965) in Geraldton and in Fremantle's WA Shipwrecks Museum (p889), where you can also see de Vlamingh's battered old plate.

The Dutch were merchants scouring the world for commodities. Nothing they saw on the dry coasts of this so-called 'New Holland' convinced them that the land or its native people offered any promise of profit. When another Dutchman named Abel Tasman charted the western and southern coasts of Australia in 1644, he was mapping not a commercial opportunity but a maritime hazard.

dropped anchor at Botany Bay, but the paradise that had so delighted Joseph Banks filled Phillip with dismay. The land was marshy, there was little fresh water, and the anchorage was exposed to wind and storm. So Phillip left his floating prison and embarked in a small boat to search for a better location. Just a short way up the coast his heart leapt as he sailed into the finest harbour in the world. There, in a small cove, in the

1804	1820s	1829	1835
In Van Diemen's Land (today Tasmania), David Collins moves the fledgling convict colony from Risdon Cove to the site of modern Hobart.	Indigenous Australians and European settlers in Van Diemen's Land clash in the Black Wars. The bloody conflict devastates the Aboriginal population – only a few survive.	Captain James Stirling heads a private company that founds the settlement of Perth on Australia's west coast. The surrounding land is arid, slowing the development of the colony.	John Batman sails from Van Diemen's Land to Port Phillip and negotiates a land deal with elders of the Kulin nation. The settlement of Melbourne is founded later that year.

idyllic lands of the Eora people, he established a British penal settlement on 26 January 1788.

He renamed the place after the British Home Secretary, Lord Sydney. The new arrivals set about clearing the trees and building shelters and were soon trying to grow crops. Phillip's official instructions apparently urged him to colonise the land without doing violence to the local inhabitants, not understanding that this dispossession of the land's custodians was death. Many were killed by warfare and new diseases such as smallpox.

The campaign to move Australia's national day of celebration to a different day than 26 January has been gaining momentum. Aboriginal Australians call this fateful date Invasion Day.

Law and order was a problem in the new colony, so in 1803 English officers established a second convict settlement, in Van Diemen's Land (later called Tasmania). Soon, reoffenders filled the grim prison at Port Arthur on the beautiful and wild southern coast near Hobart. Another prison within the penal colony was established at Norfolk Island.

So miserable were these convict beginnings that most Australians long regarded them as a period of shame and distanced themselves from their national history. The growing trend to trace one's family origins has seen more than some white Australians proudly boasting there was a convict in their family tree.

A likeable (and unforgettably named) observer of the first settlement at Sydney was Watkin Tench. His vivid journal is available as *1788*, edited by Tim Flannery. Flannery's *The Explorers* (1998) brings together excerpts from the writings of explorers across Australia.

From Shackles to Freedom

At first, Sydney and Port Arthur depended on supplies brought in by ship. Anxious to develop productive farms, the government 'granted' land to soldiers, officers and free settlers. After 30 years of trial and error, the coloniser's agriculture began to flourish. The most irascible and ruthless of these new landholders was John Macarthur. Along with his spirited wife, Elizabeth, Macarthur pioneered the breeding of merino sheep on his verdant property near Sydney.

Macarthur was also a leading member of the 'Rum Corps', a clique of powerful officers who bullied successive governors (including William Bligh of *Bounty* fame) and grew rich by controlling much of Sydney's trade, notably rum. But the Rum Corps' racketeering was ended in 1810 by a tough new governor named Lachlan Macquarie. Macquarie laid out the major roads of modern-day Sydney, built some fine public buildings (many of which were designed by talented convict-architect Francis Greenway) and helped to lay the foundations for a 'more civil' society.

At this point, word had reached England that the far away colony of Australia offered cheap land and new opportunities, so adventurous

The Dutch and British sailors weren't the first non-Aboriginal people to visit Australia. The Macassans, from the islands of what is now Indonesia, were visiting Arnhem Land (in the Northern Territory's Top End) for centuries before Europeans arrived. Read Andrew McMillan's excellent *An Intruder's Guide to East Arnhem Land* (2001).

1836	1851	1854	1861
Colonel William Light chooses the site for Adelaide on the banks of the River Torrens in the lands of the Kaurna people. Unlike Sydney and Hobart, settlers here are free and willing immigrants.	Prospectors find gold in central Victoria, triggering a great rush of youthful prospectors from across the world. At the same time, the eastern colonies exchange the governor's rule for democracy.	Angered by the hefty cost of licences, gold miners stage a protest at the Eureka Stockade near Ballarat. Several rebels are killed; others are charged with treason. Public opinion supports the rebels.	The explorers Burke and Wills become the first Europeans to cross the continent from south to north. Their expedition is an expensive debacle that claims several lives, including their own.

BENNELONG

Among the Indigenous Australians Governor Philip used as intermediaries was an influential Eora man named Bennelong, who adopted many white customs and manners. After his initial capture, Bennelong learnt to speak and write English and became an interlocutor between his people and the British, both in Australia and on a trip to the United Kingdom in 1792. His 1796 letter to Mr and Mrs Philips is the first known text in English by an Indigenous Australian.

For many years after his return to Sydney, Bennelong lived in a hut built for him on the finger of land now known as Bennelong Point, the site of the Sydney Opera House. He led a clan of 100 people and advised then Governor Hunter. Although accounts suggest he was courageous, intelligent, feisty, funny and 'tender with children', in his later years Bennelong's health and temper were affected by alcohol. He died in 1813 and was buried in the orchard of his friend, brewer James Squire.

migrants took to the oceans in search of their fortunes. At the same time the British government continued to transport prisoners.

In 1825 a party of soldiers and convicts established a new penal settlement in the territory of the Yuggera people, close to modern-day Brisbane. Before long this warm, fertile region was also attracting free settlers, who were soon busy colonising the land for farming, grazing, logging and mining.

Colonised

For Aboriginal Australians the effects of colonisation started immediately after the Europeans arrived. It began with the appropriation of land and water resources and an epidemic of diseases – smallpox killed around half of the Indigenous people who were native to Sydney Harbour. A period of resistance occurred as Aboriginal people fought back to retain their land and way of life; as violence and massacres swept the country, many were pushed away from their traditional lands. Over the course of a century, the Aboriginal population was reduced by 90%.

By the late 1800s most of the fertile land had been taken and most Indigenous Australians were living in poverty on the fringes of settlements or on land unsuitable for settlement. Aboriginal people had to adapt to the new culture, but had few to no rights. Employment opportunities were scarce and most worked as labourers or domestic staff. This cultural and economic disadvantage has continued to the present day, and even though successive government policies and programs have been implemented to assist Aboriginal people, most have had limited effect on improving lives.

Convict History Hotspots

Port Arthur Historic Site (Tasmania)

Parramatta (Sydney, NSW)

Rottnest Island (Perth, WA)

Hyde Park Barracks (Sydney)

1872	1880	1895	1901
Engineer Charles Todd builds a telegraph line from Adelaide to Darwin. It joins an undersea cable to Java, linking Australia to Europe. The age of electronic information in Australia is born.	Police capture the notorious bushranger Ned Kelly at the Victorian town of Glenrowan. Kelly is hanged as a criminal – and remembered by the people as a folk hero.	AB 'Banjo' Paterson's ballad 'The Man from Snowy River' is published. Paterson and his rival Henry Lawson lead the literary movement that creates the legend of the Australian bush.	The Australian colonies form a federation of states. The federal parliament sits in Melbourne, where it passes the *Immigration Restriction Act* – aka the 'White Australia policy'.

More Settlements & Genocide

Australia was not colonised in one event, but over a series of land grabs and skirmishes with different Aboriginal nations. In the cooler grasslands on the island of Tasmania, sheep farmers were establishing themselves and in the 1820s they waged a deadly war against the island's Aboriginal people, driving them to the edge of total annihilation.

Now these migrant settlers were hungry for more land. In 1835 an ambitious young man named John Batman sailed to Port Phillip Bay on the mainland. On the banks of the Yarra River, he chose the location for Melbourne, famously announcing 'This is the place for a village'. Batman reportedly persuaded local Indigenous Australians to sell him their traditional lands (a whopping 250,000 hectares) for a crate of blankets, knives and knick-knacks.

At the same time, a private British company settled Adelaide in South Australia. Proud to have no links with convicts, these God-fearing folks instituted a scheme under which their company sold their newly acquired land to well-heeled settlers then used the revenue to assist poorer British labourers to emigrate. When these worthies earned enough to buy land from the company, that revenue would in turn pay the fare of another shipload of labourers. This all collapsed in a welter of land speculation and bankruptcy, and in 1842 the private South Australian Company yielded to government administration. As miners found rich deposits of silver, lead and copper at Burra, Kapunda and the Mt Lofty Ranges, this settlement began to pay its way for the British.

The Search for Land Continues

Each year, settlers pushed deeper into Aboriginal territories in search of pasture and water for their stock. They became known as squatters – because they 'squatted' on Aboriginal lands – and many held this territory with a gun. To bring order and regulation to the frontier, from the 1830s the governments permitted the squatters to stay on these 'Crown lands' for payment of a nominal rent. Aboriginal history tells of white settlers killing groups of Indigenous Australians in reprisal for the killing of sheep and farmers. Across the country, there are also stories of black resistance leaders, including Yagan of Swan River, Pemulwuy of Sydney and Jandamarra, the outlaw-hero of the Kimberley.

In time, some squatters reached a compromise with local tribes. Indigenous Australians took low- (or no-) paid jobs on sheep and cattle stations as drovers and domestic help. In return they remained on their traditional lands, adapting their cultures to their changing circumstances. This continued in outback pastoral regions until after WWII.

For an introduction to Australian history: Stuart Macintyre's *A Concise History of Australia* (1999), Geoffrey Blainey's *A Shorter History of Australia* (1994) and Bruce Pascoe's *Dark Emu* (2015).

HISTORY MORE SETTLEMENTS & GENOCIDE

1915	1919	1928	1929
On 25 April the Australian and New Zealand Army Corps (the Anzacs) joins an ambitious British attempt to invade Turkey. The ensuing military disaster at Gallipoli spawns a nationalist legend.	Australian aviators Ross and Keith Smith become national heroes after they fly their Vickers Vimy biplane from England to Australia. Both receive knighthoods for their efforts.	Anthony Martin Fernando, the first Aboriginal activist to campaign internationally against racial discrimination in Australia, is arrested for protesting outside Australia House in London.	America's Great Depression spreads to Australia, where many working-class families are thrown into poverty. The violence and suffering of this period imprint themselves on the public memory.

The newcomers had fantasised about the wonders waiting to be discovered from the moment they arrived. Before explorers crossed the Blue Mountains west of Sydney in 1813, some credulous souls imagined that China possibly lay on the other side of the ranges. Explorers, surveyors and scientists began trading theories about inland Australia. Most spoke of an Australian Mississippi. Others predicted desert. An obsessive explorer named Charles Sturt (namesake of the Sturt Hwy) believed in a mystical inland sea.

The explorers' expeditions inland were mostly journeys into disappointment. But Australians made heroes of explorers who died in the wilderness (Ludwig Leichhardt, and the duo of Burke and Wills, are the most striking examples). The Victorian era romanticised these men losing their lives – even if that battle was with this unknown land itself.

Gold & Rebellion

Transportation of convicts to eastern Australia ceased in the 1840s. Soon after, in 1851, prospectors discovered gold in New South Wales and central Victoria. The news hit the colonies with the force of a cyclone. Young men and some adventurous women from every social class headed for the diggings. Soon they were caught up in a great rush of prospectors, entertainers, publicans, 'sly groggers' (illicit liquor sellers), prostitutes and quacks from overseas.

In Victoria, the British governor was alarmed – both by the way the Victorian class system had been thrown into disarray, and by the need to finance law and order on the goldfields. His solution was to compel all miners to buy an expensive monthly licence, partly in the hope that the lower orders would be unable to afford it and return to their duties in town. But the lure of gold was too great. In the reckless excitement of the goldfields, the miners initially endured the thuggish troopers who enforced the government licence. After three years, however, the easy gold at Ballarat was gone, and miners were toiling in deep, water-sodden shafts. They were now infuriated by a corrupt and brutal system of law that held them in contempt. Under the leadership of a charismatic Irishman named Peter Lalor, they raised their own flag, the Southern Cross (which depicts a constellation of stars seen in the Australian night sky), and swore to defend their rights and liberties. They armed themselves and gathered inside a rough stockade at nearby Eureka, where they waited for the government to make its move.

In the predawn of Sunday 3 December 1854, British troops attacked the stockade. It was all over in 15 terrifying minutes. The brutal and one-sided battle claimed the lives of 30 miners and five soldiers. But democracy was in the air and public opinion sided with the civilians. When 13 of

The ill-fated 1860s expedition of explorers Robert O'Hara Burke and William John Wills is well told in *The Dig Tree* (2010) by Sarah Murgatroyd and in *The Aboriginal Story of Burke and Wills: Forgotten Narratives* (2016) by Dr Ian Clark and Fred Cahir. Burke & Wills Web (www.burke andwills.com.au) has an archive of the expedition's records.

1932	1936	1938	1939
Firebrand NSW premier Jack Lang is upstaged when a right-wing activist named Francis de Groot, wearing military uniform and riding a horse, cuts the ribbon to open the Sydney Harbour Bridge.	The last captive thylacine (aka Tasmanian tiger) dies in a Hobart zoo. It's possible thylacines survived in the wild for subsequent decades, but extensive searches have failed to deliver credible evidence.	To mark the 150th anniversary of the arrival of the British, the Aborigines Progressive Association holds a meeting in Australia Hall in Sydney called 'A Day of Mourning and Protest'.	Prime Minister Robert Menzies announces that Britain has gone to war with Hitler's Germany and that 'as a result, Australia is also at war'.

the surviving rebels were tried for their lives, Melbourne juries set them free. Many Australians have found a kind of splendour in these events: the story of the Eureka Stockade is often told as a battle for nationhood and democracy – again illustrating the notion that any 'true' nation must be born out of blood. But these killings were tragically unnecessary. The eastern colonies were already in the process of establishing democratic parliaments, with the full support of the British authorities. In the 1880s Peter Lalor himself became speaker of the Victorian parliament.

The gold rush had also attracted boatloads of prospectors from China. These Asian settlers sometimes endured serious hostility from whites, and were the victims of ugly race riots on the goldfields at Lambing Flat (now called Young) in NSW in 1860–61. Chinese precincts soon developed in the backstreets of Sydney and Melbourne, and popular literature at the time indulged in tales of Chinese opium dens, dingy gambling parlours and brothels. Many Chinese went on to establish themselves in business and, particularly, market gardening. Today the busy Chinatowns of the capital cities and the presence of Chinese restaurants in towns across the country are reminders of the important role of Chinese migrants to Australia since the 1850s.

Gold and wool brought immense investment and gusto to Melbourne and Sydney. By the 1880s they were stylish modern cities, with gaslights in the streets, railways, electricity and that great new invention: the telegraph. In fact, the southern capital became known as 'Marvellous Melbourne', so opulent were its theatres, hotels, galleries and fashions. But the economy was overheating. Many politicians and speculators were engaged in corrupt land deals, while investors poured money into wild and fanciful ventures. It could not last...

Meanwhile, in the West

Western Australia lagged behind the eastern colonies by about 50 years. Though Perth was settled by genteel colonists back in 1829, their material progress was handicapped by isolation, resistance by the Noongar people and the arid climate. It was not until the 1880s that the discovery of remote goldfields promised to gild the fortunes of the isolated colony.

At the time, the west was just entering its own period of self-government, and its first premier was a forceful, weather-beaten explorer named John Forrest. He saw that the mining industry would fail if the government did not provide a first-class harbour, efficient railways and reliable water supplies. Ignoring the threats of private contractors, he appointed the engineer CY O'Connor to design and build each of these as government projects.

Many Aboriginal Australians speak traditional languages as well as English. There were once more than 300 Aboriginal language groups on mainland Australia. The loss of the majority of them represents a significant loss of culture, knowledge and history.

1941	1945	1948	1956
The Japanese attack Pearl Harbor and sweep through Southeast Asia. Australia discovers that it has been abandoned by traditional ally Britain. Instead, it welcomes US forces, based in Australia.	WWII ends. Australia adopts a new slogan, 'Populate or Perish'. Over the next 30 years more than two million immigrants arrive. One-third are British.	Cricketer Don Bradman retires with an unsurpassed test average of 99.94 runs. South African batter Graeme Pollock is next in line, having retired in 1970 with a relatively paltry average of 60.97.	The Olympic Games are held in Melbourne. The Olympic flame is lit by running champion Ron Clarke, and Australia finishes third on the medal tally with an impressive 13 golds.

Growing Calls for Nation

By the end of the 19th century, Australian nationalists tended to idealise 'the bush' and its people. The great forum for this 'bush nationalism' was the massively popular *Bulletin* magazine: its politics were egalitarian, democratic and republican, and its pages were filled with humour and sentiment about daily life written by a swag of writers, most notably Henry Lawson and AB 'Banjo' Paterson.

The 1890s were also a time of great trauma. As the speculative boom came crashing down, unemployment and hunger dealt cruelly with working-class families in the eastern colonies. However, Australian workers had developed a fierce sense that they were entitled to share in the country's prosperity. As the depression deepened, trade unions became more militant in their defence of workers' rights. At the same time, activists intent on winning legal reform established the Australian Labor Party (ALP).

Nationhood

On 1 January 1901 the six colonies of Australia became a federation of self-governing states – the Commonwealth of Australia. When the bewhiskered members of the new national parliament met in Melbourne, their first aim was to protect the identity and values of a European Australia from an influx of Asians and Pacific Islanders. Their solution was a law that became known as the White Australia policy, which would act as a racial tenet of faith in Australia for the next 70 years.

For whites who lived inside the charmed circle of citizenship, this was to be a model society, nestled in the skirts of the British Empire. Just one year later, white women won the right to vote in federal elections (South Australia had led the world by allowing women to vote in 1895). In a series of radical innovations, the government introduced a broad social-welfare scheme and protected Australian wage levels with import tariffs. Its radical mixture of capitalist dynamism and socialist compassion became known as the 'Australian settlement'.

Meanwhile, most Australians continued to live on the coasts of the continent. So forbidding was the arid, desolate inland that the great dry Lake Eyre was given a grim nickname: 'the Dead Heart' of the country. But one prime minister in particular, the dapper Alfred Deakin, dismissed such talk – he and his supporters were determined to triumph over this tyranny of the climate. Even before Federation, in the 1880s, Deakin championed irrigated farming on the Murray River at Mildura. Soon the district was green with grapevines and orchards.

Best History Museums

Rocks Discovery Museum (Sydney, NSW)

Mawson's Huts Replica Museum (Hobart, Tasmania)

Museum of Sydney (Sydney, NSW)

Commissariat Store (Brisbane, Queensland)

Entering the World Stage

Living on the edge of a dry and forbidding land and isolated from the rest of the world, many Australians took comfort in the knowledge that they

1963	1965	1967	1971
A bark petition is presented to the House of Representatives from the people of Yirrikala in the Northern Territory, objecting to mining on their land, which the federal government had approved without consultation.	Prime Minister Menzies commits Australian troops to the US war in Vietnam, dividing national opinion. A total of 426 Australians are killed in action, with a further 2940 wounded.	White Australians vote to grant citizenship to Indigenous Australians. The words 'other than the Aboriginal race in any State' are removed from citizenship qualifications in the Australian Constitution.	The Aboriginal flag first flies on National Aborigines Day in Adelaide. Designed by central Australian Harold Thomas, the flag has become a unifying symbol of identity for Aboriginal peoples.

were a dominion of the British Empire. When WWI broke out in Europe in 1914, thousands of Australians rallied to the Empire's call. They had their first taste of death on 25 April 1915, when the Australian and New Zealand Army Corps (the Anzacs) joined thousands of other British and French troops in an assault on the Gallipoli Peninsula in Turkey. It was eight months of fighting before the British commanders acknowledged that the tactic had failed – by then 8141 young Australians were dead. Before long the Australian Imperial Force was fighting in the killing fields of Europe. By the time the war ended, 60,000 Australians had given their lives in military service. Ever since, on 25 April, Australians have gathered at war memorials around the country for solemn Anzac Day services.

In the 1920s Australia embarked on a decade of chaotic change. Cars began to rival horses on the highway. Young Australians enjoyed American movies in the new cinemas, and – in an atmosphere of sexual freedom not equalled until the 1960s – partied and danced to American jazz. At the same time, popular enthusiasm for the British Empire grew more intense, as if imperial fervour were an antidote to postwar grief. As radicals and reactionaries clashed on the political stage, Australia careered wildly through the 1920s until it collapsed into the abyss of the Great Depression in 1929. World prices for wheat and wool plunged; unemployment brought misery to one in three households. Once again working people experienced the cruelty of a system that treated them as expendable, though for those who were wealthy – or who had jobs – the Depression was hardly noticeable. (If anything, the extreme deflation of the economy enhanced the purchasing power of their money.)

Against the backdrop of the Depression and economic desperation experienced by many Australians, the escape offered by cricket seemed more important than ever, and the 1932 Ashes series for a time unified the nation. The English team, under their captain Douglas Jardine, employed a violent new bowling tactic known as 'bodyline', its aim to unnerve Australia's star batter, the devastatingly efficient Donald Bradman. The bitterness of the tour provoked a diplomatic crisis with Britain, and became part of Australian legend, but Bradman batted on. When he retired in 1948 he had an unsurpassed career average of 99.94 runs.

War with Japan

After 1933 the economy began to recover. The whirl of daily life was hardly dampened when Hitler hurled Europe into a new war in 1939. Though Australians had long feared Japan, they took it for granted that the British navy would keep them safe. In December 1941 Japan bombed the US fleet at Pearl Harbor. Weeks later, the 'impregnable' British naval base in Singapore crumbled, and before long thousands of Australians and other Allied troops were enduring the savagery of Japanese prisoner-of-war camps.

> Australia Day is celebrated on 26 January in recognition of British settlement, but for many Australians (both Indigenous and otherwise) it's known as Invasion Day, Survival Day or Day of Mourning.

> The most accessible version of the Anzac legend is Peter Weir's Australian epic film *Gallipoli* (1981), with a cast that includes a fresh-faced young Mel Gibson.

1972	1973	1974	1975
The Aboriginal Tent Embassy is set up on the lawns of Parliament House in Canberra to oppose the treatment of Aboriginal peoples and the government's recent rejection of a proposal for Aboriginal land rights.	After a conflict-ridden construction, which included the sacking of Danish architect Jørn Utzon, the Sydney Opera House opens for business. This iconic building is granted Unesco World Heritage status in 2007.	Cyclone Tracy tears through Darwin on Christmas Eve, demolishing 70% of the city's buildings and killing 71 people. Much of the city is rebuilt (with stronger construction) within four years.	Against a background of radical reform and uncontrolled inflation, Governor-General Sir John Kerr sacks Labor's Whitlam government and orders a federal election, which the conservatives win.

During WWII the Northern Territory's capital, Darwin, was the front line for Allied action against the Japanese in the Pacific – and in 1942 Japan launched a devastating air attack on the city, killing 243 people and laying waste to its port. It was the only Australian city ever bombed in the war; official reports of the time downplayed the damage to buoy Australians' morale.

As the Japanese swept through Southeast Asia and into Papua New Guinea, the British announced that they could not spare any resources to defend Australia. But the legendary US commander General Douglas MacArthur saw that Australia was the perfect base for US operations in

THE STOLEN GENERATIONS

When Australia became a Federation in 1901, a government policy known as the 'White Australia policy' was put in place. It was implemented mainly to restrict non-white immigration to Australia, but the policy also had a huge impact on Indigenous Australians. Assimilation into the broader society was encouraged by all sectors of government, with the intent to eventually 'fade out' the Aboriginal race. A policy of forcibly removing Aboriginal and Torres Strait Islander children from their families was official from 1909 to 1969, although the practice happened both before and after those years. Although accurate numbers will never be known, it is estimated that around 100,000 Indigenous children – or one in three – were taken from their families.

A government agency, the Aborigines Protection Board, was set up to manage the policy, and had the power to remove children from families without consent, not even needing a court order. Many children never saw their families again; those who did manage to find their way home often found it difficult to maintain relationships. They became known as the Stolen Generations.

In the 1990s the Australian Human Rights Commission held an inquiry into the practice of removing Aboriginal children. *Bringing Them Home,* a nearly 700-page report that was tabled in parliament in May 1997, told of the devastating impact these policies had had on the children and their families. Government bureaus, church missions and welfare agencies all took part in the forced removal, and sexual and physical abuse and cruelty was found to be common in many of the institutions where children were placed. Today many of the Stolen Generations still suffer trauma associated with their early lives.

On 13 February 2008 Kevin Rudd, then prime minister of Australia, offered a national apology to the Stolen Generations. For many Indigenous people it was the start of a national healing process, and today there are many organisations working with the survivors of the Stolen Generations to bring healing and, in some cases, to seek compensation.

To learn more about the Stolen Generations and its impact upon countless Indigenous lives, the film *Rabbit-Proof Fence* (2002) and Archie Roach's classic song 'Took the Children Away' are good places to start.

1979	1979	1983	1987
Despite heated protests from environmental groups, the federal government grants authorisation for the Ranger consortium to mine uranium in the Northern Territory.	After a federal government inquiry in 1978, whaling is banned in Australian waters. The last legally hunted whale is killed in November 1979.	Tasmanian government plans for a hydroelectric dam on the wild Franklin River dominate a federal election campaign. Supporting a 'No Dams' policy, Labor's Bob Hawke becomes prime minister.	A Royal Commission investigates the high number of Aboriginal deaths in police custody and prisons. Aboriginal people remain over-represented in the criminal system today.

the Pacific. In a series of fierce battles on sea and land, Allied forces gradually turned back the Japanese advance. Significantly, it was the USA – not the British Empire – that saved Australia. The days of the nation's alliance with Britain alone were numbered.

Visionary Peace

When WWII ended, a new slogan rang through the land: 'Populate or Perish!' The Australian government embarked on an ambitious scheme to attract thousands of immigrants. With government assistance, people flocked from Britain as well as from non-English-speaking countries, including Greece, Italy, Czechoslovakia, Serbia, Croatia, the Netherlands and Poland, and, later, from Turkey, Lebanon and many others. These 'new Australians' were expected to assimilate into a suburban stereotype known as the 'Australian way of life'.

Many migrants found jobs in the growing manufacturing sector, in which companies such as General Motors and Ford operated with generous tariff support. In addition, the government embarked on audacious public works schemes, notably the mighty Snowy Mountains Hydro-Electric Scheme in the mountains near Canberra. Today environmentalists point out the devastation caused by this huge network of tunnels, dams and power stations, but the Snowy scheme was an expression of a new-found postwar optimism and a testimony to the cooperation among the labourers of many nations who completed the project.

This era of growth and prosperity was dominated by Robert Menzies, the founder of the modern Liberal Party and Australia's longest-serving prime minister, with over 18 years in office. Menzies was steeped in British history and tradition, and liked to play the part of a sentimental monarchist; he was also a vigilant opponent of communism. As Asia succumbed to the chill of the Cold War, Australia and New Zealand entered a formal military alliance with the USA – the 1951 Anzus security pact. When the USA hurled its righteous fury into a civil war in Vietnam, Menzies committed Australian forces to the battle, introducing conscription for military service overseas. The following year Menzies retired, leaving his successors a bitter legacy – the antiwar movement would split Australia.

There was a feeling, too, among many artists, intellectuals and the younger generation that Menzies' Australia had become a rather dull, complacent country, more in love with US and British culture than with its own talents and stories. In an atmosphere of youthful rebellion and emerging nationalism, the Labor Party was elected to power in 1972 under the leadership of a brilliant, idealistic lawyer named Gough Whitlam. In just four short years his government transformed the country: he ended conscription and abolished all university fees, and he introduced a free universal health-care scheme, no-fault divorce, the principle of

David Unaipon (Ngarrindjeri; 1872–1967), the 'Australian Leonardo da Vinci', is remembered as an advocate for Indigenous culture, a writer and an inventor. He took out 19 provisional patents, including drawings for a pre-WWI, boomerang-inspired helicopter. His portrait is on the $50 note.

HISTORY VISIONARY PEACE

1992	**2000**	**2000**	**2007**
Directly overturning the established principle of *terra nullius*, the High Court of Australia recognises the principle of native title in the Mabo decision.	More than 300,000 people walk together across Sydney Harbour Bridge to highlight the need for reconciliation between Indigenous and non-Indigenous Australians.	The Sydney Olympic Games are a triumph of spectacle and good will. Running champ Cathy Freeman, an Indigenous Australian, lights the flame at the opening ceremony and wins gold in the 400m event.	Kevin Rudd is elected prime minister. Marking a change of direction from his conservative predecessor, Rudd says 'sorry' to Indigenous Australians and ratifies the Kyoto Protocol on climate change.

Aboriginal Australian land rights, and equal pay for women. The White Australia policy had been gradually falling into disuse, and under Whitlam it was finally abandoned altogether. By now, around one million migrants had arrived from non-English-speaking countries, and they had filled Australia with new languages, cultures, foods and ideas. Under Whitlam this achievement was embraced as 'multiculturalism'.

By 1975 the Whitlam government was rocked by a tempest of economic inflation and scandal. At the end of 1975 his government was controversially dismissed from office by the governor-general, the Queen's representative within Australia. But the general thrust of Whitlam's social reforms was continued by his successors. The principle of Indigenous land rights was expanded, and from the 1970s Asian immigration increased, and multiculturalism became a new national orthodoxy. Not only that, but China and Japan far outstripped Europe as major trading partners – Australia's economic future lay in Asia.

Australia's first female prime minister – Labor's Julia Gillard – held the position from 2010 to 2013. In 1895 her home state of South Australia was the first colony to give women the right to run for parliament.

Modern Challenges

Today Australia faces new challenges. In the 1970s the country began dismantling its protectionist scaffolding. New efficiency brought new prosperity. At the same time, wages and working conditions, which were once protected by an independent tribunal, became more vulnerable as egalitarianism gave way to competition. And after two centuries of development, the strains on the environment were starting to show – on water supplies, forests, soils, air quality and the oceans.

Under John Howard, Australia's second-longest-serving prime minister (1996–2007), the country grew closer than ever to the USA, joining the Americans in their war in Iraq. Some Australians were dismayed by the conservative Howard government's harsh treatment of asylum seekers, its refusal to acknowledge the reality of climate change, its anti-union

PHAR LAP'S LAST LAP

In the midst of the Depression-era hardship, sport brought escape to an Australia in love with games and gambling. A powerful chestnut-coloured horse called Phar Lap won race after race, culminating in an effortless and graceful victory in the 1930 Melbourne Cup (this annual event is still known as 'the race that stops a nation'). In 1932 the great horse travelled to the racetracks of the USA, where he mysteriously died. In Australia, the gossips insisted that the horse had been poisoned by envious Americans...and the legend grew of a sporting hero cut down in his prime.

Phar Lap was stuffed and can be seen as a revered exhibit at the Melbourne Museum (p474); his skeleton was returned to his birthplace, New Zealand, where it is displayed in Wellington at the country's national museum.

2007	2009	2010	2011
The federal government suspends the *Racial Discrimination Act* to implement a large-scale intervention – the Northern Territory Emergency Response – to address child abuse in NT Aboriginal communities.	On 7 February Australia experiences its worst loss of life in a natural disaster when 400 bushfires kill 173 people in the countryside of Victoria – a day known thereafter as 'Black Saturday'.	Australia's first female prime minister, Julia Gillard, is sworn in. Born in Wales, as a child Gillard emigrated to Australia's warmer climate with her family due to her poor health.	Category 5 Tropical Cyclone Yasi makes landfall at Mission Beach on the north Queensland coast, causing mass devastation to property, infrastructure and crops.

reforms and the prime minister's lack of empathy with Aboriginal Australians. But Howard presided over a period of economic growth that emphasised the values of self-reliance and won him continuing support.

In 2007 Howard was defeated by the Labor Party's Kevin Rudd, an ex-diplomat who issued a formal apology to Indigenous Australians for the injustices they had suffered over the past two centuries. Though it promised sweeping reforms in environment and education, the Rudd government found itself faced with a crisis when the world economy crashed in 2008. In 2010 Rudd lost his position in a leadership spill.

Incoming Prime Minister Julia Gillard, along with other world leaders, now faced three related challenges: climate change, a diminishing fuel supply and a shrinking economy. Since 2013 the prime minister's chair has changed hands several times with a run of leaders after Gillard: Rudd (again); then three Liberal Party leaders in quick succession, Tony Abbott, Malcolm Turnbull and Scott Morrison. A May 2019 election saw the Morrison-led Liberal Party retain control.

Governing the nation, almost 120 years after it was created, has proven to be quite a challenge in the 21st century.

Rights & Reconciliation

The relationship between Indigenous Australians and other Australians hasn't always been an easy one. Over the years several systematic policies have been put in place, but these have often had underlying and often conflicting motives that include control over the land, destroying the population, protection, assimilation, self-determination and self-management.

The history of forced resettlement, removal of children, and the loss of land and culture can never be erased, even with governments addressing some of the issues. Current policies focus on 'closing the gap' and better delivery of essential services to improve lives, but there is still great disparity between Indigenous Australians and the rest of the population, including lower standards of education, employment, health and living conditions; high incarceration and suicide rates; and a lower life expectancy.

Throughout all of this, Aboriginal people have managed to maintain their identity and link to country and culture. Although there is a growing recognition and acceptance of Indigenous Australians' place in the country, there is still a long way to go. Most Aboriginal people have no real political or economic wealth, but their struggle for legal and cultural rights continues and is always at the forefront of politics. Any gains for Aboriginal people have been hard-won and initiated by Aboriginal communities themselves.

> When ex-prime minister Gough Whitlam died in 2014, Aboriginal leader Noel Pearson gave one of the great public speeches in Australia's history. Watch the eulogy at www.youtube.com/watch?v=JsXmY-HiuJ8s.

> British scientists detonated seven nuclear bombs at Maralinga in remote South Australia in the 1950s and early 1960s, with devastating effects on the local Maralinga Tjarutja people. Lesser known are the three nuclear tests carried out in the Monte-bello Islands in Western Australia in the '50s; a good read on the subject is Robert Drewe's *Monte-bello* (2012).

2013	2014	2015	2019
After widespread flooding in 2011, Queensland is again inundated as ex-Tropical Cyclone Oswald passes through; Bundaberg is particularly badly affected. The total damage bill is estimated at $2.4 billion.	New conservative Prime Minister Tony Abbott commits RAAF combat aircraft and army special forces advisers to a multinational military operation against Islamic extremists in Iraq.	A Barngarla native-title claim over a vast section of South Australia's Eyre Peninsula is upheld in the Federal Court.	Behrouz Boochani, an asylum seeker detained in an offshore detention centre in Papua New Guinea, wins Australia's richest literary prize in the Victorian Premier's Literary Awards for his novel *No Friend but the Mountains*.

Aboriginal Culture

Cathy Craigie

Aboriginal culture has evolved over thousands of years with strong links between the spiritual, economic and social lives of the people. This heritage has been kept alive from one generation to the next by the passing of knowledge and skills through rituals, art, cultural material and language. From the cities to the bush, there are opportunities to get up close with Australia's Indigenous people and learn from a way of life that has existed for over 50,000 years.

Cathy Craigie is a Gamilaori/Anaiwon woman from northern New South Wales. She is a freelance writer and cultural consultant and has extensive experience in Aboriginal affairs.

Indigenous Australians originally had an oral tradition, and language has played an important role in preserving Aboriginal cultures. Today there is a national movement to revive Aboriginal languages and a strong Aboriginal art sector; traditional knowledge is also being used in science, natural resource management and government programs. Aboriginal culture has never been static, and continues to evolve with the changing times and environment. New technologies and media are now used to tell Aboriginal stories, and cultural tourism ventures, through which visitors can experience the perspectives of Indigenous peoples, have been established. You can learn about ancestral beings at particular natural landmarks, look at rock art that is thousands of years old, taste traditional foods or attend an Aboriginal festival or performance.

Government support for cultural programs is sporadic and depends on the political climate at the time. However, Aboriginal people are determined to maintain their links with the past and to also use their cultural knowledge to shape a better future.

The Land

When Europeans first saw a corroboree they described it as a 'bush opera'. These festive social events combine music, dance and drama performances with body art. One of the first recorded corroborees was in 1791 at Bennelong Point, now rather appropriately the site of the Sydney Opera House.

Aboriginal culture views humans as part of the ecology, not separate from it. Everything is connected – a whole environment that sustains the spiritual, economic and cultural lives of the people. In turn, Aboriginal people have sustained the land over thousands of years, through knowledge passed on in ceremonies, rituals, songs and stories. Land is intrinsically connected to identity and spirituality; all land in Australia is reflected in Aboriginal lore, but particular places may be significant for religious and cultural beliefs. Some well-known sites are the Three Sisters in the Blue Mountains, and Warreen Cave in Tasmania, which has artefacts dated around 40,000 years old.

Sacred sites can be parts of rocks, hills, trees or water and are associated with an ancestral being or an event that occurred. Often these sites are part of a Dreaming story and link people across areas. The ranges around Alice Springs are part of the caterpillar Dreaming, with many sites including Akeyulerre (Billy Goat Hill), Atnelkentyarliweke (Anzac Hill) and rock paintings at Emily Gap. The most well known are Uluru and Kata Tjuta, which is the home of the snake Wanambi – his breath is the wind that blows through the gorge. Pirla Warna Warna, a significant site in the Tanami Desert for Warlpiri people, is 430km northwest of Alice Springs (NT) and is where several Walpiri Dreaming stories meet.

Cultural tours to Aboriginal sites can provide opportunities to learn about plants and animals, hunting and fishing, bush food or dance.

Please note that many Indigenous sites are protected by law and are not to be disturbed in any way.

The Arts

Aboriginal art has impacted the Australian cultural landscape and is now showcased at national and international events and celebrated as a significant part of Australian culture. It still retains the role of passing on knowledge, but today is also important for economic, educational and political reasons. Art has been used to raise awareness of issues such as health and has been a primary tool for the reconciliation process in Australia. In many Indigenous communities art has become a major source of employment and income.

Visual Arts

Although there is no word in Indigenous Australian languages for 'art', visual imagery is a fundamental part of Aboriginal culture and life: a connection between the past, present and future, and between Aboriginal people and their traditional homelands. The earliest forms of Indigenous visual cultural expression were rock carvings (petroglyphs), paintings on rock galleries, body painting and ground designs, with the earliest engraved designs known to exist dating back at least 40,000 years – perhaps longer.

Rock Art

Rock art is the oldest form of human art: Indigenous rock art stretches back thousands of years and is found in every state of Australia. For Aboriginal people, rock art is a direct link with life before Europeans. The art and the process of making it are part of songs, stories and customs that connect the people to the land. There are a number of different styles of rock art across Australia. These include engravings in sandstone, and stencils, prints and drawings in rock shelters. Aboriginal people created rock art for several reasons, including as part of a ritual or ceremony and to record events.

Some of the oldest examples of engravings can be found in the Pilbara in Western Australia (WA) and in Olary in South Australia (SA), where there's an engraving of a crocodile – quite amazing as crocodiles are not found in this part of Australia. Rock art in the Kimberley (WA) focuses on the Wandjina, the ancestral creation spirits. All national parks surrounding Sydney have rock engravings and are easily accessed and viewed. At Gariwerd (The Grampians) in Victoria, there are hand prints and hand stencils. There's also the Wangaar-Wuri painted rock art sites near Cooktown in Queensland.

In the NT, many of the rock-art sites have patterns and symbols that appear in paintings, carvings and other cultural material. Kakadu National Park has more than 5000 recorded sites, but many more are thought to exist across the Arnhem Land Escarpment, some of which are over 20,000 years old. There's even a depiction of a thylacine (Tasmanian tiger). World Heritage–listed Kakadu is internationally recognised for its cultural significance.

In central Australia, rock paintings still have religious significance. Here Aboriginal people continue to retouch the art as part of ritual and to connect them to stories. In most other areas, people no longer paint rock images, but instead work on bark, paper and canvas.

The Koorie Heritage Trust (www.koorieheritagetrust.com) is an excellent resource on Victorian Aboriginal culture. In Victoria, as around the country, Aboriginal art is part of a living and dynamic culture, and is a great way to engage with Indigenous Australians.

The *Macquarie PEN Anthology of Aboriginal Literature* (www.macquariepenanthology.com.au) offers over 200 years of Aboriginal culture, history and life. It starts with Bennelong's letter in 1796 and includes works from some of Indigenous Australia's best writers.

ABORIGINAL CULTURE VISUAL ARTS

If you visit rock-art sites, please do not touch or damage the art, and respect the sites and the surrounding areas.

The *Koori Mail* (www.koorimail.com) is an Aboriginal-owned national newspaper. Set up by several Aboriginal communities in 1991 to give a voice to Indigenous Australians, it provides news and information on politics, sport and social and cultural life from communities across Australia.

Contemporary Art

The contemporary Indigenous art industry started in a tiny community called Papunya (NT) in central Australia. It was occupied by residents from several language groups who had been displaced from their traditional lands. In 1971 an art teacher at Papunya school encouraged painting and some senior men took an interest. This started the process of transferring sand and body drawings onto modern mediums and the 'dot and circle' style of contemporary painting began. The emergence of dot paintings is one of the most important movements in 20th-century Australian art, and the Papunya Tula artists became a model for other Aboriginal communities.

The National Gallery of Australia (p254) in Canberra has a fantastic collection, but contemporary Aboriginal art can also be viewed at any public art gallery or in one of the many independent galleries dealing in Aboriginal work. Contemporary artists work in all media and Aboriginal art has appeared on unconventional surfaces such as a BMW car and a Qantas plane. The central desert area is still a hub for Aboriginal art and Alice Springs is one of the best places to see and buy art. Cairns is another hotspot for innovative Aboriginal art.

If you are buying art, make sure that provenance of the work is included. This tells the artist's name, the community and language group they come from and the story of the work. If it is an authentic work, all proceeds will go back to the artist. Australia has a resale royalty scheme.

Music

Music has always been a vital part of Aboriginal culture. Songs were important for teaching and passing on knowledge, and musical instruments were often used in healing, ceremonies and rituals. The most well-known instrument is the *yidaki* (didgeridoo), which was traditionally played in northern Australia, and only by men. Other instruments included clapsticks, rattles and boomerangs; in southern Australia, animal skins were stretched across the lap to make a drumming sound.

THE IMPORTANCE OF STORYTELLING

Indigenous Australians historically had an oral culture, so storytelling was an important way to learn. Stories gave meaning to life and were used to teach the messages of the spirit ancestors. Although beliefs and cultural practices vary according to region and language groups, there is a common world-view that these ancestors created the land, the sea and all living things. This is often referred to as the Dreaming.

Through stories, the knowledge and beliefs are passed on from one generation to another, setting out the community's social mores and recording events from the past. Today artists have continued this tradition with new media such as film and literature. The first published Indigenous Australian was David Unaipon (1872–1967), a Ngarrindjeri man from South Australia who was a writer, a scientist and an advocate for his people, and the author of *Aboriginal Legends* (1927) and *Native Legends* (1929) – you can see Unaipon's portrait on the $50 note.

Other early published writers were Oodgeroo Noonuccal, Kevin Gilbert and Jack Davis. Contemporary writers of note include Alexis Wright, Kim Scott, Anita Heiss and Ali Cobby Eckerman. Award-winning novels to read are Kim Scott's *Deadman Dancing* (2010) and *Benang* (1999); Alexis Wright's *Carpentaria* (2006); and Ali Cobby Eckerman's *Little Bit Long Time* (2009) and *Ruby Moonlight* (2012).

DR G YUNUPINGU

Described by *Rolling Stone* magazine as 'Australia's Most Important Voice', sight-impaired singer Dr G Yunupingu sang in his Yolngu language from Arnhem Land. His angelic voice told of identity, connecting with land and community. Gurrumul entranced Australian and overseas audiences with multi-awarded albums: *Gurrumul* (2008) and *Rrakala* (2011) and *The Gospel Album* (2015). He died in 2017 aged 46.

This rich musical heritage continues today with a strong contemporary music industry. Like other art forms, Aboriginal music has developed into a fusion of new ideas and styles mixed with strong cultural identity. Contemporary artists such as Dan Sultan, Thelma Plum and Jessica Mauboy have crossed over successfully into the mainstream, winning major music awards and seen regularly on popular programs and at major music festivals. Aboriginal radio (p1039) is the best and most accessible way to hear Aboriginal music.

Performing Arts

Dance and theatre are a vital part of Aboriginal culture. Traditional styles vary from one nation to the next; imitation of animals, birds and the elements is common across all nations, but arm, leg and body movements differ greatly. Ceremonial or ritual dances, often telling stories to pass on knowledge, are highly structured and are distinct from the social dancing at corroborees (Aboriginal gatherings). Like other Indigenous art forms, dance has adapted to the modern world, with contemporary dance groups bringing a modern interpretation to traditional forms. The most well-known dance company is the internationally acclaimed Bangarra Dance Theatre (p130).

Theatre also draws on the storytelling tradition, where drama and dance came together in ceremonies or corroborees, and this still occurs in many contemporary productions. Today Australia has a thriving Aboriginal theatre industry and many Indigenous actors and writers work in or collaborate with mainstream productions. There are two major Aboriginal theatre companies – Ilbijerri (www.ilbijerri.com.au) in Melbourne and Yirra Yakin (www.yirrayaakin.com.au) in Perth – as well as several mainstream companies that specialise in Aboriginal stories and have had successful productions in Australia and overseas.

After many years of lobbying by Indigenous Australians to have their language and culture reflected in the media, NITV (www.nitv.org.au) hit the airwaves in 2007. It broadcasts via the free-to-air TV channel SBS, with news, views and current affairs, as well as programs for children, documentaries and sports programs.

TV, Radio & Film

Aboriginal people have developed an extensive media network of radio, print and TV services. There are more than 120 Aboriginal radio stations and programs operating across Australia – in cities, rural areas and remote communities. Program formats differ from location to location: some broadcast only in Aboriginal languages or cater to specific music tastes. From its base in Brisbane, the National Indigenous Radio Service (NIRS; www.nirs.org.au) broadcasts four radio channels of Aboriginal content via satellite and over the internet. There's also Radio Larrikia (www.radiolarrakia.org) in Darwin and Koori Radio (www.kooriradio.com) in Sydney.

There's a thriving Aboriginal film industry and in recent years feature films such as *The Sapphires, Top End Wedding, Bran Nue Day, Samson and Delilah* and *Putuparri and the Rainmakers* have had mainstream success. Since the first Aboriginal TV channel, NITV (www.nitv.org.au), was launched in 2007, there has been an increase in the number of film-makers wanting to tell their stories.

CONNECTING WITH ABORIGINAL CULTURE

A study in the past decade found that six out of ten non-Indigenous Australians have had little to no contact with Aboriginal people. But this country's First Peoples have long been entrepreneurs, and the 21st century is bringing new ways for new and old Australia to connect.

Technology & Science

Did you know Indigenous Australians were the world's first bakers? There is evidence of this ingenuity in ancient grind stones discovered in what we now call New South Wales. Following this, it shouldn't surprise that Aboriginal and Torres Strait Islander people are leading efforts to revolutionise how we use technology and science in Australia today. From bringing to life ancient stories to finding new ways of understanding the world through traditional knowledges, the possibilities are endless.

Apps & Virtual Reality

You can get an app for just about anything these days – and that includes many Indigenous languages. Heading out to western NSW? Why not download the Wiradjuri dictionary app. You'll be surprised by how many language groups have jumped on board this growing trend.

Meanwhile virtual reality is fast becoming a tool to bring old knowledges into the present. The past few years have seen the emergence of experiences such as Collisions: a virtual storytelling of British nuclear testing in the South Australian desert at a place called Maralinga. Aboriginal people can now tell their version of what happened with immersive visualisations and sound effects.

But can we push technology to take us back further? New augmented reality technology allows just that, with apps like Indigital Storytelling. Download for free and simply point the camera at culturally significant sites, such as the rock paintings in Kakadu National Park that date back tens of thousands of years. You will experience a visual storytelling of that site, and each word and image has been approved by traditional owners.

This kind of virtual tour guide is gaining traction, with growing benefits for visitors to Australia. Aboriginal people view this country a bit like Europe: a continent made up of many nations. The Welcome to Country app tries to capture this complexity by sending a push notification when you cross borders and loading video of a traditional greeting that explains the protocols of distinct nations.

The app is still adding each of the more than 500 tribes and language groups, but there are plenty for you to download and get started today.

Indigenous Art Today

Nowadays you can find Aboriginal artwork spray painted on brick laneways in Melbourne and across silos in country towns. Capital cities boast galleries brimming with new-age Indigenous art and multimedia experiences that take on new dimensions. From the Fringe Festival in Perth to Melbourne's luminous White Night and Sydney's Vivid experience, there are myriad cultural events on throughout the year where you can spot new and exciting Indigenous artists.

For an event like no other check out the Winds of Zenadth (www.tsirc.qld.gov.au/news-events/events/winds-zenadth-cultural-festival) on Thursday Island, or immerse yourself in Giiyong Festival (https://giiyong.com.au) on the NSW South Coast.

Rachael Hocking

Environment

Tim Flannery

Australia's plants and animals are just about the closest things to alien life on earth. That's because Australia has been isolated from the other continents for a very long time: around 80 million years. Unlike those on other habitable continents that have been linked by land bridges, Australia's birds, mammals, reptiles and plants have taken their own separate and very different evolutionary journey. The result today is one of the world's most distinct natural realms – and among the most diverse.

A Unique Environment

The first naturalists to investigate Australia were astonished by what they found. Here the swans were black – to Europeans this was a metaphor for the impossible – and mammals such as the platypus and echidna were discovered to lay eggs. It really was an upside-down world, where many of the larger animals hopped and where each year the trees shed their bark rather than their leaves.

If you are visiting Australia for a short time, you might need to go out of your way to experience some of the richness of the environment. That's because Australia is a subtle place, and some of the natural environment – especially around the cities – has been damaged or replaced by trees and creatures from Europe. Places like Sydney, however, have preserved extraordinary fragments of their original environment that are relatively easy to access. Before you enjoy them though, it's worthwhile understanding the basics about how nature operates in Australia. This is important because there's nowhere like Australia, and once you have an insight into its origins and natural rhythms, you will appreciate the place so much more.

There are two important factors that go a long way towards explaining nature in Australia: its soils and its climate. Both are unique.

Climate

In most parts of the world outside the wet tropics, life responds to the rhythm of the seasons – summer to winter, or wet to dry. Most of Australia experiences seasons – sometimes severe ones – yet life does not respond solely to them. This can clearly be seen by the fact that although there's plenty of snow and cold country in Australia, there are almost no trees that shed their leaves in winter, nor do many Australian animals hibernate. Instead there is a far more potent climatic force that Australian life must obey: El Niño.

El Niño is a complex climatic pattern that can cause major weather shifts around the South Pacific. The cycle of flood and drought that El Niño brings to Australia is profound. Our rivers – even the mighty Murray River, which is the nation's largest and runs through the southeast – can be miles wide one year, yet you can literally step over its flow the next. This is the power of El Niño, and its effect, when combined with Australia's poor soils, manifests itself compellingly.

Professor Tim Flannery is a scientist, explorer, activist, writer and the chief councillor of the independent Climate Council. He was named Australian of the Year in 2007. He has written several award-winning books, including *The Future Eaters*, *Throwim Way Leg* (an account of his work as a biologist in New Guinea) and *The Weather Makers*.

The Coastal Studies Unit at the University of Sydney has deemed there to be an astonishing 10,685 beaches in Australia! (They define a beach as a stretch of sand that's more than 20m long and remains dry at high tide.)

WILD SYDNEY

If your Australian visit extends only as far as Sydney, don't give up on seeing Australian nature. The sandstone area extending for 150km around Sydney is one of the most diverse and spectacular regions in Australia. In springtime, beautiful red waratahs abound in the region's parks, while the woody pear (a relative of the waratah) that so confounded the early colonists can also be seen, alongside more than 1500 other species of flowering plants.

Even in a Sydney backyard you're likely to see more reptile species (mostly skinks) than can be found in all of Great Britain – so keep an eye out!

Soils & Geology

In recent geological times, on other continents, processes such as volcanism, mountain building and glacial activity have been busy creating new soil. Just think of the glacier-derived soils of North America, North Asia and Europe. The rich soils of India and parts of South America were made by rivers eroding mountains, while Java in Indonesia owes its extraordinary richness to volcanoes.

All of these soil-forming processes have been almost absent from Australia in more recent times. Only volcanoes have made a contribution, and they cover less than 2% of the continent's land area. In fact, for the last 90 million years, beginning deep in the age of dinosaurs, Australia has been geologically comatose. It was too flat, warm and dry to attract glaciers, its crust too ancient and thick to be punctured by volcanoes or folded into mountains. Look at Uluru and Kata Tjuta. They are the stumps of mountains that 350 million years ago were the height of the Andes. Yet for hundreds of millions of years they've been nothing but nubs.

Under such conditions no new soil is created and the old soil is leached of all its goodness by the rain, and is blown and washed away. Even if just 30cm of rain falls each year, that adds up to a column of water 30 million kilometres high passing through the soil over 100 million years, and that can do a great deal of leaching! Almost all of Australia's mountain ranges are more than 90 million years old, so you will see a lot of sand here, and a lot of country where the rocky 'bones' of the land are sticking up through the soil. It is an old, infertile landscape and life in Australia has been adapting to these conditions for aeons.

Uluru is often thought to be the world's largest monolith, but in fact it only takes second prize. The biggest is Burringurrah (Mt Augustus) in WA, which is 2½ times the size of Uluru.

Current Environmental Issues

Headlining the environmental issues facing Australia's fragile landscape at present are climate change, water scarcity, nuclear energy and uranium mining. All are interconnected. For Australia, the warmer temperatures resulting from climate change spell disaster to an already fragile landscape. A 2°C climb in average temperatures on the globe's driest continent will result in an even drier southern half of the country and greater water scarcity. Scientists also agree that hotter and drier conditions will exacerbate bushfire conditions and increase cyclone intensity.

Australia is a heavy greenhouse-gas emitter because it relies on coal and other fossil fuels for its energy supplies. The most prominent and also contentious alternative energy source is nuclear power, which creates less greenhouse gases and relies on uranium, in which Australia is rich. But the radioactive waste created by nuclear power stations can take thousands of years to become harmless. Moreover, uranium is a finite energy source (as opposed to even cleaner and also renewable energy sources such as solar and wind power) – and even if Australia were to establish sufficient nuclear power stations now to make a real reduction in coal dependency, it would be years before the environmental and economic benefits were realised.

Australia has seen some devastating bushfires in the last decade. The 2009 'Black Saturday' fires in Victoria claimed 173 lives. In 2015 Adelaide Hills bushfires burned 125 sq km; the same year fires along Victoria's Great Ocean Road consumed over 100 homes; and fires in Tasmania in 2013 and 2019 devastated forest and homes.

Uranium mining also produces polarised opinions. Because countries around the world are also looking to nuclear energy, Australia finds itself in a position to increase exports of one of its top-dollar resources. But uranium mining in Australia has been met with fierce opposition, not only because the product is a core ingredient of nuclear weapons, but also because much of Australia's uranium supplies sit beneath sacred Indigenous land. Supporters of increased uranium mining and export suggest that the best way to police the use of uranium is to manage its entire life cycle: that is, to sell the raw product to international buyers, and then charge a fee to accept the waste and dispose of it. Both major political parties consider an expansion of Australia's uranium export industry to be inevitable for economic reasons.

Malaise of the Murray–Darling

The Murray–Darling Basin is Australia's largest river system, flowing through Queensland, New South Wales, the Australian Capital Territory, Victoria then South Australia, covering an area of 1.05 million sq km – roughly 14% of Australia. Aside from quenching around a third of the country's agricultural and urban thirsts, it also irrigates precious rainforests, wetlands, subtropical areas and scorched arid lands.

But drought, irrigation and climate change have depleted Murray–Darling flows. Wetland areas around the Darling River that used to flood every five years are now likely to do so every 25 years, and prolific species are threatened with extinction. That the entire system will become too salty and unusable is a very real danger.

Rains and widespread flooding across eastern Australia since 2010 have increased flows, but finding the delicate balance between agricultural and environmental water allocations continues to cause political and social turmoil across five states and territories.

Environmental Challenges

The European colonisation of Australia, commencing in 1788, heralded a period of catastrophic environmental upheaval. The result today is that Australians are struggling with some of the most severe environmental problems to be found anywhere in the world. It may seem strange that a population of just 24 million, living in a continent the size of the USA (minus Alaska), could inflict such damage on its environment, but Australia's long isolation, its fragile soils and difficult climate have made it particularly vulnerable to human-induced change.

Environmental damage has been inflicted in several ways, some of the most important being the introduction of pest species, destruction of forests, overstocking range lands and interference with water flows.

Beginning with the escape of domestic cats into the Australian bush shortly after 1788, a plethora of vermin – from foxes to wild camels and cane toads – have run wild in Australia, causing extinctions in the native fauna. One out of every 10 native mammals living in Australia prior to European colonisation is now extinct, and many more are highly endangered. Extinctions have also affected native plants, birds and amphibians.

The destruction of forests has also had an effect on the environment. Most of Australia's rainforests have suffered clearing, while conservationists fight with loggers over the fate of the last unprotected stands of 'old growth'.

Many Australian range lands have been chronically overstocked for more than a century, the result being the extreme vulnerability of both soils and rural economies to Australia's drought and flood cycle, as well as the extinction of many native species. The development of agriculture has involved land clearance and the provision of irrigation; again the

World Heritage Wonders

Great Barrier Reef
(Queensland)

South West Wilderness
(Tasmania)

Uluru-Kata Tjuta National Park (NT)

Kakadu National Park (NT)

ENVIRONMENT ENVIRONMENTAL CHALLENGES

In 2016 Unesco warned that the Great Barrier Reef may be placed on its Danger List, which covers those sites considered at risk unless action is taken. Bleaching of the coral, caused by a combination of climate change and increased human activity in the area, is considered the most serious risk to the reef's future.

effect has been profound. Clearing of the diverse and spectacular plant communities of the Western Australia wheat belt began just a century ago, yet today up to one-third of that country is degraded by salination of the soils.

Just 1.5% of Australia's land surface provides over 95% of its agricultural yield, and much of this land lies in the irrigated regions of the Murray-Darling Basin. This is Australia's agricultural heartland, yet it too is under severe threat from salting of soils and rivers. Irrigation water penetrates into the sediments laid down in an ancient sea, carrying salt into the catchments and fields. The Snowy River in NSW and Victoria also faces a battle for survival.

Despite the enormity of the biological crisis engulfing Australia, governments and the community have been slow to respond. It was in the 1980s that coordinated action began to take place, but not until the '90s that major steps were taken. The establishment of **Landcare** (www. landcareaustralia.com.au), an organisation enabling people to effectively address local environmental issues, and the expenditure of over $2 billion through the federal government program 'Caring for our Country' have been important national initiatives. Yet so difficult are some of the issues the nation faces that, as yet, little has been achieved in terms of halting the destructive processes.

So severe are Australia's environmental problems that it will take a revolution before they can be overcome, for sustainable practices need to be implemented in every arena of life – from farms to suburbs and city centres. Renewable energy, sustainable agriculture and water use lie at the heart of these changes, and Australians are only now developing the road map to sustainability that they so desperately need if they are to have a long-term future on the continent.

Feral Animals

The introduction of animals from other countries in the last 200 years has contributed significantly to the fragmentation of ecosystems and the extinction of native animals in Australia. Introduced species include foxes, rabbits, cats, pigs, goats, donkeys, horses, camels, starlings, sparrows, cane toads, mosquitofish and carp. They each bring a unique suite of problems as they carve out a niche for themselves in their new environment – some as predators of native animals, others as competitors for the limited resources of food, water and shelter.

By one estimate, there are 15 million feral cats alone in Australia and the **Australian Wildlife Conservancy** (AWC; www.australianwildlife. org) warns that each cat could be eating five native animals every night (which would be 75 million across the continent per day!). While other scientists warn that these figures are too high – one recent study put the number of feral cats in Australia at closer to 2.3 million – no one argues that feral animals are an existential threat to Australia's native wildlife.

The AWC currently runs at least eight wildlife sanctuaries in Northern Territory and South Australia. Some of these sanctuaries are vast and some are fenced to keep out feral animals once they have been eradicated within the fenced areas. By then being able to restore ecosystems and, in some cases, reintroduce native mammal species, AWC hopes to repopulate parts of the Outback with species that haven't been seen in decades. One such sanctuary that you can visit is Pungalina – Seven Emu Wildlife Sanctuary (p848), up on the Gulf of Carpentaria, east of Borroloola.

The Australian Conservation Foundation (p1046) is Australia's largest nongovernment organisation involved in protecting the environment, while the Wilderness Society (p1046) focuses on protection of wilderness and forests.

Fauna & Flora

Australia's wildlife and plant species are as diverse as they are perfectly adapted to the country's soils and climate.

Birds

Australia has 898 recorded bird species, although an estimated 165 of these are considered to be vagrants, with only a handful of sightings (or occasionally even one!) recorded. Nearly half of all Australian birds are not found anywhere else on earth. A 2014 study by the Commonwealth Scientific and Industrial Research Organisation (CSIRO) warned that as many as 10% of Australia's birds could become extinct by the end of the century.

Relatively few of Australia's birds are seasonal breeders, and few migrate – instead, they breed when the rain comes. A large percentage are nomads, following the rain across the breadth of the continent.

So challenging are conditions in Australia that its birds have developed some extraordinary habits. Kookaburras, magpies and blue wrens (to name just a few) have developed a breeding system called 'helpers at the nest'. The helpers are the young adult birds of previous broods, which stay with their parents to help bring up the new chicks. Just why they should do this was a mystery until it was realised that conditions in Australia can be so harsh that more than two adult birds are needed to feed the nestlings. This pattern of breeding is very rare in places like Asia, Europe and North America, but it is common in many Australian birds.

Flora

Australia's plants can be irresistibly fascinating. If you happen to be in the Perth area in spring, it's well worth taking a wildflower tour. The best flowers grow on the arid and monotonous sand plains, and the blaze of colour produced by the kangaroo paws, banksias and similar native plants can be dizzying. The sheer variety of flowers is amazing, with 4000 species crowded into the southwestern corner of the continent. This diversity of prolific flowering plants has long puzzled botanists. Again, Australia's poor soils seem to be the cause. The sand plain is about the poorest soil in Australia – it's almost pure quartz. This prevents any single fast-growing species from dominating. Instead, thousands of specialist plant species have learned to find a narrow niche and so coexist. Some live at the foot of the metre-high sand dunes, some on top, some on an east-facing slope, some on the west and so on. Their flowers need to be striking in order to attract pollinators, for nutrients are so lacking in this sandy world that even insects such as bees are rare.

If you do get to walk the wildflower regions of the southwest, keep your eyes open for the sundews. Australia is the centre of diversity

Birdlife Australia (www.birdlife.org.au) is the nation's peak birding body; it organises birding excursions and publishes a regular newsletter. Watch its website for updates on unusual sightings.

The Field Guide to the Birds of Australia (9th ed, 2012) by Graham Pizzey and Frank Knight is our pick of the birding field guides. Another essential resource is *The Complete Guide to Finding the Birds of Australia* (2011) by Richard Thomas and others, with some specific recommendations on where to find elusive species.

ENVIRONMENT FAUNA & FLORA

PARROTS: GOOD & BAD NEWS

Australia has more than 50 parrot species. Some, like the Australian galah, the sulphur-crested cockatoo and the long- and short-billed corellas, are abundant to the point of being a pest for farmers in remote communities.

And yet, it was a parrot – the paradise parrot, last seen in the 1920s – that is widely recognised to be the first bird species to have fallen extinct on the Australian mainland. A likely candidate to follow in its footsteps is the orange-bellied parrot, which migrates between southern Victoria and southwestern Tasmania. With its numbers in the wild down to just 50 breeding pairs, it appears that their greatest hope may lie in captive-breeding programs, such as at Healesville Sanctuary (p520) just outside Melbourne.

At the same time, another parrot has come back from the dead. Until recently, the night parrot was thought to be extinct, having last been seen around the same time as the paradise parrot in the 1920s. A handful of possible sightings in the decades that followed came to nothing, until two dead specimens were found in far southwestern Queensland in 1990 and 2006.

ENVIRONMENT & CONSERVATION GROUPS

→ The **Australian Conservation Foundation** (www.acf.org.au) is Australia's largest nongovernment organisation involved in protecting the environment.

→ **Bush Heritage Australia** (www.bushheritage.org.au) and Australian Wildlife Conservancy (p1044) allow people to donate funds and time to conserving native species.

→ Want to get your hands dirty? **Conservation Volunteers Australia** (www.conservationvolunteers.com.au) is a nonprofit organisation focusing on practical conservation projects such as tree planting, walking-track construction, and flora and fauna surveys.

→ **Ecotourism Australia** (www.ecotourism.org.au) has an accreditation system for environmentally friendly and sustainable tourism in Australia, and lists ecofriendly tours, accommodation and attractions by state.

→ The **Wilderness Society** (www.wilderness.org.au) focuses on protection of wilderness and forests.

Official Floral Emblems

Common heath (Victoria)

Cooktown orchid (Queensland)

Red and green kangaroo paw (WA)

Royal bluebell (ACT)

Tasmanian blue gum (Tasmania)

Sturt's desert pea (SA)

Sturt's desert rose (NT)

Waratah (NSW)

for these beautiful, carnivorous plants. They've given up on the soil supplying their nutritional needs and have turned instead to trapping insects with the sweet globs of moisture on their leaves, and digesting them to obtain nitrogen and phosphorus.

If you are very lucky, you might see a honey possum. This tiny marsupial is an enigma. Somehow it gets all of its dietary requirements from nectar and pollen, and in the southwest there are always enough flowers around for it to survive. But no one knows why the males need sperm larger even than those of the blue whale, or why their testes are so massive. Were humans as well endowed, men would be walking around with the equivalent of a 4kg bag of potatoes between their legs!

Mammals

Of all the continents, Australia has the worst record on the extinction of mammals, with around 30 mammal species having become extinct since European settlement in 1788. The most recent, the Bramble Cay melomys, was the first mammal in Australia to go extinct due to human-induced climate change with a small sea-level rise inundating the island, killing all the animal's food resources.

Kangaroos

Australia is, of course, famous as the home of the kangaroo (aka just plain 'roo') and other marsupials. Unless you visit a wildlife park, such creatures are not easy to see, as most are nocturnal. Their lifestyles, however, are exquisitely attuned to Australia's harsh conditions. Have you ever wondered why kangaroos, alone among the world's larger mammals, hop? It turns out that hopping is the most efficient way of getting about at medium speeds. This is because the energy of the bounce is stored in the tendons of the legs – much like in a pogo stick – while the intestines bounce up and down like a piston, emptying and filling the lungs without needing to activate the chest muscles. When you travel long distances to find meagre feed, such efficiency is a must.

Koalas

Marsupials are so energy efficient that they need to eat one-fifth less food than equivalent-sized placental mammals (everything from bats to rats, whales and ourselves). But some marsupials have taken energy efficiency much further. If you visit a wildlife park or a zoo, you might notice that faraway look in a koala's eyes. It seems as if nobody is home – and this, in fact, is near the truth. Several years ago biologists announced that koalas are the only living creatures that have brains that don't fit their skulls. Instead they have a shrivelled walnut of a brain that rattles around in a fluid-filled cranium. Other researchers have contested this finding, however, pointing out that the brains of the koalas examined for the study may have shrunk because these organs are so soft. Whether soft-brained or empty-headed, there is no doubt that the koala is not the Einstein of the animal world, and we now believe that it has sacrificed its brain to energy efficiency – brains cost a lot to run. Koalas eat gum leaves, which are so toxic they use 20% of their energy just detoxifying this food. This leaves little energy for the brain, but fortunately living in the treetops – where there are so few predators – means they can get by with few wits at all.

Whales

Whaling, a driving economic force across much of southern Australia from the time of colonisation, was finally banned in Australia in 1979. The main species on the end of the harpoon were humpback, blue, southern right and sperm whales, which were culled in huge numbers in traditional breeding grounds such as Sydney Harbour, the WA coast around Albany and Hobart's Derwent River estuary. The industry remained profitable until the mid-1800s, before drastically depleted whale numbers, the lure of inland gold rushes and the emergence of petrol as an alternative fuel started to have an impact.

Over recent years (and much to locals' delight), whales have made cautious returns to both Sydney Harbour and the Derwent River. Ironically, whale watching has emerged as a lucrative tourist activity in migratory hotspots in Albany in WA, Warrnambool in Victoria, Hervey Bay in Queensland and out on the ocean beyond Sydney Harbour.

The website of the Australian Museum (www.australianmuseum.net.au) holds a wealth of info on Australia's animal life from the Cretaceous period until now. Kids can get stuck into online games, fact files and movies.

Wombats

The peculiar constraints of the Australian environment have not made everything as dumb as the koala. The koala's nearest relative, the wombat (of which there are three species), has a large brain for a marsupial. These creatures live in complex burrows and can weigh up to 35kg, making them the largest herbivorous burrowers on earth. Because their burrows are effectively air-conditioned, they have the neat trick of turning down their metabolic activity when they are in residence. One physiologist, who studied wombats' thyroid hormones, found that biological activity ceased to such an extent in sleeping wombats that, from a hormonal point of view, they appeared to be dead!

Wombats can remain underground for a week at a time, and can get by on just one-third of the food needed by a sheep of equivalent size. One day, perhaps, efficiency-minded farmers will keep wombats instead of sheep; at the moment, however, that isn't possible – the largest of the wombat species, the northern hairy-nose, is one of the world's rarest creatures, with only around 196 surviving in a remote nature reserve in central Queensland.

Other Mammals

Among the more common marsupials you might catch a glimpse of in the national parks around Australia's major cities are the species of antechinus. These nocturnal, rat-sized creatures lead an extraordinary life. The males live for just 11 months, the first 10 of which consist of a concentrated burst of eating and growing. The day comes when their minds turn to sex, and in the antechinus this becomes an obsession. As they embark on their quest for females they forget to eat and sleep. By the end of August – just two weeks after they reach 'puberty' – every male is dead, exhausted by sex and by carrying around swollen testes.

Two unique monotremes (egg-laying mammals) live in Australia: the bumbling echidna, something akin to a hedgehog; and the platypus, a bit like an otter, with webbed feet and a ducklike bill. Echidnas are common along bushland trails, but platypuses are elusive, and only seen at dawn and dusk in quiet rivers and streams.

There are numerous guides to Aussie mammals on the market, but some are more suited to your reference library than your suitcase. One excellent exception is *A Field Guide to the Mammals of Australia* (3rd ed, 2011) by Peter Menkhorst and Frank Knight, with just enough detail, maps and fine illustrations.

Reptiles

One thing you will see lots of in Australia are reptiles. Snakes are abundant, and they include some of the most venomous species known. Where the opportunities to feed are few and far between, it's best not to give your prey a second chance, hence the potent venom. Snakes will usually leave you alone if you don't fool with them. Observe, back quietly away and don't panic, and most of the time you'll be OK.

Some visitors mistake lizards for snakes, and indeed some Australian lizards look bizarre. One of the more abundant is the sleepy lizard. These creatures, which are found in the southern arid region, look like animated pine cones. They are the Australian equivalent of tortoises, and are harmless. Other lizards are much larger. Unless you visit the Indonesian island of Komodo you will not see a larger lizard than the desert-dwelling perentie. These creatures, with their leopard-like blotches, can grow to more than 2m long, and are efficient predators of introduced rabbits, feral cats and the like.

Feeling right at home in Kakadu National Park, the saltwater crocodile is the world's largest living reptile – old males can reach an intimidating 6m long.

Sharks

Shark phobia ruining your trip to the beach? Despite media hype spurred by five deaths in 2014, Australia has averaged just one shark-attack fatality per year since 1791. There are about 370 shark species in the world's oceans – around 160 of these swim through Australian waters. Of these, only a few pose any threat to humans: the usual suspects are oceanic white tip, great white, tiger and bull sharks.

It follows that where there are more people, there are more shark attacks. NSW, and Sydney in particular, have a bad reputation. Attacks in Sydney peaked between 1920 and 1940, but since shark-net installation began in 1937 there's only been one fatality (1963), and dorsal-fin sightings are rare enough to make the nightly news. Realistically, you're more likely to get hit by a bus – so get wet and enjoy yourself!

National & State Parks

Australia has more than 500 national parks – nonurban protected wilderness areas of environmental or natural importance. Each state defines and runs its own national parks, but the principle is the same throughout Australia. National parks include rainforests, vast tracts of empty outback, strips of coastal dune land and rugged mountain ranges.

Walk Among Australia's Tallest Timber

Valley of the Giants (WA)
⋯⋯⋯⋯⋯⋯
Tahune Airwalk (Tasmania)
⋯⋯⋯⋯⋯⋯
Otway Fly (Victoria)
⋯⋯⋯⋯⋯⋯
Illawarra Fly Tree Top Walk (NSW)

Public access is encouraged as long as safety and conservation regulations are observed. In all parks you're asked to do nothing to damage or alter the natural environment. Campgrounds (often with toilets and showers), walking tracks and information centres are often provided for visitors. In most national parks there are restrictions on bringing in pets.

State parks and state forests are owned by state governments and have fewer regulations. Although state forests can be logged, they are often recreational areas with campgrounds, walking trails and signposted forest drives. Some permit horses and dogs.

Food & Drink

Towards the end of last century Australians proudly survived on a diet of 'meat and three veg'. Fine fare was a Sunday roast, and lasagne or croissants were considered exotic. Not any more. Today Australian gastronomy is keen to break rules, backed up by award-winning wines, world-class coffee, an organic revolution in the importance of fresh produce and a booming craft-beer scene.

Mod Oz

The phrase Modern Australian (Mod Oz) has been coined to classify contemporary Australian cuisine: a melange of East and West; a swirl of Atlantic and Pacific Rim; a flourish of authentic French and Italian.

Immigration has been the key to this culinary concoction. An influx of immigrants since WWII, from Europe, Asia, the Middle East and Africa, introduced new ingredients and new ways to use staples. Vietnamese, Japanese, Fijian – no matter where it's from, there are expat communities and interested locals keen to cook and eat it. You'll find Jamaicans using Scotch bonnet peppers and Tunisians making tajine.

As the Australian appetite for diversity and invention grows, so does the food culture surrounding it. Cookbooks and foodie magazines are bestsellers and Australian celebrity chefs – highly sought overseas – reflect Australia's multiculturalism in their backgrounds and dishes. Cooking TV shows, both competitions and foodie travel documentaries, have become mandatory nightly viewing.

If all this sounds overwhelming, never fear. The range of food in Australia is a true asset. You'll find that dishes are characterised by bold and interesting flavours and fresh ingredients. All palates are catered for: the chilli-metre spans gentle to extreme, seafood is plentiful, meats are full-flavoured, and vegetarian needs are considered (especially in the cities).

> Etiquette hint: if you're invited to someone's house for dinner, always take a gift (even if the host tries to dissuade you): a bottle of wine, a six-pack of beer, some flowers or a box of chocolates.

Fresh Local Food

Australia is huge (similar in size to continental USA), and it varies so much in climate – from the tropical north to the temperate south – that at any time of the year there's an enormous array of produce on offer. Fruit is a fine example. In summer, kitchen bowls overflow with nectarines, peaches and cherries, and mangoes are so plentiful that Queenslanders get sick of them. The Murray River hinterland gives rise to orchards of citrus fruits, grapes and melons. Tasmania's cold climate makes its strawberries and stone fruits sublime. The tomatoes and olives of South Australia are the nation's best. Local supermarkets stock the pick of the bunch.

Seafood is always freshest close to the source; on this big island it's plentiful. Oysters are popular – connoisseurs prize Sydney rock oysters, a species that actually lives right along the New South Wales coast; excellent oysters are grown in seven different regions in SA, such as Coffin Bay; and Tasmania is known for its Pacific oysters. Australia's southernmost state is also celebrated for its trout, salmon and abalone.

> Australians consume more than 200,000 tonnes of seafood per year. Along the coast, fish-and-chip shops often get their seafood straight from the local fishing boats; ask the cook what's frozen (ie from elsewhere) and what's not.

FOOD: WHEN, WHERE & HOW

➡ Budget eating venues usually offer main courses for under $20; midrange mains are generally $20 to $40; and top-end venues charge over $40.

➡ Cafes serve breakfasts from around 8am on weekends – a bit earlier on weekdays – and close around 5pm.

➡ Pubs and bars usually open around lunchtime and continue till at least 10pm – later from Thursday to Saturday. Pubs usually serve food from noon to 2pm and 6pm to 8pm.

➡ Restaurants generally open around noon for lunch and 6pm for dinner. Australians usually eat lunch shortly after noon; dinner bookings are usually made between 7pm and 8pm, though in big cities some restaurants stay open past 10pm.

➡ Vegetarian eateries and vegetarian selections in nonveg places (including vegan and gluten-free menu choices) are common in large cities. Rural Australia continues its dedication to meat.

➡ Smoking is banned in cafes, restaurants, clubs, pubs and an increasing number of city pedestrian malls.

An odd-sounding delicacy from these waters is 'bugs' – shovel-nosed lobsters without a lobster's price tag (try the Balmain and Moreton Bay varieties). Marron are prehistoric-looking freshwater crayfish from Western Australia, with a subtle taste that's not always enhanced by the heavy dressings that seem popular. Prawns in Australia are incredible, particularly the school prawns or the eastern king (Yamba) prawns found along the northern NSW coast. You can sample countless wild fish species, including prized barramundi from the Northern Territory, but even fish that are considered run-of-the-mill (such as snapper, trevally and whiting) taste fabulous when simply barbecued.

There's a growing boutique cheese movement across the country's dairy regions – Tasmania alone now produces 50 cheese varieties.

Farmers Markets

Local farmers markets are terrific places to sample the culinary riches of the region, support local growers and enjoy the affable airs (live music, friendly banter, free food sampling). You'll find fruit, veggies, seafood, nuts, meat, bread and pastries, liqueurs, beer, wine, coffee and much more in markets all around the country. For locations, check the website of the Australian Farmers Market Association (www.farmersmarkets.org.au).

Top Food Festivals

Melbourne Food & Wine Festival (Melbourne, Victoria)

Gourmet Escape (Margaret River, WA)

Taste of Tasmania (Hobart, Tasmania)

Clare Valley Gourmet Weekend (Clare Valley, SA)

Eating with the Aussies

Most Aussies eat cereal, toast and/or fruit for breakfast, often extending to bacon and eggs on weekends, washed down with tea and coffee. They generally favour sandwiches, salads and sushi for lunch, and then eat anything and everything in the evening.

The iconic Australian barbecue (BBQ or 'barbie') is a near-mandatory cultural experience. In summer locals invite their friends around at dinner time and fire up the barbie, grilling burgers, sausages ('snags'), onions, corn on the cob, steaks, seafood, and veggie, meat or seafood skewers. If you're invited to a BBQ, bring some meat and cold beer. Year-round the BBQ is wheeled out at weekends for quick-fire lunches. There are plenty of free electric or gas BBQs in parks around the country, too – a terrific traveller-friendly option.

Cafes & Coffee

Coffee has become an Australian addiction. There are Italian-style espresso machines in virtually every cafe, boutique roasters are all the rage and, in urban areas, the qualified barista is ever-present (there are even barista-staffed cafes attached to petrol stations).

Sydney and Melbourne, the two cities arguing it out for bragging rights as Australia's coffee capital, have given rise to a whole generation of coffee snobs. The cafe scene in Melbourne is particularly hipster; the best way to immerse yourself in it is by wandering the city centre's cafe-lined laneways. You'll also find decent places in the other big cities and towns, and there's now a sporting chance of good coffee in many rural areas.

Cafes in Australia generally serve good-value food: they're usually more casual than restaurants and you can get a decent meal for around $20 to $30, although many only open for breakfast and lunch. Children are usually more than welcome.

Tipping is not mandatory in Australia, but is always appreciated if the food is great and service is on point. Around 5% to 10% is the norm.

FOOD & DRINK FINE DINING

Fine Dining

A restaurant meal in Australia is a relaxed affair. You'll probably order within 15 minutes and see the first course (called a starter or an entrée) 15 minutes later. The main course will arrive about half an hour after that. Even at the finest restaurants a jacket is not required (but certainly isn't frowned upon).

If a restaurant is BYO, you can bring your own alcohol. If it also sells alcohol, you can usually only bring your own bottled wine (no beer or cask or box wine) and a corkage charge is added to your bill. The cost is either per person or per bottle, and can be up to $20 per bottle in fine-dining places (do the sums in advance: you'll often be better off buying from the restaurant, even with their inflated prices).

Quick Eats

In the big cities, street vending is on the rise – coffee carts have been joined by vans selling tacos, burritos, baked potatoes, kebabs, burgers and more. Elsewhere around the cities you'll find fast-food chains, gourmet sandwich bars, food courts in shopping centres and market halls, bakeries, and sushi, noodle and salad bars. Beyond the big smoke the options are more limited and traditional, such as milk bars (known as delis in SA and WA) – these corner stores often serve old-fashioned

---

BUSH TUCKER: AUSTRALIAN NATIVE FOODS

There are around 350 food plants that are native to the Australian bush. Bush foods provide a real taste of the Australian landscape. There are the dried fruits and lean meats of the desert; shellfish and fish of the coast; alpine berries and mountain peppers of the high country; and citrus flavours, fruits and herbs of the rainforests.

This cuisine is based on Aboriginal Australians' expert understanding of the environment, founded in cultural knowledge handed down over generations. Years of trial and error have ensured a rich appreciation of these foods and mastery of their preparation.

The harvesting of bush foods for commercial return has been occurring for about 30 years. In central Australia it is mainly carried out by senior Aboriginal women. Here and in other regions, bush meats (such as kangaroo, emu and crocodile), fish (such as barramundi) and bush fruits (including desert raisins, quandongs, riberries and Kakadu plums) are seasonally hunted and gathered for personal enjoyment, as well as to supply local, national and international markets.

Dr Janelle White is an applied anthropologist. Her PhD focused on Aboriginal people's involvement in a variety of desert-based bush produce industries, including bush foods, bush medicines and bush jewellery. She splits her time between Adelaide, and the land 200km northwest of Alice Springs.

hamburgers (with bacon, egg, pineapple and beetroot) and other take-away foods.

There are more than a million Aussies with Italian heritage: it follows that pizza is (arguably) the most popular Australian fast food. Most home-delivered pizzas are of the American style (thick and with lots of toppings) rather than Italian style. However, thin, Neapolitan-style pizza cooked in a wood-fired oven can increasingly be found, even in country towns.

Fish and chips are still hugely popular. The fish is most often a form of shark (often called flake; don't worry, it's delicious), either grilled or dipped in batter and fried.

If you're at a rugby league or Aussie rules football match, downing a beer and a meat pie is as compulsory as wearing your team's colours and yelling loudly from the stands.

WINE REGIONS

All Australian states and mainland territories (except tropical and desert NT) sustain wine industries, some almost 200 years old. Many wineries have tastings for free or a small fee, often redeemable if you buy a bottle. Although plenty of good wine comes from big wineries with economies of scale on their side, the most interesting wines are often made by small producers. The following run-down should give you a head start.

New South Wales & the Australian Capital Territory

Dating from the 1820s, the Hunter Valley is Australia's oldest wine region. The Lower Hunter is known for shiraz and unwooded semillon. Upper Hunter wineries specialise in cabernet sauvignon and shiraz, with forays into verdelho and chardonnay. Further inland are award-winning wineries at Griffith, Mudgee and Orange. There is also a growing number of excellent wineries in areas surrounding Canberra and the ACT.

Queensland

High-altitude Stanthorpe and Ballandean in the southeast are the centres of the Queensland wine industry, though you'll find a few cellar doors at Tamborine Mountain in the Gold Coast hinterland.

South Australia

SA's wine industry is a global giant, as a visit to the National Wine Centre of Australia (p717) in Adelaide will attest. Cabernet sauvignon from Coonawarra, riesling from the Clare Valley, sauvignon blanc from the Adelaide Hills, and shiraz from the Barossa Valley and McLaren Vale are bliss in a bottle.

Tasmania

Try the Pipers River region and the Tamar Valley in the north, and explore the burgeoning wine industry in the Coal River Valley (p649) around Richmond near Hobart. Cool-climate drops are the name of the game here: especially pinot noir, sauvignon blanc and sparkling whites (our favourite is the 'Méthode Tasmanoise' made by Jansz).

Victoria

Victoria has more than 500 wineries. The Yarra Valley produces excellent chardonnay and pinot noir, as does the Mornington Peninsula; both can be done as day trips from Melbourne. Wineries around Rutherglen produce champion fortified wines as well as shiraz and durif.

Western Australia

Margaret River in the southwest is synonymous with superb cabernets and chardonnays. Among old-growth forest, Pemberton wineries produce cabernet sauvignon, merlot, pinot noir, sauvignon blanc and shiraz. The south coast's Mt Barker is another budding wine region.

Vegetarians & Vegans

Vegetarians and vegans will have no trouble finding restaurants that cater specifically to them in the urban centres. The majority of restaurants, pubs and cafes will offer some vegetarian menu choices (although sometimes only one or two) that can usually be made vegan on request.

In remote areas options can be much more limited, and in some small towns you'll struggle to find more than a salad or hot chips. A few outback towns have Chinese restaurants, where there'll likely be some vegetarian options. We strongly recommend that you bring your own supplies to make sure you don't go hungry.

Melbourne and Sydney are both great for herbivores. Unless you wander into a steakhouse by mistake, vegetarians should have no trouble finding satisfying choices on most menus, and few restaurateurs will look askance at special requests. Some leading restaurants offer separate vegetarian or vegan menus, often stretching to multiple-course degustation. Many of the more established restaurants specifically mark strictly vegetarian and vegan options on the menu.

Most Asian and Indian restaurants will have large meatless menus, but with Chinese, Vietnamese and Thai cooking you'll need to be clear that you don't want the common additives of oyster or fish sauce – they'll usually be happy to make soy-based substitutions. Casual Japanese places also have many vegetarian options, though similarly you'll need to ask if they can prepare your dish with *dashi* (stock) that hasn't been made with bonito fish (ask if they have mushroom or seaweed *dashi* instead).

Pubs & Drinking

You're in the right country if you're in need of a drink. Long recognised as some of the finest in the world, Australian wines are one of the nation's top exports. As the public develops a more sophisticated palate, local craft beers are rising to the occasion. There's a growing wealth of microbrewed flavours and varieties on offer, challenging the nation's entrenched predilection for mass-produced lager. If you're into whisky, head to Tasmania: there are a dozen distillers there now, bottling up superb single malts and racking up international awards.

Most Australian beers have an alcohol content between 3.5% and 5.5%, less than European beers but more than most in North America. Light beers contain under 3% alcohol and are a good choice if you have to drive (as long as you don't drink twice as much).

The terminology used to order beer varies state by state. In NSW you ask for a schooner (425mL) if you're thirsty and a middy (285mL) if you're not quite so dry. In Victoria the 285mL measure is called a pot; in Tasmania it's called a 10 ounce. Pints can either be 425mL or 568mL, depending on where you are. Mostly you can just ask for a beer and see what turns up.

'Shouting' is a revered custom where people drinking together take turns to pay for a round of drinks. At a toast, everyone should touch glasses and look each other in the eye as they clink – failure to do so is purported to result in seven years' bad sex (whether you believe that or not, why not make eye contact just in case...?).

Pub meals (often referred to as counter meals) are usually hefty and good value; standards such as sausages and mashed potatoes or chicken schnitzel and salad go for $15 to $30.

A competitively priced place to eat is at a club – Returned and Services League (RSL) or Surf Life Saving clubs are solid bets. Order at the kitchen, take a number and wait until it's called out over the counter or intercom. You pick up the meal yourself, saving the restaurant on staffing costs and you on your total bill.

FOOD & DRINK VEGETARIANS & VEGANS

Vegemite: you'll either love it or hate it. Barack Obama undiplomatically called it 'horrible'. It's certainly an acquired taste, but Australians consume more than 22 million jars of the stuff every year. And they're particularly pleased that ownership of this national icon recently returned to Australian hands for the first time since 1928.

In 2014 Sullivan's Cove (www.sullivanscove.com), a Tasmanian distillery, stunned the whisky world by winning the prize for the world's best single malt for its French Oak Cask variety. It took another prize in 2018 for its American Oak expression.

Sport

Whether they're filling stadiums, glued to a pub's big screen or on the sofa in front of the TV, Australians invest heavily in sport. The federal government kicks in fairly substantial funding, enough to see Australia hold its own against formidable international sporting opponents. However, it's the passion for sport in almost every Aussie that truly defines the country's sporting life.

What is Aussie Rules?

Australia's very own sport, and one of the most watched, is Australian rules football (aka 'footy' or 'Aussie rules'). While originally embedded in Victorian state culture and identity, the Australian Football League (AFL; www.afl.com.au) gradually expanded its reach into all states, though the majority of teams still hail from Melbourne. Compared at times to ballet, the play involves long elegant kicks, launching up high to catch the ball in a 'mark' and sometimes brutal full-body collisions. The roar of up to 100,000 fans cheering inside 'The G' (Melbourne's MCG stadium) is something to experience once in a lifetime.

Footy season runs from March until late September; tickets can be purchased online or at various stadiums around the country on the day for all but the biggest games. The season culminates in the AFL Grand Final (p482) at the MCG, one of Australia's most-watched sporting events. AFL is an obsession across the nation, even in remote communities. The Tiwi Grand Final (p817) in March, on the Tiwi Islands off Darwin (and about as far away from Melbourne as you can get in Australia), is another memorable example of this country's obsession with its homegrown sport.

It's Just Not Cricket

The Aussies dominated both international Test and One-Day International cricket for much of the 2000s, holding the number-one world ranking for most of the decade. But the retirement of once-in-a-lifetime players like Shane Warne, Adam Gilchrist, Ricky Ponting and the Waugh brothers sent the team into an extended rebuilding phase.

Their fortunes appeared on the rise again after winning the 2015 World Cup at home, but were derailed spectacularly when they were caught cheating by tampering with the ball with sandpaper in South

---

WOMEN'S FOOTY

In 2017 the inaugural season of Women's AFL (www.afl.com.au/womens) finally got under way after a five-year development phase. The eight-team league, modelled on the clubs and branding of AFL, kicked off with a sell-out match between Carlton and Collingwood (with a decisive victory by Carlton). The capacity 24,000 crowd that turned up forced a rethink of future venues and the audience for televised games is almost on a par with the men's league. The league plans to expand from 10 teams to 14 in 2020.

Meanwhile, the National Rugby Womens team (www.nrl.com/womens) launched in 2018 with four teams from NSW, Queensland and New Zealand, and plans for expansion.

Africa in March 2018. The fallout cost the captain, the opening batsman and his junior partner their professional reputations and the team has not since recovered.

The pinnacle of Australian cricket is the biennial Test series played between Australia and England known as The Ashes. The Ashes trophy is a tiny terracotta urn containing the ashen remnants of an 1882 cricket bail. Every year since 2005, the home side has won back The Ashes, except in 2010–11 when a strong England side beat Australia 3-2 in the five-match series in their own grounds.

If you have never been to the cricket, you're in for a treat whether you go to a county or an international level game – such tactical cut-and-thrust, such nuance, such grace! Though admittedly between cheating and an ugly reputation for 'sledging' (verbally dressing down one's opponent on the field) one does wonder why it's still called 'the gentleman's game' here.

Note: Test cricket lasts for up to five days, but children may lack the stamina to watch. Shorter versions of the game – One-Day Internationals or even better a night-time T20 match – are definitely a more accessible introduction. Go to www.cricketaustralia.com.au to find out about match fixtures and get thee to a game.

The Australian women's cricket team has been a dominant international side, winning six of the 11 one-day World Cup tournaments since 1973 and four of the six T20 World Cup tournaments played since 2009.

Rugby League vs Union

The National Rugby League (NRL; www.nrl.com.au) is the most popular football code north of the Murray River, with the annual State of Origin series between New South Wales and Queensland the highlight of the season.

The national rugby union team, the Wallabies, won the Rugby World Cup in 1991 and 1999 and was runner-up in 2003 (to England) and 2015 (to eternal rivals New Zealand).

Teams from Australia, New Zealand, South Africa, Japan (until 2020) and Argentina compete in the super-popular Super Rugby (www.super.rugby) competition, which includes four Australian teams: the Waratahs (NSW), the Reds (Queensland), the Brumbies (ACT) and the Rebels (Melbourne).

Football...or is it Soccer?

Australia's national soccer team, the Socceroos, has qualified for the last few FIFA World Cups after a long history of almost-but-not-quite getting there. They haven't had much success playing in the Cup, but pride in the national team is sky-high now – it reached stratospheric levels when the Socceroos won the Asian Cup in 2015 against South Korea.

The national A-League (www.a-league.com.au) competition, with nine teams from around Australia and one from New Zealand, has enjoyed increased popularity in recent years, successfully luring a few big-name international players to bolster the home-grown talent pool.

The women's national team, known as the Matilda's, is ranked six in the world and made it to the round of 16 in the 2019 World Cup before being knocked out by Norway.

Surfing

Australia has been synonymous with surfing ever since the Beach Boys effused about 'Australia's Narrabeen', one of Sydney's northern beaches, in *Surfin' USA*. Other surfing hotspots such as Bells Beach, Margaret River, the Pass at Byron Bay, the heavy-breaking Shipstern Bluff in Tasmania

---

SPORT RUGBY LEAGUE VS UNION

Australia's T20 Big Bash League (www.bigbash.com.au), the 20-over form of cricket, has been gaining ground on the traditional five-day and one-day formats. Fast, flashy and laced with pyrotechnics, it's thin on erudition but makes for a fun night out.

'Footy' in Australia can mean a number of things. In NSW and Queensland it's rugby league; everywhere else it's Australian rules football. Just to confuse you, football can also mean 'soccer' – the national governing body for soccer is called the Football Federation of Australia.

and Burleigh Heads on the Gold Coast also resonate with international wave addicts. Iron Man and Surf Lifesaving competitions are also held on beaches around the country, attracting dedicated fans to the sand.

More than a few Australian surfers have attained 'World Champion' status. On the women's side, iconic Aussie surfers include seven-time world champion Layne Beachley; now equal seven-time world champion Stephanie Gilmore (both from NSW); and the ex-South African, now Australian, Wendy Botha. In the men's competition, legendary Australian surfers include Mark Richards, Tom Carroll, Joel Parkinson and Mick Fanning.

Swimming

Australia is girt by sea and pockmarked with pools – its population can swim. Australia's greatest female swimmer, Dawn Fraser, known simply as 'our Dawn', won the 100m freestyle gold at three successive Olympics (1956–64), plus the 4x100m freestyle relay in 1956. Australia's greatest male swimmer, Ian Thorpe (known as Thorpie or the Thorpedo), retired in 2006 at age 24, with five Olympic golds swinging from his neck. Since then Australia's reputation as a nation of elite swimmers has taken a battering with disappointing performances at both the 2012 London and 2016 Rio Olympics.

A Racetrack Somewhere (2016) is a fascinating documentary journey around some of Australia's best country race meetings, including Birdsville, King Island, Warrnambool, Kangaroo Island and Darwin.

A Spot of Tennis?

Every January Melbourne is transformed by the Australian Open (p482), a Grand Slam tennis tournament that has been played in the Open era since 1969. The atmosphere in the precinct each summer is utterly magic. If you miss out on tickets, watch a twilight match in the warm night air on a big screen at nearby Federation Sq.

Australia's newest golden girl Ash Barty won the 2019 French Open and sensationally climbed to world No 1 shortly after. Before that Sam Stosur triumphed at the US Open in 2011. In the men's competition, the Australian Open was last won by an Australian, Mark Edmondson, way back in 1976. In the womens game, tennis legends Margaret Court and Evonne Goolagong Cawley won the Australian Open title four and three times respectively.

After an era dominated by charismatic Pat Cash (who won Wimbeldon in 1987), gentlemanly Pat Rafter (who won the US Open in 1997 and 1998), and the fiesty Lleyton Hewitt (who won the US Open in 2001 and Wimbledon a year later), Australian tennis has since been mired in by a long-standing rift between Hewitt and his mercurial successors, Nick Kyrgios and Bernard Tomic.

Netball

Despite the Australian national team winning or placing second at every Netball World Cup ever, and it being one of the most played sports in the country, netball gets neither the coverage nor the money that other sports rake in. During the April to September season, watch Sydney's teams the NSW Swifts and Giants Netball; Melbourne's Vixens and Magpies; the West Coast Fever; Adelaide Thunderbirds, and Queensland's Firebirds and Sunshine Coast Lightning. Get all the info at www.super netball.com.au.

Survival Guide

DEADLY & DANGEROUS..... 1058

Out and About 1058
Where the Wild
Things Are 1058

DIRECTORY A–Z...1060

Accessible Travel 1060
Accommodation.......1060
Customs Regulations...1063
Discount Cards........1063
Electricity 1063
Food 1063
Health................1063
Insurance.............1065
Internet Access........1065
Legal Matters 1065
LGBTIQ+ Travellers 1066
Maps.................1066
Money................1066
Opening Hours 1067
Post..................1067
Public Holidays........1067
Safe Travel............1068

Telephone 1068
Time 1068
Toilets................1068
Tourist Information 1069
Volunteering 1069
Women Travellers......1069
Work 1069

TRANSPORT 1071

**Getting There
& Away 1071**
Entering the Country... 1071
Air.................... 1071
Land 1071
Sea 1071

Getting Around...... 1072
Air.................... 1072
Bicycle 1072
Boat 1072
Bus 1072
Car & Motorcycle...... 1073
Hitching 1078
Local Transport........ 1078
Train 1078

Deadly & Dangerous

You've heard about Australia's deadly and dangerous wildlife, though you're statistically more likely to die from a selfie mishap than a shark bite. Most wild creatures (crocodlies aside) are wary of humans; the chances are the worst you'll encounter are pesky flies and mosquitoes. Cover up and carry insect repellent but be mindful of the following.

Out & About

At the Beach

Check conditions and be aware of your own limitations before entering the ocean. Strong undertows (rips) are a problem. If you find yourself being carried out from the shore, swim parallel to the land until you're out of the rip, then head for the beach, being careful not to panic or exhaust yourself. Patrolled, safe-swimming areas are indicated by red-and-yellow flags at popular beaches – always swim between them.

Several people are paralysed every year by diving into shallow waves and hitting sand bars: test the water before you leap.

Protection from the Australian sun should be a priority at the beach. Australians take many sun-smart precautions including wearing hats, UV-protected sunglasses and covering up (even in the water) with long-sleeve swimsuits called a 'rashie' – or for women a 'burkini' might be an option. Use SPF50+ sunscreen even if you are working on your tan; apply 30 minutes before going into the sun and repeat.

Bushfires

Forest fires or 'bushfires' flare up almost every summer. In hot, dry and windy weather you'll hear it is a Total Fire Ban day: don't use camping stoves, BBQs or light campfires and dispose of cigarettes very carefully. Campers and hikers should ensure they are up to date on local conditions in summer and know what to do if a fire breaks out. If you smell smoke, take it seriously.

Cold Weather

More hikers in Australia die in the cold rather than the heat. Even in summer, particularly in highland Tasmania, Victoria and New South Wales, conditions can change quickly, with temperatures dropping below freezing and blizzards blowing in. Pack appropriate clothing even for a hike. Early signs of hypothermia include the inability to perform fine movements (eg doing up buttons), shivering and a bad case of the 'umbles' (fumbles, mumbles, grumbles, stumbles). Get out of the cold, change out of wet clothing and into dry gear, and eat and drink to warm up.

Heat Exhaustion

Symptoms of heat exhaustion include dizziness, fainting, fatigue, nausea or vomiting. Skin becomes pale, cool and clammy. Treatment consists of rest in a cool, shady place and fluid replacement with water or diluted sports drinks.

Heatstroke is a severe form of heat illness and is a true medical emergency, with heating of the brain leading to disorientation, hallucinations and seizures. Prevent heatstroke by maintaining adequate fluid intake, especially during physical exertion. Listen to local advice on how much water to carry when setting off for a walk. One litre per hour is a minimum.

Where the Wild Things Are

Australia's profusion of dangerous creatures is legendary: snakes, spiders, sharks, crocodiles, jellyfish... Travellers needn't be alarmed, though – you're unlikely to see many of these creatures in the wild, much less be attacked by one.

Crocodiles

Around the northern Australian coastline, saltwater crocodiles ('salties') are a real danger. They also inhabit estuaries, creeks and rivers, sometimes a long way inland. Observe safety signs or ask locals whether that inviting-looking waterhole or river is croc-free before plunging in. This is one of a few dangerous animals that sees people as food, rather than acting in self-defence.

Jellyfish

With venomous tentacles up to 3m long, box jellyfish (aka sea wasps or 'stingers') inhabit Australia's tropical waters. They're most common during the wet season (October to March) when you should stay out of the sea in some places. Stinger nets are in place at some beaches, but always check with locals. 'Stinger suits' (full-body Lycra swimsuits) prevent stinging, as do wetsuits. If you are stung by a jellyfish, wash the skin with vinegar then get to a hospital. Note that washing the skin with fresh water just makes the sting worse.

The box jellyfish also has a tiny, lethal relative called an irukandji, which has been blamed for several deaths in the wet season in Australia.

Sharks

Despite extensive media coverage, the risk of shark attack in Australia is not

high. Check with surf life-saving groups about local risks.

Snakes

Australia has some of the world's most venomous snakes. Most common are brown and tiger snakes, but few species are aggressive. Unless you're poking a stick at or accidentally standing on one, it's extremely unlikely that you'll get bitten. If you are bitten, prevent the spread of venom by applying pressure to the wound and immobilising the area with a splint or sling. Stay put and get someone else to go for help immediately.

Spiders

Australia has several poisonous spiders, bites from which are usually treatable with antivenoms. The

deadly funnel-web spider lives in NSW (including Sydney) – bites are treated as per snake bites (pressure and immobilisation before transferring to a hospital). Redback spiders live throughout Australia; bites cause pain, sweating and nausea. Apply ice or cold packs, then transfer to hospital. White-tailed spider bites may cause an ulcer that's slow and difficult to heal. Clean the wound and seek medical assistance. The disturbingly large huntsman spider is harmless, though seeing one will affect your blood pressure!

For more information on health, see p1063.

For more information on health, see p1063.

MAINTAINING PERSPECTIVE

There's maybe one fatal crocodile attack per year in Australia, plus the occasional fatal shark attack or serious shark bite injuries. Spiders haven't killed anyone since 1979. Snakes may kill a person per annum, but so do bees. Blue-ringed octopus deaths are rare – only two last century. Jellyfish are tragically more prolific takers of life – but you realise that you're still way more likely to die from taking a selfie in the wrong place than be killed by Australia's deadly wildlife, right?

DEADLY & DANGEROUS WHERE THE WILD THINGS ARE

Directory A–Z

Accessible Travel

Australians are increasingly mindful of the people with different access needs and more operators are realising the social and economic benefits of accommodating them.

➡ Legislation requires that new accommodation meets accessibility standards for mobility-impaired travellers, and discrimination by tourism operators is illegal.

➡ Many of Australia's key attractions, including many national parks, provide access for those with limited mobility and a number of sites also address the needs of visitors with visual or aural impairments.

➡ Contact attractions you plan to visit in advance to confirm facilities available.

➡ Tour operators with vehicles catering to mobility-impaired travellers operate from most capital cities.

➡ Facilities for wheelchairs are improving in accommodation, but there are still many older establishments where the upgrades haven't been implemented. Download Lonely Planet's free Accessible Travel guides from http://lptravel.to/AccessibleTravel.

Australian Resources

Deaf Australia (www.deafaustralia.org.au)

e-Bility (www.ebility.com)

Vision Australia (www.visionaustralia.org)

IDEAS (Information on Disability & Education Awareness Services) (www.ideas.org.au)

Spinal Cord Injuries Australia (www.scia.org.au)

Air Travel

Qantas (☏13 13 13; www.qantas.com.au) entitles a disabled person with high-support needs and the carer travelling with them to a discount on full economy fares. Guide dogs travel free on Qantas, **Jetstar** (www.jetstar.com/au/en/home), **Virgin Australia** (www.virginaustralia.com) and their affiliated carriers. All of Australia's major airports have dedicated parking spaces, wheelchair access to terminals, accessible toilets, and skychairs to convey passengers onto planes via air bridges.

Public Transport

All of Australia's suburban rail networks and the vast majority of urban buses are wheelchair accessible. Guide dogs and hearing dogs are permitted on all public transport.

Accommodation

During the summer high season (December to February) and at other peak times, particularly school holidays and Easter, prices are at their highest. Outside these times you're more likely to find discounts and lower walk-in rates. Notable exceptions include central Australia, the Top End where summer is the low season and prices drop substantially, for good reason.

PRACTICALITIES

Newspapers Every major city and many regional towns have their own newspapers.

Radio ABC broadcasts national radio programs, many syndicated from the BBC, plus local regional stations. Check www.abc.net.au/radio for local frequencies.

Smoking Banned from most indoor public spaces, and in some outdoor spaces where crowds congregate or food is served.

Television The main free-to-air TV channels are the ABC, multicultural SBS, Seven, Nine and Ten. Locals are being seduced by paid TV options like Foxtel and Netflix.

Weights & measures Australia uses the metric system.

B&Bs

Australian bed-and-breakfast options include restored miners' cottages, converted barns, rambling old houses, upmarket country manors and beachside bungalows. Tariffs are typically in the midrange bracket but can be higher. In areas that attract weekenders – historic towns, wine regions, forest regions such as the Blue Mountains in NSW and the Dandenongs in Victoria – B&Bs are often booked out for weekend stays.

Some places advertised as B&Bs are actually self-contained cottages with breakfast provisions supplied. In the cheaper B&Bs there may be shared bathroom facilities. Some hosts cook dinner for guests (though notice is required).

Online resources:

Airbnb (www.airbnb.com.au) Global homestay accommodation provider with variable options.

Beautiful Accommodation (www.beautifulaccommodation. com) A select crop of luxury B&Bs and self-contained houses.

Hosted Accommodation Australia (www.australianbed andbreakfast.com.au) Local listings for B&Bs, farmstays, cottages and homesteads.

Camping & Caravanning

Camping in the bush is a highlight of travelling in Australia. Between the wildlife, the stars and sitting around a campfire, you're in for an unforgettable experience.

Costs Nightly camping in a private campground costs around $20 and $30 per site, more for a powered site. Unless otherwise stated, prices for campsites are for two people. Expect to pay $80 to $100 for a small on-site cabin with a kitchenette and up to $200 for a two- or three-bedroom cabin with a fully equipped kitchen, lounge room, TV and beds for up to six people. Staying at designated campsites in a national park normally costs $5 to $15 per person (often on a

---

SLEEPING PRICE RANGES

The following price ranges refer to a double room with bathroom in Sydney in high season (summer):

$ less than $200

$$ $200–350

$$$ more than $350

Prices are generally lower outside the metropolitan areas and we have adjusted our scale to reflect relative pricing for each region.

---

honesty permit system) but with few, if any, facilities.

Permits Bookings for popular national park camping spots are often handled online by state departments, so planning is required. Otherwise it's a case of first in gets a spot.

Facilities Almost all private caravan and holiday parks are equipped with hot showers, flushing toilets and laundry facilities, and often a swimming pool and playgrounds. Bush campgrounds might have a fire pit and a composting toilet, but no running water or lighting.

Locations Note that most caravan parks and campgrounds lie several kilometres from the town centre – only convenient if you have wheels. Some are close to beaches or other natural features.

Weather To avoid extremes of hot and cold weather, camping is best in the warmer months (October to March) in the south and during the Dry season up north (April to September).

Resources Get your hands on **Camps Australia Wide** (www. campsaustraliawide.com), a handy publication (and app) containing maps and information about campgrounds across Australia. Also check out **Go Camping** (www.gocamping australia.com), and **YouCamp** (https://youcamp.com), which offers camping on private land like farms.

Holiday Park Chains If you're doing a lot of caravanning/camping, consider joining one of the chain organisations, for member discounts such as **Big 4 Holiday Parks** (www.big4.com.

---

au), **Discovery Holiday Parks** (www.discoveryholidayparks. com.au) and **Top Tourist Parks** (www.toptouristparks.com.au).

Luxury Resorts & Lodges

Australia does a nice line in resorts and other forms of accommodation that represent destinations in their own right. So good are they that you may not even need to move, other than to enjoy the activities and excursions offered in the surrounding area. Most work so well because their locations are prized patches of real estate, often on private concessions in remote areas that are for the exclusive enjoyment of guests. Rates are high – up to $3000 per night – and most have minimum stays, but prices usually include all meals and activities.

Some of the standout options:

El Questro Homestead (📞08-9169 1777; www.elquestro. com.au; ☉r all inclusive $2000-3100; ❄️🌐❄️) Western Australia.

Hayman Island Resort (📞07-4940 1838; www.hayman. com.au; r incl breakfast $730-12,300; ❄️@🌐❄️) Queensland.

Sal Salis (Map p987; 📞08-9949 1776; www.salsalis.com; off Yardie Creek Rd, South Mandu; per person per night $900-1125; ☉mid-Mar–Oct) 🅿️ Western Australia.

Wildman Wilderness Lodge (📞08-8978 8955; www.wild manwildernesslodge.com.au; Point Stuart Rd; safari tents/

BOOK YOUR STAY ONLINE

For more accommodation reviews by Lonely Planet authors, check out http://lonelyplanet.com/hotels/australia. You'll find independent reviews, as well as recommendations on the best places to stay. Best of all, you can book online.

cabins half-board $675/795; ❄️ ⊠) Northern Territory.

Lizard Island Resort (✆1300 863 248; www.lizardisland.com.au; Anchor Bay; d $1970-3700; ❄️ @ 🛜 ⊠) Queensland.

Holiday Apartments

Holiday apartments are particularly common in coastal areas, with reservations often handled by local real estate agents or online booking engines.

Costs For a two-bedroom flat, you're looking at anywhere between $150 and $250 per night, but you will pay much more in high season and for serviced apartments in major cities.

Facilities Self-contained holiday apartments range from simple, studio-like rooms with small kitchenettes, to two-bedroom apartments with full laundries and state-of-the-art entertainment systems: great value for multi-night stays. Sometimes they come in small, single-storey blocks, but in tourist hotspots such as the Gold Coast expect a sea of high-rises.

Hostels

Backpacker hostels are exceedingly popular in Australian cities and along the coast, but in the outback and rural areas you'll be hard pressed to find one.

Costs Typically a dorm bed costs $28 to $40 per night, and a double (usually without bathroom) $80 to $100.

Facilities Hostels provide varying levels of accommodation, from the austere simplicity of wilderness hostels to city-centre buildings with en-suite rooms. Most of the accommodation is in dormitories (bunk rooms), usually ranging in size from four to 12

beds. Many hostels also provide twin rooms and doubles. Hostels generally have cooking facilities, a communal area with a TV, laundry facilities, and sometimes travel offices and job centres.

Bed linen Usually provided; sleeping bags are not welcome due to hygiene concerns. BYO towels.

Hotels

Hotels in Australian cities or well-touristed places are generally of the business or luxury-chain variety (midrange to top end): comfortable, anonymous, mod-con-filled rooms in multistorey blocks. For these hotels we quote 'rack rates' (official advertised rates – usually upwards of $220 a night), though significant discounts can be offered when business is quiet.

Lodges & Tented Camps

Out in the wilds of some national parks, safari-style lodges are slowly making their presence felt. Based around the same principles as African safari lodges, they inhabit fabulously remote (sometimes fly-in) locations and they offer a mix of semi-luxurious four-walled cabins and elevated canvas tents with en-suite bathrooms. Rates usually include all meals and may also include all activities and excursions. SSuch places are starting to appear in Kakadu National Park, Mary River National Park and Arnhem Land, all in the Northern Territory.

Motels

Drive-up motels offer comfortable basic to midrange accommodation and are

found all over Australia, often on the edges of urban centres. They rarely offer a cheaper rate for singles, so are better value for couples or groups of three. You'll mostly pay $120 to $180 for a simple room with a kettle, a fridge, a TV, air-con and a bathroom.

Pubs

Many Australian pubs (from the term 'public house') were built during boom times, so they're often among the largest, most extravagant buildings in town. Some have been restored, but generally rooms remain small and weathered, with a long amble down the hall to the bathroom. They're usually central and cheap – singles/doubles with shared facilities from $60/100, or more if you want a private bathroom. If you're a light sleeper, avoid booking a room above the bar and check whether a band is cranking out the rock downstairs that night.

Farm & Station Stays

Country farms sometimes offer a bed for a night, while some remote outback stations allow you to stay in homestead rooms or shearers' quarters and try activities such as horse riding. Some let you kick back and watch workers raise a sweat; others rope you in to help with day-to-day chores. Most accommodation is very comfortable – B&B style in the main homestead (dinner on request) or in self-contained cottages. Some farms also provide budget outbuildings or shearers' quarters.

Remember, however, that some farmstays use their accommodation for their army of seasonal fruit pickers, while we've also heard reports of some who cut corners and others out to take advantage of those who stay. Make sure you lock in rates and any extras (such as laundry) before you agree to stay, and always check for basic safety infrastructure, such as smoke alarms and fire escapes, before bedding in for the night. Try **Farmstay Camping Australia** (www.farmstaycampingaustralia.com.au).

Customs Regulations

For detailed information on customs and quarantine regulations, contact the **Department of Immigration and Border Protection** (☑1300 363 263, 02-6275 6666; www.border.gov.au).

When entering Australia you can bring most articles in free of duty provided that customs is satisfied they are for personal use. Duty-free quotas per person (note the unusually low figure for cigarettes):

Alcohol 2.25L (over the age of 18)

Cigarettes 50 cigarettes (over the age of 18)

General goods Up to the value of $900 ($450 for people aged under 18)

Narcotics, of course, are illegal, and customs inspectors and their highly trained hounds are diligent in sniffing them out. Quarantine regulations are strict, so you must declare all goods of animal or vegetable origin – wooden spoons, straw hats, the lot. Fresh food (meat, cheese, fruit, vegetables etc) and flowers are prohibited. There are disposal bins located in airports where you can dump any questionable items if you don't want to bother with an inspection, a hefty on-the-spot fine or up to 10 years' imprisonment.

Discount Cards

The internationally recognised **International Student Identity Card** (www.isic.org) is available to full-time students globally. The card gives the bearer discounts on accommodation, transport and admission to various attractions. Home country student ID cards are sometimes accepted by proprietors.

EATING PRICE RANGES

The following price ranges refer to a standard main course.

$ less than $20

$$ $20–40

$$$ more than $40

Travellers over the age of 60 may be eligible for the same concession prices as locals with **Senior Citizen cards**, though not many 60-year-olds take kindly to being called 'senior'.

Electricity

230V AC, 50Hz. Australia has a three-prong socket (it is different from the British one).

Type I
230V/50Hz

Food

Australia's culinary scene has transformed over the last few decades. Just about everywhere, the country's culinary offerings are filled with flavour and innovation, informed by a commitment to fresh ingredients and

bequeathed endless variety by the extraordinary diversity of peoples who have come here from around the world (bringing their recipes with them) and now call Australia home.

Health

Health-wise, Australia is a remarkably safe country in which to travel, considering that such a large portion of it lies in the tropics. Few travellers to Australia will experience anything worse than an upset stomach or a bad hangover and, if you do fall ill, the standard of hospitals and health care is high.

Before You Go

HEALTH INSURANCE

Health insurance is essential for all travellers. Remember that some policies specifically exclude some 'dangerous activities' listed in the policy. These might include scuba diving, skiing and even bushwalking. Make sure the policy you choose fully covers you for your activity of choice.

MEDICAL CHECKLIST

➡ insect repellent for the skin

➡ insect spray for clothing, tents and bed nets

➡ SPF50 sunscreen

➡ oral rehydration salts

➡ iodine tablets or water filter (for water purification)

➡ paracetamol or aspirin

➡ antibiotics

➡ antidiarrhoeal drugs

➡ antihistamines

➡ anti-inflammatory drugs

➡ antibacterial ointment in case of cuts or abrasions

➡ steroid cream or cortisone (for allergic rashes)

➡ thermometer

RECOMMENDED VACCINATIONS

The **World Health Organization** (www.who.int) recommends that all travellers get immunised for diphtheria, tetanus, measles, mumps, rubella, chicken pox and polio, as well as hepatitis B, regardless of their destination.

Visit a physician eight weeks before departure to Australia to ensure you're up to date for all routine vaccinations. While Australia has high levels of childhood vaccination coverage, outbreaks of these diseases do occur.

Upon entering Australia you'll be required to fill out a travel history card detailing any recent visits to regions other than your home country.

If you're entering Australia after visiting a yellow-fever-infected country as listed by World Health Organization, you'll be asked for proof of yellow-fever vaccination or instructed on what to do immediately if you display any systems in the coming days.

RESOURCES

There's a wealth of travel health advice on the internet, not all of it good for you.

The World Health Organization publishes *International Travel and Health*, revised annually and available free online.

The US-based **Centers for Disease Control and Prevention** (www.cdc.gov/travel) provides complete travel-health recommendations for every country for different types of travel and traveller. Other recommended sites include:

Australia (www.smartraveller.gov.au)

Canada (www.hc-sc.gc.ca)

UK (www.nhs.uk/conditions/travel-vaccinations)

In Australia
AVAILABILITY & COST OF HEALTH CARE

Facilities Australia has an excellent health-care system with a mix of private clinics and hospitals complementing a public system funded by the Australian government.

Medicare Covers Australian residents for essential health care. Visitors from countries with which Australia has a reciprocal health-care agreement are able to access Medicare. However, private travel insurance is recommended. See www.humanservices.gov.au/customer/subjects/medicare-services.

Medications Painkillers, antihistamines for allergies and skincare products are widely available at pharmacies throughout Australia. Some medications readily available over the counter in other countries are only available by prescription, such as the oral contraceptive pill and antibiotics.

ENVIRONMENTAL HAZARDS

See also, Deadly & Dangerous (p1058).

Heat Exhaustion & Heatstroke

Temperatures in Australia are reaching extreme levels, so always check forecasts and prepare properly. Heatstroke is a severe form of heat illness and is a true medical emergency, with heating of the brain leading to disorientation, hallucinations and seizures.

Symptoms of heat exhaustion include dizziness, fainting, fatigue, nausea or vomiting. The skin is usually pale, cool and clammy. Treatment consists of rest in a cool, shady place and fluid replacement with water or diluted sports drinks.

Prevent heatstroke by maintaining an adequate fluid intake to ensure the continued passage of clear and copious urine, especially during physical exertion. One litre of water per hour if

walking in summer is a good guide.

Surf & Sun

Some surf beaches in Australia are patrolled by volunteer surf life-saving organisations. Look out for the red and yellow flags showing where it is safest to enter the ocean. Be aware of your skill level and limitations before entering any surf.

The sun is extremely powerful in Australia and generally burns skin quickly. If you have to expose your skin, use SPF50+ sunscreen. Breathable clothing, a broad hat and sunglasses are recommended in summer.

TRAVELLERS' DIARRHOEA

If you develop diarrhoea, drink plenty of rehydration fluids containing lots of salt and sugar. Begin taking an antidiarrhoeal agent (such as loperamide). If diarrhoea is bloody, persists for more than 72 hours, or is accompanied by fever, shaking, chills or severe abdominal pain, seek urgent medical attention.

INFECTIOUS DISEASES

You'd be unlucky to pick up any on your travels, but there are some serious diseases known in Australia. For protection against insect-borne illnesses (dengue fever, Ross River fever, tick typhus, viral encephalitis), wear loose-fitting, long-sleeved clothing, and apply a tropical strength repellent to exposed skin. If bitten by a mosquito, watch for serious symptoms and seek medical advice if you're concerned.

BAIRNSDALE (BURULI) ULCER

Most likely spread by insects like mosquitoes, this infection presents as a small swelling, usually painless, but if left untreated it can result in a skin-eating ulcer. If you appear to have symptoms, tell the treating doctor where you have recently visited.

DENGUE FEVER

Dengue fever occurs in northern Queensland, particularly during the wet season. Causing severe muscular aches, it's a viral disease spread by a day-feeding species of mosquito. Most people recover quickly with treatment.

GIARDIASIS

Giardia is found in some Australian waterways. Drinking untreated water from streams and lakes is not recommended. Use top-quality water filters; or boil or treat collected water to help prevent giardiasis. Symptoms consist of intermittent diarrhoea, abdominal bloating and wind. Effective treatment is available if you do get sick.

HEPATITIS C

Blood-transfusion services fully screen all blood before use, but there are people with hepatitis in the Australian community.

HUMAN IMMUNODEFICIENCY VIRUS (HIV)

Australia's HIV rates are similar to other Western countries. Condoms are available everywhere from supermarkets to petrol stations; clean needles and syringes are available at pharmacies.

MENINGOCOCCAL DISEASE

A minor risk if you have prolonged stays in group accommodation. A vaccine exists for some types of this disease, but as yet there's no vaccine available for viral meningitis. Seek immediate medical attention if you're concerned.

ROSS RIVER FEVER

The Ross River virus is widespread in Australia, transmitted by marsh-dwelling mosquitoes. In addition to fever, it causes headache, joint and muscular pain, and a rash that resolves after five to seven days.

SEXUALLY TRANSMITTED INFECTIONS (STIS)

STI infection rates are similar to most Western countries The golden rule: always use protection, even in easy-going Australia.

TICK TYPHUS

Predominantly occurring in Queensland and New South Wales, tick typhus involves a dark area forming around a tick bite, followed by a rash, fever, headache and lymph-node inflammation. The disease is treatable with antibiotics so get to a doctor.

VIRAL ENCEPHALITIS

This mosquito-borne disease is most common in northern Australia (especially during the wet season), but poses minimal risk to travellers. Symptoms include headache, muscle pain and sensitivity to light. Residual neurological damage can occur, but no specific treatment is available.

REMOTE AREAS

In Australia's remote locations it's possible there will be a significant delay in emergency services reaching you in the event of serious accident or illness. Do not underestimate the vast distances between most major outback towns; an increased level of preparation and self reliance is essential. The **Royal Flying Doctor Service** (www.flyingdoctor.org.au) provides medical services for remote communities.

Take a comprehensive first-aid kit that is appropriate for activities you have planned in Australia.

Ensure you have adequate means of communication. Australia has patchy mobile-phone coverage beyond the city; additional radio communication (such as a satellite phone) is important for remote areas.

A safety flare or beacon is also an essential piece of kit

if you're really going off the beaten track.

TAP WATER

Water is generally drinkable in Australia and is usually signposted if it is not safe.

Insurance

A travel-insurance policy is a very good idea.

Worldwide travel insurance is available at www.lonelyplanet.com/travel-insurance. You can buy, extend and claim online anytime – even if you're already on the road.

Level of cover Ensure your policy covers theft, loss and medical problems. Some policies specifically exclude designated 'dangerous activities' such as scuba diving, skiing and even bushwalking. Make sure the policy you choose fully covers your planned (and perhaps unplanned) activities.

Health Check that the policy covers ambulances and emergency medical evacuations by air. Australia is a vast country so being airlifted to a hospital is a real possibility.

Internet Access

Wi-fi is the norm in most (not all) Australian accommodation, but it is not always good.

Cafes, bars, malls, museums and town squares sometimes provide free wi-fi access, but again don't expect fast speeds.

There remains a surprising number of black spots without mobile phone or internet coverage in Australia. Most are in rural or outback areas. Let family and friends know when you are likely to be uncontactable, and then enjoy properly switching off from the web.

Legal Matters

Most travellers will have zero contact with Australia's police or legal system; if they

INTERSTATE QUARANTINE

When travelling within Australia, whether by land or air, you'll come across signs (mainly in airports and inter-state train stations and at state borders) warning of the possible dangers of carrying fruit, vegetables and plants from one area to another. Certain pests and diseases (fruit fly, cucurbit thrips, grape phylloxera) are prevalent in some areas, but not in others: authorities would like to limit their spread.

Quarantine control between states mostly relies on honesty, but some posts are staffed and officers are entitled to search your car for undeclared items. Generally they will confiscate all fresh fruit and vegetables, so it's best to leave shopping for these items until you're in the next state.

do, it's most likely to be while driving.

Driving There's a significant police presence on Australian roads, and police have the power to stop your car, see your licence (you're required to carry it), check your vehicle for road-worthiness and insist that you take a breath test for alcohol (and sometimes illicit drugs).

Drugs First-time offenders caught with small amounts of illegal drugs are likely to receive a fine rather than go to jail, but the recording of a conviction against you may affect your visa status.

Visas If you remain in Australia beyond the life of your visa, you'll officially be an 'overstayer' and could face mandatory detention and be prevented from returning to Australia.

Legal advice It's your right to telephone a friend, lawyer or relative before police question-ing begins. Legal aid is available only in serious cases and is subject to means testing; for legal aid info see www.national-legalaid.org. However, many solicitors do not charge for an initial consultation.

LGBTIQ+ Travellers

Australia is a popular desti-nation for LGBTIQ+ travel-lers, with Sydney a big 'pink dollar' draw thanks largely to the city's annual, high-profile and spectacular Gay & Les-bian Mardi Gras. Australians are generally open-minded, but you may experience some suspicion or hostility in more conservative neigh-bourhoods or regions.

Throughout the coun-try, but particularly on the east coast, there are tour operators, travel agents and accommodation places that cater specifically for the rainbow community.

The age of consent varies by state for homosexual relationships. Same-sex marriages are now legally recognised in Australia after the question was finally put to a national vote in Novem-ber 2017.

Resources

Major cities have gay-community publications available from clubs, cafes, venues and newsagents. Lifestyle magazines include *Star Observer*, *Lesbians on the Loose (LOTL)* and *DNA*.

Gay & Lesbian Tourism Aus-tralia (Galta; www.galta.com. au) General information on gay-friendly businesses, places to stay and nightlife.

Gay Stay Australia (www. gaystayaustralia.com) A useful resource for accommodation.

Same Same (www.samesame. com.au) News, events and lifestyle features.

Maps

Good-quality road and topo-graphical maps are plentiful and readily available around Australia including at petrol stations and visitor informa-tion centres.

Hiking maps For longer walks proper topographic maps are essential. Published by **Geosci-ence Australia** (☑1800 800 173; www.ga.gov.au/data-pubs/ maps) they're usually available at shops selling specialist hiking gear and outdoor equipment.

Outback Driving Maps Hema Maps (www.hemamaps.com) publishes some of the best maps for desert tracks and regions. They're available online and from some bookshops. Don't rely on Google or Apple Maps if you're heading off road.

GPS You can hire a GPS from the major car-hire companies (sub-ject to availability), but they're unnecessary if you're sticking to the main roads in Australia as there is often just one route from A to B.

Money

Australian dollars is the only currency accepted. You won't have much trouble finding an ATM (automated teller machine, or cashpoint) but be aware that transaction fees are high.

ATMs & Eftpos

ATMs Australia's 'big four' banks – ANZ, Commonwealth, National Australia Bank and Westpac – and affiliated banks have branches all over Australia, plus a slew of 24-hour ATMs. You'll even find them in some outback roadhouses.

Eftpos Most petrol stations, supermarkets, restaurants, cafes and shops have Electronic Funds Transfer at Point of Sale (Eftpos) facilities.

Banking fees Withdrawing cash through ATMs or Eftpos may attract significant fees – check associated costs with your home bank and enquire about fee-free options.

Credit Cards

Credit cards are widely accepted for everything from a hostel bed or a restaurant meal to an adventure tour, and are essential for hiring a car. They can also be used to get cash advances over the counter at banks and from many ATMs, depending on the card, though you'll incur immediate interest. Diners Club and American Express (Amex) are not as widely accepted in Australia.

Currency

Australia's currency is the Australian dollar, comprising 100 cents. There are 5c, 10c, 20c, 50c, $1 and $2 coins, and $5, $10, $20, $50 and $100 notes. Prices in shops are often marked in single cents then rounded to the nearest 5c when you pay.

Debit Cards

A debit card allows you to draw money directly from your home bank account. Any card connected to the international banking network – Cirrus, Maestro, Plus and Eurocard – should work with your PIN, but again expect substantial fees. Companies such as Travelex offer debit cards with set withdrawal fees and a balance you can top up from your personal bank account while on the road.

Changing Money

Changing foreign currency (or travellers cheques, if you're still using them!) is rarely a problem at banks and licensed moneychangers such as Travelex in major cities and airports.

Opening a Bank Account

If you're planning on staying in Australia for a while (on a Working Holiday visa for instance), it makes sense to open an Australian bank account. You'll need a postal address and identification.

An ID points system operates. You need to score a minimum of 100 points before you can set up an account. Passports and birth certificates are worth the most points, followed by an International Driving Permit with photo, then minor IDs such as credit cards. You must have at least one ID with a photograph. Once the account is open, you should be able to have money transferred from your home account (for a fee, of course).

Before you arrive It's possible to set up an Australian bank account before you embark on your international trip and applications can be made online; check bank websites for details:

ANZ (www.anz.com.au)

Commonwealth Bank (www.commbank.com.au)

National Australia Bank (NAB; www.nab.com.au)

Westpac (www.westpac.com.au)

Taxes & Refunds

Goods & Services Tax The GST is a flat 10% tax on all goods and services included in the price. There are exceptions such as basic foods (milk, bread, fruit and vegetables etc).

Refund of GST If you purchase goods with a total minimum value of $300 from any one supplier no more than 30 days before you leave Australia, you are entitled under the Tourist Refund Scheme (TRS) to a refund of any GST paid. The scheme only applies to goods you take with you as hand luggage or wear onto the plane or ship. Check out www.abf.gov.au/entering-and-leaving-australia/tourist-refund-scheme for more details.

Income tax Nonresidents still pay tax on earnings made within Australia, and must lodge a tax return with the Australian Taxation Office. If too much tax was withheld from your pay, you will receive a refund.

Tipping

It's common, but by no means obligatory, to tip in restaurants and upmarket cafes if the service warrants it. Taxi drivers also appreciate you rounding up the fare. Tipping is not usually expected at hotels.

Opening Hours

Most attractions close Christmas Day; many also close on New Year's Day and Good Friday.

Banks & post offices 9.30am–4pm Monday to Thursday; until 5pm Friday

Cafes 7am–5pm; some close later

Petrol stations & roadhouses 8am–8pm; some open 24 hours in cities

Restaurants Lunch noon–2.30pm and dinner from 6pm; service ends early in country towns or on quiet nights

Shops 9am–5pm Monday to Saturday; sometimes on Sunday; in larger cities, doors close at 9pm on Friday

Supermarkets 7am–9pm; some open 24 hours

Post

Australia Post (www.auspost.com.au) runs a reliable national postal services; see the website for info on international delivery zones and rates. All post offices will hold mail for visitors: you need to provide some form of identification (such as a passport or a driving licence) to collect mail.

Public Holidays

New Year's Day 1 January

Australia Day 26 January

Easter (Good Friday to Easter Monday inclusive) late March/early April

Anzac Day 25 April

Queen's Birthday Second Monday in June (last Monday in September in Western Australia)

Christmas Day 25 December

Boxing Day 26 December

In addition, each state has its own public holidays from Canberra Day to the Hobart Show Day.

Safe Travel

Australia is a relatively safe and friendly place to travel, but natural disasters regularly wreak havoc. Bushfires, floods and cyclones can devastate local areas as weather events become more extreme and unpredictable.

➡ Check weather warnings and don't venture into affected areas without an emergency plan.

➡ Crime is low but don't let your guard too far down.

➡ Beware of online house rental scams in Australia. Follow best practice when transferring money overseas.

➡ Wild swimming can be dangerous here thanks to rips, sharks, jellyfish and crocodiles – always seek reliable information.

➡ Watch for wandering wildlife on roads, especially at night. Kangaroos are very unpredictable.

Government Travel Advice

The following government websites offer travel advisories and information for travellers to Australia.

Australian Department of Foreign Affairs & Trade (www.smartraveller.gov.au)

Canadian Department of Foreign Affairs & International Trade (www.voyage.gc.ca)

French Ministère des Affaires Étrangères et Européennes (www.diplomatie.gouv.fr/fr/conseils-aux-voyageurs)

Italian Ministero degli Affari Esteri (www.viaggiaresicuri.mae.aci.it)

New Zealand Ministry of Foreign Affairs & Trade (www.safetravel.govt.nz)

UK Foreign & Commonwealth Office (www.gov.uk/foreign-travel-advice)

US Department of State (www.travel.state.gov)

Telephone

Australia's main phone networks:

Optus (www.optus.com.au)

Telstra (www.telstra.com.au)

Virgin (www.virginmobile.com.au)

Vodafone (www.vodafone.com.au)

Phone Codes

Australia's country code	🖉61
Dialling international	🖉0011

Area Codes

Long-distance calls (over around 50km) are paid by time on the call, with peak and off-peak rates.

State/Territory	Area code
ACT	🖉02
NSW	🖉02
NT	🖉08
QLD	🖉07
SA	🖉08
TAS	🖉03
VIC	🖉03
WA	🖉08

Area-code boundaries don't always coincide with state borders; for example some parts of NSW use the neighbouring states' codes.

Numbers with the prefix 04 belong to mobile phones.

Mobile Phones

Either set up global roaming, or pick up a local SIM card with a prepaid rechargeable account on arrival in Australia. Shop around as deals vary depending on how much data or minutes you expect to use.

Toll-Free & Information Calls

➡ Many businesses have either a toll-free 1800 number, dialled from anywhere within Australia for free, or a 13 or 1300 number, charged at a local call rate. None of these numbers can be dialled from outside Australia (and often can't be dialled from mobile phones within Australia).

➡ To make a reverse-charge (collect) call from any public or private phone, dial 12 550.

➡ Numbers starting with 190 are usually recorded information services, charged at anything from 35c to $5 or more per minute (even more from mobiles and payphones).

Time

Zones Australia is divided into three time zones: Western Standard Time (GMT/UTC plus eight hours), covering Western Australia; Central Standard Time (plus 9½ hours), covering South Australia and the Northern Territory; and Eastern Standard Time (plus 10 hours), covering Tasmania, Victoria, NSW, the Australian Capital Territory and Queensland.

Daylight saving Clocks are put forward an hour in some states during the warmer months (October to early April), but Queensland, WA and the NT stay on standard time.

Toilets

➡ Toilets in Australia are sit-down Western style (though you mightn't find this prospect too appealing in some remote pit stops).

➡ Most public toilets are free of charge and reasonably well looked after.

➡ See www.toiletmap.gov.au for public toilet locations, including disabled-access toilets.

Tourist Information

Tourist information is disseminated by various regional and local offices. Almost every major town in Australia has a tourist office of some type and staff can be super-helpful (often retiree volunteers) providing local information not readily available online. Some also sell books, souvenirs and snacks.

If booking accommodation or tours through a local tourist offices, be aware that they usually only promote businesses that are paying members of the local tourist association.

Brisbane (Map p282; ☑07-3006 6290; www.visitbrisbane.com. au; The Regent, 167 Queen St; ⊗9am-5.30pm, to 7pm Fri, to 5pm Sat, 10am-5pm Sun; ⊠Central)

Canberra (Map p260; ☑02-6205 0044; www.visitcanberra. com.au; Regatta Point, Barrine Dr, Commonwealth Park; ⊗9am-5pm Mon-Fri, to 4pm Sat & Sun)

Darwin (Map p808; ☑08-8980 6000, 1300 138 886; www.tourismtopend.com.au; cnr Smith & Bennett Sts; ⊗8.30am-5pm Mon-Fri, 9am-3pm Sat & Sun)

Hobart (Map p640; ☑03-6238 4222; www.hobarttravelcentre. com.au; 20 Davey St; ⊗8.30am-5pm Mon-Fri, from 9am Sat & Sun)

Melbourne (Map p472; https:// whatson.melbourne.vic.gov.au; Bourke St Mall; ⊗9am-5pm)

Perth (Map p892; www. visitperth.com.au; Forrest Pl, Murray St Mall; ⊗9.30am-4.30pm Mon-Thu & Sat, to 8pm Fri, 11am-3.30pm Sun)

Sydney (Map p80; www. cityofsydney.nsw.gov.au; Alfred St, Circular Quay; ⊗9am-8pm Mon-Sat, to 5pm Sun; ⊠Circular Quay)

Visas

All visitors to Australia need a visa, except New Zealanders. There are several different visas available from short-stay visitor visas to working-holiday visas.

Volunteering

Lonely Planet's *Volunteer: A Traveller's Guide to Making a Difference Around the World* provides useful information about volunteering.

See also the following websites:

Conservation Volunteers Australia (www.conservation-volunteers.com.au) Nonprofit organisation involved in tree planting, walking-track construction and flora and fauna surveys.

Earthwatch Institute Australia (www.earthwatch.org) Volunteer expeditions focusing on conservation and wildlife.

GoVolunteer (www.govolunteer. com.au) Thousands of volunteering opportunities around the country.

Volunteering Australia (www. volunteeringaustralia.org) State-by-state listings of volunteering opportunities around Australia.

Willing Workers on Organic Farms (WWOOF: www.wwoof. com.au) WWOOFing sees travellers swap a day's work on a farm in return for bed and board. Most hosts are concerned to some extent with alternative lifestyles and have a minimum stay of two nights. Join online for a booklet listing participating enterprises.

Women Travellers

Australia is generally a safe place for women travellers, and the following sensible precautions all apply for men as well as women.

Night-time Avoid walking alone late at night in any of the major cities and towns – keep enough money aside for a taxi back to your accommodation.

Pubs Be wary of basic pub accommodation unless it looks particularly well managed. Alcohol can affect people's behaviour and compromise safety.

Drink spiking Pubs in major cities sometimes post warnings about drugged or 'spiked' drinks. Play it cautious if someone offers you a drink in a bar.

Sexual harassment Unfortunately still a fairly big problem in Australia from street harassment to 'nice guys' on dating apps.

Hitchhiking Hitching is never recommended for anyone, even when travelling in pairs. Exercise caution at all times.

Solo travel Most people won't bat an eyelid if you're female-identifying and travelling alone. Go forth and have the time of your life in Australia, without having to compromise just to have a buddy on the road.

Work

If you come to Australia on a tourist visa, you're not allowed to work for pay: you'll need a Working Holiday (417) or a Work and Holiday (462) visa – see www.homeaffairs.gov.au for up-to-date information.

Tax File Number

If you're working in Australia, apply for a Tax File Number (TFN) online through the Australian Taxation Office (www.ato.gov.au); it takes up to four weeks to be issued. Without it, tax will be deducted at the maximum rate from any wages you receive.

Finding Work

Backpacker magazines, newspapers and hostel noticeboards are good places to source local work opportunities. Casual work can often be found during peak season at the major tourist centres: places such as Alice Springs, Cairns and resort towns along the Queensland coast, and the ski fields of Victoria and NSW are all good prospects during holiday season. Other possibilities for casual employment include factory work, farm labour, bar work, waiting tables, domestic chores at outback roadhouses, nanny work, or as a fundraiser for charities. People in skilled professions from IT to building can find work temping in the major cities by registering with an industry agency.

See also the following websites, which are good for opportunities in metropolitan areas:

Career One (www.careerone. com.au) General employment site; good for metropolitan areas.

Gumtree (www.gumtree.com.au) Classified site with jobs, accommodation and items for sale.

Job Active – Harvest (www.job-search.gov.au/harvest) Harvest job specialists.

National Harvest Labour Information Service (☑1800 062 332) Info on when and where you're likely to pick up harvest work.

QITE (www.qite.com) Nonprofit Queensland employment agency operating around Cairns, Innisfail and the Atherton Tablelands.

Seek (www.seek.com.au) General employment site; good for metropolitan areas.

Travellers at Work (www.taw. com.au) Excellent site for working travellers in Australia.

Workabout Australia (www. workaboutaustralia.com.au) Gives a state-by-state breakdown of seasonal work opportunities.

Seasonal Work

Seasonal fruit-picking (harvesting) relies on casual labour – there's always something that needs to be picked, pruned or farmed somewhere in Australia year-round. It's definitely hard work, involving early-morning starts, and you're usually paid by how much you pick (per bin, bucket, kilo etc). Never put a deposit down to reserve a fruit-picking job and never pay for fruit-picking accommodation in advance.

SEASONAL WORK HOT SPOTS

NSW The NSW ski fields have seasonal work during the ski season, particularly around Thredbo. There's also harvest work around Narrabri and Moree, and grape picking in the Hunter Valley. Fruit picking happens near Tenterfield, Orange and Young.

NT The majority of working-holiday opportunities in the NT for backpackers are in fruit picking, station handing, labouring and hospitality.

Queensland Queensland has vast tracts of farmland and orchards: there's fruit-picking work to be found around Stanthorpe, Childers, Bundaberg and Cairns. Those looking for sturdier (and much-better-paying) work should keep an eye on mining opportunities in towns such as Weipa and Cloncurry.

SA Good seasonal-work opportunities can be found on the Fleurieu Peninsula, in the Coonawarra region and Barossa Valley (wineries), and along the Murray River around Berri (fruit picking).

Tasmania The apple orchards in the south, especially around Cygnet and Huonville, are your best bet for work in Tassie.

Victoria Harvest work in Mildura and Shepparton.

WA Perth usually has temporary work available in tourism and hospitality, administration, IT, nursing, child care, factories and labouring. Outside of Perth travellers can look for jobs in tourism and hospitality, plus a variety of seasonal work. For grape-picking work, head for the vineyards around Margaret River.

Transport

GETTING THERE & AWAY

Most travellers arrive on a long-haul flight. Pick your arrival city wisely. Sydney might be the obvious choice, but flights into smaller cities can make for a quicker trip through customs, and a happier transition to your accommodation. Flights, cars and tours can be booked online at lonelyplanet.com/bookings.

Entering the Country

Arrival in Australia is usually fairly quick and efficient. If you have a current passport and visa, and follow customs regulations, your entry should be straightforward.

Air

Airports & Airlines

Most major international airlines fly to/from Australia's larger cities. The national carrier is **Qantas** (☑13 13 13; www.qantas.com.au), which has an outstanding safety record, and code shares with British Airways.

Sydney and Melbourne are the busiest gateway cities, but Perth, Adelaide and Brisbane are all increasingly popular places to start your Australia adventure.

Adelaide Airport (ADL; ☑08-8308 9211; www.adelaideairport.com.au; 1 James Schofield Dr, Adelaide Airport)

Brisbane Airport (www.bne.com.au; Airport Dr)

Cairns Airport (☑07-4080 6703; www.cairnsairport.com; Airport Ave)

Darwin International Airport (☑08-8920 1811; www.darwinairport.com.au; Henry Wrigley Dr, Marrara)

Gold Coast Airport (www.goldcoastairport.com.au; Eastern Ave, Bilinga)

Melbourne Airport (MEL; ☑03-9297 1600; www.melbourneairport.com.au; Departure Rd, Tullamarine; ☎)

Perth Airport (☑08-9478 8888; www.perthairport.com.au; Airport Dr)

Sydney Airport (Kingsford Smith Airport; Mascot Airport; ☑02-9667 6111; www.sydneyairport.com.au; Airport Dr, Mascot; ☐Domestic Airport, ☐International Airport)

Land

It is not possible to travel here by land.

Sea

It's possible (though by no means easy and not necessarily safe) to make your way between Australia and places such as Papua New Guinea, Indonesia, New Zealand and the Pacific islands by hitching rides or crewing on yachts. Alternatively, **P&O Cruises** (www.pocruises.com.au) operates holiday

---

CLIMATE CHANGE & TRAVEL

Every form of transport that relies on carbon-based fuel generates CO_2, the main cause of human-induced climate change. Modern travel is dependent on aeroplanes, which might use less fuel per kilometre per person than most cars but travel much greater distances. The altitude at which aircraft emit gases (including CO_2) and particles also contributes to their climate change impact. Many websites offer 'carbon calculators' that allow people to estimate the carbon emissions generated by their journey and, for those who wish to do so, to offset the impact of the greenhouse gases emitted with contributions to portfolios of climate-friendly initiatives throughout the world. Lonely Planet offsets the carbon footprint of all staff and author travel.

DEPARTURE TAX

Departure tax is included in the price of a ticket.

cruises between Brisbane, Melbourne or Sydney and destinations in New Zealand and the Pacific. Some cargo ships allow passengers to travel on board – check out websites such as www.freighterexpeditions.com.au and www.freightercruises.com for options.

GETTING AROUND

Air

Time pressure, combined with the vastness of the Australian continent, may lead you to consider taking to the skies at some point in your trip. Australia has a few low-cost carriers, but deals on the main airlines often compete on value when you add baggage (and reliability).

Airlines in Australia

Australia's main domestic airlines service the large centres with regular flights. The major players:

Jetstar (☑13 15 38; www.jetstar.com)

Qantas (☑13 13 13; www.qantas.com.au)

Tigerair (☑1300 174 266; www.tigerair.com.au)

Virgin Australia (☑13 67 89; www.virginaustralia.com)

A number of regional airlines operate within smaller geographical parameters and fly into regional airports.

Air Passes

For the highly organised, **Qantas** (☑13 13 13; www.qantas.com.au) has a **Qantas Explorer** (www.qantas.com/us/en/book-a-trip/flights/qantas-explorer.html) deal where you link up to 30 domestic Australian destinations for less than you'd pay if you booked flights individually, though you must book them together.

Bicycle

Cycling around Australia is possible, but will take considerable fitness and excellent planning.

Transport If you're bringing your own bike, check with your airline for weight, costs and packing required. Within Australia, bus companies require you to dismantle your bike. Trains sometimes have separate bike-storage facilities on-board.

Legalities Bike helmets are compulsory in all states and territories, as are white front lights and red rear lights for riding at night.

Maps You can get by with standard road maps, but to avoid low-grade unsealed roads, the government series is best. The 1:250,000 scale is suitable, though you'll need lots of maps if you're riding long distances.

Safety In summer carry plenty of water at all times. Distances between towns can be gruellingly far. Avoid cycling in the middle of the day in hot weather. Drivers will not be expecting to see cyclists on most country roads. Wear as much high-vis outerwear as possible.

Boat

Unless you're crewing on a yacht or enjoying a Pacific cruise, boat travel isn't really a feasible way to get around Australia. Short-hop regional ferries will take you to places like Kangaroo Island and North Stradbroke Island and around the harbour of Sydney. Travel from Melbourne to Tasmania or back on the **Spirit of Tasmania** (☑1800 634 906; www.spiritoftasmania.com.au; ⏰customer info 8am-8.30pm Mon-Sat, 9am-8pm Sun).

Bus

Australia's extensive bus network is a reliable way to get around, but distances are often vast. Most Australian buses are equipped with aircon, comfortable seats and decent toilets; all are smoke-free and some have wi-fi and USB chargers.

Greyhound Australia (☑1300 473 946; www.greyhound.com.au; 🖵) Runs in every state except South Australia and Western Australia. Offers flexible hop-on hop-off fares. Discounts for seniors, students and children.

Firefly Express (☑1300 730 740; www.fireflyexpress.com.au) Runs between Sydney, Canberra, Melbourne and Adelaide.

Integrity Coach Lines (Map p892; ☑08-9274 7464; www.integritycoachlines.com.au; cnr Wellington St & Horseshoe Bridge) The main operator in WA.

Premier Motor Service (☑13 34 10; www.premierms.com.au) Does the east coast from Eden to Cairns. Has flexible hop-on hop-off fares.

V/Line (☑1800 800 007; www.vline.com.au; Southern Cross Station, Spencer St, Docklands) Covers all of Victoria with a mix of coaches and trains.

Bus Tours

Another way to get around by bus is on a tour. Some offer the whole package including accommodation and meals; others are less formal options to get from A to B and see the sights on the way.

AAT Kings (☑1300 556 100; www.aatkings.com) Big coach company (popular with the older set) with myriad tours around Australia.

Adventure Tours Australia (☑1300 654 604; www.adventuretours.com.au) Affordable, young-at-heart tours in all states.

Autopia Tours (☎03-9393 1333; www.autopiatours.com. au) One- to three-day trips from Melbourne, Adelaide and Sydney.

Groovy Grape Tours (☎08-8440 1640; www.groovygrape. com.au) Small-group, SA-based operator running tours ex-Adelaide, Melbourne and Alice Springs.

Nullarbor Traveller (☎08-8687 0455; https://nullarbortraveller. com.au) Small company running relaxed minibus trips across the Nullarbor Plain between SA and WA.

Oz Experience (☎1300 300 028; www.ozexperience.com) Packaged itineraries for younger travellers, partnering with Greyhound coaches.

Car & Motorcycle

Exploring Australia by road is the quintessential way to get around this vast nation. Whether you're focusing your visit on one state or several, road trips are a popular Australian experience. Pick up a copy of Lonely Planet's *Australia's Best Trips* for more on 2WD itineraries for cars, vans and campervans.

For 4WD or motorcycles, you'll need specialist skills, guidebooks, maps and equipment. Contact one of the automobile clubs for specific recommendations.

Automobile Clubs

Under the auspices of the **Australian Automobile Association** (AAA; ☎02-6247 7311; www.aaa.asn.au) there are automobile clubs in each state, which is handy when it comes to insurance, regulations, maps and roadside assistance. Club membership (around $100 to $150) can save you a lot of trouble if things go wrong mechanically. The major Australian auto clubs generally offer reciprocal rights in other states and territories.

Automobile Association of the Northern Territory (AANT; ☎08-8925 5901; www.aant. com.au; 2/14 Knuckey St; ⊙9am-5pm Mon-Fri, to 12.30pm Sat)

National Roads & Motorists Association (☎13 11 22; www. mynrma.com.au) New South

Principal Bus Routes & Railways

Principal Bus Routes ———
Principal Railways ———

Wales and the Australian Capital Territory

Royal Automobile Club of Queensland (☑13 19 05; www.racq.com.au)

Royal Automobile Club of Tasmania (RACT; ☑03-6232 6300, roadside assistance 13 11 11; www.ract.com.au; cnr Murray & Patrick Sts, Hobart; ◷8.45am-5pm Mon-Fri)

Royal Automobile Club of Victoria (☑13 72 28; www.racv.com.au)

Royal Automobile Club of Western Australia (RAC; ☑13 17 03; www.rac.com.au)

Buying a Vehicle

Buying your own vehicle gives you the freedom to go where and when your mood takes you, and may work out cheaper than renting in the long run.

Downsides include dealing with confusing and expensive registration rules, roadworthy certificates and insurance; forking out for maintenance and repairs; and selling the vehicle when you're done – which may be more difficult than expected.

If you're buying a second-hand vehicle, keep in mind the extra costs on top of the purchase price when deciding your budget: stamp duty, registration, transfer fee, insurance and maintenance.

PAPERWORK

Registration When you buy a vehicle in Australia you need to transfer the registration into your own name within 14 days. Each state has slightly different requirements. It is usually something you can do online. Similarly, when selling a vehicle you need to advise the state or territory road-transport authority of the sale and change of name.

Roadworthiness Sellers are required to provide a roadworthy certificate when transferring registration in most states except WA, SA and Tasmania where inspections/certificates are only required in certain circumstances

If the vehicle you're considering doesn't have a roadworthy certificate, ask for a roadworthiness check before you agree on a sales price. This can cost $100 but will save you money on unknown repair costs. Road-

transport authorities have lists of licensed vehicle testers.

Gas certificate In Queensland, if a vehicle runs on gas, a gas certificate must be provided by the seller in order to transfer the registration. In the ACT, vehicles running on gas require an annual inspection.

Immobiliser fitting In WA it's compulsory to have an approved immobiliser fitted to most vehicles (not motorcycles) before transfer of registration; this is the buyer's responsibility.

Changing state of registration Note that registering a vehicle in a different state from the one it was previously registered in can be time-consuming and expensive. It's something to be aware of when planning to sell.

Renewing registration Registration is usually paid annually Australia-wide, but most states and territories also give you the option of renewing for three or six months.

ROAD TRANSPORT AUTHORITIES

For more information about processes and costs see the following:

Access Canberra (☑13 22 81; www.accesscanberra.act.gov.au) ACT

Department of Planning, Transport & Infrastructure (☑1300 872 677; www.transport.sa.gov.au) South Australia

Department of State Growth – Transport (☑1300 135 513; www.transport.tas.gov.au) Tasmania

Department of Transport (☑1300 654 628; www.transport.nt.gov.au) Northern Territory

Department of Transport (☑13 11 56; www.transport.wa.gov.au) Western Australia

Department of Transport & Main Roads (☑13 23 80; www.tmr.qld.gov.au) Queensland

Roads & Maritime Services (☑13 22 13; www.rta.nsw.gov.au) NSW

VicRoads (☑03-8391 3216, 13 11 71; www.vicroads.vic.gov.

CHOOSING A VEHICLE

2WD Depending on where you want to travel, a regulation 2WD vehicle might suffice. They're cheaper to hire, buy and run than 4WDs and are more readily available. Most are fuel efficient and easy to repair and sell. Downsides: no off-road capability and no room to sleep!

4WD Good for outback travel as they can access almost any track for which you get a hankering, and there might even be space to sleep in the back. Downsides: poor fuel economy, awkward to park and more expensive to hire or buy.

Campervan Creature comforts at your fingertips: sink, fridge, cupboards, beds, kitchen and space to relax. Downsides: slow and often not fuel-efficient, not great on dirt roads and too large for nipping around the city.

Motorcycle The Australian climate is great for riding, and bikes are handy in city traffic. Downsides: Australia isn't particularly bike-friendly in terms of driver awareness; there's limited luggage capacity, and exposure to the elements.

ROAD DISTANCES (KM)

	Adelaide	Albany	Alice Springs	Birdsville	Brisbane	Broome	Cairns	Canberra	Cape York	Darwin	Kalgoorlie	Melbourne	Perth	Sydney	Townsville
Albany	2649														
Alice Springs	1512	3573													
Birdsville	1183	3244	1176												
Brisbane	1942	4178	1849	1573											
Broome	4043	2865	2571	3564	5065										
Cairns	3079	5601	2396	1919	1705	4111									
Canberra	1372	4021	2725	2038	1287	5296	2923								
Cape York	4444	6566	3361	2884	2601	5076	965	3888							
Darwin	3006	5067	1494	2273	3774	1844	2820	3948	3785						
Kalgoorlie	2168	885	3092	2763	3697	3052	5234	3540	6199	4896					
Melbourne	728	3377	2240	1911	1860	4811	3496	637	4461	3734	2896				
Perth	2624	411	3548	3219	4153	2454	6565	3996	7530	4298	598	3352			
Sydney	1597	4246	3109	2007	940	5208	2634	289	3599	3917	3765	862	3869		
Townsville	3237	5374	2055	1578	1295	3770	341	2582	1306	2479	4893	3155	5349	2293	
Uluru	1559	3620	441	1617	2290	3012	2837	2931	3802	1935	3139	2287	3595	2804	2496

	Bicheno	Cradle Mountain	Devonport	Hobart	Launceston
Cradle Mountain	383				
Devonport	283	100			
Hobart	186	296	334		
Launceston	178	205	105	209	
Queenstown	443	69	168	257	273

TRANSPORT CAR & MOTORCYCLE

These are the shortest distances by road; other routes may be considerably longer.

au; ⊙8am-5.30pm Mon-Fri) Victoria

WHAT TO LOOK FOR

It's prudent to have a car checked by an independent expert – auto clubs offer vehicle checks, and road transport authorities have lists of licensed garages – but if you're flying solo, here are some things to check:

➡ tyre tread

➡ number of kilometres

➡ rust damage

➡ accident damage

➡ oil should be translucent and honey-coloured

➡ coolant should be clean and not rusty in colour

➡ engine condition: check for fumes from engine, smoke from exhaust while engine is running, and engines that rattle or cough

➡ exhaust system should not be excessively noisy or rattly when engine is running

➡ windscreen should be clear with no cracks or chip marks When test driving the car, also check the following:

➡ listen for body and suspension noise and changes in engine noise

➡ check for oil and petrol smells, leaks and overheating

➡ check instruments, lights and controls all work: heating, air-con, brake lights, headlights, indicators, seat belts and windscreen wipers

➡ brakes should pull the car up straight, without pulling, vibrating or making noise

➡ gears and steering should be smooth and quiet

Car Hire

Larger car-hire companies have offices in major cities and airports. Most companies require drivers to be over the age of 21, though in some cases it's 18 and in others 25.

Suggestions to assist in the process:

➡ Read the contract cover to cover.

➡ Most companies will demand they put a 'hold' on a sum on your credit card to cover their insurance excess. This is released after the car is returned in one piece, but budget that into your finances.

➡ Ask if unlimited kilometres are included; it's almost essential in Australia as extra kilometres will add to your costs considerably.

➡ Find out what excess you'll have to pay if you have an accident; it's usually charged no matter who is at fault.

➡ Check if your personal travel insurance covers you for vehicle accidents and excess.

➡ Check whether you're covered on unavoidable unsealed roads (eg accessing campgrounds).

➡ Some companies also exclude parts of the car from cover, such as the underbelly, tyres and windscreen.

➡ At pick-up inspect the vehicle for any damage. Make a note of anything on the contract before you sign. Take photos, though they're usually not considered evidence if you get into a dispute.

➡ Make sure you know the breakdown and accident procedures.

➡ If you can, return the vehicle during business hours and insist on an inspection in your presence. The following websites offer last-minute discounts and the opportunity to compare rates between the big operators:

➡ www.carhire.com.au

➡ www.drivenow.com.au

➡ www.webjet.com.au

4WD HIRE

Having a 4WD is essential for off-the-beaten-track driving into the outback. The major car-hire companies have 4WDs.

Renting a 4WD is affordable if a few people get together – something like a Nissan X-Trail (which can get you through most, but not all, tracks) costs $100 to $150 per day; for a Toyota Landcruiser you're looking at $150 to $200, which should include unlimited kilometres.

Check the insurance conditions, especially the excess (the amount you pay in the event of accident and which can be up to $5000), as they can be onerous. A refundable bond is also often required – this can be as much as $7500. The excess and policies might not cover damage caused when travelling off-road (which they don't always tell you when you pick up your vehicle). Some also name specific tracks as off limits and you may not be covered by the insurance if you ignore this.

CAMPERVAN HIRE

Companies for campervan hire – with rates from around $90 (two-berth) or $150 (four-berth) per day, usually with minimum five-day hire and unlimited kilometres – include the following:

Apollo (☎1800 777 779; www. apollocamper.com)

Britz (☎1300 738 087; www. britz.com.au)

Hippie Camper (☎1800 777 779; www.hippiecamper.com)

Jucy (☎1800 150 850; www. jucy.com.au)

Maui (☎1800 827 821; www. maui.com.au)

Mighty Campers (☎1800 821 824; www.mightycampers. com.au)

Spaceships (☎1300 132 469; www.spaceshipsrentals.com.au)

Travelwheels (☎0412 766 616; www.travelwheels.com.au)

Insurance

Third-party insurance With the exception of NSW and Queensland, third-party personal-injury insurance is included in the vehicle registration cost, ensuring that every registered vehicle carries at least the minimum insurance (if registering in NSW or Queensland you'll need to arrange this privately). It's recommended that you extend that minimum to at least third-party *property* insurance – minor collisions can be incredibly expensive.

Comprehensive cover Consider taking out comprehensive car insurance if you want your own vehicle insured, even when the accident is not your fault. An uninsured driver will be hard to extract money from especially if you're not going to be in Australia for long.

Fuel Economy

Fuel types Unleaded and diesel fuel is available from petrol stations sporting well-known international brand names. LPG (liquefied petroleum gas) has waned in popularity with fewer places stocking refills – it's best to have dual-fuel capacity. Electric recharging spots are popping up all over Australia, making hybrid and electric road trips a viable alternative.

Costs Prices vary between the city and country and depend on the day of the week. At the time of writing petrol hovered around $1.50 a litre, but under certain conditions it can be as high as $2 per litre.

ROAD CONDITIONS

For up-to-date information on road conditions around the country, check the following:

Australian Bureau of Meteorology (www.bom.gov.au) Weather information and road warnings.

Department of Planning, Transport & Infrastructure (p1074) SA road conditions.

Live Traffic NSW (☎1300 131 122; www.livetraffic.com) NSW road conditions.

Main Roads Western Australia (☎13 81 38; www.mainroads.wa.gov.au) WA road conditions.

Road Report (☎1800 246 199; https://roadreport.nt.gov. au) NT road conditions.

Traffic & Travel Information (☎13 19 05; www.racq. com.au/cars-and-driving/safety-on-the-road/roadconditions) Queensland road conditions.

Availability In cities and towns, petrol stations are plentiful, but distances between fill-ups can be huge in the countryside so pay attention to your fuel gauge. On main roads there'll be a small town or roadhouse roughly every 200km.

Driving Licence

To drive in Australia you'll need to hold a current driving licence issued in English from your home country. If the licence isn't in English, you'll also need to carry an International Driving Permit, issued in your home country.

Road Rules

Australians drive on the left-hand side of the road and all cars are right-hand drive.

Give way An important road rule is 'give way to the right' – if an intersection is unmarked (unusual), and at roundabouts, you must give way to vehicles entering the intersection from your right.

Speed limits The general speed limit in built-up and residential areas is 50km/h. Near schools, the limit is usually 25km/h (sometimes 40km/h) in the morning and afternoon. On the highway it's usually 100km/h or 110km/h; in the NT it's either 110km/h or 130km/h. Police have speed radar guns and cameras and are fond of using them in strategic locations.

Seat belts & car seats It's the law to wear seat belts in the front and back seats; you're likely to get a fine if you don't. Small children must be belted into an approved safety seat.

Drinking & driving Random breath tests are common. If you're caught with a blood-alcohol level of more than 0.05%, expect a fine and the loss of your licence. Police can randomly pull any driver over for a breathalyser or drug test. Best just to drive sober and make it alive. Drug testing is also a possibility.

Mobile phones Using a mobile phone while driving is illegal in Australia (excluding hands-free technology).

GOING GREENER

A few simple actions can help minimise the impact your journey has on the environment.

➡ Ensure your vehicle is well serviced and tuned.

➡ Travel lightly to reduce fuel consumption.

➡ Drive slowly – many vehicles use 25% more fuel at 110km/h than at 90km/h.

➡ Stay on designated roads and vehicle off-road tracks.

➡ Drive in the middle of tracks to minimise track widening and damage, don't drive on walking tracks and avoid driving on vegetation.

➡ Cross creeks at designated areas.

➡ Consider ride sharing where possible.

➡ Check out the electric-car options at major dealers.

For more info, see www.greenvehicleguide.gov.au.

Road Safety
ANIMAL HAZARDS

➡ Roadkill is a huge problem in Australia, particularly in the NT, Queensland, NSW, SA and Tasmania. Many Australians in rural areas avoid travelling once the sun drops because of the risks posed by nocturnal animals on the roads.

➡ Kangaroos are common on country roads, as are cows and sheep in the unfenced outback. Kangaroos are most active around dawn and dusk and often travel in groups: if you see one hopping across the road, slow right down, as its friends may be just behind it.

➡ If you injure an animal while driving, call the relevant wildlife rescue line:

Department of Environment & Heritage Protection (☑1300 264 625; www.ehp.qld.gov.au) Queensland

Department of Parks & Wildlife (☑Wildcare Helpline 08-9474 9055; www.parks.dpaw.wa.gov.au) WA

Fauna Rescue of South Australia (☑08-8289 0896; www.faunarescue.org.au)

NSW Wildlife Information, Rescue & Education Service (WIRES; ☑1300 094 737; www.wires.org.au)

Parks & Wildlife Service (☑1300 827 727; www.parks.tas.gov.au) Tasmania

Wildcare Inc NT (☑0408 885 341; www.wildcarent.org.au)

Wildlife Victoria (☑1300 094 535; www.wildlifevictoria.org.au)

BEHIND THE WHEEL

Fatigue Be wary of driver fatigue; driving long distances (particularly in hot weather) can be utterly exhausting. Falling asleep at the wheel is a serious risk. Stop and rest regularly – do some exercise, change drivers or have a coffee.

Road trains Be careful overtaking road trains (trucks with two or three trailers stretching for as long as 50m); you'll need distance and plenty of speed. On single-lane tracks get right off the road when one approaches. Stones or debris can clip your car as it passes.

Unsealed roads Unsealed road conditions vary wildly and cars perform differently when braking and turning on dirt. Don't exceed 70km/h on dirt roads; if you go faster, you won't have time to respond to a sharp turn, stock on the road or an unexpected pothole.

Hitching

Hitching is never entirely safe, and we don't recommend it. Travellers who hitch should understand that they are taking a small but potentially serious risk. People who do choose to hitch should always let someone know where they are planning to go.

Local Transport

All of Australia's major towns have reliable, affordable public bus networks, and there are suburban train lines in Sydney, Melbourne, Brisbane, Adelaide and Perth.

Melbourne also has trams (Adelaide has one!), Sydney and Brisbane have ferries, and Sydney and Canberra have a light-rail line.

Taxis operate in all major cities and towns, which is especially handy if you're having a few drinks out. However, not every city has a pool of mobile app-booked taxi drivers – yet.

Train

Long-distance rail travel in Australia is something you do because you really want to – not because it's cheap, convenient or fast. That said, trains are more comfortable than buses, and there's a certain long-distance 'romance of the rails' that's alive and kicking.

Shorter-distance rail services within most states are run by state rail bodies, either government or private.

The most notable long-distance rail journeys in Australia are run by the following:

Great Southern Rail (☑08-8213 4401, 1800 703 357; www.greatsouthernrail.com. au) Operates the *Indian Pacific* between Sydney and Perth, the *Overland* between Melbourne and Adelaide, *Great Southern* between Brisbane and Adelaide, and *The Ghan* between Adelaide and Darwin via Alice Springs.

Queensland Rail (☑1300 131 722; www.queenslandrailtravel. com.au) Runs the high-speed *Spirit of Queensland* service between Brisbane and Cairns.

NSW TrainLink (☑13 22 32; www.nswtrainlink.info) Trains from Sydney to Brisbane, Melbourne and Canberra.

V/Line (☑1800 800 007; www. vline.com.au; Southern Cross Station, Spencer St, Docklands) Trains within Victoria, linking up with buses for connections into NSW, SA and the ACT.

Behind the Scenes

SEND US YOUR FEEDBACK

We love to hear from travellers – your comments keep us on our toes and help make our books better. Our well-travelled team reads every word on what you loved or loathed about this book. Although we cannot reply individually to your submissions, we always guarantee that your feedback goes straight to the appropriate authors, in time for the next edition. Each person who sends us information is thanked in the next edition – the most useful submissions are rewarded with a selection of digital PDF chapters.

Visit **lonelyplanet.com/contact** to submit your updates and suggestions or to ask for help. Our award-winning website also features inspirational travel stories, news and discussions.

Note: We may edit, reproduce and incorporate your comments in Lonely Planet products such as guidebooks, websites and digital products, so let us know if you don't want your comments reproduced or your name acknowledged. For a copy of our privacy policy visit lonelyplanet.com/privacy.

OUR READERS

Many thanks to the travellers who used the last edition and wrote to us with helpful hints, useful advice and interesting anecdotes:

Deb Burton, Pieter van Cleemputte, Bob Gasston, Ross Hartley, Martin Henner, Richard Kempton, Paula Köchling, Peter Tudor, Andrew Walter, Catharina Westrin

WRITER THANKS

Brett Atkinson

Thanks to the experts at visitor information centres and national parks around Victoria and NSW, and cheers to Greg and Francie in Echuca and the Mildura crew. Nick Cave, Mark Seymour and Mick Thomas provided the essential Australian soundtrack for long drives in red dirt landscapes, while words by Peter FitzSimons and Ian Jones illuminated history along the way. Thanks to Tasmin Waby for another opportunity to explore my Australian backyard, and to Carol.

Andrew Bain

For sharing the road, a big thanks to Anila Rao and my two junior partners in travel crime, Kiri and Cooper. A general thanks to all the tour operators and others who shared their ideas and thoughts for me. Special thanks to Sherene Somerville for a long list of suggestions, and Tracey Leitch for smoothing the way when needed.

Fleur Bainger

Thrilled and grateful to be on board, I'm eager to thank both Tasmin and Charles for their endless patience with helping me learn the guidebook writing ropes. Western Australia's epic scenery, passionate characters and inspiring produce also deserve gratitude; they constantly inspire me to share the word on this stunning, still relatively untouched part of the world.

Cristian Bonetto

An especially big thank you to Tasmin Waby for the commission and to Drew Westbrook for the generous hospitality and insight. Many thanks also to those who shared their passion for Queensland's southeast with me, among them Peter Scudamore-Smith, Monique Krause, Brooke Billett, Lauren Grounsell, Glen Robert, Angelo Puglisi, Leeanne Gangemi-Puglisi, Dylan Rhymer, Peter McGlashan, Jason Hannay, Tama Barry, Grace Dewar, Tim Crabtree and Leanne Layfield. Thanks also to my ever-diligent fellow writers, Kate Morgan, Hugh McNaughtan, and Paul Harding.

Samantha Forge

My thanks to Canberra locals Rachel, Sam, Emma, Harry and Lily for sharing all their insider tips. Thanks also to my travelling companions Karyn, Bill and Gemma for helping me cram as many meals into each day as possible. Lastly, thanks to everyone at Lonely Planet for their hard work on this title, and especially to Tasmin Waby for once again throwing me in the deep end with complete faith in my swimming abilities.

Anthony Ham

Huge thanks to Tasmin Waby for sending me to such soulful places, and for much wisdom. Imogen Bannister also brought great insight to the editing. Too many people to thank across the Territory and Queensland – thanks to everyone for welcoming me so warmly to country. Special thanks to Kath Soa and Geoff Mark in Katherine, Liam and the Border Store team in Katherine, and many more. To Valentina, Carlota and Marina – os quiero. And to Jan – you have the biggest heart in Australia.

Paul Harding

Far North Queensland is a wonderful part of Australia and I thank all the people who helped with advice, information or just a chat on this trip. Thanks to Dirk on Thursday Island, Vanessa on Horn Island and Col from AMPTO for the informative discussion about the reef in Cairns. Sincere thanks to Tasmin at Lonely Planet for gifting me these opportunities. And most of all, thanks to Hannah and Layla for always being there.

Trent Holden

First up a massive thanks to Tasmin Waby for giving me another opportunity to cover my home state for Lonely Planet; a wonderful gig! Also a big thanks to my fellow writers and the production staff who've worked hard to put this all together. Thank you to all the folk from the tourist information centres who've helped out along the way – in particular Glenn Harvey from Bendigo, Clare Hutchison from Castlemaine and Selma Kajan in Ballarat who assisted with useful tips. Finally, lots of love to all my family, and especially my fiancé Kate.

Anita Isalska

A heartfelt thank you for the many warm welcomes I received in NSW. For local knowledge I'm grateful to Shane Carriage, Chris Scroggy, Noel Butler, Jane Atkin, Kate Sullivan, Sarah Shields and Ian Hutton. Thanks also to John Kowalewski for helping me hit the Gong, Noraidah and George Atkin for being Narooma's best unlisted highlight, and Michele and Peter Williams for their attentive wine-tasting. Big thanks to Normal Matt for write-up support and enduring my long-distance photos of white-sand beaches.

Anna Kaminski

Huge thanks to Tasmin for entrusting me with a chunk of WA, fellow scribes Charles, Steve, Carolyn and Brett for the advice, and to everyone who's helped me along the way. In particular: John and Debbie in Geraldton, Barbara in Esperance, Anna in Meekatharra, my adoptive Wongutha family (Linden, Trevor and Marcia), plus Monica, Billy and Becky in Kalgoorlie, 'Capes' in Denham, Amy in Port Hedland, Maria, Kate and Michael in Denmark, Lyn in Norseman, plus all the helpful visitor centre staff

and Aboriginal artists who've shared their work with me.

Tatyana Leonov

I want to thank the locals who were kind enough to share their personal stories with me, the staff at the various attractions I visited who took their time to show me around, and the tourism marketing officers who pointed me in the right direction in each of the towns I visited.

Sofia Levin

Writing about your home city is both an honour and challenge. I am floored by the dedication and talent of those in the hospitality industry, from tiny, family-run restaurants to the big guys creating waves overseas – thank you for making Melbourne the best city in the world. To Matt: thank you for giving me support, space and encouragement chocolate. And finally, I'm ever grateful to my parents (aka my biggest fans), for instilling me with insatiable curiosity and appetite.

Virginia Maxwell

Victoria is my home turf, so I was able to interrogate innumerable friends and family members about their favourite places before setting off to research this edition. Thanks to them all. Peter and Max Handsaker accompanied me on day and overnight trips and were, as always, wonderful travelling companions. Dave McClymont and Janet Austin were particularly helpful in the Dandenongs. Thanks to Tasmin Waby for her expert briefing and project guidance, and to fellow Victoria authors Sofia, Brett and Trent for nominating their top eating and sleeping picks.

Hugh McNaughtan

My gratitude goes out to all who made this gig possible: Tasmin for the opportunity and guidance; Mum for the company in New South Wales; and most especially Tas (again) and my girls for allowing me to disappear again for many, many weeks.

Kate Morgan

Thank you to Tasmin for sending me off on a road trip of one of Australia's most beautiful stretches of coastline. To all of the friendly locals and staff at visitor information centres, and to the people at NSW National Parks & Wildlife Service, thanks for all of your help. Thanks to Caro Cooper, Leigh and Sarah for all of your excellent Gold Coast tips, and finally thanks to my partner Trent who I was lucky to travel with on part of this trip.

Charles Rawlings-Way

Boundless thanks to Tasmin for the gig, to Fleur for the inside running on Perth culture, and to all the helpful souls I met on the road in South Australia and in/around Perth who flew through my questions with the greatest of ease. Biggest thanks of all to Meg, who held the increasingly chaotic fort while I was busy scooting around in the sunshine ('Where's daddy?') – and made sure that Ione,

Remy, Liv and Reuben were fed, watered, washed, schooled, tucked-in and read-to.

Andy Symington

My research was greatly facilitated by many extremely helpful people along the way. I am particularly grateful to a range of friends for recommendations and for entertaining research company. Thanks also to my family for their support, to Kate Morgan for her suggestions and to Tasmin Waby at LP.

Steve Waters

Big thanks to John and Jan for fireside hospitality, Lauren, James, Jane, Trish, Anika and the rest of MC for (more) gorge love, Marie for vino frenzies, Leonie and Mera for tea and bikkies, Ted for unruliness, Kaz for listening, Roz and Megan for caretaking, Vicky and Pippa for letting me trash their car, and Jennifer from the RACV for getting me out of Marla on Grand Final Day.

ACKNOWLEDGEMENTS

Climate map data adapted from Peel MC, Finlayson BL & McMahon TA (2007) 'Updated World Map of the Köppen-Geiger Climate Classification', *Hydrology and Earth System Sciences*, 11, 1633–44.

Illustration pp74-5 by Javier Zarracina.

Cover photograph: Whitehaven Beach, Queensland, Maurizio Rellini/4Corners Images ©

THIS BOOK

This 20th edition of Lonely Planet's *Australia* guidebook was curated by Andrew Bain, Samantha Forge, Anthony Ham, Trent Holden, Hugh McNaughtan, Charles Rawlings-Way and Andy Symington. It was researched and written by Brett Atkinson, Andrew, Fleur Bainger, Cristian Bonetto, Samantha, Anthony, Paul Harding, Rachael Hocking, Trent, Anita Isalska, Anna Kaminski, Tatyana Leonov, Sofia Levin, Virginia Maxwell, Hugh, Kate Morgan, Charles, Andy, Tasmin Waby and Steve Waters. We would also like to thank the following people people for their contributions to this guide: Cathy Craigie, Tim Flannery and Dr Janelle White. This guidebook was produced by the following:

Destination Editor
Tasmin Waby

Senior Product Editors
Kate Chapman, Anne Mason

Regional Senior Cartographer Julie Sheridan

Product Editor
Hannah Cartmel

Book Designer Lauren Egan

Assisting Editors Sarah Bailey, James Bainbridge, Judith Bamber, Imogen Bannister, Pete Cruttenden, Jacqueline Danam, Andrea Dobbin, Emma Gibbs, Carly Hall, Gabby Innes, Kellie Langdon, Lou McGregor, Kristin Odjik, Lorna Parkes, Fionnuala Twomey

Cartographers Julie Dodkins, Michael Garrett

Cover Researcher
Brendan Dempsey–Spencer

Thanks to Jennifer Carey, Laura Crawford, Bruce Evans, Victoria Harrison, Eimear Healy, David Hodges, Amy Lynch, Catherine Naghten, Claire Naylor, Kirsten Rawlings, Vicky Smith, John Taufa, Angela Tinson, Anna Tyler, Saralinda Turner, Brana Vladisavljevic, Juan Winata

Index

4WD tours
Alice Springs 857
Cairns 411
Esperance 963
Fraser Island 353
Gibb River Rd 1008, 1009
Great Northern Hwy 1012
Great Sandy National
Parl 338
Magnetic Island 389-90
Munja Track 1010
Rainbow Beach 347
Uluru-Kata Tjuta National
Park 875

A
Aboriginal art 1039, 1040,
20
Aboriginal cultural centres
Arkaroo Rock 790
Bataluk Cultural Trail 596
Bilya Koort Boodja 928
Brambuk Cultural Centre
585
Burrinja Cultural Centre
516
Cape York 442
Cultural Centre
(Townsville) 385
Gab Titui Cultural Centre
446
Ghunmarn Culture Centre
845
Godinymayin Yijard Rivers
Arts & Culture Centre
837
Koorie Heritage Trust 467
Lockhart River Arts 442
Narana Aboriginal Cultural
Centre 540-1
Northern Territory 833
Quinkan & Regional
Cultural Centre 443

Map Pages **000**
Photo Pages **000**

Spinifex Hill Studios 992
Tjapukai Aboriginal
Cultural Park 401
Top Didj Cultural
Experience & Art
Gallery 837
Tower Hill Reserve 564
Uluru-Kata Tjuta Cultural
Centre 873-4
Walyalup Aboriginal
Cultural Centre 889
Waralungku Arts Centre
847
Warradjan Aboriginal
Cultural Centre 832
Western Cape Cultural
Centre 442
Wunthulpu Visitor Centre
442
Yarkuwa Indigenous
Knowledge Centre 250
Yeddonba Aboriginal
Cultural Site 607
Aboriginal cultural festivals
Barunga Festival 844
Darwin Aboriginal Art
Fair 806
Garma Festival 836-7
Kullarri Naidoc Week 1001
Laura Aboriginal Dance
Festival 443
Mahbilil Festival 828
Malandarri Festival 847
Parrtjima 857
Tjungu Festival 877
Wallaby Creek Festival
437
Aboriginal cultural tours
24-5
Alice Springs 857
Arnhem Highway 818
Arnhem Land 834, 835-6
Ballina 176
Blue Mountains 138
Bourke 209
Brisbane 280-1
Broken Hill 212
Broome 1001

Bunbury 935
Burketown 450
Byron Bay 182
Cooktown 438
Dampier Peninsula 1005
Darwin 803
Denmark 954
Derby 1006
Devonian Reefs National
Parks 1008
Gibb River Rd 1008-9
Kakadu National Park
825-6
Kalgoorlie-Boulder 1018
Karratha 989-90
Kings Canyon & Watarrka
National Park 871
Kununurra 1014
Malanda 425
Mandurah 924
Melbourne 481
Mungo National Park 215
Sydney 101
Thursday Island 446
Tiwi Islands 816-17
Tully 393
Ulladulla 228
Uluru-Kata Tjuta National
Park 875
Yorke Peninsula 777
Aboriginal culture 11, 26-8,
209, 721, 790, 815, 1029,
1036-40, **2**, **10**
dance 1039-40, **2**
music 1038-9, 1039
resources 1040
Aboriginal history 550, 629-
32, 1022-3, 1035
abseiling, see rock climbing
& abseiling
accessible travel 1060
accommodation 25, 1060-3
booking 807
houseboats 766
activities 54-8, 62, see
also individual activities
websites 56, 58

Adelaide 716-34, **718-19**,
722-3, **728-9**, **735**
accommodation 725-6
activities 720-3
children, travel with
38, 717
drinking & nightlife
728-30
entertainment 730-2
festivals & events 723-5
food 726-8
history 716
information 732-3
itineraries 716
shopping 732
sights 716-20
tours 723
travel to/from 733
travel within 734
Adelaide Fringe 29
Adelaide Hills 734-9, **735**
adventure tours
Agnes Water 358
Blue Mountains 138
Broken River 383
Byron Bay 182
Geeveston 657
Hollybank Wilderness
Adventures 688
Tarkine Wilderness 703
Tasmania 632
AFL 1054
Agnes Water 358-62
Aireys Inlet 549-51
air travel 48, 1071, 1072
Airlie Beach 373-7, **375**, **46**
Albany 956-60, **957**
Albury 246-7
alcohol restrictions 443
Aldgate 738-9
Alice Springs 852-62,
854-5, **868-9**
amusement parks 38
Adventure World 890
Big Banana 170
Cairns Adventure Park
403

Dreamworld 317
Luna Park (Melbourne) 478
Luna Park (Sydney) 87
Sugarworld 403
Tasmazia 694
Warner Bros Movie World 317
Wet'n'Wild 317
Wetside Water Park 342
WhiteWater World 317
Angaston 761-3
Anglesea 548-9
Angourie 174-6
animals 1044-8, *see also* wildlife, *individual animals*
antechinus 1047-8
Anzac Hill 853
Apollo Bay 554-6
apple cider 142, 923
aquariums
  Aquascene 800
  Cairns Aquarium 401
  Indo-Pacific Marine Exhibition 801
  Merewether Aquarium 155
  National Zoo & Aquarium 257-8
  Ocean Park (Denham) 973
  Reef HQ Aquarium 384-5
  Reefworld 342
  Sea Life Sunshine Coast 334
  Seahorse World 686
  Solitary Islands Aquarium 170
  Sydney Sea Life Aquarium 82
Arcadia 389
area codes 1068
Arkaroo Rock 790
Armidale 194-6
Arnhem Highway 817-20
Arnhem Land 20, 834-7, **20**
art galleries 28, *see also* Aboriginal cultural centres
  Aboriginal Exhibitions Gallery 610
  Araluen Arts Centre 852-3
  Art Gallery of Ballarat 571
  Art Gallery of NSW 79
  Art Gallery of South Australia 717
  Art Gallery of Western Australia 887

ArtGeo Cultural Complex 936
Bana Yirriji Art Centre 437
Bank Art Museum Moree 199
Bendigo Art Gallery 577
Brett Whiteley Studio 83
Broken Hill Regional Art Gallery 210
Buku Larrnggay Mulka Art Centre & Museum 836
Bunbury Regional Art Gallery 935
Bundaberg Regional Arts Gallery 350
Bungalow 998
Cairns 415
Canberra Museum & Art Gallery 257
Castlemaine Art Museum 581
Celia Rosser Gallery 589
Chambers of the Black Hand 199
Childers Palace Memorial & Art Gallery 350
Convent Gallery 524-5
Courthouse Gallery 991-2
East Pilbara Arts Centre 994
Field of Light 876
Fireworks Gallery 286
F Project Gallery 562
Fremantle Arts Centre 889
Gallery of Modern Art 276
Geelong Art Gallery 537
Girringun Aboriginal Art Centre 393
Godinymayin Yijard Rivers Arts & Culture Centre 837
Heartwalk 1018
Heide Museum of Modern Art 484
Ian Potter Centre: NGV Australia 463-6
Injalak Arts 835
Institute of Modern Art 286
Jan Murphy Gallery 286
KickArts Contemporary Arts 415
Kuku Bulkaway Gallery 438
Lismore Regional Gallery 189
Lost Ones Gallery 571

MAMA 246
Mangkaja Arts 1012
Marnin Studio 1012
Milani 286
Mildura Arts Centre 619-20
MONA 15, 635, **15**
Murray Bridge Regional Gallery 766
Museum & Art Gallery of the Northern Territory 801-2
Museum of Contemporary Art (Sydney) 79
National Gallery of Australia 254
National Portrait Gallery 254
Newcastle Art Gallery 155
NGV International 467, 470, **514**
Northam Silo Art 928
Northern Rivers Community Gallery 176
Norval Gallery 1006
Nyinkka Nyunyu 849
Old Castlemaine Gaol 581
Perth Institute of Contemporary Arts 887-8
Pillars Project 286
Pro Hart Gallery 210
Qdos Art Gallery 551
Queen Victoria Art Gallery 679
Queenscliff Gallery 543-4
Queensland Art Gallery 276
Riddoch Art Gallery 774
Rockhampton Art Gallery 364
Salamanca Arts Centre 635
Samurai Gallery 415
Sandra Bardas Art Gallery 520
Suzanne O'Connell Gallery 286
Tanks Arts Centre 415
TarraWarra Museum of Art 518
Toowoomba Regional Art Gallery 309
Top Didj Cultural Experience & Art Gallery 837
Walkatjara Art Centre 874

Waralungku Arts Centre 847
Warlukurlangu Art Centre 852
Warrnambool Art Gallery 561
White Rabbit 87
Wintjiri Arts & Museum 876
Yaama Ganu Centre 198
Yarliyil Gallery 1013
Atherton 424-5
Atherton Tablelands 421-7
ATMs 1066-7
Auburn 763
Augusta 947
Aussie Rules 1054
Australia Day 29
Australia Zoo 334
Australian Capital Territory 252-71, **253**
  accommodation 252
  climate 252
  food 252
  highlights 253
  travel seasons 252
  weather 252
Australian F1 Grand Prix 30
Australian Football League (AFL) 1052
Australian Institute of Marine Science 388
Australian Open 29
Australian Parliament House 254-6
automobile clubs 1073-4
Avoca 146
Avon Valley 927-9
Ayton 437

B
B&Bs 1061
Babinda 399
backpacker hostels 1062
Bairnsdale (Buruli) Ulcer 1064
Ballarat 571-5, **572**
Ballina 176-8
ballooning
  Brisbane 280
  Byron Bay 181
  Cairns 403
  Hunter Valley 150
banana farm 396
Bangalow 188-9
bank holidays 1067-8
Barcaldine 458-9
Bare Island 96, **93**
Barkly Tableland 845-8

Barossa Valley 16, 757-62, **758**, **16**
barramundi 449
bars 124
Batavia 1024
Batavia Coast 965-72
Batchelor 820-1
Batemans Bay 229-30
Bathurst 200-1
Bathurst Island 815
Battery Point 635
Bay of Fires 673-4
Bay of Islands Coastal Park 561
BBQs 1050
beaches 26-8, 37
  Avalon 89
  Batemans Bay 229
  Bells Beach 548
  Berry 221
  Boat Harbour Beach 700
  Bondi Beach 85, **94**
  Bronte Beach 85, **96**
  Byron Bay 179
  Cable Beach 998, **1004**
  Cactus Beach 787
  Cape Tribulation 433
  City Beach (Perth) 888
  Coogee Beach 86
  Coral Bay 979
  Cottesloe Beach 888
  Cow Bay 433
  Cylinder Beach 305
  Dampier Peninsula 1005
  Eastern Beach Geelong 537
  Ellis Beach 421
  Exmouth 985
  Freycinet National Park 669
  Garie Beach 136
  Gnaraloo Bay 977
  Great Keppel Island 367-8
  Gulf St Vincent 743-5
  Jervis Bay 225
  Johanna Beach 556
  Kalbarri 969
  Lillico Beach 698
  Lizard Island 438
  Logan's Beach 562
  Mackay 371
  Mandurah 924
  Manly Beach 88-9
  McLean Beach 250

Mission Beach 394-8
Newcastle 156
Ninety Mile Beach 597
Ninety Mile Beach (SA) 773
Noosa 326, **62**
Norman Beach 590
Ocean Beach 708
Palm Beach 89, 321
Palm Cove 419
Park Beach 170
Parsley Bay 86
Pearl Beach 146
Point Addis 548
Port Elliot 746-7
Rainbow Beach 347-9
Scarborough Beach 888
Seal Rocks 161
Seven Mile Beach 178
Shelly Beach 89
St Kilda Foreshore 478
Store Beach 89
Sydney 93-6
Tamarama 97-8, **95**
Tea Tree Bay 326
Trinity Beach 419
Wattamolla Beach 136
Whitsunday Islands 379
Wollongong 217
Yorkeys Knob 419
Beauty Point 685-6
Bedourie 461
Beechworth 606-9
beer 1053
Bellarine Peninsula 543-6
Bellinger 168-70
Bells Beach 548
Bells Line of Road 142
Bendigo 575-80, **576**
Ben Lomond National Park 689-90
Bennelong 1026
Bermagui 234
Berowra Waters 146
Berri 769
Berrima 239
Berry 221-2
Berry Springs 820
Beswick (Wugularr) 845
Bicheno 671-2
bicycle travel, *see* cycling
Big Banana 170
Big Prawn 176
Bilpin 142
Binalong Bay 673-4
Bingara 195
birds 941, 1045

bird sanctuaries
  Broome Bird Observatory 998
  Broughton Island 162
  Rainbow Jungle 969
Birdsville 461
Birdsville Track 49, 460, 794
birdwatching
  Bicheno 672
  Daintree Village 436
  Low Head 687
Birdwood 739
Blackheath 144-5
Black Saturday 523
Black Point 779
Blinman 792
Bloomfield Track 437
Blowhole 671
Blue Lake 774
Blue Mountains 138-46, **140**, **66**
boat tours & cruises 803-6
  Airlie Beach 374
  Bay of Fires 674
  Brisbane 280
  Bruny Island 653-4
  Canberra 258-9
  Coorong 747
  Devonport 691
  Echuca 626
  Esperance 963
  Exmouth 982
  Gordon River Cruises 708
  Hervey Bay 343
  Hobart 637-8, 639
  Innisfail 398
  Kununurra 1015
  Lake St Clair 705
  Magnetic Island 389
  Mallacoota 599
  Mandurah 924
  Maria Island National Park 667
  Merimbula 235
  Mildura 621
  Narooma 232
  Nelson 570
  Peels Lake Cruises 595
  Pemberton 950
  Pieman River Cruises 703
  Port Douglas 429
  Rottnest Island 916
  Strahan 708-9
  Sydney 98-100
  Tamar River Cruises 679

Tasman National Park 662
Victor Harbor 745-6
Victoria River 843-4
Waikerie 767
Walpole 951-2
Whitsunday Islands 379
Wilsons Promontory 590
Wineglass Bay 670
boat travel 1072
Bondi Beach 85, **94**
Bondi Icebergs 97, **94**
border crossings 1016
Boreen Point 339-40
Borroloola 847-8
Boulia 460-1
Bourke 209-10
Bowen 382
Bowral 239-41
Bradman Collection 719
Brambuk Cultural Centre 585
Bramwell Station 444
breakfast 113
breweries
  Barossa Valley Brewing 760
  Beer Farm 946
  Beer Garden Brewing 784
  Blizzard Brewing Co 617-18
  Boag's Brewery 679
  Bootleg Brewery 946
  Bridge Road Brewers 607
  Bright Brewery 613
  Bundaberg Barrel 350
  Cascade Brewery 637
  Caves Road Collective 946
  Coopers Brewery 720
  Forrest Brewing Company 555
  Gurneys Cider 589
  Hobart Brewing Company 646
  Kangaroo Island Brewery 753-4
  Little Bang Brewing Company 730
  Little Creatures & White Rabbit 542
  Pagan Cider 655
  Red Duck Brewery 571
  Robe Town Brewery 771
  Rutherglen Brewery 610-11
  Shambles Brewery 646

Map Pages **000**
Photo Pages **000**

Smiling Samoyed Brewery 743
Social Bandit Brewing Co 604
Sow & Piglets 560
Stomping Ground Brewery & Beer Hall 471-506
Sweetwater Brewing Company 615
Willie Smith's Apple Shed 655
Woolshed Brewery 770-1
Yarra Valley 521
Bribie Island 331
Bridgetown 948
Bright 613-15
Brisbane 273-305, **278-9**, **282-3**, **288**, **292**, **306**, 66
  accommodation 272, 283-6
  activities 277-80
  children, travel with 277
  drinking & nightlife 294-9
  entertainment 299-300
  festivals & events 281
  food 272, 286-94
  information 301-2
  LGBTIQ+ travellers 297
  markets 302
  shopping 300-1
  sights 273-7
  tours 280-1
  travel to/from 303
  travel within 303-5
Brisbane Powerhouse 276-7
Broadbeach 318-19
Broken Hill 19, 210-14, 214, **211**
Broken River 382-3
Brooklyn 146
Broome 18, 995-1003, **1000**, 7, **18**
brunch 113
Brunswick Heads 187-8
Bruny Island 652-5
Buchan 596
Buckley, William 550
Bunbury 933-6
Bundaberg 350-2
Bundeena 136
Bungle Bungle Range 1016-17
Burke & Wills 1028
Burketown 450
Burleigh Heads 319-21
Burnie 698-700

Burra 764
bus travel 1072-3, **1073**
bush tucker 1051, **10**
bushfires 523, 1042, 1058
bushwalking 28, 54-5, see also walking, walking tours
  Alice Springs 856
  Bataluk Cultural Trail 596
  Bay of Fires 674
  Ben Boyd National Park 238
  Bibbulmun Track 958
  Blue Mountains 143, 144, 145
  Bruny Island 654
  Cairns 411
  Camperdown Timboon Rail Trail 560
  Cape Naturaliste 940
  Cataract Gorge 677-8
  Coast Track 136
  Cradle Mountain 704
  East Gippsland Rail Trail 599
  Flinders Island 676
  Flinders Ranges 787
  Freycinet National Park 669
  Gold Coast 317
  Grampians 586
  Grampians Peaks Trail 583
  Great Ocean Walk 556
  Heysen Trail 743
  Hinchinbrook Island 393
  Ikara-Flinders Ranges National Park 791
  Kakadu National Park 827
  Kangaroo Island Wilderness Trail 756
  Kidman Trail 743
  Kings Canyon 870-1
  Koorie Cultural Walk 548
  Kunanyi/Mt Wellington 635-7
  Lake St Clair 704-5
  Larapinta Trail 865
  Lurujarri Dreaming Trail 999
  Maria Island Walk 667
  Marysville 522-3
  Mawson Trail 743
  Mossman 432
  Mt Beauty 615
  Mt Sorrow Ridge Walk 435
  Murray River Walk 770

  Murray to Mountains Rail Trail 614
  Narooma 232
  Newcastle 156
  Nightcap National Park 192
  Nitmiluk National Park 841
  Nourlangie 832
  Overland Track 705
  Porongurup National Park 960
  Port Augusta 782
  Port Campbell 557
  Port Davey Track 660, 712
  Port Macquarie Coastal Walk 163
  South Coast Track 660, 712
  Stirling Range National Park 961
  Surf Coast Walk 548
  Tabletop Track 822
  Tarkine Wilderness 703
  Three Capes Track 662
  Ulladulla 228
  Uluru & Kata-Tjuta 875
  Walls of Jerusalem National Park 697
  Wilsons Promontory 594
  Wineglass Bay 669
  Yaburara Heritage Trail 989
  Yorke Peninsula 777
  Yuraygir Coastal Walk 173
bushwalking tours
  Margaret River 942
business hours 1067
Busselton 936-7
Byfield 366
Byron Bay 15, 178-87, **180-1**, **15**

C

Cable Beach 998, **1004**, **18**
cable cars, see also scenic railways
  Arthurs Seat Eagle 528
  Scenic World 142-3
  Skyrail Rainforest Cableway 403
Cactus Beach 787
Cahill's Crossing 827
Cairns 399-418, **400-1**, **420**, **406**
  accommodation 412-13
  activities 403-4

  drinking & nightlife 415-16
  entertainment 416
  festivals & events 412
  food 413-15
  information 417
  shopping 416
  sights 399-403
  tours 411-12
  travel to/from 417
  travel within 417-18
Caloundra 332-4
camel tours
  Alice Springs 856
  Broome 999
camping 25, 1061
Canberra 63, **255**, **260**, **262**
  accommodation 252, 259-63
  activities 258-9
  children, travel with 38, 257
  drinking & nightlife 267-9
  entertainment 269
  festivals & events 259
  food 252, 263-7
  highlights 253
  history 254
  information 270
  itineraries 258
  shopping 269-70
  sights 254-8
  tours 258-9
  travel to/from 270
  travel within 271
canoeing 769, see also kayaking & canoeing
canopy adventures
  Dwellingup (Trees Adventure) 923
  Lorne (Live Wire Park) 551
  Mamu Tropical Skywalk 398
  Otway Fly 554, **539**
  Pemberton (Gloucester Tree) 949
  Tahune Adventures 657
  Tree Climb Adelaide 721
Cape Arid 964
Cape Borda Lightstation 756
Cape Bridgewater 567
Cape Bruny Lighthouse 652-3
Cape Conran Coastal Park 598-9

Cape Jervis 744
Cape Le Grand 964
Cape Naturaliste 15, 940
Cape Nelson 567
Cape Otway 556-7, **18**
Cape Tourville 669
Cape Tribulation 433-6, **434**
Cape Willoughby Lightstation 752
Cape York Peninsula 439-46, **440-1**
Capricorn Hinterland 368-9
Capricorn Coast 358-69, **360-1**
car travel 1073-8, see also four-wheel drive tours
buying a vehicle 1074-5
outback 48-53
road distance 1075
safety 50
caravanning 1061
Cardwell 392-3
Carlo Sandblow 347
Carnarvon 976-7
Carpentaria Hwy 846-7
Carrickalinga 744
Cassius 418
cassowaries 397
Castlemaine 581-3
Cataract Gorge 677-8
cathedrals, see churches & cathedrals
caves
Buchan Caves 596
Capricorn Caves 364
Cave Gardens 774
Crystal Caves 425
Hastings Caves 658
Jenolan Caves 145-6
Jewel Cave 947
King Solomons Cave 696
Marakoopa Cave 696
Naracoorte Caves National Park 775
Ngilgi Cave 940
Remarkable Cave 662
Yarrangobilly Caves 244
Caves Rd 945-7
Ceduna 786
cell phones 22, 1068
cemeteries
Broome 998
Cowra & Japanese War Cemeteries 204

Waverley Cemetery 86
Central Gibb 1010
central regions 64
Central Tilba 233-4
Cervantes 931-2
Channel Country 460-1
Charles Knife Canyon 988
Charleville 459-60
Charters Towers 386, 452
Childers 349-50
children, travel with 37-9
Adelaide 717
Canberra 257
Hobart 639
Chiltern-Mt Pilot National Park 607
Chinatown
Brisbane 277
Melbourne 466
Sydney 79-80
Chinese temples
Hou Wang Miau Temple 425
chocolate 395
chocolate factories
Yarra Valley Chocolaterie & Ice Creamery 519
churches & cathedrals
Abbey Church 929
Beagle Bay Church 1005
Christ Church Cathedral (Newcastle) 155
St James' Church 81-2
St Mary's Cathedral (Sydney) 81
St Monica's Cathedral 402
St Paul's Cathedral 467
Churchill Island 532
cinemas
Brisbane 301
Dromana Drive-In 528
Melbourne 506-7
Sydney 130
Clare 765
Clare Valley 762-5
climate 22, 29-32, 47, 1041, **22**
climate change 1042-3, 1071
Cloncurry 452
clubs 124
Cobbold Gorge 447
Cobourg Peninsula 836
Cockatoo Island 86
Cockle Creek 660
coffee 267, 1050-1, **514**
Coffin Bay 784-5
Coffs Harbour 170-4, **171**

Coles Bay 669-71
Collingwood Children's Farm 471
conservation groups 1046
convict sites 80, 86, 637, 661, 688, 889
Coober Pedy 794-6, **795**
Cooinda 832-3
Cook, Captain James 1023
cooking courses
Agrarian Kitchen 651
Brisbane 281
Essential Ingredient 478
Cooktown 437-9
Coolangatta 322
Cooloola Coast 338-40
Coolum 337-8
Cooma 241-2
Coonabarabran 198
Coonawarra 777
Coonawarra Wine Region 776, 777
Coorong National Park 773-4
Coral Bay 978-82
coral bleaching 404
Coral Coast, see Ningaloo Coast
coral spawning 412
Corinna 703
costs 23, 37
courses
cooking 478, 651
diving 404
Cowaramup 944
Cow Bay 433
Cowra 203-5
Cradle Mountain-Lake St Clair National Park 17, 704-7, **17**, **56**
credit cards 1067
Crescent Head 166
cricket 1054-5
Adelaide Oval 718-19
Melbourne Cricket Ground 470
Croajingolong National Park 601
crocodile jumping 819
crocodiles 61, 418, 421, 436, 1048, 1058-9, **27**, **805**
Crocodylus Park 802-3
Crocosaurus Cove 800, **805**
Croydon 447-8
cruises, see boats tours & cruises
CSIRO Parkes Observatory 207

cultural centres, see Aboriginal cultural centres
currency 22, 1067
Currumbin 321
customs regulations 1063
cycling 55-6, 1072
Adelaide 723
Alice Springs 856
Beechworth 607
Bright 613
Brisbane 277-80
Camperdown Timboon Rail Trail 560
Castlemaine to Maldon Rail Trail 581
East Gippsland Rail Trail 599
Encounter Bikeway 745
Great Victorian Rail Trail 604
Heysen Trail 743
Hobart 637
Kidman Trail 743
Mandurah 924
Mawson Trail 743
McLaren Vale 740
Melbourne 481
Merimbula 235
Murray to Mountains Rail Trail 614
O'Keefe Rail Trail 578
Outback 51
Perth 890
Riesling Trail 762
Rottnest Island 916
Sydney 91, 100
cyclones 377
Cygnet 655
Cygnet River 754-6

D
Daintree 14, 432-6, **14**
Daintree Village 436
Dales Gorge 994
Daly Waters Pub 849
Dampier 990-1
Dampier Peninsula 1004-6
dance
Aboriginal 1039-40
Dandenongs 516-18
dangers, see safety
d'Arenberg 741, **27**
Dark Point Aboriginal Place 161-2
Darwin 800-15, **802**, **808-9**, **816-17**, **804-5**
accommodation 797, 806-7

Map Pages **000**
Photo Pages **000**

children, travel with 38
drinking & nightlife 812
entertainment 812
festivals & events 806
food 797, 807-12
history 800
information 814
markets 813
safety 814
shopping 812-16
sights 800-3
travel to/from 814-15
travel within 815
Darwin region 815-24, **816-17**
Daydream Island 378
Daylesford 524-7
Death Rock 789
debit cards 1067
Deloraine 695
dengue fever 1065
Denham 972-4
Deniliquin 250-1
Denmark 953-6
Derby (Tas) 674-6
Derby (WA) 1006-7
Devil's Marbles 850
Devonport 690-4
diarrhoea 1064
dingoes 60-1, 356, **2**
Dinner Plain 617-19
dinosaurs 456
disabilities, travellers with 1060
discount cards 1063
distilleries
  Ambleside Distillers 737
  Animus Distillery 580
  Applewood Distillery 739
  Barossa Distilling Company 761
  Bundaberg Rum Distillery 350
  Cape Byron Distillery 179
  Echuca Distillery & Cafe 627
  Great Ocean Road Gin 549
  Great Southern Distillery 957
  Hellyers Road Distillery 698
  Hurdle Creek Still 606-7
  Kangaroo Island Spirits 754-5
  Kilderkin Distillery 571
  Lark Distillery 646
  Margaret River Distilling Company 942
  Nant Distillery 664

Old Kemp Distillery 664
Prohibition Liquor Co 729
Starward Distillery 475
Sullivans Cove Distillery 649
Timboon Railway Shed Distillery 560
Twenty Third Street 770
Whipper Snapper Distillery 885
Yarra Valley 522
diving & snorkelling 57, **46, 409**
  Apollo Bay 554
  Bellarine Peninsula 544-5
  Broken River 383
  Broome 999
  Bundaberg 351
  Byron Bay 182
  Cairns 404
  Cape Tribulation 435
  Coffs Harbour 172
  Coral Bay 979
  Exmouth 982-4, 986
  Geraldton 966
  Jervis Bay 226
  Magnetic Island 390
  Merimbula 235
  Mooloolaba 335
  Narooma 232
  Ningaloo Marine Park 16, 987-8, **16**
  North Stradbroke Island 305
  Rainbow Beach 347
  Sydney 91
  Whitsunday Islands 378
dog sledding
  Howling Husky Sled Dog Tours 617
dolphins 226, 545, 934, 974-5, 979
Doo Town 660
Dover 657-8
Dreaming stories 863
drinks 1049-53
  beer 1053
  coffee 1050-1
  wine 1053
driving, see car travel
drugs 1066
Drysdale River 1009
Dubbo 205-6
Dudley Peninsula 751-2
Dunalley 659-60
Duncan Rd 1014
Dunk Island 398
Dunkeld 586-92

Dunsborough 937-40
Dwellingup 923-4

E
Eaglehawk Neck 660-1
East MacDonnell Ranges 862-4
Eastern Gibb 1010-17
echidnas 1048, **11**
Echuca 624-7, **625**
Eden 236-9
eftpos 1066-7
electricity 1063
Emmagen Creek 437
Emu Bay 754
environment 1041-8
environmental issues 1042-4
  coral bleaching 404
  crocodile jumping 819
  uranium mines 828
Errinundra National Park 597-8
Esperance 962-5
Eumundi 341
Eureka Stockade 574
Eurong 355
Evandale 689
events, see festivals & events
Ewaninga 867
exchange rates 23
Exmouth 982-5, **983**
Eyre Peninsula 780-7, **781**

F
Fairhaven 549
Falls Creek 616-17
farmstays 1062-3
fauna 1044-8, see also individual animals
federation 1030-1
Federation Square 463
feral animals 1044
ferry travel 767, **75**
festivals & events 29-32, see also film festivals, food & wine festivals, LGBTIQ+ festivals, literary festivals, music festivals
  Abbey Medieval Festival 331
  Adelaide Cabaret Festival 724
  Adelaide Festival 724
  Adelaide Fringe 723
  Adelaide Hills 736
  Airlie Beach Race Week 374

Art, Not Apart 259
A Taste of Broome 1001
Australia Day Skyworks 891-2
Australian Italian Festival 392
Australian National Goanna Pulling Championships 173
Ballarat 573
Barossa Valley 757
Beer Can Regatta 806
Big Pineapple Music Festival 335
Bleach Festival 314
Blessing of the Fleet 894
Boab Festival 1006
Bowral Tulip Time Festival 240
Brisbane Comedy Festival 281
Brisbane Festival 281
Brisbane Street Art Festival 281
Cairns Festival 412
Cairns Show 412
Canberra Balloon Spectacular 259
Chinese New Year 101
Darwin Fringe Festival 806
Deniliquin Ute Muster 250
'Ekka' Royal Queensland Show 281
Enlighten 259
Falls Festival (NSW) 183
Falls Festival (Tas) 659-60
Falls Festival (Vic) 551
Floriade 259
Fringe World Festival 891
Henley-on-Todd Regatta 857
Hervey Bay Ocean Festival 343
Hobart 639-40
Kings Park Festival 894
Launceston 679
Lismore Lantern Parade 189
Market Days 954
Mary Poppins Festival 349
Melbourne 482
Mt Isa Rodeo 454
National Multicultural Festival 259
National Penny Farthing Championships 689
Ord Valley Muster 1015

INDEX F-H

festivals & events *continued*
Parkes Elvis Festival 207
Port Douglas Carnivale 429
Port Fairy Folk Festival 565
Port Lincoln 783
Red Earth Arts Festival 990
Royal Canberra Show 259
Sakura Matsuri 204
Sawtell Chilli Festival 174
Sculpture by the Sea 102
Sea Grass Monitoring 1001
Shinju Matsuri Festival of the Pearl 1002
Sunshine Festival 967
Sydney Festival 101
Sydney to Hobart Yacht Race 639-40
Ten Days on the Island 632
Vivid Sydney 102
Whale Festival 237
WOMADelaide 30, 724
Field of Light 896, **830**
Figure Eight Pools 136
film festivals
Adelaide Film Festival 724
Brisbane International Film Festival 283
CinéfestOZ 936
Melbourne International Film Festival 31, 507
Sydney Film Festival 102
Finch Hatton Gorge 382
Finke & Old Andado Tracks 51
Fish Creek 589
fishing 57
Airlie Beach 373
Cairns 411
Port Campbell 557-8
Fitzroy Crossing 1012-13
Fitzroy Island 418
Fleurieu Peninsula 739-48, **740**
Flinders Chase National Park 756-9
Flinders Island 676-84
Flinders Ranges 787-92, **788**
Flinders Street Station 466-7

Map Pages **000**
Photo Pages **000**

flora 1044-8
flying foxes 168
food 38, 1049-53, 62
bush tucker 1051, **10**
Clifford's Honey Farm 755
Milawa Gourmet Region 606
Twelve Apostles Gourmet Trail 560
food & wine festivals
Adelaide 724
Bangalow 188
Barossa Valley 757
Broome Mango Festival 1002
Canberra District Wine Week 271
Clare Valley Gourmet Weekend 762
Griffith 249
Innisfail 398
Launceston 679
Margaret River 933
McLaren Vale 741
Melbourne Food & Wine Festival 482
Mudgee Food + Wine Festival 207
Narooma Oyster Festival 232
Noosa Food & Wine 327
Orange 202
Riverland Wine & Food Festival 769
Sawtell Chilli Festival 174
Taste of Tasmania 639
food & wine tours
Adelaide 723, 740
Barossa Valley 757
Cape Naturaliste 940
Cape Tribulation 435
Hobart 638
Hunter Valley 150
Kangaroo Island 748-9
Margaret River 942
Mudgee 207
Orange 202
Perth 891
food trucks 291
football 1054, 1055
AFL Grand Final 482
Forrest 555
Fossickers Way 195
four-wheel drive tours, *see* 4WD tours
Fowlers Bay 786
Franklin-Gordon Wild Rivers National Park 710-11

Fraser Coast 341-57
Fraser Island 19, 352-7, **354**, **2**, **19**
Fremantle 889, **906**, **4**
accommodation 896-8
drinking & nightlife 908
food 903-4
Fremantle Doctor 905
Freycinet National Park 669-71

G
Gabo Island 599
gardens, *see* parks & gardens
Gascoyne Coast 976-8
gay travellers 502, 1066
Geelong 536-42, **540**
Geeveston 656-7
geology 1042
George Town 686-7
Geraldton 965-9, **966**
Ghan, the 21, 1078, **21**
giardiasis 1065
Gibb River Rd 1008-11
Gibson Steps 561
Gillard, Julia 1035
Gippsland 588-601, **590-1**
Gladstone 362
Glass House Mountains 332
Glenelg 720
Gold Coast 312-14, **313**, **315**
Gold Coast Hinterland 322-4
golden stairway 999
Goldfields 570-88
gold rush 772
golf
Opal Fields Golf Club 795-6
Port Douglas 427
Ratho Farm 664
Gondwana Rainforests World Heritage Area 192
Goolwa 747-51
Gosford 146
Grampians 583-8, **584**
Granite Belt 310-14
Granite Island 745
Great Australian Bight Commonwealth Marine Reserve 787
Great Barrier Reef 12, 40-6, 405-10, **42**, **12**, **46**, **405**, **408-9**
access towns 41
camping 43

environmental issues 43
islands 40-1
responsible tourism 43
travel seasons 40
websites 41
Great Keppel Island 367-8
Great Northern Hwy 1012-14
Great Ocean Road 18, 536-70, **536-7**, **538-9**
Green Island 418
Griffith 249-50
Griffiths Island 565
Grose Valley 145
GST 1067
Gulf Savannah 446-51
Gulf St Vincent 743-5
Gulflander 448
Gumeracha 739
Gunbalanya (Oenpelli) 834-6
Gundagai 246
Gunn, Jeannie 843
Gympie 349

H
Hahndorf 736-7
Halls Creek 1013-14
Halls Gap 585-6
Hamilton Island 381
Hancock Gorge 994
hang-gliding 217-18
Hanging Rock 527
Hartz Mountains National Park 657
Hawker 790-1
Hawkesbury River 146
Hay 251
Head of Bight 786-7
Healesville 520-2
health 1063-5
heat exhaustion 1058, 1064
Heide Museum of Modern Art 484
hepatitis C 1065
Hepburn Springs 524-7
Hermannsburg 866
Heron Island 363
Hervey Bay 342-7, **344-5**
High Country, Victoria 601-19, **602-3**
hiking 28, 54-5, *see also* bushwalking
Hinchinbrook Island 393
historic sites & buildings
Adelaide Gaol 720
Abbotsford Convent 471
Aboriginal Tent Embassy 257

Arltunga Historical Reserve 862
Battery Hill 565
Beechworth Asylum 607
Brickendon 688
Burke & Wills Camp 119, 450
Callington Mill 664
Cascades Female Factory Historic Site 637
Central Deborah Gold Mine 578
Clarendon 689
Coal Mines Historic Site 662
Como House & Garden 478
Darlington 667
Flagstaff Hill Maritime Village 561-2
Fort Queenscliff 543
Fort Scratchley 156
Fremantle Prison 889
Government House (Melbourne) 478
Heritage Blinman Mine 792
Hermannsburg Mission 866
Hobart Convict Penitentiary 634-5
Maralinga Atomic Bomb Test Site 786
Martindale Hall 764
Melbourne Town Hall 467
Myilly Point Heritage Precinct 800
Old Beechworth Gaol 607
Old Geraldton Gaol & Craft Centre 965
Old Melbourne Gaol 467
Perth Mint 885
Port Arthur Historic Site 661-2
Rio Vista 619-20
Round House 889
Royal Exhibition Building 471
Sandhurst Gaol 577-8
Saumarez Homestead 195
Sovereign Hill 571
Villa Fortuna 577
Woolmers Estat 688
WWII Flying Boat Wrecks 998
WWII Oil-Storage Tunnels 801
Wybalenna Historic Site 676

history 1022-35
  Aboriginal Australians 1022-3
  books 1023, 1025, 1026
  Canberra 254
  convict period 1023-6
  Darwin 800
  gold rush 1028
  Perth 884-5
  Rottnest Island (Madjemup) 914
  Sydney 69
  Tasmania 629-32
  WWI 1031
  WWII 1031
hitching 1078
Hobart 634-49, **636, 640-1**
  accommodation 640-3
  activities 637
  children, travel with 639
  drinking & nightlife 646-7
  entertainment 647
  festivals & events 639-40
  food 643-6
  information 648
  itineraries 638
  shopping 647-9
  sights 634-7
  tours 637-9
  travel to/from 648-9, 649
  travel within 649
holidays (public) 1067-8
Hook Island 378
Horizontal Waterfalls 1007
Horn Island 445-6
horse racing
  Melbourne Cup 482
horse riding
  Aireys Inlet 550-1
  Cape Tribulation 435
  Coffs Harbour 171
  Kununurra 1014
  Mt Bogong 615
  Snowy Mountains 242
  Tamworth 193
  Tennant Creek 849
  Warrnambool 562
Horseshoe Bay 389
Hosier Lane 463
hostels 103
hotels 1062
houseboats 766
Houtman Abrolhos Islands 968
Howard, John 1034

Howes Creek Farm 604
Hughenden 452
Hunter Valley 147-53, **148**
Huon Valley 655-6
hypothermia 1058

I
Ian Potter Centre: NGV Australia 463-6
Ikara-Flinders Ranges National Park 791-2
Ingham 391-2
Innes National Park 780-1
Innisfail 398-9
insurance 1063, 1065
internet access 1065
internet resources 41, see websites
itineraries 33-6, **33, 34, 35**
  Canberra 258
  Sydney 87

J
Jabiru 828-9
Jamison Valley 145
Jan Juc 548
jellyfish 1059
Jenolan Caves 145-6
Jervis Bay 225-7
Jindabyne 242-3
Jondaryan 309
Junee 248
Jurien Bay 932-3

K
Kakadu National Park 17, 824-33, **825, 17, 27**
Kalbarri 969-71, **970**
Kalgoorlie-Boulder 1017-20
Kalumburu 1011
Kangaroo Island 748-57, **749**
kangaroos 61, 1046, **61**
Kangaroo Valley 222-3
Karijini National Park 993-5, **993**
Karratha 989-90
Karumba 448-9
Kata Tjuta 874, **874**
Katherine 837-40, **838**
Katherine Gorge National Park, see Nitmiluk National Park
Katoomba 142-4
kayaking & canoeing
  Adelaide 722
  Angourie 175
  Apollo Bay 554

Batemans Bay 229-30
Broome 1001
Byron Bay 181
Eden 237
Exmouth 984
Freycinet National Park 669
Gold Coast 317
Hobart 638
Jervis Bay 226
Kalbarri 970
Kangaroo Island 755
Kangaroo Valley 223
Lake Pedder 710-11
Magnetic Island 390
Melbourne 481
Merimbula 235
Mildura 621
Mt Field National Park 651
Newcastle 159
Ningaloo Marine Park 988
North Stradbroke Island 305
Pemberton 950
Perth 890
Rapid Bay 744
Renmark 770
River Country Adventours 624
Rottnest Island 916
Royal National Park 136
Southwest National Park 712
Sydney 92
Tasman National Park 662
Town of 1770 358
Whitsunday Islands 379
Kenilworth 340
Kiama 220-1
Kiama Blowhole 220
Kiewa Valley 615-16
Killcare 146
Kimberley, the 995-1017, **996-7**
King Island 701-2
Kings Canyon & Watarrka National Park 870-2, **871, 831**
Kings Park & Botanic Garden 885-7
Kingscote 752-4
Kingston SE 773
kitesurfing
  Geraldton 966
  St Kilda 479
koalas 61, 190, 1046-7, **539**
Koorie Heritage Trust 467

Kosciuszko National Park 243-5
Kunanyi (Mt Wellington) 635-7
Kununurra 1014-16
Kuranda 422-4
Kyneton 580-1
Kynuna 455

L

Lady Elliot Island 362-3, **410**
Lady Musgrave Island 363
lakes
  Albert Park Lake 475
  Blue Lake 774
  Lake Ballard 1020
  Lake Burley Griffin 257
  Lake Cooroibah 339
  Lake Cootharaba 339-40
  Lake Macquarie 146
  Lake Mountain 522-4
  Lake Mungo 214
  Lake Pedder 711
  Little Blue Lake 773
  Tinaroo 426
Lakes Entrance 592-6
Lalor, Peter 574
Lancelin 930-1
landscapes 28
language 22
Larapinta Trail 865
Lasseter Highway 51, 870
Launceston 677-83, **678**, **680**, **685**
Laura 443-4, 787-8
legal matters 1065-6
Legana 684-5
Lennox Head 178
Leura 139-40
LGBTIQ+ festivals
  Brisbane Pride Festival 281
  Melt 283
  Sydney Gay & Lesbian Mardi Gras 101
  Tropical Fruits 189
LGBTIQ+ travellers 1066
  Brisbane 297
  Melbourne 502
  Perth 909
  Sydney 29, 128
libraries
  National Library of Australia 258

Map Pages **000**
Photo Pages **000**

State Library of NSW 80
lighthouses
  Barrenjoey Lighthouse 89-90
  Cape Bruny Lighthouse 652
  Cape Byron Lighthouse 179
  Cape Leeuwin Lighthouse 947
  Cape Nelson Lighthouse 567
  Cape Otway Lightstation 556, **18**
  Cape Schanck Lighthouse 528
  Cape Willoughby Lightstation 752
  Gabo Island Lighthouse 600
  Green Cape Lightstation 238
  Point Hicks Lighthouse 601
  Split Point Lighthouse 549
  Tacking Point Lighthouse 163
  Vlamingh Head Lighthouse 985
  Wadjemup Lighthouse 914
  Wilsons Promontory Lighthouse 590
Lightning Ridge 199-200
Lightning Ridge Bore Baths 199
Lillico Beach 698
Limestone Coast 771-6
Lincoln National Park 782
Lindeman Island 378
Lismore 189-90
Litchfield National Park 821-3
literary festivals
  Bellingen Readers & Writers Festival 168
  Brisbane Writers Festival 283
  Byron Bay Writers' Festival 183
  Sydney Writers' Festival 102
Lizard Island 438
lizards 1048
Lobethal 739
Loch Ard Gorge 560
lockout laws 127
Logan's Beach 562
Lombadina 1005
London Bridge 560
Long Island 381

Longford 688-9
Longreach 457-8
Lord Howe Island 216
Lorella Springs 846
Lorne 551-3
Low Head 687-8
Loxton 768-9
luxury resorts 1061-2

M

MacDonnell Ranges 862-7
Mackay 369-73, **372**
Macquarie, Lachlan 1025
Magnetic Island 389-91
Main Beach 316-18
Malanda 425
Maldon 582
Maleny 340
Mallacoota 599-601
Mallee 619
Mamu Tropical Skywalk 398
Mandalay, the 951
Mandu Mandu Gorge 989
Mandurah 924-6
Manjimup 948-9
Manly Beach 88-9
Mannum 766-7
Mansfield 604-5
Mapleton 340
maps 1066
Maralinga Atomic Bomb Test Site 786
Marble Bar 992
Mareeba 424
Maremma Project 563
Margaret River 15, 942-5, **938**, **943**, **15**
Maria Island National Park 665-7
marijuana 191
marine turtles 351, 985, **410**
markets 187
  Adelaide Farmers Market 732
  Atherton Tablelands 424
  Bangalow Market 188
  Barossa Farmers Market 762
  Bollywood Beach Bazaar 173
  Brisbane Riverside Markets 302
  Castlemaine Mill 581
  Central Market (Adelaide) 716-17
  Collective Markets South Bank 302
  Darwin 813

Eumundi 341
  farmers markets 1050
  Farm Gate Market 647-8
  Figtree Creek Markets 366
  Finders Keepers Markets 302
  Fremantle Markets 889, **4**
  Harvest 683
  Kangaroo Island Farmers Market 751-2
  Kuranda Original Rainforest Markets 422
  Malak Marketplace 813
  Mindil Beach Sunset Market 813, **804**
  Nightcliff Market 813
  northern NSW 187
  Prahran Market 478
  Queen Victoria Market 463, **514**
  Rapid Creek Market 813
  Riverland Farmers Market 769
  Rose Street Artists' Market 510
  Salamanca Market 635, 648
  South Melbourne Market 475
  Stirling Markets 739-40
  St Kilda Esplanade Market 511-16
  Sydney Fish Market 83
  Village Markets 319
  Willunga Farmers Market 742
  Young Designers Market 302
Maroochydore 334-7
Marrawah 701
Marrickville 123
Mary River 819-20
Maryborough 349
Marysville 522-4
massage
  Brisbane 280
  Byron Bay 182
Mataranka 843, 844-5
Maydena 712
McKinlay 455
McLaren Vale 740-2, **27**
measures 1060
Melbourne 14, 463-516, **468-9**, **472-3**, **476-7**, **480**, **495**, **504**, **517**, **14**, **514-15**
  accommodation 482-7
  activities 479

children, travel with 38
drinking & nightlife 499-506
entertainment 506-9
festivals & events 482
food 487-99
information 511
itineraries 479
shopping 509-11
sights 463
tours 481-2
travel to/from 511-12
travel within 512-18
walking tours 489, **489**
Melbourne Cricket Ground 470
Melbourne Cup 482
Melrose 789-96
Melville Island 815
memorials & monuments
Anzac Memorial (Sydney) 81
Australian War Memorial 256
Big Rocking Horse 739
Bon Scott Statue 889
Childers Palace Memorial & Art Gallery 350
Dinosaur Stampede National Monument 456
Dog on the Tuckerbox 246
Frenchman's Rock 751
HMAS Sydney II Memorial 965
Larry the Lobster 773
Obelisk 771
POW Campsite & Guard Tower 204
Shrine of Remembrance 475-7
Meningie 773-4
meningococcal disease 1065
Menzies, Robert 1020, 1033
Mereenie Loop Road 49, 866
Merimbula 234-6
Mermaid Beach 318-19
Mersey Bluff 691
Milawa Gourmet Region 606
Mildura 619-24, **622**
Millaa Millaa 425
Millthorpe 204
Milton 227-8
Mindil Beach Sunset Market 813, **804**

mines & mine tours
Battery Hill Mining Centre 849
Central Deborah Gold Mine 578
Day Dream Mine 210
Hannans North Tourist Mine 1018
Karrs Reef Goldmine 609
Opal Mine Adventure 199
Mintaro 764
Mission Beach 394-8
Mittagong 239-41
mobile phones 22, 1068
Moggs Creek 549
Mole Creek 695-7
Mollymook 227-9
MONA 15, 635, **15**
money 22-3, 1066-7
Monkey Mia 974-6
monotremes 1048
Mon Repos 351
Montville 340
monuments, see memorials & monuments
Mooloolaba 334-7
Moonta 778-9
Moree 198-9
Moreton Island 307-8
'morning glory' clouds 450
Mornington Peninsula 527-32
Morrison's Huon Pine Sawmill 708
Moruya 231
Mossman 432
Mossman Gorge 432
motels 1062
motor racing
Australian Formula 1 Grand Prix 482
Australian Motorcycle Grand Prix 534
Phillip Island Circuit 533-4
motorcycle tours
Uluru-Kata Tjuta National Park 876
motorcycle travel 1073-8, see also car travel
mountain biking 675
Adelaide Hills 735
Alice Springs 856
Atherton 425
Blue Mountains 138
Cairns 403
Derby 675
Forrest 555
Jindabyne 242
Margaret River 943

Maydena 675
Maydena Bike Park 712
Melrose 789
Mt Buller 605-6
Mt Hotham & Dinner Plain 617-19
Mt Wellington Descent 637
Thredbo 244
mountain climbing
Cradle Mountain Summit 704
Mt Gillen 857
Mt Kosciuszko 245
Pigeon House Mountain (Didthul) 228
Strzelecki Peaks 676
Mount Gambier 774-6
Mt Arapiles State Park 588
Mt Beauty 615-16
Mt Buller 605-6
Mt Field National Park 650-2
Mt Gillen 857
Mt Gower 216
Mt Hotham 617-19
Mt Hypipamee 425
Mt Isa 452-5, **453**
Mt Kosciuszko 243-5
Mt Lofty 738
Mt Panorama 200
Mt Remarkable National Park 789
Mt Spec 394
Mt Victoria 145
Mt Wellington 635-7
Mudgee 206-9
Mundaring Weir 926
Mungalla Station 391
Mungo National Park 214-15
Murphy's Haystacks 785
Murray Bridge 765-6
Murray River 619-27, 765-71, **620-1**
museums 38, 717, see also art galleries, historic sites & buildings
Abbey Museum 331
Agnes Water Museum 358
Albury Library Museum 246-51
Australian Age of Dinosaurs Museum 456
Australian Armour & Artillery Museum 402-3

Australian Centre for the Moving Image 466
Australian Fossil & Mineral Museum 200
Australian Museum (Sydney) 83
Australian National Maritime Museum 82-3
Australian Stockman's Hall of Fame & Outback Heritage Centre 457
Australian War Memorial 256
Australian Workers Heritage Centre 459
Axel Stenross Maritime Museum 782-3
Back O' Bourke Exhibition Centre 209
Bass & Flinders Centre 687
Bass Strait Maritime Centre 690
Bendigo Pottery 577
Bicheno Motorcycle Museum 671
Bligh Museum of Pacific Exploration 653
Blue Mountains Cultural Centre 142
Bond Store Museum 349
Broome Museum 999
Buku Larrnggay Mulka Art Centre & Museum 836
Bunbury Museum & Heritage Centre 935
Burke Museum 607
Burnie Regional Museum 698
Caboolture Warplane Museum 331
Cairns Museum 402
Canberra 18
Canberra Museum & Art Gallery 257
Cape Otway Lightstation 556
Carnarvon Space & Technology Museum 976
Cobb & Co Museum 308-9
Comet Gold Mine Museum 992
Commissariat Store Museum 276
Country Music Hall of Fame 193
Court House Museum 427

museums *continued*
Darwin Military Museum 802
Diamantina Heritage Truck & Machinery Museum 456-7
Dunera Museum 251
East Coast Heritage Museum 668
Esperance Museum 962-3
Eureka Centre 571
Flagstaff Hill Maritime Village 561-2
Fraser Coast Cultural Centre 342
Furneaux Museum 676
Golden Dragon Museum & Gardens 577
Great Aussie Beer Shed 624
Great Ocean Road Story 551
Gympie Gold Mining & Historical Museum 349
Heide Museum of Modern Art 484
Hemp Embassy 191
Hyde Park Barracks Museum 80-1
International Cricket Hall of Fame 239
James Cook Museum 438
Jervis Bay Maritime Museum 225-6
Jewish Museum of Australia 479
John Flynn Place 452
Justice & Police Museum 78-9
Kiewa Valley Historical Museum 615
Killer Whale Museum 237
Leuralla NSW Toy & Railway Museum 140
Low Head Maritime Museum 687
Mad Max 2 Museum 213
Makers' Workshop 698-9
Mallacoota Bunker Museum 599
Mandurah Museum 924
Mannum Dock Museum of River History 766

Mareeba Heritage Museum & Visitor Information Centre 424
Mary MacKillop Interpretive Centre 776
Mawson's Huts Replica Museum 634
Melbourne Museum 474-5
Meroogal 224
Military & Colonial Museum 349
MONA 15, 635, **15**
Moonta Mines Museum 778-9
Moreton Telegraph Station 444
Museum & Art Gallery of the Northern Territory 801-2
Museum of Australian Democracy 256
Museum of Brisbane 273
Museum of Central Australia 853
Museum of Sydney 81
Museum of the Goldfields 1018
Museum of the Great Southern 956-7
Museum of the Riverina 247-8
Museum of Tropical Queensland 385
National Anzac Centre (Albany) 956
National Capital Exhibition 257
National Holden Museum 624
National Motor Museum 739
National Motor Racing Museum 200
National Museum of Australia 256, **18**
National Wool Museum 537-40
Ned Kelly Vault 607
New England Regional Art Museum 195
New Norcia Museum & Art Gallery 929
Newcastle Museum 155
NGV International 467, **514**
Ningaloo Interpretation Centre 982
Nostalgia Box 887
NSW Corrective Services Museum 241

Old Timers Mine 794-5
Old Treasury Building 467
Orange Regional Museum 202
Outback at Isa 454
Phoenix Museum 522
Pioneer Village Museum 222-3
Pooseum 650
Port Macquarie Historical Museum 163
Port of Echuca Discovery Centre 624
Portland Maritime Discovery Centre 567-8
Powerstation Museum 193
Qantas Founders Outback Museum 457
Queen Victoria Museum 679
Queenscliff Maritime Museum 543
Queensland Cultural Centre 276
Queensland Museum & Sciencentre 276
Questacon 256
Reef Teach 401
Residency Museum 929
Rocks Discovery Museum 77
Rottnest Museum 914
Roundhouse Railway Museum 248
Roxy Theatre Greek Museum 195
Royal Australian Mint 258
Royal Flying Doctor Service 801
Royal Flying Doctor Service Base 853
Royal Flying Doctor Service Museum 210
School of the Air 853-6
Scitech 887
Shark Bay World Heritage Discovery Centre 973
Shear Outback 251
Silverton Gaol & Historical Museum 213
Sir Henry Parkes Memorial School of Arts 197
Snowy Hydro Discovery Centre 242
South Australian Maritime Museum 720

South Australian Whale Centre 745
Stansbury Museum 779
Steamtown Heritage Rail Centre 788-9
St Helens History Room 673
Susannah Place Museum 78
Sydney Jewish Museum 83
Tasmanian Museum & Art Gallery 634
Torres Strait Heritage Museum 446
Trial Bay Gaol 167
Umoona Opal Mine & Museum 795
Underground Hospital 454
WA Shipwrecks Museum 889
Wallaroo Heritage & Nautical Museum 778
Waltzing Matilda Centre 455
Western Australian Museum – Geraldton 965
Western Australian Museum – Maritime 889
Western Australian Museum – Perth 888
Willunga Slate Museum 742
Woodworks Museum 349
Yackandandah Museum 609
music
Aboriginal 1039, 1040
music festivals
Airlie Beach Festival of Music 374
Alice Desert Festival 858
Australian Festival of Chamber Music 386
Bello Winter Music 168
Big Pineapple Music Festival 335
Bigsound Festival 281
Byron Bay Bluesfest 183
Canberra International Music Festival 259
CMC Rocks Queensland 281
Deniliquin Ute Muster 250
Falls Festival (NSW) 183
Falls Festival (Tas) 659-60

Falls Festival (Vic) 551
Festival of Voice (WA) 954
Festival of Voices (Tas) 639
Gympie Music Muster 349
Laneway Festival 892-3
National Folk Festival 259
Port Fairy Folk Festival 565
Queenscliff Music Festival 545
Splendour in the Grass 183
St Jerome's Laneway Festival 482
Tamworth Country Music Festival 193-4
WOMADelaide 30, 724
Muttonbird Island 170
Myall Lakes National Park 161-2
Myella Farm Stay 365
Myponga 743
Mystery Bay 233

N
Namatjira Dr 864-5
Naracoorte Caves National Park 775
Narooma 231-3
Nathan River Road 51
National Gallery of Australia 254
National Museum of Australia 256, **18**
national parks & nature reserves 1048
Arakoon National Park 167
Bald Rock National Park 197
Ben Boyd National Park 238-9
Ben Lomond National Park 689-90
Berry Springs Nature Park 820
Big Brook Arboretum 949
Blackdown Tableland National Park 369
Bladensburg National Park 451
Booderee National Park 225
Boodjamulla National Park 450-1
Border Ranges National Park 192

Bouddi National Park 146-7
Brisbane Water National Park 147
Bundjalung National Park 175
Burleigh Head National Park 319
Byfield National Park 366
Cape Arid National Park 964
Cape Byron State Conservation Park 179
Cape Conran Coastal Park 598-9
Cape Le Grand National Park 964
Cape Range National Park 988-9
Caranbirini Conservation Reserve 847
Carnarvon National Park 368-9
Cathedral Rock National Park 168
Chiltern-Mt Pilot National Park 607
Coffin Bay National Park 784-5
Conway National Park 374
Corroboree Rock Conservation Reserve 863
Cradle Mountain-Lake St Clair National Park 17, 704-7, **17**, **56**
Crater Lakes National Park 426-7
Croajingolong National Park 601
Crowdy Bay National Park 163
D'Aguilar National Park 299
Dampier Archipelago 991
Dandenong Ranges National Park 516
Deepwater National Park 359
Devonian Reef National Parks 1007-8
Diamantina National Park 451
Dirk Hartog Island National Park 973
Dooragan National Park 163
Dorrigo National Park 168
El Questro Wilderness Park 1011

Elsey National Park 844
Emily & Jessie Gaps Nature Park 863
Errinundra National Park 597-8
Eungella National Park 382-3
Eurimbula National Park 359
Finke Gorge National Park 866-7
Fitzgerald River National Park 961
Flinders Chase National Park 756-9
Fogg Dam Conservation Reserve 818
Forest Discovery Centre 923
Francois Peron National Park 975
Franklin-Gordon Wild Rivers National Park 710-11
Freycinet National Park 669-71
Garig Gunak Barlu National Park 836
Geikie Gorge 1008
Granite Gorge Nature Park 424
Great Australian Bight Commonwealth Marine Reserve 787
Great Sandy National Park 338-9
Guy Fawkes River National Park 168
Hartz Mountains National Park 657
Hat Head National Park 166-7
Hell Hole Gorge National Park 451
Hepburn Mineral Springs Reserve 524
Idalia National Park 451
Ikara-Flinders Ranges National Park 791-2
Illawarra Escarpment State Conservation Area 217
Innes National Park 780-1
Jervis Bay National Park 226
Judbarra/Gregory National Park 842
Kakadu National Park 17, 824-33, **825**, **17**, **27**
Kalbarri National Park 971-2

Kanku-Breakaways Conservation Park 795
Karijini National Park 993-5, **993**
Kelly Hill Conservation Park 755
Kings Canyon & Watarrka National Park 870-2, **871**, **831**
Kosciuszko National Park 243-5
Ku-ring-gai Chase National Park 91
Kutini-Payamu (Iron Range) National Park 445
Lamington National Park 323-4
Lane Cove National Park 91
Leliyn 841
Lesueur National Park 932
Lincoln National Park 782
Litchfield National Park 821
Living Desert State Park 210
Lochern National Park 451
Lower Glenelg National Park 570
Maria Island National Park 665-7
Mariala National Park 451
Millstream Chichester National Park 991
Minnamurra Rainforest Centre 220
Montague Island (Barranguba) 231
Mornington Peninsula National Park 528
Morton National Park 240
Mt Ainslie 258
Mt Augustus National Park 976
Mt Canobolas 202
Mt Coot-tha Reserve 277
Mt Field National Park 650-2
Mt Remarkable National Park 789
Mt William National Park 674
Munga-Thirri National Park 451
Mungo National Park 214-15

national parks & nature reserves *continued*

Murramarang National Park 228

Murujuga National Park 990-1

Mutawintji National Park 211-12

Myall Lakes National Park 161

Namadgi National Park 271

Nambung National Park 931

Naracoorte Caves National Park 775

Narawntapu National Park 694

Naree Budjong Djara National Park 305

N'Dhala Gorge Nature Park 862-3

Nightcap National Park 192

Ningaloo Marine Park 16, 986-8

Nitmiluk National Park 840-2, **20**

Noosa National Park 326

North Gorge Walk 305

North Head 87-8

Olive Pink Botanic Garden 853

outback Queensland 451

Oxley Wild Rivers National Park 168

Paluma Range National Park 394

Panboola 234-5

Point Nepean National Park 527-8

Porcupine Gorge National Park 452

Porongurup National Park 960-1, **960**

Port Campbell National Park 559-61

Rainbow Valley Conservation Reserve 868-70

Rinyirru (Lakefield) National Park 443

Rocky Cape National Park 702

Royal National Park 136-7

Ruby Gap Nature Park 863

Map Pages **000**
Photo Pages **000**

Sea Acres Rainforest Centre 163

Seal Bay Conservation Par 754

Shoalwater Islands Marine Park 922

Snowy River National Park 596-7

South Bruny National Park 652

South Head 86-7

Southwest National Park 711-12

Springbrook National Park 324

Stirling Range National Park 961-2, **962-3**

Sturt National Park 215-16

Tamborine National Park 323

Tarkine Wilderness 702-3

Tasman National Park 661-3

The Neck 652

Tidbinbilla Nature Reserve 271

Tomaree National Park 159

Trephina Gorge Nature Park 862

Troubridge Island Conservation Park 779

Tuart Forest National Park 936

Tunnel Creek 1008

Tyto Wetlands 391

Uluru-Kata Tjuta National Park 12, 872-80, **12**, **830**

Umbrawarra Gorge Nature Park 823

Undara Volcanic National Park 447

Valley of the Giants 951

Walls of Jerusalem National Park 697

Walpole-Nornalup National Park 951

Warrumbungle National Park 198

Welford National Park 451

Wentworth Falls Reserve 139

William Bay National Park 954

Windjana Gorge 1008

Wollumbin National Park 192

Wooroonooran National Park 399

Worimi Conservation Lands 159, 160

Yuragyir National Park 173

National Portrait Gallery 254

nature reserves, *see* national parks & nature reserves

netball 1056

New England 193-7

New Norcia 929-30

New South Wales 62, 68-251, **70-1**, **137**
accommodation 68
children, travel with 38
climate 68
food 68
highlights 70-1
newspapers 1060
travel seasons 68
weather 68

Newcastle 153-8, **154**

NGV International 467, **514**

Nimbin 190-3

Ninety Mile Beach 597

Ningaloo Coast 978-95, **980-1**

Ningaloo Marine Park 16, 986-8, **978**, **16**

Nitmiluk National Park 840-2, **20**

Noosa 326-31, **327**, **36**, **62**

Noosa Everglades 339

Normanton 448

Normanville 744

Nornalup 951-3

Northam 928

North Coast Road 754

Northern Territory 65, 797-880, **798-9**
accommodation 797
children, travel with 38
climate 797
food 797
highlights 798-9
travel seasons 797
weather 797
websites 820

North Stradbroke Island 305-7

notable buildings 91
Abercrombie House 200
Australian Parliament House 254
Bell Tower 885
Boyd's Tower 238
Bridgedale House 948
City Hall (Brisbane) 273

Elizabeth Bay House 83-5

Elizabeth Farm 91

Experiment Farm Cottage 90-1

Lanyon Homestead 271

Main Beach Pavilion 316

Old Government House 91, 273

Parliament House (Brisbane) 273

Q Station 89

Royal Theatre (Mt Isa) 456

Sir Henry Parkes Memorial School of Arts 197

Sun Pictures 998

Sydney Opera House 72

Sydney Tower Eye 80

Vaucluse House 86

Nourlangie 829-32

Nowra 224-5

Nundroo 786

Nuriootpa 760-1

O

Oatlands 663-4

observatories, *see also* planetariums
Antarctic Journey 532
Cosmos Centre 459
CSIRO Parkes Observatory 207
Dubbo Observatory 205
Mudgee Observatory 206
Perth Observatory 926

Old South Rd 867-8

Olgas, The 874

Oodnadatta Track 19, 49, 793, **19**

Opal cards 135

opals 199, 795

opening hours 1067

Orange 201-3

orcas 979

Orpheus Island 392

Otway Fly 554, **539**

outback 19, 47-53, 792-6, **52-3**, **19**, **830-1**
New South Wales 208-16
permits 1018
Queensland 451-61
routes 1018
Western Australia 1017-20

outback driving 47-53, 793-4, 1018

Overland Track 705

P

paddlesteamers 621, 626, 767
Palm Beach 321
Palm Cove 419-21
Parachilna 792
paragliding 347
Parap Village 811
Paringa 769-71
Parkes 207
parks & gardens
  Adelaide Botanic Gardens 717
  Albany Heritage Park 957
  Australian Arid Lands Botanic Garden 781-2
  Australian National Botanic Gardens 256-7
  Ballarat Botanic Gardens 571
  Barangaroo Reserve 79
  Bicentennial Park 800
  Blue Mountains Botanic Garden Mount Tomah 142
  Botanic Gardens (Rockhampton) 363
  Brisbane Botanic Gardens 277
  Cairns Botanic Gardens 401
  Centennial Park 85
  Chinese Garden of Friendship 83
  City Botanic Gardens (Brisbane) 273
  Cooktown Botanic Gardens 438
  Cowra Japanese Garden & Cultural Centre Australia 204
  Djanbung Gardens 191
  Dubbo Regional Botanic Garden 205
  Fitzroy Gardens 470-1
  Foxglove Gardens 233
  Geelong Botanic Gardens 537
  George Brown Botanic Gardens 800
  Hyde Park 81
  Ju Raku En Japanese Garden 309
  Kershaw Gardens 364
  Kings Park & Botanic Garden 885-7
  Mackay Regional Botanical Gardens 371
  Mrs Macquaries Point 79
  Mt Gibraltar Reserve 239-40
  Mt Lofty Botanic Garden 738
  National Arboretum 258
  Paronella Park 398
  Queens Gardens 385
  Rainforestation 422
  Rosalind Park 578
  Royal Botanic Gardens (Melbourne) 475
  Royal Botanic Gardens (Sydney) 69-77
  Royal Tasmanian Botanical Gardens 635
  South Bank Parklands 276
  St Kilda Botanical Gardens 479
  Telegraph Station 853
  Whiteman Park 920
  William Ricketts Sanctuary 516
  Wollongong Botanic Garden 217
Parliament House (Melbourne) 466
parrots 1045
Pemberton 949-51
Pender Bay 1004
Penfolds 759
Penguin 697-8
penguins 61, 532, 559, 563, 698, 699
Penneshaw 751-2
Penola 776
Penong 786
Peregian Beach 337-8
permits 49
  Arnhem Land 835
  Cape York Peninsula 442
  Fraser Island 357
  Kalumburu 1011
  outback Western Australia 1018
Perth 884-913, **886-7**, **892-3, 898-9, 902**, **915**, **64**
  accommodation 881, 895-8
  activities 890
  children, travel with 38, 897
  drinking & nightlife 904-8
  entertainment 908-10
  festivals & events 891-4
  food 881, 899-904
  history 884-5
  information 911
  itineraries 891
  LGBTIQ+ travellers 909
  shopping 910-11

sights 885-9
  tours 890-1
  travel to/from 911-12
  travel within 912-13
Perth Hills 926-7
Phar Lap 1034
Phillip, Arthur 1023-5
Phillip Island 532-6, **533**
Picnic Bay 389
Pieman River 703
Pilbara 978-95, **980-1**
Pimba 793
Pine Creek 823-4
Pinnacles Desert 21, 931, **21, 36**
planetariums 277
planning
  Australia basics 22
  Australia's regions 62-6
  budgeting 23, 37
  calendar of events 29-32
  internet resources 23
  itineraries 33-6, **33**, **34, 35**
  repeat visitors 24-5
  travel seasons 22
plants 1044-8
platypus 61, 1048
Plenty & Sandover Hwys 51
Point Addis 548
Point Hicks Lighthouse 601
population 25
Porongurup National Park 960, **960**
Port Adelaide 720
Port Arthur 661-3
Port Augusta 781-2
Port Campbell 557-9
Port Campbell National Park 559-61
Port Douglas 427-32, **428**, **406**
Port Elliot 746-7
Port Fairy 564-7, **539**
Port Hedland 991-3
Port Lincoln 782-4
Port Macquarie 162-6, **164-5**
Port Pirie 787
Port Stephens 159-61
Port Vincent 779
Portland 567-9
postal services 1067
public holidays 1067-8
pubs 124, 1053, 1062
Puffing Billy 517
Purnululu National Park 1016-17, **1016**

Q

quarantine rules 1066
Queen Victoria Market 463, **514**
Queenscliff 543-85
Queensland 63, 272-461, **274-5, 306**
  accommodation 272
  children, travel with 38
  climate 272
  food 272
  highlights 274-5
  travel seasons 272
  weather 272
Queensland Cultural Centre 276
Queenstown 707-8
Quobba Coast 977-8
quokkas 914, 917
Quorn 789-90

R

radio 1060
rafting, see white-water rafting
rail tours
  Cairns 411
rail travel, see train travel
Rainbow Beach 347-9
Rapid Bay 744
Ratho Farm 664
Ravenswood 386
Raymond Island 598
Recherche Bay 660
red centre, see outback
Red Centre Way 866
Red Hill 530-43
red-tailed tropicbirds 941
religious sites
  Great Stupa of Universal Compassion 578
Renmark 769-71
reptiles 1048
responsible tourism 55, 979
Richmond 452, 649-50
Riverina 246-51
rivers
  Murray River 619-27, 765-71, **620-1**
road trains 48
roadhouses 49, 851
Robe 771-3
rock art 1037-8, **17**
  Kakadu National Park 824
  Nourlangie 832
  Ubirr 827

rock climbing & abseiling
Blue Mountains 138
Brisbane 280
Cairns 403, 411
Grampians 585
indoor 639, 890
Kalbarri 969
Margaret River 942
Mt Arapiles State Park 588
Perth 890
Tasmania 632
Rockhampton 363-5
Rockingham 922-3
Rocky Cape National Park 702
Roper Highway 846
Rosevears 684-5
Ross 664-5
Ross River fever 1065
Rottnest Island (Wadjemup) 913-20, **918**
Royal National Park 136-7
Rudd, Kevin 1035
rugby 1055
Rutherglen 610-13

S
safety 1058-9, 1064, 1068
beaches 801
bushwalking 55
car travel 50
crocodiles 801
cyclones 377
dingoes 356
sailing
Whitsunday Islands 380
Salamanca Place 635
Sapphire Coast 234-9
Savannahlander 448
Savannah Way 446
Sawtell 174
scenic drives
Cape Bauer Loop Scenic Drive 785
Coorong Scenic Drive 773
Danbulla Forest Drive 426
Fossickers Way 195
Great Forest Trees Drive 949
Great Ocean Drive 963
Great Ocean Road 536-70

Karratha 989
Mungo Track 214-15
Silo Art Trail 589
Tweed Range Scenic Drive 192
Waterfall Way 168
Whalers Way 783
scenic flights
Armidale 195
Broome 1001
Cairns 411
Carpentaria Hwy 846-7
Derby 1006
Exmouth 983-4
Fraser Island 342-3
Halls Creek 1013
Hobart 638
Kakadu National Park 826
Kalbarri 969
Kings Canyon & Watarrka National Park 871-2
Kununurra 1015
Litchfield National Park 822
Nitmiluk National Park 841
Par Avion 712
Shark Bay 973
Sydney 101
Twelve Apostles 561
Uluru-Kata Tjuta National Park 876
Whitsunday Islands 379
scenic railways, see also cable cars
Blues Train 546
Goldfields Railway 581
Gulflander, the 448
Hotham Valley Railway 923
Kuranda Scenic Railway 403
Pemberton Tramway 949-50
Puffing Billy 517
Savannahlander, the 448
West Coast Wilderness Railway 707
scenic views, see viewpoints
Schoolies Week 316
sea travel 1071-2
seasonal work 1070
Second Valley 744
Seisia 445
Seppeltsfield Road 760-1
Shark Bay 972-6

sharks 1048, 1059
Sheffield 694-5
Shipwreck Coast 558
Sikh temples 173
silo art
Northam Silo Art 928
Silo Art Trail 589
Silverton 213
Simpson Desert 51
Simpsons Gap 864
skiing 56-7
Ben Lomond 690
Dinner Plains 617-19
Falls Creek 616-17
Jindabyne 243
Lake Mountain 522
Mt Buller 605-6
Mt Hotham 617-19
Thredbo 244
skydiving
Airlie Beach 373
Brisbane 280
Cairns 403-4
Coolum 337
Hervey Bay 343
Perth 890
Rainbow Beach 347
Rottnest Island 916
Townsville 386
Tully 395
York 929
smoking 1060
snakes 1048, 1059
snorkelling, see diving & snorkelling
snowboarding 56-7, **57**, see also skiing
Snowy Mountains 241-5
Snowy River National Park 596-7
soccer 1055
solitary destinations 28
South Australia 65, 713-96, **714-15**
accommodation 713
children, travel with 38
climate 713
food 713
highlights 714-15
South Coast Road 754-6
South Stradbroke Island 323
South West Rocks 167-8
southern right whales 60
Southport 658-9
Southwest National Park 711-12
Sovereign Hill 571
Spaceship sculpture 795

spas
Burleigh Heads 320
Byron Bay 180, 181
Hepburn Springs 524
Peninsula Hot Springs 528
spiders 1059
Spit, the 316-18
Split Point Lighthouse 549
sport 1054-6
Adelaide 731-2
Sydney 131
sporting events
AFL Grand Final 482
Alice Springs Cup Carnival 858
Australian Formula 1 Grand Prix 482
Australian Motorcycle Grand Prix 534
Australian Open 482
Bathurst 1000 201
Big Bash 101
Birdsville Cup 461
Brisbane International 281
Camel Cup 857
Finke Desert Race 858
Kalgoorlie-Boulder 'Race Round' 1019
Margaret River Pro 933
Melbourne Cup 482
Sydney to Hobart Yacht Race 102
Tiwi Grand Final & Annual Art Sale 817
Uluru Camel Cup 877
sporting venues
Adelaide Oval 718-19
Blundstone Arena (Hobart) 647
Melbourne Cricket Ground 470
Sydney Cricket Ground 131
York Park (Launceston) 682
SS Yongala wreck 390
St Helens 672-3
Standley Chasm 864
stand-up paddleboarding
Cairns 404
Coffs Harbour 172
Margaret River 942
Mooloolaba 335
St Kilda 479
Sydney 92
Stanley 700-1
Stansbury 779-89
Stanthorpe 310-14

Map Pages **000**
Photo Pages **000**

stargazing 212, *see also* observatories, planetariums
Uluru 877
Stirling 738-9
Stirling Range National Park 961-2, **962-3**
STIs 1065
Stokes Bay 754
Stolen Generations 1032
storytelling 1038
Strahan 708-10
Strathgordon 711
Streaky Bay 785-6
street art **14**, **514**
Brisbane Street Art Festival 281
Hosier Lane 463
Melbourne tours 481
street food 291
Strzelecki Track 49-51, 794
Stuart Highway 48, 51, 851
Sturt, Charles 1028
Sunshine Coast 324-41, **325**
Sunshine Coast Hinterland 340-1
Surfers Paradise 314-16, **315**
surfing 57-8, 1055-6, **95**
Agnes Water 358
Anglesea 548
Angourie 175
Apollo Bay 554
Australian National Surfing Museum 546
Batemans Bay 230
Bells Beach 548
Byron Bay 181, 182
Cactus Beach 787
Coffs Harbour 170-1
Coolum 337
Denmark 954
Gold Coast 320
Jan Juc 548
Lorne 551
Merimbula 235
Mornington Peninsula 531-2
Newcastle 159
Noosa 326
North Stradbroke Island 305-6
Perth 890
Phillip Island 534
Port Elliot 747
Port Macquarie 163
Rainbow Beach 347
Robe 772

Surfers Paradise 314
Sydney 97
Torquay 546-8
Wollongong 218
Yallingup 941
Swan Valley 920-2
Swan Reach 766
Swansea 668-9
swimming 97, 479-81, 1056, **93**
Bondi Icebergs 97, **94**
Sydney 13, 69-135, 93-6, **74-5**, **76-7**, **80-1**, **84**, **88**, **90**, **92**, **108**, **111**, **114**, **120-1**, **137**, **13**, **73**, **75**, **93**
accommodation 68, 102-10, **104-5**
activities 91-8
children, travel with 38
drinking & nightlife 123-9
entertainment 129-32
festivals & events 101-2
food 68, 110-22
history 69
information 134-5
itineraries 87
LGBTIQ+ travellers 128
safety 134
shopping 132-4
sights 69-91
sports 131
tours 98-101
travel to/from 135
travel within 135
walking tours 98-9, 100-1, **99**
websites 130
Sydney Gay & Lesbian Mardi Gras 29
Sydney Harbour Bridge 73, **73**
Sydney Observatory 77
Sydney Opera House 72, 130, **72**

T

Table Cape Tulip Farm 699
Tablelands Hwy 846-7
tall trees
Four Aces 948-9
Gloucester Tree 949
Valley of the Giants 951
Tamar Valley 684-8
Tamarama 97-8, **95**
Tamborine Mountain 323
Tamworth 193-4
Tanami Road 51, 851-2

Tandanya National Aboriginal Cultural Institute 721
Tanunda 759-60
tap water 1065
Taranna 661
Tarkine Wilderness 702-3
Tasman National Park 661-3
Tasman Peninsula 658-63, **659**
Tasmania 64, 628-712, **630-1**, **653**, **666**, **692-3**
accommodation 628
children, travel with 38
climate 628
festivals & events 632
food 628
highlights 630-1
history 629-32
information 632
tours 632
travel to/from 632
travel within 633-4
wildlife 60
taxes 1067
telephone services 22, 1068
television 1060
tennis 1056
Australian Open 482
tented camps 1062
Tenterfield 196-7
termite mounds 822
Terrigal 146
Tessellated Pavement 660
The Farm 179
'The Man From Snowy River' 242
Thevenard 786
Thredbo 244, **57**
Three Sisters 142
Thursday Island 445-6
Tibooburra 215-16
tick typhus 1065
Tidal River 589-90
Timber Creek 843-4
Timboon 560
time 22, 214, 1068
tipping 1051, 1067
Tiwi Islands 815-17
toilets 1068
Toowoomba 308-10
Torquay 546
tourist information 1069
tours, *see also* 4WD tours
Adelaide 723
Airlie Beach 374

Albany 957-8
Alice Springs 856-7
Arnhem Highway 818
Arnhem Land 834
Ballina 176
Barossa Valley 757
Blue Mountains 138-9
Brisbane 280-1
Broken Hill 212
Broome 999
Bunbury 935
Byron Bay 182
Cairns 411-12
Canberra 258
Cape Tribulation 435
Cape York Peninsula 439-42
Central Coast NSW 146-7
Cervantes 931
Coffs Harbour 170-2
Coober Pedy 796
Darwin 803-6
Denham 973
Derby 1006
Eden 237
Esperance 963
Exmouth 982-4
Eyre Peninsula 780
Geraldton 967
Great Barrier Reef 411-12
Hervey Bay 342-3
Hobart 637-9
Hunter Valley 150
Ikara-Flinders Ranges National Park 791
Jervis Bay 226
Kakadu National Park 825-6
Kalbarri 969-70
Kangaroo Island 748-51
Karijini National Park 994
Kings Canyon & Watarrka National Park 871-2
Margaret River 942
Mary River 819
McLaren Vale 740
Merimbula 235
Mildura 620-1
Mooloolaba 335
Mudgee 207
Mungo National Park 215
Narooma 232
Noosa 326
Orange 202
Outback 49
Pemberton 950
Port Douglas 429

tours continued
Port Lincoln 783
Port Stephens 159
Rottnest Island 916
Swan Valley 920
Sydney 98-101
Tiwi Islands 816-17
Ulladulla 228
Uluru-Kata Tjuta
National Park 875-6
Walpole 951
Whitsunday Islands 379
Yulara 877
Tower Hill Reserve 564
Town of 1770 358-62
Townsville 383-9, **384**,
407
trains, see also road trains
train travel 1078, **1073**
Blues Train 546
Ghan, the 21, 1078, **21**
Goldfields Railway 581
Gulflander, the 448
outback 48
Puffing Billy 517
Savannahlander, the 448
West Coast Wilderness
Railway 707
trams 577
transport 1071-8
transport cards 135
travel to/from Australia
1071-2
travel within Australia 23,
1072-8
Tree of Knowledge 768
tree climbing, see canopy
adventures
treetop walks, see canopy
adventures
Trial Bay 167
Trinity Beach 419
Tropfest 29
Truffle & Wine Co 948
Tully 393-4
Turquoise Coast 930-3
turtles 351, 985, **410**
Twelve Apostle 559, **538**

U
Ubirr 827-8
Ulladulla 227-9
Uluru 48, 873-5, **873**,
12, **830**

Uluru-Kata Tjuta National
Park 12, 872-80, **12**,
830
Unaipon, David
(Ngarrindjeri) 1033
Undara 447
Unesco World Heritage
Sites
Budj Bim Cultural
Landscape 569
Convict Sites 80, 86, 637,
661, 688, 889
Daintree Rainforest
432-3
Fraser Island 352-7
Kakadu National Park
825-6
Lamington National Park
(Woonoongoora) 323
Lord Howe Island 216
Purnululu National Park
1016-17, **1016**
Shark Bay 972-6
Sydney Opera House 72
Tasmanian Wilderness
710
Uluru-Kata Tjuta
National Park 12, 872-
80, **12**, **830**
Wet Tropics World
Heritage Area 432-6
universities
University of Sydney 87
Uraidla 737
uranium mining 1042-3
urban scenes 62

V
vaccinations 1064
Van Diemen's Land 1025
vegans 25, 1053
vegemite 1053
vegetarians 1053
Victor Harbor 745-6
Victoria 63, 462-627, **464-
5**, **536-7**
accommodation 462
children, travel with 38
climate 462
food 462
highlights 464-5
Victoria Highway 48-9, 51
Victoria River Crossing 841
viewpoints
Bay of Islands Coastal
Park 561
Cambewarra Lookout
223
Captain Cook Lookout
179-80

City Lookout (Mt Isa) 453
Diamond Tree Lookout
949
Echo Point 142
Evans Lookout 144
Gantheaume Point &
Dinosaur Prints 998
Gardiner Point 701
Grassy Hill Lookout 438
Iron Blow Lookout 707
Jemmy's Point Lookout
594
Laguna Lookout 326
Marriners Lookout 554
McMahons Point 86
Mengler's Hill Lookout
759
Mt Brown Lookout 929
Mt Lofty Summit 738
Mt Parnassus Lookout
246
Mundi Mundi Lookout
213
Nobbies Centre 532-3
Nobby's Head 155-6
Oxley Scenic Lookout
193
Pylon Lookout 79
Scenic World 142-3
SkyPoint Observation
Deck 314
Sublime Point 140
Super Pit Lookout 1018
Tacking Point Lighthouse
163
Talinguru Nyakunytjaku
sunrise-viewing area
873
The Nut 700
Trinity Bay Lookout 427
Walu Wugirriga Lookout
433
viral encephalitis 1065
visas 22, 1069
volunteering 1069

W
Wagga Wagga 247-9
Waikerie 767-8
walking
Adelaide 721
Albury 247
Byron Bay 180
Hahndorf 736
Magnetic Island 389
Sydney 97-8, 100
walking tours
Alice Springs 857
Broome 999, 1001
Darwin 803

Melbourne 481-2, 489,
489
Rottnest Island 916
Sydney 98-9, 100-1, **99**
Wallaroo 778
Walls of China 214
Walls of Jerusalem
National Park 697
Walpole 951-3
Walsh Bay 78
Warrnambool 561-4
Waterfall Bay 660
Waterfall Way 168
waterfalls
Bloomfield Falls 437
Crystal Cascades 403
Erskine Falls 551
Fitzroy Falls 223
Florence Falls 822
Fruit Bat Falls 445
Gunlom 833
Horizontal Waterfalls
1007
Jim Jim Falls 832
Jourama Falls 394
Liffey Falls 696
Maguk 833
Mannum Waterfalls 766
Mitchell Falls 1009
Protestor Falls 192
Russell Falls 651
Steavenson Falls 522
Twin Falls 832
Wallaman Falls 391
Waterfall Way 168
Watsons Bay 86
Wave Rock 925
weather 22, 29-32, 47, **22**
websites 23, 25, 39, 56
activities 56, 58
Northern Territory 820
Sydney 130
weights 1060
Weipa 444
Wentworth Falls 139
We of the Never Never 843
West MacDonnell Ranges
864-7
Western Australia 65,
881-1020, **882-3**, **934**,
952-3, **987**
accommodation 881
children, travel with 38
climate 881
food 881
highlights 882-3
travel seasons 881
weather 881
Western Gibb 1009-10

whale sharks 16, 979, **16**
whale watching 947
  Dunsborough 937
  Eden 237
  Hervey Bay 342
  Kalbarri 970
  Merimbula 235
  Mooloolaba 335
  Warrnambool 562
whales 60, 346, 979, 1047
white-water rafting
  Cairns 411
  Franklin River 710
  Queenstown 707
  Tully River 395
Whitlam, Gough 1033-4
Whitsunday Coast 369-83, **370**
Whitsunday Islands 13, 377-81, **13, 407, 408**
Wildflower Way 933
wildlife 11, 26-7, 1044-8, **11, 46, 405, 408, 831**
  Kakadu National Park 824
  Kangaroo Island 753
  West MacDonnell Ranges 864
wildlife reserves & sanctuaries, see also bird sanctuaries
  Alice Springs Desert Park 852
  Bat House 435
  BatReach 422-3
  Bellingen Island 168
  Billabong Sanctuary 385
  Bonorong Wildlife Sanctuary 649-50
  Cairns Turtle Rehabilitation Centre 418
  Charleville Bilby Experience 459
  Cleland Wildlife Park 738-9
  Currumbin Wildlife Sanctuary 321
  David Fleay Wildlife Park 319
  Devils@Cradle 704
  Dolphin Discovery Centre 934
  Hamelin Pool 975
  Healesville Sanctuary 520
  Island Sanctuary 250
  Keatings Lagoon Conservation Park 438
  Koala Care Centre (Lismore) 190

Koala Hospital 163
Les Wilson Barramundi Discovery Centre 449
Monkey Mia Marine Reserve 975
Mornington Wilderness Camp 1010
Natureworld 671-2
Newhaven Wildlife Sanctuary 852
Penguin Parade 532
Platypus House 685
Pungalina-Seven Emu Wildlife Sanctuary 848
Tamworth Marsupial Park 193
Tangalooma Eco Centre 308
Tasmanian Devil Unzoo 661
Tolga Bat Hospital 424-5
Trowunna Wildlife Park 696
Window on the Wetlands Visitor Centre 817
wildlife watching 37, 59-61, 698, 699
  Cape Otway 557
  Daylesford 525
  Kakadu National Park 826
  Penneshaw Penguin Centre 752
  Phillip Island 534
  Port Fairy 565
  Raymond Island 598
  Warrnambool 562
wildlife-watching tours
  Anglesea Golf Club Kangaroo Tours 548
  Arnhem Highway 818
  Bunbury 935
  Byron Bay 182
  Cairns 403
  Devils in the Dark 672
  Kakadu National Park 826
  Mary River 819
  Willunga 742-3
  Wilson Island 363
  Wilsons Promontory National Park 21, 589-92, **593, 21**
wine 1053
  National Wine Centre of Australia 717-18
wine festivals, see food & wine festivals
wine regions & wineries 25, 27-8, 1052, **16**
  Adelaide Hills 736

Albany 959
Barossa Valley 16, 757-62, **16**
Barossa Valley
Bellarine Peninsula 544
Berry 221
Brisbane 295
Canberra district 268
Clare Valley 762-5
Coonawarra 776, 777
d'Arenberg 741, **27**
Denmark 955
Granite Belt 311
Griffith 249
Hunter Valley 148-50
Margaret River 936, 937, 942-3, 945
McLaren Vale 740-2, **27**
Mornington Peninsula 531
Mudgee 206-7
Nowra 224
Orange 201-2
Perth Hills 926
Pipers River 686
Porongurup National Park 960
Richmond 650
Riesling Trail 762
Rutherglen 611
Swan Valley 920
Tasmania's east coast 670
Waikerie 767
Yarra Valley 518-22
Winton 455-7
Wollongong 217-20, **218**
WOMADelaide 30, 724
wombats 61, 1047
women travellers 1069
Woolgoolga 173
Woolshed at Jondaryan 309
Woomera 793-4
Worimi people 160
work 1069-70
World Heritage-listed sites, see Unesco World Heritage Sites
Wye River 553-4

Y
Yackandandah 609-10
Yallingup 940-2
Yamba 174-6
Yankalilla 743-4
Yardie Creek Gorge 989
Yarra Valley 518-22
Yass 240

Yellow Water 832-3
Yeppoon 366-7
yoga
  Byron Bay 180
  Palm Cove 419
  Sydney 97
York 928-9
Yorke Peninsula 777-80, **781**
Yorkeys Knob 419
Yulara 876-80, **878**
Yungaburra 426
Yunupingu, Dr G 1039

Z
ziplining
  Broken River 383
  Cairns 403, 411
  Cape Tribulation 435
  Launceston 688
  Live Wire Park 551
zoos 59
  Adelaide Zoo 720
  Alice Springs Reptile Centre 853
  Australia Zoo 334
  Australian Butterfly Sanctuary 422
  Australian Reptile Park 147
  Cairns Zoom & Wildlife Dome 403
  Crocosaurus Cove 800
  Hartley's Crocodile Adventures 421
  Healesville Sanctuary 520
  Koala Conservation Centre 533
  Kuranda Koala Gardens 422
  Marineland Crocodile Park 418
  Melbourne Zoo 475
  Monarto Zoo 765-6
  National Zoo & Aquarium 257-8
  Natureworld 671-2
  Perth Zoo 885
  Platypus House 685
  Potoroo Palace 235
  Taronga Western Plains Zoo 205
  Taronga Zoo Sydney 86
  Territory Wildlife Park 820
  Wild Life Sydney Zoo 83
  Wildlife Habitat Port Douglas 427
  Wildlife HQ 334

Map Legend

Sights

- Beach
- Bird Sanctuary
- Buddhist
- Castle/Palace
- Christian
- Confucian
- Hindu
- Islamic
- Jain
- Jewish
- Monument
- Museum/Gallery/Historic Building
- Ruin
- Shinto
- Sikh
- Taoist
- Winery/Vineyard
- Zoo/Wildlife Sanctuary
- Other Sight

Activities, Courses & Tours

- Bodysurfing
- Diving
- Canoeing/Kayaking
- Course/Tour
- Sento Hot Baths/Onsen
- Skiing
- Snorkelling
- Surfing
- Swimming/Pool
- Walking
- Windsurfing
- Other Activity

Sleeping

- Sleeping
- Camping

Eating

- Eating

Drinking & Nightlife

- Drinking & Nightlife
- Cafe

Entertainment

- Entertainment

Shopping

- Shopping

Information

- Bank
- Embassy/Consulate
- Hospital/Medical
- Internet
- Police
- Post Office
- Telephone
- Toilet
- Tourist Information
- Other Information

Geographic

- Beach
- Gate
- Hut/Shelter
- Lighthouse
- Lookout
- Mountain/Volcano
- Oasis
- Park
- Pass
- Picnic Area
- Waterfall

Population

- Capital (National)
- Capital (State/Province)
- City/Large Town
- Town/Village

Transport

- Airport
- Border crossing
- Bus
- Cable car/Funicular
- Cycling
- Ferry
- Metro station
- Monorail
- Parking
- Petrol station
- Subway station
- Taxi
- Train station/Railway
- Tram
- Underground station
- Other Transport

Note: Not all symbols displayed above appear on the maps in this book

Routes

- Tollway
- Freeway
- Primary
- Secondary
- Tertiary
- Lane
- Unsealed road
- Road under construction
- Plaza/Mall
- Steps
- Tunnel
- Pedestrian overpass
- Walking Tour
- Walking Tour detour
- Path/Walking Trail

Boundaries

- International
- State/Province
- Disputed
- Regional/Suburb
- Marine Park
- Cliff
- Wall

Hydrography

- River, Creek
- Intermittent River
- Canal
- Water
- Dry/Salt/Intermittent Lake
- Reef

Areas

- Airport/Runway
- Beach/Desert
- Cemetery (Christian)
- Cemetery (Other)
- Glacier
- Mudflat
- Park/Forest
- Sight (Building)
- Sportsground
- Swamp/Mangrove

Virginia Maxwell

Victoria Although based in Australia, Virginia spends at least half of her year updating Lonely Planet destination coverage across the globe. The Mediterranean is her major area of interest – she has covered Spain, Italy, Turkey, Syria, Lebanon, Israel, Egypt, Morocco and Tunisia for LP – but she also covers Finland, Bali, Armenia, the Netherlands, the US and Australia. Follow her @maxwellvirginia on Instagram and Twitter.

Kate Morgan

New South Wales, Queensland Having worked for Lonely Planet for over a decade now, Kate has been fortunate enough to cover plenty of ground working as a travel writer on destinations such as Shanghai, Japan, India, Russia, Zimbabwe, the Philippines and Phuket. She has done stints living in London, Paris and Osaka, but these days is based in one of her favourite regions in the world – Victoria, Australia. In between travelling the world and writing about it, Kate enjoys spending time at home working as a freelance editor.

Tasmin Waby

Western Australia A London-born writer with Kiwi *whānau* who grew up in Australia, Tasmin loves cartography, starry night skies, and getting off the beaten track. When not on the road for Lonely Planet she lives in a narrowboat and is planning her next adventure with her two school-aged kids. Tasmin also contributed to the Plan and Understand sections of this guide.

Steve Waters

Western Australia Travel and adventure have always been Steve's life, and he couldn't imagine a world without them. He's been using LP guidebooks for over 30 years in places as diverse as Iran, Central Asia, Kamchatka, Tuva, the Himalaya, Canada, Patagonia, the Australian Outback, NE Asia, Myanmar and the Sahara. Little wonder then that he finally got a gig with the company he was supporting! Steve has contributed to *Iran*, *Indonesia* and the past five editions of *West Coast Australia*, and come any September you're likely to find him in a remote gorge somewhere in the Kimberley. Steve says, 'Travel gives you a unique view of the world. Patience, acceptance, resourcefulness and flexibility are all lessons well learnt. Plans change, where some people see obstacles, others see possibilities. Go with an open mind. But go!'

Paul Harding
Queensland As a writer and photographer, Paul has been travelling the globe for the best part of two decades, with an interest in remote and offbeat places, islands and cultures. He's an author and contributor to more than 50 Lonely Planet guides to countries and regions as diverse as India, Belize, Vanuatu, Iran, Indonesia, New Zealand, Iceland, Finland, Philippines and – his home patch – Australia.

Rachael Hocking
Rachael is a Warlpiri woman with roots in the Tanami Desert of the Northern Territory. She has been a reporter and presenter for the country's only national Indigenous TV channel since 2015, and currently co-hosts its flagship show, The Point. Her job has seen her travel to the annual Garma Festival in Arnhem Land and interview the first female mayor on Thursday Island. In her spare time she volunteers on an Aboriginal music show for community radio station 3RRR in Melbourne. Rachael is an intersectional feminist who is passionate about Aboriginal women's rights, language revival and social justice. Rachael contributed to the Plan and Understand sections of this guide.

Anita Isalska
New South Wales Anita is a travel journalist, editor and copywriter. After several merry years as a staff writer and editor – a few of them in Lonely Planet's London office – Anita now works freelance between San Francisco, the UK and any Baltic bolthole with good wifi. Anita specialises in Eastern and Central Europe, Southeast Asia, France and off-beat travel. Read her stuff on www.anitaisalska.com.

Anna Kaminski
Western Australia Originally from the Soviet Union, Anna grew up in Cambridge, UK. Her restless wanderings led her to settle briefly in Oaxaca and Bangkok and her flirtation with criminal law saw her volunteering as a lawyer's assistant in the courts, ghettos and prisons of Kingston, Jamaica. Anna has contributed to almost 30 Lonely Planet titles. When not on the road, Anna calls London home. Having travelled on every single continent barring Antarctica, Anna has had her share of memorable experiences, from seeing the sun rise from the top of Borneo's Mt Kinabalu and Jamaica's Blue Mountain peak and riding all day on horseback to visit the Tsaatan reindeer herders on the border between Mongolia and Russia, to spending the night in a Latvian Soviet-era prison and attending a Vodou ritual in Haiti.

Tatyana Leonov
New South Wales Born and bred in Sydney, when she's not traversing the globe Tatyana enjoys exploring (and writing about) her home turf. She has written about her travel adventures for a diverse range of publications both in Australia and overseas and edits a magazine for families who love to travel. See www.tatyanaleonov.com.au

Sofia Levin
Melbourne Seasoned traveller and food journalist Sofia believes that eating in a country other than one's own is the best way to understand a culture. It's why she feels so lucky to call Melbourne home, where the city's diversity allows her to eat all over the world without catching a flight. With Insta-famous toy poodle, @lifeofjinkee, on her lap, she writes for newspapers and travel magazines, acts as Lonely Planet's Melbourne Local and co-authors international guidebooks – often rewarding herself with regional Vietnamese noodle soups for dinner. Follow her culinary adventures or ask her where to eat via Instagram @sofiaklevin.

Hugh McNaughtan

New South Wales, Queensland A former lecturer and restaurant critic, Hugh is a native Melbournite with deep family roots in New South Wales and Queensland. Jumping behind the wheel (and up the gangplank) to explore New England and the Queensland coast, islands and hinterland from Fraser Island to the Whitsunday was a dream assignment, made all the more memorable by the many kindnesses he encountered.

Charles Rawlings-Way

Perth, South Australia, Western Australia Charles Rawlings-Way is a veteran travel, food and music writer who has penned 40-something titles for Lonely Planet – including guides to Singapore, Toronto, Sydney, Tonga, New Zealand, the South Pacific and every state in Australia, including his native terrain of Tasmania and current homeland of South Australia – plus too many articles to recall. After dabbling in the dark arts of architecture, cartography, project management and busking for some years, Charles hit the road for LP in 2005 and hasn't stopped travelling since. 'What's in store for me in the direction I don't take?' (Kerouac). He's also the author of a bestselling rock biography on Glasgow band Del Amitri, *These Are Such Perfect Days*. Follow Charles on the socials @crawlingsway and www.facebook.com/chasrwmusic. Charles also contributed to the Plan, Understand and Survival Guide sections.

Andy Symington

Sydney, New South Wales Andy has prowled the globe insatiably, speaks several languages and is passionate about human rights and international development issues. After studying archaeology and psychology, he worked in the navigation business and, for some time, in educational and community theatre before long travels through South America eventually saw him wind up in Edinburgh, selling whisky to the Scots. Andy first became involved in writing when someone cannily contracted him to contribute to a pub guide, and his formidable research on that title broke a man but launched a career.

Brett Atkinson

New South Wales Brett is based in Auckland, New Zealand, but is frequently on the road for Lonely Planet. He's a full-time travel and food writer specialising in adventure travel, unusual destinations, and surprising angles on more well-known destinations. Craft beer and street food are Brett's favourite reasons to explore places, and he is featured regularly on the Lonely Planet website, and in newspapers, magazines and websites across New Zealand and Australia. Since becoming a Lonely Planet author in 2005, Brett has covered areas as diverse as Vietnam, Sri Lanka, the Czech Republic, New Zealand, Morocco, California and the South Pacific.

Fleur Bainger

Perth Having worn her first backpack to Europe when she was just 10 years old, Perth-based journalist Fleur gets a heck of a buzz from being a freelance travel and food writer. As Western Australia's weekly food reviewer for *The Sunday Times Magazine,* she's constantly on the hunt for Perth's best new eateries, while her weekly 'what's on' slot on 6PR talkback radio means she's always got the lowdown on events and openings around town. She's a Lonely Planet Local, a destination expert for *The Telegraph* (UK) and regular contributor to *Australian Traveller, Escape,* ABC radio and more.

Cristian Bonetto

Queensland Cristian has contributed to over 30 Lonely Planet guides to date, covering places including New York City, Italy, Venice & the Veneto, Naples & the Amalfi Coast, Denmark, Copenhagen, Sweden and Singapore. Lonely Planet work aside, his musings on travel, food, culture and design appear in numerous publications around the world, including *The Telegraph* (UK) and *Corriere del Mezzogiorno* (Italy). When not on the road, you'll find this reformed playwright and TV scriptwriter slurping espresso in his beloved hometown, Melbourne. Follow him on Instagram @rexcat75.

OUR STORY

A beat-up old car, a few dollars in the pocket and a sense of adventure. In 1972 that's all Tony and Maureen Wheeler needed for the trip of a lifetime – across Europe and Asia overland to Australia. It took several months, and at the end – broke but inspired – they sat at their kitchen table writing and stapling together their first travel guide, *Across Asia on the Cheap*. Within a week they'd sold 1500 copies. Lonely Planet was born.

Today, Lonely Planet has offices in Franklin, London, Melbourne, Oakland, Dublin, Beijing and Delhi, with more than 600 staff and writers. We share Tony's belief that 'a great guidebook should do three things: inform, educate and amuse'.

OUR WRITERS

Andrew Bain

Tasmania Andrew prefers adventure to avarice and can usually be found walking when he should be working. His writing and photography feature in magazines and newspapers around the world, and his writing has won multiple awards, including best adventure story and best Australian story (three times) from the Australian Society of Travel Writers. Andrew has unwittingly smuggled goods across the China–Russia border, shared his bed with a crocodile in the Northern Territory, and been deported from Estonia. He lives in Hobart, a city that satisfies his need to be constantly near the mountains. His musings on the outdoors world can be found at www.adventurebeforeavarice.com.

Samantha Forge

Australian Capital Territory, Canberra Samantha became hooked on travel at the age of 17, when she arrived in London with an overstuffed backpack and a copy of LP's *Europe on a Shoestring*. After a stint in Paris, she moved back to Australia to work as an editor in LP's Melbourne office. Eventually her wanderlust got the better of her, and she now works as a freelance writer and editor.

Anthony Ham

Northern Territory, Queensland Anthony is a freelance writer and photographer who specialises in Spain, East and Southern Africa, the Arctic and the Middle East. In 2001, after years of wandering the world, Anthony finally found his spiritual home when he fell irretrievably in love with Madrid on his first visit to the city. Less than a year later, he arrived there on a one-way ticket, with not a word of Spanish and not knowing a single person in the city. When he finally left Madrid ten years later, Anthony spoke Spanish with a Madrid accent and was married to a local. Now back in Australia, Anthony continues to travel the world in search of stories.

Trent Holden

Victoria A Geelong-based writer, Trent has worked for Lonely Planet since 2005. He's covered 30-plus guidebooks across Asia, Africa and Australia. With a penchant for megacities, Trent's in his element when assigned to cover a nation's capital – the more chaotic the better – to unearth cool bars, art, street food and underground subculture. On the flipside he also writes books to idyllic tropical islands across Asia, in between going on safari to national parks in Africa and the subcontinent. You can catch him on Twitter @hombreholden

OVER PAGE | MORE WRITERS

Published by Lonely Planet Global Limited
CRN 554153
20th edition – Nov 2019
ISBN 978 1 78701 388 9
© Lonely Planet 2019   Photographs © as indicated 2019
10 9 8 7 6 5 4 3 2 1
Printed in Singapore

Although the authors and Lonely Planet have taken all reasonable care in preparing this book, we make no warranty about the accuracy or completeness of its content and, to the maximum extent permitted, disclaim all liability arising from its use.

All rights reserved. No part of this publication may be copied, stored in a retrieval system, or transmitted in any form by any means, electronic, mechanical, recording or otherwise, except brief extracts for the purpose of review, and no part of this publication may be sold or hired, without the written permission of the publisher. Lonely Planet and the Lonely Planet logo are trademarks of Lonely Planet and are registered in the US Patent and Trademark Office and in other countries. Lonely Planet does not allow its name or logo to be appropriated by commercial establishments, such as retailers, restaurants or hotels. Please let us know of any misuses: lonelyplanet.com/ip.